VARIETY'S®
FILM
REVIEWS

Contents

OF THE TWENTY-THREE VOLUME SET

Variety's® FILM REVIEWS

1993-1994

VOLUME 23

R.R. Bowker

A Reed Reference Publishing Company

New Providence, New Jersey

Variety's Film Reviews
Volume 23, 1993-1994
was prepared by the
R.R. Bowker Bibliographic Group

Leigh Yuster-Freeman, Vice President, Production - Bibliographies

Production
Doreen Gravesande, Production Director
Barbara Holton and Frank McDermott, Senior Editors

Manufacturing
Jerry Goldstein, Vice President
Delia Tedoff, Production Manager

Published by R.R. Bowker
A Reed Reference Publishing Company
121 Chanlon Road, New Providence, NJ 07974

Andrew W. Meyer, Chief Operating Officer
Peter E. Simon, Executive Vice President, Business Development and Database Publishing
Stanley Walker, Senior Vice President, Corporate Marketing
Edward J. Roycroft, Senior Vice President, Sales

Volume Twenty-Three, 1993-1994

PRINTED AND BOUND IN THE UNITED STATES OF AMERICA

ISSN 0897-4373
ISBN 0-8352-3577-7

Manufactured in the United States of America

ISBN 0-8352-3577-7

9 780835 235778

Introductory Note

The reviews contained in this volume are complete reproductions of the original reviews printed in *Variety*. Only full-length feature films, including foreign films, are included. Short subjects and made for television films are not included.

User's Guide

The main section of this volume includes actual reviews published in *Variety* during 1993-1994, arranged chronologically by publication date. The *Variety* issue date in which the review appeared shows at the top of the column. A new date above a column indicates the start of the reviews from that week.

The book also includes two special indexes. The **FILM TITLE INDEX** covers films from the years 1993-1994. The **DIRECTOR INDEX** is new to this edition.

The **Film Title Index** arranges all titles in alphabetical order with definite and indefinite articles in all languages moved to the end of the title. Foreign-language films, with the English translation title in parentheses, are sorted under the original title, as well as under the English-language title. Titles beginning with numerals are listed both in the alphabetical list (spelled out in the language of origin), and again numerically at the end of the A-Z listing. The country of origin follows in (**BOLD CAPS**), the director (*in italics*), and the review date of the original *Variety* review standardized as month (abbreviated by three letters), date, and year.

The **Director Index** lists directors, arranged alphabetically by last name, and any of their films reviewed in this edition.

Another brand new feature is the title and years of coverage—**"Variety's Film Reviews 1993-1994"** on each page throughout the main section and indexes of this edition to further enhance use.

Example

FILM TITLE INDEX

Afrique, Je Te Plumerai (Africa, I will Pluck You Clean)
   FRENCH-CAMEROON *d. Jean-Marie Teno* . . . . Apr. 19, 1993
(Africa, I Will Pluck You Clean) Afrique, Je Te Plumerai . . . . Apr. 19, 1993
(AIDS: Talking to One Another) SIDA, Paroles de L'Un A L'Autre . . . . Jan. 3, 1994
(Banderas, The Tyrant) Tirano Banderas . . . . Mar 7, 1944
Cool Runnings *d. Jon Turteltaub* . . . . Sep. 20, 1993
Crooklyn *d. Spike Lee* . . . . May 9, 1994
Eat Drink Man Woman **TAIWANESE** *d. Ang Lee* . . . . May 23, 1994
Elles N'Oublient Jamais (Love in the Strangest Way) **FRENCH**
   d. Christopher Frank . . . . May 9, 1994
Forrest Gump *d. Robert Zemeckis* . . . . Jul. 11, 1994
(Love in the Strangest Way) Elles N'Oublient Jamais . . . . May 9, 1994
More Time **ZIMBABWEAN** *d. Isaac Meli Mabhikwa* . . . . Apr. 11, 1994
Papagei, Der (The Parrot) **GERMAN** *d. Ralf Huettner* . . . . Apr. 5, 1993
(Parrot, The) Der Papagei . . . . Apr. 5, 1993
Pulp Fiction *d. Quentin Tarantino* . . . . May 23, 1994
SIDA, Paroles de L'Un A L'Autre (AIDS: Talking to One Another) **FRENCH**
   d. Paule Muxel, Bertrand de Soliers . . . . Jan. 3, 1994
'66 Was a Good Year for Tourism **ISRAELI** *d. Amit Goren* . . . . Dec. 19, 1994
Tirano Banderas (Banderas, The Tyrant) **SPANISH-CUBAN-MEXICAN**
   d. Jose Luis Garcia Sanchez . . . . Mar. 7, 1994

DIRECTOR INDEX

Altman, Robert: Ready to Wear (Pret-a-Porter)
Ishii, Takashi: Nudo No Yoru (A Night in Nude)
Lee, Ang: Eat Drink Man Woman; Hsi Yen (The Wedding Banquet)
Lewin, Ben: Lucky Break
Minkoff, Rob jt. directorship *see* **Allers, Rogers**
Speilberg, Steven: Jurassic Park; Schindler's List
Wells, Simon jt. directorship *see* **Nibbelink, Phil, et al.**
Zwigoff, Terry: Crumb

1993
FILM REVIEWS

January 4, 1993

STALINGRAD
(GERMAN)

A Senator release of a Royal/Bavaria/B.A./Perathonm production. (World sales: Vision Intl.) Executive producers, Hanno Huth, Günter Rohrbach, Bob Arnold. Produced, directed by Joseph Vilsmaier. Screenplay, Johannes Heide, with Vilsmaier, Jürgen Büscher. Camera (color), Vilsmaier, Rolf Greim, Klaus Moderegger, Peter von Haller; editor, Hannes Nikel; music, Norbert J. Schneider; production design, Wolfgang Hundhammer, Jindrich Goetz; costume design, Ute Hofinger; sound (Dolby), Milan Bor; assistant director, Milan Steindler; stunt coordination, Jaroslav Tomsa, Petr Drozda; special effects, Karl Baumgartner. Reviewed at Arri theater, Munich, Nov. 13, 1992. Running time: **138 MIN.**
Fritz . . . . Dominique Horwitz
Hans . . . . Thomas Kretschmann
Rollo . . . . Jochen Nickel
GeGe . . . . Sebastian Rudolph
Irina . . . . Dana Vavrova
General Hentz . . . . Martin Benrath
Otto . . . . Sylvester Groth
Musk . . . . Karel Hermanek

"Stalingrad," made to commemorate the 50th anniversary of the pivotal World War II battle (and designed to match the formula and success of "Das Boot"), is a marketing masterpiece and offers often gripping action scenes. More impressively, especially in a dangerous political climate in Germany, it is politically applaudable. Unfortunately, it lacks believable characters and a dramatically structured story. It's a longshot.

The battle of Stalingrad in January 1943 was Germany's first and most crushing WWII defeat: it was the beginning of the end. The 6th Army, planning on a quick jaunt through the small industrial town on its way to Iraq, was soon trapped and surrounded. Of the estimated 400,000 soldiers who marched in, only 6,000 returned. Even today, Germans call a private defeat as their "personal Stalingrad."

The battle's 50th anniversary, like the Columbus quincentennial, makes a seemingly perfect marketing peg. And the film made to exploit the situation is a hard-hitting antiwar drama.

The pic follows a group of German soldiers (played credibly by Dominique Horwitz, Thomas Kretschmann, Jochen Nickel and Sebastian Rudolph) as they go from heady victory to the hell of Stalingrad, reduced from self-important soldiers to whimpering animals who will do anything to survive. They first rebel against their cause, then their officers, and the last half of the film chron-icles their attempts to escape. They don't succeed.

Obviously, this is not a feel-good movie. But with so many long-buried rightist feelings resurfacing in Germany, any hint of soldier's honor or German heroism in a film like this would have opened up a Pandora's box of political controversy. Though the film may attract many neo-Nazis and die-hard revisionists, it will not satisfy or justify them.

Though his direction is often bumpy here, Joseph Vilsmaier has managed to abandon the usual war film concept of the little guy who overcomes terrible circumstances. His work on the script, along with that of Jürgen Büscher, is what insured this would become a true antiwar film.

But the screenplay is the film's weak point. Johannes Heide's original script was written for a TV miniseries, and the episodic source shows. The characters, hard to tell apart in the first place, are reduced increasingly to clichés. As the film progresses, they begin to seem like war-is-hell tour guides.

Ironically, the characters are watered down in part by the message; they have so much to say about the senselessness of the war they seldom get around to their immediate, and dramatically more interesting, situation.

"Stalingrad" will do well in Germany and deserves to — it is a film with integrity — and will premiere all over Europe at the same time in January. But with a budget of $12 million, it needs foreign sales, and attracting as large an audience as that for "Das Boot" without as strong a story and human characters is unlikely. — *Eric Hansen*

ARIZONA DREAM
(FRENCH)

A UGC release of a Constellation/UGC/Hachette Premiere co-production with the participation of Canal Plus/French Ministry of Culture and Communications/CNC. Executive producer, Paul R. Gurian. Produced by Claudie Ossard. Directed by Emir Kusturica. Screenplay, David Atkins, Kusturica. Camera (color), Vilko Filac; editor, Andrija Zafranovic; music, Goran Bregovic; set design, Miljen Kljakovic "Kreka"; costume design, Jill M. Ohanneson; sound, Vincent Arnardi; producer for UGC, Yves Marmion; co-producer, Richard Brick; assistant director, Sergio Mimica. Reviewed at Max Linder Panorama cinema, Paris, Nov. 24, 1992. Running time: **142 MIN.**

Axel Blackmar . . . . . . Johnny Depp
Leo Sweetie . . . . Jerry Lewis
Elaine Stalker . . . . . Faye Dunaway
Grace Stalker . . . . Lili Taylor
Paul Leger . . . . Vincent Gallo
Millie . . . . Paulina Porizkova
Also with: Candace Mason, Alexis Rena, Polly Noonan, Ann Schulman, Michael J. Pollard.

Despite gorgeous, sometimes surreal visuals and the valiant efforts of an interesting cast, Emir Kusturica's "Arizona Dream" is heavy going. The eclectic intergenerational cast, the helmer's track record ("When Father Was Away on Business," "Time of the Gypsies") and the intriguing trailer will lure curious viewers in many markets but auds are in for a diffuse, rambling piece of work. Still, the prospect of seeing Jerry Lewis in a film produced by Claudie Ossard ("Betty Blue," "Delicatessen") may prove irresistible in France, if not elsewhere.

Award-winning Sarajevo-born helmer's first English-lingo pic tackles dreams and flight only to alternately soar and crash. Johnny Depp anchors the overlong pic as an unambitious 23-year-old fish and game warden summoned, against his will, from Manhattan to Arizona. Depp's uncle (Lewis) is about to take a bride three decades his junior (Paulina Porizkova) and wants Depp to be his best man and stay on to work at his Cadillac dealership.

Depp finds himself torn between seductive, half-mad widow Faye Dunaway and Dunaway's equally unstable stepdaughter, heiress Lili Taylor. Vincent Gallo plays a womanizing aspiring actor who sells cars between auditions.

Working from a script by David Atkins, one of his students at Columbia University, Kusturica grafts his sometimes unwieldy Europe-inflected concerns onto brash American landscapes with mixed results. Much is made of dreams that, either spoken of at length or illustrated, are offered in lieu of character development.

Depp does a good job with his many expository voiceovers, but the text is a bit thick on offbeat anecdotes, Old World sayings and peculiar metaphors. Of other thesps, Taylor most successfully maintains control in a somewhat out-of-control environment.

By giving his actors enormous leeway Kusturica ends up losing a war of attrition between whimsy and tedium. Many scenes are both prolonged and pointless. Depp's difficulties with the two femmes feel trumped up rather than imperative. There is almost always a strained quality to the lyricism struggling to get out. But on the few and far between occasions when that lyrical magic does break free, it's a treat.

The arresting and recurring image of a fish swimming through thin air before spectacular shifting backdrops is both a stunning bit of process photography and a resonant indication of man's fluid but baffled place in the scheme of things.

Pic, which shot under the title "The Arrowtooth Waltz," could become a cult rental fave for the inspired comic bit during which Gallo auditions by miming the entire crop duster sequence from "North By Northwest." Helmer has fun with other American classics, including "Raging Bull" and "The Godfather, Part II," not to mention the presence of childhood idol Jerry Lewis.

Impeccably lensed in Alaska, New York and Douglas, Ariz., pic remains stuck in an awkward netherworld between slapstick and pathos. — *Lisa Nesselson*

LE GRAND PARDON II
(DAY OF ATONEMENT)
(FRENCH)

A UGC release of an Alexandre Films/TF-1 co-production. Executive producer, Robert Benmussa. Produced, directed by Alexandre Arcady. Screenplay, Arcady, Daniel Saint-Hamont. Camera (color), Willy Kurant; editor, Martine Barraque; music, Romano Musumarra; costume design, Mic Cheminal; set design, Tony Egry; sound, Roger Di Ponio. Reviewed at Forum Horizon cinema, Paris, Dec. 14, 1992. Running time: **145 MIN.**
Raymond Bettoun . . . . Roger Hanin
Maurice Bettoun . . . . Richard Berry
Roland Bettoun . . . . Gérard Darmon
Pasco Meisner . . Christopher Walken
Sally White . . . . Jill Clayburgh
Joyce Ferranti . . . . . . Jennifer Beals
Also with: Jean-François Stevenin, Jean Benguigui, Raul Davila, Philippe Sfez, Jim Moody, Christian Fellat, Robert Escobar.
(French and English soundtrack)

An ambitious saga of deadly rivalries among three generations of Franco-Algerian Jewish gangsters, Alexandre Arcady's "Le Grand Pardon II" is sabotaged by structural problems and sloppy storytelling. Since there is the original "Le Grand Pardon" to plunder, the confusion could presumably be straightened out, in which case, a revamped and shortened product could spur TV sales. Presence of Christopher Walken, Jill Clayburgh and Jennifer Beals might boost video rentals offshore.

Still, this sequel gives uninitiated auds only a faint clue as to why one brother (Gérard Darmon) is bent on humiliating another (Richard Berry). Snippets from the first film (broadcast on French TV annually since its 1982 release) show the same cast a decade younger but do little to clarify what's going on.

Shot on location in Miami, the energetically staged pic revels in local color. Shoot-'em-up scenes are bold and bloody, drug smuggling tricks are slick, and a hostage gets pushed out of a helicopter without a 'chute. Unfortunately, the continuity person in charge of narrative geography must also have met a grisly fate.

The viewer struggles to decipher what's what and what's where as the lengthy and lavish party sequence, intercut with a violent drug bust, follows a free-floating silent scene of patriarch Raymond Bettoun (Roger Hanin) and Jean-Louis Trintignant (never to be seen again) in Paris in 1982. Mind readers and members of the production company know that Trintignant is arresting Hanin while Hanin's infant grandson looks on.

Now 13, the boy (played by Arcady's cute but wooden son) is celebrating his bar mitzvah in 1992 in Miami, where his dad, Maurice Bettoun (Berry), launders drug money via legitimate interests. Celebration also honors Hanin, who has snuck into the U.S. after 10 years in a French prison.

Strapped for funds to purchase a privately owned island, Berry reluctantly partners with redoubtable druglord Christopher Walken. But many factors are aligned against the Bettouns, including Latin enemies, a mysterious drug courier and pic's obvious debt to the "Godfather" trilogy.

As a megalomaniac drug kingpin sired by a Chile-based Nazi, Walken adds another delightfully devilish bad boy to his roster of screen villains and occasions all the best intentional laughs. Hanin, Berry, Darmon and their various retainers turn in good perfs, but pic rarely rises above a choppy comic book sensibility.

Among the token Americans, Clayburgh, as a local hotel owner and Beals, as Berry's g.f., give game performances, but Jim Moody as a DEA inspector is weak, as are many plot points: The organization's security, for example, is air-tight except when, for dramatic purposes, it isn't.

Music is on the plodding, syrupy side. Editing aside, tech credits are pro. — *Lisa Nesselson*

DOUBLE THREAT

A Pyramid Distribution release of a David Winters presentation, in association with Sovereign Investment Corp. Executive producer, Winters. Produced by Kimberley Casey. Directed, written by David A. Prior. Camera (Image Transform color), Gerald B. Wolfe; editor, Tony Malanowski; music, Christopher Farrell; art direction, Linda Lewis; costume design, Valerie Finkel; sound, Sean Velour; assistant director, Teddi Rae; production manager, Todd King; stunt coordinator, Bob Ivy; associate producer, Robert Willoughby; casting, Jacov Bresler. Reviewed on AIP vidcassette, N.Y., Dec. 16, 1992. MPAA Rating: R. Running time: **96 MIN.**

Monica Martel	Sally Kirkland
Eric Cline	Andrew Stevens
Lisa Shane	Sherrie Rose
Stephen Ross	Chick Vennera
Coleman	Gary Swanson
Fenich	Richard Lynch
Crocker Scott	Anthony Franciosa
Tawny	Monique Detraz
Mugger	Ted Prior

Ingenious scripting and clever casting lift "Double Threat" above the commonplace in the erotic thriller genre. Film opened on a regional basis in the South last month and heads soon for video.

Sally Kirkland is the tongue-in-cheek choice for film's central role: A Hollywood star making her comeback in a melodrama whose producer, her ex-husband (Tony Franciosa), demands that the film must be sexy. Kirkland amusingly takes a stand with her director (Chick Vennera): She's never had to do a nude scene and she's not starting now.

Solution is to hire a body double, lovely Sherrie Rose. Rub is that Kirkland's leading man and off-screen b.f., younger Andrew Stevens, falls in love with Rose after making love to her before the cameras.

Filmmaker David A. Prior plants knowing in-jokes into his script but has the cast play everything straight, making for an entertaining package. Following up on similar "In the Heat of Passion," Kirkland is hot indeed, especially in an uninhibited masturbation sequence. Rose is well-matched as her double and subject of a final revelation that is a very satisfying plot twist.

Filmed on location in Mobile, Ala., this low-budget entry adequately conveys the atmosphere of Tinseltown and its behind-the-scenes antics. — *Lawrence Cohn*

SEÑORA BOLERO
(VENEZUELAN)

A Cinematográfica Macuto production, with the participation of Foncine. Produced, directed by Marilda Vera. Screenplay, Milagros Rodríguez, Vera, David Suárez. Camera (color), Hernán Toro; editor, Sergio Curiel; music, Carlos Moreán; sound, Josue Saavedra; art direction, María Adelina Vera, Sandy Jelambi. Reviewed at Foncine, Caracas, Venezuela, Nov. 25, 1992. Running time: **101 MIN.**

Amanda Contreras	Carlota Sosa
Pedro Linares	Marcelo Ramo
Alejandro Salazar	Héctor Myerston

Also with: Tania Sarabia, Jorge Caelón, Miguel de León, Rodrigo Romo, Estelita del Llano, Hans Cristopher, Dora Mazone, Yamilet Uzcaiga.

Embracing a 30-year period in Venezuelan history, "Señora Bolero" is an ambitious recounting of a love triangle poisoned by personal and political betrayal. The personal and at times melodramatic storyline is set against a larger political canvas and may find interest on the fest and arthouse circuit.

Pic revolves around Amanda Contreras (Carlota Sosa), the middle-aged lawyer-wife of a powerful politician campaigning for top political office (Pedro Linares). When her 25-year-old son commits suicide and her husband continues as if nothing had happened, Amanda takes stock.

Among those offering solace is former lover Alejandro Salazar, a radio and TV star and ex-political activist who had fled the country during the political turmoil of the 1950s that overthrew the long dictatorship of Marcos Pérez Gómez.

Amanda discovers that what's wrong with her current life began years previously when Alejandro and Pedro worked together in the political underground and that she must restructure her own life, returning to the point when, as a young bolero singer, she still had a choice.

The film recaptures this lost time through attention to art direction and okay acting. Though at times lacking sufficient extras to portray massive turmoil, pic's intimate portrait allows the larger background to emerge within a personal context. — *Paul Lenti*

L'INCONNU DANS LA MAISON
(STRANGER IN THE HOUSE)
(FRENCH)

An AMLF release of an Annabel Prods./Les Films Alain Sarde co-production. Produced by Alain Sarde, Jean-Paul Belmondo. Directed by Georges Lautner. Screenplay, Lautner, Bernard Stora, Jean Largeguy; from Georges Simenon's novel. Camera (color), Jean-Yves Le Mener; editor, Georges Klotz; music, Francis Lai; costumes, Paulette Breil; set design, Baptiste Poirot; sound, Harold Maury. Reviewed at Le Royal cinema, Montpellier, France, Oct. 30, 1992. Running time: **100 MIN.**

Loursat	Jean-Paul Belmondo
Fine	Renée Faure
Isabelle	Cristiana Reali
Manu	Sebastian Tavel
Binet	François Perrot
Bernadette	Genevieve Page

"Stranger in the House," a laborious, indifferently handled remake of 1942 Raimu-starrer "Strangers in the House," develops badly needed punch in final quarter when chronic alcoholic and non-practicing lawyer Jean-Paul Belmondo returns to the bar — er, the courtroom. Belmondo's many fans will find the star in okay form, but the vehicle, drawn from a Georges Simenon novel and helmed without distinction by Georges Lautner, is strictly TV caliber.

In the 10 years since his wife committed suicide, Belmondo has been working his way through the 25,000 bottles of fine wine in the cellar of the large house he shares with a persnickety housekeeper (Renée Faure) and the pretty but distant 21-year-old daughter (Christiana Reali) who blames him for mom's death.

Belmondo finds incentive to modify his predominantly liquid diet when an unknown young man is shot to death in a room of his house. Daughter claims not to know how the body got there. A record store clerk who says he's innocent is arrested.

Not unlike Joe Pesci in "My Cousin Vinny," the lawyer straightens up and flies right, dazzling those who have looked down on him, including, of course, his estranged daughter.

Belmondo, in his first screen role in five years, carries the pic. But despite his leathery skin and white hair, barrel-chested thesp still seems suspiciously robust for a vegetating wino.

Housekepper Faure is good, as is Genevieve Page as Belmondo's sister. Young thesps do their best with clichéd roles. Francis Lai's score is ordinary and mercifully unobtrusive. The voice of an omniscient narrator pops up two or three times, apparently hoping to lend a more literary tone. Lensing in bland settings is as hackneyed as the script.
— *Lisa Nesselson*

NORKURVE
(NORTH CURVE)
(GERMAN)

A Winkelmann Filmproduktion in co-production with WDR & Impuls Film. Produced by Christiane Schaefer. Directed by Adolf Winkelmann. Screenplay, Michael Klaus. Camera (color), David Slama; music, Piet Klocke; production design, Florian Haarmann; costumes, Heidi Wieser Plätz. Reviewed at Cologne Film Festival, Sept. 27, 1992. Running time: 100 MIN.
With: Renate Krössner, Daniel Berger, Hermann Lause, Bernd Stegemann, Christian Tasche, Rolf Dennemann, Walter Kreye, Michael Brandner, Wolf-Dietrich Berg, Jochen Nickel, Katherina Abt, Stefan Jürgens.

This muddled and confused soccer drama of behind-the-scenes intrigue and hooliganism — intended as a metaphor for the current German political and social situation —takes forever to get going, and then doesn't go anywhere.

Pic's first half cross-cuts aimlessly between assorted, unrelated characters in Dortmund: a couple who run a pub, a skinhead who harasses a young Turk, a wheeler-dealer type and the president of a soccer club. All of them are frantically pursuing something: love, sex, cash or power.

After a seemingly endless amount of time, all end up at a soccer match. Pic then becomes noisy and irksome, occasionally erupting into bouts of random violence that go nowhere due to an almost stubborn refusal to develop character or allow a coherent plot to make some sense of the ongoing brouhaha. Tech credits are unremarkable but competent. —*Rebecca Lieb*

KYURUN IYAGI
(WEDDING STORY)
(KOREAN)

A Shin Cine production. Executive producer, Oh Jung-won. Produced by Park Sang-in. Directed by Kim Eui-suk. Screenplay, Park Hun-soo. Camera (color), Koo Joong-mo; lighting, Son Dal-ho; editing, Park Soon-duck; music, Song Byung-joon; sound, Kang Dae-sung. Reviewed on vidcassette, Dec. 12, 1992. (In "Seoul Beauties" series, N.Y.) Running time: 96 MIN.
Kim Tae-Kyun . . . . . . Choi Min-soo
Choi Ji-Hae . . . . Shim Hye-in

"Wedding Story" is a modest but well-made anatomy of the marriage of two yuppies from wedding to breakup to reconciliation. While characters and situation are readily identifiable, film lacks the punch for a major foreign send-off. The good-natured tone and technical polish, however, make its local success easily understandable.

After a brief prologue, film speeds through the wedding of principals to a slightly dissonant version of Wagner's wedding march. Zippily edited vignettes highlight the couple's first days of marriage with a celebration of sexual discoveries and, later, some of the standard conflicts about toilet seats, bathroom cabinet space and the male's macho notions of lovemaking.

The real fissures in the marriage appear when Choi (Shim Hye-jin) begins to make career advances over husband Kim (Choi Min-soo), getting a job as a radio host at the same company.

From the opening shot, panning around a tombstone, director Kim Eui-suk suggests a darker tone to marriage rituals and there is even a clip from "Vertigo," Korean-dubbed down to Kim Novak's final scream. "Wedding Story's" emotional nadir comes with a violent outburst that stops just short of rape and ends their union. Kim ultimately recognizes his shortcomings and wages a siege for Choi's forgiveness.

Even though their reunion finally ensues in a cemetery, for the most part, director Kim keeps the mood frothy, employing such facetious devices as a food-obsessed co-worker and a philosophical shoeshine man. These and a stick-on comic ending undermine the film's sense of reality though most of the mood swings between comedy and drama are adroitly made.

Both leading players are adept at suggesting the charm beneath their flaws while atmospheric lensing and lighting by Koo Joong-mo and Son Dal-ho is also a strong plus. — *Fred Lombardi*

SUBLET
(SPANISH)

A Kaplan & Fernando Trueba P.C. production, with the participation of Televisión Española. Executive producer, Fernando Trueba. Directed, written by Chus Gutiérrez. Camera (color), Juan Molina; editor, Carmen Frias; music, Tao Gutiérrez; sets, Judy Becker; sound, Neil Dazinger. Reviewed at San Sebastian Film Festival, Sept. 20, 1992. Running time: 94 MIN.
Laura . . . . Iciar Bollain
Gladys . . . . Awilda Rivera
Eugene . . . . John Kelly
Louis . . . . Norm Anderson
Also with: Kevin Bagot, Cesar Olmos, Donna Linderman, Oona Farrel.

Most recent in a spate of vapid films made by Spaniards in New York, "Sublet" is about a Spanish tourist who decides to stay on and try to survive in Gotham. Story is rambling and inconsequential, and the acting so clumsy that the woes befalling the girl seem less than what she deserves.

Installed in a seedy building in a seedy nabe, Iciar Bollain strikes up acquaintances with various types, including a youth with whom she has a fleeting romance. The landlord, a kind of evil monster who lives in an abandoned building, hounds her for rent unpaid by the other tenant. This becomes the only drama in the humdru story.

Dialogue is partly in Spanish and partly in heavily accented English. Auds familiar with NYC will wince at this effort to "discover" the city. — *Peter Besas*

STRANGE HORIZON
(CANADIAN)

A Lightscape Motion Picture Co. production. Executive producers, William Johnston, Ronald Lilie. Produced, directed, written by Philip Jackson. Additional dialogue, Mark Alfano, Brian Goldman. Camera (color), John Dyer; editor, Tony Coleman; production design, Jim Plaxton, James Allan; costumes, Kathleen Smiley; sound, Dan Munroe; co-producer, Mary Terry; associate producer, Doug Dales. Reviewed at Montreal World Film Festival, Sept. 1, 1992. Running time: 83 MIN.
Pascal . . . . David Ferry
Dorothy/Alien Woman . Olga Prokhorova
Adm. Hardman . . . . . . Ken Lemaire
Shorty . . . . Robert Russell
Capt. Xaxx . . . . Denise McLeod
Maj. Charlie Vault . . . . Kyra Harper

"Strange Horizon" is a fuzzy-headed, low-budget sci-fi parable that will have a hard time finding an audience, even in video outlets.

Set in a 23rd century where people still use '90s slang, Toronto-shot pic stars David Ferry as awashed-up spaceship pilot who crash lands on a remote planet. He didn't know that his cargo is an illegal drug, Horizon, but he does know that his former commanding officer (Ken Lemaire) was dealing the stuff.

Director-producer-writer Philip Jackson devotes much of the first hour to Ferry's long, pseudo-philosophical tirades. Eventually, a woman (Russian emigré Olga Prokhorova) from an alien race's battleship also lands on Ferry's planet. She consumes vast quantities of the drug while her battleship (resembling an immense meatball shrouded in cobwebs) plays cat-and-mouse with Lemaire's spaceship.

Talky script vaguely refers to themes of loyalty, betrayal, spiritual redemption and sexual politics, but little is of interest. Acting is no better than it has to be, and costumes appear to have been purchased from a bankrupt airline. — *Joe Leydon*

MONTPELIER FEST

RASSAÈLLE CHAFAHYIA
(VERBAL MESSAGES)
(SYRIAN)

A General Film Organization, Damascus, production. Directed, written by Abdellatif Abdelhamid. Camera (color), Abdo Hamzé; editor, Antoinette Azarié. Reviewed at Montpellier Festival of Mediterranean Cinema, Montpellier, France, Oct. 26, 1992 (Competing). Running time: **108 MIN.**

With: Fayez Kazak, Rana Jammoul, Rami Ramadan, Assad Fiddah, Zouheir Ramadan.

Syrian scripter-helmer Abdellatif Abdelhamid's "Verbal Messages" is a crowd-pleasing farce that mixes surreal and gutter humor only to conclude on a surprisingly tender, dignified note. Comedy fest programmers should take note.

Thesping is broad, and colorful hyperbolic curses fly throughout a lively account of ugly young man's obsessive love for gorgeous neighbor girl.

Ismael, a four-eyed nerd burdened with a colossal nose, sends his best friend Ghassan as a go-between to beautiful Salma. Handsome but naive Ghassan is a teenaged bed-wetter who can't master his multiplication tables despite extreme disciplinary tactics of his soldier dad. Sexy Salma falls for the messenger, but Ghassan remains faithful to the wishes of his lovesick friend.

Talky pic set in a hilly village is indifferently lit but boasts a few striking dream sequences, including one in which Ghassan, tied to a stake, is overrun by dozens of glow-in-the-dark numbers to the accompaniment of a chant that curses the multiplication tables.

In daylight episodes, Ghassan, who gamely slides down a steep gully by the seat of his pants to deliver Ismael's declarations of love, offers to shoot his buddy's proboscis with a rifle after which plastic surgeons can fashion a smaller model.

Tech credits are merely okay but the evocative use of sound is a plus. At Montpelier fest, where pic won three prizes, Moscow-trained helmer announced in Russian that four couples met and married during the filming and expressed his wish that "an epidemic of love break out wherever the film is shown."

— Lisa Nesselson

BODY OF EVIDENCE

An MGM/UA release of a Dino De Laurentiis Communications production. Executive producers, Stephen Deutsch, Melinda Jason. Produced by De Laurentiis. Directed by Uli Edel. Screenplay, Brad Mirman. Camera (Deluxe color), Doug Milsome; editor, Thom Noble; music, Graeme Revell; production design, Victoria Paul; art direction (L.A.), Michael Rizzo; set decoration, Jerie Kelter; costume design, Susan Becker; sound (Dolby), Keith A. Wester, Kurt St. Amant (Portland); assistant director, Dennis Maguire; co-producers, Bernd Eichinger, Herman Weigel; line producer, Mel Dellar; casting, Mary Jo Slater. Reviewed at Filmland screening room, Culver City, Calif., Jan. 6, 1992. MPAA Rating: R. Running time: **99 MIN.**

Rebecca Carlson	Madonna
Frank Dulaney	Willem Dafoe
Robert Garrett	Joe Mantegna
Joanne Braslow	Anne Archer
Sharon Dulaney	Julianne Moore
Dr. Alan Paley	Jurgen Prochnow
Jeffrey Roston	Frank Langella
Charles Biggs	Stan Shaw
Dr. McCurdy	Charles Hallahan
Judge Burnham	Lillian Lehman
Detective Reese	Mark Rolston
Gabe	Jeff Perry
Detective Griffin	Richard Riehle

The bod of the moment is on ample display in "Body of Evidence," a low-rent edition of "Basic Instinct" that, like the star's bestselling "Sex" is more silly than erotic. A courtroom drama built around the charge that Madonna's body is a deadly weapon with which she "fornicated" a man to death, this showcase for the singer-thesp as femme fatale is titillating enough to lure an initially curious public and follow up as a good video title, but its theatrical endurance would seem closer to that of her victim than to Madonna's.

The ever-self-inventing one plays the g.f. of a rich older man with a heart ailment who is found dead after a night in the sack with her. That he's left her $8 million and had cocaine in his system points the finger of guilt straight at the "cokehead slut" — as the man's secretary (Anne Archer) calls her. Prosecutor Joe Mantegna sets out to prove that Madonna has an m.o.: preying upon wealthy older men in weakened conditions until, finally, she succeeded in knocking one off in a marathon sex session.

To this end, surprise witness and spurned ex-lover Frank Langella testifies that, despite his heart problems, "She was always trying to get me more and more worked up," adding that she liked to tie him up and insisted upon being in control.

Defense attorney Willem Dafoe makes the unforgettable opening argument that, "It's not a crime to be a great lay," but soon discovers that Madonna isn't into old men exclusively, even if she does call all the shots. Endangering his marriage and confusing the lawyer/client relationship, Dafoe just can't say no and the pair's several sex bouts are the film's main action set-pieces.

Each, of course, has to be offbeat in a slightly kinky way to suit the adventurous reputation of the character and star. First encounter, therefore, will probably be known as the candle wax scene, while the next explores the possibilities of broken glass.

The only sequence that seems truncated (possibly having been cut when pic received an initial NC-17) is one in which Dafoe finally turns the sexual tables; to be psychologically satisfying, it needs to go further to depict the resulting changes in attitude.

Trial begins a mere 20 minutes into the story, and most of the running time alternates between courtroom testimony — much of it racy — and Madonna-Dafoe face-offs in which they either talk about what's going on or get it on. In other words, pic is about nothing but s-e-x, very much in line with this year's Madonna, but it comes very close to making "dangerous" sex a big joke.

Decked out in a short platinum blonde haircut and fancy clothes that rip easily, Madonna has little trouble passing as a predatory tramp whose credo would seem to be, "I f---, therefore I am." Aspiring to the mantle of such screen sirens as Lana Turner and Barbara Stanwyck, here she most resembles Hanna Schygulla, and reverses the usual path of actresses who break into films by appearing nude but cover up over time.

Dafoe holds his own manfully, while remainder of the good cast is serviceable under helmer Uli Edel, who had some interesting angles on "Last Exit To Brooklyn" but whose approach here is surprisingly conventional, especially his by-the-numbers trial coverage.

Portland locations give the pic's exteriors an appealingly wet, cool feel. Tech contributions are in line with neo-noir conventions.

— Todd McCarthy

FINAL CUT REVIEW

MAP OF THE HUMAN HEART
(BRITISH-AUSTRALIAN-FRENCH-CANADIAN)

New version reviewed at Hoyts screening room, Sydney, Jan. 7, 1993. (In Palm Springs Intl. Film Festival.) Running time: **106 MIN.**

Vincent Ward's immensely ambitious multinational co-production was reviewed in VARIETY June 2, 1992, as a work in progress at last year's Cannes film fest. Expensive-looking film now has a much better chance in the international markets and what was only a potentially touching love story has become far more potent.

The final version world-premiered last week as the opening attraction at the Palm Springs film fest. The Cannes version ran 126 minutes; the epic love story, which spans 30 years and two continents was, in that cut, marred by a protracted and awkward ending and by apparent gaps in the central romance. Considerable re-editing and shortening by 20 minutes have markedly improved the pacing and development of the storyline without any essentials being lost in the process.

The addition of new scenes in the middle of the pic (featuring a romantic triangle played by Patrick Bergin, Jason Scott Lee and Anne Parillaud) flesh out what was a disappointingly sketchy series of relationships in the original. Ward has achieved this result via one day's extra shooting in London with Lee and Parillaud, and restoration of a key Bergin-Parillaud scene.

Most importantly, the ragged ending has been completely reshaped, with a character's death now movingly intercut with celebratory scenes of his long-lost daughter's wedding.

Miramax will release the film Stateside in March. Cannes version credited only film editor John Scott; final version credits a second editor, Brit George Akers, who supervised the final version. *—David Stratton*

OTHER REVIEWS

JUSTE AVANT L'ORAGE
(JUST BEFORE THE STORM)
(FRENCH-SWISS)

A Swift Prods. release of a Les Films du Phare/SGCC/Odessa Films/Les Prods. JMH/Television Suisse Romande co-production with the participation of the CNC, Dept. of the Interior (Berne)/ Canal Plus/Procirep. Produced by Sylvette Frydman. Directed, written by Bruno Herbulot, from Henry James' writings. Camera (color), Guillaume Schiffman; editor, Alica Lary; set design, Denis Champenois; costumes, Charlotte David; sound, Laurent Barbet. Reviewed at Club de L'Etoile screening room, Paris, Dec. 18, 1992. Running time: **85 MIN.**

With: Laura Morante, Christophe Malavoy, Zabou, Christophe Odent, Lola Gans, Carlo Brandt, Dominique Valadie, Redjep Mitrovitsa, Catherine Frot, Hanns Zischler.

"**L**oosely inspired" by the writings of Henry James, "Juste Avant l'Orage" is an earnest but tepid attempt to investigate why each heart has its reasons. Focus is on five men and five women whose past and present love lives overlap. Although helmer Bruno Herbulot has gathered a good cast for his maiden feature, no sparks fly.

Charlotte (Laura Morante) and her swain Ferdinand (Christophe Malavoy) invite a batch of pals from their high school days to a huge country manor to celebrate 15 years of friendship. Charlotte, an actress who makes no distinction between theater and life, was previously involved with Thomas (Carlo Brandt), who has married a very young and insecure girl (Lola Gans).

Malavoy, smitten by Gans, keeps dunking his head after Morante tells him that keeping an eye open under water will reveal the image of one's true love. Zabou, having just learned from her former b.f., a doctor, that she's pregnant by her current b.f., makes the evening a test of their relationship. Dominique Valadie injects some much-needed humor into her role as Malavoy's former g.f.

Beyond the manor, a would-be authoress (Catherine Frot) tries to snare a successful author (Hanns Zischler).

The lone topic of conversation is love, but characters pontificate rather than demonstrate their feelings. Catchy lensing of opening passages is soon sacrificed to mere recording of the proceedings.

Thesps are either shown dancing to a punchy mix of Anglo and Euro-rock tunes or else are off in some corner being ponderous, tense, confessional or all three. To its credit, pic comes across just like a long, dull party, but good continuity is no substitute for compelling intrigue.

— _Lisa Nesselson_

THE PRINCESS AND THE GOBLIN
(A HERCEGNÖ ÉS A KOBOLD)
(BRITISH-HUNGARIAN-ANIMATED)

An Entertainment Film Distributors (U.K.) release of a J&M Entertainment presentation of a Siriol Prods./ Pannonia Film Co. production, in association with S4C Wales/NHK Enterprises. Executive producers, Steve Walsh, Marietta Dárdai. Produced by Robin Lyons. Directed by József Gémes. Screenplay, Lyons, from George MacDonald's novel. Camera (color), Árpád Lessecry, György Verga, Ede Pagner, Nick Smith, Pete Turner, Steve Turner, Andreas Klawsz; editor, Magda Hap; music, István Lerch; sound (Dolby), Imre András Nyerges, John Griffiths, Clive Pendry; orchestrations, János Novák; song, Chris Stuart, Lyons; animation director, Les Orton; production coordinators, Lóránd Poich, Magdolna Sebestyén; production manager, Pete Turner; line producer, Emöke Marsovsky; preproduction visualization, Mike Wall; storyboard, Andrew Offiler, Wayne Thomas; background style, Gizella N. Csathó. Reviewed at Odeon Kensington theater, London, Dec. 22, 1992. Running time: **82 MIN.**

Voices of: Joss Ackland, Claire Bloom, Sally Ann Marsh, Peter Murray, Rik Mayall, Peggy Mount, Molly Sugden, Roy Kinnear, Victor Spinetti, Frank Rozelaar Green, William Hootkins, Maxine Howe, Steve Lyons, Robin Lyons.

(English soundtrack)

"**T**he Princess and the Goblin" is a potentially charming medieval cartoon let down by so-so technique and unimaginative plotting. Undemanding kid fare, uniting British and Hungarian animators, will fill afternoon tube slots quicker than movie theaters.

Roll-your-own story, credited to a novel by George MacDonald, has moppet princess Irene (voiced by Sally Ann March), lost in the woods, palling up with singing miner's son Curdie (voiced by Peter Murray), who discovers a plan by some grungy goblins to cause chaos by flooding the mines.

To make matters worse, hideous goblin prince Froglip (venomously voiced by Brit TV comic Rik Mayall) plans to kidnap Irene, marry her, and usurp power in the kingdom. Thanks to a magic thread from her fairy grandmother (Claire Bloom), Irene rescues Curdie and, despite the flooded mines, all live happily after.

Main problem is that pic fails to capitalize on its most interesting characters. After a standard opening, introing the wholesome leads, things pick up in the third reel with the arrival of Froglip and his gonzo family.

But the evil-smelling goblins aren't made into really scary villains and there's a lack of dramatic impetus leading to the climax. Latter is due in large part to the feeble, badly spotted symphonic score by István Lerch. Pic's effects track is also sparse.

Chris Stuart and producer-scripter Robin Lyons' recurring song (used by Curdie to stave off the goblins) is deserving of greater exploitation; but Lyons' script, though free of sermonizing, is surface stuff.

Pic lacks the visual texture of helmer József Gémes' "Heroic Times"; look and coloring are solid, but coin-saving lack of detail and of inbetweening results in jerky motion.

English version caught features a stellar lineup of mainly Brit voicers, all pro. Hero Curdie, however, is given a Yank accent. — _Derek Elley_

SISHI PUHUO
(FAMILY PORTRAIT)
(CHINESE-HONG KONG)

A Beijing Film Studio/Era Intl. (H.K.) Ltd./China Film Exhibition & Distribution Corp. co-production in association with China Film Co-Prod. Co. (Intl. sales: Era Intl., Hong Kong.) Produced by Cheng Zhigu, Andrew Leung, Wu Jian. Directed by Li Shaohong. Screenplay, Liu Heng. Camera (color), Zeng Nieping; music, Hou Muren; production design, Lin Chaoxiang; sound, Liu Heng; associate producer, Tian Zhuangzhuang. Reviewed at Festival of Festivals, Toronto, Sept. 17, 1992. Running time: **90 MIN.**

Cao Depei	Li Xuejian
Duan	Song Dandan
Xiaomu	Ye Jing

The third feature of femme director Li Shaohong is doing the fest circuit concurrently with her 2-year-old "Bloody Morning," and is a very different kind of pic. It's a probing family drama of considerable charm and distinction, and another quality item from the Chinese mainland, made in co-production with Hong Kong company Era.

The protagonist is Cao Depei (Li Xuejian), a Beijing photographer living with his second wife and 6-year-old son. He's working on an official book of photographs and, in a revealing early scene, is criticized by his editor for his pictures' political incorrectness.

Then comes a surprise: A call from the Child Welfare Dept. to inform him that a son he never knew existed has been found wandering the city streets. He discovers that his first wife hadn't told him she was pregnant when they separated years earlier and she has died, leaving their 10-year-old son, Xiaomu, virtually alone.

Afraid to tell his current wife about this unexpected development, Cao lets the boy stay in his darkroom; but soon the lad is calling at his father's apartment to play with his step-brother and the secret is out.

It's a universal theme, and Li handles it with great delicacy and feeling, extracting fine performances from her cast. She's careful to allow all the protagonists — the confused husband, his frustrated wife and the unfortunate boy — equal weight. She also includes some pertinent criticism of the authorities, especially via a news vendor who cries out sensational stories and then adds, "And Socialism is marching forward!" Such details help to make "Family Portrait" an unusually interesting pic to emerge from the People's Republic.— _David Stratton_

KICKBOXER III:
THE ART OF WAR

A Kings Road Entertainment release of a Kings Road and MPC production. Executive producer, Luciana Boa Marinho. Produced by Michael Pariser. Directed by Rick King. Screenplay, Dennis Pratt; camera (Deluxe color), Edgar Moura; editor, Daniel Loewenthal; music, Harry Manfredini; sound (Ultra-Stereo), Lee Orloff; production design, Clovis Bueno; costume design, Isabela Braga; assistant director, Vincente Amorim; associate producer, Kinga Kozdron; casting, Mary Jo Slater, Isabel Diegues (Brazil). Reviewed on Live vidcassette, N.Y., Jan. 3, 1993. MPAA Rating: R. Running time: **92 MIN.**

January 11, 1993 (Cont.)

David	Sasha Mitchell
Xian	Dennis Chan
Lane	Richard Comar
Marcos	Noah Verduzco
Martine	Ian Jacklin
Isabella	Althea Miranda
Sergeant	Milton Goncalves

Third entry in the series that four years ago helped make Jean-Claude Van Damme a star is a routine martial arts pic that benefits from attractive Brazilian location photography. Briefly released theatrically last fall, film has better-than-average chances for a video following.

Repeating from part two, Sasha Mitchell plays the uppity hero, a kickboxing champ headed to Rio de Janeiro for a tournament. Once arrived, Mitchell is befriended by street urchin Noah Verduzco and saves his young sister (Althea Miranda) from the clutches of brothel owner Richard Comar.

Coincidentally, Comar also manages evil kickboxer Ian Jacklin. Predictably Miranda is kidnapped and Mitchell is ordered to throw the big match against Jacklin to protect her. A corny happy ending sets the stage for yet another sequel.

Mitchell, unlike most of the protagonists in this genre an actor first and martial artist second, is a very personable lead and acquits himself well in the action scenes. Supporting cast is nondescript. — *Lawrence Cohn*

WE'RE TALKIN' SERIOUS MONEY

An RS Entertainment release of a Cinetel Films production. Executive producer, Harold Welb. Produced by Paul Hertzberg. Directed by James Lemmo. Screenplay, Leo Rossi, Lemmo; camera (Foto-Kem color), Jacques Haitkin; editor, Steve Nevius; music, Scott Grusin; sound (Ultra-Stereo), William M. Fiege; assistant director, Whitney Hunter; stunt coordinator, Spiro Razatos; co-producers, Lisa M. Hansen, Rossi; associate producer, Catalaine Knell; casting, Susan Bluestein. Reviewed on Columbia TriStar vidcassette, N.Y., Jan. 2, 1993. MPAA Rating: PG-13. Running time: **91 MIN.**

Sal	Dennis Farina
Charlie	Leo Rossi
Valerie	Fran Drescher
Jacubicki	Denis Arndt
Michael	Robert Costanzo
Gino the Grocer	John La Motta
Marty the Greek	John Kapelos
Rosemarie	Catherine Paolone
Frankie the Beast	Peter Iacangelo
Amelia	Jeanie Moore

This pleasant comedy about a pair of small-time operators got overlooked in the distribution wars when it was released theatrically last spring, but is well worth a look.

It's the brainchild of actor Leo Rossi, most familiar from his roles in Jonathan Kaplan pics like "The Accused" and "Heart Like a Wheel." As co-writer/co-producer he's made amusing roles for himself and Dennis Farina as Italian-American bumblers.

Farina concocts a scheme to steal bearer bonds and lets his best pal Rossi in on the deal. Borrowing front money from local tough guy Gino the Grocer (John La Motta), duo procede to bungle the job and have to flee New York for Los Angeles.

There they accidentally become involved in a blackmail scam involving old buddy Marty the Greek (John Kapelos). Though set in the world of crime, film contrives a light, happy ending of Farina's very Italian wedding.

What makes this work is the well-matched teaming of Farina, playing very straight as the dense member of the duo, and Rossi as the flaky hothead. They give a fresh look to the overworked of late Italian crime milieu.

Supporting cast is well-chosen for ethnic credibility, including brassy leading lady Fran Drescher. — *Lawrence Cohn*

LA MEMORIA DEL AGUA
(MEMORY OF THE WATER)
(SPANISH-B&W)

A Grup Cinema-Art S.L. production. Executive producer, Luis Serra Sanvicens. Directed by Hector Faver. Screenplay, Faver, Eugenia Kleber. Camera (B&W) Gerard Gormezano; editor, Faver, Manuel Alminana; music, Lito Vitale; art direction, Kleber; sound, Alminana, Daniel Fontrodona. Reviewed at Boston Film Festival, Sept. 10, 1992. Running time: **79 MIN.**

With: Boris Rotenstein, Isabel Abad, Cristina Peralta.

Amply proving that good intentions are not enough to ensure a worthy result, this film about the Holocaust perhaps should have had more of a reason to exist. What will it add to the discussion? Filmmaker Hector Faver obviously didn't bother to ask. Result is amateurish and offensive.

It purports to be a meditation on memory, focusing on the question of how a survivor of Nazi atrocities is supposed to transmit that history to the next generation without doing more harm than good. Faver and co-writer Eugenia Kleber follow the story of Joseph Gruferman (played by Boris Rotenstein) in the days leading up to his death, and his final message to his daughter.

The black & white footage ranges from photos to static shots to newsreels to pictures of the nondescript streets where Gruferman lived. There is no dialogue, only a series of monologues by Gruferman, his wife and his daughter. Several are just an actor talking at the camera.

Interspersed with this material is footage of naked corpses being thrown into pits. This and other concentration camp material is misused here, over-providing the dramatic shock Faver's own footage lacks.

Tech credits are as spotty as the script: Visuals vary from scene to scene, and editing further isolates death camp footage as if to emphasize it has no connection with the rest of the film.

In the end, pic yields no insights, just endless arty poses as life and death are compared to the endless flow of a brook. — *Daniel M. Kimmel*

SEARCH FOR DIANA
(CANADIAN)

A Twinbay Media Intl. Ltd. production. Produced, directed by Milad Bessada. Screenplay, Maissa Bessada Patton, Milad Bessada. Camera (color), Derick Underschultz; editor, Teresa Hannigan; music, Omar Khayrat; costumes, Cori Burchell; choreography, Diana Calenti. Reviewed Aug. 29, 1992, at Montreal World Film Festival. Running time: **90 MIN.**

Diana	Diana Calenti
Graves	Brett Halsey
Jenny	Janet Richardson
Malek	Jan Filips
Dr. Woodshouse	Corrine Conley

"Search for Diana" is a hopeless, laugh-out-loud ludicrous muddle of New Age mysticism and ancient Egyptian mythology. Commercial prospects are practically nonexistent.

That this "Search" was made by Milad Bessada, a veteran of the classic "SCTV" comedy series, might indicate pic is intended as some kind of joke. But no. "Diana" is painfully sincere.

Dancer-choreographer Diana Calenti, a U.S. native and Canadian resident who's reportedly a cult figure in Egypt, plays a Toronto choreographer troubled by visions of her past life as a high priestess in the days of Akhenaton. The character's name is Diana, and her specialty is Egyptian-flavored choreography. Make of that what you will.

"Search for Diana" has several long, awkwardly photographed dance sequences that aren't especially impressive. But they are far superior to the dopey drama. Calenti is a singularly inept actress, but at least her dancing is lithe and energetic.

After an hour of non-drama in Toronto, Diana flies to Egypt, where her best friend, an archaeologist (Brett Halsey) is so troubled by his own past-life visions he nearly sacrifices her to the ancient gods. No kidding. — *Joe Leydon*

NIE WIEDER SCHLAFFEN
(NEVER SLEEP AGAIN)
(GERMAN)

A Filmwelt release. Produced by Vega Film, Berlin. Directed by Pia Frankenberg. Screenplay, Frankenberg, Karin Aström. Camera (color), Judith Kaufmann; editors, Raimund Barthelmes, Angelika Sengbusch; music, Loek Dikker; production design, Uli Fischer; costumes, Irmgard Kersting; sound, Gunther Kortwich. Reviewed at Lupe 1 Cinema, Berlin, Nov. 2, 1992. Running time: **92 MIN.**

Rita	Lisa Kreutzer
Roberta	Gaby Herz
Lilian	Christiane Carstens
Followed Man	Ernst Stötzner
Matthias	Michael Altmann

This well-intentioned art film becomes as aimless as its characters: three women stranded in Berlin. Despite its title, it will bed down quickly.

The ultimately aimless trio includes Rita, single and in her 40s; Roberta, 30ish and married with a kid; and Lilian, who videotapes a lot, interviewing the people she encounters, meandering through the reunified city.

Attending a wedding, the trio lands in Berlin, wandering the streets, subways, parks and cafés of the city with little story to hang it all on. Film has a docu feel and scripting was apparently minimal. It is obvious the women are emblematic of some aspect of society and that their encounter with Berlin represents worlds, cultures and values colliding, but further explanations are not forthcoming.

The film's sound mix grates, and badly chosen musical tracks are inexpertly woven into the audio. — *Rebecca Lieb*

TO SLEEP WITH A VAMPIRE

A Concorde production. Executive producer, Roger Corman. Produced by Mike Elliott. Directed by Adam Friedman. Screenplay, Patricia Harrington. Camera (color), Michael Craine; editor, Lorne Morris; music, Nigel Holton; casting, Andrew Hertz. Reviewed on vidcassette, N.Y., Jan. 5, 1992. MPAA Rating: R. Running time: **76 MIN.**
With: Scott Valentine, Charlie Spradling, Richard Zobel, Ingrid Void, Stephanie Hardy.

"**T**o Sleep With a Vampire" is a middling horror pic, with an interesting story undermined by atrocious acting and unfocused helming. Film has had theatrical dates but is likely to head soon to video.

The premise is considerably more accomplished than the execution, chiefly since this is another of Concorde's rapid-fire remakes, the second culled from the work of ex-Roger Cormanite Katt Shea Ruben. Weirder is

Original film: DANCE OF THE DAMNED

A Concorde Pictures presentation of a New Classics production. Produced by Andy Ruben. Directed by Katt Shea Ruben. Screenplay, Ruben, Shea Ruben. Camera (Foto-Kem color), Phedon Papamichael; editor, Carole Kravetz; music, Gary Stockdale; sound, Michael Clark; production design, Stephen Greenberg; special effects, Steve Neill; choreography, Ted Lin; co-producers, Shane, Anna Rock. Reviewed on Virgin Vision vidcassette, N.Y., Mar. 29, 1989. (In AFI Festival, L.A.) MPAA Rating: R. Running time: **83 MIN.**

the fact the studio has remade a film it chose not to release in the first place.

The original film, "Dance of the Damned," was shown at the AFI's 1989 Festival of Independent Films but was not given a theatrical release. Released on videotape by Concorde's prestige label, Classic Films, pic has won a small cult and screened at N.Y.'s Museum of Modern Art.

Like the first film, "To Sleep" features a suicidal stripper (Charlie Spradling) who attracts a vampire (Scott Valentine) who only feeds on hopeless wretches no one will miss. Taking her to his apartment, he promises to end her pain by sunrise, but asks in return to be told about the daylight he can never experience.

The original film worked sensitively and sometimes poetically, mainly through the solid performances of the leads, Starr Andreeff and Cyril O'Reilly. Here, the emphasis is on Valentine's scroungy bloodsucker and Spradling's busty bod, but her line readings are flat and his thesping is mostly wild stares and "dramatic" head movements.

Helmer Adam Friedman, who won some good notices for his debut, "Medium Straight," is clearly not in his element here, using lunar imagery so persistantly the film looks like a werewolf movie. Most dialogue is taken word for word from the original, with the few additions excruciatingly poor.

Special effects are lackluster but new feature does have a clearer sound mix than its predecessor. — *Fred Lombardi*

HAWAII INTL. FEST

A WEEKEND WITH BARBARA UND INGRID

A Rabbit in the Moon Films production for IRS Media. Executive producer, Steven Lovy. Produced, directed, written by Gregory Neri. Camera (color), Steven Timberlake; editor, Dave Notowitz; music, Steven Lovy, Tim Kelly; production design, Robert Lovy; costume design, Lyda Anderson; sound, Stephen Brown; co-producer, Bruce Royer. Reviewed at Hawaii Intl. Film Festival, Honolulu, Dec. 12, 1992. Running time: **93 MIN.**
Danny Shaffer . . . . Jim Metzler
Barbara . . . . Anna Katarina
Ingrid . . . . Michelle Holms
Jerzy Louis . . . . John Fleck
Claire . . . . Megan Warner
Jack . . . . Bob Cady
Also with: Steven Reich, Ed You, Noreen Hennessy, Peter Quartaroli, Steve Hunter, Jay Adams, Lyda Anderson, Fabio Golombek.

Fans of the Jim Jarmusch school of oblique modern angst may enjoy the ennui-ridden "Weekend With Barbara und Ingrid." Unfortunately, Gregory Neri's mild story — about a lovelorn L.A. man and two German women who suddenly drop in — doesn't add up to enough to attract a wider aud.

Quizzical-looking Jim Metzler, after impressive hard-ass roles in "Delusion" and "One False Move," gets to play for sardonic laughs here. As Danny Shaffer, a poet-turned-businessman mourning his girlfriend's abrupt departure, Metzler is fun to watch, but he doesn't have enough to do after Barbara und Ingrid arrive.

These enigmatic tourists bear tidings from his idealized ex (seen only in photos and Super-8 clips) who's now in Berlin; their presence challenges Danny to reexamine his choices.

Danny's uninvited visitors may be goosing him to come out of his shell, but they're basically ciphers themselves. Dark-haired Anna Katarina invests the knowing Barbara with some earthy mystery, but Michelle Holmes' screechy Ingrid comes across as little more than an annoying child. And it doesn't help that the odd pair is hung up on a lame TV comic called Jerzy Louis — a thin joke even if the part had been better written — or that their intermittent German chatter was obviously dubbed in later.

What makes "Weekend" worth watching is Steve Timberlake's inventive lensing, which invests mundane images with magical light and blends them seamlessly with Robert Lovy's fanciful sets. Haunting piano music also adds a thoughtful tone.

Some auds may feel cheated by pic's promise of *menage-à-trois* action (there's no sex in sight), but Neri somehow makes the nonevents bouyant enough to keep patient viewers engaged. — *Ken Eisner*

HARRY BRIDGES: A MAN AND HIS UNION (DOCU)

A Cinema Guild production of an MW production. (Intl. sales: Cinema Guild, N.Y.) Produced, directed by Berry Minnott. Written by James Hamilton. Camera (color), John Knoop; editor, Veronica Selver; music, Mark Adler, Pete Seeger; sound, Leslie Schatz, Richard Boch. Reviewed at Hawaii Intl. Film Festival, Honolulu, Dec. 5, 1992. (In Sundance Film Festival.) Running time: **58 MIN.**
Narrator: Studs Terkel.

This fast-moving docu about a colorful and celebrated union man will be as interesting to those without a detailed knowledge of U.S. labor history as to those in the know, and a good antidote to "Hoffa."

Through archival footage, newspaper clips and talking heads, a significant era is well evoked: In the early '30s, workers were hired and fired on managers' whims and longshoremen toiled on San Francisco docks for a pittance. The Australian-born Harry Bridges, with his huge, crooked nose and cantankerous wit, hit this Depression scene like a bolt of lightning, organizing unprecedented strikes and making unheard-of demands.

As his power in the Intl. Longshoreman's and Warehouseman's Union grew, shipowners tried to threaten and bribe Bridges (once offering him $100,000 to go home), and later, a Cold War-gripped U.S. government tarred him as a communist and tried to deport him as a dangerous alien. Although Bridges' allies — and personal proclivities — leaned strongly to the left, the charismatic leader was always able to stay free, with even some of his former enemies speaking up for him.

Still, the years of trials and accusations took their toll, and this generally reverential profile suggests he was consumed by paranoia in the years before his death, at 89, in 1990. In the end, Bridges and his union were defeated more by automation than malice, but it was a good fight while it lasted.

One of the most fascinating aspects seen here is his extensive postwar work on behalf of Hawaiians laboring like plantation-era slaves, and his marriage to a Japanese internment-camp survivor also intrigues. It's a tribute to the late leader's success in improving his followers' lives that helmer Berry Minnott was able

to find so many articulate long-shoremen to talk, affectionately and honestly, about their hero.
— *Ken Eisner*

CAIRO INTL. FEST

DE NØGNE TRÆER
(THE NAKED TREES)
(DANISH)

A Warner-Metronome release of a Lise Lense-Möller Film/Danmarks Radio/Filmeffekt/Norsk Film/Hemdale/Studio TOR production. Executive producer, Lise Lense-Möller. Produced by Per Aarman, Lene Nielsen. Directed by Morten Henriksen. Screenplay, Henriksen, from Tage Skou-Hansen's novel. Camera (color), Dirk Brüel; editor, Ghita Beckerdorff; sound, Erik Ryr; production design, Palle Arestrup; costumes, Lotte Dandanell; music, Marc Marder. Reviewed at the Danish Film Studio, Copenhagen, Dec. 4, 1991. (In Cairo Film Festival.) Running time: **100 MIN.**
Holger Mikkelsen . . . . Ole Lemmeke
Gerda Borck . . . . Lena Nilsson
Christian Borck . . . Michael Moritzen
Leo . . . . Per Morberg
Also with: Lars Simonsen, Joy Maria Frederiksen, Sören Sätter-Lassen, John Hahn-Petersen, Waage Sandö.

This handsomely mounted, faithful adaptation of a w.k. postwar Danish bestseller offers excellent thesping, taut drama and even some action. Nevertheless home b.o. proved disappointing; imminent homevid release will likely do little to improve on it.

The talented Ole Lemmeke deservedly won best actor award at the recent Cairo fest for his stunning portrayal of a nihilistic law student who dabbles with sabotage in occupied 1943 Denmark. He graduates to major league sabotage when he is recruited by a Resistance ringleader (Michael Moritzen). Besides fighting the Nazis Holger devotes his time and effort to a passionate affair with Moritzen's wife (Lena Nilsson). However love and war turns out to be a dangerous cocktail.

"The Naked Trees" is by far the best piece of cinema among several Danish Resistance fighter pics of recent years. Helmer Morten Henriksen makes a promising bow with his tight adaptation of Tage Skou-Hansen's popular 1957 novel, offering hard-hitting dialogue and well-rounded characters.

Tech credits are fine; produced for a mere $2.5 million, pic decidedly delivers value for money.
— *Peter Risby Hansen*

INTL. HOF DAYS

DIE SERPENTINEN-TÄNZERIN
(THE SERPENTINE DANCER)
(GERMAN-HUNGARIAN)

A Dragon-Cine/Thees Klahn production in association with Hetföi Mühely/Novoskop Film/Royal Film, Budapest/SWF. Produced by Thees Klahn. Directed by Helmut Herbst. Screenplay, Herbst, Istvan Kardos. Camera, Sandor Kardos; editor, Renate Merck; sound, Janos Cski; music, Claus Bantzer; production design, Andras Gyürki; costumes, Janos Breckl; makeup, Magdolena Marta, Edit Basilidesz. Production Hungary, Pál Erdöss. Reviewed at Intl. Hof Film Days, Oct. 30, 1992. Running time: **86 MIN.**
Olga . . . . Karina Fallenstein
Bianca . . . . Eva Mattes
Viktor . . . . Ben Becker
Giovanni . . . . Wolf-Dietrich Sprenger
Clemens Conrad . . . . . . Otto Sander

A glossy attempt at a classy erotic costume film, "Die Serpentinentänzerin" is a well-photographed bore that pays off on none of its promises. Everything falls flat as the script skitters from one subject to another — passion, conflict, the early fascination of cinema — never focusing long enough to gain the slightest drama from them.

A traveling vaudeville show is the backdrop for this exploration of the opening skirmishes in the struggle between stage and screen for the mass audience at the turn of the century: a perfect opportunity to fill the screen with offbeat characters and strangely romantic moments. But it never really happens.

It's hard to say just who the main characters are here, and what their conflict is. Viktor (played woodenly by Ben Becker) is a photographer's son convinced movies have a future. Olga (an uninspired Karina Fallenstein) is a lithe, mute "serpentine" dancer in a traveling vaudeville act. Giovanni (capably acted by Wolf-Dietrich Sprenger) is the troupe's director, who knows that films will eventually put him out of business.

The drama, a love triangle that includes Fallenstein and Sprenger, begins when Becker is hired to travel with the little circus. But when Becker leaves the show, taking Olga, he also removes the conflict, which doesn't seem to bother co-scripter-director Helmut Herbst.

In fact, it seems that Herbst and co-scripter Istvan Kardos have done their best to avoid any kind of conflict, although every once in a while someone wrestles in the mud or shouts nasty names.

Production design and photography are professional and inviting, accenting bright circus colors and offbeat images, but all the acting is uninspired, including the usually fine Eva Mattes and Otto Sander. With so unambitious a script, no one can blame them. — *Eric Hansen*

ALIVE

A Buena Vista Pictures release of a Touchstone Pictures and Paramount Pictures presentation of a Kennedy/Marshall production. Produced by Robert Watts, Kathleen Kennedy. Directed by Frank Marshall. Screenplay, John Patrick Shanley, from Piers Paul Read's book. Camera (Gastown Film Labs color; Technicolor prints), Peter James; editors, Michael Kahn, William Goldenberg; music, James Newton Howard; production design, Norman Reynolds; art direction, Frederick Hole; set decoration, Tedd Kuchera; costume design, Jennifer Parsons; sound (Dolby), Eric Batut; co-producer, Bruce Cohen; assistant director, Katterli Frauenfelder; 2nd-unit director, Reynolds; special effects makeup design, Gordon Smith; visual effects producer, Jil-Sheree Bergin; casting, Michael Fenton, Valorie Massalas. Reviewed at Avco Center Cinema, L.A., Jan. 11, 1993. MPAA Rating: R. Running time: **127 MIN.**
Nando Parrado . . . . . . Ethan Hawke
Antonio Balbi . . . . . . Vincent Spano
Roberto Canessa . . . . Josh Hamilton
Carlitos Paez . . . . . . Bruce Ramsay
Tintin . . . . . . John Haymes Newton
Gustavo Zerbino . . . . . David Kriegel
Roy Harley . . . . . Kevin Breznahan
Javier Methol . . . . Sam Behrens
Lilliana Methol . . . . . Illeana Douglas
Bobby Francois . . . Jack Noseworthy
Federico Aranda . . . . Christian Meoli

Though Touchstone has made a point of marketing "Alive" as a heroic tale of survival, the bottom-line on this well-crafted effort is whether auds will line up for what can only be called an unappetizing premise. The film is neither the exploitative gross-out teens might be looking for nor quite the rousing adventure it needs to be. Pickings should be slim for this uphill marketing climb.

Producer-turned-director Frank Marshall proved his credentials in the latter regard on the underrated "Arachnophobia" but faces much the same problem here: A concept that will ward off an ample number of moviegoers, however well done.

This time, Marshall and producer-partner-spouse Kathleen Kennedy have chosen the true story (already told by the 1976 Par release "Survive!") of a 1970s plane crash in which the survivors, a rugby team, held on for more than two months in the subfreezing Andes largely by eating the corpses of the victims.

Marshall and writer John Patrick Shanley deal with the topic seriously, exploring the survivors' desperation as well as their reluctance, down to an ethical debate prior to the initial meal, to engage in cannibalism.

The filmmakers don't shy away from the issue or dwell on it excessively, and the cannibalism itself proves less off-putting than the generally grueling nature of the story (what might be called "Lorenzo's Oil" syndrome), notwithstanding Shanley's game, sometimes (but not literally) disarming efforts to dot the screenplay with gallows humor.

It's doubtful many moviegoers will be eager to endure the same ordeal, and the heroic elements, as the survivors' ranks dwindle, aren't uplifting enough to make it worthwhile.

It doesn't help that character personalities generally aren't distinct enough to keep track of who's who throughout the story, leaving the audience to empathize only generally. Heightening the problem is a strong physical resemblance among some actors, including leads Ethan Hawke and Josh Hamilton.

Marshall and company also seem to suffer some indecision as to how maudlin they can be. They give in to temptation and provide some big emotional flourishes during the early phases, for example, but end the film on a more restrained note and somewhat abruptly as well. As a result, they bypass the seemingly obligatory moment when Hawke and Hamilton — having wandered through the mountains seeking help — encounter someone, anyone, from the outside world.

For all its action elements, "Alive" also puts on some rather pretentious airs, among them a musical coda of "Ave Maria" and bookending an uncredited John Malkovich as one of the survivors, 20 years later.

Despite the film's shortcomings, one has to admire the perfs Marshall elicits from his largely unknown cast under apparently torturous conditions.

Technical achievements are also considerable, particularly the jaw-dropping crash sequence, courtesy of Industrial Light & Magic, in which the plane comes apart before our eyes, sucking out several passengers.

Peter James' cinematography captures the sweeping mountain vistas, in stark contrast to the cramped surroundings of the plane's cabin, where the survivors huddle seeking refuge from the blistering cold.

For all its good intentions, however, audiences will also likely seek refuge from "Alive," at least until it reaches the relative safety of homevideo. Or, as more than one viewer has doubtless mused, this isn't exactly a big popcorn movie. — *Brian Lowry*

LEPRECHAUN

A Trimark Pictures release. Executive producer, Mark Amin. Produced by Jeffrey B. Mallian. Directed, written by Mark Jones. Camera (CFI color), Levie Isaacks; editor, Christopher Roth; music, Kevin Kiner; production design, Naomi Slodki; costume design, Holly Davis; sound (Ultra-Stereo), Michael Florimbi, Geoffrey Patterson; assistant director, Adam Taylor; Leprechaun makeup effects, Atlantic West Effects, Gabe Z. Bartalos; animatronics, Dave Kindlon; stunt coordinator, Cole McKay; supervising producer, Jim Beggs; co-producers, Michael Prescott, David Price, William Sachs; associate producer, Barry Barnholtz; casting, Lisa London. Reviewed at 34th St. Showplace 3, N.Y., Jan. 8, 1993. MPAA Rating: R. Running time: **92 MIN.**

Leprechaun	Warwick Davis
Tory	Jennifer Aniston
Nathan	Ken Olandt
Ozzie	Mark Holton
Alex	Robert Gorman
J.D.	John Sanderford
Dan O'Grady	Shay Duffin
Leah O'Grady	Pamela Mant
Pawn shop owner	John Volstad
Sheriff Cronin	William Newman
Deputy Tripet	David Permenter

"Leprechaun" is a dull, unscary horror movie whose sole selling point is some extraneous gore footage.

Concept of making the mischievous figure of Irish legend into a pint-sized Freddy Krueger is unworkable to start with, and writer-director Mark Jones doesn't try very hard to provide anything interesting.

Prologue details greedy, drunken Shay Duffin returning home to America from Ireland with 100 gold coins he's stolen from a leprechaun. The leprechaun (Warwick Davis) is angry but with the aid of a four-leaf clover (sort of Kryptonite to the Irish fellow) Duffin traps him in a crate.

Suffering a heart attack, Duffin's put in a rest home and film proper picks up 10 years later when lovely Jennifer Aniston and her dad John Sanderford move into Duffin's vacant house.

Of course the leprechaun is set loose and he's still hankering for his gold. With local hunk Ken Olandt, his young brother Robert Gorman and others, our heroes laboriously kill the leprechaun. But a concluding voiceover indicates he'll be back.

Warwick Davis, who had a prominent role in Ron Howard's "Willow," doesn't get to act much here. He's covered with Gabe Bartalos' thick makeup and given consistently unfunny wisecracks to utter. Many risible moments have him riding a tricycle or other undersize vehicles.

The filmmakers tip their hand when ordinary violence turns to extreme gore, notably a scene of the leprechaun ripping out a cop's eye for a replacement after the heroine pokes out his own. This throwback to exploitation films is a crass aspect in a film that is otherwise squeaky clean, especially in its eschewing of sex.

Cast is effective, especially comic Mark Holton as a retarded man who helps keep the minimal plot going. — *Lawrence Cohn*

MIN STORE TJOCKE FAR
(MY BIG FAT FATHER)
(SWEDISH)

Sandrews presents a Movie Makers/Omega Film & Television/Svenska Filminstitutet/Sveriges Television TV2/Sandrew Film & Teater/Nordisk film-&-TV-fond/Mefistofilm production. Produced by Bert Sundberg & Anders Granström. Directed by Kjell-Åke Anderssen. Screenplay, Anderssen, Magnus Nilsson. Camera (color), Per Källberg; editor Susanne Linnman; production design, Birgitta Brensén, Stig Boqvist; costumes, Malin Bergendal; sound, Wille Peterson Berger, Jean-Fréderique Axelsson, Christer Furubrand; assistant directors, Bengt Widell, Nina Grunfeldt. Reviewed at Astoria Cinema, Stockholm, Nov. 16, 1992. Running time: **102 MIN.**

With: Rolf Lassgård, Ann Petrén, Nick Börjlind, Gunilla Röör, Krister Henriksson, Lena Strömdahl, Halvar Björk.

This uneven Scandi tragicomedy succeeds in part due to excellent thesps but will not travel any great distance.

Co-scripter Nilsson based his story on memories of his own father and their relationship when he was a young boy. In the film, 11-year-old Osvald worships his father (Rolf Lassgård) as a hero; however, the outwardly hopeful man with an enormous appetite for life is haunted by demons forcing him to drink excessively and openly philander.

The very uneven film chronicles Osvald's gradual realization of both his father's weaknesses and strengths, mixing moving or absurbly comic scenes with stiff stretches that need trimming. The main assets are the acting —especially Lassgård, who makes the father a very believeable, involving character — and the excellent, often moody, cinematography of Per Källberg.
— *Gunnar Rehlin*

A L'HEURE OU LES GRANDS FAUVES VONT BOIRE
(WHEN THE JUNGLE CATS GO TO DRINK)
(FRENCH-SWISS)

A Les Films Ariane release of a La Film Cie./Odessa Films/Les Prods. JMH/La Télévision Suisse-Romande co-production with the participation of Investimage 4/Sofiarp/Canal Plus/the CNC/the Federal Dept. of the Interior (Berne). Produced by La Film Cie., Odessa Films. Directed by Pierre Jolivet. Screenplay, Jolivet, Laurent Bachet. Camera (color), Bertrand Chatry; editor, Jean-François Naudon; music, Serge Perathoner, Jannick Top; set design, Laurent Allaire; costumes, Nathalie Desandre; sound, Yves Osmu; assistant director, Pablo Fréville. Reviewed at Club de l'Etoile screening room, Paris, Jan. 6, 1993. Running time: **77 MIN.**

Adrien	Eric Métayer
Yoska	Marc Jolivet
Elle	Isabelle Gélinas
The Cousin	Francçois Berléand
The Mother	Arlette Thomas

Also with: Christophe Bourseiller, Maka Kooto, Christophe de Barallon.

Returning to humor after two ambitious action dramas ("Force Majeure," "Simple Mortel"), versatile Pierre Jolivet has crafted a sweetly performed but minor pic. The jaunty, offbeat seduction comedy "A l'Heure Ou Les Grands Fauves Vont Boire" is probably too slight to move into other markets except on the tube.

Title of pic, shot in springtime Paris and on brightly hued studio sets, is that of a TV docu on African wildlife a woman known only as "Elle" (Isabelle Gélinas) wants to make. Adrien (renowned improv comic Eric Métayer), who assesses TV scripts, is haunted by a dream in which he nearly seduces Galina in a theatrically decorated bedroom.

On the theory that if he has the dream-boudoir built, she will come, Métayer enlists immigrant buddy Yoska (helmer's bro, stage comic Marc Jolivet, using a delightful put-on accent), who is a carpenter.

Support — Yoska's ailing mom, the "cousin" (François Berléand), a writer who's tailed Métayer since he rejected a script — deliver nice perfs.

But despite the good thesping, the whimsy is spread too thin and, though lensed with flair, the pic doesn't delve deeply enough into the variables that can make or break seduction.

— *Lisa Nesselson*

COMME UN BATEAU LA MER EN MOINS
(LIKE A BOAT OUT OF WATER)
(FRENCH)

A Belbo Films production. Executive Producer, Catherine Scheinman. Produced by Ludi Boeken, Jacques Fansten. Directed by Dominique Ladoge. Screenplay, Ladoge, Claude Gutman. Camera (color), Etienne Faudet; editor, Didier Ranz; music, Michel Coeuriot; production design, Dominique Maleret; sound, Jean-Louis Ducarme. Reviewed at Festival of Festivals, Toronto, Sept. 15, 1992. Running time: **99 MIN.**
With: Mathias Leny, Patrick Fierry, Alexandra Vandernoot.

Another perceptive film about childhood to emerge from France, "Like a Boat Out of Water" is a decent, intelligent debut for director Dominique Ladoge. But the emotions depicted here are very slight, and the film is unlikely to fare as well as the same production company's recent minor hit, "Cross My Heart." Racism is the implied theme here, an important subject in France (indeed in Europe) today, but tackled so gently that no feathers are likely to be ruffled.

Fabien (Mathias Leny) is a 9-year-old whose father is an itinerant worker. They live in a trailer and have been based in the South of France, but the father's work takes him to the chill, clammy north of the country. He's mocked by a teacher for his southern accent and bullied by other boys, who call him "gypsy" for the way he lives. He eventually befriends some real gypsies, which brings them unexpected trouble — and more racism.

Ladoge gets sensitive performances from his young actors, but doesn't probe the subject of racism too deeply. The result is a well-made but somewhat frustrating, overlong and predictable, film. — *David Stratton*

ETHAN FROME

A Miramax release of an American Playhouse Theatrical Films presentation produced in association with Richard Price/BBC Films. Executive producers, Lindsay Law, Price. Produced by Stan Wlodkowski. Directed by John Madden. Screenplay, Richard Nelson, from Edith Wharton's novel. Camera (Duart color), Bobby Bukowski; editor, Katherine Wenning; music, Rachel Portman; production design, Andrew Jackness; art direction, David Crank; set decoration, Joyce Anne Gilstrap; costume design, Carol Oditz; sound (Dolby), Paul Cote; associate producer, Johlyn Dale; assistant director, Allan Nicholls; casting, Billy Hopkins, Suzanne Smith. Reviewed at Palm Springs Intl. Film Festival, Jan. 8, 1993. MPAA Rating: PG. Running time: **99 MIN.**
Ethan Frome . . . . Liam Neeson
Mattie Silver . . . . . Patricia Arquette
Zeena Frome . . . . .Joan Allen
Reverend Smith . . . . . Tate Donovan
Mrs. Hale . . . . Katharine Houghton
Ned Hale . . . . Stephen Mendillo
Young Ruth Hale . . . . Debbon Ayer
Jotham . . . . George Woodard
Denis Eady . . . . Jay Goede
Young Ned Hale . . . . . Rob Campbell

"Ethan Frome" is the quintessential American Playhouse movie: careful, literary, restrained, nicely acted and more than a bit dry. Miramax should get some reviews and fair returns from its theatrical run, but this intimate tragedy of three stunted lives in rural New England may actually play better on the small screen.

Gary Cooper was ideally cast in WB's aborted 1940s effort to film Edith Wharton's pitiless short novel and Cooper comes instantly to mind upon seeing Liam Neeson in the part.

Almost a giant but possessed of a gentle, soft voice and inner reserves released only shyly and sparingly, from the outset Neeson cuts an indelible image dragging his hulking, disfigured frame across the snowy landscape.

A friend of Ethan's family (Katharine Houghton) tells a newly arrived minister (Tate Donovan) the sad story of the once-promising young man who, as we see in flashback, took over his mother's farm upon her death and married the splintery woman, Zeena (Joan Allen), who nursed her during her fatal illness.

Zeena herself soon becomes a professional invalid. When she calls upon her destitute cousin Mattie Silver (Patricia Arquette) to help her at home, Ethan becomes enraptured by the young, spirited girl, and takes advantage of his wife's overnight absence to start a romance.

But destiny, conventional morality, Ethan's hesitancy, Zeena's zeal and the frigid, paralytic New England atmosphere all insure the affair will end badly. Even if the intentionality of the "accident" that seals the lovers' fate is fudged in the telling here, the film effectively renders Wharton's horrifying climactic irony.

Most of the action involves commonplace events behind which seethes repressed love, bitterness, frustrated ambition, and a sense of lives made small by constraining social expectations and expected behavior.

Screenwriter Richard Nelson has done a solid job of adhering to the spirit and intentions, if not the letter, of Wharton's chillingly deterministic tale, but first-time feature director John Madden's pretty pictures and earnest storytelling provide neither a filter of irony nor a nearly unbearable sense of emotional suffocation, either of which would have lent the film a valid p.o.v.

This stands as a genteel, polite adaptation of a caustic, surgically precise book. No visual equivalent for her literary carving was found for pic.

Still, Neeson makes an superb Ethan, a big man made small by his willingness to submit to the mean-spirited, manipulative Zeena. In the latter part, which could have been one-dimensional, Joan Allen takes the thesping honors, as she strikes many unexpected and subtle notes in a very powerful characterization. Patricia Arquette is an eminently suitable Mattie, although one can imagine a more heartbreaking rendition of the part.

Lensed on superb authentic locations in upstate Vermont, pic looks fine, and is dramatically maximized by Rachel Portman's score, richly full-bodied with just-right hint of foreboding.
— *Todd McCarthy*

THE HARVEST

A Curb Musifilm/Mike Curb & Lester Korn presentation in association with Ron Stone Prods. of a Morgan Mason/Jason Clark production from RCA/Columbia TriStar Home Video. Executive producers, Stone, Carole Curb Nemoy, David A. Jackson. Produced by Clark, Mason. Directed, written by David Marconi. Camera (CFI color), Emmanuel Lubezki; supervising editor, Hubert C. de La Bouillerie; editor, Carlos Puente; music, Dave Allen, Rick Boston; production design, J. Rae Fox; visual consultant, Alex Tavoularis; set decoration, Graciela Torres; costume design, Ileana Meltzer; sound (Ultra-Stereo), Alex Silvi, Salvador De La Fuente; associate producers, Tammy Apana, Peter Nelson; assistant director, Sebastian Silva; 2nd-unit camera, Xavier Perez Grobet; casting, Rick Montgomery, Dan Parada. Reviewed at Chicago Intl. Film Festival, Oct. 17, 1992. (In Palm Springs Intl. Film Festival.) Running time: **97 MIN.**
Charlie Pope . . . . Miguel Ferrer
Natalie Caldwell
. . . . Leilani Sarelle Ferrer
Bob Lakin . . . . . Harvey Fierstein
Noel Guzmann . Anthony John Denison
Steve Mobley . . . . . Tim Thomerson
Hank . . . . Matt Clark
Detective Topo . . . . Henry Silva

An atmospheric but rather silly crime meller about a bunch of gringos stirring up trouble south of the border, "The Harvest" gets by, to the extent it does, on style alone. Made for video release, this first feature by David Marconi has a big-screen look, and a theatrical release is reportedly being negotiated, but the real aud for this remains at home.

Miguel Ferrer plays the latest in a long line of *yanquis* who head for Mexico only to get in way over the heads with shady characters and local intrigue. The grungy screenwriter leaps at the chance offered by his ultra-crass producer (Harvey Fierstein) to hie to Costa Azul (actually Puerto Vallarta) to do some final research on his script's ending.

Ferrer checks into a wild hotel, a real hothouse where he stumbles onto the trail of some unsolved multiple murders. Following a lead to a gay disco, he has the amazing fortune to meet sultry Leilani Sarelle Ferrer (Sharon Stone's g.f. in "Basic Instinct"), who introduces herself by putting some ice down her pants, feeding it to him and meowing, "I like to get wet."

Thus enticed, Ferrer takes her out to the beach, where he's knocked out and abducted. When he awakens five days later, he finds that he's minus one kidney. At this point, most would figure it's time to cut their losses.

But not a sucker like Ferrer, who sticks around long enough

for the bad guys to want his other kidney. Plotting in the second half is ridiculously and gruesomely farfetched; the irony of Ferrer's pulling "Alice In Wonderland" off a shelf in one scene is not lost. Trick ending is glib and not unexpected.

If hard to recount with a straight face, Marconi and lenser Emmanuel Lubezki's luminous, sweaty-looking film exults in its exotic locations and its actors' faces and bodies. This is both the real Mexico and the Mexico of the imagination, and even if the film is 200 proof pulp, it has a certain resonance on a cartoony, fanciful level.

A handsome-ugly type like Jean-Paul Belmondo or David Carradine, Ferrer is a good, off-beat choice as a congenital loser who's just smart enough to stay alive. Sarelle obviously learned a lot at the Sharon Stone School of Acting, as she comes on like a forest fire, even looking more like her former co-star.

Fierstein seems to be doing a Joel Silver imitation as the hot-headed producer, and everyone playing villains seem to be enjoying themselves immensely. Pounding score is abrasive.

— Todd McCarthy

TROUBLE BOUND

An ITC Entertainment Group presentation. Executive producer, Wm. Christopher Gorog. Produced by Tom Kuhn, Fred Weintraub. Directed by Jeff Reiner. Screenplay, Darrell Fetty, Francis Delia. Camera (CFI color), Janusz Kaminski; editor, Neil Grieve; music, Vinnie Golia; production design, Richard Sherman; set decoration, Michael Warga; costume design, Merrie Lawson; sound (Ultra-Stereo), Giovanni Di Simone, Stephan Halbert (Arizona); assistant director, Rod Smith; 2nd-unit director, Andrea Kampic; 2nd-unit director/stunt coordinator, Rawn Hutchinson; additional camera, Jan Kiesser; casting, Mike Fenton, Jory Weitz. Reviewed at Palm Springs Intl. Film Festival, Jan. 9, 1993. Running time: **89 MIN.**
Harry Talbot . . . . . Michael Madsen
Kit Califano . . . . . Patricia Arquette
Granny . . . . Florence Stanley
Santino . . . . Seymour Cassel
Danny . . . . Sal Jenco
Zand . . . . Paul Ben-Victor
Raphael . . . . Darren Epton
Coldface . . . . . . Billy Bob Thornton
Ratman . . . . . . Rustam Branaman

"Trouble Bound" is a comic Southwestern neo-noir road movie that substitutes facetiousness for conviction and

trades in smarty-pants cleverness for its own sake. A synthetic indie item inspired completely by bits and pieces of movies too numerous to contemplate, this technically accomplished effort features some behavioral and pictorial niceties, but exists entirely within its narrowly self-referential world of crime film conventions. Some auds looking for shallow kicks and easy laughs might be amused, but this road doesn't lead much of anywhere.

"Blood and Concrete" director Jeff Reiner's new film will be compared to "Detour," "Something Wild" and "Blood Simple," among other notable crime-spree pics, and tries to mix tones and subvert clichés in ways that are at least theoretically appealing.

But a kind of self-consciously hip irreverence pervades the enterprise to the exclusion of anything that feels true or genuine. Tired of the usual Mafia dons? This crime family head is a little old lady. Sick of couples on the run fueled by sexual passion? Here the male lead gets to suffer rejection for most of the running time. In large measure, the film's absurdity simply seems absurd.

Familiar plot device has young floozy Patricia Arquette escaping three goons and imposing herself on ex-con Michael Madsen, who just happens to be driving through the desert to Nevada with a dead body in the trunk of his Cadillac.

While telling Madsen she's a sociology student, Arquette is, in fact, the daughter of a mobster rubbed out by another hood (Seymour Cassel) who is now the object of her vendetta. For his part, Madsen is pursued by killers of the guy in the trunk.

So while everyone here is chasing and being chased, Arquette does one number after another on the befuddled Madsen, who several times comes close to dumping the motormouthed nutcase by the side of the road, but keeps thinking he might get lucky.

One can credit Reiner with keeping his tank filled with high-octane gas, as the performances and pacing possess a pedal-to-the-metal momentum. But even the fancy camera moves involving speeding cars look as if drawn directly from the "Thelma & Louise" shot list, and the hectic pace ultimately makes the pic feel longer than its hour and a half.

In a role that couldn't be more different from her gentle work in "Ethan Frome," Arquette is nothing if not flashy, but her character is much more obnoxious than

endearing. Looking like Robert De Niro one moment and Elvis the next, Madsen appealingly projects sweetness and vulnerability as a bad boy who wouldn't mind going straight.

Technically, film is very sharp. Vinnie Golia's score is unusual, proving effective at times but too intrusive on occasion.

— Todd McCarthy

WATCH IT

A Skouras release of an Island World presentation in association with the Manhattan Project of a River One Films production. Executive producers, David Brown, William S. Gilmore. Produced by Thomas J. Mangan IV, J. Christopher Burch, John C. McGinley. Directed, written by Tom Flynn. Camera (Technicolor), Stephen M. Katz; editor, Dorian Harris; music, Stanley Clarke; production design, Jeff Steven Ginn; art direction, Barbara Kahn Kretschmer; set decoration, Martha Ring; costume design, Jordan Ross; sound (Dolby), Allan Byer; line producer, Fran Roy; associate producers, Kit Golden, Pamela Hedley; assistant director, Vincent Lascoumes; casting, Shari Rhodes. Reviewed at Palm Springs Intl. Film Festival, Jan. 9, 1993. MPAA Rating: R. Running time: **102 MIN.**
John . . . . Peter Gallagher
Anne . . . . Suzy Amis
Rick . . . . John C. McGinley
Michael . . . . Jon Tenney
Ellen . . . . Cynthia Stevenson
Brenda . . . . Lili Taylor
Danny . . . . Tom Sizemore
Denise . . . . Terri Hawkes
Call girl . . . . Jordana Capra
Girl on videotape . . . . Taylor Render
Fan at ballpark . . . Lorenzo Clemons

Male bonding receives a comic thrashing in "Watch It," an entertaining diversion with a few serious things on its mind. This Skouras pickup feels too lightweight to become much of a contender theatrically, but curious viewers will be rewarded by some expert perfs from appealing young actors and amusing dialogue riffs.

First-time writer-director Tom Flynn does a nice little number on men in their late 20s who persist in behaving as if they were still living in freshman dorm.

Irresponsible, misogynistic, profoundly insincere and obsessed with sports and sex, ladies' man Jon Tenney, goofball salesman John C. McGinley and decidedly unbrilliant auto mechanic Tom Sizemore live in a state of macho bliss in a Chicago suburb.

Joined by Tenney's itinerant cousin Peter Gallagher, the boys particularly get off on a game from their college years called "Watch It," involving putting something over on one of the guys so he is utterly suckered and, preferably, humiliated.

The amusement value of these pranks is relatively low, and the annoyance level they maintain throughout the film never entirely dissipates. To an extent, the picture invites the audience to relish these unsavory practical jokes even as it condemns what they represent.

But beyond this nonsense, Flynn develops some real interest in the relationships he forges among his characters. Gallagher becomes fond of lovely veterinarian Suzy Amis and courts her charmingly in a scene at Comiskey Park that includes fan Lorenzo Clemons' hilarious comic turn.

Amis has just been jilted by Tenney, who hastily patches things up and dishonestly asks Amis to marry him when he finds Gallagher, whom he's always resented, is interested.

McGinley gets something promising going with bright, vulnerable Cynthia Stevenson, but later breaks it up to prove to himself and the others it's more important to be one of the boys.

Although the role is akin to Rhoda-ish comic relief, Lili Taylor brings ample freshness and humanity to the part of Amis' assistant at the animal hospital, whose own starved personal life doesn't prevent her from giving some pointed hints to her boss.

After building both comic and dramatic momentum through its middle third, pic becomes a bit windy and overloaded with predictable occurrences. Sabotaged by his buddies upon announcing his departure, Gallagher has to turn the tables in a series of "Watch It" gags that stalls the real wrap-up between him and Amis. Five minutes of trims would probably help.

Flynn the writer's sharp, observant dialogue acquits him more impressively than Flynn the director's uncertain pacing and lackluster visual style.

As she has been in a number of small, little-seen films, Amis is once again a total delight, both substantial and breezy. Gallagher acquits himself strongly as a confused young man who sees beyond his buddies' behavior even as he takes part in it.

McGinley, who also co-produced, commands the screen most of the time he's on. Tenney and

January 18, 1993 (Cont.)

Sizemore are more one-dimensional, but plenty engaging.

There's more than enough talent here, both before and behind the camera, to justify watching this pic, even if its pleasures are modest. The film is better the further it moves away from gags and shtick and toward real issues between the sexes, so one can hope that Flynn will push himself to be bolder and more adventurous next time.

— *Todd McCarthy*

VOR EEN VERLOREN SOLDAAT
(FOR A LOST SOLDIER)
(DUTCH)

A Concorde Film release of a Sigma Film Prods. B.V. production, in cooperation with Avro TV Holland. (Intl. sales: Fortissimo Film Sales, Amsterdam.) Produced by Matthijs van Heijningen. Directed, written by Roeland Kerbosch, from Rudi van Dantzig's novel. Camera (Eastmancolor), Nils Post; editor, August Verschueren; music, Joop Stokkermans; production design, Vincent de Pater; sound, Marcel de Hoogd; line producer, Guurtje Buddenberg; assistant director, Ian Ferguson. Reviewed at Festival of Festivals, Toronto, Sept. 18, 1992. (In Palm Springs Intl. Film Festival.) Running time: **93 MIN.**

Jeroen Boman (as a boy)	Maarten Smit
Walt Cook	Andrew Kelley
Jeroen Boman (adult)	Jeroen Krabbe
Hait	Freark Smink
Mem	Elsje de Wijn
Laura	Valerie Valentine
Jan	Derk-Jan Kroon

Though it handles a tricky subject with tact and avoids sensationalism, "For a Lost Soldier" may encounter severe censorship in parts of the world (like Britain) where laws forbid the depiction of sexuality involving children. This may provoke some controversy — and stir interest — in territories the pic is able to screen.

Based on a novel by Rudi van Dantzig, the autobiographical story concerns the relationship between a Canadian soldier and a 12-year-old Dutch boy in 1945, when Holland has been liberated from the Germans. Young Jeroen has been sent from Amsterdam to rural Friesland to live out the last months of the war in comparative safety. Billeted to a friendly farmer, he quickly adapts to country life, and spends much of his time with a somewhat older friend, who seems to have nothing but girls on his mind.

The arrival of a small group of Canadian soldiers is a matter of consternation, since the older girls in the area are quick to consort with the country's liberators. No one seems to notice the close attachment that forms between Jeroen and Walt Cook (Andrew Kelley), a fresh-faced Canuck instantly attracted to the boy ("As soon as I saw you, I was sure you were my kind of guy.")

Before long, soldier and boy are inseparable, and there are some intimate scenes, including a shower the two share (the boy clothed, the soldier naked) and a couple of sequences in which the couple share a bed. In this respect the fact that this is a gay relationship is really of no consequence; the intimate scenes of kissing and pillow talk would be just as disturbing between a soldier and a 12-year-old girl.

Young Maarten Smit is touching as Jeroen, whose friendship for the exotic stranger blossoms into first love, and Andrew Kelley is on the button as the naive, ingenuous young soldier. But it seems odd that no one in the village, especially the family with whom Jeroen is staying, ever comment on the goings-on.

Writer-director Roeland Kerbosch handles the delicate material with frankness but is careful not to go too far. The opening and closing scenes, however, with the adult Jeroen (Jeroen Krabbe), now a choreographer for a dance company, remembering his first love affair, are corny and extraneous. Technical credits are spot on. — *David Stratton*

MARIA'S CHILD
(BRITISH- 16m)

A BBC Drama Films production. (Intl. sales: BBC Enterprises, London.) Executive producer, Mark Shivas. Produced by Kenith Trodd. Directed, written by Malcolm McKay. Camera (color), Sean Van Hales; editor, John Stothart; music, Philip Appleby; production design, Marjorie Pratt; costume design, Anushia Nieradzik; sound, Clive Derbyshire; choreography, Anthony Van Laast; assistant director, Mervyn Gill-Dougherty. Reviewed at London Film Festival, Nov. 14, 1992. (In Palm Springs Intl. Film Festival.) Running time: **97 MIN.**

Maria	Yolanda Vazquez
Michael	David O'Hara
Pauline	Fiona Shaw
Eugene McCarthy	Alec McCowen
Melanie	Sophie Okonedo
Danielle	Linda Davidson
Jessica	Rudi Davies
Roland	Nick Woodeson
Bruna	Anita Zagaria

"**M**aria's Child" is an okay gloss on the abortion debate that works well in patches but has trouble finding a consistent tone. This will-she/won't-she light comedy-drama by pubcaster BBC is better suited to the small screen.

Writer-director Malcolm McKay, from a background in legit, sees it as the second in a loose trilogy on the subject of forgiveness. "Maria's Child" lacks the dramatic clout of his 1991 Tom Courtenay-Miranda Richardson TV drama "Redemption," about an ex-con reentering society; capper "Paul's Angel" is currently at script stage.

Looker Yolanda Vazquez plays Maria, a 30-year-old dancer who suddenly finds herself pregnant, the result, she thinks, of a birthday-party quickie with a handsome Spaniard. Fed up with her hunky actor b.f. (David O'Hara), she kicks him out after he admits sleeping with a fellow actress.

Striking up an imagined dialogue with the unborn kid, she vacillates between motherhood and abortion. An audition for a flamenco musical offers a potential way out, but her Italo relatives pressure her against terminating the pregnancy. The pic ends with her mind made up.

The film takes a while to establish its fragile mixture of comedy, semi-fantasy and debate, the "Look Who's Talking"-like loquacious fetus gambit is clumsy in its early stages. Things settle down in the second half, with auditions for the extravagent tuner (billed as "La Pasionaria — The Musical") and the intro of Maria's histrionic family.

Vazquez makes an attractive lead but is unconvincing as a dancer (despite clever editing) and not always up to the demands of the complex role. O'Hara scores better as the b.f., and Fiona Shaw is excellent as Maria's levelheaded gynecologist. Anita Zagoria steals her scenes as a gravel-voiced flamenco vet.

McKay's direction is mostly TV-drama style, with occasional visual flourishes in the dance sequences. Philip Appleby's score injects lift and feeling whenever it appears. — *Derek Elley*

NAO QUERO FALAR SOBRE ISSO AGORA
(I DON'T WANT TO TALK ABOUT IT NOW)
(BRAZILIAN)

A Producoes Cinematograficas R.F. Farias Ltda. production. Produced, directed by Mauro Farias. Screenplay, Farias, Evandro Mesquita, Melanie Dimantas. Camera (color), Marcelo Durst; editors, Roberto Mauro, Cio Farias; music, Celso Fonseca; production design, Gringo Dardia; sound, Juarez Dagoberto; assistant director, Breno Siliviero. Reviewed at Festival of Festivals, Toronto, Sept. 18, 1992. (In Palm Springs Intl. Film Festival.) Running time: **89 MIN.**

Daniel O'Neil	Evandro Mesquita
Meg	Elinan Fonseca
Also with: Marisa Orth.	

A half-hearted critique of a selfish, macho would-be artist is contained in this mild dramatic comedy. Pleasant performances can't overcome a routine screenplay.

Daniel O'Neil, played with off-hand detachment by Evandro Mesquita, is dumped by his rich g.f. and moves in with the plump, sisterly Meg (Elinan Fonseca), who obviously adores him.

Shamelessly using her hospitality and affection, the tiresome Daniel, who considers himself an artist, tries numerous means of expressing himself, attempting to be a writer, musician and photographer, never with much success. At the same time, he beds a number of attractive women. His downfall comes when he accidentally becomes involved in a drug deal and falls foul of gangsters and corrupt police.

Fonseca steals the film as the good-natured Meg, a fat girl everyone (except the wretched hero) loves. Director Mauro Farias, in his feature film debut, has some good ideas, but this familiar fare is strictly a local item with little to offer audiences outside Brazil. — *David Stratton*

January 25, 1993

SNIPER

A TriStar Pictures release of a Baltimore Pictures production. Executive producers, Mark Johnson, Walon Green, Patrick Wachsberger. Produced by Robert L. Rosen. Directed by Luis Llosa. Screenplay, Michael Frost Beckner, Crash Leyland. Camera (Atlab color, Film House prints), Bill Butler; editor, Scott Smith; music, Gary Chang; production design, Herbert Pinter; art direction, Nicholas McCallum; costume design, Ray Summers; assistant director, Colin Fletcher; stunt coordinator, Glenn Ruehland; casting, Anne Robinson, Liz Mullinar. Reviewed at Sony Pictures screening room, Culver City, Calif., Jan. 21, 1993. MPAA Rating: R. Running time: **98 MIN.**

Thomas Beckett'.	Tom Berenger
Richard Miller	Billy Zane
Chester Van Damme	J.T. Walsh
Doug Papich	Aden Young
El Cirujano	Ken Radley
Cacique	Reinaldo Arenas
Raul Ochoa	Carolos Alvarez
Cabrera	Roy Edmonds

"Sniper" is an expertly directed, yet ultimately unsatisfying psychological thriller. Luis Llosa's first-rate action direction is undermined by underdeveloped characters and pedestrian dialogue. **Macho auds should enjoy the tense manhunt scenes and particularly, the special effects sniper footage (by Brian Pearce). If sold correctly, the film — which underwent recent reshoots and reedit — could provide TriStar with modest b.o. returns.**

Tom Berenger essays a Marine sniper, oddly named Thomas Beckett, on assignment in Panama. Pic quickly establishes sniping as a lonely profession shunned even by other gung-ho Marines. On his latest assignment he's accompanied by an ambitious young Washington bureaucrat, Richard Miller (Billy Zane), who is so green he doesn't really need camouflage.

The hostile interplay between the emotionally detached veteran and the cocky youngster is strictly textbook, as is their eventual male bonding. This would be okay if they weren't virtually the only characters in the film.

But under Llosa's careful hand, the presentation is taut and lean and bears more than a passing resemblance to John Boorman's "Hell in the Pacific" or "Deliverance." Action scenes — and there are a good number of them — range from good to edge-of-your-seat. Audiences will see the finale coming from a mile away, but the pace only flags when the characters stop to make sense of their actions.

The pairing of Berenger and Zane is interesting. Berenger continues to become more intriguing as an actor — although he seems to be spending an inordinate amount of his career in the jungle ("Platoon," "At Play in the Fields of the Lord") — and has forsaken the James Dean pout he relied on in early efforts.

Zane recalls the young Berenger, trying too hard for effect via heavy smoldering. He's already such a strong screen presence the extra effort makes him appear unhinged, something wonderfully appropriate in "Dead Calm" but disconcerting here.

However, both actors are saddled with scenes that are almost impossible to play, heavy on flat-footed exposition. Michael Frost Beckner and Crash Leyland's script is good at sketching out movement and suspense, but seems to understand the jungle better than its characters.

Technical credits are superb. Production design by Herbert Pinter is a standout as is Bill Butler's lucid cinematography of the tropical forests of Queensland, Australia, which stand in for Panama. Music by Gary Chang is forceful without being overbearing and always appropriate to the action.

— _Richard Natale_

ASPEN EXTREME

A Buena Vista release of a Hollywood Pictures presentation, in association with Touchwood Pacific Partners I, of a Leonard Goldberg production. Executive producer, Fred T. Gallo. Produced by Goldberg. Directed, written by Patrick Hasburgh. Camera (Technicolor prints), Steven Fierberg, Robert Primes; editor, Steven Kemper; music, Michael Convertino; production design, Roger Cain; costume design, Karen Patch; sound (Dolby), David Brownlow; assistant director, Doug Metzger; 2nd-unit producer-director, E.J. Foerster; 2nd-unit camera, Jan Kiesser, Edgar Boyles; associate producer, Foerster; stunt coordinator, Gary Jensen; casting, Gail Levin. Reviewed at Gotham Theater, N.Y., Jan. 21, 1993. MPAA Rating: PG-13. Running time: **117 MIN.**

T.J. Burke	Paul Gross
Dexter Rutecki	Peter Berg
Bryce Kellogg	Finola Hughes
Robin Hand	Teri Polo
Dave Ritchie	William Russ
Karl Stall	Trevor Eve
Franz Hauser	Martin Kemp
Rudy Zucker	
	Stewart Finley-McLennan
Todd Pounds	William McNamara
Tina	Nicolette Scorsese

Poor scripting kills **"Aspen Extreme," an initially mild romance about finding one's self that eventually turns unconvincingly melodramatic. Buena Vista faces an uphill** climb in attracting auds beyond hardcore skiing enthusiasts.

Canadian hunk Paul Gross toplines as a Ford assembly line auto worker who heads from Detroit to Aspen and a new life. He drags along reluctant buddy Peter Berg, who works at a dinky local ski area.

Once at the fabled Colorado resort — since in the headlines due to the boycott against the state — the two fish-out-of-water heroes quickly establish their expertise and enter the lush life of ski instructors.

Debuting feature writer-director Patrick Hasburgh's screenplay gains some points for characterization and cross-talk but depends on stock situations out of a generic skiing, or for that matter surfing, film. Gross becomes the hottest thing on the slopes and eventually a gigolo for jetsetter Finola Hughes.

Berg also gets a girlfriend, Tina (stunning starlet Nicolette Scorsese), but after she's given a mysterious buildup the character suddenly disappears from the film without explanation.

Femme lead goes to lovely Teri Polo as a local d.j. who is the grudging Good Samaritan taking care of our heroes when they get in trouble. Of course, she's ultimately the right girl for Gross.

Along the way there's some attractively lensed hotdogging footage of skiers doing dangerous stunts as well as exciting scenes of a fall into a watery crevasse and an avalanche. Unfortunately, the last two reels of this overlong (nearly two hours) pic are loaded with anticlimaxes.

Most laughable and poorly directed sequence is Gross mailing his manuscript for the story "Aspen Extreme" to Powder magazine, fulfilling his dream as the mailman delivers the published cover story in the next shot.

Gross is an appealing if bland lead sabotaged mainly by Hasburgh's puffball script, which makes all his adversities and tragedies so easy to overcome. Berg, in a best-pal role similar to his "Late For Dinner" assignment, wins sympathy. Soap star Hughes is beautiful and instantly hissable while Polo is too good to be true in a thankless role.

Besides its '60s subject matter, film seems curiously dated by near total lack of minority casting, even as extras.

Film is physically well-mounted, with kudos to second-unit director E.J. Foerster and his crew for the skiing scenes.

— _Lawrence Cohn_

BLOOD IN BLOOD OUT

A Buena Vista release of a Hollywood Pictures presentation in association with Touchwood Pacific Partners I. Executive producers, Jimmy Santiago Baca, Stratton Leopold. Produced by Taylor Hackford, Jerry Gershwin. Directed by Hackford. Screenplay, Baca, Jeremy Iacone, Floyd Mutrux; story by Ross Thomas. Camera (Deluxe color), Gabriel Beristain; editors, Fredric Steinkamp, Karl F. Steinkamp; music, Bill Conti; production design, Bruno Rubeo; art direction, Marek Dobrowolski; set decoration, Cecilia Rodarte; costume design, Shay Cunliffe; sound (Dolby), Edward Tise; co-executive producer, Rene Sheridan; associate producer, Gina Blumenfeld; assistant directors, Josh McLaglen, Sean H. Ferrer; 2nd-unit director/stunt coordinator, Gary Davis; casting, Richard Pagano, Sharon Bialy. Reviewed at the Cinedome 6 Theaters, Las Vegas, Jan. 20, 1993. MPAA Rating: R. Running time: **174 MIN.**

Miklo	Damian Chapa
Cruz	Jesse Borrego
Paco	Benjamin Bratt
Montana	Enrique Castillo
Magic Mike	Victor Rivers
Bonafide	Delroy Lindo
Red Ryder	Tom Towles
Popeye	Carlos Carrasco
Wallace	Teddy Wilson
Chuey	Raymond Cruz
Frankie	Valente Rodriguez
Big Al	Lanny Flaherty

Producer-director Taylor Hackford clearly wants this to be a major cinematic exploration of the Latino experience, from its ponderous near-three-hour length to its more-than-occasional sermonizing. Unfortunately, disjointed storytelling and uneven performances undermine those aspirations, which should make it difficult for this Hollywood Pictures release (currently in selected markets and scheduled for wider distribution in late February) to tap into much of a b.o. vein.

With script help from poet and former convict Jimmy Santiago Baca, among others, Hackford — relying on a virtually unknown cast — has blended elements of "Boyz N the Hood" and "The Godfather," with all the pretentiousness that suggests. Using Hackford's role as producer of "La Bamba" as its calling card, the story seems preoccupied with capturing the feel of Latino culture and life in East Los Angeles but also has more ambitious overtones, detailing a bloody prison gang war in addition to exploring the tough choices and different paths that can lead to salvation or tragedy in the inner city.

Starting in the early '70s, the plot centers on three youths and follows them into their early 30s: Paco (Benjamin Bratt), a hot-tempered boxer; Cruz (Jesse Borrego, most recognizable from the TV series "Fame"), a gifted painter seemingly destined to escape the barrio; and Miklo (Damian Chapa), their half-white cousin who ultimately becomes the focus when he's drawn into an interracial turf war in San Quentin.

In a short span, a series of events change each of their lives. Miklo gets jailed for murdering a rival gang leader, an act of vengeance after Cruz is brutally beaten; Cruz forsakes his painting for drug addiction and becomes estranged from his family; Paco, initially the hardest case of the three, goes straight and becomes an undercover cop.

In the movie's biggest cliché, Miklo survives his prison ordeal only to return despite his determination to stay out, thanks in part to a callous parole system. The story might have ended there, but instead it continues for another hour, chronicling an intricate turf war over drugs and money that in many ways feels like an entirely different movie.

But a similarly fractured quality plagues the story throughout, as Hackford loses sight of characters, then returns to them years later with scant explanation. Bratt, the strongest presence among the three, suffers in that regard, as does Borrego, whose storyline is abandoned for too long to have much resonance.

Chapa, meanwhile, never projects the strength or charisma his role requires, and the strong supporting players (particularly among the prisoners) can't entirely prop up that deficiency.

Moreover, Hackford seems to fall victim to Spike Lee's penchant for directing every film as if it's his last, throwing in disparate elements and too often preaching to make his point. "Blood In Blood Out" (the title refers to the code of a prison gang) seems compelled to say something profound but too often stands on a soapbox to do it.

Much of the story takes place in prison, unflinchingly exploring some of the same brutal themes touched on in Edward James Olmos' "American Me." It's a sobering depiction but, with the focus on gang solidarity and warfare, probably won't have the desired deterrent effect it no doubt hopes to have.

Technical credits are sound, though the score at times slips into the melodramatic, and the use of subtitles (as the characters rapidly alternate English and Spanish) proves occasionally distracting. — *Brian Lowry*

NOWHERE TO RUN

A Columbia Pictures release of an Adelson/Baumgarten production. Executive producer, Michael Rachmil. Produced by Craig Baumgarten, Gary Adelson. Directed by Robert Harmon. Screenplay, Joe Eszterhas, Leslie Bohem, Randy Feldman; story by Eszterhas, Richard Marquand. Camera (Technicolor), David Gribble; editor, Zach Staenberg, Mark Helfrich; music, Mark Isham; production design, Dennis Washington; costume design, Gamila Mariana Fahkry; sound (Dolby), David Kirschner; associate producer, Eugene Van Varenberg; 2nd-unit director, Peter Macdonald; 2nd-unit camera, Douglas Milsome, Michael A. Benson; assistant director, Brian W. Cook; stunt coordinator, Billy Burton; casting, Jackie Burch. Reviewed at Murray Hill 4 theater, N.Y., Jan. 15, 1993. MPAA Rating: R. Running time: **94 MIN.**

Sam Gillen	. Jean-Claude Van Damme
Clydie	. Rosanna Arquette
Mookie	. Kieran Culkin
Dunston	. Ted Levine
Bree	. Tiffany Taubman
Lonnie	. Edward Blatchford
Billy	. Anthony Starke
Franklin Hale	. Joss Ackland

Action hero Jean-Claude Van Damme takes a career step backward in "Nowhere to Run," a relentlessly corny and shamelessly derivative vehicle. Other than laughing at a couple of extremely risible scenes, his fans will feel let down.

Dog-eared project, with a story credited to currently hot Joe Eszterhas and his "Jagged Edge" director Richard Marquand (who died in 1987), might seem OK for Van Damme, with its central loner role modeled after the Alan Ladd classic "Shane." However, Van Damme's inexpressiveness is embarrassing.

He's a bank robber sprung from a prison bus by partner in crime Anthony Starke, who's killed during the escape. Van Damme takes the cache of stolen money and hides out on Rosanna Arquette's farm.

She's a widow (the major plot change from "Shane") with two young kids, Kieran Culkin (younger brother of Macaulay) and Tiffany Taubman. Culkin thinks Van Damme is "E.T." come to live in his barn. He and young sister glimpse Van Damme bathing nude in a nearby lake, and before long mama Arquette has seduced the handsome stranger.

The next day the quartet are at the dinner table matter-offactly discussing Van Damme's penis size and, with many reels to go, "Nowhere to Run" has self-destructed. But patchwork plot continues, with Arquette pressured by evil land developer Joss Ackland to sell her homestead.

His henchmen, Ted Levine (a mild, unsatisfactory villain here) and young sheriff Edward Blatchford (stuck in a contradictory role), try to extricate Arquette from the property in boring scenes. At every key moment, Van Damme pops up, comicstrip style, to display heroism, but his bread and butter fight scenes are so one-sided there's no fun or catharsis in them.

To emphasize the film's Western antecedents, there's a lengthy chase scene of cops on horseback after Van Damme on a motorcycle, which abruptly switches to strictly motorized chasing midway in an apparent afterthought or additional shoot.

By Van Damme's climactic battle with no-match Levine, the audience has to be longing for the good, old-fashioned Westerns our hero and his fellow martial artists have supplanted.

Arquette, also retreating careerwise, looks great and delivers two non-prudish nude scenes but is obviously uncomfortable in a poorly written role.

Director Robert Harmon, who previously helmed "The Hitcher," does a very poor job of handling even stock scenes and throws in extraneous crane shots and other visual distractions that should have been left in film school. Sound mix on print reviewed was highly erratic.

— *Lawrence Cohn*

RIENS DU TOUT
(LITTLE NOTHINGS)
(FRENCH)

An MKL Distribution release of a Les Productions Lazennec/MK2 Prods./France 3 Cinema/Centre Europeen Cinematographique Rhone-Alpes co-production with the participation of Canal Plus/the Rhone-Alpes Region/Sofinergie 2 & 3/the CNC/Procirep. Produced by Adeline Lecallier. Directed by Cedric Klapisch. Screenplay, Klapisch, Berroyer. Camera (color), Kevin Morrisey; editor, Francine Sandberg; music, Jeff Cohen; art direction, François Renaud Laberthe; costumes, Eve-Marie Arnault; sound, François Waledisch; associate producer, Alain Rocca; casting, Frédérique Moidon. Reviewed at Club Gaumont screening room, Paris, Oct. 5, 1992. Running Time: **99 MIN.**

With: Fabrice Luchini, Daniel Berlioux, Marc Berman, Olivier Broche, Antoine Chappey, Jean-Pierre Daroussin, Aurélie Guichard, Billy Korng, Odette Laure, Elisabeth Macocco, Marc Maury, Pierre-Oliver Mornas, Jean-Michel Martiel, Maité Nehyr, Fred Personne, Lucette Raillat, Eric Rey, Nathalie Richard, Marie Riva, Sophie Simon, Marina Rodriquez-Tomée, Zinedine Soualem, Karen Viard, Coraly Zahonero.

In "Riens Du Tout" an optimistic exec attempts to reverse the fortunes of a failing Parisian department store by applying American-style training methods to a staff whose notion of service ranges from "The customer is never right" to "The customer is irrelevant." First feature from scripter-helmer Cedric Klapisch successfully juggles more than two dozen characters while exploring amusing variations on legendary French rudeness.

Ambitious ensemble piece is perhaps too scattered but should raise a chuckle from anyone who's ever tried to shop in Paris. Eclectic casting and an astute eye for quirks and foibles make this bittersweet comedy a good bet for TV sales and a ready-made casting reel for those in search of offbeat French faces.

Enthusiastic manager Fabrice Luchini has one year to whip an indifferent staff into shape. Reluctant employees are soon doing touchy-feely "trust" exercises and bungee-jumping on a "bonding" field trip. Helmer employs a subjective camera and other snappy techniques to give viewers a clear sense of the many characters and their workplace. Droll proceedings elicit steady chuckles and by pic's ironic ending, viewers identify with the store and its newly melded staff.

Memorable bits include an earnest how-to-smile course, a personnel placement officer whose conversation is peppered with terms like *"le starting block"* and *"le downtrend,"* and a classic philosophical argument in the employee's lounge. Thesps portray distinct, touching characters who resist the notion that innovative management can motivate them to embrace teamwork and love their boring jobs.

Thoughtful sound design adds extra life to pic, lensed mostly on location in an abandoned department store. Shots of cast members running are incorporated into docu footage of the Paris Marathon with mixed results. One employee's holiday break occasions a surreal scene of nudist campers doing their supermarket shopping in the buff.

Klapisch, who earned his MFA in film at NYU, has done a fine job of grafting American theories of efficiency onto French approaches to commerce. "Riens du Tout" has been holding its own at local wickets for over two months; Gallic helmer has followed through on the promise of

January 25, 1993 (Cont.)

his prizewinning short films and is a director to watch.

— *Lisa Nesselson*

VENT D'EST
(EAST WIND)
(FRENCH)

An MC4 release of an MC4/Duckstra Prods./SGGC/Prodeve/TF-1 Film Prod. co-production with the participation of Canal Plus/Slav/Cofimage/the CNC/Compagnie Lyonnaise de Cinema/Television Suisse Romande. Produced by Jean-Pierre Bailly, Jean-Jacques Grimblat, Aziz Ojjeh. Directed by Robert Enrico. Screenplay, Marc Miller, Frederic Fajardie, Enrico, from Nicolas Bethell's "The Last Secret." Camera (color), Michel Abramowicz; editor, Patricia Neny; music, Karl-Heinz Shafer; production design, Halina Dobrowolska; sound, Eric Devulder; associate producers, Jean-Bernard Fetoux, Roger-André Larrieu; historical research, Henning Von Vogelsang, Clemens Von Vogelsang. Reviewed at Celtec screening room, Paris, Jan. 11, 1993. Release date: Jan. 20. Running time: **116 MIN.**
General Smyslowosky . . . .
. . . . Malcolm McDowell
Dr. Hoop . . . . Pierre Vaneck
Father Siegler . Jean-François Balmer
Captain Barinkova . . Ludmila Mikaël
Colonel Tcheko . . . . Wojtek Pszoniak
Also with: Caroline Sihol, Catherine Bidaut, Serge Ranko, Jan Jankowski, Sarah Vanikoff, Geoffrey Bateman, Andrzej Zielinski, Elena Safonova, Clementine Celarie, Patrice Alexsandre.

Based on a little-known true incident, "Vent d'Est" is a well-acted, competently presented account of Stalin's efforts to reclaim a batch of Russian refugees from the safety of tiny but determined Liechtenstein. Pleasantly educational and morally uplifting without being smarmy, historical drama from veteran helmer Robert Enrico is perfect for TV, specialized fests and classroom use.

Pic assumes a glancing familiarity with European geography, the outcome of World War II and the difference between Red and White Russians, but remains accessible popular entertainment.

On the night of May 2, 1945, bold General Smyslowosky (Malcolm McDowell) led a convoy of 500 Russian soldiers wearing German uniforms past border sentries guarding the 12,000 citizens of neutral Liechtenstein.

The tiny principality granted asylum to the uninvited foreigners and, despite the hearty objections of the leader of parliament, Father Siegler (Jean-François Balmer), protected them from pointed and persistent demands by Stalin's emissaries that they be handed over to the Soviet government.

Smyslowosky's troops, most of whom hailed from the annexed Baltic states, had fought the Red Army on the Eastern front. Historians agree that, after Yalta, the Allies unwittingly returned some 2 million anticommunist Russians to vengeful Soviet authorities. But thanks to the support of Liechtenstein's prime minister (Pierre Vaneck), this Russian military unit wasn't.

Refugees are adopted by local farmers, leading inevitably to cross-cultural romances and family conflicts. Scenes of simple daily life are sometimes clichéd, but the maneuvering of higher-ups is always engaging.

Despite having been dubbed into French, the authoritative McDowell more than holds the screen as Smyslowosky, a Finnish-born exiled Russian whose honor and motives are left ambiguous long enough to boost suspense. Wojtek Pszoniak makes a strong impression as Stalin's sleazy emissary, sent to negotiate the refugees' return. Attractive Ludmila Mikaël shines as his cutthroat assistant who, in view of Russia's 20 million war dead, has nothing but contempt for the ethical niceties pursued by the neutral state.

Lensed in a quaint and majestic mountain setting in Poland, production makes an unfortunate blunder in one brief scene where American military police are shown wearing armbands that say "PM" instead of "MP."

— *Lisa Nesselson*

DRÖMMEN ON RITA
(DREAMING OF RITA)
(SWEDISH)

A Svensk Filmindustri presentation of a FilmLance Intl. production for Stiftelsen Svenska Filminstutet/Sveriges Television/TV-2/FilmTeknik/Kinotuotanto/FilmLance Intl./Street Movies/Nordisk Film und TV Fond. Produced by Börje Hansson. Directed by Jon Lindström. Screenplay, Lindström, Rita Holst. Camera (color), Khell Lagerroos; sound, Jan Brodin, Gail Brodin; production design, Staffan Erstam; costumes, Lenamari Wallström. Reviewed at the Riviera cinema, Stockholm, Nov. 24, 1992. Running time: **108 MIN.**
With: Marika Lagercrantz, Per Oscarsson, Philip Zandén, LIse Ringheim, Patrik Ersgard, Yaba Holst, Gertt Fylking, Tomas Norström, Mikael Segerström.

This offbeat road movie succeeds through gentle humor, excellent thesps and sensitive direction. Carefully handled, it could become a minor hit outside Sweden.

Rita of the title is both the leading character (Marika Lagercrantz) and movie star Rita Hayworth. The latter is the idol of old man Bob (Per Oscarsson), who also had a mistress who looked like her. When his wife dies, he sets off to Denmark, determined to find this woman. Since Bob is sick, his daughter Rita (Lagercrantz) is worried and goes after him, leaving her infant in the care of her husband (Philip Zandén).

Hubby is a hard-working businessman and is not pleased with the developments. Together with his daughter and infant son, he, in his turn, sets off to find Rita.

During their respective trips, they find affecting people and incidents. It all ends at a windy seaside hotel in Denmark, where Oscarsson finds his long-lost love and Lagercrantz and Zandén find each other again.

Finnish-born director Lindström previously has made mostly dramas, often with a heavy emphasis on explicit sex and violence. Here he proves that he can also direct comedies. All his characters are sympathetic, although with human faults, and in the end we root for all of them to find what they are looking for.

Lagercrantz and Zandén are excellent but overshadowed by vet Oscarsson, — Cannes winner in the '60s for the lead in Norwegian pic "Hunger" — whose somewhat nervous acting style suits Bob perfectly.

Tech credits are all up to par.

— *Gunnar Rehlin*

THE NORTHERNERS
(DUTCH)

A First Floor Features production. Produced by Laurens Geels, Dick Maas. Directed, written by Alex van Warmerdam. Camera (color) Marc Felperlaan; editor, Rene Wiegmans; production design, Rikke Jelier; sound, Bert Flantua. Reviewed at Palm Springs Intl. Film Fest, Jan. 16, 1993. Running Time:**105 min.**
With: Leonard Lucieer, Jack Wouterse, Rudolf Lucieer, Alex van Warmerdam, Annet Malherbe, Loes Wouterson, Veerle Dobbelaere, Dary Some, Jacques Commandeur.

Alex van Warmerdam, the Dutch writer-director-actor, makes a commendable splash with the witty and original comedy "The Northerners," one of the unqualified hits of the Palm Springs fest and the Netherlands entry for the Academy Awards. Peopled by vividly drawn oddball characters, "The Northerners" showcases a vision and style reminiscent of both Jacques Tati and Aki Kaurismäki. Specialized auds will get a kick out of this droll offering, and with the right handling, pic could find the mainstream public.

Set in 1960, the film's locale is the only completed street of a huge, since-abandoned, housing project next to a forest. The inhabitants lead quiet, isolated lives; the mail and the radio are their only connections with the outside world.

The citizens seem dull and ordinary, but in actuality, each one is eccentric. Thomas (Leonard Lucieer), the adolescent hero who likes to dress like his current hero, assassinated Congo leader Patrice Lumumba, is neglected by his sexually insatiable father (Jack Wouterse) and his devout, determinedly unsexual, Catholic mother (Annet Malherbe). Lucieer's parents are contrasted with their neighbors, burdened with reversed marital problems. Lucieer's only friend is Simon, the mailman (van Warmerdam), so obsessed with the inhabitants' private lives, he has no scruples about reading their mail before delivering it. And Lucieer himself develops sexual yearnings for Agnes (Veerle Dobbelaere), a mysterious Fellini-esque girl living in the forest.

The seemingly peaceful town is thrown into chaos when two priests arrive for a "missionary presentation" whose central exhibit is a black African. From there on, the ceaseless surprises are impossible to relate.

Helmer van Warmerdam, who won the 1992 Felix (European Film Award), stages long stretches of silent physical comedy and the narrative is structured as a series of tableaux, shot in long takes with stationery camera.

Similarly to Kaurismäki, van Warmerdam makes the most out of the alleged northern drabness and isolation. Like Tati, he creates complex comic structures and often uses creative sound as the ignition for his gag's machinery. But the whole presents his own distinctive cinematic sensibility. — *Emanuel Levy*

AL LUPO AL LUPO
(WOLF! WOLF!)
(ITALIAN)

A Penta Distribuzione release of a Tiger Cinematografica/Penta Film production. Produced by Mario and Vittorio Cecchi Gori. Directed by Carlo Verdone. Screenplay, Filippo Ascione, Leo Benvenuti, Piero De Bernardi, Verdone. Camera (color), Danilo Desideri; editor, Antonio Siciliano; art direction, Francesco Bronzi; costumes, Gianni Gissi. Reviewed at the Metropolitan Cinema, Rome, Jan. 8, 1993. Running time: **108 MIN.**

Gregorio . . . . Carlo Verdone
Livia . . . . Francesca Neri
Vanni . . . . Sergio Rubini
Father . . . . Barry Morse
Also with: Loris Paiusco, Gianpiero Bianchi, Cecilia Luci, Alberto Marozzi, Gillian McCutcheon.

One of Italy's smartest comics, Carlo Verdone, updates the familiar situation of adult siblings' catharsis in a family emergency. Intelligent comedy and small-scale trauma alternate in the well-packaged but superficial "Wolf! Wolf!", which comes on strong for family values after a few sly winks at transgression. A strong cast has made the Christmas release a highroller onshore, particularly in Verdone's native Rome. Full of terrific local color, it could entertain, if not startle, arthouse aficionados abroad.

Two thirtysomething brothers and their married sister have grown apart. All they have in common is a lap-of-luxury upbringing and a famous painterfather. One brother, Sergio Rubini, has become an acclaimed pianist. As an arch-conservative and solitary egoist, he's the diametric opposite of *frere* Verdone, the family's black sheep who ekes out a precarious living as a goofy d.j. Sister Francesca Neri is spoiled and temperamental, unable to decide between her boring husband and an ardent lover.

Can these ill-assorted sibs learn to love and respect each other? Of course, after they search for their suddenly missing father, traveling from a family villa in Tuscany to their beach house, from a dignified music conservatory to a giant discotheque.

Verdone effectively milks these simple contrasts for a series of on-target gags. As the reigning master of comic Roman dialect and philosophy, Verdone gives himself most of the best lines. He's a laugh in his d.j. "Dr. Music" get-up, animating a motley disco hall. Dapper Rubini (a filmmaker himself, director of "La Stazi-

one") makes a perfect foil as his straight-laced, permanently scandalized brother. Sensual and mysterious, Francesca Neri is an adorable creature doted on by her brothers, but she lacks a solid role to show off the comic gifts she's demonstrated in other films.

What's missing from this enjoyable comedy is real conflict. Verdone backs out of every potentially embarrassing situation. And their final meeting with papa, located in a remote mountain retreat, is a major letdown. Instead of confronting his lifelong desertion of the family, the sibs let him off the hook with an indulgent sigh. He draws their picture, and film concludes on a lamely sentimental role.

Danilo Desideri's camera captures the hedonistic pleasures of some exquisite homes and natural locales. — *Deborah Young*

FAMILY PRAYERS

An Arrow Entertainment release of a Sugar production. Executive producer, Larry Sugar. Produced by Mark Levinson, Bonnie Sugar. Directed by Scott Rosenfelt. Screenplay, Steven Ginsberg. Camera (color), Jeff Jur; editor, Susan Crutcher; music, Steve Tyrell; production design, Chester Kaczenski; costume design, Johnny Foam; associate producers, Ginsberg, Charmain Jago. Reviewed at Palm Springs Intl. Film Festival, Jan. 15, 1993. Running time: **108 MIN.**

Martin Jacobs . . . . . . Joe Mantegna
Rita Jacobs . . . . Anne Archer
Andrew Jacobs . Tzvi Ratner-Stauber
Aunt Nan . . . . Patti LuPone
Cantor . . . . Allen Garfield
Dan Linder . . . . Paul Reiser
Mrs. Romeyou . . . . Conchata Ferrell
Nina . . . . Shiri Appleby

Producer Scott Rosenfelt makes his feature directorial debut with "Family Prayers," a modest, well-intentioned coming-of-age story full of heart, if not ingenuity. This amiable family melodrama is well-acted, but the familiarity of its concept, undistinguished direction and mediocre production values will deter mass audiences. Slated for a February release in New York, pic should enjoy a longer life on homevideo.

Set in Los Angeles in 1969, tale depicts the effects of the Jacobs' family breakup on their son Andrew (Tzvi Ratner-Stauber), a sensitive adolescent who becomes a victim of his parents'

fights and squabbles as his father, Martin (Joe Mantegna), a compulsive gambler, promises wife Rita (Anne Archer) he'll reform, but he breaks one vow after another. Ratner-Stauber's main ambition is to keep his parents together at all costs.

Far behind in studies for his upcoming bar mitzvah, he is sent by cantor (Allen Garfield) to tutor (Paul Reiser), through whom he becomes aware of the "outside" world, specifically Vietnam.

Steve Ginsberg's writing is personal and often heartfelt, but lacks depth and subtlety. Scripter spells out too explicitly the lessons about maturity and commitment that Ratner-Stauber needs to learn.

Regrettably, the pleasant film suffers from draggy, unmodulated direction by Rosenfelt; lenser Jeff Jur's flat visual style gives the film an old-fashioned look.

Good acting, however, makes up for the unsatisfying tech credits, especially newcomer Ratner-Stauber's truly charismatic performance; appearing in almost every scene, he acquits himself as a pro. The only exception is the excessively theatrical Patti LuPone as the pragmatic (and a bit vulgar) Aunt Nan.

Still, "Family Prayers" refrains from being overly sentimental and gains additional poignancy from the parallels it draws between Andrew's personal and the country's political maturation during the Vietnam era.

— *Emanuel Levy*

ACTING IT OUT
(GERMAN)

A Scotia Film production. Produced by Harry Kugler. Directed by Sonke Wortmann. Screenplay, Wortmann, Jurgen Egger. Camera (color) Gernot Roll; editor, Ueli Christen; music, Torsten Breuer; costume design, Katharina von Martius, Natascha Curtius-Noss; sound, Simon Happ. Reviewed at Palm Springs Intl. Film Fest, Jan. 14, 1993. Running time: **91 MIN.**

With: Jurgen Vogel, Kai Wiesinger, Gedeon Burkhard, Meret Becker, Magdalene Artelt.

A disparate, eccentric young trio of would-be actors cross paths in "Acting It Out,"

a German road comedy that is structurally innovative and beautifully shot. Assured, fluid direction and charming performances give pic commercial appeal that could go beyond the art house and fest circuits.

The three protagonists of "Acting It Out" are very different, but not types: Ingo (Jurgen Vogel) works as a dishwasher, but aspires to be a writer. While returning a stool left at his restaurant to an acting academy, he is inadvertently mistaken for a student and his moody behavior taken to be an audition.

At the academy, Vogel meets Johannes (Kai Wiesinger), a passionate Method actor who has already flunked out of seven of Germany's eight acting schools due to an obsessive fear of auditions. He is planning to hitchhike to Munich, his last resort as an actor, and persuades Vogel, who has been jilted by his g.f. Margot (Magdalene Artelt), to accompany him. Along the way, they meet Ali (Gedeon Burkhard), a suave, handsome ladykiller and fellow would-be actor.

The film's first half is set on the road, where they encounter an array of odd characters — a hard-rock punk dressed in leather, an aging homosexual — that add to pic's quirky texture. The comrades eventually find their way to Munich, where they settle in and prepare their auditions, buoyed by friendship, and face the moment of truth.

Though following a clear structure, Jurgen Egger's innovative script is loose enough to seem improvised but each scene is fully orchestrated. Pic's pensive sequences are inventively interspersed with whimsical ones depicting the impassioned auditions, in which students take on everything from Faust. Hamlet and Woyczek to "The Glass Menagerie," Gene Hackman in "The French Connection," and Marlon Brando's Godfather.

Throughout, helmer Sonke Wortmann maintains a poignantly observant perspective on the lead characters and the twists in their identities; there is a good chemistry among the three young actors. Gernot Roll's camera work has a smooth but edgy quality that is perfectly complemented by Ueli Christen's seamless, unobtrusive editing.

— *Emanuel Levy*

THE MUSIC OF CHANCE

An I.R.S. release of an I.R.S. Media/
American Playhouse Theatrical Films
presentation of a Frederick Zollo production from Transatlantic Entertainment and RCA/Columbia TriStar Home
Video. Executive producers, Miles A.
Copeland III, Paul Colichman, Lindsay
Law. Produced by Zollo, Dylan Sellers.
Directed by Philip Haas. Screenplay,
Haas, Belinda Haas, from Paul Auster's
novel. Camera (Technicolor; Foto-Kem
prints), Bernard Zitzermann; N.Y. camera, Jean de Segonzac; editor, Belinda
Haas; music, Phillip Johnston; production design, Hugo Luczyc-Wyhowski;
art direction, Ruth Ammon; costume
design, Rudy Dillon; sound (Dolby), Les
Lupin; co-producer, Kerry Orent; assistant director, Greg Jacobs; casting, Bonnie Timmerman. Reviewed at Academy
Theater, North Hollywood, Calif., Jan.
11, 1993. (In Palm Springs Intl. Film
Fest.) Running time: **98 MIN.**

Jack Pozzi . . . . James Spader
Jim Nashe . . . . Mandy Patinkin
Calvin Murks . . . . . M. Emmet Walsh
Bill Flowers . . . . . . Charles Durning
Willy Stone . . . . Joel Grey
Tiffany . . . . Samantha Mathis
Floyd Murks . . . . . Christopher Penn

An outstanding cast, a coolly confident style and quirky
literary material turn "The
Music of Chance" into an auspicious feature debut for documentary filmmaker Philip
Haas. But it's ultimately more
of an intellectual tease and just
a fair bet for theatrical release

Based on a tome by w.k. New
York writer Paul Auster, story
will be called Kafkaesque because a hapless duo are caught in
a mystifying, virtually inescapable web. Yet, the piece has a
thoroughly American feel.

Most unlikely occurrence may
come at the opening, when Mandy
Patinkin, zipping along a rural
highway in his new red BMW,
offers a lift to a bloodied drifter,
James Spader. In Patinkin's room
at the Carlyle, Spader convinces
him to put up $10,000 for a poker
game with two rich pushovers.

So the pair proceed to the splendid country estate of Charles
Durning and Joel Grey, a pair of
odd ducks if there ever was one.
The fat man and little guy reveal
that they won the lottery and
are now living a life of leisure.

After initial success, Spader's
luck turns and he and Patinkin
are forced to agree to work off
their debt by reconstructing a
medieval stone wall, a job estimated to take 50 days. Intrigue
involving delays, hidden agen-
das, escape attempts and possible murder envelope the drudgery and command involvement.

But the denouement is too pat
and O. Henry-ish and the characters, too, are shallow constructs.

But within the limits, the actors
etch vivid surface portraits.

James Spader displays previously unrevealed sides of his talent in a very entertaining turn
as a no-class, sure-fire loser who
never doubts for an instant that
he's meant to be a winner.

Patinkin isn't able to endow
his ex-fireman with what isn't in
the script — i.e., motivation for
putting his trust in such a lowlife
— but his intensity, intelligence
and self-control are an excellent
contrast to his wild partner.

Director Haas has fashioned
an impeccably elegant, visually
distinguished film that demonstrates an impressive control of
tone and an ease with actors and
dialogue. — *Todd McCarthy*

OH BOY!
(DUTCH)

A First Floor Features production.
Executive producer, Hans De Weers.
Produced by Laurens Geels, Dick Maas.
Directed, written by Orlow Seunke. Cam-
era (color), Marc Felperlaan; editors,
Seunke, Hans Van Dongen; music, Maar-
ten Koopman; production design, Rikke
Jelier; art direction, Willem Klewais;
sound, Georges Bossaers; special ef-
fects, Hans Voors, Ray Purkis; make
up, Nancy Beaudoux; casting, Dorna X.
Van Rouveory. Reviewed at Palm
Springs Intl. Film Fest, Jan. 26, 1993.
Running Time: **88 min.**
With: Orlow Suenke, Kees Van Kooten,
Monique Smets, Steffen Kroon, Peer
Mascini, Tom Jansen, Jim Van Der
Wonde, Huub Stapel.

Director Orlow Suenke's
stylized satire, "Oh Boy!" aims
at being a cross between a Buster Keaton silent comedy and
Francois Truffaut's "Day for
Night." Unfortunately, neither
the movie-within-movie nor the
behind-the-scenes story in this
Dutch offering is very funny,
let alone original. Prospects
for theatrical release of what is
essentially one prolonged absurdist joke are dim, though it
may be more appreciated in
the fest circuit.

Scripter-helmer Seunke stars
in the dual role of Pim, an actor
who bears physical resemblance
to Keaton, and Boy, star of the
move-within-movie, who runs a
dilapidated gas station in the
middle of nowhere. The satire
gets off to a good start when
Buzz (Kees Van Kooten), an idealized 'Texaco Man,' builds a modern state-of-the-art gas station

next door. Of course, there is
hardly enough business for one
station, and a rivalry begins.
Seunke also soon falls in love
with Gal (Monique Smets) Buzz's
daughter.

As expected, the action alternates between watching the
movie about the one-upmanship
between the two competitors and
routine on-the-set problems. The
rivalry between the male leads
predictably extends onto the set's
gallery of stock characters: A
beautiful actress for whom both
men show amorous intentions; a
temperamental, egotistical star
who constantly fights with the
director and cast; a stingy producer mostly concerned with the
budget, and a happy ending, etc.

Seunke acquits himself better
as an actor than as writer or
director. But "Oh Boy!" does
boast an attractive, consciously
artificial, look. Art director Willem Klewais and production designer Rikke Jelier have whimsi-
cally copied the cluttered chaos
that usually dominated Keaton's
sets. — *Emanuel Levy*

IK-TSCHEMTAN
(THERE WHERE I LIVE)
(GEORGIAN)

A Studio Georgia Film production.
Written, directed by Zaza Khalvachi.
Camera (color), Dshirnscher Christes-
saschwili; editor, Leila Aschiani; music,
Jakob Bobochidse; costume design, Nato
Kandelaki; sound, Suram Gogua; pro-
duction manager, Roman Beraia. Re-
viewed at Montpellier Festival of
Mediterranean Cinema, Montpellier,
France, Oct. 28, 1992. Running time: **70
MIN.**
With: Nino Koberidse, Neto Change-
laia, Lali Meskhi, Giorgi Achwlediani,
Berdia Inzkirweli.

"Ik-Tschemtan," the
bleak tale of an extended family in the Caucasus mountains
of post-Soviet Georgia, leaves
an indelible and distressing impression. The dreary subject
and relatively brief length make
festivals the most likely outlet
for this first feature from Georgian helmer Zaza Khalvachi.

Life is hard and holds no promise for three generations of sub-
sistence farmers crammed into a
ramshackle house threatened by
mudslides and avalanche.

Considering that one of five
cohabiting brothers is a chronic
drunk, another resorts to theft,
the women are worn out, the
children are joyless and the patriarch is a little nuts, it's remarkable that all concerned behave as well as they do.

The entire clan is forced to
evacuate whenever landslides
threaten. Family exodus at night
provides a stark shot of bundled
figures against the morning mist.
The well-lensed setting of rocks,
snow and barren trees is rugged
and striking, if desolate, and its
poverty is apparent in decrepit
buildings so badly heated
thesps' breath is visible *indoors*.

The desperate family clings to
its misery until some of the group
find the courage to set off for
other pastures. Pic was runner-
up for the top prize at the Montpellier fest. — *Lisa Nesselson*

LA FEMME
DU DESERTEUR
(THE DESERTER'S WIFE)
(FRENCH-ISRAELI)

A Mimar Films/Mod Films/Solyfic
co-production with the participation of
Investimage 3. Produced by Marek Roz-
enbaum, Hugues Nonn. Directed, writ-
ten by Michal Bat-Adam. Camera (color),
Fabio Conversi; editor, Rivka Yogev;
music, Alex Kagan. Reviewed at Montpel-
lier Festival of Mediterranean Cinema,
Montpellier, France, Oct. 29, 1992 (com-
peting). Running time: **81 MIN.**
Nina . . . . Fanny Ardant
Ilan . . . . Sharon Alexander
Also with: Gidi Gove, Schamuel
Vilozni, Ruth Geller.

A compelling central con-
flict and a moving perf from
Fanny Ardant make "La Femme
du Deserteur" a suspenseful
and rewarding drama. Michal
Bat-Adam's emotionally draining account of a French concert pianist and her combat-
traumatized Israeli husband in
the months leading to the outbreak of the Gulf War has the
potential to reach specialized
and arthouse auds.

Nina (Ardant) and Ilan
(Sharon Alexander) meet in Paris
where they share an interest in
keyboards — piano for her, computers for him. They marry and
move to Israel where Alexander
is called up in the reserves.

Word soon comes that he has been wounded in an ambush and is hospitalized. Ardant finds him aphasic, dead-to-the-world and under military investigation.

Ardant strikingly conveys Nina's compassion and frustration as she struggles to communicate with her zombie-like spouse; eventually she finds that Alexander went AWOL for reasons unknown and was shot by fellow Israelis — no shame is greater than abandoning a post.

The implications of his actions are so overwhelming that Alexander remains hollow, drained and defeated for the bulk of the film, a task at which the actor excels. Since Ardant isn't a *sabra* (native-born Israeli), nobody thinks she can understand his predicament and, by extension, that of his family and friends and she begins to feel ostracized despite her apparent devotion.

Talk of Scuds, gas masks, sealed rooms, etc. is taken in stride throughout the well-paced lead-up to the Gulf War and the personal drama is served when Jan. 15 — the deadline date for Saddam Hussein to withdraw from Kuwait — is also the date of Ardant's debut as solo pianist with the Israeli Philharmonic.

To the pic's credit, the war, as seen through Ardant's oblivious eyes, is handled so well viewers may doubt whether it will happen or not. Tension is high on concert night and the musical drama of the Mozart concerto fits well, though the denouement verges on excess.

— *Lisa Nesselson*

EL LABERINTO GRIEGO
(THE GREEK LABYRINTH)
(SPANISH)

A Warner Espanola presentation of an Impala SA/Trabala Prods. production. Produced by Antonio Guillén, Manuel García. Directed by Rafael Alcázar. Screenplay, Manuel Vázquez Montalbán, Alcázar, from Vázquez Montalbán's novel. Camera (color), Tote Trenas; editor, Miguel González Sinde; music, Bernard Bonezzi; production design, Carlos Bodelón; sound, Enrique Molinere, Jose Antonio Bermúdez. Reviewed at Montpellier Festival of Mediterranean Cinema, Montpellier, France, Oct. 28, 1992. Running time: **97 MIN.**
With: Omero Antonutti, Aitana Sánchez-Gijón, Eusebio Poncela, Luis Fernando Albés, Magüi Mira.

"**E**l Laberinto Griego," a stylish suspenser peopled with

intriguing characters, loses momentum toward the end but leaves a satisfying if lightweight impression. Lensed with flair in a Barcelona scrambling to raze and rebuild for the Olympic games, Rafael Alcázar's second feature should do okay or better in arty hardtops and will play just dandy on the tube.

Barcelona private eye Omero Antonutti is approached by a stunning enigmatic French woman (Aitana Sánchez-Gijón) to find the "love of her life," a Greek model and painter who fled their love nest in Paris. She and her elegant businessman companion (Eusebio Poncela, familiar from Almodóvar pics) believe the b.f. is in Barcelona. Divorced Antonutti, taken with the gorgeous femme, accepts the case.

Creative gumshoeing leads the trio to the missing gent, who turns up dead next morn. The P.I., whose employers have split, has some explaining to do.

The hunt — in which AIDS, drugs and assorted sexual preferences are vital components — is laced with mocking humor, offbeat characters and local color. Both Antonutti's life and his city are clearly in disarray.

Antonutti is a winning combo of practiced cynicism and renewed lust. Sánchez-Gijón shines as a classic femme fatale. Supporting roles are good, particularly P.I.'s caustic ex-wife, yuppie son and lovely daughter.

Helmed with verve and lensed by night and by bright Catalan sunshine, tech credits are pro.

— *Lisa Nesselson*

AUTOMNE: OCTOBRE A ALGER
(AUTUMN: OCTOBER IN ALGIERS)
(FRENCH-ALGERIAN)

A Djanet Prod./SIA/ENPA/FR-3 Cinema/ENTV co-production with the participation of the CNC/Canal Plus/3B Prods. Produced by Tarek Lakhdar-Hamina. Directed by Malik Lakhdar-Hamina. Screenplay, Malik Lakhdar-Hamina, Arezki Bouaziz. Camera (color), Youcef Sahraoui; editor, Youcef Tobni; music, Safy Boutella; production design, Mohamed Boudjemaa; costumes, Habel Boukhari; sound, Dominique Vieillard. Reviewed at Montpellier Festival of Mediterranean Cinema, Montpellier, France, Oct. 27, 1992. Running time: **92 MIN.**
With: Malik Lakhdar-Hamina, Nina Koriz, Merwan Lakhdar-Hamina, Mustapha El-Anka, François Bourcier, Sid-Ahmed Agoumi, Rachid Fares, Halima Hanetite, Azzedine Medjoubi, Doudja.

Malik Lakhdar-Hamina's first feature, "Automne: Octobre à Alger," is an earnest, sober, intelligently lensed drama about conditions in Algiers in the weeks leading up to the popular demonstrations and violent government crackdown of October '88. Not yet released in Algeria, where it is certain to attract attention, pic is a promising debut that could play fests in addition to theatrical runs in North Africa and France.

Helmer Malik Lakhdar-Hamina is low-key and likable as a professional musician and ardent husband to his modern, working wife (Nina Koriz). He also supports his extended family, who include a rigid fundamentalist brother (who prays instead of working) and his submissive sister-in-law, until his music is censored because an accompanying videoclip is judged pornographic and dangerous by authorities.

His troubles are only beginning. Lakhdar-Hamina is beaten on several occasions — by police and by fundamentalists — and always when he is well within his rights by Western standards.

Pic avoids assigning blame while presenting overcrowded apartments, corruption and a palpable climate of repression. However, script packs in so many plot elements and grievances that it seems longer than its actual running time.

Naturalistic thesping is okay to good throughout. Except some authority figures, every character is presented with dignity.

Score by Safy Boutella is varied and rhythmic except for one syrupy exception.

Pic won the Best First Film award at the Carthage (Tunisia) fest and nabbed the Prix du Publizue at Montpellier.

— *Lisa Nesselson*

SOMMERSBY

A Warners Bros. release of a Le Studio Canal Plus/Regency Enterprises/Alcor Films presentation of an Arnon Milchan production. Executive producers, Richard Gere, Maggie Wilde. Produced by Milchan, Steven Reuther. Directed by Jon Amiel. Screenplay, Nicholas Meyer, Sarah Kernochan, from Meyer and Anthony Shaffer's story, based on "The Return of Martin Guerre," written by Daniel Vigne, Jean-Claude Carrière. Camera (Duart color, Technicolor prints), Philippe Rousselot; editor, Peter Boyle; music, Danny Elfman; production design, Bruno Rubeo; art direction, Michael Johnston; set decoration. Michael Seirton; costumes design, Marilyn Vance-Straker; sound (Dolby stereo), Chris Newman; co-producer, Mary McLaglen; 1st assistant director, Josh McLaglen. Reviewed at Warner Burbank screening room, Burbank, Calif., Jan. 25, 1993. MPAA Rating: PG-13. Running time: **112 MIN.**

Jack	Richard Gere
Laurel	Jodie Foster
Buck	Lanny Flaherty
Travis	Wendell Wellman
Orin	Bill Pullman
Little Rob	Bretty Kelley
Reverend Powell	William Windom
Esther	Clarice Taylor
Joseph	Frankie Faison
Dick Mead	R. Lee Ermey
Doc Evans	Richard Hamilton
Mrs. Eveans	Karen Kirschenbauer
Storekeeper Wilson	Carter McNeese
Tom Clemmons	Dean Whitworth
John Green	Stan Kelly
Mrs. Bundy	Stephanie Weaver
Eli	Khaz B.
Lawyer Dawson	Maury Chaykin
Judge Isaacs	James Earl Jones
Court Bailiff	Stuart Fallen
Timothy Fry	Richard Lineback
Witness	Joe Basham

"**S**ommersby" is an unabashedly romantic and at the same time morally intricate Civil War-era tale splendidly acted by Richard Gere and Jodie Foster. It's one of those rare occasions that the Americanization of a foreign property (here Daniel Vigne's "The Return of Martin Guerre") works as well as the original. Female audiences should flock to see the Richard Gere/Jodie Foster pairing and Warners appears to have a b.o. winner.

The relative merits of "Sommersby" and "Martin Guerre" are debatable. But while borrowing heavily from the original film, itself inspired by a 16th century incident, "Sommersby" stands on its own as an entertaining and engrossing moral fable.

The missing-in-action and presumed dead Jack Sommersby (Gere) suddenly reappears two years after the end of the Civil War and attempts to start life anew with his wife, Laurel (Foster), and young son. Foster breaks off her relationship with the righteous Orin (Bill Pullman) and tentatively resumes her place alongside her husband.

She quickly succumbs to her husband's charms. Sommersby returns a new man, as tender and committed to his wife and the community as he had once been distant and cruel. Naturally, this arouses suspicion about his identity.

The movie keeps the question beautifully balanced in mid-air. Audiences may suspect the truth all along, but the real crux of the story turns out to be why, not who. And that, ultimately, is what lends gravity to the film.

Helmer Jon Amiel ("The Singing Detective," "Tune In Tomorrow") is up to the challenge of the material, making it work both commercially and artistically, though perhaps not in equal measure. He gives the film both intimacy and scope; it's old-fashioned like a '30s historical drama and yet accessible to contemporary auds. It moves leisurely, but every moment is dense and the pace rarely lags.

The one cavil is a subplot about Sommersby's attitude toward racial equality which, while noble, seems more a concession to a 1990s sensibility than an 1860s reality. Dramatically, Sommersby is too evolved and enlightened, especially for someone who isn't motivated by a strong personal bond with any of the blacks.

Otherwise Nicholas Meyer and Sarah Kernochan's screenplay (from Meyer and Anthony Shaffer's story) is cogent and elegantly literate. The film's ending is entirely appropriate but will be much debated.

Original film:
LE RETOUR DE MARTIN GUERRE
(THE RETURN OF MARTIN GUERRE)
(FRENCH)

A GEF/CCFC release of a Société Française de Production Cinematographique/Société de Productions des Film Marcel Dassault/FR3 co-production. Directed by Daniel Vigne. Screenplay, Vigne, Jean-Claude Carrière. Camera (Fujicolor), Andre Neau; editor, Denise de Casablanca; music, Michel Portal; art direction, Alain Negre; costumes, Anne-Marie Marchand; sound, Michel Chamard; makeup, Didier Lavergne. Reviewed at the Paris theatre, Paris, May 27, 1982. Running time: **123 MIN.**
Martin Guerre . . . Gérard Depardieu,
. . . . .Stephane Pean,
. . . . .Bernard Pierre Donnadieu
Bertrande de Rois . . . Nathalie Baye
(as youngster) . . . . . . Sylvie Meda
Judge Coras . . . . . . Roger Planchon
Priest . . . . Andre Chaumeau
Pierre Guerre . . . . . Maurice Barrier

As good as it is, without the personal chemistry between Foster and Gere, "Sommersby" would be nowhere near as satisfying an experience. Foster is as compelling an actress as we have, telegraphing layer after layer of emotional subtext.

But Gere, whose production company developed the film, comes close to stealing the picture. It's his best performance since "Internal Affairs" and most likable since "An Officer and a Gentleman," delivering force and subtlety in equal measure.

The often underrated Bill Pullman is fine as the jilted suitor.

Technically the movie is flawless. Danny Elfman's lush orchestral score is a stand-out. Visually the film is all of a piece, muted and not overly pretty. Philippe Rousselot's lensing, Bruno Rubeo's design and Marilyn Vance-Straker's costumes adhere to a rich, earthy palate.

— *Richard Natale*

UNTAMED HEART

An MGM/UA release from MGM. Executive producer, J. Boyce Harman Jr. Produced by Tony Bill, Helen Buck Bartlett. Directed by Bill. Screenplay, Tom Sierchio. Camera (DeLuxe color), Jost Vacano; editor, Mia Goldman; music, Cliff Eidelman; production design, Steven Jordan; art direction, Jack D.L. Ballance; set decoration, Cliff Cunningham; costume design, Lynn Bernay; sound (Dolby), Matthew Quast; associate producers, Sierchio, Marci Liroff; assistant director, Babu (T.R.) Subramaniam; casting, Liroff. Reviewed at Filmland Corporate Center screening room, Culver City, Calif., Jan. 22, 1993. Running time: **102 MIN.**
Adam . . . . Christian Slater
Caroline . . . . Marisa Tomei
Cindy . . . . Rosie Perez
Howard . . . . Kyle Secor
Patsy . . . . Willie Garson

Appealing lead performances elevate this modestly scaled romantic tearjerker. If MGM can get the word out, "Untamed Heart" could pump reasonable b.o. returns into the studio's coffers, although its best prospects may come after a transplant to homevideo.

Working from a first script by Tom Sierchio, director Tony Bill doesn't spare the sentimentality but benefits from the beguiling Marisa Tomei, Rosie Perez's unique comic flair and a refreshingly understated turn by Christian Slater.

Tomei plays a Minneapolis waitress who tends to go out with jerks and fails to finish what she starts, or so co-worker/pal Perez tells her. Recently dumped, Tomei is assaulted one night by two creeps from the local diner, only to be rescued by Slater, an introverted, almost nonverbal busboy so enamored of her he regularly follows her home.

An awkward and unlikely romance develops, Tomei slowly penetrating Slater's protective shell, put up due to the orphaned youth's congenital heart ailment, which has kept him at arm's distance from people throughout his life. He also clings to a fairy tale about his heart coming from a baboon king after the death of his father (the pic's working title was "Baboon Heart").

The story sometimes seems like an excuse to get out the can opener and serve up the corn. But Sierchio's script possesses some strong romantic flourishes and Bill takes advantage of them. The perfs prove so earnest the movie largely works on its own terms, particularly for those looking for a traditional "good cry."

Following her breakthrough in "My Cousin Vinny," Tomei establishes her dramatic credentials here, projecting a very believable girl-next-door quality. Slater nicely projects Adam's longing and discomfort in social situations, while Perez remains a truly unique presence, though perhaps best in measured doses.

Tech credits are undistinguished but solid, with Minneapolis providing an appropriately drab backdrop and a melancholy score by Cliff Eidelman that keeps the angst flowing out of this "Heart." — *Brian Lowry*

IN ADVANCE OF
THE LANDING
(CANADIAN-DOCU-COLOR/B&W-16m)

A Cineplex Odeon Films release of a Cygnus Communications production. (Intl. sales: Films Transit.) Executive producer, Don Haig. Produced, directed by Dan Curtis, suggested by Douglas Curran's book. Script consultant, Jim Osborne; camera (Film House color, 16m), Don Hutchison; editor, Kevin Schjerning; music, Fred Mollin; sound, Brian Avery. Reviewed at Public Theater, N.Y., Jan. 23, 1993. No MPAA Rating. Running time: **85 MIN.**
With: Ruth E. Norman, Betty Hill, Larry W. Bryant, Gabriel Green, John Shepherd, Evan Hayworth, Paul Eichenberg, Alan Moseley, Dr. Marcello Truzzi, Sherrie Rose.

This bland documentary on UFOs is an exercise in naivete, both on the part of the subjects and the filmmaker. Copyrighted in 1991, film most closely resembles Diane Keaton's "Heaven." Similar mix of extended interviews, man-on-the-street Q&As and old, mainly B&W film footage lacks focus and consistency.

Canadian filmmaker Dan Curtis (not the U.S. horror and miniseries maestro) does not offer any narration or opinion of his own, making this feature different from the gee-whiz or government exposé approach of '70s docus like "Overlords of the UFO" and "UFOs Are Real." Traveling across the U.S. and Canada, Curtis has found goofy, often lonely people who share a need to believe.

Some are messianic figures, like the nutty 90-year-old Ruth E. Norman and her Unarius cult. She calls herself Uriel and compares herself to Jesus Christ. Alan Moseley is a priest in a weird L.A. cult known as the Aetherius Society which collects prayers in Prayer Batteries and claims to have achieved a ceasefire in Cyprus in 1974.

Two of the oddest interviewees are Betty Hill and John Shepherd. Hill, famous from supposedly having been abducted with her husband Barney by aliens (shown portrayed by Estelle Parsons in a clip from the 1975 telefilm "The UFO Incident"), discredits herself with ridiculous statements. Even more pathetic is Shepherd, who looks like a hippy and has spent 21 years transmitting signals to outer space and waiting for an answer. The audience almost calls out in unison: "Get a life!"

Less scintillating segments include Bud Hopkins, a Gotham artist who's written w.k. books on the subject, and Larry W. Bryant, a Pentagon employee who moonlights as head of "Citizens Against UFO Secrecy." Curtis fails to follow up this sober approach to the UFO craze.

Old movie trailers and excerpts from classics like "The Day the Earth Stood Still" and "This Island Earth" are fun, matched with newsreels and delightful clips from "The Arrival," a crazy, religioso special effects film made by Norman's Unarius Academy of Science.

Interludes of dumb questions asked of folks on the street elicit fatuous answers and add nothing to the film. Oddly, since the early pseudo-documentaries occasionally featured actors pretending to be real interviewees, one of the people caught on the street turns out to be B-movie actress Sherrie Rose, uncredited. Since she's being interviewed in L.A., Curtis probably suffered from the locational hazard of sticking a microphone in front of a woman without realizing she was an actress. — *Lawrence Cohn*

FORTRESS
(AUSTRALIAN-U.S.)

A Roadshow (Australia) release of a Village Roadshow Pictures/Davis Entertainment production. (Intl. sales: IAC Film Sales.) Executive producers, Graham Burke, Greg Coote. Produced by John Davis, John Flock. Directed by Stuart Gordon. Screenplay, Steve Feinberg, Troy Neighbors, Terry Curtis Fox. Camera (CFI color), David Eggby; editor, Timothy Wellburn; music, Frederic Talghorn; production design, David Copping; sound, Paul Clark; co-producers, Neal Nordlinger, Michael Lake; line producer, Irene Dobson; assistant director, Charles Rotherham; stunts, Glenn Boswell; special effects supervisor, Tad Pride; visual effects supervisor, Paul Gentry; casting (U.S.), Mike Fenton; casting (Australia), Maura Fay. Reviewed at Village Cinema City, Sydney, Jan. 20, 1993. Running time: **89 MIN.**

John Brennick	Christopher Lambert
Poe	Kurtwood Smith
Karen Brennick	Loryn Locklin
Abraham	Lincoln Kilpatrick
Nino	Clifton Gonzalez Gonzalez
D-Day	Jeffrey Combs
Stiggs	Tom Towles
Maddox	Vernon Wells

"Fortress" is a grim, sometimes bloody, futuristic prison picture that has been well produced and directed within the limitations of a predictable, uninspired screenplay. It should do modest theatrical business among the macho crowd (some scenes of violence against women will appall femmes) before a successful video career.

Fans of director Stuart Gordon's early schlock efforts ("Re-Animator," "From Beyond") will be disappointed to find the helmer working with altogether more conventional material this time around. But he still pulls off a few abrasive moments of genuine suspense despite the formula narrative and characters. Pic was shot with an Australian crew in the Warner Roadshow Movie World Studios in Queensland, and is a good ad for the facility; David Copping's production design of a privately run prison of the future built 30 stories underground is imaginatively conceived and constructed and is, indeed, the star of the film.

Operated by a multinational outfit known as the Men-Tel Corp., the prison uses lasers, computers and robots to control its male and female inmates. Discipline is maintained by so-called "intestinators," small metal objects implanted into the body of each prisoner, which can be activated to cause extreme pain or even death.

Pic is set in the U.S. after exploding population and depleted resources have resulted in a law against couples having more than one child. The Brennicks (Christopher Lambert and Loryn Locklin) lost their first baby, and now Locklin is pregnant a second time, a felony.

The couple are nabbed trying to cross into Mexico, and both wind up in the Fortress. While Lambert, a former Black Beret officer, undergoes beatings by fellow prisoners, his wife manages to charm all-seeing prison director Kurtwood Smith, who runs the giant computer that controls everything. Locklin uses every opportunity with Smith to plan her husband's escape.

None of this makes much sense, and too much of the dialogue sounds as if it were written for Dennis Hopper. There are some moments of graphic bloodshed, but the general tone of the film is rather somber, and it never emerges as a very exciting or suspenseful picture since the outcome is so predictable.

Lambert is adequate in the lead, and Locklin is appealing as the traumatized wife. The rest of the cast go through the motions, but are imprisoned in their rote roles. As sci-fi actioners go, "Fortress," despite its fine production credits, remains a middling experience. — *David Stratton*

MATINEE

A Universal Pictures release of a Renfield production. Produced by Michael Finnell. Directed by Joe Dante. Screenplay, Charlie Haas, from story by Jerico, Haas; camera (Deluxe color), John Hora; editor, Marshall Harvey; music, Jerry Goldsmith; sound (Dolby), Howard Warren; production design, Steven Legler; costume design, Isis Mussenden; assistant director, Donald P.H. Eaton; co-producer, Pat Kehoe; visual effects supervisor, Dennis Michelson; Mant/Ant design, James McPherson; stunt coordinator, Jeff Smolek; casting, Gretchen Rennell, Melvin Johnson (Florida), Simone Reynolds (U.K.). Reviewed at Universal screening room, N.Y., Jan. 25, 1993. MPAA Rating: PG. Running time: **99 MIN.**

Lawrence Woolsey	John Goodman
Ruth Corday/Carol	Cathy Moriarty
Gene Loomis	Simon Fenton
Stan	Omri Katz
Sandra	Lisa Jakub
Sherry	Kellie Martin
Dennis Loomis	Jesse Lee
Anne Loomis	Lucinda Jenney
Harvey Starkweather	James Villemaire
Howard	Robert Picardo
Spector	Jesse White
Herb	Dick Miller
Bob	John Sayles
Jack	David Clennon
Rhonda	Lucy Butler
Bill/Mant	Mark McCracken
Doctor	William Schallert
Scientist	Robert Cornthwaite
General	Kevin McCarthy

Joe Dante lovingly re-creates the monster pics of his youth in "Matinee," an okay film geared toward buffs that should have been much better. General audiences should find the pic's charms resistible.

Reminiscent of (but a vast improvement upon) the 1991 horror film "Popcorn," "Matinee" derives from a high concept (credited to Jerico and scripter Charlie Haas) in which the real-life fears of the 1962 Cuban missile crisis interact with the artificial fears of a horror film premiering at a Key West movie house.

Believably cast as a huckster/showman modeled after producer-director William Castle, John Goodman is previewing his new monster pic "Mant!" (Half Man, Half Ant, All Terror!) in hopes of impressing exhibitor Jesse White to book it at his 50 theater chain.

Castle was known for his macabre films such as the Hitchcock takeoff "Homicidal" as well as hoopla gimmickry like the Punishment Poll and Cowards' Corner. Dante pays homage to the gimmicks with Goodman's girlfriend and main actress Cathy Moriarty dressed as a nurse to have patrons sign releases regarding death by fright when entering the theater.

Goodman exploits the Cold War tensions with Atomo-Vision, another gimmick themed to his film's A-bomb genetic mutations theme. Film-in-a-film "Mant!" is a very accurate, hilarious black & white pastiche featuring (uncredited) genre vets Kevin McCarthy, Robert Cornthwaite (of the original "The Thing") and William Schallert opposite Moriarty. It has elements from the classic "The Fly" crossed with Bert I. Gordon's grasshoppers epic "Beginning of the End."

Against this rather amusing and knowing backdrop, "Matinee" makes two serious missteps that limit its overall achievement and appeal. Star John Goodman is always delightful when on screen, but is not given enough footage amid the sappy and well-worn teen romance plots. Secondly, the keen satire (a Dante specialty) evident in many well-written scenes gives way to numbing nostalgia in others.

For example, Dante stages a brief film within a film, "The Shook Up Shopping Cart," which pointedly spoofs the typically dumb Disney comedy of the period. Yet he lets his own film lapse into the excruciating clichés of both the "good teen" romances and the j.d. sagas of the '50s.

British thesp Simon Fenton is convincing as the lead character Gene, a new kid in school whose dad has been sent from his Key West military base to serve in the blockade against Soviet ships delivering offensive weapons to Cuba. He gets a crush on Lisa Jakub, a very precocious ban-the-bomb teen with cleverly stereotyped, freewheeling parents David Clennon and Lucy Butler.

Even when the film gets bogged down in romantic drivel, there are enough clever in-jokes and well-remembered period details to keep buffs happy. Casting is accurate down to employing Jesse White as the prototypically cynical exhib; he worked for Castle in the Sid Caesar comedy "The Spirit Is Willing."

Amidst the slow sections are solid comic turns by Goodman, Moriarty, Robert Picardo as the paranoid theater manager, and the unlikely team of John Sayles and Dick Miller as Goodman's shills who pretend to be outraged censors seeking decent screen entertainment. Under heavy monster makeup, Mark McCracken is delightful playing the Mant as a standup comedian.

Tech credits for this Florida-lensed effort are consistently good, including an elaborate but pointless segue into the disaster film genre when Fenton's young brother is trapped in the theater's falling balcony. Jerry Goldsmith's score amusingly mickey-mouses the action for satirical purposes without becoming cloying. — *Lawrence Cohn*

February 1, 1993 (Cont.)

NEMESIS

An Imperial Entertainment release. Executive producers, Sundip R. Shah, Anders P. Jensen, Sunil R. Shah. Produced by Ash R. Shah, Eric Karson, Tom Karnowski. Directed by Albert Pyun. Screenplay, Rebecca Charles. Camera (color), George Mooradian; editors, David Kern, Mark Conte; music, Michael Rubini; production design, Colleen Saro; art direction, Phil Zarling; costume design, Lizz Wolf; special visual effects, Fantasy II Film Effects; assistant director, George Parra; stunt coordinator, Ronny Rondell. Reviewed on Imperial vidcassette, L.A., Jan. 25, 1993. MPAA Rating: R. Running time: **95 MIN.**

Alex Rain	Olivier Gruner
Farnsworth	Tim Thomerson
Angie-Liv	Cary-Hiroyuki Tagawa
Max Impact	Merele Kennedy
Yoshiro Han	Yuji Okumoto
Jared	Marjorie Monaghan
Germaine	Nicholas Guest
Michel	Vince Klyn
Marion	Thom Mathews
Pam	Marjean Holden
Maritz	Brion James
Julian	Deborah Shelton
Billy	Tom Janes
Einstein	Jackie Earle Haley

If there's such a thing as cinematic dyslexia, "Nemesis" is it. Starring Olivier Gruner, the latest entrant in the sulking hunk action competition, the film doesn't even make a stab at logic. Set in the year 2020, "Nemesis" interbreeds "Robocop" cybernetics and "Blade Runner" cyborgs with passing references to the "Terminator" films. Combo should at least provide for a passable action exercise, but fails in almost every respect.

Film is supposedly set in Los Angeles and more exotic locales such as Brazil and the fictitious South Sea island of Shang-Loo. But it all looks like the same post-nuclear rubble heap. And it's shot with all the clarity of Oklahoma during a dust storm — deliberately.

Gruner plays a human (albeit one largely composed of mechanical replacement parts) in a world increasingly peopled by cyborgs, an LAPD cop with an indecipherable European accent. Fortunately, most of his colleagues also speak English as a second language. And they all have impeccable fashion sense, wearing only Armani/Hugo Boss style suits and designer eyewear. Whatever else, fashion obviously thrives in the future, and the LAPD leads the way.

Distaff cast members, most of them cyborgs, are all tall, lithe with great manes of hair and drop-dead physiques. Isn't science wonderful?

Direction by Albert Pyun is confusing but no one could be expected to make sense of Rebecca Charles' script. Best exchange Gruner: "I cared about you once." Former ladyfriend: "I'm synthetic."

Technical credits are adequate with only costume designer Lizz Wolf seems to have been given any latitude. Special visual effects by Fantasy II Film Effects deliver some nifty eye-crunching scenes and make hay despite what is obviously a threadbare f/x budget.

Gruner is no worse an "actor" than Van Damme or Schwarzenegger and he might catch on if he's ever surrounded by a real movie. — *Richard Natale*

HEXED

A Columbia Pictures release of a Price Entertainment/Brillstein-Grey production. Executive producers, Bernie Brillstein, Howard Klein. Produced by Marc S. Fischer, Louis G. Friedman. Directed, written by Alan Spencer. Camera (CFI color; Technicolor prints), James Chressanthis; editor, Debra McDermott; music, Lance Rubin; production design, Brenton Swift; costume design, Joan S. Thomas; sound (Dolby), Michael Haines; assistant director, Jules Lichtman; stunt coordinator, Russell Towery; casting, Cathy Henderson, Tom McSweeney. Reviewed at Manhattan 1 theater, N.Y., Jan. 22, 1993. MPAA Rating: R. Running time: **90 MIN.**

Matthew Welsh	Arye Gross
Hexina	Claudia Christian
Gloria O'Connor	Adrienne Shelly
Victor Thummell	Ray Baker
Det. Ferguson	R. Lee Ermey
Simon Littlefield	Michael Knight
Rebecca	Robin Curtis
Ms. Strickland	Brandis Kemp
Herschel Levine	Norman Fell
Jennifer	Pamela Roylance
Larry	Billy Jones
Hexina's body double	Shelley Michelle

Some surefire slapstick footage is about all that's funny in the stillborn comedy "Hexed." Writer-director Alan Spencer's debut pic makes one long for the sophistication of "Police Academy" movies.

Strictly sitcom premise finds 30-year-old hotel desk clerk Arye Gross anxious to end his rut and pump some excitement into his life. Enter beautiful French model and cover girl Hexina (Claudia Christian), with whom Gross inveigles a blind date by impersonating a guy who turns out to be blackmailing her.

Gross and Christian have sex in scenes imitating "Fatal Attraction" and "Basic Instinct," after which he finds out she's really a psychotic killer who's spent six years in a mental institution. Christian continues her murderous ways as Gross becomes more and more involved.

As the body count mounts, director Spencer spends much of his satire at the expense of the police, including a surprisingly funny spoof (with white victim Ray Baker) of the Rodney King beating incident. It's bad-taste humor like that that works here, as Spencer's dialogue and most situations are unfunny. Gross is an able farceur but hard-pressed to make any of the increasingly silly plot twists believable.

Christian's acting is way over the top, though she's well-cast as the beautiful loon. As she looks (and even, at times, talks) like a taller Kathleen Turner, Spencer typically misses a golden opportunity to spoof "Body Heat."

Adrienne Shelly, familiar from Hal Hartley films, is appealing as Gross's co-worker and would-be girlfriend, while R. Lee Ermey effectively spoofs his image playing an incredibly dumb cop.

Film looks cheap and slapdash, with nondescript lighting. Much is dully paced, especially the opening reel prior to Christian's entrance. — *Lawrence Cohn*

SUNDANCE FEST

BOXING HELENA

A Main Line Pictures presentation of a Philippe Caland production. Executive producers, James R. Schaeffer, Larry Sugar. Produced by Carl Mazzocone, Caland. Directed, written by Jennifer Chambers Lynch. Story by Caland. Camera (Technicolor; Panavision widescreen), Frank Byers; editor, David Finfer; music, Graeme Revell; art direction, Paul Huggins; sound (Ultra-Stereo), J. Bayard Carey; associate producers, Laurel Ann Selko, Bridget Caland; assistant director, Josh King; casting, Fern Cassel. Reviewed at Sundance Film Festival, Park City, Utah, Jan. 23, 1993. MPAA Rating: NC-17. Running time: **107 MIN.**

Dr. Nick Cavanaugh	Julian Sands
Helena	Sherilyn Fenn
Ray	Bill Paxton
Dr. Alan Palmer	Kurtwood Smith
Anne	Betsy Clark
China	Nicolette Scorsese

The subject of an unusual amount of advance talk due to the last-minute dropouts of prospective stars Kim Basinger and Madonna, the feature debut of 24-year-old writer-director Jennifer Lynch (daughter of David), bizarre subject matter and a very disputable NC-17 rating, "Boxing Helena" arrives with the sort of hyped-up expectations rarely helpful in appreciating what a film is actually about. As it is, this is the kind of intense, obsessive work that is easy to make fun of because it often goes too far, but is also surprising and intermittently potent enough to make it more interesting than some blander successes. Commercially, it's doubtful that this can rise out of fringe cult status, although a strong promo push by an enterprising distrib could make it into a momentary mini-sensation.

There's plenty here for audiences to hoot and holler about —hot and heavy voyeurism, pathetic sexual obsession unleavened by humor, outrageous behavior unmitigated by logic, and the spectacle of a beautiful woman surgically divested of her arms and legs and propped up on a box-like wooden perch in the middle of an opulent mansion — but there are dark, legitimate themes being mined as well and, from a directorial p.o.v., Jennifer Lynch displays a bold confidence, a tenacious grip on her style and a clear view of her objectives.

Working from a premise already explored in "The Collector," "Tie Me Up, Tie Me Down" and "Misery," tale offers up Julian Sands as a top surgeon who, as sketched, has been alternately humiliated and ignored by his wealthy parents. Involved with worshipful nurse Betsy Clark, Sands has had a one-night stand with stunning neighbor Sherilyn Fenn and now can't get the voluptuous sexpot out of his mind. Telling Clark he's going jogging, he instead climbs a tree outside Fenn's home and sweatily watches her disrobe until she gets it on with nasty new lover Bill Paxton.

Sands then throws a party just so he can once again see the aloof object of his desire, but Fenn throws his interest back in his face by taking off with a buddy of his. Bitchy, condescending and cruel, Fenn tells Sands in a hundred different ways to get lost, until a horrible accident deprives her of her legs and places her forever in the sick doctor's hands.

Remainder of the warped story plays on the notion of whether one person can force another to love him through cumulative dependence, time and the force of his own love. Fenn remains defi-

February 1, 1993 (Cont.)

antly belligerent even through Sands' unnecessary removal of her arms, but then seems to respond when he places her in the position of voyeuristically observing him making passionate love to a stunning stranger.

Ending is deflatingly contrived, to a great extent taking the edge off the points the film is making. Still, to viewers open to explorations of private and weird obsessions, "Boxing Helena" has something to offer. Without being a psychological treatise, it also charts a plausible case history for ending up as Sands does.

The numerous sex scenes are good and steamy. At the same time, they are no more explicit than those seen in innumerable R-rated films, leading one to wonder again what standards are in force at the MPAA, particularly where indies are concerned.

Film looks terrific, with kudos going to lenser Frank Byers for his darkly nuanced hues and to Lynch for strongly orchestrating the diverse design elements.

In the end, it's probably just as well that Basinger or Madonna didn't take the title role, as the presence of a star lurking powerlessly on the little platform no doubt would have been distracting and more laughable than it now, on occasion, is. Most of the festival audience lost it when, after being berated by Fenn for having mutilated her, Sands sincerely said, "I never meant for it to be like this."

But the thesps give it all the overheated conviction they can muster, and enticing dark waters are stirred, however erratically. Destined to be dismissed by most observers, it will undoubtedly be a guilty pleasure for some others. — *Todd McCarthy*

HERCULES RETURNS
(AUSTRALIAN)

A Roadshow (Australia) release of a Philm Prods. production. (Intl. sales: Beyond Films). Executive producer, Peter Winter. Produced by Philip Jaroslow. Directed by David Parker. Screenplay, Des Mangan; camera (color), David Connell; editor, Peter Carrodus; music, Philip Judd; production design, Jon Dowding; sound, Lloyd Carrick; production manager, Lesley Parker; assistant director, Euan Keddie. Reviewed at Village Roadshow screening room, Sydney, Jan. 20, 1993. (In Sundance Film Festival). Running time: **80 MIN.**

Brad McBain . . . . David Argue
Sprocket . . . . Bruce Spence
Lisa . . . . Mary Coustas
Sir Michael Kent . . . Michael Carman
King . . . . Brendon Suhr
Film Critic . . . . Margaret Pomeranz
Film Critic . . . . . . Ivan Hutchinson
   Voices: Des Mangan (Hercules, Samson, Machismo, Ursus, Testiculi), Sally Patience (Labia, Muriel, Fanny, Delilah), Matthew King (Charlie).
   With: Alan Steel (Hercules), Red Ross, Nadir Baldmor.

World preeming at a late-night screening at the Sundance fest, "Hercules Returns" follows in the footsteps of Woody Allen's "What's Up Tiger Lily?" by completely revamping and re-voicing a bad old foreign movie. Melbourne-based comics Des Mangan and Sally Patience have, via their Double Take comedy team, successfully presented live performances in Australia and the U.K., in which they re-voiced the films "Astro Zombies" and the 1964 Italo sword-and-sandal stinker "Hercules, Samson, Maciste and Ursus Are Invincible."

They've now adapted their second show, "Double Take Meets Hercules," into "Hercules Returns," with assistance from first-time director David Parker, who's better known as a screenwriter and cinematographer working in partnership with his wife, Nadia Tass. Parker has directed about 18 minutes of framing footage, but most of "Hercules Returns" consists of the re-voiced film.

Original Film:
HERCULES, SAMSON, MACISTE AND URSUS ARE INVINCIBLE
(ITALIAN, 1964)

A Senior Cinematografica production. Produced by Giorgio Cristallini. Directed, written by Giorgio Capitani. Camera, Carlo Belgero; editor, Roberto Canquini; music, Piero Umiliani.

The framing material features film buff Brad McBain (David Argue), who rents a rundown picture palace to show his favorite movies, rousing the ire of the boss of the country's most powerful cinema chain.

At the gala opening of the refurbished theater, McBain plans to screen "Hercules, Samson" etc., but his manic projectionist, Sprocket (Bruce Spence) discovers at the last moment that the print has arrived in its original Italo-language version, sans subtitles. McBain, Sprocket and publicist Lisa (Mary Coustas) frantically improvise a voiceover translation for the black-tie audience, and it's a hit (one well-known local critic rates it a 5 out of 5).

The improvisation turns the original clinker (never reviewed in VARIETY) into an hilarious romp, with Hercules now a frustrated singer sent by Zeus to perform at the Pink Parthenon nightclub where he's offered the hand of the lovely Labia, daughter of the club's owners. She, however, prefers Testiculi and rejects Hercules, who teams up with Samson (a weakling after Delilah shears off his hair), Ursus, a drunken Scottish bouncer, and the homosexual Machismo for some unspectacular mayhem in which obviously cardboard sets are frequently demolished.

The concept works very well, with the new dialogue (written by Mangan) cleverly undermining the plot of the original film (whatever it was) to often hilarious comic effect. Pic is pitched squarely at adult auds, however, with the dialogue littered with profanity and jokes involving genitalia and bodily functions.

Drawback is that the talk is full of Aussie slang and expressions. However, by the very nature of the exercise, the voices could easily be re-dubbed in foreign territories; that the voices are never in synch with the lip movements doesn't matter since they never were.

Film has an endearing, slapdash feel to it, and could well become a popular cult success. Argue, Spence and Coustas seem to be having fun in the framing footage, while the original Italo actors never have a chance.

Technically, it's excellent.
— *David Stratton*

TWENTY BUCKS

A Big Tomorrow Prods. presentation. Produced by Karen Murphy. Directed by Keva Rosenfeld. Screenplay, Leslie Bohem, Endre Bohem. Camera (Deluxe color), Emanuel Lubezki; editor, Michael Ruscio; music, David Robbins; production design, Joseph T. Garrity; art direction, Rando Schmook; set decoration, Linda Allen; co-set decoration, Kenneth Kirchner; costume design, Susie DeSanto; sound (Dolby), Douglas Axtell; line producer, Jason Clark; assistant director, Martha Elcan; casting, Pagano/Bialy/Manwiller. Reviewed at Sundance Film Festival, Park City, Utah, Jan. 22, 1993. Running time: **90 MIN.**

Angeline . . . . Linda Hunt
Baker . . . . David Rasche
Jack Holiday . . . . . George Morfogen
Anna Holiday . . . . Sam Jenkins
Sam . . . . Brendan Fraser
Sam's Mother . . . . . Concetta Tomei
Stripper . . . . Melora Walters
Mrs. McCormac . . . . Gladys Knight
Emily Adams . . . . . . Elisabeth Shue
Frank . . . . Steve Buscemi
Jimmy . . . . Christopher Lloyd
Bobby McCormac . . Kamau Holloway
Property Clerk . . . . William H. Macy
Ruth Adams . . . . Diane Baker
Chuck . . . . Matt Frewer
Priest . . . . Spalding Gray
Bank Teller . . . . . . Nina Siemaszko

"Twenty Bucks" is worth more like two bucks and change. A soft, contrived episodic piece that follows the lifespan of a $20 bill as it passes from person to person, pic ignores its opportunity to say something about society and is populated by an almost entirely blah set of characters. Commercial chances look meager.

Documentary filmmaker Keva Rosenfeld's debut fictional feature both harks back to the kind of omnibus films that Hollywood made in the 1930s and to the recent cult favorite "Slacker" in its multicharacter, cross-section-of-society format.

There is actually a good reason for the first similarity: "Twenty Bucks" originated in an unproduced script first written by Hungarian emigré scenarist Endre Bohem in 1935. The elder Bohem died in 1990, but his son Leslie updated the material to its current contemporary form.

Alas, that remains the most interesting aspect of the project. From the first scene, in which smart-mouthed streetperson Linda Hunt finds, then loses the stray bill fresh from a cash machine, the film has a case of the cutes from which it will be hardpressed to recover. It doesn't.

Among the lives into which the currency happens to pass are those of working stiff Brendan Fraser, who almost marries an Arab-American girl whose self-made zillionaire father arrived in the U.S. with exactly $20; "witch" Gladys Knight and her precocious grandson Kamau Holloway, a black teenage would-be Julia Child; oddball stick-up artists Christopher Lloyd and Steve Buscemi; and waitress/aspiring writer Elisabeth Shue.

Unfortunatley, the single memorable character is Christopher Lloyd's thief, disarmingly understated as an efficient old pro trying to teach some life lessons to hot-headed recruit Buscemi. Nor at any time is the bill used to give rise to any reflections on class, economy or society, never standing for anything more than what it is —twenty dollars.

Technically, the Minneapolis-shot picture looks just fine, with young Mexican lenser Emanuel Lubezki turning in another impressive job. But it's to little avail on a picture with so little on its mind. — *Todd McCarthy*

BODIES, REST & MOTION

A Fine Line Features release of a Fine Line Features/August Entertainment presentation of a Mindel/Shaw production (Intl. sales: August Entertainment). Executive producer, Joel Castleberg. Produced by Allan Mindel, Denise Shaw, Eric Stoltz. Directed by Michael Steinberg. Screenplay, Roger Hedden, from his play. Camera (Deluxe color), Bernd Heinl; editor, Jay Cassidy; music, Michael Convertino; production design, Stephen McCabe; art direction, Daniel Talpers; set decoration, Helen Britten; costume design, Isis Mussenden; sound (Dolby), Walt Martin; co-producers, Hedden, Jeffrey Sudzin; assistant director, Mike Topoozian. Reviewed at Sundance Film Festival, Park City, Utah, Jan. 23, 1993. Running time: **93 MIN.** .
Carol . . . . Phoebe Cates
Beth . . . . Bridget Fonda
Nick . . . . Tim Roth
Sid . . . . Eric Stoltz

Uncompelling but moderately engaging throughout due to its attractive cast and closeup look at contemporary spiritual ennui, "Bodies, Rest & Motion" is both flashy and laid-back, eventful and static. Script feels as if it knows whereof it speaks, and pic could rise above moderate b.o. expectations if it connects significantly with the late-20s generational group that is its subject.

Set in a sun-baked, fictional Arizona town called Enfield that is all malls and fast-food pit stops, the sharp-looking film looks at four young people coping with a malaise that seems neither easily diagnosable nor curable.

Although the film could as plausibly have been called "Entropy in Enfield," characters reflect the Newtonian principle evoked by the title. Adapted by Roger Hedden from his own play, piece betrays its theatrical origins by virtue of its taking place over one weekend mostly in a house shared by agitated, dissatisfied Tim Roth and his unfocused g.f., Bridget Fonda.

In the opening scene, Roth tells former g.f. Phoebe Cates, now Fonda's best friend, that they have decided to move to the "city of the future" — Butte, Montana — and are packing up.

Abruptly, however, Roth hits the road on his own, leaving the distraught Fonda alone with a pile of furniture and dope-smoking housepainter Eric Stoltz and the new couple soon get it on.

For the climax, both men square off over Fonda, who's been forced by her extreme situation to finally take her life into her own hands, however unpromising the future may appear.

Michael Steinberg, who makes his solo debut here after co-directing last year's "The Waterdance," gives the film an edge of pretension through his totemic use of Indian-like chanting music, kitschy tourist paraphernalia and towering cacti. At the same time, he's good with the actors, and the more intimate the scene, the more effectively it registers.

What's best about the film is the sense it conveys of how everyday life can remain humdrum and uneventful for the longest time, only to change seismically within a very short period. However, many scenes don't really have much going on in them, resulting in a relatively low-impact experience.

Still, when all else fails, the performers continually make it watchable. Fonda has the pivotal role and comes off as well as ever, suggesting depths of unarticulated uncertainties and embodying the lack of character definition is central to the film's concerns. Stoltz is good as the easygoing fellow who has lived in this cultural wasteland all his life and tries to get Fonda to settle down with him, while Roth's volatile mood swings introduce some welcome vigor and humor. Cates is appealing, but her role is too self-contained and self-satisfied in an unexplored way to be fully dimensional.

Bernd Heinl's lensing is very warm and colorful, and the arid locations serve as an apt correlative to the spiritual void under investigation. — *Todd McCarthy*

SILVERLAKE LIFE: THE VIEW FROM HERE
(DOCU-B&W/COLOR)

A Silverlake production in association with Channel 4 Television/J.P. Weiner Inc. Produced, directed by Tom Joslin, Peter Friedman. Camera (color), Joslin, Mark Massi, Elaine Mayes, Friedman; editor, Friedman; music, Lucia Hwong, additional music, Fred Gilde; co-producers, Doug Block, Jane Weiner. Reviewed at Sundance Film Festival, Park City, Utah, Jan. 25, 1993. (Also in Berlin Film Festival.) Running time: **99 MIN.**

"Silverlake Life," a documentary about AIDS, is one of a kind — a gay couple's harrowing record of the disease told from the time they were diagnosed to their deaths. The unflinching camera and the probing honesty with which the pair talk make "Silverlake" a unique first-hand journal but, at the same time, make it hard to watch, unfortunately confining the docu to the fest circuit and public and cable TV.

The subjects and objects of "Silverlake Life" are Tom Joslin, a former USC film professor and director, and his companion, Mark Massi. When Joslin was diagnosed with AIDS, he decided to shoot a video diary, using a small super-VHS camcorder. After Joslin's death, the docu was completed by Peter Friedman, his friend and former student.

The docu vividly and authentically portrays the magnitude and day-to-day suffering of life with AIDS, graphically imparting the exhaustion of both body and mind, the routine hospital checkups, drugs and their side effects, the preparation of prescribed food. It also renders the emotional and psychic impact of AIDS: isolation from society, anxiety about family and friends' reaction, disease-induced memory loss and depression.

Docu begins with Joslin's loading a cassette into a VCR, and talking directly to the camera about his love for Massi, followed by his treatment for Kaposi's sarcoma lesions at the hospital.

Most of docu is set inside the couple's Silverlake, Calif., house. There are a few excursions, such as a Christmas visit to Joslin's family in New Hampshire that captures the need for parental support and the anxiety involved in getting it.

Footage from Joslin's earlier docu, "Blackstar," about his life

as an openly gay man, a film that caused "a little consternation" among his family when broadcast on PBS, is poignantly integrated into the new docu.

One of docu's most harrowing scenes shows in closeup the death of Joslin and the necessary ministrations — closing his eyes, putting the 60-pound body in a mortuary bag. This is counterbalanced with Massi, after 22 years with his lover, finally being embraced as a legitimate member of Joslin's family — after Joslin's death.

Though the filmmakers are always aware of the camera, there is nothing hopeful or life-affirming about this journal — the couple make no attempt to portray their battle as heroic, a radical difference from other AIDS docus such as "Voices From the Front" or the Oscar-winning "Common Threads: Stories From the Quilt."

Some viewers may fault docu for not dealing with the broader socio-political context. But this is entirely consistent with the filmmakers' sharply focused account. What sustains Joslin and Massi during the most horrifying moments is their true love, passion and commitment. If there are any messages to be drawn from "Silverlake," they have less to do with personal courage than with the nature of this relationship. — *Emanuel Levy*

THE TRIAL

A BBC Films/Europanda Entertainment presentation. (Intl. sales: Capitol Films, London). Executive producers, Kobi Jaeger, Reniero Compostella, Mark Shivas. Produced by Louis Marks. Directed by David Jones. Screenplay, Harold Pinter, from Franz Kafka's novel. Camera (Rank Film Labs color), Phil Meheux; editor, John Stothart; music, Carl Davis; production design, Don Taylor; art direction, Jim Holloway; costume design, Anushia Nieradzik; sound (Dolby), Jim Greenhorn; assistant directors, Jake Wright, Jiri Matolin (Prague); casting, Leo Davis, John Lyons (U.S.). Reviewed at Sundance Film Festival, Park City, Utah, Jan. 24, 1993. Running time: **118 MIN.**
Josef K. . . . . Kyle MacLachlan
The Priest . . . . . . Anthony Hopkins
Dr. Huld . . . . Jason Robards
Landlady . . . . Jean Stapleton
Leni . . . . Polly Walker
Titorelli . . . . Alfred Molina
Fraulein Burstner . . Juliet Stevenson
Block . . . . Michael Kitchen
Washerwoman . . . Catherine Neilson
Court Usher . . . . . . Patrick Godfrey

This "Trial" is just that. Despite a fine cast, superior

Prague locations and a faithful Harold Pinter screenplay, this second film adaptation of Kafka's landmark 1913 novel is dull, lifeless and strictly TV-bound in its aesthetics. Prestige aspects of the production could give it a theatrical window, but this might actually play better on the tube.

Kafka's famous tale is both a paranoid vision of the authoritarian Austro-Hungarian Empire and an amazing prophecy of totalitarian regimes to come. Whereas Orson Welles, in his brilliant, if erratic, 1961 film, took an abstract approach, creating a fable that could take place anytime, anyplace, Pinter and director David Jones, whose feature debut was the superior adaptation of Pinter's "Betrayal," have set it very concretely in the pre-war central European milieu.

Pinter is on record that "The Trial," which he first read in his teens, has always represented one of the most important influences on his own work; this production came about when the BBC asked him to select the work he most wanted to adapt.

Opening scene suggests that perhaps its strength could lie in the pointed suggestiveness and humor of the language, rather than in the elaborate visuals of Welles' version. Two inspectors arrive at Josef K.'s boarding house one morning and make a surprise announcement. "You are under arrest." "Why?," K. asks. "We are not authorized to tell you," is the reply.

Unfortunately, this is to remain as the best sequence in the picture. But Josef K.'s nightmare has begun. Up against the brick wall of an authoritarian regime and an unknowable Law, K. (Kyle MacLachlan) moves experiences that are progressively illogical and evocative of modern man's absurd status in the universe. There are sexual skirmishes with an other boarder (Juliet Stevenson) and his lawyer's mistress (Polly Walker), encounters with various men who possess passing knowledge of aspects of the Law (uncle Robert Lang, attorney Jason Robards, court painter Alfred Molina) and assorted odd characters, such as a washerwoman (Catherine Neilson) who submits sexually to her detested boyfriend in front of hundreds of people at K.'s hearing.

But, as structured, the script evolves as a tedious series of mostly two-character scenes that are generally confrontational in nature, and lacking the darkly humorous edge promised in the first scene. The themes of the original work may be present, but only because of what is being discussed. They are not expressed cinematically, and the customary Pinter rhythms and depth charges of meaning never announce themselves.

Some deep focus cinematography by Phil Meheux allows the colors and architecture of Prague to take a notable place in the proceedings, but the settings remain mostly ornamental.

Performances are perfectly acceptable without being at all electrifying. MacLachlan — his lean but strong frame and general bearing reminiscent of Anthony Perkins (Welles' K.) —pushes the imprudent, feisty, sometimes overbearing aspects of his character, but is a good leading man for leaving aspects of his personality open for the viewer to invest him/herself in him.

Most of the others are on only for one or two scenes, with Anthony Hopkins arriving toward the end as a priest to explain the Law and K.'s choices to him.

Carl Davis' score is vigorous and old-fashioned in the good sense. — *Todd McCarthy*

NITRATE KISSES
(DOCU-B&W-16m)

A Barbara Hammer Prods. production. All credits (including producer, director, script, 16mm B&W camera, editor and sound), Barbara Hammer. Reviewed at Toronto Festival of Festivals, Sept. 14, 1992. Running time: **63 MIN.**

"Nitrate Kisses" fizzles as gay erotica but serves as a historical document. To gain any profile, this graphic docu needs some good censorship whiplash. Otherwise, oddly shot B&W docu is marginal. Its window is gay fests.

Pic marks feature debut for Barbara Hammer, a radical lesbian who has voiced her hardcore politics in numerous experimental shorts.

As in previous work, Hammer's "Nitrate Kisses" is clearly designed to shock. There are numerous closeup shots of genitals while elderly women make love or interracial males couple. Graphic docu will likely be considered pornographic by mainstream standards and enlightened by the radical gay community.

Relationships between various "couples" remain a mystery to the audience. But details about the exclusion of gays in contemporary history books is hammered home as texts are superimposed over images like credits, pic's most interesting low-budget technique.

As usual, Barbara hammers her fun-free p.o.v. down viewers throats, the message being that gay life exists and must be acknowledged. Point taken.

Unfortunately, images are more often repulsive (for example, of elderly women masturbating) than convincing to the outsider. Ultimately, "Nitrate Kisses" is preaching to the converted. — *Suzan Ayscough*

PAPER HEARTS

A King/Moonstone production. Executive producers, Sally Kirkland, James Brolin. Produced by Rod McCall, Catherine Wanek. Directed, written by McCall. Camera (color), Barry Markowitz; editor, Curtis Edge; music, George S. Clinton; production design, Susan Brand; art direction, Stuart Blatt; costume design, Leslie Daniel Rainer; sound, Jonathan Earl Stein; casting, Tom Kahn. Reviewed at Sundance Film Festival, Park City, Utah (in competition), Jan. 22, 1993. No MPAA rating. Running time: **90 MIN.**
Jenny . . . . Sally Kirkland
Henry . . . . James Brolin
Samantha . . . . Pamela Gidley
Tom . . . . Kris Kristofferson
Patsy . . . . Laura Johnson
Bill . . . . Michael Moore
Kat . . . . Renee Estevez

A feminist streak informs Rod McCall's directorial feature debut "Paper Hearts," a modest, sensitive and often touching family drama that poignantly dissects the effects of a dissolving marriage. But despite a robust, dominating performance by Sally Kirkland and a first-rate cast, leisurely paced pic is marred by an uneven script and lack of vital direction. Commercial outlook is fair to middling.

Kirkland stars as Jenny Stevenson, an attractive, middle-aged woman separated from her scoundrel womanizer of a husband, Henry (James Brolin), who left her a mountain of debts. Struggling to assert a new identity and build a new life for herself, Jenny tries to hold onto the house she inherited, now on the verge of foreclosure.

The family's disparate members reunite for one stormy and fateful weekend, during which Kirkland's youngest daughter (Renee Estevez) gets married. Brolin claims he came to the wedding to see his "little girl," but he's actually scheming to get the house. The oldest daughter (Pamela Gidley), a music student in New York, also shows up.

McCall uses the wedding to examine the pain of marital dissolution for a woman still clearly in love with her husband and the generational rift between mother and daughters. Kirkland, a prototype of a woman who can't exist without a man, is contrasted with Gidley, her sophisticated and sexually assertive daughter.

McCall acquits himself better as writer than as director, endowing his story with a coherent female point of view.. The moody, often somber film consists of brief scenes, usually confrontations between two characters.

Regrettably, the big climactic scene, in which Brolin is exposed by the women in his life, is overly melodramatic and contains an unnecessary nude scene by Kirkland that borders on the risible. However, Kirkland, who debuts as exec producer, gives her most forceful and modulated perf since her Oscar-nominated "Anna."

Most tech credits are proficient; lenser Barry Markowitz' captures the landscape's beauty and mythic force. — *Emanuel Levy*

February 8, 1993

THE VANISHING

A 20th Century Fox release of a Morra, Brezner, Steinberg & Tenenbaum production. Executive producers, Pieter Jan Brugge, Lauren Weissman. Produced by Larry Brezner, Paul Schiff. Directed by George Sluizer. Screenplay, Todd Graff, from Sluizer's 1988 film "Spoorloos," written by Sluizer, Tim Krabbé and Krabbé's novel "The Golden Egg." Camera (Deluxe color), Peter Suschitzky; editor, Bruce Green; music, Jerry Goldsmith; production design, Jeannine C. Oppewall; costume design, Durinda Wood; sound (Dolby), Jeff Wexler; co-producer, Graff; assistant director, Yudi Bennett; production manager, Ira Shuman; stunt coordinator, Chris Howell; casting, Risa Bramon Garcia, Juel Bestrop, Dixon/Walker Casting (Seattle). Reviewed at Coronet theater, N.Y., Feb. 3, 1993. MPAA Rating: R. Running time: **110 MIN.**

Barney	Jeff Bridges
Jeff	Kiefer Sutherland
Rita	Nancy Travis
Diane	Sandra Bullock
Lynn	Park Overall
Denise	Maggie Linderman
Helene	Lisa Eichhorn
Arthur Bernard	George Hearn
Miss Carmichael	Lynn Hamilton

Some last-reel thrills and cathartic violence provide commercial oomph to the otherwise tedious thriller "The Vanishing." This is one remake that sacrifices much of what made the original work so well. Auds hot for even a taste of slam-bang suspense might conjure good early figures, weak word of mouth will probably result in a disappearing act.

Dutch director George Sluizer, whose 1991 "Utz" opens domestically next week, had the rare chance to remake his own 1988 "Spoorloos" in America (Francis Veber's "Three Fugitives" from "Les Fugitifs" was a precedent). Unfortunately this version, scripted by Todd Graff, is schematic and unconvincing.

Scrupulously applying Alfred Hitchcock's theories of suspense, film introduces Jeff Bridges as the villain at the outset, rehearsing methods of chloroforming victims and plotting kidnappings. He's a happily married school teacher, close to his young daughter (Maggie Linderman) but with a Nietzschean complex, bent on proving he is beyond good and evil.

Parallel story has Kiefer Sutherland and g.f. Sandra Bullock on vacation from Seattle driving past Mount St. Helens when, after an row that hints at possibilities of a break-up, she suddenly disappears from a rest stop. Sutherland goes crazy looking for her; the police don't help as there's no evidence of foul play.

Fade out to three years later and Sutherland's obsession with finding her has continued, with constant posting of new "Vanished" flyers with Bullock's photos. On his rounds of the disappearance area, he meets a kindred spirit in diner waitress Nancy Travis. Another fadeout and it's months later with Travis moving into his home in Seattle.

Sluizer's elliptical approach (with frequent fadeouts for time transition) works against audience involvement in a story that relies far too much on coincidence. Changes from the original include giving Sutherland an easy commute to his obsession, losing the power (including dealing with the police) of the "foreign country" angle of a Dutch couple vacationing in France.

There's also much emphasis (and at least one continuity error) on Sutherland's Bullwinkle car key chain that Bullock takes with her and Bridges uses to demonstrate he's the kidnapper. The gimmick wasn't in the original and doesn't work well. Viewers not familiar with the foreign-language original — and that's

Original film: SPOORLOOS (THE VANISHING) (DUTCH)

A Hungry Eye Pictures release of a Golden Egg Films production. Produced by Anne Gordon, George Sluizer. Directed by Sluizer. Screenplay, Tim Krabbé, Sluizer. Camera (color) Tom Kuhn; editor, Sluizer; music, Henry Vrienten; set design, Santiago Isidro Pin; costumes, Sophie Dussaud; sound, Piotr van Dijk. Reviewed Aug. 29, 1988. Running time: **107 MIN.**

Rex	Gene Bervoets
Saskia	Johanna ter Steege
Lemorne	Bernard-Pierre Donnadieu
Also with: Gwen Eckhaus.	

the vast majority of Fox's target audience —won't know what they're missing, but it's faint solace for receiving sloppy seconds.

After seeing Sutherland make a plea on a TV show, Bridges seeks him out with the notion of taking him through the exact steps Bullock took in order to show Sutherland what happened to her. This gimmick is then run into the ground with the characters' reactions becoming increasingly unbelievable.

The ultimate, chilling climax of the original is repeated in the remake, but with 25 minutes to go and to with very little impact — it's been given away in the heavily-played trailer. Suspense is also lacking because the U.S. version has beefed up Travis' role (a sketchy, brief part in the original) to become Sutherland's rescuer for a "happy ending."

Travis' sudden ingenuity in outwitting Bridges in the last reel is the best thing about Graff's screenplay, but there are gaffes, such as a confusing emphasis on a gun, that hurt this lengthy coda. Ultimately it is this ultraviolence against the villain in the spirit of vigilantism that most markedly differentiates the U.S. from the European approach.

Unlike the subtle acting of Bernard-Pierre Donnadieu in the original, Bridges adopts an odd gait, curious manner, and an on-and-off accent that are distracting and spoil his performance.

Sutherland comes off as a wimp and Travis has no characterization at all, merely an obvious plot cog. Reunion of Bridges and Lisa Eichhorn as his wife (from "Cutter's Way") goes nowhere.

Washington state locations are attractively photographed by Peter Suschitzky and Jerry Goldsmith's score helps maintain interest and a mood of apprehension. — *Lawrence Cohn*

GROUNDHOG DAY

A Columbia Pictures release of a Trevor Albert production. Executive producer, C.O. Erickson. Produced by Albert, Harold Ramis. Directed by Ramis. Screenplay, Danny Rubin, Ramis, from Rubin's story. Camera (Technicolor) John Bailey; editor, Pembroke J. Herring; music, George Fenton; production design, David Nichols; art direction, Peter Lansdown Smith; set design, Karen Fletcher-Trujillo; costume design, Jennifer Butler; sound (Dolby) Scott R. Thomson; associate producer, Whitney White; assistant director, Michael Haley; 2nd unit director, Steve Boyum; 2nd unit photography, James Blanford, George Kohut. Reviewed at Mann's Village Theater, L.A., Feb. 4, 1993. Rating: PG. Running time: **103 MIN.**

Phil	Bill Murray
Rita	Andie MacDowell
Larry	Chris Elliott
Ned	Stephen Tobolowsky
Buster	Brian Doyle-Murray
Nancy	Marita Geraghty
Mrs. Lancaster	Angela Paton
Gus	Rick Ducommon
Ralph	Rick Overton
Doris the Waitress	Robin Duke
Anchorwoman	Carol Bivins
Man in Hallway	Ken Hudson Campbell
Piano Teacher	Peggy Roder
Neurologist	Harold Ramis
Psychiatrist	David Pasquesi

The premise of the romantic comedy "Groundhog Day" is essentially "if you had it to do over again — and again — what would you do differently?" And while you have to hand it to Harold Ramis (who co-scripted, co-produced and directed) for his stick-to-itiveness, the film is inconsistent in tone and pace; fortunately the pay-off works, bringing some much needed warmth to the area. Audiences are likely to forgive the dry spells and leave smiling. With a cast headed by Bill Murray and Andie MacDowell, "Groundhog Day" could cast a b.o. shadow for the remaining weeks of winter.

Murray, a cynical TV weatherman finds himself stuck in a private, repetitious hell: Groundhog Day in Punxsatawney, Pa., where he has come for the annual festivities. The day begins, over and over, at 6 a.m., Sonny & Cher on the clock radio, and moves on almost invariably, as Murray undergoes every conceivable emotional permutation — from confusion to anger to cockiness to despair—finally thawing into a beneficent soul.

The situation is ripe with comic potential — it's as if Mayberry were crossed with "Brigadoon" (pic even uses Nat King Cole's version of "Almost Like Being in Love"). But Danny Rubin and Ramis's script provides more chuckles than belly laughs. Some sequences are crisply paced and comically terse, some ramble and others just plain don't work.

Murray's weatherman is tailor-made for his smug screen persona, perhaps too much so. There are times when you wish the character were played by someone with the daffiness of Chris Elliott, largely wasted here, or at least the affable Murray of "What About Bob?"

Without the glow of Andie MacDowell's bemused, charming performance as Murray's producer and eventual romantic interest, it's hard to gauge the progress of his character's transformation, or know when he's still being ironically or actually attempting to be sincere.

Of the supporting players, Stephen Tobolowsky is hilarious in a loose-limbed turn as Murray's cloying ex-schoolmate.

Ramis' direction is often too cool and restrained. He wisely avoids playing into the tale's underlying sentimentality. Still, a little more genuine feeling along the way wouldn't have hurt and when it finally does give in to its Capra-esque side, it's satisfying.

Technical credits are professional and handsome. John Bailey's expert cinematography is of great service in suspending disbelief — every day has to look like exactly the same day and does. Production design by David Nichols nicely captures the feel of a Rust Belt small town.

—Richard Natale

February 8, 1993 (Cont.)

NATIONAL LAMPOON'S LOADED WEAPON 1

A New Line Cinema release of a New Line production, in association with 3 Arts Entertainment. Executive producers, Michel Roy, Howard Klein, Erwin Stoff. Produced by Suzanne Todd, David Willis. Directed by Gene Quintano. Screenplay, Don Holley, Quintano, from Holley, Tori Tellem's story. Camera (Deluxe color; Film House prints), Peter Deming; editor, Christopher Greenbury; additional editor, Neil Kirk; music, Robert Folk; production design, Jaymes Hinkle; costume design, Jacki Arthur; sound (Dolby), Marty Bolger, John Coffey; co-executive producer, Michael DeLuca; assistant directors, Ken Goch, David Womark; production manager, William Carroll; special effects coordinator, Lou Carlucci; stunt coordinator, Charles Picerni; casting, Ferne Cassel. Reviewed at Murray Hill theater, N.Y., Feb. 5, 1993. MPAA Rating: PG-13. Running time: **83 MIN.**
Jack Colt . . . . Emilio Estevez
Wes Luger . . . . . Samuel L. Jackson
Becker . . . . Jon Lovitz
Jigsaw . . . . Tim Curry
Destiny Demeanor . . . Kathy Ireland
Capt. Doyle . . . . Frank McRae
Gen. Mortars . . . . . William Shatner
Sgt. York . . . . . . Whoopi Goldberg
Harold Leacher . F. Murray Abraham
Also with: Bill Nunn, Dr. Joyce Brothers, Lin Shaye, Vito Scotti, Ken Ober, James Doohan, Richard Moll, Charlie Sheen, Denis Leary, Corey Feldman, Phil Hartman, J.T. Walsh, Erik Estrada, Larry Wilcox, Paul Gleason, Ric Ducommun, Charles Napier, Charles Cyphers, Robert Shaye, Danielle Nicolet, Beverly Johnson, Bruce Willis.

More an imitation than a parody, this would-be comedy is very short on laughs and virtually all are given away in its trailer. Comedy-starved audiences may give it a couple of weeks' life at the boxoffice.

The National Lampoon logo was last used on a movie spoof in 1981 with "National Lampoon Goes to the Movies," but that deadpan effort was so bad it never got a theatrical release. This one isn't any better.

Premise is spoofing Richard Donner's three "Lethal Weapon" movies right down to copying their logo. Unfunny script by director Gene Quintano and his co-writers assumes that the viewer will be kept awake by having scenes alternate between the three films but it's not sufficient to qualify as effective satire.

Launching point is Emilio Estevez doing a flat reading of Mel Gibson's hothead character, just like brother Charlie Sheen made fun of Tom Cruise in "Hot Shots!" To remind the viewer of this, Sheen shows up as a valet parking attendant and Jon Lovitz even brings up the ripoff question explicitly late in the film.

Unfortunately, Estevez lacks the feel for self-parody his brother demonstrates.

Ostensible plotline has evil general William Shatner (allowed to ham it up disturbingly by Quintano) and goofy-accented henchman Tim Curry in a scheme involving cocaine and Girl Scout (that's Wilderness Girl) cookies.

Investigation begins when cop Whoopi Goldberg (one of the few uncredited cameos) is murdered. Estevez is teamed with Goldberg's ex-partner Samuel L. Jackson, earmarked for the Danny Glover role. Jackson plays straight, doesn't even come close to raising a smile in the audience and merely proves that he would have been miscast opposite Mel Gibson in the first place.

The re-creation of scenes from "L.W." movies includes Jackson's pretty daughter Danielle Nicolet playing footsie with Estevez from film 1 and Estevez comparing scars with heroine Kathy Ireland a la Rene Russo in film 3. From film 2 we have Estevez's beach home blown up, only it turns out to be the home of uncredited guest star Bruce Willis (in "Die Hard" garb) by mistake.

Film digresses at length with Kathy Ireland and an uncredited actress both playing Sharon Stone in "Basic Instinct" for some cheap potshots. This is one area where the film's PG-13 rating negates the unexpurgated comedy potential of the material.

By the time "Loaded Weapon 1" ends with an imitation of "Wayne's World," its abbreviated 76-minute running time (plus 7 minutes of credits to come) has become exceedingly tedious. Scattershot sight gags and cheap action scenes obviously can't compete with the scope of the Warner Bros. Donner films, which, thanks to the stars' cross talk and Joe Pesci, have plenty of honest humor in them.

— *Lawrence Cohn*

HOMEWARD BOUND: THE INCREDIBLE JOURNEY

A Buena Vista release of a Walt Disney Pictures presentation in association with Touchwood Pacific Partners I. Executive producers, Donald W. Ernst, Kirk Wise. Produced by Franklin R. Levy, Jeffrey Chernov. Directed by Duwayne Dunham. Screenplay, Caroline Thompson, Linda Woolverton, from Sheila Burnford's book. Camera (Technicolor), Reed Smoot; editor, Jonathan P. Shaw; music, Bruce Broughton; production design, Roger Cain; art direction, Daniel Self; set decoration, Nina Bradford; costume design, Karen Patch; sound (Dolby), Bayard Carey; co-producer, Mack Bing; assistant director, Scott Cameron; head dog trainer, Gary (Sam) Vaughn; head cat trainer, Tammy Maples; special animal effects and makeup, Barry Demeter; casting, Susan Bluestein, Marsha Shoenman. Reviewed at Avco Cinema Center, L.A., Jan. 26, 1993. MPAA Rating: G. Running time: **84 MIN.**
Shadow . . Ben (voice by Don Ameche)
Chance . . Rattler (v.o. Michael J. Fox)
Sassy . . . . Tiki (v.o. Sally Field)
Bob . . . . Robert Hays
Laura . . . . Kim Greist
Kate . . . . Jean Smart
Peter . . . . Benj Thall
Hope . . . . Veronica Lauren
Jamie . . . . Kevin Chevalia

Leave it to the Disney marketing machine to dust off a venerable nature-adventure film like 1963's "The Incredible Journey" and wed it with "Look Who's Talking," creating a sprightly little entertainment that should enthrall tots without straining the patience of parents. While at times a bit heavy-pawed, enough kids should answer this call to nature to bury plenty of bones in Disney's backyard.

Working loosely from the original Disney movie (which featured a Rex Allen narration), the studio has taken that frame and built on it — applying animation principles to live-action by giving personalities to the movie's wayward dogs and cat through the clever use of the voices of Michael J. Fox, Sally Field and Don Ameche.

Although the story also gets spruced up with some '90s twists — like a "Brady Bunch"-type marriage between Robert Hays and Kim Greist bringing their kids together into one big family — the plot still centers on three pets, left with a family friend, who try to cross the wilderness and make it back home, encounter menaces from bears to porcupines on the way.

The aging Shadow (a golden retriever voiced with stately dig-

nity by Ameche) leads the way, followed by the upstart mutt Chance (Fox) and snooty feline Sassy (Field). The non-nuclear family isn't all that's new in this telling, however. The screenplay by Linda Woolverton (of "Beauty and the Beast," putting her writing-for-animation skills to good use) and Caroline Thompson ("Edward Scissorhands") develops a parallel view of family through the pet relationships, as the independent-minded Chance learns about love, trust and kinship from the old dog.

Granted, some of Ameche's boy-and-his-dog monologues are enough to tempt more jaded listeners to cough up a hairball, but its Mister Rogers-like simplicity should play extremely well with kids. For the most part, in fact, the writers have done a splendid job capturing what animals seem to be thinking without making them cognizant of what humans

Original film: THE INCREDIBLE JOURNEY

Buena Vista release of a Walt Disney (James Algar) production. Directed by Fletcher Markle. Screenplay, Algar, from Sheila Burnford's book. Camera (Technicolor), Kenneth Peach, Jack Couffer, Lloyd Beebe; editor, Norman Palmer; music, Oliver Wallace. Reviewed Oct. 10, 1963. Running time: **86 MIN.**
John Longridge . . . . . Emile Genest
Prof. Jim Hunter . . . . John Drainie
The Hermit . . . . . . Tommy Tweed
Mrs. Hunter . . . . Sandra Scott
Helvi Nurmi . . . . Syme Jago
Elizabeth Hunter . . Marion Finlayson
Peter Hunter . . . . . . Ronald Cohoon
James MacKenzie . . . Robert Christie
Nell MacKenzie . . . . Beth Lockerbie
Carl Nurmi . . . . Jan Rubes
Mrs. Nurmi . . . . . . Irena Mayeska
Mrs. Oakes . . . . Beth Amos
Bert Oakes . . . . . . Eric Clavering

are saying, except for the few words the pets recognize.

The voiceover personalities also work on a more adult level, particularly the snide asides by Fox (probably his best big-screen work since "Back to the Future") and Field. Pity the embodied human actors, completely overshadowed by those showy vocal turns and the four-footers. In this case even children should beware of scenes with dogs.

Duwayne Dunham, a veteran film editor making his directing debut, keeps "Journey's" pace brisk. Other stars, no less important than the animals and trainers, are cinematographer Reed Smoot and composer Bruce Broughton, whose terrific score creates the requisite sense of warmth and adventure.

February 8, 1993 (Cont.)

Other tech credits are strong, and if this venture works, Disney may have a fertile area to mine from its nature library. What's next, a blockbuster based on "Sammy, the Way Out Seal"? Pic is dedicated to producer Franklin R. Levy, who died during production. — *Brian Lowry*

CHILDREN OF THE CORN II: THE FINAL SACRIFICE

A Dimension release of a Fifth Avenue Entertainment presentation of a Stone Stanley production. Executive producer, Lawrence Mortorff. Produced by Scott A. Stone, David G. Stanley. Directed by David F. Price. Screenplay, A.L. Katz, Gilbert Adler, from Stephen King's short story. Camera (Foto-Kem color), Levie Isaacks; editor, Barry Zetlin; music, Daniel Licht; production design, Greg Melton; costume design, Gigi Melton; sound (Ultra-Stereo), Kim Ornitz; co-producer, Bill Froehlich; assistant director, Paul Martin; production manager, Phil Smoot; special makeup effects, Image Animation; special visual effects, Calico Ltd.; supervisor, Rob Burton; stunt coordinator, Bob Stephens; casting, Geno Havens. Reviewed at Loews 19th St. East 2 theater, N.Y., Jan. 29, 1993. MPAA Rating: R. Running time: **92 MIN.**

John Garrett	Terence Knox
Danny Garrett	Paul Scherrer
Micah	Ryan Bollman
Lacey	Christie Clark
Angela Casual	Rosalind Allen
Red Bear	Ned Romero
Mrs. Burke/Mrs. West	Marty Terry
Simpson	Joe Inscoe
Dr. Appleby	Ed Grady
Sheriff	Wallace Merck

Coming nine years after the original, this supernatural horror sequel is a competently made but uninspired effort. Gore fans should dig it.

The opening provides a quick recap of Fritz Kiersch's 1984 New World opus taken from a Stephen King short story, notable chiefly as the first leading film role for Linda Hamilton.

Over 50 adults were murdered in Gatlin, Neb., by a religious cult made up of the town's kids. Surviving kids are now being sent to live in a nearby town, including brooding Micah (Ryan Bollman), who's taken in by lovely innkeeper Rosalind Allen.

A journalist (Terence Knox), who once wrote for Newsweek but is now stuck at the World Enquirer, is driving by when he sniffs out an exploitable story (he covered the Jonestown Massacre, too). He's traveling with uppity son Paul Scherrer, who's been living with mom and has little affection for his old man.

Adults are again murdered in grisly fashion, some by supernatural forces (a few represented by nice visual effects reminiscent of "Wolfen"), some by the deranged kids led by Micah.

Chief explanation for the strange doings is offered by Red Bear (Ned Romero), an anthropology prof given to name-dropping and dumb jokes, who links the kids' cult to ancient rock paintings of a children's revolt and subsequent sacrifice.

Sure enough, the kids burn up nearly all the surviving adults and prepare to sacrifice Rosalind Allen and Scherrer's sexy blonde g.f. Christie Clark to their god, named He Who Walks Behind the Rows (presumably kin to H. Rider Haggard's She Who Must Be Obeyed).

The final reel is an anticlimax, with pointless elements including a burrowing monster that never surfaces. Micah goes through some morphing and molecular disintegration effects familiar from previous films but which have nothing to do with the matter at hand.

Acting here is unexceptional, with attractive young leads Scherrer and Clark untested by the dramaturgy. Bollman shows some promise for brooding Keanu Reeves-type assignments, but he and the evil children do not tap the scare potential of antecedents like "Village of the Damned."

Levie Isaacks' lensing on North Carolina locations (subbing for Nebraska) is well done, with director David Price (son of industry vet Frank Price) keeping the picture chugging along even when the script becomes risible. — *Lawrence Cohn*

THE CEMETERY CLUB

A Buena Vista release of a Touchstone Pictures presentation of a David Brown/Sophie Hurst/Bonnie Palef production in association with David Manson. Executive producers, Manson, Philip Rose, Howard Hurst. Produced by Brown, Hurst, Palef. Directed by Bill Duke. Screenplay, Ivan Menchell, from his play. Camera (color), Steven Poster; editor, John Carter; music, Elmer Bernstein; production design, Maher Ahmad; art direction, Nicklas Farrantello; set decoration, Gene Serdena; costume design, Hilary Rosenfeld; sound (Dolby), Willie Burton; assistant director, Warren D. Gray; casting, Terry Liebling; Reviewed at Avco Cinema Center, L.A., Jan. 28, 1993. MPAA Rating: PG-13. Running time: **106 MIN.**

Esther Moskowitz	Ellen Burstyn
Doris Silverman	Olympia Dukakis
Lucille Rubin	Diane Ladd
Ben Katz	Danny Aiello
Selma	Lainie Kazan
Paul	Jeff Howell
Jessica	Christina Ricci
John	Bernie Casey
Abe Silverman	Alan Manson
Irving Jacobs	Sam Schwartz
Larry	Wallace Shawn
Ed Bonfigliano	Louis Guss
Theresa	Irma St. Paule
Rene	Alice Eisner
Mel	Allan Pinsker
Al	Hy Anzell

The comedy/drama "The Cemetery Club" constantly threatens to turn into a full-fledged movie, but the pleasant little exercise never quite transcends its telefilm feeling, lacking the big-time treatment that made films like "Fried Green Tomatoes" and "Steel Magnolias" accessible to a wide audience. The subject matter limits demographic to the bargain matinee crowd; TV will better highlight pic's virtues.

Scripter Ivan Menchell adapted from his play about three close friends (Ellen Burstyn, Olympia Dukakis and Diane Ladd) and their experiences with widowhood. It plays as a fairly accurate, if sketchy, assessment.

For instance, except for the unkempt apartment of Danny Aiello (Burstyn's romantic interest), the characters' homes say nothing about who they are. And since all three are housewives, that's not good.

Still, the episodic, rambling quality lifts it above the sitcom level. Helmer Bill Duke, like many actors turned director, affords his players the space to flesh out the bony material.

The three actresses, particularly Burstyn, do their darnedest to ground their perfs in reality, even in the broader scenes. The interplay between Burstyn and Aiello is credible, if a bit unfocused. Lainie Kazan gets most of over-the-top business, but she's energetic and knows her way around a funny line.

Tech credits are fine. Lenser Steven Poster makes Pittsburgh look so smart and lush that one wishes the city's charms had been woven more imaginatively into the plot. — *Richard Natale*

RUBY IN PARADISE

A Full Crew/Say Yeah production in association with Longstreet Prods. Executive producers, Sam Gowan, Peter Wentworth. Directed, written by Victor Nunez. Camera (Duart color), Alex Vlacos; editor, Nunez; music, Charles Engstrom; production design, John Iacovelli; art direction, Burton Rencher; costume design, Marilyn Wall-Asse; sound design (Dolby), Pete Winter; line producer, Keith Crofford; assistant director, Jennifer Fong; 2nd-unit director, Gus Holzer; casting, Judy Courtney. Reviewed at Sundance Film Festival, Park City, Utah, Jan. 25, 1993. Running time: **115 MIN.**

Ruby Lee Gissing	Ashley Judd
Mike McCaslin	Todd Field
Ricky Chambers	Bentley Mitchum
Rochelle Bridges	Allison Dean
Mildred Chambers	Dorothy Lyman
Debrah Ann	Betsy Dowds

A wonderfully expressive character study exhibiting a thoughtfulness and concern for real life rare in American cinema, "Ruby in Paradise" rewards the care put into it and the patience it asks of audiences. After an eight-year layoff from filmmaking after "A Flash of Green," Victor Nunez has returned with the sort of film whose gentle, intelligent qualities never make for an easy sell. But with accumulated recognition from critics and fests, beginning with its shared Grand Jury Prize at the Sundance Festival, it will at least get a running start to help an enterprising distrib launch it.

Telling the sort of quiet, non-action-oriented story more often associated with literature, Nunez has pulled off several difficult things here — illuminating an out-of-the-way, easily dismissed milieu without applying a sociological microscope, commenting upon the American class system without being didactic, examining the relative roles chance and individuals will play in anyone's life and, above all, vividly portraying a young woman's inner life.

February 8, 1993 (Cont.)

In the last regard, he is incalculably aided by the extraordinary central performance of Ashley Judd. Attractive, poised and possessed of a gravity that is immensely appealing, this new actress (the younger daughter of country singer Naomi Judd) manages to rivet one's attention even when she is doing nothing. As it stands, the film is virtually unthinkable without her.

Beginning by showing her escape from small-town Tennessee, tale lands Ruby in Panama City Beach, a tourist town on Florida's "redneck Riviera." Although it's off-season, Ruby finds a job in a local souvenir shop owned by a businesslike woman whose good-looking but shallow son Ricky (Bentley Mitchum) ranks himself the local roué.

Ruby sleeps with him, but later develops a more meaningful romance with Mike (Todd Field), a smart biker who works in the local tree nursery. The two seem good together, but Ruby holds back and the way in which she lets the relationship slide is one of the more intriguing and realistic aspects of the story.

But the plot points are, in a way, the least important aspects of the film, which has more to do with the way in which one approaches life and deals with its challenges and frustrations. As her friend and sometimes coworker Rochelle puts it, the key to life is "how to survive with your soul intact."

Not the least bit intellectual, Ruby has a native intelligence that serves her well and is expressed through a journal presented in (considerable) voiceover. Ruby is very much a free spirit, but one with standards, ethics, morals and bearings.

It doesn't take long to begin feeling that Judd could be a major discovery. She has the fascinating quality of being open to all experience while at the same time maintaining a reserve; much of the film relies upon her direct gaze, her tranquility regardless of happenstance, and a fundamental seriousness that lends real weight to both her performance and the film.

There is always the possibility of condescension when sophisticated filmmakers take on working-class characters, but "Ruby" hits very close to the mark in evoking everyday life. Spring break, which occasions an invasion of the town by thousands of youths, is treated dispassionately, like an aberrant tribal ritual.

If done discreetly, film could be profitably trimmed by a few minutes. — *Todd McCarthy*

PUBLIC ACCESS

A Cinemabeam presentation of a Kenneth Kokin/Adam Ripp production. Produced by Kokin. Directed by Bryan Singer. Screenplay, Christopher McQuarrie, Michael Feit Dougan, Singer. Camera (Deluxe color), Bruce Douglas Johnson; editor, John Ottman; music, Ottman; production design, Jan Sessler; art direction, Bruce Sulzberg; sound (Ultra-Stereo), Adam Joseph; sound design, Mark A. Lanza; co-producer, Ripp; assistant director, Peter Diamond; casting, Dean Jacobson. Reviewed at Sundance Film Festival, Park City, Utah, Jan. 27, 1993. Running time: **87 MIN.**
Whiley Pritcher . . . . Ron Marquette
Rachel . . . . Dina Brooks
Bob Hodges . . . . Burt Williams
Jeff Abernathy . . . . . Larry Maxwell
Mayor Breyer . . . Charles Kavanaugh
Kevin Havey . . . . . . Brandon Boyce

"**P**ublic Access" represents a disturbing, dramatically cloudy, technically proficient feature debut from young helmer Bryan Singer. Co-winner of the Grand Jury Prize at the Sundance Film Festival, this very low-budget study of malaise lurking beneath the tranquil surface of a typical small American town is serious-minded and bounces around some provocative ideas, but is vague about such important matters as key story points, motivation and overriding theme. Commercial prospects look very iffy, although this will clearly lead to further work for its director.

Odd tale concerns a mysterious stranger who comes to town and stirs up no end of trouble in the sleepy community of Brewster. Handsome, flinty and disconcertingly creepy, Whiley Pritcher (Ron Marquette) takes a room in a small boarding house run by the grizzled former mayor (Burt Williams) and immediately takes air time on the local public access channel, where he launches a call-in show dubbed "Our Town" and poses the simple question, "What's wrong with Brewster?"

After initial gossipy exchanges, the nature of the calls becomes increasingly nasty, serious and political, and Marquette becomes an immediate local celebrity. While beginning a romance with sincere librarian Rachel (Dina Brooks), he takes some heat from other locals for getting involved in matters he knows nothing about, and openly sides

with the current, corrupt mayor when the politico is accused by a malcontent of selling the town down the river.

Polite, smiling and affable in public, Marquette allows neither other characters nor the audience behind his steely persona — he's a man with no known background, psychology or motivation. He's a cipher onto which the viewer can ascribe any attributes he imagines, although it comes as no surprise when this clean-cut man with an uptight, almost military bearing begins taking people's lives.

What Singer and co-scenarists Christopher McQuarrie and Michael Feit Dougan seem to be getting at is a critique of Reagan-era greed, hypocrisy and antihumanism, as well as a commentary on the power of the media and its ability to distract the public from issues with attractive surfaces. Unfortunately, the filmmakers don't articulate their views with much clarity.

Dark, purposeful and hardened, Ron Marquette possesses a physical allure that contributes to the film's intentions, but neither he nor Singer are able to open a door more than a crack into the mysterious impulses driving the picture.

Technically, the production is impressive, especially considering the $250,000 budget and 18-day schedule. Individual sequences are very well staged, shot and edited, the "Blue Velvet"-like mood of a small town not being what it seems is nicely conveyed, and confrontation scenes carry a fair measure of tension.

On the other hand, the music played at the beginning and end is unduly sappy — even if it was intended as irony, it comes off as banal. — *Todd McCarthy*

SILENT TONGUE

A Belbo Films/Alive Films presentation from Le Studio Canal Plus. Executive producers, Gene Rosow, Jacques Fansten, Bill Yahraus, Shep Gordon. Produced by Carolyn Pfeiffer, Ludi Boeken. Directed, written by Sam Shepard. Camera (Deluxe color; Panavision wide screen), Jack Conroy; editor, Yahraus; music, Patrick O'Hearn; production design, Cary White; art direction, John Frick, Michael Sullivan; set decoration, Barbara Haberecht; costume design, Van Ramsey; sound (Dolby), Susumu Tokunow; associate producer, Catherine Scheinman; assistant director, Matt Clark; 2nd-unit director, Yahraus; Reviewed at Sundance Film Festival, Park City, Utah, Jan. 28, 1993. Running time: **106 MIN.**
Eamon McCree . . . . Alan Bates
Prescott Roe . . . . . . Richard Harris
Reeves McCree . . . Dermot Mulroney
Talbot Roe . . . . River Phoenix
Awbonnie/Ghost . . . . Sheila Tousey
Velada McCree . . . . . Jeri Arredondo
Comic . . . . Bill Irwin
Straight Man . . . . David Shiner
The Lone Man . . . . Tim Scott
Silent Tongue . . . . . Tantoo Cardinal

Sam Shepard transplants a couple of his famously dysfunctional families to the Old West in "Silent Tongue," a bizarre, meandering and, finally, maddening mystic-oater that will find few partisans. The first Western financed entirely with French money, this hodgepodge of genres, intentions, acting styles and influences doesn't look to any rosier theatrical prospects than Shepard's first feature, "Far North."

The sins of the fathers are distinctly visited upon the sons in this loosely knit yarn, with the characters literally haunted by the ghosts of those they wronged. Result is an unpalatable combination of prairie melodrama, Greek tragedy, Japanese ghost tale and traveling minstrel show, staged with little sense of style and cinematic rhythm.

The opening immediately derails the narrative. The Kickapoo Indian Medicine Show is being performed in the middle of nowhere before a sparse audience, and a reel's worth of unfunny, off-putting antics pass before Shepard embarks on his real story.

Richard Harris arrives at the show's encampment in search of its leader, Alan Bates. A drunken Irish charlatan of the first order, Bates had sold Harris his half-Indian daughter, Sheila Tousey, who married Harris' son, River Phoenix. Tousey has since died in childbirth, driving Phoenix to the brink of madness.

Hoping to cure his son's delirium, Harris kidnaps Bates' second daughter, Jeri Arredondo, and takes her back to Phoenix, who is attacked on a regular basis by the ghost of his dead wife. Bates and his son Dermot Mulroney set out across the plains in pursuit of Arredondo, a trick rider who is Bates' top attraction, setting up long stretches for blarney-filled ranting by Bates endlessly indulged.

Predictably, it all ends back at the medicine show, although at less leisure than before. The dialogue is mostly rambling and unmemorable and, in the case of Bates and his brogue-tinged blustering, indecipherable. Nearly all the characters seem to have flipped their wigs long ago, and move quickly from merely unappealing to thoroughly tiresome.

Shot in eastern New Mexico near Roswell, Irish lenser Jack Conroy's parched, drab-looking widescreen images feature isolated characters moving across a vast, undifferentiated landscape.

Performances, led by Bates', are nearly all way over the top. In the end, pic should have taken a cue from its title and cut down on the continuous babble.

— *Todd McCarthy*

RIFT

An Off-Screen Prods. production. Executive producers, Edward S. Barkin and Gabriel J. Fischbarg. Produced by Fischbarg, Barkin, Tryan George. Directed, written by Barkin. Camera (color), Lee Daniel; editor, George; music, George, Eric Masunaga; production design, Mark C. Andrews; costumes, Karin Bereson; sound, Felix Andrew; assistant director, Linda Wilson. Reviewed at Sundance Film Festival, Park City, Utah, Jan. 25, 1993. Running time: **87 MIN.**

Tom . . . . William Sage
Bill . . . . Timothy Cavanaugh
Lisa . . . . Jennifer Bransford
Dr. Myron Messers . . . Alan Davidson

Writer-director Edward S. Barkin turns the conventions of psychological thrillers inside out in "Rift," a small-budget indie drama based on his own play that boasts fine performances and flashes of filmmaking ingenuity. Overall, however, effort is more promising than accomplished. Theatrical prospects are iffy.

Basic plot sounds like a second-rate TV pic: A blocked songwriter (William Sage) nurses a hopeless crush on the pretty wife (Jennifer Bransford) of his boorish best friend (Timothy Cavanaugh). When Sage seeks help from a vaguely sinister psychiatrist (Alan Davidson), things only get worse —the shrink begins appearing to him in what may or may not be hallucinations.

After he passes out drunk at his own birthday party, Sage dreams he enjoys a night of impulsive lovemaking with Bransford. The bad news is Sage can't be certain it was a dream and Cavanaugh, now convinced of his wife's infidelity, suspects Sage.

Barkin does an okay job of keeping viewers guessing as to what's real and what isn't. More importantly, he plays cleverly on expectations: the audience is strongly encouraged to guess that Davidson and Bransford are plotting to drive Sage crazy, making him the fall guy for a murder. The pay-off is mildly surprising, if not totally satisfying, and the comparatively upbeat ending is a genuine shock.

"Rift" is too slackly paced to be consistently gripping, but never dull and works best as a character study. Sage, last seen in Hal Hartley's "Simple Men," offers a subtle and sympathetic perf, particularly in his scenes with Bransford, who infuses her appealing warmth with an ambiguous hint of something darker. Cavanaugh is very good at finding shadings of character in his underwritten role.

Tech credits are uneven. The sound quality is less than optimum, but Lee Daniel's moody color lensing (adequately blown up from 16m) is first-rate.

— *Joe Leydon*

COMBINATION PLATTER

A Tony Chan/Bluehorse Film production. Executive producers, Jenny Lee, Man Fuk Chan. Produced, directed by Tony Chan. Screenplay, Edwin Baker, Tony Chan. Camera (color), Yoshifumi Hosoya; editors, Tony Chan, James Y. Kwei; music, Brian Tibbs; art direction, Pat Summa; sound, Bob Taz; co-producer, Ulla Zwicker; casting, Amanda Ma. Reviewed at Sundance Film Festival, Park City, Utah, Jan. 28, 1993. Running time: **84 MIN.**

Robert . . . . Jeff Lau
Claire . . . . Colleen O'Brien
Sam . . . . . . Lester (Chit-Man) Chan
Benny . . . . Colin Mitchell
Andy . . . . Kenneth Lu
Mr. Lee . . . . Thomas K. Hsiung
Noriko . . . . Eleonara Khilberg
James . . . . James DuMont

Both charm and naiveté characterize "Combination Platter," the directorial feature debut of 23-year-old Tony Chan. His pleasant melodrama, concerning the assimilation of a Hong Kong immigrant in New York, looks and sounds like a first film, but it also showcases the talent of a graceful director. Prospects for theatrical release seem fair for this small-budget pic, which has potential beyond the fest circuit.

Robert (Jeff Lau) is a Hong Kong immigrant working as a waiter in a Chinese restaurant in Flushing, N.Y., in desperate need of a green card. Lau's friend Andy (Kenneth Lu) helps by introducing him to American women: marriage is the safest, fastest way to become a citizen.

Most of the action is set in the restaurant, a kind of human laboratory since Lau's contacts with the white world are largely limited to his customers.

Though serious, the film is not devoid of comic touches or action. Some humor is provided by the misunderstandings between customers and waiters. Tension is supplied by a waiter who steals money, and the sudden raids by the immigration authorities — the ultimate fear of every illegal resident.

This is a personal, heartfelt story that at times gets too soft. But Chan takes a new angle on a familiar story. Reversing the usual mode of examining immigrants from a mainstream perspective, white society is freshly viewed from the Asians' p.o.v.

Co-scripters Chan and Edwin Baker refuse to judge any of their characters, showing immense generosity of spirit. As helmer, Chan doesn't display himself; under his guidance, all the performers, especially Lau, show an ease and self-effacement that are bracingly invigorating.

Chan creates an appropriately congenial atmosphere, though the rhythm of the different subplots is not varied enough; pic's energy is too evenly distributed. Modest tech credits are congruent with the film's intimate scale.

— *Emanuel Levy*

FEAR OF A BLACK HAT

An Oakwood Films production. Executive producer, W.M. Christopher Gorog. Produced by Darin Scott. Directed, written by Rusty Cundieff. Camera (color), John Demps; editor, Karen Horn; music, Larry Robinson; production design, Stuart Blatt; set decoration, Penny Barrett; costume design, Rita McGhee, sound (Ultra-Stereo), Oliver L. Moss; special effects, Kevin McCarthy; hair and makeup, Stacye Branche; casting, Jaki Brown, Kimberly Hardin. Reviewed at Sundance Film Festival, Park City, Utah, Jan. 30, 1993. Running time: **86 MIN.**

Tasty Taste . . . . Larry B. Scott
Tone Def . Mark Christopher Lawrence
Ice Cold . . . . Rusty Cundieff
Nina Blackburn . . . . . Kasi Lemmons
Guy Friesch . . . . Howie Gold
Marty Rabinow . . . . . Barry Heins
Jike Singelton . . . . . Eric Laneuville

Audience reaction to a late-night screening at Sundance Film Festival of Rusty Cundieff's "Fear of a Black Hat," a mock documentary about rap, confirmed its instant status as a midnight movie. But wild, irreverent humor and exuberant music may also help this spoof find a larger, hip public in urban centers.

Inspired by "This Is Spinal Tap," the new parody exposes the trials of a hardcore rap band called N.W.H. (Niggas With Hats), from "tough neighborhood, U.S.A." What little structure the film has is provided by interviewer Nina Blackburn (Kasi Lemmons), a sociology student writing a doctoral thesis about rap, who follows the group on tour.

Former standup comic Cundieff is cast as Ice Cold, the band's lead rapper and existential philosopher who argues and fights with his mates, Tasty Taste (Larry B. Scott), a weapons freak, and Tone Def (Mark Christopher Lawrence), the group's more spiritual voice. The eccentric trio gladly express their views about any issue of social ill, be it misogny, racism or violence.

Though revolving around one joke — which gets numerous mutations — pic's gags are witty and timely. In a tip of the hat to "Tap," the rappers recall how each of their previous five managers was killed in "an accident."

Good musical numbers serve as welcome punctuation to a film that grows increasingly tedious. In the last half-hour, when the movie begins to run out of steam, one wishes there were more production numbers.

Special kudos go to production designer Stuart Platt and costumer Rita McGhee for creating a visually striking film, dominated by bold colors. "Fear of a Black Hat" is a shade too repetitious, but directed by Cundieff at fever pitch, its high energy never falters. — *Emanuel Levy*

FLY BY NIGHT

A Lumiere Prods. production. Executive producers, Mark Gordon, Chris Meledandri, Clarence Jones. Produced by Calvin Skaggs. Directed by Steve Gomer. Screenplay, Todd Graff. Camera (Technicolor), Larry Banks; editor, Norman Gay; music, Sidney Mills, Dwayne Sumal, Kris Parker; production design, Ruth Ammon; art direction, Llewellyn Harrison; set decoration, Nancy Friedman; costume design, Alexander White; sound, Fred Rosenberg; co-producer, Ken Golden; casting, Pat Golden, John McCabe. Reviewed at Sundance Film Festival, Park City, Utah (in competition), Jan. 22, 1993. Running time: **100 MIN.**

Rich	Jeffrey Sams
I	Ron Brice
Kayam	Darryl (Chill) Mitchell
Naji	Todd Graff
Rickey Tick	Leo Burmester
Rock	Soulfood Jed
Lyte	Larry Gilliard
Lihad	Omar Carter
Denise	Maura Tierney
Sam	Yul Vazquez
Akusa	MC Lyte
Maurice	Christopher Michael Gerrard
Charlotte	Ebony Jo-Ann

"Fly By Night," about the New York City rap scene, is an often compelling film marked by intelligence and an undeniable urgency. But Steve Gomer's pic is too ambitious for its own good, trying to encompass too many of the issues faced by its characters, is inconsistent in mood and ends patly. Still, theatrical prospects are excellent as film boasts great music and authentic settings.

The script by Todd Graff ("Used People") centers on three young rappers who have nothing in common except passion for their music. Jeffrey Sams is a subway token clerk who leaves his job, his wife (MC Lyte) and young son to pursue his rap career. Ron Brice is an angry rapper who seeks, above all, honor and esteem. As Sams' cousin Kayam, Darryl (Chill) Mitchell is the conciliator between the often antagonistic bandmates.

"Fly By Night" vividly captures both the creation and presentation of rap music. The musical performances are the film's strongest and most exciting scenes. The film also successfully conveys the fine line between needing acceptance and fearing that commercial popularity might compromise their integrity.

However, the pic veers off course when it aims at its characters' romantic, sexual and family lives; female characterization is weak, almost stereotypical. And, regrettably, the most riveting relationship, between Sams and Brice, remains underdeveloped.

"Fly By Night" differs from most recent black movies in that it was written and directed by white filmmakers. But seldom does the film betray its white source. A more severe flaw is an ending that not only defies the logic of the narrative but negates its disillusioned tonality.

Still, the three leading men make for a enticing ensemble. Screen newcomers Sams' and Brice's work belies their lack of experience; real-life rapper Mitchell brings a natural effortlessness to the role of Kayam.

Shot on location in New York, director Gomer keeps the atmosphere raw. Larry Banks' cinematography has the snazzy restlessness of the rappers and their music. — *Emanuel Levy*

THREE OF HEARTS

A New Line release of a David Permut production. Executive producer, David Permut. Produced by Joel B. Michaels, Matthew Irmas. Directed by Yurek Bogayevicz. Screenplay, Adam Greenman, Phillip Epstein, from Greenman's story. Camera (color), Andrzei Sekula; editor, Dennis M. Hill; music, Richard Gibbs; production design, Nelson Coates; art direction, Douglas Hall; set decoration, Linda Lee Sutton; costume design, Barbara Tfank; sound (Dolby), Peter Halbert; co-producer, Hannah Hempstead; casting, Penny Perry, Annette Benson. Reviewed at Sundance Film Festival, Park City, Utah, Jan. 30, 1993. Running time: **102 MIN.**
Joe	William Baldwin
Connie	Kelly Lynch
Ellen	Sherilyn Fenn
Mickey	Joe Pantoliano
Yvonne	Gail Strickland
Allison	Cec Verrell
Isabella	Claire Callaway
Harvey	Tony Amendola

Yurek Bogayevicz's romantic comedy, "Three of Hearts," world-premiered at Sundance as a work in progress, is shallow, contrived and less than credible. But marvelously exploiting New York's downtown world, it is a commercially slick and appealing film, whose acting and tech achievements might help New Line generate moderate success with the twentysomething dating crowd.

In most American comic triangle involve two men in love with the same woman. But "Three of Hearts" offers a male prostitute and a lesbian nurse enamored of a seemingly bisexual woman.

The film gets off to a good start, when Sherilyn Fenn dumps g.f. Kelly Lynch in Washington Square Park. The heartbroken Lynch, who intended to officially come out at her sister's wedding by bringing Fenn, hires William Baldwin, a good-looking hustler, to accompany her.

Before long — with the help of a silly suspense subplot — Baldwin moves into Lynch's apartment and a new friendship is formed. To win Fenn back, they scheme to use Baldwin's professional charm to seduce Fenn, then dump her, so that she will rush back to Lynch's arms.

The predictable plot mixes elements from other popular movies. Reversing the characters from "Pretty Woman" (with Baldwin in the Julia Roberts role), the story also borrows from "American Gigolo."

But for viewers willing to suspend disbelief, this aspiring screwball is immensely likable. Scripters Adam Greenman and Phillip Epstein competently outline a friendship between two unlikely characters, Baldwin and Lynch, who become comrades-in-arms, exchanging info about how to seduce women — both use the motto: "Any woman, any time, any place. Guaranteed."

Meant to be a hip, relevant comedy about alternative lifestyles, "Three of Hearts" makes every effort not to offend anyone, though at a price. The characters are not stereotypical, but are superficial. For example, in fear of alienating lesbian auds, Fenn's sexual identity is kept vague — is she a lesbian who fell out of love, bisexual, or just confused? Another problem is while all are likable, they don't belong together — in any recoupling.

As he demonstrated in "Anna," Bogayevicz is a director with sensitivity for texture. He handles the comedy and melodrama not as separate moods but as inextricably mixed, with laughter stemming from the most painful and humiliating situations.

Helmer is also good with actors. Baldwin delivers a knockout performance in film's richest role. Lynch also shines as a droll, slightly obsessive lesbian, who reluctantly has to accept her new singleness. However, Fenn is unconvincing as a creative writing professor, even if some fault lies with the script.

Technical credits are first-rate, particularly Andrzei Sekula's vibrant lensing of noted New York locations. — *Emanuel Levy*

FALLING DOWN

A Warner Bros. release, presented in association with Le Studio Canal Plus, Regency Enterprises and Alcor Films, of an Arnold Kopelson production. Executive producer, Arnon Milchan. Produced by Kopelson, Herschel Weingrod, Timothy Harris. Directed by Joel Schumacher. Screenplay, Ebbe Roe Smith. Camera (Technicolor), Andrzej Bartkowiak; editor, Paul Hirsch; music, James Newton Howard; production design, Barbara Ling; art direction, Larry Fulton; set decoration, Cricket Rowland; costume design, Marlene Stewart; sound (Dolby), David MacMillion; co-producers, Dan Kolsrud, Stephen Brown, Nana Greenwald; associate producers, William S. Beasley, Smith, John J. Tomko; assistant director, Stephen Dunn; casting, Marion Dougherty. Reviewed at Warner Hollywood Studios, L.A., Feb. 5, 1993. MPAA Rating: R. Running time: **115 MIN.**
D-Fens	Michael Douglas
Prendergast	Robert Duvall
Beth	Barbara Hershey
Sandra	Rachel Ticotin
Mrs. Prendergast	Tuesday Weld
Surplus Store owner	Frederic Forrest
D-Fens' mother	Lois Smith

Pity the Warner Bros. marketing department for having to sell this one, which at first comes across like a mean-spirited black comedy and then snowballs into a reasonably powerful portrait of social alienation. The tone is so unremittingly dour, however, it's unlikely the public will be there at the finish; at least, not enough beyond the arthouse crowd to prevent this Michael Douglas odyssey from a b.o. stumble.

If nothing else, "Falling Down" merits honorable mention as one of the more bitter, darkly tinged major studio releases in recent times, taking on victim revenge fantasies and xenophobia with more than a little ambivalence.

Initially, Douglas' character appears to be a latter-day Howard Beale, suddenly mad as hell and not about to take it anymore. Seeking to journey "home" to Venice from downtown Los Angeles, he abandons his car in bumper-to-bumper morning traffic and sets off on foot, venting his anger and frustration at all those he encounters.

At first, the premise seems to owe a debt to "After Hours," but as it progresses, more and more is revealed about Douglas' nameless character: a laid-off defense worker, estranged from his wife and child, with a borderline propensity for violence.

In short, he isn't a character acting out fantasies of the downtrodden but rather a self-obsessed human powderkeg heading to a home no longer his while on the verge of going off.

February 15, 1993 (Cont.)

That explosion takes place in stages, as the character lashes out at various symbols (an unco-operative Korean store owner, two Latino gang members, a smirking fast-food manager, and, for balance, some rich white folks). Though he starts out protesting about his "rights as a consumer" he ends up angry at everything, until he's finally armed with a bag full of automatic weapons and disquietingly convinced that there's no turning back.

Actor-turned-screenwriter Ebbe Roe Smith and director Joel Schumacher set up a parallel structure with another powerless and frustrated character, Prendergast (Robert Duvall), a henpecked burglary cop in his last day on the job. It's Prendergast, himself about to be put out to pasture, who ultimately unravels the strange quest and seeks to stem its course.

Despite the sense of menace that follows Douglas' character one can't escape the feeling that the filmmakers have erred in such a grim set-up, making the audience follow a dispirited man across a landscape occupied by unsavory and ruthless characters. (Frederic Forrest tops the roster as a white supremacist, though his world view doesn't necessarily seem all that different from Douglas' own.)

Yet if "Falling Down" (the title is derived from the song about London Bridge) is about the destruction of one man's American dream, it feels too much like the curtain is ringing down for all of us, hardly a message people will line up to embrace. Put another way, one might feel uncomfortable sitting next to someone for whom this has the ring of truth.

Aside from the movie's pervading bitterness, Schumacher also creates a rather uneven tone that doesn't help matters, with a few darkly comic flourishes early and nothing to laugh about later on. While the denouement carries a real emotional wallop, it feels like too little, too late.

The film provides Douglas with a real performer's showcase, and he delivers a strong, intense portrayal of a walking time bomb. Duvall, as well, is at his congenial best, though Prendergast begins as such a passive figure he inspires scant empathy.

The most notable supporting players are Rachel Ticotin as Duvall's former partner and Tuesday Weld in a remarkably unflattering turn as his skittish wife. Barbara Hershey is largely wasted as the protagonist's ex.

Tech credits are solid, though the David Lynchian closeups feel a bit heavy-handed, a criticism that applies in part to the whole production. — *Brian Lowry*

SHELF LIFE

Executive producer, Bruce Critchley. Produced by Bradley Laven, Anne Kimmel. Directed by Paul Bartel. Based upon materials created by O-Lan Jones, Andrea Stein, Jim Turner. Camera (CFI color), Phillip Holahan; editor, Judd Maslansky; music, Andy Paley; production design, Alex Tavoularis; art direction, Devon Meadows; set decoration, Dawn Ferry; sound (Dolby), Pat Toma; associate producers, Douglas Lindeman, Mickey Cottrell; assistant director, Roger LaPage. Reviewed at Holiday Village Cinema, Park City, Utah, Jan. 30, 1993. (In Palm Springs Film Festival.) Running time: **83 MIN.**
Tina . . . . O-Lan Jones
Pam/Mrs. St. Cloud . . . Andrea Stein
Scotty/Mr. St. Cloud . . . . Jim Turner
Various apparitions . . . . Paul Bartel
Young Scotty . . . . . Justin Houchin
Young Pam . . . . Shelby Lindley
Young Tina . . . . Jazz Britany

"Shelf Life" is a distinctive small film, a microcosmic commentary on much-vaunted family values and the media generation. Based on an original stage piece created by the performers, who repeat their roles on screen, pic represents something of a departure from helmer Paul Bartel's usual outrageous comedies, but features some of his best direction. Work's intimate scope and conceptual nature angle for specialized auds, and Bartel's name and good reviews would be the selling points for an enterprising distrib.

The indie venture received its world preem as a basically finished work in progress at the recent Palm Springs Fest. It's sprightly, compact and quickly paced, a nifty little allegorical number about second-hand life in a fallout shelter where two sisters and their brother have spent nearly their entire lives.

A prologue set Nov. 22, 1963, shows all-American Mr. and Mrs. St. Cloud of Anaheim reacting to the Kennedy assassination by packing their three kids into their home's sealed-off chamber. "It's only a matter of time until they take over everything," says Dad, referring to unnamed enemies. Film proper begins with the title

"30 Years Later & 40 Feet Under" and offers up a presumably typical day in the lives of the siblings. With the skeletons of Mom and Pop lying nearby, Tina, Pam and Scotty, now well into their 30s, go through the motions of "real life" as they have learned it from TV, which they have managed to receive uninterrupted over the years.

The St. Cloud kids' various fantasies of life have by now become ritualized, each switch in roles understood by the siblings to the point where they can instantly assume them. A fair amount of the dialogue is chanted in unison and/or rhythmically, with the characters expressing joint or contrapuntal meanings within prescribed formats. Music plays a crucial role in giving "Shelf Life" its flavor, with contributions ranging from Andy Paley's catchy score to well known and original pop tunes.

While the sense of enclosure and theatrical origins is evident throughout, Bartel keeps things moving briskly, staging the piece with a physical imagination that borders on choreography.

Production designer Alex Tavoularis' densely cluttered set and Phillip Holahan's nuanced mobile camera keep the proceedings from becoming oppressively claustrophobic. Judd Maslansky's editing is also dynamic.

Thesp/creators O-Lan Jones, Andrea Stein and Jim Turner have their roles down pat, but, of the three, Jones has the most screen presence. Their antics sometimes resemble theater games played by collaborators of long standing and the routines here are honed to a fine point.

To be sure, this is an unusual work that will click with some people and pass by others. Artificial nature of it will put some off, while others will warm to it as its intentions become clear. But pic has been done with talent in a very particular key that could strike a chord with a loyal, if limited, following.

In a sweet gesture, pic bears a dedication "For the Garys," a reference to Filmex founders Essert and Abrahams who died last year. — *Todd McCarthy*

WEEKEND AT BERNIE'S II

An Artimm presentation of a Victor Drai production. Executive producer, Angiolo Stella. Produced by Drai, Joseph Perez. Directed, written by Robert Klane. Camera (Deluxe color, Panavision), Edward Morry III; editor, Peck Prior; music, Peter Wolf; production design, Michael Bolton; art direction, Eric Fraser; set decoration, Scott Jacobson; costume design, Fionn; sound (Dolby), Walter Hoylman; co-producer, Don Carmody; associate producer, Howard Ellis; assistant director, Ellis; casting, Jason Lapadura. Reviewed in Rome, Feb. 5, 1993. Running time: **90 MIN.**
Larry . . . . Andrew McCarthy
Richard . . . . . . Jonathan Silverman
Bernie . . . . Terry Kiser
Charles . . . . Tom Wright
Henry . . . . Steve James
Claudia . . . . Troy Beyer
Hummel . . . . Barry Bostwick

Hitching a routine rehash of the first installment's cavorting cadaver antics to a frantic hunt for the defunct's cash stash, writer-director Robert Klane delivers a mildly diverting farcical caper in "Weekend at Bernie's II." A TriStar release stateside, original pic clicked resoundingly in Italo playoff, prompting local outfit Artimm to finance this sequel and open it in advance of U.S. play. "Bernie's II" stretches a thin idea even thinner, but it offers enough puerile fun and well-executed gags to lure fans of the 1989 predecessor back to theaters before a more robust future on homevideo.

Story picks up ambitious insurance company stooges Andrew McCarthy and Jonathan Silverman, back in Gotham to check boss Bernie (Terry Kiser) into the morgue and return to work as heroes after uncovering his $2 million plunder. But instead of a promotion, they get fired, with company snoop Barry Bostwick tailing them to track down the missing loot.

Also after the cash are Kiser's mob cohorts, now in cahoots with a Virgin Islands voodoo queen. She dispatches a bumbling duo (Tom Wright and Steve James) to N.Y. to resurrect Kiser and bring him back. In a funny James Brown-style scene, they botch the voodoo rites, reanimating Kiser only when he hears music. This gives rise to sequel's best add: Where the stiff was hitherto limited to being manipulated puppet-fashion, Kiser now cuts loose like a zombie funkmeister.

Plot complications are troweled on with varying degrees of plausibility, but serve mainly as

February 15, 1993 (Cont.)

a stage for Klane's endless succession of well-timed setups, landing the corpse in increasingly cartoonish gags to which Kiser's deadpan smirk and rubberized gait are perfectly tuned.

But Klane pays scant attention to connecting scenes, which despite the affable mugging of McCarthy and Silverman, fail to keep things buoyant. Also going nowhere is a half-cooked romantic interest (Troy Beyer). She appears destined first for one lead then the other, but after saving their skins, the character is unceremoniously dumped.

Tech aspects are sound, and lenser Edward Morry III's abundant establishing shots of St. Thomas and the U.S. Virgin Islands locations should prove a boon to tourism. — *David Rooney*

AMONGST FRIENDS

An Islet presentation of a Last Outlaw Films production. Executive producer, Rob Weiss. Produced by Matt Blumberg. Directed, written by Weiss. Camera (TVC Labs color), Michael Bonvillain; editor, Leo Trombetta; music, Mick Jones; production design, Terrence Foster; co-producer, Mark Hirsch; associate producers, Jeff Sternhell, Andrew Landis, Mira Sorvino; assistant director, John O'Rourke; 2nd-unit director, Bonvillain. Reviewed at Sundance Film Festival, Park City, Utah, Jan. 27, 1993. Running time: **86 MIN.**
Andy . . . . Steve Parlavecchio
Billy . . . . Joseph Lindsey
Trevor . . . . Patrick McGaw
Laura . . . . Mira Sorvino
Friend . . . . Brett Lambson
Michael . . . . Michael Artura
Vic . . . . Frank Medrano
Eddie . . . . Louis Lombardi
Jack Trattner . . . . . . David Stepkin

The mean streets are in suburbia in "Amongst Friends," an energetic, raw, but shallow look at the 1990s generation of young toughs. Very much in the "boys will be boys" school of streetwise filmmaking, encompassing everything from Scorsese through "Laws of Gravity," Rob Weiss' debut feature offers the novel angle of focusing on rich kids who aspire to be lowlife thugs. Pic is enough of an audience pleaser to do some business on the specialized circuit, but will serve more readily as a calling card for its director.

Crammed with action, confrontations, wiseguy dialogue and a great pop score, this low-budget indie screams out for attention and succeeds in capturing it, even if it doesn't measure up artistically to its models. Weiss' screenplay covers ground that has been trod many times before: A bunch of brash young hustlers, one more macho than the other, scheme, smoke, gesture, talk tough, hang out, pack guns, ride around and occasionally pull off some scams that pull down enough coin for them to pay for their fancy wheels and threads.

The difference here is that these boys hail from the affluent Five Towns area of Long Island. Andy, Billy and Trevor, best friends since childhood, come from good Jewish homes and could have been or had anything they wanted. But that's the trouble. One of the script's best, but unfortunately undeveloped, observations is that these kids' grandfathers were bookies who worked hard so they could send their sons to law school, and the sons' desire, in turn, was to make life "comfortable" for their offspring. But, rejecting college and respectability, these kids *want* to be like their grandfathers.

Trevor gets sent up the river after getting busted for a drug deal in which all three buddies are involved; when he returns three years later, things just aren't the same.

To assert himself, little Andy pulls off a major robbery of a club owned by old-time Jewish crimelord Jack Trattner, a long-ago associate of his grandfather. Quickly apprehended, Andy and his gang are forced to work for Trattner to pay off the debt, Trevor is betrayed by Billy, and the old group of friends is further splintered, with treacherous and bloody results.

All of this is played for maximum surface impact but little depth. The scummy, brutal, animalistic behavior of the young men is portrayed with a vividness and vitality that gives the film considerable electricity, and this is hypoed even further by a dynamite score from former Clash member Mick Jones, along with astutely used pop tunes.

But missing is any evidence of reflection, perspective or irony about the irresponsible actions perpetrated by these ne'er-do-wells. Film never pauses to consider why such well-born kids prefer the thuggish street lifestyle, and the ending disappointingly sentimentalizes lost friendship rather than corrosively commenting on the stupid decisions that led to such ruin.

Weiss clearly has what it takes to make an engaging, even exciting picture, and his cast of newcomers conveys a milieu and attitude that are entirely convincing. Low-budget pic is technically sharp, notably Leo Trombetta's editing, which supplies plenty of pop. — *Todd McCarthy*

THE TEMP

A Paramount release of a David Permut production from Columbus Circle Films. Executive producer, Howard W. Koch Jr. Produced by Permut, Tom Engelman. Directed by Tom Holland. Screenplay, Kevin Falls; story by Falls, Engelman. Camera (Deluxe color), Steve Yaconelli; editor, Scott Conrad; music, Frederic Talgorn; production design, Joel Schiller; art direction, Gordon W. Clark; set decoration, Kim MacKenzie Orlando; costume design, Tom Rand; sound (Dolby), Thomas Nelson; assistant director, Michael Green; 2nd-unit director, Bud Davis; 2nd-unit camera, Michael O'Shea, David Butler; casting, Elisabeth Leustig, Judith Holstra. Reviewed at the Bruin Theater, L.A., Feb. 11, 1993. MPAA Rating: R. Running time: **95 MIN.**
Peter Derns . . . . . . Timothy Hutton
Kris Bolin . . . . . . Lara Flynn Boyle
Roger Jasser . . . . . . Dwight Schultz
Jack Hartsell . . . . Oliver Platt
Brad Montroe . . . . . . Steven Weber
Sara Meinhold . . . . . . Colleen Flynn
Charlene Towne . . . . Faye Dunaway
Lance . . . . Scott Coffey
Dr. Feldman . . . . . . Dakin Matthews
Sharon Derns . . . . . . Maura Tierney

If this "Temp" were applying for a full-time position, she wouldn't get the job. Moronic, derivative, artificial and pointless are just the first adjectives that come to mind to describe this concoction, which Par understandably declined to tradescreen until the last second. Auds enjoy humor-tinged horror stories about the workplace, but this, like its heroine, goes too far. Its only b.o. prayer lies in a hefty opening four-day weekend, as patrons will send it back to the agency once they check out its skills.

If "Basic Instinct" and "The Hand That Rocks the Cradle" hadn't existed (and been big hits), then it's safe to say neither would "The Temp" have been born. It's a hybrid of the worst sort, where not a single gesture, plot development, line of dialogue or motivation seems remotely human or believable but, rather, torn crudely from some other movie.

From the opposite end of the economic spectrum as Sharon Stone but with a background just as mysterious and skirts almost as short, Lara Flynn Boyle temps for Timothy Hutton, a junior executive at the Mrs. Appleby baked goods firm in Portland. Taking charge and quite expert at making herself indispensable, Boyle gets to keep the job after Hutton's regular assistant somehow gets his hand into the paper shredder.

Mrs. Appleby is run by the sleekly ruthless Faye Dunaway, enacting a faint echo of her high-powered exec in "Network," but is being subjected to a hostile takeover by the Bart Foods conglomerate from New York. Job uncertainty pits worker against worker, but provides room for Boyle to slither up the corporate ladder through stealth and, depending upon what you choose to believe, murder, as several top executives come to increasingly unpleasant ends.

Although she claims to be married with a kid, Boyle doesn't disguise her interest in Hutton, who has a son of his own and is half-heartedly trying to effect a reconciliation with his wife. But it's all a tease, a picture with quite a bit of foreplay but no actual sex, unless you count a silly scene in which Hutton is beaten by a neighbor for indulging in a little Peeping Tom-ism while Boyle writhes in bed alone.

So-called action finale exposes who is the most ruthless person of all in this particular corporate jungle, while the final coup de grace was greeted with hoots of derision from the large screening audience. After this one, most viewers will be happy to go back to the office the next day, if only to talk about what a bad movie they saw the night before.

Tom Holland's directorial style consists of making everyone appear busy by moving them around at twice normal speed and shoving rapidly moving Steadicams down every available hallway. Entire production looks just slightly on the chintzy side.

Every cast member has been seen to considerably better effect, when they were perhaps asked to act a bit less hysterically. Hutton's character seems too mild-mannered and undriven to belong in the dog-eat-dog world of the crass types on display, and Boyle comes across better when she is more natural and less posturing. — *Todd McCarthy*

February 15, 1993 (Cont.)

HOUSE OF CARDS

A Miramax release of a Mario and Vittorio Cecchi Gori and Silvio Berlusconi presentation of a Penta Pictures production in association with A&M Films. Executive producer, Vittorio Cecchi Gori. Produced by Dale Pollock, Lianne Halfon, Wolfgang Glattes. Directed, written by Michael Lessac from a story by Lessac, Robert Jay Litz. Camera (Technicolor; Deluxe prints), Victor Hammer; editor, Walter Murch; music, James Horner; production design, Peter Larkin; art direction, Charley Beal; set decoration, Leslie E. Rollins; costume design, Julie Weiss; sound (Dolby), Thomas Brandau; co-executive producer, Gianni Nunnari; co-producer, Jonathan Sanger; assistant director, Tony Gittelson; casting, Mali Finn. Reviewed at Sundance Film Festival, Park City, Utah, Jan. 30, 1993. Running time: **107 MIN.**
Ruth Matthews . . . . Kathleen Turner
Jake Beerlander . . Tommy Lee Jones
Sally Matthews . . . . . . Asha Menina
Michael Matthews . . . . Shiloh Strong
Adelle . . . . Esther Rolle
Lillian Huber . . . . Park Overall
Stoker . . . . Michael Horse
Judge . . . . Anne Pitoniak

Well made but narrowly one-note in its concerns, "House of Cards" plays like a top-of-the-line disease-of-the-week TV movie. Sensitive feature debut by theater/TV director Michael Lessac shows he knows his way around and boasts a few dramatically unusual sequences, but does not sufficiently distinguish itself from similar stories to command the kind of attention that will propel this Miramax pickup very far in theatrical release.

An orphan from the Penta Pictures/Fox deal that fell apart after the disasters of "Folks" and "Man Trouble," "House of Cards" has the misfortune of arriving on the heels of significantly more powerful and less formulaic afflicted child/embattled adults drama "Lorenzo's Oil." While the specifics of Lessac's script are sometimes arresting, this road has been traveled innumerable times before, resulting in a predictability and a tediousness that stems from familiarity.

Drama is triggered by the fatal plunge of an archeologist off a site in Mexico, leaving Ruth Matthews (Kathleen Turner) a widow. Returning to the U.S. with her son and daughter, Ruth soon has to deal with the fact that little Sally (Asha Menina) isn't speaking anymore.

Instead, Menina emits almost deafening, rhythmic shouts when anything seems amiss to her and begins to do weird things, such as fearlessly walking in a rooftop rain gutter, catching a speeding baseball with her bare hand and building an extraordinary tower of cards in her room.

Child psychiatrist Jake Beerlander (Tommy Lee Jones) wants to get his hands on this mysterious 6-year-old, whom he believes exhibits classic autistic symptoms, but Turner goes into heavy denial, arguing that Sally is just going through a phase. But, little by little, she sees that her daughter has entered a world of her own and undertake a major effort to try to bring her out of it.

Much of the problem lies with Turner's character. Again, particularly after the galvanically involved parents of "Lorenzo's Oil," Turner's refusal to even acknowledge anything might be wrong is a dramatic detriment.

Ruth is also an incompletely written character, and Turner does little to add to its depth or complexity. Nothing provides the kind of surprise and insight needed to individualize her or bring her in close emotional contact with the viewer. Auds are more likely to comment on the actress' noticeable weight fluctuations than her maternal plight.

Although she mainly just mutely animates one curious situation after another, Menina makes a striking Sally, impressing with the sense of power and otherworldliness she throws off. Shiloh Strong is good as her brother, while Jones quietly underplays the shrink who is as fascinated with Sally's case as Ruth is initially resistant to it.

Director Lessac seems to show special interest in all the scenes involving the autistic children, and a sympathetic fascination with their special world would appear to provide the motivating spark behind the picture. The trappings of Sally's interior landscape and the reasons for her strange behavior are surrounded in less mystery than they might be because they are laid out so clearly, but Lessac presents them in a smooth, visually pleasing way that suggests an aptitude for filmmaking.

Technically, pic is sharp, with fine lensing by Victor Hammer and notable editing by Walter Murch. — *Todd McCarthy*

CHILDREN OF FATE: LIFE AND DEATH IN A SICILIAN FAMILY
(DOCU-B&W/COLOR)

A Young/Friedson production in association with Archipelago Films. Executive producer, Robert M. Young. Produced by Adam Friedson. Co-produced, directed by Andrew Young, Susan Todd. Camera, editor, Andrew Young; music, Ted Kuhn, John La Barbera. "Cortile Cascino," 1961 NBC docu, was directed, written, edited by Robert Young, Michael Roemer. Reviewed at Sundance Film Festival, Park City, Utah, Jan. 25, 1993. Running time: **87 MIN.**

"Children of Fate," the documentary tale of one woman's indefatigable 30-year struggle to keep her children alive in a Palermo slum, would have been a great docu even if only based on the 1991 footage shot by Andrew Young and Susan Todd. Reminiscent of Luis Buñuel's masterpiece about rural Spain, "Las Hurdes," it is a natural for public TV and resource libraries, film fests and arthouses.

Like Michael Apted's landmark "7 Up" docus, "Children of Fate" is a sociological followup study. In 1961, NBC financed Robert M. Young and Michael Roemer's slice-of-life docu, set in a slum known as Cortile Cascino, as one of its "White Papers." However, the docu never aired because NBC considered it "too gritty."

Thirty years later, Andrew Young and Todd returned. Interweaving the 1961 black and white footage with the new color footage, "Children of Fate" follows three generations of a family molded by poverty and its belief their lot is simply cruel, inescapable fate.

At the center of both is Angela, a woman of enormous courage, in 1961 a naive, 23-year-old mother of three and battered wife of an abusive, alcoholic husband living amid dirty streets, noisy markets, and starving children digging in garbage for food.

Sadly, excepting Angela's running away from her husband after 35 years of marriage, there has not been much progress or change over the years. Though Angela and her children now live in cleaner apartments in a nicer neighborhood, most of her children have been to prison and are uneducated and unemployed. The division of labor is almost as sexually segregated. Men always eat first, few work, and even fewer try to improve their lot.

Using Angela as narrator lends consistancy through significantly different sets of footage: the '61 material is shot more subjectively; the '91 color footage is probing, but more impersonal.
— *Emanuel Levy*

AN AMBUSH OF GHOSTS

A Stress Fiesta Films presentation. Produced by Robert Shulevitz, Lauren Graybow. Directed by Everett Lewis. Screenplay, Quinton Peeples. Camera (CFI color), Judy Irola; editor, Claudia Hoover; music, Klive and Nigel Humberstone; production design, Vincent Jefferds; set decoration, Regina O'Brien; wardrobe design, Alexandra Welker; sound, Walt Martin; coproducer, Scott Arundale; line producer, Debbie Diaz; associate producers, Sam Sloves, Charles Myers; assistant director, Kris Krengel; casting, Ed Johnston. Reviewed at Sundance Film Festival, Park City, Utah, Jan. 22, 1993. Running time: **92 MIN.**
George Betts . . . . Stephen Dorff
Irene Betts . . . . . Genevieve Bujold
Bill Betts . . . . Bruce Davison
Christian . . . . Alan Boyce
Denise . . . . Anne Heche

A strikingly arty treatment of a relatively conventional dramatic and psychological situation, "An Ambush of Ghosts" plays like a post-modern version of "Ordinary People." Far richer in style than in substance, this ambitious indie effort looks and sounds terrific and features some strong performances in the bargain, but the sensory impressions it offers perhaps too heavily outweigh the meanings and insights it serves up. Pic deserves a place on the fest and specialized circuit, but it remains too esoteric for any assurance of success even in arthouses.

Although it bears a certain resemblance in performance style and its handling of extended one-on-one scenes, "Ambush" is still a far cry from Everett Lewis' first feature, "The Natural History of Parking Lots," which seriously divided viewers when it preemed at Sundance three years ago. Whereas the earlier work was raw and primitive, new film is elaborate in its strategies and highly polished in technique.

Screenwriter Quinton Peeples' tale is one of haunted memories and family nightmares thwarting the impulse to normalcy. As revealed in stylized flashbacks, the tragic incident that changed everything was the death of George's little brother Grover when their mother accidentally ran over him with her car.

Roughly 10 years later, Mom is crazy as a loon, while George, struggling to get through his teens, is still trying to reconcile with what happened. Suddenly, one of his classmates, Christian, shows up needing to hide out and it soon becomes apparent it because he's killed another student. Caught in the unwanted position of being able to arbitrate an evidently guilty colleague's fate, George hesitantly meets with Christian's trendy g.f. Denise, but develops feelings for her that complicate his life even further.

Pic climaxes with a sequence calling into question how much of what has come before happened and how much might have only unfolded in George's mind. Instead of feeling like a cop-out, however, ending takes on the nature of a deep, unfathomable mystery, and casts the film in a haunting, if hazy, afterglow.

This is decidedly a case not of what a film says, but how it says it. Lewis displays a sleek, muscular, brooding style some will undoubtedly find overwrought and pretentious, but it is undeniably arresting and makes the picture grippingly watchable.

Lewis and lenser Judy Irola, who won the Sundance Fest's camera award for her work, have fashioned a relentless succession of stunningly dark images and sequences. Also crucial is the extraordinary electronic score by Klive and Nigel Humberstone of the British group In the Nursery, which adds considerably to the film's emotional resonance.

Stephen Dorff gives a very strong central performance as George, a character that easily could have seemed wimpy and indecisive in lesser hands. Genevieve Bujold is eerily convincing as a woman permanently in outer orbit, and one early scene in which Dorff applies lipstick to his mother is compellingly erotic. Bruce Davison has little to do as George's father, while Alan Boyce as Christian and Anne Heche as Denise add to the intense and offbeat nature of the entire project. — *Todd McCarthy*

LILLIAN

Produced, directed, written, edited by David D. Williams. Camera (Commonwealth Film Lab color), Robert Griffith; music, H. Shep Williams; sound, Jeff Kenton; associate producer, Frank Pineno. Reviewed at Sundance Film Festival, Park City, Utah, Jan. 24, 1993. Running time: **82 MIN.**
Lillian . . . . Lillian Folley
Nina . . . . Wilhamenia Dickens
Ricky . . . . Ricky Green
Frank . . . . Steve Perez
Maria . . . . . Danita Rountree-Green
Joy . . . . Joy Buckner
Niecey . . . . Dynisha Dickens
Red . . . . Stanley Holcomb
Mrs. Evans . . . . Helen Jervey
Charles . . . . John Wise
Karen . . . . Karen Motley
Insurance Salesman . . . . . Sam Wells

An anomaly both artistically and commercially, "Lillian" could scarcely stand farther away from the mainstream of the American film industry: a fictional documentary-like study of a middle-aged black woman who is both ordinary and remarkable, played by the subject herself. Many may conceivably respond to David D. Williams' plain, simple, very human feature, but coming up with a marketing angle will require exceptional ingenuity.

Lillian is a heavy-set, gray-haired, slow-moving, fiftyish woman whose life is dedicated to caring for several young children and some old folks in her two-story house in Virginia. Over the course of one long day, pic follows Lillian through her humble, common but vital activities: seeing the kids off to school, preparing a birthday party for her granddaughter, getting the daughter of one her old boarders to remove her dying mother to a hospital; interviewing a woman about a prospective new boarder; dealing with her own daughter, who has palmed off a granddaughter; negotiating with her insurance man; cooking meals for everyone; and finally, at day's end, taking in a new foster baby.

Lillian is the sort of character one rarely sees on a screen, big or small. In any normal dramatic context, Lillian would simply fade into the background due to her commonplace activities and conversation. But as presented here, she is the sun around which many satellites revolve. Much of what the woman does is mundane, but the cumulative weight of Lillian's love and concern, and her indispensability to many other people, endow her, and the film, with dignity and value.

There is little to say about Lillian's performance other than she is utterly and completely believable playing herself. Many around her are portrayed by actors; the only missteps come in a couple of subsidiary roles.

Williams has filmed Lillian's life in an unhurried, unsentimental, straightforward way, and his film seems like a documentary of a life the viewer has unobtrusively been allowed into.

Watching Lillian calmly and resolutely tend to the elemental needs of others places a lot of more superficial concerns in perspective. It's hard to say who the audience for this would be, but the suspicion persists that it would be found among people who rarely go to the movies.

— *Todd McCarthy*

BERLIN FEST

AL-LAIL
(THE NIGHT)
(SYRIAN-LEBANESE-FRENCH)

A National Cinema Organization (Syria)/Maram for Cinema (Lebanon)/La Sept (France) co-production. Directed, written by Mohamed Malas. Camera (color), Youssef Ben Youssef; editor, Kais Al Zubaidi. Reviewed at Carthage Film Festival, Oct. 9, 1992. (In Rotterdam, Berlin Film Fests.) Running time: **120 MIN.**
Father . . . . Fares Lahlou
Mother . . . . Sabah Jazairi
Son . . . . Omar Malas
Also with: Riadh Chahrour, Maher Salibi.

From "Exodus" on, the creation of the state of Israel has often been recounted from a Western p.o.v. "The Night" fascinates because it looks at this historic event from the Arab perspective — a real and a symbolic defeat.

Directed by Syria's foremost filmmaker, Mohamed Malas, the film has a rare authority. Despite its undeniable difficulty, "The Night" is a must-see for anyone interested in Arab cinema or the history of the region. The winner of the Golden Tanit at the Carthage Film Festival of Arab and African films, it looks headed for a long festival life. But to come across to broader audiences, it requires a great deal of explanation.

Specifically, it shows the devastating effects the new nation had on Arab populations living across the border in Kenitra, Syria. Though anyone can appreciate its aesthetic qualities, "The Night" will be most meaningful to Arab viewers who already have some background on the period. One key fact nowhere mentioned in the version premiered at Carthage is that the city of Kenitra was razed to the ground — many years after the story takes place — by Israeli forces. This clearly gives added poignancy to the dusty but beautiful town of the 1940s Malas lovingly depicts in his film.

More than a history lesson, however, "The Night" is a voyage into childhood memories and emotions, family and community ties. The story begins and ends with a pompous, modern monument commemorating the narrator's father, a famed resistance fighter.

Back in the '40s, the father (Fares Lahlou) arrives in Kenitra and stays on, marrying the daughter (Sabah Jazairi) of a hostel keeper and having a son. The town is swept by a continual flow of volunteers who set off to combat in nearby Palestine — some on horseback, some on foot. The father, an impassioned, slightly crazy visionary, is one of them.

While the fighting sporadically continues, Palestinian refugees begin to appear in the border town and the years go by. One day, a new president comes to inspect the now disspirited local military post, and finds the Israelis firmly established across the border. By now even the father's sacrifice is swallowed up in meaningless speech-making.

The Lebanese-French co-prod had a tough shoot, shut down twice during the gulf war. But the result has the loving, intricate detail of an ancient Mideastern miniature.

Malas' highly pictorial style —something of a stylistic watershed in contemporary Arab cinema — is unique, but it also makes the story harder to follow by putting a distance between audience and characters. Image by image, block after block, Malas brings the period to life, showing freedom fighters and noisy family feuds that end up involving the whole community. The film leaves a strong final impression, but remains hard to pin down.

— *Deborah Young*

February 15, 1993 (Cont.)

WITTGENSTEIN
(BRITISH)

A British Film Institute release of a Channel 4/BFI presentation, in association with Uplink (Japan), of a Bandung production. Executive producers, Ben Gibson, Takashi Asai. Produced by Tariq Ali. Directed by Derek Jarman. Screenplay, Jarman, Terry Eagleton, Ken Butler. Camera (color), James Welland; editor, Budge Tremlett; music, Jan Latham-Koenig; art director, Annie Lapaz; costume design, Sandy Powell; sound (Dolby), George Richards, Toby Calder, Paul Carr; associate director, Butler; assistant director, Davina Nicholson; production managers, Anna Campeau, Gina Marsh. Reviewed at De Lane Lea preview theater, London, Feb. 3, 1992. (In Berlin Film Festival, Panorama section.) Running time: **71 MIN.**
Ludwig Wittgenstein . . Karl Johnson
Bertrand Russell . . . . Michael Gough
Lady Ottoline Morrell . . Tilda Swinton
Maynard Keynes . . . . . John Quentin
Johnny . . . . Kevin Collins
Young Wittgenstein . Clancy Chassay
Martian . . . . Nabil Shaban
Hermine Wittgenstein . . Sally Dexter
Lydia Lopokova . . . . Lynn Seymour

Derek Jarman's latest is an immaculately lensed, intellectual jape that's more a divertissement than a substantial addition to his quirky oeuvre. Shot on legit-like minimalist sets, the gabby but sophisticated riff on the tortured life of Austrian-born philosopher Ludwig Wittgenstein is a natural for fests and small-scale playoff. Gay subtext will win it extra dates.

Heavy-duty behind-the-camera roster includes producer Tariq Ali, well-known for Channel 4 political programs, and co-scripter Terry Eagleton, an Oxford prof who's a popular international authority on literary theory and criticism. Latter's input in untangling Wittgenstein's teachings on language and philosophy seems considerable, with Jarman supplying the visual framework and cinematic stamp.

Pic's opening, with young Ludwig (confidently played by 12-year-old Clancy Chassay) introducing the members of his ill-fated family, promises a Ken Russell-like irreverence that never really develops. With the appearance of the adult Wittgenstein (Karl Johnson), things settle down into a series of talky tableaux against black backdrops.

Though the script often demands a basic knowledge of Wittgenstein's work to appreciate the nuances, the general progression of his life and thought is clear enough. Born into a rich Viennese family in 1889, he quickly fled to Britain, establishing his rep at Cambridge, where he fell in with other thinkers like Bertrand Russell (Michael Gough) and economist John Maynard Keynes (John Quentin). He died in 1951 of cancer.

Philosophical sparring between the trio takes up much of the running time, with light relief provided by Russell's snooty mistress, Lady Ottoline Morrell (Jarman regular Tilda Swinton in top histrionic form), and chats on the meaning of life with a green Martian (Nabil Shaban).

Running parallel with the intellectual stuff is an exploration of Wittgenstein's repressed homosexuality, per his friendship with a handsome, working-class student (Kevin Collins) and Keynes, portrayed as a flouncing gay. On this level, the pic can also be read as an allegory of HIV-positivity, with Russell's worries about Wittgenstein "infecting too many young men [with his teachings]." (Jarman himself is an admitted carrier.)

Apart from the occasional homosexual kiss, there's nothing on a par with Jarman's previous "Edward II" to worry ratings boards. Language-wise, it's also clean as a whistle.

Johnson (Ariel in Jarman's earlier "The Tempest") draws a persuasive portrait of the screwed-up thinker, a confessed doubter of conventional philosophical wisdom who also loved Carmen Miranda and Betty Hutton musicals. The humor, when it comes, is dry and self-effacing, with Gough, Swinton and Quentin getting the peachier parts.

Pic is always visually alert, with characterful costuming by Sandy Powell, razor-sharp lighting by James Welland, and varied classical gobbits by music director Jan Latham-Koenig. Trim running time is a further plus. — *Derek Elley*

LOVE IN LIMBO
(AUSTRALIAN)

A Beyond Films release of a Palm Beach Pictures production, with the support of the Film Finance Corp Film Fund. Produced by David Elfick, John Winter, Nina Stevenson. Directed by Elfick. Screenplay, John Cundill. Camera (Eastmancolor), Steve Windon; editor, Stuart Armstrong; music, Peter Kaldor; production design, David McKay; costumes, Clarissa Patterson; sound, Guntis Sics; assistant director, Colin Fletcher; production manager, Maggie Lake; casting, Christine King. Reviewed at AFI Cinema, Sydney, Aug. 1, 1992. (In Berlin Film Fest, Panorama section.) Running time: **102 MINS.**
Ken Riddle . . . . Craig Adams
Gwen Riddle . . . . Rhondda Findleton
Max Wiseman . . . . Martin Sacks
Barry . . . . Aden Young
Arthur . . . . Russell Crowe
Maisie . . . . Samantha Murray
Ivy . . . . Maya Stange
Uncle Bert . . . . Bill Young
Aunt Dorrie . . . . Jill Perryman
Cyril Williams . . . . . . Vincent Ball
Mona . . . . Diane Jeffries

Former producer David Elfick's second try as director (after "Harbor Beat") is an amiable coming-of-age pic set in 1957 in the Western Australian city of Perth. The film has many lively moments and several strong performances, but John Cundill's screenplay takes in too much territory, deflecting attention from the central character, a sex-obsessed teenager, and his adventures. A modest commercial run is indicated before a potentially strong video career.

Ken (Craig Adams) lives with his widowed mother, Gwen (Rhondda Findelton), and his twin sister, Ivy (Maya Stange). Filled with theoretical knowledge about sex, he is able to give his uncle, summoned by his mother to talk to him on the subject, more advice than he himself receives. Expelled from school for selling nude pictures, he's given a job in his uncle's garment factory where he meets sleazy salesman Max (Martin Sacks), shy Arthur (Russell Crowe) and handsome Barry (Aden Young).

At this point the script gets schizophrenic, because instead of concentrating on Adams' attempts to lose his virginity, the film spends almost equal time on his mother's romance with the unappealing Sacks, scenes that, despite a warm Findelton, merely extend the running time.

The highlight of this basically likable film is the visit Adams, Crowe and Young pay to a whorehouse in a mining town far from the city. Although Young's encounter with a pretty prostitute with the proverbial heart of gold is standard stuff, Adams' encounter with a mature, matter-of-fact whore smacks of the truth, and is amusingly presented.

Thesping is fine, though lead Craig Adams tends to be overshadowed by his co-stars in the scenes he shares with Crowe, who is undoubtedly ready for international roles, and Young, who also registers strongly.

There's plenty of femme nudity on display during this old-fashioned teen romp, in some ways a throwback to films made in Australia 20 years ago.

David McKay's ultra-bright production design reflects the garish era. Popular music is well used, too, and vet Yank rocker Little Willie Littlefield is a bonus. Elfick has done a slick job, but further polishing of the script would have kept the pic more focused. — *David Stratton*

DEN TEUFEL AM HINTERN GEKÜSST
(THE DEVIL KISSED FROM BEHIND)
(GERMAN-DOCU-16m)

A Basis Films release of a Arpad Bondy and Margit Knapp Film co-produced by SDR. (Intl. sales: Zero film, Berlin.) Produced by Bondy. Directed by Bondy, Knapp. Screenplay, Knapp. Camera (16m, color), Norbert Bunge; editor, Bondy; music, Norbert Schultze; sound, Manfred Herold; production manager, Pimes Dörfler. Reviewed at Berlin Film Festival (Intl. Forum of Young Films), Jan. 28, 1993. Running time: **90 MIN.**

Norbert Schultze's name might not be world famous, but "Lili Marlene," which he composed, is. Pic catches up with Schultze as he recounts his life and career as a privileged Aryan artist during Hitler's regime. Geared for Euro TV auds, pic would have been tighter in a one-hour format and the lack of supporting archive material, apparently out of reach financially, would be less apparent.

The film slowly unwinds, literally, with a shot of film stock unspooling on an editing table. Filmmakers return to shots of the film in postproduction and narrative appearing on a computer screen as a repetitive device. Otherwise, pic is primarily a talking head interview with Schultze, who occasionally accompanies himself on the piano.

Following a strict, Prussian childhood and career as a musician, the modest, self-deprecating old man readily admits: "I would never have been a success if the Jews weren't gone. I filled a gap." When his first successful operetta pleased one of Hitler's propaganda ministers, Schultze explains with wide-eyed surprise, he was placed on a list exempting him from military service. He remained well behind the lines, leading a life of privilege and composing rousing Nazi propaganda songs and film scores.

February 15, 1993 (Cont.)

The question of how committed Schultze was to the messages in the lyrics (lots of "following the Führer" and "drop bombs on England") he still sings with lusty glee for the camera gradually emerges. Although a party member, Schultze denies any political leanings, saying he just wanted to compose for an audience. Later, he wrote nearly identical melodies, with different lyrics, for the American occupying forces. Title refers to a line a relative in America wrote Schultze in refusing him aid after the war.

The filmmakers do an adequate job, but would have done well to illustrate their story with more contemporary material. Technique of cutting to the editing room is innovative, but soon wears thin. — *Rebecca Lieb*

KIRA KIRA HIKARU
(TWINKLE)
(JAPANESE)

A Fuji TV/Space Bond production. (Intl. sales: Herald Ace, Tokyo.) Produced by Shinya Kawai, Haruo Umekawa, Tomoki Ikeda. Directed, written by George Matsuoka, from Kaori Ekuni's story. Camera (color), Norimichi Kasamatsu; editor, Mari Kishi; production design, Mitsuo Endo; sound, Shimpei Kikuchi; production managers, Koichi Murakami, Juichi Horiguchi. Reviewed at Berlin Film Festival (Intl. Forum of Young Films), Jan. 29, 1993. Running time: **103 MIN.**
Shoko Koyama . . Hiroko Yakushimaru
Mitsuki Kishida . . Etsushi Toyokawa
Also with: Michitaka Tsutsui, Masahiko Tsugawa, Mariko Kaga, Yusuke Kawazu, Masuyo Iwamoto.

Handsome pic about the marriage of a troubled, alcoholic young woman to a closeted gay doctor is a natural for the fest circuit, and should find additional legs in arthouses.

Shoko, recently released from a detox unit, is of the age when respectable young Japanese girls marry. Her parents arrange a union for her with Mutsuki, who has been secretly living with his gay lover Kon for years. The two are listless and uninterested in one another until each learns the other's secret. They marry, keeping Mutsuki's homosexuality a secret from her family.

Eventually the relationship becomes complex as Shoko yearns for a baby and Kon plays an ever larger role in the household. Shoko begins to hate her husband for being kind to her while withholding physical love. "It's like eating soup with a fork," Mutsuki's father says of the union.

Hiroko Yakushimaru plays Shoko with a high-tension level of sweet compusure and stubbornness. Some of the film's best and most disturbing scenes are between her and a waitress at a restaurant she frequents. Shoko vents all her anger on the virtual stranger before going home to compulsively iron her husband's sheets on the bed she doesn't share, then hit the bottle.

Other perfs are good, as is the film's spare self-confidence. Cinematography and sound are strong; sets and costumes sterile and spartan, underscoring the emotional tension.

Helmer Matsuoka, after sustaining mood and tension throughout the film, seems to run out of ideas, allowing an otherwise commendable pic to end in a whimper. — *Rebecca Lieb*

DE FORCE
AVEC D'AUTRES
(FORCED TO BE WITH OTHERS)
(FRENCH)

An SDF Prod. (Paris)/Partners Prod. (Rome) co-production, with the support of Unifrance Film Intl. Produced by Caroline Reussner, Simon Reggiani. Directed, written by Reggiani. Camera (color), Alain Choquart; editor, Catherine Bonetat; music, Celia Reggiani; sound recording, J. Michel Chauvet. Reviewed at 5th Premiere Plans, European First Film Festival, Angers, France, Jan. 24, 1993. (In Berlin Film Fest, Intl. Forum of Young Cinema.) Running time: **87 MIN.**
(Italian and French soundtrack)
Serge/Sergio . . . . . . Serge Reggiani
Simon . . . . Simon Reggiani
Also with: Ferruccio Soleri, Daniel Gelin, Pascal Vignal, Elsa Zylberstein, Denis Lavant, Antoine Chappey.

"De Force Avec D'Autres" is a peculiar but touching hybrid of fact and fiction, made by Simon Reggiani to cheer famous but ailing dad Serge. First film should draw some attention on the fest circuit and may also work as a curio TV item in markets where auds are familiar with the elder Reggiani.

Fake documentary-cum-portrait began as a 1989 book, "La Question Se Pose," which was followed by a 15-minute docu, then expanded into a fictionalized documentary when the son concluded that the lensing process "worked like a respirator" on the elder Reggiani, then undergoing a drying out spell.

Pic is the story of a son (Simon) who, on the pretext of writing a book, takes his dad (Serge) back to his native Italy where a priest convinces him that he's not responsible for the death of his infant brother 70 years earlier. Result, though sometimes scattered, is livelier than it sounds.

Unable to secure conventional financing due to Serge's precarious health, Simon mortgaged his apartment and rounded up friends to shoot extensive clinic episodes. A former leading man (famed for his 1951 role opposite Simone Signoret in Jacques Becker's "Casque d'Or") and still-beloved music hall icon, Serge is delightfully unselfconscious throughout the mostly scripted pic and oozes stage presence during a triumphant concert segment lensed at Paris' Olympia theater. Whatever his tribulations with the bottle, Reggiani still packs an expressive wallop.

Helmer is okay as the messed up son trying to be a good parent to his daughter despite his own predilection for alcohol. As a clinic nurse, Pascale Vignal does a fine turn explaining how alcoholism leads to neurological damage. Denis Lavant, chubbier than in his Leos Carax pics, convinces as an edgy clinic inmate.

Title refers to Serge's reluctance to communicate with others, a behavioral block that he eventually overcomes, although how the transformation occurs could be better explained.

The line between docu and fiction is further blurred by the polish of lenser Alain Choquart's images. Nicely punctuated by songs and recitations, pic was to undergo additional tightening before its Berlin showing.
— *Lisa Nesselson*

OKOGE
(FAG HAG)
(JAPANESE)

A Kajima Prods./Into Group production. (Intl. sales: Shibata Organization.) Produced by Yoshinori Takazawa, Masashi Moromizato. Directed, written by Takehiro Nakajima. Camera (color), Yoshimasa Hakata; editor, Kenji Goto; music, Edison, Hiroshi Ariyoshi; Reviewed at Berlin Film Festival (Panorama), Jan. 29, 1993. Running time: **120 MIN.**
With: Misa Shimizu, Takehiro Murata, Takeo Nakahara, Atsushi Fukazawa.

"Okoge," about a straight young woman's fascination with gay men in Tokyo, begins on a courageous and funny note, but becomes risible, then uproariously melodramatic. Numerous sex scenes between men will keep it off arthouse screens, and political incorrectness will not endear it to gay auds, either.

A sweet young thing, Sayoko, meets Goh and his married male lover Tochiko. As fascinated by their gayness as her girlfriend is repelled, she befriends the pair and offers her apartment, festooned with Frida Kahlo self-portraits, for their trysts.

The opening scenes are witty and cleverly shot but the film, despite serious intentions, draws characters with cartoon-like strokes. Sayoko is gay (in the original sense of the word) to the extreme, singing rousing songs to her new pals and smiling maternally as they make it upstairs.

Film rapidly loses ground after Goh and Tochiko's breakup, descending into a level of melodrama rivaled only by Douglas Sirk. Goh's mother, learning of his homosexuality, goes into a deep depression resulting in her death. In a deathbed scene, her daughter-in-law clucks that it is fortunate Goh is gay: "No straight man would take such good care of his mother."

Sayoko, trying to convice a man Goh has his eye on to sleep with her friend, is raped. In a B&W flashback apparently aimed at explaining her attraction to gay men, we learn she was raped as a child. She next pops up with a baby in her arms, which heart-of-gold drag queens vow to support. Salaryman Tochiko finally decides to come out of the closet, quit his job, leave his wife, and, in one of a series of grand finales, shows up at the wedding of a colleague with his new, corpulent transvestite lover and regale the thunderstruck guests with a song.

Although well-intentioned, helmer Nakajima has bitten off more than he can chew in trying to reconcile all aspects of Japanese homophobia. The problem is that for the target audience, it probably hits too close to home.

Tech credits are good, with lurid colors underscoring the melodrama. — *Rebecca Lieb*

February 15, 1993 (Cont.)

KRIEGSENDE
(WAR'S END)
(GERMAN-DOCU)

A Freunde Der Deutsche Kinemathek release of a Viola Stephan production. Directed, written by Viola Stephan. Camera (color), Pavel Lebeschev; editor, Yvonne Loquens; sound, Wolfgang Widmer; line producer, Alexi Artemov; adviser, Christiane Bauermeister; production manager, Renée Gundelach. Reviewed at Berlin Film Festival (New German Films), Jan. 28, 1993. Running time: **90 MIN.**

"**K**riegsende" is a very accomplished and subtle fly-on-the-wall view of the broad spectrum of Russian life in Berlin, which the filmmaker calls the "western city of the East, and the eastern city of the West." A natural for the fest circuit, pic should see Euro TV play, too.

For the most part devoid of dialogue, interviews or narration, pic leaves the viewer very much alone to make sense of the images of a varied slice of Russian life. Pavel Lebeschev's camerawork is commendable in a film that shows more than it tells.

Pic opens with Russians being subject to the indignities of a meticulous emigration inspection at the Brest customs station before moving to Germany. There, the life of the immigrant community is portrayed in detail, moving from a home for asylum seekers to army garrisons, the vacant grandeur of the Russian embassy in eastern Berlin, a disco frequented by Russians, their restaurants and bars. The life of the intelligentsia is also portrayed at dinners and gallery openings, contrasting sharply with sequences of the Red Army choir singing and trains bringing troops back to Russia at the film's end.

Characters discuss reasons for being in the West and feelings about leaving Russia, but the film is best when being voyeuristically inquisitive. Stephan's accomplishment is in infusing a minimum of external presence into a well-conceived portrait.

—*Rebecca Lieb*

HAMMERS OVER
THE ANVIL
(AUSTRALIAN)

A South Australian Film Corp./Harvest Prods. production, with the support of the Film Finance Corp. Film Fund. (Intl. sales: Beyond Intl.) Executive Producers, Janet Worth, Peter Gawler, Gus Howard. Produced by Ben Gannon. Directed by Ann Turner. Screenplay, Turner, Peter Hepworth, based on stories by Alan Marshall; camera (color), James Bartle; editor, Ken Sallows; music, Not Drowning, Waving; production design, Ross Major; sound, Phil Tipene; co-produced by Peter Harvey-Wright; production manager, Barbara Gibbs; assistant director, Chris Webb; casting, Lis Mullinar. Reviewed at Beyond Films screening room, Sydney, Jan. 21, 1993. Running time: **101 MIN.**
Grace McAlister . Charlotte Rampling
East Driscoll . . . . Russell Crowe
Alan Marshall . . . Alexander Outhred
Bushman . . . . Frankie J. Holden
Joe Carmichael . . . . Jake Frost
Nellie Bolster . . . . . Amanda Douge
Mr. Thomas . . . . . . Frank Gallacher
Mr. McAlister . . . . John Lee
Mrs. Herbert . . . . Daphne Grey
Mrs. Bilson . . . . . Alethea McGrath

"**H**ammers Over the Anvil" unfolds during the summer of 1910 in a farming community in Australia, where a crippled 14-year-old boy is the quiet observer of the problems and passions of his friends and family. Despite sensitive direction by Ann Turner ("Celia"), the film lacks a strong emotional center and the climactic developments carry little conviction. A mild theatrical career is indicated.

The screenplay, written by Turner in collaboration with Peter Hepworth, is based on stories by the late Australian author Alan Marshall (Karel Kachyna's 1970 Czech feature "I Can Jump Puddles" was based on one of his works). Marshall was brought up on a horse stud farm and was crippled by polio at an early age. According to the pressbook, no fewer than 21 of his autobiographical stories were tapped for the script, so it's not surprising the film is on the discursive side, leaving viewers wondering if the incidents will ever mesh into a dramatic climax.

The events Alan (Alexander Outhred) witnesses include: The disgrace of pretty Nellie (Amanda Douge), impregnated and forced to return to the orphanage; the death of a sweet but batty old woman; sexual awakening as his best friend Joe (Jake Frost) first dates; Outhred's doomed efforts to fulfill his greatest ambition — riding a horse —supported by his father (a robust perf from Frankie J. Holden), a former horsebreaker.

The biggest drama of the summer involves Outhred's hero, East (a tough, charming performance from Russell Crowe), admired by all the girls, who lives alone with the horses he trains. He becomes secretly involved with Grace (Charlotte Rampling), the older, aristocratic wife of a local landowner, a liaison Outhred literally stumbles on.

There are echoes here of Joseph Losey's "The Go-Between," but the characters in "Hammers" are less convincingly drawn. Crucially, though through no fault of the actors, the vital chemistry between Crowe and Rampling is lacking, and this lack leads to a somewhat mystifying climax, lessening the impact of what could have been a touching story.

On a technical level, "Hammers Over the Anvil" is beautifully designed and photographed.

— *David Stratton*

UNA ESTACION
DE PASO
(WHISTLE STOP)
(SPANISH)

An Elías Querejeta production. Directed by Gracia Querejeta. Screenplay, Elías and Gracia Querejeta. Camera (color), Antonio Pueche; editor, Nacho Ruiz-Capillas; music, Angel Illarramendi; set design, Llorenc Miquel; costume design, Maiki Marin; production manager, Primitivo Alvaro. Reviewed at Valladolid Film Festival, Valladolid, Spain, Oct. 26, 1992. (In Berlin Film Fest, Panorama section.) Running time: **92 MIN.**
Antonio (father) . . . Omero Antonutti
Miguel . . . . . . .Joaquim de Almeida
Antonio . . . . Santiago Alonso
Lise . . . . Bibi Andersson
Also with: Luis Crespo, Cralos Arias, Maria Larumbe, Fernando Valverde, Alfoso Lussón, Maria Pineda, Ana Duato, Paco Sagarzazu.

First film by producer Elias Querejeta's daughter is a sensitively made story of a young man's summer in a village outside Madrid; appeal will be for arthouses and it's a perfect entry for the fest circuit.

Helmer meticulously chronicles the solving of mysterious happenings during a summer 10 years earlier, a hidden family drama mostly told in flashbacks: key elements include a foreign woman occupying the house of a man formerly nicknamed "the Nazi"; her older brother's infatuation with the "Nazi's" wife; the "Nazi's" suicide; and the young man's realization of the truth he failed to understand as a child.

Omero Antonutti gives a fine performance as the elusive and secretive father, and Santiago Alonso makes a convincing protagonist seeking the strands of his past.

Pic copped the special jury prize at the Valladolid Film Festival. — *Peter Besas*

February 22, 1993

AMOS & ANDREW

A Columbia Pictures release of a Castle Rock Entertainment production, in association with New Line Cinema. Produced by Gary Goetzman. Directed, written by E. Max Frye. Camera (Technicolor), Walt Lloyd; editor, Jane Kurson; music, Richard Gibbs; production and costume design, Patricia Norris; sound (Dolby), John Pritchett; co-producers, Marshall Persinger, Cummins; assistant director, Henry Bronchtein; production manager, Jack Cummins; stunt coordinator, Glenn Randall Jr.; casting, John Lyons. Reviewed at Loews 19th St. 5 theater, N.Y., Feb. 4, 1993. MPAA Rating: PG-13. Running time: **94 MIN.**

Amos Odell	Nicolas Cage
Andrew Sterling	Samuel L. Jackson
Chief Tolliver	Dabney Coleman
Phil Gillman	Michael Lerner
Judy Gillman	Margaret Colin
Officer Donaldson	Brad Dourif
Rev. Brunch	Giancarlo Esposito
Dr. Fink	Bob Balaban
Waldo	I.M. Hobson
Earl	Chelcie Ross
Wendy Wong	Jodi Long
Bloodhound man	Tracey Walter
Stacy	Aimee Graham

A one-joke sketch that doesn't work as a feature, Castle Rock's "Amos & Andrew" raises the question: "How did this film ever get made?" Few audience members will sit through its entirety to ponder the issue.

Debuting director E. Max Frye, who previously penned Jonathan Demme's wildly uneven "Something Wild," attempts a satire of contemporary racism that employs strictly stereotyped characters and typecast actors.

With barely a switcheroo or comedic reversal in sight, Frye postulates a Pulitzer Prize-winning African-American writer, Andrew Sterling (played unsympathetically by Samuel L. Jackson), who buys a summer home on exclusive Watauga Island, Mass., and moves in undetected.

Neighbors Michael Lerner and Margaret Colin don't know the place has been sold and think Jackson is a burglar because he's black. They summon the cops, led by Dabney Coleman (who's running for political office), and somehow deduce, practically out of thin air, that Jackson is holding hostages. Before long, seemingly retarded deputy Brad Dourif dons camouflage makeup and opens fire.

When Coleman finds out Jackson is famous, he sees his own political career going up in flames. To cover up the police gaffe, he cajoles recently arrested car thief Nicolas Cage into posing as the shooter and breaking into Jackson's house to hold him hostage in exchange for being allowed to quietly leave town after letting Jackson go on cue.

Things continue to escalate (unconvincingly) with Coleman doublecrossing Cage and an opportunistic media circus erupting to cover the siege at Sterling's mansion. The wildly incompatible Cage and Jackson bond against a common enemy and the viewer looks at his watch with a full hour of redundant movie to go.

Scenes like the police opening fire on Jackson in his home play like a dead-serious documentary and even slapstick gags fall flat. When Jackson lapses into preachy speeches even Frye's pretense of satire is in doubt. Since bad taste is usually the savior of failed modern comedy, Frye tries to inject some, but with such timidity that even a bit of down and dirty doesn't pep things up.

Film's premise might have been mildly amusing if some twist were offered, say a fictional restricted New England town populated by Jews and African-Americans into which a WASP moves; or more logically given pic's title have both lead roles played by blacks representing different social strata. As it stands, the film has no edge and zero wit, rendering its barbs offensive.

Cage uses his patented overdone physical shtick for momentary amusement and gets to recite an endless shaggy dog story about sea monkeys that some might find amusing. Jackson is miscast; the relentless heaviness of his performance is not conducive to levity.

Besides the typecast Coleman and Dourif, are the equally typecast (and boring) Giancarlo Esposito as a black activist minister from New York who tries to exploit the situation by rabblerousing; Bob Balaban as a hostage situation expert who's a milquetoast shrink; and, briefly, Tracey Walter as a good ole boy with bloodhounds. "Amos" is unlikely to be listed on their résumés.

Film is technically competent but runs out of gas so fast it's tough to evaluate editing and atmosphere. For people who arrive late, the whole farrago is summarized in trivial terms in an out-theme rap song by Sir Mix-Alot. — *Lawrence Cohn*

LE ARBE, LE MAIRE ET LA MÉDIATHÈQUE
(THE TREE, THE MAYOR AND THE MEDIATHEQUE)
(FRENCH)

A Les Films du Losange release of a La Compagnie Eric Rohmer production. Directed, written by Eric Rohmer. Camera (color), Diane Baratier; editor, Mary Stephen; music, Sebastien Erms; sound, Pascal Ribier. Reivewed at Saint-Germain-des-Pres Cinema, Paris, Feb. 15, 1993. Running time: **111 MIN.**

Julien Dechaumes	Pascal Greggory
Berenice Beaurivage	Arielle Dombasle
Marc Rossignol	Fabrice Luchini
Blandine	Clementine Amouroux

Also with: François-Marie Banier, Michel Jaouen, Jean Parvulesco, Françoise Etchegaray, Galaxie Barbouth, Jessica Schwing.

With "Spring" and "Winter" under his belt, Eric Rohmer takes a break from his "Tales of the Four Seasons" to tell a timely tale of politics and culture, aimed squarely at his countrymen. Talky and topical fare is unlikely to enrapture non-Francophiles, but gentle goosing of self-styled authorities in tandem with Rohmer's trademark serendipity make "Le Arbe, Le Maire et Le Médiathèque" mildly entertaining, if not as magical or accessible as his best efforts. Launched on one Paris screen, pic has been well-received locally.

Main title is followed by the words: "Or Seven Chance Happenings." After smalltown teacher Fabrice Luchini leads his grammar class through the use of "the conditional," seven title cards, written out on notebook paper and each starting with "If . . . ," punctuate the proceedings.

The all-important "ifs" indicate how, through a chain of events, the teacher, the village's mayor, a Socialist with ambitions beyond regional politics (Pascal Greggory); a flighty and stylish Parisian novelist (Arielle Dombasle); a magazine journalist (Clementine Amouroux); and her editor (François-Marie Banier) go about their business only to be served or sabotaged by their interconnected actions.

The mayor, who has fallen for the novelist, intends to build a grandiose sports and cultural center in an empty field. Luchini, who loves both the unsullied horizon and the hundred-year-old willow tree that will be felled to make a parking lot, opines that, "The death penalty should be abolished except for architects."

The mayor believes that his project is a done deal and the teacher assumes that nothing can impede the disgusting march of progress. But the men don't guess that their respective daughters will strike up a friendship.

In its leisurely, non-pedantic way, pic comments on the relentless modernization of rural France, on the often ridiculous way in which funding is apportioned, and on the theory that since Paris — as any Parisian will admit — is the center of the universe, it follows that the rest of the country is lamentably devoid of culture.

Camerawork is rarely better than perfunctory and, depending on one's personal tolerance for Luchini's and Dombasle's mannered deliveries, some viewers may prefer the nonpro members of the cast to the Rohmer vets.

What may prove a stumbling block to successful export is pic's extreme topicality. It helps to know a bit about the French political system, particularly the power plays afoot between the Socialists and the Ecologists, and the fact that the Socialists are expected to lose most of their influence after March elections. What's more, the same elected official can legally hold up to three government posts, but this parenthetical information can be dispensed with by local critics if, as is regularly the case with Rohmer's work, this film is distributed to urban arthouses beyond France. — *Lisa Nesselson*

TANGO
(FRENCH)

An AMLF release of a Cinea/Hachette Premiere & Co./TF1 Films/Zoulou Films co-production with the participation of Sofinergie, Canal Plus and the Languedoc-Roussillon region. Produced by Philippe Carcassonne, Rene Cleitman. Directed by Patrice Leconte. Screenplay, Leconte, Patrick Dewolf. Camera (color, Panavision widescreen), Eduardo Serra; editor, Genevieve Winding; music, Angelique Nachon, Jean-Claude Nachon; production design, Ivan Maussion; sound, Pierre Lenoir. Reviewed at Forum Horizon Cinema, Paris, Feb. 8, 1993. Running time: **90 MIN.**

L'Elegant	Philippe Noiret
Vincent	Richard Bohringer
Paul	Thierry Lhermitte

Also with: Miou-Miou, Judith Godreche, Carole Bouquet, Jean Rochefort.

A deliciously dark comedy that revels in male observations about women and the impossibility of living with them,

February 22, 1993 (Cont.)

"Tango" will delight some viewers and infuriate others. A deliberately crass departure from "Monsieur Hire" and "The Hairdresser's Husband," Patrice Leconte's latest offering should dance its way into offshore arthouses.

Vicious and absurd, yet packed with revealing insights about human longings and behavior, pic's tone recalls the films of Bertrand Blier. Scripters were guided by statistics indicating that the majority of married men wish they were single and the majority of bachelors wish they were married, reaching the conclusion that, however much they may need and appreciate women, guys are happiest hanging out with other guys.

Obsessed by the wife who's left him, handsome ladies' man Paul (Thierry Lhermitte) decides he'd be happier if he knew she were dead. Paul's uncle, a dapper and unscrupulous judge known as "L'Elegant" (Philippe Noiret), has the perfect assassin in mind — a widower named Vincent (Richard Bohringer), who killed his own unfaithful wife accidentally-on-purpose and got away with it.

The three men pile into a car and set off to off Lhermitte's spouse. As a group, they embody most of the possible approaches to heterosexual male behavior, which paves the way for offbeat encounters and testosterone-fueled deadpan pronouncements, most of which are unfair to the fair sex. The men are reprehensible but always interesting. Helmer keeps matters off-kilter and only the end is predictable.

Miou-Miou, Judith Godreche and Carole Bouquet — whose names are deliberately absent from the opening credits — make brief but memorable appearances. Godreche, especially, is disturbingly radiant and self-possessed. Some local scribes accused pic of rampant misogyny, but they overlook the fact that the women in the cast know precisely what they want, whereas the men are bumbling and deluded.

Dialogue employs a catchy mix of elegant and slangy vocabulary to express lusty, direct sentiments, and thesps are superb across the board. Clad in boxer shorts, Noiret makes it seem classy to watch a porno video. In a fancy restaurant, Lhermitte wows his buddies by betting that he can bed any woman there in under three minutes. Bohringer can be reckless or reasonable.

Widescreen lensing is bright and appealing. Jaunty soundtrack, ranging from Wagner to North African rhythms, suits the action. — *Lisa Nesselson*

JACK THE BEAR

A 20th Century Fox release of an American Filmworks/Lucky Dog production. Executive producer, Ron Yerxa. Produced by Bruce Gilbert. Directed by Marshall Herskovitz. Screenplay, Steven Zaillian, from Dan McCall's novel. Camera (Deluxe color, Super 35m widescreen), Fred Murphy; editor, Steven Rosenblum; music, James Horner; production design, Lilly Kilvert; costumes, Deborah L. Scott; associate producer, Peter Burrell; assistant director, Nilo Otero; casting, Mary Goldberg. Reviewed at Berlin Film Festival (Panorama), Feb. 13, 1993. Running time: **98 MIN.**
John Leary . . . . Danny DeVito
Jack Leary . . Robert J. Steinmiller Jr.
Dylan Leary . . . . Miko Hughes
Norman Strick . . . . Gary Sinise
Peggy Etinger . . Julia Louis-Dreyfus
Karen Morris . . . Reese Witherspoon
Mother-in-Law . . . . Erica Yohn
Father-in-Law . . . . . Stefan Gierasch
Mitchell . . . . Bert Remsen
Mrs. Leary . . . . . Andrea Marcovicci

"**J**ack the Bear," a mostly likable first feature from "Thirtysomething" co-creator Marshall Herskovitz, concerns a boy who discovers that monsters are to be found not only on television but also in real life. A clever portrayal of eccentric fatherhood by Danny DeVito and a socko performance from young Robert J. Steinmiller Jr. as the eponymous hero are major assets, but selling this offbeater may be a tricky proposition for Fox.

Lensed in spring 1991, the film world-preemed in the noncompeting Panorama slot at the Berlin Film Fest to enthusiastic response. Based on Dan McCall's 1974 tome, and set in suburban Oakland in 1972, film mixes comedy and horror to make its points about latent evil.

Twelve-year-old Jack (Steinmiller) and his younger brother Dylan (Miko Hughes) have moved here with their oddball father, John Leary (DeVito), after the death of their mother in a car crash following a quarrel with Leary. (Andrea Marcovicci, as the mother, is glimpsed only in stylized flashbacks.)

Using the name Al Gore, Leary gets a gig as host of a latenight show that recycles old horror movies. But he drinks too much and is often on the brink of losing his job. He tends to neglect his sons, and it's Jack (whose mother nicknamed him Bear) who has to take his little brother to school on his first day.

Pic's first half rather indulgently explores the relationships among the Learys and their neighbors in a street that seems permanently under repair. Jack and Dylan mix easily with local boys, but there's also the sinister Norman Strick (Gary Sinise), a crippled, bigoted war vet and supporter of a far-right-wing candidate in the 1972 election.

In some touching scenes, Jack finds first love with a knowing schoolgirl (Reese Witherspoon), but the girl soon decides she doesn't want to be tied down. On a tougher note is when the generally decent Jack "punishes" his brother by forcing him close to a broken-down fence that holds back vicious dogs.

However, the real menace is saved for the final act, when the deranged Strick kidnaps Dylan and then, like some monster from a real horror flick, comes after Jack. Though these scenes sometimes appear to have strayed from a different film, they drive the momentum toward a satisfying conclusion.

DeVito gives an interesting portrayal as the fond father whose personal problems hinder his relationship with his sons, and it's not his fault that the smallfry steal the film. Steinmiller's performance is especially good in its range and feeling.

Use of the Super 35m widescreen format is justified by the panorama of the bustling suburban street, and James Horner's music effectively helps build the mood created by script and direction. It remains to be seen if a substantial audience will shell out for this small-scale picture.
— *David Stratton*

DIARIO DI UN VIZIO
(DIARY OF A MANIAC)
(ITALIAN)

An Italian Intl. Film release (in Italy) of a SOI/Società Olografica Italiana production. Produced by Vittorio Alliata. Directed by Marco Ferreri. Screenplay, Ferreri, Liliana Betti. Camera (color), Mario Vulpiani; editor, Ruggero Mastroianni; music, Gato Barbieri; art direction, Tommaso Bordone; costumes, Maria Camilla Righi. Reviewed at Anica screening room, Rome, Feb. 5, 1993. (In competition at Berlin Film Festival.) Running time: **88 MIN.**
Benito . . . . Jerry Calà
Luigia . . . . Sabrina Ferilli
Chiominto . . . . . . Valentino Macchi

Anguishing, exalting, tender and pathetic, Marco Ferreri's "Diary of a Maniac" is probably one of this idiosyncratic director's finest works. Its black humor traces the life of a lonely salesman as he follows a doomed love around an imaginary yet intensely real Rome. It may prove too offbeat to go wide in Italy, despite a cast aimed at drawing in local comedy fans, but pic's original modernity should capture arthouse auds offshore.

Made on a low budget, pic overflows with a feeling of stylistic freedom. The story is told in short flashes, which the hero reads from his diary.

Benito (played with unsuspected candor by popular comic star Jerry Calà), the "maniac" of the title, lives in cheap rented rooms and makes a humiliating living peddling toilet-bowl detergent to hotels. Despite having a sexually insatiable girlfriend, Luigia (Sabrina Ferilli), Calà can't resist constant, casual affairs with women of all types and ages.

At pic's center is Calà's madcap, neurotic diary, full of entries about heart palpitations, stomach acidity and other effects of meeting females who "provoke" him on trams. Its grotesque observations faithfully chronicle the life of a little man on the skids.

A knock-out beauty of humble origin and few scruples, Ferilli rises from hotel maid to striptease artist and bit parts in the movies. She loves Calà, and he loves her, though she drops him the minute a guy in a sports car turns up. They fight, make love and break up frequently, —material for his growing obsession.

Calà's dreams — recorded in his sick childish scrawl, but sometimes chillingly visualized by the camera — are filled with Ferilli, his mother and sexual fantasies.

February 22, 1993 (Cont.)

The diary takes up more and more space, while Calà's life becomes more impoverished. At last he disappears altogether, and only words remain.

Instead of the usual snotty Milanese wisecracks from the average-Joe characters he has played, here Calà is perfectly deadpan in delivering bizarre one-liners and off-the-wall diary entries. He makes Benito both surreal and achingly human.

This may be the breakthrough film for Ferilli, who throws herself into the role of the oft-disrobed sexpot with irrepressible *joie de vivre*.

One of "Diary's" most winning qualities is its affection for life's rejects and "ordinary" people who form a chorus in praise of the average man and woman.

In contrast to Calà's high-pitched anxiety, film's rhythm is pleasantly relaxed. It's a visual pleasure, thanks to Mario Vulpiani's modernistic, precision camerawork and Tommaso Bordone's slumming-chic art direction.

Gato Barbieri's sax solo (shades of "Last Tango in Paris") works surprisingly well in this completely different context.

If traces of Fellini peek out of "Diary," it may be thanks to Ferreri's co-scripter, Liliana Betti, a longtime Fellini aide-decamp. — *Deborah Young*

DEDICTVÍ ANEB KURVAHOSIGUTNTAG

(THE INHERITANCE OR FUCKOFFGUYSGOODBYE)

(CZECHOSLOVAKIAN)

A Space Films/Polytechna production. (Intl. sales: Space Films, Prague.) Produced by Jirí Ježek. Directed by Vera Chytilová. Screenplay, Bolek Polívka, Chytilová. Camera (color), Ervín Sanders; editor, Jan Mattlach; music, Jirí Bulis; art direction, Zbynek Hloch; sound, Zbynek Mikulík; assistant director, Daniela Flejsarová. Reviewed at Berlin Film Festival (Panorama section), Feb. 13, 1993. Running time: **124 MIN.**

Bohus	Bolek Polívka
Dr. Ulrich	Miroslav Donutil
Vlasta	Dagmar Veskrnová
Irena	Sárka Vojtková
Kostál	Jozef Króner
Aunt	Anna Pantucková

"**T**he Inheritance" is a loopy, sublimely un-P.C. Czech comedy that needs to lose a good half-hour. New Wave vet Vera Chytilová's post-communist satire about a rural tree-swinger who inherits a fortune could do modest arthouse biz and even better tube sales after a shears-session.

Lanky co-scripter Bolek Polívka stars as Bohus, a Moravian nerd who lives on a run-down farm and spends his days with his mouth to a plum brandy bottle. His only exercise is backroom quickies with willing barmaid Vlasta (Dagmar Veskrnová). One day, a starchy lawyer (Miroslav Donutil) from Brno arrives to tell him he's inherited a brickworks, several shops and even a five-star hotel.

Bohus sets out on a tour of his new empire, insulting everyone in sight, organizing a boozy outing with his buddies, and falling head-over-heels for spectacular hooker Irena (Sárka Vojtková). Final, fantasy twist, hardly unexpected, has an optimistic capper.

It's a one-joke movie, but keeps up a head of steam for the first hour thanks to Polívka's winning perf as an out-and-out philistine and some good set-pieces. Latter include a baiting episode with an arrogant waiter at the hotel Polívka now owns, a funny (and sexy) sequence at a whorehouse where he gets to know Vojtková, and a drunken outing at a posh restaurant. Last contains the pic's funniest (but unprintable) line, in which Polívka demolishes the lawyer's snooty wife. However, the movie seriously runs out of gas during the final half-hour.

Supporting performances are all sharp and well-timed, in true Czech style. Veskrnová and Vojtková are equally good as the raunchy barmaid and golddigging hooker, and veteran Jozef Króner makes a mark as Polívka's aged pal. Technically, pic is fine, with beautiful color lensing by Ervín Sanders.

— *Derek Elley*

HATACHI NO BINETSU

(THE SLIGHT FEVER OF A 20-YEAR-OLD)

(JAPANESE)

A PIA Corp./Pony Canyon production. (Intl. sales: PIA Corp., Tokyo.) Produced by Akira Ishigaki. Directed, written by Ryosuke Hashiguchi. Camera (color, 16m), Junichi Tozawa; editor, Hiroshi Matsuo; music, Kohei Shinozaki, Akira Isono, Ryuji Murayama; art direction, Hiroshi Yanai; sound, Masaru Usui; co-producer, Mana Katsurada. Reviewed at Berlin Film Festival (Forum section), Feb. 12, 1993. Running time: **109 MIN.**

Tatsuru	Yoshihiko Hakamata
Shin	Masashi Endo
Yoriko	Reiko Kataoka
Atsumi	Sumiyo Yamada

The emotional temperature refuses to rise in "A Slight Fever of a 20-Year-Old," a tedious haul through alienated gay subculture in contempo Japan. Despite flashes of originality, debut feature of former Super-8m filmer Ryosuke Hashiguchi is of interest only to followers of Asian marginalia.

Its four student characters are a passionless "rentboy" (hustler), a sexually screwed-up youth who thinks he loves him, and two girls who fancy them but are blind to their night jobs. The rentboy (Yoshihiko Hakamata) services elder male clients simply for the money and ignores the attentions of young gymnast Masashi Endo, who can't bring himself to declare his love. The two girls in their lives spend a lot of time grappling with the mystery of their b.f.s' coolness.

There's some interesting subject matter here about the twilight zone between friendship and love, but it keeps slipping out of focus thanks to distanced direction and empty characters. Best scene is an embarrassing evening meal at g.f. Reiko Kataoka's home, at which Hakamata recognizes her father a client.

Hashiguchi's fondness for long takes and long shots, often with a fixed camera, hammers home the alienation theme without evoking audience sympathy. Performances by the males are uninteresting; liveliest thesp is Kataoka as the bemused Yoriko.

Technically, the 16m pic is okay, and gay content visually discreet.

— *Derek Elley*

WARHEADS

(GERMAN-FRENCH-DOCU-16m)

A Max Film/Eurocréation/WDR co-production. (Intl. sales: Ex Picturis, Berlin.) Produced by Wolfgang Pfeiffer, Anne-Marie Autissier. Directed, written by Romuald Karmakar. Camera, (color, 16m), Michael Teutsch (Mississippi), Klaus Merkle (French Guiana), Reiner Lauter (Munich), Bruno Affret (Croatia); editor, Katja Dringenberg; video, Karamakar; sound, Klaus-Peter Kaiser (Mississippi), Norbert Werner (French Guiana), Eckard Kuchenbecker (Munich), Istvan Kerenyi (Croatia). Reviewed at Berlin Film Festival (Intl. Forum of Young Films), Jan. 26, 1992. Running time: **182 MIN.**

This docu exploring the lives of mercenary soldiers gets off to a promising start, but after the first third of a hefty three-hour running time, it cracks, becoming two distinct films with only tenuous links, stylistically as well as thematically. "Warheads" lacks the thesis or p.o.v. necessary to maintain viewer interest, and ultimately becomes self-indulgent, torpid and rambling when it could have been daring.

Film's strong point is its exploration of the life of Günter Aschenbrenner, a German whose family's Nazi past and strict religious upbringing compelled him to seek a life in the French Foreign Legion. In a series of interviews, Aschenbrenner recounts his life and adventures in Chad, Djibouti, Zaire and the French/Algerian war. His insights into the the hardships of life in the Legion (five in his 43-member troop committed suicide) are compelling, as are details such as tales of how organized groups of prostitutes followed the men.

Aschenbrenner is currently involved in running a private paramilitary training camp in Mississippi. Interviews with him are cross-cut with scenes from training sessions with his would-be Rambos, presumably recruited via Soldier of Fortune ads.

Pic loses its ground when Aschenbrenner begins recounting his post-Legion life. By the time he reunites with some Legion comrades in French Guiana to drink, sing and swap stories, docu is on a hopelessly aimless course.

Abruptly, the focus shifts and all traces of Aschenbrenner are dropped unceremoniously. Karl, a British mercenary, is a new focal point, but just barely. He gets only one formal interview, where he says he is both doing good for the world and points out that being a mercenery is an interesting lifestyle choice for someone with limited education.

Action dissolves into long tracking shots of bombed out buildings (we don't know where or why) and rambling encounters with soldiers and mercenaries that feel like unedited footage.

Pic ends with a rather cursory focus on female mercenaries in Croatia, where Karl is also fighting. — *Rebecca Lieb*

February 22, 1993 (Cont.)

THE BED YOU SLEEP IN

A Complex Corp. production. Produced by Henry S. Rosenthal. Directed, written, edited, designed by Jon Jost. Camera (Technicolor), Jost; music, Erling Wold; sound, John Murphey. Reviewed at Berlin Film Festival (Forum), Feb. 13, 1993. Running time: **113 MIN.**
Ray Weiss . . . . Tom Blair
Jean Weiss . . . . . . Ellen McLaughlin
With: Kathryn Sannella, Marshall Gaddis, Thomas Morris, Brad Shelton.

The prolific Jon Jost's latest pic will be a frustrating experience for all but the helmer's most loyal fans on fest and arthouse circuits. The core of an interesting, important theme is encased in an overlong and maddeningly indulgent framework that digresses, whenever possible and at length, from the business at hand.

Jost, who does just about everything on his films except record the sound and compose the music, needs a producer who will tell him when enough's enough; but for auds who find meaning in images of everyday banality, "The Bed You Sleep In" may be just the thing. Set in lush Oregon timberland, the film revolves around Ray Weiss (Tom Blair), owner of a timbermill threatened by a raw material shortage and a soft Asian market.

Jost incorporates endless documentary footage of the mill, which could be drastically sheared. The point is also made (not too subtly) that the mill has scarred the environment.

As the recession bites into his livelihood, Blair tries to escape his troubles by fly-fishing (there's a direct reference to "A River Runs Through It") and he has the sympathy of his loving wife, Jean (Ellen McLaughlin). But then comes disaster: a letter from his daughter, studying in Seattle, in which she accuses her father of incest. He denies it, and Jost never reveals the truth of the matter, but it ends in tragedy for all concerned.

Shorn of much of the redundant material that constantly interrupts the drama of the film, "Bed" might have worked as a disturbing arthouse item. The performances of Blair and McLaughlin as the doomed couple are raw but effective, and the themes the film explores are potent and relevant.

Technically, pic is adequate most of the time, though poor sound in one scene made important dialog inaudible at the screening caught. Jost's editing is pre-

sumably what he wanted, but seems very slack. Erling Wold's music is a bit self-important.

Maddeningly, the lengthy credits are not only written without punctuation, but fly past at unreadable speed, surely something of an insult to the people who worked on the film.

— *David Stratton*

LE JEUNE WERTHER
(YOUNG WERTHER)
(FRENCH)

A Les Films Alain Sarde/Home Made Movies production. Produced by Hervé Duhamel. Directed, written, edited by Jacques Doillon. Camera (color), Christophe Pollock; music, Philippe Sarde; sound, Jean-Claude Laureux; assistant director, Marie de Laubier; production manager, Sylvain Blache. Reviewed at Berlin Film Festival (competing), Feb. 13, 1993. Running time: **100 MIN.**
Ismaël . . . . Ismaël Jole
Mirabelle . . . Marie-Isabelle Rousseau
Théo . . . . Thomas Bremond
Miren . . . . Miren Capello
Faye . . . . Faye Anastasia
Pierre . . . . Pierre Mézerette
Simon . . . . Simon Clavière
Sunny . . . . Sunny Lebrati
Jessica . . . . Jessica Tharaud

Inspired by Goethe's novella "The Sorrows of Young Werther," Jacques Doillon's new film is a sympathetic look at a group of schoolchildren, all about 13, who are shattered by a (never seen) classmate's suicide. Though the youngsters are very natural in their roles, the extreme talkiness of the film, and its downbeat theme, will make it an unlikely bet for foreign-language markets.

The best friend of the dead youngster is Ismaël (Ismaël Jole.) He and his friends spend the film pondering why it happened. Was it drugs? The fault of a hated teacher, whom they punish by spraying something toxic in his face? Or unrequited love?

Ismaël becomes convinced that the dead boy was infatuated with his neighbor, the pretty and precocious Miren (Miren Capello). He follows her around, gradually finding himself drawn to her.

With its lengthy scenes in which the pubescent youngsters chat endlessly about their problems, feelings and beliefs, "Young Werther" sometimes feels like an Eric Rohmer film with a younger than usual cast. There's no doubting Doillon's sympathies for these troubled youngsters, who have to face a tragedy at a most vulnerable age.

But the writer-director does ask a lot of his audience to maintain interest in a feature film almost entirely devoted to 13-year-old talk sessions. Smartly acted by all the youngsters, and written with what appears to be an authentic ear for their jargon, "Young Werther" is an intelligent and touching film, but commercially a very difficult one.

— *David Stratton*

HUNGARIAN WEEK

GYEREKGYILKOSSÁGOK
(CHILD MURDERS)
(HUNGARIAN-B&W)

A Hétfői Műhely Studio/Magic Media production. Produced by István Kardos, Péter Barbarics. Directed, written by Ildikó Szabó. Camera (B&W), Tamás Sas; editor, Panni Kornis; music, János Másik; production design, Szabó; assistant director, Attila Herczeg; production manager, Zoltán Gulyás. Reviewed at Hungarian Film Week, Budapest, Feb 7, 1993. Running time: **82 MINS.**
Zsolt Balogh . . . . Barnabás Tóth
Bizsu (Grandmother) . . . . Ilona Kállai
Bela Andor . . . . Péter Andorai
Juli . . . . Mária Balogh
Little Girl . . . . . . Eszter Csákányi

As chilly as the wintry Danube but as bleakly beautiful, "Child Murders" is a poetic, affecting, quietly horrific pic from talented femme director Ildikó Szabó which seems bound to surface at fests and could find specialized arthouse interest. Though the subject is macabre and even shocking, the film's dispassionate calm constantly undercuts the incipient horror, and the positive aspects of the grim little tale are strongly emphasized.

Bespectacled Zsolt, played with great intelligence by young Barnabás Tóth, lives in a rundown flat by the Danube with his bedridden, alcoholic grandmother. His mother has left the country; his father is never mentioned. The old lady, a former actress who dreams of past glories, demands constant attention; the boy bathes her each morning, and helps her with her makeup.

Seemingly friendless, Zsolt finds himself drawn to a newcomer to the area, Juli (Mária Balogh), a young, pregnant gypsy girl who has moved into an abandoned railway car. The boy pays for his friendship with the out-

sider by being ostracized and beaten by other children; a jealous little girl who lives in his building is especially spiteful.

Zsolt helps Juli when she suffers a miscarriage; they consign the tiny body to the Danube. But the spiteful girl calls the police; Juli is arrested and hangs herself in prison hospital. Zsolt calmly takes his revenge (offscreen) on the informer. The last section of the film touchingly depicts the growing friendship between the boy, whose grandmother has finally been hospitalized, and the policeman (Péter Andorai) in looking into the girl's disappearance.

Within the comparatively brief running time, director Szabó creates powerful emotions with great subtlety, helped by consistently fine performances. With her talented cameraman, Tamás Sas, she has also created images of great beauty; the film is perfectly composed and designed. A haunting score by János Másik adds considerably to the mood.

The film, with its look at poverty among children, the elderly and other outsiders, is not for everyone. But pic deservedly won prizes for best feature, cinematography and actor (Tóth) from the Hungarian jury at the Film Week, as well as the Gene Moskowitz Award of the foreign press.

— *David Stratton*

ANNA FILMJE
(ANNA'S FILM)
(HUNGARIAN)

An MTV/PRO-25/Produceri Iroda production. Produced by Éva Schulze. Directed, written by György Molnár, based on Péter Esterházy's novel. Camera (color), Sándor Kardos; editor, Éva Palotai; music, László Dés; production design, Rita Dévényi; sound, György Kovács; production manager, Tamás Hámori; assistant director, Krisztina Ratai. Reviewed at Hungarian Film Week, Budapest, Feb. 9, 1993. Running time: **82 MIN.**
Anna . . . . Anna Ráczkevei
Husband . . . . György Cserhalmi
Anya . . . . Éva Timár
Father . . . . Tamás Végvári

Anna, an attractive woman with a loving husband, pleasant home and three well-behaved children, has a problem: She's pregnant, and she doesn't want a fourth child. From this familiar premise, writer-director György Molnár, working from a well-regarded novel by Péter Esterházy, has produced a self-conscious film in which very good scenes constantly collide with self-conscious, attention-seeking material. Fests might bite, but arthouse dates seem unlikely.

Like the book on which it's based, "Anna's Film" mixes reality with fantasy, past with present. Flashbacks to parents catching teen Anna having sex with her boyfriend. The b.f. is now her husband, and, by Hungarian standards, the couple live extremely well in their rather stark suburban home.

Anna's dismay at finding herself pregnant for the fourth time triggers her memories and fantasies, which include an omnipresent gent, dressed in white, forever playing a saxophone and dogging her heels. Cold reality is to be found in the grim scene where the husband (a good performance from popular Magyar thesp György Cserhalmi) visits his dying mother in hospital.

Molnár's attempts at artiness abound, however, and rebound against the film. The simplest scenes are handled with pretension; a family meal shown ominously from above, a key in a lock as a gigantic, screen-filling image, a shot from inside a toilet bowel, and so on. In a couple of scenes, half the screen is in color, the other half in black and white.

None of this visual trickiness helps the film, which is just about strong enough to survive it. Anna Ráczkevei gives a luminous performance as the troubled wife, and the supporting cast is uniformly good. A strong Hungarian irony pervades the film, with lines like "To be born here is a tragedy; what's more, it's a tragedy." The film's a bit like that, too. — *David Stratton*

A NAGY POSTARABLÁS
(THE GREAT POST OFFICE ROBBERY)
(HUNGARIAN-GERMAN-POLISH)

A Guild Film Distribution (Hungary) release of a Dialóg Filmstudio/Fero Film/Transfilm GmbH production. Executive producer, Albert Kitzler. Produced by Ferenc András. Directed by Sándor Söth. Screenplay, István Horváth, Géza Bereményi, Söth. Camera (color), Gábor Szabó, Piotr Sobocinski; editor, Maria Rigó; music, Ferenc Darvas; art direction, Gyula Pauer, János Rauschenberger; costume design, Tamás Király; sound, Tamás Márkus. Reviewed at Hungarian Film Week, Budapest, Feb. 7, 1993. Running time: **81 MIN.**

Mari	Dorottya Udvaros
The Boss	Ádám Rajhona
Balázs	Chic Ortega
Géza	Luke Mullaney
Bogdan, the cop	Jan Nowicki

A crime caper with a social edge, "The Great Post Office Robbery" is an ex-East bloc comedy that could travel further than most. Neat construction and fine ensemble playing make the time zip by quickly.

Setting is a new housing estate somewhere in Hungary at which a post office is soon to open. A trio of con artists hit on the idea of moving in a week early, collecting as much money as possible, and making a quick getaway. Things go fine until a fellow fraudster tries to move in on their turf, and a neighborhood cop starts to smell a rat.

Pic works well on several levels, both as a scam comedy and as a satire on the "new entrepreneurialism" of East Europe. An opening caption announces "the dawn of a new world ..." and thereon greed is the main motor driving all the characters.

The strict Monday-to-Friday time-frame, with each section introed by a caption, gives the movie shape and pacing, and the three scriptwriters come up with enough twists and turns to keep things moving. Hurdles include an inquisitive local drunk, an elderly couple who plant a bomb in the building, and even a general strike by post office workers. Finale is neat and ironic.

Performances by a large cast are colorful and well-drawn without descending into pratfall comedy. Hungarian thesp Dorottya Udvaros, as the femme of the central trio, brings a sophisticated edge to the proceedings, and Gérard Depardieu lookalike Luke Mullaney makes a characterful mark as the ex-jailbird who muscles in on the operation.

Despite the story's pre-Christmas setting, pic's look is bright and light, with valuable boosts from Ferenc Darvas' breezy score and trim editing by Maria Rigó. Main title graphics have a '60s look and feel. — *Derek Elley*

INDIÁN TÉL
(INDIAN WINTER)
(HUNGARIAN-B&W)

A Budapest Filmstudio production. Produced by Ferenc Kardos. Directed, written by János Erdélyi, Dezsö Zsigmond. Camera (B&W), Péter Jankura; editor, Gabriella Koncz; music, István Slamovits; production design, Károly Veér; sound, Béla Prohászka; assistant director, István Mag; production manager, Ferenc Szohár. Reviewed at Hungarian Film Week, Feb. 9, 1993. Running time: **84 MIN.**

Tamas	Károly Eperjes
Mother	Mari Töröcsik
Hajnal	Zsuzsa Németh
Friend	András Szöke
Teacher	Pál Zolnay

This is a sad little film, inspired by a real character who spent much of his time living in the woods dressed as an American Indian, and was the subject of dual helmers' 1985 docu. Top Magyar thesp Károly Eperjes brings insight to this touching middle-aged man who lives with his mother (vet Mari Töröcsik) but prefers a life in the wild, trapping rabbits and catching fish the way he imagines his Indian heroes did. It might get fest exposure and certainly the moving perfs of Eperjes and Töröcsik deserve to be seen. Commercial chances are slim, however.

Eperjes seems perfectly happy when left to his own devices. The villagers naturally think he's eccentric, but he helps a friend who's trying, in vain, to escape from the law and is gentle in his dealings with people, unlike the bullies who often torment him. He loves to watch old Westerns (especially when the Indians win) at the local cinema.

His mistake is to fall in love with beautiful gypsy girl Zsuzsa Németh, who moves in on him after breaking up with another man. He marries her, despite the misgivings of his mother. Soon after the wedding, the bride ankles, taking with her all the money Eperjes' mother has saved over the years. Németh returns later seeking help from a vengeful lover, but Eperjes refuses, and the film ends in tragedy.

Helped by striking black and white photography by Péter Jankura, directors János Erdélyi and Dezsö Zsigmond have come up with a poignant film about a simple man living on the edge of society.

— *David Stratton*

BUKFENC
(PIROUETTE)
(HUNGARIAN)

A Fiatal Magyar Filmkészítök Studio/Magyar TV/PRO-25/Fifi/Teleshop production. Produced by Márton Ledniczky. Directed, written by Róbert Pajer, based on Marcel Pagnol's screenplay. Camera (color), Frigyes Marton; editor, Júlia Kende; music, Ferenc Darvas; production design, Zsolt Csengery; sound, Gábor Rozgonyi; costumes, Katalin Juhász; production manager, Kornél Sipos; assistant director, Eleanora Petak. Reviewed at Hungarian Film Week, Budapest, Feb. 8, 1993. Running time: **79 MIN.**

Panier	Róbert Alföldi
Peluque	János Zalán
Lucie	Zsuzsa Mányi
Pomponette	Auguszta Tóth
Captain	Frigyes Hollósi

"Pirouette," a modestly staged adaptation of an original by French author Marcel Pagnol — vogueish thanks to the offshore success of "Jean de Florette" and "Manon of the Spring" — is slight material and film makes little impact.

It centers on two students, one of whom narrates and is constantly speaking directly to the camera, a device that becomes annoying. His more ebullient friend finds himself engaged to two girls at the same time, one an easygoing type, the other the straitlaced daughter of a military officer who zealously guards her honor.

The lack of many settings (about two locations are rather obviously used for what's supposed to be a variety of places) suggests a very tight budget was a constraining factor here, and as a result the film hardly passes muster even as a television movie. Acting is generally flat, and the sought-after effervescence is noticeably lacking in direction and pacing. — *David Stratton*

ÖRDÁG VIGYE
(THE DEVIL TAKE IT)
(HUNGARIAN)

A Dialog Filmstudio/Magyar TV production. Produced by Ferenc András. Directed by Róbert Pajer. Screenplay, Pajer, Sándor Fábry, László. Camera (color), Frigyes Marton; editor, Júlia Kende; music, Ferenc Darvas; production design, Károly Horváth; sound, István Wolf; costumes, Katalin Juhász; assistant director, Mária Eperjes; production manager, András Tóth. Reviewed at Hungarian Film Week, Budapest, Feb. 9, 1993. Running time: **86 MIN.**

February 22, 1993 (Cont.)

Micci	Irén Psota
Geza	Zoltán Bezerédy
Pici	György Dörner
Sanyi	Sándor Gáspár
Armin	Frantisek Pieczka

This is a ho-hum supernatural comedy in which the Devil, in the form of an aging femme, arrives in Budapest in a London taxi. Nothing that follows is particularly exciting, and the pic is strictly local fare.

The Prince(ss) of Darkness, who can change at will into an attractive young woman, is after an elixir of life, which has been discovered by an eccentric inventor. Frustrated in her attempts to secure the priceless potion, Satan/Micci (Irén Psota), hires a stuttering plumber and two incompetent Italians to get it for her. Obviously, her powers aren't quite what they used to be, for her hired help prove quite unable to fulfill their tasks.

Róbert Pajer's film has a few bright moments, but the special effects are rudimentary, most of the acting is exaggerated, and the narrative is completely without surprises. This is strictly routine work for undemanding audiences. — *David Stratton*

NYOMKERESÖ
(PATHFINDER)
(HUNGARIAN)

An Objektiv Filmstudio production. Produced by Gabriella Grósz. Directed, written by Eszter Tóth. Camera (Eastmancolor), Balázs Bélafalvy; editor, Katalin Kabdebó; music, Péter Müller; production design, Zsolt Khell; sound, István Wolf; costumes, Nóra Cselényi; production manager, Miklós Szita; assistant director, István Mag. Reviewed at Hungarian Film Week, Feb. 8, 1993. Running time: **88 MIN.**
With: Mátá Haumann, Gyula Schóbel, Eszter Csákányi, Tünde Murányi, Ági Szirtes, Andor Lukáts, Mari Csomós, Sándor Téri.

A routine film for children, "Pathfinder" (a.k.a. "Trail Seeker") centers on a boy who's read too much James Fenimore Cooper. Indulgent sprigs might go for this unenthralling item.

There's lots of rose-colored fantasy in the film. Wide open spaces, peopled by Cooper's heroes, are to be found on the other side of a school cupboard and a plump, middle-aged teacher can easily return to the way she looked when she was a child. The boy is even able to encounter his grandmother when she was younger. A little girl dies, but it just means she's reunited with her mother.

Mixed up with the fantasy are a few cautionary notes about tackling life's problems, but nothing really intrudes on the boy's hazy vision of the world.

Technically, pic is quite adequate, and the child actors are all fine. But this isn't a film youngsters are likely to remember with any great affection.

— *David Stratton*

HOLTAK SZABADSÁGA
(FREEDOM OF THE DEATH)
(HUNGARIAN-GERMAN-DOCU)

A Fórum Film/MTV (Hungary)/Satellit-Film (Germany) production. Produced by Tamás Fehéri, Barna Kabay. Directed, written by Katalin Petényi, Kabay, Imre Gyöngyössy. Camera (color), Péter Jankura, Bence Gyöngyössy; editor, Petényi; music, Zoltán Bíró; sound, Gyula Traub. Reviewed at Hungarian Film Week, Budapest, Feb. 6, 1993. Running time: **78 MIN.**
(Lithuanian and Russian soundtrack)

"Freedom of the Death" is a moving case study of an elderly Lithuanian couple returning home 40 years after being deported to Siberia under the Soviet regime. Slow-starting docu, which really delivers in the second half, is a strong item for specialized tube slots.

Pic is one of the series of recent docus by Munich-based trio Katalin Petényi, Barna Kabay and Imre Gyöngyössy looking at displaced peoples in Russia and East Europe. Like the subjects of their previous "50 Years of Silence" and "Exiles" (a.k.a. "Homeless"), the current family is human flotsam from the Hitler and Stalin years. Some 500,000 Lithuanians were carted off to Siberia by Uncle Joe and branded as "criminals." Many died in the snowy wastes.

The filmmakers zero in on a family who are planning to move their graves back to Vilnius. Interviews and dinner-table discussions reveal cross-generational differences over whether to forgive and forget: The father is still vehemently anti-Communist; the children (who consider themselves more Russian than Lithuanian) see their future where they live.

Unlike "Exiles," the film attempts no dramatic restaging of events. The closing reel, in which the parents are welcomed in Lithuania with symbolic bread and salt, is a real heart-puller after the mass of background info and archive material preceding it.

Technically the docu is okay. The filmmakers themselves just managed to get out of Vilnius on the eve of the brief-lived 1991 invasion by Soviet troops.

— *Derek Elley*

HOPPÁ
(WHOOPS)
(HUNGARIAN)

A Hunnia Film Studio/Superplan Film/Duna TV production. (Intl. sales: Cinemagyar, Budapest.) Produced by Sándor Simó. Directed, written by Gyula Maár. Camera (Fujicolor), János Vecsernyés; editor, Zsuzsa Jámbor; art direction, Tamás Banovich; costume design, Katalin Horváth; sound (Dolby), András Horváth; assistant director, Edit Fehér. Reviewed at Hungarian Film Week, Budapest, Feb. 5, 1993. (Also in Berlin Film Festival, competing.) Running time: **92 MIN.**

Ede	Dezsö Garas
Kati	Mari Töröcsik
Jenö	István Avar
Elvira	Kati Lázár
Grandmother	Erzi Pártos

"Whoops" is a subtly written, ironic look at two old people broadsided by recent changes in Magyar society that could have trouble reaching the audience it deserves. Fine dialogue and top-rate perfs by a vet cast are undersold by loose, unfocused direction. Extreme gabbiness could also prove a chore for subtitled auds.

Main characters are a couple in their 60s, Kati (Mari Töröcsik) and Ede (Dezsö Garas), who fret about how the new market-driven Hungary will affect their remaining years. She's a dreamer, still worshipping her late father's heroic image; he's a realist who's made the most of every system but never hit the big time.

One day he bumps into Elvira (Kati Lázár), his mistress of 40 years ago, who announces he fathered her son. Her attempts to get Ede to meet his son, and Kati's relentless pushing for him to adapt to the "new system," totally confuse him. Events climax at a large family gathering.

Writer-director Gyula Maár's dense script touches on a host of current talking points in contempo Magyar society: ex-Party big shots turned entrepreneurs (wittily repped by István Avar, as Töröcsik's oily brother), the older generation's nostalgia for the relative certainties of Communism and the breakdown of old social norms under the new order. Less accessible for foreign viewers are the frequent in-jokes and general tone of straight-faced comedy.

Garas and Töröcsik play off each other with practiced, easy skill. Latter (Maár's wife) gets her best role in years after being sidelined in mother parts. Lázár, as the catalyst "other woman," is a fine aggressive foil for Töröcsik's mellower style.

With a few notable exceptions, Maár's camera mostly roams around the characters as they talk and spat. Tech credits are okay, with emotive use of a solo guitar melody to heighten the movie's mystical flavored finale. Hungarian title literally means "Upsydaisy." — *Derek Elley*

SOSE HALUNK MEG
(WE NEVER DIE)
(HUNGARIAN)

A Hunnia Studio/Magic Media production. (Intl. sales: Cinemagyar, Budapest.) Produced by Sándor Simó. Directed by Róbert Koltai. Screenplay by Gábor Nógrádi, Koltai. Camera (Fujicolor), Gábor Halász; editor, Mari Miklós; music, László Dés; art direction/costume design, Gyula Pauer; sound, György Kovács; line producer, László Sipos. Reviewed at Hungarian Film Week, Budapest, Feb. 6, 1993. Running time: **89 MIN.**
With: Róbert Koltai, Mihály Szabados, Tamás Jordaán, Kathleen Gati, Gábor Mate, Andor Lukáts, László Csákányi.

This goofy comedy about a traveling salesman and his nerdy nephew in '60s rural Hungary is an agreeable time-passer. Pic may not be an easy sell in overseas markets but its sunny, feel-good tone could prove a draw where earthy comedy is appreciated.

Director-star Róbert Koltai built his local rep during the '70s and '80s with legit roles and politically risqué cabaret. Current item, his behind-the-lens bow, has been riding high at the Hungarian box office on the strength of his public following.

Koltai plays a salesman who takes his teenage nephew Mihály Szabados on a trip to the country as a birthday present. An unscheduled detour to the track lands Koltai with a hot tip and, after getting Szabados deflow- ered by a sexy local (Kathleen Gati) and teaching him some other facts of life, he returns to place his bet. Ending is sweet-sour but overall upbeat.

The movie is mostly a one-man show by Koltai, as a never-say- die bespectacled bozo who's an incorrigible skirt- and coin-chas- er. The thesp's fast-talking, antsy creation doesn't really develop, but there's enough incident and other semi-crazed characters to keep things bubbling along. Sza- bados is neutral as the nephew; Hungarian-Canadian actress Gati is colorful as the ditzy purloiner of his viginity.

Tech credits are fine, and the pic's bright look and cheeriness are an agreeable antidote to more serious Magyar fare.
— *Derek Elley*

A GOLYÁK MINDIG VISSZATÉRNEK
(THE STORKS ALWAYS RETURN)
(HUNGARIAN)

A Filmex Kft production. Produced by László Baji. Directed by Tibor Puszt. Screenplay, Ferenc Jeli. Camera (color), Gábor Halász; editors, Csilla Derzsi, Lujza Tóth; production design, Tibor Szollár, István Takács; sound, Ottó Oláh; assistant director, Veronika Oláh; pro- duction manager, Péter Rutkai. Re- viewed at Hungarian Film Week, Bu- dapest, Feb. 7, 1993. Running time: **68 MIN.**
With: Sándor Szabó, Péter Gyenes, Erika Fényes, Hédi Temessy, Gellért Raysányi, Frigyes Funtek, Barbara Hegyi, Zoltan Gera, László Szabó.

A routine kidpic that makes political points bound to be lost on most non-Hungar- ians, "The Storks Always Re- turn" is an outside bet for pro- grammers of smallfry material.

Set in 1956 in the Hungarian countryside, the film's wafer- thin plot revolves around Zoltán, an 8-year-old who lives on his grandfather's farm with his mother; his father, a political prisoner, languishes in prison.

On a solo hunting expedition, the lad accidentally shoots a stork, a protected bird. As if in punish- ment, he almost immediately gets stuck in deep mud and has to be rescued after hours of misery. While he recovers, grandfather nurses the wounded stork also.

Then comes the unseen, but talked about, uprising against Communist rule and the boy's

father is released. But life on the farm is tense as it becomes clear the Communists will be restored to power, and the father decides to flee across the border with his family. As they cross into free- dom, the recovered stork symbol- ically flies for the first time.

Scenes in which the feverish boy dreams that the farm ani- mals talk may appeal to young- sters, but are typical of the some- what desperate attempts of di- rector Tibor Puszt to expand the slim material. Pic is stilted and not even very attractive visual- ly. Hungarian sprigs may appre- ciate the political references, but offshore kids won't have a clue.

Technically, pic is of standard quality in every department.
— *David Stratton*

BLUE BOX
(HUNGARIAN)

A Motion Picture Innovation & Foun- dation (MIT) production. Produced by István Darday. Directed, written by Elemér Káldor. Camera (color), Nyika Jancsó; editor, Csilla Derzsi; music, László Melis; art direction, László Zsótér, Sándor Kállai; costume design, János Papp; sound, Tamás Márkus. Re- viewed at Hungarian Film Week, Bu- dapest, Feb. 6, 1993. Running time: **90 MIN.**
With: András Kozák, János Vetö, György Kozma, János Derzsi, László Gálffi, Tamás Cseh, Andrea Drahota, Pál Zolnay, Edit Káldor.

Some nice ideas slip the leash early on in "Blue Box," a psychological murder mystery set around a real Budapest rock club. Magyar movie buffs will groove on the in-refs but oth- ers will likely head for the exit.

Andrá Kozák, a regular in Miklós Jancsó movies for the past 30 years, plays the vodka-swill- ing Tamás, a regular in Miklós Jancsó movies. During a fracas at his cellar club, the Blue Box, the body of an actress (Andrea Drahota, another regular in Miklós Jancsó movies), is found in the street outside.

Kozák, a video junkie who's obsessed by images of Drahota and planning a movie called "Blue Box," confesses. But the cop investigating says Kozák has an unbreakable alibi.

Deep down there's the seed of an interesting psychological cat- and-mouse game between the burned-out actor and wily cop. Clips from past movies by Kozák

and Drahota, including "My Way Home," "Current" and "Red Psalm," are jumbled up with lots of introspection about Hungari- an national identity, but the brew only works intermittently. Pac- ing is slow, capped by a silly finale in which the three main characters are resurrected in a post-apocalyptic landscape.

Performances are okay, and there's a plethora of local rock songs in the club scenes. Moody lensing, blurrily transferred from vid to 35m, is by Nyika Jancsó, son of Miklós. — *Derek Elley*

GOTHENBURG FEST

DET SOCIALA ARVET
(MISFITS TO YUPPIES a.k.a. GENERATION TO GENERATION)
(SWEDISH)

A Europex presentation of a Stefan Jarl production. Produced, directed, writ- ten by Stefan Jarl. Camera (color), Per Källberg; music, Fläskkvartetten/22 Pis- tepirkko; editor, Anette Lykke Lund- berg. Reviewed at Bödakyarn cinema, Stockholm, Feb. 4, 1993. (In Gothenburg Film Festival.) Running time: **87 MIN.**

Third part of Stefan Jarl's trilogy about a pair of misfits and their offspring is powerful documentary filmmaking at its best. Fest directors should start to line up for his must-see film, a natural for fests, preferably shown with the first two films.

In his 1967 "They Call Us Mis- fits," Jarl told the story of Stock- holm youths Kenta and Stoffe, whose lives revolved around booze, drugs and girls. Anybody leading an ordinary life was abused and ridiculed by them.

In 1979, Jarl made a followup, "A Decent Life," where the happy-go-lucky lifestyle had been replaced by one of excessive drug use and petty crimes. During the shooting of the film — one of the most hard-hitting and gut-wrench- ing documentaries from Sweden — Stoffe died of an overdose.

In "Misfits To Yuppies," Jarl shows what has happened to the children of Kenta, Stoffe and their friends. Stoffe's widow wants noth- ing to do with the filmmaker, preventing him from seeing Stof- fe's son, who has been adopted, lives in the countryside and works as an auto mechanic.

On the other hand, contrary to what Jarl believed would hap- pen, Kenta's son, Patrik, and Car- ina, the daughter of their misfit friend Jalla, are on the verge of achieving success. Patrik wants to earn money and is becoming a hard-working yuppie, and Cari- na graduates from school and wants "a life that is secure."

Jarl makes expert use of foot- age from the previous films, show- ing us the characters' develop- ment. The film is both hopeful for its young protagonists but harrowing in its depiction of a Sweden where class distinctions are becoming sharper.

The Swedish title of the film literally means "the social heri- tage" — Jarl had thought the misfits' kids would also end up losers. But despite Kenta's "I'm still a misfit, and I'm proud of it" attitude, his child is completely different. — *Gunnar Rehlin*

TALA! DET ÄR SÅ MÖRKT
(TALK! IT'S SO DARK)
(SWEDISH)

A Swedish Film Institute presenta- tion of a Götafilm production in coopera- tion with Swedish Television/the Swed- ish Film Institute. Produced by Chris- ter Nilsson. Directed by Suzanne Osten. Screenplay, Niklas Rådström. Camera (color), Peter Mokrosinski; editor, Mi- chael Leszclyowski. Reviewed at Go- thenburg Film Festival, Gothenburg, Sweden, Feb. 7, 1993. (Also in Berlin Film Fest, Panorama Section.) Running time: **80 MIN.**
With: Etienne Glaser, Simon Norrthon.

Drama of a meeting be- tween an elderly Jewish doctor and a young racist is tense and well-acted, though most of what is said is predictable.

"Tala!" starts with a bang. In a fast, furious montage of pictures, a young black man at a railway station is severely beaten by young Swedish neo-Nazis. One of them (Simon Norrthon) jumps on board a train and meets a Jewish doctor (Etienne Glaser). They start talking, and despite Norrthon's hostility toward the man, he accepts an invitation to come and talk to him in what becomes analytic sessions.

The doctor wants to know what is the driving force behind the racial rage burning within the young Swede. And for Norrthon,

February 22, 1993 (Cont.)

the older Glaser gradually becomes the father symbol he has been trying to find.

The sessions are sometimes calm, sometimes explosive. Osten intercuts with scenes where he meets his companions, other young neo-Nazis, and in blurred, newsreel-like scenes we see them on the rampage, threatening and beating up immigrants. But we also see the latter react, and in one scene Norrthon is the one who's threatened and beaten.

Etienne Glaser plays the doctor in his usual low-keyed way. The find is young Norrthon, who's still in acting school. There's not a false note in his portrayal and he'll be someone to watch.

For Osten, the film technically is a departure, in the use of fast montages and a rhythm that she seems to have borrowed from some of the loud rock music on the soundtrack. Tech credits are all okay, with special mention to Peter Mokrosinski's lensing.

— *Gunnar Rehlin*

DEN ANDRA STRANDEN
(THE SECOND SHORE)
(SWEDISH-DOCU)

Folkets Bio presents a SVT/Kanal 1 Dokumentär/Manharen & Film production. Produced, directed, written by Mikael Wiström. Camera (color), Peter Östlund; editor, Annika Geijerstam; music, Peter Bryngelsson-Piirtauke; sound, Lars Palmgren, Per Strandberg. Reviewed at Gothenburg Film Festival, Gothenburg, Sweden, Feb. 7, 1993. Running time: **84 MIN.**

In his book "The First Shore," Mikael Wiström tells of preparing to go back to Peru to meet a family he first encountered 17 years ago when they were living in a garbage dump. Wiström's accompanying documentary is an uneven film that only functions when accompanied by his book. If the book is translated into English, the film might be of interest for festivals.

The director wants to make a film about his hunt to get back in touch with the family, and the book is revelatory about the different manipulations that lie behind any documentary. It becomes the story of a man who always thinks of how a given encounter might look on camera, and who sometimes starts to direct reality in order to better

suit his purposes. Which is more important for him: to make a good film or to really get to know the family once again? Wiström seems unsure.

The book is fascinating, and essential reading for anyone interested in the mechanics behind docu-making. But the film falls flat. — *Gunnar Rehlin*

DOCKPOJKEN
(BOY DOLL)
(SWEDISH-COLOR/B&W)

The Swedish Film Institute presents a Swedish Film Institute/Swedish Television Channel 1 production. Produced by Lisbet Gabrielsson. Directed by Hilda Hellwig. Script, Hellwig, from Martin Andersen Nexo's story. Camera (color/B&W), Bertil Wiktorsson; music, Jonas Lindgren; editor, Christos Kefalas; costumes, Lars Gogo Björkman; sound, Bengt Wallman. Reviewed at Gothenburg Film Festival, Gothenburg, Sweden, Feb. 7, 1993. Running time: **83 MIN.**
With: Sven Wollter, Lena Granhagen, Hampus Pettersson, Thomas Antoni, Cecilia Nilsson.

Four years in the making, "Boy Doll" is a sympathetic first feature with excellent acting from Sven Wollter. But despite its short running time, it still feels too long.

Pic was intended as a short and during its troubled years in production was extended to feature length. The story of a poor family in the snow-plagued wilderness of northern Sweden, where the father (Wolter) works in the forest and, with his wife, makes dolls that they sell to a nearby toy factory.

Their only child, a boy in his early teens, often plays what his father regards as ill-willed pranks and Wolter, in turn, responds with his only means of communication: violence. In the end, the boy runs away and does not return until he is a grown man with a family of his own.

Low-budget pic mostly takes place in the lonely cottage where the family lives. These scenes are shot in a grainy black-and-white, and are quite effective. Scenes in color, which mostly depict the boy's life as an adult, are weaker, partly due to unsatisfying acting.

— *Gunnar Rehlin*

DER ELFENBIENTURM
(THE IVORY TOWER)
(GERMAN-B&W)

A Mauvin Film production. Directed, written by Matthias Drawe. Camera (B&W), Torsten Schneider, Frank Lucas, Julia Suermann; editor, Drawe; music, Rainer Vierkötter, Till Tilmans. Reviewed at Gothenburg Film Festival, Gothenburg, Sweden, Feb. 8, 1993. Running time: **81 MIN.**
With: Matthias Drawe, Maren Lass, Rasit Tuncay, Frank Lucas.

Shot on a tiny budget, this amateurish feature tells the story of a restaurant chef who wants to write a novel. To get inspiration, he sets up house in an old tower deep in the forest. He does not find inspiration, but does gain the love of a beautiful young girl.

Pic is shot in grainy B&W, with some scenes scratched. There is no dialogue and no direct sound. What we hear is a voiceover (in English) telling the story in a slightly sarcastic manner, and some instrumental music repeated over and over again.

As a home movie, "The Ivory Tower," which is occasionally witty, might have some merits. It does not belong in a cinema.

— *Gunnar Rehlin*

HAWAII INTL. FEST

USUREYUKU KIOKU
NO NAKADE
(IN FADING MEMORY)
(JAPANESE)

A Maruhachi Shinoda production for Never Forget Films (Intl. sales: Herald Ace, Tokyo). Produced by Masan Nagai. Directed, written by Kazuyuki Shinoda. Camera, Kenji Takama; editor, Yoshinori Oota; music, You Tsuji; art direction, Takashi Sasakisound, Yositeru Takahashi. Reviewed at Hawaii Intl. Film Festival (Aikahi), Dec. 3, 1992. Running time: **96 MIN.**
Kazuhiko Sumi . . . . Masaki Hori
Kaori Kotosumi . . . . . . Maiko Kikuti
Yumiko Saotome . . . . Yuoko Tanaka
Ippei Koguma . . . . . . Touru Hibino
Kinzou Sumi . . . . Toru Tamura
Yoshiko Sumi . . . . Mie Torii
Ryohei Kotosumi . Kouzaburo Hanayama
Hatue Kotosumi . . . Tizuko Watanabe

Its theme of star-crossed lovers is far from unique, and

the tone of constant teen-suffering grows tiresome by the end, but it's hard to recall a more astonishing, or revealingly personal, Japanese debut pic in the last decade or more.

Kazuhiko (Masaki Hori) and Kaori (Maiko Kikuti) are two 17-year-olds at a suburban high school in the late 1970s (although period detail is sketchy). They don't really know each other, but at band practice one day, Hori rudely snaps Kikutu's bra strap and both know something new and strange is underway.

If the teens' parents don't actually get in the way of this Japanese Romeo and Juliet act, they're not very supportive either. Hori is about to ask his self-absorbed businessman father (Toru Tamura) for some man-to-man advice when dad turns and huffs, out of nowhere, "Don't betray me like all the others." Kikuti's folks, are gentle enough, but the way she avoids her father suggests something dark and dismaying in their history.

These details, along with trips to mountain retreats, the day-to-day minutiae of school life, and a climactic night festival on the Nagara river — celebrating the legend of Tanabata, a myth which parallels the young couple's troubled romance — are subtly and lovingly rendered by Kazuyuki Shinoda (no relation to "Double Suicide" helmer Masahiro Shinoda). It's startling to discover "In Fading Memory" is not only his first time as a helmer-scripter, but marks his beginning in filmmaking, after advanced study in atomic physics, an interest he gives to Kikuti.

Certainly, veteran lenser Kenji Takama helped, as did fine editing and other pro tech credits, which belie the pic's ultra-low budget. But Shinoda deserves the most credit for drawing superb performances from his lead thespers, who had no previous experience. Soft-eyed Hori effectively explores the passive-aggressive pull of a decent boy's first maddening crush, and introspective Kikuti gives the girl an amazing but believable range.

The only jarring note is a sudden shift to frantic conflict and psychological excess, with one character's descent into convenient amnesia. This doesn't quite mesh with such sweet beginnings, and the suffocating intensity of the last twenty minutes dispel any possibility of feel-good appeal to international auds. Still, the youthful Shinoda digs into the selfish drive of first love without ever yielding to cloying sentiment. And contrary to title, pic stays permanently in mind.

— *Ken Eisner*

ANG TOTOONG BUHAY NI PACITA M.
(THE REAL LIFE OF PACITA M.)
(FILIPINO)

A MRN Films Intl. production (Intl. sales: Syneco Ventures, Quezon City, Phillipines). Produced by Mely R. Nicandro. Directed by Elwood Perez. Screenplay, Ricardo Lee. Camera, (color) Ricardo Jacinto; editor, George Jarlego; music, Danny Tan; production designers, Raymond Bajarias, Abigail Reyes, Lita Torres, Tonette Policarpio; sound, Noel Mauricio, Lito Paet; associate producer, George Jatico; associate director, Jun Sto. Dorringo. Reviewed at Hawaii Intl. Film Festival (Varsity), Dec. 2, 1992. Running time: **108 MIN.**
Pacita . . . . Nora Aunor
Grace . . . . Lotlot De Leon
Mrs. Estrella . . Arrida Siguion-Reyna
Also with: Juan Rodrigo, Alma Moreno, John Rendez, Subas Herror, Marissa Delgado, Dexter Doria, Marilyn Villamayor, Soxy Topacio, Eddie Infante, Ernie Zarate.
(Tagalog and English soundtrack)

Filipino films tend to opt for the operatic, even at their most restrained. In fact, the Phillipines press has dubbed this multiple prize-winning opus from soap veteran Elwood Perez "a quiet film." Yeah, if you call strip-joint parties, slo-mo street shootings, courtroom histrionics, and a climactic ambulance chase "quiet." Interesting only as an example of how bad melodrama can get without being funny, it stands no chance in offshore markets.

Pacita Macaspac is a parttime singer-comic and fulltime mother, actively smothering her goody-two-shoes daughter, Grace. Grace is about to head off for college when she's accidentally shot by passing bandits, leaving her in a permanent coma and Pacita to battle the girl's patrician grandmother over pulling the plug.

The theme may sound serious, but it's undercut at every turn by over-the-top thesping, ham-fisted editing, and above all, Danny Tan's library of hackneyed synthesizer sounds. Lead thesper Nora Aunor, with her skull-like face and vacuous eyes, is an acquired taste from the start, but helmer Perez is unusually cruel to her, pushing for prolonged humiliations like an

endless (and horribly dubbed) song-and-dance number in a supermarket. Even her potentially dramatic courtroom monologue is ruined by inept shock-zooms and crashing music.

Tech credits are abysmal throughout. — *Ken Eisner*

MAD DOG AND GLORY

A Universal Pictures release of a Martin Scorsese/Barbara De Fina production. Executive producer, Richard Price. Produced by De Fina, Scorsese. Directed by John McNaughton. Screenplay, Price. Camera (Technicolor), Robby Muller; editors, Craig McKay, Elena Maganini; music, Elmer Bernstein; production design, David Chapman; art direction, Mark Maack; set decoration, Leslie Pope; costume design, Rita Ryack; sound (Dolby), James J. Sabat; co-producer, Steven A. Jones; assistant director, Amy Sayres; casting, Todd Thaler. Reviewed at Universal Studios, Universal City, Feb. 17, 1993. MPAA Rating: R. Running time: **96 MIN.**
Wayne 'Mad Dog' Dobie . . . .
. . . . Robert De Niro
Glory . . . . Uma Thurman
Frank Milo . . . . Bill Murray
Mike . . . . David Caruso
Harold . . . . Mike Starr
Andrew . . . . Tom Towles
Lee . . . . Kathy Baker
Shooter . . . . . . Derek Anunciation

A pleasurably offbeat picture that manages the rare trick of being both charming and edgy, "Mad Dog and Glory" represents a refreshing, unexpected change of pace for all the major talents concerned. Amusing premise — a poor schmoe saves a gangster's life and is given a beautiful woman for a week as thanks — ends up taking on unexpected dramatic and romantic dimensions, and leads are played to the hilt by its stellar trio. Unusual tone and low-key comedy place this Universal release from Martin Scorsese's production company rather off-center for a mass market entry, but distrib appears to be going all out to reap the benefits of Bill Murray's current hit, "Groundhog Day."

In Richard Price's terrifically colorful and imaginative script, Murray plays Frank Milo, a dapper hoodlum in the modern mode who likes to quote his analyst, owns a comedy club where he can do stand-up anytime he wants, but who is also guaranteed laughs from the goons he packs in down front.

By contrast, Robert De Niro's Wayne Dobie, ironically nicknamed "Mad Dog," is a retiring middle-aged loner who photographs crime scenes at night for the Chicago Police Dept. Nebbishy and rather proper, Wayne would seem to have given up on any further prospects in life, such as a family or promotion, although he shyly dreams of recognition as an art photographer (shades of "The Public Eye").

Like a Preston Sturges hero, however, Wayne has greatness

thrust upon him, after a fashion, when he interrupts an armed robbery in a convenience store and saves Milo from almost certain death. Invited to the club, Wayne doesn't know what to make of Milo's insistence that, "I'm the expediter of your dreams," but soon finds out, when club bartender Glory (Uma Thurman) turns up at his apartment and announces that she's staying for a week, courtesy of Milo.

What follows could easily have been cute, contrived, exploitative, crude or any combination of same. Instead, Price deepens his characters and, with the aid of the exceptional actors, the story takes on a resonance and emotional urgency that aren't initially indicated.

Wayne, who hasn't slept with a woman for two years, falls in love with the nervous, skittish Glory, who turns out to be repaying her brother's debt to Milo. Despite Wayne's less than overwhelming sexual performances, Glory seems to fall for him as well, transforming this curious comedy into a moving tale of two people who need to be saved, he from a life of loneliness and mediocrity, she from the path of being used by men and selling herself.

Genuine drama ensues when Milo wants his woman back after a week, and the climax is both funny and genuinely satisfying.

Most of the comedy stems from the strange, left-field scenes between the two men, and from the interesting tension developed through the against-type casting. One would have expected the actors to appear in opposite roles but, given the choice, De Niro opted to play Wayne, the repressed, somewhat uptight bachelor. After a series of mostly indifferent performances, De Niro delivers some of his best work in years in a role that's not as weird as Rupert Pupkin, but could well be a cousin to his great "King of Comedy" character.

As a heavy who is comical as well as threatening, Murray is highly entertaining. Immaculately groomed and concerned with style, his Milo clearly wants recognition for his wit, psychological insight and humanity, but underneath it all he's still a thug.

But the key to the film lies in the intimate scenes involving Wayne and Glory. Few major actors would care to do one particularly embarrassing sex scene here, but De Niro's enactment of it is crucial to making Wayne appealingly vulnerable. As the days go by, he's somehow able to

March 1, 1993 (Cont.)

make Glory calm down and see straight, and the interplay of De Niro and Thurman, who seems unusually invigorated here, make this couple, whose lives are so different, a pair one can root for, at least in movie terms.

One might not have expected such a sweet, tonally mixed film from the director of "Henry: Portrait of a Serial Killer," but John McNaughton has done a quietly admirable job of walking a stylistic tightrope and meeting the multiple demands of Price's rich script. Also enormously helpful in maximizing pic's potential is Elmer Bernstein's flavorful score, which nicely incorporates some pop standards into the mix.

Supporting cast is strong, notably David Caruso as De Niro's savvy partner and Mike Starr as Murray's imposing aide de camp.

Technically, film has the look of having been handcrafted to perfection, thanks in great measure to lenser Robby Muller's subtle palette and David Chapman's reality-based production design. Editors Craig McKay and Elena Maganini brought it in at a crisp, just-right running time.

— *Todd McCarthy*

THE ABYSS: SPECIAL EDITION

A 20th Century Fox release of a Gale Anne Hurd production. Directed, written by James Cameron. Special edition restoration credits: Producer, Van Ling; editor, Steven Quale; additional music, Robert Garrett; sound supervisor, Dody Dorn; additional wave composites, Industrial Light & Magic, supervisor, Dennis Muren. Reviewed at Todd-AO screening room, N.Y., Feb. 23, 1993. MPAA Rating: PG-13. Running time: **171 MIN.**

The special edition answers much of the criticism that greeted this inner space epic when it was released in 1989, but "The Abyss" remains an acquired taste.

This action/romance is still the most ambitious picture made by writer-director James Cameron and producer Gale Anne Hurd, attempting to go beyond their action and sci-fi genre expertise by incorporating a moving love story. Along the way, it accomplished innovations in the area of underwater lighting (Mikael Salomon, who since has become a director himself with Disney's "A Far Off Place"), mechanical vehicles and sound recording.

In an industry where more frequently the tail is wagging the dog, the special edition was created in response to the laserdisc release of "The Abyss." For filmgoers, as opposed to the target audience of couch potatoes and collectors, this half-hour longer film is far more satisfying than the 1989 version, representing both a grueling and exhilarating theatrical experience.

It retains the basic story of Ed Harris and estranged wife Mary Elizabeth Mastrantonio leading a crew of salvage divers to mount a last-minute rescue mission of a downed nuclear sub before a hurricane intervenes. They have to contend with a ruthless squad of Navy Seals, led by crazy Michael Biehn, operating on secret orders and technically in charge of the rescue effort.

Restored footage is spread throughout the picture but primarily appears during the final two reels, rounding out "The Abyss" with the climax that was missing in the 1989 shaggy-dog version. Notably punched up is Harris' heroic descent into the abyss (over 12,000 feet below the surface) to defuse a nuclear weapon, connected with the world by radio transmitter to Mastrantonio, who pours her heart out to keep him conscious.

Reminiscent of Steven Spielberg's "Close Encounters of the Third Kind" (and especially *its* 1980 special edition), Harris emerges into a vast underwater city where cute jellyfish/butterfly aliens communicate with him via rear-projected TV broadcasts. They recap the worldwide Cold War crisis that has erupted and then show a montage of man's inhuman behavior in warfare. The aliens create massive tidal waves threatening humanity (with shots of beaches, the Statue of Liberty and the Golden Gate Bridge for scope).

This warning to mankind, as the vast waves magically recede without doing damage, is a virtual replay of an earlier 20th Century Fox pic, Robert Wise's classic "The Day the Earth Stood Still," and is not as forceful in the retelling. The wave effects are okay (not on a par with the best of "The Abyss") and their restoration at least gives the film a point and logical conclusion. It is Harris' love for Mastrantonio and spirit of self-sacrifice that causes the aliens to relent.

Cameron baldly and boldly borrowed from the aforementioned films as well as Stanley Kubrick's "2001" and Andrei

Tarkovsky's "Solaris" to adapt outer space picture motifs to an underwater setting. Result is a technical marvel with sustained tension, exciting action footage and an emotional wallop in its nearly platonic love story (there is no sex and minimal physical contact between the principals except when Harris revives the drowned Mastrantonio).

— *Lawrence Cohn*

PUERTO ESCONDIDO
(ITALIAN)

A Penta Distribuzione release of a Penta Film/Colorado Film co-production. Produced by Maurizio Totti, Mario and Vittorio Cecchi Gori. Directed by Gabriele Salvatores. Screenplay, Enzo Monteleone, with Diego Abatantuono, Salvatores, from Pino Cacucci's novel. Camera (color), Italo Petriccione; editor, Nino Baragli; music, Mauro Pagani, Federico De Robertis; art direction, Marco Belluzzu, Alejandro Olmas; costumes, Francesco Panni. Reviewed at Fiamma Cinema, Rome, Jan. 15, 1993. Running time: **125 MIN.**
Mario . . . . Diego Abatantuono
Anita . . . . Valeria Golino
Alex . . . . Claudio Bisio
Commissioner Viola . . . .
. . . . Renato Carpentieri
Di Gennaro . . . . . . Antonio Catania

Italian Oscar-winner Gabriele Salvatores fails to recapture the other-worldly atmosphere of "Mediterraneo" in this sun-drenched but forced Mexican romp. "Puerto Escondido" is so drawn out it will take a very mellow-minded viewer not to lose patience with the cartoonish characters and their unconnected adventures. Film has scored decently at the holiday b.o. on its home turf, but is unlikely to attract the offshore success of its predecessor.

Salvatores' oeuvre is a long succession of laid-back road movies, and "Puerto Escondido" is the latest variation. Skillfully playing to the city-dweller's malaise, he proposes the impossible dream of a simpler way of life. For boringly normal bank teller Diego Abatantuono, it's witnessing one cop killing after another that forces him to go on the lam.

A lot of screen time later, Abatantuono pops up in a dusty Mexican backwater. He reluctantly teams with another Italian, hippie guitarist Claudio Bisio and his gorgeous girlfriend, Valeria Golino. The pair quickly convert priggish Abatantuono to their drop-out lifestyle, turning him onto a drug courier (the

drugs get stolen before they can cause any scripting problems).

Against all logic, but as one fears, the nutty policeman-assassin who drove Abatantuono out of Italy (Renato Carpentieri) reappears. Later when the plot needs a new turn, Golino recklessly suggests robbing her ex-husband, a nasty Mexican capitalist, of a briefcase of money.

This warmed-up version of the '60s Milanese-style leaves the entertainment largely up to the cast. Abatantuono, one of Italy's most versatile actors, carves out a role for himself as the everyman bank clerk in out of his depth, constantly struggling to adapt. Golino has little to do but exercise her magnetic screen presence. Fast-rising comic Claudio Bisio fails to crystallize here as a desert guru.

Top-notch lensing and editing give pic a pleasing surface, made familiar by Marco Belluzzi and Alejandro Olmas' cozy-warm Mexican decor. — *Deborah Young*

STEFANO QUANTESTORIE
(ITALIAN)

A Penta Distribuzione release of a Penta Film/Bambu co-production. Produced by Ernesto di Sarro. Directed by Maurizio Nichetti. Screenplay, Nichetti, Laura Fischetto. Camera (color), Maurizio Battistoni; editor, Rita Rossi; music, Sergio Conforti, Paolo Panigada; art direction and costumes, Maria Pia Angelini. Reviewed at CDS screening room, Rome, Feb. 1, 1993. Running time: **90 MIN.**
Stefano . . . . Maurizio Nichetti
Young Stefano . . . .
. . . . James Spencer Thiérrée
Toy seller . . . . Amanda Sandrelli
Hostess . . . . Elena Sofia Ricci
Wife . . . . . . Caterina Sylos Labini
Father . . . . Renato Scarpa
Mother . . . . Milena Vukotic

Italy's most eccentric actor-director, Maurizio Nichetti, offers another cheerfully offbeat comedy that should follow in the footsteps of "The Icicle Thief" and "Volere Volare" (just released in the U.S.) in making a profitable turn at the offshore boxoffice. "Stefano Quantestorie" is packed with Nichetti's very personal brand of humor that seems capable of leaping national boundaries.

Undoubtedly his training as a mime (most evident in his first, dialogueless films) has something to do with the universal quality of his work. "Quantestorie" can

March 1, 1993 (Cont.)

be read many ways — as a funny series of loosely connected skits; as philosophy (everything happens by chance); or even as an experimental form of storytelling. Literally, *"quante storie"* means "how many stories!" and is a parent's reproof to whining kids.

As Stefano, Nichetti and his teenage alter ego (James Spencer Thiérrée), silently battle a hyper-protective mom (Milena Vukotic) and manipulative dad (Renato Scarpa) over deciding on a profession. Stefano wants to study in America, or become a musician. Mama wants him to teach and marry a nice hometown girl. Papa wants him to become a soldier.

Initially, daddy's wishes have prevailed, and Stefano is a far too mild-mannered *carabiniere*. He can't believe the fetching girl in a snapshot (Amanda Sandrelli) is a bank robber. When he accidentally bumps into her, he falls head over heels in love. She really *is* a bank robber, but before he discovers the truth, he's transformed into the downtrodden husband of the nice girl his mother wanted him to marry.

Here, the shrewish Caterina Sylos Labini makes life unbearable for him and their teenage son. Life would have been better if he had gone to America to study and become an airline pilot: in this scenario, he trysts with knockout hostess Elena Sofia Ricci — who is married to another Stefano, a post-hippie highschool math teacher.

Nichetti's multiple characters (he plays six in the film) start overlapping in the same lobby, airport, disco. Naturally, nobody sees the faintest resemblance, partly thanks to Nichetti's fantastic make-overs.

At times, "Quantestorie" seems to have too much latitude to roam. Since everything happens by chance, the sense of random scripting gets a little disturbing, but Nichetti (and co-writer Laura Fischetto) master it by keeping the film rolling along at a brisk pace. Film is just the right length and, while there are few belly laughs, chuckles are practically continuous.

Vukotic and Scarpa are quietly hilarious as Stefano's parents. Sandrelli (Stefania's daughter) sparkles as toy seller/Bonnie whose Clyde is another Nichetti. Sylos Labini makes a scary homemaker-harridan, while aloof Ricci is perfect as the sex-starved air hostess who keeps winding up with the same man.

Inevitably recalling grandfather Charlie Chaplin (partly because his role is silent), James Spencer Thiérrée plays a helpless, bumbling but imaginative young Stefano, whose destiny seems to be in anybody's hands but his own.

Tech credits are up to snuff.
— *Deborah Young*

SOMETHING WITHIN ME
(DOCU)

> Executive producer, Margaret Francis Mercer. Produced by Jerret Engle. Directed by Emma Joan Morris. Camera, Juan Cristobal Cobo; editor, Jean Tsien. Reviewed at Sundance Film Festival, Park City, Utah, Jan. 25, 1993. Running time: **54 MIN.**

It's easy enough to explain the popularity of "Something Within Me," a well-made, uplifting documentary about a pioneering arts school in the South Bronx, which won the Audience Award at the Sundance. Short running time suggests public and cable TV dates, but restrict chances for even limited theatrical release.

Hopeful and inspirational, this work superbly demonstrates the power of education, specifically in the arts. In 1985, enrollment at St. Augustine, a Catholic school in the South Bronx, was so low it was about to close. The school's pastor approached Thomas Pilecki, a local music teacher, and together they designed an ingenious curriculum with a strong emphasis on art and music.

"Something Within Me" tells the story of this remarkably experimental school, mixing interviews with seventh graders and their teachers with exciting footage of interaction in the classroom, music rehearsals and public performances for parents.

Significantly, all the students at the school, which goes from kindergarten through eighth grade, are ethnic minorities, mostly African-American, but also Hispanic and Asian. Each student is required to take music theory, piano and a second instrument in addition to required classes in the humanities.

The extremely dedicated, underpaid teachers explain that students are not auditioned because the school's goal is not to produce musicians, but "disciplined and well-educated" individuals, equipped to meet the challenges of their tough surroundings.

In light of this, what is missing here is more information about the students' lives outside school. While St. Augustine functions as an educational oasis, the kids still have to live in an economically depressed region.

Technical credits of the docu, which also won the Filmmakers Trophy and a Special Jury Award, are most accomplished, particularly the crisp cinematography of Joan Cristobal Cob.
— *Emanuel Levy*

SEX AND ZEN
(HONG KONG)

> A Golden Harvest production of a Johnny Mak production. Executive producer, Mak. Produced by Stephen Siu. Directed by Michael Mak. Screenplay, Lee Ying Kit, from Li Yü's "Prayer Mat of the Flesh." Camera (color), Peter Ngor; editor, Poon Hung; music, Chang Wing Leung; art direction, Raymond Lee; sound, Kwon Wai Hung; associate producer, Virginia Lok. Reviewed at Quirinale Cinema, Rome, Feb. 10, 1993. Running time: **99 MIN.**
> With: Amy Yip, Isabella Chow, Lawrence Ng, Kent Chang.

An irreverent riff on a classic of 17th century Chinese erotica, "Sex and Zen" dishes up softcore sauce with a dose of all-out action frenzy and grotesque, goofball humor. Hong Kong item was a hit on local release, and now follows "Tokyo Decadence Topaz" as the second East Asian sizzler to heat up Italo wickets in the past year, looking set to sail over the $1 million mark. Astute marketing could concoct the required cult aura to push this frisky froth beyond Chinatown circuits in other territories.

After marrying a straitlaced rich girl (Amy Yip, busty star of a string of Hong Kong nudie pics), and breaking her in with a bout of debauched buffoonery, an aspiring Don Juan (Lawrence Ng) embarks on a mass-seduction mission but soon finds he's insufficiently endowed for the task. In a sequence reminiscent of vintage John Waters, he undergoes a slapdash transplant, trading his puny pickle for one freshly lopped from a stallion. The discarded member ends up as a snack for the surgeon's dog.

First to test-drive his equine appendage is the abused wife of barbaric silk merchant Kent Cheng, himself no slouch at sack athletics. Humiliated into leaving town when he learns of the betrayal, Cheng takes a gardening job at the residence where Yip languishes in hubby's absence, and before long, they're making whoopee in the hot tub. Shamed and cast out, Yip is sold to a deluxe bordello, where after intensive training, she becomes a sought-after love doctor.

Ng's sexual excesses have meanwhile left him decrepit and almost blind, and he's sent to Yip for an overhaul. Pic's moral about-face comes when he discovers her identity. Realizing that no man can be a slave to lust and go unpunished, he checks into a monastery to repent.

Helmer Michael Mak capably orchestrates proceedings at a rambunctious pace, tempering the steamy romp with splashes of casual silliness that almost succeed in whitewashing its encroaching repetitiveness. Perfs are enjoyably arch, and Raymond Lee's vividly colorful art direction makes pic richly visual. Sex scenes are rowdy, but relatively coy in their explicitness.
— *David Rooney*

BERLIN FEST

XIANG HUN NÜ
(THE WOMEN FROM THE LAKE OF SCENTED SOULS)
(CHINA)

> A Tianjin Film Studio/Changchun Film Studio production. (Intl. sales: China Film Export & Import Corp., Peking.) Directed, written by Xie Fei, from Zhou Daxin's short story "Xianghuntangpande xiangyou fang" ("The Sesame-Oil Mill by the Pool of Scented Souls"). Camera (color), Bao Xiaoran; editor, unavailable; music, Wang Liping; art direction, Ma Huiwu, Wang Jie; costume design, Zhang Qing, Wei Lianxiang; sound, Liu Xiaochuan. Reviewed at Berlin Film Festival (competing), Feb. 15, 1993. Running time: **105 MIN.**
> Xiang . . . . Siqin Gaowa
> Huanhuan . . . . Wu Yujuan
> Que . . . . Lei Luosheng
> Ren . . . . Chen Baoguo
> Zhier . . . . Jing Lei
> *(Mandarin soundtrack)*

A meticulously lensed, multilayered drama about a savvy peasant woman and her guilty secret, "The Women From the Lake of Scented Souls" should build a fragrant rep on the fest circuit and interest buyers from specialist webs. Arthouse playoff is also indicated, if saturation with

March 1, 1993 (Cont.)

rural-themed Chinese fare can be overcome. The pic shared Golden Bear honors at the Berlin fest with Taiwan entry "The Wedding Banquet."

Setting is a small village in Hebei province, northern China, where Xiang (Siqin Gaowa) runs a sesame-oil operation that's attracted the attentions of a hardnosed Japanese company. Hardworking, bottom-line, devoted to her family, she seems a model entrepreneur in the "new" China. Her only worry is finding a bride for her retarded son.

The goalposts suddenly shift half an hour in when it's casually revealed Xiang has a longtime lover, local transport chief Ren (Chen Baoguo), who's also married. Gradually, what started as a straight-arrow rural drama starts to reveal onion-like layers as the certainties of Xiang's ordered world peel away.

Her husband (Lei Luosheng), to whom she was sold as a child, is a drunken idler. Negotiations with a smart Japanese businesswoman reveal a whole new world of femme independence to the traditional Xiang. And the arranged match between her son and peasant girl Huanhuan (Wu Yujuan) hits the rocks early on.

The capper is when Huanhuan, whom Xiang has treated as a business investment at best, accidentally discovers the truth about her mother-in-law's lover, putting Xiang on a knife edge.

Helmer Xie Fei, who bagged a Berlin Silver Bear three years ago for his gritty city drama "Black Snow," does a stylistic somersault here, with plenty of stunning landscape shots and sunsets, backed by traditional use of off-screen Chinese songs.

What marks the pic out from the host of other cinematic scroll-paintings is its tight script and subtle perfs, the latter free of exaggeration and developing real depth in the relationship between Xiang and Huanhuan, two women with mirrored fates. Mongolian Chinese actress Siqin Gaowa ("Homecoming," "Full Moon in New York") is outstanding as the tough but essentially lonely Xiang, and she gets strong support from both Wu as her daughter-in-law Huanhuan and Chen as her smooth lover. Technically the pic is top drawer, with Bao Xiaoran's photography a standout.

Previously announced under the title "Sesame Oil-Making Woman," pic may be in for a further, snappier name change. Original Chinese refers to the local lake in which two mytho-logical lovers drowned, as well as word-playing on the main character's name, Xiang ("scented").

— *Derek Elley*

GORILLA BATHES AT NOON
(GERMAN-YUGOSLAVIAN)

An Alert Film (Berlin)/Extaza (Belgrade)/Von Vietinghoff Filmproduktion (Berlin) co-production. Produced by Alfred Hürmer, Bojana Marijan, Joachim von Vietinghoff. Directed, written by Dusan Makavejev. Camera (color), Aleksander Petkovic, Miodrag Milosevic; editor, Vuksan Lukovac; music, Brynmor Llewellyn-Jones; production design, Veljko Despotovic; sound, Uros Kovacevic; assistant director, Duda Ceramilac; production manager, Elisabeth Schwärzer; special effects, Srba Kabadajic. Reviewed at Berlin Film Festival (noncompeting), Feb. 21, 1993. Running time: **83 MINS.**
Victor Borisovich . Svetozar Cvetkovic
Miki Miki/Lenin . . . . . . Anita Mancic
German girl . . . . Alexandra Rohmig
Trandafil . . . . Petar Bozovic
Policeman . . . . Andreas Lucius
Mother . . . . Eva Ras
Turk . . . . Suleyman Boyraz
Frau Schmidt . . . Natasa Babic-Zoric
Dealer . . . . Aleksander Davic

For his first film in five years, Dusan Makavejev returns to the themes that made him famous in pics like "Innocence Unprotected" and "WR: Mysteries of the Organism." Though his new offering lacks the vigor and anarchy of his best work, it's still immensely likable and despite not competing at the Berlin fest won the Fipresci (international film critics) prize for best film in the official section. Despite thin patches, "Gorilla" could well restore Makavejev to prominence on the international arthouse circuit.

Set in Berlin, the film centers on a Russian army officer (winningly played by Yugoslav thesp Svetozar Cvetkovic) left behind when the whole of his unit deserts. With nowhere to stay and nothing to do, he wanders around town in his smart uniform, scrounging food (he steals from animals in the zoo) and making acquaintances along the way. His contacts include a friendly Berlin policeman; a dealer who deals in anything, even babies; an attractive German girl with a violent Turkish boyfriend; and a refugee girl with whom he establishes a close relationship.

This pleasant but on the whole rather aimless material is bolstered at the beginning and end of the film by considerable footage from a flag-waving Russian epic, "The Fall of Berlin" (1949), which, in livid Sovcolor, depicts the storming of the Reichstag by the Red Army in 1945. The climax of this blockbuster is a marvelously over-the-top scene in which Stalin (played by a lookalike actor) flies into defeated Berlin to be ecstatically greeted by troops from all the allies. Makavejev intercuts this old footage with a surprisingly poignant sequence shot in contemporary Berlin in which a gigantic statue of Lenin is decapitated by East German workers, and the head trucked off to some obscure destination.

This kind of juxtaposition is Makavejev, the ironic political commentator, at his best. It's a pity that, for long stretches, "Gorilla" lacks the vitality of his earlier work; even the music score is subdued, and there is none of the trademark raunchy but liberating sexual material. It is amusing, though, to see a female actor play a bearded Lenin who knits a woollen sock for the film's soldier hero, and then smothers him with comradely kisses.

But a sense of the absurd pervades the film, such as the information that a Siberian tiger in the Berlin zoo was actually born in Stuttgart, or the confession of the sad-sack hero that he was trained to kill many people, not just one. "Ich bin ein Berliner," he hollers at one point, and he's a great fan of the city's prison, though nervous that word of how good its food is might get out.

Pic is technically fine, and the running time is suitably tight.

— *David Stratton*

HSI YEN
(THE WEDDING BANQUET)
(TAIWANESE)

A Central Motion Picture Corp. production, in association with Good Machine. (Intl. sales: Good Machine, N.Y.) Executive producer, Jiang Feng-chyi. Produced by Ted Hope, James Schamus, Ang Lee. Directed by Lee. Screenplay, Lee, Neil Feng, Schamus. Camera (Duart color), Jong Lin; editor, Tim Squyres; music, Mader; production design, Steve Rosenzweig; art director, Rachael Weinzimer; costume designer, Michael Clancy; sound, Tom Paul; executive in charge of production, Cheng Shuei-chih; assistant director-line producer, Dolly Hall; additional camera, Frank De Marco; associate producer, Hsu Li-kong; casting, Wendy Ettinger. Reviewed at Berlin Film Festival (competing), Feb. 18, 1993. Running time: **107 MIN.**

Wai-tung . . . . Winston Chao
Wei-wei . . . . May Chin
Simon . . . . . . Mitchell Lichtenstein
Mr. Gao . . . . Sihung Lung
Mrs. Gao . . . . Ah-leh Gua
(English and Mandarin soundtrack)

A slickly mounted Gotham comedy about two gays who try to hoodwink the Chinese partner's parents with a phony marriage, "The Wedding Banquet" slides down easily even if it doesn't leave much aftertaste. Canny mix of feelgood elements and ethnic color could pay off in brisk foreign sales.

Commercially, the Taiwan-funded pic has the potential to go much wider than previous Amerasian items, even though it's a shallower work than helmer Ang Lee's first feature, "Pushing Hands." Latter drew admiration at last year's Berlin fest but slowish offshore theatrical sales.

Easily digestible package is clearly designed with crossover appeal. Rather than being the movie's *sine qua non*, the gay-based storyline is more a hook for a broader portrait of traditional Chinese attitudes to sex and posterity. On that level it works, mainly thanks to a grounding performance by Sihung Lung (the old master in "Hands") as the wise paterfamilias.

Central couple are Wai-tung (Winston Chao), a Taiwanese with a comfy lifestyle in Manhattan from real estate investments, and his white U.S. lover Simon (Mitchell Lichtenstein). To fend off his overseas mom's nagging to get married, Wai-tung agrees to a green-card deal with one of his tenants, ambitious but broke Wei-wei (May Chin), an illegal immigrant from Shanghai.

The proverbial hits the fan when Wai-tung's parents suddenly fly over from Taiwan to attend the marriage. Not only do they stay in the lovers' apartment but a planned quickie at City Hall becomes a full-blown wedding banquet to satisfy mom and dad's expectations.

Gradually, all characters start to change position as they get to know each other. A further complication is when a drunken Wai-tung briefly slips off the sexual wagon and makes Wei-wei pregnant on their wedding night.

Most of this is smoothly done and scripted with plenty of incident, especially in the setpiece of the enormous wedding banquet (complete with Chinese rituals) and some funny sitcom-y sequences of fooling the parents inside their son's apartment. In pacing, and handling of ensemble playing, Lee is more assured here than in "Hands."

Where the movie is less satisfying is in giving the characters enough depth for the climax to pay emotional dividends. Though succinctly sketched at the start, the gay relationship slips out of focus as Chinese issues and the escalating comedy of errors takes over. Lichtenstein's role is an early casualty. With Chao's role also developing no new wrinkles, the final payoff is milder than expected. It's also a tad glib, though in tune with the generally light tone.

For Sinophiles and East Asian auds there is masses of subtext that may pass westerners by. For example, the phony marriage of mainlander Wei-wei to Taiwanese Wai-tung is a clever take on the hot potato of Chinese unification, especially when "brokered" by the American Simon.

As the taciturn father, Lung fleshes out a largely symbolic part into the soul of the movie, encapsulated in the final scenes. Chin, a popular singer/TV thesp in her native Taiwan, is far too sexy for someone having difficulty finding a husband, but adds color and shape to an initially unsympathetic role.

Newcomer Chao, a former model and flight attendant, is okay as pig-in-the-middle Wai-tung without bringing much extra to the table. Lichtenstein ("Streamers") melds easily with the Chinese cast, and vet Taiwan actress Ah-leh Gua (better known under the name Kuei Ya-lei) has her moments as the mother.

Tech credits are pro on all fronts. Pic shared the top Golden Bear prize at Berlin with "Women From the Lake of Scented Souls," the first time entries from both sides of the divide have competed together. — *Derek Elley*

CALENDAR
(CANADIAN-GERMAN-ARMENIAN)

An Alliance Intl. (Canada) release of an Amenian National Cinema/ZDF presentation of an Ego Film Arts production. (Intl. sales: Ego Film Arts, Toronto.) Produced, directed, written, edited by Atom Egoyan. Camera (color, 16m), Norayr Kasper; sound, Yuri Hakobian, Ross Redfern; sound design, Steven Munro; producer for ZDF, Doris Hepp; co-producer, Arsinée Khanjian. Reviewed at Berlin Film Festival (Forum section), Feb. 16, 1993. Running time: **70 MIN.**

Translator . . . . . Arsinée Khanjian
Driver . . . . Ashot Adamian
Photographer . . . . . . Atom Egoyan
(English and Armenian soundtrack)

"Calendar," Atom Egoyan's first pic shot in his ancestral homeland, will delight the Canadian helmer's fans and send others screaming up the walls. The rondo-like fake-umentary is pure fest material.

Like Derek Jarman's "Wittgenstein," "Calendar" is an interesting pull-off on Egoyan's career highway lacking the depth or broader appeal of fully fledged features like "The Adjuster."

Egoyan regular Arsinée Khanjian plays the wife of a photog (Egoyan) commissioned to do a calendar of historic churches in Armenia. While traveling around, the wife gradually feels drawn to her ethnic roots and stays on after her husband returns home.

Over the next year, the photog writes a series of letters to her, and seeks inspiration in a variety of foreign women invited for dinner. End of picture.

As usual, Egoyan is slow to reveal the essentials of his storyline (which only becomes clear about halfway through) but has a lot of fun with some dry comedy on the way. It works best in the Armenian segs, as Khanjian gradually loses her patience with her husband's asinine requests and drifts off with the local driver-guide. Beneath the jokes, it's all about seperation, national identity (or lack of), and the distancing effect of the camera lens.

The 16m pic is up to Egoyan's usual fine tech standards, with mixed-media use of video and crisp lensing by Norayr Kasper. Khanjian is striking as ever, and Egoyan particularly good in their exchanges. — *Derek Elley*

DIE DENUNZIANTIN
(THE DENUNCIATION)
(GERMAN)

A Bremer Institut Film/Fernsehen Prods. (Bremen)/Lichtblick Filmproduktion (Hamburg)/DF (Mainz)/Journal Film (Berlin) production. (Intl. sales: Futura Filmverlag, Munich.) Produced by Elke Peters. Directed by Thomas Mitscherlich. Screenplay, Detlef Michel. Camera (color), Thomas Mauch; editor, Margot Neubert-Marie; music, Jens-Peter Ostendorf; production design, Christian Bussmann; sound, Benjamin Schubert; costumes, Ann Poppel; assistant director, Ulla Ziemann; production manager, Madeleine Remy. Reviewed at Berlin Film Festival (competing), Feb. 20, 1993. Running time: **96 MIN.**

Helene Schwärzel . Katharina Thalbach
Carl Goerdeler . . . . . . Dieter Schaad
Anneliese Goerdeler . . . .
. . . . Elisabeth Schwarz
Elisabeth Bethke . . . . . Dolly Dollar
Walter Bethke . . . . . . Richy Müller
Werner Krängel . Burghard Klaussner
Jean Blome/Hans Blome . . . .
. . . . Marquand Bohm
Investigator . . . . . . Hanns Zischler
Psychiatrist . . . . Doris Schade
Photographer . . . Christoph Eichhorn

This quietly impressive, somber film goes back to the theme of war guilt and the manipulation of justice in post-war Germany. The true story involves the naive young woman who fingered the w.k. civilian leader of the failed 1944 coup against Hitler. A strong performance from Katharina Thalbach is a major asset to a film that may be too rooted in specifically German concerns to find offshore audiences.

Pic opens on a sunny day in 1924 when young, impressionable Helene Schwärzel (Thalbach) meets and is politely greeted by Carl Goerdeler (Dieter Schaad), a w.k. figure in German life. A title reveals that, 20 years later, Schwärzel denounced Goerdeler as the fugitive coup leader, whom she recognized when he stopped off at a small guest house where she was a waitress. She received a reward of 1 million Reischmarks from Hitler himself. Goerdeler was executed.

But after the war, Schwärzel was considered a war criminal and brought to trial, not under German law, but under an Allied law of "crimes against humanity." She served six years in prison, all the time protesting that she only did her duty.

Director Thomas Mitscherlich paints a fascinating picture of Germany during and immediately after the war. Though Schwärzel did nothing more than point out a man the whole country was looking for, she became the reluctant focus of a Nazi propaganda campaign. Far from endearing her to the people at large, once the conflict was over many were were only too happy to make a scapegoat of someone given so much money. Ironically, she hardly touched the reward, leaving it in a bank until the Reichsmarks were worthless.

Thalbach is moving as the simple woman who remains barely aware of what's happening to her, and the supporting cast is strong. Thomas Mauch's photography, suitably gloomy in the post-war scenes, brightens for flashback sequences and ironic

original meeting between Goerdeler and his future betrayer.

The film's alternative English title is "Just a Matter of Duty." — *David Stratton*

FRAMEUP

A Complex Corp. presentation of a Henry S. Rosenthal production. Produced by Rosenthal. Directed, written, photographed (Monaco color), edited by Jon Jost. Music, Jon A. English; sound, Anne Marie Miguel. Reviewed at Sundance Film Festival, Park City, Utah, Jan. 29, 1993. (In Berlin Film Festival, Forum section.) Running time: **91 MIN.**
Beth-Ann Bolet . . . . . . Nancy Carlin
Ricky-Lee Gruber . . . Howard Swain

A jokey reworking of the standby losers-on-the-road genre, "Frameup" reveals more of the game player than the artist in director-writer-lenser-editor Jon Jost. Amusing in spots but condescending toward its scabby, outcast characters, this spunky, insubstantial low-budgeter feels like something knocked off as a lark. Commercial outlets will be few and far between.

Jost is still under the influence of hero Jean-Luc Godard, using fragmented block-letter titles and dividing the story into 12 "movements." He indulgently begins this survey of barrel-bottom Americana with eight minutes of shots of landscapes and objects.

Following, however, is his strikingly original introduction to the male protagonist, Ricky-Lee Gruber (Howard Swain). In a hilarious gambit, Jost offers contrapuntal monologues: as one mugshot rails about the stupidity of his current arrest, and the other analyzes how he got this way.

In a similar but less inspired manner, pic presents Beth-Ann Bolet (Swain's real-life wife Nancy Carlin), a woman of stupefying dullness who waxes nostalgic for her "best year" — 1977 —as artifacts from her youth are trotted out.

Unfortunately, most of the pic seems like intellectual doodling, as Jost plays with form in some frisky ways that have little to do with strengthening the meaning or impact of the story, using stop-action animation, extended takes, and other techniques.

What hurts the film even more is Beth-Ann's gratingly monotonous voice, which Jost acknowledged after the screening he had to talk Carlin into using. It forces

the viewer to look down on, not empathize with, Beth-Ann.

Things pick up a bit toward the end. Most talked-about scene — if, indeed, people ever see the film — is bound to be an episode in which the couple, in bed, decide to rob a store. Next comes the most explicit expression of the phallic impulse behind crime and gunplay, as well as some funny wordplay involving a tattoo on Ricky-Lee's private parts.

— *Todd McCarthy*

LA VIDA LACTEA
(THE MILKY LIFE)
(SPANISH-GERMAN-FRENCH)

A Cartel Films (Madrid)/Journal Film KG (Berlin)/Aries Production (Paris) co-production. Produced by Eduardo Campoy. Directed by Juan Esterlich. Screenplay, Esterlich, Chris Doherty. Camera (color), Gerard de Battista; editor, Luis Manuel del Valle; music, Mario de Benito; production design, Felix Murcia; sound, Goldstein & Steinberg; co-producer, Klaus Volkenborn. Reviewed at Berlin Film Festival (Panorama section), Feb. 17, 1993. Running time: **90 MIN.**

Barry Reilly	Mickey Rooney
Aloha	Marianne Sägebrecht
Julian Reilly	William Hootkins
Victoria	May Hatherley
Bianca	Emma Suarez
Marilyn	Michel McKaine
Steven	Thomas Heinze
Kunyo	Carlos Oda
Bruno	Feodor Atkine
Mimi	Angie Gray
Logan	Jack Taylor
Dr. Davis	Juan Luis Bunuel

(English soundtrack)

"**T**he Milky Life" is one of the more bizarre concepts in memory, and one of the worst executed. This tasteless and painfully unfunny film, a Europudding with no distinguishing features, will probably emerge as a cult item because of its very awfulness.

Mickey Rooney plays Barry Reilly, an 80-year-old millionaire who lives in a huge castle on the California coast. When his promiscuous granddaughter gives birth to a baby boy, the old man becomes attached to the cuddly sprig and decides to become a baby himself, having his lawyer draw up papers demanding his appalled family's acceptance. That's the gimmick here, and it's an unworthy one.

Things get even worse when burglars rob the mansion and hit Rooney over the head. He wakes up able to speak only baby talk.

Mark this down as a major folly. — *David Stratton*

LE BATEAU DE MARIAGE
(THE MARRIAGE BOAT)
(FRENCH)

A Compagnie Lyonnaise de Cinema production, in association with CEC/La Sept/Zagora Films. (Intl. sales: Pathé TV, Paris.) Directed by Jean-Pierre Améris. Screenplay, Améris, Caroline Bottaro, Jean Gruault, from Michel Besnier's novel. Camera (Eastmancolor), Yorgos Arvanitis; editor, Yves Deschamps; music, Pierre Adenot; production design, Jean-Pierre Clech; sound, Georges Prat; costumes, Danièle Colin-Linard; production manager, Bernard Lorain; assistant director, Pascal Deux. Reviewed at Berlin Film Festival (Panorama section), Feb. 16, 1993. Running time: **94 MIN.**

Mauve	Florence Pernel
Pierre	Laurent Grevill
Béatrice	Marie Bunel

"**T**he Marriage Boat" is a gently impressive first feature, set in a village in Vichy France. Based on a novel by Michel Besnier, and with script input from François Truffaut's old collaborator Jean Gruault, its themes will have more immediate impact on French auds, but the modestly effective film is worth seeking out.

Mauve (Florence Pernel) returns to her home village after an unhappy period of living in Paris. Reunited with her sister, Béatrice (Marie Bunel), she hints that she's left an unhappy love affair behind her.

In this quiet backwater, far from the battlefields of Europe, Mauve meets her sister's friend, Pierre (Laurent Grevill), the local teacher whom she had known as a child. A withdrawn character, Pierre is hanging on to his job despite being the subject of an investigation by the Vichy government. (Marshall Pétain's "campaign of decency" blamed Jews and Freemasons for France's malaise and teachers were suspect.)

Before long, Mauve has seduced the diffident Pierre, and they marry in a rainswept ceremony on the traditional "marriage boat" that floats down the river on festive occasions. But all too soon, the young bride realizes her marriage was a mistake.

Despite its simple outline, there's a lot going on under the surface of first-time director Jean-Pierre Améris's film, which discreetly probes old wounds.

Among the many qualities of "The Marriage Boat," is the often breathtaking photography by gifted Greek lenser Yorgos Arvanitis. — *David Stratton*

LIBERA
(ITALIAN)

A Hathor Film production. Directed, written by Pappi Corsicato. Camera (color), Roberto Meddi, Raffaele Mertes; editor, Fabio Nunziata; art direction, Corsicato; costumes, Ortensia De Francesco. Reviewed at Agis screening room, Rome, Feb. 8, 1993. (In Berlin Film Festival, Forum section.) Running time: **83 MIN.**

Aurora/Libera	Iaia Forte
Pistoletta	Ninni Bruschetta
Don Arcangelo	Enzo Moscato
Carmela	Cristina Donadio
Sebastiano	Ciro Piscopo
Tanino	Manrico Gammarota

Naples now has its own Pedro Almodóvar. "Libera," the directorial bow of Pappi Corsicato, is a three-part madcap comedy bursting with showy inventiveness. A shoestringer that gets by on wit alone, pic is bound to be a fest hit and could get some offshore bites by pitching to the right, hip audience.

Corsicato's greatest achievement — apart from offering steady entertainment — is capturing the real flavor of Naples in surreal stories. The director himself has referred to his style as "neon-realism." All three episodes are centered on women and their broken dreams, particularly in regard to men.

In the first, blonde floozy Aurora (Iaia Forte) sees her smug, nouveau-riche world crumble when her shady, never-seen husband first openly betrays her with his secretary, then skips the country to avoid arrest. Bereft of her swanky apartment, credit cards and convertible, she returns home town to revive a lost love, but that turns out to be an even greater disappointment.

Carmela (Cristina Donadio), in the second story, lives in an open-door, street-level apartment in the slums of Naples. Her handsome adolescent son (Ciro Piscopo) comes home from reform school — now he's gay and a heroin addict. He learns who his real father is in a surprise ending, guaranteed to shock.

Episode 3 sees poor, lonely Libera (Iaia Forte again) forced to run a newsstand on the outskirts of Naples by herself. When she discovers her husband (Manrico Gammarota) has been playing sick at home to make it with prostitutes, she plots revenge. His sexual exploits become the hottest-selling videotapes at her newsstand, and she becomes a rich, lonely woman.

Corsicato's tales all have an extraordinary liveliness and an exceedingly weird sense of humor. Free-and-easy role switching between the sexes is characteristic. The women are tough as nails, often sexual aggressors, while the men all loaf in bed.

Forte and Donadio make their incredible characters believable, steering clear of the stereotypes that often populate Neapolitan comedies, and have a hardcore realism that rescues the film in the rare moments when it runs out of control.

Film began as a short (the episode lensed by Raffaele Mertes) in 1991; the other two parts (shot by Roberto Meddi) were added later. Cinematography has a startling modernity throughout. — *Deborah Young*

DET PERFEKTE MORD
(THE PERFECT MURDER)
(NORWEGIAN)

A Movie Makers/Norsk Film production. Produced by Peter Bøe, Dag Nordahl. Directed by Eva Isaksen. Screenplay, Isaksen, Morten Barth, from Jan Kjaerstad's novel. Camera (color), Philip Øgaard; editor, Ake Gengenbach; music, Atve Karlsen; production design, Anne Bryhna; sound, Are Kalmar; production manager, Binne Thoresen. Reviewed at Berlin Film Festival (Market section), Feb. 12, 1993. Running time: **110 MIN.**

Pierre	Gard B. Eidsvold
Greta	Anna Lena Hemström

With: Anne Marit Jacobsen, Finn Schau, Per Jansen, Geir Kvarme, Ragnhild Hilt.

An initially intriguing, ultimately obscure thriller, "The Perfect Murder" (a.k.a. "Homo Falsus") is a frustrating tease.

The plot revolves around Greta (Anna Lena Hemström), a Garbo lookalike who models her work on the famous Swedish star. She's currently working on a film with her live-in lover, Pierre (Gard B. Eidsvold) directing, and scenes are being modeled on Garbo classics like "Queen Christina" and "Camille" (both excerpted).

In the film, Greta is playing a mysterious woman who picks up and seduces men who subsequently disappear. In real life, men similar to those she encounters in the flick also disappear. This is promising material for a thriller, but director Eva Isaksen, who made the more interesting "Burning Flowers" (1985), doesn't really deliver. The plot gets terribly convoluted, and even when it's over things are none too clear.

March 1, 1993 (Cont.)

The film is evocatively photographed by Philip Øgaard, and Hemström does a great Garbo imitation, but auds are likely to be turned off, rather than on, by this one. — *David Stratton*

UN JOUR DANS LA MORT DE SARAJEVO
(A DAY IN THE DEATH OF SARAJEVO)
(FRENCH-DOCU)

> An Odessa Films/France 3 production. Produced by Jean-Marc Henchoz. Directed by Thierry Ravalat, Alain Ferrari. Script, narration, Bernard-Henri Lévy. Camera (color), Ravalat; editor, Yann Kassile; sound, Stéphane Billiau; production manager, Sylvette Frydman. Reviewed at Berlin Film Festival (noncompeting), Feb 15, 1993. Running time: **65 MIN.**

One of the many sad things about this grim documentary about the besieged civilians of Sarajevo is that it is already out of date, having been filmed last August. But, for the record, it still paints a horrific picture of a cosmopolitan European city being steadily destroyed and its people starved, shot and terrified.

The filmmakers make no secret of where they stand: for them the Serbs, both those in Belgrade and Bosnian Serbs, are the aggressors, and their policy of ethnic cleansing is compared in the narration of Bernard-Henri Lévy to fascism.

Shot on video, and transferred to film with variable results, the film is seen mostly through the tired eyes of a French-speaking woman, a historian who mourns the loss of 90% of the city's culture in the destruction.

The viewer is taken on a grim tour of pock-marked high-rises, the shattered hospitals, the ruined streets. There is footage of street fighting, of nervous people venturing out to find food or water, of the courageous people who keep a daily newspaper going (the most threatened journalists in the world, per the narration), and of maimed and terrified women and children.

It all makes for a vivid picture of a great and senseless tragedy, but since the material is already six months old, and the conflict continues unabated, we are left with the impression that the situation in Sarajevo is now far worse than the horrors on display here. — *David Stratton*

TUHLAAJAPOIKA
(THE PRODIGAL SON)
(FINNISH)

> A Villealfa Filmproductions production. (Intl. sales: World Sales Christa Saredi, Zürich.) Produced by Aki Kaurismäki. Directed by Veikko Aaltonen. Screenplay, Iiro Küttner. Camera (color), Timo Salminen; editor, Aaltonen, Kimmo Taavila; music, Mauri Sumén; sound, Jouko Lumme; assistant director, Pauli Pentti. Reviewed at Berlin Film Festival (Forum section), Feb. 15, 1993. Running time: **94 MIN.**
>
> Esa . . . . Hannu Kivioja
> Lindstrüm . . . . Esko Salminen
> Laura . . . . Leea Klemola
> Makkonen . . . . Markku Peltola
> Ade . . . . Antti Raivio
> Salminen . . . . Sulevi Peltola
> Harri . . . . Matti Onnismaa

A dark thriller mixing S&M mindgames with Yank genre elements, "The Prodigal Son" is a real original that bites like a coiled rattlesnake. Fests are likely to snap up this Scandi bauble for latenight slots and, with careful handling, it could also beat out some cult business on the arthouse circuit.

Central character is tough excon Esa (Hannu Kivioja), who takes on paid jobs as a bruiser when he can't find regular employment. At first he just beats up street thugs; as word spreads, he takes private clients who enjoy the experience.

Enter the outwardly respectable Lindstrüm (Finnish vet Esko Salminen), a wealthy middle-aged psychiatrist who imposes more and more demands during his masochistic sessions with Esa. Soon he demands Esa's services on an exclusive basis, and has him hooked on drugs. A weird father-son relationship develops between the pair, with Lindstrüm in the psychological driving seat.

When Esa falls for a blonde (Leea Klemola) and starts to go off his new line of work, Lindstrüm retaliates with the ferocity of a cornered Dobermann, implicating Esa in a horrific murder. The finale, set in a prison hospital, is a real squirmer.

There's plenty going on here that could easily have degenerated into pure exploitation or ludicrous farce. But helmer Veikko Aaltonen, in only his second feature, keeps a strong hand on the tiller, drawing intense, focused perfs from his smallish cast (especially the silky-tongued Salminen and wild-eyed Kivioja as the cat and mouse) and corralling the movie's volatile elements with care.

Alongside the thriller elements is a strong vein of black humor that sends up the characters' foibles even as the dramatic screw tightens. Iiro Küttner's tightly written script juggles cornball elements from other genres — such as our hero refocusing his life thanks to the love of a good woman — with scant attention to reality and even less to viewer empathy. The whole is definitely more than the sum of its parts.

Tech credits are fine down the line, with special mentions for Timo Salminen's sharply lit photography and Mauri Sumén's unabashed thriller score. Pic was produced by Finnish maverick Aki Kaurismäki's Villealfa Filmproductions. Since opening in Helsinki last fall, the movie has already won a fistful of Jussi Awards, equivalent of the Oscars. — *Derek Elley*

NEW! IMPROVED! REAL-LIFE AMERICAN FAIRY TALE

> A Rhizomatic Films production. Produced by Deborah Magocsi, Rick Putnam. Directed, written, edited by Magocsi. Camera (color), Mary Ahmann, Gregg J. Levine; production design, Jaime Levy; sound, Matt Davis; choreography, Austin Beecher; assistant director, Delritta Hornbuckle. Reviewed at Berlin Film Festival (Market section), Feb. 19, 1993. Running time: **85 MIN.**
>
> Mia . . . . Via Lambros
> Captain . . . . Jeff Kearney
> Mia's father . . . . Grady Shytles
> Lovey . . . . Lovey Carey
> Bob . . . . Steve Mason
> Peggy . . . . Kathleen Rodger
> Otto . . . . Alex Magocsi
> J.F.K. . . . . Nelson Hume
> Miss U.S.A. . . . . . Chappel Westlake

An arch, self-important micro-budgeted indie, "New! Improved!'s" feminist philosophizing is extremely fuzzy, though there are a few comic moments amid the embarrassingly inept jokes. Despite strenuous efforts to be lively and funny, pic generally falls flat and commercial bookings will probably be hard to find.

The film is set in the near future when private expression of sexual expression has been declared illegal. Love Patrols check on infringements, and public sex spots are designated.

Mia's father is arrested for having sex in his apartment and explains to his daughter that he and his partner were in love; Mia

doesn't know the meaning of the word and sets out to discover what it's all about.

What follows are some sophomoric sequences that spoof all the tired old targets: consumerism, advertising, TV evangelists, etc. There are "real" interviews, murkily shot, on the question "What is love?" Since the film was made in Dallas, there's also a diversion to Dealey Plaza where a JFK-type vainly searches for those missing bullets.

Writer-director-editor Deborah Magocsi throws everything into the mix, including a half-hearted car chase, Godardian intertitles and a tiresome ending in which one of the actors proposes a different fadeout to the one scripted. — *David Stratton*

BAD BEHAVIOUR
(BRITISH)

> A Channel 4 Films presentation, with particpation of British Screen, of a Parallax Pictures production. (Intl. sales: FFI, London.) Executive producer, Sally Hibbin. Produced by Sarah Curtis. Directed by Les Blair. Screenplay uncredited. Camera (color), Witold Stok; editor, Martin Walsh; music, John Altman; production design, Jim Grant; art direction, Rebecca M. Harvey; costume design, Janty Yates; sound (Dolby), Bruce White, David Old; assistant director, Peter McAleese. Reviewed at Berlin Film Festival (Market section), Feb. 18, 1993. Running time: **100 MIN.**
>
> Gerry McAllister . . . . . Stephen Rea
> Ellie McAllister . . . . . Sinead Cusack
> Howard Spink . . . . . . Philip Jackson
> Jessica Kennedy . . . . . Clare Higgins
> The Nunn Brothers . . . . Phil Daniels
> Sophie Bevan . . . . Saira Todd
> Winifred Turner . . . . Mary Jo Randle

Stephen Rea heads a strong cast, crisply directed, in "Bad Behaviour," a delightful comedy of manners set among a group of north Londoners. Somewhere between Mike Leigh's "Life Is Sweet" and Ken Loach's "Riff-Raff" in tone, this could be a steady performer in specialized urban playoff, with Rea, hot from "The Crying Game," an extra draw.

Rea plays a district planning officer and amateur cartoonist, whose wife (Sinead Cusack) is quietly going through a midlife crisis. Between balancing a part-time job in a bookshop with the demands of raising a family, she's also being used as an emotional cushion by manic-depressive friend (Clare Higgins), a divorcée who can't communicate with her teenage daughter.

March 1, 1993 (Cont.)

In strides Ellie's greaseball ex-husband (Philip Jackson), who's operating real estate scams. Things get real complicated when Jackson tries to rip off Rea et al. for some rebuilding work, a job done by identical twins (both played by Phil Daniels) to whom Jackson already owes money.

Working, in the style of Mike Leigh, from an improvised script, helmer Les Blair juggles his small cast with great dexterity, drawing tight playing down the line with no feel of treading water. The pic is character, not knockabout, comedy, but this is a group of mild eccentrics you want to follow to the end.

Laid-back and hangdog, Rea shows a great sense of comic timing, balanced by Cusack's more straightforward perf. Jackson is terrific as the smooth-tongued schemer, and Daniels ditto as the identical builders whom everyone mixes up. Saira Todd impresses as Rea's workmate with a quiet crush on him.

A bright pop-jazz score by John Altman and good-looking lensing by Witold Stok are further pluses. — *Derek Elley*

ROTTERDAM FEST

BELLE
(DUTCH-B&W)

An Allarts production. Produced by Kees Kasander, Denis Wigman. Directed, written by Irma Achten. Camera (B&W), Nestor Sanz; editor, Marina Bodbijl; art direction, Anete Wilgenhof. Reviewed at Rotterdam Intl. Film Festival, Rotterdam, Netherlands, Feb. 5, 1993. Running time: **99 MIN.**
With: Wivineke van Groningen, Rosa Herzberg, Nelleke Zitman, Reinout Bussemaker, Do van Stek, Ulf Maria Kuhne.

"**B**elle," the feature debut of Dutch stage actress turned director Irma Achten, tells the story of a restless and independent-minded woman's lifelong search for fulfillment. Visually delectable and idiosyncratic in its narrative approach, it reveals an unmistakably personal style and an accomplished technique. It should go down well with fest- and arthouse auds, especially those with a taste for the intriguingly offbeat.

Though the exact period is left unclear, it seems to open in the early 1900s. Belle (Wivineke van Groningen), born to well-off but emotionally stunted parents, is an instinctive rebel, troubled by vague poetic yearnings. Her sole attachment is to the young housekeeper, Marthe, with whom she sets up a lesbian ménage.

Van Groningen's determination to be her own boss leads to a breach with Marthe. She founds a chain of clothing stores, marries and has children, but nothing brings satisfaction. She has become, she unhappily realizes, what she despised as a child: her own cold, withdrawn mother.

Elegantly shot by Nestor Sanz in crisp, luminous black and white, "Belle" is strikingly beautiful to look at, creating images whose lighting and compositions draw on classic Dutch art. The soundtrack makes evocative use of Mahler, and the whole film is suffused with a cool sensuality all the more erotic for its restraint. Van Groningen uses her expressive face and fetchingly toothy grin to age convincingly from schoolgirl to matron.

The end lapses into self-conscious and occasionally risible symbolism, but this apart, "Belle" marks an impressive debut.
— *Philip Kemp*

FORBIDDEN QUEST
(DUTCH)

An Ariel Film production. Produced by Suzanne van Voorst. Directed, written by Peter Delpeut. Camera (color), Stef Tijdink; editor, Menno Boerema; music, Loek Dikker; sound, Paul Veld. Reviewed at Rotterdam Intl. Film Festival, Rotterdam, Netherlands, Feb. 3, 1993. Running time: **75 MIN.**
With: Joseph O'Conor, Roy Ward.
(English soundtrack)

Surreal and enigmatic, "The Forbidden Quest" has the makings of a minor cult classic. Though a Dutch production, it's entirely in English, which should maximize its appeal among specialized auds.

In June 1905, we're told, the sailing ship Hollandia sailed from Bergen in Norway for a secret destination: the South Pole. In 1941, an interviewer tracked down and filmed the expedition's sole survivor, a ship's carpenter, in a tiny Irish cottage. The old man, who died soon afterwards, recounted the fate of his companions: an outlandish tale of obsession, murder, cannibalism and mystical redemption.

"The Forbidden Quest" is a feature film masquerading as a documentary, turning genuine factual footage to fictional use. Half-a-dozen or more myths are mixed into the plot, as though Coleridge's "Rime of the Ancient Mariner" had been rewritten by Poe and Verne, with hints of "The Flying Dutchman" and "Moby Dick." But despite derivative elements, pic exerts a haunting fascination all its own.

With deft economy, helmer Peter Delpeut constructs his film from two elements. One is a actual footage from polar expeditions of the first three decades of the century drawn from archives of the Netherlands Film Museum. (Delpeut, a programmer at the museum, put found footage to similarly ingenious use in "Lyrical Nitrate.") This footage, much of it of exceptional beauty, is woven together to illustrate the old man's story. Some of it has been tinted to good effect, but occasional touches of colorization should have been avoided.

The other is Joseph O'Conor as the survivor. In effect the film's sole actor (since the interviewer features only as a disembodied voice), he holds the attention with understated intensity. Never raising his voice, scarcely moving from his chair, he conveys all the burned-out desolation of a man blighted by his memories. — *Philip Kemp*

MALENKY GIGANT BOLSHOGO SEXA
(A SMALL GIANT OF BIG SEX)
(RUSSIAN-COLOR-MONOCHROME)

A Film Studio Krug/Mosfilm production. Directed by Nikolai Dostal. Screenplay, Alexander Borodyanski, Dostal, from Fazil Iskender's "Oh, Marat." Camera (color, B&W, sepia), Yuri Nevsky; music, Irakly Gabely; sound, Valentin Bobrovsky. Reviewed at Rotterdam Intl. Film Festival, Rotterdam, Netherlands, Feb. 4, 1993. Running time: **80 MIN.**
With: Gennady Khazanov, Irina Rozanova, Irina Sobanova, Roland Nadreshvili.

Since sexual freethinking under the long Soviet chill was almost as taboo as the political kind, bawdy Russian comedies are a fairly recent development. Which may explain a certain goofy ungainliness about "A Small Giant of Big Sex."

The story concerns the memories — or maybe the fantasies — of Marat, former seaside photographer at a Black Sea resort. In the present (filmed in dour black and white) he's in a wheelchair, pushed around the crumbling resort by a starchy nurse. His youth as a student in post-war Moscow features briefly in sepia. But the bulk of the film takes place in the full color '50s, depicted as a lush Golden Age when infinitely available women paraded in summer finery along the seafront.

Most of these beauties succumb to the diminutive hero's advances. But what saves the film from monotony is that by no means all his escapades are successful. Introduced to a houseful of women, he finds they're all lesbian. Another tryst ends abruptly when the lady proves to be the mistress of Lavrenty Beria, Stalin's feared secret police chief. Even worse, Beria's glower haunts Marat's subsequent amours, inducing impotence.

The ending — Marat, his powers miraculously restored, pleasures his now-defrosted nurse — is all too predictable, as is much else in the film. Still, anyone after a fresh perspective on Soviet life — and prepared to stomach a little naive sexism — will be pleasantly diverted, though something should be done about the title. — *Philip Kemp*

JIB-BORHA BE BEHESHT NEMIRAVAND
(PICKPOCKETS DON'T GO TO HEAVEN)
(IRANIAN)

A Farabi Film Foundation production. Produced by Ali Mohammad Saadaddin, Mahmud Sami'ie. Directed by Abolhassan Davudi. Screenplay, Sami'ie. Camera (color), Mehrdad Fakhimi; editor, Hassan Hassandoost; music, Naser Chasm-azer; sound, Mahmud Sammakbashi. Reviewed at Rotterdam Intl. Film Festival, Rotterdam, Netherlands, Feb. 2, 1993. Running time: **90 MIN.**
With: Ateneh Faghih Nassiri, Hamideh Kheirabadi, Alireza Khamseh, Gholamhossein Lotfi, Hossein Moheb Ahari, Bagher Sahrarudi, Mahmud Bahrami, Ruhollah Mofidi Nasrabadi, Atash Taghipoor.

A cheerful, undemanding comedy about a lovable rogue, "Pickpockets Don't Go to Heaven" breaks little new ground in terms either of character or plot. But what it lacks in originality it makes up for in energy

March 1, 1993 (Cont.)

and infectious good humor. It should appeal to specialized audiences and possibly beyond.

The popular comic actor Ateneh Faghi Nassiri, an Iranian Peter Sellers, plays a resilient hawker who scrapes a living selling whatever comes to hand. Seriously behind with his rent, and smitten by a pretty neighbor who's also in hock to the landlord, he sets out to make some real money. This brings him into collision with three small-time hoods who rope him into their pickpocketing racket — and then, as they grow more ambitious, into a planned bank job.

If few of the situations in "Pickpockets" are new, they're handled inventively and enjoyably. One of the best is a mismanaged heist for which the hero wears a stocking mask so thick that he has to be pointed at the cashier by helpful customers.

The film also dares to poke sly fun at the stern moral precepts of the ayatollahs' regime. At one point a megaphone descends from the sky emitting stern exhortations, and a chase scene is complicated by the ethical unthinkability of a woman riding behind a man on his motorbike.

Technically, "Pickpockets" looks than a little rough and ready, and the acting won't take many prizes for subtlety. But it contains plenty of ingenious, likeable gags, and romps along exuberantly. — *Philip Kemp*

RADIO YEREVAN
(ARMENIAN)

An Aysor-Plus Studio/Aragast/Film Festival Rotterdam production. Directed by Nariné Mkrtchian, Arsen V. Azatian. Screenplay, Mkrtchian, Azatian, A. Grigorian. Camera (color), A. Yavourian; editors, Mkrtchian, Azatian; sound, A. Sahakian. Reviewed at Rotterdam Intl. Film Festival, Rotterdam, Netherlands, Feb. 1, 1993. Running time: **80 MIN.**

With: Areg Azatian, Karen Mirijanian, Ashot Jenterejians, Armen Jenterejians, E. Shahirian, H. Abrahamian, Z. Nalbandian, F. van Dorn, N. Ghahramanian, A. Mirzakhanian.

"**R**adio Yerevan" is structured rather like the aftermath of an explosion: a whole lot of bits, some of which clearly relate to each other, and others that don't seem to have much to do with anything at all. Even arthouse and festival audiences may find their patience tried by the film's unvaried pacing and often wanton disregard for audience involvement.

The two main narrative strands, such as they are, concern a pair of French truck drivers en route to Yerevan with a load of humanitarian aid, and musical twin brothers trying to perform a piece by Wieniawski on the radio station of the title. Around these stories, Mkrtchian and Azatian dispose images, tableaux and fragmentary anecdotes.

The overall mood is deadpan humor laced with melancholy. Even so, inconsequentiality is best taken in small doses, and for all pic's brief running time it becomes wearisome well before the end. — *Philip Kemp*

SF18 FEST

AELITA
(RUSSIAN-B&W-SILENT)

A Mezrabom/Amkino production. Directed by Jakov Protazanov. Screenplay, Fedor Ozep, Aleksey Fajko, from Alexei Tolstoy's play. Camera (B&W), Yuri Zheliabovsky, Emil Schoenemann; art director, Isaak Rabinovitch, Vikto Simov, Sergei Kozlovski; costumes, Aleksandra Ekster. Reviewed at SF18 Science Fiction Marathon, Brookline, Mass., Feb. 14, 1993. Running time: **85 MIN.**

With: Yulia Solntseva, Nikolai Batalov, Igor Illinski, Nikolai Tseretelli, Vera Orlova, Pavel Pol, Konstantin Eggert, Yuri Zavadski, Valentina Kuindzi, N. Tretyakova.

This 1924 Soviet space epic has been recently revived in several fest and museum appearances but was never reviewed in VARIETY.

Seriocomic tale involves an inventor (Nikolai Tseretelli), a soldier (Nikolai Batalov) and a police informant (Igor Illinski), who take the first journey to Mars. Film is an adaptation of a play by Alexei Tolstoy, and is most notable for its production design, particularly the sets and costumes for the Martian sequences. Designers were alumni of the Kamerny Theater, known for its modernist productions.

The costumes must be seen to be believed, including Aelita's handband and her assistant's pants, both of which look like complicated TV antennas. Elaborate Martian sets prefigure the Flash Gordon and Buck Rogers serials of the next decade, with stylized design suggesting much more than actually appears.

Print, supplied by the Walker Arts Center, runs 85 minutes, although sci-fi histories report an original length of two hours. Pic was also known as "Aelita: The Revolt of the Robots."

Visuals hold up nicely, as do the performances, with only Illinski's overeager police worker playing broadly. Live musical accompaniment at SF18 was a plus — in spite of the decor, pic needed the music to propel it along.

While "Aelita" doesn't surpass Fritz Lang's 1926 classic "Metropolis," it is a major early achievement in futuristic cinema, and deserves the renewed interest. — *Daniel M. Kimmel*

BREAKFAST OF ALIENS

A Hemdale Communications release of an Eric Parkinson and Hemdale presentation in association with DVB. Executive producers, David Lee Miller, Vic Dunlop, Brian James Ellis. Produced by Ellis. Directed by Miller. Screenplay, Miller, Dunlop. Camera (Deluxe color), Marcel V. Shain; editor, Fabien D. Tordjmann; music, Mathew Ender; art direction, Steven J. Monroe; costumes, Catherine Beaumont; sound, Robert Crosby Jr.; associate producers, Paul Messier, James P. Garvey, James Olson; assistant director, Shari Genser; casting, Elizabeth Ward, Peter Looney. Reviewed at SF18 Science Fiction Marathon, Brookline, Mass., Feb. 14, 1993. MPAA Rating: R. Running time: **88 MIN.**

Walter Clydepepper . . . . Vic Dunlop
Susie . . . . Indy Shriner
Landlord . . . . John Hazelwood
Fred . . . . Steve Franken
Phil . . . . Johnny Dark
Darrell . . . . Donald R. Gibb
She-witch . . . . Jeanet Moltke
Also with: Alan Koss, Murray Langston, David Strassman.

"**B**reakfast of Aliens" was filmed in 1989, later picked up by Hemdale and preemed at SF18. The comedy is set to test the theatrical waters in early April in L.A., but its future is clearly on homevid and specialized cable venues.

Comic Vic Dunlop plays a loser pushed around by everyone and basically an overgrown child. One morning, while gorging on cereal, he swallows an alien who begins to take over his body. Eventually Dunlop becomes a hit stand-up comedian, but also a drug-addicted boor.

Humor by first-time helmer David Lee Miller (who co-wrote the script with Dunlop) is weak, with the emphasis on the loud and vulgar. A few moments are genuinely amusing, and if the filmmakers didn't constantly play down to the audience, they might have had a better shot.

Special effects are minimal since focus is on mugging rather than aliens. Tech credits are adequate. — *Daniel M. Kimmel*

March 8, 1993

SWING KIDS

A Hollywood Pictures presentation in association with Pacific Touchwood Partners I of a John Bard Manulus/Mark Gordon production. Executive producers, Frank Marshall, Christopher Meledandri. Produced by Gordon, Manulus. Directed by Thomas Carter. Screenplay, Jonathan Marc Feldman. Camera (Technicolor), Jerzy Zielinski; editor, Michael R. Miller; music, James Horner; production design, Allan Cameron; art direction, Steve Spence, Tony Reading; set decoration, Ros Shingleton; costume design, Jenny Beavan; sound (Dolby), Ivan Sharrock; choreography, Otis Sallid; co-producer, Harry Benn; 1st assistant director, David Householter; 2nd assistant director, Marcia Gay; 2nd-unit camera, Tony Spratling; casting, Deborah Aquila. Reviewed at Avco Center Cinema, Los Angeles, March 2, 1993. MPAA rating: PG-13. Running time: **112 MIN.**

Peter	Robert Sean Leonard
Thomas	Christian Bale
Arvid	Frank Whaley
Frau Muller	Barbara Hershey
SS official	Kenneth Branagh
Evey	Tushka Bergen
Willi	David Tom
Frau Linge	Julia Stemberger
Otto	Jayce Bartok
Emil	Noah Wyle

A fascinating footnote to WWII Nazi Germany is trivialized and sanitized in Hollywood Pictures' odd concoction of music and politics "Swing Kids." Apart from its appealing young cast and period score, it has precious little to entice audiences and will probably replicate the commercial performance of the company's near-catastrophic "Newsies."

Jonathan Marc Feldman's screenplay plays fast and loose with historical fact and chronology as it chronicles the development of a trio of young men whose passion for such American pop music favorites as Benny Goodman, Artie Shaw and Count Basie puts them in the unusual dilemma of embracing officially forbidden "decadent art," the film fumbles in portraying their wild attempt to create a span between the poles of free expression and totalitarian rule.

It is Peter's (Robert Sean Leonard) situation that provides the narrative line. The son of a renowned musician who was discredited and died in a work camp, his family lives under a cloud of suspicion only relieved by the intervention of a seemingly generous SS official (an uncredited Kenneth Branagh) who has romantic intentions on Peter's mother (Barbara Hershey).

The more upwardly mobile Thomas (Christian Bale) finds his musical ardor dampened after joining the Hitler Youth. Initially, he signs up to pal around with Peter (who was forced to join after committing a petty crime), but Thomas soon gives way to total conformity. The third, the physically crippled Arvid (Frank Whaley), remains unrepentant: the least capable of standing up against the tide, he is the fiercest in devotion to jazz.

A latter-day "Three Comrades," the film cannot find the right note of contemporary resonance. The main problem is that its leitmotif of rebellion rings hollow. Far more interesting, but secondary, is its presentation of the insidious, intoxicating aspects of Nazi conformity.

Tech credits are pro.

— *Leonard Klady*

SHADOW OF THE WOLF
(a.k.a. AGAGUK)
(CANADIAN-FRENCH)

A Triumph release of a Vision Intl./Mark Damon presentation in association with Transfilm/Eiffel Prods., with participation of Canal Plus. Executive producer, Charles L. Smiley. Produced by Claude Leger. Directed by Dorfmann; screenplay, Rudy Wurlitzer, Evan Jones; from David Milhaud's adaptation of Yves Theriault's novel "Agaguk." Camera (Sonlab color; CinemaScope), Billy Williams; editor, Francoise Bonnot; music, Maurice Jarre; production design, Wolf Kroeger; costume design, Olga Dimitrov; co-producer, Dorfmann; directors, 1st/2nd crews, Pierre Magny, Christian Duguay. Reviewed at the Culver Studios, Culver City, Jan. 18, 1993. MPAA Rating: PG-13. Running time: **112 MIN.**

Agaguk	Lou Diamond Phillips
Kroomak	Toshiro Mifune
Igiyook	Jennifer Tilly
Brown	Bernard-Pierre Donnadieu
Henderson	Donald Sutherland

A story of survival, revenge and murder in the frozen north, "Shadow of the Wolf" has all the subtlety of a silent movie serial. Reportedly, at $30-plus million, the costliest Canadian production ever, this wilderness epic's oddball international cast enacts the tragic confrontation of native Americans and encroaching whites in the Arctic, circa 1935. Long in production, pic is too simple-minded and cliched for adults, but probably too rough for kids. B.O. forecast is chilly.

As fashioned here by scripters Rudy Wurlitzer and Evan Jones from the much honored source novel, tale relates the maturation of a young Inuit Eskimo hunter who, out of violent hatred for whites, is banished by his shaman father, impetuously kills a trader and, in company with the local beauty, forges a difficult life on the tundra. Eventually, everything comes full circle and Agaguk returns to the village to accept the mantle of maturity from his father.

Unfortunately, the film borders on the laughable throughout due to dialogue that erases the distinction between simple and simple-minded. Some incidents are enough to leave viewers gaping with incredulity as well. One notable sequence has Agaguk jumping on board a speeding whale to escape his foes.

Led by the ferociously hot-blooded Lou Diamond Phillips as Agaguk, cast acts with a heavy seriousness that compounds the problems of the elementary dialogue. As the compromised father, Japanese great Toshiro Mifune lends his imposing presence, but is obviously dubbed. Jennifer Tilly contributes the behavioral grace notes as the young woman who bravely manages to cope with fierce elements and a less-than-congenial Agaguk.

Lensed in widescreen, pic has its moments pictorially but misses the scenic splendors of similar past films ranging from "Eskimo" to "The White Dawn." Jacques Dorfmann, in his second directorial outing after a long-career as a producer, hits the obvious dramatic notes but doesn't seem aware of the risible elements.

An array of Oscar winners, including lenser Billy Williams, editor Françoise Bonnot and composer Maurice Jarre, have been recruited to enhance the production values, but even they can't disguise the patchwork nature of the overall effort.

— *Todd McCarthy*

CB4

A Universal Pictures release of a Brian Grazer/Sean Daniel production. Executive producers, Daniel, Grazer. Produced by Nelson George. Directed by Tamra Davis. Screenplay, Chris Rock, George, Robert LoCash from Rock and George's story. Camera (Deluxe color), Karl Walter Lindenlaub; editor, Earl Watson; music, John Barnes; production design, Nelson Coates; art direction, Martin Charles; set design, Karen Steward; set decoration, Susan Benjamin; costume design, Bernie White; sound (Dolby), Jose Antonio Garcia; co-producers, William Fay, Rock; assistant director, Rip Murray; parody song producer, Daddy-O; casting, Kimberly Hardin. Reviewed at Sunset Laemmle 5 Theater, Hollywood, Feb. 22, 1993. MPAA Rating: R. Running time: **86 MIN.**

Albert	Chris Rock
Euripides	Allen Payne
Otis	Deezer D
A. White	Chris Elliott
Virgil Robinson	Phil Hartman
Gusto	Charlie Murphy
Sissy	Khandi Alexander
Albert Sr.	Arthur Evans
Eve	Theresa Randle
Trustus	Willard E. Pugh

Just as "Wayne's World" cashed in lampooning the addled heavy-metal set, this rap spoof attempt by another "Saturday Night Live" performer, Chris Rock, should mix it up pretty well at the b.o. Unfortunately, pic's appeal will be limited to fans well-versed in "Ice" etiquette, its reach blunted by juvenile humor and a scattered, disjointed narrative.

Telling the story of mythical rap trio CB4, the movie's at its best creating parodies of rap videos, but eventually falls victim to the shortcomings of that form, resulting in a series of vignettes that lack cohesion.

The problem may be a failure to decide what the movie wants to be. It starts promisingly enough like a hip-hop version of "This Is Spinal Tap," with Ice-T and Ice Cube among the well-known rappers turning up in interview-style cameos. That tactic is soon abandoned, however, in favor of a long flashback about how the middle-class trio (Rock, Allen Payne and rapper Deezer D) passed themselves off as bad-ass types (CB stands for "cell block") in order to tap into the rap audience, running afoul of the vicious club owner/drug dealer (Charlie Murphy, a dead ringer for younger brother Eddie) who served as their inspiration.

Tamra Davis, a musicvideo director with the well-received feature debut "Guncrazy" on her résumé, and writers Rock, producer Nelson George and Robert LoCash might have really had something here had they settled on any one of the many paths the movie starts down.

Some semiserious messages — among them a nice exchange between Rock's character and his father — end up muddled, as does the film's skewering the portrayal of women in hip-hop culture while it does its own exploiting of the feminine form.

Tech credits are generally okay, considering the modest scope of the production and the original musicvideos come so close they often seem more like remakes than takeoffs. All that music creates ample possibilities for marketing tie-ins and cross-

March 8, 1993 (Cont.)

promotion, but for the most part "CB4" looks too narrow to really break out. — *Brian Lowry*

FIFTY/FIFTY

A Cannon Pictures release of a Raymond Wagner/Maurice Singer production. Produced by Singer, Wagner. Directed by Charles Martin Smith. Screenplay, Dennis Shryack, Michael Butler. Camera (Rank color; Film House prints), David Connell; editors, James Mitchell, Christian A. Wagner; music, Peter Bernstein; production design, Errol Kelly; sound (Ultra-Stereo), Cameron Hamza; assistant director, Robin Oliver; stunt coordinator, Hubie Kerns Jr.; special effects supervisor, Conrad Rothman; 2nd-unit director, Eric Weston; 2nd-unit camera, Ross Berryman; casting, Ellen Lang, Anna Lim (Malaysia). Reviewed at Embassy 1 theater, N.Y., Feb. 26, 1993. MPAA Rating: R. Running time: **100 MIN.**
Jake Wyer . . . . Peter Weller
Sam French . . . . Robert Hays
Martin Sprue . . Charles Martin Smith
Suleta . . . . Ramona Rahman
Akhantar . . . . Kay Tong Lim
Gen Bosavi . . . . Dom Magwili
Col. Kota . . . . Azmil Mustapha
Liz Powell . . . . Ursala Martin

"**F**ifty/Fifty," a thoroughly mediocre actioner, fails to hit the required tongue-in-cheek tone. Obviously video-driven pic is an inauspicious return of Cannon Pictures to the theatrical marketplace after an eight-month hiatus.

Peter Weller and Robert Hays topline as soldiers of fortune in the Far East who are commandeered by the CIA for a mission to depose evil Gen. Bosavi (Dom Magwili) of Tengara. They cornily train the green troops of rebel leader Akhantar (Kay Tong Lim) while vying for the affections of his niece (Ramona Rahman). Of course the CIA double-crosses them and naturally the duo singlehandedly save the day.

Structured as an old-fashioned buddy romp, pic shamelessly imitates "Butch Cassidy and the Sundance Kid" to ill effect. Charles Martin Smith gives a very wishy-washy reading of the nominal CIA bureaucrat bad guy and directs the film in similarly "who cares?" fashion.

Weller is bland (he was far more expressive in the recent direct-to-video release "Sunset Grill"), while Hays, with perennial chin stubble, is comic relief. Stunts and other tech credits for this Malaysian-lensed opus are adequate. — *Lawrence Cohn*

ACCION MUTANTE
(MUTANT ACTION)
(SPANISH)

An El Deseo/CIBY 2000 production, with the participation of Spanish Television (TVE)/Warner Española. Executive producer, Agustín Almodóvar. Produced by Agustín and Pedro Almodóvar. Directed by Alex de la Iglesia. Screenplay, de La Igelsia, Jorge Guerricaechevarria. Camera (Fujicolor), Carlos Gusi; music, Juan Carlos Cuello; editor, Pablo Blanco; art direction, José Luis Arrizabalaga; costumes, Estibaliz Markiegi; sound (Dolby), Ricardo Steinberg, Daniel Goldstein; special effects, Olivier Gleyze, Ives Domenjoud, Jean Baptiste Bonetto, Bernard André Le Boette; special effects makeup, Hipólito Cantero; makeup, Paca Almenara. Reviewed at Cine Palacio de la Música, Madrid, Jan. 21, 1993. Running time: **90 MIN.**
Ramón Yarritu . . . . Antonio Resines
Patricia Orujo . . . . Fréderique Feder
Alex . . . . Alex Angulo
Juanito . . . . Juan Viadas
Quimicefa . . . . . . Saturnino García
Orujo . . . . Fernando Guillén
Also with: Enrique San Francisco, Teodoro Atkine, Karra Elejalde, Jon Gabella, Alfonso Martínez.

The first film produced by the Almodóvar brothers and not directed by Pedro, "Accion Mutante" bows with a cachet that should draw followers of the Spanish wunderkind. Pic is a spoof of the "Terminator" genre, elbow-deep in gore, but with touches of humor and social comment.

Neophyte helmer Alex de la Iglesia, 27, plunges into his subject with a Troma-like gusto, presenting a bumbling terrorist group calling itself "Mutant Action" and vows to decimate socialites, phonies, establishment softies, deodorant advocates and others of their ilk.

First 20 minutes is a hilarious tour de force as the deformed members of the mob bludgeon their way via a mammoth cake into a high society wedding. Thus far pic has an Almodóvarian look and even its violence is funny. But after the kidnapping of the bimbo bride and the death of some of the funniest members of the mob, pic seems to lose its direction. Its humor turns nasty.

The remaining members of the mob become increasingly repulsive and dull. Their leader, played by Antonio Resines in his usual deadpan style, sadly lacks the mobster associates who made the first part of the pic amusing. Social satire degenerates into plodding grossness as Resines, the bride and a lone survivor (a kind of Siamese twin) flee in a futuristic spaceship to another planet.

De la Iglesia wraps pic with a kind of Western barroom shootout and when TV crews zero in to cover it, pic's earlier zaniness promises to return, but it's too late to offset the previous hour.

Pic is well-directed and special effects (by the French team who did "Delicatessen") are good as are the music and design. Despite flaws, de la Iglesias's pic shows enormous promise.
— *Peter Besas*

GROSS MISCONDUCT
(AUSTRALIAN)

An R.A. Becker presentation of a PRO Film, produced in association with David Hannay Prods., Underworld Prods. and Australian Film Finance. (Intl. sales: Beyond Films.) Executive producer, Richard Becker. Produced by Richard Sheffield-MacClure, David Hannay. Directed by George Miller. Screenplay, Lance Peters, Gerard Maguire from Peters' play "Assault With a Deadly Weapon." Camera (color), David Connell; editor, Henry Dangar; music, Bruce Rowland; designer, Jon Dowding; sound, Andrew Ramage; co-producers, Peters, Maguire; associate producer, Rocky Bester; production manager, Brenda Pam; assistant director, Brian Giddens. Reviewed at G.U. Theaterette, Sydney, Feb. 18, 1993. Running time: **100 MIN.**
Justin Thorne . . . . . . Jimmy Smits
Jennifer Carter . . . . . . Naomi Watts
Laura Thorne . . . . . Sarah Chadwick
Kenneth Carter . . . . . Adrian Wright
Henry Landers . . . . . Alan Fletcher
Miriam McMahon . Leverne McDonnell

Based on a true story of a professor charged with raping one of his students, "Gross Misconduct" is a well-established relationship/courtroom drama women will find particularly challenging. While potential is there for carefully positioned theatrical exposure, aided by Jimmy Smits' presence, it's an excellent item for cable and PPV and a solid video title.

The actual case happened in the '50s, when a philosophy professor tried for 10 years to clear his name after being sacked for alleged rape. "Gross Misconduct" is set in the '90s but, as in the real case, no one comes out a winner, an essentially depressing given that may keep it from finding a wide audience.

While it strives to bring in elements of a psychological thriller, it's the play of relationships that comes across the strongest. Smits is the popular, happily married professor. One of his students (Naomi Watts) becomes increasingly infatuated with him and strives to become closer

through personal tutorials and babysitting.

She fantasizes about having liaisons with Smits, keeping a diary of the imagined encounters. She finally expresses her desire, which Smits gently but firmly rejects; then succumbs while trying to restrain her anger after a more definite denial.

By now it's clear that her obsession is driven by more than just teenage desire, with indications her father (Adrian Wright) has some form of control over her and is intensely jealous of her interest in Smits.

Not long after the encounter, the police find Watts badly beaten and claiming to have been raped by Smits, who is soon arrested. The diary, lies he's told police, and the way he met his wife (Sarah Chadwick) all add up to a guilty verdict. Pic ends with an indication of the harrowing life Watts has lead since and leaves Chadwick and Smits with a tattered relationship.

Apart from a slow development of what drives Watts' obsession, director George Miller has paced the pic well. Smits and Chadwick's marriage is clearly developed, making the later tension between them believable.

The court scenes are well-handled, and Smits is particularly effective. Watts, better-known for her TV work, is excellent — bright and sensual one moment, scared and withdrawn the next.

Technically the film is of high quality, with Miller opting for a subdued look and wintry, often rain-washed gothic settings that may surprise those used to the bright, expansive look often seen in Aussie films.
— *Blake Murdoch*

IL GRANDE COCOMERO
(THE GREAT PUMPKIN)
(ITALIAN-FRENCH)

An Italian Intl. Film release (in Italy) of an Ellepi Film (Rome)/Chrysalide Films (Paris) co-production. Produced by Leo Pescarolo, Guido De Laurentiis, Fulvio Lucisano. Directed, written by Francesca Archibugi. Camera (color), Paolo Carnera; art direction, Livia Borgognoni; costume design, Paola Marchesin; editor, Roberto Missiroli; music, Battista Lena, Roberto Gatto. Reviewed at Quirinetta Cinema, Rome, Feb. 8, 1993. Running time: **90 MIN.**
Arturo . . . . Sergio Castellitto
Pippi . . . . Alessia Fugardi
Cinzia . . . . Anna Galiena
Priest . . . . Victor Cavallo
Aida . . . . Laura Betti
Also with: Lidia Broccolino, Armando De Razza, Alessandra Panelli, Silvio Vannucci.

March 8, 1993 (Cont.)

A brilliant young child psychologist cures a difficult 12-year-old patient in "The Great Pumpkin," an old-fashioned story well-told. Francesca Archibugi's third feature is eminently watchable and a little weepy; now doing respectable business in Italy, it should make a good pickup offshore, particularly for television.

In Italy, "The Great Pumpkin" is a progressive psychiatric movement that takes its name from the Peanuts comic strip. In Archibugi's film — a lightly veiled biopic of the late neuropsychiatrist Marco Lombardo Radice, influential in Italian counter-culture of the 1970s and '80s — it is a symbol of childish yearning and adult utopianism.

Arturo (Sergio Castellitto) works in the children's psychiatric wing of Rome university hospital. A tireless doctor devoted to his young patients, Castellitto deals with his own problems, like the pain of his wife walking out on him, by marrying his work. When he spends the night sleeping in a spare bed on the ward, Big Nurse Laura Betti — a maternal figure gone partly bad — indulgently shuts an eye.

Pippi (Alessia Fugardi) is brought in almost by accident, escorted by over-protective mother Anna Galiena. As the good doctor quickly senses, Fugardi — the epileptic daughter of an ill-assorted, nouveau riche couple — needs psychiatric help. He convinces her to go into analysis, and through dissecting her family situation finds she isn't really epileptic at all.

Fugardi's treatment is a gradual process in which she alternately runs hot and cold with Arturo. To encourage her, he has a little girl suffering from a brain hemorrhage moved to the ward, to whom Fugardi devotes herself. But the child dies unexpectedly, leading to a teary funeral scene; the trauma precipitates Pippi's final crisis and cure.

Archibugi has a rare gift for simple, clear-cut storytelling, able to move the audience without fireworks. Much of the film is lensed in close shots that should play well on TV. Closely in contact with reality, "Pumpkin" naturally mixes actors and nonpros, kids and adults.

One of pic's most interesting elements is its down-to-earth depiction of the state-run hospital. The shouting matches between the personnel, the stolen toilet paper, decrepit furniture and unpainted walls seem to come out of a Romanian war film — but are all unfortunately true to life. The scene where an exasperated Betti throws a dog out a second-story window is a classic of the evil-hospital genre. But there is a paradoxically positive side, seen in a few passionately caring medics and the solidarity between the young patients.

In his finest role, Sergio Castellitto shows his ability to give comic lightness to a deadly serious character. If Arturo owes some of his solidity to the real doctor he's based on, Castellitto contributes a sense of humor and strong conviction.

Young Alessia Fugardi is so completely spontaneous that whatever she does it's hard to remember she's acting. Anna Galiena, on the contrary, is such an alive presence she seems to jump out of the screen with nervous fragility. Betti and Cavallo, in minor roles, are scene-stealers.

— *Deborah Young*

BERLIN FEST

THE CEMENT GARDEN
(GERMAN-BRITISH-FRENCH)

A Neue Constantin (Germany)/Metro Tartan (U.K.) release of a Neue Constantin (Munich)/Laurentic Film (London)/Torii (Paris) production. (Intl. sales: the Summit Group, London.) Executive producers, Bernd Eichinger, Martin Moszkowicz. Produced by Bee Gilbert, Ene Vanaveski. Directed, written by Andrew Birkin, from Ian McEwan's novel. Camera (Technicolor), Stephen Blackman; editor, Toby Tremlett; music, Edward Shearmur; production and costume design, Bernd Lepel; art direction, Amanda Grenville; sound (Dolby), Guillaume Sciama; co-producer, Steve O'Rourke; assistant director, Martin Harrison. Reviewed at Berlin Film Festival (competing), Feb. 20, 1993. Running time: **105 MIN.**
Jack . . . . Andrew Robertson
Julie . . . . Charlotte Gainsbourg
Sue . . . . Alice Coulthard
Tom . . . . Ned Birkin
Mother . . . . Sinead Cusack
Father . . . . Hanns Zischler
Derek . . . . Jochen Horst
(English soundtrack)

G allic star Charlotte Gainsbourg makes a striking English-lingo debut in "The Cement Garden," a quirky drama of sibling incest and teenage alienation from British writer Ian McEwan's 1978 debut novel. But this moody, dramatically uneven pic will need careful handling and good reviews to go wider than specialized play-off, and its unblinking portrait of teen and subteen sexuality could limit tube sales.

The movie is a family affair in more ways than one. Director Andrew Birkin ("Burning Secret") is Gainsbourg's uncle and his son Ned plays Charlotte's youngest brother in the film.

Pic's setting is a lone house amid a concrete wasteland. When the family's stern father (Hanns Zischler) dies of a heart attack, mom (Sinead Cusack) buckles under the strain of rearing her four children and becomes bedridden. When she, too, dies, the elder kids secretly bury her body in a cement box in the cellar to avoid being taken into care.

Left to their own devices, the children start to give freer vent to their sexual confusion. The eldest, Julie (Gainsbourg), 16, plays with the incestuous infatuation of 15-year-old brother Jack (Andrew Robertson), as well as inviting 'round an elder boyfriend (Jochen Horst). With her secretive younger sister Sue (Alice Coulthard), she also encourages 6-year-old Tom (Ned Birkin) in his desire to dress up as a girl.

The catalyst to the simmering sexuality between Gainsbourg and Robertson is when her b.f. starts to smell a rat about the mother's disappearance.

The pic lacks the straightforward dramatic smarts of Jack Clayton's 1967 "Our Mother's House," also about moppets hiding their mom's death. Birkin focuses more on the blurred areas between genders, and the vulnerable world of puberty blues.

Maybe aware of the danger of the whole ripe confection tipping over into farce, Birkin keeps the perfs low-key throughout, complemented by steely-gray lensing and underlit interiors. Bernd Lepel's quirky production and costume design — part '50s, part '90s, and not wholly grounded in a British "look" — add to the unreal atmosphere, compounded by two German actors cast as the English father and b.f.

Despite its sensitive subject matter, and scenes of Jack furiously masturbating, the pic is visually discreet, with only a single scene of nude lovemaking. Biggest problem is jerky dramatic development and lack of a thoroughgoing tone — faults disguised but not hidden by Edward Shearmur's textured score.

Gainsbourg makes a good showing in English, mirroring the quietly rebellious qualities of her French perfs. Newcomer Robertson matches her in androgynous appeal but is short on screen presence. Cusack is solid as the mother, and the other kids are okay.

Birkin copped Best Director prize at the Berlin fest.

— *Derek Elley*

LES VISITEURS
(THE VISITORS)
(FRENCH)

A Gaumont Buena Vista Intl. release of a Gaumont/FR-3 Cinema/Alpilles Prods./Amigo Prods. co-production with the participation of Canal Plus and the Languedoc-Roussillon region. Produced by Alain Terzian. Directed by Jean-Marie Poiré. Screenplay, Poiré, Christian Clavier. Camera (color), Jean-Yves Le Mener; editor, Catherine Kelber; music, Eric Levi; production design, Hugues Tissandier; sound, Jean-Charles Ruault; costumes, Catherine Leterrier; makeup, Muriel Baurens; assistant director, Paul Gueu. Reviewed at UGC Odeon cinema, Paris, Feb. 10, 1993. (In Berlin Film Festival (Market section); American Film Market.) Running time: **103 MIN.**
Jacquouille/Jacquart . Christian Clavier
Godefroy . . . . Jean Reno
Frénégonde/Béatrice . . . .
. . . . Valérie Lemercier
Ginette . . . . Marie-Anne Chazal
Also with: Christian Bujeau, Isabelle Nanty, Gérard Séty, Didier Pain.

"L es Visiteurs," a crowd-pleasing time-travel comedy, is doing boffo biz at Gallic wickets. Snappily paced and resoundingly silly pic follows the goofy antics of an 11th century knight and his faithful serf who are mistakenly zapped to present-day France. Wacky, nimble fare should have legs throughout Europe.

En route to his betrothed (Valérie Lemercier) in the year 1122, the brave knight Godefroy de Montmirail (a deadpan Jean Reno) captures a sorceress. The witch drugs Reno, causing him to kill his fiancée's father, putting a damper on the marriage plans and jeopardizing the continuation of his line.

Desperate to make amends, Reno and loyal serf Jacquouille La Fripouille (Christian Clavier) drink a magic potion that is supposed to turn back the clock and undo the fatal deed. Instead it propels them 871 years into the future, where they encounter their modern-day descendants.

Plenty of fish-out-of-water gags ensue as the dynamic duo, mistaken for an amnesiac relative and his peculiar sidekick, are offered hospitality by the local countess (also played by Lemercier). To Reno's horror, the chateau of yore has been converted into an exclusive luxury hotel, run by a prim dandy, Jacquart (also played by Clavier). The unnerving resemblances seem to indicate that a few centuries can alter ancestral social status in either direction.

The visitors are klutzes in refined surroundings, with less-than-genteel notions about table etiquette and positively medieval concepts of subservience, hygiene, chivalry and honor. Dopey but inventive plot is kept aloft via frantic pacing and lots of extreme camera angles.

The visitors speak a newfangled Old French that is sometimes uproarious by virtue of its incongruity. The serf's name, repeated as often as possible, runs on the same adolescent wavelength as the Monty Pythoners discussing the Roman dignitary "Biggus Dickus."

Thesps, most of whom have worked together before, seem to be having a ball. Lemercier's physical humor and upper-class elocution are particularly funny. Poking fun at the "everything must be resolved before the stroke of midnight" tradition, script provides a satisfying punchline.

Straight dramatic score and fine production design lend classy counterpoint to the silly proceedings. Costumes and special effects are also on target.

— *Lisa Nesselson*

LA PETITE APOCALYPSE
(THE LITTLE APOCALYPSE)
(FRENCH-ITALIAN-POLISH)

A K.G. Prods. (Paris)/Nickelodeon Films (Rome)/Heritage Films (Warsaw) co-production. (Intl. sales: World Marketing Film, Paris.) Executive producers, Conchita Airoldi, Dino Di Dionisio. Produced by Michele Ray-Gavras. Directed by Costa-Gavras. Screenplay, Costa-Gavras, Jean-Claude Grumberg, from Tadeusz Konwicki's novel. Camera (color, widescreen), Patrick Blossier; editor, Joele Van Effenterre; music, Philippe Sarde; production design, Philippe Chiffre; sound, Pierre Gamet, Claude Villand; co-producers, Valerio de Paolis, Lev Ryvin, Grzegorz Warchol; assistant director, Frederic Blum. Reviewed at Berlin Film Festival (competing), Feb. 22, 1993. Running time: **108 MIN.**
Jacques . . . . Andre Dussollier
Henri . . . . Pierre Arditi
Stan . . . . Jiri Menzel
Barbara . . . . . . Anna Romantowska
Arnold . . . . Maurice Benichou
Physiotherapist . . . . . . Carlo Brandt
Doctor . . . . Jacques Denis
Luigi . . . . Enzo Scotto Luiggi
Luigi's daughter . . . . . Chiara Caselli
Pitchik . . . Jan Tadeusz Stanislawski
Mme. Pitchik . . . . . Beata Tyskiewicz

After two consecutive American pics ("Betrayed" and "Music Box"), Athens-born Costa-Gavras returns to his Paris base with another political film, this time a comedy. Though based on a well-regarded book by Polish filmmaker-author Tadeusz Konwicki, the director's forte is not comedy, and despite potent themes "The Little Apocalypse" is sluggish and occasionally awkward, boding ill for the arthouse market.

The timely theme explored here is the West's attitude toward the newly "liberated" citizens of Eastern Europe, who have found that with freedom and a free market come human costs. Stan (played by the Oscar-winning Czech director Jiri Menzel), a dissident Polish author who's never been published in the West, lives in the attic of the house where his ex-wife (Anna Romantowska) lives with her wealthy second husband (Pierre Arditi). He and journalist pal Andre Dussollier are ex-leftists who've settled into conservative, comfortable middle age.

Arditi and Dussollier, convinced a drunken accident of Menzel's was a suicide attempt, find a powerful media maven (hilariously played by Maurice Benichou), who offers to publish Menzel's works on condition he commits suicide in front of a TV crew, immolating himself at St. Peter's during a papal speech.

Having set up an intriguing plot for a very black comedy, Costa-Gavras soon drops the ball with a series of flatly staged scenes that stop pic dead. Pic works better as a philosophical piece on the plight of people from countries like Poland.

The sharp widescreen lensing by Patrick Blossier is a major asset, though Joele Van Effenterre's editing could have been tighter. — *David Stratton*

LE SOUPER
(THE SUPPER)
(FRENCH)

A Trinacra production, in association with Parma Films/France 2 Cinema/Canal Plus/Soficas/Investimage 4/Cofimage 4/Procirep. (Intl. sales: Mainstream SA, Paris.) Produced by Yves Rousset-Rouard. Directed by Edouard Molinaro. Screenplay, Jean-Claude Brisville, Rousset-Rouard, Molinaro, from Brisville's play. Camera (Panavision, Eastmancolor), Michael Epp; editor, Annick Rousset-Rouard; music, Vladimir Cosma; production design, François de Lamothe; sound, Daniel Brisseau; costumes, Sylvie de Segonzac; production manager, Philippe Schwartz. Reviewed at Berlin Film Festival (Panorama section), Feb. 14, 1993. Running time: **92 MIN.**
Fouché . . . . Claude Brasseur
Talleyrand . . . . Claude Rich
Jacques . . . . Ticky Holgado
Jean . . . . Yann Collette
Carème . . . . Stéphane Jobert
Voice of Chateaubriand . Michel Piccoli

A handsomely mounted film version of a successful stage play, in which two great actors repeat their original roles, "The Supper" is elegant entertainment, although its concerns may not be of much interest outside France.

Almost a 19th century "My Dinner With Andre," the film is basically a spirited supper conversation between two powerful men at a crucial moment in French history. Claude Brasseur is the humbly born, now powerful, police minister Fouché and Claude Rich as the smoothly sinister, aristocratic former prime minister Prince Talleyrand.

This is essentially a stage piece, and it excels with witty, incisive dialog and the subtle thesping of two consummate actors who know their roles inside out. In fact, the few attempts by director Edouard Molinaro to open out the material, seem pointless and diminish rather than enhance the basically claustrophobic piece.

It is the night of July 6, 1815, three weeks after Waterloo, where France, under Napoleon, was defeated by the British. Paris is an occupied city. The question is: In what direction will the country move? As the two most powerful men in France, Fouché, who espouses a republic under the Jacobins, and Talleyrand, who wants a return to the Bourbon monarchy, must decide.

As they sample the food prepared for them by a master chef, and served by two eavesdropping servants, and as Talleyrand's "niece" waits in his bedroom, the plotters argue, threaten and cajole each other, finally coming to

an agreement described as "Vice and Crime arm in arm."

The film features such acerbic nuggets of wit as "In France, regimes pass but cuisine remains" and "Power only tires people who don't wield it." "The Supper" will be a delight for Francophiles, especially those interested in the period depicted, and all lovers of fine acting. It's not a particularly striking cinematic experience, but a fine example of a play lovingly preserved on film.

— *David Stratton*

SAMBA TRAORÉ
(BURKINA FASO-FRENCH-SWISS)

A Les Films de l'Avenir (Ouagadougou)/Les Films de la Plaine (Paris)/Waka Films (Switzerland) co-production. Produced by Sophie Salbot, Idrissa Ouédraogo, Silvia Voser. Directed by Ouédraogo. Screenplay, Ouédraogo, Jacques Arhex, Santiago Amigorena; camera (color), Pierre Laurent Chenieux, Mathieu Vadepied; editor, Joelle Dufour; music, Wasis Diop, Faion Cahen. Reviewed at the Carthage Film Festival, Oct. 8, 1992. (Competing at Berlin Film Festival) Running time: **85 MIN.**
Samba Traoré . . . . . Bakary Sangare
Saratou . . . . Mariam Kaba
Salif . . . . . . Abdoulaye Komboudri.
Binta . . . . Irene Tassembedo

One of the best-known new directors from West Africa, Idrissa Ouédraogo shows what he can do on a more substantial budget in his beautifully lensed moral tale "Samba Traoré." The Swiss-French-Burkinabé co-prod won the Silver Tanit at the last Carthage Film Festival. Though the film has been criticized by some Africans for being too "Western" in its story and style, few Western viewers will share these qualms. Pic is unquestionably more accessible than helmer's earlier works, bettering its chances for TV pick-ups and fest prizes.

After being involved in a gas-station hold-up, during which the attendant was shot and killed, Samba (Bakary Sangare) flees to his native village with a suitcase of money and a dirty secret. He tells friends and relatives he has earned the money, but cannot dispel an aura of suspicion.

Sangare brings a warm humanity to Samba, making it hard to take a firm moral stance against him. He falls in love with the beautiful Saratou (Mariam Kaba,) who has left her husband and has a young child. With the help of childhood friend Abdoulaye Kom-

March 8, 1993 (Cont.)

boudri, he courts and marries her, building a house lavish by the poor village's standards. Samba joyfully spends more money on building a bar.

He is exposed when, for fear of running into the law, he abandons his pregnant, seriously ill wife instead of taking her a city hospital. The shock and disgust the villagers and Samba's family feel finally leads to a climactic scene of great impact.

The relationship between Samba and Saratou is unusually well developed for a Burkinabé film, and has an even more unusual bedroom scene. Helmer's experiments with nontraditional storytelling give pic more emotional immediacy and characters more depth. Kaba has a quasi-feminist dignity as a single mom bravely seeking a better life. Komboudri stands out as Samba's admiring but dubious friend.

Pierre Laurent Chenieux's lush cinematography conveys a much more pleasant impression of the Burkina Faso countryside than the usual burned-out brush seen on out-of-date film stock. The advantages of good equipment and tech work are everywhere apparent, from the editing to the music. — *Deborah Young*

TELEGRAFISTEN
(THE TELEGRAPHIST)
(NORWEGIAN-COLOR-B&W)

A Nordic Screen Development production, in association with Schibsted Film, Metronome Prods., Norsk Film. (Intl. sales: Majestic Films & Television, London.) Produced by Petter Borgli, Tomas Backström. Directed by Erik Gustavson. Screenplay, Lars Saabye Christensen, from Knut Hamsun's novel "Svaermere" (Dreamers). Camera (Eastmancolor/B&W), Philip Øgaard; editor, Sylvia Ingemarsson; music, Randall Meyers; production design, Tina Schwab; art direction, Billy Johansson; costume design, Inger Derlick; sound design, Meyers; sound, Gunnar Meidell; assistant director, Marius Holst; associate producer, James Frazee. Reviewed at Berlin Film Festival (competing), Feb. 17, 1993. Running time: **101 MIN.**

Ove Rolandsen	Bjørn Floberg
Elise Mack	Marie Richardson
Mack	Jarl Kulle
Cpt. Henriksen	Ole Ernst
Miss Van Loos	Kjersti Holmen
Levion	Bjørn Sundquist
Pastor's wife	Elisabeth Sand
Pastor	Svein Sturla Hungnes
Olga	Camilla Strøm Henriksen
Fredrik	Johan H:Son Kjellgren

Also with: Knut Haugmark, Reidar Sørensen, Maria Bonnevie, Per Jansen.

"The Telegraphist" is a top-of-the-line Scandi costumer

with a quirky edge. Lushly packaged, mildly erotic tale of a fjord Romeo and the three women in his life deserves quality arthouse playdates.

In light of disappointing biz for recent Scandi fare like "The Best Intentions," this one will need heavy marketing, good reviews and careful subtitling that conveys the subtle humor in Lars Saabye Christensen's finely crafted reworking of Knut Hamsum's novel "Dreamers."

Setting is a small coastal town in northern Norway in 1903. Local telegraphist Ove Rolandsen (breezily played by Robert Redford lookalike Bjørn Floberg) moonlights as a inventor looking for the big kill. He also has eyes for Elise (Marie Richardson), lovely daughter of local tycoon Mack (Jarl Kulle), owner of a fish-glue factory.

Elise isn't immune to Rolandsen's charms but is already promised to a German ship owner, whose business connections her dad desperately needs. In between keeping his mousy fiancée happy, and seducing the local pastor's wife (Elisabeth Sand), Rolandsen tries to make himself financially more attractive to Elise and her dad by coming up with a marketable invention.

Rolandsen's elaborate plan works, resulting in an unexpected business alliance. However, the hand of the elusive Elise turns out to be another matter.

Shooting on stunning locations in northern Norway, well integrated with studio interiors, helmer Erik Gustavson gives a standard novelistic look to the story. What's fresh is the pic's strain of ironic humor, nicely handled by Floberg and Swedish vet Jarl Kulle, and a risk-taking quality already evident in Gustavson's previous "Herman."

There's a lightness of touch that marks pic out from the run of Scandi costumers and, though far from heavy-duty erotic, the long undertow of the pair's unconsummated desire is neatly maintained. Richardson, an Ingmar Bergman regular on stage and TV, is fine as the proud beauty, and the Norwegian-Swedish-Danish cast melds smoothly.

Philip Øgaard's eye-catching photography and Randall Meyer's evocative score are top drawer. — *Derek Elley*

PATUL CONJUGAL
(THE CONJUGAL BED)
(ROMANIAN)

An Alpha Film production. Produced by Oltea Munteanu. Directed, written by Mircea Daneliuc. Camera (color), Vivi Dragan Vasile; editor, Melania Oproiu; production design, Mircea Ribinschi; sound, Anusavan Salamanian; production manager, Gabriela Moruzi. Reviewed at Berlin Film Festival (competing), Feb. 14, 1993. Running time: **102 MIN.**

With: Gheorghe Dinica, Coca Bloos, Valentin Teodosiu, Lia Bugnar, Geo Costiniu, Jana Gorea, Flavius Constantinescu, Nicolae Praida, Paul Chiributa, Cristian Motriue.

This jet black comedy paints an extremely grim picture of life in contempo Romania, but does so with a smart line of absurdist humor. Probably too bleak and technically rough to find much of an audience, it deserves to play the fest circuit at the very least.

It's w.k. that life under dictator Nicolae Ceausescu was appalling; the trouble is, now it's worse. "If God has pity on us, he'll kick us in the ass!" is the motto of Mircea Daneliuc's caustic film.

His "hero" is Vasile (Gheorghe Dinica), who manages a cinema few people ever attend. He loves his mistress, Stela, more than his wife, and is horrified that the latter is somehow pregnant. To get an abortion, he needs hard to come by U.S. dollars.

To add to his woes, Stela decides to turn pro and demands money for her sexual favors. Poor Vasile winds up in a mental home, and when he comes out, discovers his wife has rented their apartment to porno filmmakers and that Stela is their leading lady.

Daneliuc adopts the time-honored theory that when times are hopelessly bad, the only thing to do is laugh. One of the sharpest jokes involves a book, titled "The Future of Romania," written by the former dictator. As most copies were burned when he was overthrown, the first edition is extremely rare and, ironically, worth thousands of dollars.

Daneliuc's abrasively funny pic might have a better chance were it not so visually ugly. The color processing is poor and the settings are drab. The male characters are unrelievedly sexist and repulsive. Audiences are likely to be more depressed than amused, and so may miss the very valid points the writer-director makes so uncompromisingly. Pic is also a shade too long. — *David Stratton*

CONTES ET COMPTES
DE LA COUR
(ACCOUNTS AND ACCOUNTING
FROM THE COURTYARD)
(FRENCH-DOCU)

A Caméras Continentales production, in association with La Sept. Directed, written, photographed by Eliane de Latour. Editor, Monique Dartonne; sound, Lardia Tchambiano. Reviewed at Berlin Film Festival (Forum section), Feb. 18, 1993. Running time: **96 MIN.**

The popular conception of a harem is wrong according to this absorbing ethnographic documentary, filmed inside a harem in rural Niger. Eliane de Latour's film should find tube slots without difficulty.

The Islamic sheikhs of Niger still have several wives. De Latour obtained permission to film in the quarters of the six wives of one sheikh, spent nine weeks gathering material, and demonstrates that times are gradually changing: The women, hitherto strictly confined to quarters, are slowly venturing outside. One even has a job as a nurse.

Their children have no inhibitions about venturing outside the courtyard that borders the harem where they're sent to sell trinkets and foodstuffs. Meanwhile, the women deal with the sheikh via a steward, whom they constantly ridicule. The women talk freely and seemingly without embarrassment to de Latour (as unseen interviewer) and the result is a fascinating portrait of a fast-disappearing lifestyle. — *David Stratton*

MUSTARD BATH
(CANADIAN)

A 9Y6S Film production, with participation of Telefilm Canada and Ontario Film Development. (Intl. sales: Films Transit, Montreal.) Produced by Darrell Wasyk, David M. York. Directed, written by Wasyk, from a story by Wasyk, Bebo Haddad. Camera (Eastmancolor), Barry Peterson; editor, Tom McMurtry; music, Rob Carroll; art direction, Ian Brock, Enrico Campana; costume design, Beth Pasternak; sound design, Alan Geldart; assistant director, David Webb; co-producer, Brian Ferstman. Reviewed at Berlin Film Festival (Panorama section), Feb. 19, 1993. Running time: **109 MIN.**

Matthew Linden	Michael Riley
Grace	Martha Henry
Mindy	Alissa Trotz
Sister Amantha	Tantoo Cardinal
Matthew's mother	Elizabeth Shepherd
Dexter	Fernando Da Silva
Rasta Fad'dah	Eddy Grant

March 8, 1993 (Cont.)

"**M**ustard Bath" doesn't cut it on any dramatic level. Guyana-set second feature of Canadian maverick Darrell Wasyk sets out as a search for identity and mislays its compass about halfway through. Indie pic may get some mileage on the fest circuit but looks to take a b.o. bath of its own.

Per Wasyk, the movie is a "more cinematic" about-face after his confined, two-person junkie drama "H" (1990). Dedicated to "the memory of my mother," it's an attempt at meditative cinema, following a Guyana-born Canadian doctor, Matthew (Michael Riley), as he revisits the land of his youth to exorcise painful memories of rejection by his mom.

In true odyssey fashion, the people he meets point up aspects of himself. Hungarian exile Grace (Martha Henry), endlessly reminiscing about the old days in Guyana, becomes a surrogate mother; local teacher Mindy (Alissa Trotz) represents the country's allure; and young orphan Dexter (Fernando Da Silva) recalls Riley's happy childhood.

Like many self-discovery pics, however, Wasyk's makes the cardinal error of falling into the same vagueness as the hero. When Trotz, after a lily-pond lovemaking sesh, starts screaming at Riley that he's afraid of something, she meets the same blank wall as the rest of the cast. Later, from a local priest (Eddy Grant) we learn Riley's problem may be "poverty of the spirit."

Poverty of the script is more like it. Vet Henry makes the most of her long monologues, especially one about a messy abortion (the title's "mustard bath"), and other supports are solid.

Wasyk and young cameraman Barry Peterson (making his feature bow) conjure up some beautiful, russet-tinged images as well as lingering over ex-model Riley's physique. Technically, the production is smooth all the way, with an emotive, churning score by Rob Carroll.— *Derek Elley*

BARABANIADA
(DRUMROLL)
(RUSSIAN-FRENCH)

A Studio of First & Experimental Film production, in association with Lenfilm (St. Petersburg)/MIK (Moscow)/Dess Prods. (Paris). (Intl. sales: Dess, Paris.) Produced by Aleksandr Donchenko, Aleksandr Golutova. Directed, written by Sergei Ovcharov. Camera (color), Aleksandr Ustinov; editor, Olga Amasova; music, Ovcharov; art direction, Viktor Ivanov; costume design, Larisa Konnikova; sound, Konstantin Zarin; assistant director, Aleksandr Vasiliev; co-producer, Dalya Dessertyn. Reviewed at Berlin Film Festival (Panorama section), Feb. 12, 1993. Running time: **99 MIN.**
    With: Aleksandr Polovtsev.

Loonily funny and packed with invention, "Drumroll" is a jewel of a movie that should have festival bookers standing in line. This silent pastiche, set in a crumbling modern-day Russia, is also perfect for adventurous TV programmers.

Central character (played with airheaded charm by Aleksandr Polovtsev) is a drummer in a group that plays at funerals. Incurably attached to his instrument, to the despair of doctors, he wanders off on an odyssey that becomes a portrait of contempo Russia's social chaos. Mostly set against snowy wastes and grungy urban landscapes, Polovtsev meets a succession of types, including venal border guards, city thugs, a buxom blonde and black marketeers.

There's more than a touch of Buster Keaton in Polovtsev's style and comic riffs, but the wild ideas and straightfaced humor are less physical than Keaton's and very Slavic in tone. Though taking a reel to hit its stride, the invention is thick and fast thereafter, capped by a breathtaking stunt with a submarine.

Funniest running joke is the uses to which Polovtsev puts the drum, including a table, TV set, giant frying pan, and even a washing machine. The ancient instrument takes on an almost human quality, panting in exhaustion after too much journeying.

Deputizing for the lack of dialogue are exaggerated sound effects and a mass of classical lollipops played at full tilt. Undercranked camerawork gives a slightly jerky, silent-movie look that manages never to become tiresome. — *Derek Elley*

HA CHAYIM ALPY AGFA
(LIFE ACCORDING TO AGFA)
(ISRAELI-B&W)

A Moviez Entertainment production. Executive Producer, Uri Sabag. Produced by Yoram Kislev, Rafi Boukaee. Directed, written by Assi Dayan. Camera (B&W), Yoav Koush; editor, Zohar Sela; music, Naftali Alter; production design, Ya'akov Tourjeman; sound, David Liss; assistant director, Uri Yerushalmi. Reviewed at Berlin Film Festival (competing), Feb. 15, 1993. Running time: **102 MIN.**
Dalia . . . . Gila Almagor
Leora . . . . Irit Frank
Benny . . . . Shuli Rand
Riki . . . . Avital Dicker
Cherniak . . . . Danny Litani
Eli . . . . Ezra Kafri
Nimi . . . . Sharon Alexander
Sammy . . . . Barak Negbi
Samir . . . . Akhram Tallawi
Mahmud . . . . Reuven Dayan

Assi Dayan's latest film, well received in Israel and which won awards for best direction and screenplay from the Israel Film Academy, is a very bleak depiction of that country's society. Following a mixed, but generally positive reaction at its offshore launch in competition at the Berlin fest, it could find arthouse distribution thanks to its challenging themes and striking perfs.

Set "a year from now" (per the opening title), the film spans 12 hours, most of them unfolding in a small Tel Aviv all-night bar owned by two women. Dalia (vet Israeli actress Gila Almagor) has had a longstanding affair with a married film producer who has cancer; when he's not around, she picks up younger men. Her partner, Leora (Irit Frank), a compulsive photographer (hence pic's title), lives with a faithless young policeman (Shuli Rand).

On this particular night, patrons at the bar include some drunken soldiers, led by Sharon Alexander); a mentally disturbed young woman (Avital Dicker) who's on doctor's orders not to spend the night alone; and a trio of drug dealers. There are also the bar's singer (Danny Litani), whose left-wing ballads annoy the soldiers; and a couple of Arabs who work in the kitchen.

As the long night wears on, tensions run high. Rand has a confrontation with the soldiers, who have been accosting Dicker, then takes the distraught girl back to Frank's apartment and heartlessly seduces her, leading to the night's first tragedy. Almagor is confronted by her lover's wife and has to come to terms with his incipient death. And

Frank finally realizes the futility of her relationship with Rand.

In production notes, Dayan (son of Israel's soldier-hero Moshe Dayan) evokes Robert Altman's "Nashville" as being the film's inspiration, but "Nashville" was a more rounded portrait of a society in trouble; there's nothing at all positive in Dayan's portrait of Israeli life, of characters who are dying before they actually die.

Fascinating as far as it goes, with stark black and white photography by Yoav Koush providing a dark mood which is accentuated by the mournful songs of Leonard Cohen on the soundtrack (another Altman link). However, Dayan literally blows it with an over-the-top finale of staggering banality, in which the soldiers attack the bar with automatic weapons, a nonsensically negative gambit.

Performances are uniformly good, with Almagor outstanding as the world-weary Dalia and Rand quietly menacing as the brutally sexist cop. Despite its flaws, this was one of the better pics in the Berlin competition.
—*David Stratton*

HEYA
(THE ROOM)
(JAPANESE-B&W)

An Anchors production. Produced by Takaharu Yasuoka, Takayuki Nakano, Ryo Matsuoka. Directed, written by Sion Sono. Camera (B&W), Yuichiro Otsuka, Shigenori Miki; editor, Kunihiko Ukai; music, Kosei Yamamoto; production design, Norimasa Wakita; sound, Hiroki Okano; assistant director, Kunifumi Yoshida. Reviewed at Berlin Film Festival (Forum section), Feb. 14, 1993. Running time: 92 MIN.
The Murderer . . . . Akaji Maro
The Real Estate Agent . . . .
. . . . Yoriko Doguchi
    With: Shiro Sano, Sayoko Takahashi, Masao Matsuda, Eiichi Uchida, Yuko Terashima, Momochan.

Sion Sono's second feature (after "Bicycle Sighs") is a black and white minimalist piece composed with formal beauty, but likely to tax the patience of all but the most dedicated fans of Asian fringe cinema. A safe bet for the fest circuit, but chances in other outlets look as empty as the various rooms in the film.

The deceptively simple premise involves a young woman real estate agent trying to find a room for a middle-aged man. He specifies that he wants a small, quiet room with a view that contains no skyscrapers, a tall order in today's Tokyo.

The odd couple travel around the ugly suburbs by train, the young woman telling the man about each room's price and available amenities, as he finds a reason not to take the place, and the search goes on. Gradually, it becomes clear that the man is a professional assassin, who needs somewhere quiet to recover from his last assignment.

Both the murderer and the agent speak in hushed monotones, and the stark, depressing apartments they visit echo the grim, sad mood of the characters. It's an interesting concept but, at 92 minutes, stretches the slim premise to the max.

The cool camerawork is a major asset, as are the implacably bland performances. — *David Stratton*

DEN RUSSISKE SANGERINDE
(THE RUSSIAN SINGER)
(DANISH-RUSSIAN)

A Nordisk Film Prod./Starlight Moscow production, in association with Danish Film Institute/TV-2 (Denmark)/ Svensk Filmindustri (Sweden)/Gorky Film Studios (Russia)/Eldorado Co. (Intl. sales: Pathé-Nordisk Film TV-Distribution, Copenhagen/Stockholm.) Executive producers, Lars Kolvig, Michael Zilberman, Hans Morten Rubin. Produced by Erik Crone. Directed by Morten Arnfred. Screenplay, William Aldridge, Leif Davidson, Arnfred, from Davidsen's novel. Camera (Eastmancolor), Alexander Gruszynski; editor, Lizzi Weischenfeldt; music, Ole Arnfred; art direction, Nikolai Terekhov, Alexander Gilyarevsky; costume design, Vera Skopinova; sound (Dolby), Jan Juhler; assistant director, Bella Dunaeva. Reviewed at Berlin Film Festival (competing), Feb. 21, 1993. Running time: **119 MIN.**
Jack Andersen . . . . . . Ole Lemmeke
Lili . . . . Elena Butenko
Gavrilin . . . . Vsevolod Larionov
Basov . . . . Igor Volkov
Piotr Demichev . . . . Igor Yasulovich
Castesen . . . . . . Jesper Christensen
C.W. . . . . Erik Mørk
(English, Russian, Danish soundtrack)

"The Russian Singer" is a no-thrills thriller: Smart production values and attractive Moscow locations can't disguise a so-what storyline and playing that fails to raise the mercury. Danish-Russo pic drew raised eyebrows for being included in Berlin fest competition, then jeers at its press screening. Theatrical chances for the polyglotter look zip in English-lingo markets, though it could eke out a dubbed career in undemanding markets.

Based on the 1986 novel by Danish journo Leif Davidsen, but seemingly set in the more immediate present, plot revolves round the bizarre murder of two hookers in a Moscow apartment. As one worked at the Danish embassy, diplomat Jack Andersen (Ole Lemmeke) is called in; things get complicated when Jack falls for singer Lili (Elena Butenko), sister of one of the corpses.

Apart from by-the-numbers plotting, and dialogue that seems stitched together from old spy movies ("I'm bad luck. I make accidents happen," Lili warns Jack), there's a real failure by director Morten Arnfred and his co-scripters to generate any kind of cumulative tension.

Additionally, having a large chunk of the dialogue in English means most of the Danish-Russian cast are acting in their second language. Lemmeke gets by on the linguistic front, though he hasn't the presence to carry a production of this size; Butenko, no great shakes as a singer, is cute but lightweight. Other performances are serviceable.

Ole Arnfred's dramatic score and Lizzi Weischenfeldt's slick editing complement handsome lensing by Alexander Gruszynski. All of the 16 million kroner ($2.5 million) budget is up on the screen. — *Derek Elley*

WIR KONNEN AUCH ANDERS . . .
(NO MORE MR. NICE GUY)
(GERMAN)

A Boje Buck production, with WDR. (Intl. sales: Cinepool, Munich.) Produced by Claus Boje. Directed by Detlev Buck. Screenplay, Buck, Ernst Kahl. Camera (Eastmancolor), Roger Heereman; editor, Peter R. Adam; music, Detlef Petersen; production design, Ute Rohrbeck; sound, Wolfgang Schukrafft; assistant director, Petra Erler; production manager, Martin Rohrbeck. Reviewed at Berlin Film Festival (competing), Feb. 17, 1993. Running time: **90 MIN.**
Rudi Kipp . . . . Joachim Król
Most Kipp . . . . Horst Krause
Viktor . . . . . . Konstantin Kotljarov
Nadine . . . . Sophie Rois
Police Chief . . . . . . Heinrich Giskes

Director Detlev Buck scored a local hit with his 1991 thriller "Karniggels," and looks to top it with his new road comedy-farce. "No More Mr. Nice Guy" had German members of the audience rolling in the aisles when it unspooled competitively at the Berlin fest. However, non-Germans didn't entirely get the joke, so despite the canny English title (the German title translates as "We Know Other Ways . . . "), pic might not find so many nice guys in offshore market.

Buck is poking fun at the attitudes of ex-West Germans to their new ex-Communist compatriots, and he socks his points through a crazy trip taken by two illiterate brothers who set out in an old truck to claim property their grandmother left them near the Russian border.

Rudi (Joachim Król) has spent years in a mental home, but always dresses in a natty, if old, suit, and his head is crammed with useless information he doesn't really understand. His brother, by contrast, is a beefy bruiser. Early on, they're joined by Viktor (Konstantin Kotljarov), a Red Army deserter with a Kalashnikov who just wants to get home to Russia, but can't speak a word of German.

Before long, they are accosted by a ragged hoodlums, but drive them off, thanks to Viktor and his gun. When two of the hoods die as a result, an ambitious local police chief starts a manhunt.

The familiar fugitive formula is reworked for humor at the expense of police, real estate agents, car salesmen, funeral directors, lonely hausfraus, et al. until the trio finally gets to their destination and a droll finale.

Unfortunately, much of the satire was lost on non-German aud members. Despite this, pic is a breezy, enjoyable jape, briskly handled and confidently acted. It should pull in plenty of marks at the local box office, but was an unlikely festival selection.

— *David Stratton*

SABABU
(THE CAUSE)
(BURKINA FASO)

A Miyougou Films production. (Intl. sales: Atriascop, Paris.) Produced, directed, written by Nissi Joanny Traore. Camera (color), Nara Keokosal; editor, Marie-Jeanne Kanyala; music, Ray Lema; sound, Issa Traore, Antoine Gueben. Reviewed at Berlin Film Festival (Forum section), Feb. 13, 1993. Running time: **88 MIN.**
With: Rasmene Ouedraogo, Kalilou Outtara, Hamarlo Nombre.
(Dioula and French soundtrack)

A slim but watchable look at social forces in a small African village when a stranger is found murdered, "Sababu" is primarily of interest to specialized fests and webs.

Set in the early '60s in Burkina Faso, in West Africa, story opens with the discovery of a visiting peddler found dead in an alley. While the authorities try standard procedures to uncover the murderer, the villagers adopt age-old methods, finally arresting and killing the guilty party. Woven into the tale is a parallel thread of the village chief sending his nephew on an initiation trek, the purpose of which only becomes clear at the end.

First feature of Burkinabé helmer Nissi Joanny Traore spreads its material pretty thin, and is slow to lay all its cards on the table. But though leisurely, pic is never boring, thanks to an interesting spread of characters, accomplished location lensing, and a lively ethnic score, of which more in the middle would have helped. Performances are naturalistic throughout.

— *Derek Elley*

March 15, 1993

A FAR OFF PLACE

A Buena Vista release of a Walt Disney Pictures/Amblin Entertainment presentation in association with Touchwood Pacific Partners I. Executive producers, Kathleen Kennedy, Frank Marshall, Gerald R. Molen. Produced by Eva Monley, Elaine Sperber. Directed by Mikael Salomon. Screenplay, Robert Caswell, Jonathan Hensleigh, Sally Robinson, from Laurens van der Post's books "A Story Like the Wind" and "A Far Off Place." Camera (Rank Film Labs color; Technicolor prints), Juan Ruiz-Anchia; editor, Ray Lovejoy; music, James Horner; production design, Gemma Jackson; art direction, Carine Tredgold, Jonathan McKinstry; set decoration, Ian White; costume design, Rosemary Burrows; sound (Dolby), Colin Charles; co-producer, William W. Wilson III; assistant director, Michael Zimbrich; casting, Shari Rhodes, Sally Stiner. Reviewed at Avco Cinema Center, L.A., March 8, 1993. MPAA Rating: PG. Running time: **105 MIN.**

Nonnie Parker	Reese Witherspoon
Harry Winslow	Ethan Randall
John Ricketts	Jack Thompson
Xhabbo	Sarel Bok
Col. Mopani Theron	Maximilian Schell
Paul Parker	Robert Burke
Elizabeth Parker	Patricia Kalember
John Winslow	Daniel Gerroll

This leisurely paced adventure is probably a better African travelogue than a movie, but it still delivers as a coming-of-age yarn that should hold the attention of kids and patient adults. Paired with a new "Roger Rabbit" short, the pic should poach the same aud as Disney's "Homeward Bound," and more spacing from its sister release might have helped.

Pic is similar thematically to Nicolas Roeg's 1971 "Walkabout,"set in the Australian outback. The action here focuses on two teens in Africa, suddenly orphaned when poachers kill their parents, journeying across the desert with the help of a Bushman who spouts "Kung Fu"-style homilies and may or may not possess mystical powers.

In not-so-hot pursuit are the poachers, led by an erstwhile family friend (Jack Thompson), while the kids seek to hook up with the grizzled Mopani (Maximilian Schell, in what amounts to a cameo), an adventurer who believes in shooting poachers first and asking questions later.

Nothing is much of a mystery in this updated adaptation of two books by Laurens van der Post, except perhaps how long it will take to cross the desert (answer: too long) and when the kids — an initially snotty New York boy (Ethan Randall) and a raised-in-the-wilderness, highly self-sufficient girl (Reese Witherspoon) — will break down and acknowledge their mutual affection.

Pushing that relationship along is Xhabbo, played sweetly by Sarel Bok, in a much more stately presentation of Bushmen than the popular but broadly comic "The Gods Must Be Crazy." Even so, "Far" mines some of the same humor, such as Xhabbo's hysterical reaction to the idea of TV.

Director Mikael Salomon shows off plenty of sweeping vistas but follows a too-leisurely path toward the final confrontation, though eliciting strong performances from his likable leads.

The PG-rated movie is stronger than standard kid fare in its depiction of the slaughter of the elephants and of the kids' parents, though the latter is no more traumatic than in "Bambi" and the kids deal with their anguish relatively quickly.

Technical credits are solid, with special kudos to cinematographer Juan Ruiz-Anchia, capturing all the usual Amblin-style over-the-moon flourishes.

The latest "Roger Rabbit" short, "Trail Mix-Up," offers the usual assault of sight gags at such a manic pace it makes the average "Looney Toon" seem sedate. The barrage is so unrelenting that more becomes less, but the crisply animated production does offer a few extremely clever moments. — *Brian Lowry*

SAVIORS OF THE FOREST
(DOCU)

A Camera Guys production. Executive producer, Todd Darling. Co-executive producer, Richard Hassen. Produced by Bill Day, Terry Schwartz. Directed by Day. Written by Schwartz. Camera (color); editors, Day, Schwartz. Reviewed at Sundance Film Festival, Park City, Utah, Jan. 27, 1993. Running time: **75 MIN.**

Inspired by Michael Moore's "Roger and Me," "Saviors of the Forest" provides an original, humorous look at the issue of rainforest destruction. Docu's fresh p.o.v. and amusing insights about ecology and filmmaking could make it a favorite in the international fest and docu circuits.

Bill Day and Terry Schwartz, self-styled "video warriors" known as "The Camera Guys," find themselves on the run from ABC News for copyright infringement after recycling the network's footage for their own environmental program. They therefore gladly accept an offer to go to Ecuador to make a film that will save the country's rainforest, only to learn that the issue is more complicated than it appears on the surface.

Most of this unorthodox film details the actions of some foreign ecologists who plan to use a computer program to number the trees, then determine how many and which ones will be selectively harvested.

Charged with humor, "Saviors of the Forest" lacks the sermonizing self-importance of other ecological docus. And while always diverting, it does capture some of the paradoxes involved in saving tropical foests around the world. Indeed, it is ironic that major consumers of rainforest plywood are Hollywood studios, which use it to build sets, including those of ecologically correct films.

Irreverent docu does take sides. In fact, it shows sympathy for the "colonos," local residents who cut trees and burn them because they need the land for grazing. As Day and Schwartz get to know the subject, they find there are no easy targets or easily identifiable villains.

Docu's raw quality and modest tech credits are congruent with its goal and suits docu's format as a diary of two wacky filmmakers in search of "something meaningful" to shoot.
— *Emanuel Levy*

MENSONGE
(LIE)
(FRENCH)

An AMLF release of a Les Films Alain Sarde/Cuel Lavalette Prods./France-3 co-production with the participation of Canal Plus/the CNC/Procirep. Produced by François Cuel. Directed by François Margolin. Screenplay, Denis Saada, Margolin. Camera (color), Caroline Champetier; editors, Martine Giordano, Catherine Schwartz; set design, Julie Sfez; costumes, Catherine Meurisse; sound, Jean-Jacques Ferran, Gerard Rousseau. Reviewed at Club de l'Etoile screening room, Paris, Jan. 14, 1993. Running time: **88 MIN.**

Emma	Nathalie Baye
Charles	Didier Sandre
Louise	Hélène Lapiower
Louis	Marc Citti
Rozenberg	Dominique Besnehard
Gégé	Christophe Bourseiller
Grandfather	Louis Ducreux

Although "Mensonge" doesn't avoid all of the pitfalls of a first film, François Margolin's involving story of a woman who discovers she's both pregnant and HIV positive intelligently treats the specter of AIDS and the issue of trust in an established couple. Fests and tube exposure beckon.

Parisian journalists Emma (Nathalie Baye) and Charles (Didier Sandre) have lived together for 10 years, have an 8-year-old son and have considered having another child. When Baye's lab test comes back "positive" with the double-whammy of pregnancy and HIV, she discovers that her best b.f. is a jerk, her closest male friend has made some crucial omissions, and that Sandre, a daring political reporter, is also a coward living a double life.

We're shown just enough of Baye before the ax falls to conclude that she's a reasonably carefree writer, spouse and mom. Her shock and anger at the news verge on unconvincing in early telephone scenes that require the thesp to deal with disembodied voices and an answering machine, but face-to-face scenes are good and sometimes gripping.

A monogamous non-drug-user who's never had a blood transfusion, Baye suspects Sandre, off on a dangerous reporting assignment. She goes through his address book and, starting on Christmas Eve, calls every woman in it to demand, point-blank, "How long have you been sleeping with Charles?" Obsessed with finding out how she got infected, Baye runs the gamut from passion to despair and her detective work sports elements of black humor.

Baye and Sandre shine in crucial scenes in which they begin to deal with their radically changed situation. Hélène Lapiower is very good as the live-in babysitter who shares Baye's secret.

Use of Paris is gritty and unromantic although lensing rarely exceeds okay.

Co-scripter Saada is a psychiatrist who specializes in HIV and AIDS patients; for educational purposes, pic crams in more variables and reactions than seems likely to befall just two people. With a background in humanitarian docus and a prize-winning short to his credit, Margolin's fiction debut takes a dramatically rich, non-morbid approach.

Pic marks the final screen appearance by versatile elderly thesp Louis Ducreux, who died in December. — *Lisa Nesselson*

March 15, 1993 (Cont.)

BEST OF THE BEST II

A 20th Century Fox release, presented by the Movie Group. Executive producers, Frank Giustra, Peter E. Strauss. Produced by Strauss, Phillip Rhee. Directed by Robert Radler. Screenplay, Max Strom, John Allen Nelson, from characters created by Paul Levine. Camera (Deluxe color), Fred Tammes; editor, Bert Lovitt; music, David Michael Frank; sound (Dolby), Kim Ornitz; production design, Gary Frutkoff; co-producers, Marlon Staggs, Deborah Scott; production manager, Steve Brown; 2nd-unit camera, Jerry Watson; stunt coordinator, Simon Rhee; casting, Eliza Rayfiel, Maureen A. Arata. Reviewed at Manhattan 2 theater, N.Y., March 5, 1993. MPAA Rating: R. Running time: **100 MIN.**

Alex Grady	Eric Roberts
Tommy Lee	Phillip Rhee
Travis Brickley	Christopher Penn
Walter Grady	Edan Gross
Brakus	Ralph Moeller
Sue	Meg Foster
James	Sonny Landham
Weldon	Wayne Newton
Grandma	Betty Carvalho
Dae Han	Simon Rhee
Greta	Claire Stansfield

A corny, below-standard martial arts pic, this sequel will barely keep Fox staffers busy for a couple of weeks. Lacking marquee bait or excitement, it's strictly for ancillary markets.

Pic is unusual as a major distrib release of a sequel to an indie pic. The first edition was a 1989 Taurus Entertainment release that did so-so at the b.o. It at least had a point, limning the heroic adventures of the national karate team. Sequel is merely a vanity film showcasing the martial arts skills of producer Phillip Rhee. He and pal Eric Roberts operate a karate school in Las Vegas but shift into vengeance mode when their third partner, Chris Penn, is murdered in an illegal gladiatorial match held at the Coliseum, heavy Ralph Moeller's secret nightspot.

With Roberts' young son Edan Gross in tow, the deadly dull duo hide out from the gun-wielding heavies at an American Indian ranch owned by the crusty woman who raised Rhee. Her son, Sonny Landham, has become a drunk after having been whupped by Moeller and agrees to train our heroes. Of course, Landham is murdered by Moeller's henchmen to increase the spirit of vengeance.

Pic takes forever to get to what the fans paid for: some OK prelim bouts in the final reel in which Rhee struts his stuff.

Unlike the original, film has an unfortunate vigilante mentality with no police or authorities ever appearing. Instead, Rhee violates the good guy rule and kills Moeller ruthlessly to finish the pic.

Rhee obviously is a pro but lacks the personality of a screen hero, while Roberts is stuck in a role that's many steps down from his promising early roles. Penn is miscast as a supposed champion who's apparently never heard the word conditioning.

Film looks and plays like a drive-in picture of 20 years ago, only less fun. — *Lawrence Cohn*

NEL CONTINENTE NERO
(ON THE DARK CONTINENT, a.k.a THE ITALIANS)
(ITALIAN)

A Penta Distribuzione release of a Trio Cinema/Penta Film co-production. Produced by Maurizio Tedesco, Mario and Vittorio Cecchi Gori. Directed by Marco Risi. Screenplay, Risi, Tedesco, Andrea Purgatori. Camera (color) Mauro Marchetti; editor, Franco Fraticelli; music, Manuel De Sica; art direction, Davide Bassan; costumes, Roberta Guidi Di Bagno. Reviewed at Fiamma Cinema, Rome, Jan. 4, 1993. (In Palm Springs Intl. Film Festival.) Running time: **122 MIN.**

Fulvio Colombo	Diego Abatantuono
Alessandro Benini	Corso Salani
Anna	Anna Falchi
Monsignor	Ivo Garrani
Don Secondino	Tony Sperandeo
Sparafico	Gianfranco Barra

Also with: Maurizio Mattioli, Nanni Tamma, Bernard Chaperon, Cinzia Monreale, Luigi Burruano.

Marco Risi is a compelling director of social dramas but seems ill at ease in "Nel Continente Nero," a comedy of bad manners that ribs the ugly Italian strutting around Africa. A weird hybrid of journalism and comedy, the film did good biz domestically but offshore auds may get less of a kick out of the film's setting.

Malindi, Kenya, on the Indian Ocean, is famous as a hangout for rich and spoiled Italians, particularly swinging politicians on vacation. "Nel Continente Nero" has two main selling points —it's the first picture to spoof the Malindi beach scene; and it pairs comic Diego Abatantuono and ernestly straight Corso Salani as friendly enemies.

Salani is a hot young sales exec who learns, in a riotous opening, that his long-lost father has just died and left him property in Africa. His journey to claim his "fortune" — he's deprived of his passport and thrown into jail practically on arrival as dad left no property, just heavy debts — puts him at the mercy of Abatantuono, a small-time boss.

Abatantuono is terrifically cast — in dark glasses and black shirt, he strongly suggests an unscrupulous soldier of fortune from the fascist period. He's the key to the parallel Risi draws between fascist colonialism and crass, contemporary tourism spiked with racist condescension. He does have a good side: He turns Salani on to the glories of nature in some breathtaking scenery. His bad side is violence. This ambuiguity, along with Abatantuono's intelligent perf, gives the character unexpected depth. Unfortunately he meets a comic-strip end, leaving Salani to return to Italy a little bit wiser.

Though the story is laden with spoof potential that would have delighted his father, Dino, Marco Risi is strangely reluctant to run with it. Reliable technical work underlines the exotic African attractions. — *Deborah Young*

FIRE IN THE SKY

A Paramount Pictures release of a Joe Wizan/Todd Black production. Executive producer, Wolfgang Glattes. Produced by Wizan, Black. Directed by Robert Lieberman. Screenplay, Tracy Tormé, from Travis Walton's book "The Walton Experience." Camera (Panavision, Deluxe color), Bill Pope; editor, Steve Mirkovich; music, Mark Isham; sound (Dolby), Henry Garfield, production design, Laurence Bennett; art direction, Mark W. Mansbridge; set decoration, Daniel L. May; costume design, Joe I. Tompkins; co-producers, Robert Strauss, Tormé, Nilo Rodis-Jamero; production manager, Glattes; assistant director, J. Michael Haynie; special visual effects, Industrial Light & Magic, supervisor, Michael Owens; stunt coordinator, Chuck Waters; additional editor, Stephen E. Rivkin; casting, Rick Pagano, Sharon Bialy, Debi Manwiller. Reviewed at Loews N.Y. Twin theater, N.Y., March 11, 1993. MPAA Rating: PG-13. Running time: **107 MIN.**

Travis Walton	D.B. Sweeney
Mike Rogers	Robert Patrick
Allan Dallis	Craig Sheffer
David Whitlock	Peter Berg
Sheriff Watters	James Garner
Greg Hayes	Henry Thomas
Bobby Cogdill	Bradley Gregg
Blake Davis	Noble Willingham
Katie Rogers	Kathleen Wilhoite
Dana Rogers	Georgia Emelin
Dan Walton	Scott MacDonald
Cyrus Gilson	Wayne Grace

A truly harrowing sequence in the final reel fails to save "Fire in the Sky," an otherwise prosaic approach to the gee-whiz genre of UFO aliens snatching a human specimen for examination. This unappealing pic is likely attract only a few curiosity seekers.

Supposedly "based on a true story," shaggy-dog film concerns ordinary, uninteresting people who happen to be enmeshed in an extraordinary phenomenon by chance. That was the starting point for Steven Spielberg's "Close Encounters of the Third Kind," but that 1977 picture exhibited the good sense to emphasize the fantastic rather than the boring aspects of everyday life (per Hitchcock's famous dictum). D.B. Sweeney portrays the real-life Travis Walton, an Arizona lumberjack upon whose book this is based. Out driving with five co-workers one night, he's zapped by a bright light from a ship hovering in the sky and left for dead by his pals. An extremely tedious probe of Sweeney's disappearance is conducted by visiting lawman James Garner, with nasty co-worker Craig Sheffer a prime suspect in what Garner views as a homicide.

Five days after being taken, Sweeney pops up naked in the rain and utterly traumatized. Eventually he flashbacks to the horrors experienced in the aliens' ship, where he awakes in a cocoon, floats weightless clutching an umbilical rope, and is subjected to a grueling physical exam and probing that rivals Laurence Olivier's dental torture of Dustin Hoffman in "Marathon Man" for gruesomeness. If only the preamble had matched this payoff, director Robert Lieberman would have had a viable picture.

Unfortunately, scripter Tracy Tormé (son of singer Mel) has no ear for the way people speak, delivering corny dialogue that sounds like a pastiche of ancient B-movie cliches.

Technical contributions are okay for this modestly budgeted ($15 million) effort, though loud music and sound effects are not sufficient to sustain one's attention during the 90 minutes of preliminaries. —*Lawrence Cohn*

EARTH AND THE AMERICAN DREAM
(DOCU)

An HBO presentation of a Couturie Co. production produced in association with the BBC. Executive producer, Cis Wilson. Produced by Bill Couturie, Janet Mercer. Directed by Couturie. Written by Ken Richards, Couturie; editor, Gary Weimberg; music, Todd Boekelheide; associate producer, Richards. Reviewed at Sundance Film Festival, Park City, Utah, Jan. 26, 1993. Running time: **78 MIN.**

March 15, 1993 (Cont.)

Readings by: Zalami Zahir, Frank Sotonoma Salseda, J.J. Paladino, Mel Gibson, E.G. Marshall, Jeremy Irons, Karl Malden, Joe Paulino, Dennis Weaver, Alec Baldwin, Anthony Hopkins, Gene Hackman, Jack Lemmon, Mary Steenburgen, Lee Grant, Jeffrey De Munn, Harrison Ford, Peter Coyote, Rod Steiger, James Caan, Vince Bointy, Jim Elk, Ed Asner, Robert Hegyes, Sam Waterston, Ed Begley Jr., Diana Salinger, Christopher Reeve, Bette Midler, Don West, Lloyd Bridges, Ned Beatty, Tom Everett, Glenn Shadix, Dustin Hoffman, Michael Keaton, David Ogden Stiers, Ellen Burstyn, Haing S. Ngor, François Marthouret, Floyd Red Crow Westerman, Graham Green.

Granola-eating tree-huggers of all persuasions will chant mantras of praise for "Earth and the American Dream," an environmental tract that could not be more one-sided if Edward Abbey had written the script. On the other hand, many viewers instinctively sympathetic to the idea that Earth's resources have been plundered beyond necessity could easily be turned off by award-winning filmmaker Bill Couturie's pile-driving style and unwavering insistence that history since 1492 has consisted of nothing but greedy, rapacious destruction.

Infinitely promotable as "important" and will no doubt be swallowed whole by emotional youth and easily outraged political types. But you don't have to be right-wing or pro-big business to find fault with this simplistic propaganda piece.

With a cascade of archival and originally shot footage conveying images of startling beauty and depressing devastation, film makes the basic argument that the environment and our planet's well-being have always taken a back seat to progress and profit, at least where the United States and its capitalistic leaders have been concerned.

To support their point, Couturie and co-writer Ken Richards lay in dozens of pertinent quotes from historical figures famous and unknown, ranging from the predictable Manifest Destiny bellowings of 19th century politicians to surprisingly foresightful ecological observations by George Washington. As in Couturie's earlier "Dear America: Letters Home From Vietnam," an all-star cast recites these utterances, yielding mixed results but providing a selling point.

The overriding problem is that, as posited by the film, all "progress" is, by definition, so evil, insidious, monstrous and vile that one begins to feel all white people of European descent should just kill themselves out of shame and that the world would be better off if human beings just didn't inhabit it.

Very well made on a technical level, "Earth and the American Dream" may be the last word in political correctness, but it's also the ultimate in manipulative filmmaking. — *Todd McCarthy*

BERLIN FEST

DE DRIE BESTE DINGEN IN HET LEVEN
(THE THREE BEST THINGS IN LIFE)
(DUTCH)

A Studio Nieuwe Gronden/NOS Televisie production. (Intl. sales: Studio Nieuwe Gronden, Amsterdam.) Produced by René Scholten. Directed, written by Ger Poppelaars. Camera (Eastmancolor), Lex Wertwijn; editor, Wim Louwrier; music, Henny Vrienten; art direction, Gert Brinkers; costume design, Linda Bogers; sound, Alex Booy; assistant director, Dan Wallagh; line producer, Will Koopman. Reviewed at Berlin Film Festival (Panorama section), Feb. 18, 1993. Running time: **100 MIN.**
Sacha van Eden . . . . Loes Wouterson
Caspar . . . . Victor Löw
Maarten . . . . Jack Wouterse
Otto . . . . Gerard Thoolen
Thomas . . . Gijs Scholten van Aschat
Jawek Vitebsk . . . .
. . . . Michel van Dousselaere
Ben de Kadt . . . . . . Pierre Bokma

"The Three Best Things" is an enjoyable Dutch comedy that deserves wider exposure than it will probably get. Short of hooks for the arthouse circuit, this romantic item about a femme violinist and two dropouts in Amsterdam is likely to get tube dates at best. Remade Stateside with a name cast, the offbeat pic could have real b.o. potential.

Sacha (Loes Wouterson) is a 25-year-old violinist who journeys to Amsterdam to break the news of her pregnancy to b.f. Ben (Pierre Bokma). On the way she meets a strange Czech (Michel van Dousselaere) who asks her to look after a cardboard box with a live duck inside. Ben not at home, mugged of her money, Sacha tries to locate the Czech and soon finds herself pursued by two heavies after the box. She's rescued by Caspar (Victor Löw), a likable bum who shares a trailer with Maarten (Jack Wouterse). Both have their eyes on her expensive violin.

That's only the start of an off-center love story that doesn't plumb any depths but proves immensely winning along the way. As the chic violinist, Wouterson is photogenic and feisty, well matched by the relaxed Löw and Wouterse as the jazz-loving dropouts. Bit parts are well cast.

It all gets glossy mounting by writer-director Ger Poppelaars, his feature debut after a series of art docus. For the record, the "Three Best Things in Life," per the two bums, are jazz, a pizza in Rome, and a turtle in a Dutch aquarium. — *Derek Elley*

SANKOFA
(U.S.-GERMAN-GHANIAN-BURKINA FASO)

A Negod Gwad Prods. (Washington, D.C.)/NDR and WDR (Germany)/National Commission on Culture (Accra)/DiProCi (Burkina Faso) co-production. Produced, directed, written, edited by Haile Gerima. Camera (color), Agustin Cubano; music, David J. White; production design, Kerry Marshall; costumes, Tracey White; co-producer, Shirikiana Aina; production manager, Charles Butler Knuckles; assistant director, Andrew Millington. Reviewed at Berlin Film Festival (competing), Feb. 19, 1993. Running time: **124 MIN.**
Mona/Shola . . . Oyafunmike Ogunlano
Nunu . . . . Alexandra Duah
Joe . . . . Kofi Ghanaba
Plantation Manager . . . . Nick Medley
Shanho . . . . Mutabaraku

Ethiopian-born, U.S.-based filmmaker Haile Gerima, whose "Harvest: 3,000 Years" played the fest circuit in the mid-'70s, has been planning "Sankofa" for years. Pic emerges as an ambitious attack on the old evil of slavery, and a call for black people worldwide to "rise up and tell your stories," per the opening narration. Film's length and repetitiveness unfortunately mitigate against an otherwise impressive indie effort.

It opens strikingly with tourists at an ancient fort on the coast of Ghana being confronted by Sankofa, an old mystic claiming contact with the spirits (in the Akan language, "sankofa" means "to return to one's past, to rescue it from oblivion, and to turn towards the future.")

Mona, an African-American model doing a photo shoot on the spot, becomes intrigued by the old man. She follows him and, in an impressive coup on the part of Gerima, suddenly finds herself in the past, the victim of slavers.

In a scene of sheer horror, she is stripped, manacled and branded.

The action now shifts to a sugar plantation in America, where Mona, now called Shola, is a house servant. She befriends the kindly Nunu (Alexandra Duah) and falls in love with the half-caste Joe (Kofi Ghanaba), whose black mother had been raped by a white man and who was raised by a fanatical priest. She also meets Shango (Mutabaraku), a visionary revolutionary leader.

There are no prizes for guessing a slave revolt climax before the film returns to the present to reveal the effect this vision has had on Mona. The trouble is that Gerima seems to have been reluctant to dispense with any of his material. After the clever opening, there are no surprises. Attacks on the Catholic church and whites in general are valid in this context, but more subtlety would have helped.

Thesping is natural and unaffected but another problem is the very thick accents of some of the actors, especially Mutabaraku's, whose Shango is quite incomprehensible; his character should be revoiced or subtitled.

On the plus side is a vibrantly exciting music score by David J. White, and the bold and inspiring concept. There's no doubt that "Sankofa" is a film a lot of people will enjoy, and, with careful pruning and other postproduction tinkering, it can be greatly enhanced. — *David Stratton*

YUME NO ONNA
(YEARNING)
(JAPANESE-B&W)

A Shochiku Co./Saison Group production. (Intl. sales: Shochiku, Tokyo.) Produced by Shigehiro Nakagawa, Toshiaki Nakazawa. Directed by Tamasaburo Bando. Screenplay, Genki Yoshimura, Taeko Sakurai, Masafumi Saito, from Mantaro Kubota's play based on Kafu Nagai's novel. Camera (B&W), Mutsuo Naganuma; editors, Akira Suzuki, Yoshiyuki Okuhara; music, Meisho Tosha, Etsugoro Kineya; art direction, Takeo Kimura; sound (Dolby), Ichiro Tsujii. Reviewed at Berlin Film Festival (competing), Feb. 19, 1993. Running time: **98 MIN.**
Onami ("Kaede") . . Sayuri Yoshinaga
Otabe . . . . . . Toshiyuki Nagashima
Osawa . . . . Sumie Sasaki
Kaede II . . . . Kyoko Kataoka
Guest at pier . . . . . Hiroyuki Nagato
Brothel owner . . Katsuhiko Watabiki
Chief clerk . . . . . Mutsuhiro Toura
Kamigo . . . . Shoji Yasui
Omatsu . . . . Kirin Kiki

"Yearning" is an exquisite, but empty, vase. This turn-of-the-century drama about the

March 15, 1993 (Cont.)

travails of an iron-willed courtesan may fool festgoers with its arty, monochrome look and studied perfs but will prove a snooze for others. TV looks like its most profitable outlet.

Onami (Sayuri Yoshinaga) is supporting her impoverished family by working at a riverside brothel in Tokyo. Under the name Kaede, she meets merchant Otabe (Toshiyuki Nagashima), who's prepared to buy out her contract at any cost.

Because her daughter is being mistreated by foster parents, Onami backs out of marrying Otabe at the last moment, causing him to commit suicide and her to hit the bottle. With the help of two femme servants, Onami finally puts her life back in order, attracting a new suitor, the wealthy Kamigo (Shoji Yasui), who's not put off by her rep.

Helmer Tamasaburo Bando, a female impersonator in *kabuki* theater who has played the Onami role himself, seems keen to create a perfect replica of period dramas by the great names of Japanese cinema. Topnotch black and white lensing by Mutsuo Naganuma is a major asset here, and there are neat devices like the story's circular construction underlined by a mirror-image opening and close.

The problem is that Bando's movie has little to offer except carefully crafted artifice. Beautiful but blank playing by Yoshinaga ("The Makioka Sisters") doesn't give the audience any help in solving the riddle of the courtesan's personality. Other perfs are standard for such fare.

Technically flawless, choice costume and set design provide a beautiful frame for a whole lot of nothing. Japanese title is "Woman of Dreams." —*Derek Elley*

CH'ING SHAONIEN NA CHA
(REBELS OF THE NEON GOD)
(TAIWAN-HONG KONG)

A Central Motion Picture Corp./ Golden Harvest Motion Picture Co. production. (Intl. sales: Anthex, Amsterdam/ Berlin.) Produced by Jiang Feng-chyi. Directed, written by Tsai Ming-liang. Camera (color), Liao Pen-jung; editor, Wang Chyi-yang; music, Huang Shu-chun; art director, Lee Pao-ling; costume design, Chen Ying-hui; sound, Hu Ting-yi; line producer, Hsü Li-kong. Reviewed at Berlin Film Festival (Panorama section), Feb. 19, 1993. Running time: **106 MIN.**

With: Lee Kang-sheng, Chen Chao-jun, Jen Chang-bin, Wang Yü-wen, Miao Tien, Lu Hsiao-lin.
(Mandarin and Hokkien soundtrack)

A neatly constructed, if distanced, drama of bored Taiwan youth, "Rebels of the Neon God" should build a solid rep at festivals and Asian weeks. But this first feature by young legit and TV director Tsai Ming-liang lacks a strong enough personality to arc over into much arthouse playoff.

Less nihilistic and self-conscious than the gun-toting, similarly themed "Dust of Angels" (also Taiwanese), Tsai's pic boasts an appealing strain of humor. Homoerotic undercurrents, too, are there for the taking. All that's missing is real dramatic clout.

Teen quartet comprises Hsiao Kang, a cab-driver's son who's being pushed to study by his parents; Ah-tzu and his brother Ah-bing, both into smashing telephone boxes and hocking stolen computer circuit boards; and Ah-kuei, Ah-tzu's g.f. who works at a roller-skating rink.

The lives of these bored young rebels start to connect when Hsiao Kang recognizes Ah-tzu as the biker who smashed his dad's cab one day. Unbeknownst to his parents, Hsiao Kang quits his university-entrance crammer and sets out to get his revenge, with bloody results.

The pic contains plenty of small incident, and some clever plotting in the latter stages. Ironic humor peeks through in running jokes like Ah-tzu's permanently flooded apartment and the elevator that always stops at the (supposedly haunted) fourth floor.

But Tsai's failure to build any major emotional bridges between characters and audience makes the final reel light on impact, despite easy playing by the principals (all novices, apart from Wang Yü-wen as the girl), and fluid direction. Veteran Miao Tien adds dramatic ballast as Hsiao Kang's bemused father.

Atmospheric lensing of downtown Taipei's demimonde of vid arcades and small hotels, and a moody bass guitar score by Huang Shu-chun, are both pluses. Pic did low-voltage business on local release last November. Chinese title means "Teenage Na Cha," a reference to the mythical pesky warrior with whom Hsiao Kang identifies.
—*Derek Elley*

MADAME L'EAU
(MADAM WATER)
(DUTCH-FRENCH-DOCU)

An NFI Prods. (Hilversum)/Sodaperaga (Paris) co-production, in association with BBC Television and the Comité du Film Ethnographique (Paris). Produced by Menno van der Molen. Directed by Jean Rouch. Screenplay, Rouch, Philo Bregstein. Camera, Rouch; editor, Françoise Beloux; music, Tallou Mouzourane; sound, Moussa Hamidou, Bert van den Dungen; co-producers, Guy Seligmann, André Singer. Reviewed at Berlin Film Festival (Forum section), Feb. 12, 1993. Running time: **127 MIN.**
With: Damouré Zica, Lam Ibrahim Dia, Tallou Mouzourane, Wineke Onstwedder.

Veteran ethnographic filmmaker Jean Rouch, now 76, has brought the Africa he loves to Europe in "Madam Water," a staged documentary that follows three men from Niger on a trip to the Netherlands to explore the ways of establishing windmills to pump water in their dry country.

The opening scenes are shot in Niger at the surgery of a doctor, Damouré Zika, the leader of the three. He and friends Lam Ibrahim Dia and Tallou Mouzourane ponder the fact that their village's river is now a dried-up bed of sand. They decide to go to Holland and seek advice on irrigation. What follows is a leisurely odyssey as the three and a female Dutch government guide, Wineke Onstwedder, wend their way around the country looking at windmills that could be adapted to conditions in Niger.

Rouch handles the material in the loosest possible way, filming improvised conversations at great length and allowing many diversions from the main theme. The result is an amiable, ambling film that lacks energy and is far too long, but with a gentle appreciation for the three Africans as they travel the Dutch landscape.
— *David Stratton*

RICHTING ENGELAND
(HEADING FOR ENGLAND)
(DUTCH)

A Bergen (Amsterdam)/NCRV (Hilversum) co-production. (Intl. sales: Bergen, Amsterdam.) Produced by Hans de Weers, Hans de Wolf, Harry Hemink. Directed by André van Duren. Screenplay, Peter van Gestel, Willem Wilmink. Camera (Eastmancolor), Theo Bierkens; editor, Rob Hakhoff; music, Mark van Platen; sound, Victor Dekker; production designer, Dirk Debou. Reviewed at Berlin Film Festival (Panorama section), Feb. 15, 1993. Running time: **62 MIN.**

Hans	Geert Lageveen
Hans's father	Peter Faber
Sonja	Maike Meyer
English teacher	Trins Snijders
Art teacher	Huib Broos
Hans's mother	Rick Nicolet
German teacher	Wim van de Grijn
Narrator	Gerard Thoolen

Winner of the Critics Prize at the 1992 Dutch Film Days, "Heading for England" is a pretentious amalgam of overdramatized, distracting voiceover, music, filters and choreographed actors that would seem to have little or no arthouse potential.

Set in provincial Holland in the '50s, film focuses on the student Hans (uninspiringly played by Geert Lageveen) who observes such dark tragedies as the last days of a lonely old teacher and a "Star is Born"-style suicide: A tranvestite barber, after being exposed by some students and paralyzing one of them with a shotgun, walks into the sea "heading for England."

When pic switches gears and moves into the Oedipal conflict between the bright Hans and his pompous but uneducated father (Peter Faber, a Max von Sydow clone), who works at the local factory, an already confusing narrative voice becomes even murkier; viewer isn't clear if he's hearing Hans in his old age or his father. Their main point of contention is whether or not Hans will attend university.

This weak plot device fails to give the pic momentum, for which helmer compensates by such outrageous scenes as father screaming at the factory complex itself and a flashback, after the father's death, of him carrying Hans off into the sea, apparently heading for England himself.
— *Howard Feinstein*

March 15, 1993 (Cont.)

SAY A LITTLE PRAYER
(AUSTRALIAN)

A Flying Films production, in association with Australian Film Finance. (Intl. sales: Beyond Films.) Executive producer, Jacki Mann. Produced by Carol Hughes. Directed, written by Richard Lowenstein, from Robin Klein's "Came Back To Show You I Could Fly." Camera (Eastmancolor), Graeme Wood; editor, Jill Bilcock; production design, Chris Kennedy; sound, Lloyd Carrick; production manager, Catherine "Tatts" Bishop; assistant director, Toby Pease; casting, Greg Apps. Reviewed at Berlin Film Festival (Panorama section), Feb. 17, 1993. Running time: **97 MIN.**
Seymour . . . . Sudi de Winter
Angie . . . . Fiona Ruttelle
Thelma . . . . Lynn Murphy
Seymour's mother . . Mickey Camilleri
Lynne . . . . Rebecca Smart
Mrs. Easterbrook . . . . Jill Forster
Mr. Easterbrook . . . . . Roger Neave
Op Shop Lady . . . . . Phyll Bartlett
Nursery manager . . Ben Mendelsohn

A curiously touching "odd couple" movie, "Say a Little Prayer" could find an appreciative audience with careful handling. Admirers of director Richard Lowenstein, who made the docudrama "Strikebound" and the lacerating antidrug pic "Dogs In Space," will find him in gentler mood this time.

Set in Melbourne, the film is seen entirely from the perspective of Seymour (Sudi de Winter), an 11-year-old boy who is spending a lonely summer. His parents are separated, and he's been palmed off on a demanding relative. He dreams of escape. That's when he stumbles into Angie (Fiona Ruttelle), a 20-year-old woman living a hippy existence in a filthy house.

Audiences will instantly grasp that Angie is on drugs, but the innocent Seymour doesn't until near the end. He accepts her friendship with gratitude and pic revolves around this odd, strangely naive relationship.

Lowenstein based his screenplay on a well-regarded book, "Came Back To Show You I Could Fly," by Robin Klein, inspired by the author's daughter's drug addiction. Some of the director's additions aren't especially helpful; Seymour's psychedelic visions become distracting. But as long as it concentrates on the Seymour-Angie relationship, the film is very effective, thanks to refreshingly natural performances by the two screen newcomers, and situations that touchingly convey the problems of the addicted girl.

Wide-eyed Seymour tags along, enjoying her hedonism and the fact that most of the time she's willing to let him share her world. One daring, but marvelously successful sequence, again seen from the boy's rose-colored perspective, has Angie suddenly break into the title song (actually miming Aretha Franklin's definitive rendition) while passers-by and bus passengers join in. It could easily have been risible, but it works magically.

Pic builds to the point at which Angie is inevitably placed in a drug rehabilitation home, but there's an upbeat finale, which includes an odd little cameo from prominent Aussie thesp Ben Mendelsohn. The supporting cast, especially Rebecca Smart as Angie's disapproving younger sister and Jill Forster as her anguished mother, are tops.

Visually, Chris Kennedy's production design perfectly contrasts Angie's flotsam-packed home with the sterile settings of the more conventional characters, and Graeme Wood's camerawork is fine. — *David Stratton*

UDZINARTA MSE
(THE SUN OF THE WAKEFUL)
(GEORGIAN)

An Adam and Eve Studio/Gruzia Film production. Directed, written, edited by Temur Babluani. Camera (color), Viktor Andrievski, Nugzar Nozadze; music, Babluani; production design, Temur Chmaladze, Tamaz Lomia; sound, Edisher Georgadze. Reviewed at Berlin Film Festival (competing), Feb. 12, 1993. Running time: **128 MIN.**
Dr. Gela . . . . Elgudsha Burduli
Dato . . . . David Kazischvili
Agnessa . . . . Eka Saataschvili
Vantschka . . . . . . Ghivi Sicharulidze
Mother . Lija Amirdshanova-Babluani
Tamara Kldiaschvili . Flora Schedania

This is an overlong meller that uneasily mixes a gangster thriller with a more interesting saga of an eccentric medico who thinks he has a cure for cancer. Interest outside the fest circuit is likely to be subdued.

Part of the trouble is that writer-director-editor-composer Temur Babluani, artistic director of the Adam and Eve studio that produced the film, badly needed a firm producer to edit the lengthy script and keep the narrative more focused.

The film opens with promise: A little old lady, lost on a crowded city street, has forgotten her name and the people at the only address she remembers died long ago. A passing doctor, Dr. Gela (Elgudsha Burduli), takes her in. Oddly, she hardly features in the film after that.

The focus shifts partly to Gela, who, for 22 years, has been working on a cure for cancer, and his son, Dato (David Kazischvili), a member of a gang of violent bandits who's plotting revenge on a prison officer, a subplot explored at far too much length, and never very convincingly.

His father's story offers more: The obsessed medico is dismissed from position after position as he spends more and more time with his laboratory rats, and he's eventually forced to do his experiments at home, to the disgust of neighbors, who naturally don't like the idea of cancer-infected rodents on the premises.

Climax is a bizarre scene in which the doc, aided by his inexperienced son, operates on himself to remove his appendix. The result is, unsurprisingly, fatal but there's an ironic finale.

Though Burduli gives a gallant performance in his unlikely role, the supporting cast is less effective. Some of the action scenes are poorly staged, and, given the great tradition of Georgian cinema, this competing Berlin fest entry was particularly disappointing. — *David Stratton*

OP AFBETALING
(THE BETRAYED)
(DUTCH)

A Lowland Series production, in association with VPRO Television. Produced by René Seegers. Directed by Frans Weisz. Screenplay, Jan Blokker, from Simon Vestdijk's novel. Camera (color), Goert Giltay; editor, Ton Ruys; music, Theo Nijland; production design, Jaap Verburg; sound, Marcel de Hoogd; costumes, Francis Hutjers; assistant director, Fabienne Hulsebos; production manager, Milly Schloss. Reviewed at Berlin Film Festival (competing), Feb. 17, 1993. Running time: **121 MIN.**
Hendrik Grond . . . .
. . . . Gijs Scholten van Aschat
Olga Grond . . . . . Renée Soutendijk
Mien . . . . Annet Malherbe
Grewestein . . . . Coen Flink
Krynie Woudema . . . Willem Nijholt
Sjef van Relte . . Wouter Steenbergen
Inspector . . . . Johan Simons

"The Betrayed" is a somber drama of obsession and revenge that starts slowly but builds to an impressive climax. Made also as a TV miniseries (it's available in three one-hour episodes), pic is elegantly made and boasts a strong perf by Gijs Scholten van Aschat as a husband who discovers his wife has been unfaithful.

Based on a novel by Simon Vestdijk, and set in a provincial town in the '50s, the film establishes Hendrik Grond (Scholten van Ashat) as a happily married lawyer with a lovely wife (Reneé Soutendijk) and son. Returning home unexpectedly one afternoon, he discovers his wife in the arms of his senior partner, Grewestein (Coen Flink). The lovers don't see him; but the incident has changed his life, and he starts plotting his revenge.

First, he's the cause of an accident in which Olga is permanently crippled. Then he refuses to help a friend in whom she has confided; the friend is being blackmailed, but Grond accepts an assignment to work for the suspected blackmailer.

Latter runs an illegal brothel in a suburban street. Soon, Grond is a regular visitor and involved with the voluptuous Mien (Annet Malherbe). But his ultimate revenge is to murder his partner, and make the crime look like a botched robbery. By this time, director Frans Weisz is really tightening the screws and, in the film's best scene, police investigators interview the couple and reveal that the dead man had a photo of Olga in his wallet.

Though the basic material covers no new ground, and the pacing is slow in the first half, "The Betrayed" emerges as a satisfying meller. The ominous mood is evoked thanks to the somber camerawork and production design, and to the appropriate music score. Fans of the luminous Soutendijk won't be disappointed in her apparently perfect wife whose faithlessness triggers the drama. —*David Stratton*

KAERLIGHEDENS SMERTE
(PAIN OF LOVE)
(DANISH-SWEDISH)

A Per Holst/Danish Film Institute/Nordic Film and TV Fund/Mekano Pictures co-production. (Intl. sales: Pathé-Nordisk Film, Stockholm.) Produced by Per Holst. Directed by Nils Malmros. Screenplay, Malmros, John Mogensen. Camera (Eastmancolor), Jan Weincke; editor, Birger Møller Jensen; music, Gunnar Møller Pedersen; production design, Søren Krag-Sørensen; sound, Niels Arild; production manager, Bodil Stenstrup; assistant director, Søren Kjoer Nielsen. Reviewed at Berlin Film Festival (competing), Feb. 19, 1993. Running time: **118 MIN.**

March 15, 1993 (Cont.)

Kirsten	Anne Louise Hassing
Søren	Søren Østergaard
Kirsten's mother	Birthe Neumann
Kirsten's father	Waage Sandø
Inge-Louise	Anni Bjørn
Anders	Peder Dahlgaard
Julie	Kamilla Gregersen
Lasse	Finn Nielsen

"**P**ain of Love" is an intelligent, beautifully made and extremely sad portrait of a manic-depressive. By the nature of its subject matter, the film may have a hard time finding an audience, but director Nils Malmros, who is also a doctor, has such sympathy for his tragic heroine and depicts her short, confused life with such tenderness that the film deserves attention and praise. The spectacularly good performance of Anne Louise Hassing in the lead is a major plus.

The film opens when Kirsten is a child; one day, she discovers the father of a friend has hanged himself, and her mother tells her that her father, too, had committed suicide when she was little.

When Kirsten is 17, she seems to have everything to look forward to. She's cheerful, open, with loving parents who support her (her mother suggests she be fitted with a diaphragm when she starts going steady with her first boyfriend, Anders), popular with teachers and fellow students.

She develops a crush on one teacher, Søren, who likes flirting with his female pupils, though he lives with a fellow teacher, Inge-Lise. At 22, she has her first major setback; she fails her exams. Søren coaches her, and she scrapes by, but the incident has shaken her self-confidence.

The night she celebrates her passing grade, she allows herself to be seduced by a womanizing TV personality. After finding herself pregnant, she has long periods of insomnia and suffers guilt over a minor incident. She attempts suicide, and spends some time in a mental home.

After the birth, she resumes her liaison with Søren, who has separated from Inge-Lise, and they move in together. But the bouts of insomnia and depression continue. The ending is, predictably, tragic.

"Pain of Love" is far from a relaxing evening at the movies, but it's not clinical, thanks to the subtle central performance and the beautifully observed characters who surround, and try to help, the troubled young woman.

The Billie Holiday standard "You Go To My Head" is made haunting use of in the credits.

— *David Stratton*

VETURIMIEHET HEILUTTAA
(GOODBYE, TRAINMEN)
(FINNISH-SWEDISH)

A FilmitaKomo/Villealfa Filmprods. (Helsinki)/Pan Film (Stockholm) co-production, supported by the Finnish Film Foundation/Nordic Film & TV Fund/ZDF. Produced by Klaus Heydeman. Directed by Kari Paljakka. Screenplay, Juha Lehtovuori. Camera (color), Timo Heinänen; editor, Alvaro Pardo; music, Jay Havanna; production design, Risto Karhula; sound, Jussi Olkinuora. Reviewed at Berlin Film Festival (Panorama section), Feb. 22, 1993. Running time: 83 MIN.

Hapa	Santeri Jinnunen
Vähy	Samuli Edelmann
Sari	Liisa Mustonen
Vähy, aged 14	Toni Limnell
Vähy, aged 7	Jarno Rajala
Hapa, aged 14	Joona Lindberg
Hapa, aged 7	Mikko Huida
Tiki	Niko Saarela

Kari Paljakka's first feature is a well-acted, downbeat drama about friendship. Honestly handled, the film is a somewhat depressing experience, but could find its way to fests as an above-average example of current Finnish cinema. Aki Kaurismäki's Villealfa company was co-producer.

Pic opens with Hapa (Santeri Kinnunen) arriving at night in pouring rain to visit the grave of his friend Vähy. Flashbacks reveal that the boys met when they were 7 years old as neighbors in an apartment building; they swear a blood oath to be friends for life. Hapa is the serious one, and Vähy the bad boy.

As years go by, Hapa slowly discovers that his fun-loving friend is really a loser. Hapa studies, and eventually gets a college degree, while Vähy just hangs out with the old gang, getting hopelessly drunk almost every night and whoring around. The friendship comes to an abrupt end when Hapa is seduced by his friend's latest girl, Sari, while Vähy is out for the count.

The former friends meet only once more, by chance, some years later, but they have nothing to say to one another, and before long Hapa hears his old friend has been murdered in a pointless, drunken brawl. Director Paljakka and scripter Juha Lehtovuori paint a sad portrait of an aimless, wasted life, and it's difficult to have much sympathy for the self-destructive Vähy, or to understand why the far more intelligent Hapa should put up with him for so many years.

Pic is technically fine, and Samuli Edelmann is all too convincing as the adult Vähy.

— *David Stratton*

RUSSIAN PIZZA BLUES
(DANISH)

A Filmkonsortiet Zanzibar production, in association with Danish Film Institute/Danemarks Radio-TV/Graested Film & Fjernsyn/Fortuna Film Prod. (Denmark)/NRK (Norway)/Nordic TV Cooperation Fund. (Intl. sales: Pathé-Nordisk Film TV-Distribution, Copenhagen/Stockholm.) Produced by Peter Aalbaek Jensen. Directed by Michael Wikke, Steen Rasmussen. Screenplay, Rasmussen, Wikke, Mikael Olsen; camera (Eastmancolor), Erik Zappon; editor, Peter Englesson; music, Billy Cross, Joakim Holbeck; costume design, Magrethe Rasmussen; sound (stereo), Preben Mortensen. Reviewed at Berlin Film Festival (Market section), Feb. 20, 1993. Running time: 88 MIN.

Sergei Gazarov	Sergei Gazarov
Elena	Marianna Roubintchik
Bjarne Bent ("B.B.")	Steen Rasmussen
Leslie Howard Hansen	Michael Wikke
Claus	Claus Nissen
Lotte	Charlotte Toft
Robert	Robert Grant
Monica Zetterlund	Herself
(Danish, English, Russian soundtrack)	

Fresh as a daisy with a script like a Swiss clock, "Russian Pizza Blues" has all the makings of a cult item. But this likable, offbeat comedy will need a hard sell to overcome foreign auds' arty preconceptions of Scandi product. Fest exposure could be the key.

TV actor-producer duo Michael Wikke and Steen Rasmussen have come up with a real original for their first helm stint. Aside from the pic's confident, laidback style, it's technically slick and full of quirky surprises.

A single night's interlocking events involve a bear-like Russian rock singer (Sergei Gazarov) and his English-speaking daughter (Marianna Roubintchik), stranded in Copenhagen en route to a Russian Pizza House in New York; a handsome Dane (Wikke) visiting his boozy long-lost brother (Rasmussen); an airline stewardess (Charlotte Toft) and a bus driver (Robert Grant).

Pic begins with them traveling on the same airport bus into town and spins off their separate stories as each disembarks. As the night progresses, full of initially weird events, the script ingeniously overlaps their stories. A heartwarming finale with local singing star Monica Zetterlund, sees the protagonists reunited on the bus next morning.

Like John Landis' 1985 "Into the Night," the pic has a jet-lag quality that lends the modern romantic fairytale a blue-note feel. Whenever things threaten to get predictable, the helmers pull another rabbit out of the hat. Even running jokes like a guy in a bear suit, and a blonde who maintains "they're pulling everything down," all click.

Performances are on the money all 'round, with Gazarov going the whole nine yards as the neanderthal Russian and the Danes supplying the straightfaced comedy. Other credits are top drawer, with glistening photography of small-hours Copenhagen by Erik Zappon, and a laidback cocktail bar score by Billy Cross and Joakim Holbeck. — *Derek Elley*

LAST CALL AT MAUD'S
(DOCU-16m)

A Maud's Project production. (Intl. sales: The Maud's Project, L.A.) Produced by Karen Kiss, Paris Poirier. Directed by Poirier. Camera (Eastmancolor, 16m), Cheryl Rosenthal, Gary Sanders; editors, Poirier, Elaine Trotter; music, Tim Horrigan; sound, Loretta Molutar; sound design, Danny Alvarez; associate producer, Amanda Brilliante. Reviewed at Berlin Film Festival (Panorama section), Feb. 15, 1993. Running time: 74 MIN.

With: Rikki Streicher, Phyllis Lyon, Del Martin, Gwenn Craig, Jo Daly, Sally Gearhart, Judy Grahn, Joann Shirley.

A short history of the West Coast lesbian scene through the filter of San Francisco's oldest lesbian bar, "Last Call at Maud's" is a well-researched, undogmatic look at a footnote in social history. Docu should have no trouble finding its target audience, judging by the packed world preem at the Berlin fest. Specialist webs should also place orders.

Brainchild of owner Rikki Streicher, Maud's closed its doors on Sept. 9, 1989. From being "the hub of everything that was happening" when it opened in April 1966, the bar had outlived its usefulness to Frisco's lesbian community. As one interviewee notes: "[The bar's] time is over. It will now become a story." Another adds, "I hope we always do stay outlaws."

First-time director Paris Poirier assembles an impressive array of photos, memorabilia and archive footage limning California's twilight lesbian world from the '40s to now. Through a raft of interviews — but notably with

March 15, 1993 (Cont.)

lesbian couple Del Martin and Phyllis Lyon, founders of the Daughters of Bilitis club and the Ladder magazine — she sketches the bar's place in that scene's history and its special flavor.

Though the docu isn't a political pamphlet, it makes salient points about lesbians' generally second-league standing to gay men, legalistic problems such as women not being allowed to be bartenders, a '70s souring of homosexual pride due to male gays' "lack of political consciousness," the shooting of Harvey Milk, etc.

Speakers are not identified until the final rollcall, an irritating but minor fault. Transfer from vid to 16m is par. — *Derek Elley*

PIMPF WAR JEDER
(EVERYONE WAS A 'PIMPF')
(GERMAN-DOCU-16m)

An EML Film-und-Fernsehproduktion (Munich)/ZDF (Mainz) co-production. (Intl. sales: EML Film-und Fernsehproduktion, Berlin.) Directed, written by Erwin Leiser in conjunction with Vera Leiser. Camera (color, 16m), Peter Warneke; editor, Yvonne Loquens; sound, Wolfang Widmer; production manager, Renée Gundelach. Reviewed at Berlin Film Festival (Intl. Forum section), Feb. 13, 1993. Running time: **90 MIN.**

A "pimpf," in the German slang of the '30s, was a member of the Hitler Youth. This record of what one ex-student calls "the silent generation" —who have only recently been able to speak about this period— is of limited interest for Euro tube markets and international Jewish organizations.

Director-writer Erwin Leiser ("Germany, Awake!"), a Jewish student in the class of 1940 at the Berlin Gymnasium of the Gray Cloisters, was certainly not a "pimpf"; he was expelled in 1938.

Now a Swiss resident, in 1990 Leiser returned to Berlin for a class reunion and began interviewing his former classmates, almost all professionals, about the politics of their schooldays.

In a time of "ethnic cleansing" and other racial violence in Europe, this docu is timely, but Leiser's dialogue between Jewish and non-Jewish talking heads, who usually contradict one another, is fairly dull. The Jews remember aggression towards them from teachers and students; the non-Jews recall none; one non-Jewish student claims "my

Hitler Youth was absolutely apolitical, humanistic. We were interested in outings." Another states, "Jews weren't very good at sports, not heroes, but I made no distinction between them and my Aryan classmates."

When Leiser loses focus and begins questioning them about the war itself — in which a third of his class lost their lives — one man says "we didn't want to do something for National Socialism, but we wanted to do something for our country."

Pic suffers from inclusion of Leiser's own family biography and thudding archival footage of Hitler, Nazi violence, and "pimpf" outings; the editing is also uninventive, slowing pic down.

— *Howard Feinstein*

SABZI MANDI KE HEERE
(DIAMONDS IN A
VEGETABLE GARDEN)
(INDIAN-DOCU-16m)

A Film Sixteen production. Produced, directed by Nilita Vachani. Camera (16m, color), Vangelis Kalambakis; editor, Vachani; music, D. Wood; sound, Suresh Rajamani. Reviewed at Berlin Film Festival (Forum section), Feb. 16, 1993. Running time: **68 MIN.**

This is a straightforward docu about the entrepreneurs who conduct their business at India's long-distance bus terminals. These colorful characters sell all manner of items, including food, trinkets and reading material. Nilita Vachani's simple but charming film could, with a little pruning, fit a one-hour TV slot with ease.

Many of the cheaply priced items appear to be useless, but the salesmen are great and confident con artists, and there seems to be no lack of customers among the bus passengers. One man, a professed doctor, sells "surma," a lotion for sore eyes, as well as various balms and other tonics. There are also peddlers of religious tracts, and singers panhandling for coins. Special attention is given to a magician who performs sleight-of-hand tricks, and then does a roaring trade in booklets explaining his secrets.

Technically, it's a bit rough and ready, but the personalities of these hucksters come across vividly. — *David Stratton*

SEX IS . . .
(DOCU-16M-COLOR/B&W)

An Outsider production (San Francisco). Produced by Marc Huestis, Lawrence Helman. Directed by Huestis. Camera (16m, color/B&W), Fawn Yacker; editors, Lara Mac, Hrafnhildur Gunnarsdottir; sound, Lauretta Molitar; music, Donna Viscuso, Pussy Tourette; art direction, Vola Ruben; production manager, Helman; erotic coordinator, Robert Kirsch. Reviewed at Berlin Film Festival (Panorama section), Feb. 20, 1993. Running time: **80 MIN.**

Coming out strongly for sexual gratification in the age of AIDS, San Francisco-based filmmaker Marc Huestis' docu "Sex Is . . . " is an uncompromising portrait of the ups and downs of gay pleasure from the '70s through the '90s. A lack of concession to certain formats, notably TV, will limit pic to specialized auds, especially at gay/lesbian or other fests.

The director relies chiefly on an eccentric, diverse and certainly politically correct assortment of talking heads to recall their sex lives — from coming out, through indulgent activity, to safe sex. He punctuates the interviews with a wide variety of graphics and flashes of erotic activity in both black and white and color. (L.A. tape-to-film lab Image Transform refused to transfer the original Betacam tapes.)

Huestis, who is HIV-positive and appears frequently in the film, also touches on such issues as racism and ageism (a couple of interviews reflect on the more closeted scene of the '40s and '50s). Unfortunately, pic sometimes rambles from subject to subject (childhood fantasies, first encounter) and, though it moves fluidly, might benefit from trims.

The music can be annoying, but well-researched archival footage is a plus, especially a '50-ish docu warning of the hazards of homosexuality in San Francisco.

— *Howard Feinstein*

ROCK HUDSON'S
HOME MOVIES
(DOCU-16m)

A Couch Potato Inc. production and presentation. Produced, directed, written, edited by Mark Rappaport. Camera (color), Mark Daniels. Reviewed at Toronto Festival of Festivals, Sept. 12, 1992. (In Berlin Film Festival, Forum section.) Running time: **63 MIN.**
With: Eric Farr.

In this clever documentary, helmer Mark Rappaport parallels Rock Hudson's screen life with the star's gay existence using precise movie clips and a sarcastic narrative to expose sublimated codes of sexuality in Hollywood during the '50s. Docu is easily accessible for festgoers, prime material for academics and ideal for specialized webs and homevideo.

Rappaport's narrative includes a first-person persona, so he has a unique, tongue-in-cheek conversation with the screen and audience much like the snide attitude of "Roger and Me."

Via on-screen Hudson lookalike (Eric Farr), Rappaport goads Hudson's screen partners (such as Doris Day or Lauren Bacall) with lines like "What do you suppose he means by that, girls?"

Film excerpts repeatedly show Hudson's characters unwilling or incapable of marriage, even of love/lust with the leading lady, Rappaport driving home the point that such obvious references to homosexuality would never pass unnoticed today.

Ultimately, pic comically deconstructs codes of accepted "masculinity" — prefaced by a briefing about Hollywood's then-sacred codes of decency — without criticizing the star, a remarkable feat, given the witticisms throughout. — *Suzan Ayscough*

March 22, 1993

THIS BOY'S LIFE

A Warner Bros. release of an Art Linson production. Produced by Linson. Executive producers, Peter Guber, Jon Peters. Directed by Michael Caton-Jones. Screenplay, Robert Getchell, from Tobias Wolff's book. Camera (Technicolor; Panavision widescreen), David Watkin; editor, Jim Clark; music, Carter Burwell; production design, Stephen J. Lineweaver; art direction, Sandy Cochrane; set decoration, Jim Erickson; costume design, Richard Hornung; sound (Dolby), Rob Young; co-producer, Fitch Cady; assistant director, Bill Westley; casting, Owens Hill, Rachel Abroms. Reviewed at Warner Bros. screening room, Burbank, March 16, 1993. MPAA Rating: R. Running time: **115 MIN.**

Dwight Hansen . . . . Robert De Niro
Caroline Wolff . . . . Ellen Barkin
Toby Wolff . . . . . Leonardo DiCaprio
Arthur Gayle . . . . . Johan Blechman
Pearl . . . . Eliza Dushku
Roy . . . . Chris Cooper
Norma . . . . Carla Gugino
Skipper . . . . Zack Ansley

"This Boy's Life" is a nicely acted but excessively bland coming-of-age memoir about a young man's escape from domestic turmoil and abuse. Numerous potent scenes of conflict between the central teenager and his violent stepfather will put this over with many critics and audiences, but treatment ultimately provides only limited insight into a familiar situation. Result is less compelling and emotionally wrenching than it means to be, and b.o. prospects look to fall in the middle range.

Advertised upfront as "a true story," tale is based on Tobias Wolff's acclaimed 1989 book of the same name and is duly narrated in writerly fashion by young Toby (Leonardo DiCaprio). Hitting the road in 1957 with his working class mother Caroline (Ellen Barkin) after she splits from her b.f. (Dad, subject of the Geoffrey Wolff memoir "The Duke of Deception," is remarried in the East), Toby begins hanging out with a bad crowd once they settle in Seattle, as he starts smoking, sports a pompadour, learns to talk dirty and indulges in petty crime.

Then mom meets Dwight (Robert De Niro), a man's man with a crewcut who courts Caroline in his own arch manner but takes a particular interest in the unimpressed Toby. Even before Dwight and Caroline marry, Toby is sent to live with Dwight in the inauspiciously named town of Concrete, Wash., where Dwight devotes himself to cutting the sullen "hotshot" down to size.

Unfortunately, after a relatively promising warmup, pic actually proceeds to flatten out the characters in the latter sections and make them less interesting than they initially seemed. After coming across as a potentially three-dimensional working woman, Barkin's Caroline is placed squarely on the sidelines once she marries Dwight; still, the disaster that is their wedding night stands as the best screen argument in memory for sex before marriage.

Dwight's three kids remain total ciphers with virtually no dialogue; given much more time is Toby's ambiguous relationship with the shamelessly flamboyant Arthur Gayle (Jonah Blechman), whom Toby initially attacks as a "homo" but later befriends. Clearly meant to reveal the sensitive, aspiring side of Toby, it is inadequately resolved.

Film's strength lies in its portrait of the father-stepson struggle, how each pushes the other toward even worse behavior. It's no accident that the two most powerful scenes depict their rivalry physically, first when Dwight teaches Toby to fight, and climactically when the two go at it no-holds-barred.

De Niro brings both a rough charm and ferocious power to Dwight, making him the intimidating, bullheaded figure he needs to be. Centerscreen almost throughout, Leonardo DiCaprio is excellent as Toby. Role demands tremendous range, and the 18-year-old thesp delivers the gamut of emotions. Barkin weighs in with plenty of spirit until her character dries up.

Screenwriter Robert Getchell and director Michael Caton-Jones have fashioned plenty of dramatically valid sequences, but they add up to less than the sum of their parts. All hands, notably production designer Stephen J. Lineweaver, costumer designer Richard Hornung and lenser David Watkin, have contributed handsomely to evoking a late-1950s atmosphere.

— Todd McCarthy

POINT OF NO RETURN

A Warner Bros. release of an Art Linson production. Produced by Linson. Directed by John Badham. Screenplay, Robert Getchell, Alexandra Seros, based on Luc Besson's "Nikita." Camera (Technicolor; Panavision widescreen), Michael Watkins; music, Hans Zimmer; production design, Philip Harrison; art direction, Sydney Z. Litwack; set design, Eric W. Orbom, James Bayliss, Sally Thornton, Roger G. Fortune; set decoration, Julia Laughlin; costume design, Marlene Stewart; sound (Dolby), Willie D. Burton; co-producer, James Herbert; associate producers, D.J. Caruso, David Sosna; assistant director, Sosna; 2nd-unit director, Caruso; 2nd-unit camera, Michael Ferris; casting, Bonnie Timmermann. Reviewed at the Bruin Theater, L.A., March 17, 1993. MPAA Rating: R. Running time: **109 MIN.**

Maggie . . . . Bridget Fonda
Bob . . . . Gabriel Byrne
J.P. . . . . Dermot Mulroney
Kaufman . . . . Miguel Ferrer
Amanda . . . . Anne Bancroft
Angela . . . . Olivia D'Abo
Fahd Bahktiar . . . . Richard Romanus
Victor the Cleaner . . . Harvey Keitel
Beth . . . . Lorraine Toussaint
Drugstore Owner . . . Geoffrey Lewis

If imitation is the sincerest form of flattery, then "Point of No Return," a soulless, efficiently slavish remake of "La Femme Nikita," creates a whole new category of homage. For those who saw Luc Besson's high-tech thriller about a female criminal transformed into a government assassin, this is almost like watching it all over again. For general audiences, hard action pic with a twist delivers the goods, which should translate into hearty b.o. and put Bridget Fonda on the map as a name to reckon with.

Following the film's reception overseas will be interesting, since Besson's 1989 international hit, originally titled "Nikita," was not ghettoized as a foreign, subtitled "art" film in the rest of the world. But offshore audiences still might enjoy seeing a new cast go through the same paces.

Mere fact of the remake is rather ironic, since "Nikita" was one of the most Americanized French films in memory: It traded in big guns, heavy attitude, amoral government, action over dialogue, and repudiated the sensitivity and humanism usually associated with French cinema.

But the premise remains a strong hook on which to peg a taut, straight-line action narrative. Sentenced to death for killing a cop in a robbery, a young, drug-addicted punk (Bridget Fonda), here named Maggie, is given a chance to live if she becomes a government hit-woman.

Under the supervision of an agent named Bob (Gabriel Byrne), Maggie the wildcat slowly comes around, accepting training in martial arts, shooting and anything else that comes in handy in the James Bond business. The elegant Amanda (Anne Bancroft) adds the feminine touch, overseeing Maggie's transformation into a sleek beauty with class, poise and table manners.

Just as Maggie comes to enjoy her new personality, she must confront the reality of having to go out and kill people. In a precise replay of "Nikita," Maggie is knocks off a man in a restaurant, and then takes on an army of bodyguards in the kitchen.

Having won her stripes, she is transferred from Washington to Venice, California, where she instantly seduces J.P. (Dermot Mulroney), the friendly young caretaker of her boardwalk apartment building. The nasty assignments keep coming, though, until her jobs get in the way of her pleasant personal life, and she determines to find a way out of her predicament. Ending is a shade more upbeat and conventional than the French version.

Possibly the best action part for a woman since Sigourney Weaver's Ripley in the "Alien" series, Maggie was understandably a highly sought-after role, ranging from streetwise toughness and cold-blooded purposefulness to sophisticated glamor and romantic vulnerability. Fonda acquits herself admirably in all departments.

Retaining a light accent, Gabriel Byrne is low-key as Maggie's lovestruck Pygmalion, and Dermot Mulroney endows Maggie's beach-dwelling boyfriend with welcome humor and a comfortable naturalism. Most amusing turn comes from Harvey Keitel, who plays a ruthless hitman nicknamed the Cleaner as if pretending to be the Terminator.

Except for a few very minor changes, screenwriters Robert Getchell and Alexandra Seros have brought nothing new to their source material. Similarly, director John Badham offers no interpretation or distinctive p.o.v., but does get the requisite action up on the screen in a straightforward manner that's a degree less stylized and poetic than the original.

Film is richly appointed in the technical department. Philip Harrison's production design warrants particular mention, in that the separate ambiences created

March 22, 1993 (Cont.)

by the disparate locations — the secret underground training center, Bancroft's opulent quarters, the unfinished Venice apartment, various hotels, homes and restaurants — all register strongly and memorably. Michael Watkins' colorful, nimble lensing, Frank Morriss' adept editing and Hans Zimmer's atmospheric score help move things along in muscular fashion.

— *Todd McCarthy*

SALT ON OUR SKIN
(GERMAN-FRENCH-CANADIAN)

A Warner Bros. Transatlantic (France) release of a Constantin Film production in association with Torii Prods./Telescene Film Group/RTL and Canal Plus. Executive producer, Edwin Leicht. Produced by Bernd Eichinger, Martin Moszkowicz. Directed by Andrew Birkin. Screenplay, Birkin, Bee Gilbert, from Benoite Groult's novel "Les Vaisseaux du Coeur." Camera (color; widescreen), Dietrich Lohmann; editor, Dagmar Hirtz; music, Klaus Doldinger; production design, Jean-Baptiste Tard, Robert Laing; costumes, Catherine Leterrier; sound, Patrick Rousseau; co-producers, Sylvia Montalti, Paul Painter, Herman Weigel. Reviewed at the Warner Bros. screening room, Paris, March 9, 1993. Running time: **110 MIN.**
George . . . . Greta Scacchi
Gavin . . . . Vincent D'Onofrio
    Also with: Anais Jenneret, Petra Berndt, Claudine Auger, Rolf Illig, Laszlo I. Kish, Shirley Henderson, Hanns Zischler, Barbara Jones.

"Salt On Our Skin" is an old-fashioned weepie about mismatched lovers whose rare, passionate encounters over 30 years make both their lives worth living. A sometimes ragged cross between "Back Street" and Ms. magazine, the romantic but borderline-silly pic's best bet is femme auds, although film could also click as a date movie for couples not given to cynicism.

The worldly, privileged daughter of a French mother and a Scots father, George (Greta Scacchi) attends school in Paris but spends each summer in Scotland, home to manly but untutored Gavin (Vincent D'Onofrio). A moonlit swim as teenagers cements the raw erotic connection that grips them forever after, although their paths diverge.

Couple's odyssey is told in flashback and v.o. by the 40ish Scacchi. Refreshing twist here is that Scacchi follows her heart as well as her intellect.

Shortly after discovering true ecstasy in D'Onofrio's arms in the late 1950s, Scacchi discovers

Camus, Sartre and — bingo! — Simone de Beauvoir's "The Second Sex." When D'Onofrio proposes, Scacchi assures him it could never work: She's a restless intellectual, he's a hunky fisherman, and a future cannot be built on sex alone. They part but end up trysting every so often.

Based on Benoite Groult's 1988 bestseller, which was hailed for its frank descriptions of female sexual desire, conventional pic relies on the two leads' personalities and does not innovate. Scacchi and D'Onofrio give game, likable perfs, and the heat and devotion between the real-life couple are convincing. (They also co-starred in Gilian Armstrong's "Fires Within" in 1991.)

Scenes in which the lovers are reunited play better than the filler between reunions; and the voiceovers are sometimes stilted and literary. George ridicules Gavin when he resorts to clichés — a charge from which the postcard-like widescreen lensing in Paris, Scotland, Montreal and the Virgin Islands does not always steer clear. Score could be more nuanced. — *Lisa Nesselson*

TEENAGE MUTANT NINJA TURTLES III: THE TURTLES ARE BACK . . . IN TIME

A New Line Cinema release of a Golden Harvest production in association with Gary Propper. Produced by Thomas Gray, Kim Dawson, David Chan. Executive producer, Raymond Chow. Directed, written by Stuart Gillard, from characters created by Kevin Eastman and Peter Laird. Camera (Technicolor), David Gurfinkel; editors, William Gordean, James Symons; music, John Du Prez; production design, Roy Forge Smith; art direction, Mayne Schuyler Berke; set decorator, Ronald Reiss; costume design, Christine Heinz; sound (Dolby), Larry Kemp, Lon E. Bender; co-producer, Terry Morse; associate producer, Roberta Chow; visual effects supervisor, Jeffrey Okun; martial arts choreographer/stunt coordinator, Pat Johnson; 2nd-unit camera, Rexford Metz. Reviewed at the Beverly Connection, L.A., March 18. MPAA Rating: PG. Running Time: **95 MIN.**
Casey Jones/Whit . . . . . Elias Koteas
April O'Neil . . . . Paige Turco
Walker . . . . Stuart Wilson
Mitsu . . . . Vivian Wu
Lord Norinaga . . . . . . Sab Shimono
Leonardo . . . . Mark Caso
Raphael . . . . Matt Hill
Donatello . . . . Jim Raposa
Michaelangelo . . . . . . David Fraser
Splinter . . . . James Murray
Kenshin . . . . Henry Hayashi
Niles . . . . John Aylward
Yoshi . . . . Travis Moon
Grandfather . . . . Tad Horino
Jailer . . . . Glen Chin

Bow-wow-abunga! The third installment of "Teenage Mutant Ninja Turtles" is a decided case of diminishing returns. On a story and craft level it borders on the unforgivably bad and were it the first in the series, might be remembered as the indie sector's "Howard the Duck." Good will from earlier outings should open pic reasonably strong, but expect a quick return to its shell.

The new episode is a time travel yarn in which the four amphibian heroes and their pal, reporter April O'Neil (Paige Turco), switch places with five 17th century samurai warriors. This is all effected with questionable scientific aplomb and a device that resembles a vintage street lamp.

In feudal Japan, they become embroiled in a supposedly fierce struggle between two dynasties: Lord Norinaga (Sab Shimono) seeks to quash the rebel faction led by Mitsu (Vivian Wu) by enlisting the aid of the English mercenary and gunrunner Walker (Stuart Wilson).

Somewhere in the subplot is a "Romeo and Juliet" thread involving Mitsu and Kenshin (Henry Hayashi), Norinaga's son. However, as he's been transported to the modern-day turtle lair beneath the IRT, it's remote and thin. Also negligible is April's involvement with Whit (Elias Koteas), a castoff member of Walker's crew who is the spitting image of NYC turtle pal Casey Jones (also Koteas).

Writer-director Stuart Gillard inappropriately paces the action at tortoise speed. There are intriguing bits of whimsy such as the Asian warrior's absorption into Manhattan's hip hop scene. But rather than being a part of the fabric, these emerge as not very amusing side gags.

Virtually every department fires wide. The music is overbearing, the lighting is too bright and obvious, and the production design borders on the cheesy. Performances range from competent to just plain embarrassing and kids everywhere ought to be encouraged to ask for their money back for being played down to so slavishly.

— *Leonard Klady*

CYBEREDEN
(ITALIAN)

An Eidoscope production with the participation of Canal Plus. Produced, directed by Mario Orfini. Executive producers, Conchita Airoldi, Dino Di Dionisio. Screenplay, Grazia Giardiello, Roberto Iannone, Orfini, Max Ember, Adriano Celentano. Camera (Cinecittá color), Luciano Tovoli; editor, Pietro Scalia; music, Giorgio Moroder, Anthony Marinelli; production design, Rolf Zehetbauer, Gianni Giovagnoni; costumes, Maurizio Millenotti; sound (Dolby), Mario Dallimonti. Reviewed at Fono Roma screening room, Rome, Feb. 22, 1993. Running time: **108 MIN.**
Furio . . . . Adriano Celentano
Prudence . . . . Kate Vernon
Cedric . . . . Christopher Lee
Madame . . . . Carroll Baker
Cosimo . . . . Totò Cascio
Swift . . . . Ben Cole
Jeffrey . . . . . . William Mannering
Violet . . . . Bryony Martin
773T . . . . Johnny Melville
    (English soundtrack)

A mesmerizingly misguided techno-tale of computer whiz brats grappling with the key to eternal youth, "Cybereden" clocks in as the year's most expensive Italo item ($12 million) and its most clamorous flop. Screen comeback for comedian/rocker Adriano Celentano was mismarketed as adult entertainment and released as "Jackpot" locally, where it blatantly defied its title. Offshore, it might work as kids' fare, especially after further snips.

Clearly borrowing from Peter Sellers' character in "Being There," Celentano plays a doltish gardener brought in to lighten up a bunch of moppet geniuses. Shifting their focus from technology to nature, he puts them back on track. Their project, to create a computer-generated Eden, seemingly strikes pay dirt until a jealous tantrum sends tot William Mannering hurtling into the menacing computer world, with Celentano and rejuvenated granny Kate Vernon in pursuit.

Helmer Mario Orfini seems clumsily out of his depth in fantasy-land and he's not helped by a script that's crammed with characters and incidents but woefully short on continuum.

Celentano's clowning is strained by an apparently limited grasp of English, and Italo tyke Totò Cascio (from "Cinema Paradiso") is positively crippled by it. Other thesps all appear to be acting in different pics.

Tech cast assembles a formidable list of names with varying success. — *David Rooney*

March 22, 1993 (Cont.)

TAXI DANCER

A Trident Release of an American New Wave Film. Produced, directed, written by Norman Thaddeus Vane. Camera (Kodak color), Richard Jones; editors, Peter Ransohoff, Reinhard Schreiner; music, Jeffrey Silverman, Larry Blank; production design, Dave Blass; set design, Heather Palmand; costume design, Marcelle McKay; sound Bob Sheridan; assistant director, Gus Ramos; casting, Larry Kogan. Reviewed at American Film Market, Santa Monica, Feb. 26, 1993. Running time: **92 MIN.**

Billie	Brittany McCrena
Diamond Jim	Sonny Landham
Miguelito	Robert Miano
Star	Tina Fite
Mercedes	Mirage Micheaux
Candy	Michele Hess
Bobby	Randall Irwin
Sparkle	Josie Boyd
Chango	Chris Cho
Hit Man	Chris Lim
Jojo	Russ Landery
Lowisa	LeOnna Small

The sleezy side of L.A.'s dance club cum hostess-for-hire scene forms the rudiments of the subpar indie "Taxi Dancers." In rather hyperbolic tones, its press kit offers "the first movie ever made about the subculture of taxi dancing." It is just one of many elements rife with sizzle and lean on substance. Flaccid sexploitationer has extremely limited theatrical potential, with video prospects only marginally better.

The barebones plot trots out the hoary saga of the innocent young girl who gets mixed up with the wrong crowd. Billie (Brittany McCrenna) walks into one of these clubs, immediately gets hired and somehow remains slightly above the fray of drugs, prostitution and serious crime, but instead, she's caught between two men — a penniless musician (Randall Irwin) and a freewheeling cowboy (Sonny Landham).

Seesawing between the banal and the embarrassing, the film provides a veritable checklist of filmmaking don'ts. Writer-director-producer Norman Thaddeus Vane encourages a shrill acting style reminiscent of 1950s exposé features and his visual technique might charitably be called inelegant. — *Leonard Klady*

SOGNANDO LA CALIFORNIA
(CALIFORNIA DREAMING)
(ITALIAN)

A Filmauro Distribuzione release of a Luigi and Aurelio De Laurentiis presentation of a Filmauro production. Produced by Luigi and Aurelio De Laurentiis. Executive producer, Mauzirio Amati. Directed by Carlo Vanzina. Screenplay, Enrico & Carlo Vanzina. Camera (Cinecittà color), Giuseppe Maccari; editor, Sergio Montanari; music, Umberto Smaila; art direction, Osvaldo Desideri; costumes, Roberta Guidi di Bagno; sound (Dolby), Tommaso Quattrini. Reviewed at Barberini Cinema, Rome, Jan. 18, 1993. Running time: **110 MIN.**

Lorenzo	Massimo Boldi
Tonino	Nino Frassica
Silvio	Maurizio Ferrini
Giovanni	Antonello Fassari
Herself	Bo Derek
Cinzia	Francesca Reggiani

A boisterous buddy movie in which four fortysomething friends realize a long-stalled dream to cross America together, "California Dreaming" aims a notch or two above the standard Italo holiday offerings. A top local earner, it could sidle into undemanding markets open to light, bawdy comic fare.

A chance encounter reunites a quartet of university chums 15 years after graduation. Three are shamelessly self-centered middle-class climbers set up in cushy medical practices and the fourth is a disillusioned Communist in a civil service job. Nostalgia for their undergrad antics puts them on the vacation trail, driving from Miami to Malibu. By unlikely coincidence, they're stuck sans cash or credit cards, and are forced to slum it, rediscovering some of life's unsullied pleasures.

Helmer Carlo Vanzina (who scripted with brother Enrico) efficiently introduces a string of comic situations; still, the pic is more story-driven than usual in gag-based Filmauro comedies.

The four leads (Italo TV comics and distinctly comedians, not actors) are eager but unmodulated, and don't attempt to bring much conviction to their characters' bonding and blossoming experience.

The clumsy sound, which cranks dialogue up to screaming pitch, also doesn't help. Elsewhere, tech work is better-judged. Visual benefits are reaped from the Yank landscape, and a well-chosen crop of pop classics helps maintain a lively pace. — *David Rooney*

PALOMITA BLANCA
(WHITE DOVE)
(CHILEAN)

A Brochitel Uno S.A. Film released by Cinematograaáfica Manutara. Produced by León Tchimino, Hugo Ortega, Elio de la Vega, Herman de la Vega & Hernán Fishman. Executive producer, Sergio Trabucco. Directed by Raúl Ruiz. Screenplay, Ruiz, from Enrique Lefourcade's novel. Camera, Silvio Caiozzi; editing, Carlos Piaggio; sound, José de la Vega, Jorge di Lauro; music, Los Jaivas; reconstruction and prints, Roberto Cheñoli. Reviewed at Cine Oriente, Santiago, Nov. 6, 1992. Running time: **122 MIN.**

With: Beatriz Lapido, Rodrigo Ureta, María Castiglione, Bélgica Castro, Mónica Díaz, Felisa González, Luis Alcarón, Manuel Aranguiz, Miriam Morales, Mónica Echeverría Fritz Stein, Nelson Fuentes, Marcial Edwards, Lila Mayo, Andrea Baksai, Rodrigo Maturana.

Shot by Raúl Ruiz in 1973, "Palomita Blanca" took 19 years to reach local screens. Surprisingly, it's not at all a dated curiosity. Local b.o. outlook is good; abroad, given Ruiz's rep, it should get fest and arthouse play.

"Palomita" takes place in 1970 during the period around the election of Salvador Allende's inauguration. Based on a bestselling novel by local author Enrique Lefourcade, it is basically a poor girl/rich boy story, placed against that turbulent background.

María, a high school senior, lives in a squalid tenement and Juan Carlos, a playboy type, in a splendid mansion. Altmanesque overlapping dialogue and the improvisational technique favored by Ruiz lets a mixed cast of nonpros (including the leads) and actors live it up. Tighter editing would benefit the film's second hour but acting is mostly good as are the tech credits.

Finished in July 1973, after the September coup it was one of many items banned by the military. In 1990, Ruiz came to Chile for a week to re-edit and to check the print. By then he had made over 50 films, but this is only the third to receive a commercial release in his own country. — *Hans Erhmann*

THE JUDAS PROJECT

An RS Entertainment release of a Judas Project production. Executive producers, James H. Barden, Edward A. Teraskiewicz. Produced by James Nelson, Ervin Melton. Directed, written by Barden. Camera (color), Bryan England; editor, Noreen Zepp Linden; music, Barden; production design, Philip Dean Foreman; visual effects produced by Richard Edlund. Reviewed at Cineplex Odeon Spectrum Theater, Houston, Feb. 28, 1993. MPAA rating: PG-13. Running time: **97 MIN.**

Jesse	John O'Banion
Jude	Ramy Zada

Also with: Richard Herd, Gerald Gordon, Jeff Corey.

Try to imagine "Godspell" without the jokes, the charm, the vigor or the terrific songs, and you have some idea what to expect from "The Judas Project," a muddle-headed allegorical drama that presents the life, death and resurrection of Christ in a contempo setting.

Indie pic posted some respectable opening-week numbers in limited Deep South and Southwest release, fueled by a canny ad campaign and direct-mail to church groups. Second-week drop-off, however, suggests trouble ahead when pic breaks wider near Easter.

Film obviously is a labor of love for James H. Barden, who's listed as writer, director and co-executive producer, and who wrote the dreadfully sincere (and sincerely dreadful) Christian-pop tunes on the soundtrack. Unfortunately, Barden's entire effort calls to mind the adage about the pavement on the road to hell.

Newcomer John O'Banion plays the Jesus Christ figure, Jesse, a charismatic fellow in blue jeans who makes the blind see, the lame walk and nonbelievers nervous. O'Banion looks like a young, beatific Alain Delon, and sounds like someone reading from the Good News Bible.

Jesse's disciples are — yes, you guessed it — fishermen. Mostly, they are sport fishermen, with at least one fly fisherman thrown in for good measure. Jude (Ramy Zada), the least dependable of Jesse's followers, betrays him for 30 pieces of silver, and is last seen skulking off with a rope.

In the gospel according to Barden, O'Banion's Jesse is the Real Thing, the long-awaited Messiah, the One and True Christ — something that, ironically, may upset many of the very devout Christian auds pic is aimed at. Barden might have overcome this by having someone remark,

March 22, 1993 (Cont.)

"You've come back!" But no. According to "The Judas Project," mankind has been quite literally godless until Jesse showed up.

Since the bad guys have an army of armed thugs, it's hard to understand why they don't simply have Jesse shot, rather than waste time with hammers and nails. But, then, why doesn't Jesse go on Larry King if he's interested in reaching the multitudes?

Embarrassingly amateur on most counts, pic's acting seldom rises above the level of religious instructional shorts for very small children. Technically, the best things are a few impressive moments of special-effects magic by Academy Award-winner Richard Edlund. — *Joe Leydon*

PAPER MARRIAGE
(BRITISH-POLISH)

A Mayfair Palace (U.K.) release of a Mark Forstater Prods. (London)/Zodiak Film Studio (Warsaw) production. Produced by Mark Forstater, Raymond Day. Directed by Krzysztof Lang. Screenplay, Lang, Marek Kreutz; additional material, Debbie Horsfield, Lise Mayer. Camera (Agfacolor; Metrocolor prints), Grzegorz Kediersky; editor, Elzbieta Kurkowski; music, Stanislas Syrewicz; production design, Allan Starski; art direction, Maciej Walczak (Warsaw); associate producer, Tracey Seaward; assistant directors, Simon King (U.K.), Krzysztof Wierzbicki (Poland); production manager, Henryk Romanowski. Reviewed at British Film Institute preview theater, Jan. 26, 1993. Running time: **84 MIN.**
Aiden . . . . Gary Kemp
Alicja . . . . Joanna Trepechinska
Lou . . . . Rita Tushingham
Red . . . . Richard Hawley
Frank Hoddow . . . . David Horovitch
Jack . . . . William Ilkley
Phyllida . . . . Ann Mitchell
Officer Crane . . . . . . Fred Pearson
Boss . . . . Gary Whelan
Also with: Martin McKellen, Sadie Frost, Ray Stubbs, David Whitaker.

"Paper Marriage" is an amiable enough variation on the "Green Card" template given more charm than the script deserves by leads Gary Kemp ("The Krays") and Polish thesp Joanna Trepechinska. Lightweight item, shot in Poland and the U.K. almost two years ago, looks headed for only brief theatrical residence but is fine for tube playoff.

Story opens in Warsaw, where beautiful young Pole Alicja (Trepechinska) is fixing her entry visa to Blighty in hope of marrying a young doc (Martin McKellen) she's fallen for. Arriving in Newcastle, northern England, she's rapidly dumped by the youth and his snooty family and in desperation arranges a mar-

riage of convenience with small-time crook Aiden (Kemp), who needs the cash to pay off some hoods he's on the run from.

After a lot of to-ing and fro-ing, with Kemp gradually insisting on his marital rights as he falls for the ambitious Pole, the pair finally team up to make a new life down south. Final twister leaves their future together in doubt till fadeout.

The movie takes a while to get going, with the inevitable sack scene (handled, in the event, with delicacy and some originality) almost an hour in. Till then, the script largely marks time.

The pair (Trepechinska holding her own in English) bond well on screen when the script gives them a chance, and there's a nice balance between his wily charm and her tunnel-vision ambition to make it big in the West. But the lack of a thoroughgoing tone — neither sparky comedy nor realistic drama — means the pic largely idles for the first half.

Supports are all solid, with an off-the-wall perf by Rita Tushingham as Trepechinska's landlady that's a real collector's item.

Polish director Krzysztof Lang, in his feature bow after a string of docus and TV work in Denmark and France, directs confidently. Interiors, mostly shot in Poland, blend seamlessly with Newcastle exteriors, which are often given a fresh look.

Tech credits are fine all round. Pic, by U.K.-based indie producer Mark Forstater, got a brief berth last month at London's National Film Theater in its "Preview" slot. Title should not be confused with the similarly themed 1988 Hong Kong production, set in Canada, directed by Alfred Cheung. — *Derek Elley*

PACCO, DOPPIO PACCO E CONTROPACCOTTO
(PACKAGE, DOUBLE PACKAGE AND COUNTERPACKAGE)
(ITALIAN)

A CDI release of a Clemi Cinematografica production. Executive producer, Bruno Ridolfi. Produced by Giovanni Di Clemente. Directed by Nanni Loy. Screenplay, Loy, Elvio Porta. Camera (Cinecittà color), Claudio Cirillo; editor, Franco Fraticelli; music, Claudio Mattone; art direction, Umberto Turco; costumes, Danda Ortoni; sound, Mario Dallimonti. Reviewed at Ariston Cinema, Rome, Jan. 25, 1993. Running time: **118 MIN.**

With: Tommaso Bianco, Enzo Cannavale, Italo Celoro, Marina Confalone, Giobbe Covatta, Isa Danieli, Nuccia Fumo, Nunzio Gallo, Leo Gullotta, Alessandro Haber, Angela Luce, Nello Mascia, Angelo Orlando, Luigi Petrucci, Giacomo Rizzo, Silvio Spaccesi, Pia Velsi, Mara Venier.

Naples habitué Nanni Loy takes an amicable swipe at the city's wily inhabitants in "Package, Double Package and Counterpackage." A paean in 10 episodes to the city's population of streetsmart wheeler-dealers, pic serves up uneven '60s-style satire that will look less dated on small screens.

Working with frequent script collaborator Elvio Porta, Loy concocts 10 situations ranging from mini-narratives to single-joke vignettes, which offer a lighthearted survival guide to a town plagued by bad administration, the Mafia and a necessarily self-serving mentality.

Drawing on innate Neapolitan theatricality, Loy targets corruption, health services, housing, education, unemployment and underworld kickbacks. Title episode refers to black market shysters' practice of switching merchandise for worthless duds mid-transaction with the aid of a staged diversion.

Standout sketch features Marina Confalone as a resourceful homemaker swindled out of her apartment by Silvio Spaccesi, who sets up shop as a medium. Outdoing his chicanery, Confalone fakes a sexually charged visitation from her "dead" husband, scaring off the usurper. Common thread shows that even the dirtiest double-dealing can be outmaneuvered with progressively more elaborate scams.

Large cast, including many well-known Neapolitan natives, can't quite stave off the overall fatigue of a glib, outmoded vehicle decidedly under par for Loy. Tech credits are functional.
— *David Rooney*

I'LL LOVE YOU FOREVER . . . TONIGHT
(B&W)

A Headliner Prods. release of a Cinema Bravo production. Produced, directed, written, edited by Edgar Michael Bravo. Camera (B&W), Jeff Crum; music, Robert Cairns; production design, John Edgar Bledsoe; set decoration, Lisa Kelly; costume design, Robert Velasquez; sound, Bill Beck, Mitchell Guttleman. Reviewed at the Monica Four-Plex, Santa Monica, Calif., Feb. 14, 1993. Running time: **77 MIN.**

Ethan . . . . Paul Marius
Dennis . . . . Jason Adams
Peter . . . . David Poynter
Steve . . . . Roger Shank
Jeff . . . . Miles Wilshire

"I'll Love You Forever . . . Tonight" is an ambitious but ultimately uncompelling exploration of ennui in the contemporary gay scene in Los Angeles. Yet the UCLA graduate thesis may serve as a calling card for its writer-director.

Opening scene, set in a Los Angeles bar, features a beginning typical of many gay films: a quick pick-up followed by impersonal sex. But it also sets the tone for a work that aspires to examine the emotional states of five young gay men whose lives seem aimless and unfocused.

Protagonist Ethan (Paul Marius) is a handsome photographer who deludes himself that he has no need for love or commitment. Emotionally scarred by a childhood trauma involving incest, it soon becomes clear Ethan needs to come to terms with himself and with his abusive father.

With the exception of the rather bland Ethan, the cast remain representatives of different lifestyles rather than individual characters, and there are too many pregnant looks among them.

Bravo's claim his is the first gay feature by a Latino may be true, but it is not especially significant, as the men on view are all white. Still, helmer shows facility with realistic scenes and in establishing a moody ambience.

Pic is more impressive technically than narratively. Jeff Crum's stylized B&W cinematography provides an interesting tension with the more naturalistic dialogue. — *Emanuel Levy*

TRYGGARE KAN INGEN VARA
(WINTER IN PARADISE)
(SWEDISH)

Sandrews presents an Omega Film & Television production in co-production with Douglas Film/FilmTeknik/Tonservice Löthner & Löthner/Sandrew Film. Produced by Peter Kropenin. Directed, written by Thomas Samuelsson. Camera (color), Mats Olofsson; editors, Hakan Karlsson, Samuelsson; music, Mikael Rickfors; production design, Anders Olausson; costumes, Malin Bergendal; sound, Oble Unnerstad. Reviewed at Sandrews screening room, Stockholm, Feb. 2, 1993. Running time: **90 MIN.**

With: Jacqueline Ramel, Frederik Dolk, Mats Hudden, Gösta Bredefeldt, Katarina Weidhagen van den Hal, Thomas Roos, Axel Duberg, Carina Jingrot.

March 22, 1993 (Cont.)

This surprisingly efficient thriller delivers the thrills it promises. Box office future in Sweden looks quite okay.

During his nightly jog in Stockholm, Peter foils a rape by knocking the rapist down. Three years later, after Peter has written a book based on the incident, the rapist is released from prison and begins stalking Peter, his wife, Elin, and their infant.

In order to finish a new book, Peter takes his family to a lonely house in the snow-drenched north of Sweden, where, of course, the rapist follows, menacing them and finally raping Elin at gunpoint. Back in Stockholm, the terror continues and in the end it's Elin who finally deals with the stalker.

This story has been told many times, but it still delivers tension and suspense. "Winter in Paradise," made on a small budget and technically a bit rough, successfully tells a straightforward story straightforwardly.

Acting is good, if not remarkable. The exception is leading actress Jacqueline Ramel, a former model, who is not only beautiful but has a promising screen presence. — *Gunnar Rehlin*

SANTA BARBARA FEST

JOEY BREAKER

A Skouras Pictures release of a Poe production. Produced by Steven Starr, Amos Poe. Directed, written by Starr. Camera (Duart color), Joe DeSalvo; editor, Michael Schweitzer; music, Paul Aston; sound design, Janet Lund Robbins; production design, Jocelyne Beaudoin; costume design, Jessica Haston; assistant director and associate producer, Dolly Hall; production manager and line producer, Louis Tancredi; casting, Deborah Aquila. Reviewed at Museum of Modern Art, N.Y., Feb. 18, 1993. (In Santa Barbara Intl. Film Festival.) MPAA Rating: R. Running time: **92 MIN.**

Joey Breaker	Richard Edson
Cyan	Cedella Marley
Alfred Moore	Fred Fondren
Hip Hop Hank	Erik King
Jennie Chaser	Gina Gershon
Wiley McCall	Philip Seymour Hoffman
Esther Trigliani	Mary Joy
Sid Kramer	Sam Coppola
Larry Metz	Michael Imperioli
Karina Danzi	Olga Bagnasco
Lester White	Laurence Mason

Of interest mainly to tradesters, "Joey Breaker" is an inside look at a New York movie talent agent. Lack of visual pizzazz plus miscasting severely limit indie pic's breakout potential.

Former William Morris agent Steven Starr makes some good points in his knowing script, but as a debuting director he ends up with more of a radio play than a motion picture. The film simply doesn't move.

Richard Edson portrays Joey Breaker, a high-powered Gotham agent juggling young clients and hoping to advance at Morgan Creative. He's eager to sign black comedian Hip Hop Hank (Erik King) and is working with colleague Jennie Chaser (Gina Gershon) on arranging a studio auction for the spec script of novice screenwriter Larry Metz (Michael Imperioli).

Breaker is styled as a user, the viewer quickly tagging him as a selfish guy. Homophobia and sexism get him into trouble but also serve as key plot devices. He begins to see the light when, after initial resistance, he starts a friendship with Alfred Moore (Fred Fondren), a man dying of AIDS. His callous remark to Hank about Hank's male lover Lester (Laurence Mason) almost costs him this client's trust, cueing more consciousness-raising.

Matters really come to a head when Breaker's offhand sexist remark about Chaser causes her to quit the agency. This occurs during the bidding war for Metz's script (termed "a cross between 'Twins' and 'The Flintstones'" by Chaser). Poor Breaker has to face his boss after Chaser sells it for $1 million for a rival agency.

Starr schematically builds a '60s-type choice for this poor man's Sammy Glick. A romance with Jamaican waitress Cyan (Cedella Marley, daughter of Bob) ends when she moves back to Jamaica to be a nurse. Breaker predictably chucks his career and exits the rat race to join her.

Edson is problematic in the central role of Joey Breaker, as he underplays the fast-talking smoothie; the part's required high energy level is sorely lacking. Marley is quite appealing as Edson's romantic interest, but they generate no heat.

As Edson's gung-ho assistant, Philip Seymour Hoffman consistently upstages the star, building on the strong impression he made as the weak-willed preppy in "Scent of a Woman."

The late Fred Fondren has a touching scene detailing his unfulfilled dream to be a writer. Best line goes to Edson's boss, Sam Coppola, who states the agent's credo: "Just remember, stars come and go, but we are forever." — *Lawrence Cohn*

THE PAINTED DESERT

A Kazuyoshi Okuyama presentation in association with New Dawn Pictures and Skyhawk. Produced by Tikki Goldberg. Executive producer, Okuyama. Directed by Masato Harada. Screenplay, Harada, Rebecca Ross, from Harada's story. Camera (color), David Bridges, Bernard Salzmann, editor, Ross; music, Masahiro Kawasaki; production design, Rae Fox; costume design, Eduardo Castro; associate producer, Wayne Yee; casting, Miguela Sandoval. Reviewed at Santa Barbara Film Festival, March 5, 1993. Running time: **106 MIN.**

Al	James Gammon
Sari Hatano	Nobu McCarthy
Jiro	Kayuza Kimura
Barbara	Priscilla Pointer
Montana	Don Keith Opper
Franco Vitali	Andreas Katsulas
Latino Scarface	Ron Joseph
Harry	Vincent Schiavelli
Griff	Rudy Diaz
Cosmo	Wayne Pere

Self-consciously mixing elements of "The Petrified Forest" and "Bagdad Cafe," the unevenly paced "The Painted Desert" also calls to mind Robert Altman's dream narrative "Three Women." This amalgam sounds like it could make for a confusing narrative, and it does. Director Masato Harada's maiden American outing is handsome but of interest mostly to festgoers and the hardcore arthouse crowd.

Action mainly transpires in a dusty old cafe in the ever-mystical American Southwest. The dilapidated dive is run by Sari (Nobu McCarthy), a cynical Japanese-American woman, and frequented by several mobster bodyguards including the crustily affable Al (James Gammon).

Sari discovers a mysterious stranger (Kayuza Kimura) — the type who only shows up in movies — who speaks little English but, we soon discover, is a knockout nouvelle Japanese chef. So far so good. But co-scenarists Rebecca Ross (who also edited) and Harada then overload the film with plot elements.

The bad guys are preyed upon by invisible but lethal rivals. Sari and her boarder Barbara (Priscilla Pointer) reveal secrets dating back to World War II, the internment of the Japanese and anti-American propaganda. And of course, Kimura has more up his sleeve than sashimi. The forced mating of all this pulls the audience out of the film long before its one-too-many endings.

The mob subplot is the most expendable; appealing James Gammon is the sole goon with any charm, though he has plenty. But it's the interplay between McCarthy, Pointer and Kimura that is the emotional core. McCarthy is a wonderful character actress with a natural grace. Pointer has few words but lends an air of palpable tension. Kimura's role isn't as well delineated but he also makes a strong impression.

Tech credits are superb. David Bridges and Bernard Salzmann capably split the duties of capturing the parched beauty of the Southwestern desert. The kitschily evocative production design is by Rae Fox and only the scoring by Masahiro Kawasaki is occasionally overripe. More refreshing are some great old Gene Autry tunes. — *Richard Natale*

THE HANGED MAN

A Lot 49 production. Produced, directed, written by Thomas Claburn. Camera (color), Kathleen Beeler; editor, Rick LeCompte; music, Alec Bartsch; production design, Richard Malerba; art direction, Lawrence Hornbach; costumes, Patricia Kazmierowski; sound, Allen Schaaf. Reviewed at Santa Barbara Film Festival, March 6, 1993. Running time: **95 MIN.**

Ray	Matthew Blomquist
Sarah	Andrea Damesyn
Ramon	Henrique Vargas
Scott	Stephen Bramfitt
Candy	Jill Burns

An impenetrable narrative, wooden performances and uninspired direction strangle "The Hanged Man," the feature debut of San Francisco State film graduate Thomas Claburn, who also produced and wrote the screenplay. Even at 95 minutes it's a tough sit and has little b.o. potential.

The germ of the story is intriguing, if more than a bit derivative. A prosperous young couple with a disintegrating marriage accidentally run over a young drifter. The mysterious young Latino is gradually integrated into their lives, which eventually leads to a dramatic climax during which everyone's dirty secrets are revealed. There's also a dark twist at the end. Unfortunately, by then the audience will have ceased to care.

Matthew Blomquist does what he can with his role as a paranoid, racist yuppie. Andrea Damesyn and Henrique Vargas try to breathe some life into their respective parts as the wife and the aspiring novelist drifter.

Kathleen Beeler's cinematography is not unpleasant to look at and Richard Malerba's production design makes the most of what was obviously a meager

budget. It at least has personality, if a rather bizarre one.
— *Richard Natale*

MASALA
(CANADIAN)

A Strand release of a Divani Films presentation. Produced by Srinivas Krishna, Camelia Frieberg. Directed, written by Krishna. Camera (color), Paul Sarossy; editor, Michael Munn; music, Leslie Winston, West India Co.; sound, Ross Redfern; production design, Tamara Deverell; costume design, Beth Pasternak; assistant director, Richard Flower; production managers, Frieberg, Sandra Cunningham; 2nd-unit director, Frieberg; casting, Linda Continenza. Reviewed at Magno Review 1 screening room, N.Y., March 15, 1993. (In Santa Barbara Film Festival.) Running time: 105 MIN.
Lallu Bhai Solanki/Mr. Tikkoo/Lord
  Krishna . . . . Saeed Jaffrey
Grandma Tikkoo . . . . . . Zohra Segal
Krishna . . . . Srinivas Krishna
Rita Tikkoo . . . . Sakina Jaffrey
Anil Solanki . . . . . . Herjit Singh Johal
Bibi Solanki . . . . . . Madhuri Bhatia
Bahadur Singh . . . Ishwarlal Mooljee
Sashi Tikkoo . . . . . . Ronica Sajnani
Gerald . . . . Les Porter
Babu . . . . Raju Ahsan
Lisa . . . . Jennifer Armstrong
Balrama . . . . Wayne Bowman
Saraswati . . . . Tova Gallimore

A severe case of first filmitis afflicts "Masala," a freewheeling satire set in Toronto's subculture of residents hailing from India. Distrib's best shot is to find a cult following.

With targets ranging as wide as stamp collecting, real estate fanatics on TV, Canadian stereotypes and assimilation-prone Indians, debuting filmmaker Srinivas Krishna scores points for originality. Unfortunately his weakness with actors and overly aggressive visual gimmicks make "Masala" tedious in the extreme.

Krishna himself plays the thoroughly dislikable rebel named Krishna who feels guilty for being a no-show when his parents and brother were killed in a plane crash. He moves in with rich Toronto relatives, the Solankis, who run a clothing boutique.

Beautiful Bibi Solanki (Madhuri Bhatia) dreams of having husband Lallu (Saeed Jaffrey) corner the world market on saris. To this end she urges him to use the shop as a front for Sikh terrorists who promise him $500,000.

Krishna is attracted to Bibi but falls in love with Rita (Sakina Jaffrey), a highly assimilated daughter of distant relative Tikkoo (also played by Saeed Jaffrey as a nerd). Tikkoo is a stamp-collecting postman who inadvertently receives a stamp worth $5

million, one the Canadian government is desperate to recover.

Numerous subplots include Krishna's obsession with retrieving the $800 owed him by drug addict former g.f. Lisa (Jennifer Armstrong); Tikkoo's mom (Zohra Segal) who communicates with the god Krishna (third role with heavy makeup for Saeed Jaffrey) via magically interactive vidcassette; Solanki's son Anil (Herjit Singh Johal) fated to an arranged marriage; and the Mounties plus SWAT team converging to bust the Sikhs.

Punctuating this messy stew (or masala) are a couple of misguided musical numbers meant to adapt the traditional Bombay musical to music video but merely stalling the action.

Krishna's mish-mash includes explicit sex (a full-frontal shot of himself that stamps this a vanity production plus highly erotic footage of Anil's betrothed Tova Gallimore) that takes pic into the underground NC-17 range. He encourages his cast to overact and pull faces in closeup, resulting in hammy fun from Saeed Jaffrey but too many bug-eyed shots of Segal and Singh Johal.

Jaffrey's real-life daughter Sakina Jaffrey is appealing as the heroine, coming off as the most naturalistic thesp in context.

Colorful photography by Paul Sarossy is as self-conscious and distracting as the heavy-handed director evidently wanted it to be. — *Lawrence Cohn*

SILENT VICTIM

A 21st Century Film Corp. presentation of a Wells Co. production. Produced, directed by Menahem Golan. Executive producer, Ami Artzi. Screenplay, Nelly Adnil, Jonathan Platnick, from Bob Spitz's story. Camera (Cine-Film Labs; Deluxe prints), David Max Steinberg; editor, Bob Ducsay; music, William T. Stromberg; set decoration, Cecilia Vettraino; sound (Dolby) David K. Neesley; associate producer, Kenneth Trotter; assistant director, Bart Patton; casting, Kathy Smith, Dan Bernstein; Georgia casting, Shay Griffin. Reviewed at Santa Barbara Film Festival, March 7, 1993. Running time: 104 MIN.
Bonnie Jackson . . . . Michelle Greene
Lauren McKinley . . . . . . Ely Pouget
Jed Jackson . . . . Kyle Secor
Carter Evans . . . . Alex Hyde-White
C. Ray Thompson . . . . Ralph Wilcox
Chrissy Lee . . . . . . Leann Hunley
Emily . . . . Rosemary Newcott
Hilda Pollack . . . . Dori Brenner
Judge Tucker . . . . . . Dan Biggers

"Silent Victim" begs the question, "Why?" The project's genesis is confusing in light of the numerous and often more penetrating dramatizations of

the abortion issue done over the past several years on TV. Shot in the fall of 1991, it's no puzzle why it's been on the shelf. Expect an if-you-blink-you'll-miss-it theatrical run.

Although it seems to take eons to get there, the central conflict of the film is intriguing: A husband sues his wife for murder in the unwitting abortion of her fetus in a failed suicide attempt.

Director Menahem Golan repeatedly underlines the fact that abortion is a legal, moral and emotional quagmire. But dramatically speaking, the film is peopled with cardboard stereotypes on the right and left, and more soap-opera elements than a month of "All My Children." Further, the Georgia setting allows for a number of implicit and explicit slams at Southerners.

The one stroke of good fortune is Michelle Greene as the victimized wife. Her part is poorly structured and she is a bit of a simp, but Greene is moving and real.

Cinematography by David Max Steinberg is too glossy, doing a disservice to Cecilia Vettraino's on-target set decoration.
— *Richard Natale*

BENNY & JOON

An MGM release of a Roth/Arnold production. Produced by Susan Arnold, Donna Roth. Executive producer, Bill Badalato. Directed by Jeremiah Chechik. Screenplay, Barry Berman, from Berman, Lesley McNeil's story. Camera (Deluxe color), John Schwartzman; editor, Carol Littleton; music, Rachel Portman; production design, Neil Spisak; art direction, Pat Tagliaferro; costume design, Aggie Guerard Rodgers; sound (Dolby), James Thornton; special effects, J.D. Streett IV; stunts, Noon Orsatti; associate producer, McNeil; assistant director, K.C. Colwell; casting, Risa Bramon Garcia, Heidi Levitt. Reviewed at Filmland screening room, Culver City, Calif., March 3, 1993. MPAA Rating: PG. Running time: 98 MIN.
Sam . . . . Johnny Depp
Joon . . . . . . Mary Stuart Masterson
Benny . . . . Aidan Quinn
Ruthie . . . . Julianne Moore
Eric . . . . Oliver Platt
Dr. Garvey . . . . C.C.H. Pounder
Thomas . . . . Dan Hedaya
Mike . . . . Joe Grifasi
Randy Burch . . . . William H. Macy
Mrs. Smail . . . . Eileen Ryan

Johnny Depp and Mary Stuart Masterson render such startling performances in the new romantic fable "Benny & Joon" they almost overcome being in a not particularly well-written or directed film. Focusing on an unusual triangle — two siblings and an outsider — this offbeat love story may rise above moderate appeal if it links with the twentysomething group that is its subject. As an actors' showcase, however, pic is destined to be more popular on video and cable.

The core of Barry Berman's script is based on a romanticized conception of mental illness, the mythology that the mentally disturbed are more sensitive and artistic than "ordinary" human beings. Masterson stars as Joon, the mentally ill sister of Benny (Aidan Quinn), an auto mechanic who takes care of her. The quick-witted Joon spends her days at home, painting with passion. Benny is overprotective, but the siblings somehow reach a balanced, if boring, lifestyle that suits both of them.

This frail equilibrium is shattered when Sam (Depp), a modern-day clown in the mold of Chaplin and Keaton, shows up and changes the rules of the game. Quinn continues to worry, but he is also freer to pursue affairs of the heart with the charming Ruthie (Julianne Moore).

An unusual story for a big studio project, the pic's strength lies more in the nuances of the relationships than in the smooth flow of an episodic narrative. The love story is superficially placed in a frame that revolves around suspense over whether Benny will institutionalize Joon.

In mood and theme, film bears some resemblance to "David and Lisa," Frank Perry's 1963 sleeper that, like the new pic, centered on the quasi-mysterious bond between two young people linked by shared marginality and temperament.

But "Benny & Joon" plays it too safe. Though a flashback of a family disaster suggests the cause of Joon's problem, it's never established just how sick she really is. This allows the narrative to have it both ways: Excepting one hysterical scene, Joon appears as "normal" as Quinn or his poker buddies.

Displaying exceptional generosity to his performers, helmer Jeremiah Chechik ("National Lampoon's Christmas Vacation") allows undramatic episodes that soar as actors' material. But he approaches the narrative with undue timidity and is ultimately unsuccessful in varying the rhythm of its comic, intimate and melodramatic sequences.

As a fairy-tale clown, Depp is playing a variation on Edward Scissorhands, a misunderstood eccentric par excellence. Both Depp and Masterson, whose screen chemistry sparkles, excel in embodying the spirits of magic. In contrast, Aidan Quinn, who continues to be typecast as the handsome and sensitive male, is stuck with a more difficult role: the representative of harsh, outside reality.

Supporting case members, particularly Oliver Platt, as Quinn's co-worker and friend, and C.C.H. Pounder, as Masterson's caring doctor, all hit their marks.

Behind-the-scenes contributions are solid, if not spectacular. With locations shot in Spokane, Wash., John Schwartzman's cinematography has an appealing look and feel, specifically in conveying the lush Riverfront Park, where Depp performs his antics.

Rachel Portman ("Used People") delivers yet another tremendous score, one fittingly tinged with romance, lyricism and melancholy. Her Nino Rota-like melodies for Depp's acrobatics poignantly underscore the film's off-center charm.

— *Emanuel Levy*

BORN YESTERDAY

A Buena Vista release of a Hollywood Pictures presentation in association with Touchwood Pacific Partners I of a D. Constantine Conte production. Produced by Conte. Executive producer, Stratton Leopold. Directed by Luis Mandoki. Screenplay, Douglas McGrath, from Garson Kanin's play. Camera (Technicolor), Lajos Koltai; editor, Lesley Walker; music, George Fenton; production design, Lawrence G. Paull; art direction, Bruce Crone; set design, Nancy Patton, Philip Toolin; set decoration, Rick Simpson; costume design, Colleen Atwood; sound (Dolby), Thomas Causey; co-producer Stephen Traxler; associate producer/assistant director, Chris Soldo; casting, Amanda Mackey, Cathy Sandrich. Reviewed at the Avco Cinema, Westwood, Calif., March 22. MPAA Rating: PG. Running time: **101 MIN.**

Billie Dawn	Melanie Griffith
Harry Brock	John Goodman
Paul Verrall	Don Johnson
Ed Devery	Edward Herrmann
JJ	Max Perlich
Senator Hedges	Fred Dalton Thompson
Cynthia Schreiber	Nora Dunn
Phillipe	Michael Ensign
Secretary Duffee	Benjamin C. Bradlee

Hollywood Pictures' updated remake of the Pygmalion-like "Born Yesterday" arrives with a credible modern resonance. The basic dynamics of the original Garson Kanin play, so well served in George Cukor's 1950 screen version starring Judy Holliday, William Holden and Broderick Crawford, have stood the test of time thanks to some clever contemporary tweaking. However, the verdict on the makeover is not all good news.

The attractive cast, individually strong, fails to coalesce as an ensemble. There's also a problem in creating a uniform tone for the yarn of a real estate speculator and his socially awkward girlfriend who invade the power elite of Washington, D.C. Getting across the obvious comedic and socio-political elements required a defter touch than is evident in this rendering, which has enough commercial pluses to make a decent showing in the current movie primaries.

Harry Brock (John Goodman), a scrap metal czar in the original, is now in real estate and hies to D.C. when the evaporation of defense contracts near his super mall threaten to undo his empire. In tow is Billie Dawn (Melanie Griffith), a former showgirl with more moxie than college knowledge. In this rarefied air she soon becomes an embarrassment.

So Harry asks lobbyist Ed Devery (Edward Herrmann) to "smarten her up." To that end he hires local reporter Paul Verrall (Don Johnson) to provide the Professor Higgins treatment and, in short order, she wises up and the sparks, romantic and otherwise, begin to fly.

Screenwriter Douglas McGrath expands his source material with the latest twists on power brokering. However, he also imbues the story with a glib, sitcom breeziness that favors cuteness over content.

While relatively faithful to the intent of Kanin's play, the film also echoes more recent cinematic assaults on the nation's capital, especially in its cribbing from "Being There." But Billie is no Chauncey Gardner, and Goodman lacks the dramatic weight of the former screen Brock, Crawford.

Following in the footsteps of Judy Holliday, who won an Oscar for her performance, Griffith provides her own credible spin on Billie Dawn and, made up to resemble Ivana Trump, provides a current touchstone. The film also gives Johnson his best role in a long time, affording him a change-of-pace bookish part and an opportunity for some effective light comic work.

In this mix, Goodman's bullying buffoonery and realistic ire stand out unfavorably. The character appears to be off-stage-commenting even when he's part of the scene.

Director Luis Mandoki invests very little that's novel in this outing. Technical credits are polished — often too much so — and he has a penchant for creating set pieces that, while diverting, also freeze the momentum of the narrative. Nonetheless, Kanin's original conception, when left to stand on its own, continues to pack a punch. — *Leonard Klady*

FIORILE
(ITALIAN-FRENCH-GERMAN)

A Penta Distribuzione release (in Italy) of a Filmtre-Gierre Film production in association with Penta Film (Italy)/Florida Movies/La Sept Cinema in association with Canal Plus (France)/Roxy-Film/K.S.-Film (Germany) co-production. (Foreign sales: SACIS.) Produced by Grazia Volpi, Jean-Claude Cecile, Luggi Waldleitner, Karl Spiehs. Directed by Paolo and Vittorio Taviani. Screenplay, Sandro Petraglia, Paolo and Vittorio Taviani. Camera (color), Giuseppe Lanci; art direction, Gianni Sbarra; editor, Roberto Perpignani; music, Nicola Piovani; costumes, Lina Nerli Taviani; associate producers, Anna Rita Appolloni, Claudio Amram. Reviewed at Anica screening room, Rome, March 16, 1993. Running time: **122 MIN.**

Corrado/Alessandro	Claudio Bigagli
Elisabetta/Elisa	Galatea Ranzi
Jean/Massimo	Michael Vartan
Old Massimo	Renato Carpentieri
Luigi	Lino Capolicchio
Juliette	Costanze Engelbrecht
Gina	Athina Cenci
Chiara	Chiara Caselli

Also with: Giovanni Guidelli, Norma Martelli, Pier Paolo Cappponi, Carlo Luca De Ruggieri, Laurent Schilling, Fritz Mueller Scherz, Laura Scarimbolo, Elisa Giani, Ciro Esposito, Giovanni Cassinelli.

The power of gold and its ability to destroy human relationships is the theme of the Taviani brothers' ambitious historical epic "Fiorile," a vast, pulsating canvas spanning two centuries of Italian history. Big-scale, thought-provoking and highly enjoyable, pic begs for major foreign art house release. It will premiere abroad at Cannes, in competition.

Co-scripted with Sandro Petraglia, "Fiorile" is one of Paolo and Vittorio Taviani's most successful attempts at mixing abstract ideas with storytelling, simplicity with inventive technique. This transposition of an old Tuscan legend echoes the social themes and rural settings that appear in all their work. At the same time, it has the elementary force of a fable.

The story is framed by a journey that takes place in the present day. The Benedetti family is driving from Paris to Tuscany to visit a grandfather the children have never seen. On the way, father Lino Capolicchio jokingly tells his son and daughter about the family legend, and why people of the region call them the "Maledetti" (cursed) instead of Benedetti (blessed). With a typical Taviani sleight-of-hand, their van becomes a time machine, and flashbacks begin.

Everything starts with the French Revolution and a chest of gold. Napoleon's army is invading the Italian peninsula, bringing an infectious trail of ideas about freedom and equality in its wake. French soldier Jean (Michel Vartan) is smitten by a peasant girl, Elisabetta (Galatea Ranzi), he meets in the woods. He nicknames her Fiorile, Italian for Floréal, the French revolutionary calendar's May.

While they make love, Jean forgets about the gold he's supposed to be guarding. Elisabetta's brother (Claudio Bigagli) makes off with the loot, aided by his elderly parents. Jean goes before the firing squad; Elisabetta dies in childbirth. Her peasant family, suddenly enriched, buys huge amounts of land.

March 29, 1993 (Cont.)

But the evil origins of the family fortune haunt Jean and Elisabetta's descendants. One hundred years later, the radiant Elisa (again played by Ranzi) is involved in another tragic love affair. Her brother Alessandro (Bigagli), one of the richest land owners in the area, is after a seat in parliament and finds her peasant lover Giovanni Guidelli too low for his ambitions. When Elisa discovers her two brothers have forced him to leave the country, she murders them. The legend of the Maledetti has begun.

In 1944, young Massimo Benedetti, played by Vartan, falls in love with fellow student Chiara Caselli. On a mission for the Italian partisans, and both are captured; the fascists spare Massimo because of his family's power, but gun down his comrades. The experience turns him into a hermit, and he refuses to see the son Chiara bears him, lest the family "curse" continue.

Film's conclusion cleverly brings all the threads together, in a spooky but touching scene between the old man and Jean's "ghost." The modern family that cheerfully arrives to take him away can't erase the legend, and destiny seems ready to dog the two children.

This complex story (beautifully edited by Roberto Perpignani) is brisker than most Taviani films. Giuseppe Lanci's cinematography has a palpable sensuality, offsetting the Tavianis' usual schematic direction. Ditto most perfs, whose concreteness lends conviction to briefly seen characters.

Nicola Piovani's wistful score is a potent motif linking the film's various parts. Gianni Sbarra's memorable sets contribute waves of atmosphere to a film that spans centuries. — *Deborah Young*

HEAR NO EVIL

A 20th Century Fox release of a David Matalon production. Produced by Matalon. Executive producer, David Streit. Directed by Robert Greenwald. Screenplay, R.M. Badat, Kathleen Rowell, from Badat, Danny Rubin's story. Camera (Technicolor), Steven Shaw; editor, Eva Gardos; music, Graeme Revell; sound (Dolby), Mark Ulano; production design, Bernt Capra; art direction, John Myhre; set decoration, Susan Mina Eschelbach; costume design, Fleur Thiemeyer; assistant director, Aaron Barsky, David Womark; production manager, Streit; stunt coordinator, Greg Elam; 2nd-unit camera, John Campbell; casting, Glenn Daniels, Jean Medley (Portland). Reviewed at Bay Cinema, N.Y., March 26, 1993. MPAA Rating: R. Running time: **97 MIN.**

Jillian Shanahan	Marlee Matlin
Ben Kendall	D.B. Sweeney
Lt. Brock	Martin Sheen
Mickey O'Malley	John C. McGinley
Grace	Christina Carlisi
Cooper	Greg Elam
Wiley	Charley Lang
Mrs. Kendall	Marge Redmond
Tim Washington	Billie Worley

A terminally dull would-be thriller, "Hear No Evil" has a perfunctory story with the gimmick of a deaf damsel-in-distress grafted on uncertainly. Oscar-winner Marlee Matlin's talents are wasted.

Matlin plays a physical trainer in Portland whose client (John C. McGinley) hides a rare stolen coin in her beeper before being nabbed by the cops.

McGinley's car blows up and corrupt cop Martin Sheen starts harassing Matlin to retrieve the coin. McGinley's pal D.B. Sweeney takes Matlin under his wing and the duo finally bring in the FBI to catch Sheen.

There's a lame-duck final twist to this trivial story, but by then nearly all TV viewers will have tuned out. At least in theaters, where the film opened without press screenings, the audience is trapped into sticking it out.

Director Robert Greenwald and his scripters show little flair for suspense, nuance or even elementary thrills; the villain and nearly all story particulars are laid out in the opening minutes. In the final reel Matlin has a cat and mouse sequence trapped in a mountain lodge with the killer, but unlike such effective films as "Wait Until Dark," her handicap (deafness) is not used as an equalizer but instead merely increases her jeopardy.

Supporting cast, particularly Martin Sheen as the zero-dimensional villain, performs with little involvement. Matlin is sexy but not given a chance at characterization. Film's technical credits are subpar in an obvious B-movie exercise to fill out Fox's release schedule with a minimum of effort or commitment.

— *Lawrence Cohn*

THE OPPOSITE SEX ... AND HOW TO LIVE WITH THEM

A Miramax Films presentation of a Once Upon a Time/Outlaw production. Produced by Robert Newmyer, Stanley M. Brooks. Executive producer, Jeffrey Silver. Directed by Matthew Meshekoff. Screenplay, Noah Stern. Camera (Deluxe color), Jacek Laskus; editor, Adam Weiss; music, Ira Newborn; production design, Alex Tavoularis; costume design, Carol Ramsey; sound (Dolby Stereo), Glenn T. Morgan, Wylie Stateman; co-producer, David Guggenheim; casting, Richard Pagano, Sharon Bialy, Debbie Manwiller. Reviewed at Loews 34th Street Showplace, N.Y., March 26, 1993. MPAA Rating: R. Running time: **86 MIN.**

David Crown	Arye Gross
Carrie Davenport	Courteney Cox
Eli	Kevin Pollak
Zoe	Julie Brown
Kenneth Davenport	Mitch Ryan
Frieda Crown	Mitzi McCall
Irv Crown	Phil Bruns
Gisella Davenport	B.J. Ward
Rabbi	Jack Carter

This conventional spin on the old Slob-meets-WASP/loses-WASP/marries-WASP plotline is too cute by half, as thesps poke strained fun at themselves rather than merely act. Despite valiant efforts by a game Kevin Pollak to liven up this tired romantic comedy, only the patient should appreciate the gross humor and sophomoric plot. This one, which opened without press screenings, is headed straight to video.

Story has libidinous Joe Six-Pack David (Arye Gross) infatuated with WASP queen Carrie (Courteney Cox), whom he meets in a bar. Despite much hesitation, the two proceed with a tumultuous — and unfunny — relationship, which is busily commented on by their respective best friends as the road to marriage looms: The satyric Eli (Pollak) and zany Zoe (Julie Brown) do their bit to make us forget that the laughs aren't coming.

One fatal gimmick that can be traced back to early John Hughes fare is thesps staring into the camera and letting the audience in on the joke. Unfortunately, punchlines here mostly involve condoms, genitalia and references to basic functions. Several dream sequences, including one where Carrie is almost gagged to death on David's mother's food, are fun but overdone.

Carrie's primness and David's locker room charm create several other unsuccessful country club-versus-matzoh ball gags that

leave the cast adrift in a sea of loose direction.

Even taking into account the $3 million budget, pic looks and feels like a hurried 1970s buddy comedy replete with "I just can't figure him/her out" lines. Interspersed animation spots want to be playful, but are so eagerly used they end up annoying.

Tech credits are okay, but title sequence is also too eager to please. The whole thing is like someone at a party telling you a loud joke you'd rather not hear.

— *Christian Mørk*

AVENTURE MALGACHE, BON VOYAGE
(FRENCH-BRITISH-B&W)

A Milestone Films release of two 1944 dramatic shorts produced by the British Ministry of Information. Directed by Alfred Hitchcock. "Bon Voyage" screenplay by J.O.C. Orton, based on an original idea by Arthur Calder-Marshall; "Aventure Malgache" screenplay uncredited. Camera (B&W), Gunther Krampf; art direction, Charles Gilbert. Reviewed March 5, 1993, at the Museum of Fine Arts, Houston. (In Berlin Film Festival.) Running times: "Aventure Malgache" **31 MIN.**; "Bon Voyage" **26 MIN.**

With: John Blythe ("Bon Voyage") and the Moliere Players.

"Aventure Malgache" and "Bon Voyage," two French-language shorts directed by Alfred Hitchcock for the British Ministry of Information during World War II, have been unearthed by the British Film Institute. The Hitchcock name and the dramas' legendary status among his devotees may be enough to ensure some theatrical exposure, but pics seem best suited for homevideo.

Without the Hitchcock imprimatur, it's debatable whether anyone (except, possibly, World War II historians) would think "Bon Voyage" worth all the bother. A briskly paced, heavily ironic drama about a downed RAF pilot smuggled out of Nazi-occupied France, pic resembles nothing so much as an above-par episode of '50s TV anthology series.

English actor John Blythe plays John Dougall, an officer being interrogated by the Free French in England after his escape. In subjective flashbacks, he recalls the heroic efforts of a fellow escapee, a Polish sergeant named Godowski, to guide him to contacts with the underground.

Trouble is, Godowsky was actually a Gestapo agent using Dougall to smoke out Resistance fighters. As soon as Dougall learns this, Hitchcock segues into a rerun of his journey, this time from the viewpoint of the Gestapo agent. Events and dialogue that previously seemed innocuous turn out to have darker alternative meanings.

It's tempting to theorize that Hitchcock's experiments with perspective here were a kind of warm-up exercise for "Vertigo." More likely is that Hitchcock was motivated more by patriotism than by experimentation.

The other short, "Aventure Malgache," was intended to reflect deep divisions in the French Resistance Hitchcock noticed during research for "Bon Voyage." But the British propagandists, preferring a more upbeat tone, shelved "Malgache" soon after its completion. Even so, pic reportedly received some theatrical exposure in France before all prints were rounded up.

Seen today, "Malgache" seems a minor but entertaining slice of Hitchcockian cheekiness. Again, most of "Malgache" is flashbacks, this time narrated by Clarousse, who recalls his days as a barrister — and his nights as a Resistance agent —in Madagascar.

After Petain's order for capitulation to the Nazi juggernaut, Clarousse helps organize an underground railway to help Resistance fighters escape. Unfortunately, Clarousse is hounded by a corrupt police chief and inadvertently betrayed. The Vichy government-run court condemns him to five years. He serves his time cheerfully, hiding a radio in his alarm clock so he can keep up with Resistance activity.

Eventually, Clarousse is rescued, and Madagascar is liberated by British forces. In the pic's funniest scene, the police chief tries to swim with the shifting political tide by taking down his office portrait of Petain, and replacing it with a portrait of — no kidding — Queen Victoria.

Like "Bon Voyage," "Aventure Malgache" is little more than a footnote to Hitchcock's career. But, then again, even footnotes to careers so remarkable are never without interest.

Blythe is the only member of the two casts identified by name either onscreen or in the production records. Other members of the cast are introduced collectively as members of the Moliere Players, a theatrical troupe formed by French actors resettled in England during the war who, fearing reprisals against friends and relatives still in Oc-

cupied France, asked that their identities not be revealed.

Tech credits, especially the first-rate black and white cinematography by former UFA cameraman Gunther Krampf, are above and beyond the call of duty. Film historian Tom Milne's English subtitles are everything they should be. — *Joe Leydon*

STREET KNIGHT

A Cannon Pictures release of a Mark DiSalle production. Produced by DiSalle. Executive producers, Yoram Globus, Christopher Pearce. Directed by Albert Magnoli. Screenplay, Richard Friedman. Camera (color; Panavision), Yasha Sklansky; editor, Wayne Wahrman; music, David Michael Frank; production design, Curtis Schnell; art direction, Michael L. Fox; set design, Archie D'Amico; costume design, Darryl Levine; sound (Dolby), Ed White; special effects, Greg Landerer; stunts, Rick Avery; co-producer, Peggy DiSalle; associate producer, Friedman; assistant director, Jerram Swartz; casting, Cathy Henderson-Blake, Tom McSweeney. Reviewed at the Mann Westwood, L.A., March 12, 1993. MPAA Rating: R. Running time: **88 MIN.**
Jake . . . . Jeff Speakman
Franklin . . . . . . Christopher Neame
Lt. Bill Crowe . . . Lewis Van Bergen
Rebecca . . . . Jennifer Gatti
Raymond . . . . Bernie Casey
Carlos . . . . Richard Coca
Santino . . . . Stephen Liska
Cisco . . . . Ramon Franco
Lucinda . . . . Ketty Lester
Emilio . . . . Santos Morales

Political correctness and unrealistic hopefulness inform "Street Knight," a formulaic actioner about gang warfare in Los Angeles. Sufficient production values and adherence to genre conventions may result in moderate b.o. success on the way to videoland.

Jeff Speakman stars as Jake, a former cop tormented by guilt over inadvertently causing the death of a young girl. Working as an auto mechanic, Speakman is doing his personal penance. Predictably, however, he is drawn back to the crime scene when a truce between two rival gangs is shattered by mysterious murders in both camps.

Scripter Richard Friedman shrewdly adds a new element to the formula: a highly organized, para-military band of mostly white professional killers, headed by a vengeful psychopath scarily played by Christopher Neame, that sets the gangs against each other to divert police attention from their own operations.

Otherwise, "Street Knight" obeys its genre imperatives with the expected number of hostages, violent deaths, stock charac-

ters and subplots. Speakman falls for Rebecca (Jennifer Gatti), the attractive sister of Carlos (Richard Coca), an innocent Hispanic adolescent who goes missing after spotting one of the killers.

Except for a chase in Griffith Park, the film lacks elaborate set pieces, but does have some excellent mano-a-manos that allow martial artist Speakman to display his expertise.

Albert Magnoli's direction is at times crude, but he handles the lurid material with verve. Tech credits are solid in every department. — *Emanuel Levy*

AKVAARIORAKKAUS
(SAARA'S LOVE)
(FINNISH)

A Finnkino (Finland) release of a Kinotuotanto production, in association with Filmlance Intl. (Sweden)/Nordic Film & TV Fund/TV2 (Finland). (Intl. sales: Finnish Film Foundation, Helsinki.) Produced, directed by Claes Olsson. Screenplay, Tove Idström, from Anna-Leena Härkönen's novel. Camera (Fujicolor), Pertti Mutanen; editors, Anssi Blomstedt, Olsson; music, Yari; art direction, Minna Santakari; costume design, Meeri Nieminen; sound, Tero Malmberg; co-producer, Börje Hansson. Reviewed at Berlin Film Festival (Market section), Feb. 20, 1993. Running time: **100 MIN.**
Saara . . . . Tiina Lymi
Joni . . . . Nicke Lignell
Irene . . . . Minna Pirilä
Marita . . . . Satu Silvo
Raikka . . . . Antti Virmavirta
Saara's mother . Riitta-Liisa Helminen
Saara's father . . . . . Olli Tuominen
Saara's brother . . . . . Mika Nuojua

Bright, slick and easy on the eyes, "Saara's Love" is an agreeable time-passer. Self-styled "modern love story" has performed well locally but lacks the personality to jump into many offshore beds.

Foxy Tiina Lymi is the eponymous Saara, a small-town girl who's outwardly independent. After meeting pony-tailed hunk Joni (Nicke Lignell) at a New Year gathering, she takes the plunge and moves in with him.

Problems start when it emerges Saara can't reach orgasm, despite Joni's herculean efforts; she's also plagued by sado-masochistic dreams involving other women. A trip home, plus an affair, sorts her out. Sort of.

As a young woman's search for identity, it's thin stuff, with a kinky detour that leads nowhere, and an ending that's pure cop-out. Lymi and Lignell get by on unforced charm.

Pic is good to look at, with beautiful-bodied leads and color-

supplement sex scenes. Finnish title literally means "Aquarium Love." — *Derek Elley*

SCHNEEWEISS-ROSENROT
(SNOWWHITEROSERED)
(GERMAN-DOCU-16m)

A Kinowelt release of a Kick Film production. Executive producer, Jörg Bundschuh. Produced by Michael Horn. Directed, written by Christa Ritter, Rainer Langhans. Camera (video to 16m), Langhans, Hans Fromm; editor, Alexander Rupp; music, Ulrich Bassenge; sound, Stefan Schindler; associate producer (WDR), Alexander Wesemann. Reviewed in Munich (special screening), Jan. 25, 1993. Running time: **84 MIN.**
With: Gisela Getty, Jutta Winkelmann, J. Paul Getty III, Dennis Hopper, Leonard Cohen, Rainer Langhans, Bob Rafelson, Sally Kirkland, Wim Wenders, Andrei Konchalovsky, Werner Herzog, Sean Penn.

"SchneeweissRosenrot" comes across as a "Lifestyles of the Rich and Famous" with a strong dash of '60s nostalgia. It tells the story of a pair of German twins who go straight from small-town anonymity to the jet set when one of them marries J. Paul Getty III. Though amateurish in places, the star cast and incredible Cinderella tale bode well for campuses and fests and may give it some video life internationally.

Twins Gisela and Jutta plumb into '60s hippiedom with all their might and systematically become part of the Beautiful People in Berlin, Rome, London and Los Angeles. Gisela (after his world-famous kidnapping) marries Getty, the grandson of one of the world's richest men. The other sister, Jutta, ends up living with co-helmer Rainer Langhans, guru of the Berlin commune scene.

However, things don't turn out as well as promised: Getty is cut off from the family fortune and turned into a vegetable by a drug-related accident. Jutta's life seems to parallel the Berlin hippie movement: floating aimlessly at first, then slowly dissolving into a puzzling unhappiness.

The docu, a collaboration between professional filmmaker Christa Ritter and Langhans, is full of nostalgia for the heady hippie days but the quality of the film is uneven. For example, the filmmakers forget to introduce the twins by name, assuming the audience knows them.

Commentary is held on an intangible personality level, as if

March 29, 1993 (Cont.)

everyone were talking to their therapists: "Nobody meant more to Gisela than Jutta, and that made me jealous back then . . ." says director Andrei Konchalovsky but the actual circumstances, background and events are wanting. How did they get to know Konchalovsky, anyway?

The docu also exagerrates the importance of its subjects' inner lives: in the end, the twins were basically ornaments; the filmmakers are too enamored of their glamour to maintain perspective.

— *Eric Hansen*

RICKY E BARABBA
(RICKY AND BARRABAS)
(ITALIAN)

A Penta Distribuzione release of a Mario and Vittorio Cecchi Gori/Silvio Berlusconi Communications presentation of an Alto Verbano production. Executive producer, Raffaello Sargagò. Produced by Mario and Vittorio Cecchi Gori. Directed by Christian De Sica. Screenplay, Leo Benvenuti, Piero De Bernardi, Alessandro Bencivenni, Domenico Salvati, Paolo Costella, De Sica. Camera (color), Sergio Salvati; editor, Raimond Crociani; music, Manuel De Sica; art direction, Gepi Mariani; costumes, Nicoletta Ercole. Reviewed at Royal Cinema, Rome, Jan. 19, 1993. Running time: **90 MIN.**
Ricky . . . . Renato Pozzetto
Barabbas . . . . Christian De Sica
Also with: Franco Fabtizi, Francesca Reggiani, Bruno Carassari, Marisa Merlini, Sylva Koscina.

Evidence, if it's really needed, that Italy's neorealist maestro Vittorio De Sica was less than magnanimous with his creative chromosomes can be had in son Christian De Sica's third directorial outing. More accomplished technically than previous efforts, "Ricky and Barabbas" is nonetheless unoriginal, uninspired and thin on laughs. Glossy comedy has performed below expectations at local wickets and seems unlikely to cross many borders.

Wearing vagrant chic, De Sica plays Barabbas, a seventh generation hobo with a taste for luxury, who unintentionally saves the life of a suicidal swell, Ricky (Renato Pozzetto). With his business empire crumbling and his scheming, shrewish wife (Francesca Reggiani) eager to ditch him, Pozzetto becomes putty in the hands of his unconventional friend. They track down and eventually outwit Reggiani, who's been sharing sheets and crucial information with hubby's grasping business rival.

Though De Sica's brash Roman vulgarian shtick (familiar from

countless film roles) is wearing decidedly thin, both he and the more measured performer Pozzetto make valiant attempts to get the material on its feet. But the script, by a committee of six, is archaically conceived with a sledgehammer sensitivity.

Cleanly edited and shot, pic uses Monte Carlo and Italo locations and a lavish costume ball to dress up the meager plot.

— *David Rooney*

ALEX
(NEW ZEALAND-AUSTRALIAN)

An Isambard Prods./Total Film and Television production, in association with the New Zealand Film Commission/NZ On Air/the Australian Film Finance Corp. Produced by Tom Parkinson, Phil Gerlach. Directed by Megan Simpson. Screenplay, Ken Catran, from Tessa Duder's book. Camera (color), Donald Duncan; editor, Tony Kavanagh; music, Todd Hunter; production design, Kim Sinclair; sound, David Madigan; costumes, Sara Beale; associate producer, Alan Witherington; line producer, Tony Winley; production manager, Tammie Painting; assistant director, Simon Ambridge; casting, Liz Mullane, Sheridan Jobbins, Heather Ogilvie. Reviewed at Leura screening room, Leura, Australia, Feb. 1, 1993. Running time: **93 MIN.**
Alex Archer . . . . . Lauren Jackson
Mr. Jack . . . . Chris Haywood
Andy Richmond . . . . . . Josh Picker
Maggie Benton . . . Catherine Godbold
Mrs. Benton . . . Elizabeth Hawthorne
Mr. Archer . . . . Bruce Phillips
Mrs. Archer . . . . May Lloyd
Mr. Benton . . . . Patrick Smith
Cyril Upjohn . . . . Grant Tilly
Enderby . . . . Greg Johnson
Female Journalist . . . . Alison Bruce

"Alex" is what used to be termed "a family film," but this uplifting tale of a talented Auckland teenager's dogged attempts to win selection to New Zealand's 1960 Olympic swimming team comes off as too slight and rose-colored to appeal to today's cynical teen auds. Prepubescent femmes would appear to be the target, and that's a limited audience. A more reasonable video and TV life is indicated.

The film's principal asset is newcomer Lauren Jackson, who seems perfectly cast as the tall (well over 6 foot) achiever. Jackson not only convinces in the numerous swimming scenes, but she also attractively plays in some restrained romantic encounters with Alex's loyal and sympathetic boyfriend, Andy (Josh Picker). Alex is so certain she's going to be selected for the Olympic team that she's already learning Italian; but her coach (Aussie thesp Chris Haywood) is frustrated because she doesn't devote herself

exclusively to swimming; she also attends ballet classes, is a member of the school hockey team, in rehearsal for a school version of "The Mikado," and about to sit for her final exams.

The girl's confidence is shattered by a new arrival on the scene, Maggie Benton (Catherine Godbold), an equally good swimmer who's been living in Singapore but whose ambitious mother is determined she'll get the official Kiwi nomination from the head of the swimming federation, Upjohn (Grant Tilly).

Here's where first-time feature director Megan Simpson shows her inexperience: the scheming Mrs. Benton and horrid Upjohn are way over the top, their motivations foggy, and their portrayals about as subtle as in a silent melodrama.

The staging of the all-important final swimming race, in which Alex has to beat Maggie to go to Rome, is poor. Still, there could be a space for this otherwise well-crafted film, especially in daytime TV slotting, but theatrical looks slow, except in New Zealand, where Tessa Duder's book is popular. The producers confidently plan a sequel depicting Alex's adventures in Rome.

Technical credits are all pro.

— *David Stratton*

LA PASSION VAN GOGH
(THE VAN GOGH WAKE)
(FRENCH-BELGIAN)

An Impex Films release of a Triplan Prods./Heliopolis Films/Alain Keytsman Prods. co-production with support from the CNC and EFDO. Produced by Georges Hoffman. Directed by Samy Pavel. Screenplay, Pavel, Jeanine Hebinck, Juliette Thiéerée, Armand Eloi. Camera (color), Nino Celeste; editor, Isabelle Dedieu; set design, Emmanuelle Sage; costumes, Monica Mucha; sound, Patrice Mendez; associate producer, Martine Kelly. Reviewed at Cine de l'Etoile screening room, Paris, Jan. 21, 1993. Running time: **92 MIN.**
Joanna . . . . Irène Jacob
Theo . . . . Jean-Pierre Lorit
Aurier . . . . Philippe Volter
Moe . . . . Maria Meriko
Also with: Juliette Thiérrée, Nicole Riston, Idil Cebula, Armand Eloi, Tatiane Verdonik.

Shot chronologically on a paltry budget in just 10 days and 10 nights, "La Passion Van Gogh" is a magnificently lit but ultimately tedious exploration of the Van Gogh clan's grief following Vincent's death. Like Vincent's canvases during his lifetime, Samy Pavel's earnest and arty exercise is likely to remain unheralded.

Though beautifully executed, a little of the pic's unrelentingly morose approach goes a long way. Irène Jacob's tiny role rules her out as a marketing hook.

Lenser Nino Celeste captures painterly tableaux (which evoke Holland though shot in Belgium) that create an atmosphere of gloom and mourning as Vincent's three sisters, brother Theo with his wife and infant son, and the journalist Albert Aurier (the painter's lone champion) gather at the family home. Together but far from united, incipient madness seems to run in this bunch.

The disconcertingly deep voice of aged Maria Meriko as the iron-willed matriarch who withheld her love, leaves an indelible impression. Her account of discarding Vincent's paintings after her husband's death is chilling.

Pic will be heavy going for those uninterested in scrutinizing carefully composed framing but, for students of superb lensing delivered on a tight schedule, it's a gorgeous exercise.

— *Lisa Nesselson*

XIN XIANG
(HEARTSTRINGS)
(CHINESE)

A Pearl River Film Studio production. (Intl. sales: Era Intl., Hong Kong.) Directed by Sun Zhou. Screenplay, Miao Yue, Sun; camera (color), Yao Li; editor, Xu Jianping; music, Zhao Jiping; music adaptation, Sun Zhao; art direction, Shi Haiying; costume design, Huang Jiakang, Sui Xiaomei; sound, Deng Qinghua, Feng Lunsheng, Lu Hong; sound effects, Zhen Fuqing; production supervisor, Di Caisheng; line producer, Lin Hai; dramaturg, Deng Yuan. Reviewed at Berlin Film Festival (Market section), Feb. 17, 1993. Running time: **97 MIN.**
Grandfather . . . . Zhu Xu
Aunt Lotus . . . . Wang Yumei
Jingjing . . . . Fei Yang
Zhuzhu . . . . He Jielin
Jingjing's mother . . . . Fu Lili
Ah Kun . . . . Li Guangneng
Old Taiwanese . . . . Qian Yifei
(Mandarin soundtrack)

A brave and involving movie dealing with feelings and intergenerational conflicts, "Heartstrings" is one of the most delicate works from mainland China in a while. Pic's theatrical career will be strictly limited to sites with a built-in following for quality East Asian product. Fest exposure and specialized TV playoff loom larger.

Modern-day story revolves around a 10-year-old Peking Opera student (Fei Yang) who, after his parents divorce, is sent to live with his grandpa (Zhu

March 29, 1993 (Cont.)

Xu), a w.k. performer of the '50s. The old man lives a ascetic life, warmed only by his friendship with Aunt Lotus (Wang Yumei), a devout Buddhist.

The kid and grandfather have a hard time finding common ground, and the former strikes up a companionship with a young girl (He Jielin) interested in Peking Opera. A further jolt to the old man's placid existence is Aunt Lotus' news that her husband, living in Taiwan for the past 40 years, can finally visit her.

Narrated by the kid, and almost entirely set in the quiet interiors and courtyards of an old-style neighborhood, the movie manages to tackle abstract concepts like tradition, memory and the bonds of family and art without losing sight of its characters.

In its grounding in the disappearing world of traditional music, buffs will note similarities with Zhang Zeming's "Swan Song" (also Canton-set), and in its fragile beauty and emotions, with Taiwan helmer Ch'en K'unhou's "The Matrimony."

Director Sun Zhou, who bowed with the contempo comedy "Put Some Sugar in the Coffee" and followed with the thriller "Blood at Dusk," maps out different territory here. Pic's measured pace never palls, with vet actor Zhu as the testy grandfather and actual Peking Opera student Fei as the antsy kid double-teaming superbly. Final scenes are genuinely throat-catching.

Visually, it's a feast for the eyes, with knockout lightplay compositions by cameraman Yao Li and atmospheric art direction by Shi Haiying. Chinese title literally means "Heart Fragrance."

— *Derek Elley*

LA FINE E' NOTA
(THE END IS KNOWN)
(ITALIAN-FRENCH)

An Artisti Associati release of a Cineritmo/RAI-TV Channel 2/Les Films Alain Sarde co-production. Produced by Giovannella Zannoni. Directed by Cristina Comencini. Screenplay, Comencini, Suso Cecchi D'Amico, from Geoffrey Holiday Hall's novel. Camera (color), Dante Spinotti; editor, Nino Baragli; music, Alessio Vlad, Claudio Capponi; art direction, Paola Comencini; costumes, Antonella Berardi. Reviewed at Anica screening room, Rome, Jan. 20, 1993. Running time: **110 MIN.**

Bernardo	Fabrizio Bentivoglio
Maria	Valerie Kaprisky
Carlo Piane	Massimo Wertmuller
Rosario	Corso Salani
Elvira	Valeria Moriconi
Lawyer	Daria Nicolodi
Elena	Mariangela Melato
The Brain	Carlo Cecchi
Also with: Valeria Milillo, Stefano Viali.	

Italian adaptations of American thrillers have traditionally met with mixed results, and "The End Is Known" is no exception. This very watchable film succeeds in transposing its story to post-terrorist Italy. But despite interesting twists, it's short on atmosphere and emotional involvement. Appeal is mostly to mystery fans, and TV sales should be in demand.

On her third feature, Cristina Comencini (daughter of director Luigi) and veteran scriptwriter Suso Cecchi D'Amico tackle a novel by Geoffrey Holiday Hall that became a bestseller in Italy thanks to its "discovery" by Leonardo Sciascia, Italy's greatest writer of political thrillers.

The story starts at an "end," when a young man (Corso Salani) falls out of a fourth floor window and lands at the feet of lawyer Fabrizio Bentivoglio. The window in question turns out to be Bentivoglio's own, and his wife (Valerie Kaprisky) the only witness to the mysterious suicide. When it is learned the dead man had a political past, Bentivoglio links it to a suspected terrorist he is defending.

Rich, smart and used to commanding, Bentivoglio is a much better sleuth than the investigating magistrate assigned to the case, plodding but honest Massimo Wertmuller. In their parallel investigations, they stumble across the same cast of characters: Valeria Moriconi as an aging bar-owner who helped hide the boy in the wilds of Sardinia; Mariangela Melato as a chic ex-comrade who has immigrated to Paris; Daria Nicolodi as the boy's one-time lawyer; Carlo Cecchi (from "Death of a Neapolitan Mathematician"), as his former cellmate in prison.

Film keeps up a good rhythm as the truth slowly emerges in flashbacks. Any alert viewer will have the mystery solved long before the film's two rival "detectives" do. But much of the fun is in watching them untangle the threads while pushing sticky personal problems to one side. Sympathy is pretty evenly divided.

Though star Kaprisky has little to do but look pretty and victimized, the other female roles are strong, as might be expected from the "Amusements of the Private Life" helmer.

Comencini keeps filmic interests in the forefront — here, the need to make a believable thriller. At times, the genre feels more like a straitjacket than a spur to her imagination and emotions.

Dante Spinotti lenses a diversity of settings; Paola Comencini's sets play an even more important role: in a neat twist, the Bentivoglios' flashy contempo apartment furnishes the solving clue. — *Deborah Young*

DIE TERRORISTEN!
(THE TERRORISTS!)
(GERMAN)

A Rechtsrheinische Verleih Cooperative release of a Philip Gröning production in association with NDR/SWF/HFF. Executive producer, Gröning. Produced by Veit Helmer. Directed, written by Gröning. Camera (color), Anthony Dod Mantle; editor, Max Jonathan Silberstein; music, Alexander Hacke, Michael Busch, Daniel Jonston; production design, Christoph Winkler, Stefan Gaffke; costume design, Maria Dimler; sound, Manuel Laval; assistant director, Michael Busch. Reviewed at Berlin Film Festival (New German Cinema section), Feb. 19, 1993. (In Sundance Film Festival.) Running time: **92 MIN.**

Claudia	Stephanie Philipp
Michael	Michael Schech
Jürgen	David Baalcke
Neighbor	Peter Cieslinski
Real Estate Agent	Gerhard Fries

"Die Terroristen!" does not know what it wants to be: a bitter satire of the rudderless left or a searing tirade against our self-destructive society. What emerges is a boring and diluted film that has a single redeeming point — an intellectually captivating premise.

In "Die Terroristen!" writer-director Philip Gröning tells the story of three young would-be terrorists (Stephanie Philipp, Michael Schech, David Baalcke) who set out to assassinate a politician (recognizable as Helmut Kohl) who regularly passes a certain house in a motorcade.

The story has but a few twists: First, after practicing maneuvering a remote-control toy car loaded with plastic explosives under the politician's limo (à la "The Dead Pool") only to have the bomb not go off on the big day. Second, the bomb later *does* go off, killing the neighbors.

When their flighty rhetorical letters, originally composed to explain the execution of their targeted politician, are printed, the terrorists get the self-confir-mation they wanted and, satisfied, return to conventional, consumer-oriented lifestyles.

Though there are spots of humor (one funny scene shows how much more Gerhard Fries' arrogant real estate agent annoys them than the abstract politics of the shadowy figure in the limo), the pic's most interesting aspects are offscreen: a bank robbery with which they finance their operations, their friends, surroundings and relationships.

Technically, instead of facilitating the story, Anthony Dod Mantle's lensing, David Hofmann and Rainer Holthoff's lighting and Max Jonathan Silberstein's editing are too busy trying to be cute. The cheap disco-light effects, odd angles and sudden cuts to consumer kitsch give one the feeling that we are all back at film school in the '60s.

— *Eric Hansen*

LEPSIE BYT BOHATY A ZDRAVY AKO CHUDOBNY A CHORY
(IT'S BETTER TO BE HEALTHY AND WEALTHY THAN POOR AND ILL)
(SLOVAKIAN)

A Mirofilm production. Produced by Miro Vostiar. Directed, written by Juraj Jakubisko. Camera (color), Viktor Ruzicka; editor, Jirí Brozek; music, Jirí Bulis, Milos Krkoska, Robert Stanke; production design, Tomás Berka, Slávo Procházka; costume design, Peter Canecky; sound, Csaba Török. Reviewed at the Viennale, Vienna, Oct. 24, 1992. (In Berlin Film Festival, Panorama section.) Running time: **108 MIN.**

Nona	Deá Horváthová
Esther	Dagmar Veskrnová
Robert	Juraj Kukura
Margita	Vilma Jamnická
Vilo	Lubomir Paulovic
Klinec	Stanislav Danciak
Saigon	Vo Dang Hoai Phuong

This inventive, warm-hearted and humorous romp through post-Cold War Bratislava comes across like a triumphant and spunky shout of "We're not dead yet!" Made basically for an indigenous market, pic will demand a lot of offshore auds, including patience with a low tech standard and a jerky cut.

When the Velvet Revolution sweeps away the previous order of things, a vacuum is left. Anything can happen, and in helmer Juraj Jakubisko's crazy world, it does. The film follows the fates of two girls, friends, robbed of their men when the state is robbed of its anchor. As their men go their ways, the women decide to go theirs — from soft porn to robbery, they try everything they can to make a little money.

Strike that: to make a lot of money. Jakubisko's wry optimistism is contagious and with Deana Horváthová as the jaded and ruthless brains of the outfit and Dagmar Veskrnová as the dumb blonde who ends up suffering as much as, but not more than, her counterpart, he has found ideal personifications. From a slow beginning, they quickly take over the screen. Though the supporting roles are well cast, the only one capable of standing up to the two of them is Vilma Jamnická as Margita, the old nun with a good relationship with the spirit world and a heartily self-forgiving attitude towards sin.

While the dynamic acting can overcome the relatively low tech standards, the jerky editing is more irritating. The idea may be to push on at a breakneck speed in the manner of many Czechoslovakian directors, but the gambit too frequently pulls the viewer out of the otherwise charming action. — *Eric Hansen*

THE SANDLOT

A 20th Century Fox release in association with Island World. Produced by Dale de la Torre, William S. Gilmore. Executive producers, Mark Burg, Chris Zarpas. Directed by David Mickey Evans. Screenplay, Evans, Robert Gunter. Camera (Deluxe color), Anthony Richmond; editor, Michael A. Stevenson; music, David Newman; production design, Chester Kaczenski; art direction, Marc Dabe; set decorator, Judi Sandin; costume design, Grania Preston; sound (Dolby), Douglas Kearns, Tom Steel; 2nd-unit director, John Moio; animal trainers, Gary Gero, Charyl Harris; casting, Shari Rhodes. Reviewed at UA Coronet, Westwood, Calif., March 25, 1993. MPAA Rating: PG. Running time: **101 MIN.**
Scotty Smalls . . . . Tom Guiry
Benjamin Franklin Rodriguez . . . . .
. . . . Mike Vitar
Hamilton "Ham" Porter . . . .
. . . . Patrick Renna
Michael "Squints" Palledorous . . . . .
. . . . Chauncey Leopardi
Al an "Yeah-Yeah" McClennan . . . . .
. . . . Marty York
Kenny DeNunez . . . Brandon Adams
Bertram Grover Weeks . . . Grant Gelt
Tommy "Repeat" Timmons . . . .
. . . . Shane Obedzinski
Timmy Timmons . . . Victor DiMattia
Mom . . . . Karen Allen
Bill . . . . Denis Leary
Mr. Mertle . . . . . James Earl Jones
"The Babe" . . . . Art La Fleur

"**T**he Sandlot" is yet another wallow in the coming-of-age stakes circa 1962. Sweet and sincere, the film is also remarkably shallow, rife with incident and slim on substance. The singular lack of true grit is a decided detriment and will impact adversely on b.o. prospects; theatrical life will be short and not so sweet and foreign prospects are limited even in baseball-loving Japan.

Scotty Smalls (Tom Guiry) arrives in some quiet piece of Americana and, without much difficulty, is recruited into the neighborhood's ad-hoc baseball team despite — to use the boys' most withering reference — the fact he "plays like a girl."

Endemic to the screenplay (by director David Mickey Evans and Robert Gunter) is its singular inability to find any dramatic resolution. Scotty's initial dilemma hints at a fractious family environment in which unstated tension bubbles between the boy and his stepfather, Bill (Denis Leary). Eventually, it is resolved, or simply goes away. But it is just one of many missed opportunities to provide some texture.

Scotty's mentor instead is Benny Rodriguez (Mike Vitar), the tallest, most charismatic and, hence, best player on the block. Don't ask for a basis for the friendship, it's pure conjecture.

Running beneath the surface of this fond remembrance is the promise of some cataclysmic event, foreshadowed in voiceover by the older Scotty (silently played by Arliss Howard and voiced by Evans, both uncredited) 30 years later. It is not the grudge match (dispersed with quickly and casually), but the a mythically feral junkyard dog who resides next to the playing field and devours all orbs, including the naive Scotty's stepfather's autographed Babe Ruth baseball, that come his way.

"The Sandlot" pretends to be about something when it really just strings together loosely connected vignettes. Worse, the setpieces are familiar retreads.

Director Evans acquits himself well in tech areas in his debut feature, enhanced by Anthony Richmond's lensing and a sprightly David Newman score.

Performances are strong but the little leaguers seem less a team than an attempt at creating the cultural mosaic in microcosm. The adult roles provide solid cameos for James Earl Jones and Karen Allen. — *Leonard Klady*

THE ADVENTURES OF HUCK FINN

A Buena Vista release of a Walt Disney Pictures presentation in association with Steve White Prods. Produced by Laurence Mark. Executive producers, Barry Bernardi, Steve White. Coproducer, John Baldecchi. Directed, written by Stephen Sommers, from Mark Twain's novel "The Adventures of Huckleberry Finn." Camera (Technicolor), Janusz Kaminski; editor, Bob Ducsay; music, Bill Conti; production design, Richard Sherman; art direction, Randy Moore; set design, Keith Neely; set decoration, Michael Warga; costume design, Betsy Faith Heiman; sound (Dolby), Steve Aaron; assistant director, Howard Ellis; casting, Mary Goldberg. Reviewed at the Avco Cinema, L.A., March 25, 1993. MPAA Rating: PG. Running time: **108 MIN.**
Huck . . . . Elijah Wood
Jim . . . . Courtney B. Vance
The Duke . . . . Robbie Coltrane
The King . . . . Jason Robards
Pap Finn . . . . Ron Perlman
Widow Douglas . . . . Dana Ivey
Mary Jane Wilks . . . . . . Anne Heche
Deputy Hines . . . . . . James Gammon
Harvey Wilks . . . . Paxton Whitehead
Dr. Robinson . . . . . . Tom Aldredge
Susan Wilks . . . . Laura Bundy

"**D**isney's remake of Mark Twain's classic "The Adventures of Huckleberry Finn" is a fine one, and writer-director Stephen Sommers has made a timely, literate and handsome film. However, the acting of the two leads fails to provide the electrifying and stirring mood that the tale deserves. Still, as a solid telling of a mainstay of American literature, Disney's film should make merry at the b.o., locally and offshore.

In the newest version of the oft-adapted book, Elijah Wood stars as the roguish Huck Finn, living with the Widow Douglas (Dana Ivey). Curiously, Huck's orchestration of his fake death and escape from his brutal father is not as emotionally riveting as it is in the book. The film improves considerably once Huck encounters Jim (Courtney B. Vance), the runaway slave whose goal is to escape to the North and buy his family's freedom. The two drifters strike up a unique friendship as they start their fateful journey down the Mississippi.

Scripter Sommers has shrewdly limited the first-person narration, letting the kaleidoscopic gallery of characters propel the tale. In tune with our times, Sommers centers his narrative on the interracial friendship, providing a thorough examination of a morally complex bond.

Sommers' faithful adaptation is successful in rendering the spirit of Twain. His direction, however, is uneven; the first half-hour is oddly flat and not very engaging. But helmer's work improves as the film progresses, and he is particularly good in rendering the life of a small rural town in the 19th century.

More problematic are the two leads. Elijah Wood is appealing, and he is especially effective when he needs to be self-reflexive. But Wood may be too cute and too tame to play a wild nature boy; his performance lacks the brashness of Mickey Rooney in the 1939 entry. Vance, who has done superb work onstage and in film ("Hamburger Hill"), is also a bit stiff and not expressive enough.

Fortunately, the two central roles are surrounded by a marvelous ensemble of supporting actors: the brilliant Jason Robards and Robbie Coltrane as the King and the Duke, respectively, Ron Perlman as the nasty Pap Finn, Ivey as the Widow Douglas and Laura Bundy as the precocious Susan Wilks.

"Huck Finn's" rich physical production, with location work done in and around Natchez, Miss., captures the look and tone of the era perfectly. Richard Sherman's production design and Betsy Faith Heimann's costumes achieve the appropriate feel. The quality of Janusz Kaminski's lensing is exquisite and evocative.

April 5, 1993 (Cont.)

Despite its faults, "Huck Finn" is superior to Michael Curtiz's 1960 or J. Lee Thompson's 1974 efforts. Authentic and enjoyable, the Disney version is richly rewarding. — *Emanuel Levy*

YOU CAN'T PUSH THE RIVER
(AUSTRALIAN)

A Sculpting Pictures production, in association with the Australian Film Commission. Produced by Robert Alcock. Directed by Leslie Oliver. Screenplay, John Reddin, Oliver. Camera (Eastmancolor), Joel Peterson; editor, Murray Ferguson; music, Carl Vine; production design, Dona Brown; sound, Counterpoint Sound; assistant director, Reddin. Reviewed at AFC screening room, North Sydney, March 9, 1993. Running time: **74 MIN.**
Joe Glass . . . . . Nollaig 'o Flannabhra
Tony . . . . Antonio Punturiero
Kohar . . . . Kathryn Chalker

Described by its producers as "a lyrical cinema essay," "You Can't Push the River" is a small, poetic film that doesn't fall into any particular category (it's neither strictly fiction nor documentary, nor is it abstract). Festivals with sections that encourage offbeat first features might take a look at "River," which could find audiences willing to respond to its unusual but attractive style. From there it might segue into small, specialist sales.

A quote from James Joyce sets the mood ("There is no past, no future; everything flows into an eternal present") for this delicate, gentle movie experience that celebrates the environment with sumptuous footage of the Australian bush. "River" is equally concerned with the procedures of teaching and learning, and with the vital importance of unpolluted water to the world.

The screenplay, by John Reddin and director Leslie Oliver, features three principal characters: an Irish schoolteacher, his Armenian-Australian lover and one of his pupils. The teacher, Joe Glass, sympathetically played by Nollaig 'o Flannabhra, instructs his class about the world's great rivers and their importance for irrigation. At the same time, flashbacks show Glass as a boy learning from a kindly Catholic priest.

A sexual element is introduced when a link is made between the teacher's blackboard diagrams and the breasts of his mistress, Kohar (Kathryn Chalker), whom he met in a public library but who eventually leaves him to return to her native Armenia. She recites Armenian poetry to Glass who, when she has left him, sings a plaintive Irish ballad as the rain pours down outside his window.

However, most of the film takes place in the schoolroom where Glass' closest listener is Tony (Antonio Punturiero), an intelligent boy who recalls lyrical summers in the bush. The film that results from this unusual blend of elements is strangely beautiful, though its appeal is likely to be limited.

Acting is unselfconsciously apt, Carl Vine's music attractive, and the soundtrack composed by Counterpoint Sound a plus. In an amusing yet apt end credit, the New South Wales Water Board is listed as a major sponsor of the film. — *David Stratton*

COP AND A HALF

A Universal release of an Imagine Films Entertainment presentation. Produced by Paul Maslansky. Executive producer, Tova Laiter. Directed by Henry Winkler. Screenplay, Arne Olsen. Camera (Deluxe color), Bill Butler; editors, Daniel Hanley, Roger Tweten; music, Alan Silvestri; production design, Maria Caso; art direction, Allen Terry; set design, Damon Medlen; set decoration, Cindy Coburn; costume design, Lillian Pan; sound (Dolby), Joe Foglia; associate producer, Elaine Hall; assistant director, Bruce G. Moriarty; 2nd-unit director, Glen Wilder; 2nd-unit camera, Frank Flynn; casting, Meg Liberman, Mark Hirschfeld. Reviewed at Universal Studios, Universal City, Calif., March 22, 1993. MPAA rating: PG. Running time: **93 MIN.**
Nick McKenna . . . . . Burt Reynolds
Devon Butler . . Norman D. Golden II
Rachel . . . . Ruby Dee
Captain Rubio . . . . . Holland Taylor
Fountain . . . . Ray Sharkey
Raymond . . . . . . Sammy Hernandez
Chu . . . . Frank Sivero
Quintero . . . . Rocky Giordani
Waldo . . . . Marc Macaulay
Rudy . . . . Tom McCleister

"Cop and a Half" is to high concept what dog whistles are to canines. Pitched at an almost intolerably calculated level, this is an inert and at times irresponsible attempt to create a funny cop action entertainment for kids. Children under the age of reason may sit still for it, but parents are advised to bring a deck of cards and try to get some poker going.

Devon Butler (Norman D. Golden II), a savvy, black 8-year-old, fantasizes about being a policeman like those he sees on TV. He can talk the talk and walk the walk. But for his fantasy to come true, he must witness a murder and become involved — and bond — with crusty, misanthropic detective Nick McKenna (Burt Reynolds). The rest, what there is of it, can easily be surmised.

The script by Arne Olsen possesses nary an original moment or believable emotion, and leaves no cliché untapped. Such torts would have been pardonable had there been even a shard of humor. That aside, the film's stance on violence (albeit mostly offscreen) and gunplay, as well as some bathroom humor even a third grader would deem immature, is a bit troubling — although certainly not as egregious as in "Kindergarten Cop."

Under Henry Winkler's direction, the coy reaction shot reigns supreme, and there are one too many overdubs of essential plot points ignored during shooting. Or maybe those scenes were cut, since the film's transitions are about as smooth as the Sierras.

As Devon, Golden is a missed opportunity. A strong directorial hand might have pulled some charm and winsomeness out of him. As it is, he doesn't steal scenes, he abducts them. Reynolds, plays the role as someone with a permanent stomachache.

Ray Sharkey's villain had possibilities but it doesn't help that he seems to be in another movie. Similarly wasted are the Holland Taylor and Ruby Dee. Apart from Bill Butler's lucid, sunny cinematography, tech credits are below par. The sound is flat and dialogue is often out of sync. Ambient noise is almost nonexistent, and Alan Silvestri's score seems to have been laid in from other movies. — *Richard Natale*

DAENS
(BELGIUM-FRANCE-HOLLAND)

A Favourite Films/Films Derive/Titane/Shooting Star production. (Intl. sales: Seawell Films, Paris.) Produced by Dirk Impens. Directed by Stijn Coninx. Screenplay, François Chevallier, Coninx, from Louis Paul Boon's novel. Camera (Technicolor), Walther Vanden Ende; editor, Ludo Troch; production designer, Allan Starski; costumes, Yan Tax; music, Dirk Brosse; sound, Henri Morelle, Jean-Paul Loublier; associate producers, Luc Dardenne, Jean Luc Ormieres, Hans Pos, Maria Peters, Dave Schram. Reviewed at AMPAS screening room, L.A., Feb. 24. Running time: **134 MIN.**
Adolf Daens . . . . Jan Decleir
Charles Woeste . . . Gérard Desarthe
Nette Scholliers . . . . Antje De Boeck
Jan De Meeter . . . . . . Michael Pas
Schmitt . . . . Johan Leysen
Eugene Borremans . . Idwig Stephane
Elisabeth Borremans . Linda Van Dijck
Pieter Daens . . . . . Wim Meuwissen
(Flemish and French soundtrack)

Oscar foreign-language nominee "Daens" provides yet another example of the talent explosion in Belgium. On the heels of such recent revelations as Felix-winning "Toto le Heros" and Cannes-prized "Man Bites Dog," comes this sumptuous, Hollywood-style period epic on the disparity between rich and poor at the turn of the century. The absence of a cultural link will make this an improbable U.S. sale, though the Venice fest entry should move beyond its immediate turf in Europe, particularly in its TV miniseries form.

Priest Adolf Daens (Jan Decleir) returns home to Flanders to find abject poverty among the locals employed at the Dickensian textile mill, a situation is frought with tension, contradiction and irony. The local Catholic church is supported by the French-speaking mill owners, something that is patently obvious to the workers. However, given the choice between socialist activists and the crusading humanism of Father Daens, most side with the latter. The priest is thrust between the teachings and politics of his order.

Director/co-writer Stijn Coninx, at least in the theatrical version, fails to illuminate the full complexity of the social, cultural, class issues at the heart of the story. His dramatic shorthand is often cloying. The French elite are cookie-cutter villains and he bridges the political factions with an all too familiar Romeo and Juliet subplot.

Yet, Decleir's central performance smooths the awkwardness to a remarkable degree. It is a towering portrait of a troubled, committed man whose own skeletons remind us of his mortal bonds. — *Leonard Klady*

EST & OUEST: LES PARADIS PERDUS
(EAST & WEST: PARADISES LOST)
(FRENCH)

A K-Films release of a Compagnie Est-Ouest production in association with Canal Plus (Intl. sales: Mercure Distribution). Executive producer, Claude Rosius. Directed, written by Pierre Rival. Camera (color, 35m, Super 16m, Super 8m), Jérome Peyrebrune, Igor Gourov; editor, Marie-Pomme Carteret; music, Michel Portal; sound, Daniel Ollivier, Alexandre Melnikov; production supervisors, Paula Stein, Galina Kouznetsova, Frank Le Wita; talent managers, Dany Jucaud, Oleg Chichkine. Reviewed at the Entrepot Cinema, Paris, March 4, 1993. Running time: **62 MIN.**
Russian Angel . . . . Aliona Antonova
Coffee shop writer . . . . Scot Kellman
Realtor . . . . Philippe Bergeron
Aspiring actress . . . . . . Cissi Saussy
Also with: Jacqueline Bisset, Zsa Zsa Gabor, José Eber, Willie (Dino) Lewis, Jonathan Lawton, Bruce Gilbert, Zalman King, Marilyn Kagan, Menahem Golan, Coco Conn, Tim Martinez.
(English, French, Russian and Japanese soundtrack)

A rather sweet semi-docu effort to draw parallels between the disintegrating "Worker's Paradise" of the ex-USSR and the disintegrating entertainment paradise of Hollywood, Pierre Rival's "Est & Ouest: Les Paradis Perdus" should find its way into fests and onto TV. Any movie that shows the Syd Field how-to bible "Screenplay" reduced to confetti after drama coach Scot Kellman opines "the paradigm is a coffin" probably stands to carve a niche on video to boot.

First-time helmer Pierre Rival was longtime editor of the French trade mag Le Film Français before he segued into producing "Taxi Blues" and "Moscow Parade." Compelling, if brief, footage of Moscow subways, video parlors, drunk tanks, saunas and strip joints, grabbed in early 1992, gives way to (pre-riots) Los Angeles.

Pic's "tour guide" is a French-speaking Russian angel (pleasantly ethereal Aliona Antonova) transplanted from disillusioned Moscow to ever-humming L.A., to see how the last utopia, the American Dream, is holding up.

Positing, with humor, that any flourishing empire is destined to fall, pic is part docu, part experimental and part just plain silly (e.g., without skipping a beat, Zsa Zsa Gabor claims she is chummy with heads of state and that her husband and her horse trade pride of place in her affections).

Hollywood types who play themselves — Zalman King on censorship in America; Jonathan Lawton on the origins of his "Pretty Woman" script; Jacqueline Bisset on the likelihood of showbiz corrupting innocence; hairdresser to the stars José Eber; talk radio host and shrink to the players Marilyn Kagan; and oleaginous orator Menahem Golan — all come off quite well.

Perfs from staged archetypes — a Beverly Hills realtor; three aspiring actresses; an opinionated cab driver — are sometimes wobbly but pic manages to be being ironic without being nasty.

Michel Portal's varied score is perfectly attuned to the shifting imagery. Lensing —Super 16 and Super 8 in L.A., 35m in Moscow — is consistently smooth.
— *Lisa Nesselson*

LUNG MIN
(CAGEMAN)
(HONG KONG)

A Filmagica Prods. production. (Intl. sales: Sil-Metropole, Hong Kong.) Executive producer, Jacob C.L. Cheung. Directed by Cheung. Screenplay, Ng Chong-chau, Yank Wong, Cheung; camera (color), Ardy Lam; editor, Henry Cheung; music, Eugene Pao; art direction, Wong, Chiu Yiu-hang; costume design, Chan Wing-wo; sound, Steve Chan; assistant directors, Benny Lau, Glory Tang. Reviewed at Berlin Film Festival (Panorama section), Feb. 15, 1993. Running time: **150 MIN.**
Fatso Koo . . . . Roy Chiao
Sissy . . . . Victor Wong
Tong Sam . . . . Teddy Robin
Luk Tong . . . . Ku Feng
Mao . . . . Wong Ka-kui
Taoist . . . . Lau Suen
(Cantonese soundtrack)

A lively, well-scripted ensembler set in a hostel for dropouts, "Cageman" is one of the strongest political items to come from Hong Kong in a long time. Extreme running time, which may prove a chore for audiences not attuned to the pic's local subtleties, will limit this challenging work to fests and Asian film weeks, though enterprising webs should snap it up.

In many ways, the pic is a throwback to Cantonese items of the '50s that dealt with pressing social issues beneath commercial surfaces. Buffs will note parallels with the classic "The House of 72 Tenants," a tenement ensembler that was Hong Kong's biggest grosser in 1973.

Setting is the 40-year-old Wah Ha Cage House, a privately owned hostel for single men in which wire-mesh "cages" do duty as regular apartments. Piled three-high, and stacked like boxes in a warehouse, they house a cross-section of young and old, local citizens and mainland Chinese, part-time workers and retired folk. Rents are minimal.

The real estate firm that owns the block wants it quietly demolished and uses a young ex-con as a Trojan horse to collect signatures from the residents agreeing to a payoff. As the tightly knit community starts to fragment, the issue turns into a media circus, with local council members currying votes by making sympathy visits. The conclusion is sudden and tragic.

Under the ensemble comedy-drama, the script has plenty to say about rapacious realtors, two-faced politicos, and loss of community values in contempo Hong Kong. The cage people are seen as the fast-vanishing diversity of the territory as modern government and conformity level out its bumps and personality.

Mobile camerawork, weaving up and down the aisles between the cages, follows the dialogue and action. Though a good 80% of the pic is set within the hostel, there's never a feeling of the setting cramping the action.

Casting is strong down the line, with an impressive lineup of experienced thesps. Roy Chiao makes a commanding presence as the cage people's de facto leader, well supported by Victor Wong (familiar from Amerasian pics by Wayne Wang and others) and local comic Teddy Robin. As the young ex-con, Wong Ka-kui blends easily with the vet cast.

Tech credits are fine, though better English subtitling than on print unspooled at the Berlin fest is needed to convey the subtleties of the Cantonese dialogue.
— *Derek Elley*

LA BRUNE
(DUSK)
(FRENCH)

A K-Films release of a Dracar Prods./Atelier Prods. co-production. Directed, written by Laurent Carcélès. Camera (color), Maurice Giraud; editor, Annick Baly; music, Jean-Pierre Sabar; production design, Sophie Sabar-Guigon; sound, Philippe Lecoeur; paintings by Guy Marie Nouvel. Reviewed at Reflet Medicis Logos cinema, Paris, France, March, 2 1993. Running time: **80 MIN.**
Anne Lassaray . . . . . Anne Marbeau
Hugo Lacombe . . . . . Michel Voletti
Also with: Patrick Laval, Alain Lionel, Sylvain Lemarie, Brigitte Carcélès, Anne Valérie Lefevre.

An intriguing premise is undercut by heavy, overly arty helming in "La Brune" docu-short maker Laurent Carcélès's first fiction feature.

Diagnosed with a fatal illness, Anne (Anne Marbeau), a mousy and apparently friendless painter, has only one year to live. She is shaken from the torpor of her doomed, depressingly mundane life by an anonymous encounter with a man (Michel Voletti) at her local library. Taken with the look in his eyes — a piercing quality that she is determined to capture on her easel — Anne begins to spy on him, only to discover that he's a murderer.

A Hitchcock or a Chabrol could have worked wonders with this setup, but promising storyline achieves only rare moments of refined tension as two doomed souls find questionable salvation.

The camera hugs the ground or hovers around its subject like a space probe. Claustrophobic images that might otherwise convey suspense and unease are often robbed of their power by the intrusive score.

Both lead thesps could stunt double for rabbits caught in the glaring headlines of an oncoming car. Marbeau is permanently shell-shocked and Voletti turns on the charm — when he's not seized with the urge to seize his dates by the windpipe.

Pic was shot in Paris in August and displays a quaint and sunny but eerily empty city.
— *Lisa Nesselson*

PAMETNIK ZNALEZIONY W GARBIE
(DIARY IN A MARBLE)
(POLISH-CANADIAN)

A Gambit Prods. (Warsaw)/Les Prods. d'Amérique Française (Montreal) co-production. (Intl. sales: Antenna, Montreal.) Produced by Jan Kidawa-Blonski, Yvon Provost. Directed by Kidawa-Blonski. Screenplay, Kidawa-Blonski, Jacek Kondracki, Zénon Olejniczak. Camera (color), Zdzislaw Najda; editor, Grazyna Jasinska-Wisniarowska; music, Michal Lorenc; production design, Barbara Komosinska; sound, Daniel A. Vermette; costumes, Renata Kochanska; assistant director, Grzegorz Okrasa; production manager, Marek Sobocinski. Reviewed at Berlin Film Festival (Panorama section), Feb. 18, 1993. Running time: **110 MINS.**
Janek . . . . Olaf Lubaszenko
Antek . . . Edward Linde Lubaszenko
Ewald . . . . Boguslaw Linda
Maria . . . . Marzena Trybala
Young Maria . . Katarzyna Skrzynecka
Apfelbaum . . . . Sergei Jurski
Nadia Apfelbaum . . . . . . Olga Kabo
Lidka . . . . Anna Majcher
Francik . . . . . . Andrzej Grabarczyk
Zdenek . . . . Aleksander Miedviediev

April 5, 1993 (Cont.)

An ambitious family saga that spans 50 years of recent Polish history, "Diary in a Marble" is marred by an extremely melodramatic and schematic final reel, but until then is an absorbing meller comparing interestingly to similar films made during the country's Communist era. Offshore commercial chances are slight, however; pic is probably more suited to TV than theatrical placement.

The opening credits place the story in the coal-mining area of Silesia in 1939. Ewald, married to the lovely Maria, joins a Polish unit to fight with the Allies against Germany; his brother Antek, who lusts after Maria, joining the German army, expecting a quick victory.

Captured by the Russians, because he's a Pole, Antek is allowed to change sides and fight with the Red Army. By war's end, he's an officer in the unit that "liberates" Poland and seizes the opportunity to make love to his sister-in-law, leaving her pregnant.

As the years go by, Antek becomes an important figure in the Polish Communist Party, while Ewald, who suspects that his crippled son, Janek, is not really his, becomes more and more depressed. Eventually, in 1953, he hangs himself.

The story continues in 1968 with Antek now married to his brother's widow and Janek studying in Moscow, where he falls for the daughter of a Jewish teacher. Antek, knowing the anti-Semitism of the Polish Party, does his best to break up the relationship, and succeeds in bringing his son back to Poland, where Janek marries a local girl and is swept up in the Solidarity campaigns that end Communism.

All this is divided into chapters with headings like "Conception," "Childhood," "Youth," etc. and many boldly directed scenes that provide a revisionist alternative to the family sagas Polish cinema has given us in the past.

Performances are variable, with the actors sometimes encouraged to overplay, especially as the film progresses to its disappointingly absurd finale. But in many respects, the film impresses, thanks to vivid production design and cinematography and a bold music score.

— *David Stratton*

DER PAPAGEI
(THE PARROT)
(GERMAN-16m)

A Filmwelt release of a Factory Entertainment production, in association with Bavarian Broadcasting. (Intl. sales, Cinepool.) Executive producer, Gloria Burkert. Directed by Ralf Huettner. Screenplay by Huettner, Andy Hoetzl, Hans Dräxler. Camera (color, 16m), Diethard Prengel; editor, Ulla Möllinger; production design, Christian Kettler; costume design, Eveline Stösser; sound Marc Parisotto; assistant director, Jan Becker; production assistance, Marco Weber, Sandra Scheucher. Reviewed at Intl. Hof Film Days, City Theater, Oct. 30, 1992. (In Berlin Film Festival, New German Films section.) Running time: 89 MIN.

Did . . . . Harald Juhnke
Rainer . . . . Dominic Raacke
Wilma . . . . Ilse Zielstorff
Helga . . . . Veronica Ferres
Alexa . . . . Daniela Lunkewitz
Karl . . . . Dietmar Mössmer

"Der Papagei" is everything people say a German film cannot be: light, funny and topical (the nationalist political movement) without getting preachy. However, offshore there may be two hurdles it is unable to jump: it is too German to translate well and, originally conceived for TV, lacks the aura of an event.

The film is a little gem. The "parrot" of the title is an out-of-work actor who gets hired by an extreme rightist political party to sugarcoat their shady platform for public consumption. The scheme works, thanks to the parrot, who proves to have a true feeling for the people — especially their unpretentious humor. However, it's not long before the otherwise mercenary front-man's developing political conscience forces him to rebel.

The story is simple, well told and light enough to let the hero win, more or less, in the end. But the gem here is not primarily Ralf Huettner's pro direction or Andy Hoetzl's script, but Harald Juhnke's performance as Did, the turned politico, happily leading the audience to a variety of morally and politically unsavory dead-ends (and back), without ever taking the danger too seriously. In "Schtonk" and here, he has rightly earned the title of "the German Walter Matthau."

Hof Days auds loved this 16m tube-bound pic so much that German distrib Filmwelt picked it up for rerelease after its airing last December. — *Eric Hansen*

NAD TYOMNOY VODOY
(OVER THE DARK WATER)
(RUSSIAN-GERMAN)

A Nikola Film production, in association with Lenfilm/Roskino/Avrova Filmproduktion. Produced by Natan Fyodorovsky, Aleksandr Bukhman. Directed by Dmitri Meskhiev. Screenplay, Valery Todorovsky. Camera (Eastmancolor), Pavel Lebeshev; editor, Tamara Lipartia; music, Sergey Kuriochin; art direction, Natalya Kochergina; costume design, Natalya Zamakhina; sound, Kirill Kuzmin; assistant directors, Yulia Sobolevskaya, Tanya Furtseva. Reviewed at Berlin Film Festival (Panorama section), Feb. 16, 1993. Running time: 98 MIN.

Lev . . . . Aleksandr Abdulov
Lena . . . . Ksenia Kachalina
   Also with: Tatyana Lyutayeva, Yuri Kuznetsov, Vladimir Ilyin, Ivan Chuznoy.

"Over the Dark Water" is a buoyant, if flimsy, slice of '60s life, sex, love and death, Leningrad-style. Markedly different in tone to young helmer Dmitri Meskhiev's previous "Cynics," pic could paddle to limited international business helped by a smart title change.

Featherweight story revolves round a group of pals led by charmer Lev (Aleksandr Abdulov), who "wins" the beautiful Lena (Ksenia Kachalina) after swimming the Neva River. After a session in the sack they part.

When one of the group is arrested by the secret police, Lev goes AWOL on a bender, and returns to find Lena in bed with a friend. After more coming and going, Lev supposedly dies after diving into the Neva again.

Framed as a reminiscence by Lev's son, the story has a light feel, accentuated by *nouvelle vague*-ish direction, carefree playing and colorful lensing. Scripter Valery Todorovsky comes up with a series of perky incidents to replace the movie's lack of a strong storyline. Pic can be read as Russian youth's critique of the myths constructed by their parents' generation.

Performances by the men are fine throughout, with Abdulov particularly charismatic as the roistering Lev. As the idealized beauty Lena, Kachalina has a less meaty part to chew on. Technically, pic is fine in all departments. — *Derek Elley*

HANASHIM MIMUL
(THE WOMEN NEXT DOOR)
(DOCU-16m)

A Filmmakers Collaborative Inc. production. (Intl. sales: Jane Balfour Films, London; Women Make Movies, N.Y.) Produced, directed, written by Michal Aviad. U.S. producer, Kevin White. Camera (Duart color, 16m), Yvonne Miklosh; editor, Era Lapid; music, Shlomo Mizrachi; sound, Israel David; assistant director, Buthina Khoury. Reviewed at Berlin Film Festival (Forum section), Feb. 21, 1993. Running time: 84 MIN.
(English, Hebrew & Arabic soundtrack)

"The Women Next Door" is a sideways look at ongoing Israeli-Palestinian tensions through a cross-section of women affected by the conflict. Emotive, focused subject matter will assure docu a warm welcome at the right houses, with TV sales also likely.

The film charts Israeli-born director Michal Aviad's journey (through Israel, the West Bank, Gaza Strip, Jerusalem) as she seeks out women with stories to tell. For auds already numbed by news footage from the region, the docu contains few surprises, despite its specialized take. Descriptions of torture, childbearing problems and casual disregard for human rights all have a familiar feel.

Cumulatively, however, the film adds up to a raw portrait of a society balanced on a knife edge, where paranoia has become the norm. Aviad, resident in the U.S. when the *intifada* broke out, brings a non-partisan perspective to the subject. Scenes of her and her crew challenged by Israeli soldiers, and an interview interrupted by gunfire, give the film a dramatic charge missing from slicker docus.

Tech credits are standard, with Shlomo Mizrahi's flavorful score binding the images together. Though the pic has been shown at cinematheques around Israel, local TV still refuses to air it, per Aviad. — *Derek Elley*

April 5, 1993 (Cont.)

SVARTE PANTERE
(REBELS WITH A CAUSE)
(NORWEGIAN)

A Favola Film production. Produced by Halvor Bodin, Thomas Robsahm. Directed, written by Robsahm. Camera (Eastmancolor), Harald Paalgard; editor, Inge-Lise Langfeldt; music, Pee Jay; production design, Crispin Gurholt; sound, Ragnar Samuelsson. Reviewed at Berlin Film Festival (Market section), Feb. 12, 1993. Running time: **89 MIN.**
Marius . . . . Henrik Mestad
Erik . . . . Bjarte Hjelmeland
Lise . . . . Guro Sibeko
Sonia . . . . Anneli Drecker
Bettina . . . . Bettina Banoun

This impassioned first feature is the work of Thomas Robsahm, the son of the late Italo thesp Ugo Tognazzi and Norwegian director Margrete Robsahm; it's dedicated to his father. Pic is a youthful tirade in favor of animal liberation, and could attract radical auds in many countries, though it's probably a case of preaching to the converted.

Five young Norwegians, two men, three women, live in an isolated farmhouse commune from which they regularly venture out to liberate labatory animals, or farm animals they believe are cruelly treated. At first, they worry because their activities garner little press, but as they become bolder they find themselves opposed by more conservative animal welfare outfits and targeted by police.

Eventually, they're tracked down and arrested, but the authorities seem to want to make an example of just one of them, Marius (Henrik Mestad), who's from a well-to-do background, turning the others against him and suggesting that he was sexually involved with the three women (actually, he was only involved with one). The fact that one is a minor adds to the wrath of the Establishment.

Robsahm handles this material with earnestness, and in an effort to widen the pic's appeal, there are lots of songs on the soundtrack, and there's a bright and lively young cast. There are also clips from the pioneering British animal liberation docu "The Animals Film."

Pic's Norwegian title translates as "Black Panthers;" title would obviously have different connotations in the U.S., and has been changed offshore.

— *David Stratton*

RONCSFILM
(JUNK MOVIE)
(HUNGARIAN)

A Budapest Filmstudio production. Produced by Ferenc Kardos. Directed by György Szomjas. Screenplay, Szomjas, Ferenc Grunwalsky. Camera (color), Grunwalsky; editor, Anna Kornis; music, Ferenc Kiss; production design, Tamás Vayer; sound, György Kovács; production manager, András Ozorai. Reviewed at Venice Film Festival (noncompeting), Sept. 1, 1992. (In Hungarian Film Week.) Running time: **90 MIN.**
With: Ági Szirtes, Zoltán Mucsi, Sándor Gáspár, András Szöke, Péter Andorai, Ildikó Bánsági.

György Szomjas is a perennial wild card, whose penetrating, anarchic films ("Bald Dog Rock," 1981; "Light Physical Injuries," 1983; "The Wall Driller," 1985) have regularly caught a precise mood of Hungarian working-class angst. His latest, "Junk Movie," is a companion piece to his earlier work, and was a hit with Magyar auds last year. It seems a good bet for the fest route at least.

Bearing the alternative title, "We Won, So What?," "Junk Movie" is a throwaway film with a message, a mix of zany humor and solid social criticism. Set in the same rundown urban milieu as his other films, it deals with the "ugly" face of contemporary, post-communist Hungary. Budapest is a city where a new under-privileged class has sprung up: poor, out-of-work proles coping with shortages as necessities are harder and harder to obtain.

The focus is on a sleazy pub and its surroundings, and the myriad characters include crooks who appear to prosper and ordinary people who barely survive. There are lovers, too, but the love story is quite marginal to the chaotic events on screen — the fights, monologues, half-hearted bouts of sex. Meanwhile, TV sets depict the changing outside world, along with ads for unobtainable things (a holiday in the Bahamas, for instance.)

Filled with vigor and energy, and challenging in its brutally honest anarchy, "Junk Movie" is as rough as a film can be, but it hardly matters because the material is so intrinsically fascinating. — *David Stratton*

LA JOIE DE VIVRE
(FRENCH)

An MKL release of a Les Prods. Lazennec production. Produced by Alain Rocca. Directed by Roger Guillot. Screenplay, Guillot, Josiane Maisse. Camera (color), Emmanuel Machuel; editor, Josie Miljevic; music, Angélique and Jean-Claude Nachon; production design, Sylvie Olive; costumes, Anne Schotte; sound, Olivier Schwob; associate producers, Adeline Lecallier, Christophe Rossignon. Reviewed at Les Acteurs A L'Ecran Festival, Saint-Denis, France, Feb. 7, 1993. Running time: **75 MIN.**
Monsieur Charme . . . Michel Bouquet
Reine . . . . . . Gwennola Bothorel
Joyeux . . . . Patrick Catalifo
Madame Jolly . . . . . Marie Mergey
Monsieur Jolly . . . . Michel Vitold
Also with: Micheline Dax, Henri Virlogeux, Kathy Kriegel, Emile Abossolo-M'Bo.

"La Joie de Vivre" is a dark comedy laced with nice surprises. Peppy and touching tale of an elderly widower who wants to be bumped off so as to join his late wife, should tickle the middle-aged to senior arthouse crowd. There's also a hint of U.S. remake potential in the perfectly cast first feature, directed and co-written by Roger Guillot.

Michel Bouquet (the acclaimed French stage and screen actor who starred in "Toto le Héros") is excellent as stern Monsieur Charme, the healthy but lonely oldster who approaches an enterprising young nurse, Reine (Gwenolla Bothorel), to kill him quickly and painlessly.

Quirky Bothorel, who bears a smaller-boned resemblance to Geena Davis, is delicious as the unconventional health care professional who makes house calls and reaps profits by accepting antique furnishings from her cash-strapped elderly clients.

Reine is delighted at the prospect of "inheriting" Charme's Paris apartment in exchange for her euthanasia services. But Charme's sole living relative, strapping young Joyeux (Patrick Catalifo), proves to be Reine's match when it comes to unscrupulous expediency.

Various schemes to kill Bouquet — among them a homemade poison from a recipe calling for live frogs and thwarted efforts to contract a dying friend's disease — are presented with industrious black humor.

Script sidesteps morbidity while making its observations about youth and old age and what makes life worth living. A far-fetched subplot about tribal magic may not click for all viewers but it does reinforce the idea that true love demands sacrifice. Although pic is not completely devoid of sentimentality, the characters have an edge that keeps things interesting.

Supporting thesps include celebrated cabaret vet Micheline Dax and noted Sartre interpreter Michel Vitold, who does a very convincing job of being at death's door.

Lensing and pacing effectively convey the contrasting environment of youth and old age. Mostly jaunty score nicely complements pic's tone.

— *Lisa Nesselson*

CAINO E CAINO
(CAIN VS. CAIN)
(ITALIAN)

A Penta Distribuzione release of a Mario and Vittorio Cecchi Gori/Silvio Berlusconi Communications presentation of a Penta Film/CG Group Tiger Cinematografica/Maura Intl. Film production. Produced by Mario and Vittorio Cecchi Gori. Directed by Alessandro Benvenuti. Screenplay, Leo Benvenuti, Piero De Bernardi, Ugo Chiti, Alessandro Benvenuti. Camera (color), Cristiano Pogany; editor, Sergio Montanari; music, Patrizio Fariselli; art direction, Eugenio Liverani; costumes, Enrico Serafini; sound, Candido Raini; associate producers, Bruno Altissimi; Claudio Saraceni. Reviewed at Metropolitan Cinema, Rome, Feb. 12, 1993. Running time: **104 MIN.**
Fabio . . . . Enrico Montesano
Franco . . . . . Alessandro Benvenuti
Also with: Daniela Poggi, Emy Kay, Giuliano Ghiselli, Novello Novelli, Eveline Gori.

Following a pair of smart ensemble outings that felicitously milked the rich dialect humor of his native Tuscany, Alessandro Benvenuti takes a disappointingly retrogressive step with the bland black comedy "Cain vs. Cain." Able performances and undeniable technical flair can't disguise a hackneyed idea given resoundingly laugh-free treatment.

Story is a workaday account of hammer-and-tongs sibling rivalry, pitting university-educated Franco (Benvenuti) against streetsmart brother Fabio (Enrico Montesano). Their father's death kicks off a scrimmage for control of his textile business, which Montesano slyly relinquishes in time to gloat as Benvenuti sweats through a tax audit.

Benvenuti strikes back by exposing Montesano's affair with his lifelong buddy's wife and so on — and on — until Benvenuti fakes his own kidnapping, swindling Montesano into forking out

April 5, 1993 (Cont.)

a whopping ransom. Revelation of the hoax sparks the inevitable physical clash in which they slug each other into total amnesia and apparent amicability.

Pic consistently strives to override its unexceptional core material with attention-getting tech work — most notably Cristiano Pogany's agile, inventive lensing — and a smattering of quirky, stylized sequences. One repeatedly used device is a chorus-like running commentary on the feud that bounces through the business world and factory personnel with the playful ebullience of a '50s musical. But the slick packaging registers hollowly.

Having shone in past efforts while working with large casts, all variously equipped with finely observed foibles, Benvenuti flounders with a narrower comedic focus in what's basically a two-hander. Supporting gallery is well populated, but insufficiently explored to give the multihued peoplescape of previous pics. Though he successfully shuns the vulgar slapstick of most mainstream Italo comedy, Benvenuti fails here to pin down a coherent style or rhythm to substantially replace it.

— *David Rooney*

ICELANDIC FEST

VEGGFODUR EROTISK ASTARSAGA
(WALLPAPER: AN EROTIC LOVE STORY)
(ICELANDIC)

An Icelandic Film Co./Icelandic Film Corp. co-production, supported by the Icelandic Film Fund. Produced by Julius Kemp, Johann Sigmarsson, Fridrik Thor Fridriksson. Directed by Kemp. Screenplay, Kemp, Sigmarsson. Camera (color), Jon Karl Helgason; editor, Steingrimur Karlsson; production design, Sigriour Sigurjonsdottir; sound, Elisabet Ronaldsdottir; costumes, Maria Olafsdottir; line producer, Vilhjalmur Ragnarsson. Reviewed at Berlin Film Fest (Market section), Feb. 21, 1993. Running time: **83 MIN.**
Lass . . . . Baltasar Kormakur
Sol . . . . Ingibjörg Stefansdottir
Sveppi . . . Steinn Armann Magnusson
Uggi . . . . Ari Matthiasson
Geirvar . . . . Flosi Olafsson

There's nothing very erotic about "Wallpaper: An Erotic Love Story," which broke b.o. records in Iceland last year but probably won't travel.

The simple tale is mainly set in a nightclub in Reykjavik. The place has been going downhill because the owner has been out of touch with teenage tastes and has consistently hired an aging rocker with no youth appeal. When the owner's smugly self-confident son, Sveppi, takes over the place he's determined to make drastic changes.

He also sees his powerful position as a way to add to his long list of female conquests; he has Polaroids of all the girls with whom he's had one-night stands displayed in his apartment. When attractive Sol (the name means "Sun" in Icelandic) arrives from the country and gets a job behind the bar, Sveppi thinks he's spotted another victim, and makes a bet with his more sensitive friend, Lass, an artist, that he'll conquer her first: The prize is to be Sveppi's red Chevy.

What follows is strictly predictable, except perhaps for a scene in which Sveppi attempts to rape Sol, who responds with violence and escapes with her virtue intact. The press material for the film boasts the presence of "Iceland's hottest bands," but they don't get much of a look in.

The male actors create minimal impression, but statuesque Ingibjörg Stefansdottir is a find as Sol, the girl determined to hang on to her virginity — until the inevitable last-reel coupling with Lass.

Technically, "Wallpaper" (the title remains obscure) bears all the hallmarks of a 16m blowup. The drab settings of downtown Reykjavik make an unusual backdrop to the familiar goings-on.

— *David Stratton*

NEW DIRECTORS

LANGER GANG
(PASSAGES)
(GERMAN-16m)

A Wild Okapi Film production. Produced by Frank Löprich, Katrin Schlösser. Directed, written by Yilmaz Arslan. Camera (Kodak color, 16m), Izzet Akay; editor, Bettina Böhler; music, Ralph Graf; sound, Michael Hemmerling; assistant director, Petra Erler. Reviewed at Museum of Modern Art, New Directors/New Films series, N.Y., March 23, 1993. (In Berlin Film Festival, New German Cinema section.) Running time: **78 MIN.**
Nedrin . . . . Nina Kunzendorf
Didi . . . . Dieter Resch
Martin . . . . Martin Seeger
Junge . . . . Marco Neumeier
Tarik . . . . Tarik Senouli
Sascha . . . . . . Alexandra Krieger
Juana . . . . Juana Volkers
Agnes . . . . Agnes Steinacker
Punk . . . . Andreas Frank
Schwab . . . . . Christian Verhoeven
Man in elevator . . . . . Yilmaz Arslan

An original dramatic film about handicapped youngsters in a German rehab center, "Passages," with proper nurturing, could attract the same U.S. audience that supported similarly visionary works by Werner Herzog in the '70s.

Debuting Turkish-born filmmaker Yilmaz Arslan, himself an alumnus of such an institution, demonstrates a flair for dramatic composition in creating a mood of loneliness and genuine strangeness within the confines of a huge institution. His cast is drawn from non-pros, friends who, like Arslan, stayed there.

Vignette structure economically introduces a diverse group of youngsters, suffering various disabilities ranging from no arms to crippled legs, each coping as best he can. Unlike the usual docu or drama on this type of subject, Arslan expresses the rage of the inmates without moralizing or sentimentality.

Best performance is by Dieter Resch, a dwarf with atrophied arms who nonetheless plays a mean drum solo, paints impressive portraits with his feet and is even a bit of a Lothario with paraplegic Nina Kunzendorf.

Film is bookended by scenes of the center's rep, Christian Verhoeven, giving civic-minded visitors a guided tour of the facility, obviously missing all the very human stories therein. Resch embodies the spirit of the place and at film's end, after he's been busted by the police for drug possession, his legacy is transferred to a sympathetic young boy with paralyzed legs, Marco Neumeier, who started out as an incorrigible playing games with elevators but was taken under Nina and Dieter's protection.

Key subplots involve an African-American singer, Juana Volkers, whose blues chants punctuate the action until she is taken away by her straitlaced military dad; also a weird boy on a bike who nearly falls in love with a spastic girl but is raped on an elevator (by director Arslan, taking a role he says everyone else turned down) and goes crazy.

Film includes considerable controversial material, especially rumbles between the patients, as well as sex scenes that are vivid and realistically grotesque. Throughout there is a strangeness that recalls some of Herzog's best work, notably in "Heart of Glass" and "Stroszek." Like Herzog, Arslan includes several non sequitur scenes of suggestive but cryptic behavior, and punctuates the picture with extremely black humor.

With moody lighting by Izzet Akay, "Passages" is remarkable in its sustained atmosphere of a constrained world, parallel to but quite different from the one inhabited by the viewer. Getting inside Arslan's vision is difficult (pic will definitely alienate audiences who can't take Tod Browning's horror classic "Freaks," for example), but well worth the consciousness expansion.

Tech credits are okay, though Ralph Graf's distorted electronic musical score is overbearing.

— *Lawrence Cohn*

MANHATTAN BY NUMBERS

A Rising Star/Pardis/Intl. Film & Video Center production. Produced by Ramin Niami. Executive producers, Bahman Maghsoudiou, Behrooz Hashemian. Directed, written, edited by Amir Naderi. Camera (color), James Callanan; music, Gato Barbieri; sound, Judy Karp. Reviewed at New Directors/New Films series, N.Y., March 19, 1993. Running Time: **88 MIN.**
George Murphy . . . . John Wojda
Chuck Lehrman . . . Branislav Tomich
Ruby . . . . Mary Chang Faulk
Fabric Store Assistant . Matt Friedson
Floyd . . . . Frank Irwin
Man in Bar . . . . Lou Galiardo
Fabric Store Owner . . . Lee Crogham
Mouse Man . . . . William Rafal
Shining Star . . . . . . Genard Small

"Manhattan By Numbers" follows an unemployed newspaperman into a Gotham heart of darkness. Pic's depressing tenor and gradual loss of conventional narrative will make it a hard mass-market sell; however, its determined grip on the pulse of the city and the nation may seize arthouse audiences.

Writer-director-editor Amir Naderi focuses on out-of-work newspaperman George Murphy (John Wojda) who has one day left to pay his rent while his wife and child stay with his in-laws.

An associate recommends that George look up another newspaper pal, Tom Ryan. George's search for Tom turns into a

Kafkaesque comedy as he is told to look for him in a decrepit apartment building where all the room numbers are missing.

In crisscrossing Manhattan's poorer neighborhoods, George learns that Tom has become a kind of ubiquitious street philosopher whom everyone knows but sees differently. Ultimately, even the search for Tom is forgotten and George becomes the focus for an "I Am a Camera" approach that permits Naderi to concentrate on the sights, sounds and people of Manhattan. Naderi returns to the plot one last time as George's Christmastime quest for money comes to an ironic conclusion in the Wall Street area.

The pic sometimes seems too much like filming by numbers with different parts of the city, e.g. Wall Street, serving for appropriate symbolic statements. However, Naderi also reminds us that the city looks like an assemblage of economic symbols. As the film meanders through the city's different neighborhoods, catches glimpses of the Times Square' Jumbotron, the Wall Street bull, flashing headlines on Newsday's Times Square "zipper," and the National Debt Clock, Manhattan begins to look like the visual aid for a cosmic H. Ross Perot.

James Callanan's lensing and Gato Barbieri's score should also be credited for their roles in establishing the city's ambience. In true operatic fashion, however, it is the appearance on the track of Puccini's "Nessun Dorma" that finally pulls out all the emotional stops.

— *Fred Lombardi*

THE GENIUS
(16m)

A Fugitive production. Produced by Joe Gibbons. Directed by Gibbons, with Emily Breer. Screenplay, Gibbons, Breer. Camera (Duart color, 16m), Mark MacElhattan, Gibbons, Peggy Ahwesh, Breer; editor, Breer; music, Henry Mancini, Ennio Morricone, Earle Hagen, Johnny Mandel, John Lurie, others; sound, Henry Hills, Keith Sanborn, Gibbons; production manager, Corinne Mallet. Reviewed at Museum of Modern Art, New Directors/New Films series, N.Y., March 22, 1993. No MPAA Rating. Running time: **95 MIN.**
Desmond Denton . . . . . Joe Gibbons
Kitty Church . . . . Karen Finley
Les Alabaster . . . . Tony Oursler
Dirk Dirkson . . . . Tony Conrad
Kiki Dirkson . . . . . . Corinne Mallet
Dr. Emmanuel Corbin . Adolfas Mekas
TV reporter . . . . Henry Hills
   Also with: Mark MacElhattan, Camden Toy, Gary Nicard, Mike Osterhout, Al McCreery, Jay Barry.

Talent scouts looking through the N.Y. underground for the next Jim Jarmusch or Beth & Scott B will likely pass on Joe Gibbons and Emily Breer's "The Genius." It's a tiresome, amateurish 16m feature preeming at the Film Society of Lincoln Center and Museum of Modern Art's New Directors/New Films series.

Gibbons, progressing very little from his previous forays in the world of Super-8m, stars as a goofball doctor of "Personality Stylings," using various patients obviously in need of a shrink as guinea pigs for his experiments in personality transplants. Film's lo-tech sci-fi content is silly rather than funny, as he copies clients' personalities on CDs and tries each one on himself, using portable equipment of his own invention. This gimmick allows Gibbons to ham it up, depressed in one scene, manic in the next.

He obsessively photographs himself with a video camera, and the video footage has been adequately transferred to 16m (but is not likely to sustain a further blow-up to 35m very well). Other scenes are shot in 16m.

Technically pic is a bit ragged, most notably in a dark night video sequence after Gibbons has ingested the personality of a psychopath. Though film almost plays on the level of genre master Frank Henenlotter's N.Y. nightmare fantasies ("Basket Case," "Brain Damage"), Gibbons' main agenda is to satirize the art establishment and types who frequent downtown galleries. Pointlessly prophetic is a subplot in which artist-bartender Kitty Church (Karen Finley) blows up paintings around town, naming her terrorist self "Eve of Destruction."

By film's end, Gibbons has adopted Church's personality and is expressing himself in similar wish-fulfillment manner. In real life, he was briefly famous in 1978 for having stolen a painting at an Oakland Museum opening as a protest against the commercialization of art.

Gibbons and his collaborator Emily Breer (a former animator who came on "The Genius" project after principal photography as a film doctor) have not provided sharp writing, with many scenes seeming crudely improvised. Acting is poor, especially Tony Conrad as an evil art gallery owner who drugs his stable

of artists to cause them to overproduce assembly-line art.

Gibbons' attitude towards art is consistent with his filmmaking ethos: The soundtrack is extracts from the work of others, ranging from Earle Hagen's "Harlem Nocturne" and a John Zorn cover version of Ennio Morricone's jaunty "Sicilian Clan" theme to using Henry Mancini's "Breakfast at Tiffany's" to back a corny romantic interlude. Similarly, one of the most effective scenes relies on Breer intercutting clips from James Whale's "Bride of Frankenstein" on TV with the unimpressive live action.

— *Lawrence Cohn*

INDECENT PROPOSAL

A Paramount release of a Sherry Lansing production. Produced by Lansing. Executive producers, Tom Schulman, Alex Gartner. Co-producer, Michael Tadross. Directed by Adrian Lyne. Screenplay, Amy Holden Jones, from Jack Engelhard's novel. Camera (Deluxe color), Howard Atherton; editor, Joe Hutshing; music, John Barry; production design, Mel Bourne; art direction, Gae Buckley; set decoration, Etta Leff; costume design, Bobbie Read, Bernie Pollack, Beatrix Aruna Pasztor; sound (Dolby), Keith Wester; assistant director, Aldric Porter; casting, Victoria Thomas. Reviewed at the Bruin Theater, L.A., April 4, 1993. MPAA Rating: R. Running time: **117 MIN.**
John Gage . . . . Robert Redford
Diana Murphy . . . . Demi Moore
David Murphy . . . . Woody Harrelson
Jeremy . . . . Oliver Platt
Mr. Shackleford . . . . Seymour Cassel
Day Tripper . . . . Billy Bob Thornton
Mr. Langford . . . . Rip Taylor
Auction Emcee . . . . . Billy Connolly

It's axiomatic in Hollywood that everyone can be bought, so it's too bad that Hollywood couldn't come up with a better way to express one of its most cherished beliefs than "Indecent Proposal." A provocative premise, megawatt star power and high-gloss production values guarantee potent early business, but aren't enough to forestall word-of-mouth that will prevent Adrian Lyne's latest from sporting the long-distance b.o. legs Paramount needs.

This is one of those high-concept pictures with a big windup and weak delivery. On paper, a film in which billionaire Robert Redford offers down-on-their-luck married couple Woody Harrelson and Demi Moore a cool million in exchange for one-night stand with Moore sounds surefire. Onscreen, the result has little sex, goes nowhere interesting or believable in the long second hour, and sports an idiotic conclusion that looks like Test Marketing Ending No. 6.

Plot somewhat resembles last year's "Honeymoon in Vegas," although it's arguable which picture has more laughs. Director Lyne spends the first reel establishing college sweethearts Harrelson and Moore as really in love and still ripping each other's clothes off. But the recession has dented his architecture career and her real estate sales. Needing $50,000 to keep their house, they head for Vegas.

But when they hit bottom, fate appears in the guise of Redford, a handsome high-roller who first calls upon Moore for good luck, sets the couple up in an opulent

April 12, 1993 (Cont.)

suite, etc., before making The Proposition. After instinctively saying no, Harrelson and Moore spend a sleepless night mulling it over, Moore finally concluding that she can do it without emotional consequence.

So off she flies in Redford's helicopter to his yacht, while Harrelson goes drunkenly off the deep end. Pic's second half similarly unravels, as Harrelson can't erase what happened from his mind, defies their prior agreement by demanding to know all about The Night and how good the sex was, and passively allows his wife to fall into the manipulative Redford's waiting arms and Rolls-Royce.

Ending is Hollywood hokum in its purest form, so silly as to undercut even the goodwill of viewers who might have bought into the story up until then, and exacerbated by John Barry's most syrupy score ever.

Despite the misfired storytelling, tale holds plenty of commercial appeal simply because the central issues involved are so compelling. Unfortunately, the script by Amy Holden Jones (who directed "Love Letters" and "Maid to Order" and co-wrote "Beethoven" and "Mystic Pizza") delves into these issues only sporadically, and Lyne is not a director to dwell meaningfully on philosophical nuances.

With their talent for making even grunge look glamorous, Lyne and lenser Howard Atherton dwell lovingly on the opulence of Las Vegas and the luxury of Redford's lifestyle. Dressed impeccably and smiling nearly all the time, Redford glides through the action like a latter-day Gatsby, a man who has it all — except a woman to love. However, Jones pilfers shamelessly from Everett Sloane's great girl-on-the-ferry monologue in "Citizen Kane" to give Redford's loneliness depth.

What emotional legitimacy the film does possess stems from Moore's performance, which is lively, heartfelt and believable until the script stops letting it.

After all the legal turmoil surrounding his hiring for the part, it's ironic that Harrelson is the weak link here. Standout support comes from Oliver Platt, who gets off some genuinely funny lines and looks as Harrelson's friend and attorney brought in to write up a contract for Moore's services. Seymour Cassel has nothing to do as Redford's aide-de-camp.

Tech credits are ultralush, although Moore has been saddled

with some silly looking shorts-and-suspenders outfits. Barry's score is spiced up by quite a few pop tunes. — *Todd McCarthy*

MR. NANNY

A New Line Cinema (U.S.)/Entertainment Film Distribtors (U.K.) release of a New Line Cinema production. Produced by Bob Engelman. Executive producers, Benni Korzen, Michael Harpster. Directed by Michael Gottlieb. Screenplay, Edward Rugoff, Gottlieb. Camera (Deluxe color), Peter Stein; editors, Earl Ghaffari, Michael Ripps; additional editing, Amy Tompkins; music, David Johansen, Brian Koonin; production design, Don DeFina; art direction, Jose Duarte; sound (Dolby), Henri López; special effects coordinator, J.B. Jones; associate producer, Carla Fry; assistant directors, Nelson Cabrera, Gary Sales; casting, Fern Champion, Mark Paladini. Reviewed at MGM Haymarket 3 theater, London, April 6, 1993. MPAA Rating: PG. Running time: **84 MIN.**

Sean Armstrong	Terry "Hulk" Hogan
Bert Wilson	Sherman Hemsley
Alex Mason	Austin Pendleton
Alex Jr.	Robert Gorman
Kate	Madeline Zima
Corinne	Mother Love
Tommy Thanatos	David Johansen

Cross "Uncle Buck" with "Home Alone," stir in the Hulkster, and you've got "Mr. Nanny," a comedy-actioner that should entertain the under-12 and couch potato sets. New Line is planning a late July release stateside.

Excuse for a plot has Hogan (billed here as Terry "Hulk" Hogan) as an ex-grappler whiling away days fishing in Florida. To help out his old trainer (Sherman Hemsley), he reluctantly takes a job as bodyguard to computer tycoon Austin Pendleton.

Twist is that Hogan, who loathes kids, has in reality been hired to protect Pendleton's brats (Robert Gorman, Madeline Zima), as well as double as nanny when the latest in a long line walks out. The anklebiters have been targeted for kidnapping by a psycho loon (David Johansen) who wants one of Pendleton's microchips, on which, naturally, world peace depends. Johansen and Hogan also have history.

Meat of the movie is the domestic war between the indestructible Hogan and the two kids, whose preferred reading is "Unusual Weapons of the Inquisition." Telegraphed finale has everyone learning mutual respect and taking on Johansen and his heavies in a warehouse finale.

Hogan's feet are on firmer ground here than in the more fantastic "Suburban Commando," and the computer-generated

script wisely doesn't try to extend him as a character actor.

As the family's acid-tongued maid, Mother Love gets most of the best lines. Johansen, sporting a steel basin on top of his skull, goes way over the top as a self-styled "average psychotic computer genius," and Zima impresses as the younger moppet.

Tech credits are average, though helmer Michael Gottlieb has turned in far classier material in the past ("Mannequin"). Cartoon violence has a slightly nasty edge, but went down gangbusters with child viewers at screening caught. — *Derek Elley*

THE CRUSH

A Warner Bros. release of a James G. Robinson presentation of a Morgan Creek production. Produced by Robinson. Executive producer, Gary Barber. Directed, written by Alan Shapiro. Camera (Technicolor), Bruce Surtees; editor, Ian Crafford; music, Graeme Revell; production design, Michael Bolton; art direction, Eric Fraser; set decoration, Paul Joyal; costume design, Sharon Purdy; sound (Dolby), Michael T. Williamson; associate producers, Marci Liroff, Joel Segal; line producer, Michael MacDonald; assistant director, Segal; casting, Liroff. Reviewed at AMC Century 14 Theaters, L.A., April 2, 1993. MPAA Rating: R. Running time: **89 MIN.**

Nick Eliot	Cary Elwes
Darian Forrester	Alicia Silverstone
Amy Maddik	Jennifer Rubin
Cheyenne	Amber Benson
Cliff Forrester	Kurtwood Smith
Liv Forrester	Gwynyth Walsh
Michael	Matthew Walker

For those "Poison Ivy" fans who haven't quite sated their appetite for psychotic yet seductive teenagers, here comes "The Crush," another by-the-numbers thriller longer on suspense than brains. Silly and predictable, the pic might squeeze out some early returns but, lacking star power, figures to peter out pretty quickly.

Writer-director Alan Shapiro says in the production notes that the idea was inspired by an incident in his own life, where "a brilliant young woman" developed a crush on him and refused to take "no" for an answer. However, the intervening rash of "Single White Female"-type hits appears to have provided further inspiration, with a touch of "The Bad Seed" for good measure.

Cary Elwes plays a writer who moves into the guest house of a wealthy couple and befriends their beautiful, precocious 14-year-old daughter, Darian (Alicia Silverstone), who starts out cute and coquettish and ends up

reminiscent of a similarly named youth from "The Omen."

Nick (Elwes) gives in to a momentary indiscretion and kisses the girl, then watches her grow gradually more obsessed, until she starts venting her wrath on him, a co-worker (Jennifer Rubin) and a teenage friend who may know too much.

Aside from the touchy aspects of a crazed teenager as sexual aggressor, the movie also flirts with uncomfortable territory via Nick's obvious ambivalence about this alluring woman-child and ultimately a false rape accusation.

Still, Shapiro (making his feature debut after directing several movies for the Disney Channel) explicably abandons any court proceedings to allow for the usual overwrought ending; however, the age of Darian, this latest variation on the crazed fill-in-the-blank, proves somewhat limiting in terms of both the actual threat and her eventual comeuppance. It even prevents the movie from qualifying as much of a male fantasy, unless one daydreams about statutory rape and prison time.

Elwes has a certain boyish charm as Nick but is so relentlessly dense he doesn't engender much sympathy. Silverstone (who has guest-starred on ABC's "The Wonder Years") brings the right mix of little-girl pouting and budding sensuality to a role that is, finally, a caricature. Other roles are equally limited.

Tech credits are generally undistinguished, though Bruce Surtees does provide some eerie moments in lensing the girl's shrine to her inamorato, as does Graeme Revell's score. Revell knows the territory, having worked on "The Hand That Rocks the Cradle" and, here, on the hand that robs it. — *Brian Lowry*

SPLITTING HEIRS
(U.S.-BRITISH)

A Universal (U.S.)/UIP (U.K.) release of a Universal Pictures presentation of a Prominent Features production. Produced by Simon Bosanquet, Redmond Morris. Executive producer, Eric Idle. Directed by Robert Young. Screenplay, Idle. Camera (Panavision 1.85; Eastmancolor; Technicolor prints), Tony Pierce-Roberts; editor, John Jympson; music, Michael Kamen; production design, John Beard; costume designer, Penny Rose; sound (Dolby), Peter Glossop; assistant director, Jonathan Benson; 2nd-unit director, Bosanquet; casting, Michelle Guish. Reviewed at Empire 1 theater, London, April 6, 1993. MPAA Rating: PG-13. Running time: **86 MIN.**

April 12, 1993 (Cont.)

Henry . . . . Rick Moranis
Tommy Patel . . . . Eric Idle
Duchess Lucinda . . Barbara Hershey
Kitty . . . . Catherine Zeta Jones
Raoul P. Shadgrind . . . . John Cleese
Angela . . . . Sadie Frost
Butler . . . . Stratford Johns
Mrs Bullock . . . . Brenda Bruce
Andrews . . . . . . William Franklyn
Doorman . . . . Eric Sykes

"**S**plitting Heirs" is a minor royalty "King Ralph." Breezy but lightweight comedy toplining Rick Moranis as a phony Yank heir to a Brit dukedom has already stiffed in Blighty but could play better in territories with a yen for English stereotypes.

Moranis plays a motormouth Yank who becomes the 15th Duke of Bournemouth and head of the family bank when his father suddenly drowns. Unbeknownst to him, the real heir to the fortune is bank underling Eric Idle, who's become his best pal.

Source of the confusion is Idle's mom, Barbara Hershey, who left him in a restaurant during the Swinging Sixties and claimed the wrong baby at the police station.

When Idle stumbles across the truth he tries every means to deep-six Moranis and claim his rightful fortune, in between fighting off the foxy Hershey who doesn't realize he's her son.

Even though it's short of true belly-laughs, the dumb-sounding storyline plays better than it reads, thanks to brisk pacing, all-out playing by the main leads, and some okay sight gags once the plot cranks up into revenge mode. Idle, who exec produced and penned the script, brings a Pythonesque flavor to much of the humor, making up in energy what it lacks in invention.

Main problem, apart from a storyline that could do with a few more twists, is that neither Idle nor Moranis, good as they are at klutzy routines, are strong enough to headline a pic of this sort. The deficit is spotlighted by the scattered appearances of John Cleese as a psychotic lawyer after a piece of the action.

Still, it's a hard pic to dislike so long as you check your brains at the door. Hershey throws herself in with such abandon it's almost churlish to note she looks 20 years too young for the part. Rising Brit glamorpuss Catherine Zeta Jones just about holds her own as a golddigger.

Rest of the cast is peppered with British stalwarts. Newcomer Sadie Frost ("Bram Stoker's Dracula") makes a brief mark early on as a yuppie bank colleague of Idle's.

Production values are smart, with locations in southern France and upper-crust English sites brightly captured by Tony Pierce-Roberts' lens. Michael Kamen's busy score and pacey editing by John Jympson make the 86 minutes breeze by.
— *Derek Elley*

FONG SAI-YUK
(HONG KONG)

A Golden Harvest release of a Zen-Dong production. Produced by Li-Young Zhong. Directed by Yuen Kwai. Screenplay, Chai Kung-Yung, change Jiang-Chung, Ji Ang. Camera (color), Ma-Tsu Cheng; production design, Ann Hui. Reviewed at Chinatown Twin theater, Sydney, April 1, 1993. Running time: **104 MIN.**
Fong Sai-Yuk . . . . Jet Li
Ting Ting . . . . Li Jia Xing
Mother Fong . . . . . . Fong Fong Siu
Father Fong . . . . Zhu Zhang
Tiger Lei . . . . Chan Sung-Yun
Lei Siu Huan . . . . Sibelle Hu

A current box office hit in Hong Kong, "Fong Sai-Yuk" is a breathtakingly energetic mixture of martial arts and comedy, lushly produced and in the best tradition of the genre. Right from the opening sequence, edited with the speed and punch of a theatrical trailer, pic delivers maximum entertainment. The crazy plot involves gender-bending and broad slapstick as well as astonishingly choreographed action.

Star Jet Li, whose Zen-Dong production outfit made the film, plays the title character, the handsome son of the Fongs, the self-styled martial arts champions of Canton. Unknown to his son, Fong Sr. is a member of a secret society dedicated to the overthrow of the Manchu emperor.

Another prominent Canton citizen, Tiger Lei, wants a strong husband for his willful daughter Ting Ting, who has already met and fallen for the younger Fong without learning his identity; he doesn't know her name either.

Ting Ting's mother, also a martial arts expert, offers to fight all comers with the man who defeats her to win her daughter's hand in marriage. Not realizing the prize is his beloved, Fong Sai-Yuk deliberately loses a fight against Mrs. Lei, but his place is taken by his mother (disguised as a man) who feels she has to uphold the honor of the Fong family. Unfortunately, Mrs. Lei falls in love with her opponent, not realizing she's a woman.

In addition to these almost Shakespearean complications, there's an evil emissary from the Emperor who arrives in Canton seeking a list of the members of the secret society. Fong Sr. narrowly escapes the guillotine in the suspenseful finale.

Great invention has gone into all the action scenes here, with a highlight being a fight in which the adversaries do battle while standing on the heads and shoulders of their supporters. Perfs do justice to the larger than life almost mythical characters.
— *David Stratton*

EL AMANTE BILINGÜE
(THE BILINGUAL LOVER)
(SPANISH)

A Lola Films/Atrium Prods./Cartel co-production with the collaboration of Sogepaq/Antena 3 TV/Intl. Dean Film (Rome). Produced by Andrés Vicente Gómez in association with Carlos Vasallo and Enrique Cerezo. Executive producer, Eduardo Campoy. Directed, written by Vicente Aranda, from Joan Marsé's novel. Camera (color), Juan Amorós; editor, Teresa Font; sets, Wolfgang Burmann; sound, Jim Willis; music, José Nieto; associate producer, Manuel Lombardero. Reviewed at Cine Benlliure, Madrid, April 3, 1993. Running time: **100 MIN.**
Norma Valenti . . . . Ornella Muti
Juan Marés . . . . Imanol Arias
Griselda Ramos Gil . . . . . Loles León
Also with: Javier Bardem, Joan Lluis Bozzo, Julieta Serrano, Felipe Hitas, Mario Pedrales.
Spanish, Catalan soundtrack)

Following the recent international success of his "Amantes," helmer-scripter Vicenta Aranda gets bogged down in a murky, rambling tale about a down-and-out street musician who mopes about and pines for his aristocratic ex-wife. The result is a flawed yawner that never gets its gums into any of the characters portrayed.

A first-person narrative introduces us to Juan (Imanol Arias), a 10th-rate accordion player and ventriloquist who, during the Franco era, meets Norma (Ornella Muti), a pretty society girl, during a sit-in protest in an art gallery. The pair are married (why is never explained), but soon she discards him, forcing him back into the streets to beg.

After being wounded and partly blinded by a Molotov cocktail, Juan starts dressing up alternatively as the "Phantom of the Opera" and "The Invisible Man." But his maimed heart still bleeds for Norma. In one droll interlude, he beds down with a myopic widow (the amusing Loles León

from the Almodóvar stable), who's trying to learn Catalan.

The bilinguality factor (Catalan and Castilian) is tangentially touched on, but the cultural and politics are vague and none of the characters is believable.

Muti, who is now 40, is still attractive; Arias and León put in good performances. But the sex scenes are clumsy, almost ludicrous. — *Peter Besas*

RECKLESS KELLY

A Warner Bros. release of A Serious production, produced with the assistance of the Australian Film Finance Corp. Produced by Yahoo Serious, Warwick Ross. Executive producer, Graham Burke. Directed by Serious. Screenplay, Yahoo Serious, David Roach, Ross, Lulu Serious. Camera (Eastmancolor, Panavision), Kevin Hayward; editors, Yahoo Serious (supervising), Roach, Robert Gibson, Antony Gray; music designer, Yahoo Serious, music, Tommy Tycho; visual design concepts, Yahoo Serious; art department head, Graham (Grace) Walker; art director, Ian Gracie; costumes, Margot Wilson; sound, Tim Lloyd; co-producer, Lulu Serious; associate producer, Roach; assistant director, Keith Heygate; production manager, Julia Ritchie; choreography, Aku Kadogo; special effects, Steve Courtley; stunts, Douglas (Rocky) McDonald; casting, Judith Cruden. Reviewed at Village Roadshow screening room, Sydney, April 1, 1993. Running time: **94 MIN.**
Ned Kelly . . . . Yahoo Serious
Robin Banks . . . . Melora Hardin
Major Wib . . . . Alexei Sayle
Sir John . . . . Hugo Weaving
Mrs. Delance . . . . Kathleen Freeman
Sam Delance . . . . John Pinette
Dan Kelly . . . . Bob Maza
Ernie the Fan . . . . . Martin Ferrero
Joe Kelly . . . . Anthony Ackroyd
Miss Twisty . . . . Tracy Mann
Newsreader . . . . Max Walker
Hank the Fan . . . . Don Stallings
Movie Director . . . J. Andrew Bilgore

Yahoo Serious' 1988 debut, "Young Einstein," was a hit in Australia and did more modestly offshore; the comic's second outing, produced on a far larger budget is full of ideas and nonsense but short on genuine laughs and zest. Still, teens might lap it up, thanks to adroit use of songs and issues.

Starting from the engaging premise that the spirit of Australia's legendary outlaw Ned Kelly (1855-1880) lives on in one of his descendents, Serious puts the new Ned Kelly (himself) and family on an island paradise where the only building appears to be a rundown pub/video outlet/brewery and where endearing Oz creatures freely roam.

Kelly motorbikes to Sydney, where he robs the bank owned by evil Sir John (Hugo Weaving), giving the money to the poor and a furious Sir John rea-

April 12, 1993 (Cont.)

son to hire Brit military expert Alexei Sayle and plot to sell Kelly's island to the Japanese.

Needing a quick $1 million, Kelly heads for the "land of opportunity for outlaws," America, accompanied by actress girlfriend Robin Banks (get it?), charmingly played by Melora Hardin.

In Hollywood, Kelly and Robin are spotted by schlock producer (John Pinette) and starred in a Vegas-based B-picture. Having earned his $1 million and survived an assassination attempt engineered by Sayle, Kelly and Robin head home to save their island and defeat the villains.

There are a lot of ideas here and a brash, go-for-it style. But star-helmer-co-writer-editor-designer Serious seems to have taken on too many chores: his own perf suffers and the script continually builds to punchlines that, when they come, fall flat.

Though there are some delights among the supporting cast, Serious allows usually reliable players like Sayle and Weaving to turn in dull perfs. The animals steal the film and the occasional visual joke lend a feeling of spontaneity the film otherwise lacks.

Nevertheless, "Reckless Kelly" could click with young auds, especially in Oz, thanks to Serious' canny use of current obsessions with the environment and plans for a new Aussie flag.

Technically, it's a top-flight production in every department.

— *David Stratton*

MORFARS RESA
(GRANDFATHER'S JOURNEY)
(SWEDISH)

Svensk Filmindustri presents a Victoria Film/Ottokar Runze Film/Svenska Filminstitutet/Defa Studios Babelsberg/Nordisk Film & TV-fond/Det Danske Filminstitut/SVT Kanal 1 Drama/Filmstiftung: Nordrhein-Westfalen/Land Berlin/Land Brandenburg production. Produced by Ole Sondberg, Soren Staerrmose, Ottokar Runze. Directed by Staffan Lamm. Screenplay, Lamm, Lars Forssell. Camera (color), Esa Vuorinen; music, Wlodek Gilgowski; editor, Darek Hodor; production design, Marlene Willman; costumes, Inken Gusner; associate producer, Hans Lönnerheden. Reviewed at the Riviera cinema, Stockholm, Jan. 25, 1993. Running time: **79 MIN.**
Simon Fromm . . . . . Max von Sydow
Elin Fromm . . . . . . Mai Zetterling
Karin Fromm . . . Marika Lagercrantz
Göran . . . . Carl Svensson
Vera . . . . . Ina-Miriam Rosenbaum
Sara . . . . Sharon Brauner

Despite superb acting from Max von Sydow, this autobiographical drama is too uneven and too loose in its construction to be satisfying. Box office prospects are slim.

Director-scriptwriter Lamm has based his story on his own memories of his grandfather, legendary literature professor Martin Lamm. It takes place in the end of 1945, when the young boy, Göran (Carl Svenson), is to spend a couple of days with his eccentric, intellectual grandfather (von Sydow). The boy's parents are divorced and his overworked M.D. mother doesn't have much time for her son.

The grandmother (Mai Zetterling) is overprotective of her husband and tries to keep everything quiet around him. This means the professor and the boy have to sneak out very quietly one night, when von Sydow discovers he has put the wrong letters into the wrong envelopes and has to exchange them. The walk through Stockholm brings Göran and his grandfather even closer together, but also tests the family's tolerance of von Sydow's odd behavior.

The ambitions behind "Grandfather's Journey" are many but unfortunately unfulfilled. Several side stories that could have turned out interestingly are left dangling and there is no real drama or tension; the film feels more embryonic than finished.

The acting is very good, especially from von Sydow, who once again shows his wide range and the depth of his emotions.

The entire film — except for a couple of establishing shots — was shot in the Defa studios outside Berlin. All tech credits are good, though little genuine Stockholm atmosphere is evoked.

— *Gunnar Rehlin*

SAN REMO FEST

SPARE ME
(16m)

A Film Crash production. Produced by Matthew Harrison, Madeline Warren. Co-producer, Christopher Cooke. Directed by Harrison. Screenplay, Christopher Grimm. Camera (Duart color, 16m), Michael Mayers; editor, Piero Mura, Hughes Winborne; music, Danny Brenner; production designer, Mark Friedberg; art direction, Tom Jarmusch; costume design, Mayers; assistant director, Jonathan Starch; casting, Meredith Jacobson. Reviewed at San Remo (Italy) Intl. Film Festival (competing), March 26, 1993. Running time: **88 MIN.**

Theo Skinner . . . . . . Lawton Paseka
Sheila Kastle . . . Christie MacFadyen
Buzz Fazeli . . . . Mark Alfred
Millie Fazeli . . . . Sunny Weil
Miles Kastle . . . Richard W. Sears Jr.
Junior . . . . Bill Christ
Sid . . . . Christopher Cooke
Breeze . . . . Sean Hagerty

N.Y. filmmaker Matthew Harrison's micro-budget debut feature steps into the seemingly innocuous bowling milieu and opens up a menacingly weird can of worms. A deadpan comedy/film noir, "Spare Me" has its share of fresh angles, but in attempting to muscle in on the terrain of indie exponents like Hal Hartley, it's knowing to the point of self-consciousness. Beyond the college circuit, it looks like a low-scorer commercially.

The basic idea is familiar Off Hollywood fodder: Mysterious out-of-town dude with cool sideburns breezes into Normalsville, kicks the lid off a cesspool of no-gooders and nutcases, and hooks up with a local bad girl.

Item's dude is ace sportsman Theo (Lawton Paseka). Suspended from pro bowling for braining an opponent, he tracks down his absentee father (Mark Alfred), hoping pa's legendary status in the sport will get him reinstated. Dad's in deep with a bowling alley-owner (Richard W. Sears Jr.), whose scams include an illegal sideline in dwarf-bowling.

While Paseka weighs the ethics of accepting sponsorship from Sears, he gets romantically entangled with his troubled daughter (Christie MacFadyen). She, in turn, is irked by the unbrotherly affections of her unhinged sib (Bill Christ), who's just escaped from a psych hospital. Paseka becomes a pawn in their insidious individual plans, but following some twisted plot subterfuge and a gruesome death on the pinstacking machine, he eventually gets back in the game.

Harrison's resourceful direction brings a sharp look and sound to the shoestring venture, playing up rather than trying to cover the raw edges imposed by limited technical means.

But the film wavers noncommittally between styles and tones. Dialogue is straight-out *noir*-speak, but the stylized camerawork, off-the-wall characters and arbitrarily over-the-top performances don't fit the mold. Result is an affable but relatively formless pastiche that gets by on reckless energy and charismatic leads. — *David Rooney*

IZGOY
(EXILED)
(UKRAINIAN-GERMAN-SWEDISH)

A Fest-Zemlya/Ukrainian Fund of Culture (Ukraine)/SSS Filmkunst (Germany)/Svea Sov Konsult (Sweden) coproduction. Directed, written by Vladimir Savelyev. Camera (color), Yuriy Garmash; music, Yevgeniy Stankovitch. Reviewed at San Remo (Italy) Intl. Film Festival (competing), March 27, 1993. Running time: 77 MIN.
With: Jossy Pollak, V. Brondukov, M. Vishnyakova, S. Stanyuta, V. Masalskis.

Starting as a folkloric field trip through 1940s rural Ukraine, "Exiled" sways gently between melancholy and euphoric moods before spiraling into nightmarish territory with the onset of World War II in the region. The 36th San Remo fest's grand prize winner may be too modest techwise for wide arthouse exposure, but its wrenching emotion and political timeliness in light of rising neo-Nazism should wrestle a long life out of specialist cultural venues and TV outlets.

The real forte of Vladimir Savelyev's film is the supple modulation of its passage through a Jewish refugee's cyclical odyssey of flight, reprieve, humiliation and destruction. Fleeing Nazi-occupied Poland, a physical dynamo (Jossy Pollak) delivers his family to a Ukrainian village, where they assimilate into the non-Jewish community.

Ethnic scene-setting and the family's idyll provide a deliberate lull that snaps neatly when, after enlisting with locals, Pollak is taken prisoner by German soldiers after a merciless attack. Exposed as a Jew, he looks earmarked for death until his ox-like strength singles him out to stand in for a Nazi big shot's dead horse, and pull the man's buggy cross-country. A cruel bet follows, forcing him to race against a real horse-drawn cart: if he wins, he can see his family; lose and he dies.

The melodramatic artifice of slow motion in the harrowing race sequence goes vaguely against the grain of pic's almost docu-style straightforwardness, but its impact resounds through to the desolate finale. Escaping back to the village to find only his newborn son remaining, Pollak's formidable strength deserts him. In a bizarre dance of death, a German tank crushes him, its 360 degree turns imitating the celebratory wedding dance that earlier marked his acceptance into the community.

Lensing of the rustic setting, and editing are simple but well-judged, and pic's only bothersome technical setback is the clumsy slapping of Russian dialogue over the original Yiddish. Pollak's robust performance admirably supplies the story's backbone. — *David Rooney*

TAK TAK
(YES, YES)
(POLISH-FRENCH)

A Studio Filmowe Perspektywa/ Flach Film Telewizja (Poland)/La Sept/ Syrena Entertainment Group (France) co-production. Director of production, Iwona Ziulkowska. Directed, written by Jacek Gasiorowski. Camera (color), Witold Adamek; editor, Ewa Smal; music, Michal Urbaniak; art direction, Teresa Gruber; costumes, Ewa Krauze; sound, Mariusz Kuczynski. Reviewed at San Remo (Italy) Intl. Film Festival (competing), March 28, 1993. Running time: **85 MIN.**
Marek . . . . . Zbigniew Zamachowski
Also with: Maria Gladkowska, Julie Japhet, Monica Bolly.

"Yes, Yes" rides an unrepentent Don Juan's roller coaster of amorous escapades in a Poland smarting under regime rule. A huge hit with San Remo festgoers, this slick, fast-paced frippery should turn up on offshore tube slates, but outmoded sexual mores will keep it from going wider.

Charting romantic territory that owes more to French cinema than Polish, pic kicks off, not illogically, in 1970s Paris, where Marek (Zbigniew Zamachowski), studying at the Sorbonne, makes his first conquest. Sexual excess virtually cripples him, but heading home, he moves in a second femme. Hospitalized back in Warsaw, he gets more than medicine from a night nurse, who finds herself pregnant.

The complications of keeping all three flames burning fuel the story as Marek negotiates between being a soldier in the sexual revolution and a one-woman man and father. Further dalliances are provided by his day job at a TV station, including one with the chief censor's girl Friday that sparks some funny digs at old-guard politics.

Zamachowski's easy charm, a bright supporting cast and nimble direction by Jacek Gasiorowski make buoyant, audience-pleasing fare out of largely passé material. Tech aspects are pro all

around, especially Ewa Smal's rhythmic editing, which threads a nonstop succession of lightning-quick scenes. — *David Rooney*

PSY
(PIGS)
(POLISH)

A Studio Filmowe Zebra production. Director of production Andrzej Soltysik. Directed, written by Wladyslaw Pasikowski. Camera (color), Pawel Edelman; editor, Zbigniew Nicinski, Wanda Seman; music, Michal Lorenc; art direction, Andrzej Przedworski; sound, Aleksander Golebiowski. Reviewed at San Remo (Italy) Intl. Film Festival (competing), March 29, 1993. Running time: **108 MIN.**
Franz . . . . Boguslaw Linda
Olo . . . . Marek Kondrat
Also with: Janusz Gajos, Zbigniew Zapasiewicz, Cezary Pazura, Jerzy Bonczak, Aleksander Bednarz, Ryszard Pietruski.

s former Eastern bloc filmmakers shake off the chains of Communist censorship, most of their commercial forays have seemed tentative at best, but this polished Polish effort leaps head-on into the ultraviolent Yank cops and corruption tradition. Often as brutally obvious as its title, "Pigs" still burns enough high-octane juice to overcome an occasionally confusing narrative and snort out limited offshore turf as a sophisticated actioner.

Once heroes but now more often classed as morally bankrupt gangsters, political police rep one of the most volatile redundancies of the old East's teething phase as new democracies. Writer-helmer Wladyslaw Pasikowski's film hinges on this ethical quandary, compellingly personified by dynamite thesp Boguslaw Linda's chilling antihero.

Linda and his fellow Stasi-collaborating cop buddy (Marek Kondrat) go before an commission on charges of destroying personnel files. Kondrat is thrown off the force, and Linda is bumped downstairs to the crime squad, where his disdainful indifference to an apparently routine assignment leads to a bloodbath for several colleagues.

Kondrat takes up with a drug-trafficking network and gets ahead fast, while Linda's remorseless application of secret service tactics is increasingly at odds with normal police duty. The duo continue working in tandem from opposite sides of the law, but conflicting interests surface and intensify, kickstarting a crescendo of bloody mayhem.

Pasikowski intermittently sacrifices clarity, especially in the story's somewhat hurried establishing scenes, and the love interest is also weak and poorly introduced. But his firm handle on the thriller is unrelenting, and despite its excessive, sometimes derivative violence, pic grips right up to its inevitable final face-off. Technically, it's top-notch. — *David Rooney*

DIE UNGEWISSE LAGE DES PARADIESES
(IN SEARCH OF PARADISE)
(GERMAN)

A Connexion Film/Vulcano M. production. Produced by Willi Bär, Rainer Bienger. Directed, written by Franziska Buch. Camera (color), Jürgen Jürges; editor, Patricia Rommel; music, Michaela Dietl; art direction, Roger Katholing; costumes, Corinna Dreyer; sound, Marco Parisotto. Reviewed at San Remo (Italy) Intl. Film Festival (competing), March 26, 1993. Running time: **113 MIN.**
Marianne . . . . Sabine Wegner
Anna . . . . Daniela Schleicher
Paula . . . . Barbara Nüsse
Vincenzo . . . . Michael Greiling
Isolde Strätter . . . . . . Isolde Barth
"Lulu" Lämmle . . . Walter Schultheis
Also with: Alexander Radszun, Franziska Herold, Benno Fürmann.

A wintry fugue played against the bleakly imposing North Sea shoreline, "In Search of Paradise" thrashes out eternally unanswerable questions concerning happiness, harmony and human contact. Unresolved, emotionally unrewarding item nonetheless marks a confident, visually handsome bow for writer-director Franziska Buch, and it should land further festival dates.

Hoping to exorcize the demons of a sour marriage, mom Sabine Wegner takes her 8-year-old daughter (Daniela Schleicher) to the rundown hotel where she grew up. Studying its menagerie of emotional fringe-dwellers; the moppet struggles to fathom the adult world, while Wegner bites at the hook of an amorous Italian (Michael Greiling), who too literally gives back her childhood.

Story unfolds like a mother-daughter shrink session, with other characters serving as shards of a shattered personality. Wegner's flamboyant sis (Barbara Nüsse) pins her hopes on rescue by a rich Swiss inamorato. Her long-suffering suitor (Walter Schultheis) hangs about selflessly, finally winning her by default. And a physically and men-

tally scarred tenant (Isolde Barth) progresses from bitter self-punishment to suicide.

Buch maps out the somber drama with measured strokes, but dialogue leans frequently toward pompous, poetic inflatedness, consequently, the lighter moments often seem like mummified exuberance within an angst-fest. Heavy-handedness is partly compensated by strong ensemble playing, superior tech-backup and smart use of a striking location. — *David Rooney*

April 19, 1993

WIDE SARGASSO SEA
(AUSTRALIAN)

A Fine Line release of a New Line Cinema presentation of a Laughing Kookaburra production. Produced by Jan Sharp. Executive producer, Sara Risher. Directed by John Duigan. Screenplay, Sharp, Carole Angier, Duigan, based on Jean Rhys' novel. Camera (color), Geoff Burton (Jamaica), Gabriel Beristain (U.K.); editors, Anne Goursaud, Jimmy Sandoval; music, Stewart Copeland; production design, Franckie D; art direction, Susan Bolles; set decoration, Ron von Blombert; costume design, Norma Moriceau; sound design (Dolby), Harry Cohen; line producer, Karen Koch; assistant director, Charles Rotheram; 2nd-unit director, Sharp. Reviewed at Magno Review 2 screening room, N.Y., April 12, 1993. MPAA Rating: NC-17. Running time: **96 MIN.**
Antoinette Cosway . . Karina Lombard
Edward Rochester . Nathaniel Parker
Annette Cosway . . . . . Rachel Ward
Paul Mason . . . . Michael York
Aunt Cora . . . . . Martine Beswicke
Christophene . . . . Claudia Robinson
Amelie . . . . Rowena King
Richard Mason . Huw Christie Williams
Young Antoinette . . . . Casey Berna
Nelson . . . . Ancile Gloudin

An exotic and erotic melodrama bearing notable literary pedigrees, "Wide Sargasso Sea" is an uneven but ultimately engrossing feature that should provide interesting counterprogramming for New Line's arthouse unit Fine Line.

Aussie director John Duigan, best known for "The Year My Voice Broke" and "Flirting," has filmed British novelist Jean Rhys' novel with stunning location photography in Jamaica and the north of England, but the editing looks like the film was put through a shredder.

The initially confusing storyline concerns a mad French woman (Rachel Ward) in Jamaica who marries an Englishman (Michael York) and is subjected to the trauma of an uprising by ex-slaves at the end of the first reel.

Her daughter, played as a youngster by Casey Berna and as adult by lovely model Karina Lombard, narrates the tale at first. Grown up, she is stuck in a marriage arranged by her uncle to Englishman Edward Rochester, the brooding hero of Charlotte Brontë's "Jane Eyre," played by Nathaniel Parker.

The couple's erotic tangles in and out of love are set against a backdrop of superstition in which the local form of voodoo seems to hold each of them in thrall.

Frequent nudity and sex scenes are mainly tastefully handled, though a couple contain the explicit content that earned "Sargasso" an NC-17 rating.

Punctuated by frequent nightmare imagery emphasizing Ward's madness or Parker imagining himself trapped underwater in seaweed, film exerts a fable-like power despite its choppy construction.

Parker is blackmailed by a native with information about Lombard's background, which turns out to be her supposedly inheriting her mother's madness.

Upshot is Parker's infidelity with a seductive servant girl (Rowena King) that sends Lombard over the top and alienates the other servants, especially Lombard's black nanny and medicine woman (Claudia Robinson).

In a hurried wind-up, Parker gets an inheritance and returns to his ancestral home in England with Lombard. She goes mad in a garret and the scene is set for "Jane Eyre."

Lombard, who has landed the role of Tom Cruise's Cayman Islands seductress in "The Firm," is a hauntingly beautiful heroine well-matched to shirt-ad handsome Parker. Their acting is not really up to some dramatic scenes, particularly those in which they may be operating under the influence of voodoo.

Thesping honors go to Robinson as the nanny, whose sharp tongue perfectly embodies the rebellious nature of the still-subjugated servant population. Martine Beswicke, herself Jamaican-born, is a treat as Lombard's loyal aunt, but her character is conveniently written out of most of the film.

The very sexy Rowena King upstages the heroine in several scenes but overplays her role.

Aussie cinematographer Geoff Burton has done an atmospheric job lensing in Jamaica, buttressed by brief, contrasting scenes in wintry England executed by Gabriel Beristain.

The varied musical score by Stewart Copeland knits together disparate scenes and excels during native dance sequences.
— *Lawrence Cohn*

SIDEKICKS

A Triumph Releasing Corp. release of a Gallery Films presentation. (Intl. sales: Vision Intl.). Produced by Don Carmody. Executive producers, Chuck Norris, Jim McIngvale, Linda McIngvale. Directed by Aaron Norris. Screenplay, Don Thompson, Lou Illar, from Illar's story. Camera (color), Joao Fernandes; editors, David Rawlins, Bernard Weiser; music, Alan Silvestri; production design, Reuben Freed; sound (Dolby), James Troutman; associate producers, Jordan Yospe, Illar; casting, Annette Benson, Penny Perry Davis. Reviewed at Cineplex Odeon Sharpstown Center Theater, Houston, April 8, 1993. MPAA rating: PG. Running time: **100 MIN.**
Chuck Norris . . . . Chuck Norris
Jerry Gabrewski . . . . . Beau Bridges
Barry Gabrewski . . Jonathan Brandis
Mr. Lee . . . . Mako
Noreen Chen . . . . Julia Nickson-Soul
Stone . . . . Joe Piscopo
Lauren . . . . Danica McKellar
Randy Cellini . . . . . . John Buchanan
Horn . . . . Richard Moll

Imagine a cross between "The Karate Kid" and "The Secret Life of Walter Mitty," and you'll know what to expect from "Sidekicks," an offbeat family-audience opus from, of all people, action star Chuck Norris. Medium-budget indie pic, shot and largely financed in Houston and now in regional release, has a chance to attract the pre-teen "Three Ninjas" crowd and might also get some teen b.o. Vid prospects are even brighter.

Norris' presence dominates pic, but the lead character is a daydreaming teen played by Jonathan Brandis ("Neverending Story II"). Brandis is an asthmatic outsider who's mocked by many of his peers, harassed by most of his teachers, and ignored by his computer-programmer dad (Beau Bridges). So the boy seeks refuge in heroic fantasies where he is the brave and resourceful sidekick of his favorite action movie hero, Norris.

Film is peppered with moderately clever daydream sequences modeled after (and featuring brief excerpts from) such Norris movies as "Missing in Action," "Lone Wolf McQuade" and "The Hit Man." There are a few more of these bits than absolutely necessary, but Norris proves a good sport about kidding his taciturn, tough-guy image.

To be sure, some parents might question whether an impressionable youngster should be allowed by his dad to watch so many of Norris' R-rated, hard-action movies. "Sidekicks" might have been a more interesting and socially responsible (albeit much darker) pic had it raised questions about the effect of a youngster's exposure to so much movie mayhem.

But that is not the picture that director Aaron Norris (the star's brother) and screenwriters Don Thompson and Lou Illar chose to make. In their lightweight but diverting effort, the fantasy violence is bloodless and non-lethal, played for cartoonish laughs rather than thrills. Brandis' obsession with Norris' movies is depicted as altogether harmless.

Coached by the sage uncle (Mako) of his only compassionate teacher (Julia Nickson-Soul), Brandis quickly picks up enough martial arts skill to compete in a karate tournament against his school's worst bully (a punkish John Buchanan).

The bad guy's mentor is an even worse fellow, a big blowhard (zestfully overplayed by Joe Piscopo) who claims he can "whip Chuck Norris' ass." So, of course, the real Norris just happens to be a guest at the karate tournament, and joins Brandis' team just to settle Piscopo's hash.

Brandis is appealing and persuasively intense; Danica McKellar ("The Wonder Years") is passably sweet as a classmate who feels sorry for, then falls for him.

Fantasy fights scenes might have been improved with some snazzier editing. Other tech credits are fine. Alan Silvestri's overblown score hits just the right note of parody in the fantasy sequences. — *Joe Leydon*

DUST DEVIL: THE FINAL CUT
(BRITISH-U.S.)

A Miramax (U.S.)/Polygram Filmed Entertainment (U.K.) release of a Palace and Film Four Intl. presentation, in association with Miramax Film Corp. and with the participation of British Screen, of a Palace production. Produced by Joanne Sellar. Executive producers, Nik Powell, Stephen Woolley, Paul Trybits. Co-executive producers, Bob Weinstein, Harvey Weinstein. Directed, written by Richard Stanley. Camera (Technicolor), Steven Chivers; editor, Derek Trigg; editor ("Final Cut"), Paul Carlin; music, Simon Boswell; production design, Joseph Bennett; art direction, Graeme Orwin, Michael Carlin; costume design, Michele Clapton; sound (Dolby) editor ("Final Cut"), Richard Rhys-Davies; special effects chief, Rick Creswell; special makeup and animatronic effects, the Dream Machine; special makeup effects supervisor, Little John; stunt coordinator, Roly Jansen; associate producers, Daniel Lupi, Stephen Earnhart; assistant director, Guy Travers. Reviewed at Scala Cinema, London, April 7, 1993. Running time: **108 MIN.**

April 19, 1993 (Cont.)

Dust Devil	Robert Burke
Wendy	Chelsea Field
Ben	Zakes Mokae
Joe	John Matshikiza
Mark	Rufus Swart
Cornelius	William Hootkins
Dr. Leidzinger	Marianne Sägebrecht

Overflowing with ideas, visual invention and genre references but saddled by a weak, unfocused script, "Dust Devil" is a brilliant mess. Pic looks destined to become an immediate cult item, but its offbeat approach and slow-burn pacing mark this for a bigger killing on vid than theatrical.

This mystical African-set slasher movie is the second feature of pop promo alum Richard Stanley ("Hardware"). Director's cut (billed as "the final cut" in cards added before end crawl) world preemed at London grindhouse Scala Cinema April 7. U.K. vid release by Polygram is set for mid-May.

The low-budget production was shot in late summer 1991 in Namibia, southern Africa, with Stanley delivering a 125-minute European cut in December. Demands by Miramax and the U.K.'s Palace Pictures for shorter versions, plus the latter's fiscal problems, left the pic in limbo.

Subsequent U.K. distrib Mayfair test-screened a shorter version last August, to ho-hum response. Mayfair has since relinquished U.K. theatrical rights. Stanley spent $45,000 of his own coin to reconstruct this version.

Miramax's U.S. cut, American-dubbed and with a new voice-over, is skedded for release in late summer or fall. Adding to the confusion, abridged version has already opened, under different titles, in France and Italy.

Story origins date back to a 16m short Stanley shot in 1984. Here, action is set in Namibia, in August 1991. The opening 45 minutes is a tour de force of elaborate cross-cutting and sustained tension as three characters compete for attention.

First is a taciturn Yank (Robert Burke) hitching across country murdering and mutilating strangers and collecting their fingers in a box. Second is black cop Ben (Zakes Mokae), haunted by nightmares of his lost family and a career blunder, who turns to the witch-doctor owner of a desert drive-in (John Matshikiza) to solve the ghastly murders. Third is Wendy (Chelsea Field), a South African who walks out on her boring hubby (Rufus Swart) and drives north to Namibia on a journey to nowhere.

Story slides into focus halfway through, as the trio's destinies crisscross and it becomes clear Burke is trying to return to the spirit world but is trapped in the present, surviving by claiming human souls. Burke hitches a ride from Field and tries to slice her; she escapes, hotly pursued by Mokae and Swart.

Working with the same key personnel as on "Hardware," Stanley turns in a good-looking product, with stunning lensing by Steven Chivers. Every cent is on the screen.

Also impressive are effects by Rick Creswell and grisly cadavers by the Dream Machine. But final impression is of a film that's run amok with too many half-baked ideas, which might have cohered with a stronger script.

Field struggles with an underwritten role. Burke is charismatic but no more. Much of the dialogue by Mokae and Matshikiza is difficult to make out.

William Hootkins has fun as a superior of Mokae's, and German thesp Marianne Sägebrecht cameos woodenly as a ghoulish coroner. — *Derek Elley*

BOILING POINT
(U.S.-FRENCH)

A Warner Bros. release of a Hexagon Films production. Produced by Marc Frydman, Leonardo de la Fuente. Executive producers, René Bonnell, Olivier Granier. Directed, written by James B. Harris, from Gerald Petievich's novel "Money Men." Camera (Foto-Kem color; Technicolor prints), King Baggot; editor, Jerry Brady; music, Cory Lerios, John D'Andrea; sound (Dolby), Russell C. Fager; production design, Ron Foreman; art direction, Russ Smith; set decoration, Rick Caprarelli; costume design, Molly Maginnis; assistant director, Jules Lichtman; production manager and line producer, Ramsey Thomas; additional editor, Dick Williams; aerial camera, David Butler, Rexford Metz; stunt coordinator, Chuck Waters; co-producer, Patrick Beaufront; co-executive producer, Philippe Maigret; casting, Al Guarino. Reviewed at Loews 34th St. Showplace 2 theater, N.Y., April 16, 1993. MPAA Rating: R. Running time: **90 MIN.**

Jimmy	Wesley Snipes
Red Diamond	Dennis Hopper
Vikki	Lolita Davidovich
Ronnie	Viggo Mortensen
Brady	Dan Hedaya
Virgil Leach	Seymour Cassel
Max	Jonathan Banks
Carol	Christine Elise
Tony Dio	Tony LoBianco
Mona	Valerie Perrine
Levitt	James Tolkan
Transaction man	Paul Gleason
Connie	Lorraine Evanoff
Sally	Stephanie Williams
Roth	Tobin Bell
Steve	Bobby Hosea

Promoted as a hard-action film for Wesley Snipes fans, "Boiling Point" turns out to be an old-fashioned police procedural. Low-key and bland in the extreme, it's strictly for film buffs, though Snipes should ensure a strong first-week sampling among action enthusiasts.

Disappointingly, writer/director James B. Harris ("Cop"), in his zeal to re-create the mood and character acting of '40s film noir, seems to have forgotten about excitement and visual flair.

Snipes toplines as a U.S. Treasury agent partnered with Dan Hedaya. The third T-man on their stakeout is killed by ruthless thug Viggo Mortensen, who gets away with partner Dennis Hopper before the feds can close in.

Because of the fatal snafu, Snipes is reassigned from L.A. to Newark. He holds out for one week's time to catch the killers; coincidentally Hopper is given a week to find the $50,000 he owes gangster Tony LoBianco.

Loaded ith false irony, Harris' mechanical script emphasizes the parallel lives of the two main characters to an almost laughable extent. Throughout the picture, Snipes keeps running into Hopper, neither knowing one is methodically hunting the other.

Because of terrific acting down to the smallest role, one's interest is maintained despite the minimalist direction and lack of story twists. Particularly through Mortensen's careful underplaying, the film builds suspense and a sense of dread, but it never pays off.

Hopper's Red Diamond is a memorable small-time rogue who's a romantic at heart. Snipes is stuck in a one-dimensional role. Valerie Perrine is touching as the woman Hopper once put out on the street to pay his debts. Lolita Davidovich, as Snipes' ex-flame turned hooker, has little to work with in a patently unbelievable part. Seymour Cassel and Jonathan Banks are on the money as criminal types.

Pic looks nondescript ;soundtrack makes repeated use of Johnny Mercer's lovely standard "Dream." — *Lawrence Cohn*

ZOO
(DOCU)

A Zipporah Films release in association with Channel 4 of a Zipporah Films production. Produced, directed, edited by Frederick Wiseman. Camera (color), John Davey. Reviewed at Cinema du Reel Festival, Studio 5 theater, Georges Pompidou Center, Paris, March 14, 1993. Running Time: **130 MIN.**

Master docu-maker Frederick Wiseman has culled just over two hours of instructive, amusing, sometimes startling footage from 100 hours of raw material lensed in bright Florida sunshine during a 42-day shoot at Miami's MetroZoo. "Zoo" world-preemed at the Cinema du Reel fest and will be telecast June 2 on PBS.

Apart from a brief lag in the middle, longish docu sustains viewer interest. Punctuated by the adventures of the zoo's lone vet, well-edited pic sports its own ebb and flow, high drama and biz-as-usual contrasts. It helps that the spacious facility, home to 2,800 animals, genuinely seems to be a nice place — only the lions and a few primates appear displeased with their surroundings.

MetroZoo is a city unto itself complete with medical emergencies (a protracted rhino birth) and "crime" (some deer are mauled to death by a feral dog).

The zoo has the balmy, benign look of a controlled environment but the cumulative effect is odd, sometimes queasy. Absence of didactic narration creates suspense. Self-contained dramas are gradually and skillfully resolved. Cutaways to zoo visitors, who seem to do more peering by intermediary of camcorder than via the naked eye, effortlessly emphasize that humans may sometimes look and act stranger than their fellow animals.

Pic never shies from gory or unsettling events, including the clinical yet convivial postmortem butchering of a stillborn rhino calf. The sunlit procedure, from laying out the deflated bubble gum-like placenta for photos to the vet rinsing the calf's severed head while co-workers chat in the background, is as surreal as "Un Chien Andalou."

The always unobtrusive and steady lensing puts viewers in a privileged position. Some events could prove frightening to young children and others may unnerve grown-ups. Even though zookeepers procure the grub, anyone who's forgotten that some animals eat others is in for a pointed refresher course. In one example, we hear a fluffy little bunny's death throes after a staffer bonks him on the head, then watch in extreme close-up as a snake gobbles the cottontail whole.

Nice touches include an episode of simian dentistry, and a meeting of zoo trustees complete with a "Komodo dragon update." — *Lisa Nesselson*

THE SNAPPER
(BRITISH-16m)

A BBC Television production (Miramax TV and video, U.S.). Produced by Lynda Myles. Executive producer, Mark Shivas. Directed by Stephen Frears. Screenplay, Roddy Doyle, from his novel. Camera (color, 16m), Oliver Stapleton; editor, Mick Audsley; art direction, Mark Geraghty; costume design, Consolata Boyle; sound, Kieran Horgan, Peter Maxwell; assistant director, Martin O'Malley; associate producer, Ian Hopkins; casting, Leo Davis. Reviewed in London, April 4, 1993. Running time: **90 MIN.**
Dessie Curley . . . . . . Colm Meaney
Sharon Curley . . . . . Tina Kellegher
Kay Curley . . . . Ruth McCabe
Jackie . . . . Fionnuala Murphy
George Burgess . . . . Pat Laffan
Mary . . . . Deirdre O'Brien
Yvonne . . . . Karen Woodley
  Also with: Eanna MacLiam, Peter Rowen, Joanne Gerrard, Colm O'Byrne, Ciara Duffy, Virginia Cole, Denis Menton, Brendan Gleeson.

Culled from the same pen as "The Commitments," Stephen Frears' "The Snapper" is a lively, likable slice of Dublin working-class comedy that could bite off small-scale theatrical returns with good reviews and strategic playoff.

Colm Meaney, who was also in the Alan Parker opus, plays the head of a clan who's floored by eldest daughter Tina Kellegher's announcement that she's in the family way. Catch is, she won't name the "snapper's" papa.

Just when Meaney has wrapped his brain around the news and decided to adopt a mature attitude, word slips out that the father is a married neighbor (Pat Laffan), who decides to disappear for a spell, as all hell breaks loose among the tight-knit community.

Smoothly adapted by Dublin author Roddy Doyle from the second of his "Barrytown trilogy" and in theory focused on the same central family as in "Commitments" (here renamed the Curleys), pic differs markedly in content, feel and style to Parker's slick, big-screen movie.

Frears' rougher, Brit TV drama helming, though fine for the tube, concentrates more on character comedy and lacks the dramatic and emotional highs of the earlier film, with its exhilarating musical content.

Still, the pic marks out its own territory and plays well within it, with much unvarnished, off-the-wall humor, plus real warmth under the rough one-liners.

Doyle draws a portrait of northside Dublin life that at any moment could tip over into violence and retribution. Sans the light comic approach, it's heavy-duty social drama.

As the Dublin paterfamilias trying desperately to be a New Man, Meaney doesn't quite have the weight to carry such a busy pic, despite plenty of huffandpuffing. But he pairs well with Kellegher, strong as the independent daughter, tough as nails for a 20-year-old.

Casting and playing are uniformly tops, with special nods to Fionnuala Murphy as Kellegher's best pal and Ruth McCabe as the quiet, long-suffering mom.

Oliver Stapleton's 16mm lensing is no-frills, and editing by Mick Audsley is tight and neat all the way. The made-for-TV pic, scheduled to open this year's Cannes Directors' Fortnight, aired April 4 on BBC2 as the last of its season of "Screen Two" offers. — *Derek Elley*

COMINCIO TUTTO PER CASO
(IT ALL STARTED BY CHANCE)
(ITALIAN)

An Istituto Luce/Italnoleggio Cinematografico release of a Rodeo Drive production. Produced by Marco Poccioni, Marco Valsania. Directed by Umberto Marino. Screenplay, Marino, Elisabetta Zincone, Ottavio Sabatucci, Maria Lourdes Camino. Camera (Cinecittà color), Alessio Gelsini; editor, Simona Paggi; music, Antonio Di Pofi; art direction, Osvaldo Desideri; costumes, Stefano Giambanco; sound, Fulgenzio Ceccon. Reviewed at Eden Cinema, Rome, March 17, 1993. Running time: **91 MIN.**
Stefania . . . . Margherita Buy
Luca . . . . Massimo Ghini
Marilù . . . . . . Barbara Jane Ricasa
Romolo . . . . Raoul Bova
Serena . . . . Laura Marinoni
  Also with: Silvana De Santis, Francesco Zenoni, Imma Piro, Ludovica Modugno, Natalia Leoni.

Prolific playwright and screenwriter Umberto Marino weighs in as director with "It All Started by Chance," a winsome but uncharacteristically wishy-washy comedy that attempts to travel an alternate route through loveland, but ultimately lacks distance from the treacly pop culture sentimentality it's ribbing. Local status of Marino and lead femme Margherita Buy promises a healthy Italo stint, and pic's shortcomings shouldn't prevent offshore TV pickup.

Parallel sentimental journeys follow the downward turn of Buy's marriage to Massimo Ghini (a nondescript stock figure of the political journalist wrestling with lapsed convictions), and the obstacle-strewn romance between their Philippine nanny (Barbara Jane Ricasa) and a sweet but stupid plumber (Raoul Bova). Stymied on both sides by family prejudice, the affair looks set to fizzle, but driven by a tenacious belief in happy endings, Buy bounces back from her own bust-up to champion their cause.

Lightheartedly mirroring the quartet's triumphs and tribulations are the schmaltzy lyrics of the lovers' favorite pop tunes (by Italo idol Claudio Baglioni) and the melodramatic mayhem of an interminable Argentinian soap opera that Buy's character dubs into Italian.

Further commentary comes (often superfluously) from her voiceovers, which frequently take on the semblance of pat sermons from Marino, the self-appointed spokesman for the disillusioned thirtysomething league. He sprinkles events with neat comic touches and wry observations on current social mores, but his storytelling style meanders.

Performances are fine, with newcomers Ricasa and Bova especially appealing. Tech aspects are uniformly slick, and with a more consistent script, Marino should eventually join Italy's smart set of young directors.
— *David Rooney*

RUPTURES
(FRENCH)

A Corto Films/Les Films Ariane co-production. Produced by Olivier Mille. Directed by Christine Citti. Written by Alexandra Deman, Citti. Camera (color), Jean-Yves Delbreuve; editor, Emmanuelle Castro; music, "chaude Lance"; sound, Pierre Excoffier. Reviewed at Les Acteurs à L'Ecran Festival, Saint-Denis, France, Feb. 7, 1993. Running time: **101 MIN.**
Lucie . . . . Emmanuelle Béart
Paul . . . . Michel Piccoli
Lucien . . . . Laurent Grévil
Marthe . . . . Anouk Aimée
  Also with: Nada Strancar, Marc Citti, Patrick Blondel, Eva Ionesco, Guilaine Londez.

"Ruptures" is a personal, fairly indulgent film whose sterling cast passes the time by talking about how most romances end badly. Nominally the story of how a group of friends and relatives behave in the aftermath of one woman's suicide, forced pic will have its staunch defenders but seems unlikely to garner much b.o.

Emmanuelle Béart and Michel Piccoli — together again after Jacques Rivette's "La Belle Noiseuse" — may spark some curiosity beyond France.

Twentysomething guys in a rock 'n' roll band try to relate to their girlfriends and vice versa. Piccoli, who was the dead femme's lover, temporarily houses several characters, including a recently separated woman, her young daughter (whose voiceover brackets the film) and baby. Also in residence is child-woman Lucie (Béart), who is involved with the band's lead singer (Laurent Grévil), although she hasn't gotten over her previous affair.

Episodic pic is sometimes peppy and fanciful but mostly resigned and morose. The entire cast gravitates to a spacious and trendy bar on the east side of Paris or loiters in a nearby park. Warm weather lensing is okay, and the set is brightly hued.

Citti wrote each role to measure for her actor pals and thesping is fine. Anouk Aimée has a brief cameo as a widow whose cat has died. Bracing French rock composed by two of the thesps is easier on the ears than some of the dialogue and one comes away with the impression that the cast enjoyed themselves. General auds are unlikely to say the same.
— *Lisa Nesselson*

SÖKARNA
(THE SEARCHERS)
(SWEDISH)

A Svensk Filmindustri release of a Sökarna/Svensk Filmindustri production. Produced by Kaska Krosny. Coproduced by Waldemar Bergendahl, Karstin Bonnier. Directed by Daniel Fridell, Peter Cartriers. Screenplay, Fridell. Camera (color, widescreen 1:1.66), Yngvar Lande; editor, Leon Framhole; music, Rob & Raz; production design, Carouschka; costumes, Marie Blom, Madeleine Lundberg; sound, Per Nyström. Reviewed at the Svensk screening room, Stockholm, March 23, 1993. Running time: **105 MIN.**
  With: Liam Norberg, Ray Jones IV, Malou Bergman, Thorsten Flinck, Nina Linden, Musse Hassevall, Jonas Karisson, Percy Bergström, Yvonne Schaloske, Marika Lindström, Christer Söderlund, Örjan Ramberg.

This violent youth movie, written and directed by a couple of 25-year-olds, is a technically inept effort that glorifies violence. The fact that it has done well in Sweden just points up the lack of quality domestic product for teenagers.

Daniel Fridell and Peter Cartriers have based "Sökarna" on

April 19, 1993 (Cont.)

their own experiences in the Stockholm underworld, where they've seen several of their friends die from drugs and gang violence. Execs at Svensk Filmindustri gave them $400,000 to make the film but obviously the pair received no advice from experienced movie-makers.

The result is a film that is either very ugly or styled to look like MTV at its worst. The actors seem to have been given no direction and even highly regarded pros sound like they've never been in front of a camera before, although making all the adults into clichés was probably the intention.

The story centers on four young guys and their graduation from petty thefts and random violence into heavy crimes and drugs. But since there is no effort at characterization, and scenes are put together without any thought of continuity, we never get to know the characters and don't care what happens to them. What's left is lots of stylized, glossy violence. The filmmakers say they wanted to make a film that shows how meaningless violence is but what they've accomplished is rather the opposite. — *Gunnar Rehlin*

EL CASO
MARÍA SOLEDAD
(THE MARIA SOLEDAD CASE)
(ARGENTINE)

A Distrifilms release of a Tercer Milenio/Aries production. Produced by Fernando Ayala. Directed by Héctor Olivera. Screenplay, Graciela Maglie, Olivera. Camera (color), Juan Carlos Lenardi; editor, Eduardo López; music, Osvaldo Montes; art direction, Aldo Guglielmone; costumes, Alicia Macchi; sound, Jorge Stavropulos; assistant director, Alberto Lecci. Reviewed at the Ocean I theater, Buenos Aires, March 25, 1993. Running time: **125 MIN.**
With: Carolina Fal, Juana Hidalgo, Valentina Bassi, Belén Blanco, Lidia Catalano, Francisco Cocuzza, Alfonso De Grazia, María José Demare, Luis Medina Castro, Juan Palomino, Ana Acosta, Villanueva Cosse, Alberto Segado.

Argentina's most shocking, still unsolved murder of recent years inspired Héctor Olivera's ("The Night of the Pencils") catching mix of fact and fiction that often looks like a docudrama. The mystery of

the crime itself is strengthened by the depiction of the powerful political forces blocking both the police and the judiciary to protect the culprits. If offshore audiences get a sense of the situation and its repercussions, they may find this case as gripping as natives do.

On Sept. 8, 1990, the mutilated body of schoolgirl María Soledad Morales was found in the outskirts of Catamarca, capital of the Andean province of same name and controlled for decades by *caudillo* Vicente Saadi and then governed by his son Ramón.

Early testimony pointed to the sons of political leaders as suspects in luring María Soledad to a fatal orgy above the disco where she was dancing. As soon as their names were mentioned, a coverup began, with destruction of evidence, intimidation of witnesses, the sowing of false leads, a smear campaign against the victim and an attempt to blame the girl's lover (maybe not entirely innocent) and his wife.

This prompted the coeds in the Catholic school attended by the slain girl, with the backing of the dean, Sister Martha Pelloni, to stage a silent march; this was followed by another, led by the nun and the victim's parents, and joined by dozens of people crying for justice. These were repeated some 60 times until they forced Argentina's President Menem to oust Gov. Saadi and call elections, which were won by the opposition candidate.

The murder, however, was never solved, the main suspect freed, and Sister Pelloni transferred. So "El Caso María Soledad," presumably to avoid slander suits, is a film whose story is known but whose bad guys helmer Olivera couldn't identify.

By fragmenting the tale in flashbacks, visualizing testimony and hypothetical situations, choosing convincing players (Juana Hidalgo stands out as Sister Pelloni), taking advantage of Catamarca locations, intertwining TV coverage of the actual marches and even using a narrator on camera, Olivera and co-scripter Graciela Maglie make viewers feel the psychopathic excesses allowed by the corrupt regime.

Technical credits are okay. — *Domingo Di Núbila*

TOUBAB BI
(FRENCH-SENEGALESE)

A Valprod production. (Intl. sales: Mercure Distribution, Paris.) Produced by Valérie Seydoux. Directed by Moussa Touré. Screenplay, Touré, Michele Armandi, Nathalie Levy. camera (LTC color by Fuji), Alain Choquart; editor, Josie Miljévic; music, Touré; sound, Dominique Levert; assistant director, Eddy Moine. Reviewed at Walter Reade Theater in "Modern Days, Ancient Nights" series, N.Y., April 4, 1993. Running time: **100 MIN.**
With: Oumar Diop Makena, Hélène Lapiower, Khalil Gueye, Cheikh Touré, Mousse Diouf, Monique Melinand, Philippe Mahon, Stephane Ferrara.

"Toubab Bi" (an untranslatable title) is a very entertaining fish out of water story that marks the arrival of a talented new director from Dakar, Moussa Touré. It's worth a look-see for U.S. distribution.

One of the most accessible films in the Lincoln Center African cinema series, "Toubab Bi" has entry points to fans of French cinema as well, recalling the well-made (though never released domestically) "Black mic-mac" in giving a glimpse of the African subculture of Paris.

Handsome Oumar Diop Makena toplines as Soriba Samb, an aspiring filmmaker who's headed to Paris from Dakar for an internship. At the airport he's saddled with a 5-year-old boy, a distant relative, whose dad Issa split for Paris seven years ago.

Flashbacks reveal that Soriba and Issa grew up together, so our hero becomes obsessed with finding his old pal. In the meantime, director Mouré (who himself apprenticed in France with Bertrand Tavernier and François Truffaut) with a light comic touch details Soriba's encounters with an assortment of quirky Parisians. Throughout, the director is even-handed in his avoidance of stereotypes and his sympathetic treatment of both African and French characters.

He finally discovers Issa successful as a pimp and vendor of porno videos and magazines. Undeterred, Soriba works to fulfill his promise to Issa's mom and tribal spells (including animal sacrifice) are conjured to aid the process of getting Issa to return.

Apart from one confusing scene when Soriba sends the boy away (he is literally written out of the picture), story is consistently interesting and well-acted. Lead

thesp Makena with his excessive politeness and warm manner is a genuine find. French leading lady Hélène Lapiower, with whom he has an interracial romance, is affecting and natural as well.

Film is differentiated from Western efforts in this genre by its emphasis on superstition, leading to a clever ending that makes the mystical content ambiguous. Technical credits are first-class, especially Alain Choquart's photography. — *Lawrence Cohn*

WHEELS AND DEALS
(TODLICHE GESCHAFTE)
(GERMAN-S. AFRICAN-B&W)

A Wild Okapi Films presentation of a Deutsch Film und-Fersehakademie production. Produced by Pierre de C. Hinch. Executive producer, Christian Hohoff. Directed, written by Michael Hammon, from Mtutuzeli Matashaba's story. Camera (B&W), Hammon; editor, Simone Brauer; music, William Ramsay; sound, Kevin Montenari, Robin Harris, Thomas Neubauer; art direction, Mark Wilby; costume design, Nicola Rauch. Reviewed at Walter Reade Theater in "Modern Days, Ancient Nights" series, N.Y., April 10, 1993. Running time: **96 MIN.**
B.T.	Sello Ke Maake-Ncube
Alsina	Kimberleigh Stark
Bandiet	Archie Mogorosi
Chippa	Ramolao Makhene
Opa Leroy	Mac Mathunjwa
Shabantu	Dominic Tyawa

Also with: Sandy Mokwena, Arthur Molepo, Neo Matsuyane
(English soundtrack)

A rough-edged but hard-hitting first feature about modern Soweto, "Wheels and Deals" reps a talented new German-trained director-cameraman from South Africa, Michael Hammon.

Backed by his Berlin film school, Deutsch Film und-Fersehakademie, the feature contains both English and local dialect dialogue but is subtitled only in German. Since even the English is heavily accented and lapses into patois, the film has some scenes that are impenetrable for American audiences.

Styled as a film noir with chiaroscuro photography by Hammon, pic depicts the downward spiral of handsome, ambitious B.T. (legit actor Sello Ke Maake-Ncube), who befriends a beautiful lawyer from America, Alsina (Kimberleigh Stark).

B.T. is involved with union leader Chippa (Ramolao Makhene) at their factory, but soon slides into a life of stealing autos. After filing off the serial number and giving it a new paint job, he even presents one of the hot

April 19, 1993 (Cont.)

vehicles to Alsina as a gift, leading to a falling out with her when she's busted by the police for the forged registration.

Chippa is driving the car when she's busted and he's thrown in jail. B.T. decides to turn over a new leaf and gets Chippa sprung, but in the process becomes more deeply involved with a ruthless (and warring) car theft ring masterminded by black political candidate Shabantu (hissable Dominic Tyawa).

Final reel leads B.T. to disaster after he's framed for the killing of a white woman in a car theft (anti-apartheid stickers on her car are pointedly shown before a black henchman shockingly shoots her) and his best friend (Archie Mogorosi) is murdered.

This bleak picture is enlivened by an expressive antihero limned by Maake-Ncube in the showy central role and the beauty of co-star Stark. Tyawa is a stock villain, recalling U.S. blaxploitation films.

Hammon's lensing is dramatic and film is tightly edited.

— *Lawrence Cohn*

AFRIQUE, JE TE PLUMERAI
(AFRICA, I WILL PLUCK YOU CLEAN)
(FRENCH-CAMEROON-DOCU-COLOR/B&W)

A Les Films du Raphia/Raphia Film Prods. production. Produced, directed, written, narrated by Jean-Marie Teno. Camera (Kodak color, B&W), Robert Dianoux, Louis Paul Nisa; editor, Chantal Rogeon, Angela Martin; music, Rax Lema, Aboubakar; sound, Francis Bon Fanti.

Militant to a fault, this documentary on the history and legacy of colonialism in Cameroon is of obvious educational value to properly motivated U.S. audiences. Director's idiosyncratic approach to the documentary form also gives it entertainment value.

Director Jean-Marie Teno, who also narrates, says he started out to do a film about Cameroon's publishing industry, but decided to expand his purview. Result is an often fascinating historical piece blending newsreels, interviews and staged scenes.

He gives a capsule history of the republic, occupied by the Germans before World War II and the French thereafter. It became independent Jan. 1, 1960, but Teno has harsh things to report

about its presidents Ahmadou Ahidjo and Paul Biya, with scary footage of beatings and killings to illustrate their harsh rule.

France is the main target of Teno's criticism, as he points out that the former colonial power is still dominating Cameroon industries, especially publishing. He makes a plea for self-reliance, stating the familiar fear of cultural domination from abroad that can wipe out a nation's heritage. For American viewers, this ironically echoes France's frequent protests against domination by Hollywood and English lingo.

Director's satirical approach is wide-ranging, even staging an interview with a TV magnate who callously rejects his request for production funds. Best segment features stand-up comic Aboubakar doing a mock press conference with very clever impressions of foreign journalists.

Though pic's focus is on Cameroon there's a segment paying tribute to assassinated leader Patrice Lumumba of the Belgian Congo. — *Lawrence Cohn*

LAAFI
(BURKINA FASO-FRENCH-SWISS)

A Les Films de l'Espoir/Thelma Film production. (Intl. sales: Amorces Diffusion.) Produced by Pierre-Alain Meir, S. Pierre Yameogo. Directed, written by Yameogo. Camera (color), Sekou Ouédraogo, Jürg Assler; editor, Loredona Cristelli; music, Pierre Akendenge, Nick Domby, Jerome Zongo, Abdoulay Cissé; sound, Issa Traoré, Johnny Traoré; production manager, Bado Babou. Reviewed at Walter Reade Theater in "Modern Days, Ancient Nights" series, N.Y., April 9, 1993. Running time: **94 MIN.**
With: Elie Yameogo, Aline Hortense Zoungrana, Denis Yameogo, Cheick Ali Kone, Laure Kaho, Yolande Belem, Jocelyne Bassolet.

A one-note film about high school grads having their pipe dreams dispelled, "Laafi" from Burkina Faso doesn't travel well. It's unlikely to have a commercial future beyond inclusion in African film series.

Joe (Elie Yameogo) has just graduated from high school in Ouagadougou with honors in mathematics; his heart is set on going to med school in France. But at registration he is told there are no spots reserved in medical school, only law school, secretarial school, etc. His only recourse is to get special permission from a government minister.

Debuting filmmaker S. Pierre Yameogo follows Joe's uninteresting battles with bureaucracy

with plenty of filler scenes involving a sandwich man named Man of the People, who dispenses folk wisdom and gets to sum up the film in a particularly anticlimactic final reel.

Naive Joe is shocked to find out that pull is what matters; film dwells redundantly on this truism and then inserts a *deus ex machina* climax in which Joe gets into a French med school.

Acting is weak and film's tech qualities are minimal.

— *Lawrence Cohn*

LA VIDA ES UNA SOLA
(YOU ONLY LIVE ONCE)
(PERUVIAN)

A Kusi Films production. Executive producer, Diana Cabrera. Directed, written by Marianne Eyde. Camera (color), César Pérez; editor, Michele André; music, Esteban Ttupa; sound, Rosa María Oliart. Reviewed at Cartagena Intl. Film Festival, Cartagena, Colombia, March 8, 1992. Running time: **84 MIN.**
Florinda . . . . . . Milagros del Carpio
El Tigre . . . . Aristóteles Picho
Meche . . . . . Rosa María Olórtegui
Marcelino . . . . Jiliat Zambrano

Second feature by Marianne Eyde, "La Vida Es una Sola" presents a harsh, unsentimental look at the guerrilla warfare being waged in Peru. Pic should find some international interest, especially for those trying to understand the complex situation in Peru. Film picked up best script award at the 33rd Cartagena Film Fest.

In a country under siege, the film is critical of both the Shining Path and the heavy-handed tactics of the Peruvian military, who see the villagers' submission as treason. There is no middle ground: You only live once and politics involve everyone.

Set in the Andean highland community of Rayopampa in 1983, story centers on Florinda (Milagros del Carpio), daughter of the village leader. She falls in love with a young man, part of a group of students visiting the area. When the students declare themselves to be Shining Path guerrillas, she decides to sacrifice everything — family, friends, social standing — for love. But the price turns out to be too high.

The guerrillas round the villagers up, declaring the town part of the new order and executing anyone who resists them.

When the military arrive, led by El Tigre (Aristóteles Pich), they are equally harsh. They suspect everyone of rebel sympathies and begin their own terror tactics.

Florinda leaves with the guerrillas but realizes that love is not enough to conquer the moral compromise demanded by political commitment. She is subjected to tests such as killing her dog and executing a longtime friend.

Eyde gives the film an authentic anthropological feel, capturing the shared atmosphere of an indigenous highland community, as well as the larger complexity of indigenous communities placed between guerrillas and the military with no escape.

— *Paul Lenti*

VIDAS PARALELAS
(PARALLEL LIVES)
(CUBAN)

An Instituto Cubano del Arte e Industrias Cinematográficas ICAIC (Cuba)/ Alter Prods. Cinematográficas/Foncine (Venezuela)/Televisión Española (Spain)/ Promotora de Inversiones y Financiamiento de Nicaragua production. Directed by Pastor Vega. Screenplay, Zoe Valdés, from Vega's idea. Camera (color), Livio Delgado; editor, Justo Vega; music, Ulises Hernández. Reviewed at Cartagena Intl. Film Festival, Cartagena, Colombia, March 10, 1993. Running time: **110 MIN.**
Andy . . . . Orlando Urdaneta
Rubén . . . . Omar Moynello
Aida . . . . Daisy Granados
Carmen . . . . Isabel Serrano

"Parallel Lives," the fifth feature by Cuban director Pastor Vega, is a lumbering rumination/thesis film that becomes snowbound en route to the big screen. With a schematic script by Zoe Valdés, it won first prize at the 1990 Havana Film Festival.

Story takes place over the course of one day, on one street: One side of the street is sunny Havana, while the other side is snowy Union City, N.J., which has a large Cuban immigrant population. (The location is never detailed, so unfamiliar audiences may wonder why a U.S. city is filled with Cubans and all signs, etc., are in Spanish.)

Tale revolves around Andy (Orlando Urdaneta), a Cuban who wants to go to the U.S., and Rubén (Omar Moynello), a U.S. resident who is nostalgic and wants to return to Cuba. Neither is happy, nor can either of them "cross the street" to get a taste of what they are pining for.

Instead of contrasting U.S. and Cuban societies, pic is a reflection on Cuban-ness, without dealing with the true depths and complications that separate those Cubans who have remained in Cuba from those in exile communities abroad.

Clichés abound: Kids dance on the festive sunny street of Havana, while decadence abounds in the frozen U.S. street, with thievery, prostitutes and one of the trashiest transvestites ever to grace the screen.

Technically, there are also major problems. Although Vega originally wanted to shoot the film in wintertime New Jersey, he was denied a visa. Instead of moving north and shooting in Canada, the U.S. scenes were filmed in Venezuela, where the snow looks like detergent powder and the actors seem to be sweating under their overcoats.
— *Paul Lenti*

FIN DE ROUND
(END OF THE ROUND)
(VENEZUELAN)

An Alter Prods. Cinematográficas/ Cine-Qua-Non production, in co-production with Televisión Española (Spain)/ Instituto Cubano del Arte e Industrias Cinematográficos/ICAIC (Cuba)/Anabase Films (France). Executive producers, Delfina Catala, Cristian Castillo. Directed by Olegario Barrera. Screenplay, Rodolfo Santana, Barrera, José Manuel Pelaez, from Santana's play. Camera (color), Mario García Joya; editor, Cacho Briceño; music, Alonso Toro; art direction, Cami García. Reviewed at Cartagena Intl. Film Festival, Cartagena, Colombia, March 9, 1993. Running time: **107 MIN.**
Perucho . . . . Raúl Vásquez
Brigido . . . . Karl Hofman
Mariana . . . . Gisvel Ascanio
Cecilia . . . . Linsabel Noguera
Gonzalito . . . . Orlando Casín
Cara E. Perro . . . . . . Frank Spano
Tico . . . . Alejandro Lugo
Also with: Jenny Noguera, Omar Moynello, Gonzalo Cubero, Freddy Pereira, Mirtha Borges, Yanis Chimaras, Juan Franquiz, Tony Padrón, Moises Correa, Romelia Aguero.

Although "Fin de Round" contains some bright lights, it is basically a competition of about four different films that never merges into a coherent whole, and ends up down for the final count.

First, there is the tale of three people — a couple and the wife's brother — who migrate from the countryside to the capital, installing themselves in a slum. One day, the brother, Perucho (Raúl Vásquez), discovers he can

fight and becomes a champion pugilist. Fighting under the name Manopla, one day he accidentally kills an opponent and is haunted for the rest of the film.

It is a familiar story of a humble man who raises himself through athletic prowess to achieve a certain fame, only to lose it at the end while gaining peace of mind.

Sandwiched in between these stories is the chronicle of the sister (Gisvel Ascanio), who goes into a trance and picks winners at the horse races. (Fortunately, this storyline is dropped about midway through.) Also, there is bungling inventor brother-in-law (Karl Hofman), who devises a glider and is fascinated by new technology.

Unfortunately, helmer Olegario Barrera doesn't stick to making a boxing movie. The story is involving and the actors are charismatic and likable. Cuban cinematographer Mario García Joya breathes life and excitement into the fight scenes. But, the overall pic fails to coalesce into a satisfying whole. — *Paul Lenti*

SUEÑO TROPICAL
(TROPICAL DREAM)
(CUBAN)

An Instituto Cubano del Arte e Industrias Cinematográficos (ICAIC) production. Executive producers, Carlos Calderón, Manuel Angueira. Directed by Miguel Torres. Screenplay, Torres, Rubén Geller. Camera (color), Raúl Rodríguez; editor, Jorge Abello, Susana Miguel; music, Jorge Aragón. Reviewed on vidcassette at the Mecla Market, Cartagena Intl. Film Festival, Cartagena, Colombia, March 8, 1992. Running time: **75 MIN.**
Hermes . . . . Alberto Pujois
Sara . . . . Hilda Rabilero
Antonia . . . . Daisy Granados
Nora . . . . Almi Alonso
Pablo . . . . Orlando Casín

In this "Year of the Woman," Cuba's diverting commercial comedy "Sueño Tropical," helmed by Miguel Torres, might find some successful play offshore. Pic will probably be most appreciated in Latin markets where the macho attributes depicted are more pronounced.

A light satire and critique of machismo, pic presents a reversal of situations: Men do the shopping and take care of the children, while women parade off to work, spend their free time playing cards in smoky bars and openly flaunt sexual conquests. You get the picture.

Message pic starts at a birthday party for Hermes (Alberto Pujois). Although his wife Nora (Almi Alonso) is tired, he demands she clean up the apartment before going to sleep, asserting his role as husband and provider. They go to bed angry and Hermes wakes up to discover a changed world.

On the whole, the story eventually gets out of hand, but pic does offer some unpretentious humorous moments. The thank-god-it-was-all-a-dream ending is an easy out, and the film does not belabor it. — *Paul Lenti*

DAVE

A Warner Bros. release of a Northern Lights Entertainment/Donner/ Shuler-Donner production. Produced by Lauren Shuler-Donner, Ivan Reitman. Executive producers, Joe Medjuck, Michael C. Gross. Directed by Ivan Reitman. Screenplay, Gary Ross. Camera (Technicolor), Adam Greenberg; editor, Sheldon Kahn; music, James Newton Howard; production design, J. Michael Riva; art direction, David Klassen; set decoration, Michael Taylor; costume design, Richard Hornung; sound (Dolby), Gene Cantamessa; associate producers, Gordon Webb, Sherry Fadely; assistant director, Peter Giuliano; 2nd-unit director, Gross; casting, Michael Chinich, Bonnie Timmermann. Reviewed at the Avco Center Cinema, L.A., April 17, 1993. MPAA Rating: PG-13. Running time: **110 MIN.**
Dave Kovic/Bill Mitchell . Kevin Kline
Ellen Mitchell . . . Sigourney Weaver
Bob Alexander . . . . . Frank Langella
Alan Reed . . . . Kevin Dunn
Duane Stevenson . . . . Ving Rhames
Vice President Nance . . Ben Kingsley
Murray Blum . . . . . . Charles Grodin
Alice . . . . Faith Prince

When it comes to tapping into a populist wave of support, Ross Perot will have nothing on "Dave," a delightful, buoyant new take on an old theme that will win at the polls because it never strikes a false chord. Displaying an unerring eye for current events, and deftly mixing political cynicism with elements of "Mr. Smith Goes to Washington," Warner Bros. figures to walk away with a major box office landslide.

Writer Gary Ross (who helped bring the same sense of wonder to "Big") and director Ivan Reitman have done a masterful job, crafting a near-perfect movie by realizing its simple goals with panache, political savvy and ample warmth and humor.

The central premise's lack of originality — explored from various angles in films as diverse as "Prisoner of Zenda," "Kagemusha" and "Moon Over Parador" — doesn't detract at all from the appeal of "Dave," the story of a run-of-the-mill guy asked to stand-in for a major leader who suddenly falls ill.

In this case, the office is President of the United States, and Dave (Kevin Kline), a sometime-presidential-impersonator and full-time struggling employment agent, gets the call to glory after the real Commander-in-Chief suffers a stroke while entertaining a comely White House aide.

Dave gets drafted by White House chief of staff Bob Alexander (Frank Langella, in a role so smarmy it would do John Sununu proud) and his communications director (Kevin Dunn), who fear a loss of their power and want to keep Dave in office long enough to engineer a sort-of coup in which Alexander can take over. Just to be safe, they dispatch the Vice President (Ben Kingsley, in a small but effective cameo) on a fool's errand to Africa.

In addition to breathing new life into what must have been a rather torpid presidency (the movie's one drawback may be that the incumbent's politics are studiously ignored), Dave also thaws the icy, for-appearances-only relationship between the President and the First Lady (Sigourney Weaver), providing a nifty romantic element.

That, in fact, forms the central core of the story and helps differentiate "Dave" from Disney's "The Distinguished Gentleman," which also had a D.C. backdrop.

Even so, the film's most-talked-about element (especially on the coasts and in D.C.) may well be its more than two dozen remarkably clever cameos, from the entire "McLaughlin Group" (the president's turnaround is scored an "8") to various senators and Oliver Stone, who's on-target with *this* conspiracy theory.

Kline stands forth as the glue that holds it all together, but he benefits from strong supporting performances all around — particularly in smaller roles, such as Ving Rhames' stony Secret Service agent, who pulls off the film's most affecting moment.

Reitman has proven his credentials as a comedy director on such money-makers as "Twins" and "Ghostbusters," but he moves to a new level here in terms of the movie's dead-on-target Capra-esque flourishes, aided immeasurably by Ross' smart, meticulously assembled script.

Technical personnel add to that winning ticket, from production designer J. Michael Riva's "western" White House (interiors were actually built on a Warner Bros. soundstage in Burbank) to James Newton Howard's fine score.
— *Brian Lowry*

THE DARK HALF

An Orion release of a Dark Half production. Produced by Declan Baldwin. Executive producer, George A. Romero. Directed, written by Romero, from Stephen King's novel. Camera (Deluxe color), Tony Pierce-Roberts; editor, Pasquale Buba; music, Christopher Young; production design, Cletus Anderson; art direction, Jim Feng; set decoration, Brian Stonestreet; costume design, Barbara Anderson; sound (Dolby), John Sutton; makeup effects created by, John Vulich, Everett Burrell; visual effects producer, VCE/Peter Kuran; computer generated birds and computer composited effects scenes, Video Image; associate producer, Christine Romero; assistant director, Nicholas C. Mastandrea; 2nd unit director, Tom Dubensky; 2nd unit camera, Robert Wagner, Mike Spiller; casting, Terry Liebling. Reviewed at the Orion screening room, L.A., March 25, 1993. MPAA Rating: R. Running time: **122 MIN.**
Thad Beaumont/George Stark . . . . .
. . . . Timothy Hutton
Liz Beaumont . . . . . . Amy Madigan
Sheriff Alan Pangborn . Michael Rooker
Reggie DeLesseps . . . . . Julie Harris
Fred Clawson . . . . Robert Joy
Mike Donaldson . . . . Kent Broadhurst
Shayla Beaumont . . . . . . Beth Grant
Miriam Cowley . . . . . . Rutyana Alda
Rick Cowley . . . . . Tom Mardirosian
Homer Gamache . . . . .Glenn Colerider
Annie Pangborn . . . : . . Chelsea Field
Digger Holt . . : . . . . . . Royal Dano

The writer's desk intriguingly becomes a gladitorial arena for warring manifestations of the same personality in "The Dark Half," George A. Romero's fine adaptation of Stephen King's 1989 bestseller. One of Orion's numerous long-on-the-shelf items during its bankruptcy hiatus, this one should actually generate some welcome coin for the beleaguered distrib.

A classic Jekyll-and-Hyde story played out in recognizably King-like terms, pic features enough gruesome killings and special effects to satisfy hardcore horror fans, but also has sufficient narrative and thematic substance to keep more mainstream viewers interested. It certainly ranks as one of the top King adaptations.

After a 1968-set prologue establishes Thad Beaumont as a precocious kid writer and a grotesque operation gives physical evidence of a twin in Thad's brain, story proper picks up in the current day, with Thad married to the solid, resourceful Liz (Amy Madigan) and the father of — natch — twins. He's penned two failed "art" novels but, under the pseudonym George Stark, authored four disreputable bestsellers, books that pay the bills but would do nothing for his standing at his Maine university.

When a grungy student discovers Thad's double life and demands money to keep silent, Thad goes public and, in the presence of a People magazine photographer, literally buries "George Stark" under the epitaph "Not A Very Nice Guy."

But Stark doesn't take too kindly to his premature death, and begins manifesting his existence in places other than the bestseller list. The People lenser is the first to go, and Thad's fingerprints are all over the murder scene. Then the student who exposed Thad is found slaughtered, and who else had a motive?

As the killings mount up, it's not hard for either Thad or the audience to figure out what's going on, that he is, in a sense, being held hostage until by his "brother" until he agrees to revive him by writing again in the Starkian vein. That Thad eludes arrest is one of the less convincing aspects, but he must remain free in order to enact the epic doppelganger confrontation.

Playing Thad/Stark represents a juicy challenge for an actor, and Timothy Hutton makes the most of it in his most impressive screen work in quite some time. Unlike most thesps, Hutton is plausible portraying a writer, and manages to give Thad solid human dimensions beyond the earnestness and distress that are the surface keynotes of the role.

His George Stark is a terrific contrast, a cowboy greaser in black who's all razor edges, cigarettes and booze. Hutton's never attempted a part like this before, and he makes the guy quite scary, a genuine threat to any and all who come under his amoral gaze.

None of the other characters has much depth, but all performers register favorably, including Madigan, Michael Rooker as the cop reluctantly on the writer's case, and Julie Harris as an eccentric academic colleague.

Aside from the assorted killings and opening-scene surgery, the major special effects effort has gone into the sporadic massing of thousands of birds, dragged in by way of an ancient Greek myth, in which sparrows were the conductors of human souls from one world to another. What their presence actually does is allow Romero the chance for some climactic ornithological gore way beyond anything Alfred Hitchcock attempted.

Director's customary Pittsburgh-area locations double adequately for King's small-town New England, and tech contributions are all solid without being ostentatious. — *Todd McCarthy*

THE NIGHT WE NEVER MET

A Miramax Films release of a Miramax, Sidney Kimmel presentation of a Michael Peyser production. Produced by Peyser. Executive producers, Kimmel, Bob Weinstein, Harvey Weinstein. Directed, written by Warren Leight. Camera (Duart color; Film House prints), John Thomas; editor, Camilla Toniolo; music, Evan Lurie; production design, Lester Cohen; art direction, Daniel Talpers; costume design, Ellen Lutter; sound, William Sarokin; co-producer/production manager, Rudd Simmons; assistant director, J. Miller Tobin; casting, Billy Hopkins, Suzanne Smith. Reviewed at Magno Review 1 screening room, N.Y., April 12, 1993. MPAA Rating: R. Running time: **99 MIN.**
Sam Lester . . . . Matthew Broderick
Ellen Holder . . . . Annabella Sciorra
Brian McVeigh . . . . Kevin Anderson
Pastel . . . . Jeanne Tripplehorn
Janet Beehan . . . . . Justine Bateman
Aaron Holder . . . . . Michael Mantell
Lucy . . . . Christine Baranski
Neighbor . . . . Doris Roberts
Neighbor . . . . Dominic Chianese
Also with: Tim Guinee, Bradley White, Greg Germann, Dana Wheeler-Nicholson, Louise Lasser, Bill Campbell, Ranjit Chowdhry, Garry Shandling, Katherine Houghton, Brooke Smith.

A quintessential New York movie, "The Night We Never Met" takes a novel premise and develops it in fits and starts. A guaranteed crowd-pleaser on its home turf, episodic effort could attract a hip audience elsewhere as well.

Debuting filmmaker Warren Leight has come up with an offbeat notion: time-sharing a Greenwich Village apartment by days of the week (practice exists, but is hardly a trend). Hissable yuppie Kevin Anderson is behind the scheme, wanting two nights out a week with his poker-playing, football watching buddies while living with patrician fiancée Justine Bateman.

One customer is Matthew Broderick, moping over losing his performance artist girlfriend Pastel (Jeanne Tripplehorn, spoofing a familiar downtown type). Broderick is sharing a flat with too many noisy, vulgar roommates and needs a crash pad.

Third tenant is frustrated housewife Annabella Sciorra, who uses it to get away from her dense husband (Michael Mantell) and spend a couple of days painting.

This format allows Leight to develop some surefire situation comedy. The three tenants never meet but are aware of their differing habits: boorish slob Anderson leaves a mess each time;

Sciorra fixes up pretty curtains and furnishings; Broderick is a gourmet cook (he works in an upscale food store) who provides fabulous leftovers for Sciorra.

Plot is set in motion when Anderson innocently switches one of his designated days with Broderick but doesn't update the posted schedule, causing Sciorra to confuse the two guys, swearing at Broderick over the phone for leaving a mess and fixing her sights on a romance with "dream guy" Anderson.

Finale has the threesome of nearly 30-year-olds finally meeting in the apartment, but not until after Sciorra has slept with Anderson, almost ruining her life, and further complications when (predictably) fiancée Bateman half-learns of the apartment and assumes Anderson carries on all week long.

Wonderfully atmospheric use of New York locations and familiar characters brings "Night" to life. Unfortunately, there are many scenes, particularly those of Anderson and his obnoxious pals, which kill time and detract from the romantic leads. Ultimately it's not really so much an ensemble piece as a film of alternating casts or vignettes.

Broderick, making a notable screen comeback after his laughless "Out on a Limb" fiasco, is utterly convincing as the hapless hero. Sciorra immediately garners sympathy, giving the film some heart and depth beyond the surface yocks. Anderson throws himself whole-heartedly into his stereotyped assignment.

Garry Shandling pops up uncredited as a wiseguy patient of dental hygienist Sciorra, while Christine Baranski is perfect as Sciorra's best friend.

Lensing by John Thomas (who photographed Gotham-set "Metropolitan") is sharp and Evan Lurie's sprightly score is a definite asset. — *Lawrence Cohn*

TEMPTING A MARRIED MAN
(AUSTRALIAN)

An Adam Lynton production. Produced, directed, written, photographed, edited, scored, designed, recorded by Lynton. Reviewed at Leura screening room, Leura, Australia, April 11, 1993. Running time: **100 MIN.**

Karen Scott	Lile Hammond
Stan Scott	Tim Baker
Peggy Lumet	Theresa Huska
Barbara Parker	Jay Gargett
Harry Parker	Matt Pritchard
Shirley Cameron	Anna Sheehan
Alan Cameron	Adam Lynton

Perth-based Adam Lynton self-financed this ultra-low-budgeter to the tune of a little over $4,000, and did just about all the chores himself. The results are as rough as could be expected, yet Lynton obviously has ideas, both as a writer and a director, and deserves the chance to show what he could do on a real budget with a pro cast and crew.

In title and theme, "Tempting a Married Man" harks back (perhaps unintentionally) to those C.B. DeMille marital comedies of the late teens and early '20s.

Three suspicious wives get together and decide to test the fidelity of their spouses, who all work for the same computer outfit. The women hire a beautiful young prostie (Theresa Huska) and dispatch her to vamp the men. One rejects her, another suffers a heart attack when she comes on to him and the third, after some hesitation, strays.

Lynton has some amusing ideas, and an original way of putting them across, though he shows an overfondness for shots taken from floor level, and a coyness in handling sexual scenes. Budgetary problems no doubt account for the inadequate soundtrack and the variable performances; though Lile Hammond, Tim Baker, Huska and Lynton himself (as the husband who says no) acquit themselves well.

In its present form, "Tempting" is going nowhere, but it indicates an embryonic talent who could be nurtured for the future. — *David Stratton*

INDIAN SUMMER

A Buena Vista release of a Touchstone presentation of an Outlaw production. Produced by Jeffrey Silver, Robert Newmyer. Directed, written by Mike Binder. Camera (Film House color; Technicolor prints; Panavision widescreen), Tom Sigel; editor, Adam Weiss; music, Miles Goodman; production design, Craig Stearns; art direction, Rocco Matteo; set design, Diane Bald; set decoration, Jane Manchee; costume design, Jane Robinson; sound (Dolby), Ed Novick, Freddy Potatohead; co-producers, Caroline Baron, Jack Binder; assistant director, Eric Heffron; casting, Richard Pagano, Sharon Bialy, Debi Manwiller. Reviewed at the Avco Cinema, L.A., April 19, 1993. MPAA Rating: PG-13. Running time: **97 MIN.**

Unca Lou	Alan Arkin
Jamie Ross	Matt Craven
Beth Warden	Diane Lane
Jack Belston	Bill Paxton
Jennifer Morton	Elizabeth Perkins
Brad Berman	Kevin Pollak
Stick Coder	Sam Raimi
Matthew Berman	Vincent Spano
Kelly Berman	Julie Warner
Gwen Daugherty	Kimberly Williams
Claire Everett	Diane Lane

Awash in romantic nostalgia for childhoods spent in summer camps, "Indian Summer" is a sentimental, TV sitcom-like film. However, graced with some humor and first-rate acting, pic is amiable enough to please thirtysomething auds, and perhaps older viewers. The cast and appeal of the genre could insure a strong opening and modest b.o. life.

Writer-director Mike Binder ("Crossing The Bridge") reconvenes the old friends in the familiar cinematic territory of "The Big Chill" et al. But this regrouping takes place in gorgeous Camp Tamakwa, the site of their 1972 summer, making "Indian Summer" less theatrical and claustrophobic.

The seven returning campers represent a vivid assortment of diverse characters, including the single and increasingly desperate Jennifer (Elizabeth Perkins), Matthew and Kelly (Vincent Spano and Julie Warner), whose marriage seems in trouble, insensitive "macho" Jamie (Matt Craven) and his much younger g.f. Gwen (Kimberly Williams).

Presiding over the group is Unca Lou (Alan Arkin), a benevolent patriarch who has devoted his entire life to the camp, who immediately treats them all like kids again, inducing them to engage in tetherball, sailing, canoeing, swimming, etc.

True to form, the tale involves revelation of personal secrets, frustrated loves, new sexual yearnings, and some unexpected truths. The most "dramatic" event is Lou's announcement of his retirement after four decades despite making no provisions for the camp's continuity.

Drawing on his personal experience in Canada's Algonquin Provincial Park, where actual lensing was done, Binder has constructed a loose series of vignettes, some funnier than others, that provide a pretext for a rather shallow look at all kinds of pre-midlife crises and often lets things get a little too cute.

Fortunately, the highly accomplished ensemble keeps this confection tasty and enjoyable, and waves of recognition will flow between the actors' escapades and the audience. Alan Arkin shows a gleaming pleasure in his moments of broad farce. And each of the younger performers registers strongly in his or her big moment, though the women, whose roles are richer and better scripted, come off better.

Of the entire cast, the three stand-out performers are Elizabeth Perkins and Bill Paxton in two showy roles and Diane Lane in a subtler and more difficult part. As the lonely singleton, Perkins gives her lines a personal rhythm and brittle snap. Paxton, so touching as the cop in "One False Move," demonstrates that he is an able physical comedian. Lane renders an entirely disciplined performance that underlies the vulnerability of her character, and also plays a small role as an elderly woman.

Tech credits are pro in every department, particularly Tom Sigel's lensing of the handsome locations and the black and white flashbacks. — *Emanuel Levy*

WHO'S THE MAN

A New Line Cinema release of a New Line production in association with Tin Pan Apple/de Passe Entertainment/Thomas Entertainment. Produced by Charles Stettler, Maynell Thomas. Directed by Ted Demme. Screenplay, Seth Greenland; from Doctor Dre & Ed Lover and Greenland's story. Camera (Technicolor), Adam Kimmel; editor, Jeffrey Wolf; music, Michael Wolff, Nic. ten-Broek; production design, Ruth Ammon; set decorator, Sue Raney; costume designer, Karen Perry; sound (Dolby), Rosa Howell-Thornhill; associate producer, Janet Grillo; assistant director, Randy Fletcher; casting, Jaki Brown-Karman, Martha Diaz. Reviewed at the Raleigh Studios, Los Angeles, April 20. MPAA Rating: R. Running Time: **87 MIN.**

Ed Lover	Ed Lover
Doctor Dre	Doctor Dre
Lionel Douglas	Badja Djola
Demetrius	Richard Bright
Nighttrain/Chauncey	Ice-T
Teesha Braxton	Cheryl "Salt" James
Nick Crawford	Jim Moody
Sgt. Bo Griles	Rozwill Young
Frankie Flynn	Colin Quinn
Sgt. Cooper	Dennis Leary
Lamar	Andre B. Blake
K.K.	Bill Bellamy
Fuji	Kim Chan

New Line's "Who's the Man?" is an enjoyable, kinetic mess of music, low comedy and social drama. No matter that it doesn't quite coalesce logically, the film has decided niche audience appeal that will generate respectable business. However, it doesn't quite have what it takes to crossover to a more mainstream crowd.

MTV rap jocks Ed Lover and Doctor Dre play vague facsimil

April 26, 1993 (Cont.)

ies of themselves, here as the world's worst tag team barbers in a Harlem tonsorial parlor. But they have bigger plans.

While the duo aspire to be music impresarios, their boss, clipper Nick (Jim Moody), tells them they have to take the police recruiting exam or they will be out on their shears. Of course, guessing wildly on the multiple choice test, they get top scores.

The buffoonishness is short-lived as the story spins out into a too familiar urban drama scenario. A real estate developer (Richard Bright) — the current reigning movie heavy — is buying up the nabe and Nick's emporium is the sole holdout. When he's murdered, the boys inherit the shop and, using their badges, set out to expose the evil speculator's scheme and put him behind bars.

Recalling the kind of films his uncle Jonathan and others made for Roger Corman two decades ago, debutant feature director Ted Demme acquits himself well with an assured, breezy style. However, he has much to overcome in Seth Greenland's sketch of a script. The balance between the physical pratfalls of the stars and the more serious social/ethnic crime drama milieu clash in an aesthetic stalemate.

Lover and Doctor Dre are a promising screen partnership but need to develop more distinct screen personae. The supporting cast is strong, elevating their basic stock characters a notch.

Imbued with a wall-to-wall music soundtrack, concert numbers and a host of cameos by such artists as Queen Latifah, Kriss Kross and Flavor Flav, "Who's the Man?" knows exactly who it wants to reach. The ragtag medley may be a poor man's "Mo' Money," yet its determined frenzy and momentum is ultimately more satisfying than slicker cousins. — *Leonard Klady*

MY HOME, MY PRISON
(DOCU-COLOR/B&W)

A My Home, My Prison production. Produced, directed by Susan Blaustein Munoz, Erica Marcus. Camera (color, b&w), John Knoop; editor, Ismael Saavedra; music, Donna Viscuso, Mustafa Kurd, Marcel Khalifeh. Reviewed at Sundance Film Festival, Park City, Utah, Jan. 29, 1993. Running time: 63 MIN.
Narrators: Martin Sheen, Gail Golden.

Set against the backdrop of the Israeli-Palestinian dis-

pute, "My Home, My Prison" centers on courageous journalist Raymonda Tawill, a woman who has devoted her life to the Palestinian cause and co-existence with Israel. Though not a well-rounded perspective on the conflict, informative docu is still a natural for public TV and other venues.

Born in Palestine in 1940, Tawill was taken away from her mother, an independent woman whose divorce was perceived as a "deviant" act. The only Arab girl in a boarding school in Haifa, she was exposed to Jewish students whose families were Holocaust survivors. Tawill showed interest in politics from an early age. One of the first Palestinians to engage Israelis in a direct dialogue after the 1967 Six Day War, she was arrested several times by Israeli authorities and finally exiled to Paris.

Docu effectively interweaves archival footage, interviews with Palestinian and Israeli politicians, dramatic reenactments of Tawill's childhood, and readings from her book, also called "My Home, My Prison," which was translated into many languages.

Despite its explicit agenda, docu's most engrossing sequences describe Tawill's status as a liberated woman in a traditional, misogynistic society. In a rare humorous moment, her husband complains that she neglected her duties as a mother, and her daughters fondly remember Tawill's house arrest because it was the only time she was at home.

Midway, docu loses Tawill and skirts toward polemics and is not even-handed: The Israeli side is not as well-represented as the Palestinian. But so long as docu focuses on Tawill's charismatic personality, it provides riveting personal and political insights. — *Emanuel Levy*

SNÖVSEN
(THE SNOOKS)
(DANISH-SWEDISH)

A Nordisk Film Prod. presentation in collaboration with Svensk Film Industri and the Danish Film Institute. Produced by Lars Kolvig. Directed by Jörgen Vestergaard. Screenplay, Benny Andersen, Vestergaard from Andersen's children's books. Camera (color), Claus Loof. Reviewed at the Palads multiplex, Copenhagen, Dec. 12, 1993. Running time: 80 MIN.
Eigil . . . . . Bjarke Smitt Vestermark
Pernille . . . . . . Amalie Ihle Alstrup
Mr. Blomme . . . . Kurt Ravn
Mrs. Blomme . . . . Sös Egelind
Eigil's Uncle . . . . Jesper Klein
Also with: Niels Olsen, Fleming Jensen, Daimi, Torben Zeller.

A sympathetic children's film combining puppet animation and live action "The Snooks" has done good business at local wickets and will be be a hot kidvid release. Appeal overseas could depend on proper dubbing.

Eigil, 7, is puzzled by some odd phrases used by his parents, such as "leaving the Snooks" (losing one's marbles) and "buying the cat in the bag" (getting a raw deal). The imaginative boy takes pity on the Snooks and the cat and he sets out on quest to find these creatures. After finding them, their friendship leads him into a number of adventures.

Bjarke Smitt Vestermark's Eigil comes across as a likable youngster and the supporting cast of experienced grown up thesps plays the whole thing tongue-in-cheek. Pic's combination of puppet animation and live action are less than perfect but okay for smaller children, likewise pic's creature designs are a bit primitive.

Pic nevertheless comes off as charming in a quaint sort of way, mostly due to good performances and the often witty dialogue. Helmer Jörgen Vestergaard has made a number of puppet animation shorts, this is his feature debut. — *Peter Risby Hansen*

THE LIFE AND TIMES OF ALLEN GINSBERG
(DOCU-B&W/COLOR)

A Jerry Aronson production. Produced, directed by Jerry Aronson. Camera, Jean de Segonzac, Roger Carter, Richard Lerner; editors, Nathaniel Dorsky, Aronson; music, Tom Capek. Reviewed at Sundance Film Festival, Park City, Utah, Jan. 27, 1993. Running time: 82 MIN.
With: Allen Ginsberg, William Burroughs, Ken Kesey, Norman Mailer, Timothy Leary, Joan Baez, Amiri Baraka, Abbie Hoffman, others.

The best thing to be said about the painstaking "Life and Times of Allen Ginsberg" is that it provides a systematic look at the poet. However, considering Ginsberg's flamboyance and the intriguing gallery of writers and artists who have been part of his life, Jerry Aronson's docu is disappointingly conventional. Still, interest in Ginsberg's poetry and renewed interest in the beatnik generation will facilitate docu's showings at film fests, universities and on public TV.

Producer-director Aronson, a film instructor in Colorado, imposes a strict chronological order on his material, with each decade serving as a chapter in Ginsberg's life. Docu begins interestingly with the handsome young Ginsberg learning the art of poetry from his father, Louis, and suffering when his mentally ill mother is institutionalized.

Ginsberg's formative years were in the 1940s and early '50s, when he met Jack Kerouac and William Burroughs, who helped him come out of the closet and establish his intellectual persona. In the '60s and '70s, he became a political activist, demonstrating against the Vietnam War and American nuclear policy. The film concludes with a portrait of the older Ginsberg as university professor.

Docu is quite methodical in covering Ginsberg's public persona, but it doesn't provide very deep insights into his private life. Ginsberg's longtime companion, Peter Orlovsky, is mentioned in the context of their "deep bond" and vows of eternal love, but not much information is conveyed about the kind of relationship they have or life together.

Regrettably, Ginsberg's friends and followers tend to be too brief and unilluminating: "Allen and Peter were true bohemians," says Timothy Leary, and Joan Baez recalls, "Allen could behave like a nut, but he was serious about things."

Though centered around a compelling figure who has defied time and fashion, Aronson's film, while succeeding in communicating his respect and love for Ginsberg, provides no focal point and nothing that challenge what is already known about the poet. Ginsberg reading his famous poems "Howl" and "Kaddish," while engrossing, might have been better if filmed during a performance. — *Emanuel Levy*

FUNES, UN GRAN AMOR
(FUNES, A GREAT LOVE)
(ARGENTINE)

A Transmundo release of a Piedra de Agua production. Produced by Guillermo Szelske. Executive producer, Raúl de la Torre. Directed by de la Torre. Screenplay, Ugo Pirro, de la Torre, from Humberto Constantini's short story "Talk to Me About Funes." Camera (color), Juan Carlos Desanzo; editor, Marcela Sáenz; music, Charly García; art direction, Miguel Angel Lumaldo; costumes, Leonor Puga Sabaté; sound, Miguel Babuini; assistant director, Santiago Carlos Oves. Reviewed at the Broadway theater, Buenos Aires, April 1, 1993. Running time: 115 MIN.

April 26, 1993 (Cont.)

With: Gian María Volonté, Graciela Borges, Andrea Del Boca, Pepe Soriano, Jairo, Nacha Guevara, Susana Rinaldi, Moria Casán, Rodolfo Ranni, Dora Baret, Beba Bidart, Alfredo Zemma, Antonio Tarragó Ros, Daniel Binelli, Juan Cruz Bordeu, Matías Gandolfo.

This tango-flavored melodrama seemingly made with an eye on European markets has Gian María Volonté heading a cast of several Argentine stars known abroad (Graciela Borges, Andrea Del Boca, Pepe Soriano, Jairo, Susana Rinaldi, Nacha Guevara) plus musical attractions and a production effort above local standards. It achieves some colorful, even catching moments, but misfires as entertainment mainly due to a disjointed script, overacting and uneven editing.

Story takes place in the '30s mostly at a bar/whorehouse near the slaughterhouse in Sárate, the hometown of helmer/co-scripter Raúl de la Torre. Volonté plays the owner, a taciturn Italian who beats a corrupt political heavy at the poker table, sleeps with the prostitutes and apparently falls for Borges, the female pianist of a tango band, but this is not certain until near the end.

Pepe Soriano, as the bartender who tells the story from a home for old people many years later, has chances to display his acting class here and there. Ditto bosomy Maria Casán as a spirited prostie. The other able professionals in the multistar cast are hampered by the screenplay's shortcomings but their personalities help to hide many holes.

Period look and atmosphere are pluses as are Desanzo's camerawork, Charlie García's score and the songs, including full renditions by Jairo of tango classics "Yuyo Verde" (Green Weed) and "Naranjo en Flor" (Flowered Orange Trees). First-class tango soloists form the band, among them bandoneonist Daniel Binelli, who also plays a grumpy character. José Colángelo is the ghost pianist for Borges. Ace tango dancer Juan Carlos Copes does a brief appearance.

Editing leaves plenty of room for further scissor work. Sound recording is faulty, especially with the voice of Volonté.
— *Domingo Di Núbila*

INGE, APRIL UND MAI
(INGE, APRIL AND MAY)
(GERMAN)

A Filmpool Köln production. (Intl. sales: Futura/Filmverlag, Munich.) Produced by Gisela Marx. Directed by Wolfgang Kohlhaase, Gabriele Denecke. Screenplay, Kohlhaase from his short story. Camera (color), Igor Luther; editor, Evelyn Carow; music, Günther Fischer; art direction, Klaus Winter, Hans-Joachim Schwarz; costume design, Rita Gawkrikow; sound, Wolfgang Schukrafft; assistant director, Irene Weigel. Reviewed at Berlin Film Festival (noncompeting), Feb. 16, 1993. Running time: **86 MIN.**
Kalle . . . . Niels-Bruno Schmidt
Inge Kaliska . . . . . Nadine Böttcher
Uschi Nietzelbach . . . . Tina Haseney
Gerdchen Pachäl . . . . . . Jens Adler
"Monkey" Lehmann . . Oliver Ahrendt
Kalle's mother . . . . Corinna Harfouch
Aunt Lisbeth . . . . . . Silke Matthias
Inge's father . . . . Otto Sander

First love meets the last days of the war in "Inge, April and May," a mildly offbeat rites of passage movie that's too TV-ish to score in offshore markets. Surprisingly, pic was accorded a prestigious out-of-competition slot at this year's Berlin fest.

The time is spring 1945, the place Berlin. The Russians are coming, food is short, and youngsters are being rounded up for army service. Against this background, 15-year-old loafer Kalle (Niels-Bruno Schmidt) meets the darkly beautiful Inge (Nadine Böttcher), and it's love at first sight for the cocky teen.

However, despite lots of groping sessions, Kalle doesn't get much beyond first base. When the Russians arrive, Inge's father (Otto Sander) tries to force her to commit suicide; meanwhile, Kalle's visiting aunt (Silke Matthias) is servicing Soviet troops. At a dance celebrating peace, Kalle's on-off relationship with the his dream girl reaches a conclusion.

The movie is more a patchwork portrait of a moment in time than a structured drama. Scenes of Kalle and his pals raiding condom machines and peeking up women's skirts are set against dour scenes of suburban Berlin life as the Reich crumbles. Latter are well-observed but lack cumulative tension.

Based on co-helmer Wolfgang Kohlhaase's own memories of the period, the movie was long nixed under the East German regime. What it lacks is a strong central line to anchor the mass of small detail and off-center humor.

Playing by the kids is okay, though Schmidt is too modern as Kalle. Böttcher, as the dark-eyed, half-Argentinian Inge, is suitably mysterious, and Matthias has her moments as Kalle's sexy aunt. Pic was clearly shot on a budget, but period detail and tech credits are all pro.
— *Derek Elley*

GUADALAJARA FEST

NOVIA QUE TE VEA
(LIKE A BRIDE)
(MEXICAN)

An Instituto Mexicano de Cinematografía (Imcine)/Prods. Arte Nuevo/Fondo de Fomento a la Calidad Cinematográfica (FFCC) production. Executive producer, Tita Lombardo. Directed by Guita Schyfter. Screenplay, Hugo Hiriart, from Rosa Nissan's book. Camera (color), Toni Kuhn; editor, Carlos Bolado; music, Joaquín Guitiérrez; art direction, Tere Pecanins; sound, Salvador de la Fuente. Reviewed at the 8th Muestra Nacional de Cine, Guadalajara, Mexico, March 14, 1992. Running time: **115 MIN.**
Oshinica Mataraso . . Claudette Maille
Sara . . . . Angélica Aragón
Rifke Groman . . . . . Maya Mishalska
Saavedra . . . . . . Ernesto Laguardia
  Also with: Mercedes Pascual, Verónica Langer, Pedro Armendáriz.

Introducing a new theme in Mexican cinema, the well produced "Novia que Te Vea" explores Mexico's Jewish community. Although first-time director Guita Schyfter can't resist throwing in the occasional message, admirable pic should pique offshore interest.

Film shows the lives of two young women through their involvement in 1960s politics and Jewish groups, flirting with Zionism, socialism, feminism, generational differences, etc.

Oshinica (Claudette Maille) is the daughter of conservative Ladino-speaking Sephardic immigrants from Turkey who have installed themselves in the *schmatte* business in Mexico City's Lagunilla market area. Her family believes a woman's sole goal in life is to get married. The ultimate compliment is the pic's title: "I see you as a bride."

Oshinica sees herself as a modern Mexican woman but her family roundly rejects her interest in pursuing a career in art. When she announces her upcoming marriage to a promising Jewish doctor, her family is ecstatic — that is, until she changes her mind.

Her liberal friend Rifke (Maya Mishalska), daughter of Eastern European refugees of the Holocaust, upsets her family when she falls in love with a goy, the revolutionary son of a local politician. Although she doesn't commit herself, she calls herself a socialist and is involved in the student movement of the '60s.

Pic does not lack its didactic side: A dinner scene at the politician's house has a journalist friend voice theories of a Jewish agenda, and the audience is told time and again that Jews are no different than everyone else. But the film also shows the complexity of Mexico's Jewish community and its internal racism between the conservative Sephardim and the liberal Eastern European Ashkenazim.

Film embraces various well-defined time periods thanks to the art direction by artist Tere Pecanins. Thesping is also very good. — *Paul Lenti*

MIROSLAVA
(MEXICAN)

An Aries Films/Instituto Mexicano de Cinematografía (Imcine)/Fondo de Fomento a la Calidad Cinematográfica (FFCC)/Tabasco Films production. Executive producer, Grazia Sade. Directed by Alejandro Pelayo Rangel. Screenplay, Vicente Leñoro, from Guadalupe Loaeza's story. Camera (color, B&W), Emmanuel Lubezki; editor, Oscar Figueroa; music, José Amozurrutia; art direction, José Luis Aguilar. Reviewed at the 8th Muestra Nacional de Cine, Guadalajara, Mexico, March 14, 1992. Running time: **100 MIN.**
Miroslava (adult) . . Arielle Dombasle
Miroslava (teen) . . . Arleta Jeziorska
Dr. Stein . . . . Milos Trnka
Mother . . . . Verónica Langer
Alex Finman . . . . Claudio Brook

Known professionally by her first name, actress Miroslava Stern appeared in around two dozen pics before her death by her own hand at age 25. Biopic, fourth feature by Alejandro Pelayo, is a beautifully shot reverential portrait that may generate some interest in the actress, who was little known outside of Mexico.

Although Miroslava (1930-55) acted in a couple of Yank ventures — including "Brave Bulls" (1951) and the western "Stranger on Horseback" (1955) — she is perhaps most known for playing the feisty Lavinia in Luis Buñuel's "The Criminal Life of Archibaldo de la Cruz" (1955).

Film ruminates on Miroslava's troubled life, beginning with her family's escape from occupied

Czechoslovakia. She is haunted by memories of her grandmother, left behind in Nazi hands and the later death of her mother by cancer, yet she is distant and cold in her efforts to find love.

After a failed first marriage, she succumbs to the allure of Spanish bullfighter Luis Miguel Dominguín, noted for his trysts with the likes of Rita Hayworth and Ava Gardner. When she is inevitably betrayed, suicide is her solution.

French actress Arielle Dombasle manages to capture Miroslava's beauty, aloofness and restrained personality but ultimately, it is exactly this detachment that distances viewers. Miroslava never shares her interior world and the film is a cold exercise in glossy surfaces.

Pelayo varies the film's texture with noteworthy camerawork, employing varying styles: hand-held camera, black and white and color, interesting angles, etc. This is complemented by rich art direction by José Luis Aguilar. — *Paul Lenti*

ENCUENTRO INESPERADO
(UNEXPECTED ENCOUNTER)
(MEXICAN)

A Clasa Films Mundiales production. Executive producer, Tita Lombardo. Produced by Pablo Barbachano, Francisco Barbachano. Directed by Jaime Humberto Hermosillo. Screenplay, Arturo Villaseñor. Camera (color), Angel Goded; editor, Ramón Aupart, Javier Patiño; sound, Fernando Cámara; music, Humberto Alvarez; art direction, Lucero Isaac. Reviewed at the 8th Muestra Nacional de Cine, Guadalajara, Mexico, March 15, 1992. Running time: **80 MIN.**
Pilar Landeros . . . . Lucha Villa
Estela . . . . María Rojo
 Also with: Ignacio Retes, Jorge Zepeda, Ari Telch.

An almost old-fashioned melodrama, Jaime Humberto Hermosillo's 18th feature, "Unexpected Encounter," is a basic two-character actress vehicle that maintains a spirited dramatic tension.

Pic is reminiscent of Hermosillo's 1982 "Confidencias," another two-character film, which concerned the relationship between a manipulative woman and her submissive maid.

"Encounter" centers on famous singer Pilar Landeros, played by w.k. *ranchero* singer Lucha Villa. In her climb to the top, Pilar has abandoned her husband and daughter and invented a new past. Now this past intrudes on her present life.

Tale begins as Pilar returns from a trip abroad, telling her household staff she is not to be disturbed. She soon finds major disturbance in the form of Estela (María Rojo), who has entered the house in a maid's uniform and subserviently asks for a job, later revealing she is a journalist in search of an interview. But this disguise also wears thin: Pilar discovers Estela is really her long-lost daughter, bitter after years of abandonment.

Both actresses have ample opportunity to change roles, going from dominant to passive and back again and they assert their respective positions, maintaining an uneasy tension.

Hermosillo introduces a few disturbing elements: When Estela opens a closet to search for a robe, a pair of handcuffs and a whip are mounted on the inside door, and Estela's revelation of how she gained entrance into the house is also unsettling.

Hermosillo uses the confined space of the house and garden to his advantage, underlining pic's claustrophobic theme. Images of Pilar's dying, devoted husband, played by Ignacio Retes, are unsuccessfully superimposed several times over the action, which tend to distract viewers from the tour-de-force acting by the two leads. — *Paul Lenti*

KINO
(MEXICAN)

A Cineclipse production, in association with RTC/Instituto Mexicano de Cinematografía (Imcine)/Fondo de Fomento de la Calidad Cinematográfica (FFCC)/TV München. Produced by Carlos Resendi. Directed by Felipe Cazals. Screenplay, Tomás Pérez Turrent, Gerardo de la Torre, Cazals. Camera (color), Angel Goded; editor, Carlos Savage; music, Amparo Rubín; art direction, Patricia Martín. Reviewed at the 8th Muestra Nacional de Cine, Guadalajara, Mexico, March 13, 1992. Running time: **120 MIN.**
Padre Kino . . . . Enrique Rocha
Lt. Mange . . . . . Fernando Balzaretti
Lt. Rincón . . . . Carlos Cardán
Admiral Atondo . . . Rodolfo de Anda
 Also with: Jorge Fegán, Leonardo Daniel, Manuel Ojeda, Ignacio Guadalupe, Adyari Cházaro, Blanca Guerra.

Never has a more lumbering treatment been given to the biography of such an interesting historical personage. Film is an exploration of the life of **Francisco Eusebio Kino (1645-1711), better known as Padre Kino, early missionary to the California territory.**

"Kino" is an old project and helmer Felipe Cazals, a veteran of more than 20 features, seems to have lost interest in it, even though pic has the sweeping panoramic cinematography and orchestral flourishes of an epic.

Story deals with Padre Kino's early explorations, yet all the action is in the text. Characters discuss Kino's determination to explore California despite the church, yet none of this passion is shown. In fact, there is no passion whatsoever; the pic's dramatic climax is when Padre Kino discovers that Baja California, till then thought to be an island, is actually a peninsula.

Acting is okay, and tech credits are strictly overkill to such a small storyline. — *Paul Lenti*

LOLO
(MEXICAN)

A Centro de Capacitación Cinematográfica/Instituto Mexicano de Cinematografía (Imcine)/Estudios Churubusco productio. Directed, written by Francisco Athié. Camera (color), Jorge Medina; editor, Tlacatéotl Mata; music, Juan Cristóbal Pérez Grobet; art diretion, Marisa Pecanins; sound, Miguel Sandoval, Salvador de la Fuente. Reviewed at the 8th Muestra Nacional de Cine, Guadalajara, Mexico, March 16, 1992. Running time: **88 MIN.**
Doña Rosario . . . . Lucha Villa
Lolo . . . . Roberto Sosa
Marcelino . . . . Damián Alcázar
Alambristo . . . . . . Alonso Echánove
Sonia . . . . Esperanza Mozo
Olimpia . . . . Artemisa Flores

Stalwart first entry by Mexican helmer Francisco Athié, "Lolo" presents an unflinching view of life in an urban slum, depicting the Darwinian pact of honor that exists in the streets. Despite flaws, pic's tough stance should attract a degree of offshore interest.

When he complains about his low pay at a foundry, 17-year-old Lolo (Roberto Sosa) is beaten and robbed, then fired because of the time spent in the hospital. When he eventually returns home, his mother Doña Rosario (Lucha Villa) insults him and calls him a good-for-nothing.

Lolo finds part-time work helping neighborhood hurdy-gurdy player Alambrista (Alonso Echánove), and falls in love with the new girl next door. Yet simple happiness is impossible in this unsentimental impoverished world, where roving punk gangs impose their own rules.

Doña Rosario hocks her watch to an avaricious neighbor to raise money. When Lolo goes to steal the watch, he can't resist stealing the neighbor's money and is caught. Something snaps and he murders the woman, leaving evidence pointing to Alambrista.

Since Alambrista had earlier been a fall guy for another crime, the neighborhood demands justice, but not the truth. Truth becomes a subjective, abstract notion; a sacrificial lamb must be thrown to the slaughter. It is the law of self-preservation.

At times, Athié shows off a few annoying film school tricks, but other techniques are used to good advantage. A final confrontation scene (lit by an altar to the Virgin) in which Lolo admits to the deed, is all shot in one take, allowing the dialogue to give its full weight to the scene. In general, however, Athié has produced a winner. — *Paul Lenti*

BARTOLOME DE LAS CASAS
(MEXICAN)

A Cooperativa José Revueltas production in association with the Fondo de Fomento a la Calidad Cinematográfica (FFCC)/IMSS/Gecisa Intl./Prods. Rosas Priego/STPC. Executive producer, Jaime Alfaro. Directed by Sergio Olhovich. Screenplay, Olhovich, Sergio Molina, from Jaime Solóm's play "Bartolomé de las Casas, una Hoguera en el Amanecer." Camera (color), Alex Phillips, Arturo de la Rosa; editor, Carlos Savage; music, Leonardo Velázquez; art direction, Gabriela Robles. Reviewed at the 8th Muestra Nacional de Cine, Guadalajara, Mexico, March 15, 1992. Running time: **120 MIN.**
Bartolomé de las Casas . . José Alonso
Antón de Montesinos . . . .
. . . . Germán Robles
Pedro las Casas . . . . Rafael Montalvo
 Also with: José Luis Padilla, Rolando de Castro, Claudette Maille, Blanca Torres, Rafael Cortés, Elizabeth Arciniega, Claudio Brook.

Often referred to as Latin America's first defender of Indian rights, Fr. Bartolomé de las Casas (1474-1566) spoke out against mistreatment of the indigenous population by its Spanish conquerors. As filmed theater, pic seems best destined for the small screen.

Tenth feature by Sergio Olhovich, pic is based on Jaime Solóm's effort "Una Hoguera en el Amanecer" (A Bonfire in the Dawn), which Olhovich directed on stage in 1990. Rather than disguising the play's trappings, Olhovich underlines it by bookending the actors and director in the studio, watching as the camera rolls. The pace is snappy, music cues are on the mark and the acting is larger than life. The soundstage locations have an artificial feel that works within the stylized approach.

Revolving around a small core of principal characters, the film attempts to follow the course of Bartolomé's life as he goes from enlightened despot to fierce advocate for equal rights. Pic also offers a revisionist p.o.v. on the legacy of colonization, with a contemporary appraisal of racism within a Christian society.

Tech credits are fine while thesping tends toward stage mannerisms. — *Paul Lenti*

UN AÑO PERDIDO
(A LOST YEAR)
(MEXICAN)

An Instituto Mexicano de Cinematografía (Imcine)/Prods. Rancho Grande production. Produced by Dulce Kuri. Directed by Gerardo Lara. Screenplay, Lara, Patricio Ruffo. Camera (color), Luis Manuel Serrano; editor, Jorge Vargas; music, Alejandro Lora, El Tri; sound, Gabriela Espinosa; art direction, Coni Jaimes, Vicente González, Esbón Gamaliel. Reviewed at the 8th Muestra Nacional de Cine, Guadalajara, Mexico, March 17, 1992. Running time: **90 MIN.**
Matilde . . . . Vanessa Bauche
Yolanda . . . . Tiaré Scanda
José Antonio . . . . Marco Muñoz
Doña Ema . . . . Ada Carrasco
Also with: Javier Zaragoza, Bruno Bichir, Miguel Rodarte, Alicia del Lago, Rocío Rodríguez.

While the intentions of Gerardo Lara's first pic, "A Lost Year," are clear, something got lost on the way to the screen and what emerges is an uneven teen pic with little to distinguish it from the herd.

Film recounts a year in the life of two high school coeds bound by their shared out-of-towner status. When small-town Matilde (Vanessa Bauche) moves to the provincial capital of Toluca to study high school, she meets the spirited Yolanda (Tiaré Scanda), who has also recently moved there. Matilde lives in a boarding house while Yolanda works as a secretary in the afternoons and wants to be a singer.

The girls find freedom away from their families as they meet boys and get involved in the 1976 student strikes in Toluca. Yet, much of the film's intentions will be lost on foreign auds due to the pic's focus on obscure local politics and failure to to universalize the experience.

Both girls also fall for José Antonio (Marco Muñoz), the son of Matilde's landlady. Rather than spark a confrontation between the two friends, José Antonio suddenly moves to Mexico City. Just as mysteriously, he later dies, without explanation.

Further confrontations between students and the authority figures are ludicrous and meant to be crowd pleasers. Lara offers no room for debate, and his pic would have benefited from more character development.

Technically, pic is okay.
— *Paul Lenti*

BODY SNATCHERS

A Warner Bros. release of a Robert H. Solo production. Produced by Solo. Directed by Abel Ferrara. Screenplay, Stuart Gordon, Dennis Paoli, Nicholas St. John, from Raymond Cistheri, Larry Cohen's story, based on Jack Finney's novel "The Body Snatchers." Camera (Technicolor, Panavision widescreen), Bojan Bazelli; editor, Anthony Redman; music, Joe Delia; sound (Dolby), Michael Barosky; production design, Peter Jamison; art direction, John Huke; set decoration, Linda Spheeris; costume design, Margaret Mohr; assistant director, Drew Rosenberg; production manager, John G. Wilson, Jack Clements; special makeup effects, Tom Burman, Bari Dreiband-Burman; special effects supervisor, Phil Cory; stunt coordinator and 2nd-unit director, Phil Neilson; 2nd-unit camera, Phil Link; additional music, Peter Fish; associate producer, Kimberly Brent; casting, Ferne Cassel. Reviewed at Warner Bros. screening room, N.Y., April 17, 1993. (In Cannes Film Festival, competing.) MPAA Rating: R. Running time: **87 MIN.**
Marty Malone . . . . . Gabrielle Anwar
Steve Malone. . . . . . . Terry Kinney
Tim . . . . Billy Wirth
Carol Malone . . . . Meg Tilly
Major Collins . . . . . Forest Whitaker
Genn Platt . . . . Christine Elise
General Platt . . . . . . R. Lee Ermey
Andy Malone . . . . . Reilly Murphy
Pete . . . . G. Elvis Phillips
Mrs. Platt . . . . Kathleen Doyle

The third screen version of Jack Finney's "The Body Snatchers" is a tremendously exciting thriller that compares favorably with Don Siegel's classic 1956 original. WB can expect a strong response from audiences and critics alike, with potential repeat business from older teens.

Film is competing in the Cannes Film Festival, an unusual slot for a horror picture but not unprecedented.

Producer Robert Solo effectively remade the picture in 1978 with Philip Kaufman directing and has carried over to the current edition several innovations, notably the shrieking sound effects (originally by Ben Burtt). In director Abel Ferrara, already highly praised for his urban studies of paranoia, he found the perfect match to the material.

Five credited scripters have retained the basics, which make Finney's 1954 story always timely: Aliens are invading Earth in the form of giant seed pods that replicate human beings while they sleep in order to replace them. The primal fear of loss of identity is the story's central theme, enhanced by the eternal war of nonconformist individuals (repping the human race) vs. a collective social mass of emotionless "pod people."

Improvements that make the third edition distinctive include having a teenage heroine (defusing any comparisons with Kevin McCarthy's classic original perf) and setting the entire film on an

Original Production
INVASION OF THE BODY SNATCHERS
(1956)

An Allied Artists release of a Walter Wanger production. Produced by Walter Wanger. Directed by Don Siegel. Screenplay, Daniel Mainwaring (and, uncredited, Sam Peckinpah), from Jack Finney's novel. Camera (B&W, Superscope), Ellsworth Fredricks; editor, Robert S. Eisen; music, Carmen Dragon. Reviewed in Hollywood, Feb. 14, 1956. Running time: **80 MIN.**
Miles . . . . Kevin McCarthy
Becky . . . . Dana Wynter
Danny . . . . Larry Cates
Jack . . . . King Donovan
Theodora . . . . Carolyn Jones
Sally . . . . Jean Willes
Nick . . . . Ralph Dumke
Wilma . . . . . . Virginia Christine
Ira . . . . Tom Fadden
Driscoll . . . . . . Kenneth Patterson
Sam . . . . Guy Way
Baggage Man . . . . Pat O'Malley
Doctor . . . . Whit Bissell

1978 Version

An United Artists release, produced by Robert H. Solo. Directed by Philip Kaufman. Screenplay, W.D. Richter, from Jack Finney's novel. Camera (Technicolor), Michael Chapman; editor, Douglas Stewart; music, Denny Zeitlin; production design, Charles Rosen; sound, Art Rochester; makeup effects, Thomas Burman, Edouard Henriques; special effects, Dell Rheaume, Russ Hessey; special sound effects, Ben Burtt; assistant director, Jim Bloom. Reviewed at MGM Studios, Hollywood, Dec. 13, 1978. MPAA Rating: PG. Running time: **115 MIN.**
Matthew Bennell . Donald Sutherland
Elizabeth Driscoll . . . Brooke Adams
Dr. David Kibner . . . Leonard Nimoy
Nancy Bellicec . . Veronica Cartwright
Jack Bellicec . . . . . . Jeff Goldblum
Geoffrey . . . . Art Hindle
Katherine . . . . Lelia Goldoni
Running Man . . . . . Kevin McCarthy

Alabama military base.

Gabrielle Anwar toplines in a star-building performance as teen Marty Malone, who has moved to an Army base with her EPA biologist dad (Terry Kinney), stepmom (Meg Tilly) and younger brother (Reilly Murphy). She also narrates the tale.

While her dad goes about inspecting the local streams and warehouses full of toxic chemicals, Anwar is befriended by the punkette daughter (Christine Elise) of the base commander, Gen. Platt (R. Lee Ermey).

Unsettling events occur early: Anwar is accosted in a gas station restroom by a black man who warns her cryptically: "They get you when you sleep." Camp

May 3, 1993 (Cont.)

medical officer Forest Whitaker tells Kinney he's received many reports of delusional fixations in people afraid to sleep.

Soldiers arrive at the Malones' home on base and deliver several boxes for Kinney — they're seed pods, one surmises. Soon the gas station man pops up, but as a soldier who doesn't remember Anwar and is completely emotionless and Elise's alcoholic mom appears "cured," leaving Elise positive she's someone else.

Anwar and her young brother soon deduce that Tilly is the enemy and flee, with Tilly letting out a wailing banshee shriek that alerts nearly the whole base to pursue the kids in the movie's central set piece.

Teaming up with their dad and, later, Anwar's soldier boyfriend (Billy Wirth), they elude the baddies, but Anwar soon discovers she can't trust anyone. Adding to the thrills are two erotic and scary scenes, one in which Anwar is confronted with her pod double. There's an apocalyptic climax and an unsettling final image plus sardonic use of "The End" title card.

Anwar is a strong heroine who provides maximum identification for the target audience. Kinney, a low-key type resembling Don Johnson, is on the money as the ambiguous father, while Wirth exudes sex appeal as Anwar's b.f. and savior. Tilly is chilling.

Ermey, the unforgettable drill sergeant of "Full Metal Jacket," is perfect casting as the pod leader. Elise delivers another natural, precocious perf following her role in "Boiling Point."

As he did in "The Crying Game," Forest Whitaker makes every screen moment count as the insomniac symbol of the indomitable human spirit. Most of the supporting cast portrays soldiers, a nice touch since one can't tell from their disciplined behavior if they're normal or pods.

A chilling sense of dread is developed in the film's first half, aided by subliminal sound effects and Anthony Redman's superb editing. (Running time is a no-flab 87 minutes.)

Returning to the widescreen format of the original, Bojan Bazelli's often backlit, monochrome silhouette shots are eerie. Other tech credits, including sound and Joe Delia's score, enhance the apprehensive mood.

Makeup effects by Tom Burman and Bari Dreiband-Burman eschew the genre's explicit gore, in favor of frightening tendrils snaking around the victims.

Ferrara keeps everything under tight control and wisely injects black humor to relieve the tension. The script's most interesting inversion stresses that mankind's ability to hate and seek revenge is a unique survival trait. — *Lawrence Cohn*

MUCH ADO ABOUT NOTHING
(BRITISH-U.S.)

A Samuel Goldwyn Co. release of a Renaissance Films production in association with American Playhouse Theatrical Films and BBC Films. Produced by Stephen Evans, David Parfitt, Kenneth Branagh. Directed by Branagh. Adapted by Branagh from Shakespeare's play. Camera (Technicolor), Roger Lanser; editor, Andrew Marcus; music, Patrick Doyle; production design, Tim Harvey; art direction, Martin Childs; costume design, Phyllis Dalton; sound (Dolby), David Crozier; assistant director, Chris Newman. Reviewed at Sony Studios screening room, Culver City, Calif., April 15, 1993. (In Cannes Film Festival, competing.) MPAA rating: PG-13. Running time: **110 MIN.**

Benedick	Kenneth Branagh
Dogberry	Michael Keaton
Claudio	Robert Sean Leonard
Don John	Keanu Reeves
Beatrice	Emma Thompson
Don Pedro	Denzel Washington
Leonato	Richard Briers
Hero	Kate Beckinsale
Antonio	Brian Blessed
Conrade	Richard Clifford
Verges	Ben Elton
Borachio	Gerard Horan
Ursula	Phyllida Law
Margaret	Imelda Staunton
Friar Francis	Jimmy Yuill

After going increasingly astray with two contemporary outings, Kenneth Branagh returns to the high and, for him, safe ground of Shakespeare with "Much Ado About Nothing," a spirited, winningly acted rendition of one of the Bard's most popular comedies. Aimed at the widest possible audience for a classic through its shrewdly selected Anglo-American cast, clarion-clear enunciation of the witty dialogue and warm-hearted expression of the piece's exalted romantic themes, this rambunctious production should find favor with most viewers disposed to attending a Shakespeare film.

Accessibility was clearly the major concern for Branagh in staging one of the playwright's more surefire works. Helmer has gone to great lengths to insure nothing is left unclear, and to make every scene as physical, playful and rollicking as possible.

Result is a film that is continuously enjoyable from its action-filled opening to the dazzling final shot, one that offers a very generous welcome to newcomers to the play, and reminds those familiar with it of its heady pleasures. Only real drawback, and not an insignificant one, is pic's visual quality, which is unaccountably undistinguished, even ugly, especially considering the sun-drenched Tuscan location.

From the outset, Branagh injects this tale of foolishness, betrayal and transcendent love with an invigorating earthiness. As a group of victorious soldiers returns from war on horseback, the lust between the men and their waiting women becomes palpable as they prepare for the evening's revelries.

All should be well in the domain of Leonato (Richard Briers): The righteous Don Pedro (Denzel Washington) helps young Claudio (Robert Sean Leonard) woo and win Leonato's lovely daughter Hero (Kate Beckinsale), while the proudly unmarried Benedick (Branagh) and the feisty Beatrice (Emma Thompson) trade barbs with such zest their teaming is inevitable.

But the fly in the ointment is the sulky, jealous Don John, who falsely convinces Claudio of Hero's unfaithfulness on the eve of their wedding, resulting in a chain reaction of insults, misunderstandings, deceptions and assaults that take most of the second half to resolve.

Branagh puts the actors through the play's intricate paces at an almost breathless clip, but with diction so clear that little verbiage will be lost on anyone. He also applies a lubricious tone that could end up making this "Much Ado" a good date movie.

In the context, it's a shame that more care was not put into the film's pictorial quality. Although Branagh's physical staging is exemplary, the visual approach is strictly utilitarian.

Still, the day is more than carried by the talented thespians and Branagh's infectious, energetic enthusiasm. Branagh and Thompson bring appealing intelligence and verbal snap to their ongoing sparring.

Looking almost as weird as Beetlejuice, Michael Keaton delivers a very alert, surprising turn as the malapropping constable Dogberry, reminding in the process that he should never stray from comedy for too long. Washington is pleasingly stalwart as Don Pedro, while Robert Sean Leonard is highly capable

in the pivotal role of Claudio. For those who might tremble at Keanu Reeves playing Shakespeare on the basis of "My Own Private Idaho" and "Bram Stoker's Dracula," his Don John reassuringly announces early on "I am not of many words" and cuts a dashingly menacing figure.

Richard Briers and Brian Blessed are rock solid as the elders of the community. It all wraps up in wondrous fashion with a long Steadicam shot that finally soars high above dozens of merrymakers to Patrick Doyle's movingly celebratory music. — *Todd McCarthy*

POSSE
(U.S.-BRITISH)

A Gramercy release of a Polygram Filmed Entertainment release in association with Gramercy Pictures of a Working Title Films production. Produced by Preston Holmes, Jim Steele. Executive producers, Tim Bevan, Eric Fellner. Directed by Mario Van Peebles. Screenplay, Sy Richardson, Dario Scardapane. Camera (Technicolor; Panavision widescreen), Peter Menzies Jr.; editor, Mark Conte; music, Michel Colombier; production design, Catherine Hardwicke; art direction, Kim Hix; set design, Mark A. Worthington; set decoration, Tess Posnansky; costume design, Paul Simmons; sound (Dolby), Don Sanders; co-executive producers, Paul Webster, Bill Fishman; co-producer, Jim Fishman; associate producer, Jim Bigwood; assistant director, Joseph Ray; casting, Pat Golden. Reviewed at the Charles Aidakoff screening room, Beverly Hills, April 21, 1993. MPAA Rating: R. Running time: **109 MIN.**

Jessie Lee	Mario Van Peebles
Little J	Stephen Baldwin
Weezie	Charles Lane
Obobo	Tiny Lister Jr.
Father Time	Big Daddy Kane
Colonel Graham	Billy Zane
Carver	Blair Underwood
Papa Joe	Melvin Van Peebles
Lana	Salli Richardson
Angel	Tone Loc
Phoebe	Pam Grier
Vera	Vesta Williams
Cable	Isaac Hayes
King David	Robert Hooks
Sheriff Bates	Richard Jordan
Mayor Bigwood	Paul Bartel
Cook	Lawrence Cook
Doubletree	Richard Gant
Jimmy Love	Stephen J. Cannell
Snopes	Nipsey Russell
Preston	Reginald VelJohnson
Storyteller	Woody Strode

Begin with a reliable pursuit-and-revenge plotline, lay on a Sergio Leone look and flashback structure, stir in some John Ford community values and Sam Peckinpah violence, tag "The Magnificent Seven" on at the end and paint it black, and you've got "Posse." Mario Van Peebles' lively pastiche of Western conventions races through its paces with

May 3, 1993 (Cont.)

little attention to nuance or characterization, but its action, hip attitude and cool cast should score with youthful general auds as well as blacks, and give Gramercy Pictures a winner with its maiden release. Pic bowed last week at the USA Film Festival in Dallas.

As told by narrator and stalwart Ford veteran Woody Strode in bookends to the action, the "posse" is more or less intact at the outset. Engaged in the Spanish-American War in Cuba in 1898, a ragtag band including strong silent type Mario Van Peebles, bespectacled Charles Lane, giant Tiny Lister Jr., cigar-chomping Tone Loc and irreverent white boy Stephen Baldwin, is betrayed by vicious, swash-buckling commanding officer Billy Zane, and flees the regiment with a large stash of gold.

Landing in New Orleans, the gang takes refuge in a bordello, where they also pick up another member, a laconic riverboat gambler with the nifty name of Father Time (Big Daddy Kane).

Initial half-hour establishes plenty of sassy attitude, which is amusing if a lot more 1990s than 1890s, but little motivation aside from Van Peebles' man with a moral code out to get revenge on the men who killed his father. Passing through snowy mountains, Monument Valley and Indian country, the band finally arrives at Freemansville, a utopian black township dedicated to peaceable living, black self-sufficiency and the principle, espoused by Van Peebles' preacher father, of "Education Is Freedom."

But the arrival of the gang doesn't sit well with venal nearby sheriff Richard Jordan and his Ku Klux Klan goons, who suddenly covet Freemansville since it lies along a future railway route. So the men are recruited, à la "Magnificent Seven," to help save the town from the marauders, who themselves receive Zane's support.

Sy Richardson and Dario Scardapane's eventful script, which evinces film buff and socially relevant awareness in roughly equal measure, packs in enough confrontations, fights and shootouts for several films, which will keep action fans happy.

But neither the writers nor Van Peebles, in his second directorial outing, modulate the drama to maximize its impact. Van Peebles gets across the humor and violence, but hasn't mastered the building of cathartic climaxes through quiet sequences and ac-

cumulated tension. As a result, even the pertinent revelations that will be most surprising and interesting to modern audiences carry more intellectual than emotional resonance.

Still, Van Peebles demonstrates the adaptability and current viability of the genre by enthusiastically employing its conventions to his own ends, and that alone should prove exhilarating to many for whom Westerns constitute a distant notion rather than a profound memory.

Of course, the guys, led by the stoical Van Peebles himself, all look ultra-sharp in cowboy duds, riding horses and firing rounds. Actors are clearly having fun, and it's contagious, although many of the familiar names in the hefty supporting cast are wasted in throwaway roles.

Tech credits and locations are solid, although Michel Colombier's score is uncharacteristically dull. — *Todd McCarthy*

THE PICKLE

A Columbia release. Produced, directed, written by Paul Mazursky. Executive producer, Patrick McCormick. Co-producer, Stuart Pappé. Camera (Technicolor), Fred Murphy; editor, Pappé; music, Michel Legrand; production design, James Bissell; art direction, Christopher Burian-Mohr, John Berger (N.Y.); set decoration, Dorree Cooper, Beth Kushnick (N.Y.); costume design, Albert Wolsky; sound (Dolby), Jim Webb, Gary Alper (N.Y.); special visual effects, Apogee Prods.; visual effects supervisor, John Swallow; assistant director, Henry J. Bronchtein; casting, Carrie Frazier, Shani Ginsberg. Reviewed at the Beekman Theater, N.Y., April 30, 1993. MPAA Rating: R. Running time: **103 MIN.**

Harry Stone	Danny Aiello
Ellen Stone	Dyan Cannon
Francoise	Clotilde Courau
Yetta	Shelley Winters
Ronnie Liebowitz	Barry Miller
Phil Hirsch	Jerry Stiller
Gregory Stone	Chris Penn
President	Little Richard
Yakimoto Yakimura	Jodi Long
Carrie	Rebecca Miller
Mike Krakower	Stephen Tobolowsky
Nancy Osborne	Caroline Aaron
Bernadette	Linda Carlson
Patti Wong	Kimiko Cazanov
Molly-Girl	Ally Sheedy
Dr. Spalding	Spalding Gray
Butch Levine	Paul Mazursky
Planet Cleveland Man	Griffin Dunne
Planet Cleveland Woman	Isabella Rossellini
Planet Cleveland Man	Dudley Moore

"**T**he Pickle" is a vegetarian turkey. Self-indulgent story about a depressed, dispirited, middle-aged film director aims for comedy and poignance that never come, and

feels wearily disenchanted and out of touch. Pic opened cold without advance screenings, and b.o. outlook is sour.

More than 20 years ago, Paul Mazursky made "Alex in Wonderland," an appealingly personal look at a creatively blocked filmmaker with a hit behind him. As flawed as the picture might be, it was witty, warmblooded and engagingly offbeat.

By contrast, the director in "The Pickle," Harry Stone (Danny Aiello), has made a string of flops and is suffering convulsions of remorse and regret over having sold out for the first time in his career by making a stupid commercial sci-fi schlocker for teenagers. "I didn't direct a movie, I committed a crime," he moans to his longtime agent (Jerry Stiller), who has accompanied him to New York for the picture's first preview.

During the couple of days Harry holes up at the Plaza, Mazursky once again summons up memories of Fellini's "$8^{1}/_{2}$" by surrounding his melancholy protagonist with two ex-wives, a 22-year-old French girlfriend, daughter, son, granddaughter, mother, predatory female fan, publicist and journalist, among others. Harry abuses almost all of his loved ones, as well as himself, as he drinks, smokes and eats heavily while sweating over his blood pressure.

Mazursky layers the mirthless tale with black and white flashbacks to Harry's youth in 1940s Brooklyn, as well as with bizarre snatches from the dreaded film-within-a-film, which concerns a space trip embarked upon by a giant pickle grown and launched by farm kids. The appalling bits revealed from this provide the only sympathy for Harry's plight in the entire picture.

Technically, film is smooth, and the thesps do agreeable, if rather relaxed, work. A number of unexpected names, including Little Richard, Spalding Gray, and Donald Trump, make uneventful cameos. — *Todd McCarthy*

DRAGON: THE BRUCE LEE STORY

A Universal Pictures presentation of a Raffaella De Laurentiis production. Produced by Raffaella De Laurentiis. Executive producer, Dan York. Directed by Rob Cohen. Screenplay, Edward Khmara, John Raffo, Cohen, from Linda Lee Cadwell's book "Bruce Lee: The Man Only I Knew." Camera (Fujicolor), David Eggby; editor, Peter Amundson; music, Randy Edelman; production design, Robert Ziembicki; art direction, Ted Berner; set decorator, Dayna Lee; costume design, Carol Ramsey; sound designer (Dolby), Leslie Shatz; fight choreographer, John Cheung; Jeet Kune Do trainer/adviser, Jerry Poteet; co-producer, Rick Nathanson; associate producers, Kelly Breidenbach, Hester Hargett, Charles Wang; assistant director, Herb Gaines; casting, Jane Jenkins, Janet Hirshenson. Reviewed at Universal Studios, Universal City, Calif., March 25. MPAA Rating: PG-13. Running time: **121 MIN.**

Bruce Lee	Jason Scott Lee
Linda Lee	Lauren Holly
Bill Krieger	Robert Wagner
Vivian Emery	Michael Learned
Gussie Yang	Nancy Kwan
Philip Tan	Kay Tong Lim
Jerome	Sterling Macer
Bruce's Father	Ric Young
The Demon	Sven-Ole Thorsen

The meteoric, tragic life of martial arts star Bruce Lee forms the basis of "Dragon: The Bruce Lee Story," an unlikely pastiche of traditional biography, Hollywood saga and interracial romance. Seemingly contrary elements and styles nonetheless mesh into an entertaining whole and the result provides extremely touching and haunting material. The combination looks commercially potent. Not truly aimed at aficionados of the action star, it will unquestionably attract that crowd. However, at its core, it is a romance and that audience will determine whether the picture is a small or a big hit.

The echoes of the more recent set death of Brandon Lee also unintentially heightens the underlying sadness of the story.

The jumping off point of the biopic finds the teenage Lee (the not related Jason Scott Lee) as a young man in Hong Kong. Somewhat awkward socially, he transforms into a confident human dynamo when he's forced to fight.

Lee's physical prowess, however, gets him into trouble with the authorities and he's sent to San Francisco for his own safety. Moreover, his father lives in fear of the peril to his son from both human and spiritual demons.

The object of racial persecution, Lee obviously holds his own against campus bullies. But the

May 3, 1993 (Cont.)

situation additionally propels him into a new career teaching students the art of self defense. One, Linda Emery (Lauren Holly), becomes the love of his life despite her mother's fierce antipathy toward the prospect of an Asian son-in-law.

The screenplay by Edward Khmara, John Raffo and director Rob Cohen, manages to provide an organic flow that is disarming without being simplistic. It also effects the very difficult sleight of hand of focusing on Lee's accomplishments rather than his early demise.

Cohen, balancing disparate visual styles, basically keeps "Dragon" pretty straightforward. Lee's metaphoric demons, visualized as a towering, faceless samurai, avoid cuteness; and potential hokum ranging from the spontaneous fights to the forays into "inner strength" sidestep the high-toned silliness associated with the kung fu era. Overall it maintains a high technical sheen.

Jason Scott Lee carries much of the weight of the production with a devil-may-care performance that embodies more the spirit than the discipline of the title character. His absorption into the role is complete to a degree rarely seen in biopics. If historically suspect, it is certainly the way the life should have been.

The supporting cast is dotted with a strong array of familiar and tyro talent. Lauren Holly brings a fresh, spunky dimension to a largely underwritten and conventional drawn role.

The ultimate artistic success of "Dragon" is in its giving viewers the iconographic Lee in novel fashion and his offstage life in a logically and dramatically satisfying manner. — *Leonard Klady*

HOW U LIKE ME NOW

A Shapiro Glickenhaus Entertainment release of an Avant Garde production in association with Woolf Vision Enterprises. Produced, directed, written by Darryl Roberts. Executive producer, Bob Woolf. Camera (Foto-Kem color), Michael Goi; editor, Tom Miller; music, Kahil El Zabar, Chuck Webb; art direction, Kathy Domokos; sound (Dolby), Mike Terry; associate producer, Sharese Locke. Reviewed at United Artists Coronet, Westwood, Calif., April 23, 1993. MPAA Rating: R. Running time: **109 MIN.**

Thomas	Darnell Williams
Valerie	Salli Richardson
Spoony	Daniel Gardner
Alex	Raymond Whitefield
Michelle	Debra Crable
B.J.	Darryl Roberts
Pierre	Byron Stewart
Sharon	Jonelle Kennedy

Darryl Roberts' "How U Like Me Now," an original satire focusing on the new black middle class, deserves better treatment it's getting from its distributor. A fresh portrait of a cross-section of black lives, the film could have had crossover appeal; however, the theatrical run got no publicity on its quick trip to videoland.

Producer-writer-director-actor Roberts departs from the recent genre of coming-of-age-in-the-ghetto black films. Set in Chicago, pic is crude and amateurish, but it also intricately weaves the lives of five African-American men and three women, who despite differences in class, profession and intellect, occasionally meet and socialize.

The male group consists of Thomas (Darnell Williams), a handsome warehouse employee; Spoony (Daniel Gardner), a cynical cab driver who is discovering the magic of sex; Alex, a phony obsessed with projecting a chic image with his convertible and fashionable clothes; B.J. (Roberts), a contemplative store owner; and Pierre (Byron Stewart), a smart gay hairdresser.

The female gallery also contains "types," ranging from Michelle (Debra Crable), an executive committed to her career, to Valerie (Salli Richardson), an upwardly mobile, slightly pretentious computer programmer.

The episodic, disjointed story consists of humorous sketches about work and leisure, courtship and dating, love and sex. As a writer, Roberts shows a keen eye for the telling detail. Though the witty satire makes strong points about relationships and mores, the humor is always decent and generous.

"How U Like Me Now" requires faster pacing and subtler shadings than Roberts' direction affords. Lacking a distinctive visual style, the film has a detached, quasi-documentary manner that doesn't enhance the material.

Excepting Gardner as the coarse and forthright Spoony, and Stewart as the witty gay barber, who are outstanding, the rest of the cast is just acceptable.

Technical credits are modest.
— *Emanuel Levy*

SODOM TO HOLLYWOOD

PRINZ IN HÖLLELAND
(PRINCE IN THE LAND OF HELL)
(GERMAN-16m)

Produced, directed by Michael Stock. Screenplay, Stock, Stefan Laarmann, Wolfram Haack. Camera (color, 16m), Lorenz Haarmann; editor, Uwe Lauterkorn; music, Alexander Hacke, Chris-lo Haas, Tom Stern, Einstürzende Neubauten; art direction, Thomas Fitzpatric; costumes, Agnes Müller; sound, Margarete Heitmüller. Reviewed at From Sodom to Hollywood Intl. Gay Film Festival, Turin (competing), April 18, 1993. Running time: **96 MIN.**

Stefan	Stefan Laarmann
Jockel	Michael Stock
Micha	Andreas Stadler
Firlefanz	Wolfram Haack
Dealer	Harry Bear

Also with: Simone Spengler, Nils-Leevke Schmidt, Alexander Schröder, Oliver Picot, Andreja Schneider.

A trio of gay men jostle with the flotsam and jetsam of reunified Berlin in "Prinz in Hölleland," a trenchant bout of sex, sleaze and drug-induced descent tethered to an intrusive fairytale frame. Despite a surfeit of shrilly theatrical artifice cluttering the more solid dramatic core, ex-Rosa von Praunheim assistant Michael Stock's debut pic shows enough know-how and bold invention to put him on the map.

The trio consists of two chums (Stefan Laarmann and director Stock) and a bedtime contender for both (Andreas Stadler). A bizarre puppeteer decked in jester garb (Wolfram Haack) narrates the story, with stock's anonymous sex- and drug-seeking character becoming the title's prince, set on marrying a miller's apprentice. Haack watches over Stadler's son, who adds another magical dimension with visions of the prince in trouble.

Stock goes on a heroin diet (supplied by one-time Fassbinder regular, Harry Baer — an evil wizard in the fairytale), and shrugs off Laarman's efforts to steer him away from addiction. Stadler floats between them, but eventually veers to the dark side, shooting up and bedding down with Stock. Jealousies and grievances surface on a trip to the countryside, and the clash propels events to a tragic end.

Set mainly in Berlin's seedy Kreuzberg neighborhood, the story builds a formidable backdrop out of the chaotic, politically volatile climate, with protest demonstrations, threats of Nazi thuggery, gay-bashing and high-gear drug-peddling moodily peppering the action. The one notably absence is AIDS, though Stock may intentionally be pointing up the unrealistically utopian notion that unsafe sex and needle-sharing are in the past.

Pic's technical rough edges are well-aligned with its plot concerns. Stock is equally surefooted at cruising the city's dimly lit nooks as at sketching an easy intimacy between the characters. Performances are convincing and appealingly relaxed.
— *David Rooney*

THANK GOD I'M A LESBIAN
(CANADIAN-DOCU-16m)

Produced by Laurie Colbert. Directed by Colbert, Dominique Cardona. Camera (color, 16m), Kim Derko, Dominique Le Rigoleur; editor, Geraldine Peroni; music, Lee Pui Ming; sound, Aerlyn Weissman, Henry Maikoff, Miroslav Bodnaruk; assistant directors, Jane Waterous, Paul Lee; associate producer, Lori Campana. Reviewed at From Sodom to Hollywood Intl. Gay Film Festival, Turin (competing), April 16, 1993. Running time: **60 MIN.**

"Thank God I'm a Lesbian" is both the vigorous affirmation of lesbian sexuality that its title promises and an informatively broad, objective spectrum of pro and con standpoints on a volley of issues pertaining to gay women. Snappy, intelligent spielfest won audience plaudits as best docu at both the Turin gay fest and the recent Films des Femmes meet in Creteil. Tidy one-hour format makes it a natural for upscale tube programming.

For what's principally a series of talking heads, the film has a remarkably variegated texture that's due partly to the well-rounded diversity of the lesbians doing the talking, and partly to first-time documakers Laurie Colbert and Dominique Cardona's skill in putting it together to maximize this diversity.

Women from various ethnic and cultural backgrounds, including writers, academics and musicians independently pronounce on subjects such as fidelity, the legitimacy of bisexuality, the butch/femme dynamic, outing, S&M and, in greater depth, lesbianism's link to the women's movement. The wealth of shared, overlapping and often wholly opposing views makes illuminating fodder.

May 3, 1993 (Cont.)

The observations are pacily intercut with well-chosen archive material and footage, further enhanced by interviewee Lee Pui Ming's music. — *David Rooney*

FORBIDDEN LOVE: THE UNASHAMED STORIES OF LESBIAN LIVES
(CANADIAN-DOCU-16m)

A National Film Board of Canada Studio D production. Produced by Margaret Pettigrew, Ginny Stikeman. Executive producers, Stikeman, Rina Fraticelli. Directed, written by Aerlyn Weissman, Lynne Fernie. Camera (color, 16m), Zoe Dirse; editor, Cathy Gulkin, Denise Beaudoin; music, Kathryn Moses; art direction, Denis Boucher; costumes, Nicoletta Massone; sound, Justine Pimlott; associate producers, Weissman, Fernie; assistant director, Vicki Frodsham; casting, Nadia Rona. Reviewed at From Sodom to Hollywood Intl. Gay Film Festival, Turin (competing), April 15, 1993. Running time: **84 MIN.**
Laura . . . . . Stephanie Morgenstern
Mitch . . . . Lynne Adams

Taking its cue from lesbian pulp novels of the '50s and '60s, "Forbidden Love" blends a savvy mix of fiction and fact to hand down tales of the sapphic experience in Canada during the period. Via recollections that are by turns celebratory, heroic and infectiously funny, this well-crafted docu unearths a fascinating subculture with a potential far wider than its target aud. Limited theatrical runs should segue to a bright TV and cable future.

Two female lovers are forced to part at a backwoods train station in a lushly cornball dramatized prologue that surges from monochromatic tones to lurid color as the eye-catching title sequence kicks off. Scanning paperback covers from the "golden age of lesbian publishing," titles like "Odd Girl Out," "Women Barracks" and "Girls' Dormitory" leap out, with copy lines like "They hid their claws under their nail polish!" against torrid art.

The dramatizations of the fugitive lovers continue at intervals, and author Ann Bannon, who churned out a slew of similar, semi-tragic romance novels, outlines their importance to gay women of the era. The books spoke to lesbians trapped in conservative towns and sham marriages, and despite the formula forcing one lover to die or be spiritually broken, they encouraged many to accept their sexuality and beat down closet doors.

Filmmakers Aerlyn Weissman and Lynne Fernie establish the socio-historical context with amusing clips that illustrate ideals of '50s womanhood. Where the docu really comes into its own though, is in interviews with nine feisty, highly individual women who came out in that decade. Undeniably compelling, the history and fictional detours pale next to the real-lifers' stories.

Interviewees recall the highs and lows of their bohemian existence: the rebel status some reveled in and others found intimidating; gay bars where brawls and police raids happened nightly; face-saving "dates" with gay men; harassment; family reactions to their chosen lifestyles. Despite the obvious pressures and denial, the prevailing mood is unfailingly buoyed by the women's wry humor and refreshing candor.

Cathy Gulkin and Denise Beaudoin's editing fluidly threads newsreels, stills, interviews and dramatac vignettes at a lively pace, though the film feels marginally overlong, and fictional chapters could perhaps be advantageously pruned. Other tech credits are clean as a whistle. — *David Rooney*

GUADALAJARA FEST

CRONOS
(CHRONOS)
(MEXICAN)

A Prods. Iguana production in association with Ventana Films/Instituto Mexicano de Cinematografía (Imcine)/Fondo de Fomento a la Calidad Cinematográfica (FFCC)/U. of Guadalajara/Grupo del Toro production. Produced by Bertha Navarro, Arthur Gorson. Directed, written by Guillermo del Toro. Camera (color), Guillermo Navarro; editor, Raúl Dávalos; music, Javier Alvarez; art direction, Brigitte Broch, special effects, Laurencio Cordero, makeup effects, Necropia. Reviewed at Muestra Nacional de Cine, Guadalajara, Mexico, March 16, 1992. (In Cannes Film Festival, Critics Week) Running time: **92 MIN.**
Jesús Gris . . . . Federico Luppi
Angel de la Guardia . . . Ron Perlman
Dieter de la Guardia . . Claudio Brook
Mercedes Gris . . . Margarita Isabel
Aurora Gris . . . . . Tamara Shanath
Also with: Daniel Giménez Cacho, Mario Iván Martinez, Juan Carlos Colombo, Faresio de Bernal.
(Spanish and English soundtrack)

"Chronos," the meritorious first effort by Guadalajara-based filmmaker Guillermo del Toro, is an absorbing, modern vampire film. Pic should capture international interest on the fest and arthouse circuit.

Film begins with a preface chronicling the flight to Mexico of an alchemist from the hands on the Inquisition in 1536. Obsessed with immortality, he invented the "chronos device," an ornate clockwork instrument with the power to grant eternal life, but giving its user a thirst for life-sustaining human blood.

When the alchemist dies in a freak explosion in the 1930s in an ancient building in downtown Mexico City, the device turns up in the base of a statue at an antique shop run by Jesús Gris (veteran Argentine actor Federico Luppi).

Intrigued by the device, he winds it up and soon pays the price. Things complicate with the entrance of aging millionaire industrialist Dieter de la Guardia (Claudio Brook). Dying of a terminal disease, he has come into possession of the alchemist's original diary and he sends his cold-hearted nephew (U.S. actor Ron Perlman) to search for the device. Perlman's character's greed naturally leads him to seek the device for himself.

Script has few loose ends — such as why some characters speak Spanish and others English, yet they all understand each other — but overall the pic offers a healthy measure of inventiveness and interest.

Tech credits are first rate. Helmer del Toro has a good feel for the material and a keen eye for detail. Brigitte Broch's art direction is well cared for.
— *Paul Lenti*

LA VIDA CONYUGAL
(CONJUGAL LIFE)
(MEXICAN)

An Instituto Mexicano de Cinematografía (Imcine)/ Fondo de Fomento a la Calidad Cinematográfica (FFCC)/Vida Films/U. of Guadalajara/Tabasco Films/Ocixem production. Produced by Fernando Sariñana. Directed by Carlos Carrera. Screenplay, Ignacio Ortiz, from Sergio Pito's novel. Camera (color), Xavier Pérez Grobet; editor, Carlos Bolado; music, Enrique Quezadas; art direction, Brigitte Broch. Reviewed at the 8th Muestra Nacional de Cine, Guadalajara, Mexico, March 17, 1992. Running time: **100 MIN.**
Jacqueline . . . . Socorro Bonilla
Nicolás . . . . Alonso Echánove
Gianni . . . . Patricio Castillo
Alicia . . . . Isabel Benet
Also with: Demián Bichir, Margarita Sanz, Alvaro Guerrero, Nora Velázquez, Eduardo López Rojas, Regina Orozco.

The second film by Carlos Carrera, "Conjugal Life" is an amusing black comedy tracing the long unhappy married life of Jacqueline and Nicolás Magdalena over a 40-year period. Like his earlier "Benjamin's Woman," Carrera controls original material with a good sense of off-beat pacing. Pic should find acceptance on the arthouse circuit.

Film begins with the happy marriage turning sour as Jacqueline burns their first meal and he declares that he doesn't want kids. The marriage has its shares of ups and downs as Nicolás devotes himself to working in a hardware store, neglecting her for trysts with his secretary as the business grows and he becomes a shady land developer. In retaliation, Jacqueline also takes on various paramours, plotting Nicolás's murder with the help of her lovers. Of course, all of her murder plans backfire.

Film's stylistic touches present a minimalistic approach to narrative and Carrera knows when to cut a scene and move on.

Bridgitte Broch's careful art direction aptly delineates the time periods depicted, complementing the pic's off-beat humor and tongue-in-cheek tone. Thesping is also very good. — *Paul Lenti*

DAMA DE NOCHE
(LADY OF THE NIGHT)
(MEXICAN)

An Instituto Mexicano de Cinematografía (Imcine)/Centro de Capacitacón Cinematográfica production. Produced by Gustavo Montiel. Directed, written by Eva López-Sánchez, from David Martín del Campo's book. Camera (color), Rodrigo Prieto; editor, Hubert Barrero; music, José Elorza; sound, Beatriz Lorge; art direction, Carlos Gutiérrez. Reviewed at Muestra Nacional de Cine, Guadalajara, Mexico, March 15, 1992. Running time: **100 MIN.**
Bruno Carrasco . . . . . Rafael Sánchez
        Navarro
Sofia . . . . Cecilia Toussaint
Mutute . . . . Miguel Córcega
Salomé . . . . Regina Orozco
Also with: Salvador Sánchez, Boris Peguero, Abel Woolrich, Lisa Owen, Arturo Rios, Moisés Manzano.

A first effort by helmer Eva López-Sánchez, "Dama de Noche" is an uneven venture with a few surprises that might arouse some attraction in spite of its unappealing main characters and absurd plot turns.

Despite pressing deadlines, popular author Bruno Carrasco (Rafael Sánchez Navarro) drops everything to run to the aid of his hopeless — and unfaithful — love Sofia (Cecilia Toussaint), who had been on vacation in Veracruz with a wealthy older businessman. When their lovemaking became a bit too energetic, the businessman keeled over with a heart attack.

Sofia doesn't want to get involved; she wants Bruno to make the problem disappear. He takes the challenge, patterning his actions after his novels' heroes.

Bruno's outlandish method to dispose of the body is simply to embalm it and stick it in the trunk. Its existence permeates the rest of the film as concealed evidence waiting to be found.

Pic's most original character is Salomé (Regina Orozco), a corpulent demimondaine in a sexy red dress, whom Bruno meets when she is kicked out of a car by an unsatisfied customer. Her swaggering confidence and hefty presence are complemented by a good sense of comic timing.

Unfortunately, pic's two principals are not as colorful. The irrational script leads them to make preposterous decisions, and they become an accident waiting to happen.

Technically, pic has some good moments, helped by a nice jazz score by Jose Elorza and director López-Sánchez feel for quirky directorial touches.

— *Paul Lenti*

CARTAGENA FEST

MASCARO, EL CAZADOR AMERICANO
(MASCARO, HUNTER OF THE AMERICAS)
(CUBAN)

An Instituto Cubano del Arte e Industrias Cinematográficos (ICAIC) production. Produced by Humberto Hernández. Directed by Constante "Rapi" Diego. Screenplay, Jorge Cedrón, Diego, Eliseo Alberto Diego, from Haroldo Conti's book. Camera (color), Luis García Mesa; editor, Roberto Bravo; music, José María Vitier; sound, Germinal Hernando. Reviewed at Cartagena Intl Film Festival, Cartagena, Colombia, March 11, 1992. Running time: **102 MIN.**
With: Reynaldo Miravalles, Victor Laplace, Mimí Laso, Omar Moynello.

Winner of top honors at the 33rd Cartagena Film Fest and based on the award winning book by Harold Conti, "Mascaró" is a meandering, confused adventure story lacking all sense of adventure. Its deconstructed approach to a classic literary form siphons off pic's basic interest level. Directed by Constante "Rapi" Diego, pic comes across as pointless and flat, and its prestige can only be explained by political solidarity with Cuba during this time of economic strife.

With references to the Spanish picaresque novel, period story is a grab-bag of exotic elements: naval voyages, seedy circus characters, mysterious black-clad figures, wandering princes, bandits and an avenging military captain. But all of this is to no avail and the supposed chase scenes ramble and lack any tension.

All of this should make for excitement, yet motivations are undefined. We are given an ample cast of stock characters set against a larger canvas lacking in personality and sufficient characterization to be engaging.

Tech elements are okay, as is the acting; but where is the story?

— *Paul Lenti*

PERFUME DE GARDENIAS
(SCENT OF GARDENIAS)
(BRAZILIAN)

A Star Filmes e Raiz production. Produced by Assunção Hernandes. Directed, written by Guilherme de Almeida Prado. Camera (color), Claudio Portoli; editor, Danilo Tadeu; music, Hermelino Neder; art direction, Luis Fernando Pereira. Reviewed at Cartagena Intl. Film Festival, Cartagena, Colombia, March 6, 1992. Running time: **116 MIN.**
Adalgia (Giza) Diniz . Christine Torloni
Danial . . . . José Mayer
Also with: Walter Quiroz, Claudio Marzo, Bettty Faria, Jose Lewgoy, Raul Gazzola.

Like his 1984 film "The Lady From the Shanghai Cinema," Brazilian helmer Guilherme de Almeida Prado plays with cinematic conventions in his new film to produce a cross between humor and tension. While "Lady" successfully parodies film noir, "Scent of Gardenias" is a confused mess that will likely leave viewers shaking their heads.

"Scent" tries too hard to incorporate national genre styles — TV soaps, "chanchadas," melodramas, etc. — yet these unfamiliar references are lost on a foreign audience as the story meanders through a variety of acting styles and tones without a vision to hold it all together.

Tale begins in 1979 with poor hard-working Daniel (José Mayer), driving a cab at night to support his wife and son. One night when a couple tries to rob him, he kills them. He tells no one and changes to a day shift, but he has become a murderer.

Meanwhile, a film crew arrives in the neighborhood to do location shots for a popular soap. Daniel's wife Giza (Christiane Torloni) is selected as an extra and eventually becomes a major star on the small screen, leaving her family for national fame. Thus, Daniel plots revenge.

There are some fun moments and the acting has its bright spots, but individual scenes get lost within the wandering plotline. Pace is slow and the "surprise" ending becomes predictable very early on.

Tech credits are all right.

— *Paul Lenti*

HONG KONG FEST

WUYANDE SHANQIU
(HILL OF NO RETURN)
(TAIWANESE)

A Central Motion Picture Corp./Zia Cheng Motion Picture production. (Intl: sales: Anthex, Berlin/Amsterdam.) Produced by Chiang Feng-ch'i, Li P'ei-kuei. Executive producer, Hsü Li-kung. Directed by Wang T'ung. Screenplay, Wu Nien-chen; camera (color), Yang Weihan; editor, Ch'en Sheng-ch'ang; music, various; song sung by Huang P'in-yüan; production-costume design, Li Fuhsiung; sound, Hsin Chiang-sheng, Yang Ching-an; line producers, Hou Chienwen, Chen Ts'un-tao, Ts'ao Wei-hua. Reviewed on CMPC vidcassette, London, March 11, 1993. (In Hong Kong Film Festival, Berlin Film Festival, Market section) Running time: **178 MIN.**
Ah-chu . . . . P'eng Chia-chia
Ah-jou . . . . Yang Kuei-mei
Ah-wei . . . . Huang P'in-yüan
Fumiko . . . . Ch'en Hsien-mei
"Red-Eye" . . . . Jen Ch'ang-pin
Madam . . . . Wen Ying
Japanese . . . . Isao Shinozaki
(Hokkien and Japanese soundtrack)

A flavorsome portrait of a Taiwanese mining community toiling under the imperial Nipponese yoke, "Hill of No Return" looks to face an uphill struggle of its own in foreign marts. Pic has nuggets a-plenty for buffs of East Asian fare but its extreme length effectively puts it off limits beyond festivals and specialized TV.

Setting is 1927, halfway through the island's 50-year stint under Japanese rule. Brothers, Ah-chu and Ah-wei, fired by stories of fabled wealth, head to Chiu-fen and sign on at the Japanese-owned gold mine. Ah-wei falls for Fumiko, a young Okinawan woman who works as a housekeeper at the town brothel. Ah-chu slowly cosies up to his gutsy landlady, widow Ah-jou, who sleeps with locals to pay the bills.

Things get worse as the Japanese raid the bordello for smuggled gold, and humiliate the Chinese workers with body-searches. Tensions roil into violence, with casualties on both sides.

Though much of the movie is sensitively played and beautifully shot, with a romantic-mystical undertow, there's a tendency for it to tip over into histrionics at key dramatic moments. For foreign auds unfamiliar with the setting, the lack of explanatory captions at the start is no help.

Still, for those willing to stay the course, experienced helmer Wang T'ung mostly delivers the goods, smoothly stitching a host of competing stories into a colorful tapestry.

Playing is sharply etched down the line, especially by TV thesp Yang Kuei-mei as the pragmatic but caring widow Ah-jou and vet actress Wen Ying as the foulmouthed cathouse owner. Stage actor Peng Chia-chia and local singer Huang Pin-yüan contrast convincingly as the brothers.

As in Wang's previous movies ("Runaway," "Strawman," etc.), pic's production and costume design are detailed and lived-in.

Pic won five gongs at Taiwan's Golden Horse Awards, including best feature, helmer and script. Local b.o. was a polite $NT5 million ($200,000). — *Derek Elley*

ZHAO LE
(FOR FUN)
(CHINESE-HONG KONG)

A Peking Film Studio/Hongkong Wan Ho Film & TV production. (Intl. sales: Ning Ying, Beijing.) Executive producers, Zheng Kainan, Cai Rubin.) Produced by Liu Yuansheng, Cheng Zhigu. Directed by Ning Ying. Screenplay, Ning Dai, Ning Ying, from Chen Jiangong's novella. Camera (color), Xiao Feng, Wu Di; editor, Zhou Meiping; music, Meng Weidong; art direction, Yang Xiaowen; costume design, Li Fengju; sound, Chao Jun; line producers, Liu Weidong, Yang Hanping. Reviewed at Berlin Film Festival (Forum section), Feb. 16, 1993. (In Hong Kong Film Festival.) Running time: **95 MIN.**
Old Han . . . . Huang Zongluo
Qiao Wanyou . . . . . . Huang Wenjie
Dong Fugui . . . . Han Shanxu
Little He . . . . He Ming
(Mandarin soundtrack)

"For Fun" is just that, an exhilarating ensemble comedy

set among a bunch of opera-mad Beijing oldsters. Low-budget indie production by young femme helmer Ning Ying has enough broad-based yocks to become a minor arthouse click, though TV sales are likely to be its more profitable route.

Main character is Old Han (Huang Zongluo), a pompous janitor at Peking Opera Academy who finds his days empty after retiring. Meeting a group of fellow retirees in a park one day, he soon finds a new outlet for his organizational skills: setting up a club so they can indulge their passion in all weathers. All hell breaks loose, however, as petty jealousies start to surface, with the group even turning on Han, viewed as a meddlesome old martinet. The crunch comes when they hear the premises are to be pulled down to make room for a karaoke club.

Scripting with her sister Ning Dai from a little-known novella by Chen Jiangong, Ning creates a marvelous self-contained world of feuding old eccentrics well advanced into their second childhood. Salty dialogue, laden with refs to Peking Opera and details of local life, needs more careful subtitling than on print world preemed at Berlin fest, but the performances alone carry the day.

Beneath the comedy, there's a deeper message about bureaucratic mindsets in communist China and the chaos resulting from "self-government." But it never deflects from the main feast of ensemble playing, observed with a naturalistic feel by Ning, in only her second feature after a seven-year studying stint in Italy.

Huang, a w.k. stage actor who's virtually the only professional in the cast, is terrif as the dour, ramrod-backed Old Han. Tech credits are par.

Original title means "Looking for Fun," with a play on the second Chinese ideogram which can also mean "music." In a first for a mainland Chinese director, Ning herself is handling world sales. — *Derek Elley*

ZHANZHI LUO BIE PAXIA
(STAND UP, DON'T BEND OVER)
(CHINESE)

A Xi'an Film Studio production. Directed by Huang Jianxin. Screenplay, Huang Xin, from Deng Gang's story. Camera (color), Zhang Xiaoguang; editor, Zhang Xiaodong; music, Zhang Dalong; art direction, Zhang Zili; costume design, Ding Ni; sound, Yan Jun, Dang Wang; assistant director, Yang Yazhou. Reviewed on videocassette in London, March 30, 1993. (In Hong Kong Film Festival.) Running time: **120 MIN.**
Gao, the writer . . . . Feng Gong
Zhang . . . . Niu Zhenhua
Liu, the cadre . . . . Da Shichang
Gao's wife . . . . Zhang Lu
Zhang's wife . . . . Fu Lili
Liu's wife . . . . Liu Xiaohui
Old Sun . . . . Ma Shuangqing
Also with: Yang Bo, Xu Lu, Qu Ying, Luo Jingmin, Yang Yazhou.
(Mandarin soundtrack)

Seven years after bowing with "The Black Cannon Incident," mainland Chinese helmer Huang Jianxin bounces back with "Stand Up, Don't Bend Over," a warm, witty, wonderfully observed ensemble item centered on an apartment block. Pic's pleasures are perhaps too subtle to equip it for theatrical playoff, but fest exposure could translate into robust tube sales.

This one should help to re-boost Huang's international rep after dipping with the over-ambitious "Dislocation" (a.k.a. "The Stand-In") and "Samsara." Setting is the seaside resort of Qingdao (where the beer comes from), though for dramatic purposes it's strictly Anytown, P.R.C. A writer (Feng Gong) and his wife (Zhang Lu) move into an average backstreets apartment block, where they're immediately dubbed as "intellectuals" and soon get caught up in the mildly loony tenants' lives.

There's no plot to speak of — more a continuous flow of small incidents, ever-changing relationships, and the ups and downs of everyday life. But by pic's end, when the couple move again, you've got to know the characters in some depth.

Like any apartment movie, the leads are a microcosm of contempo life, here repping the various strands of fast-changing '90s China. There's the fast-buck entrepreneur (Niu Zhenhua) and his blousy wife (Fu Lili); the loyal party cadre (Da Shichang) trying to keep pace with his teen daughter (Xu Lu) and the new reforms; an old tenant (Ma Shu-

angqing) who's seen it all over the years; and a sympathetic cop (Yang Yazhou).

As a high-grain snapshot of contempo urban life, pic ranks with Zheng Dongtian's 1987 portmanteau movie "Young Couples," set in a Beijing apartment building. But Huang's ironic take on human foibles, refined from his earlier movies, lifts the present item a couple rungs higher. Despite the movie's casual front, there's a fine control of mood and character that builds to a genuinely heartwarming finale, sans messages or ickiness.

Playing is best described as exaggerated naturalism, with all thesps showing a nice line in straight-faced humor. Juiciest part goes to Niu, as the get-rich-quick small businessman, but he's well complemented by the dumb-looking Feng as the block's resident "intellectual" who — in one of the pic's many sly jokes — never seems to do any actual work. (Pair are a w.k. patter act on Chinese TV.)

As the unctuous Party cadre, Da handles a tricky (and politically sensitive) role with skill. The women, apart from Fu, are less strongly drawn.

Tech credits are smooth all the way, with well-placed use of music for emotional effect and clever blending of locations in Qingdao itself and the studio's home base, Xi'an. Extra-careful subtitling is a must to convey the movie's many coded refs to foreign auds.

— *Derek Elley*

LOST IN YONKERS

A Columbia release of a Rastar production. Produced by Ray Stark. Executive producer, Joseph M. Caracciolo. Directed by Martha Coolidge. Screenplay, Neil Simon, from his play. Camera (Technicolor), Johnny E. Jensen; editor, Steven Cohen; music, Elmer Bernstein; production design, David Chapman; art direction, Mark Haack; set design, Thomas H. Paul, Mark Garner; set decoration, Marvin March; costume design, Shelley Komarov; sound (Dolby), Lee Orloff; co-producer, Emanuel Azenberg; assistant director, Randall Badger; casting, Jennifer Shull. Reviewed at Sony Studios screening room, Culver City, Calif., May 4, 1993. MPAA Rating: PG. Running time: **112 MIN.**
Uncle Louie . . . . . . Richard Dreyfuss
Aunt Bella . . . . . . Mercedes Ruehl
Grandma Kurnitz . . . . . Irene Worth
Jay . . . . Brad Stoll
Arty . . . . Mike Damus
Johnny . . . . David Strathairn
Hollywood Harry . Robert Guy Miranda
Eddie . . . . Jack Laufer
Gert . . . . Susan Merson

"Lost In Yonkers" is a carefully rendered, ultimately unexciting screen version of Neil Simon's 1991 Pulitzer Prize-winning play. Story of a domineering old woman's tyranny over two generations of offspring is adroitly structured and contains strong human elements, but what proved so affecting onstage seems a bit pat and calculated when viewed in closeup. Columbia should expect okay b.o. results.

One of Simon's most deeply felt, ungimmicky works, "Yonkers" impresses most in the way it demonstrates the different ways the cast-iron personality of a matriarch has negatively effected the lives of all those within her sphere of influence.

Set in the summer of '42, tale begins as Eddie Kurnitz (Jack Laufer) attempts to deposit his two sons with his mother, who lives above her Yonkers candy store and soda fountain. Eddie needs to go south to earn quick money to pay back a loanshark in the wake of his wife's death, but leaving them with Grandma is far from automatic.

Grandma Kurnitz (Irene Worth) has terrorized Eddie into a cowering shadow of a man, and the kids haven't been brought to see her in two years. Having two teenagers around is far from what Grandma fancies at this point in her life, as she is sufficiently tended to by her somewhat backward 36-year-old daughter Bella (Mercedes Ruehl), but she finally has little choice.

The two boys, 15-year-old Jay and Arty, two years younger, are bright, presentable, well-behaved kids, and much of the pleasure of the film lies in watching the alert, bright-eyed performances of Brad Stoll and Mike Damus. Still, they are susceptible to the brash appeal of their uncle Louie (Richard Dreyfuss), a small-time hood who lays low at Grandma's for a few days while being stalked by a thug in fancy threads named Hollywood Harry.

Meanwhile, Aunt Bella escapes as often as possible to the movies, where she watches Bette Davis pictures and hangs around a bashful, aging usher named Johnny (David Strathairn). Two of a kind in their social awkwardness, Johnny and Bella get enough of a romance going for him to propose, and the big serio-comic setpiece involves Bella's creating the right circumstances to announce her engagement.

Some disappointments later, the piece's main suspense and poignance derive from whether or not Bella will once and for all be able to liberate herself from her oppressive mother.

Simon has gently opened up the pic by adding a number of characters who didn't appear in the play, notably Johnny, and setting quite a few scenes outside the apartment and store. Despite this, the film still seems bound by its theatrical origins in the way everything is stated and spelled out, rather than implied or related through style.

Approaching the play intelligently and with precision, Martha Coolidge has done a better job than most directors with Simon material onscreen. Johnny E. Jensen's lensing, David Chapman's production design and Shelley Komarov's costumes create a strong period feeling, although the film is overdrenched in amber-hued ambience.

Performances by the leads could have been brought down a notch or two. In the role that won her a Tony Award, Ruehl can scarcely help but evoke sympathy and goodwill, but she comes off as a bit hyper and calculated at moments. Dreyfuss, in the showy but essentially supporting role that Kevin Spacey originated on Broadway, ironically gives the most theatrical performance, hitting mostly predictable notes of antic shtick and simmering rebellion. Irene Worth, who also won a Tony, memorably re-creates her role of a domestic dictator for whom the audience, at least at the very end, can still summon a measure of feeling and understanding. Strathairn puts in a very fine

turn as Bella's hot-and-cold suitor. — *Todd McCarthy*

THE MYSTERY OF EDWIN DROOD
(BRITISH)

A Mayfair Entertainment (U.K.) release of a Bevanfield Films presentation of a First Standard Media production. Produced by Keith Hayley. Executive producer, Mary Swindale. Directed, written by Timothy Forder, from Charles Dickens' unfinished novel. Camera (Agfa XT color; Metrocolor prints), Martin McGrath; editor, Sue Alhadeff; music, Kick Production; production design, Edward Thomas; costume design, Justine Luxton; sound (Dolby), Geoff Neate; associate producer, Mark Crowdy; assistant director, Rob Done. Reviewed at MGM Shaftesbury Avenue 2 theater, London, April 29, 1993. Running time: **102 MIN.**

John Jasper	Robert Powell
Helena Landless	Michelle Evans
Edwin Drood	Jonathan Phillips
Neville Landless	Rupert Rainsford
Rosa	Finty Williams
Septimus Crisparkle	Peter Pacey
Mrs. Crisparkle	Nanette Newman
Sapsea	Freddie Jones
Miss Twinkleton	Gemma Craven
Mrs. Tope	Rosemary Leach
Dean	Ronald Fraser
Grewgious	Glyn Houston
Durdles	Andrew Sachs

Second filming of Dickens' last, unfinished novel, "The Mystery of Edwin Drood" is a pedestrian costumer low on atmosphere and dramatic oomph. Tamely toplined by Robert Powell as the fiendish Jasper, pic's better fitted to the tube and English Lit classes.

Like the 1935 Universal version, starring Claude Rains, Douglass Montgomery and Heather Angel, this one opts for making Jasper, the opium-smoking village choirmaster, the murderer of his nephew, Edwin Drood. (Dickens' manuscript, only half-finished when he died in 1870, simply ends with Drood missing. Rupert Holmes' 1980s Broadway musical version let the audience vote on who the murderer was.) Motive in both pics is the same: Jasper's insane jealousy over Drood's fiancée, Rosa.

Story is set in a fictional English village, Cloisterham, where Jasper (Powell) is the local choirmaster, obsessively in love with the pert Rosa (Finty Williams), fiancée of his visiting nephew, Drood (Jonathan Phillips). When one of the local canon's lodgers, Neville (Rupert Rainsford), gets the hots for Rosa, Jasper secretly encourages him.

Original Production
MYSTERY OF EDWIN DROOD

Universal production and release. Stars Claude Rains and Douglas Montgomery. Directed by Stuart Walker. Producer, Edmund Grainger. From novel by Charles Dickens; screen play, John L. Balderston and Gladys Unger; adaptation, Leopold Atlas and Gradley King; camera, George Robinson. At Rialto week, March 20, '35. Running time: **85 MIN.**

John Jasper	Claude Rains
Neville Landless	Douglass Montgomery
Rosa Bud	Heather Angel
Edwin Drood	David Manners
Helena Landless	Valerie Hobson
Mr. Crisparkle	Francis L. Sullivan
Hiram Grewgious	Walter Kingsford
Thomas Sapsea	E.E. Clive
Tops	Vera Buckland
Durdles	Forrester Harvey
Mrs. Crisparkle	Louise Carter
Miss Twinkletoe	Ethel Griffies
Opium Den Hag	Zeffie Tilbury

One dark and stormy night, Drood disappears. Jasper throws suspicion on Neville and later declares his love to a horrified Rosa. After trying to fake Neville's suicide, Jasper is caught by the canon (Peter Pacey), who's guessed that he's the real murderer.

Writer-director Timothy Forder does a workmanlike job of compressing the existing manuscript but misses out on the noirish atmosphere that fuels Dickens' original. There's no sense here of mad, swirling passions or dark deeds; apart from a brief burst of Hitchcockian Grand Guignol showing Drood's murder, Forder's helming is dramatically flat.

As Jasper, Powell is lightweight, hardly suggesting the opium-fueled madness behind his genteel exterior. Newcomer Williams (daughter of actress Judi Dench) shows promise as the snooty Rosa but lacks experience. Best of the large supporting cast is Pacey as the smart canon. A gaggle of w.k. Brit actors are in for reliable bits, including Nanette Newman, Gemma Craven and Ronald Fraser.

Lowbudgeter, shot on deferred salaries, has an okay period look and clever use of locations, but a meller of this kind requires bigger production values to come off. Photography by Martin McGrath is generally murky and untextured; string quartet score is suitably brooding but too low-key. — *Derek Elley*

RUBY CAIRO
(U.S.-JAPANESE)

A Miramax (U.S.)/Entertainment (U.K.) release of a Kadokawa Prods. production. Produced by Lloyd Phillips, Haruki Kadokawa. Executive producer, Kadokawa. Directed by Graeme Clifford. Screenplay, Robert Dillon, Michael Thomas, from Dillon's story. Camera (Technicolor), Laszlo Kovacs; editor, Caroline Biggerstaff; additional editing, Paul Rubell; music, John Barry; ethnic music, Robert Randles; production design, Richard Sylbert; art direction, John King (supervising), Peter Smith; costume design, Rudy Dillon; sound (Dolby, THX), Don Summer; line producer, David Nichols; assistant directors, Don French, Dennis White; 2nd-unit camera, David Burr; casting, Jennifer Shull. Reviewed at Plaza 1 theater, London, April 30, 1993. MPAA Rating: R. Running time: **110 MIN.**

Bessie Faro	Andie MacDowell
Fergus Lamb	Liam Neeson
Johnny Faro	Viggo Mortensen
Ed	Jack Thompson
Joe Dick	Jeff Corey
Renee Dick	Miriam Reed
Hermes	Luis Cortes
Coroner	Paco Mauri
German	Hark Bohm

"Ruby Cairo" is an old-fashioned Yank-in-Europe mystery-adventure that squanders an interesting cast headed by Andie MacDowell and Liam Neeson. Too bad everyone forgot to pack a script along with their passports and sunscreen. This attractively lensed timewaster is strictly in-flight fare.

Japanese-financed pic pic surfaces in U.K. distribution some 18 months after start of shooting. Director Clifford is prepping a new cut for Stateside and subsequent international release, now skedded for fall '93.

MacDowell plays the wife of Viggo Mortensen, who runs an aircraft salvage company directly under a flightpath to LAX. One day, while he's off in Mexico, she receives a packet with some teeth inside, and hotfoots it to Veracruz to inspect the remains of his plane and supposed body.

Realizing he's still alive and done a runner, she sets off tracking him down using a dogeared set of his favorite baseball cards containing the key to a string of bank accounts where he's stashed over $800,000.

The trail leads from Panama and the Bahamas to Berlin, Athens and Cairo, where with the help of food aid worker Liam Neeson she uncovers a scam smuggling a chemical for making poison gas inside grain shipments. Meanwhile, some Mexican heavies are shadowing her hoping she'll lead them to Mortensen.

There's a curiously dated feel to the whole enterprise, with MacDowell as a can-do Yank battling her way through countries where the natives are unfriendly. With a half-decent script, this could have played either as a romantic comedy-thriller or as a long-limbed drama of betrayed love. Under Graeme Clifford's unfocused direction, it keeps promising both but ends up neither.

MacDowell, looking miscast, struggles gamely with a role that puts her on-screen almost the whole time. Neeson, who looks as if he doesn't believe any of it, coasts as her hunky savior. Mortensen is bland, and Aussie thesp Jack Thompson pops up briefly as a grizzled fixer in Cairo.

Where the reported $24 million budget went is anyone's guess. Tech credits are easy on the ears and eyes. — *Derek Elley*

HARMONY CATS
(CANADIAN)

An Alan Morinis-Richard Davis production, in association with BC Film/NFB/CBC. Produced by Morinis, Davis. Directed by Sandy Wilson. Screenplay, David King. Camera (color), Philip Linzey; editor, Debra Rurak, Haida Paul; music, Graeme Coleman, Bill Buckingham; production design, Lynne Stopkewich; art direction, Eric McNab; sound, Daryl Powell, R. Tim Richardson; assistant director, Robert Petrovicz; casting, Stuart Aikins. Reviewed at Vancouver Center Cinema, Vancouver, May 2, 1993. Running time: **104 MIN.**

Graham Braithwaite . . . . Kim Coates
Frank Hay . . . . Jim Byrnes
Debbie Hay . . . . Lisa Brokop
Bill Stratton . . . . Hoyt Axton
Jane Pitkeithly . . . Charlene Fernetz
Reg . . . . Alec Willows
Alma . . . . Beverley Elliott
Alan . . . . Byron Lucas
Rocky . . . . . Dave "Squatch" Ward
Sandra . . . . Tamsin Kelsey

Real affection for the suds 'n' sawdust subculture of country music marks this low-budget Canadian pic, which has enough quirky charms to win over a non-country crowd. Now in Canadian release, pic will need major U.S. backing to travel far beyond the arthouse circuit there, but will sure-as-shootin' kick up its heels in cable and video markets.

Set in Vancouver and environs, story follows priggish — and suddenly out-of-work — symphony violinist Graham Braithwaite (Kim Coates) through his descent into hillbilly hell when he's drafted to play bass in the low-rent Harmony Cats, a traveling band led by almost-washed-up Frank Hay (regional blues musician and "Wiseguy" veteran Jim Byrnes).

An instant culture-clash-on-wheels, band has a jazzhead drummer (Alec Willows), headbanging guitarist (Byron Lucas), 300-pound roadie (Squatch Ward) and rough den mother manager (Beverley Elliott). It also features Hay's sweet-voiced daughter Debbie (Lisa Brokop), in whom in the slowly unlimbering Graham sees much potential — musically and romantically. Natch, this doesn't sit well with the highfalutin fiddler's live-in g.f. (Charlene Fernetz), or her interfering sister (Tamsin Kelsey). Meanwhile, a cool Nashville producer (Hoyt Axton) is also sniffing around the young singer.

The love-and-career stuff is fairly routine. What sticks is the shuffling, edgy interplay of the mismatched musicians. First-timer Brokop isn't asked for a lot of variety, and doesn't deliver it. But when she sings, the screen lights up, and she's guided well by the pros around her, particularly the paternal and unexpectedly fiery Byrnes.

Coates departs from his typical thin-lipped baddies with remarkable comic flair. Even funnier is offbeat Willows as the deadpan drummer.

It helps that David King's script is full of witty flourishes and "Northern Exposure"-style utopianism. Director Sandy Wilson keeps the tone light without robbing the sometimes ornery pack of its humanity.

Tech credits far outstrip the $1.5 million spent. — *Ken Eisner*

MY NEIGHBOR TOTORO
(JAPANESE-ANIMATED)

A Troma Inc. release of a Tokuma Group production. Produced by Toru Hara. Executive producer, Yasuyoshi Tokuma. Directed, written by Hayao Miyazaki; editor, Takeshi Seyama; music, Jo Hisaishi; production design, Yoshiharu Sato; art direction, Kazuo Oga; special effects, Kaoru Tanifuji; English lyrics, Severin Browne. production planning supervisor, Tatsumi Yamashita, Hideo Ogata; assistant director, Tetsuya Endo. Reviewed at Sunset Screening Room, L.A., April 28, 1993. MPAA Rating: G. Running time: **87 MIN.**

Voices: Satsuki . . . . Lisa Michaelson
Mei . . . . Cheryl Chase
Dad . . . . Greg Snegoff
Kanta . . . . Kenneth Hartman
Mother . . . . . Alexandra Kenworthy
Nanny . . . . Natalie Core

Troma, purveyors of such unusual and fitfully crass entertainments as "Toxic Avenger" and "Sgt. Kabukiman," are off on a different and difficult rocky path with the animated Japanese kidpic "My Neighbor Totoro." Displaying no more than adequate TV techcraft, the simple family saga poses no threat to the commercial dominance of Disney cartoonists. U.S. box office prospects will be fleeting, likely no more than a blip among the upcoming product onslaught.

Apparently a popular household character in Japan, Totoro is a furry forest sprite with powers ranging from the mystical to the superhuman. He can only be seen by children, though adults recall his memory fondly.

The story centers on two young sisters, Satsuki and Mei, who move to rural Japan with their professor father. In a far-off city hospital, mom is recuperating from an unnamed ailment.

Not only is the tale of a rare wholesome stripe, but is virtually absent of dramatic tension. Instead, it largely concentrates on the journey of wonderment in which the girls discover a new environment and the creatures, both real and fanciful, of the region. They are indeed cuddly and have a few tricks that are mildly diverting.

Obviously aimed at an international audience, the film evinces a disorienting combination of cultures. The characters, despite obvious Japanese names, have Anglo features. But instead of a 1950s TV neighborhood, they live in unmistakably Asian dwellings set amid rice fields.

Writer-director Hayao Miyazaki has essentially padded a TV half-hour into a sluggish feature. The rigid backgrounds and limited movements appear dull and crude when viewed on a large screen. — *Leonard Klady*

112th & CENTRAL: THROUGH THE EYES OF THE CHILDREN
(DOCU-16m)

A Flatfields Inc. presentation of a film by the Children of South Central. Produced by Jim Chambers, Vondie Curtis-Hall, Hal Hisey. Executive producers, Stephon Barnatt, Cedric Broddie, David Harrell, Cleop has Jackson, Marzina Scott, Hector Soto, Violeta Soto, Darrell Straight, Lorenzo Straight, Nia Mydra Tiggs, Yolanda Woods, Gabriel Wright. Co-directed by Chambers. Camera (Fujicolor) John Simmons; editor, Michael Schultz; music, Delfeayo Marsalis; sound, Veda Campbell. Reviewed at Universal Studios screening room, Universal City, Calif., April 14, 1993. Running time: **108 MIN.**

An obvious labor of love and good will can often transcend its limitations, and "112th & Central: Through the Eyes of the Children" is just such a film. Several filmmakers and entertainers have guided Los Angeles inner-city youth through an explanatory journey into the hub of last year's riots. The 16m specialized film is rough-hewn and its pacing is often slow, but it is worthy of the small, specialized audience it will undoubtedly receive.

More document than documentary (and blessedly not a sociological treatise), this timely film is broken into sections exploring the relationship between South Central L.A. and the police, neighbors and families.

The youngsters ask questions that appear naive, but are also refreshingly non-manipulative. Because the interviews are with friends or colleagues, they often have a pleasant, discursive quality. Responses that could sound like platitudes don't, because they are obviously felt.

The film is not without its flaws. More judicious pacing and editing would have helped. But it might have interfered with the ingenuous approach of the young filmmakers, some of whom have infectious on-camera personalities and inner strength that no acting school could provide.

Johnny Simmons' photography is simple and unobtrusive and blends well with newsreel footage. Delfeayo Marsalis' cool jazz score (yes, another talented Marsalis brother) is a standout.
— *Richard Natale*

CANNES FEST

THE PIANO
(AUSTRALIAN)

A Miramax release of a CIBY 2000 presentation of a Jan Chapman Prods. film. Produced by Chapman. Executive producer, Alain Depardieu. Directed, written by Jane Campion. Camera (Eastmancolor), Stuart Dryburgh; editor, Veronika Jenet; music, Michael Nyman; production design, Andrew McAlpine; costumes, Janet Patterson; sound, Lee Smith; associate producer/assistant director, Mark Turnbull; casting, Diana Rowan, Susie Figgis, Alison Barrett. Reviewed at Gaumont screening room, Paris, Feb 24, 1993. (In Cannes Film Festival, competing.) Running time: **120 MIN.**

Ada McGrath . . . . Holly Hunter
George Baines . . . . . . Harvey Keitel
Stewart . . . . Sam Neill
Fiona McGrath . . . . Ana Paquin
Aunt Morag . . . . Kerry Walker
Nessie . . . . Genevieve Lemon

Jane Campion's fourth feature is a visually sumptuous

May 10, 1993 (Cont.)

and tactile tale of adultery set during the early European colonization of New Zealand. With Harvey Keitel daringly cast in the role of a passionately romantic lover, and Holly Hunter a knockout as a woman physically unable to articulate her feelings, the elements are in place for Miramax to reap strong arthouse coin, with crossover business also indicated. Cannes festival, where Campion's early shorts and first features, "Two Friends" and "Sweetie," were launched, will provide this special film with a strong international sendoff.

The basic plot, about an unhappily married woman who takes a lover, is a familiar one, but, as usual for Campion, the setting and the character details are most unusual.

This time, the main character's sickness isn't mental, as it was in "Sweetie" and "An Angel at My Table," but physical: Ada McGrath (Hunter) is dumb. She can hear, and can communicate in sign language through her young daughter, Fiona (Ana Paquin), but she can't talk. Apart from her child, Ada's most treasured possession is her piano.

Tale begins in Scotland, with Ada's voice heard on the soundtrack ("The voice you hear is my mind's voice") explaining that she's about to marry a man she's never met, a pioneer settler in far-off New Zealand who believes that God loves dumb creatures and so should he.

However, when Ada and Fiona arrive on a stormy, bleak shore on the other side of the world, the marriage gets off to a bad start when Stewart (Sam Neill) isn't there to meet them, and, when he does arrive, refuses to transport Ada's piano to his settlement. Later, he allows George Baines (Keitel) to take the piano.

Baines, who has "gone native" (he lives with a Maori woman and even tattooed his face), is instantly attracted to the diminutive, crinolined Ada, and offers to return the piano to her — if she gives him some lessons.

These "lessons" become stages in an increasingly erotic courtship that ends in a passionate affair, shown in frank and boldly handled sequences with the lovers spied upon, first by Fiona, then by Stewart.

At this point, another characteristic Campion element is introduced: Ada "mutilates" her piano in sending a message to Baines; but her daughter betrays her secret, and Stewart takes gruesomely calculated revenge.

Campion unfolds this striking story with bold strokes, including flashes of unexpected humor. The settlement looks like the township in Robert Altman's "McCabe and Mrs. Miller" — a chilly, muddy, rainswept place where civilization is barely making an impact. Stuart Dryburgh's fine camerawork finds the terrain's maximum pictorial splendor.

Composer Michael Nyman provides a robust score, and the credits note that Hunter herself played solo piano and acted as piano coach on the production. The actress also gives one of her finest performances.

Keitel, unexpectedly cast as the lover, acquits himself with brilliance, while Sam Neill, in the less showy role of the undemonstrative husband, is also fine. Young Ana Paquin brings plenty of complexity to Fiona.

Great care was obviously taken on authentic details, and it pays off in a totally convincing milieu. Production design by Andrew McAlpine and costumes by Janet Patterson are major plus factors.

— *David Stratton*

BEDEVIL
(AUSTRALIAN)

A Southern Star presentation of an Anthony Buckley production, produced with the participation of the Australian Film Finance Corp. Produced by Buckley, Carol Hughes. Directed, written by Tracey Moffatt. Camera (Atlab color), Geoff Burton; editor, Wayne Le Clos; music, Carl Vine; production design, Stephen Curtis; art director, Martin Brown; sound, David Lee; choreography, Stephen Page; production coordinator, Maggie Lake; assistant director, P.J. Voeten; casting, Susie Maizels. Reviewed at Film Australia screening room, Sydney, April 28, 1993. (In Cannes Film Festival, Un Certain Regard section.) Running time: **90 MIN.**

MR. CHUCK
Shelley . . . . Diana Davidson
Rick . . . . Jack Charles
CHOO CHOO CHOO CHOO
Ruby Morphet . . . . . Tracey Moffatt
Stompie Morphet . . . . Banula (David) Marika
Jack . . . . Pauline McLeod
Older Ruby . . . . . . Auriel Andrews
Maudie . . . . . Mawuyul Yanthalawuy
Old Mickey . . . . Les Foxcroft
Bob Malley . . . . Cecil Parkee
LOVIN' THE SPIN I'M IN
Dimitri . . . . Lex Marinos
Voula . . . . Dina Panozzo
Spiro . . . . Riccardo Natoli
Beba . . . . Pinau Ghee
Minnie . . . . Patricia Hardy
Emelda . . . . Debai Baira

Distinctly different from any other Australian feature film to date, Tracey Moffatt's first feature is a frequently dazzling tapestry in which three supernatural stories unfold against stylized settings amid the heat and bizarre landscapes of northern Queensland. With its fragmented narrative structure, apparent carelessness of form and unusual themes, "Bedevil" will certainly pose a marketing challenge but could fascinated specialized audiences.

With this film, Moffatt earns the distinction of being the first aboriginal woman to direct a feature, though she's already made a couple of well-regarded shorts. Current item draws on childhood memories of ghost stories told by members of her family.

After some jazzy credits, pic segues into the first story, "Mr. Chuck," set near a sinister-looking swamp located on an idyllic island. In the present, a white woman (Diana Davidson) and an old aboriginal man (Jack Charles) recall their childhood when the swamp was haunted by the ghost of an American soldier who'd accidentally driven into it. Later, a cinema was built above the site; now, the island is covered with ugly suburban houses, one occupied by the woman.

Story two, "Choo Choo Choo Choo," again cuts between the past and the present, and, as with the first episode, the present is shot like a documentary and the past is filmed on stylized sets. A woman remembers her youth when she lived with her husband and child near a railway track which was haunted by the ghost of a blind girl who'd been killed there. Moffatt herself plays the narrator as a young wife.

The last story, "Lovin' the Spin I'm In," is set in a small coastal town. The local tradesman and landlord, a Greek-Australian (Lex Marinos), is trying to evict tenants who are behind with their rent; one woman refuses to leave. Marinos' teenage son discovers that his father's warehouse is haunted by the ghosts of the woman's son and his lover.

None of the three stories unfolds in conventional form. All are fragmented and broken up with humorous diversions.

Geoff Burton's camerawork is outstanding both in the semi-docu depictions of Queensland life and in its lighting of Stephen Curtis' sets. The intricate editing of Wayne Le Clos is first rate and Carl Vine's bouncy score is also of major import in propelling the film. — *David Stratton*

PADMA NADIR MAJHI
(THE PADMA BOATMEN)
(INDIAN-BANGLADESHI)

A West Bengal Film Development release of a Government of West Bengal/Ashirbad Chalachchitra (Bangladesh) production. Directed, written (from Manik Bannerji's novel) and photographed (Eastmancolor) by Goutam Ghose. Editor, Moloy Bannerji; music, Ghose, Alauddin Ali; art direction, Ashoke Bose, Mohiuddin Moroque; sound, Anup Mukherji. Reviewed at Indian Film Festival, New Delhi, Jan. 18, 1993. (In Cannes Film Festival, Directors Fortnight section.) Running time: **135 MIN.**
Kuber . . . . Asaad
Mala . . . . Champa
Kapila . . . . Rupa Ganguly
Hossain Mian . . . . Utpal Dutt

Goutam Ghose, one of the premier directors of India's "Parallel Cinema" or arthouse scene — all his films have reached the festival circuit over the last decade — has chosen a difficult novel to adapt for the screen in Manik Bannerji's Bengali classic. But, cut down from its original length to a more manageable two hours, "The Padma Boatmen" is sure to make its mark as quality arthouse and fest fare.

Pic looks ravishing — Ghose was an awardwinning lenser before he became a director — and tells an epic story about Kuber, a humble fisherman whose life is changed by Hossain, a wealthy trader with a mission: populating a remote island in the Padma delta, employing the people to clear its dense forests and then persuading them to settle in an ideal society free from sectarian strife. The time is 1947, before the partition of Bengal.

Kuber meets one of the settlers who has run away, who tells him of the hardship and desolation on the island. But, deprived of his livelihood by a great storm, the fisherman accepts the trader's offer of captaining Hossain's cargo boat. When he reaches the island, he sees for himself his benefactor's attempt to achieve a better world.

Returning, Kuber becomes increasingly discontented with his former lot, infatuated with his seductive sister-in-law, and is framed for theft by the disappointed suitor of his daughter, forcing him to leave for the island and a new life. The trader has won the boatman's soul.

The film has many incidental threads and doesn't explain much about the odd island. But it provides a magnificently authentic-looking portrait of life on the

May 10, 1993 (Cont.)

Padma. And, as an allegory, it is a timeless view of communal strife in India: Kuber is a Hindu, Hossain a Muslim, but each finally loses his suspicion of the other.

Ghose, assisted by a good cast of relatively unknown actors, pours heart and soul into the film, using all his considerable technical skill while displaying a clearsighted warmth.

— *Derek Malcolm*

EL PAJARO DE LA FELICIDAD
(THE BIRD OF HAPPINESS)
(SPANISH)

A Central de Prods. Audiovisuales production, with the collaboration of Sogepaq. Executive producers, José Luis Olaizola, Rafael Diaz-Salgado; associate producer, Diego Hidalgo. Directed by Pilar Miró. Screenplay, Mario Camus. Camera (color), José Luis Alcaine; editor, José Luis Matesanz; art director, Felix Murcia; costumes, Javier Artiñano; sound, Carlos Faruolo; music, Jordi Savall; production manager, Juan Carlos Caro. Reviewed at Cine Alphaville, Madrid, April 16, 1993. Running time: **115 MIN.**
Carmen . . . . . . Mercedes Sampietro
Nani . . . . Aitana Sánchez-Gijón
Eduardo . . . . José Sacristán
Also with: Carlos Hipólito, Lluis Homar, Daniel Dicenta, Mari Carmen Prendes, Jordi Torras, Asunción Balaguer, Ana Gracia.

As in several earlier Pilar Miró films, this subtle and sensitive film zeroes in on the solitude and estrangement of a middle-aged woman who ultimately prefers her own cultural resources to the company of men. Pic probably will find most appeal with femme audiences in arthouse circuits.

With a superb lead performance by Mercedes Sampietro, who has become a kind of alter ego for Miró, pic eschews any kind of hardline feminist stand, concentrating mostly on a woman's quest for a purpose in life after breaking up with her live-in companion. Carmen, whose job is restoring old master paintings, can relate neither to her grown son, nor to her conservative Catalan parents, nor to a winsome ex-Spanish literature prof she meets in a vacation house she rents.

Carmen is clearly a "difficult" person who relishes her privacy, but also has a guarded soft side. Latter quality ultimately wins out. At the inconclusive end she chooses virtual isolation, with only her baby grandchild and a puppy sent by her ex-husband.

Pic is superbly lensed by José Luis Alcaine, and Mario Camus's script is literate and intelligent. Occasional refs to local politics and literature and brief poetry readings are not obtrusive.

— *Peter Besas*

DON'T CALL ME FRANKIE

Produced by Sam Braslau. Executive producers, Michael Alden, Sam Braslau, Marvan Nabili. Directed, written by Thomas A. Fucci. Camera (color), Barbu Marian, Barbod Taheri; editor, Jacqueline French; music supervisor, Virginia S. Ellsworth; production design, Silvana Alfonso; sound, Austin Beck. Reviewed at Passage du Nord-Ouest cinema, Paris, April 27, 1993. (In Cannes Film Festival, Intl. Critics Week section.) Running time: **105 MIN.**
Frank . . . . Peter Van Nordan
Barbara . . . . Elizabeth Anne Bowen
Also with: Martin Beck, Thomas Prisco, Nan Moog, Krista Eulberg.

The laid-back situational humor in "Don't Call Me Frankie" will be tedious to some and hilarious to others. Minimalist tale of a distraught man who is interrupted while attempting to do himself in sports a few original ideas and a carefully chosen soundtrack that could appeal to midnight movie auds.

Tubby, middle-aged Frank (Peter Van Nordan) is about to shoot himself in a cheap hotel room when an earthquake erupts, making a steady hand impossible. During the darkly funny and well-staged emergency, Frankie meets the prostie next door. It's the beginning of a peculiar relationship throughout which Frank, who has an aversion to being called Frankie, invokes the pic's title until the rather wry but very leisurely payoff.

Pic, set mostly at night, sports a gloomy decor and lighting to match. Although there's more atmosphere than content, the two lead thesps are good. The mood and behavioral cues are established as much by the mostly vintage songs as by anything else. — *Lisa Nesselson*

LA ARDILLA ROJA
(THE RED SQUIRREL)
(SPANISH)

A Sogetel production, with the collaboration of Sogepaq. Executive producer, Fernando de Garcillán. Directed, written by Julio Medem. Camera (Agfacolor), Gonzalo Berridi; editor, María Elena Saiz de Rozas; sets, Alvaro Machimbarrena; sound, Julio Recuero; music, Alberto Iglesias; production manager, Ricardo García Arrojo. Reviewed at Cine Roxy A (Madrid), April 24, 1993. Running time: **108 MIN.**
Jota . . . . Nancho Novo
Lisa . . . . Emma Suárez
Carmen . . . . María Barranco
Félix . . . . Carmelo Gómez
Also with: Karra Elejalde, Cristina Marcos, Mónica Molina, Ana Gracia, Txema Blasco, Ane Sánchez, Eneko Irizar, Sarai Noceda.

Some imaginative lensing, odd dream sequences and a seemingly mysterious amnesia plot give "The Red Squirrel" a promising opening fillip. But item rambles on, never making its point and ending in such bathos auds are left laughing.

Plot concerns a former rock musician who, as he seems to be contemplating a watery suicide, sees a motorcycle crashing over the ledge of the boardwalk in San Sebastian and catapulted onto the beach. The man, Jota, goes over to help, sees victim is a pretty girl, and accompanies her in the ambulance. The girl has amnesia, and Jota tells the doctor her name is Lisa and that he's lived with her four years.

Lisa apparently believes hium, and they set off for a camping site called "The Red Squirrel." Mixed in are dream sequences of Jota performing with his band; a squirrel's POV running through the bushes; a young boy who seems to have hypnotic powers; a husband whose face remains unseen searching for the girl and other poorly explained elements.

Dialogue and scenes move along fairly well and thesp Emma Suárez has some appeal. However, the physical unattractiveness of Nancho Novo as Jota, the even less likable husband and a repulsive taxi driver who is their neighbor at the camp further undermine the plot, which, when finally shorn of its mystery, is a total letdown. — *Paul Besas*

HOUSTON FEST

EDDIE PRESLEY
(16m)

A Laika Films/Eddie Prods. and Fauve Cinema presentation of a William Burr/Tom Denolf production. Produced by Burr, Denolf. Executive producer, William Brantley. Directed by Jeff Burr. Screenplay, Duane Whitaker. Camera (color, 16m), Tom Callaway; editors, Jay Woelfel, Jeff Burr; music, Jim Manzie; production design, Robert Eberz; costumes, Stacy Delbick; sound, Bob Sheridan; makeup, Judy Mathai; associate executive producer: Bruce Critchley; co-producer: Chuck Williams; associate producers: Stephen Hunter Flick, Bill Rojas. Reviewed at WorldFest/Houston, April 29, 1993. Running time: **105 MIN.**
Eddie Presley . . . . . Duane Whitaker
Doc . . . . Roscoe Lee Browne
Sid . . . . Clu Gulager
Tyranny . . . . Stacie Bourgeois
Becky . . . . Harri James
Nick . . . . Willard E. Pugh
Scooter . . . . Ted Raimi
West . . . . Lawrence Tierney
Starch . . . . Ian Ogilvy
Keystone . . . . Daniel Roebuck
The Shock Comic . . . Tim Thomerson
Foxey . . . . Julie Rohde-Brown
Also with: Tom Everett, Larry Lyles, Leon Edwards.

There may be a cult audience for "Eddie Presley;" it will be hard going for this oddball indie to find life beyond the fest circuit. Pic is an eccentric mix of minimalist humor and downbeat near-tragedy, half-Jim Jarmusch and half-psychodrama. It doesn't quite come off, but it's never dull.

Much like the recent "Johnny Suede," "Eddie"is a drastically expanded adaptation of a one-character theater piece. In this case, the protagonist is Eddie Presley (Duane Whitaker), an overweight L.A. security guard who once had minor success as an Elvis imitator.

Pic drops broad hints in early scenes that Eddie is recovering from a nervous breakdown, an event described in full detail during the extended climactic sequence. Bulk of the story details Eddie's ill-fated career as a rent-a-cop, his camaraderie with other guards, his dogged courtship of a pretty waitress (Stacie Bourgeois) and, eventually, his seemingly miraculous chance to revive his Elvis routine at a seedy nightclub for a one-night stand.

Predictably, the nightclub gig is a disaster, as the tape of Eddie's music is chewed up by faulty equipment. Not so predictably, the snafu triggers a long, rambling monologue in which Eddie describes his past (including his

May 10, 1993 (Cont.)

divorce, his bankruptcy and his mental breakdown) and his hunka-hunka burning love for Elvis.

Whitaker, who adapted the script from his own play, makes an agreeable impression in the early scenes. He presses his luck during the climactic monologue, which no doubt worked better on stage, but director Jeff Burr manages to inject visual variety with apt use of flashbacks.

Standouts in cameo bits and supporting roles include Clu Gulager as a sleazy talent agent with what appears to be the world's rattiest toupee; Roscoe Lee Browne as the urbane owner of the seedy nightclub; and, briefly but memorably, Tim Thomerson as a ferociously foul-mouthed comic who swears he used to use clean material when he toured with the Cowsills. Harri James has some sweetly klutzy moments as a tongue-tied security guard with a crush on Eddie.

Photographer Tom Callaway and production designer Robert Eberz do a good job of evoking Skid Row cheesiness without making the movie itself look cheap.

— *Joe Leydon*

THE TRUST

A Quadrangle Films, Ltd. production. Produced by Gary Chasen. Directed by J. Douglas Killgore, Neil Havers. Screenplay, Killgore, from his play. Camera (color), Claudia Raschke; editor, Brian Beasley; music, George Burt; production design, Trudy Sween; art direction, Tom Dornbusch; costume designer, Sigrid Insull; sound, Tim Himes; associate producer, Carolyn Killgore. Reviewed at WorldFest/Houston, April 23, 1993. Running time: **120 MIN.**
James Baker . . . . Sam Bottoms
Maria Vandermeer . . . . Karen Black
William Marsh Rice . . . Harold Suggs
Albert Patrick . . . . Jon Bruno
Charlie Jones . . . . . . Michael Petty
    Also with: Jim Bernhardt, James Black, Ira J. Black, Cyril Lavender, Luis Lemus, Suzanne Savoy, Bonnie Gallup, Jeff Millar.

"**T**he Trust" is a hopelessly stiff and uninvolving period pic that makes the least of a potentially intriguing real-life drama. Theatrical and homevid prospects are spotty, though pic might have some future as TV fodder.

Handsomely produced on a small budget, indie effort suffers from a lack of narrative momentum and prosaic storytelling that demystifies what might have been an arresting mystery. Pic has all the wit, charm and spontaneity of the audiovisual aids produced for American History classes during the 1950s.

Drama focuses on the life and, more important, mysterious death of Texas philanthropist William Marsh Rice, who bequeathed his immense fortune to the founding of Houston's Rice University. Shortly after the garrulous Rice (Harold Suggs) dies in New York in 1900, Rice's Houston attorney, James Baker (grandfather of the recent Secretary of State, played by Sam Bottoms), is told of a new will in which Rice leaves the bulk of his estate to a disreputable New York lawyer, Albert Patrick (Jon Bruno).

Baker suspects foul play. But the audience is way ahead of him, since co-director and screenwriter J. Douglas Killgore (adapting his own play) details every step of the conspiracy spun by Patrick and valet Charlie Jones (Michael Petty), who finally poisons his elderly employer.

Yes, that's right, the butler did it.

The real-life Rice case was the focus of national attention, given the potent mix of money, sex (Rice was the platonic friend of a lovely young widow, Maria Vandermeer, played by Karen Black) and scandal. Patrick's trial was notable for being one of the first where handwriting analysis was accepted as anything more authoritative than palm reading.

But what might have seemed like hot stuff to newspaper readers in 1900 comes off as tepid talking-head tedium in 1993.

Killgore, a commercial/industrial director making his feature debut, never figures out an interesting way to tell his interesting story — co-director Neil Havers reportedly helped out only during rehearsals.

Killgore gets little help from Bottoms, who is stolid and bland, and Black, whose overplaying is just a few degrees short of hysteria. Petty and Bruno have been directed to suggest a homoerotic undercurrent to their relationship.

Sigrid Insull's costume design and Tom Dornbusch's art direction greatly enhance the period ambience. Other tech credits are acceptable. — *Joe Leydon*

THE WEBBERS

A Blue Ridge Filmtrust presentation of a DEN Films production. Produced by Mike Erwin, J. Max Kirishima. Executive producer, Taro Tanabe. Directed, written by Brad Marlowe. Camera (Foto-Kem color), Irv Goodnoff; editor, Jonas Thaler; music, Anthony Guefen; production design, Michael Helmy; costumes, Robyn Reichek; sound (Ultra Stereo), Ed White; choreography, Maurice Hines. Reviewed at WorldFest/Houston, April 24, 1993. Running time: **118 MIN.**
Gerald Webber . . . . . Jeffrey Tambor
Emma Webber . . . . . . Rita Taggart
Miranda Webber . . . . . Jennifer Tilly
Johnny Webber . . . . David Arquette
Josh . . . . Brian Bloom
Roger Swade . . . . . . Robby Benson
    Also with: Luke Perry, Alyssa Milano.

"**T**he Webbers" is a shrill and foolish comedy that misses its satirical target (reality TV) by a country mile. Theatrical prospects are zilch, vid potential is scarcely better. If pic has any future, it's as late-night filler for cable nets.

Indie effort's premise is rife with comic possibilities: A slick, slimy network exec (Robby Benson) signs an "average" American family to a lucrative contract, whereby the family will move to a palatial new home and remain under constant vid camera surveillance.

Rather than develop comic situations from an average family's sudden fame, writer-director Brad Marlowe goes the easy route by making the Webbers appear ridiculous even before they go on camera.

Dad (Jeffrey Tambor) is a psychiatrist whose patients include a mass murderer who, in pic's most bizarre, least funny sequence, admits to killing his own mother. Mom (Rita Taggart) is undersexed and feels neglected, though she becomes a role model to her loyal viewership. Teenage son Johnny (David Arquette) is a moody sort who pines for his late g.f., who died in an auto wreck.

And sister Miranda (Jennifer Tilly) is a voluptuous dingbat and would-be artist who's obsessed with male genitalia. She sleeps with a variety of hunks, making a plaster cast of each lover's most attractive attribute — face, legs, torso, etc. — to build her version of the perfect man. Naturally, her erotic interludes become the most popular segment of the TV series.

None of this is terribly amusing. Still, some of it could have been diverting had Marlowe not encouraged his actors to gesticu-late wildly, mug shamelessly and generally "act funny."

Production values are handsome, more so than pic merits.

— *Joe Leydon*

EYE OF THE STRANGER

A Silver Lake Intl. Pictures presentation of a Hero Films production. Produced, directed, written by David Heavener. Executive producer, Gerald Milton. Camera (color), Paul Edwards; editor, Chris Roth; music, Robert Garrett; art direction, George Peirson; associate producer, Vidette Schine. Reviewed at WorldFest/Houston, April 23, 1993. Running time: **96 MIN.**
Stranger . . . . David Heavener
Mayor Howard Baines . Martin Landau
Lori . . . . Sally Kirkland
Rudy . . . . Don Swayze
    Also with: Stella Stevens, Sy Richardson, Joe Estevez, John Pleshette.

"**E**ye of the Stranger" is a thoroughly unremarkable, by-the-numbers timekiller that strives to be a modern-day version of such revisionist Western morality plays as "A Fistful of Dollars" and "High Plains Drifter." Vid audiences may respond, but only on nights when there's nothing else on the "New Releases" shelf.

Pic's ambitions are severely cramped by an obviously limited budget, and by the low-wattage charisma of writer-director David Heavener. The prolific B-movie mogul cast himself in the lead as an Eastwooden "Man With No Name" type who drifts into Harmony, a dying small town where dark secrets fester.

Martin Landau, Harmony's genially corrupt mayor, rules with a warm smile and a steel fist, methodically forcing the townspeople to sell their oil-rich land to him. The few holdouts are terrorized or killed.

It turns out the stranger is the brother of a lawyer killed by Landau's goons. Even so, it takes the stranger a long time to plot revenge — just long enough, in fact, for him to have time for a gratuitous romantic tussle with Sally Kirkland, the ex-girlfriend of the late lawyer.

Kirkland's performance is better than the material deserves, and the same can be said for Landau's surprisingly subdued co-starring bit. Supporting cast includes Don Swayze as Landau's chief enforcer, Stella Stevens as the town's hard-drinking doctor, Joe Estevez as the gutless sheriff and, most impressively, Sy Richardson as a store owner who stands up to Landau.

May 10, 1993 (Cont.)

Heavener works up little excitement and no suspense whatsoever. As an action lead, he looks tough enough, but radiates little in the way of star power.

Tech credits are adequate.

— *Joe Leydon*

NERIA
(ZIMBABWEAN)

> A KJM3 Entertainment Group release of a Media for Development Trust production. Produced by Louise Riber, John Riber. Directed by Godwin Mawuru. Screenplay, Riber, from Tsitsi Dangarembga's story. Camera (Central Film color), John Riber; editor, Louise Riber; music, Oliver Mtukudzi; sound, Esko Metsola; art direction, David Guwaza; assistant director, Isaac Mabhikwa; production manager, Tiyane Chitero. Reviewed at Walter Reade Theater, in "Modern Days, Ancient Nights" series, N.Y., April 16, 1993. Running time: **103 MIN.**
> Neria . . . . Jesesi Mungoshi
> Phineas . . . . . . Dominic Kanaveti
> Patrick . . . . Emmanual Mbrimi
> Jethro . . . . Oliver Mtukudzi
> Ambuya . . . . Violet Ndlovu
> Mavis . . . . Tsitsi Nyamukapa
> Shingi . . . . Manyika Kangai
> Connie . . . . Kubi Indi
> Mr. Machacha . . . . . Claude Maredza
> Mr. Chigwanzi . . Anthony Chinyanga
> *(English soundtrack)*

An old-fashioned crowd-pleaser, the Zimbabwe feature "Neria" is a strong film about an indomitable woman. Already a big hit on its home turf, film looms as an unusual attraction for African-American audiences tired of Hollywood exploitation (pic was recently released in Washington, D.C.).

Debuting director Godwin Mawuru harks back to a form resembling 19th century melodrama, replete with a lip-smacking villain who all but twirls his mustache. However, the *tsuris* piled on the long-suffering heroine leads to a satisfying climax right out of a "Billy Jack" movie.

Jesesi Mungoshi is Neria, a happily married woman who sews clothing and lives in the city with her husband (Emmanual Mbrimi) and two kids.

His family, under matriarch Violet Ndlovu, still lives in their small village and follows ancient traditions. When Neria's husband is killed in a car accident, his relatives use tradition to exploit the tragedy and the widow.

The eldest surviving brother no longer lives nearby, so another brother, Phineas (Dominic Kanaveti), takes it upon himself to "protect" Patrick's family, taking the family car, her furniture and even her children. Yet, when her daughter gets appendicitis, he won't even drive her to a hospital, so Neria literally has to carry her there on her back.

Final straw comes when Phineas and his wife move into Neria's city house and he starts bribing her kids to turn them away from mama. Neria finally blows up, putting herself in a bad light.

Fortunately, a modern neighbor, Connie (Kubi Indi), hips Neria to a lawyer, Mr. Machacha (Claue Maredza), and she sues.

Exceptionally sharp writing, credited to editor/co-producer Louise Riber, spells out all the issues evenhandedly in two courtroom scenes. Thanks to having a shrewd lawyer of his own (Anthony Chinyanga), Phineas mounts a convincing case for his own POV. After some suspense, a judge sets things right.

Heartwarming coda has Neria assert her newfound feminism and defy the culture by refusing to marry one of her brother-in-laws after a year of mourning has passed. Her reconciliation with mother-in-law Ambuya is a touching finale.

Wearing the weight of the world on her face, Mungoshi is a find as the earth mother Neria, though one would be hard-pressed short of "Stella Dallas" to think up a contemporary western equivalent to the role.

Of course Kanaveti overplays his rotter role, even laughing in cruel glee when the other characters are out of earshot, but that's part of the fun. Supporting cast is solid, particularly Ndlovu as the cranky but good-hearted mother-in-law.

Film is enlivened by the musical score by Oliver Mtukudzi.

— *Lawrence Cohn*

RABI
(BURKINA FASO-BRITISH-FRENCH)

> A Cinecom Prod. (Ouagadougou) production for BBC TV (London), in association with TVE (Paris). Produced by Peter Firstbrook. Executive producer, Robert Lamb. Directed, written by Gaston J.M. Kaboré. Camera (Bry-Sur-Marne color), Jean-Noel Ferragut; editor, Marie-Jeanne Kanyala; music, René B. Guirma, Wally Badarou; costume design, Mariame Sidibe; sound, Marc Nouyrigat; assistant director, Ismaël Ouédraogo. Reviewed at Walter Reade theater, "Modern Days, Ancient Nights" series, N.Y., April 18, 1993. Running time: **63 MIN.**
> With: Joseph Nikiema, Colette Kaboré, Yacouba Kaboré, Tinfissi Yerbanga, Josephine Kaboré.

A very slight children's fable, "Rabi" is a Burkina Faso film that resembles a short subject padded out to feature length. It's flat and of little interest to western audiences.

Using a cast of mainly family members (with little acting talent), filmmaker Gaston J.M. Kaboré limns the very boring saga of young Rabi (Yacouba Kaboré), a kid growing up in a remote part of Burkina Faso.

His mom makes pottery that his dad sells in town. Flimsy story premise has dad breaking his load of pottery when he almost runs over a tortoise. He takes the tortoise home to show his wife why he loused up their business and Rabi immediately bonds with the pet.

Following the corny format of a thousand children's films, Rabi isn't allowed to keep the pet and goes into an emotional tailspin. With the help of his friendly grandpa (Tinfissi Yerbanga), he finds a giant tortoise and brings it home to further objections.

Key subplot has Rabi becoming the romantic go-between between his aged grandpa and a long estranged woman who loved him but to whom gramps never popped the question.

Cast barely can recite their lines; Kaboré exhibits an okay visual sense but fails to shape his material. — *Lawrence Cohn*

CASA DIN VIS
(THE HOUSE FROM THE DREAM)
(ROMANIAN)

> A Romania Film release. Directed by Ioan Carmazan. Screenplay, Fanus Neagu, Carmazan. Camera (color), Cristian Comeaga; editor, Amau Teclui; music, Radu Zumtivrscui; art direction, Maria Miu; sound, Constantine Catanchtin. Reviewed at "Cinema in Transition" series, The New School, N.Y., April 27, 1992. Running time: **96 MIN.**
> With: Gheorghe Dinica, Maia Morgenstern, Horatiu Malaele, Sofia Vicoveanca, Llorin Tauase, Tasa Berea.

Focusing on a strong-minded cantankerous old man and his resistance to change, Ioan Carmazan's "The House From the Dream" may pique interest in its quaint depiction of regional life in Romania.

Plot is set around the large birthday party a rural town throws for village elder Chivu, who hides indoors and rejects festivities as a pretext to get him out of the house; the town wants to demolish the house and put Chivu in a modern apartment. As he rails against those present, a series of flashbacks show why relations with family and friends are strained.

Things begin when the dominating Chivu arranges the marriage of his eldest son, the feeble-minded Babulete, to an unmarried woman from a neighboring town who has recently given birth. When she runs off with the youngest son, Chivu loses both his control over the family and his standing in the community.

Pic is notable for portrait of charming folk eccentricities, such as the mother who dreams that her dead daughter is searching for a bridegroom, or the blue-winged man overseeing all like an angel of misfortune.

Radu Zumtivrscui's score is an effective blend of bucolic airs and plaintively sung folk melodies. Other tech credits are all right. — *Paul Lenti*

SPIRKA ZA NEPOZNATY
(STOP FOR STRANGERS)
(BULGARIAN)

> An E.R. Prods. release of a Boyana Film Studio production. Directed by Ivan Rossenov. Screenplay, Peter Iskrenov. Camera (color), Svetla Ganeva; editor, Evgenia Tasseva; music, Bojidar Petkov. Reviewed at "Cinema in Transition" series, The New School, N.Y., April 28, 1992. Running time: **80 MIN.**
> Maria . . . . Katya Paskaleva
> Ivan . . . . Anton Raditchev

Ivan Rossenov's uneasy romance "Stop for Strangers" would have made a good short, but as a slow-paced 80-minute feature it outstays its welcome by about an hour. Film was banned when it was produced in 1989 and was only released after the fall of Bulgaria's Communist government.

Slight tale concerns a rundown, out-of-the-way train station, where no passenger has gotten on or off in over two years. The government has it slated for closure, but the strong-willed station master vows to defend it.

Her husband is in the hospital and she lives with her grandson, Sashko. Every day, she puts on her uniform, signals the train as it roars past and tries to maintain the illusion of a functioning station.

One day, a stranger emerges and wants to by a ticket. Since the train will not arrive until early the next morning, he dawdles around the stark waiting room, observing the woman.

When the train comes, he pretends to be asleep and must stay on. When the major calls, warning her about an escaped murderer, she shields the stranger out of loneliness and because, by buying a ticket, he is a validation of her job as station master.

Film is unsettling and has some nice moments, but as a feature, the story wears thin. Acting and tech credits are fine.

— *Paul Lenti*

LOLUL SUD
(THE SOUTH POLE)
(ROMANIAN)

A Romania Film release of a Studioului de Creatie Profilm production. Directed, written by Radu Nicoara. Camera (color), Relu Morariu; editor, Mircea Ciorciltei; art direction, Mircea Tofann; sound, Silviu Camil. Reviewed at "Cinema in Transition" series, The New School, N.Y., April 26, 1992. Running time: **112 MIN.**
With: Claudiu Bleont, Ioana Pavelescu Sion, Ruxandra Bucescu, Dana Dembinski, George Constaniu, George Alexandru.

A study of Eastern European angst or, more aptly, a reflection of Sartre's existential nausea, helmer Radu Nicoara's "The South Pole" reflects the emptiness of Romania's former intellectual community. Slow-paced pic offers a harsh look at the changes taking place in contemporary Romania and may find select offshore interest.

Film centers on Stefan Sirbu (Claudiu Bleont), a 35-year-old once-promising young writer and former recipient of the national writers guild's award for a bold first novel. Since then, he has basked in government favor while suffering from chronic writer's block.

Sirbu spends much of the film in his underwear, as if he wants to strip himself of his emotional angst. He barely tolerates his wife and daughter and carries on a clandestine affair with the wife of an important man. He sits amid a jumble of books at his desk, moaning about not selling out, while his paramour reminds him that if he wants the benefits, he has to play by the rules.

When Ceausescu's communist government falls, he is further alienated and it is not until the end, when even his underwear is shed, that he finds freedom.

Nicoara inserts some interesting directorial quirks: When Sirbu finally begins a new novel, he watches himself at a distance with a bemused look as if he were removed from even this.

Pic allows us a peek into the bankrupt artistic milieu of Romania's intellectuals who, after years of being coddled, are now forced to define their roles in post-Communist society.

Tech credits are okay and acting is good, especially Bleont.

— *Paul Lenti*

CARUGA
(CHARUGA)
(CROATIAN)

A Maestro Films (Zagreb)/Viba Film (Ljubljana)/Hrvatska TV (Zagreb) production. Produced by Mladen Koceic. Directed by Rajko Grlic. Screenplay, Ivan Kusan, Grlic. Camera (Jadran Film color), Slobodan Trninic; editor, Andrijia Zafranovic; sound (Dolby), Mladen Perun; art direction, Zeljko Svecic. Reviewed at "Cinema in Transition" series, The New School, N.Y., April 20, 1993. Running time: **108 MIN.**
Jovo Charuga . . . . . . Ivo Gregurevic
Lt. Gile . . . . Petar Bozovic
Svilena . . . . Ena Begovic
Also with: Davor Janjic, Dusan Acimovic, Bronislaw Lecic, Dusan Jovanovic.

Haphazardly scripted and obnoxiously vulgar, Rajko Grlic's "Charuga" is a misguided attempt at a folk epic in the form of disconnected vignettes. It's a tough slog to sit through and probably unexportable.

Grlic's last film was the successful international effort "That Summer of White Roses," which won the top prize at the Tokyo Film Festival. For "Charuga" (the "h" is added to original title for translation pronounciation), he limns the legend of a bandit who returned from the war in Russia in 1918 to Slovenia.

His lusty adventures robbing, killing and raping are portrayed in almost random scenes conveniently separated by fadeouts. This sloppy approach affords no continuity or character progression, with actor Ivo Gregurevic (a Giancarlo Giannini type) looking different in each scene and behaving arbitrarily. There's no one to root for in Grlic's violent, mean-spirited satire.

First seen running naked through the woods pursued by local gendarmes, Charuga returns to his home village to have sex with an old sweetheart and kill the squire who's been bedding her while he was at war.

He soon teams up with a local revolutionary, Bozo the Red, for a series of violent encounters with the dogged gendarme leader Lt. Gile (Petar Bozovic). Unfunny running gag has Gile dead-set on a sexual tryst with daffy Austrian aristocrat Svilena a.k.a. "Silky" (Ena Begovic), whom Charuga is regularly *shtupping*, most notably a noisy, slapstick encounter under her piano.

Punctuated by awkwardly staged battle scenes and gratuitous male and female nudity, "Charuga" slavishly imitates the style of a Sergio Leone Western.

Yocks are both simple-minded and treacherous, as when Charuga gets a makeover that styles him like Lenin to apparently feed Svilena's sexual fantasies.

After several years (supposedly off in America) Charuga reemerges with a new identity so that Lt. Gile improbably doesn't recognize him, until an arbitrary arrest scene that, like everything before, goes unexplained.

The acting is broad and the use of Dolby sound effects is distracting. — *Lawrence Cohn*

UNDE LA SOARE E FRIG
(OUTBACK)
(ROMANIAN-B&W)

A K-Films release of a Filmex-Romania production. Produced by Titi Popescu. Directed, written by Bogdan Dumitrescu. Camera (B&W), Doru Mitran; editor, Adina Georgescu Obrocea; music, Adrian Enescu; sound, Mihai Orasani. Reviewed in "Cinema in Transition" series, The New School, N.Y., April 27, 1992. Running time: **90 MIN.**
With: Oana Pellea, Gheorghe Visu.

First feature by Bogdan Dumitrescu, "Outback" is a slow-paced love story with a twist "bad joke" ending that comments on the threat of the uniformity of urban life. With careful handling, pic may spark some arthouse interest.

Film begins with a silent preface, showing vacationers on Romania's Black Sea coast. When a woman and her male companion get into a fight, he gets into a car and drives off.

The woman eventually hitches a ride from a stranger, who has several stops en route. When he stops to make a delivery at a remote lighthouse, the woman gets out of the car to drink some water. The driver returns, assumes the woman has found another ride and takes off, abandoning her miles from the nearest highway.

The lighthouse keeper has no telephone and his motorcycle has a flat tire. And so the two characters — neither of their names are ever exchanged — share several days slowly getting to know each other. However, their isolation is broken when the woman's companion comes to look for her.

Doru Mitran's black and white photography is wisely used and Dumitrescu narrates various scenes without depending on dialogue: Key scenes show characters at a distance talking while foreground sounds or music dominate the soundtrack. The reactions are easy to judge and the unsettling device works.

Insistent score by Adrian Enescu has some interesting moments but at times tends to overwhelm the proceedings. — *Paul Lenti*

May 17, 1993

MA SAISON PRÉFÉRÉE
(MY FAVORITE SEASON)
(FRENCH)

An AMLF (France) release of an Alain Sarde presentation of a Les Films Alain Sarde/TF-1 Films Prods./D.A. Films co-production with the participation of Soficas/Cofimage 4/Investimage 4/La Region Midi Pyreness/Canal Plus. (Foreign sales: Le Studio Canal Plus.) Produced by Sarde. Directed by André Téchiné. Screenplay, Téchiné, Pascal Bonitzer. Camera (color; widescreen), Thierry Arbogast; editor, Martine Giordano; music, Philippe Sarde; art direction, Carlos Conti; costume design, Claire Fraisse, Bernadette Villard; sound (Dolby), Remy Attal, Jean-Paul Mugel; assistant director, Denis Bergonhe. Reviewed at the Cannes Film Festival (Opening Night, noncompeting), May 13, 1993. Running time: **125 MIN.**

Emilie	Catherine Deneuve
Antoine	Daniel Auteuil
Berthe	Marthe Villalonga
Bruno	Jean-Pierre Bouvier
Anne	Chiara Mastroianni
Khadija	Carmen Chaplin
Lucien	Anthony Prada
Woman at bar	Ingrid Caven

Andre Téchiné's Cannes Fest opener "Ma Saison Préférée" is a dull exposition of the glacial shifts in the emotional alignments within a dysfunctional middle-class family. Star names and director's rep will mean more in France than offshore, where commercial outlook is negligible.

Slickly made but deliberately less stylized than most of Téchiné's previous pics, this somber drama focuses on estranged sibs Catherine Deneuve and Daniel Auteuil, forced together during the final decline of their ailing mother, Marthe Villalonga.

Broken down novelistically into four chapters, this very French story reunites middle-aged brother and sister for the first time in several years. Erratic and immature, Auteuil prefers to avoid dealing with family issues that make him uncomfortable, notably his mother's desire to discuss her estate. In a childish fit, Auteuil strikes Deneuve's husband (Jean-Pierre Bouvier), which manages to lead to the couple splitting. Their daughter, played by Deneuve's real-life daughter Chiara Mastroianni in her screen debut, is upset by this, while adopted son Anthony Prada is preoccupied with his affair with Carmen Chaplin, who works for the family business.

At this, Deneuve hits a low point, confessing, "I hate what I've become," a remark that has reverberations later on, when Villalonga, in a potent death speech, relates that her late husband's overriding concern in raising their kids was for them to be "modern." Script's concerns are apparent, but Téchiné and co-scripter Pascal Bonitzer do little to rouse viewer interest in these drab personalities.

As it is, Auteuil plays only the most unappetizing character among a thoroughly sour lot. A rather stifling quality surrounds all the decorum and efforts to maintain a prescribed version of normal family life, and if this dissection of the Toulousian bourgeoisie means something to a French public, it doesn't translate with any impact.

While attractive and accomplished, Téchiné's mounting here is plodding, and while Deneuve, Auteuil and Villalonga all have their moments, they cannot overcome the maddeningly uninsightful and selfish nature of their characters. Young Chiara Mastroianni looks more like her father, Marcello, than like her mother, and the beginnings of a private friendship subplot between her and the free-spirited young Moroccan played by Carmen Chaplin goes undeveloped.

Pic looks handsome.
— *Todd McCarthy*

BROKEN HIGHWAY
(AUSTRALIAN-B&W)

A Black Ray Films production, in association with the Australian Film Commission and Queensland Film Development Corp. Produced by Richard Mason. Directed, written by Laurie McInnes. Camera (Panavision widescreen, B&W), Steve Mason; editor, Gary Hillberg; music, David Faulkner; production design, Lesley Crawford; art director, Lisa Thompson; sound recording, Paul Brincat; audiographer, Penn Robinson; stunts, Danny Baldwin; line producer, Julie Forster; associate producers, Meredith King, Gaby Mason; production supervisor, Lynn Gailey; assistant director, Bruce Redman; casting, Liz Mullinar. Reviewed at Film Australia screening room, Sydney, March 18, 1993. (In Cannes Film Festival, competing.) Running time: **97 MIN.**

Angel	Aden Young
Tatts	David Field
Wilson	Bill Hunter
Catherine	Claudia Karvan
Elias Kidd	Norman Kaye
Max O'Donnell	Dennis Miller
Woman	Kris McQuade
Roger	William McInnes
Jack	Stephen Davis
Night Manager	Peter Settle

Femme writer-director Laurie McInnes' first feature, "Broken Highway" is a poetic, astonishingly audacious and, for the most part, impressive work.

It boasts outstanding performances, camerawork and soundtrack, and creates a mordant, bleakly beautiful mood unlike anything previously seen in Australian cinema. Solid international arthouse acceptance is indicated for this trailblazer.

McInnes, who won the Golden Palm at Cannes in 1987 for her short film "Palisade," has, for her feature debut, conceived a plot that is a cross between the American Western and film noir genres, with richly poetic dialogue resonant at times of Tennessee Williams. She has bravely chosen to shoot the film in widescreen and black and white, a decision that pays off in cinematographer Steve Mason's haunting, stark, inventively framed visuals.

The opening scenes are set aboard a merchant ship plowing through dark waters towards an Australian port. Angel (Aden Young) realizes that his dying friend, Max (Dennis Miller), isn't going to make it home; Max claims to hear "lost souls" calling him. He bequeaths Angel a pair of cowboy boots and instructs him to visit the small town of Honeyfield and deliver a package to someone he calls "The Dead Man," explaining that the package contains "what he's been hungry for — the sweet things money can't buy."

Max's death in no way affects the sinister Tatts (David Field), another member of the crew. So when Angel sets off to deliver his package, Tatts follows him at a discreet distance to Honeyfield, a desolate place that time has passed by and the bitter opposite to conventional images of coastal Australia.

In Honeyfield, Angel encounters "Dead Man" Elias Kidd (Norman Kaye), a bitter, evil old character who owns most of the area, and delivers his package, which contains opium. He also meets Wilson (Bill Hunter), a fisherman who works for Kidd, and Catherine (Claudia Karvan), Wilson's young mistress. And he pays a visit to the rotting, cobwebbed house where Max's wife, now dead, had awaited his return in vain.

From these mysterious elements, McInnes has fashioned a classical "stranger in town" narrative, his arrival bringing long simmering passions to a head; and the later arrival of the brutal Tatts brings those passions to a roiling boil.

After a tremendous build-up, the ending of the film is a touch problematic, and though there's a cathartic physical confrontation between Good (Angel) and Evil (Tatts), "Broken Highway" lacks a sock final clincher.

Despite this, the film should garner positive critical support. Aden Young has his strongest role to date as Angel; Claudia Karvan (the girl in "High Tide") is sweetly vulnerable as Catherine; David Fields is genuinely menacing as Tatts; Bill Hunter is moving as a stubborn man who discovers he's losing what little he had; Norman Kaye makes Kidd a genuinely malevolent figure; and Dennis Miller brings distinction to the dying Max.

The soundtrack, the atmospheric music of David Faulkner and the "audiographics" of Penn Robinson; and is a major contributor to the mood. — *David Stratton*

LES DEMOISELLES ONT EU 25 ANS
(THE 'YOUNG GIRLS' TURN 25)
(FRENCH-DOCU-16m)

A Ciné Tamaris production with the participation of the CNC and the support of the Procirep Television Commission and Laure Adler of France 2. (Intl. sales: Ciné Tamaris.) Produced by Ciné Tamaris. Directed, written by Agnès Varda. Camera (color), Stéphane Krausz, Georges Strouve, Varda; video camera (color), Alexandre Auffort, Patrick Mounoud; editors, Varda, Anne-Marie Cotret; music, Michel Legrand, Jacques Loussier; sound, Thierry Ferreux, Jean-Luc Rault Cheynet, Bernard Seidler; documentation, Christian Chaudet; journalist, Michel Boujut; assistant director, Yves Caumon. Reviewed at Carré Seita screening room, Paris, April 30, 1993. (In Cannes Film Festival, Un Certain Regard section.) Running time: **62 MIN.**

With: Mag Bodard, Catherine Deneuve, Bernard Evein, Jean-Louis Frot, Michel Legrand, Jacques Perrin, Bertrand Tavernier.

Delightful is the word for Agnès Varda's magically well-edited docu tribute to her late husband Jacques Demy's classic widescreen musical "Les Demoiselles de Rochefort" 25 years after its release. A touching, amusing and buoyant mix of "then" and "now" footage, sure to be a sentimental favorite at Cannes, "Les Demoiselles Ont Eu 25 Ans" will be telecast on France 2 May 19.

Perfectly paced gem is an essential companion piece to revival screenings of Demy's playful and beloved "Young Girls of Rochefort," but stands on its own as a loving and fanciful docu.

Since Demy's "Demoiselles" bowed in 1967, the French port

May 17, 1993 (Cont.)

city of Rochefort has been synonymous with song and dance and with some of composer Michel Legrand's most ubiquitous theme music.

While on location in Rochefort in 1966, Varda took 16m "home movies" of the cast and crew —including Catherine Deneuve and her older sister and co-star, Françoise Dorleac. Although Varda had abandoned the material when Dorleac was killed in a 1967 car accident, she dug some of the rushes out of Pathè's vaults after Demy died in 1990.

Camera crew in tow, Varda returned to Rochefort in 1992 for a star-studded (in a comically undercranked scene, Deneuve and other dignitaries arrive in a chartered plane) yet sweetly provincial tribute to the pic that put it on the map, then let her unique sensibility fly in the editing room. Varda also skillfully incorporates portions of a vintage "making of" docu lensed by Belgian helmer André Delvaux.

Tender testimony from Deneuve, Legrand, actor Jacques Perrin, helmer Bertrand Tavernier (who was a publicist at the time) and other leading film professionals is informative, but more so are Varda's interviews with locals who were extras. Examples: the now-grown boys who shared a dance number with Gene Kelly; twin brothers who secretly and independently kept boyhood diaries during the shoot; youngsters who met on the set and later wed.

Varda's witty voiceovers sometimes heighten the humor exponentially as in a vintage clip of Demy putting on a pullover sweater "at his own speed."

Four of the featured performers in the original film, George Chakiris, Danielle Darrieux, Gene Kelly and Michel Piccoli, are absent. Although their reflections might have been interesting, the 62-minute pic is sufficiently chock-full of material.

Pic's aura of upbeat nostalgia, which is cemented by the final tracking shot, will delight established fans of the film, and pique the interest of viewers who haven't seen Demy's musical.
— *Lisa Nesselson*

PIKKUJA JA PIKKUHOUSUJA
(LYRICS AND LACE)
(FINNISH)

A Dada-Filmi Oy (Helsinki)/Film-Teknik/Swedish Film Institute/Nordic Film-and-TV-Fund co-production. Directed by Matti Ijas. Screenplay, Heikki Reivila, Ijas; Camera (color, widescreen), Kari Sohlberg; editor, Irma Taina; music, Raoul Bjorkenheim; production design, Anu Maja; sound (Dolby), K.J. Koski, Matti Kuortti. Reviewed at Club de l'Etoile screening room Paris, May 6, 1993. (In Cannes Film Festival, Directors Fortnight.) Running time: **85 MIN.**
Tauno Lintunen . . Paavo Pentikainen
Tomi . . . . Mikko Reitala
Also with: Liisa Mustonen

"**L**yrics and Lace" (literally, "Commas and Underpants") is a modestly entertaining semi-comic portrait of a dissolute poet. Sometimes crass depiction of Finland's fictional answer to Charles Bukowski starts off reasonably well but grows tiresome, tapering off into arbitrary episodes, like an epic poem about nothing.

Although scraggly-pated and dissipated Tauno Lintunen (Paavo Pentikainen) hasn't published a line for 10 years, he is so keen an observer he can predict a woman's sexual tastes, her underpants' color, what her next gesture will be and talks himself in and out of situations, some ribald, some extremely far-fetched.

Spry instrumentals punctuate different episodes as the poet and his callow assistant undertake a tour of backwater retirement homes and cultural centers. Such bits as the Salvation Army singing "Hey Jude" at their mission are too rare to salvage the pic. — *Lisa Nesselson*

ANCHORESS
(BRITISH-BELGIAN-B&W/COLOR)

A British Film Institute/Corsan Prods. co-production in association with the Ministry of the Flemish Community/BRTN/ASLK-CGER/National Loterij/CR Television. Produced by Paul Breuls, Ben Gibson. Executive producer, Angela Topping. Directed by Chris Newby. Screenplay, Judith Stanley-Smith, Christine Watkins. Camera (B&W, color), Michel Baudour; editor, Brand Thumin; production design, Niek Kortekaas; costume design, Annie Symons; sound, Andre Patrouillie; associate producer, Catherine Vandeleene. Reviewed at Carré Sieta screening room, Paris, April 30, 1993. (In Cannes Film Festival, Un Certain Regard section.) Running time: **106 MIN.**
Christine Carpenter . . Natalie Morse
The Reeve . . . . . Eugene Bervoerts
Pauline Carpenter . . . . Toyah Wilcox
Priest . . . . . . Christopher Eccleston
Also with: Peter Postlethwaite, Michael Pas, Brenda Bertin, François Beukelaers.

An earthy, well-integrated sensuality meshes with medieval spirituality in "Anchoress." The strikingly lensed 14th century tale of a young woman who chooses to be sealed into the wall of her village church to chastely live out her days — only to change her mind — could lay anchor beyond fests to arthouses.

Natalie Morse is suitably radiant as Christine, so smitten with the Virgin she wishes to dwell permanently "in Her house." Bricking her in thrills the ambitious and hypocritical priest because Christine will not be available to wed the menacing local overseer (Eugene Bervoerts).

Toyah Wilcox gives a bold perf as Christine's mother, a secular-minded midwife and herbalist who is eventually accused of witch-craft with harrowing results.

Evocatively designed period pic creates a long ago world yet remains relevant on such issues as what recourse women have in a man's world and how faith grounded in nature fares against faith dictated by the clergy.

Convincingly medieval landscape (lensed on an air base in Belgium) is finely rendered in black and white. Once sealed in (her cell has windows) Christine sees fields in a loaf of bread, an entire pond in a bowl of water. The only swatch of color appears after a female leper advises cloistered Christine to "embrace your body." In a poetically sexy scene she makes love to the earth.

Despite pic's occasional lusty humor and Wilcox's defiant attitude, some viewers will find the subject matter slow going. Still, helmer Chris Newby's first feature — also the BFI's first Belgian co-production — is an imaginative and thoughtfully textured tale that bodes well for the director's future. — *Lisa Nesselson*

ABISSINIA
(ABYSSINIA)
(ITALIAN)

An Istituto Luce/Italnoleggio Cinematografico release of an Iterfilm production in association with RAI-2/Istituto Luce/the Ministry of Tourism & Entertainment. (Intl. sales: Sacis.) Produced by Laurentina Guidotti. Directed by Francesco Martinotti. Screenplay, Fulvio Ottaviano, Martinotti, from Michele Corsi's story. Camera (color), Mauro Marchetti; editor, Annalisa Forgione; music, Fiorenzo Carpi; art direction, Giantito Burchiellaro; costumes, Sergio Ballo; sound, Fabio Felici. Reviewed at Anica screening room, Rome, May 7, 1993. (In Cannes Film Festival, Intl. Critics' Week.) Running time: **87 MIN.**
Antonio . . . . Enrico Salimbeni
Enzo . . . . Mario Adorf
Francesca . . . . . Grazyna Szapolowska
Armida . . . . Milena Vukotic
Marco . . . . Luca Zingaretti
Renato . . . . Paki Valente

A shiftless stranger gets drawn into the firing line of another man's pathological jealousy in "Abissinia," a bleak, slow-burning tragedy quirkily recounted in an appealingly discordant key. Film noir-styled tale of lethargy gone lethal will need critical support to overcome its nameless cast domestically, but it should make a healthy traveler, wangling fest dates and some specialized offshore release.

Set in the Adriatic coastal town of Riccione, pic immediately establishes its balancing act of lightness and sobriety, with a coffin moving down the flash/trash tourist mecca's main street. Backtracking, it recaps the events leading to the death, saving the contents for a final-reel surprise.

Turfed out of his restaurant job, and roughed up by the boss' flunkies for pilfering his outstanding wage, indolent waiter Enrico Salimbeni is taken in by gruff restauranteer Mario Adorf, whose unpopular eatery's location is so out of the way, it's nicknamed Abyssinia. Salimbeni settles right into the place's all-consuming inertia, piecing together the once-illustrious pasts of Adorf and his fiery femme Grazyna Szapolowska through tidbits from the bone-idle staff.

Director Francesco Martinotti slyly maintains the sense of dread as more an unnerving hint than a promise, quietly milking the setting's stifling oppressiveness. Helping him keep a tight rein on the smoldering events is Salimbeni's easy mix of awkwardness and cool nonchalance. Other thesping is mostly strong, but one detour into histrionics briefly upsets the balance.

Pic is smoothly edited and shot, and Fiorenzo Carpi's music nicely reinforces the mood. Art director Giantito Burchiellaro captures the dusty, kitsch decadence of unfashionable beach resorts.

— *David Rooney*

MOI IVAN, TOI ABRAHAM
(ME IVAN, YOU ABRAHAM)
(FRENCH-CIS-B&W)

A Pan-Européene release of a Hachette Premiere/UCG Images/Les Films Balenciago/La Sept Cinema/Vitt (CIS)/Europa Plus (CIS) co-production. (Intl. sales: Président Films.) Produced by René Cleitman, Jean-Luc Ormieres. Directed, written by Yolande Zauberman. Camera (B&W, widescreen), Jean-Marc Fabre; editor, Yann Dedet; music, Ghedalia Tazartes; production design, Alexandre Sagoskin; sound, Jean-Pierre Duret, Dominique Hennequin. Reviewed at Club de l'Etoile screening room, Paris, May 6, 1993. (In Cannes Film Festival, Directors Fortnight section.) Running time: 105 MIN.
With: Sacha Iakovlev, Roma Alexandrovitch, Vladimir Machkov, Maria Lipinka, Hélène Lapiower, Daniel Olbrychinski, Oleg Iankovski.
(Yiddish, Polish, Russian soundtrack)

Slow and disjointed but visually and thematically rich, "Moi Ivan, Toi Abraham" demands patience. Tale of unshakable Jewish-gentile friendship in a tension-wracked 1930s Polish village portrays deep-seated ethnic and religious intolerance. Fest exposure seems mandatory. Striking black and white widescreen lensing may suffer on TV.

In her first fiction outing, documaker Yolande Zauberman steers clear — perhaps too clear — of the didactic approach. Helmer drops us into a bygone world without a map. Village residents are introduced pell-mell and the connections among them are slow to emerge. To the dismay of their respective families, Jewish youngster Abraham and slightly older gentile Ivan are inseparable.

Abraham's grandfather Nachman, who rules with an iron fist, wants to spirit him away from his friend for good. But, having overheard Nachman's plan, Abraham convinces Ivan to run away with him. Further persecution ensues during their odyssey when Abraham is taken for a gypsy.

Lead thesps and plentiful extras (pic was shot in Ukraine and Belarus) have interesting faces that serve to convey unspoken travails. Jean-Marc Fabre's lensing stuffs plenty of local color

into the frame and contrasts tawdry, long-ago atmosphere with barren landscapes. The soundtrack includes strident music blended with foreign babble that surfaces jarringly now and then.

— *Lisa Nesselson*

MENACE II SOCIETY

A New Line Cinema release and production. Produced by Darin Scott. Executive producer, Kevin Moreton. Directed by Allen and Albert Hughes. Screenplay, Tyger Williams. Camera (Foto-Kem color), Lisa Rinzler; editor, Christopher Koefoed; music, QD III; music supervisors, Bonnie Greenberg, Jill Meyers; production design, Penny Barrett; set decorator, Adel Mazen; costume design, Sylvia Vega-Vasquez; sound (Dolby), Veda Campbell; co-producers, Allen and Albert Hughes, Tyger Williams; assistant director, Tyrone Mason. Reviewed at Aidikoff Screening Room, L.A., April 27, 1993. MPAA Rating: R. Running Time: 107 MIN.
Caine Lawson . . . . Tyrin Turner
Ronnie . . . . Jada Pinkett
Sharif . . . . Vonte Sweet
O-Dog . . . . Larenz Tate
A-Wax . . . . Mc Eiht
Stacy . . . . Ryan Williams
Lew-Loc . . . . Too $hort
Tat Lawson . . . . . Samuel L. Jackson
Mr. Butler . . . . Charles Dutton
Pernell . . . . Glenn Plummer
Detective . . . . Bill Duke

A grim, nihilistic trip to the inner city is what's in store for the stout-hearted who enter into "Menace II Society." Fierce, violent and searing in its observation, the film makes all previous excursions seem like a walk in the park. The unrelenting tale marks a dynamic debut for brothers Allen and Albert Hughes and the film premieres as part of Cannes' Directors Fortnight.

Certain to be the subject of heated debate, it has both ethnic and highbrow appeal and should carve quite a niche for itself in the marketplace. While commercial prospects don't compare to "Boyz N the Hood," "Menace" should readily escape the ghetto of specialized minority films and play well in urban areas.

The story centers on Caine (Tyrin Turner), a black teenager who grew up amid drugs and guns. In the opening moments he witnesses his friend O-Dog (Larenz Tate) murder an Asian shopkeeper and his wife for change and a glancing insult.

Set in contemporary Watts, Caine, O-Dog, Sharif (Vonte Sweet) and Stacy (Ryan Williams) hang together in the brutal environment. They sell drugs, get involved in carjacking and wreak violent retribution on those who cross their path.

Nonetheless, there are glimmers of hope. Caine is urged to join Stacy, whose football scholarship will take him to Kansas. His sometime g.f., Ronnie (Jada Pinkett), encourages him to join her and her son and go to Atlanta. Mr. Butler (Charles Dutton), a teacher and Sharif's father, extols the virtues of education in an unsermonizing manner.

The problem is Caine is numb and crippled from the pain of his upbringing. Like the Korean couple, he will eventually do the wrong thing at the wrong time and wind up a casualty.

The unsparing nature of the portrait is ironically relieved by its seeming authenticity. Working from a script by Tyger Williams, the Hughes brothers eschew most stylistic flourishes yet there is a poetry to the images that is immediate and visceral.

Turner, in the lead, has a natural, unflashy ease that keeps you watching when better judgment suggests you look away. Also particularly noteworthy are Tate as the hair-trigger O-Dog and Pinkett as the woman who's been through it and wants to push on.

— *Leonard Klady*

E PERICOLOSO SPORGERSI
(DON'T LEAN OUT THE WINDOW)
(ROMANIAN-FRENCH)

A Filmex (Romania)/Compagnie des Images (France) co-production. (Intl. sales: Mainstream/Hotel Majestic, Suite 540.) Executive producer, Titi Popescu. Directed, written by Nicolae Caranfil. Camera (color), Christian Comeaga; editor, Victorita Nae; music, Nicolae Caranfil; art direction, Gloria Papura; costume design, Maria Peici; sound, Anusavan Salamanian; Reviewed at Club de l'Etoile screening room, Paris, April 29, 1993. (In Cannes Film Festival, Directors Fortnight.) Running time: 104 MIN.
Horiatu . . . . Marious Stanescu
Cristina . . . . Natalie Bonifay
Dino . . . . Giorgin Alexandru
(Romanian soundtrack)

"E Pericoloso Sporgersi," a deft, "Rashomon"-style tale shot through with resigned humor, is a good bet for fests and arthouses. It pegs first-time helmer-scripter Nicolae Caranfil as a talent to watch.

Fine thesping and good production values garnish the slyly spun interlocking stories of three young people in Romania in the early 1980s. Pic is in three sections — The High School Girl, The Actor and The Soldier — all

of which nicely dovetail in a well-calibrated finish. High schooler Cristina is preoccupied with auditioning for acting school and withholding sex from soldier b.f. Horiatu until he gives her a ring. Horiatu is obsessed with getting laid and getting out of the army.

Cristina finds herself drawn to Dino, a cynical actor who bucks authority and does his best to bed young ladies. Dino is receiving love notes from an anonymous admirer but also receives a menacing phone call that may or may not be connected to his vague plans for defecting.

Frustration runs rampant and irreverence flourishes before the overall design is revealed; package is boosted by a pleasant score.

— *Lisa Nesselson*

SAN FRANCISCO

BELLS FROM THE DEEP: FAITH AND SUPERSTITION IN RUSSIA
(RUSSIAN-GERMAN-DOCU)

A Momentous Events Inc. presentation of a Werner Herzog production in collaboration with Moscow Film and Television. Directed by Herzog. Camera (color), Jorg Schmidt-Reitwein; editor, Rainer Standke;' sound, Vyacheslav Belozerov; assistant director, Rudolph Herzog; mixing engineer, Max Ramler-Rogall. Reviewed at San Francisco Intl. Film Festival, May 5, 1993.) Running time: 57 MIN.

Werner Herzog's latest slice of nonfiction exotica is an amused yet admiring look at facets of spirituality throughout Russia. First in six projected hourlong outsider's views of the nation (other committed helmers include Jean-Luc Godard, Lina Wertmüller and Ken Russell), it should make the festival rounds until the completed series is ready for broadcast sometime next year.

Short feature begins with a view of pilgrims crawling across a barely frozen lake, hoping for a view of the legendary Kitezh — a village believed sunken intact by God to save it from Mongol raiders. Other eccentric practices glimpsed include "transmission of cosmic energy" into bottled water hawked by faith healer Alan Chumack; wailing women under the spell of "sorcerer/exorcist" Yurit Tarassov; and followers of a robed, Christ-like man known as "The Redeemer."

May 17, 1993 (Cont.)

Of more aesthetic than devotional interest are the unearthly sounds of several Siberian "throat singers." An arresting find is ex-movie projectionst Yuri, who now plays a jerry-rigged complex of church tower bells with remarkable dexterity.

Film offers no overview of the vast religious differences in Russian territories; it simply offers up these curious slices of superstition, shamanism, et al., as an end in itself. Helmer's tone of affectionate fascination avoids any whiff of condescension. The results are bizarrely entertaining, sometimes lyrical.

Camerawork is expectedly fine, sound work crystalline. Herzog provides English voiceover translation of interviewees. While lacking the majestic impact of his last subject, the Kuwait oil field requiem "Lessons of Darkness," "Bells From the Deep" is a worthy addition to his log of spectral ethonographic musings.

— *Dennis Harvey*

MY LIFE'S IN TURNAROUND

An Islet presentation of a Third Step production in association with Frontier Prods. Produced by Daniel Einfeld. Co-produced, directed, written by Eric Schaeffer, Daniel Lardner Ward. Camera (color), Peter Hawkins; editor, Susan Graff; music supervisor, Susan Cirillo; original score, Red Hays. Reviewed at San Francisco Intl. Film Festival, April 21, 1993. Running time: **84 MIN.**
Split . . . . Eric Schaeffer
Jason . . . . Daniel Lardner Ward
Sarah Hershfeld . . . . . Lisa Gerstein
Shrink . . . . .John Dore
Amanda . . . . Debra Clein
Rachel . . . . Dana Wheeler Nicholson
With: Phoebe Cates, Casey Siemaszko, Martha Plimpton, Chris America, John Sayles.

Yet another movie about first-timers making a movie, "My Life's in Turnaround" is an obvious calling-card feature that nonetheless has genuine, flippant comic appeal. Affability of creators/stars is enough of a selling point that, given proper selling, modest specialized biz seems assured.

Allegedly "true" narrative has cab driver Split (Eric Schaeffer) and bartender Jason (Daniel Lardner Ward), erstwhile high school buds now struggling in NYC and both in pursuit of the ideal girlfriend, as generally funny/dim/pop-culture-obsessed boomers at the 30-year-old crisis point.

Having met with resounding defeat in the realm of experimental theater, they hit on the genius idea of making a film. Problem is, they have no idea what film to make. In fact, coming up with a concept, script, et al., barely occurs to them. Generously set up for meetings with actual biz types by their long-suffering agent friend Sarah (Lisa Gerstein), the duo expose their ignorance for all (including John Sayles and Casey Siemaszko as sleazy bizzers and Phoebe Cates and Martha Plimpton as themselves) to see.

Their naive zeal doesn't fade, until a personal falling out, followed by a be-true-to-yourselves reconciliation. Film ends with stock full-circle shooting of earlier sequences. Subplots involve stumble-courting of actual perfect girls. Split gets the lawyer who'd gotten him out of scrape, Jason meets an assumedly fellow patient of his psychiatrist.

Schaeffer and Ward's amusing Mutt 'n' Jeff act tends to overshadow their competent input as writer/helmers. Shaeffer has the greater comic savvy, though Ward's spacier presence pays off nicely in hilarious sequences with his consummately passive shrink. Gerstein scores as a reality grounded female counterpoint.

Tech work is OK. Amid good use of several songs, an occasionally drippy synth score seems incongruous. — *Dennis Harvey*

BOKUTO KIDAN
(THE STRANGE STORY OF OYUKI)
(JAPANESE)

A Toho presentation of a Jiro Shindo/Manabu Akashi production, presented by Japan Art Theater Guild, co-distributed by ATG/Toho. Produced by Kindai Eiga Kyonkai. Planned by Shosuke Taga. Directed, written by Kaneto Shindo, from Kafu Nagai's books. Camera (color), Yoshiyuki Miyake; music, Hikaru Hayashi; art director, Shigemori Shigeta; editor, Yukio Watanabe; sound, Susumu Take; lighting, Hiroshi Yamashita. Reviewed at San Francisco Intl. Film Festival, April 21, 1993. Running time: **116 MIN.**
Kafu Nagai . . . . . Masahiko Tsugawa
Oyuki . . . . Yuki Sumida
Ohisa . . . . Yoshiko Miyazaki
Outa . . . . .Tomomi Seo
Kimi Surosawa . . . . Yasuko Yagami

Veteran helmer Kaneto Shindo ("Onibaba") checks in with an erotically angled pic that belies his 80 years. Deftly crafted work might coax international arthouse biz given proper exploitation.

Based on a novel by an honored Japanese novelist, "The Strange Story of Oyuki" incorporates elements from the writer's diary to create a pseudo-biographical narrative. We first meet wealthy author Kafu Nagai (Masahiko Tsugawa), already notorious for writing only of "geishas and prostitutes," at the brink of middle age in the 1920s

Early sequences take Nagai rapidly past various submissive/blackmailing/unreachable mistresses to his chance meeting with the perky Tokyo prostitute Oyuki (Yuki Sumida). Nearly 60 at this point, he's enthralled at the seemingly gauche girl's reawakening of his desire.

This involvement uneasily straddles commerce and romance. When the World War II arrives, disparate expectations — she wants a marital path out, he skittishly protects his bachelor independence — end matters sadly amid historical melodrama.

The dry humor of the film's first half gradually fades into melancholy; "The Strange Story of Oyuki" is ultimately quite touching and it's all managed with consummate acting/tech precision by Shindo. — *Dennis Harvey*

DAS TRIPAS CORACAO
(TWIN FLAMES)
(PORTUGUESE)

A Paulo Brancho presentation of a Televisaeo Portuguesa/La Sept/Madragon Filmes co-production. Produced by Brancho. Directed, written by Joaquim Pinto. Camera (color), Sophie Maintigneux; editor, Claudio Martinez; set design, Ana Vaz Da Silva; sound, Francisco Veloso; costumes, Matilde Matos. Reviewed at the San Francisco Intl. Film Festival, May 2, 1993.) Running time: **65 MIN.**
Armando . . . . Manuel Wiborg
Beatriz . . . . Elsa Batalha
Leonor . . . . Leonor Silveira

"Twin Flames" is helmer Joaquim Pinto's innocently sensual fantasy on the theme of "fire," originally commissioned as part of Portuguese series "The Four Elements." Despite its short length, it has enough odd charm to win further fest exposure.

Twenty-year-old twins Armando and Beatriz share a parentless home and a new vocation — they've just passed exams as apprentice firefighters. But their curious exclusive union is broken by the beautiful older career woman downstairs, who begins a flirtation with Armando.

Unamused, Beatriz immediately begins experiencing a novel symptom of jealousy. She constantly hears nonexistent fires crackling in her ears, "flames" only put out by kisses, preferably from attractive strangers.

Her kissing-bandit forays begin to produce rumors of promiscuity, while tension with her bro continues to ferment. The strange "happy" ending suggests that their hitherto vaguely incestuous relationship may become more literally so.

Tale is told with drolly humorous touches from the actors and the attractive cinematography. While "Twin Flames" ultimately seems a parable without a point, its slender progress is diverting.

— *Dennis Harvey*

SOY CUBA/JA KUBA
(I AM CUBA)
(CUBAN-RUSSIAN-1964-B&W)

A co-production of ICAIC (Miguel Mendoza, Simon Mariajin) and Mosfilm. Directed by Mikhail Kalatozov. Screenplay, Yevgeny Yevtushenko, Enrique Pineda Barnet. Camera (B&W, widescreen), Sergei Urusevsky; editor, Lida Turina; music, Carlos Farinas; design, Evgueni Svidietelev; sound, Vladimir Sharum. Reviewed on vidcassette, San Francisco, April 26, 1993. (In San Francisco Intl. Film Festival.) Running time: **141 MIN.**
With: Luz María Collazo, Jean Bouise, Sergio Corrieri, Jose Gallardo, Raul Garcia, Salvador Wood, Alberto Morgan, Fausto Mirabal, Roberto García York, Maria M. Diez, Silia Rodriguez, Barbara Dominquez, Iris del Monte, Rosendo Lamardriz, voice of Raquel Revuelta.

This massive propaganda "friendship project" between the USSR and Cuba was apparently despised by both sides in 1964 — branded revolutionary kitsch Eastside, and scornfully dubbed "I Am NOT Cuba" in Havana. First unveiled outside the former blocs at last year's Telluride Fest, it's much more than a Cold War curio. If carefully marketed as a newly discovered classic, visually staggering pic could find appreciative arthouse auds.

What director Mikhail Kalatozov ("The Cranes Are Flying") has engineered is an epic hymn to romantic Communism, a living agitprop mural more deliriously choreographed than "1900." It moves from one unrelated narrative to another, linked by a female voiceover portraying the soul of a Mother Cuba despoiled by capitalist pigs, then rescued by its intellectuals and peasants.

First episode shows the titillating decadence of Havana nightlife in a "La Dolce Vita" nightmare. Aged cane worker Pedro is seen setting fire to his fields rather than turn them over to United Fruit Co. thugs. Back in the city, student radicals attempt a cop's assassination, then combat government troops in a harrowing riot. Finally, guerrillas unite with peasants in closing glory-of-comradeship tableaux.

Anti-U.S. sentiments are pronounced, and characters are drawn in broad ogre/martyr strokes nearly devoid of dialogue. "I Am Cuba" is fascinating enough as a time piece, with its odd mix of Sovfilm humorlessness and Latin exoticism (helped by a rhythmically rich score). But its textural brillance would be astounding in any context.

Shot in shimmering deep-focus, high-contrast B&W, the movie is one gorgeous image after another. Some of the endless shots defy belief — especially an incredible early track through a bikini-cluttered party that ends up literally underwater.

Film's Eisensteinian roots are obvious, but it also borrows freely from the New Wave. Sergei Unsevsky's work remains a high water mark for the possibilities of cinematography. Taken as either historical footnote or a mad aesthetic flight, "I Am Cuba" is remarkable. — *Dennis Harvey*

I VOZRASCAETSJA VETER
(AND THE WIND RETURNETH)
(RUSSIAN-COLOR/B&W)

A Filmstudio Zodiak production in association with Benjajev Construction Co., Moscow and USA. Executive producer, Ruvin Sapiro. Directed, written by Michail Kalik. Camera (color/B&W), Jevgenij Potievskij, Vsevolod Suprun; editor, Janina Bogolepova; music, Mikael Taverdiev; sound, Dmitrij Bogolepov; costumes, Tamara Kasparova; makeup, Aleksandr Zurba, Ljudmiola Kuznecova. Reviewed at San Francisco Intl. Film Festival, April 30, 1993. Running time: **133 MIN.**
With: Alla Balter, Boris Brondukov, Vladimir Valov, Emanuil Vitorgan, Stanislav Govoruchin, Oleg Guscin, Sergej Desnickij, Oleg Jefremov.

A former USSR dissident helmer who emigrated to Israel in 1971, Michail Kalik has found his projects variously banned or unfinanced for decades. Unfortunately "And the Wind Returneth" tries to make up for lost time by jamming several films together — it's a dramatized autobio; a semi-docu look at 40 years of Russian history; and an homage to Soviet cinema itself. Cineaste

angle will attract fests, but would-be epic is too disjointed for theatrical play.

Kalik's alter ego, Misha, starts out as the precocious brat of showbiz parents; his early penchant for questioning authority proves prophetic. As years leap by, Misha abruptly lands in a gulag. He's eventually freed to enter the state cinematography school, where his experimental and realist leanings anger the Party censors.

Much more happens here, but the large-scale narrative is just a series of disconnected Big Scenes sandwiched between footage from newsreels, classic Sov flicks and Kalik's own works. The story gaps are amazing — we're never even told why Misha is imprisoned. Hero's Jewish heritage is ignored until it suddenly takes over the film's last part.

Despite much interesting material (especially archival), the clueless pacing soon wears down patience. About six successive false endings provide the last exasperating straw.

While acting and most tech qualities are good, camerawork disappoints at times with excessive zooming and arbitrary black and white/color switches.
— *Dennis Harvey*

CACHAO ... COMO SI RITMO NO HAY DOS
(CACHAO ... LIKE HIS RHYTHM THERE IS NO OTHER)
(DOCU)

A Cineson Prods./Atlantico Films presentation. Produced by Fausto Sanchez, Andy García. Directed by García. Camera (color), Al "Tiko" Lopez; editor, Alan Geik; musical director, Israel Lopez "Cachao"; associate producers, George Hernandez, Joe Drago. Reviewed on projected videotape at San Francisco Intl. Film Festival, April 26, 1993. Running time: **108 MIN.**

A labor of love but not much skill, Havana-born actor Andy García's helming bow "Cachao" pays homage to the legendary Cuban composer-bassist of its title. For all the sensuous dance rhythms heard here, film itself lacks any structural tempo. Visually dull, rarely straying from concert footage, it could easily be cut to an hour's length. While specialty houses may bite, such trimming for telecast could be the likeliest play path.

The 74-year-old Cachao, né Israel Lopez, wrote the original

"Mambo" song. His infectious music borrowed from and affected trends in African, Latin, jazz, classical and pop music from the 1930s onward. But aside from the odd anecdote or archival photo, docu does little to educate crossover auds about the history of Cuban music. Mostly it's just one full-length number after another, intercutting rehearsal and public performances by an all-star band, the music is delightful. Yet the lifeless presentation induces boredom before long.

Sitting in, playing emcee and interviewer, or humbly accepting Cachao's praise for "preserving our roots," García manages to put himself centerstage to a rather superfluous degree.

Sound recording is very good, tech qualities otherwise mediocre. — *Dennis Harvey*

NO DIA DOS MUES ANOS
(ON MY BIRTHDAY)
(PORTUGUESE)

A Paulo Brancho presentation of a Televisaeo Portuguesa/La Sept/Madragon Filmes co-production. Produced by Brancho. Directed, written by Joao Botelho. Camera (color), Dominique La Rigoleur; editor, Manuela Viegas, Jose Nascimento; set design, Ana Vaz Da Silva; costumes, Matilde Matos; sound, Vasco Pimentel. Reviewed at San Francisco Intl. Film Festival, May 2, 1993. Running time: **60 MIN.**

Laura	Jessica Weiss
Father	Joao Lagarto
Miguel	Andre Costa
Joana	Madalena Rodriguez
Grandfather	Artur Ramos
Rafael	Victor Norte
Aviator	Paulo Matos
Aviator's wife	Leonor Silveira

Director Joao Botelho's arresting miniature, originally planned as part of a four-director series of musings on "The Four Elements," mixes irony, mysticism and melodrama with exquisitely stylized detachment. Despite short running time, fests should bite.

Narrative is a series of barely overlapping complications between disparate characters. Miguel, on the verge of his seventh birthday, and his dysfunctional family are at the center. Grandpa is ailing, mom is depressed, sis is undergoing adolescent pique, and father is in prison for homicide (presumably of a romantic rival). Next door, a pilot and his wife battle. Other figures drift through the digressive scenario until a surprisingly reconciliatory close.

Low on dialogue, "On My Birthday" entertains the element of "air" as metaphor for the enormous yet conquerable gaps that separate modern urbanites. Botelho's stark imagery freezes actors in compositions at once expansive and stifled. Yet there's queasy humor as well — inspired by the director's amusement with Brazilian soap operas. The mood is complemented by excellent acting/tech work, and wittily employed excerpts from 20th century composers. — *Dennis Harvey*

ALLAH TANTOU
(GOD'S WILL)
(GUINEAN-FRENCH-DOCU)

An Archibald Films/David Achkar presentation. Produced by Edmee Milot. Directed by Achkar. Camera (color), Anne Mustelier; editor, Anne Guerin Castell; music, Lumumba Marrouf Achkar Jr., François Corea; sound, Frederic Gourment; narrators, David Achkar, Mohamed Camera, Ali A.K. Kaba, Nabi Diakite. Reviewed on vidcassette, San Francisco, April 24, 1993. (In San Francisco Intl. Film Festival.) Running time: **62 MIN.**
With: Michel Montanary.

An earnest but dour effort, "God's Will" is first-time helmer David Achkar's investigation into the demise of his African statesman father. Short running time and a sometimes tricky negotiation between docu/dramatized elements limits its outlook to educational markets and some fests.

Marof Achkar had a brilliant career, first as a 1950s member of the "Ballets Africains," later as Guinea's ambassador to the U.N. and chair of its apartheid commission. Archival photos and footage show him alongside Castro, Malcolm X, even Marlon Brando. But in 1968, governmental power plays led to his seizure by authorities; he was hazily charged with "treason" after months of imprisonment.

Only after a military coup in 1984 was the long-exiled family informed that Achkar had died from "shooting" 13 years earlier. Narration is apparently taken from his letters and other writings. New footage (with actor Michel Montanary) starkly pictures Achkar in his dank cell —starved, tortured, forced to "confess," hanging on to his religious and intellectual faiths.

Mix of elements doesn't always work, as we're sometimes unclear whether info is based on existing materials or conjecture.

May 17, 1993 (Cont.)

The essential human rights message comes through clearly even if the political backdrop could be better articulated.

Tech aspects are competent.

— *Dennis Harvey*

THE SEVENTH COIN
(U.S.-ISRAELI)

An Orbit Entertainment/April Communications production. Produced by Lee Nelson, Omri Maron. Executive producers, James E. Nelson, Shimshon Rafaeli, Dov Strikofksy. Directed by Dror Soref. Screenplay, Soref, Michael Lewis. Camera (Deluxe color), Avi Karpik; editor, Carole Kravetz; music, Misha Segal; production design, Yoram Shayer; sound (Ultra Stereo), Yohai Mosche; casting, Lisa London. Reviewed at WorldFest/Houston, April 19, 1993. Running time: **92 MIN.**
Emil Saber . . . . Peter O'Toole
Salim Zouabi . . . . . Navin Chowdhry
Ronnie Segal . . . . Alexandra Powers
Captain Galil . . . . John Rhys-Davies
Lisa . . . . Ally Walker
Julius Washington . . . Whitman Mayo

Call it "Nancy Drew Goes to Jerusalem," and you won't be far off the mark. "The Seventh Coin" is a mildly diverting **adventure that, minus a few seconds of graphic violence, would be well-suited for the Disney Channel. Theatrical prospects are iffy, but pic could prosper in vid and international TV markets.**

Handsomely produced in Jerusalem, medium-budget indie has an American teenage tourist (Alexandra Powers) drawn into danger when her camera case is swiped by a young Arab pickpocket (Navin Chowdhry). The plucky girl finds the more mischievous than menacing boy and convinces him to return what he stole. Unfortunately, the boy's grandfather has hidden the legendary seventh coin of King Herod the Great in the case and effete British baddie Peter O'Toole, who has the other six, will kill to complete the set.

Most of "Seventh Coin" is an extended chase through the Old City of Jerusalem; a subplot involves an ambitious rookie Israeli cop (Ally Walker) who wants to impress her police chief uncle (John Rhys-Davies) by finding the killer of a rare coin dealer strangled by O'Toole.

Director and co-screenwriter Dror Soref keeps things moving, with periodic pauses for a bud-

ding (and entirely chaste) romance between his attractive protagonists. Powers and Chowdhry are well cast and engaging, which could attract the teen date crowd.

For older aud, the splendidly malevolent hamminess of O'Toole hits the perfect balance of eccentricity and self-parody. Most of the other perfs are pitched at a tongue-in-cheek level; Walker in particular provides spunky comic relief. In this context, the occasional bloody violence seems jarringly inappropriate.

Avi Karpick's cinematography and other tech credits are first-rate. — *Joe Leydon*

NIGHT TRAP
(MARDI GRAS FOR THE DEVIL)

A West Side Studios production. Produced by Jill Silverthorne. Executive producer: David Winter. Directed, written by David A. Prior; Camera (Kodak color), Don E. Faunt LeRoy; editor, Tony Malanowski; music, Christopher Farrell; sound, David Neesley. co-executive producer: Diane Daou; associate producers: Robert Willoughby, Bret McCormick, Sadie Winters. Reviewed at WorldFest/Houston Film Festival, April 25, 1993. MPAA rating: R. Running time: **95 MIN.**
Mike Turner . . . . Robert Davi
Bishop . . . . Michael Ironside
Christine Turner . Lesley-Anne Down
Miss Sadie . . . . . . Margaret Avery
Captain Hodges . . . . . . John Amos
Valerie . . . . Lydie Denier
Detective Williams . . . . . Mike Starr

"Night Trap" is a flat and unconvincing supernatural thriller that will spend little time haunting theaters. Vid prospects are iffy, despite exploitable cast and even more exploitable elements of nudity and mayhem. (Pic reportedly is already set for a July 7 vid release by Prism, under the title "Mardi Gras for the Devil.")

Director-writer David A. Prior fared much better last year with the twisty-turny machinations of his conspiracy melodrama "Center of the Web." Here, once again working with actor Robert Davi, he ploddingly directs a derivative and muddled story about a demonically possessed serial killer who carves up New Orleans women during Mardi Gras.

Michael Ironside is the bad guy, ironically named Bishop, evidently some sort of ancient witchfinder general who has lived and killed for centuries. Davi, cast as an N.O. police detective, is torn between his obsession with finding the killer and his yearning for his ex-wife (Lesley-Anne Down). That yearning, it should be noted, doesn't prevent him

from bedding the beautiful roommate (Lydie Denier) of a victim.

Ironside expertly underplays, in contrast to Davi and Down, and manages a few moments of genuinely creepy menace.

Prior has done a reasonably effective job of stitching together footage shot in and outside New Orleans, so that only a native would notice. Christopher Farrell's overheated music makes some scenes seem even sillier, but Don E. Faunt LeRoy's moody lensing is a definite asset. Other tech credits are competent.

—*Joe Leydon*

THE CONTENDERS

A Royal Cinema Group presentation of a Tobias Meinecke production in co-production with Infafilm (München) and Matima Film Prod. (Montreal). Produced by Kevin J. Foxe, Tobias Meinecke. Executive producer: Michael Hausman. Directed, written by Meinecke. Camera (color), Laszlo Kadar; editor, Michael Gorchow; music, David Yazbek; production designer, Debbie DeVilla; sound, Jac Rubenstein; co-executive producer: Manfred Korytowski. Reviewed at WorldFest/Houston, April 23, 1993. Running time: **90 MIN.**
Anton Menescu . . . . . . Davide Manuli
Ivo Popescu . . . . Tom Gallop
Pedro Perusia . . . . Jon Polito
Anja . . . . Avital Dicker
Also with: Stuart Rudin, Vasek Simke, Andre Belgrader and Jake Dengel.

Painfully sincere but ultimately pointless, Tobias Meinecke's "The Contenders" is a **frail and fuzzy drama about two Romanian immigrants bent on making it big in New York showbiz. Small-budget indie, begun as a Columbia University film school thesis, has no evident commercial prospects.**

Davide Manuli and Tom Gallup are the ambitious young men from Romania. They share a seedy apartment, work as dishwashers in a second-rate restaurant, and cherish golden dreams of success. Manuli wants to be a filmmaker, but his pretensions get in the way. Gallup wants to be an actor, but he sounds hopelessly silly whenever he does an "On the Waterfront" monologue at auditions.

Manuli finally borrows from a loan shark (a juicy supporting perf by Jon Polito) to make his magnum opus. But success — or, the possibility of success — spoils him. He goes back on his promise to cast Gallup in the lead, playing the role himself.

Meanwhile, Gallup falls in love with a sweetly innocent actress (Avital Dicker) who says she

won't do nude scenes. Trouble is, she isn't capable of any kind of in-character intimacy.

Somewhere around the midpoint of "The Contenders," pic loses what little focus it has. Since neither of the Romanians is conspicuously talented, it's hard to tell whether their ambitions are meant to seem pathetic or comical. Manuli and Gallop give straightforward, heartfelt performances, but they can do little to clear up this muddle.

Tech credits are unremarkable.

— *Joe Leydon*

May 24, 1993

SLIVER

A Paramount Pictures release of a Robert Evans production. Executive producers, Howard W. Koch Jr., Joe Eszterhas. Produced by Evans. Directed by Phillip Noyce. Screenplay, Eszterhas, from Ira Levin's novel. Camera (DeLuxe color), Vilmos Zsigmond; editor, Richard Francis-Bruce, William Hoy; music, Howard Shore; production design, Paul Sylbert; art direction, Peter Lansdown Smith; set decoration, Lisa Fischer; costume design, Deborah L. Scott; sound (Dolby), Tom Nelson; co-producer, William J. Macdonald; associate producer, Laura Viederman; assistant director, Christopher T. Gerrity; 2nd-unit director, David Ellis; casting, Amanda Mackey, Cathy Sandrich. Reviewed at Mann National Theater, L.A., May 20, 1993. MPAA Rating: R. Running time: **106 MIN.**

Carly . . . . Sharon Stone
Zeke . . . . William Baldwin
Jack . . . . Tom Berenger
Vida . . . . Polly Walker
Judy . . . . Colleen Camp
Samantha . . . . . . Amanda Foreman
Alex. . . . . Martin Landau
Lt. Victoria Hendrix . . CCH Pounder
Mrs. McEvoy . . . . Nina Foch
Gus Hale . . . . Keene Curtis

After all the hype about unbridled sexuality, ratings board strife and last-minute reshoots, "Sliver" proves all flash and no sizzle — a thriller that simply changes gender on the "Basic Instinct" formula to "did he or didn't he?" Curiosity should generate strong opening numbers, but once word-of-mouth spreads, pic could lose steam amid fast-on-its-heels summer fare.

Working from Ira Levin's novel, writer Joe Eszterhas and director Phillip Noyce have ultimately crafted a cold, inaccessible yarn about murder and voyeurism that's too leisurely about getting where it needs to go and doesn't fully develop what should be its core: a just-divorced woman (Sharon Stone) drawn into a kinky, voyeuristic relationship with mysterious younger man (William Baldwin).

What you get, however, is considerably less, with the third side of the triangle never really filled in and the voyeurism boiling down to little more than a high-tech homage to "Rear Window," with the central character's response to it all decidedly unclear.

Carly (Stone) is a book editor who moves into the new building and catches the eye of both Zeke (Baldwin), a computer whiz, and Jack (Tom Berenger), a burned-out writer who comes on strong right away.

Flattered, Carly is drawn to both of them but ultimately ends up with Zeke, only to discover that he owns the building, has each unit wired with intrusive video cameras and that there's been a series of murders there — including a woman to whom she bears an unerring resemblance and who occupied her unit.

Blame it on the editing and reediting, but even the sex scenes aren't all that steamy, and the movie suffers from some choppy moments and highrise-size lapses in logic.

For Stone fans, the actress shows a lot less here, both literally and figuratively, than she did in her menacing and alluring turn in "Basic Instinct." While she's equal to the task, she makes a far more compelling vamp.

Zeke, meanwhile, emerges as a sort of sexual Batman. Eerie and wealthy, he oversees his building from a lofty perch, occasionally even swooping down to right the wrongs he witnesses. Baldwin brings the requisite creepy-yet-alluring quality to the role, while Berenger proves the odd man out, sleepwalking through an underdeveloped character.

Technically, the narrative suffers from the reshoots and editing, and the murky video images never prove as titillating as they should be in order to convey the sense that Carly might be drawn into this shadowy world. Howard Shore provides a vibrant, memorable score, but when all's said and done that proves about the only facet of "Sliver" that gets under your skin.

— Brian Lowry

HOT SHOTS! PART DEUX

A 20th Century Fox release. Executive producer, Pat Proft. Produced by Bill Badalato. Directed by Jim Abrahams. Screenplay, Abrahams, Proft. Camera (Deluxe color), John R. Leonetti; editor, Malcolm Campbell; music, Basil Poledouris; production design, William A. Elliott; art direction, Greg Papalia; set decoration, Jerie Kelter; costume design, Mary Malin; sound (Dolby), Thomas Causey; associate producers, Greg Norberg, Michael McManus; assistant director, Denis L. Stewart; 2nd-unit director/stunt coordinator, Ernie Orsatti; visual effects supervisor, Erik Henry; casting, Jackie Burch. Reviewed at GCC Galaxy Theater, Hollywood, May 14, 1993. MPAA Rating: PG-13. Running time: **89 MIN.**

Topper Harley . . . . . . Charlie Sheen
Tug Benson . . . . Lloyd Bridges
Ramada Rodham Hayman . . . .
. . . . Valeria Golino
Col. Denton Walters . Richard Crenna
Michelle Rodham Huddleston . . . . .
. . . . Brenda Bakke
Harbinger . . . . Miguel Ferrer
Dexter Hayman . . . Rowan Atkinson
Saddam Hussein . . . . . Jerry Haleva

If the first mission made roughly $50 million domestically, the sky could be the limit for this much better sequel — a clever spoof of "Rambo" and a dozen other movies that employs the usual scattershot "Airplane!" approach but boasts a higher shooting percentage than its forebear.

While the first movie got too caught up in "Top Gun" parody and relied on gags that were bordering on stupid, not just silly, the latest raid uses the "Rambo" and "Missing in Action" series to pull the audience along on a movie-parody funhouse ride. Along the way, director Jim Abrahams and executive producer Pat Proft, who co-wrote the screenplay, find time to throw in clever skewerings of numerous other films, among them "Apocalypse Now," "Casablanca," "Star Wars," "The Wizard of Oz," even "Lady and the Tramp."

Charlie Sheen, with wild locks and a buffed-up physique, returns as Topper Harley, recruited by a former commander (Richard Crenna, a brilliant bit of casting due to his "Rambo" role) and a stunningly limber CIA agent (Brenda Bakke) to try to rescue U.S. servicemen held prisoner after Desert Storm.

Sheen seems more comfortable playing this sort of role, with tongue way in cheek, than he does when playing it straight (as in "Navy SEALs"), while genre regular Lloyd Bridges again demonstrates what a good sport he can be as the daft, dim-witted president, though that's one area where the movie at times tediously overplays its hand.

Valeria Golino also returns as Sheen's former love interest ("because," she explains, "it's the sequel"), though Bakke, with her impossibly short dresses, serves as the primary ice cube-melting surface this time around.

Technically, "Hot Shots!" doesn't cut corners just because it's a parody — a key point, since convincing depictions of the various battles, shootouts and explosions are crucial in making the gags work by coming close to the originals before veering into the absurd.

Still, with a mold this familiar it's impressive to encounter so many belly laughs, and for that "Part Deux" will no doubt be amply rewarded — including, one assumes, a "Part Tres." By the way, if you haven't seen "The Crying Game," don't read the closing credits. In this comic minefield, nothing is sacred.

— Brian Lowry

CLIFFHANGER

A TriStar release of a Mario Kassar presentation of a Carolco/Le Studio Canal Plus/Pioneer production in association with RCS Video. Produced by Alan Marshall, Renny Harlin. Executive producer, Kassar. Directed by Harlin. Screenplay, Michael France, Sylvester Stallone, from France's story, based on John Long's premise. Camera (Technicolor; Panavision widescreen), Alex Thomson; editor, Frank J. Urioste; music, Trevor Jones; production design, John Vallone; art direction, Aurelio Crugnola, Christiaan Wagener; set decoration, Bob Gould; costume design, Ellen Mirojnick; sound (Dolby), Tim Cooney; sound design supervisors, Wylie Stateman, Gregg Baxter; visual effects producer, Pamela Easley; visual effects supervisors, Neil Krepela, John Bruno; special visual effects in 65m, Boss Film Studios; climbing coordinator, Mike Weis; co-producers, Gene Hines, James R. Zatolokin, David Rotman; co-executive producer, Lynwood Spinks; associate producers, Tony Munafo, Jim Davidson; assistant director, Terry Miller; 2nd-unit director/camera, Philip Pfeifer; aerial coordinator, David Paris; aerial camera, Adam Dale; casting, Mindy Marin. Reviewed at Cannes Film Festival (noncompeting), May 20, 1993. MPAA Rating: R. Running time: **112 MIN.**

Gabe Walker . . . . Sylvester Stallone
Qualen . . . . John Lithgow
Hal Tucker . . . . Michael Rooker
Jessie Deighan . . . . . Janine Turner
Travers . . . . Rex Linn
Kristel . . . . Caroline Goodall
Kynette . . . . Leon
Walter Wright . . . . . Paul Winfield
Frank . . . . Ralph Waite
Delmar . . . . Craig Fairbrass
Ryan . . . . . Gregory Scott Cummins
Heldon . . . . Denis Forest
Sarah . . . . Michelle Joyner
Evan . . . . Max Perlich
Brett . . . . Trey Brownell

"Cliffhanger" lives up to its title as a two-hour roller-coaster ride that never stops from first minute to last. A high-octane action suspenser with thrilling vertiginous footage unlike anything seen before in a feature, this is an ideal summer popcorn picture that will keep the audience's collective palms sweaty and give Sylvester Stallone his first major international hit in some time.

TriStar release received its world premiere out of competition at the Cannes fest as part of a benefit evening for the American Foundation for AIDS Research.

May 24, 1993 (Cont.)

With a good guy seeking redemption and bad guys 200 percent evil, the battle lines are as clear as in a cartoon or a World War II movie. But where most rugged he-man films feature a few action sequences scattered throughout, director Renny Harlin keeps the adventure in this reputed $65 million production coming at an astonishing pace.

Each scene may not top the last — in fact, the two most amazing passages occur early on — but despite its simplistic script, "Cliffhanger" has few peers in the sheer quantity of visceral thrills it delivers. Nineminute opening sequence is a heart-stopping stunner. Rocky Mountain Rescue pro Gabe Walker (Stallone) has climbed up a needle peak to help rescue an inexperienced climber, the girlfriend of his partner Hal Tucker (Michael Rooker). But in a grippingly detailed succession of events, the rescue goes awry, and the young woman slips out of Gabe's grasp to her death thousands of feet below.

When Gabe returns to Colorado a year later, he's unable to patch things up with his own g.f., Jessie (Janine Turner), and Hal still blames him for causing the accident. Having disengaged from friends and career in the interim, Gabe isn't sure he's ready to rejoin the living, and gets more than he bargained for by the challenge that is immediately foisted upon him.

In the next gasp-quality sequence, a private Treasury Dept. jet is hijacked by turncoat T-Man Travers (Rex Linn), who slips across a cord to another jet commandeered by the nefarious Qualen (John Lithgow), whose gang of mostly Brit baddies is expecting to collect $100 million from the heist. But the three suitcases containing the cash fall to the ground and the jet (in another amazing scene) makes a crash landing on a mountain, stranding the band of villains in a gathering storm.

Enter Gabe and Hal, who arrive to rescue the group but are promptly captured and forced to lead them through the snowy, icy terrain to the loot. So it's the masters of the mountains versus well-armed and particularly nasty adversaries. Many variations of cat-and-mouse are played, as Gabe escapes and beats the others to some of the money, Jessie choppers in, and the nasties begin quarreling among themselves as they also begin to be picked off one by one.

But the picture has got to scale the peaks one more time for the finale, a literal cliffhanger involving Gabe and Qualen and a helicopter. It's another doozy, but perhaps sensing that the audience has just about had its fill by this time, Harlin keeps it short and wraps things up rapidly.

It was no doubt a lot more fun to think up all these scenes than to shoot them, but on both counts the filmmakers have done their jobs admirably. Given the basic black-and-white story, plenty of imagination has gone into the conception of the individual interludes. Harlin's headlong approach and breathless pacing maintain continual excitement, but what really puts this in a class of its own is the verisimilitude of the action. Despite credits to stunt and climbing doubles and the occasional process shot, there is no doubt that Stallone and other actors were really up on the sides of mountains and hanging precariously over gorges and ravines.

Looking great, Stallone is clearly into this one, and it pays off in one of his most rugged screen appearances. Rooker, Turner and Ralph Waite are fine as the other good guys, while the baddies — Lithgow, in what could be called the Alan Rickman role, Linn, Leon, Craig Fairbrass, Caroline Goodall, Denis Forest and Gregory Scott Cummins — all try to outdo each other in defining pure evil.

Although set in Colorado and partly filmed in Durango, most of the picture was lensed in Italy, both near Cortina D'Ampezzo in the Alps and in Rome. Locations are spectacular, and tech contributions throughout are aces, with Alex Thomson's lensing, Frank J. Urioste's editing and Trevor Jones' score all charging things up along with the virtuoso visual effects and stunt work.

— *Todd McCarthy*

NAKED
(BRITISH)

A First Independent (U.K.) release of a Film Four Intl. presentation, in association with British Screen, of a Thin Man production. Produced by Simon Channing-Williams. Directed, written by Mike Leigh. Camera (Agfacolor; Metrocolor prints), Dick Pope; editor, Jon Gregory; music, Andrew Dickson; production design, Alison Chitty; art direction, Eve Stewart; costume design, Lindy Hemming; sound (Dolby), Ken Weston; assistant director, Rupert Ryle-Hodges. Reviewed at Cannes Film Festival (competing), May 14, 1993. Running time: **131 MIN.**

Johnny . . . . David Thewlis
Louise . . . . Lesley Sharp
Sophie . . . . Katrin Cartlidge
Jeremy . . . . Greg Cruttwell
Sandra . . . . Claire Skinner
Brian . . . . Peter Wight
Archie . . . . Ewen Bremner
Maggie . . . . Susan Vidler
Woman in window . Deborah MacLaren
Cafe girl . . . . Gina McKee

A Stygian comedy on '90s London social angst, Mike Leigh's "Naked" will come as a major surprise to those reared on lighter fare like "Life Is Sweet" and "High Hopes." Shot through with sudden, psychotic mood shifts, from comedy to violence to, finally, a strangely moving love story, pic could build to solid specialized biz among urban auds given a critical fair wind.

Though recognizably a Leigh movie, with its gallery of Brit eccentrics, "Naked" dwarfs everything the director has yet done, with a resonant, beautifully modulated script that builds to a bleak but basically optimistic portrait of post-'80s Blighty. Leigh's gallery of haves and have-nots, of emotional anorexics and exploited deadbeats, carries a strong political charge, but also plays as a black, offbeat comedy with a romantic undertow.

Center of Leigh's script — as with prior movies, the result of several months of improvisation and rehearsal — is an unemployed philosopher-bum, Johnny (David Thewlis), who's fled south from Manchester and initially stays with former g.f. Louise (Lesley Sharp). After bedding her loopy flatmate, punkette Sophie (Katrin Cartlidge), he suddenly ups and leaves on a weird nocturnal odyssey on the streets on London.

Pic's middle section is a series of encounters with various oddballs dos, as Johnny motormouths his way through dialogues of almost Socratic proportions. First to cross his path are a feuding, foul-mouthed Scots couple (Ewen Bremner, Susan Vidler); next comes a sesh with an equally philosophical night janitor (Peter Wight); and finally a shy waitress in a grungy diner (Gina McKee), who abruptly boots him out after inviting him home.

Leigh saves the strongest stuff for the last leg, as Johnny, beaten up in the street, returns to Louise and Sophie's apartment, where their sicko yuppie landlord has pitched his tent and made a sex slave of Sophie.

Despite the sudden changes of mood and atmosphere of incipient violence (signaled in a raw, handheld opening of violent date-rape), "Naked" plays lighter than it reads, thanks to wonderful straight-faced thesping of Leigh's dry, humor-filled script.

Anchored by a confident tour de force from Thewlis ("Life Is Sweet"), perfs by the hand-chosen cast mesh splendidly, with Cartlidge (recalling the Jane Horrocks character in "Life") delivering a wonderful array of one-liners, sharp filling out a tough straight role as Thewlis' Manchester g.f. and McKee strong as the emotionally starved waitress. On the male side, Cruttwell is suitably fearsome as the arrogant yuppie, and Wight well cast as the janitor.

Pic would benefit from 10 to 15 minutes tightening, especially in its slacker central section. Otherwise, things keep moving smartly along, with a dramatic, propulsive score by Andrew Dickinson and some fine nocturnal lensing by Dick Pope of London's shabbier quarters.

Dialogue is four-letter stuff all the way, and some regional accents could prove tough going for North American auds.

— *Derek Elley*

KING OF THE HILL

A Gramercy release of a Wildwood/Bona Fide production. Produced by Albert Berger, Barbara Maltby, Ron Yerxa. Executive producer, John Hardy. Directed, written by Steven Soderbergh, based on A.E. Hotchner's memoir. Camera (Deluxe color; Filmhouse prints; Panavision widescreen), Elliot Davis; editor, Soderbergh; music, Cliff Martinez; production design, Gary Frutkoff; art direction, Bill Rea; set design, Erik Olson; costume design, Susan Lyall; sound (Dolby), Larry Blake; assistant director, Gregory Jacobs; casting, Deborah Aquila. Reviewed at the Aidakoff screening room, Beverly Hills, May 6, 1993. (In Cannes Film Festival, competing.) MPAA Rating: PG-13. Running time: **102 MIN.**

Aaron Kurlander . . . . Jesse Bradford
Mr. Kurlander . . . . . Jeroen Krabbé
Mrs. Kurlander . . . . . Lisa Eichhorn
Miss Mathey . . . . Karen Allen
Mr. Mungo . . . . Spalding Gray
Lydia . . . . Elizabeth McGovern
Ben . . . . Joseph Chrest
Lester . . . . Adrien Brody
Sullivan . . . . Cameron Boyd
Billy Thompson . . . . . Chris Samples
Christina Sebastian . . Katherine Heigl
Ella . . . . Amber Benson
Patrolman Burns . . . John McConnell
Mr. Desot . . . . Ron Vawter
Mr. Sandoz . . . . John Durbin
Arletta . . . . Lauryn Hill
Front Desk Clerk . . . . David Jensen

"King of the Hill" has all the rich satisfactions of a fine novel. A marvelous comeback for writer-director Steven Soderbergh after his problematic sophomore effort, "Kafka," this densely detailed, superbly acted evocation of a resourceful boy's life during the depths of the Depression animates another time and place, while quietly underlining the parallels to contemporary problems. Film's qualities will please specialized, sophisticated viewers more than the general public, but careful marketing could generate an audience for it.

It only takes Soderbergh a few minutes to establish a feeling of total authority over his material in deftly etched scenes that illuminate the imaginative world of his young protagonist and define the desperate straits of his characters.

Drawing upon A.E. Hotchner's 1972 book about his St. Louis childhood, Soderbergh creates a vibrant picture of the Middle American social fabric while maintaining sharp focus on the changing fortunes of 12-year-old Aaron Kurlander (Jesse Bradford), and his disintegrating family.

Living in the seedy Empire Hotel in a working-class section, the Kurlanders find themselves financially forced to send away the younger son, Sullivan (Cameron Boyd), to live with a relative; consumptive mom (Lisa Eichhorn) needs a sanatorium cure.

While Mr. Kurlander (Jeroen Krabbé) scrapes by, awaiting word of a good job, Aaron excels at school and becomes involved with some of the down-and-outers at the hotel. Ella (Amber Benson) is a nervous, bespectacled, epileptic girl. Mr. Mungo (Spalding Gray) is a formerly wealthy alcoholic who eases his pain with prostie Lydia (Elizabeth McGovern). The grungy bellboy (Joseph Chrest) keeps an eagle eye on everyone.

At film's midpoint, Mr. Kurlander gets a job as a traveling salesman, leaving Aaron alone at the Empire without financial resources, which winning the top award for achievement at school does nothing to alleviate.

Slowly, however, the splintered family begins pulling back together, giving the story an upbeat ending tempered by the main portrait of life's severity.

Soderbergh's approach is shot through with an appreciation for both school and street smarts, and an unsentimental nostalgia for a time when there was a belief anything was possible in America. Down to the smallest roles, all the characters are indelibly drawn, a brilliant gallery of types from all social levels.

But despite all its excellences, the film wouldn't work nearly so well without Jesse Bradford. His Aaron is an exemplar of the limitless potential that can exist in children before they are damaged, limited or brought down. As a boy increasingly forced to apply his creativity to his life rather than his imaginative world, Bradford simply gives one of the best pre-teen perfs in memory.

Entire ensemble cast is first-rate. Along with those already mentioned, Adrien Brody is notable as a young Jewish fellow who helps Aaron through some of his more difficult jams.

St. Louis, with its brick streets, vast turn-of-the-century mansions and remnants of industrial-revolution America, is splendidly used to evoke a particular aspect of the nation's history. Working on a relatively modest budget for such an ambitious period piece, production designer Gary Frutkoff, costume designer Susan Lyall and lenser Elliot Davis have made outstanding contributions. Soderbergh himself edited adroitly and tightly, while Cliff Martinez's score is lively. — *Todd McCarthy*

THE BABY OF MÂCON
(DUTCH-FRENCH)

An Allarts production with UGC, in association with Cine Electra, Channel 4 (U.K.)/Filmstiftung NRW (Germany)/ La Sept Cinéma (France). (Intl. sales: Cine Electra, London.) Produced by Kees Kasander. Executive producer, Denis Wigman. Directed, written by Peter Greenaway. Camera (Panavision widescreen, Technicolor), Sachy Vierny; editor, Chris Wyatt; production design, Ben Van Os, Jan Roelfs; costume design, Dien Van Straalen; sound (Dolby), Garth Marshall; co-producer, Yves Marmion; assistant director, Jeroen Planting. Reviewed at Cannes Film Festival (non-competing), May 17, 1993. Running time: **122 MIN.**

The Daughter	Julia Ormond
The Bishop's Son	Ralph Fiennes
The Bishop	Philip Stone
Cosimo Medici	Jonathan Lacey
The Father Confessor	Don Henderson
The Major Domo	Jeff Nuttall
Midwives	Jessica Stevenson, Kathryn Hunter, Gabrielle Reidy
Wet Nurse	Anna Nieland
Cantor	Frank Egerton
Famine	Graham Valentine
(English soundtrack)

Peter Greenaway's "The Baby of Mâcon" is all fluff and no filling. Visually sumptuous and laden with religious refs and Brechtian devices, this elaborate but overlong film-of-a-play about the birth of a 17th-century miracle child and his short-lived period of grace plays like a tired rerun of the director's previous extravaganzas. "Mâcon" probably won't bring home the b.o. bacon.

Pic's sexual and gross-out elements — similar to "Prospero's Books" and "The Cook, The Thief, His Wife and Her Lover" — could attract frisky early biz, but this one doesn't look like developing the longer arthouse legs of earlier Greenaway items.

Entire film takes place in a single giant set that includes audience and performers, gathered for an elaborate theatrical masque is held before local dignitaries to celebrate fertility — the community is plagued by barrenness, seen as God's punishment for letting the local cathedral fall into disrepair.

Opening act features a hideously bloated pregnant woman delivering a beautiful boy, immediately dubbed a miracle-child after poking through the afterbirth. The sprig quickly becomes an icon for the region's barren mothers, and one of its sisters (Julia Ormond) uses the window of opportunity to claim to be its rightful mother. The fact she's still a virgin (verified by numerous on-stage exams) doesn't cramp her style: the Virgin Mary is a strong enough precedent.

Subsequent acts chart the rise and fall of the young woman and the baby. After imprisoning her mother and paying off her father, she sets about seducing the son (Ralph Fiennes) of the bishop (Philip Stone) in a gut-splattered sexual/religious travesty of Mary and Joseph in the stable, complete with manger.

However, peeved at the way the Church is prospering from selling off the baby's liquids as fertility aids, the woman suffocates the kid and claims religious immunity under local laws that virgins can't be executed. Solution of the bishop, in cahoots with teenage dignitary Cosimo (Jonathan Lacey), is to sentence her to being raped 217 times.

Greenaway, whose script till now has played with Brechtian ideas of actors confusing their roles with real life, springs his most audacious twist, with the phalanx of priapic male thespians actually raping the woman/actress, who dies. The church authorities carve up the baby's corpse for more religious icons.

As in previous Greenaway costumers, the movie is a visual feast, with the extra fillip of regular lenser Sacha Vierny giving a candlelit look to his richly textured photography, resplendent in widescreen. Where Greenaway uncharacteristically falls down is in the script: While his previous movies have been a cornucopia of challenging ideas and intellectual *jeux*, this one quickly starts going round in circles once the board has been laid out.

Helmer himself says the movie is about child exploitation, modern and historical. The pic certainly lays on its message with a trowel — and looks set to prove deeply offensive to Catholic groups — but Greenaway fails to come up with enough variation or fresh ideas to sustain two hours. Still, as a master of the ornate Greenaway is firing on all cylinders. Production design by Holland's Ben Van Os and Jan Roelfs is eye-boggling; ditto Dien Van Stralen's costuming.

Performances are lusty throughout, with legit actress Ormond generally holding her own as the ambitious daughter, the experienced Stone well cast as the ruthless bishop and Fiennes (Heathcliffe in the recent remake of "Wuthering Heights") in for a bit as his son. Nudity is frank but not excessive in the circumstances; blood and offal content is lighter than in "The Cook, The Thief." — *Derek Elley*

IN WEITER FERNE, SO NAH!
(FARAWAY, SO CLOSE!)
(GERMAN-B&W-COLOR)

A Sony Pictures Classics (U.S.) release of a Road Movies/Tobis Filmkunst presentation. Produced, directed by Wim Wenders. Executive producer, Ulrich Felsberg. Screenplay, Wenders, Ulrich Zieger, Richard Reitinger, dialogue by Zieger. Camera (B&W/color), Jurgen Jurges; editor, Peter Przygodda; music, Laurent Petitgand; production design, Albrecht Konrad; costume design, Esther Walz; line producer, Michael Schwarz. Reviewed at Cannes Film Festival (competing), May 17, 1993. Running time: **164 MIN.**

Cassiel	Otto Sander
Peter Falk	Himself
Tony Baker	Horst Buchholz
Raphaela	Nastassja Kinski
Konrad	Heinz Ruhmann
Damiel	Bruno Ganz
Marion	Solveig Dommartin
Phillip Winter	Rudiger Vogler
Lou Reed	Himself
Emit Flesti	Willem Dafoe
Special Guest	Mikhail Gorbachev

Wim Wenders the amateur philosopher gets the better of Wim Wenders the filmmaker in the awkwardly titled "Faraway, So Close!," a meandering, erratic follow-up to his beguilingly poetic "Wings of Desire." Overlong and ultra-slow meditation on the sad state of things will tax the patience of even dedicated Wenders fans, presenting domestic distrib Sony Pictures Classics with a big marketing challenge.

Beginning with remarks by Mikhail Gorbachev on the need for harmony in the world, Wenders fitfully builds toward his themes of trying to make something good out of life and saving the world from the disunified impulses that increasingly guide people's behavior. But pic never stays on track for more than a few moments, and the ideas and dramatics remain hazy and unsatisfactorily developed.

In "Wings," the angel Damiel (Bruno Ganz) turned human after falling in love with trapeze artist Marion (Solveig Dommartin), leaving his companion Cassiel (Otto Sander) alone atop the Angel of Victory tower in Berlin. That's where Cassiel is first seen here, surveying a city that has changed in unimaginable ways in the intervening six years, not necessarily for the better.

As his angelic companion Raphaela (Nastassja Kinski) stands by passively, Cassiel gives in to his impulse to join the ranks of humanity when he saves a little girl who falls from a balcony.

Tedious digressions abound, in the form of the reflections of an old man (Heinz Ruhmann) whose position as a chauffeur has afforded him a certain view of the century's history; the strange, out-of-nowhere appearances of the bluntly philosophical Emit Flesti (Willem Dafoe); deadpan musical performances by Lou Reed; and even the return of Peter Falk, who was more effectively used the first time.

Access to the former East Berlin has given Wenders a host of monumental new locations to work with, but despite the constant movement of Jurgen Jurges' camera and the repeated switching from black and white to color (with monochrome generally reflective of the angelic state), pic has a static, arid quality. Further cutting would lighten the load for audiences but would be unlikely to clarify or goose up the film much.

Many shots are individually striking, but they generally lack the resonance and quirky sense of invention of Wenders' best work. Speaking of the world at large, Dafoe at one point announces, "Now everything's out of balance," which is unfortunately true of the film as well.
— *Todd McCarthy*

BAWANG BIE JI
(FAREWELL TO MY CONCUBINE)
(HONG KONG)

A Miramax release of a Tomson (H.K.) Films Co. production, in association with China Film Coproduction Corp. and Beijing Film Studio. (Intl. sales: Shu Kei's Creative Workshop, Hong Kong.) Produced by Hsu Feng. Executive producers, Hsu Bin, Jade Hsu. Directed by Chen Kaige. Screenplay, Lilian Lee, Lu Wei, from Lee's novel. Camera (color), Gu Changwei; editor, Pei Xiaonan; music, Zhao Jiping; production design, Chen Huaikai; art direction, Yang Yuhe, Yang Zhanjia; costume design, Chen Changmin; sound (Dolby), Tao Jing, Hu He; Peking Opera director, Shi Yansheng; Peking Opera music designer, Tang Jirong; makeup, Fan Qingshan, Xu Guangrui; associate producer, Donald Ranvaud; assistant director, Zhang Jinzhan. Reviewed at Cannes Film Festival (competing), May 18, 1993. Running time: **170 MIN.**

Cheng Dieyi ("Douzi") .	Leslie Cheung
Duan Xiaolou ("Shitou") .	Zhang Fengyi
Juxian	Gong Li
Guan Jifa	Lu Qi
Na Kun	Ying Da
Master Yuan	Ge You
Laizi	Li Dan
Red Guard	David Wu

Also with: Ma Mingwei, Yin Zhi, Fei Yang, Zhao Hailong, Jiang Wenli, Zhi Yitong, Li Chun, Lei Han, Tong Di.
(Mandarin soundtrack)

A seductively lensed but emotionally uninvolving drama about two male Peking Opera stars and the ex-prostie who comes between them, Chen Kaige's fourth feature, "Farewell to My Concubine," reps a stylistic U-turn compared with his earlier abstract parables like "Life on a String" and "Yellow Earth." Pic's easily digestible narrative, production values and name Mainland Chinese actress Gong Li ("The Story of Qiu Ju") should prove strong marketing cards, but Miramax will need good word-of-mouth and critical bouquets to lure more general clients to the near-three-hour item.

Much-ballyhooed production is a high-profile blending of money and talent from the three Chinese territories. Though entirely shot in Beijing, the $4 million-plus coin came entirely from the Hong Kong affil of Taiwan-based Tomson Films, run by former actress Hsu Feng ("A Touch of Zen"), with the Mainland side simply providing facilities. Cast blends Mainland stars with former Hong Kong pop singer Leslie Cheung — to the point that pic has been passed for exhibition in China but banned by Taiwan because of majority of Mainland actors. Hong Kong b.o. earlier this year was a solid but unspectacular $HK10 million.

Long-arc-ed storyline spans 50 years of modern Chinese history, from the warlord period of the '20s, through Japanese occupation during WWII, to Communist rule and the turmoil of the Cultural Revolution. Against this tumultuous fresco unwinds an essentially simple tale of love and betrayal among a handful of characters involved in the traditional Peking Opera.

From the earliest scenes, with the young Douzi's mother (Jiang Wenli) battling her way through Peking's chaotic streets to deposit her son (Ma Mingwei, later Yin Zhi as an adolescent and Leslie Cheung as the adult female-roles star) at the Peking Opera training school, Chen's helming is consciously operatic in style.

With frequent use of Steadicam, and abetted by lenser Gu Changwei's almost Storaro-like play with diffused light, there's a stagy, unreal quality that mirrors the tight, enclosed universe in which the homosexual Douzi's friendship and rift with fellow student and eventual male-roles star Shitou (Zhang Fengyi, Fei Yang as a child, Zhao Hailong as a teen) over his marriage to Juxian (Gong Li) is played out.

Combined with the relatively small number of leading characters (especially given the story's scope), Chen's hermetically sealed world plays every aspect of production and performance in the same key. There's little attempt to dig deep into the political and historical background.

Somewhere along the line, however, a sense of balance got lost. Though fascinating in its detail, the kids' training is too long in relation to the time expended on the more important adult relationships later. And though the pic's emotional center is Douzi's sense of betrayal at being cut out of Shitou's affections when he marries Juxian, the script skirts around any real examination of Douzi's sexual identity.

As the "male" half of the duo, Mainland actor Zhang anchors the movie in a powerful, shaded performance. Cheung, though well cast as the tragic gay, does his best in an underwritten part. Gong, strong in several scenes, such as a well-written confrontation with Douzi's lover Master Yuan (Ge You), is also shackled by a script that's too stop/go.

Supporting roles, especially a creepy perf by talented Mainland actor Ge, are solid. Combined effect, however, is lopsided, only Zhang really making a strong emotional connection.

Tech credits are tip-top, with every dollar up on the screen. Makeup, costuming and production design are immensely detailed, and though the plethora of opera scenes may tax some general viewers' patience, the filmers have made a major effort to make their content clear for Western auds. — *Derek Elley*

MAGNIFICAT
(ITALIAN)

A Duea Film production, in association with Istituto Luce-Italnoleggio Cinematografico/Penta Film/Union P.N. (Intl. sales: Cine Electra, London.) Produced by Antonio Avati. Directed, written by Pupi Avati. Camera (Technovision, Eastmancolor), Cesare Bastelli; editor, Amedeo Salfa; music, Riz Ortolani; art direction, Giuseppe Pirrotta; costume design, Sissi Parravicini; sound, Raffaele De Luca; assistant director, Gianni Amadei. Reviewed at Cannes Film Festival (competing), May 16, 1993. Running time: **96 MIN.**

Lord of Malfole	Luigi Diberti
Folco	Arnaldo Ninchi
Margherita . . .	Eleonora Alessandrelli
Baino	Massimo Bellinzoni
Roza	Dalia Lahav
Venturina	Lorella Morlotti
Margherita's father	Massimo Sarchielli
Lord of Campodose .	Brizio Montinaro
Agateo	Marcello Cesena
Abbess	Consuelo Ferrara
Lord of Manfole	Andrea Scorzoni
Bagnaro	David Celli

A collection of low-key vignettes in a medieval Italian town during Passion Week, "Magnificat" should please faithful acolytes of helmer Pupi Avati's distanced style but won't raise many hallelujahs beyond arty *salles.*

Set in Tuscany, A.D. 926, picture zeroes in, after a discursive start, on a group trekking to Malfole, site of an abbey with links to the Virgin Mary. Intertwining of various stories builds to a patchwork portrait of 10th-century faith and manners.

The motley collection of pilgrims includes a heavily pregnant royal concubine (Dalia Lahav), hoping to produce a male heir to the throne; a local lord (Luigi Diberti), who's had premonitions of death and decides to roll over on his late wife's burial spot; a 14-year-old girl (Eleonora Alessandrelli) being handed over to a monastery by her family; and the regional executioner and his apprentice (Arnaldo Ninchi, Massimo Sarchielli), for whom it's business as usual.

In its mixture of ritualism and genuine locations, pic partly recalls the early Pasolini — without that director's political sub-

May 24, 1993 (Cont.)

texts. Avati focuses on faces and the routine grind of everyday life; dialogue, when it comes, is mostly built out of procedure, incantations, religioso jargon, etc.

The only types who get a real shot at building personalities are the pretty teenage girl, mutely accepting the monastic life, and the executioners, who share pleasantries with a wife-murderer en route to hacking him up. Visuals in the latter sequence are discreet but powerful.

Though nominally concerned with the characters' search for faith, the picture can also be read more cynically in agnostic terms. God dumps pretty frequently on these Italian peasants.

Despite measured pacing and a tendency not to explain things for general viewers, pic has a calm, serene quality (plus sly humor in places) that staves off boredom. It's always a pleasure to watch, thanks to Cesare Bastelli's attractive lensing of the crumbling, sun-baked Tuscan locations, and editing that doesn't linger needlessly. Costume design is a further plus, especially given the movie's obviously limited budget. — *Derek Elley*

THE WRONG MAN

A Polygram Filmed Entertainment presentation of a Viacom Pictures presentation of a Beattie/Chesser production. (Intl. sales: Manifesto.) Produced by Alan Beattie, Chris Chesser. Executive producer, Frederick Schneier. Directed by Jim McBride. Screenplay, Michael Thoma, from Roy Carlson's story. Camera (CFI color), Affonso Beato; editor, Lisa Churgin; music, Los Lobos; production design, Jeannine Oppewall; art direction, Hector Romero; costume design, Tracy Tynan, Rudy Dillon; co-producer, Carlson; line producer, Ted Swanson; associate producer, Anna Roth; assistant directors, Jack Baran, Miguel Lima. Reviewed at Cannes Film Festival (Un Certain Regard section), May 16, 1993. Running time: **110 MIN.**
Missy Mills . . . . . Rosanna Arquette
Alex Walker . . . . . . Kevin Anderson
Phillip Mills . . . . John Lithgow
Captain Diaz . . . . . Jorge Cervera Jr.
Detective Ortega . Ernesto Laguardia
Felix Crawley . . . . . Robert Harper

A sultry sex-suspenser about gringos on the run south of the border, "The Wrong Man" teeters back and forth over the line between good, dirty, genre fun and outright silliness. Although there is too much of the latter, enough remains in the way of offbeat scenes, potent atmosphere and overt sexuality to keep red-blooded viewers interested. Hotsy Viacom entry will be premiered domestically on Show-

time in the fall, and should be a decent bet for theatrical sales offshore.

Story is as familiar as any in the film noir genre, with elements of "The Postman Always Rings Twice" and "The Big Steal," among many others.

A blue-eyed Yank in a white suit (Kevin Anderson) is in the wrong place at the wrong time, standing in a grubby room with a gun in his hand over a dead man who robbed him of his wallet — which gives the pursuing police positive I.D. of their suspect.

Innocent of any crime but looking guilty as hell, Anderson dives into an old American convertible belonging to Rosanna Arquette and older hubby John Lithgow. The couple agree to let the stranger hitch a ride, and at their first rest stop, Arquette immediately gets their guest heated up by frolicking topless in the surf.

With the youngsters mooning and drooling over each other from the outset, it's only a matter of time until they ignite, but the way they combust — publicly and almost oblivious to Lithgow — reps one of the pic's most interesting wrinkles as they endlessly heat each other up to near-boiling, but always stop short of consummation.

Through all this, Lithgow displays a curious variety of reactions, from jealous rage to aged resignation and manly camaraderie with his youthful rival. And it is one of the film's jokes that, when the passionate duo finally do get it on, coupling happens off camera.

Michael Thoma's script, from a story by Roy Carlson, is low on believability and high on goofy contrivance; there's so little realistically at stake that no tension is generated. The Mexican cops, while not derided in an old-fashioned way, are destined not to catch up with their prey until the end, and overlong pic often is lax when it should have more snap.

These deficiencies make it incumbent upon director Jim McBride to goose up matters however he can, which he does through a heavy dose of colorfully seedy atmosphere.

Much like his "The Big Easy," also shot by Affonso Beato, "The Wrong Man" seethes with languid humidity, sexy sweat and the grime of crime.

Even more notably, however, McBride has made Rosanna Arquette the inarguable centerpiece of the picture. Watching her voluptuous bimbo, it is impossible not to regard the film, as much as

anything else, as a documentary tribute to the actress' breasts.

Lithgow gives a memorable reading of a volatile man with a seismically shifting sense of self, while Anderson could perhaps have brought more energy to his romantically burned expatriate who almost passively sets off the sexual *sturm und drang*.

In the end, pic stands as a modest exercise in style that will find favor among aficionados of the form. — *Todd McCarthy*

MADADAYO
(NOT YET)
(JAPANESE)

A Daiei Co. Ltd./Dentsu Inc./Kurosawa Prods. co-production. (Intl. sales: Daiei Co. Ltd.) Directed, written by Akira Kurosawa. Camera (color), Takao Saito, Masaharu Ueda; editor, Kurosawa; music, Shin'ichiro Ikebe; production design, Yoshiro Muraki. Reviewed at Cannes Film Festival (noncompeting), May 14, 1993. Running time: **134 MIN.**
Professor Hyakken Uehida . . . .
. . . . Tatsuo Matsumura
Professor's Wife . . . . Kyoko Kagawa
Takayama . . . . Hisashi Igawa
Amaki . . . . George Tokoro
Kiriyama . . . . Masayuki Yui
Sawamura . . . . Akira Terao

At age 83, Japan's Akira Kurosawa, who directed his first film 50 years ago, has come up with a serene, leisurely item about old age. Relatively talky pic will entrance Kurosawa aficionados the world over, but may have difficulty finding its niche in the arthouse market.

Evidently a very personal picture, it is tempting to see this, at least to some degree, as an autobiographical reflection, though the events in the film begin in 1943, the year Kurosawa directed his first film, "Judo Saga." His protagonist is a university professor who, during the war, decides to drop out of academia and concentrate on his writing.

The film is divided into unidentified chapters, separated by long fades to black. Early on, the professor loses his home in a wartime bombing raid; he and his wife move into pitifully small premises. After the war, a new home is built on the site.

Very little happens in "Not Yet" (the title is a reference to the professor's regular assertions to Death that he's "not yet" ready). There are two lengthy scenes of birthday celebrations, the first, when the old man is 60, during the American post-war occupation, and the second 17

years later in more relaxed and prosperous times.

The first is a gathering for men only in a functional beer-hall, where the prof's former students reminisce about him and sing songs; the second is in a smart restaurant with women and children present, and during this function the old man collapses and has to be helped away from the festivities.

Longest segment in the film involves the prof's distress when a stray cat he'd adopted goes missing. It may seem indulgent to spend almost an hour on the futile search for a missing feline, but somehow it works in the context of the film, and comes across, as does the pic as a whole, as touching and charming.

Throughout his long retirement, the professor is regularly visited by former students who are always ready and willing to help him whenever he needs them. Their loyalty, and the devotion of his wife (who usually stays discreetly in the background), are the sources of his support over the years.

Tatsuo Matsumura gives a dignified, sometimes quite comic, performance as the old man, and is given strong support.

Production values are on the simple side, and the culminating vision of death is a tad naive. But the film is never boring, thanks to the director's affection for his characters and the innate humanity he brings to the material. — *David Stratton*

DOUBA-DOUBA
(RUSSIAN)

A Pan Europeenne (France) release of an Ask/Intercross production. Directed by Alexandre Khvan. Screenplay, Piotr Loutsik, Alexei Samoriadov. Camera (color), Anatoly Soussekov; editor, Albina Antipenko; art direction, Grigori Chirokov. Reviewed at Cannes Film Festival (competing), May 17, 1993. Running time: **130 MIN.**
Andrei . . . . Oleg Menchikov
Tania . . . . Angela Belianskaya
Viktor . . . . Grigori Konstantinopolski
Igor . . . . Alexandre Tioutine
Kolia . . . . Alexandre Negreba
Also with: Vladimir Golovine, Viktor Terelia, Ramil Sabitov, Roman Grekov, Gyorgy Taratorkine.

Alexandre Khvan's feature debut "Douba-Douba" lies uneasily between a Russian gangster tale and a collage of undigested moods. The story of a student filmmaker who turns to crime to save his ex-girlfriend is often incomprehensible, earmarking the all-

Russian production for fest play and a few specialty outings.

Andrei (brooding Oleg Menchikov), the director, struggles to get his former g.f. (pouting Angela Belianskaya) out of jail. To get money, he begins mugging men in public toilets then moves on to armed robbery and to swiping stashes of drug money from other gangsters. When at last he has enough dough to smuggle the girl out of the country to New York, he discovers she detests him, and all his crimes were meaningless.

Viewers will find following the plot a challenge. Not only are scenes ill-connected but Khvan offers few clear signs about how to interpret the characters, whose personalities shift like quicksand. Belianskaya goes from looking shell-shocked to having outbursts of hysteria; instead of being grateful to Andrei, she's spacy enough to get herself arrested again.

Virtually the only thing holding pic together is top Russian stage star Menchikov as the scholar-turned-criminal. He has an unsettling intensity able to overshadow the banality of his Mr. Cool character.

Khvan reveals a lot of unchained talent that could be put to more disciplined use. He's strong at depicting the brutality of Andrei's hometown, somewhere along the banks of the melancholy Volga River.

Less successful is the complicated editing, which includes incomprehensible flash-forwards and other examples of first-film bravado. Cinematographer Anatoly Soussekov does a high-profile job, full of shadows and atmospheric effects.

— *Deborah Young*

LA SCORTA
(THE BODYGUARDS)
(ITALIAN)

An Istituto Luce/Italnoleggio Cinematografico (Italy) release of a Claudio Bonivento production. (Intl. sales: Intra Films.) Produced by Claudio Bonivento. Directed by Ricky Tognazzi. Screenplay, Graziano Diana, Simona Izzo. Camera (color), Alessio Gelsini; editor, Carla Simoncelli; music, Ennio Morricone; art director, Mariangela Capuano. Reviewed at Adriano Cinema, Rome, May 4, 1993. (In Cannes Film Festival, competing.) Running time: **95 MIN.**
Angelo . . . . Claudio Amendola
Andrea . . . . Enrico Lo Verso
Judge . . . . Carlo Cecchi
Fabio . . . . Ricky Memphis
Raffaele . . . . Tony Sperandeo

Ricky Tognazzi's "La Scorta" topped the Italian box office charts for weeks, thanks to its skill in capturing the country's current political climate in an entertaining action film format. Though local references to real people and newspaper headlines are most meaningful to Italians, pic has a strong reservoir of energy and a fast American rhythm that can carry over to offshore auds.

Most memorable for its convincing characterizations and its relentless atmosphere of tension, the story is told from the point of view of a team of four dedicated young policemen — depicted as the unsung heroes who risk their lives protecting Mafia targets. They don't always succeed.

When a state attorney working on a sensitive political case is blown away, along with one of his bodyguards, magistrate Carlo Cecchi is sent to Sicily from northern Italy to replace him.

Tognazzi skillfully juggles the team's personal lives with their selfless dedication to the magistrate. The members of Cecchi's escort are carefully individualized, building up sympathy — and apprehension — for each.

Enrico Lo Verso ("The Stolen Children") braves his young wife's wrath to lead the team. Claudio Amendola has a personal grudge against the hitmen who killed the last state prosecutor, whom he considered a friend. Tony Sperandeo has a comic love interest; neophyte Ricky Memphis is so scared he wants to transfer out.

The ice between Cecchi and his bodyguards is quickly broken and the team goes from respecting the man to identifying with his work.

Given the film's theme, there is actually very little violence, gunfights or bombings. Tognazzi keeps the tension high simply by showing the daily stress involved in guarding the life of a high-profile investigator. These generally culminate in action sequences edited "all'americana."

Following a recent trend toward greater realism in the dialogue, "La Scorta" characterizes each guard by his accent and regional "personality." Though it will be largely lost offshore, the technique has given pic a leg up in Italy, where auds are delighted by Memphis' Roman cynicism, Amendola's Sicilian temper and so on. Stage thesp Carlo Cecchi, in contrast, plays the prosecutor with a timeless Shakespearean nobility that is a little over the top. — *Deborah Young*

FRANÇOIS TRUFFAUT: PORTRAITS VOLÉS
(FRANÇOIS TRUFFAUT: STOLEN PORTRAITS)
(FRENCH-DOCU)

An AAA (France) release of a Chrysalide Films presentation co-produced by France 2 Cinema/INA Entreprise/Maecenas Films/Premiere with the participation of Canal Plus. Produced by Monique Annaud. Directed by Serge Toubiana, Michel Pascal. Camera (color), Maurice Fellous, Jean-Yves Le Mener, Michel Sourioux; editor, Dominique B. Martin. Reviewed at Cannes Film Festival (Un Certain Regard section), May 14, 1993. Running time: **93 MIN.**
With: Gerard Depardieu, Ewa Truffaut, Claude Chabrol, Jean-Louis Richard, Jean Gruault, Alexandre Astruc, Claude de Givray, Jean Aurel, Annette Insdorf, Olivier Assayas, Marcel Berbert, Madeleine Morgenstern, Eric Rohmer, Robert Lachenay, Janine Bazin, Bertrand Tavernier, Marcel Ophüls, Monique Lucas, Albert Duchesne, Liliane Siegel, Laura Truffaut, Marie-France Pisier, Yann Dedet, Claude Miller, Nathalie Baye, Fanny Ardant.

Film critics Serge Toubiana and Michel Pascal have made a revealing but far from definitive docu study of the life and career of the late François Truffaut. Interviews with an impressive lineup of friends, associates and family members peel away layers of the onion to unveil aspects of the French director's personality largely undiscussed during his lifetime. But absence of some of his closest collaborators and much film of Truffaut himself produces frustration along with the insights. Nicely mounted production should find a little niche on the international fest and rep house circuit.

Truffaut's daughter Ewa points out, "He took great care of his image," and the filmmakers seem to take their cue from screenwriter Jean Gruault, who states, "Like all men, he was a lie." Pic than snakes into areas of Truffaut's life he tended to conceal while building his reputation.

For anyone with an interest in Truffaut, the succession of important figures from his early days brings a lot of personal history to life, as they tell of an unloved boy who became something of a delinquent, took refuge in the cinema, was imprisoned for going AWOL and began his brilliant career as an outspoken critic.

Film rightly identifies the equally important serious and mischievous sides of Truffaut, alludes to his seductiveness to women, and uses clips from his films mainly for their most overtly autobiographical aspects.

But pic begins navigating in deeper and more mysterious water when it takes on his deeply resentful feelings toward his mother, ambivalent attitude toward psychoanalysis and religion, lifelong search for father figures among great older directors, and ultimately successful hunt for his real father, a lover of his mother's who turned out to be a Jewish dentist.

Impressive as the participants may be, one deeply misses several of Truffaut's closest collaborators, most notably actor Jean-Pierre Leaud, perennial assistant and sometime screenwriter Suzanne Schiffman, any of his cinematographers, and other important thesps, such as Jeanne Moreau and Catherine Deneuve.

Toubiana (who as a critic was not always sympathetic to Truffaut) and Pascal made a deliberate decision not to use interviews with the director himself, preferring to create a group portrait painted by others. As revealing as many of their remarks are, result is a mixed blessing, since what's ultimately missing here is Truffaut's engaging voice and personality, as well as explanations of his working methods and evaluation of his talents.

Fine use has been made of private photographs and behind-the-scenes footage, and some of the most potent observations, from Fanny Ardant, his final companion, have been saved for last.

— *Todd McCarthy*

LA PLACE D'UN AUTRE
(THE PLACE OF ANOTHER)
(FRENCH)

A Les Films Alyne/Crrav co-production with the participation of Canal Plus and Sofiarp. (Intl. sales: Les Films Alyne.) Produced, written, directed by René Féret. Camera (color), Gilberto Azevedo; editor, Fabienne Camara, Sabine Emiliani; set design, José Froment; costume design, Patricia Rabourdin; sound, Christine Charpail, Claude Villand. Reviewed at CNC screening room Paris, March 4, 1993. (In Cannes Film Festival, Cinemas en France section.) Running time: **88 MIN.**
Thomas . . . . Samuel Le Bihan
Marie . . . . Cécile Bois
Thomas' father . . . Philippe Clevenot
Thomas' mother . . . Suzy Rambaud
Also with: Fréd–rin, Frédéric Hulne, Elsa Zylberstein, Jacques Bonnaffe, Carme Costa, Michèle Gleizer.

"La Place d'Un Autre," writer-producer-director René Féret's autobiographical account of compound misfortune, taps into melodrama to project hard-earned emotional truth. Buried demons and bad luck gang up to produce a mental and physical breakdown from which the protagonist eventually emerges through the healing power of art.

At pic's outset, 23-year-old Thomas (Samuel Le Bihan) is performing in a Shakespeare play while his proud father beams from the audience. In rapid succession the thesp's g.f. leaves him for a married man, he accidentally runs over and kills a cyclist, his father dies of cancer and he develops a chronic balance disorder that causes him to black out and fall. A long repressed identity problem surfaces with a vengeance and (in a darkly amusing scene) a shrink advises Thomas to abandon acting and get a job paying enough to underwrite at least six years of full-bore psychoanalysis.

Saving grace is his brief but torrid tryst with a Swiss woman, Marie (Cécile Bois), to whom he writes as the pressures of so many bad breaks accumulate.

Every phase of the intense and wearing tale of woe actually befell the helmer 20 years ago. Pic seems to exceed its actual running time as Thomas attempts suicide, becomes clinically paranoid and ends up anorexic and catatonic in a mental hospital where he experiences visions of storming a cemetery by night. The protagonist's eventual salvation through art is welcome, but verges on tedious by the time his recitation of Schonberg's "Warsaw Survivor" with full orchestra stamps his recovery.

Le Bihan convincingly shoulders a difficult role and supporting thesps are fine.

— *Lisa Nesselson*

THE NOSTRADAMUS KID
(AUSTRALIAN)

A Ronin Films (Australia) release of a Beyond Films presentation of a Simpson/Le Mesurier production, with the participation of the Australian Film Finance Corp. (Intl. sales: Beyond Films.) Produced by Terry Jennings. Executive producers, Roger Simpson, Roger Le Mesurier. Directed, written by Bob Ellis. Camera (Eastmancolor), Geoff Burton; editor, Henry Dangar; music, Chris Neal; production design, Roger Ford; sound, David Lee; assistant director, Bob Donaldson; casting, Liz Mullinar. Reviewed at Village screening room, Sydney, April 21, 1993. (In Cannes Film Festival, market section.) Running time: **120 MIN.**

Ken Elkin . . . . Noah Taylor
Jennie O'Brien . . . . . Miranda Otto
McAlister . . . . Jack Campbell
Wayland . . . . Erick Mitsak
Meryl . . . . Loene Carmen
Esther Anderson . . . . Alice Garner
Sarai Anderson . . . . . . Lucy Bell
Christy . . . . Jeanette Cronin
Pastor Anderson . . . . Arthur Dignam
American Preacher . . . . Colin Friels
The Shepherds Rod . . . Peter Gwynne
Pastor Dibley . . . . . Hec McMillan
Black Man . . . . Bob Maza
Also with: Bartholomew Rose, Robyn Gurney, Marie Lloyd, Jim McClelland, Claudia Karvan, Imogen Annesley, Norman Kaye, Evan Williams, Bob Ellis, Kate Fitzpatrick, Denny Lawrence, Tony Llewellyn-Jones, Drew Forsythe, Margaret Blinco, Liddy Clark, Patrick Cook.

Blending melancholy humor with hard-edged nostalgia, "The Nostradamus Kid" is an autobiographical film of distinction. It should do excellent arthouse biz in Australia and find auds in selected exposure elsewhere, with fest bookings also indicated.

Writer-director Bob Ellis' third feature brings this long-cherished project (announced as a Paul Cox project 11 years ago) to the screen. It's a fictionalized vision of two formative years in the life of the filmmaker: 1956, when he was a sex-starved teenager and unwilling disciple of Seventh Day Adventists in northern New South Wales; and 1962, in Sydney, when he got his first job and lost his virginity.

Noah Taylor, familiar from the John Duigan films "The Year My Voice Broke" and "Flirting," is perfectly cast as Ken Elkin, a character closely modeled on Ellis in his youth. Elkin is singlemindedly determined to cut loose from his country bumpkin/ultrareligious background, and is not a popular member of a 1956 Adventists' summer camp during which he ogles one of the pretty daughters (Alice Garner) of visiting preacher Arthur Dignam, and makes a nuisance of himself asking "heretical" questions at prayer meetings. A residue of Elkin's upbringing is an in-built feeling that the end of the world may, indeed, be near.

Six years later in Sydney, he has a lowly job on a university newspaper, sharing scrounged accommodations with former schoolfriend McAlister (Jack Campbell), a would-be filmmaker and Robert Mitchum buff. Elkin, described by Ellis as "a human cockroach," is a scruffy, often grubby character whose air of seedy depravity seems to attract women. He loses his virginity in a hilarious sequence with a drunken pickup (Jeanette Cronin).

However, he soon becomes involved with the lovely, virginal Jennie O'Brien (Miranda Otto), daughter of a prominent newspaper editor who, not surprisingly, strongly disapproves of his daughter's relationship. Matters come to a head when Elkin decides that Sydney is about to be destroyed in a nuclear attack triggered by the Cuban Missile Crisis, and insists that Jennie drive him in her father's car to safety across the mountain range west of the city.

There's also a coda, set in the present, when Elkin, now a successful playwright, meets by chance some childhood friends.

The resulting, constantly amusing and perceptive film plays almost like a cross between Woody Allen and François Truffaut but with a distinctly Australian tone. Ellis himself narrates the film in the style of early Truffaut and has his young lovers go to see "Jules and Jim." At the same time, his self-deprecating sexual jokes and obsessions are reminiscent of the Woodman, but without the one-liners.

Though long at two hours, "Kid" doesn't overstay its welcome, since Ellis and Taylor create an exceptionally interesting sad-sack hero. The strong supporting cast includes a glowing perf from Otto as the girl from another social world who is both strongly attracted and repelled by Elkin; Loene Carmen as a "bad girl" who leaves her religious background behind and becomes a stripper/hooker; Campbell and Erick Mitsak as Elkin's two, contrasted, friends; Peter Gwynne as a false prophet; and Bob Maza, memorable as a black philosopher in a bar.

Ellis himself makes an amusing appearance. In Australia, Ellis is known and (mostly) admired for his witty journalism, his outspoken political commentaries, his plays and film scripts, and his willingness to comment perceptively on almost any aspect of public life. Specialized overseas auds should also respond to the distinctive blend of wistfulness and anarchy.

Geoff Burton, who also shot the Duigan films, has done a fine job lensing and Roger Ford's unobtrusive production design is commendable. Chris Neal provides an attractive score.

— *David Stratton*

FAUSTO
(FRENCH)

An Amorces Diffusion release of a Lili Prods./BBD Prods./France 2 Cinema co-production in association with Investimage 4/Sofinergie 3 and the participation of the CNC/Canal Plus. Produced by Joeel Poulon, Daniel Daujon. Directed by Rémy Duchemin. Screenplay, Richard Morgiève, Duchemin, from Morgiève's novel. Camera (color, widescreen), Yves Lafaye; editor, Maryline Monthieux; music, Denis Barbier; production design, Fouillet and Wieber; art direction, Gilbert Druart; costume design, Annie Perier; sound (mono), Michel Kharat, Thierry Delor; Fausto's special fashions created by Philippe Guillotel; assistant director, Jérôme Navarro. Reviewed at CNC screening room, Paris, May 3, 1993. (In Cannes Film Festival, Cinemas en France section.) Running time: **81 MIN.**
Fausto Barbarico . . . . . Ken Higelin
Mitek Breslauer . . . . . . Jean Yanne
Raymond . . . . François Hautesserre
Tonie . . . . Florence Darel
Also with: Maurice Bénichou, Bruce Myers, Marianne Groves, Maité Nahyr, Arthur H.

As charming as it is improbable, "Fausto" is the peppy and well-acted tale of a shy orphan boy who, under the supportive tutelage of a crusty Jewish tailor, blossoms into a likable fashion innovator in mid-1960s Paris. Modern fairy tale leaves viewers refreshed and entertained. Fest and tube programmers should take note.

Lean and appealing Ken Higelin stars as Fausto Barbarico, the newly orphaned 17-year-old who is apprenticed to feisty and good-hearted Mitek Breslauer. Jean Yanne (the police chief in "Indochine") is ideal as Mitek, a well-dressed hunchback whose take on the human condition is leavened by humor and pinking shears. ("Did you see what the Italians did with the pope? You think it's normal to garb a man like a pregnant woman?")

Deciding that it pays to advertise, Fausto makes a suit out of real grass and flowers. He attracts a French pop star for a customer and, via imagination and hard work, is soon on his way to fame and fortune as neighborhood merchants and residents warmly cheer him on.

No real rationale is offered for Fausto's sudden transformation from meek to fearless, but once he hits his stride, the oddball garments are a visual treat. They were designed by French wiz Philippe Guillotel, who works with "Delicatessen" helmers Jeunet and Caro, and also clad the opening and closing ceremonies of the Albertville Winter Olympics.

May 24, 1993 (Cont.)

Fausto's friendship with a fellow orphan and his budding romance with a Jewish mechanics daughter round out the upbeat account of initiative rewarded. Beethoven has a fanciful hand in Fausto's sexual initiation and the plucky designer incorporates bank notes into his diet. Any hint of tragedy (the best friend is struck by a car, jealousy rears its head) works out fine.

First-time helmer Duchemin's sweet and spirited rendering of friendship and coming of age shows bite when needed but remains "nice" in the best sense of the word. — *Lisa Nesselson*

LE MARI DE LÉON
(LEON'S HUSBAND)
(FRENCH)

A Koala Films release of a Koala Films/Lonely Pictures co-production with the participation of Canal Plus and Bymages. (Intl. sales: Bybli 3000.) Directed by Jean-Pierre Mocky. Screenplay, Mocky, Frédéric Dard (a.k.a. "San Antonio") based a novel by San Antonio. Camera (color), Edmond Richard; editor, Mocky, Stéphane Schohn; music, Vladimir Cosma; production design, Clorinde Méry; sound, Louis Gimel. Reviewed at CNC screening room Paris, May 4, 1993. (In Cannes Film Festival, Cinemas en France section.) Running time: **97 MIN.**
Boris . . . . Jean-Pierre Mocky
Léon . . . . Serge Riaboukine
Nadia . . . . Laura Grandt
Nadège . . . . Brigitte Hansen
    Also with: Pascale Roberts, Dora Doll, Pierre Kameneff.

Deliberately brash, vulgar, over-the-top portrayal of the master-slave complicity between a flamboyant actor-director and his passionately devoted male secretary, Jean-Pierre Mocky's "Le Mari de Léon" creates an intimate and tyranical universe. The 34th pic by the iconoclastic helmer, who also plays lead, is from the love-it-or-hate-it school.

Tech credits border on crude as Mocky plunges into the baroque, extreme relationship between Léon (Mocky) and factotum Léon (Serge Riaboukine). Perverse tale is adapted with raw expediency from prolific novelist San Antonio's book, admittedly is loosely based on his own admiration for popular legit director Robert Hossein.

Léon, whose wife is catatonic, is utterly, selflessly in thrall to Boris. Boris is a shameless larger-than-life womanizer who humiliates and ignores his gorgeous wife, Nadia (Laura Grandt). The factotum succeeds in eliminating the wife, but Léon's young sister-in-law poses an unanticipated threat to his continued bliss in Boris' limelight.

A noodle king and his raucous wife complement the slate of mostly grotesque characters. Coarse seductions, cod pieces, cunnilingus, and a bevy of bare bottoms round out the proceedings.

Perfs are surprisingly touching considering the excessive, devil-may-care atmosphere. Tech aspects, apart from Cosma's score, are utterly perfunctory, even careless. But Mocky's full-bore energy in the service of a cruel tale will probably please his many fans and perhaps win new ones. — *Lisa Nesselson*

CUISINE ET DEPENDANCES
(KITCHEN WITH APARTMENT)
(FRENCH)

A Gaumont Buena Vista Intl. release of a Gaumont Intl./Gaumont/Le Studio Canal Plus/EFVE co-production. Produced by Alain Poiré. Directed by Philippe Muyl. Screenplay, Jean-Pierre Bacri, Agnès Jaoui, from their play. Camera (color), Willy Kurant; editor, Françoise Berger-Garnault; music, Vladimir Cosma; production design, Jacques Dugied; set decoration, Michel Autheman; costume design, Jackie Budin; sound, Yves Osmu; Reviewed at Gaumont Ambassade theater, Paris, April 28, 1993. (In Cannes Film Festival, market section.) Running time: **95 MIN.**
Martine . . . . Zabou
Georges . . . . Jean-Pierre Bacri
Charlotte . . . . Agnès Jaoui
Jacques . . . . Sam Karmann
Fred . . . . . . Jean-Pierre Darroussin
    Also with: Laurent Benoit, Marine Labouyssaire, Quentin Hue.

Despite presence of the talented original cast, the successful play "Cuisine et Dependances" emerges as an earnest but tedious film that retains the theatricality — in perfs and setting — of its stage roots. Pithy semi-comic revelations about petty human motivations seem strained, and the tidy denouement is long in coming.

Social conventions take their toll on a comfortably bourgeois Parisian couple Martine (Zabou) and Jacques (Sam Karmann) the night they invite a now successful TV personality to their apartment for dinner. It's been 10 years since they've seen their old friend. The celeb — never shown onscreen — is married to Charlotte (co-scripter Agnès Jaoui), a fact which continues to annoy ex-b.f. Georges (co-scripter Jean-Pierre Bacri), an uptight, bitter, non-prolific writer who, between jobs, who has been camping out in the living room for two months.

Before the night is out, Zabou's debt-ridden brother Fred (Jean-Pierre Darroussin) will have lured the celebrity into a high stakes poker game, Bacri's welcome will have worn to the breaking point, Zabou will bemoan the futility of her housewife life, Charlotte's marriage will be deglamorized and Karmann will rue the day his wife extended the invitation.

Pic has the compartmentalized stops and starts of a play transferred to the screen. Apart from opening and closing scenes, entire pic takes place in the apartment. Lion's share of activity is set in the kitchen, hence the title.

Congregating in the kitchen to gossip, characters are away from the guest of honor for what seems like hours, a device that kills all credibility.

Although some dialogue is amusing and a few isolated scenes are touching, the overall enterprise is dragged down by ponderous pacing. — *Lisa Nesselson*

TESTE RASATE
(SKINHEADS)
(ITALIAN)

A Chance Film release (in Italy) of a Century Film Europa production. (Intl. sales: Sacis.) Produced by Carmine De Benedittis. Executive producer, Caterina De Benedittis. Directed by Claudio Fragasso. Screenplay, Rosella Drudi. Camera (color), Luigi Ciccarese; editor, Ugo De Rossi; music, Eugenio Bennato, Sergio Cammariere; art direction, Claudio Bissattini; costumes, Giovanna Russo; sound (Dolby), Carlo Palmieri. Reviewed at Cola di Rienzo Cinema, Rome, May 5, 1993. (In Cannes Film Festival, market.) Running time: **94 MIN.**
Marco . . . . Gianmarco Tognazzi
Roberta . . . . Franca Bettoja
Zaira . . . . Fabienna Gueye
Riccardo . . . . Flavio Bucci
Beppe . . . . Stefano Molinari
The Führer . . . . Giulio Base

Suburban blues leave an aimless Italian kid prey to the swastika's stepped-up lure in the disturbing contempo drama "Skinheads." Directed with music-vid punchiness by seasoned horror hand Claudio Fragasso, pic lacks the sensitivity and critical distance to shake its vaguely repellent sensationalism. But heavy-duty violence and urban grit should click on video in many territories.

Major asset is Gianmarco Tognazzi's tough performance, which provides space, alongside his obtuseness, for character sympathy not explicit in the script. Able playing in his scenes with on- and offscreen mom Franca Bettoja also adds subtle depths to the fatherless boy's quest for direction and ideals.

Disgruntled with his braindead chums, and ma's haranguing to get a job, Tognazzi is at permanent loose ends, till a neighborhood neo-Nazi honcho known as the Führer (Giulio Base) goosesteps into his unmotivated existence. Without undue persuasion, the group's discipline and conviction win him over, and he's lining up for a haircut.

While he's embracing the thug ethic, things start heating up with the Somalian domestic from downstairs (Fabienne Gueye — a tad too beautiful and poised to be entirely credible as a humble immigrant worker). Tognazzi juggles the demands of his double life for a time, but as his Fascist fervor really takes wing, conflicts become insurmountable.

Rosella Drudi's script is arguably unbalanced in showing the local slackers as going utterly nowhere, while contrasting the Nazis as a model of purposeful organization and — apart from the final crunch — group support. As such, the film might even be accused of swaying susceptible tykes in the wrong direction. But it succeeds in tying the rise of neo-Fascism to the absence of a tangible youth culture in 1990s Italy.

Fragasso's direction hits its mark when the main force is visual (gym workouts, Hitlerian dancefloor displays, violent nighttime expeditions — given the requisite electricity by Ugo De Rossi's editing), but it falters in personal moments. Tognazzi's scenes with Gueye are less convincing than his passionate exchanges with Base, who's chillingly on-target. Also, the tolerance bid is clutzily introed via a Jewish jeweler (Flavio Bucci), whose warning speech is little more than a humanitarian infomercial.

Technically, pic gets by in all departments, but Luigi Ciccarese's lensing looks flat and underlit. — *David Rooney*

May 24, 1993 (Cont.)

JONA CHE VISSE NELLA BALENA
(JONAH WHO LIVED IN THE WHALE)
(FRENCH-ITALIAN)

A Mikado Film release (Italy) of a Jean Vigo Intl./French Prod. Focusfilm production in association with RAI-1. Produced by Elda Ferri. Directed by Roberto Faenza. Screenplay, Faenza, Filippo Ottoni, from Jonah Oberski's book "Kinderjaren." Camera (Technicolor), Janos Kende; editor, Nino Baragli; music, Ennio Morricone; art direction, Maria Ivanova, Laszlo Gardonyi; costumes, Elisabetta Beraldo; sound (Dolby), Bernard Rochut; associate producer, Aron Sipos. Reviewed at Mignon Cinema, Rome, April 12, 1993, Running time: **94 MIN.**
Max Oberski . . Jean-Hugues Anglade
Hanna Oberski . . . . . . Juliet Aubrey
Jonah . . . . Jenner Del Vecchio
Younger Jonah . . . . . Luke Petterson
Also with: Francesca De Sapio, Djeke Rosic, Simona Faceva.

Dutch physicist Johan Oberski's autobiographical account of his childhood years in Nazi concentration camps gets straightforward, effective treatment in "Jonah Who Lived in the Whale." Focusing less on horrific suffering than on workaday hardship, this child's-eye-view of persecution and the deprivation of human rights is especially attuned to smallfry sensibilities and it should travel widely in kidpic forums and family-oriented TV slots.

Director Roberto Faenza skillfully sets the mood with the opening passage in Amsterdam in 1943, as the Oberski family's cozy existence takes an inexorably bitter turn. Anti-Semitism's strengthening foothold is thriftily depicted through the innocently subjective and largely uncomprehending observations of 4-year-old Jonah (Luke Petterson).

The family endures escalating humiliations, as they are forced to wear yellow stars, kept from working or buying groceries, and bullied by hostile strangers. Clinging to the belief they're being relocated to Palestine, Jonah and his mother (Juliet Aubrey) are dumped in a neighboring camp to dad (Jean-Hugues Anglade), where they spend years in a gray, dehumanized limbo.

Jenner Del Vecchio steps in as the slightly older Jonah, and the young thesp's bruised intensity makes a sturdier fulcrum than way-too-adorable Petterson. The unwitting inappropriateness of his efforts to enter the hierarchy of older prison kids while Anglade succumbs to illness and Aubrey to madness underscores the bleak recollections with quiet, unforced desolation. With similar restraint, Faenza avoids caricaturing prison officers as monsters, going instead for faceless, barking authority figures.

Holding back somewhat less is Ennio Morricone's sometimes stridently overstated score, which, coupled with the early reels' cloying nursery-time voiceovers, steers pic dangerously close to calculated treacledom.

Other tech facets are on target, with much impact owing to Magyar lenser Janos Kende's warmly nostalgic images, gradually drained of color and depth as tragedy sets in. Perfs are generally strong, with Anglade especially touching in a delicate, low-key turn. — *David Rooney*

SAN FRANCISCO

RUNNING LATE
(BRITISH)

A Cinema Verity production for BBC Films in association with Peter Bowles Prods. Produced by Verity Lambert. Executive producer, Richard Broke. Directed by Udayan Prasad. Written by Simon Gray. Camera (color), Jason Lehel; editor, Barrie Vince; music, Richard Hartley; sound, Albert Bailey; production designer, Michael Pickwoad; art director, Henry Harris; makeup, Carolyne Walsh; associate producer, Peter Bowles. Reviewed at the San Francisco Intl. Film Festival (Golden Gate Awards section), April 14, 1993.) Running time: **75 MIN.**
George Grant . . . . Peter Bowles
Sally Grant . . . . . . Carole Nimmons
Clitheroe . . . . Michael Byrne
Michael Mitchrum . . . Adrian Rawlins
Carol . . . . Suzette Llewellyn
Mr. Humphrey . . . . . . Roshan Seth

Scenarist Simon Gray's "Running Late" rings some sly minor-key notes on a familiar comic theme. Basically one long fantasy-comeuppance gag (not unlike "Groundhog Day"), film is clever but uneven until a letdown finale. Evident telepic origins will further limit theatrical exposure.

Impossibly arrogant TV interviewer George Grant (Peter Bowles) is barely finished with yet another tabloid-style grilling before the certifiable Worst Day of His Life starts rolling. First his long-suffering wife takes off for greener pastures. Then car theft, lost house keys and other indignities conspire to humble the obnoxious "personality."

Playwright Gray has contrived an amusing knot of situations, although the early media satire could be more fully explored. Director Udayan Prasad too often goes for slapstick. The funniest moments are the most subtle — the photos in George's office (he's seen glad-handing both Queen Elizabeth and Elizabeth Taylor), and Roshan Seth's insinuating turn as a "loving and caring" bank manager.

It would be best if cretinous George were sent off to purgatory at the end. But the close settles for a more sentimental strain of supernaturalism. The "Love redeems all" message doesn't play, given preceding action's bilious tenor.

Acting is fine, tech aspects OK. But while 16m blowup looks smart, reliance on closeups and the broad touch betray its BBC birth. — *Dennis Harvey*

LE QUATOR DES POSSIBLES
(THE QUARTET OF THE POSSIBLES)
(FRENCH-SWISS-DOCU)

An Arcanal presentation of a Contrechamps/Krystal production with Television Suisse Romande/La Sept/Arcanal. Directed by Edna Politti, with Philippe Albera. Camera (color), Axel Brandt, Patrice Cologne; editor, Elizabeth Waelchli; music, Luigi Nono; sound, Marc-Antoine Beldent; texts, Friedrich Holderlin. Reviewed on vidcassette, San Francisco, May 1, 1993. (In San Francisco Intl. Film Festival, Golden Gate Awards section.) Running time: **88 MIN.**
With: Le Quatuor Arditti (Irvine Arditti, David Alberman, Garth Knox, Rohan de Saram).

Late Italian serialist composer Luigi Nono is the ostensible subject, but Edna Politti's "Quartet of the Possibles" noodles with no end of "possible" focal points. Resulting tedious intellectual exercise will have a hard time drumming up interest outside Euro TV and academic musical interests.

Politti planned to make a presumably straightforward docu about Nono, but was only able to film him briefly once before the ailing master died in 1990. So instead, the feature spends most of its time on a dull rehearsal process as members of the Arditti Quartet grapple with Nono's sole string quartet, "Fragmente-Stille, an Diotima."

Then there's the filmmaker herself vapidly musing on the relations between time, space and music; interviewing an astrophysicist; reading literature (particularly Holderlin, who inspired the Nono piece); staring pensively into the distance etc. Handsomely shot views of Venice and the Abbey of Royaumont, plus well-recorded performing excerpts, don't alleviate the level of pompous boredom.

Bruno Ganz contributes a brief voiceover. — *Dennis Harvey*

SUPER MARIO BROS.

A Buena Vista release from Hollywood Pictures of a Lightmotive/Allied Filmmakers presentation, in association with Cinergi Prods. Produced by Jake Eberts, Roland Joffé. Directed by Rocky Morton, Annabel Jankel. Screenplay, Parker Bennett & Terry Runté, Ed Solomon, based on the Nintendo game concept and characters created by Shigeru Miyamoto, Takashi Tezuka. Camera (Technicolor), Dean Semler; editor, Mark Goldblatt; music, Alan Silvestri; production design, David L. Snyder; art direction, Walter P. Martishius; set decoration, Beth Rubino; costume design, Joseph Porro; sound (Dolby Digital), Richard Van Dyke; production manager/co-producer, Fred Caruso; assistant director, Louis D'Esposito; special visual effects, Christopher Francis Woods; narrator, Dan Castellenetta; choreography, Barry Lather; stunt coordinator, Gary Jensen; special effects coordinator, Paul Lombardi; 2nd-unit directors, James Devis, Semler; 2nd-unit camera, Devis; associate producer, Brad Weston; casting, Mali Finn, Don Finn. Reviewed at Murray Hill Theater 4, N.Y., May 28, 1993. MPAA Rating: PG. Running time: **104 MIN.**

Mario Mario . . . . Bob Hoskins
Luigi Mario . . . . . . John Leguizamo
King Koopa . . . . Dennis Hopper
Daisy . . . . Samantha Mathis
Iggy . . . . Fisher Stevens
Spike . . . . Richard Edson
Lena . . . . Fiona Shaw
Daniella . . . . Dana Kaminski
Toad . . . . Mojo Nixon
Scapelli . . . . Gianni Russo
Bertha . . . . . . Francesca Roberts
The King . . . . Lance Henriksen
Old Lady . . . . Sylvia Harman
Angelica . . . . . . Desiree Marie Velez

Wildly overproduced and derivative, "Super Mario Bros. is 1993's answer to "Howard the Duck." Some brief kiddie business and eventual video rentals can't justify its nearly $50 million negative cost.

The task of converting a non-narrative Nintendo videogame into a motion picture was too much for a trio of scripters, a pair of (married) directors and a couple of high-profile producers. What set them in motion was obviously the success of the "Teenage Mutant Ninja Turtles" movies, which "Mario" imitates when it's not into "Star Wars" riffs or "Batman" pastiche.

Awkwardly constructed pic, featuring two prologues and two epilogues, starts with the premise of a parallel world to New York created 65 million years ago by a meteorite that also killed off the dinosaurs. A miscast (he's not the only one) Dennis Hopper is the villain ruling the other world and intent upon retrieving a meteorite fragment and a young princess (Samantha Mathis) sent with it to our world. If the princess reunites the rock with the meteorite she will refuse the two dimensions.

Mathis is kidnapped by Hopper's bumbling assistants and pursued into his world by the Mario Bros., two Brooklyn plumbers beloved by Nintendo game fans over the past decade. If you're over the age of 5 and can believe that Bob Hoskins and John Leguizamo are brothers, let alone Italian, the rest of the film's leaps of faith are child's play.

After a fairly realistic opening reel, picture segues into Hopper's world of oversize sets and mechanical slapstick. There are plenty of gags, but not one laugh.

As stiffly directed by Annabel Jankel and Rocky Morton, "Mario" occasionally attempts to career along like a videogame with chases, fireballs and narrow escapes. However, the action is generally photographed in unexciting closeups and telephoto shots.

While Hopper overacts and condescends to the comic strip material, Fiona Shaw as his Joanna Cassidy-esque partner in evil is an impressive, larger-than-life villainess. Down-to-earth Hoskins and Leguizamo vainly try to humanize their strictly functional central roles, while Mathis is an overly plain heroine.

The technicians have done an okay job here, delivering decent morphing effects, a cute little dinosaur pet named Yoshi, quality sound effects (given impressive separation via Dolby Digital Stereo) and some striking sets.
— *Lawrence Cohn*

MADE IN AMERICA

A Warner Bros. release of a Le Studio Canal Plus/Regency Enterprises/Alcor Films presentation of a Stonebridge Entertainment/Kalola Prods./Arnon Milchan production. Produced by Milchan, Michael Douglas, Rick Bieber. Executive producers, Nadine Schiff, Marcia Brandwynne. Directed by Richard Benjamin. Screenplay, Holly Goldberg Sloan; story by Brandwynne, Schiff, Sloan. Camera (Deluxe color, Technicolor prints), Ralf Bode; editor, Jacqueline Cambas; music, Mark Isham; production design, Evelyn Sakash; set decoration, Hilton Rosemarin; costume design, Elizabeth McBride; sound (Dolby), Richard Lightstone; co-executive producer, Steven Reuther; co-producer, Patrick Palmer; associate producer, Suzanne Rothbaum; assistant directors, L. Dean Jones Jr., Newton Arnold; 2nd-unit directors, Patrick Palmer, David R. Ellis; casting, Reuben Cannon & Associates. Reviewed at Universal City Cineplex Odeon Theaters, May 25, 1993. MPAA Rating: PG-13. Running time: **110 MIN.**

Sarah Mathews . . . Whoopi Goldberg
Hal Jackson . . . . Ted Danson
Tea Cake Walters . . . . . . Will Smith
Zora Mathews . . . . Nia Long
Jose . . . . Paul Rodriguez
Stacy . . . . Jennifer Tilly
Alberta . . . . Peggy Rea

Reminiscent of old Hollywood, this uneven comedy is probably more interesting for the off-screen grist it provided the tabloid mill than anything on-camera. Still, with its undeniable "feel-good" elements, Whoopi Goldberg's heavenly glow from "Sister Act" and Ted Danson still basking in the "Cheers" finale, pic could make some OK early deposits before more interesting summer fare forces its withdrawal.

At least "Made in America" has the distinction of being better than the last movie involving a sperm bank, "Frozen Assets," though at times the humor — overplayed to nearly shrill levels — seems to come from the same test tube. The plot has Zora (Nia Long), a high-school honors student, discovering her mother Sarah (Goldberg) conceived her after her father's death using a donor from a sperm bank.

Wanting to find her biological dad, Zora raids the sperm bank files and finds the name of Hal Jackson (Danson) — a Cal Worthington-like car salesman who cavorts on-air with elephants, bears and chimps and, to the chagrin of both mother and daughter, turns out to be white. Hostile toward each other at first, an unlikely relationship develops between Hal and Sarah.

The setup has obvious comedic and romantic possibilities, but director Richard Benjamin, whose career has generally been on a downward arc since his impressive 1982 debut with "My Favorite Year," plays the first half of the movie at such an over-the-top, cartoonish pitch it's hard to relate to the characters.

Then, in an effort to bring Sarah and Hal's relationship to a crisis point, the action suddenly veers into a heavy-handed, semi-serious mode that doesn't mesh with the screwball opening.

If there's chemistry between Danson and Goldberg, it's certainly not allowed to unfold adequately or with any sense of pacing in Holly Goldberg Sloan's script. The race issue, for example, quickly dissipates, which would be fine if Sarah and Hal hadn't each made such a point of it early on.

In fact, both Danson and Goldberg are better than this material, and perhaps as a result it's the supporting players who end up stealing much of the film, particularly rapper Will Smith as Zora's nerdy friend and a golden-locked Jennifer Tilly as Hal's airheaded aerobics instructor girlfriend.

Also meriting honors is the adorable Long, who brings the requisite sweetness and determination to a role that, again, at times deserts her on paper, where the audience can only look at Zora's reaction and say "Huh?"

Mark Isham's score proves overbearing at times as Benjamin lays on the corn, while other tech credits are generally undistinguished. Pic does wind up with a jaunty, closing-credit rap number that provides a more energizing mix than much of what preceded it. — *Brian Lowry*

CANNES FEST

HSIMENG JENSHENG
(THE PUPPETMASTER)
(TAIWANESE)

An Era Intl. presentation of a City Films production. (Intl. sales: Era Intl., Hong Kong.) Produced by Chiu Fusheng. Executive producers, Michael Yang, H.T. Jan. Directed by Hou Hsiaohsien. Screenplay, Wu Nien-jen, Chu Tien-wen, from Li Tien-lu's memoirs. Camera (color), Lee Pin-bing; editor, Liao Ching-sung; music, Chen Mingchang; art direction, Chang Hung, Lu Ming-jin; costume design, Chang Kuanghui, Juan Pei-yun; sound (Dolby), Du Du-jih, Meng Chi-liang; associate producer, Chang Hwa-kun; assistant director, Chen Hwai-en. Reviewed at Cannes Film Festival (competing), May 22, 1993. Running time: **142 MIN.**

Adult Li . . . . Lin Chung
Teenage Li . . . . . Cheng Kuei-chung
Child Li . . . . Cho Ju-wei
Father . . . . Tsai Chen-nan
Stepmother . . . . Yang Li-yin
Wife . . . . Hwang Ching-ru
Police Officer . . . . I Toshiro
Grandfather . . . . Li Hei
Also with: Li Tien-lu, Kao Tung-hsiu, Li Wen-chang, Tsai Yi-hwa, Chen Yishan.

(Hokkien soundtrack)

A slow but mesmerizing biopic doing double duty as social/cultural document, "The Puppetmaster" is an assured return by Taiwan helmer Hou Hsiao-hsien after his Venice Golden Lion-winner "A City of Sadness" four years ago. Those not attuned to Hou's distanced, controlled style, will be turned-off; enthusiasts, however, will relish its greater refinement, painterly visuals and deeply humanistic approach. Theatrically, it will prove a tough sell.

Movie is based on the memoirs of Taiwan-born Li Tien-lu, a famed exponent of traditional hand puppetry, whose early life is used as a mirror of Taiwan under Japanese colonial rule during the first half of this century.

Li himself, a feisty 84-year-old who's played supporting roles in three Hou pics, is also appears occasionally in on-camera interviews.

Story begins with Li's birth in 1909 into a large, traditionally run Chinese family who, believing the baby has "the evil eye," assigns him his mother's rather than father's surname. After she dies and father marries a brittle ex-hooker, Li takes refuge from the latter's bullying in learning the craft of puppeteering.

In his '20s, he leaves home and sets up his own troupe. On the outbreak of the Sino-Japanese war in 1937, however, the colonial Japanese government bans all street theater, and Li is forced to work as an actor in straight vaudeville. After retreating to the countryside at the end of WWII, his family is struck by malaria. Film ends elegiacally in 1945, with Taiwan finally free of Japanese rule after 50 years. ("City of Sadness" opens soon after.)

In the hands of Hou and regular scripters Wu Nien-jen and Chu Tien-wen, the dramatic ingredients of Li's life are pulped down and distilled into a series of tableaux, beautifully lit and composed but statically shot, that function as pinpoints in time. Major narrative events are referred to in Li's v.o. rather than shown on screen; when someone leaves the room it's a major event. Takes are generally on the long side, with the image segmented by shadows or objects.

In Hou's "A City of Sadness," this minimalist approach often worked against audience comprehension by withholding basic info. In "Puppetmaster," which lacks the previous pic's political complexities and narrative content, it's much more successful. Basic relationships are clear from the start, and the film, with its large gaps in continuity, doesn't pretend to present a cohesive storyline. Pic's deeper subtext is the restriction on personal expression and freedom provided by the double whammy of traditional Chinese family life and Japanese colonialism.

Performances, as usual, are highly contained, with the most natural playing often coming from the children. Taiwan rock singer Lin Chung makes an impressive screen bow as the adult Li, experienced actress Yang Li-yin is fine as Li's waspish stepmother, and songwriter Tsai Meng-dang is good as the testy father. Li, himself, who suddenly appears unannounced some 50 minutes in, comes over as a lively, straight-

talking character with a personality diametrically opposite to that of Hou's movie. Deliberate contrast works well.

Tech credits are top drawer, with locations in Fujian province, mainland China, repping pre-war Taiwan. Lensing by Lee Pin-bing, who worked on Hou's "Dust in the Wind," is outstanding, contrasting sunlit landscapes with cramped, shadowy interiors. Occasional music is soothing, and the relatively few puppet performances are no chore for nonspecialists. — *Derek Elley*

FRIENDS
(BRITISH-FRENCH)

A Friends Prods. (London)/Chrysalide Films (Paris)/Rio Films (Paris) co-production. (Intl. sales: The Sales Co., London.) Produced by Judith Hunt. Directed, written by Elaine Proctor. Camera (Technicolor), Dominique Chapius; editor, Tony Lawson; music, Rachel Portman; production design, Carmel Collins; art director, Mark Wilby; costumes, Moira Meyer; sound, Robin Harris; production manager, Sheila Fraser Milne; assistant director, Domonique Combe; casting, Mooyeenn Lee. Reviewed at Cannes Film Festival (competing), May 22, 1993. Running time: **109 MIN.**
Sophie . . . . Kerry Fox
Thoko . . . . Dambisa Kente
Aninka . . . . Michele Burgers
Johan . . . . Marius Weyers
Jeremy . . . . Tertius Meintjes
Innocentia . . . . Dolly Rathebe
Iris . . . . Wilma Stockenstrom
Rheinhart . . . . Carol Trichardt
Sophie's mother . . . . . Anne Curteis
Sophie's father . . . . . Ralph Draper

The tense, divided realities of life in contemporary South Africa are vividly brought to the screen in "Friends," a provocative pic from first-time writer-director Elaine Proctor. Despite intriguing characters and good performances, however, the film is saddled with a schematic screenplay that leaves many questions unanswered. Despite this, the film stands a decent chance to perform in international arthouses thanks mainly to a strong, gutsy central perf from Kerry Fox in the lead role as a young white member of a terrorist organization.

Proctor's screenplay is structured around the three titular friends, representatives of three key factions in the South African tragedy. Fox is Sophie, who comes from a privileged, white English-speaking family; Michele Burgers is Aninka, a Boer, whose family live in a rural area; and Dambisa Kente is Thoko, a black woman whose mother lives in a township.

A major problem is that, for a film titled "Friends," the audience is asked to take the friendship of the three women entirely on trust; we know nothing about their relationship except that they met at university. Sophie and Thoke have both been married, and now the three share a large house in Johannesburg.

Sophie is Proctor's principal concern, and the young woman's combative attitude toward apartheid is indicated early on at the wedding of Aninka to a liberal, older man. A librarian, Sophie is secretly involved with an anti-apartheid terrorist organization; on their behalf, she plants bombs in public places. When a parcel bomb she left at Jan Smuts Airport explodes killing two people, including an elderly black cleaning woman, Sophie is devastated. Aninka's husband discovers her involvement, and Sophie is forced to leave the house; unable to turn to her dissolute ex-husband or her uncomprehending parents, she gives herself up.

Proctor's screenplay has too many rough edges and contrivances, but "Friends" is so well acted that the occasional flaws can be easily overlooked. New Zealander Fox gives a brave, feisty performance as Sophie; the actress, previously seen in "An Angel at My Table" and "The Last Days of Chez Nous," is completely captivating in her difficult and demanding role.

Burgers, as the slightly remote Aninka, and Kente, as the moderate Thoke (who teaches school in a black township where her students are becoming increasingly more radical) have less to do, but are also completely convincing.

There are some telling performances among the supporting characters; Anne Curteis, as Sophie's faded, anguished mother, conveys in a few glances volumes of pain and worry.

The prison scenes in the second half of the film are grueling, but the film raises questions about the use of terrorism as a weapon against apartheid that it never really confronts. It could be said that the film is about personal relationships, not politics; but the political events are inescapable, and Sophie's violent behavior is accepted too easily. But Proctor's depiction of the uneasy atmosphere of Johannesburg between 1985 and 1990 is vivid enough that auds should be caught up in the drama.

French cinematographer Dominique Chapuis, who also shot the South African-themed "A Dry

White Season," does a tremendous job of on-location shooting in different parts of Johannesburg and its environs, and Carmel Collins' production design also contributes strongly to the film. Other technical credits are very fine. — *David Stratton*

FRAUDS
(AUSTRALIAN)

A Live Entertainment/J&M Enterprises presentation of a Latent Image production, in association with the Australian Film Finance Corp. Produced by Andrena Finlay, Stuart Quin. Executive Producer, Rebel Penfold-Russell. Directed by Stephan Elliott. Camera (Eastmancolor), Geoff Burton; editor, Frans Vandenburg; music, Guy Gross; production design, Brian Thomson; art director, Robert Dein; costumes, Fiona Spence; sound, Ross Linton; stunts, Bernie Ledger; production manager, Sandra Alexander; assistant director, Keith Heygate; casting, Alison Barrett. Reviewed at Hoyts screening room, Sydney, May 3, 1993. (In Cannes Film Festival, competing). Running time: **92 MIN.**
Roland Copping . . . . Phil Collins
Jonathan Wheats . . . . Hugo Weaving
Beth Wheats . . . . . Josephine Byrnes
Michael Allen . . . . . . Peter Mochrie
Margaret . . . . . . Helen O'Connor
Mother . . . . Rebel Russell
Mrs. Waterson . . . . Colleen Clifford
Detective Simms . Nicholas Hammond
Detective Alan . . . . Kee Chan
Judge . . . . Vincent Ball
Barry Gribble . . . . Al Clark
Lawyer . . . . Martin Cooper

First-time director Stephan Elliott breaks a lot of the rules with his wayward first feature, "Frauds," cheerfully mixing suspense with comic-strip comedy. Boasting a top-flight performance from Phil Collins as a con-man insurance investigator with a child-like sense of humor, pic could attract audiences in search of way-out entertainment.

Elliott's gung ho approach masks a rather thin concept, and his style may not be to everyone's taste. But the film contains enough surprises and invention to ensure it a place in the market.

The film opens with a prologue establishing the character of Roland Copping as a frustrated child who plays a cruel trick on his brother. Pic then leaps forward in time to an urban limbo where characters speak in a jumble of accents designed to prevent identification with any particular city or country.

The home of a yuppie couple, Jonathan (Hugo Weaving) and Beth (Josephine Byrnes), who like to play games, is burgled by a masked intruder; the panicky Beth shoots the stranger with an

June 7, 1993 (Cont.)

arrow from an antique crossbow only to discover that he was a family friend. He had an accomplice, however, which is the cue for an insurance investigator to enter the picture.

This is the adult Roland Copping (Collins), who makes decisions via throws of the dice his mother gave him on a fateful birthday years before. Copping discovers that Jonathan was the burglar's accomplice (he'd needed the money) and proceeds to play games with the couple, who are at first amused, then annoyed, and finally terrified by his strange, childish antics.

As Elliott unfolds his story, he changes the mood and texture of the film from the thriller format of the early scenes to frenetic farce in the closing reel, as Jonathan tries to rescue Beth from Roland's strange house, so filled with toys and gadgets it looks like a leftover set from "Toys." But there's a deliberately nasty edge to the humor.

Elliott flings these disparate elements together with sublime confidence, driving the film along at a brisk pace (Frans Vandenberg's editing is assured) and creating a strange and deliberately unreal world for his eccentric characters. He's aided immeasurably by the clever production design of Brian Thomson and by Geoff Burton's usual sterling job of lensing.

Guy Gross' music also plays an important role here but is overinsistent in a couple of scenes. British singing star Collins has already proved (notably in "Buster") that he's no mean actor, and he's terrific here as the strange man-child. As the threatened couple, Hugo Weaving and Josephine Byrnes give him good support, though some will find the latter's unexplained Yank accent a distraction. — *David Stratton*

RAINING STONES
(BRITISH)

A Film Four Intl. presentation of a Parallax Pictures production for Channel Four. Produced by Sally Hibbin. Directed by Ken Loach. Screenplay, Jim Allen. Camera (color), Barry Ackroyd; editor, Jonathan Morris; music, Stewart Copeland; production design, Martin Johnson; art director, Fergus Clegg; sound, Ray Beckett; production manager, Lesley Stewart; assistant director, Tommy Gormley. Reviewed at Cannes Film Festival (competing), May 23, 1993. Running time: **90 MIN.**

Bob . . . . Bruce Jones
Anne . . . . Julie Brown
Tommy . . . . Ricky Tomlinson
Father Barry . . . . Tom Hickey
Coleen . . . . Gemma Phoenix
Tansey . . . . Jonathan James
Jimmy . . . . Mike Fallon

Repeating more or less the same formula as their 1991 success "Riff Raff," director Ken Loach and writer Jim Allen have come up trumps with "Raining Stones," a sad-funny portrayal of working class stiffs battling the recession in northern England. Though designed for the TV screen, the film contains more truth and humor than many a large-screen picture, and is sure to captivate audiences who seek it out.

From his earliest films ("Poor Cow," "Kes") and TV productions ("Cathy Come Home") Loach has always been the champion of Britain's working class, and scripter Jim Allen is obviously a kindred spirit, writing about real characters whose everyday lives are filled with comedy and suspense. Loach's perfect casting and remarkable way with actors turn Allen's words into small-scale cinema gems.

"Raining Stones," set in Manchester suburb of Middleton, centers on Bob (Bruce Jones), an out-of-work plumber who desperately needs money to pay for the expensive white dress he feels his small daughter deserves for her first communion. His attempts to earn much-needed cash include the bizarre (rustling a sheep and selling pieces of mutton at the local pub) to the comic (going door to door offering to fix faulty drains and winding up cleaning out the foul-smelling waste toilet pipes of the local Catholic Church for no payment) to the dangerous (borrowing money from a loan shark.)

Like Bette Davis in "The Catered Affair," Bob stubbornly insists his daughter have the best for her Big Day, even though she doesn't really need it and he can't afford it; and, like the father in "The Bicycle Thief," is forever optimistic, even in the face of humiliation and despair.

Loach and Allen alternate comedy (some of it spoken in broad enough Manchester accents to warrant the use of subtitles) with suspense and tragedy; at times, the film almost plays like one of those 1940s Hollywood pics in which a beleaguered Everyman struggles against an almost crushing system. A climactic scene between Bob and his parish priest (Tom Hickey) provides the

entirely satisfying, yet quite unexpected, conclusion.

Bruce Jones is perfectly cast as the rumpled hero whose luck seems to have run out, and Ricky Tomlinson (the guy caught in the bath in "Riff Raff") is a scream as his loyal, sardonic friend whose wisecracks provide much of the film's rich vein of humor. As the unorthodox priest, Tom Hickey is properly placid for the most part, but is given the film's most unexpected — and for the faithful probably shocking — line of dialogue.

Barry Ackroyd's grainy lensing is in keeping with the film's mood and setting, and Stewart Copeland's bright music score is intelligently used. Jonathan Morris edited to a lean 90 minutes.

The title is derived from a comment made by Bob's socialist father-in-law: "When you're a worker, it rains stones seven days a week." It's an apt moniker for a feisty, hugely enjoyable film.

— *David Stratton*

MAZEPPA
(FRENCH)

An MK2 production. (Intl. sales: MK2 Diffusion.) Produced by Marin Karmitz. Directed by Bartabas. Screenplay, Claude-Henri Buffard, Bartabas, Homerick, from Bartabas' idea. Camera (color), Bernard Zitzermann; editor, Joseph Licide; music, Jean-Pierre Drouet; production design, Emil Ghigo. Reviewed at Cannes Film Festival (competing), May 23, 1993. Running time: **111 MIN.**
Theodore Gericault . . . . Miguel Bose
Franconi . . . . Bartabas
Mouse . . . . Brigitte Mary
Alexandrine . . . . . Eva Schakmundes

All "poetic" atmosphere and no dramatic substance, "Mazeppa" is a pretentious, overlong meditation on the creative act of painting, irrational love for horses and horses' superiority to human beings. Intensely pictorial, film provides interesting re-creation of historical locale and minor visual pleasures sufficient only for the most patient arthouse auds; others will avoid this dull film.

The slim narrative is constructed as a series of painterly tableaux, most set within the Franconi Circus, where the mythic tale unfolds. Story concerns the complex, ambiguous relationship between Theodore Gericault (Miguel Bose), the famous Romantic painter of horses, and Franconi (Bartabas), the w.k. master trainer and circus director. In their first, combative encounter, the obsessed trainer charges

the painter with drawing horses as if he had never seen real ones in action. Gericault takes matters to heart and spends all his time at the circus observing.

Lord Byron's 1819 poem "Mazeppa," which inspired a small painting by Gericault, is reconstructed — providing the film with a literary cachet that it otherwise lacks. Byron's poem describes a Polish gentleman tied naked to a wild horse after being caught in an adulterous affair with a noblemen's wife.

Making his directorial debut, Bartabas shows more than anything else unreasonable obsession — actually fetishism — with horses' graceful and elegant movement. Regrettably, the dialogue, co-written by Bartabas, is all mumbo jumbo on the order of, "Have you ever felt a horse quivering between your thighs?" Though the painter and trainer appear to be different, the script offers hints, but doesn't develop the idea, that they actually share many attributes — and neuroses — in common. Even more fatal to the drama is the fact that most of the vital information is ponderously narrated offscreen.

As Gericault, Miguel Bose wears a perpetually intense expression meant to convey brooding anguish and suffering. As Franconi, Bartabas is masked throughout, but seems to have an impressive, if a bit monotonous, voice. — *Emanuel Levy*

SONATINE
(JAPANESE)

A Bandai Visual/Shochiku Dai-ichi Kogyo co-production, in association with Right Vision/Right Vision Entertainment/Office Kitano. (Intl. sales: Shochiku, Tokyo.) Produced by Masayuki Mori, Hisao Nabeshima, Takio Yoshida. Executive producer, Kazuyoshi Okuyama. Directed, written by Takeshi Kitano. Camera (color), Katsumi Yanagishima; editor, Kitano; music, Joe Hisaishi; art direction, Osamu Sasaki; sound (Dolby), Senji Horiuchi; assistant director, Toshihiro Tenma. Reviewed at Cannes Film Festival (Un Certain Regard section), May 15, 1993. Running time: **94 MIN.**
Murakawa . . . . "Beat" Takeshi
Miyuki . . . . Aya Kokumai
Uechi . . . . Tetsu Watanabe
Ryoji . . . . Masanobu Katsumura
Ken . . . . Susumu Terashima
Katagiri . . . . Ren Ohsugi
Kitajima . . . . Tonbo Zushi
Takahashi . . . . Kenichi Yajima
Hit man . . . . Eiji Minakata

Fourth feature of multifaceted Japanese maverick Takeshi Kitano, "Sonatine" plays like a condensed riff on his previous works. Story of a loose-cannon yakuza on a one-way ticket to hell mingles the casual violence and straight-faced humor of his earlier gangster pics with the childlike simplicity of the recent "A Scene at the Sea." Fest dates could translate into limited arthouse biz, with enterprising webs airing his quartet as a package.

As in "Violent Cop" and "Boiling Point," Kitano himself (under his stage moniker "Beat" Takeshi) plays the central role, a ruthless Tokyo mobster who's sent to Okinawa to help a gang against a rival group. When all hell breaks loose, Kitano and his underlings hole up in a house by a beach and await instructions from Tokyo. Gradually, they realize they were pawns in a larger game, and Kitano sets out singlehandedly to level the playing field.

Pic's combo of dry humor, sudden bursts of violence, and world-weary romanticism will take a while to build for first-time viewers of Kitano's movies, and the jigsaw of plot and characters only takes recognizable shape about halfway in. Once the board is set, however, the elaborate game of killings and counter-killings develops a powerful momentum that leads smoothly to the explosive finale and quiet coda. There's more than a hint of "The Killers" or "Point Blank," Japanese-style.

Heart of the movie is the central interlude by the beach, as Kitano and his faithful band of young hoods play games and mess around with guns, all the while realizing that death may be only just around the corner. Kitano's spare script and cool helming style are curiously involving, continuously catching the audience off-guard and pulling the rug from under its sympathies. Basically, everyone is a total lowlife.

As the shambling, expressionless hood with a private death wish, Kitano repeats his act from earlier pics. As the young femme who falls for him, Aya Kokumai draws a small but frightening portrait of brainless devotion, notably in a sequence where he teaches her how to fire a machine gun. The multitude of yakuza types are convincingly cast, and tech credits are precision in all departments.

— *Derek Elley*

TOXIC AFFAIR
(FRENCH)

A Gaumont release of a Camera One/France 2/Lilith Films production. Produced by Michel Seydoux. Executive producer, Armand Barbault. Directed, written by Philomène Esposito. Camera (Fuji color), Pierre Lhomme; editor, Noelle Boisson; art direction, Daniel Chevalier; costumes, Olga Berluti; music, Goran Bregovic; sound (Dolby Digital), Pierre Lenoir; casting, Françoise Menidrey. Reviewed at Cannes Film Festival (closing night film, noncompeting), May 23, 1993. Running time: **89 MIN.**
Penelope . . . . Isabelle Adjani
Sophie . . . . Clementine Celarie
Mr. Ray-Ban . . . . . Sergio Castellitto
Georges . . . . . . Hippolyte Girardot
Clumsy Man . . . . Michel Blanc
Psychiatrist . . . . . . Fabrice Luchini

Isabelle Adjani returns to the screen after a four-year absence with the too appropriately titled "Toxic Affair." The shrill comedy is an excruciatingly banal and ill-conceived look at modern relationships. Adjani's name may stir some initial interest in France, but the effort will do nothing to enhance her international reputation, and foreign sales will likely be extremely limited.

Writer-director Philomène Esposito chronicles the neurotic adventures of ex-model Penelope (Adjani). Now looking to a career in writing, she allows her entire life to come to a stop with the departure of b.f. Georges (Hippolyte Girardot).

She contemplates revenge and she contemplates suicide — in the process nearly driving her best friend, Sophie (Clementine Celarie), to do the deed herself. It's not a pretty personal picture, and despite the actress' charisma, the character builds suitable cause for euthanasia.

Though Adjani is more than capable of carrying every frame of the movie, the script simply isn't there. Dominated by a hysterical edge, the comedy is noticeably absent.

The actress is the least well served in the cast. Michel Blanc, in a brief cameo, provides a few moments of well-observed levity which rapidly evaporate into a hopeless attempt to wring humor from a patently unfunny situation. Director Esposito demonstrates an amazing lack of resourcefulness in conveying any evidence she inhabits a known earthbound society.

Technically handsome, the film features Dolby's new digital system. The good word on this is separate high-decibel dialogue and music tracks can be heard distinctly and simultaneously. The very bad news is that, in "Toxic Affair," both are an affront. — *Leonard Klady*

MI VIDA LOCA

A Sony Pictures Classics (U.S.) release of an HBO Showcase/Odyssey Distributors Ltd. presentation in association with Film Four Intl. of a Cineville production. Produced by Daniel Hassid, Carl-Jan Colpaert. Executive producers, Christoph Henkel, Colin Callender. Directed, written by Allison Anders. Camera (Deluxe color), Rodrigo Garcia; supervising film editor, Richard Chew; editors, Kathryn Himoff, Tracy Granger; music, John Taylor; production design, Jane Stewart; art direction, Bradley Wisham; set decoration, Chris Miller; costume design, Susan Bertram; sound (Dolby), Mary Jo Devenney; sound design, Leonard Marcel; co-producers, William Ewart, Francine Lefrak; line producer, Whitney R. Hinton; assistant director, Matthew J. Clark; casting, Betsy Fels. Reviewed at Cannes Film Festival (Directors Fortnight), May 21, 1993. Running time: **95 MIN.**
Sad Girl . . . . Angel Aviles
Mousie . . . . Seidy Lopez
Ernesto . . . . Jacob Vargas
Giggles . . . . Marlo Marron
Whisper . . . . Nelida Lopez
El Duran . . . . Jessie Borrego
La Blue Eyes . . . . . Magali Alvarado
Big Sleepy . . . . Julian Reyes
Rachel . . . . Bertilla Damas
Shadow . . . . Art Esquer
Baby Doll . . . . Christina Solis
Gata . . . . Salma Hayek
Joker Bird . . . . . . Panchito Gomez
Los Lobos . . . . Los Lobos

A portrait of young Latino women in the Los Angeles barrios, Allison Anders' "Mi Vida Loca" is a particularly disappointing follow-up to "Gas Food Lodging." Dramatically fuzzy and very flat visually and in performance, this slice-of-life look at the gang culture will automatically attract some interest on the basis of Anders' name and the subject matter, but is scarely a satisfying treatment. Pic could generate limited b.o. in specialized theatrical release, and will debut on HBO later this year.

"We girls need new skills 'cause by the time our boys are 21, they're either in prison, disabled or dead," says one of the main characters, more or less repping the jumping-off point for the picture, but writer-director sophomore Anders has not done nearly enough to animate her subjects or to place them in a meaningful context vis-à-vis American society.

Filmmaker essentially sinks herself at the outset, as instead of dramatizing things, a great portion of the opening reel is blanketed by voiceover narration that explains relationships and events. Dully functional v.o. from numerous characters continues to pop up throughout, and in many instances seems suspiciously like a desperation measure to patch over poorly developed scenes and inexpressive acting.

The drama focuses on two gang girls, Sad Girl (Angel Aviles) and Mousie (Seidy Lopez), lifelong friends who nearly come to blows after discovering they have been sharing the same man. The three-part tale then follows the lives of these women and several of their friends as they have babies, pursue relationships with invariably unreliable men, strike attitudes and try to figure out what to do with their lives.

The only woman with any real illumination about a positive life course is Giggles (Marlo Marron), who on release from prison announces she is going to go into computers, a remark met with derisive incomprehension.

Unfortunately, the vignettes Anders has developed of life in Echo Park never coalesce into a proper structure or even a vivid fresco. Most of the dialogue, when it prevails over the voiceover, consists of banal everyday conversation or attitudinizing, and Anders' staging of scenes is listless and unimaginative.

Acting is also a liability, as the realistic performances undoubtedly desired are not heightened by the revelations and insights one hopes for, and the actress' range seems limited at best.

Camera of Rodrigo Garcia (son of Gabriel Garcia Màrquez) boringly approaches subjects head-on, with no visual depth or movement. — *Todd McCarthy*

L'HOMME SUR LES QUAIS
(THE MAN ON THE SHORE)
(FRENCH-CANADIAN-HAITIAN)

A Les Productions du Regard/Froma Films Intl. production. (Intl. sales: Motion Media.) Executive producer, Pascal Veroust. Directed by Raoul Peck. Screenplay by Peck, Andre Grail. Camera, Armand Marco; editor, Jacques Comets; music, Amos Coulanges, Dominique Dejean; production design, Gilles Aird. Reviewed at Cannes Film Festival (competing), May 15, 1993. Runing time: **106 MIN.**
Sarah . . . . Jennifer Zubar
Grandmother Desrouillere . . . .
. . . . Toto Bissainthe
Gracieux/Sorel . . . . Patrick Rameau
Janvier . . . . Jean-Michel Martial
Aunt Elide . . . . . . Mireille Metellus

The horrors of Haiti's Papa Doc Duvalier era of the 1960s

June 7, 1993 (Cont.)

form the basis of "The Man on the Shore." As seen through the eyes of young Sarah (Jennifer Zubar), the film unfolds as a memory tinged with pain, fantasy and a kind of justice. A strong festival entry, the serious-themed film will nonetheless find rough sailing in commercial waters.

An odd melange of political and personal awakening, "Shore" trips on its own ambition. Though a vivid and frightening environment, the arm's length allegorical quality is more frustrating than informative.

Though the grown Sarah narrates, it is the 8-year-old girl who inhabits the screen, the split being the film's strongest asset. The daughter of politically disgraced parents, Sarah finds herself in the care of her grandmother. The opening frames reveal just one of many shocks to come as a man is beaten by *Tontons Macoute* outside her window. Escape from the pervasive horror is simple: Sarah invents an imaginary world where the title character poses the only physical threat.

This second fiction feature of Haitian-born Raoul Peck demonstrates an assured, if didactic, directorial hand. His familiarity with the milieu seems to be both an asset and a stumbling block.

Technical credits are pristine, with a lively music score and an extremely handsome visual style.
— *Leonard Klady*

VALE ABRAO
(VALLEY OF ABRAHAM)
(PORTUGUESE-FRENCH-SWISS)

A Madragoa Filmes (Portugal)/Gemini Films (France)/Light Night Production (Switzerland) co-production, in association with IPC/FC Gulbenkian/SEC/CNC/Canal Plus/Office Federal de la Culture (Berne)/TSR/Eurimages. Produced, written by Manoel de Oliveira. Directed, written by Paulo Branco, from Agustina Bessa-Luis' novel. Camera, Mario Barroso; editor, de Oliveira, Valerie Loiseleux; art direction, Maria Jose Branco; costumes, Isabel Branco; sound, Henri Maikoff. Reviewed at Cannes Film Festival (Directors Fortnight), May 20, 1993. Running time: **187 MIN.**
Ema . . . . Leonor Silveira
Young Ema . . . . Cecile Sanz De Alba
Carlo De Paiva . . . Luis Miguel Cintra
Paulino Cardeano . . Rui De Carvalho
Pedro Lumiares . . Luis Lima Barreto
Simona . . . . Micheline Larpin
Fernando Osorio . . . . . . Diogo Doria
Also with: Jose Pinto, Filipe Cochofel, Joao Perry, Gloria De Matos, Antonio Reis, Isabel Ruth.

"**V**alley of Abraham," the most accessible of Manoel de Oliveira's work to date, will win new fans for Portugal's diffi-

cult art film director. Though over three hours long, pic's strong storyline makes it as engrossing as a rich 19th century novel. Pic should make headway into larger arthouse markets while it tours festivals.

Certainly one of the richest, most cultured directors alive, de Oliveira begins "Valley" with a Biblical citation linking its breathtaking northern Portuguese locations with Abraham's exploitation of his wife Sarah's body. The expectation that this is a film about female victimization is strengthened when the young heroine, Ema (Cecile Sanz De Alba), begins wistfully reading "Madame Bovary." As a woman (Leonor Silveira), she even marries a passive doctor (Luis Miguel Cintra) she doesn't love, and begins to have affairs.

But de Oliveira (who, at 85, has hit his stride) throws viewers a curve ball full of mischievous irony. Film is adapted from Agustina Bessa-Luis' novel, itself a reflection on Flaubert. "Abraham" deliberately confuses the Bovary comparison, forcing viewers to keep rethinking literary and cultural givens.

During a privileged childhood with her doting father, Ema discovers she has enormous power over men. She causes car crashes just by standing by a country road, and has many suitors. But her hold over men isn't enough to satisfy her, and pic ends with Ema's carefully prepared death.

The film's great device is an off-screen narration, constantly commenting on the images and giving them a different slant. The idea that Ema is a dazzling, menacing beauty — underlined by the narrator — is something else from Silveira's quiet, slightly awkward charm. Perfs reflect the narration's arch irony. De Oliveira regulars Silveira and Cintra are perfectly in step with this distanced acting, so deadpan it gets a laugh.

The narrator keeps busy advancing the plot and interjecting heavy bouts of psychological and social analyses. Auds are forced to read enough subtitles to fill a small 19th-century novel, but happily, the effect is more stimulating than soporific.

Uniformly stunning locations in the Portuguese countryside are rendered expressive by Mario Barroso's silken cinematography. Costumes and decor give pic a magical atemporal quality that makes it a shock every time a car drives by. — *Deborah Young*

SOMBRAS EN UNA BATALLA
(SHADOWS IN A CONFLICT)
(SPANISH)

A Cayo Largo Films production. (Intl. sales: Sogepaq, Madrid.) Produced by Carlos Ramon. Directed, written by Mario Camus. Camera (color), Manuel Velasco; editor, Jose Maria Biurrun; music, Sebastian Marine; production design, Carlos Dorremochea, Rafael Palmero; costumes, Javier Artinano; sound, Julio Recuero. Reviewed at Cannes Film Festival (Directors Fortnight), May 18, 1993. Running time: **97 MIN.**
Ana . . . . Carmen Maura
José . . . . Joaquim de Almeida
Dario . . . . Fernando Valverde
Blanca . . . . Sonia Martin
Fernando . . . . Ramon Langa

A sombre drama set in barren countryside near the Spanish border with Portugal, "Shadows in a Conflict" lacks the dramatic highlights that might have found it a niche in the international arthouse market. Despite the formidable presence of Carmen Maura, the film is unlikely to travel outside Spanish-lingo territories.

Writer-director Mario Camus specializes in literary adaptations, like "The House of Bernarda Alba." Here he tries an original screenplay, about a fiercely independent woman veterinarian (Maura) who lives in an old farmhouse with her young daughter. She has what appears to be a platonic relationship with a colleague (Fernando Valverde) who regularly drops by for meals, and she seems to have settled into a placid middle age.

But events from her past catch up with her when she meets a handsome Portugese (Joaquim de Almeida) and they become lovers. He reveals that he'd served a prison term for arms smuggling, and Maura finds herself caught up in his somewhat murky affairs.

Camus unfolds this basically simple story at a steady pace, relying on his fine actors and the spectacularly bleak settings to create an ominous mood. Despite a sterling performance, Maura's character proves, in the end, to be a rather shallow one, and audiences are unlikely to be drawn into her bitter world. As the men in her life, de Almeida and Valverde give solid perfs, and young Sonia Martin is charming as her intelligent, talented daughter.

The film is extremely handsome, with top-notch camerawork and production design.
— *David Stratton*

REMOTE CONTROL
(ICELANDIC)

An Angelika Films release of a Skifan/Icelandic Broadcast Corp./Icelandic Film Fund production. Produced by Jon Olafsson. Directed, written by Oskar Jonasson. Camera (color), Sigurdur Sverrir Palsson; editor, Valdis Osarsdottir; music, Sigurjon Kjartansson; art director, Thor Vigfusson; sound, Kjartan Kjartansson. Reviewed at Cannes Film Festival (Un Certain Regard section), May 18, 1993. Running Time: **82 MIN.**
Axel . . . . Bjorn Fridbjornsson
Moli . . . . Helgi Bjornsson
Aggi Flinki . . . . Eggert Thorleifsson
Unnur . . . . Soley Eliasdottir
Maja . . . . . . Margret Gustavsdottir
Mamma . . . . . Thora Fridriksdottir
Brjansi . . . . . Stefan St. Sigurjonsson
Elli . . . . Throstur Gudbjartsson

A truly madcap romp, "Remote Control" is an unusually fresh and unexpected treat from Iceland. Driven by a bouncy rock score, the youth comedy has an infectious quality and sound that should translate into specialized appeal in selected foreign markets.

The fun fest kicks off as a result of a missing television remote control unit. Axel (Bjorn Fridbjornsson), a twentysomething Reykjavik mechanic, gets the panic call from his couch potato mother that it's nowhere to be found. In no uncertain terms he's to retrieve it or the family bathtub where his goldfish resides will be unstopped.

The seemingly innocent call sets off a series of wild and improbable events. The unit, stolen by Axel's sister's boyfriend, has melted in a small house fire. But not to worry, her friend, a local bootlegger and black marketeer, has dozens in his storehouse. Like a perfect arrangement of dominos, the pieces of the script cascade into a novel chaos.

Axel gets deeper and deeper into the mire as he desperately attempts to extricate himself from the mess. Antic druggies, hustlers and self-styled mobsters pop up as Icelandic punk rock blares on the soundtrack.

Already a monster success in its homeland, "Remote Control" provides writer-director Oskar Jonasson with an opportunity to unleash his somewhat ragtag bag of tricks, his style and observation builds up more than enough goodwill to overcome much of the banal comedy of its second half. Energy is certainly a major part of the low-budget effort. Additionally, Jonasson has assembled a vivid cast that brings enough authenticity to the proceedings to hit a chord that will

resound with many cultures far from the Northern community.
— *Leonard Klady*

OHIKKOSHI
(MOVING)
(JAPANESE)

A Herald Ace/Argo Project production. Produced by Hiroshisa Mukuju, Hiroyuki Fujikado. Executive producers, Kei Ijichi, Masahiro Yasuda. Directed by Shinji Soomai. Screenplay, Satoko Okudera, Satoshi Okonogi, from Hiko Tanaka's novel. Camera (color), Toyomichi Kurita; editor, Yoshiyuki Okuhara; music, Shigeaki Saegusa; production design, Narinori Shimoizaka; sound, Hidetoshi Nonaka. Reviewed at Cannes Film Festival (Un Certain Regard section), May 19, 1993. Running time: **117 MIN.**
Renko . . . . Tomoko Tabata
Nazuna (Mother) . . . Junko Sakurada
Kenichi (Father) . . . . . . Kiichi Nakai
Kimekome (Teacher) . . . .
. . . . Shofukutei Tsurubei
Yukio . . . . Taro Tanaka
Wakako . . . . Mariko Sudo

An 11-year-old girl is devastated when her parents decide to separate and does everything in her power to bring them back together. That's the familiar premise of this beautifully made and sometimes touching film that, however, breaks no new ground and seems distinctly old-fashioned.

Tomoko Tabata gives a natural performance as the troubled child unable to accept the fact that her beloved parents no longer want to live together. The separation affects her school work (she even sets fire to the chemistry lab) and her obsession becomes quite painful.

She tries to bring her parents together by arranging a family holiday near a lake, but, when she realizes that all her efforts are in vain, she wanders off into the nearby town, driving her parents frantic.

Director Shinji Soomai, best known for his 1984 award-winner "The Typhoon Club," handles this theme with sympathy but little sense of the child's traumatic obsession. The result is a film full of picture postcard images (every shot is of pristine beauty) but little substance or sense of loss. — *David Stratton*

I LOVE A MAN IN UNIFORM
(CANADIAN)

An Alliance Films release of a Miracle Pictures production. Produced by Paul Brown. Executive producer, Alexandra Raffe. Directed, written by David Wellington. Camera (color), David Franco; editor, Susan Shipton; music, Ron Sures, the Tragically Hip; production design, John Dondertman; set decorator, Susan Less; costume design, Beth Pasternak; casting, Susan Forrest. Reviewed at Cannes Film Festival (Directors Fortnight), May 17, 1993. Running Time: **97 MIN.**
Henry Adler . . . . . . Tom McCamus
Charlie Warner . . . . . Brigitte Bako
Frank . . . . Kevin Tighe
Father . . . . David Hemblen
Bruce . . . . Alex Karzis
Mr. Pearson . . . . Graham McPherson

With a nod to "Taxi Driver," the Canuck "I Love a Man in Uniform" provides a chilling saga of a sociopath that's certain to work its way under your skin. With a strong central perf by newcomer Tom McCamus, the film should ellicit strong arthouse and fest response. But it falls short of mainstream appeal, largely due to a screenplay that cannot find a satisfying conclusion.

The central character, Henry Adler (McCamus), is one of those quiet ones we've been warned to avoid. A bank employee by trade, he moonlights as an actor and his life gets a dramatic twist when he lands the role of a self-righteous cop on a TV series.

While early scenes tip us to his fascination with law enforcement, nothing can forewarn us of the madness to his Method. Slowly and steadily the lines between his make-believe cop and the real thing merge and things get weird.

It is a truly unsettling experience, all the more unnerving in that he begins as a seemingly ordinary, decent guy. When an off-screen attraction begins between Henry and Charlie (Brigitte Bako), there's the hope for a bright romance. Instead, his intensity builds to violence.

Writer-director David Wellington, despite adopting a seemingly cheery title, never sidesteps the violence of his piece. The very first scene is a brutal, senseless murder. Later, when Henry's bank is robbed, the bandits graphically demonstrate how far they're willing to go for money.

McCamus is a genuine find and carries virtually every scene in the picture. An unusual chameleon, he organically develops

Henry and his alter ego into a single, fused entity that's a fearsome terror. Among the supporting cast, Kevin Tighe does a quietly sinister bad cop to a turn. It's the picture's pivotal moment — the instant where Henry can no longer distinguish between right and wrong.

Ultimately though the parts are much more effective than the whole. The nihilism of the finale feels empty amid what had otherwise been a horrifyingly credible odyssey. — *Leonard Klady*

EL ACTO EN CUESTION
(THE ACT IN QUESTION)
(ARGENTINIAN-B&W)

An Allarts production. (Intl. sales: Allarts). Produced, directed, written by Alejandro Agresti. Camera (color), Nestor Sanz; editor, Stefan Kamp; music, Toshio Nakagawa; production design, Wilbert van Dorp, John Bramble. Reviewed at Cannes Film Festival (Un Certain Regard section), May 19, 1993. Running time: **114 MIN.**
Quiroga . . . . Carlos Roffe
Rogelio . . . . Lorenzo Quinteros
Liguori . . . . . . Sergio Poves Campos

A flashy, often dizzying style marks "The Act in Question," the tragic saga of the rise and fall of Miguel Quiroga, the famous Argentinian magician. The strikingly arty treatment of the material, which is more illustrative than dramatic, makes pic a natural entry for film fests and arthouse auds.

Defying linear development or coherent storytelling, "The Act in Question" is structured as a disjointed, surrealistic travelogue. Using narration and jumping back and forth between past and present, tale recounts Quiroga's poor childhood and his addictive habit of stealing books and reading them, cover to cover, in all-night sessions.

When Quiroga finds an obscure book of magic and occult, it literally changes his life. He discovers a secret formula for an vanishing act that works for both objects and human beings. The rest is devoted to the magician's rise to celebrity and his worldwide tours, including a performance that involves the disappearance of the Eiffel Tower.

Far stronger in style than substance, ambitious pic has possibly larger themes on its mind, such as the neurotic psyche of artists and their fear of losing their special skills. Indeed, among the film's most powerful episodes

is Quiroga's surrealistic nightmare in which his secret book is stolen and reprinted in mass.

Using the circus as its main locale — and metaphor — pic borrows heavily from Fellini, specifically "8½" and "The Clowns." But as impressive as Agresti's cinematic pyrotechnics are, they often overwhelm the thematic concerns and preclude emotional involvement in the potentially interesting saga.

Still, "The Act in Question" boasts terrific expressionistic lighting by Nestor Sanz and evocative music by Toshio Nakagawa. Carlos Roffe renders a robust, multishaded performance as the egocentric, womanizing and ultimately self-destructive magician.
— *Emanuel Levy*

DESPERATE REMEDIES
(NEW ZEALAND)

A James Wallace Prods. production, in association with New Zealand Film Commission/NZ On Air/Avalon-NFU Film Studios. Produced by Wallace. Directed, written by Stewart Main, Peter Wells. Camera (Agfacolor), Leon Narbey; editor, David Coulson; music, Peter Scholes; production design, Michael Kane; art director, Shane Radford; costume design, Glenis Foster; associate producer, Trishia Downie; sound, Graham Morris; production manager, Katherine Curtis; assistant director, Greg Stitt. Reviewed at Cannes Film Festival (Un Certain Regard section), May 22, 1993. Running time: **93 MIN.**
Dorothea Brook . . . .
. . . . Jennifer Ward-Lealand
Lawrence Hayes . . . . . Kevin Smith
Anne Cooper . . . . . . Lisa Chappell
Fraser . . . . Cliff Curtis
William Poyser . . . . . Michael Hurst
Rose . . . . Kiri Mills
Mary Anne . . . . . Bridget Armstrong

An extravagant, opulent and mostly enjoyable exercise in high camp (or low kitsch), "Desperate Remedies" has "cult item" written all over it. A feast for the eyes and ears, this knowingly over-the-top melodrama will delight the limited audience at which it's obviously aimed, with some crossover possibilities.

This ambitious first feature from Stewart Main and Peter Wells received a mainly positive sendoff in the Un Certain Regard section, with many hooting cheerfully at pic's wild extravagancies and gay abandon.

Set in the mythical colonial seaport of Hope some time during the 19th century where Dorothea, an elegantly beautiful draper who likes to dress entirely in scarlet, lives with her assistant, Anne, and worries about her young sister, Rose, addicted

June 7, 1993 (Cont.)

to opium thanks to a liaison with the sinister Fraser.

Dorothea hires a handsome, penniless immigrant, Lawrence, to seduce Rose away from Fraser; instead, Lawrence falls for Dorothea, who instead marries a scheming politician, before eventually winding up in the loving arms of Anne.

All this is played out against a background of extravagantly stylized sets, magnificently designed costumes, and deafening opera music by Verdi and Berlioz. The corn is high, but the film is lots of fun, and, while probably primarily appealing to a gay crowd, it may also amuse straights seduced by the sheer fun of it all.

Jennifer Ward-Lealand cuts an impressive figure as the imperious Dorothea, while Lisa Chappell suffers beautifully as the jealous Anne. Kevin Smith is a muscular and handsome Lawrence, while Cliff Curtis is suitably dastardly as Fraser.

The technical credits are sumptuous, despite the obviously limited budget; all the money is up there on the screen, flaunting itself. — *David Stratton*

MUI DU DU XANH
(THE SCENT OF THE GREEN PAPAYA)
(FRENCH)

An MKL (France) release of a Productions Lazennec/La SFP Cinéma/La Sept Cinéma production, in association with Canal Plus/Centre National de la Cinématographie/Fondation GAN pour le Cinéma/Procirep. (Intl. sales: President Films, Paris.) Produced by Christophe Rossignon. Directed, written by Tran Anh Hung. Camera (color), Benoit Delhomme; editor, Nicole Dedieu, Jean-Pierre Roques; music, Ton That Tiêt; production design, Alain Negre; costume design, Jean-Philippe Abril; sound, Michel Guiffan, Joël Faure; associate producers, Adeline Lecallier, Alain Rocca; assistant director, Nicolas Cambois. Reviewed at Cannes Film Festival (Un Certain Regard section), May 16, 1993. Running time: **104 MIN.**
Mùi (aged 20) . . . . Tran Nu Yên-Khê
Mùi (aged 10) . . . . Lu Man San
The mother . . . . . . Truong Thi Lôc
Old Thi . . . . Nguyen Anh Hoa
Khuyen . . . . Vuong Hoa Hôi
The father . . . . . . Tran Ngoc Trung
Also with: Souvannavong Keo, Do Nhat, Gérard Neth.
(Vietnamese soundtrack)

An exquisite exploration of a Vietnamese servant girl's private world in '50s Saigon, "The Scent of the Green Papaya" marks a striking feature bow by 30-year-old helmer Tran Anh Hung. French-funded movie, entirely shot in a studio

outside Paris, could chew off small but fragrant arthouse biz with careful handling, and is a natural for specialized webs.

First hour, set in 1951, limns the everyday chores and small joys of Mùi (Tran Nu Yên-Khê), a peasant girl engaged by a family headed by a feckless, spendthrift father. Working alongside old servant Thi (Nguyen Anh Hoa), she learns cooking and cleaning, plus the inner workings of the extended family, with its three spoiled sons, a hardworking mother (Truong Thi Lôc), and the children's grandparents.

One night, the father disappears with the family's savings, and the mother is left to hold things together with the meager pickings from her small fabric shop. Mùi slowly develops a secret liking for Khuyen (Vuong Hoa Hôi), a friend of the eldest son, Trung (Souvannavong Keo).

Pic's second seg, 10 years later, finds the family on hard times and Mùi, now a true beauty, is sent to work at the house of Khuyen, a talented classical pianist. Though he has a flirtatious g.f., Khuyen starts to notice Mùi's devotion, and love flowers.

Though visually more rigorous, Hung's movie in some ways recalls the early works of Indian helmer Satyajit Ray in its portrayal of childhood dreams and the invisible walls between kids and adults. It's a film of small events, often quietly humorous, that builds to a moving but undogmatic portrait of quiet female strength.

Dialogue, especially in the second part, is sparse, with events often recounted simply through music and Hung's constantly tracking camera. Though slowly paced, pic never dawdles unnecessarily, and Hung's emphasis on things like the girl's fascination with plants, insects and the minutiae of life gives the movie an amazing richness.

Star of the movie is production designer Alain Negre's main set of the rambling family house and street outside, both with a natural, lived-in look and packed with detail. Though the studio lighting is clearly artificial, effect heightens the feel of a self-contained world whose only concessions to reality are occasional sounds of airplanes and script refs to curfews. (Period is during the Vietminh's war of independence from the French.)

Precision lensing by Benoit Delhomme and charming, contained playing by the amateur cast add to a tasty morsel. — *Derek Elley*

O FIM DO MUNDO
(THE END OF THE WORLD)
(PORTUGESE-FRENCH)

A Madragoa Filmes/Radiotelevisao Portuguesa/La Sept co-production. Produced by Paulo Branco. Directed by Joao Mario Grilo. Screenplay, Grilo, Paulo Filipe. Camera (color), Antoine Heberle; editor, Christian Dior; music, Jorge Arriagada; production design, Jorge Calvet; sound, Frederic Ullman. Reviewed at Cannes Film Festival (Un Certain Regard section), May 21, 1993. Running time: **64 MIN.**
Augusto . . . . Jose Viana
Conceicao . . . . Adelaide Joao
Violante . . . . Zita Duarte
1st Policeman . . . . . . Santos Manuel
2nd Policeman . . . . Heitor Lourenco

Though preemed in the Un Certain Regard section of the Cannes Film Festival, "The End of the World" is strictly small-screen fare and was, in fact, designed to be the first of a TV series titled "The Four Elements" (this one's "Earth"; two other sections were at the San Francisco fest).

The extremely simple tale involves a 65-year-old farmer in a dispute over water rights with an elderly woman neighbor. During a violent quarrel, he accidentally kills her with a hoe. Though he doesn't really consider himself to be guilty (she'd moved her head at just the wrong moment), he dresses in his best suit and turns himself in. Though this was his first crime, he gets a fairly stiff sentence.

Jose Viana gives a placid performance as the old farmer but few of the other characters in the drama register. Director Joao Mario Grilo keeps this sad little story straightforward and brief, but it's hard to imagine even dedicated television viewers becoming terribly enthralled with this morbid, mundane tragedy. — *David Stratton*

WENDEMI, L'ENFANT DU BON DIEU
(WENDEMI)
(BURKINA FASO)

A Laafi Prods. (Paris)/Les films de l'espoir (Ouagadougou)/Thelma Film (Zurich) co-production. Directed by S. Pierre Yameogo. Screenplay, Yameogo, Rene Sintzel. Camera (color), Jurg Hassler; editor, Michelle Darmon; music, Mahmoud Tabrizizadeh. Reviewed at Cannes Film Festival (Un Certain Regard section), May 16, 1993. Running time: **95 MIN.**

Wendemi . . . . . Sylvain Minoungou
Also with: Abdoulaye Komboudri, Sylvie Yameogo, Aida Diallo, Celestin Zongo, Sotigui Kouyate.

A charming fable about a boy in search of his identity, "Wendemi, L'enfant du Bon Dieu" gently communicates director S. Pierre Yameogo's warning against the temptations of a moral fall. Its simplicity is matched by surprising candor about sexual mores in Burkina Faso. Pic's leisurely pace and repetitive structure recall fairy tales and will have a lullaby effect on many viewers. Festival and specialty audiences should be interested abroad.

In a classic opener, set in a dusty country backyard, a family powwow is being held to discuss the advanced pregnancy of daughter Cecile. The girl refuses to reveal who the baby's father is and runs off and abandons her newborn in a field. A neighbor who finds the baby brings him up as Wendemi, "child of the Good God." When he's still young, the boy is cruelly taken from his foster parents and put in a remote village. As a young man, he sets off to find his mother in the city and learn his true identity.

In Ouagadougou, the capital, Wendemi stumbles across a shepherd from his village and finally locates Cecile, who has married and moved to town. She now repents of having abandoned her son, and together they return to Wendemi's native village to find his father. Cecile reveals the culprit is a man above suspicion — the hypocritical parish priest. In a beautifully understated finale, the villagers indignantly confront the servant of God with the unhappiness he has caused.

This simple story sometimes gets away from Yameogo, who resorts to the most outrageous coincidences to get himself out of a tight spot. Wendemi's meeting with his mother may be destiny, but the ease with which he finds her, thanks to an ordinary looking bracelet he wears, is exasperatingly amateurish.

The lensing has a similar naivete, but luckily it's in tune with the story's elemental separation of good and evil.

Young Sylvain Minoungou has the right handsomely innocent face to play Wendemi, while the rest of the cast is professional. Technical work is adequate.

— *Deborah Young*

REQUIEM POUR UN BEAU SANS-COUER
(REQUIEM FOR A HANDSOME BASTARD)
(CANADIAN)

An Allegro Films release of a Coop Video/Lux Films production. Produced by Nicole Roberts, Lorraine Dufour. Directed, written by Robert Morin. Camera (color), James Gray; editor, Lorraine Dufour; music, Jean Corriveau; art direction, Marie-Carole De Beaumont, Marie-Christiane Mathieu; costumes, Nicoletta Massone; sound, Marcel Chouinard; assistant director, Pierre Plante. Reviewed at Cannes Film Festival (Intl. Critics Week), May 15, 1993. Running time: 93 MIN.
Regis Savoie . . . . Gildor Roy
Tonio . . . . Jean-Guy Bouchard
Maki . . . . Klimbo
Cindy . . . . Sabrina Boudot
Jean-Pierre Trudel . . . . Stephan Cote
Madame Savoie . . . . Sabrina Boudot
Denise . . . . Brigitte Paquette
Mike Di Palma . Louis-Georges Girard

Already a cult hit in Quebec, "Requiem for a Handsome Bastard" should score international specialized success. A clever, audacious account of the rise and fall of a small-time thug, the film could be this year's more sober-sided "Man Bites Dog."

Ostensibly centered around an unrepentant thief and murderer, first-time feature helmer Robert Morin effects an unusual narrative style to convey the rise and fall of his punk protagonist. The device, baffling to the casual moviegoer, is well worth it for those who stick out the chase and carnage.

Regis Savoie (Gildor Roy) is serving 25 years in a Montreal lockup. In a misguided sense of compassion, the authorities allow him a visitation from his young son. It's the chance he's been waiting for and in a moment of confusion, Savoie grabs a gun and makes a break for it.

Savoie collects an old crony and, after an interlude of brutal revenge, grabs his girlfriend and hies for the hinterlands. Not far behind is Maki (Klimbo), a city detective every bit as ferocious as his quarry. Effectively, it's now a cat and mouse game where one has to ultimately take a fall.

While a brief synopsis would suggest a fairly straightforward narrative, the structure is considerably more complex and random. Incidents occur out of time and the disjointedness is often a challenge, only making sense when all the pieces come together at the end.

Roy pulls out all the stops as a Kray-zed criminal whose bravura and brutishness lends him equal parts of menace and humor, riveting work worthy of the cinema's rogues gallery.

A talent to watch, Morin executes a very difficult premise with aplomb. Tech credits are frighteningly assured.

— Leonard Klady

LA FLORIDA
(CANADIAN)

An Aliance Vivafilm release of a Films Vision 4/Prods. Pierre Sarrazin production. Produced by Pierre Sarrazin, Claude Bonin. Executive producers, Bonin, Sarrazin, Jacques Bonin, Suzette Couture. Directed by Georges Mihalka. Screenplay by Couture, Sarrazin. Camera (color), Rene Ohashi; editor, François Guill, Yves Chaput; production design, Perri Gorrara; art direction, Barbra Matis; costumes, Paul-Andree Guerin; sound, Douglas Ganton, Jane Tatersall. Reviewed at Cannes Film Festival (market section), May 16, 1993. Running time: 111 MIN.
Leo . . . . Remy Girard
Ginette . . . . Pauline LaPointe
Big Daddy . . . . Raymond Bouchard
Rheal Lariviere . . . . Gildor Roy
Rheaume Lariviere . Martin Drainville
Carmen . . . . Marie-Josée Croze
Sylvain Sylvestre . . Dennis Bouchard
Jay Lamori . . . . Jason Blicker
Vivy Lamori . . . . . . Margot Kidder
Romeo Laflamme . . Michael Sarrazin

The annual flight of the "snowbirds" — the winter escape of Canadians to the sunnier clime of Florida — is the comic subject of "La Florida." While this provincial comedy has been eliciting big laughs in French Canada, it simply doesn't travel.

Despite a more polished look than one expects from such piffle and a generally excellent cast, the material and direction is broad and simplistic. The by-the-numbers plot centers on Leo (Remy Girard), a retiring Montreal bus driver who's saved all his cash to move the family to the transplant community and open a modest motel. Then the story breaks down into the political dynamics in the Canadian community itself and the machinations of a developer (Margot Kidder) who needs Leo's property for a major development.

Amid the mild dramatics there's plenty of buffoonery and sexy girls strutting their stuff in the sun. It's predictable, predictable, predictable.

A straight programmer in its domestic market, "La Florida" could spawn a healthy series if subsequent chapters are reined in on a tight budget. With a little more creative thought it might also tap a nerve for other cultures. — *Leonard Klady*

LE PRESSENTIMENT/ PREDTCHOUVSTVIE
(FOREBODING)
(RUSSIAN-ROMANIAN-B&W/COLOR)

A Delta-Film production. (Intl. sales: Valeriu Jereghi, Russia). Directed, written by Valeriu Jereghi. Camera (B&W/color), Vivi Dragan-Vasile; editor, Nita Kivulescu; music, Liudmila Jereghi; production design, Daniel Radutsa. Reviewed at Cannes Film Festival (Un Certain Regard section), May 22, 1993. Running time: 90 MIN.
La femme . . . . Maria Ploae
Le garcon . . . . Daniel Ionescu
La vache . . . . Lunaia

A visionary film about the Apocalypse, "Foreboding" is a pretentious exercise in abstract, imagistic cinema. Judging by the public's reaction at Cannes (a huge walk-out), nearly-silent pic may please only the most serious and committed fest and arthouse viewers.

Director Valeriu Jereghi also gets credit as writer, though the script comprises perhaps 100 words. It takes about half an hour before the first one is uttered, by a woman who seems to be the only survivor of a catastrophic, possibly ultimate, war.

Heavy-handed allegory has only four characters: a nameless woman, a naked, speechless boy, a wandering cow, and a destructive tank that occasionally threatens to kill the pair.

Atrociously slow, film documents the extraordinary strength of the will to survive, observing in an almost anthropological manner how the woman and boy take care of their basic needs (food, clothes, shelter).

The woman, Maria Ploae, possesses an attractive, expressive face. But, for the most part, her thesping consists of sighs, moans, cries and whispers, which provide the film's sound; there is minimal use of music.

Jereghi demonstrates greater talent in establishing a visual tonality of doom and gloom than in re-creating life and rebirth, which appear at the very end. Vivi Dragan-Vasile's stylized cinematography, which smoothly changes from black and white to color (often within the same shot) is breathtaking. One wishes this grand, arty design decorated a less metaphorical narrative.

—Emanuel Levy

FAUT-IL AIMER MATHILDE?
(SHOULD MATHILDE BE LOVED?)
(FRENCH)

A 3B production. Produced by Jean Brehat. Directed by Edwin Baily. Screenplay, Luigi de Angelis, Baily. Camera (Color), Pierre-Laurent Chenieux; editor, Dominique Gallieni; music, Arno; sound, Philippe Fabbri. Reviewed at Cannes Film Festival (Intl. Critics Week), May 15, 1993. Running time: 100 MIN.
Mathilde . . . . Dominique Blanc
Charlie . . . . Andre Marcon
Papy . . . . Paul Crauchet
Lucien . . . . Victor Garrivier
Jean-Pierre . . . . . Jacques Bonnaffe
Mano . . . . Marc Doret

"Should Mathilde Be Loved?" is a French melodrama centering on the midlife crisis of a sensitive working-class woman. Sharply observed psychological study should be of interest to female viewers and Franco-cinephiles.

Mathilde (Dominique Blanc), is an attractive middle-aged woman, left to raise her children when her husband suddenly disappears. Desolate, Mathilde sees that time is passing her by. The impetus for change is provided by an accident at work that forces Mathilde to reevaluate her relationships.

Shot in Northern France, melancholy pic provides a good sense of place in observing Mathilde's interactions with four men: husband Jean-Pierre; Charlie, her dull current beau who has loved her since childhood; the married Jacques, who fathered her illegitimate son; and Mano, a Spanish immigrant who volunteers to rebuild her house.

As Mathilde, Dominique Blanc, holds the narrative together, carries off her role with physical grace and verbal charm, displaying a great range of emotion and intelligence that helps establish the film's shifting moods.

Helmer Edwin Baily's direction is at times low-key, though he is good at locating the gentle humor in the most painful episodes. — *Emanuel Levy*

June 7, 1993 (Cont.)

CARNOSAUR

A Concorde-New Horizons Corp. production and release. Produced by Mike Elliott. Executive producer, Roger Corman. Directed, written by Adam Simon. Camera (color), Keith Holland; editor, Richard Gentner; music, Nigel Holton; production design, Aaron Osborne; visual effects supervisor, Alan Lasky; creature designer/creator, John Carl Buechler, Magical Media Industries. Reviewed at Cannes Film Festival (market section), May 15, 1993. MPAA Rating: R. Running time: **82 MIN.**

Dr. Jane Tiptree . . . . . . Diane Ladd
"Doc" Smith . . . . . Raphael Sbarge
Thrush . . . . Jennifer Runyon
Sheriff . . . . Harrison Page
Trucker . . . . Clint Howard

It would be a very long stretch to suggest that Concorde's "Carnosaur" was raising the anxiety level at Universal, whose "Jurassic Park" opening in two weeks. A market quickie that is guaranteed a fast two weeks in regional playoff, the contemporary dino tale harks back to '50s monster epics in style and sophistication. The ever-vigilant Roger Corman film factory is once again first in the marketplace with an exploitable sensation.

Replete with scientific mumbo jumbo, this breezy outing is a not-very-filling popcorn treat. Predictably plotted with bargain-basement effects, it's a serviceable programmer destined for a quick trip to the tar pits of video shelves and cable screenings.

Somewhere in the Nevada desert, genetic scientist Dr. Jane Tiptree (Diane Ladd) is hatching diabolical experiments with chickens. Exactly what it's all leading to, not even her employers know. As best as can be gleaned early on, Tiptree has cross-fertilized chicken eggs with T-Rex DNA. The result is a lethal little pecker that dines on the Southwest smorgasbord of truckers and military/industrial support staff. But bigger horrors are to come.

The unwitting hero is "Doc" Smith (Raphael Sbarge), a plant operations employee who hooks up with Thrush (Jennifer Runyon), a member of a commune of eco-freaks. Together they dodge the rapidly growing prehistoric terror, eventually winding up in the underground lab of the off-kilter scientist.

There the full horror is revealed. Tiptree's next step is to fertilize her dinos via the human reproductive system. What appears to be a fever is a prelude to an unwanted pregnancy.

Ladd chews up the scenery as the mad doctor; her *raison d'etre* is to end the lousiest species. Sbarge and Runyon are not called on for anything more than obvious characterizations.

Writer-director Adam Simon keeps the action about a step or two ahead of the silliness. But it's a real footrace for this fleeting diversion. — *Leonard Klady*

LE PAYS DES SOURDS
(LAND OF THE DEAF)
(FRENCH-DOCU)

An MKL release of a Les Films d'Ici/La Sept Cinema/Le Centre Européen Cinématographique Rhône-Alpes co-production in association with Rhône-Alpes region/Canal Plus/the CNC/La Foundation de France/the Ministry of Foreign Affairs, RAI-3/BBC/RTSR and support from the Gan Fondation. Produced by Serge Lalou. Directed by Nicolas Philibert. Camera (color), Frédéric Labourasse; editor, Guy Lecorne; sound, Henri Maïkoff; production supervisor, Françoise Buraux; assistant director, Valéry Gaillard; assistant editor, Anja Lüdke. Reviewed at Club Publicis screening room, Paris, Feb. 18, 1993. Running time: **99 MIN.**

With: Jean-Claude Poulain, Odile Ghermani, Babette Deboissy, Denis Azra, Aboubakar, Anh Tuan, Betty, Floret, Frédéric, Jalal, Karen, Tomo.

A completely inspiring if not consistently riveting documentary, "Le Pays des Sourds" shows that while the deaf are "just like everybody else" they also inhabit a culturally distinct world of their own. The informative film, which has already won fest acclaim, is tailor-made for international tube sales, should have a long life and could inspire similar projects in other countries.

The parallel universe of the deaf is shared by 130 million people worldwide, 3.5 million of them in France. Those presented are so cheerful, expressive and thoughtful that one is left with the impression that, in terms of emotional balance, it's practically an advantage to be deaf.

The viewer gains an immediate appreciation for the beauty, precision and humor of signing, reinforced by anecdotes. Delightful teacher Jean-Claude Poulain traces and defines the "frame" for gestures — which is the obvious connection between sign language and film. Eloquent, accurate signing uses "establishing shots," "closeups," etc.

Well-adjusted, productive adults are contrasted with a small class of youngsters whose firm but patient teachers prod and encourage the kids as they struggle to make the sounds that drive ingenious computer games.

The wedding of a young deaf couple is unduly awkward as the well-meaning minister puts the bride and groom through the ordeal of exchanging their vows aloud. When they go apartment hunting, the viewer gets one of the pic's few concrete glimpses of how difficult it can be to function in a hearing world.

Otherwise, everyone is unflaggingly supportive. Pic is so careful to put across "normal" lives that what are, after all, extraordinary situations finally take on the tediousness of normalcy.

Pic took the Grand Prix at the 1992 Belfort (France) fest as well as top prize at the Festival dei Popoli. — *Lisa Nesselson*

TEENAGE BONNIE AND KLEPTO CLYDE

A 21st Century presentation of a Grove Park Intl. production. Produced by Steve Jankowski. Executive producers, Menahem Golan, Ami Artzi. Directed by John Shepphird. Screenplay, Shepphird, Jankowski. Camera (Alpha-Cine color), Neal Brown; editor, Brent White; music, Terry Plummer; production design, Paul Nibley; sound, Joe Judd; production manager, Bryce W. Fillmore; assistant director, Robert A. Reeves; postproduction supervisor, Mark S. Hoerr; 2nd-unit director, Robert Eker. Reviewed at Cannes Film Festival (market section), May 17, 1993. Running time: **87 MIN.**

Bonnie Baker . . . Maureen Flannigan
Clyde . . . . Scott Wolf
Kirk . . . . Bentley Mitchum
Peter Baker . . . . Tom Bower

A low-voltage updating of the Arthur Penn classic, "Teenage Bonnie and Klepto Clyde" is a natural for undemanding video freaks. Numerous nods to the 1967 pic add nothing to the unconvincing mayhem.

In this version of the yarn, Clyde (Scott Wolf) and Bonnie (Maureen Flannigan) are both small-town high-school students. He works in a fast-food joint at night, while she's the spoiled daughter of the local hard-line police chief (Tom Bower).

They meet when Bonnie's b.f. (Bentley Mitchum) trashes Clyde's eatery, and before long they're off on a crime spree, using her Daddy's substantial armory, until they're gunned down near the Mexican border.

This is strictly routine fare, in which the by-the-numbers screenplay by director John Shepphird and producer Steve Jankowski asserts that sexual fulfillment comes from participation in violent crime. As in the Penn pic, Clyde is not at first turned on by the well-endowed Bonnie, though in this version the sexual hijinks commence sooner.

The young actors are adequate, though Maureen Flannigan pouts rather too much. Pic, mostly shot in Utah, takes a very routine approach, but it's technically adequate. —*David Stratton*

BRAIN SMASHER

A Kings Road production. Produced by Tom Karnowski. Directed, written by Albert Pyun. Camera (color), George Mooradian; editor, Lauren Schaffer; music, Tony Riparetti; production design, Phil Zarling; casting, Cathy Henderson Blake. Reviewed at Cannes Film Festival (market section), May 15, 1993. Running time: **85 MIN.**

Ed Malloy . . . . . . Andrew Dice Clay
Sam Crain . . . . Teri Hatcher

"Brain Smasher" is an assault on the viewer's brain. The small-budget actioner, ridiculously subtitled "A Love Story," won't generate any box office coin and may find only few advocates on video.

Set in Seattle, the pic concerns the adventures of two sisters involved in the smuggling and possession of "the Red Lotus," a rare flower from China supposed to hold the secret to world domination. Constructed as clichés, the sisters' characters could not be more different: The elder is a botanist, and therefore less attractive; the younger (Teri Hatcher) is a model, which also means she is weaker and naive.

Enter Ed Malloy (Andrew Dice Clay), nicknamed Brain Smasher, a macho disco bouncer. Younger sister gives him an expensive watch (from an old b.f) in exchange for protecting her. As it happens, the gorgeous model only seems to be a bimbo. After one brief lesson from Brain Smasher, she is almost as skillful a fighter as her mentor.

The witless script uses the same joke over and over: The black-masked villains are continuously referred to as Ninjas, despite their protests that they are Chinese, not Japanese. And in the midst of the chases and shootings, the guilt-stricken Ed stops to visit his mother.

Helmer Albert Pyun does his best to move the story fast, but not fast enough. Proficient technical credits can't overcome pic's deficiencies; prominent among them is Teri Hatcher's awkward acting. — *Emanuel Levy*

June 7, 1993 (Cont.)   **June 14, 1993**

THE PUNK
(BRITISH)

A Videodrome production. Produced, directed by Mike Sarne. Executive producer, Robin Mahoney. Screenplay, Sarne, from Gideon Sams' book. Camera (Panavision widescreen), Alan M. Trow; editor, Gwyn Jones; associate producers, David Goldstein, William Sarne; assistant director, William Beaton. Reviewed at Cannes Film Festival (market section), May 18, 1993. Running time: **96 MIN.**
David . . . . Charlie Creed-Miles
Rachel . . . . Vanessa Hadaway
David's Father . . . . David Shawyer
Rachel's Father . . . . . . Jess Conrad

After a long absence from the screen, director Mike Sarne, best known for "Myra Breckinridge," makes an impressive comeback with "The Punk," a gritty, contempo take on "Romeo and Juliet." Theatrical prospects are excellent for the vibrant, visually stunning movie, clearly made with an eye on the youth market.

Sarne's script is based on Gideon Sams' 1976 book, originally scribbled as an essay in an English class. The irony is that Sams, who died in New York from pneumonia when he was 21, reputedly never read Shakespeare.

In the new film, which firmly stands on its own and departs from the original, the Montagues and Capulets are transformed into the Punks and the Rockers. David (Charlie Creed-Miles), a working-class punk, calls himself Adolph just to annoy his obnoxious policeman father (David Shawyer), whose hobby is watching "stamps programs" on TV. David is closer to his victimized mother, who is mentally ill and sent to the hospital.

David spends his time shooting pool and wandering in the streets. He accidentally meets Rachel (Vanessa Hadaway), a product of a rich and pompous family, in a local theater where she is performing Shakespeare.

Set for the most part around Notting Hill Gate, Sarne brings a narrative looseness and immediacy to his love story. But by embracing wholeheartedly the youth's point of view, the portraiture of the adult world comes off as a stereotypical caricature.

Sarne elicits perfectly natural performances from his two youngsters, particularly Creed-Miles. The actors' youth, freshness, and romantic passion overcome the trappings of most other screen "Romeo and Juliets."

Technical credits are superior, particularly Alan M. Trow's exhilarating photography and Gwyn Jones' seamless editing. Shot in an impressively fluid way, with a mobile, often hand-held camera, "The Punk" is visually distinguished and always maintains a high energy level and an amiably eccentric tone.
— *Emanuel Levy*

JURASSIC PARK

A Universal release of an Amblin Entertainment production. Produced by Kathleen Kennedy, Gerald R. Molen. Directed by Steven Spielberg. Screenplay, Michael Crichton, David Koepp, from Crichton's novel. Camera (Deluxe color), Dean Cundey; editor, Michael Kahn; music, John Williams; production design, Rick Carter; art direction, Jim Teegarden, John Bell; set design, John Berger, Lauren Polizzi, Masako Masuda; set decoration, Jackie Carr; sound (Dolby; The Digital Experience), Ron Judkins; sound design, Gary Rydstrom; full-motion dinosaurs, Dennis Muren; live-action dinosaurs, Stan Winston; dinosaur supervisor, Phil Tippett, special dinosaur effects, Michael Lantieri; full-motion dinosaurs and special visual effects, Industrial Light & Magic; stunt coordinator, Gary Hymes; associate producers, Lata Ryan, Colin Wilson; assistant director, John T. Kretchmer; aerial unit director, David Nowell; "Mr. D.N.A." animation, Kurtz and Friends; casting, Janet Hirshenson, Jane Jenkins. Reviewed at Universal Studios, Universal City, Calif., June 2, 1993. MPAA Rating: PG-13. Running time: **126 MIN.**
Dr. Alan Grant . . . . Sam Neill
Ellie Sattler . . . . Laura Dern
Ian Malcolm . . . . . . Jeff Goldblum
John Hammond . . . .
. . . . Richard Attenborough
Robert Muldoon . . . . Bob Peck
Donald Gennaro . . . . Martin Ferrero
Dr. Wu . . . . B.D. Wong
Tim . . . . Joseph Mazzello
Lex . . . . Ariana Richards
Arnold . . . . Samuel L. Jackson
Dennis Nedry . . . . . . Wayne Knight
Park Tour Voice . . . . . Richard Kiley

"Jurassic Park" will at least disabuse anyone of the idea that it would be fun to share the planet with dinosaurs. Steven Spielberg's scary and horrific thriller may be one-dimensional and even clunky in story and characterization, but definitely delivers where it counts, in excitement, suspense and the stupendous realization of giant reptiles. Having finally found another set of "Jaws" worthy of the name, Spielberg and Universal have a monster hit on their hands.

Very cleverly, the film positions itself both as a dark look at a theme park gone awry, and as a theme park itself. Merchandising, Universal tour attractions and sequels will extend the profits enormously. The only thing that will keep this properly PG-13-rated extravaganza from approaching rarefied "Star Wars" and "E.T." b.o. heights is its inappropriateness for kids under 10 or 12 — it's just too intense.

The $60 million production (a bargain at the price) follows the general idea if not the letter of co-scriptor Michael Crichton's 1990 bestseller.

Basis of this hi-tech, scientifically based, up-to-date version lies in the notion that living, breathing and eating full-sized dinosaurs can be biologically engineered using fossilized dino DNA. Having accomplished this in secret on an island off Costa Rica, zillionaire entrepreneur/tycoon John Hammond (Richard Attenborough) brings in a small group of experts to view and, he hopes, endorse his miracle, which is to be the world's most expensive zoo-cum-amusement park.

Arriving to inspect the menagerie are paleontologists Dr. Alan Grant (Sam Neill) and Ellie Sattler (Laura Dern), as well as oddball mathematician Ian Malcolm (Jeff Goldblum), advocate of the Chaos Theory, a sort of numerical equivalent of Murphy's Law. Also along for the look-see are Donald Gennaro (Martin Ferrero), a hardnosed attorney repping the park's investors, and Hammond's two fresh-faced grandchildren, Lex (Ariana Richards) and Tim (Joseph Mazzello).

Introductory scenes are surprisingly perfunctory and even sloppy, as there are several bad cuts unworthy of a filmmaker of Spielberg's skill, and the script wouldn't pass muster in Screenwriting 101. Equally surprisingly, Spielberg lets the dinosaurs out of the bag very early, showing some of them in full view after only 20 minutes.

Still, none of these problems ends up mattering once the film clicks into high gear. When a storm strands two carloads of Hammond's guests in the middle of the park at night, a Tyrannosaurus rex decides it's dinnertime. Suddenly, after a fitful first hour, Spielberg pulls off one of the most exciting set pieces of his career, highlighted by a stunning shot of a T-Rex in a rearview mirror and climaxed by a gag lifted from Buster Keaton's "Steamboat Bill Jr."

Events from here on frighteningly verify the mathematician's view of an unpredictable universe. With command central's computer and power systems shut down, the dinosaurs are free to run amok, thanks to the treachery of rotund hacker Dennis Nedry (Wayne Knight).

Grant and the two kids are forced to make their way back across the park to the compound, and their adventures are spiked by arguably the most beautiful and awe-inspiring scene in the film, in which a herd of speedy small dinosaurs sweep toward the characters across a plain and away from a hungry T-Rex, who ultimately enjoys a meal. The outdoor perspectives here, after

June 14, 1993 (Cont.)

the nocturnal studio work, prove particularly refreshing. The reptiles here are brilliantly convincing — lifelike, crafty, smooth of movement and numerous. Taking special bows in this department are special effects wizards Stan Winston, Dennis Muren, Phil Tippett, Michael Lantieri and hundreds of technicians, at Industrial Light & Magic and elsewhere.

In fact, the monsters are far more convincing than the human characters. Saddled with skin-deep roles, the actors are not in much of a position to distinguish themselves. Sam Neill's paleontologist comes off rather like a bland Indiana Jones, while Laura Dern considerably overdoes the facial oohs and ahhs. The kids are basically along for the ride, while Jeff Goldblum, attired in all-black, helpfully fires off most of the wisecracks.

As for Richard Attenborough, agreeably back onscreen for the first time since 1979, his role has been significantly softened from the book, turned from single-mindedly malevolent developer into a profit-minded grandpa willing to acknowledge his folly.

While the gore of the novel has been toned down to unbloody levels, and the body count is notably lower (as if with the wave of a hand, the vast number of workers at the park are made to disappear when convenient), Spielberg nevertheless turns the screws very tight in the film's second hour, having evidently decided to sacrifice the youngest potential viewers in order to give everyone else a good scare.

Technically, the film is sometimes more than it needs to be. As in some of Spielberg's previous outings, Dean Cundey's lensing overdoes the back illumination and shafts of light at times, and John Williams' score gets unnecessarily bombastic. But the dinosaurs rule here, and Spielberg and his team of special effects aces have put something on the screen that people have never seen before, which is the surest way to create a blockbuster.

— *Todd McCarthy*

WHAT'S LOVE GOT TO DO WITH IT

A Buena Vista release of a Touchstone Pictures presentation of a Krost/Chapin production. Produced by Doug Chapin, Barry Krost. Executive producers, Roger Davies, Mario Iscovich. Directed by Brian Gibson. Screenplay, Kate Lanier, from Tina Turner and Kurt Loder's book "I, Tina." Camera (Kodak color), Jamie Anderson; editor, Stuart Pappe; music, Stanley Clarke; music supervisor, Daniel Allan Carlin; production design, Stephen Altman; art director, Richard Johnson; set decorator, Rick Simpson; costume design, Ruth Carter; sound (Dolby), John Stacy, Jane Carpenter Wilson; co-producer, Pat Kehoe; choreographer, Michael Peters; assistant director, Barry Thomas; casting, Reuben Cannon & Associates. Reviewed at Cinerama Dome, L.A., June 3, 1993. MPAA Rating: R. Running Time: **118 MIN.**

Tina Turner . . . . . . Angela Bassett
Ike Turner . . . . Laurence Fishburne
Jackie . . . . . . Vanessa Bell Calloway
Zelma Bullock . . . . . . Jenifer Lewis
Alline Bullock . . . .
. . . . Phyllis Yvonne Stickney
Darlene . . . . .Khandi Alexander
Leanne . . . . Pamela Tyson
Lorraine . . . . Penny Johnson
Young Anna Mae . . . . Rae'ven Kelly
Fross . . . . Chi

Touchstone's "What's Love Got to Do With It" looks like a surefire winner. The musical biography of songstress Tina Turner is a passionate personal and professional drama that hits both the high and low notes of an extraordinary life and career. An immensely enjoyable saga, the film should score across the board with audiences and ring up big numbers for the summer.

It's also one of those star-is-born roles for lead Angela Bassett, who would be well advised to buy her Oscar gown now.

From the outset, there's a sense of specialness in Kate Lanier's screenplay. Young Tina, a.k.a. Anna Mae Bullock, is first seen as a precocious youngster whose bluesy interpretation of gospel drives a proper choirmaster to extremes. Closer to home, she is left in the care of her grandmother after her mother (Jenifer Lewis) goes off to the big city. Years will pass before they are reunited in St. Louis.

It's also in St. Louis, circa 1958, that she encounters charismatic R&B singer-songwriter Ike Turner (Laurence Fishburne). Part of his act involves coaxing comely women to the mike. Most of the participants are pretty dreadful but when Anna Mae lets loose, Ike sees a potent meal ticket.

Though capable of great charm,

Ike chiefly coerces his renamed Tina to work to the breaking point. When tact succumbs to vice and ambition, he abuses her, becoming a master of cruelty.

Nothing in Bassett's earlier repertoire suggested the consummate skill she brings to the part. It is a full-bodied, nuanced portrayal. While her physical resemblance is glancing, it is truly one of the most convincing embodiments of a living performer.

The only sour note comes at the finale with a jarring switch from the fictional to the real life Tina in concert. It's unnecessary and a slap to Bassett's efforts.

Fishburne as Ike Turner is also pitch perfect. An actor of considerable resources, he never balks at the challenges in creating an ultimately despicable man. Yet, he maintains the humanity that keeps the character outside the danger zone of caricature.

The supporting cast is uniformly strong, with Jenifer Lewis worthy of special note as Tina's slyly treacherous mother.

Director Brian Gibson easily surpasses his work in "The Josephine Baker Story." He is in sync with the subject matter to an extent few contemporary filmmakers have demonstrated. The technical work, especially the musical elements, are peerless.

— *Leonard Klady*

LIFE WITH MIKEY

A Buena Vista Pictures release of a Touchstone Pictures presentation of a Scott Rudin production. Produced by Teri Schwartz, Rudin. Directed by James Lapine. Screenplay, Marc Lawrence. Camera (Film House color, Technicolor prints), Rob Hahn; editor, Robert Leighton; music, Alan Menken; production design, Adrianne Lobel; art direction, Dennis Davenport; set decoration, Gordon Sim; costume design, William Ivey Long; sound (Dolby), David Lee; co-producer, Marc Lawrence; assistant director, J. Stephen Buck; casting, John Lyons. Reviewed at Avco Center Cinema, L.A., May 22, 1993. MPAA Rating: PG. Running time: **91 MIN.**

Michael Chapman . . . . Michael J. Fox
Angie Vega . . . . Christina Vidal
Ed Chapman . . . . Nathan Lane
Geena Briganti . . . . . . Cyndi Lauper
Barry Corman . . . . David Krumholtz
Mr. Corcoran . . . . David Huddleston
Brian Spiro . . . . Victor Garber

What happens to a child star (at least, the ones who don't wind up in jail) when he grows up? In this unassuming

little comedy, he runs a kids' talent agency, discovers a wayward waif oozing natural talent and, in the process, finds himself. A better version of "Curly Sue," this Michael J. Fox vehicle screams "cute" from every pore but should play well with kids and won't insult the intelligence of adults. Disney may have a quiet success here, assuming the little guy isn't lost amid brassier summer fare.

Michael Chapman (Fox) was once the star of his own sitcom, "Life With Mikey," making him one of the best-known tykes in America. Unfortunately, he topped out at age 15, and now suffers from a serious case of Peter Pan-itis, unwilling to take on responsibility while his patient brother (Nathan Lane) runs their business.

Then a streetwise 10-year-old steals Michael's wallet and puts on a Meryl Streep-quality performance when caught. A light bulb goes off over Michael's head, and an uneasy alliance is forged. Thief-ette Angie (newcomer Christina Vidal) actually does have a sob story; she's forced to live with her inattentive sister because her parents are gone.

She quickly lands a major commercial gig and moves in with Michael, compelling him to confront some of his own inadequacies, while the fate of his agency hangs in the balance.

This is all very stock, predictable stuff, but director James Lapine and writer/co-producer Marc Lawrence bring an easy charm to most of the proceedings.

Fox turns in an extremely likable, believable performance sans camp or melodramatics (even when the script leans in that direction), and Vidal emerges as an engaging child actor without resorting to the shameless mugging characteristic of so many children's roles, even if her precociousness at times overdone.

Lane is properly harried as the brother, while Cyndi Lauper — after an ill-fated star turn in "Vibes" — is better-suited to her supporting role as a ditzy secretary. Ruben Blades also shows up in an uncredited cameo.

"Mikey" does have a rather flabby midsection but rallies at the finish. Tech credits are solid, with Oscar-winner Alan Menken providing a nifty score.

Kudos also to the art direction on the various commercial spoofs, which should have even tots smiling with a sense of recognition. — *Brian Lowry*

June 14, 1993 (Cont.)

GUILTY AS SIN

A Buena Vista release of a Hollywood Pictures presentation. Produced by Martin Ransohoff. Executive producers, Don Carmody, Bob Robinson. Directed by Sidney Lumet. Screenplay, Larry Cohen. Camera (Eastman color; Technicolor prints), Andrzej Bartkowiak; editor, Evan Lottman; music, Howard Shore; production design, Philip Rosenberg; set decoration, Enrico Campana; costume design, Gary Jones; sound (Dolby Digital), Bruce Carwardine; assistant director, Martin Walters; production manager, Joyce Kozy King; stunt coordinator, Dwayne McLean; associate producers, Lilith Jacobs, Jolene Moroney; casting, Lynn Stalmaster, Stuart Aikins (Canada). Reviewed at Cinema 1, N.Y., June 1, 1993. MPAA Rating: R. Running time: **104 MIN.**

Jennifer Haines	Rebecca DeMornay
David Greenhill	Don Johnson
Phil Garson	Stephen Lang
Moe	Jack Warden
Judge Tompkins	Dana Ivey
Diangelo	Ron White
Emily	Norma Dell'Agnese
Nolan	Sean McCann
Lt. Martinez	Luis Guzman

It takes too long for the courtroom thriller "Guilty As Sin" to heat up and engage an audience. Despite some intriguing plot twists and a visceral windup, Sidney Lumet's study of a war of wills is of very limited b.o. interest.

The prolific director scored his last hit over a decade ago with "The Verdict," and elements here (primarily Andrzej Bartkowiak's moody lighting and Jack Warden's similar support role) that conjure up memories of that superior Paul Newman-starrer.

Don Johnson is effectively cast as the literal ladykiller, who's just been accused of throwing his rich wife out a highrise window. Like a stalker, he's become fixated on hotshot criminal lawyer Rebecca DeMornay and uses reverse psychology to get her to take his case.

Johnson's upfront sexism and smug role reversal as a narcissistic gigolo generate comic relief and unintentional risibility in equal measure. DeMornay gets top billing but is saddled with a functional, reactive part. Viewer is immediately intrigued with Johnson's showy character and has to wait four or five reels for DeMornay to wake up and battle him in earnest.

Early on she is convinced Johnson is guilty and trying to manipulate her. However, judge Dana Ivey forces her to continue his defense, locking DeMornay into an untenable situation.

Soon fearing for her very life when it becomes apparent that Johnson's killing spree is open-ended, DeMornay has detective Jack Warden gather evidence of Johnson's previous unsolved murders. She can't use it because of client confidentiality so, in Cohen's most questionable ploy, plants evidence incriminating Johnson in the current case.

He figures out what she's up to and produces a surprise alibi, resulting in a hung jury. Gory climax locks the stars in a frightening dance of death that gives "Sin" its only commercial zing. Like the monster sometimes added to an atmospheric Val Lewton thriller of the '40s, finale seems imposed on an otherwise tasteful and bloodless exercise.

Bartkowiak's compositions and lighting add menace to the urban locations, lensed in Canada as a convincing double for Chicago settings. Score by Howard Shore is exceedingly spare.

Johnson is at his best oozing oily charm but muffs a dramatic freakout scene midway through the picture. DeMornay does little more than keep a straight face no matter how farfetched the proceedings become.

Film is almost a two-hander, with supporting cast led by Warden and DeMornay's boyfriend Stephen Lang literally (and sometimes comically) expendable.
— *Lawrence Cohn*

THE HEARTBREAK KID
(AUSTRALIAN)

A Roadshow (Australia) release of a View Films production, in association with the Australian Film Finance Corp. Produced by Ben Gannon. Executive producer, Andrea Asimov. Directed by Michael Jenkins. Screenplay, Jenkins, Richard Barrett, from Barrett's play. Camera (Eastmancolor), Nino Martinetti; editor, Peter Carrodus; music, John Clifford White; production design, Paddy Reardon; sound, John Phillips; co-produced by Barbara Gibbs; production manager, Gibbs; assistant director, Ian Kenny; postproduction supervisor, Barbara Biggs; casting, Alison Barrett. Reviewed at Village screening room, Sydney, April 27, 1993. (In Sydney Film Festival.) Running time: **97 MIN.**

Christina Papadopoulos	Claudia Karvan
Nick Polides	Alex Dimitriades
Dimitri	Steve Bastoni
George Polides	Nico Lathouris
Southgate	William McInnes
Evdokia	Doris Younane

"The Heartbreak Kid," which has no connection with Elaine May's homonymous 1972 pic, has major b.o. potential in Australia, where it should click with teens and their parents, and there are decent possibilities in offshore arthouses for this warmhearted, liberating love story. It opens the Sydney Film Festival on June 11.

Set in the ethnically mixed suburbs of Melbourne, pic establishes Claudia Karvan as 22-year-old Christina, a well-educated Greek-Australian with wealthy parents. She's just become engaged to the upwardly mobile Dimitri (Steve Bastoni), the type who talks into a cellular phone while undressing for sex.

Just embarking on a teaching career, Christina has been assigned to a rowdy high school in a working-class area. At the school there's a conflict between the racist sports master (William McInnes), who's only interested coaching boys willing to play Australian Rules Rugby, and students, who prefer to play soccer. Christina sides with the latter group, and especially spunky 17-year-old Nick (Alex Dimitriades); she agrees to coach the soccer team herself, until Nick's father (Nico Lathouris), who once played for Greece, steps in.

Just when it seems the film is going to be about rivalry between the two different sports teams, the main subject emerges: Nick makes it clear that he has the hots for his teacher and she, gradually, responds, eventually borrowing her girlfriend's apartment for secret afternoon trysts with her willing pupil.

Inevitably, the secret gets out, and Christina finds herself in trouble at school and with her shocked parents and outraged fiancé. It's the way she resolves her dilemma that makes the film so honest and likable.

"Kid" started life as a stage play, though you'd never guess it, thanks to the skillful adaptation of playwright Richard Barrett and director Michael Jenkins, aided by fine work from lenser Nino Martinetti.

Karvan, effective in the Cannes competing entry "Broken Highway," plays her role with distinction, capturing the moral dilemma of choosing between a secure but dull marriage or an unwise, ardent relationship. Dimitriades, who has never acted before, is a find as her passionate young lover, while Bastoni avoids turning the role of the fiancé into a caricature. As Karvan's girlfriend, Doris Younane is outstanding, bringing natural comic talent to all her scenes.

The film's b.o. success Down Under will no doubt be enhanced by the shrewd choice of contemporary songs and music. The compact running time is another asset. — *David Stratton*

PÉTAIN
(FRENCH)

An AMLF release of a Mod Films/ France 2/France 2 Cinema co-production with the participation of La Compagnie Audiovisuel Phenix/Canal Plus/ Sofica Creations and the French Ministry of Education and Culture. Produced by Jacques Kirsner. Directed by Jean Marboeuf. Screenplay, Jean-Pierre Marchand, Alain Riou, Marboeuf, from Marc Ferro's biography; Camera (color), Dominique Bouilleret; editor, Anne-France Lebrun; music, Georges Garvarentz; production design, Jérome Clement; costume design, Odile Sauton; sound, Philippe Arbez, Catherine D'Hoir, Gérard Lamps. Reviewed at Forum Horizon cinema Paris, May 6, 1993. Running time: **133 MIN.**

Pétain	Jacques Dufilho
Laval	Jean Yanne
Dumoulin	Jean-Claude Dreyfus
Hans Roberto	Jean-Pierre Cassel

Also with: Christian Charmetant, Denis Manuel, André Penvern, Julie Marboeuf, Clovis Cornillac, Pierre Cognon, Antoinette Moya, Frédérique Tirmont, André Thorent, Jean-François Perrier, Vincent Gauthier.

"Pétain" is a major accomplishment. Taboo-breaking and ideologically irreproachable pic about Vichy and its legacy is a clear yet nuanced — and long overdue — view of crucial French history. Unfailingly cinematic, intelligently structured and beautifully cast, pic is essential viewing for Gallic auds and deserves to be shown everywhere.

Occupation saga is something much more useful than a biopic: It is a compelling, dramatic examination of how France, having capitulated to Germany in 1940, zealously embraced official anti-Semitic policies.

Reassuring myths of France's collective amnesia about the era are laid waste — Marshal Philippe Pétain's election was not a fluke. He was duly and legally installed and many of the men who voted for him and enforced his policies, went on to illustrious postwar political careers.

Pétain was 84 when invested with absolute power as head of the Vichy government in 1940. In appearance, voice and gesture, distinguished veteran thesp Jacques Dufilho inhabits Pétain with stiff formal composure. Jean Yanne, casual and direct, gives a stupendous performance as Vichy henchman Pierre Laval, a career politician whose thinking so pleased Hitler that Pétain was forced to take him back into the fold after having dismissed him for chronic insubordination.

Lensed on location in Vichy, in the actual Hotel du Parc where the government resided, much of pic is pale and slightly overexposed, as if hand-colored and about to fade from memory. Other scenes are dark and crisp.

Helmer Jean Marboeuf brings a rigor and accessibility to the story, told from both the corridors of power and the vantage of the Hotel du Parc's ordinary staff — the cook who joins the Resistance, the chambermaid who finds Pétain endearing, the bandleader whose Jewish musician is asked to leave. The secondary characters never overstep the line into caricacture, although they sometimes come close.

When Vichy broadcasts a speech about "collaborating," the word, in context, seems to have temporarily reverted back to mean nothing more sinister than "cooperating and helping out." It is precisely this restored spin that makes it possible to grasp how official France and many of its citizens fell so far so quickly.

After the Germans cross the demarcation line between Occupied and Unoccupied France on Nov. 11, 1942 — marking the end of Pétain's direct influence — the story skips ahead to August 1944. Flash forward is jarringly abrupt and the tail end of the war is condensed. (Pic will apparently run longer on TV.)

Pic is not only lensed with verve but written with flair. Depicting a time when words truly could spur deeds, each (authentic) speech, each turn of phrase, each upper-echelon encounter, sings with the precision of French well spoken.

Faced with squeamish reluctance at every turn, producer Jacques Kirsner toiled for over six years to get the film off the ground. (Alain Corneau was slated to direct an early draft.) As it turns out, Jean Marboeuf was a fine choice. — *Lisa Nesselson*

CANNES FEST

LIBERA ME
(FRENCH)

A UGC (France) release of a UGC/Le Studio Canal Plus/La Sept Cinema co-production in association with Canal Plus/Centre National de la Cinematographie. Produced by René Fauvel. Directed by Alain Cavalier. Screenplay, Cavalier, Bernard Crombey, Andrée Fresco. Camera, Patrick Blossier; editing, sound, Marie-Pomme Carteret; set design, Claire Seguin; costumes, Monique Parelle Renaud. Reviewed at Cannes Film Festival (competing), May 19, 1993. Running time: **80 MIN.**

Mother . . . . Annick Concha
Father . . . . Pierre Concha
Older son . . . . Thierry Labelle
Younger son . . . . Christophe Turrier
Helper . . . . Philippe Tardif
His girlfriend . . . . Cecile Haas
Butcher . . . . Michel Labelle
Blonde woman . . . . . Claire Seguin
Photographer . . . Michel Quenneville
Also with: Louis Becker, Catherine Caron, François Christophe, Jean Monot, Paul Chevillard.

One of France's most rigorous, experimental directors, Alain Cavalier ("Therese") lays good claim to being the heir of intensely spiritual filmmaker Robert Bresson in "Libera Me." All that's missing from this unique film without words is the emotional impact of the master. Created piece by piece like a semiological puzzle, pic's pleasure lies in deciphering the meaning of its finely photographed images. Though surprisingly brisk, this specialty item lacks a final payoff and needs a patient, dedicated aud willing to do some brainwork.

Dialogue is actually superfluous in pic's river of brief, symbolic scenes. They succinctly illustrate a terrible social drama in an unspecified, modern-day society where a totalitarian military junta has taken power and rules the state through terror and bloodshed. The population is forced to toe the line, or be killed.

Using closeups — of a butcher chopping meat or two men peeling potatoes — Cavalier boils his narrative down to essential elements. Patrick Blossier's lighting further isolates these "ideograms," against an unnatural, neutral background.

Mysteriously torn photographs of children (sinisterly missing from the film) turn out to be a password by which opponents of the regime recognize each other. Two brothers (Thierry Labelle, Christophe Turrier) from an ordinary working family are part of the underground organization. So is photographer Michel Quenneville, who secretly forges passports for the rebels.

Objects take on a strong symbolic value. A pair of handcuffs, a metal chair and table, a blow torch stand for all the horrors of (offscreen) torture. In a vignette that recalls "The Godfather," the rebels put a pig's head in one of the ruler's beds. Violence is signaled by just a trickle of blood.

Cavalier gives viewers enormous leeway in interpreting the meaning of his images, which requires recognizing conventional film symbols and making astute connections. Perfs are deadpan, though cast's faces are quietly expressive.

Marie-Pomme Carteret's clipped, no-nonsense editing and canny use of ambient sound are always in the foreground. But, after 80 minutes of creativity, "Libera Me" ends a little lamely with a symbolic rebel gesture, but the regime seems far from over. — *Deborah Young*

NO WORRIES
(AUSTRALIAN-BRITISH)

A Film Four International presentation, with the participation of British Screen, of a Palm Beach Pictures (Sydney)/Initial Films (London) co-production. Produced by David Elfick, Eric Fellner. Executive Producer, Kim Williams. Directed by Elfick. Screenplay, David Holman. Camera (Eastmancolor), Stephen F. Windon; editor, Louise Innes; music, David A. Stewart, Patrick Seymour; production design, Michael Bridges; costumes, Clarrissa Patterson; sound, Guntis Sics; production manager, Anne Bruning; assistant director, Chris Webb; casting, Christine King. Reviewed at Cannes Film Festival (market section), May 15, 1993. Running time: **92 MIN.**

Matilda Bell . . . . Amy Terelinck
Ben Bell . . . . Geoff Morrell
Ellen Bell . . . . Susan Lyons
Anne O'Dwyer . . . . Geraldine James
Clive Ryan . . . . . . John Hargreaves
Burke . . . . Harold Hopkins
Old Burke . . . . Ray Barrett
Tim . . . . Gary Cooper
Gary . . . . Steve Vidler
Maggie . . . . Rhonda Findleton

The devastating impact of drought and recession on rural Australia is unflinchingly depicted in this unsentimental family drama of an 11-year-old girl whose world collapses around her. Some last-reel contrivances mar this otherwise sensitive David Elfick pic, which, with proper handling, could attract New Age families in good numbers.

Australia's climate is notoriously extreme and the effects of the current drought, which covers much of the country, have been exacerbated by the international recession and agricultural trade wars. British writer David Holman's screenplay brings all these abstractions down to a very personal level as he describes the lives of Matilda Bell (Amy Terelinck) and her struggling parents Ben (Geoff Morrell) and Ellen (Susan Lyons) on a sheep property.

Matilda attends the small local school which is threatened with closure as attendance dwindles because families are being forced to leave the land. She helps her parents by driving their tractor and feeding the sheep; despite the hardships, she loves the farm life and, especially, her beloved cattle dog, Dingo.

Early scenes depict Matilda's sympathy for a school friend. The crisis facing her own parents proves to be even harder: The Government is forced to lower the price of wool just at shearing time, and a violent storm does heavy damage to the Bell property. Ben comes to the tough but inevitable decision; he kills his last, starving stock and heads for the city. He even shoots Dingo who, he knows, won't survive in an urban environment.

In Sydney, the Bells stay with relatives in a crowded, racially mixed neighborhood. Ben finds work as a cab driver, and Matilda is sent to a school where her only friend is a Vietnamese girl whose parents were killed by pirates. Matilda retreats into silence and finally runs away.

The first half of the film, is powerful stuff and the natural, unforced performances from the entire cast help create a convincing, if very sad, world. City scenes are suitably grim, though the film's resolution, which really solves none of the family's basic problems, seems contrived.

Elfick's staging of key scenes is excellent, and there's atmospheric lensing from Stephen F. Windon. — *David Stratton*

ABSENT WITHOUT LEAVE
(NEW ZEALAND)

A Meridian Films production, in association with the New Zealand Film Commission/NZ On Air/Avalon-NFU Studios. Produced by Robin Laing. Directed by John Laing. Screenplay, James Edwards, Graeme Tetley. Camera (Eastmancolor), Allen Guilford; editor, Paul Sutorius; music, Don McGlashan, David Long, Mark Austin; production design, Rick Kofoed; costumes, Glenis Foster; sound, Ken Saville; production manager, Jan Haynes; assistant director, David Norris; casting, Diana Rowan. Reviewed at Cannes Film Festival (market section), May 17, 1993. Running time: **96 MIN.**

James "Ed" Edwards . . . .
. . . . Craig McLachlan
Daisy Edwards . . . . . Katrina Hobbs
Peter Wilson . . . . Tony Barry
Ella Wilson . . . . . . Judie Douglass
Betty . . . . Robyn Malcolm
Claude . . . . David Copeland

John Laing's "Absent Without Leave" tells the true story of a confused young man who deserted from the New Zealand Army in 1942 to be with his wife. Boasting superb period production design and affecting performances in the lead roles, this is a modest but quite appealing film of a painfully naive couple ill-equipped to face the reality of conscription and separation in wartime. But there's little sense of urgency; the film will have difficulty finding theatrical outlets away from its home turf.

Director Laing says he first heard the story of Ed and Daisy Edwards when Ed was interviewed on radio.

Ed and Daisy marry because she's pregnant. He starts his enforced military training soon after the wedding ceremony, but his young wife suffers a miscarriage. Told (falsely, it turns out) that his unit is about to be posted overseas without leave, Ed deserts to help Daisy find somewhere to live, intending to be AWOL only a short while.

However, circumstances extend the length of his desertion, and when he's finally arrested he's given a hefty sentence while Daisy's left to fend for herself.

This is a slight story, but Laing and his screenwriters succeed in creating a believable wartime atmosphere in which Ed's foolish absence without leave seems close to treason.

Aussie TV soap actor Craig McLachlan acquits himself well as the foolish young soldier on the run, and former child actress Katrina Hobbs is touching in her first adult role. Very strong support is provided by Tony Barry and Judie Douglass as farmers who give the young runaways assistance and shelter.

Always watchable thanks to the excellent re-creation of wartime New Zealand, via top-flight production and costume design, film's music is often used inappropriately, and could have filled a stronger role in building up tension. — *David Stratton*

TRAUMA

An Overseas Filmgroup presentation of an ADC production. (Intl. sales: Overseas Filmgroup, Los Angeles.) Produced by Dario Argento. Executive producer, Andrea Tinnirello. Directed by Argento. Screenplay, Argento, T.E.D. Klein, from Franco Ferrini, Giovanni Romoli, Argento's story. Camera (Eastmancolor; Technicolor prints; widescreen), Raffaele Mertes; editor, Conrad Gonzalez; music, Pino Donaggio; production design, Billy Jett; art direction, Nance Derby; costume design, Leesa Evans; sound (Dolby), Paul Coogan; special makeup effects, Tom Savini; assistant director, Rod Smith; casting, Ira Belgrade. Reviewed at Cannes Film Festival (market section), May 15, 1993. Running time: **105 MIN.**

David . . . . Christopher Rydell
Aura . . . . Asia Argento
Adriana . . . . Piper Laurie
Judd . . . . Frederic Forrest
Also with: Laura Johnson, James Russo, Brad Dourif.

"**T**rauma" is a by-the-numbers stalker thriller for undemanding genre fans only. Minneapolis-shot item by cult Italo scare-meister Dario Argento is traumatically short on the helmer's usual Grand Guignol flair. Vidbiz looms likely.

Helmer's daughter Asia plays a screwed-up anorexic who's rescued from jumping off a bridge by a local TV employee (Christopher Rydell). She's taken back to her mother (Piper Laurie, with a scenery-chewing Italian accent), a medium who runs the mysterious Faraday Clinic.

At a seance one dark and stormy night, Laurie is about to reveal the name of a killer who's been decapitating locals — nicknamed the Head Hunter by the media — but is seemingly murdered first. Argento runs away and contacts Rydell, and together the pair try to uncover the truth as the body count mounts.

Pic settles down into a low-key romance between Rydell and Argento, punctuated by p.o.v. sequences of the Head Hunter and his cord saw. Former is capsized by a blah script and Argento's stiff performance in English. Latter conspicuously lack tension, despite a busy score by Pino Donaggio and director Argento's straining after visual flair.

The movie only delivers in the final reel, with a coda revealing the true murderer and some stops-out baroque horror that briefly recalls the Dario Argento of old. Tech credits are fine, with good-looking widescreen lensing by Raffaele Mertes. — *Derek Elley*

LAN FENGZHENG
(THE BLUE KITE)
(HONG KONG-CHINESE)

A Longwick Production presentation of a Longwick/Beijing Film Studio co-production. (Intl. sales: Fortissimo, Amsterdam.) Line producers, Luo Guiping, Cheng Yongping. Directed by Tian Zhuangzhuang. Screenplay, Xiao Mao. Camera (color), Hou Yong; editor, Qian Lengleng; music, Yoshihide Otomo; art direction, Zhang Xiande; costume design, Dong Juying; sound (Dolby), Wu Ling; assistant directors, He Jianjun, Zhong Weiyong. Reviewed at Cannes Film Festival (Directors Fortnight section), May 21, 1993. Running time: **139 MIN.**

Chen Shujuan . . . . Lu Liping
Lin Shaolong . . . . Pu Quanxin
Li Guodong . . . . Li Xuejian
Old Wu . . . . Guo Baochang
Chen Shusheng . . . . . . Zhong Ping
Chen Shuyan . . . . . Chu Quanzhong
Sister . . . . Song Xiaoying
Zhu Ying . . . . Zhang Hong
Teenage Tietou . . . . . Chen Xiaoman

A moving, politically frank look at a family torn apart by China's social turmoil of the '50s and '60s, through the eyes of a young Beijing kid and his thrice-married mom, "The Blue Kite" looks unlikely to fly very high theatrically but should build a solid fest rep that will lead to specialized tube sales.

After wrapping in Beijing in March '92, pic world-preemed in the Cannes fest's Directors Fortnight following a tortured history of roadblocks by China's censors at script and workprint stages, and final postproduction in Japan done from director Tian Zhuangzhuang's detailed notes. The movie has still to be okayed for local exhibition. Tian's earlier "Horse Thief" (1986) also had political trouble at home.

Story stretches from 1953 to 1967, from the first heady years of Communist rule and nationalization, through endless political campaigns of the late '50s, to the start of the Cultural Revolution in the mid-'60s. At each stage, change or tragedy strikes the woman's large, extended family.

Setting is mostly a rambling courtyard house in backstreets Beijing (flavorsomely recreated by the movie's art team), where newlyweds Chen Shujuan, a teacher, and Lin Shaolong, a librarian, live. Other members of the family include her two brothers and older sis, the last a Party hardliner. Soon after the birth of their son, Tietou, a mass drive towards nationalization begins, and neighborhood committees are already extending the Party's reach into everyday life.

In 1957, during the backlash of the Hundred Flowers movement encouraging free criticism of the Party, Shaolong gets carted off to a labor camp. Shaolong later dies, and Shujuan and her kid are cared for by a family friend, Li Guodong, whom she marries three years later.

Final half-hour limns Shujuan's third marriage, to an old Party member, Wu Leisheng, after Guodong has died. Tietou, now a restless teen, can't get on with his new stepfather, but with the dawn of the Cultural Revolution in 1966 all their lives are irreversibly changed.

Major surprise of the movie is that, despite a story and multi-character cast that looks more fitted to a miniseries, it works on a simple emotional level as a feature film. Characters emerge as real people rather than political stereotypes, and thanks to the narrow focus and lack of spectacle there's a real feel for everyday life during the turbulent period covered.

Auds with prior knowledge of the complex politics will get an extra charge, but the story's overall trajectory is clear enough for general viewers. Family relationships are no more complex than in similar Chinese movies.

The offbeat approach by Tian and scripter Xiao Mao ("Bloody Morning," "Five Girls and a Rope") of having the yarn recounted through the child's eyes gives an ironic spin to the whole thing, as Tietou provides naive voiceover summaries of events he witnesses but only partly comprehends.

Performances are strong down the line, with beautifully textured playing by actress Lu Liping ("Old Well") as the mother for all seasons, and a specially moving character study by Guo Baochang as her third husband. Final scenes between the two are real grippers. The three kids portraying Tietou are seamlessly cast.

Production design, clearly drawing on Tian's own memories of the period, is true and unshowy, as is Tian's no-frills helming. Music is simple but effective, generally pointing up the movie's kid's-eye-view approach, symbolized by his hobby of kite-flying. — *Derek Elley*

PIERSCIONEK Z ORLEM W KORONIE
(THE RING WITH A CROWNED EAGLE)
(POLISH-BRITISH-GERMAN-FRENCH)

A Perspektywa Film Studio (Warsaw)/Heritage Films (London)/Regina Ziegler Filmproduktion (Berlin)/Erata Films (Paris) co-production. (Intl. sales: Cine Electric, London.) Directed by Andrzej Wajda. Screenplay, Wajda, Maciej Karpinski, Andrzej Kotkowski, from Aleksander Scibor-Rylski's book. Camera (Eastmancolor), Dariusz Kuc; music, Zbigniew Gorny; editor, Ewa Smal; production design, Allan Starsky; production manager, Barbara Pec-Slesicka. Reviewed at Cannes Film Festival (market section), May 18, 1993. Running time: **105 MIN.**

```
Marcin . . . . . . . . Rafal Krolikowski
Wiska . . . . . . . . . . Agnieszka Wagner
Janina . . . . . . Adrianna Biedrzynska
Kosior . . . . . . . . . . Cezary Pazura
Zbigniew Cybulski . Tomaz Koniczky
Also with: Miroslaw Baka, Maria Ch-
walibog, Jadwiga Jankowska-Clesak.
```

Veteran Polish director Andrzej Wajda returns to the scene of early triumphs "Kanal" and "Ashes and Diamonds" to take another look at the tragic period of the Polish uprising against the Germans in 1944 and the complicated aftermath of war. Film is fascinating, but knowledge of the complex political situation of the period is required — a limiting factor to a substantial arthouse release.

When Wajda made his early films in the mid-'50s, he was unable to tell the complete story. The Communist authorities of the period downplayed the role the anti-Communists played in the Warsaw uprising and its aftermath, and Wajda was forced to make his positive characters toe the Party line. "The Ring With a Crowned Eagle" is based on a long-banned novel by the director's old collaborator, Aleksander Scibor-Rylski, and its hero, Marcin (newcomer Rafal Krolikowski) is a member of the non-Communist Home Army.

Pic opens with a vivid recreation of the bitter 63-day last struggle of Polish patriots against overwhelming German forces, at the end of which, many of the Polish resistance fighters mingle with refugees in order to escape.

Among them is Marcin, along with his beautiful g.f., Wiska (Agnieska Wagner), who gives him a ring with a design of the Polish royal crest (the crowned eagle) before being dragged off and raped (offscreen) by Germans. Marcin winds up in hospital and is unable to locate Wiska as the war ends. Helped by the devoted Janina (Adrianna Biedrzynska), he endeavors to steer a middle course through the chaotic political events as the Russians oust the Germans and Poland becomes a Communist state.

The central section of the film is filled with intrigue and debate that, while it's vividly staged, will mean little to non-Polish audiences. Also, Krolikowski, though a very adequate actor, lacks the charisma that Zbigniew Cybulski brought so memorably to "Ashes and Diamonds," which dealt with similar events from a different perspective.

In one memorable scene, Wajda re-creates a scene from the earlier film. A Cybulski lookalike (Tomaz Koniczyky), complete with dark glasses, sets fire to glasses of vodka in a bar in memory of fallen comrades just as in "Ashes and Diamonds."

Production design and camerawork are excellent in this ultimately moving film, but the result lacks the dramatic urgency needed to give the dense story of betrayal and patriotism a contemporary relevance.

— *David Stratton*

ED AND HIS DEAD MOTHER

An ITC Entertainment Group presentation. Produced by Wm. Christopher Gorog. Directed by Jonathan Wacks. Screenplay by Chuck Hughes. Camera (CFI color), Francis Kenny; editor, Lisa Day; music, Mason Daring; production design, Eve Cauley; costume design, Julie Rae Engelsman; co-producer, Nancy Rae Stone; special effects, KNB EFX Group; casting, Jory Weitz. Reviewed at Cannes Film Festival (market section), May 16, 1993. MPAA Rating: PG-13. Running time: **89 MIN.**

```
Ed Chilton . . . . . . . . Steve Buscemi
Uncle Benny . . . . . . . . Ned Beatty
Mabel Chilton . . . . Miriam Margolyes
A.J. Pattle . . . . . . . . John Glover
Storm Reynolds . . . . . Sam Jenkins
Lar . . . . . . . . . . . . Gary Farmer
Mr. Abner . . . . . . . Eric Christmas
Reverend Praxton . . . Rance Howard
```

Not quite dark or bizarre enough to earn cult status, "Ed and His Dead Mother" has modest theatrical potential on its merry way to the video shelf.

An arch comedy, the film takes the Oedipal complex way beyond the grave. The result is fitfully amusing rather than a full-tilt gut-busting romp.

The morose Ed (Steve Buscemi) runs the family hardware store in an American town still lost in the 1950s. Though his mom passed away a year earlier and his Uncle Benny (Ned Beatty) uses everything but dynamite to coax him out of his shell, he refuses to release his grief.

But help is unexpectedly on its way in the form of fast-talking cryogenics salesman A.J. Pattle (John Glover). For $1,000 his company is willing to resurrect and re-animate the old doll. Though skeptical, the young man finds it an offer he can't refuse. So, when mom (Miriam Margolyes) arrives on the front porch, harmony would momentarily appear to have returned.

It is fleeting. Soon mom's need to sleep in the fridge and eat live bugs escalates into an appetite for human flesh. And getting rid of her proves twice as hard as plucking her from the grave.

Chuck Hughes script proves tame in taking on the darker aspects implicit in the materal. Juxtaposing the sanitary picket fence environment and a seemingly traditional boy meets girl subplot against the night-of-the-living-dead mother yarn is about as complex as things get. It's often fun but never really a satisfying munch.

The largely over the top ensemble certainly livens things up. Beatty, Margolyes and Glover take delight in chewing the scenery and Buscemi is an engaging deadpan foil. Newcomer Sam Jenkins as the sexy neighbor has a thankless part.

Director Jonathan Wacks adopts a breezy style that keeps the antics above water. Tech credits brightly enhance an odd little time capsule. — *Leonard Klady*

KARLAKORINN HEKLA
(THE MEN'S CHOIR)
(ICELANDIC-GERMAN-SWEDISH)

A Umbifilm (Iceland)/Artiel (Germany)/Filmfotograferna (Sweden) co-production. (Intl. sales: Angelika Film Intl., New York.) Produced by Halldor Thorgeirsson, Ariane Metzner, Stefan Hencz. Directed, written by Gudny Halldorsdottir. Camera (color), Jurgen Lenz; editor, Uli Leipold; music, Sigurdur R. Jonsson; production design, Arni Pall Johansson; sound, Michael Diekmann; production managers, Ulfur H. Hrobjartsson, Barbara Scholler; assistant director, Kristin Palsdottir. Reviewed at Cannes Film Festival (market section), May 16, 1993. (In New York Icelandic Film Festival.) Running time: **92 MIN.**

```
Magga . . . . . Ragnhildur Gisladottir
Max . . . . . . . . . . . . Gardar Cortes
Gunnar . . . . . . . . . Egill Olafsson
Jonas . . . . . . . . . Rurik Haraldsson
Kalli . . . . . Sigurdur Sigurjonsson
Viggo . . . . . . . . . . . Orn Aranson
Britta . . . . . . . . . . . . Lena Nyman
```

"The Men's Choir" is a gentle comedy in which members of an enthusiastic amateur singing group from a small Icelandic town set off on a tour of Sweden and Germany — all of them men, except for their charming accompanist. What follows is quietly amusing, but not very robust, and although the warblers travel around a lot, the film in which they appear probably won't.

At the outset there's a self-imposed problem in that one of the most interesting characters in the pic, and the choir's enthusiastic leader, Max (Gardar Cortes), a rose gardener in love with accompanist Magga (Ragnhildur Gisladottir), never goes on the tour; he dies of a heart attack on the eve of the trip. Cortes creates such a strong and likable character his death casts a pall on the comedy that follows.

The misadventures of these naive Icelanders in Sweden and Germany provide some gentle but, finally, unenthralling amusement, with the whole film pitched on a very low key. Lena Nyman, the notorious star of "I Am Curious (Yellow)," crops up as an accommodating mother of twins in the Swedish sequence.

The rest of the cast is adequate, with Gisladottir charming as the bereaved Magga. Pic is technically crisp and the music, actually performed by the Fostbraeour Men's Choir and the Icelandic Symphony Orchestra, is attractive, which much emphasis given to the Romberg-Hammerstein standard "Stouthearted Men."— *David Stratton*

WHERE THE RIVERS FLOW NORTH

A Ulysse Entertainment release of a Caledonia Pictures presentation. Produced by Bess O'Brien, Jay Craven. Directed by Craven. Screenplay by Don Bredes, Craven, from Howard Frank Mosher's novel. Camera (Technicolor), Paul Ryan; editor, Barbara Tulliver; production design, David Wasco; set decorator, Sandy Wasco; costume designer, Stephanie Kerley; co-producers, Mark Yellen, Lauren Moye. Reviewed at Cannes Film Festival (market section), May 16, 1993. Running time: **106 MIN.**

```
Noel Lourdes . . . . . . . . . Rip Torn
Bangor . . . . . . . . . Tantoo Cardinal
Quinn . . . . . . . . . . . Bill Raymond
Farnsworth . . . . . . . Michael J. Fox
Henry Coville . . . . . John Griesemer
New York Money . . . . Mark Margolis
Sheriff . . . . . . . . . Dennis Mientka
Judge . . . . . . . . . . . . . Sam Lloyd
Champ's manager . . . Treat Williams
```

Rip Torn plays an older, crustier version of his role in "Cross Creek" as he assails the forces of encroaching civilization in 1920s Vermont in the indie "Where the Rivers Flow North." A well-meaning yarn that's handsomely mounted, it's stopped short of success by a dollop too much preachiness and the absence of salable stars and subject matter. Though visually stunning on the big screen, it has the feel of something destined for "American Playhouse"; the film probably has a marginal theatrical career with its primary audience to come from television.

Torn, as Noel Lourdes, finds his livelihood in timber products threatened by the construction of a new dam. The power authorities come calling with bags of cash but he's mule-headed about retaining his life lease. Naturally he's the sole holdout.

However, this is not some altruistic stand. As the story unfolds we discover he's playing a badger game. He wants to trade his plot of land for another with a plentiful supply of pine he'll then cut down and sell for a richer price, in order to move his household to still pristine Oregon.

More De Maupassant than Greenpeace, "Rivers' " sense of irony and justice is too clever for its own good. Noel and his Indian companion Bangor (Tantoo Cardinal) discover to their chagrin that the trees they've acquired are literally rotten. The best laid plans come unglued and tragedy is the inevitable conclusion.

Jay Craven, the director, co-producer and co-writer, shows an assured hand in creating just the right environment, with sterling tech work from cameraman Paul Ryan and production designer David Wasco.

Torn's playing is right on the nose and, while it's a treat to watch, it's also predictable. The heavies, including Vermont resident Michael J. Fox, are stock villains and the good folk of the region are lily white. Only Cardinal as Torn's outcast companion has much depth or range.

"Where the River Flows North" makes a valiant attempt to be current but winds up an anachronistic paean to an earlier, gentler era of moviemaking.
— *Leonard Klady*

WSZYSTKO CO NAJWAZNIEJSZE ...
(ALL THAT REALLY MATTERS ...)
(POLISH-BRITISH)

A Powszechny Zakland Ubezpieczeri/ Marek Nowowiejski Film production, in association with Animex, Elektrim. (Intl. sales: Cine Electra, London.) Produced by Nowowiejski. Directed by Robert Glinski. Screenplay, Dzamila Ankiewicz-Nowowiejska, from Ola Wat's memoir. Camera (Eastmancolor), Jaroslaw Szoda; editor, Elzbieta Kurkowska; music, Jerzy Satanowski; production design, Wojtek Babiak; costumes, Ewa Krause; sound, Mariusz Kuczynski; production managers, Iwona Ziulkowska, Jozef Jarosz. Reviewed at Cannes Film Festival (market section), May 20, 1993. Running time: **103 MIN.**
Andrzej Wat . . . . Adas Siemion
Ola Wat . . . . Ewa Skibinska
Alexander Wat . . . Krzysztof Globisz
Prezydet . . . . Grazyna Barszczewska
Tadeusz Boducki . . . Boguslaw Linda
Ivan . . . . Viktor Czebotariev
Viera . . . . Natalia Kolakanova
Adam . . . . Krzysztof Stroinski
Zofia . . . . Marzena Trybala
NKVD Officer . . . . Lev Ryuin

Polish filmmakers have over the years thoroughly explored the personal tragedies of World War II and its aftermath, but Robert Glinski's impressive film, based on the memoir of Ola Wat, transported by the Russians to Kazakhstan in Soviet Central Asia with her small son, is a different. Grueling but ultimately moving, it has had some fest exposure and deserves a wider audience.

When the film begins, it is 1939 and Ola (Ewa Skibinska), is married to Alexander (Krzysztof Globisz), a Jewish poet and political activist; they have a 10-year-old son, Andrzej (Adas Siemion). Preferring to place his fate with the Russians rather than await certain death at the hands of the invading Germans, Alexander takes his family into the Ukraine despite not being a member of the Communist Party. Betrayed by a journalist friend (Boguslaw Linda), he is arrested by the Soviet secret police, NKVD.

Ola and Andrzej are transported, along with refugee Poles of differing backgrounds, to a remote part of Kazakhstan, where conditions are appalling. The deportees are forced to do hard manual labor, food and water are scarce, and Ola is constantly threatened with rape by the camp commandant (Viktor Czebotariev).

Luckily, young Andrzej becomes a tower of strength for his mother, even learning a little of the Kazakh language so that he can communicate with local people and obtain additional food.

The horrific plight of these displaced Poles is unflinchingly presented by Glinski, who obtains strong performances from his actors. Location shooting near Alma Alta is a plus.

Pic's downbeat theme is leavened by an improbable — but true — happy ending in which the family is reunited.
— *David Stratton*

BITTER HARVEST

A Prism Pictures presentation of a Crystal Sky Communications production. (Intl. sales: Prism, Los Angeles.) Produced by Steven Paul, Gary Binkow. Executive producer, Barry Collier. Directed by Duane Clark. Screenplay, Randall Fontana. Camera (Foto-Kem color), Adam Kane; supervising editor, Garry Ulmer; editor, Paul M. Petschek; music, Michael Tavera; production design, Leonardo; costume design, Kathy Russo; sound design (Ultra-Stereo), Ulmer; sound, Tony Smyles, Rob Janiger; executive in charge of production, Barbara Javitz. Line producer, Eric M. Breiman. stunt coordinator, Michael R. Long; assistant director, Paul Childs; casting, Dorothy Koster. Reviewed at Cannes Film Festival (market section), May 19, 1993. Running time: 98 MIN.
Jolene . . . Patsy Kensit
Travis . . . . Stephen Baldwin
Kelly Ann . . . . Jennifer Rubin
Bobby . . . . Adam Baldwin
Sheriff Bob . . . . . . M. Emmet Walsh

A cornball sex meller-cum-crimer about two lookers and the dumb hunk in their clutches, "Bitter Harvest" is entertaining schlock. Sexy, good-looking item could reap a few bales of theatrical hay before segueing to cable and vid.

Pic bears no relation to the 1985 Angieska Holland opus, the 1982 Emmy-nommed TV-pic starring Ron Howard, or the 1963 British sex drama with Janet Munro. Smalltown setting has shy hayseed Stephen Baldwin inheriting the family farm but plagued with bad dreams about his domineering father. Enter loose-limbed blonde Jennifer Rubin, who's hitching to Hollywood but stays overnight and beds our shy hero.

Next blonde in town is horny realtor Patsy Kensit, who claims to be after Baldwin's property but eventually hops in the shower with him as well. Soon, the trio have a cosy *ménage à trois* down on the farm.

Things turn darker when Rubin is almost raped by some bank robbers who've been working the area, but she dispatches them with prejudice. After disposing of the bodies, the two women suggest taking their place and robbing a bank for fun. Final twist is silly but neat.

Duane Clark, who helmed the low-budget Chicago buddy movie "Shaking the Tree," lets Randall Fontana's okay script play for what it's worth, easily sliding from sardonic comedy via softcore sex to psycho-drama.

Rubin, showing an easy, natural style, sizzles as the more complex of the femmes. Kensit, though striking, is miscast and

can't match Rubin in screen presence or voltage. Baldwin hunkers around as their sexual plaything, and brother Adam Baldwin is lightly menacing as a cop.

Technical credits on the pic, shot in and around L.A. earlier this year, are tip-top, with atmospheric scoring by Michael Tavera and sharp, clear lensing by Adam Kane. — *Derek Elley*

JACK BE NIMBLE
(NEW ZEALAND)

An Essential Prods. production in association with New Zealand Film Commission. Produced by Jonathan Dowling, Kelly Rogers. Executive Producers, Murray Newey, John Barnett. Directed, written by Garth Maxwell. Additional screenplay material, Rex Pilgrim. Camera (Eastmancolor), Don Duncan; editor, John Gilbert; music, Chris Neal; production design, Grant Major; costumes, Ngila Dickson; sound, Dick Reade; associate producer, Judith Trye; stunt coordinator, Peter Bell; production coordinator, Therese Curran; assistant director, Robin Murphy. Reviewed at Cannes Film Festival (market section), May 20, 1993. Running time: 93 MIN.
Jack . . . . Alexis Arquette
Dora . . . . . . Sarah Smuts Kennedy
Teddy . . . . Bruno Lawrence
Clarrie . . . . Tony Barry
Bernice . . . . . Elizabeth Hawthorne
Mrs. Birch . . . . . . Brenda Simmons
Mr. Birch . . . . Gilbert Goldie
Anne . . . . Tricia Phillips
Kevin . . . . Paul Minifie

First-time writer-director Garth Maxwell shows potential in "Jack Be Nimble," a brooding tale of siblings separated when young and reunited in an uneasy and ultimately violent relationship as adults. This mixture of the supernatural and the revenge thriller sags a bit in the middle, but could find a theatrical niche and looks like a strong video bet.

Pic opens brilliantly with a strange scene in which the mother of a small boy and girl succumbs to a nervous breakdown during a windstorm. The ominous sequence sets the stage for subsequent dark doings to come.

The children, Jack and Dora, are adopted by different families. Dora, though teased at school and almost killed in a violent incident as a teen, otherwise has a more or less normal childhood. Jack, meanwhile, is brutalized by his adopted father (Tony Barry), who beats him with barbed wire, and constantly menaced by his four strange, identically dressed sisters.

The adult Dora (Sarah Smuts Kennedy) discovers she is psychic and is determined to locate her long-lost brother as Jack (Alexis Arquette) takes his revenge on his parents by hypnotizing them and forcing them to suicide. By the time the siblings are reunited, Dora has become involved with a kindly older man, Teddy (Bruno Lawrence), making Jack jealous. Jack is determined to take revenge against his real parents, and the film tips over into the realm of violent psycho thriller for the final suspenseful reel.

Despite a few flat stretches, Maxwell acquits himself well with this tall tale, though "Jack" may prove to be ultimately too intense for arthouse auds, and not consistently thrilling enough for action/horror fans. There's a talent here, though, and the film is strikingly lensed (by Don Duncan) and scored (by Chris Neal).

Arquette, speaking with a convincing Kiwi accent, is a potent presence as the deranged Jack, while Kennedy effectively portrays Dora and Lawrence lends his usual authority as her sympathetic lover.

Pacing could have been a little brisker, but in general this is a modestly accomplished debut.
— *David Stratton*

TICKS

A First Look Pictures production. Produced by Jack F. Murphy. Executive producer, Brian Yuzna. Directed by Tony Randel. Screenplay, Brent V. Friedman. Camera (color), Steve Grass; editor, Leslie Rosenthal; music, Daniel Licht; production design, Anthony Tremblay; special visual effects, Doug Beswick. Reviewed at Cannes Film Festival (market section), May 15, 1993. Running time: **83 MIN.**
With: Rosalind Allen, Ami Dolenz, Seth Green, Virginya Keehne, Ray Oriel, Alfonso Ribeiro.

"Ticks," a dim and clichéd horror pic, concerns a group of inner-city adolescents who spend a disastrous weekend in the wilderness. Rehashing themes, characters and effects from other horror flicks, "Ticks" may be enjoyed by the genre's most ardent buffs. However, there are few pleasures for the rest of the audience.

Holly Lambert and b.f. Charles Block give a bad name to their professions (social worker and research sociologist, respectively), showing complete insensitivity to the problems of their ethnically diverse group of six teens, all troubled, who prove right in their reluctance to go on a consciousness-raising trip.

Once in the woods, their ordeal begins: a huge egg sack covered with mucous is found in the closet, a large bug crawls up a kid's leg and burrows into his flesh — huge bugs mutated by the steroid fertilizers used by two creepy marijuana farmers.

In the film's climax, aptly orchestrated by helmer Tony Randel, thousands of mutated, bloodthirsty ticks advance towards the cabin where the kids hide, while a huge fire from all the chemicals blazes out of control.

The embarrassing dialogue is all clichés, and with few exceptions, thesping is amateurish. Special effects are skillfully done, though ultimately they are more appalling and gross than truly scary. — *Emanuel Levy*

TANGUITO
(ARGENTINIAN)

A Kuranda Films production. Produced by Katrina Bayonas, Claudio Pustelnic. Directed by Marcelo Pineyro. Screenplay, Aida Bortnik, Pineyro. Camera (color), Alfredo Mayo; editor, Miguel Gomez; music, Oswaldo Montes; production design, Jorge Ferrari; sound (Dolby), Anibal Libenson. Reviewed at Cannes Film Festival (market section), May, 18, 1993. Running time: **121 MIN.**
Tango . . . . Fernan Miras
Marianna . . . . Cecilia Dopazo
Lobo . . . . Hector Alterio

Based on a true story, "Tanguito" marks the directorial debut of Marcelo Pineyro, better known as the Oscar-winning producer of the popular Argentinean film "The Official Story." Though not as emotionally powerful as the 1985 film, Tanguito's political alertness and relevant message, dealing with individual oppression under military dictatorship, will appeal to viewers interested in the kind of political cinema practiced by Costa-Gavras et al.

Set in Buenos Aires in the late 1960s, tale is based on the true story of the popular Argentinian rock singer who died during the military's "dirty war."

As co-written by Aida Bortnik and Pineyro, tale revolves around Tango (Fernan Miras), a rebellious young singer who sees his music as a medium for personal and political expression. Arrested by the cops while joining a student demonstration, Tango meets Mariana (Cecilia Dopazo), a beautiful philosophy student. Without uttering a single word, the youngsters passionately fall in love, triumphantly overcoming their class differences: Tango

is a slum kid, and Mariana is a rich colonel's daughter.

Idealistically committed to his music, Tango turns down a lucrative record contract because he refuses to sing other people's songs in English. He is imprisoned again when he refuses to collaborate with Lobo (Hector Alterio), a cop who offers him protection if he'll talk. At the inevitable end, Tango's medical records are altered and he is subjected to shock treatment.

First-time helmer Pineyro punches out the many brief scenes emphatically, each making its strong point and ending. But this is also a weakness: Too ambitious in scope, "Tanguito's" shifting locales and changing moods are not easily reconcilable, resulting in a narrative that, despite its urgent relevancy, is engaging without being stirring.

The acting, however, is uniformly accomplished. As Tango, Fernan Miras, the talented actor-singer, sparkles, keeping the movie afloat even in its weaker moments. — *Emanuel Levy*

SLEEPLESS IN SEATTLE

A TriStar Pictures release of a Gary Foster production. Produced by Foster. Executive producers, Lynda Obst, Patrick Crowley. Directed by Nora Ephron. Screenplay, Ephron, David S. Ward, Jeff Arch, from Arch's story. Camera (Technicolor), Sven Nykvist; editor, Robert Reitano; music, Marc Shaiman; production design, Jeffrey Townsend; art direction, Gershon Ginsburg, Charley Beal; set decoration, Clay Griffith; costume design, Judy Ruskin; sound (Dolby), Kirk Francis; associate producers, Delia Ephron, Jane Bartelme, James W. Skotchdopole; assistant director, Skotchdopole; casting, Juliet Taylor. Reviewed at WGA Theater, Beverly Hills, June 4, 1993. MPAA Rating: PG. Running time: **104 MIN.**
Sam Baldwin . . . . Tom Hanks
Annie Reed . . . . Meg Ryan
Walter . . . . Bill Pullman
Jonah Baldwin . . . . . . Ross Malinger
Becky . . . . Rosie O'Donnell
Jessica . . . . Gaby Hoffmann
Greg . . . . Victor Garber
Suzy . . . . Rita Wilson
Victoria . . . . Barbara Garrick
Maggie Baldwin . . . . . Carey Lowell
Jay . . . . Rob Reiner

Having achieved her greatest success writing "When Harry Met Sally," director-co-writer Nora Ephron tries a slightly new riff on that theme in this shamelessly romantic comedy. Pic delivers ample warmth and some explosively funny moments in its quest for "sleeper" status as a summer alternative to dinosaurs and action heroes; still, it's so self-consciously what Tom Hanks' character calls "a chicks' movie" it may limit box office potency, falling short of "Harry's" heartwarming heights.

In fact, Ephron and fellow writers Jeff Arch and David S. Ward have almost cynically made "Sleepless in Seattle" as purposefully schmaltzy as one can imagine — as if auds can't be trusted to buy into good, old-fashioned romance without trappings like skies *cum* shooting stars.

That said, there's inherent appeal in the set-up, Hanks and Meg Ryan fare considerably better than their last pairing (the sputtering "Joe Versus the Volcano"), and young Ross Malinger is one of the most appealing and real moppets since Justin Henry, whom he resembles. The biggest problem may be the leisurely pace with which Ephron gets to a foregone conclusion.

Sam (Hanks) is still grieving over the death of his wife (Carey Lowell, seen in flashback) when his son Jonah (Malinger) phones a latenight radio call-in show saying he thinks the solution is for dad to remarry. Sam reluctantly gets on the line and ends up spilling his guts, showing such sensitivity that thousands of women write in offering to cure his sorrowful insomnia.

Among those listening is Annie (Ryan), a just-engaged newspaper reporter whose husband-to-be, Walter (Bill Pullman), is sensible but not very exciting. She finds herself increasingly obsessed with "Sleepless in Seattle," Sam's on-air handle, fearing she may be settling for "OK" instead of finding "magic."

The movie pursues a parallel structure, with Sam's friends and son pushing him toward opening up while Annie voices her own doubts only to her co-worker Becky (Rosie O'Donnell) and creating a strain on her relationship with her fiancé.

There are some extremely amusing explorations of dating mores, plus more somber moments that provide Hanks an opportunity to strut Sam's almost tangible grief. Yet for all the enjoyable flourishes, and there are many, Ephron keeps pausing to remind us that this is a movie, making it hard for anyone to really get lost in the story. And since the big question isn't "if," but "when" and "how," the film loses considerable momentum about two-thirds through before rallying for a heart-tugging finale.

More than anything else, "Sleepless" may be a boon to 20th Century Fox, spurring rentals of "An Affair to Remember," used not only as a key plot device but as a running gag — a movie whose squishy romantic elements appeal to women more than men.

Hanks certainly figures to increase his stock as a well-rounded actor and not just a comic, while Ryan essentially plays the same character as "Sally," with pleasing if predictable results.

Other supporting roles are generally strong, though Pullman is a bit less annoying than he should have been to prevent audiences from feeling undue sympathy toward his character.

On the tech side, Sven Nykvist's lensing does the romance justice, while Marc Shaiman's music and carefully chosen song score evoke their share of laughs but at times prove overbearing.

Tuned-in viewers may also be aware of the editing due to the truncated appearances of some players, though it's also clear "Sleepless" is as long as it needed to be. — *Brian Lowry*

EXCESSIVE FORCE

A New Line Cinema release in association with Ian Page Prods./3 Arts Prods. Produced by Thomas Ian Griffith, Erwin Stoff, Oscar L. Costo. Executive producer, Michael Harpster. Directed by Jon Hess. Screenplay, Griffith. Camera (Deluxe color), Donald M. Morgan; editor, Alan Baumgarten; music, Charles Bernstein; music supervisor, Kevin Benson; production design, Michael Z. Hanan; art director, Charlie Lagola; sound (Dolby), Henri Lopez; 1st assistant director, Jerry Ketcham; casting, Jane Alderman (Chicago), Doreen Lane (L.A.). Reviewed at Loews Saks Theater, Houston, June 6, 1993. MPAA Rating: R. Running time: **90 MIN.**
Terry McCain . . . Thomas Ian Griffith
Devlin . . . . Lance Henriksen
Jake . . . . James Earl Jones
Anita Gilmour . . . . . Charlotte Lewis
Frankie Hawkins . . . . . . Tony Todd
Sal DiMarco . . . . Burt Young
Vinnie DiMarco . . . . . W. Earl Brown

Even though New Line is going through the motions with a spotty, regional theatrical release, "Excessive Force" appears headed down the express lane to homevid, where it may find favor with undiscriminating action fans.

The best that can be said for the Chicago-shot, medium-budget opus: It certainly lives up to its title. During the course of this otherwise unremarkable cops-and-killers melodrama, gang boss Burt Young expresses his displeasure by shoving a ballpoint pen into an underling's ear; another mobster crushes the legs of a captive cop with a baseball bat; and nominal hero Thomas Ian Griffith, playing a martial-arts-trained cop, breaks enough arms, dislocates enough shoulders and cracks enough heads to keep an emergency room staff gainfully employed for weeks.

There's even a scene in which James Earl Jones — usually treated with a modicum of respect even while picking up easy money in B-movies — gets slapped around when he arouses Griffith's worst suspicions.

Griffith and his two partners are marked for death by Young, who thinks one of the cops pilfered $3 million during a raid on a Young-financed drug deal. After the other cops are reported dead, Griffith decides to launch a preemptive strike against Young's HQ. In this, he gets surprising support from his superior (Lance Henriksen), who normally disapproves of Griffith's maverick tactics.

It comes as no great surprise that Henriksen has good reason to want Young dead or that he wants to frame Griffith for the crime. In fact, the only surprising thing about this by-the-numbers effort is the talent squandered in supporting roles.

In addition to Young, Henriksen and Jones (owner of the jazz club where Griffith hangs out), cast includes Charlotte Lewis as the mandatory estranged girlfriend, and Tony Todd ("Candyman") as one of the marked-for-death cops. All perform well beyond the call of duty.

Griffith wrote and co-produced the pic, which he no doubt hoped would be his ticket to the major leagues of action stardom. Right now, though, he's strictly a minor-league heavy hitter — less graceful than Jean-Claude Van Damme, and not as personable as Steven Seagal.

Tech credits, including Donald M. Morgan's exceptional cinematography, are first-rate.

— *Joe Leydon*

SEATTLE FEST

DAZED AND CONFUSED

A Gramercy Pictures release of an Alphaville production in association with Detour Films. Produced by Jim Jacks, Sean Daniel, Richard Linklater. Directed, written by Linklater. Camera (color), Lee Daniel; editor, Sandra Adair; production design, John Frick; art direction, Jenny C. Patrick; costume design, Katherine (K.D.) Dover; sound, Jennifer McCauley; assistant directors, John Cameron, Sarah Addington; 2nd-unit camera, Layton Blaylock; casting, Don Phillips. Reviewed at Seattle Film Festival, June 4, 1993. Running time: **94 MIN.**
Pink . . . . Jason London
Mitch . . . . Wiley Wiggins
Don . . . . Sasha Jenson
Slater . . . . Rory Cochrane
Michelle . . . . Milla Jovovich
Cynthia . . . . Marissa Ribisi
Mike . . . . Adam Goldberg
Tony . . . . Anthony Rapp
Sabrina . . . . Christin Hinojosa
Daria . . . . Parker Posey
Wooderson . . Matthew McConaughey
O'Bannion . . . . Ben Affleck
Coach Conrad . . . . . Terry G. Kross
Also with: Michelle Burke, Cole Hauser, Jason O. Smith, Nicky Katt, Catherine Morris, Jeremy Fox, Deena Martin, Joey Lauren Adams.

The teenage wasteland, 1976-style, of "Dazed and Confused" is smack-dab between "The Brady Bunch" and "Children of the Damned," and it's a scary, if sometimes giddily amusing, place to visit. Richard Linklater's followup to his no-budget "Slacker" is sure to attract support from urban Gen-X-ers, but the pic's unrelieved nihilism may keep it out of mallplexes, where its most appropriate auds are found.

All the action takes place within 24 hours, as listless Austin, Texas, teens endure their last day of school, making bongs in shop and cataloguing every episode of "Gilligan's Island" in history (while teachers doze or recall their exploits in Nam or at Woodstock), before the summer's serious business of drinking, fighting and generally humiliating each other and themselves.

In this suburban delirium, a few personalities emerge: Pink (Jason London) is a gentle, hunky quarterback unsure about his future in football; his pal Don (Sasha Jenson) is less interested in sports than in developing his gal-getting patter, and O'Bannion (Ben Affleck) takes the ritualistic paddling of new freshmen to psycho-sexual extremes.

One victim is the slight, scraggly haired Mitch (Wiley Wiggins), who gets invited to join the older boys in their graduation-night debauchery. Roughly the age of helmer Linklater in those Bicentennial days, Mitch is intended to be our semi-innocent guide, but with more than 30 recurring roles, it's a wonder even he can keep track of them.

One-liners and dry sight gags still abound, but the ennui-sodden formlessness of "Slacker" doesn't fly as well in this $6 million, smoothly lensed package, which calls for shapelier narrative and resolution. Reaction to "Dazed" can be expected to divide along gender and generational lines, with older auds turned off by the tale's hollow emotional center, and women offended by Linklater's lack of interest in his female characters.

Few, though, would contest its pivotal song-selection, with everyone from Foghat and Peter Frampton to Joan Jett and War setting the stage perfectly. (Just as the film world-preemed in Seattle, Linklater got permission to use the title Led Zep song, sure to show up in future prints.)

Katherine Dover's beige-flared, butterfly-collared costuming is also dead-on . . . unfortunately. What the pic is most likely to be remembered for, however, is the consistently fine quality of its too-large ensemble, with the helmer notably adept at mixing professionals with rank first-timers (linchpin Wiggins was spotted in an Austin coffee shop).

— *Ken Eisner*

June 21, 1993 (Cont.)

LATCHO DROM
(SAFE JOURNEY)
(FRENCH)

A K.G. Prods. production with the participation of the CNC/Sofiarp/Investimages/Canal Plus/the Sacem Fund. (Intl. sales: World Marketing Film.) Produced by Michèle Ray-Gavras. Directed, written by Tony Gatlif. Camera (color, Cinemascope), Eric Guichard, Claude Garnier; editor, Nicole Berkmans; musical adviser, Alain Weber; production design, Denis Mercier; sound, Nicolas Naegelen; assistant, Alexandre Gavras. Reviewed at Cannes Film Festival (Un Certain Regard section), May 21, 1993. Running time: **103 MIN.**

A captivating musical journey that resonates with lively and haunting instrumental, vocal and dance performances, "Latcho Drom" limns the historic odyssey of the Gypsies from India to Egypt and beyond. Although the individual musical numbers are miles beyond the average video clip, skillfully staged self-contained segments would not be out of place on MTV-style programs.

Impeccably lensed and crisply recorded widescreen panorama dispatches age-old prejudices by presenting its subjects as proud, defiant people who treasure their communal nomadic life. The compact seven-member crew spent a full year lugging 800 kilos of equipment through eight countries to capture rousing and moving performances of Gypsy music. Tech aspects are superlative.

Experienced helmer Tony Gatlif — himself an Algerian-born French citizen with Gypsy blood — drew storyboards and staged every scene so as best to convey dignity and resillience. Although pic flows like a documentary, nothing was shot docu-style. Indeed, the Cinemascope images are too polished and well lit to have been improvised. The overriding impression is one of grace and beauty plucked from nothing in the middle of nowhere.

"Latcho drom" is an expression in Romany meaning "Have a safe journey." Universal scapegoats, rejected whever they roam, the Gypsies have ironically become a roving depository of musical and cultural influences — true ambassadors of "world music" and consumate musicians.

Whether Gypsies perform barefoot in the desert or wearing suits and ties in a city restaurant it is the communal virtuoso sound

that prevails. Lyrics tell of love and wanderings, of being banished and decimated. A toothless Romanian violinist sings about Ceausescu. An elderly woman's lovely tune turns out to be about starving at Auschwitz (as many as 500,000 Gypsies were liquidated by Hitler).

Free of narration save the songs themselves, pic relies on aud's knowledge of architecture and musical styles to distinguish one country from the next. An ethnographic marvel for those drawn to Gypsy music, pic risks being soporific for others.

Winner of the Prix Gervais following the close of Un Certain Regard at Cannes, pic was given a gala premiere at the Paris Opera on June 6. — _Lisa Nesselson_

JE M'APPELLE VICTOR
(MY NAME IS VICTOR)
(FRENCH)

A Bac Films release of a Les Prod. Dussart/France 2 Cinema/Spica Prods. (Paris)/PDG & Partners (Brussels)/Fidibus Film (Cologne) co-production with the collaboration of Westdeutscher Rundfunk and the participation of Canal Plus/RTL/TVI. (Intl. sales: Mainstream.) Produced by Bertrand Dussart, Catherine Dussart. Directed by Guy Jacques. Screenplay, Jacques, Emmanuel List. Camera (color), Jerome Robert; editor, Susana Rossberg; music, Jean-Claude Vannier; art direction, Jean Rabasse; costume design, Monika Bauert; sound, Jean-Paul Loublier; associate producers, Pierre Drouot, Dany Geys, Tharsi Vanhuysse, Marcia Flakenberg; Reviewed at Vidéothèque de Paris, May 27, 1993. (In Cannes Film Festival, Cinemas en France section.) Running time: **100 MIN.**
Rose . . . . Jeanne Moreau
Luce . . . . Micheline Presle
Bernard . . . . Dominique Pinon
Basile . . . . Claudio Bucella
Cecile . . . . Brigitte Bémol
 Also with: Julien Guiomar, Maria Schrader, Ernst Jacobi.

T he lovely bittersweet conclusion is long in coming in "Je M'Appelle Victor," a carefully crafted but contrived intergenerational tale whose few memorable highlights include a sweet perf by Jeanne Moreau as a radiantly kind invalid. Fests and tube sales seem likely for leisurely pic set in a rural French town in autumn 1978.

All the grown-ups dote on 11-year-old Basile (Claudio Bucella), except his flaky mom. He lives with grandma Micheline Presle and an eccentric granddad, whose crocodile farm leads to thigh-high household floods. Basile's pals include a fun-loving uncle (Dominique Pinon) and the local stationmaster.

But Basile's closest confidante is Presle's elderly half-sister Rose (Moreau). Wheelchair-bound and (in one of pic's thinnest conceits) believed dead, she's lived in the attic for over 30 years.

Imaginative Basile appropriates Moreau's pre-war memories of her long-dead sweetheart, Victor (hence pic's title) to romance 16-year-old Cecile. Claiming to be Victor reincarnated, Basile obtains mixed results.

In an initially comic scene, Moreau releases a crocodile into unsuspecting Presle's kitchen. Revealing showdown between the two strong-willed femmes is pic's dramatic high point.

Production design conveys a sleepy town; dainty score suits the story. — _Lisa Nesselson_

LOUIS, ENFANT ROI
(LOUIS, THE CHILD KING)
(FRENCH)

A Les Films du Losange release of a Les Films du Losange/Le Centre Europeen Cinematographique Rhone-Alpes/TSF Prods./Telema/La Sept Cinema/France 2 Cinema co-production with the participation of Canal Plus/French Ministry of Culture & Communication/CNC/Sofiarp/Investimage 3/Procirep/Avanti (Barcelona)/Sabre TV (Madrid). Produced by Margaret Menegoz. Directed by Roger Planchon. Screenplay, Planchon, Katharina Baranyai. Camera (color, widescreen), Gerard Simon; production design, Ezio Frigerio; costumes, Franca Squarciapino; music, Jean-Pierre Fouquey; editor, Isabelle Devinck; sound (Dolby), Vincent Arnardi. Reviewed at 14 Juillet Odeon Cinema, Paris, May 11, 1993. (In Cannes Film Festival, competing.) Running time: **160 MIN.**
Anne of Austria . . . . . Carmen Maura
Mazarin . . . . Paolo Graziosi
Louis XIV . . . . . . Maxime Mansion
Philippe . . . . Jocelyn Quivrin
 Also with: Serge Dupire, Michele Laroque, Regis Royer, Irina Dalle, Herve Briaux, Isabelle Gelinas, Isabelle Renaud.

E uropeans may be able to identify the conniving players of 17th-century France in "Louis, Enfant Roi" without a scorecard, but non-history buffs offshore will be baffled. Central perf by Maxime Mansion as adolescent Louis XIV is excellent, and $11 million budget is all on screen.

A lavish and lengthy portrait of the extended dysfunctional family and constant upheaval that influenced the Sun King in his intrigue-filled youth, pic is an initially confusing but sometimes enthralling succession of scenes peopled by historic figures.

Betraying one's friends and relatives was a national pastime

in the War of the Fronde (1648-52), a time of scheming rivalries, decadence and a civil war so complex even the best historians have trouble explaining it. Director-cowriter Roger Planchon's brave but perhaps ill-advised tactic is to present the shifting allegiences helter-skelter, the way young Louis would have seen them. Matters grow clearer, mirroring Louis's growing political sophistication, but opening confusion will throw most auds.

Pic does, however, effectively convey the events' unmistakable lasting effects on Louis, who is shown growing from a giggly child to a heavy-hearted young monarch aware of the uses and drawbacks of power.

Foreigners — Louis's mother, the Spanish Anne of Austria (highly capable Carmen Maura), and Prime Minister Mazarin (Paolo Graziosi), who was Italian — ruled France in tandem until Louis took over on his 13th birthday in late 1651.

Predominantly stage-trained ensemble cast is fine across the board. Serge Dupire cuts a dashing figure as Conde, whom Louis was obliged to betray. Femmes, from classy to vulgar, capture the range of womanly influence.

Louis's younger brother, Philippe, Duke of Anjou (Jocelyn Quivrin), addresses the camera with clever, somewhat snotty comments about how the grown-ups carry on. More of his irreverent spin would have been welcome.

Wide-screen lensing is often academic but plays up fine production design at court and on the battlefield. Sprightly baroque score is used sparingly.

Planchon, incidentally, has cast himself as the fellow in charge of chamber pots. — _Lisa Nesselson_

GRAND BONHEUR
(GREAT HAPPINESS)
(FRENCH)

A Les Acacias Ciné Audience release of a Ognon Pictures production. (Intl. sales: UGC Intl.) Produced by Humbert Balsan. Written and directed by Hervé Le Roux. Camera (color), Antoine Roch; editor, Nadine Tarbouriech; music, Michel Pallasse, Bernard Gérard; production design, Patrick Durand; costume design, Nathalie Raoul, Maud Blanc-Fleury; sound (Dolby), Gérard Rousseau; assistant directors, Michel Dubois, Dominique Perrier, Stephane Riga; Reviewed at the Vidéothèque de Paris, May 30, 1993. (In Cannes Film Festival, Cinemas en France section.) Running time: **165 MIN.**

June 21, 1993 (Cont.)

Caroline . . . . Charlotte Léo
Paul . . . . Pierre Berriau
Judith . . . . Marilyne Canto
Charly . . . . Nathalie Richard
Nanou . . . . Christine Vouilloz
Luc . . . . Lucas Belvaux
Also with: Pierre Gérard, Olivier Cruveiller, Laszlo Szabo, Eva Ionesco, Bernard Ballet, Arielle Dombasle, Alain Bergala, Philippe Fretun, Rosette.

Indulgent but endearing comic tale of a group of French film and theater students taking it easy in summertime Paris, "Grand Bonheur" weaves low-key pranks, silly musical numbers and convincing perfs into an entertaining portrait. With trimming of unfocused final third, pic could be a real crowdpleaser with student and fest auds.

Scripter-helmer Hervé Le Roux's first feature shows assured direction and a nice feel for casual comedy. Resourceful, likable band of students at the tail end of their studies is nicely delineated as they pursue romances, mock their pretentious teachers, worship or ridicule the classics and hang out in cafés.

Pic captures the lazy banter of artsy college students — by turns self-important and self-deprecating. A few of their existential pranks are almost up to Jean-Pierre Leaud's standards in Jean-Eustache's classic "The Mother and the Whore." But mostly, pic is a pleasantly rambling contemporary account of a group of friends before they disband.

The all-purpose morosity of Paul (Pierre Berriau), a sensitive filmmaker who always sports a goatee and a long coat, is a running joke with his easygoing comrades. Caroline (Charlotte Léo) is always up for romance, screenwriting couple Luc and Nanou end up compromising when a baby enters the picture, Judith (Marilyne Canto) falls for an older actor only to sense trouble; Charly (Nathalie Richard) does a bang-up job of scaring off a buddy's ex-g.f.

As a peppy stage revue takes shape in rehearsal, corny production numbers woven around old-fashioned cabaret songs are silly and fun. Veterans of buff-run film societies will take delight in a gem-like spoof of earnest-but-ill-attended retrospectives.

Pic grows disjointed in final 45 minutes and could be trimmed to excellent effect, starting with the unnecessary singing at a drawn-out party. — *Lisa Nesselson*

LES HISTOIRES D'AMOUR FINISSENT MAL EN GENERAL
(LOVE AFFAIRS USUALLY END BADLY)
(FRENCH)

A CTV Intl. release of a Prods. Desmichelle/Cinéa co-production. (Intl. sales: Cinéa) Produced by Hughes Desmichelle. Directed by Anne Fontaine. Written by Claude Arnaud, Fontaine. Camera (color), Christophe Pollock; editor, Sylvie Gadmer; music, Said Houmaoui, Jean-Pierre Castelain; art direction, François-Renaud Labarthe; sound, Thierry Delor. Reviewed at Cannes Film Festival (Cinemas en France section), May 20, 1993. Running time: **84 MIN.**
Zina . . . . Nora
Slim . . . . Sami Bouajila
Fredric . . . . Alain Fromager
Also with: Jean-Claude Dreyfus, Eric Metayer.

As a slightly cross-eyed second-generation Arab immigrant who can't decide between two guys, newcomer Nora makes flightiness appealing in "Les Histoires d'Amour Finissent Mal En General." With this assured maiden effort, helmer-co-scripter Anne Fontaine became the first woman to win the prestigious Jean Vigo Prize. Fests and TV beckon.

Twenty-year-old theater usherette Zina (Nora) is engaged to Slim (Sami Bouajila), a fellow "beur" — a term for a French-born child of North African immigrants — and a hard-working law student who drives a cab to make ends meet. As the wedding date nears, Zina becomes involved with the theater's enigmatic leading man (Alain Fromager) and begins to think that taking to the Paris stage — despite her conspicuous lack of training — might be more interesting than marriage.

Like many a French movie heroine before her, Zina, while not out to hurt anyone's feelings, doesn't understand what's wrong with having her cake and eating it, too. She senses she's too young to settle down but is ill-equipped to live more than one day — perhaps one hour — at a time.

Viewers will find Zina's behavior either endearing or annoying. She excuses her own cavalier conduct by proclaiming, "For the time being, the love of my life is me." Male thesps do a fine job of convincing us that not one, but two men might put up with her. — *Lisa Nesselson*

NIGHT TRAIN TO VENICE
(GERMAN)

A Take Munich Filmproduktion. Produced by Toni Hirtreiter. Supervising producer, Wiktor Grodecki. Directed by Carlo U. Quinterio. Screenplay, Leo Tichat, Hirtreiter. Camera (color), Armando Nannuzzi; editor, Grodecki; music, Alexander Bubenheim; production design, Heinz Eickmeyer; art direction, Markus Penth, Peter Kaser; set decoration, Bernhard Henrich, Guido Salsilli (Venice); costumes, Ernestine Hipper, Jolanta Kammer; sound (Dolby), Martin Muller; assistant director, Mike Zens; 2nd-unit directors, Grodecki, Hirtreiter; 2nd-unit camera, Rodger Hinrichs; casting, Paul Werner Pochath. Reviewed at Cannes Film Festival (market section), May 20, 1993. Running time: **97 MIN.**
Martin . . . . Hugh Grant
Vera . . . . Tahnee Welch
Stranger . . . . Malcolm McDowell
Eufemia . . . . Kristina Soderbaum
Pia . . . . Rachel Rice
Tatjana . . . . Evelyn Opela
Pedro . . . . Samy Langs

This train enters a tunnel and never comes out. Painfully reminiscent of the worst international co-productions of days gone by, slipshod German venture "Night Train to Venice" is too deadeningly awful to be enjoyably bad. The obviously patched together effort won't see many screens in any country, or even cut it as a video title in the U.S.

Plot has so many holes, unaccountable events, deeds with no repercussions and unknowable character motivations that it would be useless to belabor them.

Supercilious journalist Hugh Grant takes the Orient Express to deliver a disk containing his explosive book on the European neo-Nazi movement. Onboard he falls for actress Tahnee Welch, who's traveling with her daughter and mother-in-law. Remainder of the flamboyant passengers are going to the Venice Carnivale, and all are surveyed with a mean-spirited eye by mysterious stranger Malcolm McDowell, who just may be in charge of the gang of skinheads who take over the train.

Amazingly, the passengers take little notice of the violent punks even after they throw the conductor overboard, and the train conveniently never stops.

But this is actually the good part of the movie. With its ghastly dubbing, papered over musical score and pervasive feeling of irreality, pic has the look of something that's spent a long time in postproduction trying in vain to become presentable. Technical quality alone makes it subpar for Yank audiences.

Cast members should be glad this one will go mostly unseen.

Welch, making her first appearance since the "Cocoon" features, is given a British accent, does a couple of brief nude scenes, and looks like Cindy Crawford. A graceful and amusing actor under reasonable circumstances, Grant should stop playing such wimps if he wants to forge a decent career. — *Todd McCarthy*

QUICK

A Promark Entertainment Group and Academy Entertainment presentation of a Fleabite Prods. production. (Intl. sales: Promark, L.A.) Produced by David Lancaster. Executive producers, Martin F. Gold, Carol M. Rossi. Directed by Rick King. Screenplay, Frederick Bailey. Camera (Foto-Kem color), Geza Sinkovics; editor, Stan Salfas; music, Robert Sprayberry; music supervision, Carol Sue Baker; production design, Ivo Cristante; art direction, Ken Larson; costume design, Daniel Orlandi; sound (Ultra-Stereo), Steuart Pearce; executives in charge of production, Steve Beswick, Trisha Robinson; associate producer, Amy Krell; assistant director, Jeffrey Wetzel. Reviewed at Cannes Film Festival (market section), May 19, 1993. Running time: **94 MIN.**
Muncie . . . . Jeff Fahey
Quick . . . . Teri Polo
Davenport . . . . Robert Davi
Herschel . . . . Martin Donovan
Janet Sakamoto . . . . . . Tia Carrere
Hellman . . . . Michael McGrady

"Quick" is a mildly offbeat actioner lifted by above-average playing from Teri Polo and Martin Donovan as a sexy hitwoman and her hostage. Quick theatrical playoff should lead to healthy vidbiz.

Pic starts with a bang with a mysterious brunette ventilating a hood and his bodyguard in a chic L.A. clotherie. Bewigged assassin turns out to be blonde Quick (Polo), an emotionally fragile hitwoman who's fed assignments by her sadistic DEA agent b.f. (Jeff Fahey).

Plot proper cranks up when Polo takes an assignment from mobster Robert Davi to waste an accountant (Donovan) who's made off with $3 mil. Donovan is holed up in a safe house guarded by Fed agent Tia Carrere.

After a shootout, Polo suspects a double-cross and kidnaps Donovan herself. The pair work their way back to L.A. and the loot, pursued by Davi's men and Carrere, latter now a tad suspicious of colleague Fahey's motives.

Frederick Bailey's catch-all script doesn't amount to a hill of beans, but Polo and Donovan bring substance to the comic-dramatic love story. Polo ("Mystery Date") moves well in the action bits and handles the rapid

June 21, 1993 (Cont.)

switches from tough-sexy to comic-girlish with confidence, recalling a younger Jodie Foster. She's well supported by Donovan's ironic, laidback perf.

Fahey and Davi give it the full genre play, and Rick King's helming is smooth, suggesting more sex and violence than ever ends up on screen. Technically, it's fine. — *Derek Elley*

SHOTGUN WEDDING
(AUSTRALIAN)

A Beyond Films presentation of A David Hannay Prods. production, in association with the Australian Film Finance Corp. (Intl. sales: Beyond Films.) Produced by Hannay, Charles Hannah. Directed by Paul Harmon. Screenplay, David O'Brien. Camera (Agfacolor), Kim Batterham; editor, Wayne Le Clos; music, Allan Zavod; production design, Michael Philips; costumes, Clarrissa Patterson; sound, Ross Linton; stunts, Grant Page; casting, Alison Barrett. Reviewed at Cannes Film Festival (market section), May 16, 1993. Running time: **95 MIN.**

Jimmy Becker . . . . Aden Young
Helen Llewellyn . . . . . . Zoë Carides
Police Comm. Andrews . . Bill Hunter
Det. Frank Taylor . . . . . John Walton
Det. Dave Green . . . Marshall Napier
Supt. Frank Church . . . John Clayton
Ben Quill . . . . Warren Coleman
Geoffrey Drinkwater . . . Paul Chubb
Peter Bingham . . . . . . Yves Stening
Det. Craig Haker . . . . . . Sean Scully
Det. Ted Jones . . . . . . Jeff Truman
Rev. Arthur Hickey . . . . Max Cullen
Dr. Craig Kelvin . . . . . Brian Adams
Dr. Wainwright . . . . . . Mary Regan

Truth is a lot stranger than fiction according to this bizarre hostage comedy-drama, which was, according to the opening credits, inspired by an incident that occurred in Sydney in 1968. Scriptor David O'Brien seems to have taken some liberties, but not enough: It's not suspenseful nor funny enough to work as a genre piece, nor does it play comfortably as "torn from the headlines" realism. Modest results can be expected, despite Aden Young's formidable perf.

This is the film that should have established the brooding young actor, first seen in "Black Robe," as a bankable star. He plays Jimmy, a handsome young ex-con who, discovering his girlfriend, Helen (Zoë Carides) is pregnant, gets a prison sentence reduced by naming a crooked cop, Frank Taylor (John Walton); he's promised protection, but it never materializes.

Jimmy and Helen rent a rundown house miles from anywhere and try to start a new life, but Taylor and his partner, Dave Green (Marshall Napier) come

after them. A long siege, with lotsa media attention à la "The Big Carnival," ensues, during which Helen's baby is born and Jimmy persuades the Police Commissioner (Bill Hunter) to organize a wedding ceremony. Eventually, the couple, plus sprig, give themselves up, though a final twist is added to boost the otherwise anticlimactic resolution.

Director Paul Harmon, making his first feature in eight years, treats this real-life material too reverentially; the film simply fails to deliver on any level. Almost nothing is made of the character of the vengeful cop, robbing the film of a requisite dark edge.

This is a shame, because Young is riveting as the besieged hero. A severely deglamorized Carides, who has to appear heavily pregnant during most of the film, is also good, and there is solid support from the ever-reliable Hunter, Napier, and Sean Scully as a redneck detective.

Production values are fine, although the film has the feel of a play since, after some brief opening scenes, it entirely unfolds in or around the hostage house. Michael Philips' set looks like one; Allan Zavod's music is bright.

—*David Stratton*

EVERY BREATH

A Motion Picture Corp. of America presentation of a Brad Krevoy & Steve Stabler production. Produced by Krevoy, Stabler. Executive producers, Anthony Poll, Steve Bing. Directed by Bing. Screenplay, Andrew Fleming, Bing, Judd Nelson. Camera (Foto-Kem color), Chris Taylor; editor, Eric Beason; music, Nils Lofgren; production design, Stuart Blatt; art direction, Carey Meyer; set decoration, David A. Konoff; sound (Ultra-Stereo), Peter V. Meiselmann; co-producer, Brad Jenkel; line producer, Cristen Carr; assistant director, Chris Edmonds; casting, Ed Mitchell, Robyn Ray. Reviewed at Cannes Film Festival (market section), May 18, 1993. MPAA Rating: R. Running time: **85 MIN.**

Jimmy . . . . Judd Nelson
Lauren . . . . Joanna Pacula
Richard . . . . Patrick Bauchau
Bob . . . . Willy Garson
Mimi , ... Rebecca Arthur
Hal . . . . John Pyper Ferguson
Kris . . . . Cynthia Brimhall
Kim . . . . Kathleen Beaton

"Every Breath" is a particularly sour and unpleasant sexpenser, one in which a distasteful set of characters plays out a succession of unpalatable acts. Pic has little going for it as a theatrical possibility, although cast members and a lurid campaign could help it make a dent on video.

Jimmy (Judd Nelson) could hardly be more of a loser: In the opening scene, the broke actor suffers the ignominy of being fired from a condom commercial, and, at a party, behaves with all the charm of Quasimodo at a dress ball. As he accurately sums up, "My life sucks."

But he doesn't know how bad things can get until he meets the sultry Lauren (Joanna Pacula), who takes the lad to her palatial Hollywood Hills home and announces that her husband is trying to kill her.

Hubby turns out to be Richard (Patrick Bauchau, playing a rich variation on his part in "The Rapture"), a jaded European into sex games and paying strangers to make love to his wife. Sucked into his patrons' sick scene, in which it's supposed to be interesting to figure out who's manipulating whom, Jimmy nearly suffers the fate of the protagonists of "The Premature Burial" and "The Vanishing," but he and Lauren are finally able to turn the tables on the voyeuristic, impotent Richard.

The problems here are very basic — the characters are all completely unlikable, their acts utterly unconvincing and unappetizing. After the appalling "The Dark Backward," one might have thought Nelson would hesitate before playing another nerdy no-talent, but he had a hand in *writing* this role. The only thing that could have salvaged this ridiculous part — a comic touch — is not on the menu.

Pacula shows both a very in-shape body and acute embarrassment in an impossibly paradoxical role. Bauchau walks through his amoral part as if he's played it before, which he has.

First-time helmer and co-writer Steve Bing approaches the material in a wide-eyed manner as if it really were sophisticated, intriguingly kinky and suspenseful. — *Todd McCarthy*

HUMAN RIGHTS FEST

SERTSCHAWAN (BEI MEINEN AUGEN)
(UPON MY EYES)
(SWISS-DOCU)

A Filmkollektiv Zurich/Suissimage production. Produced by Hans Stürm. Directed by Beatrice Michel Leuthold, Hans Stürm. Screenplay, Leuthold. Camera (color), Strüm; editors, Leuthold, Stüm; sound, Leuthold. Reviewed at Human Rights Watch Film Festival, Loews Theater IV, N.Y., May 15, 1992. Running time: **90 MIN.**

In March 1988, 25 Iraqi planes descended on the village of Halabja and released a deadly cargo of chemical gas, killing hundreds of Kurds. Using the incident as a departure point, this docu's examination of Kurdish culture is particularly relevant as world attention currently focuses on "ethnic cleansing" in other parts of the globe.

Kurdistan exists within the borders of three different countries, but is as ancient as the cultures surrounding it. Yet, the Kurdish minority has been disenfranchised. Starting with a news photo of a dead Kurdish man holding a child in his arms, filmmakers Beatrice Michel Leuthold and Hans Stürm offer a sensitive look at Kurdish history, culture and continued persecution under Saddam Hussein.

Narration tends to be sympathetic and offers filmmakers' impressions and observations about what they encounter, punctuated by talking head interviews of survivors of Iraqi attacks now living in Iranian Kurdistan. Per the film, approximately 4,000 Kurdish villages have been attacked over the past 15 years in Iraq.

Film depicts the Kurds as they go about their daily life, raising sheep, preparing food and clothing, living as they have for thousands of years.

The culture is also explored: the Legend of Mam and Zin, by poet Ahmade Kane, is narrated at intervals throughout the pic, supplying a sense of tragic destiny that exists beyond time.

Use of folk rhythms on the soundtrack is also particularly effective. — *Paul Lenti*

June 21, 1993 (Cont.)

TEATER ATTONDE DAGEN/TEATR OSMEGO DNIA
(EIGHTH DAY THEATER)
(SWEDISH-DOCU)

A Kino Koszyk production in association with SVT Kanal 1/Svenska Filminstitutets B2/ABF/Kulturradet/TCO. Produced, directed by Joanna Helander, Bo Persson. Camera (color), Jacek Petryeki, Jacek Blawut, Thomas Albrecht, Fulvio Grubissich, Zdzlslaw Kaczwarek, Horst Kandeler, Peter Mokrosinski, Ulf Simonsson, Bogdan Stachurski, Alain Weill; editors, Krzysztof Suchodolski, Bogustawa Klopotowska; sound, Owe Svensson. Reviewed on vidcassette, New York, May 20, 1993. (In Human Rights Watch Film Festival.) Running time: **78 MIN.**

Documakers Joanna Helander and Bo Persson produced this chronicle of the Polish dissident troupe "Eighth Day Theater" during five years of exile in Europe, before returning to a democratic Poland. Docu should attract some interest for those viewing the shifting political currents in Eastern Europe preceding the fall of Communism.

Founded by Poland's student association ZSP in 1964, the troupe notes that God made the world in seven days, but on the eighth day he created theater. Working with improvisational techniques developed by legendary Polish director Jerzy Grotowski, the group took questioned and denounced Poland's Communist state.

In 1976, the government began to repress the troupe, jailing members and restricting travel; by 1986, Eighth Day was forbidden to perform and no longer officially existed. Various troupers decided to emigrate and this docu covers five years of European tours in Sweden, Italy, France, Spain, Switzerland and Germany. They meet and find kinship with other experimental troupes such as a Theatro Nucleo, etc.

In a way the film is a travel diary, recording the troupe's work, their confrontations with Europe, their finding affinity in Catalonia, and their shifting relationship with Poland.

Interviews and rehearsals are varied by excerpts from performances, including a dramatization of Albert Camus's "The Plague."

With only five members, their repertoire is limited, and they wait through most of the film to be joined by member Marcin, whose request for a passport is rejected 23 times before he is finally allowed to leave.

As a document concerning freedom of expression within the former Soviet Bloc, "Eighth Day Theater" is an engaging chronicle of the final throes of Polish political repression.—*Paul Lenti*

AL-IRHAB WAL KABAB
(TERRORISM AND KEBOB)
(EGYPTIAN)

Produced by Essam Emam. Executive producer, Mohamed Zein. Directed by Sherif Arafa. Screenplay, Wahid Hamad. Camera (color), Mohsen Nasr; editor, Adel Mounir; music, Moudy Elemam; sound, Gamil Aziz. Reviewed on vidcassette, New York, May 16, 1993. (In Human Rights Watch Film Festival.) Running time: **105 MIN.**
With: Adel Imam, Youssra Kamal el Shenawy.

Winner of top prize at the Cairo Intl. Film Festival and a hit at Egyptian wickets, Sherif Arafa's "Terrorism and Kebab" begins as a broad comedy, mugging for laughs, before losing its shrillness to end up as a thoughtful reflection on the value of the individual. Film stars Adel Imam, Egypt's most popular comedian.

Story centers around the character of Ahmed (Imam), an Everyman who must work two jobs in order to keep his family at middle-class level. When he takes a day off to move his children to a school closer to home, he discovers he must return because of government red tape and petty bureaucrats. Yet a second visit is no more successful than the first.

Unable to bear the bureaucrats any further, he protests and somehow ends up with a machine gun and a floor full of hostages. Led by the interior minister, the government building is surrounded by police agents while the media report a crazy terrorist has taken over.

Ahmed is soon joined by others fed up with the system, and both sides enter into negotiations. When asked his demands, Ahmed insists on shish kebobs for everyone, and a little respect.

Film is replete with eccentric characters and Arafa has a nice feel for the material. Thesping is also good, especially Imam.
— *Paul Lenti*

DER SCHWARZE KASTE
(THE BLACK BOX)
(GERMAN-DOCU)

A BerlinBerlin Dokfilm production, in association with Max Film. Produced by Wolfgang Pfeiffer. Directed by Johann Feindt, Tamara Trampe. Camera (color), Feindt; editor, Sybille Windt; sound, Paul Oberte. Reviewed on vidcassette, New York, May 18, 1993 (In Human Rights Watch Film Festival). Running time: **97 MIN.**

To make "The Black Box," documakers Johann Feindt and Tamara Trampe spent about a year and a half conducting a psychological profile — or what they call a "psychograph" — of Dr. Jochen Girke, former lieutenant colonel of the Stasi, East Germany's secret police. Girke's cooperation and sincerity is coupled with the filmmakers' relentless and sometimes belligerent efforts to understand how he decided to enter the secret service.

The filmmakers build up their case study while Girke discusses the possibility that a vitamin deficiency might be the culprit for his antisocial behavior. They likewise dissect Girke's life to find the one key factor that might explain his decisions. A once aspiring documentary filmmaker, Girke later decided to switch careers by joining the service and teaching operative psychology at the Stasi school.

Girke's family describes him as "sensitive," yet it is not until Stasi is officially disbanded that he even began to question its role. As Girke puts it, his sense of justice was "underdeveloped."

The filmmakers talk to former teachers, family members, friends and even a dissident friend, jailed in part because of Girke's testimony.

Both filmmakers display a *parti pris*, inserting their quirks into this document: Johann Feindt's camera calls attention to itself, even reshooting its own images replayed on a video monitor.

Co-director Tamara Trampe poses pointed questions in extended takes, reversing roles as her questions force Girke to defends himself. "I don't believe you," she tells him, exasperated. "You aren't listening to me," he counters.

Trampe finally admits, "Your secret service mentality is too much for me." Perhaps this admission is the film's bottom line.
— *Paul Lenti*

PREMIER CONVOI
(THE FIRST CONVOY)
(FRENCH-DOCU)

A Ex Nihilio/Paradiso Prods/La Sept production. Executive producers, Hervé Nisic, Patrick Sobelman. Directed by Pierre Oscar Lévy. Camera (color), Roman Winding; editor, Pascal Lordan; sound, Pierre Ecoffier; research, Suzzette Bloch. Reviewed on vidcassette, New York, May 11, 1993. (In Human Rights Watch Film Festival.) Running time: **102 MIN.**

A powerful document that recreates the passage of a group of survivors of the first convoy of Jews from occupied France to Eastern concentration camps, "Premier Convoi" offers a stirring first-hand account of the Holocaust.

A half-century after this convoy departed on March 27, 1942, destined for Auschwitz and Birkenau, French documaker Pierre Oscar Lévy accompanied a dozen survivors as they follow the same route. (Of the initial shipment of 1,112, only 104 survived; about half were French, the rest refugees from elsewhere.)

Set against a backdrop of real locations, this insightful film documents the survivors' stories as they ride the train eastward or walk through the now-empty grounds of the camps. Pic captures the immediacy of memories sparked by this direct confrontation with the past.

One man tells of meeting his father in the camps and being unrecognized. They all tell of avoiding death only through incredible resourcefulness or because of some lucky break. Everyone here is a witness and has a story.

Lévy's incessant camera captures these men as they move through time and space, from real locations to the vivid memories evoked by words and images as they retake this painful odyssey. Thanks to Lévy, these words and images will not be easily forgotten. — *Paul Lenti*

SIYABEND Û XECÊ
(SIYABEND AND XECÊ)
(TURKISH)

A Senar Film production. Directed by Sahin Gök; screenplay, Hüseyin Erdem. Camera (color), Kamal Saydo, Georg Berg; editor, Margot Löhlein; music, Ken B. Wood. Reviewed on vidcassette, New York, March 10, 1993 (In Human Rights Watch Film Festival). Running time: **100 MIN.**

June 21, 1993 (Cont.)   **June 28, 1993**

Siyabend . . . . Tarik Akan
Xecê . . . . Mine Çayiroglu
Siyabend (as boy) . Menderes Samancila
Queda . . . . Yaman Okay
Aya . . . . Kazim Kartal
Merike Kal . . . . Bûlent Oran
  Also with: Mesut Çakarli, Cemal Gen-
der, Duygu Ankara, Hûlya Erçel,
Hikmet Kargôz, Metin Çkmez, Mustafa
Suphi, Cengiz Sezici.
    (Kurdish soundtrack)

Astory within a story, Sahin Gök's "Siyabend and Xecê"
deals with the sometimes dangerous nature of preserving cultural identity within an ethnic
minority. Blatant social message is driven home in a conversation at pic's end, where
two characters discuss the ban
on speaking their language in
their own homeland.

Shot in Kurdish, tale is structured around a secret meeting
that the children of an isolated
Turkish Kurdish community have
with a raconteur, who regularly
relates old Kurdish legends to
preserve tradition. While an old
woman watches out for soldiers,
the children gather round the
storyteller for "Siyabend and
Xecê," a tragic love story.

Meandering tale revolves
around the character of
Siyabend (Tarik Akan), an orphan and nephew of the village
leader, whose cruel and selfish
antics make life so miserable that
the villagers drive him out. One
day, lightening hits a tree and
deposits a lightening bolt, which
Siyabend has forged into an in-
destrictible dagger and shield.

During his travels through the
mountains, he encounters Xecê
(Mine Çayiroglu), a beautiful
young woman who lives with her
seven brothers. She has spurned
the amorous attentions of a local
prince, who later sends his men
to kidnap her. Of course,
Siyabend goes to the rescue with
his dagger and shield.

As a folk tale, story wanders
and incorporates side plots that
are later abandoned. The actual
love story doesn't even appear
until three-quarters of the way
in. A further problem is that
Siyabend is so antisocial and unlikable that it is difficult to feel
any sympathy for him when he
suffers eventual tragedy.

Shot under difficult conditions
in Turkey (with postproduction
in Germany), pic has an authentic anthropolitical feel. Acting is
okay. — *Paul Lenti*

VIDEOGRAMME EINER REVOLUTION
(VIDEOGRAM OF A REVOLUTION)
(GERMAN-DOCU-16m)

A Harun Farocki Filmproduktion
Berlin/Bermer Institut Film/Fersehen
production. Produced by Ulrich Sirchio.
Directed, written by Harun Farocki,
Andrei Ujica. Editor, Egon Bunne; nar-
rator, Elisabeth Neiman. Reviewed at
Human Rights Watch Film Festival,
N.Y., May 16, 1992. Running time: **107
MIN.**

"Videogram of a Revolution" presents a mannered look
at Romania's popular overthrow of the government of Nicolae Ceausescu from Dec. 21,
1989, the day of Ceausescu's
final public speech, to Dec.
26, the day of his trial and
execution. Subject is fascinating despite occasional exasperation with filmmakers' decon-
structive approach.

Documakers Harun Farocki
and Andrei Ujica operate with
the contention that video has put
the means of recording history
into everyone's hands. Thus, docu
incorporates video footage from
about 100 sources (transferred
to 16m) to show that the Romanian revolution truly belonged
to everyone. While some of this
footage is illustrative and gives a
behind-the-scenes look at a revolution in the making, much of the
jerky nonprofessional camerawork is dizzyingly out of focus
and desperately searches for a
center of attention.

To give credit, much of this
unedited and formless footage
gives the film an immediacy, mirroring the chaos and 'formlessness of the revolution itself. It
was not a coup d'etat; it was a
revolution whose only plan is to
get rid of Ceausescu.

There are some interesting attempts at analysis, especially
when presenting material from
the state TV Televiziunea Ro-
mana Libera. While Ceasescu
gives his final speech, we are
simultaneously shown what was
shot and what the public saw.
Later, officials discuss the role
and responsibility of national TV
in presenting the revolution, without sparking further violence.

"Videogram of a Revolution"
is an unavoidable document yet
its tech shortcomings will limit
wide distribution. — *Paul Lenti*

LAST ACTION HERO

A Columbia release of a Steve Roth/
Oak production. Produced by Roth, John
McTiernan. Executive producer, Arnold
Schwarzenegger. Directed by McTiernan. Screenplay, Shane Black, David
Arnott, from Zak Penn, Adam Leff's
story. Camera (Technicolor; Panavision
widescreen), Dean Semler; editor, John
Wright; music, Michael Kamen; production design, Eugenio Zanetti; art direction, Marek Dobrowolski, Rick Heinrichs, John Wright Stevens (N.Y.); set
design, Peter J. Kelly, Natalie Richards,
Carl Stensel, Elizabeth Lapp; set decoration, Cindy Carr, Debra Shutt (N.Y.);
costume design, Gloria Gresham; sound
(Dolby; SDDS), Lee Orloff; visual effects consultant, Richard Greenberg;
visual effects supervisor, John Sullivan;
co-producers, Robert E. Relyea, Neal
Nordlinger; associate producer, Robert
H. Lemer; assistant directors, Brian W.
Cook, Richard Baratta (N.Y.); 2nd-unit
director, Fred M. Waugh; 2nd-unit cam-
era, David B. Nowell; casting, Jane Jen-
kins, Janet Hirshenson. Reviewed at
Sony Studios, Culver City, Calif., June
11, 1993. MPAA Rating: PG-13. Run-
ning time: **130 MIN.**
Jack Slater . . Arnold Schwarzenegger
John Practice . . . F. Murray Abraham
Frank . . . . Art Carney
Benedict . . . . Charles Dance
Dekker . . . . Frank McRae
Ripper . . . . Tom Noonan
Nick . . . . Robert Prosky
Vivaldi . . . . Anthony Quinn
Mom . . . . Mercedes Ruehl
Danny Madigan . . . . Austin O'Brien
Death . . . . Ian McKellen
Tough Asian Man . . Prof. Toru Tanaka
Teacher . . . . Joan Plowright
Lt. Governor . . . . Jason Kelly
Rookie . . . . Noah Emmerich
The Mayor . . . . Tina Turner
Whitney/Meredith . . Bridgette Wilson
  Cameos: Keith Barish, Jim Belushi,
Chevy Chase, Chris Connelly, Karen
Duffy, Larry Ferguson, Leeza Gibbons,
Hammer, Little Richard, Robert Pat-
rick, Maria Shriver, Sharon Stone, Jean-
Claude Van Damme, Melvin Van Pee-
bles, Damon Wayans.

"Last Action Hero" is a
joyless, soulless machine of a
movie. This $80 million-plus
mishmash of fantasy, industry
in-jokes, self-referential parody, film-buff gags and too-big
action set-pieces will test the
clout of a humongous, super-
star-driven marketing campaign to put over a picture people won't much like, with the
possible exception of early-teen
boys. After the big opening,
word of mouth will likely send
b.o. down on a steeper-than-
desired slide.

In a PG-13 picture that reps
Arnold Schwarzenegger's self-
proclaimed attempt to soften his
image and reduce the violence in
his work, the body count and
sadism quotient remain remarkably high. But far more staggering is the total imbalance between the money and effort lavished on every scene and the
utter lack of emotion or human
interest to latch on to.

Schwarzenegger plays the indestructible screen superhero
Jack Slater, and at one point his
young charge tells him, "You
can't die until the grosses go
down" (repeated by the star himself at the end, and likely to be
quoted frequently), but his prophetic signature phrase to his
enemies when they try to harm
him is "Big mistake."

That's what he's made here. It
may have been alluring to give
his persona a tweaking by essentially playing himself, and the
appeal of an 11-year-old boy joining in his he-man exploits can
also be understood. But the central problem is that the picture is
based on a gimmick rather than a
story, so the viewer is presented
with a succession of arbitrary
scenes in which nothing is at
stake because, in context, it's
almost all "fiction" anyway.

Watching a Slater opus in a
Times Square grindhouse, little
Danny Madigan (Austin O'Brien)
is invited by old projectionist
friend Nick (Robert Prosky) to
return at midnight for a private
screening of "Jack Slater IV."

Before showing it, however,
Nick presents Danny with a gold-
en ticket, a magic "passport to
another world" handed down
from Houdini but never used by
the Nick. With it, Danny passes
into the world onscreen, plunked
right down in the 1966 Pontiac
convertible in which Slater is
being pursued by some machine-
gun toting baddies.

Because of what he's already
seen of the film in progress,
Danny is able to lead Slater to
the home of the chief mobster
(Anthony Quinn) and his sinister
triggerman Benedict (Charles
Dance), yet another cruel British villain. This leads to one shootout after another, each more elaborate and tiresome than the last,
interrupted only by visits to the
gargantuan, futuristic police station where Slater's boss (Frank
McRae) can shout at him for his
unorthodox methods.

This being a "movie," much is
made of the fantasy element:
Slater can survive all manner of
firepower without injury, cars
are capable of impossible stunts,
and all the women are hot babes.
At one point, Slater and Danny
enter a videostore (heavily stocked with Columbia/TriStar product) only to encounter a display
for "Terminator 2" starring
Sylvester Stallone. Sad to say,
this represents the high water
mark of the film's wit.

At a crucial juncture, the crafty
Benedict comes into possession
of the magic ticket and takes his

June 28, 1993 (Cont.)

evil ways into the "real" world of Times Square, followed by Danny and Slater, who is dismayed to discover that violence can actually hurt and that his entire "life" has been lived in movies. It just so happens that "Jack Slater IV" is opening in New York, allowing the "real," Planet Hollywood-plugging Arnold Schwarzenegger, accompanied by wife Maria Shriver and surrounded by a host of celebs in cameos, to be threatened at his own premiere and saved by his fictional counterpart.

The basic conceit of a "real" character joining "fictional" characters up onscreen was possibly done first, and certainly best, by Buster Keaton in his brilliant "Sherlock Jr." (1924). The fanciful script here, contributed to by several uncredited hands (including William Goldman's), certainly leaves a lot to be desired, and director John McTiernan nowhere displays the deft, whimsical touch required to pull this off. To the contrary, it's all heavy, empty and exceptionally noisy. There are too many guns, too many cars, too many explosions, too many extras, too many villains (at least four prominent ones) and no heart.

Almost everything about the film has annoying aspects, beginning with the heavy metal score that is uniquely strident. Many of the settings look murky and unattractive, and their lensing lacks the muscular grace that best suits ambitious actioners.

On a character level, Arnold is Arnold, and there's not really much else to be said about his performance. Everyone else seems to have checked in for a nice payday.

Unfortunately, Austin O'Brien, who is onscreen most of the time, is far from being a charming or endearing kid. Jabbering incessantly and always badgering his hero, he delivers a one-note perf that adds considerably to the already deafening soundtrack, and is best characterized as a perpetual insistence upon being seen and heard.

"Last Action Hero" is enough to make one nostalgic for "Hudson Hawk." — *Todd McCarthy*

DENNIS THE MENACE

A Warner Bros. release of a John Hughes production. Produced by Hughes, Richard Vane. Executive producer, Ernest Chambers. Directed by Nick Castle. Screenplay, Hughes, from characters created by Hank Ketcham. Camera (Technicolor), Thomas Ackerman; editor, Alan Heim; music, Jerry Goldsmith; production design, James Bissell; art direction, Michael Baugh, Steve Wolff; set design, Karen Fletcher; set decoration, Eve Cauley; costume design, Ann Roth, Bridget Kelly; sound (Dolby), Jim Alexander; associate producer, William Ryan; assistant director, Joe Camp III; 2nd unit director, Freddie Hice; 2nd unit camera, Steve Yaconelli, Reed Smoot, Flemming Olsen; casting, Jane Jenkins, Jane Hirshenson. Reviewed at the Mann Westwood Theater, L.A., June 9, 1993. MPAA Rating: PG. Running time: **94 MIN.**

Mr. Wilson	Walter Matthau
Dennis Mitchell	Mason Gamble
Martha Wilson	Joan Plowright
Switchblade Sam	Christopher Lloyd
Alice Mitchell	Lea Thompson
Henry Mitchell	Robert Stanton
Chief of Police	Paul Winfield
Margaret Wade	Amy Sakasitz
Joey	Kellen Hathaway

In contrast to "Jurassic Park," "Dennis The Menace" isn't really appropriate for anyone over the age of 12. Very young children may find the numbskull, by-the-numbers gags here amusing, but teens will consider this kids' stuff and adults will be pained. B.o. for the debut release from Warner's new Family Entertainment label will depend upon how much of the family market automatically trails along by virtue of its brand name subject, but results will fall way, way short of the "Home Alone" stratosphere likely dreamed of at project's inception.

Producer-screenwriter John Hughes continues his march down the age-scale from adolescence to babyhood with the antics of five-year-old Dennis Mitchell, for more than 40 years the star of Hank Ketcham's comic strip, for four years of an early 1960s TV series and now of a syndicated animated series. A new cartoon series debuts on CBS-TV this fall.

Hughes prepared for his writing by going through the entirety of Ketcham's comic strips and trying to distill the highlights. One would have thought this process would yield a cache of comic nuggets, but what's onscreen is a parade of meek outrages perpetrated upon an irascible old coot by a little kid who can't help himself.

There's no plot per se, just one lame gag after another. Opening scene has little blond Dennis (Mason Gamble) casually torturing next-door neighbor Mr. Wilson (Walter Matthau) in bed, a scene climaxed by the kid shooting aspirin into the man's mouth with a slingshot.

Natch, Dennis' parents (Lea Thompson and Robert Stanton) admonish their sprig to cool it, but soon he's back to his tricks, vacuuming up spilled paint which ends up in Mr. Wilson's hamburgers, fiddling with his false teeth, pouring toilet cleanser into his mouthwash and creating havoc at a garden party.

In an attempt to introduce some notion of suspense, Hughes drags in a sinister looking stranger named Switchblade Sam (Christopher Lloyd) who stalks the idyllic town for awhile before kidnapping the little tyke. But the evil Sam doesn't know who he's tangling with in Dennis, and the sentimentality is laid on thick when Dennis is enthroned as a town hero and good kid after all.

The one real pleasure for adults in the film comes from watching Matthau. His challenge in playing Mr. Wilson lay in inventing an infinite number of reactions to Dennis' pranks, and Matthau has reached deep into his bag of tricks to deliver a huge assortment of slow burns, simmering grimaces, delayed howls and intolerant glances. It's a performance worthy of a real Sunshine boy, calling as it does on a repertoire developed by the great vaudevillians and executed delectably by this highly skilled disciple of that tradition.

Gamble has the expected toussled looks and mischievous attitude in the lead, but lacks the charismatic watchability of this generation's real Dennis, Macaulay Culkin. Lloyd's scraggly ghoul seems like a brother to Freddy, and eveyone else in the cast play mild, benign characters who generate no interest.

Basically, Hughes and director Nick Castle have delivered the safest, most innocuous "Dennis the Menace" possible, applying little imagination to an old-fashioned vision of America where the biggest problems are little kids with impish senses of fun. Unfortunately, this "fun" isn't contagious.

Tech credits for this small-scale production are smooth.
— *Todd McCarthy*

ONCE UPON A FOREST
(ANIMATED)

A 20th Century Fox release of a Hanna-Barbera production in association with HTV Cymru/Wales Ltd. Produced by David Kirschner, Jerry Mills. Executive producers, William Hanna, Paul Gertz. Directed by Charles Grosvenor. Screenplay, Mark Young, Kelly Ward, from a Welsh story created by Rae Lambert. CFI color; animation director, Dave Michener; voice direction, Ward, Young; music, James Horner; production design, Carol Holman Grosvenor, Bill Proctor; art direction, Carol Holman Grosvenor; supervising film editor, Pat A. Foley; character design, Judith Holmes Clarke; visual effects supervisor, Glenn Chaika; additional animation by Wang Films, Lapíz Azúl Animación, Jaime Diaz Studio, A-Film, The Hollywood Cartoon Co., Phoenix Animation Ltd., Matias Marcos Animation; sound (Dolby), Larry Hoki; casting, Mike Fenton, Judy Taylor, Allison Cowitt. Reviewed at National Theater, L.A., June 13, 1993. MPAA Rating: G. Running time: **80 MIN.**

Voices:

Cornelius	Michael Crawford
Phineas	Ben Vereen
Abigail	Ellen Blain
Edgar	Ben Gregory
Russell	Paige Gosney
Michelle	Elizabeth Moss

"Once Upon a Forest" is an OK ecologically themed animated entry from "An American Tail" creator David Kirschner. While an agreeable enough effort in most respects, pic is a bit dark and somber to be wholly appealing to kids, and could have used bigger doses of humor and music. Fox should be able to generate respectable b.o. from this briskly told fable.

Introductory section nicely sets up the idyllic forest world of Dapplewood, where a variety of cuddly animals live in perfect harmony. Four kids, or "furlings" — Abigail the cute mouse, Edgar the nerdy mole, Russell the pudgy hedgehog and Michelle the adorable badger — study with Michelle's uncle, wise old inventor Cornelius, who's just developed a model of his greatest creation, the flying flapper-wing-a-ma-thing.

On one of their treks, the furlings come upon a highway, and Cornelius warns them to stay away from the hostile outside world. But humankind won't leave the creatures alone, as a chemical truck crashes nearby and releases poisonous gas into Dapplewood, decimating the foliage and infecting its inhabitants.

With Michelle gravely ill, Cornelius sends the three others on a journey to find the rare herbal cure in a far-off meadow. Along the way, the little critters grow up fast, fighting off a hungry

June 28, 1993 (Cont.)

owl, encountering a rambunctious preacher and gospel group, sneaking past the "yellow dragons" (bulldozers and cranes at a construction site), and finally building a full-scale flying machine in order to snatch the medicinal herb off the mountainside.

Highly ecologically sensitive film does a good job of creating an us-against-the-world feeling. Until a late sequence shows human beings as capable of some kindness, civilization is portrayed as the ever-looming source of evil. This threatening cloud hangs over most of the action, lending a rather gloomy mood despite the furlings' upbeat personalities.

Periodic attempts are made to lighten the tone and inject some juice into the proceedings, notably with the gospel number (created by Andrae Crouch and performed by Ben Vereen) and mild clowning. But pic has only three songs, not really enough to qualify as a musical. More jokes and gags would have helped, too.

The furlings are genuinely appealing without being cloyingly cute, and Cornelius, very nicely voiced by Michael Crawford, quickly emerges as a thoroughly lovable source of wisdom and guidance. Character animation is pleasing without being overly complex, and backgrounds are nicely filled in, though not on par with the most ambitious animation.

Script wisely wraps things up quickly when the upbeat ending is in sight, and small children's endurance will not be overly tried by the reasonable running time.
— *Todd McCarthy*

TIME INDEFINITE

A First Run Features release. Producer, director, camera, editor, sound, Ross McElwee. Assistant editors, Claudia Gonson, Andrea Lelievre. Reviewed at Film Forum, N.Y., May 6, 1993. Running time: **117 MIN.**

With "Time Indefinite," indie filmmaker Ross McElwee continues the autobiographical journey begun with the cult hit "Sherman's March" (1986). While that film chronicled McElwee's failed romances and the nature of romance, the new film plunges into more metaphysical questions as McElwee explores the cycle of life and death as it affects his family. This powerful and personal statement stays with the viewer longer after leaving the cinema.

Like his earlier films, helmer's distinctive narration soothes the aud and carries us along on his personal journey. Pic picks up where "March" leaves off: McElwee is a 39-year-old unmarried Southerner living in the Boston area. At a family reunion, McElwee announces plans to marry filmmaker Marilyn Levine and the family rejoices.

Yet, this happiness does not last long: The couple first suffers a miscarriage, then McElwee's father, a prominent doctor, and his grandmother both die, ending the generational link.

Film becomes an intimate rumination on the mystery of life and death. McElwee makes characteristic associations, such as mulling over the fate of a fish that connects to the death of his brother and his own relationship with his father.

McElwee seeks out advice from others and again returns to his longtime friend and mentor Charleen, who questions his methods: "This is life and not art," she states exasperatedly, bringing McElwee to the observation: "It's hard to film your life and live it at the same time."

Yet it is precisely this effort to pursue his own demons, to breach Southern etiquette and confront death head-on that gives "Time Indefinite" its diary-like vitality, its self-mocking gentle humor and even its questioning of the filmmaking process itself.

Title emerges from a phrase uttered by a visiting Jehovah's Witness. Yet, McElwee notes, his film also keeps his family "alive" into time indefinite.

The visual texture is varied with the insertion of old home movies and video. Camerawork has a cinéma vérité feel, using available light to document an immediate reality. — *Paul Lenti*

CE QUE FEMME VEUT...
(WHAT A WOMAN WANTS...)
(FRENCH)

A Rezo Films release of a Rezo Films/Rio co-production. Produced by Jean-Michel Rey, Jean Gontier. Executive producer, Philippe Liègeoise. Directed by Gérard Jumel. Screenplay, Sulvie Randonneix, Jumel. Camera (color), Hélène Louvart; editor, Marion Monestier; music, Philippe Eidel; sound, Pascal Ribier; sound mixing, Thomas Gauder; assistant director, Sylvie Randonneix. Reviewed at Club de l'Etoile screening room, Paris, June 1, 1993. Running time: **75 MIN.**
Isabelle . . . . . . Caroline Chaniolleau
Cécile . . . . Karin Viard
Pierre . . . . Gérard Jumel
Hubert . . . . François Siener

A quirky tale of an expectant father sharing a country house with his young wife and former g.f., "What a Woman Wants ... " is amusing and memorable. It's a modest, perfectly controlled exercise.

When 35-year-old Pierre (helmer co-scripter Gérard Jumel) and his six-months-pregnant wife Cécile (Karin Viard) visit a hospital emergency room, the doc on duty turns out to be Isabelle (Caroline Chaniolleau) who was Pierre's g.f. 10 years previous.

Adventurous, independent Isabelle, back from a humanitarian stint in Colombia, is living with her parents. Pierre offers the spare room and the lady doc — at 35, determined to have a baby of her own — moves in.

Pic contrasts two generations of French women: Although not yet 20, Cécile seems more grounded and mature than experienced Isabelle. While plagued with sympathetic pregnancy symptoms, Pierre juggles his feelings about his past with Isabelle and his future with Cécile.

Perfectly rendered awkward moments include Pierre's gauche banter when Isabelle invites a prospective "inseminator" to dinner and a scene in which hubby and wife argue with mouths full of toothpaste.

Thesping is all on the nose, lending an unexpected richness to bare bones narrative. Lensing has a light summery feel. The jaunty score rounds out the sweet comedy. — *Lisa Nesselson*

WONG FEI-HUNG TSI SAM: SIWONG TSANGBA
(ONCE UPON A TIME IN CHINA III)
(HONG KONG)

A Golden Harvest presentation of a Film Workshop production. Produced by Raymond Chow. Executive producer, Tsui Hark, Ng See-yuen. Directed, written by Tsui. Camera (Panavision widescreen), Lau Wai-keung; editor, Mak Chi-sin, Lam On-yi; music, Wu Wai-lap; art direction, Timmy Yip; costume design, Ching Tin-kiu; sound (Dolby), Tsau Kam-wing; martial arts director, Yun Pan; associate producer, Mak; 2nd-unit camera, Chou Man-keung. Reviewed at Metro 2 theater, London, May 8, 1993. Running time: **105 MIN.**
Wong Fei-hung . . . . Jet Li
Aunt Yee ("Peony") . Rosamund Kwan
Leung Fun . . . . Mok Siu-cheung
Wong Kei-ying . . . . Lau Shun
"Club Foot" . . . . Hung Yan-yan.
Tumanovsky . . . . . . John Wakefield
(Cantonese soundtrack)

Third leg of Tsui Hark's "Once Upon a Time in China" series, centered on Cantonese hero Wong Fei-hung, is an upper-case comedy actioner flawed by signs of sequel-itis. Result should please fans of martial arts star Jet Li but doesn't match the high points (or historical resonances) of the two earlier outings.

Unlike the Canton-set "I" and "II," "III" is set in Beijing, northern China. Pre-title sequence, showcasing the Forbidden City, has the Empress Dowager persuaded by her premier to hold a Lion King Competition to strengthen Chinese spirit against growing western incursion.

Enter Wong (Jet Li), with secret love Aunt Yee (Rosamund Kwan) and pesky disciple Leung Fun (Mok Siu-cheung), up on a visit to his father (Lau Shun), head of the local Cantonese Association. Turns out local triad groups are heavy-hitting Wong Sr., a veteran lion dance trainer, into not entering the meet so they can win the prestigious prize.

Plot rapidly settles down into a series of rival-schools confrontations, with Wong Jr. as peacemaker. Aunt Yee, meanwhile, is being romanced by a suspicious Russian (John Wakefield) plotting to kill the premier at the competition. Climax is the meet itself, with Wong Jr. saving the day and making a neat speech about government responsibility.

Pic's connections with "II" — which ended with Aunt Yee sailing off to Hong Kong — are remote at best. Tsui's script neatly develops the ongoing shy romance between Wong and Aunt Yee, plus the theme of the growing sway of western technology (here repped by the steam engine), but ditches most of the nationalist passion and historical grounding stoking "I" and "II."

Still, much refs to China's imminent takeover of Hong Kong, notably in the Cantonese vs. northerners subtext and implicit links between government and triads.

Setpieces — a fight on an oily floor, a pre-meet tryout and the final match — provide a fine showcase for Li's talents but lack cumulative tension. Nothing here equals the ladder fight of "I" or final reels of "II." The punning humor doesn't translate, either.

Period details, like Kwan's early movie camera and projector, are up to scratch and neatly included. Perfs and tech credits on the partly Beijing-lensed item are all par, though the music score is weaker than usual. Pic was socko at the Hong Kong b.o. earlier this year. — *Derek Elley*

SWEET KILLING
(CANADIAN-FRENCH-BRITISH)

A 20th Century Fox France release of a Canada/France/U.K. co-production with the participation of Canal Plus, the CNC and Telefilm Canada. Produced by Suzanne Girard, Eddy Matalon, Timothy Burrill. Directed by Matalon. Screenplay, Dominique Roulet, Matalon, from Angus Hall's novel "Qualthrough." Camera (color), Hugues de Kaeck; editor, Debra Karen; music, Jean Musy; production design, Claude Bere; art direction, Andre Chamberland; costume design, Nicoletta Massone; sound (Dolby), Alain Rivard. Reviewed at MGM screening room, Paris, June 7, 1993. Running time: **90 MIN.**
Adam Crosse . . . . . Anthony Higgins
Eva Bishop . . . . Leslie Hope
Zargo . . . . F. Murray Abraham
Garcia . . . . Michael Ironside
Also with: Andrea Ferreol, Aron Tager, Kathleen Fee, Ian Finlay, Terry Haig.

An entertaining black comedy/suspenser in which the perfect murder leads the guilty party into nerve-wracking new relationships, "Sweet Killing" is unlikely to make a box office killing but stands out as dandy tube and video fare. Genre fans will enjoy a wry twist or two.

Adam Crosse (Anthony Higgins) handles client relations for a bank but is able to make excellent use of his twin passions for comic books and handmade electronic toys in doing away with his nagging wife (Andrea Ferreol). Firmly establishing a house call on a fictional client named Zargo as his alibi, clever Higgins rigs things to look like a burglar bumped Ferreol. But driven inspector Garcia (Michael Ironside) remains skeptical — particularly when Higgins starts a passionate affair with Eva Bishop (Leslie Hope), the radiantly sexy divorcée he happened to meet the night of the murder.

Having borrowed the name "Zargo" from a detective comic book, Higgins is very spooked when tough customer F. Murray Abraham barges in claiming to *be* Zargo. Higgins' perfect crime and at-first perfect romance are compromised by sinister, increasingly demanding Zargo. But serendipity and zany karma may yet be on Higgins' side.

"Crime and Punishment" is the date movie at the local rep house and script features a handful of amusingly bad visual puns. Dialogue is sometimes stagier than need be ("You're my bottle of

champagne — I want to pop your cork") but perfs — with the exception of blatantly dubbed Ferreol — are all enjoyable, particularly stunning Hope as a maneating career woman who knows her own mind.

Tech credits are adequate, with Canadian locations standing in for unspecified American city.
— *Lisa Nesselson*

BRANDBILEN SOM FÖRSVANN
(THE FIRE ENGINE THAT DISAPPEARED)
(SWEDISH)

Svensk Filmindustri presents a Victoria Film production of a Victoria APS/Rialto Film Berlin/SVT Kanal 1 Drama/Nordiska Films & TV-fonden/SF Film. (Intl. sales: J&M.) Produced by Hans Lonnerheden. Executive producers, Ole Sondberg, Soren Staermose, Bertil Ohlsson. Directed by Hajo Gies. Screenplay, Rainer Berg, Beate Langmaack, from Maj Sjöwall and Per Wahlöö's novel. Camera (color, widescreen), Achim Poulheim; editor, Héléne Berlin; music, Stefan Nilsson; production design, Micke Kinning; costume design, Lenamari Wallström; sound, Mats Lindskog; stunts, Kimmo Rajala. Reviewed at Svensk screening room, Stockholm, April 28, 1993. (In Cannes Film Festival, market section.) Running time: **86 MIN.**
Martin Beck . . . . . . Gösta Ekman
Lennart Kollberg . . . Kjell Bergqvist
Gunvald Larsson . . . . Rolf Lassgärd
Benny Skacke . . . . Niklas Hjulström
Einar Rönn . . . . Bernt Ström
Evald Hammar . . Torgny Anderberg
Kristiansson . . . . P G Hylen
Kvant . . . . Birger Österberg
Greta Hjelm . . . . Agneta Ekmanner
Gun Kollberg . . . Eng-Marie Carlsson
Also with: Sandra Bergqvist, Tova Magnusson-Norling, Holger Kunkel, Rolf Jenner, Daniela Ziegler, Gunvor Ponten, Peter Schroder, Maria Heiskanen, Lena Thorsen, Bjarne Hildebrand, Ulla Akselson, Lina Lindblom.

The first of a series based on the police procedural novels of Maj Sjöwall and Per Wahlöö is a well-crafted, atmospheric thriller that makes good use of its Stockholm locale. Pic should be an easy sell abroad, especially for TV.

There have been several films made of the bestselling novels by Sjöwall/Wahlöö; the most w.k. are Bo Widerberg's "The Man on the Roof" and Stuart Rosenberg's "The Laughing Policeman." "The Fire Engine That Disappeared" is the first of six films shot back-to-back over a year.

The novels were written in the '60s and '70s, and the stories have been updated for the '90s. In the first film, a mysterious fire that kills several people puts the Stockholm police on the tracks of a narcotics syndicate.

Almost by chance, the hard-working policemen stumble onto the truth, which leads to a violent showdown at Arianda airport.

As helmed by German director Hajo Gies, who made several episodes of the German TV series "Tanort," the story hews a steady course through all the developments and knows where to place the short but, for a Swedish film, brutal action sequences.

The film also manages to establish the main characters and give them flesh and bones. Central character Martin Beck (Gösta Ekman), however, is a little too downplayed, and the emphasis instead is on his colleague Gunvald Larsson, played with powerful presence by the excellent Rolf Lassgard.

Pic is an efficient entry in the genre. Although not as tightly paced as "The Man on the Roof," it still delivers and does justice to the novel. — *Gunnar Rehlin*

EIGHT HUNDRED LEAGUES DOWN THE AMAZON

A Concorde Pictures presentation. Produced by Luis Llosa. Executive producer, Roger Corman. Directed by Llosa. Screenplay, Laura Schiff, Jackson Barr, from Jules Verne's novel. Camera (color), Pili Flores-Guerra; editor, Gwyneth Gibby; music, Jorge Tafar; art direction, Javier Duran; costume design, Teo Toro; sound, Edgar Lostaunau; associate producers, Schiff, Margarita Macedo; assistant director, Michelle Alexander. Reviewed at Cannes Film Festival (market section), May 14, 1993. MPAA Rating: PG-13. Running time: **88 MIN.**
Minha . . . . Daphne Zuniga
Garral . . . . Barry Bostwick
Koja . . . . Adam Baldwin
Manoel . . . . Tom Verica
Frolgoso . . . . E.E. Ross

A bad case of sleeping sickness floors "Eight Hundred Leagues Down the Amazon," a lethargic version of the Jules Verne adventure that's strictly moppet fare. Fans of Luis Llosa's "Sniper" won't recognize the director here. Pic is a homevid release on Roger Corman's New Horizons label.

Brazil-set period story has Barry Bostwick as a plantation owner with a past who travels down river with daughter Daphne Zuniga and her fiancé Tom Verica to attend their wedding. Hitching a free ride is bounty hunter Adam Baldwin, who's after Bostwick's money and also has eyes for Zuniga.

Lame development has Bostwick arrested halfway on a false

charge of jewel theft, and Zuniga and Verica trying to prove his innocence as the noose tightens.

Flatly lensed pic features a cheesy alligator attack, a pathetic storm sequence and Zuniga's best horse gobbled by joke piranhas. As an adventure movie, it's about as exciting as a bout of food poisoning.

Performances are routine, with Zuniga, who's meant to be an ace markswoman and equestrienne, stuck with lines like "You vile beast!" when Baldwin gets horny.
— *Derek Elley*

COLD SWEAT
(CANADIAN)

A Norstar Entertainment production, with the assistance of Ontario Film Investment Program. (Intl. sales: Norstar, Toronto.) Produced by Peter R. Simpson. Directed by Gail Harvey. Screenplay, Richard Beattie. Camera (color), Vic Sarin; editor, Nick Rotundo; music, Paul Zaza; production design, Andrzej Halinski; art direction, Jasna Stefanovic; costume design, Ruth Secord; sound, Richard Nicholl; co-producers, Ray Sager, Ilana Frank; assistant director, Charles Braive. Reviewed at Cannes Film Festival (market section), May 16, 1993. Running time: **88 MIN.**
Mark Cahill . . . . Ben Cross
Mitch . . . . Adam Baldwin
Beth . . . . Shannon Tweed
Larry . . . . Dave Thomas
Sean . . . . Henry Czerny
Ghost . . . . Lenore Zann
Joanne . . . . Maria del Mar

A surreal black comedy masquerading as an erotic thriller, "Cold Sweat" is an okay time-waster that should please fans of Adam Baldwin and former Playboy playmate Shannon Tweed. For mature markets, it's a vidbin title.

Multi-character plot revolves around a spooked-out hitman (Ben Cross) haunted by the ghost of an innocent woman (Lenore Zann) he's accidentally shot. When he's hired by a pusher (Baldwin) to ice the business partner (Henry Czerny) of a sleazebag businessman (Dave Thomas), he fumbles the job and is seemingly killed by the businessman's calculating wife (Tweed).

Complications include the fact that both Baldwin and Czerny are Tweed's lovers and Tweed thinks Baldwin was hired by her jealous hubby to kill *her.* Cross' hang-up is also affecting his love life with wife Maria de Mar.

In her second feature — and first commercial outing — Canadian director Gail Harvey, a former photog, steers a careful

June 28, 1993 (Cont.)

course through the over-ripe plotting and sexy inserts showcasing the Tweed bod. Aside from Thomas' manic performance as the businessman, most of the cast play Richard Beattie's formula script straight. Britisher Cross isn't required to do much other than look glazed.

Technically, the Toronto-shot pic is fine. — *Derek Elley*

CHAINED HEAT II
(CANADIAN)

A New Line (U.S.) release of a North American Releasing presentation, in association with New Line Cinema, of a North American Pictures/Public 21 Cinema production. (Intl. sales: NAR, Vancouver.) Produced by Lloyd Simandl, John Curtis. Executive producer, Simandl. Directed by Simandl. Screenplay, Chris Hype. Camera (Fujicolor), Danny Nowak; editor, Vera Flak; music, Bruce Curtis; production design, Stefan Exner; sound (Dolby), Vlastimil Kulisek; line producer, Michael Mazo; assistant director, Robert E. Lee. Reviewed at Cannes Film Festival (market section), May 16, 1993. Running time: **95 MIN.**
Magda Kassar . . . . . Brigitte Nielsen
Franklin Goff . . . . Paul Koslo
Alex Morrison . . . . Kimberley Kates
Suzanne Morrison . . . . Kari Whitman
Rosa . . . . Jana Svandova

"**C**hained Heat II" is a Z-grade women's prison schlocker that's for hardcore fans of Brigitte Nielsen and trashvid couch potatoes only. Listless bargain-basement item, shot in Prague, has no plot ties with the decade-old original.

Nielsen toplines as the sadistic Magda, head of the postcommunist privatized Razik Correctional Facility that doubles as a coke-packing plant and supplier of femme flesh for porn vids. When Yank tourist Alex (Kimberley Kates) ends up there on a fake drugs charge, her sister (Kari Whitman) comes looking for her.

The whole shebang is co-run by the local U.S. ambassador (Paul Koslo). When things start to go wrong, Magda decides to get rid of him, as well as her butch lover (Jana Svandova).

T&A content is mild, and there's precious little heat. Nielsen's statuesque perf is the only one to hit the right campy tone. Others range from plain awful to embarrassing.

Tech credits are cheesy, most seemingly shot in an abandoned factory. — *Derek Elley*

MONOLITH

An EGM Film Intl. production. (Intl. sales: EGM, L.A.) Produced by Geoff Griffiths, John Eyres. Executive producers, Rudiger von Spies, Griffiths, Eyres. Directed by Eyres. Screenplay, Stephen Lister; additional dialogue, Eric Poppen. Camera (Eastmancolor; CFI Color prints), Alan M. Trow; editor, Joel Goodman; music, Frank Becker; production design, Mark Harris; costume design, Meg Goodwin; special visual effects, Introvision (producer, Nick Davis); special visual effects supervisor, John Mesa; special effects, Ultimate Effects; line producer, Michael Polaire; associate producer, Stan Wertlieb; assistant director, Robert Lee; casting, Ulrich-Dawson & Associates. Reviewed at Cannes Film Festival (market section), May 14, 1993. Running time: **95 MIN.**
Tucker . . . . Bill Paxton
Terri Flynn . . . . Lindsay Frost
Villano . . . . John Hurt
Capt. MacCandless . Louis Gossett Jr.

Buddy-cop movie meets alien lifeforms in "Monolith," a high-voltage sci-fi actioner saddled with low-voltage dialogue. Slick, goodlooking genre item should scarf some fast cash in undiscriminating sites before shape-shifting into rental.

Bill Paxton and Lindsay Frost are two spatting LAPD cops who stumble on a high-level coverup by John Hurt, ruthless head of the blandly titled Dept. for Historical Research. Hurt's project of harnessing a shapeless alien force has gone awry, and the Thing is hopping from human to human en route to a massive recharge at its buried spaceship.

Pic's knock-'em-dead opening, as the duo confront a Russian scientist and alien-ized kid in the streets, segues to a familiar "Hunter"-style teaming of the two tecs as they ignore their exasperated boss (Louis Gossett Jr.) and take on Hurt and his goons. Over-the-top finale has Paxton taken over by the lifeforce and Frost doing a Sigourney Weaver number deep below L.A.

Director-producer team of Brits John Eyres and Geoff Griffiths ("Project: Shadowchaser") come up with a handsome product on a posted $8 million budget; fine visual effects by Introvision only occasionally betray their miniature origins. Action sequences deliver in spades, with good use of Dolby and tight cutting that shows Eyres and Griffiths' vid background.

As the grunt cops, Paxton and Frost double-team okay, but with no sparks, thanks to lackluster dialogue by Stephen Lister that isn't half as hard-assed as it thinks. Hurt hams as the villain,

and Gossett is his usual commanding presence. Title of pic, shot as "Tucker and Flynn," is meaningless. — *Derek Elley*

A HOUSE IN THE HILLS

A Live Entertainment/Delux Prods. presentation of a Seraglio Films production. (Intl. sales: Adriana Chiesa Enterprises, Rome.) Produced by Patricia Foulkrod, Ken Wiederhorn. Executive producers, Richard N. Gladstein, Adriana Chiesa, Wiederhorn. Directed by Wiederhorn. Screenplay, Wiederhorn, Miguel Tejada-Flores. Camera (Eastmancolor; CFI Color prints), Josep Civit; editor, Peter Teschner; music, Richard Einhorn; production design, Morley Smith; art direction, Peter Powis; costume design, Marcy Craig; sound (Ultra-Stereo), Victor Deckker ; assistant director, Javier Chinchilla. Reviewed at Cannes Film Festival (market section), May 16, 1993. Running time: **91 MIN.**
Mickey . . . . Michael Madsen
Alex Weaver . . . . Helen Slater
Ronald Rankin . . . . James Laurenson
Sondra Rankin . . . . . Elyssa Davalos
Willie . . . . Jeffrey Tambor
Susie . . . . Toni Barry

Michael Madsen and Helen Slater go head to toe in "A House in the Hills," an oddball light drama-thriller about a burglar and small-time actress in a Bel Air manse. Initially intriguing mix of styles goes to pieces in the final reels, signaling a tough sell theatrically for this leaky property.

Slater is a young actress who takes a weekend housesitting job at a swanky Canyon retreat to study lines for a TV soap audition. Next door a girl was recently murdered by a psycho.

Enter Madsen, posing as an exterminator, who thinks she's the owner's wife and holds her hostage. He's after his share of a $2 million insurance swindle by the owner, who had double-crossed him, landing him in jail.

Pic's first half settles down into an impressive, legit-style two-hander as Madsen and Slater play cat and mouse. Fragile construction starts to take on water, however, with the intro of the psycho (Jeffrey Tambor) and return of the house's owners (James Laurenson, Elyssa Davalos). Subsequent mayhem and shootouts verge on black farce.

Slater and Madsen are well matched in the early running, the former showing a neat line in dippy-smart and the latter serving up another of his trademark lightly menacing hunks. Slater handles some brief nude scenes naturally, and a central sex sesh between the pair is hot.

Other performances are standard, with Tambor eye-rolling as

the psycho, Laurenson a one-dimensional villain, and Davalos a straight rich bitch.

Helmer-co-scripter-producer Ken Wiederhorn ("Return of the Living Dead Part II," "Meatballs Part II," etc.) turns in a glossy-looking package and shows talent to spare in the well-paced early stages. Other credits are smooth, neatly disguising interiors shot in Luxembourg under the duchy's tax-shelter scheme. — *Derek Elley*

SEATTLE FEST

ACTING ON IMPULSE

A Spectacor Films production. Produced by David Peters. Executive producers, Joe Cohen, David Newlon, Jon Kramer, David Lewine. Directed by Sam Irvin. Screenplay, Mark Pittman, Alan Moskowitz, from Sol Weingarten's story. Camera (color), Dean Lent; editors, James Mitchell, Neil Grieve; music, Dan Licht; production design, Gary Randall; costume design, Jill Ohanneson; sound, Giovanni Di Simonil; line producer, Jat Sedrish; assistant director, Adam C. Taylor; casting, Gale Salus. Reviewed at Seattle Film Festival, June 3, 1993. Running time: **92 MIN.**
Susan Gittes . . . . . Linda Fiorentino
Paul Stevens . . . . C. Thomas Howell
Cathy Thomas . . . . Nancy Allen
Gail Black . . . . Judith Hoag
Dave Byers . . . . Adam Ant
Yoram Sussman . . . . Patrick Bachau
Detective Stubbs . . . . . Isaac Hayes
Brunop . . . . Paul Bartel
Leroy . . . . Don Most
John . . . . Miles O'Keeffe
Also with: Dick Sargent, Charles Lane, Mary Woronov, Zelda Rubinstein, Nicholas Sadler, Peter Lupus, Kim McGuire, Cassandra Peterson, Brinke Stevens, Michael Talbot, Robert Alan Golub, Cliff Dorfman, Craig Shoemaker, Scott Thompson Stevens.

After an awkward start, "Acting on Impulse" accelerates into a nonstop delight, poking affectionate fun at the cheap-thrills sex 'n' gore genre while creating believable characters and original twists. Too flippant for action auds, and a tad in-jokey for general tastes, pic preems on Showtime in July.

Linda Fiorentino toplines as Susan Gittes, a self-described "scream queen" buckling under the weight of too many Z-grade chainsaw epics. Already known as erratic, she casually brushes off her director (Paul Bartel) and her b.f.-manager (Adam Ant) in the middle of a quickie shoot, but when her slimy producer (Patrick Bachau) turns up dead in her trailer, the police are called.

Checking into a deluxe hotel outside of L.A. (and using the name DeeDee Slaughter), the on-

June 28, 1993 (Cont.)

the-lam actress sidles up to Paul (C. Thomas Howell), a straight-arrow salesman who struggles to remain faithful to his left-behind fiancée. In town for a pharmaceutical convention, Paul also hooks up with Cathy (Nancy Allen), a goody-two-shoes saleswoman looking to loosen up.

Once this unlikely trio is in place, the story takes off with edgy precision, powered by sexual and value-system tensions among the three. There's also a snappy subplot with Tom Wright (the script capitalizes on his resemblance to Sugar Ray Leonard) as a buttoned-down buppie who becomes Paul's biggest rival, and nominal nods to the thriller theme, with Susan/ DeeDee stalked by an obsessed fan while Paul remains ignorant of her identity and alleged crime.

This latter aspect is less effective, but it gives helmer Sam Irvin a chance to intercut droll scenes with Isaac Hayes as an unflappable homicide detective, and indulge in a variety of red herrings and amusing side trips.

With left-field curves in lensing and editing, and the note-perfect thesping of its three leads (especially Fiorentino, who makes her harsh character likable), pic really clicks as a parody loyal to its subject while establishing its own smart identity.

Occasionally, all its best elements come together brilliantly, as in the much-anticipated carnal encounter between intermittently meek Paul and definitely dangerous Susan. Highly charged by any standard, the scene takes on "Basic Instinct" overtones when audience sees (and Paul doesn't) the actress surreptitiously fishing under the bed for . . . a condom.

Funny, suspenseful, surprisingly lyrical moments like this could tickle adult auds — if "Acting on Impulse" can slash its way out of the midnight-cult ghetto.

— *Ken Eisner*

EIGHT-TRAY GANGSTER: THE MAKING OF A CRIP
(DOCU-16m)

An ETG-Saramatt production. Produced, directed, written by Thomas Lee Wright. Camera (color, 16m), Jean de Segonzac; editor, Pat Barber. Reviewed at Seattle Intl. Film Festival, May 19, 1993. Running time: **70 MIN.**

A powerful slice of current urban African-American

life, "Eight-Tray Gangster" should attract immediate fest and theatrical interest for its sensational content — and respect for its sober treatment of same. Yet gaps in editorial/ explanatory logic will limit future televid exposure as surely as the unexpurgated language.

Doc centers on Kershaun "Li'l Monster" Scott, who with brother "Monster Kody" (allegedly so named for an extremely brutal adolescent attack on a foe) grew up in a tranquil SoCal suburb. But their move with mom to L.A.'s South Central in 1972 "changed everything," according to Kershaun. The brothers "became adults suddenly," forcibly introduced to violent gang ways.

On New Year's Eve 1981, Kody was shot point-blank three times at a convenience store. Li'l Monster, then 14, immediately set in motion an all-night drive-by shooting spree in the 'hood suspected of sponsoring the original attack. Both brothers have done hard time; Kody, 29, remains there on an assault rap even as his book, "Monster: The Autobiography of 'Monster Kody,' " is published to monster hype.

Li'l Monster a.k.a. Kershaun now does community service work with South Central kids. But his activities (including visits to his g.f. and their child) have to be managed on the sly for fear that old gang ties may yet carry violent consequences.

"Eight-Tray Gangster" is strong stuff on several levels. Both brothers have obviously evolved over time into thoughtful, articulate spokesmen for an embattled community. They discuss the teachings of Malcolm X and the need for African-American youth to "stop shooting each other." Yet we see Kershaun with fellow "New African Militia" members target-shooting, discussing "the right to defend ourselves by any means necessary," and disparages Dr. Martin Luther King's nonviolence.

The film could be much better organized to reveal these seeming contradictions as part of an actual, organized philosophy. Chronology is also confused by scant differentation of footage — some shot in the summer of '89, some in the wake of the Rodney King verdict much later.

In evident sympathy with the subjects, first-time helmer (and "New Jack City" scenarist) Thomas Lee Wright sometimes willfully omits crucial elements of their milieu. What point does it serve to completely avoid the

issue of drug trafficking/use in lower-class black neighborhoods? Editing adjustments and perhaps intertitles or narration would help clear up the more nagging questions. Tech credits are otherwise rough-hewn but competent.

For both inner-city and general auds, "Eight-Tray" will certainly provide a hard-hitting forum for discussion. When Kershaun's current best friend/bodyguard cooly says, "I figure I can kill about 20 more motherf---ers, then go get a job and get married," the intimacy leaves little room for viewer comfort. Wright suggests the real "monster" is the country's neglect of its marginalized citizens. The consequences are right here on screen, in harsh and often scarifying form.

— *Dennis Harvey*

A FOREIGN FIELD
(BRITISH)

A Fingertip Film production. Produced by Martyn Auty, Steve Lanning. Executive producer, Richard Brooke. Directed by Charles Sturridge. Screenplay, Roy Clarke. Camera (color), Richard Greatrex; editor, John Bloom; music, Geoffrey Burgon; production design, Simon Holland; art direction, Dominic Masters; costume design, Nic Ede; sound, Simon Kaye; assistant director, David Tringham. Reviewed at the AFI/L.A. Intl. Film Festival, June 12, 1993. Running time: **90 MIN.**

Amos	Alec Guinness
Cyril	Leo McKern
Waldo	John Randolph
Angelique	Jeanne Moreau
Lisa	Lauren Bacall
Beverley	Geraldine Chaplin
Ralph	Edward Herrmann

"A Foreign Field" is a slow, embarrassingly sentimental comedy-melodrama about three World War II veterans revisiting the battlefield. The all-star film aimed at senior citizens is technically pedestrian and more suitable for TV and video than for theaters.

Pic begins as a comic tale of Amos (Guinness) and Cyril (Leo McKern), two British vets who fought heroically in the D-Day landing and are returning to Normandy for the first time. Their "mission" is twofold: to visit the grave of a wartime buddy, and to look up Angelique (Jeanne Moreau), the French girl Cyril was enamored of back in '44.

At their hotel, they run into Waldo (John Randolph), an American vet traveling with his bickering daughter (Geraldine Chap-

lin) and her CPA husband (Edward Herrmann). To his surprise and dismay, Cyril realizes the Yank is there for the same reason: to revisit Angelique. Lauren Bacall, as a mysterious lady who appears to be an American widow, is also at the hotel.

TV writer Roy Clarke's predictable script consists of brief scenes in which each of the characters makes revelations about his/her past and share some painful and/or joyful memories.

It is always a pleasure to see Guinness, who does some marvelous things as a long-wounded vet. But most of the other actors play clichés rather than individuals, particularly Chaplin and Herrmann's uptight, unpleasant couple, who seem to be there only to make the older actors appear more sympathetic.

As the retired prostie now in a home, Moreau brings life to her stereotypical role and delivers a stirring rendition of Edith Piaf's "La vie en rose." Bacall, as a boozy widow whose national identity is the film's only real mystery, looks elegant, but gets nothing memorable to do or say.

Charles Sturridge, who established some reputation as co-director of "Brideshead Revisited" and helmer of the "Where Angels Fear to Tread," here exhibits an unaccountably draggy, unmodulated style that lacks visual distinction, subtlety or nuance. — *Emanuel Levy*

IT WAS A WONDERFUL LIFE
(DOCU-16m)

A Cinewomen production. Produced by Tammy Glaser. Executive producers, Elisa Rothstein, Kimberly Marteau. Directed by Michele Ohayon. Camera (color), Theo Van de Sande, Jacek Laskus, Bruce Ready; editors, Anne Stein, Lisa Leeman; music, Melissa Etheridge; sound, Margaret Duke, Giovanni Di Simone. Reviewed at the AFI/ L.A. Intl. Film Festival, June 14, 1993. Running time: **84 MIN.**
Narrator: Jodie Foster.

Dedicated to the "hidden homeless," "It Was a Wonderful Life" is a devastating but ultimately unsatisfying docu about middle-class women who have fallen from riches to rags. Presentation of a relevant, previously unchronicled problem is marred by lack of sharp focus, overly stressed feminist agenda, and mediocre tech credits. Still, the timely issue and narration by Jodie Foster will be

helpful in luring pubcasters, video, schools and other orgs.

Aptly titled pic traces the daily lives of six homeless women, all formerly affluent, as they struggle to survive.

Group is varied enough in age, ethnicity and occupational status to sustain viewer interest. Typically, these women were left destitute by an inequitable divorce settlement, recessionary job market, sudden illness and bad health insurance. As a category, the women defy society's image of the homeless: They don't sleep on the street, are educated, clean, well-dressed, and too proud to receive public handouts.

The women's strength and creativity are riveting. One uses her artwork as payment to a chiropractor; another is a law student. Homelessness also brings to the surface some unexpected positive values: incredibly intimate family life, indefatigable fortitude, even humor.

The first — and best — part of the docu provides a compassionate look at each woman; however, the second, more ideological part presents its information rather selectively, in a manner that emphasizes its feminist agenda: Men walking out on their wives and children, ineffective legal protection for divorced women, inadequate child-support enforcement. All of these factors are present, but are part of larger, more complex structures that include government and city policies, the recessionary economy, and evolving social values.

Foster's minimal narration is effectively matter-of-fact.

— *Emanuel Levy*

THE FIRM

A Paramount release of a John Davis/ Scott Rudin/Mirage production. Produced by Rudin, Davis, Sydney Pollack. Executive producers, Michael Hausman, Lindsay Doran. Directed by Pollack. Screenplay, David Rabe, Robert Towne, David Rayfiel, from John Grisham's novel. Camera (Technicolor; Deluxe prints), John Seale; editors, William Steinkamp, Frederic Steinkamp; music, Dave Grusin; production design, Richard Macdonald; art direction, John Willett; set decoration, Casey Hallenbeck; costume design, Ruth Myers; sound (Dolby), David MacMillan; assistant director, David McGiffert; casting, David Rubin. Reviewed at the National Theater, L.A., June 24, 1993. MPAA Rating: R. Running time: **154 MIN.**

Mitch McDeere . . . . Tom Cruise
Abby McDeere . . Jeanne Tripplehorn
Avery Tolar . . . . Gene Hackman
Oliver Lambert . . . . . . Hal Holbrook
Lamar Quinn . . . . Terry Kinney
William Devasher . . . Wilford Brimley
Wayne Tarrance . . . . Ed Harris
Tammy Hemphill . . . . . Holly Hunter
Ray McDeere . . . . . David Strathairn
Eddie Lomax . . . . Gary Busey
F. Denton Voyles . . . . . Steven Hill
The Nordic Man . . . . Tobin Bell
Kay Quinn . . . . Barbara Garrick
Royce McKnight . . . . . Jerry Hardin
Thomas Richie . . . . . . Paul Calderon
Sonny Capps . . . . . Jerry Weintraub
Barry Abanks . . . . . Sullivan Walker
Nathan Locke . . . . John Beal
Woman on Beach . . . Karina Lombard

"The Firm," a very smooth adaptation of John Grisham's giant bestseller, is destined to be one of the summer's strong audience pleasers. Tom Cruise's hotshot lawyer bent on toppling his corrupt bosses could be a brother to his "A Few Good Men" character and grosses should approach, if not equal, those of the actor's winter hit.**

The millions of readers who made Grisham's novel the bestselling book of 1991 are in for a few extra twists in the final third of the story, as director Sydney Pollack and his trio of high-powered screenwriters have added some dramatic and ethical complexity to this yarn.

The story is of the artificial, instantly disposable variety that doesn't warrant much serious discussion or provoke thought afterward, but there is sufficient conviction from everyone before and behind the camera to provide an absorbing, pulpy, old-fashioned movie experience.

Cruise portrays Mitch McDeere, a sought-after Harvard grad who shuns offers from big city law offices in favor of a small, lucrative Memphis concern that promotes itself as a family. Mitch's teacher wife Abby (Jeanne Tripplehorn) smells a rat from the outset, since the firm imposes unusually rigid codes of personal behavior, but Mitch jumps in with the enthusiasm of a puppy, working all hours, currying favor with the boss (Hal Holbrook) and lunching with mentor Avery Tolar (Gene Hackman).

After two of the firm's attorneys die in a mysterious boating accident, Mitch and Avery head to the Cayman Islands to investigate. Later, Mitch begins to suspect that the firm could be responsible for the deaths of four of its employees over the years.

When he is informed by the Justice Department that not only is the firm under investigation, but that no one has ever left its employ alive, Mitch finds himself in a vise: Either get the proof the government needs to nail the firm, or stay on and go down with the ship.

Rebounding from "Havana," his biggest career flop, Sydney Pollack has done an ultra-pro job in giving spit and polish to this star-driven, sure-fire commercial project. Close attention has been paid to story structure, the narrative is advanced in every sequence, and types of scenes are alternated carefully.

A few Hitchcockian touches are inserted in the late-going, and the film takes on a different feel as Pollack begins cross-cutting among three sets of action. As an examination of high-level conspiracy, film is a tad soft and lacks the snap and grit of Pollack's "Three Days of the Condor." The more than 2½ hour length is also a bit indulgent.

But pic retains its grip, despite the inevitable success of its hero's endeavors and the familiarity of its themes. The Tyrone Power of his generation, Cruise hits notes of determination, all-nighter energy and gradually develops standards and smarts he has hit before, but one couldn't imagine anyone better at this sort of star turn except Robert Redford 25 years ago.

At times uncannily resembling Genevieve Bujold, Jeanne Tripplehorn gets to do a bit more than hold down the home front and express doubt and fury at Mitch's long hours. Hackman (curiously unbilled in the advertising, though credited onscreen) turns in another sterling perf as a top lawyer with unexpected depths of pain and remorse.

Supporting cast is stellar indeed. Most indelible etchings are offered by David Strathairn as Cruise's insightful convict brother; Holly Hunter as P.I. Gary Busey's tartish, resourceful secretary; Busey himself as an engagingly down-home detective; Ed Harris, shaven bald as a tough, frequently frustrated FBI agent; and Wilford Brimley as the firm's ruthless enforcer.

Holbrook, Terry Kinney, Jerry Hardin and John Beal effectively limn remaining hierarchy at the firm, Tobin Bell is the eminently hissable silent villain, and Paul Sorvino turns up uncredited as a mobster.

All tech hands have contributed to the unimpeachable Hollywood veneer, although the percussive, non-orchestral score by Dave Grusin proves effectively different at times and intrusive at others. — *Todd McCarthy*

SON-IN-LAW

A Hollywood Pictures presentation of a Rotenberg/Lenkov production. Produced by Michael Rotenberg, Peter M. Lenkov. Executive producer, Hilton Green. Directed by Steve Rash. Screenplay, Fax Bahr, Adam Small, Shawn Schepps; story by Patrick J. Clifton, Susan McMartin, Peter Lenkov. Camera (Technicolor), Peter Deming; editor, Dennis M. Hill; music, Richard Gibbs; production design, Joseph T. Garrity; art direction, Pat Tagliaferro; set design, Barry Chusid; set decoration, Dena Roth; costume design, Molly Maginnis; sound (Dolby), Bruce Bisenz; assistant director, Jerram A. Swartz; 2nd-unit camera, Paul D. Hughen; casting, Cheryl Bayer. Reviewed at Regency II Theater, San Francisco, June 20, 1993. MPAA Rating: PG-13. Running time: **95 MIN.**

Crawl . . . . Pauly Shore
Rebecca Warner . . . . . Carla Gugino
Walter Warner . . . . Lane Smith
Connie Warner . . . . . Cindy Pickett
Walter Warner Sr. . . . . Mason Adams
Zack . . . . Patrick Renna
Theo . . . . Dennis Burkley
Tracy . . . . . Tiffani-Amber Thiessen
Travis . . . . Dan Gauthier

Show Jerry Lewis some respect. Leave Don Knotts out of it. Even Jim "Ernest" Varney deserves better. No, you'd have to dig way back to the likes of Sleep 'n' Eat and the Bowery Boys' Huntz Hall to find a moron-funnyman persona as aggressively irksome as Pauly Shore's. Amid heavy summer competition, his bland, witless soph big-screener "Son-in-Law" looks set to divert just a few theatrical bucks before retiring to rental-land.**

Treacly opening has smalltown valedictorian Rebecca Warner (Carla Gugino) bidding adieu to the folks in favor of California college kicks. Life in the fast lane proves alienating, however, until dorm resident adviser "Crawl" (Shore) shows her the ropes of wacky living — apparently requiring a Sunset Boulevard 'do and going to mudwrestling bouts.

Rebecca takes her new bud home to the South Dakota farm for Thanksgiving, where his obnoxious antics rapidly get on the wrong side of Dad (Lane Smith), Mom (Cindy Pickett), bratty little brother and cantankerous grandpa. Some sub-Kettle slapstick ensues: Crawl puts face to fertilizer, gets urinated on by a cow and broadsided by pigs, among other barnyard treats.

Plot-motivating conflict arrives in the form of Rebecca's jealous boyfriend (Tom Cruise lookalike Dan Gauthier), who plots Crawl's downfall before the predictably happy fade. The lowjinks are lame enough, but someone felt compelled to dump some icky sentimentality into the brew. Crawl "bonds" with the kid bro, does a tartish makeover on Mom that revives Dad's hormones and plays Mr. Fix-it for Gramps' sagging popularity. In a sloppily realized scene, he wins over the town by turning a country club square dance into a slam pit.

Shore's brain-damaged surfer-dude act was wisely relegated to support-banana status in last year's modest subteen success "Encino Man," but he's the whole show here and his puny bag of tricks is likely to quickly weary even youthful auds. There's the remote possibility that Shore has a broader range. But vehicles like this may milk his 15 minutes dry before anyone finds out.

Director Steve Rash ("The Buddy Holly Story") punches the clock with understandably minimal enthusiasm. Lensing is slick but as faceless as the material.

While the soundtrack includes songs by Queen, Goo-Goo Dolls, Belly and Spin Doctors, country tunes are more heavily employed for mood. But use of the "Green Acres" theme raises an unfortunate comparison: Hooterville had more hicksville wit than this rote no-brainer. — *Dennis Harvey*

IL GIOVANE MUSSOLINI
(A MAN NAMED BENITO)
(ITALIAN-GERMAN-SPANISH)

A Beta Film release of a RAI-2/RTVE/Zweitze Unitel (Kirch Group)/Mirofilm (Prague) co-production, in association with PROGEFI. (Intl. sales: Beta Film.) Produced by Gianluigi Calderone, Mimmo Rafele, under the supervision of Vincenzo Cerami. Directed by Calderone. Screenplay, Lidia Ravera, Rafele, Calderone. Camera (color), Jaromir Sofr; music, Nicola Piovani; art director, Tomas Moravec; set designer, Bruno Amalfitano; costume designer, Mariolina Bono; line producer, Fernando Franchi. Reviewed at Cinémathèque Française, Paris, June 9, 1993. Running time: **110 MIN.**
Benito Mussolini . . Antonio Banderas
Angelica Balabanoff . . Susanne Lothar
Renzi . . . . Meè Perlini
Giacinto Serrati . . . Ivano Marescotti
Rachele . . . . Claudia Koll
Eleonora . . . . Anna Geislerova

As a free-standing feature, "Il Giovane Mussolini," the elongated first installment of a three-part miniseries, gets its historical points across but doesn't generate much excitement. Although thesps — particularly Antonio Banderas — and settings are attractive, pic never rises above broad strokes, making it a good bet for TV but less certain for theatrical dates.

Spanning 1901-07 (Mussolini was born in 1883), pic follows the tyro tyrant as the brash young schoolteacher is run out of town for seducing his benefactor's married daughter, then emigrates to Switzerland to toil in a stone quarry, where he tastes exploitation and unsafe conditions.

Two Russian women influence him: stern Socialist Party leader Angelica Balabanoff (Susanne Lothar), whom he antagonizes, and luscious well-born medical student Eleonora (Anna Geislerova), whom he loves. Benito supports himself as a construction worker, dabbles in journalism and polishes his oratory skills. He has run-ins with the authorities but is indulged and rescued by his fellow Socialists.

Bulk of pic covers 1901-03, then skips ahead five years, where Benito renews ties with lovely wife-to-be Rachele (Claudia Koll).

Banderas plays the budding fascist as a lovable rascal, impudent and cocksure. Thesp conveys Mussolini's charisma; the script doesn't really capture his fatal lust for power.

Lensing and editing are adequate. Nicola Piovani's score features some pleasant music-box style melodies. Extras (much of pic was lensed in Czechoslova-kia) have an authentic period look, reinforced by costumes and handsomely appointed sets.

Women bare their breasts and Banderas displays his buns, but except for brief love scenes, pic is staid. — *Lisa Nesselson*

DAY OF THE DOG
(BLACKFELLAS)
(AUSTRALIAN)

A Barron Films production, in association with the Australian Broadcasting Corp./Australian Film Finance Corp./Australian Film Commission. (Intl. sales: Beyond Films.) Executive Producers, Paul D. Barron, Penny Chapman. Produced by David Rapsey. Directed, written by James Ricketson, from Archie Weller's book. Camera (Eastmancolor), Jeff Malouf; editor, Christopher Cordeaux; music, David Milroy; production design, Bob Ricketson; art director, Sue Vivian; costumes, Ron Gidgup; stunts, Peter West; production manager, Bernadette O'Mahony; assistant director, Michael Faranda. Reviewed at Cannes Film Festival (market section), May 20, 1993. Running time: **98 MIN.**
Doug Dooligan . . . . John Moore
'Pretty Boy' Floyd Davey . . . .
. . . . David Ngoombujarra
Polly . . . . Jaylene Riley
Valerie . . . . Lisa Kinchela
Mrs. Dooligan . . . . . Julie Hudspeth
Detective Maxwell . . John Hargreaves
Tiny . . . . Trevor Parfitt
Silver . . . . Attila Ozsdolay
Nanna . . . . . Judith Margaret Wilkes
Percy . . . . Ernie Dingo

"Day of the Dog," which vividly depicts the problems facing a part-aboriginal teenager in his efforts to stay out of prison, is a darker version of Bruce Beresford's "The Fringe Dwellers." Based on a book by aboriginal writer Archie Weller scripter/helmer James Ricketson's film is an honest and unsensational look at a depressingly familiar problem.

Set in Perth, pic opens with bushland scenes depicting an aboriginal artist painting in the traditional way while a couple of black children ironically play cowboys and Indians. Years later, the children, cousins, have grown into teenagers. Doug (John Moore), son of a drunken black father and a white mother (Julie Hudspeth) is released from prison after serving time for a stabbing. He longs to go straight, and to save enough money to buy his father's old farm.

But, inexorably, he's pulled back into a life of crime by his cousin "Pretty Boy" Floyd (David Ngoombujarra), a handsome, charismatic petty thief (cars mainly) but who is always lucky enough to get away with it. Doug also falls for Polly (Jaylene Riley), a feckless young shoplifter.

Every time it seems as though Doug will succeed in his dream, he finds his loyalties torn between his past and his future, with Pretty Boy constantly taunting him with the reminder that "we're you're people." Pic builds to the inevitable tragic climax: a botched armed robbery.

John Moore, who made his mark in "Deadly," and David Ngoombujarra give electric performances as the two young protagonists, while Jaylene Riley is touching as the easily tempted Polly. As a vicious white cop, John Hargreaves is effective.

Pic suffers from a ragged structure, indicating some postproduction tampering (it preemed 10 months ago at the Brisbane film fest, but has yet to obtain Oz release), and too many key scenes are shot at night. It's being sold offshore under its original title, but be called "Blackfellas" at home. — *David Stratton*

MY FORGOTTEN MAN
(AUSTRALIAN)

A Boulevard Films presentation. Produced, directed by Frank Howson. Executive producers, Peter Boyle, Malcolm Olivestone. Screenplay, Howson, Alister Webb. Camera (Cinevex Film Lab color), John Wheeler; editors, Peter McBain, Peter Carrodus; music, Anthony Marinelli, Billy Childs; production design, Brian Dusting; costume design, Rose Chong; sound (Dolby), John Rowley; 2nd-unit director, Brian Kavanaugh; casting, Liz Mullman Co. Reviewed at Cannes Film Festival (market section), May 15, 1993. Running time: **104 MIN.**
Errol Flynn . . . . Guy Pearce
Klaus Reicher . . . . . Steven Berkoff
Penelope Watts . . . . Claudia Karvan
Joe Stromberg . . . . . . John Savage

A look at the pre-Hollywood life of Errol Flynn, "My Forgotten Man" represents a mild-mannered telling of some wild exploits. Indie Australian effort will hold viewers disposed to the subject, but TV-style approach doesn't make the most of potentially rich material. Modest offshore prospects loom.

Similar projects dealing with the star's reckless youth were announced over the years, and this one's production history is unusually checkered. Under the title "Flynn," pic started shooting in 1990 under Brian Kavanaugh's direction. Lensing was halted after a few weeks and, with a new leading lady and Steven Berkoff added, resumed with Frank Howson at the helm.

Rather than exhibiting signs of behind-the-scenes havoc, however, result is altogether too placid and well-mannered, given the nature of its leading character. A childhood prologue has little Errol catching his mother committing adultery, only to be told, "Sometimes you have to lie."

The kid seems to have taken the advice to heart, as, by the time he's in his early 20s, he's committed most of the seven deadly sins and has done a good job getting away with it.

Down on his luck and living on the streets, Flynn decides to try his luck in the New Guinea gold rush (Fiji subs for location), and in the process gets mixed up with a mysterious Hitlerite, Klaus Reicher (Steven Berkoff), who endeavors to indoctrinate his protégé into his own sexual and political persuasions. Instead, Flynn gets involved with a local girl and is charged with the murder of a native man. He is found guilty, only to be rescued by his Nazi buddy.

Back in Sydney, Flynn becomes a back alley fighter and hustler, but shortly develops theatrical ambitions which quickly lead to his stage debut. The rest is history, covered in an infinitely worse American telefilm.

Co-writer-director Frank Howson has related Flynn's wicked, wicked ways with a reasonable amounts of raunch and intelligence, but limited flair. Much rides, of course, on his leading man, and in Guy Pearce, 23, popular on Aussie TV, he has an actor who's appropriately fine looking and callow, but lacks the crucial devilish charm.

Berkoff is vigorously rascally, but the role has been curiously fictionalized from the real-life Dr. Herman Erben, Howson would seem to have hedged a bit on reality. Similarly, Claudia Karvan plays a composite role as a young lady who tempts the irrepressible womanizer to settle down but can't manage it.

Although clearly low budget, production looks good. Lensing, art direction and costumes are all plusses. — *Todd McCarthy*

HAVANERA
(SPANISH)

An Imatco production, with the collaboration of Televisió de Catalunya/ICAIC (Cuba)/ICAA/Generalitat de Catalunya/Comisió America i Catalunya 1992. Exec producer, Carles Jover. Directed by Antoni Verdaguer. Screenplay, Jaume Cabre, Jaume Fuster, Vicenñ Villatoro, Verdageur. Camera (color), Macari Golferichs; editor, Ernest Blasi; music, Carles Cases; production designer, Josep M. Espada; production manager, Modesto Pérez Redondo; special effects, José Ramón Molina; casting, Sandra Sánchez. Reviewed at Casa de las Americas, Madrid, May 11, 1993. Running time: **152 MIN.**
Amelia Roig . . . Aitana Sanchez-Gijon
Alfons Rovira . . . .
　　　　　　Fernando Guillen Cuervo
Ton Massana . . . . Abel Folk
Francesc Valen . . . . . Jordi Dauder
Mr. Johnson . . . . . . Patrick Bauchau
Yvonne Duchamp . . Assumpta Serna
　　Also with: Ikay Romay, Aristides Bringues, Xabier Elorriaga, Patxi Bisquert, Angels Moll, Fernando Guillen, Josep M. Domenech, Teresa Cunilla.

This long period pic, set in 1820, in Havana and Spain, tries to broach it all: the slave trade, a reactionary but honest Catalan shipper and his scoundrel son, an unscrupulous Havana plantation owner, soft sex with mulattas and prostitutes, a Yank trader trying to peddle steamboats, a British antislavery official, a rebellious slave leader. Result is a confused and tiresome hodgepodge best suited for TV fodder as a three-hour miniseries.

Tale concerns a young girl of fashion, Amelia, married by proxy in Spain to a brutal and dissipated Havana plantation owner, Ton. Amelia is shipped off to Cuba on the same vessel as Ton's friend Alfons, son of the ship company's owner. After instigating a mutiny on board and setting the captain afloat in a dingy, Alfons picks up a boatload of slaves in Africa, tries to seduce Amelia and sails merrily to Havana.

The ensuing story is so convoluted that it would take pages to describe its rudiments. Included are two slave revolts; a duel to the death; the relations between Amelia, Ton and Alfons; the antislavery efforts of the Brit; the business deals between the Yank and the Catalan shipowner; the intrigues of a French *femme fatale*, and a dozen other tangents that might detract from the central theme if there were one.

Efforts to make film look like a superproduction are unconvincing; action segs are disjointed and episodic. —*Peter Besas*

CIBLE EMOUVANTE
(WILD TARGET)
(FRENCH)

An AFMD release of a Les Films Pelleas/Locofilms/France 2 Cinema/M6 Films co-production in association with Investimage 4/Canal Plus/Procirep. Produced by Philippe Martin. Directed, written by Pierre Salvadori. Camera (color), Gilles Henry; editor, Helene Viard; music Philippe Eidel; set design, Yan Arlaud; sound, Paul Pertault. Reviewed at Cannes Film Festival (market section), May 14, 1993. Running time: **86 MIN.**
Victor Maynard . . . . Jean Rochefort
Renée Dandrieux . . Marie Trintignant
Antoine . . . . . Guillaume Depardieu
Mme. Meynard . . . . Patachou

Most gags hit the bull's-eye in "Wild Target," a dry comedy about a middle-aged hit man who falls for the younger con woman he's supposed to rub out. Comedy fests and TV sales seem assured.

Jean Rochefort is nicely cast as meticulous gun-for-hire Victor Meynard. When a talking parrot and a bicycle messenger (Guillaume Depardieu) happen to witness a hit, childless Rochefort takes on Depardieu as an apprentice. Contract killing is the family business: Victor's baby mobile featured guns and coffins and his redoubtable mom (Patachou) proudly keeps a scrapbook of his "assignments" — including an allusion to JFK.

Rochefort and Depardieu flinch when hired to kill Renée (Marie Trintignant), a sort of Holly Golightly who fences art forgeries and specializes in the five-finger discount. Duo becomes a trio and ensuing comedy of errors is well-timed, right up to the final showdown.

Thesps are all fine. Young Depardieu ends up in the buff in two bathtub sequences. The jaunty cello and accordian score is used sparingly. Pic's plot will invite inevitable comparisons to the recent "Max and Jeremie," but Trintignant as the spirited love interest makes all the difference in this lighter, sillier outing.
— *Lisa Nesselson*

DE FRIGJORTE
(FISH OUT OF WATER)
(DANISH)

An ASA Film Prod./Nordisk Film production. (Intl. sales: Pathe-Nordisk Films.) Produced by Henrik Møller-Sørensen. Directed by Erik Clausen. Screenplay, Clausen, Sanni Sylvester, Søren Skjaer, John Nehm, from Nehm's book. Camera (Fujicolor), Claus Loof; editor, Camilla Skousen; music, Kim Larsen; production design, Thorkil Slebskager; sound, Preben Mortsensen; assistant director, Birthe Frost. Reviewed at Cannes Film Festival (market section), May 15, 1993. Running time: **93 MIN.**
Viggo Hansen . . . . Erik Clausen
Oda Hansen . . . . Helle Ryslinge
Iversen . . . . Leif Sylvester
Karen . . . . Anne Marie Helger
Lone . . . . Gitte Rugaard
Lars . . . . Thor Heddemann
Claus . . . . Lars Lippert
Snedker . . . . Bjarre Lille
Carlsen . . . . Torben Zeller

Versatile actor-director Erik Clausen's new film about a factory closing will touch a painful nerve with audiences in most industrialized countries of the world, and the knowing humor with which Clausen sweetens his bitter pill should ensure his film gets some fest and specialized TV scheduling.

Pic is based on a book by co-scripter John Nehm, and the original title means "the released." This is the euphemism used by the owners of a Copenhagen engineering factory when it throws workers out of their jobs — they aren't "fired," they're "released." The implication is that a new factory will open in Portugal, where labor is cheaper.

Clausen plays Viggo Hansen, who's been a welder in the factory for 25 years. A loyal leftist and ardent union member, he's never come to terms with the collapse of Eastern Europe's Communist regimes, and the loss of his job coincides with other mid-life crises; he quarrels bitterly with his daughter and her smug ad-agency husband; he discovers his son is gay; and he gradually loses interest in his wife (gamely played by Helle Ryslinge).

Inevitably, he starts an affair with another woman (Anne Marie Helger) and they go off on vacation to Majorca together. But the tryst is a disaster, and Viggo returns home to discover that his wife accurately suspects what he's been up to.

Clausen's middle-aged working-class stiff, poleaxed by the worldwide recession, is finely drawn and the actor-director imbues Viggo with enough warmth and sentiment to make him sympathetic even when he behaves badly. Supporting actors are fine, and there are a number of telling vignettes. The ending is upbeat.

Fine production dress, and jolly music, are also assets.

— *David Stratton*

AMOK
(FRENCH)

An AB Films (France)/MGN (Portugal)/NEF Filmproduktion (Germany) co-production. (Intl. sales: Claude Nouchi, WMF.) Produced by Frédéric Bourboulon. Executive producer, Agnes Le Pont. Directed by Joel Farges. Screenplay by Dominique Rousset, Catherine Foussadier, Farges, from Stefan Zweig's story. Camera (color), Fabio Conversi; editor, Ludo Grunenwaldt; music, Nicola Piovani; set design, Danka Semenowicz; costumes, Claire Fraisse; sound, Bernard Aubouy; associate producers, Tino Navarro (MGN), François Duplat (NEF). Reviewed at Cannes Film Festival (market section), May 15, 1993. Running time: 85 MIN.
The Woman . . . . Fanny Ardant
Dr. Steiner . . . . . Andrzej Seweryn
The Traveler . . . . . Bernard Le Coq
The Lover . . . . Joaquim De Almeida

"**A**mok" is a well-intentioned but occasionally clumsy adaptation of a Stefan Zweig story about a once-respected German doctor whose misguided pride and obsessive love for a French woman in the Portuguese West Indies leads to ruin. Exotic locations, Andrzej Seweryn's lead perf and an okay turn by Fanny Ardant make the pic suitable for international TV sales and video.

In March of 1939, during the sluggish boat journey from Goa to Cochin in Southern India, scruffy, liquor-guzzling Dr. Steiner (Seweryn) confides the tragic tale of his downfall — in flashback — to a traveler en route back to Europe (Bernard Le Coq).

Disgraced for embezzling from a German hospital, reformed ladies' man Steiner had put in years manning a remote clinic in the Portuguese colonies when Fanny Ardant appeared, an arrival that also spins the somewhat stilted and literary pic into a much more compelling mode.

Ardant's hubby, a Portuguese diplomat, has been in Europe on business for five months. Alas, Ardant is three months pregnant. She offers Steiner a fortune for a discreet abortion. Dazzled by the sight of a white woman after so long, he makes a crude counter-offer. Their relationship goes downhill from there.

Fearing the consequences of a back alley abortion, hopelessly

smitten Steiner tries to redeem himself but ends up going "amok" — a frenzy brought on by palm liquor and tropical heat. Awkward coda implies that Europe, too, had gone amok in 1939.

Thesps lend approximately the right tone but can't give the story the haunting depth it requires. Nicola Piovani's hearty score sometimes stands out more than it should. Good period production design plays up locations in India and Portugal. — *Lisa Nesselson*

YOUNG GOODMAN BROWN

A 50th Street Films release of a The Institute presentation in association with Desert Music Pictures. Produced by Robert Tinnell. Executive producers, Margaret Hoey, Peter George, Mary Ella Galbraith. Co-produced by Jeffrey Tinnell. Directed, written by George, from Nathaniel Hawthorne's story. Camera (Duart color), Roxanne di Santo; editors, Lauren Schaffer, Randy Vandegrift; music, Jon McCallum; production design, Jennifer Long; art direction, Garrick Manninen; set decoration, Anne F. Bugatch; costumes, Julie Carnahan; sound, Mario L. Cardenas; associate producer, Larry Rice; assistant director, Maria Melograne; 2nd-unit director, Robert Tinnell; casting, Michael Orfanos, Raquel Osbourne Casting. Reviewed at Cannes Film Festival (market section), May 15, 1993. Running time: 81 MIN.
The Devil . . . . John P. Ryan
Goodman Brown . . . . Tom Shell
Bridget Bishop . . . . . . Judy Geeson
Sarah Good . . . . Dorothy Lyman
George Burroughs . . . . Gregory Itzin
Goody Cloyse . . Mary Grace Canfield
Faith Brown . . . . Mindy Clarke
Joseph Ring . . . . Miles Chapin
William Stacey . . . . . . Matt Adler

Troma subsid 50th Street Films gets off to an inauspicious start with "Young Goodman Brown," a hokey, static rendition of the Nathaniel Hawthorne story augmented with the Salem witchhunts. Ultra-low-budget period effort resembles a student film both in earnestness and production values, and has an exceedingly limited market outside of old-fashioned classroom situations.

Director Peter George, producer Robert Tinnell and some of the cast and crew previously teamed on Troma's legendary 1987 "Surf Nazis Must Die," so have thus far proved themselves versatile if nothing else.

But their reason for telling this tale of devilish temptation in the late 1600s is not in evidence onscreen, as the clumsily staged drama just sits there waiting for a point of view or dramatic rationale to announce itself.

Opening reels establishing life in the Puritan community give an accurate indication that the film, even with its short running time, is going to be a long haul. Sequences are covered with an emphasis on master shots that show no sense of shot sequencing, rhythm or pacing. This is compounded by stilted, old-fashioned dialogue that is not made to sound natural or even easy to deliver by the actors.

When the title character (Tom Shell) heads through the woods on an errand, he is shortly set upon by some cackling fools who engage in what can only be called unearthly goings-on. This provides the occasion for some cheap-looking special effects, all attendent to a communion of evil presided over by the Devil himself (John P. Ryan), who predicts that he will prevail over the dull forces of good.

There's a lot of warmed-over hocus pocus and mumbo jumbo about witchcraft and the struggle for souls, all done in the style of overacted amateur provincial theatricals. What a modern film audience is supposed to take away from this stilted and portentous mish-mash will remain the most minor of eternal mysteries.

— *Todd McCarthy*

RIPA RUOSTUU
(RIPA HITS THE SKIDS)
(FINNISH-B&W)

A Villealfa Filmprods. production. Produced by Aki Kaurismäki, Klaus Heydemann. Directed, written by Christian Lindblad. Camera (B&W), Ilkka Ruuhuärvi; editor, Ulli Enckell; music, Björn B. Lindström; production design, Marjaana Rantama; sound, Risto Iissalo, Jouko Lumme. Reviewed at Cannes Film Festival (market section), May 22, 1993. Running time: 80 MIN.
Ripa . . . . Sam Huber
Tiina . . . . Mari Vainio
Pirjo . . . . Merja Larivaara
Irma . . . . Leena Uotila
Lynkkynen . . . . Kari Väänänen
Lindgren . . . . Jussi Lampi
Antti . . . . Leo Raivio
Father . . . . Vesamatti Loiri

The eponymous antihero of this raffish first feature by writer-director Christian Lindblad is a scroungy would-be filmmaker hooked on beer, sex and idleness. He's the sort of guy you'd run a mile from in real life, but on screen, Sam Huber is funny in a gross sort of way. It's a film that may repel many people, but could become a cult item.

Lindblad's references to Jean-Luc Godard's "Breathless" are

clear; Ripa is just as feckless as Jean-Paul Belmondo in that New Wave trailblazer and meets a similar fate; but certainly lacks Belmondo's Gallic charm.

This lank-haired, oafish character with beer gut and permanent hangover is a would-be film director, but his projects contain too much sex and violence for government funding bodies or indie producers. He lives on money scrounged from his bitter ex-wife, who wants repayment, and handouts he gets from a gay porno filmmaker pal; when he's expected to pay him off by taking part in a hardcore gay film, Ripa he draws the line. Meanwhile, he's having an affair with a sexually insatiable bank teller (Mari Vainio) and trying to prevent his beloved '63 Mercedes from being repossessed along with his other belongings.

Sam Huber narrates the film in the sardonic Raymond Chandler style and is strangely likable as this outrageous slob. The film is full of chuckles as it depicts Ripa's gradual fall from grace during the span of a week. Finale is way over the top as Ripa shoots the husband of a woman he's having sex with, is betrayed by his girlfriend, gunned down by the cops, and re-appears as an angel, complete with ironic Wenders-wings.

Writer-director Lindblat, working for Aki Kaurismäki's Villealfa outfit, has a disarmingly laidback style and Ilkka Ruuhijärvi's black and white images are atmospheric. Technically it's fine, with a smart score by Björn B. Lindström. — *David Stratton*

SYDNEY FEST

MEMORIES AND DREAMS
(AUSTRALIAN-B&W/COLOR)

A Milburn Stone production, in association with Australian Film Commission. Produced by Julie Stone. Directed by Lynn-Maree Milburn. Screenplay, Milburn, Stone. Camera (B&W/color), Andrew de Groot; editor, Milburn; music, Eddy Zlaty, Paul Schutze; production/costume design, Jacqui Everitt; sound, Peter Clancy; postproduction supervisor, de Groot; associate producer (postproduction), Tony Helman. Reviewed at Melbourne Film Festival, June 5, 1993. (In Sydney Film Festival.) Running time: 60 MIN.
With: Johanna Kimla Ocenaskova, Joanna Weir, Jeremy Stanford, Alexandra Chapman, Scott Murray.

This astonishingly beauti-

July 12, 1993 (Cont.)

ful and moving combination of documentary, fiction, animation and experimentation is, quite simply, a thrilling experience. Five years in the making, it's a considerable achievement for the young filmmaking team of producer-writer Julie Stone and director-writer Lynn-Maree Milburn. Specialized distribution is certainly indicated, and this will also be sought-after by festivals and a natural for quality TV programming.

The film is structured around the recollections of an elderly Czech woman, Johanna Kimla Ocenaskova, who is seen on-camera and also heard on the soundtrack as narrator. Quietly, but with considerable suppressed emotion, she describes her life. She grew up in Prague in the 20s, became a keen motorcycle rider (unusual for a woman at the time) and then a journalist. When the Germans annexed Czechoslovakia, her lover executed and she herself was placed in a concentration camp (she wasn't Jewish, but her papers weren't fully in order).

She managed to escape, faked suicide, and wound up working at the Barrandov film studios as an extra under an assumed name. The Communist takeover brought even greater hardship and, eventually, in 1949, she escaped, crossing the mountains into Germany and eventually emigrating to Australia.

The story Kimla Ocenaskova tells is by no means a unique one, but it's given very special treatment by the filmmakers. Key moments are beautifully staged by sensitive actors; impressionistic use is made of newsreels, fragmented images of the narrator's idol, Marlene Dietrich, and animation. There's also an immensely inventive soundtrack.

The film opens with the words: "Two things are forgotten only in Death — and the face of our cities." Pic is not only an extremely original biography, but is also a paean to the beauty of the city of Prague, glimpsed in tantalizingly beautiful images.

— *David Stratton*

GLAMAZON: A DIFFERENT KIND OF GIRL
(DOCU-COLOR/B&W)

> Produced by Maria Demopoulos. Directed, written by Rico Martinez. Camera (color, B&W), David Morrison. Co-produced by Jodi Bell. Editor, Jim Makiej; production designer, Kvin Adams; original music, Kristen McCord; post-production sound, effects, Skywalker Sound. Reviewed on vidcassette, San Francisco, Feb. 10, 1993. (In the New Festival, N.Y.; Asian American Intl. Film Festival Showcase, S.F.) Running time: 83 MIN.

As docu portraiture goes, "Glamazon" has personality plus: Its subject is Barbara LeMay, a 62-year-old ex-carnival star of ambiguous transgender status.

Returning to her native West Virginia after 30 years, Barbara's roots still stick out with a vengeance (via such colorful enunciations as "homorphrodite" and "doclamentry"). She's an amazing enough find to lend this otherwise sketchy, padded work potential midnight aud appeal.

Born Sammy Hoover, Barbara regales us with stories of her myriad "admirers" during a glorious "perfayshunnel" career as kootch dancer. "I useta carry a hunnert dollar bill under both my knockers," she notes. She more recently lived in Hollywood, where a zesty latterday near-strip act was presumably shot.

Barbara LeMay is relentlessly chatty and entertaining. But the movie doesn't even try to qualify her likely delusions of past grandeur, or impose a chronological shape on her reminiscences. There's probably a more interesting real hard-knock history behind the cheerful facade.

While encounters with her former "rust belt" pals (exclusively female) are amusing, seemingly inevitable issues of homophobia et al. are simply bypassed. We never find out whether Barbara was a full post-op transsexual, or why she apparently died just after filming ended (noted only in a close-credit dedication). While "Glamazon" pretends to be a thorough portrait, its limited scope ultimately seems lazy and timid.

It's also heavily padded, with pointless recurrent B&W countryside views and amateurishly acted "flashback" sequences. Among the latter, a narrative of carny-staff vengeance on a prej-

udiced co-worker is interesting if choppily told; the rest are pure low-grade vanity camp. Tech credits are fairly good, with suitably gaudy color. — *Dennis Harvey*

TURNABOUT: THE STORY OF THE YALE PUPPETEERS
(DOCU-COLOR/B&W-16m)

> A Shire Films production. Produced, directed, written by Dan Bessie. Camera (color/B&W, 16m), Matt Burgess, Victor Nelli, Robb LaRussa, Edvardas Yurchis; editing, Helen Garvy; sound, Susumu Tokunow, Richard Strickland; songs, Forman Brown; production assistant, Eva Andrews; main titles, Mallory Pearce; online editing, Spotlight Video, Mark Shuttuck. Reviewed on vidcassette, San Francisco, May 5, 1993. (In San Francisco Lesbian & Gay Intl. Film Festival.) Running time: 60 MIN.
> With: Harry Burnett and His Marionnettes, Forman Brown, Elsa Lanchester, Lotte Goslar, Odetta, Dorothy Neumann.

"Turnabout" is a charming slice of antiquated American theater life. Beyond possible fest plays, its natural shelf life lies in educational/nostalgia broadcast programming.

Filmmaker Dan Bessie chronicles the life and times of his uncle Harry Burnett, cousin Forman Brown, and Brown's lifelong partner Roddy Brandon. (Brandon died before shooting began; Burnett died May 28). The trio toured for some 70 years as the Yale Puppeteers, crafting marionettes gently parodying celebs from Harold Lloyd and Aimee Semple MacPherson to Hitler, FDR and Albert Einstein.

Called to Hollywood for a film gig, the trio ran their Turnabout Theater there from 1941 to 1956. Elsa Lanchester was a co-headliner; folksinger Odetta got her start under Burnett's wing.

Burnett and Brown, both 92 at the time of filming, are gentlemanly company, Brown playing several of his charmingly antique revue tunes. Director Bessie is clearly interested in their history as gay men. But having "come out" only in their old age, the twosome are rather reticent. (Brown, however, in 1933 wrote a pseudonymous gay novel, recently republished.)

This mix of celebrity anecdotes and archival photos/footage reveals a nearly forgotten corner of the showbiz world. Tech quality is up to PBS-worthy grade.

— *Dennis Harvey*

SMOKE
(16m)

> Produced, directed, written, edited by Mark D'Auria. Camera (color), Teodoro Maniaci; music, Arnie Bieber. Reviewed at San Francisco Lesbian/Gay Intl. Film Festival, June 4, 1993. Running time: 90 MIN.
> With: Mark D'Auria (Michael), Nick Discenza, Tom Dorsey, Maryjane Chalaire, Barbara Andrews, David Philips, Jeffrey D'Auria, Joe Colaccio, Tom Lee Sinclaire, David Interrante.

Mix curiously retro, guilt-ridden gay sexuality with equally antique symbolism of the flaming-crucifix experimental school, and what you've got is just "Smoke," writer-director-star-producer-editor Mark D'Auria's all-too-private portrait of one man's bottomless angst. Painfully earnest but low on illumination, pic's theatrical prospects look as cheerless as its unfortunate protagonist.

Michael (D'Auria) is on the brink of middle age. After an older presumed ex-lover punches him in the stomach, he wakes up in the hospital, masturbates while gazing at his obese roommate, and flees.

So it goes. Michael works as a bathroom attendant at a posh hotel, whose owner humiliates him. He protests — yet this seems to be his sexual metier. Attracted to stout older men, he pursues public loo encounters, a seedy personals-ad interlude, and repeated dismissal by a married policeman he's stuck on.

Taking his agony to church, he's shot by a disturbed woman, wakes up and flees the hospital again. His elderly Italian mom keeps beckoning him back to hearth and home, and sepia flashbacks point to a gloomy, father-deprived childhood.

D'Auria comes up with the odd striking visual, such as racing buck-naked on a winter morning down a Manhattan street. But despite okay acting and tech work, heavy-handedness finally becomes silly. Where Gus Van Sant's "Mala Noche" hero's questionable pursuit of love and lust was tempered by humor, there's no such luck here: Michael is presented as a full-on martyr.

No one makes a movie as insistently joyless as "Smoke" without some profound personal commitment. But D'Auria fails to communicate his passion in digestible terms. He's pastiched together a personal language hardly anyone will want to translate.

— *Dennis Harvey*

July 12, 1993 (Cont.)

FEED THEM TO THE CANNIBALS!
(AUSTRALIAN-DOCU-16m)

A Dangerous to Know production. Produced, directed by Fiona Cunningham Reed. Co-producer, Martin Coucke. Camera (color, 16m), Reed; editor, Rodney Sims; music, Diane McCloughlin; sound, Coucke. Reviewed on vidcassette, San Francisco, May 10, 1993. (In San Francisco Intl. Lesbian & Gay Film Festival.) Running time: **67 MIN.**

"**F**eed Them to the Cannibals!" is a delightful tribute to Australia's apparently open-minded acceptance of gays, at least within cosmopolitan Sydney. Colorful doc is limited by its principally regional interest; the historical/political themes played out here are delayed echoes of Euro-North American gay-lib currents. But as an alternative Chamber of Commerce plug, it's undeniably persuasive.

Focus centers on a one-year period leading to 1992's Sydney Mardi Gras, "the biggest gay event in the world." Organizational efforts glimpsed in behind-the-scenes footage include orchestration of the spectacular fundraising "Sleaze Ball," related AIDS activism, etc.

Most of "Cannibals" (its title drawn from an early Euro settler's attitude toward homosexuals) is giddily affirming, offering candid glimpses of a bountiful drag scene and a strong, politically motivated lesbian/gay milieu. A poignant moment occurs when the Mardi Gras parade pauses before a hospital AIDS ward in respectful silence. Aussie officials (including a police chief and parliament member) seem refreshingly genuine in their enthusiasm for the gay community.

Yet there are indications that life Down Under isn't entirely liberated: When we drop in on an AIDS quilt "naming," not a single commemoratee's surname is spoken aloud. And these hugely money-spinning festivities have yet to see a bit of promotion from the government's skittish tourist bureau. Representing the moral naysayers, a fundamentalist Christian reverend prays for rain to cancel the "obscene and blasphemous" annual parade.

Despite such moments, the mood here is more party-hearty than political, with plenty of spectacular costumes and bared skin. Cinematography and editing are zippy, sound generally good.

—*Dennis Harvey*

VERZAUBERT
(ENCHANTED)
(GERMAN-DOCU-16m)

A Trigon Film production. Directed by Dorothee van Diepenbroick, Jörg Fockele, Jens Golombek, Dirk Hauska, Sylke Jehna, Claudia Kaltenbach, Ulrich Prehn, Johanna Reutter, Katrin Schmersahl. Camera (16m, color), Vera von Wilcken; editor, Martin Ekert. Reviewed at the New Festival, New York, June 8, 1993. Running time: **89 MIN.**

Although Weimar Germany was known for some enlightenment in regards to homosexuality, this openness was shattered in 1933 when the Nazis enacted Article 175, making homosexuality illegal. When a postwar German constitution was written in 1949, Article 175 was retained.

Produced by nine different filmmakers, this powerful docu focuses on a baker's dozen of German gays and lesbians from Hamburg who describe survival during this dangerous period when homosexuality could warrant death in concentration camps or, in the postwar period, police sweeps and witch hunts.

Since most of the words to describe homosexuals in German are harsh or derogatory, one lesbian in the film blushingly refers to gays as "verzaubert" ("enchanted"). This use of euphemisms is evident in many of those interviewed, so scarred that even today they find it difficult to talk openly. (Two even refuse to show their faces.)

Among those interviewed: Edith, interrogated by vice cops after her married lover committed suicide and left an incriminating letter. Rudolf was caught in the act at age 14; his friend was pressured by his "dishonored" family to join the army where he was killed weeks later.

Arno discusses the three years he spent in Auschwitz for violating Article 175. Perhaps the most frightening story is that of Wally, a lesbian raped by her stepfather and later sterilized by the state.

But, there are other stories: Heiner and Peter have lived together openly for 38 years and they report no problems with acceptance by landlords or neighbors. There is also Werner, who ran a gay bay with his mother and did drag shows under the same Thérèse.

"Enchanted" is a fascinating glimpse into a frightening period. — *Paul Lenti*

ONE NATION UNDER GOD
(DOCU-COLOR/B&W-16m)

A 3 Z/Hourglass production. Produced, directed, edited by Teodoro Maniaci, Francine Rzeznik. Camera (color/B&W, 16m), Mark Voelpel, Maniaci. Music, Robert Mitchell. Associate producer, Zinka Benton. Reviewed on vidcassette, San Francisco, May 9, 1993. (In the New Festival, N.Y.; San Francisco Lesbian & Gay Intl. Film Festival.) Running time: **83 MIN.**

Religion and psychiatry have rarely been perceived as sympathetic to the homosexual cause; centering mostly on the bizarre collusion of these two forces in gay "cure" groups, "One Nation Under God" is a fascinating doc hampered by somewhat muddy focus. Theatrical future is modest, broadcast potential high.

Interview and archival footage are mixed to give an overview of the psych field's frequent moralizing stand against gay lifestyles. While the APA deleted homosexuality from its "disorder" list in 1974, that decision hasn't killed off the existence of organizations like Exodus Intl., which mixes Christian ministry with dubious "therapy" to fix "sexual brokenness."

Pathetically funny sequences feature "experts" discussing the benefits of beauty shop makeovers for repentant lesbians and football games for gay men. One born-again heterosexual takes a blunter approach: "God hates homosexuals, and so do Christians."

An articulate male couple of "ex-ex-gays" explain the "brainwashing" techniques of these groups, having once been leaders themselves. Therapeutic training films from as late as the early '70s offer one misguided "treatment" after another, including an electroshock "organismic reorientation" method right out of "A Clockwork Orange."

All this material is powerful. By the time Nazi medical experiments are cited, the comparison hardly seems inapt. But in straining to encompass the vast histories of Christianity and modern psychiatry as connected to the subject — plus that of the Gay Liberation Movement — "One Nation" sometimes loses clarity, covering terrain already exhausted by other docs.

Editing could improve matters by either fleshing out the sprawl out to a less cluttered comfortable length, or by excis-

ing non-church/shrink themes. Otherwise, tech qualities are all high-grade. — *Dennis Harvey*

THE EAST IS RED
(SWORDSMAN III)
(HONG KONG)

A Golden Princess/Rim Film Distributors Inc. presentation of a Film Workshop production. Produced by Tsui Hark. Directed by Ching Siu-Tung, Raymond Lee. Screenplay, Tsui Hark, Roy Szeto, Carbon Cheung. Camera (color), Lau Moon-Tong; editor, Chiang Chuen-Tak; music, Wu Wai-Lap; art direction, Eddie Ma; costumes, William Chang, Mark Chiu; martial arts direction, Ching Siu-Tung; associate producers, Lee, Tung. Reviewed at San Francisco Lesbian & Gay Intl. Film Festival, June 4, 1993. (In the New Festival, N.Y.) Running time: **95 MIN.**
With: Brigitte Lin, Joey Wang, Yu Rong-Guang, Jean Wang.

The latest "Swordsman" sequel is daft, energetic fun sure to entertain regular HK action customers around the globe. Narrative incoherence won't assist crossover appeal in Western territories, though. Gender-bending content won pic a slot in bicoastal lesbian and gay fests, though interp of these aspects as liberating or merely exploitive is strictly in the eye of the beholder.

The frenzy commences with a recap of "Swordsman II's" final bout, in which supernaturally cross-gendered Asia the Invincible (Brigitte Lin) was ostensibly vanquished by smitten Koo (Yu Rong-Guang). Shepherding a trecherous Spanish military ship, Koo soon discovers his contentious former flirtation-object has only been playing dead.

Asia is a dangerous, Kali-like super-antihero, alternatively merciless and sympathetic. This reconstituted lesbian warrior-wizard takes vengeance on a slew of "pretend Asia the Invincibles" across the country; former lover Snow (Joey Wong), is principal among the adherents, and the most anxiously repentant.

One fanciful battle follows another, colorfully embodied in the increasingly cheesy special effects — flying characters, unconvincing nautical miniatures, etc. Story confusion reigns. Anti-Western sentiments are heavily thumped, as Asia giddily orders the Spaniards to replace God's name in the Bible with her own.

Acting is appropriately florid, photo/editing aspects dizzy but tightly wound. This chaotic entertainment machine has plenty of oomph. Yet more scripting care would do "Swordsman IV" a big favor. — *Dennis Harvey*

IN THE LINE OF FIRE

A Columbia release of a Columbia and Castle Rock presentation of an Apple/Rose production. Produced by Jeff Apple. Executive producers, Wolfgang Petersen, Gail Katz, David Valdes. Co-producer, Bob Rosenthal. Directed by Petersen. Screenplay, Jeff Maguire. Camera (Technicolor; Panavision widescreen), John Bailey; editor, Anne V. Coates; music, Ennio Morricone; production design, Lilly Kilvert; art direction, John Warnke; set design, Jann K. Engel; set decoration, Kara Lindstrom, A. Charles Carnaggio (Washington, D.C.); costume design, Erica Edell Phillips; sound (Dolby; SDDS), Willie Burton; assistant director, Peter Kohn; campaign unit camera, Mark Vargo; casting, Janet Hirshenson, Jane Jenkins. Reviewed at Sony Studios, Culver City, June 25, 1993. MPAA rating: R. Running time: **128 min.**

Frank Horrigan	Clint Eastwood
Mitch Leary	John Malkovich
Lilly Raines	Rene Russo
Al D'Andrea	Dylan McDermott
Bill Watts	Gary Cole
Harry Sargent	Fred Dalton Thompson
Sam Campagna	John Mahoney
President	Jim Curley
First Lady	Sally Hughes
Jack Okura	Clyde Kusatsu
Tony Carducci	Steve Hytner
Mendoza	Tobin Bell
Pam Magnus	Patrika Darbo
Sally	Mary Van Arsdel
Professor Riger	John Heard

A solidly commercial contemporary thriller in its own right, "In the Line of Fire" makes one appreciate the extra shadings and textures Clint Eastwood brings to his own films. The star's first outing since his Oscar-winning "Unforgiven" is, by current standards, a proficiently made thriller pitting Eastwood's vet Secret Service agent against John Malkovich's insidious would-be presidential assassin. B.O. promises to be sturdy worldwide.

Castle Rock release via Columbia is Eastwood's first venture away from Warner Bros. since "Escape From Alcatraz" in 1979, and his first as an actor for another director since "Pink Cadillac" in 1989. His role is pretty familiar, a maverick enforcement officer of flawed character who could be a brother to Eastwood's characters in "Tightrope," "Heartbreak Ridge" and even the "Dirty Harry" series.

But Frank Horrigan's flaw approaches tragic dimensions, as he has been haunted since Nov. 22, 1963, by the possibility that he could have saved John F. Kennedy's life. As JFK's favorite Secret Service agent, Horrigan was with the president in Dallas, and was closest to him when the first shot rang out. But Horrigan didn't react, and has spent the intervening 30 years trying to live with his failure to cover him before the fatal bullet hit.

It's this weakness that is manipulated by Mitch Leary (Malkovich), a professional assassin who makes no secret of his intention to kill the current president sometime before the election, which is six weeks away at the start of the action.

Horrigan wins an assignment to cover the chief of state while he tries to nail Leary, who calls every so often to taunt him, and at the same time must endure the gibes of his colleagues, who consider him "a borderline burnout with questionable social skills" and "a dinosaur."

There are signs that Horrigan might soon want to consider hanging it up. He huffs and puffs and practically passes out when required to run alongside the president's limo in a Pennsylvania Avenue motorcade, and can't keep up with Leary when chasing him on foot.

But his saving grace is his sense of humor about himself, and his vulnerability is especially appealing to fellow agent Lilly Raines (Rene Russo), who hesitates for quite awhile before getting involved with an older man who makes such crude jokes, but who finally gives him an unfortunately abbreviated tumble, the lead-up to which provides film's comic highlight.

What neophyte scripter Jeff Maguire's plot comes down to, however, is the cat-and-mouse game between Horrigan and Leary. The craftiness and strategies involved on both sides, while not exactly ingenious, are tantalizing enough to compel interest.

Cleverly withheld from full view early in the picture, Malkovich's Leary is established as a master of disguise, an entirely demented soul who admires John Wilkes Booth for having had "panache" and viciously kills a few people along the way just to assert his credentials.

When Horrigan loses his cool at a Chicago rally and sets off panic by yelling out, "Gun!" he is dismissed from the presidential detail. But Horrigan continues his hunt anyway and, in perhaps the film's tensest scene, the aging agent chases his prey across some D.C. rooftops, misses a jump between buildings and must take his nemesis' extended hand if he has a hope of surviving.

This thematic situation is reversed in the film's action climax, a pseudo-Hitchcockian sequence set on board a glass elevator at L.A.'s Bonaventure Hotel, where Leary has finally hunted down the president. Script's only moral concern relates to an agent's willingness to take a bullet to save the person he's meant to protect, something Horrigan claims he's willing to do but which he didn't prove in Dallas.

Director Wolfgang Petersen sends the story efficiently down its straight and narrow track, indulging Horrigan a few endearing character traits such as a taste for jazz, a minimal apartment (his wife left along with the kids years ago) and a preference for public transportation, and deftly engineering the battle of wills between two desperately committed men heading for a collision.

Pic doesn't pretend to be anything other than what it is, but previous Eastwood films have shown that,

given his own head, the actor will explore dark, shadowy, even somewhat kinky aspects of generally stable, capable characters.

Here, Eastwood splendidly gives Horrigan humor, grit and imagination along with the wounded quality, but the specter of Nov. 22 stands alone as his psychological motivator.

Such pictures are often made by virtue of their villains, and Malkovich provides a delicious one, a true psychopath so sure of himself that he's willing to give his pursuer half a chance of catching him. The actor's weird looks are given full play here with his variety of disguises, and his relish in playing such a creep is rather contagious.

Fresh from her turn opposite Mel Gibson last year in "Lethal Weapon 3," Russo is pleasant but has little to work with and can't entirely stand up to her accomplished co-stars. Supporting perfs are basically one-note affairs, although Patrika Darbo makes a strongly sympathetic impression as a friendly bank clerk who has the misfortune of meeting Leary.

Lenser John Bailey, editor Anne V. Coates, production designer Lilly Kilvert and composer Ennio Morricone contribute heavily to the ultra-pro sheen of the production.

—*Todd McCarthy*

FREE WILLY

Warner Bros. presents, in association with Le Studio Canal Plus, Regency Enterprises and Alcor Films, a Donner/Shuler-Donner production. Produced by Jennie Lew Tugend, Lauren Shuler-Donner. Executive producers, Richard Donner, Arnon Milchan. Co-producers, Penelope L. Foster, Richard Solomon, Jim Van Wyck. Directed by Simon Wincer. Screenplay, Keith A. Walker and Corey Blechman. Story by Walker. Camera (Technicolor), Robbie Greenberg; editor, O. Nicholas Brown; music, Basil Poledouris; production design, Charles Rosen; art direction, Diane Yates, Chas. Butcher; set decorator, Mary Olivia-McIntosh; costume design, April Ferry; sound (Dolby), Clark King; sound design, Tim Chau; whale effects supervisor, Walt Conti; wildlife cinematography, Bob Talbot; casting, Judy Taylor, Lynda Gordon. Reviewed at Burbank Studios, June 23, 1993. MPAA Rating: PG. Running time: **111 MIN.**

Jesse	Jason James Richter
Rae Lindley	Lori Petty
Annie Greenwood	Jayne Atkinson
Randolph Johnson	August Schellenberg
Glen Greenwood	Michael Madsen
Dial	Michael Ironside
Wade	Richard Riehle
Dwight Mercer	Mykelti Williamson
Perry	Michael Bacall
Gwenie	Danielle Harris

"Free Willy" is an exhilarating drama of boy and nature that unabashedly pulls at the heartstrings. Thankfully, its creators know just what to do emotionally and technically to pull off this old-fashioned sentimental yarn.

Cued to Jesse (Jason James Richter), an abandoned child in his umpteenth foster home, the story begins with a tough edge. He's running with a gang of outsiders who are into petty theft and random vandalism. But on one outing, he's nabbed at a Portland amusement park and winds up doing community service.

In true movie fashion, we discover "there's no such thing as a bad boy." The sullen Jesse soon becomes enthralled by Willy, a killer whale who's the unwilling and unresponsive main attraction of the resident aquatic show. They are kindred souls. The analogy is perhaps a tad cute and convenient but the filmmakers largely succeed in muting it with more pressing drama.

When Jesse gets wind of the evil park owner's (Michael Ironside) intentions for the whale, he enlists his friends to do the right thing as the story hurtles to its exciting conclusion.

An astute, intelligent family picture, the film is a potent reminder that you can have your heart in the right place and still produce a gripping, satisfying entertainment.

—*Leonard Klady*

BENEFIT OF THE DOUBT

A Miramax release of a Monument Pictures production in association with CineVox Entertainment. Produced by Michael Spielberg, Brad M. Gilbert. Executive producers, Bob Weinstein, Harvey Weinstein. Co-producer, Dieter Geissler. Directed by Jonathan Heap. Screenplay, Jeffrey Polman, Christopher Keyser, based on a story by Michael Lieber. Camera (Deluxe color), Johnny Jensen; editor, Sharyn L. Ross; music, Hummie Mann; production design, Marina Kieser; art direction, David Seth Lazan; set decoration, Larry Dias; costume design, Ann Foley; sound (Ultra Stereo), Reinhard Stergar; casting, Rachel Abroms, Owens Hill. Reviewed at the Raleigh Studios, L.A., June 30, 1993. MPAA Rating: R. Running time: **90 MIN.**

Frank	Donald Sutherland
Karen	Amy Irving
Pete	Rider Strong
Dan	Christopher McDonald
Calhoun	Graham Greene
Gideon Lee	Theodore Bikel
Suzanna	Gisele Kovach

Suspense is not the strongest suit of "Benefit of the Doubt," a lackluster psychological thriller that uses the format of a TV-styled family melodrama but fails to target the gut or the mind. Predictable concept and mediocre production values should result in modest B.O. results, though a strong performance by Amy Irving might translate into potent video rentals.

Initially interesting setup has Frank Braswell (Donald Sutherland) paroled after 22 years in prison. Accused of killing his wife, Sutherland's conviction was helped by the testimony of his daughter Karen (Amy Irving), who still believes he is guilty.

A single mother working as a cocktail waittress in a strip joint, Irving dreads the return of her father to Cottonwood, a small Arizona town. The idea of seeing him again not only revives haunting childhood nightmares, but also threatens the new life she has built with young son Pete (Rider Strong) and b.f. Dan (Christopher McDonald). It turns out that Sutherland is mainly concerned with maintaining the unity of his nuclear family. Early on, in narration that may reveal too much, he expresses his motto: "The strength of this nation lies in the strength of its families." Before going to prison, Sutherland told his daughter, "Daddy won't forget this," and now it remains to be seen what exactly he meant.

Centering on the rural working class, "Benefit of the Doubt" cleverly deviates from the much exploited "yuppie-in-peril" urban thriller that has saturated American screens over the last couple of years. But Jeffrey Polman and Christopher Keyser's B-movie plot devices constantly drag the material down to a perfunctory level.

The chief problem is that a half-hour into the movie, the pivotal dirty family secrets are disclosed and the story has nowhere to go. When the first murder makes its scheduled stop, one can sniff red herring a mile away. The audience is ahead of the story, nullifying genuine suspense.

There are also plausibility problems: A key bedroom scene in the middle of the film simply doesn't ring true, and some intriguing details, including the possibility Irving's testimony against her father was coached by the prosecutor (Theodore Bikel), are dropped in but never developed.

The movie aspires to the ambience and tonality of "The Stepfather," with which it shares some common themes, but it lacks the nasty irony and frightening undertones of that film. One waits for the plot to become more clever, but instead it gets more pedestrian.

Novice director Jonathan Heape doesn't possess the savvy technique or manipulative skills required for a taut thriller. The climax, involving a chase scene at gorgeous Lake Powell and its surrounding mountains, is ineptly staged and poorly photographed.

Cast against type, Amy Irving gives a startling performance, conveying the vulnerability of a single mother and suspicious daughter without begging for audience sympathy or indulging in undue hysterics. Looking sexy and down-to-earth, Irving holds interest even under improbable circumstances.

As her loving yet menacing father, however, the usually reliable Sutherland is surprisingly timid and inexpressive. Despite the fact that he has played ambiguous and creepy roles before, Sutherland's portrayal here lacks nuance, a problem in the film overall.

McDonald as the fiance, Graham Greene as the benevolent sheriff, and Bikel as the prosecutor are all excellent actors wasted in roles that are basically plot functions.

—*Emanuel Levy*

8-A
(U.S.-CUBAN)

A P.M. Films production. Produced by Mary Garcia-Pimienta. Directed by Orlando Jimenez-Leal. Written by Jose Huguez, Jimenez-Leal, David Tedeschi. Camera (color), Garcia-Pimienta; editor, Tedeschi; music, Daniel Freiberg. Reviewed at AFI screening room, L.A., June 27, 1993 (in AFI/L.A. FilmFest). Running time: **83 MIN.**
(In Spanish; English subtitles)

An effective demonstration of how Fidel Castro's ideological apparatus works is provided by "8-A," a reconstruction of the 1989 trial and execution of Gen. Arnaldo Ochoa Sanchez. Docu's relevance and interesting format make it a likely bet for PBS, cable and other venues.

Ochoa, the highest-ranking general of the Cuban revolution and commander-in-chief in the Angolan and other military campaigns, was one of the country's most beloved heroes before his arrest in 1989. 8-A, a code for his name in Spanish, appeared in street graffiti at the time of the trial. Ochoa was part of a group that was convicted and executed for drug trafficking, a crime labeled by Castro as "compromising the dignity and honor of the country."

Docu's point of departure — and the event that precipitated the collective arrest — is a dinner party at which Ochoa and other members of the power elite were secretly recorded while reportedly expressing their discontent with Cuba's political and economic conditions. Two weeks later, they were arrested, though the drug charges were made later, suggesting that Castro was trying to conceal the real issues of political schism and conspiracy.

At the trial, which aired on Cuban state TV, the accused not only confessed to all the charges against them, but also expressed repentance for "betraying the Fatherland and the Revolution." While focusing on the trial, docu raises provocative questions concerning human rights in a dictatorial regime. In its structure, urgency and tone, "8-A" resembles "Z" and other Costa-Gavras political thrillers. Constructed from trial tapes from the Italian web RAI, docu presents its case in an orderly, yet always stimulating, manner.

—*Emanuel Levy*

ROAD SCHOLAR

A Samuel Goldwyn Co. release of a Public Policy production. Produced, directed by Roger Weisberg. Associate producer, Daniel Klein. Co-director, camera (Duart color), Jean de Segonzac; editor, Alan Miller; music, North Forty Music, Wave Band Sound; sound, Scott Breindel, Mark Roy. Reviewed at the Sundance Film Festival, Park City, Utah, Jan. 22, 1993. Running time: **81 MIN.**
With: Andrei Codrescu.

America "seems to be discovered over and over and never definitively," Andrei Codrescu muses at the start of "Road Scholar," as he launches on a journey in search of the nation's spirit and his own relationship to it.

The commentator for National Public Radio's "All Things Considered" offers a look at the United States that is far more idiosyncratic than definitive, but this zippy, witty docu is sophisticated and amusing enough to carve out a small place in the theatrical market on its way to a healthy life in TV and video.

Admittedly inspired by "On the Road," the Romanian-born Codrescu, accompanied by producer-director Roger Weisberg and co-helmer-lenser Jean de Segonzac, set out from New York to San Francisco in December 1991 (after a dry run by the filmmakers alone). But first, Codrescu had to learn how to drive, providing a funny prologue.

The intellectual writer and poet grew up with the European romanticism for the American road, and would drive nothing less than a cherry red, extravagantly finned vintage Cadillac convertible.

To fortify himself, he feasts on meat at Sammy's Romanian restaurant on the Lower East Side, acknowledges some Haitians living in a wall, then pays homage to Walt Whitman's home in Camden, N.J., on his way to a utopian community where a small group pursues an ascetic existence as Jesus is imagined to have lived, utterly without modern conveniences.

From there it's up to Niagara Falls, to his Caddy's birthplace in Detroit, and on to the Chicago area, where he visits the Board of Trade, the original McDonald's, black Holy Rollers and a "junk" artist whose creations offend neighbors in suburban Glencoe.

Codrescu finds the Old West intact in Colorado, where a hot female shooting instructor provides a lesson in firing a machine gun. In New Mexico he opines that "the '60s never died in Santa Fe," where he has some riotous encounters with New Age types, notably a psychic who manhandles him pretty handily.

After speeding past the schlock on Route 66 and winning at poker in

Vegas, the poetic wayfarer finally arrives in San Francisco, where matters turn a bit more serious, as Codrescu reflects on the value of freedom, which has made possible the lifestyles of those he's met along the way.

While Weisberg's P.O.V. certainly leans toward the humorous, the film doesn't indulge in cheap shots. De Segonzac's camera is exceptionally alert to the ironies of the diverse situations. Most viewers will have traveled down this road before, but Codrescu's distinctive perspective makes the trip worth taking.

—*Todd McCarthy*

GRIEF

A Grief Prods. production. Produced by Ruth Charny, Yoram Mandel; Executive producer, Marcus Hu. Directed, written by Richard Glatzer. Camera (16mm, color), David Dechant; editors, Bill Williams, Robin Katz; music, Tom Judson; production design, Don Diers; set decoration, David Carpender; costumes, Laser N. Rosenberg; sound, Thomas Jones. Reviewed at the San Francisco Lesbian & Gay Intl. Film Festival, June 26, 1993. Running time: **88 MIN.**

Mark	Craig Chester
Joe	Jackie Beat
Leslie	Illeana Douglas
Bill	Alexis Arquette
Jeremy	Carlton Wilborn
Paula	Lucy Gutteridge
Kelly	Robin Swid
Bill No. 2	Bill Rotko
Ben	Shann Hoffman

With: Paul Bartel, Mickey Cottrell, John Fleck, Johanna Went, Mary Woronov.

Likely to be pegged as a gay "Soapdish," writer-director Richard Glatzer's "Grief" actually has a good deal more heart and wit. Modestly mounted indie will need solid word of mouth to attract a deserved arthouse aud — as comic elements gradually fade to surprisingly effective drama, it's too complex for easy selling. But terrific script and performances should ensure those good vibes.

The setting is a former prostitutes' hotel now supplying offices for a TV production company. They crank out episodes of "The Love Judge," a tacky tabloid-style syndicated series.

Flashback action takes place during a Monday-Friday work week, framed by head writer Mark's (Craig Chester) suicide contemplation on the first anniversary of his lover's death of AIDS.

It's a hairy five days. The imminent departure of no-nonsense exec producer Jo (Jackie Beat, aka Kent Fuher, in an initially disconcerting but deft piece of cross-gender casting) sets Mark and serious-minded divorcee Paula (Lucy Gutteridge) against one another as competing successors.

Emotionally vulnerable Mark has a crush on writer Bill (Alexis Arquette), who's recently broken up with his girlfriend and is sending out

flirtation signals in all directions. Career ambitions of Jo's assistant Leslie (Illeana Douglas) are distracted by romantic attentions from a cute copy machine repairman.

Tensions are compounded by homophobia of the (unseen) exex upstairs, as they decide who ultimately gets the big promotion. Mark's gloom is further pressed by discovery that his best friend/story editor Jeremy (Carlton Wilborn) has already launched a secret affair with baby "closet case" Bill. Best running gag is Jo's mortification upon discovering evidence — stains, used condoms, a bit of unused lube — of their trysts on her office couch.

Scenario starts out looking rather insular, just another amusing look at behind-the-scenes Hollywood incestuousness. But the familiar satire soon develops no end of healthy wrinkles.

"Grief" is ultimately about the redemptive value of friendship. It credibly conveys (in strong confrontation/monologue scenes) that these characters really do care about each other.

The barbed verbal wit is sometimes muddied by tinny sound recording. But video-shot glimpses from the ersatz "Love Judge" series are hilarious — featuring such L.A. underground staples as Paul Bartel, John Fleck, Mary Woronov and Johanna Went in ludicrous yet apt parodies of televid "docudrama" scenarios.

Central performances are excellent. Chester's melancholy Mark is understated and enormously appealing. Douglas nearly steals the show as genially "burnt-out party girl" Leslie. While visually nondescript, Glatzer's direction is perfectly attuned to his lovingly fostered ensemble rhythms.

"Grief" isn't a dazzling debut technique-wise, but its drollery and genuine warmth are of another, perhaps deeper stripe. As "feel-good" sleepers go, this one is funny, smart and sweet.

—*Dennis Harvey*

ZERO PATIENCE
(CANADIAN)

A Zero Patience Prods. Ltd. presentation, produced with the participation of Telefilm Canada and Ontario Film Development Corp. in association with Channel Four Television, U.K., with the assistance of Cineplex Odeon Films Canada/Ontario Arts Council/Canada Council/Canadian Film Centre/The CRB Foundation. Produced by Louise Garfield, Anna Stratton. Executive producer, Alexandra Raffe. Directed, written by John Greyson. Camera (color), Miroslaw Baszak; editor, Miume Jan; music, Glenn Schellenberg; lyrics, Schellenberg, Greyson; production design, Sandra Kybartas; costumes, Joyce Schure; choreographer, Susan McKenzie; casting, Dorothy Gardner. Reviewed at the San Francisco Lesbian & Gay International Film Festival, June 25, 1993. Running time: **100 MIN.**

Sir Richard Burton	John Robinson
Zero	Normand Fauteux
Mary	Dianne Heatherington
George	Richardo Keens-Douglas
Dr. Placebo	Bernard Behrens
Monkey	Maria Lukofsky
Miss HIV	Michael Callen
Maman	Charlotte Boisjoli
Dr. Cheng	Brenda Kamino

John Greyson's new feature is a cheekily agitating "AIDS musical." Juggling MTV-style numbers, intellectual in-jokes and very sexual politics, "Zero Patience" is — like the Canadian director's prior "Urinal" and "The Making of 'Monster'" — often more impressive in conceptual daring than execution. Still, the climate is right for Greyson to expand his festival cult following to a limited arthouse audience.

Freewheeling scenario pivots around the controversial "Patient Zero" theory popularized in Randy Shilts' 1987 book "And the Band Played On." Some evidence (since heavily argued against by researchers) pointed toward a French-Canadian airline steward as the messenger whose sexual promiscuity first brought the disease to North America. Screenplay offers "Zero" (Normand Fauteux) as a "gay ghost" who abruptly materializes in a jacuzzi several years after his death. He sees old friends succumbing to illness and fighting back via activism.

But most of the action centers on his confrontation with Sir Richard Francis Burton (John Robinson), the 19th century English explorer-writer-translator. The latter has lived an extra 100 years to become chief "taxidermist and dioramacist" of Toronto's Natural History Museum. Burton plots a Patient Zero exhibit as part of the Hall of Contagion. His initial motives are a crass affirmation of homo/AIDS-phobia, designed to "perpetuate bigotry and fetishize blame."

But when the real P.Z. shows up, only Burton can see and hear him. As they become lovers, more enlightened views slowly dawn. In Greyson's revisionist view, Patient Zero is revealed as the "heroic slut who inspired safe sex."

The best song in Glenn Schellenberg's generally frisky and well-sung rock score is the first: "Tell Me the Story of My Life," a deliciously catchy pop tune neatly visualized with underwater ballet.

Finale scores with a well-edited musical ACT-UP museum invasion and rather poignant coda. Despite such episodes, "Zero Patience" suffers from somewhat monotonous cinematic imagination. Serious excess of closeups compound a claustrophobic feel. Cast is attractive but short on strong personalities and comic flair. Fauteux's awkward Quebecois line readings are a liability.

Despite these flaws, "Zero Patience" is like little else in recent gay-themed cinema.

—*Dennis Harvey*

THE SILVER BRUMBY
(AUSTRALIAN)

A Roadshow (Australia) release of a Media World Features production, with the participation of the Australian Film Finance Corp. and the assistance of Film Victoria. Produced by John Tatoulis, Colin J. South. Executive producer, William T. Marshall. Line producer, Brian Burgess. Directed by Tatoulis. Screenplay, Tatoulis, Jon Stephens, Elyne Mitchell, based on Mitchell's book, "The Silver Brumby." Camera (color), Mark Gilfedder; editor, Peter Burgess; music, Tassos Ioannides; production design, Phil Chambers; art direction, Peter Kendall; sound, John Wilkinson; stunts, Chris Anderson; assistant director, Stephen Saks; casting, Greg Apps. Reviewed at Village Cinema City 2, Sydney, June 27, 1993. Running time: **92 MIN.**

Elyne	Caroline Goodall
The Man	Russell Crowe
Indi	Ami Daemion
Jock	Johnny Raaen

A superbly crafted family film for animal lovers, "The Silver Brumby" should earn solid coin during school vacations everywhere and have a long video life.

Pic is based on a book written in the 1950s by a single mother for her teenage daughter, and the filmmakers have retained the original period, although this is really a timeless story of the life of a legendary wild horse (or brumby).

Elyne Mitchell's story is inspired by real events occurring in the spectacularly beautiful Victorian High Country where she lives with her daughter.

However, Mitchell embellishes the truth for dramatic effect as she tells of a silver brumby stallion who quickly learns the ways of survival in the wild and who eventually replaces his father as leader of a pack of wild horses that roams the mountains.

Simple tale has the Man (Russell Crowe), a mountain horseman, coveting the magnificent silver stallion and trying to capture it. Later, he pays a large sum of money for a mare, which the stallion later rescues from captivity. In revenge, the Man and a tracker set out to capture the stallion once and for all, and yarn ends as the stuff of legend, with the silver brumby now a ghost horse that haunts the mountain ranges.

Most of the film is taken up with magnificently staged and photographed footage of the horses in their natural environment. Filming took place over a year around Mount Hotham and Dinner Plain in Victoria, and cinematographer Mark Gilfedder has breathtakingly captured the rugged beauty of the High Country. Major kudos are clearly due horse trainer Evanne Chesson.

The human actors have less to do but acquit themselves well. Russell Crowe, in a very different role from the one he essayed in "Romper

Stomper," is excellent as the tenacious bushman. Caroline Goodall brings sensitivity to the role of the lonely woman, and Ami Daemion is charming as her strong-willed daughter.

Director and co-writer John Tatoulis (whose previous feature was the underrated private eye thriller "In Too Deep") sensibly doesn't try to beef up the uncomplicated story with contrived narrative. There are thrilling scenes, not least a stunning helicopter shot that reveals the stallion and the men hunting it down galloping straight toward a cliff.

The unusual but strikingly apt music score by Tassos Ioannides is a major asset. All other tech credits are excellent. —*David Stratton*

FULL CONTACT
(HONG KONG)

A Rim Film Distributors Inc. release of a Golden Harvest production. Directed by Ringo Lam. Camera (color), Tony Chau. Reviewed at Roxie Cinema, San Francisco, Feb. 9, 1993. Running time: 96 MIN. Jeff ..... Chow Yun-Fat
Judge .... Simon Yam
Virgin .... Bonnie Fu
Sam .... Wong Chow-Sang
Mona .... Anne Park

Fast, fierce and gleefully tasteless, "Full Contact" is a Hong Kong actioner sure to capitalize in Asian markets here and abroad. Lacking the transcendent style of star Chow Yun-Fat's John Woo-directed vehicles, it compensates with a brutality that may alienate some crossover markets intrigued by the cult allure of other recent Hong Kong features.

But the violence is pulse-quickening at the least. It starts with a wicked robbery sequence in which bad guy Judge stabs a young Thai female clerk for no reason beyond satisfying his passing sadistic urge.

Back in Bangkok, club bouncer Jeff (Chow) incites underworld anger by rescuing his loan shark-indebted pal Sam from the clutches of thugs. Sam suggests hooking up with gay cousin Judge and his crew to procure needed international getaway money.

Trouble is, Judge and his cronies are even more morally bankrupt than the loan shark's minions. His companions soon slaughtered, Sam must betray his own loyalties to stay alive.

Left for dead, invincible Jeff rouses himself to plot revenge against all. He alarms the bad guys and confuses erstwhile g.f. Mona (who's taken up with Sam after Jeff's "demise") with phantom-like appearances before a climactic disco shootout.

"Full Contact" is formula Hong Kong gangster stuff. Which is to say it's basically one improbable but wildly energetic climax after another, with familiar minor refrains of sentimentality (Jeff takes responsibility for a child bystander fire-scarred by the villains) and quasi-

mysticism. The results may be crass, but they sure aren't dull. More disturbing than the film's eager blood-shedding is its dicey sketching of the principal villainous trio. They're a bizarre combo — hulking, mean-spirited Rambo-types; his extremely sluttish girlfriend, Virgin; and their mastermind, the foppish, heartless Judge.

While not fondling some younger comfort-boy, the Judge is making sarcastic goo-goo eyes at the hero, smirking, "Your eyes are so charming and attractive!" "Well! Masturbate in hell!" is one of Jeff's comebacks. Meanwhile, Virgin tries to get intimate with every man in sight. "Check if there's a hole in my underwear," she suggests to Jeff. "No, I saw a vomiting crab there," Jeff replies.

Good taste is not the prevailing virtue of "Full Contact"; pic hits the gutter at a sprint. Tech aspects are tops; acting turns make the most of the script's crass humor.
—*Dennis Harvey*

CADILLAC GIRLS
(CANADIAN)

A Cineplex Odeon Films Canada Release (Canada) of an Imagex Ltd. production, in association with Orca Productions Ltd./Telefilm Canada/NFB/Nova Scotia Film Development Corp./The Movie Network. (Intl. sales: Saban International Inc., Burbank). Produced by Nicholas Kendall, Christopher Zimmer, Christian Bruyere. Directed by Nicholas Kendall. Screenplay, Peter Behrens. Camera (color), Glen McKenna; costume design, Lin Chapman; sound, Paul Sharpe. Reviewed at the Seattle Film Festival, June 1, 1993. Running time: 96 MIN.
Sally .... Jennifer Dale
Page .... Mia Kirshner
Sam .... Gregory Harrison
Will .... Adam Beach
Aunt Grace .... Anna Cameron
Donald .... Mike Crimp
Also with: Benita Ha, Nancy Marsh, Deborah Allen, Ronald Bourgeois, Martha Irving, Morrissey Dunn, Rachel Clark, Carmen Diges.

Another addition to the growing catalogue of blame-the-career-woman pics, this soft-edged family saga will seem overly familiar to CBC-saturated auds, and not exotic enough for Americans. After a brief cable life, "Cadillac Girls" could move to European and Japanese markets, where maritime settings may hold fresh appeal.

Title refers to the yellow convertible left behind by college prof Jennifer Dale when she departed Nova Scotia for Berkeley's sunnier climes. Its backseat is where now grown-daughter Mia Kirshner was conceived, and after many meller-mixups involving their strained relationship, this very literal *deus ex machina* becomes central to bringing them back together. Another passenger is Scotch-guzzling poetry prof Gregory Harrison, who doesn't much care which woman is driving.

Scripter Peter Behrens starts off well enough, with mother and daughter wittily locking horns — teenage Kirshner's been picked up for auto theft and says, "This should interest you, mother ... at least intellectually" — just as Dale is called back to Canada by her own father's death. The bicoastal transplant also intrigues, since helmer Nicholas Kendall establishes their strait-laced, one-horse Nova Scotia town with a former documaker's eye.

That's as good as it gets, though, since the characters remain closely tethered to the surface symbols defining them. A whirling dervish in a red-leather miniskirt, Kirshner is handed some temporary humility by a handsome native lad (Adam Beach), but her whining selfishness proves unbearable.

It's hammered home that bad-mother Dale keeps all her buttons tight thanks to her unfeeling family, but we never glimpse the qualities that make her a good teacher (she's up for a gig at Harvard) or even an interesting person. Harrison drinks, womanizes, and wears bad ties because, well, that's what poets do.

Equal automotive blame belongs to Behrens, who hurls this initially attractive vehicle straight into a no-escape bog, and Kendall, who asks too little of the always-reliable Dale and far too much of young Kirshner — no one should have to pout, scream and cry this much.

Former MOW hunk Harrison, here going by the "Simpsons"-esque name of Sam LaRiviere, is just about right, and smaller roles are well handled, with John Goodman lookalike Mike Crimp a standout as the town's jolly, bagpipe-puffing cop.

Regional lensing is exceptionally good, although marred somewhat by substandard editing and dull, TV-predictable music.
—*Ken Eisner*

BONES

A Chery's Filmworks production. Produced, directed, written, edited by Yves Chery. Co-producer, Brenda Westbrooke. Camera (Color), Thomas E. Oetzell; music, Jacques Richmond, Chris Monroe, Anthony Jefferson; production design, Lisa Linden. Reviewed June 16, 1993 at AFI/L.A. Film Fest. Running time: 62 MIN.
Bello .... Terence Riggins
Simbi .... Devika Parikh
Wendell .... Reginald Hobbs
Renee .... Vicky Rise
Doctor .... David G. Thomas

Yves Chery makes quite an impressive debut as producer-writer-director of "Bones," a contemporary AIDS drama situated in a middleclass black community. Indie pic is flawed by uneven writing and preachy dialogue, but its realistic context, smooth style, and amiable cast should increase its chances for a limited theatrical

showing beyond the festival circuit.

Set in present-day L.A., "Bones" is the story of a sexy, newlywed black couple who suddenly have to face the realization that they are afflicted with the AIDS virus. Bello (Terrence Riggins), is a compassionate counselor and loving husband of Simbi (Devika Parikh), a beautiful real-estate loan officer.

The first part of the cautionary tale traces Bello's daily routine: love-making with his wife, sensitive sessions with his AIDS patients, socializing with his buddy Wendell (Reinald Hobbs), a macho man who has hard time accepting the fact that he had lost his younger brother to the lethal disease. The second, more dramatic, part documents the inevitable tragic effects of the illness on the couple and their close friends.

Chery's greatest achievement is in defying excessive melodramatics and easy sentimentality. Though utterly shocked and devastated when his loyal doctor (David G. Thomas) informs him he has tested HIV-positive, there is no hysterics or self-pity in Riggins' reaction, only the natural and expected "Why me? What have I done?"

In his benign, informed philosophy, scripter Chery goes out of his way to fight facile stereotyping of the fatal ailment (that it's a strictly gay disease, that blacks afflicted with the virus are mostly drug addicts). But this liberal, well-intentioned approach sometimes results in uninventive writing that functions as instructive sermons.

In its best moments, "Bones" resembles Paul Mazursky's realistic "slice of life" comedies, but in its weakest, it's a morality tale with an overtly "messagey" agenda. Still, acquitting himself better as helmer than scripter, Chery's direction is always vibrant and fluent, showing a particular facility in establishing the right tonality for each and every scene of his film.

It helps a great deal that the two leading actors, Terrence Riggins and Devika Parikh, are extremely attractive, appealing and sympathetic. Thomas E. Oetzell's camera is informal and unobtrusive; even the occasional interludes of tedium are nicely photographed.
—*Emanuel Levy*

MAUVAIS GARCON
(BAD BOY)
(FRENCH)

A.G.I.E. Les Films Noirs-Thunder Films International S.A. production. (Foreign sales: WMF - Claude Nouchi) Produced, directed by Jacques Braal. Screenplay, Braal, Jean-Paul Leca. Camera (color), Jacques Assuerus, Jean Mosigny; editor, Braal; music, Stephan Delplace, based on a theme by Francisco Tarrega; art direction, Denis Mercier; costume design, Olga Pelletier; sound, Gerard Dacquay, Gerard Barra. Reviewed June 18, 1993 at Paris Film Festival — competing). Running time: 88 MIN.

Thomas .... Bruno Wolkowitch
Lea .... Delphine Forest
Also with: Ludmile Mikael, Gabrielle Forest, Josy Bernard, Marie-Josee Legault, Patricia Malvoisin, Anne Clelia-Salomon, Hugues Quester, Jean Francois Balmer.

Jacques Braal puts an engaging and original, grace-tinged spin on boy-meets-girl in "Mauvais Garcon," his first film in 10 years. Handsome young leads are aces in contemporary love story set in Paris. Pic could perform nicely at Gallic wickets, if good word of mouth develops. Fest programmers should take note.

The morning he's paroled from prison, petty thief Thomas (Bruno Wolkowitch) discovers his girlfriend in bed with another man. Appealing, soft-spoken Thomas — whose lifestyle amounts to taking what he wants — burgles an apartment or two and expediently seduces a few women before endeavoring to pick up stern, highly attractive Lea (Delphine Forest), who tries to shake her new admirer but eventually succumbs to his persistent charm.

Wolkowitch mixes wry and devilish charisma as the selfish no-goodnik who can shoplift a live lobster and scale the outside of a building with equal aplomb.

Forest shines as the don't-mess-with-me beauty who has reasons of her own for resisting such a diligent suitor. Classical-style score is sometimes overbearing and camerawork occasionally calls attention to itself. But the tone is so intriguing that the narrative doesn't suffer.

Protagonist's redemption echoes pix from Bresson's "Pickpocket" to Paul Schrader's "Light Sleeper," yet Braal makes the outcome humorous and just new enough to satisfy.

Inside joke — when couple goes to the movies together, the pic on screen is Sam Fuller's "Street of No Return," which Braal produced.
—*Lisa Nesselson*

THE GREAT UNPLEASANTNESS

A Crescent Pictures production. Produced by Wendy Fishman. Directed, written, edited by Dorne M. Pentes. Camera (color), Mick McNeely; music, Jake Berger, Buzzoven, Pervis Lee; production design, Dominic Masters; art direction, Jim Gloster; Sound, Jack Rainsford; casting, Linda Newcomb, Vinnie Woods. Reviewed June 18, 1993 at AFI/L.A. Film Fest. Running time: **77 MIN.**
Errol .... Peter Carrs
Isabel .... Collyn Gaffney
Parks .... C.K. (Chuck) Bibby
Sally .... Elizabeth Orr
Darla .... Paige Johnston
Johnny .... Jim Gloster

There's nothing new in Dorne M. Pentes' "The Great Unpleasantness," a naive, simple-minded melodrama about youth angst and alienation. Despite impressive acting by the two leads, overly familiar concept and unexciting direction should confine this indie to minor film festivals and possibly video.

Set in a large Southern city, story concerns Errol (Peter Carrs), an angry young man estranged from his divorced parents and living in a run-down building with his g.f. Isabel (Collyn Gaffney). The two lovers make a scrappy living, taking odd jobs and committing petty burglary, and socialize with their feuding gay neighbors and friend Darla (Paige Johnston), who is married to an abusive husband. Together, they form some kind of communal bond, one that proves helpful in fighting their eviction.

Regrettably, Pentes' melodrama is not only commonplace but contrived. The building where they live belongs to Errol's greedy capitalist father (C.K. Bibby), a modern symbol of the old, exploitive plantation owner. And after years of estrangement, Errol's mother (Elizabeth Orr) suddenly shows up at the restaurant where he works.

For the most part, the writing is bland and immature — almost every scene ends in yelling and screaming. The small arguments and fights lead to the ultimate confrontation between irresponsible father and long-suffering son.

Pentes shows talent in handling his young actors. As the couple, Carrs and Gaffney are always credible, bringing much-needed energy and liveliness to their pedestrian roles. But their work is surrounded with mediocre, colorless performances, particularly by Bibby and Orr, who seem to act completely from the outside. —*Emanuel Levy*

POETIC JUSTICE

A Columbia Pictures release. Produced by Steve Nicolaides, John Singleton. Directed, written by Singleton. Camera (Technicolor), Peter Lyons Collister; editor, Bruce Cannon; music, Stanley Clarke; production design, Keith Burns; art director, Kirk Petruccelli; set decorator, Dan May; costume design, Darryle Johnson; sound (Dolby), Roby Eber; associate producer, D. Alonzo Williams; casting, Robi Reed; poetry, Maya Angelou. Reviewed at Sony Pictures, Culver City, July 8, 1993. MPAA Rating: R. Running time: **110 MIN.**
Justice .... Janet Jackson
Lucky .... Tupac Shakur
Iesha .... Regina King
Chicago .... Joe Torry
Jessie .... Tyra Ferrell
Heywood .... Roger Guenveur Smith
Aunt June .... Maya Angelou
Markell .... Q-Tip
J Bone .... Tone Loc
Maxine .... Miki Howard
Dexter .... Keith Washington

John Singleton's followup to "Boyz N the Hood" and the screen debut of Janet Jackson cannot sustain the scrutiny and expectation that inevitably follow a conspicuous first film. "Poetic Justice" is a hermetic inner city love story elevated by resonant social commentary. It has an obvious appeal to a core ethnic audience but faces a considerable challenge in tapping into the mainstream.

The film begins promisingly enough with the central character, Justice (Jackson), at the local drive-in with her boyfriend. The momentary idyll quickly disintegrates when a nabe hothead recognizes the young man as someone who crossed his path. The firebrand kills the beau while in the girl's embrace. The violent setup looms over the narrative without tying in to the rest of the story. Justice, chastened by the incident, has cut herself off from the world outside the beauty salon where she works. Lucky (Tupac Shakur), the young letter carrier on the shop's route, attempts to break the ice with brittle consequences.

This second section is also a bit of a dead end. While we learn something of the environment and background of the two characters, it is no more than a prologue for what ultimately turns into the heart of the film. Singleton has chosen a most awkward and confusing way to develop his story.

Things finally get into gear when Justice's planned trip from South Central L.A. to Oakland is fouled up by a dead car battery. Her friend Iesha (Regina King) arranges a last-minute ride with Chicago (Joe Torry) and his buddy from work. The pal turns out to be Lucky, the mailman.

The trip north in a U.S. Postal truck is a gem that begins as a variation of the classic romantic comedy — two people who can't stand each other are thrust into close quarters and wind up in love.

And the road provides some choice opportunities for digression, including clever stops that involve crashing a family reunion and attending an African fair. But auds may be distanced by the disjointed nature of the ramble. Singleton proves himself an adept director, fascinated with the echoes beneath the narrative. But his writing skills are less assured.

Another misfire is the filmmaker's effort to weave Justice's poetry into the soundtrack. In reality the work of Maya Angelou, it is a forced device that strains to provide another level for the character. The literal implications are often just plain embarrassing.

Jackson proves herself a natural in front of the camera in a thoughtful rather than dynamic performance. This is not a "star is born" role but it places her in the mold of faces to watch.

Shakur has the juicier part and turns in truly outstanding work. The vignette structure also allows a considerable number of actors to shine in brief but memorable turns — perhaps the most bizarre being Billy Zane and Lori Petty as the performers in the drive-in feature.

Though aiming to create a feel for the locale, Singleton periodically loses sight of audiences unfamiliar with the colorful lingo. "Poetic Justice" has a lot to commend but discipline is not high on the list. That flaw will be a major stumbling block toward wide appeal, and overseas prospects seem particularly remote.
—*Leonard Klady*

HOCUS POCUS

A Buena Vista release of a Walt Disney Pictures presentation of a David Kirschner/Steven Haft production. Produced by Kirschner, Haft. Executive producer, Ralph Winter. Co-executive producer, Mick Garris. Co-producer, Bonnie Bruckheimer. Directed by Kenny Ortega. Screenplay, Garris, Neil Cuthbert; story by Kirschner, Garris. Camera (Technicolor prints), Hiro Narita; editor, Peter E. Berger; music, John Debney; production design, William Sandell; art direction, Nancy Patton; set decoration, Rosemary Brandenberg; costume design, Mary Vogt; sound (Dolby), C. Darin Knight; associate producer, Jay Heit; assistant director, Ellen H. Schwartz; visual effects supervisor, Peter Montgomery; casting, Mary Gail Artz, Barbara Cohen. Reviewed at the Mann Bruin Theatre, L.A., July 10, 1993. MPAA Rating: PG. Running time: 95 **MIN.**
Winifred .... Bette Midler
Sarah .... Sarah Jessica Parker
Mary ....Kathy Najimy
Max .... Omri Katz
Dani ....Thora Birch
Allison .... Vinessa Shaw
Thackery .... Sean Murray
Ernie ("Ice") .... Larry Bagby III
Jay .... Tobias Jelinek
Jenny .... Stephanie Faracy
Dave .... Charles Rocket

July 26, 1993 (Cont.)

With Bette Midler and her on-screen sisters shamelessly hamming things up, it looks as if those involved in making this inoffensive flight of fantasy had more fun than anyone over 12 will have watching it. Still, the blend of witchcraft and comedy should divert kids without driving the patience of their parents to the boiling point, leaving a chance to conjure up a little box office magic among that contingent before the pot tips over.

Actually, without a heavily made-up Midler (and perhaps the hot-off-"Honeymoon in Vegas" Sarah Jessica Parker) at its center, "Hocus Pocus" wouldn't seem out of place on the Disney Channel, and perhaps belongs there. As it is, even with souped-up special effects, the premise feels a bit wispy to sustain a feature, and the action sags at times as a result.

That tried-and-true storyline has a teen-age boy (Omri Katz) feeling out of place having moved to a new town — in this case venerable Salem, Mass. — with his parents and kid sister. Stuck with taking moppet Dani (Thora Birch, one of the pic's major assets) trick-or-treating on Halloween night, he meets up with his dream-girl classmate (Vinessa Shaw) and ends up traveling to a musty old museum where, inadvertently, he conjures up three children-hungry witches from the dead.

They are, in fact, the Sanderson sisters: the cruel Winifred (Midler), the daft Mary (Kathy Najimy of "Sister Act") and the positively dense, boy-crazy Sarah (Parker).

According to Mick Garris and Neil Cuthbert's script, from a story by Garris and producer David Kirschner, the trio must suck the life-force out of children by dawn or risk being scattered forever.

Max (Katz) and the two girls find help in seeking to undo the wrong they've done in the form of an immortal black cat, actually a boy cursed by the witches during an OK pre-credit sequence.

"Hocus Pocus" suffers from inconsistency, careening aimlessly between a sense of menace and a comedic sort of Three Stooges on broomsticks.

Choreographer-turned-director Kenny Ortega, whose own last flight was on the ill-fated Disney musical "Newsies," can't quite pull off this tap dance, even with the ripe comedic possibilities in the setup that finds these witches on Halloween with no one taking them seriously.

There are a few inspired moments from the witches, but for the most part the movie belongs to the kids, with Katz appropriately earnest as Max, Birch cute and wisecracking as the sister and Shaw spunky and well-cast as the quintessential dream girl.

Tech credits are modest yet solid, with creditable visuals from Buena Vista Visual Effects, some nifty costuming and a sharp look from cinematographer Hiro Narita.

Unfortunately, like the zombie revived by Winifred, the film keeps losing its head, particularly during the final sequence, when it's hard to ascertain exactly what the heroes hope to accomplish. For all its "E.T."-type flourishes — from John Debney's score to one particular line of dialogue at the end — these broomsticks won't give anyone that sort of lift. *—Brian Lowry*

ROOKIE OF THE YEAR

A 20th Century Fox release. Produced by Robert Harper. Executive producers, Jack Brodsky, Irby Smith. Directed by Daniel Stern. Screenplay, Sam Harper. Camera (Technicolor), Jack N. Green; editor, Donn Cambern, Raja Gosnell; music, Bill Conti; production design, Steven Jordan; art direction, William Arnold; set decoration, Leslie Bloom; costume design, Jay Hurley; sound, Scott Smith; associate producer, Joan Aguado; baseball adviser, Tim Stoddard; casting, Linda Lowy. Reviewed at the Cineplex Century City, Los Angeles, June 26, 1993. MPAA Rating: PG. Running time: **103 MIN.**

Henry Rowengartner	Thomas Ian Nicholas
Chet Steadman	Gary Busey
Martinella	Albert Hall
Mary Rowengartner	Amy Morton
Larry (Fish) Fisher	Dan Hedaya
Jack Bradfield	Bruce Altman
Bob Carson	Eddie Bracken
Phil Brickman	Daniel Stern

"Rookie of the Year" aspires to be a pint-sized "It's a Wonderful Field of Dreams," and largely succeeds in minor league fashion. A warm, comic "what if" yarn, it's rife with humor and sentimentality but is just one run away from the game-winning score. As such the film is solidly played and should rank among the summer's top second-stringers without quite reaching Hall of Fame status.

The premise is engaging. Preteen Henry Rowengartner (Thomas Ian Nicholas) is your typical single-parented, enthusiastic baseball-playing Chicago kid who's unaware of life's crueler realities. Then the accident happens. Henry breaks his arm in a baseball mishap.

Months later, Henry discovers the fracture has healed in a curious way. His tendons have tightened, allowing him to hurl a ball faster than a speeding bullet. Circumstance brings this to the attention of his beloved Chicago Cubs. Soon the contracts are signed and the peewee player is on his way to delivering his franchise World Series berth.

Essentially a one-gag premise, Sam Harper's screenplay valiantly attempts to enhance the yarn by fleshing out characters and injecting splashes of madcap comedy. It connects more often than it fans in the hands of rookie helmer Daniel Stern, who lacks the seasoning to ground the fantasy in a realistic setting.

The film is about Henry's maturation as well as the game. There's also a subplot involving his mother (Amy Morton) and a creepy new boyfriend (Bruce Altman) who has dollar signs for pupils. This nicely segues into management treachery in which Henry is seen as the means to sell off the sagging franchise.

Stern and Harper, however, fail to make the team coalesce. Most of the players get scant screen time, with the exception of the team's former pitching star (Gary Busey), who's forced to take Henry under his wing.

"Rookie of the Year" conveys a true love of the game. Stern has adroitly chosen his technical team, with ace credits throughout, especially Jack Green's gliding camera and Bill Conti's big, emotional score.

The principal cast also shines. Youngster Nicholas effects the role of a good kid without being cloying. There's plenty of the bratty and brainy in his character to provide a well-rounded performance. Also strong are the ever-reliable Busey and Morton. With little script help, she provides old-fashioned warmth to the modern mom.

Supporting roles, including an uncredited turn by John Candy as an announcer, fall into archetype. Some, like Dan Hedaya's as a manipulative suit, are too on-the-nose, while Albert Hall's team manager finds a novel edge. Eddie Bracken, as the dotty team owner, suggests a tip of the hat to Sturges comedy. The most obvious role in that mold, the Cubs' inept pitching coach, played by Stern, is a total misfire.

The fantasy-comedy breezes home with so much goodwill that audiences will unabashedly cheer it on to the finish. *—Leonard Klady*

AFI / L.A. FEST

JAMES ELROY
DEMON DOG OF AMERICAN CRIME FICTION
(AUSTRIAN-DOCU)

A Fischer Film production in association with ORF. Produced by Markus Fischer. Directed by Reinhard Jud. Script, Jud, Wolfgang Lehner. Camera (color), Lehner; editor, Karina Ressler; music, Deedee Neidhart, Sam Auinger; sound, Auinger; narrator, Phil Tintner. Reviewed at AFI/L.A. Film Fest, June 21, 1993. Running Time: **89 MIN.**

Novelist James Elroy proves himself the energetic subject of a film portrait subtitled "Demon Dog of American Crime Fiction." But the Austrian-produced documentary allows him to run on through his guided tour of the seamy side of Los Angeles without benefit of context, reflection or standing. The resulting film is for the aficionado and best suited for television and videocassette sales.

Densely packed with autobiographical detail and commentary from Elroy, the profile is wall-to-wall narration, punctuated only by vaguely related travelogue montage. The author is smart, glib — in short, supremely entertaining. Nonetheless, the filmmakers' failure to challenge Elroy's narrative or lend it specificity makes the project feel incomplete.

Elroy's personal saga is especially riveting. He was born and raised in less fashionable sections of the city. His mother was murdered, the killer never found. He succumbed to alcohol and drugs, joined the Navy and settled into a marginal lifestyle as a caddie. Elroy began to write around his 30th birthday and five years later had the confidence to turn his passion into his profession.

Only slightly less commanding are the author's observations about the city, crime fiction, the police and criminals.

The film is a true fan letter from director Reinhard Jud and producer Markus Fischer. But ultimately its approach short-changes its subject, who, in the absence of a good challenge, retains his crown without a fight. *—Leonard Klady*

NIGHT OWL

A Franco film production. Produced, directed, written, edited by Jeffrey Arsenault. Camera (b&w), Pierre Clavel, Howard Krupa, Neil Shapiro; music, Mark Styles, Rubio Hernandez. Reviewed at AFI screening room, L.A., June 26, 1993 (In AFI/L.A. FilmFest). Running time: **77 MIN.**

Jake	James Raftery
Angel	John Leguizamo
Frances	Lisa Napoli
Zohra	Karen Wexler
Dario	David Roya
Anne	Ali Thomas
Barfly	Holly Woodlawn
Screamin' Rachel	Herself
Caroline Munro	Herself

A modern take on the familiar vampire mythology, "Night Owl" is a disappointing horror film that is neither scary nor funny. Amateurish pic will be of interest only to horror completists and avid searchers for new faces on the American indie scene.

Set in New York's East Village, Jeffrey Arsenault's tale centers on Jake (James Raftery), an attractive modern-day vampire who targets his female victims in a sleazy neighborhood bar. Film begins rather promisingly with an intense sex scene between Jake and his first victim, Zohra (Karen Wexler).

Following are other murders and a tender romance with Anne (Ali Thomas), a beautiful girl Raftery resists killing. Some tension is injected into the otherwise routine story when Angel (John Leguizamo), Zohra's brother, decides to look for his missing sister.

Arsenault fails to develop a clear structure to contain his ideas, such as the interesting link they suggest between sex and blood-thirst. Lacking a coherent story, or real characters for that matter, "Night Owl" feels like an exercise in noir style and mood.

—Emanuel Levy

CONEHEADS

A Paramount Pictures release of a Lorne Michaels production. Produced by Lorne Michaels. Executive producer, Michael Rachmil. Co-producers, Dinah Minot, Barnaby Thompson, Bonnie Turner. Directed by Steve Barron. Screenplay, Tom Davis & Dan Aykroyd and Bonnie & Terry Turner. Camera (color), Francis Kenny; editor, Paul Trejo; music, David Newman; production design, Gregg Fonseca; art direction, Bruce Miller; set decoration, Jay Hart; costume design, Conehead makeup, David B. Miller, Marie France; casting, Lora Kennedy. Reviewed at the Mann National Theatre, L.A., July 21, 1993. MPAA Rating: PG. Running time: **88 MIN.**

Beldar Conehead	Dan Aykroyd
Prymaat Conehead	Jane Curtin
Connie Conehead	Michelle Burke
Gorman Seedling	Michael McKean
Larry Farber	Jason Alexander
Lisa Farber	Lisa Jane Persky
Ronnie	Chris Farley
Eli Turnull	David Spade
Marlax	Phil Hartman
Highmaster	Dave Thomas
Otto	Sinbad
Gladys	Jan Hooks

Cones phone home. Those "Saturday Night Live" cranial wonders have arrived on the big screen, and the result is a sweet, funny, anarchic pastiche that should find broad-based popularity. The film's sly combination of the outrageous and the mundane is a surprisingly appealing screen entertainment that transcends the one-joke territory it inhabited on television.

Chief among "Coneheads' " assets is a clean storyline. For anyone who ever wondered how this aberrant family unit blended into the American topography without entering the radar sceen of Immigration and Naturalization, the answer is finally at hand. Briefly, it wasn't easy.

The script, written by Tom Davis, Dan Aykroyd, and Bonnie and Terry Turner, begins when the Remulakian scout ship of Beldar (Aykroyd) and Prymaat Conehead (Jane Curtin) runs afoul of USAF fighter planes. Aground in alien territory, the illegals accept fugitive status and employment. Beldar is, briefly, a wizard appliance repairman and a cab driver, changing jobs whenever the INS operatives close in.

When the Coneheads are finally able to contact their planet, they are told that a rescue craft should be arriving several eons later. For the nonce it's a matter of holding tight and improving upon their social-blending skills.

So, after Prymaat reveals that she is with Cone, the two settle into suburban bliss. They buy a bungalow, barbecue with the neighbors, join the country club and confront the typical travails of parents who have teenage daughters.

The unexpected strength in this foolishness is the sheer glee in watching other characters relate to the visitors from another universe as if they were the Donna Reed family.

And when that element begins to flag, the filmmakers can neatly throw in the goofy romance between daughter Connie (Michelle Burke) and local lunkhead Ronnie (Chris Farley). There's also the sporadic menace supplied by an INS official (Michael McKean) and his supplicant assistant (David Spade).

Aykroyd and Curtin have evolved their cartoonish TV-skit characters into figures whose robot-like demeanor just barely hides emotions sparked by human contact. Burke also proves herself as both a face and brow to watch.

The supporting cast is nicely laced with dozens of present and past SNL regulars. There are even uncredited turns by Jon Lovitz and Tom Arnold.

Director Steve Barron keeps the shaggy-dog yarn sprightly. His light touch, which launched the first "Ninja Turtles," never falters.

"Coneheads" seems certain to please fans, win converts and develop into a successful comic franchise. Live long and prosper! Oops, wrong galaxy.   *—Leonard Klady*

RISING SUN

A 20th Century Fox release of a Walrus & Associates Ltd. production. Produced by Peter Kaufman. Executive producer, Sean Connery. Line producer, Ian Bryce. Directed by Philip Kaufman. Screenplay, Philip Kaufman, Michael Crichton, Michael Backes, based on the novel by Crichton. Camera (Deluxe color), Michael Chapman; editors, Stephen A. Rotter, William S. Scharf; music, Toru Takemitsu; production design, Dean Tavoularis; art direction, Angelo Graham; set design, Peter Kelly, Robert Goldstein; set decoration, Gary Fettis; costume design, Jacqueline West; Connery's wardrobe, Giorgio Armani; sound (Dolby), David MacMillan; sound design, Alan Splet; special visual effects, Industrial Light & Magic; assistant director, Matthew Carlisle; casting, Donna Isaacson. Reviewed at 20th Century Fox Studios, L.A., July 7, 1993. MPAA Rating: R. Running time: **129 MIN.**

John Connor	Sean Connery
Web Smith	Wesley Snipes
Tom Graham	Harvey Keitel
Eddie Sakamura	
	Cary-Hiroyuki Tagawa
Bob Richmond	Kevin Anderson
Yoshida-san	Mako
Senator John Morton	Ray Wise
Ishihara	Stan Egi
Phillips	Stan Shaw
Jingo Asakuma	Tia Carrere
Willy "the Weasel" Wilhelm	
	Steve Buscemi
Cheryl Lynn Austin	Tatjana Patitz

Part two of the Michael Crichton summer, "Rising Sun" waters down the more contentious aspects of the controversial bestseller about Japanese influence in the United States, while remaining faithful to its mechanical plotting and superficial characterizations. Pre-sold title, star power and public curiosity should give Fox's biggest seasonal release a solid launch, although downbeat word of mouth could spread from readers disappointed by the changes wrought in the storyline.

A thriller spurred by the murder of a white party girl at the opening of a Japanese office tower in Los Angeles, Crichton's novel ruffled feathers due to its alleged Japan-bashing, its blunt discussion of Japanese mores, aggressive and exclusionary business practices and purportedly racist attitudes.

But once again, the writer can be credited with having tapped into an unusual subject of widespread interest in an enormously clever, if artistically pedestrian, way, and his observations about Japanese conglomerates and unfair trade policies obviously struck a responsive chord.

Following the cut-and-dried police procedural structure of the book, co-writer and director Philip Kaufman has soft-pedaled the critique of Japanese behavior stateside, which may reduce justification for protests against the film, but also removes much of the material's bite. What remains is a moderately interesting mystery without much cultural resonance or character depth.

Lt. Web Smith (Wesley Snipes), a liaison officer with the LAPD, is called upon to investigate the strange death of a beautiful young woman in the boardroom of the giant new Nakamoto skyscraper during the course of a swank opening-night bash.

He is advised to bring with him a man of both legendary and slightly dubious status within the force, Detective John Connor (Sean Connery), who is so expert on the Japanese that he is suspected of having been co-opted by them.

Although company executives are eager to sweep the apparent homicide under the rug so as to minimize negative publicity, the cops go about the business of pursuing their leads, which point to Japanese playboy Eddie Sakamura (Cary-Hiroyuki Tagawa), who was involved with the dead girl and with her that night.

But one can be sure that the case won't be that simple, and as the pair run down numerous other possibilities, Connor and Smith develop a "senpai-kohai" (older guide-younger student) relationship that allows the senior man to expound on Japanese ways.

Crichton's structure tiresomely flip-flops investigative scenes with interludes of the men driving through the wet night as Connor imparts his wisdom to his less experienced partner, and there is nothing Kaufman can do to make these sequences dramatic or visually inventive.

But the mystery itself begins to exercise a certain pull. A critical

August 2, 1993 (Cont.)

surveillance tape of the murder

Kaufman has soft-pedaled the critique of Japanese behavior stateside, removing much of the material's bite.

scene would seem to have been doctored to alter the identities of the people who appear to have been present, and a U.S. senator might be central to the case due to a key upcoming congressional vote concerning Nakamoto's purchase of an American company active in defense matters.

The distinct spirits behind the book and film can be defined as the difference between suspicious, almost hostile detente and liberal-minded peaceful coexistence.

While acknowledging the long tentacles of Japanese business interests, the film takes a more humanistic view of the relationship between the world's economic giants and makes at least one whopping plot change that decisively shifts the onus off the Asians.

Unfortunately, crudeness has seeped in elsewhere, notably in two scenes that are without precedent in the work of the normally sophisticated Kaufman.

One is a gratuitously exploitative scene in which Eddie eats sushi off the naked body of one woman and licks sake off the breasts of another. Other is an entirely implausible episode in which Smith recruits some of his brothers in the hood to terrorize some Japanese pursuers. Sequence is played in an embarrassingly jocular way that seems particularly inappropriate given recent black-Asian tensions in L.A.

Idea of casting a black actor as Lt. Smith, who was white in the novel, appeared likely to add an intriguing dimension to the tale, but in the event it hasn't altered matters much.

Compared to some of his earlier performances, Snipes seems lax and unfocused here, his intense physicality is given little outlet, and beyond plot function his character is given too little personality and background to fill out even a one-paragraph description.

Detective Connor was reputedly written with Connery in mind, and the brawny veteran thesp brings plenty of authoritative, fatherly appeal to the role, issuing sage aphorisms and expressing scorn, approval and, most often, bemusement at the behavior and mental

processes of Smith and others. Still, even he has been denied any real depth, such as might have been provided by the book's brief but acute monologue as to why he moved back to the States from Japan.

When working in genre territory before, the idiosyncratic Kaufman ("The Right Stuff," "Invasion of the Body Snatchers") has shown a marked tendency to debunk or subvert conventions. Playing it straight here, he brings little to the table except a taste for interesting settings and an impulse to soften the ideological roughness of Crichton's book, which might have been fine in theory but instead makes the material more bland.

A couple of car chases are executed in a perfunctory, abbreviated fashion that only points up the film's lack of significant action. Even if the director was keen on doing a thriller exercise, his creative instincts don't seem to have been fully ignited.

Supporting peformances are functionally intense, and behind-the-scenes contributions, notably Dean Tavoularis' opulent production design, are elaborate and highly professional.

—Todd McCarthy

ANOTHER STAKEOUT

A Buena Vista release of a Touchstone Pictures presentation. Produced by Jim Kouf, Cathleen Summers, Lynn Bigelow. Executive produced, directed by John Badham. Co-producer, D.J. Caruso. Screenplay, Kouf, based on his characters. Camera (Gastown color, Technicolor prints), Roy H. Wagner; editor, Frank Morris; music, Arthur B. Rubinstein; production design, Lawrence G. Paull; art direction, Richard Hudolin; set design, Richard Harrison; set decorator, Rose Marie McSherry; costume design, Stephanie Nolin; sound (Dolby stereo), Rick Patton; associate producers, Justis Greene, Kristine J. Schwarz; assistant director, David Sosna; casting, Carole Lewis. Reviewed at the Avco Cinema, Los Angeles, July 14, 1993. MPAA Rating: PG-13. Running time: **109 MIN.**

Chris Lecce	Richard Dreyfuss
Bill Reimers	Emilio Estevez
Gina Garrett	Rosie O'Donnell
Brian O'Hara	Dennis Farina
Pam O'Hara	Marcia Strassman
Lu Delano	Cathy Moriarty
Thomas Hassrick	John Rubinstein
Tony Castellano	Miguel Ferrer
Barbara Burnside	Sharon Maughan
Maria	Madeleine Stowe

A purely escapist entertainment, John Badham's "Another Stakeout," a sequel to his 1987 hit "Stakeout," is sillier and less plausible than the first movie, but it's also funnier. Adding a woman to the Richard Dreyfuss-Emilio Estevez detective team, and stressing the comedy elements instead of the suspense, pic is broad enough to have across-the-board appeal. B.O. prospects for lighthearted

summer pic are good in quick, wide playoff.

Scripter Jim Kouf's new comedy-adventure picks up Chris Lecce (Dreyfuss) and Bill Reimers (Estevez), the two Seattle police detectives, six years later. Estevez is now married and the father of two, but still wears his mustache, the subject of some Freudian humor.

Dreyfuss, who is clean-shaven, lives with Maria (Madeleine Stowe, uncredited), the woman he was assigned to observe and fell in love with the first time out. But he suffers from a commitment problem and, in what is possibly the film's broadest scene, Stowe walks out on him.

The eternally feuding cops are appointed to locate Lu Delano (Cathy Moriarty), a missing key witness in the trial of a Las Vegas mobster. This time around, their team also includes Gina Garrett (Rosie O'Donnell), an assertive, tough-talking assistant D.A., who insists on bringing along her dog.

Once the "Three Stooges" situate themselves in an elegant house in an upscale neighborhood, pretending to be one big happy family, the real movie — and frolic — begins.

Most of the humor revolves around comic exchanges between Dreyfuss as Dad, O'Donnell as Mom and Estevez as their grown son. O'Donnell actually plays the "nagging wife" role that Estevez had in the 1987 movie. As a result, the Neil Simon-like odd couple routines of Dreyfuss and Estevez are secondary here, submerged in the main tale of a chaotic, dysfunctional household.

There's one hilarious scene, a dinner party hosted by Dreyfuss and O'Donnell for their neighbors (Dennis Farina and Marcia Strassman). The fluency of wisecracks and sight gags in this sequence, which would do Blake Edwards proud, overshadows everything that follows.

Dreyfuss and O'Donnell successfully exploit their physiques (Dreyfuss is shorter and smaller than O'Donnell), with a spirited rivalry that produces rowdy jokes and raucous fun. Playing a quieter and more limited role, Estevez nonetheless holds his own in an engaging perf.

Suspense takes a back seat to comedy. When the story cuts to the suspense plot, the movie loses its momentum. The incongruity between the boisterous comedy and the standard action is problematic.

Badham's work is, as usual, polished if impersonal. He gives the film a shining gloss, greatly assisted by Roy H. Wagner's sharp lensing and Frank Morris' energetic editing.

Despite some dopey, cloying skits and a derivative plot, "Another Stakeout" is very amusing.

—Emanuel Levy

SO I MARRIED AN AXE MURDERER

TriStar Pictures presents a Fried/Woods production. Produced by Robert N. Fried and Cary Woods. Executive producer, Bernie Williams. Co-producer, Jana Sue Memel. Directed by Thomas Schlamme. Screenplay, Robbie Fox. Camera (Technicolor), Julio Macat; editors, Richard Halsey, Colleen Halsey; music, Bruce Broughton; production design, John Graysmark; art director, Michael Rizzo; set decorators, Peg Cummings, Jim Poynter; costume design, Kimberly Tillman; sound (Dolby), Nelson Stoll; casting, Mindy Marin. Reviewed at Sony Pictures, Culver City, July 16, 1993. MPAA Rating: PG-13. Running time: **93 MIN.**

Charlie and Stuart Mackenzie	Mike Myers
Harriet Michaels	Nancy Travis
Tony Giardino	Anthony LaPaglia
Rose Michaels	Amanda Plummer
May Mackenzie	Brenda Fricker
Susan	Debi Mazar
Alcatraz Guide	Phil Hartman
Commandeered Driver	Charles Grodin
Pilot	Steven Wright
Obit Writer	Michael Richards
Heed	Matt Doherty

Don't expect to see gobs of gore in TriStar's "So I Married an Axe Murderer." The comedy is a hip slice of life about the dilemma of marital commitment with just a pinch of Hitchcock providing the cutting edge. Fueled by an anarchic style and a winning cast, it looks like an appealing commercial prospect perfectly aimed at the twentysomething crowd.

The San Francisco-set yarn finds poet Charlie Mackenzie (Mike Myers) glibly fashioning a verse (supported by multimedia trappings) concerning his umpteenth failed relationship. Both his weird Scottish family and his best friend, Tony (Anthony LaPaglia), understand Charlie's fear of commitment is irrational. He's desperately in need of a strong centering influence.

So, by chance, his eye catches Harriet Michaels (Nancy Travis), a butcher at the not-too-elegant Meats of the World. Quicker than you can say "hae ya got any haggis?" they are kindred souls.

But Charlie's evasive pattern is soon in play. He begins to believe that Harriet might be an uncaught husband killer. The supposed three victims have alarming similarities to the men from her past. Is it just paranoia or is the young versifier apt to be the mystery killer's next statistic?

Robbie Fox's screenplay finds a telling modern metaphor linking society's physical and emotional perils. The emphasis is on the latter but the script never abandons hope that the unkindest cut might be lethal.

Director Thomas Schlamme milks the ambiguity for all it's worth. Despite a few narrative lulls and some humor in questionable taste, the film has an oddball spirit of invention. It aspires to the deft deadpan style of Bill Forsyth with splashes of Monty Python and Grand Guignol. It's not surprising a few ingredients fail to jell.

The look of the piece is also quite unusual, with Julio Macat's camerawork and John Graysmark's design opting for a casually surreal quality. Even the costumes by Kimberly Tillman have a comic inventiveness.

Myers does well as both Charlie and his father. His Scottish elder comes off as the more assured, but his vulnerable leading man is pretty convincing. Travis pulls off an acting sleight of hand that keeps the audience guessing.

"So I Married an Axe Murderer" should click with those looking for slightly upscale humor that's not averse to a few well-placed cheap shots. It's a delightful and unexpected surprise. —*Leonard Klady*

A CAUSE D'ELLE
(BECAUSE OF HER)
(FRENCH)

An AMLF release of a Camera Noire-TF1 Films Production-Ciby 2000 coproduction. Produced by Ciby 2000. Directed, written by Jean-Loup Hubert. Camera (color), Claude Lecomte; editor, Raymonde Guyot; production design, Thierry Flamand; costume design, Annick Francois; sound (Dolby), Bernard Aubouy, Claude Villand, Bernard Leroux. Reviewed at AMLF screening room, Paris, June 8, 1993. Running time: **110 MIN.**

Antoine	Antoine Hubert
Olivia	Olivia Munoz
Mrs. Hervy	Therese Leotard
Mr. Hervy	Jean-Francois Stevenin
Olivia's mother	Ludmila Mikael
Francoise	Romane Bohringer

"**A** Cause d'Elle" is a moving, impeccably acted account of a modest young man's maturing via chaste tutoring by a sober upper-class girl. "Le Grand Chemin" ("The Grand Highway") Jean-Loup Hubert's semiautobiographical pic perfectly captures life in the French provinces, circa 1963, and conveys nascent adolescent love and ambition with rare power.

"Professional dreamer" Antoine (beautifully portrayed by helmer's son) is almost 15 in the summer of 1963. He cares little for school and has been left back a grade, preferring to tinker in the attic with a homemade electric guitar.

Antoine's sudden interest in an aloof, well-to-do only child named Olivia (eerily self-possessed Olivia Munoz) is rewarded when he breaks his legs and studious, serious Olivia takes it upon herself to tutor him in literature. Their awkward formality, as she introduces him to the world of lofty sentiments and classical music, is convincing and affecting. Reading the classics she gives him, Antoine

realizes that he's fallen in love with his privileged young teacher.

Story is lovingly built out of the small details that mark both a communal era and individual psyches. Helmer has stated that his films examine a milieu that was once at the heart of French cinema — ordinary families trying to get by, modest protagonists hoping to carve a place in the world. —*Lisa Nesselson*

MUNICH FEST

EINE UNHEILIGE LIEBE
(AN UNHOLY LOVE)
(GERMAN-16m)

A Sentana production. Produced by Michael Verhoeven. Executive producer, Helmut Rasp (ZDF). Directed, written by Verhoeven. Camera (color, 16m), Axel de Roche; editor, Barbara Hennings; production design, Wolfgang Hundhammer; costume design, Heidi C. Wujek; sound, Johannes Rommel; assistant director, Christine Ruppert; line producer, Christine Rothe. Reviewed at Munich Film Festival, July 2, 1993. Running time: **93 MIN.**

Georg Mittenzwey	Timothy Peach
Eva Buschbaum	Heike Falkenberg
Bishop	Alexander May
Housekeeper	Barbara Gallauner
Franz	Robert Giggenbach
Monika	Elena Rublack
Mother	Luise Deschauer

After "The Nasty Girl," Michael Verhoeven disappoints with a great topical subject, fine direction and performances, but a story that dips off into pedantry and anticlimax. Meant to dramatize the love affair of a priest, pic ends up feeling more like an open letter against celibacy to the Catholic Church. Subject and Verhoeven's reputation could draw enough moviegoers for theatrical and festival release in Germany, but drab word of mouth will work against it.

Story's two biggest sins are didacticism and lack of structure. As it begins, the affair between the young priest, Georg (Timothy Peach) and a member of his flock, Eva (Heike Falkenberg), is already in full swing. Their dilemma now is over how not to get caught.

The drama has trouble climbing. When Eva discovers she is pregnant the film dissolves into a tirade against celibacy. Those interested in the characters will feel cheated.

But the film is not without merits. Small graces attest to Verhoeven's abilities. In one throat-clutching scene an elderly woman gives the priest a handmade baby jacket... but it turns out to be a covering for a hot water bottle. Other nice moments include the less than alarmed reactions to Georg's transgression on the part of his bishop and his best friend, a Jesuit. —*Eric Hansen*

THE FUGITIVE

Warner Bros. presents a Keith Barish/Arnold Kopelson production. Produced by Arnold Kopelson. Executive producer, Roy Huggins. Co-producer, Peter MacGregor-Scott. Directed by Andrew Davis. Screenplay, Jeb Stuart and David Twohy, from a story by Twohy based on characters created by Roy Huggins. Camera (Technicolor), Michael Chapman; editors, Dennis Virkler, David Finfer, Dean Goodhill, Don Brochu, Richard Nord, Dov Hoenig; music, James Newton Howard; production design, Dennis Washington; art direction, Maher Ahmad; set decoration, costume design, Aggie Guerard Rodgers; sound (Dolby), Scott D. Smith; visual effects supervisor, Bill Mesa; second unit directors, Terry Leonard, Mike Gray; casting, Amanda Mackey, Cathy Sandrich. Reviewed at the Mann Bruin, Westwood, July 29, 1993. MPAA Rating: PG-13. Running time: **127 MIN.**

Dr. Richard Kimble	Harrison Ford
U.S. Marshal Samuel Gerard	Tommy Lee Jones
Helen Kimble	Sela Ward
Cosmo Renfro	Joe Pantoliano
Dr. Charles Nichols	Jeroen Krabbe
Sykes	Andreas Katsulas
Dr. Anne Eastman	Julianne Moore
Biggs	Daniel Roebuck
Poole	L. Scott Caldwell
Newman	Tom Wood

"**T**he Fugitive" is in for one hell of a run. The movie, inspired by the vintage television series, is a giant toy-train entertainment with all stops pulled out. A consummate nail-biter that never lags, it leaves you breathless from the chase yet anxious for the next bit of mayhem or clever plot twist. Commercial prospects for the thriller are huge.

This is one film that doesn't stint on thrills and knows how to use them. It has a sympathetic lead, a stunning antagonist, state-of-the-art special effects, top-of-the-line craftsmanship and a taut screenplay that breathes life into familiar territory.

Hard to believe, but it's been more than a quarter-century since David Janssen's Dr. Richard Kimble stopped running from Barry Morse and disarmed the real murderer of his wife. The new screenplay retains the essence of Roy Huggins' (who serves as exec producer) original concept and characters. Once again Kimble (Harrison Ford) returns home to find his wife (Sela Ward) murdered. He struggles with a one-armed man lurking in his house.

As the new edition opens, he's being interrogated by the police, who have designated him the prime suspect. After a trial built on circumstantial evidence, he's found guilty and sentenced to death.

But fate steps in when prisoners on the bus transporting him to death row stage a daring escape that backfires. Kimble escapes in

the course of a show-stopper bus-train wreck that alone is worth the price of admission.

Enter Marshal Gerard (Tommy Lee Jones) and his crack investigative team. The deputy sizes up the situation and quickly sets his trap.

Director Andrew Davis manages to sustain an ongoing chase for two hours in which hunter and prey are virtually within arm's reach of each other. In lesser hands the reliance on coincidence and close calls would be ludicrous.

The opening section borrows liberally from such classics as "Rashomon" and "Last Year at Marienbad" with elliptical editing that reveals just enough information to send audience in the wrong direction.

Then there are the set pieces, beginning with the fateful crash. Davis takes us through storm drains, into the midst of Chicago's St. Patrick's Day parade, down hospital wards, on elevated trains and into the county lockup. It's a vigorous obstacle course.

As Kimble embarks on his own investigation, the guts of the story is the confrontation between wronged man and his tracker. It's another opportunity for Jones to remind us of his acting chops. Aided by a shrewdly modulated script, Jones embodies the sang-froid of a man part Mountie, part maniac who loves his job, respects his team and thrives on the hunt.

Ford, in contrast, has the non showy role. He portrays Kimble with such conviction that the idea that he is succeeding a small-screen predecessor is forgotten. The large supporting cast works like a beautifully oiled machine.

In addition to the handsome ef-

> **Director Davis manages to sustain a chase for two hours in which hunter and prey are within arm's reach of each other.**

fects work from Introvision, special note is due James Newton Howard's score, which slips in just enough hints of the TV theme to bridge the years. The film also employs some of the most imaginative sound mixing in recent years.

This screen version of "The Fugitive" had a fractious history, and the cool heads who doubted its box office potency are probably going mad for a way to create a sequel. —*Leonard Klady*

August 9, 1993 (Cont.)

ROBIN HOOD: MEN IN TIGHTS

A 20th Century Fox release of a Brooksfilms production in association with Gaumont. Produced by Mel Brooks. Executive producer, Peter Schindler. Directed by Brooks. Screenplay, Brooks, J. David Shapiro and Evan Chandler, from a story by Shapiro and Chandler. Camera (Deluxe), Michael D. O'Shea; editor, Stephen Rivkin; music, Hummie Mann; production design, Roy Forge Smith; art direction, Stephen Myles Berger; set decoration, Ronald Reiss; costume design, Dodie Shepard; sound (Dolby), Jeff Wexler, Don Coufal, Gary Holland; sword/fight coordinator, Victor Paul; archery master, Jack Verbois; casting, Lindsay Chag, Bill Shepard. Reviewed at the Mann Plaza, Westwood, Calif., July 16, 1993. MPAA Rating: PG-13. Running time: **102 MIN.**

Robin Hood	Cary Elwes
Prince John	Richard Lewis
Sheriff of Rottingham	Roger Rees
Maid Marian	Amy Yasbeck
Ahchoo	David Chappelle
Blinkin	Mark Blankfield
Latrine	Tracey Ullman
Little John	Eric Allan Kramer
Broomhilde	Megan Cavanagh
Rabbi Tuckman	Mel Brooks
Don Giovanni	Dom DeLuise
Abbot	Dick Van Patten
Will Scarlet O'Hara	Matthew Porretta
Asneeze	Isaac Hayes
Hangman	Robert Ridgely
King Richard	Patrick Stewart

Robin Hood: Men in Tights" marks a return to the wild, anarchic scatological comedies that made Mel Brooks a marquee name around the world. It is a film for both his diehard fans and a new generation who know Mad Mel only from legend. Virtually a primer of all the familiar visual and literal jokes in his bag of tricks, the film is a paean to the obvious that is more delight than retread. It should sail through the summer on steady business aimed at the funny bone like no other film in the marketplace.

Brooks' fascination with the denizens of Sherwood Forest is honest if hard to figure. In 1975 he covered the territory in the television series "When Things Were Rotten." Here he has managed to mangle the legend so that it essentially resembles his biggest hit, "Blazing Saddles." Even purists will find it difficult not to doff their hats in much the same way respect was accorded Dr. Frankenstein for his warped creation.

For the somnambulists in the crowd, the tale involves nobleman Robin of Loxley (Cary Elwes), who ventures with King Richard to the Crusades. He escapes and returns to England, where he finds the kingdom in disarray in the hands of Prince John (Richard Lewis) and his evil henchman, renamed here the Sheriff of Rottingham (Roger Rees).

Adopting outlaw ways, Robin enlists the good country folk to join his cause and rid the kingdom of the scourge. He also finds romance with Maid Marian (Amy Yasbeck).

Brooks takes considerable liberties with the traditional story. Friar Tuck has been reinvented for Brooks to play as Rabbi Tuckman, and the characters include a black foreign-exchange student and plenty of anachronistic modern references.

The manic ensemble is grounded by Elwes' virtually straight-faced interpretation of Robin with a glib assuredness that hits the target dead center.

Rather slier is Yasbeck's Marian, who gets great comic effect from being the girl too good to be true.

The supporting cast features many members of Brooks' stock company. Best of all are the comic snivelings of Rees' sheriff and the haggish Latrine as embodied by Tracey Ullman.

Taste, never a factor to be considered seriously in the filmmaker's work, is appropriately questionable. There is tremendous glee to be derived from the spontaneity of his outrageous antics. It's blunted only when he steals shamelessly from past successes.

One size of these "Tights" won't fit all, but Brooks remains a talent whose audience is amazingly elastic.
—*Leonard Klady*

JOSH AND S.A.M.

A Columbia Pictures release of a Castle Rock Entertainment in association with New Line Cinema presents a City Lights Films production. Produced by Martin Brest. Executive producer, Arne Schmidt. Co-producers, Alex Gartner, Frank Deese. Directed by Billy Weber. Screenplay by Deese. Camera (Technicolor); Don Burgess; editor, Chris Lebenzon; music, Thomas Newman; production design, Marcia Hinds-Johnson; art direction, Bo Johnson; set decoration, Jan Bergstrom; costume design, Jill Ohanneson; sound, Douglas Axtell; casting, Carrie Frazier, Shani Ginsberg. Reviewed at the AMC Century 14, L.A., July 14, 1993. MPAA Rating: PG-13. Running time: **98 MIN.**

Josh	Jacob Tierney
Sam	Noah Fleiss
Alison	Martha Plimpton
Thom Whitney	Stephen Tobolowsky
Caroline	Joan Allen
Derek Baxter	Chris Penn
Pizza Man	Maury Chaykin
Jean-Pierre	Ronald Guttman
Salon Manager	Udo Kier
Curtis	Sean Baca
Leon	Jake Gyllenhaal
Ellen	Anne Lange

A pastiche of contemporary youth traumas and on-the-road movies, "Josh and S.A.M" rambles along good-naturedly if aimlessly. It twists and turns along the route, too often utilizing gimmickry and jettisoning its reality base. By the time it reaches its destination, however, the film has scored enough good points for viewers to forgive much of its dopiness and misguided emphasis on the cute and corny.

One senses that writer Frank Deese loved the challenge of taking a stock situation and spinning it out to its illogical conclusion. The basic germ unquestionably infected the film's producers and first-time helmer Billy Weber. Yet there's the overriding feeling that, apart from possibly its creator, no one quite got the point of the tale.

Josh (Jacob Tierney) and Sam (Noah Fleiss) are brothers, 12 and 7 years old, respectively. They live with their mother (Joan Allen), a woman who has been largely focused on finding a new husband.

The elder son has learned to use a quick wit and native intelligence to mask his crippling insecurity. Sam is even less fortunate. He is a despondent child prone to bouts of silence and violence.

When they are shipped off to Florida to spend the summer with their dad (Stephen Tobolowsky) and his new family, matters slowly build to a boil. Deeply troubled about his ultimate fate, Josh concocts, with the help of cleverly fabricated evidence, a wild scenario to enlist his brother to action. He tells Sam that he is a "Strategically Altered Mutant" — the creation of a government program. Soon his genetically designed super powers will be utilized in a secret war about to begin in Africa.

It is a rather slim device to get the youngsters on the road.

The foundation continues to wobble as Josh invents a wild story at a high school reunion he's managed to crash that convinces one attendee (Chris Penn) he's Josh's father. Credulity is strained to the limit when they take the man to Josh's supposed grandparents' home and accidentally knock him unconscious, believing he has been killed. So, they do the obvious thing. They steal his car and head for Canada, hoping to find the fictional Liberty Maid — according to Josh, the sole person capable of protecting Sam from being sent to the impending war.

Placing an inordinate emphasis on coincidence stalls the endeavor before it can shift into top gear.

But it begins to redeem itself en route. This is largely accomplished with the introduction of Alison (Martha Plimpton), a hitchhiker who Sam believes is the so-called Liberty Maid. It is a role she willingly adopts to reach her destination.

The preposterous underpinnings give way to some real emotions. The interdependence of the trio is both desperate and touching. Their self-serving manipulations ultimately reveal an ingrained humanity that allows the story's larger concerns to surface in powerful ways. The family unit in this bizarre configuration proves dramatically potent.

Plimpton's finely etched performance is an enormous asset. Weber doesn't quite know how to incorporate Deese's black comic vision into the script's more sober concerns.

He's also at sea with his neophyte actors but glides past this difficulty with a technical facility for pacing and a keen ability to establish a sense of place.

As a commercial vehicle, "Josh and S.A.M." suffers by not clearly defining itself. A tad too highbrow to be considered a kids' picture, it lacks a hip metaphor that might appeal to a more sophisticated crowd. Finally, it emerges as a curiosity that's fascinating to watch more for its ambition than for the pleasure of being drawn into its off-kilter consciousness.
—*Leonard Klady*

YOUNGER AND YOUNGER

A Kushner-Locke presentation of a Pelemele Film/BR/Duckster/Leora production. Produced by Percy Adlon, Eleonore Adlon, Aziz Ojjeh. Executive producers, Dietrich V. Watzdorf, Jonathan Gans. Directed by Percy Adlon. Screenplay, Percy Adlon, Felix O. Adlon. Camera (color), Bernd Heinl; editor, Suzanne Fenn; music, Hans Zimmer, Bob Telson; production design, Steven Legler; art direction, Nancy Roberts; set decoration, Barbara Cassel; costume design, Sharen Davis; sound, Jose Araujo; line producer, Beverly J. Graf; associate producer, Christopher Webster; choreographer, Patsy Swayze; SFX makeup, Todd Masters; casting, Jerold Franks. Reviewed at Cannes Film Festival (market section), May 15, 1993. Running time: **99 MIN.**

Jonathan Younger	Donald Sutherland
Penelope	Lolita Davidovich
Winston Younger	Brendan Fraser
Melodie	Julie Delpy
ZigZag Lilian	Sally Kellerman
Frances	Linda Hunt

The iconoclastic oeuvre of Percy Adlon expands by another unusual human comedy with "Younger and Younger." Superficially a family drama of an errant, philandering father, the yarn spins out from its simple premise into fantasy, music, black comedy and innumerable offbeat digressions. It's a mad, wild souffle served up by actors at the top of their form. Too quirky for the mainstream, it needs a carefully considered campaign to ensure strong specialized results.

While the film isn't quite a bull's eye, it is chockablock with intriguing elements and echoes of Adlon's earlier "Bagdad Cafe." His latest American microcosm is set in a storage facility where the forgotten and marginal mingle with the hoi polloi.

Jonathan Younger (Donald Sutherland) is the titular overseer of the activity. Comporting himself in the manner of some exiled European royal, he greets both regulars and new accounts as if they were entering some grand estate. He's expert at providing the illusion that the dark cubicles are the key attractions of an amusement park. He is all artifice. The real work falls upon his dowdy, badly neglected wife, Penelope (Lolita Davidovich). She abides his transgressions, his indolence and selfishness, because she truly holds the reins.

Jonathan seems to care only about their son, Winston (Brendan Fraser), who is studying economics in England. He dreams of Winston's graduation and subsequent return to carry on the family business.

Not one for conventional narrative, Adlon, who co-wrote the script with his son Felix, dots the story with numerous subplots and colorful characters. Sally Kellerman and Julie Delpy pop up as a mother and daughter who are the subject of media scrutiny when Kellerman's husband dies under curious circumstances.

There is also considerable attention given a pipe organ located in the bowels of the establishment, rabbits and other flights of fancy.

Though free-flowing in the way he swings from drama into, for instance, a musical production, Adlon eschews the culty and kitschy. His unique method of tackling everyday life has been both the greatest strength and the most problematic aspect of his commercial appeal.

The helmer consistently elicits fine performances and creates distinctive looks for his films. "Younger and Younger" is no exception.

—Leonard Klady

THE SECRET GARDEN

A Warner Bros. release of an American Zoetrope production. Produced by Fred Fuchs, Fred Roos, Tom Luddy. Executive producer, Francis Ford Coppola. Directed by Agnieszka Holland. Screenplay, Caroline Thompson, based on the book by Frances Hodgson Burnett. Camera (Technicolor), Roger Deakins; editor, Isabelle Lorente; music, Zbigniew Preisner; production design, Stuart Craig; supervising art director, John King; art direction, Peter Russell; set decoration, Stephanie McMillan; costume design, Marit Allen; sound (Dolby), Drew Kunin; associate producer, Thompson; assistant director, David Brown; additional camera, Jerzy Zielinski, Dick Pope; casting, Karen Lindsay-Stewart. Reviewed at Warner Bros. screening room, Burbank, Aug. 4, 1993. MPAA Rating: G. Running time: **101 MIN.**

Mary Lennox	Kate Maberly
Colin Craven	Heydon Prowse
Dickon	Andrew Knott
Mrs. Medlock	Maggie Smith
Martha	Laura Crossley
Lord Craven	John Lynch
Ben Weatherstaff	Walter Sparrow
Mary's Mother/Lilias Craven	Irene Jacob

As the company did with "The Black Stallion" 14 years ago, American Zoetrope has produced another exquisite children's classic in "The Secret Garden." Executed to near perfection in all artistic departments, this superior adaptation of the perennial favorite novel will find its core public among girls but should prove satisfying enough to a range of audiences to make it a solid performer for Warner Bros.' Family Entertainment banner.

Although she has worked in English before, this marks a significant stride into the mainstream for Polish-born director Agnieszka Holland after the acclaim for her most recent pics, "Europa, Europa" and "Olivier, Olivier." But there is no hint of compromise or pandering to a wide market, as the film betrays a rigorous, sophisticated sensibility that will encourage viewers to meet it on its own level.

Best known of late as a Broadway musical, "The Secret Garden" has been a success ever since English-American author Frances Hodgson Burnett wrote it in 1911. A solid, darkly Gothic, psychologically slanted film version starring Margaret O'Brien was made by MGM in 1949, and the BBC and Hallmark Hall of Fame each produced telefilms of the metaphorical fantasy.

Like that other undying favorite "The Wizard of Oz," this story carries the central theme that the answers to life's mysteries and possibilities lie in your own back yard. But "The Secret Garden" trades in the private world of children, their early experiences with profound emotions and their battles with contrary, often irrational adults.

An exotic title sequence conjures up the unhappy childhood of 10-year-old Mary Lennox (Kate Maberly) in British colonial India. When her parents are killed in an earthquake, the orphan is sent to live in the gloomy, 100-room Yorkshire mansion of her reclusive uncle, Lord Craven (John Lynch).

A shell of a man since the death of his beloved wife a decade before, Craven ignores both Mary and his crippled son, Colin (Heydon Prowse), whose bedridden life is tyrannically run by the estate's housekeeper, Mrs. Medlock (Maggie Smith).

Rude and disagreeable at first, Mary, who laments that "I've never had any friends," soon becomes intrigued by the existence on the grounds of a secret garden that has supposedly never been entered since Lady Craven's death.

In league with down-to-earth local boy Dickon (Andrew Knott), Mary begins nurturing the unkempt garden, just as she begins an edgy, illicit friendship with Colin.

Initially a bossy crybaby of the first order, Colin begins to be convinced that he won't necessarily become a hunchback like his father and die young, and is eventually taken on his first exhilarating outing by Mary and Dickon.

Although the wrath of Mrs. Medlock continues to threaten the children, Colin grows to health in the embrace of the magical garden, which teems with all manner of colorful life, leading to a heartwarming reconciliation with his father and the liberation of the inner spirits of all concerned.

There is nary a misstep along the way in telling this potentially precious but intelligent tale.

Screenwriter Caroline Thompson ("Edward Scissorhands," "The Addams Family," "Homeward Bound") has structured the piece impeccably and has also fashioned particularly memorable dialogue scenes between Mary and Colin, conveying the impression of children having adult-style arguments on serious issues for the first time. These kids grow up before one's eyes.

This is also a tribute, of course, to Holland and her youthful players. Using all British thesps of proper age (unlike the earlier Hollywood version, which seemed cast too old), the director displays an unerring instinct for obtaining truthful performances from child actors, who are playing abandoned children left to their own devices to learn and grow up.

As Mary, Maberly has a beauty and direct gaze that grow on the viewer as the film progresses, and proves absolutely up to the demand of carrying the picture.

Unlike the quite healthy-looking Dean Stockwell in the earlier film, little Prowse (who had never acted before) has an ashen, haunted quality as Colin that is quite affecting, and this makes his slow rise from pathetic confinement all the more involving.

Knott conveys earthy, easygoing appeal as Dickon, while Laura Crossley is winning as Mary's teenage servant girl.

Maggie Smith gets off to a great start as Mrs. Medlock, gnawing chicken legs while transporting Mary across the forbidding moors, and brilliantly sustains the character of an all-seeing, dictatorial witch who will no doubt terrify younger viewers.

This is the most graceful, elegant and assured filmmaking that Holland has ever done, and the same adjectives can be applied to every physical aspect of the British-lensed production.

Ace production designer Stuart Craig has made the secret garden as densely verdant and glorious as he has the Misselthwaite mansion frigid and haunted.

Cinematographer Roger Deakins has possibly topped his considerable previous work with his richly atmospheric lighting and compositions here, and Isabelle Lorente's editing gives the story a subtle urgency.

Zbigniew Preisner's score is timelessly melodic and unsentimentally expands the emotional range of the film. Special nods should also be made in the direction of the animal handlers, whose work with a diverse range of creatures was extensive, and to the film's special effects experts.

During an era of many pointless remakes, this is one that proves it's worth every minute of its running time.

—Todd McCarthy

MANHATTAN MURDER MYSTERY

A TriStar release of a Jack Rollins and Charles H. Joffe production. Produced by Robert Greenhut. Executive producers, Rollins, Joffe. Co-producers, Helen Robin, Joseph Hartwick. Directed by Woody Allen. Screenplay, Allen, Marshall Brickman. Camera (DuArt color; Technicolor prints), Carlo Di Palma; editor, Susan E. Morse; production design, Santo Loquasto; art direction, Speed Hopkins; set decoration, Susan Bode; costume design, Jeffrey Kurland; sound (Dolby), James Sabat; associate producer-assistant director, Thomas Reilly; casting, Juliet Taylor. Reviewed at TriStar screening room, Culver City, Aug. 3, 1993. MPAA Rating: PG. Running time: **105 MIN.**

Ted	Alan Alda
Larry Lipton	Woody Allen
Marcia Fox	Anjelica Huston
Carol Lipton	Diane Keaton
Paul House	Jerry Adler
Marilyn	Joy Behar
Sy	Ron Rifkin
Lillian House	Lynn Cohen
Helen Moss	Melanie Norris

August 16, 1993 (Cont.)

Woody Allen once described himself as "thin but fun," and the same could be said for his latest effort, "Manhattan Murder Mystery." Light, insubstantial and utterly devoid of the heavier themes Allen has grappled with in most of his recent outings, this confection keeps the chuckles coming and is mainstream enough in sensibility to be a modest success. The commercial wild card, of course, remains whether the public, and even longtime Allen fans, have turned off the idea of seeing his films in the wake of recent events. In an unprecedented move for one of his pictures, TriStar held nationwide sneaks over the weekend in advance of the Aug. 18 opening.

Aside from his "Oedipus Wrecks" episode from "New York Stories," this represents Allen's first flat-out comedy in nearly a decade. In its feather-weight frivolity and disconnection from any recognizable reality, it resembles nothing so much as the goofy backstage murder mellers of the 1930s, complete with vanishing corpses, high society settings, bickering leads and self-consciously theatrical denouement.

Writing with Marshall Brickman for the first time since the great duo of "Annie Hall" and "Manhattan," Allen opens with an echo of the latter film as he backdrops the glittering Gotham skyline with Bobby Short's rousing rendition of Cole Porter's "I Happen to Like New York."

Allen and Diane Keaton play Larry and Carol Lipton, a long-married pair whose next-door neighbors are the chatty middle-aged couple Paul and Lillian House (Jerry Adler and Lynn Cohen). Suddenly, Lillian drops dead of a heart attack, but Carol is suspicious of how cheerful Paul seems afterward and, having just seen "Double Indemnity," becomes obsessed with the idea that he actually murdered his wife.

Snooping around in Paul's apartment, Carol finds evidence to support her suspicions. When Mrs. House turns up dead again in another location, things become stranger still, and it is up to fiction writer Marcia Fox (Anjelica Huston) to explain it all to the audience.

A great many of the scenes are devoted to Carol spinning her wild theories about what actually happened and pursuing her hunches, while her husband grudgingly accompanies her, complaining all the while that she's crazy.

Carol finds a more sympathetic ear in bachelor writer friend Ted (Alan Alda in the old Tony Roberts part), who suspects she may not be happy with Larry and gently comes on to her. For his part, Larry deflects the interest of the sex-minded Marcia and sets Ted up with her.

"Manhattan Murder Mystery" is as neurotic a farce as can be imagined, and Allen and Brickman have amusingly festooned the plot with an array of topical and psychological concerns. The heart attack that sets the story in motion, for example, unleashes a flood of jokes about diet, exercise and cholesterol, and Allen's typical phobias are on display as prominently as ever.

In fact, the one-note nagging of Allen's character becomes grating, and while the film doesn't invite deep scrutiny of the characters, the apparent sexlessness of the Liptons' marriage and their negligible, unbelievable relationship with their college-age son do open up some dead-end avenues of inquiry.

Stylistically, Allen and lenser Carlo Di Palma persist here in the overboard hand-held, verite look they initiated on "Husbands And Wives," and it seems more inappropriate and pointless this time out.

Diane Keaton nicely handles her sometimes buffoonish central comedic role, but few strenuous demands are placed on the rest of the agreeable cast. Almost continuously humorous to varying degrees, pic can be forgotten as easily as it can be digested. —*Todd McCarthy*

THE METEOR MAN

An MGM release of a Tinsel Townsend production. Produced by Loretha C. Jones. Directed, written by Robert Townsend. Camera (Deluxe color), John A. Alonzo; editors, Adam Bernardi, Richard Candib, Andrew London, Pam Wise; music, Cliff Eidelman; production design, Toby Corbett; art direction, Greg Papalia; set design, William J. Newmon II, Stephanie J. Gordon; set decoration, Kathryn Peters; costume design, Ruth Carter; visual effects supervisor, Bruce Nicholson; special visual effects, Industrial Light & Magic; sound (Dolby), Mark Weingarten; assistant directors, Richard A. Wells, Joseph Ray; casting, Eileen Mack Knight. Reviewed at the AMC Century 14, L.A., July 21, 1993. MPAA Rating: PG. Running time: **99 MIN.**

Jefferson Reed	Robert Townsend
Mrs. Reed	Marla Gibbs
Michael	Eddie Griffin
Mr. Reed	Robert Guillaume
Mr. Moses	James Earl Jones
Simon	Roy Fegan
Mrs. Harris	Cynthia Belgrave
Mrs. Walker	Marilyn Coleman
Goldilocks	Don Cheadle
Uzi	Bobby McGee
Marvin	Bill Cosby
Pirate	Big Daddy Kane
Byers	Frank Gorshin
Malik	Sinbad
Mrs. Laws	Nancy Wilson
Jamison	Luther Vandross
Jr. Lords	Another Bad Creation

There's a universe that divides actor-director-writer Robert Townsend's debut, "Hollywood Shuffle," and his current "The Meteor Man." The seemingly hip, irreverent and street-savvy talent has evolved into a kinder, gentler, rather too polite storyteller who is oddly out of step with the times. This allegorical fantasy is a cute skit expanded out of all proportion for the big screen.

The fairy tale nature of "The Meteor Man" flies in the face of contemporary sensibilities, particularly those of a young, niche audience. With a cast full of familiar television names, it feels dangerously like sitcom. Commercial theatrical prospects are decidedly brief and slim, with foreign prospects providing an even less rosy picture.

Set in Washington, D.C., yarn centers on schoolteacher and aspiring musician Jefferson Reed (Townsend). An advocate of nonviolence and flight in the face of danger, he is only marginally more timid than his family and neighbors.

One evening Jeff runs afoul of the peroxided Golden Lords and just barely escapes their clutches. Emerging from his hiding place, he walks into the path of a falling meteor fragment, and when he awakes realizes that he's gained super powers. He's enlisted into service to clean up the streets in a uniform lovingly sewn by his mother.

The idea of a street-smart though awkward superhuman crime fighter ought to have been a rich mine from which to excavate laughs. But Townsend seems strangely out of place in this milieu. His characters are stereotypes culled from two decades of television viewing.

"The Meteor Man" is a comedy with a true paucity of humor. It is neither social satire or broad farce, but a sweet, earnest effort that would pass muster as a citizenship class essay.

Given access to higher-profile talent, Townsend shows little maturation as a filmmaker. Both his use of actors and his staging of action are flat and mundane. It is far too great a stumbling block to overcome with charm, a smile and good intentions. "The Meteor Man" may be coming to a theater near you, but it will be streaking right on pretty darn quick. —*Leonard Klady*

SEARCHING FOR BOBBY FISCHER

A Paramount Pictures release of a Scott Rudin/Mirage production. Produced by Rudin, William Horberg. Executive producer, Sydney Pollack. Coproducer, David Wisnievitz. Directed by Steven Zaillian. Screenplay, Zaillian, based upon the book by Fred Waitzkin. Camera (DeLuxe prints), Conrad L. Hall; editor, Wayne Wahrman; music, James Horner; production design, David Gropman; art direction, Gregory P. Keen; set decoration, Steve Shewchuk; costume design, Julie Weiss; sound (Dolby), David Lee; assistant directors, Tony Gittelson, Burtt Harris; casting, Avy Kaufman. Reviewed at the Mann Regent Theatre, L.A., July 30, 1993. MPAA Rating: PG. Running time: **110 MIN.**

Fred Waitzkin	Joe Mantegna
Josh Waitzkin	Max Pomeranc
Bonnie Waitzkin	Joan Allen
Bruce Pandolfini	Ben Kingsley
Vinnie	Laurence Fishburne
Jonathan Poe	Michael Nirenberg
Poe's Teacher	Robert Stephens
Kalev	David Paymer

Earnest and well-acted, Steven Zaillian's directorial debut explores the price of being a child prodigy while seeking to bring excitement to chess — becoming a kind of cerebral "The Karate Kid." It's a tall order, and while the film makes lots of good moves, that mild schizophrenia, its subject matter could check box office performance, heralding a relatively quick jump to its most logical playing field, homevideo.

The movie does possess some of the softer, old-fashioned values that have struck a chord of late, as evidenced by "Sleepless in Seattle." On the flip side, the pic will have to overcome being labeled "that chess movie" and does a poor job of making the game itself accessible.

Based on a true story written by the father depicted in the film, "Searching for Bobby Fischer" focuses on Josh Waitzkin (Max Pomeranc), a relatively normal 7-year-old who, his parents discover, possesses a stunning aptitude for chess. Max starts honing that talent, playing a sped-up form of the game known as "blitz" with street hustlers. Soon after, his father, Fred (Joe Mantegna), takes him to a chess coach (Ben Kingsley) who says that Josh could well be the second coming of Bobby Fischer, the legendary former chess champ.

"Searching" is at its best when exploring the tension between wanting to develop a child's abilities and allowing him to remain a child.

Unfortunately, as scripter, Zaillian (who wrote "Awakenings") also feels compelled to throw in "Karate Kid"-type flourishes, a rather stale genre to begin with that doesn't lend itself all that well to chess.

The narrative is ruthlessly edited, jumping around in a manner that skips needed exposition and abandons characters (Laurence Fishburne's role as a "blitz" master, in particular, feels truncated).

Zaillian does a better job with his actors. Mantegna adds to his portfolio with a fine, subdued performance as the suddenly driven father, while Joan Allen is strong as the protective mom.

Newcomer Pomeranc is wonderfully real and wide-eyed as Josh, with a raspy voice and slight lisp recalling Linus from the "Peanuts" cartoons. One of the movie's best devices involves the use of grainy, documentary-style snippets of Fischer, narrated by Josh and backed by James Horner's characteristically uplifting score.

Technical players attack the board with gusto, from the deft incorporation of the Fischer footage to editor Wayne Wahrman and cinematographer Conrad L. Hall's near-impossible challenge to try to make a chess match move like an NBA playoff game. —*Brian Lowry*

August 16, 1993 (Cont.)

HEART AND SOULS

Universal Pictures presents an Alphaville/Stampede Entertainment production. Produced by Nancy Roberts, Sean Daniel. Executive producers, Cari-Esta Albert, James Jacks. Co-producers, Erik Hansen, Gregory Hansen. Directed by Ron Underwood. Screenplay and screen story by Brent Maddock & S.S. Wilson and Gregory and Erik Hansen. Camera (Deluxe), Michael Watkins; editor, O. Nicholas Brown; music, Marc Shaiman; production design, John Muto; art direction, Dan Webster; set decoration, Anne Ahrens; costume design, Jean-Pierre Dorleac; sound (Dolby), Richard Bryce Goodman; visual effects producer, Julia Gibson; casting, Dixie Capp. Reviewed at the AMC 14, Century City, July 31, 1993. MPAA Rating: PG-13. Running time: **104 MIN.**

Thomas Reilly	Robert Downey Jr.
Harrison Winslow	Charles Grodin
Penny Washington	Alfre Woodard
Julia	Kyra Sedgwick
Milo Peck	Tom Sizemore
Hal	David Paymer
Anne	Elisabeth Shue
Young Thomas	Eric Lloyd
Mr. Reilly	Bill Calvert
Mrs. Reilly	Lisa Lucas
Max Marco	Richard Portnow

It may be a tad premature for the sap to be flowing in Maine, but it's flooding through the lightweight comedy "Heart and Souls." Recalling such vintage fantasy fare as "Topper" and "Here Comes Mr. Jordan," the current incarnation lacks an all-important element from the past — namely, charm. While it may garner initial steam from its enchanting cast, the film's ongoing prospects amount to little more than vapor.

The elaborate setup begins in San Francisco circa 1959, when a bus carrying four passengers veers off an overpass to avoid colliding with a car driven by a couple on their way to the hospital to have their first child. The driver and passengers of the urban transport are killed, but the passengers are divinely assigned to guard the welfare of the boy born to the couple.

The task becomes more problematic when the boy (Thomas Reilly) enters school, and it's assumed his discussions with invisible friends mask an emotional problem. So the angels decide to disappear.

The filmmakers might have been well advised to end their yarn here.

Instead, they speed to the present, where young Tom has evolved into a yuppie-scum bankruptcy banker played by Robert Downey Jr. The invisible cadre feel just awful about what he has become. At about the same time, the heavenly bus driver — steering his way though a hole in the plot you can, well, drive a bus through — returns to take them onward.

It turns out someone at the front office was sleeping, and though a little late, the driver's back to give the four a chance to redeem their past through their temporal host.

This is delicate material that requires a considerably lighter hand than the one wielded by director Ron Underwood. Moreover, co-writers S.S. Wilson and Brent Maddock, who teamed with Erik and Gregory Hansen, prove on the basis of this and their earlier "*batteries not included" that they are not masters of whimsy.

That the effort is at all watchable is a tribute largely to its performers. The angels embodied by Charles Grodin, Alfre Woodard, Kyra Sedgwick and Tom Sizemore breathe credibility into the tale. Downey is an amazingly pliant performer, and Elisabeth Shue is radiant if underused. Collectively they deserve medals for retaining their dignity in extreme circumstances.

—Leonard Klady

MY BOYFRIEND'S BACK

A Buena Vista release of a Touchstone Pictures presentation. Produced by Sean S. Cunningham. Directed by Bob Balaban. Screenplay, Dean Lorey. Camera (DeLuxe color, Technicolor prints), Mac Ahlberg; editor, Michael Jablow; music, Harry Manfredini; production design, Michael Hanan; art direction, Charles Lagola; set design, John A. Frick, Jonathan Short; costume design, Kimberly Tillman; sound (Dolby), Darrell Henke; makeup, Kimberly Greene; associate producer, Deborah Hayn-Cass; assistant director, Donald P.H. Eaton; casting, Julie Hughes, Harry Moss. Reviewed at General Cinema's Hollywood Galaxy, Aug. 4, 1993. MPAA Rating: PG-13. Running time: **84 MIN.**

Johnny	Andrew Lowery
Missy	Traci Lind
Eddie	Danny Zorn
Mr. Dingle	Edward Herrmann
Mrs. Dingle	Mary Beth Hurt
Dr. Bronson	Austin Pendleton
Sheriff McCloud	Jay O. Sanders
Big Chuck	Paul Dooley
Murray	Bob Dishy
Maggie	Cloris Leachman
Judge in Heaven	Paxton Whitehead
Buck Van Patten	Matthew Fox

Touchstone Pictures attains the nadir of this summer season (and probably the entire year) with Bob Balaban's "My Boyfriend's Back," an idiotic offbeat comedy about an obsessive teenage love. Lacking any redeeming quality, it's a matter of days before this tasteless pic is buried without a trace in the sands of Hollywood.

"My Boyfriend's Back" is so moonbeam-silly and so embarrassingly offensive — to the ear and to the eye — that it's hardly worth talking about. Still, for the record: Scripter Dean Lorey uses the concept of a fairy tale — a kind of reworking of "Beauty and the Beast" — setting his quirky fantasy in a white picket-fenced small town meant to look like a Norman Rockwell painting with a touch of David Lynch.

Missy (Traci Lind), the most attractive and desirable girl of her class has a b.f. (Matthew Fox), but is obsessively pursued by Johnny Din-

gle (Andrew Lowery), a shy daydreaming classmate whose ultimate desire is to take her to the prom. To prove his sacrificial love and heroic valiance, Lowery stages a robbery at the convenience store where Lind is working so he can save her life. But the ill-conceived caper backfires and he loses his life. The relentless Lowery then comes back from the dead — as a frail and decaying zombie.

Napkin-thin pic starts falling apart in the first reel, as soon as Lowery is buried, and then keeps unraveling in an unremitting stream of false notes, which includes body parts falling off, cannibalism, vampirism and lynching.

Balaban's direction repeats ideas and jokes more effectively used in his 1989 "Parents," which was also thin-plotted but at least managed a level of black humor and an interesting visual style — elements that are totally missing from his new pic.

The real mystery is how helmer Balaban managed to recruit his talented ensemble of actors. Pic is a wasteland for everyone.

Attention must be paid when a picture is as aggressively horrible as "My Boyfriend's Back," yet more proof that just because an idea is outrageously audacious doesn't necessarily mean it's good — or funny.

—Emanuel Levy

BOYS' SHORTS: THE NEW QUEER CINEMA

Frameline presents six short films: "Resonance," directed by Stephen Cummins, written by Cummins and Simon Hunt; "R.S.V.P.," directed, written by Laurie Lynd; "Anthem," directed by Marlon Riggs; "Relax," directed, written by Christopher Newby; "Billy Turner's Secret," directed, written by Michael Mayson; and "The Dead Boys' Club," directed, written by Mark Christopher. Reviewed at the Village East Cinemas, New York, Aug. 2, 1993. No MPAA rating. Running time: **119 MIN.**

If diversity is the point behind the selection of the six short films grouped under the title "Boys' Shorts: The New Queer Cinema," consider the point taken. Each entry in this sextet of gay-themed shorts has done the festival circuit. Only half of the six films (at most) offer much more than the promise of more fully developed works. Still, all have a clear take on their chosen subject matter that should entice arthouse audiences when the bill makes its way to other cities this fall.

First on the roster is Australian Stephen Cummins' "Resonance," the most experimental (and least satisfying) of the lot. An impressionistic black-and-white film that examines, in a largely symbolic and imagistic style, the aftermath of a

gay-bashing incident, "Resonance" is an intellectual exercise that, despite its title, fails on a visceral level. Even its most arresting sequence — a choreographed boxing match that blurs the line between violence and eroticism, sport and dance — is more film-school obvious than resonant.

By contrast, Laurie Lynd's "R.S.V.P." discovers its considerable poignance in simplicity. This Canadian entry has a startlingly somber premise: Arriving home from the funeral of his AIDS-stricken lover, a man hears on a classical radio station the song his lover requested before dying. As the beautiful "Le Spectre de la Rose" is performed by Jessye Norman, Lynd's austere camera captures the various reactions of the deceased man's friends and family.

"R.S.V.P.," with very little dialogue included in its 23 minutes, contains some of the most haunting images of the entire program: A sister sobbing alone in her kitchen; the pained reaction of a young student as she reads her teacher's obit that other students have scrawled with an anti-gay epithet.

Marlon Riggs, whose "Tongues Untied" caused a stir when PBS planned an airing a couple of seasons back, contributes "Anthem," a nine-minute hip-hop hodgepodge of poetry, percussion and African-American homoerotic imagery spliced together in quick-cut MTV fashion. This is familiar terrain for Riggs, and not as affecting or interesting as his more famous work.

"Relax," a 25-minute film by London's Christopher Newby, combines the impressionistic style of "Resonance" with a more conventional narrative in tracing the torturous 10-day waiting period between an HIV blood test and its results. A young man's nerve-wracked, nightmarish imaginings are intercut with scenes from his day-to-day life as he awaits the fateful news. Newby is particularly adept at building tension through sound and editing, even if the technique is more than a little self-conscious at times.

Michael Mayson's playful "Billy Turner's Secret" is the most mainstream of the six, with an obvious debt to Spike Lee. His comedy about two Brooklyn roommates — one a sexist homophobe, the other a closeted gay — has fun taking jabs at stereotypes and macho posturing, but the character development is rushed and too tidy.

Program ends with the most ambitious of the films, "The Dead Boys' Club," Mark Christopher's paean to the bygone era of pre-AIDS Manhattan. Film cleverly thrusts Toby (Nat DeWolf), a naive, young gay man from Wisconsin visiting his older New York cousin, into that bygone era via a pair of leather boots that belonged to the cousin's recently deceased lover. Whenever Toby, frightened but intrigued, dons the shoes, he sees images of the enticingly uninhibited gay disco scene of the 1970s. Jonathan Demme reportedly is considering inserting the flashback footage of "The Dead Boys' Club" into his upcoming "Philadelphia."

—*Greg Evans*

NEEDFUL THINGS

A Columbia Pictures release of a Castle Rock Entertainment presentation in association with New Line Cinema. Produced by Jack Cummins. Executive producer, Peter Yates. Directed by Fraser C. Heston. Screenplay, W.D. Richter, based on the novel by Stephen King. Camera (Technicolor), Tony Westman; editor, Rob Kobrin; music, Patrick Doyle; production design, Douglas Higgins; set decoration, Dominique Fauquet-Lemaitre; costume design, Monique Prudhomme; sound (Dolby), Eric Batut; associate producer, Gordon Mark; assistant director, Anthony Brand; special effects coordinator, Gary Paller; casting, Mary Gail Artz, Barbara Cohen. Reviewed at the AMC Century 14 Theater, L.A., Aug. 4, 1993. MPAA Rating: R. Running time: **120 MIN.**

Leland Gaunt	Max von Sydow
Sheriff Alan Pangborn	Ed Harris
Polly Chalmers	Bonnie Bedelia
Nettie Cobb	Amanda Plummer
Danforth Walsh III	J.T. Walsh
Dep. Norris Ridgewick	Ray McKinnon
Hugh Priest	Duncan Fraser
Wilma Jerzyk	Valri Bromfield
Brian Rusk	Shane Meier

Stephen King's name seems to bring an audience to even the poorest adaptations of his work, which should provide some comfort to the filmmakers here.

Nearly choking on its tongue-in-cheek approach, this darkly comic picture proves a sadistic, mean-spirited, overlong exercise that should have a devilish time sustaining any box office fire once the King-induced spark wears off.

Fraser C. Heston (yes, Charlton's son) certainly had the plate set for his feature directing debut, working from a script by W.D. Richter ("The Adventures of Buckaroo Bonzai") based on a King best-seller about the devil opening a curio shop in a seemingly benign small town.

Set appropriately in King's fictitious Castle Rock, Maine, the story has similarities to everything from the "Friday the 13th" TV series to Ray Bradbury's "Something Wicked This Way Comes," which also involved dark forces seducing simple townsfolk by granting their deepest desires.

In this case, fatherly-looking Leland Gaunt (Max von Sydow) is the proprietor of Needful Things, a new shop providing objects to the town's residents in exchange for each doing him "a favor.' Gaunt successfully uses those prankish deeds to prey on petty jealousies and set the good people of Castle Rock homicidally at each other's throats.

Only the town sheriff (Ed Harris) seems to realize something is rotten in the state of Maine, while even his fiancee (Bonnie Bedelia) falls under Gaunt's promise-fulfilling spell.

Moviegoers aren't likely to be similarly spellbound, as Heston employs a too-slow buildup to an explosion of mayhem that incorporates gruesome violence with awkward attempts at dark humor.

Heston and Richter can't seem to make their minds up as to what genre the film is. When Gaunt calls someone a "wussy," for example, it's obvious they're trying to play "Things" both ways by courting a high-school mentality as well as a more discriminating palate. That brand of comedy doesn't play well alongside the horror, however, except perhaps among the most undemanding pubescent minds.

The actors suffer from the same schizophrenia, with Harris playing things perfectly straight as the sheriff while many other performers (among them J.T. Walsh as an embezzling town elder) are cartoonishly over the top.

Von Sydow emerges as the picture's least-needy asset with his toothy embodiment of Old Ned, impishly humming "My Favorite Things" or swaying to strains of "Ave Maria" while almost tangibly absorbing the carnage.

From "The Greatest Story Ever Told" to this, it can now be said that the Swedish actor's film career has run the full gamut.

Besides the familiar elements of the story, certain technical contributions are equally derivative, particularly Patrick Doyle's heavy-handed "Omen"-like score. Special effects are understated but for the most part effective.

Interestingly, the best recent adaptations of King's work have been for television, as ABC miniseries like "It" and "The Tommyknockers" have been able to more fully develop characters and milk the suspense.

Castle Rock, in fact, probably scored the last major King feature with "Misery."

"Needful Things'" dark shopkeeper seems to sum up this effort when, surveying his most recent handiwork, he acknowledges, "I would hardly call it a rousing success."

—*Brian Lowry*

JASON GOES TO HELL: THE FINAL FRIDAY

A New Line Cinema release of a Sean S. Cunningham production. Produced by Sean S. Cunningham. Line producer, Deborah Hayn-Cass. Directed by Adam Marcus. Screenplay, Dean Lorey, Jay Huguely, story by Huguely, Marcus. Camera (Deluxe color), William Dill; editor, David Handman; music, Harry Manfredini; production design, W. Brooke Wheeler; set decoration, Natali K. Pope; costume design, Julie Rae Engelsman; sound (Dolby), Oliver L. Moss; special visual effects, Al Magliochetti; special makeup effects, Kurtzman, Nicotero and Berger EFX Group; assistant director, Francis R. (Sam) Mahony III; casting, Hughes/Moss, David Giella. Reviewed at Murray Hill Cinemas, N.Y., Aug. 13, 1993. MPAA Rating: R. Running time: **88 MIN.**

Steven Freeman	Jon D. LeMay
Jessica Kimble	Kari Keegan
Jason Voorhees	Kane Hodder
Creighton Duke	Steven Williams
Robert Campbell	Steven Culp
Diana Kimble	Erin Gray
Joey B	Rusty Schwimmer
Coroner	Richard Gant
Shelby	Leslie Jordan
Sheriff Landis	Billy Green Bush

Jason goes to hell, and not a moment too soon. His descent has been far too long in coming, as the exhausted, witless "Jason Goes to Hell: The Final Friday" demonstrates. But that's about all that the ninth, allegedly final and supposedly explanatory chapter in the popular "Friday the 13th" series makes clear. B.O. outlook appears modest, unless the last-installment angle unexpectedly disinters longtime series fans.

With one or two exceptions, freshman director Adam Marcus forgoes the camp humor and inside jokes that marked the tail end of the slasher craze, opting instead for a straightforward Saturday night drive-in approach. It worked for John Carpenter's "Halloween," but it doesn't work here. Blame Marcus for the film's complete lack of tension and style, but point a machete or two at a bland, occasionally inept cast and scripters unable to contribute a single innovation to the genre.

"Jason" attempts to explain Jason — his origins, his secrets for a long, long life and the means by which he can be sent to his just rewards. That it's all remarkably silly is to be expected and perhaps even relished, but pic doesn't even play by its own rules. Aside from some somber mumbo jumbo about Jason's family tree, the film doesn't even make a stab at explaining the supernatural goings-on.

Following a plot twist that occurs within pic's first 15 minutes, Jason Voorhees (Kane Hodder) is slaughtered by an Uzi-toting SWAT team. Later, a gruesome autopsy reveals an oversize, malformed heart beating and oozing black bile. Within seconds, the coroner is chowing down on the grotesque ticker, thus allowing the spirit of Jason to enter him and explaining, sort of, how the hockey-masked slasher outwits death.

This time around, Jason is after his only living relatives — a sister, a niece and the niece's infant. Enter Creighton Duke (Steven Williams), a bounty hunter specializing in serial killers, who inexplicably knows that Jason can only be killed by blood kin. If the killer dispatches the last of his relatives, he'll live forever.

Plot, of course, is merely an excuse to see Jason julienne his way through a series of scantily clad teenage campers, stupid cops and, best of all, a sleazy tabloid TV reporter. The killings seem fairly tame by slasher standards, although their number and the gratuitous skin shots warrant the R rating.

Marcus and screenwriters Dean Lorey and Jay Huguely toss in more than a little "Alien," as the slimy creature apparently meant to represent Jason's spirit enters and exits any number of humans. Marcus tips that he's aware of the thieving by showing a crate marked "Arctic expedition" during a particularly "Thing"-like episode.

Tech credits, especially the grainy focus, betray the film's modest budget, and even the special effects seem second-rate. Zombie makeup looks about as convincing as the original "Night of the Living Dead." After this one, even Jason die-hards won't mourn his passing.

—*Greg Evans*

TOUT CA ... POUR CA!

(ALL THAT ... FOR THIS?!)

(FRENCH/COLOR)

A Bac Films release of a Les Films 13-TFI Films co-production in association with Sofiarp, CNC Rhone-Alpes and the participation of Canal Plus. (Foreign sales: Jean-Paul de Vidas, Les Film 26.) Produced, directed, written by Claude Lelouch. Camera (color), Lelouch; editor, Helene de Luze; music, Francis Lai, Philippe Servain; set decoration, Laurent Tesseyre; costume design, Mimi Lempicka; sound (Dolby), Harald Maury, Gerard Rousseau, Eric Tisserand; lighting, Philippe Pavans de Cecatty. Reviewed at UGC Odeon cinema, Paris, July 20, 1993. Running time: **116 MIN.**

Cast: Marie-Sophie L., Vincent Lindon, Gerard Darmon, Jacques Gamblin, Evelyne Bouix, Francis Huster, Alessandra Martines, Fabrice Luchini, Charles Gerard, Salome Lelouch.

Adultery and its consequences, fellatio in tight quarters and inspired fraud loom large in one-man band Claude Lelouch's latest confection, "Tout Ca ... pour ca!" Congenial thesping gets higher marks than contrived tale that interweaves the romantic imbroglios of five couples. Lelouch's 33rd film has been a steady draw since its June release.

Lelouch opted for a light contemporary story after "La Belle histoire," his biblical times-to-the-present epic about Christ, gypsies, bees and the transmigration of souls, failed to set the world on fire.

New pic celebrates the serendipity that life may well offer, but with, one hopes and prays, a better soundtrack. (Although Lelouch has a fine eye for buoyant widescreen camera work and a fair knack for dialogue, he has a tin ear when it comes to gauging how much audiences might want to hear tone-deaf thesps break into song.)

At pic's outset, three working-class schnooks — cab driver Gerard Darmon, hairdresser Jacques Gamblin and waiter Vincent Lindon — are in prison, where lawyer Marie-Sophie L. is trying to get their con-

voluted stories straight. It is gradually revealed that all three, driven slightly nuts by bad breaks related to the women in their lives, ended up on the lam in vacation-time France, fleecing tourists via an ingenious series of improvised scams.

Parallel saga concerns judge Francis Huster, who is married to gorgeous and adoring ballerina Alessandra Martines but is having an affair with Marie-Sophie L., who is married to unsuspecting fellow lawyer Fabrice Luchini. Elaborate interlocking flashbacks reveal that while the hard-luck trio were getting into hot water, the two upscale couples were scaling Mont Blanc and straining their marriages.

Pic sets out to show that Huster cannot presume to judge the love-addled trio in quite the same way after his own motivations were put to the test by thoughtlessly alienating his devoted wife. As always, Lelouch takes glee in lensing his actors in improbable situations and, as the narrative careens around, his enthusiasm is contagious. But the whole thing hangs together by cotton candy threads that exhaust the viewer's suspension-of-disbelief mechanism.

Although pic is riddled with contextual references to oral sex — an awkwardly amusing episode with the tent-confined climbers earned some local notoriety — it is the prison-bound trio's clever schemes for acquiring money, meals and luxury accommodations that entertain best.

There is a frankly middle-aged, strangely wholesome undercurrent of voyeurism in the scenes of Martines rubbing oil into her shapely breasts or dancing in the nude. Lindon's wounded puppy-dog expression grows tiresome, as does the closing waltz. But Lelouch's energetic, often clumsy determination to tell broad human stories wins out in the end.

—*Lisa Nesselson*

PESARO FEST

AHLAM SAGHIRA

(LITTLE DREAMS)

(EGYPTIAN-GERMAN/COLOR)

An MISR International films (Egypt), ZDF (Germany) co-production. Directed, written by Khalid al-Haggar. Camera (color), Samir Bahzan; editor, Adel Mounir; music, Rageh Daoud; art direction, Hamed Hemdan; sound, Gasser Gabr. Reviewed at 29th International Festival of New Cinema, Pesaro (Italy), June 13, 1993. Running time: **90 MIN.**

With: Mervat Amin, Salah Al Sadany, Raga'a Hussein, Seif Abdel Rahman, Tamer Ashraf, Maher Selim, Hassan Al Adl, Ibrahim Hassan.

A 13-year-old boy follows his father's ghost to the front line in

"Little Dreams," a sure-footed first feature by Egyptian Khalid al-Haggar. Powerfully conveying a generation's disenchantment with popular late-'60s leader Gamal Abdel Nasser, pic strays occasionally into manipulative overstatement, but remains a compellingly human wartime drama that should feature widely on the festival trail.

Set in Suez, in the period leading up to and during the six-day war against Israel in 1967, the story pivots on plucky youngster Ghareb. Captivating, dreamlike opening scenes unfurl with vivid splashes of color, recapping his parents' wedding, his birth and early childhood and his father's death as a Resistance hero in the 1956 Suez conflict.

Reality takes on a grittier tone as the boy's mother, Hoda, unable to support them on her earnings as a seamstress, sends Ghareb to work in a printer's shop. The overbearing boss, Salah, carries a torch for Hoda, but she turns down his repeated marriage proposals. Ghareb also rejects him as a father figure, forming a bond instead with Mahmood, an ex-comrade of his father's, who prints propaganda at the shop.

Ghareb is soon swept up by political fervor, secretly printing Mahmood's tracts after hours and distributing them in town. His ongoing clash with Salah causes conflict as his mother is gradually won over. As war breaks out, he arrives home to catch the tail end of their wedding ceremony, and runs away to join the war effort.

From here on, al-Haggar pulls out a few too many stops in his attempt to harness the boy's plight to a wider-reaching political and historical framework. Unable to keep Egypt from defeat, Nasser steps down, and the resulting popular uprising literally crushes Ghareb. The scene's emotional resonance is considerable, despite the muffling effect of a distinctly *de trop* coda showing the birth of his baby brother, with his own set of hopes, ideals and dreams.

The off-kilter finale, however, doesn't undermine al-Haggar's boldly confident storytelling skills. Pic is similarly sharp in looks and sound, with Samir Bahzan's lensing and Rageh Daoud's music both deserving of a nod. —*David Rooney*

HARD TARGET

A Universal release of an Alphaville/Renaissance production. Produced by James Jacks and Sean Daniel. Executive producers, Moshe Diamant, Sam Raimi, Robert Tapert. Co-producers, Chuck Pfarrer, Terence Chang. Directed by John Woo. Screenplay, Pfarrer. Camera (Deluxe color), Russell Carpenter; editor, Bob Murawski; music, Graeme Revell; production design, Phil Dagort; art direction, Philip Messina; set decoration, Michele Poulik; costume design, Karyn Wagner; sound (Dolby), Al Rizzo, Kenny Delbert; special effects coordinator, Dale Martin; special sound effects, John Pospisil; stunt coordinator, Billy Burton; associate producer, Eugene Van Varenberg; assistant director, Dennis Maguire. Reviewed at the Writers Guild Theater, Beverly Hills, Aug. 11, 1993. MPAA Rating: R. Running time: **94 MIN.**

Chance Boudreaux	
	Jean-Claude Van Damme
Fouchon	Lance Henriksen
Van Cleaf	Arnold Vosloo
Natasha Binder	Yancy Butler
Carmine	Kasi Lemmons
Douvee	Wilford Brimley
Mr. Lopacki	Bob Apisa
Binder	Chuck Pfarrer
Frick	Douglas Forsythe Rye
Frack	Michael D. Leinert
Elijah Roper	Willie Carpenter

John Woo, cult director of the new Hong Kong Cinema, makes his eagerly awaited American debut with "Hard Target," a briskly vigorous, occasionally brilliant actioner starring Jean-Claude Van Damme. However, hampered by a B script with flat, standard characters, and subjected to repeated editing of the violent sequences to win an R rating, pic doesn't bear the unique vision on display in Woo's recent "The Killer" and "Hard-Boiled." Van Damme and the director's reputation should ensure initial commercial kick on the way to solid if not spectacular box office.

Chuck Pfarrer, who also co-produced and plays a small role, fashions his script as a variation of "The Most Dangerous Game," a classic story that has received numerous film versions, such as the 1932 Joel McCrea vehicle, Robert Wise's 1946 "A Game of Death" and Roy Boulting's 1956 "Run for the Sun."

With locale switched from a remote island to urban New Orleans, tale centers on a sadistic band of hunters, headed by amoral chief Fouchon (Lance Henriksen) and his deputy, Van Cleaf (Arnold Vosloo), who operate a profitable "safari game" in which the prey are homeless combat veterans.

Van Damme plays Chance Boudreaux, a down-on-his luck merchant sailor, who comes to the rescue of Natasha Binder (Yancy Butler), a young woman searching for her missing father, the latest victim. At first, Van Damme is willing to help her just for money; he needs $217 to pay his union dues to get work. Gradually, however, he becomes morally and emotionally committed to the cause.

August 30, 1993 (Cont.)

Unfortunately, "Hard Target's" script is too schematic, populated with standard thug villains. By now, Henriksen has played so many cold-blooded heavies that just his appearance suggests all there is to know about his deviant, nefarious venture. The tale's social subtext, pitting the rich hunters against victims willing to bet their lives against a $10,000 prize, also gets lost.

Ultimately, "Hard Target" is a compromised work, a stylistic hybrid of the American and Hong Kong action pics. But Woo's distinctiveness is still in evidence. He is a virtuoso at staging and editing intricate set pieces with precision, visual inventiveness and humor.

The pacing, in fact, is so fast that Woo manages to cover Van Damme's usual inexpressiveness. While Van Damme's line delivery is still stiff, Woo helps his star display his specialty — high-powered martial arts skills — with greater panache and stylization than before.

The casting of Butler as the ingenue is inexplicable. Lacking screen presence or charm, she gives an embarrassing perf.

In contrast, Wilford Brimley brings offbeat humor to his role as Van Damme's salty Cajun uncle.

The disjointed storytelling, occasional chopped editing and uneven performances undermine what could have been a much better picture. But "Hard Target" still packs a lot of punch and, by American action standards, contains some strikingly impressive set pieces.

Tech credits are polished in every department. Still, what's missing from "Hard Target" is Woo's poetic style and hyperkinetic force, his visceral jaw-dropping stunts that are as gracefully elegant as balletic movement.
—*Emanuel Levy*

WILDER NAPALM

A TriStar release of a Baltimore Pictures production. Produced by Mark Johnson, Stuart Cornfeld. Executive producer, Barrie Osborne. Directed by Glenn Gordon Caron. Screenplay, Vince Gilligan. Camera (Technicolor), Jerry Hartleben; editor, Artie Mandelberg; music, Michael Kamen; production design, John Muto; art direction, Dan Webster; set decoration, Leslie Bloom; costume design, Louise Frogley; sound (Dolby), Les Lazarowitz; visual effects supervisors, Stephen Brooks, Harrison Ellenshaw; elephant trainer, Bill Morris; casting, Louis DiGiaimo. Reviewed at Sony Studios, Culver City, Aug. 5, 1993. MPAA Rating: PG-13. Running time: **109 MIN.**
Vida Foudroyant .... Debra Winger
Wallace Foudroyant .... Dennis Quaid
Wilder Foudroyant .... Arliss Howard
Fire Chief .... M. Emmet Walsh
Rex .... Jim Varney
Snake Lady .... Mimi Lieber
Deputy Sheriff Spivey ....
.... Marvin J. McIntyre
The Singing Firemen ....
.... The Mighty Echoes

If nothing else, "Wilder Napalm" deserves a special mention

in the history books as the first and only pyrokinetic romantic comedy-drama. Beyond that, there's little to recommend in the slow-moving, fuzzy-minded yarn. Like many shaggy-dog tales, it reads better than it plays, with the drollery more apt to raise a few smiles than ignite laughter. Commercial prospects for the long-on-the-shelf TriStar release are ashen.

The Foudroyant brothers — Wallace (Dennis Quaid) and Wilder (Arliss Howard) — have that oh-so-special gift of thinking real hard and making things explode in flames. It's great for party tricks like lighting cigarettes. In fact, Wallace has managed to incorporate such shenanigans into a clown act he performs in a low-grade traveling carnival.

In sharp contrast, Wilder has spent decades avoiding the spotlight. He works quietly and alone in one of those shopping mall film-processing joints. Yet he's married to the spunky, brash Vida (Debra Winger).

The brothers are hopelessly estranged, and there's mysterious bad blood involving a prank Wallace inflicted on his brother, and deeply ingrained tension over Vida's affections.

But that might change when the carnival arrives in town and parks itself in the very mall where Wilder plies his trade.

If this all sounds like gobbledygook, one can only say that the filmmakers have worked diligently at rendering the material incomprehensible. The very title suggests something quirky and unusual. While Vince Gilligan's screenplay certainly provides enough anecdotal material, director Glenn Gordon Caron foolishly assumes there's some logic to be gleaned here. The moral really isn't any more brilliant than "Don't play with matches."

Winger and Quaid appear at a loss to make sense of their characters and it's painful to watch such gifted actors struggling to maintain their dignity. Howard emerges slightly better if only because one can see the semblance of a character arc. However, it's a part that calls for an absence of flamboyance — the one thing the film so desperately needs.
—*Leonard Klady*

THE BALLAD OF LITTLE JO

A Fine Line Features release of a Fine Line and Polygram Filmed Entertainment presentation of a Fred Berner/JoCo production. Produced by Fred Berner, Brenda Goodman. Executive producers, Barry Bernardi, Ira Deutchman, John Sloss. Directed, written by Maggie Greenwald. Camera (Technicolor), Declan Quinn; editor, Keith Reamer; music, David Mansfield; production design, Mark Friedberg; costume design, Claudia Brown; sound (Dolby), Felipe Borrerro; associate producer, Anne Dillon; casting, Judy Claman, Jeffery Passero. Reviewed at the Charles Aidikoff screening room, Beverly Hills, Aug. 12, 1993. MPAA Rating: R. Running time: **120 MIN.**

Little Jo .... Suzy Amis
Frank Badger .... Bo Hopkins
Percy Corcoran .... Ian McKellen
Tinman Wong .... David Chung
Ruth Badger .... Carrie Snodgress
Streight Hollander ... Rene Auberjonois
Mary Addie .... Heather Graham

Suzy Amis' superlative performance dominates every frame of "The Ballad of Little Jo," an earnest drama about a woman who disguises herself as a man to survive hardship in the Old West. But this well-intentioned, revisionist frontier saga is too solemn and dramatically unexciting to generate wide appeal beyond a core of female viewers and ardent followers of indie pics.

Inspired by a true story, writer-director Maggie Greenwald's fascinating story is set in 1866, during the Gold Rush. Josephine Monaghan (Amis) is a wealthy woman from the East, cast out by her family after giving birth out of wedlock.

Heading west, she meets Hollander (Rene Auberjonois), a peddler who initially befriends her but then sexually harasses her. Realizing her only chance for freedom in the West is as a man, Josephine proceeds to cut her long hair, scar her face, put on trousers — and change her name to Little Jo.

She begins her new life in Ruby City, a frontier mining outpost populated by fortune-seeking adventurers. Miraculously, she is accepted as a man by everyone, including macho Percy Corcoran (Ian McKellen), who provides practical advice, and Frank Badger (Bo Hopkins), who instructs her in sheepherding. Before long, she learns how to mine, hunt and manage a self-sufficient existence.

Jo's solitary life changes after she saves Tinman Wong (David Chung), an Asian outcast, from lynching. In an intriguing role reversal, Wong is assigned to cook, mend and take care of her needs, while she functions as the breadwinner. But once he discovers her identity, an affair ensues and they secretly set up house.

Scripter-helmer Greenwald brings a contemporary feminist vision to the saga. But despite her efforts to demystify the Old West, Greenwald ends up mythologizing her heroine as a symbol of pioneering endurance.

Ultimately, what makes "The Ballad of Little Jo" worthy is Amis' full-bodied performance in what may be her most challenging role to date. She never makes a false move.
—*Emanuel Levy*

THE MAN WITHOUT A FACE

A Warner Bros. release of an Icon production. Produced by Bruce Davey. Executive producer, Stephen McEveety. Co-producer, Dalisa Cohen. Directed by Mel Gibson. Screenplay, Malcolm MacRury, based on the novel by Isabelle Holland. Camera (DuArt color; Technicolor prints), Donald M. McAlpine; editor, Tony Gibbs; music, James Horner; production design, Barbara Dunphy; art direction, Marc Fisichella; set design, Vicki Fraser; set decoration, Donald Elmblad; costume design, Shay Cunliffe; sound (Dolby), Michael Evje; associate producers, Donald Ginsberg, Bob Schulz; assistant director, Matt Earl Beesley; special makeup created by Greg Cannom; casting, Marion Dougherty. Reviewed at the National Theater, L.A., Aug. 18, 1993. MPAA Rating: PG-13. Running time: **114 MIN.**
McLeod .... Mel Gibson
Chuck .... Nick Stahl
Catherine .... Margaret Whitton
Gloria .... Fay Masterson
Megan .... Gaby Hoffmann
Chief Stark .... Geoffrey Lewis
Carl .... Richard Masur
Douglas Hall .... Michael DeLuise

Mel Gibson's directing debut reinforces his status as a genuinely fine actor, a fact often lost amid the explosions and car crashes in the "Lethal Weapon" and "Mad Max" trilogies. This simple, sappy film lacks those flashy trappings but compensates with ample heart, promising a solid mid-range box office earner on the order of Gibson's last foray into such sentimental territory, "Forever Young."

Flanked by a fine performance from newcomer Nick Stahl, Gibson's well-calculated production tills the same ground as "Dead Poets Society" without overly exploiting its gimmick — namely, that Gibson's character goes through the movie in heavy makeup, the result of a mysterious accident that left him seriously deformed.

The action begins with a "Cinderella"-type setup: 12-year-old Chuck (Stahl) lives in a Maine coastal village with his uninterested, often-married mother (Margaret Whitton) and two difficult half-sisters.

Having romanticized the image of his late father, an Army pilot, Chuck dreams of getting into Dad's old military academy but has already failed the entrance exam. Needing a tutor, he enlists the aid of Mr. McLeod (Gibson), a gruff, mysterious recluse — known as "the freak" among the small-minded locals — whose teaching career was ended by the accident that scarred him and took the life of one of his students.

Malcolm MacRury's script comes off a bit sitcom-ish in the early going, with a precocious younger sister (Gaby Hoffmann) and contrived strokes in establishing the central relationship.

Still, the words become more compelling as the action moves along, with Chuck finding a mentor and father figure while McLeod rekindles his contact with the outside world — a place where the teacher-student bond prompts suspicions of molestation, jeopardizing the relationship.

Gibson's direction meanders in places but for the most part is clear and unaffected. In addition to the charm of the two main characters, the movie manages to glorify education without being heavy-handed and provides a wry take on the more "groovy" aspects of the late 1960s, when the action takes place.

Greg Cannom's convincing make-up proves surprisingly unobtrusive as the story wears on, a point made explicitly by Chuck in case the audience misses the lesson. In fact, with his face marred, what really shines through is Gibson's resonant voice, though ardent fans may feel the unsullied half of his head would be enough for them.

Other technical aspects exhibit considerable care, from Dennis McAlpine's languid shots of the idyllic coastal town to the period costumes and interchangeable strains of the ubiquitous James Horner's latest uplifting score.

With "Hamlet" and other recent roles, Gibson appears to be well on his way toward emulating Sean Connery, establishing an appeal not totally reliant on his action hunk status. "The Man Without a Face" continues that push for Gibson the actor, and even with its corny trappings, Gibson the director has no cause to hide his face, either. —*Brian Lowry*

SURF NINJAS

A New Line Cinema release. Produced by Evzen Kolar. Executive producers, Sara Risher, Dan Gordon, Kevin Moreton. Directed by Neal Israel. Screenplay, Gordon. Camera (Deluxe color; Filmhouse prints) Arthur Albert, Victor Hammer; editor, Tom Walls; music, David Kitay; production design, Michael Novotny; art direction, Curtis W. Baruth; set decoration, Janis Lubin; costume design, Deborah La Gorce Kramer; sound, Ike Magal; associate producer, Ernie Reyes Jr.; assistant director, J. Stephen Buck; second unit director, Ernie Orsatti; casting, Annette Benson. Reviewed at Loews Copley Place, Boston, Aug. 20, 1993. MPAA Rating: PG. Running time: **86 MIN.**

Johnny	Ernie Reyes Jr.
Iggy	Rob Schneider
Adam	Nicolas Cowan
Colonel Chi	Leslie Nielsen
Lt. Spence	Tone Loc
Zatch	Ernie Reyes Sr.
Baba Ram	Keone Young
Ro-May	Kelly Hu
Gum-Bey	Tad Horino
Mac	John Karlen
Mr. Dunbar	Neal Israel

"Surf Ninjas" is a juvenile comedy-action pic for audiences too young to get into the R-rated "Hard Target." Action is relatively mild for the genre and, unfortunately, so are the jokes.

Two California surfing dudes (Ernie Reyes Jr., Nicolas Cowan) discover they are long-lost crown princes of the obscure nation of Patu San after a royal family retainer (Ernie Reyes Sr.) arrives to inform them of their true identities. To regain the throne, they must overthrow the dictator (Leslie Nielsen looking like a cross between a samurai and "Star Trek's" Borg). Joining them on their adventure is a spaced-out friend (Rob Schneider), an L.A. cop (rap star Tone Loc) and a prospective bride (Kelly Hu).

While the martial arts choreography by Reyes Sr. can't be totally dismissed, the PG target ensures it's pretty tame stuff. Given the near-supernatural abilities attributed to most onscreen ninjas, the bad ninjas here seem almost amateurish.

The humor is pretty lame as well. Instead of going all out for comedy in the manner of "Bill and Ted's Excellent Adventure," director Neal Israel and writer Dan Gordon want us to take the characters seriously enough to care what happens to them. Audiences won't.

Chief drawing card for the younger set is likely to be Reyes Jr., who was a stunt double in "Teenage Mutant Ninja Turtles" and then got his own role in the sequel.

Tech credits are OK. Nothing will be lost when the pic makes its inevitable transition to the small screen. —*Daniel M. Kimmel*

SON OF THE PINK PANTHER

An MGM release of a United Artists presentation in association with Filmauro S.R.L. Produced by Tony Adams. Executive producer, Nigel Wooll. Directed by Blake Edwards. Screenplay, Edwards, Madeline and Steve Sunshine, based on Edwards' story and characters created by Edwards and Maurice Richlin. Camera (Deluxe color), Dick Bush; editor, Robert Pergament; music, Henry Mancini; production design, Peter Mullins; art direction, David Minty, John Siddall, Leslie Tomkins; costume design, Emma Porteous; sound (Dolby), Ken Weston; assistant director, Terry Needham; casting, Nancy Klopper (U.S.), Davis & Zimmerman (U.K.). Reviewed at the Avco Cinema, L.A., Aug. 26, 1993. MPAA Rating: PG. Running time: **93 MIN.**

Jacques	Roberto Benigni
Dreyfus	Herbert Lom
Maria	Claudia Cardinale
Princess Yasmin	Debrah Farentino
Yussa	Jennifer Edwards
Hans	Robert Davi
Chief Lazar	Anton Rodgers
Cato	Burt Kwouk
Dr. Balls	Graham Stark

Blake Edwards, Hollywood's one-time ingenious *farceur*, desperately tries to bounce back with "Son of the Pink Panther," the eighth episode in the series that began in 1964. Starring Italian comedian Robert Benigni as the new bumbling inspector, it is a tired pastiche of recycled sketches and gags. Pic will generate some coin opening week as a curio item for nostalgic viewers, but will rapidly lose its draw after dismissive reviews and negative word of mouth.

It must have sounded like a valid concept to revive the series, a decade after the last installment, with a gifted comedian like Benigni as a new hero. But Edwards has nothing fresh or funny to add to the old ideas.

This time around, twitching Commissioner Dreyfus (Herbert Lom) is investigating the disappearance of Princess Yasmin (Debrah Farentino), kidnapped by a nasty terrorist (Robert Davi). Also assigned to the case is Jacques Gambrelli (Benigni), a second-class gendarme who doesn't initially realize he's the illegitimate son of the famed Inspector Clouseau. Nor, to his dismay, does Lom.

Too bad that Edwards' specialty, the elaborate orchestration of sight gags with hilarious payoffs, is almost absent here, replaced by vulgar slapstick humor and a few effective gags.

Benigni is the major asset, but his vast talents are underutilized. It's nice to see the series' veterans again, although, under these circumstances, neither Lom, usually so pathetically laughable, nor Burt Kwouk as Cato — whose brawls with Sellers were always a high point — excel.

Except for the cute credit sequence, production values are mediocre, making pic feel as if it were quickly put together. Judging by the results, it may be a good idea to put the Pink Panther to rest. —*Emanuel Levy*

THE THING CALLED LOVE

A Paramount release of a John Davis production. Produced by Davis. Executive producer, George Folsey Jr. Co-producer, Darlene K. Chan. Directed by Peter Bogdanovich. Screenplay, Carol Heikkinen. Camera (Deluxe color), Peter James; editor, Terry Stokes; music supervisor, G. Marq Roswell; executive music consultant, J. Steven Soles; production design, Michael Seymour; art direction, Thomas D. Wilkins; set decoration, Cloudia; costume design, Rita Riggs; sound (Dolby), James Edward Webb Jr.; associate producer, Steve Foley; assistant director, Jerry L. Ballew; casting, Dianne Crittenden. Reviewed at Paramount Studios, L.A., Aug. 23, 1993. MPAA Rating: PG-13. Running time: **116 MIN.**

James Wright	River Phoenix
Miranda Presley	Samantha Mathis
Kyle Davidson	Dermot Mulroney
Linda Lue Linden	Sandra Bullock
Lucy	K.T. Oslin
Billy	Anthony Clark
Ned	Webb Wilder
Floyd	Earl Poole Ball
Trisha Yearwood	Trisha Yearwood

A fairly typical tale of young talent on the rise in Nashville is given nicely nuanced treatment in "The Thing Called Love." Perhaps there's not much new to say about the dues and disappointments involved in breaking into the country music scene, but the scenes are fresh and the emotions real in Peter Bogdanovich's tune-laden, mixed-mood drama.

Paramount is showing less than total assurance in the picture by releasing it in 490 prints in the South, Southwest and parts of Canada, where distrib has determined country music appeal is strongest, and avoiding most major-city markets. To have any kind of B.O. chance against higher-profile entries, film would need a special push.

Debuting screenwriter Carol Heikkinen's story seems familiar from the outset, as cute aspiring singer-songwriter Miranda Presley (Samantha Mathis) Greyhounds from New York City to Nashville in search of her dream. Her first stop is the Bluebird Cafe, where "open mike" night attracts hundreds of hopefuls all looking for the same break.

Taking a waitress job when her first audition doesn't land her a gig and shortly moving in with the buoyantly untalented Linda Lue Linden (Sandra Bullock), Miranda attracts the attention of two good-looking dudes, the moody, gifted James Wright (River Phoenix) and soulful Kyle Davidson (Dermot Mulroney), who writes better than he sings.

Partial to writing alone in the diner across the road from her motel, Miranda can't reciprocate Kyle's earnest emotions, and is alternately tantalized and infuriated by James' hot-and-cold routine. Characters hit the crossroads at a big country dance to which the romantically hopeful Kyle brings Miranda, but loses her

September 6, 1993 (Cont.)

after James, who is unexpectedly performing that night, invites her up onstage to join in one of his numbers.

While Kyle's jealousy is partly mollified when Trisha Yearwood records one of his tunes, Miranda and Kyle head for Memphis to see Graceland but end up getting married in an oddball ceremony conducted at an all-night convenience store. This hasty union quickly comes to no good, and among the film's most potent scenes are those detailing the quick unraveling of this immature relationship.

Refusing cloying sentimentality and reassurance, wrap-up pleasingly, and realistically, leaves all the main characters at different places on the road between success and failure, and only partly reconciled to their fates and each other. Even if it doesn't present anything resembling a comprehensive view of the Nashville music scene, it credibly enters into the mind-sets of the struggling artists and imparts a good sense of their mixed camaraderie and competitiveness.

Brought on to replace another director on relatively short notice, Bogdanovich hasn't been able to transcend such fundamental script problems as its predictability and the conventional, thinly conceived secondary characters. But, like good country songwriters and singers, he and his leading actors have been able to locate authentic emotion in a standard format, and the director displays a visual confidence that is all the more impressive for its refined subtlety. His staging, camera setups and cutting have a suppleness and fluidity that are quite rare, and would be well employed on more substantial material.

Alert and game, Mathis nicely carries the picture, drawing the viewer in without pleading for sympathy. Phoenix sharply etches a self-styled, hard-to-reach tough guy who's really a scaredy-cat, and Mulroney registers well as a sensitive Eastern cowboy.

Unfortunately, Bullock can only hit familiar notes with her cheerful second banana role, and other supporting thesps are one-dimensional.

That all the performers do their own singing is a very agreeable plus, and the vast song score has been imaginatively and enjoyably worked into the proceedings. Tech contributions on the relatively low-budget production are all solid.

—Todd McCarthy

TRUE ROMANCE

A Warner Bros. release of a Morgan Creek production in association with Davis Film. (Foreign sales: August Entertainment.) Produced by Bill Unger, Steve Perry, Samuel Hadida. Executive producers, James G. Robinson, Gary Barber, Bob and Harvey Weinstein, Stanley Margolis. Directed by Tony Scott. Screenplay by Quentin Tarantino. Camera (Technicolor), Jeffrey Kimball; editors, Michael Tronick, Christian Wagner; music, Hans Zimmer; production design, Benjamin Fernandez; art direction, James Murakami; set decoration, Thomas Roysden; costume design, Susan Becker; sound (Dolby), William Kaplan; casting, Risa Bramon Garcia, Billy Hopkins. Reviewed at the Mann Westwood, L.A., Aug. 13, 1993. MPAA rating: R. Running time: **116 MIN.**
Clarence Worley .... Christian Slater
Alabama Whitman ..... Patricia Arquette
Clifford Worley .... Dennis Hopper
Drexl Spivey .... Gary Oldman
Floyd .... Brad Pitt
Vincenzo Coccotti . Christopher Walken
Mentor .... Val Kilmer
Elliot Blitzer .... Bronson Pinchot
Dick Ritchie .... Michael Rapaport
Lee Donowitz .... Saul Rubinek
Nick Dimes .... Chris Penn
Cody Nicholson .... Tom Sizemore
Big Don .... Samuel L. Jackson

The footprints of dozens of classic thrillers are imprinted on the slick, violent and energetic "True Romance." One of the endless variations on the couple-on-the-run subgenre, yarn provides some amazing encounters, bravura acting turns and gruesome carnage. But it doesn't add up to enough, as preposterous plotting and graphic violence ultimately prove an audience turnoff and will limit pic's commercial prospects.

The odd couple here are Clarence (Christian Slater) and Alabama (Patricia Arquette), a young man working in a comic-book store and a gal on the job on the streets of Detroit. Their not-so-chance encounter blossoms into true love and marriage.

Clarence, on the pretense of picking up Alabama's suitcase, walks into the lair of her former pimp (Gary Oldman). Better judgment would have him steer clear of the haunt, but this is a movie. During a scuffle Clarence kills Drexl and grabs his wife's suitcase — except it's the wrong one. Opening the Pandora's box reveals a fortune in uncut cocaine. The young man is smart enough to know he's in a lot of trouble. He also foolishly believes he can skip town, sell the stash and escape to some remote paradise — in this case, Hollywood.

Building on a shaky premise, "True Romance" rides along largely on the power of its colorful rogues' gallery. Besides Oldman's gleeful incarnation of evil, there's dopey fun in Brad Pitt's space cadet and Saul Rubinek as a Hollywood producer whose ego transcends morality, law and common sense. Slater and Arquette lend the proceedings a charged sexuality, elevating the essentially inane material.

Sure to elicit the most notice is a scene between Mafioso Chris Walken and Dennis Hopper as Clarence's ex-cop dad. It is a testament to the two actors that their superlative work transcends racist dialogue and in-your-face brutality.

Movie mavens have a veritable field to plow in the Quentin Tarantino screenplay. Cinematic references are rife, but the story's downfall can be credited in part to the writer's wholehearted embrace of both the best and worst of the noir canon. Pic also suffers because its reality base is other films, with only glancing reference to the outside world.

Tony Scott's slick style is visually arresting if too obvious. Entire film is an elegantly packaged affair on all levels. Still, it doesn't blunt the inevitable disappointment when unwrapped.

—Leonard Klady

KALIFORNIA

A Gramercy Pictures release of a Polygram Filmed Entertainment presentation produced by Propaganda Films with Kouf Bigelow productions. Produced by Steve Golin, Aris McGarry and Joni Sighvatsson. Executive producers, Lynn Bigelow, Jim Kouf. Co-producers, Mitch Sacharoff, Kristine Schwarz. Directed by Dominic Sena. Screenplay, Tim Metcalfe. Story by Stephen Levy and Metcalfe. Camera (Deluxe), Bojan Bazelli; editor, Martin Hunter; music, Carter Burwell; production design, Michael White; art direction, Jeff Mann; set decoration, Kate Sullivan; costume design, Kelle Kutsugeras; sound (Dolby), Jose Antonio Garcia; casting, Pat Golden, Carol Lewis. Reviewed at the Northstar Screening Room, Los Angeles, Aug. 17, 1993. MPAA Rating: R. Running time: **117 MIN.**
Early Grayce .... Brad Pitt
Adele Corners .... Juliette Lewis
Brian Kessler .... David Duchovny
Carrie Laughlin .... Michelle Forbes
Mrs. Musgrave .... Sierra Pecheur
Walter Livesy ..... Gregory Mars Martin
Parole Officer .... Judson Vaughn
Eric .... David Rose

The name Early Grayce (Brad Pitt) deceivingly suggests the patience and understanding of a sympathetic cleric. But the only preacher the laconic Grayce resembles is the vengeful and driven faux minister incarnated by Robert Mitchum in "The Night of the Hunter." The vintage thriller and the intriguing "Kalifornia" are cut from the same cloth but ultimately steer different paths.

The fascination with the homicidal urge and the inability to recognize it in ourselves and others provides the chilling core of this road movie. Though somewhat overplayed and coy about its destination, the film, which is unspooling in competition at the Montreal Film Festival, packs a wallop and should do solid business on the specialized circuit.

Though Early commands much of our attention, it is magazine writer Brian Kessler (David Duchovny)

who relates the harrowing saga. After completing an assignment on a serial killer, Kessler decides his research on similar psychos would make a nifty coffee-table book. He concocts a cross-country tour of nefarious murder sites to collect info that will be augmented by photos shot by girlfriend Carrie Laughlin (Michelle Forbes). Early, meanwhile, happens upon Brian's rideshare ad on a bulletin board at the university where he works as a janitor. No doubt he's intrigued by the invitation to visit ghoulish haunts.

The film cross-cuts between the relatively mundane lives of the yuppish Pittsburgh couple and scenes of Early with his significant other, the bedraggled, naive Adele Corners (Juliette Lewis), portraying a white-trash trailer-park life in which fragile circumstances tend to erupt into unpleasant consequences. Early and Adele are familiar caricatures, but so are Brian and Carrie. It's how each breaks from the mold that brings the juice to Tim Metcalfe's script and director Dominic Sena's interpretation.

When Brian cozies up to Early's easy machismo, his susceptibility and our own identification with the lure of danger are palpable and disquieting.

The charismatic Pitt explores his character with quiet resolve, venting both horror and darkly comic implications. Duchovny is strong in a thankless part, and Forbes is a unique presence in her major-role screen debut. But Lewis steals the show with an affectless performance that registers pity, pathos and pluck.

"Kalifornia" is an extremely handsome production imbued with a chilling surrealistic sensibility. Bojan Bazelli's camera work is more than aptly complemented by the Carter Burwell score. The film will certainly send Sena's artistic stock up the charts.

—Leonard Klady

FATHER HOOD

A Buena Vista release of a Hollywood Pictures presentation. Produced by Nicholas Pileggi, Anant Singh, Gillian Gorfil. Executive producers, Jeffrey Chernov, Richard H. Prince. Directed by Darrell James Roodt. Screenplay, Scott Spencer. Camera (Technicolor), Mark Vicente; editor, David Heitner; music, Patrick O'Hearn; production design, David Barkham; art direction, Dins Danielsen; set decoration, Suzette Sheets; costume design, Donfeld; sound (Dolby), J. Bayard Carey; assistant director, George Parra; second-unit director/stunt coordinator, Charles Picerni; casting, Michael Fenton, Allison Cowitt. Reviewed at the GCC Beverly Connection, L.A., Aug. 25, 1993. MPAA Rating: PG-13. Running time: **94 MIN.**
Jack Charles .... Patrick Swayze
Kathleen Mercer .... Halle Berry
Kelly Charles .... Sabrina Lloyd
Eddie Charles .... Brian Bonsall
Jerry .... Michael Ironside
Rita .... Diane Ladd
Lazzaro .... Bob Gunton

A train wreck from start to finish, despite Patrick Swayze's marquee value this title in search of a movie will have a hard time scaring up any business, even among the trailer-park set.

Hollywood Pictures calls this as "an action/adventure" in the press notes, indicating the publicity department didn't know what to make of it any more than production execs did. "Father Hood" is a basic road movie — small-time criminal takes his kids across country and they bond — handled so ham-fistedly one can't wait for the journey to end.

Swayze plays a hustler whose kids are in an evil foster-care home. On his way to New Orleans to rob a drug dealer, Jack, who's taken no interest in the children despite their mother's death, in a fit of pique snatches them from the home and reluctantly drags them along on his trek.

In transit, the teenage daughter (Sabrina Lloyd) and young son (Brian Bonsall) fret about their dad abandoning them while Jack carries on a phone correspondence with a reporter (Halle Berry) who's intent on busting the foster-care operation.

"Father Hood" may be most notable for the unusual assemblage of talent — director Darrell James Roodt ("Sarafina!"), writer Scott Spencer (the novel "Endless Love") and producer Nicholas Pileggi ("GoodFellas") — and how horribly that mix misfires.

Swayze appears too young for his role, Lloyd is equally miscast as the teenage daughter and Bonsall (the baby brother on "Family Ties," having outgrown his "cute" phase) proves a thoroughly obnoxious child. It's difficult to imagine three more unpleasant characters, let alone being trapped in a car with them.

It also bears noting how casual the kids are about Dad's vocation, which includes waving guns around, stealing three cars and a boat and leading them on multiple car chases, to which the nipper reacts with cries of "faster, Dad, faster."

If Jack is supposed to be a lovable scoundrel, Swayze captures the swagger and none of the likability, and the kids prove at best grating. Part of that, admittedly, may have to do with Spencer's mundane dialogue and Roodt's unsteady direction.

Tech credits include choppy editing, blase chases, peculiar wardrobe and an inappropriate score heavy with Smokey Robinson and Marvin Gaye tunes. Gaye's most applicable title, "What's Goin' On?," didn't make the list.   —*Brian Lowry*

ONLY THE STRONG

A 20th Century Fox release presented in association with Freestone Pictures & Davis Films. Produced by Samuel Hadida, Stuart S. Shapiro, Steven G. Menkin. Executive producer, Victor Hadida. Directed by Sheldon Lettich. Screenplay, Lettich, Luis Esteban. Camera (Eastmancolor), Edward Pei; editor, Stephen Semel; music, Harvey W. Mason; production design, J. Mark Harrington; art direction, Annabel Delgado; costume design, Patricia Field; sound (Dolby), Henri Lopez; associate producer, Robert D. Simon; supervising producer, Conrad L. Ricketts; assistant director, Simon; stunt coordinators, Artie Malesci, Frank Dux; fight coordinator, Dux; casting, James F. Tarzia. Reviewed at the UA Westwood Theatre, L.A., Aug. 20, 1993. MPAA Rating: PG-13. Running time: **96 MIN.**

Louis Stevens	Mark Dacascos
Dianna	Stacey Travis
Kerrigan	Geoffrey Lewis
Silverio	Paco Christian Prieto
Cochran	Todd Susman
Orlando	Richard Coca
Philippe	Jeffrey Anderson Gunter
Shay	Roman Cardwell
Donovan	Ryan Bollman

Only the simple-minded will find much to cheer in this martial arts actioner, which has the queasy feel of a movie slapped together by the marketing department — i.e., let's double our pleasure by putting those nifty kicks and leaps to a Lambada beat. With a Jean-Claude Van Damme epic already in circulation, Fox will face a tough fight for B.O. turf.

Pic does provide a major-studio vehicle for Mark Dacascos, whose impressive look and athletic ability could position him for bigger things after paying his dues in the likes of "American Samurai" and "Ninja Academy."

Here, working with co-writer/director Sheldon Lettich, a three-time Van Damme collaborator, Dacascos has to overcome a lot more than just a neighborhood full of hostile types — like the unintentional giggles evoked by some of the other performers and the script.

Dacascos plays Louis, a special forces officer who has mastered capoeira — a Brazilian form of kung fu that relies on a musical beat — while stationed overseas. Returning to Miami, he seeks out an old teacher (Geoffrey Lewis), who suggests he use that skill to take the 12 toughest kids in school and instill discipline in them — the thought being, if it'll work with them, it'll work on anybody.

Unfortunately, two of those kids are related to neighborhood drug lords — the most menacing being Silverio (Paco Christian Prieto), a ponytailed lummox who, conveniently, is also a capoeira master, giving Louis someone to play with.

Lettich and co-writer Luis Esteban don't waste much time on winning these allegedly lost-cause kids over, the better to get to Louis' showdown with the bad guys.

Still, the lapses in logic are wide enough to drive a graffiti-tagged school bus through, and lead baddie Prieto, while physically imposing, consistently sounds like he's doing a bad impersonation of Desi Arnaz.

Dacascos bears some physical resemblance to the late Brandon Lee and possesses some of the same easy charm, though there's scant outlet for the latter except for a brief liaison with a former classmate (Stacey Travis) who wears rather amusingly short dresses for a young woman working in a tough inner-city school.

Technically, the action scenes are athletic but relatively unimaginative when they're not downright ridiculous, and the music proves so persistent, someone must have forgotten that those two Lambada movies didn't exactly set the world on fire.

"Only the Strong" does push a "Just say no" theme, with an additional message that might be translated "kick butt, stay in school." Staying in theaters should be an equally formidable challenge.

—*Brian Lowry*

SHORT CUTS

A Fine Line Features release and presentation in association with Spelling Films Intl. of a Cary Brokaw/Avenue Pictures production. Produced by Brokaw. Executive producer, Scott Bushnell. Directed by Robert Altman. Screenplay, Altman, Frank Barhydt, based on the writings of Raymond Carver. Camera (Deluxe color; Panavision widescreen), Walt Lloyd; editor, Geraldine Peroni; music, Mark Isham; music producer, Hal Willner; production design, Stephen Altman; art direction, Jerry Fleming; set decoration, Susan J. Emshwiller; costumes, John Hay; sound (Dolby), John Pritchett; associate producers, Mike Kaplan, David Levy; assistant director, Allan Nichols. Reviewed at TriStar screening room, Culver City, Aug. 9, 1993. (In Venice Film Festival.) MPAA Rating: R. Running time: **184 MIN.**

Ann Finnigan	Andie MacDowell
Howard Finnigan	Bruce Davison
Marian Wyman	Julianne Moore
Dr. Ralph Wyman	Matthew Modine
Claire Kane	Anne Archer
Stuart Kane	Fred Ward
Lois Kaiser	Jennifer Jason Leigh
Jerry Kaiser	Chris Penn
Honey Bush	Lili Taylor
Bill Bush	Robert Downey Jr.
Sherri Shepard	Madeleine Stowe
Gene Shepard	Tim Robbins
Doreen Piggot	Lily Tomlin
Earl Piggot	Tom Waits
Betty Weathers	Frances McDormand
Stormy Weathers	Peter Gallagher
Tess Trainer	Annie Ross
Zoe Trainer	Lori Singer
Paul Finnigan	Jack Lemmon
Andy Bitkower	Lyle Lovett
Gordon Johnson	Buck Henry
Vern Miller	Huey Lewis

Exploding Raymond Carver's spare stories and minimally drawn characters onto the screen with startling imagination, Robert Altman has made his most complex and full-bodied human comedy since "Nashville" in "Short Cuts."

Crisscrossing 22 significant characters through an impressively constructed web of interconnected plots and subplots, this is a bemused contemplation of the unaccountable way people behave when fate deals them unexpected hands, embracing everything from slapstick comedy to devastating tragedy. Top reviews and terrific cast will get this Fine Line release off to a strong start in specialized situations, sparked by its world premiere at the Venice Film Festival and U.S. bow as opener of the New York Film Festival. Prime marketing challenges entailed in putting the picture over with a wider public include the three-hour running time, fragmented structure and emotional distance stemming from Altman's characteristic skepticism about the human animal.

Few films have tried to detail so much, to chart so many trajectories, to drop so many little truths while not insisting upon some grandiose overall statement.

While the filmmaking mastery is evident in every area, the two things that are finally most impressive are the way Altman and co-screenwriter Frank Barhydt have expanded the stories, and the offhandedness of it all. Most films have trouble enough telling one story, but Altman makes juggling a trunk load of them seem easy.

Set mostly in the Pacific Northwest and populated by working class characters, Carver's stories deal with convulsions in commonplace lives, how people react to the sudden intrusion of setbacks, infidelity, violence and death.

By shuffling the deck of stories, Altman has importantly magnified the elements of chance, randomness and luck as determinants in the cosmic scheme of things. Net effect is that of eavesdropping upon very carefully selected slices of life.

Shifting the action effectively to the blandly anonymous outlying areas of Los Angeles, Altman raises the curtain with Medfly spray being rained down on the city's inhabitants, a metaphor some will read more into than others. With economical simplicity, he brings on his enormous troupe of players.

They include married couple Bruce Davison and Andie MacDowell, whose young son is hit by a car driven by waitress Lily Tomlin, a trailer park denizen whose marriage to chauffeur Tom Waits has hit choppy water. Attending to the injured boy is doctor Matthew Modine, who still wonders if artist wife Julianne Moore had an affair a few years back. They meet married couple Anne Archer, who works as a clown at children's parties, and Fred Ward at a concert and invite them to dinner, but first Ward is due to take a fishing trip with buddies Buck Henry and Huey Lewis, during which they make the shocking discovery of a dead woman's body in a river.

Performing at the concert is classical cellist Lori Singer, a loner whose mother Annie Ross sings jazz and ballads at a local club. Among the hangout's habitues are pool serviceman Chris Penn and wife Jennifer Jason Leigh, who indelibly gives phone sex from home while feeding her kids, and their friends Robert Downey Jr., a special-effects makeup artist, and Lili Taylor, who make the most of a housesitting opportunity.

Medfly chopper pilot Peter Gallagher has split from wife Frances McDormand, who in turn has been having an affair with L.A. cop Tim Robbins, whose wife Madeleine Stowe models for Moore.

Conclusion loosely ties the disparate characters together by way of a unifying event, although it doesn't unite them physically in one place a la "Nashville."

Altman has used Carver's stories as a vehicle for presenting a vast panorama of life problems that are humorous, grim and absurd in equal measure. Viewer interest in the goings-on is generated not by artificial melodrama or hyped-up filmmaking technique, but by the recognition factor of the human foibles on display.

As the grand ringmaster, it's here that Altman passes the baton to his actors, whose behavioral insights are critical to the film's success.

MacDowell excels as a mother agonizing over the prolonged hospitalization of her injured son; with his fascistic glare and manipulativeness, Robbins crystallizes why a lot of people don't like L.A. cops; Penn subtly registers a limited man going over the edge, and Moore is arresting as the spunky artist (she also stars in what will no doubt be the most discussed scene, in which she casually performs naked from the waist down).

Also noteworthy are Archer, as a woman outraged by her husband's casual response to finding a corpse; Lemmon, who has a showpiece monologue in which he reveals a dark secret to long-estranged son Davison, and McDormand and Gallagher, the former showing no quarter as a spiteful estranged wife, the latter taking gleeful vengeance on her furniture with a chain saw.

But there are ways in which the film comes up short. Some uncomfortable traces of condescension toward the characters creep in, and film may not be as funny as it sometimes strives to be.

As in any multi-episode film, some vignettes work better than others. The price it pays for being an observant character piece, rather than narrative-driven, is that its length is fully felt.

Altman and lenser Walt Lloyd keep the camera alertly moving but simple, often starting with establishing shots, then closing in on the actors. Editor Geraldine Peroni has done a stupendous job juggling the story lines, never losing sight of one for too long, and expertly judging when to resume another.

Mark Isham's effective score is abetted by a torrent of source music, notably Ross' throaty jazz vocals and Singer's cello playing.

For the record, the Carver stories drawn upon are "Jerry and Molly and Sam," "Will You Please Be Quiet, Please?," "Collectors," "Neighbors," "A Small Good Thing," "So Much Water So Close to Home," "They're Not Your Husband," "Vitamins" and "Tell the Women We're Going," and the narrative poem "Lemonade."

—*Todd McCarthy*

THE AGE OF INNOCENCE

A Columbia release of a Cappa/De Fina production. Produced by Barbara De Fina. Co-producer, Bruce S. Pustin. Directed by Martin Scorsese. Screenplay, Jay Cocks, Martin Scorsese, based on the novel by Edith Wharton. Camera (Technicolor; Super 35 widescreen), Michael Ballhaus; editor, Thelma Schoonmaker; music, Elmer Bernstein; production design, Dante Ferretti; art direction, Speed Hopkins; set decoration, Robert J. Franco, Amy Marshall; costume design, Gabriella Pescucci; sound (Dolby), Tod Maitland; special visual effects, Illusion Arts, Syd Dutton, Bill Taylor; associate producer-assistant director, Joseph Reidy; casting, Ellen Lewis. Reviewed at Sony Studios screening room, Culver City, Aug. 26, 1993. (In Venice Film Festival — non-competing.) MPAA rating: PG. Running time: **136 MIN.**

Newland Archer	Daniel Day-Lewis
Ellen Olenska	Michelle Pfeiffer
May Welland	Winona Ryder
Mrs. Mingott	Miriam Margolyes
Larry Lefferts	Richard E. Grant
Sillerton Jackson	Alec McCowen
Mrs. Welland	Geraldine Chaplin
Regina Beaufort	Mary Beth Hurt
Julius Beaufort	Stuart Wilson
Mrs. Archer	Sian Phillips
Mr. van der Luyden	Michael Gough
Mrs. van der Luyden	Alexis Smith
Letterblair	Norman Lloyd
Monsieur Riviere	Jonathan Pryce
Janie Archer	Carolyn Farina
Ted Archer	Robert Sean Leonard
Narrator	Joanne Woodward

An extraordinarily sumptuous piece of filmmaking, "The Age of Innocence" is a faithful adaptation of Edith Wharton's classic novel, which is both a blessing and a bit of a curse. Director Martin Scorsese has met most of the challenges inherent in tackling such a formidable period piece, but the material remains cloaked by the very propriety, stiff manners and emotional starchiness the picture delineates in such copious detail. Despite all the talent involved, this portrait of an impossible romance set in the upper reaches of New York society in the 1870s has a finite audience, more or less defined by the $25 million to $30 million grosses achieved by such tony releases as "Howards End" and "Dangerous Liaisons."

Even if it does that well, this prestige entry, with its reported $40 million-plus price tag, will be a long way from break-even. Film premiered Aug. 31 at the Venice Film Festival.

For sophisticated viewers with a taste for literary adaptations and visits to the past, there is a great deal here to savor. The sets, costumes, cinematography, music and attention to the mores and customs of the time are almost unimaginably luxurious and evocative, giving evidence of tremendous research and a feel of extreme authenticity. The screenplay is intelligent and economical, and the casting and acting, from the leads to the smallest roles, are as fine as one could want.

But it is difficult to picture general audiences warming up to these representatives of the old ruling class, whom Wharton brilliantly illustrated in her 1921 Pulitzer Prize-winning novel.

Present rendition (Irene Dunne and John Boles starred in a forgotten 1934 version) begins with a lovely floral-and-lace title sequence by Elaine and Saul Bass, then plunges the viewer into the hotbed of high society — the opera, where the real action is in the boxes, not onstage. The focus of most lorgnettes this evening is Ellen Olenska (Michelle Pfeiffer), a beautiful American recently returned from Europe after leaving her aristocratic husband.

Ellen is a cousin of lovely young May Welland (Winona Ryder), who is just now announcing her engagement to socially prominent lawyer Newland Archer (Daniel Day-Lewis).

Although related to a distinguished family, Ellen is much whispered about due to the free-thinking ideas she appears to have acquired in Europe, and because she is rumored to have lived with her male secretary.

In this world of formal balls, dinners and other ritualized social engagements, propriety is all, and Countess Olenska doesn't conform to the letter of New York's standards. But Newland Archer, who at moments dares to express unorthodox ideas about acceptable behavior for women, defends her and, with the help of his mother, orchestrates her acceptance into society.

But just as he is urging May to move up the date of their wedding, Newland becomes entranced by the bewitching Ellen, who is tantalizingly different from everyone else in his sphere. With the excuse of advising her legally on her impending divorce, he is able to call on her frequently, and when he finally reveals his feelings, it's almost too much for both of them.

The real subject of the film is Newland's adhering to his prescribed role rather than following his heart, and while this is apparent, the emotion is, crucially, not deeply felt or conveyed. The obsessive central love story is repressed on all levels, which serves to parch the film more than intensify it. Nor does a rather flat coda, set in Paris years

September 13, 1993 (Cont.)

later, deliver the intended poignance.

The picture's other subject is the re-creation of an era, and in this the film is almost overwhelmingly successful. The repeated close-ups of 1870s place settings, food preparation, cigar trimmers, fabrics, clothes, paintings and decor, to the accompaniment of appropriate music, bespeaks an immersion in time and place that some may feel goes beyond the necessary to the fanatical, but which actually constitutes a pleasure in its own right.

Dante Ferretti's production design and Gabriella Pescucci's costume design are practically beyond compare, and Michael Ballhaus surpasses himself with his resplendent widescreen cinematography (he and Scorsese get in a good little joke about aspect ratios in a scene in which Newland inspects some of Ellen's unusually shaped paintings).

In his attempt to define an era through a thwarted romance set among the trappings of the very rich, Scorsese conjures up the cinematic worlds of Max Ophuls, notably "Madame de ... ," and Luchino Visconti, particularly "Senso" and "The Leopard."

For a director previously associated mostly with the violence of the lower classes of New York, it's a notable attempt to stretch, and admirable in many ways.

Day-Lewis cuts an impressive figure as Newland, and it may be that he is playing something of a thankless part: a character who invariably makes decisions that disappoint.

The two principal female roles are superbly filled. For any actress to make the transition from Catwoman to Ellen Olenska would be impressive, and that Pfeiffer succeeds here as she did in that role is the most conclusive proof yet of her widening talents. Ryder is also perfect as the child-woman with a more tenacious instinct than her retiring manner would indicate.

A great roster of superior actors fills out the supporting roles, and seeing the likes of Alec McCowen, Sian Phillips, Richard E. Grant, Miriam Margolyes, Geraldine Chaplin, Mary Beth Hurt, Norman Lloyd, Michael Gough, Jonathan Pryce and, in her last role, the late Alexis Smith pop up throughout reps a connoisseur's delight.

Thesps generally affect a mid-Atlantic accent that would seem appropriate to the time, so it is jarring to hear Joanne Woodward's plain contemporary American delivery of the narration, which is oppressively abundant at the outset but fortunately recedes later on.

Scorsese brings great energy to what could have been a very static story, although his style is more restrained and less elaborate than usual. Script by the director and former film critic Jay Cocks judiciously trims the story down to

manageable length while retaining its essential elements.

Elmer Bernstein's score is full-bodied and richly romantic, and Thelma Schoonmaker's editing is very finely tuned. This is no doubt one of the few films ever to credit a table decoration consultant, etiquette consultant and chef for 19th-century meals, and these credits are well earned.   —*Todd McCarthy*

THE JOY LUCK CLUB

A Buena Vista release of a Hollywood Pictures presentation of an Oliver Stone production in association with Ronald Bass. Produced by Wayne Wang, Amy Tan, Bass, Patrick Markey. Executive producers, Stone, Janet Yang. Directed by Wang. Screenplay, Tan, Bass, based on Tan's novel. Camera (Monaco Film Lab color; Technicolor prints), Amir Mokri; editor, Maysie Hoy; music, Rachel Portman; production design, Donald Graham Burt; art direction, Diana Kunce; art direction (China), Kwan Kit (Eddy) Kwok, Jian Jun Li; set decoration, Jim Poynter; costume design, Lydia Tanji, Shu Lan Ding (China); sound (Dolby), Curtis Choy; sound design, Tim Chau; associate producer (China), Jessinta Liu Fung Ping; assistant director, Josh King; assistant directors (China), Kong Hon (Cub) Chien, De Gen Yang; casting, Heidi Levitt, with Risa Bramon Garcia. Reviewed at the Beverly Connection Theater, L.A., Sept. 2, 1993. (In Telluride, Toronto Film Festivals.) MPAA rating: R. Running time: **138 MIN.**

Lindo	Tsai Chin
Suyuan	Kieu Chinh
An Mei	Lisa Lu
Ying Ying	France Nuyen
Rose	Rosalind Chao
Lena	Lauren Tom
Waverly	Tamlyn Tomita
June	Ming-Na Wen
Harold	Michael Paul Chan
Ted	Andrew McCarthy
Rich	Christopher Rich
Lin Xiao	Russell Wong
Old Chong	Victor Wong
An Mei's Mother	Vivian Wu
Mr. Jordan	Jack Ford
Mrs. Jordan	Diane Baker

Wayne Wang's fine adaptation of Amy Tan's best-selling "The Joy Luck Club" will no doubt mark a breakthrough for films about Asians in America. Beautifully made and acted and emotionally moving in the bargain, this dramatic study of trying relationships between Chinese mothers and daughters through the century will be widely accessible to all viewers, although women will certainly comprise the base audience. A surprising entry from Hollywood Pictures, via Oliver Stone's company, this lovely production should generate strong support in many quarters and perform well through the fall. Pic received its world preem over the weekend at the Telluride Film Festival.

Conventional Hollywood wisdom offered many excuses why Tan's

novel, the No. 1 fiction bestseller of 1989, would not make a viable film: It centered on Asian women, the names and faces would be confusing, there were too many stories jumping around in time, and much of the dialogue would need to be in Chinese.

Quite impressively, screenwriters Tan and Ronald Bass and director Wang have basically solved all these potential problems in a very lucid explication of the major tales related in the book.

Even more importantly, from a commercial p.o.v., they have retained, and perhaps even magnified, the universal emotional qualities of the material, making this story of innumerable hardships and sacrifices one that the mainstream general public will very likely embrace.

The central occasion of a festive farewell party for June, one of the daughters, on the eve of her departure for China, is skillfully used like the hub of a wheel, with the individual stories its spokes.

As flashbacks illustrate the events, June relates how her late mother left two babies behind during her flight from her war-torn country, and adds background about their own estrangement, which introduces one of the central themes of mothers' expectations for, and disappointment in, their daughters.

Attention then turns to one of June's mahjong-playing "aunties," Lindo, who tells of how she was sold into marriage by her mother at 15, and how she and her daughter Waverly endured many rocky years before a touching reconciliation.

Another older woman, Ying Ying, had a son by a playboy husband in China and endured events so tragic that her American daughter Lena remains hounded by her mother's depression.

And young Rose, whose marriage to a white American has come unglued, reveals the devastating saga of her mother An Mei, who was one of several wives to a rich man in China and sacrificed herself so that her daughter might acquire strength.

Tying things together is June's climactic trip to China, and her ultimate reunion with her lost sisters will leave millions teary-eyed at the powerful, if sentimental, fadeout.

After years of ups and downs as an independent filmmaker, Wayne Wang has made a dramatically confident move into the mainstream here, on his own terms, and with highly congenial material. The focus remains as intimate as in his previous work, but the emotions and concerns are much bigger.

Visually, film is splendid, with Amir Mokri's luminous lensing, Donald Graham Burt's production design and Lydia Tanji's costumes fusing into a rich, but not overly

self-conscious, look. Thesping from the vast cast is top-notch across the boards.

Quibbles might relate to slight pacing problems at times, a bit of a sag around the two-hour mark and, most of all, the similarity of some of the stories, which makes the lives of these women seem surprisingly uniform. But the film contributes a strong and exceedingly rare view of a different cultural experience to the American screen, and in a way that will reach a wide public.

—*Todd McCarthy*

CALENDAR GIRL

A Columbia Pictures release of a Parkway production. Produced by Debbie Robins, Gary Marsh. Executive producers, Penny Marshall, Elliot Abbott. Directed by John Whitesell. Screenplay, Paul W. Shapiro. Camera (Technicolor), Tom Priestley; editor, Wendy Greene Bricmont; music, Hans Zimmer; production design, Bill Groom; art direction, Sarah Knowles; costume design, Erica Edell Phillips; sound (Dolby), Don Hall; associate producer, Amy Lemisch; assistant director, Tony Gittelson; casting, Lisa Beach. Reviewed at TriStar screening room, Culver City, Aug. 16, 1993. MPAA Rating: PG-13. Running time: **90 MIN.**

Roy Darpinian	Jason Priestley
Ned Bleuer	Gabriel Olds
Scott Foreman	Jerry O'Connell
Harvey Darpinian	Joe Pantoliano
Roy's father	Steve Railsback
Arturo Gallo	Kurt Fuller
Antonio Gallo	Stephen Tobolowsky
Becky O'Brien	Emily Warfield
Marilyn Monroe	Stephanie Anderson
Monroe's voice	Cortney Page
Chubby Checker	Himself

Masquerading as a wild romantic adventure, "Calender Girl" is actually a dull, sanctimonious morality tale about the meaning of friendship and manhood in the manner of James Dean's melodramas. The timing for Columbia's youth comedy is all wrong, as pic should have been released in late spring or early summer. This may initially appeal to fans of "Beverly Hills, 90210" heartthrob Jason Priestley, who makes his feature film debut, but will be quickly forgotten following a brief theatrical run.

Awkward narration intros the three heroes, who are fated to form a lifelong bond. They first meet at a Howdy Doody look-alike competition, at age 6, and at 12 experience their initial sexual urgings via Marilyn Monroe's famous nude calendar.

Main story is set in June 1962, right after Monroe was fired from Fox's "Something's Got to Give," with the three high school grads now experts on the star's life and career. Preying on his friends' fantasy of meeting the actress, Roy Darpinian (Priestley) talks his pals (Jerry O'Connell and Gabriel Olds) into a crazy plan: Why not leave their boring Nevada town and drive

September 13, 1993 (Cont.)

to Hollywood in his father's sky blue Galaxy 500 convertible?

Regrettably, once the trio lands in Hollywood and starts a vigil outside Monroe's house, pic settles into a static mood. Staying with Priestley's uncle Harvey (Joe Pantoliano), an aspiring actor whose day job is selling bomb shelters, provides some amusing moments, but they aren't enough. Chief problem is Paul W. Shapiro's unfunny, schematic script, which consists of the boys' interminable machinations to meet Monroe. One such effort is placing a cow in the star's yard because of her alleged love of animals.

So long as Monroe is seen from afar and only her voice is heard, her charismatic mystique is maintained. But pic makes the mistake of letting the boys fulfill their dream; the "date" with Monroe (Stephanie Anderson) is a particularly weak sequence.

What Shapiro and first-time director John Whitesell do get right is the dynamics of the group, specifically Priestley's leadership as a combination of persuasion, intimidation and manipulation. He is a misunderstood and rebellious son, and his emotional reconciliation with his father brings to mind "Rebel Without a Cause" and "East of Eden." In its sticky sentimentality, pic bears the signature of Penny Marshall, who co-executive produced, though it lacks the shrewd savvy of her work.

"Calendar Girl" is afflicted with wholesome, beefy moralism: In an old-fashioned manner, everything is laid out and messages don't flinch from the banality of the film's "end of innocence" theme as the boys go their separate ways at the end.

Priestley looks handsome in a bland TV manner, but he's not particularly interesting to watch. Olds and O'Connell register better, but all are hampered by uninspired writing and plodding direction.

Tech credits are adequate, the only energetic element being the pop songs of the era.

—*Emanuel Levy*

THE LAST PARTY

A Triton Pictures release of a Campaign Films Inc. & the Athena Group production. Produced by Eric Cahan, Donovan Leitch, Josh Richman. Executive producers, Samuel D. Waksal, Elliott Kastner. Co-producer, Garth Stein. Directed by Mark Benjamin, Marc Levin. Camera, Benjamin; editor, Wendey Stanzler; music coordinator, Diane DeLouise Wessel; sound, Pamela Yates; associate producer, Serena Altschul. Reviewed at the Raleigh Studios screening room, Hollywood, Aug. 11, 1993. Running time: **95 MIN.**

This video chronicle of Robert Downey Jr.'s trip to the 1992 Democratic National Convention wants to issue a call-to-arms to Generation X but plays like a pretentious vanity piece as much as a political

tract. Pic is opening in limited release, but box office should be limited even on the arthouse circuit, enjoying less circulation than the last out-of-focus video featuring a young actor at a political convention four years earlier.

There is some irony, of course, that the 1988 convention became infamous for the pirate Rob Lowe video, taken by many as a symbol of the decadence of the '80s. "The Last Party" may represent a recoil effect toward greater political consciousness, but no less self-gratification.

Directed by Mark Benjamin and Marc Levin, documentarians whose credits include some of Bill Moyers' PBS specials, the film could have been an intriguing behind-the-scenes look at the Democratic and Republican conventions but keeps getting sidetracked by focusing on Downey and how everything affects him, to which we can only reply, "Who cares?"

Emphasis on the actor's life and recollections, in fact, raises the question whether this is supposed to be about issues facing a post-Cold War America or about Downey, the suddenly conscious political animal, who lacks the kind of massive star appeal needed to justify this kind of vehicle.

Downey and crew certainly put considerable time into the effort, engaging in a vast array of interviews — with everyone from angry rappers to Wall Street types, from ardent feminists to militant right-to-lifers. Unfortunately, what's lacking is any real connecting theme, other than who's asking the questions.

Hollywood denizens turn up as background players, adding to the self-aware, home-movie feel. Those on hand include Mary Stuart Masterson (Downey's co-star in "Chances Are," her apparent qualification to serve as spokeswoman for her generation), Sean Penn, Richard Lewis, Spike Lee, Oliver Stone, Christian Slater and William Baldwin.

Aside from the lack of a linear through-line there are more basic foul-ups. The filmmakers, for example, only sporadically identify subjects, a particular disservice to those who might not recognize Sen. John Kerrey or G. Gordon Liddy. For all the preoccupation about awakening twentysomethings, the older generation steals the show — namely, the gruff, foul-mouthed Robert Downey Sr., who cuts to the core of political issues while displaying a genuine affection for his son that, alas, belongs in a better (or at least different) movie.

"The Last Party" does capture a few ironic sidelights to the conventions, such as a stripper who proclaims herself "a registered Republican" while hosing off between numbers. More profound moments are spread sparingly among the detritus, but it's nothing you couldn't see some variation of nightly on "The CBS Evening News."

Clearly, there's room for an intelligent documentary delineating the fractious nature of modern America and where young citizens fit in, but

this isn't close to being it; instead, we're served up a poor-man's version of MTV's "The Real World," documenting the summer vacation of a young actor who's decided he wants to make a difference.

The aim is understandable and even laudable, but from an entertainment standpoint, that Rob Lowe video has this "Party" beat hands down. —*Brian Lowry*

SUGAR HILL

A 20th Century Fox release of a Beacon presentation of a South Street Entertainment Group production. Produced by Rudy Langlais, Gregory Brown. Executive producers, Armyan Bernstein, Tom Rosenberg, Marc Abraham. Line producer, Steven R. McGlothen. Directed by Leon Ichaso. Screenplay, Barry Michael Cooper. Camera (Deluxe color), Bojan Bazelli; editor, Gary Karr; music, Terence Blanchard; production design, Michael Helmy; art direction, J. Jergensen; set decoration, Kathryn Peters, Elaine O'Donnell (N.Y.); costume design, Eduardo Castro; sound (Dolby), Malcolm Morris, Rolf Pardula (N.Y.); assistant directors, Randy Carter, Bruce Greenfield (N.Y.); casting, Mary Gail Artz, Barbara Cohen. Reviewed at 20th Century Fox screening room, L.A., Aug. 31, 1993. MPAA Rating: R. Running time: **123 MIN.**
Roemello Skuggs .... Wesley Snipes
Raynathan Skuggs ...... Michael Wright
Melissa .... Theresa Randle
A.R. Skuggs .... Clarence Williams III
Gus Molino .... Abe Vigoda
Harry Molino .... Larry Joshua
Lolly Jonas .... Ernie Hudson
Doris Holly .... Leslie Uggams
Ella Skuggs .... Khandi Alexander
Sal Marconi .... Raymond Serra
Tony Adamo .... Joe Dallesandro
Mark Doby .... Vondie Curtis-Hall

A self-indulgent drama about a Harlem drug kingpin trying to go straight, "Sugar Hill" plays like a dreary variation on "New Jack City." Heavy on simplistic psychology and light on plausibility, pic exists in a netherworld between art and action films that makes it the least commercially viable Wesley Snipes entry since he hit the big time. Not skedded for domestic release until January, it is premiering at the Montreal Film Festival.

Riddled with flashbacks, the script by former journalist and "New Jack City" co-writer Barry Michael Cooper tells of two brothers with giant chips on their shoulders. Having witnessed their mother overdose and white mobsters shoot their addict father, Roemello and Raynathan Skuggs (Snipes and Michael Wright) long ago decided to get their own by becoming the biggest dealers in Harlem.

But while Raynathan remains an ambitious hothead, Roemello, who has all the worldly possessions he could desire, has become bored and wants out. But, natch, that's easier said than done, since the old-time Mafia hoods in the hood have

brought in new blood from Brooklyn to muscle in on the local action.

When not brooding in lonely luxury, Roemello persistently courts the beautiful young Melissa (Theresa Randle), a proper lady who wants nothing more to do with him when she discovers his metier, but who can't ignore him either. It all ends in predictably bloody violence, but with a particularly sappy and unbelievable coda that seems tacked on to relieve what would otherwise have been total grimness.

Best known for his 1985 indie musical "Crossover Dreams," director Leon Ichaso opts for a straightforward presentational approach utterly lacking in dynamics and excitement. Staging is conventional and dialogue scenes are lethargically paced, which, combined with unnecessary and protracted scenes, results in a tiresomely long picture. In particular, the final reels are filled with digressions when they should build to a streamlined climax.

Looking just too cool in his expensive threads and elegant Jaguar, Snipes invests little energy in his performance until the end, when the urgency of his situation seems to wake him up. As his brother, Wright is called upon mostly to deliver hysterical, violence-threatening tirades, which grow tiresome after awhile. Randle is lovely in a standard role, and Abe Vigoda is a welcome presence as a veteran lieutenant whom the mob posted in Harlem decades before.

Tech contributions are fine, distinguished by Bojan Bazelli's well-defined lensing and Terence Blanchard's moody jazz score.

Designed to show the drug trade as a dead-end, no-win field, pic is undoubtedly well-intentioned, but territory is so familiar by now that some new angles are needed to command viewer attention. "Sugar Hill" provides too little in the way of either insight or excitement.

—*Todd McCarthy*

MONTREAL FEST

LE SEXE DES ETOILES
(THE SEX OF THE STARS)
(Canadian)

A CFP (Quebec) release of a Les Productions du Regard & Bloom Films production, with the participation of the National Film Board of Canada, Telefilm Canada, SOGIC. (International sales: Cinepix.) Produced by Jean-Roch Marcotte, Pierre Gendron. Directed by Paule Baillargeon. Screenplay, Monique Proulx, based on her novel. Camera (color), Eric Cayla; editor, Helene Girard; music, Yves Laferriere; production design, Real Ouellette; sound, Richard Besse, Viateur Paiement; associate producer, Doris Girard; line producer, Yves Richard; assistant director, Mireille Goulet. Reviewed at World Film Festival, Montreal (competing), Aug. 26, 1993. Running time: **104 MIN.**

September 13, 1993 (Cont.)

Camille
.... Marianne-Coquelicot Mercier
Marie-Pierre .... Denis Mercier
Lucky .... Tobie Pelletier
Michele .... Sylvie Drapeau
J. Boulet .... Luc Picard
Jacob .... Giles Renaud

Selected to open the 1993 Montreal World Film Fest, "The Sex of the Stars," from distaff helmer Paule Baillargeon, proves an interesting, worthy but strangely uninvolving selection. Offbeater, about a 12-year-old girl who has to come to terms with the fact that her beloved father is a transsexual, never really engages the emotions, despite sensitive handling. It's unlikely to be much of an arthouse attraction, despite a titillating, and misleading, ad campaign.

On paper, the story, adapted by Monique Proulx from her own 1987 novel, has plenty of possibilities. Camille (Marianne-Coquelicot Mercier) is a bright youngster, a few weeks short of her 13th birthday. She's obsessed with astronomy, and claims she likes star gazing because stars have no sex.

Her problem is not only that her dad walked out on her and her mother, Michele (Sylvie Drapeau), some years before and that she longs for him to come back; it's that when he does come back, it's as a not very attractive woman, Marie-Pierre (Denis Mercier). "Father" and daughter strike up a tentative relationship, and she persuades him to stay on in Montreal instead of returning immediately to New York as he'd planned. But she wants her old father back, and Marie-Pierre isn't about to change. Growing up fast, Camille is taken in hand by Lucky (Tobie Pelletier), a crippled kid her age, who snorts cocaine and knows more than he should about the wilder side of sex.

It's a pity that, having set up this intriguing premise, Proulx and Baillargeon do very little with it. What should have been an emotionally draining experience plays, instead, as unexciting, with little variation in mood. Part of the problem is the awkward performance of Denis Mercier, who never convinces as Marie-Pierre. Marianne-Coquelicot Mercier is somewhat more successful in depicting the daughter's pain, but by far the best performance comes from Drapeau as the angry, anguished mother.

Pic was greeted coolly by the opening-night audience, and it won't travel far. Tech credits are all excellent.   —*David Stratton*

IL LUNGO SILENZIO
(THE LONG SILENCE)
(Italian-French-German)

A UIP (Italy) release of an Evento Spettacolo (Rome)-Union P.N. (Rome)-K.G. Prods. (Paris) co-production, in collaboration with Bioskop Film (Munich). Produced by Felice Laudadio. Directed by Margarethe Von Trotta. Screenplay, Laudadio. Camera (Telecolor), Marco Sperduti; editors, Ugo De Rossi, Nino Baragli; music, Ennio Morricone; production design, Antonello Geleng; sound, Remo Ugolinelli; associate producer, Giorgio Leopardi; assistant director, Beatrice Banfi. Reviewed at World Film Festival, Montreal (competing), Aug. 29, 1993. Running time: **93 MIN.**
Dr. Carla Aldrovandi .... Carla Gravina
Judge Marco Canova .... Jacques Perrin
Carla's Mother .... Alida Valli
Rosa .... Ottavia Piccolo
Tommaso Pesce .... Guiliano Montaldo
Francesco Mancini .... Paolo Graziosi
Maria Mancini .... Agnese Nano
Fantoni .... Ivano Marescotti
Fantoni's wife .... Antonella Attili

Margarethe Von Trotta's agonizingly up-to-the-minute political thriller, "The Long Silence," is a devastating depiction of a society almost in the grip of anarchy. Poignant and grim, film nevertheless ends on a note of muted optimism, and could well make an impact internationally. It's one of Von Trotta's best.

The very first image sets the mood: A middle-aged couple stroll down a beach at dusk; the camera pulls back to reveal they're surrounded by heavily armed bodyguards.

The husband, Marco (Jacques Perrin), is an investigating judge on the verge of prosecuting senior government ministers and businessmen for corruption and arms trafficking. The wife, Carla (Carla Gravina), is a successful gynecologist who is wracked with fear for her husband's safety.

Pic's first half beautifully depicts the scary, restricted lifestyle of the couple for whom a trip to a favorite restaurant is a logistical nightmare. As Marco turns up more and more evidence, through an informer held in a secret place, his life is constantly threatened via anonymous phone calls. Security is tightened further, but, as it turns out, in vain.

At midpoint, the inevitable occurs. Marco and the informer are assassinated and, soon afterward, Marco's colleague also is murdered. At first devastated, Carla gradually resolves to continue her husband's work, using notes and documents he'd hidden away, and with the help of the informer's widow. She gives stories to the press and helps produce a TV docu in which widows of assassinated judges speak out. But now her life, too, is in danger.

Gravina is excellent as the initially frightened, ultimately angry and vengeful woman, and there are strong supporting performances from Perrin as her dedicated, doomed husband, Ottavia Piccolo as her best friend, Guiliano Montaldo as Marco's boss and Alida Valli as Carla's troubled mother.

Von Trotta creates a genuinely frightening atmosphere in which the investigators and their families live in constant dread. Snippets of near-current news items add to the film's air of authenticity. Director paces the film with unerring precision, and the result is a thriller that never relaxes its grip during a very tight 93 minutes. A typically vibrant Ennio Morricone score helps a lot.

Ending may at first glance seem too bleak for some, but a coda suggests that Italy's salvation lies in its women. The film, which is dedicated to the late producer Franco Cristaldi, seems designed to rouse public opinion against organized crime and official corruption.

All tech credits are first-rate.
—*David Stratton*

THE MOZART BIRD
(DUTCH)

A Spellbound production. (International sales: Intl. Art Film, Amsterdam.) Produced, directed by Ian Kerkhof. Screenplay, Kerkhof, Daniel Daran. Camera (color), Joost van Gelder; editor, Wendela Scheltema; music, Rosalind George; sound, Fokke van Saane. Reviewed Aug. 28, 1993, at World Film Festival, Montreal. Running time: **75 MIN.**
Howard .... Daniel Daran
Selene .... Stacey Grace

The explicit sex and explicit talk about sex throughout "The Mozart Bird" may turn off many viewers and, in fact, there were lots of walkouts at the Montreal Fest screening. But this steamy, intellectual gabfest could still find a niche on the arthouse circuit.

Howard (Daniel Daran) and Selene (Stacey Grace), a couple of English-speaking foreigners living in Amsterdam, begin a casual affair that turns serious and then begins to deteriorate. Howard is a fledgling fiction writer, and both suffer from the tendency to over-intellectualize — typical of over-educated, underemployed university grads.

"You were the first man I met who actually liked talking about sex," observes Selene at one point, and that neatly sums up the film. There's endless analysis of their sex lives, which is saved from self-indulgence by the tough, true-to-life humor of the script by Daran and director Ian Kerkhof.

But Kerkhof's attempt to deliver a "Last Tango in Amsterdam" isn't for everyone: Almost all the action takes place in one apartment, and the claustrophobic setting is reinforced by the stark, gloomy photography. The first 15 minutes take place in almost total darkness.

Pic also features lots of nudity and sex scenes guaranteed to land it in ratings hot water. Tech credits are average.   —*Brendan Kelly*

TAORMINA FEST

DIE MACHT DER BILER: LENI RIEFENSTAHL
(THE POWER OF THE IMAGE: LENI RIEFENSTAHL)
(DOCU/GERMAN-BRITISH-FRENCH/ COLOR-B&W)

An Omega Film/Nomad Films/ZDF/Channel Four Television/Arte coproduction. (Foreign sales: Omega Film.) Produced by Hans-Jurgen Panitz, Jacques De Clercq, Dimitri De Clercq. Directed, written by Ray Muller. Camera (color/b&w), Walter A. Franke, Michel Baudour, Jurgen Martin, Ulrich Jaenchen; underwater camera, Horst Kettner; editors, Beate Koster, Stefan Mothes, Vera Dubsikova; music, Ulrich Bassenge, Wolfgang Neumann; historical consultants, Kevin Brownlow, David Culbert, Martin Lolperdinger. Reviewed at the Taormina Film Festival (Italy), Aug. 1, 1993. Running time: **181 MIN.**

In her native Germany, filmmaker Leni Riefenstahl is still a taboo topic for many, as witnessed by the number of German directors who not only turned down the opportunity to make this film, but refused to comment on her work onscreen. Documaker Ray Muller accepted the assignment, and though three hours long, the intriguing result has scarcely a dull moment and should be received with absorbed interest at fests and in specialized theatrical and TV slots.

One of the great filmmakers, Riefenstahl made her most memorable films in the service of the Nazi cause, and this paradox between good art and bad politics remains a painful enigma for film theorists.

Part of the fascination of this docu lies in the way Muller puts the woman and her work before the audience, without imposing reassuring evaluations. The burden of judgment rests with the viewer, and it isn't an easy task. In the end, the film leaves many questions unanswered.

Perhaps in the hope of filling this gap, Channel Four is adding further material about Riefenstahl's childhood and youth before airing the film in the U.K., though one wonders if this will shed any light on the dark riddle of political responsibility she has always refused to address.

Riefenstahl — now a hyperactive 90-year-old — began her career as a dancer and actress; in 1932 she directed "The Blue Light."

September 13, 1993 (Cont.)

Fascinated by the atmosphere of a Nazi rally she attended, she was introduced to Hitler, who is supposed to have pegged the beautiful young Riefenstahl as the embodiment of his mythic ideal of a heroic German superwoman. Although she judged a film she made about him a failure, the *Fuhrer* was pleased enough to give her carte blanche on "Triumph of the Will," lensed at the Nazis' Nuremberg rally in 1934.

This film, like her subsequent "Olympia," about the 1936 Berlin games, exemplifies an unbearable contradiction between powerfully moving filmmaking and the way it aesthetically mirrors Nazi ideology. Her masses of regimented soldiers and love for monumental theatricality have been much plundered by grandiose filmmakers in the years since.

Riefenstahl's images of a triumphant Hitler create uncomfortably mixed emotions. Muller cleverly incorporates long excerpts from these docus, narrated by Riefenstahl, as she explains how she argued with the organizers of the Nuremberg rally about planting her cameras onstage, or how she was the first to use multiple camera setups to capture the thrill of the *Fuhrer's* arrival in the city.

Though she speaks a great deal about technical questions, Riefenstahl goes from touchy to livid when Muller poses questions about her political responsibility in making these films. She denies ever being a Nazi or going out socially (as Goebbels' diaries insist) with Nazi bosses.

She unconvincingly claims she was ignorant of the death camps. She protests her films reflect what all Germans felt about Hitler at the time. "What blame do I have?" she queries, adding that she claims "not to know what the aesthetics of fascism means."

After the war, Riefenstahl was briefly incarcerated and put on trial. Though acquitted of war crimes, she was barred from directing films, and her career came to an abrupt end. For that reason alone — being "boycotted" — she says she regrets having made "Triumph of the Will." And as Muller points out, she was in some respects a victim of a nation's bad conscience.

Vain, egotistical and quick-tempered, always ready to tell Muller he's got his camera in the wrong place, Riefenstahl comes across as a tough-minded woman, but one with more than a few qualities to admire.
— *Deborah Young*

LE JOURNAL DE LADY M

(THE DIARY OF LADY M)

(SWISS-BELGIAN-SPANISH-FRENCH)

A Filmograph release (Switzerland) of a Filmograph (Geneva)/Nomad Film (Brussels)/Messidor Films (Barcelona)/Les Productions Lanzennec (Paris) co-production. (World sales: Metropolitan Film.) Produced by Alain Tanner, Jacques De Clercq, Dimitri De Clercq, Gerardo Herrero, Marta Esteban, Christophe Rossignon. Executive producer, Gerard Ruey for Cab Prods. Directed by Tanner. Screenplay, Myriam Mezieres. Camera (color), Denis Jutzeler; editor, Monica Goux; music, Arie Dzierlatka. Reviewed at the Taormina (Italy) Film Festival (competing), July 31, 1993. Running time: **113 MIN.**
Lady M .... Myriam Mezieres
Diego .... Juanjo Puligcorbe
Nuria .... Felicite Wouassi
Also with: Antoine Basler, Carlotta Soldevilla, Nanou, Marie Peyrucq-Yamou, Gladys Gambie, Makeda.

After directing Myriam Mezieres in "A Flame in My Heart," Alain Tanner takes a plunge into the actress's world with "The Diary of Lady M." Mezieres wrote the screenplay based on her own diary, and result is an intense love story performed in the first person. Besides the limited art-film circuit, pic should have a shot at wider markets due to its red-hot sex scenes and overall erotic charge.

Mezieres, a sultry, bewitching red head, identifies herself only as Lady M, a sexy singer in exotic Parisian bistros. One night a Spanish painter, Diego (Juanjo Puligcorbe), catches her act and waits for her after the show. After a night with her walking around Paris, he leaves for Spain. Their love affair begins when Lady M impulsively goes to Barcelona to see him again. Diego drives her around Catalonia, where the two alternate torrid lovemaking with surprisingly delicate conversation. Mostly it's Mezieres talking in lyrical voiceover, poetically expressing her feelings about her lover and the rest of the world.

If M's feelings are minutely described, the painter's are hidden behind a veil of reticence. His secret emerges when a photo of his black wife, Nuria (Felicite Wouassi), and their little girl drops out of his wallet. Lady M is crushed, and soon leaves. But back in Paris, she misses him so much she invites him to come, even if it means bringing his family. Soon everybody is living awkwardly in her small apartment until passion draws the adults into a threesome.

Pic loses altitude at this point, as events are hurriedly told, and story ends in an improbable coda that is instantly forgettable.

Mezieres is a consummate performer, and Lady M's nightclub numbers are most enjoyable. She radiates sensitivity and intelligence and is riveting to the point of overwhelming the film.

"Diary" is at its best when it opens a curtain on the backstage world of singers and artists. Mezieres calls it an outlaw's life, and she is painfully conscious that she is different from normal folk. Her introspective acceptance of this difference is unexpectedly moving.

Pic's extremely frank sex scenes have a shocking realism and seem a natural outgrowth of Mezieres' honesty in recounting her feelings. A scene in which Lady M shaves her pubic hair and dances for her lover clothed only in a long, dangling earring must set some kind of art-film precedent. — *Deborah Young*

KADISBELLAN

(THE SLINGSHOT)

(SWEDISH-COLOR)

A Svensk Filmindustri presentation of a Svensk/SVT Kanal 1 Drama/Nordisk Film A/S/Filminstitutet production. Produced by Waldemar Bergendahl. Directed, written by Ake Sandgren, based on the novel by Roland Schutt. Camera (color), Goran Nilsson; editor, Grete Moldrup; music, Bjorn Isfalt; production design, Lasse Westfelt; costumes, Inger Pehrsson; sound, Wille Peterson-Berger, Jean-Frederik Axelsson. Reviewed at the Svensk screening room, Stockholm, Sweden, Aug. 9, 1993. Running time: **101 MIN.**
Roland Schutt .... Jesper Salen
Fritiof Schutt .... Stellan Skarsgard
Zipa Schutt .... Basia Frydman
Bertil Schutt .... Niclas Olund
Teacher Lundin . Ernst-Hugo Jaregard
Hinke Bergegren .... Reine Brynolisson
Bitt-Margit .... Frida Hallgren

The best Swedish film of its kind since "My Life as a Dog," "The Slingshot" is an exquisite period piece, combining humor, tragedy and uplifting optimism. It has definite potential to become a big hit in Scandinavia and legs strong enough to carry it throughout the world.

Pic is based on an autobiographical novel by Roland Schutt about his life in Stockholm in the 1920s and '30s. Tome's unusual structure led most observers to consider it unfilmable, but writer-director Ake Sandgren has done a terrific job of extracting episodes and moods from the book so as to preserve its essence.

That essence consists of burlesque comedy, brooding atmosphere and optimism. Roland's father is a devoted socialist with a bad leg and no desire to do real work. Mother, a Jewish refugee from Russia, runs a tobacco shop where she also secretly sells condoms, which were outlawed in Sweden at the time.

As both a Jew and a socialist, Roland suffers from prejudice at school and from his mates, but he has a spirit that always keep him going, even when things turn black. He's also an inventive young man, making slingshots from steel and condoms that he peddles to neighborhood boys, and eventually managing to take revenge on his sadistic teacher and principal.

Acting is superb, especially young Jesper Salen as Roland and the leering Ernst-Hugo Jaregard as his racist, sadistic teacher. Production design, in particular, is also tops, creating a realistic picture of a Stockholm that no longer exists.

Although a couple of side stories are not sufficiently developed, Sandgren has created a film that is thoroughly entertaining and that has enough levels to keep it resonant with viewers long after the credits roll. — *Gunnar Rehlin*

UN DEUX TROIS SOLEIL

(1, 2, 3, SUN)

(FRENCH)

A Gaumont Buena Vista International release of a Gaumont/Cine Valse/France 3 Cinema co-production with the participation of Canal Plus. Produced by Patrice Ledoux. Directed, written by Bertrand Blier. Camera (color, Panavision widescreen), Gerard de Battista; editor, Claudine Merlin; music, Khaled; production design, Theobald Meurisse, Jean-Jacques Caziot, Georges Glon; costume design, Jacqueline Bouchard; sound (Dolby), Pierre Befve, Paul Bertault. Reviewed at Gaumont Kinopanorama, Paris, Aug. 23, 1993. (In Venice Film Festival competing.) Running time: **103 MIN.**
Victorine .... Anouk Grinberg
Constantin .... Marcello Mastroianni
The mother .... Myriam Boyer
Petit Paul .... Olivier Martinez
Maurice .... Jean-Michel Noirey
Also with: Claude Brasseur, Jean-Pierre Marielle, Patrick Bouchitey, Denise Chalem, Irene Tassembedo, Eva Darlan.

Persistent iconoclast Bertrand Blier brings his patented irreverence to the topic of immigrant-heavy suburban housing projects and the aspirations of their inhabitants in "Un Deux Trois Soleil." Outrageous from the first frame, unsettling pic is marbled with hard truths treated in a fanciful time-hopping manner. Fests and art-houses should embrace this one.

Anouk Grinberg, who's in her early 20s, stars winningly as Victorine, who grows up among the vacant lots and public housing of north Marseilles. Startling opening scene — a tight 'Scope close-up of Grinberg as she sloppily eats breakfast, coached and crowded by her looming, disheveled mother (Myriam Boyer) — establishes that full-grown Grinberg is playing little Victorine at age 6 or so.

Thesp, who deploys her quirky voice and astute body language to limn Victorine from childhood to age 25 — but not in chronological order — conveys youthful joy and apprehension in "little girl" mode but has no trouble conveying nononsense womanhood. Victorine is a role literally written to order for Grinberg, who has been helmer's companion since starring in his previous pic, 1990's "Merci la Vie."

Her cloying mom is a source of embarrassment to her, although she loves her alcoholic dad (a grizzled, touching Marcello Mastroianni), who's so far gone on the local elixir that he can't find his own apartment.

Blier toys with notions that will raise the hackles of the politically correct crowd. A teacher tells the gang of boys about to attack, "Don't rape me, you idiots — I'm a consenting adult. Let's go to my place." After a fleshy African woman resuscitates a boy by clutching him to her naked breasts and thrusting hips, Victorine asks the healer to "be her mother" and is soon strutting her stuff in cornrows and batik.

Blier populates rooms, beds and corridors as if the Marx Brothers' stateroom in "A Night at the Opera" were the zoning board's model for housing. Everywhere the camera turns, there are plaintive young mouths to be fed and people of all ages in search of affection and encouragement.

Thesps are aces. Jean-Pierre Marielle and Claude Brasseur have striking cameos as well-off citizens with radically conflicting views on how to handle burglars.

When, in the final scene, Mastroianni gets a movie-cliche send-off, it becomes clear how unencumbered by cliche are the components of Blier's cinematic universe that went before.   —*Lisa Nesselson*

BAD BOY BUBBY

(AUSTRALIAN-ITALIAN)

A Bubby P/L (Adelaide)-Fandango (Rome) co-production, with the participation of the Australian Film Finance Corp., in association with the South Australian Film Corp. Produced by Domenico Procacci, Giorgio Draskovic, Rolf De Heer. Directed, written by De Heer. Camera (color; Technovision widescreen), Ian Jones (and 30 others); editor, Suresh Ayyar; music, Graham Tardif; production design, Mark Abbott; art direction, Tim Nicholls; costumes, Beverley Freedan; sound design, James Currie; casting, Audine Leith; production consultant/assistant director, Paul Ammitzboll. Reviewed at Mandolin theater, Sydney, Australia, Aug. 9, 1993. (In Venice Film Festival — competing.) Running time: **112 MIN.**

Bubby	Nicholas Hope
Mam	Claire Benito
Pop	Ralph Cotterill
Angel	Carmel Johnson
Cherie the Salvo	Natalie Carr
The Scientist	Norman Kaye
Rachael	Rachael Huddy
Angel's mother	Bridget Walters
Angel's father	Graham Duckett
Mercedes Woman	Celine O'Leary
Paul (Band Singer)	Paul Philpot
Violinist	Emma West
Gayle	Betty Sumner-Lovett
Vicki	Nellie Egan

Rolf De Heer's "Bad Boy Bubby" is a very original dramatic comedy with something to offend just about everybody. Provocative, stylistically daring and inventive, pic was to be launched at the Venice Film Fest and could ride a crest of controversy to become a challenging arthouse item in many territories. A great performance by newcomer Nicholas Hope in the lead is a major plus.

"Bubby" starts off like a modern variation on "The Wild Child" or "Kasper Hauser," but then veers off into the sci-fi territory of "Starman" or John McNaughton's "The Borrower," in which an alien acquires knowledge and power from the people who cross his path.

Bubby's crazy mother (Claire Benito), a religious freak, has kept her son in isolation from the outside world for the first 35 years of his life.

Living in a grubby, windowless room, they bathe each other and even have sex together, an act Bubby has been raised to regard as normal. The mother occasionally ventures outside, wearing a gas mask to protect her from the supposedly poisoned environment.

This strange existence is interrupted by the arrival of Bubby's long-lost father (Ralph Cotterill), a ragged priest heavily into booze and sex. He quickly displaces Bubby in mom's bed, and the younger man's jealousy and frustration erupts in violence: Hardly knowing what he's doing, he suffocates his parents in cellophane, whereupon he finally leaves home for the first time.

Up until this point the action unfolds in the cramped room. Out in the city, Bubby encounters a number of "normal people," whose language, speech patterns and actions he memorizes and repeats, often at inappropriate moments.

No less than 30 different cameramen and women filmed these sequences, the idea being to depict Bubby's experiences in different visual styles, though the end result is visually seamless. James Currie has provided an intricate stereo soundtrack of unusual quality.

Using Bubby as a kind of human sponge who absorbs the people and sights he encounters, De Heer is able to comment on many aspects of contemporary society in a totally uncompromising manner.

Among those likely to be outraged by at least some aspects of the film are the devoutly religious, feminists, animal lovers and the Salvation Army. Yet ultimately, this dark mirror on the world provides an extraordinary panorama of humanity and the environment in the 1990s, and it is very much to the credit of writer-director De Heer (whose work includes the intriguing sci-fi thriller "Incident at Raven's Gate" and the Miles Davis musical "Dingo") that he has presented such an unflinching vision.

Hope gives a brave and sometimes astonishing performance as the naive "wild child."

The supporting cast, a mixture of professional and amateur actors, is uniformly excellent, with standout perfs from Benito and Cotterill as Bubby's amazing parents and Carmel Johnson as the patient Angel.

Shot in the widescreen Technovision process, pic is extremely handsome and transcends the modest budget. Running time is a shade long, but the pace never seriously flags. Though an Australian-Italian production, the film is entirely Australian in every respect.

—*David Stratton*

M. BUTTERFLY

A Warner Bros. release of a Geffen Pictures presentation. Produced by Gabriella Martinelli. Executive producers, David Henry Hwang, Philip Sandhaus. Directed by David Cronenberg. Screenplay, Hwang, based on his play. Camera (color), Peter Suschitzky; editor, Ronald Sanders; music, Howard Shore; production design, Carol Spier; art direction, James McAteer; set decoration, Elinor Rose Galbraith; costume design, Denise Cronenberg; sound (Dolby), Bryan Day; asssistant director, John Board; casting, Deirdre Bowne. Reviewed at Festival of Festivals, Toronto, Sept. 9, 1993. MPAA Rating: R. Running time: **100 MIN.**

Rene Gallimard	Jeremy Irons
Song Liling	John Lone

Ambassador Toulon	Ian Richardson
Frau Baden	Annabel Leventon
Comrade Chin	Shizuko Hoshi
Embassy Colleague	Richard McMillan
Agent Etancelin	Vernon Dobtcheff

This butterfly just doesn't fly. Icy, surprisingly conventional and never truly convincing, David Cronenberg's screen version of David Henry Hwang's hit Broadway play gets all dressed up in fancy threads but goes nowhere, due to lack of chemistry and heat on the part of the two leads. Without top reviews, this class release, which world preemed at the Toronto Fest on Sept. 9, won't venture too far beyond specialized situations.

Inspired by the true story of a French diplomat in China during the 1960s who conducted an 18-year affair with a native man he always thought was a woman and who was later convicted of espionage, "M. Butterfly" worked onstage because the artifice and distance created by the theatrical setting allowed the audience to accept the rather far-fetched premise.

But as much as one tries to buy the notion that Jeremy Irons' Rene Gallimard is so smitten with John Lone's Song Liling that he overlooks the hefty frame, masculine fingers and moustache stubble beneath the makeup, it just doesn't wash. Disbelief is never suspended, resulting in the unfortunate but continuous sense of two fine actors never really becoming comfortable inside the skin of their characters.

However unfair, comparisons to "The Crying Game" are inescapable, and it is clear that Neil Jordan's smash pulled off a similar gambit both first and better. "The Crying Game" proved that you could present a man who passed as a woman onscreen, and the one key comparable scene — in which the character reveals the truth about his body — is far more powerful in the earlier film.

Set in Beijing in 1964, tale begins with French Embassy accountant Gallimard being enchanted with Song Liling's performance of excerpts from Puccini's "Madama Butterfly." Enticed by a brief conversation in which Song Liling cleverly challenges his notions of Western males and Asian females, the married Gallimard conspicuously attends the Chinese Opera to see her again and advances things toward an affair.

With Song Liling pleading traditional modesty and shyness, Gallimard accepts his mistress's wish never to completely disrobe. Cronenberg shows just enough sex between them to suggest how such a charade was pulled off, although the crucial passion between the two is notably missing.

Once Gallimard is promoted to vice consul, in which capacity he is privy to confidential intelligence, Song Liling is able to become an effective spy for the Communist regime, passing along advance word on U.S. plans in Vietnam, among other information.

The pair refer to their racially and culturally perscribed sex roles, with Song Liling a "slave" and Gallimard a "white devil," but when the Frenchman insists upon seeing his mate naked, Song Liling announces that she's pregnant and disappears to the country to have their "son."

Seventy minutes in, action jumps to Paris 1968. Gallimard attends a performance of "Butterfly" at the Paris Opera, but is soon revealed to be a burnt-out case, living alone in a small apartment decorated in quasi-Oriental style and pining over his lost love.

"When I left China, everything fell apart," he drunkenly confesses before beholding the spectacle of French students parading through the streets in the name of Mao.

To his astonishment, Song Liling suddenly appears at his door. But Gallimard, now a mere diplomatic courier, is soon arrested and becomes the center of a sensational trial in which the depths of his deception are revealed. Ending works an ironic and highly theatrical twist on the "Madama Butterfly" theme.

Irons gave possibly his greatest screen performances in his previous outing with Cronenberg, "Dead Ringers." Here, however, his sang-froid and dissolute air don't work for the role. Irons can't be as gullible as Gallimard needs to be. British to the core, he doesn't easily reveal headlong passion or the sense of throwing caution to the wind.

Lone is a similarly superb actor, but all the effort in the world can't prevent him from looking like a man in drag here. This can be rationalized ad infinitum, but the problem remains, and it isn't helped by a voice that,

in an attempt to hit a neutral zone between male and female, sometimes sounds strangely disembodied, almost electronic.

Other thesps have limited demands placed upon them, although Ian Richardson shines in his scenes as the impeccable French ambassador.

Lensed in China, Hungary and France, this is Cronenberg's first film shot outside Canada. Unfortunately, nothing manages to disguise the feel of artifice that surrounds the entire production.

—*Todd McCarthy*

VENICE FEST

HELAS POUR MOI

(OH, WOE IS ME)

(SWISS-FRENCH)

A Vega Film (Zurich)/Les Films Alain Sarde, Periphiria (Paris) production. (International sales: World Marketing Film, Paris.) Produced by Ruth Waldburger. Directed, written by Jean-Luc Godard. Camera (color), Caroline Champetier; editor, Godard; music, extracts from Bach, Shostakovich, Beethoven, Tchaikovsky, Honegger; sound, Francois Musy; assistant director, Frederic Jardin; production manager, Pierre-Alain Schatzmann. Reviewed at Venice Film Festival (competing), Sept. 9, 1993. Running time: **85 MIN.**
Simon Donnadieu .... Gerard Depardieu
Rachel Donnadieu ... Laurence Masliah
Abraham Klimt .... Bernard Verley
Max Mercure .... Jean-Louis Loca
The Pastor ....Francois Germond
The Other Pastor .. Jean-Pierre Miquel
The Pastor's Wife .... Anny Romand
The Teacher .... Roland Blanche
The Doctor .... Marc Betton

Only those very hip to Jean-Luc Godard will easily translate the obscure ramblings of his latest work, "Oh, Woe Is Me." Despite the presence of Gerard Depardieu, this aptly titled pic is unlikely to perform any better that Godard's 1990 Alain Delon starrer, "New Wave."

Film is inspired by lofty sources: The Greek legend of Alcmene and Amphitryon, about a god who wants to experience human desire, pleasure and pain, and a text by Italian poet Leopardi about the anguish of man's journey through life.

It will be left to theoreticians, or those on the director's increasingly obscure wavelength, to decipher any kind of narrative. Depardieu plays a godlike character who drifts into a village by a Swiss lake with a floppy hat, raincoat, English newspaper and bemused expression.

He also seems to have an alter ego, with a rasping voice similar to the computer in Godard's 1965 sci-fi classic, "Alphaville."

Pic is a series of unresolved encounters between various charac-

ters, with overlapping dialogue, solemnly amusing inter-titles and occasionally soaring music. Those wandering aimlessly include students, a teacher, a couple of pastors, a doctor and the wife/mistress of the Depardieu character.

Scenes unfold in or near the lake, or at a station where passing trains drown out the dialogue, consisting of banalities, aphorisms and the occasional profundity. There are puns (many difficult to translate into English), political comments and refs to the current Bosnian crisis.

All this is elegantly photographed and recorded but lacks the incisive wit and visual daring of Godard's pioneering early work. "Woe" won't win any new converts.

—*David Stratton*

EVEN COWGIRLS GET THE BLUES

A Fine Line Features release of a New Line Intl. Releasing Co. production. Produced by Laurie Parker. Directed, written by Gus Van Sant, based on the novel by Tom Robbins. Camera (color), John Campbell, Eric Alan Edwards; editor, Curtiss Clayton; music, k.d. lang, Ben Mink; production design, Missy Stewart; art direction, Dan Self; costume design, Beatrix Aruna Pasztor; associate producer, Mary Ann Marinno. Reviewed at Venice Film Festival (competing), Sept. 2, 1993. Running time: **106 MIN.**
Sissy Hankshaw .... Uma Thurman
The Countess ....John Hurt
Bonanza Jellybean .... Rain Phoenix
The Chink .... Noriyuki "Pat" Morita
Delores Del Ruby ...... Lorraine Bracco
Julian .... Keanu Reeves
Miss Adrian .... Angie Dickinson
Marie Barth .... Sean Young
Howard Barth .... Crispin Glover

American counterculture and early '70s values come flooding back like a peyote-induced dream in Gus Van Sant's "Even Cowgirls Get the Blues," a far-out, meandering fantasy set on a ranch run by lesbians, from Tom Robbins' 1973 cult novel. Unless the Fine Line release takes off as a cult item itself — which is doubtful — it will have trouble expanding the minds of those who lack a hippie past. Among the film's many themes, the heroine's search for sexual identity should appeal especially to female patrons.

Seen through the lens of the present, the mystical utopianism and women's battle for sexual freedom look about a century old. "Cowgirls" doesn't get a clear enough bead on the period, with the result that all its narrative risk-taking and stylistic fireworks frequently confuse rather than enlighten.

Missing from "Cowgirls" is the poetry of yearning and desperation running through Van Sant's "My Own Private Idaho." Pic stays on

the surface without attempting any exploration of painful depths. Result is at best amusing; at worst, uninvolving, often confusing and sometimes a little boring.

Main character, Sissy (Uma Thurman), is a 29-year-old virgin hippie whose delicate beauty is marred only by giant, phallus-like thumbs. Sissy has a contract with the Countess (John Hurt), a prancing drag queen, to model for feminine hygiene ads.

Leaving behind the flashy New York scene populated by the asthmatic Julian (Keanu Reeves) and his swinging pals, Sissy hitches cross-country to the Countess' Oregon beauty farm, the Rubber Rose Ranch, to shoot another commercial.

At the ranch, however, a pack of rebellious, unwashed cowgirls, led by Bonanza Jellybean (Rain Phoenix), foment an uprising against the Countess and his authoritarian hireling (Angie Dickinson), and kick out the guests.

Sissy, who's sided with the cowgirls, finds love in the arms of Bonanza and friendly sex with the Chink (Noriyuki "Pat" Morita), a weird old Japanese-American who was raised by some Native Americans known as the Clock People and now awaits the Eternity of Joy.

The ideal community of work and friendship is disrupted when the cowgirls feed peyote to migrating flocks of cranes, causing an ecological scandal. The White House sends out the Army to wrest the ranch away from the femmes' control, leading to a heroic confrontation.

Ending has Sissy preparing to parthenogenically reproduce a giant-thumbed race of superior beings with visionary feminist cowgirl Delores Del Ruby (Lorraine Bracco).

Thurman's sensual, little-girl presence keeps auds firmly on her side, no matter how absurd the rough-and-tumble situations. The cowgirls (many played by non-pros) have a surreal concreteness, especially brave, grinning Phoenix, playing like a female version of a genre cowboy star.

In this upside-down context, professional thesps like Dickinson and Bracco stand out less. Morita's armchair philosopher — like all the characters, talking in sententious literary phrases — makes little impact.

John Campbell and Eric Alan Edwards' imaginative visuals offer a new interpretation of the psychedelic spirit of the period. Soundtrack by k.d. lang and Ben Mink is playful and ironic.

—*Deborah Young*

September 20, 1993 (Cont.)

THE REAL McCOY

A Universal Pictures release of a Bregman/Baer production. Produced by Martin Bregman, Willi Baer, Michael S. Bregman. Executive producers, Ortwin Freyermuth, William Davies, William Osborne, Gary Levinsohn. Co-producer, Louis A. Stroller. Directed by Russell Mulcahy. Screenplay, Davies, Osborne. Camera (Technicolor), Denis Crossan; editor, Peter Honess; music, Brad Fiedel; production design, Kim Colefax; art direction, Paul Huggins; set design, Jonathon Short; set decoration, Richard Charles Greenbaum; costume design, Donna O'Neal; sound (Dolby), Mary H. Ellis; associate producer/unit production manager, Allan Wertheim; assistant director, Joel Tuber; stunt coordinator, Dick Ziker; casting, Mary Colquhoun. Reviewed at Writers Guild of America Theater, Beverly Hills, Sept. 7, 1993. MPAA Rating: PG-13. Running time: **104 MIN.**

Karen McCoy	Kim Basinger
J.T. Barker	Val Kilmer
Jack Schmidt	Terence Stamp
Gary Buckner	Gailard Sartain
Patrick	Zach English
Baker	Raynor Scheine

Kim Basinger finds herself boxed up after all in this vehicle about a female bank robber, which isn't bad but gets where it's going very slowly. With Basinger and Val Kilmer generating little romantic chemistry, and the action uninspired, pic seems unlikely to steal away with a major box office haul.

Surprisingly, former video director Russell Mulcahy ("Highlander") offers little flash in what turns out to be a standard caper pic with a dose of old-fashioned motherhood thrown in for calculated good measure.

Just paroled after six years in prison, cat burglar Karen McCoy (Basinger) is like Michael Corleone in "The Godfather, Part III" — no matter how hard she tries to get out of the safe-cracking biz, they keep pulling her back.

In this case, big-time criminal Jack Schmidt (Terence Stamp) kidnaps Karen's son (Zach English) as a means of compelling her to knock off an Atlanta bank.

With a parasitic ex-husband, Karen's lone ally is J.T. (Kilmer), a none-too-bright small-timer whose m.o. includes robbing convenience stores with a faulty gun and stealing Betamax equipment, apparently unaware that virtually nobody uses it anymore.

Writers William Davies and William Osborne ("Stop! or My Mom Will Shoot") don't provide much firepower in the laughs department and build an inherent flaw into the movie's setup — namely, why go through the lengthy process of having parolee Karen rejected by employers when Jack ends up simply blackmailing her into returning to crime anyway?

Mulcahy's direction provides scant suspense, and the final bank job doesn't blaze any trails for anyone who's seen caper movies. Similarly, the payoff may satisfy the undemanding, but most viewers will see it coming a mile off.

Projecting smarts in addition to her good looks, Basinger proves a reasonably effective lead, although this crime-oriented take on balancing work and motherhood has at best an inadvertently amusing feminist bent.

Kilmer provides a few laughs but has little to work with, playing a character so consistently dense it's hard to see where an attraction between the two could develop. Stamp, meanwhile, trips over a truly awful Southern accent — perhaps belated payback from across the water for Kevin Costner's off-and-on stab at a British brogue in "Robin Hood: Prince of Thieves."

Tech credits are generally sound, from Brad Fiedel's sleek score to the bank vault's cathedral-like design. It bears noting, however, that Universal's marketing crew has pulled a fast one on viewers: Basinger never dons a skin-tight spandex outfit like the one prominently featured in the movie's ad.

For that matter, when it comes to capers, "The Real McCoy" proves something of a misrepresentation as well: Anyone who really wants to see the real McCoy in this genre should rent "Thief." —*Brian Lowry*

UNDERCOVER BLUES

A Metro-Goldwyn-Mayer presentation of a Lobell/Bergman/Hera production. Produced by Mike Lobell. Executive producers, Herbert Ross, Andrew Bergman. Directed by Ross. Screenplay, Ian Abrams. Camera, Donald E. Thorin; editor, Priscilla Nedd-Friendly; music, David Newman; production design, Ken Adam; art direction, William J. Durrell Jr.; set design, James R. Bayliss; set decoration, Jeff Haley; costume design, Wayne Finkelman; sound, Dennis L. Maitland; associate producers, Kim Kurumada, Adam Merims, Steve Warner; first assistant director, Barry K. Thomas; stunt coordinator/second unit director, Glenn H. Randall Jr.; casting, Hank McCann. Reviewed at Bruin Theater, Westwood, Sept. 9, 1993. MPAA Rating: PG-13. Running time: **89 MIN.**

Jane Blue	Kathleen Turner
Jeff Blue	Dennis Quaid
Novacek	Fiona Shaw
Muerte	Stanley Tucci
Halsey	Larry Miller
Sawyer	Obba Babatunde
Vern Newman	Tom Arnold
Bonnie Newman	Park Overall
Leamington	Ralph Brown
Axel	Jan Triska
Mr. Ferderber	Saul Rubinek
Cab driver	Jenifer Lewis
Jane Louise Blue	Michelle Schuelke

The moderately enjoyable "Undercover Blues" plays like a big-screen, big-budget pilot for a TV series. As such, it should draw respectable coin from those seeking an undemanding, fun time at the movies, but the cartoony style and disconnected set pieces should play best on the home-video/cable circuit.

Former spies Jane and Jeff Blue (Kathleen Turner, Dennis Quaid) are relaxing in New Orleans with their 11-month-old baby when they're lured back into the espionage business to help foil an international terrorist ring led by Novacek (Fiona Shaw), who's a cross between Cruella de Vil and Lotte Lenya in "From Russia With Love."

The film spends about four of its 89 minutes on plot, with the rest devoted to comic scenes of Quaid and Turner playing kissy-face and cooing over their baby, fending off attackers, sidestepping the New Orleans police and brushing aside the assaults of persistent street mugger Muerte (Stanley Tucci, who garners the lion's share of laughs in a role that's a variation of Burt Kwouk's Cato in the "Pink Panther" series).

Script by first-timer Ian Abrams doesn't cover any new ground, but aims at one of the most difficult targets — lighthearted fun — and hits it. Story occasionally wanders off on tangents, like Quaid foiling a bank robbery, but has some good scenes, such as Turner and Quaid interrogating Saul Rubinek, and Tucci in the alligator pit at the zoo.

However, the baby (played by cutie pie Michelle Schuelke) is basically an accessory, adding little to the plot except the novelty factor. Script might have benefited from exploring the couple's feelings about the toddler and their work. And while there's nothing wrong with showing romantic/sexual feelings of new parents, aren't there ways to display affection for one's partner other than sucking face?

Herbert Ross' camera setups are good and his tone consistent, but he evidently decided to forgo subtlety when he took on the project.

MGM is no doubt hoping for a new franchise here (as every studio does with just about every new film) but the modest stunts, juxtaposed against equally low-key family scenes, indicate film could more logically be translated to a TV series. The publicity may evoke "The Thin Man," but pic's style is more like "The Girl From U.N.C.L.E."

Turner is immensely appealing, tossing off the comedy and jumping into the action scenes with equal ease. Quaid is OK, but isn't up to her level, trying too hard to lay on the charm in the comic scenes.

The always terrific Tucci steals the show as the self-styled tough guy. The usually dependable Larry Miller resorts to a "funny" voice and speech impediment as the latest in Hollywood's long line of idiotic cops, while Obba Babatunde is fine as the latest in Hollywood's long line of smart-but-dull black cops. Shaw seems to be having fun as the latest of Hollywood's long line of terrorists with East European accents.

Film is technically superior, moving briskly under Priscilla Nedd-Friendly's sharp, tight editing; score by the underrated David Newman is outstanding, as are the cinematography of Donald E. Thorin and Ken Adam's production design.

Somebody unfortunately changed the pic's title from the coy-but-descriptive "Cloak and Diaper." Maybe they can change it back for the series. —*Timothy M. Gray*

MONEY FOR NOTHING

A Buena Vista Pictures release of a Hollywood Pictures presentation of a Tom Musca production. Produced by Musca. Executive producers, David Permut, Gordon Freedman, Matthew Tolmach. Co-producer, Cyrus Yavneh. Directed by Ramon Menendez. Screenplay, Menendez, Musca, Carol Sobieski. Camera (DuArt color, Technicolor prints), Tom Sigel; editor, Nancy Richardson; music, Craig Safan; production design, Michelle Minch; art direction, Beth Kuhn; set decoration, Susan Raney; costume design, Zeca Seabra; sound (Dolby), Dennis Maitland II; assistant director, Babu Subramaniam; casting, Victoria Thomas. Reviewed at the Disney Studios screening room, Burbank, Sept. 8, 1993. MPAA Rating: R. Running time: **100 MIN.**

Joey Coyle	John Cusack
Monica Russo	Debi Mazar
Detective Laurenzi	Michael Madsen
Dino Palladino	Benicio Del Toro
Kenny Kozlowski	Michael Rapaport
Vincente Goldoni	Maury Chaykin
Billy Coyle	James Gandolfini
Mrs. Coyle	Fionnula Flanagan
Eleanor Coyle	Elizabeth Bracco
Katie Coyle	Ashleigh Dejon
Hrbek	Lenny Venito

The team behind "Stand and Deliver" has delivered Disney a difficult marketing proposition: a predominantly serious film about a subject matter that seems rife with humor. As a result, this uneven true story about an out-of-work longshoreman who finds $1.2 million lying in the street seems destined for no such luck at the box office, despite the strong performance by John Cusack at its core.

Cusack plays Joey Coyle, a none-too-bright blue-collar guy who, at 26, is watching the American Dream slip by: He's living with his family in South Philadelphia, estranged from his girlfriend (Debi Mazar, from TV's "Civil Wars"), and he can't even get his straight-arrow brother to give him work at the docks.

Driving along with one of his pals, Joey finds a bundle of money that has fallen out of an armored car, and he starts dreaming of the good life. Unfortunately, his ill-advised use of the cash creates an easy trail for a local detective (Michael Madsen) to follow, while Joey gets in deeper and deeper over his head by trying to launder the loot through the mob.

September 20, 1993 (Cont.)

Director Ramon Menendez and producer Tom Musca, who co-wrote the script with Carol Sobieski, never bring much life to this production, in part because Joey's efforts are so inept and misguided from the get-go.

Surrounding the lead with various unattractive characters, the filmmakers don't exploit Joey's initial exultation, instead turning out a thinly veiled political tract about haves and the hopelessness of have-nots — barely articulated through the reaction of the caring cop, nicely played by Madsen, who grew up in the neighborhood and understands the desperation those environs can produce.

That approach certainly distinguishes "Money for Nothing" from the TV-movie tack that might have been used — showing Joey going on a "Home Alone 2"-type shopping spree, for example — but it isn't particularly entertaining, and the fact that Joey is destined not to enjoy his accidental gains never seems in doubt.

If there's a moral lesson here it's lost in the movie's general ambivalence, with lots of people telling Joey to give the money back but, based on the way his life is depicted, little incentive for him to do so.

Cusack plays essentially the same character he created in "Say Anything" — a directionless 20-something type with, for the most part, a good heart. His efforts to win back his gal prove endearing, although her reactions also convey the indecision that generally plagues the whole production.

Menendez does deliver some flashes of what might have been, such as the warmth of a late exchange between Joey and his brother (James Gandolfini), but the movie keeps drawing back to its title through darkly comedic flourishes — fostering images of a light-hearted Dire Straits song that ends with the refrain "and your chicks for free."

Tech credits exhibit blue-collar craftsmanship, as cameraman Tom Sigel and production designer Michelle Minch capture the squalor of Joey's life in pastel-gray tones.

Pic carries a dedication to the late Joey, who died recently. Like the character himself, "Money for Nothing" has an opportunity for better things but, despite good intentions, can't quite get it right.

—Brian Lowry

RED ROCK WEST

A Polygram Filmed Entertainment presentation of a Propaganda Films production. Produced by Sigurjon Sighvatsson, Steve Golin. Executive producers, Michael Kuhn, Janie Mc-Cann. Directed, written by John Dahl. Camera (Deluxe color), Mark Reshovsky; editor, Scott Chestnut; music, William Orvis; production design, Rob Pearson; art direction, Don Diers; costume design, Terry Dresbach; sound (Dolby), Mark Deren; associate producers, Rick Dahl, Lynn Weimer; casting, Carol Lewis. Reviewed at Paramount Studios, L.A., Aug. 25, 1993. Running Time: **97 MIN.**

Michael	Nicolas Cage
Lyle	Dennis Hopper
Suzanne	Lara Flynn Boyle
Wayne	J.T. Walsh
Deputy Greytack	Timothy Carhart
Deputy Bowman	Dan Shor
Truck Driver	Dwight Yoakam
Old Man	Bobby Joe McFadden

A wry thriller with a keen edge, "Red Rock West" is a sprightly, likable noirish yarn with very definite specialized appeal. Already in release in the U.K. and Germany, the larkish indemnity piece received its North American launch at the Toronto Film Festival.

Centered on a case of mistaken identity, the internecine plot becomes progressively more complex without losing its sense of fun. Essentially a bumbler, Michael (Nicolas Cage) finds himself in a nest of vipers and only through dumb luck manages to elude getting bitten.

Michael has headed to the oil fields of Wyoming in his vintage Cadillac on the promise of a job. But an old knee injury sends him to the sidelines, and in the town of Red Rock he's presumed to be a hired gun commissioned to rub out the wife of a local barkeep.

The saloon owner, Wayne (J.T. Walsh), wafts the long green in front of Michael's nose, and the near destitute man takes a deep whiff. Playing along for a moment, he confronts the woman (Lara Flynn Boyle) only to have the original offer doubled. He grabs it but decides to bail out before things get worse.

Of course, nothing's that easy.

After sending a note to the local sheriff, he heads out of town. As the rain beats on his windshield, Michael plows into a stranded motorist. When the police arrive things get mighty uncomfortable as the sheriff turns out to be Wayne. He's taken into custody but manages to escape, only to be rescued by Lyle (Dennis Hopper), the gunman he'd been impersonating.

The ping-pong plot, concocted by writer-director John Dahl, is not to be taken seriously or metaphorically. Though it vaguely resembles a droll Bunuel construction, it owes more to hard-boiled thrillers of the 1940s, albeit with a very large tongue-in-cheek quotient.

Cage plays his dumb-guy role with aplomb. He's virtually as thick-headedly resilient as a cartoon character but manages not to lose audience sympathy. Logically, he's no match for the icy precision of Walsh or the hair-trigger temper evinced by Hopper. However, this is deeply rooted in movie reality.

Dahl, who earlier made the slick, steamy "Kill Me Again," demonstrates an affection and understanding of the genre. His sense of the environment is shrewdly incorporated in the very handsomely mounted production. He also gets added texture from William Orvis' clever, romantic music score.

Modest only in budget, the tightly constructed "Red Rock West" has upbeat prospects if it can secure the type of niche that propelled "One False Move" to cult status last year.

—Leonard Klady

WARLOCK: THE ARMAGEDDON

A Trimark Pictures release of a Tapestry production. Produced by Peter Abrams, Robert Levy. Co-producer, Natan Zahavi. Directed by Anthony Hickox. Screenplay, Kevin Rock, Sam Bernard. Camera (color), Gerry Lively; editor, Chris Cibelli; music, Mark McKenzie; production design, Steve Hardie; art direction, John Chichester; set decoration, David Koneff; costume design, Leonard Pollack; sound (Dolby), Don Johnson; makeup special effects, Bob Keen; casting, Alison Kohler. Reviewed at Cannes Film Festival (market), May 19, 1993. MPAA Rating: R. Running Time: **93 MIN.**

Warlock	Julian Sands
Kenny Travis	Chris Young
Samantha Ellison	Paula Marshall
Will Travis	Steve Kahan
Ethan Larson	Charles Hallahan
Franks	R.G. Armstrong
Kate	Micole Mercurio
Andy	Craig Hurley
Ted Ellison	Bruce Glover
Amanda Sloan	Dawn Ann Billings
Douglas	Zach Galligan
Paula Dare	Joanna Pacula

J ulian Sands remains unrepentantly evil as he assails familiar territory in "Warlock: The Armageddon." Though not specifically linked to the earlier horror thriller, the new outing echoes the first foray sufficiently to satisfy fans of hokum-filled good-and-evil conflict. It should have good initial B.O. impact and thrive in subsequent ancillary exploitation.

The current mumbo jumbo involves the struggle for control of six 17th century Druidic rune stones. The baubles not only have the ability to summon Satan's emissary but also have the power to quell his nefarious activities. So when the Warlock pops up in the contemporary world, his task is to seek out and secure the pieces and commence a relentless evil reign. Just for fun he dispatches the current owners with gleeful delight.

His path leads to a Northern California hamlet that is one of the last known enclaves of the virtually extinct sect. The descendants sense the coming of evil but remain somewhat distanced from the onslaught, secure in the knowledge they have two warriors in their midst. The problem is that the young designated defenders — Kenny (Chris Young) and Samantha (Paula Marshall) — are neither aware of nor trained in their chosen roles.

To paraphrase the venerable Mammy Yokum: "Good is better than evil 'cause it's nicer." However valid that contention, it serves little purpose here. Dramatically, these scrubbed, wholesome teens are bland beside Sands' sinister histrionics.

Director Tony Hickox, too, seems more at home with the bad guy. The strutting and posture of the title character is considerably more entertaining than the picture-book world of the idealized community.

Chewing up the landscape with great relish, Sands almost erases all thought of his colorless adversaries. He's also given additional ammo with some very effective special effects work.

"Warlock: The Armageddon" certainly has enough fire and brimstone to burn up the screen. All the franchise requires is a healthy threat to keep this diabolical creature alive. *—Leonard Klady*

TROIS COULEURS: BLEU

(THREE COLORS: BLUE)

(FRENCH)

A Miramax (U.S.)-MKL (France) release of an MK2 Production SA. CED Prods.-France 3 Cinema (Paris)-CAB Prods. (Lausanne)-Tor Production (Warsaw) co-production with the participation of Canal Plus, the Eurimages Fund and the CNC. (Foreign sales: John Kochman, MK2.) Produced by Marin Karmitz. Directed by Krzysztof Kieslowski. Screenplay, Krzysztof Piesiewicz, Kieslowski. Additional screenwriting, Agnieszka Holland, Edward Zebrowski, Slawomir Idziak. Camera (color), Idziak; editor, Jacques Witte; music, Zbigniew Preisner; art direction, Claude Lenoir; sound (Dolby), Jean-Claude Laureaux, William Flageollet; assistant director, Emmanuel Finkiel; casting, Margot Capelier. Reviewed at Club 13 screening room, Paris, Aug. 16, 1993. (In Venice — competing, Telluride, Toronto festivals.) Running time: **97 MIN.**

Julie	Juliette Binoche
Olivier	Benoit Regent
Sandrine	Florence Pernel
Lucille	Charlotte Very
The mother	Emmanuelle Riva

Also with: Helene Vincent, Philippe Volter, Hugues Quester, Florence Vignon, Yann Tregouet, Julie Delpy, Zbigniew Zamachowski, Alain Decaux.

"T rois Couleurs: Bleu," the first installment in Krzysztof

September 20, 1993 (Cont.)

Kieslowski's trilogy inspired by the French tricolor, falls short of the mystical perfection that characterized "The Decalogue," but boasts a riveting central performance by a carefully controlled, lovingly lit Juliette Binoche.

Dramatic tale of a woman who streamlines her life after surviving the accident that kills her young daughter and composer husband retains traces of the puzzle-piece serendipity that distinguishes helmer's most captivating work. But in this outing (as, to a lesser extent, in "The Double Life of Veronique") Kieslowski's French characters are watered-down icons compared to their Polish counterparts.

Like Wim Wenders with "Far Away, So Close!," Kieslowski (along with co-scripter Krzysztof Piesiewicz and other credited hands including Agnieszka Holland) seems to be grappling with a diluted variation on his own greatest moments and insights, suggesting, as does Wenders, that all you need is love.

Post-accident, bereaved but businesslike Julie (Binoche) instructs her lawyer to sell every last shred of property. She's methodical about disposing of the evidence of her former life, but is she truly at liberty to discard the "Concerto for Europe" that her late husband left unfinished?

Julie is determined to live anonymously and do "absolutely nothing," but when someone touches an emotional nerve in her, the screen literally goes blank and snippets of powerful music surge forth. It's a risky but effective device for blowing Julie's facade of indifference.

Zbigniew Preisner's music, whose thundering chords evoke memory, limn loss and hail the tenuous promise of European unity, is a character in its own right, making up in expressiveness what taciturn Julie seems to lack.

Binoche goes from banged-up to smashing, but rarely smiles or sheds her reserve. As the camera lingers, trying to get at the character's innermost thoughts, filmmaker puts his faith in the planes of his leading lady's face as few directors have since the silent era.

Julie wants only to blend into Paris, but a sex-attuned neighbor (Charlotte Very, as a sensitive sinner) and her late husband's assistant (Benoit Regent) exert a pull on her.

Kieslowski, whose "Camera Buff" (1979) seized on the power of image-making machines, here casts TV in a sly, pivotal role as everything from companion and solace to a medium of betrayal. Hunched under the covers like a bruised but resolute child, Julie watches her famous husband and daughter's televised funeral on a tiny portable set. Julie's senile mother (a cameo by careworn Emmanuelle Riva) assures her daughter that everything is fine because "I have the TV." A TV monitor glimpsed at a Pigalle sex joint sets a vital trail of discovery in motion.

Bold final sequence is a visual and aural crescendo calibrated to show that while each person is fundamentally alone, every life inevitably touches other lives — like it or not.

Jean-Claude Laureaux's evocative sound design and Slawomir Idziak's tiptop lensing are practically peerless.

It remains to be seen whether the trilogy — "Blue" (liberty), "White" (equality), "Red" (brotherhood) — will take on cumulative power. Viewers who enjoy gazing at omnipresent Binoche will drink their fill in this free-standing episode. Others may have trouble connecting with her internalized grief and stubborn resolve. —_Lisa Nesselson_

TELLURIDE FEST

LOVE AND HUMAN REMAINS
(CANADIAN)

A Max Films (Canada) release of a Max Films presentation in co-production with Atlantis Films Ltd., produced with the participation of Telefilm Canada/La Societe Generale des Industries Culturelles-Quebec/Ontario Film Development Corp./The Movie Network-First Choice/Foundation to Underwrite New Drama for Pay Television/Super Ecran. (International sales: Max Films Intl.) Produced by Roger Frappier. Executive producers, Frappier, Pierre Latour. Co-producer, Peter Sussman. Line producer, Richard Lalonde. Directed by Denys Arcand. Screenplay, Brad Fraser, based on his play "Unidentified Human Remains and the True Nature of Love." Camera (color), Paul Sarossy; editor, Alain Baril; music, John McCarthy; production design, Francois Seguin; set decoration, Jean Kazemirchuk; costume design, Denis Sperdouklis; assistant director, David Webb; second unit director, Oliver Asselin; casting, Deirdre Bowen (Toronto), Lynn Kressel (N.Y.), Lucie Robitaille (Montreal), Stuart Aikins (Vancouver). Reviewed at Telluride Film Festival, Sept. 5, 1993. (Also in Toronto Film Festival.) Running time: **98 MIN.**
David .... Thomas Gibson
Candy .... Ruth Marshall
Bernie .... Cameron Bancroft
Benita .... Mia Kirshner
Jerri .... Joanne Vannicola
Kane .... Matthew Ferguson
Robert .... Rick Roberts

Denys Arcand's "Love and Human Remains" is a bawdy and spirited comedy about a group of mostly 30ish urbanites trying to get a grip on their sexuality and place in the world. Coming in the wake of his international arthouse hits "The Decline of the American Empire" and "Jesus of Montreal," the Quebecois filmmaker's first English-language feature is a more mainstream affair, and its attempts at serious commentary about the modern world's ills seem jarring in the otherwise vastly entertaining context.

There's no reason this couldn't score with hip young audiences, but an enterprising distrib would still have to work hard to help this cross over to wider release.

Based on the hit play "Unidentified Human Remains and the True Nature of Love," by Canadian playwright Brad Fraser, pic instantly grabs viewer attention because the subject is Sex with a capital S, and in many of its alternative forms.

Lead character is David (Thomas Gibson), a charismatic, devilishly good-looking young Lothario who used to act but now defiantly insists that he's found his true calling in waiting tables. For David, love doesn't exist, and he's made an art form of the casual relationship.

Just returned to an unnamed big city (pic was lensed in Montreal), David attracts nearly everyone whose path he crosses including his male sex partners and the women who bemoan his gay status.

David lives with Candy (Ruth Marshall), a former g.f. whose disenchantment with men makes her susceptible to the avid attentions of cute lesbian Jerri (Joanne Vannicola). Overlapping this tryst is a flirtation with bartender Robert (Rick Roberts), who angers Candy when he doesn't want to bed her.

David hangs out some with old friend Bernie (Cameron Bancroft), a raging misogynist, but spends more time with admiring 17-year-old busboy Kane (Matthew Ferguson), who wants to be like David so much he considers becoming gay. Another friend is Benita (Mia Kirshner), a young S&M specialist who, in one extreme and hilarious case, calls upon David to help her out.

This roundelay of ambisexual desires and experiments keeps matters almost continuously sparking and libidinous. The specter of AIDS is invoked through recurring references to condoms and the repeated presence of blood, although it doesn't slow the characters down a whit.

Weighing too heavily on the story is a backdrop of serial murders of young women which may or may not be the work of one of the principal characters. Resolution of this framing device proves overly melodramatic and angst-ridden.

Many of Fraser's lines possess a pungent humor, and Arcand moves the action through many colorful locations at a propulsive clip.

Unknown cast is excellent. Gibson's David is knowingly sexy and jaded without being narcissistic, and he looks like a good bet for important film work.

Production looks and sounds sharp, and is enhanced by terrific end titles that move attractively from right to left, rather than up.
—_Todd McCarthy_

MONTREAL FEST

TRAHIR
(BETRAYAL)
(FRENCH-ROMANIAN-SWISS-SPANISH)

A Parnasse Prods. (France)-Filmex (Romania)-Cactus Films (Switzerland)-Xaloc Film (Spain) co-production. Produced by Eliane Stutterheim, Sylvain Bursztejn. Directed by Radu Mihaileanu. Screenplay, Mihaileanu, Laurent Moussard. Camera (color), Laurent Dailland; editor, Catherine Quesemand; music, Temistocle Popa; production design, Christian Niculescu; costumes, Viorica Petrovici; sound, Dominique Warnier, Jean-Pierre Laforce; casting, Nathalie Cheron; assistant director, Olivet Jacquet. Reviewed at World Film Festival, Montreal (competing), Sept. 1, 1993. Running time: **104 MIN.**
George Vlaicu .... Johan Leysen
Laura Cocea .... Mireille Perrier
The Inspector .... Alexandru Repan
Cristea .... Razvan Vasilescu
Woman in Prison .... Maia Morgenstern
Vlad .... Radu Beligan

A gripping drama that spans 30 years of recent Romanian history, "Betrayal," which won the Grand Prix of the Americas at the Montreal Fest, is solid arthouse fare.

It opens in 1948, with anticommunist journalist George Vlaicu (very well played by Dutch actor Johan Leysen) writing a provocative article about the death of democracy in his country. For his pains, he serves 11 punishing years in a waterlogged prison cell.

In 1959, a smooth police inspector, played by Raymond Burr lookalike Alexandru Repan, offers him a deal: He can go free if he signs a weekly statement, but is guaranteed he'll never have to reveal in these statements anything the inspector doesn't already know. Reluctantly, he agrees.

Once out of prison, he finds and marries his former typist, Laura (Mireille Perrier), who, unknown to him, had herself been imprisoned for typing the piece he wrote. They have a son. He continues to meet the inspector once a week, but otherwise all goes well, and he's able to publish poetry and is even acclaimed as the country's national poet. But when a friend tells him he plans to defect and is killed soon afterwards, Vlaicu realizes he's been used all along by the state, and starts making plans to leave the country himself.

Filmed almost entirely in Romania (apart from some scenes set in Paris near the end) but entirely spoken in French, this is a lucid and intelligent drama about the way a police state controls its artists and writers. It's not as depressing as perhaps it sounds, and boasts fine performances as well as top-class technical credits. —_David Stratton_

September 20, 1993 (Cont.)

COOL RUNNINGS

A Buena Vista release of a Walt Disney Pictures presentation. Produced by Dawn Steel. Executive producers, Christopher Meledandri, Susan Landau. Directed by Jon Turteltaub. Screenplay, Lynn Siefert, Tommy Swerdlow & Michael Goldberg, from a story by Siefert and Michael Ritchie, based on the true story of the 1988 Jamaica Bobsled team. Camera (Technicolor), Phedon Papamichael; editor, Bruce Green; music, Hans Zimmer; production design, Stephen Marsh; art direction, Rick Roberts; costume design, Grania Preston; sound (Dolby), Larry Suton; second unit director, Micky Moore; casting, Chemin Bernard, Jaki Brown. Reviewed at World Film Festival, Montreal (Hors Concurs), Sept. 4, 1993. MPAA Rating: PG. Running Time: **97 MIN.**

Derice Bannock	Leon
Sanka Coffie	Doug E. Doug
Yul Brenner	Malik Yoba
Junior Bevel	Rawle D. Lewis
Irv Blitzer	John Candy
Kurt Hemphill	Raymond Barry
Larry	Larry Gilman
Josef Grool	Peter Outerbridge
Roger	Paul Coeur

The travails and triumph of the 1988 Jamaican Olympic bobsled team deliver a highly entertaining combination in "Cool Runnings." The offbeat, fact-based saga is enlivened by the perfect balance of humor, emotion and insight and should be one of the true sleepers among fall box office releases.

One can now see why producer Dawn Steel tenaciously pursued the subject matter. In addition to its intrinsic novelty, the yarn effortlessly draws us into the spirit of competition and the sheer delight of the Olympian ethos. Unlike most sports-based films, this is one tale with universal appeal.

The filmmakers have taken some dramatic liberties, though the essential facts are intact. Derice Bannock (Leon) is, like his Olympian father, a leading runner in the small island republic. But at the local trials for the 1988 event, he stumbles when another competitor falls in his path, and Derice fails to qualify.

When he vainly appeals to the local board for reinstatement, Derice hears a wild tale of an American gold medal bobsledder living in Jamaica. The man had attempted years ago to recruit Derice's father for an island team, believing that world-class runners would take to the sport like penguins to ice.

The germ of an idea begins to grow. The runner recruits his friend Sanka (Doug E. Doug) — a go-cart driver — and they go off to convince Irv Blitzer (John Candy), the former Winter Olympian, to coach the fledgling team. Blitzer is coerced into the job, and the team is completed when two other runners scratched from the trials show up.

The idea is preposterous, and were it not for the fact that it actually happened, even cockeyed Hollywood would have taken a pass.

The requisite details for this type of endeavor are much in evidence as Blitzer whips his athletes into form despite a decided absence of snow. Both the local committee and business leaders look upon the pursuit as hilarious if somewhat embarrassing. But the team ekes out enough money to get to Calgary and acquire a barely useable sled cast off by the American team.

Director Jon Turteltaub has a fresh, uncluttered approach to the story that allows its natural warmth and humor to dominate. The classic underdog script provides a positive minority perspective without the usual downside, self-conscious righteousness.

The cast, like their real-life counterparts, work marvelously as a team. Doug provides the comic foil while Leon emerges as a charismatic leader in the type of role that should lead to more prominent work.

Candy gets the opportunity to create a real character and remind us of his facility for pathos — regrettably so rarely employed.

The whole experience is a tonic that's sure to delight viewers.

—*Leonard Klady*

CENTURY

A BBC Films production is association with Beambright. Foreign sales: the Sales Company. Produced by Therese Pickard. Executive producers, Mark Shivas, Ruth Caleb. Directed, written by Stephen Poliakoff. Camera (Agfa), Witold Stok; editor, Michael Parkinson; music, Michael Gibbs; production design, Michael Pickwoad; art direction, Henry Harris; costume design, Anushia Nieradzik, Daphne Dare; sound (Dolby), Hugh Strain; medical adviser, Dr. Ghislaine Lawrence; casting, Joyce Gallie. Reviewed at World Film Festival, Montreal (competing), Sept. 4, 1993. Running time: **112 MIN.**

Professor Mandry	Charles Dance
Paul Reisner	Clive Owen
Clara	Miranda Richardson
Mr. Reisner	Robert Stephens
Mrs. Whitweather	Joan Hickson
Felix	Neil Stuke
Miriam	Lena Heady
Theo	Graham Loughridge
James	Carlton Chance

The dawn of a new era imbues Stephen Poliakoff's provocative "Century." Centered on a time of great strides in scientific and medical discovery, the film seamlessly incorporates such pertinent issues of turn-of-the-century England as race, religion and sexuality. Still, the pedigree production will have a difficult time swimming against mainstream tastes and will require special handling to find an arthouse niche.

The film opens on the eve of 1899 in rural England. Reisner (Robert Stephens), a Romanian Jew by way of Scotland, is a prosperous textile mill owner grudgingly tolerated by the local gentry. His garish ways —

including a lavish electrical sign to bring in the new year — have served him well in commerce but not in society.

Reisner's son Paul (Clive Owen) is a recent medical school grad whose position at a London research hospital proves more commendable than tactical. Medicine has yet to be embraced as a science and the resident physicians are viewed with amusement and skepticism. Nonetheless, Paul shines in this new setting, emerging as the star medical researcher and confidant of the operation's chief, Mandry (Charles Dance). He also finds romance with Clara (Miranda Richardson), a lab assistant with a veiled past.

The turning point occurs when Paul defies Mandry, who he believes is purposely ignoring vital experiments developed by another doctor. The breach of etiquette costs Paul dearly. While it's difficult to tell the scoundrels from the gentlemen, truth is ultimately the young man's guide and greatest weapon.

Woven into the moral tale is an unabashed romanticism. The relationship between the two men, Paul's love for Clara and an affection for a time past combine for a breathtaking emotional experience. Handsomely crafted and cleverly adorned, "Century" gives the sense of an honest perspective on the bygone era. The performers, particularly Dance and Richardson, provide superlative turns, grounding the drama in real terms.

Sure to elicit strong response, the film will have to capitalize quickly on whatever heat it can generate. That it is decidedly outside the "Masterpiece Theatre" mode proves both an entertainment asset and a bit of a marketplace obstacle.

—*Leonard Klady*

TORONTO FEST

THE SECRET RAPTURE

Channel Four Films with the participation of British Screen present a Greenpoint Film. Produced by Simon Relph. Directed by Howard Davies. Screenplay, David Hare, based upon his stage play. Camera (Kodak), Ian Wilson; editor, George Akers; music, Richard Hartley; designer, Barbara Gosnold; art direction, Fiona McNeil; costume design, Consolata Boyle; sound (Dolby), Danny Hambrook; casting, Janey Fothergill. Reviewed at World Film Festival, Montreal (competing), Sept. 3, 1993. Running time: **96 MIN.**

Isobel Coleridge	Juliet Stevenson
Katherine Coleridge	
	Joanne Whalley-Kilmer
Marion French	Penelope Wilton
Patrick Steadman	Neil Pearson
Tom French	Alan Howard
Max Lopert	Robert Stephens
Norman	Hilton McRae
Jeremy	Robert Glenister

A broad family melodrama, "The Secret Rapture" is a fitfully

successful adaptation (by the author) of the David Hare play. Making his film directing debut, the theater's Howard Davies provides an appropriate somber tone for the tale of blood rivalries and emotional manipulation. Yet the relentless weightiness of the proceedings ultimately wears down the viewer and limits the film's appeal to a specialized audience.

The film jettisons much of the play's politically specific underpinnings and bolsters the Shakespearean-style tragedy.

Isobel (Juliet Stevenson), whose father has recently died, is torn apart when she discovers her bereavement for the dead man isolates her from friends and family. Sister Marion (Penelope Wilton) remains icily detached, concerned only with the family fortunes. Their young stepmother, Katherine (Joanne Whalley-Kilmer), has inured herself to alcohol.

While Isobel grapples with a sense of loss, Marion is quick to establish her reign. Katherine puts Isobel under her younger sister's care and moves to seek partners in the family graphic-design operation. The latter is neatly effected with the treacherous consent of Isobel's lover, Patrick (Neil Pearson).

Of course, the neat little package quickly unravels. Human frailties plague the orderliness Marion so fiercely attempts to create.

Hare's screenplay delineates a frightening precision and alarming logic in the machinations that bring the principals to the breaking point. But the story's catharsis is never satisfyingly resolved. It's as if the characters have been left adrift for eternity.

Existing in a holding room between upscale kitchen sink reality and allegory, "The Secret Rapture" challenges the director and performers to find their ground. Stevenson effects a powerful, strident and unpleasant pose that ultimately works against the material. Others in the cast are less successful in finding a balance, though Kilmer gains our sympathies in an eccentric, bravura performance.

—*Leonard Klady*

INTRUSO

(INTRUDER)

(SPANISH-COLOR)

A Pedro Costa P.C.S.A., Atrium Prods. S.A., Promociones Audiovisuales Reunidas S.A. production, with the collaboration of Antena 3-TV. Produced by Enrique Cerezo, Pedro Costa, Carlos Vasallo. Directed by Vicente Aranda. Screenplay, Alvaro del Amo, Aranda, based on a story by Costa. Camera (color), Jose Luis Alcaine; editor, Teresa Font; music, Jose Nieto; sets, Josep Rosell; sound, Carlos Faruolo. Reviewed at Madrid Film, Aug. 12, 1993. (In Festival of Festivals, Toronto.) Running time: **85 MIN.**

Luisa .... Victoria Abril
Angel .... Imanol Arias
Ramiro .... Antonio Valero
Also with: Alicia Agut, Eufemia Roman, Susana Buen, Carlos Munoz, Alicia Rozas, Nain Thomas, Alejandro Fernandez, Rebeca Roiza.

In "Intruder," as in his recent hit "Lovers," director Vicente Aranda delves with consummate skill into a quirky triangular relationship. Set in modern Spain in the northern coastal city of Santander, pic features top-notch thesping, especially from Imanol Arias, and the gloomy, often morbid story is handled with wit and expertise. Pic's downbeat thrust may put off some audiences, making it a possible but tricky bet for the international art market.

Luisa (Victoria Abril) spots her ex-husband, Angel (Arias), wandering about the city in complete destitution. She takes him into her house, where she lives with her husband, Ramiro (Antonio Valero), a doctor, and two small children. Once ensconced in the house, the terminally ill Angel decides to wreak vengeance on Ramiro by reclaiming his ex-wife, physically and emotionally.

Plot thickens as Angel sees in the couple's young children, a boy and a girl, the reflection of his own youth and his erstwhile friendship with Luisa and Ramiro. As Angel's health worsens, Luisa insists upon caring for him in the house rather than sending him off to a hospital.

The confrontations and Angel's menacing manner seem to be building to a violent climax, but the ending's grim twist is rather too low-key and abrupt. The occasional sex scenes are tame. Pic nonetheless holds audience interest and is well-limned, albeit ultimately depressing.
—*Peter Besas*

LOCARNO FEST

TWO SMALL BODIES
(GERMAN)

A Daniel Zuta Filmproduktion production. Executive producers, Daniel Zuta, Brigitte Kramer. Directed by Beth B. Screenplay, Neal Bell, Beth B, based on Bell's play. Camera (color), Phil Parmet; editors, Andrea Feige, Melody London; music, Swans; art direction, Agnette Schlosser. Reviewed at Locarno Film Festival, Aug. 13, 1993. (Also in Toronto festival.) Running time: **80 MIN.**
Eileen Mahoney .... Suzy Amis
Lt. Brann .... Fred Ward
(English dialogue)

The third feature of New York "New Wave" helmer Beth B (who co-directed "Vortex" and "Salvation" with Scott B), "Two Small Bodies" is a two-actor theater piece skillfully transposed to film but cramped by its single setting.

Though story line — a cop accuses a young cocktail waitress of killing her own children — is strong, pic's extreme faithfulness to the one-set play has an old-fashioned feel likely to limit its appeal. After a few theatrical playoffs, this one will be ready for the small screen.

The dynamics between a nasty, sexist cop and a sexually inhibited, fragile-but-tough young woman offer screenwriters Neal Bell (play's author) and Beth B an emotional field day. "Bodies" is a powerful exercise in female humiliation, with the woman turning the tables on her aggressor before they achieve some kind of equal standing.

Lt. Brann (Fred Ward), a cross between Richard Gere, Columbo and Mickey Spillane, is convinced that blond Eileen Mahoney (Suzy Amis) is a criminal the moment he sees her wearing only a slip. His interrogations soon turn to badgering and outrageous insinuations.

Mahoney stands her ground, tauntingly calling herself a slut. She paints the worst-case scenario herself: She and her one-night stand have sex in front of the kids, suffocate them and cold-bloodedly dispose of the bodies.

Though it's clear Brann has no case, he becomes so obsessed with her he returns day and night for "additional questioning." Finally he tells her they've found her children strangled not far from the house, and confronts her with a police photo of the bodies.

Mahoney takes this punishment on the chin and dishes it back. She, too, is clearly hooked on the snarling lieutenant, who even undresses in her kitchen to unnerve her.

As the mother who's grieved over losing her children but is rather glad to be free of constricting family life, Amis is measured and witty. Veteran thesp Ward, all wild surmises and flailing insults, is allowed few flashes of vulnerability, far too little to endear him to auds.

Despite its high pitch, film gets a little boring once its structure becomes clear. Pic would have benefited from a few visual surprises. As it is, characters are limited to a couple of costume changes and an angry striptease by each.
—*Deborah Young*

WHEN PIGS FLY
(DUTCH-JAPANESE-GERMAN-U.S.)

An Allarts/NDF Sumitomo/Pandora Film/Sultan Driver production. (International sales: Odyssey.) Produced by Kees Kasander, Denis Wigman. Directed by Sara Driver. Screenplay, Ray Dobbins. Camera (color), Robby Mueller; editor, Jay Rabinowitz; music, Joe Strummer. Reviewed at Locarno Film Festival (competing), Aug. 9, 1993. (Also in Toronto festival.) Running time: **97 MIN.**
Marty .... Alfred Molina
Lilly .... Marianne Faithfull
Sheila .... Maggie O'Neill
Frank .... Seymour Cassel
Ruthie .... Rachel Bella
(English dialogue)

Sara Driver's third film is a low-budget, German-shot indie that could succeed as family entertainment. A ghost story in the "Topper" mold, it gives an original, scruffy twist to all the main cliches of the genre, while softpedaling tale's grimmer implications. Instead of the indie audiences that went for Driver's arty "Sleepwalk," "Pigs" could fly with mainstream and TV viewers.

Pic's grungy, post-punk signature gives a modicum of style more comic than disturbing. Film was shot in a nameless German wasteland that convincingly mimics a hip New Jersey no-man's land.

Slobby bachelor Marty (Alfred Molina), a young, wasted jazz musician, lives in a run-down haunted house with his equally spacey dog. The dwelling is on the edge of a town that seems not to exist, in a mysterious Irish-American community on the verge of extinction.

Action alternates between the house and a sleazy bar, the Rose of Erin, where bored, buxom Sheila (Maggie O'Neill) dances on the counter for owner Frank's (Seymour Cassel) deadbeat customers.

Sheila has a soft spot for Marty, and brings over a rocking chair that's "inhabited" by two playful but harmless spooks — the wife (Marianne Faithfull) who Cassel beat to death and a Victorian child (Rachel Bella) straight out of Charles Addams. They help Sheila and Marty get off the skids, and use them to take revenge on the brutal Cassel, who wanted to throw the chair out.

Pic is stuffed with small jokes and treats, like the dog's dream and Molina flying over fields with a pint-sized piano student. Pic's scenic squalor is a laugh in itself.

Acting is OK, dialogue's a snooze. Faithfull has a gentle, reassuring screen presence, and gets to sing one number, but has little range to develop her character as the slightly teed-off ghost.

Music ranges confidently from "Rose of Erin" and "Danny Boy" to Thelonious Monk.
—*Deborah Young*

A LIFE IN THE THEATRE

Turner Pictures presentation of a Beacon Communications and Bay Kinescope production in association with Jalem Prods. Produced by Patricia Wolff and Thomas A. Bliss. Executive producers, David Mamet, Marc Abraham. Associate producers, Connie McCauley and Paddy Cullen. Directed by Gregory Mosher. Script, David Mamet, based on his play. Camera (color), Freddie Francis; editor, Barbara Tulliver; production design, David Wasco; set decoration, Sandy Reynolds-Wasco; costume design, Jane Greenwood; first assistant director, Michael Zimbrich; second assistant director, Stuart Brian Hagen. Reviewed at Festival of Festivals, Toronto, Sept. 14, 1993. Running time: **78 MIN.**
Robert .... Jack Lemmon
John .... Matthew Broderick

David Mamet's "A Life in the Theatre" is a disappointment on the screen, despite the presence of high-pedigree talent on both sides of the camera. The Turner Broadcasting presentation, world premiered at the Toronto fest, will have its cable TV debut Oct. 9 on TNT. Foreign theatrical prospects appear slim, but lead players Jack Lemmon and Matthew Broderick will likely guarantee some shelf life via homevid.

At best, pic is a slight improvement over the play's previous TV adaptation, an unfortunately literal-minded videotaping (produced in the late 1970s for PBS) that's memorable only for recording the brilliant performances of Ellis Rabb and the late Peter Evans, stars of the original 1977 Chicago production.

Lemmon and Broderick are the stars here, playing two members of a second-rate repertory company in an unnamed modern-day city. Robert (Lemmon) is a grandiloquent old pro who clearly senses, but never acknowledges, his career is in decline; John (Broderick) is a talented newcomer whose awed respect for Robert curdles into impatience and annoyance while they share a dressing room during a long theatrical season.

"Life in the Theatre" alternates between excerpts from onstage productions (some very amusingly evocative of Chekhov and other greats) and elliptical episodes of offstage conversations between the two actors. The film, like the play, can be read as a metaphor for teacher-student and parent-child relationships. Or, it can simply be enjoyed as Mamet's love letter to the temple where he works his magic.

On either level, this film version of "Life in the Theatre" is a misfire.

For his first effort as a filmmaker, Gregory Mosher, the veteran legit director who staged the play's first Chicago production, has done his best to open up Mamet's two-character, two-set drama. With the considerable assistance of production designer David Wasco and cinematographer Freddie Francis, Mosher creates a low-rent universe of neighborhood bars, seedy hotels and backstage dressing rooms in vividly realistic detail.

This turns out to be major miscalculation, however, in that Mamet's meticulously stylized dialogue sounds jarringly off-key — and, occasionally, downright ludicrous — in such a realistically drawn environment. Worse, by taking a realistic approach, Mosher underscores the artificiality of having Lemmon and Broderick be the only characters onscreen who speak dialogue.

Mosher also has erred in tipping the play's balance of sympathy so obviously in favor of the older actor essayed by Lemmon. But Lemmon, too, merits criticism for relying so heavily on pathos-inducing shtick and for being so transparent in his efforts to make Robert a tragic figure. The performance is all the more dismaying when compared to Lemmon's wonderful work last year in the Mamet-scripted "Glengarry Glen Ross."

With the deck stacked so heavily in favor of his co-star, Broderick provides a genuinely pleasant surprise with his fine, effectively sharp-edged performance. His evolution from callow, eager-to-please acolyte to self-assured, nakedly ambitious professional is quietly impressive in non-showoffy manner, much like Broderick's seriously underrated performance in "Glory."

The best parts of this "Life in the Theatre" are the sure-fire comedy bits — the brief scenes of onstage disasters involving missed cues and defective props. But these are rare moments in a 78-minute production that seems much longer than it is.

—*Joe Leydon*

THE SAINT OF FORT WASHINGTON

A Warner Bros. release of a David V. Picker/Nessa Hyams production in association with Carrie Prods. Produced by Picker, Hyams. Exec producers, Lyle Kessler, Carl Clifford. Directed by Tim Hunter. Screenplay, Kessler. Camera (Technicolor), Frederick Elmes; editor, Howard Smith; music, James Newton Howard; production design, Stuart Wurtzel; art direction, Steve Saklad; set decoration, Debra Schutt; costume design, Claudia Brown; sound (Dolby), Bill Daly; associate director, Vebe Borge; casting, Hyams. Reviewed at Festival of Festivals, Toronto, Sept. 10, 1993. MPAA Rating: R. Running time: **108 MIN.**

Jerry .... Danny Glover
Matthew .... Matt Dillon
Rosario .... Rick Aviles
Tamsen .... Nina Siemaszko
Little Leroy .... Ving Rhames
Spits .... Joe Seneca

The Saint of Fort Washington" takes a soft, benign look at the homeless. Sympathetic performances from Danny Glover and Matt Dillon somewhat compensate for the mildness of the material, but can't disguise the fact that the film has little to say about a major societal problem. World preemed at Toronto, this looks like a short-termer for Warner Bros. in theatrical release.

A Vietnam vet with shrapnel in his leg, Jerry (Glover) is out on the streets of New York after his business partner has frittered away their money. Cut off from his wife and kids, he washes car windows and has a plan to climb back up the economic ladder.

Matthew (Dillon) is offered up as a disturbed schizophrenic estranged from his mother and newly on the streets after being jerked around by the government bureaucracy. He likes to take photographs, the only problem being that he doesn't put any film in his camera.

Early scenes at the humongous Fort Washington Armory vividly illustrate what it's like at a facility where 700 men are sheltered each night. Taking the touchy kid under his wing, the generous Jerry shows him how to wash windows, save money and deal with life on the mean streets. In his most insightful gesture, he also gives him a roll of film.

For a time, the men stay in an abandoned building with three friendly folks, played by the late Joe Seneca, Rick Aviles and Nina Siemaszko, the latter two as a couple expecting a baby. After Matthew turns the tables in the relationship by pulling Jerry up from the gutter, he is fatefully forced to return to Fort Washington, leading to a bittersweet end.

Shot all over Manhattan, pic benefits from integrating the actors into such soberingly authentic locations as the cavernous armory and a potter's field.

But despite the emotional validity of a father-son dynamic between the two leads, the particulars of playwright Lyle Kessler's script often seem phony, contrived and far too polite for the harshness of the conditions on display.

With the exception of Little Leroy (frighteningly played by Ving Rhames), the house villain at Fort Washington who terrorizes Matthew, all the characters here are virtual sweethearts, good people on a run of bad luck. Drugs, alcohol and crime are never mentioned, and the filmmakers offer no clues as to how they think society should regard and, in turn, deal with the homeless.

Instead of a point of view, pic advances the half-baked concept of Matthew having some sort of holy or healing power for those who come in contact with him, hence the title. But except for the help he extends to Jerry, there is not much evidence of this, as the world is little changed for his presence in it.

Tim Hunter's direction is solidly straightforward with an emphasis on character. There are some unbelievable details, however, including the incredible swiftness of police response in several instances, and the extremely conspicuous Little Leroy's apparent freedom to stalk Fort Washington menacingly with a knife in his hand. Surely the authorities would be on to this guy before too long.

Glover and Dillon get some good things going in some scenes, but the latter's schizophrenia is forgotten, and the vapid sincerity of the project finally overtakes them both.

Production values are appropriately modest and unflashy.

—*Todd McCarthy*

A BRONX TALE

A Savoy release of a Price Entertainment presentation in association with Penta Entertainment of a Tribeca production. Produced by Jane Rosenthal, Jon Kilik, Robert De Niro. Executive producer, Peter Gatien. Directed by De Niro. Screenplay, Chazz Palminteri, based on his play. Camera (DuArt color; Technicolor prints), Reynaldo Villalobos; editors, David Ray, R.Q. Lovett; music supervisor, Jeffrey Kimball; music director, Butch Barbella; production design, Wynn Thomas; art direction, Chris Shriver; set decoration, Debra Shutt; costume design, Rita Ryack; sound (Dolby), Tod Maitland; associate producer-assistant director, Joseph Reidy; casting, Ellen Chenoweth. Reviewed at Festival of Festivals, Toronto, Sept. 10, 1993. (Also in Venice Film Festival.) MPAA Rating: R. Running time: **122 MIN.**

Lorenzo .... Robert De Niro
Sonny .... Chazz Palminteri
Calogero (age 17) ...... Lillo Brancato
Calogero (age 9) .... Francis Capra
Jane .... Taral Hicks
Rosina .... Kathrine Narducci
Jimmy Whispers .... Clem Caserta
Bobby Bars .... Alfred Sauchelli Jr.
Danny K.O. ..... Frank Pietrangolare
Carmine .... Joe Pesci
Tony Toupee .... Robert D'Andrea
Eddie Mush .... Eddie Montanaro
JoJo the Whale .... Fred Fischer
Frankie Coffeecake .... Dave Salerno

A "GoodFellas" with heart, "A Bronx Tale" represents a wonderfully vivid snapshot of a colorful place and time, as well as a very satisfying directorial debut by Robert De Niro. Overflowing with behavioral riches and the flavor of a deep-dyed New York Italian neighborhood, the film also trades intelligently in pertinent moral and social issues that raise it above the level of nostalgia or the mere memoir. First release from Savoy Pictures should be able to carve a nice niche for itself through the fall.

Adroitly expanded by Chazz Palminteri from the one-man play he wrote and performed successfully in Los Angeles and New York, tale charts the growing-up of a youngster named Calogero amidst the small-time hoods and wiseguys of the Bronx in the 1960s. While serving up a wealth of anecdotal material, script never strays far from its potent dramatic focus, which pits the influence of the boy's hard-working, highly principled father against the allure and power of the local mob strongman.

At first, it seems we've seen it all before — the street-corner thugs in shiny suits, the strutting and gesticulating, the heavy New York accents, the gambling and drinking, the constant swearing, the macho culture, the period music, the primacy of thuggish cool.

But, as seen from the p.o.v. of 9-year-old Calogero, it doesn't take too long for the film to get beneath these trappings to establish its own rhythm and texture. The neighborhood in 1960 is ruled by Sonny (Palminteri), who's always on the corner or at the local bar looking after business.

Everything changes after the boy sees Sonny shoot down a man in the street. When Calogero doesn't identify the killer to the police, Sonny takes the kid under his wing, letting him in on craps games from which he takes home more money than his bus driver father Lorenzo (De Niro) makes in weeks.

Lorenzo has no use for a slimebag like Sonny and tries to argue the virtues of hard work and moral values, but Calogero eventually comes to think of his dad as a sucker and Sonny as a winner.

Eight years later, Calogero and his buddies have their own social club, Sonny is a much bigger shot, and black neighborhoods have edged close to Italian turf. Very much under Sonny's sway, Calogero has followed his surrogate father's advice to get two educations, in school and on the street, but his friends all seem like an accident waiting to happen, as they taunt and beat up black kids as they pass on the street.

For his part, Calogero takes a fancy to a black girl and dares to date her against a backdrop of escalating racial tension. Climax is fittingly violent, given the nature of the characters, and Calogero is left with any number of lessons well learned.

Not surprisingly, the film boasts nothing but splendid performances from the leads down to the smallest character bits. As the 9-year-old Calogero, Francis Capra shows both feistiness and obedience. This is magnified by Lillo Brancato, who takes over at 17, as Calogero develops into a young man in whom one can clearly see the dawning of moral

September 27, 1993 (Cont.)

sense and mature judgment. Brancato is also utterly believable physically as De Niro's son.

De Niro has cast himself in the script's least showy role, as the responsible, upright man amidst a carnival of flashy hoods, but he delivers some great scenes, particularly a hilarious one in which he warns his son about letting the little head think for the big head. It's also given to him to repeatedly deliver pic's theme — "The saddest thing in life is wasted talent."

A vaguely familiar face from assorted small roles in films and on TV, Palminteri is terrific as the charismatic Sonny, his quicksilver mood changes keeping everyone on their toes. His henchmen, including the memorable Clem Caserta as his first lieutenant, and the various neighborhood layabouts are pricelessly cast, and Taral Hicks is winning as the black girl who reciprocates Calogero's interest.

Beyond the performance level, however, De Niro has shown impressive sensitivity to the irrational roots of racism and violence. A spectacularly funny scene in which the older wiseguys beat up a bunch of insolent bikers who invade their bar serves as prelude to the young Italians' savage attack on some black kids, and the feel for racial matters is acute without stepping outside the narrative's established p.o.v.

Pic abounds in flavorful, unforced humor, and the penetrating impression of neighborhood life is reinforced by De Niro's decision to shoot entirely on location on a modified block in Queens, as well as by the naturalistic tech contributions.

Film takes a little time getting started, and a final development between Calogero and his girlfriend strains credulity, but this is an impressive first-time outing from many angles. —*Todd McCarthy*

BOPHA!

Paramount Pictures presents an Arsenio Hall Communications production in association with Taubman Entertainment Group. Produced by Lawrence Taubman. Executive producer, Arsenio Hall; co-producer, Lori McCreary. Directed by Morgan Freeman. Screenplay, Brian Bird and John Wierick, based on the play by Percy Mtwa. Camera (Deluxe), David Watkin; editor, Neil Travis; music, James Horner; production design, Michael Philips; art direction, Tracey Moxham; set decoration, Dankert Guillaume; costume design, Diana Cilliers; sound (Dolby), Richard Lightstone; technical adviser, Gregory Rockman; casting, Leo Davis, Jane Warren. Reviewed at Paramount Studios, L.A., Aug. 18, 1993. MPAA Rating: PG-13. Running time: **121 MIN.**
Micah Mangena .... Danny Glover
De Villiers .... Malcolm McDowell
Rosie Mangena .... Alfre Woodard
Van Tonder .... Marius Weyers
Zweli Mangena .... Maynard Eziashi
Pule Rampa .... Malick Bowens
Solomon .... Michael Chinyamurindi
Naledi Machikano
.... Christopher John Hall
Thokozile Machikano ... Grace Mahlaba

Percy Mtwa's contemporary saga of political/personal strife in a South African township, "Bopha!" has been transferred to the screen with tremendous emotional power and integrity. The theatrical directing debut of actor Morgan Freeman is a handsomely crafted, potently played drama that brings the issue of apartheid down to a visceral human dimension. However, the charged nature of the material tends to limit appeal to a partisan crowd.

Commercial prospects remain rarefied. This is a quality production with direct appeal to a small moviegoing segment. It should score in urban, ethnic areas fueled by strong reviews, but secondary life in smaller centers and foreign response can be expected to be erratic.

Set in 1980, the story revolves around the Mangena family. Micah (Danny Glover) is the senior black police officer in his township. He takes great pride in the peace and order evident in the small community and believes in the South Africa that has existed for decades under white British and Afrikaner rule.

His son, Zweli (Maynard Eziashi), is cut from different cloth. A student, his generation is striving to make a country of majority native rule. As wife and mother, Rosie Mangena (Alfre Woodard) finds herself primarily in the role of conciliator.

With growing unrest being experienced already in other townships, De Villiers (Malcolm McDowell), an officer in the country's Special Branch, is charged with keeping the Mangenas' township calm. The irony is that De Villiers' hard-nosed tactics provoke a situation in an essentially tranquil environment.

Since, thanks to media coverage, the real-life events are so familiar, the script's fire derives from the fractious relationship between father and son. The country's evolution is codified in their divergent views. Micah's basic tenets of nonviolence may be sound, but the politics it serves is out of step with his son's struggle for freedom, and this is the saga's deeply felt tragedy.

The painful truth that good intentions do not necessarily translate into a happy ending is key to the plot. "Bopha," from the Zulu language, means to arrest or detain. In this tale, that constraint translates into a stasis that can be resolved only by violent force.

Freeman has a natural feel for environment and a not surprising facility with his performers. Glover's work verges on the Shakespearean as he portrays a man of power undone by blindness and tradition. Eziashi has the charisma and energy of youth, and even Woodard, in a thankless role, provides a little gem of a performance. The youthful supporting cast is also strong, as is Marius Weyers as the township's knowing white police administrator.

The only misstep comes from an all too familiarly painted depiction of bigotry as embodied by McDowell. The Brad Bird-John Wierick adaptation simply cannot find the flesh and blood of this character.

"Bopha!" is a heartfelt and anguished cry. Though moored in historic/geographic specificity, it is an easily understood and universal tale. —*Leonard Klady*

STRIKING DISTANCE

A Columbia Pictures release of an Arnon Milchan production. Produced by Milchan, Tony Thomopoulos, Hunt Lowry. Executive producer, Steven Reuther. Co-producer, Carmine Zozzora. Directed by Rowdy Herrington. Screenplay, Herrington, Martin Kaplan. Camera (Technicolor), Mac Ahlberg; editors, Pasquale Buba, Mark Helfrich; music, Brad Fiedel; production design, Gregg Fonseca; art direction, Bruce Miller; set decoration, Jay Hart; costume design, Betsy Cox; sound (Dolby), John Sutton III; associate producer, Kaplan; assistant director, Nicholas C. Mastandrea; second-unit director, Todd Hallowell; special effects, Allen L. Hall; stunt coordinator, Mickey Gilbert; casting, Pam Dixon. Reviewed at the Hollywood Pacific Theatre, Hollywood, Sept. 9, 1993. MPAA Rating: R. Running time: **101 MIN.**
Tom Hardy .... Bruce Willis
Jo Christman ...... Sarah Jessica Parker
Nick Detillo .... Dennis Farina
Danny Detillo .... Tom Sizemore
Det. Eddie Eiler .... Brion James
Jimmy Detillo .... Robert Pastorelli
Tony Sacco .... Timothy Busfield
Vince Hardy .... John Mahoney
Frank Morris .... Andre Braugher

Columbia apparently dragged the river to come up with the script for this Bruce Willis vehicle — an OK action movie until it sinks under the weight of implausible plotting and over-the-top direction. While the high-testosterone promos may be enough to attract genre fans, it's doubtful this powerboat ride will be able to maintain much box-office flow, with better sailing ahead in homevideo.

Director and co-writer Rowdy Herrington, the guy responsible for all those unintentional laughs in the irresistibly campy "Road House," nearly tops himself here, directing a high-ticket action yarn that casts Willis as a Pittsburgh cop on the trail of a serial killer. The all-over-the-map plot opens with square-jawed Tom Hardy (Willis) "ratting" on his partner (Robert Pastorelli) in an excessive-use-of-force case, alienating himself from other members of the department.

Still, that's just the hors d'oeuvre, as Hardy soon loses his chief of detectives dad (John Mahoney), who was pursuing a serial killer, and is subsequently drummed out of the force after insisting that the actual culprit is not the derelict the police apprehended but another cop.

Flash forward two years, and we find Hardy a near-alcoholic working for the city's River Rescue squad, until the supposedly incarcerated killer begins striking again — this time exclusively at women with some connection to Hardy.

An outcast because of the trial, Hardy receives scant support from his uncle (Dennis Farina) — another cop in the family's five-generation line — but discovers a softer shoulder on his comely new partner, Jo (Sarah Jessica Parker).

The convoluted script by Herrington and Martin Kaplan tries to be full of surprises, but mostly they're either obvious (anyone who can't guess the killer's identity must be sucking boat exhaust) or downright ridiculous. Some of the best guffaws stem from Willis' exchanges with Parker, whose character decides to tell him they shouldn't become "involved" *while* the two are lying in bed together.

Herrington does have a flair for action, as the pic begins with a terrific car chase (Hardy and his dad chat casually while darting through traffic), followed by a taut shootout aboard a garbage scow and, ultimately, a dimly lit boat chase reminiscent of "Patriot Games."

That finale, however, underscores the movie's problems, milking the "Fatal Attraction," back-from-the-dead gimmick well beyond its limits, to the point where the urge to giggle buries the suspense.

Willis plays his "Die Hard" riff effectively enough, while the supporting cast is largely wasted, including Mahoney in a brief turn as his dad, Brion James as a one-note detective and Timothy Busfield in what amounts to a cameo as Willis' obnoxious partner. Parker gets in a few amusing one-liners but, to use an old line, looks a little short (among other things) to be a cop.

Tech credits are generally top-notch, though Brad Fiedel's score seems to echo his previous work on "Terminator 2: Judgment Day" in more than a few places; then again, it's hardly the only part of "Striking Distance" that feels recycled. —*Brian Lowry*

ROMEO IS BLEEDING

A Gramercy release from Polygram Filmed Entertainment of a Working Title/Hilary Henkin production. Produced by Henkin, Paul Webster. Executive producers, Eric Fellner, Tim Bevan. Co-producer, Michael Flynn. Directed by Peter Medak. Screenplay, Henkin. Camera (color), Dariusz Wolski; editor, Walter Murch; music, Mark Isham; production design, Stuart Wurtzel; art direction, W. Steven Graham; set decoration, Beth A. Rubino; costume design, Aude Bronson-Howard; sound (Dolby), Gary Alper; assistant director, Mark McGann; casting, Bonnie Timmerman. Reviewed at the Northstar screening room, L.A., Aug. 28, 1993. MPAA Rating: R. Running time: **108 MIN.**

September 27, 1993 (Cont.)

Jack Grimaldi	Gary Oldman
Mona Demarkov	Lena Olin
Natalie Grimaldi	Annabella Sciorra
Sheri	Juliette Lewis
Don Falcone	Roy Scheider
Scully	David Proval
Martie	Will Patton
Joey	Larry Joshua
Skouras	Paul Butler
Cage	James Cromwell
Sal	Michael Wincott
John	Gene Canfield
Jack's Attorney	Ron Perlman

The blood and grunge run thick on the mean streets in "Romeo Is Bleeding." This heavy dose of ultra-violent neo-noir gives Gary Oldman a face-first trip through the gutter that would make Mickey Rourke drool, but the far-fetched plotting eventually goes so far over the top that pic flirts with inventing a new genre of film noir camp.

Gramercy release will find a cadre of devotees who will groove on the hot cast, high style and low-down macho fantasies, but more people will be turned off by the excessive gore and progressive facetiousness.

Perhaps the most interesting angle here is that the story represents a tough working man's wet dream, and yet it was written by a woman. Determined to make it big financially, Oldman's New York police sergeant, Jack Grimaldi, does his job on the organized crimes task force while accepting payoffs from the mob. He also has it both ways in the sack, knowing his lovely wife (Annabella Sciorra) awaits him at home while he makes time with his sultry mistress (Juliette Lewis).

But that's before he meets a member of a Moscow crime family, Mona Demarkov (Lena Olin), who has just been nabbed after wiping out some Feds and a government witness. Grimaldi is entrusted with guarding her at a safe house but she's got him disarmed and sexually compromised before the Feds even arrive to pick her up.

As narrated in the third person by Oldman's character in traditional hard-boiled fashion, tale knots up considerably from there.

Cultivated gangster Don Falcone (Roy Scheider) orders Grimaldi to eliminate Mona, who in turn offers Grimaldi six times as much money to let her flee the country but tell Falcone he's killed her.

Grimaldi takes Mona's cash, but when the she-devil tries to kill him, all hell breaks loose, and pic flies into darkly absurdist territory that finally gets grotesquely out of hand.

A scene of the two struggling in a car about to crash will have viewers laughing if they aren't already, and other scenes, including the ultra-bloody climactic shootout, push matters ever further into silliness.

Ultimately, the prevailing impression is one of an unrestrained fantasy of perverse sex and violence.

Screenwriter and co-producer Hilary Henkin has delivered some pungent dialogue, vivid characters and wild scenes, and director Peter Medak has responded by creating a stylishly warped environment for it all.

One of pic's prime motives would seem to be the creation of the most astoundingly, memorably vicious and sexy female villain in movie history, and who better than Olin to play her?

With her deep, husky voice, hot bod and intimations of limitless depravity, she would convince anyone that she has already chewed up and spit out the men of one empire and is working on her second.

For his part, Oldman clearly has a taste for the wild side, but he outdoes himself here as a self-deluding cop whose weakness for sex and money lets him tolerate no end of beatings, mutilations, humiliations and defeats.

Sciorra registers well in the limited role of the wife at the end of her patience; Lewis' role is a throwaway. Remainder of the cast fits snugly into the tough-talking mold.

Where style is substance, craft contributions are crucial, and all hands, notably lenser Dariusz Wolski, production designer Stuart Wurtzel, editor Walter Murch and composer Mark Isham, have made strong marks on the prevailing mood. *—Todd McCarthy*

A DANGEROUS WOMAN

A Gramercy release from Amblin Entertainment in association with Island World of a Rollercoast production. Produced by Naomi Foner. Executive producer, Kathleen Kennedy. Line producer, Patricia Whitcher. Directed by Stephen Gyllenhaal. Screenplay, Foner, based on the novel by Mary McGarry Morris. Camera (Foto-Kem color), Robert Elswit; editor, Harvey Rosenstock; music, Carter Burwell; production design, David Brisbin; set design, Mary Finn, Renato Franceschelli; set decoration, Margaret Goldsmith; costume design, Susie DeSanto; sound (Dolby), Stephen Halbert; casting, Amanda Mackey, Cathy Sandrich. Reviewed at the Northstar screening room, L.A., Sept. 2, 1993. MPAA rating: R. Running time: **101 MIN.**

Martha Horgan	Debra Winger
Frances	Barbara Hershey
Mackey	Gabriel Byrne
Getso	David Strathairn
Birdie	Chloe Webb
Steve Bell	John Terry
Make-up Girl	Jan Hooks
Tupperware Salesman	Paul Dooley
Mercy	Viveka Davis
John	Richard Riehle
Anita	Laurie Metcalf

Both absorbing and exasperating, "A Dangerous Woman" is such a small-scale character piece that it might have been more at home on the small screen. Film's main attraction is totally change-of-pace lead performance by Debra Winger that some will find heartbreaking and others will consider amusing, but this will probably not be enough to make this Gramercy release a B.O. contender.

Winger has transformed herself considerably to play Martha, a pudgy, goggle-eyed nerd who dresses like a high school wallflower and has probably never had a date, much less a boyfriend. Martha works at a small town cleaners, and lives with her aunt Frances (Barbara Hershey), a wealthy California widow rancher.

Aside from her lack of social graces, Martha's distinguishing trait is that she cannot lie. This lands her in hot water on the job, for when she rightly accuses white trash employee Getso (David Strathairn) of stealing money, the "screwball" cannot stand up for herself when no one believes her, and she's canned.

Back on the ranch, itinerant handyman Mackey (Gabriel Byrne) has begun hanging around in hopes of some work. With time on her hands, Martha befriends him and, in the first of several off-putting scenes, the two make love.

Naturally, Martha decides that she's in love with the scoundrel. But when Mackey gets it on with her sexy aunt, Martha violently takes out her rejection on Getso.

This lands the picture right in TV-movie land, as a pregnant Martha winds up in jail and is forced to decide between telling a lie that will enable her to escape a murder rap and sticking to the truth and its more serious consequences.

Adapted by Naomi Foner from Mary McGarry Morris' well-received 1991 novel, the film carries some fundamental contradictions. The mostly leisurely pace established by director Stephen Gyllenhaal is the tradeoff for the accumulation of character detail, but the lurches into outright melodrama feel jarring in this context, particularly in the final reel.

The three notable men — Byrne's amoral wanderer, Strathairn's sleazy thief and John Terry's pragmatic politico — are thoroughgoing SOBs. Hershey similarly remains one-dimensional.

This leaves Winger's performance as the central point of interest. After any number of sexy outings in her career, it is fascinating to see her take on this awkward, sexually innocent character. Her graceless, insecure movements are right on target. But there is an element of the stunt to the performance that can also prompt a detached, if admiring, amusement.

Strathairn adds further proof that he's one of the great contemporary character actors. His slow and underplayed expiration after Winger attacks him stands out as the most striking sequence in the film and one of the most distinctive death scenes in memory.

small screen. Film's main attraction is totally change-of-pace lead performance by Debra Winger that some will find heartbreaking and others will consider amusing, but this will probably not be enough to make this Gramercy release a B.O. contender.

An unusual entry from Amblin Entertainment, pic will register deeply with some viewers, especially women, but it's the kind of odd and muted tale for which it is difficult to drum up theatrical interest these days.

Tech credits are strong.
—Todd McCarthy

TELLURIDE FEST

SUTURE

A Kino-Korsakoff production. Produced, directed, written by Scott McGehee, David Siegel. Executive producers, Steven Soderbergh, Michael Halberstadt. Co-producers, Laura Groppe, Buddy Enright, Alison Brantley. Camera (Foto-Kem B&W, Deluxe prints; Panavision widescreen), Greg Gardiner; editor, Lauren Zuckerman; music, Cary Berger; production design, Kelly McGehee; costume design, Mette Hansen; sound (Dolby), David Chernow; sound design, Mark Magini; associate producer, Eileen Jones; assistant director, Groppe; casting, Sally Dennison, Patrick Rush. Reviewed at Telluride Film Festival, Sept. 3, 1993. (Also in Festival of Festivals, Toronto.) Running time: **96 MIN.**

Clay Arlington	Dennis Haysbert
Renee Descartes	Mel Harris
Dr. Max Shinoda	Sab Shimono
Alice Jameson	Dina Merrill
Vincent Towers	Michael Harris
Lt. Weismann	David Graf
Mrs. Lucerne	Fran Ryan
Sidney Callahan	John Ingle

"Suture" is an exceedingly smart and elegant American indie in a very unusual vein. Part mystery thriller, part psychological investigation and part avant-garde experiment, first feature from the team of Scott McGehee and David Siegel will be a fest favorite and put them on the map as filmmakers. An adventurous distrib should be able to situate this nicely in specialized slots, but pic's chilliness and formalism will make it an unlikely bet for commercial breakout.

The young writer-directors, both of whom have advanced college degrees, are upfront about their influences here, citing the striking but rarely discussed 1960s psychological suspensers "Seconds" and "Mirage," as well as the more familiar work of Hitchcock and Hiroshi Teshigahara. Picture was shot in black-and-white 'Scope, which creates a great look and itself represents a selling point to a certain audience, even if it poses a problem for some ancillary markets down the line.

Focusing on a strange case of amnesia prompted by an attempted murder, pic takes an analytical, clinical look at the issues of memory, identity and personality. Story is given a surreal twist from the outset by a central, unremarked-upon incongruity, and its stylistic strategies tilt it more in the direction of a

September 27, 1993 (Cont.)

rarefied art film than a mainstream thriller.

A brilliant, attention-getting opening tersely presents the lead-up to a dramatic confrontation between a white intruder and a black man hiding with a shotgun, all to the disorienting accompaniment of narration concerning memory and amnesia.

Suddenly jumping back in time, the narrative introduces Vincent Towers (Michael Harris), a wealthy but cold white man living in an opulent home in Phoenix.

Vincent has initiated a reunion with his half-brother, Clay Arlington (Dennis Haysbert), whom he hasn't seen in years, and both men comment upon their remarkable physical resemblance. The surreal joke here is that Clay is black.

Vincent plots to blow up his own car with Clay in it, and assumes a new identity after having planted his own papers with Clay. Clay survives the explosion, but must undergo long hospitalization for a program of plastic surgery as well as treatment for his amnesia.

Naturally, he is assumed by his shrink (Sab Shimono) to be Vincent and begins being fed images and memories of the other man.

Remainder of the film has a cool fascination, as Clay attempts to rebuild his memory from scraps of assorted evidence, as well as figure out what happened to him and seek revenge. Handling of the story is intelligent and precise, although the pacing is too static and the plotting too elliptical for those not attuned to art films.

What will impress discerning viewers most is the style. Greg Gardiner's almost glowing black-and-white images of the parched Arizona locations and blank hospital settings create a semi-hallucinatory look that is astutely linked to the subject matter. Filmmakers have drawn upon some experimental film techniques in their unusual editing and sound work, and pic's physical qualities are distinctive in all respects.

Performances are functionally low-key. Steven Soderbergh came aboard as exec producer after lensing was completed to help navigate the film through post-production.
— *Todd McCarthy*

THE BOYS OF ST. VINCENT

(CANADIAN — 16mm)

A Les Productions Tele-Action production in co-production with the National Film Board of Canada in association with Canadian Broadcasting Corp. with the participation of Telefilm Canada. (Foreign sales: Alliance Intl., Toronto.) Produced by Sam Grana, Claudio Luca. Executive producers, Luca, Colin Neale. Directed by John N. Smith. Screenplay, Des Walsh, Smith, Grana. Camera (color), Pierre Letarte; editors, Werner Nold (part one), Andre Corriveau (part two); music, Neil Smolar; production design, Real Ouellette; chief decorator (Montreal), Claire Alary; set decoration (Newfoundland), Annie McLeod; costume design, Denis Sperdouklis; sound, Serge Beauchemin; line producer, Martine Allard; associate producer, Nicole de Rochemont; assistant director, Pierre Plante; casting, Elite Prods., Nadia Rona, Rosina Bucci. Reviewed at Telluride Film Festival, Sept. 3, 5, 1993. (Also in Festival of Festivals, Toronto.) Running time: part one, **92 MIN.**; part two, **93 MIN.**
Peter Lavin .... Henry Czerny
Kevin Reevey, age 10 ... Johnny Morina
Kevin Reevey, age 25 ....
.... Sebastian Spence
Steven Lunny, age 10 .... Brian Dodd
Steven Lunny, age 25 ... David Hewlett
Eddie Linnane .... Jonathan Lewis
Mike Sproule .... Jeremy Keefe
Mike Finn .... Phillip Dinn
Detective Noseworthy ... Brian Dooley
Brother Glackin .... Greg Thomey
Brother MacLaverty .... Michael Wade
Chantal Lavin .... Lise Roy
Sheilah .... Kristine Demers
Brian Lunny, age 30 . Timothy Webber
Brian Lunny, age 16 ...... Ashley Billard
Brother Glynn .... Alain Goulem
Tom Kennedy .... Ed Martin
Monsignor .... Sam Grana
Archbishop .... Maurice Podbrey

"The Boys of St. Vincent" is a powerful, sociologically and politically important two-part Canadian telefilm that is beginning to make a splash in film circles. Drama concerning the molestation of young boys in a Catholic orphanage won the grand prize at the Banff Television Festival earlier this year, and was first seen on the big screen at the Telluride Film Festival, where it caused a sensation. Possible cutting and consolidation of the three-hour running time, along with blowup from 16mm to 35mm with an eye to theatrical run, are now being mulled.

Inspired by, but not directly based upon, an infamous case at Mount Cashel in St. John's, Newfoundland, in the late 1980s, this insistently fictional film has already provoked considerable controversy in Canada. This is due not only to its touchy subject matter, but to a court injunction blocking its CBC broadcast in Ontario and parts of Quebec on the basis that it might prejudice similar court cases still in progress. Pic was a last-minute addition to the Toronto fest, and only the French-lingo version has been shown on Ontario TV.

Taking on such material clearly presented a daunting challenge in both the writing and performance, but the Canadian team has proven up to the task. The approach is intelligent and controlled, allowing much to remain implicit but nevertheless well understood.

Set in 1975, part one quickly establishes the physical intimacy of the St. Vincent orphanage, as well as its close ties to the local town life in Eastern Canada. The institution is presided over by the young, good-looking Brother Peter Lavin (Henry Czerny), who exhibits the expected paternalistic attitude toward his charges but also betrays a stern manner and short temper.

The first sign that things aren't right comes when 10-year-old Kevin Reevey (Johnny Morina) is returned to St. Vincent after running away. So intensely does Lavin feel for little Kevin that he showers him with impassioned, borderline lustful embraces and kisses. But when Kevin protests, Lavin turns on the lad and beats him severely.

All this would pass unnoticed except for the suspicions of the orphanage's janitor, who spirits the terrorized kid off to the doctor. For this transgression, he is fired by the furious Lavin, but the gesture is enough to start tongues wagging and for the janitor to hire a detective to look into what might be going on at St. Vincent.

Discreet but unmistakable scenes show other Catholic Brothers sneaking into the boys' dorm room after dark to join them in bed. Finally a police interrogation of the boys reveals a horrifying catalogue of abuse.

Script by Des Walsh, director John N. Smith and co-producer Sam Grana sensitively play out the power relationships among the Brothers and boys but are also excellent at suggesting the conspiracy of silence and inaction forged by the local government and church hierarchy. Despite the evidence, the investigation is shown as being blocked at the highest administrative level, allowing the perpetrators to get away.

Part two picks up 15 years later. Lavin is living in Montreal with his wife and two boys when a cop abruptly arrives at his door to arrest him and transport him to St. John's to face charges of sexual assault and gross indecency and misconduct.

In the end, it's a tossup as to which half is the more disturbing — the first, showing the actual abuse, or the second, detailing the possible ruination of many lives in order to see justice done.

Part one is marked by the poignant, naturalistic playing of the young boys, all of whom convey fear and pitiful deprivation. The quotidian life of both the orphanage and the town is economically suggested under Smith's firmly straightforward and concentrated direction, and it is commendable that such a story could be told without a trace of homophobia.

Dominating it all, however, is the central performance of Czerny as Brother Lavin. A Toronto stage actor with scant screen experience, Czerny superbly limns the layers of authority, control and irrepressible rage within the man, suggesting deep deprivation and shortcomings in his own past that might have led him to such behavior. Striding swiftly in his long black frock, Czerny cuts a frequently terrifying figure, and he is not afraid to inject a little melodrama into the performance to help get the audience to hate him even more.

Admirably solid and irreproachable rather than dazzlingly inspired, "The Boys of St. Vincent" has a lot to keep people talking, and is one of those occasional phenomena (like the Anita Hill-Clarence Thomas hearings) that can change public awareness and perception of an issue. If it doesn't go theatrical in the U.S., it at least deserves prominent airing on cable and PBS.
— *Todd McCarthy*

CLEAN, SHAVEN

A DSM III Films presentation. Produced, directed, written by Lodge Kerrigan. Executive producer, J. Dixon Byrne. Camera (DuArt color), Teodoro Maniaci; editor, Jay Rabinowitz; music, Hahn Rowe; production design, Tania Ferrier; sound, John Kelsey, Matthew Perry (Miscou Island), Michael Parsons (N.Y.); special effects makeup design and creation, Rob Benevides; associate producer, Melissa Painter; assistant directors, Eliot Rockett (Miscou Island), Antek Walczak, Matthew Boccaccio (N.Y.). Reviewed at Telluride Film Festival, Sept. 5, 1993. Running time: **77 MIN.**
Peter Winter .... Peter Greene
Jack McNally .... Robert Albert
Mrs. Winter .... Megan Owen
Melinda Frayne .... Molly Castelloe
Nicole Frayne ...... Jennifer MacDonald

"Clean, Shaven" is an almost unbearably intense, exceedingly concentrated study of schizophrenia by a clearly talented new filmmaker. Using a fragmented narrative and some avant-garde techniques, pic is so unsettling that many viewers won't be able to tolerate it, and there is no doubt that the graphic gruesomeness of two or three scenes goes well beyond what any audience would want to see. Still, this could find a place on the more adventurous fringe of the specialized scene, and marks Lodge Kerrigan as a talent to watch.

A young cinematographer, Gotham-based producer-director-writer Kerrigan lensed this short feature in fits and starts beginning in 1990 on remote Miscou Island in Eastern Canada. Both the razor-sharp focus on the subject matter and the strong filmmaking discipline bespeak a tenacious commitment to the project.

First dialogue doesn't occur until 12 minutes in, and Kerrigan puts the viewer ill at ease almost at once.

September 27, 1993 (Cont.)

His central figure, Peter Winter (Peter Greene), is a blond young man who is clearly very disturbed and is probably a murderer.

Simple story line of Peter searching the windswept, sparsely populated island for his daughter while pursued by a detective presents a string upon which to hang numerous scenes in which it appears that Peter's head might literally explode.

At one point, he cuts himself up with a razor, and while driving down the road starts digging bloodily into his skull. There are also some vivid autopsy shots, but worst of all is a prolonged scene of Peter digging out a fingernail with a knife. In the end, it turns out there was a reason for all this, but that doesn't help while watching it.

This aside, Kerrigan and Greene present a close study of an unbalanced mind perhaps unprecedented in its artistic concentration and clinical detail. Character seems so beyond the pale, so incapable of doing anything normally, that it's hard to believe he could have made it this far and been part of a family. But as the deconstructed facts of his life are pieced back together, a plausible portrait emerges.

Film has a powerful impact for both the right and wrong reasons. But even without the blood, Kerrigan instantly grabs the attention and makes the viewer squirm for the full running time. The visuals possess an exceptional clarity, the precise editing keeps one off balance, and the soundtrack is of an exceptional complexity and density.

Ultimately, pic puts the viewer in agonizingly close proximity to a character one would like to get as far away from as possible, but it conveys his pressurized state of mind with impressive skill.

—*Todd McCarthy*

BLUE

(BRITISH)

A Channel Four presentation in association with Arts Council of Great Britain, Opal and BBC Radio 3 of a Basilisk Communications/Uplink production. Produced by James Mackay, Takashi Asai. Directed, written by Derek Jarman. Associate director-producer, David Lewis. (Technicolor.) Music, Simon Fisher Turner; sound design (Dolby), Marvin Black. Reviewed at Telluride Film Festival, Sept. 6, 1993. Running time: **76 MIN.**

Voices: John Quentin, Nigel Terry, Derek Jarman, Tilda Swinton.

Perhaps not since Andy Warhol's "Sleep" and "Empire State" has there been a film quite like Derek Jarman's "Blue." This conceptual essay/meditation/memoir on the director's deteriorating condition with AIDS consists of a dense soundtrack accompanied visually by 76 minutes of blue screen. The high-art crowd and Jarman partisans will find ways to rationalize and

defend this sporadically gripping piece, but the audience will, by definition, be extremely limited, and the stunt aspect of it will cause it to be more talked about than actually sat through.

For those who will want to debate its artistic merits, there are numerous levels to be considered. Is something in which the only visual kick comes from the reel changes in fact a film at all? Would this deeply personal but still rather objectively written commentary be more or less effective listened to on radio or tape?

Very early in the experience, there is a tendency to look away from the screen, as staring continuously at the bright, almost glowing blue Technicolor hue proves both too boring and too intense. Better to look at the ceiling, walls, floor or the inside of one's eyelids while taking in the text. Joined occasionally on the track by three close collaborators and backed by Simon Fisher Turner's rich score and Marvin Black's complex sound design, Jarman ponders numerous subjects and aspects of his disease.

Most affectingly, and at greatest length, he speaks of going blind because his retina is being destroyed. "If I lose half of my sight, will my vision be halved?" he asks.

"Blue" has moments of power, but its many digressions prompt the mind to wander, giving one the chance to think about anything — Jarman's other films, how other artists have reacted to their own AIDS, what's playing down the street.

Sticking with this will entirely be a question of individual tolerance and patience for an art artifact that is personal, political and conceptually extreme.   —*Todd McCarthy*

TORONTO FEST

HOUSEHOLD SAINTS

A Fine Line Features release of a Jonathan Demme presentation of a Jones Entertainment Group/Newman-Guay production. Produced by Richard Guay, Peter Newman. Executive producer, Demme. Directed by Nancy Savoca. Screenplay, Savoca, Guay, based on the novel by Francine Prose. Camera (DuArt color), Bobby Bukowski; editor, Beth Kling; music, Stephen Endelman; production design, Kalina Ivanov; art direction, Charles Lagola; set design, Jeff McDonald; set decoration, Karen Wiesel; costume design, Eugenie Bafaloukos; sound (Dolby), William Sarokin; assistant director, J. Miller Tobin; casting, John Lyons, Julie Madison. Reviewed at Festival of Festivals, Toronto, Sept. 12, 1993. MPAA Rating: R. Running time: **124 MIN.**

Catherine Falconetti	Tracey Ullman
Joseph Santangelo	Vincent D'Onofrio
Teresa	Lili Taylor
Carmela Santangelo	Judith Malina
Nicky Falconetti	Michael Rispoli
Lino Falconetti	Victor Argo
Leonard Villanova	Michael Imperioli
Young Teresa	Rachael Bella
Evelyn Santangelo	Illeana Douglas
Frank Manzone	Joe Grifasi

"Household Saints" has so many changes of mood, pacing and focus that it is impossible to know what it is aiming at. After building up some cockeyed charm through the first half, Nancy Savoca's third feature peels off into obscure and particularized religious mysticism, leaving the viewer grasping in vain for a handle to hold onto for the second hour. This is a very offbeat project that would need to have been brilliant to work; that it isn't means Fine Line has a difficult marketing task beyond initial specialized dates.

A tale of misfits in postwar Little Italy, film has a peculiar structure that does not unfold smoothly. Spanning more than 20 years and embracing three generations of strange women, this is, among other things, a look at different kinds of faith within the context of otherwise unexceptional lives. Unfortunately, the flights of fancy never stay aloft for long.

Yarn opens during a heat wave in 1949. The local butcher of Mulberry Street, Joseph Santangelo (Vincent D'Onofrio), wins the hand of Catherine Falconetti (Tracey Ullman) in a pinochle game with her father, and marries her despite the misgivings of his witchlike mother, Carmela (Judith Malina).

Catherine's daughter, Little Teresa, exhibits a precocious fascination with saints and Catholic legends that grows stronger and more weird in her teens. Determined to become the bride of Christ, she frustrates her parents as well as a boyfriend (Michael Imperioli) with her obsession. The best things in the film are the many oddball touches — sudden apparitions, details of a horrible meal, Carmela's curious religious observances, Teresa's tireless ironing of checkered shirts. But the more these accumulate, the less they hang together, leaving the film incoherent as it lurches toward the end.

Beyond the lack of focus, numerous other elements irritate, such as the virtual disappearance of Joseph and Catherine in the second half, the choppy pacing in the film's second section, and an unsatisfactory and irrelevant subplot involving Catherine's brother.

Looking uncannily like the young Orson Welles, D'Onofrio unleashes a good deal of charm as the friendly butcher. As his wife, Ullman is forced to be uncommunicative in the early going and never expands much beyond that, while Malina gives a lively account of the nightmare mother-in-law.

But Lili Taylor, as Teresa, has the most perplexing part. Entering the scene only after 70 minutes, she has, in a way, an unplayable part, in that her character's only dimension is unexplained religious fanaticism.

The cramped interiors of Little Italy are well represented, but one sees little of the streets, and Bobby Bukowski's lensing is on the drab side. Other tech credits are OK.

—*Todd McCarthy*

FREAKED

20th Century Fox presents a Tommy production. Produced by Harry Ufland and Mary Jane Ufland. Co-produced, written by Tim Burns, Tom Stern, Alex Winter. Directed by Stern and Winter. Camera (Deluxe), Jamie Thompson; editor, Malcolm Campbell; music, Kevin Kiner; production design, Catherine Hardwicke; art direction, Kim Hix; costume design, Malissa Daniel; creature/visual effects supervisor, Thomas Rainone; sound (Dolby), Lee Orloff; casting, Artz & Cohen. Reviewed at Festival of Festivals (Midnight Madness), Toronto, Sept. 10, 1993. MPAA Rating: R. Running time: **79 MIN.**

Ricky Coogin	Alex Winter
Julie	Megan Ward
Ernie	Michael Stoyanov
Elijah C. Skuggs	Randy Quaid
Dick Brian	William Sadler
Bearded Lady	Mr. T
Skye Daley	Brooke Shields
Stuey Gluck	Alex Zuckerman
Worm	Derek McGrath

Now is the Alex Winter of our discontent. "Freaked" showcases Ted (or is it Bill?) of the "Excellent Adventure" as star, co-director, co-producer, co-writer and conspirator. An anarchic mix of hip comedy, vague, socially correct eco politics and overstated makeup effects, Winter's pic might just eke by as a cult curiosity. However, mainstream chances are dim, with offshore prospects likely to reach no farther than Puerto Rico.

Loud and flamboyant, pic takes a few shots at societal sacred cows but more often misses the target. The effort comes off much in the prankish manner of a student film. "Freaked" thumbs its nose at the status quo, but few will find themselves on the filmmakers' side when the last laughs are counted.

Former child star Ricky Coogin (Winter) has entered into adulthood as a vain, obnoxious, amoral vulgarian. He's wooed and succumbs to a multimillion-dollar offer to be the spokesman for industrial giant EES (Everything Except Shoes). Specifically, he's sent to banana republic Santa Flan to squelch rumors about the deadly side effects of its Zygrot-24 chemical.

Ricky is blind to everything but the money. When he encounters eco radicals, all he can think about is effecting a disguise to romance protester Julie (Megan Ward). With

September 27, 1993 (Cont.)

the assistance of buddy Ernie (Michael Stoyanov), he whisks her away from the throng but soon blows his cover.

The trio's discord deepens when they arrive at the ghoulish theme park Freek Land and encounter its maniacal mastermind, Elijah J. Skuggs (Randy Quaid). Skuggs lures them into his lair and, employing Zygrot, turns Julie and Ernie into Siamese twins while Ricky becomes half man, half monster. Showing exceptionally good judgment, actor Keanu Reeves appears uncredited and visually unidentifiable as the Dog Boy.

Unlike Tod Browning's 1932 "Freaks," the new outing has precious little to convey about the nature of physical deformity. It's weighed down by a staccato of fitfully funny gags; the filmmakers simply try too hard to displease.

Not as brisk as its running time might suggest, "Freaked" disproves the old saw that brevity is the soul of wit. —*Leonard Klady*

THIRTY-TWO SHORT FILMS ABOUT GLENN GOULD

(CANADIAN — DOCU-DRAMA)

Rhombus Media present a Max Film with the participation of Telefilm Canada, OFDC in association with the NFBC, CBC, Nos-Television, RTP-Portugal, Oy Yleisradio Ab and Glenn Gould Ltd. Produced by Niv Fichman. Directed by Francois Girard. Screenplay, Girard, Don McKellar. Research, Nick McKinney, Chantal Neveu. Camera (Kodak), Alain Dostie; editor, Gaetan Huot; design consultant, Charles Dunlop; art direction, John Rubino; costume design, Linda Muir; sound (Dolby), Stuart French; artistic consultants, Charles Dunlop, John Rubino; casting, Deidre Bowen. Reviewed at Festival of Festivals (Gala), Toronto, Sept. 11, 1993. Running Time: 93 MIN.
Glenn Gould .... Colin Feore
Also with Gale Garnett, Katya Ladan, David Hughes, Gerry Quigley, Carlo Rota, Peter Millard, Yehudi Menuhin, Bruno Monsaingeon.

While the title is deceiving, "Thirty-two Short Films About Glenn Gould" is a thirtysomething, impressionistic approach to the life and times of the iconoclastic classical pianist. An assured melange of dramatic recreation, archival material and interviews, it is a uniquely entertaining venture. One need not know Gould's artistry or be attuned to the music to respond to the material. It has definite upscale appeal and ancillary prospects are decidedly upbeat.

Director/co-writer Francois Girard is neither particularly interested in fashioning a Hollywood-style bio nor in conducting clinical dissection. His take on Gould is rather like a tone poem, and is unquestionably reverential. He comes up with intriguing and unusual ways of cozying up to genius.

Apart from the requisite biographical details, the so-called short films run the gamut. There are a couple of Gould's non-musical ventures for radio and a segment of his film collaboration with the animator Norman MacLaren.

There's also dramatic reconstruction of key events in his life, including his last live performance. Woven into an already rich tapestry are a handful of recollections, often bland, from real-life colleagues and friends.

The personal qualities that made Gould unique and a seminal force are never fully defined. But in this instance that proves a satisfying tact; any conclusion about the driven, chronically unwell artist who died at 50 undoubtedly would have been glib and banal.

Girard and co-writer Don McKellar effect an organic mixture of fact, drama and points in between that, if not stamped Canadian, at least reflects an artistic format at which the country's filmmakers excel. The blurring of real and reconstructed elements is seamless, heightened by pristine visuals and naturalistic performances.

Though arguably a one-man show for actor Colin Feore, an army of performers tramp through the life story providing memorable turns, particularly Gale Garnett and David Hughes. But it is Feore at the front and center, creating music and orchestrating lives with the same facility with which he commands orchestras. A memorable dramatic bridge segues from a series of overheard conversations in a diner to his offbeat method of conveying images of the north in a radio doc.

"Thirty-two Short Films About Glenn Gould" is music for the heart of adventurous filmgoers. Definitely in a high class of its own, it is one of the few pictures to capture the nature of the artist and his craft. —*Leonard Klady*

RUDY

TriStar Pictures presents a Fried/Woods Films Production. Produced by Robert N. Fried and Cary Woods. Executive producer, Lee R. Mayes. Directed by David Anspaugh. Screenplay, Angelo Pizzo. Camera (Technicolor), Oliver Wood; editor, David Rosenbloom; music, Jerry Goldsmith; production design, Robb Wilson King; art direction, set decorator, Martin Price; costume design, Jane Anderson; sound (Dolby), Curt Frisk; football technical assistants, Paul Bergan, Bill Bergan; consultant, Daniel Ruettiger; casting, Richard Pagano, Sharon Bialy, Debi Manwiller. Reviewed at Sony Pictures, Culver City, Aug. 24, 1993. MPAA rating: PG. Running time: 113 MIN.

Rudy Ruettiger .... Sean Astin
Daniel Ruettiger .... Ned Beatty
Fortune .... Charles S. Dutton
Sherry .... Lili Taylor
Ara Parseghian .... Jason Miller
Father Cavanaugh .... Robert Prosky
D-Bob .... Jon Favreau
Mary .... Greta Lind
Frank .... Scott Benjaminson
Coach Yonto .... Ron Dean
Dan Devine .... Chelcie Ross

"Rudy" is one of those beating-the-odds tales that no one does better than Hollywood. A film that hits all the right emotional buttons, it's an intelligent, sentimental drama that lifts an audience to its feet cheering. In the current filmgoing climate, this is an easy winning touchdown that should score big returns.

Based on the life story of Joliet, Ill., native Rudy Ruettiger (Sean Astin), it chronicles Ruettiger's battle to overcome the seemingly impossible educational and physical handicaps in his path.

From the get-go, Rudy has been filled with tales of Notre Dame's legendary Fighting Irish football champions. It matters little to him that his slight stature and below-average scholastic standing make him a highly unlikely candidate for the school or the squad. His brother mocks his ambition and his father (Ned Beatty) vainly attempts to bring him down to earth.

His future would seem to be a job in the local smelter. But when his only friend and ally dies in a freak accident, Rudy packs his bags and heads for the South Bend campus.

A priest (Robert Prosky) impressed by his determination gets Rudy into an allied college, and, against all odds, he succeeds. Along the route he learns other valuable life lessons. A primary guiding influence is Fortune (Charles S. Dutton), the stadium grounds manager who reminds him that whether he makes the football squad or not, he has the golden opportunity to get a quality education.

"Rudy" is rife with insights about the nature of ambition and the caste system that pervades American society. Angelo Pizzo's screenplay is a heartfelt paean to the working class. Pizzo and director David Anspaugh are working on familiar emotional turf, having earlier explored the thrill of victory in "Hoosiers." "Rudy" is richer, less obvious material. That it gives the impression of a by-the-books tale only makes its unexpected turns more satisfying.

Astin works as hard to shake off his bland image as his character strives to achieve his ambition; his youthful zeal is perfect for the role. The large supporting cast is excellent, particularly Dutton and Jason Miller as legendary Fighting Irish coach Ara Parseghian. There are also ample opportunities for its cast of newcomers to excel. —*Leonard Klady*

ROOSTERS

A KCET theatrical presentation of an American Playhouse Theatrical Films and WMG production, in association with Olmos Prods. Produced by Susan Block-Reiner, Norman I. Cohen, Kevin Reidy. Executive producers, Lindsay Law, Hans Brockmann, Sandra Schulberg, Justin Ackerman. Co-executive producers, Ricki Franklin, Phyllis Geller. Directed by Robert M. Young. Screenplay, Milcha Sanchez-Scott, based on her play. Camera (Foto-Kem color), Reynaldo Villalobos; editor, Arthur Coburn; music, David Kilay. Reviewed at Festival of Festivals, Toronto, Sept. 14, 1993. Running time: 93 MIN.

Gallo .... Edward James Olmos
Juana .... Sonia Braga
Chata .... Maria Conchita Alonso
Hector .... Danny Nucci
Angela .... Sarah Lassez
Adan .... Valente Rodriguez

Centering on a classic father-son conflict, "Roosters" is an absorbing family drama marked by Freudian symbolism and the fatalism of a Greek tragedy. Superb acting, particularly by Sonia Braga, almost makes up for the lack of sustained dramatic interest and some rough shifts between the film's realistic scenes and its more poetic ones. Prospects for theatrical release for this Latino intergenerational drama, set in the Southwest, are good.

Narrative begins with the coming home of Gallo Morales (Edward James Olmos), a legendary breeder of fighting cocks, after seven years in prison for manslaughter. His return is anxiously anticipated by his sturdy wife, Juana (Sonia Braga), 20-year old rebellious son Hector (Danny Nucci) and, especially, adolescent daughter Angela (Sarah Lassez), who suffers, in her own words, from "acute neglect." Also living in the house is Chata (Maria Conchita Alonso), Gallo's sister, whose overt sensuality soon ignites her libidinous nephew.

The conflict that haunts and eventually tears the family apart revolves around a prize-fighting cock that Hector inherited from his grandfather, to the utmost resentment of his father, for whom the cock is a symbol of his macho, patriarchal power. Wishing to escape the drudgery of farm work, Hector is determined to win a cockfight and forge a new life for himself and his family.

The film's central and most moving figure is the sensitive daughter, who wears handmade wings and lives her fantasy life in a lair beneath the front porch. A dedicated Catholic, she holds conversations with her favorite saints and plays with religious icons in a miniature graveyard.

Adapting her 1987 stage hit to the screen, Milcha Sanchez-Scott has opened up her compelling play without sacrificing its dramatic in-

September 27, 1993 (Cont.)

tensity. However, in pic's second part, a few of the one-on-one confrontational scenes reveal the theatrical origins of the material.

Robert M. Young, who last co-directed the landmark documentary "Children of Fate," endows the film with the haunting, doomed feel of a genuine Greek tragedy, but he is less successful in providing smooth transitions between the drama's realism and its poetic imagery. Nonetheless, as usual, "Roosters" reflects Young's compassionate humanism and his great work with actors.

As the long-suffering but strong matriarch who keeps the family together through all its crises, Braga gives one of her quietest — and best — performances. She is supposed to look plain, but Braga is stunning even without makeup.

Debutante Lassez is heartbreaking as the daughter who desperately needs her father's love and attention. Playing an ambitious role, and providing the film's most lyrical — and comic — moments, Lassez acquits herself magnificently. As the stubborn patriarch, Olmos is not as good as the women, though his acting here is less mannered and monotonous than in previous outings.

Production values are first-rate in every department. Reynaldo Villalobos, who recently lensed Robert De Niro's "A Bronx Tale," scores another triumph, effectively capturing the desolate beauty and bone-dry heat of the Southwest.

—*Emanuel Levy*

JUSTINIEN TROUVE, OU LE BATARD DE DIEU

(JUSTINIEN TROUVE, OR GOD'S BASTARD)

(FRENCH)

A Gaumont Buena Vista International release of an FCF-Solo Prods. co-production with the participation of Canal Plus. (Foreign Sales: Roissy Films). Produced by Bernard Artigues. Directed by Christian Fechner. Screenplay, Fechner, Michel Folco, based on Folco's novel "Dieu et nous seuls pouvons." Camera (color), Claude Agostini; editors, Roland Baubeau, Nadine Muse; music, Germinal Tenas; production design, Jacques Bufnoir; art direction, Marc Balzarelli; costume design, Pierre-Yves Gayraud; sound (Dolby Spectral), Pierre Excoffier, Gerard Lamps. Reviewed at Gaumont Ambassade cinema, Paris, July 21, 1993 (also in World Film Festival, Montreal). Running time: **162 MIN.**
Justinien .... Pierre-Olivier Mornas
Beaulouis .... Ticky Holgado
Martin Coutouly ....
.... Bernard-Pierre Donnadieu
Baron Raoul .... Patrice Valota
Galine .... Roland Blanche

Gloriously entertaining, fast-paced and absorbing, "Justinien Trouve, ou le batard de Dieu" is a spirited French-lingo cross between "The Name of the Rose" and "Young Indiana Jones." Lengthy but riveting pic has everything one could wish for in an adventure yarn — including humor — except high-profile stars.

Properly marketed, first pic directed by famed Gallic producer Christian Fechner ("Les Amants du Pont-Neuf," "Camille Claudel") should perform nicely wherever auds clamor for a strapping good legend, but on French turf the handsomely staged medieval saga will face an uphill battle in the crushing fall lineup of mostly U.S. mega-releases.

July 26, 1683, in the French countryside is a dark and stormy night as only the movies can offer. As hyperbolic thunder and lightning pierce the heavens (Germinal Tenas' sometimes mocking, sometimes inspirational score is perfection from the first note), a lone rider deposits a newborn babe on the steps of a monastery. The masked horseman bites off the infant's nose, leaves a coin purse in its bunting and vanishes.

Dubbed Justinien Trouve (meaning "found"), baby no-nose is given to a compassionate wet nurse and her loving spouse, an ex-pirate who teaches his adopted son to fence and joust, read, write and count. A free spirit, raised in love, who sports the right mix of humility and wit — along with a wooden nose — Justinien is ordered by the local baron to report to a seminary that would make a penal colony look cushy, but soon rebels and makes an ingenious action-packed escape.

Incorporating the plot twists and turns of an old-fashioned serial without skimping on character development, pic traces the runaway lad's path as it intersects with lepers, skeletons, dungeons, slimy noblemen, conniving gypsies, an unrepentant serial killer, an enterprising sorceress and several excursions to death's door.

Once seated, auds aren't likely to care about the absence of major stars — casting is excellent. Pierre-Olivier Mornas as Justinien is a winning hero. When it comes to improvising with the material at hand, Justinien could give MacGyver a run for his medieval money. Not since Pinocchio has a kid with a wooden nose been so appealing.

Most gore is implied, but what is shown is never gratuitous. Pic abounds with darkly amusing folklore such as the distinction between a torturer and an executioner. (The former is a poor but respected member of the community, the latter a well-paid pariah.)

All production elements conspire to spirit the viewer to another place and time. Dialogue, peppered with terms from the Middle Ages, is forthright and chipper. From rousing debut to gratifying conclusion,

Jacques Bufnoir's ("Indochine") wide-ranging production design is aces. Claude Agostini's painterly lensing shows off hundreds of extras in Pierre-Yves Gayraud's apt costumes. Although one or two early passages are mildly confusing, pic is edited with flair — particularly in the cross-cut nail-biting finale during which God's Bastard's true parents are revealed.

—*Lisa Nesselson*

THE HAWK

(BRITISH)

A BBC Films presentation of an Initial Production, in association with BBC Enterprises/Screen Partners. (International sales: the Sales Co., London.) Produced by Ann Wingate, Eileen Quinn. Executive producers, Mark Shivas, Eric Fellner, Larry Kirstein, Kent Walwin. Directed by David Hayman. Screenplay, Peter Ransley, based on his novel. Camera (color), Andrew Dunn; editor, Justin Krish; music, Nick Bicat; art direction, Charmian Adams; costume design, Pam Tait; sound (Dolby SR), Kant Pan; assistant director, Mary Soan; casting, Leo Davis. Reviewed at Cannes Film Festival (market), May 15, 1993. (Also in Edinburgh Intl. Film Festival; Festival of Festivals, Toronto.) Running time: **84 MIN.**
Anne Marsh .... Helen Mirren
Stephen .... George Costigan
Mother-in-law .... Rosemary Leach
Brother-in-law .... Owen Teale
Norma .... Melanie Hill

The Hawk" is a mild serial-killer suspenser hooded by a stop-go script and telefilm-style direction. The tube looks like the coziest nest for this BBC Films effort, which is making the fest rounds.

Helen Mirren toplines as Anne Marsh, a housewife with two kids in northeast England who gradually suspects spouse Stephen (George Costigan) of being "The Hawk," the media name for a sicko who has raped six women in the East Lancashire area. Stephen has been out of town on business each time a murder has been committed, and there's the strange matter of a missing hammer from the toolshed.

After much to-ing and fro-ing, Anne kicks Stephen out of the house. Double-twist finale is clever but dramatically weak, more like an afterthought when the main action has peaked.

David Hayman's direction has its cinematic moments, but they seem more spliced into a suburban drama than part of a bigger movie. Mirren does what she can with Peter Ransley's poor script (from his own novel) but sends mixed dramatic signals. Costigan and Teale come off better. Technically, the production is solid.

—*Derek Elley*

THE INNOCENT

BRITISH-GERMAN

A Jugendfilm (Germany) release of a Lakehart/Sievernich-Film/Defa Studios Babelsberg production, in association with Film Kredit Treuhand, Filmstiftung Nordrhein-Westfalen. (International sales: World Film Inc.) Produced by Norma Heyman, Chris Sievernich, Wieland Schulz-Keil. Executive producer, Ann Dubinet. Directed by John Schlesinger. Screenplay, Ian McEwan, based on his novel. Camera (Eastmancolor), Dietrich Lohmann; editor, Richard Marden; music, Gerald Gouriet; production design, Luciana Arrighi; costume design, Ingrid Zore; sound (Dolby), Axel Arft; assistant director, David Tringham; casting, Noel Davis, Jeremy Zimmerman. Reviewed at Astra cinema, Royal Air Force Base, Gatow, Berlin, Sept. 16, 1993. Running time: **107 MIN.**
Maria .... Isabella Rossellini
Bob Glass .... Anthony Hopkins
Leonard Markham .... Campbell Scott
Otto .... Ronald Nitschke
Russell .... Hart Bochner
MacNamee .... James Grant
Cpt. Lofting .... Jeremy Sinden
Black .... Richard Durden
Lou .... Corey Johnson
Piper .... Richard Good
(English dialogue)

John Schlesinger's "The Innocent" rings hollow, underutilizing both its top-drawer talent and some compelling Berlin locations. Despite a close screen translation by Ian McEwan of his novel of intrigue, espionage, betrayal and love, pic lacks a sense of real drama. Name cast headed by Anthony Hopkins and Isabella Rossellini looks likely to attract auds only briefly.

Pic double world preemed Sept. 16 in Berlin, with English and German-dubbed versions unspooling in separate locations.

A bespectacled Campbell Scott plays the central role of Leonard Markham, a young, naive and virginal British engineer sent to Berlin in 1955, at the height of the Cold War, for reasons he does not know. His commanding officer, Lofting (Jeremy Sinden, in a spunky perf), is warily cooperative with U.S. forces.

Lofting turns Markham over to Bob Glass (Hopkins), a CIA officer overseeing Operation Gold, a British-West German espionage project to intercept communications between East Germany and the Soviet Union.

Glass is a reserved type who repeatedly reiterates to Markham his own obsessions and the film's dramatic crux: Everyone is a potential spy or informant, nothing and no one is as it seems. Glass' mistrust also extends to Maria (Rossellini), who picks up Markham in a dance hall and with whom he soon falls in love.

Having set the scene, both McEwan's script and Schlesinger's direction forge ahead to resolve the conflicts established in the first two reels. So intent is the film on its narrative purpose that it fails to

September 27, 1993 (Cont.)

build tension or suspense. The main characters develop no idiosyncrasies, or even fleshed-out personalities, that can later be debunked. When story threads are unexpectedly concluded, there's no sense of catharsis.

When Markham finally enters a secret tunnel dug by the allies deep under the Soviet sector to tap phone lines, the assignment is deftly finished using a pair of pliers — a weak resolution to the script's setup of a delicate, top secret mission, as well as Markham's alleged talents as an engineer.

The Maria-Markham story satisfies even less, especially in light of Schlesinger's usual sure hand in portraying relationships. Rossellini's Maria comes across unevenly, with abrupt character shifts. The shocking murder that climaxes their story in the novel is stripped of passion here, as it's unclear what the lovers mean to each other.

Bookending the film with scenes of the Berlin Wall's fall seems a gratuitous touch, with a bathetic ending of the lovers reuniting 34 years later.

Performances in the pic are mostly understated, with Hopkins' Glass muted and one-dimensional, a character who's never allowed to penetrate into the story's foreground. As Markham, Scott carries the film well but gets no chance to fill out his role.

Dietrich Lohmann's lensing is fluid and assured, eloquently using many eastern Berlin locations that convey the menacing atmosphere of postwar Germany. Along with well-cast supporting roles, many of them native Germans, these help to buoy an otherwise bland film.

—Rebecca Lieb

L'ENFANT LION

(SIRGA)

(FRENCH)

A UGC release (France) of an RGP Prods./Odessa Films/Skyline/Jean-Rene de Fleurieu/Studio Canal Plus production, with participation of Filmafrica Investments, Sofinergie, Sofinergie 2, Sofica Lumiere, CNC, Procirep. (International sales: Odyssey.) Produced by Patrick Grandperret, Yannick Bernard. Executive producer, Luc Besson. Directed by Grandperret. Screenplay, Catherine K. Galode, based on the novel "Sirga la Lionne," by Rene Guillot. Camera (color, Technovision), Jean-Michel Humeau; editors, Sean Barton, Yann Dedet; music, Salif Keita; art direction, Nikos Meletopoulos; costume design, Were Were Liking; sound (Dolby), Julien Cloquet, Pascal Armant. Reviewed at UGC Montparnasse theater, Paris, Sept. 6, 1993. (In Venice and Toronto fests.) Running time: **90 MIN.**

Oule .... Mathurin Sinze
Lena .... Sophie-Veronique Toue Tagbe
Also with: Souleyman Koly, Were Were Liking, Salif Keita, Jean-Rene de Fleurieu.

Twenty-five weeks of widescreen lensing in Ivory Coast, Zimbabwe, Niger and Morocco is all up on the screen in "L'Enfant Lion," a family-oriented yarn about an African kid who bonds from birth with a lion cub. Pic has been a steady draw at Gallic wickets since roaring on to screens in mid-June.

Presold by Odyssey in many territories, it should delight youngsters and impress adults. Large amount of voiceover narration makes foreign dubbing a snap.

Two African children, Oule and Lena (winningly played by non-pros cast in Ivory Coast), are enslaved, sold to a desert prince and held in his walled palace. Via a long flashback narrated by Lena, we learn of Oule's childhood in Pama village. He became inseparable from a lion, Sirga, born the same day he was, as well as becoming pally with all members of the animal kingdom, from snakes and scorpions to antelopes and bees. He also communicated with trees, wind and fire.

Narrative comes full circle 45 minutes later when evil horsemen descend on the village, slaughter the adults and enslave the children. Oule, who can also roar like a lion, uses his special powers to escape from bondage.

Tricks include summoning a swarm of bees to heal his festering shoulder wound, and an impressive desert tornado to rescue Lena.

Creature sequences have a wonderful spontaneity and are completely convincing. Although the v.o. narration is sometimes choppy, visuals are stunning throughout. Fine sound design complements the displays of Oule's magical powers, and pic offers pleasant African songs and chants overseen by Malian musician Salif Keita.

—Lisa Nesselson

THE GOOD SON

A 20th Century Fox release. Produced by Mary Anne Page, Joseph Ruben. Executive producers, Ezra Swerdlow, Daniel Rogosin. Co-producer, Michael Steele. Directed by Ruben. Screenplay, Ian McEwan. Camera (Deluxe color), John Lindley; editor, George Bowers; music, Elmer Bernstein; production design, Bill Groom; art direction, Rusty Smith; set decoration, George DeTitta Jr.; costume design, Cynthia Flynt; sound (Dolby), Susumu Tokunow; unit production manager, Thomas Kane; assistant director, Steele; second unit director/stunt coordinator, Jack Gill; casting, Deborah Aquila. Reviewed at the UA Westwood Theater, L.A., Sept. 15, 1993. MPAA Rating: R. Running time: **87 MIN.**

Henry .... Macaulay Culkin
Mark .... Elijah Wood
Susan .... Wendy Crewson
Jack .... David Morse
Wallace .... Daniel Hugh Kelly
Alice .... Jacqueline Brookes
Connie .... Quinn Culkin

The "Home Alone" kid as an amoral, psychotic killer? What next, Barney leveling Tokyo? The bizarre prospect of Macaulay Culkin as a latter-day "bad seed" should prompt enough curiosity to generate initial box office visits, but this rather peculiar thriller doesn't deliver enough jolts to leave the audience screaming, and without a kid audience for this "R"-rated entry, expect a relatively quick trip to the foster care of homevideo.

Though Culkin will accrue most of the ink — and no doubt a few complaints about casting this childhood icon as the embodiment of evil, as if he desperately needed to expand on his repertoire — the action centers around another prominent moppet, Elijah Wood ("Avalon," "Forever Young"), playing a young boy with some very bad luck.

Not only does Mark (Wood) watch his mother die at an early age, but he then gets shipped off to spend a couple of weeks with his aunt and uncle, only to discover that he's sharing a room with a prepubescent psychopath.

At first, Henry (Culkin) seems only a bit eccentric, but the stunts gradually become more outrageous, until he hints that he did away with his brother (the kid drowned in the bathtub) and tries to off his baby sister (Quinn Culkin, making her debut as yet another sprig, along with brothers Macaulay and Kieran, on the Culkin money tree).

With his dad away on business, Mark tentatively turns to a few adults for help, but no one wants to believe him — including Henry's mom (Wendy Crewson), eventually a target herself of Henry's supposition that once you've done evil and gotten away with it, you're capable of anything.

Working from a script by novelist Ian McEwan, producer-director Joseph Ruben pulls some of the same hackneyed strings as in his "Sleeping With the Enemy" but runs across the pitfall of mixing suspense with day care.

In a nutshell, Culkin's cold, dispassionate performance will evoke too many laughs of the derisive kind, not just the genre's characteristic release of nervous tension.

Indeed, the filmmakers hold back too long in establishing the depths to which Henry will sink, and when the action does boil over it too often feels silly — if, in some respects, strangely compelling, particularly the perverse climactic sequence.

The film also pushes the rather dispiriting conclusion, as in "The Bad Seed," that there's such a thing as inherent evil with a capital "E" — but for convenience's sake, without examining the more chilling aspects of that hypothesis.

Reading lines with the same detachment as in the "Home Alone" movies, Culkin projects soullessness but not the darkness we need to see behind those eyes. Wood fares better in the easier role of Mark, while Crewson ("The Doctor") is the only real standout among the adult roles.

With its low-caliber thrills, "The Good Son's" greatest asset may be its spectacularly shot scenery by cinematographer John Lindley, from mesas of Arizona to the snowy climes of New England. Unfortunately, that's also about the only territory of any note the pic explores.

—Brian Lowry

SNAKE EYES

A Mario & Vittorio Cecchi Gori presentation of A Maverick-Eye Films production, in collaboration with Pent-America Pictures. (International sales: Penta Intl., London.) Produced by Mary Kane. Executive producers, Freddy Demann, Ron Rotholz. Directed by Abel Ferrara. Screenplay, Nicholas St. John. Camera (Deluxe color), Ken Kelsch; editor, Anthony Redman; music, Joe Delia; production design, Alex Tavoularis; costume design, Marlene Stewart; sound, Greg Sheldon; assistant director, Terry Miller; production manager, Diana Phillips. Reviewed at Venice Film Festival (competing), Sept. 9, 1993. Running time: **107 MIN.**

Eddie Israel .... Harvey Keitel
Sarah Jennings .... Madonna
Francis Burns .... James Russo
Madlyn Israel .... Nancy Ferrara

For his second pic of the year, following his slick sci-fi remake "Body Snatchers," maverick helmer Abel Ferrara returns to the mood and, to some extent, the theme of his controversial cult item "Bad Lieutenant," also toplining Harvey Keitel. Perfs, as usually in Ferrara's movies, are powerful but, despite the presence of Madonna, "Snake Eyes" is another abrasive, confrontational downer likely to appeal only to a marginal audience.

As pic deals with the process of moviemaking and features Keitel as a filmer apparently not unlike Ferrara himself, "Snake Eyes" will be seen as one of the director's most personal efforts. Added to which, Nancy Ferrara (helmer's spouse) also portrays Keitel's loyal but betrayed wife, in a very sympathetic performance.

Pic opens in wintry New York, as filmmaker Eddie Israel (Keitel) leaves his wife (Ferrara) and small son to fly to the Coast to work on a new movie, "Mother of Mirrors," starring actors Sarah Jennings (Madonna) and Francis Burns (James Russo) as a couple whose marriage is disintegrating.

Jennings' character, Claire, has found religion and wants to halt a destructive lifestyle of booze, drugs and sexual experimentation. Burns' character, Russell, rejects her change of attitude angrily and with increasing violence.

Regular Ferrara scripter Nicholas St. John has devised a screenplay in which the stresses of filming spill into private lives. As the director goads the volatile Burns to extremes of violence in his role, Jennings becomes increasingly distraught and victimized, both on and off-screen.

Jennings sleeps with her co-star and director, both of whom treat her appallingly. In one of the movie's most shocking scenes, the director even encourages what amounts to on-camera rape.

The director's attempt to confess his multiple infidelities and wild behavior to his wife is met with her horror and disgust. As filming nears its close, the director finds his personal traumas intruding more and more into the fictional material. (A final scene, set at the premiere of the completed movie, is described in the Venice fest catalogue but was not in the version unspooled.)

"Snake Eyes" is raw, intense material, with an aura of authenticity. But despite extensive four-letter dialogue, pic plays down the sexual content, and Madonna remains clothed almost throughout.

As the director, Keitel, in another remarkable performance, again proves he's one of the finest actors around. Russo's angry, anguished actor is a knockout. Madonna, in the least showy role of the three leads, acquits herself well: This is probably her best screen perf to date.

Pic is a most pessimistic depiction of the filmmaking process. A last-reel clip from Les Blank's docu "Burden of Dreams," in which Werner Herzog talks about the "madness" of making movies, is, presumably, a distillation of Ferrara's disenchanted theme.

—*David Stratton*

DISPARA!

(SHOOT!)

(SPANISH-ITALIAN)

An Arco Films (Madrid)/Metrofilms (Rome) production. (International sales: Adriana Chiesa, Rome.) Produced by Galliano Juso, Jaime Comas. Directed by Carlos Saura. Screenplay, Saura, Enzo Monteleone, based on a short story by Giorgio Scerbanenco. Camera (Technicolor, Panavision widescreen), Javier Aguirresarobe; editor, Juan Ignacio San Mateo; music, Alberto Iglesias; art direction, Rafael Palmero; sound in Dolby. Reviewed at Venice Film Festival (competing), Sept. 3, 1993. Running time: **100 MIN.**
Ana .... Francesca Neri
Marcos .... Antonio Banderas
Manuel .... Walter Vidarte
Mother .... Eulalia Ramon

Updating a bizarre short story about a rape victim turned vigilante, Carlos Saura's "Shoot!" is an unmoving mix of modern psychology applied to a world of freaks and outsiders. Arthouse fans of Spanish director Saura will wonder what's up, but action markets may bite.

Ana (played by Italo thesp Francesca Neri) is a dazzling circus performer who has a sharpshooting

act on horseback. Reporter Marcos (Antonio Banderas) fast becomes a regular in Ana's caravan and he discovers a sensitive, affectionate heart behind her tigerish exterior.

Their romance reaches a turning point, with the circus due to move on and Marcos having distant assignments. The night before their crucial rendezvous, Ana is brutally raped by three young mechanics.

Seriously wounded and mentally deranged, Ana shoots the rapists dead and drives off into the Spanish countryside, growing weaker by the minute. The law finally tracks her down, holed up in a farmer's cottage with three hostages.

The pic tries to justify Ana's murderous rampage through psychologically extenuating circumstances. But the sequence of her killing two motorcycle cops on her trail is clumsily handled, neither suspenseful nor believable.

Much of the tale's dramatic potential drains away in filmic cliches, such as the exasperating around-the-clock updates on the case by every TV and radio station.

Saura's personal touches emerge from time to time, like the long opening aerial shot of Madrid's outskirts, finishing on a zoom into a circus tent, that sets the story in its social context.

As the lovelorn but practical journo, Banderas blends into the woodwork. Neri, however, is a sheer delight in her chameleonlike changes from glam circus star to vulnerable woman in love to a tough, mentally detonated sharpshooter, stripped of pride, hope and humanity. —*Deborah Young*

YOU SENG

(TEMPTATION OF A MONK)

(HONG KONG)

A Tedpoly Films production. (International sales: Tedpoly Films, Hong Kong.) Produced by Teddy Robin. Executive producer, Kay Wong. Directed by Clara Law. Screenplay, Eddie Fong, Lillian Lee. Camera (Cine Art color), Andrew Lesnie; editor, Jill Bilcock; music, Tats Lau; production design, Timmy Yip, Yang Zhanjia, William Lygratte; sound, Gary Wilkins, Ross Linton; action director, Leung Siuhung; line producer, Lam Ping-kwan; production manager, Cheung Chi-kwong; assistant director, Ma Po-than. Reviewed at Venice Film Festival (competing), Sept. 7, 1993. Running time: **118 MIN.**

Princess Scarlet/Violet .... Joan Chen
General Shi .... Wu Hsin-kuo
General Huo .... Zhang Fengyi
Old Abbott .... Michael Lee
Shi's mother .... Lisa Lu

In contrast to her contempo "Autumn Moon," which made its mark on the international fest circuit, Hong Kong director Clara Law's latest, "Temptation of a Monk," is a visually bold saga of rival generals, revenge, betrayal and love, handled with skill and excitement. With the current surge of interest in Chinese cinema, this one could gain acceptance by specialized auds worldwide.

Film has a different look from most Hong Kong period pics. Law used an Australian camera team, led by d.p. Andrew Lesnie, whose use of filters gives an unusual sheen. Costumes and staging also evoke Japanese samurai movies rather than H.K. martial arts epics.

Set during the Tang dynasty over a thousand years ago, story has as its theme a disgraced man's journey into self-discovery.

Central character, General Shi (Wu Hsin-kuo), finds himself in a dilemma when the old emperor is close to death: The heir to the throne is perceived to be weak; his brother would be a stronger ruler.

Shi cuts a deal with fellow general Huo (Zhang Fengyi, who played the macho actor in Chen Kaige's "Farewell My Concubine"), but the unscrupulous Huo, instead of protecting the rightful heir, oversees a massacre of the prince and his men.

The disgraced Shi takes refuge first with his mother (veteran Lisa Lu, in a striking cameo) and, after she commits suicide, with Princess Scarlet (Joan Chen), who falls victim to a violent encounter with Huo. Shi decides on the monastic life and winds up serving an elderly abbot in a dilapidated mountain-top temple.

In one of the film's most striking scenes, a beautiful assassin (also played by Chen) is sent to eliminate Shi. Posing as a nun, she has her head shaved before seducing him in a weirdly erotic sequence just prior to her assassination attempt. This is kinky stuff. Pic ends with the inevitable confrontation between Shi and Huo.

Shot on remote locations in mainland China in wintry conditions, "Monk" boasts strong characters, bold performances (Chen is good in both her roles), sumptuous costumes and settings, and vivid action with lots of slo-mo battles.

Editing by Aussie Jill Bilcock, who cut "Strictly Ballroom," is slick, and the sound mix (also by Aussies) excellent.

—*David Stratton*

FUSA

(JAPANESE)

A Fuji Television Network production. Executive producers, Yoichi Nomura, Ryunosuke Endo. Produced by Akira Sakai, Toshiro Kamata. Directed by Kon Ichikawa. Screenplay, Ichikawa, Tsutomu Nakamura, from the story "Passing Through the Wooden Gate," by Shuguro Yamamoto. Camera (color), Takeo Akiba; editor, Chizuko Osada; music, Kensaku Tanigawa; production design, Masanori Umeda; sound, Tetsuya Ohashi. Reviewed at Venice Film Festival (non-competing), Sept. 3, 1993. Running time: **91 MIN.**
Seishiro Hiramatsu .... Keiichi Nakai
Fusa .... Yuko Asano
Gonemon Tahara .... Frankie Sakai
Yoshizuka .... Hisashi Igawa
Mura .... Kyoko Kishida
Kageyu Iwai .... Koji Ishizaka
Kajima .... Shigeru Kohyama

"Fusa" is a glowing late work from master director Kon Ichikawa, now 78. It's one of those elegiac Japanese period films that tells a supernatural story with uncanny resonance. High-quality vid-to-film transfer has definite small-screen appeal, with theatrical possibilities also.

Based on a classic story by Shuguro Yamamoto set in the 16th century, the film tells of an ambitious young samurai, Seishiro (Keiichi Nakai), who is adopted into the Iwai household to attain the necessary status to marry the daughter of the castle warden.

Plans for the marriage are jeopardized when a beautiful, bedraggled young woman (Yuko Asano) arrives, claiming to have lost her memory. He names her Fusa, and finally marries her instead. They have a daughter, but Seishiro lives in fear that Fusa will recover her memory.

Simple, beautifully told tale is visually impressive, with perfect framing and lighting. Final product in no way betrays its video origins. Pic was recorded on hi-def 1125-60 tape and transferred to 35mm using HDTV laser recording equipment. Process enabled Ichikawa to compose some striking images, such as using color and monochrome in the same scene. —*David Stratton*

October 4, 1993

GETTYSBURG

A New Line Cinema release of a Turner Pictures and Mace Neufeld/Robert Rehme presentation of an Esparza/Katz production. Produced by Robert Katz, Moctesuma Esparza. Co-producer, Nick Lombardo. Directed, written by Ronald F. Maxwell, based on the novel "The Killer Angels," by Michael Shaara. Camera (Foto-Kem color), Kees van Oostum; editor, Corky Ehlers; music, Randy Edelman; production design, Cary White; art direction, Mike Sullivan; costume design, Michael T. Boyd; sound (Dolby), Stephen Halbert; assistant director, Skip Cosper; second unit director, Steve M. Boyum; second unit camera, Eddy ven der Enden; casting, Joy Todd. Reviewed at Loews Cheri, Boston, Sept. 20, 1993. (In Boston Film Festival.) MPAA Rating: PG. Running time: **254 MIN.**

Lt. Gen. James Longstreet .... Tom Berenger
Gen. Robert E. Lee .... Martin Sheen
Major Gen. George E. Pickett .... Stephen Lang
Brig. Gen. Lewis A. Armistead ...... Richard Jordan
Col. Joshua Lawrence Chamberlain .... Jeff Daniels
Brig. Gen. John Buford .... Sam Elliott
Lt. Thomas D. Chamberlain .... C. Thomas Howell
Sgt. Buster Kilrain .... Kevin Conway
Brig. Gen. Richard B. Garnett .... Andrew Prine
Col. Strong Vincent .... Maxwell Caulfield
Lt. Col Arthur Freemantle .... James Lancaster
Brig. Gen. James L. Kemper .... Royce Applegate
Major Gen. Winfield Scott Hancock .... Brian Mallon

Ted Turner doesn't do anything in a small way. The premiere entry for his new feature production unit is a 4¼-hour epic on the biggest battle of the Civil War, and it will prove a hit with history buffs. Regular filmgoers should be captivated, too, especially those who made Ken Burns' "The Civil War" into a TV event. World preemed at the Boston Film Festival, pic will go out theatrically Oct. 8 in advance of TV airing.

"Gettysburg" concentrates on the three days of fighting, with about 45 minutes devoted to the day before. Gen. Robert E. Lee (Martin Sheen) believes that he can end the war with a decisive victory over Federal troops by taking Gettysburg, then marching on Washington with an offer to President Lincoln of terms for peace. The rebel leader and his men are tired after three years of fighting a war most thought would be over in a month.

The Northern troops are in disarray. The military leadership keeps changing, some of the commanders lack battle experience and there are stirrings of rebellion among the troops.

Thus, the stage is set for a battle that would see more than 53,000 American soldiers killed, more casualties than there were during the entire Vietnam War. Writer-director Maxwell, adapting the Michael Shaara novel "The Killer Angels" and relying on historical research and documents of the era, tries to reconstruct what happened on both sides during the fateful events of early July 1863.

The first day is seen through the eyes of Brig. Gen. John Buford (Sam Elliott), whose actions prevent the South from gaining an early advantage. Elliott presents us with a portrait of the professional soldier, doing his job quietly and efficiently.

On the Northern side, the chief point of reference is provided by Col. Joshua Lawrence Chamberlain (Jeff Daniels), a Maine college professor so ill-suited to his role that he has to keep reminding his aide-de-camp — and brother (C. Thomas Howell) — to stop referring to him as "Lawrence" instead of by his military title. Chamberlain's moment of truth comes on the second day at the Battle of Little Round Top. As depicted here, Chamberlain's efforts to hold the Northern line against the Southern forces could have made a movie all by itself. It is a fitting climax to the first half of the film.

Among the rebels, the chief conflict is between Lee, who wants a decisive victory, and Lt. Gen. James Longstreet (Tom Berenger), who argues that the risks are astronomical, and that they can win tactical advantages by continuing to fight defensively. It is little solace to him that he is proved right in the final day of battle, which takes up the second half of the movie.

In spite of its length, pic works on several levels. First, there's the sense of this being as close as an audience can come to seeing what the Battle of Gettysburg was like. The final credit scroll runs 10 minutes, with an impressive list of historical advisers and Civil War organizations that helped stage the reenactments.

Second, there's the cast. Daniels walks away with the film as the mild scholar who, when tossed into battle, rises to the occasion. He wins audience sympathy with an early speech about what the North is fighting for.

Whereas the North is fighting for principle — freeing the slaves and preserving the Union — the representatives of the South voice several viewpoints, with the "state's rights" argument given to a politician who is laughed at by the other Southerners. The most eloquent call to arms is a speech late in the film by Brig. Gen. Lewis Armistead (the late Richard Jordan), arguing that his troops, at least, are there to defend the honor of Virginia.

If the film can be criticized on any level, it is that its focus is almost entirely on the officers. Howell's lieutenant has a poignant scene talking with captured rebels about why they're there, but the only real representative of the non-officer class is Sgt. Buster Kilrain (Kevin Conway), a loyal and battle-scarred sidekick.

Among the Southerners, acting honors go to Sheen and Berenger, with Sheen giving some idea of why Lee remained a general respected by soldiers on both sides during the war. Stephen Lang and Jordan provide other perspectives of the Southern aristocracy, with Jordan especially moving in a scene talking about a comrade-in-arms who is leading the Northern forces in the coming battle.

In a bit of in-joke casting, both documentarian Ken Burns and Ted Turner have brief cameo bits. Burns plays an aide to Major Gen. Hancock, urging him to get off his horse during the final battle, while Turner is shot right after answering Brig. Gen. Armistead's call to advance on the Northern position.

Credit has to go to writer-director Maxwell, as well as to stunt coordinator/second unit director Steve M. Boyum, for capturing the madness of the battle scenes. There is a real sense of the wanton slaughter and of the perseverance of both sides against incredible odds. One can see why Lee would take a gamble that he thought could end the bloody war.

Maxwell has tried to make this something that works on the big screen as well as on TV. In addition to the theatrical release version, he has also cut a 4½-hour edition (six hours with commercials) that will run on Turner's TNT cable channel in 1994 as a three-part miniseries, and has also prepared a 5½-hour version for homevideo release. There are also plans to set up a venue in the Gettysburg area that would become a permanent showplace for the theatrical version of the film.

"Gettysburg" succeeds as a motion picture event, and as a recreation of a pivotal chapter of American history. After a summer of flash and sizzle, audiences may be ready for a healthy dose of substance. —*Daniel M. Kimmel*

THE REMAINS OF THE DAY

A Columbia release of a Mike Nichols/John Calley/Merchant Ivory production. Produced by Nichols, Calley, Ismail Merchant. Executive producer, Paul Bradley. Directed by James Ivory. Screenplay, Ruth Prawer Jhabvala, based on the novel by Kazuo Ishiguro. Camera (Technicolor, Panavision widescreen), Tony Pierce-Roberts; editor, Andrew Marcus; music, Richard Robbins; production design, Luciana Arrighi; art direction, John Ralph; set decoration, Ian Whittaker; costume design, Jenny Beavan, John Bright; sound (Dolby), David Stephenson; associate producer, Donald Rosenfeld; assistant director, Chris Newman; casting, Celestia Fox. Reviewed at Sony Studios screening room, Culver City, Sept. 20, 1993. MPAA Rating: PG. Running time: **135 MIN.**

Stevens .... Anthony Hopkins
Miss Kenton .... Emma Thompson
Lord Darlington .... James Fox
Lewis .... Christopher Reeve
Father .... Peter Vaughan
Cardinal .... Hugh Grant
Dupont D'Ivry ....Michael Lonsdale
Benn .... Tim Pigott-Smith
Spencer .... Patrick Godfrey
Sir Leonard Bax .... Peter Cellier
Harry Smith .... Paul Copley
Lord Halifax .... Peter Eyre
Lizzie .... Lena Headey
Baroness .... Brigitte Kahn
Publican .... Ian Redford
Doctor Carlisle .... Pip Torrens
Sir Geoffrey Wren .... Rupert Vansittart

All the meticulousness, intelligence, taste and superior acting that one expects from Merchant Ivory productions have been brought to bear on "The Remains of the Day." This curious, cloistered piece, which examines the life of a very proper English butler who sacrifices anything resembling a personal life in total dedication to his master's needs, is continuously absorbing, but lacks the emotional resonance that would have made it completely satisfying.

Top performances from Anthony Hopkins and Emma Thompson, as well as the Merchant Ivory cache, make this a class late-fall entry for Columbia, although appeal may not be as deep or long-lasting as that of "Howards End."

Based on the 1989 Booker Prize-winning novel by Kazuo Ishiguro, this impeccably made film wears its literary origins a bit more obviously than the team's recent E.M. Forster adaptations, and some structural problems, particularly in the late going, have not been worked out.

But if it doesn't quite reach the brass ring, film still possesses plenty of riches to beguile the discriminating viewer. As faithfully adapted by Ruth Prawer Jhabvala, story provides an uncanny point of entry into a particular and unusual mindset, that of a man entirely devoted to service, as well as into a specific and fascinating historical milieu, that of the upper-class British partial to the Nazis during the 1930s.

October 4, 1993 (Cont.)

Told in flashbacks via narrated letters, story begins with the aging butler Stevens (Hopkins) traveling across Britain to see his former co-worker, Miss Kenton (Thompson).

Stevens' employer at the palatial Darlington Hall is now an American ex-Congressman, Mr. Lewis (Christopher Reeve), and in the course of his journey, Stevens recalls life at the great estate in its heyday.

Fastidious in every detail and mindful of every nuance and nicety, Stevens places dignity and decorum at the top of life's values and his own emotional needs at the bottom. The latter are never seriously called into question, but are tested a bit in his relationship over several years with Miss Kenton. In key scenes, she tries to break through Stevens' wall of reserve, only to find that it is not to be transgressed.

But then, nothing can ruffle Stevens, not even the death of his father, who inconveniently expires during a major political conference hosted by Lord Darlington (James Fox). An affable single gentleman, Darlington harbors German sympathies. Only much later does Stevens recognize that he may have spent the prime of his life in the service of a man whose intentions were misguided at best and evil at worst.

His recognition of a missed opportunity with Miss Kenton spurs him to take the cross-country journey to meet her. It is clear that she came to love him deeply, and only his unbending rigidity forced her to marry someone else.

The thematic and dramatic similarities of "The Remains of the Day" to Columbia's other prestige fall release, "The Age of Innocence," can hardly go without remark. Drawn from distinguished literary properties, both portray an insular, stultifying upper-class milieu that suffocates potential romance, causing regret years later.

The pictures are also notable for the preponderance of formal dinners, fancy clothes and rich decor. Like Martin Scorsese's film, James Ivory's is exquisitely made, although on a less lavish and costly scale. Four English country houses were used to summon up Darlington Hall, a fabulous estate that beautifully represents an all but vanished way of life. The film can't dwell on the minutiae of service to the extent that the book does, and a bit more humor might have been applied to detailing it, but the all-encompassing nature of the job is solidly conveyed.

All the Merchant Ivory behind-the-scenes regulars — lenser Tony Pierce-Roberts, production designer Luciana Arrighi, costume designers Jenny Beavan and John Bright, composer Richard Robbins and editor Andrew Marcus — deliver their customary top-drawer goods.

But more than ambience, this is a film of acting. Continuing his recent roll of sterling performances, Hopkins creates a superbly observed and nuanced Stevens. A man ruled by

propriety, he relaxes slightly only in private with a cigar and a cheap novel. Hopkins cunningly toys with the audience at times, hinting that the character might crack a bit or drop his reserve, but he never does, as the actor offers up a man who is sadly defined by his job rather than by his needs or desires.

Pic also reps another career highlight for Thompson, who expertly reveals the conflicting feelings of her conventional, if occasionally spirited, character. If the ending feels emotionally flat it isn't the fault of the lead actors, but of the script's somewhat lumpy construction, which causes the film to seem to evaporate rather than conclude.

Fox is ideal as the distracted, fatally sentimental Lord Darlington, Reeve brings authority and Yankee energy to the one dissenting voice in the collaborationist circle, and Peter Vaughan is astounding as the elder Mr. Stevens, who continues in service even after he begins losing his faculties. One can see in him almost everything one needs to know about why his son turned out the way he did. —*Todd McCarthy*

THE PROGRAM

A Buena Vista Pictures release of a Touchstone Pictures and the Samuel Goldwyn Co. presentation. Produced by Samuel Goldwyn Jr. Executive producers, Duncan Henderson, Tom Rothman. Directed by David S. Ward. Screenplay, Ward, Aaron Latham. Camera (Technicolor), Victor Hammer; editors, Paul Seydor, Kimberly Ray; music, Michel Colombier; production design, Albert Brenner; art direction, Carol Winstead Wood; set design, Harold Fuhrman; set decoration, Kathe Klopp; costume design, Tom Bronson; sound (Dolby), Robert J. Anderson Jr.; assistant director, Josh McLaglen; second unit director, Allan L. Graf; casting, Lynn Stalmaster. Reviewed at Avco Center Cinema, L.A., Sept. 21, 1993. MPAA Rating: R. Running time: **114 MIN.**

Coach Winters	James Caan
Autumn	Halle Berry
Darnell Jefferson	Omar Epps
Joe Kane	Craig Sheffer
Camille	Kristy Swanson
Bud-Lite	Abraham Benrubi
Alvin Mack	Duane Davis
Bobby Collins	Jon Maynard Pennell
Steve Lattimer	Andrew Bryniarski
Ray Griffen	J. Leon Pridgen II

Director/co-writer David S. Ward ("Major League") **may find baseball has been better to him than football, as the** signals get crossed a bit in this all-over-the-field sports drama. At-tractive leads and the subject matter may generate some interest from gridiron enthusiasts, but **Disney still doesn't figure to light up the box office scoreboard much with this recruit.**

"The Program" starts in a fourth-down situation by being a sports movie with virtually no one for whom the audience can root — a major drawback, no matter how

hackneyed those "Rocky"-ized finishes have become.

Instead, Ward and co-writer Aaron Latham seek to indict big-time college football through a collection of cliches (money-doling boosters, steroid abuse, academic negligence, shady recruiting practices) and still want us to care about whether these players and coaches — who've been made to look so unappealing — win the big game.

The action centers on fictitious Eastern State University, whose coach (James Caan, top-billed in a relatively minor role) is coming off two subpar seasons, feeling the heat to turn things around.

In addition to a Heisman Trophy candidate quarterback in Joe Kane (Craig Sheffer), ESU lands a promising young small-town running back (Omar Epps, from "Juice") with his sights set on a starting job.

Pursuing those players' romantic liaisons (with Kristy Swanson and Halle Berry, respectively) as a soapy sidebar to all the bashing and crunching, "The Program" doesn't develop either part of the story very well; indeed, those two facets keep colliding off each other, diffusing any concern as to how ol' ESU performs on the field. Although he's supposed to engender sympathy as the son of an uncaring alcoholic, Joe comes off as a self-centered boor so reckless it's hard to understand why Camille (Swanson, last seen skewering the undead in "Buffy, the Vampire Slayer") puts up with him. The pompous Darnell (Epps) isn't particularly endearing either.

The strongest characters toil in smaller roles, particularly Duane Davis as a bruising linebacker intent on making the pros and Andrew Bryniarski as a steroid-injecting behemoth who personifies the danger of a win-at-all-costs mentality.

Yet if there's an alternative to that approach you won't find it here, with Caan's gruff coach clearly willing to look the other way at any excess short of murder as long as it keeps him in his job. That may make for good copy in a Sports Illustrated expose, but watching the team's various offenses (against society, not opposing defenses) doesn't exactly spur much support.

The football scenes prove reasonably convincing, although the use of slow-motion is far too extensive, robbing the sport of its collision-oriented excitement and speed.

Most of the focus is on Sheffer, whose character is too enigmatic, while Epps, Berry and Swanson gamely try to pull for extra dramatic yardage but can't do much with their underwritten roles.

Interestingly, several real college powers (among them Michigan, Georgia Tech and Iowa) lent their actual monikers and uniforms to this unflattering portrait.

Aside from the slo-mo woes, technical crew and cast convincingly capture the football scenes and col-

lege environs, with lensing at Duke and the University of South Carolina. —*Brian Lowry*

MALICE

A Columbia release of a Castle Rock Entertainment in association with New Line Cinema production. (International distribution: New Line Intl. Releasing). Produced by Rachel Pfeffer, Charles Mulvehill, Harold Becker. Executive producers, Michael Hirsh, Patrick Loubert. Co-executive producer, Peter Brown. Directed by Becker. Screenplay, Aaron Sorkin, Scott Frank. Story by Sorkin, Jonas McCord. Camera (Technicolor), Gordon Willis; editor, David Bretherton; music, Jerry Goldsmith; production design, Philip Harrison; art direction, Dianne Wager; set design, Sydney Litwack, Alan Manzer, Hugo Santiago, Harold Fuhrman; set decoration, Garrett Lewis, Tracey Doyle (Boston); sound, Robert Eber; associate producer-assistant director, Thomas Mack; casting, Nancy Klopper. Reviewed at Sony Studios screening room, Culver City, Sept. 14, 1993. MPAA Rating: R. Running time: **107 MIN.**

Jed	Alec Baldwin
Tracy	Nicole Kidman
Andy	Bill Pullman
Dana	Bebe Neuwirth
Dr. Kessler	George C. Scott
Ms. Kennsinger	Anne Bancroft
Dennis Riler	Peter Gallagher
Lester Adams	Josef Sommer

The immaculately crafted **"Malice" is a virtual scrap-book of elements borrowed** from other suspense pics, but no less enjoyable for being so familiar. **Pic should tickle audiences who want to be entertained without being challenged, and will probably drum up healthy business for Columbia and Castle Rock.**

The film starts slowly, with college dean Bill Pullman concerned over the mysterious rapist who's attacked several students in the sleepy New England college town, and worrying about the mysterious abdominal pains plaguing his wife (Nicole Kidman).

Enter polished, self-assured surgeon Alec Baldwin, who is new to the area and moves into the third floor of the house Pullman and Kidman are restoring. (The script never addresses the issue of why a presumably highly paid doctor would feel the need to share a house with virtual strangers, but if the filmmakers didn't worry about this, neither should you.)

After about 40 minutes, the pic shifts into high gear when Baldwin performs emergency surgery on Kidman, which kicks off a series of revelations, plot reversals and character twists.

Script by Aaron Sorkin and Scott Frank, from a story by Sorkin and Jonas McCord, touches on big topics like fear of doctors, but doesn't explore them, choosing instead to simply give the audience a piece of escapism.

To its credit, pic takes the high road in not going for cheap effects — though a thriller, there's not one big scream in the whole movie — which may frustrate some horror fans, but the plotting and, especially, the execution maintain interest.

"Malice" makes nods to specific films, such as "Marnie" and "Pacific Heights," and collects a lot of elements familiar from recent suspense pics: the sinister janitor, the bloody-rubber-gloves operating room scenes, grappling bodies crashing through the banister, as well as some familiar plot twists that won't be repeated here.

Some of the plotting gets plodding — bits involving a mysterious neighbor and a hypodermic needle are particularly dubious — but on the whole, the script does what it set out to do, and if the filmmakers didn't worry about these things, neither should you.

"Malice" boasts a polished crew — scorer Jerry Goldsmith, lenser Gordon Willis, editor David Bretherton, production designer Philip Harrison and soundman Robert Eber all do first-class work. Kudos to director Harold Becker and his producer partners Rachel Pfeffer and Charles Mulvehill for assembling such a classy, tight package and making it work so well.

The actors play amusing variations on past roles — Baldwin as the self-assured charmer with dark and fragile undercurrents (as in "Miami Blues"), Kidman as the threatened wife with reservoirs of strength (as in "Dead Calm"), Peter Gallagher as an unctuous lawyer ("sex, lies, and videotape") and Bill Pullman as a likable, confused schlub (just about everything he's ever been in).

All the thesps, including George C. Scott and Anne Bancroft in brief cameos, are fine, with Baldwin and Kidman the standouts. After listless performances in such pics as "Days of Thunder" and "Far and Away," Kidman, who here uses a flawless American accent, proves her strengths as an actress, and Baldwin mixes menace, sex and humor in another terrific performance.

Scripter William Goldman is listed as "consultant," a credit that's unexplained. But if Mr. Goldman didn't worry about it, neither should you. —*Timothy M. Gray*

AIRBORNE

A Warner Bros. presentation of an Icon production. Produced by Bruce Davey and Stephen McEveety. Directed by Rob Bowman. Screenplay, Bill Apablasa. Story by Apablasa and McEveety. Camera, Daryn Okada; editor, Harry B. Miller III; music, Stewart Copeland; production design, John Myhre; sound (Dolby), Christopher Sheldon, Dane A. Davis; casting, Robert J. Ulrich C.S.A., Eric Dawson C.S.A. Reviewed at Loews 84th Street, N.Y., Sept. 17, 1993. MPAA rating: PG. Running time: **89 MIN.**

Mitchell	Shane McDermott
Wiley	Seth Green
Nikki	Brittney Powell
Jack	Chris Conrad
Aunt Irene	Edie McClurg
Uncle Louis	Patrick O'Brien

There's plenty of wheel-spinning in "Airborne," and rollerblades account for only a fraction of it. Kids might enjoy this teenage fish-out-of-the-surf comedy, but anyone approaching the high school age of the movie's characters will spot the obvious formula within 15 minutes of opening credits.

Why Warner Bros. chose an early fall release is a puzzlement. "Airborne" might have gotten lost among the summer releases, but at least its only possible audience wouldn't have been in math class. Even goosed by the rollerblading fad, B.O. prospects look modest.

Premise has California teen Mitchell Goosen (Shane McDermott) sent to Cincinnati to live with extremely unhip relatives while his parents spend six months in Australia on a research grant. While he and cousin Wiley (Seth Green) become pals, Mitchell's surfer dude lingo, pretty face and ultracool L.A. demeanor make him the target of the requisite young toughs at his new school.

The toughs, in this case, are a group of hockey players who hate Mitchell nearly as much as they hate the "preps" from a rival school. That hockey is about as much a part of Cincinnati culture as surfing doesn't matter to the filmmakers, who chose the sport apparently so Mitch could show off his rollerblade skills, lead his classmates to victory and win the respect of those Ohio ruffians, not to mention the love of the pretty Nikki (Brittney Powell).

Younger children probably won't notice that the film has fewer visible teachers and coaches than a "Peanuts" cartoon, and they might even enjoy the lengthy rollerblade race down the hilly mean streets of Cincinnati that caps the action. Director Rob Bowman and lenser Daryn Okada do OK with the action sequence despite a weakness for such obvious tricks as slow-motion air jumps and screechy auto crashes. The Cincinnati locale is put to good use.

What Bowman can't seem to manage is anything but the most by-the-numbers character development, and he fumbles most of the comedy. A bland cast doesn't contribute, with McDermott showing little more than a nice smile and dreamy eyes in his portrayal. The surfer lingo comes and goes, and it's never believable from the one-note thesp. Then again, even a more polished or charming actor would have problems with screenwriter Bill Apablasa's Malibu Zen dialogue ("You don't have to fight the shark to fight for the wave.").

Green gets off a bit easier as the wimpy heavy-metal cousin, although he seems to owe more than a nod to Anthony Michael Hall's perf in "Sixteen Candles." Rest of the cast is given little to work with and proceeds accordingly.

Stewart Copeland's mediocre rock score won't fill any seats either, although a heavy television ad blitz might show some initial results. Homevideo should be just around the corner. —*Greg Evans*

MORNING GLORY

An Academy Entertainment release of a Dove Audio production. Produced by Michael Viner. Executive producer, Jerry Leider. Directed by Steven Stern. Screenplay, Charles Jarrott, Deborah Raffin, based on the novel by LaVyrie Spencer. Camera (color), Laszlo George; editor, Richard Benwick; music, Jonathan Elias; art direction, David Hiscox; set decoration, Barry Kemp; costume design, Maureen Hiscox; sound, Eric Batut; associate producer, Richard Hack; assistant director, David Markowitz; casting, Stuart Aikins. Reviewed at Charles Aidikoff Screening Room, Beverly Hills, Sept. 13, 1993. MPAA Rating: PG-13. Running time: **95 MIN.**

Will Parker	Christopher Reeve
Elly Dinsmore	Deborah Raffin
Bob Collins	Lloyd Bochner
Miss Beasly	Nina Foch
Lula Peaks	Helen Shaver
Sheriff Reese Goodloe	J.T. Walsh

Morning Glory," toting a script with more clunks than the 1930s Fords its characters drive, plays like a TV miniseries rather than a feature pic. It's got some heart, a rustic tone and Superman star appeal of Christopher Reeve, but B.O. looks to be lukewarm.

The story, based on LaVyrie Spencer's 1989 novel of the same name, shows sparks of originality, with Reeve as down-and-out ex-con Will Parker who answers a newspaper classified ad for a husband. But weak scripting and a choppy, uninspired narrative turn the Depression-era yarn into a garbled collection of predictable soap opera scenes against an albeit nicely lensed backdrop of rural Canadian farmland. Pic moves at a decent clip, but sacrifices character and sense as it whooshes along.

Plot starts simply, then gets lost in its own twists. Recently widowed Elly Dinsmore (Deborah Raffin) is not looking for love, just someone to share the chores. She's got two kids, with one more on the way, but she's shunned as a crazy recluse by her small Georgia town. Parker, broke and fresh from a murder rap, appears on her doorstep to take the "husband" job. At first they are sweetly nervous together, stumbling over each other in the tiny house. But after a cloying musical montage of chopping wood, milking cows and fixing up the backwoods cabin, they drop anchor, culminating in a love scene that feels outrageously out of place.

Then, as if imported from a different pic, sheriff Reese Goodloe (J.T. Walsh) roughs up Parker and local floozy Lula Peaks (Helen Shaver) pesters him with seduction attempts. Suddenly Lulu's dead, the sheriff is mad and Parker is back in jail.

What might have been an intriguing tale of two lovers coming together under oddly adverse circumstances turns into a flashy murder trial drama resolved by a ridiculous *deus ex machina*.

Despite flaws, helmer Steven Stern ("Money," "Rolling Vengeance") periodically shows a delicate touch. In Elly's childbirth scene, he trains the lens on her other children, bored at the kitchen table, unsure what's happening. Lenser Laszlo George offers requisite rural vistas, sunlit grassy fields in soft breezes.

Reeve is a sturdy, if not stiff, leading man. But his Man of Steel history plagues the blue-eyed hunk. No matter how much they smudge his face, he looks like Clark Kent. He gives Parker a pensive demeanor that's incongruous with his prison time, but appeals.

Raffin, who co-scripted and whose hubby, Michael Viner, produced, uses small, affected gestures and ticks to convey her questionable madness. She's stunningly beautiful in the setting sun, but doesn't have the dramatic weight necessary to carry the pic.

The ever-solid Walsh offers a small-town sheriff at his sleaziest, despite floating in and out of his Southern accent.

Pic may have better luck in cable and homevid. —*Dan Cox*

SPLIT

An E.F.T. release of an E.F.T. production. Produced by Ellen Fisher Turk. Directed by Fisher Turk, Andrew Weeks. Screenplay, Dan Chayefsky. Camera (color), Jacqueline Escolar, Mirjana Gall, Nick Manning, Josh Pease, Hank Rifkin, Fisher Turk; editors, Peter Ringer, Keith Brown; narrator, Wes Kent. Reviewed at Quad Cinema, N.Y., Sept. 3, 1993. Running time: **60 MIN.**

With: Brian Belovitch, David Burns, Amy Coleman, Jimmy Camica, Justin Davis, Michael Degenhardt, Gerald Duval, David Glamamore, Ron Jones, Codie Leone, Jeremiah Newton, Teri Paris, Rodney Pridgen, Maggie Ruzo.

Split" is a surprisingly unsentimental celebration of a life that was as much a self-creation as it was a product of the times. Subtitled "William to Crysis: Portrait of a Drag Queen," hourlong pic delves into the life of International Crysis (1951-90), an infamous Gotham drag queen, performer, confidant of Salvador Dali and regular habitue of Studio 54.

October 4, 1993 (Cont.)

Not only was Crysis a product of her own creation, but she was also its victim: She died at age 39 of cancer, caused by seepage from wax and silicon breast implants. Yet the film never waxes sentimental. When Crysis is told of her cancer she sneaks into the hospital bathroom to smoke a cigarette.

Booted out of her home at age 14 for what she calls "differences in taste" with her family concerning her wardrobe, Crysis arrived in a fashionable Manhattan gay scene where cross-dressing was made chic by Warhol superstars Holly Woodlawn and Candy Darling and glitter groups like the New York Dolls; discos like Studio 54 celebrated androgyny and "La Cage aux Folles" was a hot ticket on Broadway.

Pic uses fragments from Crysis' monologues, performances and interviews counterpointed with talking-head comments from friends and cohorts. There is also ample footage — transferred from video — from New York's annual Wigstock, a public drag fest celebrated on Labor Day.

Also discussed is acceptance of gay lifestyles and the difference between being a drag queen and a transsexual; Crysis lived as a woman 24 hours a day, taking female hormones and having breast enlargement, and yet didn't make the final decision to endure a complete sex change.

Tech credits are OK, and theme is a natural for gay and lesbian film festivals. —*Sylvester Joachim*

GERMINAL

(FRENCH)

An AMLF release (France) of a Renn Prods., France 2 Cinema, DD Prods. (Paris)/Alternative Films (Brussels)/Nuova Artisti Associati (Rome) production, with participation of Nord-Pas-de-Calais Region, French Ministries of Culture & Education, CNC, Canal Plus, Sofiarp, Investimage 2, Groupe Pinault, and Eurimages. (International sales: President Films, Paris.) Produced, directed by Claude Berri. Executive producer, Pierre Grunstein. Screenplay, Arlette Langmann, Berri, based on the novel by Emile Zola. Camera (color, widescreen), Yves Angelo; editor, Herve de Luze; music, Jean-Louis Roques; production design, Than At Hoang, Christian Marti; costume design, Sylvie Gautrelet, Caroline de Vivaise, Bernadette Villard; sound recordist, Pierre Gamet; sound mixer (Dolby SR), Dominique Hennequin; associate producer, Bodo Scriba; assistant directors, Frederic Aubertin, Eric Bartonio; second unit director, Natalie Engelstein. Reviewed at Gaumont Grand Ecran Italie theater, Paris, Sept. 20, 1993. Running time: **158 MIN.**

Etienne Lantier .... Renaud
Maheu .... Gerard Depardieu
Maheude .... Miou-Miou
Bonnemort .... Jean Carmet
Catherine Maheu .... Judith Henry
Chaval .... Jean-Roger Milo
Souvarine .... Laurent Terzieff
Also with: Jean-Pierre Bisson, Bernard Fresson, Jacques Dacqmine, Anny Duperey, Pierre Lafont, Annik Alane, Frederic Van Den Driessche, Gerard Croce, Cecile Bois.

Though commendable and ambitious, Claude Berri's reverent adaptation of the Emile Zola mining saga "Germinal" is strangely flat and matter-of-fact. This earnest depiction of class struggle will be a struggle for many viewers as well.

With Gallic awareness of pic running high, and a cast of local favorites including Gerard Depardieu (from Berri's earlier "Jean de Florette") and renegade folk singer Renaud in his screen bow, local auds are likely to embrace this dignified telling of Zola's 1885 classic. Those in search of lighter fare may give this longish pic the shaft, but foreign coin, needed to offset the record 172 million franc ($30 million) budget, should be forthcoming from offshore arthouses.

Story of the brutal conditions in Gallic coal mines in the 1870s is immediate and accessible, even to those with no prior knowledge of the book, which delineates the strained interdependence between starving miners and their well-fed overlords.

Unemployed mechanic Etienne Lantier (Renaud) stumbles into the hellish pre-dawn bustle of the Montsou mine complex, in northern France, and is drafted by miner Maheu (Depardieu) to replace a deceased worker on his crew.

Maheu's daughter, Catherine (Judith Henry), shows Etienne kindness but ends up in an abusive relationship with the selfish Chaval (Jean-Roger Milo). Maheu's wife, Maheude (Miou-Miou), has 10 mouths to feed.

Due to management's time-consuming safety demands, tensions are running high. Etienne spreads the idealistic vision of a Workers' Paradise and, when management lowers the per-bin fee, encourages the men to strike. Result is a chain reaction of tragic events.

Zola's meticulously detailed account of deep-seated inequalities and miserable living conditions has been diluted in its transfer to the widescreen. Pic's major shortcoming is that characters speak of poverty and hunger but their privations are not strongly conveyed at a visual level.

Lenser Yves Angelo, who gave "Tous les Matins du monde" its painterly beauty, sidesteps the temptation to make poverty glossy but the overall results stir a sense of neither pity nor indignation.

There's no sense of claustrophic back-breaking labor; rather, a series of hints that mining is probably not a very pleasant job. Though never dull, pic seems dramatically arbitrary rather than inevitable and right.

Book's omnipresent drinking and coupling are implied with deft strokes, with casual nudity always appropriate. Scenes of freewheeling dances at the village fair have genuine verve, and those of miners on the rampage are powerful.

A sequence in which women take their revenge on a lecherous grocer ranks as the most vivid depiction of castration since Nagisa Oshima's "In the Realm of the Senses."

Performances are strong down the line. Although a trained actor may have better anchored the epic tale, singer-turned-thesp Renaud, whom Berri spent a decade convincing to accept the role of Etienne, delivers as the wan and pensive catalyst with Messianic overtones.

As Maheu, Depardieu gives a reined-in performance as a man made weary by hard labor and chronic injustice. Jean Carmet is touching as his father, whose coal-black spittle bears witness to half a century in the mine.

Petite Henry ("La Discrete") is fine as the underfed child-woman. But the script underplays the mutual longing between her and Renaud to a point where what should be the pic's strongest romance is so subdued as to go unnoticed.

Milo makes a hissable villain as Chaval, and Miou-Miou, as Depardieu's wife, delivers an award-caliber perf in the plum role of a practical woman struggling to make ends meet.

Production design is impressive, and music fitting and unobtrusive. Extras, drawn from modern mining families, provide an arresting display of faces. —*Lisa Nesselson*

TORONTO FEST

TOTALLY F***ED UP

A Desperate Pictures production with Blurco/Muscle & Hate Studios. Produced by Andrea Sperling, Gregg Araki. Directed, written, edited by Araki. Camera (color), Araki; sound, Marianne Dissard; postproduction sound design, Alberto Garcia; associate producer, Garcia. Reviewed at Festival of Festivals, Toronto, Sept. 16, 1993. (Also in N.Y. Film Festival.) Running time: **79 MIN.**
Andy .... James Duval
Tommy .... Roko Belic
Michele .... Susan Behshid
Patricia .... Jenee Gill
Steven .... Gilbert Luna
Deric .... Lance May
Ian .... Alan Boyce
Brendan .... Craig Gilmore

Gregg Araki ladles up a rather stale serving of gay teenage angst in "Totally F***ed Up." Somewhat surprisingly slated for the New York Film Festival in the wake of its Toronto Fest world preem, this ultra-low-budget, Godardian "homo movie" feels like a step backward to his earlier group mopes rather than an advance beyond his provocative last film, "The Living End." Commercial prospects are limited to gay and highly alternative venues.

Dubbed by its director as "a kinda twisted cross between avant-garde experimental cinema and a queer John Hughes flick," this boasts neither the excitement of the former at its best nor the entertainment value of the latter. Pic was written concurrently with "The Living End" and shot just after it but shelved for two years as Araki edited and promoted his most successful film to date.

In the manner of his 1989 feature "The Long Weekend (O' Despair)" but with a pinch more filmmaking flair, new effort wallows in the terminal ennui of a handful of marginally articulate L.A. kids. Their conversations focus upon sex or how totally f***ed up everything is in their lives. Working deeply in the shadow of Godard's landmark "Masculine-Feminine," which pictured "the children of Marx and Coca-Cola," Araki presents "lifestyles of the bored and disenfranchised" in fragmented, disconnected scenes that are regularly interrupted by titles in the style of his artistic mentor.

Alienation rules the lives of six young gay friends — the utterly confused, good-looking Andy, aspiring videomaker Steven and his artist b.f. Deric, skateboarding dude Tommy and two ditzy lesbians, Michele and Patricia. Opening couple of reels are devoted to their alternately vapid and vaguely amusing complaints about life in the 1990s, during which it becomes clear that there is a dichotomy between Araki's radical, activist attitude and the passive, victimized mind-set of his characters.

After 25 minutes, a clever title card announces, "Start Narrative Here" and, lo and behold, something actually happens. The directionless Andy meets a slightly older guy named Ian who lights his fire, and their nocturnal wanderings around a chillingly desolate L.A. do generate some mood and interest.

But whatever tenuous acquaintance most of the characters have with optimism is extinguished by gaybashing, homophobia and, more than anything, failed love affairs.

Like Araki's previous work, pic undeniably conveys a strong sense of a certain attitude toward life. But arbitrary structure and lack of interesting characters prove off-putting, and the virtual disappearance of the two women in the second half underscores their marginal importance to the film. Ultimately, the desperation here seems like an artistic pose compared to the genuine anarchic nihilism born of utter hopelessness in "The Living End."

Visually, this guerrilla-style production, which mixes some transferred Super 8 video material with the 16mm footage, is murkier and

harder to watch than Araki's last picture. This would seem like the time for the filmmaker to move on to more varied subjects and budgets if he is to broaden his palette.
—*Todd McCarthy*

SMALL PLEASURES

A Wondrous Light production. Produced by John Sutton, Keith Lock. Directed, written by Lock. Camera (color), Maurizio Belli; editor, Anna Pafomow; music, Kirk Elliot, An-Lun Huang; art direction, Bill Koon, Brenda Joy Lem, Henry Wang; sound, Steve Munro, Henry Embry; associate producers, Yan Cui, Leslie Padorr. Reviewed at Festival of Festivals, Toronto, Sept. 12, 1993. Running time: **85 MIN.**
Sally .... Lily Zhang
Zhao .... Reimonna Sheng
Li An .... Andy X. Xu
Jack Kelly .... Phillip MacKenzie
Mr. Ying .... David Chant

Keith Lock's feature debut, "Small Pleasures," is a raw but decent addition to a growing body of films ("Combination Platter," "The Wedding Banquet") dealing with multiculturalism and the experience of Asian immigrants in North America. Reportedly the first film ever written and directed by a Chinese-Canadian, timely, if also naive, pic may be of interest to viewers in urban centers, where Asian immigrants reside.

Set in the spring of 1989, during the tumultuous events of Tiananmen Square, story centers on Sally (the extremely beautiful Lily Zhang), a young, ambitious woman determined to make the most of her new life in Toronto. She is contrasted with her roommate, Zhao (Reimonna Sheng), also a recent immigrant, but one who still clings to the traditions of the old world.

Pic chronicles their daily existence: work in a restaurant owned by a rigid Mr. Ting (David Chant), and affairs of the heart. Rebelling against the notion of an arranged marriage back home, Zhao ends up having an affair with Li An (Andy Xu), a dissident professor who works as a waiter in the same restaurant because he can't practice his profession.

A leisurely first half establishes the setting's context in Toronto's Chinatown. In the second, however, story becomes overly melodramatic when the two women experience detachment. In what appears to be a reversal of stereotypes, Li turns out to be a married man with a wife in China. And Sally is forced into sudden maturity when her white Canadian beau (Phillip MacKenzie) goes abroad.

For the sake of accuracy, Beijingers were cast as Beijingers, and assimilated CBC (Canadian-born

Chinese) play characters born there. The melange of accents promotes pic's authenticity, a crucial but often missing ingredient from other immigrant sagas.

"Small Pleasures" contains charming perfs by the two women (Zhang and Sheng), but it's the kind of heartfelt film in which characters spell out everything and mean exactly what they say. Still, in this first film, scripter-helmer demonstrates generosity of spirit and ample talent in handling his actors.
—*Emanuel Levy*

TOP OF THE WORLD

A Denver Center production. Produced by Beth Harrison. Executive producer, Brockman Seawell. Directed by Cort Tramontin. Screenplay, Jamie Horton, Seawell. Camera (color), Bernd Heinl; editor, William A. Anderson; music, Bruce Odland; production design, Christopher Nowak; costume design, Nancy Bassett; sound (stereo), Richard Jenkins; casting, Judy Henderson, Alycia Aumuller. Reviewed at Festival of Festivals, Toronto, Sept. 11, 1993. Running time: **109 MIN.**
Brad .... Gregg Almquist
Suzy .... Kayla Black
Ali .... Margaret Gibson
Megan .... Alice Haining
Bill .... Jamie Horton
Greg .... John Ottavino

"Top of the World," Cort Tramontin's impressive directorial debut, belongs to the "reunion" genre of "The Big Chill," "Return of the Secaucus 7" and "Peter's Friends." Angst-ridden tale examines the ennui of six characters in search of themselves during a Thanksgiving weekend in the Colorado mountains. Commercial prospects for indie pic, the first to come from the Denver Center for the Performing Arts, are very good, as it deals with the midlife crises of the thirtysomething crowd.

Pic doesn't borrow its title from "White Heat," in which James Cagney dies while uttering "Top of the world, Ma," nor from the last, ironic scene of Mike Leigh's "High Hopes." Instead, title is used as both a geographic and symbolic metaphor for being on the edge.

Scripters Jamie Horton and Brockman Seawell have woven a complex "relationship" tale with characters representing a cross-section of white, middle-aged professionals. Central figure is Ali (Margaret Gibson), a frustrated artist unhappily married to Bill (Jamie Horton), a psychologist who tends to carry his doctor-patient dynamics into his personal ties.

Megan (Alice Haining), Ali's sister, arrives with her new lover, Brad (Gregg Almquist). The foursome are entertained by Greg (John Ottavino), a writer who has fled to the family ranch with the excuse of settling his late father's estate. Ali, Greg's ex-girlfriend, soon realizes

that her design to rekindle her old flame won't work, since Greg has fallen for Suzy (Kayla Black), his father's young and beautiful widow.

Like the individuals in "The Big Chill" and "Peter's Friends," locked in one place over a weekend, the characters are forced to deal with their raw, often disturbing, feelings. Pic consists of illuminating interactional scenes that are at once painful and liberating, and admirably doesn't shy away from being ambitious.

First-time director Tramontin shows a sensitive ear for realistic dialogue, though he has problems establishing the appropriate pacing for this wordy piece. Tempo, particularly in the first part, is too slow and deliberate, though the film improves considerably in its second half.

Most of the actors acquit themselves with decent, natural performances. The one notable exception is Gibson, who is photogenic but tends to pose too much and deliver her lines in a mannered, often monotonous, mode.

Production values are proficient, particularly Bernd Heinl's lensing of the winter mountains and Bruce Odland's evocative music.

At times, the characters come across as pretentious and too self-absorbed, but they also capture problems that most career-driven, success-oriented individuals face when they reach middle age. Ultimately, pic may be more relevant to women, as it depicts the eternal career-vs.-marriage conflict and the strains involved in trying to be desirable women, accomplished professionals and "fitting" wives and mothers. —*Emanuel Levy*

DE DOMEINEN DITVOORST
(THE DITVOORST DOMAINS)
(DUTCH — DOCU — B&W/COLOR)

A CineTe Filmproduktie production. Produced by Willem Thyssen, Hans Otten. Directed, written by Thom Hoffman. Camera (color), Peter de Bont; editor, Danniel Danniel; music, Sofia Gubaidulina, Franz Liszt; art direction, Harry Anumeriaan; sound, Piotr van Dijk. Reviewed at Festival of Festivals, Toronto, Sept. 15, 1993. Running time: **112 MIN.**
With: Bernardo Bertolucci, Gerard Brach, Robby Muller.

Visually striking but intellectually pretentious and a bit vague, "The Ditvoorst Domains" presents a gloomy portrait of Adriaan Ditvoorst, the gifted Dutch filmmaker who committed suicide in 1987. Docu offers valuable insights about Ditvoorst and the Dutch cinema, but lack of familiarity outside Holland with his work will restrict its appeal to the fest circuit.

Born in 1940, Ditvoorst graduated from Amsterdam's Film Academy, where he was influenced by the French New Wave; Jean-Luc Godard reportedly thought of him as a kindred soul. Ditvoorst's dream was to build a local industry modeled on the French. Indeed, in the late 1960s and 1970s, the New Dutch Cinema was lively and original, brimming with talent.

Producers, colleagues and friends who went to school with Ditvoorst talk about him as a director and a man. Representative clips from his films are interspersed, illustrating his surrealistic style and expressionistic lighting.

A complex, problematic personality, Ditvoorst dealt in motifs of despair and death. According to friends, "imagination, poetic melancholy and gloomy interior" characterized his vision. He was instinctively drawn to Kafka and the absurd; self-destruction was a leitmotif—every pic was a *cri de coeur*.

In the 1970s, Ditvoorst made "The Blind Photographer," "The Idiot" and "Flanagan," the latter a gangster flick with the structure of a Greek tragedy. These films showed innovation, but they all failed commercially. When his wife left him, he sank into severe depression.

Financing was always a nightmare for Ditvoorst. His peers concur that he was out of place in Holland, that had he lived in France, his talent would have blossomed. Ditvoorst had "aesthetic purity" but lacked the pragmatic skills to fulfill it. Docu takes a romantic view of the director as a solitary artist who refused to compromise his vision for the sake of mass appeal. "The Ditvoorst Domains" is the tragedy of a man who never fully exploited his talent, an artist who never found his audience.

Though docu puts the blame on the lack of "cultural climate," what's missing is a consideration of the broader context of Dutch cinema, beyond such generalities as declining financial resources. Thus, no mention is made of Ditvoorst's contemporary, Paul Verhoeven, who made great films at the same time and later became Holland's best-known export to the U.S. It's also unclear why Ditvoorst never moved to Paris or another film center.

First-time director Thom Hoffman played the lead — a mother-adoring drug addict — in "White Madness," a 1983 film that turned out to be Ditvoorst's last.

Ultimately, docu is more forceful as a personal tribute to an interesting director than as a manifesto of the declining *cinema d'auteur* in Holland. —*Emanuel Levy*

PANO KATO
KE PLAGIOS

(UP, DOWN AND SIDEWAYS)

(GREEK)

A Michael Cacoyannis Films production. Produced, directed, written, edited by Cacoyannis. Executive producer, Yannoulla Wakefield. Camera (color), Andreas Sinanos; music, Stefanos Korkolis; art direction, Yannis Metzikof; sound, Marinos Athanassopoulos. Reviewed at Festival of Festivals, Toronto, Sept. 18, 1993. Running time: 108 MIN.
Maria .... Irene Papas
Stavros .... Stratos Tzortzoglou
Anestis .... Panos Mihalopoulos

Michael Cacoyannis emerges from semi-retirement with "Up, Down and Sideways," an amusing farce about the wild and crazy inhabitants of modern-day Athens. Featuring his favorite leading lady, Irene Papas, and good-natured humor, it's Cacoyannis' first film since "Sweet Country" seven years ago, and his most accessible project since his 1964 international hit, "Zorba the Greek." Focusing on the very contemporary, hip lives of a mother and her gay son, comedy has good chances for limited theatrical release.

Sex farce has a great opener that sets the tone for the whole film: a traffic jam in Athens, with people losing their temper, and a bank robbery with the wrong gangsters caught. However, nothing that follows this sequence matches its irreverent mood, fast pace and masterly *mise en scene*.

At comedy's center is Papas, a middle-aged, prosperous widow who shares an elegant house with her handsome gay son, Stratos Tzortzoglou. Enjoying an open, amiable relationship, mother and son also share great passion for the opera. Enter Panos Mihalopoulos, a young gym instructor, who claims to be Maria Callas' nephew and manages to confuse both mother and son.

At the climax, directed in the best tradition of a Feydeau bedroom farce, Papas entertains her athletic beau upstairs while her son courts a sailor downstairs. They are, of course, unaware of each other's activities. Doors open and close, and lovers are caught with their pants down, when a transvestite arrives at the house under circumstances too convoluted to describe.

The three lead characters are always credibly vivid and sympathetic. At 67, the still-beautiful Papas gives a charming performance as the open-minded, amorous widow — and dream-mother of every gay man. It's a welcome change of pace for an actress mostly known for essaying Greek tragedies, including Cacoyannis' films of "Electra" and "The Trojan Women."

The handsome Tzortzoglou and the romantic Mihalopoulos lend reliable support as the sensitive son and macho instructor, respectively.

Light on its feet even in its weak moments, "Up, Down and Sideways" is Greece's refreshing contribution to a growing body of films about the ever-changing lifestyles in big, cosmopolitan cities. It's also a welcome move from Cacoyannis, whose erratic and sporadic career has included a number of pretentious films. —*Emanuel Levy*

THE LAST BORDER

(FINNISH)

A Last Border/Connexion Films/Sandrews/MC4 production. Produced, directed, edited by Mika Kaurismaki. Executive producers, Willy Baer, Klas Olofsson, Pia Tikka. Camera (color), Timo Salminen; music, Anssi Tikanmaki; art direction, Tony De Castro; sound, Kikeono. Reviewed at Festival of Festivals, Toronto, Sept. 12, 1993. Running time: 105 MIN.
Jake .... Jolyon Baker
Doavia .... Fanny Bastien
Duke .... Jurgen Prochnow
Borka .... Kari Vaananen
Dimitri .... Matti Pellonopaa

Directed by Mika Kaurismaki, the older but less famous brother of Aki Kaurismaki, "The Last Border" is a rare film — a spoof of the "Mad Max" cult films that also works as a futuristic adventure in its own right. Subtle humor and moderate violence (by today's standards) may disappoint viewers expecting excessive treatment of such matters. Nonetheless, impressive visual design and strong perfs by Matti Pellonopaa and Jurgen Prochnow could broaden satire's commercial prospects beyond the midnight circuit.

Narrative is set in the desolate near-future of 2009, when toxic waste has pushed the remaining civilization to the frigid Arctic Circle. The place is terrorized by a band of motorcycle cutthroats, led by Duke (Prochnow), who round up rebellious guerrillas and sell them to the dictatorial military government.

Pic begins when Jake (Jolyon Baker), an escaped army prisoner, is captured by Duke's men, but then manages to escape. Running away, Jake encounters and rescues Dimitri (Pellonopaa), a long-haired peddler whose motorcycle and trailer have crashed. To reciprocate, Dimitri blasts Jake's handcuffs with a blunderbuss and sets him free. Every once in a while, Dimitri, a Santa Claus figure, reappears, endowing the tale with his comic and humanistic persona, magnificently embodied by Pellonopaa.

Spoof actioner is decorated with a "love story" of sorts between Jake and a tough female prisoner (Fanny Bastien), who also escaped from Duke's camp. The unconventional courtship of Jake and Doavia, who has mysteriously lost her memory, gives new meaning to romanticism.

Baker is not as sexy or handsome as Mel Gibson, but his voice is similar, creating the double effect of spotlighting his acting and at the same time relating to Gibson's Mad Max. Kari Vaananen also excels as Borka, a mute, 30-year-old lunatic.

The ambience here is just as weird and the characters just as eccentric as those of George Miller's landmark 1980s actioners. The production values, particularly Timo Salminen's dark lensing of the open, uninhabited vistas, are polished.

Overall, however, pic lacks the kinetic energy, astounding stunt work and exhilarating motorcycle chases of the "Mad Max" trilogy. The climactic fight between Jake and Duke is too leisurely paced and not rousing enough. At the end, an old woman's prophecy of revenge against Duke, which began the story, is fulfilled — a flashback to Jake's childhood explains the motivation for his vengeance.

Though not as uniquely inventive as his brother Aki's movies, Mika Kaurismaki's "The Last Border" still stands at the forefront of a burgeoning new wave of Finnish cinema. —*Emanuel Levy*

SENKIFOLDJE

(WHY WASN'T HE THERE?)

(HUNGARIAN)

A Dailogu Filmstudio/AB Films/Dom Filmowe production. Executive producer, Derta Laszlo. Directed, written by Andras Jeles. Camera (b&w/color), Tibor Mathe; editor, Margit Galamb; music, Laszlo Melis; art direction, Tamas Breier; sound, Cyorgy Kovacs. Reviewed at Festival of Festivals, Toronto, Sept. 13, 1993. Running time: 104 MIN.
With Gyorgy Berkhoffer, Tamas Baumholczer, Janos Csikesz, Jozsef Buczko.

A film of great pictorial beauty, "Why Wasn't He There?" is a major contribution to the cinematic literature about childhood and the Holocaust. Set in Hungary during World War II, riveting tale focuses on the coming of age of a Jewish girl. Subtle, contemplative, stylized picture should be embraced by film festivals and arthouse audiences.

The protagonist of this epic film is Eva, a 13-year-old who lives in the countryside with her extended family. Narrating from her diary, Eva begins with the astute observation that she didn't get her customary birthday party because her grandmother felt that "we don't need Jewish kids showing off when our country is bleeding." Writer-director Andras Jeles uses Eva's point of view to relate the shattering events that took place in Hungary during the war. Story is of a rich Jewish family whose life is devastated when the Nazis invade and the Jews are sent to labor and, later, concentration camps.

At first innocent of the changing political setting, Eva tries to live a normal, routine life. But she is forced into rapid maturation as soon as some of her family members are arrested and others are obliged to wear the Yellow Star. The crucial scene in which her bicycle is confiscated provides a turning point and one of the film's most ravishing images.

Structure is episodic, unfolding as a series of bittersweet, at times humorous, tableaux of family life. Avoiding melodramatic treatment, Jeles' greatest achievement is in making a stylized, somehow detached film that doesn't lose the immediate relevance of its message.

This quiet, delicate story takes the form of a surreal dream that turns into a haunting nightmare. Tibor Mathe's expressionistic cinematography facilitates this transition by using both b&w and color imagery.

The viewer's knowledge of the Holocaust only adds to the emotional experience of "Why Wasn't He There?," a landmark film that captures the *zeitgeist* of the era in a vivid and most arresting manner. —*Emanuel Levy*

TWO BROTHERS,
A GIRL AND A GUN

(CANADIAN)

A Black Market Motion Picture production. Produced by Kate Holowach, William E. Hornecker. Directed by Hornecker. Screenplay, Grant Dryden, Hornecker. Camera (color), John Tarver; editor, Ken Berry; music, The Imagineers, Mike Shields; art direction, Hornecker; sound, Rick Youck. Reviewed at Festival of Festivals, Toronto, Sept. 10, 1993. Running time: 93 MIN.
Wes .... Shaun Johnson
Ruby .... Kim Hogan
Cliff .... David Everhart

Yet another version of the Cain and Abel story, "Two Brothers, a Girl and a Gun" fuses conventions of Hollywood's family melodrama of the 1950s and road movies of the late 1960s. Overfamiliar concept, plot and characters of this modern Canadian Western should limit its theatrical appeal, though pic showcases William Hornecker's considerable talents in his feature directorial debut.

Drawing on such American writers as John Steinbeck and Arthur Miller, and numerous films, this is Canada's attempt at a Western road movie, set in the spectacular badlands of southern Alberta.

Wes (Shaun Johnston), a stud in jeans and black leather jacket, and his girlfriend, Ruby (Kim Hogan), are on the run from the police for manslaughter. When Wes finds out that his mother has died, they head to the home of Cliff (David Everhart), his sensitive baby brother. Once siblings reunite, tension surfaces and confrontations about family secrets ensue.

Unfortunately, the contrasts between the "good-soft" and the "bad-bully" brothers are too schematic, including their looks, values and personal characteristics. Humor of the kind that fellow Canadian helmer Bruce McDonald uses in his own road films is totally missing from this literal effort.

Predictable climax is set in a farmhouse, where the boys grew up and which is now up for sale. Cliff is literally forced to dig a hole in the ground, while Wes digs at some painful truths about their childhood and the identity of their biological father.

Framed by Ruby's narration, the commentary never goes beyond such cliches as "nobody knows shit" or "you kill or get killed." The whole film amounts to a series of platitudes, exchanges of recycled dialogue and a lot of posing against the desolate Alberta prairies, which are beautifully lensed by John Tarver.

One wishes pic's skillful tech credits, energetic music and impressive directorial talent could have been applied to more original material. As it stands, this could be enjoyed only by viewers who have not seen any road or outlaw-on-the-run movies.
—*Emanuel Levy*

DEUX ACTRICES

(TWO CAN PLAY)

(CANADIAN)

A Max Films Communications presentation of a Stopfilm production in association with Arts Council of Canada and the National Film Board. Produced, directed, written, edited by Micheline Lanctot. Camera (color), Andre Gagnon; music, Kate and Anne McGarrigle; sound, Hans Peter Strobl. Reviewed at Festival of Festivals, Toronto, Sept. 15, 1993. Running time: **94 MIN.**
Solange .... Pascale Bussieres
Fabienne .... Pascale Paroissien
Charles .... Francois Delisle
Mother .... Louise Latraverse
Florist .... Suzanne Garceau

Though her film ambles into its story, actress-turned-filmmaker Micheline Lanctot ultimately delivers a hard-hitting drama of sibling bonding in "Deux Actrices."

The raw, unconventionally told tale is unquestionably for a high-brow crowd and therefore can only benefit from festival exposure.

That, coupled with the absence of a name cast, will necessitate a review-driven campaign, and sadly suggests very limited theatrical exposure.

Story begins when Fabienne (Pascale Paroissien) arrives at Solange's (Pascale Bussieres) door and announces they are sisters.

Solange, the younger of the two, feels there must have been some mistake — and turns the woman away.

It is a rather perfect beginning for what is to follow. Movie logic demands that the surprising news is either true or the start of some horrible, twisted plot. Thankfully, this is not a thriller, so the latter option is eliminated.

Bussieres and Paroissien are acutely attuned to the emotional investment their roles require. Solange allows Fabienne to move into the apartment she shares with Charles (Francois Delisle). But while she becomes increasingly accepting of her newfound sister, there's always a subtle underlying note of skepticism.

Fabienne, conversely, is a woman who masks a repressed, hidden nature with fervent outbursts of emotion. The explosions are invariably fixed to some sudden revelation, such as the existence of a 7-year-old daughter who's been taken from her by the child welfare department, or the lesbian love affairs in her past.

Lanctot, who handles four key positions on the film — producer, director, writer and editor — effortlessly conveys her commitment to the subject matter.

What is more complicated to fathom is the structure she chose to adopt. Sandwiched between the fictional scenes are sequences with the performers discussing their lives and the roles they play in the film.

While the videotaped behind-the-scenes footage doesn't directly elucidate the narrative, it does provide an effective emotional counterbalance.

"Deux Actrices" is an assured, clever, potent outing. Adroitly crafted and performed, the film derives its power honestly — from integrity and passion.
—*Leonard Klady*

KASPAR HAUSER

(GERMAN)

A Multimedia production. (Foreign sales: Cinepool, Munich.) Produced by Wolfgang Esterer. Executive producer, Dietrich von Watzdorf. Line producer, Andreas Meyer. Co-producers, BR, WDR, ORF, Arte, SVT, LfA. Directed, written by Peter Sehr. Camera (color), Gernot Roll; editor, Susanne Hartmann; music, Nikos Mamangakis; production design, O. Jochen Schmidt, Karel Vacek; costume design, Dietmut Remy; sound (Dolby), Haymo Heyder; assistant director, Eva Kadankova; special effects, Heinz Ludwig; casting, Sabine Schroth. Reviewed at Munich Film Festival, June 27, 1993. (Also in Festival of Festivals, Toronto.) Running time: **182 MIN.**
Kaspar Hauser .... Andre Eisermann
Daumer .... Udo Samel
Stanhope .... Jeremy Clyde
Feuerbach .... Hermann Beyer
Stephanie von Baden .... Cecile Paoli
Countess Hochberg ....
.... Katharina Thalbach
Ludwig von Baden ....
.... Uwe Ochsenknecht
Meyer .... Johannes Silberschneider
Hennenhofer .... Hansa Czypionka
Carl von Baden .... Tilo Nest
Ludwig I .... Dieter Laser

Three-hour costume drama based on the 19th century legend/mystery is not inspired, but it's helped by epic feel, good performances, plenty of pathos and the status of Kasper Hauser as one of Germany's favorite legends of the Romantic Age. Echoes of the most famous film rendition of the story — Werner Herzog's 1974 outing with Klaus Kinski — may bode well for theatrical business in a shortened version.

In 1828, a "wild boy" was found in Nuremberg. Rate at which the apparent half-idiot learned to talk, read and write excited all of Europe, and as he began remembering parts of his youth — he claimed he was kept in a prison-like hole his first 16 years — several theories arose about his origins.

While some said he was a fake, another theory evolved that he was the true heir to the Dukedom of Baden and the victim of a complicated court intrigue. He was murdered under mysterious circumstances some years later, which inspired even more speculation.

Hauser's true identity remains unknown. That the Baden court, to this day, will not release the documents generated in the original investigations has inspired director-writer Peter Sehr to compare the case to the JFK assassination.

Unlike Oliver Stone, however, Sehr attempts to tell the story from both perspectives. He starts with the struggle for the Baden throne and reveals the intrigues that spirited away the infant heir. Thus he solves the mystery before it arises, then goes on to tell the story of Hauser, the ultimate victim of circumstances beyond his control.

Weak points include a number of plodding stretches (most notably Hauser's education), the recurring question of who is the main character — Hauser or his torturers — and confusion toward the end, when intrigues, supporting characters and subplots pile up so high that it's not clear which of the many parties actually kills Hauser. For the most part, however, the story works in an unambitious, functional way.

Ironically, since it was originally intended for TV, main attraction is the pic's epic scope, which is achieved in large part by expanding a relatively small unsolved mystery to include a number of warring dukedoms. Costuming, lensing and score are all excellent.

Though Kaspar Hauser looks like an unappetizing human vegetable, in many scenes Andre Eisermann manages to inject the role with snappy, unexpected humor and downplayed pathos. Fact that character is completely passive, a victim who never once figures out what's going on and can't even try to fight against his fate, makes Eisermann's performance all the more noteworthy.
—*Eric Hansen*

MONTREAL FEST

WINDS OF GOD

(JAPANESE)

A Sachie Oyama production. (International sales: Shochiku Dai-Ichi Kogio Co., Ltd/KSS Inc., Tokyo.) Produced by Nobotsugu Tsubomi, Thoshihiro Osato, Satsuku Haruyama. Executive producer, Sachie Oyama. Directed by Yoko Narahashi. Written by Masayuki Imai. Camera (color), Kiyoshi Nishiura; editor, Hajime Okauashu; music, Michiru Oshima; production design, Tatsuo Suzuki, Yoshio Unno; art direction, Yuji Maruyama; sound, Sususmu Take. Reviewed at World Film Festival, Montreal, Sept. 5, 1993. Running time: **99 MIN.**
Makoto .... Masayuki Imai
Kinta .... Shota Yamaguchi
Lt. Yamamoto .... Tsunehiro Arai
Lt. Terakawa .... Takanori Kikuchi
Lt. Matsushima .... Kunihiko Ida
Group Leader Ota .... Tetsuya Bessho
Chiho .... Noriko Ogawa
Also with: Yoshiyuki Omori, Togo Shimura, Naomasa Musaka, Kengakussha Akiyama.

A Kamikaze sitcom? That's the setup as two inept comedians in modern Tokyo find themselves — via an Eddie Cantor-style crackup — in the closing days of World War II, as part of an elite corps of gung-ho suicide pilots. While it's no effects-laden blockbuster, the odd combination of culture-clash comedy, airplane action and *zeitgeist* soul-searching touches an unusual nerve and gives pic more off-island appeal than usual.

"Winds of God" began life as a play written by charismatic lead thesp Masayuki Imai, who expected it to fill first-time helmer Yoko Narahashi's colorful vision. By turns farcical and sentimental, pic follows the misadventures of Makoto (Imai) and his not-so-bright sidekick Kinta (Shota Yamaguchi), who flub their way through a Tokyo talent contest, head out into heavy traffic and, when the bandages come off, find they've traded in their Honda scooter for a couple of vintage Zeros, loaded with TNT.

It's August 1945, and the lads are the spitting image of the most respected fliers in the squadron. Naturally, no one believes those wild stories about a neon-lit future, and their lame routines — filled with references to the unbridled materialism of the 1990s — soon get on everyone's nerves, including a tough group leader (Tetsuya Bessho) who knows he must send his young charges off to certain death. Eventually, the ceremonial portentousness of the place and time gets to our feeble heroes, and their loyalties to Japan — old and new — are put to an unexpected test.

Although the pic aims for variety of tone, the alternation of nerdy humor with somber drama sometimes proves jarring. Narahashi's trick works best, surprisingly, when the two are combined in the same scene, as when Makoto plays Hendrix-style air guitar along with a kamikaze drinking song, or when his "prediction" of an atomic drop on Hiroshima comes true.

Narahashi (who has helmed legit in Canada and the U.S., as well as at home) could have made more of the stylized, artificial staging that sets the tone at pic's start, but Kiyoshi Nishiura's lensing keeps things appropiately bold and bright throughout, and aerial sequences, shot in Texas with restored fighter planes, add production luster.

All thesps are memorable. The music, however, veers disconcertingly between inspired exotica and Muzak-like lushness. —*Ken Eisner*

DA SA BA
(AFTER SEPARATION)
(CHINESE)

A Beijing Film Studio production. (International sales: China Film Export and Import Corp., Beijing.) Produced by Tian Yuping, Liu Yungchang. Directed, edited by Xia Gong. Written by Feng Xiao Gang, Zhen Xiaolong, after Wu Sang's novel "Da Sa Ba." Camera (color), Wa Xtaoming; music, Liang Gang; sound, Li Bojiang. Reviewed at World Film Festival, Montreal, Sept. 3, 1993. Running time: **94 MIN.**
Gu Yan .... Ge You
Lin Zhouyan .... Xu Fan

Something of a quiet departure for Beijing cinema, "After Separation" is a coolheaded, compassionate look at the semi-romantic entanglement of two middle-class city dwellers, each of whom has lost a spouse to the Chinese travel bug. An arthouse find for those partial to Chinese films, pic is probably too slight to travel well.

Baseball-capped photographer Gu Yan (played with tense reserve by soulful-eyed Ge You) is first seen saying goodbye to his wife, who's heading off to English school in Vancouver. Stoical while parting, he's soon in the airport lounge, practically weeping in his Tsing Tao, when another would-be emigrant's mate faints; the man runs to catch his plane, leaving pregnant Lin Zhouyan (feisty Xu Fan) in the startled Gu's arms.

He takes her to the hospital and then home, but the two don't quite hit it off. Instead, Lin starts her search for a magic exit visa, and Gu — a great cook and deft decorator — imposes his overweening charity on newly married friends who are soon screaming for him to "help" somebody else.

Despite their first impressions, Gu and Lin keep meeting accidentally, and when their other halves have been away for three years, they agree to spend the Spring Festival together, pretending (chastely) to be a married couple. All this coyness works, as firsttime helmer Xia Gang keeps a dry, Ozu-like eye on his sour-sweet, chemistry-free romance while moving it through its tentative paces, leading smoothly to a subtly emotional payoff.

Tech credits are generally fine, with Wa Xtaoming's understated framing of figures against tacky art, richly textured books and oversized buildings especially vivid. Dialogue looping, however, is of the earscraping, swallow and chew variety. —*Ken Eisner*

ARE THEY STILL SHOOTING?

An It Takes Two production. Produced by Lori Terrizzi. Directed, written by Tomislav Novakovic. Camera (Technicolor), Tony Cucchiari; editor, Suzanne Griffin; music, Dylan Maulucci; production design, Sharon Lynch; sound, Kelly Neese; associate producer, Glen Trotiner; assistant director, Sabin Streeter. Reviewed at World Film Festival, Montreal (non-competing), Aug. 29, 1993. Running time: **65 MIN.**
Boja .... Anthony Alessandro
Moshinka .... Isabelle Townsend
Mirko .... Anthony Nikolich
Father Miro .... Tomas Arana
Mile .... Robert Funaro
Bearded Gunman Tomislav Novakovic

Produced out of the Fine Arts department at Columbia University, where Croatian-born writer-director Tomislav Novakovic has been studying for a Masters degree, "Are They Still Shooting?" is a small but impassioned film that brings the conflict in Yugoslavia to the streets of New York. Though passion and some talent are evident here, pic is too small-scale to provoke much interest outside the Croatian community.

Boja (Anthony Alessandro) has escaped the bloodshed back home and lives in the Big Apple, while his brother, Mile, is in the thick of the fighting. Boja writes lengthy letters to his brother, who doesn't reply. Mile's girlfriend, Moshinka (Isabelle Townsend), has also made it to America, and she's drawn to Boja, even though she's a confirmed pacifist and he longs to get involved in the fighting by smuggling arms back to Croatia.

Plot is minimal, and is intercut with what appears to be home-movie footage shot one summer day in Croatia when the family was together and happy before the war began. There's also a soundtrack of rousing Croatian music and songs.

It's a pity that Novakovic, who evidently has commitment, wasn't able to fashion his anti-war film into a more polished package, but there should still be a limited big-city audience for this modest item. It's technically on the crude side, and performances are also rough. Pic is dedicated "to all victims of war." —*David Stratton*

CONSUMING SUN
(CHINESE-U.S.)

A Dali Intl. Co.-Zhejiang TV Film Studio co-production. (International sales: Dali Intl., Venice, Calif.) Produced, directed, written by John Zhang. Executive producer, Wenhao Zheng. Camera (color), Xiaolie Wang; editor, Haidi Ge; music, Liu Yuan; production design, Zongsi Min; sound, Deyao Feng; assistant director, Songlin Ma. Reviewed at World Film Festival, Montreal (non-competing), Aug. 28, 1993. Running time: **104 MIN.**
Mai Kebo .... Sun Min
Tumeido .... Cheng Xi
Sukeo .... Xiaoxu Dai
Hisaku .... Chu Xiao
Ueki .... Weijun Wang

"Consuming Sun" claims to be "a fictionalized account based on the life of Chinese literary giant Yu Da Fu." As biography, it fails to provide much information about Yu, or even to describe the kind of literature he wrote. Instead, it's a rather murky tale of intrigue and passion, mostly set in Japanese-occupied Sumatra toward the end of World War II. Commercial prospects in the West are slim.

Emulating Billy Wilder's "Sunset Boulevard" device of having the film narrated by a dead man who describes his own murder, this first feature by UCLA-trained writer-producer-director John Zhang is given a complicated flashback-within-flashback structure that makes an underwritten biopic appear even murkier. However, it seems that Yu, called Mai Kebo in the film, studied in Japan in the 1920s, became fascinated with Japanese culture, and fell in love with a Japanese woman, Tumeido.

Back home in China, he is forced into an arranged marriage by his autocratic mother. As his fame as a writer spreads (on this point the film is annoyingly reticent), he speaks out against Japanese imperialism. He's in Singapore when the Japanese take over, and discovers that the Japanese commanding officer, Sukeo, is a former university classmate and that his mistress is none other than Tumeido. Sukeo hires Mai as an interpreter, and the writer bigamously marries a Sumatran woman to save her from

forced prostitution at Japanese hands.

How much of this is fact or fiction is hard to determine, but the film speculates that, with the end of the war inevitable, Sukeo ordered Mai's execution before committing ritual hara-kiri.

With lavish production values, film looks handsome, but it's dramatically unsatisfying on almost every level. Thesping is adequate, though Sun Min never conveys much magnetism as the supposedly charismatic protagonist.

Thanks to a lush music score recorded by the Shanghai Symphony Orchestra, pic isn't hard to take, but just frustratingly insubstantial. Zhang seems more interested in his supposedly celebrated hero's sexual adventures than in other potentially more interesting aspects of what was, by all accounts, an unusual life. —*David Stratton*

SECONDLOJTNANTEN
(THE SECOND LIEUTENANT)
(NORWEGIAN)

A Norsk Film production. Produced by Harald Ohrvik. Executive Producer, Esben Hoilund Carlsen. Directed by Hans Petter Moland. Screenplay, Axel Hellstenius. Camera (color, widescreen) Harald Paalgard; editor, Einar Egeland; music, Randall Meyers; production design, Karl Juliusson; sound, Jan Lindvik; casting, Aamund Johannesen; assistant director, Harald Zwart. Reviewed at World Film Festival, Montreal, Aug 27, 1993. (Also in Venice Film Festival.) Running time: **102 MIN.**
Thor Espedal .... Espen Skjonberg
Bjelland .... Lars Andreas Larssen
Merstad .... Gard B. Eidsvold
Krogh .... Bjorn Sundquist
Audun .... Morten Faldaas
Ingolf .... Ove Christian Owe
Anna .... Rut Tellefsen
Bjarne .... Bjarne Thomsen
Ebba .... Camilla Strom Henriksen

This well-crafted and entertaining first feature from Hans Petter Moland reflects on the treacherous and confusing months in 1940 when Germany unexpectedly invaded Norway. Likely to spark controversy on its home turf, film boasts an interesting, exciting story and a top performance from veteran actor Espen Skjonberg. It could well find international commercial interest.

Skjonberg plays a craggy old Naval officer who has retired from the sea at about the same time as the April invasion of his country. He's the horrified witness to Germany's bombing of Oslo and skirmishes outside his own apartment building.

Determined to fight for king and country, the old-timer leaves his wife behind, dons a long out-of-date uniform (with the rank of second lieutenant, which no longer actually exists) and attempts to enlist. He discovers to his amazement that

Norway has officially surrendered to the invaders. Unwilling to accept the situation, he heads out of the city and rallies around him a ragged civilian army of partisans with the aim of guarding a strategic bridge.

Against the odds, he becomes a hero. A strict disciplinarian, he gains the confidence of his untrained men, and a first encounter with the enemy is entirely successful, with prisoners taken. But the eventual conclusion is never in any doubt, though in the end the old man is left to face the advancing Germans alone.

This very handsome $2.9 million production, also known as "The Last Lieutenant," is another fine example of classy Norwegian cinema. It's handsomely photographed for the wide screen by Harald Paalgard, and the action scenes are confidently staged. The script is intelligent and well structured, and the editing, after a slightly rocky first reel, is on the mark.

But above all this is a performance film, and Skjonberg is memorable as the tenacious old soldier who, though not a nationalist, still refuses to allow his country to be overrun without a fight. Standouts among the supporting cast are Bjorn Sundquist, as a vet of the Spanish Civil War who becomes the old man's deputy, and Lars Andreas Larssen as a regular army officer who is shamed by the old man's example.

All production credits are first class. Pic was selected to open the recent Norwegian fest at Haugesund.
—*David Stratton*

ENCONTROS IMPERFEITOS

(LIGHT TRAP)

(PORTUGUESE)

An S.P. Filmes production. (International sales: S.P. Filmes, Lisbon.) Executive producer, Pedro Correia Martins. Directed by Jorge Marecos Duarte. Screenplay, Doc Comparato. Camera (color), Edgar Moura; editor, Jose Manuel Lopes; music, Wagner Tiso; sound, Vasco Pimentel. Reviewed at World Film Festival, Montreal, Aug. 28, 1993. Running time: **90 MIN.**
Mario .... Diogo Infante
Matilde .... Paula Guedes
Alice .... Fatima Belo
Also with: Nicolau Breyner, Joao Perry, Joao Grosso, Maria Joao Luis, Fernando Curado Ribeiro, Chica Xavier, Canto e Castro, Fernando Heitor, Cecilia Guimaraes, Laurent Moine, Jose Laplaine.

For his first fictional feature, documentary helmer Jorge Marecos Duarte has attempted to construct a smart thriller that combines action and psychological twists and turns, but "Light Trap" doesn't deliver on either count. The leaden pacing and somewhat confused plot ensure that this Portuguese pic won't garner a wide audience.

Mario (Diogo Infante) has been involved in a bloody terrorist attack somewhere in Africa — though like much in this movie, it's never made clear exactly what these terrorists were up to — and, at the start of the film, he is hiding out in rural Portugal. Various villains are searching for Mario, but he seems more concerned with finding his old girlfriend Alice (Fatima Belo) than eluding the bad guys.

The film turns from a thriller into the tale of a jealous love triangle halfway through, when Mario meets the mysterious, sexy Matilde (Paula Guedes), whose sports car happens to break down near Mario's hideaway. The action virtually grinds to a halt at this point, as the brooding, intense-looking Mario tries to enlist Matilde in his search for Alice.

It sounds convoluted — and it is. Drama hinges on a much-talked-about incident in which Alice and Mario failed to meet after the terrorist incident, but, again, the script doesn't explain why this is such a big deal. The only sparks come from the sultry Guedes, who lights up the screen with her passionately jealous performance.

Wagner Tiso's score tends to the overly dramatic. Edgar Moura's shots of rural Portugal are more haunting and evocative than anything else in the film.
—*Brendan Kelly*

THE LOTUS EATERS

(CANADIAN)

A Malofilm Distribution (Canada) release of a Mortimer & Ogilvy Production, with the participation of Telefilm Canada, British Columbia Film and the National Film Board of Canada. Produced by Sharon McGowan. Executive producer, Alexandra Raffe. Co-Producer, Peggy Thompson. Directed by Paul Shapiro. Screenplay, Thompson. Camera (color), Thomas Burstyn; editor, Susan Shipton; music, John Sereda; production design, David Roberts; costumes, Sheila Bingham; sound, Michael McGee; associate producer, Armand Leo; assistant director, Jacques Hubert; casting, Stuart Aikins. Reviewed at World Film Festival, Montreal (competing), Aug. 30, 1993. (Also in Festival of Festivals, Toronto.) Running time: **101 MIN.**
Diane Kingswood ...... Sheila McCarthy
Hal Kingswood .... R.H. Thomson
Anne-Marie Andrews ....
.... Michele-Barbara Pelletier
Zoe Kingswood .... Aloka McLean
Cleo Kingswood .... Tara Frederick
Flora Kingswood .... Frances Hyland
Jo Spittle .... Andrea Libman
Dwayne Spittle .... Gabe Khouth
Tobias Spittle .... Paul Soles

A generally likable pic about a family living on a small island off the coast of British Columbia in the 1960s, "The Lotus Eaters" could attract audiences willing to go along with the gentle mood and the sometimes awkward mixture of domestic drama and comedy. Prospects are hard to predict, but it will probably play better on the small screen than it will theatrically.

Paul Shapiro's first feature centers on the Kingswood family and the small school of which Hal Kingswood (R.H. Thomson) is the rather old-fashioned headmaster. Hal and wife Diane (Sheila McCarthy) have two daughters, teenage Cleo (Tara Frederick), who is frustrated at not being allowed to go with b.f. Dwayne Spittle (Gabe Khouth) to the Beatles concert in nearby Vancouver, and 10-year-old Zoe (Aloka McLean), who's impressionable and romantic.

When the junior class teacher suddenly dies while supervising an exam, he's replaced by an attractive young Quebecer, Anne-Marie Andrews (Michele-Barbara Pelletier), whom Zoe instantly adopts as a role model.

But Anne-Marie gradually drifts into an affair with Hal, which the horrified Zoe discovers. The secret is revealed at a disastrous Christmas Day family gathering, temporarily splitting the family apart. At about the same time, Cleo announces she's pregnant and that she doesn't believe in marriage.

With its mixture of comedy and drama, romance and magic, nostalgia and disenchantment, "The Lotus Eaters" tries a bit too hard to be charming, which it is as long as McLean is onscreen — the young actress makes a very favorable impression as the grave, sensitive Zoe. As the disruptive young woman from the East, Pelletier is also fine, though the character's motivations are murky at times.

Less successful is the usually reliable Thomson in the pivotal role of the philandering Hal; the actor seems unsure how to handle some scenes, especially the crucial Christmas Day sequence in which a situation of high drama is played as though it were farce — an interesting concept, but one that doesn't work. As the betrayed wife, McCarthy is unusually subdued. The "happy ending" seems tacked on.

Apart from the performances of McLean and Pelletier, the film's chief asset is the attractive evocation of the island community and the feeling that, with the imminent onset of the hippie era, things will never be quite the same again.

Thomas Burstyn's camera work is attractive, and tech credits are all pro.
—*David Stratton*

KOLEJNOSC UCZUC

(SEQUENCE OF FEELINGS)

(POLISH)

A Tor Film Studio production. Produced by Krzysztof Zanussi. Directed, written by Radoslaw Piwowarski. Camera (Agfacolor), Witold Adamek; editor, Wanda Zeman; music, Jerzy Satanowski; sound, Krzysztof Jastrzab; assistant director, Anna Kasperkiewicz. Reviewed at World Film Festival, Montreal, Aug. 30, 1993. Running time: **87 MIN.**
Rafal Nawrot .... Daniel Olbrychski
Julia Kasprusia .... Maria Seweryn
Kochanka .... Ewa Kasprzyk
Radek .... Konrad Kujawski
Father .... Eugeniusz Priwieziencew

A wry comedy-drama about a dissolute middle-aged actor's relationship with a virginal teenager, "Sequence of Feelings" is modest but enjoyable. Polish writer-director Radoslaw Piwowarski's last effort was the altogether less subtle "Train to Hollywood."

Daniel Olbrychski gives one of his best perfs in a while as Rafal, a jaded, womanizing actor who arrives in a small mining town in Silesia to play the lead in a local legit production of "Romeo and Juliet." This stint in the sticks interrupts his latest affair, with a married woman he frequently calls.

When visited by a shy young music student, he assumes she'll be an easy conquest. But Julia (played with grave serenity by newcomer Maria Seweryn) is a virgin who needs some convincing before she'll allow the actor she idolizes to become her first lover.

Against the odds, Rafal falls hopelessly in love with her. But when Julia slips away from home to visit the actor in the middle of the night, she finds his married mistress, whom Rafal was too weak to turn away when he paid an unexpected visit. Julia's naive dreams of romantic love are shattered.

It's a simple enough story, but it works to perfection, thanks to excellent performances by Olbrychski and the delightfully natural Seweryn (daughter of Polish actors Krystyna Janda and Andrzej Seweryn). Humorous and touching by turns, pic is subtly directed, with the small town's drab streets and tacky theater amusingly observed.
—*David Stratton*

October 4, 1993 (Cont.)

L'OMBRE DU DOUTE
(A SHADOW OF DOUBT)
(FRENCH)

A Ciby 2000 release (France) of a Ciby 2000/TF1 Films production, in association with Cofimage 4, Investimage 4. (International sales: Ciby Sales, London.) Directed, written by Aline Issermann. Camera (color, Cinema-Scope), Darius Khondji; editor, Herve Schneid; music, Reno Isaac; art direction, Cyr Boitard; costume design, Maritza Gligo. Reviewed at Venice Film Festival (competing), Sept. 2, 1993. (Also in Festival of Festivals, Toronto.) Running time: **107 MIN.**

Alexandrine .... Sandrine Blancke
Father .... Alain Bashung
Mother .... Mireille Perrier
Sophia .... Josiane Balasko
Pierre .... Luis Issermann
Grandfather .... Michel Aumont
Grandmother .... Emmanuelle Riva

"**A** Shadow of Doubt" is a riveting exploration of how a father's presumed abuse of his young daughter destroys each member of a middle-class French family, and how society deals with incest. Director Aline Issermann's carefully observed characters are consistently engrossing, and her story well told. "Shadow" will interest distribs looking for a treatment of this delicate theme that can reach larger audiences.

Alexandrine (Sandrine Blancke) is a sensitive, quiet 11-year-old who appears strangely afraid of her father (Alain Bashung). She shrinks from his touch, and becomes anxious when her nurse mother (Mireille Perrier) has to work late. Her teacher is the first to suspect the handsome, blustering father of harboring incestuous desires but, after filing a complaint at the police station, the girl backs down when confronted with her dad.

From the beginning Issermann instills a doubt (but only a shadow) that the girl may be lying or imagining things. The father is disturbingly nonchalant about the accusations, the mother always backs him up, and grandpa and grandma deny all evidence.

Pic has no on-camera sex or nudity, but its subject matter is too chilling for immature auds. The one false note is a closing title full of TV-style stats about incest.

Cast is superbly chosen, with Blancke, Perrier and Bashung coming under scrutiny one by one in intensely emotional scenes. Darius Khondji's lensing keeps the viewer up close to the characters. Cutting by Herve Schneid is briskly modern, avoiding all unessential details.
—*Deborah Young*

IL SEGRETO DEL BOSCH VECCHIO
(THE SECRET OF THE OLD WOODS)
(ITALIAN)

A Penta Distribuzione (Italy) release of a Penta Film/Aura Film co-production. (International sales: Penta Intl., London.) Produced by Mario and Vittorio Cecchi Gori, Roberto Cicutto, Vincenzo De Leo. Directed, written by Ermanno Olmi, based on a short story by Dino Buzzati. Camera (Telecolor), Dante Spinotti; editor, Paolo Cottignola, Fabio Olmi; music, Franco Piersanti; art direction, Paolo Biagetti; costume design, Maurizio Millenotti; sound, in Dolby. Reviewed at Venice Film Festival (non-competing), Sept. 6, 1993. Running time: **134 MIN.**

Col. Procolo .... Paolo Villaggio
Bernardi .... Giulio Brogio
Benvenuto .... Riccardo Zannantonio
Overseer .... Lino Pais Marden
Giaco .... Luciano Zandonella
Archivist ....
Ernesto De Martin Modolado
Teacher .... Silvano Cetta

Arthouse vet Ermanno Olmi ("The Tree of Wooden Clogs") undertakes a noble defense of nature against man's destructiveness in the fable "The Secret of the Old Woods." While not a bad movie, it's one that may never find an audience.

Pic's language and imagery suggest Olmi is targeting an under-14 audience. But at 134 minutes, and far too leisurely a pace, this won't hold kids' interest, and adults will be distanced from the forest creatures with Bambi-like voices. There's a nice 90-minute kidpic lurking here, which a courageous cutter ought to look for.

Dino Buzzati's cute short story takes place in the mountains of northern Italy around the turn of the century. Retired military man Col. Procolo (played against type by stout comedian Paolo Villaggio) has inherited a majestic forest, which he is to manage until his little nephew (Riccardo Zannantonio) comes of age.

The only condition is to respect the Old Woods and its centuries-old trees. The grumpy, Dickensian colonel moves into a lodge and hatches a plan to cut down the trees and sell the wood.

He receives a stern warning from a tree spirit disguised as a forest ranger, Bernardi (Giulio Brogio), that each tree is inhabited by a benevolent genie who can help man. When Procolo fells the first, the forest becomes populated by men and women who have come to bid adieu to their sylvan companion.

Villaggio brings a gentleness to the cynical colonel that helps deepen a one-dimensional role, though he hasn't too much room to operate.

As the young nephew, Zannantonio, with a much smaller part, offers a strong character for kids to identify with.

If time is no object, it's pleasant to sit back and enjoy Olmi's vision of the magnificent living forest. Talking foxes with Disney-like voices are a little harder to take, not to mention poetic magpies and mean but chatty winds.

Lenser Dante Spinotti ("The Last of the Mohicans") turns the San Marco woods — a national forest reserve near Cortina d'Ampezzo — into a natural wonder, one that needs no genies to radiate a magical aura.
—*Deborah Young*

METISSE
(FRENCH-BELGIAN)

An MKL release for Lazennec Diffusion of a Les Productions Lazennec-SFP Cinema-Nomad Films co-production with the participation of Canal Plus and the CNC. Produced by Christophe Rossignon. Co-producers, Boudjemaa Dahmane, Jacques and Dimitri de Clerq. Directed, written by Mathieu Kassovitz. Camera (color), Pierre Aim, Georges Diane; editors, Colette Farrugia, Jean-Pierre Segal; music, Assassin, Marie Daulne, Jean-Louis Saulne; production design, Pierre Andre Roussotte; sound, Norbert Garcia, Thomas Gauder; associate producers, Adeline Lecallier, Alain Rocca; assistant director, Eric Pujoll. Reviewed at Club Gaumont screening room, Paris, Aug. 5, 1993. (In Venice Film Festival.) Running time: **95 MIN.**

Lola .... Julie Maudech
Jamal .... Hubert Kounde
Felix .... Mathieu Kassovitz
Also with: Vincent Cassel, Tadek Lokcinski, Jany Holt, Marc Berman, Jean-Pierre Cassel, Brigitte Bemol.

"**M**etisse," a hip interracial comedy with jaunty rap-inflected score, is bound to generate good word of mouth in France. Grounded in the reality of multi-ethnic city life, streetwise 100% French answer to "She's Gotta Have It" is shot like a long urgent video report (credits include a nod to the "Shakycam") only to mutate into an open-ended fairy tale.

First feature from 25-year-old scripter-helmer-actor Mathieu Kassovitz doesn't develop its characters so much as it defines them by playing against racial and cultural stereotypes.

Kassovitz stars as scrappy, aggressive Felix, a wiry Jewish bike messenger who worships the driving beat of rap music. He and his working-class relatives are crammed into a tiny run-down apartment in a housing project. Jamal (Hubert Kounde), the pampered son of African diplomats, is a wealthy, well-groomed law student who can't shoot hoops. Mulatto beauty Lola (Julie Maudech) summons her two lovers — pasty-faced Felix and ebony-black Jamal — to announce that she's pregnant and intends to have the baby although she doesn't know which guy is the father.

Two rivals are at each other's throats but eventually reconcile in order to cater to Lola's needs. Laid-back Lola, from Martinique, is not so much a fully formed character as she is an attitude with a winning smile. But this will probably be good enough for young auds, who will be pleased to see their fashions, their music and their concerns on-screen in a home-grown pic.

Jamal drops out of law school to take a minimum-wage job as a short-order cook, Felix is unemployed and Lola earns nothing, yet the trio live well in the sprawling luxury apartment that Jamal's absentee parents have conveniently left.

Helmer presents his racial, class and cultural melting pot as a simultaneously loving and belligerent milieu.

While some laughs — such as Felix's eternal clutziness on his bike — are strained, scene in which Felix brings Jamal and Lola home for Shabbat dinner ("So, it seems you're black?") an episode in which two gents compare notes on how they wooed Lola, ring both true and funny. Pic hammers home it's anti-racist message when Felix and Jamal are taken for car thieves on a midnight run to satisfy Lola's food cravings.

Rap lyrics address the fear of "watering down" one's racial roots while praising the mix-'n'-match approach to daily life and romance. Although pic is set in Paris, it could be any metro area with ethnic neighborhoods and housing projects.
—*Lisa Nesselson*

LETTRE POUR L...
(LETTER FOR L...)
(FRENCH)

A Le Poisson Volant/La Sept/Arte/Les Films du Losange production. Produced, directed, written by Romain Goupil. Camera (color), Romain Winding, William Watterlot; editor, Franssou Prenant; music, Philippe Hersant; production design, Jean-Baptiste Poirot; sound, Sophie Chiabaut; casting, Richard Rousseau. Reviewed at Venice Film Festival (non-competing), Sept. 3, 1993. Running time: **105 MIN.**

He .... Romain Goupil
L... .... Franssou Prenant
She in Berlin .... Regine Provvedi
She in Belgrade .... Anita Mancic
She in Sarajevo .... Alenka Mandic
Himself .... Ademir Kenovic

Director Romain Goupil made a modest impact at Cannes in 1982 when his first feature, the docu "To Die at 30," about growing up a militant in late '60s

October 4, 1993 (Cont.)

France, won the Camera D'Or. A decade on, he comes up with a frustratingly diffuse item that would have had more clout if better shaped and scripted.

International exposure will be extremely limited, although the pic's climactic scenes in shattered Bosnia have some impact.

Film takes the form of a letter to a former girlfriend, L..., who's written, asking, "When will you make a good film?" Goupil never really answers the question, but asks it of various people during his journey.

Pic opens in Moscow, where he receives L...'s letter, then moves to Paris, Venice, Berlin, the Gaza Strip (where stone-throwing Palestinian youths confront armed Israeli soldiers) and finally to Belgrade and war-torn Bosnia.

In Belgrade, Goupil confronts a popular Serb actress who's against the war. She becomes irritated with his following her around with a camera. In Sarajevo, he meets filmmaker Ademir Kenovic, who movingly tells what it's like to live in a once-great, multicultural European city. Goupil clearly had a lot of courage in going to Sarajevo, but the film is so haphazardly constructed that the impact is greatly reduced. Homages to Jean-Luc Godard, including a direct ref to his latest, "Oh, Woe Is Me," don't add much.
— *David Stratton*

TELLURIDE FEST

STELLA POLARIS

(NORWEGIAN)

An Oslo Film production. (International sales: Norwegian Film Institute, Oslo.) Produced by Egil Odegard. Directed, written by Knut Erik Jensen. Camera (color), Svein Krovel; editor, Trygve Hagen; music, Arne Nordheim; Dolby sound. Reviewed at Cannes Film Festival (market), May 21, 1993. (In Edinburgh, Telluride film festivals.) Running time: **86 MIN.**
Woman .... Anne Krigsvoll
Man .... Ketil Hoegh
Children .... Eirin Hargaut, Vegard Jensen

Skillfully blending docu inserts with an abstract art movie approach, "Stella Polaris" is a slim but moving portrait of a Norwegian fishing village forever changed by the Nazi occupation of World War II. First feature of documentarian Knut Erik Hansen is a choice bauble for fests and arthouse webs.

Set in Finnmark, land of the midnight sun, pic focuses on a couple and two children.

It's a film of small events: The couple make love in the fjords; a German soldier shoots the kids' cat; the women labor in the fish factory.

When the Germans raze the village to the ground during their retreat in 1944, the villagers are evacuated south.

Latter section shows a postwar freedom parade in Oslo (convincingly doubled by St. Petersburg), and the villagers' return north to rebuild their lives, capped by ironic modern-day footage of factories and intensive fishing techniques.

Pic grew out of Jensen's mammoth eight-hour docu on the region, "Finnmark Between East and West" (1986).

Though details are often vague — thanks to the almost complete lack of dialogue, with the passage of time marked only by glimpsed newspapers — the general line is clear enough.

The raw beauty of the locale, plus Arne Nordheim's churning score, build to an arresting elegy on a simple way of life forever changed by history and modernism.
— *Derek Elley*

LOCARNO FEST

BEIJING ZAZHONG

(BEIJING BASTARDS)

(HONG KONG-CHINESE)

A Beijing Bastards Group production, with aid from the Hubert Bals Fund, the French ministries of National Education, Culture and Foreign Affairs. (Foreign sales: Fortissimo Film, Amsterdam.) Produced by Cui Jian, Zhang Yuan, Shu Kei, Christopher Doyle. Directed by Zhang Yuan. Screenplay, Zhang Yuan, Tang Dalian, Cui Jian. Camera (color), Zhang Jian; editor, Feng Shungyuan; art direction, Liu Zhaodong; music, Cui Jian, Dou Wei, He Yong. Reviewed at Locarno Film Festival (competing), Aug. 12, 1993. (Also in Festival of Festivals, Toronto.) Running time: **95 MIN.**
Rock singer .... Cui Jian
Also with: Li Wei, Wu Gang, Bian Tianshuo, Tang Dalian, Bian Jing, Wen Li, Yu Feihong.

"Beijing Bastards" earns an assured niche for itself, along with an international arthouse life, for being the first film to tackle the anger and frustration of today's youth in China. The 30-year-old helmer Zhang Yuan hits hard at the frail social structures that offer no satisfaction to the post-Cultural Revolution generation growing up with sex, drugs and rock 'n' roll.

The film's Achilles' heel is a repetitive narrative structure that wears viewers out. Despite fest fanfare, it appears chiefly aimed at Chinese audiences, who will no doubt appreciate the film more than anyone else if they get a chance to see it.

Like Zhang's first film, the award-winning "Mama," "Beijing Bastards" was nixed for fest screenings by Chinese authorities, despite its Hong Kong production base. When Locarno refused to withdraw the picture from competition, China pulled its national entry from the meet in retaliation. Given the unsympathetic attitude of officialdom, it remains one of the contradictions of contemporary China that Zhang is able to continue making films, with independent financing and artistic control, about controversial topics.

Equally surprising is film's emphasis on rock music, and the fact Zhang cut his directing teeth making MTV video clips (he was the first in the country) for Chinese rock star Cui Jian. Though frowned upon, rock has been around for almost a decade in China, where it has become as much an anti-establishment force as it was years ago in the West.

Cui Jian, who helped write and finance "Beijing Bastards," appears a great deal in the film, both as performer and actor. The rocker's sound is a rhythmic, hard-rock punch in the stomach, and lyrics like "I only believe in myself" speak strongly about the emptiness of being 20 years old in China.

The young people here lead purposeless lives like disaffected kids everywhere. Pic implies they are spiritually caught between the Tiananmen Square trauma and the pull of economic liberalization, which allows the private sector to grow and presumably brings a measure of freedom. Thus, the main character Karzi is the owner of a pub featuring live music.

Reducing story line to a minimum, Zhang shows his characters one by one in unconnected actions whose common denominator is anger and resentment. Karzi has a fight with his pregnant girlfriend, Maomao, in the opening scene, and she disappears in the rain. For years, Cui Jian's band has been refused permission to perform a public concert — rock is tolerated only at private parties and clubs. Now they're losing their rehearsal room.

Karzi, continuing to search for Maomao, ends up raping one of her friends. Then, in a marijuana daze, he imagines her having an abortion. But one day he finds her in a deserted building with the baby she has given birth to — a bizarre note of hope that ends the film.

The film is structured around a long succession of beer-drinking sessions filled with banal dialogue that sounds improvised, intercut with small rock concerts. Though awfully repetitive, the gigs — like the fights, drinking and swearing — have a raw, primal realism that makes them highly convincing. For the same reason, the dark, grubby apartment buildings scattered through the film convey an image of Beijing life quite different from that normally shown.

"Bastards" communicates a strong sense of squalor and brutishness, a depressing lack of purpose and lack of contact between people. All told, pic is quite a downer. It is finely lensed by cinematographer Zhang Jian. — *Deborah Young*

SMUKKE DRENG

(PRETTY BOY)

(DANISH)

A Zentropa Entertainments Aps production. (International sales: Nordisk Film.) Produced by Peter Aalbsek Jensen, Ib Tardini. Directed, written by Carsten Sonder. Camera (color), Jackob Banke Olesen; editor, Henrik Fleischer; music, Joachim Holbek; production design, Soren Henriksen; sound, Nino Jacobsen; assistant director, Jannik Johansen. Reviewed at Screening Room, Leura, Australia, Aug. 18, 1993. (In Cannes Film Festival market.) Running time: **82 MIN.**
Nick Marcussen ..... Christian Tapdrup
Renee .... Benedicte W. Madsen
Max .... Rami Nathan Sverdlin
Ralph .... Stig Hoffmeyer
Mortensen .... Niels Jorgensen
Mother .... Kit Goetz
Grandmother .... Birgit Bruel

Apoignant tale of a 13-year-old runaway boy who turns to prostitution to survive, "Pretty Boy" explores a tricky theme with some delicacy. An unaffected performance from Christian Tapdrup, as the youngster, and Carsten Sonder's sensitive direction are pluses.

Nick has left home because (it's suggested) he hates the men his mother gets involved with. He latches on to Ralph (Stig Hoffmeyer), who lets him stay in his apartment and then seduces him. But when Ralph's female partner returns, Nick is unceremoniously thrown out.

For a while he lives on the street via his wits and his body, and then he becomes a member of a gang led by the androgynous Renee (Benedicte W. Madsen). After a while, Nick and Renee become lovers, but their happiness is short-lived, and the film ends with a violent confrontation between Nick and Ralph.

This sad little film, obviously produced on a modest budget, is likely to be of interest only to a minority audience. It's technically good, well acted, and commendably concise.
— *David Stratton*

AS AN EILEAN
(FROM THE ISLAND)
(BRITISH)

A Comataidh Telebhisein Gaidhlig/ Channel 4 presentation, in association with Grampian TV/Ross & Cromarty District Council, of a Pelicula Films production. (International sales: Jane Balfour Films, London.) Produced by Douglas Eadie, Mike Alexander. Executive producer, Rod Stoneman. Directed by Alexander. Screenplay, Eadie, based on "The Last Summer" and "The Hermit," by Iain Crichton Smith. Camera (color), Mark Littlewood; editor, Fiona Macdonald; music, Jim Sutherland; production design, Andrew Semple; costume design, Kate Carin; sound (Dolby), Phil Croal; Gaelic adviser, Tormod C. Domhnallach; associate producer, Eric Coulter; assistant director, Eric Coulter. Reviewed at Cannes Film Festival (market), May 18, 1993. (In Edinburgh Film Festival.) Running time: **99 MIN.**
McAllister .... Ken Hutchison
Callum Matheson .... Iain F. Macleod
Colin .... D.W. Stiubhart
Janet Campbell .... Wilma Kennedy
"The Hermit" .... Brian Croucher
Kirsty .... Donna Macleod
(Gaelic & English dialogue; English subtitles)

A neatly observed still life of a group of characters in a remote Scottish village, "From the Island" is a solid fest item that looks unlikely to make the crossing to theatrical.

Principals are a soccer-mad teen (Iain F. Macleod) torn between studies that will get him to a mainland university and first love with a girl (Donna Macleod); a retired schoolmaster (Ken Hutchison) chronicling village life who becomes obsessed with a silent stranger; and a nurse (Wilma Kennedy) due to get hitched to a local go-getter just back from Texas. Helmer Mike Alexander shows a surer hand here in juggling moods than in his scattershot Scottish comedy "Dreaming," made for pubcaster BBC in 1990. There's a nice blend of ironic comedy (small-town mentality) and simmering sexuality (the teens' confused love, plus the schoolmaster's secret passion for the nurse) that fuels the pic even when there's not much going on onscreen. Leisurely pacing, however, may prove a turnoff for some auds.

Performances and tech credits are all solid, with the Wester Ross, Scotland, locations looking fine in the blowup from Super-16mm.
—*Derek Elley*

THE WAR ROOM

A Pennebaker Associates production. Produced by R.J. Cutler, Wendy Ettinger, Frazer Pennebaker. Executive producers, Ettinger, Pennebaker. Directed by D.A. Pennebaker, Chris Hegedus. Camera (DuArt color), Nick Doob, D.A. Pennebaker, Kevin Rafferty; editors, Hegedus, Erez Laufer, D.A. Pennebaker; sound (Dolby), Charles Arnot, David Dawkins, Hegedus, Judy Karp; associate producer, Cyclone Films. Reviewed at Festival of Festivals, Toronto, Sept. 13, 1993. (Also in New York Film Festival.) Running time: **94 MIN.**
With: James Carville, George Stephanopoulos.

I f "The War Room" were a fictional feature, it would be a sure-fire star-making vehicle for James Carville. President Clinton's crafty, straight-talking campaign manager dominates this absorbing but basically unrevelatory behind-the-scenes look at the former Arkansas governor's long push for the presidency, which should see a good life wherever political documentaries are shown.

Like so many successful docus, D.A. Pennebaker and Chris Hegedus' first political work since 1977's "The Energy War" was the beneficiary of exceptional good luck, in that the only campaign that would allow the filmmakers exclusive access went on to be the winning team.

With Clinton as a sort of secondary character who pops in periodically, pic charts the nine-month pregnancy of his battle for the White House from the perspective of his key strategists, Carville and communications director George Stephanopoulos.

From frigid New Hampshire to the inner sanctum of their Little Rock h.q. on election night, the two young men and their staffs could almost as easily pass for grad students plotting a campus event as professionals whose hunches and whims will profoundly mark the world political landscape.

Pennebaker and Hegedus came on board in time for the Democratic Convention in New York, but previous material involving the primaries, the Gennifer Flowers controversy and other incidents has been seamlessly added to provide a strong overriding arc for the film. Presentation of the candidate's major campaign points and promises, along with such factors as the "character problem," the Tsongas and Brown challenges, the Perot threat and Clinton's disappearing voice toward the end, will revive the issues surrounding the election race for the first time for most viewers, thus creating a historical p.o.v. very soon after the fact.

With his country boy Cajun accent, fast thinking and frank talking, Carville is a disarming presence from the get-go. Sneering that "I think of an old calendar when I look at George Bush's face," Carville is usually seen on the phone or addressing his troops, and he follows a very emotional speech on election eve with a mocking concession speech. Camera also briefly catches him with his g.f., Bush campaign coordinator Mary Matalin, but no further insight is gained into their most irregular relationship.

Not at all the typical political backroom type in his T-shirt and jeans, Carville radiates energy and intelligence and inspires confidence by never getting rattled, temperamental or belligerent.

By contrast, Stephanopoulos comes off as low-key and guarded, but still smart and clever. The negative aspects of his personality alluded to by the press after Clinton took office and then reassigned him are not readily apparent here.

The frenzy and excitement of the campaign effectively propel the film, which doesn't reveal any astonishing new information about tactics or strategies. Still, one of the most interesting sequences details Carville's efforts to interest the press in his discovery that some Bush-Quayle campaign materials were printed in Brazil. This miniscandal never even became a news item simply because it didn't make it onto television.

Cinema verite pioneer Pennebaker, whose early work included the landmark political docus "Crisis" and "Primary," has, with his wife, Hegedus, and their collaborators, valuably added to the official record with this fresh angle on the U.S. political process. Even if it doesn't offer any major surprises, it's effectively upfront and in close.

Martin Scorsese's name is misspelled in the closing thank-you credits. —*Todd McCarthy*

SHIMMER

An American Playhouse Theatrical Films presentation in association with WMG and Kinowelt. Produced by Peter Deegan. Executive producers, Lindsay Law, Sandra Schulberg, Hans Brockman, Rainer Kolmel. Directed by John Hanson. Screenplay, John O'Keefe, based on his play. Line producer, Jeff Buchanan. Camera (color/ b&w), Stephen Lighthill; editor, Lisa Fruchtman; music, Todd Boekelheide; production design, David Lubin; sound mixer, Dan Gleich. Reviewed at the Roxie Cinema, San Francisco, Sept. 20, 1993. (In Festival of Festivals, Toronto; Mill Valley Film Festival.) Running time: **95 MIN.**
Spacy Callahan .... Marcus Klemp
Gary Finch .... Elijah Shepard
Mother .... Mary Beth Hurt
Mr. Speck .... Tom Bower
Teats Bower .... Clem Tucker Jr.
Tony Kelmer .... Patrick LaBrecque
Richard Halverson .... Jake Busey
Also with: Michael Hyland, Robert Breuler, Mary Forcade, Benjamin Salisbury, William Francis McGuire.

S tage writer-actor John O'Keefe's acclaimed monologue "Shimmer" inevitably loses magic in translation to conventionally dramatized screen form. But this American Playhouse production translates the source's verbal lyricism well enough to court arthouse attention, despite familiarity of theme. Cable and vid sales will likely prove a better long-term bet.

Autobiographical narrative is set in 1956. Hero Spacy Callahan (Marcus Klemp) has been stuck for years at an Iowa juvenile home whose bucolic setting masks harsh treatment from employees and an even more brutal hierarchy among "inmates." Transgressions might mean an isolated stretch in "lockup" under Bible-reciting molester Mr. Kibby.

Spacy befriends a new arrival, the equally plucky and imaginative Gary (Elijah Shepard). When the lockup release of a dim-bulb imperils their health, the two boys plot and execute an escape.

B&W memories define Spacy's troubled childhood as sole offspring of a low-income couple; one harrowing flashback shows his drunken, violent father in action. But Spacy yearns to rejoin his embattled, now single mom (Mary Beth Hurt).

Centerpiece is the boys' flight to Hurt's abode. Director John Hanson realizes this journey by means that are familiar yet capture scenarist O'Keefe's lilt — via time-lapse skyscapes and handsome nighttime vistas, one gets an adolescent sense of the world as mysterious yet magical.

Juve performances are a bit awkward at the outset, but gain assurance as pic progresses. The briefly utilized Hurt and others do well as adult archetypes. While basic coming-of-age theme provokes *deja vu*, the uniquely bleak period setting works nicely, and the writer's poetical leanings are adequately realized.

One might imagine a more deeply poetical/surreal "Shimmer" in the hands of Gus Van Sant, whose sympathy to misunderstood-baby-boy melodrama routinely assumes the spectral dimension required here. Yet Hanson manages poignancy well enough to draw a tear of empathy at O'Keefe's transcendent, ambiguous conclusion.
—*Dennis Harvey*

THE MAKING OF ...
AND GOD SPOKE

A Brookwood Entertainment production. Produced by Mark Rothman, Richard Raddon. Directed by Arthur Borman. Screenplay, Greg Malins, Michael Curtis. Camera (color), Lee Daniel; editor, Wendy Stanzler; music, John Masarri; art direction, Joe Tintfass; sound (Stereo), Brian Tracy. Reviewed at Festival of Festivals, Toronto, Sept. 17, 1993. Running time: **90 MIN.**

Clive Walton .... Michael Riley
Marvin Handleman ....
Steven Rappaport

By standards of new, irreverent documentaries, the humor in "The Making of ... And God Spoke" is too sane and too safe to qualify as a midnight movie, as it was shown at the Toronto fest. The always good-natured frolic and nearly always funny mock docu should appeal to young, hip viewers in major urban centers.

The versatile Michael Riley is perfectly cast as Clive Walton, director of a humongous biblical epic, produced by Marvin Handleman (Steven Rappaport). It's one step up the ladder for the two, after teaming together on a number of B-movies on the order of "Dial S for Sex" and "The Nude Ninjas."

Caper follows their film's execution phase by phase, from pre-production to theatrical release. Chief problems with this loose, anecdotal comedy are that its humor is predictable and that it basically revolves around the mutations of one good joke. There have been so many accounts, both serious and comical, about behind-the-scenes filmmaking shenanigans that most viewers are not going to be surprised by the disasters and mishaps that this made-in-heaven team faces.

Satire's first, and best, part details the preparation of the screenplay and casting. When the script proves too long, major but depressing characters like Job are omitted without a blink. Other highlights include the casting sessions for Jesus and Virgin Mary, and the lensing of Adam and Eve, with the latter unexpectedly revealing a huge tattoo. When Moses descends from the mountain, a six-pack of Coca-Cola is detected by the distressed director; he's told that product placement was a financial necessity.

Fast pacing, blend of accents and acting styles, and some hilarious one-liners compensate in a comedy that doesn't boast too many spurts of inspiration.

One weak sequence involves the securing of funds for the film's completion. Miraculously, however, pic regains its initial verve and gusto and concludes on a euphoric note, when the biblical epic assumes a cult status like the notorious midnight flick "The Rocky Horror Picture Show."

Best possible scenario would have this following the fate of that 1975 cult hit, with lines of people, all dressed in biblical regalia, waiting to see the film and participate in its "religious" experience.

—*Emanuel Levy*

D'EST
(FROM THE EAST)
(FRENCH-BELGIAN-PORTUGUESE)

A Paradise Films/Lieurac Prods. presentation. (Foreign sales: Lieurac Prods., Paris.) Produced by Francois Le Bayon. Executive producer, Marilyn Watelet. Directed, written by Chantal Akerman. Camera (color), Raimond Froment, Bernard Delville; editor, Claire Atherton; sound, Pierre Mertens. Reviewed at Festival of Festivals, Toronto, Sept. 14, 1993. Running time: **106 MIN.**

Applying her minimalist approach to the changing reality of Eastern Europe, avant-garde director Chantal Akerman's "From the East" is one of her most demanding "semi-fictional" documentaries. Even by standards of her own work, the utterly wordless film is one of Akerman's least accessible. At the same time, pic is a must-see for cinephiles concerned with the unique language of cinema.

Taking her relentless cameras from East Germany to Russia, Akerman delivers an impressionistic report from the new front. Displaying her distinctive visual style, influenced by structuralism and minimalism, her journal unfolds as a procession of postcards that record empty landscapes and people positioned against them.

Akerman's dialectical strategy consists of a series of oppositions, including the seasons and time of the day. Spanning summer to winter, docu chronicles the countryside of East Germany, the beaches of the Baltics, the traffic of Poland, the snowy streets of Moscow.

Alternating a studiously static camera with lengthy tracking shots, and using no dialogue or commentary and very little music, Akerman captures the essence, if not the historical particulars, of a region on the move. The dominant visual motifs — people marching and people waiting in large train stations — reinforce the sense of uncertainty in the face of continuous change.

As with every Akerman work, the new film is as much about a specific subject as about the relationship between narrative, space and time. However, this may be one of her few films without astute consideration of gender or discussion of women's role in modern society.

As a filmmaker, Akerman is full of surprises: Those who thought that her work would become more "commercial" after "The Golden Eighties," a satire of musicals with plot and fast pacing, or "Histoires d'Amerique" will be disappointed. Befitting the film that received the most walkouts at the Toronto fest, some viewers will complain that it's a boring, meaningless minimalist exercise. Akerman's fans, however, will be awed again by her visual aesthetics and consider it a footnote in the career of a truly innovative artist.

—*Emanuel Levy*

ICH WILL NICHT NUR, DASS IHR MICH LIEBT
(I DON'T JUST WANT YOU TO LOVE ME)
(GERMAN — DOCU)

A Pro-ject Filmproduktion im Filmverlag der Autoren production. Produced by Theo Hinz. Directed, written by Hans Gunther Pflaum. Camera (color/b&w), Werner Kurz, Manfred Burkie; editor, Ingrid Wolff; sound, Martin Muller, Manuel Laval, David Heinemann. Reviewed at Festival of Festivals, Toronto, Sept. 12, 1993. Running time: **96 MIN.**
With: Rainer Werner Fassbinder, Hanna Schygulla, Karlheinz Boehm, Ingrid Caven, Andrea Ferreol, Kurt Raab, Volker Schloendorff, Peter Zadek, Dietrich Lohmann, Harry Baer, Lilo Eder, Michael Ballhaus.

The late Rainer Werner Fassbinder, arguably the most important director of the New German Cinema, deserves better treatment than he gets in "I Don't Just Want You to Love Me," a disappointing documentary that contains too many glaring omissions. Nonetheless, being the first docu about Fassbinder, who died in 1982 at the age of 37, and offering some valuable insights about his work, if not personal life, it has good chances for a limited theatrical release, particularly in connection with Fassbinder retrospectives, and later on public TV, cable and video.

Written and directed by Hans Gunther Pflaum, who has also published a book on the subject, docu might as well have been titled "Observations on Fassbinder," for it's not a chronological or systematic account of the filmmaker's career or life. Instead, its awkward structure consists of nine chapters, divided along thematic lines.

Fassbinder's mother, Lilo Eder, provides some anecdotal material about his childhood, most notably his stubbornness ("He would not be ignored"), loneliness and sensitivity, and there is useful information about his stage career and the "Anti-Theater" company he established in 1967.

Actress Hanna Schygulla claims that Fassbinder wasn't spontaneous or instinctual, but precise, conscious and calculating. "He was just faster than most," she says, "he always had the cuts in his head." One reason why Fassbinder was so prolific was his competitive urge — if Jean-Luc Godard made three films in one year, he had to make four. In a career that spanned 15 years, Fassbinder directed over 50 films and TV dramas.

Other actors, including an AIDS-ridden Kurt Raab, talk about the vital function of his stage troupe, and later cast and crew, as family substitutes. For his part, Fassbinder, who is heard from in several interviews, relates how all his life he was around people "looking for both father and mother."

Docu includes several film excerpts, with visual and textual analysis. But despite the fact that a whole sequence is shown from "Fox and His Friends," one of the first gay German films, in which Fassbinder played the lead, there is no discussion of the director's homosexuality and how it was reflected in his distinctive sensibility.

Other conspicuous oversights include failure to acknowledge the influence of Hollywood's melodramas and Douglas Sirk on Fassbinder's style. Finally, even though it was public knowledge that Fassbinder died of a cocaine overdose, only his excessive drinking — and never drugs — is mentioned as an integral part of his lifestyle.

Flawed as it is, "I Don't Just Want You to Love Me" deserves to be seen — until a better, more thorough docu is made about the versatile director, who revolutionized post-WWII German cinema and helped put it on the international film map. —*Emanuel Levy*

DER OLYMPISCHE SOMMER
(THE OLYMPIC SUMMER)
(GERMAN — B&W)

A Film und Fernsehproduktionen GbR (Heidelberg) production. Executive producer, Gordian Maugg. Produced by Suzanne Binninger. Directed, written by Maugg, based on the novel "The Apprentice," by Gunther Rucker. Camera (b&w), Andreas Giesecke; editors, Monika Schindler, Behzad Behestipour; music, Heidi Aydt, Frank Will; production design, Gunter Reisch; costume design, Klaus Geidis, Hanjoachim Kathen, Klaus Kirchner; set decoration, Angelika Kraus; sound, Guido Kuhn, Omid Azmi; special effects, Hans Moser, Thomas Rosie; narrator, Otto Sander. Reviewed at Seattle Film Festival, June 3, 1993. (Also in Festival of Festivals, Toronto.) Running time: **85 MIN.**
Apprentice .... Jost Gerstein
Widow .... Verena Plangger
Butcher .... Otto Ruck
Student .... Uwe Mauch
SA Man .... Christoph Rapp
Also with: Johanna Maugg, Gordian Maugg Sr., Werner Schmetzer, Marcus Hambsch, Uwe Juppe, Astrid Warnken, Chris Krikellis, Andreas Giesecke.

Bound to baffle auds other than committed students of early cinema or German history, "The Olympic Summer" is nonetheless an audacious stylistic experiment and a valuable document. Wrapping a silent film-like scenario around rarely seen images of everyday life in Nazi-era Berlin, it earns a unique place in the libraries of film schools and universities.

Shot in staccato b&w on a 1927 Askania camera (and blown up to 35mm), pic could pass for a genuine artifact from between the wars. With its brooding close-up, off-kilter compositions and pastoral, if disconcertingly sped-up, long shots, it more than glancingly recalls the rolling, hypnotic mood of silents such as "Pandora's Box" and early talkies like "L'Atalante."

Clearly, that's only the starting point for young Heidelberg helmer Gordian Maugg (he was born in 1966), who fashions an allegory for the Third Reich around the elemental tale of a naive butcher's apprentice (Jost Gerstein) and his prolonged fall from innocence.

Leaving his characters unnamed and mute (the pic is narrated, sonorously, by "Wings of Desire" angel Otto Sander) may have been a commercially disastrous choice, but Maugg's pictures, courtesy of lenser Andreas Giesecke, take on the quality of half-remembered myth — although not the kind that Leni Riefenstahl had in mind.

In this scratchy, herky-jerk context, deftly intercut footage of real Berlin street scenes from the period leading up to the 1936 Olympics appear oddly modern (it's unnerving to see the smiles, the ice cream cones and the German and American flags fluttering side by side).

Unfortunately, the archival material is so strong it slowly overwhelms the slim saga of the apprentice, his troubled relationship with a homely widow (Verena Plangger) and his subsequent slide into urban despair — including an ill-fated friendship with a homosexual SA man and, after the war is under way, a return to his butchering skills as horses die in the charnel house called Berlin.

Some of the "romantic" material (the Vaterland's star-crossed affair with Herr Hitler?) is recycled so often that the pic's 85 minutes feel padded, and the final quarter — set in various prisons — is appropriately claustrophobic, if dramatically unengaging.

Still, "The Olympic Summer" is as much to be listened to as looked at, since it collects genuine radio broadcasts, pop songs and other aural ephemera from a setting that's already been combed for meaning in more obvious ways. This time-capsule-in-reverse will never set any B.O. records, but it does represent a quiet triumph of its own.　*—Ken Eisner*

SEVEN SONGS FOR MALCOLM X

(BRITISH—DOCU—COLOR/&W-16mm)

A Black Audio Film Collective (London) production. (Foreign sales: Jane Balfour Films Ltd., London.) Produced by Lina Gopaul. Directed by John Akomfrah. Screenplay, Akomfrah, Edward George. Camera (color7&w), Arthur Jafa; editor, Joy Chamberlain; music, sound, Trevor Mathison. Reviewed at Seattle Film Festival, June 3, 1993. (Also in Festival of Festivals, Toronto.) Running time: **52 MIN.**
Narrators: Giancarlo Esposito (from texts by Malcolm X), Toni Claude Bambara.
With: Betty Shabazz, Spike Lee, Thulani Davis, Greg Tate, Wilfred Little.

Brit helmer John Akomfrah, who made the profoundly impressionistic "Handsworth Songs" with the Black Audio Film Collective, manages to find fresh angles on the now-familiar saga of Malcolm X, but he makes auds work hard for their rewards.

Festival life should be healthy, but the short pic's artsy mix of stark, interpretive tableaux and tersely cut talking heads may keep it out of mainstream educational circuits. A more timely release would have helped this stylish docu, but X-followers will seek it out anyway.

Shuffling from arrestingly color-tinted b&w interviews to emblematic, elegantly static moments from Malcolm's life, pic takes too long to find an engaging rhythm. Scholars will be able to glean some brief but probing quotes from (poorly identified) subjects, such as writers Thulani Davis and Greg Tate, as well as seldom-heard sources such as the subject's brother, Wilfred Little.

Spike Lee, just releasing his "Malcolm X" at the time he was interviewed, comes across as glib, and Malcolm's widow, Betty Shabazz, is represented by stunningly feeble utterances.

Where film succeeds best is in its subtle evocation of the emotional hangover left by this complex figure's spiritual transformations and untimely demise.　*—Ken Eisner*

FOR LOVE OR MONEY

A Universal Pictures release of an Imagine Films Entertainment presentation. Produced by Brian Grazer. Executive producer, David T. Friendly. Directed, co-produced by Barry Sonnenfeld. Screenplay, Mark Rosenthal and Lawrence Konner. Camera (Deluxe), Oliver Wood; editor, Jim Miller; music, Bruce Broughton; production design, Peter Larkin; art direction, Charley Beal; set decoration, Leslie Rollins; costume design, Susan Lyall; sound (Dolby), Peter Kurland; assistant director, Mark McGann; casting, John Lyons. Reviewed at the Writers Guild Theater, Sept. 22, 1993. MPAA Rating: PG. Running Time: **94 MIN.**

Doug Ireland	Michael J. Fox
Andy Hart	Gabrielle Anwar
Christian Hanover	Anthony Higgins
Harry Wegman	Michael Tucker
Mr. Drinkwater	Bob Balaban
Mr. Himmelman	Udo Kier
Gene Salvatore	Dan Hedaya
Milton Glickman	Fyvush Finkel
Mrs. Vigushin	Paula Laurence
Julian Russell	Isaac Mizrahi
Gary Taubin	Patrick Breen

Michael J. Fox has charm to burn in his latest screen outing, "For Love or Money." A contemporary spin on bygone romantic comedies, the tale of an ambitious young man and the seemingly elusive woman in his life has a definite emotional pull. It falls short on story, however, and no amount of good humor can deter the thin tale from evaporating before the final clinch.

This is unquestionably a film designed for a movie star and, therefore, will be a true test of Fox's appeal. The likely conclusion is that the actor has not yet reached a level where popularity can overcome the quality of his material.

Doug Ireland (Fox) takes on the role of head concierge at an upscale Manhattan hotel with the zeal of a Sammy Glick. What makes Doug tick is the dream of putting together the financial package for a luxury hotel.

Unlike the fictional prototype, Doug wouldn't step over someone to reach his goal. The only trouble can come from his association with charismatic financier Christian Hanover (Anthony Higgins). But the "love" aspect of the title is indeed complex. Hanover just happens to be deep into an extramarital affair with Andy (Gabrielle Anwar), the very woman for whom Doug would actually take time out in his busy schedule.

Naturally, the dilemma is the juggling act. He wants to reciprocate Hanover's financial largesse by running interference with Andy, Mrs. Hanover and the Hamptons crowd. Just how much crow can Doug eat for $5 million? Healthy guy that he is, quite a bit.

Call it screwball, call it zany, call it just a bit too convenient for comfort. But this shouldn't necessarily be a detriment. Writers Mark Rosenthal and Lawrence Konner lack the deft touch of Preston Sturges or Billy Wilder, and director Barry Sonnenfeld has not quite perfected a modern Lubitsch touch.

The central flaw of "For Love or Money" is focus. Fox is charming and, as one character aptly notes, his hustling at the hotel is not about money; what he does comes from the heart. Still, what ought to be an intriguing triangle comes off less than bubbly. The real fun comes from watching Fox skillfully navigate treacherous waters at the hotel and come out a winner, with the aid — conscious or otherwise — of a motley, if colorful, staff.

Higgins is a nicely observed evil foil; Anwar is not very interesting in a sketchily realized role.

Sonnenfeld's style appropriately verges on the elegant. By nature, this is a souffle. Unfortunately its chief ingredient — the script — deflates the whole concoction.
　—Leonard Klady

LA SOIF D'OR
(THE THIRST FOR GOLD)
(FRENCH)

A Gaumont Buena Vista Intl. release (France) of a Gaumont/G Films/TF1 Films Prod. production, with participation of Canal Plus. (International sales: Gaumont Intl.) Produced by Alain Poire. Directed by Gerard Oury. Screenplay, Oury, Marcel Jullian, Christian Clavier. Camera (color), Tonino Delli Colli; editor, Pierre Gillette; music, Vladimir Cosma; production design, Willy Holt; costume design, Catherine Leterrier; sound (Dolby), Alain Sempe; special effects, Jean-Louis Trinquier. Reviewed at Bretagne Cinema, Paris, Sept. 5, 1993. Running time: **84 MIN.**
Urbain Donnadieu .... Christian Clavier
Grandma Zezette .... Tsilla Chelton
Fleurette .... Catherine Jacob
Jacques .... Philippe Khorsand
Also with: Marine Delterme, Bernard Haller, Pascal Greggory.

"The Thirst for Gold" is a frenetic and excessive comedy about greed that should do biz on the strength of comedy helmer Gerard Oury's rep and comedy staple Christian Clavier's increased marquee value after boffo local hit "Les Visiteurs."

Following cute Monty Pythonesque opening credits, pic's tone is set with a madcap sequence of Clavier chasing a 500-franc note through traffic at Place de la Concorde and finally nailing the wind-borne bill on a pile of dog excrement.

Clavier plays an avaricious cheapskate who's embezzled a fortune from his prefab-home company before the business reverts to his estranged wife (Catherine Jacob), a former tax-fraud inspector who roped him into marriage.

In cahoots with his equally greedy grandma (Tsilla Chelton, who played "Tatie Daniele"), he plans to smuggle to Switzerland his stash of gold bars, hidden in the wall of a model home transported on a trailer. Clavier's wife and trusted chauffeur, who have secretly been an item for years, realize they've been rooked and set out to intercept the gold.

Result is a prolonged, often bawdy chase that sports good, if not inspired, gags and adequate comic timing, though full-bore perfs can't keep the intrigue from flagging toward the end. Oury settles for giggles and a few well-executed stunts, with no subtext to deepen the slapstick humor. All the characters are basically unpleasant.

Lensing is perfunctory but makes good use of Paris locations.
　—Lisa Nesselson

October 11, 1993 (Cont.)

LOCARNO FEST

BHAJI ON THE BEACH

(BRITISH)

A Film Four production. (International sales: Film Four Intl., London.) Produced by Nadine Marsh Edwards. Directed by Gurinder Chadha. Screenplay, Meera Syal. Camera (color), John Kenway; editor, Oral Ottley; music, John Altman, Craig Preuss. Reviewed at Locarno Film Festival (competing), Aug. 10, 1993. (Also in Edinburgh, Toronto fests.) Running time: **100 MIN.**
Ginder .... Kim Vithana
Ranjit .... Jimmi Harkishin
Hashida .... Sarita Khajuria
Oliver .... Mo Sesay
Asha .... Lalita Ahmed
Simi .... Shaheen Khan
Also with: Peter Cellier, Zohra Segal, Shaheen Khan.

Director Gurinder Chadha makes a splashy feature bow with the comedy-drama "Bhaji on the Beach," a kind of "Mississippi Masala" set in England about a group of Indian women who take a day off at the beach. Humanly appealing and quite feminist, it should encounter few difficulties on the art-film circuit.

Chadha sets a huge cast of characters in motion, with as little fuss as Simi (Shaheen Khan) runs the Saheli Asian Women's Center. She musters crabby old ladies, gadabout teens and warring families with big secrets on an all-femme day excursion to the northern working-class resort of Blackpool, a kind of British Coney Island.

Ginder (Kim Vithana), an attractive young mother, is going through a painful divorce from her husband (Jimmi Harkishin), a sentimental wife-beater. He and his brothers follow her to Blackpool to drag her and their little boy back to the oppressive family hearth. Hashida (Sarita Khajuria) is getting ready for university when she discovers she's pregnant by her black boyfriend, Oliver (Mo Sesay), who also takes off after her.

The day proves cathartic for everyone. Severe, tradition-bound aunt Asha (Lalita Ahmed) discovers new emotions when an old English actor squires her around. A chic relative from Bombay scoffs at their saris and outmoded traditions, reminding them they're out of touch with today's India.

"Bhaji" gets a lot of laughs at the expense of the extended Anglo-Indian family, which resembles big ethnic families anywhere. Sexism and racism are treated comically, without losing their sting — such as the taunting of some punks, whom Simi almost runs over in revenge.

At times the hypocritical old ladies are a little too easy a target for Chadha's irony, but their Technicolor fantasies about Indian ro-

mance, or about the loose morals of the younger women, strike a note of high hilarity.

Pace is fast, lensing sure-footed and the whole cast fetching. John Altman and Craig Preuss' lively score wittily underlines the contrast between traditional Indian and modern Western culture.

—*Deborah Young*

STARTING PLACE/ POINT DE DEPART

(FRENCH — DOCU)

A Film d'Ici/Ruben Korenfeld/Richard Copans production. Directed, written, edited by Robert Kramer. Camera (color), Kramer. Reviewed at Locarno Film Festival, Aug. 12, 1993. (Also in Telluride Film Festival.) Running time: **90 MIN.**
(In French)

In "Starting Place/Point de depart," militant American documaker Robert Kramer movingly revisits Vietnam and the people he filmed in his 1969 short "People's War." A favorite with auds at Locarno, where it premiered, "Starting Place" should find a welcome home on TV, after an extensive run at fests and in specialized theatrical venues.

Docu is the work of a mature filmmaker. It's both more open to reality and more critical, with far less propagandistic appeal, than the 40-minute "People's War,"which passionately championed North Vietnam, an underdeveloped country whose success against U.S. technical sophistication, he suggests, depended on the mobilization of the entire population to the war effort.

Two decades later, Kramer finds Vietnam poised between its communist past and the beginnings of a market economy. The images are edited eclectically, mixing past and present, and viewers are free to draw their own conclusions.

A strong counterpoint to Kramer's Vietnam-today footage is his interview with anti-war activist Linda Evans, who went to Hanoi with him in 1969. Now serving a 40-year sentence in a California prison, Evans articulates an astonishing commitment to her ideas, despite the evident strain of prison life, which leads her at one point to break down in tears.

Kramer's intense involvement with the country during the war years lends the docu great poignancy. Even the simplest shots — slow pans over the landscape, a war-damaged Hanoi bridge, people going about their business — ring out with relevance, like a painful, half-buried memory brought to the surface. Filming is of a high technical standard. —*Deborah Young*

AU NOM DU CHRIST

(IN THE NAME OF CHRIST)

(IVORY COAST-SWISS)

A Les Films Abyssa (Ivory Coast)/ Amka Films Prods. (Switzerland) production. Executive producer, Tiziana Soudani. Directed by Roger Gnoan M'Bala. Screenplay, Gnoan M'Bala, Jean-Marie Adiaffi, Bertin Akaffou. Camera (color), Mohammed Soudani; editor, Djangoye Ahoussy; music, Paul Wassaba; art direction, Jean-Baptiste Lerro. Reviewed at Locarno Film Festival (competing), Aug. 6, 1993. Running time: **90 MIN.**
Magloire the First .... Pierre Gondo
Bewitched Woman .... Akissi Delta
Also with: Naky Sy Savane, Lauceni Hasssane, Gazeknagnon.
(French dialogue)

Shyster religion spells power in "In the Name of Christ," a sobering fable on the growing clout of aberrant sects and the changing structures in African village life. With elements of caricature and satire, Ivory Coast director Roger Gnoan M'Bala gives pic a fresh quality that will be appreciated by specialized auds.

Christianity comes to a little West African village after an outcast swineherd (Pierre Gondo) falls into the river and has a vision of a black baby Jesus, who tells him he has been chosen to save his people.

Dubbing himself Magloire the First, the swineherd claims to be "the cousin of Christ." The villagers' scorn turns to awe when Magloire works some trumped-up miracles — like personally impregnating a "sterile" woman and curing a mad woman (Akissi Delta) possessed by a sorcerer.

At first, Magloire's preaching has the comic edge of social satire. (Why are there rich and poor, good and evil, on the Earth? "For balance," he replies.) But as his power grows, so does the evil he perpetrates "in the name of Christ."

In one horrifying scene, he has the childless woman's husband castrated off-screen. Claiming himself incapable of sin, he sleeps with numerous married women, who then dress like nuns and feed him from their hands.

Though cinematically unsophisticated, the film is a pleasure to watch. Some of Mohammed Soudani's cinematography is stirring, like the night lensing of red-gowned singers and emerald forests. Paul Wassaba's score takes its cue from the liturgical music of native sects. Pic won top prize at the Pan-African Film Festival in Ouagadougou earlier this year.

—*Deborah Young*

MARCIDES

(MERCEDES)

(EGYPTIAN-FRENCH)

A Misr Intl. Films/Paris Classics Prod./La Sept production. Produced by Gabriel Khoury, Humbert Balsan. Directed, written by Yousry Nasrallah. Camera (color/b&w), Ramses Marzouk; editor, Rachida Abdel Salam; music, Mohamed Nouh; art direction, Onsi Abou Seif. Reviewed at Locarno Film Festival (competing), Aug. 11, 1993. (Also in Festival of Festivals, Toronto.) Running time: **108 MIN.**
Warda/Afifa .... Yousra
Noubi .... Zaki Abdel Wahab
Rawheya .... Abla Kamel
Mohamed Taher .... Seif Eddine
Raifa .... Menha Batraoui
Gamal .... Magdi Kamel
Achraf .... Bassem Samra

Fans of helmer Yousry Nasrallah's first feature, "Vols d'Ete," will be disappointed by his change of gear in "Mercedes." This wise, would-be political, off-the-wall soap opera has an outrageous fascination of its own, but outside Egypt the pic's appeal looks limited to select fest auds.

Pic opens splendidly (in black-and-white) at a high-society party in Cairo some 20-30 years ago. A beautiful woman (Yousra), sitting properly beside her mother and the aged man she's pledged to marry, informs her mother she's pregnant.

Mama hastily marries her off and the woman gives birth to a son, Noubi. In the space of a single sequence, her husband dies, she secretly gets pregnant by her brother and abandons the baby, Gamal.

Now a man, Noubi (stiffly acted by an overage Zaki Abdel Wahab) is both a Marxist and extremely rich. In one of its sporadic moments of wit, pic explains he has been living in a mental hospital because he tried to give his fortune to the Communist Party.

Noubi sets off in search of Gamal, whom he thinks is his cousin, hoping to give him some money. He glimpses him in a flea-bitten cinema frequented by gays, but Gamal and his boyfriend, Achraf, elude him. Instead he falls for a virgin belly dancer from the slums (also played by the lively Yousra) who looks like his mother. As a background to all this nonsense, Nasrallah stirs in the World Soccer Games, the Gulf crisis, the birth of a violent fundamentalist movement and the fall of socialism in Eastern Europe. It's a heady cocktail which, kept under control, could have ended with a bang instead of bewilderment.

—*Deborah Young*

BOSTON FEST

BANK ROBBER

An IRS Releasing release of an IRS Media Inc. and Initial Groupe presentation. Produced by Lila Cazes. Executive producer, Jean Cazes, Paul Colichman, Miles Copeland III. Directed, written by Nick Mead. Camera (Fotokem color, Panavision), Andrzej Sekula; editors, Richard E. Westover, Maysie Hoy; music, Stewart Copeland; production design, Scott A. Chambliss; art direction, Bradley Wishan; set decoration, Karen Manthey; costume design, Dana Allyson; sound, (Ultra-Stereo) Chuck Buch; assistant director, James B. Rogers; second unit camera, Alan Sherrod; casting, Donald Paul Pemrick. Reviewed at Loews Copley Place, Boston, Sept. 10, 1993. (In Boston Film Festival.) Running time: **91 MIN.**

Billy	Patrick Dempsey
Priscilla	Lisa Bonet
Officer Gross	Judge Reinhold
Officer Battle	Forest Whitaker
Selina	Olivia D'Abo
Marisa Benoit	Mariska Hargitay
Night Clerk 1	Michael Jeter
Night Clerk 2	Joe Alaskey

Debut by Brit helmer Nick Mead is a one-joke movie, and the joke isn't especially funny. Theatrical prospects are dim, but undraping of Olivia D'Abo, Lisa Bonet and star Patrick Dempsey might give this title some life on video and cable. Nudity is pretty mild, but femme leads are exploitable names from television.

Script by Mead has to do with a bank robber (Dempsey) whose mask slips during a small-time hold-up. A video camera catches a glimpse of his face and now everyone is looking for him. After Dempsey holes up at a seedy hotel, nearly everyone who comes into contact with him wants hush money for not revealing where he is. This includes the night clerks (with Michael Jeter utterly wasted in a nothing part) and various delivery people. Forest Whitaker and Judge Reinhold are incomprehensible as two philosophizing, pot-smoking cops trying to find him. Script never answers obvious question of why Dempsey doesn't simply move to another hotel once he's discovered.

The two women are his shallow girlfriend (D'Abo), who beds down with Dempsey's friends after the holdup, and the cliched hooker-with-a-heart-of-gold (Bonet) who falls in love with him. Neither brings her two-dimensional character to life, and Dempsey's not up to the burden of carrying the film on his own.

Tech credits are solid for a low-budget film that's confined mostly to one set, and credit must go to cinematographer Andrzej Sekula and the art department for keeping the film visually interesting despite the emptiness of the plot and characters. —*Daniel M. Kimmel*

THE CUSTODIAN

(AUSTRALIAN)

A Beyond Films Ltd. release of a J D Prods. and John Dingwall presentation. Produced by Adrienne Read. Executive producers, Gary Hamilton, Mikael Borglund. Directed, written by Dingwall. Camera (color) Steve Mason; editor, Michael Honey; music, Phillip Houghton; production design, Philip Warner; art direction, Ian Gracie; set decoration, Kerrie Brown, Alky Avramides; costume design, Terry Ryan; sound (Dolby), Ben Osmo; assistant director, Adrian Pickersgill; second unit camera, Simon Smith; casting, Alison Barrett. Reviewed at Loews Copley Place, Boston, Sept. 15, 1993. (In the Boston Film Festival.) Running time: **109 MIN.**

Quinlan	Anthony LaPaglia
Church	Hugo Weaving
Ferguson	Barry Otto
Reynolds	Kelly Dingwall
Jilly	Essie Davis
Josie	Gosia Dobrowolska
Managing Director	Bill Hunter

Stateside audiences may be intrigued at prospect of seeing streetwise Anthony LaPaglia return to his Australian roots, but uneven film about police corruption Down Under gives him the least interesting role in the picture. Theatrical prospects look limited, but LaPaglia's presence insures ancillary afterlife.

LaPaglia usually scores in easy-going roles on either side of the law, but his character here, Quinlan, is offputtingly uptight. At the outset, Quinlan is on the verge of a nervous breakdown, his marriage has disintegrated, and he's realized that virtually everyone in the police department is on the take, including his partner.

Quinlan decides to go on the take himself to get the evidence to break the ring of corruption. He anonymously tips off a TV reporter (Kelly Dingwall), who brings in an honest lawyer on the force (Barry Otto).

Dingwall and Otto are the ones who get to emote here, with both of their characters clearly out of their depth trying to police the police. They score in roles that are much more interesting than the remote Quinlan. Indeed, LaPaglia disappears for a good portion of the film, reduced largely to a distorted voice on the phone pulling the strings to keep them on track.

Newcomer Essie Davis manages to invest the thankless role of Quinlan's love interest with some intelligence and independence.

Director-writer John Dingwall (father of actress Kelly Dingwall) handles suspense scenes with aplomb, but is a little slow setting story in motion. Extended scenes are devoted to breakup of Quinlan's marriage and his session with police

shrink, yet neither has any real impact on the story. He also favors dramatic lighting, often used to good effect, and stylized soundtrack, which gets distracting. —*Daniel M. Kimmel*

SKIN ART

An ITC Entertainment Group presentation of a New Gaelic Films/Live-Heart production. Produced by Ron McGee. Executive producer, Craig B. Coogan. Directed, written by W. Blake Herron. Camera (Duart color), Rick Putnam; editor, Wendy Scheir; music, James Legg; production design, Beth Curtis; set decoration, Karen Nicole; costume design, Lisa Kent, Anastasia Macris; sound (Dolby), Annette Danto; tattoo artists, Steve Ferguson, Paul Booth; assistant director, Gretel Enck; second unit director, Debra Major; second unit camera, Julie Doynow. Reviewed at Loews Copley Place, Boston, Sept. 8, 1993. (In Boston Film Festival.) Running time: **88 MIN.**

Will	Kirk Baltz
Richard	Jake Weber
Sophia	Hil Cato
Lily	Nora Ariffin
Lin	Ariane

"Skin Art" wants viewers to figure out what makes Will (Kirk Baltz) tick. He's a tattoo artist who specializes in elaborate works on the backs of Asian prostitutes. While the film transcends its seedy milieu, it still ends up being little more than a mystery resolved through an all-too-convenient flashback. Look for quick playoff on the fest circuit.

Story covers two tracks. Present-day story has Will working for Richard (Jake Weber), a procurer for the brothel across the street from Will's loft. Will shuns sex with the women, as he is haunted by memories of Vietnam.

In progressive Vietnam flashbacks, Will is tortured to reveal troop placements, then ministered to by Sophia (Hil Cato), a sophisticated and somewhat bitter young Vietnamese-French woman. Eventually it becomes clear that Will's behavior with his latest tattoo subject (Nora Ariffin) represents an attempt to work through his unresolved conflicts related to Sophia.

Story is pretty schematic and not half so erotic as it would like to be. Thesping is par, with Baltz a ringer for a younger Treat Williams, and Weber suitably slimy as the procurer. Find is newcomer Cato, who has some rough edges in her delivery but who deftly handles the contradictory cynicism and romanticism of her character.

Writer-director W. Blake Herron tries to convey with arty camera work what his script lacks, and it doesn't always do the job. Tech credits are adequate for low-budget feature, but time might have been better spent figuring out why anyone should care about Will's sublimated search for his lost innocence. —*Daniel M.Kimmel*

HERESAY!

A Willpower production. Produced, directed, written by Willpower (Will Berliner). Camera (Alpha Cine color), Berliner; editors, Berliner, Brad Jacques; sound, Berliner; Michele Kanche. Reviewed at Loews Copley Place, Boston, Sept. 9, 1993. (In Boston Film Festival.) Running time: **85 MIN.**

"Heresay!" — a pun on both "hearsay" and "heresy" — is more a polemic than a documentary. Subject is nuclear power, and the pseudonymous "Willpower" (New Hampshire filmmaker Will Berliner) is very clearly against it. Prospects beyond fest circuit will be limited to benefit screenings and brief engagements at specialty houses that can draw activist audiences. Some public TV stations may pick it up, especially where nuclear power is a local issue, but obvious slant makes this a likely no-go for PBS.

There's little pretense of balance, although spokespeople for the U.S. Nuclear Regulatory Commission and the industry do get their limited say. Emphasis is on the activists who opposed the Three Mile Island and Seabrook nuclear power plants, with a series of talking heads railing against incompetency, greed, danger, nuclear poisoning and two-headed calves.

Not much effort is made to back up the assertions. The two-headed calf is attributed to the 1979 accident at Three Mile Island, but all that's shown is a photograph someone holds up.

Even viewers who agree with the film's viewpoint are likely to weary of this non-stop lecture. Instead of attempting objectivity, or even quiet persuasion, film is more apt to preach to the choir.

After an hour of being harangued by various activists and hearing from scientists, Dr. Helen Caldicott, Ralph Nader and former Massachusetts Gov. Michael Dukakis, it's a relief when the film shifts gears. Final third focuses on the success stories of alternative energy sources utilizing sun and wind power, and the economic benefits of conservation. Segment on how Sacramento found solar power more cost-effective than nuclear power is most convincing point of the film, precisely because it doesn't feel like a club beating the viewer over the head. —*Daniel M. Kimmel*

October 18, 1993

TIM BURTON'S THE NIGHTMARE BEFORE CHRISTMAS

A Buena Vista release of a Touchstone Pictures presentation of a Burton/Di Novi production. Produced by Tim Burton, Denise Di Novi. Coproducer, Kathleen Gavin. Directed by Henry Selick. Screenplay, Caroline Thompson. Adaptation by Michael McDowell, based on a story and characters by Burton. Camera (Monaco Film Lab color; Technicolor prints), visual effects supervisor, Pete Kozachik; editor, Stan Webb; music, lyrics, score, Danny Elfman; Dolby sound; animation supervisor, Eric Leighton; art direction, Deane Taylor; visual consultant, Rick Heinrichs; armature supervisor, Tom St. Amand; mold maker supervisor, John A. Reed III; character fabricator supervisor, Bonita de Carlo; set construction supervisor, Lee Bo Henry; model shop supervisor, Mitch Romanauski; associate producers, Elfman, Philip Lofaro, Jill Jacobs, Diane Minter; casting, Mary Gail Artz, Barbara Cohen. Reviewed at Walt Disney Studios screening room, Burbank, Oct. 7, 1993. MPAA Rating: PG. Running time: **75 MIN.**

Voices:
Jack Skellington	
(sung by)	Danny Elfman
Jack (speaking)	Chris Sarandon
Sally	Catherine O'Hara
Evil Scientist	William Hickey
Mayor	Glenn Shadix
Lock	Paul Reubens
Shock	Catherine O'Hara
Barrel	Danny Elfman
Oogie Boogie	Ken Page
Santa	Ed Ivory

If it were a normal holiday animated film, "Tim Burton's The Nightmare Before Christmas" would be an entertaining, amusing, darker-than-usual offering indicating that Disney was willing to deviate slightly from its tried-and-true family-fare formula. But the dazzling techniques employed here create a striking look that has never been seen in such sustained form before, making this a unique curio that will appeal to kids and film enthusiasts alike. This explains its presence in the New York Film Festival, where the very brief feature had its world premiere the weekend of Oct. 9.

Calling upon several of the same key talents he has worked with on his live-action features, along with innovative stop-motion director Henry Selick, Burton has conceived a film that is definitely of a piece with his other work, but one step to the side. Unlike normal animation, this has a fully dimensional look, as fabulously creative model figures move within constructed sets in concert with animated effects, all to the rhythm of Danny Elfman's melodious, rambunctious score.

A wonderfully weird opening number introduces the inhabitants of Halloweentown, a demented community entirely devoted to annually inventing freshly frightening ways of scaring the bejesus out of people. However, the leading citizen, the spindly, elegant Jack Skellington, or the Pumpkin King, has tired of the old routine. On a brooding stroll through the forest, he comes upon a tree with a door to Christmastown, where he finds the radiant joys of Santa's workers in frenzied preparation for their own upcoming holiday.

Jack lays plans to kidnap Santa Claus and himself become the overlord of Christmas. In perhaps the film's outstanding sequence, the spidery Jack, bedecked in beard and red outfit, takes to the night skies drawn by three reindeer skeletons, and proceeds to distribute presents that terrify their recipients — a shrunken head, a snake that devours a Christmas tree, and so on.

For his part, Santa is nearly dined upon by Halloweentown's evil Oogie Boogie man, but Jack has a change of heart that rescues Christmas' rightful overseer and reasserts the proper commission of the holidays in an ending that is about the only thoroughly conventional aspect of the film.

The dark Halloweentown instantly recalls "Beetlejuice" and the "Batman" entries, as they are replete with spiders, bats, killing machines, strange vehicles and no end of ugly creatures who look like the extended family of the Penguin. Jack himself is an exceptional creation, a skeleton in formal attire with a hollowed-out baseball for a head, a cultivated man with a hungry soul and an impeccable way with words.

The backgrounds and sets look like surreal takeoffs on 19th-century engravings and etchings, and the characters inhabiting them are endlessly inventive, as in a Bosch painting. The film's visual style has its basis in initial sketches Burton did more than a decade ago when he formulated the project while working as an animation trainee and assistant at Disney. The studio was clearly not ready at that time for this venturesome a departure from its norm.

But neither did the means then exist to produce a result this technically perfect.

In production for more than two years, the film relied upon a painstaking stop-motion technique that involved animating each movement of each figure frame-by-frame, and took about a week to shoot a minute's worth of film. "Performances" were thus created by animators actually on the set.

For those with an aversion to conventional animation, this represents something refreshingly different. The many transitions from one bizarre scene to another, and one musical interlude to the next, are handled seamlessly. There are precious few cloying or boring moments, and it moves along at a breathless clip, propelled in great measure by Elfman's superb score, which includes 10 songs. Attitude behind the story's telling is iconoclastic and a bit twisted, but not at all subversive. Hats off to the more than 120 animators, technicians and other hands whose combined efforts have produced a decidedly singular vision.

—Todd McCarthy

FEARLESS

A Warner Bros. release of a Spring Creek production. Produced by Paula Weinstein, Mark Rosenberg. Coproducers, Robin Forman, William Beasley. Directed by Peter Weir. Screenplay, Rafael Yglesias, based on his novel. Camera (Technicolor), Allen Daviau; editor, William Anderson; music, Maurice Jarre; production design, John Stoddart; art direction, Chris Burian-Mohr; set decoration, John Anderson; costume design, Marilyn Matthews; sound (Dolby), Charles Wilborn; associate producers, Christine A. Johnston, Alan B. Curtiss; assistant director, Curtiss; second unit director, Beasley; second unit camera, Tom Cannole; casting, Howard Feuer. Reviewed at Warner Bros. screening room, Burbank, Aug. 27, 1993. MPAA Rating: R. Running time: **121 MIN.**
Max Klein	Jeff Bridges
Laura Klein	Isabella Rossellini
Carla Rodrigo	Rosie Perez
Brillstein	Tom Hulce
Dr. Bill Perlman	John Turturro
Manny Rodrigo	Benicio del Toro
Nan Gordon	Deirdre O'Connell
Jeff Gordon	John de Lancie
Jonah Klein	Spencer Vrooman

As a mainstream film about profound issues and emotions, "Fearless" will deeply effect some viewers who will personally respond to its serious consideration of mortality in a way that combines the psychological, mystical and spiritual. Others, however, will find that Peter Weir's distinctive study of the aftermath of a plane crash breaks apart thanks to undue symbolism and pretension, as well as a central relationship that doesn't pay off dramatically. Warner Bros. appears to be aiming this away from an art film niche toward a wider public and, with some top reviews, could get good mileage out of this from discriminating general audiences.

In one of his very best performances, Jeff Bridges portrays Max Klein, a man who, after walking away from a plane crash that kills his business partner and many other passengers, enters an exalted state in which he feels that he has "passed through death" and believes that nothing can harm him. The crash, he says, is "the best thing that ever happened to me," and he is suddenly afraid of nothing and compelled to speak bluntly on every subject.

Weir's handling of the six-minute opening sequence is hauntingly good, with Bridges emerging from a central California cornfield, handing a baby to its hysterical mother, then wandering away from the smoking chaos.

After an odd visit with a childhood friend, he defies expectations by insisting upon flying home to San Francisco, where the architect is written up as a heroic good Samaritan who saved many lives. His new distracted, brutally honest air is disturbing to his ballet teacher wife Laura (Isabella Rossellini), but things could be far worse.

Three months later, a shrink who specializes in group therapy for accident victims (John Turturro) brings Max together with Carla (Rosie Perez), a conventionally religious Catholic who still blames herself for the death of her young son in the crash. Aside from having been on the plane, the two have nothing in common, but they spend a lot of time together, and Max abruptly announces to his wife that he feels an overwhelming love for Carla.

This is where the film becomes muddled, although despite his odd behavior, Max has a hold on audience interest from the outset, and what he's going through remains psychologically compelling. His relationship with Carla doesn't evolve in the expected manner. Essentially introduced way down the line, Carla doesn't have a fighting chance, and the fact that she's a difficult, abrasive personality doesn't help one take to her (fact that it's very hard to understand Perez much of the time reps a further detriment).

Symbolism begins intruding when it's evident that Max was injured on his side in the same place as Jesus. Max gets weirder and weirder, particularly when he indulges in a tiresome shopping spree on behalf of the dead in his life, and film itself begins to feel like therapy with the accumulation of portentous details backed up by large doses of classical music and paintings. Rafael Yglesias' script is impeded in its grand intention of weighing attitudes toward mortality by its concentration on the strange specifics of one odd couple's particular situation.

After a long murky stretch, pic regains momentum and clarity toward the end when Max, finally going off the deep end as he breaks through his denial, returns from the edge by finally envisioning the plane crash. Presentation of this as flashes of horrifying glimpses of the plane breaking apart is a great example of impressionistic montage, and is as cathartic for the audience after the wearying midsection as it is supposed to be for Max.

October 18, 1993 (Cont.)

Especially in the ethereal early moments, Bridges is transportingly fine, and he manages throughout to convey, without exaggeration, an altered state of mind that rivets the viewer. As his confused wife, who tries to proceed cautiously with the marriage despite no helpful indications from her husband as to what she should expect from him in his transformed incarnation, Rossellini gives by far the best performance of her uneven career. As interest in the Max-Carla interaction wanes, attention increasingly turns to the wife, and Rossellini rewards it with sensitive, impassioned work. Perez, unfortunately, comes off as grating and out of key with the other thesps.

Film is beautifully made in all respects. Weir handles certain scenes with exceptional grace and others with great muscular control, and no doubt achieves exactly what he intended. Allen Daviau's lensing has a lovely clarity, and the soundtrack is outstandingly dense and rich.

—*Todd McCarthy*

DEMOLITION MAN

A Warner Bros. presentation of a Silver Pictures production. Produced by Joel Silver, Michael Levy, Howard Kazanjian. Executive producers, Faye Schwab, Aaron Schwab, Steven Bratter, Craig Sheffer. Co-producers, James Herbert, Jacqueline George, Steven Fazekas. Directed by Marco Brambilla. Screenplay, Daniel Waters, Robert Reneau, Peter M. Lenkov, story by Lenkov, Reneau. Camera (Technicolor, Panavision widescreen), Alex Thomson; editor, Stuart Baird; music, Elliot Goldenthal; production design, David L. Snyder; art direction, Walter Paul Martishius; set design, Mark Poll, Natalie V. Richards, Carl Stensel; set decoration, Robert Gould, Etta Leff; costume design, Bob Ringwood; sound (Dolby), Tim Cooney; visual effects, Michael J. McAllister, Kimberly K. Nelson; associate producer, Tony Munafo; assistant director, Louis D'Esposito; second unit director, Charles Picerni; additional camera, Matthew F. Leonetti; second unit camera, Tom Priestly; casting, Joy Todd, Ferne Cassel. Reviewed at the Village Theater, L.A., Oct. 6, 1993. MPAA Rating: R. Running time: **114 MIN.**

John Spartan	Sylvester Stallone
Simon Phoenix	Wesley Snipes
Lenina Huxley	Sandra Bullock
Dr. Raymond Cocteau	Nigel Hawthorne
Alfredo Garcia	Benjamin Bratt
Chief George Earle	Bob Gunton
Associate Bob	Glenn Shadix
Edgar Friendly	Denis Leary

Though not as irksome as "Last Action Hero," "Demolition Man" is a similar kind of film: a noisy, soulless, self-conscious pastiche that mixes elements of sci-fi, action-adventure and romance, then pours on a layer of comedy replete with Hollywood in-jokes. With Sylvester Stallone and Wesley Snipes toplined, and a woman in a major role, this incoherent concoction aims to appeal to all viewers but ultimately may fall short of satisfying any. Pic will enjoy a strong opening, but long-term prospects may be inhibited by lukewarm word of mouth.

The impressive pre-credits sequence, set in L.A. in 1996, gets right to business by contrasting LAPD Sgt. John Spartan (Stallone) with his nemesis, Simon Phoenix (Snipes). Nicknamed "Demolition Man," Spartan is trying to save 30 hostages held by the psychopathic Phoenix in an armed compound. As a result of their fight, the whole area goes up in flames and Spartan is convicted of involuntary manslaughter and sentenced to 70 years of "rehabilitation" as a frozen inmate of CryoPenitentiary.

Story then jumps to 2032, when Phoenix, who has also been imprisoned, is thawed out for a mandatory parole hearing and orchestrates an ingenious escape. He finds himself in San Angeles, a kinder and gentler L.A., now run as "a beacon of order."

Most of the solid, absurdist jokes are situated in this subplot, which depicts L.A. as a clean, safe city where the police are ill-equipped to deal with violence and the worst offense is graffiti that defaces Ethical Plaza. In this "perfect" future, life is sterile and devoid of joy — people eat no meat, refrain from smoking and have no sex. Communication is mostly impersonal, via computers that have soothing voices, and there are severe penalties for using foul language. The place to spend a nice evening is Taco Bell, "the only restaurant that survived the franchise war."

In this boring world, feisty, attractive cop Lenina Huxley (Sandra Bullock) is desperate for some action. An expert on the past, she is convinced that only the "barbarian savage" Spartan is a match for Phoenix and arranges to spring him from prison.

Some of their romantic exchanges are genuinely amusing, including virtual-reality sex and a scene in which Stallone, spoofing his macho image, knits her a sweater. Daniel Waters, Robert Reneau and Peter Lenkov's uneven script also contains one nasty, somehow ironic quip alluding to "Schwarzenegger's presidential library."

Underlying it all is the usual nostalgic right-wing ideology that clings to the good ol' days, when a kiss was a kiss, men were men, and strong old-fashioned avengers like Stallone could resolve all societal problems with physical force and heroic personality.

First-time helmer Marco Brambilla reveals his TV commercials background in both the positive and negative aspects of the film. The screen is flushed with blue lighting, the pacing is swift and there is a lot of montage and fast cutting. However, most of the action set pieces are poorly staged: Keeping the camera too close to the fights and chases allows viewers no sense of space or where the antagonists stand in relation to each other.

Snipes, who has proven his versatility over the last three years, is too gifted to be playing such a one-dimensional villain. Yet sporting short blond hair and given one blue and one green eye, he brings his customary vibrant energy to the schematic role.

As for Stallone, he is not as embarrassing in delivering his comic lines as he has been in some previous outings. But as "Cliffhanger" recently demonstrated, the less Stallone talks the more effective he is as an action hero.

Ultimately, the real star is neither Stallone nor Snipes, but the high-tech, metallic look created by production designer David L. Snyder and his accomplished team. The new film is a veritable compilation of such landmark sci-fiers as "Aliens," "Star Trek" and "Blade Runner," and also seems inspired by the imagery — and some ideas — of Fritz Lang's expressionist masterpiece, "Metropolis."

In terms of its humor, "Demolition Man" works better as a comic-book adventure than did "Last Action Hero," but the witty lines become progressively scarce as the story moves along. If the design and look of the film (aptly lensed by Alex Thomson) is always fun to watch, what's badly missing is a guiding intelligence to lift this disjointed pic from its derivative status.

—*Emanuel Levy*

MR. JONES

A TriStar release of a Rastar production. Produced by Alan Greisman, Debra Greenfield. Executive producers, Richard Gere, Jerry A. Baerwitz. Directed by Mike Figgis. Screenplay, Eric Roth, Michael Cristofer, story by Roth. Camera (Technicolor), Juan Ruiz Anchia; editor, Tom Rolf; music, Maurice Jarre; production design, Waldemar Kalinowski; art direction, Larry Fulton; set design, Gae Buckley; set decoration, Florence Fellman; costume design, Rita Ryack; sound (Dolby), Gene S. Cantamessa; assistant director, J. Stephen Buck; casting, Carrie Frazier, Shani Ginsberg. Reviewed at TriStar screening room, Culver City, Sept. 28, 1993. MPAA Rating: R. Running time: **112 MIN.**

Mr. Jones	Richard Gere
Dr. Libbie Bowen	Lena Olin
Dr. Catherine Holland	Anne Bancroft
Patrick	Tom Irwin
Howard	Delroy Lindo
David	Bruce Altman
Amanda	Lauren Tom
Susan	Lisa Malkiewicz

Mixing therapy and romance is a no-no in real life, and it proves problematic as well as the subject of "Mr. Jones." A high-energy performance by Richard Gere and an intensely brooding one from Lena Olin engage attentive viewer interest, but the stars are forced to overcompensate for a rather slow pace and lack of plot. B.O. prospects look moderate for this TriStar release.

The various impulses behind the story — to explore the thin line between professional help and personal assistance in a cure, to focus on the not-uncommon affliction of manic depression, to develop an unusual attraction between opposites — have dramatic potential in theory. But in practice, a great deal of the film consists of Richard Gere's title character either carrying on in wildly unpredictable ways (manic) or submitting to treatment when his past gets the better of him (depressive). The dramatic structure is simply too weak and predictable to propel the picture on its own.

Opening scene has the buoyant Jones talking his way into a job at a construction site just so he can tightrope walk on a high beam. Building is situated on the flight path close to San Diego Airport, which creates some arresting shots of jets practically giving Jones a buzz cut, but also gives rise to the script's specious metaphor concerning Jones' desire to fly.

Gere's cocky charm carries the first half-hour, as Jones, on a manic high, hands out hundred-dollar bills, tests out pianos at a music showroom, has a playful afternoon tryst with a blonde pickup at a fancy hotel and, in an amusingly audacious scene, marches down the aisle at a packed symphony hall in a burst of enthusiasm and shows the conductor a thing or two about conducting Beethoven.

This naturally gets him carted away as a loony. While Jones protests "I'm a kid," he is diagnosed as a bipolar manic depressive. But he's soon released, against the wishes of Dr. Libbie Bowen (Olin), who thinks the guy poses a real threat, particularly to himself.

With nothing else going on, screenwriters Eric Roth and Michael Cristofer can do only the predictable — have doctor and patient fall in love. Script warms up the romance very slowly, beginning with embarrassingly innocuous scenes of the pair cavorting at the seaside. Suddenly, Jones takes a dive into depression, which leads to therapy in which Dr. Bowen catches Jones in lies about his past, as well as to an intimate bond in which the doctor oversteps her ethical and legal bounds.

Scenario's dramatic progression offers no particular surprises, and many future developments are plainly obvious from the outset: Jones starts out on such a high that his subsequent plunge is inevitable; Dr. Bowen's personal loneliness and alienation make her vulnerable to a wild card like Jones, even though she should know better; and the love-conquers-all theme sits squarely within Hollywood convention from the beginning of time.

Still, despite the familiarity of the film's attitudes and destination, many sequences play rather well on a moment-to-moment basis. Early on, director Mike Figgis and lenser Juan Ruiz Anchia's constantly roving camera effectively convey the

October 18, 1993 (Cont.)

nervous state of the characters, particularly Jones. There is also a tart, vibrant quality to the dialogue exchanges that make the scenes come alive, although not on a level with Figgis' previous collaboration with Gere, "Internal Affairs."

Gere's effervescence in his manic phase endows the film with an engaging energy, but one can never really see the character and forget the actor. This is one of Gere's showiest, most verbal roles, and his enjoyment is contagious in a certain way, but it more often feels like a showcase for Gere's infrequently seen antic, playful side rather than a penetrating performance.

A different type of thesp entirely, Olin gives a deeply serious reading of an intelligent, somewhat brittle woman who trusts her intuition as much as her logical decisions. Her soulful introspection and stunning beauty often call to mind her countrywoman Ingrid Bergman, which prompts one to imagine what a great star Olin might have been, and what roles she might have played, had she been around in the 1930s and 1940s.

Lauren Tom has some gripping moments as a suicidal mental patient, and Delroy Lindo weighs in sympathetically as a construction worker who befriends Mr. Jones. Anne Bancroft has a perfunctory role as the head of a psychiatric institution. —*Todd McCarthy*

FATAL INSTINCT

A Metro-Goldwyn-Mayer release of a Jacobs/Gardner production. Produced by Katie Jacobs, Pierce Gardner. Executive producer, Pieter Jan Brugge. Directed by Carl Reiner. Screenplay, David O'Malley. Camera (Deluxe color), Gabriel Beristain; editors, Bud Molin, Stephen Myers; music, Richard Gibbs; production design, Sandy Veneziano; art direction, Daniel Maltese; set decoration, Chris A. Butler; costume design, Albert Wolsky; sound (Dolby), Peter Hliddal; assistant director, Marty Ewing; second unit director, M. James Arnett; casting, Renee Rousselot. Reviewed at the Mann Westwood Theater, L.A., Oct. 6, 1993. MPAA Rating: PG-13. Running time: **88 MIN.**
Ned Ravine .... Armand Assante
Laura .... Sherilynn Fenn
Lana Ravine .... Kate Nelligan
Lola Cain .... Sean Young
Frank Kelbo .... Christopher McDonald
Max Shady .... James Remar
Judge Skanky .... Tony Randall

The filmmakers have provided critics ample artillery by prominently featuring a skunk in this thuddingly flat spoof of erotic thrillers. Based on the lukewarm reception for other recent parodies — from "Robin Hood: Men in Tights" to "Loaded Weapon" and the second "Hot Shots!" — the skunk should generate the only kind of B.O. this MGM release will muster.

Director Carl Reiner and writer David O'Malley cast their nets too far and wide in this grating sendup, which proves crude without being clever or even remotely funny.

The story, in fact, includes not just passing shots but actual ongoing spoofs of "Basic Instinct," "Fatal Attraction," "Body Heat," "Sleeping With the Enemy" and "Cape Fear." What's lacking is any wit or subtlety, as if it should be enough that the audience recognizes what movies the filmmakers are trying to lampoon.

Armand Assante gets the thankless job of playing Ned Ravine (if that sounds familiar, William Hurt's moniker in "Body Heat" was Ned Racine), a cop and lawyer who busts bad guys and then defends them in court, while his wife and her lover (Kate Nelligan and Christopher McDonald) plot his death.

O'Malley tries to pack too much into the screenplay, and the few gags of any merit (such as Young's tendency to catch gum, toilet paper and other objects on her high heels, or saxophonist Clarence Clemons' plodding through the background playing the bluesy score) are pounded flat through repetition.

Reiner doesn't seem to have his heart in this effort, and, with the exception of Sean Young, who plays her sex-kitten role to the hilt, neither does the cast.

Sherilynn Fenn, for example, a classic femme fatale, is sparingly used, while Assante gamely endures his role without much to show for it.

Tech credits painstakingly recreate aspects of the thriller genre, particularly Richard Gibbs' score and Albert Wolsky's costumes. Too bad the same care wasn't put into saving what's called a "killer comedy" in MGM's ad campaign from its suicidal tendencies. —*Brian Lowry*

THE BEVERLY HILLBILLIES

A 20th Century Fox release. Produced by Ian Bryce, Penelope Spheeris. Directed by Spheeris. Screenplay, Lawrence Konner, Mark Rosenthal, Jim Fisher, Jim Staahl, story by Konner, Rosenthal, based on the television series created by Paul Henning. Camera (Deluxe color), Robert Brinkmann; editor, Ross Albert; music, Lalo Schifrin; production design, Peter Jamison; art direction, Marjorie Stone McShirley; set design, Lawrence A. Hubbs, Evelyne Barbier; set decoration, Linda Spheeris; costume design, Jami Burrows; sound (Dolby), Thomas Causey; assistant director, Matt Earl Beesley; casting, Glenn Daniels. Reviewed at the Cineplex Odeon Fairfax, L.A., Sept. 24, 1993. MPAA Rating: PG. Running time: **93 MIN.**
Jethro/Jethrine .... Diedrich Bader
Mr. Drysdale .... Dabney Coleman
Elly May .... Erika Eleniak
Granny .... Cloris Leachman
Woodrow Tyler .... Rob Schneider
Laura Jackson .... Lea Thompson
Miss Hathaway .... Lily Tomlin
Jed Clampett .... Jim Varney
Aunt Pearl .... Linda Carlson
Margaret Drysdale .... Penny Fuller
Morgan Drysdale .... Kevin Connolly
Barnaby Jones .... Buddy Ebsen
Herself .... Zsa Zsa Gabor
Herself .... Dolly Parton

The flood of hit films based on popular old TV shows should continue unabated with "The Beverly Hillbillies." Just as corny and stupid as the long-running series, pic version has been cleverly cast and shrewdly skewed to appeal jointly to original fans of the show and younger viewers only vaguely familiar with it. Result should be a profitable B.O. geyser for Fox.

No matter the updating, new cast and big screen — the comic effect of the Clampett clan, 1993, is nearly identical to the one it had during its heyday on CBS from 1962-71 (it has remained in syndication almost continuously since then). The actors, for the most part, are so similar to the originals that, a couple of days after viewing the film, they virtually blend together in the mind, while the humor is the same sort of down-home, fish-out-of-water stuff that's so silly you can't help laughing at it. The delight-in-recognition factor, starting with the immortal "Ballad of Jed Clampett," will be very high, while just enough edge and hip contempo references have been applied to keep kids from regarding this as a relic.

In fact, zippy current rendition feels like scraps from numerous old TV shows thrown into a pot and spiced up with new seasoning.

Taking officious control of the newly rich family's affairs when they arrive in BevHills are toadying banker Mr. Drysdale and prim secretary Miss Hathaway, roles neatly filled by TV-friendly Dabney Coleman and Lily Tomlin. Latter is given the assignment of finding a suitable wife for the widowed Jed, who is now one of the most eligible men in America.

Latter development provides most of what passes for a plot. It's not much, but then storyline was a similarly irrelevant afterthought in helmer Penelope Spheeris' previous outing, the not excellent comedy "Wayne's World," and look how much difference it made at the box office.

Intrigue cooked up by a quartet of screenwriters involves the efforts of the nefarious Laura (Lea Thompson), assisted by bank employee Woodrow (Rob Schneider), to trick Jed into marriage and run off with his loot.

It's all pretty thin, scattershot stuff, but the ingratiating naivete of the characters and the aw-shucks friendliness of the cast are disarming, and it becomes as easy to just let this go down as a country tune with some moonshine on the side.

Gullible but common-sensical as ever, Jed has found a worthy new interpreter in Jim Varney, who feels like the genuine article and weighs his words and decisions with good comic timing. As the stubborn Granny, Cloris Leachman is a near-dead ringer for the late Irene Ryan and conveys the right antic, anarchic spirit, but the character is seriously shortchanged by the script,

which neglects her almost entirely until the final reel.

Instead, much of the running time is given over to Jethro and, even more so, to Elly May. Diedrich Bader as Jethro is leaner and more self-consciously comic than was Max Baer Jr., while Erika Eleniak, who made an impression in "Under Siege," will make more of one here in Donna Douglas' original part, as her conspicuously featured attributes sorely test her jeans buttons and bow only to those of Dolly Parton, who turns up in a party scene to sing "Happy Birthday" to Jed.

Most pointed satire comes at the easy expense of Beverly Hills High, replete with a cash machine and cappuccino cart, where Elly May is sent with Drysdale's teenage son, a role Kevin Connolly plays as the screen's first human imitation of Beavis and Butt-Head.

Knowingly camping up her role more than the others, Tomlin is a delight as the industrious but often baffled Miss Hathaway. Zsa Zsa Gabor appears in an in-joke police lineup as "someone involved in a drive-by slapping," while the original Jed, Buddy Ebsen, briefly pops up as an aged Barnaby Jones.

Robert Brinkmann's lensing is as brightly lit as any TV show, and Ross Albert's editing adroitly gets this over with in barely over 90 minutes. —*Todd McCarthy*

SAN SEBASTIAN

HUEVOS DE ORO

(GOLDEN BALLS)

(SPANISH)

A Lolafilms S.A./Iberoamericana Films/Ovideo TV/Film Auro production by Andres Vicente Gomez. Directed by Bigas Luna. Screenplay, Luna, Cuca Canals. Camera (color), Jose Luis Alcaine; editor, Carmen Frias; music, Nicola Piovani; art direction, Antxon Gomez; sound, Marc A. Beldent; associate producers, Manuel Lombardero, Pepo Sol. Reviewed at San Sebastian Film Festival, Sept. 18, 1993. Running time: **92 MIN.**
Benito .... Javier Bardem
Claudia .... Maribel Verdu
Marta .... Maria de Medeiros
Rita .... Elisa Touati
Ana .... Raquel Bianca
Miguel .... Alessandro Gassman
Also with: Francesco Maria Dominedo, Albert Vidal, Angel de Andres Lopez, Benisio del Toro.

The same producer, director and thesp who served up "Jamon, Jamon" try to give one further turn of the screw in this tasteless, meandering film about the adventures of a boorish macho type who strives to rise from construction peon to real estate speculator.

Oozing with gratuitous sex, pic is about as subtle as its title and its promotional poster — Javier Bardem clutching his crotch.

October 18, 1993 (Cont.)

Worse, its rags-to-riches story gets lost about halfway through, after the oversexed lout has an accident and the scene shifts to Miami. This will go as far commercially as a sexy sell alone can take it.

The thin story concerns bumptious bumpkin Benito, doing his military service in northern Africa, who dreams of sports cars, Rolex watches and a mini-harem. After landing in Benidorm, Spain, and after his naive deceptions fail to fool the real sharpies in the construction business, he marries a magnate's daughter (how he does this is never explained), and work on his phallic dream-skyscraper begins.

Amidst orgies (story is a thinly veiled pretext to shoot the sex scenes), and just as his priapic architectural visions take shape, his car crashes and he's left partially paralyzed. Finally tiring of his aberrations, his wife (Maria de Medeiros) throws him out, and our antihero moves to Miami with a floozy he has picked up in a disco. Pic ends with Benito sitting on a bed in a Miami room, a ruined man, sobbing.

But pity for this repulsive character cannot be wrung from audiences. Script is weak, with numerous false leads that are never followed up. The sex scenes may help pic chalk up some sales for this meretricious and ultimately non-erotic film. The "balls" of the title are never shown. —*Peter Besas*

TORONTO FEST

HALF JAPANESE: THE BAND THAT WOULD BE KING

(DOCU — B&W/COLOR/16mm)

A Morganville Films production. Produced, directed, written by Jeff Feuerzeig. Camera (color), Fortunato Procopio; editor, Peter Sorcher; music, Half Japanese; sound, Bill Drucklieb. Reviewed at Festival of Festivals, Toronto, Sept. 15, 1993. Running time: **90 MIN.**
With: Jad and David Fair, Maureen Tucker, Byron Coley, Penn Jillette, Phil Milstein.

Celebrating the 20th anniversary of the innovative music band, "Half Japanese" is a mockumentary a la "This Is Spinal Tap" that just "happens" to be about a real band. Mildly entertaining, though not as zany or original as one might expect, pic is a good bet for public TV, cable and video after limited theatrical release on university campuses and in big cities, where the band is popular. It opened commercially in New York on Oct. 8.

Composed of musical footage and interviews with the duo's parents, musicians and associates, docu reconstructs the history of Half Japa-

nese as the first punk rock band. The siblings' mother proudly relates how exciting it was "that our house of 200 years has been called the birthplace of punk rock."

The most revelatory info comes from David and Jad Fair, who convey the chutzpah that it takes to do what they did. Initially, neither could play a single note on any instrument, but the two somehow knew on a gut level how to carve a niche for themselves and display their gifts. Says David, "We decided to do two kinds of songs, love songs and monster songs."

At its best, the uneven effort provides a humorous journey into the world of underground music, contrasting it with the rigid mainstream press and record industry; MTV, Rolling Stone magazine, commercial radio and major record labels are trashed in the process.

One interviewee sums up succinctly what it takes to enjoy the revolutionary band: "Most people lack the intestinal fortitude to concentrate and listen to Half Japanese." This is followed by a poignant history of their first release, "1/2 Gentlemen/Not Beasts," a triple-LP box with a lyric sheet, a pink leopard-skin pamphlet and an alligator poster designed by David Fair.

Making it sound easy to form a band and succeed in the competitive music world, the film doesn't stress strongly enough that the band struck a chord with audiences of the 1970s because it clearly had something new to offer.

Overall, moderate tech credits and quality of 16mm lensing don't do justice to the music of Half Japanese and its place in the history of punk rock. —*Emanuel Levy*

PARIS, FRANCE

(CANADIAN)

An Alliance Communications Co.-Lightshow Communications production. Produced by Eric Norlen, Allen Levine. Executive producer, Stephane Reichel. Directed by Gerard Ciccoritti. Screenplay, Tom Walmsley, based on his novel. Camera (color), Barry Stone; editor, Roushell Goldstein; music, John McCarthy; production design, Marian Whihack; sound, Manse James; casting, John Buchan. Reviewed at Festival of Festivals, Toronto. Sept 17, 1993. Running time: **111 MIN.**
Lucy .... Leslie Hope
Sloan .... Peter Outerbridge
Michael .... Victor Ertmanis
William .... Dan Lett
Minter .... Raoul Trujillo

Despite some steamy sex and frontal nudity, male and female, "Paris, France" is a silly farce with few amusing moments and many more boring ones. Pretentious yarn concerns a novelist who, in order to overcome her writer's block, engages in wild sexual fantasies and escapades. Intermittently titillating, if also overly long, comedy might have some commercial potential

for limited theatrical release on the basis of its racy nature.

Lucy (Leslie Hope), a young married woman suffering from a severe case of creative block, decides to take matters into her hands and finish her semi-autobiographical novel, "Paris, France," at all costs. Lucy hasn't written one word since returning from Paris, where she was involved with the seductive Minter (Raoul Trujillo) in an *amour fou* that tragically ended with his death.

Back in Montreal, Lucy engages in yet another dangerous liaison with Sloan (Peter Outerbridge), a handsome bisexual poet, as a means for personal redemption and artistic renewal. At the same time, Michael (Victor Ertmanis), her ordinary-looking husband-publisher, faces his own phobia, dominated by an obsession with John Lennon's assassination.

Viewers who thought that Anais Nin, the model for the hedonist Lucy, was pretentious in "Henry & June" are bound for a real treat just listening to Lucy's pompous statements about art, literature, music, marriage and other "existential" issues.

Almost everything here is derivative and secondhand, beginning with the Wim Wenders-derived title. As scripted by Tom Walmsley and directed by Gerard Ciccoritti, the narrative registers as an agenda film in both personal and cultural ways. The filmmakers seem to be venting their own sexual fantasies as well as attempting to change the stereotype of Canadians as conservative, depicting them as more eccentric and sex-minded than they usually have been portrayed.

For a while, the attractiveness of Leslie Hope and Peter Outerbridge, whose angelic face recalls the young Terence Stamp, and their hot erotic scenes (some involving funny S&M sex), help redeem the redundant nature of the material and its questionable thesis of how to overcome creative problems.

The proficiency of the technical credits surpasses the quality of writing and direction of a feature film that would have worked much better at much shorter length.
—*Emanuel Levy*

UN MURO DE SILENCIO
A WALL OF SILENCE

(ARGENTINE)

A Lita Stantic film production, co-produced with ALEPH Prods., Instituto Mexicana de Cinematografia and Channel 4. Produced by Dolly Pussi. Executive producer, Pablo Rovito. Directed by Lita Stantic. Screenplay, Graciela Maglie, Stantic. Camera (color), Felix Monti; editor, Juan Carlos Macias; music, Nestor Marconi; art direction, Margarita Jusid; sound, Nerio Barberis, Abelardo Kuschnir. Reviewed at Festival of Festivals, Toronto, Sept. 14, 1993. Running time: **106 MIN.**

Kate Benson .... Vanessa Redgrave
Silvia Cassini .... Ofelia Medina
Bruno Tealdi .... Lautaro Murua
Also with: Lorenzo Quinteros, Andre Melancon.

Lita Stantic's Argentine political drama, "A Wall of Silence," is a kind of sequel to the 1985 Oscar-winning "The Official Story." Focusing on the effects of the former military dictatorship on the contemporary lives of a mother and daughter, the film tackles the important issue of how individuals deal with traumatic past events. But pic's awkward structure, slow pacing and unexciting direction result in a moderately absorbing drama that will appeal mainly to viewers interested in political cinema.

Sporting short blond hair, Vanessa Redgrave plays Kate, a British director making a movie in Buenos Aires about a married couple whose lives have been torn apart by the repressive military regime. Struggling with how to approach her material and guide her actors, Kate finds out that Silvia Cassini (Ofelia Medina), the woman whose life is being portrayed in the film, is now remarried, trying to forget her haunting past, particularly the disappearance of her first husband.

Revolving around the issue of personal and collective memory, tale describes the inevitable impact of the past on contemporary lives, suggesting that there is no escape from history, and that sooner or later one must come to terms with the most horrible events in one's life.

Regrettably, this riveting subject is treated with an awkward narrative structure, one that prevents emotional involvement with the characters' fascinating stories. First-time helmer Stantic switches back and forth between the filming of the political saga, which is rather dull, and the lives of the real-life counterparts, told through flashbacks. An unmodulated pacing makes the transition between subplots all the more maladroit.

Making a valiant effort to speak in Spanish, Redgrave is nonetheless miscast as the English director who inadvertently becomes the catalyst for the ensuing melodramatic events. Redgrave is simply too intelligent to convince as a filmmaker who walks around during rehearsals helplessly, not knowing how to direct her actors. As the film's emotional center — and best asset — the beautiful Medina captures the tragic price of historical forgetfulness and the urgent need for remembrance of things past.

Moderate technical credits, including newsreel footage, enhance the look of the film but are not sufficient to make it a compellingly touching drama. —*Emanuel Levy*

MONTREAL FEST

THE MYTH OF THE MALE ORGASM

A Telescene Communications production, in association with Doodskie Film Corp. (International sales: Telescene, Montreal.) Produced by Robin Spry. Executive producer, Paul Painter. Directed by John Hamilton. Written by Hamilton, David Reckziegel. Camera (color), John Berrie; editor, Denis Papillon; music, Ray Bonneville, Michel Pelletier; production design, John Meighen; costume design, Paul-Andre; sound, Gabor Vadnay; associate producer, Reckziegel; line producer, David McInnes Robertson; assistant director, Jennifer Jonas; casting, Vear Miller, Nadia Rcna. Reviewed at World Film Festival, Montreal, Sept. 2, 1993. (Also in Toronto Festival of Festivals, Vancouver Festival.) Running time **90 MIN.**

Jimmy Ruvinsky	Bruce Dinsmore
Jane Doe	Miranda de Pencier
Mimi	Ruth Marshall
Sean	Burke Lawrence
Tim	Mark Camacho
Paula	Macha Grenon
Gregory	Gianpaolo Bini
Allison	Felicia Shulman

Reducing the battle between the sexes to a witty war of words, "The Myth of the Male Orgasm" is a rare Canadian export that's both timely and jocular enough to make it ripe for moderate cross-border shopping.

Winsome but woebegone college prof Jimmy Ruvinsky (Bruce Dinsmore) is turning 30, and the need to figure out his failure with women drives him to participate in an on-campus study of male attitudes, run by psych-department feminists a tad predisposed against their subjects. Initial scenes of blindfolded Jimmy defending himself against relentless interrogation by a woman identified only as Jane Doe lay out a guide to the current sexual *zeitgeist*. It's done as neatly as French-lingo "The Decline of the American Empire" did for the less-paranoid 1980s.

The writing is definitely from the male perspective, which could prompt negative responses from female viewers, but it's brutally, hilariously honest. The real problem is that the women aren't as well cast or handled as the men, and their potentially intriguing characters pay the price. Ruth Marshall is too bland as Jimmy's best pal (and secret love), while Miranda de Pencier comes on all saucy, TV-ad purrs as the supposedly neutral inquisitor; her scenes with Felicia Shulman, as the harsh department head, consist of little more than bleak yelling and cigarette waving. Macha Grenon, however, is perfect as Jimmy's bitchy, supremely superficial ex-g.f.

Burke Lawrence is notable as Jimmy's bumptiously womanizing roommate, and Mark Camacho gets many of the funniest lines as the other roomie: a sensitive, liberated health-freak on the outside but a horny, smoke-sneaking demon underneath. Legit veteran Dinsmore, an ingenuous Kyle McLachlan type, is terrific throughout, carrying his debut lead with impressive ease.

Tech credits are adequate, with so-so lensing offset by fresh Montreal settings. Rock tunes by Quebecer Ray Bonneville also add local verve. Still, it's not urban exotica but universality that is offered here. In fact, erroneous sexist rap (along with ironic title) could stir enough controversy to attract multiplex crowds who'll find that pic doles out no politically correct answers, but raises all the pertinent questions. *—Ken Eisner*

WHITE ANGEL

(BRITISH)

A Living Spirit Pictures Ltd. production. (International sales: Living Spirit Pictures/The Old Picture House, Througham, Gloucestershire). Produced by Chris Jones. Screenplay, Jones, Jolliffe. Camera (color), Jon Walker; editor, John Holland; music, Harry Gregson-Williams; sound, Tim Cavagin. Reviewed at World Film Festival, Montreal, Sept. 6, 1993. Running time: **95 MIN.**

Leslie Steckler	Peter Firth
Ellen Carter	Harriet Robinson
Inspector Taylor	Don Henderson

This amateurish thriller wants to plumb some "Silence of the Lambs" depths, but silly plot and lame thesping will soon send it straight to video prison.

Cheapo production banks everything on solid skills of Peter Firth, as Leslie Steckler, a seemingly mild-mannered London dentist who is actually the brutal killer of blond-haired women who happen to wear white. The methodical murderer has his reasons, though, and the desire to express them proves his — and the film's — undoing, when he chooses pulp writer Ellen Carter as his vehicle.

Steckler hopes to bond with the brunet scribbler (whose specialty is serial killers, natch) when he figures out that she has bumped off her abusive husband. Harriet Robinson's flat Yankee accent may sound amusing to some Brit ears, but it's hard to imagine a more grating, gawky presence in this co-lead role, which is the cold-blooded pic's only touchstone for aud identification (oddly, Robinson was fine in a small part in "Utz").

Pedestrian tech values, with bad cuts enervating already dull images, don't help, and a few clever lines (as when veteran Don Henderson, as a wily policeman on Carter's trail, blithely warns, "Catch you later") only point up the amateurish emptiness of the rest. Racial and religious themes implied by the title never come into play.

This is the kind of tale that boils down a supposedly complex psychopath's motivation to a single triggering quirk: His first wife (a white-wearing blonde!) bossed him around … quite a lot. *—Ken Eisner*

VENICE FEST

UN'ANIMA DIVISA IN DUE
(A SOUL SPLIT IN TWO)
(ITALIAN-FRENCH)

A Darc release (Italy) of an Aran/Pic Film/Mod Films production, in association with Reteitalia, SSR/RTSI Swiss Television. (International sales: Intra Films.) Produced by Roberto Sessa. Executive producer, Daniele Maggioni. Directed by Silvio Soldini. Screenplay, Soldini, Roberto Tiraboschi, based on an idea by Umberto Marino. Camera (Agfa and Kodak color; Telecolor prints), Luca Bigazzi; editor, Claudio Cormio; music, Giovanni Venosta; art direction, Elvezio V.D. Meijden, Sonia Peng; costume design, Franca Zucchelli; sound, Henry Roux. Reviewed at Venice Film Festival (competing), Sept. 9, 1993. Running time: **127 MIN.**

Pietro De Leo	Fabrizio Bentivoglio
Pabe	Maria Bako
Miriam	Philippine Leroy-Beaulieu
Helene	Jessica Forde
Savino	Felice Andreasi
Lidia	Silvia Mocci
Son	Edoardo Moussanet
Abid	Zinedine Soualem
Lawyer	Sonia Gessner

Director Silvio Soldini confirms he's one of Italy's rising new talents with "A Soul Split in Two," about a lonely department store detective's infatuation with a free-thinking gypsy girl. Sensitive, well-observed film is beautifully lensed and acted, and should find its way to arthouse circuits abroad after multiple fest screenings.

"Soul" is also a film split in two. First half, set in Soldini's own dark, gloomy Milan, is near perfect in creating the atmosphere of a smooth-as-silk city where individuals who fall out of the system, like Pietro (Fabrizio Bentivoglio), are lost souls.

Pietro, separated, sees his kid only on weekends. His flirtation with a makeup consultant brings him no joy, while his job of catching shoplifters is fast becoming a pathological obsession.

He becomes infatuated with the teenage Pabe (Maria Bako), one of many gypsies living in Italian cities by begging and stealing. He gives her money and falsely testifies in her favor in court to keep her out of jail.

Film's high point is his plan to kidnap the girl and "marry" her on the road, gypsy-style. Bentivoglio brings a comic intensity to the struggle to make off with Pabe, aided by Giovanni Venosta's ironic musical score (a kind of gypsy pizzicato), and editor Claudio Cormio's cutting, which gives pic a nervous energy.

The second part of "Soul" changes register, lighting and mood. The odd couple go south along the Italian coast and get married. Pietro finds work as a truck driver and Pabe as a factory hand and hotel maid. Relatives and friends appear who make life easier. But the cultural divide just won't go away.

Soldini's elliptical style, skipping obvious links between scenes (like the preliminaries leading to Pietro and Pabe's wedding), gives pic a modern, nervous edge. But second half contains a few false steps, and struggles to maintain continuity and flow.

Non-pro Bako, a half-gypsy Hungarian student, brings freshness and conviction to Pabe. Acting in Italian for the first time, she has an unschooled spontaneity which contrasts well with the more measured style of Bentivoglio, whose perf won an acting award at Venice. *—Deborah Young*

LE FILS DU REQUIN
(THE SON OF THE SHARK)
(FRENCH-BELGIAN-LUXEMBOURGIAN)

A Gaumont/Compagnie des Images/France 3 Cinema/Premiere Heure/Saga Films/In Visible Films production. (International sales: Gaumont Buena Vista Intl., Paris.) Produced by Francois Fries. Directed by Agnes Merlet. Screenplay, Merlet, Santiago Amigorena. Camera (widescreen, color), Gerard Simon; editors, Guy Lecorne, Pierre Choukroun; music, Bruno Coulais; production design, Laurent Allaire; sound, Henry Morelle, Jean-Pierre Laforce; production manager, Ginette Mejinsky. Reviewed at Venice Film Festival (Critics Week), Sept. 6, 1993. Running time: **88 MIN.**

Martin	Ludovic Vandendaele
Simon	Erick Da Silva
Marie	Sandrine Blancke
The Father	Maxime Leroux

Agnes Merlet's impressive first feature (inspired by a newspaper story) is a scary portrait of potentially very violent youngsters who have scarcely reached the age of puberty. Compassionate but unflinching depiction of the abandoned kids' day-to-day existence will probably prove too downbeat to find a substantial audience, though fest exposure is indicated.

Set in winter in an unattractive coastal area, film opens with the homeless brothers, Martin (Ludovic Vandendaele) and Simon (Erick Da Silva), driving a stolen bus, which they later roll off a cliff into the sea. The pair survive by stealing food and money; they also vandalize and destroy.

There is no one to give them genuine love and affection. Though the older boy fancies a girl (Sandrine Blancke) he knew at school, he has no idea how to approach her in a non-violent way.

A recurrent theme is the boys' fascination with fish, first in an undersea film they view, and later in a fish market where they see decapitated fish still gasping for air. The kids see themselves as young sharks, predators who will terrorize society.

Merlet has obtained frighteningly natural performances from her two young actors. With its absolute realism, the film pulls no punches and isn't at all sentimental, which is its great strength but may also prevent its acceptance by a large audience. —*David Stratton*

N.Y. FEST

IT'S ALL TRUE

(DOCU — FRENCH-U.S. — B&W/COLOR)

A Paramount release of a Les Films Balenciaga production in association with the French Ministry of Education and Culture/French National Center for Cinematography/Canal Plus/R. Films/La Fondation GAN pour le Cinema. Produced by Regine Konckier, Richard Wilson, Bill Krohn, Myron Meisel, Jean-Luc Ormieres. Directed by Wilson, Meisel, Krohn. Based on an unfinished film by Orson Welles. Written by Krohn, Wilson, Meisel. Camera (b&w/color), Gary Graver; editor, Ed Marx; music, Jorge Arriagada; production sound, Jean-Pierre Duret; sound design, Dean Beville; narrator, Miguel Ferrer; special consultant, Elizabeth Wilson; associate producer, Catherine Benamou; assistant directors, Amaury Candido Bezerra, Jose Verissimo de Oliveira (Fortaleza), Rogerio Sganzerla, David Neves (Rio). "Four Men on a Raft": Directed by Welles. Camera (b&w), George Fanto; associate producer, Richard Wilson. Reviewed at Paramount Studios, L.A., Oct. 13, 1993. MPAA Rating: G. Running time: 85 MIN.

After 51 years in limbo as one of the most legendary of all "lost" films, Orson Welles' "It's All True" has finally emerged in lovingly resurrected partial form within the framework of a documentary about Welles' entire 1942 Latin American misadventure. World premiered over the weekend at the New York Film Festival and now entering commercial release, this is a film buff's delight and should score in limited specialized bookings ahead of a long life in ancillary markets.

French-backed docu is essentially divided into two parts. First half-hour effectively sketches the events surrounding Welles' trip to Brazil to shoot a major documentary as part of the U.S. government's Good Neighbor Policy at the start of World War II. Nearly an hour is then devoted to the presentation of "Four Men on a Raft," which was to have been the centerpiece of Welles' never-finished, multi-part docu.

The scene is set by Welles himself in excerpts from various interviews, as well as by numerous collaborators, including lenser Joseph Biroc, assistants Shifra Haran and Elizabeth Wilson, and associate producer Richard Wilson, who devoted many years to the current project before his death in 1991.

Recruited by the State Department, Welles reluctantly agreed to contribute his services as a special filmmaking ambassador. The boy wonder was just 26, flush with the acclaim and controversy of "Citizen Kane," when he left for Brazil literally the day after wrapping his second film, "The Magnificent Ambersons," with the understanding that

his editors would follow him south.

Welles had to rush in order to arrive in time to shoot Carnaval. The longer he stayed and figured out just what his film would be about, the more he pushed into territory that pleased neither the bosses at his studio, RKO, nor Brazil's military regime; Welles wanted to trace the origins of the samba, which led him to the poverty-ridden *favelas* and to black performers, and also was drawn to the plight of the country's poor fishermen.

As Welles confesses onscreen, the entire episode "destroyed" him. In the midst of a management change, RKO ordered Welles to stop shooting, and cut 45 minutes out of "Ambersons" behind his back. Fired when he finally returned to Hollywood, Welles found his previously golden reputation irreparably harmed by charges of financial waste and an inability to finish his work, even though "It's All True" was never designed as a commercial undertaking in the first place. Welles cites a curse put on the film by a Brazilian voodoo witch doctor when lensing had to be canceled.

This history has been variously recounted in numerous articles and books, and while there is considerable interest in seeing the wonderful archival footage that Wilson and his director-writer collaborators Myron Meisel and Bill Krohn have unearthed, the main fascination here is to finally see as much of Welles' own footage as still exists, much of it having been destroyed years ago.

Offering snippets of colorful Carnaval material and an entire sequence from another intended "It's All True" episode, "My Friend Bonito," which was directed under Welles' supervision by Norman Foster in Mexico, the filmmakers, remarkably, have been able to reconstitute "Four Men on a Raft" virtually intact. Crucially bearing in mind that Welles never edited the material and that he intended to narrate the silent footage himself, the result is nevertheless very pleasing, and represents a crucial insight into the evolution of Welles' style from studio virtuosity and long takes to location work and montage orientation.

Story recounts the astonishing two-month journey of four fisherman on a tiny raft, or *jangada*, from Fortaleza, on Brazil's northeast coast, 1,650 miles to Rio, where they successfully pleaded for social benefits for all Brazilian fishermen. The *jangadeiros* were national heroes, but when Welles re-created their arrival in Rio harbor, a giant wave overtook their raft and the leader, Jacare, drowned, which invests the entire episode with great poignance.

Stirring sequences recount the building of the raft, the send-off by a close-knit community, their struggles to sail the little craft, and stops at Recife and Salvador before their triumphal entry into Rio. There is also a modest love story between teenagers.

The images, shot by George Fanto, are reminiscent at times of Murnau's in "Tabu" and "Moana," and at others of Eisenstein. While there is the occasional awkwardness found in untrained performers, much more pervasive is the sense of great dignity, a respect for the subjects' lives and work. This is a respect returned by the local interview subjects, who speak of Welles with reverential awe to this day.

Two sequences stand out. First is one in which a little girl runs from the ocean to the village and becomes encumbered in large fish nets, which has the makings of a Wellesian tour de force. Second is a massive funeral scene, done mostly in stunning silhouette, which anticipates images in "Othello" and other later work by the director.

There are narrative gaps, to be sure, whether on account of material Welles never got to shoot or footage that remains missing. But the filmmakers have indisputably honored Welles with their sensitive handling of his beautiful pieces of film, in a way that the Spanish personnel who attempted to assemble another unfinished Welles film, "Don Quixote," did not.

The ever-present music by Jorge Arriagada isn't all it could be, proving helpful at times and annoying at others. Printing of some black-and-white excerpts, notably "Ambersons," is mediocre, but the main images of interest look fine.

Even if it doesn't do Welles any good, the "curse" on "It's All True" seems finally to have lifted, and anyone interested in one of the cinema's great creators will be thankful for it. —*Todd McCarthy*

MR. WONDERFUL

A Warner Bros. release of a Samuel Goldwyn Co. production. Produced by Marianne Moloney. Coproducer, Steven Felder. Directed by Anthony Minghella. Screenplay, Amy Schor, Vicki Polon. Camera (Technicolor), Geoffrey Simpson; editor, John Tintori; music, Michael Gore; production design, Doug Kraner; art direction, Steve Sakland; set decoration, Alyssa Winter; costume design, John Dunn; sound (Dolby), Chris Newman; assistant director, Steve E. Andrews; casting, David Rubin, Debra Zane. Reviewed at the Warner Hollywood Studios, L.A., Sept. 28, 1993. MPAA Rating: PG-13. Running time: 98 MIN.

Gus	Matt Dillon
Leonora	Annabella Sciorra
Rita	Mary-Louise Parker
Tom	William Hurt
Dominic	Vincent D'Onofrio
Pope	David Barry Gray
Dante	Bruce Kirby
Harvey	Dan Hedaya
Juice	Luis Guzman

Warner Bros. faces a tricky marketing proposition with this charming, almost sedate little romantic comedy, which is short on

October 25, 1993 (Cont.)

laughs but tinged with a pleasant European flavor courtesy of British director Anthony Minghella ("Truly, Madly, Deeply"). Those arthouse elements don't bode all that well for box office, but pic has the makings of a homevideo hit for those seeking a thinking man's entry in the "Sleepless in Seattle" vein.

Working from a script by Amy Schor and Vicki Polon, Minghella offers an appealing array of characters lacking a villain or heavy — just a lot of well-meaning folks stumbling their way through life, trying to find a soulmate.

The hook, which almost makes "Mr. Wonderful" sound like the screwball comedy it's not, centers on the efforts of blue-collar worker Gus (Matt Dillon) to marry off his ex-wife, Leonora (Annabella Sciorra), as a means of escaping his alimony payments, only to rekindle his feelings for her in the process.

Unfortunately, Gus is already involved with Rita (Mary-Louise Parker), while Leonora — in the midst of an affair with her married professor (William Hurt) — reluctantly agrees to go on a few blind dates, eventually meeting a truly nice guy, Rita's friend Dominic (Vincent D'Onofrio).

Story begins slowly — indeed, almost sluggishly — as an increasingly frustrated Gus grapples with Rita's insecurity about their relationship, his fear of commitment and his divorce-induced financial woes, preventing him from joining his buddies in fulfilling their dream of buying and renovating a local bowling alley.

When things pick up, it's clear that "Mr. Wonderful" has more to do with texture and character than its central premise — creating a real marketing challenge in a world inured to the grand flourishes and simple endings of traditional Hollywood romances.

Minghella does give in to some of those conventions, but by avoiding easy stereotypes (Hurt's professor, for example, would have been a one-dimensional slime in most other movies), the director adroitly manages to keep the audience off guard until the end.

That isn't to say the pic is without flaws, including a herky-jerky feel and some mundane stretches of dialogue in a script that also includes its share of insightful gems.

What sets the pic apart is the richness of its characters and the top-to-bottom strength of its cast, with Dillon confused yet likable, both Sciorra and Parker radiantly appealing, and Hurt, D'Onofrio and various pals all crafting clear portraits despite, in most instances, limited screen time.

More than anything, "Mr. Wonderful" explores the romantic ties that bind, the domino-like effect relationships have on one other and whether there's actually enough happiness to go around. If the answers aren't entirely convincing, there's certainly some thought to be derived from the way Minghella and company pose the questions.

Tech credits, particularly Michael Gore's breezy score, add to the bittersweet ambience, with Geoffrey Simpson's camera work and Doug Kraner's production design helping convey both the grit and romance of New York — a duality that "Mr. Wonderful," at its best, also captures.

—Brian Lowry

JUDGMENT NIGHT

A Universal Pictures release of a Largo Entertainment production in association with JVC. Produced by Gene Levy. Executive producers, Lloyd Segan, Marilyn Vance. Directed by Stephen Hopkins. Screenplay, Lewis Colick, story by Colick, Jere Cunningham. Camera (Deluxe color), Peter Levy; editor, Timothy Wellburn; music, Alan Silvestri; production design, Joseph Nemec III; art direction, Dan Olexiewicz; costume design, Marilyn Vance; sound (Dolby), Don Johnson; stunt coordinator, Walter Scott; assistant director, David Sardi; casting Judy Taylor, Lynda Gordon. Reviewed at Universal Studios, Universal City, Oct. 8, 1993. MPAA Rating: R. Running time: **109 MIN.**

Frank Wyatt	Emilio Estevez
Mike Peterson	Cuba Gooding Jr.
Fallon	Denis Leary
John Wyatt	Stephen Dorff
Ray Cochran	Jeremy Piven
Sykes	Peter Greene
Rhodes	Erik Schrody
Travis	Michael Wiseman

The most chilling aspect of the urban thriller "Judgment Night" is truly how infinitely superior its craft is to its art. This is an exceedingly well directed, cleverly filmed and edited, tension-filled affair. It is also a wholly preposterous, muddled, paranoid view of the inner-city nightmare where the slightest misstep is sure to have a fateful result.

Ultimately, the drama is neither believable nor satisfying. There's something innately phony about the story. "Judgment Night" is a slight, pretentious programmer that really doesn't work for the action crowd, and while concept and cast should open the picture, it has no sustaining box office force.

The action pivots around a boys' night out in which four young men head from the suburbs to a big boxing match in downtown Chicago. En route they run into gridlock and take an offramp into a really bad neighborhood. It doesn't take much to guess what happens next.

One character is dead-on when he observes, "Nothing about tonight makes much sense." For starters, Ray (Jeremy Piven) has comandeered a gigantic, high-end RV which we are to believe he fast-talked a dealer into lending him on the prospect of selling several to his supposed company. It exists, in true movie fashion, only to be destroyed in the course of the story.

However, more troubling is the composition of the quartet. Apart from where they live, their age, vocation and attitude provide no linking bond. Frank (Emilio Estevez) is married, has a child and may or may not be out of work. His brother John (Stephen Dorff) is alienated by something that is never defined, and Mike's (Cuba Gooding Jr.) presence has no other explanation apart from racial diversity.

Lewis Colick's script is one long line of falling dominoes defined more by gravity than logic. The descent begins when the van hits someone in the otherwise deserted streets. On closer inspection, it turns out the fallen youth has been shot. When the perps return to complete the unfinished business, they decide there are too many complications with four living eyewitnesses.

The search-and-destroy and turn-the-tables-on-the-hunters scenario is standard stock of the genre. The new wrinkle of setting the action in the poor side of town is the shorthand to raise middle-class anxiety to a fever pitch quickly. In addition to "Judgment," Universal released the inner-city actioners "Trespass" and "Hard Target" in the past year. This format has yet to be intelligently exploited.

Amid the rubble, Estevez and Denis Leary, as the chief goon, comport themselves with some dignity and skill. Without falling into caricature, each manages to embody the forces of good and evil. The fact both have baby-face looks nicely emphasizes the two sides of the psychological coin.

Director Stephen Hopkins once again proves himself a shrewd manipulator of the medium. This is a handsome and cleverly made production with particular strong visuals from cameraman Peter Levy. However, there is nothing beneath its surface other than air — very thin air. *—Leonard Klady*

THE YOUNG AMERICANS

(BRITISH)

A Gramercy (U.S.)/Rank (U.K.) release of a PolyGram Filmed Entertainment/Live Entertainment presentation, with the participation of British Screen, of a Working Title Films/Trijbits Worrell Associates production, in association with Le Studio Canal Plus. Produced by Paul Trijbits, Alison Owen. Executive producers, Richard N. Gladstein, Ronna B. Wallace, Philippe Maigret. Directed by Danny Cannon. Screenplay, Cannon, David Hilton. Camera (Rank color; Panavision widescreen), Vernon Layton; editor, Alex Mackie; music, David Arnold; production design, Laurence Dorman; art direction, Neil Lamont; costume design, Howard Burden; sound (Dolby), Clive Winter, Paul Hamblin; stunt coordinator, Terry Forrestal; associate producer, Andrea M. Franden; assistant director, Waldo Roeg; casting, Sheila Tresize. Reviewed at Odeon West End 1, London, Sept. 8, 1993. Running time: **103 MIN.**

John Harris	Harvey Keitel
Edward Foster	Iain Glen
Richard Donnelly	John Wood
Sidney Callow	Terence Rigby
Jack Doyle	Keith Allen
Christian O'Neill	Craig Kelly
Rachael Stevens	Thandie Newton
Frazer	Viggo Mortensen
Carnegie	Dave Duffy
Carver	Geoffrey McGivern

Harvey Keitel hits the mean, mixed-race streets of London in "The Young Americans," a high-octane, in-your-face cop thriller that's got everything going for it except a well-rounded script. Slick feature bow by young director Danny Cannon should find a solid following with young urban auds on the strength of Keitel's name and with sharp marketing to the MTV crowd. Now in U.K. release, pic is due for stateside openings early next year.

Cannon, 25, landed the movie on the strength of his 65-minute film school grad work, "Strangers," shot in L.A. for $20,000 with aid from Propaganda Films. "Americans" is being touted locally as the biggest broadside yet by Blighty's "multiplex-generation" directors against an industry seemingly dominated by staid costumers and low-key, TV-style kitchen-sinkers.

Tone is set straightaway with a moody pre-credits sequence of mysterious young punks blowing away two mobsters outside the backstreets Temple nightclub. Enter N.Y.-out-of-L.A. cop John Harris (Keitel), who's been seconded from the DEA as an "adviser" to London's boys in blue on the current spate of London clubland killings.

Harris suspects the real villain is psychotic Yank drugster Frazer (Viggo Mortensen), whom he's been trailing from the U.S. and who is trying to move in on the London drug scene. Meanwhile, Harris dutifully follows around two British detectives, Carnegie (Dave Duffy)

and Carver (Geoffrey McGivern), who are secretly on the take from Temple boss Doyle (Keith Allen).

When C & C get firebombed in their car one day, Harris persuades a young bartender at the Temple, Chris (Craig Kelly), to help him. Coming clean to the British cops about his fears of Frazer, Harris persuades Chris to carry a wire at work. Final shootout finds whole cast converging on the nightclub.

Pic's strength (and its strong card for international markets) is its vivid sense of place and identity, making it more a souped-up version of pics like "Get Carter," "Villain" and "The Long Good Friday" than a 1990s Yank-in-London "Brannigan." Thanks to a reined-back perf, Keitel blends in rather than dominates the Brit ambience of gruff cops, multicolored youth and grungy, back-streets villainy.

Where the pic's reach exceeds its grasp is in the script department. Cannon and co-writer David Hilton spread their net wide, throwing in a cross-race love story between Kelly and a black friend's cousin (a restless, edgy Thandie Newton), personal problems back home for Keitel and fleeting refs to the changing nature of contempo London crime.

Movie's basic theme is referred to in the title: the new order in London crime that's leaving old-style Cockney mobsters dead on the streets as ruthless dudes like Mortensen exploit rootless black and white youths for their own ends.

Mortensen plays his psychotic character smoothly, but best shot here comes from Terence Rigby as a longtime hood rapidly being sidelined by the young thugs. His scenes with Keitel carry more dramatic weight than any of the pic's other crisscrossing relationships.

As a visual stylist, Cannon shows talent to burn, handling the Panavision screen with confidence and (in tandem with David Arnold's operatic score) going for the big effect with often breathtaking chutzpah. If the finale comes over as less of a capper than seemingly intended, it's because Cannon has shot most of his big bolts in earlier set pieces.

Technically, all departments are tip-top, with Vernon Layton's rich, color-noir lensing evoking a living, breathing city. Alex Mackie's cutting is seamless, and well-chosen locations balance the city's grime and glitter. —*Derek Elley*

FONG SAI-YUK TSUKTSAP

(FONG SAI-YUK II)

(HONG KONG)

A Golden Harvest (H.K.) release of an Eastern Prods. production. Produced, directed by Cory Yuen. Screenplay, Kei On, Chan Kin-tsung. Camera (color), Lee Ping-pan; editor, Lam On-yi; music, Lowell Lo; production design, Leung Wa-sang; art direction, Tsung Yi-fung; costume design, Cheung Sai-wang; martial arts direction, Cory Yuen, Yuen Tak. Reviewed at Mongkok Broadway 2 theater, Hong Kong, July 25, 1993. Running time: **97 MIN.**
Fong Sai-yuk .... Jet Li
His mother .... Josephine Hsiao
Chen Jialuo .... Adam Cheng
Also with: Michelle Lee, Amy Kwok, Cory Yuen, Chan Lung.
(Cantonese & Mandarin dialogue).

Chinese action star Jet Li powers back to the screen in "Fong Sai-Yuk II," a rapid follow-up to the spring B.O. hit that's actually far better than the original. Witty, smartly constructed actioner, also helmed by the experienced Cory Yuen, should score equal points with martial arts fans and follow its elder sibling along the fest trail.

Original pic grossed a brawny HK$30 million locally this spring. "II" previewed in late July in Hong Kong to SRO houses prior to full-scale release.

Set during the 18th century when China was ruled by the Manchu Ching dynasty, yarn cleverly taps the nationalistic vein of the "Once Upon in China" series (also starring Li), as well as satirizing 1950s Cantonese movies with b&w inserts and anachronistic slang.

This time out, the ingenuous Fong (Li) joins the anti-Manchu Red Flower Society, led by "godfather" Chen Jialuo (Adam Cheng). After botching an assignment to grab a secret document en route to the local governor, Fong is given a second chance to retrieve it by competing for the hand of the governor's daughter. When the document reveals that Chen is actually the emperor's brother, all hell breaks loose, with a thuggish member of the Society also ousting Chen.

Thanks to a stronger script, and better balance between comedy and action, present item avoids the original's dramatic dips. Action set pieces, including a riverside encounter with some Japanese samurai and a tour de force finale played out on a pyramid of stools, are fully the equal of the first pic's.

Li makes the most of his limited talents in the acting department, playing Fong as a sexual innocent dominated by his martial-artist mom. As the latter, vet actress Josephine Hsiao encores in spades her feisty perf from the original, stealing every scene she's in with a brilliant blend of comedy and *cojones*. Other roles are all flavorsomely

cast, and production values (using mainland Chinese locations) high. —*Derek Elley*

CHUNG ON TSOU

(CRIME STORY)

(HONG KONG)

A Golden Harvest (H.K.) production and release. Produced by Leonard K.C. Ho. Executive producer, Choi Lam. Directed by Kirk Wong. Screenplay, Cheun Tin-nam, Chan Man-keung, Cheung Lai-ling, Cheung Tsi-sing, Chan Tak-sam. Camera (color), Leu Wai-keung, Lam Kok-wa, Poon Hang-seng, Arthur Wong, Joe Chan; editor, Peter Cheung; music, James Wong; song, Li Tsung-sheng; art direction, Tony Au, Lui Cho-hung, Luk Tsi-fung; costume design, Tsong Tsi-leung, Cheung Hok-yeun, Ng Chui-wa, Siu Man-lai; stunt coordinators, Jackie Chan's Stunt Group; post-production supervisor, Chen Chi-hua. Reviewed at Mongkok Broadway 1 theater, Hong Kong, July 7, 1993. Running time: **100 MIN.**
Inspector Eddie Chan .... Jackie Chan
Hung .... Kent Cheng
Also with: K'o Shou-liang, Ng Wing-mei, Poon Ling-ling, Lo Ka-ying, Auyeung Pui-san, Lou Wai-kwong.
(Cantonese dialogue)

Jackie Chan takes a career swerve with "Crime Story," a dark-edged cop thriller in which the megastar's stunts play second fiddle to plot and mood. Stylish direction by former New Waver Kirk Wong makes this a fresh entry in the Chan oeuvre.

Pic is a clear attempt by Chan, now 39, to broaden his range away from purely stunt-driven blockbusters, though on present evidence he still needs more time with his drama coach. Chan buffs will note similarities with the angry tone of the first in the "Police Story" series, since softened into exotic comedy-actioners.

Supposedly based, per final crawl, on a recent hushed-up case, "Crime Story" has Chan as a member of H.K.'s Serious Crimes Squad (the pic's Chinese title) recently bent out of shape by a botched shootout. He's assigned to protect a millionaire real-estate developer threatened with kidnapping by a powerful triad of groups.

In a well-staged car chase recalling classic Chan, the millionaire is kidnapped and held for a ransom of $60 million. The brains behind the op is one of Chan's superiors, bent cop Hung (Kent Cheng). Rest of pic is Chan unraveling the case in Hong Kong and Taiwan, climaxing in a tense finale in a burning building.

Playing by Chan is straight, sans his usual boyish humor, and he's well framed by Wong's moody lighting and direction, all diffused light and Ridley Scott-like interiors. Action set pieces and firepower are both high caliber, with a simmering tension that holds the whole together. A standout sequence of the

millionaire's wife handing over the ransom loot while being tracked by the cops is a tour de force of cross-cutting and direction.

Tech credits are all fine, with a well-paced synth score by composer James Wong. —*Derek Elley*

DAIHAO 'MEIZHOUBAO'

(CODE NAME 'COUGAR')

(CHINESE)

A Xi'an Film Studio production, in association with Xi'an Modern Science & Technology Cultural Development Board. Produced by Wang Dongfeng, Zong Feng. Directed by Zhang Yimou, Yang Fengliang. Screenplay, Cheng Shiqing. Camera (color), Gu Changwei, Yang Lun; editor, Du Yuan; music, Guo Feng; song, Guo, Tao Lung; art direction, Cao Jiuping, Tong Huamiao; sound, Gu Changning; assistant directors, Zhou Youren, Gu Changning. Reviewed on China Film Movies videocassette, London, Oct. 11, 1993. Running time: **79 MIN.**
Liang Zhuang .... Liu Xiaoning
Huang Jingru .... Wang Xueqi
Zheng Xianping .... Ge You
He Li .... Gong Li
Qu Xiaozhen .... Gu Lan
Deputy commander ...... Yu Rongguang
Zhou, the secretary .... Xu Yao
(Mandarin dialogue)

Zhang Yimou's 1988 hijack drama, "Code Name 'Cougar,'" is a highly watchable, often fascinating glimpse at the hidden flipside of China's premier arthouse director. Unshown outside East Asia, and passed over by Zhang himself in discussions of his *oeuvre*, pic makes a tasty item for Sinophiles and the curious.

Zhang shot the movie, his second, for his home studio Xi'an while on a roll from the success of his directing debut, "Red Sorghum." In the pre-Tiananmen year of 1988, many directors of his generation turned to commercial subjects as studios joined the rush to market caused by the country's economic overheating.

Like his subsequent "Ju Dou," which returned him to the arthouse fold, the movie is officially credited to both him and co-helmer Yang Fengliang, a.d. on "Red Sorghum." Tech team, however, is virtually identical to that on Zhang's surrounding films, and all publicity at the time focused on Zhang himself as prime creator.

Politically cheeky yarn has to do with a private aircraft, en route from Taipei to Seoul, hijacked by group calling itself the Taiwan Revolutionary Army Front. When the plane is forced to make an emergency landing in mainland China, Beijing's authorities secretly link up with Taiwan's to try to sort out the embarrassing mess.

Whole thing takes place during 12 hours one hot September day, with most of the action set in a large

October 25, 1993 (Cont.)

field in which the aircraft has landed. Taiwan sends over its own anti-terrorist squad to link up with China's military, as the hijackers demand the release of one of their number from a Taiwan jail and safe passage to Manila.

Action cuts back and forth between the hijackers and their businessman hostage sweltering inside the craft, and the troops roasting in the field outside.

Using a newsy, v.o. narration, and rapid picture montages showing meetings in Beijing, Hong Kong and Taipei, the film has a restless, pseudo-docu style, heightened by lotsa compressed-zoom shooting in the grassy field, with the camera cast as almost a spectator to events. Topbilled Liu Xiaoning impresses as the cool but human Mainland commander.

Scenes inside the plane are more standard, with Ge You hamming as the loony terrorist leader and Zhang's regular muse, actress Gong Li, wooden in a throwaway part of a hijacker posing as a nurse.

Pic covers itself politically with an opening caption stressing "this is a fictional story" and a closer that "reporters from various countries tried to find out whether Beijing and Taipei had ever secretly cooperated. Both sides of the Taiwan Strait denied it."

Tech credits are acceptable, with most laurels going to the edgy lensing by Gu Changwei, who's done distinguished work for both Zhang and fellow Fifth Generation director Chen Kaige. Pic had a lackluster weeklong run in Hong Kong in October 1989, under the title "Operation 'Cougar'" ("Meizhoubao xing-dong").
—*Derek Elley*

DET FORSOMTE FORAR

(THE STOLEN SPRING)

(DANISH)

A Regner Grasten Film Aps production. (International sales: Nordisk Film). Produced by Grasten. Directed by Peter Schroder. Screenplay, Peter Bay, based on a novel by Hans Scherfig. Camera (color), Dirk Bruel; editor, Jorgen Kastrup; music, Jan Glaesel; production design, Viggo Bentzon; sound, Stig Sparre Ulrich; casting, Jette Termann; assistant director, Tom Hedegaard. Reviewed at Screening Room, Leura, Australia, Aug. 18, 1993. (In Cannes Festival market.) Running time: **89 MIN.**

With: Frits Helmuth, Tomas W. Jensen, Jesper Langborg, Adam Simonsen, Hugo Oster Bendtsen, Rene Hansen, Lars Lohmann, Ken Vedsegaard, Stig Hoffmeyer, Lisa Lach Nielsen.

"The Stolen Spring" harks back in theme to Alf Sjoberg's 1944 "Torment," which was scripted by the young Ingmar Bergman. Both films deal with a sadistic schoolteacher whose perverted idea of discipline leads to the torture of his students. This carefully made pic doesn't have the impact of the earlier film, but deserves solid attention for its theme and fine performances.

Peter Schroder's film is based on a 1940 novel by Hans Scherfig, which was described in the New York Times Book Review as "a stinging indictment of an absurd and stultifying school system." The film opens with the death of the hated teacher, Blomme (Frits Helmuth), who appears to choke on some candy while strolling in the street; a passing policeman thinks he's drunk, and he dies with a Latin phrase on his lips.

In the present, former students of Blomme, who include a judge, a drifter and the school's present headmaster, gather for a reunion and recall how much they hated the man. Flashbacks depict Blomme's terror campaign against his students and his thinly disguised homosexual advances to one of them. The boys form a "secret society" to punish him, and it's suggested that one of them does, in fact, poison him.

A low-key pic, "The Stolen Spring" evocatively presents a school system that belongs in the past. Its concerns will seem remote from today's audiences, but it's sufficiently well acted and directed to merit attention on the fest circuit. Production credits are tops.
—*David Stratton*

LA CAVALE DES FOUS

(LOONIES AT LARGE)

(FRENCH)

An AFMD release (France) of a Fideline Films/France 2 Cinema/Sofiarp/Investimage 4 production, with participation of Canal Plus. (Intl. sales: Roissy Films, Paris.) Directed by Marco Pico. Screenplay, Olivier Dazat, Pierre Richard. Camera (color), Francois Lartigue; editor, Yousef Tobni; music, Olivier Defays, Christophe Defays; art direction, Dominique Andre; sound, Jean-Louis Ughetto, Jean-Bernard Thomasson. Reviewed at Vevey Comedy Film Festival (competing), Vevey, Switzerland, July 28, 1993. Running time: **91 MIN.**

Bertrand Daumale .... Pierre Richard
Henri Toussaint .... Michel Piccoli
Angel .... Dominique Pinon
Also with: Florence Pernel, Edith Scob, Patrice Alexandre, Helene Surgere.

"La Cavale des fous" is an easygoing, featherweight comedy about a sweet psychotic and a wily manic-depressive on a furtive field trip with a shy psychiatrist. Pic dishes up intermittent chuckles but never really takes off. Behavior ascribed to the characters is clinically accurate, but trio's antics won't hit a universal funny bone. Less hammy U.S. movie "The Dream Team" covered similar territory in 1989.

Michel Piccoli plays an eminent university prof who, after trying to strangle his adulterous wife, has spent six years in a luxury loony bin under the care of a mild-mannered shrink (Pierre Richard). When the terminally ill wife wants to reconcile with Piccoli, Richard decides to escort him to her bedside.

Despite his mood swings and uncouth sexual mumblings, Piccoli can pass for sane. But what should be a simple weekend excursion is soon derailed. A psychotic stowaway from the asylum (Dominique Pinon) becomes a bottomless source of inappropriate behavior.

Pinon (the offbeat-looking hero of "Delicatessen") is supremely convincing as a lovable weirdo, but Piccoli and Richard seem to be going through the motions.

Few gags or rejoinders hit the mark, although Piccoli's knack for second-guessing people yields a few bright moments. A cruel sendup of the Paris literary set is amusing.

Pic won top prize (the Golden Cane) at the Vevey Festival of Comedy Films in Switzerland this summer.
—*Lisa Nesselson*

N.Y. FEST

BIRTHPLACE

(DOCU — POLISH — 16mm)

A Kronika Film Studio production, in association with Polish Television Channel 1, Film School in Lodz and the Batory Foundation. Directed by Pavel Lozinski. Camera (color), Arthur Reinhart; editor, Katarzyna Maciejko-Kowalczyk; sound, Joanna Napieralska, Mariusz Kuczynski; art direction, Andrzej Brzozowski. Reviewed at New York Film Festival, Oct. 12, 1993. Running time: **47 MIN.**

In Pavel Lozinski's "Birthplace," a Polish-born American Jew returns to the small village where his father and baby brother fell victim during the Holocaust.

As one elderly peasant after another is asked for memories about the family and the deaths, the documentarian's shrewd objective is slowly and subtly revealed: "Birthplace" is less interested in solving a family mystery than in detailing the guilt, anger and shame harbored for 50 years by those who know the answers. Short length will limit theatrical possibilities, but docu will find a place in programs relating to the Holocaust and possibly on public TV and specialized cable outlets.

Ostensible subject is writer Henryk Grynberg, a man who, as a young boy, escaped with his mother to America, never again to see the father and brother who stayed behind. The 47-minute docu doesn't address how or why Henryk and his mother were able to flee, but endeavors to determine the fates of those who stayed. Prompted by the straightforward questions of the stoical, expressionless Grynberg, the old villagers recall in often amazing detail what they saw. Lozinski structures the interviews so that the story of Grynberg's family is told virtually chronologically, with each interview yielding information that leads to the next.

Tale reveals the villagers' complicity with and resistance to the Germans. The murders, it is learned early on, were committed not by Nazis but by Poles, and even those villagers who attempted to aid their Jewish neighbors (in ways that now seem remarkably limited) carry an unmistakable shame. "Birthplace" can be faulted for Lozinski's reliance on those villagers who both agreed to answer questions and had the memories to do so. Director has stated that most villagers refused to discuss the matter, and their absence gives the erroneous impression that Grynberg's birthplace is a welcoming place indeed.

Nevertheless, the reminiscences and chunks of information offered by these weathered survivors are captivating. Film's unsentimental style — with Arthur Reinhart's unflinching camera moving from close-ups of wrinkled faces to long shots of the harsh Polish winter — mirrors the villagers' matter-of-fact delivery of their long-remembered horror stories.

Uniformly understated, "Birthplace" still has several stand-out moments, as when an old woman recognizes Grynberg as the sick little boy she harbored many decades before. That interview is topped, however, by Grynberg's confrontation with a man who almost certainly had a hand in his father's murder. An old farmer who now protests, "I was just a boy in my teens," this possible murderer and certain accomplice is the banality of evil incarnate.

Film climaxes with a literal unearthing, the only point in which Grynberg displays any emotion, and it packs a punch. The grisly footage is handled with some taste, but since Lozinski doesn't indicate when the grave site was discovered, the question arises of whether the filmmaker was incredibly lucky or if the entire episode was staged. Lozinski insists on the former, and while there's no reason to doubt him, a bit of clarification would be in order.

Whatever its shortcomings, Lozinski's film gradually emerges as an effective group portrait of neighbors both then and now. Despite the 50-year time span, the "then" for these people is as real and present as this afternoon.
—*Greg Evans*

PAN AFRICAN

SIMEON

(MARTINIQUE-FRENCH)

An AMLF release (France) of a Saligna production in association with France 2 Cinema and Canal Plus. Produced by Jean-Lou Monthieux. Directed by Euzhan Palcy. Screenplay by Palcy, Jean-Pierre Rumeau, based on an original story by Palcy. Camera (color), Philippe Welt; editor, Marie-Josephe Yoyette; music, Bruno Coulais; production design, Bernard Vezat; costume design, Annie Quesnel; sound (Dolby), Bernard Bats; assistant director, Jerome Navarro. Reviewed at Pan African Film Festival, L.A., Oct. 10, 1993. Running time: **111 MIN.**

Simeon	Jean-Claude Duvorger
Isidore	Jacob Desvarieux
Orelie	Lucinda Messager
Roselyne	Jocelyn Beroard
Albert	Albert Lirvat
Philo	Jean-Michel Martial
Ernest	Pascal Legitimas
Fire Lady	Lisette Malador

Director Euzhan Palcy gets a mixed report card with "Simeon," a whimsical, musical-fantasy. Caribbean-set yarn has a vibrant, authentic pulse, but its script and musical components prove to be weak links in this artistic chain. Though rife with potential mainstream elements, the film winds up a uniquely specialized item, even in territories seemingly more receptive to its style and rhythms.

The title character, played by Jean-Claude Duvorger, is a sage, longtime music teacher in Martinique. A former jazz drummer in Paris, Simeon returned to his birthplace about 20 years earlier and has become the much beloved music guru for two generations of islanders.

His dream is to see his brand of calypso-jazz-salsa-swing travel far and wide. But just as one of his ex-pupils, Isidore (Jacob Desvarieux), appears primed to land a European recording contract, Simeon dies in a freak accident. He nonetheless remains earthbound and a voice Isidore and his daughter Orelie (Lucinda Messager) continue to hear.

Is his need to see a musical legacy fulfilled that strong?

Apparently not. Local superstition stipulates that Simeon cannot step beyond until he's in possession of all his temporal physical parts. And Orelie just happened to snip off a crucial braid of hair.

Palcy and co-scenarist Jean-Pierre Rumeau attempt a fusion of folkloric traditions and new music that never quite meshes. Still, both aspects have their charms.

Orelie's devotion to Simeon in life and death is touching. Her battle with the devilish Fire Lady for his soul works because of her essential innocence. Less successful is Simeon's growing attachment with Roselyne (Jocelyn Beroard), a flesh-and-blood singer who joins Isidore's band.

The cast is uniformly excellent. The director has drawn well from music, acting and local ranks in assembling her players. This very assured film also demonstrates that her technical prowess has grown and been refined since "Sugar Cane Alley." However, the soundtrack and song score remain a disappointment. They are never as original or diverse as befits the essence of the piece. —*Leonard Klady*

DINARD FEST

THE HOUR OF THE PIG

(FRENCH-BRITISH)

A Miramax (U.S.) release of a Ciby 2000/BBC Films production, with participation of British Screen and European Co-production Fund. Produced by David M. Thompson. Executive producers, Michael Wearing, Claudine Sainderichin. Directed, written by Leslie Megahey. Camera (color), John Hooper; editor, Isabelle Dedieu; music, Alexandre Desplat; production design, Bruce Macadie; costume design, Anna Buruma; sound (Dolby), Daniel Brisseau; associate producer, Dave Edwards. Reviewed at Dinard Festival of British Cinema (non-competing), Dinard, France, Sept. 25, 1993. (Also in London festival.) Running time: **115 MIN.**

Richard Courtois	Colin Firth
Albertus	Ian Holm
Pincheon	Donald Pleasence
The Seigneur	Nicol Williamson
Filette	Lysette Anthony
Samira	Amina Annabi
Mathieu	Jim Carter
Gerard	Justin Chadwick
Magistrate Boniface	Michael Gough
Jeannine	Harriet Walter
(English dialogue)	

Any lawyer who has ever taken his client for swine will have the last laugh watching "The Hour of the Pig," a droll, deftly acted period piece based on the fact that in medieval France animals were accused of crimes and tried in court with counsel. Franco-British production's offbeat storyline could help to carve a nice slice of bacon at international arthouses.

Set in the Middle Ages, pic kicks off with a witty sequence of a man and his she-ass about to be hanged for inter-species carnal activity, only to have the latter pardoned (and her good reputation restored by decree) in the nick of time. The man hangs.

An industrious young defense lawyer, Courtois (Colin Firth), has left Paris for the allegedly purer framework of the boondocks. In the village of Abbeville where he settles, intending to use his smarts for the greater good, there's a long-established prosecuting attorney (Donald Pleasence). Courtois soon learns that superstition, the Church and the local nobleman (Nicol Wil-liamson) have enormous influence. He strikes up a useful friendship with a hypocritical local clergyman (Ian Holm).

When a band of Jewish gypsies enters the town, and their prize pig is arrested and accused of killing a young boy, exotic dark-skinned Samira (Amina Annabi) implores Courtois to get the pig acquitted, offering her womanly charms in exchange. At first flabbergasted by the inanity of applying due process to a dumb animal, Courtois becomes hellbent on proving his porcine client's innocence.

The scapegoat theme is handled well and lends contemporary resonance to the long-ago story. The interracial romance between Firth and Annabi smacks a little too much of 20th century posturing, but this (and a slightly overlong conclusion) is the only false note in the comic, intellectually stimulating proceedings.

U.S. distrib Miramax is reportedly tightening both the love scenes and the ending, prior to pic's screening at the London fest in November.

Despite French co-prod money, the movie wisely sticks to an all-Brit cast, creating a homogeneous screen universe. Clever dialogue, laced with frank and bawdy observations, is delivered in ultra-dry style. Scripter-helmer Leslie Megahey gets in some well-placed digs about the ignorance of anti-Semites. The lusty interludes are sweet and full of humor.

Holm and Williamson are excellent in their roles, and supports are spirited, particularly Jim Carter as Firth's ironic law clerk and Lysette Anthony as Williamson's goofy daughter. Alexandre Desplat's score is pleasant to the ear, and production design by Bruce Mackie easy on the eye. —*Lisa Nesselson*

TOKYO FEST

SPARROW

(ITALIAN)

A Mario and Vittorio Cecchi Gori presentation in association with Nippon Film Development & Finance Inc. of an Officina Cinematografica production. Produced by Mario and Vittorio Cecchi Gori. Executive producers, Rita Ruzic Cecchi Gori, Luciano Luna. Directed by Franco Zeffirelli. Screenplay, Zeffirelli and Alain Baken, based on a novel by Giovanni Verga. Camera (color), Ennio Guarnieri; editor, Richard Marden; music, Claudio Cappani, Alessio Vlad; art direction, Giantito Burchiellaro; set design, Raimonda Gaetani; costume design, Piero Tosi; sound (Dolby), Godfrey Kirby. Reviewed at Tokyo Intl. Film Festival (non-competing), Oct. 3, 1993. Running time: **114 MIN.**

Maria	Angela Bettis
Nino	Jonathon Schaech
Matilde	Sinead Cusack
Giuseppe	John Castle
Sister Agata	Vanessa Redgrave
Giuseppe	John Castle
(English dialogue)	

This film about a 19th century nun-in-the-making has all the markings of Franco Zeffirelli's talent — it is dramatic, grand in scope, and tragic in its tale of unfulfilled love and lives. Unfortunately, the plot is almost tortuously slow, and the film ends up neither emotionally nor intellectually gripping. "Sparrow" will disappoint commercial and arthouse audiences alike and is not destined to go down as one of Zeffirelli's successes.

Zeffirelli has brought to the film his passion for the classics, but his co-authored screenplay — based on a contemporary Italian novel — does not have the structural or lyrical strength of Shakespeare. Whether derived from a weak script, cliched imagery and visual direction, or over-acting — or a combination of them all — net effect is dully melodramatic.

While many of the minor supporting roles are well acted (such as Vanessa Redgrave's Sister Agata), film relies almost exclusively on the presence of the two leads, Angela Bettis and Jonathon Schaech. Both lack emotional depth, though they err in opposite ways: Bettis is overdone, superficial and cliched, while Schaech is somewhat flat, although he indisputably has the physical qualifications for the tall-dark-handsome leading man.

The visual style is another culprit; while the scenery is gorgeous, images such as Bettis and Schaech at a steaming volcano or Bettis running her dog through fields are so stereotypical as to be nauseating.

Story revolves around Maria (Bettis), a novice at a convent in mid-19th century Italy. Because of a cholera outbreak, she must return to her home at Mount Etna. There she discovers the joys of freedom and of falling in love with the handsome Nino (Schaech). However, she remains true to her training and rejects Nino's offers of love.

Cholera threat over, Maria returns to the convent, where she becomes tortured by her conflicting emotions of love for Nino and religious commitment. When Nino ends up marrying Maria's sister, Maria goes to the brink of insanity. She runs to Nino and there finds the strength to continue the religious life that she sees as her destiny.

The best is undoubtedly saved for last, partly because it signifies the end of a slow and frustrating tale, but also because the ending possesses an intensity and visual starkness that is almost haunting. However, this last bit is not enough to overcome the shortcomings of the previous 113 minutes.

—*Karen Regelman*

October 25, 1993 (Cont.)

LA NUIT SACREE
(THE SACRED NIGHT)
(FRENCH)

A Flach Film production. (Foreign sales: Mercure Distribution.). Produced by Flach Film and Film Ariane. Directed by Nicolas Klotz. Screenplay, Elisabeth Perceval. Camera (color), Carlo Varini; editor, Jean-Francois Naudon; music, Coran Bregovic; art direction, Didier Naert; costume design, Jacques Schmidt, Emmanuel Peduzzi; sound (Dolby), Jean-Pierre Ruh, Maurice Laumain. Reviewed at Tokyo International Film Festival (competing), Sept. 29, 1993. Running time: 110 MIN.
Ahmed-Zahra .... Amina
The Consul .... Miguel Boss
The Seated Woman .... Maite Nahyr
The Father .... Francois Chattot

The Sacred Night" is a bizarre melodrama sure to please pretentious pseudo-intellectuals and vaguely baffle the rest. Set in Morocco from the 1920s to 1950s, it is an examination of gender issues strange enough to rival "The Crying Game" with a soap opera's worth of angst-ridden, tortured characters. But it's both weird enough and French enough to possibly squeak by on art-house circuit.

Pic follows the story of the seventh daughter in a girls-only Muslim family, who is raised as a boy named "Ahmed" (Amina) due to the strict Islamic inheritance laws. Her identity crisis comes to a boil after she not only starts shaving, but also decides to grow a moustache and take a wife — both of which are clearly out of the question.

On his deathbed, Ahmed's father, who is tortured by Ahmed's near-insanity and wishes to die at peace, gives Ahmed a new life by renaming her "Zahra" and telling her to go out and live a true life as a woman.

She takes off across Morocco, under privileges afforded to a Muslim man, but without identity papers or records. Eventually, she finds a position in the weirder-than-weird household of the Consul (Miguel Bose), a blind man tortured by sudden, agonizing headaches, and his sister (Maite Nahyr), a bath owner whose interest in her brother borders on the incestuous.

Zahra tends to the Consul, but their mutual affection sends the sister into jealous rages. She discovers Zahra's past, which sends the young girl to her demise, as she is essentially left without an identity.

The film is scripted and acted strongly, perhaps too strongly. Every word, every look is so infused with meaning and heavy drama that it's exhausting to listen to and watch.

Photography, set design, and costumes all combine to excellent effect, transporting the viewer into an exotic world. While the content may be a bit short on believability, the setting is both realistic and entrancing. *—Karen Regelman*

NAKED IN NEW YORK

A Fine Line Features release of a Fine Line and Pandora Cinema presentation. (Foreign sales: Pandora Cinema.) Produced by Frederick Zollo. Executive producer, Martin Scorsese. Coproducer, Carol Cuddy. Directed by Daniel Algrant. Screenplay, Algrant, John Warren, based on an idea by Algrant. Camera (color), Joey Forsyte; editor, Bill Pankow; music, Angelo Badalamenti; production design, Kalina Ivanov; costume design, Julie Weiss; sound, Dennis Maitland; associate producers, Katy Bolger, John Penotti; assistant director, Gregory Jacobs; casting, Bonnie Timmermann, Judy Henderson. Reviewed at Tokyo International Film Festival (in Young Cinema Competition), Sept. 29, 1993. Running time: 86 MIN.
Jake .... Eric Stoltz
Joanne .... Mary Louise Parker
Chris .... Ralph Macchio
Jake's mother .... Jill Clayburgh
Carl Fisher .... Tony Curtis
Dana Coles .... Kathleen Turner
Elliot Price .... Timothy Dalton
Mr. Ried .... Roscoe Lee Browne
Helen .... Lynne Thigpen
Face on the Theater
Wall .... Whoopi Goldberg

Naked in New York" is a charming, creative, but slightly inconsistent look at the dreams and loves of the artsy twentysomething set in contemporary America. Despite its affectations, it speaks to a broad cross-section of Generation X-ers. Despite one or two inappropriate casting choices, film's charm and the strength of many of the names behind this just-out-of-film-school feature could poise it for a decent run in specialized release.

Martin Scorsese offered his support for the project after reading the script, which is based on Algrant's own life. This and several short film awards landed Algrant some big-name stars, most of whom are believable and appealing, notably Mary Louise Parker, Eric Stoltz and Kathleen Turner. Several surprise cameos make for plenty of fun for star gazers.

Of these, only one — Ralph Macchio — is out of place and out of his league. Cast in a pivotal and emotionally deep role, Macchio is too, well, Macchio for his own good, doing nothing to shatter aud's "Karate Kid" preconceptions.

Story revolves around Jake (Stoltz), who grows up in a house with his mother, her friend Helen, lots of neuroses and candles, but no father. Related by Jake in flashbacks, narrative has him grow up and become interested in the performing arts rather than sports.

Most of his young adult life has been spent writing plays in which friend Chris (Macchio) stars, or experiencing first love with Joanne (Parker). After college, he ultimately must choose between trying to further his profession in N.Y. with Chris, or making his relationship with Joanne last.

The tug of Gotham wins, though there he must confront a whole new set of challenges: unexpected sexual advances from both Chris and theater star Dana Coles (Kathleen Turner). In an example of art-mirrors-life, Coles is miscast in the play-within-the-film based on her commercial draw, much as Macchio is miscast in the film itself.

One of the odder bits in the film is the statue of a frog that talks to Jake; the amphibian monument's imputed musings are even subtitled so the audience can understand as well. It doesn't seem to fit with the rest of the film, suddenly jolting the audience out of the pic's real-life quirkiness into a moment of hokey staging. But the film overcomes this and Macchio's performance and is basically enjoyable, if somewhat imperfect. *—Karen Regelman*

TORONTO FEST

DER KINOERZAEHLER
THE MOVIE TELLER
(GERMAN)

A co-production of Allianz Film Produktion with ABS Film/Roxy Film/Bioskop Film/ZDF. (Foreign sales: Weltvertrieb in Filmverlag der Autoren, Munich.) Produced, directed, written by Bernhard Sinkel, based on the novel by Gert Hofman. Executive producer, Gunther Fenner. Camera (color), Axel Block; editor, Heidi Handorf; music, Gunther Fischer; art direction, Olaf Schiefner; sets, Gotz Weidner; costumes, Barbara Baum; sound (Dolby), Michael Kranz; line producers, Norbert Schneider, Wolfgang Tumler, Udo Heiland; co-line producers, Luggi Waldleitner, Eberhard Junkersdorf. Reviewed at Festival of Festivals, Toronto, Sept. 8, 1993. Running time: 98 MIN.
Movie Teller .... Armin Mueller-Stahl
Herr Theilhaber .... Martin Benrath
Paul .... Andrej Jautze
Grandmother .... Tina Engel
Frau Fritsche .... Eva Mattes
Mother .... Katharina Tanner
Herr Lange .... Udo Samel
Salzmann .... Otto Sander

A hitherto forgotten chapter in the history of movies is the springboard for the delightful and engaging "The Movie Teller." The German memory tale skillfully weaves the stories of its principles with the era when films began to talk and a nation dug itself out of one war only to stockpile for the next. This is a deceptively simple saga made of rich fabric and imbued with often chilling and resonant echoes.

Aside from the inherent problems faced by all small, artfully produced films in the international marketplace, "Movie Teller" is confronted by another hurdle. While set in another time and another place, the film is too uncomfortably reminiscent of "Cinema Paradiso."

Commercially, it suffers from the comparison and will most assuredly need festival recognition to break into worldwide specialty release. As with the Italian Oscar winner, the story is told through the eyes of a child. Or, more accurately, a man looking back upon his youth. However, the cornerstone of both films is the older, much-adored father figure — in this instance, the boy's grandfather and title character.

Paul (Andrej Jautze) initially recalls the heyday of the Apollo, a crowded movie house in a quaint provincial town. As images of the silent "Hands of Orlac" paint the screen, grandfather (Armin Mueller-Stahl) plays his violin, pausing often to expertly interject his color coverage of the action and emotions being played out on film.

This movie teller is so consumed with his skill, all other elements of life evaporate into the ether. As the rumblings of sound film draw nearer, he avidly argues quality over audience size to an increasingly nervous theater owner. A new government takes power and while people are being stripped of possessions and power, the old man worries only for the Apollo and the return of silent features.

Lesser talents would probably have brought the Gert Hofman novel to the screen as a grand tragedy. What is skillfully realized in Bernhard Sinkel's vision and Mueller-Stahl's interpretation is the character's charm and the boy's adoration. There is little doubt that a type of emotional blindness is in play. What elevates the material is the artists' ability to convey why that was and the vital purpose it served for some.

Tech credits handsomely recreate the period. "The Movie Teller" is a labor of love not averse to showing the dark side of humanity. It's a work of great subtlety and quiet authority. *—Leonard Klady*

TALLINN PIMEDUSES
(DARKNESS IN TALLINN)
(FINNISH-U.S. — B&W)

A FilmZolfo production, in association with Upstream Pictures, Film-Lance Intl., Film Teknik and ExitFilm. (Intl. sales: Upstream Pictures, New York.) Produced by Lasse Saarinen. Executive producer, Ilkka Jarvilaturi. Directed by Jarvilaturi. Screenplay, Paul Kolsby. Camera (b&w), Rein Kotov; editor, Christopher Tellefsen; music, Mader; sound, Jussi Vantanen. Reviewed at Cannes Film Festival (market), May 19, 1993. (In Festival of Festivals, Toronto.) Running time 99 MIN.
Toivo .... Ivo Uukkivi
Maria .... Milena Gulbe
(In Estonian)

"Darkness in Tallinn" is an ambitious, suspenseful thriller that makes effective use of the Estonian capital as a backdrop to a farfetched tale in which the mob attempts to steal the country's entire gold reserves. Black-and-white lensing for this film noir is strikingly effective, and while fest and limited arthouse exposure is indicated, lack of color may prove a limitation in some ancillary markets.

It seems that, before the German invasion of Estonia in 1940, the prewar government stashed the small country's gold stocks in a Paris bank for safekeeping. The loot was never retrieved during the postwar Soviet occupation but now, with independence, it is due to be returned to its rightful place.

Some well organized and high-powered mobsters have decided to grab the haul, however, and hire an impoverished young electrician to cut all power to the city on the night Estonians are celebrating their independence and pull off the heist under cover of darkness. Ivo Uukkivi plays the electrician who needs the money for his pregnant wife who, wrongly believing he's been killed, goes into premature labor just as her husband manages to shut off the city's power. What follows is suspenseful stuff, with Finnish director Ilkka Jarvilaturi setting a brisk pace and building tension and mayhem to a cathartic finale. In all, a modest but quite ingenious genre pic with an unusual setting and plenty of authentic atmosphere. Credit titles are in color.

—*David Stratton*

BECAUSE WHY

(CANADIAN)

An Aska Film production in association with Cinoque Films. Produced by Claude Gagnon, Yuri Yoshimura-Gagnon, Francois Pouliot. Directed, written by Arto Paragamian. Camera (color), Andre Turpin; editor, Christine Denault; music, Nana Vasconcelos; art direction, Patricia Christie; sound, Yvon Benoit; casting, Jocelyne Trudeau. Reviewed at Festival of Festivals, Toronto, Sept. 11, 1993. Running time: **104 MIN.**
Alex .... Michael Riley
Arto .... Doru Bandol
Alya .... Martine Rochon
Anne .... Heather Mathieson
Albert .... Victor Knight
Andre .... Hank Hum

"**B**ecause Why," Arto Paragamian's directorial feature debut, is an offbeat romantic comedy starring Michael Riley, who is rapidly becoming one of Canada's best-known actors. Intermittently entertaining, pic features deadpan, sophisticated humor of the Jim Jarmusch-Aki Kaurismaki school. Comedy's urban locale, twentysomething triangle and contemporary feel for modern relationships should appeal to young, hip viewers.

The versatile Riley plays Alex, a wanderer who returns to Montreal only to find out that his best friend, Arto (Doru Bandol), is about to depart for Cairo. This is only the first in a series of disappointments, which include running into his ex-girlfriend in a supermarket and realizing she has married and settled down. Alex seems to "specialize" in complex romantic entanglements: an affair with Alya (Martine Rochon), his best friend's lover, and then a romance with neighbor Anne (Heather Mathieson), an attractive single mother with two kids.

Alex's building is populated by eccentric characters, beginning with his landlord. Nonetheless, the random aggregate of tenants gradually becomes a meaningful social unit, a commune of people who really like — and help — each other through various crises.

"Because Why" boasts an exhilarating beginning and some funny, unexpected turns. But it's burdened with repetitive set pieces, such as a landlord always seen in the same position, as he's about to install a smoke detector in his building. Comedy also suffers from overly deliberate pacing and self-conscious, often cutesy humor; all the characters' names, for example, begin with an A.

Yet, as scripter and helmer, Paragamian demonstrates humanistic vision in the way he depicts the emotional bonds among his disparate characters (which also include an elderly gay couple) and their function as a substitute family. Pic's central piece, a lovely picnic in the woods, reflects the kind of communal ties that rarely exist — and are seldom depicted — in American urban comedies.

Holding the film together, the enormously talented Riley excels as a classic clown, a man who doesn't really know what he wants in life and yet beguiles everybody. Riley is ably supported by an ensemble of half-a-dozen fetching performers.

Production values are proficient, particularly Andre Turpin's handsome lensing and Nana Vasconcelos' romantic, melancholy score.

—*Emanuel Levy*

MAYA MEMSAAB

(MAYA: THE ENCHANTING ILLUSION)

(INDIAN)

A National Film Development Board of India/Channel 4 presentation in association with Video Cinema 13 Prods. and Film Four Intl. (Foreign sales: Film Four Intl.) Produced, directed by Ketan Mehta. Executive producer, Vikram Merotra. Screenplay, Sitanshu Yashashchandra, Mehta, based on "Madame Bovary" by Gustave Flaubert. Camera (color), Anoop Jyotwani; editor, Renu Saluha; music, Hridaynath Mangeshkar; art direction, Meera Lakhia, Ashish Lakhia; costume design, Monica Dutta; sound, Rajat Dholakia. Reviewed at Festival of Festivals, Toronto, Sept. 15, 1993. Running time: **120 MIN.**
Maya .... Deepa Sahi
  Also with: Farooque Sheikh, Raj Babbar, Shah Rukh Khan, Satyadev Dubey.

"**M**aya: The Enchanting Illusion" is a corny romantic meller that awkwardly attempts to airlift Flaubert's "Madame Bovary" to postcolonial India. Waffling uncontrollably between self-consciously poetic romanticism and facetious, nearly campy humor, Ketan Mehta's treatment of the tale never develops an integrity of its own that could pull the viewer through the morass of erratic scenes. Prospects in the West are negligible.

Pic's one saving grace is the exquisitely beautiful Deepa Sahi, who throws herself into the title role with the abandon that it deserves.

Unfortunately, like Garbo in one of her lesser vehicles, she is so radiant to begin with that one can only bemoan the pathetic succession of men with whom she is forced to cope and the shabby circumstances of the production in which she is trapped.

Framed by a police investigation looking into "the Maya scandal," story sees the title character take the first wrong step by marrying a buffoonish doctor.

Even though she admits she has everything she could want with her daughter and material possessions, she still feels empty and dissatisfied, and hooks up with a number of generally bumbling men who predictably do her wrong, including a playboy for whom she falls hard.

A compelling presence early on, Maya becomes increasingly uninteresting as she insists upon throwing herself away on unworthy men and presses further down the road of a silly, dissolute lifestyle.

Mehta's direction is loaded with poetic flourishes, but he's hampered by a style that is more crude than fluid, and his effects are far from precise and emotionally involving.

Aside from Sahi's performance, pic is marked by one brief sex scene that is rather hot and revealing by Indian standards.

—*Todd McCarthy*

KANEHSATAKE: 270 YEARS OF RESISTANCE

(CANADIAN — DOCU)

A National Film Board of Canada presentation of a Studio B production. Produced by Alanis Obomsawin, Wolf Koenig. Executive producer, Colin Neale. Directed, written by Alanis Obomsawin. Camera (color), Roger Rochat, Jean-Claude Labrecque, Philippe Amiguet, Susan Trow, Francois Brault, Barry Perles, Zoe Dirse, Jocelyn Simard, Andre-Luc Dupont, Savas Kalogeras; editor, Yurij Luhovy; music, Claude Vendette, Francis Grandmont; sound, Raymond Marcoux, Marie-France Delagrave, Robert Verebely, Ismael Cordeiro, Catherine Van Der Donckt, Serge Fortin, Juan Gutierrez. Narrated by Obomsawin. Reviewed at Festival of Festivals, Toronto, Sept. 15, 1993. Running time: **118 MIN.**

The 78-day standoff between members of the Mohawk nation and Canadian government forces in 1990 informs the powerful chronicle "Kanehsatake: 270 Years of Resistance." More than just a thoroughgoing piece of direct cinema, the film — through its observation and narration — comments eloquently on the relationship between the native population and "the invaders" who have come to rule their domain. Film was a Toronto Fest prizewinner.

The details of this incident are not particularly unusual in contemporary history. When the town of Oka, outside of Montreal, announced plans to expand a golf course and develop a proposed housing project, Mohawk leaders called for a moratorium on all land development. Some 40 years earlier, the town had expropriated land for the original golf course, and the expansion would venture into disputed land claim territory.

The disagreement snowballs from legal channels to informational pickets, barricades, injunctions, local police, provincial and federal intervention, and the arrival of the Canadian army. If the real life issues were not so painful and longstanding, one could easily mistake the scenario for a political farce on the order of "The Mouse That Roared."

Filmmaker Alanis Obomsawin, whose screen career has largely addressed issues of native culture, steps into the fray as a quiet, reasoned observer. While hardly an unbiased spectator, Obomsawin is adroit at conveying the stupidity, the outrage and the shame of the Oka conflict and placing it in both a modern and historical context. It is riveting in great part due to its lack of histrionics and its wider analysis, which avoids a descent into a politically correct whitewash.

Obomsawin had wide access behind the barricades over the length of the ever-intensifying battle. The combination of her footage, news coverage and archival material is exhaustive and impressive. However, ultimately it is what is stated rather than documented which provides "Kanehsatake's" lasting impact. This should truly enhance international television sales and some limited theatrical opportunities. —*Leonard Klady*

TAORMINA FEST

HONARPISHEH

(THE ACTOR)

(IRANIAN)

Areen Film House production. (International sales: Farabi Cinema Foundation.) Produced by Abbas Ranjibar. Directed, written by Mohsen Makhmalbaf. Camera (color), Aziz Sa'ati; editor, Makhmalbaf; music, Ahmad Pezhman; art direction, Reza Alaghmand, Saeed Motarassed. Reviewed at Taormina Film Festival (competing), July 27, 1993. Running time: **88 MIN.**
Akbar .... Akbar Abdi
Wife .... Fatemeh Motamed-Aria
Gypsy girl .... Mahaya Petrossian

Fans of Iranian helmer Mohsen Makhmalbaf will be surprised at "The Actor," a light comedy, albeit with a social message, centered on a popular idol and his hysterical wife. Even though it's self-satirizing, pic's strong flavor of local comedy will leave foreign viewers in the cold.

Akbar (played by local comedy king Akbar Abdi) is a pudgy slob who has grown rich making commercial trash. He now wants to make "art films" — like his hero, Charlie Chaplin — but his agent is against it.

His half-mad wife is obsessed with the fact they can't have children, and decides he must marry a deaf-mute gypsy girl and have the child she can't give him. The girl lives in a gypsy camp outside the city, where pic's most striking scenes take place.

The squalor in which the gypsies live recalls Makhmalbaf's finest work, like "The Peddler" and "The Cyclist." But perhaps because he's reaching for laughs, an element of folkloristic voyeurism at times intrudes in his generally compassionate depiction of the motley crew.

The actor and his wife reside in a goofy, gadget-ridden home built for laughs. The walls, papered with stills from silent movie classics, are a constant reminder that Makhmal-

baf is aiming to model his film on the highest art comedies.

The couple's marital spats — culminating in a traffic-stopping sequence on a highway involving hundreds of "extras" who think Akbar is shooting a movie — soon become more irritating than hilarious. Makhmalbaf reaches his more familiar ground of pathos in pic's closing scenes, where Akbar takes leave of the gypsy girl and rescues his wife from a ghostly insane asylum.

As the wife, Fatemeh Motamed-Aria is versatile in showing her shrilly "comic" descent into psychosis. Mahaya Petrossian has enormous dignity as the gypsy, forced to hide her intelligence along with her speaking voice. —*Deborah Young*

COITADO DO JORGE

(POOR JORGE)

(PORTUGUESE-SPANISH-FRENCH)

An Inforfilmes/Ariane Filmes (Madrid)/Les Films d'Ici (Paris) production. (International sales: Inforfilmes.) Produced by Acacio De Almeida. Directed by Jorge Silva Meio. Screenplay, Silva Meio, Manuel Mozos, Evelyne Pieiller, based on a novel by Paula Fox. Camera (color), William Lubtschansky; editor, Nelly Quettier. Reviewed at Taormina Film Festival (competing), July 29, 1993. Running time: **110 MIN.**
Jorge .... Jerzy Radziwilowicz
Ema .... Angela Molina
Also with: Manuel Wiborg, Graziella Galvani, Luis Rego, Joana Barcia, Ana Padrao, Isabel Ribas.

A character study with tragic overtones, "Poor Jorge" is a literate European art film, heavy on psychology and with a few rough edges. Transplanting an English novel to a Portuguese setting, result has enough class to find cultured admirers on both the fest and arthouse circuits.

Jorge (Jerzy Radziwilowicz) and Ema (Angela Molina) are a professional pair with standard middle-class problems. Ema may have to move to Boston on a grant, Jorge may be able to stop teaching if he plays up to a Japanese industrialist. The two may also get married.

One day, their life is turned upside down by a young punk. Jorge discovers the boy, Ernesto, calmly hanging out in their lovely suburban home. Instead of calling the police, he talks to the youth, and becomes fascinated by the innocence behind his bad-boy bravado.

Ema is much less taken with Ernesto, especially when he starts turning up at the house with an uncouth g.f. Slowly, Jorge's personality starts coming unglued.

Helmer Jorge Silva Meio, who has worked with every major Portuguese director as an actor or assistant, has a sophisticated, classical approach to his actors and material that sometimes seems a trifle old hat. Polish thesp Radziwilowicz (from Wajda's "Man of Iron") skillfully shifts through multiple mood

swings within a scene. Spanish beauty Molina inspires sympathy as a modern woman expected to juggle her personal and working lives.

Their psychological drama is played out against a background of miniature forest fires that have inexplicably broken out in the area, and which firemen are strangely unable to put out. Clunky as a device, the fires at least furnish the story with some badly needed visual tension. Tech work is fine.

—*Deborah Young*

SAN SEBASTIAN

TAFELSPITZ

(GERMAN)

A TV-60 Filmproduktion/IndunaFilm (Kirch Group)/WEGA-Filmproduktionsgesellschaft production. Produced, directed by Xaver Schwarzenberger. Screenplay, Ulrike Schwarzenberger. Camera (color), Xaver Schwarzenberger; editor, Ulrike Schwarzenberger; sets, Elisabeth Klobassa; music, Cristian Kolonovits; sound, Rainer Wiehr, Heiko Hinderks. Reviewed at San Sebastian Film Festival, Sept. 18, 1993. Running time: **92 MIN.**
Karoline Gschwantner
.... Christiane Horbiger
William .... Otto Schenk
Thomas Jefferson .... Jan Niklas
Lilli Gschwantner .... Anika Pages
Also with: Michelle Becker, Edward Brigadier, Fritz Eckhardt, Lotte Ledl, Lorraine Landry.

This slight but amusing Austrian romantic comedy is a delight to watch, despite its evident flaws and pastiche views of life in New York. Coming on the tail of other films with gastronomic themes, "Tafelspitz" (the name of an Austrian meat dish) could cull some specs on the international circuits.

Yarn concerns a pretty young girl living in a small Austrian village, the scion of a long line of restauranteurs. Her mother, seeing the girl bored and idle, makes a deal: the daughter is to learn the intricacies of becoming a chef, and as a reward the mother will pay for a year's vacation.

After managing to prepare a sumptuous meal for an attractive Yank investment banker, latter hires her sight unseen and brings her back with him to New York where, of course, they eventually fall in love. The romance is handled with a light touch, and, of course, the German track when they're in Gotham is ludicrous (even the local super and butcher speak fluent German), but these concessions can be overlooked, as can the weddingbells ending in what is otherwise a tasty strudel of a film.

—*Peter Besas*

TOMBES DU CIEL

(FALLEN FROM HEAVEN/ IN TRANSIT)

(FRENCH)

An Epithete (Paris) — Filmania (Madrid) co-production of Bymage/CNC/Canal Plus/Procirep/Sogepaq. Executive producers, Gilles Legrand, Frederic Brillon. Directed by Philippe Lioret. Screenplay, Lioret, Michel Ganz. Camera (color), Thierry Arborgast; editor, Laurent Quaglio; music, Jeff Cohen; sets, Aline Bonetto; sound (Dolby), Eric Devulder; associate producer, Enrique Posner. Reviewed at San Sebastian Film Festival, Sept. 20, 1993. Running time: **90 MIN.**
Arturo .... Jean Rochefort
Suzanne .... Marisa Paredes
Also with: Ticky Holgado, Laura del Sol, Ismaela Meite, Sotigui Kouyate.

Jean Rochefort, the French thesp obsessed with hairdressers in a recent film, here pulls off a charming tour de force as a tourist who has lost his passport (and shoes) and is forced to live for several days in a kind of surrealistic limbo within the confines of the Charles de Gaulle airport. Alternately poignant and hilarious, pic should have strong B.O. appeal on the arthouse circuit and will further endear Rochefort to audiences as the prototype of the Gallic charmer, in the vein of Tati.

Having had all his papers stolen in Montreal, Arturo, who has Canadian and French citizenship, lives in Rome but is married to a Spaniard, confounds the airport authorities and is told to sleep on a bench in the waiting room until his case can be clarified the following morning. After protesting in vain, he resigns himself to his confinement, while his wife desperately hunts for him on the other side of customs.

Arturo's dilemma takes a droll, surrealistic turn. While wandering about the deserted airport at night, he discovers a strange group of outcasts who have somehow permanently settled into a back room at the airport and eat, sleep and live there. There's a small black African boy, an Abyssinian who speaks an incomprehensible language, a pretty girl from nowhere and a Frenchman who claims to have written a book about his many hair-raising international adventures.

When Arturo's papers are held up for several days, just before New Year's, he starts to adapt to life within the group.

Coming at a time of increasing xenophobia in Europe, pic is a touching appeal for comprehension of foreigners, with wry digs at French bureaucracy. Anyone who has ever lost wallet or run into trouble at airports can easily empathize with this winsome character and should enjoy this lighthearted, bittersweet film. —*Peter Besas*

VENICE FEST

DONERSEN ISLIK CAL

(WHISTLE IF YOU COME BACK)

(TURKISH)

A Mine Film (Turkey) release of an Ugur Film production. Produced by Memduh Un. Directed by Orhan Oguz. Screenplay, Cemal San. Camera (color), Oguz; editor, Nevzat Disiacik; music, Ohnay Oguz; art direction-costumes, Esra Avci; sound, Ergan Oran. Reviewed at Venice Film Festival (noncompeting), Sept. 1, 1993. Running time: **85 MIN.**
Dwarf .... Mevlut Demiryay
Transvestite ....: Fikret Kuskan
Pimp .... Menderes Samancilar

A wrenching story of friendship and loss between a dwarf and a transvestite in the back streets of Istanbul, "Whistle If You Come Back" takes an offbeat but sympathetic look at society's rejects. Moving tale has strong fest possibilities.

Turkish helmer Orhan Oguz casts an embracing eye on the lonely after-hours lives of his outcasts. The dwarf (Mevlut Demiryay) is a gentlemanly bartender who pours drinks in a fancy night spot. He rents a wretched apartment in the ill-famed Beyoglu district and carries a police whistle for protection.

One night, blowing on his whistle, he rescues a young hooker from a beating, and takes her home. When he discovers she's actually a he (Fikret Kuskan), his first reaction is disgust. But the transvestite's strong, taunting personality prevails and the two end up fast friends.

The stage is clearly set for tragedy, but Oguz puts in enough twists to keep the story from turning banal. Demiryay gives a moving perf as the dwarf whose much-offended dignity makes him lead a life of loneliness.

In pic's grueling climax, the dwarf, believing he's lost his only friend, agonizes over whether to commit suicide, and foolishly throws away the whistle that has often saved his life.

Kuskan's perf is more opaque as the flighty, live-for-the-day transvestite. He reveals a deeper side only at pic's end, when he's forced to come to terms with his feelings for the dwarf who sheltered him.

Oguz views the night world of loud-mouthed hookers and violent pimps with commiseration but no sentimentality. Without masking their faults, pic creates a feeling of solidarity with these denizens.

Night lensing by director Oguz, himself an award-winning cinematographer, gives the story an otherworldly tone. *—Deborah Young*

ME AND THE KID

An Orion Pictures release. Produced by Lynn Loring, Dan Curtis. Directed by Curtis. Screenplay, Richard Tannenbaum, based on the novel "Taking Gary Feldman," by Stanley Cohen. Camera (CFI color), Dietrich Lohmann; editor, Bill Blunden; music, Bob Cobert; production design, Veronica Hadfield; art direction, Roger King; set decoration, Penelope Rene Stames; costume design, Deborah Lancaster; sound (Ultra-Stereo), Pat Mitchell; associate producer, Tracy Curtis; assistant director, Robert J. Wilson; casting, Mary Jo Slater. Reviewed at Orion screening room, Beverly Hills, Oct. 11, 1993. MPAA Rating: PG. Running time: **94 MIN.**
Harry .... Danny Aiello
Gary .... Alex Zuckerman
Roy ....Joe Pantoliano
Rose .... Cathy Moriarty
Victor Feldman .... David Dukes
Mrs. Feldman .... Anita Morris

D anny Aiello's considerable talents are wasted in "Me and the Kid," a trivial comedy-adventure about the friendship between a con man and a lonely upper-class kid. Pandering to children's wildest dreams, comedy may appeal to this age group, though parents may resent a film that describes the entire adult world as witless and insensitive.

"Home Alone" would have been a more accurate title for this pedestrian item, as hero Gary Feldman (Alex Zuckerman), an isolated rich kid in an upscale New York suburb, doesn't even go to school. Instead, his self-absorbed parents (David Dukes and Anita Morris) have arranged for a personal tutor, a nice housekeeper and a battery of doctors to take care of his various allergies and ailments.

An odd couple of con men, Harry (Aiello) and Roy (Joe Pantoliano), break into this insulated, boring life, aiming to rob the father's safe, only to find it empty. The more aggressive Roy impulsively kidnaps the kid, and a road adventure — of the most familiar kind — ensues.

But the precocious boy turns out to be brighter than Roy and just as shrewd as Harry. In fact, as soon as he discovers Harry's weak spot — human compassion and the good heart of a Santa Claus — he manipulates him and the situation. Being a kidnap victim and on the run with such a charismatic criminal proves to be greater fun than he has ever experienced.

Once on the road, with the FBI after them, all of Gary's allergies and phobias miraculously disappear, and he's transformed into a healthy, adventurous boy ready to meet any challenge. He even saves Harry, who in the meantime has become his surrogate father.

Preposterous ending amorally suggests that socializing with a con man and running away to Mexico is more alluring — and educational — than going to school or staying at home with uncaring parents.

Making his feature debut, TV helmer Dan Curtis ("The Winds of War," "War and Remembrance") turns in work that is just serviceable. Using fast tempo in pic's first part, Curtis succeeds in concealing what is basically a fraudulent tale.

As the good-hearted slob, Aiello brings his customary charm and authority to the kind of role that 20 years ago would have been played by Walter Matthau, and 60 years ago by Wallace Beery. But the real revelation is red-haired Zuckerman, whose unaffected acting in his second film (after "Hook") makes up for routine pic's shortcomings.

The always reliable Pantoliano, Moriarty (as a "Woodstock dropout" who has a brief fling with Aiello), Dukes and Morris all have stereotypical parts that make them appear and sound ridiculous.

—Emanuel Levy

A HOME OF OUR OWN

A Gramercy Pictures release. Produced by Dale Pollock, Bill Borden. Executive producer, Patrick Duncan. Directed by Tony Bill. Screenplay, Duncan. Camera (Deluxe color), Jean Lepine; editor, Axel Hubert; music, Michael Convertino; production design, James Schoppe; costume design, Lynn Bernay; sound (Dolby), Steven Laneri; associate producer, Helen Bartlett; assistant director, Babu Subramanian; casting, April Webster, Paul Venture (L.A.), Cate Praggastis (Utah). Reviewed at Aidikoff screening room, L.A., Sept. 29, 1993. MPAA Rating: PG. Running time: **102 MIN.**
Frances Lacey .... Kathy Bates
Shayne Lacey .... Edward Furlong
Mr. Munimura .... Soon-Teck Oh
Norman .... Tony Campisi
Lynn Lacey .... Clarissa Lassig
Faye Lacey .... Sarah Schaub
Murray Lacey .... Miles Feulner
Annie Lacey .... Amy Sakasitz
Craig Lacey .... T.J. Lowther

A tale of a poor, spunky widow and her six children, "A Home of Our Own" is a tepid 1990s combo of "Alice Doesn't Live Here Anymore" and "Places in the Heart." Audiences will likely find no particular reason to see such a family drama on the big screen, since in scope, scale and production values it perfectly befits TV, where similar inspirational country tales are often shown.

As Frances Lacey, Kathy Bates plays a variation on the roles that won Oscars for both Ellen Burstyn and Sally Field. In 1962 L.A., Bates gets fired from her assembly line job after stirring up chaos as the result of a sexually charged prank played on her. It seems like the right time to begin a new life, as Bates thinks L.A. is a "toilet of a city."

She thus hits the road with her six moppets, ranging in age from 5 to 15, feeding them the usual egg salad sandwiches. One day, spotting a dilapidated house in the middle of nowhere in Idaho, Bates stops the car, determined to buy it — even though she has no job or money. But she soon overcomes such problems with her tough talking and resourcefulness, at one point trading her wedding ring for car repair.

The only new element in this formulaic tale is the language. Bates' kids know their mother so well that when she merely mentions her dead husband, they all say, as a well-rehearsed chorus, "goddamn vagabond Irish Catholic sonofabitch."

Scripter Patrick Duncan borrows quite a few ideas from "Places in the Heart," such as the need for strong family ties and the efforts it takes to establish a community. If, in the Robert Benton saga, the group consisted of Sally Field, her kids, a blind man and a black man, here the extended family is composed of Bates, her children and a benevolent Japanese-American neighbor and land owner (Soon Teck-Oh).

"A Home of Our Own" is yet another mythic evocation set in 1962, a turning point in modern American history, except this time the focus is not youth, but the indomitable spirit of the working class. Director Tony Bill specializes in sentimental, old-fashioned movies "with a heart." Though he isn't as condescending to his bluer-collar protagonists as in his former outing, "Untamed Heart," he still ends up glorifying their indefatigable soul and pride — the Lacey motto is "We don't accept charity, we pay our own."

But former actor Bill is good with his cast. Bates renders a solid, if not distinguished, performance in the meaty part of the dauntless mother.

Unfortunately, the handsome Edward Furlong, who was so impressive in "Terminator 2: Judgment Day" and "American Heart," doesn't have a role that tests his talent. Still, as the eldest son and man of the house, he gives his best to the easily anticipated situations and conflicts.

Excepting notable lensing by Jean Lepine, other tech credits are OK. A handkerchief or two may be necessary for the Christmas sequence and other excessively melodramatic scenes. *—Emanuel Levy*

TOKYO FEST

ZIKKIMIN KOKU

(BULLSHIT)

(TURKISH)

A Mine Film production. (Foreign sales: Mine Films.) Produced by Kadri Yurdatap. Directed by Memuduh Un. Screenplay, Un, Macit Koper, based on the novel by Muzaffer Izgu. Camera (color), Orhan Oguz; editor, Nevzat Disiacik; music, Cahit Berkay; art direction, Erse Tuncer Avci. Reviewed at Tokyo Intl. Film Festival, Sept. 29, 1993. Running time: **90 MIN.**
Little Muzo .... Emre Akyildiz
Muzo ....Gunay Girik
Father .... Menderes Samancilar
Mother .... Meric Bacaran

November 1, 1993 (Cont.)

From one of Turkey's veteran directors, this very human film is a gentle tale of love, poverty, ambition, adversity and growing up. "Bullshit" is not exciting enough to make it far in the international market, even as an arthouse entry, but it is infused with wit, intelligence and images of regular Turkish life that are exotic to the outsider patient enough to sit through a slow, real-life tale.

The film mostly focuses on 9-year-old Muzo, occasionally flashing back to the present day, when Muzo is a young man who has chosen his academic career over the girl he loves. Two actors portray the sensitive, clever Muzo with great finesse

The weight of his family's poverty is demonstrated through numerous episodes: the homemade shoes he must wear to school, the balloons he longs for but cannot buy, the work he must do selling corn to pay for his education, the reconstruction of their house's rain-ruined wall.

Muzo and his family's life does not earn pity so much as sympathy. The intermittent flash-forwards to the young bride across the street are the result of Muzo's fateful decision.

Production has admirable qualities in direction, lensing, editing and acting, but is a bit slow. Old film clips are skillfully worked in, as one of young Muzo's money-making schemes is to show other children old reels on a hand-driven, home-rigged box. —*Karen Regelman*

LAST SONG

(JAPANESE)

A Toho Pictures and Fuji Television presentation of a Koichi Murakami and Jitsuzo Horiuchi production. (Foreign sales: Toho Co. Ltd.) Produced by Kazuhiko Seta, Tomoki Ikeda. Executive producers, Takashi Nakagawa, Yoshiaki Yamada. Directed by Shigemichi Sugita. Screenplay, Hisashi Nozawa. Camera (color), Katsuhiro Kato; editor, Chizuko Osada; music, Nicky Hopkins; art direction, Fumio Ogawa; sound (Dolby), Kenichi Benitani; assistant director, Kensho Yamashita. Reviewed at Tokyo Intl. Film Festival (competing), Oct. 1, 1993. Running time: **119 MIN.**
Shukichi Yazumi .... Masahiro Motoki
Kazuya Inaba .... Hidetaka Yoshioka
Riko Shoji .... Narumi Yasuda
Shoko Aoki .... Mitsuko Baisho

Director Shigemichi Sugita's extensive background in made-for-TV movies is glaringly apparent in his second feature film, "Last Song," which is overblown, overacted and overhyped until, after two long hours it is, thankfully, just plain over. This may do well in Japan thanks to the appeal of bubble-gum pop and film stars, but foreign appeal is nil.

Thesps in this music film do all their own singing. This would be fine if they were singers, but they're not. It's nearly too much of a stretch to believe they are actors.

Familiar coming-of-age yarn centers on two musicians, a pretty journalist-turned-groupie and their four-year journey from small-town Hakata to the top of pop in Tokyo.

Shukichi, affectionately called Shu-chan, is the leader of the Shoe-less Four band. He is challenged and ultimately won over by a young railroad worker-cum-guitarist named Inaba who joins the band. Though Shu-chan is the emotional driving force, Inaba is the real talent.

Main conflict stems from Shu-chan's dilemma: Should he keep trying for stardom or sacrifice his own fame to manage Inaba? He is forced into the latter, but his personality seemingly never recovers its full strength.

Meanwhile, Inaba is also in love with Shu-chan's pretty g.f. Shu-chan, an emotional roller coaster of a young man, does not treat her, or anybody, as well as he should. This causes the inevitable disintegration of the band, of this triangle of best friends and, ultimately, of the movie itself. —*Karen Regelman*

KYOSO TANJO
(MANY HAPPY RETURNS)
(JAPANESE)

A Right Vision Corp. and Pony Canyon production. (Foreign sales: Toho Co. Ltd.) Produced by Takio and Narihiko Yoshida. Executive producers, Hisao Nabeshima, Susumu Tanaka. Directed by Toshihiro Tenma. Screenplay, Yuji Kato, based on the novel by Beat Takeshi. Camera (color), Koichi Kawakami; editor, Shizuo Arkawa; music, Naoyuki Fujii; art direction, Norihiro Isada; sound (Dolby), Hisayuki Miyamoto. Reviewed at the Tokyo Intl. Film Festival (Young Cinema competition), Sept. 26, 1993. Running time: **94 MIN.**
Kazuo Takayama ..... Masato Hagiwara
Tetsuharu Komamura ...... Koji Tamaki
Daisuke Shiba .... Beat Takeshi
Go .... Ittoku Kishibe

"Many Happy Returns" is an atypical modern Japanese film that comes as a surprise for both what it is (a slow, thoughtful look at religion and spirituality) and what it isn't (melodramatic, romantic, violent, peopled with superfluous beauties). Comedian-actor-director Beat Takeshi is one of Japan's most famous faces, and the fact that he stars in the film and also penned the bestselling novel on which it is based virtually ensures a large Japanese audience. Offshore prospects are chancier.

Kazuo (Masato Hagiwara) is a young man who encounters a religious group traveling around Japan performing "miracles." Kazuo sees that a supposedly wheelchair-bound old woman who has been "healed" is, in fact, a fully mobile member of the troupe. Showmanship of this hoax intrigues him, and he joins the group for a lark.

Gradually, Kazuo draws closer to the unit's inner workings. He is liked by both factions: The one led by religious master Komamura believes in spiritual teachings and sees that Kazuo works hard, while the one led by Shiba (Takeshi) and Go uses the facade of religion to scam money and views Kazuo as, essentially, a fellow non-believer.

Much of the humor of the film relies upon the irony of the next move: When the business faction kicks out the old master, Shiba and Go choose Kazuo to lead the religion. Fatal infighting reshuffles the group yet again, and a clever and humorous ending shows Shiba's return to the world of spiritual fakery with none other than the old holy man he fired before.

Among pic's most notable assets is the soundtrack. Composer Noayuki Fujii was saxophonist in Japan's recently dissolved super-pop group the Checkers, and score reflects his talent, with the recurring sax refrain neatly expressing the film's quirky, simple, humor-tinged personality.

Film is intelligent and amusing, if somewhat flawed by a slow pace and some overused visual and verbal punch lines. Acting is believable and sympathetic, and the characters are exaggerated enough to be interesting without ringing false. All in all, it is a thought-provoking and cynical look at organized religion through the eyes of the Japanese. —*Karen Regelman*

ANKOR, ESCHYO ANKOR!
(ENCORE, ONCE MORE ENCORE!)
(RUSSIAN)

A Krug Studio of Mosfilm Studios production. (Foreign sales: Mosfilm Intl.) Directed, written by Pyotr Todorovsky. Camera (color), Yuri Raisky; editor, Irina Kolotikova; music, Todorovsky; art direction, Valentin Konovalov; costume design, Svetlana Luzanova. Reviewed at Tokyo Intl. Film Festival (competing), Sept. 25, 1993. Running time: **96 MIN.**
Col. Vinogradov .... Valentin Gaft
Lyuba Antipova .... Irina Rozanova
Lt. Poletaev .... Eugeny Mironov
Tamara .... Larisa Malevannaya

If it's a Russian film, it must be political, angst-ridden, slow and larger than life, right? Wrong. "Encore, Once More Encore!" is fast-paced, filled with humor, lively music, illicit affairs and lots of vodka. Charming, well-acted, thought-provoking picture stands a better chance in the international marketplace than most Russian films of late.

Set in mid-century Soviet Union, story revolves around the young Lt. Poletaev (Eugeny Mironov) and his attempts to liven up military life by womanizing, drinking and seeking out fun assignments such as accompanying the base's chorus on his accordion. Mironov acts his role with overflowing charisma and skill.

He achieves one of his goals, which is to add women to the ranks of the chorus. He falls for one of them, Lyuba Antipova (delightfully played by Irina Rozanova). Lyuba returns his love, but matters are complicated by the fact that Lyuba is the live-in mistress of Poletaev's superior, Col. Vinogradov (Valentin Gaft).

Film's fabric is much richer and deeper than just this simple love triangle, thanks to a strong script by writer-director Pyotr Todorovsky ("Wartime Romance," "Intergirl").

Todorovsky has added in various other affairs, a bit of *coitus interruptus*, and an especially funny recurring theme of drunken romance: Poletaev's bunkmate regularly drinks himself into oblivion, writes melodramatic love letters to two women and posts them. He then wakes up and, in desperation, chases through the snow after the mailman.

Todorovsky also provides the music, deftly woven throughout pic. It is at once very Russian and totally borderless, ranging from the grand political manifestos in choral harmony to tap-dancing folk ditties that make the audience smile just to hear them.

Pic's far-from-happy ending may leave many unsatisfied. The dramatic change from lighthearted optimism to a rather cynical hopelessness is unsettling, but even audience members who don't find this ending intellectually appealing will forgive it based on the film's overall strength. —*Karen Regelman*

LIVES IN HAZARD
(DOCU)

An Olmos Production of an Archipelago film. Produced, directed by Susan Todd, Andrew Young. Executive producer, Edward James Olmos. Camera (color), Young; editor, Jonathan Oppenheim; sound, Todd; narration, Olmos; associate producers, Nick Athas, Daniel A. Haro. Reviewed at Mill Valley Film Festival, Oct. 10, 1993. Running time: **57 MIN.**

This strong docu was shot primarily during filming of Edward James Olmos' directorial bow, the Latino gangland drama "American Me." But it eschews familiar making-of fodder in favor of a gritty examination of real-life violence dramatized in that earlier pic. Short running time will limit theatrical potential, but the tough, inspirational "Lives in Hazard" seems a sure bet for TV and long-term educational play.

Susan Todd and Andrew Young followed Olmos to his home turf in East L.A.'s barrios. Many gang members appeared in "Me," which starred Olmos as the archetypal, lifelong victim/perpetrator of crime.

Elaborate negotiations with rival gangs allowed filming to proceed without incident, although drive-by shootings continued as usual in the neighborhoods. An even more tense environment was Folsom State Prison, where Olmos won permission to lens sequences.

Despite the dangerous atmosphere in both locales, "Hazard" finds their inhabitants open and eager to discuss the problems draining blood from the Latino communities — drug dealing, proliferation of guns, endless retaliatory violence between gangs. Most poignant among these frank interviews is the young man left paralyzed after a shooting. He's not alone; wheelchairs for teens seem to be rife in the barrio.

Humanity and intelligence of participants shine through enough to make "Hazard" more than a simple exercise in "Scared Straight"-style lecturing. Film's cautious optimism at close is qualified by sad news that former gang member-turned-mediator Ana Lizarraga (who played a role in "Me") was slain in May 1992.

While "Me's" brutally downbeat saga may have been too much for many customers, "Lives in Hazard" delivers an arguably stronger punch at half the length. (A few four-letter words aside, it's also more suitable for viewers of all ages.)

Olmos & Co. have already engaged an NBC playdate, have devised a school study guide and juvenile hall outreach program for the doc, and are hoping to enlist the White House in publicly supporting film's pro-education, anti-gang/violence message. —*Dennis Harvey*

OEROEG
GOING HOME
(DUTCH)

An Added Films, B.V. presentation. Produced by Paul Voorthuysen, Added Films; Erwin Povoost, Multimedia; Helga Bahr, Lichtblick Filmproduktion. Directed by Hans Hylkema. Screenplay, Jean van de Velde, based on a novel by Hella S. Haasse. Screenplay edited by Trevor Griffiths. Camera (color), Walther vanden Ende; editor, Ot Louw; production design, Roland de Groot; sound, Erik Langhout; line producer, Voorthuysen. Reviewed at the Roxie Cinema, S.F., Sept. 23, 1993. (In Mill Valley Film Festival.) Running time: **100 MIN.**.

Johan .... Rik Launspach
Oeroeg .... Martin Schwab
Hendrick .... Jeroen Krabbe
Twan .... Tom van Bauwel
Van Woerkom ... Francois Beaukelaers
Also with: Peter Faber, Josee Ruiter, Ivon Pelaula, Aus Greidanus, Marjon Brandsma.

The Dutch "Oeroeg" (retitled "Going Home" in English-subtitled version) is a strong colonialism drama that scores both as action meller and conscience-torn political commentary. Offshore theatrical possibilities are good but will require careful, review-based marketing.

Action is roughly divided between the 1930s and years immediately following WWII, intercutting toward moments of epiphany in each era. Johan is the son of an Indonesian plantation owner, happily raised on a land he realizes only much later is not truly his.

Best friend is Oeroeg, child of the farm's foreman. The two boys are innocent enough to figure themselves equals, but racial prejudices drive a slow, inevitable wedge between them as adulthood approaches. In one poignant sequence, they attend a "Tarzan" movie "together" — only Oeroeg must sit *behind* the screen with the other "natives."

Johan returns from several years in Holland as a young man, in the company of other Dutch soldiers warring against indigenous freedom fighters. His loyalties are torn by the brutal attitude of his superiors toward local "wogs," and by suspicion that Oeroeg (now a rebel leader) may have killed his father. As Johan ventures into familiar countryside to find his old friend-cum-enemy, a "Heart of Darkness" mood balances flashbacks with a series of complex, surprising moral dilemmas.

Sentimentality is excluded from even the childhood sequences, though anti-colonialist sentiments aren't belabored with a heavy hand, either. Cultural divides are evoked subtly, as the characters discover them for themselves.

Rik Launspach is an attractive, credible adult Johan; Martin Schwab conveys Oeroeg's increasing sense of injustice in fewer sequences. Jeroen Krabbe essays the part of a hard-nosed Dutch commander. Excellent color lensing captures the beauty and sometime menace of the Indonesian landscape. All other tech aspects of $4.5 million production (well edited down from a three-hour version for broadcast) are top-notch.

Indonesian-raised author Hella S. Haasse's original novel "Oeroeg" has gone through some 28 editions since 1948, including several foreign translations. While it may not possess much lit tie-in oomph abroad, director Hans Hylkema's finely paced and felt adaptation merits broader exposure from resourceful distribs.—*Dennis Harvey*

TE Y MENYA ODNA
(YOU ARE MY ONE AND ONLY)
(RUSSIAN)

An Informpresservice presentation of a Lenfilm Film Studio production. Produced by Arkadij Tulchin. Directed by Dmitrij Astrakhan. Screenplay, Oleg Danilov, Astrakhan. Camera (color), Jurij Voroncov; editor, Astrakhan; music, Aleksandr Pantykin; sound, Alexsandr Dudraiev; art direction, Mosha Petrova. Reviewed at Mill Valley Film Festival, Oct. 13, 1993. Running time: **97 MIN.**
Evgenij
Timoshin .... Alexander Esbruyev
Anya .... Marina Neolova
Natasha .... Svetlanna Ryabova

Using the chaotic advent of "jungle law capitalism" as background for a novel romantic triangle, helmer Dmitrij Astrakhan's second feature assuredly juggles comedy and poignance. But its export chances would be much improved if an over-the-top episode in the last stretch were toned down or eliminated.

Opening montage of photos and flashbacks gives us the shorthand dope on engineering student/sometime boxer Timoshin, his bride Natasha, and his best friend's little sister Anya in the early 1970s. Latter's adolescent crush on Timoshin is revealed to him only moments before her emigrating flight to the U.S.

Twenty years later, Timoshin slaves by day at an office, by night as a deliveryman. Natasha is a marital sex therapist; a teenage daughter has romantic problems of her own. They're all happy enough, despite their dismally cramped flat and precarious stature in the new free-market economy.

Only two engineers among 30 are expected to survive a planned multinational merger at Timoshin's firm. But in a stroke of luck, one of the arriving U.S. negotiators is no less than a very grown-up Anya, who has been carrying that torch for Timoshin all along and can hardly wait to reclaim her true love.

Taking place over 48 hectic hours, story delightfully juggles social critique, slapstick and dramatic conflict, but the tone becomes seriously jarred; the rejected Anya's reaction is far too melodramatically overblown to work in this context.

Pic recovers somewhat with a beautifully managed finale. Still, hitherto deft balance remains upset. A couple editing snips and/or a new climatic sequence would work wonders.

Some less significant bits also ring false, like the heavy-handed late use of a transvestite prostitute to symbolize all that's corrupt about the dawning capitalist era. But overall, feature is a big leap in subtlety from helmer-writer's prior

work, the noisily seriocomic Jewish pogrom piece "Get Thee Out!"

Popular Russian actor Alexander Esbruyev anchors the flick with his harried, charmingly understated Timoshin. Two female leads strike more histrionic notes, while supporting characters are often hilarious.

So much of "You Are My One and Only" is insightful, funny and bittersweet that it would be a shame if these virtues remained qualified by one plot miscalculation.

—*Dennis Harvey*

SHAMELESS
(SIN VERGUENZA)
(B&W — 16mm)

A King Tomato Productions presentation. Produced, directed, written by Robert Byington. Co-produced by Scott Perry, Grace Smith. Camera (B&W), Brian O'Kelly; editor, Scott Rhodes; production design, Mark Bristol; music, Bradley Williams, Kronos, Daniel Johnston, the Reivers, Cotton Mather; production design, Mark Bristol; sound, Kyle Rosenblad; associate producers, Jason Silverman, Nancy Schafer. Reviewed at Mill Valley Film Festival, Oct. 16, 1993. Running time: **82 MIN.**
Amalia .... Natalie Karp
Myers .... Scott Rhodes
Arcadio .... Carmen Nogales

Taken as a semester's-end project in AmerIndie Feature Production 101, "Shameless (Sin Verguenza)" wins passing marks — given the $35,000 budget, it's technically competent and low on vanity-flick indulgence. But enthusiasm ends there. Blandly noncommittal in characterization, plot and directorial perspective, pic will probably best serve 26-year-old helmer Robert Byington as a hopeful calling card for bigger/better projects.

Myers (Scott Rhodes) is a pleasant, rather dull teaching assistant who falls passively into the orbit of two attractive college roommates. Half-Mexican Amalia (Natalie Karp) is a minor-league sociopath and klepto; Arcadio (Carmen Nogales), who primarily speaks Spanish, is just, well, nice. She and Myers go along for the ride as Amalia rips off a frat Halloween party, breaks into thrift stores, steals lawn sculptures and skips out on restaurant bills, among other lackluster stunts.

While watchable, loosely strung narrative doesn't build much interest. Sexual tensions among threesome are no better fleshed out than any other motivations. Byington says his movie is about relationship/cultural communication gaps (Spanish-lingo sequences between two femmes are left untranslated). Yet central character interplay is too dramatically vague to punch across even that basic point.

Decent B&W lensing does little to exploit Austin, Texas, setting. Sound quality is middling; perfs naturalistic but shy on verve. Editor/actor Rhodes performed same duties for Richard Linklater's "Slacker," along with other members of that movie's hometown crew. Further comparisons are moot — lacking "Slacker's" originality or drive, the most vivid thing about "Shameless" is its title.

—*Dennis Harvey*

PHANOUROPITTA

(SAINT PHANOURIOS' PIE)

(GREEK)

A Greek Film Centre production. Produced, directed, written by Dimitrios Yatzouzakis. Camera (color), Philipos Koutsaftis; art direction, Hero Zervaki; music, Nikos Mamgakis; editing, Georgios Triantafyllou; sound, Nikos Papadimitriou; casting, Aristeidis Phatouros. Reviewed at Mill Valley Film Festival, Oct. 12, 1993. Running time: **62 MIN.**
Georgista .... Despina Bolla
Evanthia .... Ifigenia Makati
Papa Giannis .... Lambros Tsagkas
Angelos .... Patis Loutsaftis

Ribbing religious traditions of Greek rural life, director Dimitrios Yatzouzakis' debut, "Phanouropitta," will attract a few fests with its increasingly wild streak of humor. But film's symbols and storyline are too diffuse, its execution too rough-hewn, to attract further offshore interest.

Extremely bratty young Georgista, a struggling farmer's daughter, does everything to distract her mother from the task at hand — making a pie as ritual offering to St. Phanourios on his holy day. As a result, mom whips up a most unorthodox pie; this apparently triggers a chain reaction of bad-luck incidents ending on a curious mystical note.

Humor gets more rude as film progresses, building from early bits of absurdity to hilariously tasteless slapstick involving the blind, infirm and otherwise handicapped. Satire here resembles Luis Bunuel's scathing "Viridiana" in externals, but without its clarity of intent. Despite short running time, movie will feel digressive and obtuse to most foreign viewers. Thus sum effect is minor, despite diverting mood and inventive aspects. —*Dennis Harvey*

LE TOMBEAU D'ALEXANDRE

(THE LAST BOLSHEVIK)

(FRENCH — DOCU — VIDEO)

A Les Film de l'Astrophore/Mr. Kustow Prods./La Sept-Arte production. Directed, written, edited by Chris Marker. Camera (color/b&w), Marker, Andrei Pachkevitch. Reviewed at Locarno Film Festival, Aug. 12, 1993. Running time: **120 MIN.**

Though Chris Marker's "The Last Bolshevik" is ostensibly about the life and work of the late Russian filmmaker Aleksandr Medvedkin (1900-89), this erudite, witty docu is really a portrait of Soviet cinema and the history of the USSR.

Medvedkin's courage and humor, illusions and compromises are wrenchingly measured against the collapse of the Soviet regime.

In addition to TV airings, pic could find specialized audiences if transferred from video to film.

As a young man, Medvedkin espoused the Bolshevik cause. At 18 he commanded a division of the ferocious Red Cavalry; at 30 he made agitprop shorts for Sovkino.

His career spanned half a century of world-shaking events in the Soviet Union.

Taking as his motto "It's not the past that dominates us, but images of the past," Marker, via interviews, film footage and newsreels, builds a complex picture of Soviet life, from the dreams of the revolution to the nation's current vulgarity and dissolution.

Film is structured as a series of audiovisual "letters" to Medvedkin. Many threads lead to notable filmmakers and artists of the time.

Pic explores the influence of revolutionary directors Dziga Vertov and Sergei Eisenstein, with historian Marina Goldovskaya offering an acute analysis of Vertov's relation to Medvedkin, describing Vertov as a dour and friendless soul.

Glimpsed for the first time are the extraordinary "film-train movies" made by Medvedkin and his group in 1932, and long believed lost. A train was outfitted to shoot, process and edit agitprop films and newsreel footage. On six journeys through Ukraine and Crimea, the filmmakers documented the poverty of peasants and miners, the fury of Stalin's censors.

Medvedkin's next films (including his 1934 comic masterpiece about collective farmers, "Happiness") were banned, but he continued working.

During World War II, he invented a camera attached to a sawed-off rifle, with which soldiers could film actual battle scenes.

He finally died — luckily, notes Marker dryly — during "the euphoria of perestroika," convinced social justice was finally at hand.

Generally fast-moving, "The Last Bolshevik" includes an interview with Medvedkin at 84 and longer talks with his English-speaking daughter.

Latter notes that her father, though a communist, believed in God and knew prayers by heart.

Marker, who in 1971 made a docu about the film-train (narrated by Medvedkin), is careful to place his subject in context, using him to portray an entire generation.

He doesn't shrink from examining inglorious episodes in the director's life, like a bizarre celebratory film he made for the regime in the 1950s. —*Deborah Young*

BEWOGEN KOPER

(BRASS UNBOUND)

(DUTCH — DOCU)

An ID TV Film & Video Prods./Nos/ La Sept presentation in association with Rob Boonzajer Flaes. Produced by Peter Van Juijstee, Harry De Winter, ID TV Film & Video Prods. Directed by Johan Van Der Keuken. Screenplay, Van Der Keuken, Flaes, based on Flaes' study "Frozen Brass." Camera (color), Van Der Keuken; editors, Jan Dop, Van Der Keuken; sound, Noshka Van Der Lely; music, Krishna Das, Modern Light Music Brass Band, Naumati Baja Murkhu, Royal Nepalese Army Band (Nepal), Baas Mal Music Bambu Klarinet Berlian (Minahassa), John Collins and Friends, Peace Brass Band (Ghana). Reviewed at Mill Valley Film Festival, Oct. 9, 1993. Running time: **106 MIN.**

Why, yes — as a matter of fact, they do play the tuba in Nepal, Surinam, Ghana and the Minahassa peninsula of Indonesia.

Those pining for this info will rejoice at the arrival of "Brass Unbound." Otherwise, this extremely loose series of Third World snapshots has no play potential beyond Euro TV and anthro/docu showcases.

Vet docmeister Johan Van Der Keuken employs his customary poetic style here, abstaining from narration or any other explanatory intrusions. The area of scrutiny is too broad to provide any ingrained organizational principal. Pic merely jumps among the four aforementioned territories, observing weddings, funerals and other aspects of everyday life; linking thread is the colonial-era legacy of brass bands.

Historical background rarely surfaces. In fact, one frequently doesn't know which country one's in. Some sights are striking, like a group of merrily dancing pallbearers. Much of the music, mixing Western and local idioms, is cacophonous; think of it as exotic free jazz, and it improves. Helmer's bemused take on Westernization peaks as bands test their chops on "It's a Long Way to Tipperary."

Once viewer adjusts to pic's utter formlessness, it provides a quite pleasant form of stimulus. Sound qualities are very good. Lensing is OK, a bit grainy at times in evident 16mm blowup. Editing offers a few wry contrasts, but demurs from rising to soundtrack's occasional level of energetic frenzy.

—*Dennis Harvey*

MANOUSHE: THE LEGEND OF GYPSY LOVE

(BRAZILIAN)

A Horizonte Filmes presentation in association with Blow-Up/Embrafilme/ Sky Light/Rio Filmes. Produced, directed, written by Luiz Begazo. Camera (color), Helio Silva; editors, Marta Kuz, Helio Lemos; music, Paco De Lucia; sound (Dolby), Lemos; production design, Irenio Maia; choreography, Alberto Turina; additional camera, Renato Padovani. Reviewed at Mill Valley Film Festival, Oct. 9, 1993. Running time: **73 MIN.**
Saltimbanco .... Breno Moroni
Garota .... Drica Moraes
Also with: Thelma Reston, Alfredo Murphy

Starting off like a Carlos Saura tango movie, then veering through Fellini-isms and Brothers Grimm whimsy, Luiz Begazo's debut feature does earn points for novelty. But while handsomely done, this oddball fantasy won't travel easily — it's too eccentric for kids and, ultimately, too icky-sweet for adults.

Framing device is an old woman's reminiscence at her husband's wake. Tango dancers whirl out their mourning (in less-than-seamless tracking shots) before the elderly gypsy's corpse. In flashback, the woman (Drica Moraes) recalls her fairy-tale courtship by the traveling gypsy-magician (Breno Moroni).

Tenor up to this point is surreal quasi-satire, featuring barnyard noises from the local bourgeoisie, a chicken with baby-doll head and other absurdist touches. But once the young lovers escape into a magical forest, it's all a bit much — what with gnomes, sprites and all manner of straight-up cuteness, The odd spot of nudity or pole-frottage suggests Begazo didn't have children in mind as a primary audience. But just who he was thinking of is anyone's guess.

Never as funny or charming as it means to be, pic holds attention as a curio. Fantasy aspects are quite accomplished on the $200,000 budget, with attractive sets, costumes and color lensing. Lead actors are rather less attractive. Haunting guitar music early on outclasses synth score in forest sequences.

Whatever else one can say about "Manoushe," it is not recommended for the whimsy-phobic.

—*Dennis Harvey*

VIRTUAL LOVE

A HOTwire Prods. presentation. Directed, written, edited by Lynn Hershmann Leeson. Camera (color, video-to-16m), Kathleen Beeler; camera/effects editor, Skip Sweeny; music, Earwax (John Di Stefano, Kolonica McQuestin, Ear3); commissioning editor, Claudia Tronnier, ZDF Fernsehspiel. Reviewed at the Roxie Cinema, S.F., Sept. 17, 1993. (In Mill Valley Film Festival.) Running time: **73 MIN.**

Chip/Barry Rosenthal ...	Rinde Eckert
Valerie Vogel	Jean Mullis
Marie Lang	Ingrid Hardy
Dennis	Michael Edo Keane

Also with: Paule West, Michelle Handelman, Chris Brophy, Chrystene Ells, Rachel Rosenthal.

Subtitled "A Love Story for the 1990s," this playful meditation on the technological invasion of personal terrain is too obviously vid/experimental in origin for theatrical release. But its sometimes witty progress will win attention from cinematheque circles and certain fests.

Valerie (Jean Mullis) is a wallflowerish worker in the Productive Technologies Dept. of a computer firm. Her social life apparently barren, she fixates on bald-headed twins (both played, in seamless occasional two-shots, by Rinde Eckert) who are programming geniuses in the Northern California "virtual reality laboratory."

Chip is a nice, romantically interested guy; Barry is coldly disengaged from any such contact, thus becoming the focus of her fascination.

Hacker Valerie misguidedly contrives a way into Barry's consciousness — programming blond, conventionally gorgeous local 976-operator/public access TV hostess Maria (Ingrid Hardy) as her E-Mail "alter ego."

Meanwhile, disenfranchised loner Dennis (Michael Edo Keane) obsesses over Maria, his frustration suggesting an inevitable explosion of violence.

"Virtual Love" undercuts its mainstream erotic-thriller structure with contextualizing doc interviews that put intermedia authorities like Todd Gitlin, Jaron Lanier, R.U. Serius and Arthur and Mary Louise Kroker on the hot seat.

They expound on the horizons and repercussions of hyper-tech advancement.

Pic echoes the annoying Godardian qualities of Leeson's prior "Shooting Script: A Transatlantic Love Story" only in its last-act waf-

fle. Otherwise, pic has a disarming mix of experimental and knowing pulp elements.

Acting by S.F. theater-scene vets (plus performance guru Rachel Rosenthal as the twins' mom) is quite charming. Vid-to-16mm qualities are OK but remain viddish.

—*Dennis Harvey*

LUDWIG 1881

(SWISS-GERMAN)

A Filmproduktion Dubini/Tre Valli production. Directed by Donatello Dubini, Fosco Dubini. Screenplay, Donatello Dubini, Fosco Dubini, Barbara Marx, Martin Witz. Camera (color), Matthias Kalin; editor, Donatello Dubini; music, Heiner Goebbels; sound, Andreas Wolki. Reviewed at Locarno Film Festival (competing), Aug. 10, 1993. (Also in Montreal, Chicago, Vienna fests.) Running time: **90 MIN.**

King Ludwig II	Helmut Berger
Josef Kainz	Max Tidof

Also with: Dietmar Mossmer, Michael Schiller, Herbert Leiser, Nina Hoger.

(German dialogue)

A delicately poetic film full of fine music and breathtaking landscapes, "Ludwig 1881" recounts the true story of King Ludwig II of Bavaria's trip to Switzerland in the company of a young actor. Big plus is a surprisingly moving perf by Helmut Berger, reprising his title role from Luchino Visconti's 1973 classic. Berger's presence could help the film circulate in art circuits after fest runs.

Film's starting point is a historic photograph of Ludwig and Josef Kainz, an actor from his court in Munich. Known with good reason as the "mad king," Ludwig conceives a yearning to hear Kainz (Max Tidof) recite Schiller's play "William Tell" in its Swiss settings.

Letting affairs of state be damned, Ludwig sets out with Kainz, posing as the Marquis de Saverny and Monsieur Didier, two characters from a Victor Hugo play. With them go a pair of know-it-all servants and a state counselor who sporadically tries to interest the monarch in weightier matters.

Swiss sibling directors Donatello and Fosco Dubini have an aesthetic orgy with their amusing premise. The inspiring mountains around the Lake of the Four Cantons offer a set worthy of a king (thanks to Matthias Kalin's sensual, almost 3-D cinematography), while stylized use of color recalls Visconti's operatic interpretation of Ludwig's life.

From his first reading of the play's prologue, it's clear Kainz is a disastrous actor. When Ludwig demands Kainz "prepare" for his role by climbing mountain passes to drink in the sunrise, Kainz oversleeps or simply refuses. The journey ends in disappointment.

Pic suggests that behind Ludwig's eccentricity was a desire to achieve an ideal fraternal union

with a subject far below him in class and rank. To do this, he tries to alter not only their identities, but bend time and place to his will. To the film's credit, Ludwig's failure gives the viewer a pang of regret.

Berger's Ludwig naturally looks more mature than in the 20-year-old Visconti film, but there's an eerie continuity of bearing and manner. Though the Dubinis play off the earlier film, their ideas are original enough to make citation a game, not a crutch.

Film is completely bereft of homosexual innuendo or any kind of physical contact between the two characters. Instead, Ludwig shows enormous, almost comic sensuality toward literature and art, the real inspiration for his emotions. Pic reflects his longings in superb imagery and a stirring classical score (blessedly, no Wagner).

—*Deborah Young*

ZGHVARDZE

(PUSHED TO THE LIMIT)

(GEORGIAN — B&W)

A Shvidkatsa Film Company production. Directed, written by Dito Tsintsadze. Camera (b&w), Michael Magalashvili; editor, Eka Guramishvili; art direction, Guia Rigvav; sound, Guram Gogua. Reviewed at Locarno Film Festival (competing), Aug. 10, 1993. Running time: **80 MIN.**

Nika	George Nakashidze
Lika	Lika Guntsadze
Wife	Marika Giorgobiani

Also with: Vajha Gelashvili.

Like a time bomb waiting to explode, "Pushed to the Limit" describes the days immediately preceding the outbreak of a civil war. In deliberately grainy, bleary-eyed b&w, this second feature by Dito Tsintsadze goes beyond the tension in Georgia to conjure up other seemingly senseless conflicts. Though pic won a Silver Leopard at Locarno, it falls down in an unconvincing ending of abstract violence, and is likely to be limited to fest and specialty outings.

Nika (George Nakashidze), the apathetic hero, is a gym teacher whose school has been closed in anticipation of civil unrest. The town is full of militiamen in training; affection and family ties are eroded in an atmosphere of growing hostility.

Nika has left his beautiful but taunting wife (Marika Giorgobiani) for a plain ballet teacher (Lika Guntsadze) who likes to make love in acrobatic positions. In ironic *cinema verite*, Tsintsadze's camera shows several of these amorous exercises in all their joyless banality.

Pic's b&w film stock seems of extremely poor quality, helping cinematographer Michael Magalashvili to capture grainy, blurred images that look like newsreel footage and to create a haunting prewar

landscape of abandoned buildings and barricades. —*Deborah Young*

TRAVOLTA ET MOI

(TRAVOLTA AND ME)

(FRENCH)

An IMA Prods./La Sept-Arte/SFP Production/Sony Music production. Produced by Georges Benayoun, Paul Rozenberg. Executive producers, Francoise Guglielmi, Elisabeth Deviosse. Producer for Arte, Pierre Chevalier. Series director, Chantal Poupaud. Directed by Patricia Mazuy. Screenplay, Yves Thomas, Mazuy. Camera (color), Eric Gautier; editor, Benedicte Brunet; music, Yarol Poupaud; art direction, Louis Soubrier. Reviewed at Locarno Film Festival (competing), Aug. 7, 1993. (Also in Montreal fest.) Running time: **68 MIN.**

Christine	Leslie Azzoulai
Nicolas	Julien Gerin
Karine	Helene Eichers
Igor	Igor Tchiniaev
Jerome	Thomas Klotz

"Travolta and Me" captures that rare sense of being a teenager, frustrated by the adult world and slave to new emotions. Patricia Mazuy's striking second feature, just 68 minutes of incisive observation and flabbergasting twists, should see brisk TV sales, its short length the only obstacle to an arthouse run.

Pic is part of a 10-film French TV series, "All the Boys and Girls of Their Time," dealing with adolescence and music. It's set in the Champagne district of France in the 1970s, when "Saturday Night Fever," the Bee Gees and the Clash made teens dream.

On a bus, 17-year-old Nicolas (Julien Gerin), a long-haired boy who reads Rimbaud and Nietzsche, makes a bet he can have any girl he wants. His choice falls on the intense Christine (Leslie Azzoulai), 16, whose parents run a bakery.

Mistaking Nicolas' interest for a great romance, Christine falls hard for him. They make a date for the next day, but Christine's parents leave town and she has to watch the bakery.

In a long, superbly orchestrated sequence drawing comedy out of Christine's exasperation, Mazuy (who worked as a film editor) swiftly intercuts an unending stream of clients and croissants with the girl's frantic efforts to see Nicolas. Amusing naturalistic dialogue and rapid-fire pace hold the attention, even though little happens.

Film concludes with an exceptional sequence at the local ice-skating rink, where a mating dance ensues between Nicolas (caught flirting with another girl) and Christine (who forgets herself for a moment in the arms of pro skater Igor Tchiniaev). The climax is totally unexpected.

Young Azzoulai communicates a frightening willpower behind her vulnerable, girl-in-love exterior.

Also touchingly real is Helene Eichers as her plump, gentle friend. Gerin makes a dangerously attractive Nicolas, whose self-destructive streak rubs off on everyone.

Mazuy depicts a kaleidoscope of teenage emotions pushed to the extreme and, in all their raw passion, never psychologized away. Eric Gautier's camera stays close to the characters, except in a few lyrical long shots that punctuate the film.

—*Deborah Young*

PETRIFIED GARDEN

(FRENCH-GERMAN)

Produced by Laurent Truchaut, Eleonore Feneux for Agav Films (France), in association with Simon Aranovitch, Gilles Sandoz, Felix Kleman. Directed, written by Amos Gitai. Camera (color), Henri Alekan, Luc Drion, Edouard Timline; music, Simon and Marcus Stockhausen. Reviewed at Taormina Film Festival (competing), July 31, 1993. Running time: **87 MIN.**
Daniel .... Jerome Koenig
Woman .... Hanna Schygulla
Sam .... Sam Fuller
Also with: Masha Itkina, Natasha Silentieva, Arkadi Dreiomochtchenko.

Petrified Garden" is Israeli director Amos Gitai's second part of a trilogy on the golem — an artificially created being of Jewish legend. Shot largely in Russia, it has the look of a hastily stitched-together work whose intriguing concept never has a chance to get off the starting line.

Gitai focuses his attention on the symbolic resonance of the golem legend, forgetting to attach it to a coherent story. The result is a frustratingly incomplete film.

Daniel (Jerome Koenig) is a suave, worldly-wise art dealer who runs a gallery in Paris with partners Sam Fuller (appearing in a hilariously tongue-in-cheek cameo) and Hanna Schygulla. When Daniel learns he has inherited an important modern art collection from a long-lost Russian uncle, they insist he go get it. The problem is that the collection is at the Chinese border of Siberia.

Instead of simply flying to Vladivostok, Daniel starts his odyssey at the other end of the country, in St. Petersburg. He also decides to take along a 10-foot stone hand, presumably from a golem sculpture. This unwieldy impediment to travel is only the beginning of a long series of maddeningly loose plot ends.

In passing, Gitai piques viewers' curiosity about Birobidjian, the Jewish Autonomous Region created in Siberia in 1928 as a place for Jews to live together and develop their culture.

After wasting much time describing Daniel's tedious dealings with post-Soviet bureaucracy, film is almost over when Daniel gets on the trans-Siberian express, the giant hand roped down to a flatbed. Frustratingly, this is practically the end of the Russian visuals. The rest is narrated by Daniel to Schygulla on his return to Paris.

Koenig makes Daniel a wry, sympathetic hero, while Schygulla is a scary figure who radiates a sphinx-like star quality, but doesn't create a credible character. Perhaps her performance is meant to refer to her role in "Golem: The Spirit of Exile," but those who haven't seen the first part of Gitai's trilogy can only guess. Camerawork by Henri Alekan, Luc Drion and Edouard Timline is excellent. —*Deborah Young*

JARDINES COLGANTES

(HANGING GARDENS)

(SPANISH)

A La Banera Roja production. Directed, written by Pablo Llorca. Camera (color), Gerardo Gormezano; editor, Llorca; music, Saimon Simonet; art direction, Monica Bernuy. Reviewed at Taormina Film Festival, Italy (competing), Aug. 1, 1993. (Also in San Sebastian festival.) Running time: **110 MIN.**
Tailor .... Luis Flete
Bar Owner .... Feodor Atkine
Girl .... Iciar Bollain
Also with: Rafael Diaz, Andres Lima, Elisabeth Watling, Manolo Calderon.

A bespectacled tailor falls for a lady of the night in "Hanging Gardens," a post-Freudian fairy tale with the starkness of a captured nightmare. This second feature of Spanish director Pablo Llorca runs on imagination, with mucho potential to strike the fancy of the off-off-arthouse circuit.

Like his tailor hero who abhors the superfluous, Llorca empties his scenes of decor as he empties his characters of names and personality. They have no past, no human relations, almost no psychology.

The tailor (Luis Flete), who works in leather, goes to town to purchase a hide. He ends up in a surreal warehouse filled with bins that contain everything under the sun. Its brutish owner (Feodor Atkine) also runs the local bar and owns numerous apartments in a run-down labyrinthine building.

Atkine prides himself on his masculinity but can't seduce a haughty girl (Iciar Bollain) who's one of his tenants. He and the tailor recognize they're bound by their desire for the elusive femme.

In exchange for one of Atkine's apartments, Flete agrees to make him a special suit to win the girl over. In a kinky S&M bedroom scene, spied on by the tailor, she agrees to marry Atkine, and the tailor realizes he has lost her. The last sequence is uninterrupted carnage.

As the tailor, non-pro Flete (who was Llorca's film teacher) lends a potentially laughable role conviction and a kind of mad dignity. Atkine's magnetic presence and sexual force make the side of evil almost attractive.

Though obviously shot on a shoestring, the film makes the most of its limitations: Faces shot against a black background help to emphasize the tale's symbolic force.

—*Deborah Young*

DIE SONNENGOTTIN

(THE SUN GODDESS)

(GERMAN)

A Moana Film production (Berlin). (Foreign sales: Filmverlaug der Autoren.) Directed, written by Rudolf Thome. Camera (color), Reinhold Vorschneider; editor, Dorte Volz; music, Chico Hamilton. Reviewed at Taormina Film Festival (competing), July 30, 1993. Running time: **110 MIN.**
Richard Todd .... John Shinavier
Martha .... Radhe Schiff
Also with: Susan Chesier, Marie Soranno, Chico Hamilton, Robert Rutman.

With "The Sun Goddess," Rudolf Thome ("Love at First Sight") confirms himself as high priest of the banal. Thome's uniquely punishing style of filmmaking, which insists on describing stereotyped relationships in minute, meaningless detail, will drive a large segment of any audience this film finds up the wall. Its future on the festival circuit deserves to be short-lived, as even die-hard fans of Thome's better films like "Der Philosoph" will discover to their sorrow.

Richard (John Shinavier), a New York-based film critic who bears an odd resemblance to Mel Gibson, gets a grant to write a book about director F.W. Murnau. His research takes him to Berlin, where he reunites with ex-g.f. Martha (Radhe Schiff).

At Murnau's grave, they notice a tombstone sculpture of a girl with her arms raised, which reminds them of Martha. The old grave tender just happens to know it represents the Greek sun goddess Akatirer. Next scene, the young couple is off to Greece, where they become mutually obsessed with the dumb idea that Martha is a reincarnation of the goddess.

Through no fault of the very fine lensing by cinematographer Reinhold Vorschneider, or the dazzling Greek island most of pic is shot on, "The Sun Goddess" is a uniquely tedious film.

Recurrent scenes of bathing, teeth-brushing and unnaturally tidy decor underline the boring cleanliness and order of this fictional world. In this pic, a brief excerpt from Murnau's "Tabu" is a breath of fresh air in a stifling room.

Shinavier and Schiff make a fine-looking couple, but have no scope. Stilted dialogue is sandwiched between long, meaningful looks. Bedroom scenes generate as much passion as a singles bar. Pic also abounds in self-conscious nudity, particularly after Richard discovers his mission in life is to photograph Martha nude with her arms upraised. This idyll has the abrupt, inconclusive ending one would expect.

—*Deborah Young*

MI HERMANO DEL ALMA

(MY SOUL BROTHER)

(SPANISH)

A Sogetel S.A. and Fernando Colomo P.C. production. Produced by Fernando de Garcillan. Directed by Mariano Barroso. Screenplay, Barroso, Joaquin Oristell. Camera (color), Flavio Martinez Laviano; editor, Miguel Angel Santamaria; music, Bingen Mendizabal; sets, Vincente Ruiz; sound, Julio Recuero. Reviewed at Fotofilm, Madrid, Oct. 7, 1993. Running time: **93 MIN.**
Toni .... Juanjo Puigcorbe
Carlos .... Carlos Hipolito
Julia .... Lydia Bosch
Sebastian .... Juan Echanove
Also with: Jordi Molla, Walter Vidarte, Chema Munoz.

This is a well-limned, often engaging story about two brothers and their struggle to get the same girl. Pic is well paced with fine thesping all around, but weak ending undermines the plot.

After successfully displacing his brother for the affections of a girl, the "good" brother, Carlos, has married and settled down comfortably with Julia and works as an insurance salesman. Ten years elapse and Toni, who hangs around the dog races, mixes with Mafiosi and is in generally wretched condition, suddenly turns up to torment his brother and his wife.

Toni is erratic, irascible, unscrupulous, irredeemably nasty. But he wheedles himself into Toni's life again, sleeps with Julia and puts the jinx on Carlos' insurance sales until matters come to a violent end.

Though story sometimes lacks oomph, this first pic by Barroso holds the interest and augurs well for future efforts. —*Peter Besas*

EL ALIENTO DEL DIABLO

(THE DEVIL'S BREATH)

(SPANISH)

An Elias Querejeta production, presented by Tesauro S.A. in collaboration with Eurimages and ESICMA. Coproduced by Bastille Films S.A. (France) and C.N.C (Belgium). Produced by Elias Querejeta. Executive producer, Tadeo Villalba. Directed by Paco Lucio. Screenplay, Lucio, Querejeta, Manuel Gutierrez Aragon. Camera (color), Alfredo Mayo; editor, Nacho Ruiz Capillas; music, Angel Illarramendi; sets, Ion Arretxe; costumes, Maiki Marin. Reviewed at San Sebastian Film Festival, Sept. 22, 1993. Running time: **90 MIN.**

Damian	Alexander Kaidanovski
Priscila	Valentina Vargas
Don Rodrigo	Fernando Guillen

Also with: Alfredo Zafra, Fernando Valverde, Ester Bizcarrondo, Francisco Maestre, Al Victor, Diane Salcedo.

This ponderous allegory about a group of immigrants in medieval times arriving on the shores of a mysterious lake is laden with symbolism and allusions that are never really explained. Though pic has some moments of great beauty, thanks to fine lensing by Alfredo Mayo, slow pacing and wooden direction of Paco Lucio impede this from ever generating any emotions.

A small family of travelers, after voyaging for a long time, arrives at a hut. Amidst obscure omens and symbols (the moon, a stag whose eyes shed tears after it is killed, drowning rats that presumably bring the plague), Damian, the mute father, fights back against the encroachments of a feudal lord who eyes Damian's wife.

Production values are kept to the barest minimum. Lucio never really gets into his characters, and the outcome, despite a few tame action sequences, is extraordinarily anemic. —*Peter Besas*

MADREGILDA

(SPANISH)

A Tornasol and Marea Films (Madrid) coproduction with Road Movies Dritte Produktionen (Germany) and Gemini Films (Paris). Produced By Gerardo Herrero, Adrian Lipp, Ulrich Felsberg. Directed by Francisco Regueiro. Screenplay, Regueiro and Angel Fernandez-Santos. Camera (color), Jose L. Lopez Linares; editor, Pedro del Rey; music, Jurgen Knieper; art direction, Luis Valles; sound, Jean-Paul Mugel; associate producer, Paulo Branco. Reviewed at San Sebastian Film Festival, Sept. 20, 1993. Running time: **120 MIN.**

Longinos	Jose Sacristan
Franco	Juan Echanove
Angeles/Madregilda	Barbara Auer
Hauma	Kamel Cherif

Also with: Fernando Rey, Juan Luis Galiardo, Coque Malla, Antonio Gamero, Hark Bohm, Sandra Rodriguez Garcia, Israel Biedma, Manuel Alexandre.

Director/co-scripter Francisco Regueiro strives for sarcasm in this parody of Madrid in the 1940s, the latest Spanish film to use Gen. Francisco Franco as a central character. But what is intended as whimsical is instead laden with long palavers in the ironic vein, most of which will be lost to those not very familiar with the Franco period.

Thesp Juan Echanove, who looks more like Mussolini that Franco, does a tongue-in-cheek version of the Generalisimo, and Jose Sacristan does a nice bit of overacting as a fascist colonel whose wife has been raped by his own troops before a key battle in the Civil War.

The wife, who appears to the protagonists in the guise of Rita Hayworth's "Gilda;" their child, who is now a street urchin; and other personages who doubtless have symbolical meaning to the scripters but are unintelligible to most viewers, are paraded into the episodes of this non-story. Camerawork is strikingly bad, as is quality of the sound. —*Peter Besas*

SUFLOOR

(THE PROMPTER)

(ESTONIAN)

A Freyja Film production. (International sales: Ajend, Talinn). Produced by Madis Tramberg. Directed by Kaljo Kiisk. Screenplay, Juhan Viiding. Camera (color), Valeri Blinov; editor, Kersti Miilen; music, Margo Kolar; sound, Mati Schonberg. Reviewed at World Film Fest, Montreal (non-competing), Aug 28, 1993. Running time: **96 MIN.**

Melissa	Epp Eespaev
Robert	Elmo Nuganen
Martin	Jaan Tate
Karl	Marko Matvere

This Estonian item is a disappointingly stolid drama about jealousy and rivalry among members of a small theater company. It will have an audience among Estonians worldwide, but otherwise is just a tame item.

During the final dress rehearsals of a new play, it becomes clear that lead actor Martin is distracted by the presence of Melissa, the statuesque wife of the play's director, Robert. He keeps fluffing his lines. Seems that Martin and Melissa have been having a secret affair. Eventually, Robert is forced to set up a prompt box to enable him to jog Martin's memory.

These theatrical intrigues are given glum treatment by vet helmer Kaljo Kiisk, with political comments kept minimal. Despite classic themes

of love and betrayal, Kiisk keeps it all remote and uninvolving, with the actors just going through their paces. It's a modest, even rather drab, production, but technically adequate. —*David Stratton*

L'HONNEUR DE LA TRIBU

(THE HONOR OF THE TRIBE)

(ALGERIAN-FRENCH)

A Neuf de Coeur production. Produced by Claude Phillippot. Directed, written by Mahmoud Zemmouri, from the book by Rachid Mimouni. Camera (color), Mustafa Belmihoub; editor, Jacques Gaillard; music, Jean-Marie Senia; sound, Philippe Senechal, Claude Villand. Reviewed at World Film Festival, Montreal (competing), Aug. 28, 1993. Running time: **90 MIN.**

With: Said Amadis, Thierry Lhermitte, Brigitte Rouan, Ticky Holgado, Mouss, Rabah Loucif, Ahmed Mazouz, Kader Kada, Nael Kervaas.

"The Honor of the Tribe" is a quirky comedy-drama that unfolds in a remote Algerian village over a 25-year period. A mixture of politics and ribald humor, this virtually demands some knowledge of Algeria's war against the French and its aftermath, and so is unlikely to find wide acceptance internationally, despite the talent of established director Mahmoud Zemmouri, whose work includes the amiable comedy "The Mad Years of the Twist."

Pic opens with an odd scene in which a traveling showman challenges a villager to fight his trained bear; the man is killed by the animal, leaving his children, Omar and Ourida, orphans.

Twenty years later, Algeria is fighting a war of liberation against France, and the siblings are involved in an incestuous relationship until Ourida catches the eye of the French officer in charge of the village. Omar takes off, Ourida dies in childbirth, the war ends and the French leave. Omar, who has apparently been in the Soviet Union in the interim, returns to Algeria on an Aeroflot jet with a Russian wife in tow; he's appointed mayor of his old village and sets about modernizing the place.

The ramshackle plot, with its cheerful satire of Algerian politics, is intercut with vivid newsreel footage of the period, some of it quite shocking, including scenes of Arabs being gunned down casually by French soldiers. But for the uninitiated, it doesn't add up to much, and certainly lacks the appeal of Zemmouri's earlier work.

Said Amadis is a rather charmless protagonist, and Thierry Lhermitte has little to do as the French officer. Production credits are excellent, and the film is dedicated to

the late film publicist Simon Mizrahi. —*David Stratton*

LA MADRE MUERTA

(THE DEAD MOTHER)

(SPANISH)

A Gasteizko Zinema (Vitoria, Spain) production. (Foreign sales: Sogepac, Madrid.) Produced by Juanma Bajo Ulloa. Directed by Bajo Ulloa. Screenplay, Bajo Ulloa, Eduardo Bajo Ulloa. Camera (color), Javier Aguirresarobe; editor, Pablo Blanco; music, Bingen Mendizabal; art direction, Satur Idaretta; sound, Gilles Ortion; special effects, Poli Catero. Reviewed at Vancouver Intl. Film Festival, Sept. 13, 1993. Running time: **107 MIN.**

Ismael	Karra Elejalde
Maite	Lio
Leire	Ana Alvarez
Blanca	Silvia Marso

This atmospheric thriller, about a semi-psycho killer who can't escape the eyes of one crucial witness, is long on baroque, widescreen style and short on psychological payoff. Powerhouse perfs and a strong directorial hand, however, almost compensate for a plot that gets more muddled as it goes along.

Pic starts with a small-time Madrid hood rifling through possessions of a Christian-themed painter. In fact, he has just slashed a smiling madonna's blood-red heart when the artist walks into her studio. The perp shoots without hesitation, then discovers his victim's small daughter has seen the whole thing.

About 10 years later, the cleaned-up, urbane-looking Ismael (pockmarked, sad-eyed Karra Elejalde) is working in a back-street bar when he happens to see a young, raven-haired woman walk by and becomes convinced that she's his inevitable accuser.

Turns out the i.d. is right, but the irony is that Leire (Ana Alvarez) is an asylum-bred ward of the state. Still, she eyeballs him once and Ismael is off and running.

Next thing you know, he has kidnapped the mute witness and chained her to the upstairs bed. At first, Leire's g.f. Maite (Lio) can't see why her unpredictable b.f. feels threatened by this near-vegetable child-woman, but it's not long before she's the one who feels put out.

Sophomore helmer Juanma Bajo Ulloa, who's only 26 (and had to share his best director prize at Montreal with veteran Claude Lelouch), has mixed his Oedipal metaphors so brazenly in "The Dead Mother" that it's hard to know what anything means. There are lots of Pinter-like role reversals, as the characters toy with different kinds of dependency, and Maite is revealed to have the coldest nerves around. Religious symbols are everywhere, culminating in the unholy trio's encampment in a boarded-up cathedral. Scatological elements are stronger than anything sexual or spiritual.

Overall, pic's claustrophobic, beige-colored artiness proves wearing. A final attempt to pick up the pace increases the body count, as well as the number of laughable gaffes. The meller-heavy ending fatally undermines Bajo Ulloa's tony mood, although memorable lensing and an intensely controlled male lead will give this "Mother" life on the festival circuit, if not ever after.
—*Ken Eisner*

REPORTAJE A LA MUERTE
(REPORTS OF DEATH)
(PERUVIAN)

A Casablanca Films production. Produced by Esther Alvarez de Gavidia, Juan Gavidia, Stefan Kaspar. Directed by Danny Gavidia. Screenplay, Jose Watanabe. Camera (color), Eduardo Davila; editor, Gianfranco Annichini; music, Miky Gonzales; sound, Francisco Adrianzen; assistant director, Esteban Mejia. Reviewed at World Film Festival, Montreal (non-competing), Aug. 31, 1993. Running time: **95 MIN.**
Alfredo .... Diego Berti
Anel .... Marisol Palacios
Supae .... Aristoteles Picho
El Conde .... Juan Suelpres
Alcaide .... Carlos Gassols
Venezuelan
  ambassador .... Martha Figueroa

Danny Gavidia's often exciting first feature, inspired by a 1984 uprising in a Peruvian prison, tries to have it both ways. It attacks the role of TV's live coverage of a violent event, but at the same time takes the form of a violent entertainment itself.

The setup is classic suspense. In a Lima prison, which houses rival gangs of terrorists and radicals, a riot breaks out during a visit from the (female) Venezuelan ambassador, who is taken hostage, along with two others and a prison guard. Police and army immediately surround the prison, with dozens of TV crews carrying the action live.

A young woman TV reporter from Caracas, well-played by Marisol Palacios, teams with a local cameraman (Diego Berti) whose regular cameraman and lover has been wounded (fatally, as it turns out) in the line of duty. At first, there's tension between the two, due to Berti's chauvinist ideas about working with a woman. But personalities are put aside as the hostage crisis intensifies.

Pic builds to an implausible though undeniably exciting climax, but the film's attacks on the TV network execs, who insist on continuing live coverage of the siege despite the fact that the prisoners have access to television and are getting a kick out of seeing themselves, ring a bit hollow.

Despite some garish color, pic is technically good, with the action scenes frighteningly well staged.
—*David Stratton*

L'ARGENT FAIT LE BONHEUR
(MONEY BRINGS HAPPINESS)
(FRENCH)

A France 2/Cameras Continentales production, with the participation of the Centre National de la Cinematographie. (Foreign sales: K-Films, Paris.) Produced by Takis Candilis. Directed by Robert Guediguian. Screenplay, Guediguian, Jean-Louis Milesi. Camera (color), Bernard Cavalie; editor, Bernard Sasia; music, Fatima Laourassia, Peter Gabriel, Johnny Hallyday, Gianna Nanini, G. Villard, Zao, Rossini; sound, Laurent Lafran; assistant director, Jacques Reboud. Reviewed at World Film Festival, Montreal (non-competing), Aug. 30, 1993. Running time: **90 MIN.**
Simona Viali .... Ariane Ascaride
The priest .... Jean-Pierre Darroussin
Mr. Degros .... Pierre Banderet
The prostitute .... Daniele Lebrun
Jackpot .... Roger Souza
Mr. Munoz .... Gerard Meylan
Mrs. Degros .... Frederique Bonnal
Mrs. Munoz .... Lorella Cravotta

This French made-for-TV movie could do well theatrically in some territories, including Quebec, thanks to an innovative, funny script and a top-notch ensemble cast. But it may be too closely rooted in the culture of southern France to travel well in English-language markets.

Pic tackles all the usual urban ills — including drug abuse, AIDS, rampant crime, violence and racism — but co-writer-director Robert Guediguian treats the material with a refreshing sense of humor, turning what could easily have been a solemn drama into an offbeat, postmodern fairy tale.

This 1990s update of Robin Hood is set in a squalid, tough, multiethnic suburb of Marseilles. Most of the men are alcoholics, criminals or chronically unemployed, and their kids run small-time theft operations to pay for their drug habits. The local parish priest (Jean-Pierre Darroussin), who narrates, is a streetwise activist who wanders the streets picking up used syringes and handing out condoms.

When rival gangs divide the town in two, neighborhood mothers join forces to reclaim their community by taking over the local crime trade and forcing their kids to help them steal from richer folks outside their neighborhood.

The colorful characters come to life in the hands of these actors, especially Darroussin as the grizzled, somewhat bemused priest and Ariane Ascaride as a tough, no-nonsense woman leading the crusade to bring the community back to life.
—*Brendan Kelly*

NA TEBIA UPOVAYU
(IN THEE I TRUST)
(RUSSIAN)

A 12-A Studio production. Produced by Alexander Mikhailov. Directed by Elena Tsiplakova. Screenplay, Nadejda Pokornaya. Camera (color), Ilia Diomin; editor, Natalia Volchek; music, Valery Miagkih; sound, Valery Golovnitsky. Reviewed at World Film Festival, Montreal (non-competing), Aug. 30, 1993. Running time: **86 MIN.**
Alla .... Evgenia Dobrovolskaya
Ira .... Irina Rozanova
  Also with: Natasha Sokorova, Vladimir Ilyin.

A bleak, compassionate film about the plight of orphaned children in today's Russia, "In Thee I Trust" deserves to be widely seen, but will be just too depressing for most audiences.

Evgenia Dobrovolskaya gives an astonishingly good performance as a young unmarried mother who, without a home or money, abandons her baby in a toilet and lives to regret it. Consumed with guilt, she accepts the advice of a priest and gets a job in an orphanage. But here she discovers a nightmare world, in which little children are regularly beaten for minor offenses, and food and supplies meant for them are stolen by the staff.

· Director Elena Tsiplakova presents this appalling state of affairs with justifiable anger and passion, and the film's message is socked home without pulling any punches.

The visuals are grainy, but this only adds to the authenticity of a film about a national tragedy.
—*David Stratton*

GE LAO YE ZI
(OLD MAN GE)
(CHINESE)

A Changchun Film Studio production. Directed by Han Gang. Screenplay, Jiang Yi. Camera (color), Jin Zi, Zhang Weimin; editor, Han; music, Mo Fan; sound, Wu Hao. Reviewed at World Film Festival, Montreal (non-competing), Aug. 31, 1993. Running time: **93 MIN.**
Ge .... Li Baotian
Grandson .... Jiang Wu
  Also with: Ma Xialqing, Fang Shu, Meng Jin, Liu Jian.

A simple tribute to the tenacity and courage of the older generation, "Old Man Ge" might contain political allusions (to Chinese leader Deng, perhaps), but is just as likely to reflect the reverence the Chinese have for old age.

Old Ge is retired and sickly. His grandson, who has built up what appears to be a successful business as a bar owner, has placed him in the hospital. But Ge refuses to lie down; he leaves the hospital, determined to spend one last winter gathering and selling junk so that he can afford to buy a mule and head for the countryside where he grew up.

Despite his grandson's objections, that's exactly what he does. There's really no more to the film than that, but the charming performance from veteran Li Baotian, as the determined old-timer, is constantly watchable.

Technical credits are all OK.
—*David Stratton*

MAVI SURGUN
(THE BLUE EXILE)
(TURKISH-GERMAN)

A Kenmovie-Kentel Films-Stefi 2 coproduction. Produced by Kenan Ormanlar. Directed by Erden Kiral. Screenplay, Kiral, Ormanlar, Elly Scheller-Ormanlar; camera (Eastmancolor), Ormanlar; editor, Karin Fischer; music, Timur Selcuk; sound, Simon Happ. Reviewed at World Film Festival, Montreal (competing), Aug. 31, 1993. Running time: **113 MIN.**
Cevat Sakir .... Can Togay
The Actress .... Hanna Schygulla
Hatce .... Ayse Romey
  Also with: Ozay Fecht, Tatiana Papamoskou, Halil Ergun.

A film about the political exile of a prominent Turkish journalist of the 1920s, Erden Kiral's "The Blue Exile" is a moody, leisurely pic with few dramatic highs. International exposure is unlikely outside the fest circuit.

Kiral, best known for "A Season at Hakkari" (1983), tells the story of Cevat Sakir, a writer who, just after Turkey's defeat in World War I, fell afoul of the authorities when he wrote about deserters from the army. At first sentenced to hang, he was later sent to a distant part of the country to serve a prison sentence.

Much of the film is taken up with his long train journey to exile in a remote, picturesque village by the sea, where it seems the local prison has fallen into disrepair and he's allowed to live in a rented house provided he reports regularly to the police. Here he marries and finds a kind of isolated peace.

Flashbacks to his youth portray the mother he adored, the father he hated, and his first wife's infidelity with her father-in-law.

In a very marginal role, German thesp Hanna Schygulla has a couple of rather odd scenes as a traveling actress.

This is a handsome but rather insubstantial production, and it probably won't mean much outside Turkey, where Sakir's writing is well known. He died in 1973.
—*David Stratton*

LOS ANOS OSCUROS

(URTE ILUNAK/THE DARK DAYS)

(SPANISH)

A Jose Maria Lara P.C.-Euskal Media S.A. production. Produced by Lara. Directed, written by Arantxa Lazcano. Camera (Eastmancolor), Flavio M. Labiano; editor, Julia Juaniz; music, production design, Inaki Eizagirre; costume design, Josune Lasa; sound, Julio Recuerdo; production manager, Javier Arsuaga. Reviewed at World Film Festival, Montreal (noncompeting), Aug. 30, 1993. Running time: **91 MIN.**
Iciar as a child .... Eider Amilibia
Iciar as a teenager .... Garazi Elorza
Father .... Carlos Panera
Mother .... Klara Badiola
Miren .... Amaia Basurto
Jose Luis as a child ....
.... Gorka Iruretagoyena
Jose Luis as a teenager ... Asier Arriola
Sofia .... Andrea Toledo
Cosme .... Joxe Lizaso

A hauntingly beautiful Basque film, "The Dark Days," with its theme of childhood oppressed by a harsh political regime, evokes memories of Victor Erice's "The Spirit of the Beehive." "The Dark Days" lacks the dramatic impact of that film, however, and though subtle and intelligent, may find it difficult to attract international arthouse audiences.

The "dark days" are the years between 1946 and 1965. The film begins with a secret meeting in which a group of Basque separatists plan to attract international support for their fight for independence from Franco's Spain — to no avail. One of the separatists (Carlos Panera) becomes, a few years later, the father of Iciar, through whose innocent eyes the rest of the story unfolds.

As a child of the '50s, Iciar attends a Catholic school where education is based on punishment and a sense of guilt. The speaking of the Basque language is officially outlawed, but continues in secret.

There are no big dramatic scenes here, just a series of beautifully lit and composed sequences in which Iciar and her friends discover the world and try to come to terms with the restrictions of the time. There are classroom scenes, a visit to the cinema (to see the Spanish classic "Marcelino Bread and Wine"), vows of eternal friendship. Eventually, Iciar is sent away to boarding school and returns seven years later, a teenager.

Writer-director Arantxa Lazcano and his fine cinematographer, Flavio M. Labiano, tell their deceptively simple story through luminous images. The film may be too slow and seemingly uneventful for many viewers, but it carries its own charge and resonance.

Performances are natural and unaffected. There's a lush score by Inaki Salvador, and production design is first class. This is a quiet, unassuming film for connoisseurs to seek out.
— *David Stratton*

AMIGOMIO

(ARGENTINE-GERMAN)

A Cheiko Producciones SRL (Buenos Aires)/Malena Films Gmbh (Berlin)/Telefilm Saar Gmbh (Saarbrucken) co-production. Produced by Martin Buchhorn, Mirta Reyes. Directed, written by Jeanine Meerapfel, Alcides Chiesa. Camera (color), Victor Gonzalez; editor, Andrea Wenzler; music, Osvaldo Montes; sound, Paul Oberle, Jorge Stavropulos. Reviewed at World Film Festival, Montreal (competing), Sept. 1, 1993. Running time: **115 MIN.**
Carlos Lowenthal .... Daniel Kuzniecka
Amigomio .... Diego Mesaglio
Grandfather .... Mario Adorf
Also with: Atillo Veronelli, Manuel Tricallotis, Deborah Brandwajnman, Christoph Baumann, Hugo Pozo, Gabriela Salas.

A film about exile and displacement, "Amigomio" is fascinating for much of its length but ultimately is a little overextended and confusing. Some trimming would help a great deal.

The tense opening scenes are set in Buenos Aires during the grim period of the military dictatorship (although no title explains this, and audiences have to work it out for themselves). Carlos, of German extraction, has recently separated from his wife, Negra, a leftist radical; he has custody of their son, whom he calls Amigomio ("my friend"). When Negra disappears, presumably abducted by the police, Carlos decides to leave the country.

He and the boy head northwest across the Andes, first into Bolivia and eventually into Ecuador, where they start a new life. Long central section is virtually a road movie, as father and son trek through the mountains and stop off in picturesque towns, encountering eccentrics, bandits, corrupt police, revolutionaries, a Jesus freak and others along the way. It's great material but seems haphazardly constructed, giving the film surprisingly little forward momentum. Daniel Kuzniecka is effective as the nervous hero, while young Diego Mesaglio is a charmer as the son. Vet German actor Mario Adorf does a bit as Carlos' father.

All production credits are excellent, though editor Andrea Wenzler has allowed too much slack.
— *David Stratton*

OCHENJ VERNAJA ZHENA

(A VERY FAITHFUL WIFE)

(RUSSIAN)

A Mosfilm Concern-Rhythm Studio production. Directed by Valery Pendrakovski. Screenplay, Razikov Rogosin. Camera (color), Valentin Makarov; editor, Natalia Dobrunova; music, Edison Denisov; sound, Boris Vengerovsky. Reviewed at World Film Festival, Montreal (competing), Aug. 30, 1993. Running time: **75 MIN.**
Tanya .... Natalia Chernyavskaya
Zhenia .... Valery Nikolaev
Iskrin .... Victor Proskurin
Polina .... Olga Ostroumova
Verka .... Valeria Ustinova
Dina .... Tatiana Yegorova

A modest little film about a romance that goes sour, "A Very Faithful Wife" is decently made but really too slight to make much of an impact with audiences.

Familiar story concerns Tanya (Natalia Chernyavskaya), a young Muscovite who gets pregnant by superficially charming go-getter Zhenia (Valery Nikolaev). They marry, but soon after their son is born Zhenia heads for Siberia, planning to get rich quick; instead, he gets a five-year jail sentence for an unspecified petty crime.

Living with her disapproving mother, Tanya makes ends meet as a stenographer, and gets extra work helping a middle-aged journalist (Victor Proskurin), who falls in love with her. Eventually, she succumbs. Meanwhile, Zhenia is paroled, but is not allowed to leave the remote village.

When the journalist asks Tanya to accompany him to Australia for two years, she goes to see Zhenia and discovers that he's living with another woman. Pic ends before she decides what to do with her life.

Chernyavskaya gives an attractive, sensitive perf as the young woman who tries to be loyal to her feckless husband, but finds the odds well and truly stacked against her. Film could have gone into her situation in more depth, but its depiction of contempo Russian life is always interesting, if a bit depressing.

Visuals are very grainy, but otherwise tech credits are good, and an attractive, old-fashioned, romantic music score is a plus.
— *David Stratton*

MATAR AL ABUELITO

(KILLING GRANDDAD)

(ARGENTINE)

An Aura Producciones S.R.L.-Kankun S.A.-TVE production. Produced by Pablo Rovito. Directed by Luis Cesar D'Angiolillo. Screenplay, D'Angiolillo, Ariel Sienra, Eduardo Mignona; camera (Fujicolor), Miguel Abal; editor, D'Angiolillo; production design, Maria Favale; music, Litto Nebbia; sound, Abelardo Kuschnir; costumes, Cristina Tavano; associate producer, Claudia Kohen; production manager, Juan Vera; assistant director, Sona Karpiuk. Reviewed at World Film Festival, Montreal (non-competing), Aug. 31, 1993. Running time: **114 MIN.**
Don Mariano Aguero ... Federico Luppi
Rosita .... Ines Estevez
Ferchu .... Alberto Segado
Ramon .... Emilio Bardi
Fabiana .... Laura Novoa
Amelita .... Mirta Busnelli
Jeff .... Horacio Pena

"Killing Granddad" has arthouse potential, and will probably be compared to "Like Water for Chocolate." Like that Mexican hit, this is a plush, entertaining trifle with lots of sex and fantasy.

Don Mariano (Federico Luppi) has been miserable since the death of his wife, and his fractious family can't wait to inherit his loot. He lies, bedridden, in a large house, and is given regular injections and pills by an unsympathetic nurse.

His loyal servant Ramon (Emilio Bardi) is distressed to see the old man in this state, and introduces his stepsister, Rosita (Ines Estevez) into the household. This lovely young woman, it's revealed, has spent time in a mental home; but she sets about bringing Don Mariano back to life by means of love and even sex, slipping naked into bed with him. The therapy works, and, to the dismay of his family, Don Mariano makes a rapid recovery and starts a passionate affair with Rosita, who's young enough to be his granddaughter. His family conspires to end this state of affairs, and the film ends in a scene of lyrical escape that is lifted shamelessly from "Thelma & Louise."

This flaw aside, "Killing Granddad" is a thoroughly entertaining pic, with top-class production values and an excellent cast. Luppi is splendid as the old man who gets a new lease on life, while Estevez is a delight as the literally bewitching young girl. Other characters, including the old man's grasping sons and daughter-in-law, and his granddaughter (who has a lesbian lover), are very well limned.

This is a film with no pretension other than to entertain, something it achieves most successfully.
— *David Stratton*

November 1, 1993 (Cont.)

GOLEM BAMA'AGAL

(BLIND MAN'S BLUFF)

(ISRAELI)

A Chaim Sharir production, with the assistance of the Fund for Israeli Quality Films. (Foreign sales: the Golem Partnership, Tel Aviv). Produced by Chaim Sharir. Directed by Aner Preminger. Written by Preminger, Tal Zilbertain, based on Lilly Perry Amitai's novel. Camera (color), Ya'acov Eisenman; editor, Tova Asher; music, Haim Permont; production design, Eitan Levi; costume design, Ada Levin; sound, Shabtai Sarig. Reviewed at World Film Festival, Montreal, Sept. 5, 1993. (Also in Vancouver Festival.) Running time: **95 MIN.**

Miki Stav	Hagit Dasberg
Mrs. Stav	Nicole Casel
Mr. Stav	Gedalia Besser
Marlen	Anat Waxman
Amnon	Dani Litani
Grandfather	Albert Cohen
Uri Rozes	Ichio Avital

A disappointing coming-of-age pic, "Blind Man's Bluff" looks through the eyes of a Tel Aviv pianist trying to break the shackles of her demanding family. Unfortunately, after initial sparks, the script fails to flesh out this familiar setup, and auds are left whistling in the dark. Prospects are limited to Jewish fest circuit, where it will strike a mild chord with adolescent females and older auds.

Hagit Dasberg has subtle gamine appeal as Miki, a budding musician who abruptly moves from her parents' suburban home and into a noisy, working-class apartment house. There she meets some unusual neighbors, including a promiscuous Bohemian and a cool-headed lawyer who moonlights as a nightclub folkie and part-time Lothario.

Unfortunately, this intriguing mix — with its implied clash between old-world values and new — is quickly subsumed by battles with her hypochondriac mother (Nicole Casel), a once-beautiful Holocaust survivor, now taking out a lifetime of disappointments on her cowed daughter, passive husband and aged, wisdom-dispensing papa.

What the pic lacks in drive it almost makes up for with character and texture, But Miki's love of music is not sufficiently established, and her climactic recital sequence is excruciatingly rote. Finally, the story recalls too many artist-stifled-by-sick-moms sagas to play well away from home.

First known in English as "Dummy in a Circle," the pic's Hebrew handle refers to the mythical Golem's shapeless potential, and thus reflects both the young pianist's plight and the unfinished nature of the movie. Current title means nothing. —*Ken Eisner*

ASHAKARA

(TOGOLESE)

A Koulinga production in association with Television Suisse Romande/ADAVI/DiProCi/Togo Ministry of Culture. Produced, written by Phillippe Souaille. Directed, adapted by Gerard Louvin. Camera (color), Yves Poulquan; editor, Nelly Meunier; music, Louis Crelier, Sally Nyoto; sound, Gilbert Hamilton. Reviewed at Pan African Film Festival, L.A., Oct. 9, 1993. Running time: **97 MIN.**

Dr. Kara	James Campbell-Badine
Jerome Blanc	Jean-Marc Pasquet
Koffi	Willy Monshongwo
Also with: N. Bamela, E. Pinda.	

An unusual and sprightly tale of modern Africa, "Ashakara" is a colorful blend of social, political and cultural elements wrapped up in a thriller format. Although narrative is somewhat clunky, the unfamiliarity of the terrain provides an enjoyable, bumpy ride. It adds up to limited theatrical prospects but deserved exposure on the festival beat.

The essential story centers on a local homeopathic cure for a virus that's crept into Europe. Dr. Kara (James Campbell-Badine), a respected medical researcher, literally goes back to his roots in a remote Togo village to find the remedy. Then, when a French pharmaceutical company — with its own fitfully successful medicine — gets wind of the African discovery, it dispatches rep Jerome Blanc (Jean-Marc Pasquet) to secure the commercial rights.

Phillippe Souaille's script expands the simple premise into an intricate cat's cradle with fascinating, if not always successful, results. The unexpected turns include Blanc's growing allegiance to the Africans and the treachery of Kara's assistant, who's been blinded by the prospect of a financial windfall from the sale of the patent. That dream evaporates when Kara suspects the Europeans want only to suppress the remedy's entry into the marketplace. That spins out into an elaborate kidnapping ruse. Director Gerard Louvin demonstrates more energy than focus in this adventure. He's abetted by an appealing, personable cast, but tech achievements fall into an uncomfortable limbo between smooth professionalism and gritty realism.

—*Leonard Klady*

LIVING PROOF: HIV AND THE PURSUIT OF HAPPINESS

(DOCU — 16mm)

A First Run Features release of a Short Films production. Produced by Kermit Cole, Beth Tyler, Anthony Bennett. Directed by Cole. Written by Jameson Currier. Camera (Duart color), Richard Dallett; editor, Michael Gersh; music, James Legg, Mark Suozzo; sound, Richard Brause, Kira Smith, Felix Andrew, John Murphy; associate producer, Chiemi Karasawa. Reviewed at Loews Copley Place, Boston, Sept. 9, 1993. (In Boston, London fests.) Running time: **72 MIN.**

An AIDS documentary that has audiences cheering with happiness seems like an unlikely occurrence — short of the announcement of a cure — but filmmaker Kermit Cole has pulled it off. This chronicle of people who are HIV-positive and who refuse to play victim has been picked up by First Run Features and should prove a real crowd pleaser in art and specialty houses.

Premise is that the media has given the world an image of those infected with AIDS as desiccated and covered with lesions, briefly clinging to life before succumbing to the disease. In conjunction with a project by photographer Carolyn Jones, Cole speaks to HIV-positive people of all ages and walks of life who clearly haven't given up living.

He interviews them both at Jones' photo shoot and elsewhere, and only rarely do their stories bring a tear to the eye. (A man relating how he came out to his "conservative Southern grandfather" as both HIV-positive and gay is easily the most moving moment in the film.) For the most part, these are people who have accepted their fate and are getting on with their lives, trying to live it to the fullest knowing that their time may be cut short.

Often, the people interviewed have taken the opportunity to make changes in their lives, switching careers, focusing on their families, becoming involved in the community or merely rethinking what's important to them. Indeed, the film is so relentlessly upbeat that Cole provides some balance: Some of his subjects qualify their optimism by noting that they'd trade their present happiness for HIV-negative status in a moment.

Tech work is top-notch for a 16mm docu. Many production costs were donated, from film stock and equipment to title design and post-production editing.

—*Daniel M. Kimmel*

LA PROSSIMA VOLTA IL FUOCO

(NEXT TIME THE FIRE)

(ITALIAN-FRENCH-SWISS)

An Istituto Luce-Italnoleggio release (Italy) of a Gam Film (Rome)/Erato Films (Paris)/Frama Films Intl. (Lugano) production, in association with the Ministry of Entertainment, Istituto Luce-Italnoleggio Cinematografico and Canal Plus. Produced by Gherardo Pagliei, Elisabetta Riga. Directed by Fabio Carpi. Screenplay, Carpi, Luigi Malerba. Camera (color), Renato Berta; editor, Alfredo Muschietti; art direction, Gilberto Del Tedesco, Ruggero Magrini; costumes, Silvana Carpi. Reviewed at Venice Film Festival (competing), Sept. 7, 1993. Running time: **78 MIN.**

Amedeo	Jean Rochefort
Elena	Marie-Christine Barrault
Mother	Lila Kedrova
Gloria	Jacqueline Lustig
Diana	Lidia Koslovich
Malvina	Patrizia De Clara
(French dialogue)	

"Next Time the Fire" is a sophisticated game that begins well but turns out not much fun to play. A college prof decides to switch the roles of the women in his life (daughter, wife, mother) to make himself feel younger. Helmer Fabio Carpi doesn't draw the conceit out far enough to rouse any emotion stronger than mild surprise. Despite a sterling cast, pic has very limited appeal.

A Sorbonne semantics teacher (Jean Rochefort) drives his wife (Marie-Christine Barrault) to Italy for a holiday in his mother's (Lila Kedrova) country house. The wife's classic beauty is beginning to wane, and so is the prof's interest. His feisty invalid mother seems so ancient he even entertains the idea of putting her out of her misery.

When prof finds his unwed daughter Gloria (Jacqueline Lustig) in the tub with her newborn child, her unselfconscious nudity apparently strikes a chord: In the garden he kisses her deeply on the mouth, in front of his wife, who decides to go along with her husband's absurd whim and assumes the role of his mother, who conveniently dies of a heart attack. Gloria also humors her father, and quickly becomes his lover/wife.

There should be more outright comedy or acid irony in a story like this. Instead, there is an aloofly intellectual, gently joshing tone, and a dreamlike atmosphere that precludes passion or any other emotion. By the end, the women assume their usual places in the prof's life.

Acting is the strongest suit here. Rochefort and Barrault make a delightfully witty team, with his Freudian slips and her know-it-all repartee. Kedrova is a splendidly nasty mother.

Despite Italian title, director and setting, original dialogue is in French, so actors could perform in their native lingo.

—*Deborah Young*

LOIN DES BARBARES

(FAR FROM BARBARY)

(FRENCH-ITALIAN-BELGIAN)

A K.G. Productions (Paris)/Urania Films (Rome)/Prima Vista (Brussels) production. (Foreign sales: World Marketing Film, Paris.) Produced by Michele Ray-Gavras. Directed by Liria Begeja. Screenplay, Begeja, Olivier Douyere. Camera (color), Patrick Blossier; editor, Luc Barnier; music, Piro Cako; sound, Eric Vaucher. Reviewed at Venice Film Festival (non-competing), Sept. 8, 1993. Running time: **95 MIN.**
Zana Peza .... Dominique Blanc
Selman Peza .... Sulejman Pitarka
Vladimir .... Timo Flloko
Omer .... Piro Mani
Vincent .... Ronald Guttmann

A modest but well-made film about a French woman of Albanian origin whose well-ordered world is disrupted by an illegal refugee from the old country, "Far From Barbary" starts in leisurely fashion but becomes more intriguing as it unfolds. Modest biz looms.

Dominique Blanc plays Zana, every inch a sophisticated Parisienne, who plans to leave with her boyfriend to live in New York. She has few scruples about leaving behind her elderly uncle, Selman, who raised her, though she's still haunted by nightmares about her parents, who were killed smuggling her out of Albania as a baby.

Zana's plans are changed when she hears an Albanian refugee, Vladimir (Timo Flloko), is being held by immigration authorities because he doesn't have the necessary documents. He promises information about her father, who may not be dead after all.

When Vladimir escapes (somewhat unconvincingly) from the authorities, he joins Zana in a search for people who may know her father's whereabouts. Meanwhile, love blossoms between the sophisticated woman who can't speak a word of Albanian and the refugee who can't get used to the fact that in Paris the tap water is never cut off and there's no need for a black market.

Femme helmer Liria Begeja directs smoothly, and is well served by her cast. Pic lacks tension, but it's well mounted and intriguing enough to seduce minority audiences. —*David Stratton*

ZA ZUI ZI

(CHATTERBOX)

(CHINESE)

A Children's Film Studio production. Directed by Liu Miaomiao. Screenplay, Liu, Yang Zhengguang. Camera (color), Wang Jiuwen; editor, Feng Sihai; music, Wen Zhongjia; production design, Liu Jian, Liao Yongjun; sound, Huang Siye. Reviewed at Venice Film Festival (competing), Sept. 8, 1993. Running time: **94 MIN.**
Min Sheng .... Li Lei
Shu Ying .... Cao Cuifen
Qun Sheng .... Yuan Jing
Yan Mai .... Lu Xiaoan
Wang Laoshi .... Guo Shaoxiong

On the surface, "Chatterbox" is a simple children's film, set in a Chinese mountain village, about a feisty moppet who's forever getting into trouble for speaking his mind. Well-crafted pic is a natural for kids' programming but too insubstantial to make much impact internationally.

If there's a political subtext in distaff helmer Liu Miaomiao's movie — the danger of speaking out against the Establishment — it's pretty well concealed.

Little Min Sheng is nicknamed "za zui zi" ("chatterbox") because he can't stop talking and usually says more than he should. His troubles begin when his father, the village treasurer, is accused of embezzlement and his family is ostracized. Also, his brother's fiancée is pregnant, though the wedding arrangements aren't finalized.

Liu's depiction of wintry village life is both affectionate and penetrating, and young thesp Li Lei gives a confident perf as the talkative youngster who sorts out all his family's problems by fade-out.

Pic was originally skedded to compete at the Locarno fest in August but was pulled by the Chinese authorities to protest helmer Zhang Yuan's indie effort, "Beijing Bastards," also in competition.
—*David Stratton*

VIGYAZOK

(THE WATCHERS)

(HUNGARIAN)

An Objektiv Filmstudio production. Directed by Sandor Sara. Screenplay, Sara, Miklos Domahidy; camera (Eastmancolor), Balazs Sara; editor, Eva Szentandrassy; music, Zoltan Jeney; production design, Jozsef Romvari; sound, P. Laczkovich. Reviewed at Venice Film Festival (non-competing), Sept. 8, 1993. Running time: **94 MIN.**
With: Eszter Nagy-Kaloczy, Gabor Mate, Anna Rackevei, Peter Andorai, Mari Torocsik, Laszlo Mensaros.

Sandor Sara's "The Watchers" deals with the way the lives of ordinary Hungarians were af-

fected during the darkest days of communism, but does so in a flat, uninvolving fashion. Pic is too talky and uninventive to make an impact on the big screen. TV exposure is possible.

Film opens promisingly enough during a dinner party attended by seven friends in a Budapest apartment. The hostess finds an anonymous State Security ID card, apparently fallen from someone's pocket. One of the friends is a spy for the authorities, but which?

Instead of exploring this theme in an interesting way, Sara settles for a series of routine confrontations in which each of the seven in turn becomes a suspect. Despite his background as a cinematographer, Sara makes nothing cinematic out of these chatty scenes.

Only toward the end, when the hostess, Eva (Eszter Nagy-Kaloczy), embarks on a secret love affair with one of her guests, does the picture break away from its static formula. By then, it's too late.

On the plus side, all the thesping is fine, and the film is technically excellent in every department.
—*David Stratton*

AQUI NA TERRA

(HERE ON EARTH)

(PORTUGUESE)

A Uniportugal release (Portugal) of a Companhia de Filmes do Principe Real production. Produced by Antonio Da Cunha Telles. Executive producer, Maria Joao Mayer. Directed, written by Joao Botelho. Camera (color), Elso Roque; editor, Jose Nascimento; music, Antonio Pinho Vargas; art direction, Ana Vaz Da Silva. Reviewed at Venice Film Festival (competing), Sept. 4, 1993. (Also in Festival of Festivals, Toronto.) Running time: **105 MIN.**
Miguel .... Luis Miguel Cintra
Isabel .... Jessica Weiss
Antonio .... Pedro Hestnes
Cecilia .... Rita Dias
Mother .... Isabel De Castro
Prostitute .... Ines Medeiros
Housekeeper .... Laura Soveral

Meticulous Portuguese helmer Joao Botelho misses the mark in "Here on Earth," a structurally ambitious, visually refined art movie flawed by an uncertain tone. Its two unrelated stories, contrasting the woes of a rich and poor couple, merge in a forced ending with mystical Catholic overtones. Festivals will be the most open to this interesting but failed experiment.

At the peak of success, a rich financier (Luis Miguel Cintra) begins to hear sounds that nobody else can — squeaking, shrieking, roaring and drilling that make his head throb. He gives up his job and becomes a recluse. His wife (Jessica Weiss) considers leaving him.

Simultaneously, in a remote mountain area, a saintly young cowherd (Rita Dias) is raped by an old

man and becomes pregnant. The boy she loves (Pedro Hestnes) kills the old man and flees the village.

The three characters meet in the final sequence, when the financier, driving in the mountains, gives the boy a lift. The two find Dias among the rocks with her infant son, every inch a Madonna and Child. The vision of the baby cures Cintra of his madness, and he returns to the arms of his still-faithful wife, a joyful man. Botelho's talent for intriguing storytelling ("Hard Times," "On My Birthday") falters here. Long before the "miracle" occurs, auds will tire of Cintra's problems. The saga of the young lovers, on the other hand, seems lifted out of an old religious tear-jerker. Botelho's gamble is to tie these two film styles together, but pic's rhythm suffers from the constant intercutting.

Even a veteran as seductively inventive as Cintra can't retain his dignity during scenes of vomiting, walking around with his ears taped up and ecstatically romancing an aging housekeeper. By the time he jumps up in a transvestite nightclub with cries of "I see the light!," many viewers will already be heading for it. —*Deborah Young*

THE HOLLOW MEN

(POLISH)

A Million Frames (Warsaw) production. (International sales: Pinnacle Pictures, London.) Produced by Jerzy Skolimowski. Directed, written by John Yorick, Joseph Kay. Camera (color), Krzysztof Ptak; editor, Kay; music, Verdi, Krzesimir Debski; production design, Krzysztof Stefankiewicz; sound (Dolby), Piotr Knop; costume design, Jolanta Wlodarczyk; casting, Louise Elman. Reviewed at Venice Film Festival (non-competing), Sept. 7, 1993. Running time: **95 MIN.**
Matthew .... John Yorick
Mark ....Joseph Kay
Rita .... Agnes Wagner
Agnes .... Barbara Kosmal
Father .... Michael Sarne
Lena .... Violetta Klimczewska
(English dialogue)

A brooding drama of youthful angst, inspired by Jungian philosophy, "The Hollow Men" is a visually striking but dramatically muddled pic which faces an uphill battle to find an audience.

Writer-director-leads John Yorick, 24, and Joseph Kay, 22, are the sons of well-known helmer Jerzy Skolimowski, who produced this Polish-made, English-language effort. Yorick also appeared, under the moniker Michael Lyndon, in Skolimowski's "Success Is the Best Revenge" and "The Lightship."

Story is set in a small seaside town where an open-air play by an anonymous writer is to be performed. Kay plays Mark, an actor, who's discomfited when his brother, Matthew (Yorick), the play's secret author, arrives.

Problem is there's little genuine conflict or drama, as the characters just drift around the town in endless, aimless wandering, interrupted only by the occasional encounter, argument or sexual dalliance.

Kay and Yorick look a lot like their father, have the youthful, brooding arrogance of a James Dean, and could cut themselves careers in front of the camera. As directors, they had the benefit of a fine cameraman (Krzysztof Ptak) and the film always looks good. As writers, they have a lot to learn: This is a script that needed a lot more work before shooting.

Agnes Wagner and the late Barbara Kosmal (to whom the film is dedicated) are strikingly beautiful as two of the town's enigmatic women. Casting British actor-director Michael Sarne as the brothers' father is odd: This would surely have been the perfect role for Skolimowski himself.

Verdi's "Requiem" is used with pretension, and the overkill Dolby soundtrack has every footstep sounding like a crash of thunder.

—*David Stratton*

TOUCHIA
(SONG OF ALGERIAN WOMEN)
(ALGERIAN-FRENCH)

A National Enterprise for Audiovisual Production (Algiers)/Les Films Singuliers (Paris) production. Produced by Neil Hollander. Directed by Rachid Benhadj. Screenplay, Benhadj, Cristina Paterlini. Camera (color), Zine Bessa; music, Mezoum H'sine; production design, Omar Hamoul; sound, Kamel Mekesser; assistant director, Keltoum Mazif. Reviewed at Venice Film Festival (Critics' Week), Sept. 10, 1993. Running time: **73 MIN.**
Fella .... Nabila Babli
Fella, age 11 .... Lylia Ait Kaci
Anissa .... Cristina Fioretti
Mother .... Dalila Helilou

A woman's-eye drama opposing Algeria's growing Islamic fundamentalism, "Touchia" makes its points forcefully but is thin and underdeveloped dramatically. Pic may scrape a few fest outings, more for its theme than for its qualities as a film.

A 40-ish spokeswoman for Algeria's feminists, Fella (Nabila Babli) is nervously prepping for an important TV interview. In the street outside her apartment, Muslims parade against democracy and all she stands for.

In flashback, she remembers when she was 11 and Algeria won its war against colonialist France. For Fella and her friend Anissa, celebrations were shattered when they were attacked and raped by

three men. Back in the present, Fella begins her TV interview with a cry of protest.

The film is interesting as far as it goes, but it leaves the viewer wanting a lot more info — about Fella's life and the current conflict in Algeria between modernism and fundamentalism.

Pic is modestly, somewhat scrappily made, as though good intentions were enough.

—*David Stratton*

DOVE SIETE?
IO SONO QUI
(WHERE ARE YOU? I'M HERE)
(ITALIAN)

An Italian International Film (Italy) release of a San Francisco Film production, in association with RAI-TV Channel 1 and Sacis. (Foreign sales: Sacis, Rome.) Produced by Giovanni Bertolucci. Directed by Liliana Cavani. Screenplay, Cavani, Italo Moscati. Camera (color), Armando Nannuzzi; editor, Angelo Nicolini; music, Pino Donaggio; art direction, Luciano Ricceri. Reviewed at Venice Film Festival (competing), Sept. 1, 1993. (Also in World Film Festival, Montreal.) Running time: **148 MIN.**
Fausto ....Gaetano Carotenuto
Elena .... Chiara Caselli
Mother .... Anna Bonaiuto
Aunt .... Valeria D'Obici
Maria .... Ines Nobili
School principal .... Paola Mannoni
Latin teacher .... Carla Cassola

Liliana Cavani's "Where Are You? I'm Here" tackles with sympathy and warmth the subject of a deaf boy who rejects his mother's desire for him to lead a "normal" life. But mostly it's too predictable and flat to work beyond a superficial level, and faces an uphill struggle for offshore distribution.

Pic is Cavani's first since "Francesco," the 1989 Mickey Rourke-Helena Bonham Carter starrer about Francis of Assisi.

Though deaf from birth, Fausto (Gaetano Carotenuto) has been forbidden by his mother (Anna Bonaiuto) to use sign language or mix with other deaf people.

Fausto carries out his mother's wishes, working in a bank and going out with the sexy Maria (Ines Nobili). Mama urges the bank director to transfer him to a cushy job in London and, despite an embarrassing dinner in which Fausto gets too flustered to speak, everything seems to be on course.

Then he meets Elena (Chiara Caselli), a poor high school drop-out. With Fausto's encouragement, Elena returns to class and convinces the hostile school board she's good enough to stand for her final exams. Fausto later achieves his own victory against his mother's psychological dominance.

Cavani several times brings the film to emotional peaks, but the total lack of irony and easy crisis-overcome ending give it an old-fashioned feel of TV drama.

Carotenuto is convincing as the rich deaf boy whose other senses are vibrantly alive. In her most mature performance to date, the high-strung Caselli makes her every scene vibrate with nervous tension.

Excellent in supporting roles are Bonaiuto as the iron-willed, over-loving mother (perf won an acting award at Venice fest) and Valeria D'Obici as her sister, who taught Fausto sign language.

—*Deborah Young*

IL TUFFO
(THE DIVE)
(ITALIAN)

A Riverfilm production, with the co-operation of Centro Sperimentale di Cinematografica. Produced by Dario Formisano. Directed by Massimo Martella. Screenplay, Martella, Roberto De Francesco, Maurizio Fiume. Camera (color), Paolo Ferrari; editor, Ilaria De Laurentiis; music, Peter D'Argenzio, Mario Tronco; production design, Renato Lori; sound, Luigi Melchionda; assistant director, Gianfranco Pannone. Reviewed at Venice Film Festival (Critics' Week), Sept. 6, 1993. Running time: **98 MIN.**
Matteo .... Vincenzo Salemme
Elsa .... Carlotta Natou
Giulio .... Arturo Paglia
Gianluca .... Francesco Apolloni
Monica .... Elisabetta Cavallotti
Giulio's mother .... Annalisa Foa
Matteo's father .... Gianni Cajafa
Matteo's mother .... Elisa Mainardi

"The Dive" is a straightforward relationships film about a teacher and two teenage students in a small Italian town in the heat of summer. Modestly appealing small-budgeter will play comfortably on small screens.

Matteo, 30, is looking after his sickly father, but he agrees to spend part of the summer vacation coaching Giulio and Elsa in physics. Elsa is a brash, sparkling, self-confident young woman; Giulio is painfully shy and withdrawn.

Matteo finds himself attracted to Elsa, and so does Giulio. Matters come to a head when Matteo takes the two students to an all-night party by the sea at the end of the holidays.

This is a very gentle comedy-drama, with few dramatic highlights, and seems unlikely to boost the reputations of either actors or director. It's technically well made, but the familiar subject offers no original insights.

—*David Stratton*

CONDANNATO
A NOZZE
(CONDEMNED TO WED)
(ITALIAN)

A Penta Distribuzione (Italy) release of a Mario & Vittorio Cecchi Gori, Silvio Berlusconi Communications presentation of a Penta Film/Esterno Mediterraneo production. Produced by Mario & Vittorio Cecchi Gori, Gaetano Daniele. Directed by Giuseppe Piccioni. Screenplay, Piccioni, Franco Bernini, Fabrizio Bettelli. Camera (color), Roberto Meddi; editor, Esmeralda Calabria; music, Antonio Di Pofi; art direction, Lorenzo Baraldi; costume design, Marina Campanale; sound, Tommaso Quattrini. Reviewed at Penta Film screening room, Rome, Sept. 2, 1993. (In Venice Film Festival, Italian Panorama.) Running time: **110 MIN.**
Roberto .... Sergio Rubini
Sandra .... Margherita Buy
Gloria .... Valeria Bruni Tedeschi
Olivia .... Asia Argento
Enrica .... Patrizia Piccinini

A Romeo bitten by pre-wedding nerves gets his wish granted for a double life as both family man and philanderer in "Condemned to Wed." From this not entirely fresh notion, director Giuseppe Piccioni delivers a sophisticated romantic parable that, with tightening, could be a contender for offshore exposure. Pic is doing sprightly biz in Italy.

Piccioni is one of a handful of young Italo helmers to tap intelligent middle ground between art-house and commercial fare. His 1991 road romance, "Ask for the Moon," pepped up local wickets and was a popular fest entry. New effort is more ambitious but less fully realized. A 20-minute trim would tighten pic's meandering narrative and eliminate some confusing plot digressions.

Sergio Rubini plays a verbose divorce lawyer whose amorous uncertainty causes him to split into two warring halves while asleep one night. One half pursues monogamous marriage and fatherhood with an architect (Margherita Buy). The other becomes a diehard Don Giovanni, sharing his favors chiefly with a TV presenter (Valeria Bruni Tedeschi) and a homicidal/suicidal teen temptress (Asia Argento).

Setup starts to crumble when the husband-half starts tirelessly preaching against the evils of infidelity. He tosses his career away by promoting marital harmony to potential divorcees, and drives his wife away with his unfounded jealousy.

His bed-hopping twin falls foul of his own ardor. Unable to sway him from sex to sentiment, his conquests fight back and eventually dump him. Hardship and loneliness inexorably push Rubini's wayward halves together.

Looking more than ever like an emaciated, low-rent Al Pacino, Rubini (director and star of the 1990 "The Station") stretches credibility as a sexual terminator. But he expertly balances affable charm with the character's consistently questionable behavior.

Even more winning is the film's dynamite femme lineup, from whom Piccioni coaxes a richly textured assortment of naturalistic perfs. Buy is sympathetic in a relatively low-key role; Bruni Tedeschi and Argento (daughter of scaremeister Dario) get to shine more brightly.

Also appealing is Patrizia Piccinini as a colleague at Rubini's law firm. She has pic's funniest scene, in which Rubini exposes her extramarital fling during a dinner party. Elsewhere, comedy takes on darker tones, serving up wry jibes at the male animal's idiosyncrasies.

Tech work is impeccable all round, including pristine direct sound recording (still hit-and-miss in Italian movies). —*David Rooney*

KOSH BA KOSH

(ODDS AND EVENS)

(TADJIK-JAPANESE-SWISS)

A VVYS Feature Film Production Co. (Dushanbe)/Euro Space (Tokyo)/ Sunrise Filmvertriebs (Zurich) production, in collaboration with Pandora Film, Tadjikgaz Trigon Film, Tadjik Film Studios. Produced by Bakhtiyar Khudojnazarov, Kenzo Horikoshi. Executive producer, Christa Saredi. Directed by Khudojnazarov. Screenplay, Khudojnazarov, Leonid Mahkamov. Camera (color), Georgy Dzalaiev; editor, Khudojnazarov; music, Achmad Bakaev; production design, Negmat Jouraiev; sound, Roustam Achadov; assistant director, Dominique de Rivaz. Reviewed at Venice Film Festival (competing), Sept. 8, 1993. Running time: **103 MIN.**
Mira .... Paulina Galvez
Daler .... Daler Madjidav
Farhad .... Alisher Kasimov
Mira's father ...... Bokhodur Djurabajev
Daler's mother ...... Albardji Bakhirova
Daler's father ... Rahmonkul Kurbanov

"Odds and Evens" is an old-fashioned love story with a potent extra dimension, as it was filmed in the middle of the ongoing civil war between opponents and defenders of Islamic fundamentalism in Dushanbe, capital of Tadjikistan (a former region of the U.S.S.R. near the Afghanistan and Pakistan borders). Result is very rough at the edges, but has considerable power and poignancy.

Screenplay was written before the war erupted, and the conflict isn't really part of the story. Still, with gunfire heard in practically every scene, the night sky lit up with tracer bullets, and scenes of refugees, the film has an urgency that presumably wasn't planned.

Story involves a young Tadjik woman, Mira, who's been living in western Russia, but who returns home to visit her dissolute father. He's just "lost" her in a game of "odds and evens" (kosh ba kosh) that he obsessively plays with his friends.

She's disgusted by these macho goings-on, but then meets Daler, who operates a cable car used to transport things up a hillside overlooking the city. It also becomes the location for his trysts with Mira.

"Odds and Evens" is strangely schizophrenic, as the horror of the real war that's going on around the actors overwhelms the modest story being told. Perfs are naturalistic and, given that production was interrupted from time to time, it's no wonder the film is technically uneven. —*David Stratton*

YOUCEF, OU LA LEGENDE DU SEPTIEME DORMANT

(YOUCEF, OR THE LEGEND OF THE SEVENTH SLEEPER)

(ALGERIAN-FRENCH)

A C.A.A.I.C. (Algeria)/K Films (Paris) production. Produced, directed, written by Mohamed Chouikh. Camera (color), Allel Yahiaoui; editor, Yamina Chouikh; music, Khaled Barkat; production design, Rachid Diguer; sound, Rachid Bouafia. Reviewed at Venice Film Festival (non-competing), Sept. 7, 1993. Running time: **109 MIN.**
Youcef .... Mohamed Ali Allalou
Aicha .... Shiraz Selma
Amin .... Youcef Benhadouda
Fatima .... Dalila Helilou
Ali .... Benguettaf M'Hamed

Via a tale about an Algerian who "awakes" after more than 30 years to discover the ideals for which he once fought have been subverted, writer-producer-director Mohamed Chouikh has made a provocative, wryly amusing pic. "Youcef" should be seen widely at fests, with specialized distribution also indicated.

Chouikh, who made the 1988 "The Citadel," an indictment of patriarchal Arab society, is a courageous filmmaker. "Youcef" violently opposes the Islamic fundamentalists who have become a powerful force in Algeria.

Youcef (Mohamed Ali Allalou) fought against the French colonialists in the 1950s, and because of a head wound has since been an amnesiac. Kept for many years in a mental asylum, he regains his memory, escapes and begins a vain, single-handed struggle against the country's leaders.

This is strong stuff, though non-Arab audiences may have difficulty getting a grip on the material. Pic is dedicated to the writer Tahar Djaout, who defended Chouikh's screenplay against the country's censorship commission, and to former president Mohamed Boudiaf, an ex-freedom fighter. Both were recently assassinated.
—*David Stratton*

MILLE BOLLE BLU

(ITALIAN)

A Penta Distribuzione (Italy) release of a Mario & Vittorio Cecchi Gori, Silvio Berlusconi Communications presentation of a Sorpasso Film production. Produced by Marco Risi, Maurizio Tedesco. Directed by Leone Pompucci. Screenplay, Filippo Pichi, Pompucci, Paolo Rossi. Camera (color), Massimo Pau; editor, Mauro Bananni; music, Franco Piersanti; art direction, Maurizio Marchitelli; costume design, Catia Dottori; sound, Gaetano Carito. Reviewed at Penta Film screening room, Rome, Sept. 23, 1993. (In Venice Film Festival — Italian Panorama.) Running time: **80 MIN.**
With: Claudio Bigagli, Paolo Bonacelli, Nicoletta Boris, Antonio Catania, Stefano Dionisi, Denise Du Chene, Matteo Fadda, Cesare Gelli, Evelina Gori, Stefano Masciarelli, Maurizio Mattioli, Ludovica Modugno, Stefania Montorosi, Clelia Rondinella, Orazio Stracuzzi.

Photographer and adman Leone Pompucci makes a glossy but lightweight directing bow with "Mille Bolle Blu," a comedic nostalgia trip intertwining the stories of the inhabitants of a Rome apartment block in 1961. Audience prize as best of the Italo Panorama at this year's Venice fest has helped pic's entree onto local screens, but its innocuous pleasures look to be more contagious offshore as TV fare.

Title (which means "thousands of blue bubbles") comes from a 1960s pop tune by legendary local singer Mina. The film strives for the same kind of campy buoyancy.

Pompucci achieves this with the help of Maurizio Marchitelli's colorful art direction and Massimo Pau's agile lensing, which weaves in and out of the various apartment windows. But the film is all style and no substance, with flimsy characters and plotting.

The most substantial story strands concern an inheritance-hungry clan gathering for a funeral; an impending wedding, with a bride who's opted for a dependable dullard over her passionately unpredictable ex, and a young blind man forced to wait until the bandages are removed from his eyes to know if his operation is a success.

No character or plot element is given enough depth or screen time to come adequately into focus. However, using a tack not unlike Robert Altman's earthquake in "Short Cuts," Pompucci effectively brings the characters together with a total eclipse of the sun that coincides with their respective outcomes.

The large cast is winsome and energetic given their limited scope. Behind-the-lens backup is similarly sharp. Pau's camera caresses the terracotta reds of residential Rome, making the pic a consistently agreeable eyeful. —*David Rooney*

BONUS MALUS

(ITALIAN)

An Istituto Luce-Italnoleggio Cinematografico release (Italy) of a Cavadaliga production, in association with with Surf Film, Istituto Luce. Executive producer, Maurizio Mattei. Directed by Vito Zagarrio. Screenplay, Francesco Bruni, Luigi Guarnieri, Enzo Monteleone, Zagarrio. Camera (Cinecitta color), Renato Tafuri; editor, Cecilia Zanuso; music, Antonio Di Pofi; art direction, Paola Bizzarri; costume design, Maria Giovanna Caselli; sound, Bruno Pupparo; casting, Valentina Conti. Reviewed at Greenwich Cinema, Rome, Sept. 17, 1993. (In Venice, Toronto fests.) Running time: **93 MIN.**
Marco .... Claudio Bigagli
Andrea .... Gigio Alberti
Marco's father .... Felice Andreasi
Baldini .... Claudio Bisio
Valeria .... Giulia Boschi
Marco's boss .... Athina Cenci
Marco's mother .... Lorella De Luca
Also with: Claudio Botosso, Francesca D'Aloja, Antonella Fattori, Maddalena Fellini, Carlo Monni, Novello Novelli, Leonardo Pieraccioni, Massimo Sarchielli.

Vito Zagarrio's "Bonus Malus" is the latest excursion into young Italo director's favorite theme of escaping from soul-destroying yuppiedom. So low-key it's almost comatose, this pallid comedy is more Malus than Bonus, but is partly saved by its intelligent approach and watchable cast. Result looks to remain a minor-league fest item.

Charting two weeks in the obsessively ordered life of insurance inspector Marco (Claudio Bigagli), pic follows his various encounters while touring the firm's Tuscan branches.

Marco's upwardly mobile existence starts going askew when an ex-flame gets married, a current lover unloads him and an extramarital fling by his mother sparks a parental rift. Work assignments become irksome and, as uncertainty spirals into borderline hysteria, Marco opts out of the rat race for a fresh start.

With three "Mediterraneo" alumni (Bigagli, Claudio Bisio, Gigio Alberti) in the most prominent roles, and that pic's writer (Enzo Monteleone) among the four scripters here, Zagarrio's film makes a studied attempt to harness a similar ensemble effect.

But the non-stop vignettes don't build to a satisfying mosaic, not least because the characters are rarely incisive enough to be memorable.

Lenser Renato Tafuri's visuals match the yarn's gray tone, and even manage to make the Tuscan landscape look drab. Despite frequent intercutting of traveling spells, pic's editing lacks both rhythm and forward motion. Sound recording is way under par.

—*David Rooney*

DONNE IN UN GIORNO DI FESTA

(WOMEN ON A HOLIDAY)

(ITALIAN)

A Chance Film (Italy) release of a Tip Techno Image production. Produced by Alessandro Verdecchi. Directed by Salvatore Maira. Screenplay, Maira, Frida Aimme. Camera (color), Maurizio Calvesi; editor/music, Alfredo Muschietto; art direction, Marina Pinzuti; costume design, Luigi Bonanno. Reviewed at Cinecitta lab, Rome, July 25, 1993. (In New Italian Cinema Events, New York Film Festival.) Running time: **93 MIN.**

Sister Faustina	Flora Mastroianni
Sabrina	Sabrina Ferilli
Marta	Bettina Giovannini
Lorella	Lorella Morlotti
Claudia	Claudia Muzzi
Francesca	Francoise Fabian
Sister Esperanta	Daniela Giordano
Sister Marina	Valentina Lainati
Sister Clara	Marzia Villani
Grandpa	Guido Alberti

Halfway on the road to melodrama, "Women on a Holiday" is a feast of female acting that vaguely recalls a 1940s Hollywood weepie. Graced by sophisticated lensing and intriguing perfs, film portrays the group as a family substitute, with all its accompanying traumas and joys. Something different, this Italian fest entry has an old-fashioned warmth that could appeal to wider audiences.

An old Roman orphanage run by nuns is in danger of closing. While the nuns, led by aged Sister Faustina (Flora Mastroianni), reconcile themselves to inevitable change, on Faustina's birthday four young women return to the site where the nun reared them.

Each is a mess. The charms of Sabrina (Sabrina Ferilli) are just enough to get her entangled with the wrong men. Marta (Bettina Giovannini), who has struggled to become a lawyer, has been left by her married lover. Lorella (Lorella Morlotti) has a childish streak of thievery that keeps her in and out of reformatories. Claudia (Claudia Muzzi) is tormented by an elderly grandfather who wants to live with her.

The nuns have problems, too. Faustina's health is fading fast, and she finds religion isn't much of a comfort. A younger nun, unable to deal with the heartbreak of raising orphans, has requested a transfer to Africa.

Director Salvatore Maira smoothly mixes these stories into a cocktail of individual drama and human solidarity. Contributing to film's past-times look is its nonchalance toward realism, which is simply ignored when it gets in the way of the story.

Mastroianni (wife of Marcello) is standout as the wise old head of the orphanage. Ferilli is irrepressible as the bombshell nobody wants. For attentive viewers, Maurizio Calvesi's lensing quietly incorporates some whopper shots.

—*Deborah Young*

SUD

(SOUTH)

(ITALIAN)

A Penta Film (Italy) release of a CG Tiger Cinematografica/Penta Film/Colorado Film production. Produced by Mario and Vittorio Cecchi Gori, Maurizio Toti. Executive producer, Marina Gefter. Directed by Gabriele Salvatores. Screenplay, Franco Bernini, Angelo Pasquini, Salvatores. Camera (color), Italo Petriccione; editor, Massimo Fiocchi; music, Federico De Robertis; art direction, Gian Carlo Basili; costume design, Francesco Panni; sound, Tullio Morganti. Reviewed at CDS screening room, Rome, Oct. 13, 1993. Running time: **92 MIN.**

Ciro	Silvio Orlando
Lucia	Francesca Neri
Elia	Antonio Catania
Michele	Marco Manchisi
Mounir	Mussie Ighezu
Canavacciuolo	Renato Carpentieri
TV interviewer	Claudio Bisio
Military police colonel	Antonio Petrocelli
Boyfriend	Gigio Alberti

Finally moving on after a string of mellow Euro pix ("Mediterraneo," "Puerto Escondido"), Italian helmer Gabriele Salvatores smoothly changes gears with "Sud," about a protest by four homeless, unemployed men that temporarily disrupts Italy's corrupt political system.

Film's timely theme, hip irony and pulsating audiovisual energy should score big at home, where "Puerto" was the top Italian draw last season. Offshore, where viewers are unlikely to get emotionally involved with the movie's social issues, "Sud" will have to rely on auds interested in the current Italian situation.

Film's opening leaps into the thick of things. In a sleepy Sicilian town, devastated by an earthquake, public elections are unfolding as usual: Each ballot has a double, already marked in favor of a fat-cat pol. Suddenly a rag-tag "commando" of four, led by mild-mannered Ciro (Silvio Orlando), barricades itself in a school being used as a polling station. Their goal is to protest the misspending of public funds and demand jobs and a roof over their heads.

Only thing that keeps the military police from using force is that the four have inadvertently locked themselves in with the pol's daughter and her rich Milanese boyfriend. Latter tricks a tough-guy member of the band into giving himself up, but the rest stay. By day's end, citizens have occupied other polling places, following their example.

Filmically, "Sud" is no earth-shaking breakthrough, but for Italy it's unusual in being a political film that asks the viewer for agreement and participation, as in a Brecht play. Characters are grounded in Italy's social chaos: They lose their jobs when the factory closes, lose their homes in an earthquake and never see the state money allocated for the disaster.

Like Daniele Lucchetti's acclaimed "The Factotum," in which Orlando also starred, "Sud" has as its motor an Everyman caught up in the national mess and, for local auds who know the scene, his revolt assumes heroic dimensions.

Cast works well together, all perfs hovering in a hip comic limbo between realism and caricature.

Unnamed town looks as eerie as a lost Incan civilization. Lenser Italo Petriccione bathes the film — shot entirely in the school and the square in front of it — in hot "Mediterraneo"-like light. Rapid-fire cutting produces an effect of almost cartoonlike speed, while a punchy soundtrack integrates Federico De Robertis' original score with Italian neo-rap by a Roman band, Assalti Frontali, and a Neapolitan group, 99 Posse. —*Deborah Young*

MANILA PALOMA BLANCA

(ITALIAN)

An I Cammelli production. (Foreign sales: Intrafilms, Rome.) Produced by Enrico Verra. Executive producer, Mario Alessio. Directed by Daniele Segre. Screenplay, Davide Ferrario, Segre. Camera (color), Luca Bigazzi; editor, Claudio Cormio; music, Giuseppe Napoli; art direction, Elena Bosio; sound, Marco Tidu. Reviewed at Festival of Festivals, Toronto, Sept. 17, 1993. Running time: **88 MIN.**

Carlo	Carlo Colnaghi
Sara	Alessandra Comerio
Bianca	Laura Panti
Guido	Lou Castel
Maria Luisa	Barbara Valmorin
Esther	Eugenia D'Aquino
Paolo	Leone Ferrero

Practically a one-man show, "Manila Paloma Blanca" is the kind of theatrical film that is very seldom made nowadays. A chronicle of the life of a homeless, mentally ill actor, depressing pic has no commercial prospects in the U.S. or elsewhere, and it's not a festival entry either. Only way to exhibit curio item is in a retrospective of the new Italian cinema.

Carlo Colnaghi, a severe-looking performer, plays Carlo, a middle-aged, out-of work actor, in and out of psychiatric hospitals. Living on welfare but still dreaming of a better life and career, Carlo plans a grand comeback with a new, highly personal monologue. The frustrations of an actor who has not performed for a decade and lives in horrible conditions manifest themselves in bouts of anger, hostility, and self-inflicted suffering.

Monotonous monodrama is somehow enlivened by a strange relationship that Carlo develops with Sara (Alessandra Comerio), a wealthy Jewish museum curator. Indeed, Sara's friends can't understand what she is doing with the eccentric, disturbingly volatile Carlo.

Ultimately, the film's philosophical ambitions to provide insights about the human condition, aging and loneliness remain unfulfilled, because the observations are not sufficiently illuminating or original. Only redeeming quality is Colnaghi's grand performance, which dominates the somberly dreary tale in its tragic lyricism and pathos.

—*Emanuel Levy*

November 8, 1993

FLESH AND BONE

A Paramount release of a Mirage/Spring Creek production. Produced by Mark Rosenberg, Paula Weinstein. Executive producer, Sydney Pollack. Co-producer, G. Mac Brown. Directed, written by Steve Kloves. Camera (Deluxe color), Philippe Rousselot; editor, Mia Goldman; music, Thomas Newman; production design, Jon Hutman; art direction, Charles Breen; set decoration, Samara Schaffer; costume design, Elizabeth McBride; sound (Dolby), Danny Michael; assistant director, Cara Giallanza; casting, .Risa Bramon-Garcia. Reviewed at Paramount Studios, L.A., Oct. 21, 1993. MPAA Rating: R. Running time: **124 MIN.**

Arlis Sweeney .... Dennis Quaid
Kay Davies .... Meg Ryan
Roy Sweeney .... James Caan
Ginnie .... Gwyneth Paltrow
Elliot .... Scott Wilson
Reese Davies .... Christopher Rydell

Despite arresting images and moments, writer-director Steve Kloves doesn't quite fill the vast Texas landscapes of "Flesh and Bone" with enough dramatic blood and muscle. While very different in tone, this haunted tale of fate and coincidence actually resembles his impressive debut outing "The Fabulous Baker Boys" to a surprising extent, but delivers less audience satisfaction. Commercial prospects are middling.

Prologue is a stunner and, unfortunately, remains by the end as the best scene in the picture. Tautly and quietly, Kloves presents an isolated family insidiously invaded by outsiders, first a seemingly bereft little boy, then his evil father, who proceeds to wipe out nearly the entire clan on a botched robbery.

Thus soberingly launched, tale jumps ahead by 25 years or so and begins moseying up on Sam Shepard territory of blood ties, betrayals and dues being paid. Arlis (Dennis Quaid) is a solitary guy who lives in a motel room and traverses the endless highways tending to vending machines.

Before long, Kay (Meg Ryan), in an entrance not quite the equal of Michelle Pfeiffer's in "Baker Boys," but memorable all the same, stumbles into his life, and despite his diffidence and her wedding ring, it's only a matter of time until they roll in the hay.

An hour in, the evil father, Roy (James Caan), pops up, although it has long been clear that Arlis was, in fact, the little boy from the prologue, and that Kay was the infant survivor.

Since the tale is not played for melodrama or surprise, the unlikelihood of this coincidence doesn't stop the film in its tracks, but in the long run it does detract from its basic credibility.

Roy's presence eventually proves fatally disruptive, and Kloves winds up the offbeat but emotionally stunted piece with an annoyingly cliched crane shot that mashes the curious yarn as flat as the Texas prairie.

As a portrait of human shells both refusing and hoping to be filled set within a giant frame of sky and earth, pic had the potential for poetic reverberations concerning futures lost and fates tangled across the generations.

But this possibility fades as it becomes clear that Kloves is trying to shoehorn a cute romance of tempermental opposites into an essentially somber, violent format.

Compared with Quaid's impressively self-contained, withdrawn man, Ryan's boisterous little Texas tart comes off as just too much.

No matter how hard she tries at times, Ryan is just too adorable, pert and effervescent to entirely convince as a young woman ground down by a bad marriage and few prospects.

Quaid commands attention, but the psychological contours of his part remain too underwritten to make the part entirely full-bodied and dimensional.

In what could be called the Dennis Hopper part of the charmingly deranged con man, Caan has the scary, unpredictable side down pat, but comes off as somewhat mannered when he's trying to be ingratiating. Gwyneth Paltrow steals every scene she's in as Caan's bad-girl sometime companion, a young woman compelled to make a score wherever she goes.

On a craft level, film is impeccably made in every respect. Philippe Rousselot's lensing is aces, and Thomas Newman's score contains some strikingly unusual instrumental effects.
—*Todd McCarthy*

KIKA

(SPANISH)

MADRID An El Deseo S.A. and Ciby 2000 production. Executive producer, Agustin Almodovar. Directed, written by Pedro Almodovar. Camera (color), Alfredo Mayo; editor, Pepe Salcedo; sets, Alain Bainee, Javier Fernandez; costumes, Jose Maria Cossia; makeup, Gregorio Ros; hairstyles, Jesus Moncusi; sound (Dolby), Jean Paul Mugel. Reviewed at Cine Palacio de la Musica (Madrid), Oct. 26, 1993. Running time: **115 MIN.**

Kika .... Veronica Forque
Nicholas .... Peter Coyote
Andrea .... Victoria Abril
Ramon .... Alex Casanovas
Juana .... Rossy de Palma
Also with: Anabel Alonso, Bibi Andersson, Jesus Bonilla, Karra Elejalde, Charo Lopez, Santiago Lajusticia, Manuel Bandera.

Pedro Almodovar has pulled off another unqualified winner that should delight his aficionados all over the world with its dazzling, stylized sets and costumes, fast pacing, irreverent sendups and zany antics. Pic is imbued with the Almodovar "look," and the story lurches from improbable histrionics to mock melodrama.

What is unclear is how much of the scintillating, fast dialogue — steeped in the very marrow of Madrid slang — will be fully appreciated in subtitles. And some of the scenes, especially a long tongue-in-cheek rape sequence, may run into censorship/classification problems if not cut.

Much of the charm of "Kika" comes from a hilarious performance by Veronica Forque in the title role. A dizzy dame hairdresser, Kika gets involved with a homicidal but attractive expatriate Yank writer (Peter Coyote) and his bewildered stepson (Alex Casanovas); a vampish, oddball femme TV reporter (Victoria Abril) who's constantly on the lookout for "reality" scoops and who wears a strange uniform with a revolving video camera mounted on her head; and a bedraggled maid (Rossy de Palma) and her criminal brother, out of prison for the day so he can attend a religious procession. A host of other loony Almodovarian characters interact verbally and physically with dizzying speed.

There are moments in the middle of the film when the laughs taper off and the going is a bit slow, and the aforementioned rape sequence, when the escaped convict assaults Kika in her bed, comes close to crossing the line from funny to tasteless, yet pic is laden with plenty of irreverent humor, using snappy down-to-earth dialogue that reflects the reality of modern Spain.

Beautifully crisp lensing by Alfredo Mayo, adept editing and Almodovar's unusual verve and eye for the amusingly outrageous are bound to make "Kika" a surefire hit around the world. —*Peter Besas*

GIOVANNI FALCONE

(ITALIAN)

ROME A Columbia/TriStar Italia release of a Clemi Cinematografica production. Produced by Giovanni Di Clemente. Directed by Giuseppe Ferrara. Screenplay, Armenia Balducci, Ferrara; camera (color), Claudio Cirillo; editor, Ruggero Mastroianni; music, Pino Donaggio; art direction, Nino Formica; costumes, Danda Ortona; sound, Mario Dallimonti. Reviewed at CDI screening room, Rome, Oct. 19, 1993. Running time: **127 MIN.**

Giovanni Falcone .... Michele Placido
Francesca Morvillo .... Anna Bonaiuto
Paolo Borsellino ..... Giancarlo Giannini
Ninni Cassara .... Massimo Bonetti
Chinnici .... Nello Rivie
Tommaso Buscetta .... Giovanni Musy

In chronicling the buildup to the assassinations of anti-Mafia crusader Giovanni Falcone, his wife and fellow judge Paolo Borsellino last year, director Giuseppe Ferrara delivers an earnest and inevitably disappointing news recap. The impact of this densely journalistic, rigorously uncinematic pic hinges in part on familiarity with Italy's political panorama, placing it largely out of reach to offshore auds.

Anti-Mafia activists, politicos and relatives of victims denounced the pic at various stages of production.

Prior to its release, lawsuits were being threatened by public figures irked by over-explicit refs, and producer Giovanni Di Clemente was reportedly protecting himself by imposing minor cuts.

Pic's clinical tone saps events of their inherent tension, and dialogue lifted from legal documentation and official statements also makes the account dramatically static. Only as the climactic assassinations loom closer is any kind of visceral punch felt.

Overall tone is more matter-of-fact than this year's similarly themed Cannes entry "La Scorta." Pic opens with a rare cinematic flourish — Falcone (Michele Placido) being sworn in as a judge while a mafioso is sworn into Cosa Nostra.

It then retraces a decade-long investigation into underworld activity that succeeded in delineating the Sicilian Mafia's power structure and came close to exposing links with top-level pols.

Helmer Ferrara makes quiet but acute points about the frequently insubstantial credit given Falcone during his career, in sharp contrast to the quasi-hero status accorded the current crop of corrupt judges.

Performances are solid but somewhat shortchanged by a script that's low on personal insights into its characters. As Falcone's colleague, Giannini has singularly powerful moments in the aftermath of Falcone's death and the prelude to his own.

Ruggero Mastroianni's even-handed editing capably threads together the high dosage of facts, but does little to distract from the script's inability to satisfyingly flesh them out into a full-bodied narrative. —*David Rooney*

RETURN OF THE LIVING DEAD 3

A Trimark Pictures release. Produced by Gary Schmoeller, Brian Yuzna. Executive producers, Roger Burlage, Lawrence Steven Meyers. Directed by Yuzna. Screenplay, John Penney. Camera (Foto-Kem color), Gerry Lively; editor, Christopher Roth; music, Barry Goldberg; production design, Anthony Tremblay; art direction, Aram Allen; sound (Dolby), Geoffrey Lucas Patterson; special effects, Steve Johnson, Tim Ralston, Kevin Brennan, Christopher Nelson, Wayne Toth; assistant director, Tom Milo. Reviewed at Wilshire Courtyard screening room, L.A., Oct. 21, 1993. MPAA Rating: R. Running time: **97 MIN.**

November 8, 1993 (Cont.)

Julie	Mindy Clarke
Curt	J. Trevor Edmond
Col. Reynolds	Kent McCord
Riverman	Basil Wallace
Sinclair	Sarah Douglas

Playing it straight, sans humor, "Return of the Living Dead 3" departs from the first two films of the horror series that began in 1985. In an effort to capture the youth market, this B-pic emphasizes a love story gone awry at the expense of constructing a scary plot. Opening on Halloween weekend, pic will benefit from the timing of its release and some support of genre aficionados, but will soon join its predecessors in videoland.

Tale begins with two attractive lovebirds, Curt (J. Trevor Edmond) and Julie (Mindy Clarke), sneaking into his father's Army research lab, where experiments are conducted with Trioxin, a chemical capable of bringing the dead back to life, which was introduced in the series' first installment. When Julie dies in a tragic motorcycle accident, the heartbroken Curt is determined to keep her alive by exposing her to the "magical" chemical.

What ensues is a pedestrian and gruesome, but never really scary, story of how the "undead" zombies interact with the living. Serving as background is the yarn of a military scientist and insensitive father (Kent McCord), about to be relieved from his top-ranking position by the Pentagon's new female chief (Sarah Douglas) even as he's losing the affection of his son, whom he had severely neglected after his wife's death.

In a desperate attempt to hold viewer interest, most of the pic consists of special effects that include piercing, vampirism and cannibalism. Once individuals become "living dead," they are constantly hungry, craving the flesh of others and, if worse comes to worst, their own. As producer-director, Brian Yuzna demonstrates technical competence and a good sense of tempo, but he's ultimately defeated by uninvolving, mechanical script.

"Return of the Living Dead 3" boasts the dubious achievement of using five different special effects experts — the superior Sam Raimi's "Army of Darkness" reportedly held the previous record of a four-member crew. This may be why, after the story reaches its climax and resolution, pic goes on for another act, entirely composed of special effects that are excessive in every way, if also well-executed.

Judging by the final results, it might have been a mistake to eliminate the comedy; the two previous installments, which spoofed George Romero's 1968 classic "Night of the Living Dead," are much more entertaining. —*Emanuel Levy*

BLOCKADE

(CANADIAN — DOCU — 16m)

A Canada Wild Prods. film. Produced, directed by Nettie Wild. Executive producer, Christian Bruyere. Camera (color), Kirk Tougas; editor, Jeff Warren; music, Roy Forbes; sound, David Husby, Gary Marcuse. Reviewed at Festival of Festivals, Toronto, Sept. 13, 1993. Running time: 90 MIN.

Nettie Wild's "Blockade" is a solemn, politically correct documentary about the conflict over land rights between the Gitksan tribe and the white community in northern British Columbia. Conventional, unexciting treatment of a potentially engrossing issue will restrict appeal of overly long docu to minor film festivals and specialized TV slots.

Main protagonist in the strife is Art Loring, a Gitksan chief of the Eagle clan, who has been a logger for 17 years. When the conflict erupts, he and his comrades set a blockade that prevents the Hobenshield brothers' logging crews from cutting the trees. Wild's camera crews followed the battling parties for 15 months, chronicling their differing cultures and ideologies and the Gitksans' ultimately successful attempt to force the government to the negotiating table.

Chief problem with docu is tedious treatment, some of which stems from the almost gentlemanly manner of the contestants, who engage in quiet protest with no violence or screaming and yelling. Still, Wild could perhaps have chosen more vibrant interviewees to present the rather complex concerns in a more engaging way.

Wearing its heart on its sleeve, "Blockade" doesn't compare favorably with the recent wave of more dynamic and vigorous eco documentaries. —*Emanuel Levy*

VELENO

(POISON)

(ITALIAN)

A Minnie Ferrara & Associati production, in association with Reteitalia. Directed by Bruno Bigoni. Screenplay, Bigoni, Fabio Carlini; camera (color), Luca Bigazzi; editor, Claudio Cormio; music, Davide Masarati; art direction, Carlo Sala. Reviewed at Locarno Film Festival (competing), Aug. 8, 1993. Running time: 90 MIN.

Tonino Strano	Carlo Colnaghi
Ida, his wife	Ida Marinelli
Bruno Strano	Elio De Capitani
Cristina, his wife	Marina Confalone

Also with: Matteo Bigoni, Valeria D'Onofrio, Fabio Modesti.

A caustic half-comedy, half-drama about two brothers who hate each other to death, "Poison" is often amusing but never completely convincing. Made without stars, it will have to scramble to do better on the Italo market than Mario Monicelli's recent (and superior) "Parenti Serpenti" (Relatives: Snakes), which failed to take off.

The Strano brothers (Carlo Colnaghi, Elio De Capitani) start quarreling at their father's funeral when one accuses the other of having used cheap wood for the coffin. Division of the sprawling country mansion does not proceed smoothly, and each brother moves into a separate wing with his family.

The house becomes a theater of war for the latter-day Cain and Abel, who go at each other day and night until the escalating violence involves the whole family. One day, De Capitani disappears, and Colnaghi is thrown into prison for his apparent murder.

Debuting helmer Bruno Bigoni fails to keep his admirable cast rowing together. Colnaghi reprises his poignant victim role from "Manila Paloma Blanca"; De Capitani (who resembles him not at all) goes overboard on comic routines; and Marina Confalone ("Parenti Serpenti") plays in yet another key as a vain, egotistical wife for whom money is everything. A half-developed romance between two of the brothers' kids further dilutes the dramatic waters.

Result is an emotionally confused picture graced by an occasional good gag. A solid crew led by cinematographer Luca Bigazzi makes it all watchable. —*Deborah Young*

LA RIBELLE

(THE REBEL)

(ITALIAN)

A Taodue Film/Banda Magnetica/Reteitalia production. Produced by Pietro Valsecchi, Camilla Nesbitt. Directed, written by Aurelio Grimaldi, based on his novel "Storia di Enza." Camera (color), Maurizio Calvesi; editor, Claudio Di Mauro; music, Carlo Crivelli; art direction, Pasquale Germano; costumes, Claudio Cordaro. Reviewed at Cinecitta lab, Rome, July 25, 1993. (In Locarno festival, competing. Also in N.I.C.E. fest, N.Y.) Running time: 88 MIN.

Enza	Penelope Cruz
Franchino	Stefano Dionisio
Sister Valida	Laura Betti
Rosaria	Lorenza Indovina
Sebastiano	Marco Leonardi

A year after his controversial film bow "Acla," director Aurelio Grimaldi returns with another story about the poor and disenfranchised in his native Sicily. Set in a girls' reform school, "The Rebel" has less shock value and more technical savvy than "Acla." Its commercial chances will be boosted by the intense screen presence of Spanish starlet Penelope Cruz in the lead role.

A generally fast-moving story introduces tough, streetwise Enza (Cruz) as she tries to steal a wallet with her sister (Lorenza Indovina). A judge sends the girls, both minors, to a religious institute, where Sister Valida (amusingly camped up by Laura Betti) gives Enza enough slack to make some discoveries for herself.

Enza plays hookey to have her first sexual experience with curly-haired Sebastiano (Marco Leonardi), but later turns to handsome Franchino (Stefano Dionisio), with whose help she obtains her freedom from the institute. Final twist is ironic.

Grimaldi, a working teacher who also penned the Marco Risi prison-school film "Forever Mery," treads a dangerous line in the reform school genre. The cliches are all here — the girls fight, get punished, exchange confidences, plot escape. Happily, much of the tale unfolds outside the institute's walls.

In the lead role, Cruz, whose expressionless mask can be interpreted as sullen or mysterious, deep or shallow, has the magnetism to push film through its more deja-vu moments. Pic's extensive use of fades and its elliptical style give it a contemporary appeal.

Carlo Crivelli's score ranges from gently pungent to full-blown operatic. Maurizio Calvesi's lensing gives the visuals a clean, classy look. —*Deborah Young*

CAP TOURMENTE

(CANADIAN)

C/FP Distribution (Quebec) release of a ACPAV Inc. production in association with National Film Office of Canada and Telefilm Canada. Produced by Bernadette Payeur, Marc Daigle. Directed, written by Michel Langlois. Camera (color), Eric Cayla; editor, Jean-Claude Coulbois; art direction, Normand Sarrazin; costumes, Denis Sperdouklis; sound (Dolby), Claude Beaugrand. Reviewed at Festival of Festivals, Toronto, Sept. 12, 1993. Running time: 115 MIN.

Alex	Roy Dupuis
Alfa	Elise Guilbault
Jeanne	Andree Lachapelle
Jean-Louis	Gilbert Sicotte
Barbara	Macha Limonchik

"Cap Tourmente" is a tepid psychosexual drama that's unlikely to earn either critical interest or arthouse coin once it completes a go-round on the fest circuit.

Script by Montreal-based screenwriter Michel Langlois ("La Femme de l'hotel," "Straight to the Heart") is an original, but it plays like a slightly opened-up adaptation of a one-set stage play, as Langlois, making his feature directing debut, emphasizes almost nonstop talk and only perfunctory action.

November 8, 1993 (Cont.)

Drama is triggered by the return of Alex (Roy Dupuis), a hunky ne'er-do-well who washed out while trying to follow in his late father's footsteps as a merchant seaman. Alex retreats to the riverside bed-and-breakfast operated by his indulgent mother, Jeanne (Andree Lachapelle), and sister Alfa (Elise Guilbault). By coincidence, Jean-Louis (Gilbert Sicotte), an old friend of the family, shows up for a visit just as Alex arrives.

It turns out that Jean-Louis used to have something going with Alfa, and something else going with Alex. Alfa isn't averse to sharing Jean-Louis' bed again, but it seems that she's really pining for her brother. And just to make the air of incest a little heavier, Jeanne indicates that she, too, thinks her son is a hot number.

Trouble is, Alex is too wrapped up in self-regarding ennui, and too strung out on drugs, to remain interested very long in anyone.

After a while, however, Alex's childish behavior places an impossible demand on the audience's sympathies, even as he remains the darling of those around him.

The performances are wildly uneven, ranging from Guilbault's unfortunately comical overplaying to Dupuis' jeans-ad posturing.

Lachapelle works hard at creating a flesh-and-blood character, Sicotte works even harder, and both succeed more often than not.

Eric Cayla's moody lensing and Normand Sarrazin's apt art direction go a long way toward giving the pic some visual variety.

—*Joe Leydon*

LEY LINES

(CANADIAN — DOCU)

A Noema Prods. Inc. production. Produced, directed, written, edited by Patricia Gruben. Camera (color), Kirk Tougas, Bob Aschmann, Gruben; music and sound, Martin Gotfrit. Reviewed at Festival of Festivals, Toronto, Sept. 17, 1993. Running time: **80 MIN.**

Intended as a fanciful collage of autobiography and introspection, "Ley Lines" instead comes off as a ponderous and self-indulgent vanity production that will go nowhere beyond fest circuit.

Pic by Texas-born, Canada-based Patricia Gruben begins with her admitting that, as a little girl, "I thought of myself as the center of the universe." Apparently, time has not diminished her opinion of herself.

Title comes from pre-Christian legends about unseen lines that connect significant points of spiritual and psychic interest throughout the world. Pic itself is a free-association attempt by Gruben to trace diverse branches of her family tree, from Germany to Texas, then to Canada. While in the Fatherland, Gruben takes time to raise questions about

the influence of the occult on Nazi philosophy, a subject that is much more interesting than anything Gruben conveys about her relatives.

"Ley Lines" is the sort of pretentious one-person show in which various unseen actors, each representing some aspect of the filmmaker's personality, provide voice-over narration and commentary. Result is as cloyingly precious as it sounds.

The climactic scenes have Gruben traveling to Tuktoyaktuk, in the Canadian Arctic, to search for alleged relatives. Long before she gets there, unfortunately, both she and "Ley Lines" lose their way.

—*Joe Leydon*

THIS WON'T HURT A BIT!

AUSTRALIAN

A Dendy Films release of an Oilrag Prods. production, with the participation of the Australian Film Finance Corp. Produced, directed, written by Chris Kennedy. Camera (color), Marc Spicer; editor, Peter Butt; music, Mario Grigoriv; production design, Ken Muggleston; sound, David Glasser; assistant director, Butt; casting, Kennedy. Reviewed at Screening Room, Leura, Australia, Sept. 30, 1993. Running time: **85 MIN.**

Gordon Fairweather	
	Greig Pickhaver
Vanessa Prestcott	
	Jacqueline McKenzie
Mrs. Prestcott	Maggie King
George Prestcott	Patrick Blackwell
Riley	Dennis Miller
Farrow	Adam Stone

Also with: Gordon Chater, Alwyn Kurts, Colleen Clifford, Ralph Cotterill, Peter Browne, Kate Smith, Lisa Peers, Ghandi McIntyre.

A comedy about a dishonest dentist won't be everyone's idea of a good joke, but writer-producer-director Chris Kennedy, himself a former dentist, delivers quite a few laughs in this modestly budgeted item. A basic problem in construction detracts from the film, however, and commercial results will be mild.

This is Kennedy's second feature, after the little-seen "Glass" (1989), a direct-to-vid release Down Under. Here, Greig Pickhaver plays Gordon Fairweather, an Aussie dentist wanted by the British police. Flashbacks, fragmented and non-sequential, fill in the story, touching on Fairweather's troubled boyhood, his student years, a bout of insanity and his eventual departure for Britain.

Setting up a modest dental practice in Portsmouth, he soon becomes very rich, but he also seems to be an incompetent dentist, judging from the evidence of patients who suffer at his hands, especially George Prestcott (Patrick Blackwell), whose teeth are gradually ruined by Fairweather.

This doesn't stop Prestcott's daughter, Vanessa (Jacqueline McKenzie), from becoming Fair-

weather's nurse and eventually announcing she'll marry him, but Fairweather skips the country.

Almost all of this droll story is told from the viewpoint of various people who knew Fairweather, but this structure means that very little screen time is given to Fairweather himself, making it tough to know whether to root for himf.

Another result is that Pickhaver barely registers as a comedy performer. This gap at the center of the film is partly offset by the clever perfs of most other cast members.

Production values are modest, although footage was lensed in four countries (there is a coda set in Paris). Within its limited framework, pic works perfectly well, but it seems that a funnier and more accessible film probably could have been made without additional effort.

—*David Stratton*

BREAD AND ROSES

(NEW ZEALAND)

A Preston Laing release of a Preston Laing Production. (Foreign sales: New Zealand Film Commission; TV: Beyond Distribution.) Produced by Robin Laing. Executive producer, Dorothee Pinfold. Directed by Gaylene Preston. Screenplay, Graeme Tetley, Preston. Camera (color), Allen Guilford; editor, Paul Sutorius; music, John Charles; production design, Rick Kofoed; art direction, Mark Robins, Matt Murphy; costume design, Chris Elliot; sound, Tony Johnson; associate producer, Preston. Reviewed at New Zealand Film Commission screening room, Wellington, Aug. 27, 1993. Running time: **193 MIN.**

Sonja Davies	Genevieve Picot
Achie Barrington	John Laing
Red	Erik Thomson
Maisie	Frances Kewene
Joan	Emily Perkins
Dot	Laissa Matheson
Peggy	Theresa Healey
Ruth Page	Janet Fisher

Following Jane Campion's "An Angel at My Table," originally made as a miniseries but released first in a feature version, "Bread and Roses" is another biographical New Zealand offering — this time about women's rights activist Sonja Davies — made for TV but now packaged for theatrical release.

Released theatrically in N.Z., pic has received hefty acclaim locally. But despite a fabulous leading performance by Genevieve Picot, the parochial and plodding nature of "Bread and Roses' " subject matter makes big-screen interest beyond Australasian shores unlikely apart from the fest circuit.

Davies is a well-known commentator and politician in N.Z., and "Bread and Roses" follows the first half of her life. Much of this concerns her struggle with tuberculosis, and nicely sets the scene of a society in which women are not expected to speak their mind or buck the system.

Davies does both, marrying and divorcing young, having an illegitimate child and agitating for a nurses' union. When asked by her child why she's different from other mothers, she answers, "Because things have to be done."

But with TB holding her back, it's not until the mid-1950s, while participating in a women-only strike against the demise of a railway service that she starts holding influential positions and becomes better known.

And that's where the film ends, despite Davies' achievements over the next 30 years, and it's taken three hours to get there.

It's a well-evoked story, but slow going and overly detailed. Matters aren't helped by a somewhat colorless performance from John Laing, playing husband Archie.

However, Picot holds the film together, giving a fine perf that nicely combines Davies' often tempestuous spirit and the frustration she feels as an invalid.

Like most N.Z. offerings, tech credits are top-notch, but the lingering nature of "Bread and Roses" is probably best suited to viewing over a few nights on the small screen.

—*Blake Murdoch*

THE BURNING SEASON

(CANADIAN)

An Astral Communications release (Canada) of a Primedia Pictures and Siren Films production. Produced by Annette Cohen, Amarjeet S. Rattan. Executive producer, W. Patterson Ferns. Directed by Harvey Crossland. Screenplay, Crossland, Cohen. Camera (color), Vic Sarin; editor, Crossland, Michelle Bjornson, Lara Mazur; music, Gordon Durity; production design, Tamara Deverell; costume design, Aline Gilmore; sound, Gael Maclean; casting, Sid Kozak (Vancouver), Jennifer Jaffrey (U.K.), Jiten Varma (India). Reviewed at Festival of Festivals, Toronto, Sept. 16, 1993. Running time: **104 MIN.**

Sanda	Akesh Gill
Pat	Ayub Khan Din
Rajiv	Om Puri

Harvey Crossland's directorial feature debut, "The Burning Season," is a disappointingly shallow romantic epic decorated with a David Lean-like grand visual treatment. Beautiful sunrises and sunsets make the semi-feminist saga of an Indian-Canadian woman's identity crisis less meaningful than it should be, severely limiting its commercial appeal outside Canada.

Sanda (Akesh Gill) is a modern-day kindred soul to Sarah Miles' heroine in Lean's "Ryan's Daughter." Rebelling against family tradition and arranged marriage, this young Vancouver wife and mother engages in an adulterous affair with high-born college instructor Pat (Ayub Khan Din).

November 8, 1993 (Cont.)

When Pat is unexpectedly recalled to India to care for his dying father, Sanda follows him, risking all for passion. Once in India, however, Sanda painfully observes Pat's inner struggle between his love for her and his duty as a Rajput prince, dictated by family honor. Caught in a desperate situation, and haunted by the emptiness of her life, Sanda must face the truth and make fateful decisions. Unfortunately, the screenplay by Crossland and Annette Cohen is derivative, never delving deeply enough into the complex web of family relationships and divergent historical contexts of Vancouver and India. The politics of the characters — and film — remain unclear.

Worse yet, mixing the traditions of romantic epic cinema, National Geographic and Masterpiece Theatre and the mysticism of anthropological rituals, "The Burning Season" never finds the appropriate voice or tone for its potentially moving story.

Gill and Din are both attractive actors, but the trite and hackneyed dialogue works against them. Vic Sarin's handsome cinematography and Gordon Durity's impressive music manage to drown the tale's intimate scale and human emotions.
—*Emanuel Levy*

EXILE AND THE KINGDOM

(AUSTRALIAN-DOCU)

A Snakewood Films production. Produced by Frank Rijavec, Noelene Harrison. Directed by Rijavec. Camera (color), Rijavec, Peter Kordyl; editor, Liz Goldfinch; music, David Milroy; narrator, Roger Solomon. Reviewed at Sydney Film Festival, June 19, 1993. Running time: **112 MIN.**

Many documentaries have been made about Australia's tribal aboriginal people; this is one of the better ones. Filmed at Roebourne, in the northwest of Western Australia, the film vividly depicts the history and contemporary lifestyle of the Injibandi people and their tribal neighbors. Documentary is a natural for docu fests worldwide.

What's especially fascinating here is Australia's colonial history as told through aboriginal eyes. The current lifestyles of the Injibandi, Ngarluma, Banjima and Gurrama people are candidly explored.

Roebourne is notorious because it was the location of the 1987 death of John Pat, an aboriginal, while in police custody.

The film touches on this as part of a comprehensive, revealing and well-done study.

Pic scored high in the vote for best docu by the film festival audience.
—*David Stratton*

92 HAK MUIGWAI DUI HAK MUIGWAI

(92 LEGENDARY LA ROSE NOIRE)

(HONG KONG)

A Hoventin Films production. (International sales: Hoventin, Hong Kong.) Produced by Fau Lok-lin. Executive producer, Fau. Directed by Joe Chan. Screenplay, Kei On. Camera (color), Chan Yun-kai; editor, Hai Kit-wai; music, Lowell Lo; art direction, Chan A-tsou; costume design, Luk Ha-fong, Tsui Tsung-kwan; action director, Leung Siu-hung; associate producer, Joe Chan; assistant director, Yiu Man-kei. Reviewed on Star Entertainment vidcassette, London, Aug. 21, 1993. (In Festival of Festivals, Toronto, Asian Horizons section.) Running time: **90 MIN.**
Wong .... Maggie Shiu
Chow .... Teresa Mo
Yim-fan .... Wong Wan-si
Piu-hung .... Feng Po-po
Lui Kei .... Tony Leung Kar-fai
(Cantonese dialogue)

A happy hunting ground for Sinophiles but a likely head-scratcher for most everyone else, "92 Legendary La Rose Noire" is a clever, slickly shot satire on Cantonese movies of the 1960s that's so daft it's enjoyable.

With careful subtitling and explanatory material, pic could score among festival auds in tune with Asian fare. For those with the decoding manual, "Rose Noire" is an homage-laden laugh fest with more levels than a club sandwich. Debut feature by Joe Chan, associate producer on the cult fave "Days of Being Wild," was a sleeper at H.K. wickets last year, grossing a bright $HK22 million over its six-month run.

Anything-goes story line, set in the present, revolves around a young woman writer (Maggie Shiu) who's frustrated in her career. When she and her best friend (Teresa Mo) get accidentally involved in a gangland bloodbath, she leaves a note at the scene signed "La Rose Noire" (The Black Rose), name of a well-known fictional 1960s femme avenger.

Chan and scripter Kei On's loving parody of 1960s cliches — handsome matinee idols, lovers' duets, cliff-hanging sequences and magical martial arts — moves at a fast clip, propelled by a knowing, 1990s-style irony and bright production design and costumes. Tech credits are assured down the line.

Leung (from "The Lover") has fun mimicking the acting style and funny voice of 1960s H.K. heart-throb Lui Kei, while bob-haired Feng parodies her own background as a child star from the period.

Chinese title literally means "92 La Rose Noire vs. La Rose Noire." Pic's success has already spawned a further riff, Pang Yi-wa's "Rose, Rose, I Love You," also with Leung.
—*Derek Elley*

THE SUMMER HOUSE

(BRITISH)

A Samuel Goldwyn release (U.S.) of a BBC Films production. Produced by Norma Heyman. Executive producer, Mark Shivas. Directed by Waris Hussein. Screenplay, Martin Sherman, based on the novel "The Clothes in the Wardrobe" by Alice Thomas Ellis. Camera (color), Rex Maidment; editor, Ken Pearce; music, Stanley Myers; production design, Stuart Walker; costume design, Odile Dicks-Mireaux, Leah Archer; sound, John Pritchard; associate producer, Derek Nelson; assistant director, Daphne Phipps; casting, Susie Figgis. Reviewed at the Hamptons Intl. Film Festival, East Hampton, N.Y., Oct. 23, 1993. Running time: **82 MIN.**
Lili ....Jeanne Moreau
Mrs. Monro .... Joan Plowright
Monica .... Julie Walters
Margaret .... Lena Headey
Syl .... David Threlfall
Mrs. Raffald .... Maggie Steed
Robert .... John Wood
Cynthia .... Gwyneth Strong
Derek .... Roger Lloyd Pack
Marie-Clair .... Catherine Schell

Jeanne Moreau has a field day in a showboating, grande dame role in "The Summer House," a comic audience pleaser about older women sabotaging the unwise wedding plans of a confused young lady in stuffy 1950s England. Played broadly for laughs, this slight, genteel but spunky BBC Films production, which has already been telecast in the U.K. and will be released domestically by Goldwyn at Christmas, could shake loose some B.O. coin if marketing reaches its prime target among older women.

In the primly middle-class London suburb of Croydon, lovely but listless teenager Lena Headey is engaged to foppish 40-year-old David Threlfall, who still lives with ma Joan Plowright. Headey and her divorced mother Julie Walters had lived in Egypt, the exotic and erotic memories of which provide the young woman with an active fantasy life. Enter Moreau, Walters' best friend from Egyptian days, a half-French, half-English whirlwind of mischief and feminine wiles whose notorious romantic life has been unencumbered by typically British conventions concerning appropriate ladylike behavior.

It's easy to see a mile away that Moreau's Mediterranean influence will thaw the others out and convince Headey not to fall into a passionless marriage, but there is still plenty of lowdown fun to be had in watching it all play out.

Chain-smoking, guzzling booze and spouting worldly epigrams about love and life, Moreau fits into Croydon like a peacock in Antarctica, sashaying around and imposing her seductive will on everyone. While working her ways on Headey, she even unstraps the cloistered Plowright, getting her rip-roaring drunk on an outing. The sight of these two women falling down in inebriated hilarity is a comic highlight.

Scenarist Martin Sherman ("Bent") has festooned this safely domesticated item with a healthy measure of zippy dialogue and character humor, extended by the extravagantly talented cast. For anyone who enjoys Moreau, this is a feast, as she struts her stuff in a deliciously theatrical manner seldom afforded her onscreen.

As the initially retiring old mum, Plowright delivers moments of caustic deadpan wit as well as rambunctious comedy, while Walters, constrained by the most routine role, still conveys strong character.

Headey, who caught the eye as the young lover in "Waterland" last year, has the burden of playing near-total passivity for most of the running time, but holds sufficient promise of eventual beauty, sensitivity and fulfilled womanhood to sustain interest. What happened to her character back in Egypt is less clearly and meaningfully worked out.

Threlfall is frequently hilarious as the oafish fiance, while remaining roles are deftly caricatured.

Made on a low budget, pic has basic but adequate production values.
—*Todd McCarthy*

November 15, 1993

CARLITO'S WAY

Universal Pictures and Epic Prods. present a Bregman/Bear production. Produced by Martin Bregman, Willi Baer, Michael S. Bregman. Executive producers, Louis Stroller, Ortwin Freyermuth. Directed by Brian De Palma. Screenplay, David Koepp, based on the novels "Carlito's Way" and "After Hours," by Edwin Torres. Camera (Eastman, Panavision), Stephen H. Burum; editors, Bill Pankow, Kristina Boden; music, Patrick Doyle; production design, Richard Sylbert; art direction, Gregory Bolton; set decoration, Leslie Pope; sound (Dolby), Les Lazarowitz; assistant director, Daniel Stillman; casting, Bonnie Timmerman. Reviewed at Universal Studios, Oct. 29, 1993. MPAA Rated: R. Running time: **144 MIN.**

Carlo Brigante .... Al Pacino
David Kleinfeld .... Sean Penn
Gail .... Penelope Ann Miller
Pachanga .... Luis Guzman
Benny Blanco .... John Leguizamo
Steffie .... Ingrid Rogers
Norwalk .... James Rebhorn
Vinnie Taglialucci .... Joseph Siravo
Lalin .... Viggo Mortensen
Pete Amadesso ....Richard Foronjy
Saso .... Jorge Porcel
Frankie .... Adrian Pasdar

The surprise for many upon seeing "Carlito's Way" is that it's a throwback to the kind of ethnic gangster pics of the '30s like "Scarface" with Paul Muni, and not rife with the modern social spin of the later "Scarface" made by "Carlito's" principals. In that respect it's a true reminder of the enduring vibrancy of the immigrant-crime-does-not-pay genre.

On its own terms, the new film is a lively saga of the rise and fall of a Puerto Rican criminal, rich with irony and keen in its attention to detail. Handsomely made, expertly directed and colorfully acted, it should satisfy action buffs and slightly more sophisticated audiences. That adds up to solid commercial prospects at home and abroad that are just shy of blockbuster returns.

The saga is bookended by scenes of Carlito (Al Pacino) being rushed to the hospital after he's shot at close range in a subway station. So, how did this particular fate befall him?

It's 1975 and, after serving five years, Carlito has had his drug-related sentence reversed due to improper evidentiary procedures. He addresses the court and, in grand style, explains how he's been rehabilitated and will not be going back to the street.

What we don't know or suspect is that he means it; his cant sounds as if it's all for show. But Carlito is a bit like Gregory Peck's "Gunfighter," savvy from experience, lucky to be alive and ready to move on gracefully.

The problem is that there's no retirement plan in his former line of work. Throw in the fact that everyone around him expects Carlito to continue where he left off five years earlier, and you begin to understand his frustration. His plan to save enough money to open a car rental agency in the Caribbean has his former associates practically doubled up with laughter.

Additionally, trouble follows him like an obedient lap dog. A car ride with a young cousin evolves into a bloody, botched drug deal. A favor for a friend threatens to become his death sentence. And on and on it goes.

The great strength of David Koepp's adaptation of two books by Manhattan judge Edwin Torres is a comic strain as unexpected and unpredictable as the hair-trigger personalities of its underworld figures. Carlito is continually placed into situations he honestly would rather avoid. He can rightfully say, "Just when I thought I was out, they pull me back in," but thankfully the sentiment remains tacit.

Eventually he agrees to manage a disco that's a haunt of gangster high rollers. Though meant to be his ticket out of that environment, it proves to be the means to his end. He insists that he lives by the credo "You got no friends in this business," but he's become sentimental, and it's a fatal flaw. Trusting the wrong people is his undoing.

Pacino plays the title role with broad strokes. It's an audience-pleasing performance of grand

There's perhaps no director better than De Palma at maintaining tension in extended action set pieces.

gestures, posturing and humor. The bigness of his interpretation takes the film out of the specific and realistic into an almost mythic arena.

Sean Penn, in his first major screen role since directing 1991's "The Indian Runner," reminds us of what we've been missing in his performance as Carlito's ambitious, amoral lawyer.

Without stooping to caricature, he effortlessly captures what is most heinous in the profession. His David Kleinfeld is someone naturally capable of the most vile acts when strung out on cocaine.

The supporting cast is strong, including John Leguizamo as a strutting, up-and-coming hood, Luis Guzman as Carlito's thick-headed bodyguard and Paul Mazursky as the barely contained, slow-burning judge presiding over the opening trial. Penelope Ann Miller does the most with the underwritten girlfriend role and hits an effective emotional note when she explains the pleasure and agony of being a dancer in love with show business.

Brian De Palma is in top form with "Carlito's Way." There's perhaps no director better today at maintaining a level of tension and anxiety in extended action set pieces. He works hard at making his backgrounds both interesting and complementary to the main action.

Tech credits are peerless, with Richard Sylbert's production design cleanly and precisely capturing the bygone era. Frequent De Palma collaborator Stephen Burum adopts some unusual angles to give his camera work an extra boost, and Patrick Doyle's score suggests his ascendance into the niche vacated by the late Bernard Herrmann. Period disco selections have been cleverly conceived by Jellybean Benitez.

"Carlito's Way" is ample evidence that it's still the same old story when it comes to gangster movies. The other truth is that the good ones provide fertile ground worth tilling for another season.

—*Leonard Klady*

MY LIFE

Columbia Pictures presents in association with Capella Films a Zucker Brothers production. Produced by Jerry Zucker, Bruce Joel Rubin, Hunt Lowry. Executive producer, Gil Netter. Directed, written by Bruce Joel Rubin. Camera (Technicolor), Peter James; editor, Richard Chew; music, John Barry; production design, Neil Spisak; art direction, Larry Fulton; set decoration, Anne McCulley; costume design, Judy Ruskin; sound (Dolby), John Sutton III; casting, Janet Hirshenson, Jane Jenkins, Roger Mussenden. Review at Sony Studios, Culver City, Oct. 30, 1993. MPAA Rated: PG-13; Running time: **114 MIN.**

Bob Jones .... Michael Keaton
Gail Jones .... Nicole Kidman
Paul Ivanovich .... Bradley Whitford
Theresa .... Queen Latifah
Mr. Ho .... Haing S. Ngor
Bill Ivanovich ...... Michael Constantine
Rose Ivanovich .... Rebecca Schull
Doris .... Toni Sawyer
Anya Stasiuk .... Romy Rosemont
Carol Sandman .... Lee Garlington

Writer Bruce Joel Rubin's fascination with death knows no temporal bounds. It reached back from the grave in "Ghost" and struck out into the future in "Jacob's Ladder." "My Life," his directorial debut, is his most cozy brush with the final journey. It's an emotional, spiritual odyssey centered on a man confronting terminal cancer and, coincidentally, the birth of his first child.

The sincere, often touching story tugs shamelessly at the heartstrings. Nonetheless, its subject matter will prove a daunting marketing challenge. It's a film in dire need of tender loving care, slow nurturing and critical kudos to earn a place in the mainstream.

The writer/director's conceit is a videotape being prepared by Bob Jones (Michael Keaton) for his unborn child. Jones has been diagnosed with inoperable cancer, and his doctor doubts he will live to see the arrival of the infant. So he sits in front of the camera to explain some pretty banal things, like how to walk cool, which way to hold a razor and tips on sports.

This is, thankfully, the jumping-off point for considerably weightier issues. Rubin is a confirmed believer that people ought to put their houses in order prior to that final breath. Jones experiences the emotions often associated with the confrontation of death — denial, anger and acceptance.

What is of particular interest to the filmmaker is the opportunity for the character — a workaholic — to step back and get some perspective. His wife (Nicole Kidman) gently cajoles him into seeing a healer (Haing Ngor), and it is at these sessions that he begins to get in touch with what's really ailing him: his roots.

At first the prospect that he cannot remember his youth is amusing. However, once he begins to unblock the past, we discover that his seething hostility toward his father (Michael Constantine) was so intense, changing his name was his least vengeful act. The memory of a schoolboy dream is so vivid and painful for him that you have to believe it literally ate away at his insides.

There's nothing essentially wrong with the manipulative nature of "My Life." Rubin's inexperience, however, makes his footprints a lot more obvious than those of others who have walked down this road before.

Keaton as Jones/Ivanovich gives a textured performance that goes a long way to smooth the narrative's rough edges. His fine work is a reminder of his range and versatility. He is unquestionably a natural comic, but he can also deliver the goods without cracking when it comes time to bring on the heavy drama.

Essentially the story is at the service of Keaton's character but allows for moving supporting turns. Kidman, Ngor, Constantine and Bradley Whitford all register with emotional work. Rubin orchestrates a level of concern and pain in the performances that seems real and is easily accessible.

Technical ambitions are kept simple and effective. John Barry's score may be a dot too obvious, but

November 15, 1993 (Cont.)

this is a minor quibble in an otherwise impressive directorial debut.

While the entire production teeters on the corny and the cliched and falls into that trap from time to time, more often it hits a sensitive nerve and makes us stop, think and feel.

—*Leonard Klady*

ROBOCOP 3

An Orion Pictures release. Produced by Patrick Crowley. Co-producer, Jane Bartelme. Directed by Fred Dekker. Screenplay, Frank Miller, Dekker; story by Miller. Based on characters created by Edward Neumeier, Michael Miner. Camera (DuArt color, DeLuxe prints), Gary B. Kibbe; editor, Bert Lovitt; music, Basil Poledouris; production design, Hilda Stark; art direction, Cate Bangs; set decoration, Robert J. Franco; costume design, Ha Nguyen; sound (Dolby), Kirk Francis; assistant director, Steve Fisher; associate producer, Andy Lamarca; second-unit director/stunt coordinator, Conrad E. Palmisano; special effects supervisor, Jeff Jarvis; RoboCop designed and created by Rob Bottin; stop-motion animation, Phil Tippett; casting, Steven Jacobs. Reviewed at the Mann Bruin Theatre, L.A., Nov. 1, 1993. MPAA Rating: PG-13. Running time: **104 MIN.**
RoboCop .... Robert John Burke
Anne Lewis .... Nancy Allen
The CEO .... Rip Torn
McDaggett .... John Castle
Dr. Marie Lazarus .... Jill Hennessy
Bertha .... CCH Pounder
Kanemitsu .... Mako
Sergeant Reed .... Robert DoQui
Nikko .... Remy Ryan
Otomo .... Bruce Locke
Zack .... Stanley Anderson

This latest widget off the "RoboCop" assembly line is a bit better than the first sequel, which amounts to damnation with faint praise. Limiting the gore, but not the carnage, in pursuit of a PG-13 rating and more youngsters, pic remains a cluttered, nasty exercise that seems principally intent on selling action figures. As with "RoboCop 2," video prospects could be explosive, but after an initial burst, box office looks rusty.

Relying on heavy makeup and the trademark costume, Robert John Burke replaces Peter Weller — star of the first two films — in the title role of the murdered cop who returns as a crime-fighting cyborg.

Still, by downplaying the character's Murphy side to accommodate the change, the filmmakers also lose some of the original's humanity, skimming over the battle for identity that helped elevate Paul Verhoeven's superior 1987 pic, next to which both sequels pale.

This time, ubiquitous conglomerate OCP is trying to evict poor tenants from a run-down neighborhood to erect Delta City, a pet project of the massive Japanese corporation run by tycoon villain Kanemitsu (Mako) that now owns the company.

Director Fred Dekker ("The Monster Squad") wrote the screenplay with comic-book writer-illustrator Frank Miller — who also scripted the series' second installment — and helps bring some flashes of broad humor to the otherwise dour proceedings.

The RoboCop action figures that frequent the background also provide a constant reminder why the film was made — with a new innovation that has RoboCop flying, apparently designed to be the big holiday accessory.

In fact, the marketing gurus seem to be working overtime, introducing an orphaned, computer-hacking moppet (Remy Ryan) to try reaching a younger demographic and, for their older brothers, a dishy doctor (Jill Hennessy) who also joins the Robocause.

Burke gamely handles his thankless task, hiding within the costume to emulate Weller, while Nancy Allen, Robert DoQui and Felton Perry provide continuity with the earlier films.

Most of the performances, however, are cartoonishly overplayed, with Rip Torn and Mako wasted as ruthless execs, Allen appearing in what amounts to a cameo, and Hennessy and Ryan attractive and obnoxiously spunky, respectively, as the featured newcomers.

The series' enduring stars remain Rob Bottin's knockout RoboCop suit and Basil Poledouris' musical score.

Most special effects are topnotch, though the ninja tricks feel a bit incongruous with the rest of the action — as if they were borrowed from a dubbed latenight entry on local TV.

That's perhaps appropriate, since that's where fans will soon find the character, with a RoboCop TV series oiling up for syndication. The arrival of that vehicle is timely, since the movie franchise looks like it's running out of gas.

—*Brian Lowry*

LOOK WHO'S TALKING NOW

A TriStar Pictures release. Produced by Jonathan D. Krane. Executive producer, Leslie Dixon. Co-producers, Amy Heckerling, Fitch Cady. Directed by Tom Ropelewski. Screenplay, Ropelewski, Dixon. Camera (color), Oliver Stapleton; editors, Michael A. Stevenson, Harry Hitner; music, William Ross; production design, Michael Bolton; art direction, Alexander Cochrane; set decoration, Jim Erickson; costume design, Molly Maginnis, Mary E. McLeod; assistant director, Peter D. Marshall. Reviewed at the Beverly Connection Cinema, L.A., Oct. 17, 1993. MPAA Rating: PG-13. Running time: **97 MIN.**
James .... John Travolta
Mollie .... Kirstie Alley
Rosie .... Olympia Dukakis
Samantha D'Bonne ... Lysette Anthony
Mikey .... David Gallagher
Julie .... Tabitha Lupien
Rocks (voice) .... Danny DeVito
Daphne (voice) .... Diane Keaton

Stretching a premise that one might say has gone to the dogs, "Look Who's Talking Now" runs feebly on the calculated steam of its forebears, "Look Who's Talking" and "Look Who's Talking, Too." Pic could glean small carryover B.O., but expect it to make quick and painless rollover to the video shelf.

Once again, pic derives yuks from wisecracking inner monologues of non-talking characters. First, it was the baby boy, then the baby girl. Now, it's the dogs. What's next, the refrigerator? Still, scripters Tom Ropelewski and Leslie Dixon find droll if not witty voices in Danny DeVito's street-smart mutt and Diane Keaton's prissy poodle.

A physically unlikely couple, DeVito and Keaton vocally conjure up a nouveau Nick and Nora, spitting insults faster than their canine counterparts can lap up water from the bowl. Problem is that they have little to do with ho-hum storyline, which has little to do with anything.

Taxi driver James (John Travolta) and wife Mollie (Kirstie Alley) decide to buy a pooch from the pound for their curious child, Mikey (David Gallagher), who has recently been disillusioned by a drunken Santa Claus.

Meantime, James' new boss, the sultry, corporate Samantha D'Bonne (Lysette Anthony), dumps her over-coiffed poodle on James' children before making a serious seduction play for him. Mollie suspects James is fooling around with his blond boss and a jealousy triangle ensues. Somehow, through it all, the dogs save the day.

Ropelewski, who also helmed, keeps the pic moving, and he cleverly puts to use Travolta's dancing past, with coy references to "Saturday Night Fever" and even "Grease." But he would have been better served to leave the humans out altogether. The dog-meets-dog, dog-loses-dog, dog-gets-dog-back scenario provides a much more watchable film than the overworked jealousy theme. At least the dogs are funny.

Reprising their original roles, Travolta and Alley are serviceable, but why are they wasting time in a sequel destined to be so short-lived? Gallagher and newcomer 5-year-old Tabitha Lupien tap the cute-deviant-lovable formula that Hollywood demands for kids. And Olympia Dukakis growls as well as she ever did in her third stab at the supporting mother.

One nagging point: Pic seems aimed at kidvid market, but it revels in its ongoing references to open sexuality, including opening credits that run over a microscopic view of squirming sperm. Very tasteful.

—*Dan Cox*

THE NOVEMBER MEN

Arrow Releasing presents a Rohd House Investments and Sun Lion Films production. Produced by Rodney Byron Ellis and Paul Williams. Directed by Paul Williams. Screenplay, James Andronica. Camera (Foto-Kem), Susan Emerson; editor, Chip Brooks; music, Scott Thomas Smith; sound, James Dehr, Vince Garcia; assistant director, Rick Nanis. Reviewed at Chicago Intl. Film Festival, Oct. 20, 1993. MPAA Rating: PG. Running time: **98 MIN.**
Arthur Gwenlyn .... P.W. Williams
Duggo .... James Andronica
Elizabeth .... Leslie Bevis
Agent Granger .... Beau Starr
Clancy .... Rod Ellis
Robert Davi .... Robert Davi
Morganna .... Lexie Shine

Just when you thought no one was more paranoid than Oliver Stone, along comes "The November Men" — the ultimate in conspiratorial presidential assassination films. The slyly comic saga marks the welcome return of filmmaker Paul Williams, who carved out a niche two decades ago with such films as "Out of It" and "Dealing." Age has deteriorated neither his wit nor skill at packing considerable entertainment punch without benefit of a big budget.

The film just might be that rare, quirky item that can transcend the specialized arena and creep into wider release. It certainly works well as both thriller and black comedy. Only its modest production values could keep it from attaining mainstream appeal.

The filmmaking is wild and unconventional, as befits the subject matter. Noted Stone-like cineaste Arthur Gwenlyn (Williams) is the kind of guy who gets mad as hell and puts that venom on celluloid. What's gotten under his skin lately is the fact that there hasn't been an assassin from the left in recent American history. In the months leading up to the 1992 U.S. elections, he contemplates just what impact such an event might have on the political climate and a raft of societal ills.

He doesn't exactly know where that scenario might lead in script form. But very quickly he learns conventional Hollywood isn't interested anyway. He'll just have to roll up his sleeves, mortgage the house and adopt guerrilla tactics to get this little epic off the ground.

People, of course, think he's a lunatic. His girlfriend and collaborator, Elizabeth (Leslie Bevis), isn't even particularly sure he isn't serious about taking the fiction into a

November 15, 1993 (Cont.)

more realistic arena. After all, he's turned his back on the actors' union and is soliciting his cast from the ranks of the disaffected — Vietnam vets, the homeless, unemployed and terminally ill.

Duggo (James Andronica), a disgraced Marine, is horrified about the movie plot but desperate for any kind of work. Others in the cast and crew appear to have different and personal scenarios in mind. One even convinces the Secret Service to use him as a mole and plants the seed of a much bigger conspiracy that might lead to a big career promotion for Agent Granger (Beau Starr).

"The November Men" is rife with plots within plots within plots. While it maintains a stone-sober facade, there can be little doubt that director Williams and writer Andronica are subtly applying pinholes to the great gasbag of American hypocrisy. Nothing is too politically correct to evade their droll scorn.

None of this would work without the fierce, airtight wacko logic of Gwenlyn's pursuit. The very edginess of the story, combined with appropriately off-kilter performances and *cinema verite* techniques, keep the audience off guard and riveted. Up to the very last moment, one remains unsure whether the movie's assassination script is only a movie or some horrible extreme of ego and dementia.

Williams beefs up the film's credibility with footage of the real candidates, including material of himself with George Bush. There's also an interesting disclaimer that at least sounds legally valid.

Vibrant, original and nervy, "The November Men" should hit the right chord with critics and have solid specialized response.

—*Leonard Klady*

ABGESCHMINKT!

(MAKING UP!)

(GERMAN)

A TiMe (Germany) release of a Vela-X/HFF production, in association with Arnold & Richter and Bayerischer Rundfunk. Produced by Ewa Karlstroem. Directed by Katja von Garnier. Screenplay by von Garnier, Benjamin Taylor, Hannes Jaenicke. Camera (color), Torsten Breuer; editor, von Garnier; music, Peter Wenke, Tillmann Hoehn; art direction, Irene Edenhofer, Nikolai Ritter; costume design, Birgit Aichele; sound (Dolby), Rainer Plabst. Reviewed at Fantasia theater, Munich, Germany, Oct. 13, 1993. (In Chicago, London festivals.) Running time: **55 MIN.**

Frenzy	Katja Riemann
Maischa	Nina Kronjaeger
Rene	Gedeon Burkhard
Mark	Max Tidof
Susa	Daniela Lunkewitz
Editor	Peter Sattmann
Party Animal	Jochen Nickel

A 55-minute student film that's been an unexpected success in Germany since being picked up by a small distrib, "Making Up!" is an above-average single-women's date comedy that could score overseas in tube sales. It shows a promising new German talent in young helmer Katja von Garnier.

Film tells the story of two friends, Frenzy (Katja Riemann) and Maischa (Nina Kronjaeger), the former preoccupied with professional troubles as a strip-cartoonist, the latter continually on the lookout for a partner.

At a party, Maischa picks up dreamboat Rene (Gedeon Burkhard), who turns out to be an arrogant pig; Frenzy, meanwhile, falls head over heels for charming, funny and unassuming Mark (Max Tidof).

Most of the humor revolves around poking gentle fun at what fools women make of themselves when falling in love — or trying to. But the moral is clear: Love is found in unexpected places and at unexpected moments.

The pic's lightness is unusual for a German movie. Riemann plays Frenzy with a wry jadedness; as Maischa, Kronjaeger has a certain ironic sexiness the camera loves.

Tech credits are all above average for a student production, with camera work and editing modest but slick. Blowup from 16mm is OK.

Film has a heavy admixture of Yank refs and culture, with some jokes direct translations of Americanisms.

Frenzy smears "Life's a bitch and then you die" on a wall in German; one character describes another as "Pippi Longstocking on acid." Co-scripter Benjamin Taylor is American.

Local distrib TiMe programmed the film with a 15-minute student film "Der schoenste Busen der Welt" (The Most Beautiful Breasts in the World), from the short story by Roland Topor. By mid-October, "Making Up!" had been in the German top 10 for 17 weeks, for a cume of $4.8 million in no more than 100 prints. "Singles," by comparison, had grossed just under $4 million since its April release.

—*Eric Hansen*

DIGGER

(CANADIAN)

A Norstar release of a Circle Northwood (Vancouver) production, in association with WIC Inc. (International sales: August Entertainment, L.A.). Executive producers, Chris Bowell, Dale Andrews. Produced by Robert MacLean. Directed by Rob Turner. Screenplay, Rodney Gibbons. Camera, Michael Buckley; editor, Michael Chandler; music, Todd Boekelheide; production design, Mark S. Freeborn; costume design, Susan deLaval; sound, Jay Boekelheide; assistant director, Don French; casting, Georgianne Walker (U.S.), Trish Robinson (Canada). Reviewed at Vancouver Intl. Film Festival, Sept. 30, 1993. Running time: **95 MIN.**

Digger	Adam Hann-Byrd
Billy	Joshua Jackson
Sam	Timothy Bottoms
Anna	Barbara Williams
Bea	Olympia Dukakis
Arthur	Leslie Nielsen
Rosemary	Gabrielle Miller

A rare Canadian family drama that strikes out in an original direction, "Digger" overcomes its thin script and heavy subject — children facing mortality — to deliver a memorable mood piece with style and conviction.

Set in a rural part of Vancouver Island, the tale centers on the growing friendship between 10-year-old Digger (Adam Hann-Byrd) and his slightly older neighbor, Billy (Joshua Jackson). The latter suffers from a weak heart, but that doesn't keep him from revealing the literary treasures (mainly Jules Verne) and natural spirits that inspire him — and lenser Michael Buckley — to flights of lyrical fancy.

What makes Digger himself tick isn't so apparent, although we see the odd garden-shovel hobby that got him his nickname. It's clear that the city lad is riding out his parents' crumbling marriage by visiting his aunt and uncle (Barbara Williams and Timothy Bottoms) for the summer, but their sullenness takes even longer to explain than his.

Writer Rodney Gibbons doesn't invest enough time in the Williams character to make auds care why she gives the kid the cold shoulder. Bottoms doesn't have much to do, either.

Olympia Dukakis, as the boy's sympathetic grandmother, and Leslie Nielsen, as her good-natured admirer, also seem dropped tangentially into the story, but at least these old pros use every minute of screen time to liven things up. Nielsen appears thrilled to be, for once, a bearer of jokes, instead of the butt of them.

It's a pity that the script, and first-time helmer Rob Turner, didn't weave these fragmented characters into a more satisfying whole; an overall shortage of dialogue weakens the emotional impact, and Hann-Byrd, who stole hearts in "Little Man Tate," is overwhelmed by the compelling, clear-voiced Jackson.

That lack of dialogue turns into a strength when leftover space is given to the terminally ill boy's interior world (courtesy of Mark Freeborn's ornately detailed set design) and his imaginative connection with animals, trees and native mythology.

The locations are fresh, and Todd Boekelheide's Celtic-flavored score is a major plus.

The pic's slow pacing and serious theme will make it a tough sell to laugh-hungry toddlers, but it could have a brief-but-healthy theatrical life if pitched to families in search of gentler pictorial fare. On tape, it's sure to burrow a unique niche as something to help parents explain a recent or impending loss — and how many movies can make a claim like that? —*Ken Eisner*

FEMME FATALE

(BRITISH — 16mm)

A BBC Enterprises production for Screen 2. Executive producer, Mark Shivas. Produced by Kenith Trodd. Directed by Udayan Prasad. Written by Simon Gray. Camera, Graham Frake; editor, Ken Pearce; music, Stephen Warbeck; production design, Grenville Horner; costumes, Kate O'Farrell; sound, Jane Greenwood, Debbie Pragnell; associate producer, Julie Scott; assistant director, Brett Fallis; casting, Gail Shreeves. Reviewed at Vancouver Intl. Film Festival, Oct. 17, 1993. Running time: **80 MIN.**

Maddalena	Sophia Diaz
Vicar Ronnie	Simon Callow
Victor Harty	Donald Pleasence
Martin Harty	Colin Welland
Mary-Jane	Jaqueline Tong
Davey Harty	Jason Durr
Algie	James Fleet

Recalling the Ealing heyday of "Kind Hearts and Coronets" and "The Ladykillers," this pubcast production marries England's key comic virtues — broad slapstick, rampant xenophobia, blinding fear of sex and mordant self-loathing — in a hilarious, if only skin-deep, package.

Legit writer Simon Gray's bon-mot-filled script turns the title cliche on its head by creating a heroine so virtuous, her only crime is the lust she triggers in others. In fact, Sicilian-born Maddalena (raven-haired Sophia Diaz) has moved to England to get away from volatile sexual tempers, and when she marries a nice rural lad, it looks like her new home in a quaint Devonshire village will be above such earthy matters.

The unctuous voiceover recollection of befuddled Vicar Ronnie (Simon Callow in a sly turn) quickly tells us this is not to be. Men and women only have to gaze on Maddy's beatific visage — and the breasts that keep popping out of her peasant blouse — to drop over dead. Soon the villagers are actively helping each other out of the picture.

Auds looking for depth won't find it in the main character, who serves only to point up hypocritical provincial attitudes and infantile male impulses. Still, the Benny Hill-meets-"Jane Austen" dialogue is a relentless scream, with the cynical clergyman (Maddy calls him "Vicaroni") particularly acerbic in his easily distracted search for "God, or His equivalent."

Donald Pleasence makes the most of his small but key part as a blind accordion player with no good word for man nor beast, and all other players are tops.

Lensing is attractive, but prints need to be brightened, with improved sound, for the 16mm pic to have even a limited arthouse life. "Femme Fatale" will, however, knock 'em dead in the Brit-com section of bigger videostores.

—*Ken Eisner*

CHUT SARANG

(FIRST LOVE)

(SOUTH KOREAN)

A Sam-Ho Film Co. production. (International sales: Korean Motion Picture Promotion Corp, Seoul.) Executive producer, Kang Hui-Young. Produced by Park Hyo-Sung. Directed by Lee Myung-Se. Screenplay, Lee, Yang Sun-Hee. Camera, Yu Young-Gil; editor, Kim Hyun; music, Song Byung-Joon; art direction, Cho Yung-Sam; costume design, Ahn Soung-Sun; sound, Kim Won-Young; line producer, Kim Tae-Kyun. Reviewed at Vancouver Intl. Film Festival, Oct. 2, 1993. Running time: **108 MIN.**
Young-Shin .... Kim Hye-Soo
Chang-Wook .... Song Young-Chang
Mun-Su .... Cho Min-Gi
Young-Shin's father .... Choi Jong-Won
Young-Shin's mother .... Ahn Hae-Sook
Young-Sun .... Kim Hye-Young

I t's hard to imagine a more poignant evocation of adolescent crush-ville. Only overreach mars this generally delightful view of "First Love," as seen through the eyes of an impressionable young Korean woman.

Animation, stop-action effects and gorgeous, legit-like staging are just some of the clever devices director Lee Myung-Se uses to flesh out this (literally) timeless study of a teenager's fixation on her college drama teacher. Kim Hye-Soo is perfect as Young-Shin, who initially finds her chain-smoking, hard-drinking prof a major pain, but then can't get him out of her pixie-haired head. Somehow the teen endures countless humiliations in her quest for the slightest recognition from him — even while bullying her kid

sister — but never totally loses her cloud-nine dignity.

The tale is set in a small-town milieu resembling — thanks to irony-rich pop music and candy-colored clothes — both the early '60s and the present. The helmer tips his sentimental hand by having the middle-class collegiates performing "Our Town." That bit of nostalgic Americana informs the film, and an abruptly telescoped version of the play is only one among many forced-elegy sequences Lee crams into the closing quarter.

Of course, many a puppy-love tryst sputters impotently after a happy start, but unless this seemingly endless denouement is trimmed, offshore auds won't flip for "First Love." —*Ken Eisner*

DEADFALL

A Trimark release of a Ted Fox Prods. production. Executive producers, Mark Amin, Gerson Fox, Gertrude Fox. Produced by Ted Fox. Directed by Christopher Coppola. Screenplay, Coppola, Nick Vallelonga. Camera, Maryse Alberti; editor, Phillip Linson; music, Jim Fox. Reviewed at Vancouver Intl. Film Festival, Oct. 13, 1993. Running time: **113 MIN.**
Joe Donan .... Michael Biehn
Mike/Lou Donan .... James Coburn
Eddie .... Nicolas Cage
Diane .... Sarah Trigger
Pete .... Peter Fonda
Steve Lebett .... Charlie Sheen
Sam .... Talia Shire

W atchable only for camp value, "Deadfall" is at its best when cameo-laden anarchy reigns. As a tribute to film noir, it won't make it to the late late show.

This feature bow from Christopher Coppola, Francis F.'s nephew, is a haphazard run at "Grifters"-type fun. It is rife with overripe writing — as in "Every time you fleece a sucker, it eats another piece of your soul" — and the Spillane-isms amuse but grow wearying, especially in the mouth of lead thesp Michael Biehn.

Blond, bland Biehn plays Joe Donan, the son of a veteran New York con man (James Coburn). When dad goes down in a sour scam, Joe heads out to Santa Monica to look up his estranged Uncle Lou (Coburn again) and runs into a new set of games involving crazed henchman Eddie (the director's brother, Nicolas Cage) and his hot-stuff girlfriend Diane (Sarah Trigger).

Trigger probably has what it takes for comedy, but she's as insubstantial as Biehn in the heat department. Call it "True Romance" syndrome, but the leads are forgettably blah next to the grotesques around them. Coburn and Cage aren't exactly control freaks to begin with, and Coppola turns them utterly loose.

Unfortunately, when Cage's character dies, so does the movie.

An attempt to revive his sleazoid factor, via Charlie Sheen as a too-smooth pool shark, does more for Sheen's comic rep than for the pic's flagging momentum. By the end, the tale is so laden with red herrings and forced repartee that even die-hard genre-freaks will have dropped their frozen smiles.

Tech credits are OK, with jazzy music a plus, although lensing and design are not quite up to those ready references to Hitchcock, Welles and, well, Coppola. Losing a few minutes of deadwood might help block the bloated pic's free fall from limited theatrical run, but it's likely to end its days as a video oddity, saved for at-home Nicolas Cage retrospectives. —*Ken Eisner*

JUSTIZ

(JUSTICE)

(GERMAN-SWISS)

A GFF Munich/Luna Film AG (Zurich) co-production. Produced, directed by Hans Geissendorfer. Executive producer, Patrick Baumann. Co-producer, Rudolf Santschi. Screenplay, Geissendorfer, based on the novel by Friedrich Durrenmatt. Camera (Fuji), Hans-Gunther Bucking; editor, Annette Dorn; music, Frank Loef; art direction, Hans Gloor, Susanne Jauch; costume design, Katharina Von Martius; sound (Dolby), Jorg Von Allmen; assistant director, Holger Barthel; casting, Horst Schiel, Judith Kennel. Reviewed at the Aidikoff Screening Room, Beverly Hills, Oct. 23, 1993. Running time: **107 MIN.**
Isaak Kohler .... Maximilian Schell
Felix Spat .... Thomas Heinze
Helene Kohler .... Anna Thalbach
Stussi-Leupin ...... Norbert Schwientek
Police Chief .... Matthias Gnadiger
Ilse Freude .... Ulrike Kriener
Daphne Winter .... Susanne Borsody
Lienhard .... Christoph Lindert
Dr. Benno .... Dietrich Siegl
Prof. Winter .... Hark Bohm

G ermany's foreign-language Oscar submission is a worthy, somewhat dry adaptation of novelist Friedrich Durrenmatt's last novel, "Justiz." The very nature of justice and its elusive qualities provide the film with rich, philosophical questions to ponder. Simultaneously, the clinical nature of the script robs the film of a vital degree of humanity.

It all adds up to a very high-brow affair headed for specialized, upscale distribution. The film will desperately need critical hosannas to make a commercial dent, and that prospect seems highly unlikely.

The story revolves around Swiss businessman and politician Isaak Kohler (Maximilian Schell), who for no apparent reason walks into a crowded restaurant and fatally shoots his presumed friend Winter. Kohler offers no motive when he's brought to trial. Nor does he protest his sentence of 20 years.

But as a seeming act of largess to his daughter Helene (Anna Thalbach), he hires struggling advocate Felix Spat (Thomas Heinze) to reopen his case. "Create a fiction," he advises the young man.

"Justiz" inhabits extremely oblique, ironic territory. As with previous adaptations of Durrenmatt — including the Schell-directed "End of the Game," based upon "The Judge and His Hangman" — it doesn't quite jump cleanly from page to screen. Its notions of fair play and vengeance engage the intellect, but, without a proper thriller format to keep one guessing, the exercise is rendered cold, distant and tutorial.

Writer-director Hans Geissendorfer's weakness for adaptation is poorly serviced here, suggesting the source material was intrinsically untranslatable. It's a shame, because he remains one of Germany's foremost craftsmen, and his latest film shows him at his most technically sublime.

Schell and Heinze seem slightly ill at ease with their roles. Neither appears to have found the center of his character's power or weakness.

The effort remains a sometimes amusing intellectual exercise with extremely limited box office appeal.

—*Leonard Klady*

November 22, 1993

THE THREE MUSKETEERS

A Buena Vista release of a Walt Disney Pictures presentation in association with Caravan Pictures. Produced by Joe Roth, Roger Birnbaum. Executive producers, Jordan Kerner, Jon Avnet. Co-producers, Ned Dowd, William W. Wilson III. Directed by Stephen Herek. Screenplay, David Loughery, based on the novel by Alexandre Dumas. Camera (Technicolor; Panavision widescreen), Dean Semler; editor, John F. Link; music, Michael Kamen; production design, Wolf Kroeger; supervising art director, Richard Holland; art direction, Herta Hareiter-Pischinger, Neil Lamont (U.K.); set decoration, Bruno Cesari; costume design, John Mollo; sound (Dolby), Colin Charles; assistant director, David Tomblin; second unit director, Micky Moore; casting, Jeremy Zimmermann, Davis & Zimmermann (U.K.), Lucky Englander, Fritz Fleischhacker (Austria, Germany). Reviewed at the El Capitan Theater, L.A., Nov. 10, 1993. MPAA Rating: PG. Running time: **105 MIN.**

Aramis	Charlie Sheen
Athos	Kiefer Sutherland
D'Artagnan	Chris O'Donnell
Porthos	Oliver Platt
Cardinal Richelieu	Tim Curry
Milady	Rebecca De Mornay
Queen Anne	Gabrielle Anwar
Rochefort	Michael Wincott
Girard	Paul McGann
Constance	Julie Delpy
King Louis	Hugh O'Connor

Fifth major screen version of Alexandre Dumas' classic swashbuckling saga is a handsome but pallid affair aimed squarely at a young Disney audience. Those who have never seen a previous "Musketeers" adaptation or a truly exciting Hollywood adventure in the grand style may be swept along, but the mechanical, paint-by-numbers feel of this outing is too evident to ignore. The Disney marketing combine and "Young Guns With Swords" angle will generate some good initial B.O., but hanging on solidly until the new year looks like an iffy proposition.

Although filmed on beautiful locations in Austria and elsewhere, pic has an Americanized slant, with the good guys all speaking in Yank vernacular and the baddies sporting British accents. No doubt the straightest, and possibly most faithful rendition of the perennial favorite, it is quite tame compared with Richard Lester's wild and woolly 1974 version.

In many ways the prototypical romantic adventure tale, filled with innumerable fights, flights, rescues, close shaves and derring-do, "The Three Musketeers" also offers up enjoyably edifying notions about loyalty, patriotism, camaraderie and a devil-may-care attitude about life. All of this is present on the surface of this outing, but that's where it remains, as the film manages the unusual feat of being both breezy and tedious.

Set in 16th century France, yarn begins as the noble Musketeers, guardians of the king, are disbanded by Cardinal Richelieu (Tim Curry), who is conniving to wrest the throne from the weak teenaged monarch. Dashing D'Artagnan (Chris O'Donnell), whose late father was a Musketeer, is hoping to join their ranks, but the only ones left are renegades Aramis (Charlie Sheen), Athos (Kiefer Sutherland) and Porthos (Oliver Platt).

Soon after proving his worth to them with his swordplay, D'Artagnan is captured, but upon his rescue is able to inform his friends about Richelieu's dastardly plot to form an alliance with Britain. Chased to Calais, they intercept his eminence's messenger, the crafty Milady (Rebecca De Mornay), and eventually return to Paris to disrupt Richelieu's plans.

All these incidents provide innumerable opportunities for energetic action, blazing duels, horseback escapes and nonchalant bravado, but after the first 10 minutes one has seen enough jumping on and off moving objects and bodies conveniently falling into haystacks for five pictures. The moves are staged and executed proficiently, but generally without true flair, wit or imagination, investing the legendary tale with no new resonance or emotion.

Where the picture falls short can be seen very simply in the casting, as precisely two of the leading players get the tone deliciously right, thereby showing up the deficiencies of the others and demonstrating that, when performing a familiar text, it helps to have style and attitude. Curry steals the film as the evil Richelieu, bringing lip-smacking glee to his naughty deeds and pronouncements, and making the intended bon mots in David Loughery's workmanlike script sound much better than they actually are. Film comes alive whenever Curry's onscreen.

Also aces is Platt, always the one to watch when all the young Turks are working in ensemble. A bit portly and unusual looking, Platt has the sense of relish, experience and tossed-off humor that defines a Musketeer.

By contrast, Sheen and Sutherland mostly contribute a hardiness and athleticism, while O'Donnell's bland D'Artagnan epitomizes the Disneylandish side of this production.

A treacherous villainess at the outset, De Mornay eventually brings out other aspects of the icily beautiful Milady, while the lovely Gabrielle Anwar, as the queen, and Julie Delpy, in the very minimized role of Constance (played so memorably by Raquel Welch in 1974), are present for strictly decorative purposes.

Enacting a stereotype to memorable effect is Michael Wincott, who out-Rathbones Basil as Richelieu's sadistic, black-eyepatched, blade-wielding henchman.

Production values are strong, with Dean Semler's fluid camera nicely capturing the diverse European locations, notably including Vienna's Hofburg Palace. Wolf Kroeger's production design and John Mollo's costumes are resplendent, Michael Kamen's score is nothing if not energetic, and John F. Link's editing is snappy within scenes, even if the picture overall feels a bit long. —Todd McCarthy

GEORGE BALANCHINE'S THE NUTCRACKER

A Warner Bros. release of an Elektra Entertainment/Regency Enterprises presentation of a Krasnow/Milchan/Hurwitz production. Produced by Robert A. Krasnow, Robert Hurwitz. Executive producer, Arnon Milchan. Line producer, Catherine Tatge. Directed by Emile Ardolino. Adapted from the New York City Ballet production by Peter Martins. Story by E.T.A. Hoffmann. Camera (DuArt color; Technicolor prints), Ralf Bode; lighting design, Alan Adelman; editor, Girish Bhargava; music, Peter Ilyitch Tschaikovsky; choreography, Balanchine; narrator, Kevin Kline; narration written by Susan Cooper; scenery, Rouben Ter-Arutunian; costume design, Karinska; sound (Dolby), Frank Stettner; sound design, Randy Thom; special visual effects, Industrial Light & Magic; coordinating producer, Merrill Brockway; associate producer, Amy Schatz; assistant director, Thomas Reilly. Reviewed at Hamptons Intl. Film Festival, East Hampton, N.Y., Oct. 24, 1993. MPAA Rating: G. Running time: **92 MIN.**

The Sugarplum Fairy	Darci Kistler
Her Cavalier	Damian Woetzel
Dewdrop	Kyra Nichols
Drosselmeier	Bart Robinson Cook
The Nutcracker	Macaulay Culkin
Marie	Jessica Lynn Cohen

With: The New York City Ballet.

This rendition of George Balanchine's perennial Christmastime ballet attraction proves attractive but unexciting as a screen offering. Basically a representation of the stage production with little added in terms of cinematic flair, Warner Bros. release will pull families on the basis of the property's reputation as a holiday classic and the Macaulay Culkin casting coup, but will likely remain a modest earner.

The Tschaikovsky-Marius Petipa ballet, which celebrated its 100th birthday last year, illustrates E.T.A. Hoffmann's tale of a little girl who, on Christmas Eve, is transported to a magical world of giant toys, animated mice and glittering spectacle under the escort of a young prince who was once a nutcracker doll.

First scene warmly evokes a festive Old World Christmas, teeming with relatives in fancy dress and many kids brimming with eager anticipation. Marie's subsequent trip to the enchanted land provides the occasion for numerous virtuoso balletic turns, both from soloists and the corps de ballet, to the accompaniment of several of the composer's most famous passages, which are a pleasure to re-experience at the hands of conductor David Zinman and the New York City Ballet Orchestra.

But as gracefully and professionally executed as Peter Martins' production may be, the film retains a stagebound feel that delivers neither the excitement of a live performance nor a transporting movie experience.

Under the direction of Emile Ardolino, who made his reputation with the PBS series "Dance in America" and frequently collaborated with Balanchine, camera maintains the objective viewpoint of an audience member, albeit a very mobile one. The sumptuous original Rouben Ter-Arutunian sets and Karinska costumes are supplemented by a modicum of film-style special effects.

Balletomanes may revel in the respect and fidelity shown the source, but suspicion that more mainstream audiences may not respond as readily is addressed by the casting of Culkin in the central role of the Nutcracker Prince. Part doesn't require the child superstar to dance per se, but more to mime and move purposefully, which he does perfectly well. Culkin studied at the School of American Ballet and appeared onstage (as Marie's younger brother) in "Nutcracker" productions in 1989 and 1990.

Regardless of pic's pedigree, "The Nutcracker" is about as sticky and sweet as a Christmas fruitcake, and not that appetizing to a sizable public outside of culturally minded parents.

Technically, film is exceedingly polished, even if tame and earthbound. Some low-key narration by Kevin Kline, which was added late in the game and has been a bone of contention between the Culkin clan and producers, will help orient viewers not accustomed to ballet or films without dialogue.
—Todd McCarthy

DIRTY WEEKEND

(BRITISH)

A UIP release (U.K.) of a Scimitar Films production. Produced by Michael Winner, Robert Earl. Executive producer, Jim Beach. Directed by Winner. Screenplay, Winner, Helen Zahavi, based on Zahavi's novel. Camera (color), Alan Jones; editor, "Arnold Crust" (Winner); executive editor, Chris Barnes; music, David Fanshawe; production design, Crispian Sallis; sound (Dolby), David Brill; associate producer, Ron Purdie; assistant director, Purdie. Reviewed at MGM Oxford Street 2 theater, London, Oct. 29, 1993. Running time: **102 MIN.**

Bella	Lia Williams
Reggie	David McCallum
Nimrod	Ian Richardson
Tim	Rufus Sewell
Charles	Shaughan Seymour
Norman	Michael Cole
Mr. Brown	Mark Burns
Mrs. Crosby	Sylvia Syms
Marion	Miriam Kelly

Michael Winner aims low and half-misses with "Dirty Weekend," a jet-black genre-bender of femme vengeance from the British bestseller by Helen Zahavi. Those expecting a female, Anglo version of Winner's earlier "Death Wish" outings will be disappointed. "Weekend" is more rooted in everyday drama than high-octane thrillers.

Pic has attracted plenty of column inches in Blighty thanks to the original "feminist" novel's rep and Winner's own tub-thumping. (Producer-director is also reported to be ponying up his own P&A coin.)

In territories where book and helmer are less well known, "Weekend" will need careful handling, though should tick over nicely on vid marketed as a sexploitationer. Pic also has the seeds of a cult movie down the tracks.

Setting is Brighton, where the introverted Bella (Lia Williams) has moved after being dumped by a b.f. in London. Renting a small basement apartment, she's soon prey to an obscene phone-caller (Rufus Sewell) who spies on her from a window opposite.

After an empowering visit to an Iranian fortuneteller (Ian Richardson), she brains the peeper with a hammer in his bed one night.

High on the experience, she sets out on a weekend killing spree of male porkers. Dressed like a hooker, she asphyxiates a businessmen (Michael Cole) during an S&M sesh. Next day, she runs down a sadistic dentist (David McCallum) after some forced fellatio in an underground parking lot, and later shoots three punks about to incinerate a bag lady. Finale has her coming face to face with a serial killer.

Zahavi's much-hyped 1991 novel (compared at the time to "American Psycho") presents major challenges for any screen adaptation, being composed mostly of an interior reverie by the central character. Most of its special qualities stem from obsessive, repetitive play with words and a deliberately unreal, sarcastic tone that can be interpreted in several ways. Ironically, Winner's version (scripted with Zahavi herself) is most successful when sticking closely to the original.

After an opening caption of the novel's famous first sentence ("This is the story of Bella, who woke up one morning and realized she'd had enough"), the movie's first half-hour largely hangs fire with dreary exposition and lackluster dialogue, and would benefit from heavy scissoring.

Thereafter, pic sticks slavishly to the novel, with whole chunks of dialogue and v.o. by Williams that conjure up much of the book's blackly comic tone and irreverent approach to highly PC, feminist issues.

Winner plays up the unreality with off-center framing and careful use of lenses, recalling Polanski's efforts to give a heightened, jet-lag feel to "Frantic," although flat lighting and grubby color give the whole thing a bargain-basement look. Cutting is sharp and unlingering, and David Fanshawe's melodramatic score pumps up genre elements already present in Zahavi's original.

As the worm who turns, newcomer Williams tent-poles the movie with a fine perf that catches the work's bitter-sardonic tone and pulls off some tricky dialogue. (Since making the film in summer '92, actress has carved a career in TV and legit.) Richardson, McCallum, Cole and Sylvia Syms (the last in a waspish cameo as an employment agency boss) play their stereotypes to the hilt.

Visuals in the sex scenes and bloodletting are discreet by contempo standards, verging more on the cartoony. —*Derek Elley*

<hr>

LONDON FEST

<hr>

HIFAZAAT

(IN CUSTODY)

(BRITISH)

A Merchant Ivory Prods. Ltd. production, in association with Channel 4 Films. Produced by Walid Chowhan. Executive producers, Paul Bradley, Donald Rosenfeld. Directed by Ismail Merchant. Screenplay, Anita Desai, Shahrukh Husain, based on Desai's novel. Camera (Technicolor), Larry Pizer; editor, Roberto Silvi; music, Zakir Hussain, Ustad Sultan Khan; production design, Suresh Sawant; costume design, Lovleen Bains; sound (Dolby), Mike Shoring, John Hayward; assistant director, Henry Tomlinson, Shah Jehan. Reviewed at Curzon Mayfair Theater, London, Nov. 5, 1993. (In London Film Festival.) Running time: **125 MIN.**

Nur	Shashi Kapoor
Imtiaz Begum	Shabana Azmi
Deven	Om Puri
Safiya Begum	Sushma Seth
Sarla	Neena Gupta
Murad	Tinnu Anand
Jain	Prayag Raj
Siddiqui	Ajay Sahani
(Hindi & Urdu dialogue; English subtitles)	

Producer Ismail Merchant makes a smooth and confident move to the director's chair with "In Custody," an elaborate shaggy-dog tale about a teacher's bruising relationship with an admired Urdu poet that's given stature and resonance by its central trio of marvelous perfs. Merchant's name should ensure the pic a smooth entree to fests and upmarket salons, though further tightening of its two-hour-plus running time would bring dramatic benefits to its specialized subject matter.

Pic is a much more assured work, in look and structure, than Merchant's previous sortie behind the lens, the rococo, semi-docu short feature "The Courtesans of Bombay" (1983). Though Merchant's style is conservative — largely fixed-camera setups and textbook cutting — there's a clean, easy flow to both the movie and the playing that's in sharp contrast to many of the works of his longtime partner James Ivory. Setting is north central India, in the state of Madhya Pradesh, where Deven (Om Puri) is a small-town teacher who's urged by a goofy publisher friend to interview the poet Nur (Shashi Kapoor), the greatest living exponent of the dying Urdu language.

After scrabbling together some money and putting his teaching job on the line, Deven travels to scenic Bhopal to meet his hero, now an obese, broken wreck, surrounded by hangers-on and bullied by an ambitious second wife (Shabana Azmi) who's plagiarized his works for her own ends.

Deven's attempts to record Nur's memories and recitations turn into a tragicomedy of bizarre proportions. Nur is mostly drunk or incoherent, his second wife hostile, his first wife jealous and money-grubbing. Deven returns almost empty-handed, his dreams shattered — though a final twist restores his faith. Co-scripted by Anita Desai from her own 1987 novel (written in English), the movie essentially spins on a dime: the breaking of one man's blinkered idealism. Around this the movie weaves a fabric of relationships and cultural riffs — the dying art of majestic Urdu poetry, the lack of modern respect for tradition, and the sheer impossibility of achieving anything lasting in India's social and economic setup.

It's a rich feast, sometimes too rich for viewers not attuned to the cultural and linguistic subtleties, though the sheer strength of the main perfs manages to hold the attention even in the burgeoning musical and poetic sequences.

As the burnt-out, roly-poly bard, Kapoor, almost unrecognizable from his slim, matinee-idol days, limns a commanding presence, halfway between an Indian Laughton and Greenstreet. Playing neat and tight as the teacher, Puri treads a fine line between comic bemusement and dogged veneration.

Azmi, as Kapoor's beautiful second wife, skillfully manages the difficult switch from cynical regality in the early stages to an object of some sympathy. Playing in a host of other roles is sharp and full of character.

The pic is a delight to behold, with standout lensing of Mughal-style locations near Lake Bhopal by British-born Larry Pizer ("The Europeans") and deft use of music to carry the tragicomic mood. Roberto Silvi's cutting is unobtrusive, and costuming and production design are consistently eye-catching.
—*Derek Elley*

<hr>

GENGHIS COHN

(BRITISH — 16mm)

A BBC production, in association with Arts & Entertainment Network. (International sales: BBC Enterprises, London.) Produced by Ruth Caleb. Executive producer, Mark Shivas. Directed by Elijah Moshinsky. Screenplay, Stanley Price, based on the novel "The Dance of Genghis Cohn," by Romain Gary. Camera (color), John Daly; editor, Ken Pearce; music, Carl Davis; production design, Tony Burrough; art direction, Peter Findley; costume design, James Keast; sound, Martyn Clift; assistant director, Daphne Phipps. Reviewed at London Film Festival, Nov. 9, 1993. Running time: **79 MIN.**

Otto Schatz	Robert Lindsay
Genghis Cohn	Antony Sher
Frieda von Stangel	Diana Rigg
Dr. Eckhardt	John Wells
Police chief	Robert Lang
Dr. Helen Feuchtwanger	Frances de la Tour
Interior Minister	Paul Brooke

A loopy idea diffused by a loose script and even looser direction, "Genghis Cohn" should attract some offshore attention from the sheer outrageousness of its premise and the roster of name players. But this BBC telemovie, about a former Nazi haunted by the pesky ghost of a Dachau victim, is more fitted to fests and Jewish events than broader theatrical situations. Item is due to air early next year in the British pubcaster's Screen Two season.

Based on Romain Gary's novel "The Dance of Genghis Cohn," pic opens in lively, colorful style with a montage of anti-Nazi stage shtick by Jewish ventriloquist Cohn (Antony Sher) in 1930s Europe. Cohn finally ends up in a Dachau lime pit.

Cut to Bavaria, 1958, where Cohn's executioner, Schatz (Robert Lindsay), is police commissioner in a small town and still carrying a secret torch for the late, lamented *Fuhrer*. Cohn's ghost starts to haunt Schatz, who gradually develops a taste for chopped liver and gefilte fish between trying to solve a string of serial murders of *in flagrante* males.

Though the film targets broader racism and bigotry beyond anti-Semitism, the obviousness of much of the humor works more against than for its serious subtext. A one-joke movie like this needs more visual style and richer production values than either helmer Elijah Moshinsky (better known as a theater and opera director) or a TV budget can bring to it.

Playing is solid by the experienced cast, with Lindsay fine as the koshered ex-Nazi, Sher throwing himself into the tragicomic *farceur* Cohn, and Diana Rigg having a ball as a horny *haute bourgeoise*. Carl Davis' bouncy fairground score livens up Ken Pearce's routine 16mm lensing, and German locationing is used to generally good effect.

—*Derek Elley*

BODY MELT

(AUSTRALIAN)

A Dumb Films presentation of a Body Melt production, in association with the Australian Film Commission, Film Victoria. (International sales: Beyond Films, Sydney.) Produced by Rod Bishop, Daniel Scharf. Directed by Philip Brophy. Screenplay, Brophy, Bishop. Camera (color), Ray Argall; editor, Bill Murphy; music, Brophy; production design, Maria Kozic; costumes, Anna Borghesi; sound, Gary Wilkins; special effects makeup, Bob McCarron; associate producer, Lars Michalak; assistant director, Euan Keddie; casting, Greg Apps. Reviewed at Village-Roadshow screening room, Sydney, Oct. 19, 1993. (In London Film Festival.) Running time: **84 MIN.**

Det. Sam Phillips	Gerard Kennedy
Johnno	Andrew Daddo
Dr. Carrera	Ian Smith
Pud	Vince Gil
Shaan	Regina Gaigalas
Gino	Maurie Annese
Sal	Nick Polites
Paul Matthews	William McInnes
Brian Rand	Brett Climo
Thompson Noble	Adrian Wright
Cheryl Rand	Lisa McCune
Kate	Suzi Dougherty
Angelica Noble	Jillian Murray

First-time feature director Philip Brophy comes up with a shlocky, tongue-in-cheek gore pic in "Body Melt," a moderately enjoyable item for fans of the genre. This loopy tale, about a mad doctor whose invention — a new kind of vitamin pill — has horrific side effects, should have a decent life on video shelves, but theatrical chances are iffy.

Brophy seems to be following in the footsteps of Kiwi Peter Jackson, director of "Brain Dead," but he's not yet in the same league: "Body Melt" is full of gruesome deaths but is also cluttered with too many characters and needs a surer touch to sock over this brand of cheerfully sick humor.

Plot, which is not always clear, turns on the invention, by doctor-scientist Carrera (Ian Smith), of vitamins that cause bodies to crack open, melt or explode. In the past, tests of the treatment have had disastrous results, and Carrera's former partner (Vince Gil), who had experimented on himself, now lives on an isolated farm with his deformed, half-mad family, a creepy clan whose threatening attitude toward outsiders evokes memories of "The Texas Chainsaw Massacre."

Against Carrera's wishes, the vitamins are now being marketed, in pill and powder form, by an ambitious woman (Regina Gaigalas) who runs a kinky health farm; free samples have been sent to a "typical" city suburb, with disastrous results. The suburbanites who try the samples start to hallucinate and then disintegrate in a variety of spec-

tacular ways. In one grisly scene, the stomach of a very pregnant woman explodes.

Special effects makeup by Bob McCarron is revolting enough to please the fans, but more care with the convoluted screenplay would have made for a more commercial package. Still, there will be plenty of small-screen fans for this gorefest.

Despite a large ensemble cast, this isn't an actor's film. More might have been expected from Brophy, whose provocative short film "Salt Saliva Sperm and Sweat" made its mark a while back. Connoisseurs of bizarre credits will note that Brophy himself provided the testicles and production designer Maria Kozic the buttocks for a brief but graphic sex scene glimpsed on TV in a clinic sequence. Other tech credits are pro. —*David Stratton*

VANCOUVER

DARWIN

(BRITISH-FRENCH — VIDEO)

A Telemax/Les Editions Audiovisuelle co-production. (International sales: Les Editions Audiovisuelles, Paris.) Produced by Kees Kasander. Executive producer, Andre Djaoui. Directed, written by Peter Greenaway. Camera (color, video), Chris Renson, Reinier van Brummelen; editor, Chris Wyatt; music, Nicholas Wilson; art direction, Ben van Os, Jan Roelfs; set decoration, Ben Zwydwijk; costume design, Ellen Lens, Bernadette Corstens; sound, Tjeenl van Zanen; associate producer, Ritza Brown; assistant director, Jerven Planting; casting, Edit Hazelbach. Reviewed on videcassette at Vancouver Intl. Film Festival, Oct. 17, 1993. Running time: **52 MIN.**

With: Bert Svenhujsen.

A must-see for history buffs and Greenaway completists, "Darwin" sports an awkward format and length may make post-fest survival fitful at best.

Broken into 18 elaborately staged tableaux, the story of Charles Darwin and his carefully nursed theories centers on his cluttered workplace. A desk flanked by two towering windows, this ever-changing stage (for a dark-suited Moses and his church-shaking commandments) takes on the monumental, ersatz solidity of a painting by Jacques-Louis David — the kind 19th-century men and boys gazed on with religious awe.

Greenaway is actually pricking that pretense, sandwiching the formal Victorian speech of the pic's precise narration (extended from section headings like "16: in which Darwin's relevance to our present understanding of ourselves is considered") with the increasingly orgiastic accumulation of extras, props and lighting effects.

There's droll humor in this approach: Darwin is seen shooting quail (in his study, natch) while we're told his father picked theol-

ogy as "a reliable sinecure for a not very bright second son." For all the baroque formalism, though, pic could probably be enjoyed just as well as an audio-only combo of words and propulsive music.

Quite simply, the dense and often spectacular imagery, even with deceptively static lensing, is often lost on the small screen (it was made for Euro TV). Tuned-up 35mm transfers would be required for "Darwin" to evolve past its pubcasting origins. —*Ken Eisner*

PART TIME GOD

(DUTCH — DOCU — 16mm)

A DNU Film/VPRO Television production. (International sales: De Nieuwe Unie BV/Orthel Filmproductie.) Produced by Rolf Orthel. Directed, written by Paul Cohen. Camera (color), Cohen; editor, Sytse Kramer; music, Henny Vrienten; sound, Hugo Helmond; computer animation, Teun van Tubergen; special effects, Adrian Hill. Reviewed at Vancouver Intl. Film Festival, Oct. 7, 1993. Running time: **80 MIN.**

The lackadaisical deity of "Part Time God" is director Paul Cohen, who takes great pains to reveal the filmmaker's usually unseen touch in the editing-and-organizing process. The central device in this provocative Dutch docu is literally his hand, which repeatedly intrudes into the frame to choose between parallel stories shot (on video) in seven countries and transformed (on film) into a computer-like collage.

Although not obvious at first, pic is toying with the notion of free will vs. such forces as chance, destiny and you-know-Who. Jumping from a lovelorn grape-picker to a nuclear physicist to a pensioner surrounded by clocks, from a Surinam duck breeder and his evangelical wife to a Danish lighthouse keeper to a New York artist facing a radical mastectomy (with grueling footage of the operation), Cohen occasionally hits fast-forward or rewind to make a point. He is aided by hypnotic music and the tiny, black-and-white heads of philosophical pundits — like biologist Richard Dawkins and Nobel laureate Ilya Prigogine — popping up at the bottom of the screen, ready to chat at the touch of a finger. A woman's voice would have been useful here. Pic is utterly fascinating, and, most intriguing, it points to interactive, seams-exposed storytelling from documakers, mostly in the educational arena. Theatrically, "Part Time God" will find few parishioners, but look for countless disciples in the coming millennium.

—*Ken Eisner*

YUEGUANG SHAONIAN

(MOONLIGHT BOY)

(TAIWANESE)

A Shutter Pictures/Fire Sky Pictures production. Produced by Wu Wukung, Yu Wei-yen. Executive producers, Yang Li-hsing, Hou Te-chien. Directed by Yu. Screenplay, Yu, Jerry Sun, from a screen story by Yeh Hsiang-hua. Camera (color), Li Yi-hsu, Chu P'ei-chi; editor, Wen Yi-hui; music, music direction, Hou; art direction, Yu; costume design, Liao Chuan-ling; sound, Su Li-hsin, Kuo Wen-fu; animation director, Yu Wei-cheng; assistant director, Ts'ai Kuo-hui. Reviewed on videcassette, London, Sept. 11, 1993. (In Venice, San Sebastian, Montreal, Toronto, Tokyo, Vancouver fests.) Running time: **98 MIN.**

Hsiao-feng	Wang Ch'i-tsan
Hsiao-ch'i	Caroline Lu
Mother	Ni Shu-chun
Grandmother	Elaine Jin
Old man	Eric Tsang
(Mandarin dialogue)	

Downbeat and frustratingly obscure, "Moonlight Boy" is a dreamlike, existential puzzler on memory and changes in Taiwanese society that won't survive long beyond the oxygen tent of the fest circuit.

Helmer-art director Yu Wei-yen, whose impressive directorial bow, "Gang of Three Forever," made the fest rounds four years ago, here serves up a complex structure and local references that look to baffle all but the faithful.

Title character is a young kid (Wang Ch'i-tsan) who roams the streets of nighttime Taipei and follows the singer (Caroline Lu) in an all-girl band, calling her "sis."

The girl's life is a mess: her married b.f. won't leave his wife, her mother (Ni Shu-chun) is an obsessive Christian, and her uncle is a bedridden vegetable after a traffic accident some 30 years ago. Only her grandmother (Elaine Jin) is sympathetic.

Knitted into the fabric are occasional sequences of the boy talking to his late father (played by Hong Kong actor Eric Tsang), initially portrayed as a toon.

Things get complex when the film roams down memory alley, with the kid (un-aged) playing the girl's uncle prior to his accident. When the girl realizes the boy is actually her uncle's spirit, the family starts to unglue.

Yu's movie has a soulless, introverted quality familiar from several other recent Taiwan productions. Beneath its arty obscurities, script seems to plead for a return to old-style values — also touched on in the girl's favorite song, "Why Not Change Things Round?"

But flat acting and dialogue make this a tough one to endure. None of the self-obsessed characters engenders much sympathy.

Film has a claustrophic feel from being shot mostly at night or in half

November 22, 1993 (Cont.)

shadow. Sound, often directly recorded, is low-key. Live-action-blended animation by helmer's brother Yu Wei-cheng is clever but could be more fluid. —*Derek Elley*

DONG-CHUN DE RIZI

(THE DAYS)

(CHINESE — B&W — 16mm)

An Image Studio production. (International sales: Shu Kei's Creative Workshop, Beijing.) Produced by Liu Jie, Zhang Hongtao, Wang Yao. Directed, written, edited by Wang Xiaoshuai. Camera, music, Liu, Wu Di. Reviewed at Vancouver Intl. Film Festival, Oct. 16, 1993. Running time: **80 MIN.**
With: Liu Xiaodong, Yu Hong, Lou Ye.

Part of a new wave of Chinese independents eschewing social observation (and government approval) in favor of European-style introspection, "The Days" is a subtle look at Beijing twentysomethings who can't quite put their fingers on what's missing from their no-pressure lives.

It's pertinent that the story's married, longtime sweethearts are named Dong (winter) and Chun (spring), since their personalities are complementary without being entirely compatible. Low-level academics from out-of-favor families, Dong (stoical Liu Xiaodong) chain-smokes, listens to Hendrix and creates unsalable paintings in his copious spare time, while Chun (pretty Yu Hong) has grudgingly put aside her art to keep up the threadbare household.

With passion lacking in marriage and career departments, the two drift apart emotionally, and Chun considers joining her transplanted parents in New York. By now, her hangdog hubby is too stuck to stop her, but he does rouse himself to propose one last trip together, to his childhood home in Manchuria. The nostalgic but tense reunion with his peasant family forms the redeeming heart of the tale, with leisurely black-and-white lensing effectively conveying the generation-X ennui of the main characters and their unspoken yearning for something deeper.

Young helmer Wang Xiaoshuai set himself a tough task, capturing modern torpor without losing solid form or aud interest, and he does this strikingly well. But the cool subject and tightly bridled thesping will number "The Days" outside fest calendars. A sexy opening sequence, by mainland standards, may help video circulation, but mostly pic will be remembered by budding Chinese filmmakers as a quiet, but firm, door-opener.
—*Ken Eisner*

MUNGSING SIFAN

(MARY FROM BEIJING)

(HONG KONG)

A Golden Harvest/Art & Talent Group production. Produced by Anthony Chow. Executive producer, Hon Pou-chu. Executive in charge of production, Victor Chu. Directed, written by Sylvia Chang. Camera (color), Christopher Doyle; editors, Yu Shum, Kong Chi-leung; music, Music Factory; songs, Lo Ta-yu; art direction, William Chang; costume design, Luk Ha-fong; associate producer, Zhang Yimou; assistant directors, Bill Yip, Crystal Kwok; Peking location camera, Jingle Ma. Reviewed on Universe Laser & Video vidcassette, London, Aug. 29, 1993. (In Festival of Festivals, Toronto, Asian Horizons section.) Running time: **96 MIN.**
Ma Li	Gong Li
Wong Kwok-wai	Kenny Bee
Peter	Wilson Lam
Yip	John Chiang
Elizabeth	Cynthia Cheung
(Cantonese & Mandarin dialogue)	

Hot Chinese star Gong Li shows more wardrobe than acting talent in "Mary From Beijing," a good-looking but lightly scripted romancer about a Mainland woman adrift in glitzy Hong Kong.

Item could spur minimal interest among buffs curious to see Gong ("The Story of Qiu Ju") in a non-Zhang Yimou vehicle, but is more fitted to Asian weeks than the arthouse circuit. Pic performed mildly on H.K. release in late 1992.

Gong is Ma Li (wrongly dubbed "Mary" by Westernized Hong Kongers), a Hong Kong-born but Peking-raised woman living with a wealthy, daddy's-boy jeweler and trying to get an H.K. identity card to fulfill her own sense of identity.

Enter Wong (Kenny Bee), a rich businessman back from a long spell in Blighty, who wants to plug a gap in the Mainland China toilet-tissue market and moves into the apartment opposite.

Director-scripter Sylvia Chang resurrects the out-of-fashion genre of relationship movies, while stitching in resonant observations on mainland-Hong Kong prejudices, emotional statelessness and the colony's transient lifestyle. But one is often left hungry for more.

Highlights include a very funny seg in Beijing, satirizing mainland bureaucracy, plus an on-target description by Bee's character of Hong Kong as a much-pursued beauty for whom "only money can enable her to live with dignity."

With less wooden, mannequin-like playing by Gong, pic might have gained more dramatic momentum. Rest of the cast is fine, with Bee sympathetic as the boyish charmer, Wilson Lam OK as the milquetoast b.f. and Cynthia Cheung sharp as Bee's waspish ex-wife.

Technically, pic is smooth, helped by Chris Doyle's easy-on-the-eyes photography. Chinese title literally means "half-dreaming, half-waking," referring to the unsettled status of Gong's character. As on several of the actress's outings, Zhang cops a token associate producer credit. —*Derek Elley*

SHIBA

(18)

(TAIWANESE)

A Taiwan Film Culture Co./King's Video production in association with Creative Communication. Produced by Li Shu-ping, Lu Mu-ts'un. Executive producers, Wang Pao-min, Hsu An-chin, Lu Chih-tzu. Directed by Ho P'ing. Screenplay, Kuo Cheng, Ho, from the novel by Kuo. Camera (color), Tom Ryan; editors, Ch'en Po-wen, Chou Hsu-wei; music, Jim Shum; production design, Fu Ch'ang-feng; art direction, Li Ching-hua; costume design, Roger; sound design, Shum. Reviewed on vidcassette, London, Aug. 19, 1993. (In Festival of Festivals, Toronto.) Running time: **106 MIN.**
Pearl/Ah-chiao	Monica Lu
"Weirdo"	Wu Hsin-kuo
Ah-hai	T'o Tsung-hua
Red Fish	Turnip
O-liang	Crooked Chin
Weirdo's wife	Lin Ch'i-lou
The Kid	Chen Yi-fan
Weirdo's daughter	Lin Chia-chen
(Mandarin & Hokkien dialogue)	

Bold and always watchable, "18" is an ultimately over-coded slice of existential Taiwan cinema that won't travel far offshore beyond specialized fest slots.

Title refers to a winning combo at dice, to which a city type (Wu Hsin-kuo) becomes attached when he visits a seaside village in rural Taiwan.

When his frosty wife (Lin Ch'i-lou) and brattish daughter hie back to town, the man, nicknamed "Weirdo" by the locals, gets drawn into the community's simmering sexuality and violence, which ends with several people dead and the chaos blamed on the visitor.

Second feature of young Ho P'ing (not to be confused with Mainland Chinese helmer He Ping, of "Swordsman in Double-Flag Town" repute) is a self-consciously arty detour after his baseball biopic "A Son Remembers."

Pic's fractured style, off-center compositions and pretensions don't sit easily on the thin script, which flirts with themes like Taiwanese identity and tensions between Chinese of different backgrounds, but will baffle most auds.

Perfs are OK within their limits, with lusty playing by the experienced Monica Lu (aka Lu Hsiao-fen) as a brassy hotelier-cum-hooker. Tech credits are peachy, with fine, sharp location lensing by Tom Ryan. —*Derek Elley*

SAFE

(BRITISH)

A BBC Screenplay production. Produced by David M. Thompson. Executive producer, George Fabre. Directed by Antonia Bird. Screenplay, Al Ashton. Camera (color), Fred Tammes; editor, Arden Fisher; music, Billy Bragg; production design, Ken Starkey; costume design, Jill Taylor; Dolby sound; associate producer, Joanna Newbery. Reviewed at Dinard Festival of British Cinema (competing), Dinard, France, Sept. 24, 1993. (Also in Edinburgh festival.) Running time: **64 MIN.**
Gypo	Aidan Gillen
Kaz	Kate Hardie
Nasty	Robert Carlyle
Sean	George Costigan
Duggie	Andrew Tiernan

A supremely convincing slice of life leavened by the dark humor of resignation, "Safe" is an almost unrelentingly bleak and violent portrait of homeless youths in London. Intense pic will be a deeply unpleasant experience for many, but is a good shake-'em-up tool for TV auds and an urgent item both for fests and civic leaders. After copping two awards at the Edinburgh fest and the Prix du Jury (Silver Hitchcock) at the Dinard British Cinema fest, item aired Oct. 13 in BBC2's "Screenplay" slot.

Kaz (Kate Hardie) and Gypo (Aidan Gillen) are intelligent but homeless twentysomethings adrift in London's West End. Rather than settle for spare change, they pose as pimp and prostie, fleecing men for hunks of cash.

One risky scam leads to brutal consequences. The toll that street people take on those who try to help them is well conveyed in scenes at a youth shelter, whose long-suffering staff have their patience exhausted each night by the unruly behavior of misfits, wastrels and psychic burnouts.

Full-throttle thesping gives the compact tragedy an impact that outlasts the brief running time. Robert Carlyle, unrecognizable from his role as the soft-spoken lead in Ken Loach's "Riff-Raff," is first-class as a street-dwelling gent who could be a cousin to Gary Oldman's evil pimp in "True Romance," terrorizing his mates and plunging broken bottles into his chest to earn a hospital stay.

Lensing captures the ultra-gritty bustle of city streets and the forlorn chill of makeshift digs on the sidewalk. A defiant episode in which Gillen frolics full-frontally in the shelter could pose problems in some markets. —*Lisa Nesselson*

ZOHAR: MEDITERRANEAN BLUES

(ISRAELI)

A New Films production. Produced by Michael Sharfstein, Amitai Manelzon. Directed by Eran Riklis. Screenplay, Moshe Zonder, Amir Ben-David. Camera (color), Amnon Alait; editor, Einat Glaser-Zarhin; music, Avihu Medina; production design, Jacob Turgeman; costume design, Rona Doron; sound, Israel David. Reviewed at the Royal Theater, L.A., Oct. 11, 1993. (In Israeli Film Festival.) Running time: **116 MIN.**
Zohar Argov .... Shaul Mizrahi
Bracha .... Dafna Dekel
Reuveni .... Gaby Amrany
Avihu Medina .... Menahem Einy
The Mother .... Cochava Harari

Despite being the story of the rise and fall of a popular singer, "Zohar: Mediterranean Blues" is not formulaic in the manner of most biopics. Endowed with a distinct flavor of Israeli culture and politics, this is an honorable representative of the new Israeli cinema and as such should be a welcome addition to any festival or retrospective of Israeli films.

Story begins with the release of Zohar (Shaul Mizrahi) from prison, where he's spent one year for assault on a woman. Still attached to his former wife (Dafna Dekel) and their young boy, he hopes to rekindle their love, though she is now dating another man.

Most of the narrative concerns Zohar's struggle to establish a name for himself as a folk singer who performs moody, soulful Sephardic songs in an industry dominated by Western music. Set in the 1980s, "Zohar" draws an interesting analogy between an ethnic singer's rising popularity and the Sephardic community's call for greater recognition of its distinctive culture.

Chief problem is that the screenwriters, Moshe Zonder and Amir Ben-David, wish to play the tale as both personal and national tragedy. But the script never makes it clear to what extent Zohar's drug addiction and eventually senseless death, at the age of 32, derived from his personal frustrations over unrequited love for his ex-wife. Ultimately, the film works better as a psychological study of a singer who became a victim of drugs than as a metaphor for the long-enduring clash between Israel's Ashkenazic and Sephardic communities.

Gifted helmer Eran Riklis, who directed "Final Cup," one of the more riveting Israeli films of the last decade, keeps his camera close to Zohar, his family and associates. Visual style is modest and unobtrusive, effectively serving the personal drama. Similarly, Mizrahi, who appears in almost every scene,

renders a natural, most touching performance.

Truly depressing in its portrait of self-degradation induced by drugs, "Zohar" is a demanding film that may not be to everyone's taste. But always honest and realistic, pic is a good sample of the new, more critical and sophisticated contemporary Israeli cinema. —*Emanuel Levy*

FANFAN

(FRENCH)

A Gaumont Buena Vista Intl. release of a Gaumont-France 3 Cinema coproduction with the participation of Canal Plus. Produced by Alain Terzian. Directed by Alexandre Jardin. Screenplay, Alexandre Jardin, based on his novel. Camera (color), Jean-Yves Le Mener; editor, Joelle Hache; music, Nicolas Jorelle; set decoration, Hugues Tissandier; costume design, Lyvia D'Alche; sound (Dolby), Gerard Lamps. Reviewed at Gaumont Marignan cinema, Paris, July 25, 1993. Running time: **69 MIN.**
Fanfan .... Sophie Marceau
Alexandre .... Vincent Perez
Laure .... Marine Delterme
Maude .... Micheline Presle
    Also with: Gerard Sety, Bruno Todeschini, Ariel Semenoff, Marcel Marechal, Gerard Caillaud.

"**Fanfan**" is a forced and unconvincing romantic comedy that has done well at Gallic wickets thanks to the drawing power of Sophie Marceau coupled with first-time helmer Alexandre Jardin's popularity as a novelist. Bland pic, adapted by Jardin from his own bestseller, tries hard to be magical but is unlikely to fool anyone over the age of 14.

Jardin, whose book "Le Zebre" was the basis for Jean Poiret's hit in which Thierry L'hermitte played nonstop pranks on his adored wife in order to keep their romance fresh and unpredictable, mines similar territory in "Fanfan."

Already bored with the longtime g.f. he's about to marry, Alexandre (Vincent Perez, Catherine Deneuve's love interest in "Indochine") is attracted to sexy, free-spirited Fanfan (Marceau), but fears the inevitable decline of passion. His new strategy for avoiding routine and sustaining desire is to orchestrate wildly inventive dates on a "best friend" basis, sans sex.

Approach is exasperating and, ultimately, anti-romantic. Mired in an eternal courtship with no payoff, Fanfan is baffled by Alexandre's refusal to hop in the sack.

Alexandre's self-righteous celibacy comes across as just plain ornery and misguided. Where there should be delicious tension, helmer — who seems to think that directing actors consists mostly of getting them to smile a lot — dishes up half-baked temerity.

"Fanfan" has been translated into 23 languages, which should assure a built-in international market for so-so pic. —*Lisa Nesselson*

COLORADO COWBOY: THE BRUCE FORD STORY

(DOCU — B&W)

An Arthur Elgort Production. Produced by Ronit Avneri. Directed by Elgort. Camera (b&w), Morten Sandtroen; edited by Paula Heredia. Reviewed at Denver Intl. Film Festival, Oct. 17, 1993. Running time: **78 MIN.**

Arthur Elgort's docu on the life of a million-dollar winner, five times a national rodeo champion, presents an energetic, precise profile of Bruce Ford, the unassuming cowboy from Greeley, Colo., with a unique gift for staying aboard bucking broncos.

Elgort's film has been superbly shot by Morton Sandtroen in black-and-white to achieve a touching, often exciting, always personable account of the life of a generous-spirited man in an old tradition. A second-generation rodeo cowboy whose teenage son is already a Little Britches rodeo champion, Ford appears to be floating above the 1,200 pounds of rebellious horse beneath him, his fringed chaps flying.

Ford speaks in latter-day terms like "ego-builder" and teaches six classes a year in the art of riding bucking broncos. It is the mastery of "something wild" that he seeks.

Sandtroen's photography is terrific, whether catching Ford in his life-threatening rides, the treeless sweeps of Eastern Colorado beneath great thunderheads, horses running in the corral, Ford's family at play or the excitement of rodeo time.

Film does not endeavor to make Ford a paragon of human behavior but leaves him as he is, a man who strives to excel in rodeo action in a completely professional manner.
—*Allen Young*

MRS. DOUBTFIRE

A 20th Century Fox release of a Blue Wolf production. Produced by Marsha Garces Williams, Robin Williams, Mark Radcliffe. Executive producer, Matthew Rushton. Co-producer, Joan Bradshaw. Directed by Chris Columbus. Screenplay, Randi Mayem Singer, Leslie Dixon, based on "Alias Madame Doubtfire," by Anne Fine. Camera (Deluxe color; Panavision widescreen), Donald McAlpine; editor, Raja Gosnell; music, Howard Shore; production design, Angelo Graham; art direction, W. Steven Graham; set design, Steve Saklad, Steve Wolff, Robert Goldstein, Harold Fuhrman; set decoration, Garrett Lewis; costume design, Marit Allen; sound (Dolby), Nelson Stoll; associate producer, Paula DuPre'; assistant director, Geoff Hansen; special makeup created by Greg Cannom; animation by Chuck Jones; casting, Janet Hirschenson, Jane Jenkins. Reviewed at the Samuel Goldwyn Theater, Beverly Hills, Nov. 12, 1993. MPAA Rating: PG-13. Running time: **125 MIN.**
Daniel Hillard/
    Mrs. Doubtfire ..... Robin Williams
Miranda Hillard .... Sally Field
Stu .... Pierce Brosnan
Frank .... Harvey Fierstein
Gloria .... Polly Holliday
Lydia Hillard .... Lisa Jakub
Chris Hillard ..... Matthew Lawrence
Natalie Hillard .... Mara Wilson
Mr. Lundy .... Robert Prosky
Mrs. Sellner .... Anne Haney
Jack .... Scott Capurro

Fox's only major holiday offering should stuff its stockings with a favorite holiday color — green. Although overly sappy in places and probably 20 minutes too long, this Robin Williams-in-drag vehicle provides the comic a slick surface for doing his shtick, within a story possessing broad family appeal. With those elements and a little luck, "Mrs. Doubtfire" may even cover the tab for Williams' last Fox outing, "Toys."

Director Chris Columbus shrewdly brings together many of the same selling points as in his "Home Alone" movies, mixing broad comedic strokes with heavy-handed messages about the magical power of family.

Foremost, however, the director and writers Randi Mayem Singer and Leslie Dixon have crafted a showcase for Williams (who also produced the film) that allows the comic to display his machine-gun-like wit and still play a character — without, for the most part, bringing the action to a screeching halt each time he goes off.

While the concept screams "Tootsie," the tone is more "Mr. Mom." Williams plays a flaky, unemployed actor (the inspired opening has him voicing original animation provided by the venerable Chuck Jones) who quickly botches his son's birthday party and ends up getting tossed out by his wife (Sally Field).

Enormously attached to his kids but limited to weekly visitation, Daniel (Williams) and his brother (Harvey Fierstein), a gay makeup artist, hatch the plan of having Williams masquerade as a matronly nanny — the better to steal precious hours with his three adorable moppets.

Columbus and the writers provide all the expected broad strokes, from Williams' agonizing over the misogynist who invented high heels to his manfully warding off a would-be purse-snatcher, and including an obligatory montage that smacks of "Risky Business" in a skirt.

The pic does reveal occasional inspiration, however, in terms of sharp dialogue — particularly Daniel's costumed efforts to dissuade Miranda (Field) from acting on her attraction to an old beau (Pierce Brosnan) — and in scenes of well-choreographed slapstick lunacy, among them an unexpected visit from a court-appointed supervisor and a crowning scene in which Daniel/Mrs. Doubtfire fulfills two dinner engagements at the same time.

Williams seems most comfortable playing such childlike characters, but few of his films — other than "Dead Poets Society," "Good Morning, Vietnam" and, perhaps most notably, the animated "Aladdin" — have as deftly allowed the comic to strut his comedic stuff and still create a character.

That said, "Mrs. Doubtfire's" warm-fuzzy aspects prove a bit much, from the raspy Sally Brown voice on the wide-eyed youngest daughter (Mara Wilson) to the ham-fisted and plentiful "You're OK even if your parents aren't together" speeches.

Indeed, the filmmakers bend over backward to make the mom and her boyfriend sympathetic — apparently another pseudo-public-service announcement that you don't need bad people to have a bad marriage. Still, it's hard to imagine Miranda not wanting to pummel the exposed Daniel after pouring her heart out to him, as Mrs. Doubtfire, about their life.

Greg Cannom warrants kudos for the amusing body makeup (someone should have told De Niro about this before "Raging Bull"), while the usually reliable Howard Shore lays the powder on a bit thick with his saccharine score. One tastes that too-sweet flavor periodically in "Mrs. Doubtfire," but not enough to spoil the mixture. —*Brian Lowry*

A PERFECT WORLD

A Warner Bros. release of a Malpaso production. Produced by Mark Johnson, David Valdes. Directed by Clint Eastwood. Screenplay, John Lee Hancock. Camera (Technicolor; Panavision widescreen), Jack N. Green; editors, Joel Cox, Ron Spang; music, Lennie Niehaus; production design, Henry Bumstead; art direction, Jack Taylor Jr.; set design, Charlie Vassar, Antoinette Gordon; set decoration, Alan Hicks; costume design, Erica Edell Phillips; sound (Dolby), Jeff Wexler; assistant director, L. Dean Jones; casting, Phyllis Huffman, Liz Keigley (Texas). Reviewed at Warner Bros. screening room, Burbank, Nov. 16, 1993. MPAA Rating: PG-13. Running time: **137 MIN.**

Butch Haynes	Kevin Costner
Red Garnett	Clint Eastwood
Sally Gerber	Laura Dern
Phillip Perry	T.J. Lowther
Terry Pugh	Keith Szarabajka
Tom Adler	Leo Burmester
Dick Suttle	Paul Hewitt
Bobby Lee	Bradley Whitford
Bradley	Ray McKinnon
Gladys Perry	Jennifer Griffin
Mack	Wayne Dehart
Eileen	Linda Hart

Star Kevin Costner and director Clint Eastwood deliver lean, finely chiseled work in "A Perfect World," a somber, subtly nuanced study of an escaped con's complex relationship with an abducted boy that carries a bit too much narrative flab for its own good. Dazzling marquee combination of leading male stars from two generations will provide a hefty initial draw, but audiences and critics are likely to be divided between those moved by the unusual surrogate father-son bonding and viewers put off by the whole subject of child kidnapping. Ultimate B.O. looks to be solid but less than smash.

In his directorial follow-up to the Oscar-winning "Unforgiven," Eastwood once again touches upon certain subjects he has been drawn to in the past, such as ruptured families, bereft children, loner outlaws pushed to the brink, and working people in rural America. This is a disturbing, intimate, noirish road movie paradoxically lensed in widescreen across the vast, sunbaked Texas landscape, its impact made through oblique dialogue and the finesse of performance rather than by broad action and suspense.

Framed by haunting images of its sweaty protagonist lying in the grass as money stirred up by helicopter blades wafts over him, John Lee Hancock's story centers on Butch Haynes (Costner), a lifelong loser toughened up by many years in the pen. With a nod to "Escape From Alcatraz," Butch and his nasty partner Terry (Keith Szarabajka) break out of the joint on Halloween night in 1963, commandeer a car and, after briefly terrorizing a family, make off with 7-year-old Phillip Perry (T.J. Lowther) as a hostage.

Quickly taking up the chase is Texas Ranger Red Garnett (Eastwood), a seasoned, instinctive pro who gets saddled with an unwanted contingent of man hunters, including Laura Dern's state criminologist and Bradley Whitford's odious sharpshooter. Faintly amusing touch has the law gang traveling in a silver mobile trailer loaded with high-tech gizmos with which they hope to track Butch's movements.

Remainder of the picture crosscuts between the hunters and the prey, with heavy emphasis on the latter. Even so, it was not heavy enough, as the scenes among the cops prove uniquely uneventful impediments to forward progress.

After a nervous gas station interlude in which Butch disposes of the menacing Terry, little Phillip begins admiring his abductor for his cool, manly, take-charge ways and his friendly, liberating words of encouragement, things he never hears from his severe, Jehovah's Witness mom.

Phillip can hardly help but begin to see in Butch the father he doesn't have. Fortunately, the sympathetic Butch doesn't have any windy speeches explaining his own unlucky childhood. The most he says is, "I ain't a good man. I ain't the worst neither. Just a breed apart."

Film is strongest in building this erratic, potent and unusually complicated link between man and boy. Resulting emotions pull on the viewer in diverse, disturbing and increasingly involving ways, justifying the protracted finale in which the two play out their relationship under the scrutiny of a phalanx of armed authorities.

Film's major surprise is Costner's performance, which is undoubtedly the best of his career to date. Sporting short hair, shades and a perpetual cigarette, the actor trades in taciturnity here for major dividends, as the slow rate at which his character is revealed produces mounting interest, much in the fashion of some of Eastwood's slow-burn characterizations in the past. Costner skillfully indicates the glimmerings of good instincts buried somewhere deep in Butch that have rarely, if ever, been articulated or brought to the surface.

As the kid, who spends the latter-going running around in a Casper the Friendly Ghost suit, T.J. Lowther is exceptionally good. Engaging company despite adverse circumstances, he achingly conveys the contradictory feelings his experience with Butch summons up.

For once, Eastwood the director has served other actors significantly better than he serves himself. His tough cop role resembles many others he's played before, but this time remains a strictly one-dimensional supporting figure who doesn't really do much. Similarly, Dern's initially adversarial smartypants shows the potential to flower into one of Eastwood's periodic female sparring partners whom he

grows to respect, but role never goes beyond the annoyingly sketchy.

Director brings strong tact and intelligence to the human story, and elaborates it with many grace notes. A climactic scene involving Butch, the kid and a black sharecropper family is brilliantly staged for maximum dread, ambiguous intent and key, but subtle, revelation of Butch's personality.

Pic would have benefited from at least 20 minutes of tightening, nearly all in the police scenes. Fact that tale is set three weeks before JFK's fateful trip to Dallas is fortunately not belabored, but will be noted in light of Eastwood's most recent outing in "In the Line of Fire."

Behind-the-scenes contributions are strong, notably Henry Bumstead's evocative but unstressed period production design, Jack N. Green's sensitive but unshowy lensing and Lennie Niehaus' resourceful score. Eye-catching supporting turns are delivered by Wayne Dehart as the threatened farmhand and Linda Hart as a lustful waitress. —*Todd McCarthy*

ADDAMS FAMILY VALUES

Paramount Pictures presents a Scott Rudin production. Produced by Scott Rudin. Executive producer, David Nicksay. Directed by Barry Sonnenfeld. Screenplay by Paul Rudnick, based on the characters created by Charles Addams. Camera (Deluxe color), Donald Peterman; editors, Arthur Schmidt, Jim Miller; music, Marc Shaiman; production design, Ken Adam; art direction, William Durrell Jr.; set decoration, Marvin March; costume design, Theoni V. Aldredge; visual effects supervisor, Alan Munro; sound (Dolby), Peter Kurland; associate producer, Susan Ringo; assistant directors, Burtt Harris, Mark McGann; casting, David Rubin, Debra Zane. Reviewed at Paramount Studios, Nov. 13, 1993. MPAA Rating: PG-13. Running time: **93 MIN.**

Morticia Addams	Anjelica Huston
Gomez Addams	Raul Julia
Fester Addams	Christopher Lloyd
Debbie Jellinsky	Joan Cusack
Wednesday Addams	Christina Ricci
Granny	Carol Kane
Pugsley Addams	Jimmy Workman
Pubert Addams	Kaitlyn and Kristen Hooper
Lurch	Carel Struycken
Joel Glicker	David Krumholtz
Thing	Christopher Hart
Margaret	Dana Ivey
Gary Granger	Peter MacNicol
Becky Granger	Christine Baranski
Amanda Buckman	Mercedes McNab

They're back!!! Yes, Charles Addams' gloriously macabre characters have returned in "Addams Family Values," and the big-screen sequel looks to be on a commercial par with its inspiration, which scared up $200 million at movie houses around the world.

Nonetheless, the new outing, written by Paul Rudnick and again directed by Barry Sonnenfeld, shares many of the pluses and minuses of the 1991 excursion. It remains perilously slim in the story department but glides over the thin ice with technical razzle-dazzle and an exceptionally winning cast. Chief among its virtues is an anarchic spirit that embraces and delights in all that is politically incorrect.

The screen equivalent of a Rube Goldberg invention kicks into action as Morticia (Anjelica Huston) informs devoted hubby Gomez (Raul Julia) that they are expecting a child — right now. The new spawn, the cuddly, mustachioed Pubert (Kaitlyn and Kristen Hooper), immediately becomes the object of offspring Wednesday (Christina Ricci) and Pugsley Addams' (Jimmy Workman) lethal jealousy.

So the couple try to recruit a nanny. Naturally, the candidates are horrified by their encounter with this unique household. Everyone, that is, except the nauseatingly perky Debbie Jellinsky (Joan Cusack). We soon discover that her bottomless taste for the bizarre is promoted by a desire to woo, wed and murder hapless, lovesick Fester Addams (Christopher Lloyd) and abscond with his considerable financial assets.

When Debbie gets wind that the kids have picked up on her scheme, she devises a clever ruse to pack them off to the snobbishly elite Camp Chippewa.

The story is merely functional. It may be foolhardy to expect a film culled from cartoons and sitcom to have an organic, feature-length plot. The source material, after all, affords seemingly limitless opportunities to hold up a mirror to society and present its converse with humorous bite.

The success of the Addams family in all its incarnations is that subtle balance between normality and the outrageous. Somehow this family unit, which embodies so many wrong values, still has as its bedrock the sanctity of hearth and home.

Huston and Julia are one of the truly magical screen couples; it is a sublime pairing of effortless grace. Their masterful deadpan sincerity makes it impossible to imagine any other combination of actors in the roles.

The cast is uniformly wonderful, with young Ricci providing a depth to her character well beyond her years. Cusack is a lively addition, playing her black widow character as a princess with an attitude. Also notable is Peter MacNicol as the suitably loopy, vane, misguided camp leader, and a raft of cameos from a rogue's gallery that includes Nathan Lane, director Sonnenfeld and Mr. "Mission Impossible," Peter Graves.

Designer Ken Adam creates a rich, textured environment to set the scene. It is a handsome foundation for the other tech credits and such inspired wackiness as Gomez and Morticia's wild, masochistic tango.

"Addams Family Values" rates high on the commercial tote board. It's the kind of wickedly delicious comedy one can savor without adding the proviso of guilty pleasure.
—*Leonard Klady*

THE ICE RUNNER

A Borde Film Releasing release of a Gold Leaf Intl. and Johan Schotte presentation of a Jeffrey M. Sneller production of a Monarch Picture. (International sales: Trident Releasing.) Produced by Sneller. Executive producer, Samuel S. Sneller. Co-producers, Richard Strickland, Jane Ballard. Directed by Barry Samson. Screenplay, Joyce Warren, Clifford Coleman, Joshua Stallings. Camera (Foto-Kem color), Brian Capener; supervising editor, Roy Watts; editor, Stallings; music, Emilio Kauderer; additional music, Jim Goodman; production design, Victor Zenkov, Eric Davies; art direction, Alexei Speransky; set design, Svyatoslav Gavrilov; costume design, Svetlana Borborova; line producer, Eva Andrews; sound (Ultra-Stereo), Sergei Karpenko, Tom Varga; assistant directors, Strickland, Oleg Grigorovitch, Davies; casting, Estelle Tepper, Steve Snyder. Reviewed at the Wilshire Courtyard Screening Room, L.A., Nov. 9. 1993. MPAA Rating: R. Running time: **116 MIN.**

Jeffrey West	Edward Albert
Fyodor	Victor Wong
Lena	Olga Kabo
Kolya	Eugene Lazarev
Petrov	Alexander Kuznitsov
J.C. Kruck	Basil Hoffman
Ed Ross	Bill Bordy
Gorsky	Sergei Ruban

"The Ice Runner" is a strange, minor-key attempt to make an old-fashioned, Cold War-style American thriller in the new Russia. Lensed more than two years ago during the turmoil of the coup attempt against Yeltsin, pic features the trappings of a standard prison camp escape yarn, but with various political and cultural twists that at least lend it a distinctive personality. Being released modestly in L.A. against the holiday biggies, this hasn't got a prayer theatrically but could emerge as a passable vid item.

Mostly English-lingo suspenser has Edward Albert as Jeffrey West, a U.S. government functionary who, in a 1988-set prologue, is caught making a payoff to the Soviet finance minister in Red Square for weapons headed for the Afghan insurgents. With embarrassed Yank diplomats washing their hands of their pawn, West receives a stiff sentence of 12 years at hard labor.

A train wreck on the way to Siberia, however, enables West to assume the identity of one of the accident's casualties and land in a much more benign detention camp in the northern wilderness. In short order, he attaches himself to local sage Fyodor (Victor Wong) and is allowed to take up quarters in an old mill, although he remains under the suspicious eye of prison commandant Kolya (Eugene Lazarev), who abhors the changes his country is undergoing.

Thinking he can trip up West, Kolya brings in the widow of the wreck victim, but it turns out she loathed her boorish mate and chooses to protect West's secret as she shacks up with him. Still, the American jogs incessantly to whip himself into shape for his planned epic run across the ice into home territory.

Despite its fair share of dramatic incident, pic is short on narrative oomph, and too many scenes dwell unnecessarily upon Fyodor dispensing "Karate Kid"-like aphorisms, and on West and the sweet young widow, Lena (Olga Kabo), trying to assess their relationship. Overlong running time is also rife with awkward silent sequences wallpapered by music, often a tell-tale sign of difficulties in scene coverage, sound or performance.

Despite the undoubted rigors of a Russian shoot on remote, frigid locations, tech quality is otherwise OK, and pic gives a plausible picture of a rarely glimpsed area bypassed by time. Cast is similarly acceptable, with Albert grimacing mightily and generally looking not too happy to be where he is, which fortunately is appropriate to his character's situation. —*Todd McCarthy*

ERNEST RIDES AGAIN

An Emshell Producers Group presentation. Produced by Stacy Williams. Executive producer, Coke Sams. Co-producer, Tom Rowe. Directed by John R. Cherry III. Screenplay, Cherry, William M. Akers. Camera (CFI color), David Geddes; editor, Craig Bassett; music, Bruce Arntson, Kirby Shelstad; production design, Chris August; art direction, Helen Veronica Jarvis; set decoration, Mary Lou Storey; costume design, Martha Snetsinger; sound (Dolby), Rich Schirmer; assistant director, Patrice Leung; casting, Sid Kozak. Reviewed at Loews Charles, Boston, Nov. 12, 1993. MPAA Rating: PG. Running time: **92 MIN.**

Ernest P. Worrell	Jim Varney
Abner Melon	Ron K. James
Nan Melon	Linda Kash
Dr. Glencliff	Tom Butler
Frank	Duke Ernsberger
Joe	Jeffrey Pillars

The fifth in the series of slapstick comedies about Ernest P. Worrell (Jim Varney) will please his fans but is unlikely to convince anyone else as to it merits. Self-distributed film should get quick playoff while letting viewers know — through an end-of-pic teaser — that "Ernest Goes to School" is already set for release next August.

Story involves a college professor (Ron K. James) who believes that the British crown jewels were hidden in a Revolutionary War cannon. How and why is never explained, but with Ernest's help he is proven right.

What ensues is a long chase as they and the runaway cannon are pursued by a villainous collector of antiquities, the professor's wife, British secret agents and two vacuum cleaner salesmen. Even Varney says at one point that it's little more than a live-action cartoon.

Humor is broad, with Varney getting in several of his trademark "KnowwhutImean?" comments, but also allowing him to show a gift for comic characterization far beyond the moronic Ernest.

Tech credits are solid and locations in British Columbia, doubling for Virginia, provide colorful backgrounds for the action.

Film is preceded by the short "Mr. Bill Goes to Washington." Like Ernest, Mr. Bill keeps mining the same material for an aud that likes it that way. —*Daniel M. Kimmel*

THE PHILADELPHIA EXPERIMENT 2

A Trimark release of a Mark Levinson production. Produced by Mark Levinson, Doug Curtis. Executive producer, Mark Amin. Co-producer, Andrew Hersh. Line producer, Paul Hellerman. Directed by Stephen Cornwell. Screenplay, Kevin Rock, Nick Paine. Camera (color), Ronn Schmidt; editor, Nina Gilberti; music, Gerald Couriet; production design, Armin Ganz; art direction, Kirk Petruccelli; costume design, Eileen Kennedy; sound (Dolby), Ed White, Ken Mantlo; special effects, Frank Ceglia; stunts, Rawn Hutchinson; assistant director, Chris Krengel; casting, Linda Phillips Palo. Reviewed at the Manhattan 2 Theater, N.Y., Nov. 17, 1993. MPAA Rating: PG-13. Running time: **97 MIN.**

David Herdeg	Brad Johnson
Jess	Marjean Holden
Dr. William Mailer/	
Friederich Mahler	Gerrit Graham
Professor Longstreet	James Greene
Logan	Geoffrey Blake
Decker	Cyril O'Reilly
Benjamin	
Herdeg	John Christian Grass

Trimark's "Philadelphia Experiment 2" is a middling sci-fi sequel to the middling 1984 New World original. Although the current opus has some marketable and even clever elements, there are not enough of them to make a dent at the B.O. prior to its quick flight to videoland.

Original pic dealt with a World War II radar experiment that went awry and sent a U.S. warship adrift in the space-time continuum. In spite of inane plot developments and numbing car chases, director Stewart Raffill managed to impart some vulnerability to the protagonists.

"P.E. 2," however, plunges into melodrama with abandon. The son of a scientific adviser to the Nazis, Gerrit Graham is an American government scientist intent on producing a super stealth bomber, even though this risks continued tampering with the s-t continuum as well as afflicting the surviving sailor of the original (Brad Johnson taking over from Michael Pare).

Johnson finds himself transported to a nightmare world of internment camps and Orwellian

November 29, 1993 (Cont.)

brainwashing. A neat plot twist reveals that Graham's experiment sent the fighter plane into the past, where it landed in Nazi Germany. The metaphysical time-playing, however, plays second fiddle to a humdrum action plot.

Johnson is OK as the beleaguered hero, while Graham strikes the right notes as the megalomaniac villain without going over the top. Marjean Holden briefly enlivens things as a guerrilla heroine before returning in a self-consciously sappy coda.

Ronn Schmidt's lensing and Armin Ganz's production design provide some visual menace to the Nazi netherworld, but Stephen Cornwell's direction could have used more dramatic consistency.

Pic abounds in a number of mild in-jokes, references to the Nazi empire as the New World Order, and such gags as naming the Nazi scientist Mahler. A more intriguing prank is that, per the credits, the Nazi propaganda film of pastoral paternalism was taken from WPA documentaries. —*Fred Lombardi*

LONDON FEST

IS THAT ALL THERE IS?

(BRITISH — 16mm)

A Yaffle Films production for BBC Scotland. (International sales: BBC Enterprises, London.) Produced by Trevor Ingman. Executive producer, John Archer. Directed, written by Lindsay Anderson. Camera (Metrocolor), Jonathan Collinson; editor, Nicolas Gaster; music, Alan Price; sound, John Anderton. Reviewed at London Film Festival, Nov. 15, 1993. Running time: **54 MIN.**

With: Lindsay Anderson, Alexander Anderson, Bernard Kops, David Sterne, Mark Sigsworth, Brian Pettifer, Andrew Eaton, Tom Sutcliffe, David Sherwin, Jocelyn Herbert, David Storey, Alan Price, Murray Anderson.

Lindsay Anderson's typically eclectic contribution to "The Director's Place," the BBC Scotland's series of self-portraits, shows the septuagenarian helmer alive and well and feisty. Anderson's first venture behind the lens in three years will delight buffs and find a ready niche on specialized webs.

The series has already yielded fascinating, offbeat works by Nagisa Oshima, John Boorman and Susan Seidelman. Anderson's "Place" is not a town but his north London apartment, where friends and colleagues come to vent their spleen, discuss work or chew the fat on the state of 1990s Britain. Anderson's dry take on his own marginalized situation is also an ironic commentary on his own place as a director in the media world.

The film starts with a quote from the 1956 Free Cinema Manifesto, in which Anderson was a prime mover: "Perfection is not an aim." Thereafter, it shows him getting up in the morning, lying in the tub surrounded by one-sheets from his movies, receiving relatives and colleagues and traveling by public transport (with his pensioner's travel pass) for a heart checkup. A celeb-studded boat trip along the Thames, during which the ashes of actresses Jill Bennett and Rachel Roberts are belatedly scattered on the waters, forms a moving finale, supported by Alan Price's music.

It is never clear which parts of the film are scripted, and this blurring of lines lends pic a teasing feel. In this staged reality, Anderson clearly relishes his role of puppet master, drawing out colleagues' views and dispensing his own with knowing, crusty humor.

A discussion about John Ford with a BBC producer leads to an assessment of Archie Stout's lensing on "Fort Apache." Later, Anderson opines that David Lean is "overpraised," and he likes Michael Powell only "up to a point." In a funny sequence with longtime scripter David Sherwin, Anderson reads aloud rejection slips on submitted projects (including a treatment for "If ... 2") from companies like the BBC and Channel 4.

Production values are modest but neat, with trim editing by Nicolas Gaster and OK 16mm photography by Jonathan Collinson.

—*Derek Elley*

FEARLESS: THE HUNTERWALI STORY

(INDIAN — DOCU)

A Wadia Movietone production. (International sales: Wadia Movietone, Bombay.) Produced, directed, written by Riyad Vinci Wadia. Executive producer, Farhad A. Ostavari. Camera (color), R.M. Rao, Anil Mehta, Faroukh Mistry; editor, Arunabha Mukherjee; music, Shiv Mathur; production design, Seema Sawhny; sound, Indrajit Neogi. Reviewed at London Film Festival, Nov. 11, 1993. Running time: **61 MIN.**

With: Mary Evans-Wadia, John Cavas, Homi Wadia, Shyam Benegal, Firoze Wangoola, B.K. Karanjia.

An obscure corner of Indian popular cinema is entertainingly excavated in "Fearless: The Hunterwali Story," an hour-long docu about a stunt star of Bombay cinema who made Pearl White look like a wimp. Item is a natural for fests and enterprising webs, and camp subject has crossover potential to gay fests.

Subject is one Mary Evans, born 1910 in Perth, Western Australia, to a soldier father. Moving to India when her dad was transferred, she worked in the circus and as a singer before striking lucky in the 1935 pic "Hunterwali," playing a big, butch Zorro-type who socked men in the jaw and leapt around with a whip.

"Hunterwali" was a B.O. sensation, spawning the tacky action/ stunt genre in Hindi cinema and a career for Evans (billed as "Fearless" Nadia) that stretched to the late 1950s and some 40 pics with titles like "Diamond Queen," "Jungle Princess" and "Tigress."

Docu is as much a portrait of Bombay's voracious movie industry as of Evans. Director Riyad Vinci, grand-nephew of Evans and inheritor of Wadia Movietone, draws freely on the company's archives for an entertaining collection of clips. Sound in some of the interviews needs improving (or subtitling) but otherwise the film's 35mm values are OK. —*Derek Elley*

JUST FRIENDS

(BELGIAN-FRENCH-DUTCH)

A Wajnbrosse Prods. production. (International sales: Mercure, Paris.) Produced by Marc-Henri Wajnberg. Executive producer, Nicole La Bouverie. Directed by Wajnberg. Screenplay, Pierre Sterckx, Alexandre Wajnberg. Camera (color), Remon Fromont; editor, Ludo Troch; music/musical arrangements, Michel Herr, Archie Shepp; production design, Emmanuelle Batz; art direction, Frederic Roullier-Gall; costume design, Tamara Jongsma; sound (Dolby), Jean-Bernard Thomasson, Bernard Morelle. Reviewed at London Film Festival, Nov. 11, 1993. (Also in San Sebastian fest.) Running time: **99 MIN.**

Jack	Josse de Pauw
Lucy	Ann-Gisel Glass
Anita	Sylvie Milhaud
Andre	Charles Berling
(French dialogue)	

Likable performances and some off-the-wall humor bring a fresh glow to "Just Friends," an easygoing tale of two pals and their girls against a late 1950s jazz background. Confident directorial bow of Belgian scripter-actor Marc-Henri Wajnberg looks a cert for TV playoff but could also get limited theatrical gigs with good reviews.

Set in 1959 Antwerp, the movie gets off to a punchy start with saxophonist Jack (Josse de Pauw) and his g.f., singer Anita (Sylvie Milhaud), rehearsing a bebop number in a small hall. Jack, who works on the docks to pay the rent, idolizes Bird and dreams of making it in New York but is stuck in ultra-conventional Belgium playing to afternoon tea parties.

His friend and neighbor Andre (Charles Berling) is an avant-garde sculptor whose oars aren't all in the water. Andre takes up with the equally loopy Lucy (Ann-Gisel Glass), who causes a split between the two friends when she shares her bed platonically with Jack one night. Later, Jack gets a chance to make his Stateside dream come true.

There's nothing particularly new in the storyline, which has a strong Gallic flavor to its emotional makeup. But the characters are interesting, the humor is gently anarchic, and Wajnberg's direction has shape and a feel for the big screen.

Playing by the four principals meshes well, with De Pauw especially convincing as the Flemish reed-lover and Berling a light foil as his Walloon friend. Milhaud brings a mature sexiness to the role of the singer, and Glass an otherworldly, waiflike charm.

Technically, pic is excellent, with hunky Dolby sound for the musical moments and period art direction that doesn't look pinched.

—*Derek Elley*

LA GENTE DE LA UNIVERSAL

(THE PEOPLE AT UNIVERSAL)

(SPANISH-COLOMBIAN-BULGARIAN)

An Igeldo Zine Produkzioak (Spain)/ Fotoclub-76 (Colombia)/Tchapline (Bulgaria) production, in association with Channel 4/TVE/Euskai Media. (International sales: Igeldo Zine, San Sebastian.) Produced by Angel Amigo. Executive producer, Carlos Guerrero, Manuel Arias, Kroum Manoilov. Directed by Felipe Aljure. Screenplay, Aljure, Arias, Guillermo Calle. Camera (color), Kalo F. Berridi; editor, Antonio Perez Reina; music, Pascal Gaigne; production design, Inaki Ros; art direction, Charlotte Haeger; costume design, Luis Jairo Retrepo; sound (Dolby), Valentin Kirilov; assistant director, Rodrigo Espina. Reviewed at London Film Festival, Nov. 6, 1993. Running time: **127 MIN.**

Diogenes Hernandez	Alvaro Rodriguez
Fabiola	Jennifer Steffens
Clemente Fernandez	Robinson Diaz
Margarita	Ana Maria Aristizabal
Gaston	Ramon Aguirre
Begona	Aitzpea Goenaga
Francois	Francois Bassile

A raunchy black comedy centered on a spitball Bogota p.i. agency, "The People at Universal" marks a lively debut by Colombian director Felipe Aljure. Tightened by some 20 minutes, especially from its discursive latter reels, pic could prove a tasty item for tube buyers and even cross over to some arthouse biz.

Film moves at a fast lick, with a cleverly worked out wheels-within-wheels plot that has everyone doing the dirty on everyone else. Central characters are the sexually insatiable trio of the Universal Detective Agency, run by ex-cop Diogenes (Alvaro Rodriguez) with his sexy wife Fabiola (Jennifer Steffens) and handsome nephew Clemente (Robinson Diaz). Clemente and Fabiola go at it like bunnies whenever the boss isn't around.

November 29, 1993 (Cont.)

When Diogenes is hired by a jailed Spanish mobster (Ramon Aguirre) to find out who's sleeping with his porn-star mistress (Ana Maria Aristizabal), the sexual and financial double-crossing moves into high gear.

Playing is straight-faced but colorful, heightened by antsy camera work, a perky score and large dollops of Latin machismo and sexuality. Final reels lack verve and overdo the violence; nudity throughout is frank but natural. Performances are excellent down the line, led by Rodriguez as the simian Diogenes.

Tech credits are fine, with postproduction (done in Bulgaria) up to scratch.
—*Derek Elley*

GADAEL LENIN

(LEAVING LENIN)

(BRITISH)

A Gaucho Cyf/S4C Television (Wales) production, in association with Lara Globus Intl. (St. Petersburg). (International sales: Mentrau Cyf, Cardiff.) Produced by Pauline Williams. Directed by Endaf Emlyn. Screenplay, Sion Eirian, Emlyn. Camera (color), Ray Orton; editor, Chris Lawrence; music, John Hardy; art direction, Vera Zelenskaya; costume design, Noelle Rees Rowlands; sound, Jeff Mathews. Reviewed at London Film Festival, Nov. 5, 1993. Running time: **93 MIN.**

Eileen Jenkins	Sharon Morgan
Mostyn Jenkins	Wyn Bowen Harris
Merv	Ifan Huw Dafydd
Sharon	Shelley Rees
Rhian	Catrin Mai
Sasha	Ivan Shvedov
Spike	Steffan Trefor

(Welsh dialogue; English subtitles)

Welsh-language cinema adds another feather to its cap with "Leaving Lenin," an engaging light comedy about a group of teachers and high school students on a snafu-riddled trip to Russia. Commissioned by Welsh web S4C, result has the look and feel of a theatrical feature and could enjoy modest outings at specialized sites, though use of subtitled Welsh dialogue could limit it commercially.

Simple story starts with the motley band being split up when the Russian train on which they're traveling is divided in the middle of the night. The youngsters go on to St. Petersburg while their three teachers are carted off down a branch line to the countryside.

One sensitive student (Steffan Trefor) has a homosexual awakening with a Russian (Ivan Shvedov), despite the attentions of a Welsh girl (Catrin Mai). Meanwhile, the adult teachers are having their own interpersonal problems as they make their way to St. Petersburg.

The film is very different in style from director Endaf Emlyn's previous feature, the semi-mystical "One Full Moon." Though the use of Welsh dialogue for a foreign-set pic seems unnecessarily fastidious, the overall tone is light and easy, with not too much soul-searching: The spirit of Czech comedy is never far away. Only weakness is the script's failure to make the adults' adventures as involving as the kids'.

Performances are fine all around, with Sharon Morgan a standout as a wise, knowing teacher. Editing is smooth, and Ray Orton's good-looking 35mm lensing of the Russian locations betrays no signs of the hasty five-week shoot.
—*Derek Elley*

I AM A SEX ADDICT

(U.S.-BRITISH — DOCU — 16mm)

A Dox Deluxe production for BBC Television. (International sales: Dox Deluxe, L.A.) Produced by Vikram Jayanti. Executive producer, Andre Singer. Directed, written by Jayanti, John Powers. Camera (DuArt color), Maryse Alberti; editor, Ila von Hasperg; music, Charlie Skarbeck; sound, Scott Breindel. Reviewed at London Film Festival, Nov. 13, 1993. (Also in Locarno, Sao Paulo fests.) Running time: **81 MIN.**

More is definitely less in "I Am a Sex Addict," which takes an intriguing idea (sex junkies) and grinds it into the ground with repetitive talking-head interviews and silly visual inserts.

Main subjects are a nurse, actor, college student, accountant, computer consultant and performance artist who talk frankly about their past and present addictions across the whole range of sexuality, including some intriguing byways. Language and visuals are ultraupfront, with one man taking the viewer through his album of genital worship and a woman parading a body that would give Jabba the Hutt pause for thought.

At 50 minutes or so, and minus its extraneous inserts, this could have made a witty, sometimes sad, shock item. But apart from a bedside interview with a couple whose sheer joy in matters carnal is almost inspirational, these aren't people you'd want to be trapped in a ski lift with.

L.A.-based documaker Vikram Jayanti and co-director film critic John Powers fail to get further than the lobby in trying to penetrate the inner sanctums of their subjects' compulsions. Intellectual ballast comes in the form of occasional readings by Hubert Selby from his sex-urge novel "The Demon."

Film was commissioned by British pubcaster BBC for its docu series "Fine Cut" but pulled just prior to its skedded March 1993 airdate as too controversial. Filmmakers have since cut 32 minutes for TV broadcast, but retain rights to distribute this full version. Tech credits are average.
—*Derek Elley*

PARAKALO YINIKES MIN KLETE

(PLEASE LADIES, DON'T CRY)

(GREEK)

A Greek Film Centre production. Produced by Yannis Gavrilos, Stavros Tsiolis. Directed, written by Tsiolis, Christos Vakalopolous. Camera (color), Vassilis Kapsouros; editor, Kostas Iordanidis; music, Makis Bekos. Reviewed at Vancouver Intl. Film Festival, Oct. 7, 1993. Running time: **89 MIN.**

With: Argiris Bakirtzis, Dimitris Vlachos, Dora Masklavanou, Nicholas Kekkos, Emily Papachristou.

A wistful comedy of Balkan manners, "Please Ladies, Don't Cry" concerns a pair of traveling icon restorers who never quite get around to their work. Instead, they root around for small joys and philosophize incessantly about the decay of ancient treasures (like themselves). The pic is gentle, nostalgic, very pretty and curiously unnecessary.

Deep-voiced, hound-faced Argiris Bakirtzis makes a strong impression as the younger of the two quasi scam artists — his ministrations to the old master (Dimitris Vlachos) are full of tender regard and quiet resentment. The pair flit from one mild and pleasantly predictable adventure to the next as they head toward a vague contract in an Arcadian mountain village.

When an attractive young painter (Dora Masklavanou) insists on joining them at their hilltop encampment, Bakirtzis is torn between lusty and paternal inclinations; he eventually manages to scare the woman — and what remains of the storyline — away.

The music and lensing are consistently sweet, but the pic feels dragged-out at less than 90 minutes. Co-helmer Stavros Tsiolis — using some of the same core ensemble featured in his solo ventures — has so much affection for his characters that he can't bear to bring any discipline to their meanderings.
—*Ken Eisner*

BAODAO DA MENG

(BODO)

(TAIWANESE)

A New Taiwan Pictures (Taipei) production. Produced by Tzou Bukam. Directed by Huang Mingchuan. Screenplay, Mingchuan, Angel Chen. Camera (color), Mingchuan, Huang, J.J. Chen; music, ToMoMoTo, Shi Chenlan. Reviewed at Vancouver Intl. Film Festival, Oct. 7, 1993. (Also in Hawaii fest.) Running time: **80 MIN.**

Aki	Huang Zhiqi
Kanghua	Shi Nanhua
Yisan	Tsai Yi
Yisan's Father	Huang Hongbin
Bodo	Bodo

This heavy-handed metaphor for life and politics in Taiwan — with the "action" moved to a microcosmic island off its own coast — will be slow going for all but the most studious Asia-watchers. And for them, it will just be boringly obvious.

Helmer Huang Mingchuan's greatest strength is his interest in the little-known aboriginal folk culture of the region — something he explored at (considerable) length in "The Man From Island West."

Here he's content to interweave Formosan ghost tales (mostly via interesting sound effects) with the spare saga of a military outpost.

The fortress is a place so dull, officers order enlisted men to shoot beer cans off their heads. When a captain dies in this jolly sport, private Yisan (Tsai Yi) heads for the bush, where he encounters a haughty prostitute (Shi Nanhua) and a longhaired rebel gun-runner called Bodo (the actor, character and film are all named after Taiwan's Prosperity Island cigarettes).

There's also a less-than-engaging subplot about a soldier (Huang Zhiqi) who is obsessed with a weirdly illustrated notebook the captain left behind — providing the most arresting images in an otherwise flat-looking pic.

Only thesp who makes an impression in this static, close-upladen imbroglio is Huang Hongbin, as Yisan's Polynesian-looking father.

He never finds the lad, but his crinkled stare at the far horizon says volumes about what's been lost in the South China Sea.
—*Ken Eisner*

BOKURA WA MINNA IKITEIRU

(WE ARE NOT ALONE)

(JAPANESE)

A Shochiku Co. production, in association with the Melies Co. (Intl. sales: Shochiku Company Ltd., Tokyo). Produced by Toshio Kobayashi. Directed by Yojiro Takita. Screenplay, Nobuyuki Isshiki. Camera (color), Takeshi Hamada; editor, Isao Tomita; music, Yasuaki Shimizu. Reviewed at Vancouver Intl. Film Festival, Oct. 13, 1993. Running time: **115 MIN.**

With: Harry Sanada, Tsutomu Yamazaki, Kyusaku Shimada, Ittoku Kishibe, Bengaru, Rakuko Tane.

"Made in Japan" is the battle cry of the businessmen competing for international building contracts in this globe-trotting comedy-adventure from Yojiro Takita, who hit homeland pay dirt with "The Yen Family."

Things start with a prototypical go-getter (Harry Sanada) embarking on his first trip to Talckistan, a tin-pot Southeast Asian dictatorship (Thailand, in a bit of geographical typecasting). There he hooks up with a jaded older company man (Tsutomu Yamazaki, the milk-truck cowboy from "Tampopo") who appears to have gone native but actually maintains a cynical detachment from everything around him.

As does the movie, which holds Nippon materialism, corrupt military governments and insurgent opportunism in equal contempt. While that keeps the tale emotionally cool, it does give it satirical bite — who wouldn't laugh at the sight of Japanese suits trying to protect themselves from gunfire by handing out business cards?

The attractive pic's patently insular title will mean plenty in its parochial island base, but it needs to be rethought to move beyond marginal foreign consumption. "Made in Japan" springs to mind.

—*Ken Eisner*

THE PERFECT MAN

(CANADIAN)

An Alliance (Canada) release of a Midnite Cafe Prods. (Calgary) production in association with Telefilm Canada and the Alberta Motion Picture Development Corp. Produced, directed by Wendy Hill-Tout. Screenplay, Hill-Tout, Lynda Shorten. Camera (color), Peter Wunstorf; editor, Lenka Svab; music, George Blondheim; art direction, Ken Remple; costume design, Delores Burke; sound, Rick Youck; associate producer, Fe Wills; line producer, Tom Benz. Reviewed at Vancouver Intl. Film Festival, Oct. 12, 1993. Running time: **94 MIN.**
Mother .... Phyllis Diller
Melissa .... Michelle Little
Michael .... Garwin Sanford
Also with: Janice Ungaro, Brian Jensen.

Straining hard to hit the pulse of contemporary urban relationships, this slight Canadian comedy offers a few engaging moments that are as familiar as an old couple's favorite spats. The presence of Phyllis Diller in a largely dramatic part is the pic's only convincing hook.

Although it's a supporting part, Diller toplines as the neurotic, secretly drinking suburban mom to would-be artist Melissa (Michelle Little), who's not sure whether she wants to chuck dependable, live-in boyfriend Michael (Garwin Sanford) for the more bohemian lifestyle represented by worldly gallery owner Peter (Brian Jensen). The script stacks the deck so heavily toward the status quo, it's hard to empathize with ditzy Melissa, much less be bothered about her plight.

Nicely lensed and staged, with fresh Calgary settings, the pic makes some stabs at quirky texture, but incidental characters aren't fleshed-out enough to give off sparks. Comic thesp Janice Ungaro, for example, is wasted as Melissa's gal pal, whose rampant promiscuity is raised for laughs, then used against her without explanation. Diller's scenes also intrigue but never pay off with significant revelations in character or story.

All thesps acquit themselves well, but helmer and co-scripter Wendy Hill-Tout bets everything on the wan charm and chirpy timing of Little, who will strike some as a Meg Ryan without the big-time hair. Sanford's amiably urbane presence ultimately serves to undercut the repeated assertion that his character is an insensitive boor (and an American "cultural imperialist," although his accent sounds more Canadian than hers, eh). Unintentionally bad grammar mars already struggling dialogue.

Far from perfect, but friendly enough to make a decent TV date, this "Man" shouldn't expect many nights out.

—*Ken Eisner*

LOST CAUSE

A Tobia Prods. presentation. Produced by Karin Dichiara, Lawrence Silverstein. Directed by Silverstein. Screenplay, Dmitri Ragano. Camera (color, 16mm), Daniel Robin; editor, Scott Petersen; sound, Anthony Muzik; art coordinator, Don Dichiara. Reviewed on vidcassette in San Francisco, Oct. 21, 1993. (In Cinequest, San Jose Film Festival.) Running time: **75 MIN.**
Rufus Zapruder .... Mike Hansel
Jerry Kingdom .... Joe Briggs
Ellman Louis ..... Lawrence Silverstein
Dulcinea .... Cindy Morales
Zero .... Greg Current

Good use of San Francisco location shooting and backing music are the main virtues of this indie drama. Such superficial niceties on a $20,000 budget aren't enough to compensate for glib script and shallow characters.

Dragging out the familiar and forced young-white-Turk/wise-black-mentor buddy formula, pic has troubled Pacific Heights brat Rufus stomping out when dad insists he attend Dartmouth. (Given the lad's apparent dim-bulb status, this option stretches credulity.) He lands at the pad of pal Ellman (director Silverstein), guitarist in the rock band for which Rufus is the inept drummer.

Ellman stumbles upon fortyish pianist Jerry at a bar, luring the taciturn musician to join a band rehearsal. Jerry is bitter from a prior brush with jazz-circuit fame.

Dialogue in Dmitri Ragano's script is cloddish, but real problem is Rufus' personality. Witless, tantrum-prone, irresponsible, he's like Keanu Reeves' "Ted" minus humor — in short, a moron. Despite one stilted speech pointing blame at his unloving parents, we don't find Rufus remotely sympathetic, nor can we believe level-headed Jerry would. Since that relationship is film's crux, story never lifts above contrivance. Perfs are only as good as the context allows.

Tech credits are decent, though. Lensing nicely exploits S.F.'s varied backgrounds; lots of soundtrack tunes (blues, jazz, rock) provide needed pacing and nuance. It's unclear, however, whether the retread blues-rock of Rufus' band is actually meant to be as lame as it sounds.

—*Dennis Harvey*

SANDRA, C'EST LA VIE
(SANDRA: A LOVE STORY)
(SWISS)

A Television Suisse Romande and Gaumont Television co-production with the participation of M6/RCS/Cinevista-Nos/Kunst en Kino. Produced by TV Suisse Romande. Executive producers, Philippe Berthet, Alain Bloch, Raymond Voullaimoz. Directed by Dominique Othenin-Girard. Screenplay, Michel Viala, Denise Fusco, with Philippe Conil. Dialogue, Fusco. Camera (color), Jacky Mahrer; editor, Suzanne Lang-Willar; music, Beatrice Lapp; production design, Luc Marelli; costumes, Nadia Ceunoud; sound, Michael Kharat; casting, Florence Dugowson. Reviewed on vidcassette in San Francisco, Oct. 21, 1993. (In Cinequest, San Jose Film Festival.) Running time: **92 MIN.**
Sandra .... Lisa Fusco
Marie .... Imogen Stubbs
Julien .... Jean-Philippe Ecoffey
Fred .... Frederic Van Den Driessche
Veronique .... Valeria Bruni-Tedeschi
Marcel .... Franck Rousselet
Mme. Chevalier .... Veronique Silver
Voice of Sandra
(French version) .... Zouc

Aslick but predictably sentimental retread of "Rain Man" and its ilk, "Sandra C'est la vie" adds no new wrinkles to screen portraiture of the mentally handicapped. While some fests may bite, Euro TV is where this middling project was conceived and where it's bound to stay.

Born with Down's syndrome, Sandra is the liveliest resident at the pleasant state-run institution she has inhabited as long as she can remember. But having reached 16, she must be released into the care of mother Marie. Latter has scarcely dealt with her offspring over the years and is unprepared to accept this new responsibility. Fearing reaction of loutish fiance Fred, Marie tries to pass her "secret" daughter off as a sister.

It takes no more than a day for cretinous Fred to blow his top while Marie's at work. Hitherto sheltered from such emotional stress, Sandra runs away — straight to the houseboat of artist Julien, whom she'd met and "fascinated" just recently.

This last quasi-romantic strand plays a mite queasy. But pic's main problem is familiar among such scenarios — the central idiot savant figure is too good to be true, straining credibility and exaggerating black-and-white moral divisions. Sandra is independent-minded, wise, good-humored. So what if she can't wash dishes properly?

By creating such an idealized persona, pic muddies any clear understanding of Down's syndrome. It also undercuts dramatic tension.

Imogen Stubbs is good in the uncomplicated role of Marie, who bore a child when she was just a teen herself. Other perfs are pro, though contrived script precludes much depth.

Bright lensing echoes Sandra's upbeat p.o.v.; other tech aspects are solid. One problem in French version (another is available in English) is Zouc's vocal turn as Sandra. Her dubbed characterization is so adult and assured that it further distances reality of figure's disability.

Co-scenarist Denise Fusco is the sister of leading actress Lisa, who has Down's syndrome. While the narrative is pointedly not autobiographical, its brew of wish-fulfillment and earnestness makes one wish D. Fusco had hewed closer to actual experience.

—*Dennis Harvey*

OCEANO ATLANTIS
(ATLANTIS OCEAN)
(BRAZILIAN)

A Sky Light Cinema and Naive Films presentation. (International sales: Naive Producoes Artisticas Ltda., Sao Paulo.) Executive producers, Rene Bittencourt, Maria Figueiredo, Isa Castro. Directed by Francisco de Paula. Screenplay, Ciro Pessoa, de Paula. Camera (color), Dib Lutfi, Pedro Farkas; editor, Renato Nena Moreira; music, Pessoa; assistant directors, Helena Lenos, Philis Huber. Reviewed at Sao Paulo Intl. Film Festival, Nov. 1, 1993. Running time: **84 MIN.**
With: Nuno Leal Maia, Dercy Goncalves, Antonio Abujamra.
(English and Portuguese dialogue)

Evidently produced on a budget that would have crimped Roger Corman's style in the 1950s, this incoherent Brazilian indie has the will but not the way to present an alternative fantasy world populated by survivors of a devastating tidal wave that wiped out Rio de Janeiro. Sorry effort succumbs to all its limitations of talent and production values, so that even the most indulgent sci-fi fans would have trouble getting through it. Export potential is nil.

With an apparent nod to the international market, this thoroughly Brazilian production is played largely in English, but the bad sound and worse dialogue delivery ironically make it that much more difficult to figure out what happens in the course of the numbingly obscure story.

Camera remains mostly focused on a middle-aged gent named Dionysus who, after a spell in some sort of detention center/loony bin, makes periodic underwater diving trips, meditates on the legend of Penelope and finally ends up with a hippy-dippy cult that speaks an incomprehensible language and hopes to impress upon the modern world the benign goodness of the ancient society it reveres.

Filmmakers' noble motive would appear to be to assert the need for a new order based on agrarian, peaceful and spiritual ideals, but there are ways to do this other than to show meagerly costumed actors uttering gibberish in front of black curtains as in some junior high school production. Amateur-night venture truly possesses the vaguely disembodied feel of the cheapest off-Hollywood efforts of 30-40 years ago.

Due to the woefully apparent language barrier, film is edited so as to mostly avoid showing actors as they are speaking, resulting in a narrative largely composed of cutaways.

Helmer Francisco de Paula keeps introducing new characters whose identity and function forever remain a mystery, and applicability of the Atlantis legend is purely conjectural.
— *Todd McCarthy*

HOF

DIE TOEDLICHE MARIA

(DEADLY MARIA)

(GERMAN)

A Sputnik release (Germany) of a Liebesfilm production. Produced by Stefan Arndt, Tom Tykwer. Co-producer (for ZDF), Liane Jessen. Directed, written by Tykwer, from a story by Tykwer, Christiane Voss. Camera (color), Frank Griebe; editor, Katja Dringenberg; music, Tykwer; art direction, Jeanne Waltz, Alexander Manasse; set decoration, Sybille Kelber, Attila Saygel; costume design, Monika Jacobs; sound, Arno Wilms; associate producer, Milanka Comfort; assistant director, Lih Janowitz. Reviewed at Intl. Hof Film Days, Hof, Germany, Oct. 29, 1993. Running time: **106 MIN.**
Maria .... Nina Petri
Maria's father .... Josef Bierbichler
Heinz .... Peter Franke
Dieter .... Joachim Krol
Maria, aged 16 .... Katja Studt
Maria, aged 10 .... Juliane Heinemann

As slick and multifaceted as anything by David Lynch or the Coen Bros., though without their humor, "Deadly Maria"

reps the debut of a major new German talent in director Tom Tykwer. However, the depressing and ultimately predictable story of an oppressed wife's revenge makes the pic more suitable for TV, video and festival outings than general situations.

Maria (played well but dispassionately by Nina Petri) has been neglected and oppressed all her life, both by her invalid father (Josef Bierbichler) and by her cold husband (Peter Franke).

When her husband takes away the household money she has been squirreling away, Maria kills him and her father.

The film ends there, the last image being the uneasy expression on the face of her new lover (cuddly Joachim Krol, last seen in "No More Mr. Nice Guy") as he discovers the crime.

Though viewers are supposed to identify with Maria, Tykwer's psychodrama script is too predictable and the woman's personality too introverted. Character quirks like her killing and collecting dead flies are less insightful than just plain boring.

As a technician, though, Tykwer shows talent, with none of the "realistic" style favored by many young German filmmakers.

One of the interesting things about the pic is its grafting of commercial techniques onto an arthouse theme.

Tech credits are highly developed. Frank Griebe's photography is precise and controlled, with color and lighting maintaining a line between realism and fantasy. Production design is immaculate.

Music, by Tykwer himself, is high-powered, lending the depressing story the urgency of a Hitchcock thriller.
— *Eric Hansen*

ADAMSKI

(GERMAN)

A Senso Film production. Produced by Georg Kilian. Directed, written by Jens Becker. Camera (color), Aicke Fricke; editor, Ines Bluhm; music, Rainer Boehm; art direction, Katrin Steinmann; costume design, Gertraud Wahl; sound, Lutz Schoenherr; assistant director, Sabine Weyrich. Reviewed at Intl. Hof Film Days, Hof, Germany, Oct. 29, 1993. Running time: **89 MIN.**
Adamski .... Steffen Schult
Lili .... Nadja Engel
Wolf .... Axel Werner
Erika .... Petra-Maria Cammin
Fraulein
  Ziglinski .... Deborah Kaufmann
Milchgesicht .... Daniel Morgenroth
Barsch .... Udo Kroschwald
Brauer .... Frank Lienert

The charming story of a quirky love affair between a security guard and a shoplifter in low-rent Berlin, "Adamski" is east Germany's answer to west Germany's

sleeper date-movie hit, "Making Up!" Though technically unappealing, this understated, character-driven comedy could see good returns locally and do well offshore at festivals, specialized slots and on TV with the right sell.

Horst Adamski (sad-faced but sly Steffen Schult), a guard in an east Berlin department store, spies Lili (wide-eyed Nadja Engel) shoplifting, and falls for her. His courtship is a trifle offbeat: He videotapes her at work, follows her at night, and his declarations of love are more like obscene phone calls. Lili, however, turns out to be just as strange.

Writer-director Jens Becker makes his unlikely heroes too sympathetic to ignore, and the film comes alive thanks to the slyly funny performances of Schult, Engel and the rest of the cast.

Pic's soul is thoroughly east German. Where a west German writer might have pitted Adamski and Lili against the oppressive system, or had them make big bucks and escape the drabness of east Berlin, none of these plot devices occurs to Becker. His characters live in spite of the system and their own circumstances, and their goals are ultimately personal — love.
— *Eric Hansen*

DIALOGUES WITH MADWOMEN

(DOCU)

A Light-Saraf Films presentation. Produced by Allie Light, Irving Saraf. Directed by Light. Camera (color; video-to-16mm transfer), Saraf; sound, Deborah Brubaker, Sara Chin; editors, Saraf, Light; still photography, Jim Block; sound, Deborah Brubaker; additional camera, Frances Reid, Fawn Yacker; dialogue editing, Millie Iatrou; film-to-tape transfers, John Carlson, Monaco Video; on-line editing, Ed Rudolph, Video Arts Inc; sound mix, Jeff Roth, Focused Audio. Reviewed at the U.C. Theatre, Berkeley, July 23, 1993. Running time: **89 MIN.**
With: Deedee Bloom, Allie Light, Mairi McFall, Karen Wong, Susan Pedrick, R.B., Hannah Ziegellaub.

Allie Light and Irving Saraf's 1991 Oscar-winning feature doc "In the Shadows of Stars" focused on chorus members of the San Francisco Opera, some of whom seemed quite eccentric. Their new "Dialogues With Madwomen" plunges more seriously into the realm of mental illness, focusing on seven subjects with diversely troubled histories. Generally powerful effort should win some theatrical interest before hitting the broadcast market.

The women here — including director Light herself — are candid, angry and often amused as they relate some harrowing stories. While their "recovery" is obviously an ongoing project, most seem reasonably adjusted to everyday life.

(More information about their current jobs and relationship status would help fill out these portraits.)

The past is another matter. The women cover an illustrative range of diagnosed problems, as well as race, class and sexual preference, without the film trying to "explain" mental illness or argue over treatments.

Many of the themes here, from alcoholic and abusive parents to childhood incest, are familiar. Chinese-American and black women discuss the alienating pressures of being raised among Caucasian peer groups. Nearly all can point toward psychiatrists, doctors, drug therapies and institutional experiences more disorienting than helpful.

Skillfully edited feature breaks up the talking-head focus by illustrating incidents and hallucinations via silent dramatized segs, archival footage, stills and artwork. Sometimes this goes over the top, as in the kitschy image of a woman go-go dancing before a huge rising moon. The ending, an oceanside film-within-film interlude, offers a strong final image but otherwise seems muddily conceived.

Video transfer to 16mm and other tech factors are top-notch. A sad postscript informs that Chinese-American subject Karen Wong was raped and murdered in her home after filming was complete; the assailant remains unknown.
— *Dennis Harvey*

EXCHANGE LIFEGUARDS

(AUSTRALIAN)

A Beyond Films release of an Avalon Films production, with the participation of the Australian Film Finance Corp. Produced, written by Phil Avalon. Executive producers, MPM and Beyond Films. Directed by Maurice Murphy. Camera (color, Panavision widescreen), Martin McGrath; editor, Alan Trott; music, John Capek; production design, Richard Hobbs; costume design, Jenny Campbell; sound, Bob Clayton; stunts, Richard Bone; assistant director, Dennis Kiely. Reviewed at Hoyts Centre 4, Sydney, Australia, Oct. 26, 1993. Running time: **93 MIN.**
Bobby McCain .... Christopher Atkins
Mike McCain .... Elliott Gould
Mick .... Julian McMahon
Julie Thomas .... Rebecca Cross
Richard Grey .... Christopher Pate
Cheryl .... Vanessa Steele
Tishi .... Peter Gow
Donna .... Amanda Newman-Phillips
Max .... Mark Hembrow

Described by writer-producer Phil Avalon as "Porky's on the Beach," "Exchange Lifeguards" falls short of even that modest aim. With a cliched screenplay and almost complete lack of zest and comic invention, it's a tired throwback to the beach films of the past, but might grab video sales and latenight cable exposure on the names of Elliott

November 29, 1993 (Cont.)

Gould and Christopher Atkins and some mildly titillating nudity.

Cornball plot has L.A. developer Gould, who's being sidelined by his faithless wife and his business partner, plotting to take over an Australian surfing beach for a high-rise resort. He sends his son (Atkins) down to Oz to check out the situation. Atkins, posing as an exchange lifeguard, is soon accepted by the laid-back locals and finds himself a lissome sexual partner in pretty Rebecca Cross, who owns the land his father needs for the development.

Naturally, Atkins' true identity is revealed just as he's decided to support his suntanned Aussie mates, and he finds himself on the outside. But all ends well when his repentant father arrives and proposes an environmentally friendly cooperative development, which pleases everyone except the unrepentant capitalist villains.

All this is just an excuse for a string of mostly unfunny jokes involving nude bathers, a farting dog, condoms and ugly Americans who mostly turn out to be not so ugly after all. Maurice Murphy's direction is routine, but given a script composed of wall-to-wall cliches, this is hardly surprising.

Gould and Atkins go through the motions, but there are a couple discoveries among the supporting cast, notably Julian McMahon (son of a former Australian prime minister), who oozes charisma as the boss of the surf club, and Cross, who makes the most of her thin material.

—*David Stratton*

POLIS POLIS POTATISMOS

(MURDER AT THE SAVOY)

(SWEDISH)

A Svensk Filmindustri presentation of a Victoria Film production of a Victoria APS/Rialto Film Berlin/SVT Kanal 1 Drama/Nordiska film and TV fonden/SF Film co-production. Produced by Hans Lonnerheden. Executive producers, Ole Sondberg, Soren Staermose, Bertil Ohlson. Co-producer, Matthias Wendtlandt. Directed by Pelle Berglund. Screenplay, Jonas Cornell, Berglund, based on the novel by Maj Sjowall and Per Wahloo. Camera (color), Tony Forsberg; editor, Carina Hellberg; production design, Mike Kinning; costume design, Lenamari Wallstrom; sound, Mats Lindskog. Reviewed at the Swedish Film Institute, Stockholm, Sept. 2, 1993. Running time: **90 MIN.**
Martin Beck .... Gosta Ekman
Lennart Kollberg .... Kjell Bergquist
Gunvald Larsson ....Rolf Lassgard
Benny Skacke .... Niklas Hjulstrom
Per Mansson .... Ingvar Andersson
Bertil Svensson ...... Thommy Johnsson
Stig Malm ....Jonas Falk
Helena Hansson .... Marie Richardson
Also with: Lena T. Hansson, Claes Sylwander, Arthur Brauss, Agneta Ekmanner, Gorel Crona, Lena Nilsson, Reine Brynollsson, Anders Ekborg, Jonas Bergstrom.

The least interesting of the 10 Sjowall-Wahloo novels, "Murder at the Savoy" also provides the basis for what so far is also the least interesting film adaptation in the series. It might work on television, though.

A famed industrialist is gunned down while having dinner at a posh Malmo hotel. The investigations lead Martin Beck and his colleagues to people involved in illegal gun-running, but the killer is to be found in other circles.

Although well acted and not without merits, pic never manages to create any suspense. It's by far the weakest of the three films in the series readied to date.

—*Gunnar Rehlin*

ROSEANNA

(SWEDISH)

A Svensk Filmindustri presentation a Victoria Film production of a Victoria APS/Rialto Film Berlin/SVT Kanal 1 Drama/Nordisks Film and TV-London/SF Film co-production. Produced by Hans Lonnerhden. Executive producers, Ole Sondberg, Soren Staermose, Bertil Ohlson. Co-producer, Matthias Wendtlandt. Directed by Daniel Alfredson. Screenplay, Jonas Cornell, based on the novel by Maj Sjowall and Perr Wahloo. Camera (color), Dan Myhrman; editor, Helene Berlin; production design, Micke Kinning; costume design, Lenamari Wallstrom; sound, Mats Lindskog. Reviewed at the Swedish Film Institute, Stockholm, Sept. 2, 1993. Running time: **94 MIN.**
Martin Beck ....: Gosta Ekman
Lennart Kollberg .... Kjell Bergquist
Gunvald Larsson ....Rolf Lassgard
Benny Skacke .... Niklas Hjulstrom
Asa Torell .... Lena Nilsson
Per Mansson .... Ingvar Andersson
Also with: Berndt Strom, Torgny Anderberg, Jacob Nordenson, Anita Ekstrom, Tova Magnusson-Norling, Ingmari Carlsson, Anna-Lena Bergendahl, Donald Hogberg.

First to be shot, but second to be released, this entry in the Sjowall-Wahloo series is an efficient police-procedural story, although more suited for TV than for cinema screens.

Filmed in Sweden, "Roseanna" was the first of the 10 Sjowall-Wahloo novels about Martin Beck and his colleagues at the Stockholm police. It establishes the characters, and since pic does the same, it's rather odd to see it released after "The Fire Engine that Disappeared," whose action takes place after the events in "Roseanna."

Yarn deals with the murder of a young American tourist who has been killed aboard a tourist boat and dumped in the water. It seems impossible for the police to find any clues at all. When they finally do, they stake a trap for the killer in which a young policewoman is almost killed. This final sequence is the best in the film, working up nail-biting suspense. "Roseanna" is competently made, its acting tops,

especially the perf by Gosta Ekman, whose Martin Beck is as non-glamorous and hard-working as he should be. —*Gunnar Rehlin*

CAPITALISMO SALVAGEM

(SAVAGE CAPITALISM)

(BRAZILIAN)

A Cinematografica Superfilms Ltda. production. Produced by Flavio Tambellini. Executive producer, Zita Carvalhosa. Directed by Andre Klotzel. Screenplay, Klotzel, Djalma Batista. Camera (color), Pedro Farkas; editor, Danilo Tadeu; music, David Tygel; art direction, Roberto Mainiero. Reviewed at Festival of Festivals, Toronto, Sept. 17, 1993. Running time: **86 MIN.**
Elisa Medeiros .... Fernanda Torres
Hugo Assis .... Jose Mayer
Also with: Marisa Orth, Marcelo Tas.

Inspired by Pedro Almodovar's quirky, offbeat films, the originally titled "Savage Capitalism" is a Brazilian soap opera about a frenzied romance, with political and environmental issues in the background. Good acting by leading lady Fernanda Torres and sporadic amusing moments should make pic part of Latin American film surveys, but its humor isn't riotous enough to qualify for commercial release in the U.S.

Torres plays a young journalist engaged in an investigative report on a mining company run by Jose Mayer. In the midst of her research she realizes that Mayer is a survivor of an Indian tribe, a revelation that has implications for both his political identity and her feelings toward him.

A wild liaison ensues, only to be interrupted when Mayer's presumably "dead" wife comes back with greedy ambitions that involve extracting gold from the Indians' land. This leads to Torres' growing consciousness as an environmentalist and protector of Indians' rights. Soon, the media turns the issue into a grand public scandal.

Helmer Andre Klotzel is successful in making "Savage Capitalism" the cinematic equivalent of a Brazilian TV soap opera, but he is less adept in using this format as a political metaphor for modern-day Brazil, which is pic's ultimate goal.

Torres, who made her mark in the 1986 "Love You, For Ever and Ever," has the energy and temperament necessary for a comic melodrama. She's not conventionally beautiful but exudes immense erotic appeal. Her wild sex scene with Mayer in the woods is worthy of Almodovar.

In mode, the film aspires to be an Almodovar comedy-melodrama, though it lacks the Spaniard's skillfulness in rapid gear shifts and mood changes. The bold color

scheme is most appropriate for the tale's soap operatic tone.

—*Emanuel Levy*

PERDIDO POR PERDIDO

(NOTHING TO LOSE)

(ARGENTINE)

A Cipe Fridman production in association with Negocios Cinematograficos S.A. Executive producer, Luis Sartor. Directed by Alberto Lecchi. Screenplay, Lecchi, Daniel Romanach. Camera (color), Jose Luis Garcia; editor, Alejandro Alem; music, Julian Vat; production design, Guillermo Pilosio; art direction, Clara Notari; costumes, Monica Torschi; sound, Jose Luis Diaz; assistant director, Fernando Bassi. Reviewed at Festival of Festivals, Toronto, Sept. 17, 1993. Running time: **93 MIN.**
Ernesto Vidal .... Ricardo Darin
Mattesutti .... Enrique Pinti
Veronica .... Carolina Papaleo
Pierotti ....Jorge Schubert
Clara .... Ana Maria Picchio
Del Bono .... Fernando Siro
Garces .... Alberto Segado
Arregui .... Julia Von Grolman
Also with: Walter Santa Ana, Jose Maria Lopez, Alberto Busaid, Cristina Fridman.

Argentine screenwriter Alberto Lecchi makes a competent but unexciting feature directing debut with "Perdido Por Perdido," a routine caper drama that's best suited for international TV markets.

Seemingly inspired by, but not so inspired as, Elmore Leonard and Jim Thompson, script has Ernesto (Ricardo Darin), a salesman for a glass company, pressured by mounting debts and Argentina's skyrocketing inflation to seek help from loan shark Pierotti (Jorge Schubert). Latter draws the salesman into an insurance scam that has Ernesto filing a claim for his "stolen" car.

Trouble begins when Mattesutti (Enrique Pinti), an ex-cop who works for the insurance company, smells a rat. He investigates the claim, links Pierotti to major-league white-collar criminals, and blackmails Ernesto into helping him shake down Pierotti's boss, a corrupt industrialist who counts real-estate dirty dealings as well as insurance scams among her crimes.

Lecchi's straightforward, if not slapdash, approach tends to dilute any suspense the familiar material might have generated. But the performances, including Carolina Papaleo as Ernesto's initially ditzy but ultimately feisty wife, are good. Pinti is particularly noteworthy as the cynical ex-cop who wants revenge against a corrupt system more than any monetary reward.

Jose Luis Garcia's attractive color lensing is pic's standout production value. —*Joe Leydon*

VSETKO CO MAMA RAD

(EVERYTHING I LIKE)

(SLOVAKIAN)

A Charlie's/Slovak Television Bratislava production. (Intl. sales: Filmexport, Prague.) Produced by Rudolf Biermann. Directed by Martin Sulik. Screenplay, Sulik, Ondrej Sulaj. Camera (color), Martin Strba; editor, Dusan Milko; music, Vladimir Godar; art direction, Frantisek Liptak; costumes, Mona Hafsahl; sound, Peter Mojzis. Reviewed at Festival of Festivals, Toronto, Sept. 16, 1993. Running time: 101 MIN.
Tomas .... Juraj Nvota
Ann .... Gina Bellman
Magda .... Zdena Studenkova
Vaclav .... Jiri Menzel
Andrej .... Jakub Ursini
Father .... Anton Sulik
Mother .... Viera Topinkova
Writer .... Rudolf Sloboda

"Everything I Like" presents an existential hero of sorts caught in the emotional rubble of the new Eastern Europe. Part homage to the free-spirited human Czech tales of the 1960s and part modern political post-mortem, film founders badly as it attempts to bring its disparate strands to a cohesive conclusion. Commercial prospects are negligible.

At the center of the story is Tomas (Juraj Nvota), a thirtysomething, unemployed, divorced quasi-intellectual. Thrust of his life is to comment on the sorry state of the world and to wrap himself up in the problems of those around him while sidestepping personal dilemmas. It all becomes tiresome and weighty very quickly.

Tomas grapples with a son who may be even more opaque than he is, an ex-wife who gives him no quarter and parents who are role models in passive aggression. When Ann (Gina Bellman), a forthright English teacher, arrives in his life it ought to be cause for celebration. She's the tonic that momentarily enlivens the patient.

Filmmaker Martin Sulik adopts a darkly ironic tone that often fails to translate. There's the suggestion of a comic emotional roller coaster ride at every turn, as he structures the film in vignettes and introduces characters with just a hint of the humorous. It would also seem likely that he has a contemporary political parable to relate which may hit home only on the local front. There's lots of promise and scant delivery.

While clearly a skilled craftsman, Sulik needs remedial help in his casting and story choices. Nvota is fatally charmless as Tomas, and supporting roles reflect bland or unconventional decisions. The script starts strong, ends strong and disappears somewhere in between.

There are occasional flashes, but little ultimately develops onscreen.
—*Leonard Klady*

SWEET 'N' SHORT

(SOUTH AFRICAN)

A U.I.P. release of a Torkon-Koukos-Troika production. Produced by Andre Scholtz, Carl Fischer. Executive producer, Edgar Bold. Directed by Gray Hofmeyr. Screenplay, Hofmeyr, Leon Schuster. Camera (color), James Robb; editor, Johan Lategan; music, Don Clarke, Wendy Oldfield, Kalla Bremer; production design, JonJon Lambun; costumes, Loli Repanis; sound, Rudiger Payrhuber; stunts, Rolly Jansen; assistant director, Graham Hickson. Reviewed at Hoyts Centre 2, Sydney, Australia, Aug. 12, 1993. Running time: 90 MIN.
Sweet Coetzee .... Leon Schuster
George .... Casper De Vries
Sandy Stewart .... Joanna Weinberg
Alfred Short .... Alfred Ntombela
Bossie .... Ivan D. Lucas

A cheerfully simple slapstick comedy from South Africa, this 1991 pic was a hit on its home turf and is now getting its first international bookings in Australia. Much of the humor depends on knowledge of South African politics, which puts the pic on a rockier road than the country's previous breakout hit, "The Gods Must Be Crazy."

This said, co-writer and director Gray Hofmeyr unquestionably knows how to stage slapstick sequences, and there are many genuine laughs in the picture. But there are a good many yawns as well.

Co-writer Leon Schuster plays Sweet, a hard-drinking, hard-living, sexist TV sports commentator. The opening scenes are set in 1989, "before the changes." Sweet behaves badly toward his g.f. (Joanna Weinberg) and is on the point of losing his job to a rival sportscaster (Casper De Vries). A blow to the head just as he's won a large sum of money results in a coma that lasts almost three years; when Sweet awakens, Nelson Mandela is president, F.W. De Klerk is leader of the opposition and right-wing Boers live in white townships (it all turns out to be a dream).

With the help of Alfred Short (Alfred Ntombela), an ultra-cute black boy, Sweet sets about getting back his job, his money and his girl. The jokes include a long sequence in which Sweet disguises himself as a black African, some broad comedy at the expense of the arch-conservative Boers, and an over-long rugby match which Sweet attempts to sabotage by a variety of means, including the use of itching powder and laxatives.

This is simple stuff for undemanding audiences, but indicates that a comedy tradition is alive and well in South Africa. Still, international B.O. results are likely to be modest for this ramshackle, uneven farce. Performances are pro,

though the film could have benefited from a funnier performance in the lead; Schuster, though often amusing, lacks a confident comic persona. Pic is technically adequate.
—*David Stratton*

FAR AWAY FROM ST. PETERSBURG

(LATVIAN)

A Latvian Independent Film Studio production. Directed by Alexander Hahn. Screenplay, Sascha Zhukowski. Camera (color), Henrik Pilipson; editor, Jutta Brante; music, Edward Artemiew; sound, Leb Korotejeew. Reviewed at AFI/L.A. Film Fest, L.A., June 18, 1993. Running time: 79 MIN.
With: Dzintars Belogrudovs, Igor Klass, Zhenja Krjukowa, Larisa Tatunowa.
(English and Russian dialogue)

"Far Away From St. Petersburg" is a chaotic, messy farce that at once evokes and mocks Russian history of the last century. Despite inventive premise and breezy pace, it isn't easy to watch, let alone enjoy, this Latvian curio.

Born in St. Petersburg, Fla., Iwan Rabczynski, the hero of Alexander Hahn's movie, writes Russian epics under the pen name of John F. Romanoff. His new novel begins with his Russian great-grandfather in St. Petersburg in 1882 and follows three generations as they endure the country's political upheavals.

Made in a free form, as a pastiche with absurdist undertones, adventure is narrated by the author in a semi-humorous vein. As Russian history of the last hundred years could fill many lengthy volumes, the movie jams in as many hilarious — and tragic — events as possible. Bodies pile up as family members die from incurable diseases, revolutions, wars and accidents. Many familiar cliches about Russian culture and soul are on display.

Historical tale is intercut with the contemporary story of the author, who is flying to Moscow to get "inspiration" for a new saga and manages to irritate all the passengers with his incessant chat. Unfortunately, the modern scenes, which draw parallels between past and present, not only fail to invigorate the film but also halt the little flow it has.

The tone shifts radically fron scene to scene, though chief problem is pic's disastrous execution: Production is badly photographed, clumsily edited and amateurishly acted. Its only real distinction — and it is a rare one — is that it's Latvian.
—*Emanuel Levy*

BLACK BOMBER

(YUGOSLAV)

A Zabava Miliona Fivet production. Produced by Raka Dokic. Directed by Darko Bajic. Screenplay, Aleksander Barisic, Bajic. Camera (color), Radan Popovic; editor, Vuksan Lukovac; music, Srdan Gojkovic Gile. Reviewed at American Film Institute, L.A., June 11, 1993 (in the AFI/LA Film Fest). Running time: 116 MIN.
Black .... Dragan Bjelogric
Luna .... Anica Dobra
(Serbo-Croatian dialogue)

"Black Bomber" is a boisterous, energetic, all-out celebration of Yugoslavia's "Anti-Establishment" youth culture. The politics of this futuristic film are a bit abstract, but the timeliness of this sex-music-drug saga, and the poignant love story at its center, should appeal to young viewers beyond the international fest circuit.

Set in Belgrade in 1999, the story concerns an underground radio station, "Boom 92," which possesses a single mike but plenty of rebellious attitude. The handsome hero, DJ Black (Dragan Bjelogric), a James Dean-type in looks and demeanor, is not beyond selling drugs or tape recorders to keep his vigorous station alive.

When Black meets Luna (Anica Dobra), a beautiful rock singer who is even tougher than he is, he falls head over heels. Their love affair is set against a background of institutional oppression, censorship and violence. When Boom 92 is declared dangerously subversive by the state, Black forms a pirate radio station named Black Bomber in a pickup truck.

The broader political contexts of the film somehow remain vague — no specific issues or figures are identified. In fact, the only representative of the ruling class (and adult world) is a cop who spends most of the time chasing the defiant deejay in armed police cars or helicopters. As co-written by Aleksander Barisic and director Darko Bajic, tale doesn't make much use of its futuristic setting either. Pic would have been much more powerful had it been set in the present, as the current situation in Yugoslavia is certainly bleak enough to warrant it. Futuristic setting is particularly strange in that the film reportedly reconstructs a huge, violent student demonstration that took place in 1991.

Structural problems are a likely result of this being a condensation of a four-hour film planned to air on TV in four episodes. Helmer Bajic rushes the action from one brief scene to another, resulting in a truncated narrative that doesn't fulfill its potential and lacks emotional resonance.

Overall, "Black Bomber" is less interesting for its ideas than for the offbeat, buoyant energy of its two charming performers. Never dull, film works best as an allegory about the power of love and the indefatigable resourcefulness of youth in totalitarian societies.

—*Emanuel Levy*

KO ZAPREM OCI

(WHEN I CLOSE MY EYES)

(SLOVENIAN)

A TV Slovenia and Binweed Sound-vision presentation of a Mladina Film. Directed by Franci Slak. Screenplay by Slak, Silvan Furlan. Camera (color), Sven Pepeonik; editor, Neva Fajon; music, Mitja Vrhovnik-Smrekar; production design, Tomaz Marolt; costume design, Dunja Zupancic, Suzana Sisernik; sound (Dolby), Hanna Preuss. Reviewed at Chicago Intl. Film Festival, Oct. 17, 1993. Running time: **99 MIN.**

Ana Resnik	Petra Govc
Ivan	Valter Dragan
Aunt	Mira Sardoc
Inspector	Pavle Ravnohrib
Thief	Mario Selih
Man with Hat	Ludvik Bagari
Postal Chief	Dusan Jovanovic
Boris	Gojmir Lesnjak

If "When I Close My Eyes" is a precursor of things to come, then expect to see some exciting new talent emerging from the newly constituted Slovenian Republic. This psychological thriller, the first indie production to emerge from the nation, is a resourcefully made, emotionally gripping and unnerving entertainment that will translate effortlessly to other cultures. With effective marketing it has reel playability internationally and potential crossover appeal in sophisticated situations.

Filmmaker Franci Slak has deftly woven the conventions of genre into the evolving social contract of his nation and fashioned a haunting scenario. Story centers on Ana (Petra Govc), a young post office worker. As luck would have it, the day she substitutes at a rural depot, a man on motorcycle arrives and robs the station.

However, internal and police response to the incident would suggest something far from routine was involved. The investigating officer questions her in an icily cynical way that implies she is a prime suspect. Her supervisor also tosses out a cloud of suspicion and culpability.

The climate is rife with paranoia. We learn that Ana has been imbued with guilt since she was a child and discovered her father hanging from a tree in a ritual, political murder. In her state of mind anything is possible — even her unwitting complicity in the robbery.

Slak, who co-wrote the script with Silvan Furlan, devises a structure that provides the illusion of a logical progression. It is fiendishly clever in doling out choice tidbits to guide the viewer down the wrong primrose path. Virtually nothing proves to be what it seems.

Of particular note is the high technical sheen of the production. Sven Pepeonik's super 16mm camera work is a handsome, eerie complement to the off-center storyline. Score by Mitja Vrhovnik-Smrekar is evocative and stylized, suggesting the subtle flourish of a young Ennio Morricone.

"When I Close My Eyes" is a thoroughgoing deception of the highest order. Slak accomplishes a rare feat of sleight of hand where the enjoyment is derived from being totally bamboozled by a master cinemagician. —*Leonard Klady*

AMERICAS FEST

ORDINARY MAGIC

(CANADIAN)

A Film Works production, in association with Telefilm Canada/Ontario Film Development Corp./Eastern Moonlight Movies/FUND/Rogers Telefund. Produced by Paul Stephens, Eric Jordan. Directed by Giles Walker. Screenplay, Jefferson Lewis, based on the novel "Ganesh," by Malcolm Bosse. Camera (color), Paul Sarossy; editor, Ralph Brunjes; music, Mychael Danna. Reviewed on vidcassette as part of seventh Americas Film Festival, AFI, Washington, D.C., Oct. 24, 1993. Running time: **104 MIN.**

Charlotte	Glenne Headly
Jeffrey	Ryan Reynolds
Joey Dean	Paul Anka

Also with: David Fox, Heath Lamberts.

An inspirational tale of individualism and assimilation, "Ordinary Magic" has the scope and texture of made-for-TV fare. Amiable small film seems aimed to the youth-oriented small-screen market and should spark some international interest there.

Pic deals with Jeffrey (Ryan Reynolds), a 15-year-old orphan who, upon the death of his parents, travels to a small Ontario town to live with his aunt Charlotte (Glenne Headly). As expatriates, Jeffrey's parents had lived for many years in India fighting social injustice.

As young Jeffrey tries to integrate himself into the local community, he discovers that he also can continue his parents' cause when his aunt receives an eviction notice. The family home is skedded to be demolished to make way for a ski resort complex.

Following Gandhi's principle of passive resistance, the boy and his aunt begin a hunger strike. Needless to say, their independent spirit eventually wins over the town.

Singer Paul Anka does a turn as the heavy, playing a smarmy real estate baron.

Tech credits are OK, replete with colorful flashbacks to India. While the actors work hard, script's overall facile characterizations and predictable plot development detract from real tension. —*Paul Lenti*

SECUESTRO: A STORY OF A KIDNAPPING

(COLOMBIAN-U.S. — DOCU — 16mm)

An E.M. Films production. Produced by Camila Motta, Barry Ellsworth. Directed, written by Camila Motta. Camera (color/b&w), Ellsworth; editor, Holly Fisher; music, German Arrietta, Nicolas Uribe; sound, Heriberto Garcia. Reviewed at Americas Film Festival, AFI, Washington, D.C., Oct. 30, 1993. Running time: **92 MIN.**

Debut docu by Camila Motta deals with the complex problem of kidnapping in Colombia, which can be classified as a business venture. Every seven hours someone in Colombia is kidnapped, 90% of them for money. "Secuestro" (Kidnapping) centers on one case, that of Motta's sister Silvia, who was held from March-June 1985.

Besides selected stylized re-enactments, docu features interviews with Silvia, her influential banker father, the police and even one of the kidnappers, along with audio tapes of negotiations by phone with the kidnappers, who eventually received about 10% of their original $600,000 asking price.

Docu takes a step-by-step chronological approach, and Motta maintains tension as she extends Silvia's case to further concerns: The kidnapper justifies his actions in sociopolitical terms as a way to redistribute wealth; the mother is rejected as a negotiator simply because she is a woman, and the police view everything as a mere business deal.

The methodology of the kidnappers is surprisingly professional: Their research includes a complete review of the father's assets and those of his friends, and of the individual routines of each of the five children. Nothing is left to chance.

Although Silvia's presence is felt throughout in the form of voiceover descriptions of her captivity and tapes to her father, Motta deliberately keeps Silvia's image absent until negotiations are completed and she is freed. In a highly textured soundtrack of voices, Silvia's words permeate the film, often intruding upon the talking-head commentaries by those involved in her liberation. Her very absence becomes a type of presence.

The rich photography counterpoints this soundtrack with a montage of images, interviews, recreations, still photos, slow-motion and hand-held camera work and alternating use of color and b&w.

With "Secuestro," Motta shows a firm hand, avoiding easy sentimentality and creating a document that functions as an indictment of a system that has established itself between the haves and the have-nots. As a result of the sensitive subject matter, merely screening the film has been problematic in its country of origin. —*Paul Lenti*

SERPIENTES Y ESCALERAS

(SNAKES AND LADDERS)

(MEXICAN)

A Mexican Film Institute (Imcine) release of an Imcine/Prods. Romelia/Fondo de Fomento a la Calidad Cinematografica/U. Iberoamericana production. Produced by Jorge Cortes Rocha. Executive producer, Georgina Teran. Directed by Busi Cortes. Screenplay, Cortes, Alicia Molina, Carmen Cortes. Camera (color), Francisco Bojorquez; editor, Federico Landeros; music, Jose Amozurrutia; art direction, Gabriela Reigadas; sound, Miguel Sandoval. Reviewed at Americas Film Festival, AFI, Washington, D.C., Oct. 24, 1993. Running time: **95 MIN.**

Gregorio	Hector Bonilla
Adelaida	Diana Bracho
Valentina	Arcelia Ramirez
Rebeca	Lumi Cavazos
Raul	Bruno Bichir
Alfonso	Ernesto Rives

Also with: Josefina Echanove, Pilar Medina, Luis de Tavira.

This ambitious second feature by Mexican helmer Busi Cortes concerns such explosive themes as love, betrayal and political intrigue, yet it meanders through a muddled soap opera plot that eventually leaves viewers indifferent to the plight of its characters. Commercial possibilities are vague at best.

Set in the provincial city of Guanajuato, post-revolutionary tale chronicles the friendship between two young women, Rebeca and Valentina, from childhood to early womanhood.

Rebeca (played by "Like Water for Chocolate" star Lumi Cavazos) discovers that she was born out of wedlock when she and her mother are evicted from their home upon her father's death. Gregorio, father of her friend Valentina and a skirt-chasing corrupt politician seeking the state governorship, offers to help Rebeca secure her former home through political machinations. He further seduces the young woman, getting her pregnant.

Of course, the politician's dirty dealings eventually come to a head. Conflicting emotions of love and betrayal, as well as questions concerning women's roles, come into play, as do condemnations of political corruption and the plight of local miners, but all of it seems mere grist for the mill.

Leisurely paced film seems tediously long due to scenes that lack focus and the overall flatness of tone. Period re-creation is very good, as are other tech credits.

—Paul Lenti

GOLPES A MI PUERTA

(KNOCKS AT MY DOOR)

(VENEZUELAN-ARGENTINE-CUBAN-BRITISH)

An Alejandro Saderman Prods.-Foncine (Venezuela) production in co-production with the Instituto Cubano del Arte e Industrias Cinematograficos (Cuba)-ASP (Argentina), in association with Channel 4 (England). Produced, directed by Alejandro Saderman. Executive producer, Antonio Llerandi. Screenplay, Juan Carlos Gene, Saderman, based on the play by Gene. Camera (color), Adriano Moreno; editor, Claudia Uribe; music, Julio D'Escrivan; art direction, Marietta Perroni; sound, Raul Garcia. Reviewed on vidcassette, Americas Film Festival, AFI, Washington, D.C., Oct. 25, 1993. Running time: **106 MIN.**
Ana .... Veronica Oddo
Ursula .... Elba Escobar
Mayor Cerone .... Juan Carlos Gene
Monsenor .... Jose Antonio Rodriguez
Severa .... Ana Castell
Also with: Frank Spano, Mirta Ibarra, Eduardo Gil, Dimas Gonzalez.

Based on the Venezuelan play of the same name, "Knocks at My Door" presents a political and moral polemic that questions the role of the Catholic Church within a politically repressive society. Although politically relevant, film ultimately fails due to its faithful adherence to the legit source material, making it schematic, static and talky.

Set in an unnamed Latin American country (with parallels to El Salvador), pic deals with how a repressive political situation forces those uncommitted to take sides.

The film offers a thesis on liberation theology when a political refugee enters the dwelling of two nuns. Knowing he will be tortured and killed, the nuns hide him even though they face execution if caught.

While the military displays an open contempt for the clergy, the town mayor understands the negative p.r. that would result from executing two nuns. Thus the dilemma and the makings of a discourse on political involvement and a questioning man's moral and charitable principles.

Acting is particularly strong, especially Veronica Oddo and Elba Escobar as the nuns. Other tech credits are good, but the film needs to be opened up further with less dependence on dialogue to carry the plot.

—Paul Lenti

VAGAS PARA MOCAS DE FINO TRATO

(UNDER ONE ROOF)

(BRAZILIAN)

A Vitoria Cinema e Video Producoes production. Produced by Glaucia Camargos. Directed by Paolo Thiago. Screenplay, Alcione Arauj, based on the play of the same name. Camera (color), Antonio Penido, editor, Marco Antonio Cury; music, Tulio Mourao; sound, Jorge Sanldehna. Reviewed at Americas Film Festival, AFI, Washington, D.C., Oct. 22, 1993. Running time: **94 MIN.**
Lucia .... Lucelia Santos
Gertrudes .... Norma Bengell
Magdalena .... Maria Zilda Bethlem

"Under One Roof," second feature by Paolo Thiago, presents a curious tale that deliberately leaves the viewer worrying over too many loose ends. While the film may provoke some interest, auds will ultimately be frustrated by its overall shortcomings.

Story concerns a trio of women who share a flat in Vitoria, Brazil. Gertrudes, a former music teacher, wants to shut herself off from the rest of the world when she is abandoned by a lover. The freewheeling Magdalena works in a mental hospital during the day and spends her nights looking for men.

The third roommate, Lucia, is a young woman who fakes mental illness to take advantage of Gertrudes' maternal nature. While she envies Magdalena's wildness, she and Gertrudes play mother-and-daughter games when Magdalena is gone.

Playing with perception and offering a plethora of red herrings that are never explained, Thiago approaches this material with a jolting editing style and an overwhelming musical score. In a film that deals vicariously with insanity, one is often left wondering which characters are sane and what is real.

Although the story has been opened up, the snappy repartee betrays pic's legit origins. Tech credits are fine and thesping is good, especially Norma Bengell and the feisty Maria Zilda Bethlem.

—Paul Lenti

LATIN NIGHTS

(CANADIAN — DOCU — 16mm)

A Cineroutes production, in collaboration with the CBC-Vision TV and Saskatchewan Communications Network. Produced, directed by Anthony Azzopardi. Camera (color, 16mm), Michael Boland; editor, Jacques Holender; sound, Stuart French. Reviewed at Americas Film Festival, AFI, Washington, D.C., Oct. 23, 1993. Running time: **77 MIN.**
With: Ramiro's Latin Orchestra, Banda Brava, Cocada, Dario Domingues, Hugo Torres Group, Memo Acevedo's Latin Jazz Band, Nazka, Onda Latina, Romulo Larrea Tango Ensemble, Tito Puente, Gonzalo Rubalcaba, Dave Valentin.

Documenting Canada's growing Latin music scene, "Latin Nights" focuses on nine musicians or groups, using both interviews and concert footage. Presenting a spectrum of Latin music — tangos, salsa, folk, jazz and experimental — pic could do OK on small-screen cultural format.

Each act is introduced and allowed a complete tune, followed by a talking-head interview about the national market. Although the pic mentions them in passing, it does not delve into the deeper expatriate issues; many of the musicians ended up in Canada as political or economic refugees. Film also doesn't explore how influx of immigrant groups has enriched Canada's cultural mosaic.

Background info is supplied by a female radio announcer, who is supposedly broadcasting the music on a radio program. Device doesn't work; a more traditional narrative would be more effective.

Photography has some exciting moments, with various cameras catching the action. Sound is also good.

While "Father of the Mambo" Tito Puente has a special guest turn with Memo Acevedo's orchestra, fellow guest Gonzalo Rubalcaba is shown briefly at the concert without playing. For salsa fans, this is like announcing Eric Clapton's participation at a rock concert and only offering a brief clip of him sitting backstage. *—Paul Lenti*

WE'RE BACK! A DINOSAUR'S STORY

A Universal release of a Steven Spielberg presentation of an Amblin Entertainment and Universal production. Produced by Stephen Hickner. Executive producers, Spielberg, Frank Marshall, Kathleen Kennedy. Co-producer, Thad Weinlein. Directed by Dick Zondag, Ralph Zondag, Phil Nibbelink, Simon Wells. Screenplay, John Patrick Shanley, based on the book by Hudson Talbott. (Rank Labs and Foto-Kem/Foto-Tronics color; Deluxe prints); supervising editors, Sim Evan-Jones, Nick Fletcher; music, James Horner; art direction, Neil Ross; character design, Carlos Grangel; sound (Dolby), Albert Romero. Reviewed at Loews Cheri, Boston, Nov. 20, 1993. MPAA Rating: G. Running time: **72 MIN.**
Voices:
Rex .... John Goodman
Buster .... Blaze Berdahl
Mother Bird .... Rhea Perlman
Vorb .... Jay Leno
Woog .... Rene LeVant
Elsa .... Felicity Kendal
Dweeb .... Charles Fleischer
Captain NewEyes ..... Walter Cronkite
Louie .... Joey Shea
Dr. Bleeb .... Julia Child
Professor ScrewEyes ... Kenneth Mars
Cecilia .... Yeardley Smith
Stubbs the Clown .... Martin Short

"We're Back! A Dinosaur's Story" can be seen as "Jurassic Park" for kids who were too young to attend the summer blockbuster. Given the Spielberg name and that Disney's animated feature for the season — "Tim Burton's The Nightmare Before Christmas" — was released a month ago, it should be smooth sailing at the B.O. for these cartoon dinosaurs.

In spite of narrative problems in this adaptation of the children's book by Hudson Talbott, the film's chief appeal is its central conceit — that giant prehistoric monsters can be transformed into intelligent, talking tourists who like to play with children. ("Jurassic Park" is even plugged on a marquee as the lumbering creatures pass by.)

The source of this miracle is a special cereal invented by Captain New-Eyes (voice of Walter Cronkite), who brings Rex (John Goodman) and his friends to New York so that children who want to see a real dinosaur can have their wish come true. Problems ensue when the addled Dr. Bleeb (Julia Child) fails to meet them and they instead are trapped by the Captain's evil brother, Professor ScrewEyes (Kenneth Mars).

Film gets off to a slow start, first with a framing story and then the back story of how the dinosaurs make it to New York. Eventually things click, especially in the film's best sequence, in which the dinosaurs pretend to be floats in Macy's Thanksgiving Day Parade.

The danger from ScrewEyes is both convoluted and an unseemly attack on the handicapped. It's stated that the cause of his evil behavior is

December 6, 1993 (Cont.)

that he lost one eye. One doesn't have to be politically correct to question the wisdom of teaching children to be fearful of the disabled.

The animation is a bravura mix of traditional cel animation and computer-generated material.

Among the voice cast, Goodman and Martin Short are the standouts, with Mars and Yeardley Smith, among others, handling their chores well. While it's a kick for adults to hear the familiar voices of Cronkite and Child coming from cartoon characters, Jay Leno seems to be on board mostly for his marquee value and has little to do.

Prospects are solid because of the subject matter and the lack of competition. Universal is holding off its other holiday family picture — "Beethoven's 2nd" — so as not to compete. —*Daniel M. Kimmel*

MAN'S BEST FRIEND

A New Line Cinema release of a Roven-Cavello Entertainment production. Produced by Bob Engelman. Executive producer, Robert Kosberg, Daniel Grodnick. Directed, written by John Lafia. Camera (Deluxe color; Film House prints), Mark Irwin; editor, Michael N. Knue; music, Joel Goldsmith; production design, Jaymes Hinkle; art direction, Erik Olson; set design, Sharon E. Alshams; set decoration, Ellen Totlebren; costume design, Beverly Hong; sound (Dolby), Steve Nelson; animal trainer, Clint Rowe; special makeup effects, Kevin Yagher; associate producer, Kelley Smith; assistant director, Benita Allen; casting, Valorie Massalas. Reviewed at Loews Cinema 57, Boston, Nov. 19, 1993. MPAA Rating: R. Running time: **87 MIN.**

Lori Tanner .... Ally Sheedy
Dr. Jarret .... Lance Henriksen
Detective Kovacs .... Robert Constanzo
Perry .... Fredric Lehne
Detective Bendetti .... John Cassini
Rudy .... J.D. Daniels
Ray .... William Sanderson
Annie .... Trula M. Marcus

New Line trots out a potential new horror franchise with "Man's Best Friend," story of a genetically engineered guard dog on the loose. It should take a healthy nibble at the box office at first, but get quickly banished to the doghouse by onslaught of major holiday releases.

Chief problem is that Max the dog — a Tibetan mastiff — is easily the most likable character in the movie. Ally Sheedy plays an airhead lifestyle reporter looking for a "real" story. When her source at the animal research lab inconveniently disappears, she breaks in with her assistant to get the story on her own.

In liberating Max and taking him home, not once does Sheedy's character wonder if the dog is unhealthy, much less dangerous. Her lackadaisical attitude is matched by the incompetence of the police (Robert Constanzo, John Cassini), who are unable to locate the killer dog.

Lance Henriksen's scientist offers the best bet for a sympathetic character since he is the one who has been wronged, but he eventually emerges as a modern "mad scientist" who is willing to expend animal — and human — lives for what he considers a more worthy cause.

A large chunk of the running time is spent waiting for Max's sedative to wear off so that the hulking guard dog can start wreaking havoc. Violence is brief but notable, including the beast's swallowing a cat whole and urinating acid in the face of Sheedy's b.f. (Fredric Lehne). Although much of the violence is depicted with special effects, animal trainer Clint Rowe (credited with "Max's behavior") gets the real dog to deliver the film's best performance.

Sequel is set up by killing virtually every character in the film except Sheedy's and having Max leave behind a litter of puppies. As with most shaggy dog stories, it'll be hard to stop. —*Daniel M. Kimmel*

LUSH LIFE

A Showtime presentation of a Chanticleer Films production. (International sales: Chanticleer Films, L.A.) Produced by Thom Colwell. Executive producers, Jana Sue Memel, Jonathan Sanger. Co-producer, Ron Colby. Directed, written by Michael Elias. Camera (Agfacolor; Foto-Kem prints), Nancy Schrieber; editor, Bill Yahraus; music/music director, Lennie Niehaus; production design, John Jay Moore; costume design, Mary Kay Stolz; sound (Dolby), Peter V. Meiselmann; assistant director, Michelangelo Csaba Boller; casting, Leslee Dennis. Reviewed at London Film Festival, Nov. 18, 1993. Running time: **104 MIN.**

Al Gorky .... Jeff Goldblum
Buddy Chester .... Forest Whitaker
Janis Oliver .... Kathy Baker
Sarah .... Tracey Needham
Lucy .... Lois Chiles
Beanstrom .... Zack Norman
Jack .... Don Cheadle
Lester .... Alex Desert

The free-floating world of the N.Y. session musician forms a richly textured background to Michael Elias' directorial bow, "Lush Life," a moving celebration of friendship and the joy of music-making. Lit up by sympathetic ensemble playing from leads Jeff Goldblum, Forest Whitaker and Kathy Baker, this Showtime presentation will find a ready niche with jazz and music lovers, and with good reviews and careful handling could cross over from its cable origins to limited theatrical biz among discerning international audiences.

World premiered at the London Film Festival, pic is skedded for an April Showtime airdate, though it really deserves to be seen on the big screen.

Goldblum and Whitaker play, respectively, a tenor saxophonist and trumpeter, top sidemen and session players in the business, though not stars in their own right. Goldblum is married to Baker, a singer-turned-teacher who wants to leave Manhattan behind.

Goldblum is still married to his job, however — a world of casual dope-smoking, musical camaraderie and one-night stands (musical and carnal). Relations with Baker are loving but under strain: She starts to suspect him of extramarital affairs and can't break his spiritual bond to the hip 1960s. Worse, he's also starting to take his music less than seriously.

When Whitaker, who's been getting headaches from his high notes, finds he has a malignant brain tumor and only weeks to live, the trio's tight relationship is put to the test. Whitaker agrees to a final party-cum-jazz session, which all of Gotham's best session musicians will attend, on condition that no one is told of his problem and that Goldblum sharpen up his musical act.

TV writer/producer Elias, who wrote the script eight years ago, knows his jazz and its world. A patchwork of short scenes separated by musical sessions, pic has an easy, loose structure that nicely mirrors the characters' "lush life," as per the title of the Billy Strayhorn number.

Film's major strength lies in conveying the real joy of making music together, of wordless communication. In that respect, it's on a par (though in a different century and beat) with the French Gerard Depardieu starrer "Tous les Matins du monde."

Both Goldblum (doubled by the late, great Bob Cooper) and Whitaker (by Chuck Findley) convincingly rep their parts, especially the latter, with the camera carefully disguising their finger movements.

In a difficult middle role, Baker comes up aces, and gets her own chance to shine in a nightclub scene where she sings (dubbed by Sue Raney) one last time. There's a peachy bit by Lois Chiles as a sexy Manhattanite who's hot for both musicians. Other roles are notable, especially Zack Norman as a hard-hearted fixer.

Though the film could benefit from some trims in the second half — especially the interior monologuing by Whitaker as his illness starts to impinge (and a silly, out-of-style fantasy sequence) — the relationships are sufficiently strongly drawn to bypass disease-of-the-week cliches.

Aside from exteriors, most of the pic was in fact shot in L.A., with West Coast players in many of the background roles. Film still has a convincing New York feel and looks handsome despite its rapid 20-plus-day shoot and $4 million budget.

Tech credits are fine down the line, with Lennie Niehaus contrib-

bing powerful musical arrangements and Nancy Schrieber's camera alert and textured. Bill Yahraus' editing, especially of the musical montages, is on the money. Sole glitch is some indistinct, mumbled dialogue passages between Goldblum and Whitaker, which need to be clearer. —*Derek Elley*

NECRONOMICON

A Davis Film production. (International sales: August Entertainment, L.A.) Produced by Samuel Hadida, Brian Yuzna. Executive producer, Taka Ichise. Co-producer, Aki Komine. Screenplay, Brent V. Friedman. Production design, Anthony Tremblay; art direction, Aram Allen; set decoration, Claire Kaufman; costume design, Ida Gearson; sound (Dolby SR), Geoffrey Patterson, Ken Ross; makeup special effects supervisor, Thomas C. Rainone; mechanical effects, Doug Beswick; miniatures, David Sharp; line producer, Gary Schmoeller; second unit camera, Jerry Watson; casting, Jeffery Passero. Reviewed at Planet Hollywood screening room, London, Nov. 19, 1993. (In London Film Festival.) Total running time: **96 MIN.**

Wraparound ("The Library")
Directed by Brian Yuzna. Camera (Foto-Kem color), Gerry Lively; supervising editor, Chris Roth; music, Joseph Lo Duca; makeup special effects, Todd Masters; assistant director, Ed Licht.

H.P. Lovecraft .... Jeffrey Combs
Librarian .... Tony Azito
Attendant .... Juan Fernandez
"The Drowned"
Directed by Christophe Gans. Camera, Russ Brandt; editor, Chris Roth; makeup special effects, Tom Savini, Optic Nerve (John Vulich); assistant director, Bill Barry. Running time: **27 MIN.**
Edward De La Pore .... Bruce Payne
Jethro De La Pore .... Richard Lynch
Nancy Gallmore .... Belinda Bauer
Clara .... Maria Ford
Jethro's son .... Peter Jasienski
Emma De La Pore ...... Denice D. Lewis
Doctor .... William Jess Russell
Villager .... Vladimir Kulich
"The Cold"
Directed by Shu Kaneko, based on H.P. Lovecraft's "Cool Air." Camera, Gerry Lively; editor, Chris Roth; makeup special effects, Screaming Mad George, Chris Robbins, Misa Gardner; assistant director, Ed Licht. Running time: **24 MIN.**
Dr. Madden .... David Warner
Emily Osterman .... Bess Meyer
Lena .... Millie Perkins
Dale Porker .... Gary Graham
Mr. Hawkins .... Curt Lowens
Cops James Paradise, Sebastian White
"Whispers"
Directed by Brian Yuzna, based on H.P. Lovecraft's "The Whisperer in the Darkness." Camera, Gerry Lively; editor, Keith Sauter; makeup special effects, Todd Masters; assistant director, Ed Licht. Running time: **25 MIN.**
Sarah .... Signy Coleman
Paul .... Obba Babatunde
Mr. Benedict .... Don Calfa
Mrs. Benedict .... Judith Drake

In-your-face goremeister Brian Yuzna makes a game attempt to revive the portmanteau horror flick with "Necronomicon," a three-parter (plus wraparound) based on stories and themes drawn from the deep well of H.P. Lovecraft. Result, using a raft of international directors, is diverting but uneven, though pic will see brisk biz in vid-bin afterlife. Theatrical chances in mature territories look chancier beyond quick-play splatter venues.

Yuzna himself helms the fanciful wraparound ("The Library"), set in fall 1932, in which H.P. (Jeffrey Combs) visits a library run by strange monks where resides a copy of the famed Necronomicon, a book that contains "the very secrets of the universe." H.P. is low on inspiration, so, locked up in a vault with the magical tome, he jots down notes for stories.

Segue to first seg ("The Drowned"), a "House of Usher"-like variation set in a remote, coastal New England hotel with a ghostly rep.

Jethro (Richard Lynch, serviceable), returning from abroad to claim his inheritance, is shown around the dump by a sexy realtor (Belinda Bauer, terrific) who advises him to sell it straightaway. Jethro demurs and finds his late uncle made a pact with the devil. Eventually, history repeats itself.

Set in Boston, "The Cold" centers on an aggressive reporter (Gary Graham, twitchy) researching a spate of killings. His digging leads him to a house owned by Emily (Bess Meyer, flavorsome), who lives in subcryonic temperatures and relates the story of her mother, victim of a mad scientist (David Warner, over the top) who needed a constant supply of human spinal fluid to maintain eternal life. Final twist is signaled early on.

"Whispers," set in a vaguely futuristic Philly, follows a feisty female cop (Signy Coleman, OK) who crashes her car in an urban hell and is drawn into a pit full of monsters by a folksy old couple (Don Calfa, Judith Drake, cleverly menacing). Double-punch twist ending is neat but nothing new.

Yuzna's wraparound rolls down the curtain in grand F/X style, with H.P.'s dabbling with the Necronomicon causing the netherworld to demand a victim. The author lives to write another batch of stories, natch.

Overall jokey tone of the film is precariously maintained, given the wide spread of genres. Best of the bunch is, in fact, the most serious, "The Drowned," in which French director Christophe Gans trades on but finds more modern equivalents of the Roger Corman legacy. Effects and atmosphere are stylishly handled, with a dreamlike quality that doesn't simply rely on gore.

Japanese helmer Shu Kaneko's "The Cold" is competently handled but degrades early on into a retread of Yuzna's own "Re-Animator," capped by gruesome F/X. Millie Perkins balances Warner's hammy boffin with more controlled menace.

Yuzna's own seg, "Whispers," is the weakest of the three, a straight linear tale whose only interest lies in how far he'll go with rotting corpses and bodily fluids to cap the previous episodes. After 80 minutes or so, *deja vu* looms.

Tech credits are fine, with iron-hard Dolby sound and an intense, driving score in "The Drowned" and the wraparound by Joseph Lo Duca ("Evil Dead") that's a real plus. Russ Brandt's lensing of "The Drowned" has a stylish edge, and effects throughout, by a battery of names, are up to scratch, especially in the showcase final minutes.

—*Derek Elley*

DOLLAR MAMBO

(MEXICAN-SPANISH)

A Programa Doble (Mexico)/Igeldo Zine Produkzioak (Spain) production. (International sales: Igeldo Zine, San Sebastian.) Produced by Arturo Whaley. Executive producers, Alejandro Springall, Alejandra Liceaga. Directed by Paul Leduc. Screenplay, Jaime Aviles, Jose Joaquin Blanco, Leduc, Hector Ortega, Juan Tovar, from an original idea by Leduc inspired by real events published in the international press April 5, 1990. Additional material, Fernando Lijan. Camera (color), Guillermo Navarro; editor, Guillermo S. Maldonado; music, Eugenio Toussaint; art direction, Arturo Nava; costume design, Claudia Fernandez, Jimena Fernandez; sound (Ultra-Stereo), Juan Carlos Cid, Andres Franco, David Barsht; choreography, Marco Antonio Silva; additional choreography, Tito Vasconcelos; associate producers, Berta Navarro, Angel Amigo. Reviewed at London Film Festival, Nov. 18, 1993. Running time: **78 MIN.**
Jenny .... Dolores Pedro
Roberto .... Roberto Sosa
Raul .... Raul Medina
  With: Litico Rodriguez, Tito Vasconcelos, Eduardo Lopez Rojas, Kandido Uranga, Silvestre Mendez, Gabino Diego, Monica Castillo.

A musical without dialogue set in a Panamanian cabaret-bar during armed American invasion, "Dollar Mambo" fires blanks in almost all departments. Listless direction by Mexican helmer Paul Leduc ("Reed: Mexico Insurgente") and eye-gougingly obvious political sniping sink a potentially peppy idea early on. Commercial chances beyond hardcore Caribbeanophiles are zip.

Setting is the tacky Salon Panama, where a group of blowzy singers, chorus girls, magicians and actors entertain longshoremen and assorted barrio riffraff. Performers' routines are cross-cut with a group breaking into and plundering a warehouse full of electronic goods.

Some 45 minutes in, the Americans arrive, rape one of the artistes (Dolores Pedro) and colonize the joint. Pic ends with the cabaret resuming amid U.S. flags and dollar icons.

Colorful opening titles and a shock special effect during the (mimed/danced) rape scene are pic's only eye-openers. Lineup of well-known artistes is squandered by Paris-trained Leduc's uninventive visual style, a dully recorded soundtrack and cramped 1.33 visuals. Pedro makes a sassy lead but deserves better. —*Derek Elley*

THE LINE, THE CROSS & THE CURVE

(BRITISH)

A Novercia production. (International sales: Novercia, Welling, Kent, U.K.) Produced by Margarita Doyle. Directed, written by Kate Bush. Camera (Technicolor), Roger Pratt; editor, Julian Rodd; music, Bush; production design, Roger Hall; art direction, Hall, Ben Scott; costume design, Hazel Pethig; sound (Dolby digital), Steve Jones, Ian Silvester; special effects, Bob Hollow; assistant director, Laurie Borg. Reviewed at London Film Festival, Nov. 13, 1993. Running time: **44 MIN.**
Dancer .... Kate Bush
Male dancer .... Stewart Arnold
Mysterious
  woman .... Miranda Richardson
Guide .... Lindsay Kemp

Shyly retiring British pop diva Kate Bush, 35, steps behind the lens with mixed artistic results in "The Line, the Cross & the Curve," a music promo flick high on whimsy and low on content. Cinematic values (and demo-quality Dolby digital sound) make this a solid bet for special events, however, with eight numbers sure to please Bush aficionados.

Written and directed by Bush herself to promote her new album, "The Red Shoes," the pic (played at ear-splitting volume) got a warm welcome at its SRO London Festival screening at a large downtown theater. It goes out on U.K. homevideo later this year. Story is a snappy variation on the 1948 Michael Powell-Emeric Pressburger classic "The Red Shoes," with Bush as a dancer who's given a pair of red ballet shoes that won't stop dancing by a mysterious woman (Miranda Richardson) in exchange for three magical symbols (pic's title).

Richardson, reprising her "Crying Game" Irish accent, steals the acting stakes as a kind of wicked witch. When not warbling, Bush is colorless. Mime artist Lindsay Kemp, under whom Bush studied, is reliable. Pic's visual style is relatively conservative, far from the usual musicvid fare. Aspect ratio is also a conservative 1.33.

—*Derek Elley*

LES MARMOTTES
(THE GROUNDHOGS)
(FRENCH)

A President Films presentation of a 7 Films Cinema and TF1 Films production in association with Canal Plus. Produced by Robert Benmussa. Directed by Elie Chouraqui. Screenplay, Daniele Thompson, Chouraqui. Camera (color), Robert Alazraki; editor, Martine Giordano; music, Gabriel Yared; sets, Patrice Biarent; costumes, Mimi Lempicka; sound, Francois Musy. Reviewed at Sarasota French Film Festival, Nov. 13, 1993. Running time: **103 MIN.**
Stephane ....Jean-Hugues Anglade
Frederique .... Jacqueline Bisset
Marie-Claire .... Christine Boisson
Simon .... Andre Dussollier
Max .... Gerard Lanvin
Lucie .... Marie Trintignant
Francoise .... Anouk Aimee
Leo .... Daniel Gelin
  With: Anne Roussel, Christian Charmetant, Christopher Thompson, Virginie Ledoyen, Patricia Malvoisin, Nita Klein, Julia Maraval, Yves Gavard, Edith Vernes, Pierre Yves Gallenne, Dany Gallenne, Elodie Tairraz, Renaud Musy.

Elie Chouraqui offers a deft mix of comedy and melancholy with the help of a strong ensemble cast in "Les Marmottes," a lightweight but likable opus about an eventful Christmas ski vacation. Pic covers familiar territory well enough to ensure some offshore exposure.

The "Marmottes" of the title are friends, relatives and couples who enjoy an annual yuletide get-together in Chamonix. But they spend little time on the slopes and devote most of their energies to affairs of the heart.

Leo (Daniel Gelin), the widowed gray eminence of the group, chooses the occasion to announce his marriage to longtime companion Francoise (Anouk Aimee) — much to the discomfort of Max (Gerard Lanvin), his middle-aged son, whose marriage to Marie-Claire (Christine Boisson) is crumbling. Simon (Andre Dussollier), Max's brother, seems to enjoy a much better time of it with his wife, Frederique (Jacqueline Bisset), but still sneaks his mistress along for the holiday.

Meanwhile, family friend Stephane (Jean-Hugues Anglade) is repeatedly guilt-tripped by his suicidal girlfriend, Lucie (Marie Trintignant), who wants him to make a commitment.

Other subplots include a rocky romance between Simon's twenty-something son and Max's teenage daughter, and Max's infatuation with a resort employee.

Chouraqui would have done better to make it easier (and faster) for an audience to understand who's related by birth or marriage, and who's just a good friend. It says much about the charm of the characters and the actors playing them that, even as one scrambles to figure out the interconnections, the occasional confusion is at worst a minor distraction.

Dussollier and Bisset are standouts in the large cast, in large part because they have the meatiest roles and the most affecting dramatic moments. Anglade and Lanvin also make solid impressions.

Tech credits, including Robert Alazraki's attractive lensing of the wintry Chamonix climes, are first-rate.
—*Joe Leydon*

LE NOMBRIL DU MONDE
(I, BAJOU)
(FRENCH)

A Le Studio Canal Plus/AJO Distribution/Partner's Prods./Odessa Films/Cerito Films co-production. Produced by Yannick Bernard. Directed, written by Ariel Zeitoun. Camera (color), Eric Gauthier; editor, Hugues Darmois; production design, Bernard Vezat; costumes, Edith Vesperini; sound, Gerard Lecas; assistant director, Yvon Rouve. Reviewed at Sarasota French Film Festival, Sept. 11, 1993. Running time: **145 MIN.**
Bajou .... Michel Boujenah
Habiba .... Delphine Forest
Marcel .... Thomas Langmann
Amina .... Souad Amidou
Marie .... Natacha Amal
Oumi .... Marie-Josee Nat
With: Roger Hanin, Mustapha Adouani, Laurent Natrela, Victor Haim, Bruno Todeschini, Jean-Marie Winling, Hichem Rostom, Bernard Vezat, Alberto Canova, Phil Barney, Olivier Sitruk, Marc Saez, Yoan Hayoun, Stephane Cohen.

Michel Boujenah's full-bodied (in every sense of the term) and fearless lead performance dominates "Le Nombril du monde," an engrossing period drama also known by the more wieldy, less idiomatic title "I, Bajou." By any name, it's a first-rate achievement by writer-director Ariel Zeitoun that will doubtless enjoy prominent exposure on global fest circuit, and might also earn respectable coin in select urban markets.

Set in the French protectorate of Tunisia from the early 1930s through the postwar period, pic focuses on Bajou (Boujenah), an obsessively driven Jew who rises from sharecropper to entrepreneur through dint of hard work, mathematical skills and occasionally sheer ruthlessness. Always mindful of his precarious status in an Arab-dominated culture, and quietly resentful of remarks about his enormous bulk, he slowly gains power and influence, if not respect, after moving to the capital city of Tunis.

Along with his hotheaded cousin Marcel (Thomas Langmann), Bajou joins the Resistance movement during the German Occupation —

motivated as much by economics as patriotism. Later, he decides to claim the beautiful Habiba (Delphine Forest), daughter of the now-bankrupt landowner who once employed Bajou, as a wife. That Habiba doesn't want to marry him, and already has a lover, is of little consequence to Bajou. He pays off Habiba's father, drives the lover out of town and settles down to what he thinks will be a lifetime of domestic bliss.

The most impressive thing about Boujenah's multilayered performance is the way he manages to retain some audience sympathy, without any obvious pandering or soft-pedaling, even when Bajou's being most selfish. The character is complex and deeply flawed, yet also tremendously loyal and, in his own way, deeply in love with Habiba. All he really wants is a family. Trouble is, he will stop at nothing to achieve that goal. Boujenah's brilliant portrayal shines a mercilessly bright light on every dark corner of Bajou's soul.

But even though he's the main attraction, Boujenah isn't the whole show. "I, Bajou" is as rich in incident, character and ambiguity as a classic novel, with just a touch of Pagnol's "The Baker's Wife" thrown in for good measure. (Zeitoun slyly acknowledges the influence during one of Habiba's trips to the local cinema). Despite a certain choppiness to the continuity in the final reels, the narrative drive is consistently compelling for pic's nearly 2½-hour running time.

As Habiba, Forest evidences impressive range and depth, making a persuasive progression from hate to resignation to a kind of love. More strong support is offered by Langmann as Marcel, Marie-Josee Nat as Bajou's stern mother and Roger Hanin as the former landowner who sells his daughter to Bajou.

Bountiful period flavor is provided by costumer Edith Vesperini, production designer Bernard Vezat and cinematographer Eric Gauthier. Makeup artist Dominique Colladant deserves credit for deftly aging Bajou and other characters.
—*Joe Leydon*

COUPLES ET AMANTS
(COUPLES AND LOVERS)
(FRENCH)

A Providence Films production in association with La Sept Cinema and Canal Plus. Produced by Yves Gasser. Directed by John Lvoff. Screenplay, Pascal Bonitzer, Lvoff, Catherine Breillux. Camera (color), Jean-Claude Larrieu; editor, Jacqueline Counor; music, Charlie Couture; sets, Therese Ripaud; sound, Christian Fontaine, Jerome Thiault. Reviewed at Sarasota French Film Festival, Sept. 14, 1993. Running time: **90 MIN.**
Isabelle .... Marie Bunel
Paul .... Jacques Bonaffee
Also with: Bruno Todeschi, Sara Guiran, Isabelle Candelier.

John Lvoff's "Couples et amants" is a well-acted and competently made drama of adultery that offers little in the way of fresh ideas or compelling plot eccentricities. Commercial prospects appear dim for this unremarkable pic, despite fine performances by leads.

Isabelle (Marie Bunel), a psychoanalyst, and Paul (Jacques Bonaffee), an ophthalmologist, are attractive and successful professionals who, in the eyes of their friends, have the perfect marriage. In pic's opening moments, however, it's revealed that Isabelle is enjoying afternoon trysts with a temperamental writer, and suffering only the mildest pangs of guilt.

Paul is faithful only until a beautiful but neurotic young patient captures his fancy. The woman, who restores antique screens, is the one who makes the first move. But it doesn't take long for Paul to follow.

Lvoff's point seems to be that even someone who's happily married might find it irresistible to have an affair with someone more troublesome, even more dangerous, than one's "perfect" spouse. In contrast to the leads, Lvoff presents a squabbling couple on the verge of divorce. Their open hostility may be intended as some sort of ironic counterpoint, but it doesn't work very well as such.

"Couples et amants" has more than a trace of Ingmar Bergman — specifically, "Scenes from a Marriage" — particularly when Paul turns angrily brutal after learning of Isabelle's infidelity. But the best moments are bits of comic relief, most of them provided by Isabelle's most surly patient, a German who finds nothing charming about France.

Bonaffee and Bunel are good within the limits of their material, even though their characters never establish a firm grip on the audience's sympathies. Tech credits are average.
—*Joe Leydon*

VANCOUVER

IKI KADIN
(TWO WOMEN)
(TURKISH)

A Z Film production. Produced, directed, written by Yavuz Ozkan. Camera (color), Orhan Oguz; editor, Mevlu Kocak; music, Muzikotek. Reviewed at Vancouver Intl. Film Festival, Oct. 15, 1993. Running time: **132 MIN.**
With: Zuhal Olcay, Serap Aksoy, Haluk Bilginer.

On paper, "Two Women" looks like a sure-fire winner. With a plot centering on the friendship between a high-priced prostitute and the wife of the politician who raped her, it promises to tackle Turkish machismo, class-crossing feminism and government corruption at one go. Result, however, is a sudsy mess, obscuring as many issues as it raises.

Triple-hatted filmmaker Yavuz Ozkan first establishes the inarguable niceness of the lead character, played by European-looking Zuhal Olcay: she has a calm, art-filled house and dotes on her sweet little daughter, who's doubly handicapped since she's blind and her voice is obviously dubbed by a goo-goo-talking adult.

Then, quicker than you can say Lesley Ann Warren, Olcay's being led to the hotel lair of hotshot minister Haluk Bilginer. When the embarrassed politico tries to cancel their "date," she taunts him relentlessly until he responds with an inevitable, if highly unpleasant, rebuttal. Without examining her own ambiguous motives — entirely lost on Ozkan — she decides to sue the minister for sexual assault, becoming a tabloid *cause celebre*, and causing her aged father to actually say, "Where did we go wrong?"

The politico uses all his slick skills to wriggle out of the growing scandal, while his dignified, too-sheltered wife (Serap Aksoy) is increasingly unimpressed by his machinations. After a seeming eternity, she seeks out Olcay for some heart-to-heart talks, complete with a coyly implied lesbian undercurrent (mainly, Aksoy wears slacks).

Considering the serious "no-means-no" subject, especially in the context of a developing Islamic culture, pic is a curiously timeless, placeless mishmash, played for glossy sentiment more than social comment. Thesping and lensing are OK (even if both go out of focus on occasion), but the best scenes are crushed by a hideous synthesizer score, credited to the Muzikotek library, and edited with a blunt cleaver. Even among open-minded festgoers, "Two Women" can't expect much respect.
—*Ken Eisner*

December 6, 1993 (Cont.)

SURAJ KA SATVAN GHODA
(SEVENTH HORSE OF THE SUN)
(INDIAN)

A National Film Development Corp. production. Produced by Doordarshan. Directed by Shyam Benegal. Screenplay, Shama Zaida. Camera (color), Piyush Shah; editor, Bhanudas Divkar; music, Vanraj Bhatia. Reviewed at Vancouver Intl. Film Festival, Oct. 6, 1993. Running time: **124 MIN.**
With: Amrish Puri, Neena Gupta, Ila Arun, K.K. Raina, Pallavi Joshi.
(In Bengali; English subtitles)

A colorful compendium of Indian folk tales and modern-day polemics, "Seventh Horse of the Sun" is as expertly told as a favorite campfire saga and as haunting as a dimly remembered love song. It will take a bold market-minded rider, however, to get this horse to run in foreign orbits.

"Don't tell the kind of story where events just pile up on top of each other," pleads one of the young professional men who gather frequently to hear tales spun by Manek Mulla (soulfully handsome Amrish Puri).

But Manek takes his own sweet time spinning stories that veer between the intensely personal and the mythically grand. And whether he's talking about his own harsh school days or the gilded carriage of an unhappy princess, the tales always seem to involve sharp longing and sudden separation — along with digressions into Marxist dialectic.

Vet helmer Shyam Benegal imbues each flashback section with a different tint of color and mood, but never gets too schematic about it.

There are dark moments in the most farcical passages, and hints of comedy even in quasi-mystical parts: an apparently devoted servant suggests impotence-curing tasks to his master that are Herculean to the point of absurdity (that's where the equestrian title comes in).

Stunningly lensed events are moved along nicely by Vanraj Bhatia's synth 'n' sitar score. Most of the characters and tones come together in the wildly climactic section in which Manek woos a feisty Gypsy woman ("Gypsy," for these Bengalis, actually means Iranian) and ends up so troubled by her loss, his objectivity as a raconteur is ultimately subverted. Clever, richly understated stuff, and it never feels long. —*Ken Eisner*

KUSA NO UE NO SHIGOTO
(WORK ON THE GRASS)
(JAPANESE — 16mm)

A Pictures Up production. Produced by Tetsuo Shinohara, Akemi Sugawara, Shogo Ueno. Directed, written by Shinohara. Camera (color), Ueno; editor, Yoko Nishioka; music, Hiroyuki Murakami. Reviewed at Vancouver Intl. Film Festival, Oct. 5, 1993. Running time: **42 MIN.**
With: Naoki Goto, Hikari Ota.

Content, form and execution are perfectly married in this miniature meditation on labor, desire and individuality, which grabbed the grand prize at this year's short-pic fest in Kobe.

Story throws together two grass-cutters, assigned to mow an untamed field so huge that it recedes into the far horizon. One's a veteran greensman (Naoki Goto) with a working-class background, military bearing and authoritarian inclinations; the other's a middle-class novice (Hikari Ota) on leave from college, and infuriatingly passive when it comes to learning his task.

They don't hit it off. Still, the vet's browbeating produces a curious obstinacy in the student, and he begins to suspect there's more going on than bourgeois laziness. When they break for lunch, the mismatched pair form an uneasy, mildly sensual rapport.

Lensing and other tech values are merely adequate, but helmer Shinohara (who earned his stripes as an assistant director in Japan's collapsed apprentice system) makes masterful use of luxuriant rhythms and oblique humor to build his quirky parable.

The two young leads provide top-notch thesping. Pic's odd length and format indicate an unlikely art-house traveler, but the classy "Work" is a natural for pubcasting packages worldwide.
—*Ken Eisner*

CRACK ME UP
(CANADIAN)

An Oneira Pictures Intl. production. Produced by Bashar Shbib, Janet Cunningham. Executive producer, Michael Kolin. Directed by Shbib. Screenplay, Shbib, Daphna Kastner, Maryse Wilder. Camera (color), Stephen Reizes; editors, Vincent Lauzon, Shbib; music, Emilio Kauderer; art direction, Janet Campbell; costume design, Thomas G. Marquez; sound, David Chornow, Manse James; associate producers, Didier Farre, Gregor Bismarck, Wendy Rittermal; casting, Cunningham. Reviewed at Vancouver Intl. Film Festival, Oct. 12, 1993. Running time: **76 MIN.**.

Louie B.	Tim Brazzil
Billy Jean	Daphna Kastner
Stacey	Mary Crosby
Det. Harry Bork	David Charles
Elizabeth	Arma Lou Divine
Loretta	Anita Olanick

Ostensibly a *verite* romp on the sleazy side of Hollywood, "Crack Me Up" never gets its story — about a naive filmmaker's chance encounter with crack cocaine — into high gear. And it never drops it long enough to let the pic's documentary instincts take over.

In "Julia Has Two Lovers" and "Lana in Love," renegade Canadian helmer Bashar Shbib found a workable balance between slick and spontaneous. Here, he's lost the precarious knack in a misguided attempt to up the ante by combining slummy camp, porno spoof and slice-of-life realism.

To begin with, Tim Brazzil is intended to have Gary Cooper dignity — but comes off like a cigar-store Indian — as the video-toting Louis B. Trying to get Angelenos to kiss for his camera, he accidentally tapes a bank holdup in progress. The gang leader turns out to be Mary Crosby, joshing her own "Dallas" role. Her boys soon find Louis and "crack him up." Suddenly sightless, he wanders into the arms of gold-hearted hooker Billy Jean (Daphna Kastner), who takes him home to her dormlike bordello.

In this red-filled house the best scenes occur, as the blind filmmaker (oh the irony!) turns his camera over to male and female sex workers to tell their own stories, which are by turns bitchy, funny and sad. Most of these non-pro pros were found on L.A. streets, and they act rings around the "real" cast (with the notable exception of Anita Olanick, as Billy Jean's buddy and would-be lover). Apart from these affecting vignettes, pic tries hard for farce, but only veteran Kastner's perf gets boffo laughs — of the glaringly unintentional kind.

Shbib should hold out for better scripts or make like Louie B. and skip them altogether if he wants to open theater doors more than the smallest crack. Could be worth a few video chuckles, though.
—*Ken Eisner*

KOI NO TASOGARE
(BREAKABLE)
(JAPANESE — 16mm)

A Far East Films production. Produced by Koji Hirata. Directed, written by Takayoshi Yamaguchi, from a story by Hirata. Camera (b&w), Akihito Shiota; editor, Toshihide Hukano; music, Shinsuke Honda; sound, Masami Nishioka; associate producers, Hiorokazu Akiyama, Satoshi Umezawa; assistant directors, Kazunori Nishimura, Yasuhara Suido. Reviewed at Vancouver Intl. Film Festival, Oct. 8, 1993. Running time: **70 MIN.**

Minoru	Hironobu Hirabayashi
Kyoko	Satoko Abe
Yumi	Keiko Sugano
Emi	Koru Soya
Nanae	Yumi Wagai
Fumiko	Tubama Mita

A subtle new direction for Japanese indie production, "Breakable" takes an unblinking, Euro-style look at urban twentysomethings and their vague search for meaning. Remarkably, the quietly satisfying pic neither condescends nor succumbs to their torpor, but small scale and lack of "Less Than Zero" histrionics will probably keep it from cracking offshore B.O.

First-time helmer Takayoshi Yamaguchi says Woody Allen is his fave, but Eric Rohmer is a closer model for his breezy, docu-style story, which follows the low-key exploits of Minoru (long-faced Hironobu Hirabayashi), the laconic editor of a dumb comic book called "Maiden's Dream."

Minoru has grown comfy in his unquestioned relationship with serious Kyoko, but this is shaken by a chance meeting with pretty Yumi, the sister of an almost pathologically uncooperative illustrator. Soon he's indulging, among other things, Yumi's taste for occidental oddities like jam on toast. Eventually, he's forced to reevaluate his primary affair when Kyoko gets a chance to work at a sushi house in Brazil, but his conclusions remain elusive.

All this romantic flummoxing sounds fairly spare, but it's frequently enlivened by droll humor (as when a friend totals Kyoko's car, and everyone is too polite to talk about it) and incisive, yet compassionate, jabs at Japanese materialism and its dispirited offspring.

A nifty surf-guitar score gives a Jarmusch-like kick to Akihito Shiota's cool b&w lensing. Twentysomethings themselves, Shiota, Yamaguchi and producer Koji Hirata comprise the maverick collective Far East Films, and each is slated to helm future pix. —*Ken Eisner*

HWA-OM-KYONG
(SOUTH KOREAN)

A Tae Hung Prod. Co. production, with Korean Films Associates (International sales: Korean Motion Picture Promotion Corp., Seoul). Produced by Lee Tae-Won. Directed, written by Jang Sun-Woo, based on the novel by Ko Eun. Camera (color), Yu Young-Gill; editor, Kim Hyun; music, Lee Chong-Ku; production design, Chun Yung-Haeng; costume design, Lee Eun-Kyung; sound, Kim Won-Yong; assistant director, Moon Myung-Hee; special effects, Kim Chul-Suk. Reviewed at the Vancouver Intl. Film Festival, Oct. 8, 1993. Running time: **110 MIN.**

December 6, 1993 (Cont.)

With: Oh Tae-Kyung, Kim Hye-Sun, Lee Ho-Jae, Chung Soo-Young, Shin Hyun-Joon, Lee Dae-Ro, Dogko Young-Jae, Huh Byung-Sub, Lim Chang-Dae, Kim Eun-Mi, Um Chun-Bae, Lee Hye-Young, Won Mi-Kyung.

This gorgeous, tender, and warmly funny update of a famous Buddhist tract manages the seemingly miraculous: to translate religious literature to the modern screen, and in terms catholic enough to make true believers of selected arthouse auds.

Helmer Jang Sun-Woo moves Ko Eun's novel — already a retelling of the fifth century Avatamsaka Sutra — into the present by following one youngster on his Siddhartha-like journey. After Sonje (Oh Tae Kyung) loses his father, he wanders the craggy peaks and trash-strewn inlets of the Korean peninsula in search of the mother he never knew.

He meets a rascally monk, a saintly blind prostitute, a tough-talking doctor, a boy astronomer and a kind lighthouse-keeper. Sonje remains the same age as others grow old. The script doesn't push any particular dogma to explain this phenomenon, and is, in fact, awash with contradictory impulses (hence the surprising amount of humor); few films have presented human life as a kind of erotic Oedipal death dance.

But even those puzzled by this episodic storyline will go gaga over Yu Young-Gil's supernatural lensing, and all acting is entertainingly high gear. The only minus is that Lee Chong-Ku's stately string music eventually gives way to soapy, all-too-secular synthesizers.

Korean lingo will make pic a tough sell to distribs even if high quality begs a try. Tape will prove a rare boon to theology students, but it will take a marketing crusade to give general auds religion. —*Ken Eisner*

RAMAYANA: THE LEGEND OF PRINCE RAMA

(INDIAN-JAPANESE)

A Nippon Ramayana Films/Malati Tambay Vaidya and Assoc. (Bombay) production. (International sales: Carnegie Film Group, L.A.) Produced, directed by Yugo Sako. Screenplay, Narendra Sharma, Koichi Sasaki, Rani Burra, Hiroshi Onogi, Ram Mohan, Sako, based on the book by Valmiki and conception of Sako, Vijay Nigam. Camera (color), T. Nishimura; music, Vanraj Bhatia. Reviewed at Vancouver Intl. Film Festival, Oct. 17, 1993. Running time: 120 MIN.

This is an animated retelling of the famous Indian saga, in which an earthly incarnation of Vishnu does battle with the forces of dark not-niceness. Relentlessly paced, pic has no heart for general auds to cotton to, and is not even great to look at.

The classic "Ramayana," originated around 500 B.C. and usually credited to the poet Valmiki, was continuously censored and altered by touchy Brahmins, fearing even a secular retelling of the life of the privileged Prince Rama, who hit the theosophical big time as the Gautama Buddha. They needn't have bothered, if they'd known it would end up in the hands of these Japanese and Indian animators; picture Schwarzennegger as a well-armed cartoon Jesus ("Ah'll be back") and you've got some idea of the moral tone of this action-crammed epic.

It's like reducing "War and Peace" to a series of disjointed battle scenes, with most of the females jettisoned from the plot. With one violent confrontation after another, there's little of the reflection necessary to get even a hint of spiritual underpinning. Instead, traditional notions of masculinity, courage and filial piety are drummed home, between noisy clashes of metal and wood.

The art itself places flatly drawn, rigidly moving central characters (in the "Clutch Cargo" style of mass-prod Japanese cartooning) against richly painted Indian backgrounds. One of the few times these elements are integrated is in a climactic sequence pitting hundreds of monkey-warriors against an awesome, sky-filling giant.

Even with English dialogue, the results won't find B.O. nirvana on the animation circuit. It will, however, play well with laserdisc-owning boys, unlikely to notice, or care, that the good guys have the lightest skins, or that Rama and his buddies speak in hushed Oxford tones, while the lesser beings have plain Indian accents. —*Ken Eisner*

KE-YEOJA, KE-NAMJA

(THAT WOMAN, THAT MAN)

(SOUTH KOREAN)

An Ik-Young production. (Intl. sales: Korean Motion Picture Promotion Corp., Seoul). Produced by Park Sang-In. Directed by Kim Ui-Seok. Written by Park Heon-Su. Camera (color), Koo Chung-Mo; editor, Park Sun-Deok; music, O15B; production design, Cho Yung-Sam, Yu Jin-Sang; sound, Lee Byeong-Ha. Reviewed at Vancouver Intl. Film Festival, Oct. 11, 1993. Running time: 115 MIN.
With: Kang Soo-Yeon, Lee Kyeong-Young, Ha Yu-Mi, Kim Sung-Su.

Poignant, colorful and frequently hilarious, this romantic comedy of errors would be instant boffo B.O. in the U.S. if its mixed-up lovers spoke English. As it is, you can't get much more universal than this playfully convoluted tale of Kuppies (Korean urban professionals) who move into the same building, are instantly repelled, then hate each other more once they get involved.

In fact, a smart Hollywood producer could lift the Ben Hecht-like byplay of "That Woman, That Man" intact, with only the political references changed: The characters sing along with Puccini, hang trendy Matisse prints, fight over a Michael Bolton CD (talk about a loser's game) and kiss with Audrey Hepburn on the vidscreen, all while scrambling for position in their careers and beds.

"That Man" Chang (Kang Soo-Yeon) is a self-centered TV journalist (he's in charge of editing obituaries on people who never die); "That Woman" Eun (Lee Kyeong-Young) is a maternity nurse without much interest in babies. When they "meet cute" in the apartment elevator, each is preoccupied with dumping a longtime b.f./g.f., and they don't connect for some time. When they finally do, more than sparks fly, as their temperaments are strictly chalk and kim-chi.

What raises the comic eventualities above the average TV pic is the ironic unpredictability of the script, which doesn't have a lot of sentimental attachment to which way the romance goes. Instead, with the aid of constantly percolating thesping and snappy editing, it concentrates on the habituated foibles and petty resentments that keep these attractive urbanites apart and make them who they are.

Along the way, light-handed helmer Kim Ui-Seok ("Marriage Story") and clever lenser Koo Chung-Mo have immense fun with elaborate set-pieces showing the Seoul "Man" and "Woman" in side-by-side rooms, lost in their own high-rise worlds, banging on the walls or longing to be somewhere else. —*Ken Eisner*

UNE NOUVELLE VIE

(A NEW LIFE)

(FRENCH)

An Arena Films/La Sept Cinema/Lumiere co-production with the participation of Vega Film/Alia Film/Canal Plus/Cofimage 4/Investimage 4/C.N.C. (Paris)/Television Suisse/D.F.1. (International sales: Pyramide Intl., Paris.) Produced by Bruno Pesery. Directed, written by Olivier Assayas. Camera (color; Panavision widescreen), Denis Lenoir; editor, Luc Barnier; set design, Francois-Renaud Labarthe; costumes, Francoise Clavel; sound (Dolby), Francois Musy. Reviewed at Festival of Festivals, Toronto, Sept. 12, 1993. Running time: 122 MIN.
Tina .... Sophie Aubry
Lise .... Judith Godreche
Constantin .... Bernard Giraudeau
Laurence .... Christine Boisson
Fred .... Philippe Torreton
Ludovic .... Bernard Verley
Nadine .... Nelly Borgeaud
With: Antoine Basler, Roger Dumas.

Writer-director Olivier Assayas impressively sustains a highly controlled mood for more than two hours in "Une Nouvelle Vie," but what a mood. This tale of a disenfranchised young woman trying to piece together the jigsaw puzzle that is her personal life is loaded with uniformly sullen characters morosely expressing nothing but ugly emotions. Well-made picture is too slow and temperamentally off-putting for offshore success.

Tina (Sophie Aubry) is a typically pouty French 20-year-old whose blank expression remains the same whether she's having sex or working at her job in a supermarket warehouse. Living desultorily with her pathetic mother and going out with a loser b.f., Tina decides to break a lifelong taboo by seeking out her father, about whom she knows nothing.

Search initially leads to her half-sister Lise (Judith Godreche), a strange girl who's involved in a weird S&M relationship with their father's lawyer Constantin (Bernard Giraudeau).

Pic's strongest scene is an initial confrontation between Tina and her powerful, piggish father (Bernard Verley), a collision of raw emotion in which he tells her she'll never see him or Lise again, upon which she draws blood hitting him.

In the protracted course of things, matters become infinitely more complicated, as Tina's mother dies; Constantin, who's been dumped by both Lise and his wife, takes up with Tina and informs her he once slept with her mother; Laurence (Christine Boisson), Constantin's lovely wife, unaccountably lets Tina's old b.f. have his way with her, and Tina and Lise decide to work out their complicated relationship.

Basically, everyone seems to dislike everyone else, but they have a strange compulsion to automatically want to sleep with one another regardless. The characters ooze poisonous emotions, expressed in hushed, ultra-serious monotones that do not allow for the variety of moods found in real life.

Worse, all humor is banished, to the point where its rigorous exclusion seems ridiculous. Assayas' method is most apparent in a moment in which someone tells the two sisters something that makes them laugh. However, the scene is covered from outside a window, so as to not let the viewer in on the joke.

Two of the former critic's previous pictures, "Desordre" and "Paris s'eveille," were good, gritty looks at fringe youth in contempo France. This outing sees him too immersed in an unpleasant, negative mood to communicate much for an audience to grab onto. Perhaps it's time for him to move on to a subject he can handle more objectively.

Widescreen lensing, deliberately drained of color, creates a determinedly drab environment in which the characters play out their sad, nasty-spirited games.

—*Todd McCarthy*

THE PROS AND CONS OF BREATHING

A Chi-Boy production. Produced by Steve Hart. Directed, written by Robert Munic. Camera (Technicolor), Steve Adcock; editor, Michael Waterhouse; production design, Donna Kaczmarek; costumes, Phillip Mershon; sound (Ultra Stereo), David Aron; assistant director, Joan Bostwick. Reviewed at Chicago Film Festival, Oct. 17, 1993. Running Time: **89 MINS.**
Shirley .... Joey Lauren Adams
Tippy .... Phillip Brock
Tony .... Joey Dedeo
Bradley .... Ira Heiden
Troy .... Philip Tanzini
Ira .... Barry Sobel
Canbi .... Noelle Parker
Homeless Vet .... Robert Munic

"**T**he Pros and Cons of Breathing" is the latest incarnation of the several-guys-sitting-around-talking subgenre. It is neither the worst nor the best of the breed. Rather, it shows first-time writer-director Robert Munic's technical prowess and his need for some remedial storytelling classes. The imbalance does not bode well for the venture's commercial life. Limited theatrical prospects could muster modest interest in ancillary areas.

The basic focus is on four twenty-something young men who hang out at a subdued Los Angeles club. The entertainment equivalent of the multiethnic platoon in war movies, the group is comprised of an actor (Joey Dedeo), an agent (Ira Heiden), a standup comic (Phillip Brock) and a director (Philip Tanzini).

Essential to this type of endeavor is a crisp script, brimming with wit and etched with vivid characterization. It should be noted that this element falls into the "Cons" section of the title.

Munic's narrative vision is almost uniformly bleak, in sharp contrast to the slick, sharp images of the club and its surroundings. It is fraught with lost jobs, lost roles and financial catastrophe. Coupled with characters dogged by self-doubts, the overall mood is not exactly something to snuggle up with on a chilly night. Worse, the tale provides little insight into the human condition under pressure circumstances.

Curiously, the story is narrated by someone outside the group — Shirley (Joey Lauren Adams), a waitress at the club and onetime girlfriend of one of the members of the quartet. If the four men appear callow, the young woman is downright grating as she reports the mundane details of individual fortunes as if reading a news report. A bit more irony would have sweetened the recipe.

While the material is rooted in the banal and melodramatic, Munic effects a rather savvy visual style. Technically, he avoids the obvious pitfall of claustrophobia in his scene construction. Though produced on a modest budget, the film's ills have little to do with surface polish.

Apart from Adams, the cast rises at least to the level of the script and generally a notch or two above. The actors have the exceedingly thankless task of attempting to make their flawed and unsympathetic losers at least semi-palatable.

—*Leonard Klady*

HOMELANDS

(AUSTRALIAN — DOCU)

A Jotz Prods. production, with the participation of the Australian Film Finance Corp., in association with the Special Broadcasting Service. Produced, directed by Tom Zubrycki. Camera (color), Joel Peterson; associate producer/editor, Ray Thomas; music, Jan Preston; sound, Gary O'Grady. Reviewed at Sydney Film Festival, June 13, 1993. Running time: **79 MIN.**

Tom Zubrycki, one of Australia's top docu directors, has come up with a candid and moving portrait of a married couple who relocated to Australia from El Salvador at the height of that country's civil war. Result is not only a study of displaced people, but a portrait of a marriage that is profoundly affected by the changes in circumstances. It's a gripping docu.

Zubrycki, himself the son of Polish refugees in Australia, is extremely sympathetic to both his protagonists, Maria and Carlos Robles. Film commences on Feb. 1, 1992, in Melbourne, as the Robles and their four daughters celebrate the end of the war in their far-off homeland. It's revealed that both Maria and Carlos had participated in the struggle for freedom, and that Maria had been tortured and raped by the military.

Carlos immediately decides to return home. Maria, left alone in Australia with her children, speaks English far better than her husband, is aware that her daughters have become completely Australianized, and is torn between her new home and her native land.

Eventually she returns to El Salvador to find that her husband has been involved with another woman. Still, she acknowledges he's been doing great work in a poor village, and she's prepared to forgive him if he returns to his family.

Even if Carlos comes out second best, both display courage, especially Maria, who bares her soul to the camera with startling candor.

Zubrycki and editor Ray Thomas have shaped the material into a seamless drama, and result is an accessible and moving documentary. Technical credits are all first-rate.

—*David Stratton*

HIGH LONESOME: THE STORY OF BLUEGRASS MUSIC

(DOCU — COLOR/B&W — 16mm)

A Tara release of a Northside Films production. Produced by Rachel Liebling, Andrew Serwer. Directed, written by Liebling. Camera (color), Buddy Squires, Allen Moore; editor, Tody Shimin. Reviewed at the Red Victorian Movie House, San Francisco, Nov. 18, 1993. Running time: **95 MIN.**
With: Bill Monroe, Ralph Stanley, Mac Wiseman, Jimmy Martin, Earl Scruggs, the Osborne Bros., Jim and Jesse McReynolds, the Seldom Scene, San Bush, Alison Krauss & Union Station, the Nashville Bluegrass Band, others.

A well-assembled mix of interview, archival and concert footage, "High Lonesome" charts the evolution of bluegrass music as a uniquely American art form. Limited theatrical play should dovetail toward vid marketing to music fans, with educational and foreign specialty play to follow.

Frame is the career of "father of bluegrass" Bill Monroe. He grew up amid eight Kentucky coal-mining sibs to become leader of a new music movement born from "hillbilly" filtering of inherited Scots-Irish folk traditions.

Through the 1920s and 1930s, rural infiltrations of phonograph, radio and motion pictures brought doses of ragtime, jazz, swing and blues. They spiced the "folk music with overdrive" Monroe eventually brought to a mass audience via the Grand Ole Opry broadcast.

Pic nicely traces the ever-shifting weight history laid on musical evolution — from urban-migrational hardships of the Depression through "devastation" wrought by Elvis Presley's electrified popularity, to the hippie reawakening of interest in bluegrass craft.

The form has persevered with a new generation of gifted purists — notably the gorgeously high-voiced Alison Krauss, who gets more footage here than most. Elsewhere, performance glimpses are short but satisfying.

Film succeeds in locating a musical progress both innately grassroots and connected to larger social changes. While some of the color archival footage is now pinked out, antiquated feel adds to overall authenticity.

Pic presents 84-year-old Monroe in a less stiff-necked forum than recent direct-to-vid doc feature "Bill Monroe: Father of Bluegrass," in which a similar historical perspective seemed stultified by worship of its subject.

—*Dennis Harvey*

CARO DIARIO

(DEAR DIARY)

(ITALIAN-FRENCH)

A Lucky Red release (Italy) of a Sacher Film (Rome)/Banfilm/La Sept Cinema (Paris) production, in association with RAI-1 and Canal Plus. Produced by Nanni Moretti, Angelo Barbagallo. Directed, written by Moretti. Camera (color), Giuseppe Lanci; editor, Mirco Garrone; music, Nicola Piovani; art direction, Marta Maffucci; costume design, Maria Rita Barbera; sound, Franco Borni. Reviewed at Nuovo Sacher Cinema, Rome, Nov. 9, 1993. Running time: **100 MIN.**
Giovanni Moretti .... Nanni Moretti
Gerardo .... Renato Carpentieri
Stromboli Mayor ..... Antonio Neiwiller
Film Critic .... Carlo Mazzacurati
With: Jennifer Beals, Alexandre Rockwell, Conchita Airoldi, Raffaella Lebboroni, Marco Paolini.

A major film in a slow Italian season, Nanni Moretti's three-parter "Dear Diary" is an intensely personal work one step away from an autobiographical docu. Consistently stimulating and amusing (two segs are comedy), "Diary" speaks forcefully to Italian auds, and domestic outlook looks strong. Fest outings, for which film has excellent prospects, could help it break through to offshore screens, though it will require special handling.

As in his previous six features, which have earned him cult status in Italy, Moretti the actor occupies center stage with his lanky frame, handsome pout and sudden De Niro-like grin.

The inner universe of Moretti the writer/director — mixing current newspaper clippings with his own thoughts and feelings and events from his life — unfolds in three different stories.

In the breezy "On My Vespa," Moretti rides around a lush summertime Rome, checking out obscure neighborhoods and admiring their architecture.

He meets actress Jennifer Beals and her companion, U.S. indie director Alexandre Rockwell; goes to see "Henry: Portrait of a Serial Killer," and sets out to kill the critic (a hilarious Carlo Mazzacurati) who recommended it.

Real-time driving is accompanied by a hip African beat, but the segment does finally drag.

In "Islands," Moretti humorously examines how the politically committed late-1960s generation has become cynical and isolated. Looking for peace and quiet in which to work, he ferries round the magnificent Aeolian islands off Sicily with his friend (Renato Carpentieri), a monastic intellectual who's retired

December 6, 1993 (Cont.)

from the world to study James Joyce's "Ulysses."

On one isle, the people are so willfully secluded they won't answer the door. Carpentieri discovers he can't live without TV soaps, and he and Moretti climb into a remote volcano to quiz American tourists about upcoming episodes of "The Bold and the Beautiful."

Concluding seg, "Doctors," is in a darker vein, opening with a chilling view of Moretti in bed receiving chemotherapy for cancer. After months of visits to dermatologists and acupuncturists, a malignant tumor is diagnosed — now cured, he stresses.

This true story is told lightly, but the film remains disquietingly open, perhaps intentionally. Viewer is left with a raw feeling of anger at the Italo medical-pharmaceutical industry.

Co-produced by Italian and French TV companies for $2.7 million, "Dear Diary" retains an honest, small-picture feel that directly connects with auds. Offering intimate self-exposure, Moretti solders his bond with fortysomethings who have lived through years of political disenchantment.

But Moretti's sarcastic voiceover comments challenge viewers' political correctness while sanctimoniously asserting his own.

"I'm not guilty!" he announces as he tools around Rome on his moped. "You all shouted horrible things in demonstrations and you've grown old! I shouted the right things, and now I'm a splendid 40-year-old."

Pic has a deceptively casual look, painstakingly constructed by cinematographer Giuseppe Lanci and editor Mirco Garrone. Nicola Piovani's music is lighthearted and witty. —*Deborah Young*

IMAGINING INDIANS

(DOCU — 16mm)

An ITVS (Independent TV Service) production, in association with the Corporation for Public Broadcasting. Produced, directed, written, edited by Victor Masayesva Jr. Camera (color), Masayesva. Second camera, David Leitner; music, Jerry Hunt, E. Vincent Warren; narrator, Robb Webb. Reviewed at Margaret Mead Film Festival, Museum of Natural History, N.Y., Oct. 5, 1993. Running time: **90 MIN.**

Although the message of "Imagining Indians" is valid, pic's fanciful approach and occasionally shrill tone become off-putting over the long haul.

Pic — written, directed, shot, edited and produced by well-known Hopi indie producer Victor Ma-

sayesva Jr. — explores Hollywood's insensitivity in its portrayal of Native Americans: Peoples and sacred rituals are used merely for background color with no understanding or perception of emotional depths.

Talking-head interviews feature actors and extras from many films, including "Dances With Wolves" and the two "Man Called Horse" pics, punctuated by clips from such pics as "The Plainsman," "Battle at Elderbush Gulch," "War Party" and "The Last Hunt."

In between are repeated random scenes of a Native American woman at the dentist's office, tongue-in-cheek narration, postmodern titles and a handful of fanciful fades and effects that distract from pic's more serious intent. Unfortunately, "Imagining Indians" tries hard but ends up caught in its own cleverness. —*Paul Lenti*

AGA NI IKIRU

(LIVING ON THE RIVER AGANO)

(JAPANESE — DOCU — 16mm)

A Jay Film Co. release of a Living on the River Agano Committee production. Directed, edited by Satoh Makoto. Camera (color), Kobayashi Shigeru; music, Kyoumaro; sound, Suzuki Shouji; additional sound, Kikuhi Nobuyuki. Reviewed at Margaret Mead Film Festival, Museum of Natural History, N.Y., Oct. 6, 1993. Running time: **115 MIN.**

Four years in the making, "Living on the River Agano" is a powerful indictment of Japanese government policies. Pic focuses on the destruction of traditional communities and lifestyles by chemical pollution in the Agano River Valley and the continued disregard for its inhabitants' suffering. Film's intimate approach brings viewers into the daily lives and concerns of those affected, making their plight all the more palpable.

Docu explores communities along the river, which runs through the country's northern Snow Region. After a dam was constructed in 1929, the Showa Electric Co. began to dump organic mercury into the river until residents began to come down with Minamata disease. Fish were poisoned, and fishing and related sources of livelihood for generations came to an end.

Before filming, second-time documaker Satoh Makoto and a crew of six lived in the community for a year, helping residents with farming and fishing. This was followed by two years of filming and another year to shape the material. Makoto sold shares to more than 1,400 investors from around the country to cover post-production costs.

What emerges is an intimate glimpse of the people and their lives as they try to live as they have for

centuries. Most young people have opted to move to the larger cities, leaving their often crippled parents and grandparents to carry on with tradition. We follow the futile attempts of these sexagenarians and septuagenarians to acquire official recognition of their affliction (only 650 of the thousands of applicants have been so recognized in a decade).

"Living on the River Agano" is a powerful and unflinching document that extends into larger issues, ones that deserve to be heard. —*Paul Lenti*

PAS D'AMOUR
SANS AMOUR
(S.O.S. WOMAN IN DISTRESS)
(FRENCH)

An Artedis release (France) of an SED/France 2/INA production, with participation of Soficas Investimage 4 and Valor 2, CNC, and Canal Plus. Produced, directed, written by Evelyne Dress. Executive producer, Louis Duchesne. Camera (color), Bertrand Chatry; editor, Jacques Gaillard; production design, Pierre Voisin; sound, Dominique Viellard. Reviewed at Club de l'Etoile screening room, Paris, Oct. 7, 1993. (In Intl. Festival of Women's Images, Marseille, France; Ghent Intl. Film Festival, competing.) Running time: **92 MIN.**

Michel	Patrick Chesnais
Eva	Evelyne Dress
Francois	Jean-Luc Bideau
Bruno	Gerard Darmon

With: Aurore Clement, Dora Doll, Michel Duchaussoy, Martin Lamotte, Valerie Steffen, Tanya Lopert, Cecile Pallas, Jacques Penot, Henri Gruvman.

In "S.O.S. Woman in Distress," first-time helmer Evelyne Dress presents an uneven, comic look at the downside of liberated womanhood. Dress, who also produced, scripted and stars, makes an appealing center and obviously has talent, but pic's approach is too scattered to thrive beyond fests and TV.

Eva (Dress) is a vivacious, fortyish businesswoman who hasn't had sex in the three years since breaking up with Bruno (Gerard Darmon). Her gynecologist tells her to "use it or lose it," but the men Eva meets are duds.

Michel (Patrick Chesnais), her grumpy partner in an Outward Bound-style adventure agency, seems to care more for bonsai trees than for her. But the mere idea of her bedding clients to secure contracts makes him jealous.

Eva's three female buddies, who run the gamut from randy divorcee to contented housewife, spout dialogue only slightly less subtle than blinking neon signs. Few characters in the pic, save Eva herself, evolve beyond caricature.

Roster of Gallic thesps helps to offset the clumsy narrative, and lensing makes good use of Paris locations, but each scene seems to

start from scratch rather than flow from what came before.

Female viewers may prove forgiving, as the film explores a rocky road that many will identify with. Pic won the Prix du Public at the 10th Intl. Festival of Women's Images, Marseille. —*Lisa Nesselson*

GREEN ON THURSDAYS

(DOCU — B&W/COLOR — 16mm)

A Red Branch production. Produced, directed, edited by Dean Bushala, Deirdre Heaslip. Camera (B&W/color), Bushala, Heaslip; music, Leo Crandall, Michael Bondert; still photography, Allen Nepomuceno, Paul Vosdic, Paul Roesch; video artist, Charles Christensen. Reviewed at AFI/L.A. Film Fest, June 15, 1993. Running time: **76 MIN.**

Gay and lesbian bashing in the Chicago area is the focus of "Green on Thursdays," a docu that is both a cautionary tale and an urgent call for activism. The increasing homophobia and other hate crimes in the U.S. should make pic relevant to viewers on PBS, cable and in schools.

For the most part, pic consists of interviews with the victims and survivors of gay-directed violence. Title refers to a 19th century practice by which gay men secretly identified each other by wearing green ties on Thursdays.

Film's most interesting section deals with gay activists' determination not to react as "an oppressed and passive community." Out of this grew a network of organizations.

What's missing here is an exploration of the sources and causes of bashing and how these hate crimes fit into the broader issues of racism and sexism. —*Emanuel Levy*

TEMPUS DE BARISTAS

(TIME OF THE BARMEN)

(ITALIAN-BRITISH — DOCU)

An Istituto Superiore Regionale Etnografico/Regione Autonoma della Sardegna production with Fieldwork Films, in association with BBC-TV. Produced by Paolo Piquereddu. Directed by David MacDougall. Camera (color), MacDougall; editor, Dai Vaughan; sound, Dante Olianas; technical assistants, Jaime McCoan, Ignazio Figus, Virgilio Piras. Reviewed at Margaret Mead Film Festival, Museum of Natural History, N.Y., Oct. 9, 1993. Running time: **100 MIN.**

After years of making distinguished films about Africa and Aboriginal peoples, vet Australian anthropological documaker David MacDougall turns his camera to Europe with this ambitious study of mountain goatherds in eastern Sardinia. Effective docu shows those caught in a world where their way of life is being displaced by modernization.

Docu focuses on three generations of goatherds: The eldest, Franchiscu, grew up at a time when herding goats was a noble profession; his 17-year-old son Pietro helps his father, but he has yet to decide whether to follow family tradition or pursue other interests; Miminu is a bachelor in his 40s who tends his large herd alone and feels trapped by history.

The title refers to the fact that today's goatherds are a dying breed while tourism becomes the island's principal source of income. Even Pietro considers pursuing hotel management training after graduation.

Sensitive pic is important for its depiction of those caught in the dilemma of deciding whether to continue a tradition that has become anachronistic in today's world.

—*Paul Lenti*

SCHINDLER'S LIST

A Universal release of an Amblin Entertainment production. Produced by Steven Spielberg, Gerald R. Molen, Branko Lustig. Executive producer, Kathleen Kennedy. Co-producer, Lew Rywin. Directed by Spielberg. Screenplay, Steven Zaillian, based on the novel by Thomas Keneally. Camera (b&w, Deluxe prints), Janusz Kaminski; editor, Michael Kahn; music, John Williams; violin solos, Itzhak Perlman; production design, Allan Starski; art direction, Ewa Skoczkowska, Maciej Walczak, Ewa Tarnowska, Ryszard Melliwa, Grzegorz Piatkowski; set decoration, Ewa Braun; costume design, Anna Biedrzycka-Sheppard; sound, Ronald Judkins, Robert Jackson; associate producers, Irving Glovin, Robert Raymond; assistant directors, Sergio Mimica-Gezzan, Marek Brodzki (Poland); casting, Lucky Englander, Fritz Fleischhacker, Magdalena Szwarcbart, Tova Cypin, Liat Meiron, Juliet Taylor. Reviewed at Universal Studios, Universal City, Nov. 18, 1993. MPAA Rating: R. Running time: **195 MIN.**

Oskar Schindler .... Liam Neeson
Itzhak Stern .... Ben Kingsley
Amon Goeth .... Ralph Fiennes
Emilie Schindler .... Caroline Goodall
Poldek Pfefferberg Jonathan Sagalle
Helen Hirsch .... Embeth Davidtz

After several attempts at making a fully realized, mature film, Steven Spielberg has finally put it all together in "Schindler's List." A remarkable work by any standard, this searing historical and biographical drama, about a Nazi industrialist who saved some 1,100 Jews from certain death in the concentration camps, evinces an artistic rigor and unsentimental intelligence unlike anything the world's most successful filmmaker has demonstrated before. Marked by a brilliant screenplay, exceptionally supple technique, three staggeringly good lead performances and an attitude toward the traumatic subject matter that is both passionately felt and impressively restrained, this is the film to win over Spielberg skeptics.

How the general public will take to a three-hour, fifteen-minute, black-and-white epic about the Holocaust with no major stars is another matter. Even with the cards of conventional wisdom stacked against it, top reviews, off-entertainment page coverage, possible awards and the Spielberg name should stir enough interest to turn release into an event, elevating it to must-see status for discerning audiences worldwide. The gamble should pay off financially as well as artistically.

Besides being familiar, the Nazi persecution of the Jews is perilous subject matter since it can so easily elicit automatic reactions of moral outrage, personal horror, religious self-righteousness and dramatic extremes, not to mention severe depression.

Taking their cue from Australian writer Thomas Keneally's 1982 book of the same name, Spielberg and scenarist Stephen Zaillian have overcome the problem of familiarity by presenting innumerable details of this grim history that are utterly fresh and previously unexplored, at least in mainstream films. And they have triumphed over the most obvious potential pitfalls by keeping as their main focus a man whose mercenary instincts only gradually turned him into an unlikely hero and savior.

Oskar Schindler (the imposing, impeccably groomed Liam Neeson) is masterfully introduced in a rowdy nightclub sequence that instantly builds interest and mystique around him as he curries favor with the Nazis, who have completed their lightning conquest of Poland in September 1939.

With Jews being registered and entering Krakow at the rate of 10,000 per week, Nazi Party member Schindler arranges to run a major company that will be staffed by unpaid Jews. Itzhak Stern (Ben Kingsley) becomes his accountant and right-hand man and helps build the concern into a major supplier of pots, pans and cookware for troops at the front.

In near-documentary fashion and often using a dizzyingly mobile, hand-held camera, Spielberg (who operated his own camera for many of these sequences) deftly sketches the descent of the Jews from refugee settlers in Krakow to their con-

A remarkable work by any standard, this searing drama is the film to win over Spielberg skeptics.

finement within 16 square blocks by 1941, to the creation of a Plaszow Forced Labor Camp in 1942, to the brutal liquidation of the ghetto the following year. In fascinating detail, and using a plethora of vivid characters, the film shows how the black market worked, how previously well-to-do families were forced into miserable dwellings, how the Judenrat — Jews nominally empowered by the Germans — oversaw and carried out Nazi law, how some managed to survive and others didn't.

In these sequences, the seed is planted for one of the picture's superbly developed great themes — that the matter of who lived and died was completely, utterly, existentially arbitrary. As one of the characters observes, the casu-alness and randomness of Nazi cruelty was such that at no point could one develop a strategy for survival; there was no safe way to behave, and even extreme cleverness couldn't save you in the long run. All morality, justice and personal worth was erased.

With the clearing of Krakow, most of the action shifts to the labor camp, which is set in an extraordinary location at the base of a cliff. Looming above it is the opulent chateau of Commandant Amon Goeth (Ralph Fiennes), from which invited revelers can look down upon the prisoners during glittering parties and, in shocking scenes that, again, are unlike anything previously seen, from the balcony of which the commandant randomly shoots helpless inmates as if taking target practice.

The commandant is a fascinating creation, as evil as any Nazi presented onscreen over the past 50 years, but considerably more complex and human than most. He is deeply and, he admits, disturbingly attracted to the young Jewish woman he keeps as his personal maid. Tellingly, both he and Schindler drink a great deal, but Goeth admires Schindler for not, unlike him, being a drunk. "That's control," he says, "and control is power."

Schindler must use utmost diplomacy in dealing with Goeth and other top-ranking Nazis in order to get his way, gently suggesting that their murderous policies are bad for business and that to bestow a pardon confers even greater power on a ruler than constantly meting out death. Schindler is permitted to continue operating his Krakow factory as a "sub-camp," which becomes a virtual haven for hundreds of Jews in that they are basically assured they won't die there.

Still, with the Final Solution being implemented with ever-greater dispatch by 1944, Schindler must finally buy, with his tremendous war profits, the leftover Jews to prevent them from being shipped to Auschwitz. In a harrowing sequence, women he has arranged to rescue wind up at the extermination camp by mistake. For Schindler as well as the Jews, it remains a question of which will last longer, his money or the war.

After listening to Churchill's announcement of the German surrender, Schindler delivers an extraordinary speech of his own in the presence of both Nazi guards and Jewish workers before fleeing with nothing more than a suitcase. Throughout the mesmerizing narrative so masterfully orchestrated in Zaillian's faultlessly intelligent screenplay, there are many opportunities for heart-tugging, obvious plays for sympathy and hate, maudlin sentiments and cheap indulgences. Not only because Spielberg resisted every one of them, but also because this film is so different,

December 13, 1993 (Cont.)

and so much tougher, than anything else he's done, if not forewarned as to its director's identity, even a well-schooled critic could watch virtually the entire picture and never suspect it was Spielberg.

On reflection, some of the themes relating to greed, corruption and inadvertent heroism have been present in his work from early on, but nothing before has been anywhere near this deep or resonant. Images, moments and scenes stay in the mind and become even stronger, well after viewing the film.

Despite its 3¼-hour length, the film moves forward with great urgency and is not a minute too long for the story it is telling and the amount of information it imparts. It is, naturally, full of violence and death, but Spielberg makes this both memorable and somehow bearable by staging it all with abrupt, shocking suddenness, which adds to the feeling of arbitrariness.

This is not, strictly speaking, a concentration camp movie but a densely woven personal drama with the most striking of historical backdrops, which is what will get mainstream audiences through it.

The only debatable choice is the brief color epilogue, which depicts many of the surviving "Schindler Jews" filing by his grave in Israel accompanied, for the most part, by the much younger actors who have portrayed them in the film. This will have many viewers crying their eyes out, but it also smacks, on a certain level, of direct emotional manipulation, the only such instance in the work.

Another device that uses color is also questionable, that of a little girl whom Schindler notices and whose red coat stands out against the prevailing black-and-white. What this is supposed to signify is anyone's guess, although it's so minor that it doesn't matter.

From top to bottom, the performances from the enormous cast are impeccable. Whereas most major stars would have wanted to tip the audience off early on that Schindler was actually a sensitive, caring guy underneath it all, Neeson leaves no doubt through most of the film that his character was driven foremost by profit. In a superlative performance, Neeson makes Schindler a fascinating but highly ambiguous figure, effectively persuasive and manipulative in one-on-one scenes where he's determined to get what he wants, and finally rising to dramatic heights with his courageous and stirring farewell speech.

Kingsley must act within much more rigid constraints as his trusted accountant Stern, a man who feels he must never make a misstep. Role is reminiscent of Alec Guinness' deluded Col. Nicholson in "The Bridge on the River Kwai"; in his compulsion to do a perfect job for Schindler, he often seems to forget that he's working for the enemy.

The extraordinary Fiennes creates an indelible character in Goeth. With paunch hanging out and eyes filled with disgust both for his victims and himself, he's like a minor-league Roman emperor gone sour with excess, a man in whom too much power and debauchery have crushed anything that might once have been good.

The dozens of small roles, many of which figure in the action only briefly, have been superbly filled by faces that invariably register immediately and with terrific effectiveness.

Shot mostly on location in Poland, the picture captures in exceptional detail the nightmare world of 50 years ago. Allan Starski's production design blends imperceptibly with natural locations. This is a film that could have been made only in black-and-white, and yet it is solely because of Spielberg's commercial stature that it was able to be made that way. Lensing by Janusz Kaminski, a young Polish-American cinematographer whose previous credits include "The Adventures of Huck Finn," Diane Keaton's made-for-cable "Wildflower" and some Roger Corman efforts, is outstanding. Lighting is mostly very simple, camera moves are agile and perceptive, and palette features many shades of gray rather than high-contrast black-and-white.

Michael Kahn's editing moves with dynamic swiftness when desired and holds on scenes when required, making the running time seem shorter. John Williams' score is atypical, especially in the context of his work for Spielberg, as it's low-key, soulful and flecked with ethnic flavors.

Dedicated to the late Time Warner chairman Steve Ross, "Schindler's List" has a deep emotional impact that is extraordinarily well served and balanced by its intelligence, historical perspective and filmmaking expertise.

—*Todd McCarthy*

GERONIMO: AN AMERICAN LEGEND

A Columbia release of a Walter Hill/Neil Canton production. Produced by Hill, Canton. Executive producer, Michael S. Glick. Directed by Hill. Screenplay, John Milius, Larry Gross, story by Milius. Camera (Technicolor; Panavision widescreen), Lloyd Ahern; editors, Freeman Davies, Carmel Davies, Donn Aron; music, Ry Cooder; production design, Joe Alves; art direction, Scott Ritenour; set decoration, Richard C. Goddard; costume design, Dan Moore; sound (Dolby), Lee Orloff; assistant director, Josh McLaglen; second unit director-stunt coordinator, Allan Graf; second unit camera, Michael D. O'Shea; casting, Reuben Cannon. Reviewed at Sony Studios, Culver City, Nov. 29, 1993. MPAA Rating: PG-13. Running time: **115 MIN.**

Lt. Charles Gatewood .... Jason Patric
Brig. Gen. George
 Crook .... Gene Hackman
Al Sieber .... Robert Duvall
Geronimo .... Wes Studi
Lt. Britton Davis .... Matt Damon
Mangas .... Rodney A. Grant
Brig. Gen. Nelson Miles .... Kevin Tighe
Chato .... Steve Reevis
Sgt. Turkey .... Carlos Palomino
Ulzana .... Victor Aaron
Sgt. Dutchy Stuart Proud Eagle Grant
Schoonover .... Stephen McHattie

Sad, stately and ideologically *au courant,* "Geronimo: An American Legend" relates the final stages of the U.S. government's subjugation of the West's native population in absorbing, detailed fashion. Neatly turning long-standing genre conventions upside down while working squarely within them, director Walter Hill has fashioned a physically impressive, well-acted picture whose slightly stodgy literary quality holds it back from an even greater impact.

Strong campaign and continued interest in Westerns and Native American matters should combine for solid business, although it's impossible to know how TNT's concurrent, rushed-to-air telefilm on the same subject will detract from B.O. While the cardboard TNT version hopped, skipped and jumped between key moments in the Apache warrior's long, eventful life, this large-scale feature intriguingly concentrates on 1885-86, when the U.S. Army devoted 5,000 men, or one-quarter of its entire troop strength, to the effort to stamp out Indian resistance once and for all. Of course, the result is a foregone conclusion, but it's a tremendously resonant story, full of courage, tenacity, tragedy, regret, duplicity and historical weight, one that will give anyone plenty to think about.

In movie terms, it's a fine tale of resistance and struggle, with plenty of confrontations, action and violence, all played against a stunningly beautiful backdrop. Somehow, this "Geronimo" rarely becomes quite as stirring as it seems it should, but it still offers an intelligent, respectful reading of a key

historical chapter that has too often been trivialized, sanitized and revised by Hollywood.

Pic is framed by the words of a secondary character, Lt. Britton Davis (Matt Damon), a freshly scrubbed lad straight from West Point who arrives in Arizona territory just in time for the Geronimo push. Narration clearly establishes the film's p.o.v. as that of sympathetic whites and provides plenty of useful information over the course of things, but its strictly 19th century diaristic style seems at odds with the way the characters talk (unlike a similar device in Robert Benton's underrated "Bad Company") and sets a kind of square, lecturing, overly reverential tone.

Closer to the center of matters is Lt. Charles Gatewood (Jason Patric), a young Virginian who, after an opening skirmish between the cavalry and the last remaining Chiricahua Apaches, takes Geronimo into custody and peacefully escorts him to Brig. Gen. Crook (Gene Hackman), a veteran Indian fighter who is overseeing the settlement of natives on reservations.

A liberal by 1880s standards who respects Geronimo and would protect him against the many blood-thirsty avengers lurking about, Crook declares the Indian wars over and announces that the former nomads must learn farming. All is quiet for awhile, but when some soldiers violently attack a group of rebellious braves, Geronimo and some followers escape and head for Mexico.

With Geronimo on a wild, if justifiable, rampage through small villages and settlements, the Army again takes up its pursuit with the aide of grizzled scout Al Sieber (Robert Duvall). When Crook is unable to persuade Geronimo to surrender again, he is replaced by Brig. Gen. Miles, a martinet who institutes a no-compromise, full Indian pacification policy and orders Gatewood to bring Geronimo in once and for all.

A cipher at first, Gatewood remains an ambiguous figure whose innate sympathy for Geronimo is counterbalanced by his patriotic and professional obligations. The thick-skinned Sieber accurately points out, "You don't love who you're fighting for, and you don't hate who you're fighting against." Little by little, however, Patric makes him an intriguing character. He's good on horseback, and his soft, lulling accent is strikingly reminiscent of Marlon Brando's when he played Southerners.

Wes Studi is a rugged, commanding, admirably defiant Geronimo, convincing as a leader and, once he surrenders, a man who knows his life is over. Only problem with all the young actors — white and Indian — is a total lack of humor seemingly imposed on them by the script. Pic's tone is kept in a dour straitjacket that Hackman and Duvall manage somewhat to escape with their irony and seasoned humanity.

December 13, 1993 (Cont.)

Working on stunning locations around Moab, Utah, Hill no doubt deliberately resurrects the indelible iconography of John Ford's Westerns, some of which were shot in basically the same places, only to slyly and totally reverse their political meanings. Many of the same scenes are present — the Indian raids, the cavalry battles, the Indians' long march, the removal of an Army officer, younger officers doing their duty — but their import is inverted, even if the ultimate aim in both cases is to limn the passing of an era.

Ironically, the single sequence of greatest tension and narrative economy is a barroom standoff between good guys and bad guys that is uncannily Hawksian in the way it quietly escalates to a resolution of terrible swiftness.

Rich and majestic production values demand big-screen viewing rather than video consumption. Lloyd Ahern's grand widescreen lensing is actually too colorful at times due to the overuse of filters, especially on landscape shots. Sets and costumes are densely textured, and Ry Cooder's generally fine score goes slightly overboard at a couple of points. —*Todd McCarthy*

LITTLE BUDDHA

A Miramax release (U.S.) of a Recorded Pictures Company and CIBY 2000 presentation. Produced by Jeremy Thomas. Directed by Bernardo Bertolucci. Screenplay, Rudy Wurlitzer, Mark Peploe, story by Bertolucci. Camera (Technicolor; Technovision widescreen), Vittorio Storaro; editor, Pietro Scalia; music, Ryuichi Sakamoto; production and costume design, James Acheson; sound (Dolby SR), Ivan Sharrock; special effects supervisor, Richard Conway; casting, Howard Feuer (L.A.), Joanna Merlin (N.Y.), Priscilla John (London). Reviewed at the Aidikoff Screening Room, Beverly Hills, Nov. 29, 1993. Running time: **140 MIN.**
Prince Siddhartha .... Keanu Reeves
Dean Konrad .... Chris Isaak
Lisa Konrad .... Bridget Fonda
Jesse Konrad .... Alex Wiesendanger
Lama Norbu .... Ying Ruocheng
Champa .... Jigme Kunsang
Raju .... Raju Lal
Gita .... Greishma Makar Singh
The Abbot .... Khyongla Rato Rinpoche
Kenpo Tensing .... Sogyal Rinpoche
Sanjay .... Thupten Kalsang
Ani-La .... Doma Tshomo
Maria .... Jo Champa

"**Little Buddha**" is a visually stunning but dramatically underwhelming attempt to forge a bridge between the ancient Eastern religion and modern Western life. Bernardo Bertolucci's second foray into remote Asian territory is considerably less successful than his first, "The Last Emperor," as the double narrative is awkwardly structured and never comes into sharp focus. Opened Dec. 1 in Paris and set to bow in April domestically, the lavish $35 million-plus production is like a long art film for kids, which puts it in a tricky commercial position that will test the resources even of Disney-backed Miramax.

In fashioning his least intellectual work, and the one least preoccupied with politics, Freud or sex, Bertolucci has created a picture that is half a picture-book history of the origins of Buddhism and half a consideration of the possibilities of reincarnation in the context of contrasting value systems. Unfortunately, he and his screenwriters have failed to provide a driving dramatic impetus or enough conflict to fuel the story, which is largely populated by underdrawn, dull characters that don't serve its exalted aims.

Bertolucci once intended to undertake an actual biographical drama of the Buddha, but he opted to channel his interest in the religion into this curiously bifurcated tale of a young American boy who is considered the possible reincarnation of a great lama, intertwined with the life of the Buddha-to-be, Prince Siddhartha, 2,500 years ago.

Modern story sees the aged, august Lama Norbu (Ying Ruocheng) traveling from the Himalaya kingdom of Bhutan to Seattle in search of the reincarnation of his order's revered late teacher. Path leads to the home of Dean and Lisa Konrad (Chris Isaak and Bridget Fonda), an upscale couple with a fancy but soulless new house whose energetic son, Jesse (Alex Wiesendanger), is the suspected enlightened one.

Norbu and his fellow monks spend a good deal of time with little Jesse, who, along with the audience, is told of the life of Siddhartha (a strikingly darkened Keanu Reeves), a handsome prince who abandoned his charmed existence to live in poverty and search for the true path. Initially a pageant of stunning palace sets, colorful royal costumes and crowded spectacle, this ancient saga evolves into a small-scale portrait of an ascetic lifestyle punctuated by a magic serpent, genuflecting trees and briefly rampaging special effects.

Bertolucci's sweeping, choreographic camera style is fine for the first part of this, but operatic cinema is perhaps the opposite of what is needed to convey the simplicity and serenity critical to the second part of Siddhartha's life.

Seeking some answers of his own, Dean agrees to Norbu's request to bring Jesse to Bhutan, where the boy will be sized up against two other candidates to determine who is truly the reincarnate.

A touristic visit to Katmandu precedes a long ceremonial climax at the previously unfilmed Paro Dzong monastery in Bhutan. Film fizzles and even cops out during the final half-hour, with a terribly vague resolution that satisfies neither dramatically nor thematically.

Despite the multitude of unsatisfactory elements, "Little Buddha" generally holds the interest due to its unusual subject, exotic settings, filmmaking skill and intrigue as to where it might all be leading. Aside from its pictorial beauties, Vittorio Storaro's Technovision lensing creates a bold duality between the vibrant, emotional color of the Eastern settings, whether ancient or modern, and the washed out, spiritually drained blues and grays of contempo Seattle.

In all respects, Western people and buildings (in the case of the Konrads' home and Dean's unoccupied office building) are presented as empty vessels needing to be filled, an arguable notion that, unfortunately, is not presented with any depth or analytical acuity. The Konrads are given no particular backgrounds and vastly uninteresting personalities; their little life crises smack of artificial inventions to fill out some kind of biographical profile.

It would have taken enormously resourceful actors to bring such thin roles to life, so the casting of musician Isaak as the father proves a further liability. Isaak is wan and unable to communicate the fruits of introspection. Fonda is OK but overly smiley as his fastidious wife, and Wiesendanger doesn't register much as the son who is propelled on a curious journey, especially compared with some of the terrific child performances seen onscreen earlier this year.

Although his ethnic appropriateness may be questioned by some P.C. police, Reeves makes for a surprisingly watchable and dashing Siddhartha. Ying Ruocheng, who also appeared in "The Last Emperor," brings a welcome, light gravity to the principal monk.

However the screenwriting duties split up, Bertolucci never synthesized the work of Rudy Wurlitzer and Mark Peploe into a script that functions meaningfully for both children and adults, which seems to have been the aim.

As expected from any Bertolucci film, production values are tops, notably Storaro's work and James Acheson's endlessly inventive production and costume designs.

—*Todd McCarthy*

SIX DEGREES OF SEPARATION

An MGM release of a Maiden Movies/New Regency production. Produced by Fred Schepisi, Arnon Milchan. Executive producer, Ric Kidney. Directed by Schepisi. Screenplay, John Guare, based on his play. Camera (Deluxe color; Panavision widescreen), Ian Baker; editor, Peter Honess; music, Jerry Goldsmith; production design, Patrizia von Brandenstein; art direction, Dennis Bradford; set decoration, Gretchen Rau; costume design, Judianna Makovsky; sound (Dolby), Bill Daly; assistant director, Amy Sayres; casting, Ellen Chenoweth. Reviewed at MGM Screening Room, Santa Monica, Nov. 11, 1993. MPAA Rating: R. Running time: **111 MIN.**
Ouisa Kittredge .... Stockard Channing
Paul .... Will Smith
Flan Kittredge .... Donald Sutherland
Geoffrey .... Ian McKellen
Kitty .... Mary Beth Hurt
Larkin .... Bruce Davison
Dr. Fine .... Richard Masur
Trent Conway ... Anthony Michael Hall
Elizabeth .... Heather Graham
Rick .... Eric Thal
Ben .... Anthony Rapp
Woody Kittredge .... Osgood Perkins
Tess Kittredge .... Catherine Kellner
Mrs. Bannister .... Kitty Carlisle Hart

The connection between any two people in the world — so we are told in "Six Degrees of Separation" — is no farther than a half-dozen human associations away. Pauper or king and anywhere in between can be traced via no more than six intermediary sources. The trick, of course, is to find those precise links.

Scientific sociology aside, the screen version of John Guare's award-winning stage hit is an elaborate mousetrap where getting caught can be delightful fun. But the central scam dissipates into self-analysis and moralization. The more serious it becomes, the more of a pedestrian path it takes, and the tug of war between the rational and the absurd draws no victor. That won't matter to the sophisticated viewer but poses serious commercial limitations for this classy entertainment.

The tale within a tale is related by the Kittredges (Stockard Channing and Donald Sutherland), chic Fifth Avenue folk who deal and speculate in high-society art. They have an incredible story to relate about a young black man who arrived at their doorstep late one evening bleeding from a knife wound and claiming to have been a mugging victim. Identifying himself as Paul (Will Smith), a friend and classmate of their children at Harvard, he enters their life for a moment.

In that brief period, he proves himself immaculately seductive. Posing as the son of Sidney Poitier, he captivates the couple and a visiting friend (Ian McKellen) with his candor, intelligence and passion. He also cooks up a spectacular meal and by the end of the evening has established such a warm bond that the Kittredges insist he sleep over.

The bubble promptly bursts when Ouisa Kittredge awakens the next morning and finds their guest cavorting with a male hustler. Paul flees and his hosts begin to hyperventilate. Was something stolen? Worse yet, they might have been murdered.

They sense they were taken advantage of and resent how easily they fell for his patter. It doesn't become any clearer when friends relate a carbon-copy experience. The police are called but make it very clear that taking advantage of gullibility is not a felony offense.

But the incident weighs heavily on the Kittredges' minds. They simply must get to the root of why anyone would go to such elaborate lengths to create such an elegant ruse for no tangible profit. Paul's importance diminishes as the Kittredges begin to look in the mirror for the essential answers.

The transition from farce to thriller to moral inspection does not flow organically. Guare and director Fred Schepisi are intent on changing the rules as the story proceeds. While it provides the material with an edge and uncertainty, the wildly black comic elements evaporate as the script attempts to make sense of the human condition. The promise of an exciting journey is run aground by rather routine, banal explanations.

"Six Degrees of Separation" is in essence an examination of artifice. On that level it has few equals. It is a choice, elegant production, pristine in its craft and attention to detail.

The central cast complements the story. Smith proves himself an extremely charismatic presence, convincing in his sincerity and cunning in conveying his character's talents as a human sponge. Channing, who created her role on Broadway, has the less flashy part. Ultimately she must anchor everything and provide the human, realistic perspective. Watching that unfold on her face is a frighteningly withering experience.

Caught between in a tour de force performance is Sutherland as Flan Kittredge. He is the embodiment of the educated, glib and superficial Manhattan social lion who Guare loathes. The combination of intelligence and blindness has never seemed so funny and tragic. It is sublime work.

Guare undoes much of his story by insisting on making his points crystal clear. The transition from stage to screen is accomplished in a literal manner in which asides in the theater cut away to the actual location onscreen. "Six Degrees" is magical when addressing the preposterous. Like any good storyteller, Paul is deft at knitting eyes with wool. Somehow explaining that gift destroys the illusion in a most unpleasant fashion.

—Leonard Klady

SHADOWLANDS

(BRITISH-U.S.)

A Savoy release. Produced by Richard Attenborough, Brian Eastman. Executive producer, Terence Clegg. Co-producer, Diana Hawkins. Directed by Attenborough. Screenplay, William Nicholson, based on his play. Camera (color), Roger Pratt; editor, Lesley Walker; music, George Fenton; production design, Stuart Craig; art direction, Michael Lamont; set decoration, Stephanie McMillian; costume design, Penny Rose; sound (Dolby), Simon Kaye, Jonathan Bates; associate producer, Alison Webb; assistant director, Patrick Clayton; casting, Lucy Boulting. Reviewed at the Aidikoff screening room, Beverly Hills, Nov. 30, 1993. MPAA Rating: PG. Running time: 130 MIN.

Jack Lewis	Anthony Hopkins
Joy Gresham	Debra Winger
Warnie Lewis	Edward Hardwicke
"Harry" Harrington	Michael Denison
Christopher Riley	John Wood
Dr. Craig	Peter Firth
Douglas Gresham	Joseph Mazzello

Anthony Hopkins delivers yet another towering performance in "Shadowlands," a touching, somewhat fictionalized account of a late-in-life love between eminent English writer and scholar C.S. Lewis and Joy Gresham, an American poet. Positive word-of-mouth and favorable reviews are crucial in making Richard Attenborough's sensitive exploration of love popular beyond the circle of viewers who frequent literary British cinema.

Contrary to popular notion, "Shadowlands" shows that there are second acts — and significant ones at that — in people's lives. Set in the early 1950s, it's a quiet, pensive tale of two eccentric individuals whose personae, lifestyles and cultures couldn't have been more different.

A middle-aged bachelor, Lewis is a reserved, repressed intellectual who lives an orderly life with his brother Warnie (Edward Hardwicke) and spends his leisure time with his male colleagues in a most habitual manner. For years, he's been the literary hero of Gresham (Debra Winger), a feisty, straightforward American who's in the process of recovering from a failed marriage to an alcoholic.

After years of quiet admiration and correspondence with Lewis, Gresham decides to take her son Douglas (Joseph Mazzello) and visit him in London. At first, the relationship is formal and restrained, but gradually it evolves into intimate friendship, romantic love and, ultimately, marriage.

Their liaison causes something of a stir, however, for Gresham is an outsider par excellence: She's not only a woman, but an American Jew whose outspoken, uninhibited behavior defies Oxford's rigid sensibility. By today's standards, Gresham's trips to England may not be daring, but at the time she was perceived as an adventurous woman who refused to be intimidated by a sexist, male-dominated bastion and challenged its notion of a "woman's place."

Focusing on their private lives, "Shadowlands" doesn't provide much info about the creative process; as the story unfolds, one almost forgets that Lewis is a world-renowned author. The film effectively captures the isolation and insulation — intellectual and emotional — of British academic life. But it also suggests that the act of reading can provide solace and comfort and even change one's life.

Up to the last reel, the film resists sentimentality, but then it succumbs to a level of a slow, old-fashioned — even heavy-handed — melodrama that negates its earlier matter-of-fact tone. Still, even when Gresham is stricken with a fatal disease, the movie emphasizes the hopeful, strong dimensions of the mutual attraction. Indeed, both individuals change radically as a result of their bond: In deep crisis when they meet, the spirited Gresham finds a new direction in her life, and Lewis lets his guard down.

It's a testament to the nuanced writing of William Nicholson, who adapted his stage play after successful productions in London and Broadway, that the drama works effectively on both personal and collective levels. Lewis and Gresham represent divergent cultures: The reserved and controlled British vs. the open and emotional American.

Ultimately, though, the film's greatest achievement is that neither comes across as an abstraction of type. Attenborough opts for modest, unobtrusive direction that serves the material — and actors.

Production values are accomplished in every department, particularly Roger Pratt's on-location lensing of Oxford, Magdalen College and its old chapel.

Hopkins adds another laurel to his recent achievements. As always, there's music in his speech and nothing is over-deliberate or forced about his acting. In fact, Hopkins renders a more emotional and flexible performance than in "The Remains of the Day," his previous, equally impressive, work.

Coming off years of desultory and unimpressive movies, Winger at last plays a role worthy of her talent, though her character is less complex than Hopkins'. Occasionally, as in a scene in which she tells off a sexist instructor, Winger uses her sarcastic voice to great advantage.

The entire British supporting cast is glorious, from Hardwicke as the quiet brother to Michael Denison as the Reverend, Peter Firth as the doctor and, particularly, John Wood as the acerbic professor.

A mature film for grown-ups, "Shadowlands" demonstrates the emotional fear of love but also its magical power to transform one's life. The film says that to experience happiness and intimacy, one must risk exposure, vulnerability — and pain.

—Emanuel Levy

WHAT'S EATING GILBERT GRAPE

A Paramount release of a Matalon Teper Ohlsson production. Produced by Meir Teper, Bertil Ohlsson, David Matalon. Exec producers, Lasse Hallstrom, Alan C. Blomquist. Directed by Hallstrom. Screenplay, Peter Hedges, based on his novel. Camera (Technicolor; Deluxe prints), Sven Nykvist; editor, Andrew Mondshein; music, Alan Parker, Bjorn Isfalt; production design, Bernt Capra; art direction, John Myhre; set decoration, Gretchen Rau; costume design, Renee Ehrlich Kalfus; sound (Dolby), David Brownlow; assistant director, David Householter; casting, Gail Levin. Reviewed at Paramount screening room, L.A., Nov. 18, 1993. MPAA Rating: PG-13. Running time: 118 MIN.

Gilbert Grape	Johnny Depp
Becky	Juliette Lewis
Betty Carver	Mary Steenburgen
Arnie Grape	Leonardo DiCaprio
Momma	Darlene Cates
Amy Grape	Laura Harrington
Ellen Grape	Mary Kate Schellhardt
Mr. Carver	Kevin Tighe
Tucker Van Dyke	John C. Reilly
Bobby McBurney	Crispin Glover
Becky's Grandma	Penelope Branning

"What's Eating Gilbert Grape" is an offbeat middleweight charmer that is lent a measure of substance by its astute performances and observational insight. A modest effort of uninsistent qualities but many felicitous moments, this is not the sort of self-trumpeting, broadly commercial release normally associated with the year-end holidays. But word of mouth, probably starting with teenage girls but potentially extending to a wide variety of audiences, could reward distrib patience with good long-term results.

Based on playwright and actor Peter Hedges' 1991 novel and adapted by him, small-scale film depicts the Grapes, a rural family that has every right to qualify as dysfunctional. After all, Dad hanged himself in the basement years ago, Momma weighs 500 pounds and hasn't left the house for seven summers, Amy and Ellen are teenage sisters who probably need a husband and father, respectively, and Arnie is an unpredictable 17-year-old mental case who wasn't supposed to survive childhood and requires constant supervision.

Under the circumstances, however, the family copes reasonably well due to the princely, self-sacrificial ministrations of eldest son Gilbert (Johnny Depp), who works at the local grocery, carries on a discreet affair with an older woman and can't even think of leaving due to how much Momma (Darlene Cates) and Arnie (Leonardo DiCaprio) depend upon him.

Arnie's refrain, "We're not going anywhere," is thrown into pointed relief with the arrival of Becky (Juliette Lewis), who, with her grandmother, pitches tent outside town in a shiny trailer. More worldly and sophisticated than the local rubes, Becky gently entices the reticent, unassertive Gilbert into a tentative romantic relationship just as his lover (Mary Steenburgen) is moving away.

Through it all, the center of Gilbert's life, and of the film, remains his selfless, fatherly bond with Arnie. The evidently autistic, goofily childlike Arnie, who (attempting to charm Becky) announces, "I could go at any time," particularly likes to climb the town's water tower so that the cops have to retrieve him, and is the object of family attention due to the grand party planned for his upcoming 18th birthday.

Gilbert is so good, benign and self-effacing in his devotion to those around him that one wonders when he's going to snap, and indeed he does, but in a comparatively mild manner.

Dramatic climax, involving the fate of Momma and the family, is piercingly poignant, although actual ending feels soft and artificially upbeat.

In other hands, this sort of quirky, low-key material could have veered in numerous objectionable directions — toward the cutesy, the inspirational, the sentimental or the banal, just for starters. But Swedish director Lasse Hallstrom and his fine cast have endowed the story with a good deal of behavioral truth, as well as investing it with beguilingly unstressed comedy that expresses an engagingly bemused view of life.

This is best seen in the treatment of the two seriously afflicted characters, Momma and Arnie. Weighing in at a quarter of a ton, Momma gets her children to do her bidding from her permanent perch on the living room couch. Two key sequences, one in which the dangerously weakened floor under her sofa is repaired without her knowing it, and another in which she finally emerges from the house to demand that the police release Arnie, could have been meanly derisive or superficially ennobling. Instead, under Hallstrom's sympathetic direction of first-time actress Cates, who was discovered on a TV talkshow about overweight women, both interludes evoke multiple emotions, which pay moving dividends in her gentle final scene.

Even trickier is Arnie's character, whose spastic movements and infantile rantings could easily make viewers uncomfortable. DiCaprio's remarkable performance doesn't stint on the erratic behavior, but also brings the kid alive as a human being who must be cared for and nurtured — as difficult a task as that might be — thereby justifying Gilbert's devotion to him.

Working with an opaque character who is almost a cipher where desires, emotions and ambitions are concerned, Depp manages to command center screen with a greatly affable, appealing characterization. Only bothersome detail is his pointlessly hennaed hair, which doesn't match anyone else's and proves distracting.

Lewis provides some nice moments of well-timed interchange but might have brought a bit more edge and vitality to her outsider role. Given much less attention than the boys, Laura Harrington and Mary Kate Schellhardt can only hurriedly sketch in the Grape sisters. Steenburgen must mostly convey desperate longing, while Crispin Glover is amusing as the town's predatory undertaker.

Set in Iowa but lensed in central Texas, pic has an unassuming, even surprisingly plain look, given Sven Nykvist's eye behind the camera.

— *Todd McCarthy*

GRUMPY OLD MEN

A Warner Bros. release of a John Davis/Lancaster Gate production. Produced by Davis, Richard C. Berman. Executive producer, Dan Kolsrud. Directed by Donald Petrie. Screenplay, Mark Steven Johnson. Camera (Technicolor), Johnny E. Jensen; editor, Bonnie Koehler; music, Alan Silvestri; production design, David Chapman; art direction, Mark Haack; set decoration, Clay Griffith; costume design, Lisa Jensen; sound (Dolby), Russell Fager; associate producers, Darlene K. Chan, Kathy Sarreal; assistant directors, Randy Suhr, Doug Wise; casting, Sharon Howard-Field. Reviewed at Warner Bros. screening room, Burbank, Nov. 30, 1993. MPAA Rating: PG-13. Running time: **104 MIN.**

John	Jack Lemmon
Max	Walter Matthau
Ariel	Ann-Margret
Grandpa	Burgess Meredith
Melanie	Daryl Hannah
Jacob	Kevin Pollak
Chuck	Ossie Davis
Snyder	Buck Henry
Mike	Christopher McDonald

On the Jack Lemmon-Walter Matthau scale, "Grumpy Old Men" comes closer to the languor of "Buddy, Buddy" than the inspired lunacy of "The Odd Couple" or "The Fortune Cookie," saddling the two old pros with so-so material. Still, under Donald Petrie's direction, the pic emerges as light, reasonably pleasant and undoubtedly sappy holiday entertainment, though box office appeal may be limited to those who saw the duo's more legendary pairings in their initial release.

Warner Bros. added the film to its year-end arsenal at the last minute, and the move makes sense. All of the action takes place from Thanksgiving to Christmas, and the movie at times feels like a Hallmark holiday special when it isn't painting in broad slapstick strokes.

Looking craggy and dour, Lemmon and Matthau play aging Minnesota neighbors whose decades-old feud is rekindled when they become enamored with a fetching widow, the aptly named Ariel (Ann-Margret), who moves in across the street.

Ariel literally barges into both of their lives, spouting New Age aphorisms about lost opportunity and seizing the moment in a sort of near-dead poets society. In the process, she breathes life into John (Lemmon) and Max (Matthau), who at the start seem content to live out their lives alone watching TV, fishing off the frozen lake and insulting each other.

There are subplots, though not so you'd notice. John's daughter (Daryl Hannah) is estranged from her husband, and Max's son (Kevin Pollak) harbors a long-standing crush on her. John also faces the threat of losing his house because of an irksome IRS agent (Buck Henry) and receives romantic advice from his randy 94-year-old father (Burgess Meredith, a hoot in the film's showiest role).

Petrie, who directed "Mystic Pizza," oscillates a bit awkwardly between humorous and bittersweet moments during the first two acts, and the film provides few big laughs before rushing to its warm, fuzzy and overly tidy conclusion.

Part of the problem is the script by newcomer Mark Steven Johnson, whose dialogue proves a bit pedestrian. John and Max repeatedly snap "moron" and "putz" at each other, for example, as if no one could come up with more creative invectives.

Both Matthau and Lemmon are appropriately crotchety, but the almost unseemly childishness of their behavior never shows either actor at his best — a situation exacerbated by the unflattering photography and bleak, bitterly cold backdrop.

The film doesn't truly shine, in fact, until a fabulous, worth-the-price-of-admission outtake sequence over the closing credits, displaying a connection between the performers that isn't made anywhere near as well during the preceding 100 minutes.

In the same vein, Ann-Margret has little to work with as the merry widow, so ditzy at the outset it's hard to take her seriously in more poignant scenes. Hannah, Pollak and Ossie Davis all receive relatively little screen time in support but make the most of it.

Tech credits are satisfactory, though Alan Silvestri's score shovels sentimentality as thick as the snow, underscoring tonal similarities between "Old Men" and its most obvious competition this season, Fox's "Mrs. Doubtfire" — both films to which one could take parents, kids or unwelcome guests in a pinch.

Maybe if Warner Bros. had talked Lemmon into doing his drag number again, they'd really have something here. — *Brian Lowry*

LONDON FEST

JEAN RENOIR

(BRITISH — DOCU — 16mm)

A BBC production. (Intl. sales: BBC Enterprises, London.) Executive producer, Roger Thompson. Directed by David Thompson. Series editor (for Omnibus), Nigel Williams. Camera (color), Colin Waldeck; editor, Colin Minchin; sound, Michael Whitehouse; consultant, Ronald Bergan; narrator, Harriet Walter. Reviewed at London Film Festival, Nov. 17, 1993. Running time: **120 MIN.**

With: Francoise Arnoul, Maurice Baquet, Bernardo Bertolucci, Peter Bogdanovich, Leslie Caron, Claude Chabrol, Paulette Dubost, Rumer Godden, Hurd Hatfield, Norman Lloyd, Louis Malle, Burgess Meredith, Pierre Olaf, Alain Renoir, Catherine Rouvel, Alexander Sesonske, Bertrand Tavernier and others.

The late, great Jean Renoir (1894-1979) is nobly served by this first full-length docu that leaves you hungry for more. Due to air next fall in British pubcaster BBC1's "Omnibus" arts slot, on the centenary of Renoir's birth, the two-parter should travel well on the fest trail and clock up cable and specialized tube sales.

First seg ("From La Belle Epoque to World War II") follows Renoir from his youthful love of movies, aerial photography work in the French air force, marriage, first pix with actress-wife Catherine Hessling, early sound films like "Boudu Saved from Drowning" and "The Crime of M. Lange," to the string of classics "La Marseillaise," "A Day in the Country," "Grand Illusion," "La Bete Humaine" and "Rules of the Game."

Second part ("Hollywood and Beyond") begins with his 1941 arrival in Hollywood, unhappy experiences at 20th Century Fox and subsequent scattergun career that produced titles like "This Land Is Mine," "The Diary of a Chambermaid," "The Southerner," "The Woman on the Beach" (recut by its producer) and the Indian-set "The River."

Sad ending notes that on his final film, the portmanteau "Le Petit Theatre de Jean Renoir" (1969), he was initially refused an *avance sur recettes.*

Though clearly limited by availability of archive material (especially from France), and the relatively few survivors from a long-gone age, director David Thompson does a thorough job of rounding up the usual suspects.

Biggest coup is nabbing the director's normally camera-shy son,

December 13, 1993 (Cont.)

Alain, who is revealing about his father's attitude to America and the snub by the French intelligentsia when he stayed Stateside after World War II.

Just as the humanistic magic of Renoir's movies is difficult to dissect, so Renoir the man proves equally elusive, beyond the chubby, *echt*-Gallic bon vivant that emerges in several 1960s interviews.

Faced with a formidable number of classics to cover, especially during the productive 1930s, Thompson has little space for Renoir's intriguing private life (such as his relationship with the left-wing cutter Margueritte Houlle) or working methods.

A rare criticism of "le patron" comes in a resurrected quote by actor Jean Gabin who called Renoir "as an artist, a genius; as a man, a prostitute."

Clips are plentiful and acceptable in quality, including Renoir's rarely seen, "L'Atalante"-like debut "La Fille d'Eau" and the loopy "Charleston" with the feisty Hessling. Helmers like Chabrol, Tavernier, Bertolucci and Bogdanovich supply critical acumen, the last most penetratingly when describing Renoir's mastery of nuance.

Interviews were shot on film, with post-production done on vid, subsequently transferred to 16mm for theatrical showings. Results on the big screen retain an electronic flavor, but are OK. Voiceover narration by actress Harriet Walter lacks punch, more like a cozy fireside chat.
—*Derek Elley*

XUAN LIAN
(RED BEADS)
(CHINESE — B&W)

Produced with the support of China Eastern Cultural Development Center. (International sales: Fortissimo, Amsterdam.) Produced by Xiao Ming. Executive producer, Xiao. Directed by He Yi. Screenplay, Liu Xiaojing, You Ni. Camera (b&w), Nie Tiejun, Yu Xiaoyang; editor, Liu; music, Guo Xiaohong; art direction, Wang Wangwang; costume design, Yun Fang; sound, Guan Jian; assistant director, Hu Zhi. Reviewed at London Film Festival, Nov. 13, 1993. (Also in Vancouver fest.) Running time: **88 MIN.**
Jing Sheng .... Liu Jiang
Jiyun .... Shi Ke
Dr. Sha .... Tian Gechen
With: Hu Zhi, Wang Yongsheng, Li Huo, Meng Yan, Han Jingru, Liu Zhiyi.

A dreamlike fantasy about a young porter in a stark Peking loony bin and the beautiful young patient he befriends, "Red Beads" looks set for only limited unspoolings on the fest circuit but announces a talent of some conviction and technique.

Director He Yi (real name, He Jianjun) graduated from Peking Film Academy in 1990 and worked as an assistant to both Zhang Yimou (on "Raise the Red Lantern") and Tian Zhuangzhuang ("The Blue Kite"). Present item is a totally indie production, shot over 12 days in late 1992 in b&w, free of government controls.

Slow-burning relationship between the disturbed girl (played by popular actress Shi Ke) and young man (Liu Jiang) gathers genuine warmth, ending with a chaste cuddle on a bed and his assuming her dementia of dreaming of "red beads."

Pic can be read as a political allegory on social controls in China — inmates are a cross-section of society, reduced to zombies, and the hospital head (Tian Gechen) boasts they all get "special care."

Style is consciously arty, with exaggerated sound effects, repeated scenes of routine, a discreet *musique concrete* soundtrack, and low-key perfs. Lapses into pretentiousness are rare. A framing device ends the film on an upbeat note.

Tech credits are fine for a no-budgeter. Original title literally means "Suspended Love."
—*Derek Elley*

DARK SUMMER
(BRITISH)

A 2C Prods./Activate production. (International sales: Activate Prods., London.) Produced, directed, written, edited by Charles Teton. Additional material, Bernie Deasy, Steve Cheers, Bernd Luebke. Camera (color, widescreen), Teton; music, Clive Chin; production design, Elouise Attwood; art direction, Kate Jones; sound, Joss Jotham; associate producers, Derrin Schlesinger, Mary Calderwood. Reviewed at London Film Festival, Nov. 19, 1993. Running time: **71 MIN.**
Abe Wilson .... Steve Ako
Jess Sheppard .... Joeline Garner-Joel
Bernie Deasy .... Bernie Deasy
Alan Sheppard .... Chris Darwin
Chris King .... Dave Rooney
Johnny Wild .... Jimmy Fitz

First-time filmmaker Charles Teton, 32, scores high for initiative but lower on results with "Dark Summer," a visually accomplished but highly distanced cross-tracks love story set in Liverpool. Commercial chances look slim for the no-budgeter, though Teton clearly has the know-how and chutzpah for future projects.

A former photog, Teton brought the film in for some £40,000 ($60,000) after four years in production. Aspect ratio is a bold, visually refreshing 2.35.

Central characters are young black boxer Abe (Steve Ako), who works in a scrap-metal yard, and young white girl Jess (Joeline Gar-ner-Joel), daughter of the yard's owner. Jess moves in with Abe, who's since been fired by her father; she later has a miscarriage, gets depressed and vanishes one day.

Using a fixed camera, and lots of fade-outs/fade-ins, Teton presents a kind of moving photo album of the young couple's summer affair. Race (or even class) is not an issue: The pic's metaphysical bent is more Gallic than Anglo-Saxon.

With a stronger script (dialogue is minimal and everyday), and stronger lead perfs (best described as low-key), the pic could have generated some onscreen passion to equal the bouncy, Afro-flavored pop score heard offscreen. But after the opening reels, Teton's rigid, over-intellectualized style and reluctance to go with the flow quickly start to pall.

Apart from some indistinct dialogue passages, tech credits are fine, and Teton's widescreen lensing of Merseyside locales is characterful.
—*Derek Elley*

JACK L. WARNER: THE LAST MOGUL
(DOCU — VIDEO)

A Gregory Orr production. (Intl. sales: Gregory Orr Prods., Beverly Hills.) Produced, directed, written by Gregory Orr. Camera (color), various; editor, Don Priess; music, Herman Beeftink; narrator, Efrem Zimbalist Jr. Reviewed at London Film Festival, Nov. 15, 1993. Running time: **104 MIN.**
With: Efrem Zimbalist, Jr., Shirley Jones, Debbie Reynolds, Jack Warner Jr., Neal Gabler, Rudy Behlmer.

The man Jack Benny said would rather tell a bad joke than make a good movie gets a warm, personal appreciation from his grandson, Gregory Orr, in "Jack L. Warner: The Last Mogul." OK vid item looks a good bet for tube playoff.

Film is partly structured as a personal odyssey by Orr, 39, to come to terms with the memory of a man whose vast estate he would visit as a kid — "a little like visiting royalty." Orr's ingenuous, look-at-me approach (which gets in the way after a while) yields high-chutzpah scenes of him driving to the Warner manse and even talking like an interviewee on camera.

Most interesting material is in the first half, where Orr draws on fascinating family photos and other material to show how Jack, the "rebellious," problem child of the four Warner brothers (the children of first-generation Polish Jewish immigrants), rose to head the studio almost by accident.

The film doesn't gloss over Warner's weaknesses — his womanizing, capitulation to the House Un-American Activities Committee and betrayal of brother Harry to become sole head of WB in the 1950s. But with the passage of time, there's a romantic affection for Warner's love of playing the mogul, his swashbuckling qualities and sad self-realization after being eased out in 1969 that, without a studio, he was just another nobody in town.

Even WB's reputation for "squeezing pennies till they shouted" is viewed almost wistfully, with the caveat that it was a cut-price but not a cut-rate studio. As veteran director Vincent Sherman notes, "If you could make a picture at Warner Bros., you could make it anywhere."

Not much time is spent on individual titles, save those that had a key historical/political place in WB's development ("The Jazz Singer," "Confessions of a Nazi Spy," "Mission to Moscow"). Best clips are from Warner's home movies (in color), showing Jack L. relaxing with his family or at play. Tech credits are OK. —*Derek Elley*

WARREN OATES: ACROSS THE BORDER
(DOCU — 16mm)

A Tom Thurman/Fly By Noir production. (International sales: FBN Films, Danville, Kentucky.) Produced, directed by Thurman. Executive producer, Chris Iovenko. Screenplay, Tom Marksbury. Additional script material, David Thomson. Camera (color) Walter Brock; editors, Thurman, Bruce R. Ogden; music, Frank Schaap; sound, Arthur Rouse; associate producer, Rouse; narrator, Ned Beatty. Reviewed at London Film Festival, Nov. 10, 1993. Running time: **52 MIN.**
With: Peter Fonda, Ned Beatty, Stacy Keach, Harry Dean Stanton, Ben Johnson, Millie Perkins, Monte Hellman, Thomas McGuane, Robert Culp.

Peckinpah icon Warren Oates (1928-82) is warmly saluted in "Warren Oates: Across the Border," fellow Kentuckian Tom Thurman's technically modest but well-meaning bio-tribute to the flavorsome character actor. As befits Oates' career as a supporting player, the film is as interesting for its luminary interviewees as for insights into its subject but should find a welcome among buffs, especially in Europe, where Oates has a solid following.

Ned Beatty, who also narrates, gets closest to Oates' appeal when he says he played "negative" guys (i.e., losers) in a way that allowed audiences to identify with them. Born in western Kentucky during

December 13, 1993 (Cont.)

the Depression, Oates made it to movies in the late 1950s via the Marines, stage work, N.Y. and TV.

Writer David Thomson succinctly notes that Oates was maybe "the common element" in the great period of U.S. cinema from 1965 to 1977, when challenging movies were made that would never get studio support today. Fellow free spirits Monte Hellman, Peter Fonda and Harry Dean Stanton (latter only briefly) touchingly recall an age that's forever gone. Robert Culp describes Oates as "a glorious failure that demands our love and respect."

Made with the Oates family's cooperation, but with little industry clout, pic uses vid extracts from the actor's work that are often not of best quality. Disappointingly, clips from "The Wild Bunch" were not available.

Though Oates himself emerges as an essentially simple character, the film wisely makes the point that he was never a star actor who could shape a pic. Peckinpah's "Bring Me the Head of Alfredo Garcia" was the only vehicle he led, and the jury is still out on that one. —*Derek Elley*

YIU SAU DOUSI

(THE WICKED CITY)

(HONG KONG)

A Film Workshop production, with participation of Edko Films. (International sales: Film Workshop, Hong Kong.) Produced by Raymond Lee, Mak Chi-sin. Executive producer, Tsui Hark. Directed by Peter Mak. Screenplay, Tsui, Roy Szeto, from the comic strip by Hideyuki Kikuchi. Camera (color), Andrew Lau, Joe Chan; editor, Mak Chi-sin; music, Richard Yuen; art direction, Eddie Ma; costume design, Chris Wong; sound, Mak Chi-sin; action directors, Lee Kin-sang, Cheung Yiu-sing. Reviewed at BFI screening room, London, Oct. 22, 1993. (In London, Vancouver festivals.) Running time: **88 MIN.**
Ken .... Jacky Cheung
Taki .... Leon Lai
Windy .... Michelle Li
Also with: Tasuya Nakadai, Yuen Woo-ping, Roy Cheung, Carmen Lee, Lisa Jane Burnett, Reiko Hayawa, Sophia Crawford.
(Cantonese dialogue)

Political allegory runs riot in "The Wicked City," a roller-coaster blend of Nipponese *manga*, H.K. actioners and choice cuts from "Blade Runner" that has everything except a sense of pacing. However, pic has the makings of a robust performer as a dubbed homevideo, and could do limited theatrical biz offshore as a cleverly marketed culter.

In a nod to its adaptation from a popular Japanese comic strip, film opens in Tokyo, where cop Ken

(Jacky Cheung) has just saved his colleague Taki (Leon Lai) from being gobbled by one of the "raptors," sexy women who are monsters in disguise and bent on taking over the East.

Back in H.K., the Anti-Raptor Bureau is busy defending the city from takeover, especially as "1997 will be a good time for raptors to invade." A Japanese corporation has been lulling the population with a drug called Happiness, and the boss' son, Shudo (Roy Cheung), is in cahoots with the raptors.

Just to complicate matters, Ken reveals he's only half-human, Taki falls for a beautiful, kindhearted raptor (Michelle Li), and the baddies have a spy in the bureau. Delirious finale has the good guys battling Shudo atop I.M. Pei's Bank of China building, where he's having fun turning back time and playing King Kong with jumbo jets.

Helmer Peter Mak, whose earlier non-action credits include the sharp Taiwan satire "The Hero, the Loser" and inventive "All Night Long," changes career gear with a vengeance. No time is wasted on backgrounding or explanations: The ride's the thing. But with no pause for breath or characterization, the film squanders its invention in the long run.

Technically, the Tsui Hark (Film Workshop) production is good but not outstanding. Playing by the star cast is reliable, with Jacky Cheung stealing the personality honors. Pic performed pleasantly on H.K. release in late 1992. —*Derek Elley*

TURIN FEST

MATI SHENG SUI

(DISTANT TRAMPLING OF HORSES)

(CHINESE)

A Xiaoxiang Film Studios production. Directed by Liu Miaomiao. Screenplay, Jiang Qitao. Camera (color), Zhang Li, Yan Yuanzhao; editor, Wang Xiaoming; music, Wen Zhongjia; art direction, Yang Li; sound, Huang Siye. Reviewed at Turin Intl. Young Cinema Festival, Italy, Nov. 15, 1993. Running time: **90 MIN.**
With: Bianba Danzi, Yang Qiong, Zhang Yimei, Xu Zhiqun, Yang Lei.

"Distant Trampling of Horses" revisits the historic 1935 Long March by Chinese communists in disenchanted terms. Arduousness, injustice, prolonged hardship and human loss are intimately depicted through the struggle of an eight-woman detachment roaming the icy, inhospitable highlands along the Tibetan border.

Debut feature by femme helmer Liu Miaomiao (youngest of the "Fifth Generation" gang fronted by Chen Kaige and Zhang Yimou) was made in 1987 but is only now being shown outside China. By turns dolefully expressive, quietly acerbic and frustratingly remote, this challenging pic should notch up a crowded calendar of festival and Asian film week dates on the strength of its curio value and heavily censored history alone.

After years of refusals to Western programmers, Chinese authorities OK'd the Turin screening following this fall's Venice fest showing of Liu's third feature, "Chatterbox." But Liu still had to organize documentation, translation and print shipment herself.

Pic's starting point is a power conflict between communist Liberation Army chiefs, prompting a faction to break away from the march in an abortive attempt to set up bases on the border between Tibet and Sichuan province. Sent out from the dissident regiment on a misguided mission, a small women's platoon, low on everything except revolutionary ideals, finds itself isolated.

Tracking their dogged efforts to rejoin the troops, Liu ably conveys conditions of extreme discomfort, borderline starvation and physical danger. But her real focus — and the pic's most persuasive element — is examining events via their effect on the women.

She sketches a steely revolutionary determination often born less of informed political conviction than as a way out of lifelong poverty and servitude.

The film's intended tone is sometimes baffling. In one scene, the malnourished platoon (diminished by two deaths) breaks into a rousing Party anthem which sends them striding uphill like cheery Von Trapp children. Elsewhere, irony is clearer, as in a closing v.o. hinting that the most enduring memory of the Long March is the sound of 10,000 soldiers coughing in unison.

Though it doesn't quite have the crystalline communicative power of some of her classmates' early work, Liu's pic stands as a confidently executed, grand-scale feature bow that warrants attention in surveys of quality Chinese cinema. Original title means "The Broken Sound of Horses' Hooves." —*David Rooney*

NUDO NO YORU

(A NIGHT IN NUDE)

(JAPANESE)

A New Century Producers production. Produced by Kaoya Karita, Taketo Kiitsu. Directed, written by Takashi Ishii. Camera (color), Yasushi Sasakibara; editor, Akimasa Kawashima; music, Goro Yasukawa; art direction, Teru Yamazaki; sound, Atsuki Sugiyama. Reviewed at Turin Intl. Young Cinema Festival, Italy, Nov. 17, 1993. Running time: **110 MIN.**
Jiro Kurenai .... Naoto Takenaka
Nami Tuchiya .... Kimiko Yo
Also with: Kippei Shiina, Yoshiko Shimizu, Ryo Iwamatsu, Hiroshi Kobayashi.

In his last feature, "Original Sin," Takashi Ishii sliced, diced and completely recooked "The Postman Always Rings Twice." This time around, he offers another dizzying orgy of prime noir ingredients, Nipponized and underscored by pounding rain and throbbing neon. "A Night in Nude" has cult potential stamped all over it.

Scheming to unload her sadistic lover, a floozy (Kimiko Yo) poses as a tourist in Tokyo, hiring an unsuspecting jack-of-all-trades (Naoto Takenaka) to act as her guide. He checks her into a hotel, rejects her drunken advances and clears off before lover boy arrives.

A rigorous slap-and-tickle session follows that's decidedly heavier on the former. Afterwards, Yo joins her bedmate in the bathroom, and the grisliest shower scene since Norman Bates first wielded a knife ensues.

Next day, Takenaka finds Yo gone, removes her lover's body and sets about tracking her down. The lover's psychopath partner also steps in, threatening to make sushi first out of Takenaka, then Yo.

Wild excesses of cartoon sex and violence are played almost for laughs. At one point, instead of coming to Yo's rescue, a fresh-faced suitor slaps her about with a bunch of roses; at another, a surreal nightmare has a gun literally being bored through Takenaka's skull.

Ishii also plays with the pic's tone musically, laying inappropriate cocktail tunes over a tearful repentance scene and bubble-gum pop over dramatic exchanges. Regular lenser Yasushi Sasakibara's low, skewed camera angles and kinky compositions again contribute significantly to the flamboyantly stylish feast. —*David Rooney*

HALBE WELT

(HALF WORLD)

(AUSTRIAN)

An Allegro Filmprods. production. Produced by Helmut Grasser. Directed by Florian Flicker. Screenplay, Flicker, Michael Sturminger. Camera (color), Jerzy Palacz; editor, Berhard Weirather; music, Andreas Haller; art direction, Andreas Donhauser, Renate Martin; costume design, Anette Schroder; sound, Weirather. Reviewed at Turin Intl. Young Cinema Festival (competing), Italy, Nov. 14, 1993. Running time: 85 MIN.

Herzog	Rainer Egger
Katz	Dani Levy
Sunny	Maria Schrader
Sina	Mercedes Echerer
Repro	Goran Rebic

Though this inventive meeting of "Total Recall" and "Alphaville" probably won't keep Paul Verhoeven awake at night, Florian Flicker's grunge sci-fi "Half World" shows a fertile imagination running rings round a slender budget. Pic loses itself slightly amid narrative digressions but should find a core of genre admirers.

Flicker conjures up a festering future world where the sun's harmful rays force people to live by night. However, the rebellious Herzog (Rainer Egger) risks arrest and his health for a regular fix of sunlight.

For high payers, exposure to nature is available through computer-generated experiences of an earlier world. The cheaper alternative is panoramic postcards illegally sold by a street hawker.

Themes of artificial existence and self-serving society are intelligently illustrated. But Flicker shifts tracks too frequently, focusing on a succession of sketchy characters (Herzog being the most constant) and muddling the mechanics of his story of survival under a coercive regime.

Performances are nondescript, but the film's shoestring effects are varied and convincing, among them a virtual-reality option for mountain climbers. Scenes of blinding sunlight were achieved by repeatedly copying original footage before switching to negatives.
—*David Rooney*

YA NEKUDA TEBYA NE OTPUSCU

(I'LL NEVER LET YOU GO)

(RUSSIAN)

Produced by Nina Batetnikova. Directed, written, edited by Elena Konstantinovna Tonunc. Camera (color), Yevgeni Sokolov; music, Gabriel Faure; sound, Aleksandr Zakrzevsky. Reviewed at Turin Intl. Young Cinema Festival (competing), Italy, Nov. 16, 1993. Running time: 63 MIN.

With: Angelika Nevolina, Andrei Rostovsky, Igor Bokin, Vsevold Silovsky.

Communist-controlled Russia looks like a party compared with the post-*glasnost* chaos of "I'll Never Let You Go," the work of thesp-turned-director Elena Konstantinovna Tonunc.

Made with a crew of two on coin allocated for a 20-minute short, pic has a lacerating intensity, harnessed to a compelling turn by Angelika Nevolina as a luckless waif. But the film's technical rawness will limit post-fest exposure to specialized cultural venues.

Nevolina plays a young Muscovite who flees home at age 16 after her mother's death leaves her at the mercy of an alcoholic father. Recounting her experiences later to an unseen listener, she recalls a life as sad and stark as the concrete apartment blocks it's lived in.

Police brutality, pitiless exploitation at work, a bad marriage and the death of her children prompt a slide into theft and virtual prostitution. Despite Nevolina's narration, the story unfolds disjointedly. But Tonunc redresses the balance with observations on the grim alternatives available in a Moscow plagued by poverty and crime and stripped of human solidarity.

Intermittent use of jarring Western pop tunes also adds to the withering portrait of modern Russia's unresolved identity. Tonunc's VGIK film school graduation work won best film and acting plaudits, respectively, from Fipresci (international critics) and competition juries at Turin.
—*David Rooney*

LONGE DAQUI

(FAR FROM HERE)

(PORTUGUESE)

A Madragoa Filmes production. Produced by Paolo Branco. Directed by Joao Guerra. Screenplay, Guerra, Jorge Silva Melo. Camera (color), Vladymir F. Brilyakov; editor, Manuela Viegas; art direction, Miguel Mendes, Manuel Lobao; costume design, Isabel Branco; sound, Francisco Veloso. Reviewed at Turin Intl. Young Cinema Festival (competing), Italy, Nov. 15, 1993. Running time: 97 MIN.

Vitor	Canto e Castro
Manuel	Filipe Cochofel
Artur	Antonio Pedro Figueiredo
Maria Joao	Maysa Marta

With: Glicinia Quartin, Manuela De Freitas, Luis Santos, Armando Branco Alves, Rui Luis, Rui Gomes, Manuel Mozos.

An agreeably loose-limbed, unfettered road movie, "Far From Here" demands certain concessions that arthouse auds may not be willing to make. But festgoers willing to shrug off its jumble of confused narrative points and go with its easy rhythms and relaxed sense of humor will find much that's seductive in Portuguese helmer Joao Guerra's debut.

Catalyst in the story of crossed paths is a 1957 Ford Fairlane being driven through Portugal's Alentejo region to a new owner. Film's overly protracted opening has car's drivers (Filipe Cochofel, Antonio Pedro Figueiredo) joy riding the night away until the roadster breaks down. Momentum picks up at sunrise with their attempts to fix the car.

A retired mechanic-turned-beekeeper with a heart condition (Canto e Castro) does the trick and convinces Figueiredo to take him cross-country on a motorbike to look up an old friend.

Cochofel and the mechanic's alarmed niece (Maysa Marta) follow in pursuit. The old man dies peacefully on the road, but Figueiredo, having wholeheartedly grasped his deliverance mission, keeps going.

Beginning with the mechanic's death, the four characters' motivations become decidedly fuzzy, but the strong cast's comradely interplay keeps things moving. Some night segs are underlit, but tech aspects are generally pro.
—*David Rooney*

TADA HITO TABI NO HITO

(THE SINGING BAMBOO)

(JAPANESE — 16mm)

A JJS Plan Sequence production. Produced by Fumio Hamada, Harumi Kato. Directed by Tetsu Kato. Camera (color), Yoshiaki Miyatake; editor, Chikako Fukuda; music, Yukihiko Mitsuka; sound, Yutaka Tsurumaki. Reviewed at Turin Intl. Young Cinema Festival (competing), Italy, Nov. 18, 1993. Running time: 105 MIN.

Namihiko	Namihiko Omura
Mother	Sachiko Hidari
Grandfather	Michio Kida
Sister	Kaoru Okunuki

Also with: Yoko Katori, Tsuyoshi Itoh, Emiko Yamamoto.

It's hard to imagine a gentler, more contemplative riff on the industrialized world's incompatibility with the artistic temperament than "The Singing Bamboo."

Inhabiting a Zen plane somewhere between documentary and narrative, this languorous Japanese tract requires ascetic reserves of patience it's unlikely to find beyond the fest circuit. World preemed at the Turin Young Cinema meet, soulful pic was duly lauded by jury and critics.

Entirely improvised from a four-page outline, story concerns a young bamboo-flautist (Namihiko Omura), intro'd in a long jazz-concert sequence. Leaving Tokyo to attend his sister's hometown wedding, he agrees to stick around and take a factory job. But his musical calling lures him back to the city.

Dumped by his g.f. and turfed out by his harridan landlady, he wanders the streets. Pic's remaining half flows almost totally without dialogue, with the amiably unruly, mostly hand-held camera trailing Omura as he narrowly escapes being hauled in for vagrancy. He finally finds his nirvana with a band of street musicians.

Fly-on-the-wall director Tetsu Kato is well served by the unselfconscious presence of Omura (himself a musician). One of the few seasoned thesps on hand, Sachiko Hidari has standout scenes as his single-minded mother. Music written by Yukihiko Mitsuka and performed by his Tone trio is a consistent pleasure. Kato has already announced plans for a sequel.
—*David Rooney*

POSLEDNIYE KHOLODA

(THE LAST COLD DAYS)

(KAZAKH)

A Katarsys Studio production. Directed by Bolat Kalymbetov, Bulat Iskakov. Screenplay, Albert Likhanov, based on his short story. Camera (color/b&w), Sergei Ossenikov; music, T. Muhametjanov; art direction, Marxen Gaukhman-Sverdlov, M. Sarsenbayev. Reviewed at Turin Intl. Young Cinema Festival (competing), Italy, Nov. 17, 1993. Running time: 70 MIN.

Akezhan	Nariman Bekturov
Vadik	Vitaly Gusyev
Masha	Kseniya Baranova

With: Vasily Galganov, B. Zhangaliyeva, L. Polokhov.

Childhood candor and resilience are seamlessly wedded with adultlike pragmatism in the affecting young leads of "The Last Cold Days." Directing duo Bolat Kalymbetov and Bulat Iskakov pack a poetic punch that underlines Kazakhstan as a growing force in world cinema. Extensive fest rounds look certain.

Set near the end of World War II, story centers on two evacuee siblings befriended by a tyke in a remote Kazakh outpost far from the battle front. Learning his mother has died in hospital, Vadik tries to conceal the news from his younger sister, Masha, and from authorities

December 13, 1993 (Cont.)

who'll pack them off to an orphanage. His friend Akezhan begins skipping school to help him beg, steal food and stay clear of a violent band of urchins.

The film's arresting editing structure reruns key moments to heighten their impact and interrupts events with flashes of both past and future scenes. In the opening segment, editing is used to impart information economically: A soldier steps from a train and is stabbed and robbed by young thugs; coffins are unloaded; and a defenseless kid has food stolen from his bowl.

Moral questions surface naturally, as does a sense of charity and shared destiny between the kids. Their need to feel part of the harsh world around them is left implicit. In their discussions of what hunger and cold can drive them to, the young non-pro cast approaches neorealist excellence.

A color title sequence showing a cloudy sky gives way to melancholy monochrome. Lenser Sergei Ossenikov lingers frequently over memorably bleak images, from factory smokestacks against the barren landscape, through skeletons of wrecked boats along the beach, to a dwarf leading a camel-drawn cart loaded with coffins. T. Muhametjanov's music adds a poignant complement. —*David Rooney*

LILLY

(CANADIAN — B&W — 16mm)

A Psychosomatic production. Produced by Stacey Donen. Directed, written by David Marcoux. Camera (b&w), Joseph Micomonaco; editors, David Axelrad, Aaron Shuster; art direction, Jerry Drozdowsky; sound, Russell Walker; assistant director, Prakash Younger; casting, Jeff Marshall. Reviewed at Turin Intl. Young Cinema Festival (competing), Italy, Nov. 17, 1993. Running time: **105 MIN.**
Lilly	Shelly Hong
Mother	Shirley Cui
Aunt	Agnes Guia
Uncle	K.K. Ho
Donald	Ben Teh
Hank	Wayne McNamara
Julia	Thea Gill
Mrs. Curr	Deanne Judson

A brief encounter sets an emotionally isolated girl's life in motion in "Lilly," first feature of Canadian director David Marcoux. Blending oddball melodrama, soap-operatic angst and earnest introspection on a threadbare $18,000 budget, Marcoux serves up a wealth of catchy ideas that's somewhat let down by indifferent thesping and sporadic humor. Still, pic should give him a firm foot in the door for future outings.

Title character is a 19-year-old Asian girl (Shelly Hong) stuck in the family dry-cleaning store. After a vaguely romantic brush with a stranger, she learns he's been found dead, goes to claim the body and is accused of murder. She clams up, but

the truth surfaces during visits from a neighborly kook (Deanne Judson).

Sketched in short scenes punctuated by fade-outs and brief musical comments, the conflicts between Lilly and her family are more successfully wrought than the central murder mystery.

Judson's flat, unmodulated turn makes story anything but a mystery soon after she hits the screen. Similarly bland perfs from store regulars make Lilly's urge to become part of the world seem less urgent.

But Marcoux strikes wryly original notes in other areas, making clever digs at the media's power (fatuous glossy mags, in particular) to inform public opinion.

A keen sense of humor emerges as various locals theorize on what drove Lilly to kill, offering low blood sugar, sexual thrill-seeking, a prostie's vendetta and lesbian manhatred as probable explanations.

Tech work, including Joseph Micomonaco's b&w lensing, is modest but clean. —*David Rooney*

THESSALONIKI

ONIREVOME TOUS FILOUS MOU

(I DREAM OF MY FRIENDS)

(GREEK)

A Stefi/Greek Film Center production. Directed, written by Nikos Panayotopoulos, based on Dimitris Nollas' short stories. Camera (color), Giorgos Frentzos; editor, Giorgos Triantafylou; music, Stan Getz, Dizzy Gillespie, Sonny Stitt; art direction, Dionyssis Fotopoulos, Maria Kaltsa; costume design, Marianne Spanoudaki; sound (Dolby), Andreas Achlidis, Thanassis Georgiadis. Reviewed at Thessaloniki Film Festival, Greece, Nov. 13, 1993. Running time: **114 MIN.**

With: Lefteris Voyatzis, Akilas Karazissis, Yannis Karatzoyannis, Stathis Livathinos, Alekos Kolipoulos, Minas Hatzisavas.

A pleasurable reflection on everything and nothing, "I Dream of My Friends" is right up there in minimalist heaven. Story of a strong, silent Euro dude's four ambivalent, inconclusive encounters over 25 years has an indulgently unhurried pace that will hinder commercial prospects, but veteran Greek helmer Nikos Panayotopoulos' unfailing finesse should steer it to wide fest exposure.

Despite his scant interest in conventional narrative, Paris-trained Panayotopoulos has crafted four short stories by contempo Greek writer Dimitris Nollas into an elliptical but engaging personal assessment of his own generation that displays technical prowess and a coolly pan-European aesthetic.

Opening in 1965 with a series of loving, leisurely camera-prowls around Berlin's hazy cityscape, story picks up the laid-back Kyriakos (Lefteris Voyatzis), who is involved with a fellow Greek in a scam to unload encyclopedias on U.S. army bases.

In 1973, he shares a ride with an insistently communicative truck driver heading from the Yugoslav border down to Greece. In 1981, he gets drunk with a bartender in a Greek airport during a blackout. Final encounter, in 1990, is in the opulent marble bathroom of an Athens hotel, where during a wedding reception he smokes a joint with two colleagues, one of whom subsequently drops dead.

Panayotopoulos appears as concerned with inanities as truths. He doesn't hedge at dipping into periods of silence, idleness and boredom as a means of adding nuance to his focal character, played with precision and detachment by Voyatzis. What emerges is a minor-key riff on disillusionment and displacement.

Giorgos Frentzos' graceful camera work stands out in an unerringly pro technical field. The four time brackets are introed with jazz interludes by Stan Getz, Dizzy Gillespie and Sonny Stitt. —*David Rooney*

HADASHI NO PICNIC

(DOWN THE DRAIN)

(JAPANESE — 16mm)

A PIA Corp./Pony Canyon production. Produced by Binbun Furusawa, Mana Katsurada. Directed by Shinobu Yagushi. Screenplay, Yagushi, Takuji Suzuki, Yasunobu Kanagawa. Camera (color), Furusawa, Kazuhiro Susuki; editor, Yagushi; music, Unohana; art direction, Akihiro Inamura; sound, Youichi Kinami. Reviewed at Thessaloniki Film Festival (New Horizons section), Greece, Nov. 6, 1993. Running time: **92 MIN.**

With: Saori Serikawa, Mr. Okure, Miwako Kazi, Akane Asano, Kotaro, Shigeru Izumiya, Morio Agata.

A Japanese schoolgirl unwittingly sets off a catastrophic chain of events in 26-year-old Shinobu Yagushi's appealingly off-kilter debut, "Down the Drain." Rough-edged, unpredictable black comedy should turn heads in fest outings, particularly those devoted to emerging talent.

Nabbed for train-fare evasion and fearing disciplinary repercussions at home and school, Junko heads for cover at grandma's, but finds out she's recently died. Entrusted with granny's ashes, Junko klutzily drops the urn in the path of a street-sweeping vehicle.

Grief-stricken, she gate-crashes a stranger's memorial service to mourn, but accidentally sets fire to

the altar. A walking disaster area, Junko wanders cross-country, wreaking havoc on family, schoolmates and anyone else in her path.

Yagushi's tack of constantly switching narrators creates mild continuity strife (especially in the sloppily subtitled print caught). Still, he compensates with irrepressible energy and quietly subversive comic charm, even as events spark increasingly grave and often violent results.

Pic winningly taps the humorous possibilities offered by fresh-faced schoolies driven to be bad girls.

Yagushi (whose background is in graphic design) shows a keen compositional eye that enlivens the multitude of static shots. Made for what appears to be a handful of yen, pic's only bothersome tech note is Unohana's mostly melodic music, ill-matched with the presidingly off-the-wall tone. —*David Rooney*

A LA BELLE ETOILE

(UNDER THE STARS)

(FRENCH-SWISS)

An FRP/La Vie Est Belle Films Associes/Groupe TSF (Paris)/PCT Pierre-Andre Thiebaud (Geneva) production, with the participation of Canal Plus. Produced by Frederic Robbes. Directed, written by Antoine Desrosieres. Camera (color), Georges Le Chaptois; editor, Catherine Bonetat; music, Bojan Zulfikarpasic, Julien Lourau; art direction, Cyr Boitard; sound, Marc Nouyrigat. Reviewed at Thessaloniki Film Festival (competing), Greece, Nov. 11, 1993. Running time: **95 MIN.**
Thomas	Mathieu Demy
Hannah	Julie Gayet
Marion	Aurelia Thierree
Claire	Chiara Mastroianni
Rebecca	Camila Mora

Adolescent amour gets a spirited but uneven once-over in "Under the Stars," a neatly packaged feature bow by 22-year-old Antoine Desrosieres. Director's gifts for physical comedy, coupled with those of energetic lead Mathieu Demy, are let down by excessive displays of cine-literacy, which make it all seem numbingly familiar. Still, pic makes a chirpy calling card, and a breezy entry for young cinema meets.

Demy plays a klutzy late-teenster who develops a crush on a perfect stranger (Aurelia Thierree). His dogged pursuit of her is aided by his best friend's girl (Chiara Mastroianni) and obstructed by the unsolicited attentions of another girl (Camila Mora). Chaos reigns until an aspiring tightrope walker (Julie Gayet) shimmies onto the scene.

After its bouncy opening, pic gradually runs out of steam. Spontaneity and off-the-cuff humor give way to studied cuteness.

Desrosieres gets affable turns from the bright young cast. Gallic critic and filmmaker Luc Moullet appears as an art professor and, in a neat touch of black comedy, Desrosieres himself plays a class nerd who kills himself, allowing the cash-strapped Demy to re-work a funeral wreath into a floral gift for Thierree.

—*David Rooney*

AP' TO HIONI

(FROM THE SNOW)

(GREEK)

A Hyperion Prods./Greek Film Center/Sotiris Goritsas production. Executive producer, Panos Papahadzis. Directed, written by Sotiris Goritsas, based on Sotiris Dimitriou's short story. Camera (color), Stamatis Yannoulis; editor, Takis Koumoundouros; music, Nikos Kypourgos; art direction, costume design, Youla Zoiopoulou; sound, Nikos Papadimitriou. Reviewed at Thessaloniki Film Festival (competing), Greece, Nov. 11, 1993. Running time: 90 MIN.

With: Gerassimos Skiadaresis, Vassilis Eleftheriadis, Antonis Manolas, Mania Papadimitriou, Sophia Olympiou.

The fruitless odyssey of a trio of refugees from Albania to Greece provides a potent dramatic core to "From the Snow," but writer-director Sotiris Goritsas keeps his subject at arm's length emotionally, limiting audience involvement.

Technically polished entry is best suited to the tube, especially in Europe, where the parallel plights of non-E.C. immigrants will fuel its immediacy.

Considered Greek by Albanian authorities and Albanian by Greeks, refugees from the Northern Epirus region were initially given virtual carte blanche to enter Greece as cheap labor, 'till the Greek government began slashing the influx. Clandestine immigration continues, however, creating a flourishing climate for worker exploitation, police harassment, homelessness and the sale of refugee children for adoption.

Goritsas skillfully incorporates this background into the story of two villagers and a recently orphaned boy who flee first to Corfu and then to the Greek mainland. Their dreams of socialism's opportunities quickly dissolve as they endure a hopeless bout of adversity that eventually sends them homeward.

Despite an able cast, the protagonists remain remote figures, and pic has a vague, underlying flatness that intrudes on the drama. "Snow" took best feature prize in the Thessaloniki fest's international competition, as well as nods for best film,

screenplay, cinematography and the Fipresci (international critics') award in the national lineup.

—*David Rooney*

I EPOHI TON DOLOFONON

(A TIME TO KILL)

(GREEK)

A Hyperion Prods./Greek Film Center/Nikos Grammatikos/Les Productions Bagheera production. Produced by Panos Papahadzis. Directed by Nikos Grammatikos. Screenplay, Grammatikos, Achilleas Kyriakides. Camera (color), Costis Gikas; editor, Giorgos Giannopoulos; music, Kyriakos Sfetsas; art direction, costume design, Youla Zoiopoulou; sound, Antonis Samaras, Dimitris Galanopoulos. Reviewed at Thessaloniki Film Festival (competing), Greece, Nov. 7, 1993. Running time: 110 MIN.

Nikos	Giorgos Giannopoulos
Kostas	Akis Sakellariou
Daphne	Betty Livanou
Andreas	Minas Hadzisavas

Matters of conscience and loyalty are challenged when two longtime friends confront the ethics of murder in "A Time to Kill." Though it's overlong and no groundbreaker, young Hellenic helmer Nikos Grammatikos' sober sophomore feature packs enough dramatic weight to muscle in on Euro tube slates.

Ace target-shooter Nikos (Giorgos Giannopoulos) is approached by shifty stranger Andreas (Minas Hadzisavas), offering him big bucks to become a hit man. When his reckless shooter buddy Kostas (Akis Sakellariou) is roughed up by gambling heavies, Nikos accepts the job to clear his chum of debt.

Nikos balks at the crucial moment, but the target gets felled by an unknown assailant, Daphne (Betty Livanou). Seeing the boys as her ticket out of a sour relationship with Andreas, Daphne slips into a romantic clinch with Kostas, causing problems all round.

Pic opens with the T.S. Eliot lines "This is the way the world ends. Not with a bang but a whimper." More of a bang is what's missing from the movie: Grammatikos' direction is confident but shies away from displays of violence and too often dilutes tension with ponderous reflective stretches when concrete character motivation is needed.

Acting and tech contributions are all solid, however, and judicious further editing could carve out pithier results. Sakellariou and Livanou won awards at the Thessaloniki fest's national competition for their roles.

—*David Rooney*

EN MEDIO DE LA NADA

(IN THE MIDDLE OF NOWHERE)

(MEXICAN)

A Hugo Rodriguez/Ladron de Besos SA de CV/Instituto Mexicano de Cinematografia production. Directed by Hugo Rodriguez. Screenplay, Rodriguez, Marina Stavenhagen. Camera (color), Guillermo Granillo; editor, Rodriguez; music, Eduardo Gamboa; art direction, Gloria Carrasco; sound, Juan Carlos Prieto, Nerio Barberis. Reviewed at Thessaloniki Film Festival (competing), Greece, Nov. 8, 1993. (Also in Turin Young Cinema fest.) Running time: 93 MIN.

Joaquin	Manuel Ojeda
Susana	Blanca Guerra
Raul	Guillermo Garcia Cantu
Claudia	Gabriela Roel
Ernesto	Emilio Cortes
Ramon	Alonso Echanove
Alejandro	Ignacio Guadalupe

More smoldering glances than bullets are exchanged in the sweaty, Mexican siege movie "In the Middle of Nowhere." First-time helmer Hugo Rodriguez keeps the tension humming and cleverly sustains a taut if familiar atmosphere thick with possibilities. He leaves too many of them underexplored for the result to make much of a mark commercially. But the slick pic's watchable, sharply directed cast could help open inroads into vid markets.

A desert rose (Blanca Guerra) and her husband (Manuel Ojeda), an ex-trade unionist with a spotty past, run a truck stop miles from nowhere. Dust-bowl ennui and minor marital friction are interrupted when a fugitive trio turns up—a gravely wounded criminal (Guillermo Garcia Cantu), his dangerously sexy wife (Gabriela Roel) and his trigger-happy, none-too-smart brother (Emilio Cortes). With no getaway car handy, *banditos* and hostages settle in for the day.

While the claustrophobic situation slow-burns to an inevitable (but surprisingly low-voltage) gun-slinging conclusion, the superior thesps continually seem poised to break out of their relatively stock characterizations.

But despite some promisingly edgy confrontations — such as one between the stoical Guerra and tough enchilada Roel — Rodriguez and co-scripter Marina Stavenhagen never veer off at the psychological turning points on offer.

—*David Rooney*

CHAKMEH

(THE BOOTS)

(IRANIAN)

A Shahed Group production. Directed, written by Mohammad-Ali Talebi, based on H. Moradi Kermani's short story. Camera (color), Farhad Saba; editor, Hassan Hassandoust; music, Mohammad-Reza Aligholi; sound, Mahmud Sammakbashi. Reviewed at Thessaloniki Film Festival (New Horizons section), Greece, Nov. 10, 1993. Running time: 60 MIN.

Sameneh	Sameneh Jafar-Jalali
Ali	Ali Atashkar
Sameneh's mother	Raya Nasiri

Essentially a sprightly moral lesson for tots, "The Boots" presents a smart, sweet and crisply concise parable that adults will get a kick out of too. Classy kidpic forums on large and small screens should look up this Iranian item.

Struggling to keep in line her capricious moppet, a doting but frazzled seamstress (presumably a war widow) shells out for a new pair of red boots. But when the kid's euphoria subsides, and she nods off on the bus, one boot slips off and is lost. The boot's tortuous path round the city is amusingly tracked.

Scripter-director Mohammad-Ali Talebi colors the warmly human yarn with gently infectious humor and soft-sell sentimentality that stays the right side of syrupiness. The hardship and poverty ingrained into everyday Iranian life are evidenced without being unduly hammered, as is the importance of community and mutual consideration.

—*David Rooney*

December 20, 1993

THE PELICAN BRIEF

A Warner Bros. release. Produced by Alan J. Pakula, Pieter Jan Brugge. Directed, written by Pakula, based on the novel by John Grisham. Camera (Technicolor), Stephen Goldblatt; editors, Tom Rolf, Trudy Ship; music, James Horner; production design, Philip Rosenberg; art direction, Robert Guerra; set design, Sarah Stollman, Monroe Kelly (New Orleans); set decoration, Lisa Fischer, Rick Simpson; costume design, Albert Wolsky; sound (Dolby), James J. Sabat; associate producer, Donald Laventhal; assistant director, Peter Kohn; casting, Alixe Gordon. Reviewed at the Warner Bros. screening room, Burbank, Dec. 8, 1993. MPAA Rating: PG-13. Running time: **141 MIN.**

Darby Shaw	Julia Roberts
Gray Grantham	Denzel Washington
Thomas Callahan	Sam Shepard
Gavin Verheek	John Heard
Fletcher Coal	Tony Goldwyn
Denton Voyles	James B. Sikking
Bob Gminski	William Atherton
President	Robert Culp
Khamel	Stanley Tucci
Justice Rosenberg	Hume Cronyn
Smith Keen	John Lithgow

The title is certainly a misnomer. This crackling thriller will have a long, prosperous box office flight and promises quite literally to give the first John Grisham film adaptation, "The Firm," a run for its money. With perfect casting and stellar work by writer-producer-director Alan J. Pakula that eliminates most of the novel's flaws, "The Pelican Brief" should fill Warner Bros. with holiday cheer straight through to St. Patrick's Day.

Tilling some of the same conspiracy turf he explored in "All the President's Men," Pakula has actually improved on Grisham's book by excising much of the detritus, crafting a taut, intelligent thriller that succeeds on almost every level.

Playing a part written with her in mind, Julia Roberts is sensational as law student-on-the-run Darby Shaw, and Denzel Washington proves her equal in a laudable example of color-blind casting.

As those who watched more than 2½ hours of "The Firm" discovered, adapting Grisham is no picnic. Although he writes cinematically, despite his brilliant setups the author tends to meander in the second half of his books and gets caught up in technical gobbledygook that isn't action-packed enough to sustain the typical thriller audience.

That compels the filmmakers to rectify those shortcomings, and Pakula has managed to do so even more effectively — with nearly every deviation necessary and on target, all the while remaining quite true to the book.

The story opens with two Supreme Court justices murdered on the same night by a contract killer named Khamel (Stanley Tucci). Engrossed by the bizarre events, 24-year-old Tulane law student Darby researches and drafts a brief detailing an obscure case eventually destined for the court docket that could provide inspiration for the dual murders.

Darby's professor boyfriend, Thomas Callahan (Sam Shepard, in a solid cameo) passes the brief along to a friend at the FBI (John Heard). When Thomas' car explodes, the game of cats-and-mouse is on — with both the government and the perpetrators pursuing Darby, even as the president (Robert Culp) and his chief of staff (Tony Goldwyn) fret that the conspiracy could implicate the White House.

Pushed to the limit, Darby contacts newspaper reporter Gray Grantham (Washington), already chasing the story through an anonymous source, seeking to save herself by shining a light on the shadowy doings.

Pakula does a remarkable job weaving and making sense of these complex strands. Although there's plenty of suspense as Darby and Gray evade her pursuers, the director eschews the cheaper tricks of the trade, respecting the audience's ability to keep track of what's going on. Also, "Brief" is a relatively gore-free thriller, with most of the violence effectively conveyed offscreen.

With all the descriptions of a long-legged, red-haired beauty in the book, it's not hard to figure out who Grisham had in mind, and Roberts is simply terrific, expressing Darby's initial bewilderment, followed by resourcefulness and steely resolve.

Washington also impresses as Gray, whose personality remained vague in the novel, allowing the actor to put his own stamp on the part. With his concurrent role in "Philadelphia," Washington's stock should be so high by January that the best advice would be to buy now.

Casting in supporting roles is equally meticulous, with top-notch performances all around — even in such limited exposure as that afforded Shepard and Heard. Culp is dead-on as the president (an apparent cross between Gerald Ford and George Bush), and Goldwyn wonderfully smarmy as his cool chief of staff, while Tucci projects considerable yet restrained menace as the assassin.

Tech credits are also impeccable, from James Horner's evocative, understated score to Philip Rosenberg's sumptuous production design, ranging from the White House to stark corporate law offices to New Orleans' Bourbon Street. Washington is attired a bit more nattily than most reporters one encounters, but to point that out is picking nits — about the only sort of flaw one can find in this "Brief."

—*Brian Lowry*

PHILADELPHIA

A TriStar release of a Clinica Estetico production. Produced by Edward Saxon, Jonathan Demme. Executive producers, Gary Goetzman, Kenneth Utt, Ron Bozman. Directed by Demme. Screenplay, Ron Nyswaner. Camera (DuArt, Technicolor), Tak Fujimoto; editor, Craig McKay; music, Howard Shore; production design, Kristi Zea; art direction, Tim Galvin; set decoration, Karen O'Hara; costume design, Colleen Atwood; sound (Dolby), Chris Newman; associate producer-second unit director, Zea; assistant director, Bozman; casting, Howard Feuer. Reviewed at TriStar screening room, Culver City, Nov. 30, 1993. MPAA Rating: PG-13. Running time: **122 MIN.**

Andrew Beckett	Tom Hanks
Joe Miller	Denzel Washington
Charles Wheeler	Jason Robards
Belinda Conine	Mary Steenburgen
Miguel Alvarez	Antonio Banderas
Bob Seidman	Ron Vawter
Walter Kenton	Robert Ridgely
Judge Garnett	Charles Napier
Lisa Miller	Lisa Summerour
Sarah Beckett	Joanne Woodward

Also with: Obba Babatunde, Andre B. Blake, Robert Castle, Daniel Chapman, Roger Corman, Ann Dowd, David Drake, Karen Finley, Charles Glenn, Peter Jacobs, Paul Lazar, John Bedford Lloyd, Roberta Maxwell, Warren Miller, Dan Olmstead, Joey Perillo, Lauren Roselli, Bill Rowe, Anna Deavere Smith, Lisa Talerico, Daniel von Bargen, Tracey Walter, Bradley Whitford, Chandra Wilson, Kathryn Witt, Julius "Dr. J." Erving.

"**P**hiladelphia" is an ideal film for people who have never known anyone with AIDS. In other words, this extremely well-made message picture about tolerance, justice and discrimination is pitched at mainstream audiences, befitting its position as the first major Hollywood film to directly tackle the disease. Intelligent but too neatly worked out in its political and melodramatic details, Jonathan Demme's follow-up to his Oscar-winning "The Silence of the Lambs" is fronted by a dynamite lead performance from Tom Hanks, but will need top reviews and a superior marketing campaign to make it a must-see for members of the general public whose idea of a night out might not be to see a movie about a man dying of AIDS.

Even if the format and arc of Ron Nyswaner's script constitute a familiar one of outraged justice resolved by courtroom fireworks, the story is seductive, its concern for humanity unavoidably stirring. The picture feels compelled to signal in a hundred ways that its heart is in the right place, although that doesn't change the fact that it is. The impulse behind the film seems to be to make people who haven't had to deal with AIDS face up to the illness, and it dramatizes the issue grippingly enough to probably succeed at that aim.

Hanks stars as Andrew Beckett, a rising young attorney at a powerful Philadelphia law firm. But as soon as he's made an associate and assigned to an extremely important case, he displays the first visible signs of AIDS. Suddenly and shockingly, he's fired by the firm over a bit of alleged incompetence that might have cost them the case, but Andrew knows he was dismissed because of his illness.

Determined to spend the rest of his life, if necessary, fighting this gross injustice, Andrew, in desperation, is finally able to recruit Joe Miller (Denzel Washington) as his attorney. A somewhat flashy lawyer who advertises on TV, Joe initially refuses the case and goes in panic to his doctor to see if he's in danger merely from superficial contact with Andrew. "I admit it. I'm prejudiced," Joe confesses. "I don't like homosexuals."

Nevertheless, Joe begins to see that discrimination is discrimination, and signs on, even if he still can't buy Andrew's lifestyle.

By the time the trial begins, at the 45-minute point in the film, Andrew has lost weight and gone gray. In court, Joe broadens the issue to talk about the public climate of prejudice, while the defense remains adamant that Andrew didn't measure up professionally.

On a scene-by-scene basis, in terms of performance and the grave issues under consideration, the film is quite absorbing. Through the character of Joe, Nyswaner and Demme have found a shrewd way of dealing with the audience's discomfort with the subject of AIDS, and it's both realistic and dramatically admirable that Joe never comes around entirely to an enlightened perspective.

Filmmakers have also neatly avoided showing the conventional emotional moments that would be the designated high points of a by-the-numbers TV movie — the announcement of the verdict, the big death scene, and so on. The screenplay has been extremely well worked out, but too much so, because every piece fits so perfectly that there are no rough edges, no moments when the raw, devastating reality of the situation registers with total force.

Pic's rainbow coalition of sympathies is impeccably tidy — Andrew's lawyer is black, his "partner" is Spanish, one trial witness is a woman who contracted AIDS "innocently" through a transfusion, the defense attorneys are a woman and a black man, Andrew's family is unfailingly loving and supportive, and the bad guys are big-shot WASP lawyers anyone can root against.

Film's biggest gap is its non-portrait of Andrew's private life. The basic outline of his biography is easily surmised, but there are no intimate scenes between him and his mate, Miguel (Antonio Banderas), to illuminate the personal side of his struggle. Rather, in a sequence that's intended as a tour de force but really doesn't work, Andrew plays his favorite operatic aria for Joe and wrenchingly attempts to explain what it means to him.

December 20, 1993 (Cont.)

Still, Hanks makes it all hang together in a performance that triumphantly mixes determination, humor, perseverance, grit, energy and remarkable clearheadedness. Whatever else might nag about the film's treatment of a difficult subject, Hanks constantly connects on the most basic human level.

Washington is also first-rate as the attorney dragged reluctantly to an awareness of others' sensibilities and problems.

With his increasingly craggy face, gravelly voice and cigar clamped between his teeth, Jason Robards is positively Hustonian as a legal kingpin who can't believe he's been called to the mat on this issue, while Mary Steenburgen is all smiles and honeyed insinuations as her boss's go-for-the-jugular defender. Huge cast delivers well down the line.

Demme's direction is constantly inventive, from the opening credit montage backed by a superb Bruce Springsteen song, the first he's written expressly for a film, to the superior use of colorful locations and the particularly fine subjective evocation, through manipulation of camera and sound, of Andrew's deterioration during the trial's final stages.

Behind-the-scenes contributions are top-drawer, notably Craig McKay's fleet editing and Howard Shore's lively score, which is abetted by numerous tunes old and new. Kristi Zea's production design and Tak Fujimoto's lensing successfully capture the diverse lifestyles encompassed by the story. Title not only refers to the film's setting, but is supposed to reverberate with meanings relating to brotherly love and the cradle of American values.

—Todd McCarthy

WRESTLING ERNEST HEMINGWAY

A Warner Bros. release of a Joe Wizan/Todd Black production. Produced by Black, Wizan. Co-producer, Jim Van Wyck. Directed by Randa Haines. Screenplay, Steve Conrad. Camera (Technicolor), Lajos Koltai; editor, Paul Hirsch; music, Michael Convertino; production design, Waldemar Kalinowski; art direction, Alan E. Muraoka; set design, Carlos Arditti; set decoration, Florence Fellman; costume design, Joe I. Tompkins; sound (Dolby), Michael R. Tromer; makeup, Manlio Rocchetti; associate producer, Danna Blesser; assistant director, Jim Van Wyck; casting, Lora Kennedy. Reviewed at Warner Bros. Studios, Burbank, Nov. 6, 1993. MPAA Rating: PG-13. Running time: **122 MIN.**

Walter	Robert Duvall
Frank	Richard Harris
Helen	Shirley MacLaine
Elaine	Sandra Bullock
Bernice	Nicole Mercurio
Ned Ryan	Marty Belafsky
Georgia	Piper Laurie

A poignant tale of intimate friendship between two elderly, eccentric men, "Wres-

tling Ernest Hemingway" serves mostly as a showcase for its two stars, Robert Duvall and Richard Harris. Aimed at the "Fried Green Tomatoes"/"Used People" audience, Randa Haines' drama may achieve moderate success, provided a shrewd marketing campaign hits its older target audience.

Set in a small Florida town, this bittersweet, often lyrical story is based on the age-old theory that opposites attract.

Duvall, a retired Cuban barber, and Harris, a flamboyant ex-sea captain, accidentally meet in a public park in what turns out to be a fateful encounter that will change their lives. The two men are dissimilar, even incongruous, in almost every respect, from their nationalities to their professions, personalities and philosophies of life.

But they share two characteristics that can — and do — overcome any other disparities: aging and loneliness.

Scripter Steve Conrad's strategy is to first establish the idiosyncratic lifestyle of each man alone, then to cross their paths with a series of interactions set mostly in a park or a local restaurant, which Duvall frequents daily for his favorite bacon sandwich.

Shy, dignified and gentlemanly, Duvall leads a quiet, orderly life marked by the absence of women — or friends. He's secretly enamored of a much younger waitress (Sandra Bullock), though the film never explains his lack of knowledge or experience with the opposite sex.

In contrast, the often-married Harris is still an amorous daredevil, who tries to make it with his motel manager (Shirley MacLaine) and in a local movie house with a proudly reticent woman (Piper Laurie) who rejects him time after time.

Harris exhaustingly relishes telling the story of how as a youngster he wrestled Ernest Hemingway.

Script has a few inspired scenes and some poignant dialogue, but not enough to conceal the clanky machinery of the schematic plot.

In one of the film's highlights, Duvall finally lets down his guard, takes off his clothes and swims in the nude — following his jubilant mentor. Harris, in turn, learns kindness, gentleness and compassion from Duvall.

Well-intentioned story, which progressively becomes too sappy and message-laden, overstresses the invigorating dimensions of friendship among the elderly.

"Wrestling" bears a strong thematic resemblance to Haines' previous films, "Children of a Lesser God" and "The Doctor," in which she also explored complex relationships between individuals with different backgrounds, though the novelty here is that both characters are of the same sex. Haines' direction is proficient but also too expansive and leisurely; the film would have benefited from at least 15 minutes of tightening. As in her previous work, however, Haines shows great facility with the actors.

Though Duvall gets top billing, pic belongs to Harris, who turns his role into an overloaded tour de force. Beginning with a nude scene, Harris throws himself into every situation with too much gusto and bravura.

Wearing a wig and heavy makeup and sporting a thick Cuban accent, Duvall renders a quieter, more effective performance, though ultimately his understated work also comes across as excessive. Duvall's graceful dancing is one of several touching, euphoric moments, reminiscent of Al Pacino's in "Scent of a Woman."

The three women play sketchy roles that primarily serve the plot. Still, MacLaine, Laurie and Bullock acquit themselves with modest, unassuming performances.

Tech credits are impressive, particularly lenser Lajos Koltai's sun-drenched palette that captures Florida's landscape and contributes to the film's occasional poetic moments.

—Emanuel Levy

IO SPERIAMO CHE ME LA CAVO
(ME LET'S HOPE I MAKE IT)
(ITALIAN)

A Penta Distribuzione release (Italy)/Miramax (U.S.) of a Mario and Vittorio Cecchi Gori, Silvio Berlusconi Communications presentation of a Eurolux Produzione/Cecchi Gori Group Tiger Cinematografica/Penta Film production. Produced by Ciro Ippolito, Mario and Vittorio Cecchi Gori. Directed by Lina Wertmuller. Screenplay, Wertmuller, Leo Benvenuti, Piero De Bernardi, Alessandro Bencivenni, Domenico Saverni, based on Marcello D'Orta's book. Camera (color), Gianni Tafani; editor, Pierluigi Leonardi; music, D'Angio Greco; art direction, Enrico Job; costume design, Gino Persico. Reviewed at Penta screening room, Rome, Dec. 2, 1993. Running time: **99 MIN.**

Marco Sperelli	Paolo Villaggio
The principal	Isa Danieli
Caretaker	Gigio Morra
Cardboard dealer	Sergio Solli
Esterina	Esterina Carloni
Ludovico	Paolo Bonacelli

Miramax looks to be in a distinctly Disney frame of mind with its stateside pickup "Me Let's Hope I Make It," a winsomely bittersweet schoolroom lark whose social dissection is colored with disarming sentimentalism. This mainstream departure for veteran Italo helmer Lina Wertmuller won straight A's at national wickets and should earn decent grades in U.S. playoff if carefully pitched to sophisticated auds.

As in Wertmuller's 1975 international breakthrough, "Swept Away," the initial conflict and much of the humor stems from North-South antagonism, more pertinent than ever given the current swell of secessionism in Italian politics.

Source material is a bestselling collection of school compositions by barely literate Neapolitan tykes. Wertmuller and a team of seasoned comedy scripters have cleverly woven these into a familiar but amply functional story.

A computer hiccup lands a Northern elementary school teacher (Paolo Villaggio) in a run-down, inefficient school outside Naples. While waiting to be reassigned, he tries to instill order, clashing with the school's laissez-faire principal (Isa Danieli), its crooked janitor (Gigio Morra) and the kids themselves.

Funny opening sequence has Villaggio entering an almost empty classroom, then heading out to round up the truants, variously employed as everything from barmen to barbers to pint-size black marketeers. Villaggio eventually wins their confidence and becomes their teacher, counselor, doctor and confidant.

En route to a heart-tugging conclusion in which he's transferred back up north, Villaggio shepherds the kids through changes and undergoes a few himself, culminating with his stealing a car and manhandling an uppity nun.

Pic touches humorously on things like shoddy health care, sanitation, education and public services, but with a grim note of truth. Entry of drugs and the Mafia into the kids' consciousness is also fluidly intro'd, along with their wretched family situations.

Though the pic frequently seems on the point of sermonizing, the scripters step back from the soapbox each time. But Wertmuller mildly oversteps the cutesiness boundary at times, with one doe-eyed gaze too many from the moppet cast.

A local icon — thanks to his long-running series of "Fantozzi" flicks — Villaggio forgoes his trademark buffoonery to play foil to the wily kids and indolent locals. Some of the laughs stemming from his tenuous grasp of Neapolitan dialect may be lost on offshore auds, but Southern histrionics are neatly played against his Northern reserve.

Backup adult cast is fine all around, with Danieli hilarious as the chaotic school's imperturbable chief. Kids are especially delightful when at their rowdiest, as when

December 20, 1993 (Cont.)

they supply Villaggio with a lexicon of vulgar insults.

Technically, pic is solid but undistinguished, with some visibly post-synched dialogue a minor blight.

—*David Rooney*

WAYNE'S WORLD 2

A Paramount release of a Lorne Michaels production. Produced by Michaels. Executive producer, Howard W. Koch Jr. Co-producers, Barnaby Thompson, Dinah Minot. Directed by Stephen Surjik. Screenplay, Mike Myers, Bonnie Turner, Terry Turner, based on characters created by Myers. Camera (Deluxe color), Francis Kenny; editor, Malcolm Campbell; music, Carter Burwell; production design, Gregg Fonseca; art direction, Richard Yanez; set design, Stephanie Gordon, Mark Poll, Gary Sawaya; set decoration, Jay R. Hart; costume design, Melina Root; sound (Dolby), Keith A. Wester; assistant director, Matt Earl Beesley; second unit directors, Beesley, Thompson; second unit camera, Robert Brinkmann; additional camera, Laszlo Kovacs; casting; Lora Kennedy. Reviewed at the Samuel Goldwyn Theater, Beverly Hills, Dec. 3, 1993. MPAA Rating: PG-13. Running time: **94 MIN.**

Wayne Campbell	Mike Myers
Garth Algar	Dana Carvey
Bobby Cahn	Christopher Walken
Cassandra Wong	Tia Carrere
Del Preston	Ralph Brown
Honey Hornee	Kim Basinger
Milton	Chris Farley
Mr. Wong	James Hong
Jim Morrison	Michael Nickles
Naked Indian	Larry Sellers
Glen	Ed O'Neill
Betty Jo	Olivia D'Abo
Jerry Segel	Kevin Pollak
Bjergen Kjergen	Drew Barrymore
Aerosmith	Themselves

The latest chapter in the saga of Aurora, Ill., twosome Wayne and Garth is a puerile, misguided and loathsome effort ... NOT! The SNL icons of vapid youth have come up with an exceedingly clever mixture of pure juvenilia and hip, social comedy for "Wayne's World 2." The combination produces hilarious results, is sure to generate strong B.O. and warrants invoking the duo's war cry, "party on."

For the clueless, Wayne Campbell (Mike Myers) and Garth Algar (Dana Carvey) are the stars of a cable access show deep in the American heartland. They play music badly and expound — they believe — on deep subjects.

Since the last episode, they have graduated or been turfed out of high school and have entered the big world. But Wayne has an empty hole in the pit of his being. Where is the purpose in his life?

Then it happens!

He is visited in his dreams by a Native American guide who leads him into the desert where he encounters late rock star Jim Morrison (Michael Nickles). The singer tells him to put on a concert. He sagely advises, "If you book them, they will come." Thus is born Waynestock.

Myers, with co-writers Bonnie and Terry Turner, has created a simple, effective through-line on which to hang miles of assorted plot laundry. The mad pursuit to put on the show fuels subplots, asides, digressions and 100%, unadulterated non sequiturs.

The stream of conscious unconsciousness includes Wayne's anxiousness about girlfriend Cassandra's (Tia Carrere) growing attachment to record producer Bobby Cahn (Christopher Walken) and Garth's initiation into manhood by hungry housewife Honey Hornee (Kim Basinger). But that's just scratching the surface. We learn how to be a rock concert roadie from desiccated vet Del Preston (Ralph Brown) and get a Village People showpiece that tops original pic's "Bohemian Rhapsody" seg.

The trap for the filmmakers, including debuting feature helmer Stephen Surjik, is keeping the melange from becoming just plain dumb and arbitrary. The incredible sleight of hand is largely accomplished thanks to a deft script and extremely shrewd casting. Walken and Basinger, for instance, know how to use the extremes of their screen personae without succumbing to caricature.

"Wayne's World 2" has an amazingly good nature. There's genuine affection accorded the characters and situations, and that lack of mean-spiritedness elevates this mad romp. That it's technically well made and demonstrates more than a soupcon of wit just has to make one's heart *schwingggg.*

—*Leonard Klady*

RESCUE ME

A Cannon release produced in association with Apollo Pictures. Produced by Richard Alfieri. Executive producers, Jere Henshaw, David A. Smitas. Directed by Arthur Allan Seidelman. Screenplay, Mike Snyder. Camera (color), Hanania Baer; editor, Bert Glatstein; music, Al Kasha, Joel Hirschhorn, David Waters; production design, Elyne Barbara Ceder; set decoration, Gary Moreno; costume design, Lennie Barin; sound (Ultra-Stereo), Richard Birnbaum; associate producers, Russ Chesley, Joseph M. Eastwood, Greg Johnson, Mike Snyder; assistant director, Robert Sonntag; casting, Nancy Lara Hansch. Reviewed at the Pacific Hollywood theater, L.A., Dec. 4, 1993. MPAA Rating: PG. Running time: **90 MIN.**

Daniel (Mac) MacDonald	Michael Dudikoff
Fraser Sweeney	Stephen Dorff
Ginny	Ami Dolenz
Rowdie	Peter DeLuise
Kurt	William Lucking
Sarah Sweeney	Dee Wallace-Stone

Gifted actor Stephen Dorff should not be wasted in films like "Rescue Me," a dull, formulaic coming-of-age saga that masquerades as an adventure actioner. Theatrical release is just a warm-up en route to video for this embarrassingly inept picture.

Set in an unidentified Nebraska town, story centers on smart adolescent Fraser Sweeney (Dorff), who lives with his mother (Dee Wallace-Stone) but never knew his father, a Vietnam hero.

The never-been-kissed Dorff is infatuated with attractive class queen Ginny (Ami Dolenz), who is engaged to another boy.

When Dolenz is kidnapped in a silly plot involving two dumb thugs (Peter DeLuise and William Lucking), Dorff joins forces with tough-but-sensitive Vietnam vet Michael Dudikoff, who becomes his surrogate father and thus instructs him how to behave like a man.

Every element in Mike Snyder's screenplay is a recycled cliche, from the naive-but-handsome kid who needs to get laid to the sentimental father-son saga that evolves between Dorff and Dudikoff. Dorff's personal charm and natural talent help, but Dudikoff plays a disturbingly stereotypical role.

Helmer Arthur Allan Seidelman stages the story, including its chase scenes, in a slow, monotonous tempo. Tech credits are flat and on the raw side, particularly Hanania Baer's murky lensing and Bert Glatstein's jarring editing that occasionally truncates scenes before they're over.

—*Emanuel Levy*

A LINHA DO HORIZONTE

(THE LINE OF THE HORIZON)

(FRENCH-PORTUGUESE)

A K-Films release (France) of a CTN Prods./Cameras Continentales/Origen Prods. Cinematograficas production, with the participation of CNC/French Ministry of Culture & Education/Instituto Portugues de Cinema/Radiotelevisao Portuguesa/Fundacao Gulbenkian/Channel Four Films/Cofimage 3/Canal Plus. Produced by Maria Joao Mayer. Executive producers, Antonio Da Cunha Telles, Jean Nachbaur, Antonio Cardenal. Directed by Fernando Lopes. Screenplay, Christopher Frank, Nachbaur, based on Antonio Tabucchi's novel, "Il filo dell'orizonte." Camera (color), Javier Aguirresarobe; editor, Jacques Witta; music, Zbigniew Preisner; production design, Jasmim De Matos; sound (Dolby), Vasco Pedroso. Reviewed at Le Latina cinema, Paris, Nov. 27, 1993. Running time: **90 MIN.**

Spino	Claude Brasseur
Francesca	Andrea Ferreol
Prostitute	Ana Padrao
Alvaro	Antonio Valero
(French dialogue)	

A morose morgue attendant confronts a cadaver with his own face (30 years younger) in "The Line of the Horizon," a willfully enigmatic French-lingo pic set in Portugal that's heavy on atmosphere and low on narrative coherence. Item belongs on graveyard-shift TV and at shaggy-dog-story film fests.

Spino (Claude Brasseur) worries his long-suffering g.f. (Andrea Ferreol) and her police inspector brother (Antonio Valero) as he tries to trace the identity of the 25-year-old murder victim. Corpse is a dead ringer for Brasseur at that age, down to his custom-sewn tweed jacket and distinctive key ring.

Classic film noir signposts and the enticing premise lead nowhere slowly, until Brasseur is lured to a dull date with destiny.

Alain Corneau's 1989 "Nocturne Indien," about a man searching for a missing friend in India, fared far better at adapting novelist Antonio Tabucchi's specialty of following a loner obsessed with a mystical quest.

Evocative latenight lensing in Lisbon is well served by Zbigniew Preisner's spare and eerie score. Brasseur and Ferreol have a few OK scenes together, but overall this would-be philosophical/metaphysical pic remains D.O.A.

—*Lisa Nesselson*

SISTER ACT 2: BACK IN THE HABIT

A Buena Vista release of a Touchstone presentation of a Scott Rudin/Dawn Steel production. Produced by Steel, Rudin. Executive producers, Laurence Mark, Mario Iscovich. Co-executive producer, Christopher Meledandri. Directed by Bill Duke. Screenplay, James Orr, Jim Cruickshank, Judi Ann Mason, based on characters created by Joseph Howard. Camera (Technicolor), Oliver Wood; editors, John Carter, Pem Herring, Stuart Pappe; music, Miles Goodman; music supervisor, Marc Shaiman; production design, John De Cuir Jr.; art direction, Louis M. Mann; set design, Lauren Cory, Sandy Getzler; set decoration, Bruce Gibeson; costume design, Francine Jamison-Tanchuck; sound (Dolby), Jim Webb; choreographer, Michael Peters; associate producers, Shaiman, Ron Stacker Thompson; assistant director, Barry Thomas; casting, Aleta Chapelle. Reviewed at the El Capitan Theater, L.A., Dec. 6, 1993. MPAA Rating: PG. Running time: **106 MIN.**

Deloris	Whoopi Goldberg
Sister Mary Patrick	Kathy Najimy
Father Maurice	Barnard Hughes
Sister Mary Lazarus	Mary Wickes
Mr. Crisp	James Coburn
Father Ignatius	Michael Jeter
Sister Mary Robert	Wendy Makkena
Florence Watson	Sheryl Lee Ralph
Joey Bustamente	Robert Pastorelli
Father Wolfgang	Thomas Gottschalk
Mother Superior	Maggie Smith
Rita Watson	Lauryn Hill
Father Thomas	Brad Sullivan
Maria	Alanna Ubach
Ahmal	Ryan Toby
Sketch	Ron Johnson

Two trips to the convent is one too many. Suffering a bad case of sequelitis, this "Sister Act" follow-up is too formulaic and frequently pauses to sermonize at the expense of entertaining. Though

December 20, 1993 (Cont.)

there's clearly a built-in audience eager to clap along, pic lacks the charm and buoyancy that made the first "Act" a mass-appeal hit, and a heavenly opening B.O. glow could fade quickly as the holiday sweepstakes wear on.

"Back in the Habit" is a clever subhead but also truer than may have been intended, as "Act 2" habitually seeks to rekindle elements from the original but lacks its inspiration.

The major shift involves the setting — a run-down high school as opposed to a decrepit convent, a milieu seemingly designed to allow the filmmakers to push an agenda counseling youths to stay in school, which would be fabulous if this were a public service announcement.

The action opens with Deloris (Whoopi Goldberg) headlining in Vegas, rattling off a medley that by itself probably pushed the music-rights budget into the stratosphere. Almost immediately, however, she's doing the nun thing again at the request of the Mother Superior (Maggie Smith), who needs help reaching her young flock.

Unfortunately, having Deloris shack up with the nuns voluntarily limits the comedic possibilities, and the lone menace this time around is rather pallid, coming in the form of an officious administrator (James Coburn) intent on closing the school.

Deloris turns the rather tame group of kids into a choir in a nebulous effort to save good ol' St. Francis. Director Bill Duke ("A Rage in Harlem") and writers James Orr, Jim Cruickshank and Judi Ann Mason devote themselves to reaching the younger audience segment at the expense of keeping the narrative moving.

The action gets bogged down, for example, in a subplot involving the talented Rita (impressive newcomer Lauryn Hill), whose mother (Sheryl Lee Ralph) objects to her joining the choir. Rita's story could be the basis of a better, more serious movie, but here merely creates a lull during the film's soft midsection.

Terrific as she was the first time around, Goldberg seems to mail in this performance, with laughs generated mostly by the mirthful Kathy Najimy and dour Mary Wickes.

Hill is the only real standout among the younger performers, while Michael Jeter and Barnard Hughes supply nice supporting turns as slightly daft clergy.

Tech credits hit a flat note as well, with nothing magical about the choreography and awkward editing that attempts to meld the subplots. There is some sparkle in a playful video sequence under the closing crawl, but by then it's too late.

"Sister Act 2" accents the fact that certain films don't readily lend themselves to sequels, no matter how successful they were on the first pass. The audience may ulti-mately disagree, but creatively, at least, it seems time to break this habit.

—*Brian Lowry*

LE DONNE NON VOGLIONO PIU
(WOMEN DON'T WANT TO)
(ITALIAN)

A Penta Distribuzione release (Italy) of a Mario and Vittorio Cecchi Gori/ Silvio Berlusconi Communications presentation of a Penta Film/Oficina Cinematografica production. Produced by Mario and Vittorio Cecchi Gori. Executive producers, Luciano Luna, Rita Cecchi Gori. Directed by Pino Quartullo. Screenplay, Quartullo, Claudio Masenza, Luca D'Ascanio. Camera (Cinecitta color), Danilo Desideri; editor, Angelo Curi; music, Stefano Reali; art direction, Mariangela Capuano; costume design, Raoul Settimelli; sound (Dolby), Massimo Loffredi. Reviewed at Fiamma Cinema, Rome, Dec. 4, 1993. Running time: **94 MIN.**
Luca .... Pino Quartullo
Francesca .... Lucrezia Lante
Della Rovere
Ricky .... Antonella Ponziani
Claudia .... Rosalinda Celentano
Marta .... Francesca Reggiani
Sandro .... Giuseppe Antonelli

Second foray behind the lens by actor, playwright and legit director Pino Quartullo is a vigorous role-reversal comedy centered on a thirtyish banker's obsession with becoming a father. Attractively cast and stylishly packaged, "Women Don't Want To" sashayed to moderate hit status locally and could find a commercial niche offshore with the right push.

The urge of Luca (Quartullo) to produce progeny isn't shared by his partner (Lucrezia Lante Della Rovere). They split up, and Luca's quest for a potential propagator has him resurrecting old dates, then puncturing condoms before bedding one-night-stands. In a clever jab at technology's headway into emotional territory, his paternal desires are temporarily assuaged by a video baby.

A parallel story follows a lesbian floriculturist couple (Antonella Ponziani, Rosalinda Celentano) on the hunt for some male parenting. Luca meets the duo when, having reluctantly engaged a surrogate mother, he checks into a McDonald's-like insemination center to deposit sperm for the job. The trio strike a deal, but all the anxiety has made him sterile.

Aside from momentary lapses into good-natured vulgarity, the comedy is fresh, sexy and fast. The chaos that reigns while Quartullo holds the center at gunpoint gives rise to big laughs as the two women ransack vaults for the most desirable donors.

Jauntily appealing perfs by Ponziani and Celentano as the lesbian duo make the easygoing treatment of same-sex couples (rare in Italian mainstream comedy) even more refreshing.

As Quartullo's partner, Lante Della Rovere swiftly captures the obsessive 1990s urbanite, and Francesca Reggiani is archly funny as a bank colleague with rabid homemaking ambitions.

Quartullo also scores, likably contrasting his brash, smooth-guy appearance with the character's broody fixation.

Stefano Reali's music, along with songs by Queen and the Spin Doctors, keeps things moving at a sustained clip. Crisp lensing and snappy production design lend a slick visual sheen, and costumer Raoul Settimelli outfits the cast in effortless Italo chic. —*David Rooney*

DEATH & TAXES
(DOCU)

A Country People production. (Intl. sales: Country People Prods., Venice, Calif.) Produced by Jeffrey F. Jackson. Executive producer (for Channel 4), Angela Kaye. Directed, written by Jackson. Camera (color), Tracy Adams, Jackson, Allison Hoffman; editors, Adams, Jackson, Martyn Hone; music, Adams; art direction, Jim Haddon, Peter Lloyd; sound, Jackson, Adams. Reviewed at London Film Festival, Nov. 20, 1993. Running time: **113 MIN.**
With: Gordon Kahl, Toots Mathis, Joan Kahl, Yorie Kahl, Jack McLamb.

Indie documaker Jeffrey F. Jackson sticks it to the IRS and the Feds in "Death & Taxes," a hard-hitting reinvestigation of the 1983 Gordon Kahl case, about which questions still linger. Jackson's unfazed, investigative reporting-style approach and inventive handling of familiar material make this a controversial item for fests and progressive webs. Non-U.S. viewers will also get a charge out of its conspiracy theme.

Docu's intriguingly non-linear structure starts with un-introed cross-cutting between recent footage of Kahl's exhumation, news footage of the 1983 shootout and interviews with relatives and friends. Though initially confusing for those not closely acquainted with the affair, Jackson's slow-burning approach yields dividends later as the mists clear and the pieces fall into place with a vengeance.

Through interviews and archive material, Jackson traces Kahl's background from North Dakota farmer-turned-WWII hero, to disillusionment with Roosevelt and the postwar welfare program, to his unilat-eral opt-out from the country's social security system in 1968 and subsequent harassment by the IRS.

As Kahl's opposition to the federal system became more vocal, encouraging people to start "township governments," the authorities slowly moved in, prompted by the area's new marshal. Final shootout and manhunt in summer 1983 ended at a remote Arkansas farmhouse, with a body claimed to be Kahl's burnt beyond recognition.

Though Jackson's sympathies for the maverick Kahl are never in doubt, he presents a persuasive armory of evidence, eyewitness reports and fundamental questions that support his cage-rattling approach (which even includes a sideswipe at Bill Clinton, then Arkansas governor).

Lack of captions identifying interviewees is initially annoying, but Jackson's technique of letting them identify themselves through what they say is ultimately involving. Visual style for these interviews is straight talking-head, though pointedly cut and never dull. Occasional use of music is flavorsome, underscoring the snowballing conspiracy atmosphere.

Docu includes a brief clip from the 1991 NBC telepic "In the Line of Duty: Manhunt in the Dakotas," in which Rod Steiger played Kahl.

Pic is the result of three years of videotaped interviews, subsequently transferred to film. Result on the big screen is OK but far from high-def quality.

At London Fest world preem, Jackson revealed he was still in dispute with the U.K.'s Channel 4, which provided some of the original coin but now wants pic recut in a more linear structure. Jackson currently plans U.S. release around the fiscally sensitive date of April 15.

—*Derek Elley*

DANS LA VALLEE DU WUPPER
(IN THE VALLEY OF THE WUPPER)
(FRENCH — DOCU — 16mm)

An Agav Films/La Sept-Arte production, in association with Channel 4/ RAI-3/IPS. (International sales: Agav Films, Paris.) Produced, directed, written by Amos Gitai. Camera (color), Max Rheinlander, Nurith Aviv; editor, Eric Carlier; music, Simon Stockhausen; sound, Joest Bernhard, Daniel Ollivier. Reviewed at London Film Festival, Nov. 6, 1993. Running time: **96 MIN.**

As hard as he tries, Amos Gitai fails to come up with anything fresh in "In the Valley of the Wupper," an unfocused docu on the problem of growing racism in

Germany. **Result is specialist fest/tube fare at best.**

Starting point is a barroom brawl in the town of Wuppertal, northwest Germany, in November 1992, that ended in two right-wing German skinheads setting fire to a man who claimed to be half-Jewish.

Gitai quizzes a cross-section of inhabitants about what they remember of the incident (not much), and zeros in on the deputy public prosecutor (impeccably polite) and other parties. Photos and press reports are never shown, which lends a distanced air to the work.

The event emerges more as a drinking contest that turned ugly than a racist attack per se, despite Gitai's earnest attempts to expose a legal coverup. Clearly running out of gas on that approach, the film switches tack halfway through and starts interviewing discontented young Germans and foreigners. Gitai's attempt to paint Wuppertal as a microcosm of Germany, and one with dark industrial/anti-semitic associations, seems strained.

At half the length, and with a clearer focus, docu would make a mildly interesting snapshot of social woes in Germany. But Gitai's starting point is too shaky to support an extrapolation of this kind.

Pic is padded with endless traveling shots of the town from its raised railway. Tech credits are functional.
—*Derek Elley*

BERLIN IN BERLIN

(TURKISH)

A Plato Film Prod. production. (International sales: Wild Okapi Film, Berlin.) Produced by Sinan Cetin. Executive producer, Cemalettin Cetin. Directed by Sinan Cetin. Screenplay, Cetin, Umit Unal. Camera (color), Rebekka Haas; editor, Omer Sevinc; music, Clemens-Maria Haas, Nazih Unen, Fahir Atakoglu; production design, Zeynep Tercan; costume design, Sebnem Uguz; sound, Tom Neubauer. Reviewed at London Film Festival, Nov. 13, 1993. Running time: **98 MIN.**
Dilber .... Hulya Avsar
Murtuz .... Cem Ozer
Thomas .... Armin Block
Ugu, the grandmother .... Aliye Rona Ekber,
  the grandfather .... Esref Kolcak
Zehra, the mother .... Nilufer Aydan
Mehmet .... Zafer Ergin
Bea .... Susa Kohlstedt
(Turkish and German dialogue)

A neat idea doesn't quite go the distance in "Berlin in Berlin," a claustrophobic cross-racial drama about a German man trapped in an apartment owned by hostile Turks. **Pic could find a quiet berth in specialized webs' film slots.**

Thomas (Armin Block) is an amateur photog who hangs around Berlin's Turkish quarter and secretly snaps a beautiful woman (Hulya Avsar) with whom he's obsessed. When her husband is accidentally killed, and his brother (Cem Ozer) gives chase, Thomas takes refuge in an apartment — only to find it's the very one in which the extended Turkish family lives.

Though the opening stretches credibility, pic starts to develop its own character, with a smart twist: Turkish tradition demands that anyone taking refuge in someone's home can't be harmed by the occupants. So the young German holes up in the apartment, where he's fed and watered by his very enemies. As soon as he steps outside, he's dead meat.

The varying tensions are cleverly layered, from the brother's rabid hatred, through the parents' neutral respect for tradition, to the sympathy of the young woman for the love-struck German.

But largely thanks to a script that relies more on lingering glances (the woman) or snarling hatred (the brother) than solid dramatic development, the intriguing premise starts to show stretch marks about an hour in.

With little backgrounding, the German emerges as a weak center of the drama. The final showdown, in the street, is more worthy of Turkish mellers.

Performances and tech credits are adequate, and director Sinan Cetin keeps his camera setups within the confined apartment consistently interesting. —*Derek Elley*

HAWAII FEST

SEO-PYON-JAE

(SOPYONJE)

(SOUTH KOREAN)

A Tae-Hung Production Co. production. (International sales: Korean Motion Picture Promotion Co., Seoul.) Produced by Lee Tae-Won. Directed by Im Kwon-Taek. Written by Kim Myung-Gon, based on the novel by Lee Chung-Joon. Camera (color), Jung Il-Sung; editor, Park Sun-Duk; music, Kim Soo-Chul. Reviewed at Hawaii Intl. Film Festival, Nov. 7, 1993. Running time: **112 MIN.**
Yu-Bong .... Kim Myung-Kon
Song-Hwa .... Oh Jung-Hae
Dong-ho .... Kim Kyu-Chul

The biggest hit in South Korean B.O. history, this emotional tribute to Korean folk culture has been seen by almost a million people — and many are going back for seconds. **Quality is tops on all counts, but content may prove too parochial for Western auds.**

To recount the passing of a hearty southwest Korean music called *pansori* — a powerful storytelling form not unlike the most wailing blues — the pic offers the wanderings of Yu-Bong, an itinerant balladeer who takes suffering for his art all too seriously.

In compound flashbacks, we see Yu-Bong (played spectacularly by scripter Kim Myung-Kon) almost accidentally adopt two children on the road. He attempts to teach them the drum-and-voice music, already dying out in the 1950s, but eventually the boy, Dong-Ho (Kim Kyu-Chul), rebels against his master's martinet ways. Brilliantly gifted "daughter" Song-Hwa (Oh Jung-Hae) sticks around for the full course, which includes going blind as she enters adulthood.

The plot is as downbeat as the tunes, but the film has a majestic undertow rare for tales about art, let alone about such an ephemeral one. Part of its sustained impact comes from the fact that the songs are delivered live (or appear to be) instead of the usual slick-but-deadening lip-syncs. Helmer Im Kwon-Taek takes heady risks along with his performers, most notably in a breathtaking nine-minute take in which the camera never moves but the singing "family" approaches it from a distance.

It's a joyous, nervy moment, but life is no Yellow Brick Road for these ghostly remnants of an antique culture. Yu-Bong is a harsh stand-in for what's been lost while the small peninsula has been trampled by one power after another; Song-Hwa is the suffering heart that has survived, and the sensitive Dong-Ho — whose recollections frame the story — may represent a new path (and a new kind of masculinity) for buffeted Koreans.

Whether that metaphorical, and deeply affecting, journey will touch others remains to be seen, but fest kudos and persistent marketing could make it the first tentative breakout of the dazzling Korean film renaissance. —*Ken Eisner*

AN UNFORTUNATE FORTUNE

(MONGOLIAN — 16mm)

A Mongol Kino production. (Intl. sales: Tumendemberelin Sarantuya, Dept. of Cinematography, Ministry of Culture, Ulan Bator.) Directed by N. Nyamdawaa. Written by D. Namsarai. Camera (color), N. Zondoi; art direction, P. Sosorbaram; music, H. Biligjargal. Reviewed at Hawaii Intl. Film Festival, Nov. 10, 1993. Running time: **67 MIN.**
Monkhetenger .... E. Monkherdeni
Donjaa .... D. Tserendarzav
Lunden .... L. Jamsaranjav
Nerenkhuu .... Sh. Tsetseg

Ancient folklore come to cinematic life, this wry slice of Mongolian culture says plenty about religious desperation, even if its one-note treatment of a lad's obsession with becoming a "living Buddha" won't make many converts.

Short pic centers on a fatherless shepherd (E. Monkherdeni) who endures the taunts of wealthy neighbor boys by running to his mother's skirts. Hanging around the yurt one day, he spies some passing wise men and runs after them, yelling that he's choice messiah material. The blase Lamaists don't even see him and, deeply frustrated, mama's little Buddha passes out in the summer sun.

Frothing at the mouth, he wakes up convinced the transformation is complete, and he proceeds to freak out the neighborhood with his crazed fixation. Already scraping by, his long-suffering mom (D. Tserendarzav) gives up everything to cope with this in-house god with atrocious table manners. Things get worse.

Tale is rich with ethnographic material, and veteran kidpic helmer N. Nyamdawaa throws in painted backgrounds and fanciful lighting to imaginative effect. But few auds will be able to tolerate the boy thesp's gaga grin for even the brief time required. And the bleak resolution, while suitably ironic, is less than uplifting. —*Ken Eisner*

BYOIN DE SHINUTO IUKOTO

(DYING IN A HOSPITAL)

(JAPANESE)

A production of the Japanese Workers' Cooperative Union/Opt Communications/Space Mu Co./Shufu No Tomo Co./Television Tokyo Channel 12, in association with Kindai Eiga Kyokai Co. (International sales: Opt Communications, Tokyo.) Produced by Tetsuo Satonaka. Executive producers, Koichi Ito, Shogo Sekiya, Toshio Tsukamoto. Directed, written by Jun Ichikawa, based on a book by Fumio Yamazaki. Camera (color), Tatsuhiko Kobayashi; editor, Yukio Watanabe; music, Fumi Itakura; art direction, Shigeo Mano; sound, Yasuo Hashimoto; associate producers, Yoshiko Imai, Shingo Iijima, Akio Kikuchi, Makiki Shimuzu; assistant director, Koji Mori. Reviewed at Hawaii Intl. Film Festival, Nov. 11, 1993. Running time: **100 MIN.**
With: Ittoku Kishibe, Masayuki Shionoya, Ikuyo Ishii, Akira Yamanouchi, Tae Hashimoto, Reiko Nanao, Yutaka Matsushige, Hiroshi Tamura, Daikichi Sugawara, Nobuhiro Nakaji, Mutsumi Matsushita, Yoko Ishihara.

Despite a title that couldn't be more off-putting if it tried, "Dying in a Hospital" is an edifying model of delicate restraint. Its poignant, coolly compassionate view of life and death in a big-city hospice ward deserves to be seen by anyone ... well, mortal.

The docu-like feature opens with a medium-length lens fixed on an empty bed. Eventually, a feeble old man (Akira Yamanouchi) inhabits it, and film slowly draws in on his fading days. Other patients, in varying states of decline or revival, come and go, but the camera keeps its distance. Months pass in time-lapse fashion, and a young businessman (Masayuki Shionoya), who's already been in for an operation, returns for a longer stay — long enough to view his stalwart wife's emotional deterioration.

Most of the dialogue consists of the deceptively polite conversation between patients and nurses and doctors, doubly formal, since they're Japanese. There are also v.o. diary entries and letters, usually from a mild-mannered doctor (the well-known Ittoku Kishibe) — the script is based on a doctor's memoirs — but sometimes from other quarters. This quiet flow of language and almost opaque imagery is regularly punctuated by Fumi Itakura's piquant music, accompanying vignettes snatched from everyday life. These lovely, fleeting moments (a trip to the zoo, children in sprinklers, assembling origami, etc.) are the fragments common to the failing lives that intersect in the hospital's antiseptic wards.

Pic maintains its clean, fugue-and-variations quality until the very end, when a posthumous narrator goes over the top into pure emotion. But whether seen as austere or sentimental, this literally life-and-death saga will be a tough sell in any market, except the pubcasting one where it was born. "Dying" is also likely to live on in medical and educational circles, where its unblinking honesty — and subtly reassuring warmth — will be savored. —*Ken Eisner*

TOOKI RAKUJITSU

(FARAWAY SUNSET)

(JAPANESE)

A Shochiku Films production. (U.S. sales: Shochiku Films of America, L.A.) Produced by Renji Tazawa, Masao Nagai. Executive producers, Kazuyoshi Okuyama, Kyuemon Oda. Directed by Seijiro Kayama. Written by Kaneto Shindo, from books by Shindo, Junichi Watanabe. Camera (color), Masahiko Iimura; editor, Osamu Inoue; music, Tetsuji Hayashi; art direction, Yoshinaga Yoko-o; sound, Kenichi Benitani, Masaji Hosoi. Reviewed at Hawaii Intl. Film Festival, Nov. 11, 1993. Running time: **119 MIN.**
Shika Noguchi .... Yoshiko Mita
Hideyo Noguchi .... Hiroshi Mikami
Yoneko .... Riho Makise
Yago .... Takahiro Tamura
Dr. Kitasato .... Hiroyuki Nagato
Dr. Watanabe .... Shingo Yamashiro
Mary .... Julie Dreyfus

A smash hit at home, where it's still playing with 2.5 million tix already sold, "Faraway Sunset" is a glossy historical weepy with better-than-usual off-shore sales potential — on paper.

Syrupy production and an empty story, however, will make its glow short-lived.

This ambitious biopic sketches the twist-of-fate life and career of Hideyo Noguchi, whose childhood accident led him to study medicine; because his hand was badly burned, the world lost a poor shrimp-picker and gained a first-rate bacteriologist.

Unfortunately, the filmers found his dawn-of-the-century struggles with immunization to be insufficiently interesting, and focused instead on the low-down woes of his left-behind mom — which is a bit like turning "The Story of Louis Pasteur" into "Stella Dallas."

Not that topliner (and Japanese fest award winner) Yoshiko Mita doesn't make the most of this Stanwyckian opportunity: With the aid of exceptionally convincing make-up, she plays the poverty-stricken Mrs. Noguchi from 16 to 66, milking her character's lack of fulfillment for all its Kleenex-soaking potential. The dominant tone, though, is grimly smiling determination, and Westerners may find such womanly submission all too familiar, if not downright regressive.

More problems arrive when the action switches to the American university where Hideyo (Hiroshi Mikami) heads for post-graduate work, and some disastrous English-lingo scenes: His mentor is played by a wooden amateur; his future wife is a Philadelphian named Mary (Julie Dreyfus), although her accent is obviously French, and Mikami's English is phonetic at best.

Worst of all, when the young scientist makes his most significant breakthrough — isolating syphilis bacteria — the script hasn't bothered to say what he was looking for (his exultant "I've got it! I've got it!" may raise more jeers than cheers). A v.o. ending, explaining how Noguchi succumbed to yellow fever in Africa, feels tacked-on and unsatisfying after a long two hours.

Nonetheless, lensing is often spectacular, and most small parts are well handled, with the daily texture of long-ago Japanese village life revealed in loving detail. From the start, however, intrusive TV-style music underscores the pic's shallow intentions. This "Sunset" may look nice on the fest circuit, but it won't go down with wider auds. —*Ken Eisner*

XUONG RONG DEN

(BLACK CACTUS)

(VIETNAMESE)

A Liberation Films (Ho Chi Minh City) production. Directed by Le Dan. Written by Pahm Thuy Nhan, Nguy Ngu. Camera (color), Dinh Anh Dung; editor, Cam Van; music, Phu Quang; sound, Le Nghia. Reviewed at Hawaii Intl. Film Festival, Nov. 8, 1993. Running time: **90 MIN.**

With: Viet Trinh, Vo The Vy, Le Cung Bac, Thuy Lien, Kim Xuan, Diem Kieu.

T ackling a serious subject, "Black Cactus" explores the mistreatment of Amerasians left behind by the Yank pullout. Unfortunately, this theme is thoroughly undercut by a routine soap approach and laughably inept tech credits.

The 20-year-old son of a local farm woman and an unknown African-American soldier, Lai (Viet Trinh) responds to village ostracism by becoming the best damn Vietnamese around. Of course, his penchant for illegal activities and self-mutilation sets him apart, too, but that doesn't deter pretty Ma (Vo The Vy), who goes against family and social convention to be with him — prompting an unforgettably frenzied line from her mother: "Ma, did Lai lay you?"

He did, and since the folks won't let them wed, Lai seeks the wealth of Ho Chi Minh City (everyone calls it Saigon), where the local equivalent of Joan Collins makes short work of him. Illiterate, he tries to make fumbling contact with Ma — and with his dad, somewhere in the States — but he's in the dark when their baby is born.

So is helmer Le Dan, who daubs what looks like gray-green shoe polish on the babe to make him look more multiracial (with frequent close-ups yet). This clunky touch goes with lenser Dinh Anh Dung's three modes: shock-zoom intensity, washed-out daylight and reflector-crazed night shots. It's also hard to tell whether the hokey script or sloppy subtitles are more responsible for the tale's many howlers: After a character gets blown up in an old American mine field, someone yells, "Hey, don't go in there ... it's dangerous!"

Even so, pic engages, thanks to the sweet, naive tone set by its appealing leads (Viet Trinh is a real Amerasian, sans shoe polish), and its value as an ethno-political curiosity could give it some currency on educational circuits. Regular festival outlets, let alone arthouse distribs, won't touch this "Cactus." —*Ken Eisner*

SEILAMA

(THE CITY)

(SRI LANKAN)

An EAP Films (Colombo) production. Produced by Soma Edirisinghe. Directed by H.D. Premaratne. Screenplay, Simon Nawagattegama. Camera (color), Andrew Jayamanna; editor, Elmo Halliday; music, Rohana Weerasinghe, Prof. Sunil Ariyaratne; sound, Edward Jayakody, Sriya Kariyawasam; assistant director, L.S. Chandrasekera. Reviewed at Hawaii Intl. Film Festival, Nov. 12, 1993. Running time: **105 MIN.**

Woman .... Anoja Weerasinghe
Driver .... Ravindra Randeniya
Hunter .... Daya Thennakoon
Bande .... Cyril Wickramage
Mudalali .... G. Goonawardena
Jumbo .... Dilani Abeywardena

Y et another village pic in which Third Worlders go urban and discover it's not so nice, "The City" adds nothing new to the bulging genre and can't expect to find new demographics elsewhere.

A prototypical back-country woman (the ever-suffering Anoja Weerasinghe) goes along with her farmer-husband's plan to open a roadside shop, even though their tiny village already has one, and she accurately smells trouble. Seems hubby has the patronage of a relatively affluent — and strikingly Anglo-Indian — trucker (Ravindra Randeniya), who trades urban goods for the ganja grown by the couple's laconic, always-stoned buddy (Daya Thennakoon).

Unfortunately, booze is also part of the bargain, and the rural types are soon besotted, besieged or worse. Things (including the sound, lensing and editing) get so ugly, that the woman ends up moving with Mr. Driver to Colombo, where she discovers such newfangled comforts as rent, public toilets and rock videos.

The pic's always watchable; as many memorable characters show up as there are illogical twists in the script. But helmer Premaratne appears to have tricked up the tale with a complex flashback structure simply because he could — this form never serves the tale in any way that straight chronology wouldn't improve on. Subtitles cover maybe half the dialogue. —*Ken Eisner*

SURABI DENA

(WOMB FOR HIRE)

(SRI LANKAN)

A National Film Corp. of Sri Lanka (Colombo) production. Produced by Lakshman Jananatha. Directed, written by Chandraratne Mapitigama. Camera (color), Andrew Jayamanna; editor, Elmo Halliday; music, Rohana Weerasinghe, Prof. Sunil Ariyaratne; sound, Edward Jayakody, Sriya Kariyawasam; assistant director, L.S. Chandrasekera. Reviewed at Hawaii Intl. Film Festival, Nov. 11, 1993. Running time: **140 MIN.**
Soma .... Anoja Weerasinghe
Kirthi .... Ravindra Randeniya
Sama .... Somi Ratnayake
(Sinhalese dialogue; English subtitles)

T his Sri Lankan soaper about a poor woman paid to carry a child for barren landowners may speak to class conflicts on the troubled isle. To Westerners, it will look as laughably out of date as old reruns of "Oprah."

Lowly vegetable seller Soma initially resists the plan to bear a lucrative baby for self-important aristocrat Kirthi and his equally cold-blooded, and sterile, wife, Sama. Her gruff husband, however, grabs for the money and drowns his qualms in drink with a local chorus of ne'er-do-wells.

Once everyone agrees, things really turn sticky: Rich stud and peasant breeder are soon fogging up the master bedroom (chastely lensed, of course), while grim Sama vacuums the horribly decorated villa, and a mute butler smirks. Dutifully, the mismatched pair continue to "try," even after Soma is declared pregnant.

Apart from this gimmicky, and increasingly implausible, plot device, "Womb" occasionally evinces the raw power of an oft-told folk tale, especially once Soma's down-trodden hubby starts unraveling violently. As the sex-hungry big shot, Ravindra Randeniya hams it up with a lot of presumably romantic sniffing, while Anoja Weerasinghe (Sinhalese cinema's leading lady) shows remarkable restraint in the main role — even if the in-your-face dubbing consistently over-amps all emotions.

Other tech credits are fairly rough (music, for example, is always chopped when a scene is), and it's hard to support pic's absurd 140 minutes.
—Ken Eisner

KLING WAI KON POR SORN WAI

(THE TIME NOT BEYOND)

(THAI)

A Tai Entertainment Co. (Bangkok) production. Produced by Visute Poolvoralux. Directed by Somching Srisupap. Written by Chaninthon Prasertprasat. Camera (color), Arnuparp Buajan; editor, Sunit Asvinikul; music, Jingel Bell Co. Reviewed on vidcassette at the Hawaii Intl. Film Festival, Nov. 12, 1993. Running time: **105 MIN.**
With: Mos Patipan, Saksit Tangtong, Nutsima Kooptawatin, Vitid Ladd, Teerawat Aranyanag, Saksil Suwanket, Pramot Sangsorn, Sagaewal Yongjaiyoot.

This "Thai Graffiti" follows a group of high school students more interested in adolescent high jinks than academic achievement. Swiftly paced and cleverly mounted, the frothy comedy has surprisingly universal appeal, although it's far too frank for its logical audience.

Khan (Mos Patipan) is the acknowledged ringleader of a middle-class gang calling itself the Rolling Stones. Forever pulling gags and impressing or bullying the younger kids, Khan and Co. are in for rude surprises as graduation approaches, and they're more or less told to shape up or expect to be pulling guard duty on the Cambodian border.

Eventually, the boys do the rite-of-passage thing and learn to conform and have fun, in the time-honored TV afterschool special tradition. But helmer Somching Srisupap, still in his 20s, has a blast showing their confusion along the way. Even if the slapstick action is frequently over-orchestrated, he's particularly adept at building sequences of cleverly contrasted widescreen close-ups interspersed with moody breathing spaces and pop-culture sendups familiar to teens everywhere.

In fact, the colorful coming-of-age pic would play well in Western schools — if the script wasn't so scatological: The lads break up a school meeting by breaking wind in unison, and they're more likely to watch "Debbie Does It All" on dad's VCR than hit the books.

Fortunately, the un-p.c. undertone makes a quirky counterpoint to the upbeat ending, at a talent night in which everybody overcomes their hang-ups in one fell swoop — and the girls learn to rock. Enjoyable and remarkably polished, it's nicely acted, even if no one stands out.

Pic's mildly head-scratching title — surely the result of the same semi-translation that plagues its subtitles — is a hint of the quizzical reception it will receive from educators and fest programmers.
—Ken Eisner

DIKI VOSTOK

(THE WILD EAST)

(KAZAKH)

A Studio Kino production (Alma Ata). Produced by Mourat and Rashid Nougmanov. Directed, written, edited by Rashid Nougmanov. Camera (color), Mourat Nougmanov; music, Alexander Aksyonov; art direction, Rustem Abdrashev, Baurzhan Aldekov; sound, Andrei Vlaznev. Reviewed at Vancouver Intl. Film Festival, Nov. 7, 1993. Running time: **100 MIN.**
With: Konstantin Fyodorov, Zhanna Isina, Gennadi Shatunov, Alexander Aksyonov.
(Russian dialogue; English subtitles)

A cockeyed nod to Sergio Leone and "Mad Max" movies, "The Wild East" doesn't add much except stark Central Asian locales to the dusty, apocalyptic genre.

Here, the Man With No Name (played by Konstantin Fyodorov, a white-haired Alexander Godunov type) is an amoral drifter in a vaguely futuristic post-Soviet wasteland. He's tracked down by a member of the Solar Children — a band of circus midgets and dwarves hiding out in the desolate Tian-Shan mountains — who want him to help defend their rocky enclave against

roving bands of bikers and ex-military types.

Faster than you can say "Seven Samurai," the cheroot-puffing anti-hero finds an ape-suited daredevil, a hard-drinking sharpshooter, and a smart-cookie driver named Marilyn (non-blond Zhanna Isina) to aid in the uneven struggle.

Nothing new happens, but several set pieces, including a nighttime confrontation with the death's-head-festooned biker-king (his minions wear SS regalia and listen to loud Russian rock), are handled with flair.

No-budget pic is too underplotted and underpopulated (most of the crew shows up onscreen) to raise Western pulses, save in the most specialized midnight circuits. Allegorical references to the collapse of the Soviet military, including a subplot about a renegade, won't travel at all.

But helmer Nougmanov — elected head of Kazakh filmers after the 25-million-viewer success of his first effort, "The Needle" — has talent to burn, and his recent move to France bodes well for next-round exposure.
—Ken Eisner

IN THE NAME OF THE FATHER

(IRISH-BRITISH-U.S.)

A Universal release of a Hell's Kitchen/Gabriel Byrne production. Produced, directed by Jim Sheridan. Executive producer, Byrne. Co-producer, Arthur Lappin. Co-executive producer, Terry George. Screenplay, George, Sheridan, based on the autobiographical book "Proved Innocent," by Gerry Conlon. Camera (Technicolor), Peter Biziou; editor, Gerry Hambling; music, Trevor Jones; original songs, Bono, Gavin Friday, Maurice Seezer; production design, Caroline Amies; art direction, Rick Butler, Tom Brown (U.K.); costume design, Joan Bergin; sound (Dolby), Kieran Horgan; assistant directors, Gerry Toomey, Peter McAleese (U.K.); second unit director, George; casting, Patsy Poloock, Nuala Moiselle. Reviewed at Universal Studios, Universal City, Dec. 4, 1993. MPAA Rating: R. Running time: **132 MIN.**

Gerry Conlon	Daniel Day-Lewis
Giuseppe Conlon	Pete Postlethwaite
Gareth Peirce	Emma Thompson
Paul Hill	John Lynch
Robert Dixon	Corin Redgrave
Carole Richardson	Beatie Edney
P.O. Barker	John Benfield
Benbay	Paterson Joseph
Sarah Conlon	Marie Jones
Belfast Detective Pavis	Gerard McSorley
Ronnie Smalls	Frank Harper
Paddy Armstrong	Mark Sheppard
Joseph McAndrew	Don Baker
Annie Maguire	Britta Smith
Trial Judge	Aidan Grennell
Prosecutor	Daniel Massey
Defense Counsel	Bosco Hogan

Miscarried justice often provides the vehicle for emotionally wrenching drama and histrionic fireworks, and such is the case in spades with "In the Name of the Father." The award-winning "My Left Foot" duo of writer/director Jim Sheridan and star Daniel Day-Lewis have reteamed to tell the real-life story of Gerry Conlon, an Irish man who spent 15 years in a British prison before his wrongful sentence was overturned. Star power, strong reviews and absorbing nature of the case should overcome various potential commercial negatives to secure a solid B.O. verdict.

This is not the sort of film one normally expects from a Hollywood major at Christmastime: It's highly political, inflammatory, partisan, foreign and far from comforting. It also deals with a subject — the ongoing struggle over the fate of Northern Ireland — that is hardly appealing to many viewers, although, ironically, Universal could benefit from the current headlines about possible breakthroughs in the peace process.

Gerry Conlon was arrested for the 1974 bombing of a bar in Guild-

December 27, 1993 (Cont.)

ford, London, that killed five people. On the basis of coerced confessions, Conlon, his friend Paul Hill and two others who came to be known as the Guildford Four were convicted and sentenced to long terms, as were other completely innocent bystanders, including Conlon's own father and aunt, who were charged with conspiracy.

It wasn't until 1989 that the convictions were overturned, forced by the revelation that crucial evidence that would have exonerated the defendants had been deliberately withheld by the Crown. The legal ramifications of this malfeasance are still pending.

In unfolding this outrage, Sheridan and co-scenarist Terry George are stuck with the basic liability of the format — a built-in predictability of the dramatic arc encompassing table-setting, the crime itself, false arrest, trial and imprisonment, needless suffering, resolve to fight back against the odds, new trial and eventual vindication.

But the filmmakers have invigorated and enriched the story through the use of a thousand details, a strong sense of time and place, outstanding characterizations and a display of energy and cinematic flair that marks an advance on "My Left Foot."

In an excitingly staged action sequence, Conlon (Day-Lewis) is first seen as a rebellious youth on the streets of Belfast, caught up in a pitched battle between British troops and locals. Sent to London by his father, Conlon, along with Paul Hill (John Lynch), falls in with some hippies and befriends flower children Paddy Armstrong (Mark Sheppard) and Carole Richardson (Beatie Edney).

On the night of the Guildford bombing, Conlon and Hill are shown to be resting in a park, where they meet a homeless man. Later they rob a prostitute's flat. Picked up by police, they are held under the newly enacted Prevention of Terrorism Act and eventually knuckle under to days of interrogation.

Day-Lewis engagingly conveys the breezy, devil-may-care quality of the youthful Conlon, whose indulgence in petty crime and casual brushes with politics in no way made him a terrorist but whose profile precisely fits the British prescription for one.

Shockingly, Conlon's father, the incongruously named Giuseppe (Pete Postlethwaite), is not only convicted but is imprisoned in the same cell with his son, which provides the film with a strange, emotionally potent, unanticipated extra dimension. Gerry has never respected or felt close to his father, and initially spurns his patient, dogged tactics of fighting the long legal fight to clear their names.

Much more attractive is the real bombing culprit Joseph McAndrew (a wonderfully steely Don Baker), whose admission of guilt has proven useless to the Guildford Four's appeal and who continues his troublemaking in prison.

But the close quarters eventually draw father and son together, and the tenacious work of committed solicitor Gareth Peirce (Emma Thompson) finally exposes the government's lies and earns the victims a new trial.

Given the blatant outrageousness of the injustice under examination here, Sheridan has little trouble getting the viewer's blood boiling on behalf of his protagonists. Conlon is seen as an essentially sweet, if sometimes wayward, guy in no way prepared for the political and legalistic maze he's plunged into. But prison brings out surprising sides to him, from a taste for the drugs he shares with a friendly Rastafarian inmate to an ability to care for his father in a way he never could have guessed.

Pic reaches its actorly heights in the intense, intimate scenes between Day-Lewis and Postlethwaite, as the former conveys Gerry's growth in the face of deep despair and frustration while the latter reveals innate qualities previously unsuspected. Both thesps are utterly first-rate.

In a decidedly secondary role, Thompson is the picture of a single-minded crusader, and Corin Redgrave scores as the hissable British heavy who railroads the Irish suspects. Other supporting players register in spirited fashion.

Film's tangy, rough quality is aided by Peter Biziou's vibrant, not overly composed location lensing, Gerry Hambling's dynamic editing and the effective and loud rock score by Trevor Jones, with original songs by Bono, Gavin Friday and Maurice Seezer.

Many similar stories have been told before on the big and small screens, but the particulars here have been related with such authority and conviction as to fully warrant their airing.

—*Todd McCarthy*

HEAVEN AND EARTH

A Warner Bros. release presented in association with Regency Enterprises/ Le Studio Canal Plus/Alcor Films of an Ixtlan/New Regency/Todd-AO/TAE production. Produced by Oliver Stone, Arnon Milchan, Robert Kline, A. Kitman Ho. Executive producer, Mario Kassar. Co-producer, Clayton Townsend. Directed, written by Stone, based on the books "When Heaven and Earth Changed Places," by Le Ly Hayslip with Jay Wurts, and "Child of War, Woman of Peace," by Le Ly Hayslip with James Hayslip. Camera (Technicolor; Panavision widescreen), Robert Richardson; editors, David Brenner, Sally Menke; music, Kitaro; production design, Victor Kempster; supervising art director (Thailand), Alan R. Tomkins; art direction, Stephen Spence, Leslie Tomkins, Chaiyan (Lek) Chunsuttiwat (Thailand), Woods Mackintosh (L.A.); set design, Jack G. Taylor Jr. (L.A.); set decoration, Ted Glass (Thailand), Merideth Boswell (L.A.); costume design, Ha Nguyen; sound (Dolby), Bill Daly; associate producers, Risa Bramon Garcia, Christina Rodgers, Richard Rutowski; assistant directors, Herb Gains, Sompol Sungkawess (Thailand); second unit camera, Philip C. Pfeiffer; casting, Garcia, Billy Hopkins, Heidi Levitt. Reviewed at Skywalker Sound, Santa Monica, Nov. 19, 1993. MPAA Rating: R. Running time: **140 MIN.**
Sgt. Steve Butler .... Tommy Lee Jones
Mama .... Joan Chen
Papa .... Haing S. Ngor
Le Ly .... Hiep Thi Le
Eugenia .... Debbie Reynolds
Sau .... Dustin Nguyen
Bernice .... Conchata Ferrell
Madame Lien .... Vivian Wu
Larry .... Dale Dye
With: Liem Whatley, Robert Burke, Michael Paul Chan, Timothy Carhart, Tim Guinee, Catherine Ai.

The U.S. stayed in Vietnam too long, and Oliver Stone has returned to the subject one time too many with "Heaven and Earth." Final installment in the director's trilogy of films on the nation's convulsive recent history represents an attempt to show the war and its aftermath from a Vietnamese POV, but the sledgehammer approach to storytelling merely results in audience numbness and distance from the potentially moving material. Critical and commercial response will be muted.

This is also Stone's first film centering upon a female protagonist, but, unlike his first two powerful Nam sagas, "Platoon" and "Born on the Fourth of July," this one won't win him any Oscars. Drawing upon two autobiographical works by his central figure, Stone presents nearly 40 years in the life of Le Ly as a succession of events with a melodrama quotient that might have challenged even Joan Crawford or Lana Turner.

The vessel for Stone's latest agitated history lesson is a Vietnamese Buddhist peasant who, in the way she is soiled, dominated, exploited, raped, brutalized, colonized, transformed and torn apart from her family, is no doubt supposed to represent Vietnam itself. Unfortunately, the analogy works better than the personal, emotional story that, even if true down to the smallest detail, as related here comes off as conventional and cliched.

An early-1950s prologue presents the rice-farming community of Ky La, in central Vietnam, as a simple paradise, "the most beautiful village in the world," and indeed it looks to be, a patch of green situated gloriously amid towering limestone peaks. But the French destroyed the quiet hamlet, and subsequently, per the heroine, "everything changed forever" with the arrival of the Viet Cong in 1963.

Le Ly (Hiep Thi Le) sees her two brothers run off to join the Communists, who eventually torture and rape her. To escape the turmoil in the midlands, she flees to Saigon at 18, where she joins a wealthy household but promptly becomes pregnant by the master.

Kicked out of the house but supported financially, Le Ly moves to Da Nang, where her sister has become a cheap whore, then back to her village, where her parents are in dire straits and she's perceived as a tramp.

Back in Saigon, she meets Yank Sgt. Steve Butler (Tommy Lee Jones), who just needs someone to talk to but, of course, is interested in something else from Le Ly as well. He proposes immediately, vowing to take her away from all this and settle her down in San Diego, but it takes three years, and the final evacuation of Americans from the country, for his promise to come true.

At the 90-minute mark, Butler, Le Ly, their son and her previous son arrive in suburbia, and perhaps the film's most effective moments catalogue her experiences seeing American middle-class lifestyles and consumerism for the first time. Butler's family and home are lightly and amusingly caricatured, just enough to let Americans see how others might see them and to create an alien feeling that would take some getting used to.

But over time, which sees the birth of another son, things go better for Le Ly than for Butler, the latter a classic case of a soldier who's kept his wartime atrocities bottled up and cracks under the pressure of normal life. While his wife slowly works her way up the professional and economic ladder, and finds sustenance in Buddhism, he implodes, resulting in irrational and emotional acts of violence that doom the family as a unit.

Finale, which has Le Ly making her first visit to her native village in many years, provides a way to say that if the U.S. suffered a great deal because of the traumatic war, Vietnam suffered much more and is still suffering.

All this plays just about as melodramatically and simplistically as it sounds, but there are numerous other problems as well. Lecturing tone is set from the beginning, and

December 27, 1993 (Cont.)

the accents of the Asian performers, some thicker than others, are not only intermittently hard to wade through, but result in their characters speaking a sort of pidgin English that makes them seem more simple and less natural than they should.

Worst of all is the score by Japanese composer Kitaro, which thunderously announces and then underlines the film's every occurrence. It's almost a parody of a self-importantly dramatic soundtrack, and its incessant insistence upon communicating the picture's import allows for no moments of quiet insight or intimacy.

In writing this screenplay, foreign to him in more ways than one, Stone has taken no overt political position, and consequently adds very little to either the general discussion of Vietnam or his own.

Despite the different perspective, and unlike his two previous pix on the subject, this story doesn't provide him with a forum to say much new or interesting. Nor, despite the intensity of the dramatic situations, does he make it feel personal or impassioned.

Newcomer Hiep Thi Le goes through all the histrionic motions as the beleaguered Le Ly, but the effect of the performance is mostly surface sweat and little inner suffering. Jones tries to hit some unusual notes by emphasizing the vulnerable aspects of a professional killer, but that part of the tortured vet never becomes fully dimensional.

Joan Chen is aged and made deliberately ugly to play Le Ly's long-suffering mother in what ultimately seems like serious miscasting. Haing S. Ngor, an Oscar winner for "The Killing Fields," is seen to considerably less effect here as Le Ly's father. Debbie Reynolds has a throwaway in her first screen role in more than 20 years.

Shot mostly in Thailand, with some background views having been grabbed on location in Vietnam, pic looks impressive. Production designer Victor Kempster and his team have done a memorable job recreating the village as well as teeming Saigon, and lenser Robert Richardson has once again fashioned some colorfully dense widescreen images of the recent past.

But the net effect is that Stone and his audience have been here before, and that the point of diminishing returns has definitely been reached. —*Todd McCarthy*

BEETHOVEN'S 2ND

A Universal Pictures release of an Ivan Reitman presentation. Produced by Michael C. Gross, Joe Medjuck. Executive producer, Reitman. Co-producer, Gordon Webb. Directed by Rod Daniel. Screenplay, Len Blum, based on characters created by Edmond Dantes, Amy Holden Jones. Camera (Deluxe color), Bill Butler; editors, Sheldon Kahn, William D. Gordean; music, Randy Edelman; production design, Lawrence Miller; art direction, Charles Breen; set decoration, Cloudia; costume design, April Ferry; sound (Dolby), Gene S. Cantamessa; associate producer, Kahn; Beethoven trainers, Glen D. Garner, April Morley; Missy and puppy trainers, Karin McElhatton, Paul A. Calabria; casting, Steven Jacobs. Reviewed at the Universal City Cinemas, Universal City, Dec. 4, 1993. MPAA Rating: PG. Running time: **88 MIN.**
George Newton .... Charles Grodin
Alice Newton .... Bonnie Hunt
Ryce .... Nicholle Tom
Ted .... Christopher Castile
Emily .... Sarah Rose Karr
Regina .... Debi Mazar
Floyd .... Chris Penn
Taylor .... Ashley Hamilton
Seth .... Danny Masterson

Universal unleashes what should be a big, slobbering hit with this reasonably entertaining sequel, certainly a more pleasing tale than the one that sired it. Facing relatively weak competition for its kid-oriented family audience, pic figures to outscore the first movie and bury a whole lot of bones in the studio's backyard.

The producers don't stray far thematically from their first composition, where reluctant family patriarch George Newton (Charles Grodin) had to be won over to keeping a monstrous mutt around.

To its credit, though, "Beethoven's 2nd" does better than just double up its mediocre forebearer, creating what amounts to a live-action cartoon with a strong "101 Dalmatians" riff that should play particularly well among moppets.

Pic begins with a lonely Beethoven meeting his dream-dog and having puppies, only to have the pooch taken away by her evil owner, Regina (Debi Mazar), who hopes to use the St. Bernard to fleece her husband in their divorce settlement.

The Newton kids start raising the puppies, concealing them from Dad, before Regina becomes determined to cash in on a second front by selling the pure-bred litter. After a section based largely on kid-dog antics, the climax occurs at a mountain retreat where both the Newtons and Regina, conveniently, are vacationing.

As in the first film, the dog exhibits the strangely prescient ability to solve all the family's problems, and one wishes there were less reliance on peeing puppies as the basis for comedy.

Even so, those elements are less obtrusive this time, as director Rod Daniel (whose credits include the man-and-dog comedy "K-9") and writer Len Blum ("Stripes") capture the simple feel of a solid animated children's film, mixing in identifiable coming-of-age crises that the dog helps the Newton kids resolve.

Mazar, of TV's "Civil Wars" and "L.A. Law," adds necessary menace as a flesh-and-blood version of "Dalmatians' " Cruella de Vil — her piercing, Stepford-wife eyes helping distinguish her as the sort of villain kids can immediately recognize.

Grodin and Bonnie Hunt also manage a few sitcom-style moments that will provide even jaded adults a chuckle, and Nicholle Tom, Christopher Castile and Sarah Rose Karr are OK as the kids — Karr the closest runner-up to the puppy quartet on the adorable meter.

Not surprisingly, the trainers merit the biggest kudos, as the dog actors (more than 100 play the puppies at various stages, per the production notes) out-emote their two-footed counterparts.

Tech credits are also well-groomed, with Montana's Glacier National Park providing a lush backdrop as the fictitious town of Glen Haven.

The producers, meanwhile, can start considering what to play for an encore. It doesn't take a bloodhound's scent to ascertain that this dog will have yet another day.
—*Brian Lowry*

MATUSALEM

(CANADIAN)

An Allegro Films Distribution release of a Films Vision 4 production, with the participation of the National Film Board of Canada/Telefilm Canada/SOGIC. (International sales: Films Transit, Montreal.) Produced by Claude Bonin. Directed, written by Roger Cantin. Camera (color), Michel Caron; editor, Yves Langlois; music, Milan Kymlicka; art direction, Vianney Gauthier; costume design, Francesca Chamberland; sound, Dominique Chartrand; associate producer, Yves Rivard; line producer, Louise Ranger; assistant director, Ginette Guillard. Reviewed at Theatre Maisonneuve, Place des Arts, Montreal, Dec. 14, 1993. Running time: **105 MIN.**
Philippe
de Beauchene .... Marc Labreche
Olivier
St-Pierre ...... Emile Proulx-Cloutier
Claude Petit .... Jod Leveille-Bernard
Benoit Painchaud .... Maxime Collin
Helene
Lafleur .... Marie-France Monette
Laurent St-Pierre .... Steve Gendron
Carole Bonin .... Jessica Barker
Capitaine Monbars .... Gabriel Gascon
El Diablo .... Raymond Cloutier
El Cachiporra .... Claude Desparois
El Moribundo .... Rodrigue Proteau
Evelyne Monbars .... Annette Garant

"Matusalem" is an engaging, fantasy-filled adventure for kids of all ages that will almost certainly draw strong auds on its home turf in Quebec, where it will benefit from one of the biggest marketing campaigns in the history of French-Canadian cinema. Pic opened on more than 40 screens across the province and is the first Quebec film to be officially sponsored by McDonald's.

This imaginative, often funny story from writer-helmer Roger Cantin could also do business in other Franco territories, but is unlikely to cross over to English-speaking North America.

With time-traveling pirates and lots of special effects, "Matusalem" is squarely aimed at the grade-school set, but Cantin's tongue-in-cheek sense of humor and a strong performance from adult lead Marc Labreche will keep the parents entertained too.

The tall tale starts in the village of Ste-Lucie de Bagot, with 11-year-old daydreamer Olivier St-Pierre (Emile Proulx-Cloutier) being chased by two of his schoolmates. Olivier ends up bumping into the ghost of an 18th-century pirate, Philippe de Beauchene (Labreche), who enlists the kid's aid in his quest for the long-lost pardon that he promised to bring to his uncle.

With his eyebrows arching into incredible contortions, theater vet Labreche lights up the screen as the somewhat goofy pirate-ghost with a taste for fine wine and rum, and pic's first half generates lots of laughs as he attempts to elude the gang of bad-guy pirates, led by El Diablo (Raymond Cloutier).

Pacing slows to a crawl at the midway point, but again picks up steam when a group of village kids and Beauchene jump through a time-machine wall into 18th-century Cuba in search of Olivier and the nefarious El Diablo. The chase climaxes with a hilarious battle on a giant pirate ship that involves heavy-metal music and some silly special effects.

The mostly young cast tends to be upstaged by Labreche and the other cartoonlike pirates, though Steve Gendron stands out with his performance as Olivier's nerdy brother Laurent. Tech credits are first-rate throughout, though the special effects may seem a tad ordinary for audiences used to Industrial Light & Magic-style onscreen fireworks. —*Brendan Kelly*

SISTA DANSEN
(THE LAST DANCE)
(SWEDISH)

A Sandrews presentation of a Sandrews/TV2 Gothenburg/Schibsted Film (Oslo)/Metronome (Copenhagen) production, with assistance from Eurimages/ Nordisk Film & TV Fund/ Swedish Film Institute. Produced by Katinka Farago. Executive producers, Klas Olofsson, Steen Priwin. Directed, written by Colin Nutley. Camera (color), Jens Fischer; editor, Perry Schafter; music, Eddy Grant, Abba, Denis King and others; production design, Mona Theresia Forsen; sound, Eddie Axberg, Lars Liljeholm. Reviewed at Astoria cinema, Stockholm, Sweden, Dec. 13, 1993. Running time: **114 MIN.**

Tove Sarlefalk	Helena Bergstrom
Claes Sarlefalk	Reine Brynolfsson
Liselott Waltner	Ewa Froling
Lennart Waltner	Peter Andersson
Preacher	Rikard Wolff
Police Inspector	Philip Jackson

Darker and more tragic than his previous hit, "House of Angels," Swedish-based Brit director Colin Nutley's eagerly awaited latest work is a less comforting look at Swedish jealousy and envy through the story of two pairs of competing dance couples. Fine pic looks set to score locally (if not on the scale of "Angels") and is a natural for major fests and specialized offshore distribution.

Whereas "Angels" was set in the Swedish countryside, "Dance" takes place in the very different surroundings of Stockholm, Barbados and the northern U.K. resort town of Blackpool. Main characters are two married couples, Tove/Claes and Liselott/Lennart, friendly rivals in the world of ballroom dancing.

Tove is jealous that Liselott/Lennart always win and, following an incident in Oslo, hasn't spoken to them for nine months. A further cause for tension is the fact that Tove can't have kids, whereas Liselott repeatedly gets pregnant and has abortions.

The four are brought together again by the death of Claes' mother, but, during a joint vacation to Barbados, strains resurface both between and within the couples. Final resolution is set at a masters competition in Blackpool.

Pic opens with Liselott lying dead on the Blackpool seafront at night. Story is then told in flashbacks, interspersed with scenes of ballroom dancing in which Tove/Claes seem to be on their way to their first victory.

Thanks to lots of small, everyday comic touches and fine performances by all the principals — especially Reine Brynolfsson as Tove, the most sympathetic of the four — Nutley manages to create moving, human portraits of vulnerable people who are unhappy in their personal lives and want out. Smaller character roles, such as a Blackpool police inspector (Philip Jackson), also are well-drawn.

Tech credits are tops, with Jens Fischer's superb lensing, especially of Stockholm during early summer mornings, rating special mention.
— *Gunnar Rehlin*

SORT HOST
(BLACK HARVEST)
(DANISH)

A Nordisk Film presentation of a Nordisk Film/Danish Film Institute/ Svensk Filmindustri/Danmarks Radio production. Produced by Lars Kolvig. Directed by Anders Refn. Screenplay, Flemming Quist Moeller, Refn, based on Gustav Wind's novel "And the Fathers Eat the Grapes." Camera (color, widescreen), Jan Weincke; editor, Jesper W. Nielsen; art direction, Gunilla Allard; costume design, Henrik Garnov, Niels Arnt Torp. Reviewed at Nordisk Film screening room, Copenhagen, Denmark, Oct. 21, 1993. Running time: **125 MIN.**

Niels Uldahl-Ege	Ole Ernst
Clara Uldahl-Ege Line	Sofie Graaboel
Uldahl-Ege	Marika Lagercrantz
Isidor Seeman	Philip Zanden
Anna Uldahl-Ege Charlotte	Anna Eklund
Uldahl-Ege	Mette Ahrenkiel
Frederikke Uldahl-Ege	Cecilie Brask

A dark, turn-of-the-century family drama set amid the beautiful Danish countryside, Anders Refn's "Black Harvest" has a haunting fascination, plus some of the same epic qualities that made the Danish pic "Pelle the Conqueror" a winner. Despite the grim goings-on, Refn's movie could reap business at foreign arthouses.

Well-known Danish actor Ole Ernst plays Niels, a wealthy landowner who's the evil center from whom corruption and meanness fan out like ripples in the water. With his beautiful wife and four lovely daughters, he's talked about as a putative government minister, despite his constant womanizing and several illegitimate offspring among his servants.

A brutal and violent man, he at one point demands that his mistress share the family dinner table at Christmas. When others oppose this, he spends the holiday with his servants instead.

The only family member who consistently defies him is his feisty 17-year-old daughter, Clara (Sofie Graaboel), who's also secretly in love with her married cousin, Isidor (Philip Zanden). Latter, clearly tempted by her affections, turns to drugs in his confusion.

Pic is both violent and tragic, with suicides, beatings, murders and rape (among other things). But while not easy to digest, it rises above its general grimness thanks to beautiful widescreen lensing by Jan Weincke and superb acting, especially by Graaboel as the rebellious daughter. — *Gunnar Rehlin*

STELLE DI CARTONE
(CARDBOARD STARS)
(ITALIAN)

A Flipper Cinematografica production. Produced by Romano Di Bari. Directed by Francesco Anzalone. Screenplay, Anzalone, Dario Bonomolo. Camera (color), Paolo Camera; editor, Roberto Schiavone; music, Francesco De Luca; art direction, Alfonso Rastelli; costume design, Innocenza Coiro; sound, Glauco Puletti. Reviewed at Sorrento Festival, Italy (competing), Dec. 11, 1993. Running time: **90 MIN.**

Stephanie	Francesca De Rose
Marco	Massimiliano Franciosa
Elena	Federica Mastroianni
Arturo	Angela Sorino
Fra Gustavo	Daniele Formica
Sergio	Mattia Sbragia

Small-town inertia weighs heavily on the 20-ish protagonists of "Cardboard Stars," a gentle reflection on the dreams and ambitions of middle-class youth in the Italian provinces. Unassuming charm, appealing performers and restrained use of splendid Spoleto locations should ensure Euro tube sales for Francesco Anzalone's first feature.

Two Blues Brothers-fixated chums, Marco (Massimiliano Franciosa) and Arturo (Angelo Sorino), co-host a latenight regional radio show which reps the only spark of achievement in their humdrum lives. Parents and other older-generation locals seem as archaically Etruscan to them as the town's forefathers. When their boss (Mattia Sbragia) tries squeezing their talents for questionable ends, they quit and are forced to confront a basically empty future. Arturo checks out with a homeward-bound Californian (Francesca De Rose), while Marco makes an unwitting transition to sedentary adulthood with his g.f. (Federica Mastroianni).

The pic's male characters are much better defined than the females. Franciosa and Sorino have an easy, complementary rapport that keeps the material coasting along despite an occasional hint of blandness due largely to the script's dearth of tangible conflicts. Well-edited effort is technically clean on all counts. — *David Rooney*

IL TEMPO DEL RITORNO
(TIME OF THE RETURN)
(ITALIAN)

A Technovisual/Falso Movimento production. Produced by Alberto Pisa, Gherardo Pagliei. Directed, written by Lucio Lunerti. Camera (color), Raffaele Mertes; editor, Gino Bartolini; music, Roberto Ciotti; art direction, Mario Fontana Arnaldi; costume design, Luisa Taravella; sound, Massimo Pisa. Reviewed at Sorrento Festival, Italy (competing), Dec. 10, 1993. Running time: **86 MIN.**

Luca	Stefano Abbati
Giovanni	Alberto Di Stasio
Giulia	Barbara Nay
Simona	Fiammetta Carena
Matteo	Giovanni Visentin
Marco	Francesco Capitano

With: Anna Lelio, Vittorio Duse, Raimondo Penne.

The story of a lapsed activist's reinvolvement with his political past, "Time of the Return" breaks with the seemingly endless number of Italo pix dealing with the disenchantment of the former protest generation in purely abstract, introspective terms. Lucio Lunerti's debut feature should land further fest exposure before turning up in quality TV slots.

Film's pivotal figure is Luca (Stefano Abbati), who works as a radio deejay and is involved in a noncommittal relationship. He gets hauled out of his self-imposed insularity when TV documaker friend Giovanni (Alberto Di Stasio) enlists his help on a film inquiry into the "leaden years" of terrorism in 1970s Italy.

Pic takes an existential road-movie turn with Luca first visiting his hometown, for some emotionally unrewarding sessions with his estranged parents and former fellow activists, and later meeting old friend Matteo (Giovanni Visentin), who's in hiding after informing on terrorists. A thriller element creeps in as it becomes apparent that Giovanni's own past brush with terrorists has left scars.

Writer/director Lunerti's approach remains low-key and solemnly intelligent where a more suspenseful tack wouldn't have been amiss. Also, some late plot developments lack clarity. Still, the pic's assessment of the price paid for coming to terms with one's choices gets through undimmed.

Perfs are quietly focused and understated. Raffaele Mertes' camera work and Roberto Ciotti's only occasionally intrusive music are both significant contributions. Other tech credits are sound.
— *David Rooney*

GALERES DE FEMMES

(WOMEN IN PERPETUAL HELL)

(FRENCH — DOCU)

A Les Films Grain de Sable release and production, with funding from the French government agencies for Combatting AIDS and Combatting Drug Addiction/Ministry of Youth & Sports/Ministry of Justice/UNESCO/Ministry of Culture & Communications/CNC. Directed by Jean-Michel Carre. Camera (color), Gilles Clabaut, Jean-Marie La Rocca; editor, Sarah Matton; sound, Bruno Lecoeur; line producers, Marie-Claude Reverdin, Marie-Agnes Azuelos. Reviewed at Reflet Medicis Cinema, Paris, Dec. 3, 1993. Running time: **94 MIN.**

Jean-Michel Carre's "Women in Perpetual Hell" is an emotionally devastating, keenly assembled docu that follows seven inmates of France's Fleury-Merogis women's prison, the world's largest, during two years. A must for festivals and issue-oriented TV, pic deserves a long international career as a model of insightful, non-judgmental filmmaking and a capsule education in penal (and societal) failures.

Film portrays the reality of the subjects' lives with sober grace and unforced dignity. Each articulate, self-aware prisoner comes across as a complex "character" that most novelists would kill to have created.

At the same time, pic's a stunning indictment of the pointless cycle of imprisoning women for relatively minor offenses while failing to address the underlying problems that lead to criminal behavior.

Per film, 60% of the prison population uses hard drugs and nearly half are HIV-positive. The women, who range in age from barely 20 to mid-30s, reveal childhoods littered with incest, rape and suicide.

What makes the film doubly searing is that the camera also follows the women's fortunes when confronted with the challenge of rebuilding their lives after doing time. Lensing and editing are consistently fine: Within the prison, static framing accentuates the women's confinement; outside, free-wheeling tracking shots emphasize their range of movement.

At one point, the film cuts from an AIDS-afflicted prostitute, who says her only regret is not having a child, to another inmate whose infant daughter is brought to visit her. The mother, HIV-positive, says she'll kill herself before her strength and beauty decline, but is seen hollow and failing two years later.

In situations like the prostitute's running into brick walls when trying to secure lodging on release, it is the case workers and assorted do-gooders who come across as deluded.

Given that the docu has nothing positive to say about France's penal system — except that it sometimes saves heroin addicts from death thanks to forced withdrawal — it is remarkable the authorities cooperated in the filming.

Final news that four of the seven women are now dead comes like a body blow after sharing their sad lives. Pic is dedicated to their memory.
—*Lisa Nesselson*

FANTOZZI IN PARADISO

(FANTOZZI IN HEAVEN)

(ITALIAN)

A Penta Distribuzione release (Italy) of a Mario and Vittorio Cecchi Gori/Silvio Berlusconi Communications presentation of a Cecchi Gori Group Tiger Cinematografica/Maura Intl. Film production. Produced by Mario and Vittorio Cecchi Gori. Directed by Neri Parenti. Screenplay, Leo Benvenuti, Piero De Bernardi, Alessandro Bencivenni, Domenico Saverni, Paolo Villaggio, Parenti. Camera (Cinecitta color), Alessandro D'Eva; editor, Sergio Montanari; art direction, Maria Stilde Ambruzzi; costume design, Fiamma Bedengo; associate producers, Bruno Altissimi, Claudio Saraceni. Reviewed at Sorrento Festival, Italy, Dec. 11, 1993. Running time: **92 MIN.**

Ugo Fantozzi	Paolo Villaggio
Pina Fantozzi	Milena Vukotic
Filini	Gigi Reder
Signorina Silvani ... Anna Mazzamauro Mariangela	
Uga Fantozzi	Plinio Fernando

"Fantozzi in Heaven," the eighth and, perhaps, final installment of the downtrodden Italo hero's adventures, dishes up a customary dose of slapstick and puerile humor that shouldn't disappoint the series' legions of fans. With several local Christmas contenders delayed, the pic could end up the season's biggest local money spinner.

The name Fantozzi has entered the nation's vocabulary as a synonym for the luckless, ugly underdog. What sets the series apart from most other comic schlock is the able actors' affection for characters they've been playing for nearly 20 years.

Major development this time round is that retired accountant Ugo Fantozzi (Paolo Villaggio) finally gets his shrewish, man-eating former co-worker (Anna Mazzamauro) into the sack during a skiing weekend that amusingly apes "Doctor Zhivago."

A string of office colleagues drop dead, followed by Fantozzi's final demise. But his arrival in a Buddhist heaven, with reincarnation decided by a wheel of fortune, means further sequels aren't entirely ruled out.
—*David Rooney*

DROMKAKEN

(THE DREAM HOUSE)

(SWEDISH)

A Svensk Filmindustri presentation of a Cinema Art Productions AB/AB Svensk Filmindustri/Piscon AB/Dalle Manus & Regi AB/Sveriges Television Kanal 1 production. Produced by Christer Abrahamsen. Directed by Peter Dalle. Screenplay, Dalle, Bengt Palmers. Camera (color), Esa Vuorinen; editor, Jan Persson; music, Bengt Palmers; production design, Bengt Froderberg; costumes, Malin Bergendahl; sound, Bo Persson, Jan-Erik Lundberg. Reviewed at Saga Cinema, Stockholm, Oct. 26, 1993. Running time: **104 MIN.**

Goran	Bjorn Skifs
Tina	Suzanne Reuter
Petra	Zara Zetterquist
Anton	Mikael Haack
Sanna	Lena Nyman

Also with: Jan Malmsjo, Pierre Lindstedt, Jan Blomberg, Gunnel Fred, Pontus Gustafson, Johan Ulveson, Claes Mansson, Peter Dalle.

Already a B.O. success in Sweden, this mix of "The Money Pit" and "Home Alone" is amiable entertainment for the moment, strictly for local use. Traveling opportunities are slim.

Leading man Bjorn Skifs is a popular singer/entertainer/actor, and his films are always centered around his sympathetic character. In "The Dream House," he plays a family man who buys an old house.

Abode, however, turns out to be in more than urgent need of repair and, along the lines of "The Money Pit," Skifs soon loses both his job and his family. He also discovers that a band of burglars is searching the house for something they've hidden there, and when he decides to strike back at them, pic becomes a clone of "Home Alone."

First part is the most satisfying, with Skifs coping with workmen demanding more and more money. The "battle scenes" are less interesting, especially when they take on a touch of unnecessary sadism.

Tech credits are fine, as is most of the acting.
—*Gunnar Rehlin*

NEITRALNIYE VODY

(NEUTRAL WATERS)

(RUSSIAN — B&W)

A Sovexportfilm presentation of a Maxim Gorky Studio production. Directed, written, edited by Vladimir Berenstein. Camera (b&w), Mikhail Kirillov; music, Kirill Molchanov. Reviewed at Sorrento Festival, Italy, Dec. 10, 1993. Running time: **102 MIN.**

With: Kirill Lavrov, Vladimir Chetverikov, Gennadi Karnovich-Valua, Vladimir Samoilov.

An authentic Cold War curio that milks suspenseful melodrama from the moral/politi-

cal conflict between Soviet and U.S. navy ships, "Neutral Waters" boasts solid craftsmanship, impressive b&w lensing and frequent touches of unintentionally hokey humor. Result should warm the hearts of daredevil festival and TV programmers.

Made in 1969, pic was promptly banned for its supposedly subversive pacifist content. The restriction was recently lifted following Russian prez Boris Yeltsin's bestowal of an award for artistic achievement on director Vladimir Berenstein. Helmer was to have attended the pic's world preem at the Sorrento fest but died of a stroke in Moscow a week prior.

Opening is almost documentary in style, with Mikhail Kirillov's dynamic location shooting capturing military drills at sea, a commemorative service followed by r&r at a Yugoslav port and homecoming festivities in Moscow.

A brief, relatively uninteresting stretch of shore drama follows, before pic gears up into glorious adventure/meller mode as the Russian ship ("Pride") crosses paths with an American vessel in neutral waters.

During both parties' displays of one-upmanship while destroying a stray German mine, a case holding top-secret Soviet papers falls overboard. A young officer dives in after it, and the pic's second half has him bobbing in the water awaiting rescue as all sorts of memories and fantasies swirl in his head.

These include a synchronized swimming sequence that would make Esther Williams proud, a frolic with dolphins and a rescue by a chiffon-clad maiden. All are set to lush kitsch music by Kirill Molchanov. Vaguely campy tone is echoed elsewhere by a shower scene in which sailors whip each other with birch branches, and twee philosophical exchanges between deck hands draped over a gun barrel.

Also adding to the humor is some disastrous English dialogue from an American sailor (clearly played by a Russian) who picks up the floating officer.
—*David Rooney*

ZHIZN S IDIOTOM

(LIVING WITH AN IDIOT)

(RUSSIAN)

A Trinity Bridge production. Produced by Mikhail Kirilyuk, Oleg Konkov. Directed by Aleksandr Rogoshkin. Screenplay, G. Ostrovsky, based on Viktor Yerofeyev's short story. Camera (color), S. Yurizditsky; art direction, O. Tagel; sound, Nikolai Ostakhov. Reviewed at Sorrento Festival, Italy, Dec. 9, 1993. (Also in Thessaloniki fest.) Running time: **67 MIN.**

With: Angelika Nevolina, Anatoli Romantsov, Sergei Migitsko.

Sanity is a strictly relative concept in "Living With an Idiot," a tragicomic essay on human nature and Everyman's dark side that takes its cue from the Russo literature of Gogol, Tolstoy and Dostoevsky. Curious concoction of absurd farce and repugnant antics in a claustrophobic domestic setting marks this strictly for rarefied fests.

A humanist intellectual (Anatoli Romantsov) visits a state clinic and, partly to punish himself for lack of concern over his first wife's death, picks a seemingly sedate lunatic (Sergei Migitsko) to be a live-in inspiration for his writing.

The loony's congenial behavior appears to support the writer's theory that only circumstances separate a sound mind from an unsound one. However, a rampage of destruction and defecation, followed by the violent rape of the writer's languid second wife (Angelika Nevolina), unhinges his theory.

Later transformed into an almost gentlemanly man of the house, Migitsko rejects the now-smitten Nevolina for a slam-dunk bathtub seduction of her husband. Murder, abandonment and further descent into madness follow.

Director Aleksandr Rogoshkin ("The Chekist") fashions the yarn into a bizarre three-act opera in which the power points, and mental faculties of the three principals, are in continual flux. Unfortunately, the middle act's intense grip is framed by a choppy, uninvolving opening and a political subtext that remains overly obscure. Tech credits are modest. —*David Rooney*

POJKDROMMAR

(THE SACRED MOUND)

(ICELANDIC-SWEDISH)

Svensk Filmindustri presents a F.I.L.M./Viking Film/Islanske Filmfund/Sveriges Television Kanal 1/ Svensk Filminstitutet/Svensk Filmindustri/Film Teknik AB/Nordisk Film and TV fund production. Produced by Bo Jonsson. Directed by Hraln Gunnlaugsson. Script by Jonsson, Gunnlaugsson. Camera (color), Per Kallberg; editor, Vidar Vikingsson, Gunnlaugsson; production design, Tor Vigtusson; costumes, Karl Juliusson; sound, Sigurdur HR Sigurdsson/Gunnar Smari Helgason. Reviewed at the Svensk screening room, Stockholm, Sweden, Oct. 15, 1993. (In Stockholm Film Festival.) Running time: **88 MIN.**
Gestur ...... Steinthor Rafn Matthiasson
Helga .... Alda Sigurdardottir
The boyfriend .... Valdimir
Orn Flygenring
The father .... Helgi Skulason

Drama about a young boy's passion for an older girl is at times both cute and menacing. Box office prospects are so-so, and pic seems more destined for festival exposure.

Director Hraln Gunnlaugsson, who's previously directed three violent Viking epics, has based his new film on his own experiences as a young boy. Nine-year-old Gestur goes to live with relatives on a remote island off the Icelandic coast. Their 20-year-old daughter is pretty and not shy about taking long baths in the boy's presence. He quickly falls in love with her.

Shot on location on a low budget, "The Sacred Mound" is a curious film. At times, it's close to being sweet in its depiction of a young boy's gradual sexual awakening, and at other times it's dark and threatening, especially when depicting his furious jealousy.

Perfs by mostly unknowns are quite good, especially Alda Sigurdardottir's as the daughter. She walks a narrow line, being part of a young boy's fantasies, without crossing into a questionable realm.

The open nudity and fairly graphic scene of oral sex could give the film ratings — or censorship — problems in certain countries. —*Gunnar Rehlin*

MIDNIGHT EDITION

A Shapiro Glickenhaus Entertainment presentation of a Libov/Epstein production. Produced by Ehud Epstein, Jonathan Cordish. Directed by Howard Libov. Screenplay, Michael Stewart, Yuri Zeltser, Libov, based on the autobiography "Escape of My Dead Man," by Charles Postell. Camera (color), Alik Sakharov; editor, Yosef Grunfeld; music, Murray Attaway; production design, Guy Tuttle; costume design, Mary-An Ceo; sound, Palmer Norris; associate producer/assistant director, Eric Mofford; casting, Pagano/ Bialy/Manwiller, Ann Mongan. Reviewed at Chicago Intl. Film Festival, Oct. 19, 1993. (Also in Hamptons Film Festival.) Running time: **97 MIN.**
Jack Travers .... Will Patton
Darryl Weston .... Michael DeLuise
Sarah Travers .... Clare Wren
Becky .... Sarabeth Tucek
Maggie .... Nancy Moore Atchinson

"Midnight Edition," the fact-inspired tale of a reporter who becomes enthralled with a death-row killer, is marred by pacing and continuity problems. Downright confusing indie production should do OK at fests and on video but might see its prospects improve via judicious re-editing.

Pic displays good intentions and often inventive lensing but fails to build or sustain a plausible mood. After two years away from his wife and daughter, semi-defeated newspaper reporter Jack Travers (Will Patton) returns to a tiny Georgia town just in time for some sensational local murders. Violence is tastefully and chillingly portrayed, as 19-year-old Darryl Weston (Michael DeLuise) slaughters a family in cold blood.

Charismatic Gary Gilmore wannabe Weston is caught, tried and sentenced to die in the electric chair, prompting Travers to conduct a series of interviews with the charming felon. After resulting profiles create a stir, spotlight-hungry Travers spends most of his time at the prison, increasingly drawn in by his menacing and manipulative subject.

In a poorly developed digression, muddled elements of an apparently unrelated murder fuel mutual animosity between Travers and a black cop.

Although scattered scenes ring true, human interactions tend to be all over the map. DeLuise puts the right spin on the evil hunk, and Sarabeth Tucek scores as his groupie Becky, but direction of other characters, particularly Travers and his wife (Clare Wren) is frustratingly uneven. Travers' co-workers at the paper run hot and cold without sufficient explanation.

Tech crew gets a lot of visual bang for low bucks on Georgia locations, with prison set a convincing plus. —*Lisa Nesselson*

1994
FILM REVIEWS

January 3, 1994

TOMBSTONE

A Buena Vista release of a Hollywood Pictures/Andrew G. Vajna presentation of a Sean Daniel/James Jacks/Cinergi production. Produced by Jacks, Daniel, Bob Misiorowski. Executive producers, Buzz Feitshans, Vajna. Directed by George P. Cosmatos. Screenplay, Kevin Jarre. Camera (Technicolor; Panavision widescreen), William A. Fraker; editors, Frank J. Urioste, Roberto Silvi, Harvey Rosenstock; music, Bruce Broughton; production design, Catherine Hardwicke; art direction, Chris Gorak, Kim Hix, Mark Worthington; set design, Tom Benson, Richard Prantis, Siobhan Roome; set decoration, Gena Serdena; costume design, Joseph Porro; sound (Dolby), Walt Martin; special effects coordinators, Dale Martin, Paul Stewart; associate producers, Fraker, John Fasano, Michael Sloan; assistant director, Adam C. Taylor; second unit director/stunt coordinator, Terry J. Leonard; second unit camera, Lenny Hirschfield; casting, Lora Kennedy. Reviewed at the Disney Studio Theatre, Burbank, Dec. 21, 1993. MPAA Rating: R. Running time: **127 MIN.**

Wyatt Earp	Kurt Russell
Doc Holliday	Val Kilmer
Johnny Ringo	Michael Biehn
Curly Bill	Powers Boothe
Frank McLaury	Robert Burke
Josephine	Dana Delany
Virgil Earp	Sam Elliott
Ike Clanton	Stephen Lang
Mayor Clum	Terry O'Quinn
Kate	Joanna Pakula
Morgan Earp	Bill Paxton
Billy Breckenridge	Jason Priestley
Sherman McMasters	Michael Rooker
Behan	Jon Tenney
Mattie Earp	Dana Wheeler-Nicholson
Mr. Fabian	Billy Zane
Turkey Creek Jack Johnson	Buck Taylor
Marshall Fred White	Harry Carey Jr.
The Priest	Pedro Armendariz Jr.
Henry Hooker	Charlton Heston
Narrator	Robert Mitchum

A decent addition to the current cycle of screen and TV Westerns, "Tombstone" is a tough-talking but soft-hearted tale that is entertaining in a sprawling, old-fashioned manner. Hollywood Pictures won the race to be the first to offer a 1990s version of the oft-told adventures of legendary Wyatt Earp and Doc Holliday, as Lawrence Kasdan's Warner Bros. release starring Kevin Costner won't be ready until next summer. Unburdened by the somber, politically correct tone of a Western like "Geronimo," this never-dull oater should do brisker B.O., particularly with younger viewers.

As written by Kevin Jarre, who was replaced as director early in the shoot by George P. Cosmatos, "Tombstone" is not so much a revisionist view of the Old West as a retelling of the famous story that blends drama, comedy, action and romance the way 1950s movies did. Story begins in 1879, when Wyatt Earp (Kurt Russell), retired marshall of Dodge City, arrives in the lawless boomtown of Tombstone, Ariz., determined to settle down into domesticity with his wife (Dana Wheeler-Nicholson) and open a business with his brothers Virgil (Sam Elliott) and Morgan (Bill Paxton).

But Earp is soon forced to drop his ideology of non-involvement, as the town is terrorized by a bunch of fearless, corrupt villains, headed by the McLaurys and Clantons. Like Clint Eastwood's character in "Unforgiven," Earp is depicted as a reluctant hero, a man who resists the use of violence as a means of establishing law and order until it becomes absolutely necessary. The high price of senseless violence thus becomes the powerful motif of the film's last chapters, which re-create the famous 1881 O.K. Corral battle and its aftermath.

Earp is assisted by the unpredictable Doc Holliday (Val Kilmer), who's portrayed as a boozy intellectual and womanizer dying of tuberculosis, yet fast on the draw. As it has in other films on the subject, the friendship between Earp and Holliday, the town's most intriguing and mysterious figure, provides the story's most poignant angle.

The most visibly modernist touch concerns the demythification of its heroes — unlike previous screen versions, pic focuses on Earp's and Holliday's darker, personal sides. A light feminist streak also runs through the female characters, especially Mattie, Earp's drug-addicted wife, and Josephine (Dana Delany), an actress for whom room service epitomizes the "good life."

As in many other Westerns and period dramas, Jarre's dialogue is often anachronistic, combining a campy contemporary edge with a more realistic dialect. Despite the lack of emotional center and narrative focus, his script contains enough subplots and colorful characters to enliven the film and ultimately make it a fun, if not totally engaging, experience.

Resisting the temptation of creating a reverential tribute to John Ford, whose version of the story was the classic "My Darling Clementine," director Cosmatos instead opts for the more operatic, gritty style of Sergio Leone, particularly in his cutting and use of mega-closeups during the legendary gunfight at O.K. Corral. After a weak initial half-hour, Cosmatos judiciously finds the most audience-appealing dimensions of his tale.

Ultimately, pic's chief virtue is that its handsome actors show a gleaming pleasure in being cast against type. Russell brings a measure of authority and sensitivity to Wyatt Earp, a man tormented by family problems and conflicting values. But it's Kilmer who delivers the standout performance, giving fresh shadings to the lethal but humorous Doc Holliday. Delany as the romantic performer, Elliott as Earp's stoic brother and Michael Biehn as Johnny Ringo also have impressive moments.

Excepting Bruce Broughton's bombastic music, production values are accomplished. Filmed on location around Tucson, Ariz., where the story's major incidents occurred, "Tombstone" boasts the visuals of an epic thanks to William A. Fraker's luminous widescreen lensing.

Though lacking the star magnetism that Burt Lancaster and Kirk Douglas brought to John Sturges' 1957 "Gunfight at the O.K. Corral," film is filled with just as many tense action sequences. Moreover, Robert Mitchum's laconic narration, which frames the story, and the presence of such vets as Charlton Heston, Harry Carey Jr. and Pedro Armendariz Jr. add credible continuity to the film, another in the grand Western tradition that has seen many ups and downs but is still the most unique American genre.
—*Emanuel Levy*

THE HOUSE OF THE SPIRITS

(GERMAN-DANISH-PORTUGUESE-U.S.)

A Miramax (U.S.) release of a Bernd Eichinger presentation of a Neue Constantin production in association with Spring Creek. Produced by Eichinger. Executive producers, Edwin Leicht, Paula Weinstein, Mark Rosenberg. Co-producer, Martin Moszkowicz. Directed, written by Bille August, based on the novel by Isabel Allende. Camera (color; Panavision widescreen), Jorgen Persson; editor, Janus Billeskov Jansen; music, Hans Zimmer; production design, Anna Asp; art direction (Portugal), Augusto Mayer; set decoration, Soren Gam; costume design, Barbara Baum; sound (Dolby SR), Niels Arild Nielsen; makeup supervisor and special effects makeup, Horst Stadlinger; line producer, Thomas Lydholm; assistant director, Guy Travers; casting, Billy Hopkins, Suzanne Smith. Reviewed at Raleigh Studios, L.A., Dec. 23, 1993. Running time: **138 MIN.**

Esteban Trueba	Jeremy Irons
Clara	Meryl Streep
Ferula	Glenn Close
Blanca	Winona Ryder
Pedro	Antonio Banderas
Transito	Maria Conchita Alonso
Esteban Garcia	Vincent Gallo
Satigny	Jan Niklas
Segundo	Joaquin Martinez
Pancha	Sarita Choudhury
Rosa	Teri Polo
Nana	Miriam Colon
Severo	Armin Mueller-Stahl
Nivea	Vanessa Redgrave

A stellar cast, lavish production values and an epic storyline combine for blue-blooded suds in "The House of the Spirits." Bille August's high-toned reduction of Isabel Allende's 1985 worldwide best-seller aims to be a bittersweet historical romance on a grand scale, along the lines of "Gone With the Wind," "The Leopard" or "Doctor Zhivago." While the narrative pull and work of the actors maintain viewer involvement, the herky-jerky meller mostly bumps from one dramatic highlight to the next, with a final effect akin to a stone bouncing along the surface without indicating the depth of the water beneath.

This ambitious European co-production has clicked on the Continent, having grossed nearly $20 million in Germany alone since its bow there Oct. 18. Prospects look OK but somewhat less robust for Miramax release stateside, with inherent value of the star names and pre-sold title likely to be offset somewhat by mixed reviews and word of mouth.

Rushed to completion to meet the German opening date, pic runs 145 minutes in version showing in Germany, Switzerland, the Netherlands and Scandinavia. In the interim, the director continued to fine-tune his work, and it is his 138-minute version that will open in the U.S. and, reportedly, in all remaining territories.

Fronted by narrated sentiments about how life is fragile and brief, pic proceeds to chart 45 eventful years in the lives of the Trueba family in a South American country very much like Chile. At the outset in 1926, Esteban Trueba (Jeremy Irons) is a struggling young man who promises to become worthy of the beautiful, aristocratic Rosa (Teri Polo), whose parents (Armin Mueller-Stahl, Vanessa Redgrave) support the match. But by the time Esteban strikes gold, Rosa mysteriously dies, an event foreseen by her little sister Clara.

Clara is so amazingly clairvoyant that the townspeople line up to hear her insights. But Rosa's death proves so traumatic that Clara turns mute for years, during which time Esteban becomes the most powerful rancher in the area. It is only when he returns 20 years later that Clara (Meryl Streep) again opens her mouth, and the two marry.

But private bliss is not to be theirs, as living with them at the remote hacienda is Esteban's spinster sister Ferula (Glenn Close), a severe woman who always dresses in black and takes feverish interest in spying on the couple in the sack. As time goes on, they have a daughter, Blanca, while Esteban shuts the door on a peasant woman he raped years before who presents him with a kid she maintains is his son.

Jump ahead to 1963, and the lovely 17-year-old Blanca (Winona Ryder) is in love with handsome Pedro (Antonio Banderas), the rebellious son of her father's chief ranch hand. Having encrusted into an intolerant tyrant, Esteban goes after Pedro with a whip, then a gun, banishes his sister from the ranch when he catches her innocently in bed with his wife, and tries to force Blanca to marry an effete European aristocrat.

By 1971, the seriously reactionary Esteban is a senior member of the conservative government, which is threatened by a leftist movement in which one of the chief agitators is — you guessed it — the firebrand Pedro.

The film's protracted final section shows the old order crumbling around the calcified Esteban, as an army coup puts the desperate Blanca and Pedro in great peril from which perhaps only influential old Esteban can rescue them. But the chief inquisitor and torturer of the new regime is none other than — Esteban's massively resentful bastard son.

In its dramatic, if abrupt, progressions, the story as presented here is of a man who systematically and tragically pushes away his loved ones. Through his proud, rigid attitudes and abusive behavior, Esteban manages to profoundly estrange his wife, sister and daughter, as well as his illegitimate son, his workers and the voters of his country. His attempts

August's sensibility is clearly in the epic realist camp rather than with the Latin fabulists.

to mend his ways at the end of his life make for some reasonably moving final moments, although the soap opera trappings nearly smother any real insights into a highly contradictory man.

Just as the characters' motivations are mostly crude rather than complex, and the view of class politics superficial and romantic rather than acute or intelligent, so is the film's treatment of the novel's magical realism on the mundane side. The Danish August's sensibility is clearly in the epic realist camp rather than with the Latin fabulists, and Clara's visions come off more as uncanny coincidences than as part of a larger fabric.

Performances by the terrific cast are variable. Playing a largely loathsome character who salvages some redemption by the end, Irons adopts a vaguely swarthy look and does as well as he can while putting both the other characters and the audience at a distance. Sporting radiant red hair, Streep is a bit mature for her role as a virginal bride at first, but increasingly convinces as a woman possessed by spirits and by love for an impossible man.

Best of all is Close as the repressed but utterly devoted Ferula; her confession to a priest of what she saw in the bedroom is a highlight. Ryder is fetching and fine as the spirited romantic but, like the rest, has no subtext to play with.

Some of the performers, notably Mueller-Stahl, are clearly dubbed into English by other actors, and delivery of the dialogue seems stilted and off at times. Another questionable factor is that the characters don't seem to age at the same rate.

Portuguese locations stand in very serviceably for South American settings, although Lisbon streets and buildings will be recognizable to anyone who's been there. Jorgen Persson's widescreen lensing, Anna Asp's production design and Barbara Baum's costumes are all superior, while Hans Zimmer's score does what it can to smooth over all the narrative abridgments.

—*Todd McCarthy*

GHOST IN THE MACHINE

A 20th Century Fox release of a Paul Schiff production. Produced by Schiff. Co-producers, William Osborne, William Davies, Barry Sabath. Directed by Rachel Talalay. Screenplay, Davis, Osborne. Camera (Deluxe), Phil Meheux; editors, Janice Hampton, Erica Huggins; music, Graeme Revell; production design, James Spencer; art direction, Jim Truesdale; set decoration, Sarah Stone; costume design, Isis Mussenden; visual effects supervisor, Richard Hollander; makeup effects/animatronics, Tony Gardener; sound (Dolby), Mark Weingarten; assistant director, Mike Topoozian; casting, David Rubin, Debra Zane. Reviewed at 20th Century Fox Studios, L.A., Dec. 28, 1993. MPAA Rating: R. Running time: **95 MIN.**
Terry Munroe	Karen Allen
Bram Walker	Chris Mulkey
Karl Hochman	Ted Marcoux
Josh Munroe	Wil Horneff
Elaine Spencer	Jessica Walter
Frazer	Brandon Quintin Adams
Phil	Rick Ducommun
Landlord	Nancy Fish
Elliott	Jack Laufer
Carol	Shevonne Durkin

In the 1950s, terror struck out from the screen in the form of deformed animals, insects and

the like. It's in that spirit that Fox's "Ghost in the Machine" arrives as a late-year chiller. But the new horror comes via scientific gadgetry — specifically, the computer. The so-called ghost is the soul of a serial killer loose in a mainframe and adept at traveling on electrical current to mete out lethal revenge.

It's an effective, if predictable, paranoid fantasy. The film's social statement may be hopelessly muddy but its adroit sense of fun and thrills cannot be discounted. This devilish outing looks to score some fast money from a genre crowd prior to the onslaught of new titles in 1994.

The filmmakers stay pretty much with convention, beginning the yarn with some gruesome, unexplained carnage to get things rolling. What finally turns the action is a car wreck on a rainy night. The victim, a computer store employee named Karl Hochman (Ted Marcoux), is rushed to the hospital and put in a brain scanner. When lightning causes a citywide power surge, his body is lost but his spirit escapes into the core of the Datanet Corp. system.

And wouldn't you just know it, Hochman happens to be the notorious "Address Book" killer. He's been lifting people's personal phone books and murdering those listed within. His latest acquisition belongs to single mom Terry Munroe (Karen Allen) and, though physically disembodied, he has the spirit to continue his killing spree.

Using the phone lines, he can literally dial M for murder and does so in a variety of chilling and stomach-turning ways. It takes Munroe, her son and computer wiz Bram Walker (Chris Mulkey) some time to realize those accidents were planned and that the killer can't be identified in a conventional police lineup.

The screenplay is inspired by genre fare ranging from the good to the bad to the mundane. But director Rachel Talalay livens it up with clever computer-generated visuals that nicely obscure the thinness of plot. Pictorially, it is an engrossing undertaking neatly embellished by the skillful lensing of Phil Meheux.

The skilled cast has precious little to do other than present fear and confusion. Ultimately it all boils down to finding a way to destroy a seemingly unstoppable maniac. This is, after all, a concept thriller.

"Ghost in the Machine" can't be faulted for its ability to hit the appropriate scare buttons. It's a straight-ahead programmer without pretension or much ambition. For the course of its running time, it keeps viewers cowering under the covers, and that should work out just fine in subsequent video life.

—*Leonard Klady*

BATMAN: MASK OF THE PHANTASM

A Warner Bros. release. Produced by Benjamin Melniker, Michael Uslan. Executive producer, Tom Ruegger. Co-producers, Alan Burnett, Eric Radomski, Bruce W. Timm. Directed by Radomski, Timm. Screenplay, Alan Burnett, Paul Dini, Martin Paso, Michael Reaves, story by Burnett. Batman created by Bob Kane. (Color: Technicolor.) Sequence directors, Kevin Altieri, Boyd Kirkland, Frank Paur, Dan Riba; editor, Al Breitenbach; music, Shirley Walker; casting/voice supervision, Andrea Romano. Reviewed at Warner Bros., Burbank, Dec. 23, 1993. MPAA Rating: PG. Running time: **76 MIN.**
Voices:	
Batman	Kevin Conroy
Andrea Beaumont	Dana Delany
Arthur Reeves	Hart Bochner
The Joker	Mark Hamill
Phantasm/	
Carl Beaumont	Stacy Keach Jr.
Alfred	Efrem Zimbalist Jr.
Sal Valestra	Abe Vigoda
Chuckie Sol	Dick Miller
Buzz Bronski	John P. Ryan

Recalling the animated "Superman" shorts of the 1940s, "Batman: Mask of the Phantasm" is a baroque, melodramatic tale of good and evil that's a tad too sophisticated for its intended youthful audience. The shrill thriller is a throwback to a bygone time more appealing to adults. This series of misconnections doesn't add up to terrific box office potential. Expect quick playoffs for the noble effort.

Much in the vein of the avenger's Dark Knight persona, "Mask of the Phantasm" finds Batman mistaken for the title villain, a mysterious killer with presumed superhuman strength and wiles. The evil presence is systematically knocking off crime czars, with both the police and the gangsters assuming it's the work of Batman.

Complicating the puzzle is the arrival of Andrea Beaumont, a former flame of alter-ego Bruce Wayne. She disappeared years earlier, the night after accepting his marriage proposal. Only now is the reason beginning to come clear, implicating the woman in the lethal proceedings.

The high pitch of the drama, the earnest quality of its characters and a deafening score combine for a fun, fatal romp. The filmmakers lean heavily on Tim Burton's first Batman feature for its German Expressionist look, but the story is pure pulp fiction. The moral underpinnings are pretty obvious, though thankfully a step up from the banal.

The outing also benefits mightily from a strong cast of voices, including Kevin Conroy as the crime fighter, Dana Delany as Andrea and Mark Hamill as the Joker. But the level of the animation work, though acceptable, is clunky to the point of self-parody.

It's often impossible to decipher how much of the story should be taken seriously and what part is meant to be comic relief.

A hit on television, the animated "Batman" does not flow to the big screen gracefully. While the script and pedigree of actors are commendable, the craft level is too close to the small-screen offering to get audiences into theaters.
—*Leonard Klady*

SMOKING/ NO SMOKING

(FRENCH)

A Pyramide release of an Arena Films/Camera One/France 2 Cinema production, with participation of Canal Plus/CNC/Procirep/Alia Film (Rome)/ Vega Film (Zurich) and Eurimages. (Intl. sales: Pyramide Intl., Paris.) Produced by Bruno Persey, Michel Seydoux. Directed by Alain Resnais. Screenplay, Jean-Pierre Bacri, Agnes Jaoui, based on Alan Ayckbourn's octet of plays "Intimate Exchanges" as translated by Anne and Georges Dutter. Camera (color), Renato Berta; editor, Albert Jurgenson; music, John Pattison; production design, Jacques Saulnier; set decoration, Jacques Quinternet, Marc Pinquier; costume design, Jackie Budin; sound (Dolby), Bernard Bats, Gerard Lamps; title card illustrations, Floc'h; assistant director, Daniel Deforges. Reviewed at Gaumont Hautefeuille Cinema, Paris, Dec. 21-22, 1993. Running times: **135 MIN.** ("Smoking"), **142 MIN.** ("No Smoking").

SMOKING
Celia Teasdale/Sylvie Bell/
  Irene Pridworthy ...... Sabine Azema
Toby Teasdale/Miles Coombes/
  Lionel Hepplewick/
  Joe Hepplewick .... Pierre Arditi

NO SMOKING
Celia Teasdale/Rowena Coombes/
  Sylvie Bell/Irene Pridworthy/
  Josephine Hamilton .. Sabine Azema
Toby Teasdale/Miles Coombes/
  Lionel Hepplewick ...... Pierre Arditi
(French dialogue)

"Smoking" and **"No Smoking"** light up the screen and rev up the intellect. In having the vision and audacity to compress Alan Ayckbourn's variation-loaded octet of plays into two free-standing but richly complementary feature films, Alain Resnais may have made the first self-regulating interactive movie. It may not require a joystick, but there's joy aplenty for venturesome auds and arthouse patrons.

Duo can be thought of like a suit: You can wear the pants or jacket separately, but they're designed to go together. Gallic plexes are unspooling the pix simultaneously on different screens, leaving it to viewers to choose which they see first. Showtimes are arranged so patrons can view back-to-back if desired. Offshore exhibs should consider the same option, rather than tampering with the formula by programming one at a time on a lone screen.

Local consensus seems to prefer the second pic, whichever one that happens to be. Certainly, the two works taken together are greater than the sum of their parts.

Resnais' duo is drawn from eight Ayckbourn plays (with 16 possible denouements) that require eight consecutive nights to realize onstage. (Plays were premiered at Ayckbourn's home base of Scarborough, England, in 1982 and were first staged in London in 1984.) Screenwriters have dropped two of the plays, resulting in six tales with 12 potential conclusions.

The ingenious premise is to eavesdrop on the lives, loves, aspirations and disappointments of the nine characters (all played by versatile thesps Sabine Azema and Pierre Arditi), abruptly backing up at crucial junctures to ask, "What if ...?" and to veer off in another direction.

Forks in the road are signposted by distinctive title cards (by Gallic cartoonist Floc'h), and each trajectory labeled by illustrations announcing "Five days later," "Five weeks later" and "Five years later."

Both pix begin identically, with an English-accented narrator introing the Yorkshire town of Hutton Buscel and the nine characters who live there. Each is illustrated by a stylized Floc'h portrait.

Each film flows from a similar opening sequence: Faculty wife Celia Teasdale goes onto the terrace, eyes a pack of cigarettes and (according to pic's title) either lights up or doesn't. At about the 55-minute point, after recounting one story straight, each pic then asks "what if?" and explores a parallel universe peopled by the same characters. Original time intervals of five days, weeks and years are still respected. Frustration or fulfillment, and sometimes life or death, hang in the balance.

"Smoking" emphasizes the tottering marriage of alcoholic school director Toby Teasdale and his insecure wife Celia; Celia's tentative relationship with cocky jack-of-all-trades Lionel Hepplewick; and the transformation of Eliza Doolittle-like punkette employee Sylvie Bell.

Lionel falls in love with Celia and either starts an ill-fated business partnership or pursues her incognito to a seaside hotel. Celia either goes off the deep end or summons untold initiative. In a further variation, Lionel and Sylvie are an item, and Sylvie either ties the knot or outgrows the community.

"No Smoking" favors the tottering marriage between wimpish gentleman Miles Coombes and his hot-to-trot wife Rowena, and the friendship between Miles and Toby.

Though the pix brim with theatrical artifice — no more than two characters are visible at a time — they are also 100% cinematic. One of many ongoing delights is that the two thesps change costumes, hair and makeup at a clip that would be impossible onstage.

For example, in "No Smoking," Miles and Rowena are supposed to dine at Celia and Toby's home, but conveniently Toby is at the corner pub. When the slightly tipsy Celia exits to check the oven, her discreet mother, Josephine Hamilton, emerges seconds later.

In addition, characters talk to other characters hidden behind retaining walls or off-camera in a house or shed.

Sets by Jacques Saulnier, who has designed all of Resnais' films since "Stavisky" in 1974, reinforce the jokey tone with consummate artistry. Both pix, though set exclusively in exteriors, were shot totally on soundstages, with sets including a seaside hotel with a cloudswept horizon ("Smoking") and a coastal cliff with rippling tide and rising fog ("No Smoking"). Seasons and times of day are conveyed via masterly lighting.

The films also mock their sometimes soap opera-ish melodramatics. As Celia gets carried away with hyperbole over the prospect of opening a bakery with Lionel, John Pattison's music swells to match the increasingly corny, overwrought dialogue. Resnais counterbalances the language transfer by reinforcing British details. Ambient sounds, clothing and accessories couldn't be more English.

Azema and Arditi, who appeared together in Resnais' earlier "La Vie est un roman," "L'Amour a mort" and "Melo," are aces.

Azema exudes fretful midlife anxiety as Celia, spinsterish clout as school administrator Irene Pridworthy and prim discretion as Josephine Hamilton, yet still convinces as twentyish Sylvie and flamboyant live wire Rowena. Arditi employs defeated posture as the dour Toby, polite restraint as Miles, bottomless vigor as Lionel and crotchety resignation as Joe, Lionel's 77-year-old wheelchair-bound father.

Overall, Resnais' audacious exercise is just about perfect within the boundaries it sets itself. But some viewers may find the form loses its initial charm through familiarity. One possible pathway is theoretically as good as another — the characters live, die, better their situations or settle for less, but viewers are rarely given enough information to root for one denouement over another.

Pix have already nabbed France's prestigious Prix Louis Delluc and seem likely candidates for multiple noms for next spring's Cesar Awards. —*Lisa Nesselson*

TOUT LE MONDE N'A PAS EU LA CHANCE D'AVOIR DES PARENTS COMMUNISTES

(NOT EVERYBODY'S LUCKY ENOUGH TO HAVE COMMUNIST PARENTS)

(FRENCH)

A Bac Films release of a Salome/Bac Films/Les Prods. de 3eme Etage/TF1 Films/M6 Films/General d'Images/ Films Flam/Mafilm Europa/Limbo Films/Sofica Sofinergie 2 & 3 production, with participation of CNC and Eurimages. (Intl. sales: Bac Films, Paris.) Produced by Maurice Bernart. Executive producer, Alain Centonze. Directed by Jean-Jacques Zilbermann. Screenplay, Zilbermann, Nicholas Boukhrief. Camera (color), Bruno Belbonnel, Thierry Jault; editor, Joelle van Effenterre; music, Serge Franklin; production design, Jean Vincent Puzos; costume design, Fabienne Katany; sound (Dolby), Pierre Lorrain; associate producers, Jean Labadie, Michel Propper; assistant director, Thierry Binisti. Reviewed at Max Linder Panorama Cinema, Paris, Dec. 19, 1993. Running time: **88 MIN.**
Irene .... Josiane Balasko
Bernard .... Maurice Benichou
Uncle Charlot ..... Jean-Francois Derec
Ivan .... Victor Nieznanov
Little Leon .... Jeremy Davis
  With: Catherine Hiegel, Alexandre Piskariov, Alexis Maslov, Christine Dejoux, Jacques Herlin, Andre Oumansky, Patrick Burgel.

A comic childhood reminiscence by first-time helmer Jean-Jacques Zilbermann, "... Communist Parents" is a sweet but slight anecdotal enterprise carried by a radiant central perf from Josiane Balasko as a commie-loving Auschwitz survivor and nostalgic period detail of late 1950s working-class Paris.

Honorable freshman effort would have benefited from a richer script with a little more bite, but what pic lacks in means and scope it makes up for in heart. Jewish and history-themed fests should bite, and tube sales should be brisker than Red Square in January. This affecting portrait of one woman's sincere belief in a better world through communism is a modest local hit thanks to good reviews, national affection for Balasko and, no doubt, a significant pool of current and former communist sympathizers.

Catchy title is a bit of a misnomer. Central conflict between otherwise loving spouses Irene (Balasko) and Bernard (Maurice Benichou) is that she's a militant commie and he isn't.

Setting is September 1958, a time when French political life was split into Gaullist and communist camps. Irene was interned at Auschwitz and liberated by the Red Army, so her love for all things Soviet is complete and uncritical. Pragmatic, apolitical Bernard, whose shoe shop is failing, craves respite from Marxist rhetoric and the Russian music and tchotchkes that overrun their puny apartment, also shared by their son and Irene's gangly brother.

Most of all, Bernard would like his exuberant wife to pay as much attention to him as she does to the Cause. Flushed with excitement over Paris concerts by the Red Army Choir, Irene is in seventh heaven when three of its number befriend her. Victor Nieznanov is suitably dashing here as Ivan, the virile soloist who embodies the grandeur and promise of Russia for Irene and encourages her in a way Bernard can't.

Thesping is fine throughout. Delightful score is a bittersweet blend of Russian classics. Cramped by limited locations and decor, lensing is tentative, as if the camera is worried about accidentally capturing any 1990s detail. —_Lisa Nesselson_

SIDA, PAROLES DE L'UN A L'AUTRE

(AIDS: TALKING TO ONE ANOTHER)

(FRENCH — DOCU)

A Pierre Grise Distribution release of an M de S Films production, with participation of French Agency for Combating AIDS, Agnes B. and AIDES. Directed, written, edited by Paule Muxel, Bertrand de Solliers. Camera (color), Agnes Godard; music, Uakti Mapa; sound, Sophie Chiabaut, Jean-Pierre Laforce. Reviewed at Saint-Andre-des-Arts Cinema, Paris, Dec. 4, 1993. Running time: **70 MIN.**

"**A**IDS: Talking to One Another" is a frank and refreshing talking-heads docu in which a cross-section of HIV-positive men and two women articulate their reactions and feelings. Intimate and informative pic, which puts many human faces on the disease, is down to earth and touching in its immediacy.

France has the highest rate of HIV-positive cases in Europe. Cohelmers found their subjects by placing an ad in the daily Liberation: former drug addicts, gay and straight men of several generations, a preteen hemophiliac contaminated in a blood-transfusion scandal. Interviews were filmed in April 1993.

Subjects describe, with candor and eloquence, how they found out they were infected, how they envision the future, how their sex lives and daily relationships have been affected. Photography and editing are straightforward.

A father who learned he was HIV-positive from the blood test for a marriage license says his first concern was for the health of his child and wife-to-be. One young man, when diagnosed, called his adoptive parents and then set off in search of his biological mother.

Only tearful moment comes from an HIV-positive mother who still hasn't found the words to tell her 11-year-old son that he'll be an orphan one day. (Father died of AIDS in 1989.) "I have to find him a family," she says. "I have to stockpile memories for him."

Subjects evince little faith in politicians. One contends that "cadavers dumped on the health ministry's doorstep wouldn't make a difference." The hemophiliac's mother asserts that, after officials responsible for "the greatest health scandal of this century" only had their wrists slapped, her belief in the nation's institutions has been so shattered that she refuses to rise when a judge enters the courtroom. Doctors at the hospital where her son receives blood assured her that being HIV-positive was no big deal.

A drug addict diagnosed 10 years ago says the impression in his circle was that AIDS was something people got "an ocean away, over in America."

Though self-pity is strikingly absent, many voice the fear of a lingering, disfiguring death. A few are convinced they've become better, spiritually richer beings as a result of having to cram a lifetime into a shorter time frame.

—_Lisa Nesselson_

TEL-AVIV STORIES

(ISRAELI)

A Dream Entertainment production. Produced by Ehud Bleiberg, Yitzhak Ginsberg. Directed by Nirit Yaron, Ayelet Menahemi. Screenplay, Yaron, Menahemi, Shemi Zarhin. Camera (color), Amnon Zlavet, Jorge Gurevitz; editor, Menahemi; music, Ari Frankel, Shlomo Gronich; associate producer, Shuki Friedman. Reviewed at Cannes Film Festival (market), May 19, 1993. (In Israel Film Festival, L.A.) Running time: **95 MIN.**

Sharona .... Yael Abecassis
Sophie .... Ruthi Goldberg
Tikva .... Anat Waxman

"**T**el-Aviv Stories" is Israel's response to Pedro Almodovar's "Women on the Verge of a Nervous Breakdown." Mildly entertaining anthology of three short stories, each focusing on a hysterical woman in a state of crisis, provides some insights about the psyche of modern Israeli women. But uneven writing and amateurish production values will limit its appeal to those interested in the new Israeli cinema.

In the first story, "Sharona Honey," a stunningly beautiful woman (Yael Abecassis) is relentlessly pursued by four men, all madly in love with her, all interested in fathering her baby. At the center of "Operation Cat," the second and weakest segment, is Sophie (Ruthi Goldberg), a woman dumped by her husband who spends most of her time fighting bureaucratic obstacles in her attempt to save a kitten caught in the sewer. The third, and most hysterical, episode, "Divorce," revolves around Tikva (Anat Waxman), a policewoman who loses her temper and takes hostages in order to prevent her husband from leaving the country before granting her a divorce.

The premise is amusing, but the execution of this low-budgeter leaves a lot to be desired. Still, all three actresses are charming and interesting to watch, even when the script lacks wit. Singly and collectively, they provide a glimpse of the changing morality and sexuality of the Israeli woman.

—_Emanuel Levy_

ZHI YAO WEI NI HUO YITIAN

(TREASURE ISLAND)

(TAIWANESE)

A City Films production. Produced by Yang Teng-kuei, Chang Hua-kun. Executive producer, Hou Hsiao-hsien. Directed by Chen Kuo-fu. Screenplay, Chen, Chen Shih-chieh. Camera (color), Chang Ta-lung; editor, Chen Po-wen; music, Baboo; art direction, Li Wan-lin; costume design, Chu Ching-wen; sound, Tu Tu-chih; associate producer, Chan Hung-chih. Reviewed at National Film Theater (Films From Taiwan season), London, Dec. 14, 1993. (Also in Locarno, Toronto fests.) Running time: **105 MIN.**

Chen Chih-feng .... Lin Chung
Tang .... Veronica Yip
Ah-ping .... Tracy Su
Chao .... Jack Gao
Maggie .... Amy Lee
Polo .... David Lee
(Hokkien, Mandarin & Cantonese dialogue)

An offbeat, stylish riff on the recent spate of urban alienation pix from Taiwan, "Treasure Island" looks unlikely to mine much gold outside the fest circuit but reps an interesting sophomore bauble from critic-turned-director Chen Kuo-fu.

Story this time round involves a group of young Taipei residents drawn into the city's underworld through the growing obsession of one, the boyish Ah-feng (Lin Chung), for the sexy Cantonese mistress (Veronica Yip) of a gang boss (Jack Gao).

Others involved include Ah-feng's vacant g.f. (Tracy Su), his feisty friend Maggie (Amy Lee) and womanizing cool dude Polo (David Wu). Final reels and climactic, semisurreal shootout leave only a couple alive.

Sinophiles familiar with titles like "Rebels of the Neon God" and "Dust of Angels" will spot intriguing grace notes recalling those pix. And in its portrayal of casual violence and designer gangsters in Taipei's underbelly, there's more than a few echoes of Hou Hsiao-hsien's late-1980s "Daughter of the Nile." Hou himself exec produced current item through his own City Films.

Though much of the pic's dry humor (and flavorsome switching between Chinese dialects) will pass general auds by, the movie's high-sheen packaging, careful compositions and right-on casting set this on a separate level from most of its kind.

Relationships are clearer, and the clever working-out of the complex plot shows unusual care at script stage. Plus, when quietly trading on commercial genres, ex-critic Chen knows whereof he speaks.

Performances are fine, headed by local pop star Lin (the young lead in Hou's "The Puppetmaster") as the kid, Gao (from "Dust of Angels") as the saturnine mob boss, and Lee, strong as his spunky friend Maggie. Hong Kong sex star Yip, in her first arty role, is decorative.

Technically, pic is first-rate, with striking city and nightscapes by Chang Ta-lung. Chinese title literally means "Only Want to Live a Day for You." English title is strictly ironic. —_Derek Elley_

TONG FONG SAM HOP

(THE HEROIC TRIO)

(HONG KONG)

A Gordons Film Co. Ltd. (Hong Kong) and Rim Film Distributors (U.S.) release. Produced by Ching Siu Tung. Executive producers, Brian Yip, Coca Cheng. Directed by Johnny To. Screenplay, Sandy Shaw. Camera (color), Poon Hang Seng, Tom Lau; editor, Kum Wah Production Co., music, William Hu; art direction, Bruce Yu; set direction, Raymond Chan; costume design, Bruce Yu; martial arts director; Ching Siu Tung. Reviewed at the Cinema Village, N.Y., Dec. 7, 1993. Running time: **88 MIN.**

Tung (Wonder Woman) .... Anita Mui
Chat
  (Thief-Catcher) .... Maggie Cheung
Ching/San
  (Invisible Woman) ..... Michelle Yeoh
Kau .... Anthony Wong
  (In Cantonese with English and Chinese subtitles)

"The Heroic Trio" is a flashy kung fu superheroine adventure full of solid production values but marred by some disturbingly gratuitous plot elements. Hard-core kung fu fans, however, will probably be unfazed by such indelicacies.

Although the chief superheroine is called Wonder Woman (Anita Mui), she's far removed from the Lynda Carter TV character. In both costumes and ambience, "Trio" is closer to "Batman" and takes an even more noirish tone. The other two heroines are more ambiguous characters, one a reckless Rambo-type (Maggie Cheung), the other (Michelle Yeoh), at the outset, a henchwoman of the story's master villain.

Plot revolves around the villain's demented scheme to breed future emperors of China; at film's opening, 18 babies have been mysteriously kidnapped. For those who find children-in-peril stories in questionable taste, pic carries the concept considerably further, with infants often endangered and one baby killed.

Some of the stolen children are shown grown to early adolescence and, in preparation for their bloodthirsty future, are fed human flesh. Adding to some of the less digestible plot aspects, two of the heroines decide that these boys are now beyond rehabilitation and proceed to annihilate them.

Other plot and thematic developments include: two sisters separated early in life before being reunited as supercomrades, a doom-laden romance, a superheroine married to a cop — in short, enough goings-on to support not only a sequel but a kung fu soap opera series.

Film's ambitious plot range, however, does not always mesh with recurring comic-book tone. Full-blown climax has heroines battling their nemesis both above and below ground as the villain, as in "Terminator 2," continues to struggle even when reduced to skeletal remains.

Sets by Bruce Yu and Raymond Chan and lensing by Poon Hang Seng and Tom Lau provide moody evocations both for the evildoers' subterranean hideout and the exteriors and interiors of the city above. Lead actresses all acquit themselves well, with the ubiquitous Cheung still faring best.
— *Fred Lombardi*

TAIGIK CHEUNG SAM-FUNG
(THE TAI CHI MASTER)
(HONG KONG)

A Golden Harvest release (Hong Kong) of an Eastern production. Executive producer, Lee Yeung-tsung. Executive in charge of production, Chui Po-tsu. Directed by Yuen Woo-ping. Screenplay, Yip Kwong-kim. Camera (color), Lau Mun-tong; editor, Lim On-yi; music, Woo Wai-lap; art direction, Lee King-man (H.K.), Fu Delin (Peking); martial arts directors, Yuen Woo-ping, Yuen Cheung-yan, Kuk Hin-chiu; makeup, Man Yun-ling. Reviewed at Metro 2 Cinema, London, Dec. 20, 1993. Running time: **92 MIN.**
Zhang Junbao .... Jet Li
Qiuxue .... Michelle Yeoh
Dong Tianbao .... Chin Siu-hou
Little Melon .... Fennie Yuen
  With: Yuen Cheung-yan, Lau Seun, Yu Hoi.

Teaming of Hong Kong top-dollar action stars Jet Li and Michelle Yeoh pays dividends in "The Tai Chi Master," a costume martial arter that should find plenty of play on Asian circuits. Film opened strongly in H.K. in early December.

Plot is the old chestnut about two Shaolin Temple pupils who make their way into the wicked outside world and take divergent paths. Ambitious Dong Tianbao (Chin Siu-hou) joins up with the nasty Royal Eunuch's forces, while wholesome Zhang Junbao (Li) allies with feisty femme Qiuxue (Yeoh) against imperial oppression.

After Dong betrays his friends and almost kills Zhang, latter convalesces in the countryside, studies tai chi and takes on Dong and the Eunuch in a final set-to in their army encampment. In line with genre rules, (native Chinese) Taoist-based fighting styles are shown to triumph over (imported) Buddhist ones.

Pic, shot in mainland China, lacks the slickness and artier values of the best H.K. product but compensates with old-style, no-nonsense direction by vet Yuen Woo-ping and fine action sequences choreographed with his brother Yuen Cheung-yan, also responsible for the recent "Iron Monkey."

Yeoh is overshadowed by the plot's male rivalry but holds her own in several sequences. Li shows glimmers of personality in the recuperative section, played for laughs. Chin makes a fine villain.

Film's music track plays on Li's association with the "Once Upon a Time in China" series, even though the actor has since moved on. Color processing lacks sparkle, but production values are otherwise fairly generous. — *Derek Elley*

PICCOLO GRANDE AMORE
(PRETTY PRINCESS)
(ITALIAN)

A Columbia/TriStar Italia release of a Video 80 production in association with Reteitalia. Produced by Carlo and Enrico Vanzina. Directed by Carlo Vanzina. Screenplay, Carlo and Enrico Vanzina, Cesare Frugoni. Camera (Telecolor), Luigi Kuveiller; editor, Sergio Montanari; music, Simon Boswell; art direction, Tonino Zera; costume design, Roberta Guidi Di Bagno; sound (Dolby), Tommaso Quattrini, Ettore Mancini. Reviewed at Europa Cinema, Rome, Dec. 16, 1993. Running time: **111 MIN.**
Sofia .... Barbara Snellenburg
Marco .... Raoul Bova
Prince Max .... David Warner
Queen Christina .... Susannah York
Otto Von Dix .... Paul Freeman
Queen Mother .... Liz Smith
  With: Alessio Avenali, Francesca Ventura, Adam Barker, Sarah Alexander, Bettina Giovannini.

The Vanzina brothers' Italo hit factory has struck pay dirt again with "Pretty Princess." Locally, this soporific spin on "Roman Holiday" for brain-dead mall rats is riding high with an under-18 crowd starved for home-grown entertainment. Teens elsewhere should find it palatable as tube fare.

Despite a smattering of 1990s plot ingredients — Euro royalty scandals, womanizing tennis pros, the supermodel arena as an antidote to recessionary blues — and a soundtrack crowded with last summer's dance hits, pic feels about as in sync with the times as a reissue of "Chitty Chitty Bang Bang."

To rescue his near-bankrupt fairytale principality of Liechtenhaus, Prince Max (David Warner) tries to marry off his rebellious daughter Sofia (Claudia Schiffer look-alike model Barbara Snellenburg) to a neighboring kingdom's cloddish heir (Adam Barker). But Sofia takes off for a Sardinian vacation village, where she falls for a hunky windsurf instructor (Raoul Bova).

Meanwhile, a royal louse (Paul Freeman), eager to sell the palace to American developers for a casino-cum-amusement park, orchestrates Sofia's kidnapping, and the surfer takes the rap. Ending is pure happy-ever-after.

Snellenburg and Bova's looks can't compensate for their wooden presence and lack of chemistry. Susannah York as an earthy Anglo queen and Liz Smith as her boozy mother make a game stab at enlivening the torpid material. However, Warner sleepwalks through

it, and Freeman's villainy is indifferently insipid. Tech credits are par. — *David Rooney*

MANEN PA BALKONGEN
(THE MAN ON THE BALCONY)
(SWEDISH)

A Svensk Filmindustri presentation of a Victoria Film production, in association with SVT-1 Drama, Svensk Filmindustri/Rialto Film (Berlin), with support from Nordisk Film & TV Fund. Produced by Hans Lonnerheden. Executive producers, Ole Sondberg, Soren Staermose, Bertil Ohlsson. Directed by Daniel Alfredson. Screenplay, Alfredson, Jonas Cornell. Camera (color), Peter Mokrosinski; editor, Helene Berlin; music, Stefan Nilsson; production design, Kaj Larsen; sound, Mats Lindskog, Michael Lechner. Reviewed at Svensk Filmindustri screening room, Stockholm, Sweden, Oct. 20, 1993. Running time: **94 MIN.**
Martin Beck .... Gosta Ekman
Lennart Kollberg .... Kjell Bergqvist
Gunvald Larsson .... Rolf Lassgard
Benny Skacke .... Niklas Hjulstrom
Einar Ronn .... Bernt Strom
Stg Ake Malm .... Jonas Falk
Ake Persson .... Ulf Friberg
Gun Kollberg .... Ingmarie Carlsson
Putte Beck .. Tova Magnusson-Norling
Susanne Grassman .. Magdalena Ritter

Fourth entry in the current series of crimers from the novels of Maj Sjowall/Per Wahloo is by far the best. Already a hit on home ground, it's an efficient police procedural thriller, told with skill and taste. Pic (not to be confused with Bo Widerberg's 1976 "The Man on the Roof," also from a Wahloo novel) could do well on foreign soil, too.

Grim storyline centers on a string of murders of young girls who have also been raped. Only witness to one of the crimes is a violent robber.

Daniel Alfredson, who helmed the series' first entry, "Roseanna," tells the story swiftly and with mounting suspense. Pic doesn't exploit its seedy subject matter: Only the murders' aftermaths are shown.

Acting and tech credits are very good. Only real minus is the creation for co-production reasons of a police psychologist role for German actress Magdalena Ritter. Thesp is badly dubbed and her character lacks motivation. — *Gunnar Rehlin*

INTIMITE

(INTIMACY)

(FRENCH)

A Serenade production. Produced by Benedicte Mallac, Vincent Dietschy. Directed, written by Dominik Moll, based on a short story by Jean-Paul Sartre. Camera (color), Pierre Milon; editor, Thomas Bardinet; sound, Francois Maurel, Camille Chenal. Reviewed at La Rochelle Intl. Film Festival, France, July 7, 1993. Running time: **96 MIN.**

Lucie .... Christine Brucher
Francoise .... Nathalie Krebs
Henri .... Francois Chattot
Pierre .... Christian Izard

A blandly indecisive married woman is buffeted by the actions and opinions of her lumpy husband, her dashing lover and her closest girlfriend in "Intimate." Nicely paced first film — inspired by a story by Jean-Paul Sartre — is full of telling little comic touches about how people really behave.

Attractive blonde Lucie (Christine Brucher) is married to older, condescending Henri but starts an affair with independently wealthy Pierre when urged to do so by Francoise, a store clerk who has no love of her own.

What Henri lacks in possessiveness he makes up for in didacticism. Henri chides his wife for watching TV at random without consulting the program guide. In one winning sequence at his mother's house, what should be a harmless game of Trivial Pursuit is a perfect reflection of familial tensions.

Lucie tells hubby she's leaving him, but resolve is one thing and reality another.

Thesps are fine, particularly Brucher as the wife made dull by routine, who has no handle on what she really wants.

Lensed at the height of summer, pic sports crisp, bright colors. Helmer infuses modest pic with a quirky, appealing tone that should make it welcome at fests.

—*Lisa Nesselson*

KARLEKENS HIMMELSKA HELVETE

(MAGIC - STRONGER THAN LIFE)

(SWEDISH)

Giraff Film AB presents a Sveriges Television TV2/Stillelsen Svenska Filminstitutet/Nordisk Film-TV-Fond/OV Filmfotograferna AB/Filmpool Nord production. Produced by John O. Olsson. Directed by Agneta Fagerstrom-Olsson. Screenplay, Staffan Gothe. Camera (color), Olsson; editor, Christian Loman; music, Erik Petersen; production design, Ulla Kassius; sound, Jan Brodin, Asa Lindgren-Dawidson. Reviewed at the Victoria Cinema, Stockholm, Sweden, Oct. 12, 1993. Running time: **110 MIN.**

Manfred .... Johan Hagglund
Momma .... Marita Nordberg
Eilert .... Asko Sarkola
Tage .... Rolf Skoglund
Ingrid .... Rea Mauranen
Jules .... Charles Barton
Kicki .... Agneta Ahlin
Ritz .... Krister Henriksson

O verbearing comedy about a wedding in the north of Sweden is a failed attempt at the kind of seemingly improvised pix that film innovators Emir Kusturica and Fellini have made. Pic is doomed to B.O. failure both in Sweden and abroad.

Made by husband-and-wife team Agneta Fagerstrom-Olsson and John O. Olsson, pic was born out of wish to make a film outside of Stockholm. It was written by Staffan Gothe, an acclaimed playwright, and made in collaboration with a theater group in the north of Sweden. While all this is commendable, it's a pity the result isn't better. Focusing on an outside wedding, where the groom is a man from the big city, pic tries to give entertaining portraits of a group of odd people. But the loud-mouthed over-acting kills any audience interest, and in the end this is a party one wishes one had not been invited to.

—*Gunnar Rehlin*

SHACKLES

(MONGOLIAN — B&W — 16mm)

A Mongolian Ministry of Culture production. (International sales: Tumendemberelin Sarantuya, Dept. of Cinematography, Ministry of Culture, Ulan Bator.) Directed, written by N. Uranchimeg. Camera (b&w), J. Binder; art direction, T. Goosh; music, Ts. Chinzorig. Reviewed at Hawaii Intl. Film Festival, Nov. 10, 1993. Running time: **75 MIN.**

Toguldur .... S. Gombo-Ochir
Grandpa .... N. Tsegmid
Enkhee .... E. Monkherdeni
Sainaa .... Kh. Tomur
Nergui .... N. Badral

W hat's that sweeping out of the grassy plains of Mongolia? Golden Hordes? A race of Khans? No, it's the return of Italian neo-realism. Part of the first wave of films made without Russian control, this stark study of a hardscrabble urchin recalls Rossellini in his postwar phase — and that may be fitting, considering the remote nation's starting-over status.

Moscow-trained helmer N. Uranchimeg's first effort has the gritty, bombed-out look of "Germany: Year Zero," but she's not immune to lyrical touches a la "The 400 Blows" in this downbeat saga of a sensitive lad forced onto the mean streets of Ulan Bator and into a life of crime. Toguldur (S. Gombo-Ochir) wants to do good, but his physical adeptness has him roped (the Mongolian title also means "Bondage") into a gang of thieves who depend on the wiry lad to climb into high-rise windows and then let them in to smirk and snaffle the occupants' samovars and such.

Why these hoods are so mesmerizing is never explained, and it doesn't help when the soundtrack jumps from evocative string music to sci-fi organ swirls whenever they appear. Still, these silly missteps don't hinder the warmth of crisply lensed scenes with an aged farmer (N. Tsegmid) who takes the boy under his grizzled wing, if only temporarily.

This central metaphor — for an orphaned land that seeks its faded Buddhist soul — isn't hammered home.

The ending is undeniably a downer, though, whether "Shackles" is parable or straight retro-drama; only the most specialized exhibs will want to unchain it.

—*Ken Eisner*

TSUKI WA DOCHI NI DE TE IRU

(ALL UNDER THE MOON)

(JAPANESE)

A Cine Qua Non production. (International sales: Lee Bong Ou, Tokyo.) Produced by Lee Bong Ou, Katsuhiko Aoki. Directed by Yoichi Sai. Written by Sai, Chong Wui Sin. Camera (color), Junich Fujisawa; music, Yuukadan, Compostera. Reviewed at Hawaii Intl. Film Festival, Nov. 10, 1993. Running time: **109 MIN.**

Tadao .... Goro Kishitani
Connie .... Ruby Moreno

O stensibly a black comedy about the plight of Koreans in modern Japan, "All Under the Moon" tries to cram too much into its taxicab microcosm. Confusion will dominate laughs for offshore auds.

With a glib hauteur somewhere between Toshiro Mifune and Kevin Bacon at their smirkiest, Goro Kishitani makes an appropriately nasty splash as anti-hero Chung Nam, a Japan-born Korean going by the more assimilated name Tadao. Working for a Korean-run cab company — alongside a near-psychopath, a quiet alcoholic and an illegal Iranian, among others — Tadao meets, and tends to dislike, all kinds.

To round things out, he's not fond of his dragon-lady mother, either, who runs a sleazy nightclub aimed at immigrants. Still, he starts to bring himself out of his funk when mom hires Connie (Ruby Moreno), a pretty Filipina with a mind of her own.

The course of love isn't smooth, and work gets dicey. No one knows quite what to do, and this includes viewers, who will be intrigued by hints of dissent and ambivalence in seemingly monolithic Japan (the pic's also known as "Rearview Mirror"), but left cold by the complete lack of anyone substantial to identify with.

Bright, inventive lensing and brassy swing music are entertaining pluses, and veteran TV helmer Yoichi Sai (himself Korean-Japanese) keeps his thesps in smooth motion, especially during the openly comic passages.

But much like the effete cabbie who never knows where he is, even when he's parked directly in front of Mt. Fuji, "All Under the Moon" is a story that tends to get more and more lost at every turn.

—*Ken Eisner*

January 10, 1994

THE AIR UP THERE

A Buena Vista Pictures release of a Hollywood Pictures presentation of an Interscope Communications/PolyGram Filmed Entertainment production in association with Nomura Babcock & Brown and Longview Entertainment. Produced by Ted Field, Rosalie Swedlin, Robert W. Cort. Executive producers, Lance Hool, Scott Kroopf. Co-producer, Conrad Hool. Directed by Paul M. Glaser. Screenplay, Max Apple. Camera (Technicolor), Dick Pope; editor, Michael E. Polakow; music, David Newman; production design, Roger Hall; art direction, Leigh Ridley, Hans van der Zanden; set decoration, Karen Mary Brookes; costume design, Hope Hanafin; sound (Dolby), David Lee; assistant director, Martin Walters; basketball technical advisor, Bob McAdoo; casting, Mali Finn, Donn Finn. Reviewed at the Avco Cinema Center, L.A., Jan. 3, 1994. MPAA Rating: PG. Running time: **108 min.**

Jimmy Dolan	Kevin Bacon
Saleh	Charles Gitonga Maina
Sister Susan	Yolanda Vazquez
Urudu	Winston Ntshona
Nyaga	Mabutho (Kid) Sithole
Ray Fox	Sean McCann
Father O'Hara	Dennis Patrick
Mifundo	Ilo Mutombo
Halawi	Nigel Miguel

Working a bit too hard to send the crowd into a frenzy, the action in this basketball-oriented yarn isn't exactly fantastic, but it is mildly entertaining. Still, with the limited star power in its lineup, Hollywood Pictures should have a hard time running up much of a box office score, though this Interscope production figures to shoot a higher percentage in homevideo.

Novelist and first-time screenwriter Max Apple may not have written a movie before, but he's certainly seen a lot of them, as this story of a college coach seeking a prized recruit in Africa contains elements ranging from "The Gods Must Be Crazy" to "A Man Called Horse" to every basketball movie you've ever seen.

Still, "The Air Up There" isn't quite as stale as the numerous cliches it launches, nor as condescending as it could have been in its portrayal of a white savior leading a bunch of native people to the promised land.

Rather, it's simply a traditional fish-out-of-water tale — where the fish learns from as well as teaches his charges — drawing its inspiration from African players like Houston Rockets center Hakeem Olajuwon (who hails from Nigeria) or the baseball scout who stumbled upon former Dodger pitching ace Fernando Valenzuela in Mexico.

Kevin Bacon plays Jimmy Dolan, a one-time college great who's now an assistant coach at his alma mater, St. Joseph's. Having let his pride result in the loss of a blue-chip recruit (in perhaps the film's most effective sequence), Jimmy has a revelation when he sees a tape of the 6-foot-10-inch answer to the school's prayers and takes off to Kenya after him.

Unfortunately, Saleh (newcomer Charles Gitonga Maina, who possesses Michael Jordan's leaping ability and Magic Johnson's smile) has his own problems, since his tribe, the Winabi, is being pushed off its land by an evil developer, Nyaga (Mabutho "Kid" Sithole).

Saleh's father, tribe chief Urudu (Winston Ntshona), objects to his son leaving to try and cash in on his basketball prowess, but through a series of reasonably preposterous circumstances ultimately proposes a basketball game between Nyaga's team and the village to settle matters, with Jimmy acting as player/coach.

Director Paul M. Glaser (the former TV star whose directing credits include "The Running Man" and "The Cutting Edge") brings a certain energy to the predictable proceedings — aided immeasurably by cinematographer Dick Pope and composer David Newman — that captures some of the beauty and majesty of the African wilderness.

Bit pic doesn't reach for the lights in its efforts to entertain, using ample lower-brow comedy, from Jimmy suffering the "Winabi trots" to enduring local culinary delights.

Bacon does a solid job, displaying Jimmy's growth toward considering goals higher than the Final Four, and Maina and others exhibit real charm as the tribesmen. Hoopaholics will also note former UCLA standout Nigel Miguel (previously seen in "White Men Can't Jump") and Ilo Mitumbo (elder brother of NBA center Dikembe) in key roles.

Other tech credits are well-drilled, with lensing in South Africa, Kenya, Toronto and Vancouver. From a marketing standpoint, pic also deserves kudos for its clever title and logo, the prominently displayed word "Air" doubtless capitalizing on the celebrity of a certain Mr. Jordan. — *Brian Lowry*

BYZANTINE BLUE

(SERBIAN)

A Vans Film & Video Distributors (Belgrade) release of a Star 6/Balkan Film Co. production, in association with Ministry of Culture. Produced by Dejan Vrazalic. Directed by Dragan Marinkovic. Screenplay, Milorad Pavic, Nada Markovic-Bebler, Marinkovic, based on Pavic's short stories. Camera (color), Predrag Todorovic; editor, Petar Markovic; animation, Gama Electronics. Reviewed on vidcassette, Rome, Jan. 4, 1994. Running time: **92 MIN.**

Liza	Katarina Zutic
Arandjel	Lazar Ristovski

It is amazing that, in the midst of war, Serbia continues to produce films like "Byzantine Blue" (original title), an escapist fantasy set in no particular place or time. Superbly shot by director Dragan Marinkovic, pic describes the passing infatuation of a bored rich girl for a monk-like painter. Item is worth a look as a curio.

Liza (Katarina Zutic), a beautiful "babe" who's also got brains, is prepping for a big math exam at college. In her futuristic home, she designs complicated experiments with numbered turtles. One day, a blue stain mysteriously appears on her hands, leading her to the lab of Arandjel (Lazar Ristovski), who's spent his life searching for the formula to the indelible blue paint used in Byzantine icons.

Older, bearded and spiritual, Arandjel contrasts favorably with Liza's rich, fashion-conscious b.f. The two consummate their mutual attraction atop a white ox at the seaside — a typically stunning image that verges on high kitsch.

Pic is meticulously made, stuffed with eye-catching visuals (including some amusing animation) and edited at a consistently snappy pace. Young Zutic is a smart and sexy lead, able to carry the whole film on her bare shoulders. Like the rest of the cast, she seems to have stepped out of an erotic-adventure comic book.

Oblique refs to the present grim reality are almost nil, though at one point characters discuss "the world beneath the world of appearances." However, pic lifts its fig-leaf in the final shot where, after the painter is dead and Liza has resumed her social obligations, a tag line informs us: "Her real name is Europe. His is the Balkans." — *Deborah Young*

HEONGGONG YA FUNGKWONG
(CRAZY HONG KONG)
(HONG KONG)

An Edko Communications/First Distributors (H.K.) presentation of a Golden Flare Films/Edko Classics Films production. (Intl. sales: Edko, H.K.) Produced by Hoi Wong. Executive producers, Edwin Kong, Po-chih Leong, Peter Shepherd. Directed by Wellson Chin. Screenplay, Kong Fung, Lau Tseun-wai. Camera (color), Kwan Pak-sun; music, Lau Yu-tat. Reviewed at Cannes Film Festival (market), May 20, 1993. Running time: **90 MIN.**

N!xau	N!xau
Shirley Huang	Carina Liu
Winnie	Cecilia Yip
Jack	Conrad Janis
John	Lau Ching-wan
(English version)	

Jamie Uys can rest easy over "Crazy Hong Kong," a good-natured variation on "The Gods Must Be Crazy" that dumps South African bushman N!xau in money-mad Kowloon. Completists and exotica buffs will want to seek this one out, but fans of Uys' two comedies may well decide enough's enough.

Plot device of getting N!xau to the Orient is having him save yuppie businesswoman Carina Liu from a lion in South Africa and getting trapped in the luggage on her private jet back home. Rest of the film has N!xau tracking down Liu in H.K., sorting out her personal and business problems and converting her to the joys of a non-materialistic lifestyle.

Action sequences are plentiful and handled with nice comic style. Whenever the pace slackens, a subplot of two dumb jewel thieves who think N!xau has their diamonds resurfaces for another chase sequence. Subtext of the evils of Coca-Cola culture isn't pushed.

N!xau makes a natural performer, even when wandering round Hong Kong in a loincloth. Local stars Liu and Cecilia Yip (as Liu's ditzy friend) bring a touch of class to the proceedings. Direction by action-comedy journeyman Wellson Chin is pro.

Color in American-dubbed version is below par, especially in the bookending African scenes. Parts of original soundtrack survive in N!xau's "click" dialogue and one Cantonese song. Film took an unassuming $HK5 million on release in February 1993. — *Derek Elley*

CABIN BOY

A Buena Vista release of a Touchstone Pictures presentation of a Burton/Di Novi production. Produced by Tim Burton, Denise Di Novi. Executive producers, Steve White, Barry Bernardi. Directed, written by Adam Resnick. Story, Chris Elliott, Resnick. Camera (Fotokem color, Technicolor prints), Steve Yaconelli; editor, Jon Poll; music, Steve Bartek; production design, Steven Legler; art direction, Nanci B. Roberts, Daniel A. Lomino; set design, Stephen Alesch; set decoration, Roberta J. Holinko; costume design, Colleen Atwood; sound (Dolby), Edward Tise; assistant director, Thomas Irvine; visual effects supervisor, Michael Lessa; casting, Rik Pagano, Sharon Bialy, Debi Manwiller. Reviewed at the GCC Beverly Connection, L.A., Jan. 5, 1994. MPAA Rating: PG-13. Running time: **80 min.**

Nathanial Mayweather	Chris Elliott
Captain Greybar	Ritch Brinkley
Paps	James Gammon
Skunk	Brian Doyle-Murray
Big Teddy	Brion James
Trina	Melora Walters
Calli	Ann Magnuson
Chocki	Russ Tamblyn
Figurehead	Ricki Lake

Call this one "The Nightmare After Christmas." Obnoxious, snide and pointless, this ill-fated spoof carries the bonus of being as crude and gamy as the hold of an old fishing barge.

Still, that aroma probably won't linger, as this fish figures to sail out of theaters quickly.

Although Tim Burton's company produced the film, the filmmaker clearly left the creative carnage to the team of Chris Elliott and writer-director Adam Resnick, both former "Late Night With David Letterman" scribes (they share story credit here) before collaborating on the short-lived Fox Broadcasting series "Get a Life."

Elliott, sadly, may have topped out with his two-minute appearances on "Late Night," since subsequent exposures of any greater length have proven grating at best. Think of this as a bad version of an old "Saturday Night Live" sketch, stretched to an interminable 80 minutes.

Elliott plays a finishing school snob who, en route to his father's hotel in Hawaii, accidentally boards the wrong boat. Instead of an elegant yacht, he ends up on a schooner, The Filthy Whore, populated by a quintet of surly, grizzled fishermen who delight in abusing him.

But wait, it gets worse. The ship nears an island called Hell's Bucket, which leads to the inexplicable addition of several fantasy elements lifted from old Sinbad movies, from a snow beast to the six-armed dominatrix Calli (Ann Magnuson). Elliott's character also discovers a love interest, Trina (Melora Walters), who runs afoul of the boat while seeking to swim around the world.

Russ Tamblyn turns up in a silent cameo as a half-man, half-shark named Chocki, as does Ricki Lake playing the boat's figurehead — both parts that suggest considerable editing was done in an effort to reduce the damage. Even old pal Dave Letterman, listed in the credits as "Earl Hofert," turns up briefly and, indicative of the general malaise, draws barely a chuckle.

Elliott either can't act or seems unwilling to try, preventing the film from deviating for a moment from its churlishly broad tone. The rest of the cast, including such capable character actors as James Gammon and Brion James, are left mostly to fend for themselves under Resnick's slapdash direction.

In addition to Elliott and Resnick, "Get a Life" alumni Brian Doyle-Murray and Bob Elliott (Chris' dad) also join the voyage (as does Andy Richter, latenight host Conan O'Brien's sidekick), creating the impression we're watching a reunion from a failed, little-seen sitcom. According to the production notes, producers Burton and Denise Di Novi were big fans of the show, which seems admirable by comparison.

Purposely shoddy sets and special effects only add to the mess. Elliott might be best served by a return to Letterman's show, where he could reprise such sketches as "the guy under the seats." In this case, anywhere but in them would be an improvement.

—Brian Lowry

AUX PETITS BONHEURS

(LIFE'S LITTLE TREASURES)

(FRENCH)

An AMLF release of an Elefilm/France 3 Cinema/AMLF production. (International sales: Studio Canal Plus, Paris.) Produced by Rosalinde Deville. Directed by Michel Deville. Screenplay, Rosalinde Deville; camera (color), Martial Thury, Eric Faucherre; editor, Raymonde Guyot; music, selections from works of Louis Moreau Gottschalk; production design, Thierry Leproust; set decoration, Isabelle Arnal; costume design, Cecile Balme; sound (Dolby), Jean Minando, Francois Groult. Reviewed at AMLF screening room, Paris, Dec. 20, 1993. Running time: **102 MIN.**

Helene	Anemone
Marc	Xavier Beauvois
Pierre	Andre Dussollier
Ariane	Nicole Garcia
Cecile	Sylvie Laporte
Sabine	Michele Laroque
Matthieu	Francois Marthouret
Lena	Hanna Schygulla
Michel	Victor Miletic
Bertrand	Patrick Chesnais

Michel Deville's latest pic is a sly, sexy ensemble piece that should make international arthouse owners happy. Leisurely, sometimes whimsical tale of four women Easter vacationing with the men in their lives unspools in a spacious country house, tailor-made for voyeurism, overheard conversations and creaking bedsprings.

Catalyst to events is Helene (Anemone), 43, returning to the house where as a teenager she spent one memorable night of romance. Arriving, she spies Ariane (Nicole Garcia) and Matthieu (Francois Marthouret) making passionate love against a piano while Lena (Hanna Schygulla) sobs behind a door.

Taking such proceedings in stride, Helene is soon made to feel at home by Ariane's husband, amateur photog Pierre (Andre Dussollier). Helene is intent on locating the love of her life 25 years after the event, and all of the house's occupants agree to join in the manhunt.

The rest of the crowd includes Matthieu's young wife, Sabine (Michele Laroque), desperate to have a child despite her husband's refusal; Lena's lover, Marc (Xavier Beauvois), 23 years her junior; Lena's precocious son, Michel; and Cecile (Sylvie Laporte), a bright inquisitive black woman who, summoned to babysit by mistake, stays on to pepper the proceedings with jaunty keyboard melodies by 19th century composer Louis Moreau Gottschalk.

Thanks to scripter Rosalinde Deville having the entire cast introduce themselves for Helene's benefit, viewers know in one fell swoop who's sleeping with whom, plus their professions, ages and aspirations. One can then sit back and enjoy the interlocking plot machinations that are at once deceptively simple and deliciously complex.

Narrative spans four days, tagged on-screen as "Helene's Arrival," "Ariane's Day," "Sabine's Day," and "Lena's Day." Though the camera pays special attention to the designated character in each seg, the full cast weaves in and out of each.

As the characters lounge around, shop, prepare meals and plan a party, Anemone is the catalyst to promiscuous Garcia, lovesick Schygulla, broody Laroque, faithful Dussollier, youthful Beauvois and reluctant Marthouret figuring out what they truly want.

Pic has the relaxed, lyrical pace of a continuous vacation among friends, with a strong undercurrent of sex. There's much partial disrobing, and trading and borrowing of clothing, by both sexes.

Deville trademark of spirited wordplay is much in evidence, including an elaborate group discussion of gradations of meaning between "slut," "bitch" and "bimbo." Anemone and Laroque also have their verbal way with a hapless male victim.

Perfs and lensing are fine. Use of pleasant music by Gottschalk helps to make the couplings and uncouplings appear fitting and inevitable.

—Lisa Nesselson

PER AMORE, SOLO PER AMORE

(FOR LOVE, ONLY FOR LOVE)

(ITALIAN)

A Filmauro release of a Filmauro production. Produced by Aurelio De Laurentiis. Executive producer, Maurizio Amati. Directed by Giovanni Veronesi. Screenplay, Ugo Chiti, Veronesi. Camera (color), Giuseppe Ruzzolini; editor, Nino Baragli; music, Nicola Piovani; art direction, Enrico Fiorentini; costume design, Gabriella Pescucci; sound, Massimo Loffredi, Giulio Viggiani; assistant director, Gianni Arduini. Reviewed at Multiplex Savoy, Rome, Jan. 2, 1994. Running time: **114 MIN.**

Joseph	Diego Abatantuono
Mary	Penelope Cruz
Socrates	Alessandro Haber
Dorotea	Stefania Sandrelli
Cleofa	Renato De Carmine
Sara	Valeria Sabel
Child Mary	Eliana Giua

Also with: Mariangela D'Abbraccio, Gianni Musy, Ugo Conti, Antonio Juorio, Massimo Pittarello, Laura Roncaccia.

"For Love, Only For Love" is an offbeat Christmas film in which St. Joseph gets top billing over the Virgin Mary, and baby Jesus doesn't even appear in the credits. Fabricated biopic about the practically unknown Joseph features piquant casting of comedian Diego Abatantuono and Spanish starlet Penelope Cruz that largely overcomes a trite storyline. Pic's money-making run in Italy since late last year could be duplicated elsewhere, given the tale's universal appeal.

However, for those looking for an uplifting Bible yarn, "For Love" may seem a bit lacking in piety. There's very little of the divine, though the brief appearance of a glowing boy Jesus confirms the film's underlying orthodoxy. Helmer Giovanni Veronesi's superficial treatment of the gospels is mainly aimed at entertainment, where it scores.

An unlikely saint, Abatantuono (the macho Sgt. Lo Russo in "Mediterraneo") is an imposing thesp with fiery eyes and a blustering tone which he easily turns into laughs. He spends a restless youth traveling around Palestine with faithful sidekick Socrates (Alessandro Haber), until the two set up a carpentry shop outside the bustling town of Nazareth.

Though mightily attracted by the ladies, Joseph finds a steady date in retired Syrian courtesan Dorotea (Stefania Sandrelli, caricaturing her seductress roles). His heart is steadily drawn, though, to an eight-year-old tomboy, Mary. Years later, she turns up at the more suitable age of 14 or so, played with defiant splendor by Penelope Cruz.

Against her guardian's wishes, Mary has set her sights on Joseph, and much screen time is devoted to their comical courtship. Just when things look arranged, Mary mysteriously disappears for several months. Her pregnancy is traumatic for everyone concerned, but as the villagers believe Joseph is the father, his face is saved and they marry anyway.

Oddly, pic shuns all the Famous Moments: no Annunciation (just Mary's word it happened), no Wise Men following the star to Bethlehem (just a bunch of locals staring at the newborn in a manger). Poor Joseph never has a divine revelation to help him accept a life of celibacy; in the end, he goes mad, even while claiming to believe that Mary's son is God.

In an exceptionally fine perf, Haber brings to life the undocumented character of Joseph's assistant (who also narrates the story), as well as rounding out Joseph's private life with a strong and convincing friendship. As Mary, Cruz transforms her natural sex appeal into an intense but chaste passion. She makes a spirited match for Abatantuono, who slips into pathos for film's quiet finale.

Technically, pic is a pleasure to watch. Tunisian locations double dramatically for Palestine under Giuseppe Ruzzolini's straightforward lensing. —*Deborah Young*

PARISERHJULET

(THE FERRIS WHEEL)

(SWEDISH)

A Sandrews presentation a Cinetofon AB/Sandrew Film AB/Sveriges Television TV2 AB/Lindberg & Landoff Film/Joson AB/Tonservice Lothner & Lothner AB/Vintergatan Film & Television AB/Tomas Lindahl Musikprod AB production. Produced by Lennart Duner. Directed, written, edited by Clas Lindberg. Camera (color), Andra Lasmanis; music, Thomas Lindahl; production design, Lena Billingskog; costume design, Kim Astrom; sound, Olle Unnerstad. Reviewed at the Sandrews screening room, Stockholm, Sweden, Sept. 17, 1993. Running time: **105 MIN.**
Marten .... Jakob Eklund
Kickan .... Helena Bergstrom
Risto .... Claes Malmberg
Raymond .... Christer Banck
Inspector Stark .... Peter Huttner
The Foreman .... Goran Boberg

A breakthrough part for young actor Jakob Eklund is the most memorable aspect of "The Ferris Wheel," an uneven but sympathetic comedy with lots of dark touches.

Helmer-scriptwriter Clas Lindberg won several prizes for his moody "The Secret of the Under-

ground" two years ago. New effort is more erratic, but certainly not without merits.

Marten (Eklund) is released from prison and goes to visit his cellmate Risto's girlfriend, Kickan. He soon talks himself into her bed. When Risto is released, the result is an odd triangle, where both men claim to be the father of the child Kickan is expecting.

Trio dreams about buying a big ferris wheel to take around Sweden in summertime. To raise money, the men steal Christmas trees in the forests and sell them in the streets of Stockholm. When caught, Risto kills the owner of the trees. The men are now murderers, sought by the police.

"The Ferris Wheel" is difficult to classify; it's both comedy and tragedy, and very unpredictable. This is an asset, but can also lead to some audience confusion. Overall, pic is an entertaining story of three people using extreme methods to survive, but it lacks the magic touch that made "Secret of the Underground" so enchanting.

Acting is tops, especially by Eklund, previously seen in Colin Nutley's "House of Angels," and Helena Bergstrom, who is now the actress most heavily in demand in Sweden. —*Gunnar Rehlin*

LES GENS NORMAUX N'ONT RIEN D'EXCEPTIONNEL

(THERE'S NOTHING SPECIAL ABOUT NORMAL PEOPLE)

(FRENCH)

A Pierre Grise Distribution release of a Gemini Films/BC Films/BVF production, with participation of CNC and Canal Plus. Produced by Paulo Branco. Executive producer, Monod. Directed by Laurence Ferreira Barbosa. Screenplay, Ferreira Barbosa, Santiago Amigorena, Berroyer, Cedric Kahn. Camera (color), Antoine Heberle; editor, Emmanuelle Castro; music, Cesaria Evora, Cuco Valoy, Melvil Poupaud; set design, Brigitte Perreau; costume design, Francois Clavel; sound, Francois Waledisch, Jacques Thomas-Gerard. Reviewed at Gaumont Hautefeuille Cinema, Paris, Dec. 25, 1993. Running time: **102 MIN.**
Martine .... Valeria Bruni-Tedeschi
German .... Melvil Poupaud
Pierre .... Marc Citti
Anne .... Claire Laroche
Francois .... Serge Hazanavicius
Mr. Jacquet .... Barroyer
Also with: Frederic Diefenthal, Sandrine Kiberlain, Marianne Groves, Michel Bos.

"There's Nothing Special About Normal People" is a quirky, enjoyable portrait of a flake who plays matchmaker

during her 10-day stay in a psychiatric ward peopled by memorable misfits. Debut pic by Laurence Ferreira Barbosa marks helmer as a talent to watch.

Valeria Bruni-Tedeschi glows in a nicely nuanced perf as Martine, a 25-year-old telephone sales employee who can't get a grip on things since being dumped by her boyfriend of three years. Often told she should "have her head examined," Martine bluntly demands explanations where others would let matters slide.

After confronting her b.f., who curtly says that he no longer loves her, Martine smashes her head against a glass door and, contracting amnesia, winds up in a psychiatric ward.

There, she creates a whirlwind of unsolicited activity, mostly centered on getting dysfunctional lovebirds together.

Character's energetic and naive penchant for organizing other people's lives is both wacky and endearing. Pic is a series of offbeat moments, some tender and some literally out-to-lunch, such as the misfits' picnic Martine assembles by hijacking players from two institutions.

Thesps on both sides of the sanity curve are exemplary. Blend of handheld and traditional camerawork suits the episodic, intimate tale. Production design neatly captures the essence of urban indifference and the scruffy, utilitarian atmosphere of working-class apartments and haunts. —*Lisa Nesselson*

THE SECRET ADVENTURES OF TOM THUMB

(BRITISH - ANIMATED)

A Manga Entertainment release of a bolexbrothers production for BBC Bristol/La Sept (France)/Manga Entertainment, in association with Lumen Films. Produced by Richard "Hutch" Hutchison. Executive producers, Thierry Garrel (for La Sept), Colin Rose (for BBC). Directed, written, edited by Dave Borthwick. Camera (color), Borthwick, Frank Passingham; music, Startled Insects; title theme, John Paul Jones; production design, Borthwick; sets, costume design, makeup, the bolexbrothers; sound design, Andy Kennedy; sound, Paul Hamblin; key animators, Borthwick, Passingham, Lee Wilton; character models, Justin Exley, Jan Sanger; additional models & set dressing, Cathy Price, Beverley Knowlden; script associate, John Schofield; associate producer, Hengemeh Panahi; second unit director, Passingham. Reviewed in London, Jan. 5, 1993. Running time: **60 MIN.**
Pa Thumb .... Nick Upton
Ma Thumb .... Deborah Collar
Two men .... Frank Passingham
.... John Schofield
Woman in bar .... Mike Gifford
Voices: Brett Lane, Helen Veysey, Paul Veysey, Peter Townsend, Marie Clifford, Tim Hand, Andrew Bailey, Nick Upton, John Schofield.

A triumphant demonstration of animation techniques, but weakened by thin plotting that doesn't quite hold the attention, "The Secret Adventures of Tom Thumb" is a high-grunge, post-industrial meltdown of elements from the traditional yarns "Tom Thumb" and "Jack the Giant Killer." Hourlong feature should find a home in adventurous TV programmers' skeds, though item and subject matter is too outre for afternoon kidslots.

Production is the brainchild of U.K. animator Dave Borthwick, co-founder of Bristol-based production house bolexbrothers with Dave Riddett, a cameraman from claymation specialists Aardman Studios. Pic mixes their pixilation technique (frame-by-frame animation of live actors) with standard model and clay animation, all done in-camera. Result has an unreal, time-lapse feel, perfectly suited to the film's David Lynch-like, industrial-Gothic atmosphere.

Slim story, set in a kind of 1950s British working-class ambience, has a hairless, earless, tiny sprig (resembling the Star Child in Kubrick's "2001") born to a poor couple in a bug-ridden apartment. Christened Tom Thumb by his parents, the kid is taken away by Kafkaesque goons for testing in a lab, whence he escapes down a chute to discover an alternative society of

Little People scraping a living among the garbage and industrial waste.

The medieval-like society is led by Jack, who goes on raids among the Giants (humans), felling them with blowdarts. Tom's father tracks him and Jack down but is accidentally killed by a drinking partner in a fight. The tiny duo make their way to the lab, where they smash a secret, mystical power source. Surreal ending is ironic (and obscure).

Though the pic's technique is often awesome, the relentlessly downbeat tone, with the screen suffused by bugs, creepy-crawlies and dank imagery, proves a turn-off after a while. Dialogue is mostly grunts, with occasional key words highlighted to aid comprehension.

The project started as a 10-minute series pilot, screened by pubcaster BBC during Christmas 1988. When the BBC went cold on more funding, the producers raised their own coin for a feature version, finally re-interesting the BBC. Following a screening at last year's London fest, and a brief theatrical outing, pic aired Dec. 23 in an evening slot on the U.K. pubcaster's minority channel, BBC2.

—*Derek Elley*

IRON WILL

A Buena Vista release of a Walt Disney Pictures presentation. Produced by Patrick Palmer, Robert Schwartz. Co-producers, James Ployhar, George Zepp. Directed by Charles Haid. Screenplay, John Michael Hayes, Djordje Milicevic, Jeff Arch. Camera (Technicolor), William Wages; editor, Andrew Doerfer; music, Joel McNeely; production design, Stephen Storer; art direction, Nathan Haas; costumes, Betty Madden; sound (Dolby), Richard Lightstone; assistant directors, Gary M. Strangis, Chris Stoia; second unit directors, David Ellis, Palmer; casting, Jennifer Shull. Reviewed at AMC Meyer Park 14, Houston, Jan. 8, 1994. MPAA Rating: PG. Running time: **108 MIN.**

Will Stoneman	Mackenzie Astin
Harry Kingsley	Kevin Spacey
J.P. Harper	David Ogden Stiers
Ned Dodd	August Schellenberg
Angus McTeague	Brian Cox
Borg Guillarson	George Gerdes
Jack Stoneman	John Terry
Maggie Stoneman	Penelope Windust
De Fontaine	Jeffrey Allen Chandler
Simon Lambert	Michael Laskin
Peter Swenson	James Cada
Joe McPherson	Rex Linn
Albert Carey	Allan "RJ" Joseph

Disney stands to take a healthy bite out of the box office with "Iron Will," a rousingly old-fashioned dog-sled adventure that's entertaining enough to draw even adolescents who normally avoid "wholesome" family fare. Backed by a carpet-bombing TV ad campaign, pic should easily surpass domestic grosses for studio's recent "White Fang." Foreign, vid and TV prospects are just as bright.

Pic began life as a 1971 first-draft screenplay by John Michael Hayes, a two-time Oscar nominee ("Rear Window," "Peyton Place") and frequent Alfred Hitchcock collaborator. Hayes — whose last documented onscreen credit was 1966's "Nevada Smith" — subsequently wrote a second draft that was optioned in 1988 by producer Robert Schwartz. Later, writers Djordje Milicevic ("Runaway Train") and Jeff Arch ("Sleepless in Seattle") were brought aboard to make their own contributions.

The end result is a seamless albeit frequently cornball scenario based on a real-life event, a 522-mile dog-sled race between Winnipeg, Canada, and St. Paul, Minn., in winter 1917.

Youngest and least experienced of the competing mushers is 17-year-old Will Stoneman (Mackenzie Astin), a South Dakota farm boy who enters the race to save his family from financial ruin after the accidental death of his father (John Terry). With the reluctant support of his mother (Penelope Windust), who wants Will to use part of the $10,000 prize to attend college, Will trains for the ordeal with Native American handyman Ned Dodd (August Schellenberg).

J.P. Harper (David Ogden Stiers), the flamboyant mogul who's underwriting the race, is initially unwilling to permit the youth to risk life and limb while competing under such harsh physical and climatic conditions. But Harry Kingsley (Kevin Spacey), a hard-charging yellow journalist, shames the mogul into accepting Will. Kingsley's motives, of course, are not altruistic — he plans to exploit the boy's adventures for his own career advancement.

As the overland race begins, Will finds he must be extra mindful of an opponent even more dangerous than the snow-blanketed terrain: Scandinavian champ Borg Guillarson (George Gerdes), an egotistical and underhanded blowhard. To make matters worse, Borg has the behind-the-scenes support of Angus McTeague (Brian Cox), a wealthy sports fan who doesn't want to lose a side bet he made against Will.

That's the bad news. The good news is, Will has courage to burn and fortitude to spare. Better still, he also has his father's best dog, Gus, at the head of his sled team.

Under the smooth and solid direction of first-time feature helmer Charles Haid (the actor still best known for his "Hill Street Blues" TV role), "Iron Will" sustains interest, excitement and period flavor for all of its well-paced 108 minutes. The sled-race scenes appear authentic — sometimes harrowingly so — and lead to a suitably cheer-worthy climax. William Wages' superior lensing greatly enhances the impressive action, which was shot on location in Minnesota and Wisconsin.

Astin — brother of Sean, son of John Astin and Patty Duke — does a fine job of registering pure-hearted pluck and idealistic fervor without coming across as bland or campy. He also does himself proud in scenes where it's obvious that the filmmakers didn't fake his dashing (and tumbling) through the snow.

Script does trot out a few howlers, such as: "Don't let fear stand in the way of your dreams, son" and "That boy has the heart of a bear."

On the plus side, though, "Iron Will" makes clever use of a media-savvy subplot. Kingsley's stories about Will's exploits are taken to heart by readers in an anxious America on the verge of entering World War I. As a result, Will becomes an instant hero who is greeted by flag-waving fans at various stops on his journey. And just to make sure the story can be milked even more, Kingsley, who coins the "Iron Will" nickname in the first place, has a colleague track down Will's family for an exclusive interview.

Obviously, some things haven't changed much since 1917.

—*Joe Leydon*

HOUSE PARTY 3

A New Line Cinema release in association with Doug McHenry and George Jackson. Produced by Carl Craig. Executive producers, Doug McHenry, George Jackson, Janet Grillo. Directed by Eric Meza. Screenplay, Takashi Bufford, based on a story by David Toney, Bufford, based on characters created by Reginald Hudlin. Camera (Foto-Kem color), Anghel Decca; editor, Tom Walls; music, David Allen Jones; music supervisor, Dawn Soler; production design, Simon Dobbin; set decoration, M. Claypool; costume design, Mel Grayson; makeup, hair, Judy Murdock; sound (Dolby), Darryl Linkow; associate producer, Helena Echegoyen; assistant directors, Don Wilkerson, Rodney Allen Hooks; casting, Robi Reed, Tony Lee, Andrea Leed. Reviewed at the Hollywood Galaxy cinema, L.A., Jan. 12, 1994. MPAA Rating: R. Running time: **93 MIN.**

Kid	Christopher Reid
Play	Christopher Martin
Stinky	David Edwards
Veda	Angela Means
Sydney	Tisha Campbell
Immature	Themselves
Aunt Lucy	Betty Lester
Uncle Vester	Bernie Mac
Showboat	Michael Colyar
Johnny Booze	Chris Tucker
Janelle	Khandi Alexander

In spite of New Line's ads promising "the best house party yet," "House Party 3" is the worst, which explains why it was not press-screened in advance. Lacking the genially goofy and infectious, good-natured tone that marked the initial 1990 entry (and to a lesser extent the second), and hampered by a disjointed structure, the comedy should appeal only to the most ardent fans of the previous pix and Kid N' Play's animated TV series.

Meant as a natural progression of the escapades of the hip-hop duo from the 'hood, new installment revolves around the engagement of Kid (Christopher Reid) to beautiful Veda (Angela Means), who replaces ex-girlfriend Sydney (Tisha Campbell). Kid's anxieties and fears of matrimony serve as weak glue to a loosely structured comedy composed of uninspired vignettes about Kid's management company, his lifelong friendship with the now threatened Play (Christopher Martin), meeting his disapproving in-laws, and so on.

The pleasure-loving, upbeat original "House Party" contained comic highlights and hilarious mishaps involving a watchful father, vicious dogs, inept cops and neighborhood bullies, all obstacles to Kid's attending Play's latenight jam. The less imaginative and weaker 1991 sequel turned socially conscious and preached for education among black suburban teenagers.

The material for the series was always ephemeral and episodic, but the chief problem here is fragmentation and self-consciousness about its humor, characters, fashion — and just about everything. Under these circumstances, David Edwards' Stinky, Ketty Lester's Aunt Lucy, Bernie Mac's Uncle Vester and especially Michael Colyar's Showboat come across as broad caricatures.

Ultimately, the success of each party film depends on the quality of its guests and the fun they generate. It's therefore perplexing that, despite some promising talent drawn from hot clubs and TV shows, "House Party 3" drags along, without fully utilizing its varied cast of performers.

Pic comes to life only in the last 15 minutes, when everybody shows up at Kid's bachelor party, orchestrated by Immature's three shrewd kids.

However, pandering to the younger viewers, scripter Takashi Bufford and helmer Eric Meza allow these kids excessive screen time, at the expense of the far more entertaining and gifted team of Kid N' Play.

Technical credits are solid.

—*Emanuel Levy*

BLINK

A New Line Cinema release. Produced by David Blocker. Executive producers, Robert Shaye, Sara Risher. Directed by Michael Apted. Screenplay, Dana Stevens. Camera (Deluxe color, Filmhouse prints; widescreen), Dante Spinotti; editor, Rick Shaine; music, Brad Fiedel; additional music, Michael Kirkpatrick; production design, Dan Bishop; art direction, Jefferson Sage; set design, Amy J. Smith; set decoration, Dianna Freas; costume design, Susan Lyall; sound (Dolby), Chris Newman; digital effects supervisor, Art Durinski; line producer, Barry Watkins; assistant director, David Sardi; casting, Linda Lowry. Reviewed at Warner Hollywood Studios, L.A., Jan. 6, 1994. (In Palms Springs Film Festival.) MPAA Rating: R. Running time: **106 MIN.**
Emma Brody .... Madeleine Stowe
Det. John Hallstrom .... Aidan Quinn
Candice .... Laurie Metcalf
Det. Thomas Ridgely ..... James Remar
Dr. Ryan Pierce .... Peter Friedman
Lt. Mitchell .... Bruce A. Young
Officer Crowe .... Matt Roth
Neal Booker .... Paul Dillon
The Drovers .... Michael Kirkpatrick,
Sean C. Cleland,
Craig Winston Damon,
David Callahan, Jackie Moran

High concept blurs the bedrock of plot and plausibility in "Blink." A thriller steeped in scientific research, its focus is too often bogged down in lab-room mumbo jumbo. The result is that

what should be a straightforward genre outing becomes a cumbersome scientific digression in which somewhere lurks a killer.

Being neither fish nor fowl, this New Line release adds up to spotty theatrical prospects. The craft and gloss may provide some initial business, but its primary vitality will be as a video rental title.

Not to be confused with "Jennifer 8's" story of a blind woman in jeopardy, the new outing is about a formerly blind woman in peril from a killer whom she may or may not have seen. Musician Emma Brody (Madeleine Stowe) has recently regained her eyesight following a corneal transplant. But the coordination between what her brain registers and what she actually sees isn't quite aligned. Skewed images that she experiences one day become clear a day later. Her doctor explains that she's experiencing that rare phenomenon known as an ocular flashback.

So, one evening upon hearing noise in the hallway of her apartment building, she goes to investigate. All she can discern is a form until the next morning, when she hallucinates a man's face. As her upstairs neighbor was murdered the night before, it doesn't take a genius to figure out what the killer might look like.

If you find this a bit far-fetched, you're in good company. The police are highly skeptical of this witness's credibility. The only reason John Hallstrom (Aidan Quinn) — the detective in charge of investigating the presumed serial killer — begins to rely on Emma is because she's his only witness and he's sexually attracted to her. The latter element appears to be the bane of all contemporary movie cops.

Writer Dana Stevens just doesn't know how to transmit her fascination with things optical and maintain the minimum amount of tension necessary for a thriller. However, her zeal has rubbed off on director Michael Apted, who concocts some clever visual devices to simulate Emma's condition. It provides for some arresting sights but proves no substitute for the script's blind spots.

"Blink's" major problem is a reliance on gimmick. There is no scientific payoff, no metaphor to be played out. In fact, once all the eye stuff becomes too cumbersome, the backdrop shifts to the equally undramatic arena of organ transplants. "Blink" may never screen in a film studies department, but it does seem destined to be a must-see in medical school.

The picture is not improved by the presence of some very good actors attempting to make sense of their characters and situations.

Stowe simply is not good in the role of a somewhat dumb woman in jeopardy, though she has more range here than in "Unlawful Entry." Quinn is just barely capable of keeping a straight face confronted with his cop steeped in cliche.

About the only interesting aspects of the film are such marginal elements as the depiction of a certain squad room vulgarity and some nuts-and-bolts elements surrounding the music scene that Emma's contempo folk group inhabits.

This flash-in-the-pan entertainment will not have the type of rapid movement a title like "Blink" suggests. Expect no more than a commercial flutter. —*Leonard Klady*

AMERICAN CYBORG: STEEL WARRIOR

A Cannon Pictures release of a Yoram Globus and Christopher Pearce presentation of a Global Pictures production. Produced by Mati Raz. Executive producers, Amnon Globus, Marcos Szwarcfiter. Directed by Boaz Davidson. Screenplay, Brent Friedman, Bill Crounse and Don Peqingnot, based on a story by Davidson, Pearce. Camera (color), Avi Karpick; editor, Alain Jakubowicz; music, Blake Leyh; production design, Kuly Sander; sound (Dolby), Eli Yarkoni; stunt coordinator, Clay Boss; assistant director, Shaul Dishy; casting, Nancy Lara-Hansch; Alecia C. Dixon, Shaul Dishy. Reviewed at Cineplex Odeon Sharpstown Center, Houston, Jan. 8, 1994. MPAA Rating: R. Running time: **94 MIN.**
Austin .... Joe Lara
Mary .... Nicole Hansen
Cyborg .... John Ryan
Akmir .... Yoseph Shiloa
Leech .... Uri Gavriel
Carp .... Helen Lesnick
Arlene .... Andrea Litt
Dr. Buckley .... Jack Widerker

Coming soon to a video store near you: "American Cyborg: Steel Warrior," a plodding and hackneyed B-movie adventure that's currently going through the motions of regional theatrical release. Only the least discriminating action fans will take notice.

Low-budget, filmed-in-Israel Cannon release is yet another reworking of riffs from the "Mad Max" and "Terminator" pix. Set in the bleak, blue-grayish ruins of an American city — Charleston, according to an early visual cue — story begins 17 years after a devastating nuclear war. Human survivors, most of them rendered sterile by radiation exposure, are ruled by computers and policed by killer cyborgs.

Underground scientists manage to produce a viable fetus through in vitro fertilization, thanks to Mary (Nicole Hansen), a plucky and bo-

somy young woman who may be "the only source of ova" left on Earth. After the meanest of the cyborg meanies (John Ryan) attacks the rebel lab, Mary escapes, carrying away the fetus in a portable incubator.

Heroine's only hope is to make it across the devastated city, to rendezvous with European rebels during their brief docking at a coastal port. Heroine's only help comes from Austin (Joe Lara), your standard-issue, post-apocalypse herohunk. Austin defends Mary against mutant cannibals, transvestite muggers and assorted other riffraff while the killer cyborg relentlessly pursues them both.

It's supposed to be a big surprise when, two-thirds of the way through, Mary and Austin discover that Austin himself is a cyborg. As it turns out, however, Lara (best known as the star of the 1989 telepic "Tarzan in Manhattan") seems a lot more human than Hansen, whose stiff, awkward line readings provide the pic's only comic relief.

Neither the supporting performances nor the production values are any better than they have to be.

According to production notes, director Boaz Davidson ("Lemon Popsicle") shot most of "American Cyborg" in "a deserted factory complex outside Tel Aviv." And that's exactly what it looks like onscreen, despite game efforts by set dressers to provide some visual variety. Indeed, two or three different scenes appear to have been shot inside the same room. But maybe that's just because once you've seen one room in a deserted factory complex, you've seen them all. —*Joe Leydon*

DEATH WISH V: THE FACE OF DEATH

A Trimark Pictures release of a 21st Century Film Corp. production. Produced by Damian Lee. Executive producers, Menahem Golan, Ami Artzi. Associate producer, Helder Goncalves. Directed, written by Allan A. Goldstein, based on characters created by Brian Garfield. Camera (color), Curtis Petersen; editor, Patrick Rand; music, Terry Plumeri; production design, Csaba A. Kertesz; sound (Ultra Stereo), Valentin Pricop; casting, Kathy A. Smith, Anne Tait; executive in charge of production, Yael Golan. Reviewed at Cineplex-Odeon Spectrum Cinema, Houston, Jan. 13, 1994. MPAA Rating: R. Running time: **95 MIN.**
Paul Kersey .... Charles Bronson
Olivia Regent .... Lesley-Anne Down
Tommy O'Shea .... Michael Parks
Tony Hoyle .... Saul Rubinek
Lt. Mickey King .... Kenneth Welsh

It's been 20 years since pacifist-turned-vigilante Paul Kersey blasted his way through the first "Death Wish" melodrama, and "Death Wish V: The Face of Death" finds both the character and the franchise looking mighty tired. Charles Bronson returns once again as the impassive avenger, but even that won't be enough to keep pic in theaters long. Vid and pay TV prospects are marginally brighter.

By this point in his career, Bronson — still fit and fearsome at 72 — could play Kersey in his sleep. Indeed, there are one or two scenes here where he appears to be doing just that. And who can blame him? Canadian filmmaker Allan A. Goldstein ("The Outside Chance of Maximilian Glick") may be new to the "Death Wish" series, but he's provided little that's new in the way of revivifying plot innovations.

Once again, Bronson is trying to live a reasonably nonviolent life, having promised D.A. Saul Rubinek and police detective Kenneth Walsh that he's hung up his guns for good. Once again, he has found the love of a good woman — in this case, fashion designer Lesley-Anne Down — and hopes to make a permanent commitment.

And, once again, Bronson's lady love meets a sudden and violent end shortly after he makes his tender feelings known to her.

The only difference this time is, instead of muggers, street gangs or drug dealers, the villains are slightly more upscale creeps. Down is killed by the goons of her ex-husband (Michael Parks), a smooth-talking mobster who's bent on taking over the Manhattan garment district. The police, as usual, can't prove anything. Worse, they can do nothing when the mobster reclaims his late ex-wife's young daughter.

That's when Bronson gets the old revolver out of the wall safe.

As "Death Wish" pix go, this one — set in New York but filmed mostly in Toronto — has a surprisingly small body count. Action fans likely will be disappointed to see Bronson kill only six bad guys. Granted, he tortures information out of a seventh by wrapping up the guy with clinging plastic. But somebody else delivers the *coup de grace*.

Slackly paced and unexciting, "Death Wish V" comes off as a flat-footed, by-the-numbers programmer that, judging from what's on-screen, failed to spark much enthusiasm among the people who made it. Except for Parks, who livens up his scenes with some juicy hamminess, supporting players simply go through the motions and pick up their paychecks. Tech credits are adequate.

Maybe they should have called it "Death Warmed Over: The Bottom of the Barrel" instead.

—*Joe Leydon*

PALM SPRINGS

CHINA MOON

An Orion Pictures release of a Tig production. Produced by Barrie M. Osborne. Directed by John Bailey. Screenplay, Roy Carlson. Camera (Deluxe color), Willy Kurant; editors, Carol Littleton, Jill Savitt; music, George Fenton; production design, Conrad E. Angone; art direction, Robert W. Henderson; set decoration, Don K. Ivey; costume design, Elizabeth McBride; sound (Dolby), Jim Webb; special effects, Lawrence J. Cavanaugh; associate producers, Roy Carlson, Carol Kim; assistant director, Eric Jewett; casting, Elizabeth Leustig. Reviewed at the Orion screening room, Beverly Hills, Jan. 5, 1994. (In Palm Springs Film Festival.) MPAA Rating: R. Running time: **99 MIN.**
Kyle Bodine .... Ed Harris
Rachel Munro .... Madeleine Stowe
Lamar Dickey .... Benicio Del Toro
Rupert Munro .... Charles Dance
Adele .... Patricia Healy
Fraker .... Tim Powell
Pinola .... Rob Edward Morris

Ed Harris' stellar performance as the fall guy in "China Moon" elevates John Bailey's noir mystery to a cut or two above the usual Hollywood thriller. Despite some plot holes, the thematic mixture of passion and danger and the pleasure of visual style should prove alluring enough to make this genre item (which was shot in 1992) more popular with audiences than the recent slate of Orion films.

On the surface, "China Moon" seems too explicitly conscious of its genre's themes, signs and visual strategy. Set in small-town Florida, it immediately recalls Lawrence Kasdan's "Body Heat" as well as Victor Nunez's Florida tale of greed and corruption, "A Flash of Green," which also starred Harris. And the triangle involving Harris, a lonely homicide detective who falls for Madeleine Stowe, a beautifully seductive married woman, bears resemblance to such noir classics as "Double Indemnity" and "The Postman Always Rings Twice."

Here, however, the appealing, mysterious lady is not married to an old or crippled man, but to a young and successful banker (Charles Dance). This is just the first of a number of alterations and twists that cast fresh light on the time-honored genre. Indeed, this version humanizes Stowe's femme fatale by making her husband physically abusive and engaged in his own adulterous affair.

The tension in Roy Carlson's efficient, pared-down narrative derives from the complex relationship between Harris and ambitious rookie detective Benicio Del Toro, once Harris gets drawn into a murder scheme.

The well-developed characters, with whom the audience feels an immediate, emphatic connection, are distinctively pungent, the way they were in noir thrillers of the 1940s.

Bailey, a first-rate cinematographer making his fictional feature directorial debut, knows that it's not plot but characterization that carries viewers through the best thrillers — the bits of personality as filtered through the story's turns. He therefore takes his time in establishing the specific context of each of the four major figures.

Like other good thrillers, "China Moon" depends on long silent moments and acute observation of physical milieu. To make the story more gripping, Bailey relies on the emotional pull of such forces as psychological obsession and domination rather than graphic violence.

He's at his best in scenes where the characters reveal some quirks and hide others in an intriguing web of steamy sex and ominous evil. But some viewers may be bothered by the tale's underlying cynicism, which is reflected in the conduct of its law officers.

Harris brings his customary quiet, focused intensity to a tailor-made role, one that calls for equal measure of virility and vulnerability. Endowed with the glamorous looks of the old movie queens, Stowe is also well cast as a dreamy femme fatale with an active imagination and strong feelings.

There is moody, evocative cinematography by vet French lenser Willy Kurant of the Lakeland-Ocala-Tampa area, a region that reportedly has not been used in film before. With the expert editing of Carol Littleton and Jill Savitt, "China Moon" moves along smoothly, setting up the situations and delivering the payoffs.

Shrewd viewers may be able to detect at least one major plot development that telegraphs itself well before it arrives. And the final 15 minutes are weak — a concession to the genre's current requirements for desperate violence and quick resolutions.

Nonetheless, unlike thrillers that target the viscera, "China Moon" avoids slick montage and the cheap thrills of shock cuts and instead aims for the eyes — and heart.

—*Emanuel Levy*

RHINOSKIN: THE MAKING OF A MOVIE STAR

(DOCU — 16mm)

A Hopwood Production. Produced, directed, written by Tod De Pree, Dina Marie Chapman. Camera (Fotokem color), John Bishop; editor, Robert Hoffman; music, Ian Christian Nickus, Thomas Morse; sound, Jon Ailetcher; associate producer, Robert Hoffman. Reviewed at Palm Springs Intl. Film Festival, Jan. 8, 1994. Running time: 90 MIN.

High on spunk and sincerity, if rather short on tech credits and follow-through, "Rhinoskin" is an amiable and wide-eyed documentary on the struggles of a young, aspiring actor in today's Hollywood. With a roving camera and sound crew documenting his own (and every other showbiz wannabe's) worst Tinseltown rejection nightmares, the film's subject, co-director and co-writer, Tod De Pree, manages to turn humiliation into a badge of honor, and a very amusing film.

Perhaps not "serious" enough for many festivals, pic should nonetheless please public TV audiences and perhaps European arts channels hungry for a funny contemporary look at life on the bottom rungs of the American entertainment industry.

As struggling thesp De Pree tries gamely to break into the business, co-writer/director/producer Dina Marie Chapman is on hand questioning the wisdom of investing her time and gas money in what looks increasingly like a portrait of pathetic, abject failure. De Pree is continually shut down by a beautiful young actress, given the bum's rush in casting land and relentlessly hustled by agents, head-shot artists, physical trainers, stylists, acting coaches, colonic therapists and cosmetic surgeons.

But as in the best Hollywood tradition, failure has a funny way of turning into a cockeyed triumph, and many of the characters that first appear crass or deluded wind up displaying real interest in the kid, his quest and his talent. The camera crew also visits Tod's Midwestern hometown, and the Diane Arbus/Richard Avedon-type portraits of small-town life make the case for taking the first Greyhound west.

While diverting and often engaging, eventually "Rhinoskin" becomes a little like watching a friend's home movies. Other than some shrewd work by the editor in finding ways to assemble the scramble of off-the-cuff shots, the film never develops a viewpoint much beyond De Pree's own as he ventures out on his dogged quest to get one line of dialogue on a network sitcom.

It's a measure of De Pree's good-natured, implacable screen persona and scrappy determination that the film plays as well as it does. If you're rooting for him to get on "Doogie Howser," then he's justified his partner's Texaco bill. For longtime observers of Hollywood's mean streets, doc is packed with genuinely strange and wonderful locals.

—*Steven Gaydos*

LOOKIN' ITALIAN

A Vision Quest Entertainment presentation of a Wing and a Prayer production. Produced, directed, written by Guy Magar. Line producer, Brian J. Smith. Camera, (Pacific Film Labs color), Gerry Lively; editor, Gregory Harrison; music, Jeff Beal; production design, William Matthews; set decoration, Laurie Scott; costume design, Susanna Puisto; sound (Ultra-Stereo), James R. Einolf, Pat Toma; SFX makeup, Howard Berger; associate producer, Mickey Cottrell; assistant director, Anthony Fiorno; casting, Susan Scudder. Reviewed at Palm Springs Intl. Film Festival, Jan. 9, 1994. Running time: **100 MIN.**

Vinny Pallazzo	Jay Acovone
Anthony Manetti	Matt LeBlanc
Danielle	Stephanie Richards
Don Dinardo	John La Motta
Manza	Ralph Manza
Willy	Lou Rawls

Vet TV director Guy Magar takes an able cast and solid tech support through the paces of a story that feels stitched together from too many well-worn sources. The story of an ex-Mafioso who tries to start a new life but finds family allegiances and his violent past difficult to shake, "Lookin' Italian" fails to overcome the script's familiar turns and hoary cliches. Inconsistencies in tone, ranging from "Revenge of the Nerds" humor to bloody Tarantino-style mayhem and "Bronx Tale" domestic melodrama, only further distance pic from theatrical contention. The attractive leads and colorful supporting characters may help only enough for "Italian" to find its place on video.

Both Jay Acovone and TV hunk Matt LeBlanc work overtime to flesh out the relationship of a former mobster and his brash, reckless young nephew whom he has taken under his wing. Flashbacks fill in the uncle's dark history; after a deadly confrontation with gangland rivals in New York, Acovone has settled in L.A., where he finds peace toiling as a clerk in a musty bookshop and paying daily visits to the local church.

Sexually charged and strutting his looks in a variety of muscle shirts, LeBlanc challenges his uncle's efforts to provide guidance, and along the way also confronts Acovone's self-imposed retreat from life. As the story progresses through a series of unconvincing events ranging from godfather warnings to unprovoked L.A. street gang attacks, both thesps are called on to hit fever-pitch emotions that might connect in a better-sketched scenario.

Here, however, their sincerity becomes maudlin, and uneven direction by Magar, who helmed the 1987 horror item "Retribution" as well as "Stepfather III" for HBO, too often stops the burgeoning relationship in its tracks.

Along the way to the film's wrap, which involves dark secrets, street gang revenge and wistful love interludes graced with lines like "Is it possible to fall in love after only 24 hours?," crooner Lou Rawls turns up as an unlikely hero, and interracial romance emerges as a key plot element just in time for the fade.

Pic looks and sounds fine, but could use some judicious editing, especially in the draggy first act, and an excess of repetitive dialogue could use pruning as well.

—*Steven Gaydos*

FROSH: NINE MONTHS IN A FRESHMAN DORM

(DOCU — 16mm)

A Geller/Goldfine Production. Produced, directed by Daniel Geller, Danya Goldfine. Camera (video-to-16mm)/sound, Geller, Goldfine; additional camera, Ashley James, Jon Else, John Knoop; editors, Goldfine, Geller, Deborah Hoffman; music, Don Hunter/Overtone Prods.; sound re-recording and mix, Stuart Dubey. Reviewed on vidcassette, San Francisco, Jan. 11, 1994. Running time: **97 MIN.**

The engaging doc "Frosh" follows a dormful of Stanford University students through their first year, offering a limited but well-observed perspective on today's youth/tomorrow's probable leaders. TV-style aspects of vid-transfer feature will limit theatrical play to fests and college-town theatrical circuit, but broadcast sale prospects are bright.

Coed Trancos Hall houses 40 male and 40 female newcomers to the Northern California institution, eight of whom dominate the filmmakers' loose focus. From move-in day to start of summer break, these 18-year-olds log familiar rites of passage — partying, bonding, arguing, dating, studying and gossiping for the first time on adult terms.

Pressure-cooker atmosphere is captured with admirable filmic concision and participatory candor. While the kids' travails will ring bells for anyone with collegiate background, "Frosh" fascinates in its reflection of the shifting 1990s cultural/academic landscape. Tolerance vs. political correctitude is a constant underlying theme. Notions of homophobia, racism, feminism, religious beliefs and so on occupy so much screentime that p.o.v. sometimes seems skewed. But directors Daniel Geller and Danya Goldfine succeed in conveying the excitement of a period when personalities, goals and values are changed, often for life.

They also succeed in nailing more mundane aspects of campus life in getting us to care about protagonists. Central figures cut a swath across sex-pref, ethnic and class grounds, though presentation rarely feels schematic. Lack of any external commentary is both blessing and dilemma — while one may leave with questions regarding universality given Stanford's elite stature, tight focus on students pays off emotionally. They're an endearing, articulate bunch, with plenty of warts viewers with empathetic *deja vu* can cringe over.

Lensing is good, editing ace; pull-quote title cards separating segs tend to underline vid origins, as does some mediocre vid scoring.

As one woman puts it, "Everyone's so insecure about everything" in dorm society. At the end of "Frosh" these fledglings have weathered their first real-world gauntlet in touching microcosm. What's cheering is the belief that they'll now use those fundamental discoveries to make the off-campus world a better place.

—*Dennis Harvey*

DER BESUCHER

(THE VISITOR)

(GERMAN)

A Wild Okapi Film presentation of a Zahavi Film/Duetscher Fersehfunk DSF-TV production. Produced by Horst Kiaulehn. Directed by Dror Zahavi. Screenplay, Andre Hennicke. Camera (color), Matthias Tschiedel; editor, Christine Schone; music, Peter Hilier; art direction, Gunter Pezolod; costumes, Karin Pas; sound, Christfried Sobczyk. Reviewed at World Film Festival, Montreal, Sept. 3, 1992. (In Jews in New Europe fest, N.Y.) Running time: **88 MIN.**

Leon	Andre Hennicke
Almuth	Silke Matthias
Mother	Anne Moll
With: Peter Hiller, Volker Ranisch.	

Return of fascist sentiments within the reunited German territories is a hot subject. But you couldn't beat a colder path to that door than the regurgitated 1970s New German Cinema cliches of "The Visitor."

Traveling to his maternal homeland for the first time, Israeli Jew Leon (played by scenarist Andre Hennicke) finds his train mysteriously stopped in a tunnel, where all passengers are ordered out and detained indefinitely. There, a mini-society has grown sheepish with fear and boredom. They passively accept all police abuse while amusing themselves with their own "street" musicians, press conferences, useless politicians and evangelists.

Leon meanders through, witnessing predictably degraded local color. Symbolism is laughably crude, including the requisite chorus line of high-kicking Nazi-ettes. Eventually Leon simply walks through an unguarded exit, leaving the cowed populace behind.

The societal metaphor is obvious within 10 minutes, leaving plenty of time to be padded with pretentious dialogue and ersatz decadence a la the most mannered excesses of the sub-Fassbinder school.

Picking the silliest sequence is difficult. Perhaps the big smokers' rights rebellion. Or the gay man forced to "sodomize" a woman who keeps her undies on. Director Dror Zahavi seems to think all of this is quite devastating. Any humor is strictly of the unintentional stripe.

Sallying forth with pure *cineaste* noodling, "The Visitor" comes off as just another Weimar Republic dress-up cabaret, with the usual leering faces standing in for the Collective Evil.

Performances are mechanically stylized, tech aspects adequate.

—*Dennis Harvey*

PROFIL BAS

(LOW PROFILE)

(FRENCH)

An AMLF release of a Films 7/Film par Film/TF1 Films production, in association with Sofica Investimage 2 and participation of Canal Plus. (International sales: Roissy Films, Paris.) Produced by Claude Zidi, Jean-Louis Livi. Directed by Zidi. Screenplay, Simon Michael, Didier Kaminka, Zidi. Camera (color), Francois Latonne; editor, Nicole Saunier; music, Gabriel Yared; production design, Francoise de Leu; costume design, Saphira Adam; sound (Dolby), Pierre Gamet. Reviewed at Montparnasse Cinema, Paris, Jan. 5, 1994. Running time: **110 MIN.**

Julien	Patrick Bruel
Claire	Sandra Speichert
Carre	Didier Bezace
Plana	Jean Yanne

Also with: Jacques Rosny, Jean-Louis Tribes, Jean-Pierre Castaldi, Arnaud Giovaninetti.

"Low Profile" is an uneven police thriller about a burnt-out cop who dupes a corrupt superior by masterminding a one-man crime spree. Pic will entertain auds with low expectations, plus femme fans of likable actor/singer Patrick Bruel's buns. Bruel's following has helped the movie make a dent

January 17, 1994 (Cont.)

at the Gallic B.O., and pic will play dandy on the tube.

Helmer Claude Zidi, who marshaled fine comic timing in the law-enforcement comedies "Les Ripoux" ("My New Partner") and "La Totale," here delivers an intriguing opening, lame middle, OK third act and a fair dose of action.

Traitorous inspector Carre (Didier Bezace, unsubtle), in league with big-time dope dealer Roche (Jean-Louis Tribes), is intent on framing disillusioned but honest cop-on-the-beat Julien Segal (Bruel) to look like a turncoat. When Carre's plan misfires, Segal resolves to fight evil with evil, moonlighting as an invincible thief.

His ally in crime, lovely young nightclubber Claire (Sandra Speichert), insists on bedding Segal in record time, turning an initially gritty tale into a ludicrously trumped-up romance awash with cliched dialogue. Plot hinges on a few convenient developments, which Bruel's mild manners and puppy-dog eyes almost carry off.

As the masked Segal finds hold-ups to his liking, Carre squirms in the face of a crime wave he's powerless to stop. Amusing and suspenseful stunts include a payroll heist in an elevator shaft.

Bruel acquits himself well as the soft-spoken tough guy transformed from unenthusiastic loser to take-charge winner. Lensing and editing suit the nighttime atmosphere of Paris' working-class suburbs.

—*Lisa Nesselson*

TAXI DE NUIT

(NIGHT TAXI)

(FRENCH)

An Oliane Prods. release of an Oliane Prods./TF1 Films production, with participation of Canal Plus. (International sales: Claude Nouchi, WMF, Paris.) Produced by Marie Laure Reyre. Directed, written by Serge Leroy. Camera (color), Andre Domage; editor, Francois Ceppi; music, Philippe Sarde; production design, Jean-Pierre Bazerolle; costume design, Monique Giarard; sound, Claude Bertrand. Reviewed at Images d'Ailleurs Cinema, Paris, Dec. 27, 1993. Running time: **85 MIN.**

Taxi Driver .... Bruno Cremer
Carole .... Laure Marsac
Dubrovsky .... Didier Bezace
Jim "The Black" .... Maka Kotto
Also with: Jacqueline Guenin, Bernard Verley, Marianne Groves, Aurore Clement.

"**T**axi de Nuit" is a pleasantly diverting thriller set in Paris in late 1999, by which time the City of Light has evolved into an AIDS- and unemployment-weary police state. Tube programmers should flag this taxi down.

Setting the modest but effective tale in the near future presents ample opportunities for well-incorporated, often wry social commentary about everything from the decline of smoking to the state-enforced triumph of family values. Mothers wishing to divorce are forcibly returned to their spouses, gainful employment is mandatory, political activism is outlawed. Society runs smoothly at the expense of personal freedoms.

Story is set during one long October night. Plucky young blonde Laure Marsac breaks up with an unseen b.f. and hails a cab driven by 20-year vet Bruno Cremer. However, having left in a huff without her wallet, Marsac lacks the cash to pay her fare, plus the all-important "code card" for transactions and identity checks.

Cremer gets Marsac a room in a hotel where his black African buddy Maka Kotto is the night clerk. Pic soon demonstrates that, if Gallic standbys tobacco and alcohol have been curbed, racism and anti-semitism haven't. Didier Bezace, an underground communist the duo met earlier, shows up uninvited, drawing police.

Arrested on a trumped-up morals charge, protagonists are hauled off to the hoosegow and given blood tests. Pic implies the cops are not above planting HIV-positive status on a suspect. Suspenseful visit to the police precinct, and a more disturbing sojourn at the Big Brother-ish Ministry of Security, give the central quartet a chance to show solidarity and buck the system.

The film sustains a sinister tone, which the music reinforces, by adjusting key aspects of behavior without altering the physical appearance of the city. Formal modes of address ("monsieur," "madame") are still entrenched, but a sense of malevolence reigns.

With her waiflike beauty, Marsac contrasts nicely with the grizzled Cremer. Other characters are close to stereotypes but keep things moving at a watchable clip. Lensing dishes up plenty of otherworldly blue-and-yellow-hued night atmosphere.

—*Lisa Nesselson*

LA NAGE INDIENNE

(HEADS ABOVE WATER)

(FRENCH)

An AFMD release of a Film Par Film/BVF/Orly Films/Sedif/France 3 Cinema/Centre Europeen Cinematographique Rhone-Alpes production, with participation of Canal Plus and CNC. (International sales: Roissy Films, Paris.) Produced by Jean-Louis Livi. Executive producer, Bernard Verley. Directed, written by Xavier Durringer, based on his novel. Camera (color), Laurent Macheul; editor, Delphine Desfons; production design, Jean-Pierre Kohut Svelko; sound, Claudine Nougaret, Francois Musy; assistant directors, Arnaud Esterez, Jean-Luc Mathieu. Reviewed at Gaumont Hautefeuille Cinema, Paris, Jan. 3, 1994. Running time: **93 MIN.**

Clara .... Karin Viard
Max .... Gerald Laroche
Loockeed .... Antoine Chappey
Also with: Eric Savin, Sherif Scouri, Aude Amiot, Florence Joubert.

Playwright and theater director Xavier Durringer's "La Nage Indienne" is a leisurely character study of argumentative underachievers in search of a low-rent oasis in their rudderless lives. Despite fine perfs, offshore prospects beyond fests seem limited.

Central threesome is attractive stripper Clara (Karin Viard), mild-mannered auto mechanic Max (Gerald Laroche, in an affecting, memorable perf) and Clara's temperamental b.f., Loockeed (Antoine Chappey). With Clara in tow, the two men set off south for a better, if more precarious, life beside Lake Annecy in the Alps, where an army-bound buddy guards pleasure boats in dry dock.

Pic strings together episodes including Clara's toothache-plagued brother and his combative g.f.: Max's banal yet bittersweet courtship of a perky grocery cashier, and the tragicomic slaughter of a baby lamb at the mountain retreat.

The bond of friendship between the men — in their own little world of a car, a woman, cigarettes and a bit of money — is difficult to grasp. Plucky Max, whose inner strength is gradually revealed, makes endless concessions to the congenitally jealous, sort-tempered Loockeed. Clara takes her lumps.

Pic is like a working-class 1990s skeleton of "Jules and Jim," stripped of charm and charisma — a story of one woman and two fast friends without the flair for epic betrayal. Taunting and baiting are the primary modes of expression by the three leads, with Max the closest thing to a *mensch*. Photography conveys a true sense of place, to

which crummy bric-a-brac and mismatched garb add bull's-eye authenticity. The well-incorporated score of contempo tunes ranges from soothing to grating. French title literally means "Sidestroke" (the swimming style), but also carries connotations of getting by on one's wits. —*Lisa Nesselson*

WONG FEI-HUNG TSI TITGAI DAU NGGUNG

(LAST HERO IN CHINA)

(HONG KONG)

A Wins' Movie Prods./Eastern Prods. production. (International sales: Wins' Movie, H.K.) Produced by Heung Wa-keung, Heung Wa-sing. Executive producer, Lee Yeung-tsung. Directed, written by Wong Jing. Camera (color), Jingle Ma, Lau Mun-tong; editor, Poon Hung; music, Lui Tsung-tak, James Wong; art direction, Ying Siu-kei; costume design, Tony Au; sound, Tsu Tsi-ha; action director, Yuen Woo-ping; martial arts director, Yuen Cheung-yan; associate producer, Lo Kwok. Reviewed on vidcassette, London, Jan. 7, 1993. Running time: **108 MIN.**

Wong Fei-hung .... Jet Li
Yin-er .... Sharla Chang

Chopsocky action star Jet Li looks a whole lot more relaxed in "Last Hero in China," a semi-comic, well-mounted gloss on his Wong Fei-hung character (from "Once Upon a Time in China") that keeps all its plates spinning from start to finish. There's plenty of entertainment here for more general auds, as well as genre nuts.

Back-of-a-coaster plot has martial arts ace Wong (Li) returning from Hong Kong to his training school in Canton, only to find his rent hiked. Local governor Lui, no slouch at the fighting arts himself, has it in for the saintly Wong, as well as being in cahoots with Western businessmen.

Prolific comedy director Wong Jing keeps the pratfalls and goofy stuff on a tight rein and seems happy to turn most of the pic over to action specialist Yuen Woo-ping and his brother. From the opening set-to in a Hong Kong ticket office, through the inventive tournament sequences, to the *mano a mano* showdown between hero and villain, the fight scenes are lively and full of character, expressing plot tensions as well as sheer technique.

Ensemble playing is fine, and tech credits par. Chinese title means "Huang Fei-hung: Iron Chicken vs. Centipede," referring to the combat styles in the final tournament. H.K. box office last spring was a slick $HK18 million.

—*Derek Elley*

OUT OF SIGHT

(DOCU)

A David Sutherland production in association with the WGBH Educational Foundation. Produced, directed by David Sutherland. Executive producer, David Ticchi. Co-producer, Nancy Sutherland. Camera (color) Joe Seamans, A. J. Dimaculangan; editor, Michael Colonna; music, Reeves Gabrels; sound, Zack Krieger, Flora Moon; second camera, Eric Trageser. Reviewed at Museum of Fine Arts, Boston, Jan. 9, 1994. Running time: **85 MIN.**

Boston-based docu filmmaker David Sutherland has spent the past decade trying to redefine the stylistic limits of the documentary. With "Out of Sight" he goes further, creating what one interview subject suggests is closer to soap opera than the traditional talking-head documentary. After a test run at Boston's Museum of Fine Arts, pic heads to the Berlin Film Festival, which should be the first of many stops on the fest and arthouse circuit.

Film's subject is Diane Starin, a 34-year-old blind woman living on a ranch in Northern California. While part of the story is her blindness — she is seen doing everything from cleaning her artificial eyes to serving as a role model for others — it's not really the main point.

As she notes, "I think people are ready for a story about a blind woman who's raising a family, having a career, or both. What I wonder is if they're ready for a blind woman who's in her 30s living with a man who's in his 60s, in a relationship that deals with alcohol and infidelity."

The people in her life are gradually introduced in both interviews and real-life situations. In a somewhat unusual technique for docus, Sutherland shows re-enactments of incidents from Starin's past using the actual people playing themselves, including a scene where her boyfriend nearly burns them both alive inside their camper.

Sutherland doesn't try to force sympathy for Starin. She comes across as someone all too human, with much to admire but also much to criticize.

After she breaks up with her older b.f., he is diagnosed with cancer. She comes back to live with him in a new house they will share. When he does better than his doctors anticipated, Starin calculates whether she can afford to wait for him to die so she will inherit his share of the house.

Sutherland's cast of real-life characters aren't freaks but simply folks trying to make the best of the hand that life has dealt them. In the end, the complex relationships carry the film, not any maudlin and easy concern for a "handicapped" person.

Sutherland's gritty *cinema verite* style is aided by the understated stylization of the flashbacks, which use a washed-out, nearly black-and-white look to convey the sense of recollection. Western-style music is provided by Reeves Gabrels, a guitarist/songwriter with David Bowie's band Tin Machine.

—*Daniel M. Kimmel*

INTERSECTION

A Paramount release of a Bud Yorkin production in association with Frederic Golchan. Produced by Yorkin, Mark Rydell. Executive producer, Golchan. Co-producer, Ray Hartwick. Directed by Rydell. Screenplay, David Rayfiel, Marshall Brickman, based on the novel by Paul Guimard and the screenplay by Guimard, Jean-Loup Dabadie, Claude Sautet. Camera (Deluxe color), Vilmos Zsigmond; editor, Mark Warner; music, James Newton Howard; production design, Harold Michelson; art direction, Yvonne Hurst; set design, Marco Rubeo; set decoration, Dominique Fauquet-Lemaitre; costume design, Ellen Mirojnick; sound (Dolby), Eric Batut; associate producer/assistant director, Alan B. Curtiss; second unit director, Christopher Wilkinson; second unit camera, Laszlo George; casting, Lynn Stalmaster, Stuart Aikins (Canada). Reviewed at Paramount Studios, L.A., Jan. 19, 1994. MPAA Rating: R. Running time: **98 MIN.**

Vincent Eastman	Richard Gere
Sally Eastman	Sharon Stone
Olivia Marshak	Lolita Davidovich
Neal	Martin Landau
Richard Quarry	David Selby
Meaghan Eastman	Jenny Morrison

"Intersection" represents a misguided attempt to retool a French art film as a Hollywood big-star vehicle. On the most elementary commercial level, this lushly appointed meller about a wealthy man caught between his wife and new girlfriend will severely let down audiences hoping for steamy encounters between Richard Gere and Sharon Stone, resulting in quick falloff from whatever its initial weekend B.O. may be.

More significantly, however, Mark Rydell's first film since "For the Boys" three years ago never gets a narrative head of steam going precisely because it's based on material whose nature is utterly at odds with the way American films normally tell stories. Claude Sautet's 1970 Michel Piccoli-Romy Schneider starrer "Les Choses de la vie" (The Things of Life), like many French films, was more concerned with character and life's texture than with plot. This very loose adaptation (acknowledgement of the sources is buried in the end credits) attempts to goose things up here and there, but original's essentially meditative nature is left quite unfulfilled by the new approach and glamour cast.

Set in the bracing, gray locale of a wintry Vancouver, the David Rayfiel-Marshall Brickman script has trendy architect Vincent (Gere) enjoying sack time with groovy journalist Olivia (Lolita Davidovich) while working at the firm he founded with his refined wife, Sally (Stone).

Not only do the two women still adore Vincent, but so does his 13-year-old daughter (Jenny Morrison). The man is rich, designs the most exciting new buildings in B.C. and is fawned over by beautiful females, but his life's still a mess and he pouts whenever any of his women puts any pressure on him. Flashbacks begin to reveal the past: Daddy's girl Sally, whom Vincent married years ago, has probably always been too cold and high-society-minded for her husband, who explains his situation with, "We weren't a family. We were a corporation with a kid"; Vincent started his affair with Olivia somewhat reluctantly, but their hot nights finally hooked him, and he has managed to have his g.f. and daughter get along.

Vincent remains on the fence until the end, when he finally decides which woman he really wants. But a car wreck, telegraphed by the opening sequence, puts him on an unanticipated detour, leaving it to the women to sort things out.

Highly decorous pic is cloaked in allusions and metaphors about the quick passage of time and how one should seize and cherish what's most important in life. But, save Vincent's relationship with his lovely daughter, there's precious little in the film that would seem to represent anything worth holding onto, rendering the already facile philosophical content even more superficial.

As the man at an emotional crossroads, Gere increasingly indulges some easy mannerisms to diminishing returns. Whenever confronted with something he doesn't like, he looks away or closes his eyes and exhales with impatience or disgust as a way of communicating his tortured soul. He also narcissistically bathes in the attentions of the three women in his life in a manner that eventually grates, given how negligently he treats them.

Choosing to play the scorned wife rather than the other woman, Stone is all tension and welled-up eyes. She acquits herself nicely in her few dramatic opportunities, but after "Sliver" this is the second consecutive victim role that she has played, and she's just not the victim type. Some better judgment in role selection seems in order.

As the temptress, Davidovich comes off as too flighty and insubstantial to make a middle-aged man both leave his family and ponder the meaning of life. Registering best is Morrison as the bright, agreeable daughter.

Production values are almost too deluxe, from Ellen Mirojnick's ultra-elegant costumes and production designer Harold Michelson's pampered settings to Vilmos Zsigmond's cool lensing.

Pic reportedly had test-marketing screenings that included two hot sex scenes between Gere and Davidovich, but there is not a trace of them left. One flashback quickie between Gere and Stone is played fully clothed and mostly for laughs. —*Todd McCarthy*

SUNDANCE

FOUR WEDDINGS AND A FUNERAL

(BRITISH)

A Gramercy Pictures release of a Polygram Filmed Entertainment and Channel Four Films presentation of a Working Title production. Produced by Duncan Kenworthy. Executive producers, Tim Bevan, Eric Fellner. Co-executive producer, Richard Curtis. Directed by Mike Newell. Screenplay, Curtis. Camera (Metrocolor), Michael Coulter; editor, John Gregory; music, Richard Rodney Bennett; production design, Maggie Gray; set decoration, Anna Pinnock; costume design, Lindy Hemming; sound (Dolby), David Stephenson; assistant director, Kieron Phipps; casting, Michelle Guish, David Rubin (U.S.). Reviewed at the Sunset Screening Room, L.A., Jan. 13, 1994. (In Sundance Film Festival.) Running time: **116 MIN.**

Charles	Hugh Grant
Carrie	Andie MacDowell
Fiona	Kristin Scott Thomas
Gareth	Simon Callow
Tom	James Fleet
Matthew	John Hannah
Scarlett	Charlotte Coleman
David	David Bower
Hamish	Corin Redgrave
Father Gerald	Rowan Atkinson
Henrietta	Anna Chancellor

Truly beguiling romantic comedy is one of the hardest things for a modern film to pull off, but a winning British team has done it in "Four Weddings and a Funeral." Frequently hilarious without being sappily sentimental or tiresomely retrograde, this Gramercy release, which bowed as the opening night attraction at the Sundance Film Festival, holds strong appeal as a date and couples-oriented entry and should be a good vid title as well.

Whether they acknowledge their antecedents (as "Sleepless in Seattle" did) or not, romantic comedies these days have a great deal of trouble not looking like pale copies of the dizzy and enchanting entertainments that Hollywood did so well in the 1930s. Another problem is that the screen's increased frankness makes adherence to the traditional standards seem coy or naive, but foisting too much lewdness on old-fashioned conventions often produces coarse and unconvincing results.

Screenwriter Richard Curtis ("The Tall Guy," many award-winning BBC productions) has hit just the right balance with this story, which is original in every sense of the word. The splendidly performed account of how an unlikely match is made across the bridge provided by the five title events, Mike Newell's pic is knowingly funny about sex and structurally unusual enough to set it apart from countless other films in the genre, old and recent.

Charles (Hugh Grant) is a charming bumbler whose natural elegance, wit and good looks give him a certain advantage over the other men in his circle of friends, but who still suffers from the same self-doubts as everyone else.

At an English country wedding he meets and, after a series of missed connections, is very willingly seduced by another guest, the gorgeous and exceedingly accommodating American Carrie (Andie MacDowell).

At another wedding three months later, the mere sight of Carrie sets Charles' heart aflutter, but his hopes are dismally dashed when Carrie announces that she's engaged.

Back in London, in the film's only non-ceremonial interlude, the love-struck Charles sits at a cafe as Carrie reels off a chronological and rather lengthy enumeration of her lifetime's worth of bed mates, and then can't help but blurt out his profound feelings for her even as she's heading to the alter with a wealthy older Scotsman (Corin Redgrave).

So it's with wistful resignation that Charles journeys to the knight's northern castle for Carrie's wedding. A sudden death at the reception precipitates the funeral, at which the heretofore unknown diversity and depth of Charles' inner circle is revealed.

Just when it seems that the scenarist has boxed himself into a corner by climaxing matters with Charles' own wedding (to one of his former girlfriends), out come a string of nifty surprises that may lead to a predictable end but make the viewer squirm with delightful anxiety through the final reel.

Like a good deal of first-rate screwball fare, much of this can be characterized as the comedy of frustration and humiliation. Through the entire first reception, a succession of amusingly imposing guests and restricted situations make it agonizingly difficult for Charles and Carrie to even speak to one another.

At the posh second wedding, not only does Charles have to swallow his disappointment over Carrie's engagement, he must endure a torrent of verbal abuse from his ex-girlfriends, all seated at his table. He then suffers the indignity of being stuck in a bedroom while the nuptial couple sneaks in for a noisy, post-ceremony quickie.

As always, the success of such lighthearted nonsense depends upon the appeal, adeptness and timing of the cast, and it is here that the film really soars.

Since first making his mark in "Maurice," Grant has scored mostly in deftly etched supporting roles, but here he emerges as a first-class romantic *farceur* who, in his ability to absorb innumerable comic arrows with grace, recalls a fellow Briton with the same surname who excelled at this sort of thing some 60 years ago. Grant's got just the combination of good looks, rueful self-disparagement, quickness and bespectacled nerdiness to carry off refined, sophisticated screen comedy.

MacDowell gives her role everything it needs — allure, warmth, a natural breeziness and a worldliness enhanced by romanticism.

As they should in comedy, the supporting players cut vivid figures at the outset and seem like old friends by the end. Simon Callow, James Fleet, John Hannah, Kristin Scott Thomas and Charlotte Coleman all have memorable moments as regulars in the traveling company of celebrants, and David Bower has a couple of choice scenes as Charles' deaf brother. Best of all is Rowan Atkinson, uproarious as a priest who can't quite get the names of the wedding party right.

Displaying full responsiveness to the nuances of the script, director Newell sets a sly tone at once and keeps the characters' humor and libidos bubbling throughout. Tech crew has supplied the film with a lush look that boosts the material. —*Todd McCarthy*

SIRENS

(AUSTRALIAN-BRITISH)

A Miramax release of a WMG-British Screen presentation of a Samson Prods. Two P/L (Sydney)-Sarah Radclyffe Prods.-Sirens Ltd. (London), with the participation of the Australian Film Finance Corp. and the assistance of the N.S.W. Film and Television Office. Produced by Sue Milliken. Executive producers, Justin Ackerman, Hans Brockmann, Robert Jones. Co-producer, Sarah Radclyffe. Directed, written by John Duigan. Camera (color), Geoff Burton; editor, Humphrey Dixon; music, Rachel Portman; production design, Roger Ford; art direction, Laurie Faen; costumes, Terry Ryan; sound, David Lee; assistant director, P.J. Voeten; casting, Liz Mullinar. Reviewed at Village-Roadshow screening room, Sydney, Jan. 13, 1994. (In Sundance Film Festival.) Running time: **94 MIN.**

Rev. Anthony Campion	Hugh Grant
Estella Campion	Tara Fitzgerald
Norman Lindsay	Sam Neill
Sheela	Elle Macpherson
Giddy	Portia de Rossi
Pru	Kate Fischer
Rose Lindsay	Pamela Rabe
Lewis	Ben Mendelsohn
Tom	John Polson
Devlin	Mark Gerber
Jane	Julia Stone
Honey	Ellie MacCarthy
Bishop of Sydney	Vincent Ball

"Sirens," the latest Miramax pickup from the Antipodes, is a deliciously sexy and hedonistic comedy of morals and manners, filmed amid some of Australia's most spectacular scenery. The blend of eroticism and humor, plus the formidable presence of supermodel Elle Macpherson, who is seen regularly in the buff in her featured role as an artist's model, will ensure wide interest in this engaging yarn from writer/director John Duigan.

Though the story here is fictional, it's based on real characters and situations. Sam Neill plays Norman Lindsay, who was, until his death in 1969, a celebrated and controversial Australian painter, sculptor, cartoonist, novelist and writer of children's books (notably the much-loved "The Magic Pudding").

Lindsay's lifelong penchant for featuring voluptuous nude women in his work occasionally got him into hot water. In the early 1930s, when "Sirens" is set, he became embroiled in a controversy over an etching, "The Crucified Venus," which depicted a naked beauty on the cross. (Michael Powell's 1968 film "Age of Consent" was based on a Lindsay book about a painter and his model.)

In Duigan's story, the outraged Anglican Bishop of Sydney (Vincent Ball) is determined to have the offending etching removed from an important art exhibition and instructs a newly arrived Oxford graduate, the Rev. Anthony Campion (Hugh Grant), to journey to Lindsay's home in the picturesque Blue Mountains to convince him the painting must be removed.

Campion, who considers himself a bit of a free thinker, and his young, naive wife, Estella (Tara Fitzgerald), arrive to find the unrepentant artist living with his wife/model, Rose (Pamela Rabe), and three models. Sheela (Macpherson) and Pru (Kate Fischer) are statuesque, supremely self-confident women who enjoy flaunting their frequent nudity, while the younger and shyer Giddy (Portia de Rossi), originally a household servant, refuses to disrobe for a new painting, "Sirens," on which Lindsay is working.

The pompous, patronizing English couple, who are soon stranded because of a train derailment, are at first mildly scandalized at the Lindsays' bohemian lifestyle, the more so as Sheela (an aspiring painter herself) and Pru (a radical socialist) set about provoking them in every way possible. Gradually, however, Estella becomes drawn to the liberated lifestyle of the other women; she befriends the virginal Giddy and, like her, is attracted to Lindsay's male model, a supposedly blind Adonis (Mark Gerber) whose nakedness Estella finds exciting.

Though the film lacks a strong dramatic line, its comic clashes between conservatism and bohemianism in these lush surroundings are beautifully observed. Grant, in a role not dissimilar from the one he played in Polanski's "Bitter Moon," is very funny as the upper-crust Englishman who isn't nearly as enlightened as he thinks he is. Fitzgerald, as the uptight wife who gradually loses her inhibitions, manages the shift from shy to bold with class. Macpherson, who added some weight to play the role of Sheela (Lindsay's models were distinctly Rubenesque) is funny and saucy, and both she and Fischer are stunningly beautiful as the principal models. De Rossi is lovely as the shy girl who gradually drops her guard (and her clothes), and Rabe, as Lindsay's knowing wife, is tart and amusing.

Somewhat less satisfying is Neill's Lindsay, not because of any fault on the part of the actor, but because the role is surprisingly underwritten, so that Lindsay, who should surely have been the central character, is too often shunted to the sidelines.

Duigan injects plenty of humor into this sensual saga, and particularly has fun with Australia's fauna and with the way the local mountain folk behave toward the outrageous Lindsays and their house guests. After "Flirting" and "Wide Sargasso Sea," Duigan must now lay claim to be the reigning sensualist of the Australian cinema, and in this

context his own cameo performance as an earnest village minister, who delivers a pompous sermon, is deliciously funny.

Cinematographer Geoff Burton does a magnificent job in capturing the texture of the place and the time; the film should be a big tourist boost for the Blue Mountain area. Using Lindsay's old home, now an art gallery, for exteriors, Roger Ford's production design convincingly creates the period settings. Rachel Portman's music is delightful, and Humphrey Dixon's editing couldn't have been sharper.

Though totally different in style and mood, "Sirens" echoes "The Piano" in its theme of female emancipation and sexual liberation. It may not score as highly as Jane Campion's prize winner, but there are plenty of elements on which Miramax can pin an enticing campaign for this droll and sexy comedy. —*David Stratton*

KILLING ZOE

A Samuel Hadida presentation of a Davis Film production. (International sales: PFG.) Produced by Samuel Hadida. Executive producers, Becka Boss, Quentin Tarantino, Lawrence Bender. Directed, written by Roger Avary. Camera (CFI color), Tom Richmond; editor, Kathryn Himoff; music, Tomandandy; production design, David Wasco; art direction, Charles Collum; set design, Michael Armani; set decoration, Sandy Reynolds-Wasco; costume design, Mary Claire Hannan; sound (Dolby), Giovanni Di Simone; assistant director, John Vohlers; casting, Rick Montgomery, Dan Parada. Reviewed at the Raleigh Studio, L.A., Dec. 17, 1993. (In Sundance Film Festival.) MPAA Rating: R. Running time: **96 MIN.**

Zed	Eric Stoltz
Zoe	Julie Delpy
Eric	Jean-Hughes Anglade
Oliver	Gary Kemp
Ricardo	Bruce Ramsay
Jean	Kario Salem
Francois	Tai Thai
Claude	Salvator Xuereb
Bank Manager	Gian Carlo Scandiuzzi
Martina	Cecilia Peck
(English and French dialogue)	

If there's a hint of Tarantino in "Killing Zoe," it's well deserved, as the tyro talent shepherded this indie project. However, writer/director Roger Avary is no clone, and "Zoe" is a vivid thriller of a different, more considered tone than anything yet seen from his mentor.

While the comprehension of violence in the film is acute, ironically it represents both its biggest marketing asset and a potential commercial stumbling block. The current domestic moviegoing mood has been cool to this type of action fare, regardless of craft or intelligence. The new offering has both in spades, which can't hurt, and should certainly benefit in ancillary and foreign exploitation.

The yarn finds recently released con Zed (Eric Stoltz) arriving in Paris to do a "job" for a friend. His specialty is cracking safes, and Eric (Jean-Hughes Anglade), the mastermind, has selected a particularly difficult one for him at a large bank. Adding to the degree of difficulty is a plan to hit the establishment in broad daylight, do the deed and get to another continent quickly.

But before getting down to mapping out the details, Zed takes some long overdue R&R with a Parisian professional named Zoe (Julie Delpy). As things later evolve, he could easily have stayed in bed longer. Eric's idea of an orchestrated plan is to walk in, pull out guns and take the money.

The exercise program leading up to the next day's heist is a night of debauchery and abandon. Whoring, alcohol and drugs are all part of the diet. It's not exactly what Zed had envisioned. And while this section seems protracted, it provides an enormous payoff for the subsequent assault.

The bank siege is a botch from the word go. Most of the seven-member team are at less than peak performance following their long night, and the concept of a clean operation is quickly erased when someone is killed. For Zed — whisked away to work on the basement vault and oblivious to the mayhem — matters are complicated when he spots Zoe in her day job as a bank teller.

Obviously an aficionado of the genre, Avary culls from some classics and twists the material into a new form. Though we've seen bank jobs and the like go awry before, it's rather unique to be confronted by an operation so clearly doomed to failure.

The truly chilling aspect of "Killing Zoe" is the correlation Avary makes between the gang's nihilistic attitude and its penchant for violence. He pinpoints the schism in a precise and unnerving manner.

Though set in the French capital, the film was largely filmed on L.A. soundstages to great effect. Tom Richmond's camera work and lighting is particularly outstanding, contributing handsomely to the high-gloss look of the production.

Stoltz is adept as the slightly naive Zed. He transmits a sense of dread that's ably coupled with equal parts of guile and blindness. Delpy displays dignity in a thankless sketch of a character. Zoe exists more as a plot contrivance than an actual plot motor. Also disappointing is Avary's inability to provide clear distinctions and traits among other gang members.

But Anglade proves such a dynamo of energy, these and other shortcomings are quickly obscured. Though Eric is an unquestionably showy role, Anglade is exact in the

weight he invests at every turn of the narrative.

"Killing Zoe" isn't quite a lethal prescription for entertainment. Still, Avary has concocted one of the most assured directing debuts in recent years with a film that demonstrates a one-of-a-kind sensibility well worth watching.

—*Leonard Klady*

BLESSING

A Starr Valley Films production. Produced by Melissa Powell, Paul Zehrer. Executive producer, Christopher A. Cuddihy. Co-executive producer, Mark Bardorf. Directed, written by Zehrer. Camera (Duart color), Stephen Kazmierski; editors, Andrew Morreale, Zehrer; music, Joseph S. Debeasi; production design, Steve Rosenzweig; costume design, Janie Bryant; sound, Derek Felska; associate producer, Joseph Marger; assistant director, Peter D. Bove; casting, Sheila Jaffe, Georgianne Walken, Cassandra Han. Reviewed at Raleigh Studios, L.A., Jan. 11, 1994. (In Sundance Film Festival.) Running time: **94 MIN.**

Randi	Melora Griffis
Arlene	Carlin Glynn
Jack	Guy Griffis
Clovis	Clovis Siemon
Lyle	Gareth Williams
Fran	Randy Sue Latimer
Snuff	Tom Carey
Early	Frank Taylor

A heartfelt, well-characterized study of a hemorrhaging Midwestern farm family, "Blessing" remains too safe and predictable in its naturalistic melodrama to stir reaction beyond sympathy and respect. First feature by writer/director Paul Zehrer creates an utterly believable picture of limited horizons and frustrated desires in America's dairyland, but it lacks the dramatic dimensions to draw much of a paying public. PBS seems a much more congenial destination.

A rural Minnesota native who has most recently worked as a documentary film editor in New York, Zehrer at once establishes a strong affinity for his setting and characters, and the anguish he feels for the restricted options and dried-up lives he depicts is well communicated and never in question.

In this perpetually dark, wet and cold corner of southwestern Wisconsin in early winter, the world is composed of two types of people: those old enough to have already let life pass them by and those still waiting for it to happen.

At 23, Randi (Melora Griffis) is past the point of adolescent rebellion and could easily continue forever milking the cows every morning and waitressing in the local roadhouse.

January 24, 1994 (Cont.)

But exerting the strongest hold is her attachment to her 10-year-old brother Clovis (Clovis Siemon), a sprightly kid who desperately needs her as a buffer between him and their parents.

Ornery and uncommunicative when sober and downright cruel and abusive when drunk, Dad (Guy Griffis, Melora's real father) regularly climbs the silo and spies off into the gray distance, sometimes snapping photos.

Mom (Carlin Glynn) sparks a family crisis by accusing her husband of going up there to spy on the neighbor woman, but otherwise dotes on her cheap religious icons, dreams of winning the lottery and pathetically asks why everyone just can't get along.

Dad has already pushed his eldest son away from home, and when Randi takes a fancy to amiable milkman and astrologer Lyle (Gareth Williams), it doesn't take much more of Dad's meanness to make her want to flee the misery of family life. Simple narrative comes off as both convincing and familiar, as this basic storyline of unbearable familial tensions vs. the intractability of blood ties has been played out countless times before.

What compels the interest is the integrity of the characterizations in both their writing and performance. Not just a farm girl, Randi is very much a product and a symptom of the dysfunctional 1990s, attracted to the basic values of family life but in flight from the intolerable realities of her suffocating parents.

Robustly attractive and with an outgoing nature, Melora Griffis centers the film commendably, believably amplifying the deep conflicts indicated by the script and never seeming preening or theatrical.

Williams is pleasantly appealing as a standard-issue drifter type who rather too pointedly symbolizes Randi's chance of escape. Glynn catches the mother's sad futility, and Guy Griffis cuts a ceaselessly menacing figure as the father. Siemon nicely elicits the hope one needs to have for the youngster.

Tech values are modest.

—*Todd McCarthy*

FLOUNDERING

A Front Films, Inc. presentation. Produced, directed, written by Peter McCarthy. Camera (Foto Kem color); Denis Maloney; editors, Dody Dorn, McCarthy; music, Pray for Rain; production design, Cecilia Montiel; set decoration, Lisa Monti; costumes, Keron Wheeler; sound (Ultra Stereo), Aletha Rodgers; associate producers, Greg Eliason, Kevin Morris; assistant director, Angie Brown; casting, Jeanne McCarthy. Reviewed at the Aidikoff Screening Room, Beverly Hills, Jan. 11, 1993. (In Sundance Film Festival.) Running time: **97 MIN.**
John Boyz	James Le Gros
JC	John Cusack
Jimmy	Ethan Hawke
Jessica	Lisa Zane
Ned	Steve Buscemi
Commander K	Sy Richardson
Gun Clerk	Billy Bob Thornton
Unemployment Clerk	Kim Wayans
Elle	Maritza Rivera
Chief Merryl Fence	Nelson Lyon

Also with: Nina Siemaszko, Jeremy Piven, Ted Raimi, Alex Cox, Brian Wimmer, Biff Yaeger, Jo Harvey Allen, Viggo Mortensen, Exene Cervenka.

There's an appropriate aimless quality to the Sundance entry "Floundering." While the disjointed tale of contemporary alienation doesn't always connect the dots, it has a raw energy and sense of fun that's infectious. The off-kilter nature of the yarn fits nicely into the specialized arena and should find good results domestically and in upscale foreign venues (it's also headed for Berlin's Panorama).

The film also provides actor James Le Gros with a tour-de-force opportunity as the non-hero of the piece. It's a rigorous obstacle course of emotion and incident anchored by a performance of unerring integrity.

John Boyz (Le Gros) is unguided and unemployed in Venice, Calif. He is classically constipated. However, life has somehow begun to intrude and is shaking him to his very core.

The dominoes tumble one by one. First, Internal Revenue freezes his bank account. Then his unemployment benefits run out. Add to the mix a drug-dependent brother in desperate need of rehab, a two-timing girlfriend and a series of closed doors for the complete and dire picture.

This ought to be extremely depressing stuff. But writer/first-time director Peter McCarthy is more interested in allegory than *cinema verite*. Boyz's situation is an amalgam of youthful travail and he is, initially, more observer than participant in this modern "Pilgrim's Progress." That distance, combined with the colorful, if dehumanized, members of civilization he encounters, is absurd and blackly comic.

Just as Boyz must cede to the world he inhabits, it's wise to go with the flow of "Floundering." Though seemingly illogical and complex, the rogue's gallery of revolutionaries, bigots, dead spirits and human automatons makes perfect sense to the pic's protagonist. When the tide turns and he decides to take charge, the result is equally bizarre. The fates have conspired to make the impact of his action as feeble as when he assumed a lethargic pose.

The film is virtually wall-to-wall with dialogue suggesting a lot is being said when the script's thesis is considerably more modest. The rough-hewn nature of the story dovetails snugly with a rather brash visual style. No doubt much of this was accomplished by the decision to shoot on Super 16mm, which also allowed for a quality theatrical blowup.

McCarthy has rounded up quite a stellar cast to populate the tale, with such familiar faces as John Cusack, Ethan Hawke and Steve Buscemi providing effective cameo support. "Floundering" standouts include Lisa Zane as a predatory type and a Brechtian turn from Nelson Lyon as a corrupt police chief.

Though contemporary in setting, the film harks back to the anti-heroes of the 1970s. To the filmmakers' credit, there's no hint of nostalgia. Rather, the appropriate modern nerve has been hit squarely and effectively. —*Leonard Klady*

MARILYN MONROE: LIFE AFTER DEATH

(DOCU — B&W/Color)

A Showtime Networks TV presentation of a Freedman/Greene production. Produced by Anthony Greene. Executive producer, Steven Hewitt. Co-producer, Peter Marshall. Directed, written by Gordon Freedman. Camera (color), Bing Sokolsky; visual consultant, Joshua Greene; editors, Gib Jaffe, Joe Saccone; music, Peter Carl Ganderup; production design, Alan Roderick-Jones; sound, Troy Wilcox; associate producer, Amy McCubbin. Reviewed at Palm Springs Intl. Film Festival, Jan. 14, 1994. Running time: **75 MIN.**
Narrated by Roscoe Lee Brown.
With: Dr. Joyce Brothers, David Brown, Amy Greene, Hugh Hefner, Leon Katz, Norman Mailer, Liz Smith, Donald Spoto, Susan Strasberg, others.

A tribute to the star and sex symbol, "Marilyn Monroe: Life After Death" is an uncritical celebration of the actress's beauty, talent and continuous allure for generations of viewers. Though Gordon Freedman's documentary doesn't shed new information about Monroe's career or life, it contains fabulous stills, some never seen before, by photographer Milton H. Greene. Showtime, which produced the film, will air it this year, and the subject's international fame might warrant limited theatrical release.

Director/writer Freedman, who produced Errol Morris' impressive docu "A Brief History of Time," shrewdly avoids a tedious chronological approach to Monroe's life and instead focuses on some selective issues, such as her gradual rise to stardom and her immortality.

Hugh Hefner discusses how Monroe's nude pictures inspired him to use them as the first Playboy magazine centerfold. Columnist Liz Smith talks about how Hollywood never took Monroe seriously as an actress and poked fun at her when she left for New York and enrolled in acting classes at the Actors Studio. Biographer Donald Spoto highlights Monroe's acting achievements, particularly in "Bus Stop."

Docu's most interesting section details how Monroe's persona has lived on for 30 years after her death — and shows no signs of stopping — beginning with Andy Warhol's pop art and continuing with repeated screenings of her movies. Pic vividly documents the thriving of a merchandising industry — dolls, posters, paintings, mugs, even wine — that has cashed in on and continues to exploit the star's iconographic appeal.

Regrettably, there's no explanation of why Monroe has become such an icon, and pic doesn't distinguish between her various roles as movie star, sex symbol, cultural icon and myth. After 45 minutes or so, docu just repeats — albeit with majestic photos — what was said and shown before.

Producer Anthony Greene and visual consultant Joshua Greene succeed in paying homage to the unique talents of their father, the late Milton H. Greene, as a photographer — and as Monroe's business associate and longtime friend. Digital video enhancement of formerly unprinted stills magnifies Monroe's luminous photogenic qualities.

Ambitious docu aims at honoring Monroe with the respect and dignity she never had, but ultimately it amounts to a handsome presentation of what's already known about the star from numerous articles, books, and exposes.

—*Emanuel Levy*

LA PREDICTION

(THE PREDICTION)

(FRENCH-RUSSIAN)

An AFMD release of a Film Par Film (Paris)/Film Studio Slovo (Moscow) production. Directed, written by Eldar Ryazanov, based on his novel. Camera (color), Valeri Chuvalov; editor, Valeria Berlova; music, Andrei Petrov; art direction, Aleksei Aksenov; sound, Semyon Litvinov; assistant director, Viktor Skuibin. Reviewed at Images d'Ailleurs cinema, Paris, Jan. 7, 1994. Running time: **112 MIN.**

January 24, 1994 (Cont.)

Oleg Gorunov .... Oleg Bassilashvili
Lyuda .... Irene Jacob
Young Oleg .... Andrei Sokulov
Oksana .... Caroline Sihol
Poplavsky .... Aleksei Kharkov
    Also with: Aleksandr Paovtin, Zoya Zelinskaya, Sergei Hartsibachev, Irina Morosova.
    (Russian dialogue)

"The Prediction" is a suspenseful Russian-lingo tale of one eventful day in the life of a famed Moscow writer after a gypsy predicts he's got only 24 hours to live. Good perfs, the glowing presence of actress Irene Jacob ("The Double Life of Veronique") and an intriguing if unevenly executed metaphysical premise should translate into fest showings and specialized tube sales.

The gypsy fortuneteller also predicts that 50-ish Oleg (Oleg Bassilashvili) will have a unique encounter. Returning to his apartment, he finds a handsome, faintly menacing 25-year-old (Andrei Sokulov) who's also a writer, shares his birthday, name and parents, and even has an identical scar over one eye. This youthful alter-ego of Oleg announces he's leaving for Israel the next morning but until then is at the older man's disposal.

As part of the gypsy's prediction has already come true, Oleg senior decides to *carpe diem* like crazy in case the day proves his last. He expresses a desire to avenge his father's murder, and the pair visit the presumed killer, a former KGB thug who's now a decorated professor and whom the fearless young Oleg corners into confessing.

Oleg senior then tracks down young bank teller Lyuda (Jacob), a onetime adoring fan whom he hasn't seen since her marriage to a possessive racketeer. They consummate their love in his country *dacha*, where Jacob strips tenderly by moonlight and the camera sometimes observes from a God's-eye view in the clouds.

Most of the pic's social commentary about how Mother Russia is doomed arrives in force toward the end. The young Oleg offers his travel documents to Oleg senior so he and Lyuda can escape her jealous hubby. The couple make a mad dash to the airport, where a palm-reading gypsy makes another surprising prediction.

The sometimes heavy-handed pic by veteran helmer Eldar Ryazanov can either be read straight as a mystical interlude or be taken as a symbolic treatise on the temptations to abandon a troubled nation. Script implies that young and old together can create something new.

Lensing favors fog and gloom. Arresting images include an eerie funeral procession of taxis for a slain cabby. Comic relief involves a loon who believes Oleg senior should immolate himself in protest and has bought a can of gasoline to facilitate the public sacrifice.
    —Lisa Nesselson

LA LUMIERE DES ETOILES MORTES
(THE LIGHT FROM DEAD STARS)
(FRENCH-GERMAN)

A Les Acacias Cineaudience release of an Ognon Pictures/La Sept Cinema/Varuna Prods. production, with participation of Canal Plus, CNC (France)/Factory Entertainment, Filmstiftung Nordrhein Westfalen, Petit Paris Filmproduktion, Film Forderungsanstalt, Bayerische Landesanstalt fur Aufbaufinanzierung (Germany). Produced by Humbert Balsan. Co-producers, Gloria Burkhert, Andreas Bareiss. Directed by Charles Matton. Screenplay, Charles and Sylvie Matton. Camera (color), Jean-Jacques Flory; editor, Catherine Poitevin; music, Nicolas Matton; production design, Charles Matton; set decoration, Pierre Sicre; costume design, Isabelle Blanc; sound, Dominique Vieillard; model makers, Blanc, Patricia Jouvencel; assistant directors, Christophe Marillier, Nadine Chaussonniere (autumn/winter), Joel Lecussan, Jeremie Joubert (spring/summer). Reviewed at Arlequin Cinema, Paris, Jan. 9, 1994. Running time: **107 MIN.**
Pierre .... Jean-Francois Balmer
Magdeleine .... Caroline Sihol
Beyerath .... Richard Bohringer
Charles .... Leonard Matton
Karl .... Thomas Huber
    (French and German dialogue)

Painter Charles Matton's "The Light From Dead Stars" is artistic in the best sense of the word, melding memory and imagery with bark and bite. Gorgeous, deeply affecting autobiographical account of the 9-year-old helmer's cohabitation with German soldiers when the family home was requisitioned during World War II is the first truly outstanding French pic of 1994.

Film belongs in offshore arthouses but could prove a hard sell to overcome perceptions that it is yet another WWII occupation tale. Matton, a former Esquire illustrator whose two previous pix ("L'Italien des roses" and "L'Amour est un fleuve en Russie") date from the early 1970s, has come up with the kind of movie Proust might have made if he had a Louma crane instead of a fountain pen. Helmer had a hand in everything from casting to color timing, and his search for perfection is consistently rewarded.

Pic begins its trajectory into memory with a fluid pan above a dressed set on a soundstage. Camera lands in the painter's studio, where Matton's voice describes the scene to come as his finger points to a canvas of a lawn, which then transforms into a three-dimensional location, circa June 1940.

Camera swoops around the exterior of a lovely chateau, which it then enters and examines like a hovering spirit. Director as a 9-year-old boy is winningly played by Matton's son Leonard, 10, a pale redhead who renders his father's childhood delights and fears with casual ease.

Young Charles lives with his religion-obsessed older sister, his slightly clairvoyant mother (Catherine Sihol) and two female servants. His father, Pierre (Jean-Francois Balmer), stumbles in, having walked almost 200 miles from Paris. The German occupation of France has just begun.

Balmer (the hapless hubby in Chabrol's "Madame Bovary") is excellent as the Verdun veteran with no further stomach for war who politely welcomes the delegation of German soldiers demanding to be lodged in the family's expansive manse. Until they are called to the Russian front two years later, the Germans share daily life with the Mattons.

Charles becomes close to Karl (Thomas Huber), a French-speaking soldier who believes that killing, though sometimes necessary, is never just. Latter's gifts to the boy include a scale model of a zeppelin and a notebook (from which film gets its title) on the wonders of the cosmos.

Charles' tutor, a Jewish woman who did delicate hand-shadow shows in Germany before the war, teaches her young charge about the magical uses of light and shadow.

Household conflicts are few in the idyllic setting. The housekeeper starts a romance with one of the Germans, but the gap between peaceful coexistence and cruel reality doesn't register until the family's Jewish neighbors are dragged from their stately home and the building is torched.

French thesp Richard Bohringer limns the local casino director, who seems to be a suave capitalist but personally transports Jews into unoccupied France at considerable risk. All other actors, both French and German, are superb.

Jean-Jacques Flory's elegant, expressive lensing honors artifice in the service of memory. Closing sequence, an audacious visual feat, sums up Matton's influences and artistic convictions. *—Lisa Nesselson*

CHACUN POUR TOI
(EVERY MAN FOR YOURSELF)
(FRENCH-GERMAN-CZECH)

A Pan-Europeene release of a MACT Prods., Studio Canal Plus, SFP Cinema, Saris/Lichtblick Produktion/Wega Film production, with participation of Canal Plus/Sofinergie 1 & 2/Cofimage 4/Eurimages. Produced by Antoine and Martine Clermont-Tonnarre. Executive co-producers, Michel Nicolini, Helga Bahr. Directed by Jean-Michel Ribes. Screenplay, Philippe Madral, Ribes. Camera (color), Bernard Dechet, Jean-Paul Meurisse; editor, Olivier Mauffroy; music, Philippe Chatel; art direction, Richard Cunin, Ludvik Siroky; costume design, Juliette Chanaud; sound, Eric Tisserand; hair design, Ghislaine Tortereau; artistic adviser, Dieter Flimm; assistant director, Florence Strauss. Reviewed at MGM/Cannon screening room, Paris, Jan. 6, 1994. Running time: **101 MIN.**
Georges Flavier .... Jean Yanne
Gus .... Albert Dupontel
Roland .... Roland Blanche
Fernande .... Michele Laroque
Louisa .... Catherine Arditi
Botha .... Heinz Schubert
    Also with: Pamela Knaack, Jean Rougerie, Laurent Gamelon, Frank Lapersonne, Marc Andreoni, Roxiane, Milan Dvorak.
    (French, German, Czech and English dialogue)

The fanciful tale of a grizzled hairdresser and the surrogate son he fishes out of a Paris canal, "Chacun pour Toi" sports a delightfully kitsch demeanor and boasts a lovable cast of flamboyant, offbeat characters. Stylish enterprise is an upbeat fest item with possible arthouse potential.

This buoyant buddy film offers an idealized Paris neighborhood full of good-hearted citizens. There's legendary but morose hairdresser Georges (Jean Yanne, in a rock-solid, understated perf), who owns signed photos of Grace Kelly, Ava Gardner and other beauties he once styled; a roly-poly butcher (Roland Blanche) who can't resist mile-high hair on his mistress (Michele Laroque); and a customer who thinks his remaining strands can be convincingly combed over his forehead.

When Georges jumps into a canal to rescue recently jilted plumber Gus (Albert Dupontel) but ends up being rescued himself, it's a soggy start to a beautiful comic friendship in which two defeated men convert resignation into hope.

Georges leads Gus on a tour of the Louvre in which he critiques famous canvases for their hairstyles. He also bawls out a necking couple, declaring that public displays of affection are disheartening for others.

When a colleague breaks his arm, Georges reluctantly agrees to represent France (assisted by Gus) in the World Hairdressing Championships, held in the Czech Republic.

Pic goes practically psychedelic here, with obsessed tress-tweakers whose creations include an Eiffel Tower, a battleship and a burning building.

Certain characterizations on the pic's periphery (two feuding gay hairdressers, a vulgar American femme stylist) will be too broad for some tastes, but this sweet-spirited third feature from prolific playwright Jean-Michel Ribes is as refreshing and appealing as its protagonists.

Philippe Chatel's jaunty score reinforces the far-fetched proceedings. And with his dark, chiseled good looks and slightly spooked gaze, Dupontel recalls a Gallic Monty Clift. —*Lisa Nesselson*

FAREWELL USSR, FILM I, PERSONAL

(RUSSIAN — DOCU)

An Innova Films production. Directed, written by Alexander Rodnyansky. Camera (color), Igor Ivanov; sound, Israel Moizhes. Reviewed at Tradition and Renewal: Jews in the New Europe Intl. Film Series, Lincoln Center, N.Y., Jan. 15, 1994. Running time: **62 MIN.**

The obscure, awkward title of Alexander Rodnyansky's 1992 documentary "Farewell USSR, Film I, Personal" can only hint at the frustrating shortcomings of this occasionally penetrating film. American audiences mining its 62 minutes for insight into the state of Soviet Jewry in the post-Gorbachev era almost certainly will be disappointed.

Film made its New York bow at the annual film series co-sponsored by the Jewish Museum and the Film Society of Lincoln Center. Poorly subtitled and burdened with an impressionistic style that befuddles more than it illuminates, "Farewell USSR" does little to communicate its theme of identity in time of flux.

Rodnyansky focuses his camera on five of his Ukrainian friends — a child-care worker, a Jewish activist, a folk singer, a politician and a pop music stage designer — who, by turns, ponder their commitment to a land that thousands of fellow Jews are fleeing.

Among the filmed interviews and too-lengthy segments of these friends at their respective jobs, Rodnyansky intercuts archival footage of several landmark events.

The images are definitely haunting: A devastating 1961 flood or the mass graveyard of Babyj Jar near Kiev, site of the 1943 massacre of Ukrainian Jews. But their significance will just as certainly be lost on American audiences. Rodnyansky clearly made his film (financed by German television) for an Eastern European audience well-versed in its own history, and pointedly does not provide even the slightest of historical information to accompany the archival footage.

Perhaps, as suggested by the final word of the title, Rodnyansky intended his film as personal musing. Perhaps the subtitles, which even Rodnyansky has conceded are abominable, are at fault. Whatever the case, "Farewell USSR," well-received at last year's St. Petersburg Film Festival, won't find much of an audience Stateside.

—*Greg Evans*

MONTPARNASSE-PONDICHERY

(FRENCH)

A Gaumont Buena Vista Intl. release of a La Gueville/Gaumont/Gaumont Production 2/TF1 Films production, with participation of Canal Plus. Produced by Daniele Delorme, Alain Poire. Directed by Yves Robert. Screenplay, Robert, Frederic Lasaygues. Camera (color), Robert Alazraki; editors, Pierre Gilette, Monique Andre; music, Vladimir Cosma; production design, Jacques Dugied; art direction, Martin Drescher; costume design, Marie-Claude Herry; sound, Pierre Lenoir, William Flageollet; assistant director, Luc Goldenberg. Reviewed at UGC Danton Cinema, Paris, Jan. 15, 1994. Running time: **103 MIN.**
Julie .... Miou-Miou
Leo .... Yves Robert
Bertin .... Andre Dussollier
Raoul Marquet .... Jacques Perrin
Felix .... Maxime Leroux
Mme. Chamot .... Judith Magre

A saccharine, bighearted tale about characters returning to school at an advanced age, Yves Robert's "Montparnasse-Pondichery" is a wholesome tribute to public education that brims with praise for growth and change at every stage of life. Naive but watchable pic should do nicely at Gallic wickets and on the Euro tube.

Julie (Miou-Miou), 40-year-old single mom to a ravishing young daughter, is a successful wallpaper designer who never received her high school diploma. When a dashing commercial consul (Jacques Perrin) invites her to teach print design near his post in Pondichery, India, Julie goes back to school to get the qualification to enable her to accept the job. The students couldn't be nicer, and the class clown sweetly courts her.

Julie breaks up with her devoted but condescending b.f., Felix (Maxime Leroux), gets drunk, then gets lost in the labyrinthine Montparnasse subway station, where she meets Leo (director Robert), a former trumpeter with the Paris Opera. At age 70, he's also studying for a high school diploma, by correspondence, and the two begin a deeply supportive but chaste relationship.

Nearly everything about the story is too good to be true, but characters are appealing and pic's messages of tolerance, anti-ageism and unqualified love are conveyed with energy. The only truly nasty character is a chic, no-nonsense math teacher (Judith Magre) whose name, Chamot, also sounds like the French word for "camel."

Nice touches include teary-eyed Julie and Leo telling their life stories while peeling onions. Ill-advised ones include a rap song that tries way too hard and highlights of the Julie-Leo relationship flashing by at pic's end.

As Julie, Miou-Miou gives a nicely nuanced perf, and 73-year-old helmer Robert ("My Father's Glory") sparkles as the easygoing, grandfather-figure musician. As a devoted philosophy prof, Andre Dussollier in fact gets the most screen time, though the tone of the classroom lectures is mostly prankish and light.

Vladimir Cosma's lively, sometimes dissonant melodies are occasionally invasive. Plentiful close-ups add intimacy and will work well for TV showings. —*Lisa Nesselson*

SIUNIN WONG FEI-HUNG TSI TITMALAU

(THE IRON MONKEY)

(HONG KONG)

A Golden Harvest presentation of a Long Shong Pictures/Film Workshop production. Executive Producer, Tsui Hark. Directed by Yuen Woo-ping. Screenplay, Hark, Tang Pik-yin, Cheung Tan, Lau Tai-muk. Camera (color), Arthur Wong; editor, Mak Chi-sin; martial arts directors, Yuen Woo-ping, Yuen Cheung-yan; associate producer, Raymond Lee. Reviewed at Hoover Cinema 2, Sydney, Dec. 28, 1993. Running time: **87 MIN.**
With: Yu Wing-kwong, Donnie Yen, Wong Tsing-ying, Yam Sai-kun.

This is a spirited but basically familiar martial arts effort that seems to have been inspired by Robin Hood and Zorro pix. It's efficiently made but lacks the originality needed for exposure outside the world's Chinatown circuits.

A corrupt official near the end of the Ching Dynasty period is being harassed by "The Iron Monkey," a masked avenger who steals from the rich and gives to the poor.

The official employs Wong, a stranger who agrees to trap the Monkey in return for a reward, but when Wong discovers the Monkey's identity and realizes he's a good guy, the two team up to clobber the real bad guys.

The plot's just an excuse for almost non-stop chopsocky action, all of it fairly routine. The climactic battle during a fierce fire is the extremely effective action highlight.

Tech credits are par for the course, and the English subtitles are as dire as usual.

—*David Stratton*

BETTER THAN ESCAPE

(YUGOSLAV)

A Klapa (Belgrade) production. (International sales: Vans, Belgrade.) Produced by Jasna Dukic. Directed by Lekic Miroslav. Screenplay, Miroslav, Sinisa Kovacevic. Camera (color), Boris Gortinski; music, Ksenija Zecevic; art direction, Veljko Despotovic; costume design, Mira Cohadzic. Reviewed on vidcassette, Rome, Jan. 11, 1994. Running time: **100 MIN.**
Aleksa .... Zarko Lausevic
Stamena .... Claire Backman
Tale .... Aleksandar Bercek
Isidora .... Renata Ulmanski
Barmaid .... Mirjana Karanovic

A film as technically well made as "Better Than Escape" deserves a better script. This 1991 Yugoslav pic about a talented actor whose life crumbles due to alcoholism verges on melodrama yet lacks the emotional punch that would make it a good weepie.

Pic may have some historical value in highlighting ethnic differences between Serbs and Americans. An American girl of Serbian origin (the adequate Claire Backman) falls for an ambitious young actor (clean-cut hunk Zarko Lausevic) during a vacation in Belgrade. Thanks to her pidgin Serbo-Croatian, much of the dialogue between the two is in English.

Though in general "Escape" contains far too little dramatic conflict, the couple does have a few cultural clashes. She wants to work, he wants her to stay home with the baby. He drinks too much of the local liquor; she wants him to stop.

Lausevic becomes rich and famous from a TV series, while he's esteemed for his brilliant theatrical work. But when the government shuts down a controversial play, he turns to the bottle again and is involved in a fatal car accident. He goes to jail, while his coldhearted wife leaves him and takes their son back to the States.

Though a maudlin conclusion leaves a faint ray of hope, viewers may decide it was better to escape than get this far. —*Deborah Young*

HARIFRAN TILL KOM

(FROM HERE TO KIM)

(SWEDISH)

Sonet Film Ab presents a Kraakbacken Film & TV AB/AB Filmteknik/ Nordiska Film & TV-fond/Spice Entertainment/Spice Filmfinans production. Produced by Lars Egler, Mats Egler. Directed by Lars Egler. Screenplay, Sten Holmberg, Anders Ohlin, based on the novel by Bernt Danielsson. Camera (color), Holmberg; music, Bengt-Arne Wallin; editor, Mats Egler; costumes, Hedvig Ander; sound, Peter Eklund, Jorgen Hasselblad. Reviewed at Rigoletto Cinema, Stockholm, Aug. 10, 1993. Running time: **103 MIN.**

With: Aida Jercovic, Jonas Karlsson, Kristian Almgren, Rolf Skoglund, Lena Dahlman, Lis Nilheim, Reuben Sallmander.

This youth movie with a troubled production history is sympathetic and appealing enough to hit its young target audience.

Director Lars Egler fell ill during the shooting of the film and died shortly thereafter. His brother Mats Egler took over and cut it according to his late brother's wishes.

Result is a film that, unlike other recent Swedish entries aimed at a young audience, treats the youths and their anxieties and problems seriously. Lead character Per is a restless soul who moves to Stockholm from a small country town. He goes to school, befriends the mannerly but mysterious Roffe and, from a distance, falls in love with the beautiful Kim — and finally becomes sufficiently sure of himself to approach the girl of his dreams.

Considering the troubled production, "From Here to Kim" is surprisingly well told. It has its weaknesses; some of the grown-up characters, especially, are more cliches than portraits. But overall tone is so sympathetic, and the depiction of young people's feelings so sincere, that it manages to overcome its faults. —*Gunnar Rehlin*

THE HUDSUCKER PROXY

A Warner Bros. release presented in association with Polygram Filmed Entertainment of a Silver Pictures production in association with Working Title Films. (International distribution: Manifesto.) Produced by Ethan Coen. Executive producers, Eric Fellner, Tim Bevan. Co-producer, Graham Place. Directed by Joel Coen. Screenplay, Ethan Coen, Joel Coen, Sam Raimi. Camera (color), Roger Deakins; editor, Thom Noble; music, Carter Burwell; production design, Dennis Gassner; art direction, Leslie McDonald; set design, Gina Cranham, Tony Fanning, Richard Yanez; set decoration, Nancy Haigh; costume design, Richard Hornung; sound (Dolby), Allan Byer; visual effects supervisor, Michael McAlister; assistant director, Victor Malone; second unit director, Raimi; casting, Donna Isaacson, John Lyons. Reviewed at Sundance Film Festival, Park City, Jan. 27, 1994. MPAA Rating: PG. Running time: **111 MIN.**

Norville Barnes	Tim Robbins
Amy Archer	Jennifer Jason Leigh
Sidney J. Mussberger	Paul Newman
Waring Hudsucker	Charles Durning
Chief	John Mahoney
Buzz	Jim True
Moses	William Cobbs
Smitty	Bruce Campbell
Lou	Joe Grifasi
Benny	John Seitz
Beatnik Barman	Steve Buscemi
Vic Tenetta	Peter Gallagher

"The Hudsucker Proxy" is no doubt one of the most inspired and technically stunning pastiches of old Hollywood pictures ever to come out of the New Hollywood. But a pastiche it remains, as nearly everything in the Coen brothers' latest and biggest film seems like a wizardly but artificial synthesis of aspects of vintage fare, leaving a hole in the middle where some emotion and humanity should be.

In an unlikely pairing of two of America's most idiosyncratic artists with Joel Silver's production company, and costing somewhere in the vicinity of $40 million, this reps by far the Coens' biggest commercial roll of the dice. Some top reviews and strong support from Warner Bros. should lead to decent mid-level B.O. upon pic's release March 11, but its pleasures are a tad esoteric for widespread mainstream acceptance.

The Coens' one distinct commercial success, "Raising Arizona," was their one film most recognizably set in a real world inhabited by working-class characters. The rest have taken place in a relatively stylized and remote gangster milieu ("Blood Simple," "Miller's Crossing") or a brilliantly designed capital of industry (Hollywood in "Barton Fink," New York here) in which little people are manipulated and buffeted about by the string pullers.

"Hudsucker" plays like a Frank Capra film with a Preston Sturges hero and dialogue direction by Howard Hawks. Startling opening sequence recalls "Meet John Doe" and "It's a Wonderful Life," as a desperate young man prepares to jump from a Manhattan skyscraper at midnight on a snowy New Year's Eve, 1958-59.

Flash back a few months and the same young man, Norville Barnes (Tim Robbins), literally bright-eyed, bushy-haired and straight off the bus from Muncie, Ind., is hitting the pavement looking for work. He lands a mailroom job at the enormous Hudsucker Industries just as the successful company's founder (Charles Durning) less decorously hits the pavement after pirouetting out of the boardroom's 44th-floor window.

In a pristine example of one of Sturges' dufus heroes having "greatness thrust upon him," Norville is installed as the firm's president by the cigar-chomping Machiavellian executive Sidney J. Mussberger (Paul Newman), who intends to forestall a public takeover by lowering investor confidence, thereby driving down the price of shares and allowing the board to purchase a controlling interest.

Initially, this strategy works well, especially when hot-shot, tough-talking, Pulitzer Prize-winning reporter Amy Archer (Jennifer Jason Leigh), after worming her way into Norville's confidence and employ, exposes him in an article headlined "Imbecile Heads Hudsucker."

Twisting him around her little finger a hundred times, this dizzyingly clever impostor is Barbara Stanwyck's "Lady Eve" to Norville's Henry Fonda in Sturges' romantic comedy classic, right down to the very verbal seduction. But Norville surprises one and all when, after having baffled everyone with the design of his brainstorm — a simple circle on a piece of paper — he pushes through on his invention "for kids," the hula hoop.

The huge success of "the dingus" deals an unexpected setback to Mussberger's scheme, but for him, "business is war," and it isn't long before he hatches another plot to bring Norville down for good.

Plotwise, it's all been done before: The little man goes up against the evil titans of big business (or government) and gets ground up, only to prevail through his own native ingenuity and decency, and the hard-bitten career woman rediscovers her vulnerability through the love of a simple, good-hearted man. The Coens, and their co-screenwriter this time out, Sam Raimi, aren't saying anything new here.

So it's the way they say it that commands attention, and for connoisseurs of filmmaking style and technique, "Hudsucker" is a source of constant delight and occasional thrills. The Coens' approach, in large measure, consists of the fabulous and ornate elaboration of small details and moments; they make entire jaw-dropping sequences out of incidents that other directors would slide right by.

Three such scenes are an outrageous memory flashback in which Mussberger, literally hanging by a thread over the street far below, becomes sure he won't fall by recalling how his tailor double-stitched his pants; the movement of pneumatic mail capsules through tubes lacing Hudsucker h.q. and, best of all, an incredible episode detailing how the hula hoop became a national sensation.

Throughout, the rhythms of Thom Noble's editing are extraordinary, the montage on a par with just about any classic examples one could cite. This, on top of the orchestration of the other superior elements — Dennis Gassner's formidable architectural production design, Richard Hornung's impeccable costume designs that draw upon diverse periods, Roger Deakins' moody yet vivid cinematography and, perhaps best of all, Carter Burwell's sumptuously supportive score — must certainly establish the Coens among the most imaginative and supple craftsmen of the cinema.

But rehashes of old movies, no matter how inspired, are almost by definition synthetic, and the fact is that nearly all the characters are constructs rather than human beings with whom the viewer can connect. With his gangly frame and appealing pie face, Robbins calls to mind Gary Cooper and Jimmy Stewart, but there's no authentic sweetness or strength underneath all his doltishness to make him seem like a good guy the audience can get behind.

Partly for this reason, no rooting interest develops in the curious romance between Norville and Amy. Leigh skillfully plays the latter with a Katharine Hepburn accent, Rosalind Russell's rat-a-tat-tat speed in "His Girl Friday" and Stanwyck attitude in a lot of things, but the character never seems quite right, although her habit of slugging guys whenever they make the slightest suggestive remark is good for a number of laughs.

Beautifully decked out and speaking with a pronounced rasp in his voice, Newman is elegant and mean but never seems entirely, deeply evil in the old Edward Arnold fat-cat role. Durning has delicious fun with his few moments as the departing tycoon and does his share to make the climactic sequence — when the film returns to see what happens to Norville on the ledge — a doozy.

William Cobbs has some wonderful moments as the man who runs

Hudsucker's giant clock and knows all, and Peter Gallagher, all too briefly, is uproarious as a Dean Martin-like singer.

—*Todd McCarthy*

I'LL DO ANYTHING

A Columbia Pictures release of a Gracie Films production. Produced by James L. Brooks, Polly Platt. Executive producer, Penney Finkelman Cox. Directed, written by Brooks. Camera (Technicolor color), Michael Ballhaus; editor, Richard Marks; music, Hans Zimmer; production design, Stephen J. Lineweaver; art direction, Bill Brzeski; set decoration, Cheryl Carasik; costume design, Marlene Stewart; sound (Dolby), David M. Kelson; associate producer, Marks; assistant director, Ned Dowd; unit production manager, John D. Schofield; casting, Paula Herold. Reviewed at the Cary Grant Theatre, Culver City, Jan. 14, 1994. MPAA Rating: PG-13. Running time: **115 MIN.**

Matt Hobbs .... Nick Nolte
Jeannie Hobbs .... Whittni Wright
Burke Adler .... Albert Brooks
Nan Mulhanney .... Julie Kavner
Cathy Breslow ...... Joely Richardson
Beth Hobbs .... Tracey Ullman
Male D Person .... Jeb Brown
Female D Person .... Joely Fisher

Destined to be known forever in industry circles as the musical that wasn't, James L. Brooks' showbiz comedy hits occasional high notes on the laugh scale but suffers from a choppiness that betrays its history. While reasonably entertaining and sharply written, "I'll Do Anything" never appears certain what it aims to do and may be best suited to the art-house circuit, making its $40 million production tab a major liability.

Given its origins, the movie is better than one might have anticipated yet has to be viewed as a disappointment relative to Brooks' earlier features.

For those who've been living in a cave or, worse, not reading the trades, Brooks — having raised eyebrows initially by casting such dubious crooners as Nick Nolte and Albert Brooks — finally junked the musical numbers after test audiences voted thumbs down, shooting new material and turning "Anything" back into a multitiered romantic comedy.

While what survived the editing room is watchable, there's an inescapable sense that something's missing, as the movie lacks smoothness in making transitions from scene to scene and relationship to relationship.

Nolte plays a rarely employed actor, Matt Hobbs, who's saddled with his 6-year-old daughter (Whittni Wright) after his ex (Tracey Ullman) is shipped off to prison.

Desperate to make a living, and uncomfortable tending to the fit-prone moppet, Matt settles for work chauffeuring around Burke Adler (Albert Brooks) — a self-obsessed, hyperkinetic producer of schlocky blockbusters — in the process becoming entangled with comely if insecure development executive Cathy (Joely Richardson).

Producing, writing and directing his first feature since "Broadcast News" in 1987, Brooks displays his characteristic ear for dialogue, particularly in lines spouted by the other Brooks, who inexplicably becomes involved with a divorced test-marketing researcher, Nan (Julie Kavner).

The story, however, flits awkwardly between Matt's relationship with his daughter, his budding ties to Cathy and the Burke-Nan pairing, often with little to connect those strands.

While the father-and-daughter reunion serves as the film's core, the child is so unpleasant at first it's hard to root for things to work out. In addition, that premise — out-of-work actor raising smart-alecky daughter — at times feels like a wacky sitcom struggling to get out, even if the material operates on a higher plane.

Brooks fares better milking laughs from his depiction of Hollywood eccentricities, though some of those keenly observed moments may not play well east of the San Bernardino Mountains. While not as fiercely inside as "The Player," it's doubtful a Des Moines housewife, for example, will appreciate the indignity of having one's phone calls returned during the lunch hour.

The ongoing obsession with research also proves more than a little ironic, as Burke tinkers with his latest cranked-up exercise in cinematic machismo. In fact, Brooks uses a smarmy development exec (Jeb Brown) to evince disdain for those who bring such a passionless approach to filmmaking, though the scenes appear to be there more to make that point than service the plot.

Nolte solidly conveys Matt's acting fervor, but his character, in particular, seems to have suffered from the editing process. Wright, discovered via a months-long talent search, looks adorable but says little to make her seem that way, and her ultimate conversion feels too quick and hollow.

On the plus side, almost every moment with Brooks' Burke provides a terrific howl, and Richardson is extremely appealing as the wide-eyed and confused Cathy — a character, again, who demonstrates the business's artistic bankruptcy,

lacking the courage to support convictions and ideas.

Though both are gifted comic actresses, Kavner and Ullman (who, along with Harry Shearer, have been players in Brooks' TV empire) each seem a bit miscast. Rosie O'Donnell, Woody Harrelson and Ian McKellen turn up in cameos.

Tech credits are top-notch, capturing such discrepancies as Burke's posh abode and Matt's grungy apartment. Hans Zimmer provides an effective score, albeit one that works too hard in places at turning up the emotional volume.

Although the pic at one point included tunes penned by Prince and Sinead O'Connor, the only song remaining of any note — "You Are the Best," written by Carole Bayer Sager and sung by Wright — sounds like a Sesame Street ditty, providing jaunty accompaniment to the closing credits but hardly reason to pine for the missing soundtrack.

—*Brian Lowry*

CAR 54, WHERE ARE YOU?

An Orion Pictures release of a Robert H. Solo production. Produced by Solo. Supervising producer, John M. Eckert. Directed by Bill Fishman. Screenplay, Erik Tarloff, Ebbe Roe Smith, Peter McCarthy, Peter Crabbe; story by Tarloff. Based on the TV series created and produced by Nat Hiken. Camera (Deluxe color), Rodney Charters; editors, Alan Balsam, Earl Watson; music, Pray for Rain, Bernie Worrell; production design, Catherine Hardwicke; art decoration, Gregory P. Keen; set decoration, Anthony Greco; costume design, Margaret M. Mohr; sound (Dolby), Peter Shewchuk; assistant director, Michael Zenon; casting, Eliza Simons. Reviewed at the Orion screening room, L.A., Jan. 10, 1994. MPAA Rating: PG-13. Running time: **89 MIN.**

Gunther Toody .... David Johansen
Francis Muldoon ...... John C. McGinley
Velma Velour .... Fran Drescher
Capt. Dave Anderson ... Nipsey Russell
Lucille Toody .... Rosie O'Donnell
Don Motti .... Daniel Baldwin
Herbert Hortz .... Jeremy Piven
Carlo .... Bobby Collins
Nicco .... Louis Di Bianco
Leo Schnauzer .... Al Lewis

At least we know now why this latest big-screen version of a vintage TV series was parked on the shelf more than two years. Crude, virtually laughless and aimed at a target audience that's probably never heard of the source material, "Car 54" should have a short patrol of theaters before being towed away to the vacant lot of "10 worst" lists. Translate the show's trademark "Oo! Oo!" into an "Uh-oh" for Orion.

Based on the goofy NBC series starring Joe E. Ross and Fred Gwynne that ran from 1961-63, the movie seems misguided from the

start, since the show never enjoyed the lingering appeal of other, higher-profile sitcoms. Efforts to "contemporize" the series only demonstrate how little there was on which to build a movie and the creative bankruptcy of the filmmakers, who rely on bad puns, an abusive rap score and scads of crotch-level humor.

David Johansen plays Gunther Toody, a none-too-bright patrolman in Brooklyn's tough 53rd precinct who gets paired with straight-laced Francis Muldoon (John C. McGinley) after his partner, Leo (Al Lewis, a holdover from the original series along with Nipsey Russell), retires.

Toody tries to loosen up Muldoon by introducing him to a femme fatale, Velma Velour (Fran Drescher). Meanwhile, the pair get involved in protecting a witness (Jeremy Piven) being held to testify against claustrophobic Mafia kingpin Don Motti (Daniel Baldwin).

Director Bill Fishman, who made his motion picture debut with the quirky "Tapeheads," and a quartet of writers can't stick with a plot, so half the scenes are incomprehensible. In the same vein, the closing credits include moments seemingly excised from the movie that aren't outtakes — although, admittedly, it would be hard to ascertain what is. Johansen — an odd choice for the lead, aside from his vague resemblance to Ross — and Rosie O'Donnell, as Mrs. Toody, perform at such a shrill level they're nearly unwatchable, and the rest of the cast fares little better. Even the series' quaint song never appears in its entirety, with snippets of it merged into a bastardized rap version. Johansen does utter one "Oo! Oo!," albeit in off-color fashion. Tech credits, from the dank lighting to drab sets, underscore the general sense of torpor. Barring a major tuneup, "Car 54" should have been left on the blocks. —*Brian Lowry*

January 31, 1994 (Cont.)

SUNDANCE

BACKBEAT
(BRITISH)

A Gramercy Pictures release of a Polygram Filmed Entertainment and Scala Prods. presentation in association with Channel Four Films of a Scala/Woolley/Powell/Dwyer and Forthcoming production. Produced by Finola Dwyer, Stephen Woolley. Executive producer, Nik Powell. Line producer, Paul Cowan. Directed by Iain Softley. Screenplay, Softley, Michael Thomas, Stephen Ward. Camera (color), Ian Wilson; editor, Martin Walsh; original score composed, produced by Don Was; music supervisor, Bob Last; production design, Joseph Bennett; art direction, Michael Carlin, Joseph Plagge (Hamburg); costume design, Sheena Napier; sound (Dolby), Chris Munro; assistant director, Mary Soan; casting, John and Ros Hubbard, Dianne Crittenden, Vicky Hinrichs (Hamburg).
Reviewed at the Aidikoff Screening Room, Beverly Hills, Dec. 21, 1993. (In Sundance Film Festival.) MPAA Rating: R. Running time: **100 MIN.**
Astrid Kirchherr .... Sheryl Lee
Stuart Sutcliffe .... Stephen Dorff
John Lennon .... Ian Hart
Paul McCartney .... Gary Bakewell
George Harrison .... Chris O'Neill
Pete Best .... Scot Williams
Klaus Voormann .... Kai Wiesinger
Cynthia Powell .... Jennifer Ehle

The early, pre-fame days of the Beatles are a great subject for a film, but the potential has been only partly realized in "Backbeat." This energetic, dramatically potent look at the band's Hamburg days, with special emphasis on the little-known original fifth Beatle, Stuart Sutcliffe, has quite a bit going for it in the way of cultural and musical history but lacks a crucial, heightened artistic quality and point of view that would have given it real distinction. Various promotable elements should translate into decent B.O., perhaps more so in the U.K. and Europe and on video than in U.S. theaters.

Spanning the years 1960-62, just before Beatlemania broke out in Britain, rock video and docu director Iain Softley's first feature looks at how the world's first supergroup got it together musically, personally and image-wise during its wild days and nights in Germany.

More intensely, the screenplay focuses on John Lennon's relationship with his best friend, Sutcliffe, a young man of James Dean looks but little musical ability who left the group to pursue his muse as a painter and his love affair with Astrid Kirchherr, a young German photographer who had a lot to do with creating the long-haired look that shortly swept the world.

It's a tumultuous tale, populated by soon-to-be mega-celebrities in the early throes of love, jealousy, the dawning of talent and genius and the discovery of self, all set against a backdrop enormously pregnant with the promise of what came after — namely, all of pop culture from the 1960s to the present. The strong feeling that this is where it all began is inescapable throughout. Opening reel is set in Liverpool, 1960, where John and Stu are beat up outside a nightclub and then organize their trip to Hamburg to play in a band with Paul McCartney, George Harrison and drummer Pete Best.

Next 45 minutes unspool in Hamburg, where the boys begin their careers in a sleazy bar in the Reeperbahn. When artist Klaus Voorman brings his girlfriend, Astrid, to the club, she and Stu immediately connect, and Astrid introduces the Englishmen to her avant-garde existentialist scene, a forerunner of 1960s trends toward drugs, bisexuality and anything-goes cool.

Railing against the pretenses of these self-conscious hipsters, John develops a resentment of Astrid, who shortly throws Klaus over for dreamy Stu.

As the group begins moving up via better gigs and an offer to record, Paul begins insisting that Stu shape up or get out of the group. Stu eventually gets in deeper with his art and with Astrid. Finally admitting that Paul is a much better bass player than he is, Stu leaves the band without regrets, although John reproaches him: "They'll say, 'There goes Stu Sutcliffe. He could have been in the Beatles.'"

All of this holds the interest, but the film's looming shortcoming is the lack of a solid point of view on these culturally momentous events.

For the most part, pic has been well cast. Returning as Lennon after his successful outing in "The Hours and Times," Ian Hart is again terrifically effective, catching John's rebellious attitude (his catch-all putdown is "It's all dick"), and this time including his demanding professionalism and sense of destiny.

American actor Stephen Dorff also scores strongly as Sutcliffe, a cool cat, ladies' favorite and tortured soul who chooses his own, more difficult and lonely road.

More problematic is Sheryl Lee (Laura Palmer of "Twin Peaks") as Astrid. Lee looks too much like the well-scrubbed Midwestern cheerleader type to be truly convincing as an alluring, off-the-map sophisticated Continental bohemian, which robs the film of some essential mystery and heat at its core.

Gary Bakewell and Chris O'Neill provide good representations of Paul and George, while Scot Williams' Best remains opaque.

A power group comprised of Greg Dulli, Don Fleming, Dave Grohl, Mike Mills, Thurston Moore and Dave Pirner does almost too good a job covering the rock 'n' roll standards the Beatles played in those years, in that it's hard to believe the band was as accomplished in 1960 as it's made out to be here.

Production values are a bit threadbare, and pic lacks a strong visual style.   —*Todd McCarthy*

GO FISH

A Can I Watch Pictures production in association with KVPI. Produced by Rose Troche, Guinevere Turner. Executive producers, Tom Kalin, Christine Vachon. Directed, edited by Troche. Screenplay, Turner, Troche. Camera (b&w), Ann T. Rossetti; music, Brendan Dolan, Jennifer Sharpe, Scott Aldrich; sound, Missy Cohen; associate producer, V.S. Brodie; assistant director, Wendy Quinn. Reviewed at Sundance Film Festival, Park City, Utah, Jan. 22, 1994. Running time: **85 MIN.**
Ely .... V.S. Brodie
Max .... Guinevere Turner
Kia .... T. Wendy McMillan
Evy .... Migdalia Melendez
Daria .... Anastasia Sharp

Rose Troche makes an auspicious debut as director, co-writer and editor of "Go Fish," a fresh, hip comedy about contemporary lifestyles within the lesbian community. Theatrical prospects are excellent for an all-female picture that is sharply observed, visually audacious and full of surprising charms. A shrewd marketing campaign should broaden the appeal of enormously likable comedy beyond the gay and lesbian markets, particularly among young urban viewers.

The most refreshing dimension of "Go Fish" is that it's not dealing with coming out and is not burdened with the stiff, sanctimonious tone of such lesbian films as "Claire of the Moon." Instead, the point of departure of scripters Troche and Guinevere Turner is that women can — and do — live emotionally fulfilling lives in lesbian communities, without being stigmatized.

The comedy is off to a good start when Kia (T. Wendy McMillan), a mature black professor, is speculating with her students about who might be lesbian in American society. Kia, who is romantically involved with Evy (Migdalia Melendez), a divorcee, would like Max (Turner), her younger, energetic roommate, to meet a girl. She decides to set her up with Ely (V.S. Brodie), an ex-student of hers who's in the process of terminating a long-distance relationship.

Through cross-cutting between the Max and Ely households, the well-written comedy conveys the folklore that women share when there are no men around — sort of a current, lesbian version of Gregory La Cava's "Stage Door," though a far cry from George Cukor's "The Women," two Hollywood classics dominated by women.

The whole story builds up to an hilarious date between Ely and Max, with their friends insisting on getting all the dirty details. In one of the film's strongest — and most political — scenes, a woman who committed the "sin" of sleeping with a man is abducted by militant lesbians and subjected to trial.

Small in scale but full of truthful insights, "Go Fish" is charged with a fierce intelligence about how lesbians actually live. The narrative unfolds as a series of vignettes that chronicle the daily routines of these women: their hopes, anxieties, romances — and sex lives. Troche's lovely touches are especially evident in the way she shows the characters' healthy sensuality. It's to her credit that sex in the 1990s is treated in the most natural fashion, without condescending to any of the characters, including the perpetually horny Daria (Anastasia Sharp).

As director, Troche elicits perfectly natural performances from her mostly non-professional ensemble. The performers' mixture of strong physical presence and light self-mockery helps set the film's quirky, offbeat mood. As the central couple, Turner and Brodie inhabit rather than play their roles by projecting an inner verve and verbal charm. Their self-absorption and zany antics add up to something marvelously inventive — and authentic.

Tricked out with a kinetic wit, "Go Fish" is replete with flashy montages and dissolves, yet the tempo is swift and smooth. As editor, Troche brings snap to the storytelling, particularly in her letter-perfect intercutting of the various glances — lusty, duplicitous, suspicious — that the women exchange. She's greatly assisted by Ann Rossetti's stylized black-and-white cinematography. Though stylish flourishes are everywhere, the film manages to maintain its semblance of humanity and compassion.

In moments, "Go Fish" turns too cutesy for its own good — some one-liners are thrown in just because they're funny. And the film's last sequence, a montage of beautiful women making love, is unnecessarily long and turns the comedy into an agenda movie, which otherwise it is not.

These are minor complaints, however, for a film whose characters are so likable and sympathetic that it's bound to win over viewers who might initially be suspicious of an all-out lesbian film. Highly entertaining and always light on its feet, "Go Fish" is unmistakably one of the Sundance Festival's popular hits.   —*Emanuel Levy*

CLERKS

(B&W — 16mm)

A View Askew production. Produced by Kevin Smith, Scott Mosier. Directed, written by Smith. Camera (b&w), David Klein; editors, Mosier, Smith; music, Scott Angley; sound, Mosier. Reviewed at Sundance Film Festival, Park City, Utah, Jan. 22, 1994. Running time: **103 MIN.**

Dante	Brian O'Halloran
Randal	Jeff Anderson
Veronica	Marilyn Ghigliotti
Caitlin	Lisa Spoonhauer
Jay	Jason Mewes
Silent Bob	Kevin Smith
Willam the Idiot Manchild	Scott Mosier

The "Slacker" generation is alive and well in "Clerks," a randy, irreverent, slice-of-life no-budgeter that's played for laughs and gets them. This view of the world from behind the counter at a no-account convenience store is both appealingly minimalist and amusingly deadpan, and will strike a sympathetic chord with Generation Xers and indie film buffs, indicating a reasonable future on the urban and college-town specialized circuit.

Allegedly the cheapest picture in Sundance this year at $27,000 and made by a film school dropout who was actually working at a convenience store during production, pic chronicles a day in the life of Quick Stop Groceries, a pit stop for assorted loafers, layabouts, weirdos, ne'er-do-wells and derelicts in Springsteen Country, or Asbury Park, N.J.

Called to fill in at the store on his day off, 22-year-old Dante (Brian O'Halloran) barely has the place open at 6 a.m. before being confronted with an anti-smoking maniac who scares off a slew of potential patrons with his tirades.

Shortly, Dante's girlfriend, Veronica (Marilyn Ghigliotti), turns up and incites a huge argument when she informs him how many men she's had oral sex with. More customers are put off by Dante's antagonistic friend Randal (Jeff Anderson), who runs the adjacent video store, and before the day is over a circus's worth of mangy humanity has paraded through the establishment seeking sustenance of the edible, physical and emotional varieties.

At first, given the naturalistic environment, non-pro actors and bargain-basement black-and-white look, the rapid-fire comic delivery of the abundant dialogue sounds rather jarringly artificial; what with the films of Richard ("Slacker") Linklater, Jim Jarmusch, Hal Hartley and Spike Lee as influences acknowledged in the credits, one doesn't expect banter that seems as though it was honed in vaudeville.

But once the adjustment is made, pic sails along smoothly, as what amount to blackout sketches run the gamut from absurdist comedy and low-key social commentary to outrageously smutty gags and rude, off-the-wall remarks.

Although arbitrarily divided into sections sporting such chapter headings as "Syntax," "Vagary" and "Malaise," pic feels much more slapdash and less self-consciously aesthetic than its spiritual forebears. With no narrative per se and nothing holding it together except unity of time and place, it's surprising that "Clerks" plays as well, and consistently, as it does, with very little down time.

Based on the quick, attitudinally attuned humor the script reveals in abundance, writer/director Kevin Smith could probably as easily get a job writing for "Saturday Night Live" as make another film. But he's obtained fine timing from his amateur cast, and the impudence and boldness of his comic strategies are impressive, especially sustained over a slightly overlong feature running time.

Technically elementary but still perfectly watchable, "Clerks" is a grunge movie par excellence.

—*Todd McCarthy*

THE INKWELL

A Buena Vista release of a Touchstone presentation of an Irving Azoff production. Produced by Azoff, Guy Riedel. Executive producer, Jon Jashni. Directed by Matty Rich. Screenplay, Tom Ricostronza, Paris Qualles. Camera (Continental Labs color; Technicolor prints), John L. Demps Jr.; editor, Quinnie Martin Jr.; music, Terence Blanchard; production design, Lester Cohen; art direction, Daniel Talpers; costume design, Ceci; sound (Dolby), Robert L. Warner; associate producer, Matthew Baer; assistant director, Tyrone L. Mason; casting, Chemin Sylvia Bernard. Reviewed at Sundance Film Festival, Park City, Utah, Jan. 25, 1994. Running time: **110 MIN.**

Drew Tate	Larenz Tate
Kenny Tate	Joe Morton
Brenda Tate	Suzzanne Douglas
Spencer Phillips	Glynn Turman
Francis Phillips	Vanessa Bell Calloway
Heather Lee	Adrienne-Joi Johnson
Harold Lee	Morris Chestnut
Lauren Kelly	Jada Pinkett
Jr. Phillips	Duane Martin
Evelyn	Mary Alice
Dr. Wade	Phyllis Yvonne Stickney

Matty Rich struggles through the sophomore jinx in "The Inkwell," a conventionally plotted, often buffoonish coming-of-age tale that nevertheless imparts a distinctive flavor. Both the storyline and the filmmaking are routine, even awkward at times, but this look at an upscale black enclave on Martha's Vineyard, circa 1976, unarguably provides a look at an aspect of the black experience that neither black nor white audiences have seen before. Disney won't be able to use reviews to help sell this one, and it's not funny enough to market it as an outright comedy, so only B.O. chances rest with blacks on the lookout for something different and possibly with crossover teen viewers.

The youthful Rich, who scored at Sundance a couple of years back with the heartfelt, autobiographical "Straight Out of Brooklyn," about the difficulties of family life in the projects, goes far afield from his own background for this odd, mixed-tone outing that, at its embarrassing worst, plays like a combo of "Summer of '42" and "Porky's," but at other moments has a curious, if limited, cultural poignance.

After accidentally burning down his parents' house, 16-year-old Drew Tate (Larenz Tate) is taken from his lower-middle-class upstate New York environs to spend two weeks with relatives on Martha's Vineyard. His parents, Kenny (Joe Morton), a still-militant former Black Panther, and Brenda, are concerned about their boy's social awkwardness and infantile behavior (he always carries around a little doll he talks to), a problem put in greater relief when they arrive in Massachusetts.

Drew's uncle Spencer (Glynn Turman) and aunt Francis (Vanessa Bell Calloway) are so Republican that they even keep a portrait of Richard Nixon on the wall of their opulent beachside home. Their teen-age son (Duane Martin) is a self-styled ladies' man who tools around with two loutish buddies and tries to provoke poor Drew to come on to every girl they see.

Anyone who enjoyed the hilarious mid-1970s art direction and costumes in "Dazed and Confused" will get a double dose of pleasure here, as the Inkwell, a section of the island inhabited by blacks who have made it ("boogie niggers as far as the eye can see," as the jaundiced Kenny puts it), offers up a wonderful collection of "Soul Train" fashions and blinding color schemes, all in an anachronistically genteel setting.

While the two older men argue politics, Jr. and his stooges lead Drew on some silly escapades, such as to a nudist beach. On his own, Drew befriends Heather (Adrienne-Joi Johnson), a nice lady whose husband, Drew discovers, is flagrantly cheating on her, and also spends a lovely day and night with the town's reigning teen beauty, Lauren (Jada Pinkett), leading him to develop some far-reaching romantic fantasies. A la "Summer of '42," things work out for Drew, but not in the way he anticipated.

The unusual cultural backdrop aside, the story's unfolding is wildly routine, as it's packed with the sort of teen-age pranks, emotional shocks and dawning recognitions that rep the usual baggage of the coming-of-age genre. Nor does Rich stage the comedy very well, so that when the laughs don't come, there's a lot of unwanted dead air.

Similarly, the disputes among the adults are handled in an over-the-top, ham-fisted way, particularly when it involves the manically caricatured Spencer, who sports a cigarette holder and struts about, in Turman's mugging performance, as if he owns the secret of the world because he's managed to separate himself from other blacks.

Pic's dullest moments, which could profitably be excised, involve Drew's completely uninteresting therapy with a local lady doctor.

Still, despite all the missteps, predictability and general clunkiness, there's a certain sweetness behind the story and its handling that elicits viewer sympathy and goodwill. It's also nice to see a broadening of the range of black stories on the screen, and this one certainly takes audiences to a destination never before visited.

Newcomer Tate has an easy, open presence as Drew, while remainder of the cast is proficient.

Project's schizophrenia can largely be ascribed to its screenwriting history. Credited co-scenarist "Tom Ricostronza" is a pseudonym for Trey Ellis, a black novelist who removed his name from the project once Rich and new writer Paris Qualles moved too far away from his original, more dramatic, intentions.

Actually shot in Swansboro, N.C., rather than on Martha's Vineyard, pic boasts nice settings but a rather garish look. Rich still has quite a ways to go to become a sophisticated filmmaker, but the second feature is very often the hardest.

Next time out will be the occasion to make a real jump.

—*Todd McCarthy*

NINA TAKES A LOVER

A Sharona Prods. presentation. Produced by Jane Hernandez, Alan Jacobs. Executive producers, Graeme Bretall, Shelby Notkin. Directed, written by Jacobs. Camera (Monaco Labs color), Phil Parmet; editor, John Nutt; music, Todd Boekelheide; production design, Don De Fina; set decoration, Victoria Lewis; costume design, Marianna Astrom-De Fina; sound, Dan Gleich; associate producer, Clarisse Perrette; assistant director, Frank Simeone; casting, Richard Pagano, Sharon Bialy, Debi Manwiller. Reviewed at Sundance Film Festival, Park City, Utah, Jan. 22, 1994. Running time: **100 MIN.**

Nina	Laura San Giacomo
Photographer	Paul Rhys
Journalist	Michael O'Keefe
Friend	Cristi Conaway
Paulie	Fisher Stevens

"**N**ina Takes a Lover" is a nicely made, very slight little trick of a love story. A meditation on the eternal question of what happens to passion over the course of a marriage, Alan Jacobs' directorial debut displays intelligence and professional sheen, but the story lacks excitement and consequence. Commercial prospects look slim.

Told in a time-jumping manner that encompasses flashbacks and flashbacks-within-flashbacks in the guise of a journalistic investigation into marriage in the 1990s, tale charts the slow burn of an affair between Nina (Laura San Giacomo), a foxy San Francisco lady whose husband is never around, and a strikingly handsome Welsh photographer (Paul Rhys) who's also married.

As Nina relates her story, which she insists at the outset is truly different from others, to a newspaperman (Michael O'Keefe), there are secondary glimpses of another affair, between Nina's more reckless blond friend (Cristi Conaway) and goofy Italian Paulie (Fisher Stevens).

Most of the touches consist of lightly amusing observations about romance and adultery that are generally cute without being cloying. Neither, however, are they particularly acute or memorable, making for a wisp of a film that leaves no indelible impression save a general attractiveness and civilized sensibility.

San Giacomo has proven she can be awfully good when called upon to be tempestuous and feisty ("sex, lies, and videotape") or funny ("Pretty Woman"), but she's not the sort of actress who commands attention when alone onscreen and trying to be naturalistic; she needs someone else to strike sparks with. She's onscreen by herself a great deal here, and Rhys, who's amply magnetic, conveys a gentle nature that doesn't bring out the zest and fire in his co-star.

For a story of a sizzling affair, in fact, Jacobs gingerly avoids sex scenes for the longest while, and when they finally arrive, they are disappointingly genteel. The polite surfaces could have used some disruptive heat. The journalistic interrogations prove to be a cumbersome narrative device, while the trick ending proves Nina right about her story's uniqueness.

Playing a major role in drawing the viewer into the film is Todd Boekelheide's gorgeous guitar and orchestral score. Jacobs ends up depending on it too much by the end, but the music is lovely.

Shot in S.F. and Oakland, with comfy-looking interiors, pic looks lush on what was surely a tight budget.
—*Todd McCarthy*

REALITY BITES

A Universal Pictures release of a Jersey Films production. Produced by Danny DeVito, Michael Shamberg. Executive producers, Stacey Sher, Wm. Barclay Malcolm. Directed by Ben Stiller. Screenplay, Helen Childress. Camera (CFI), Emmanuel Lubezki; editor, Lisa Churgin; music, Karl Wallinger; music supervision, Karyn Rachtman; production design, Sharon Seymour; art direction, Jeff Knipp; video sequences producer, James Jones; costume design, Eugenie Bafaloukos; sound (Dolby), Stephen Halbert; assistant directors, Allan Wertheim, Keri McIntyre; casting, Francine Maisler. Reviewed at Universal Studios, University City, Jan. 20, 1994. MPAA Rating: PG-13. Running time: **98 MIN.**
Lelaina Pierce	Winona Ryder
Troy Dyer	Ethan Hawke
Michael Grates	Ben Stiller
Vickie Miner	Janeane Garofalo
Sammy Gray	Steve Zahn
Charlane McGregor	Swoosie Kurtz
Tom Pierce	Joe Don Baker
Grant Gubler	John Mahoney

The *verite* of this saga of Generation X is that it is no more fierce than a peck. "Reality Bites" begins as a promising and eccentric tale of contemporary youth but evolves into a banal love story as predictable as any lush Hollywood affair.

A wall-to-wall pop-song score and some fancy camera angles do little to disguise the old-fashioned nature of the drama. While one can commend tyro director Ben Stiller for some adroit work with actors, he's yet to display much grasp of narrative. The target audience should quickly smell a rat and signal a fast theatrical fade for the effort.

The story centers on four recent Texas college grads, including valedictorian Lelaina Pierce (Winona Ryder). Her parting comment to the class and parents is that the answer is, "There's no answer."

Such aimlessness infects these lives. Her roomie Vickie (Janeane Garofalo) manages a heavy-denim clothing store, while Troy (Ethan Hawke) and Sammy (Steve Zahn) appear to have no profession. Lelaina's work, as a television intern on a chatty morning show with a two-faced host (John Mahoney), seems very adult in comparison.

But grappling with finding direction and meaning winds up a secondary concern in Helen Childress' script. She employs the quite labored device of having the heroine meet a romantic interest in a fender bender. Michael (Stiller) is a high-strung exec on an MTV-style cable web.

The device descends into a three-way sexual tension, with Troy the third point in the mix. It also allows the young woman to show off her homevideos, which Michael believes his outlet will snap up.

Shrill and obvious, "Reality Bites" quickly turns blunt and dull. The screenplay telegraphs virtually every character move, leaving the audience impatient for the story to move on.

Despite these shortcomings, Ryder maintains her dignity in a thankless role. She is genuine when all around her is patently synthetic.

She also appears to have been shortchanged in the suitor department; Hawke certainly is convincing as an unlikely bully and Stiller is equally repellent as a classic neurotic workaholic. Thankfully, some levity is brought to the fore by Joe Don Baker and Swoosie Kurtz as Ryder's estranged parents and from Mahoney as a thoroughgoing rotter who gets his comeuppance.

Tech credits are good, if a bit on the showy side. But that's somehow in keeping with the air of phoniness and lack of reality inherent in the piece. If nothing else, it serves as a logical extension of America's idealized and unreal view of youth that extends from Andy Hardy through a string of TV sitcoms. The precursors, however, were infinitely more palatable. —*Leonard Klady*

RISK

A Northern Arts release of a Hank Blumenthal presentation in association with Naked Eye Prods. Produced by Gordon McLennan. Directed, written by Deirdre Fishel. Camera (Duart color), Peter Pearce; editors, Fishel, McLennan; music, John Paul Jones; production design, Flavia Galuppo; sound, Steuart Pearce; associate producers, Blumenthal, Andrew Weeks; assistant director, Risa Koren. Reviewed at Sundance Film Festival, Park City, Utah, Jan. 21, 1994. Running time: **85 MIN.**
Maya	Karen Sillas
Joe	David Ilku
Nikki	Molly Price
Karl	Jack Gwaltney

If only "Risk" had anything to say about its implied subject, it might be worth a look. But this desperate romance between an irredeemable loser and the woman who vainly tries to save him goes through familiar lovers-on-the-run motions without adding a single new interesting twist. Few paying customers will risk this one.

First feature by writer/director Deirdre Fishel presents a parade of implausible, silly or just irritating decisions and actions by the characters that make one want to go spend time with just about any other characters in any other film.

It's doubtful that many women in New York City would allow a complete stranger to enter their apartment and immediately proceed to take a bath with him, but that's precisely what Maya (Karen Sillas) does when the creepy Joe (David Ilku) turns up at her door.

Having met Maya briefly on the bus, Joe has followed her home, and once their affair has begun, the penniless fellow thinks nothing of getting the frustrated artist fired from her job as a model, stealing a car and driving them out to the country.

It's not hard to guess why Joe is the last person his pregnant sister, Nikki (Molly Price), and her husband, Karl (Jack Gwaltney), want to see, since Joe messed up the last job he did for them. When Joe messes up again, the needy couple moves on, taking a job shoveling manure.

What Fishel hoped an audience might take away from this woebegotten tale will remain an unsolved mystery, and there are no compensations offered in the way of stylistic grace notes or pleasure in performance. Pic is threadbare both imaginatively and technically.
—*Todd McCarthy*

GOLDEN GATE

A Samuel Goldwyn Co. presentation in association with American Playhouse Theatrical Films. Produced by Michael Brandman. Executive producer, Lindsay Law. Co-producer, Stan Wlodkowski. Directed by John Madden. Screenplay, David Henry Hwang. Camera, Bobby Bukowski; editor, Sean Barton; music, Elliot Goldenthal; production design, Andrew Jackness; art direction, Edward Rubin; costume design, Ingrid Ferrin; sound (Dolby), Andy Wiskes; casting, Risa Bramon Garcia, Juel Bestrop, Mary Vernieu. Reviewed at Sundance Film Festival, Park City, Jan. 26, 1994. Running time: **90 MIN.**
Kevin Walker	Matt Dillon
Marilyn Song	Joan Chen
Ron Pirelli	Bruno Kirby
Cynthia	Teri Polo
Chen Jung Song	Tzi Ma
Bradley Ichiyasu	Stan Egi
FBI Chief	Jack Shearer
Byrd	Peter Murnik
Meisner	George Guidall

The collision of culture, politics and mysticism imbues Goldwyn's noirish "Golden Gate." Though the film doesn't stint on ambition, its ultimate conclusion comes up short and an unsatisfactory ending will work against its commercial acceptance.

Definitely an upscale venture, it touches upon a number of distinct interest groups without truly tapping into a particular viewing segment. Finally, its arthouse sensibility will prevail theatrically with a potentially greater crowd in ancillary exposure. That still falls far short of coming anywhere near the mainstream.

The core of the tale is pretty straightforward. Kevin Walker (Matt Dillon) is a go-getter fresh out of law school and an eager recruit with the San Francisco office of the FBI. Thrust into the hysteria of communist witch hunting in 1952, he's assigned to ferret out subversives among the city's Chinese community.

While the Hoover honchos may be keen, no substantive evidence can be found implicating groups or individuals. Though essentially a decent type, Kevin nonetheless succumbs to head office pressure to get indictments. He devises a case in which money sent to relatives via Hong Kong lands a trio in jail.

What fascinates scripter David Henry Hwang is how this injustice affects someone who acutely understands the difference between justice and the law.

The film begins to buckle when the action is spread out over a span of two decades. The lapses in time (its three acts occur in 1952, 1962 and 1968) result in rough transitions.

Ten years after the fact, Song (Tzi Ma) is released but emotionally ill-prepared for freedom. Kevin is assigned to track him but gets too close. Song jumps from the title structure with the departing curse that Kevin become a Chinaman. Rather, he becomes the protector and, later, lover of the blameless laundry man's daughter Marilyn (Joan Chen).

This is a grand tragedy in which no amount of repentance can erase a single, if definitive, lapse of judgment. The consequences nonetheless seem too extreme. This is amplified by a hastily contrived final act that suggests a more complex denouement was scrapped in the editing process.

Once again, Dillon provides the bedrock to the piece in a wonderfully conceived and modulated performance. He is eminently engaging and far superior to the meandering material. The supporting cast is also first-rate, as are technical credits, particularly the lighting and camera work of Bobby Bukowski.

But the artistry can surmount only so much of what's lacking in the script's failure to focus and consolidate. There is no gold ring for "Golden Gate," only the promise of an intriguing premise unfulfilled.

—*Leonard Klady*

TROIS COULEURS: BLANC

(THREE COLORS: WHITE)

(FRENCH-SWISS-POLISH)

An MKL release of an MK2 Prods., France 3 Cinema (Paris)/Cab Prods. (Lausanne)/Tor Prod. (Warsaw) production, with participation of Canal Plus and Eurimages. (International sales: MK2, Paris.) Produced by Marin Karmitz. Executive producer, Yvon Crenn. Directed by Krzysztof Kieslowski. Screenplay, Krzysztof Piesiewicz, Kieslowski; camera (color), Edward Klosinski; editor, Urszula Lesiak; music, Zbigniew Preisner; art direction, Halina Dobrowolska, Claude Lenoir; set decoration, Magdalena Dipont; sound (Dolby), Jean-Claude Laureux; script consultants, Agnieszka Holland, Edward Zebrowski, Edward Klosinski; assistant director, Pawel Lozinski; casting, Margot Capelier, Teresa Violetta Buhl. Previewed at 14 Juillet Odeon cinema, Paris, Dec. 16, 1993. (Also in Berlin Film Festival, competing.) Running time: **89 MIN.**
Karol .... Zbigniew Zamachowski
Dominique .... Julie Delpy
Mikolaj .... Janusz Gajos
Jurek .... Jerzy Stuhr
Also with: Juliette Binoche, Florence Pernel.
(Polish and French dialogue)

The entertaining second seg of Krzysztof Kieslowski's "Three Colors" trilogy, "White" is involving, bittersweet and droll. A fine lead perf from Zbigniew Zamachowski anchors an ingenious rags-to-riches tale of revenge filtered through abiding love. Mostly in Polish, with a smattering of French, this successor to "Blue" should produce plenty of black ink at Gallic and offshore arthouses. (Pic also competes at next month's Berlin fest.)

Those put off by the glossy aesthetics of "Blue" will find "White" a fairly straightforward black comedy that skirts pretentiousness and goes easy on the symbolism while retaining Kieslowski's eerie gift for spinning mystical narrative gold from the simplest of ingredients. Where "Blue" dealt with Liberty, "White" focuses on Equality (per the colors of the French flag, repping concepts of Liberty, Equality and Fraternity).

Although mostly set in Warsaw, pic begins in a Paris law court where cruel French beauty Dominique (Julie Delpy) is finalizing her divorce from somewhat bumbling Polish hubby Karol (Zamachowski), on the grounds that their bond was never consummated. Karol, who runs a hairdressing salon with his spouse, has only a sketchy understanding of French and needs an interpreter. Within the day he's divested of wife, home, credit card and business.

Stuck in Paris, with just a large suitcase and tissue paper comb to his name, Karol is offered a lucrative job by fellow countryman Mikolaj (Janusz Gajos) of killing an unnamed Pole. He declines, but the two become friendly and Mikolaj agrees to smuggle Karol back home as "checked baggage."

Spirited away inside the suitcase by corrupt baggage handlers, Karol gets a rude introduction to the new Poland in which anything and everything can be bought and sold. He returns to the hair salon, tended by lumpy brother Jurek (Jerzy Stuhr, also Zamachowski's brother in the rollicking 10th episode of Kieslowski's "Decalogue"), and, through a mixture of luck and determination, becomes a wealthy big shot.

At the pinnacle of his career, Karol hatches a plot to fake his own death and leave his financial empire to his ex-wife. A riveting chain of events begins that is almost impossible to second-guess.

In line with the second watchword of the French Republic, the scripters set about "equalizing" the metaphorical playing field between Karol and his ex-wife, with the former determined to impress the latter.

She lingers on in his life in the form of two talismans salvaged from France — a two-franc coin and a cracked alabaster bust of a woman. Evoking shades of Kieslowski's earlier "The Double Life of Veronique," when Karol handles the coin in Warsaw, Dominique feels uneasy in Paris.

The title color is favored in ethereal flashbacks to the wife on her wedding day and in a cathartic sequence of the two brothers giddily playing on a frozen pond in Warsaw.

As the resourceful underdog, Karol ("Charles") is meant as an homage to Chaplin, with the worldly Mikolaj a perfect friend and foil to the Little Tramp. Although Delpy is fine as the wife, the pic is Zamachowski's through and through.

Lensing and editing are aces, as is Zbigniew Preisner's score. Fans of Kieslowski's earlier work will be delighted to find him back at work in his native language, with the cream of Polish thesps peopling bit parts.

Third seg, "Red" (Fraternity), with Irene Jacob and Jean-Louis Trintignant, is skedded for Cannes fest. Heroines Juliette Binoche ("Blue"), who's fleetingly on show here, Delpy and Jacob will all cross paths in the final tale of the trilogy.

—*Lisa Nesselson*

MY FATHER, THE HERO

A Buena Vista release of a Touchstone Pictures presentation of a Cite Films/Film Par Film/D.D. Prods. production in association with the Edward S. Feldman Co. Produced by Jacques Bar, Jean-Louis Livi. Executive producer, Feldman. Co-producer, Ted Swanson. Directed by Steve Miner. Screenplay, Francis Veber, Charlie Peters, based on "Mon Pere, ce heros," by Gerard Lauzier. Camera (Continental Labs color, Technicolor prints), Daryn Okada; editor, Marshall Harvey; music, David Newman; production design, Christopher Nowak; art direction, Patricia Woodbridge; set decoration, Don K. Ivey; costume design, Vicki Sanchez; sound (Dolby), Joseph Geisinger; assistant director, Dennis Maguire; second unit director, David Ellis; casting, Dianne Crittenden. Reviewed at the Avco Center Cinema, L.A., Jan. 31, 1994. MPAA Rating: PG. Running time: **90 MIN.**
Andre .... Gerard Depardieu
Nicole .... Katherine Heigl
Ben .... Dalton James
Megan .... Lauren Hutton
Diana .... Faith Prince
Mike ....Stephen Tobolowsky
Stella .... Ann Hearn
Doris .... Robyn Peterson
Fred .... Frank Renzulli

In addition to providing a fabulous feature-length ad for Bahamas tourism, this latest U.S. remake of a French film offers some of the same breezy charm as its environs. Those winds could blow some solid box office returns Disney's way, assuming the low-octane cast can attract enough vacationers to fill its sails with word-of-mouth air.

In an intriguing twist, French megastar Gerard Depardieu — who made his English-language debut in Disney's "Green Card" — reprises a role he played in a 1991 French feature, "Mon Pere, ce heros," for a U.S. version of the same story.

Depardieu stars as an absentee father who takes his willful, resentful 14-year-old daughter, Nicole (Katherine Heigl), on a tropical vacation, only to have her concoct a lie about Dad being her lover to impress a slightly older boy (Dalton James).

That simple premise provides a fertile planting ground for comedy, as word of the liaison spreads among the hotel's increasingly outraged vacationers and staff, who view the oblivious Andre (Depardieu) as the worst sort of dirty old man. Nicole, meanwhile, keeps amplifying her story to keep the charade — and, in her eyes, the boy's interest — alive, eventually recruiting her father into the act.

There's also a warm, fuzzy, Hallmark-card angle stemming from the unresolved feelings between father and daughter, as well as Andre's own uncertainty about his relationship with an unseen girlfriend back in Paris. The film offers a dose of the same reassuring if decidedly 1990s message as "Mrs. Doubtfire" —

namely, that parents and kids don't have to stop loving each other after being separated by divorce.

As with his most recent feature, "Forever Young," director Steve Miner gets the most out of formulaic material, working from a script by Francis Veber and Charlie Peters based on writer/director Gerard Lauzier's original.

Depardieu, having been over this terrain before, is perfect as the bewildered dad, while the lovely Heigl — previously seen in "King of the Hill" — brings the right mix to her role as innocent, boy-crazy coquette and compulsive liar all in one.

The picture is also well cast in terms of supporting players, including James as Nicole's dreamboat, Faith Prince as an on-the-prowl vacationer and the various scowling couples populating the resort, who provide two or three howling laughs.

The location itself also plays a major role, and cameraman Daryn Okada's vistas of crystal-blue water and stark white beaches — enhanced by David Newman's snazzy score — will doubtless make many wish they could make a beeline from the theater to their travel agent.

Production and costume design also lend some island spice to this U.S. souffle, which, despite dragging in places, makes the most of its basic ingredients. —*Brian Lowry*

SUNDANCE

WHAT HAPPENED WAS

A Good Machine Production of a Genre Film. Produced by Robin O'Hara, Scott Macaulay. Executive producers, Ted Hope, James Schamus. Directed, written by Tom Noonan, based on his play. Camera (DuArt color), Joe DeSalvo; editor, Richmond Arrley; music, Lodovico Sorret; production design, Dan Ouelette; set decoration, Andras Kanegson; costume design, Kathy Nixon; sound, Rick Stevenson; assistant director, Steve Apicella. Reviewed at the Sundance Film festival, Park City, Jan. 26, 1994. Running time: **91 MIN.**
Jackie .... Karen Sillas
Michael .... Tom Noonan

Off Broadway actor Tom Noonan emerges as a talented writer and director in "What Happened Was," an intriguing, often mysterious drama about a date between two lonely misfits. This intense chamber piece for two features strong performances, particularly by Karen Sillas. This appealing and disturbing movie, winner of the Grand Jury Prize

at this year's Sundance Festival, holds some potential on the fest and specialized theatrical circuits.

There's nothing in common between this movie for grown-ups and Hollywood's teenage pix, except their central, universal situation: Dating as a culturally celebrated custom in American life. It's Friday night and Jackie (Sillas), a secretary in a law firm, leaves work early to prepare for a dinner date at her New York loft with paralegal colleague Michael (Noonan).

The film's first five minutes, which focus on Jackie's nervous behavior and frequent dress changes, are superbly observed by Joe DeSalvo's restless camera. Every viewer will be able to relate to Jackie's contradictory feelings of tension, anticipation, excitement and fear.

It doesn't help much that Jackie and Michael know each other from work, for when he arrives at the door, it's a new ball game with a new set of rules.

Indeed, "What Happened Was" presents a most authentic chronicle of how people actually behave on a date: the discreet moves and countermoves, the fine line between image projection and negative exposure. It's to Noonan's credit as scripter and helmer that he captures in minute detail the uncomfortable feelings, awkward pauses and forced smiles.

Jumping from one topic to another, Michael tells Jackie that he went to Harvard Law School but didn't graduate and that he has been engaged in writing an expose about the firm. Jackie is impressed, but then reveals that she has written children's fairy tales.

Puzzled, Michael asks her to read one of them aloud, and the couple moves to her dressing room, a candlelit magical kingdom decorated with dolls and toys. Dealing with child abuse, violence and terror, her story disturbs Michael.

Contrasting behavior in public and private and the difference between appearances and identities, it turns out that most of the characters' self-descriptions are inaccurate.

There are plenty of shocking role reversals and twists, but the script's most illuminating insights show how well-intentioned and potentially pleasurable encounters can turn disastrous and humiliating as a result of differing expectations. Michael neither pretends to fully understand his persona nor

tries to provide facile motivation for their conduct.

The beauty and originality of "What Happened Was" rests on defying the melodramatic conventions of Hollywood's psychodramas.

Though based on a play, there's nothing theatrical or claustrophobic about the narrative. "What Happened Was" becomes a thoroughly cinematic experience thanks to Noonan's superlative *mise en scene*. Changes in time and physical space are transmitted with remarkable subtlety.

It's rare nowadays to see two-character movies that depend entirely on dialogue and gestures. Some viewers might find the pacing too slow and the story too stagnant, as there's almost no background music and no fast cuts between or within scenes.

Both Noonan and Sillas give startling performances as the bruised, isolated individuals. This film should establish Sillas, who has done splendid work for Hal Hartley ("Trust," "Simple Men"), as a dramatic actress of the first order.

Production values are first-rate, particularly Dan Ouelette's remarkable production design of the loft — the film's single locale — and DeSalvo's nuanced camera movement and lighting.

Whether "What Happened Was" imparts an urban nightmare or the reality of alienation is up to each viewer to decide. But it's significant that the film begins and ends with a view of huge, threatening buildings, in which each window might conceal a human mystery.
—*Emanuel Levy*

THREESOME

A TriStar release of a Motion Picture Corp. of America production in association with Brad Krevoy and Steve Stabler. Produced by Krevoy, Stabler. Executive producer, Cary Woods. Co-producer, Brad Jenkel. Line producer, Tracie Graham Rice. Directed, written by Andrew Fleming. Camera (Foto-Kem color), Alexander Gruszynski; editor, William C. Carruth; music, Thomas Newman; production design, Ivo Cristante; art direction, Ken Larson; set decoration, Tim Colohan; costume design, Deborah Everton; sound (Dolby), Giovanni Di Simone; associate producer, David Stein; additional camera, Jacek Laskus; assistant director, Jack Breschard; casting, Ed Mitchell, Robyn Ray. Reviewed at Sundance Film festival, Park City, Utah, Jan. 28, 1994. MPAA Rating: R. Running time: **93 MIN.**

Alex .... Lara Flynn Boyle
Stuart .... Stephen Baldwin
Eddy .... Josh Charles
Dick .... Alexis Arquette
Renay .... Martha Gehman
Larry .... Mark Arnold
Kristen .... Michele Matheson

Cute, sexy and funny, "Threesome" also manages to deftly capture the working out of personality and sexual identity that is part and parcel of the college years. Slickly mounted, polished off with witty one-liners and a calculated audience pleaser, this TriStar release is satisfyingly blunt and truthful under all the pranks and sexual mischief, and could click strongly with young audiences if smartly marketed.

At very least, pic should establish writer-director Andrew Fleming as a talent to watch. There have been many films over the years about kids' sexual confusion, fears, experimentation and just fooling around, and this one does better than most in expressing the sex-saturated state-of mind of 20-year-olds while maintaining psychological verisimilitude.

The external package is too glossy, overtly sexy and plain fun for some critics to take the film seriously, and some gays may feel that the gay character's status is fudged or trivialized, but Fleming tenaciously holds his sharp focus on his leading characters' mutual obsessions while keeping the proceedings vastly entertaining on the surface.

Because of a silly technicality involving her male-sounding name, sharp-looking Alex (Lara Flynn Boyle) is assigned a room in the same UCLA dorm suite already shared by hot-looking party boy Stuart (Stephen Baldwin) and handsome intellectual Eddy (Josh Charles), himself a recently arrived junior transfer student.

Characters' close physical proximity quickly leads to emotional ties and eruptions. The first to surface is Alex's infatuation with Eddy, which is spurred by his literary bent. Alex literally jumps him, but Eddy instantly backs off and soon must acknowledge that he's actually attracted to Stuart, not Alex.

For his part, the aggressively macho Stuart tries to seduce Alex, but she in turn spurns him, still distracted by Eddy's sexual ambivalence and intent upon molding him into a heterosexual.

It doesn't take long for Stuart to realize that Eddy's staring at him rather too often, but he's cool about it, and since all three have thwarted passions, they agree that none of them will have sex within the circle.

Fat chance of that, however. Each of the three leads is briefly shown in the course of a dismal outside date, and before long the trio is almost constantly locked in three-way embraces and gropings, supplemented by separate sessions between Alex and the two young men.

Eventually, this web of emotional and physical entanglements becomes too complicated, weighty and frustrating for any of them to bear, but it does give them something they all want and helps clarify a lot of issues for them.

Some of the early going smacks of overly convenient contrivance and cuteness. But the film gets past this quickly and with ease, notably due to its wonderfully attractive casting.

Beauty can make one forgive a lot, and the three leads here are sexy, smart and funny as the need arises, invariably a pleasure to be around and quite agreeable to watch rolling around together.

For a short time, it appears that the two men are hopelessly irreconcilable polar opposites — Stuart the lust-crazed animal and Eddy the uptight bookworm. But even if he never develops a keen intellect, Stuart soon opens up to reveal unexpected levels of sensitivity and flexibility.

Baldwin, the third of the talented brothers to break through notably on the screen, expands these corners of character in a rambunctiously sexy and thoroughly winning performance.

Seen in some dismal pictures recently, notably "The Temp," Flynn Boyle rebounds here with some spirited, spunky, passionate work. Alex is not meant to be a woman of legendary allure, such as Jeanne Moreau in the obliquely referred-to *menage a trois* "Jules and Jim," but a healthy college student who knows she's attractive and takes a long time to figure out why she can't get what she wants.

In the repressed, uncertain Eddy, who narrates the piece, Charles has the most difficult role and does a splendid job of it, even if some of his motivations are not easy to pinpoint.

After resisting physical intimacy with Alex, seeing an old French film suddenly inspires him to rush to her room and take her to bed, and he's still terrified to act on his impulses long after he admits he's interested in men. But Charles seems fully as intelligent as his character, and he embodies Eddy's uncertainties very believably.

Fleming, whose previous feature was "Bad Dreams," has kept a tight rein on his storytelling, from the script through performance and editing, and only occasionally indulges an effect for its own sake. Script is savvy about relations and what people are thinking.

Solid contributions by the behind-the-scenes team has made an independently produced feature look like a bigger-budget studio effort.
— *Todd McCarthy*

SHOPPING

(BRITISH)

A Film Four Intl. presentation in association with Polygram, Kuzui Enterprises and WMG of an Impact Pictures production. Produced by Jeremy Bolt. Line producer, Laurie Borg. Directed, written by Paul Anderson. Camera (Metrocolor), Tony Imi; editor, David Stiven; music, Barrington Pheloung; production design, Max Gottlieb; art direction, Chris Townsend; costume design, Howard Burden; sound (Dolby), Colin Nicolson; assistant director, Alan J. Wands; second unit camera, Arthur Wooster; casting, Jane Frisby. Reviewed at Sundance Film Festival, Park City, Utah, Jan. 21, 1994. Running time: **106 MIN.**
Jo .... Sadie Frost
Billy .... Jude Law
Tommy .... Sean Pertwee
Be Bop .... Fraser James
Bev .... Marianne Faithfull
Venning .... Sean Bean
Conway .... Jonathan Pryce

An all-style, no-content attitudinal actioner, "Shopping" is as blank-minded as its vapidly rebellious leading characters. Set in a vaguely futuristic Britain exclusively populated by valueless kids and fascistic police, this slick, sleek and empty joyless ride is immediately unhinged by its lack of credible forces of opposition; there's nothing colliding here except cars. A candidate for cultdom in theory only, these would-be rebels without a cause will remain rabble without applause.

Along with "The Young Americans," also showing at Sundance, "Shopping" stands at the forefront of fare by the so-called multiplex generation of new British filmmakers. Repudiating the genteel, literary, Masterpiece Theater aesthetic, these directors admire and aspire to the commercial big time as best represented by highly tooled American pictures. Or, as "Shopping" producer Jeremy Bolt put it, "We're part of a new wave of British filmmakers who are not afraid of saying we like 'Lethal Weapon' and are impressed by big action directors."

Still, "Shopping" has its sights set more on reworking aspects of "A Clockwork Orange" and "Blade Runner." A sock opening, consisting of stunning aerial industrial landscapes accompanied by a pulsating score, wonderfully summons up a devastated, depersonalized world. Unfortunately, this remains by far the pic's best sequence, as matters quickly devolve into silly plotting and violence devoid of meaning.

At the outset, when 19-year-old pretty boy Billy (Jude Law) is being released, he's asked, "What's prison taught you, Billy?" He replies, "Don't get caught," and that's as philosophical as the picture gets.

Without missing a beat, Billy and his partner, Jo (Sadie Frost), steal and trash a BMW in a profound bit of anti-yuppie crime as they head back into their nocturnal netherworld of street punks.

An "adreneline junkie" who lives in a tiny trailer by the river, Billy is intent upon regaining his status as top dog in his anarchic world, which he can do by stealing cars and "shopping." This consists of crashing vehicles into store windows, stealing a few things and generally trashing the outward manifestations of consumer society.

This plot setup opens the door on an orgy of extravagant destruction, spurred on by Billy's macho battle with Tommy (Sean Pertwee) to be the town's best shopper, characterized by numerous wild car rides and tempered only by Jo's growing desire to take Billy away from all this.

Lamenting "I'm 22, I'm an old woman," Jo finally corners Billy and puts the make on him, but he lowers the boom, warning, "This is the 1990s. Sex isn't safe anymore." So much for romance. But Jo still hangs around for one last score, an assault on the seemingly impregnable Retailand.

Along with aping American actioners, tyro writer-director Paul Anderson, who comes out of TV, would appear to aspire to the mantle of the British Luc Besson, as his faith in the power of heavy atmospherics and thick style seems unlimited. Hardly a shot goes by without large amounts of smoke, fire and steam wafting over everything, all to the accompaniment of the usual rock music wallpaper.

Random violence and aimless kids may be symptoms of the times, but "Shopping's" formulation of crime against department stores comes off as stupid and hardly formidable as a narrative foundation.

Newcomer Law seems more like a candidate for a British technorock group than screen stardom, and Frost, fresh from "Bram Stoker's Dracula," strikes a tough-girl pose throughout. Marianne Faithfull pops up momentarily as the proprietress of a video arcade, while Jonathan Pryce is obliged to supply world-weary opposition as a police chief.

Pic has put a big look on limited means to no good use.
— *Todd McCarthy*

FRESH

(U.S.-FRENCH)

A Miramax release of a Lumiere Pictures presentation of a Lawrence Bender production. Produced by Bender, Randy Ostrow. Executive producer, Lila Cazes. Co-producer, Chrisann Verges. Directed, written by Boaz Yakin. Camera (Deluxe color), Adam Holender; editor, Dorian Harris; music, Stewart Copeland; production design, Dan Leigh; costume design, Ellen Lutter; sound (Dolby), Michael Barosky; associate producer, Joann Fregalette Jansen; assistant director, J. Miller Tobin; casting, Douglas Aibel. Reviewed at Sundance Film Festival, Park City, Utah, Jan. 27, 1994. Running time: **112 MIN.**
Fresh .... Sean Nelson
Esteban .... Giancarlo Esposito
Sam .... Samuel L. Jackson
Nicole .... N'Bushe Wright
Corky .... Ron Brice
Jake .... Jean LaMarre
Chuckie .... Luis Lantigua
Chillie .... Yul Vasquez
Aunt Frances .... Cheryl Freeman

"Fresh" is the story of one young boy's way out of the vicious circle of drug violence that defines the world in which he has grown up. Skillfully made and involving, first feature by Boaz Yakin stands to generate considerable controversy, not over its artistic qualities but in regard to its morality and positioning of a child as an instigator of widespread crime and bloodshed. Ensuing debate could lead to plenty of off-entertainment-page and chatshow attention, which, in addition to some top reviews, should give Miramax enough to nicely launch this French-financed pickup in April. How the mass public responds down the line is an open question.

Dismayingly unforgettable opening scenes show the black, 12-year-old Fresh (Sean Nelson) showing up late for school because he's running behind on his morning rounds as a drug courier. Living with 11 female cousins in New York under the care of his Aunt Frances, Fresh keeps his own counsel as he delivers for local heroin kingpin Esteban (Giancarlo Esposito) and does freelance work for assorted sidewalk and backroom dealers.

As long as he stays straight and keeps quiet, Fresh has it made, as he's smart, honest and, most important, too young to arouse suspicion. As one of his fond bosses tells him: "The only reason you ain't the man, you too goddamned little. When you get bigger, you be the man."

Although forbidden to see him, Fresh surreptitiously meets his father, Sam (the excellent Samuel L. Jackson), in Washington Square for sessions of speed chess. Apparently a brilliant near-derelict, Sam proves a tough taskmaster, lectur-

February 7, 1994 (Cont.)

ing Fresh about discipline and brutally upbraiding him for stupid moves and lack of concentration.

What chess has to do with the rest of Fresh's life only slowly becomes apparent. In a shocking sequence, a pickup basketball game turns deadly as well-known crack dealer Jake (a very scary Jean LaMarre) shoots dead an opponent and also fatally wounds a little girl who's sweet on Fresh.

A clear witness to the crimes, the taciturn Fresh can't say anything to authorities if he wants to stay alive, but the incident begins turning the gears that result in the high-wire act of the last couple of reels.

Much like the leading character of Akira Kurosawa's "Yojimbo," Fresh cleverly begins pitting against each other all his employers, those responsible for the violence and death all around him. As the chess metaphor settles in, Fresh, through a series of lies, deceptions, tips and alibis, springs the traps into which all the evil adversaries will step and watches, impassively, as they do each other in.

As in any Western or crime film, there is a certain visceral satisfaction in seeing these ultrabad dudes get their just desserts, and "Fresh" will be embraced by some as a satisfying fictional portrait of how one kid outwitted the evil kings, rooks, bishops and knights at their own game.

But even while they are drawn in by the undeniably potent, even mesmerizing story, others will feel a queasiness about the spectacle of a little boy setting other people up for the kill. No matter how smart and sympathetic Fresh may be, he is still part of the problem, not the solution, in his extension of the drug-and-death cycle. Pic's p.o.v. on this seems ambivalent but vaguely endorsing, allowing viewers to take up the issues while questioning the film's presentation of them.

Still, Yakin has put some powerful drama up on the screen, and he has been assisted by no one more significantly than young Nelson, who plays Fresh. A blank slate much of the time, he seems to take everything in, storing up information and street smarts that he can finally use to his own advantage.

This portrait of a childhood both incredibly resourceful and tragically deprived is memorable in an era of numerous outstanding preteen performances, and the final image of Fresh cracking, for the first time, from the cumulative pressure of his life is indelible.

Performances are terrifically intense from top to bottom. Esposito is particularly riveting as the sinewy drug baron, and Ron Brice also scores as a rival dealer.

Producing team has made this look like a big, polished film on a no-doubt limited budget. Adam Holender's lensing achieves a vividly colorful look on mostly ghetto loca-

tions, and Dorian Harris' editing has real snap and verve. Eschewing a predictable rap soundtrack, Yakin recruited Stewart Copeland, whose varied score lends unexpected textures to the film but does become overblown at moments.

—*Todd McCarthy*

RIVER OF GRASS

A Plan B Pictures presentation. Produced by Jesse Hartman, Kelly Reichardt. Directed, written by Reichardt, story by Reichardt, Hartman. Camera (Duart color), Jim Denault; editor, Larry Fessenden; sound, Matthew Sigal; sound design, Fessenden; associate producer, Ralph McKay; assistant director, Greg Webb. Reviewed at Sundance Film Festival, Park City, Utah, Jan. 21, 1994. Running time: **75 MIN.**
Cozy .... Lisa Bowman
Lee .... Larry Fessenden
Jimmy Ryder .... Dick Russell

An outlaw-lovers-on-the-run saga in which the leads don't commit a crime, fall in love or ever hit the road, "River of Grass" works much better as a jokey, theoretical piece of genre revisionism than as a real movie. A modern, ennui-laden film noir turned inside out and filmed in bright colors under the Florida sun, this ultra-low-budget indie will appeal exclusively to film academics and genre specialists.

New York writer-director Kelly Reichardt returned to her native area of suburban Miami to make her first feature, and she clearly knows her way around the neighborhood as well as around film conventions.

Unfortunately, the energy working on the leading characters, and by extension upon the story itself, is almost entirely negative. A terminally bored housewife and mother whose husband is perpetually absent, Cozy (Lisa Bowman) doesn't know what to do with herself until she meets Lee (Larry Fessenden), an entropy specialist who still lives at home at 29 and whose ambition is to "just drink."

Lee has come into possession of a gun found on the road, one lost by Cozy's detective (and jazz drummer) father, Jimmy (Dick Russell). When Cozy accidentally fires the gun, she and Lee believe they've shot a black man and bolt to a motel to decide what to do.

Without as much as pocket change between them, the pair can't even get on the toll road to leave town, and with the perfect opportunity to become wild, even legendary outlaws on the lam, they can't get it together to do a thing. "If we weren't killers, we weren't anything," Cozy realizes upon learning that their "victim" wasn't hit after all.

Despite the intellectually clever notions in play, the film is all about what the characters are not, and what doesn't happen. Unlike most entries in this genre over the decades, the leads are not attractive and have no romantic chemistry, and the formerly swampy world they inhabit is utterly devoid of mystery and appeal.

Reichardt and her collaborators have devised a vivid color scheme for the film, and this, in combination with the rigor involved in working out the anti-plot, will give certain film-wise viewers something to latch onto. But the pleasures are too esoteric and narrowly channeled.

Bowman and Fessenden (who also edited) occasionally generate some deadpan humor but generally make for lackluster centers of attention. Russell gives the father, desperate to recover his weapon, some welcome style and pizazz.

With the tiniest of budgets at their disposal, filmmakers have gotten a reasonably good-looking picture on the screen.

—*Todd McCarthy*

THE SECRET LIFE OF HOUSES

A Tainbreaker Films production. Produced by Crocker Coulson. Co-producer, Charles E. McKittrick III. Directed, edited by Adrian Velicescu. Screenplay, Velicescu, Scott Bradfield, based on Bradfield's short story. Camera (Foto-Kem color), Velicescu; production design, Sergio Onaga; coordinating producer (for ITVS), James Schamus. Reviewed at Sundance Film Festival, Park City, Utah, Jan. 29, 1994. Running time: **91 MIN.**
Margret .... Remy Ryan
Ann .... Laurie Metcalf
Aunt Fergie .... Shirley Knight
David .... Joseph Culp
Head Nurse .... Catherine Coulson

Slow, ponderous and a bit pretentious, Adrian Velicescu's "The Secret Life of Houses" is yet another examination of a dysfunctional family, this time seen from the perspective of a lonely young girl. As a portrait of a daughter coming to terms with her mother's sudden death, the film is more impressive in its expressionistic visuals and evocative ambience than in its dramatic elements. Chances for theatrical release of this tawdry art film, which was initially made for TV, are middling.

Director, co-scripter, lenser and editor Velicescu explores the complex relationship between Margret (Remy Ryan) a sensitive 9-year-old, and her harsh, frustrated single mother (Laurie Metcalf). When her mother is abruptly rushed to the hospital, Margret not only decides

to fend for herself but manages to conceal from the authorities that she lives by herself.

For the first half-hour or so, this moody drama rather effectively chronicles the solitary existence of Margret, who simply refuses to believe that her mother is going to die. As she rushes back and forth from her home to the hospital, Margret's life is presented as a mysterious, often intriguing, labyrinth of childhood memories, wishful dreams and painful realities.

Margret's secret, imaginative life is terminated by the arrival of Aunt Fergie (Shirley Knight), a greedy, rational, down-to-earth woman, who's determined to take care of business as quickly and efficiently as possible, which includes liquidating the house, cremating the body, taking the remaining money and sending Margret to her unstable father in Detroit.

Defying a linear structure, Velicescu captures convincingly — in sporadic moments even poetically — the inner working of a girl's psyche and soul when faced by abrupt, traumatic events. Keeping his camera close to Ryan's beautifully expressive face, helmer shows the subjective perception — and reconstruction of reality — from her point of view.

But the juxtaposition of Margret's lyrical world with the surrounding, unfeeling adult world is schematic and overly stressed. Though most of the grown-up characters are intended as caricatures, the farcical humor they bring to the story is often forced and external, and it clashes with the narrative's rather gloomy nature, making the film jarringly incongruous.

As helmer, Velicescu exhibits a draggy, unmodulated style that ultimately becomes too detached and formal for such an intimate story. But he shows some talent in evoking mood: The film is marked by a European artistic sensibility.

Funded and produced by the Independent Television Service as part of its "TV Families" series, "The Secret Life of Houses" probably worked better in its shorter TV version.   —*Emanuel Levy*

THE FIRE THIS TIME
(DOCU)

A Blacktop Films production. Produced, directed, written by Randy Holland. Camera (color), Jurg Walther; additional camera, David May, Sal Paradise; editor, Barbara Kaplan; music, James Verboort; sound, Walther, May, Diane Hall, Tark Abdul Wahid; associate producers, Albert Lord, Jack Smith. Reviewed at Sundance Film Festival, Park City, Utah, Jan. 23, 1994. Running time: **90 MIN.**
Narrator: Brooke Adams.

A searing, touching documentary about the 1992 civil unrest in Los Angeles, "The Fire This Time" is also the first work to place the riots in the context of the black community's history in L.A. Viewed from inside by residents of South Central, and containing invaluable interviews with Betty Shabazz (Malcolm X's widow) and former U.N. Ambassador Andrew Young, this important and timely docu deserves theatrical bookings before airings on public TV and other outlets.

It's ironic and prophetic that the 1992 L.A. riots occurred precisely 25 years after the commission appointed by Lyndon Johnson came up with its 25-year Master Plan to restore the city in the wake of the Watts riots. As one resident comments, blacks were missing from the plan, and the report itself has disappeared from the archives.

Randy Holland's docu examines the riots not as a sudden reaction to verdicts in the first Rodney King beating trial, but from a historical perspective, beginning with the arrival of the first blacks in California in 1850, the evolution of the inner-city ghetto, the 1965 Watts riots, the rise and fall of the Black Panthers and the emergence of violent street gangs in the 1970s and 1980s.

What comes across most powerfully is the consistent breakup of what used to be a lively community, through the sabotage of the Watts Writers workshop, the decimation of the Black Panthers, the harassment of the community's black leadership by the FBI and L.A.P.D.

If "The Fire This Time" is less emotionally exciting or stirring than its explosive subject matter warrants, it's due to its conventional style and even tempo. The excessive, often dull narration spoken by Brooke Adams creates an unnecessary distance between viewers and the screen, lending pic the aura of a clinical survey.

Though technical credits are accomplished and the footage used is most satisfying, at times Jurg Walther's camera wanders instead of highlighting the personal experiences shared by the residents.

That said, in its fastidious attention to historical background, "The Fire This Time" is a provocative documentary, a wake-up call and a warning that the riots can happen again — in L.A. and elsewhere. —*Emanuel Levy*

SPANKING THE MONKEY

A Fine Line Features release of a Buckeye Communications presentation of a Dean Silvers production. Produced by Silvers. Executive producers, Stanley F. Buchthal, David O. Russell. Line producer, Jon Resnik. Directed, written by Russell. Camera (DuArt color), Michael Mayers; editor, Pamela Martin; songs, Mark Sandman; production design, Susan Block; costume design, Carolyn Greco; sound, William Tzouris; associate producer, Cheryl Miller Houser; assistant director, John O'Rourke; second unit camera, Mark Schmidt; casting, Ellen Parks. Reviewed at Sundance Film Festival, Park City, Utah, Jan. 21, 1994. Running time: **106 MIN.**
Raymond Aibelli .... Jeremy Davies
Susan Aibelli .... Alberta Watson
Tom Aibelli ..... Benjamin Hendrickson
Toni Peck .... Carla Gallo
Nicky .... Matthew Puckett
Aunt Helen .... Judette Jones

Some notably touchy material receives erratic treatment in "Spanking the Monkey." David O. Russell's first feature, which won the Audience Award at the Sundance Film Festival and was picked up there by Fine Line, embellishes a tale of parent-son power plays and incest with good performances and intriguing psychological nuances, but falls victim to wildly varying tone and frustrating plot developments. Low-budgeter will generate controversy on both the moral and artistic levels, although probably not clamorously enough to make it into a significant B.O. entry.

Russell, who previously directed two shorts that were shown at Sundance, invests this story of a smart college kid forced to spend the summer with his bedridden mother with considerable personal feeling, which is for better and for worse. In fact, it has a lot in common with many autobiographical first novels, in the sense of working out certain psychological and emotional problems in a sometimes uncomfortable way, of distancing oneself from traumatic events by trying to transform them into art.

Although he is supposed to go to Washington, D.C., for a prestigious internship during his summer vacation from MIT, Ray Aibelli (Jeremy Davies) is told by his tyrannical, traveling father (Benjamin Hendrickson) that he's going to have to stay home to play nurse to his mother (Alberta Watson), who has a fractured leg.

Initially, Mom is just as bossy as Dad has been, as she constantly criticizes and degrades her son, but the situation soon becomes ambiguous and queasy when Ray is required to carry his attractive mother to the toilet and shower, rub her down with creams and carry out other tasks rather beyond the physical norms of mother-son intimacy.

The only break Ray gets from Mom is walking the dog, in the process of which he meets high schooler Toni (Carla Gallo), with whom he develops a slow-cooking romance of sorts but of whom Mom naturally strongly disapproves.

Still hoping to get down to Washington, Ray engineers the arrival of Aunt Helen (Judette Jones) to look after Mom. Helen is too square to accept what now appears to be happening in Mom's bedroom, since Ray has obviously spent the night there.

With the tone becoming more blackly comic, Ray, after telling Dad what's going on, feels compelled to pull a Harold (as in Maude) but, failing this, takes his fury out on Mom herself while Dad tries to intervene.

The story is undoubtedly weird, but perhaps more so on paper than on the screen, since Russell and his actors have played it mostly straight in attempting to confer psychological validity on all the untoward developments.

Crucially, the steps in Ray's relationship with his mother are all believable, thanks in large measure to the quietly observed performance by Davies and the quicksilver one by Watson. There are many moments when, based on the tension and vagueness in the air, relations between the two characters could go any which way, and the two thesps make even the most unlikely of these dramatic jumps relatively credible.

On the other hand, there are many times when the father's, and even the mother's, behavior is so absurd and dictatorial that one can't believe that Ray doesn't just tell them to go stuff it. While the central action is presented seriously, things on the periphery are caricatured and one-dimensional, which helps contribute to the widely roving tone.

The two main performances may be nuanced, but the visuals are not, as Russell doesn't really know where to put the camera for maximum effect and control of his material. Images don't proceed in a smooth, logical or attractive manner, creating erratic pacing and making plot developments seem more abrupt and indigestible than necessary.

Lensed in Pawling, N.Y., pic is clearly the work of a creative intelligence, but one that doesn't yet have full command of the tools and fine points of the craft. As with many first novels, it's sometimes necessary to get compulsive stuff out of one's system before moving on to more mature work.
—*Todd McCarthy*

COMING OUT UNDER FIRE

(DOCU — B&W — 16mm)

A Deep Focus production. Produced, directed by Arthur Dong. Written by Allan Berube, Dong, based on Berube's book. Camera (B&W), Stephen Lighthill; editor, Veronica Selver; music, Mark Adler; sound, Lauretta Molitor. Reviewed at Sundance Film Festival, Park City, Utah, Jan. 24, 1994. (Also in Berlin Film Festival.) Running time: **70 MIN.**
Narrator: Salome Jens.

Arthur Dong's powerful documentary, "Coming Out Under Fire," informs the current debate over gays and lesbians in the military by viewing the issue from a historical perspective. By focusing on undaunted homosexuals who served as soldiers in World War II, the film provides some context for President Clinton's 1993 effort to lift the ban on gays in the military and the ongoing national debate. Many viewers may want to see this timely, informative, technically accomplished docu in theaters before it's shown on public TV and in other venues.

Fascinating docu is based on the acclaimed 1990 book "Coming Out Under Fire: The History of Gay Men and Women in World War II," by Allan Berube, who served here as historian and co-writer. Director and co-writer Dong masterfully interweaves the tales of nine courageous men and women, all sharing in detail their personal memories of daily military life.

"They made you lie," says one man. "They made you live an invisible life." Indeed, "don't ask, don't tell" became by necessity the motto of patriotic homosexuals.

Despite their varied backgrounds, motivations to join the war effort and military careers, the stories are united by the individuals' strength and willingness to serve the country in the face of oppression and humiliating treatment. Docu shows that the military proved most resourceful in its methods, subjecting known gays and lesbians to dehumanizing interrogations, medical examinations, incarceration in "queer stockades" and hospitals for the criminal and mentally insane, and stigmatization as "sex perverts."

Though pic's overall tone is serious and investigative, it also contains compelling personal stories that make it riveting and entertaining. Some talk about how they devised subtle ways to identify other gays and communicate through newsletters that used campy Dorothy Parker lingo; one publication was called Myrtle Bitch; a former WAC fondly recalls her infatuation and first romance with another woman. Being black and gay was a "double whammy," one member mournfully testifies.

Dong, who made the 1983 Oscar-nominated "Sewing Woman," a touching portrait of his mother's emigration from China to the U.S., properly balances his work between serious, matter-of-fact illumination of a shameful chapter in American history and lighter, though sensitive, treatment of the human stories.

Framing the docu are dramatic scenes from the 1993 Senate hearings, which expose how the American government continues to perpetuate and reaffirm its ideology — and practice — of discriminating against homosexual soldiers. This contemporary evidence lends greater poignancy to the numerous cases of dishonorable discharge of valiant homosexuals.

Tech credits are first-rate, particularly Stephen Lighthill's polished lensing and Veronica Selver's seamless editing of invaluable archival footage of medical examinations, psychiatric sessions, sex education lectures, statistics and interviews. Deservedly cited by the Sundance jury for its technical distinction, "Coming Out Under Fire" is accomplished and satisfying emotionally and politically.

—*Emanuel Levy*

MARTHA & ETHEL

(DOCU — B&W/COLOR)

A Sony Pictures Classics release of a Canobie Films production. Produced, directed by Jyll Johnstone. Co-producer, Barbara Ettinger. Camera (B&W, color), Joseph Friedman; editor, Toby Shimin; associate producers, Gretchen McGowan, Christina Houlihan. Reviewed at Sundance Film Festival, Park City, Utah, Jan. 24, 1994. Running time: **78 MIN.**

Highly personal and original, "Martha & Ethel" deals with a subject rarely seen on screen before: nannies and their long-lasting influence on the children they raise. Criss-crossing the paths of the filmmakers' own nannies, a German-Catholic and a Southern black woman, this remarkable docu provides a piercing yet subtle look at the inner workings of two families as they change over five decades of American history and politics.

Though Martha and Ethel are of similar age, they couldn't have had more diverse backgrounds — and personalities. Born in Germany in 1902, Martha trained as a baby nurse and worked as a nanny for a Jewish family. In 1936, she escaped Nazi Germany and emigrated to the U.S. Five years later, she began working for the Johnstones, where she remained until she retired 30 years later.

Ethel is just as eccentric as Martha but displays a greater sense of drama and humor when she speaks. She was born in 1903 in South Carolina to a sharecropper family. Like Martha, she totally embraced the responsibility of raising someone else's family — in this case, the Ettingers — serving as its cornerstone through divorce, relocations and marriages.

Though intimately focused, "Martha & Ethel" embodies a universal dimension in its challenge to the conventional definition of family, summed up by Ethel as: "You don't have to birth a child to love her." Docu shows effectively that it's possible to be closer as a surrogate than a biological mother. Indeed, the children in both families ultimately absorbed the value systems of their nannies: Martha's authoritarian discipline and Ethel's warm kindness.

As youngsters, the Ettingers and Johnstones were so used to their nannies' presence and comfort that they were "offended" upon learning that a fee was paid for their services. Taking for granted their privileged status, they also naively assumed that every American family has its nanny.

Stylistically, "Martha & Ethel" employs traditional methods, mostly lengthy interviews with the nannies and their respective households. But what gives this docu a distinctive flavor is the personal odyssey that director Jyll Johnstone and producer Barbara Ettinger have undergone, as they continue to define and redefine the meanings and effects of their relationships with their nannies.

"Martha & Ethel" assumes greater relevance by placing its unique personae in a broader political context. The vast changes in American society's expectations of women as wives and mothers have dramatically affected the younger generation. It's a testament to the lasting power of their bond that Ethel continues to live with Ettinger, though none of the children is at home, and that Martha moved to California to be closer to the Johnstones.

For the most part, "Martha & Ethel" presents its heroines from the children's point of view. Docu glides over the emotional price and personal loss that these women might have experienced, as neither had romantic attachment once they assumed their positions. Analysis of the class differences between nannies and employers is lacking.

Still, earning every minute of its uplifting, life-affirming quality, "Martha & Ethel" raises provocative questions and is genuinely entertaining.

—*Emanuel Levy*

THE PORNOGRAPHER

A Charlie MoPic Co. production. Produced by Michael Nolin, Julie Bilson Ahlberg. Directed, written by Patrick Sheane Duncan. Camera (DuArt color), Michael G. Wojciechowski; editors, Joan Zapata, Troy Takaki, Rick Blue; music, Don Schiff; production design, Vincent Jefferds; art direction, Lauren Sharfman; set decoration, Ann Johnstad White; costume design, Jenny T. Jefferds; sound, Thomas Gregory Varga; associate producers, Steve Flick, Jefferds; assistant director, Michael Pariser; casting, Justine Jacoby. Reviewed at Sundance Film Festival, Park City, Jan. 24, 1994. Running time: **105 MIN.**

Greyson Robey	Jason Tomlins
E. Conrad Zabo	Nicholas Cascone
Sasha Leon Hoffner	Melora Hardin
Angel	Alix Koromzay
Irene	Margot Kidder

A viable idea for a movie is buried inside "The Pornographer," an intellectually pretentious meditation on art vs. commerce in American life, centering on a nasty, frustrated, unfeeling artist. The core melodrama is so maladroitly written and most of the acting so amateurish that it might be a tough challenge to place this pic in the theatrical market.

As helmer and scripter, Patrick Sheane Duncan shows little trace of the talents he evidenced in "84 Charlie MoPic," one of the more remarkable films about Vietnam. The anti-hero of his new film is Greyson Robey (Jason Tomlins), a painter who seems to be commercially successful and artistically fulfilled, but only on the surface. In reality, he is a bitter, angry young man who's incapable of love and whose agenda is to exploit the gifts and goodwill of those around him.

The gallery of people manipulated by Greyson include his college buddy Connie (Nicholas Cascone), a porn filmmaker who helped launch his career; Sasha (Melora Hardin), the attractive daughter of the publisher of an influential arts magazine; and even Oscar (Hector Elias), an underpaid Hispanic day laborer who's actually creating Greyson's sculptures and is also expected to provide "stimulating" gruesome stories.

When Connie falls in love with Angel (Alix Koromzay), a prostitute he rescues from the streets, the insanely jealous, self-loathing Greyson devises a mean scheme to destroy him. This includes an unbearable scene in which Greyson tortures Irene (Margot Kidder), Connie's ex-lover who's now dying of AIDS.

Regrettably, Duncan's uninventive writing consists of too many stereotypes and cliches about the art world and its inhabitants. The juxtaposition between Connie, a paragon of goodness reconciled to making the most of his life even if it means directing porn, and Greyson, an obnoxious, talentless success, is embarrassingly simplistic.

Production values of this low-budgeter are serviceable. But considering that the narrative is situated in the art/porn worlds, "The Pornographer" offers little by way of voyeuristic pleasure; in fact, one wishes the ambience were wilder, more titillating.

Duncan acquits himself better as a director than writer, particularly in the film's first half-hour, which is promising in the way it sets the arena for the major conflicts. But as the story unfolds, the movie falls victim to a Freudian melodrama of jealousy. What the script needs is dramatic streamlining — the personalities and dialogue are too banal to provoke much interest.

In the lead role, Tomlins brings a convincing physical presence and some authority to his deplorable character. The rest of the cast, however, is unimpressive, particularly Cascone as the kind and loyal Connie, and Hardin as the bystander witness, who finally summons courage and walks out on Greyson.

Ultimately, the film can't disguise the fact that it's a camouflage for "artistic" vs. "commercial" filmmaking in Hollywood. Indeed, "The Pornographer" is a disingenuous film that suffers from too many familiar generalities about real creativity and selling out.

—*Emanuel Levy*

ACE VENTURA, PET DETECTIVE

A Warner Bros. release of a James G. Robinson presentation of a Morgan Creek production. Produced by Robinson. Executive producer, Gary Barber. Co-producers, Peter Bogart, Bob Israel. Directed by Tom Shadyac. Screenplay, Jack Bernstein, Shadyac, Jim Carrey, story by Bernstein. Camera (color), Julio Macat; editor, Don Zimmerman; music, Ira Newborn; production design, William Elliott; art direction, Alan E. Murakoa; set design, Rich Fojo; set decoration, Scott Jacobson; costume design, Bobbie Read; sound (Dolby), Russell C. Fager; animal coordinator, Cathy Morrison; stunt coordinator, Artie Malesci; assistant director, Terry Miller; casting, Mary Jo Slater. Reviewed at AMC Old Pasadena 8, Jan. 29, 1994. MPAA Rating: PG-13. Running time: **93 MIN.**

Ace Ventura	Jim Carrey
Melissa	Courteney Cox
Einhorn	Sean Young
Dan Marino	Dan Marino
Riddle	Noble Winningham
Podacter	Troy Evans
Woodstock	Raynor Scheine
Camp	Udo Kier
Emilio	Tone Loc

Built as a slapstick vehicle for Jim Carrey, "Ace Ventura, Pet Detective" may hit a few bumps when it veers outside the lanes of its core audience of

February 7, 1994 (Cont.)

under-20s and aficionados of the "In Living Color" star. While clearly following a path carved by anarchic clowns such as Jerry Lewis and Peter Sellers, "Ace" doesn't display the comic pedigree needed for the rubber-faced-and-limbed comedian to collar breakthrough dollars. That said, dumb good times still wield a strong lure for the Saturday night date crowd.

Directed with vigor if not spades of style or polish by vet TV thesp-director Tom Shadyac in his feature debut, "Ace" spoofs the detective genre by positing Carrey as a goofball private gumshoe whose specialty is finding missing pets.

Unlike famous bumbling sleuths such as Inspector Clouseau and Lt. Frank Drebin, there's no consistency to Ace's character, and pic shifts in tone from social satire to sophomoric pranks and cop-show plotting as Ventura sets out to solve the kidnapping of the Miami Dolphins' lovable dolphin mascot, Snowflake.

Along the trail he befriends and beds the Dolphins' beautiful flak (Courteney Cox), perplexes top cop Einhorn (Sean Young) and stumbles onto a nefarious revenge plot that involves Dolphins quarterback Dan Marino and a mythical Super Bowl misplay of the past.

"Ace" is briskly paced and graced with Carrey's ceaseless energy and peculiar talents, such as the ability to act out a football play in slow motion *and* rewind.

Pic scores points for its peppy, unpretentious quest to wrest laughs out of less than sparkling material. Best gags involve Ventura's menagerie-packed apartment and animal-like qualities, including high-revved senses of taste, smell and sexual appetite. Unfortunately, there are too few to fill out the film's 90-plus minutes.

Supporting players Cox, Warhol alumnus Udo Kier as mysterious billionaire Camp and rapper Tone Loc as a sympathetic cop have little to do but watch Carrey riff. Young grimaces and growls as she is subjected to an endless barrage of indignities. Her Einhorn is the kind of role that makes it even clearer why she fought so hard for a shot at Catwoman.

Film sputters and eventually slows to a trot due to the script's inability to give Carrey anything more than a free rein to mug and strut, and a third-act payoff that takes the film's generally inoffensive tastelessness into a particularly brutal and unpleasant stew of homophobia and misogyny. This misstep, after a midplot turn involving a key character's bloody (and confusing) murder, throws the good-natured high jinks of Carrey off course.

Seemingly clueless as to how best to utilize Carrey, or make humorous hay out of its pet-loving shamus' central character, "Ventura" fails to place either Carrey or "Ace" in the winner's circle of memorable screen crazies.   —*Steve Gaydos*

GUNMEN

A Miramax/Dimension Films release. Produced by Laurence Mark, John Davis, John Flock. Executive producers, Lance Hool, Conrad Hool. Co-producers, James Gorman, John Baldecchi. Directed by Deran Sarafian. Screenplay, Stephen Sommers. Camera (Deluxe color), Hiro Narita; editor, Bonnie Koehler; music, John Debney; production design, Michael Seymour; art direction, Hector Romero Jr.; set decoration, Ian Whitaker, Enrique Estevez; costume design, Betsy Heimann; sound (Dolby), Fernando Camara; special effects, Jesus (Chucho) Duran; assistant director, Sebastian Silva; casting, Terry Liebling. Reviewed at the Laemmle Sunset 5, L.A., Jan. 7, 1994. MPAA Rating: R. Running time: **90 MIN.**

Dani Servigo	Christopher Lambert
Cole Parker	Mario Van Peebles
Armor O'Malley	Denis Leary
Loomis	Patrick Stewart
Izzy	Kadeem Hardison
Bennett	Sally Kirkland
Chief Chavez	Richard Sarafian
Rance	Robert Harper
Maria	Brenda Bakke

Cashing in on the appeal of stars Mario Van Peebles and Christopher Lambert, "Gunmen" is a routine, vacuous actioner that tries to mix thrills with humor. Saddled with an uninvolving B plot, pic will be more popular in Europe, where Lambert is a marketable star, than domestically, and it may prove to be a better video rental than a big-screen presentation.

Scripter Stephen Sommers, who last year wrote and directed "The Adventures of Huck Finn," constructs a formulaic tale of chase and revenge that combines elements of both the action and Western genres. Cole Parker (Van Peebles), a N.Y. special forces agent working with the Drug Enforcement Agency, is sent to an unnamed South American country to confiscate the illegal gains stolen from a drug dealer who murdered his father.

The adventure begins when Parker busts out of jail Dani Servigo (Lambert), an offbeat outlaw who is supposed to know the site of the huge fortune. The two men are soon pursued by Armor O'Malley (Denis Leary), a ruthless killer hired by drug lord Peter Loomis (Patrick Stewart) to halt Parker and recover the money.

As written by Sommers and directed by Deran Sarafian, "Gunmen" suffers from serious storytelling problems: The violent sequences erupt senselessly without much attention to logic or continuity. Sarafian gives the picture an erratic, high-strung pace.

Van Peebles' considerable acting talents are largely wasted on what's basically a stereotypical, under-written role; in most scenes he's allowed to utter no more than one sentence. Lambert, usually a bland action hero, lacks the necessary skills to pull off what's intended as light and humorous dialogue.

Stewart, who's been impressive in his TV work ("Star Trek: The Next Generation"), registers strongly as a physical presence but plays a cliched archvillain. As the tough, foulmouthed villainess, Brenda Bakke is given an embarrassing sex scene that is meant to be amusing.

Production values, particularly Hiro Narita's lensing around Puerto Vallarta, are proficient, though Bonnie Koehler's editing is abrupt and lacks fluidity.

Mindlessly cartoonish, "Gunmen" lacks the expected frills and spiteful tension of a serviceable actioner.   —*Emanuel Levy*

MOUVEMENTS DU DESIR
(DESIRE IN MOTION)
(CANADIAN-SWISS)

An Alliance-Vivafilm release of a Cinemaginaire Inc./National Film Board of Canada/Catpica Co-productions Ltee (Zurich) production, with the participation of Telefilm Canada and SOGIC. (International sales: Alliance.) Produced by Denise Robert. Co-producers (Switzerland) Alfi Sinniger, Peter Baumann. Directed, written by Lea Pool. Camera (color), Pierre Mignot; editor, Michel Arcand; music, Zbigniew Preisner; artistic director, Serge Bureau; costumes, Sabina Haag; sound, Florian Eidenbenz; line producer, Daniel Louis; line producer (National Film Board), Leon G. Arcand; associate producer (National Film Board), Yves Rivard. Reviewed at the Astral screening room, Montreal, Feb. 1, 1994. (In Rendez-Vous du Cinema Quebecois Film Festival.) Running time: **94 MIN.**

Catherine	Valerie Kaprisky
Vincent	Jean-Francois Pichette
Charlotte	Jolianne L'Allier-Matteau
Tom	William Jacques
Tadzio	Mathew Mackay

Also with: Elyse Guilbault, Mimi D'Estee, Nadia Paradis, Yvon Roy, Michael Rudder, Jean Marchand, Sheena Larkin, Jacques Girard, Sylvie Legault, Serge Christiansens, Doru Bandol

Selected to open this year's Rendez-Vous du Cinema Quebecois fest, veteran helmer Lea Pool's "Mouvements du desir" is an ultra-steamy up-date of the classic romance-on-a-train theme that adds new zing to the storyline with the help of some hot train-car sex scenes and Pool's hyperactive visual imagination.

The pic will likely do well with adult audiences in French Canada, where it opened Feb. 4. It could also generate serious arthouse action in Europe, where the Swiss-born, Montreal-based Pool is well-respected, and could have a shot in the U.S. The presence of Euro siren Valerie Kaprisky ("Breathless," "La Femme publique") in the lead role won't hurt the film's commercial prospects either.

Pool — whose previous pix include 1984's "La Femme de l'hotel" and 1988's "A Corps perdu" — is known for a moody, introspective style of filmmaking that frequently employs innovative formal flourishes. All those qualities are still to be found in "Mouvements du desir," but it is easily her most accessible, viewer-friendly outing to date.

The story couldn't be more straightforward. Catherine (Kaprisky), with her spunky 7-year-old daughter, Charlotte (Jolianne L'Allier-Matteau), is taking the cross-Canada train from Montreal to Vancouver in an attempt to forget about a failed relationship. Vincent (Jean-Francois Pichette) is also on the train, on his way to meet up with the woman he loves.

The melancholic Catherine and the shy, unassuming Vincent don't hit it off at first, but the sensual sparks begin to fly somewhere west of Toronto, and by the time the train hits the Rockies, they're steaming up the windows with lusty abandon.

The sultry Kaprisky shows impressive range in her portrayal of this complex character who is swept up in an almost magnetic attraction. Pichette also deserves top marks for his perf, though the real scene stealer is L'Allier-Matteau as the little girl who's not amused by her mother's torrid railway romance.

Pool is still fond of throwing in funky, avant-garde twists, and she spices up this meditation on love and desire with a series of surrealistic, Fellini-esque dream sequences, which ensure that this won't be mistaken for a standard romantic drama. She also adds to the quirky atmosphere by populating the train with eccentric characters, including a thief who steals cameras and Walkmans and then redistributes them among the passengers.

Cinematographer Pierre Mignot, who's worked extensively with Robert Altman, nicely juxtaposes hand-held shots of the tight, claustrophobic interiors with broad outdoor vistas, and the images of the Canuck landscape haunt this intimate love story. Polish composer Zbigniew Preisner provides a subtle, eclectic score. All other tech credits are first-rate.

—*Brendan Kelly*

February 7, 1994 (Cont.) **February 14, 1994**

DECADENCE

(BRITISH-GERMAN)

A Mayfair Entertainment release (U.K.) of a Delux Prods. production, in association with Vendetta Films and Schlammer Prods., with assistance from Filmstiftung NRW (Germany). Produced by Lance W. Reynolds, Christoph Meyer-Wiel. Executive producers, Fred Bestall, Frank Henschke, Romain Schroeder. Co-producer, Wieland Schulz Keil. Directed, written by Steven Berkoff, from his play. Camera (Fujicolor; Technicolor prints), Denis Lenoir; editor, John Wilson; music, Stewart Copeland; production design, Yolande Sonnabend, Simon Holland; art direction, Wilbert van Dorp, Ulli Hanisch; costume design, David Blight; sound (Dolby SR), George Richards, Peter Smith; choreography, Rodolpho Leoni, Thorsten Kuth; assistant director, Eric Bartonio; casting, Sue Jones. Reviewed at MGM Haymarket 1 theater, London, Feb. 2, 1994. Running time: **112 MIN.**
Helen/Sybil .... Joan Collins
Steve/Les/
  Helen's Couturier .... Steven Berkoff
  Also with: Christopher Biggins, Michael Winner, Marc Sinden, Edward Duke, Robert Longdon, David Alder, Trim Dry, Imogen Bain, Susannah Morley, Ursula Smith, Veronica Lang, Mathilda Ziegler, Terence Beesley.

Actor/playwright Steven Berkoff's own film of his stage play "Decadence" is a ripe, belching, heaving, power-drill satire of 1980s Thatcherite Britain that's as full of excesses as the passe targets it parodies. Essentially a two-hander, with Berkoff himself and Joan Collins in multiple roles, pic has some fine moments but finally sinks under the weight of its own ego. Brit legit bad-boy Berkoff looks set for a B.O. clunker here.

Berkoff and Collins play two couples at the extremities of the English social scale. Steve is having an affair with Mayfair socialite Helen; meanwhile, Steve's nouveau riche wife, Sybil, who lives in the 'burbs, is canoodling with working-class Les, an investigator she's hired to follow her philandering husband.

Story, such as it is, cross-cuts between the two pairs as the former romp in Helen's ritzy apartment and fashionable restaurants while the latter plot between the sheets how to get rid of their socially mobile nemeses.

It's clear by about the second reel that the pic is essentially the biggest ego outing by a renaissance spirit since Anthony Newley's 1969 "Can Hieronymus Merkin Ever Forget Mercy Humppe and Find True Happiness?" (which also, coincidentally, lassoed Collins in a supporting role).

When Berkoff slows down his motor, or hands over the screen to Collins, the qualities of the script take on an aspect of almost Shakespearean bawdy humor. (It's written in generally discreet rhym-

ing couplets and a mix of archaisms and modern four-letter words). Though the targets of the play — first staged in the mid-1980s when Berkoff-mania was at its peak in Blighty — are long gone in the safe, recessionary '90s, there's often much to enjoy in Berkoff's rotund dialogue.

Though Collins was a late choice — after the pic's backers nixed Berkoff's stage partner, Linda Marlowe, and Miranda Richardson and Helen Mirren declined — she emerges with the greatest credit in a role tailor-made for her talents, moving effortlessly between the high-glam, bored socialite queen and lower-middle-class slag. Her sexual monologues, especially one astride a kneeling Berkoff as they play rider and horse, are alone almost worth the price of admission.

Actor Berkoff's over-the-top pastiching of Bob Hoskins in the Les role, and a Jack Hawkins-like character in the twit part, often does his own script a disservice. In his first big-screen directing stint, he shows an OK command of the medium — notably in a semi-choreographed eatery scene, with "Hello, Dolly!"-like gliding waiters — that occasionally overreaches into obviousness.

Among several familiar British faces, Michael Winner cameos as a cigar-chomping true Brit in an embarrassing sequence set in a London gentleman's club.

Camera work by Denis Lenoir is often unsubtly over-lit, and production design shows budget limitations. For a pic in which the words are everything, soundtrack could be much cleaner as Berkoff's words are often obscured by distortion. Film was produced in Luxembourg and Germany, with only some establishing material actually lensed in London. —*Derek Elley*

THE GETAWAY

A Universal release from Largo Entertainment in association with JVC Entertainment of a Turman-Foster Company/John Alan Simon production. Produced by David Foster, Lawrence Turman, John Alan Simon. Directed by Roger Donaldson. Screenplay, Walter Hill, Amy Jones, based on the novel by Jim Thompson. Camera (Deluxe color; Panavision widescreen), Peter Menzies Jr.; editor, Conrad Buff; music, Mark Isham; production design, Joseph Nemec III; art direction, Dan Olexiewicz; set design, Wm. Law III; set decoration, R.W. "Inke" Intlekofer; sound, Richard Bryce Goodman; stunt coordinator, Glenn R. Wilder; associate producer, Marilyn Vance; assistant director, Joel B. Segal; second unit camera, Peter Levy; casting, Michael Fenton, Allison Cowitt. Reviewed at the UA Westwood, L.A., Feb. 8, 1994. MPAA Rating: R. Running time: **115 MIN.**
Doc McCoy .... Alec Baldwin
Carol McCoy .... Kim Basinger
Rudy Travis .... Michael Madsen
Jack Benyon .... James Woods
Jim Deer Jackson .... David Morse
Fran Carvey .... Jennifer Tilly
Harold Carvey .... James Stephens
Slim .... Richard Farnsworth
Frank Hansen .... Philip Hoffman
Gollie .... Burton Gilliam
Gun Shop
  Salesman .... Royce D. Applegate
Mendoza .... Daniel Villareal

"The Getaway" is a pretty good remake of a pretty good action thriller. Although the attributes and drawbacks of this well-outfitted retelling of Jim Thompson's edgy crime meller and Sam Peckinpah's gritty 1972 rendition lie in different places, the net effect of this tale of innumerable deceptions, betrayals and double-crosses is more or less the same. With Alec Baldwin and Kim Basinger toplining, this Universal release delivers enough high-octane kicks to make off with some solid coin.

While it may seem pointless to redo a 22-year-old film that wasn't bad to begin with (with a writer and producer from the original doing encores, no less), the first version was hardly a classic that should never have been tampered with. At the time, in fact, it seemed like a routine commercial assignment in the midst of Peckinpah's great run from "The Wild Bunch" through "Pat Garrett and Billy the Kid."

Still, initial outing featured attractively terse storytelling, plenty of authentic Southwestern good ol' boys and, most of all, a brooding, tightly coiled lead performance by Steve McQueen.

On the other hand, the original's attitude toward women was decidedly dicey, a problem exacer-

bated by Ali MacGraw's blandness and Sally Struthers' shrillness. Along with redressing the balance between the sexes, director Roger Donaldson has cooked up two or three suspense scenes that surpass their earlier equivalents. All comparisons aside, the new film simply engages attention by virtue of its nasty narrative, duplicitous characters and tough action, which puts it a cut above the norm among Hollywood crime sagas these days.

Peckinpah's protracted original credit sequence, with McQueen's Doc McCoy in a prison surrounded by deer, was wonderful, but Donaldson has one-upped him with a startlingly fresh prologue, turning on two criminal betrayals, showing how Doc (Baldwin) landed in jail. Early action also firms the characters of Doc's sharpshooting wife, Carol (Basinger), and their early partner and eventual nemesis, Rudy (Michael Madsen).

Plot clicks in as Doc is released from a Mexican slammer courtesy of slick crime lord Jack Benyon (James Woods), who recruits the master thief and explosives expert to head a heist of a Phoenix dog track vault.

Reassuring his wife with the well-worn promise that this will be their last job, Doc succeeds in nabbing the cash, but things go awry when a guard is killed. Rudy is nearly snuffed himself in a shootout with Doc, who then honorably goes to split up the loot with Benyon. Taunting the younger man, Benyon oozingly informs him exactly what his wife did to get him released from the pen, and how much she enjoyed it. Enter Carol pointing a pistol, not quite sure whom she intends to shoot.

From this point on, as the McCoys uneasily make their way to El Paso and the Mexican border in a variety of cars, with an unplanned detour by train, "Getaway" '94 becomes increasingly identical to the original, down to specific incidents and lines of dialogue. Some police car chase stuff seems a bit tired and perfunctory, but Donaldson puts the pedal to the floor for the climactic border-town hotel shootout.

With momentary exceptions, pic clicks along neatly, as Donaldson reasserts the talent he displayed for rugged action and contentious relationships earlier in his career, but which seemed dissipated in some of his more recent projects. For the most part, screenwriters Walter Hill (whose second screen credit was the original) and Amy Jones ("Indecent Proposal") have made an effort to retain and expand what was dramatically effective in the Peckinpah, and to revise or prop up the obvious weak points.

In particular, the character of Carol has been strengthened considerably. Doc here considers her a valuable partner in crime, in addition to being a lusty wife, and she gets to come through in a pinch on more than one occasion. Even Basinger bashers might find themselves rather taken with her gritty turn here, which certainly reps one of the film's more pleasant surprises.

Baldwin fills the bill perfectly well as the smart, tenacious criminal ready to hang up his hat, but McQueen came with a magnetism and fascination Baldwin doesn't have — at least not yet. Like a Mickey Rourke crazy with a rock 'n' roll fright wig, Madsen fashions a villain you love to hate, while Woods hits a repetitious note of smug superiority as the plot's mastermind.

Jennifer Tilly seems just feeble-brained as the wimpy vet's wife kidnapped and enslaved by Rudy, which is somewhat preferable to Struthers' gross floozy. Hard as it was to imagine who could replicate Slim Pickens' unique humor in the crucial role of the truck driver who spirits the couple to Mexico, Richard Farnsworth pulls it off, and is even called "Slim" in tribute.

Tech credits are solid, notably the extensive stunt work. Sex scenes between the married co-stars begin with promisingly spicy atmosphere and foreplay, but are cut before things really get cooking. Lucky foreign audiences reportedly will see several minutes more of the apparently too-hot-for-R-rating footage.
—*Todd McCarthy*

YOU SO CRAZY

A Miramax release of an HBO Independent Prods. presentation in association with You So Crazy Prods. Produced by Timothy Marx, David Knoller. Executive producer, Martin Lawrence. Co-producer, Michael Hubbard. Directed by Thomas Schlamme. Camera (color), Arthur Albert; editors, John Neal, Stephen Semel; production design, Richard Hoover; art direction, John Gisondi; lighting design, Allen Branton; associate producer, Ken Buford; assistant director, Emily Cohen. Reviewed at Raleigh Studios screening room, L.A., Feb. 9, 1994. MPAA Rating: NC-17. Running time: **85 MIN.**

Riding a hit Fox sitcom and regular HBO host role, **Martin Lawrence** is a very hot property right now, and this energetic concert film should cash in on his loyal if somewhat limited following. Using language so bawdy as to make a Friars roast look like a church sermon, Lawrence doesn't figure to expand his ap-

peal here, but the existing "Martinized" audience should be enough to make this pic "go" for Miramax.

Lawrence is clearly trying to follow in the footsteps of Eddie Murphy and particularly Richard Pryor through this standup vehicle, while HBO (which also produces his sitcom) provides itself with a savvy marketing tie-in as it seeks to elevate the comic to that level.

Like Murphy, with whom he co-starred in "Boomerang," Lawrence is perhaps a less gifted standup comic than he is a comic actor, playing multiple characters as he paces and occasionally sprints around the stage.

As a result, the material — from an opening routine about racism (a particularly funny moment has Lawrence likening Rodney King to Kunta Kinte of "Roots") to extensive talk about sex and differences between the sexes — isn't as strong as the manner in which Lawrence presents it, seamlessly shifting from being the smooth nightclub operator to the "crazy, deranged" boyfriend that operator becomes a few months later.

Punctuating practically each sentence with the same four- and 12-letter words, Lawrence certainly works as dirty as Pryor, but lacks the observational skills Pryor possessed in his heyday, relying too heavily on blue material to prop up his act.

That may delight easily impressed teenagers, but it inhibits Lawrence from expanding his reach, though, as noted, his talents seem well-suited to moving up to headline a scripted comedy vehicle.

Director Thomas Schlamme, a veteran of numerous comedy specials, does a fine job in giving the moviegoing audience the best seat in the house, making particularly deft use of editing techniques when Lawrence plays more than one character.

Pic was shot at the Majestic Theatre in Brooklyn, with Lawrence nattily attired in leather pajamas, all dressed up and clearly looking for his next big showcase.
—*Brian Lowry*

SUNDANCE

HOOP DREAMS

(DOCU—16mm)

A Kartemquin Films/KCTA-TV production. (Sales: Iltis Sikich, Chicago.) Produced by Fred Marx, Steve James, Peter Gilbert. Executive producers, Gordon Quinn, Catherine Allan. Directed by James. Camera (color), Gilbert; additional camera, Quinn, Ed Scott, Sid Lubitsch, Kevin McCarey, Mirko Popadic, Jim Morrissette, Jim Fetterley; editors, Marx, James, Bill Haugse; music producer, Ben Sidran; creative consultant, Quinn; sound, Adam Singer, Tom Yore. Reviewed at Sundance Film Festival, Park City, Jan. 25, 1994. Running time: **174 MIN.**
With: William Gates, Arthur Agee, Emma Gates, Curtis Gates, Sheila Agee, Arthur (Bo) Agee, Earl Smith, Gene Pingatore, Isiah Thomas, Patricia Weir, Luther Bedford, Shannon Johnson, Tomika Agee, Joe (Sweetie) Agee, Jazz Agee, Catherine Mines, Willie Gates, Dick Vitale, Kevin O'Neill, Bobby Knight, Spike Lee, Bo Ellis, Tim Gray, others.

A prodigious achievement that conveys the fabric of modern American life, aspirations and, incidentally, sports in close-up and at length, "Hoop Dreams" is a documentary slam dunk. This intimate epic chronicles 4½ years in the lives of two black inner-city Chicago kids, both of whom harbor legitimate hopes of making it as professional basketball players, from neighborhood play at 14 to high school tournaments, college recruiting and their eventual departure from home. A dual approach of screenings at fests and for specially targeted urban audiences would trigger plenty of start-up word of mouth, and limited theatrical runs would seem warranted in advance of broadcast on public TV, where it could easily be positioned as a major event.

In its most specific sense, this film by Steve James, Fred Marx and Peter Gilbert follows teenage hoopmeisters William Gates and Arthur Agee as they go through the steps all prospects must take on the way to the National Basketball Assn.

Of the 500,000 kids who play high school basketball every year, only about 25 ever play as much as one season professionally, but it is clear that the dream of success motivates the lives, not only of the players themselves but of their families and much of the economically depressed communities in which they live.

By keeping their cameras in close over such a long period, however, the filmmakers have also rendered a remarkable portrait of growing up in the city today, of the fragility and resilience of the family, of the dif-

ficulty of escaping the ghettos and projects, of the negative pressures on decent people applied by society and criminality, of the perception of successful athletes as something other than normal human beings.

The three-hour running time makes for a long sit, and some will argue that sections could be lost without heavy damage, but the wide-ranging, comprehensive approach ultimately pays dividends that decidedly reward the investment of time.

High school scout Earl Smith leads the filmmakers to Gates and Agee, who, as 14-year-old eighth-graders, are already considered blue-chip prospects. Both are lured out of Chicago to attend St. Joseph's, a suburban Catholic high school of which NBA superstar Isiah Thomas is the most illustrious alumnus. Both are offered financial support and perform well on the court during freshman year, but Agee is forced to leave for financial reasons.

Agee enrolls in the all-black public high school Marshall, where he becomes so despondent that both his academic and sports careers falter. Adding to his woes is the departure of his father, forcing the family onto welfare for the first time. One of the film's most startling sidelights, which speaks volumes about the fatherhood problem in the inner cities, is the weaving in and out of Bo Agee; in a shocking scene, Arthur sees his father, now a crack-addicted street person, making a drug buy on the very playground where he's shooting baskets.

The players' high school careers progress in surprising ways: Agee, who seems on the verge of closing up and possibly turning bad, rebounds and helps lead unranked Marshall to the state championship tourney. Gates suffers the setback of a knee injury that ultimately requires two operations. Despite this, he is invited to the prestigious Nike Basketball Camp at Princeton, where the nation's leading college coaches check out the season's top prospects.

The pressures and personal aspects of college recruiting are seen in detail, as Gates, who is suddenly shown to have a girlfriend and baby, is induced to sign a scholarship with Marquette, while Agee is virtually ignored despite his great play. After the tension of their senior-year games, and especially after one of them is held up at gunpoint in the neighborhood, they are looking forward to getting out, although the future for both is questionable.

Few works in any medium have been able to show so concretely all the ways kids change during adolescence. The process is exaggerated here because of the tremendous pressure on all fronts, but the fact that it is real, not dramatized, makes the spectacle of the kids being worn down, and forced so young to face life's disappointments and realities, so compelling.

Filmmakers shot some 250 hours of film (and, it would appear, video) to cover this saga. The fact that they always seem to have been on the spot when it counted speaks to their tenacious commitment, as well as to the tremendous cooperation of their subjects, who had to put up with the invasion of their lives (often at uncomfortable moments) for more than four years. Pic will provoke interesting comment from many different quarters for its innumerable artistic, sociological and sports-related qualities.

—*Todd McCarthy*

THEREMIN: AN ELECTRONIC ODYSSEY

(DOCU — B&W/COLOR)

A Kaga Bay production. Produced, directed, written by Steven M. Martin. Camera (b&w, color), Frank De Marco, with Robert Stone (Moscow), Cris Lombardi (Los Angeles), Ed Lachman (Clara Rockmore concert); editor, David Greenwald; music, Hal Wilner; sound, Andy Green. Reviewed at Sundance Film Festival, Park City, Utah, Jan. 29, 1994. Running time: 83 MIN.
With: Leon Theremin, Clara Rockmore, Robert Moog, Nicholas Slonimsky, Paul Shure, Henry Solomonoff, Brian Wilson, others.

Brilliant in moments, but basically flawed, "Theremin: An Electronic Odyssey" revolves around Leon Theremin, the genius scientist/artist who revolutionized modern music with his invention of the world's first electronic instrument. Gliding over crucial issues, director Steven M. Martin conveys only glimpses of the eccentric life, politics and art of Theremin, who died in Moscow in 1993, at the age of 97. Shown last fall on British TV, "Theremin" is similarly a likely item for American TV, though docu might also warrant a limited theatrical release due to its subject's fascinating life and long-lasting influence on popular culture.

Labeled "the prophet of the future of music" and "the Soviet Edison," Theremin was born in Russia in 1895. Docu doesn't provide much information about his childhood, education or the intellectual influences on his vision, other than saying that in 1918 he invented the theremin, an electronic instrument that produced, as one interviewee says, "strange ethereal sounds from the air, without even touching it." Lenin was reportedly so impressed that he summoned Theremin to the Kremlin for a demonstration, after which he exclaimed, "Communism equals socialism plus electrification!"

Martin chronicles Theremin's 1928 demonstration of his new instrument at a sold-out Carnegie Hall concert,

which led to his acceptance into the American artistic elite. But, unfortunately, not much is said about Theremin's controversial interracial marriage to the black ballerina Lavinia Holmes; docu just states that "his friends dropped him."

The most bizarre event in Theremin's life occurred in 1938, when he was abducted by Stalin's agents from his New York apartment. Charged with treason, Theremin was imprisoned in a Magadan Gulag. Later, during World War II, he was put to work on electronic research at the Moscow KGB headquarters. For his invention of the "bug," the first miniature electronic device that helped the Soviets spy on foreign embassies, Theremin was awarded the Stalin Prize.

Docu's most systematic aspect concerns Theremin's vast impact on the music world, including Hollywood movies that used his invention for their eerie scores, illustrated by excellent footage from Hitchcock's "Spellbound," Billy Wilder's "The Lost Weekend" and sci-fi pix such as "The Day the Earth Stood Still." Jumping to the 1960s, Brian Wilson talks about Theremin's effect on his work, specifically in composing the Beach Boys' landmark song "Good Vibrations."

Considering the flamboyant life that the handsome Theremin lived, the intellectual circles he belonged to and his invention of the world's first electronic security system (for Sing Sing prison), "Theremin: An Electronic Odyssey" suffers from too many information gaps and an awkward structure.

Despite all the problems, the man that "Theremin" celebrates lived such an outlandish life that it's always absorbing to watch his near-century-long odyssey. Here is a documentary that should have been longer — and fuller.

—*Emanuel Levy*

FREEDOM ON MY MIND

(DOCU — B&W/COLOR — 16mm)

A Clarity Film Prods. film. Produced, directed by Connie Field, Marilyn Mulford. Written, edited by Michael Chandler. Camera (b&w, color), Michael Chinn, Steve Devita, Vicente Franco; music, Mary Watkins; sound, Don Thomas, Larry Loewinger, Curtis Choy; associate producer, Hardy Frye. Reviewed at Sundance Film Festival, Park City, Jan. 28, 1994. Running time: 104 MIN.
Narrator: Ronnie Washington.

Telling the dramatic story of the Mississippi voter registration project from 1961 to 1964, "Freedom on My Mind" is a landmark documentary that chronicles the most tumultuous and significant years in the history of the

civil rights movement. Though its style and format may be a bit conventional for exploring such a riveting topic, the importance of the issue, which is placed in a broader political context, should make Connie Field and Marilyn Mulford's documentary a must-see, particularly for students. Pic won top docu prize from the jury at the Sundance fest.

Saga is told through the recollections of a few courageous blacks, mostly local Mississippi sharecroppers, who joined forces with committed organizers. Their personal stories are truly mesmerizing, showing how "second class" citizens — without any formal education, political power or experience — changed their lives as a result of their membership in the movement.

Feature's best chapter documents the fateful summer of 1964, when white middle-class students from all over the country went to Mississippi to work. The black members stress the novelty of those encounters, and how they were not used to being called by their first names by Southern whites; racism and segregation had become institutionalized down to the most personal interactions.

Pic shows that aside from putting cracks in a calcified society, the movement also performed vital personal functions, by helping to forge identities and supplying meaningful membership in larger collectives than one's own family. As one member puts it: "All my life I felt odd, and then I felt like home." Docu records how activists had to fight racism on two fronts: American society at large and the Democratic Party itself. It details the creation of the Mississippi Freedom Democratic Party and its plan to unseat the all-white segregationist delegates to the Democratic Convention in Atlantic City.

Ultimately, Field and Mulford's feature serves as a testimony to the power of grassroots politics, for the 68-member MFDP delegation consisted of sharecroppers, maids and day laborers. Even though the battle didn't result in immediate victory, it still demonstrated how the highest political authority can be challenged when the struggle concerns such values as equality and justice.

Tech credits are excellent: Intimate personal interviews are augmented by archival footage, some of which has not been seen since it was first shot in the 1960s. What's missing is some kind of epilogue to update the lives of the dozen or so individuals whose lives it celebrates.

—*Emanuel Levy*

FUN

A Neo Modern Entertainment Corp. and Damian Lee production. Produced, directed by Rafal Zielinski. Executive producers, Rana Joy Glickman, Jeff Kirshbaum. Co-producer, Lee. Screenplay, James Bosley, based on his play. Camera (Deluxe color), Jens Sturup; editor, Monika Lightstone; music, Marc Tschanz; production design, Vally Mestroni; costume design, Renee Johnston; sound (Ultra-Stereo), Arnold Brown, Laurent Wassmer; associate producers, Jeff Sackman, Lightstone; assistant director, Rick Baer; second unit camera, Donald Luczak; casting, Cathy Brown, Markie Costello. Reviewed at Sundance Film Festival, Park City, Jan. 23, 1994. Running time: 105 MIN.
Bonnie .... Alicia Witt
Hillary .... Renee Humphrey
John .... William R. Moses
Jane .... Leslie Hope
Mrs. Farmer .... Ania Suli

Startlingly good lead performances by two new actresses give some distinction to "Fun," an absorbing study of crime and absent values among contempo teenagers that nonetheless feels unjelled and schizophrenic. Director Rafal Zielinski holds the interest with some intriguing artistic strategies, brutal subject matter and live-wire characterizations, but pic's tendency to repeatedly wobble between honest reporting and faintly exploitative voyeurism casts the proceedings in an uneasy light. The acting and touchy, timely topic, give critics and certain audiences something to respond to here, but reactions will be divided and commercial chances look iffy.

Zielinski, Polish-born helmer who has spent most of his career on commercial fodder such as "Screwballs" and "Spellcaster" but had one previous Sundance entry in "Ginger Ale Afternoon," tries hard to give this theatrical adaptation an edgy, artistic veneer and succeeds up to a point.

Skipping back and forth in time and cinematic styles to recount how two teenage girls immediately bonded and committed a senseless murder, resourceful low-budgeter conveys seriousness and immediacy, but ends up having less to say about its contentious issues than the filmmakers might like to imagine.

James Bosley's screenplay, which is based on his play, delineates the exceedingly brief criminal careers of Bonnie and Hillary, two girls whose idea of a good time gets rather out of hand. Meeting by chance on a California roadside, they start sharing intimacies and secrets that are largely lies, and finally knock off a little old lady just for the hell of it.

This narrative, which is shot in vibrant color, is broken up and set in relief by an equal amount of raw, black-and-white material set in the juvenile detention facility where the girls are being held. Hillary (Renee Humphrey), a stubborn brunette, is under questioning by a male interviewer from a trendy magazine, while Bonnie (Alicia Witt), a hyper redhead, receives the third degree from a hard-bitten female case counselor.

Together in the day-in-the-life color section, the girls are quicksilver, emotionally eager and anxious to one-up each other with confessions of lurid experiences. If one says that she was raped by her father, the other feels compelled to claim the same violation by her brother. Any traits smacking of normalcy are shunned and denied, while anything that makes them seem fashionably victimized, or special by virtue of deprivation, is enthusiastically embraced and conspiratorially shared.

The *verite*-like interrogation sessions, by contrast, reveal resentful, immature kids who reject all values except for their motto, "Fun is No. 1." The reason for their detention is cleverly kept a mystery for virtually half the running time, but once revealed, the girls express no remorse for their crime, as it was bigtime fun in their book. Bonnie is less concerned for her victim than about whether Drew Barrymore will play her when their story is filmed.

Some time ago, such a story would have been utterly shocking. But while the externals of the case are undeniably potent, the tale is not sufficiently fleshed out or analyzed to get chillingly under the skin, and the rendering is too schematic to make it emotionally affecting.

If the film had some particularly telling insight into the behavior of the girls, a point of view that provided some unusual understanding, its raison d'etre would be clear. But running through the film there is a creepy, if subtle, feeling of surreptitious peering into the lives of naughty, wild young ladies, done under the guise of artistic seriousness, that creates a nagging discrepancy between the film's presumed intentions and its visceral effect.

Still, the performances by Witt and Humphrey go a long way toward giving the film a stinging legitimacy. Making their characters frighteningly grown-up in some ways and nearly infantile in others, the young actresses are vital and electrifying, and certainly bear watching in the future.

As the counselor, Leslie Hope provides an intriguingly brittle foil for her charge's impudence, while William R. Moses is hamstrung by an unsympathetic part as the writer looking to cash in on the girls' sensationalistic act.

Cinematographer Jens Sturup exhibits expertise in two styles, the luminous color narrative and the mostly hand-held, docu-style black-and-white, although the novelty of the approach wears a bit thin by the end.
—*Todd McCarthy*

FIRE EYES

(DOCU)

Executive produced, directed, written by Soraya Mire. Camera (color), Nancy Morita; editors, Lillian Benson, Joe Staton; music, Katherine Quittner; associate producer, Barry Ellsworth. Reviewed at Sundance Film Festival, Park City, Utah, Jan. 21, 1994. Running time: **60 MIN.**

"**Fire Eyes**," made by Somali filmmaker Soraya Mire, is a rare documentary that is equally effective as a personal and a political statement. Dealing with female genital mutilation, a widespread phenomenon in many African countries but little known in the West, this informative docu should be well-received on public TV, film festivals and wherever women's issues are aired.

Hourlong film focuses on female genital circumcision, which in its extreme form creates a chastity belt made of the girl's own flesh as she is literally stitched shut until marriage. Docu begins with a demonstration of a 7-year-old Somali girl about to undergo circumcision — her mother tells her that the "evil piece of flesh" between her thighs must be removed for her to become pure and worthy of a husband.

Mire makes a clear and useful distinction between male circumcision and its female version, which is much more drastic and excruciatingly painful. Pic gains poignancy and personal meaning when she relates how, at 13, she underwent this operation, which was framed as a necessary rite of passage.

As a mature woman, however, Mire perceives this mutilation as a manifestation of child abuse and an ideological mechanism designed to perpetuate women's sexual, economic and cultural inferiority.

Using a direct, uncompromisingly investigative strategy, Mire examines the wide range of results of this procedure: medical and physiological complications, psychological traumas and so on.

The filmmaker is sober enough to know that, as a ceremonial tradition still supported by many men, female genital mutilation might continue to prevail as it's transmitted from one generation to the next. But she also knows that without raising the consciousness of African women and without bringing the issue to the Western medical establishment, no change would be possible at all.
—*Emanuel Levy*

MY GIRL 2

A Columbia Pictures release of a Brian Grazer/Imagine Films Entertainment production. Produced by Grazer. Executive producers, David T. Friendly, Howard Zieff, Joseph M. Caracciolo. Directed by Howard Zieff. Screenplay, Janet Kovalci, based on characters created by Laurice Elehwany. Camera (color), Paul Elliott; editor, Wendy Greene Bricmont; music, Cliff Eidelman; production design, Charles Rosen; art direction, Diane Yates; set design, Harold Fuhrman; set decoration, Mary Olivia McIntosh; costume design, Shelley Komarov; sound (Dolby), John Sutton III; assistant director, Jerry Sobul; associate producer, Devorah Moos-Hankin; casting, Alan Berger. Reviewed at Loews Memorial City Mall Cinema, Houston, Feb. 9, 1994. MPAA Rating: PG. Running time: **99 MIN.**

Hary Sultenfuss	Dan Aykroyd
Shelly Sultenfuss	Jamie Lee Curtis
Vada Sultenfuss	Anna Chlumsky
Nick Zsigmond	Austin O'Brien
Phil Sultenfuss	Richard Masur
Rose Zsigmond	Christine Ebersole
Jeffrey Pommeroy	John David Souther
Maggie Muldovan	Angeline Ball
Alfred Beidermeyer	Aubrey Morris
Dr. Sam Helburn	Gerrit Graham
Stanley Rosenfeld	Ben Stein
Daryl Tanaka	Keone Young
Arthur	Anthony R. Jones
Hilary Mitchell	Jodie Markell
Peter Webb	Richard Beymer

"**My Girl 2**" is pleasant, painless and, as sequels go, genuinely ambitious in its efforts to be a continuation rather than just a retread of its surprise-hit 1991 predecessor. That may not be enough for pic to broaden its appeal beyond its obvious target audience of preteen and young adolescent girls (and, of course, tag-along parents and boyfriends). But while B.O. likely won't be anywhere near the worldwide $120 million gross for "My Girl," sequel should perform modestly well before doing even better on homevid and pay cable.

Screenwriter Janet Kovalcik (working from characters created by Laurice Elehwany) picks up the story two years after "My Girl," in 1974. Opening scenes return to original pic's setting, the fictitious town of Madison, Pa., with same lead actors reprising central roles. Precocious Vada (Anna Chlumsky), now 13, still lives with her father, Harry (Dan Aykroyd), operator of the town's funeral parlor. Harry has married g.f. and co-worker Shelly (Jamie Lee Curtis), who's now very pregnant. Vada accepts the new domestic situation agreeably enough but still wonders about the mother she never knew, who died from childbirth complications.

After a leisurely paced but amiable start, "My Girl 2" leaves Madison (and Aykroyd and Curtis) and moves to Los Angeles, where Vada wants to research her mother's past for a school project. In L.A., she stays with Uncle Phil (Richard Masur, another "My Girl" alumnus), a mechanic who's living with g.f./boss Rose (Christine Ebersole) and her young teenage son, Nick (Austin O'Brien).

Nick reluctantly serves as her tour guide through L.A. as Vada searches for people who knew her mother in high school and college. Her investigation puts her in contact with a by-the-book cop (well played by Keone Young), a sickly poet (a witty turn by Aubrey Morris) and a self-absorbed film director (a nifty cameo by Richard Beymer).

Vada learns her mother was married, then divorced, long before meeting Harry. This leads to pic's emotional payoff, as the ex-husband (John David Souther) shows Vada a home movie of her mother (Angeline Ball of "The Commitments").

"My Girl 2" is often mildly amusing, and never less than engaging, but it lacks a strong narrative drive.

Director Howard Zieff, who helmed the original, places a great deal of stock in the charm of his players, and they rarely let him down. Zieff's best films ("Hearts of the West," "Slither") are more plot-than character-driven, so it's not surprising to find here that Vada's search is presented more as a methodical journey of self-discovery than a race against time.

But the lack of urgency tends to work against the film, since there are stretches when the viewer is very aware of time passing. That impression is only reinforced by a subplot (Rose's flirtation with a suave customer played by Gerrit Graham) that plays like so much padding.

Still, even without the presence of Macaulay Culkin, whose character was killed off in the original pic, "My Girl 2" has enough going for it to entertain and satisfy. In the lead role, Chlumsky has developed into an even more appealing young actress for the sequel. She establishes a nicely persuasive rapport with co-star O'Brien ("Last Action Hero"), who probably will set many fair hearts aflutter in shopping-mall multiplexes everywhere.

Despite their top billing, Aykroyd and Curtis are around for less than a third of the film. But they make their moments count, as do Masur and Ebersole. Souther offers an affecting mix of wistful regret and resigned serenity in his small role.

Cinematographer Paul Elliott, costumer Shelley Komarov and production designer Charles Rosen do a bang-up job of evoking early 1970s period flavor without letting it get in the way of the story. Well-chosen top-40 tunes from the era are used effectively. Given the current '70s nostalgia, pic's soundtrack could click on the charts.

February 14, 1994 (Cont.)

To offer "My Girl 2" the highest possible praise: It doesn't make one fear the prospect of a "My Girl 3."
—*Joe Leydon*

8 SECONDS

A New Line Cinema release of a Jersey Films production. Produced by Michael Shamberg. Executive producers, Cyd LeVin, Jeffrey Swab. Co-producer, Tony Mark. Directed by John G. Avildsen. Screenplay, Monte Merrick. Camera (Foto-Kem color; Film House prints), Victor Hammer; editor, J. Douglas Seelig; music, Bill Conti; production design, William J. Cassidy; art direction, John Frick; set decoration, Jenny C. Patrick; costume design, Deena Appel; sound, Michael Scott Goldbaum; stunt coordinator, Mike McGaughy; assistant director, Clifford C. Coleman; casting, Caro Jones. Reviewed at the Aidikoff screening room, Beverly Hills, Feb. 4, 1994. MPAA Rating: PG-13. Running time: **104 MIN.**

Lane Frost	Luke Perry
Tuff Hedeman	Stephen Baldwin
Clyde Frost	James Rebhorn
Elsie Frost	Carrie Snodgress
Cody Lambert	Red Mitchell
Carolyn Kyle	Ronnie Claire Edwards
Martin Hudson	Linden Ashby
Kellie Frost	Cynthia Geary
Teenage Lane	Dustin Mayfield
Young Lane	Cameron Finley

"8 Seconds" takes a smooth, sappy ride through the life of a great bucking bull rider. Sweet, sentimental and rose-colored to a fault, this family-oriented biopic has none of the grit, dust and bruises that virtually define the sport in question, and plays more like a reassuring, inspirational TV movie than a big-screen attraction. Audience for this, if it still exists en masse, is the Middle American one that supported four-walled "Wilderness Family"-type sagas 15-20 years ago, although New Line should be able to generate some coin on the basis of star Luke Perry and a "true rodeo 'Rocky'" promotion of director John G. Avildsen.

In his feature starring debut, Perry plays Lane Frost, an Oklahoma boy who became world champion bull rider in 1987 but was tragically killed in a rodeo accident two years later. Virtually all the characters in Monte Merrick's painting-by-numbers script are based on real people, which is no doubt partly responsible for the caution and reverence with which the film approaches virtually every scene.

From the outset, it is apparent that the main challenge here should be finding a new way to relate the familiar premise of a young man's attempt to turn his dream of sports triumph into reality. A secondary goal might have been discovering a fresh approach to lensing rodeos.

Unfortunately, the picture rises to neither occasion. The sketch of Frost's life and career arc could not be more perfunctory: early training by his former riding champ dad; hitting the circuit with best pals Tuff Hedeman (Stephen Baldwin), who reps his toughest competition, and Cody Lambert (Red Mitchell), who's better at scribbling cowboy poetry; shy courtship and marriage with Kellie ("Northern Exposure's" Cynthia Geary), the only girl he ever loved; winning the championship; dealing with fame, which leads to temptations on the road, a bitter separation from Kellie but eventual mature reconciliation, and a climactic series of rides on a fearsome bull that's never been ridden in more than 300 attempts.

Treatment of all this, particularly the domestic scenes, is exceedingly polite, making for little conflict even when the characters are arguing. Frost's ascent to the top of his profession feels more like a glide than a struggle, and his only nagging frustration is that his reserved father (James Rebhorn) can never express his love and support.

Although the riding is expectedly impressive and the atmosphere authentic, Avildsen and lenser Victor Hammer don't come up with any new visual angles on the rodeo, certainly nothing to compare, for instance, with the stunning images in the new documentary "Colorado Cowboy: The Bruce Ford Story." The elaborate preparation for a rider's quick trip in the arena are largely glossed over, and the vivid immediacy of the man-vs.-beast contests is softened by the gross extension of the rides; even the film's title is false, in that the rides are made to last upwards of 25 seconds before the buzzer sounds.

Part of the mild impact is also due to Frost's lightweight personality, at least as written and enacted here. Early on, when Tuff, who thinks he's John Wayne, is lecturing Frost on how "you can't be a cowboy and be a nice guy," Frost is standing in their motel room flossing his teeth, which pretty much sums up his character.

Although his role is one-dimensional, Baldwin again registers strongly as the aptly named sidekick, who in real life has won three world titles himself. Remainder of cast is vanilla.

Tech contributions are pro. Film features one of the most egregiously overextended end-credit sequences ever devised, thanks largely to the liberal amount of Frost family home movie footage the filmmakers felt compelled to serve up. —*Todd McCarthy*

BLANK CHECK

A Buena Vista Pictures release of a Walt Disney Pictures presentation of an Adelson/Baumgarten production. Produced by Craig Baumgarten, Gary Adelson. Executive producers, Hilary Wayne, Blake Snyder. Directed by Rupert Wainwright. Screenplay, Snyder, Colby Carr. Camera (Technicolor), Bill Pope; editors, Hubert C. de La Bouillerie, Jill Savitt; music, Nicholas Pike; production design, Nelson Coates; art direction, Burton Rncher; set decoration, Cecilia Rodarte; costume design, Deborah Everton; sound (Dolby), David Kirschner; stunt coordinator, Patrick Romano; associate producer, Charles Skouras III; assistant directors, Michael Daves, Dennis Maguire; second unit director, David R. Ellis; second unit camera, Don Reddy, Layton Blaylock; casting, Reuben Cannon. Reviewed at AMC Meyer Park 14, Houston, Feb. 5, 1994. MPAA Rating: PG. Running time: **93 MIN.**

Preston Waters	Brian Bonsall
Shay Stanley	Karen Duffy
Quigley	Miguel Ferrer
Fred Waters	James Rebhorn
Juice	Tone Loc
Sandra Waters	Jayne Atkinson
Henry	Rick Ducommun
Yvonne	Debbie Allen
Damian Waters	Chris Demetral
Ralph Waters	Michael Faustino
Butch	Alex Zuckerman
Biderman	Michael Lerner

"Blank Check" is a low-yield Disney programmer that may generate some interest among pre-teen and young adolescent audiences. Theatrical B.O. likely will amount to small change, but pic may do better when deposited in homevid outlets.

With more than a wink and a nod in the direction of the "Home Alone" blockbusters — and a preemptive hint of the forthcoming "Richie Rich" — director Rupert Wainwright and writers Blake Snyder and Colby Carr bend over backwards to contrive a fantasy-fulfillment scenario for pic's target audience.

Eleven-year-old Preston Waters (Brian Bonsall) feels badly put-upon by his penny-pinching, aphorism-spouting father (James Rebhorn) and pushed around by his bullying older siblings (Michael Faustino, Chris Demetral). The final straw comes when Preston is invited to a classmate's amusement-park birthday party but lacks enough money to join other guests on the A-ticket rides. After that, Preston wishes aloud that he had his own money and his own house.

Quicker than you can say "I made my parents disappear!" Preston runs into fugitive criminal Quigley (Miguel Ferrer). Or, to be more precise, Quigley runs into Preston's bike, with his car. Anxious not to arouse police interest, he gives the boy a half-completed check to pay for the damage, then drives off.

Preston gleefully fills in the amount of the check — $1 million,

the exact sum Quigley has deposited in the money-laundering bank operated by a former cohort (Michael Lerner) — and cashes it.

Palming himself off as the young aide of a fictitious "Mr. Macintosh"— an alias taken from his home computer — Preston buys a palatial home in his neighborhood, then stocks it with high-tech games.

Tyro director Wainwright made his mark as an award-winning maker of commercial spots, and his experience serves him well here: Seldom has conspicuous consumption been made to seem so exhilarating.

"Blank Check" wallows in the exuberance of excess so enthusiastically, for so long, that even naive youngsters may have trouble buying pic's ultimate "money can't buy happiness" message.

It takes more than an hour to get to the real payoff — Preston's "Home Alone"-style defense of his home against a siege by Quigley and his cohorts. Unfortunately, the sequence is too short to live up to its buildup, and not ingenious enough in its slapstick situations.

Bonsall is believable without being particularly memorable. Rick Ducommun offers an adequate John Candy impersonation as the chauffeur hired by the young millionaire.

Ferrer is savvy enough to play it straight, and makes a wonderfully menacing foil. Debbie Allen overdoes the flustery hysterics as a caterer hired by "Mr. Macintosh."

Although plot is set in small-town Indiana, pic was shot in central Texas. Tech credits are unremarkable. —*Joe Leydon*

TIME IS MONEY
(FRENCH)

A Les Acacias Cineaudience release of a Chorus Films presentation of a Chorus Films/Beri Finance/July Films production, with participation of Cofimage 4, CNC, Canal Plus and GAN Cinema Foundation. Produced by Yves Lombard. Directed by Paolo Barzman. Screenplay, Paolo Barzman, Yoyo Barzman. Camera (color, widescreen), Bernard Lutic, Sabine Lancelin; editor, Veronique Parnet; music, Gerard Torikian; production design, Marc Petitjean; costume design, Marilyn Fitoussi; sound (Dolby), Pierre Lorrain, Claude Villand, Christian Fontaine; assistant directors, Pablo Freville, Douglas Law; casting (U.S.), Hank McCann. Reviewed at Premiers Plans, European First Film Festival (non-competing), Angers, France, Jan. 27, 1994. Running time: **91 MIN.**

Joseph Kaufman	Max von Sydow
Irina Kaufman	Charlotte Rampling
David Hirsh	Francois Montagut
Mac	Martin Landau

Enthusiasts for provincial French vistas will be pleased, but fans of Max von Sydow and

Charlotte Rampling's meatier roles will feel cheated by "Time Is Money," a belabored, quasi-comic examination of the household machinations of a revered (but broke) writer who no longer wants to write. Tube sales beckon.

Aging novelist and Oscar-winning screenwriter Joseph Kaufman (von Sydow) lives with his wife, Irina (Rampling), on an estate in the French countryside. Though he's spent the last advance on an unwritten novel and the tax authorities are poised to seize his property, Joe is more interested in creating new strains of hypochondria than fulfilling editorial obligations.

Irina, a former concert pianist, can't get Joe to face the typewriter. Nor can longtime friend and agent Mac (Martin Landau), who flies in from New York. Mac hires budding young writer David Hirsh (Francois Montagut) as a live-in secretary to prod Joe into completion. But it's uphill all the way as the admiring David combats Joe's raging cynicism concerning life and art.

Helmer/co-writer Paolo Barzman, son of the late Yank screenwriter Ben Barzman, establishes the basic premise, then keeps paraphrasing and restating it without moving the story forward. Though the underlying themes are interesting, dialogue is frequently didactic.

Though von Sydow would not be everyone's first choice for a crotchety literary lion named Kaufman, the Swedish thesp is on the money as the aged scribe who wants only to drowse, mope and issue pronouncements. The radiant Rampling, as his casually stunning, much younger wife, shows subtlety and is a pleasure to watch. To the actors' credit, the pair come across as a longtime couple with their respective memories and grievances.

The usually fine Landau overplays the harried, foul-mouthed New Yorker role he's been dealt. Montagut is likable, if innocuous, as David.

Widescreen summertime lensing shows ample consideration for earthy provincial hues, and the leads look wonderful.

—*Lisa Nesselson*

ROTTERDAM

WU KUI
(THE WOODEN MAN'S BRIDE)
(TAIWANESE)

A Long Shong Intl. production. Produced by Wang Ying Hsiang. Executive producers, Yu Shi, Li Xudong. Directed by Huang Jianxin. Screenplay, Yang Zhengguang, based on the novel by Jia Pingau. Camera (color), Zhang Xiaoguang; editor, Lei Qin; music, Zhang Dalong; art director, Teng Jie; costume design, Du Longxi; sound (Dolby), Yan Jun; assistant directors, Yang Yazhou, Yi Xiaozhong. Reviewed at Rotterdam Intl. Film Festival, Feb. 5, 1994. Running time: **114 MIN.**
Kui	Chang Shih
Young mistress	Wang Lan
Brother	Ku Paoming
Madame Liu	Wang Yumei
Sister Ma	Wang Fuli
Chief Tang	Kao Mingjun

Though it retreads ground that's by no means new to Chinese cinema, "The Wooden Man's Bride" offers hugely entertaining melodrama coupled with potent emotional pull, a firm grasp of Hollywood-style pacing and narrative conventions and a non-stop blitz of visually ravishing spectacle. One of the Rotterdam fest's most rousing crowd-pleasers, this handsomely crafted Taiwan production from mainland Chinese helmer Huang Jianxin could eat up a greedy slice of the mainstream arthouse market with the right push.

Pic reps a pronounced (and, to some, disappointing) directional swing for Huang after the acutely observed contempo comedy of his 1986 debut pic "The Black Cannon Incident" and, more recently, "Stand Up, Don't Bend Over." But the director seems equally at home with this stirring historical folk tale of violent uprising against cruelly oppressive tradition.

Set in the 1920s in a remote part of northwest China, the operatic yarn's opening will inevitably spark comparison with "Red Sorghum." A simple-minded worker, Kui (Chang Shih), is enlisted to carry the bride of an arranged marriage (Wang Lan) in an eye-popping wedding procession on camels across the desert. Attacked by marauding bandits, he defends her fearlessly, but the bride gives herself up to save his life.

News travels back to her intended groom, and in his haste to rescue her, he rushes for his gun and sets off an explosion which kills him. Kui storms into the kidnappers' hideout, where his loyalty and belligerent courage touch a chord in the willowy, recently bereaved bandit chief (Taiwanese pop idol Kao Mingjun), prompting him to release them unharmed.

Back at the groom's family mansion, the bride gets an icy welcome from his mother Madame Liu (veteran Wang Yumei), before being subjected to a humiliating virginity test in which she's forced to squat naked over ashes and sneeze. Determining that she's still worthy of her dead son, Madame Liu arranges a solemn wedding-cum-funeral ceremony, pledging the young bride to a carved wooden man to ensure her ongoing fidelity.

The bride's attempts at rebellion and escape are harshly punished. She befriends Kui, and kindness soon gives way to tentative intimacy, then to hot passion. Catching them in the act, Madame Liu banishes Kui and orders the bride's ankles to be broken to guard against further marital infractions.

Looking for allies, Kui heads for the bandits' headquarters, but arrives to find them freshly wiped out. The film's political bite is tidily lassoed in its climactic scene, where he rides back to the mansion a year later, having rallied his own revolutionary brigade together to overthrow the despotic Madame Liu. Ordering his band to string her up, he resumes his initial task and carries the crippled bride away.

Perfs by the thwarted lovers are finely wrought (even if Chang's transition from clumsy simpleton to steely, Schwarzenegger-like victor is a little hard to swallow), but pic's thesping strength lies in the supporting ranks. Wang Yumei regally plays the bitter dowager as a complex tyrant, firmly convinced her actions are the only available course. Also memorable is Wang Fuli as her fanatically devoted housekeeper, and Kao is a knockout as the effeminate, opera-singing head bandit.

With all the rich pageantry, intricate ceremony, sweeping landscapes and full-tilt epic quality on view from scene one, pic cries out for widescreen. Zhang Xiaoguang's stately lensing nevertheless looks consistently arresting, if a little crowded, on standard 35mm. "Bride" is the first feature to be shot in mainland China on 100% Taiwan coin.

— *David Rooney*

I DON'T HATE LAS VEGAS ANYMORE
(16mm)

A Complex Corp. production. Produced by Henry S. Rosenthal. Directed by Caveh Zahedi. Camera (color), Greg Watkins; editor, Suzanne Smith; sound, Denise Montgomery. Reviewed at Rotterdam Intl. Film Festival, Feb. 1, 1994. Running time: **83 MIN.**

With: Steve Ausbury, Denise Montgomery, Greg Watkins, Amin Zahedi, Caveh Zahedi, George Zahedi.

Part docu-diary, part theological quest, part family therapy session and part improvised comedy, Caveh Zahedi's second feature, "I Don't Hate Las Vegas Anymore," is a one-of-a-kind talkfest that's as compelling as it is abrasive. Infectiously funny, morally questionable and excruciatingly egocentric, this elaborate home movie stands to cleave any audience neatly down the middle.

Like Zahedi's earlier "A Little Stiff," new pic relies in no small way on the director's singular onscreen personality: a meeting of unquenchable philosophical inquisitiveness and mesmerizing, anxiety-ridden verbosity. And like its predecessor, "Vegas'" ingenuity triumphs over meager means. No-budget exercise will be hard to place beyond the fest circuit, but will undoubtedly serve to further stoke expectations as Zahedi moves on to bigger projects.

Opening with a direct-to-camera spiel, Zahedi recounts his original intention to make a scripted movie based on conversations that took place during a family trip to Vegas. But after two years of scraping for funding, the idea turned sour and he decided to transform the project into an experiment in faith.

Setting out for Vegas again with his father, George, teenage half-brother Amin, and a small crew frequently drawn into the on-camera action, Zahedi starts shooting a scriptless film. His theory is that if God exists, He'll make it entertaining, perhaps even allowing them to catch divine intervention on film and thereby reaffirm the world's faith.

Deep-seated parental and sibling resentment is touched upon along the way, but once the group arrives in Vegas, familial animosity takes a back seat to the sound recordist's romantic woes. Zahedi's willingness to make her anguish (and later her drinking problem) grist to his mill implants a prickly double edge that's sharpened when he reveals a plan to open taciturn George and petulant Amin's hearts with Ecstasy tablets.

A static camera records the filmmaker's tireless battle to convince them to do the drugs, much of it in real time. Zahedi's unbending focus on his film project, to the point of ignoring warnings about his father's heart condition, creates almost unbearable tension and boldly risks setting up a wall of hostility between himself and the audience. The taut atmosphere is somewhat alleviated by Amin's amusing self-righteousness and unveiled antagonism.

Zahedi eventually takes the drug alone, and its mellowing effect encourages the others to follow. When the Ecstasy hits, George's immediate reaction is to hand out cash to the crew and send them downstairs to gamble.

Amin also becomes more congenial, but the subsequent discovery of a discarded Ecstasy tab suggests he was faking, and his venomous dismissal of his brother's filmmaking efforts is hilariously vindictive.

Large helpings of Godspeak and pop psychobabble will prove tough to digest for some auds, though they're clearly colored with a subtle streak of self-irony that's not hard to tap into. Counterbalancing the soul dredging to great effect is the continual acknowledgement and clever incorporation of the filmmaking process and all its nightmarish unpredictability, from lost sound tapes to double-exposed footage.

Technically, perhaps the film's most valuable asset is Suzanne Smith's swoon-inducing editing, using leisurely dissolves that allow images to flutter gently into one another, considerably cushioning some potentially grating moments.

—David Rooney

THE LISA THEORY

A Farallon Pictures production in association with Colossal Pictures. Produced, directed, written, edited by Steven Okazaki. Executive producer, Peggy Orenstein. Co-producers, Doreen Lorenzo, Roy Kissin. Camera (color), D. Matthew Smith; music, Jim Matison; art direction, Julie Slinger, Zand Gee; costume design, Anne Etheridge; sound, Michael Emery; associate producer, Zand Gee; assistant directors, Harry Yoon, Joan Bierman. Reviewed at Rotterdam Intl. Film Festival, Feb. 1, 1994. Running time: **80 MIN.**

Devon	Devon Morf
Lisa	Honey O. Yates
Adam	Avel Sosa II
Jimbo	Jim Matison
Bob	Mark Gorney
Mark	Bucky Sinister

With: Julie Slinger, Natanya Moore, Alicia Rose, Jill Parker.

Oscar-winning documaker Steven Okazaki ("Days of Waiting") does a resolute about-face with his second feature, "The Lisa Theory," a dollop of John Hughes-style teenage romantic angst beamed up into a hipper, early-20s stratosphere. Though it's missing the verdant peoplescape of "Singles," pic's airy comedy, affable cast and barrage of West Coast sounds should lure young auds in selected playdates.

The Lisa theory (an infinitesimal variation on the Jennifer theory) states that women called Lisa invariably mean trouble. This Lisa (Honey O. Yates) is a p.c. groover who, against her better judgment, gets hitched to Devon (Devon Morf), the nerdy lead singer of a punk band. She moves into his co-op apartment, transforming it from anarchic mess to socialist collective, and then moves out again without warning, pushing Devon into lovelorn limbo.

From first encounter through awkward courtship, the relationship is engagingly recounted, with the co-op inhabitants providing plenty of agreeably goofy humor. But the inarticulate-and-unwashed-spells-cool equation threatens to wear thin until pic shifts focus to chart the romantic aspirations of Devon's Winona Ryder-fixated roommate Adam (Avel Sosa II).

In terms of screen time, Adam is only marginally more visible than pic's other, less immediately sympathetic characters, but the actor breezily injects his scenes with enough truth to shove other plotlines into the periphery. His crusade to rouse Devon out of hibernation in his fetid room runs parallel to a misguided plan to seduce a self-assured band manager (Jill Parker), and a slow-spiraling flirtation with a comic-bookstore clerk (Natanya Moore).

Okazaki has a good feel for casual, deadpan humor that partly whitewashes much of the material's nagging familiarity. Frequently witty incidental observations on such things as the stunted mental faculties of comic book readers and adolescent hell act as winning distractions to some of the story's more trifling aspects. Romantic conclusions are sweetly low-key, with Lisa reaffirming her decision and Devon accepting his abandonment in a way that compromises neither character.

Clearly a thrifty operation, pic nonetheless looks and sounds sharp. D. Matthew Smith's camera cruises the San Francisco locations without featuring them to any degree that distracts from the characters and their various pursuits. Okazaki's editing is a touch indulgent at times, particularly in the lengthy musical segs, which present problems of halting rhythm for non-aficionados of the slew of local bands on view. End credits carry an apology to all the nice Lisas and Jennifers of the world.

—David Rooney

BAD APPLES

(B&W — 16mm)

A You Betcha production. Produced by Ray Lein, Amy Hobby. Directed, written by Lein. Camera (b&w), Hobby; editors, Lein, Scott Riddle, Steve Adrienson; art director, Andrea Roach; sound, Sian Roderick, Riddle; assistant director, Riddle. Reviewed at Rotterdam Intl. Film Festival, Jan. 30, 1994. Running time: **84 MIN.**

Ronnie	Alex Wolfe
Josy	Madeleine Gavin
Rocky	Jeffrey Vance

First-timer Ray Lein shrugs off the shackles of a $30,000 budget and dishes up an off-hand, unassumingly edgy take on the modern American outlaw movie in "Bad Apples." Technical rawness and an erratic narrative motor are largely overshadowed by a mood that ambles flavorsomely between soulful desperado turf and almost comic flippancy, and pic should land exposure in fests surveying new directing talent.

Unintelligible recorded dialogue in the opening scene gives a somewhat uncertain start, but speed picks up when easygoing drifter Ronnie (Alex Wolfe) falls in with hotheaded Rocky (Jeffrey Vance), who's just murdered his boss at an apple orchard. Momentum is stepped up another notch when they hook up with gun-toting Josy (Madeleine Gavin), also fresh from a kill.

Instantly miffed at his back-seat position to Rocky and Josy's romance, Ronnie becomes increasingly distanced, idly strumming his ukelele while conflict festers effectively on a low flame. Their escalating crime spree propels them through an atmospheric string of faded central California towns, tailed by cops revealed to be primarily after Josy for having shot one of their men.

Rocky slips out of the picture when Josy's allegiance shifts to Ronnie, and she helps him carve out an honest living with his ukelele act. But Rocky resurfaces with a self-serving plan that steers the trio to a well orchestrated, fatal final punch.

Lein's unfettered direction and script let the characters coast toward their fate while consistently underplaying the dramatic urgency of the events. The tack is mostly successful, giving the impression of being right at home in the lawlessness realm, though it does periodically threaten to stall the action.

The three leads are uniformly strong, playing concisely defined characters and slotting easily into pic's unforced approach. Amy Hobby's black-and-white lensing opts for functional simplicity. Amusing musical quirks are peppered throughout, from frantic Mexican pop and Ronnie's tinny ukelele tunes to a leaden funeral dirge.

—David Rooney

AT GROUND ZERO

(16mm)

A Proletariat Pictures/Roadfilm Prods. production. Produced, directed, written by Craig Schlattman. Camera (color), Bubba Bukowski; editor, Les Fatt; music, Fran Banish; sound, Konstantin Von Krusenstieren, Mikki Stitz, Mark Gaddis, Tim Timbruell; associate producer, Ivon Vassali. Reviewed at Rotterdam Intl. Film Festival, Jan. 31, 1994. Running time: **118 MIN.**

Thomas Quinton

Pennington	Tom Elliott
Aysha Almouth	Aysha Hauer
Carman	Brian Brophy
Bubba	Craig Schlattman
Rudy	Frank Kinikin
Micky	Mikki Skitz
Mr. Pennington	James Hanvik
Mrs. Almouth	Tonei Sackey

An unrewarding addition to the already bulging canon of doomed-junkie tracts, "At Ground Zero" marks an inauspicious entry into the feature arena for photographer, actor and short-film director Craig Schlattman. Sporadic flashes of visual savvy and unexpected humor can't cover for long stretches of pointless posing, and ultimately this is an excursion into nihilistic misery that few will care to take.

After the harrowing drug-world tour of "Bad Lieutenant" and the more contemplative foray of "Drugstore Cowboy," the reverential detail given to prepping syringes and shooting up here seems hackneyed and gratuitous; pic has nothing new to add.

Schlattman's direction is more than able, but he's saddled himself with a script that rarely penetrates beneath the surface of his characters' on-the-edge existences, and entrusted the central duo to actors who don't meet the challenge of fleshing real people out of the thin material. Tom Elliott brings occasional depth to the addict trying to save his relationship and moderate his drug use, but as his self-destructing g.f., Aysha Hauer (daughter of Rutger Hauer) is morosely one-dimensional.

The couple high-tails it out of town after Elliott's character brains a dealer and takes his stash. A patently dangerous redneck (Schlattman) picks them up, and when he moves in on Hauer, they pull a gun on him and snatch his car. Some overdue humor creeps in when another downwardly mobile stooge (Brian Brophy) is taken on board and hilariously recaps his bungled suicide attempt.

Schlattman lets stylized sequences take over from plot continuum for an overly extended period as the trio trips across a barren desert landscape intended to echo their state of mind. When Brophy decides to return to reality, Elliott and Hauer are left to tackle their dwindling bond.

They head for their hometown, where one incisively on-target exchange between Elliott and his unforgiving father (James Hanvik) precedes a violent denouement that's insubstantial in terms of both the tension that should come before it and the resonating visceral kick that should follow.

In execution, pic is one step ahead of its content, with some minor sound problems the only blight on an otherwise lean but clean tech slate. Less frugal use of Fran Banish's music might have helped beef up the unconvincingly flimsy atmosphere. — *David Rooney*

DOMENICA

(GERMAN)

A Corazon Film production, in association with Lisa Film/Cine Images. Produced by Axel Glittenberg. Directed, written by Peter Kern. Camera (color), Manfred Scheer; editor, Helga Borsche; music, Iwan Harlan; production design, Uli Hanisch; art direction, Nicola Schudy; costume design, Tabea Braun; sound, Michael Felber; makeup, Heidi Hass; assistant director, Herms Mueller. Reviewed at Hof Film Festival, Hof, Germany, Oct. 28, 1993. (Also in Rotterdam, Chicago, Sao Paulo fests.) Running time: **92 MIN.**
With: Andrea Ferreol, Sandra Molik, Nicolette Krebitz, Domenica Niehoff, Rita Lengyal, Karina Fallenstein, Max Kellermann, Wolf Dieter Sprenger, Christoph Schlingensief, Juergen Vogel.

Amateur from the word go, the only thing this biopic from a 12-time director has going for it is the sensationalism associated with the title. "Domenica" is the name of Germany's most famous and most outspoken sadomasochism prostitute/activist, but this is less her story than a trivial, insightless hagiography. Though the subject will get it some fest play, neither audience nor makers will profit.

With her activism over prostitutes' rights, and with her amazing reputation (she was one of the major factors in making S&M trendy in Germany), Domenica is a fascinating personality. But director/writer Peter Kern doesn't explore his subject, he merely makes use of it, pushing his view of her as noble victim.

Domenica plays herself as an adult and in parts breaks into docu-style monologues. But the film never gives any in-depth account of the world in which she lived.

As Domenica's mother, Andrea Ferreol bounces happily through, but her non-committal attitude suggests that she knows her character isn't round enough to warrant a proper investment of her talent. Other perfs are fairly amateur, including Nicolette Krebitz as a young Domenica. Only exception is Hans Michael Rehberg, who plays Domenica's tasteless, jet-set pimp with a hollow-eyed, decadent intensity that is genuinely scary.

Technical credits are above-average at times. —*Eric Hansen*

ALPE ADRIA

DEZERTER

(DESERTER)

(YUGOSLAV)

A Centar Film/RTV/Tropodium (Belgrade) production. Directed, written by Zivojin Pavlovic, based on Fyodor Dostoevsky's story "The Eternal Husband." Camera (color), Aleksandar Petkovic; editors, Olga Skrigin, Lana Vukobratovic; art direction, Dragoljub Ivkov; costumes, Mirjana Ostojic. Reviewed at Alpe Adria Cinema Festival, Trieste, Italy, Jan. 23, 1994. Running time: **118 MIN.**
Aleksa .... Rados Bajic
Pavle .... Rade Serbedzija
Mother .... Renata Ulmanski
Girl .... Milena Pavlovic

The Serbian film "Deserter," by veteran Zivojin Pavlovic, is one of the most moving, depressing films to come out of the war in Yugoslavia. Subtle but sharp as a razor, the film follows two old friends, officers in the Yugoslav army, whose ways have parted. It won the Golden Leaf at the last Mediterranean film festival in Bastia. Though the international embargo against Serbia will prevent the film from being bought by many countries, it should thrive on video after finishing the fest rounds.

The story is actually based on a short story by Dostoevsky which gives the plot its backbone — a love triangle. But the personal drama of the two military men, who are both in love with a dead woman, is heightened to an anguishing pitch when viewed against the backdrop of the war.

Like in a wartime "Jules and Jim," the story's joyous laughter of youth turns to a chain of endless funerals, battles and death.

In the early part of the film, the mixed Croatian/Serb city of Vukovar is seen as it was in 1981, a normal town where the trio of characters live and love. In the film's memorable final horizontal tracking shot, Vukovar appears today, razed to the ground by bombs. This shot, a chilling conjunction of fiction and documentary, leaves a deep impression.

The war is explicitly visualized only in one early scene, a city battle made terrifying by noise, smoke and the tension of the Serbian soldiers. An officer breaks under the stress of battle, and as he flees in panic, he shoots a pregnant girl.

Rados Bajic is introduced as the gentlemanly major who has to court-martial the killer. Bajic himself is on the verge of a nervous breakdown and is sent home to Belgrade for some rest.

There he bumps into an old buddy (Rade Serbedzija), now a drunken deserter with an 11-year-old daughter on his hands.

In memory of their friendship and Serbedzija's dead wife (who was Bajic's lover), Bajic tries to lend a hand, but only sinks into a moral quagmire. Serbedzija informs him the child is really Bajic's daughter, and dumps her on the bachelor major.

Recovering from the shock, Bajic is just beginning to enjoy being a father when the girl dies. Her funeral comes close on the heels of that of another army buddy, killed in battle.

Pavlovic's spare, sensitive direction condenses this lugubrious tale to its emotional essence. He draws out moral problems with great finesse. Serbedzija is a heel, a child beater, a liar and a deserter, but he has a basic loyalty that is touching.

The morally irreproachable Bajic, on the other hand, repeats his adulterous betrayal by stealing Serbedzija's new girlfriend (Milena Pavlovic) out from under his nose. In the end, when Bajic judges Serbedzija to be the better man, it's not such a far-fetched conclusion.

Excellent perfs by Serbedzija and Bajic round out the two characters and make them both pitiable. Aleksandar Petkovic's understated lensing forcefully conveys a desolate, wintertime atmosphere that numbs body and soul.

—*Deborah Young*

VRIJEME ZA ...

(A TIME FOR ...)

(CROATIAN-ITALIAN)

A Jadran Film (Zagreb)/RAI-3, Ellepi Film (Rome) production. Produced by Zdravko Mihalic, Leo Pescarolo, Giancarlo Santalmassi. Directed, written by Oja Kodar. Camera (color), Gary Graver; music, Franco Piersanti; art direction, Ivo Husnjak, Nenad Pecur; costume design, Jelena Matic-Mihalic. Reviewed at Alpe Adria Cinema Festival, Trieste, Italy, Jan. 22, 1994. Running time: **99 MIN.**
Marija .... Nada Gacesic-Livakovic
Darko .... Zvonimir Novosel
Bane .... Ivan Brkic
Zgoljo .... Dusko Valentic
With: Vinko Kraljevic, Dorde Rapajic, Franjo Jurcec, Andrea Bakovic, Eduard Perocevic, Slavko Brankov, Damir Mejovsek, Jasna Palic.

Oja Kodar's emotional account of the war in Croatia illustrates the danger of trying to tell a war story while the conflict is still going on. Scripted more than two years ago, when Croatia was seen internationally as a victim of Serbian aggression, "A Time for ..." takes up the Croatian banner so passionately it can easily pass for propaganda today.

The changing face of the war has given Italian co-productions RAI-3 and Ellepi Film cold feet, and no date has been fixed for its Italo release.

In Croatia, picture has been an enormous hit. With government blessing, it's been screened even in war-torn towns in practically underground conditions to avoid attracting Serbian bombs on assembled filmgoers. But the extreme emotions surrounding the war have made the film controversial among Croatian hawks, who object to the presence of a positive, peace-loving Serb character.

Though Croat herself, Kodar — Orson Welles' final companion, who worked on many of his last films — is a longtime California resident. Admirers of "Jaded," her interesting first pic set among the low-lifes of Venice, Calif., will find it hard to believe the same director opted for the sentimental style and patriotic theme on show here.

Story revolves around Marija (Nada Gacesic-Livakovic), who flees with her teenage son when their village is attacked by the ruthless Serbian militiamen known as Cetniks. Film's often-confused style actually works in this powerful scene of rape, torture and killing, as the villagers scatter in terror and the Cetniks cruelly turn against their former neighbors in an orgy of bloodshed.

A working knowledge of the Yugoslav conflict is practically essential to be able to follow the characters and the rapid succession of

February 14, 1994 (Cont.)

events. But things calm down quickly into everyday routine.

Marija finds a job in a hospital laundry in town. Her son, Darko (Zvonimir Novosel), falls for a pretty girl whose mother is missing.

Everything is told with the crushing predictability of old-style Soviet war pictures, in which all the characters are unbelievably good or bad, with no motivations needed or allowed. Darko slips away against his mother's entreaties and joins the Croat partisans. After a battle with the Cetniks, he is believed to be killed, and an unrecognizable corpse is delivered to a despairing Marija.

The film boasts one powerful archetypal image — Marija pulling a wooden cart loaded with a coffin bearing her son's body through the devastated countryside. This arresting icon has a universal antiwar resonance that briefly raises "A Time for ..." to the level of its lofty ambitions.

Croatian viewers have found the film extremely moving, in part because it was lensed in ruined churches and on real battlefields, with gunfire heard from the set. The problem for other filmgoers will be in overcoming Kodar's lack of emotional distance from her subject and deciphering her codes.

For example, the film's distinction between the good Serb and the evil Cetniks means little to the uninitiated, but it is a radical message for some Croats.

Gacesic-Livakovic creates a memorable portrait of a Croatian Mother Courage, strong enough to raise a son alone and bury him by herself. Despite its technical mediocrity, this passionate, emotionally charged film will remain a disconcerting document of the Yugoslav tragedy, seen from the point of view of a particular place and time.

—Deborah Young

MESTEM CHODI MIKULAS

(ST. NICHOLAS IS IN TOWN)

(CZECH REPUBLIC)

A Czech Television/Mirage production. (International sales: Telexport.) Produced by Helena Sykorova, Karel Skorpik. Directed by Karel Kachyna. Screenplay, Jan Prochazka, Iva Prochazkova, Kachyna. Camera (color), Vladimir Smutny; editor, Jiri Brozek; music, Petr Hapka; sound (Dolby), Pavel Jelinek. Reviewed at Alpe Adria Cinema Festival, Trieste, Italy, Jan. 19, 1994. Running time: **85 MIN.**
Doctor .... Jiri Abrham
Head nurse .... Eliska Balzcrova
Alenka .... Alena Mihulova
With: D. Douda, K. Hrachovcova.

Veteran Czech helmer Karel Kachyna, whose long-banned "The Ear" made a splash at Cannes two years ago, churns out a fairly pedestrian hospital drama in "St. Nicholas Is in Town." Made for TV, pic is at least professionally directed with some lively characters and could interest offshore TV buyers for the Christmas season.

Story takes place in a children's ward on Christmas Eve. A spunky 12-year-old boy is the leader of the ward, cheering up a homesick little girl and sneaking cigarettes in the bathroom. A young nurse has a crush on Dr. Jiri Abrham, who's drunk most of the time.

Adding a surreal note are three kids who roam the streets dressed up as St. Nicholas, an angel and the devil. For a few crowns, they visit people's homes, like Santa Claus. The boy borrows the St. Nick costume to surprise the ward.

Kachyna demonstrates a Spielberg-like knack for choosing cute blond kids who steal the show from the adults. Cast does a fine job of fleshing out the stereotyped characters. Abrham is amusingly unrepentant as the wastrel doctor who is capable of finding a hiding place for a bottle of booze in the barest hospital room. His affairs with the two nurses are obvious, without being offensive to family auds. Shooting is elegantly pro throughout.

—Deborah Young

VERLASSEN SIE BITTE IHREN MANN

(LEAVE YOUR HUSBAND, PLEASE)

(AUSTRIAN)

An MR-Film (Vienna)/Star-Film (Salzburg) production, in association with ORF television and WWF Wiener Filmfinanzierungsfonds. Produced by Kurt Mrkwicka. Directed by Reinhard Schwabenitzky. Screenplay, Knut Boeser, Schwabenitzky. Camera (color), Gerard Vandeberg; editor, Ingrid Koller; music, Arthur Lauber, Andy Radovan; art direction, Fritz Hollergschwandtner; costumes, Uli Fessler; sound (Dolby), Walter Fiklocki. Reviewed at Alpe Adria Cinema Festival, Trieste, Italy, Jan. 20, 1994. Running time: **95 MIN.**
With: Elfi Eschke, Helmut Griem, Michael Scheidl, Rudolf Buczolich, Uschi Wolff, Jan Fedder.

The broad Austrian humor of "Leave Your Husband, Please" won't be everyone's cup of tea, but pic could have wide appeal in German-lingo markets. Its main drawing card is plump, oft-disrobed actress Elfi Eschke, who sparkles as a rich housewife in search of independence. Veteran TV helmer Reinhard Schwabenitzky puts across an upbeat, upscale message for armchair feminists and voyeurs who like plump figures unclothed.

Eschke is at the beach, photographing herself in the buff, when some boys swipe her clothes and camera. Michael Scheidl ineffectually comes to her rescue, and it's love at first sight. Years later, she is comfortably married to the rich Scheidl, who has political ambitions. For poorly fleshed-out reasons, she rebels against being used as a prop in his campaign.

Frothy as chocolate mousse, pic offers a lot of easy laughs. Its unique quality, however, lies in its delightfully unrepressed heroine. Least convincing is comic premise that Eschke's brazen behavior is capable of shocking the good Austrian bourgeoisie — which, perhaps because of mediocre perfs, doesn't look all that surprised.

Schwabenitzky's small-screen experience shows in pic's fluid storyline and easy-to-identify characters. For once it's the men who are shallow and boring, while the heroine whoops it up. Lensing is warmly inviting and the Home Beautiful art direction is a middle-class dream.

—Deborah Young

NEUES DEUTSCHLAND

(NEW GERMANY)

(GERMAN)

A Colon Filmproduktion/WDR Cologne with Fool Filmproduktion/Neue Sentimental Film/Dokfilm Babelsberg/Philip Groning Filmproduktion coproduction. (In color, b&w.) Reviewed at Alpe Adria Cinema festival, Trieste, Italy, Jan. 21, 1994. (Also in Rotterdam fest.) Running time: **100 MIN.**

**OHNE MICH
(WITHOUT ME)**
Produced by Mark Schlichter, Micha Terjung. Directed, written by Dani Levy. Camera (color), Charly F. Koschnik; editors, Levy, Andreas Herder; music, Bobby McFerrin, Klaus Wagner.
Simon Rosenthal .... Dani Levy
Girlfriend .... Maria Schrader
Also with: Wim Wenders, Joachim Krol, Georg Tryphon.

**EIN ORT, EIN SELBSTMORD
(A PLACE, A SUICIDE)**
(DOCU)
Produced by Micha Terjung. Directed, written by Maris Pfeiffer, from the diary of Gunter Schirmer. Camera (color), Gerhard Hirsch, Iris Weber; editors, Ueli Christen, Elena Bromund.

**KURZSCHLUSS
(SHORT CIRCUIT)**
Produced by Sabine Lenkeit, Uwe K. Schade, Micha Terjung. Directed, written by Gerd Kroske. Camera (b&w), Sebastian Richter; editor, Ingeborg Marszalek.
With: Daniel Graf, Steffen Schult.

**OPFER. ZEUGEN
(VICTIMS, WITNESSES)**
(DOCU)
Produced by Micha Terjung, Hubertus Siegert. Directed, written by Philip Groning. Camera (color), Hito Steyerl, Benedict Neuenfels; editor, Alexandra Pohlmeier.

**HEILIGE KUHE
(SACRED COWS)**
Produced by Micha Terjung, Ulrike Hauff. Directed by Uwe Janson. Screenplay, Oliver Szeslik. Camera (color), Jurgen Jurges, Hagen Bogdanski; editors, Patricia Rommel, Hansjorg Weisdbrich.
With: Ulrich Muhe, Heino Ferch, Dorte Lyssewski.

"New Germany" is a five-episode, five-director trip through a nightmare. Though segments are uneven in technical work and highly diverse in style, seen together they create one scary portrait of contemporary Germany. The unifying theme is the revival of Nazi violence. Though as heavy as bratwurst, it's a powerful, if not a pretty, picture, and accessible to TV auds everywhere.

Dani Levy wields an effective cudgel of self-irony in "Without Me," directing himself as "a little Jew with short legs" (his girlfriend's description) who lives in squalor while he attends film school (Wim Wenders cameos as a prof who falls asleep during screenings.) Levy's docu on skinheads fire-bombing Turkish houses goes unap-

February 14, 1994 (Cont.) February 21, 1994

preciated. Meanwhile, his mounting paranoia about his own safety leads him to literally move to the moon.

"Short Circuit" skillfully uses archival footage from Helmut Kohl's triumphal visit to Leipzig at the time the two Germanies reunited. By cutting this repertory material into a fanciful account of what was going on behind the scenes, director Gerd Kroske shows a heroic little man systematically sabotaging the wiring to interrupt Kohl's speech twice before he's caught. The effect is a comical presage of the problems to come.

Less clever and more overtly fictional is Uwe Janson's "Sacred Cows." He imagines a famed docu-maker kidnapped by a Hitler-loving couple who force him to film them while they do nasty things like mutilate his foot. The episode's bizarre tone of black comedy leaves the viewer scratching his head.

Two docu segments are the most powerful, because their ghastly non-fiction is the hardest to write off. Both suffer from heavy-handed treatment and are stuffed with repetition. Maris Pfeiffer's "A Place, a Suicide" is a sad elegy to Gunter Schirmer, a happy, bearlike man who struggled to pick up his life after losing a leg in a car accident. After some boys spit on him in his wheelchair, shouting that Hitler would have had him gassed, he kills himself. In Philip Groning's "Victims, Witnesses," an unseen interviewer talks to a young factory hand and his buddy, both punk rockers, who were attacked and nearly killed by neo-Nazi skinheads.

Technically, episodes vary from wobbly 8mm blown up to 35mm to the more refined lensing and staging of Janson's "Sacred Cows."
—*Deborah Young*

BLUE CHIPS

A Paramount release of a Michele Rappaport production. Produced by Rappaport. Executive producers, Ron Shelton, Wolfgang Glattes. Directed by William Friedkin. Screenplay, Shelton. Camera (Technicolor), Tom Priestley Jr.; editor, Robert K. Lambert, David Rosenbloom; music, Nile Rodgers, Jeff Beck, Jed Leiber; production design, James Bissell; art direction, Ed Verreaux, William Arnold (Indiana, Chicago); set design, John H.M. Berger, Lauren Polizzi; set decoration, Thomas L. Roysden; costume design, Bernie Pollack; sound (Dolby), Kirk Francis; basketball coordinator, Rob Ryder; assistant director, Newt Arnold; casting, Louis Di Giaimo. Reviewed at Paramount Studios, L.A., Feb. 14, 1994. MPAA Rating: PG-13. Running time: **108 MIN.**
Pete Bell .... Nick Nolte
Jenny .... Mary McDonnell
Happy ................................J.T. Walsh
Ed .... Ed O'Neill
Lavada McRae .... Alfre Woodard
Vic .... Bob Cousy
Neon .... Shaquille O'Neal
Butch . Anfernee (Penny) Hardaway
Ricky .... Matt Nover
Father Dawkins ..... Louis Gossett Jr.
Slick .... Cylk Cozart
Tony .... Anthony C. Hall
Jack .... Kevin Benton
Freddie .... Bill Cross
Mel .... Marques Johnson
Marty .... Robert Wuhl

The venerable all-American pastimes of greed, cheating and winning at all costs take it on the chin in "Blue Chips," a deafness-inducing but otherwise ho-hum would-be expose of shady recruiting practices by college basketball programs. From a sports point of view, this fast-moving production has gone to great lengths to achieve an impeccable verisimilitude, as the cast is loaded with real-life on-and-off-the-court hoop personalities. But Paramount had better hope the avid basketball public will ante up to see their heroes in sufficient numbers to at least give this a good couple of weekends, since other viewers are likely to be underwhelmed.

The combination of Nick Nolte's ranting, agitated performance as a beleaguered coach, director William Friedkin's compulsive style and the frantic pace of the basketball action itself provides an overdose of stimulation that is more numbing than exciting. But the main problem is that the film, which was written by the very sports-savvy Ron Shelton 12 years ago, offers audiences no rooting interest, no way to cozy up to any of the characters.

Because everyone is, to varying degrees, complicit in a corrupt system of illegal payoffs, one couldn't care less what happens to them and their team. Point of the picture, other than to so bravely condemn illegal or at least unethical behavior, is hard to pin down.

Opening scene has Nolte bawling out his players after a game for their godawful play. A winner of two national championships with Western U., Nolte is on the verge of his first losing season and knows he's got to perform some kind of miracle to right his sinking ship and save his job.

The only way he can do this is through recruiting, so as soon as the season dribbles to its desultory end, he hits the road to find those elusive low-profile greats who aren't already heading for the top Eastern schools. (Basketball purists will object that recruiting generally takes place a year ahead, not the summer before a student's freshman year.)

Amusingly getting there one step ahead of some competing coaches (including such recognizable faces as Jerry Tarkanian and Jim Boeheim), Nolte comes up with three winners: a Chicago sharpshooter played by Anfernee (Penny) Hardaway; a towering farmboy (Matt Nover) from Larry Bird's hometown of French Lick, Ind.; and, especially, Shaquille O'Neal, playing a ne'er-do-well of monster talents who has been languishing unnoticed in the Army, Mexico and the Louisiana backwater.

Knowing he'll have a dynamite team with these three, Nolte believes he's convinced them to attend WU, but then come the demands: Hardaway's mother (Alfre Woodard) requests a new home and a fancy office, and Nover asks for $30,000, with a new tractor for his dad tossed in. The big innocent, O'Neal, doesn't want anything, but they throw a Lexus at him anyway.

With a cloud of alleged point-shaving by his team some years back hovering over him, Nolte wants no part of any of this, but a wealthy, overbearing alumni organization leader (J.T. Walsh) forces the issue and takes care of things himself. So with the team all set, it's only a question of how Nolte deals with it, and for how long.

Pic holds some interest for the look it affords at real players, the way they are accommodated regardless of academic abilities and the way others behave in relation to them. It also provides some incidental pleasures, such as former Celtic great Bob Cousy, in to play WU's athletic director, casually

making free throw after free throw during a chat with Nolte; Larry Bird caught shooting baskets on home turf; any number of college and pro players seen up close in practice and in games, and Shaq dunking repeatedly.

But there's also Nolte's totally boring relationship with his ex-wife (Mary McDonnell), who acts as his conscience's sounding board and agrees to tutor O'Neal; a curious narrative structure that offers little dramatic buildup and ends on a very abrupt note; and a vagueness about business-as-usual in recruiting practices.

With the exception of the cool young players, performances, led by Nolte's, are full-throttle. Pro athletes involved may not be great actors, but they're generally relaxed and likable.

To say that O'Neal has presence would be the understatement of the year: His smile and manner are ingratiating, and the main problem with his appearance here is that it's hard to frame him in the same shot with other performers.

Soundtrack, which is peppered with many pop tunes from assorted eras, has the decibel level of a Who concert. Lensing is distractingly lusterless, and Friedkin has shot much of the basketball action in so tight that it sometimes comes off as fuzzy and a bit herky-jerky. —*Todd McCarthy*

BERLIN FEST

OKNO V PARIZH
(WINDOW TO PARIS)
(RUSSIAN-FRENCH)

A Sony Classics (U.S.) release of a Fontaine (St. Petersburg)/Sodaperaga (Paris) production, in association with La Sept Cinema. (International sales: Sodaperaga, Paris.) Directed by Yuri Mamin. Screenplay, Arkadi Tigai, Mamin. Camera (color), Sergei Nekrasov, Anatoli Lapshov; editor, Olga Andrianova; supervising editor, Joelle Van Effenterre; music, Mamin, Aleksei Zalivalov; art direction, Vera Zelinskaya; costume design, Natalya Zamakhina; sound, Leonid Gavrichenko. Reviewed at Berlin Film Festival (Panorama section), Feb. 13, 1994. Running time: **90 MIN.**
Nicole .... Agnes Soral
Nikolai Chizhov .... Sergei Dontsov
Gorokhov .... Viktor Mikhailov
Vera .... Nina Ousatova
Gorokhov's
   mother-in-law .... Kira
                          Kreylis-Petrova
Gorokhov's
   daughter .... Natalya Ipatova
Kuzmich .... Viktor Gogolev
(Russian and French dialogue)

International co-productions never looked so natural as in "Window to Paris," the joyously funny story of a group of Russian bozos who find they can jump direct to the City of Light from a window in their appalling St. Petersburg apartment. Inventive, big-hearted, off-the-wall pic may be difficult to market to the English-language arthouse crowd but should be sought out by minority webs. Reception at its Berlin fest screenings was enthusiastic.

St. Petersburg-based director Yuri Mamin sprang to attention with the 1988 comedy-fantasy "The Fountain," and there's some of the same lunatic feel (plus a typical St. Petersburg lightness of touch) to his third feature.

Lead-up to the central idea is well paced, first introing Nikolay (Sergei Dontsov), an unconventional teacher who leads his pupils into class like the Pied Piper, and then Nikolay's uncouth neighbors, led by the tubby Gorokhov (Viktor Mikhailov). Climbing onto the roof one night through a concealed window, the duo get drunk in a local bar, trash the studio apartment of artist Nicole (Agnes Soral) on the way home, and realize only the next day they were actually in Paris.

Gorokhov and family use the window for increasingly ambitious looting sessions of Western goods, even managing to hoist a car into their living room. Meanwhile, Nicole, driven nuts by crazed Ruskies using her apartment as a throughway, climbs through the window and finds herself in modern-day St. Petersburg, a city of derelicts, street violence and political chaos. Nikolay manages to save her from the local cops by bluffing she's Edith Piaf on a Russian tour.

Upbeat (and strangely moving) finale has Nikolay arranging a trip through the window for his pupils in exchange for their calling off a strike at school. Twist is that they don't want to go back to dreary old St. Pete, and the "window" is about to close for the next 20 years.

Mamin's pic sets itself apart from other recent high-octane Russian comedies with its unflagging invention and performances that don't rely on caricature. Extra-tight cutting and frequent disposal of linking scenes keep the ideas coming thick and fast. Set pieces, like Gorokhov's family hawking Russo baubles in the Paris streets, are minor gems in themselves.

Occasional eruptions into music-making and dance seem such a natural part of the picture that Mamin is able to keep pushing the envelope without going over the top. Above all, these are characters you'd love to share a vodka or two with.

Tech credits and performances are fine without being overly smooth. Pic's French title is "Salades Russes." —*Derek Elley*

ON DEADLY GROUND

A Warner Bros. release of a Seagal/Nasso production. Produced by Steven Seagal, Julius R. Nasso, A. Kitman Ho. Executive producers, Robert Watts, Jeffrey Robinov. Co-producer, Edward McDonnell. Directed by Seagal. Screenplay, Ed Horowitz, Robin U. Russin. Camera (Technicolor), Ric Waite; editors, Robert Ferretti, Don Brochu; music, Basil Poledouris; production design, William Ladd Skinner; art direction, Lou Montejeno; supervising set design, Nick Navarro; set decoration, John Anderson, Ronald R. Reiss; costume design, Joseph G. Aulisi; sound (Dolby), Edward Tise; special effects coordinator, Thomas Fisher; stunt coordinator, Glenn Randall; associate producers, Peter Burrell, Doug Metzger; assistant director, Doug Metzger; second unit director, Glenn Randall Jr.; second unit camera, John M. Stephens; casting, Pamela Basker. Reviewed at the Bruin, Westwood, Feb. 17, 1994. MPAA Rating: R. Running time: **101 MIN.**

Forrest Taft .... Steven Seagal
Michael Jennings .... Michael Caine
Masu ....Joan Chen
MacGruder ....John C. McGinley
Stone .... R. Lee Ermey
Liles .... Shari Shattuck
Homer Carlton ...... Billy Bob Thornton
Hugh Palmer .... Richard Hamilton
Silook .... Chief Irvin Brink

Even before the first imposing images of hero Forrest Taft (Steven Seagal) register on the screen, the audience is fully aware of the signature that will codify "On Deadly Ground." On three separate title cards we are informed that this is a "Seagal/Nasso Production," of a "Steven Seagal Film" starring Steven Seagal. The rest is window dressing in this filigree thriller with eco trappings and a decibel and body count that strains mind and matter.

At its core the film is a vanity production parading as a social statement. It nonetheless has enough sound, fury and flash to satisfy the action crowd who have propped up Seagal's career. It should perform on the level of his earlier efforts, but marks a decided step backward from his previous pic, "Under Siege," in both quality and commercial appeal.

Seagal is a Red Adair-style trouble shooter and fire quasher for Aegis Oil Co. in Alaska. After imploding one fire, he comes to the alarming discovery that it was preventable. The greed of chairman Michael Jennings (Michael Caine) is responsible for the orders to install substandard equipment. To meet a deadline and complete a project, Jennings has put lives and the environment in jeopardy.

As Taft is of pure heart — and graphically beats the crap out of bigots and bullies on several occasions to make that point — he shifts sides to the noble, if primitive Inuit. The holy people recognize him as the Spirit Warrior and soon he is in mortal combat with the forces of evil from the corporate world.

It's later revealed that Taft is a former CIA operative. He's not just any agent, though, but the ultimate terminator who dropped out in favor of the purity of the last frontier. When that's sullied, he gets mad and naturally inflicts the maximum retribution.

"On Deadly Ground" shares a lot with other first works by action stars-turned-auteurs. The output from Cornel Wilde to Sylvester Stallone and beyond is unerringly narcissistic. The heroes are imbued with a touch of the messiah and the ability to lead — usually allegorically — from the desert and into the promised land.

Seagal, both as actor and director, filches heavily from "Billy Jack." However, this is a pale facsimile. He lacks Tom Laughlin's acting technique and the ability behind the camera to keep the story simple and direct. When he ventures into the mystic and folkloric, the result is patently inauthentic.

Nonetheless, he presses on, dropping little pearls about the environment (and stopping the plot momentum in its tracks) in between set pieces that allow him to dispatch dozens and dozens of goons without breaking into a sweat.

Horrifying rumors of a concluding 10-minute speech prove unfounded, with that turn whittled down to a near four-minute infomercial about being good to Mother Nature.

The film is slick and hollow. The work of the supporting cast ranges from uncomfortable (Caine) to loony (John C. McGinley's heavy) to improbable (Joan Chen as an Inuit activist).

All this can be forgiven in light of the fact that absolute movie power corrupts movies absolutely. Hopefully, Seagal will get back to basics and won't make "A Spokesman Is Born" next time out.

—*Leonard Klady*

INEVITABLE GRACE

A Silverstar Pictures release of a Christian Capobianco production. Produced by Capobianco. Executive producer, John Canawati Sr. Directed, written by Alex Canawati. Camera (color), Christian Sebaldt; editor, Grace Valenti; music, Christopher Whiffen; production design, Marc Rizzo; art direction, Christina Shellen; set decoration, Allison McVann; costume design, Alison Edmond; sound (Ultra Stereo), Sean Sullivan; assistant director, John Richard Glasser. Reviewed at the Laemmle Sunset 5, L.A., Feb., 11, 1994. Running time: **103 MIN.**

Adam Cestare .... Maxwell Caulfield
Lisa Kelner .... Stephanie Knights
Veronica .... Jennifer Nicholson
Dr. Marcia Stevens .... Tippi Hedren
Simone .... Sylvia B. Suarez
Philip .... John Pearson
Britt .... Samantha Eggar

There is nothing graceful about Alex Canawati's directorial feature debut, "Inevitable Grace," an amateurish, derivative would-be thriller that owes its entire existence to Hitchcock. Clumsily conceived and directed, this inept melodrama, about the disturbing relationship between an innocent psychiatrist and her patient's psycho husband, is a dud that is likely to disappear from the screen as soon as its negative reviews get printed.

A recent graduate of the University of Southern California's film school, Canawati has obviously seen many pictures by the Master of Suspense, for his noirish melodrama is replete with ideas and stylistic touches from "Rear Window," "Vertigo" and other Hitchcock classics.

Tale begins when Veronica (Jennifer Nicholson, Jack's daughter), a sultry redhead, rushes out of a revival moviehouse in a fit of hysteria. She wakes up to find herself in an asylum, supervised by Dr. Marcia Stevens (Tippi Hedren). The severe medic decides to put her under the care of Dr. Lisa Kelner (Stephanie Knights), a naive psychiatrist doing her residency at the hospital.

During their first session, Veronica mumbles something about being abused and running away from her husband, Adam Cestare (Maxwell Caulfield). Intrigued by the case above and beyond professional concern, and defying hospital regulations, Lisa finds out where the handsome husband lives and pays him a visit. Once this setup is established in the first half-hour, the movie rapidly falls apart, with its protagonists behaving stupidly and against their best interests.

"Inevitable Grace" is the kind of film that gives a bad name to psychiatrists, here portrayed as less stable and more problematic than their patients. Worse yet, all the women who work at the hospital soon forget that they are gainfully employed and spend their time in obsessive cat-and-mouse pursuits.

Most of the narrative consists of one-on-one encounters between the seductive Adam and the passive, masochistic Lisa. After witnessing a murder she inadvertently commits, Adam begins to blackmail Lisa and to transform her image to suit his desires. This subplot is lifted straight from "Vertigo," though the heroine's name, hairdo and clothes are more in the manner of Grace Kelly in "Rear Window."

Screenplay consists of banal generalities about men and women. One wishes the movie were sleazier and more titillating, but Canawati's direction is scattered, lacking visual distinction and craft in staging suspenseful or sexually suggestive scenes.

Caulfield looks good, but his would-be regal air makes him off-puttingly pompous. As the tormented psychiatrist, former model Knights is attractive but makes her character neither credible nor appealing. Hedren, a quintessential Hitchcock heroine, is miscast and is given the most embarrassing lines to utter.

Tech credits are on the raw side.
—*Emanuel Levy*

MON AMIE MAX

(CANADIAN-FRENCH)

A C/FP Distribution (Canada) release of a Les Productions du Verseay/Les Productions Lazennec production, with the participation of the National Film Board of Canada/Telefilm Canada/Sogic/Ministere de la Culture et de la Francophonie/the Centre National de la Cinematographie. (International sales: Cinepix.) Produced by Amiee Danis. Co-producer, Carole Ducharme. Directed by Michel Brault. Screenplay, Jefferson Lewis. Camera (color), Sylvain Brault; editor, Jacques Gagne; music, Francois Dompierre; artistic director, Anne Pritchard; costumes, Francois Laplante; sound, Patrick Rousseau; associate producer (National Film Board), Yves Rivard; line producer, Daniele Bussy; assistant director, Normand Bourgie. Reviewed at the Imperial Cinema, Montreal, Feb. 10, 1994. (In the Rendez-Vous du Cinema Quebecois Film Festival.) Running time: **107 MIN.**

Marie-Alexandrine
 Babant (Max) .... Genevieve Bujold
Catherine Mercier .... Marthe Keller
Marie-Alexandrine
 (teenager) ....Johanne McKay
Catherine (teenager) .... Marie Guillard
Denis Lajeunesse .... Michel Rivard
Madame Brabant .... Rita Lafontaine
With: Veronique Le Flaguais, Jean-Louis Roux, Patrice Bissonnette, Rosa Zacharie, Jean-Rene Ouellet, Francious Dompierre, Ari Snyder, Michel Sinelnikoff, Jeanne Quintal Beaulieu, Michel Daigle, Marie-Helene Poulin.

Quebec helmer Michel Brault's "Mon Amie Max" is a slow-moving melodrama about a woman's search for a long-lost son that fails to rise above its predict-

able plot. Brault has attracted international attention before — notably for the mid-1970s political drama "Les Ordres" and the more recent "Paper Wedding" — but his latest effort is unlikely to stir up much B.O. action outside Quebec. Featuring a weak script and a tired performance by star Genevieve Bujold, pic opened locally Feb. 18.

Bujold plays Marie-Alexandrine (Max) Babant, a burned-out, middle-aged former classical pianist who returns to her native Quebec City after 25 years of self-imposed exile. Max comes crashing back into the life of her old friend Catherine Mercier (Marthe Keller), now a successful concert pianist, who was Max's inseparable mate when they were teenagers studying at the Conservatoire de Musique.

In an extended flashback, the rebellious Max and the more subdued Catherine are shown winning the top spots at the school's competition, and both seem destined for music careers. But Max's life goes into a 25-year tailspin when she admits to her domineering mother, played with relish by stage vet Rita Lafontaine, that she is pregnant.

Her mother forces the 15-year-old to give up the baby boy for adoption, and Max's career prospects — and her friendship with Catherine — go down the drain when she runs away from school and home in a fury.

When she finally returns to Quebec a couple of decades later to try to find her son, Catherine immediately agrees to help out her old school friend even though Max has renewed the relationship by breaking into Catherine's apartment late one night. The plot takes a turn for the maudlin when Max also enlists the aid of Denis (local pop singer/actor Michel Rivard), who just happens to be a garage mechanic searching for his mother, who abandoned him early in life.

Bujold's performance consists mostly of an endless series of sour expressions that peek out from behind ever-present dark shades. Keller is a bit more lively, but Jefferson Lewis' script leaves her no room for character development. The real flaw here is that it's never made clear why these girls were best friends in the first place, since they have almost nothing in common. Worse, the final dramatic reunion of mother and son doesn't pack any emotional punch whatsoever thanks to a bizarre plot twist that will only confuse audiences. Lensing by Sylvain Brault — the director's son — is first-rate, and his atmospheric snapshots of Old Quebec rep one of the pic's few pleasures. Other production values are first-rate.
—*Brendan Kelly*

L'ENFER

(HELL)

(FRENCH)

An MKL release of an MK2 Diffusion presentation of an MK2 Prods./CED Prods./France 3 Cinema/Cinemanuel production, with participation of Canal Plus and support from Procirep and Conseil Regional Midi Pyrenees. (International sales: MK2.) Produced by Marin Karmitz. Directed, written by Claude Chabrol, from an original screenplay by Henri-Georges Clouzot with additional dialogue by Jose-Andre Lacour. Camera (color), Bernard Zitzermann; editor, Monique Fardoulis; music, Matthieu Chabrol; art direction, Emile Ghigo; set decoration, Denis Sieglan; costume design, Corinne Jorry; sound (Dolby), Jean-Bernard Thomasson; assistant director, Anne Guillemard. Reviewed at 14 Juillet Odeon Cinema, Paris, Jan. 21, 1994. Running time: **105 MIN.**
Nelly .... Emmanuelle Beart
Paul .... Francois Cluzet
Martineau .... Marc Lavoine
With: Nathalie Cardone, Andre Wilms, Christiane Minazzoli, Dora Doll, Mario David, Jean-Pierre Cassel, Sophie Artur.

With "Hell," Claude Chabrol brings to the screen a script about obsessive jealousy that the late Henri-Georges Clouzot ("The Wages of Fear," "Diabolique") was forced to abandon 30 years ago. The essentially two-character, husband-and-wife tale is winningly told, and fine perfs, including a patient-and-pulpy turn by Emmanuelle Beart, bode well for offshore arthouse sales.

Clouzot began shooting on July 3, 1964, with Romy Schneider and Serge Reggiani in the leads, but production stopped when latter fell ill on the third day. While rehearsing with replacement Jean-Louis Trintignant, Clouzot suffered a heart attack. Though helmer lived until 1977, pic was never resumed. His widow gave the orphaned script to Gallic producer Marin Karmitz, who drafted Chabrol.

Beart is Nelly, wife of Paul (Francois Cluzet), who's taken on massive debt to buy and manage an idyllically situated resort hotel he's worked at for 15 years. She's good-natured, devoted, vivacious. In a whirlwind, storybook opening sequence, the pair wed and become parents.

With her delectable combo of innocent face and killer contours, Beart plays the character's beauty to the hilt. Nelly enjoys her status as fulfilled young wife and mom, but once stressed-out Paul gets it into his head she's cheating on him with garage mechanic Martineau (Gallic singer Marc Lavoine), irrational jealousy sets in. He starts to hear nagging voices in his head, which he answers aloud.

Nelly is initially pleased at Paul's jealousy, which she sees as concrete proof of his love. But his volatile, apparently unfounded behavior soon renders their life hellish. His use of alcohol and sleeping pills fans the flames.

A stumbling block for offshore auds may be the absence in the script of any acknowledgment that therapy has become widespread in the three decades since original was written. As the symptoms of Paul's mental illness pile up, viewers could be constantly tempted to shout, "Get professional help, already!" prior to the devilishly ambiguous conclusion.

A hard-to-swallow development occurs after Paul is finally diagnosed. Though he's clearly got a screw loose, plus a propensity toward violence, the doctor blithely sends the couple home to spend the night together, simply because the local loony bin hasn't got a room free till the next day.

In his fourth outing with Chabrol, Cluzet convincingly conveys his character's percolating paranoia, maddened by every move Beart makes. Jean-Pierre Cassel and Christiane Minazzoli are amusing as a flagrantly hot-to-trot elder couple.

Chabrol's buffish humor is in evidence in one sequence in which Paul advises a guest with a 16mm camera to get a camcorder instead, to be met with the reply, "Nothing compares with film and the big screen." The camera buff's viewfinder is sometimes used to give the audience p.o.v. shots, a technique Chabrol also used in the opening sequence of his 1985 mystery-thriller, "Cop au vin."

Peppy lensing in the sun-drenched setting creates an ironic contrast to Cluzet's stormy outbursts.
—*Lisa Nesselson*

HEXAGONE

(FRENCH)

A Cine Classic release of an Alhambra Film presentation of an Idriss/Ministere de la Ville/Ministry of Youth & Sports/Ministry of Social Affairs/Caisse des Depots & Consignations/Femis/Fund for Immigrant Workers & Their Families production, with support from ACID. Produced, directed, written by Malik Chibane. Executive producer, Antonio Olivares. Camera (color), Patrice Guillou; editor, Alice Lary; music, Daniel Thirard, Ricardo Serra; art direction, costume design, Eliane Magrina; sound, Marc-Antoine Beldent; technical adviser, Gerard Mordillat; script consultants, J.P. Lenoir, Thomas Gilou. Reviewed at Club Publicis screening room, Paris, Jan. 20. 1994. Running time: **83 MIN.**

February 21, 1994 (Cont.)

Slimane	Jalil Naciri
Samy	Farid Abdedou
Staf	Hakim Sarahoui
Ali	Karim Chakir
Nacera	Faiza Kadour

With: Kame Allah, Driss El Haddaqui, Corinne Colas.

A modest but convincingly tailored "Arabz N the Hood," newcomer Malik Chibane's "Hexagone" traces the mostly thwarted aspirations of young, second-generation north Africans in the dead-end housing projects outside Paris. Engaging, festready pic examines contemporary dilemmas with humor, poignance and verve.

Film's characters, children of a cultural mix of restraint and resignation overseen by devout Muslim parents, are far less volatile than their American gang counterparts. Use of vivid slang, however, gives dialogue punch.

Though only a short commute from the City of Light, setting of Goussainville is a world apart from the French capital. Pic's narrator, Slimane, is a polite, upstanding young man who looks like a 1920s Latin lover but is a modern child of Algerian immigrants. He's eager to escape the stifling boredom of chronic unemployment and life in his still-traditional mother's home.

Older brother Samy is a heroin addict who spends his days shoplifting. Slimane is secretly dating the prettiest girl in the neighborhood, Nacera, who wants a greater commitment.

Pic spans five days leading to the climactic Islamic feast of Abd El Kebir, during which Slimane's circumscribed world is shaken to its foundations.

Lensed on location in areas helmer Chibane clearly knows inside out, this low-budgeter has the ring of truth throughout, with resourceful characters hemmed in by invisible walls of discrimination. It remains to be seen whether Chibane has other urgent tales to tell, but this debut is a promising new voice from Arab immigrants on French soil.

Pic's title is a synonym for France itself, taken from the shape of the country on maps. —*Lisa Nesselson*

HUANGJIN DAOTIAN
(THE NOBLEST WAY TO DIE)
(TAIWANESE)

A Yun Hung Film Co./Fu Yuan Film Co. production. Produced by Shang Yun-chiang. Executive producers, Chang Chih-hung, Chou Tan. Directed, written by Chou. Camera (color), Ch'en Chung-yuan; editor, Ch'en Po-wen; sound, Lin Shun-lang; associate producer, Chung Hao. Reviewed at Cannes Film Festival (market), May 16, 1993. Running time: **108 MIN.**

With: Shao Hsin, Lin Te-yu, Tony Wang, Ch'u Hung, Wang Hsiao-shih, Tai Li-jen, Yen Chung.
(Mandarin, Shanghainese and Japanese dialogue)

An old-fashioned Sino-Japanese war drama in pseudo-modernist wrappings, "The Noblest Way to Die" will do just that beyond home base Taiwan. Opening promise of a thoughtful reassessment of yesterday's enemies soon degrades into phony moral posturing and jawbreaking hysteria.

Film is basically a huge flashback, narrated by the grandson of Inegawa, an aged Japanese who returns to southern China in 1990 to pay his respects to the Chinese dead of World War II. Back in 1939, Inegawa, then a young lieutenant, had captured a Chinese guerrilla, T'ien Shih, and locked him up with an old Shanghainese, Uncle Ch'uan.

Inegawa slowly gains respect for T'ien and promises him he'll live if he admits he's a spy. But his superior, Inoue, a neo-samurai loon, is more interested in breaking his prisoners, finally sodomizing T'ien and raping Inegawa's half-Manchu g.f.

Despite some careful, often good-looking direction, pic is fatally flawed by its melodramatic script and cardboard characters. Second half is largely a lip-smacking succession of torture scenes. Acting by the no-name cast is standard. Tech credits are OK. —*Derek Elley*

BERLIN FEST

JEANNE LA PUCELLE
1: LES BATAILLES
2: LES PRISONS

(JOAN THE MAID
1: THE BATTLES
2: THE PRISONS)

(FRENCH)

A Pierre Grise production, in association with La Sept Cinema/France 3 Cinema/Canal Plus/CNC. (International sales: Cine Electric, London.) Produced by Martine Marignac. Directed by Jacques Rivette. Screenplay, Christine Laurent, Pascal Bonitzer. Camera (color), William Lubtchansky; editor, Nicole Lubtchansky; music, Jordi Savall; production design, Manu de Chauvigny; costumes, Christine Laurent, Daniele Boutard; sound, Florian Eidenbenz; assistant director, Dominique Arhex. Reviewed at Berlin Film Festival (Panorama section), Feb. 13, 1994. Running time: **336 MIN.** (Part 1: **160 MIN.**, Part 2: **176 MIN.**)

Joan	Sandrine Bonnaire
Dauphin/Charles VII	Andre Marcon
La Tremoille	Jean-Louis Richard
Regnault de Chartres	Marcel Bozonnet
Raoul de Gaucourt	Didier Sauvegrain
Jean d'Alencon	Jean-Pierre Lorit
Dunois	Patrick Le Mauff
Jean d'Aulon	Jean-Pierre Becker
Louis de Coutes	Mathieu Busson
La Hire	Stephane Boucher
Jeanne de Bethune	Edith Scob
Charlotte	Claire Bacot
Yolande d'Aragon	Martine Pascal
Jean de Metz	Olivier Cruveiller
Catherine de la Rochelle	Nathalie Richard

The inspiring tragedy of the 15th-century teenager who persuaded the French Establishment to give her an army with which to fight the British, only to be betrayed, tried and burned at the stake, has enticed filmmakers since the silent era. Such diverse directors as Cecil B. De Mille, Victor Fleming, Otto Preminger, Carl Dreyer and Robert Bresson all tackled the subject. Though Ingrid Bergman (in the Fleming) and Jean Seberg (in the Preminger) were both impressive, it's generally conceded that the definitive Joan was played by Falconetti in Dreyer's great 1928 film "The Passion of Joan of Arc," which dealt only with Joan's trial and execution.

Jacques Rivette's ambitious, enormously long and detailed production toplines Sandrine Bonnaire as the Maid, and though she's too old for the role (Joan died at 19), she gives a mostly impressive performance, especially in the trial scenes; she also rides a horse and carries a banner with style. But she lacks the glowing charisma that the real Joan must surely have had.

The film itself is also lacking. With a running time of almost six hours, the pic should have an inner tension and momentum with which to grip audiences over such a long and demanding period. This is especially true considering the film was designed to screen in two parts, with tickets for each sold separately. Attendance patterns will be interesting; the bet is that there will be a marked drop-off.

Simplicity is the main element here. Rivette tells the story of Joan in meticulous detail with spare sets and costumes, and refers in the narrative to precise dates and times of day. The action is regularly punctuated by "witnesses" who face the camera and quietly fill in gaps in the story; this makes the political and religious machinations much clearer than before, but also slows the personal drama of Joan's brief career.

The titles of the two parts of the film are misleading. Part 1, "The Battles," is almost entirely composed of scenes in which Joan tries to convince French officials that she is indeed sent from God and can save France

from the English and make the Dauphin king. The last half-hour contains some desultory battle scenes, structured around the siege of Orleans, though it looks as though no more than about 30 extras were used in any one shot. Other filmmakers working on a budget, notably Orson Welles in "Chimes at Midnight," have been more successful in creating the feeling of medieval armed conflict.

The battles continue at the beginning of Part 2, "The Prisons," which then describes in exhausting detail the shifting politics that culminated in Joan's trial and execution.

Bonnaire's Joan is diminutive, determined, unsophisticated; the actress dominates the film but never makes as much of an impression as she should. The large supporting cast gives her ample backup, with no real standouts except perhaps Stephane Boucher as a soldier who can't stop swearing (something that offends the straight-laced Joan).

Jordi Savall has composed a beautiful score that is used too sparingly; most of the film plays with natural sound, which is effective in the final, restrained sequence at the stake, but which leaves a void elsewhere.

It seems certain that there'll be divergence among critics over Rivette's extremely demanding film, which isn't nearly as successful as his previous effort, "La Belle Noiseuse." Given the latter's enthusiastic reception, it was surprising when Rivette later produced a shorter version; "Joan" offers up a much more plausible argument for cutting, which could make it more accessible. —*David Stratton*

FEDERAL HILL

An Eagle Beach production. Produced by Michael Corrente, Libby Corrente, Richard Crudo. Executive producers, Ron Kastner, Randy Finch, Leroy Leach. Directed, written by Michael Corrente. Camera (b&w), Crudo; editor, Kate Sanford; music, David Bravo; production design, Robert Schlienig; sound, Matt Sigal; assistant director, Gregory Allan Webb. Reviewed at Berlin Film Festival (Panorama), Feb. 12, 1994. Running time: **100 MIN.**

Ralph	Nicholas Turturro
Nicky	Anthony DeSando
Frank	Michael Raynor
Joey	Robert Turano
Bobby	Jason Andrews
Wendy	Libby Langdon
Sal	Frank Vincent
Fredo	Michael Corrente

Producer/director/scripter Michael Corrente manages to bring freshness to basically derivative material in "Federal Hill," thanks to a number of excellent performances and some evocative black-and-white images of a world he knows intimately. It's a modest entry, but an appealing one.

The "Federal Hill" of the title is a district of Providence, R.I., where Corrente grew up. It's unfamiliar screen territory, but the characters in Corrente's atmospheric first film are familiar from a score of other pix about young Italo-Americans, from "Mean Streets" on down.

Pic centers on five young men, friends from school days, who still hang out together for a weekly card game at the home of one of them, Joey, who got married and probably regrets it.

The others are Bobby, a perennial loser; Frank, son of a locally feared gang boss; Nicky, the intelligent, sensitive one; and Ralph, erratic and prone to violence.

Ralph (Nicholas Turturro) is a burglar who robs and trashes houses in the smart parts of the city; he's devoted to his sickly father and to Nicky, his best friend.

Turturro (brother of actor/director John) is very effective in what has to be termed the Robert De Niro role. Nicky sells dope on the street, and that's how he meets pretty preppie Wendy, who needs the stuff for her frat party, which Nicky and Ralph later crash (one woman gives Ralph a hilarious brushoff that's typical of the film's brash humor).

In one of the film's best scenes, Nicky (Anthony DeSando) invites Wendy (Libby Langdon) on a date and, when he can't get the service he wants at an Italian restaurant, takes her home and cooks her pasta, romancing her during the cooking and ending the meal with a bedroom frolic, inevitably interrupted by Ralph.

The film's dramatic impetus stems both from the besotted Nicky's decision to leave the gang and Ralph's determination to prove to him that, for Wendy, he's only a pleasant interlude, and from Ralph's running afoul of Frank's gangster father when he tries to help Bobby get desperately needed cash. The climax is a tad conventional, with a public assassination awkwardly staged.

But Corrente, who makes a brief appearance as foreman on a building site, shows talent and has created an interesting bunch of characters whose lives unfold in recognizable day-to-day situations.

The decision to film in black-and-white pays off artistically with some fine imagery shot by Richard Crudo. —*David Stratton*

FRESA Y CHOCOLATE

(STRAWBERRY AND CHOCOLATE)

(CUBAN-MEXICAN-SPANISH)

An ICAIC (Havana)-IMCINE-Tabasco Films (Mexico City)-Telemadrid-SGAE (Madrid) co-production. (International sales: ICAIC.) Directed by Tomas Gutierrez Alea, Juan Carlos Tabio. Screenplay, Senel Paz, Alea. Camera (color), Mario Garcia Joya; editors, Miriam Talavera, Osvaldo Donatien; music, Jose Maria Vitier; production design, Fernando O'Reilly; sound, Germinal Hernandez; assistant director, Mayra Segura. Reviewed at Berlin Film Festival (competing), Feb. 12, 1994. Running time: **111 MIN.**

Diego .... Jorge Perugorria
David .... Vladimir Cruz
Nancy .... Mirta Ibarra
Miguel .... Francisco Gattorno
German .... Jorge Angelino
Vivian .... Marilyn Solaya

This new comedy from Cuba is a gem. Filled with malicious swipes against the Castro regime, it's a provocative but very humane comedy about sexual opposites and, with proper handling, could attract the "Wedding Banquet" crowd in cinemas worldwide.

David (Vladimir Cruz) is a macho but naive and inexperienced youth who believes passionately in communism and the Cuban Revolution. He's an idealist who has accepted the official line on everything, but his knowledge of the world, especially of art, music and literature, is scanty. Depressed because his girlfriend has married another man (in a clever, funny opening sequence), he's at loose ends when he runs into Diego.

Diego (Jorge Perugorria) is an effeminate gay who revels in his gayness. He's instantly attracted to the handsome David when they share a table at an outdoor cafe, and he manages to persuade David to come to his apartment on a pretext. The homophobic David is most uneasy during this first encounter, especially when Diego prattles on about the ills of Cuban society.

He decides it's his duty to expose this most unrevolutionary Cuban, especially when Diego mentions he's working on an art exhibition with the help of a foreign embassy. So he visits the apartment again, and again — and the inevitable happens. He finds his outlook on life being changed by the warm, crazy Diego, and the two become friends. Their final hug lends the film an immensely satisfying windup.

Though the film's a bit long, vet director Tomas Gutierrez Alea and his partner Juan Carlos Tabio (director of the hilarious "Plaff," who was brought in when Alea was taken ill) have come up with a winner here,

with much credit going to the two lead actors. Cruz is perfect as the uptight, tunnel-visioned David, while Perugorria is indeed a class act as the extravagantly funny Diego. Minor characters, who include Diego's spacey next-door neighbor (Mirta Ibarra), are well limned.

"Strawberry and Chocolate" looms as the international breakthrough film for Cuban cinema, thanks to its great good humor and wit. Its cheerful debunking of many of the sacred tenets of communism should also be of interest.

Technical credits are OK, though the color processing in the print caught was rather muddy.

—*David Stratton*

EXILE

(AUSTRALIAN)

A Beyond Films release of an Illumination Films production, in association with Film Victoria and the Australian Film Finance Corp. (International sales: Beyond Intl.) Produced by Paul Cox, Santhana Naidu, Paul Ammitzboll. Executive producer, William T. Marshall. Directed, written by Cox, based on the novel, "Priest Island," by E. L. Grant Watson. Camera (color), Nino Martinetti; editor, Cox; music, Paul Grabowsky; production design, Neil Angwin; costume design, Gosia Dobrowolska. Reviewed at Village Roadshow screening room, Sydney, Jan 27, 1994. (In Berlin Film Festival — competing.) Running time: **95 MIN.**

Peter Costello .... Aden Young
Mary .... Beth Champion
Jean .... Claudia Karvan
Timothy Dullach .... David Field
Ghost Priest .... Norman Kaye
Village Priest .... Chris Haywood
MacKenzie .... Nicholas Hope
Jean's Father .... Tony Llewellyn-Jones
Sheriff Hamilton .... Barry Otto
Midwife .... Gosia Dobrowolska
Innes .... Hugo Weaving
Alice .... Tammy Kendall

With this, his second adaptation of a book by E.L. Grant Watson (after last year's "The Nun and the Bandit"), Australian auteur Paul Cox moves another step away from the kind of urban relationship film that first established him on the international arthouse circuit. "Exile" is an ambitious, sometimes hallucinatory, drama that tackles themes difficult to bring off successfully in the cinema. Responses are likely to be mixed.

Based on Grant's novel "Priest Island," pic unfolds in a kind of timeless limbo, which could be the last century or even earlier, and with a setting not specifically Australian. A young man, Peter (Aden Young), has been caught stealing sheep he needed as a dowry in order to marry his sweetheart, Jean (Claudia Karvan).

His punishment is to be exiled to an uninhabited island, with only rudimentary tools to support him. He

thus becomes a kind of Robinson Crusoe who lives a miserable, lonely existence only a few hours from his home, but with the knowledge he'll be killed if he tries to return.

The early scenes are extremely leisurely, as Nino Martinetti's camera lovingly explores the rugged coastline of the island (pic was shot in a national park in southern Tasmania) and Peter begins to carve out a primitive life for himself. Meanwhile, Jean has been forced to marry another man (Nicholas Hope, star of "Bad Boy Bubby," again scoring well) and soon becomes pregnant, but she loses her baby in an agonizing childbirth sequence.

The slender narrative takes off when Mary (Beth Champion), a servant at the village inn, becomes so intrigued by gossip about the handsome exile that she decides to join him, taking with her a few chickens and a goat. The pair soon become lovers, though Peter is still haunted by visions of Jean, and eventually Mary has a baby son. A friend brings the village priest (Chris Haywood) to the island for a baptism and marriage ceremony.

With "Exile," Cox poses a few challenges for his audience. Story is slim, dialogue is minimal, and much time is spent simply exploring the inhospitable coastal terrain. As in "The Nun and the Bandit," the writer/director is interested in the spiritual elements of the piece. Patience is required in the early scenes, and the film clearly isn't for everyone, but gradually it exerts a spell.

The three young principal actors are new to the Cox fold. Young, who registered strongly in "Black Robe," has the right physical presence as the lonely exile. Champion radiates innocence and determination as the woman who defies convention to join the outcast on the island, and Karvan is touching as the woman forced to marry a man she despises.

Haywood's bald, prissy priest injects the film with a touch of welcome humor, but another Cox regular, Norman Kaye, is stuck with the film's weakest character, that of the philosophizing ghost of a priest once banished to the same island.

Paul Grabowsky's music is beautifully mood-setting. Cox's own editing is a touch indulgent, and some tightening, especially in the first reel, would have been beneficial.

—*David Stratton*

LENINGRAD COWBOYS MEET MOSES

(FINNISH-GERMAN-FRENCH)

A Sputnik Oy (Helsinki)-Pandora Film (Frankfurt)-Pyramide Production/La Sept Cinema (Paris) co-production. (International sales: Christa Saredi, Zurich.) Produced, directed, written, edited by Aki Kaurismaki. Executive producers, Paula Oinonen, Reinhard Brundig, Fabienne Vonier. Camera (color), Timo Salminen; music supervision, Mauri Sumen; production design, John Ebden; sound, Jouko Lumme, Timo Linnasalo; assistant director, Erkki Astala. Reviewed at Berlin Film Festival (Forum section), Feb. 16, 1994. Running time: **91 MIN.**
Moses/Vladimir .... Matti Pellonpaa
The Mute .... Kari Vaananen
Lazarus/Johnson/
Elijah .... Andre Wilms
American Cousin .... Nicky Tesco
Bingo Hostess .... Nathalie Helies
Singer of Babylon ... Kirsi Tykkylainen
  Leningrad Cowboys: Twist-Twist Erkinharju, Ben Granfelt, Sakke Jarvenpaa, Jore, Marjaranta, Ekke Niiva, Lyle Narvnanen, Pemo Ojala, Silu Seppala, Mauri Sumen, Mato Valtonen
  (English dialogue)

Aki Kaurismaki's numbingly unfunny sequel to his 1989 cult success, "Leningrad Cowboys Go America," is a major disappointment. Those who responded to the quirky humor and offbeat characters of the first film may come back for more but are unlikely to have a very good time, while newcomers to the Finnish franchise will wonder what on earth made the Cowboys fun in the first place.

The problem lies not only in the fact that, inevitably, the freshness and originality of the basic joke are missing here (these lousy musicians with their strange hair and long, pointy shoes are no longer funny in themselves); it's also that Kaurismaki's script, which is basically a road movie starting in Mexico and ending in Siberia, needed a whole lot more work.

Pic starts promisingly with an amusing title card that fills in what happened to the Cowboys ("the worst rock 'n' roll band in the world") since the first film. They've been in Mexico, and even made it to the Top 10 there, until affected by "a snake in paradise — tequila," which apparently killed most of them.

The survivors, who have "gone Mexican" and are reduced to cooking cactus for food, decide to go north for a gig in Coney Island, where they meet their long-lost and still sneaky manager, Vladimir (Matti Pellonpaa), who now claims to be Moses and vows to lead them home to Siberia, "the Promised Land."

Kaurismaki's celebrated deadpan humor is just dead this time around; scene after scene plays utterly flat. The one great gag, a perfectly timed "walk on water" joke, only shows what might have been.

The music doesn't keep things bubbling, either, because most of it's also pretty bad. The brightest musical interlude has a femme singer join the band for a sweet rendition of "Rivers of Babylon"; industry insiders may recognize her as Kirsi Tykkylainen, longtime rep of the Finnish Film Foundation.

Production values are high, with excellent on-the-road location camera work and sound. The actors do their best with their familiar and routine assignments, though there are no amusing guest appearances as there were in the first film.

Kaurismaki reportedly will have another film ready in time for Cannes, and his fans can hope that the next one will turn out better than this. —*David Stratton*

EKSPRES-INFORMATSIA

(INFORMATION EXPRESS)

(GEORGIAN)

A Lileo Arts production, in association with Saarlandischer Rundfunk. (International sales: Telefilm Saar, Saarbrucken, Germany.) Produced by Alexander Sharashidze. Directed by Eldar Shengelaya. Screenplay, Revaz Cheishvili. Camera (color), Lomer Achvlediani; editor, Gari Kuntsev; production design, Dimitri Eristavi; sound, Leila Ashiani. Reviewed at Berlin Film Festival (Panorama section), Feb. 11, 1994. Running time: **93 MIN.**
  With: Zurab Kipshidze, Nana Shonia, Mikheil Yashadze, Tamaz Khutsishvili, Teimuraz Chircadze.

A fiercely funny farce about the glasnost era and its aftermath in Georgia, "Information Express" is a natural for fests looking for a comedy slot that could spark wider commercial interest if properly handled. More Marx Brothers than Karl Marx, the film had a difficult production history and has been in the works for seven years, frowned on by the previous post-communist regime in Georgia; it's director Eldar Shengelaya's first pic since his amusing "Blue Mountains" 10 years ago.

The title is that of a fictitious TV show that spotlights crime and corruption in Georgian society. The main target is a fruit-juice bottling company; it's alleged some poison has found its way into the juice, and the company boss is on the carpet, live on TV.

But that's only the starting point for an often wildly funny grab bag of jokes about life today in Georgia, where political and corporate allegiances shift wildly back and forth, gun-toting bandits battle one another from moving cars and everyone spies on everyone else.

Some of the jokes are old faves, and others will probably mean more to Georgian audiences than to outsiders. But the fast-paced comedy has something for everyone who likes to laugh at corrupt, bumbling officialdom.

Technical credits are modest, but there's a flawless cast of comics, and Shengelaya knows his stuff. The result is a most delightful diversion.
—*David Stratton*

STANTSIA LYUBVI

(LOVE STATION)

(KAZAKH)

A Kazakhfilm Studio, Alem Group production. (International sales: Kazakhfilm Studio, Alma-Ata.) Directed by Talgat Temenov. Screenplay, Temenov, Leila Akhimshanova, from Temenov's novella "Gulnaz." Camera (color), Aleksei Berkovich; editor, A. Kistauova; music, Tolegen Mukhametshanov; art direction, Aleksandr Rorokin; costume design, Aiman Bakanova; sound, Zinaida Mukhamedkhanova. Reviewed at Berlin Film Festival (Panorama section), Feb. 14, 1994. Running time: **87 MIN.**
  With: Bayan Mukhitdenova, Kuanykhbek Adylov, Bopesh Shandayev.
  (Russian dialogue)

"Love Station" is a Kazakh charmer that should win over all but the hard of heart. Central Asian yarn of a girl torn between two contrasting Romeos has a fresh, ingenuous appeal that won't conquer mountains but should prove a small-scale hit on the fest circuit.

Setting is the village of Mahabbat in 1977, when Kazakhstan was still under Soviet rule. Arriving from out of town to enroll in high school, cute teen Gulnaz locks eyes with Oral, and for the latter it's love at first sight. Fly in the ointment is Oral's smooth friend Zhenis, who also makes tracks toward the girl, finally marrying her when Oral decides to leave for army service. There's nothing here that hasn't been done a thousand times before, but director Talgat Temenov, co-adapting his own 10-year-old novella, gets unaffected playing from his young actors and wraps the whole confection in a persuasive stylistic package.

Using soft filters, an eclectic, upbeat music track and plenty of heightened light-play, Temenov creates an almost fairy-tale atmosphere. Discreet use of crane shots shows a technical savvy at odds with the apparently naive style.

Performances, especially by Bayan Mukhitdenova as the pretty Gulnaz, are on target. Pic was also shot in a Kazakh-language version ("Mahabbat beketi"), not ready in time for Berlin fest unspooling.
—*Derek Elley*

IL GIUDICE RAGAZZINO

(LAW OF COURAGE)

(ITALIAN)

A RAI-TV Channel 2/RCS TV & Films production. Produced by Maurizio Tedesco for Trio Cinema e Televisione. Directed by Alessandro di Robilant. Screenplay, Ugo Pirro, Andrea Purgatori, with di Robilant, loosely based on the novel by Nando Dalla Chiesa. Camera (Technicolor), David Scott; editor, Cecilia Zanuso; music, Franco Piersanti; art direction, Giancarlo Muselli; costumes, Catia Dottori. (In Dolby.) Reviewed at Warner Bros. screening room, Rome, Feb. 4, 1994. (In Berlin Film Festival, competing.) Running time: **96 MIN.**
Rosario Livantino .... Giulio Scarpati
Father .... Leopoldo Trieste
Mother .... Regina Bianchi
Angela .... Sabrina Ferilli
Marshall Guazzelli .... Paolo De Vita
Migliore .... Renato Carpentieri
Saetta .... Roberto Nobile
  With: Ninni Bruscetta, Turi Scalia, Salvatore Puntillo, Pippo Pattavina, Marcello Perrachio.

Based on the 1990 murder of a young magistrate in Sicily, "Law of Courage" (literally, "The Boy Judge") nobly salutes an unsung hero in Italy's ongoing battle against the Mafia. Though the story will have most resonance in Italy, its anguishing atmosphere could make it work as a genre thriller offshore.

Avoiding the tense, action-packed scripting that made a national hit of the TV series "The Octopus" (also produced by RCS), young helmer Alessandro di Robilant and his scripters, Ugo Pirro and Andrea Purgatori, concentrate on the mundane, day-to-day life of young judge Rosario Livantino (played by boyish thesp Giulio Scarpati.) A four-square, churchgoing fellow who lives with his aged parents, Rosario takes his work as a public prosecutor very seriously. He believes that justice must be carried out at all costs and that the foundation for his work is not in people's opinions but in the law.

In the small, Mafia-ridden town of Canicatti, this is revolutionary thinking. Rosario's determination frightens his parents, annoys his boss and estranges his fiancee. Finally it isolates him even from the other young public prosecutors, who are more cautious than he.

At that point Mafia boss Renato Carpentieri knows he has Rosario where he wants him. Two youths on a motorcycle gun him down on the road to Agrigento.

Scarpati portrays Rosario as a closed person who takes few risks on the personal plane — though his hesitation about marrying lawyer Angela (Sabrina Ferilli) is also motivated by his belief he'll die young.

His idealism is strikingly out of key with the rest of Canicatti, and even becomes irritating in a fire-and-brimstone speech he gives to an assembly of town dignitaries. This harangue is refrained several times in the course of the film, with elephantine heaviness.

What saves the film is Rosario's admirably unshakable conviction that he represents Good, which wins its own victories over Evil, and which can die but never disappear. Outwitting the politicians in Rome, who try to protect the Mafiosi, Rosario succeeds in bringing the bosses to trial. His cold authority in interrogating the criminals, be they brutes or charming next-door neighbors like Carpentieri, is exhilarating to watch.

Supporting cast is high-quality, notably the excellent Regina Bianchi and Leopoldo Trieste as Rosario's folks. As the girlfriend, the oddly cast Ferilli (launched in "Diary of a Maniac") constantly has to fight down a sex-kitten image to be credible as the only female lawyer this side of Palermo.

David Scott's cinematography underlines the scorched, melancholy beauty of Sicily, while Franco Piersanti's harsh, unmelodic score creates much of the film's tension. Film's pace is speedy, sometimes overly so, allowing no time for reaction shots to reap an emotional harvest.
—*Deborah Young*

ANNA 6-18

(RUSSIAN-FRENCH)

A Studio Tri T (Moscow)-Camera One (Paris) co-production. (International sales: Pyramide Intl., Paris.) Produced by Nikita Mikhailkov, Michel Seydoux. Directed, written by Mikhailkov. Camera (color), P. Lebeschev, E. Karavayev, V. Yusov, V. Alisov; editor, E. Praskina; music, Eduard Artemjev. Reviewed at Berlin Film Festival (Panorama section), Feb. 16, 1994. Running time: **99 MIN.**

Russian director Nikita Mikhailkov, known for pix like "Urga"/"Close to Eden" and "Dark Eyes," has come up with an utterly fascinating and charming combination of home movie/valentine to his daughter and personal commentary on events taking place in his country in recent years in "Anna 6-18." Pic deserves specialized distribution and fest exposure and should be of considerable public appeal.

The project began illegally in the old Soviet Union in 1980. Mikhailkov, scion of a well-respected family of Russian artists (his half-brother is director Andrei Konchalovsky) decided to make a home movie of his daughter, Anna, then 6 years old. Home movies were illegal in the USSR, so the director worked in secret with a few friends.

Every year he'd ask his daughter questions: What do you want most? What do you fear? What do you hate? At first, she answers like any child anywhere in the world (she wants a crocodile as a pet, she hates beet root soup). As the years go by, she becomes guarded, and answers like a true Soviet citizen.

Then, with perestroika, glasnost and democracy, and also her development as a teenager, she blossoms before our eyes. If this were all, it would be of limited interest, a kind of Russian "35 Up" concentrating on one child only. But Mikhailkov uses the personal material as a basis for responding to the changes in his country, including newsreel material to chart the end of the Brezhnev era.

The director's warmth and sense of humor are evident throughout in his choice of material, as, for instance, in a funny scene at an official ceremony in which a befuddled old man has great difficulty pinning a medal on the already medal-laden chest of the equally befuddled Brezhnev.

It adds up to a collage film of considerable interest and charm, a mixture of recent histories, some personal, some political. It's patched together with Mikhailkov's own perceptive commentary and is very good technically.
—*David Stratton*

ROTTERDAM

BERUF: NEO NAZI

(PROFESSION: NEO-NAZI)

(GERMAN — DOCU — 16mm)

An OST-Film/Hoffmann & Loeser production. Produced by Andrea Hoffmann. Directed, written by Winfried Bonengel. Camera (color), Johann Feindt; editor, Wolfram Kohler; sound, Paul Oberle, Ronald Gohlke. Reviewed at Rotterdam Intl. Film Festival, Feb. 3, 1994. Running time: **83 MIN.**

The cause of considerable ruckus since it first screened in Germany late last year, "Profession: Neo-Nazi" takes a cold, hard look at spotlight-seeking young fascist agitator Ewald Althans. Director Winfried Bonengel's purported failure to take an explicitly disapproving

stance is a matter open to debate, and despite a relatively routine documaking approach, the gravity of his subject should command attention in public TV airings. Thorny item has been banned in several German cities and states.

The 27-year-old Althans' political activity is matter-of-factly tracked, from duties as German liaison with a pamphleteering Holocaust revisionist in Canadian exile to networking with reps from likeminded Euro groups to cross-country recruitment tours. Nuts-and-bolts aspects of the movement's operations and economic base are well covered. Curiously, the propagandizing efforts duplicate methods pioneered by the Ayatollah Khomeini to override the Iranian government's boycott.

Bonengel avoids overt shock tactics, showing few violent demonstrations or blanket racial slurs. Instead, he lets Althans and his cronies expound on their projects for insurrection and endorse Hitler's aims with chilling composure.

Coverage of German government intervention or an official position on fascism's resurgence is missing; it's unclear whether this omission reflects government inaction concerning extremist politicking.

In perhaps pic's most disturbing seg (also its most talked-about), the camera follows Althans to Auschwitz, where he challenges visiting U.S. Jews to disprove his death-camp denial theories. Walking in the grounds later, he casually makes extermination jokes while swatting flies.

Though Bonengel capably places Althans in an unflattering light, he does so by unwaveringly subtle means, and anti-fascist aversion to the docu in Germany undoubtedly stems from its dearth of clearly defined negative reactions to its subject. Concern over its circulation seems unjustifiable but not surprising given that failure to read between the lines could lead to certain sections being misconstrued as uninterrupted Nazi rhetoric.

Arguably the most pointed indication of Bonengel's position is pic's title. The overall assessment of Althans is one of an exhibitionistic opportunist, cashing in on Aryan good looks and oratory skill more for personal glory than political conviction. Final shot of him washing his hands after a youth rally seems in line with this view. Similarly, interviews with his parents, who are ideologically opposed to Althans' politics, reveal a history of extreme behavior, but their vague detachment appears to discredit the depth of their son's involvement.

In addition, following showings at the Rotterdam fest (as part of the FilmFree program fighting screen censorship), reports in Dutch newspapers linked Althans to the Amsterdam gay scene. That could cast

doubts over his continuing rise within the rabidly anti-homosexual neo-Nazi movement.
—*David Rooney*

TERMINAL USA

(16mm)

An Independent TV Services presentation of a Killing Kulture production. Produced by Andrea Sperling. Directed, written by Jon Moritsugu. Camera (color), Todd Verow; editor, Gary Weimberg; music, Brian Burman; production design, Jennifer Gentile; art direction, Peter Calvin; costume design, Elizabeth Canning; sound, M and M Prods., Monte Cazazza, Michelle Handelman; associate producer, Timothy Innes; coordinating producer (for ITVS), James Schamus; assistant director, Erica Marcus. Reviewed at Rotterdam Intl. Film Festival, Feb. 2, 1994. Running time: **54 MIN.**

Ma	Sharon Omi
Dad	Ken Narasaki
Grandpa	Lenny Lang
Holly	Jenny Woo
Kazumi/Marvin	Jon Moritsugu
Tom Sawyer the Lawyer	Victor Aquitaine
Eightball	Amy Davis

With: Timothy Innes, Peter Friedrich, Bonnie Dickenson.

San Francisco filmmaker Jon Moritsugu turns the American sitcom family on its head with "Terminal USA," a post-punk, psychedelic picnic brimming with wholesome depravity and playfully twisted stereotypes. Part of the Independent Television Service's "TV Families" series, this rambunctious volley of flagrantly tasteless humor could whip up a minor cult following, especially in the U.K. and Europe.

Moritsugu plays up the incongruousness of Asian ethnicity wedged into a soap operatic, all-white TV entertainment mold, with a seriously problem-plagued Japanese-American family whose delivery is pure Dick and Jane. His contorted take on staple small-screen drama ingredients like drugs, incipient sexuality, discrimination, infirmity and parenting angst never goes much beyond droll trivialization, but still, it offers a tongue-in-cheek alternative to "Beverly Hills, 90210."

Ma (Sharon Omi) sits around in glamorous boudoir garb, staying sweet thanks to life-support drugs meant for bedridden Grandpa (Lenny Lang). Dad (Ken Narasaki) is a model of earnestness and solid family values with a pent-up urge to annihilate the old man.

Begging parental concern are their pregnant, nymphomaniacal cheerleader daughter (Jenny Woo), and twin sons (both played by Moritsugu), Kazumi, a nihilistic junkie with a g.f. from another planet (Amy Davis), and Marvin, a computer nerd nursing a secret passion for men in uniform. Vicious debt-collecting drug-dealers, neighborhood neo-Nazis, vengeful cheerleading cohorts and a family lawyer recruiting for the child porn industry round out the picture.

Perfs are appropriately large throughout, with standout input from Omi and Narasaki as perfect embodiments of unctuously righteous TV parents mutated by a splash of venal duplicity.

Jennifer Gentile's inventive production design re-creates the suburban picket-fence home in a garish comic-strip realm that's cleanly shot by Moritsugu's fellow West Coast underground cinema exponent Todd Verow. While the antics are generally well-sustained, they could perhaps have benefited from being cut to a marginally tighter rhythm. Frivolous sex and gore content is far from explicit, and hard to take offense at. A self-censored version nevertheless exists for TV. —*David Rooney*

HARTVERSCHEUREND

(LOVE HURTS)

(DUTCH)

A Studio Nieuwe Gronden production. Produced by Rene Scholten. Executive producer, Rene Goossens. Directed by Mijke de Jong. Screenplay, Jan Eilander, de Jong. Camera (color), Joost Van Starrenburg; editor, Menno Boerema; art director, Jolein Laarman; costume design, Nicky Schmitz; sound, Ben Zijlstra; assistant director, Doreth Matheeuwsen; casting, Hans Kemna. Reviewed at Rotterdam Intl. Film Festival, Feb. 2, 1994. Running time: **85 MIN.**
Lou .... Marieke Heebink
Bob .... Mark Rietman
Johnny .... Andre-Arend Van Noord
Marcia .... Mientje Kleijer
Kemal .... Tanar Catalpinar
Maarten .... Roef Ragas

Charting the volatile trajectory of an irreconcilable relationship against the backdrop of countercultural Amsterdam, "Love Hurts" (aka "Heartrending") channels electric lead performances into a seismic visitation of passion's outer limits. Incisive sophomore feature from Mijke de Jong should forge a considerable rep for the Dutch femme helmer as it continues to travel the fest trail.

Repeatedly blurring the line separating love and hate, de Jong and co-scripter Jan Eilander piece together a forcefully persuasive, head-on examination of a couple in their mid-30s agonizing between undeniable love and insurmountable conflict.

Fringe dweller Lou (Marieke Heebink) juggles immigration rights activism with singing gigs. Her partner, Bob (Mark Rietman), is a lawyer in a small firm that jars with Lou's scheme of social commit-

ment. Disagreements are initially low-key. His yen for physical comfort clashes with her reluctance to give up or renovate her ramshackle houseboat. He wants children while she shies away from any compromise to her freedom.

But fractiousness skyrockets into virtual war as circumstances outside their relationship combine to increasingly threaten Lou's security, and Bob retreats into his work. Gentrification of the docks area is steadily eating up her stomping ground; a refugee friend (Tanar Catalpinar) is drowned in a police skirmish; her HIV-positive singing partner (Andre-Arend Van Noord) starts pragmatically planning for death. Her unwelcome pregnancy further aggravates the rift.

What sets this tour of the romantic battlefield apart from commonplace love's-a-bitch sagas is that nothing in the script or direction implies observation from an outside vantage point. Dramatic pyrotechnics and posturing speeches are rigorously avoided in favor of focused, unobtrusive direction that severs all distance from the couple via total immersion in their rocky rapport.

The story's setting also smacks agreeably of an insider's position, offering both a nostalgic salute to Amsterdam's heyday as a libertarian paradise and a solemn acknowledgment of the inevitable changes inflicted by AIDS, racial tension and rampant development.

Joost Van Starrenburg's edgy camera work admirably mirrors the up-close attitude shown elsewhere, crowding in on the actors like a second skin and unequivocally inviting in the audience. Menno Boerema's tight editing shows similarly sharp alignment.

Perfs are refreshingly free from artifice. Neither Heebink nor Rietman has a false moment, and their fights really send out sparks, exploding in what often seems like spontaneous improvisation. Backup thesping is solid all round.
—*David Rooney*

CHAKA

(THE WHEEL)

(BENGALI)

A Chalachitram Film Society presentation. Produced by Syed Rafiqur Rahim. Directed, written by Morshedul Islam, based on Selim-Al-Deen's story. Camera (color), Anwar Hossein; editor, Nazrul Islam; music, Pulak Gupta. Reviewed at Rotterdam Intl. Film Festival, Feb. 3, 1994. Running time: **65 MIN.**
With: Amirul Huq Chowdhury, Ashish Khondoker, Ruhul Amin Rubel, Atuar Rahman.

A simple, sorrowful parable that stealthily accelerates its wrenching emotional thrust, "The Wheel" eloquently chronicles a humble quest for dignity in the face of denial. Modest, gently modulated entry from Bangladesh should roll into festival dates and specialist cultural venues.

Passing by an isolated healthcare center while transporting a load of rice, the driver of an ox-drawn cart and his companion are bullied into delivering a dead body to relatives in a distant village. A commotion of dread and morbid curiosity greets their arrival at the instructed destination, but no claimants to the corpse come forward. Forced to continue their haul, they try another, similarly named village in the hope of a mix-up, but an identical reception exacerbates their quandary.

As the debilitating odyssey proceeds, their initial resentment of the task and indifference to their cargo is steadily replaced by distressed respect for the unwanted dead man. Their attempts to give him a decent burial meet with further refusals on the grounds of his uncertain faith, and in the end, they bury him themselves in a remote stretch of land.

The story progresses unhurriedly from the journey's jaunty outset through its many acrid false finishes to its resonantly doleful conclusion, and director Morshedul Islam invests the desolate tale with a fluid, hypnotic rhythm, discordantly underscored by the harsh drone of the cart's wheels. Anwar Hossein's lensing of both countryside and poverty-stricken village locations is unembellished but effective. —*David Rooney*

NIKOTIN

(NICOTINE)

(RUSSIAN — B&W)

A Lenfilm production. Produced by A. Tsentr Salamat. Directed by Evgeni Ivanov. Screenplay, Dobrotvorsky, Maxim Pezhemski. Camera (B&W), Valerij Martynov; music, Sergej Kuryokhin; art direction, V. Yukhazov. Reviewed at Rotterdam Intl. Film Festival, Jan. 30, 1994. Running time: **67 MIN.**
With: Igor Chernevitch, Natalia Fisson.

Luminous short-film material gets unjustifiably stretched beyond an hour's length in Russian Evgeni Ivanov's feature debut "Nicotine," an impressive fusillade of technical prowess within a moodily ripe atmosphere that's glibly squandered on a weightless parody of Jean-Luc Godard's "Breathless." Slick but

slight outing should nonetheless saunter into fest dates and hip TV slots.

Storywise, "Nicotine" remains reasonably pally with its inspiration: A reckless romantic (Igor Chernevitch) stalked by assailants picks up a footloose journalist (Natalia Fisson), who eventually informs on him before torn loyalties compel her to give him an unheeded chance to run.

But consonance with the landmark Godard pic's plot is secondary to Ivanov's knowing take on its outwardly slapdash character construction and casual manipulation of the city settings into a tangible presence. More pointed nods, such as a press conference aping Jean Seberg's encounter with Jean-Pierre Melville and a detour to a screening of "Breathless" replete with introductory lecture, feel more like labored overstatement than jokey homage.

Ivanov's direction consistently eclipses the narrowness of his material, revealing a wry sense of humor and visual vitality that suggest capabilities far beyond this academic genre-bending. A richly complex soundtrack fusing unrefined jazz comments with a wide-ranging haul of noises contributes significantly. —*David Rooney*

WUREN HEGAI

(NO MORE APPLAUSE)

(CHINESE)

A Jimmy Wu, Vivian Song, Chen Zhigu presentation of a JV Century Intl. Inc./Beijing Films Corp. production. Produced by Cynthia Wu, Song Ziaojun, Cai Rubin. Directed by Xia Gang. Screenplay, Wang Shuo, Meng Zhu. Camera (color), Xing Shumin; art direction, Cui Junde. Reviewed at Rotterdam Intl. Film Festival, Jan. 31, 1994. Running time: **90 MIN.**
Xiao Keping .... Gai Xiaoling
Li Mian Ning .... Xie Yuan
Han Liting .... Ding Jiali
Qian Kan .... Fang Zige

Scratching beneath the surface of "No More Applause" won't yield many hidden depths, but what meets the eye is a warmly entertaining Eastern spin on a contempo comedy of tangled relationships. One of the past year's mightiest B.O. performers on its home turf, this engagingly played Chinese item should provide appetizing fodder for specialized tube programmers scouting upbeat international product.

Center stage is the rocky marriage of Xiao (Gai Xiaoling), a classical flautist struggling in a pop-saturated market, to Li (Xie Yuan), a brilliant engineer reduced to working as a guard in the Forbidden City. Career frustration and mutual resentment lead to divorce proceedings, but the

February 21, 1994 (Cont.)

Beijing housing shortage forces the couple to continue sharing the same apartment.

Partly to rile Xiao, Li brings home an unsophisticated hick (Ding Jiali) whose main interest is finding an alternative to living with her in-laws. Xiao refuses to be baited, however, solicitously playing hostess instead, and retaliating by encouraging the attentions of an infatuated ex-schoolmate (Fang Zige).

Amusingly decked out in universally familiar foibles, the quartet's finely etched characterizations and briskly timed comic interplay are well tuned to the script's jocular run of conflicts. Absence of any underlying punch becomes a shortcoming only when the characters each face their own sense of resignation. The conclusions they reach lack the poignancy required to cap off their romantic wanderings.

Xia Gang (whose "Letting Go" was 1992's biggest draw at Chinese wickets) directs with a light touch, letting the actors dominate and not tampering with the structural formula for such fare. Technically, the same efficient but largely by-the-numbers approach is also on view.

—*David Rooney*

SUNDANCE

THE HEART OF THE MATTER

(DOCU)

Produced, directed by Gini Reticker, Amber Hollibaugh. Executive producer, Reticker. Camera (color), Ellen Kuras, Maryse Alberti; editor, Ann Collins; music, Gregg Mann, Leo Colon; associate producer, Tracey Loggia. Reviewed at Sundance Film Festival, Park City, Jan. 23, 1994. (Also in Berlin Festival). Running time: 56 MIN.

"The Heart of the Matter," the first documentary to examine the complex issue of AIDS among women, makes a significant contribution to the growing body of films about the lethal disease. Docu's structure is a bit amorphous, but the central interviewee, Janice Jirau, is so charismatic and so honest about her struggle with AIDS that she makes this work a must-see for all interested viewers, particularly younger women.

Producer/directors Gini Reticker and Amber Hollibaugh have selected an interesting cross-section of women (blacks, lesbians, housewives) who talk most candidly about the implications of being afflicted with AIDS, and specifically about the myths surrounding the virus. Influenced by irresponsible articles in popular magazines, initially most of these women innocently felt they were outside the high-risk categories.

Ultimately, what makes the film emotionally affecting is its detailed case study of one woman as she goes through the phases, from being diagnosed HIV-positive to her death, just months before the docu was completed. Jirau relates how, as a loyal, obedient wife, she consented to her husband's wish not to use condoms, even after he was treated for AIDS at a hospital. "I loved my husband," she says, "and felt that I needed to prove that, so whatever he needed I gave him."

After his death, however, Jirau's consciousness was raised and she became politically active, recruiting the support of her extended family, challenging outdated religious preaching and right-wing myths, lecturing to female groups and testifying in Washington before the Federal AIDS Commission.

Jirau's story is interspersed with comments by a half-dozen women about their experiences, an approach that tends to diffuse the emotional impact of the central story. Still, framing the personal interviews with vital, if gloomy, statistics that AIDS is now the top killer of young black women and that it's one of the leading causes of death for all women between 18 and 44 makes this film extremely relevant, even urgent.

Winning the Sundance Film Festival's Freedom of Expression Award, "The Heart of the Matter" is an uplifting documentary that could not have made a stronger case for its motto: "We're in a race between education and catastrophe."

—*Emanuel Levy*

BOATMAN

(DOCU — B&W)

Produced, directed by Gianfranco Rosi. Camera (B&W), Rosi; editor, Jacopo Quadri; sound, Rosi. Reviewed at Sundance Film Festival, Park City, Jan. 21, 1994. Running time: 55 MIN. With: Gopal Maji.

Set entirely at Benares on the Ganges, the sacred river of the Hindu, "Boatman" captures the unique nature of this bizarre place, which is visited by Indians as well as tourists from all over the world. Original and eccentric, this highly entertaining documentary, told in English, Hindu and Italian, should be embraced by the international film festival circuit, before public TV and cable airings.

Using Benares as a microcosm of Hinduism, short pic chronicles the people who live and conduct business there, the various rituals and ceremonies observed, and the tourists who flock there year after year.

Every day, numerous bodies are cremated by the river's banks, or just sunk into its waters. And there are always masses of people in the river, bathing, praying, drinking the holy water. In one of the most revealing moments, a boy washes his bicycle, while next to him a beggar's body is dumped into the water, because cremation is too expensive.

At the center of the piece is Gopal, the charismatic boatman who serves as protagonist and narrator of this unconventional docu. While various characters appear only briefly, Gopal's presence contributes unity and a constant reference point. His running commentary — including stories of how tourists are cheated and manipulated by the locals — lends a humorous tone to a film that exhibits a non-traditional vision.

Gianfranco Rosi, an Italian who studied film at NYU, observed the strange life at Benares during his extensive visits there over a three-year-period. Shooting a good deal of footage from within the boat, he creates the illusion of a moving point of view. Sporting a Fellini-esque sensibility — the Benares as a circus — "Boatman" assumes the shape of a road movie, though it's a journey without clear destination.

Film's power is achieved through the accumulation of bits and pieces of information, encounters between businessmen and visitors, random comments by foreigners from all over the world — and above all an unblinking camera that observes the most bizarre incidents one can imagine happening by the bank of this river.

—*Emanuel Levy*

FAST TRIP, LONG DROP

(DOCU — 16mm)

Produced, directed, written by Gregg Bordowitz. Executive producer, Sara Diamond. Camera (color), Bob Huff, Jean Carlomusto, Jason Simon; music, Frank London, Lorin Sklamberg, Alicia Sviglas. Reviewed at Sundance Film Festival, Park City, Jan. 24, 1994. Running time: 54 MIN.

"Fast Trip, Long Drop" is a touching personal diary of Gregg Bordowitz, an angry young man afflicted with AIDS, and how the disease has influenced him as a video artist and political activist. Unusual in its format, docu freely and sometimes absorbingly mixes autobiographical musings on daily existence with AIDS, his Jewish identity and family life and the joys and sorrows of political involvement. The ideal exhibition for this non-traditional docu would be in a program of personal shorts about AIDS, but film also

has potential for specialized TV and cable airings.

In 1988, New York videomaker Bordowitz tested HIV-positive, a traumatic event that prompted him to drop alcohol and drugs and come out of the closet. This distressing news, he says, had some positive, if ironic effects: "At 23, I found what I've been looking for all my life — a sense of belonging."

Soon thereafter, a close friend was diagnosed with breast cancer and Bordowitz's grandparents were killed in a car crash. The cumulative result of these events was to challenge his sense of identity and force him to revisit his Jewish roots.

Bordowitz's life has been marked by countless deaths of relatives and friends that forced him to reassess his illness and his future. Prevalence of death no doubt explains docu's dominant visual motif: footage of car and airplane crashes, daredevil stunts and other disasters.

Combining personal and collective history, Bordowitz chronicles the gay community's response to government inaction on AIDS during the Reagan and Bush administrations, voicing his frustrations not only with the government's policy, the medical establishment and media coverage, but also with institutionalized gay activism.

"I don't want to be a hero or model," the filmmaker says about his new philosophy. "Survival is my only concern." That said, he must also realize that his response to having AIDS is not as peculiarly subjective as it might appear on the surface.

—*Emanuel Levy*

CUBA VA: THE CHALLENGE OF THE NEXT GENERATION

(SPANISH — DOCU — 16mm)

A Cuba Va Film Project production. Produced, directed, edited by Gail Dolgin, Vicente Franco. Camera (color), Franco and Jessie Block; lighting, Charles Griswold, Alan Steinheimer; sound, Marcio Camara; associate producer, Judith Montell. Reviewed at Sundance Film Festival, Park City, Jan. 26, 1994. Running time: 59 MIN.

"Cuba Va" is an intriguing, if not entirely successful, attempt to reassess Cuba's current socioeconomic crisis as seen by its youthful generation born after Castro's 1959 revolution. Docu suffers from an unclear structure and coverage of too many issues for its short running time, but its fascinating subject, balanced approach and direct strategy should facilitate showings on the festival circuit, public TV, at universities and in other educational venues.

The novelty of Gail Dolgin and Vicente Franco's film is that it tries to present a spectrum of opinions on Cuba's current problems that includes both the fervent socialists and the disillusioned opponents. All the interviewees were born — and have lived their entire lives — in socialist Cuba, which means that, unlike their ancestors, they have no means of comparing Castro's regime with the former one.

The youths debate the merits of socialism vs. capitalism, the need for economic reform, the fear of American — and other foreign — intervention in Cuba's internal affairs. "Our greatest dream is to determine our own future," says one Cuban with utmost conviction.

As could be expected, Castro's admirers vow allegiance and commitment to continue his revolution. They stress the free education, guaranteed jobs and non-existent unemployment. In contrast, disenchanted dissidents complain about economic rationing, scarcity of basic products — and political repression.

As one university student says, tuition may be free, but education isn't — the price is ideological. The proof: Cuba is one of the few countries in which student organizations actively support the government.

The chief problem of "Cuba Va" is that it's too short to encompass the full spectrum of opinions on such a wide range of issues. The fast pacing of the interviews and the quick jumps from one topic to another contribute to an incoherent structure and also clash with the filmmakers' serious intent.

Docu also glosses over the issue of the United States' vast influence on Cuba's popular culture, as evidenced in the country's fashion and rap music.

Still, the vigor, diversity and commitment of Cuba's younger generation is most impressive.

— *Emanuel Levy*

ASWANG

A Young American Films in association with Purple Onion Prods. Produced, directed, written by Barry Poltermann, Wrye Martin. Executive producers, Frank Anderson, Steve Farr. Camera (color), Jim Zabilla; editor, Poltermann; music, Ken Brahmstedt; art direction, Margot Czulewicz; sound, Paul Dickinson; special effects, Tim Brown; associate producers, David Dahlman, John Biesack; assistant director, Paul Johnson. Reviewed at Sundance Film Festival, Park City, Jan. 23, 1994. Running time: **82 MIN.**
Peter Null .... Norman Moses
Katrina .... Tina Ona Paukstelis
Dr. Roger Harper .... John Kishline
Olive Null .... Flora Coker
Cupid .... Mildred Nierras
Sheriff .... Victor Delorenzo
Claire Null ......,.. Jamie Jacobs Anderson

"**A**swang" tells the bizarre but unoriginal story of a young pregnant woman terrorized by a family of vampires who feed on the unborn. As a pastiche of classic horror films ("Rosemary's Baby," "Alien," "The Shining"), this low-budget item is so derivative and awkwardly acted that it might not even hold surprise for its potential audience of movie buffs and college students. Neither scary nor funny enough, "Aswang" is a self-reflexive exercise that hardly qualifies as a midnight attraction, the slot it was shown in at Sundance.

Peter Null (Norman Moses), the heir to the prosperous Null estate, desperately needs to have a child to fulfill his mother's wish and the family's will. Opportunity knocks when he meets Katrina (Tina Ona Paukstelis), a young, unwed woman needing to deal with her unwanted pregnancy. But the new couple must convince the eccentric matriarch, Mrs. Null (Flora Coker), that Katrina is Peter's wife and that their match is made in heaven.

Following genre conventions, story is entirely set in the deserted Null estate, a haunted house surrounded by a forest. Upon arrival, Katrina is introduced to its residents, who are mostly female: the crippled and nasty Mrs. Null, the doting Filipina maid Cupid (Mildred Nierras) and the mentally ill sister Claire (Jamie Jacobs Anderson), who's locked in a cabin.

Barry Poltermann and Wrye Martin, the novice scripters and helmers, have obviously seen a lot of schlock horror movies, but they don't provide many jolts and thrills along the way.

Using the legend of Aswang, the mythic Filipino vampire, pic aspires to be a modern update of classic vampire tales, but the predictable plot doesn't contain the requisite twists; one by one, unwelcome visitors to the house are eliminated in grisly ways.

Technical credits are OK, though the production lacks shrewd humor and visual style. A good horror entry needs a novel, creepy central idea or some terrifying special effects, which this movie doesn't have. Ultimately, "Aswang" is more gruesome and gross than frightening. — *Emanuel Levy*

HUNGARY

WOYZECK

(HUNGARIAN — B&W)

A Magic Media production, in association with Hetfoi Muhely Studio, Magyar Televizio. (International sales: Cinemagyar, Budapest.) Produced by Peter Barbalics. Directed, written by Janos Szasz, from the play by Georg Buechner. Camera (b&w), Tibor Mathe; editor, Anna Kornis; music, various; art direction, Peter Mandoki; costume design, Agnes Jodal; sound (Dolby), Istvan Sipos. Reviewed at Hungarian Film Week, Feb. 7, 1994. Running time: **94 MIN.**
Woyzeck .... Lajos Kovacs
Marie .... Diana Vacaru
The Doctor .... Peter Haumann
The Officer .... Aleksandr Porokhovchikov
The Policeman .... Sandor Gaspar
The Child .... Sandor Varga

Bleak but beautiful, "Woyzeck" is an involving, moving, intelligent transposition of the Georg Buechner play that should see plenty of fest and specialized tube play, with limited arthouse mileage also a possibility.

Pic is very different in look and feel from the best-known previous film version, Werner Herzog's 1979 outing. Though sticking closely to the play's text, action here is transferred from the original's army base setting to a Hungarian railroad yard, where unshaven, sweat-stained lug Woyzeck (magnificently played by Lajos Kovacs) drags out an existence as a point man in a small sentry box, his dreary life regulated by train schedules and orders barked over a p.a. system by his disciplinarian boss (Aleksandr Porokhovchikov).

Woyzeck's personal life is equally unsatisfactory: His beautiful young wife, Marie (Diana Vacaru), rejects his animal attempts at sex, preferring the embraces of a local policeman (Sandor Gaspar). Woyzeck's

only friends are the station doctor (Peter Haumann) and a young ragamuffin (Sandor Varga) who lives in the railroad sidings.

The incessant catalog of humiliations finally tips Woyzeck over the edge: He slits the throat of his boss during one of his regular shaving sessions and later knifes Marie in a deserted quarry.

Though the pic sounds unremittingly depressing on paper, young Magyar helmer Janos Szasz, in only his second feature, turns the material into an intense, almost poetic chorale to the dispossessed underdog, with confident handling of his mixed-nationality cast and a true sense of knowing exactly where the pic is headed.

Precision lensing by Tibor Mathe, exploiting the rich blacks and graded grays of genuine b&w stock and processing, and atmospheric use of smoke effects in exteriors, is a major plus throughout. More involving on an emotional level are the rich performances and a music track of soothing extracts from Baroque composers Purcell and Pergolesi.

As the dumb, half-comprehending, bull-like Woyzeck, well-known Hungarian thesp Kovacs anchors the movie with a striking performance of suppressed power. Vacaru (voiced by Hungarian actress Eva Igo) is just right as the beautiful, dissatisfied Marie, and Porokhovchikov is commanding as Woyzeck's arrogant boss.

Pic copped five awards at the 25th Hungarian Film Week in Budapest, including best actor (Kovacs), shared best director, cameraman and the foreign critics' Gene Moskowitz Award, named after the late *Variety* scribe. Tech credits are all tops. — *Derek Elley*

VASISTENEK GYERMEKEI

(CHILDREN OF CAST-IRON GODS)

(RUSSIAN-HUNGARIAN)

A Mosfilm (Russia)/Hunnia Studio (Hungary) production. (International sales: Cinemagyar, Budapest.) Directed by Tamas Toth. Screenplay, Pyotr Lutsik, Aleksandr Samoryadov. Camera (color), Sergei Kozlov; editor, Irma Tsekovaya; music, Mikhail Orlov; art direction, Vladimir Korolyov; costume design, Lena Usakova; sound, Yulia Vzorova. Reviewed at Hungarian Film Week, Feb. 9, 1994. Running time: **77 MIN.**
With: Yevgeny Sidikhin, Aleksandr Kalyagin, Aleksandr Feklustov, Nikolai Kornoikhov, Yuri Yakovlev, Larisa Borodina.
(Russian dialogue)

February 21, 1994 (Cont.)

A kind of arty "Mad Maxim Beyond Smelterdome," Hungarian-born helmer Tamas Toth's freshman feature melds Soviet industrial grunge with striking visuals and pacing to visceral effect. This largely Mosfilm-financed pic heralds a talent of considerable promise and merits serious attention from specialized outlets and webs in search of the fresh and offbeat.

Setting is a colossal steelworks in a remote, snow-covered corner of Siberia, producing armor alloys for the military. Working conditions are tough, bordering on the subhuman.

Episodic, loosely knit story pivots on one of the men at the plant, Ignat, whose only kicks come from escapades off the base, such as stealing sheep from nomads or (in a particularly exciting sequence) robbing a train at gunpoint. Out of sheer boredom, Ignat enters the annual fight between the region's strongest metalworker and strongest miner, a knock-down, drag-out slugfest that's the movie's climactic set piece.

Budapest-born Toth, 27, moved to Moscow in the early 1980s and studied film at the state VGIK school, finally getting "Children" off the ground in spring 1991. Pic has a strong Russian flavor, tempered by a Hungarian distancing, with muted color lensing by Sergei Kozlov creating a living, snorting monster from the mini-city of steel in which the characters exist.

Performances are all vivid, but the movie is essentially a concept item, trimly put together and with an otherworldly feel that lifts its potentially depressing subject matter. Pic also cries out for widescreen, rather than standard-ratio, composition. Above title is the Hungarian one used at Budapest Film Week unspooling, despite fact that all dialogue is in Russian.

—*Derek Elley*

SATANTANGO

(SATAN'S TANGO)

(HUNGARIAN-GERMAN-AUSTRIAN — B&W)

An MIT (Budapest)/Von Vietinghoff Filmproduktion (Berlin)/Vega Film (Zurich) production, in association with Magyar Televizio, TV Suisse Romande. (International sales: Cinemagyar, Budapest.) Produced by Gyorgy Feher, Joachim von Vietinghoff, Ruth Waldburger. Directed by Bela Tarr. Screenplay, Laszlo Krasznahorkai, Tarr, based on Krasznahorkai's novel. Camera (b&w), Gabor Medvigy; editor, Agnes Hranitzky; music, Mihaly Vig; costume design, Gyula Pauer, Janos Breckl; sound, Gyorgy Kovacs; assistant directors, Andras Kecza, Janos Hollos, Zoltan Gazsi. Reviewed at Hungarian Film Week, Budapest, Feb. 8, 1994. (Also in Berlin Film Festival/Forum section.) Running time: **450 MIN.**

With: Mihaly Vig, Putyi Horvath, Janos Derzsi, Miklos B. Szekely, Erika Bok, Erzsebet Gaal, Laszlo Lugossy Jr., Eva Almasi Albert, Iren Szajki, Alfred Jarai, Peter Berling, Barna Mihok.

The marathon "Satan's Tango" is a magnum opus to end all magna opera, a dark, funny, apocalyptic allegory of the Hungarian psyche that stimulates, irritates, soothes and startles with blinding strokes of genius in equal turn. Seven-hour-plus pic represents an impossible marketing exercise on any commercial level, but with good word of mouth could become a cult item as a "film event" on the fest circuit. TV sales remain a possibility, though the film demands to be seen on the big screen to work its mesmeric magic.

At its packed Budapest world preem, as part of the 25th Hungarian Film Week, pic drew general nods for the startling quality of its vision and intensely cinematic style. Director Bela Tarr was still shooting only weeks before the unspooling, with the final print arriving wet from the labs.

Adapted from a novel by Laszlo Krasznahorkai, film started out several years ago as a regular-length project but expanded as Tarr became obsessed with the content. Production, on a reportedly high budget in Hungarian terms, was spread over two years (115 shooting days), with Tarr showing an uncompromising perfectionism.

Result shows in pic's immaculate b&w compositions, a major feather in the hat of young cinematographer Gabor Medvigy, student of the famed Lajos Koltai, regular cameraman for Istvan Szabo.

Movie has a long-limbed, almost rondo construction, opening with a seven-minute take that introduces the rural setting and functions as a kind of overture. Thereafter, the film is divided into segments of various lengths (usually a half-hour or so), with chapter headings such as "The News That They Are Coming," "We, the Resurrected," "The Freeze," "Only Problems and Work." Final section is titled "The Circle Is Completed."

Setting for most of the action is an abandoned agricultural machinery plant in the vast Hungarian plain, where an assortment of deadbeats (including three couples and an alcoholic doctor) eke out a hopeless existence. Each is planning, or dreams of, some kind of escape, and the air is thick with betrayal and counter-betrayal.

Catalyst to events is the charismatic Irimias (read: Jeremiah), a former member of the community who's in fact a small-time con man

and former police informer. With a comic Romanian acolyte in tow, Irimias sweeps into town (in a sequence of Leone-ish bravura) and promises a new life to those willing to chance an exodus to other parts.

Meanwhile, the liquor-soaked doctor, holed up in his Dickensian room before a rain-streaked window, laboriously catalogs the comings and goings of the characters in a collection of exercise books.

Final chapter — in which he returns to his room, admits "I'm confused," and boards up his window-on-the-world till screen goes black — satisfyingly wraps up the pic in ironic style.

Set during a brief time span, the movie partly reruns the same events from different characters' perspectives (such as the doctor's nocturnal perambulation in search of alcohol) and partly goes down blind alleys that gloss over rather than advance the storyline (such as a long single take of two cops hammering out a fanciful report on the main characters at the local station).

Pic's magic stems from the accumulation of its jigsaw pieces, which makes viewing at a single sitting *de rigueur*. (Budapest screening started late afternoon, with two intermissions.)

Auds familiar with Tarr's 1987 "Damnation" will get a buzz of recognition out of the present item. Helmer's liking for long takes, gliding tracking shots, striking play with foregrounds and backgrounds (plus apocalyptic use of incessant rain and mud) is on display here in spades. There's also much dry Magyar humor to lighten events.

Some knowledge of Hungarian history is necessary to get the most out of the film, though its general theme — of a people riven by lack of self-confidence and internal feuding who are duped by a false messiah — is accessible enough. Animal lovers should steer clear of a graphic segment in which a village ragamuffin beats up on and then poisons her cat.

Performances are thoroughly lived-in, and tech credits tops in all departments, with special praise for Medvigy's monochrome lensing and Mihaly Vig's highly atmospheric, gently susurrating score. Film, which won a Special Award at the Magyar Film Week, is dedicated to the late Alf Bold, longtime co-worker with Ulrich Gregor, boss of the Berlin fest's Forum section, in which pic has its international preem.

—*Derek Elley*

A MAGZAT

(FOETUS)

(HUNGARIAN-POLISH)

A Budapest Film Studio, Magyar Televizio (Hungary)/Telewizja Polska (Poland) production. (International sales: Cinemagyar, Budapest.) Produced by Ferenc Kardos. Directed by Marta Meszaros. Screenplay, Meszaros, Eva Pataki. Camera (color), Nyika Jancso; editor, Eva Karmento; music, Michal Lorenc; art direction, Zsolt Juhasz Budai; costume design, Katalin Jancso; sound, Istvan Sipos; script consultant, Zoltan Jancso. Reviewed at Hungarian Film Week, Budapest, Feb. 5, 1994. (Also in Berlin fest — competing.) Running time: **107 MIN.**

Anna .... Adel Kovats
Terez .... Aliona Antonova
Terez's Husband .... Jan Nowicki
Anna's Husband .... Laszlo Bolyki
  With: Barbara Hegyi, Eniko Borcsok, Teri Torday, Zsuzsa Czinkoczi, Miklos B. Szekely, Lili Monori, Silveszter Siklosi.

"Foetus" miscarries on most fronts. Despite a radiant central perf by Adel Kovats as a young, pregnant wife whose unwanted baby will be adopted by a childless businesswoman, Hungarian helmer Marta Meszaros' latest pic stalls due to an unconvincing script and weak supporting turns. Competing at the Berlin fest, pic drew a polite reception from locals at the opening night of the 25th Hungarian Film Week in Budapest.

Pic partly looks back to subjects covered by Meszaros during her golden period of the 1970s, notably the great motherhood/female bonding trilogy of "Adoption," "Nine Months" and "The Two of Them." But with its glossy visuals and somewhat soft script, "Foetus" often more closely resembles B-league Meszaros like the 1982 "Anna" (aka "Mother and Daughter").

Protagonist here is Anna (Kovats), a young mother of two who suddenly discovers she's six weeks pregnant. Financially strapped already, it doesn't take Anna long to accept an offer from Terez (Russian actress Aliona Antonova), hard-nosed boss of the store in which she works — $50,000 if she'll go into seclusion, have the child and sign it over to Terez at birth.

Though there's enough material so far for a whole film, the script pushes on. Using frequent child-filled dream sequences and shots of a fetus suspended within a womb, Meszaros is mainly interested in Anna's emotional to-ing and fro-ing during confinement and her symbiotic relationship with Terez.

That's where the pic never really gets its wheels off the ground: Despite lots of heart-to-hearts, and even a scene in which the two women share a tub, there's a fatal lack of screen chemistry between Kovats and Antonova, largely thanks to stiff playing by the latter (voiced by Hungarian thesp Agi Szirtes) and dialogue that reduces potentially dramatic material to the level of a glossy soap.

Conflict, much to the fore in Meszaros' earlier, more gritty pix, is lacking. Anna's husband is quickly sidelined, easily duped by Terez's elaborate scheme to make him believe his wife is in the U.S. Terez's role is further trivialized by the cliched character of her bonehead husband, histrionically played by Polish actor Jan Nowicki (voiced by Gabor Revicky).

Left to her own resources, Kovats invests the film with a kind of dreamy grace that fits the bright, immaculate visuals — by Meszaros' lenser son, Nyika Jancso — and Michal Lorenc's attractive, featherlight score. But it's essentially a fine performance on an empty stage, with most of the real drama piled up in the wings.

Other perfs are OK, with longtime Meszaros regular Zsuzsa Czinkoczi (who started as a brat in the 1978 "Just Like at Home" and matured impressively in the recent "Diary" trilogy) in a smallish, intriguing role as a maid.

—*Derek Elley*

LIPSTICK

(AUSTRIAN-HUNGARIAN)

A Sternstundefilm (Vienna)/Quality Pictures, MOVI, Dialog Studio (Budapest) production. (International sales: Austrian Film Commission, Vienna.) Produced by Niki Neuspiel, Golli Marbow, Gabor Sarudi, Sandor Buglya. Directed by Robert-Adrian Pejo. Screenplay, Pejo, Reinhard Jud. Camera (color), Tibor Klopfler; editor, Csilla Derzsi; music, Paul Winter; art direction-costumes, Michaela Mueck, Gerhard Veismann; sound, Frigyes Wahl; assistant director, Markus Pega. Reviewed at Hungarian Film Week, Budapest, Feb. 6, 1994. Running time: 88 MIN.
Arpad .... Peter Andorai
Vesna Cirpancic ...... Sinolicka Trpkova
Alyosha .... Janos Ban
Vesna's mother .... Katalin Takacs
Draga .... Eszter Hamori
(Hungarian, German, Russian and Serbian dialogue)

Though it doesn't leave many traces, "Lipstick" is a pleasant enough gloss on the socially fluid situation in present-day Central Europe, centering on the story of a young Yugoslav woman stranded in Hungary over New Year's Eve. Pic is well suited for specialized airings.

Story opens Jan. 1, 1993, in a Budapest apartment where Vesna (Sinolicka Trpkova) has spent the night with Arpad (Peter Andorai).

Returning by train to Vienna, she's arrested at the Austrian border for having a now-invalid Yugoslav passport. Pic then flashes back to the previous day: her arrival in Budapest, meeting with a boisterous Russian (Janos Ban) and eventual one-night stand with boozy bar pianist Arpad.

Essentially a light relationship movie given a contempo edge by its underpinnings of Balkan rootlessness, pic never gets under the skin of its main character, despite misty flashbacks to the young woman's youth.

In the lead role, Trpkova is photogenic but blank, outclassed in the personality stakes by Magyar thesps Andorai as the hangdog musician, and Ban, as the likably boyish Russian. Tech credits are OK, the blowup from 16mm obvious but acceptable. —*Derek Elley*

ABEL A RENGETEGBEN

(ABEL IN THE FOREST)

(HUNGARIAN-ROMANIAN)

A Budapest Film Studio/Magyar Televizio/Clamatel/Profilm/Mokep production. Produced by Arpad Lukacs, Janos Drabik, Dumitru Puhus, Tanase Dinu. Directed by Sandor Mihalyfi. Screenplay, Sandor Kanyadi, from the novel by Aron Tamasi. Camera (color), Vivi Dragan Vasile; editor, Mircea Ciocaltei; music, Gyorgy Selmeczi; art direction, Sandor Nagy; costume design, Gabriella Nicolaescu; sound, Andrei Papp. Reviewed at Hungarian Film Week, Budapest, Feb. 8, 1994. Running time: 106 MIN.
With: Levente Ilyes, Sandor Hejja, George Constantin, Vlad Radescu, Anna Szeles.

"Abel in the Forest" is an OK Balkan kidpic that would be even better if it were a tad shorter. Attractively lensed and locationed yarn of a young teen and his mutt in 1920 Transylvania could get offshore mileage as a dubbed item in youth slots.

Based on the novel by Hungarian writer Aron Tamasi (1897-1966), film is set in the richly forested Hargita Mountains, handed over to Romania under the World War I peace treaty. Abel, forced to work as a logging guard away from his poor parents' home, soon cuts a deal whereby he gets to keep any trees felled by natural causes. Abel tweaks the arrangement by using unexploded bombs to blast down more arbors.

Canny kid soon gets the better of various types who reckon he's an easy mark, from oily monks after his soul to city slickers with forged bank drafts. By the following spring he's ready to stay on, swearing on his mother's grave to always support the poor and oppressed. At pic's close, he and his woofer walk

into the sunset proudly proclaiming, "We'll bark at the world."

Magyar director Sandor Mihalyfi, using a mixed Hungarian-Romanian cast and crew, keeps things moving along most of the time, with some gentle comedy, fine photography of the russet-green landscape and a pleasant symphonic score by Gyorgy Selmeczi. Preachier final section, and a slackening of tempo, could easily be solved by tightening. Perfs are all fine.

—*Derek Elley*

SZEKELYKAPU

(WEDDING SERVICE)

(HUNGARIAN-FRENCH)

A Mafilm Alkotoi Egyesules (Budapest)/Son et Lumiere (Paris) co-production. Produced, directed by Janos Szombolyai. Screenplay, Akos Kertesz. Camera (color), Sandor Kardos; editor, Hajnal Sello; music, Laszlo Benko; production design, Eva Martin; sound, Tamas Markus. Reviewed at Hungarian Film Week, Budapest, Feb. 8, 1994. Running time: 59 MIN.
With: Eszter Nagy-Kalozy, Jozsef Toth, Edit Vlahovics, Geza Kaszas, Olga Koos.

This Magyar variation on the "Green Card"/"Wedding Banquet" theme is a touching romantic comedy-drama well suited to the small screen because of its brief running time (though it unspooled on 35mm at the review screening.)

Director Janos Szombolyai tackled the subject before in "Duty Free Marriage" (1981) and doesn't have a great deal to add this time around, though attractive performances are a plus.

The story's set in 1989; the communist era is coming to an end in Hungary, but neighboring Romania is still under a strict dictatorship. A dying old woman leaves her apartment to a young man (Jozsef Toth) on condition he marry her Romanian niece so that she can legally come to live in Hungary.

Trouble is, Toth is engaged to, and very much in love with, another woman (Edit Vlahovics). But he agrees to the arrangement, and Vlahovics even accompanies him to Romania and acts as witness at his wedding to beautiful Eszter Nagy-Kalozy.

After some tense scenes with the Romanian security police — especially an officer who seems sexually attracted to both women — the trio is allowed to cross back into Hungary. The evolving triangular relationship is based on real-life experiences, per the director, who appears on camera at the end to assert that this is a true story.

—*David Stratton*

KISS VAKOND

(THE LITTLE MOLE)

(HUNGARIAN)

A Budapest Filmstudio production, in association with Hungarian TV, Movi-Duna. Produced by Ferenc Kardos, Marta Szabo, Sandor Buglya. Directed by Andras Szoke. Screenplay, Szoke, Gyorgy Palos. Camera (color), Palos; editor, Andrea Szakacs; production design, Szoke, Laszlo Hudi. Reviewed at Hungarian Film Week, Budapest, Feb. 8, 1994. Running time: 81 MIN.
With: Janos Hersko, Eszter Gyalog, Andras Szoke, Sandor Badar, Ferencne Papp, Lea Tolnai.

Andras Szoke makes offbeat comedies ("Cotton Chicken," "Lemon Pig") that produce guffaws with Hungarian audiences but don't travel. "The Little Mole" is his most wayward effort, a bizarre tale in which the director plays the underground creature who crawls out of his hole to explore the real world.

It's a concept that lends new meaning to the word "unsophisticated," but Szoke's jokes remain all his own, and his fans will probably welcome his latest low-budgeter.

Apart from the myopic mole, the other principal characters are a bickering human couple (the wife played by an actor in drag) who may somehow be the mole's parents. Much use is made of the mole's family photo album, whose contents come alive to talk to the audience.

Tech credits are extremely modest. Outside Hungary, audiences for this strange farce are likely to be few and far between.

—*David Stratton*

FENYERZEKENY TORTENET

(A LIGHT, SENSITIVE STORY)

(HUNGARIAN)

A Budapest Filmstudio production in association with TV2/ZDF/ARTE. (International sales: Cinemagyar, Budapest.) Produced by Ferenc Kardos. Directed by Pal Erdoss. Screenplay, Erdoss, Kardos. Camera (color), Ferenc Pap; editor, Klara Majoros; music, Janos Masik; production design, Laszlo Makai; sound, Istvan Sipos. Reviewed at Hungarian Film Week, Budapest, Feb. 8, 1994. Running time: 93 MIN.
With: Erika Ozsda, Attila Racz, Dani Szabo, Ilona Kallai, Adam Rajhona, Eszter Szakacs, Gyula Kormos.

A film about the everyday problems facing Hungarians in the post-communist era, this aptly titled pic is undoubtedly a minor item, but could find attentive audiences at fests and on TV in some countries. A lovely lead performance from Erika Ozsda is a major plus.

Ozsda plays Juli, a 30-year-old divorced woman who is working as a freelance photographer and bringing up her 11-year-old son whose father has been living for some years in Munich. Juli has a lover, a student a bit younger than she is, but their relationship is difficult because of the everyday problems (lack of accommodations, difficulty of earning money) they face.

One day, Juli is approached by her former in-laws, who want to take her boy to Munich for Christmas to see his father. She reluctantly agrees, but her worst fears are realized when the couple return to Budapest without the boy. Unable to make contact with her former husband and her son, Juli is forced to sell her most precious possession — her camera — in order to fly to Munich to find them.

Director Pal Erdoss tells this sad, everyday story with a gentle humanity that allows the viewer to identify completely with Juli's situation. At the same time, the film is filled with detail about life in Hungary today for a single woman (sexual harassment being only one of Juli's problems).

This modestly produced item isn't overly ambitious, but it provides a satisfying, moving experience.   —David Stratton

UTRIUS

(HUNGARIAN)

A Magyar Televizio, Magic Media production. Produced by Jolan Arvai. Directed, written by Ferenc Grunwalsky. Camera (color), Grunwalsky; editors, Andras Nagy, Klara Majoros; art direction, Tamas Vajer; costume design, Zsuzsa Stenger; sound, Andras Vamosi. Reviewed at Hungarian Film Week, Budapest, Feb. 7, 1994. Running time: 81 MIN.
With: Mihaly Szabados, Ildiko Szucs, Istvan Szabo, Peter Andorai, Mari Csomos, Agnes Csere, Bela Eles, Laszlo Csere, Peter Szilagyi, Andras Stohl, Karoly Nemcsak, Adrienn Zovath.

A blackly ironic look at the current knife-edge situation in the Balkans, "Utrius" reps an only partly successful attempt by maverick Magyar director Ferenc Grunwalsky to meld experiment and allegory. This vid-to-35mm transfer is of interest only to recherche fests and students of the offbeat.

Film begins in 1914 with the teenage Pal Utrius being drafted into the military. Before leaving, he consummates an incestuous love for his sister, to whom letters home form the basis of his inner turmoil and desires.

The combo of rigorous barracks life and the outbreak of World War I makes him seek escape via an appendix operation. Twist is that he gets blood poisoning from unsterilized instruments and dies. Bleak coda posits the wheel of history turning anew, with an outbreak of world war in summer 1994.

Unspoken parallels between Hungary's attempts at a "new life" and the current bloody situation in the former Yugoslavia (where the Sarajevo assassination spawned WWI), are there for the taking but hung on a weak, oblique storyline. Episodes of raunchy sex and misty missives to the sister/lover lack Grunwalsky's usual Godardian verve.

Performances are OK within the film's limitations, and buffs will note an intriguing cameo by well-known director Istvan Szabo as an army doctor. Vid transfer process, supervised by Grunwalsky himself, is excellent in close-ups but loses definition in longer shots. Extracts from WWI newsreels pepper the pic in a rather obvious way.

—Derek Elley

PRIVATHORVAT ES WOLFRAMBARAT

(PRIVATE HORVATH AND FRIEND WOLFRAM)

(HUNGARIAN — B&W)

A Fiatal Magyar Filmkeszitok Studio-Quality Pictures production. Produced by Matyas Godros. Directed, written by Frigyes Godros, Dr. Putyi Horvath. Camera (b&w), Tibor Klopfler, Sandor Kardos; editor, Maria Rigo; music, Gabriel Magos, Ferenc Darvas; production design, Gyula Pauer; sound, Istvan Sipos. Reviewed at Hungarian Film Week, Budapest, Feb. 8, 1994. Running time: 88 MIN.
With: Frigyes Godros, Dr. Putyi Horvath, Katalin Godros, Peter Doczy.

This is a strange autobiography in which the writer/directors appear as eccentric Everymen who behave like children.

One of them, Horvath, shows his friend apparently authentic 8mm home movies of his childhood; the friend responds with re-enacted autobiographical sequences.

All this material is extremely ordinary and uneventful, which makes the "real" scenes, in which the friends evoke the early, surreal short films of Roman Polanski, even stranger.

It's hard to see what audience the black-and-white film is aiming for, but outside Hungary its chances seem to be nil, unless it becomes a cult item on the fest circuit.

Technical credits are modest.

—David Stratton

BALKAN! BALKAN!

(BALKANS! BALKANS!)

(HUNGARIAN-FRENCH-TURKISH)

A Focusfilm-Objektiv Filmstudio (Budapest)/47th Parallel Prods. (Paris)/Par Prods. (Istanbul) co-production, with the support of Eurimages. (International sales: Cinemagyar, Budapest.) Produced by Denes Szekeres, Zafer Par, Jean-Paul Dekiss. Directed by Gyula Maar. Screenplay, Maar, Panait Istrati, based on Istrati's novels "Codin" and "Kyra Kyralina." Camera (color), Janos Vecsernyes; editor, Zsuzsa Jambor; production design, Tamas Banovich; costumes, Svetlana Mihailescu; sound, Andras Horvath, Janos Reti. Reviewed at Hungarian Film Week, Budapest, Feb. 6, 1994. Running time: 117 MIN.
With: Frigyes Funtek, Tora Vasilescu, George Calin, Alina Nedela, Mitica Popescu, Gheorghe Dinica, Leopoldina Balanuta, Ileana Predescu, Valentin Popescu, Serban Ionescu, Remus Margineau, Dorine Hollier, Razvan Vasilescu, George Alexandru.

A lively, vibrant film could have been made from these stories by Panait Istrati, which are set in a small town on the Danube in the second half of the last century. But Gyula Maar's direction fails completely to bring the material to life and the result is a dull rendering of what should have been most exciting.

Right from the first shot it's clear that Maar, who's done decent, if rather academic, work in the past, was the wrong choice for this hedonistic, exotic yarn. His use of ponderous long takes destroys the rhythm the material so obviously needs, and his staging of potentially vibrant scenes falls utterly flat.

The town in question is Braila, where a melting pot of Romanians, Turks and Greeks co-existed. The story centers on 17-year-old Dragomir (Frigyes Funtek), a narcissistic youth whose wild mother and sister regularly participated in orgies while the youth's father and older brother were absent; the father would return to beat his wife and daughter, and the former eventually loses an eye as a result of one such beating. Dragomir and Kyra, beloved sister, pay to have their father and brother murdered; the brother is killed, but the father escapes, and so mother and siblings hit the road.

They're eventually separated (the pretty Kyra is allegedly sold into prostitution) and Dragomir latches on to the charismatic Codin, a raffish fellow who turns out to be a multiple murderer. A relationship develops between them which could be sexual, though this is never clear; they become "blood brothers."

Costumes, locations and camera work evoke a colorful bygone world, and it's sad that the director is unable to inject any life into the

promising material. The actors, mostly Romanians dubbed into Hungarian, don't stand much of a chance. The music, derived from Romanian traditional songs, is lively, and technical credits are generally on a high level.

—David Stratton

JO EJT, KIRALYFI

(GOOD NIGHT, PRINCE)

(HUNGARIAN)

An Objektiv Filmstudio production. Produced by Gabriella Grosz. Directed by Janos Rozsa. Screenplay, Istvan Kardos. Camera (color), Tibor Mathe; editor, Zsusza Csakany; music, Gabor Presser; production design, Jozsef Romvari; sound, Andras Vamosi. Reviewed at Hungarian Film Week, Budapest, Feb. 6, 1994. Running time: 80 MIN.
With: Szabolcs Hajdu, Dorottya Udvaros, Csaba Ujvari, Csilla Gevai, Henriett Bernath, Andras Szoke, Zsolt Gazdag, Bela Spindler.

Would-be filmmakers working on a vidpic in the streets of Budapest is the subject of the latest slice of life from Janos Rozsa, whose work has often dealt sympathetically with young people ("Sunday Daughters," "Brats"). Here, he captures the mood of a clutch of cinephiles whose efforts are inevitably doomed, but a stronger screenplay was sorely needed.

Rozsa's young hero is Szabolcs Hajdu, newly arrived in Budapest ("the city of refugees") from the provinces; he flunked his exams, but the aspiring actor brings with him a video of his performance as Hamlet in a school production.

He goes to stay with relatives, including a still-attractive aunt (Dorottya Udvaros), and is soon playing the lead in a no-budget vid flick being shot, without permission, on the city streets. The resourceful team even sets up a police car chase for the purpose of filming, without letting the cops in on the secret.

It all ends in tragedy (as is foreshadowed by the film's title, a misquote from the end of "Hamlet"), but not before Hajdu has entered into an unexpected, and quite sensual, affair with his aunt.

A better-constructed screenplay could have made much more of these interesting characters and situations, but Rozsa does an efficient job of direction given the weak material. Performances are all fine, especially vet Udvaros as the middle-aged woman who blossoms visibly after sex with a boy who's young enough to be her son.

Technical credits are all pro.

—David Stratton

MI YEDEM V AMERIKU

(WE ARE GOING TO AMERICA)

(RUSSIAN)

A Lenfilm/Unifilm production. Produced by Yelena Amshinskaya. Directed by Efim Gribov. Camera (color, b&w), Pavel Barsky, Denis Shchiglovsky; music, Mikhail Gluz; chief designer, Amshinskaya; art direction, Alexander Yurov, Irina Surogina; sound, Alikper Gasan-Zade. Reviewed at the Roxie Cinema, San Francisco, June 22, 1993. (In Jewish Film Festival.) Running time: **118 MIN.**
Motl .... Dima Davydov
With: Lyubov Runiantseva, Semion Strugachov, Danuta Slavgorodskaya, Vadim Danilevsky, Baiba Kranats, Larisa Polyakova, Vladimir Rozhin, Rafail Mishulovich, Marina Karasyova, Maria Barbanova.

The turn-of-the-century characters in "We Are Going to America" take two hours to complete just the first leg of their title journey — from a pogrom-menaced Russian village to the European border. Based on a story by Sholom Aleichem, this look at familiar Jewish historical themes won't cross many theatrical borders. It's too shrilly comic in tone, too haphazardly assembled for extensive travel.

Son of a slain choirmaster, 11-year-old Motl provides the p.o.v., one too often literalized by randomly plotted hand-held camerawork.

The story meanders as well. Fleeing persecution, Motl's mother, older brother, sister-in-law and their intellectual relation ("I'm a free man according to Kant, Hegel and Spinoza!" he shouts after a beating) depart for the New World with nervously high hopes.

After a chaotic train journey, the family is detained in a border town. As authorities dicker with their fate, Motl has a series of enigmatic encounters, including a curiously sexual one with a "*shtetl* witch."

There are flashes of clear narrative focus, as when a despairing, orphaned young woman is driven to attempted suicide. But too much of the running time seems adrift amid heavy symbols (birds figure prominently as harbingers of freedom), disjointed episodes and noisy comic business. Performances are broadly etched to a fault. Despite OK period flavor, tech aspects are uneven. Color/sepia-toned processing shifts seem arbitrary, and the frequently yelled dialogue post-syncing is not precise.

Director Efim Gribov obviously wanted to leaven this familiar story with ample humor. But "We Are Going to America" mostly vacillates between the crude and the inchoate. —*Dennis Harvey*

MI NISMO ANDJELI

(WE ARE NOT ANGELS)

(SERBIAN)

A Yes Avala Film Intl. DD Production. (International sales: Vans, Belgrade.) Produced by Ranko Petric, Gojko Kastratovic. Executive producer, Miodrag Djordjevic. Directed, written by Srdjan Dragojevic. Camera (color), Dusan Joksimovic; editor, Branka Ceperac; music, Vampiri; art direction, Aleksandar Denic; sound, Marko Rodic. Reviewed on vidcassette, Rome, Jan. 9, 1994. Running time: **98 MIN.**
Nikola .... Nikola Kojo
Marina .... Milena Pavlovic
Also with: Branka Katic, Srdjan Todorovic, Uros Djuric, Sonja Savic, Zoran Cvijanovic, Miki Manojlovic, Vesna Trivalic.

Good and Evil slug it out in "We Are Not Angels," an Avala Film comedy featuring a rock-and-rolling devil and angel. Serbian pic's somewhat forced surrealism feels appropriate enough, considering the conditions under which it must have been made. It topped the Belgrade box office in 1992, just ahead of Goran Paskaljevic's "Tango Argentina," but looks trivial for fest use.

Helmer Srdjan Dragojevic is entertainingly cynical in the well-made yarn about a spacey teenage fashion student (Milena Pavlovic) who succeeds in bringing confirmed swinger Nikola Kojo to the altar. He can't even remember their one-night stand.

When Pavlovic discovers she's expecting, she and her best friend devise a series of impossible schemes to capture first the attention, then the heart and bachelorhood of the rake. The fact that Kojo finally puts aside girls, parties, drugs and booze to become a father has little logic, but the story is pleasantly told.

Technical work is pro throughout, whole cast included, and filmers are tops in making a small budget go a long way. A coke-sniffing devil and effeminate angel are meant to be outrageous, pairing up in 1960s rock numbers. Film buffs will note with a jolt a joke thrown in by two boys humming a gypsy theme, who delight that "Kusta (Bosnian filmmaker Emir Kusturica) is back at work in the States." —*Deborah Young*

FLODDER IN AMERIKA

(FLODDER DOES MANHATTAN!)

(DUTCH)

A United Intl. Pictures release of a First Floor Features production. Produced by Laurens Geels, Dick Maas. Directed, written by Dick Maas. Camera (Fujicolor), Marc van Felperlaan; supervising editor, Hans van Dongen; production design, Peter Jansen; art direction, Alfred Shaarf; costume design, Annie Verhoeven; sound (Dolby SR), Georges Bossaers; assistant director, Myrna van Gylst; production supervisor (N.Y.), Richard Coll. Reviewed at Cannes Film Festival (market), May 19, 1993. Running time: **114 MIN.**
With: Huub Stapel, Nelly Frijda, Rene van't Hof, Tatjana Simic.
(English soundtrack)

A bunch of Dutch tree-hangers cause cross-cultural confusion in "Flodder Does Manhattan!," a gross-out comedy that picks up speed once it hits Gotham but is never as funny as it ought to be.

Pic is a belated follow-up to the 1986 Dutch record-breaker "Flodder," also directed by Dick Maas ("Amsterdamned," "The Lift"). Current item zoomed to the top of the local B.O. charts in 1992 (beating "Basic Instinct" into second place), and has already played in some Euro territories. But major shearing would be necessary for this to work even as a curio in English-speaking markets.

Labored opening in the Netherlands has the Flodder family (a cross between Li'l Abner's brood and the Beverly Hillbillies) getting a trip to New York City as part of a yearlong government exchange of Dutch and American families.

Mistaken at the airport for a Russian delegation, they're carted off to the Plaza Hotel, wreck the joint, and later land a deal with a businessman to redecorate his nightclub in Dutch style. Subplot has the U.S. president's spoiled son falling for the Flodders' pneumatic daughter, Casey (Tatjana Simic), who's working as a stripper at the niterie.

Best bits are the action sequences (including a clever effect of a car crashing onto the floor of the New York Stock Exchange), generally done with a panache missing from the verbal comedy. Latter relies heavily on jokes about Simic's breasts. Occasional nudity reaches a nadir in a fantasy sequence involving women basketball players.

Performances are robust and tech credits OK. In English version, all the Dutch have funny accents. —*Derek Elley*

EL MISTERIO DE LOS OJOS ESCARLATA

(THE MYSTERY OF THE SCARLET EYES)

(VENEZUELAN)

A Cine Seis Ocho production. Produced, directed, written by Alfredo J. Anzola. Camera (color), Harnan Toro; editors, Luisa de la Valle, Olegario Barrera, Anzola; sound, Mario Nazoa. Reviewed at Museum of Modern Art, N.Y., Aug. 2, 1993. Running time: **80 MIN.**
With: Elba Esobar, Kristina Wetter, Julio Mota, Eduardo Gadea Perez, Chile Veloz.

"The Mystery of the Scarlet Eyes" is a charming compilation film that chronicles the first half of the 20th century through the eyes of a Venezuelan entrepreneur. With an English-dubbed voiceover, pic could be a natural for cultural or cable small-screen fare.

Entrepreneur Edgar J. Anzola seemed to be fascinated with modern technology. Whenever anything happened anywhere in Venezuela, he was on the spot. He was an avid photographer, a pioneer in newsreels, fiction filmmaker, radio and records. When the first automobiles were exported to Venezuela, he bought one and toured the country, documenting his trip with thousands of photos.

When Edgar died, his immense archive ended up in the hands of his son Alfredo J. Anzola, who has compiled this rich visual and audio material, counterpointing it with a voiceover commentary culled from his father's many diaries and letters. (Pic's title comes from one of Anzola's radio plays that is recreated in the studio.)

Result is a fascinating chronicle that captures the innocence and excitement of a country moving into the technological century, recounted with infectious charm and exhilaration. —*Paul Lenti*

February 28, 1994

GREEDY

A Universal release of an Imagine Entertainment production. Produced by Brian Grazer. Executive producers, David Friendly, George Folsey Jr. Directed by Jonathan Lynn. Screenplay by Lowell Ganz, Babaloo Mandel. Camera (Deluxe color), Gabriel Beristain; editor, Tony Lombardo; music, Randy Edelman; production design, Victoria Paul; art direction, Dan Webster; set decoration, Anne Ahrens; costume design, Shay Cunliffe; sound (Dolby), Robert Anderson Jr; assistant director, Matthew Rowland; casting, Karen Rea. Reviewed at the Beverly Connection, L.A., Feb. 23, 1994. MPAA Rating: PG-13. Running time: **113 MIN.**

Daniel McTeague	Michael J. Fox
Uncle Joe McTeague	Kirk Douglas
Robin Hunter	Nancy Travis
Molly Richardson	Olivia d'Abo
Frank	Phil Hartman
Carl	Ed Begley Jr
Glen	Jere Burns
Patti	Colleen Camp
Ed	Bob Balaban
Douglas	Jonathan Lynn
Muriel	Joyce Hyser
Nora	Mary Ellen Trainor
Tina	Sioghan Fallon

There's an ambition to "Greedy" one simply has to admire. The concept — that a small army of potential heirs will stoop lower than a limbo dancer to pick up the pelf of a stinking-rich relative — is both timeless and timely. Yet the idea quickly goes awry as the filmmakers find themselves at sea deciding whether this is a notion to disdain or embrace.

The push-me, pull-you nature of the tale ultimately results in an artistic tie that is emotionally unsatisfying. Still, the appealing ensemble rogues' gallery, the darkly satisfying humor and the sensitive universal nerve touched by the material should provide an initial boost that just might be enough to sell the picture into medium-sized success.

The yarn centers on the McTeague brood (a cinematic reference to the protagonist of von Stroheim's silent masterpiece "Greed," based upon Frank Norris' novel "McTeague"), who live for the death of wheelchair-bound Uncle Joe (Kirk Douglas), a snarly, reprehensible curmudgeon who made a fortune in scrap metal. The spawn of three siblings — Joe never married or had embarrassing accidents — the four second-generation families bow, scrape, back-bite and give their children ridiculous names like Joette and Jolene to get into the old man's good graces.

Joe barely veils his contempt for the sycophants. But the big bombshell is the arrival of Molly (Olivia d'Abo), a nubile Brit who graduated from delivering pizza into becoming Joe's so-called nurse. The normally warring clan, sensing millions slipping away, initially panics but quickly mobilizes into a unified front in search of a counterbalancing weapon.

The little ace they turn up is Daniel McTeague Jr. (Michael J. Fox), son of the brother who called Joe a weasel and turned in his platinum card for a life working with the oppressed and needy. Daniel, remembered as an adorable cherub who did a great Durante impression, is about to give up the pro bowler tour as a result of a developing arthritic wrist. He's susceptible to the lure of money.

So, the factions in the Lowell Ganz-Babaloo Mandel script include a viper, a potential mongoose, a pack of vultures and a naif training to be a cheetah. In this zoo atmosphere, Daniel's inherent decency is strained to the limit and certainly buckles and cracks from several seismic shocks.

Director Jonathan Lynn knows exactly what elements to emphasize when the action moves through breakneck drawing-room comedy. But the script aims higher, embracing pathos even when the results are pure bathos. Uncle Joe's behind-the-scenes machinations or revelations of fear never quite reach the level of fun they were meant to provide, and every time Daniel stops to consider a moral dilemma, the momentum seizes up cold.

Despite some memorable turns, most of the cast is underutilized or merely asked to effect a character trait. The avaricious thirtysomethings pretty much work as a single unit, though Phil Hartman and Ed Begley Jr. get the best lines and situations. Marginally better used is Nancy Travis as Fox's girlfriend and conscience, and Lynn casts himself very effectively as the quintessentially obsequious British butler.

The principles are basically paradigms. As the threat, d'Abo invests her role with a refreshing wit, and Douglas' iron man has just enough humanity and canniness to keep the audience off-balance and alert. But Fox's sincerity and goodness is wearing mighty thin. He seems stuck in the role of the nice guy who's tempted, waivers, and always, always winds up doing the right thing.

While tech credits are nicely polished, the production would have benefited from adopting something a little less bright and obvious.

"Greedy" hearkens back to those classic Elizabethan or Restoration comedies that get dusted off and updated, like "Volpone/Sly Fox."

Ganz and Mandell certainly understand the vintage structure, but what's sadly missing — unlike in Jonson or Moliere — is some moral for our times.
—Leonard Klady

BERLIN FEST

LADYBIRD, LADYBIRD

(BRITISH)

A Film Four Intl. presentation of a Parallax Pictures production. (International sales: Film Four Intl., London.) Produced by Sally Hibbin. Directed by Ken Loach. Screenplay, Rona Munro. Camera (color), Barry Ackroyd; editor, Jonathan Morris; music, George Fenton; additional music, Mauricio Venegas; production design, Martin Johnson; art director, Fergus Clegg; sound (Dolby), Ray Beckett; assistant director, Tommy Gormley. Reviewed at Berlin Film Festival (competing), Feb. 19, 1994. Running time: **102 MIN.**

Maggie Conlan	Crissy Rock
Jorge Arellano	Vladimir Vega
Simon	Ray Winstone
Mairead	Sandie Lavelle
Adrian	Mauricio Venegas
Jill	Clare Perkins
Sean	Jason Stracey
Mickey	Luke Brown
Serena	Lily Farrell

Far removed from the boisterous, dryly comic "Raining Stones," Ken Loach's "Ladybird, Ladybird" is a tough, steamrolling, semi-*verite* look at (non-) family life in 1990s Britain through the eyes of a battered but ballsy unmarried mother caught between her own willfulness and an intrusive nanny state. Propelled by a natural, gutsy performance by newcomer Crissy Rock (who won best actress at the Berlin fest), pic looks set to be a hot fest favorite and should translate into robust arthouse and tube sales, though public appetite for this emotional bone-shaker could prove limited in certain territories.

In tone and content, Loach hasn't directed anything this emotionally powerful since his earlier work of the 1960s and early 1970s. Main character here recalls the battling women of his 1966 telepic "Cathy Come Home" and first feature "Poor Cow" (1968), with the nihilism of the 1972 "Family Life" updated to the falsely caring 1990s.

Though Loach stressed at its Berlin fest world preem that pic is not simply a frontal assault on Britain's over-intrusive social services, but rather a wider look at the poverty trap into which single mothers can fall, the film still carries a strong anti-establishment flavor that chimes well with the rest of his work.

Based on a true story, pic has Maggie (Rock), a tough Liverpudlian mother of four, meeting gentle Paraguayan Jorge (Vladimir Vega) in a London bar where she sings. The pair bond fast, with flashbacks pasting in Maggie's history, first as a child with an abusive father and later as a battered mother forced to move into a women's refuge after being hospitalized due to an attack by one of her lovers (a sequence of sudden, shocking violence).

Scenes of her and Jorge together, underscored by warm Latino guitar music, function almost as romantic interludes between the chunks of history. Almost an hour in, pic's focus settles on this current relationship, cranked into a higher gear by the news that she's expecting another child.

Loach then progressively tightens the screws as the authorities take her baby girl into care, Jorge gets heat from the immigration authorities after his visa expires, and the relationship comes under strain as Maggie's insecurities resurface. Ending seems to offer little escape from the vicious circle, until a postscript updating the real Maggie's story.

Though the movie sounds irredeemably depressing on paper, there's a real warmth to the central relationship that lifts "Ladybird" above similar-sounding exercises in Brit self-loathing. Loach's theme seems to be that, left alone, most people are more than capable of sorting out their own problems, or at least finding a *modus vivendi*.

Villains of the piece are clearly defined as economic circumstances and legalistic do-gooders rather than any inherent British character trait for self-abuse. In its portraits of everyday working-class characters, pic also sports a low-key black humor that may be lost on some auds but is there for the taking.

A Liverpool standup comedian with no acting experience, Rock exudes a no-nonsense, working-class sensibility, moving easily from acerbic Merseyside wit to sequences of emotional violence that carry a docu charge. Vega, an exiled Chilean based in London since 1978, is also on the money in a role that could easily have deteriorated into a lovelorn wimp.

Other roles are small but cast (and scripted) with an accuracy that's often chilling.

Pic inhabits the gray area between docudrama and *verite* filming

February 28, 1994 (Cont.)

that Loach made his own more than two decades ago.

If this outing has faults, it's that the story essentially springs few surprises once the board is laid out, and that Rock's breakdowns and screaming sessions lose some of their power as familiarity with her character deepens. Pic could easily be tightened by 10 minutes with no loss of clout.

Tech credits are OK, with discreet cutting by Jonathan Morris and unshowy lensing by Barry Ackroyd. Sound has a caught-on-the-run quality that fits the movie's style but makes no concessions to Rock's thick Liverpudlian accent, which could prove troublesome for some viewers. —*Derek Elley*

THE LAST SEDUCTION

An ITC Entertainment Group presentation. Produced by Jonathan Shestack. Co-producer, Nancy Rae Stone. Directed by John Dahl. Screenplay, Steve Barancik. Camera (CFI color), Jeffrey Jur; editor, Eric L. Beason; music, Joseph Vitarelli; production design, Linda Pearl; costume design, Terry Dresbach; sound (Ultra-Stereo), Mark Deren; assistant director, Eric N. Heffron. Reviewed at Berlin Film Festival (Panorama section), Feb. 18, 1994. (Also in Palm Springs Film Festival.) Running time: **109 MIN.**
Bridget Gregory .... Linda Fiorentino
Mike Swale ....Peter Berg
Clay Gregory .... Bill Pullman
Frank Griffith .... J.T. Walsh
Harlan .... Bill Nunn
Bob Trotter .... Herb Mitchell
Chris .... Brien Varady
Shep .... Dean Norris
Stacy .... Donna Wilson

This well-paced, cleverly written and quite diabolical thriller is director John Dahl's classy follow-up to last year's generally well-received "Red Rock West." Linda Fiorentino toplines as one of the screen's most formidable femmes fatales ever in a sexy and polished performance. With proper handling and critical attention, word of mouth should make this a seductive attraction.

The film is utterly amoral and centers upon a ruthless and self-centered woman who single-mindedly manipulates for her own ends everyone unlucky enough to cross her path. She's a monster alongside whom all the male characters are pitifully inadequate.

Bridget Gregory (Fiorentino) is an intelligent N.Y. insurance exec who has conned her medic husband, Clay (Bill Pullman), into doing a dangerous but lucrative drug deal. In a cleverly structured opening sequence, the foul-mouthed Bridget bullies her underlings at the office while the nervous Clay faces a cou-

ple of unstable hoods for the drug transaction.

Bridget rewards him by simply ankling with the money, heading for Chicago. Along the way she stops at a one-horse town for fuel and sexual replenishment. Latter comes from the bruised Mike (Peter Berg), whom she picks up in a bar (her direct approach to the subject of sex is something of an eye-opener).

When her lawyer (J.T. Walsh) advises her that Clay has heavyweight muscle on her trail, she decides to lie low in the town, takes an assumed name and immediately manages (in the only contrived bit of plotting in an otherwise top-notch screenplay) to get an exec position in a local insurance company.

When a private eye (Bill Nunn) tracks her down, she's able to dispose of him without too much bother, but realizes Clay must be dealt with permanently. She plots to involve Mike in Clay's murder; writer Steve Barancik's development of the narrative is skillful and original.

Dahl keeps his direction relatively simple this time around; he has good material and a top cast, and he knows it. Pacing is on the button, and the film moves inexorably, without any flat moments, toward the suspenseful, if morally indefensible, finale.

Fiorentino is quite wonderful as the diabolical Bridget, who uses her beauty and her body to get what she wants without qualms. Sex scenes are moderately steamy, the more so for being so matter-of-fact. Berg is well cast as the patsy, and Pullman is quite touching as the husband who is no match for his ruthless wife.

"The Last Seduction" has a professional gloss. It should quickly earn a reputation as a top-class thriller and be a solid earner for ITC, in the process adding to the reputations of all involved.
—*David Stratton*

SANDRA BERNHARD: CONFESSION OF A PRETTY LADY

(BRITISH — DOCU — 16mm)

A BBC-TV production. (International sales: BBC Enterprises, London.) Produced by Sarah Mortimer. Executive producers, Nigel Finch, Anthony Wall. Directed, written by Kristiene Clarke. Camera (color), Fawn Yakker; editor, Julia Meadows; sound, John Vincent. Reviewed at Berlin Film Festival (Panorama section), Feb. 19, 1994. (Also in London Lesbian & Gay Film Festival.) Running time: **46 MIN.**
With: Sandra Bernhard, Martin Scorsese, Camille Paglia, Jeanette Bernhard, Mo Gerow, Zelda Gerow, John Boscovic, Jeff Yarborough, Abel Zaballos.

The Queen of Appropriation gets full-frontal exposure in "Sandra Bernhard: Confession of a Pretty Lady," a mid-length docu that's short on confessions but comes as close as any film is likely to get to the sassy entertainer-cum-gay icon. Packed screenings at the Berlin fest testify to its long legs in specialized situations.

Core of the pic is excerpts from a 1992 N.Y. nightclub routine, whose tone is already familiar from John Boskovich's semidocu "Without You I'm Nothing." Bernhard's one-liners like "My father's a proctologist and my mother's an abstract artist, so that's how I see the world" provide a jumping-off point for director Kristiene Clarke's nonjudgmental probing into the star's myth-laden background.

Though turned down by Bernhard's former close friend Madonna, Clarke finally gained access to both the star herself and her mother Jeanette, both of whom give good value without actually saying a lot. More interesting are family photos of Bernhard as an ugly duckling in Scottsdale, Ariz., and explicit footage of the artiste during her nude shoot for Playboy.

Media mavens like Camille Paglia expound on Bernhard's position as a performer, linking her to the neurotic Jewish school pioneered by Lenny Bruce during the 1950s. Martin Scorsese also offers a brief tribute. On the much-discussed question of Bernhard's private sexuality, however, the docu never succeeds in cracking the glass wall the star herself has constructed.

Commissioned by British pubcaster BBC for its arts program "Arena," the film was yanked at the last minute from its slot last year and has yet to air in the U.K. Clarke says she has enough material to expand it to a feature-length documentary, but Bernhard herself has so far nixed requests for theatrical showings outside fests.
—*Derek Elley*

L'ARTICOLO 2
(ARTICLE 2)
(ITALIAN)

A Bambu Srl-SIRE production. (International sales: Italtoons Corp., N.Y.) Produced by Ernesto di Sarro, Maurizio Nichetti, Marcello Siena. Directed, written by Maurizio Zaccaro. Camera (color), Pascale Rachini; editor, Rita Rossi; music, Alessio Vlad, Claudio Capponi; production design, Giovanna Zighetti; sound, Candido Raini; assistant director, Piergiorgio Gay. Reviewed at Berlin Film Festival (Panorama section), Feb. 11, 1994. Running time: **102 MIN.**

Said .... Mohammed Miftah
Fatma .... Rabia Ben Abdallah
Malika .... Naima El Mcherqui
Lawyer .... Susanna Marcomeni
Factory worker .... Fabio Bussotti
Saverio .... Fabio Sartor
Immigration
 Officer .... Massimo Mesciulam

The title refers to Article 2 of the Italian Constitution, which allows citizens to live according to the dictates of their religion. Maurizio Zaccaro's heartfelt but measured film attacks a loophole in that law in the personal story of a Muslim factory worker who has two wives. The result is a modest, decent film that could find a niche in cinemas and on TV screens in some territories.

"Article 2" covers territory similar to that of the Swiss Oscar winner "Journey to Hope," as it details the problems facing Middle Eastern immigrants trying to enter and live in a European country. But this film lacks the dramatic highlights of the earlier pic, despite a contrived, heavily ironic, ending.

Said works in a Milan steel factory and lives in a small apartment with his wife, Malika, and three children, the eldest an increasingly precocious teenage girl. He's a hard worker, accepted by his mates, who still unthinkingly upset him with leering tales about compliant Arab women.

He has left behind in his Algerian village his second wife, Fatma, who has been caring for his elderly father. When the father dies, Fatma and her three sons embark on the long journey, by decrepit bus and boat, for Italy. But when they arrive in Genoa, they face a problem with immigration officials; having two wives in Italy is bigamy, even if it's allowable under Muslim law.

Writer/director Zaccaro sympathetically relates the plight of Said and his two families, exposing the hypocrisies and compromises of the Italian legal system. He's a little too gentle, though, and the film could have done with a few more dramatic highlights. Italian racism seems mostly confined to schoolboys telling dirty stories or the occasional mindless thug (Said gets beaten up while trying to place a call to Algeria from a phone booth). Otherwise, most Italians are generous and kind to these Algerian immigrants, including Said's boss, a woman neighbor and even the immigration officials. Muslim attitudes are also criticized, as Said at first balks to discover he's been assigned a femme lawyer by the court.

The ending comes across as far too pat, tying up the loose ends with a *deus ex machina* and a dose of too-heavy irony. Zaccaro says his story is based on the experiences of several Italo-Muslims, but the screenplay fails to pull the threads together with complete satisfaction.

Production values are modest for this unsensational picture, and per-

February 28, 1994 (Cont.)

formances are natural and unforced, especially Mohamed Miftah as Said. Some very cute children have been cast as the younger members of Said's families. The humanist message is certainly socked home, and for this reason alone the film will be of considerable appeal.

—*David Stratton*

TIGRERO: A FILM THAT WAS NEVER MADE

(FINNISH-GERMAN-BRAZILIAN)

A Marianna Films (Helsinki) production, in co-production with Premiere (Hamburg)/Sky Light Cinema-Mira Set (Rio de Janeiro)/Lichtblick (Cologne). Produced, directed, written, edited by Mika Kaurismaki. Co-producers, Bruno Stroppiana, Carl-Ludwig Rettinger. Camera (color), Jacques Cheuiche; music, Nana Vasconcelos, Chuck Jonkey, the Karaja; associate producers, Christa Fuller-Lang, Hartmut Klenke, Eila Werning. Reviewed at Berlin Film Festival (Forum section), Feb. 18, 1994. Running time: **75 MIN.**
With: Samuel Fuller, Jim Jarmusch, the Karaja.

Part Hollywood film lore, part ethnographic documentary, "Tigrero" never quite decides what kind of film it's going to be, as viewers interested in the Karaja people of Brazil's Mato Grosso may not be the same viewers fascinated by hearing Sam Fuller tell Jim Jarmusch about a 1950s project that was never made. This is a genuine oddity.

It seems that in 1954, after he made "Hell and High Water" and before "House of Bamboo," Fuller was asked by Darryl F. Zanuck to tackle a book, "Tigrero," which had been purchased by 20th Century Fox. Zanuck wanted only the title, not the plot of the book, and sent Fuller to Brazil to get some ideas for a screenplay. Taking with him a 16mm camera, 75 boxes of cigars and two cases of Polish vodka, Fuller arrived at a village between two rivers, the Araguaia and the Rio das Mortes; he was one of the first "gringos" to meet the Karaja people, who greeted him cordially and allowed him to film their village and their ceremonies.

He returned to Hollywood and wrote a screenplay designed for a formidable cast. John Wayne would play Tigrero, a guide and hunter; Tyrone Power would be a convict whose loyal wife, played by Ava Gardner, frees him from a Brazilian prison after killing a guard. They flee to the jungle with Tigrero as their guide, and there Gardner discovers that Power "loves himself a little more than he loves her."

This sounds like fascinating stuff, and Fuller — working at his peak at the time — might have made a marvelously offbeat adventure on the exotic location (he asserts there would have been no romance between Gardner and Wayne in the film). But Fox's insurance company balked at the idea of three big stars working on such a dangerous location, and the project was abandoned, although some of the footage Fuller shot in 1954 was used as color inserts in his later mental-hospital thriller, "Shock Corridor."

Feisty, excitable and brimming with enthusiasm, Fuller relates this story, and other ideas he had for "Tigrero," to an ultracool Jarmusch (who, if he wanted to, could start inheriting the kind of screen role once played by Lee Marvin) as they sit in the Karaja village or wander by the river, with Jarmusch towering over the diminutive Fuller. But most of the film is taken up with Jarmusch's reaction to the Karaja, and with Fuller's talking to villagers who recognize now-dead relatives after a screening of the 1954 footage. The odd couple also chat about Fuller's rep as an outsider in Hollywood, his penchant for location filming, and about religion.

It's all fascinating, if a little overextended. A must for the fest route, with limited distribution indicated, but possibly a life on video and certainly on television, "Tigrero" brings to light a forgotten footnote in Hollywood history in an unusual and exotic format. —*David Stratton*

ABSCHIED VON AGNES

(FAREWELL TO AGNES)

(GERMAN)

An Ost Film production, with Filmhaus Munchen, Dok Film, Babelsberg. Produced, directed, written by Michael Gwisdek, from the book "The Silence Under The Sea," by Hans Loffler. Camera (color), Roland Dressel; editor, Rita Reinhardt; music, Detlef Petersen; production design, Paul Lehmann; sound, Paul Oberle; assistant director, Marlies Butzlaff. Reviewed at Berlin Film Festival (non-competing), Feb. 19, 1994. Running time: **99 MIN.**
Heiner .... Michael Gwisdek
Stefan .... Sylvester Groth
Old
  Man ... Gerhard Straus-Joachimsthal
Girl .... Heide Kipp

This is a somber little film which, with its limited settings and cast (it's virtually a two-hander), would probably have played better onstage or on television. There's an intriguing idea here, but pic takes too long to get to the point.

Set in what used to be East Berlin, it centers on Heiner, a retired scientist who lives alone mourning his beloved wife, Agnes, though it's not entirely clear whether she died or left him. One night, a young man, Stefan, asks to be let into Heiner's apartment, and once inside, refuses to leave. It seems he was a former member of Stasi (East German secret police) and that he knows all about Heiner because the Stasi had a file on him, a file containing the most intimate details of his fears and dreams, details that could surely have come only from his beloved Agnes.

The film plods along on this theme until near the end, when it becomes intriguing (Stefan dresses up in Agnes' clothes), but by then, interest in the outcome has pretty much waned. Michael Gwisdek, who scripted and then took over the film's direction when the original helmer became ill, gives a solid performance as the mournful Heiner, while Sylvester Groth is more interesting as the edgy, possibly still dangerous, Stefan.

Technical credits are modest.
—*David Stratton*

PRINCE OF JUTLAND

(FRENCH-BRITISH-DANISH-GERMAN)

A Les Films Ariane presentation of a Films Ariane (Paris)/Woodline Films (London)/Kenneth Madsen Filmproduktion (Copenhagen) production in association with Films Roses (Hamburg). (International sales: Vine Intl. Pictures, London.) Produced by Kees Kasander. Executive producers, Terry Glinwood, Sylvaine Sainderichin, Denis Wigman. Co-producer, Kenneth Madsen. Directed by Gabriel Axel. Screenplay, Axel, Erik Kjersgaard, based on the chronicle of Saxo Grammaticus. Camera (color), Henning Kristiansen; editor, Jean-Francois Naudon; music, Per Norgaard; production design, Sven Wichmann; set decoration, Torben Backmark; costume design, Gisele Tanalias; sound (Dolby), Volker Zeigermann, Mike Dawson; assistant director, Peter Baekkel; casting, Kate Dowd. Reviewed at Berlin Film Festival (market), Feb. 16, 1994. Running time: **106 MIN.**
Fenge .... Gabriel Byrne
Queen Geruth .... Helen Mirren
Prince Amled .... Christian Bale
Aethelwine,
  Duke of Lindsey .... Brian Cox
Ribold .... Steven Waddington
Ethel .... Kate Beckinsale
Bjorn .... Freddie Jones
Caedman .... Brian Glover
  (English dialogue)

Billing itself "the first telling of the true legend of Hamlet," 75-year-old Danish director Gabriel Axel's "Prince of Jutland" is a lovingly made, ultra-small-scale yarn that successfully evokes the saga tradition at the cost of jettisoning most audiences in the process.

Well-meaning effort represents an almost impossible marketing challenge for any distrib bold enough to sign on. Despite a sturdy English-speaking cast, and a director whose rep with the 1987 "Babette's Feast" still carries arthouse echoes, pic is a deliberate deconstruction of the Shakespeare play, shorn of familiar elements. As a subtitled item in Danish, it might have scraped by as an exotic art movie in Anglo markets.

The movie's style is very different from that of the warmer, emotionally involving "Babette," more often recalling Axel's only other international success, the 1967 Icelandic saga "The Red Mantle." Dispassionate, event-laden content perfectly mirrors the chronicle tradition on which it draws, but beyond extra-special situations and study classes, this looks like a pic without a public.

Set in sixth-century Jutland, "an ancient Danish kingdom," story opens with the king and his son murdered by evil Prince Fenge (Gabriel Byrne), who assumes the throne and the bed of the queen, Geruth (Helen Mirren). Fenge's nephew, Amled (Christian Bale), witness to the killing, pretends he's barking to escape death, but secretly plans an elaborate revenge.

Suspecting Amled is not half as nuts as he seems, Fenge arranges for a beautiful blonde to pry the truth out of him. When that fails, and his co-conspirator Ribold (Steven Waddington) ends up as pig food, Fenge sends Amled to a Scottish friend, Aethelwine (Brian Cox), with orders to kill him on arrival.

Amled doctors the orders, wins Aethelwine's confidence by beating a rival duke in battle, marries his daughter (Kate Beckinsale) and secretly returns to Jutland to slay Fenge.

Looking uncannily like a younger Peter O'Toole in robes, Byrne dominates the early going with his glowering presence and flavorsome Irish enunciation. Bale, recalling the long-tressed Tom Cruise in "Legend," is slow to emerge but fits the profile of the young prince thrust by events into greatness.

Mirren, in a relatively reactive part as the queen, is solid, with Cox excellent as the confident, fulsome Aethelwine. Beckinsale is colorless as Bale's love interest.

As in "The Red Mantle," Axel's portrait of the Dark Ages is unstinting on detail, but its spare look will come as a shock to audiences schooled in lusher, larger-scale Yank versions of the era. Only concession to mainstream entertainment values is Per Norgaard's bright score in the pic's first half. Scenes of violence, though brief, have an offhand brutality that's jolting in the circumstances.
—*Derek Elley*

February 28, 1994 (Cont.)

PRIVESTE INAINTE CU MINIE
(LOOK FORWARD IN ANGER)
(ROMANIAN)

A Profilm, Cinerom production. (International sales: Romaniafilm, Bucharest.) Produced by Dinu Tanase. Executive producer, Ioan Iuga. Directed by Nicolae Margineanu. Screenplay, Petre Salcudeanu. Camera (color), Alexandru Solomon; editor, Nita Chivulescu; music, Petre Margineanu; art direction, Dan Toada; costume design, Andrea Hasnas; sound, Silviu Camil; assistant director, Alexandra Movileanu. Reviewed at Berlin Film Festival (Panorama section), Feb. 14, 1994. Running time: **78 MIN.**
With: Remus Margineanu, Luminita Gheorghiu, Cristian Iacob, Simona Ciobanu, Ion Haiduc, Laurentiu Albu, Gheorghe Dinica, Virgil Adriescu, Stefan Sileanu, Valentin Teodosiu.

A multifaceted look at present-day Romania through a family progressively torn apart by social and economic tensions, "Look Forward in Anger" is well worth a look by specialized webs. Strongly scripted, consistently interesting pic was warmly received at its screenings in the Berlin fest's Panorama section.

Central character is Fane, a laborer in Braila, a drab town on the banks of the Danube some 100 miles northeast of Bucharest, who's summarily fired by his factory boss, a former Securitate (secret police) stooge during communist times. Unable to get a new job, Fane spends his days hanging out in bars and the countryside with his pals, former freedom fighters now trying to scrape a living in the new market-oriented Romania, riven by unemployment and inflation.

Meanwhile, his teen daughter, Vali, has been working nights to save money to study in the capital, and his younger son, Nilu, has joined a street gang. When Viorel, Fane's elder son, finds his sister is actually working as a prostitute in a seedy bar run by a Greek, he trashes the place and ends up in prison.

Vali and Nilu ankle for Bucharest, where they eke out a living. Fane, in a final outburst of anger at the new system, leads a strike against his factory's bosses, with tragic results.

One of pic's strengths is its forthright look at "new-style" Romania, where the December 1989 people's revolution is shown to have led to economic chaos, with former communists changing clothes and idealists like Fane left on the sidelines.

Though grim on paper, the script melds many moods — funny, dramatic, lyrical, violent — with a full range of characters, an undemonstrative tone (apart from a melodramatic finale) and an appreciation that post-revolutionary disillusionment may be one thing but, for the younger generation, life still must go on.

Performances mesh well, and there's a strong sense of purpose and direction to the pic that avoids preachiness. Scripter Petre Salcudeanu has since taken a job in the Culture Ministry but, per helmer Nicolae Margineanu, made no objections to the latter's changes to reflect ongoing events. Tech credits are good considering the $100,000 (state coin) budget, with Petre Margineanu's music rating a special nod. —*Derek Elley*

PAODA SHUANG DENG
(RED FIRECRACKER, GREEN FIRECRACKER)
(HONG KONG)

A Yung & Associate Co. (Hong Kong) production, in association with Xi'an Film Studio, Beijing Salon Films (China). (International sales: Era Intl., Hong Kong.) Produced by Chan Chunkeung, Weng Naiming. Executive producer, Weng. Directed by He Ping. Screenplay, Da Ying, from the novel by Feng Jicai. Camera (color), Yang Lun; editor, Yuan Hong; music, Zhao Jiping; art direction, Qian Yunxiu; costume design, Ma Defan; sound (Dolby), Gu Changning, Zhang Wen; assistant director, Yu Xiaobin. Reviewed at Berlin Film Festival (Panorama section), Feb. 20, 1994. Running time: **116 MIN.**

Cai Chunzhi	Ning Jing
Niu Bao	Wu Gang
Man Dihong	Zhao Xiaorui
Old Butler	Gao Yang

(Mandarin Chinese dialogue)

A simple yarn of sexual longing raised almost to a ballad level, "Red Firecracker, Green Firecracker" is a Chinese costumer that has the extra smarts to attract limited theatrical distribution beyond fest and TV bookings, which should be brisk. Though the theme is hardly new for the genre, this one has enough new wrinkles to entertain those willing to go with the semi-stylized approach.

Setting is a remote town on the banks of the Yellow River, during the early years of post-1911 Republican China. Enter handsome Niu Bao, an itinerant painter, who's hired by the powerful Cai family to decorate its sprawling manse on the other side of the river.

The most famous fireworks manufacturer in northern China, the Cai family is now headed by Chunzhi, a 19-year-old girl who's been raised in men's clothes. Almost as soon as he arrives, Niu Bao starts breaking the family's strict rules (such as silence in the household), and the severe-looking but cute Chunzhi finds things other than production schedules on her mind.

After a severe beating from Man Dihong, the family foreman who's had his eyes on Chunzhi for some time, Niu Bao leaves town, returning later to consummate the relationship. Climax is a dangerous contest in firework-wielding skills between Niu Bao and Man Dihong for Chunzhi's hand.

Mainland Chinese director He Ping (not to be confused with Taiwan's Ho P'ing, helmer of "18") first drew fest attention with his "Fistful of Dollars"-like "Swordsman in Double-Flag Town," and there's some of the same wild, operatic quality to parts of "Firecracker."

Though much of the pic is shot in a beautifully controlled, burnished style reminiscent of parts of Zhang Yimou's "Raise the Red Lantern," he frequently opens the sluice gates with sequences of extravagant romantic imagery (backed by Zhao Jiping's lush orchestral score) that raise the pic almost to the level of a mythic ballad.

Final firecracker contest, which climaxes with Niu Bao risking his manhood, doesn't quite measure up to expectations and requires a leap in auds' imaginations that many may be unprepared to make. But there's no doubting the director's skill at evoking character and atmosphere, from the tiniest flickers of sexual stirring by the wonderfully cast Ning Jing as Chunzhi to the charismatic playing of Wu Gang as the doggedly independent Niu Bao.

Technically, pic is top-drawer, with precise, wintry lensing of barren locations in Shanxi province, China, by cinematographer Da Ying that cries out for widescreen rather than 1.66 treatment, and a fine Dolby effects track that plays with silence and offscreen sound. English subtitles, however, are often over-colloquial, and would benefit from revision.
—*Derek Elley*

A TERCEIRA MARGEM DO RIO
(THE THIRD BANK OF THE RIVER)
(BRAZILIAN)

A Regina Filmes production, in association with the Centre of Cultural and Educational Production (Brasilia)/ Institute of Brazilian Art and Culture/ Ministry of Culture (Cinema). Produced by Ney Sant'Anna, Dora Sverner. Directed, written by Nelson Pereira Dos Santos, based on five stories by Joao Guimaraes Rosa. Camera (color), Gilberto Azevedo, Fernando Duarte; editors, Carlos Alberto Camuirano, Luelane Correa; music, Milton Nascimento; production design, Jurandir Oliveira; sound, Chico Bororo; assistant director, Waldir Onofre. Reviewed at Berlin Film Festival (competing), Feb. 20, 1994. Running time: **98 MIN.**

Liojorge	Ilya Sao Paulo
Alva	Sonjia Saurin
Mother	Maria Ribeiro
Nhinhinaha	Barbara Brandt
Rigerio	Chico Diaz
Rosario	Mariane Vicentini
Herculinao Dagobe	Henrique Rovira

Cinema Novo veteran Nelson Pereira Dos Santos is back with a strange, difficult fantasy in which he seems to be attacking low moral values in Brazilian society. But the message is heavily coated inside a strange story about a child who performs miracles, and it seems unlikely to arouse much interest outside Latin territories.

Part of the problem is the screenplay, which has been derived from five short stories — it doesn't feel fully cohesive, nor is the film as visually exciting as the director's work used to be. Indeed, the images are surprisingly flat.

Pic opens by a river. A man says farewell to his wife and two children and rows out into the stream, the wife ordering him not to return. But the son, Liojorge, leaves food for his father every night in a secret place by the river, and every morning the food is gone. Years go by. The daughter marries and moves to the city.

One day, Liojorge follows a stray cow, which leads him to the home of beautiful Alva, whom he quickly marries. On his wedding day, he "introduces" his bride to his unseen father by the river bank. A year later, Liojorge and Alva have a daughter, and when the child gets to be about six, they discover she can perform miracles, such as breaking a drought by wishing for rain, or getting herself the cookies she wants. A quartet of gangsters comes by, and one of them seems to be attracted to Alva. Liojorge decides to move his family to the city in case of trouble.

In the slums of Brasilia, the precocious child continues her miracles, and soon is known as the Little Saint. But the gangster kidnaps Alva, and Liojorge is forced to take extreme measures to retrieve his wife. The film ends on the same note of mystery with which it began, but by fadeout, it hardly seems as though the writer/director has taken the viewer on an inspiring journey.

No doubt there are political and social allusions hidden in the film which will mean more to the Brazilian viewer, but for international audiences, this is a rather puzzling fantasy without a satisfactory resolution. Film was lensed a couple of years ago, but only bowed in Brazil late last year.

Tech credits are adequate, with a good music score by Milton Nascimento. There's a very prominent example of product placement as a brand of beer is heavily promoted in a barroom scene. —*David Stratton*

HUO HU
(SPARKLING FOX)
(HONG KONG-CHINESE)

A Simpson Prods. (Hong Kong)/ Chang Chun Film Studio (China) production. (Intl. sales: Simpson Communication H.K.) Produced by Willy Tsao. Executive producer, Jacob C.L. Cheung. Directed by Wu Ziniu. Screenplay, Wu, Wang Chunbo. Camera (color), Yang Wei; editor, Wang Xiaoming; art direction, Wu Yang; sound, Zhang Lei; associate producer, Fan Kim-hung. Reviewed at Berlin Film Festival (competing), Feb. 11, 1994. Running time: **99 MIN.**
The Thin One .... Gong Hanlin
The Bearded One .... Tu Men
Guizhi, His Wife .... Sharen Gaowa
(Mandarin dialogue)

A basically simple yarn of two different types pursuing an elusive beast (and each other) in the snowy mountains, "Sparkling Fox" is a generally successful stab at metaphysical cinema by "Fifth Generation" Chinese director Wu Ziniu. Pic lacks the extra dramatic smarts for offshore theatrical outings, but fests and some TV sales should beckon.

Wu is best known in the West for the World War II drama "Evening Bell," which copped a Special Jury Prize at Berlin in 1989 after being taken off the shelf by China's censors, and 1988's "The Last Day of Winter." Current movie fits well into his *oeuvre* of inner psychological dramas without topping them in dramatic clout.

Film is first out of the hopper of Hong Kong-based Simpson Prods.' four-picture slate assembling talent from the three Chinese territories. Others in the works are new films by the mainland's Huang Jianxin ("Enchanted Autumn"), Hong Kong's Derek Chiu ("Mr. Sardine"), and Taiwan's Chang Tso-chi ("Midnight Revenge"). All are exec produced by H.K. helmer Jacob Cheung ("Cageman").

"Fox" starts in buffish style with a nerdy theater projectionist (Gong Hanlin) announcing to patrons the final show at his family-owned cinema, due to close thanks to commercial pressures in contempo money-mad China. After a checkup with his doc, he decides to head for the mountains for a spot of hunting. His obsession with movies has already capsized his marriage to an ambitious beautician.

After firing at a mountain hunter (Tu Men), whom he mistakes for a fox, the two men strike up a cat-and-mouse relationship, pursuing each other through the snowy forests in between hunting a legendary red fox that nobody's actually seen. A violent storm, impressively filmed, in which the hunter saves the nerd's life, finally bonds them

before the latter heads back to the city. Final scene, of the nerd meeting another city type on the way up, provides a neat ending.

In true "Hell in the Pacific" style, the duo are shown to be fighting the enemy within rather than anything more tangible, each drawn by an illusion that gives them some purpose in life. The city nerd proudly boasts he's "in the film industry," whereas his wife (in a withering, direct-to-camera monologue) describes him as basically stupid, with no redeeming qualities at all.

Aside from regular displays of one-upmanship between the two men, played in almost childlike fashion, the script contains few extra wrinkles to freshen the familiar subject matter. Ending is signaled early on, and the drama rarely plumbs the grim depths of Wu's earlier works. *—Derek Elley*

CHARACHAR
(SHELTER OF THE WINGS)
(INDIAN)

A Gope Movies production. Produced by Shankar Gope, Gita Gope. Directed, written by Buddhadeb Dasgupta. Camera (color), Soumendu Roy; editor, Ujjal Nundy; music, Biswadeb Dasgupta; production design, Shatadal Mitra; assistant director, Biswadeb Dasgupta. Reviewed at Berlin Film Festival (competing), Feb. 18, 1994. Running time: **83 MIN.**
Lakhinder .... Rajit Kapoor
Sari .... Laboni Sarkar
With: Sadhu Meher, Shankar Chakraborty, Monoj Mitra, Indrani Halder.

This Bengali-track feature is the sort of gentle, deceptively simple film whose qualities can easily be overlooked during film fests. Though it has little chance of commercial release outside India, it deserves exposure on the fest route for its refreshingly different vision.

Writer/director Buddhadeb Dasgupta has made interesting films before, including "Distance" (1978) and "The Tiger Man" (1989). This time he tells an apparently allegorical story about a man hopelessly ill-equipped for the work he performs in society. It could be seen as a parable for any number of things, but works well enough on its face value.

Lakhinder catches exotic birds in the woods of Bengal for sale in the markets of Calcutta. The trouble is, he loves the birds so much he can't bear to see them in cages; so he lets most of them go, and earns very little money as a result. Indeed, he's in debt because he owes the man who employs him money from an advance. Understandably, his wife, Sari, becomes increasingly frus-

trated with her husband, and, to his distress, she embarks on an affair with the man who comes to collect the birds to take them to market.

Though Lakhinder gets some sympathy from the daughter of his partner, who understands him better than his wife, it's really his beloved birds that console him. In scenes reminiscent of a benign variation on Hitchcock's "The Birds," Lakhinder awakens to discover his bird friends have visited him in his hut.

This is hardly more than an anecdote, really, but with exceptionally beautiful photography by Soumendu Roy and sensitive performances and direction, plus a commendably brief running time, the film succeeds in taking us into the world of an eccentric of great charm and determination.

—David Stratton

ROTTERDAM

HET IS EEN SCHONE DAG GEWEEST
(IT'S BEEN A LOVELY DAY)
(DUTCH — DOCU)

A Stichting Dieptescherpte production. Produced, directed by Jos de Putter. Camera (color), Stef Tijdink, Melle van Essen; editors, Nathalie Alonso Casale, Riekje Ziengs; sound, Paul Veld, Martijn van Haalen. Reviewed at Rotterdam Intl. Film Festival, Feb. 3, 1994. Running time: **70 MIN.**

Recording the final harvest year on his aged parents' wheat farm, Dutch film critic Jos de Putter quietly but stirringly venerates a disappearing way of life. Pastoral lyricism powered by authenticity, humanity and a direct line to its subject, "It's Been a Lovely Day" is a riveting study in the purest documentary filmmaking tradition that merits extensive festival, cinematheque and public TV exposure.

Beginning on New Year's Day 1992 and ending exactly one year later, de Putter takes in the day-to-day running of the property. His parents' tacit acceptance of hard work in all weather and their pragmatic preparations for retirement are solemnly accentuated by the acknowledgement that the farm — a family-run concern for more than a century — has reached the end of its hereditary line.

Humor creeps in via the oldsters' dry, sparsely worded exchanges on subjects ranging from changing times and work attitudes to fish that won't bite, while something miraculously approaching drama

emerges from seemingly inconsequential dilemmas such as how to work a newfangled ear-tagging device to number cattle for sale.

But the rich texture is less the result of what's actively said or chronicled than what's gently observed in a carefully juxtaposed parade of images that forms a simple yet acutely affecting mosaic. Nothing intrudes on the soulful picture of Arcadian toil, and despite the entirely unstated tenderness suffusing conversations between de Putter (who remains unseen) and his folks, there's no trace of maudlin regret or reproach over the abandonment of cherished tradition.

Elegant, uncluttered camera work frames subjects from considerable distances in beautifully composed, sustained shots that function almost as a series of tableaux. When it does occur, movement of the camera is practically imperceptible. Sharply judged editing and pristine sound add further polish.

The film played theatrically and was televised in Holland, winning Rotterdam's prize for best debut of 1993, and is being compared in both concept and achievement to Gallic documaker Georges Rouquier's milestone "Farrebique" and its companion piece, "Biquefarre."

—David Rooney

AZGHYIN USHTYKZYN AZABY
(A PLACE ON THE TRICORNE)
(KAZAKH)

A Kazakhfilm Studios production. Directed by Ermek Shinarbaev. Screenplay, Nikita Jhilkybaev. Camera (color), Serguey Kosmanev; editor, Kulan Dusenbaeva; sound, Gulsara Mukataeva. Reviewed at Rotterdam Intl. Film Festival, Feb. 4, 1994. Running time: **82 MIN.**
With: Adilkhan Essenbulatov, Saule Suleymenova, Yulia Sukhova.

In the case of "A Place on the Tricorne," less is decidedly more. Working from a script that strips away everything but the bare bones of its voyage into suspended existence, Kazakh director Ermek Shinarbaev conjures a penetrating mood that lingers long after the end credits have rolled. Winner of the Golden Leopard at Locarno last summer, this contemplative slice of Generation X ennui in Alma-Ata should continue to roam the festival map, but a less obscure title might take it further.

The film tracks one summer in the life of an indolent 20-year-old

February 28, 1994 (Cont.)

poet (Adilkhan Essenbulatov), whose days are spent writing, talking, listening to Maria Callas and floating in a drug-induced stupor. Ignoring his mother's reprimands about idleness, he drifts between encounters with friends and various lovers, consciously opting to pull back and mull over the world from a distance rather than grapple with the uncertain realities of living in the post-Soviet Kazakh capital.

Disengagement extends to his relationships with women, causing ripples of conflict. The uncomplicated camaraderie of sharing a joint with a friend is the closest thing to satisfying human contact in his life. But a darker edge sidles into his prolonged reflection, gradually steering him to a suicide attempt.

With his sharp, angular features and gaunt frame, Essenbulatov gives the melancholy, psychological scrutiny a worthy focus. Dialogue is minimal, but the actor superbly limns the character's shifting states of mind using little more than his piercing gaze.

Shot mostly in warmly lit interiors, with the camera lavishing detail onto ostensibly routine acts, the film's quiet power owes as much to Serguey Kosmanev's graceful lensing as to Shinarbaev's controlled, sensitive direction.

—*David Rooney*

XINGHUA SAN YUE TIAN

(THE STORY OF XINGHUA)

(CHINESE)

A Youth Studio of the Peking Film Academy production. Directed by Yin Li. Screenplay, Shi Ling. Camera (color, widescreen), Li Jianguo; music, Liu Weiguang. Reviewed at Rotterdam Intl. Film Festival, Feb. 2, 1994. Running time: **90 MIN.**
Xinghua .... Jiang Wenli
Wanglai .... Zhang Guoli
Fulin .... Tian Shaojun
Also with: Zhang Haiyan, Niu Xingli

A feisty feminist spirit serviceably cloaks the whiff of old-school stagnancy surrounding "The Story of Xinghua," an allegorical meller about greed and blind opportunism in modern rural China that remains absorbing despite its occasional prosaic obviousness. Helmer Yin Li's background in kidpix informs his widely accessible storytelling style, making this a likely candidate for programming in upscale international webs.

The upsurge in free enterprise under the liberalization gradually reshaping China's economy is intriguingly manifested here: Crooked grocer Wanglai (Zhang Guoli) runs a profitable sideline hawking souvenir stones lifted from the stretch of the Great Wall running through his mountain village. He is obsessed with the legend of a golden treasure said to be buried under the once-strategic tower that dominates the area. At the opposite extreme is Fulin (Tian Shaojun), a sensitive, educated neighbor scraping for spiritual rewards with his plantation of saplings.

Unable to bear him a son even after being plied with fertility medicine, Wanglai's 5,000-yuan bride, Xinghua (Chen Kaige regular Jiang Wenli), is abused, beaten and cheated on. She finds a soul mate in Fulin, who coyly confesses his attraction by commenting on the beauty of apricot blossoms (also the meaning of her name).

More coyness follows when they take shelter from a rainstorm, and the action cuts from a torrid clinch to their twin pitchforks thrust into a crop-bearing field. Having swiftly fallen pregnant, Xinghua proposes divorcing Wanglai for Fulin, but he reacts nervously, unveiling ethics only marginally less ruled by tradition than her husband's.

Learning of the fling, Wanglai all but destroys Fulin's plantation and batters him into submission before heading home to do the same to Xinghua. But she turns the tables on him, using proof of his sterility as her sword, although he's delirious at the thought of an heir and unconcerned about its parentage.

Though it's short on subtlety, the saga's sweeping emotional strokes and broad universality offer effortless enjoyment. Jiang turns in a forceful, not too showy performance, ably flanked by her contrasting but equally unworthy bed mates. Li Jianguo's unerringly efficient widescreen lensing doesn't quite sport the sumptuousness of many other Chinese dramas but still serves up enough majestic vistas to satisfy landscape fanciers.

—*David Rooney*

XIN BULIAO QING

(C'EST LA VIE, MON CHERI)

(HONG KONG)

A Film Unlimited production. Produced by Ng Yui-ming. Executive producer, Chan Mong-wa. Directed, written by Yee Tung-shing. Camera (color), Tam Tsi-wai; editors, Mei Fung, Kwong Tsi-teung; music, Peter Pau; art direction, Hai Tsung-man; sound, Stephen Chan. Reviewed at Rotterdam Intl. Film Festival, Jan. 28, 1994. (Also in Berlin Film Festival.) Running time: **100 MIN.**
With: Andy Lau, Yuen Wing-yi, Carina Liu, Carrie Ng, Fong Bo-bo, Cheun Pui, Sylvia Chang.

Hong Kong B.O. smash "C'est la Vie, Mon Cheri" earns curiosity status primarily in that it eschews high-kicking action for heart-tugging romantic tragedy. Catchy sentimental fare is easy to be swept along by but just as easy to forget and looks unlikely to tickle tear ducts beyond Chinatown circuits.

Local heartthrob Andy Lau plays Ah Kit, a talented but frustrated jazz musician held back by his own quick temper. Testiness with the music industry invades his private life, causing him to split with chart-topping singer Tracy (Carina Liu). Moving into a low-rent neighborhood, he encounters childlike Ah Man (Yuen Wing-yi), and her unflagging exuberance gradually drags the jaded loner out of his shell.

Ah Man imitates popular singers (including Tracy) on pirate tapes for additional earnings. Though Yuen's performance registers a little heavily on the expansive side, this midsection has a buoyant tempo and a fair share of contagious charm that makes its syrupiness palatable.

As friendship upgrades to romance, a ray of hope creeps into the couple's respective careers, only to be promptly tarnished when Ah Man's childhood brush with bone cancer resurfaces. Her anger gives Ah Kit the chance to match her earlier inspirational behavior, and even go-getting career girl Tracy makes a sympathetic showing as pic soars to its unabashedly weepy finale.

Lau's sensitive but measured turn keeps the material from becoming risibly saccharine. Use of music is less even-handed. Cantonese opera brackets (directed by Lee Fung) are entertainingly played by an engaging supporting cast, and also help to elevate pic above mush level. Tech credits are par.   —*David Rooney*

MINOTAUR

An RFPL production. Produced by Kris Krengel. Co-producer, Shelly Strong. Directed, written by Dan McCormack. Camera (Foto-Kem color), Dan Gillham; editor, Martin Hunter; music, William T. Stromberg; production design, Michael Krantz, Martha Rutan Faye; art direction, Ann Johnstad White; set decoration, Mary Gullickson; costume design, Penny Rose; sound (Ultra-Stereo), David Barr Yaffe, Giovanni Di Simoni. Reviewed at Foto-Kem screening room, Burbank, Feb. 10, 1994. (In Sundance Film Festival.) Running time: **55 MIN.**
The Minotaur .... Michael Faella
Mink .... Ricky Aiello
Cindy .... Holley Chant
Woman .... Willo Hausman
Paul .... Tom Kurlander
Father .... Jack Wallace

A remarkable talent and distinctive sensibility are evident in Dan McCormack's directorial debut, "Minotaur," an intelligent meditation on the nature and effects of celebrity in American popular culture. The intellectual intent, demanding artistry and ambiguous tone of this short feature present a marketing challenge in its likely round of fests, arthouses and midnight shows.

The puzzling, often cryptic story traces the meteoric rise and fall of the Minotaur (Michael Faella), a popular singer in the mold of Elvis Presley or Frank Sinatra late in their careers. Episodic, non-linear and self-reflective, pic follows the Minotaur as he looks back on his childhood, rise to superstardom in the 1950s, concert performances to multitudes of fans, drug addiction, self-absorption and his tragic demise in the 1970s.

It is to McCormack's credit, as writer and director, that the tone of his complex meditation is not easily decipherable. On the surface, pic has the air of classic camp, but as the peculiar tale unfolds, it assumes a dark, even Gothic, mood.

"Minotaur's" major achievement is in finding the pertinent visual strategy to match its narrative. The first scene, which is as visually stunning as it is emotionally disturbing, sets the ambience of the work. Sitting in his living-room swimming pool, shaped like a huge champagne glass, Minotaur is "socializing" with the sexy Cindy (Holley Chant). She is mumbling and giggling in the water when he suddenly strangles her, in an obsessive, out-of-control, drug-induced frenzy.

Faella gives a disturbing performance in the demanding role of the fat, bald, unattractive singer. The rest of the ensemble just play secondary roles, sort of signposts along the character's torturous road.

February 28, 1994 (Cont.)

Beautifully shot by Dan Gillham and subtly edited by Martin Hunter, "Minotaur" is an art film par excellence. Special kudos go to Michael Krantz and Martha Rutan Faye, whose wonderfully stylized sets are designed in bold, formal compositions that heighten the tale's sordid elements. Nothing is casual about the movie, whose text and subtext are extraordinarily dense for a running time of 55 minutes. Intelligent and provocative, "Minotaur" is a film that assumes the same qualities in its audience.

—*Emanuel Levy*

CANCER IN TWO VOICES

(DOCU — 16mm)

Produced, directed, edited by Lucy Massie Phenix. Executive producer, Sandra Butler. Original video footage, Annie Hershey. Reviewed at Sundance Film Festival, Park City, Jan. 22, 1994. Running time: **43 MIN.**

As a personal chronicle of what it means to live with a fatal disease, for both the person afflicted and her longtime companion, "Cancer in Two Voices" is always engaging and often insightful. What distinguishes this documentary is its practical, matter-of-fact approach, showing the determination of two intellectual lesbians to make the most of their relationship while facing the impending gloomy news. In both subject matter and form, docu is perfectly suited for public TV.

Barbara Rosenblum and Sandy Butler, two Jewish academics, were engaged in a loving long-term relationship when the former was diagnosed with breast cancer in 1985. In a series of interviews, mostly conducted at their San Francisco home, the women reveal the shifts in their relations over the next three years.

Among docu's most illuminating observations is Barbara's realization that she was just the first among their friends to have cancer and that "many of my friends will see their future in the way I handle mine."

As her lover, Sandy is most candid when she expresses her anger that Barbara won't be there for her in her old age. A touch of humor inflects the basically serious expose when Sandy voices resentment at the reactivation of her heterosexual instincts, instincts that she had fought for decades.

The project began as a set of journals published in 1991 and augmented by original videos, made by Annie Hershey. The final interview with Barbara was taped just three weeks before her death, in 1988.

Tech credits are modest, given that the materials consist of homevideos. Still, there are some painful truths to be learned here about the more universal issue of coming to terms with death, whether natural or premature. —*Emanuel Levy*

NEUF MOIS
(NINE MONTHS)
(FRENCH)

An AFMD release of an Anne Francois and Christophe Lambert presentation of an AFCL Prods./UGC Images/ France 2 Cinema co-production with the participation of Canal Plus and Sofinergie 2 & 3. (International sales: UGC DA.) Produced by Anne Francois. Executive producer, Christophe Lambert. Directed, written by Patrick Braoude. Camera (color) Jean-Yves Le Mener; editor, Georges Klotz; music, Jacques Davidovici; set design, Emmanuel Sorin; costume design, Mimi Lempieka; sound (Dolby), Harald Maury, Paul Berthault; assistant directors, Guila Braoude, Paul Gueu. Reviewed at UGC Danton cinema, Paris, Feb. 22, 1994. Running time: **107 MIN.**
Mathilde .... Philippine Leroy-Beaulieu
Dominique .... Catherine Jacob
Samuel .... Patrick Braoude
Georges .... Daniel Russo
Marc .... Patrick Bouchitey
New Ob/Gyn .... Pascal Legitimus

Game thesping propels the contrived and predictable plot of "Nine Months," a broad comedy about pregnancy that feels like waiting out the gestation period of an elephant. Auds who warm to the characters will find some belly laughs. Pic is procreating lots of little francs at French wickets.

Pic plays up nausea, bursting bladders and other full-bore discomforts with Gallic frankness, while examining the nine-month ordeal from the expectant father's p.o.v.

The message that pregnancy is a physically disgusting and anguish-riddled experience gives way to the stale revelation that it's all worth it when the bundle of joy arrives.

Interpreter Philippine Leroy-Beaulieu announces to her older shrink b.f. Patrick Braoude (who also scripted and directed) that she's pregnant, freaking him out.

His pal, painter Patrick Bouchitey, has just broken up with his wife since she wants kids and he doesn't. Bouchitey's sister, buxom and bulky Catherine Jacob, is expecting a fourth child.

She and her beefy lug of a hubby Daniel Russo adore kids and relish

the overheated sex that pregnancy hormones prompt.

Haunted by nightmares of predatory insects munching on their mates, Braoude wrestles with his reluctance to become a dad, while Bouchitey dates a series of shapely nymphettes and Jacob helps Leroy-Beaulieu over the hurdles of her crumbling relationship with wimpy Braoude.

As the passing months flash on the screen, indifferent lensing and ham-handed staging reveal gags about incompetent public hospital gynecologists, cruel sonogram facilities, impractical food cravings, chronic insomnia and a fearful aversion to sex.

By the time the fetus kicks, in month four, the pic is barely kicking. Final birth extravaganza is laid on thick with spatula and forceps.

Apart from the fact that it steadfastly confronts the icky aspects of pregnancy, pic's greatest merit is its jaunty Klezmer-style score.

—*Lisa Nesselson*

LA VENGEANCE D'UNE BLONDE
(REVENGE OF A BLONDE)
(FRENCH)

An AMLF release of a Les Films de la Colline/TF1 Films Production/Lumiere co-production with the participation of Canal Plus, Cofimage 4 and Investimage 4. (International sales: President Films, Jacques-Eric Strauss.) Produced by Marie Meunier. Executive producer, Robert Benmussa. Directed by Jeannot Szwarc. Screenplay, Valentine Albin, Marie-Anne Chazel, Bernard Murat, Michel Delgado. Camera (color), Jean-Yves Le Mener; editor, Catherine Kelber; music, Eric Levi; set design, Dominique Maleret; set decoration, Lise Peault; costume design, Catherine Leterrier; sound (Dolby), Frederic Hamelin; associate producer, Richard Grandpierre; assistant director, Henri Grimault; casting, Francoise Menifrey. Reviewed at UCG Odeon Cinema, Paris, Feb. 22, 1994. Running time: **91 MIN.**
Gerard Breha .... Christian Clavier
Corine Breha .... Marie-Anne Chazel
Marie-Ange
de la Baume .... Clementine Celarie
Gilles Favier .... Thierry Lhermitte
With: Annie Cordy, Marc De Jonge, Philippe Khorsand, Angelo Infanti, Maurice Lamy.

Laughs are few and far between in "Revenge of a Blonde," a shallow sendup of a nightly news-powered TV-ratings chase that devolves into a half-hearted lovers' quarrel. Gallic auds have been drawn in by "Les Visiteurs" star Christian Clavier, and other

Euro territories will probably behave otherwise, but hearty perfs can't save overwrought and underwritten plot.

When the primetime news anchor on ratings-hungry private station TV8 has a crippling accident, minor market newscaster Gerard Breha (Clavier) is promoted to the choice slot.

Ratings soar when Breha — initially summoned to Paris only because his face echoes the composite reached in a poll of what a trustworthy anchor should look like — forcefully interviews a politician about the YAM gang (a French acronym for "We're Fed Up"), whose ongoing violent attacks on gun shops spread terror.

With sudden fame, Clavier's wife Corine (the title blonde and co-scripter, Marie-Anne Chazel) and two kids see less and less of him. Sexually aggressive news producer Marie-Ange (bitchy powerhouse Clementine Celarie), whose libido is linked to ratings, seduces Clavier. Wife gets her revenge when she and hubby appear live on the station's sleazy truth-or-dare show hosted, in an over-the-top pastiche perf, by Thierry Lhermitte. The YAM gang storms the studio and takes hostages. Script is as by-the-numbers as it sounds.

Next-to-nothing is done with the Berlusconi-like media magnate who owns the station, and broad humor is carried mostly by frantic editing. Paris-born helmer Jeannot Szwarc, who sports a long career in U.S. television ("Kojak," "Columbo") and features ("Jaws 2," "Supergirl"), brings a certain breathless quality to the proceedings. Thesps remain watchable throughout, but plausibility quotient is low.

Major Gallic pubcaster TF1 co-produced pic, which may partially account for satire's blunt edge.

—*Lisa Nesselson*

March 7, 1994

THE REF

A Buena Vista release of a Touchstone Pictures presentation of a Don Simpson/Jerry Bruckheimer production. Produced by Ron Bozman, Richard LaGravenese, Jeff Weiss. Executive producers, Simpson, Bruckheimer. Directed by Ted Demme. Screenplay, Richard LaGravenese, Marie Weiss, story by Weiss. Camera (Film House color; Technicolor prints), Adam Kimmel; editor, Jeffrey Wolf; music, David A. Stewart; production design, Dan Davis; art direction, Dennis Davenport; set decoration, Jaro Dick; costume design, Judianna Makovsky; sound (Dolby), Bruce Carwardine; assistant directors, Andrew Shea, William Spahic; casting, Howard Feuer. Reviewed at Beverly Connection, L.A., March 3, 1994. MPAA Rating: R. Running time: 93 MIN.
Gus .... Denis Leary
Caroline .... Judy Davis
Lloyd .... Kevin Spacey
Jesse .... Robert J. Steinmiller Jr.
Rose .... Glynis Johns
Huff .... Raymond J. Barry
Murray .... Richard Bright

As with the recent breakthrough success of comedian Jim Carrey in "Ace Ventura: Pet Detective," bets in Hollywood have been placed on edgy, acerbic funnyman Denis Leary to hit the bigscreen jackpot. If anything, Touchstone's dark comedy "The Ref" would look to be an even longer shot than "Ace" to turn its star into a $7 million man. While "Ace" proves anything is now possible, unrelenting rough language, bitter, caustic humor and unbearable grotesqueries in place of characters seem unlikely elements to generate feel-good numbers for Simpson-Bruckheimer's first production for Disney.

A high-concept comedy that mixes O. Henry's chestnut "Ransom of Red Chief" with touches of "Home Alone" and Bunuel's "Exterminating Angel," "The Ref" mines a few laughs from the case of a high-strung cat burglar named Gus (Leary), who, after a bungled second-story job on Christmas Eve, grabs Connecticut yuppie couple Caroline (Judy Davis) and Lloyd (Kevin Spacey) as hostages while he plots his escape.

The plot-driving problem is that these are two of the most grating, unrelentingly angry neurotics one could find in this otherwise placid L.L. Beancouture paradise. Gus essentially becomes hostage to their bickering, as his hapless, largely off-screen partner in crime, Murray (Richard Bright), tries over the course of the evening to get an escape plan under way.

Co-scripted and co-produced by Richard LaGravenese, whose "The Fisher King" screenplay also mixed up seemingly disparate elements of black humor, contemporary social and psychological dysfunction with a life-affirming fade-out, "The Ref" works virtually none of the miracles of his previous mix 'n' match effort. Somewhere in this rueful mishmash there was a quirky episodic romp about the therapeutic opportunities for personal growth while being held prisoner. While it may have played as a zany guest shot for Leary on, say, "Married ... With Children," "Roseanne" or any of a dozen other sitcoms with squabbling couples, as a bigscreen vehicle the material feels stretched beyond its limits.

Odd in its premise, execution and even its release date — a winter holidays comedy in mid-March? — this pulverization of Christmas-season sentimentality and family ties takes a one-note premise and claustrophobic setting so far that its eventual message — communication and commitment are good things — arrives DOA after the third or fourth time Leary has carped his disgust at all things yuppiefied.

Unfortunately, this is early in the action and there's little to follow except repetition of the same points and the addition of more unpleasant characters, in the form of stock in-laws from hell who are dropping in for the standard, awkward yuletide gathering.

With Leary now masquerading as the couple's marriage counselor, and with the couple's teen son home from the military academy, where he has worked up a nice business blackmailing his superiors, the complications should kick up a frenzy of farcical opportunities for director Ted Demme ("Who's the Man") and Leary's signature stressed-out Everydude act. Instead it becomes a license for more verbal abuse and ugliness, as the bon mots between the leads become less and less bon, and action stagnates into a drawing-room dish session.

Judy Davis is essentially retreading her earlier shrewish role in Woody Allen's corrosive "Husbands and Wives," while Spacey fills out his milquetoast-becomes-a-man role serviceably. Vet character player Bright ("Pat Garrett and Billy the Kid") connects more strongly in his few moments on-screen, and that's probably the clearest indication how desperately the pic needs the real humanity he earnestly projects. Leary does have screen presence and a consistent bite to his bark, but with "The Ref" it's wasted on the wrong tree. —*Steven Gaydos*

ANGIE

A Buena Vista release of a Hollywood Pictures presentation in association with Caravan Pictures of a Morra-Brezner-Steinberg-Tenenbaum production. Produced by Larry Brezner, Patrick McCormick. Executive producers, Joe Roth, Roger Birnbaum. Co-producer, Todd Graff. Directed by Martha Coolidge. Screenplay, Graff, based on the novel "Angie, I Says," by Avra Wing. Camera (Technicolor; Panavision widescreen), Johnny E. Jensen; editor, Steven Cohen; music, Jerry Goldsmith; production design, Mel Bourne; art direction, Gae S. Buckley; set decoration, Etta Leff, Leslie Bloom (N.Y.); costume design, Jane Robinson; sound (Dolby), Ed Novick; sound design, Leslie Shatz; assistant director, Randall Badger; casting, Juliet Taylor. Reviewed at the Avco Cinema, L.A., Feb. 25, 1994. MPAA Rating: R. Running time: 107 MIN.
Angie Scacciapensieri ...... Geena Davis
Noel Riordan .... Stephen Rea
Vinnie .... James Gandolfini
Tina .... Aida Turturro
Frank .... Philip Bosco
Kathy .... Jenny O'Hara
Jerry .... Michael Rispoli
Joanne .... Betty Miller

"Angie" is a skin-deep feel-good movie about such less-than-breezy issues as a broken engagement, childbirth, single motherhood, infant infirmities and discovering brutal truths about your parents. By stressing the warm and giggly aspects of this viewer-friendly character study of an independent-minded Brooklyn lady, filmmakers would seem to have insured themselves a solid commercial berth at the B.O., but in the process have suppressed the psychological and dramatic potential with which the material is pregnant.

On the bright side is a star performance from Geena Davis in which the dazzling actress remains centerscreen virtually at all times, as well as an appealing turn by Stephen Rea as a wry Irish suitor who sticks around as long as it suits him. On the downside, pic goes mushy soft when confronted with its assorted heavy issues, leaving it incapable of delivering the goods required in the last reel or two.

Davis plays Angie Scacciapensieri, a spirited working girl from Bensonhurst, Brooklyn, who finds herself pregnant by her b.f., Vinnie the plumber (James Gandolfini). For a while she goes through the wedding-plan motions expected of her, but after a meet-cute with the raffish Noel (Rea), she dumps Vinnie and starts dating Noel, without any assurances the Irishman is going to be there when she needs him.

The stages of Angie's pregnancy, from the nausea to the doctor's examinations, are amusingly if lightly detailed, on the way to story's center-

piece, a childbirth scene that's played mostly for laughs.

Entertaining on a superficial level up to here, film falls entirely flat thereafter, as director Martha Coolidge is unable to successfully shift the tone to something graver and more substantial. Todd Graff's script (originally written for Madonna) clearly aspires to be deeply moving and deliver a life's-arc catharsis, but the best the film manages is to hit an occasionally touching chord.

Still, there are enough moments of recognition and heartfelt humor to keep auds on Angie's side, and Davis is a pleasure to watch throughout even though the script provides no psychological depth or complexity to her character. In his American film debut, Rea perks matters up considerably whenever he appears.

Abetted by a number of pop tunes, Jerry Goldsmith's score is effective, and tech credits are solid.
—*Todd McCarthy*

GUARDING TESS

A TriStar release of a Channel production. Produced by Ned Tanen, Nancy Graham Tanen. Directed by Hugh Wilson. Screenplay by Wilson, Peter Torokvei. Camera (Technicolor), Brian Reynolds; editor, Sidney Levin; music, Michael Convertino; production design, Peter Larkin; art direction, Charley Beal; set decoration, Leslie Rowlins; costume design, Ann Roth, Sue Gandy; sound (Dolby), James Sabat; associate producer, Jonathan Filley; assistant director, Henry Bronchtein; casting, Aleta Chappelle. Reviewed at the Avco Cinema, L.A., March 2, 1994. MPAA Rating: PG-13. Running time: 96 MIN.
Tess Carlisle .... Shirley MacLaine
Doug Chesnic .... Nicolas Cage
Earl Fowler .... Austin Pendleton
Barry Carlisle .... Edward Albert
Howard Shaeffer .... James Rebhorn
Frederick .... Richard Griffiths
Tom Bahlor .... John Roselius
Lee Danielson .... David Graf
Charles Ivy .... Dale Dye
Neal Carlo .... James Handy
Kimberly Cannon .... Susan Blommaert

There's a little gem of an idea in "Guarding Tess." The premise has a young, ambitious Secret Service agent stuck in the thankless job of protecting the widow of a U.S. president. Neither truly likes the situation but they like one another, despite constant bickering and endless infractions of protocol.

Aided and abetted by two charismatic performers and an underlying sweetness, the film is indeed likable. But director Hugh Wilson, who co-wrote the script with Peter Torokvei, just skims the surface of potentially rich territory. Comedy, pathos and thrills alternately collide, creating problems in both pacing and developing a consistent tone. Ultimately, its thinness works against it and will account for only modest theatrical returns.

Story opens with Doug Chesnic (Nicolas Cage) bidding adieu to his charge of three years, presidential widow Tess Carlisle (Shirley Mac-Laine). He returns to D.C. to take on a new assignment after the usual discreet and diplomatic debriefing session. But when told Carlisle has personally asked the president to charge him with another tour at her Ohio home, he breaks, confiding that it's the sector's worst assignment.

But if it has to be, he steels himself with the resolve to get the upper hand with the uppity former first lady. He lays down new rules as set out in the service handbook.

Doug's triumph lasts about two hours. While chowing down at a local diner, he crows to the other agents about his new rules. But moments later, when he gets a phone call from the president, Doug's expression tells all — he is out of his depth when tangling with Tess.

The battle of wills provides pic with its most amusing moments. MacLaine applies her prickliest persona and Cage embodies the ramrod, by-the-books agent. A prisoner of state and celebrity, her means of expression is defiance, whether it be sitting on the wrong side of a limo or bringing the local market to its heels on a grocery outing.

The problem is that the story develops in the most uninteresting manner. It's not about power and perception as outlined in "Being There" (and whose echoes are felt with MacLaine's presence), and it barely touches the unsettling nature of what reveals itself as essentially a mother-son relationship. Rather, it wanders into the preposterous, shifting and stripping gears when Tess is kidnapped and Doug and his men have to dig her up or wear the mantle of shame. You can be assured the conclusion yields a bumper crop of corn played out to a vapid, florid score.

MacLaine's not asked to do much more than the shrill, iron-willed matron she's come to personify. She does it well, if obviously. Cage has more fun, delineating his character right down to the way he gingerly sips alcohol or absolutely never fails to buckle his seat belt. There's also a nice little bauble from Richard Griffiths as the lady's personal nurse.

Wilson puts together a slick package that doesn't quite fit. Overall, tech credits are a little too loud and bend toward realism when fancy is wanted. But "Guarding Tess" isn't quite sure how to best accent itself, valiantly proceeding scene by scene, winning some, missing others, and finally losing the day.

—Leonard Klady

THE CHASE

A 20th Century Fox release of a Capitol Films presentation of an Elwes/Wyman production. Produced by Brad Wyman, Cassian Elwes. Executive producers, Eduard Sarlui, Charlie Sheen. Co-producer, Elliot Lewis Rosenblatt. Supervising producer, Brian Cook. Directed, written by Adam Rifkin. Camera (Film House color), Alan Jones; editor, Peter Schink; music, Richard Gibbs; production design, Sherman Williams; art direction, Jack Cloud; set decoration, Craig Loper; costume design, Yvette Correa; sound (Dolby), Tim Himes; stunt coordinator, Buddy Joe Hooker; associate producers, Hannah Leader, Romi Stepovich; assistant director, Laura Groppe; casting, Jakki Fink. Reviewed at the National Theatre, L.A., March 1, 1994. MPAA Rating: PG-13. Running time: **88 MIN.**

Jack Hammond	Charlie Sheen
Natalie Voss	Kristy Swanson
Officer Dobbs	Henry Rollins
Officer Figus	Josh Mostel
Chief Boyle	Wayne Grace
Byron Wilder	Rocky Carroll
Liam Segal	Miles Dougal
Dalton Voss	Ray Wise
Ari Josephson	Marshall Bell

Call this "The Getaway Lite." Despite considerable energy and occasional laughs, this latest effort from youthful writer/director Adam Rifkin too often feels like it was written by Beavis and Butt-Head and, as a result, should have difficulty catching up with moviegoers, except perhaps along the shoulder of the MTV crowd.

Presented virtually in real time, the story shifts into gear immediately, as an escaped convict (Charlie Sheen) kidnaps the heiress to a Donald Trump-type fortune (Kristy Swanson) in a convenience store and takes off for Mexico in her shiny red BMW. Virtually the rest of the action, believe it or not, has them in that car, as the two build a grudging relationship, with the police — as well as local TV stations — in hot pursuit.

Rifkin takes refuge from that claustrophobia sparingly, cutting back and forth to a police car occupied by two officers who are involved in the chase, a "Cops"-style film crew and, most effectively, the various media vultures trying to cash in on the story.

The opening chase sequence, with its jerky, dizzying editing techniques, feels like a fun-house ride with no exit or — with its pounding score — the worst heavy-metal video one could imagine.

"The Chase" briefly appears to right itself, offering some surprisingly big, if lowbrow, laughs — one involving carsickness, the other a truckful of medical cadavers.

Rifkin exhibits some wit in his clever skewering of TV news, with stations here engaged in an escalat-ing contest to one-up each other with the biggest "live" broadcast coup, often speculating wildly — and wrongly — about what's happening. (That local L.A. on-air talent Bree Walker and Paul Dandridge participate adds to the sense that the idiocy being lampooned isn't all that far-fetched.)

For the most part, however, "The Chase" goes nowhere, wearing out its welcome with musicvideo techniques and an equally repetitive, percussive score that will put off those who don't own a Metallica T-shirt.

Playing up its sense of teenage rebellion, Jack (Sheen), a nice guy who was wrongly convicted, wins Natalie (Swanson) over in part by telling off her dad (Ray Wise) and thumbing his nose at the authorities. The modern-day princess, meanwhile, starts to relish the idea of breaking with what's expected of her, becoming a rebel without a cause but at least possessing a tankful of gas.

While adorable, Swanson doesn't benefit from the whining Valley girl aspects of her role, which could easily be characterized as "Buffy, the Hostage." On the flip side, Sheen continues to strike the same sullen, Jack Nicholson-wannabe pose he's employed with varying degrees of success — and sporadic, self-effacing charm — in recent projects ranging from "Navy SEALs" and the "Hot Shots!" movies to "Major League."

Considering the level of high-speed carnage, tech credits are generally subpar, with the exception of the dead-on news parodies. As a closing-credit outtake featuring Sheen (who also exec produced) indicates, this is one of those projects where everyone seemed to have a better time making it than the audience will watching it.

—Brian Lowry

BERLIN FEST

UMBRELLAS

(DOCU — 16mm)

A John Kaldor and Carl Flach presentation of a Maysles Films Production. (International sales: Maysles Films, N.Y.) Produced by Henry Corra. Co-producer (California), Deborah Dickson. Directed by Corra, Grahame Weinbren, Albert Maysles. Camera (color), Maysles with Robert Richman, and Robert Leacock, Gary Stelle, Don Lenzer, Richard Pearce; editor, Weinbren; music, Phillip Johnston; sound, Corra, Ron Yoshida, Merce Williams, Roger Phenix, Bruce Perlman, Peter Miller. Reviewed at Berlin Film Festival (Forum section), Feb. 18, 1994. Running time: **90 MIN.**

Veteran *verite* helmer Albert Maysles adds his name to this highly original and structur-ally flawless collaboration between Henry Corra and Grahame Weinbren. An ambitious documentary about an ambitious environmentalist arts project by renowned New York-based "wrap" artist Christo, "Umbrellas" unfolds as an increasingly suspenseful drama.

Christo and wife Jeanne-Claude spent $26 million to raise more than 3,100 20-foot-high umbrellas along stretches of valleys in Japan and California to stunning effect for a two-week period in 1991, but nature provided some unexpected resistance.

Festival berths, web slots and specialized theatrical sites are certain for this pic, but audience response will depend on one's tolerance for the artists' unbelievable hubris, as well as one's feeling as to whether the directors have finked out by ultimately celebrating the pair more than critiquing them. (Maysles Films has shot several Christo docus and will most likely film the recently approved wrapping of the Reichstag next year.)

Pic opens in 1987, with Christo lecturing Japanese school children about his upcoming project in rural Ibaraki and California kids about his parallel effort in the Tejon Pass north of L.A.

Cut to 1991, as workers in Japan hoist blue umbrellas, their colleagues in California yellow ones. (Christo eschews sponsorship, financing much of the project through sales of drawings.) Christo and Jeanne-Claude seem to have an EST-like hold on the hordes of groupie volunteers, some of whom cloyingly mime umbrella movements.

Conflict arises when heavy rains hit Japan, and, in one of the doc's many ironies, an obstinate Christo keeps the umbrellas closed. Once they are open and Christo departs for the California site, a typhoon strikes, and an extremely bossy Jeanne-Claude takes over. (She rudely shoves aside a translator to wave goodbye to her husband.)

From the deceptive calm of California, Christo urges her to "save the project!" rather than temporarily fold up the umbrellas. Safety last seems to be his motto, and it will haunt him. In an eerie series of fades and news clips, the filmmakers show a fierce storm suddenly striking the West Coast project, and reveal how a woman was killed by a flying concrete umbrella base.

After 3 million people visited the sites, Christo agreed to close the umbrellas three days early (a Japanese construction worker was electrocuted during their removal two days

March 7, 1994 (Cont.)

later). With extraordinary chutzpah, Jeanne-Claude explains: "Christo loves his wife. He put himself in the place of the man who had just lost *his* wife. And then he said, 'We must close all the umbrellas.'"

Helmers sprinkle enough colorful talking heads and quirky behavior by locals (a California couple got married among the umbrellas) to add some humor to the somewhat somber proceedings. Maysles' camera work shows that his astute eye is still strong, Weinbren's editing is elegantly rhythmic, and Phillip Johnston's original score, which ranges from blues to bounce to big beat, is a strong plus.

—*Howard Feinstein*

DER BLAUE
(THE BLUE ONE)
(GERMAN)

A Journal Film Klaus Volkenborn, Studio Babelsberg production, in association with WDR, BR, MDR. (International sales: Journal Film Klaus Volkenborn, Berlin.) Produced by Klaus Volkenborn. Co-producer, Ernst Alexander von Eschwege. Directed, written by Lienhard Wawrzyn, from his novel. Camera (color), Martin Kukula; editor, Bettina Boehler; music, Wolfgang Hammerschmid; art direction, Dieter Doehl; costume design, Aenne Plaumann; sound (Dolby), Wolfgang Schukrafft, Manfred Arbter. Reviewed at Berlin Film Festival (competing), Feb. 18, 1994. Running time: **104 MIN.**
Dr. Otto Skrodt .... Manfred Krug
Kalle Kaminski .... Ulrich Muehe
Isabelle Skrodt .... Meret Becker
Mandy Skrodt ...... Marijam Agischewa
Werner .... Klaus Manchen
    Also with: Hanns Zischler, Margret Voelker, Jean Claude Mawila, Ralf Hirsch, Lienhard Wawrzyn.

A neatly turned script, engaging performances and smooth direction mark "The Blue One" as an accessible German item that could find a niche in offshore TV slots. Dominated by a fine study in political Machiavellianism by Manfred Krug, this cat-and-mouse drama about a former Stasi agent and his resurrected victim reps a satisfying return to features by writer/director Lienhard Wawrzyn after some eight years.

Krug, looking every inch the part, plays an oily German pol, Otto Skrodt, who's on the brink of attaining the front ranks of government. Though distanced from his daughter, Isabelle (Meret Becker), and formerly from the East, he's seemingly as clean as a whistle.

Enter youngish, affable Kalle (Ulrich Muehe), an old friend Skrodt hasn't seen since someone snitched on him when he tried to escape from East Germany. Kalle was also in love with Isabelle. After

years in jail, Kalle has two things in mind — to find out who betrayed him and to see Isabelle again.

Rest of pic is an entertaining game of bluff and counterbluff as the two men, under the guise of friendship, circle each other like vultures. Skrodt, anxious to avoid scandal, calls in the services of the former Stasi apparatchik (Klaus Manchen) who first blackmailed him into spying. Final plot twist is weak and smacks of desperation.

Pic opens with aerial shots and a driving score, and nails its colors to the non-arthouse mast. Wawrzyn avoids a straight thriller style in favor of sardonic black humor, propelled by strong characters rather than any abiding air of menace.

Main flaw is that the former friendship between the two very different men not only seems unlikely, but also has to be taken on trust.

Krug, a former East German actor who moved to West Berlin in 1977, is on the money as the Magus-like Skrodt, a seasoned survivor with six balls permanently in the air. Muehe, also from the East, matches him well as victim-turned-hunter, and there's rich playing from Manchen as a former Stasi agent who's fallen on hard times. As the daughter in the triangle, Becker is photogenic but underdrawn.

Pic is good-looking. Its title, which isn't explained till late on, refers to the nickname for unofficial Stasi informers, from the color of their files.

—*Derek Elley*

CARI FOTTUTISSIMI AMICI
(DEAR GODDAMNED FRIENDS)
(ITALIAN)

A Pentafilm-Officina Cinematografica production. Produced by Mario and Vittorio Cecchi Gori. Executive producer, Luciano Luna. Directed by Mario Monicelli. Screenplay, Monicelli, Suso Cecchi D'Amico, Leo Benvenuti, Piero de Bernardi. Camera (color), Antonio Nardi; editor, Ruggero Mastroianni; music, Renzo Arbore; production design, Franco Velchi; costumes, Lina Taviani; sound, Maurizio Argentieri. Reviewed at Berlin Film Festival (competing), Feb. 17, 1994. Running time: **118 MIN.**
Dieci (Ten) .... Paolo Villaggio
Martini .... Massimo Ceccherini
Callicchero .... Vittorio Benedetti
Calamai .... Marco Graziani
Taddei .... Giuseppe Oppedisano
Washington .... Chris Childs
Shaved Head .... Beatrice Macola
Wilma .... Antonella Ponziani
Topana .... Eva Grimaldi
Fortini .... Paolo Hendel
Zingaro .... Novello Novelli

Mainstream, grassroots Italian comedy has never exported very well, and though

veteran Mario Monicelli's "Dear Goddamned Friends" may mop up in Italy and a couple of other Euro territories, it probably won't travel, unlike its energetic characters. This World War II road movie is filled with familiar comedy ingredients and is fitfully funny, but the journey goes on much too long.

Monicelli, now in his 79th year, has been directing comedies for six decades. He started out working with the celebrated clown Toto, and is best known for "Big Deal on Madonna Street" (1958) and "The Great War" (1959). He teams here with the popular Italo comic Paolo Villaggio, a rotund thesp who worked for years on the "Fantozzi" series and who co-starred with Roberto Benigni in Federico Fellini's little-seen last film, "Voice of the Moon."

It's August 1944, and Italy has been liberated by the Allies, but in Florence there's a shortage of all essentials. Villaggio plays a former boxer nicknamed Dieci (Ten) because he always went down for the count. He dreams up the idea of gathering a few layabouts and traveling the back roads of Tuscany putting on boxing bouts to raise a little cash, or even food and wine. The fact that none of his troupe has any boxing experience doesn't much matter.

The ragged bunch, accompanied by a stray dog, set off in a ramshackle bus with no brakes and are joined along the way by a black deserter from the American Army (winningly played by Chris Childs); a woman they call Shaved Head (Beatrice Macola) because she'd slept with a German and her hair had been shaved by partisans; and, ultimately, the vengeful Wilma (Antonella Ponziani), who seeks revenge on the partisan who'd wronged her.

Comic highlights include a couple of boxing bouts, one against American soldiers in which the Italians are routed and a riot ensues. There are also running gags, like the guy who's lost his wife and his leather boots; when he finally finds the man who stole his boots, he shoots him. Basically, the film's jokes are as old as the Tuscan hills.

The countryside and small towns through which the characters pass are breathtakingly beautiful, even though scarred by war (and the war still goes on with the occasional gun battle or explosion). But the leisurely pacing, familiar material and broad comic acting won't be to the taste of many outside Italy, and the attitude toward women, though no doubt reflecting the way it was then, is also a problem.

Nevertheless, the film shows a grand old director still capably doing a professional job, and an ensemble cast who enter into the spirit of the piece.

Technical credits are all very fine, and though Renzo Arbore is the official music composer, much of the music on the soundtrack comes from the American big bands of the era — Glenn Miller, Benny Goodman, Harry James and the Dorseys.

—*David Stratton*

TIRANO BANDERAS
(BANDERAS, THE TYRANT)
(SPANISH-CUBAN-MEXICAN)

An Ion Films S.A. production, in association with Iberoamericana Films Produccion, S.A./Atrium Producciones, S.A./Promociones Audiovisuales Reunidas, S.A. in collaboration with Luz Directa S.A./I.C.A.I.C. (Cuba)/ Cinematografica del Prado (Mexico). Produced by Andres Vicente Gomez, Enrique Cerezo, Carlos Vasallo. Executive producers, Victor Manuel San Jose, Andres Vicente Gomez. Directed by Jose Luis Garcia Sanchez. Screenplay, Garcia Sanchez, Rafael Azcona, based on the novel by Ramon del Valle-Inclan. Camera (color, Panavision), Fernando Arribas; editor, Pablo G. del Amo; music, Emilio Kaudere; production design, Felix Murcia; sound, Ricardo Iztueta, Francisco Peramos. Reviewed at Cine Penalver, Madrid, Jan. 16, 1994. (In Berlin Film Festival, Panorama section.) Running time: **89 MIN.**
Santos Banderas ... Gian Maria Volonte
Lupita .... Ana Belen
Nacho Verguillas .... Juan Diego
Colonel de la
    Gandara .... Ignacio Lopez Tarso
Quintin Pereda .... Fernando Guillen
    Also with: Javier Gurruchaga, Patricio Contreras, Enrique San Francisco, Gabrilla Roel, Manuel Banderas, Daysi Granados, Omar Valdes.

Shot in Havana and Mexico, pic is presumably intended to be a sweeping period study of a bizarre Latin American tyrant in the 1920s but instead wheezes out as a disjointed, boring and superficial exercise in non sequiturs. It's as if a four-hour mini-series had been patched together as a feature, leaving out every second scene.

It's a tossup whether the "action" sequences or the yacky dialogue evokes greater tedium. None of the characters is ever explained, and though Gian Maria Volonte does a nice bit of Caligula-like thesping in the central role, his character's motivations are never explained and his ultimate death is as meaningless as the revolutionaries' huzzah.

The non-plot loosely concerns a Latin dictator in an unidentified country, one of whose daily sports is signing execution orders. He has a demented daughter who spends her time tied to a bed; a group of Spanish colonials are bullied, one of them a kind of buffoon; and there's a woman (Ana Belen) who goes into trances, a general (Lopez Tarso) who rebels and an effete Spanish ambassador. But all are skimmed

March 7, 1994 (Cont.)

over and remain paper-thin. There is never any onscreen violence, and barely a drop of blood is spilled in the revolution.

This obviously expensive and ambitious film is a total non-starter.

— *Peter Besas*

MUSIC FOR THE MOVIES: TORU TAKEMITSU

(U.S.-FRENCH-JAPANESE)

An Alternate Current (U.S.)/Les Films D'Ici, La Sept-Arte (France)/NHK (Japan) presentation. (International sales: Alternate Current, N.Y./Les Films D'Ici, Paris.) Produced by Margaret Smilow. Executive producers, Yves Jeanneau, Smilow. Directed by Charlotte Zwerin. Camera (color), Toyomichi Kurita; editors, Bernadine Colish, Zwerin; sound, Takao Itoya, Nobuyuki Tanaka, Jonathan Porath; executive producer for NHK, Tak Yamada; co-producer, Peter Grilli; co-producer for NHK, Nobuo Isobe; co-producer for La Sept-Arte, Gabrielle Babin Gugenheim; associate producers, Christine Le Goff, Sonoko Aoyagi Bowers. Reviewed at Berlin Film Festival (market), Feb. 14, 1994. Running time: **58 MIN.**

With: Toru Takemitsu, Hiroshi Teshigahara, Nagisa Oshima, Masahiro Shinoda, Masaki Kobayashi, Donald Richie.

Upscale movie buffs as well as film-music aficionados will get a charge out of this second installment in the ongoing "Music for the Movies" portraits of celluloid composers. Hourlong item is as much a reflection on '60s-'70s Japanese new wave cinema as a slice 'n' dice job on musician Toru Takemitsu himself.

Cleanly shot on Hi-Vision (with a 35mm transfer in the works), pic is from the opposite end of the spectrum to Joshua Waletzky's series opener, "Bernard Herrmann." Where the latter was an exhilarating, head-to-toe portrait of a late icon, propelled by Herrmann's motor-rhythmic music, director Charlotte Zwerin, who made the first-rate 1988 jazz docu "Thelonious Monk: Straight No Chaser," takes her stylistic cue from the still-living Takemitsu's spare sonorities and authentic Nipponese responses.

Beyond a final sliver of biography — which movingly recalls how he was inspired to compose by hearing the French song "Parlez Moi d'amour" when working in the mountains during the end of World War II — the docu records nothing of the composer's birth, background, childhood, education or non-work life.

Japan-based critic Donald Richie is the sole non-industryite to comment on Takemitsu's work. Docu also omits any mention of a short film Takemitsu himself made about a well-known Japanese drummer.

Instead, there's an abundance of top-quality clips from 16 titles, repping Takemitsu's work from the early '60s to the present, plus quality time with the self-effacing composer and interviews with name helmers like Teshigahara, Shinoda, Kobayashi and Oshima.

The relaxed reminiscences of this loose-knit group, who rebelled against the Westernized, commercial style of postwar Japanese cinema, are a fascinating document in their own right. Of particular interest are interviews with the rarely interviewed Teshigahara ("Woman in the Dunes") and Kobayashi ("Kwaidan," "Samurai Rebellion").

Clips run the gamut of Takemitsu's musical palette, from percussive scores imitating the sounds of nature (a prime source of inspiration) to offbeat orchestration (a Turkish flute in Shinoda's "Double Suicide") and the Mahlerian melancholy of Kurosawa's "Ran." Kurosawa, with whom Takemitsu had artistic differences on "Ran," is notably absent.

Takemitsu comes over as a friendly but withdrawn aesthete, with a love of movie composing equaled only by the extraordinary latitude granted by his employers. In a charming confession, he notes he'd really like to do more comedies, as most of his pix are "so dark and heavy, about murders and suicides." — *Derek Elley*

ALLES AUF ANFANG
(BACK TO SQUARE ONE)
(GERMAN)

A Von Vietinghoff Filmproduktion, with WDR (Cologne). (International sales: Matropolis Film/Cine Electra, London.) Produced by Joachim von Vietinghoff. Directed, written by Reinhard Munster. Camera (color), Axel Block; editor, Tanja Schmidbauer; music, Brynmor Llewellyn Jones; production design, Thomas Schappert; costumes, Rosi Jurat; sound, Andreas Wolki; assistant director, Heike Hempel. Reviewed at Berlin Film Festival (competing), Feb. 14, 1994. Running time: **85 MIN.**

Riki Rote	Katharina Thalbach
Lore Kuballa	Christiane Horbiger
Georg Kuballa	Harald Juhnke
Viktor Rote	Udo Samel
Nina Piel	Theresa Hubchen
Richard Rote	Florian Martens
Frank	Detlev Buck

Like most European film industries, the German one has its problems, so it's good to see a pic that encourages audiences to laugh at the local film scene. "Back to Square One" is a genuinely amusing comedy that should perform merrily at the local wickets with possible international distribution via selected fest exposure.

Writer/director Reinhard Munster has fun with the cliches of movie making and has a top cast at his disposal. He's also not at all long-winded and handles the narrative at express speed, winding up the film at a cheerful 85 minutes.

Opening and closing with a Berlin film premiere, "Square One" has elements of "All About Eve" and other showbiz yarns, with its tale of the professional rivalry between two actresses, the interference of producers, the indulgence of directors and the way everyone tends to ignore the writer. Malevolent bankers, able to shut down a production or even a film studio, also figure.

Film being preemed at the outset is "The Tin Cat," which toplines popular Riki Rote (Katharina Thalbach), wife of director Viktor Rote (Udo Samel). Viktor's socially inept but talented brother, Richard (Florian Martens), wrote the flick but isn't even allowed inside for the preem. Nor is Viktor's starlet mistress, Nina (Theresa Hubchen), an ambitious young woman who latches onto Richard as a way of getting a foot on the fame ladder.

With "Tin Cat" an instant success, producer and studio head Georg Kuballa (Harald Juhnke) gives the greenlight to the next Rote project, and the behind-the-scenes machinations begin in earnest; Georg's wealthy, and often spurned, wife Lore (Christiane Horbiger) pulls many of the financial strings when she's not dallying with her young, ambitious chauffeur (Detlev Buck).

With funny dialogue that kept Berliners happy at the screening caught, and often savagely comic situations (the vengeful Riki destroying Viktor's beloved Jaguar is a highlight), "Square One" delivers the comic goods. It needs lots of help to travel beyond German-lingo territories, however, but the effort may pay off to get this likable, though minor, pic more widely seen.

Production values are excellent.

— *David Stratton*

DAS LETZTE SIEGEL
(THE LAST SEAL)
(GERMAN)

A Jost Herring Film production, in association with NDR, WDR. Produced by Jost Herring. Directed, written by Stefan Daehnert. Camera (color), Juergen Juerges; editor, Dagmar Lichius; music, Tassilo Jelde; art direction, Volker Schaefer; sound, Rolf Hapke. Reviewed at Hof Film Festival, Hof, Germany, Oct. 28, 1993. (In Berlin Film Festival — New German Cinema.) Running time: **93 MIN.**

Priest	Josef Ostendorf
Girl	Marion Reuter

Also with: Evelyn Matzura, Nikola Weisse, Bhasker.

A comedy about trying to make a saint out of a slut, "The Last Seal" has just enough charm and gags to get auds through the first half, but after that they'll start wishing there was a storyline they could follow or a character that developed. Writer/director Stefan Daehnert's jab at the Catholic church is cute but can't seem to put any flesh on its bones, and in the end the director forgets the point he's trying to make. Don't expect great word of mouth on this one.

Pic purports to be about a small-town priest with doubts (Josef Ostendorf) who's assigned to find proof that one of his former sheep (Marion Reuter), whom he knows to have been a loose woman, really did perform the miracles that have become attached to her posthumously.

The town is dependent on her saintly reputation for additional income, and the priest, in an odd way, managed to fall in love with her. This was a woman who not only lived on the edge of society but also had the advantage of being a humanitarian whose good deeds included helping illegal immigrants.

The priest sets out on a journey of discovery in which he is intended to discover not only the truth about the woman but also anti-denominational truths about himself and life in general. Here the storyline gets entangled in too many subplots and eventually gets lost. When the priest finally decides against the church, the audience isn't quite sure why.

What helps save the film, especially in the first half, is Daehnert's oddball sense of humor. Though his uneven directing and inadequate sense of timing often don't do justice to his understated, quirky gags, they still come across.

Coupled with this is cameraman Juergen Juerges' sometimes loud, extravagant sense of color and light, at times reminiscent of "Harold and Maude."

Perfs are just this side of sparkling, however. Ostendorf's lead is fat and sweaty enough to break the image of a priest, but he isn't buoyant enough to make himself likable. Reuter's saint/slut tries too hard as a woman on the edge to be funny. Honorable mention goes to silent charmer Bhasker as an East Indian illegal immigrant flower vendor who magically pops up when he is least expected and who, though understanding nothing, saves the day every time. — *Eric Hansen*

March 7, 1994 (Cont.)

SARAHSARA

(THE WATERBABY)

(ITALIAN)

An Istituto Luce/Italnoleggio release. A Martinelli Film Co. International/RAI-TV Channel 1/Istituto Luce production. Produced, directed by Renzo Martinelli. Screenplay, Martinelli, Maurizio D'Adda, Giulio Paradisi. Script supervision, Nadine Gordimer. Camera (color), Fabio Cianchetti, Giuliano Giustini; camera operator, Martinelli; editor, Osvaldo Bargero; music, Mauro Pagani; art direction, Lisa Hart, Graeme Germond, Ada Legori; costumes, Titti De Micheli. Reviewed at International Recording, Rome, Feb. 8, 1994. (In Children's Film Festival, Berlin.) Running time: **112 MIN.**

Sarah .... Kim Engelbrecht
Gershe .... Giulio Brogi
Ciro .... Ciro Esposito
Enzo .... Lucio Allocca
Karima .... Denise Newman
Vernon .... Ricky Rudolph
Lucky .... Ray Ntlokwana
Abdul .... Gershon Palmer
(English dialogue)

A true story about a handicapped African girl who becomes a champion swimmer, "The Waterbaby" is dignified family entertainment with particular appeal for kids. Though it's mainly a heroic sports story, its South African setting lets filmmakers slip in an anti-racist message. Pic should interest TV and children's markets.

"Waterbaby" is producer/director Renzo Martinelli's first feature, but his long experience in sports documentaries and commercials explains film's slick, pro look. Especially exciting are the swimming scenes, lensed underwater and above with special equipment that allows the cameraman to move at high speed.

Tale is based on the exploits of a Sudanese girl, Gadalla Gubara, who swam 22 miles at the 1974 Capri-Naples long-distance race and came in fourth — despite being crippled in one leg. With the help of Nobel Prize winner Nadine Gordimer, who revised the script, Martinelli switches the setting to South Africa.

Sarah (Kim Engelbrecht) is the daughter of well-to-do parents who send her to an elite school and encourage her to swim. She suffers from the double discrimination of being "colored" and having a handicap.

Gershe (Giulio Brogi), a badly worn sportswriter and drunk, becomes Sarah's trainer after an hour of screen time and infinite coaxing. But once he gets started, Sarah is ready for the Capri-Naples race in no time. Though the South African Swimming Federation refuses to enroll her (for both of the aforementioned reasons), Gershe and his pint-sized sidekick (Ciro Esposito) refuse to take no for an answer. They follow Sarah through the grueling race and on to victory.

The characters are clearly drawn and appealing. Lithe, fresh Engelbrecht is a discovery as the heroine, demure and a little mysterious yet emotionally communicative. The Neapolitan-born Esposito, playing a 12-year-old mechanic who runs a garage in Capetown, adds a much-needed note of comic skepticism to an often saccharine storyline. Brogi does a good job of individualizing the cliche-ridden role of a down-and-out Italian who has become "buried in the sand" bumming around Africa. Denise Newman also rises above stereotypes as Sarah's loving, courageous mother.

Though script is generally absorbing, it sometimes gets sidetracked — the dramatically unnecessary murder of Sarah's father is a blatant example. Also, South Africa's racial problems come in for some gross simplifications, marking "Waterbaby" as a children's film. But these shortcomings shouldn't hurt it commercially.

Pic's fancy cinematography and art direction create a bright, attractive environment dominated by light blue — the color of the pool, but also of African walls and murals. A trip across the desert gives lensers a chance to show off some breathtaking natural scenery. The only false note is Mauro Pagani's "We Are the Children"-style music track. On the rare occasions that local African sounds are used, pic benefits 100%.

Exploiting his advertising connections, Martinelli has worked out an innovative scheme for launching the film in Italy. The national swimming federation will sponsor its premiere in Rome, social-minded sportswear manufacturer Benetton is sponsoring screenings in elementary schools, and controversial ad king Oliviero Toscani designed the posters. —*Deborah Young*

BOXER REBELLION

(DOCU — B&W)

Executive producer, David Lawrence. Directed, edited by Celia Cotelo. Camera (b&w), Jean Marie Meyer; music, Meyer, Mark Linden; sound, Linden. Reviewed at Sundance Film Festival, Park City, Utah, Jan. 25, 1994. Running time: **73 MIN.**

Drowned in striking visuals and dizzying sounds, but devoid of much substance, "Boxer Rebellion" is an impressionistic documentary about a Wall Street yuppie who became a professional boxer in middle age. Celia Cotelo's ambitious effort to portray the inner workings of an obsessive psyche is so intense and hard to watch that it might be limited almost exclusively to the festival and arthouse circuits.

David Lawrence, a wealthy and powerful stockbroker, was quite content with his life until he discovered the allure, risk and challenge of the boxing world. At 44, Lawrence was not young, but with the assistance of a great trainer — and obsessive urge to succeed in a milieu totally different from his own — he mastered the necessary skills and even excelled at the brutal sport.

Cotelo should be congratulated for resisting a traditional form to tell the bizarre odyssey of her unusual hero. In moments — but only in moments — she achieves brilliance, as when Lawrence is dressed as a surreal clown who fondles a Barbie doll, or when he hangs dollar bills on a clothesline to dry while expressing his inner thoughts and emotions about boxing.

Though innovative in style, "Boxer Rebellion" falls short of its goal of exploring a complex mind and provoking viewers about their own anxieties and aggressions. Clearly, Cotelo has tried to make an innovative film, the cinematic corollary of a poem, but Lawrence's statements never go beyond the fraudulent existentialism of "boxing makes me feel young" or addressing the audience directly with "I am what you're afraid to be."

Indeed, after 30 minutes or so, the surreal imagery and distorted sounds become so repetitious, and the disjointed symbols and metaphors pile up so voluminously, that it's understandable that "Boxer Rebellion" had the largest number of walkouts of any documentary shown this year at Sundance.
—*Emanuel Levy*

MAMA AWETHU!

(DOCU — 16mm)

A Tapestry Intl. production. Produced, directed by Bethany Yarrow. Camera (color), Yarrow; editors, Bethany and Mary Beth Yarrow. Reviewed at Sundance Film Festival, Park City, Jan. 24, 1994. Running time: **53 MIN.**

Original in intent but flawed in structure and lacking analytic focus, Bethany Yarrow's first documentary, "Mama Awethu!," follows the lives of five black African women as they face the daily realities of the apartheid regime in Cape Town. Despite its shortcomings, however, the opportunity to listen to firsthand information, from a strictly female perspective, about oppression in South Africa should insure this docu screenings on the film festival circuit, public TV and in political venues.

What makes pic distinctive is its spotlight on ordinary, grass-roots women rather than the leaders of the South African resistance movement. Yarrow sees her docu as a corrective to works that have centered on men.

The women's personal observations are always interesting. Iris, a community health-care worker, recalls how she lost two children in violent incidents and talks about her arduous struggle to put five others through school.

The beautiful and articulate Sheila discusses her political activism, ever since she was in high school, where she would hide banned documents in her bible. In contrast, Dinah, who lives in a tiny house with her family of nine, became politically engaged only when her neighbor was murdered.

First-time director Yarrow, daughter of folk singer Peter Yarrow, lensed this in summer 1992 while a student at Yale. Her lack of experience shows, for her film offers only glimpses of these women's existence.

It also fails to provide the political context that would give broader meaning and significance to the often fascinating stories. As it stands, "Mama Awethu!" doesn't delve deeply enough into these women's lives or motivations, which is partly a function of its short running time.

Some of the footage is remarkable, but overall quality is uneven. Pic also lacks analytic control as it shifts from one woman to another, talking about different issues.
—*Emanuel Levy*

PAS TRES CATHOLIQUE

(SOMETHING FISHY)

(FRENCH)

An AB Films/3eme Etage/M6 Films/
Planetes & Compagnie production, in
association with Cite Films/Legende
Prods., with participation of Bymages
2/Canal Plus. (International sales:
CIBY Sales, London.) Produced by
Michel Propper, Frederic Bourboulon.
Directed, written by Tonie Marshall.
Camera (color), Dominique Chapuis;
editor, Jacques Comets; art direction,
Marie-Pierre Bourboulon; costume de-
sign, Valerie Pozzo Di Borgo; sound,
Alix Comte, Gerard Lamps; assistant
director, Alain Peyrollaz. Reviewed at
Berlin Film Festival (competing), Feb.
12, 1994. Running time: **100 MIN.**
Maxime Chabrier .... Anemone
M. Paul .... Roland Bertin
Baptiste .... Gregoire Colin
Jacques Devinais .... Michel Didym
Martin .... Denis Podalydes
Vaxelaire .... Bernard Verley
Florence .... Christine Boisson
Mme. Loussine .... Micheline Presle

Though dominated by a striking, lived-in performance
from Gallic comedienne
Anemone, "Something Fishy" is
too easygoing for its own good.
Gently comic portrait of a 40ish
female gumshoe whose personal
life is as loose-fitting as her wardrobe, this sophomore effort from
Tonie Marshall (daughter of actors Micheline Presle and William Marshall) has many fine moments but would have benefited
from tighter scripting and dramatic focus. Pleasant pic looks
unlikely to net many arthouse
sales offshore.

Anemone is Maxime, a chain-
smoking, slobby private investigator who's estranged from her son
and ex-husband and occasionally
jumps in the sack with her elegant
friend Florence (Christine Boisson)
for some womanly tender loving
care. Unconventional but good at
her job, she suddenly starts to hear
hetero music again after literally
being swept off her feet by handsome, laid-back economist Jacques
(Michel Didym).

Among the many cases on which
she's working, one implicates her
smoothie ex-husband in an insurance scam and draws her closer to
her grown-up son, Baptiste (Gregoire Colin). In personal terms,
however, it's still a dead end, and
she's finally forced to choose whether to throw caution to the wind and
go off with Jacques on a lovefest or
stick with the solo life.

Anemone, with more than a passing resemblance to Bette Midler, is
excellent as the woman at a crossroads and puts to good use her dry
humor and ballsy putdowns. Equally good at goofy comedy and more
intimate scenes — and bringing an
easy sexuality to her sack sessions
with both Boisson and Didym — the
actress seems made for the role.

She's well supported by a galaxy
of character actors in background
parts, plus Colin as her independent, off-center son and Denis Podalydes as her confused, gay colleague. Presle herself pops up briefly in a disposable cameo as a grieving widow. Though technically OK,
film lacks a strong directorial presence and visual style, with scenes
strung together rather than individually advancing the storyline.
Color processing also has a somewhat steely, unwelcoming look.
—*Derek Elley*

ELS DE DAVANT

(THE WINDOW ACROSS THE WAY)

(SPANISH-FRENCH)

A Massa d'Or (Barcelona)-Le Sabre
(Paris) co-production. (International
sales: Revcom Intl., Paris.) Produced
by Pierre Javaux, Isona Passola. Directed by Jesus Garay. Screenplay,
Louis Gardel, from a book by Georges
Simenon. Camera (color), Carles Gusi;
editor, Albena Katerinska; music, Beat-
rice Thiriet; production design, Llorenc
Miquel; costumes, Patricia Marne;
sound, Antonietta Georgieva. Re-
viewed at Berlin Film Festival (compet-
ing), Feb. 13, 1994. Running time:
99 MIN.
Adil Bey .... Juanjo Puigcorbe
Sonia Koline .... Estelle Skornik
John .... Ben Gazzara
Nejla .... Carme Elias
Fikret .... Gricha Tchernov
Mme. Pendelli .... Ifka Zafirova
M. Pendelli .... Boris Loukanov

This is a strange, somber
drama, derived from a book by
Belgian writer Georges Simenon, set in a harbor town in Soviet Georgia in 1932. Mixture of
intrigue and sex pulls its punches
and never really jells, and the central character is hard to root for,
making this 1992 Catalan production problematic.

Juanjo Puigcorbe gives a morose
performance as Adil Bey, a Turkish
diplomat assigned as consul at the
Black Sea city of Batum after the
mysterious death of his predecessor. From his run-down office/
apartment, he looks across the
street into the window of an apartment housing a security cop, his
wife and sister.

The sister, Sonia (Estelle
Skornik), turns out to have been the
secretary/mistress of Adil's predecessor, and he's soon lusting after
the innocent-looking beauty himself. He also suspects he's being poisoned, which may have been how
his predecessor died.

Director Jesus Garay filmed this
strange tale on location in Sofia, Bulgaria, which convincingly stands in
for Batum; the film's main asset is the
hot, fetid atmosphere of this obscure
town, where the only other diplomats
are a pair of snobbish Italians and a
Persian with a faithless wife.

Skornik is appealing as the somewhat mysterious woman from across
the street, and Ben Gazzara registers
in an odd role as a local official.

Production values are all very
fine for this curious, ultimately disappointing item. —*David Stratton*

GRANDE PETITE

(THE TALL LITTLE ONE)

(FRENCH)

A Pierre Grise Prods. release
(France) of a Paris New York Prods.
production in association with CNC,
Canal Plus. (International sales: Mercure Distribution, Paris.) Executive
producer, Claude Kunetz. Directed,
written by Sophie Fillieres. Camera
(color), Benoit Delhomme; editor, Lise
Beaulieu; music, Rene-Marc Bini; art
direction, Antoine Platteau; costume
design, Ounie Lecomte; sound, Frederic Ullman, Jean-Pierre Laforce; assistant director, Alain Olivieri. Reviewed at Berlin Film Festival (Forum
section), Feb. 13, 1994. Running time:
105 MIN.
Benedicte .... Judith Godreche
Henri .... Hugues Quester
Paul .... Emmanuel Salinger
Pierre .... Philippe Demarle
Laurence .... Helene Fillieres
With: Marie-Christine Questerbert,
Roger Knobelspiess.

"Grande petite" is an exasperating slice of intro-
verted cinema. Direction-
less tale about a screwed-up
young femme who can't get it together on any level in her life
looks set for the B.O. bin. Pic
opens in France March 23.

Audience at pic's Berlin fest preem
started out grande but was petite by
the time the lights came up.

Benedicte (Judith Godreche) is a
reserved 20-year-old living with an
older man (Hugues Quester). She
still carries a torch for her ex-b.f.
Pierre (Philippe Demarle) and can't
shake off the curbside attentions of
another former boyfriend, Paul
(Emmanuel Salinger).

One day, her life looks poised to
be transformed when she stumbles
across a bag containing a gun and
500,000 francs. However, as in other
areas, indecision rules: She herself
can't decide whom to tell or whether to return the money, and her best
friend (Helene Fillieres) and mother (Marie-Christine Questerbert)
aren't any help. The men in her life
are equally hopeless. Ending returns the story to ground zero.

In its portrait of a painfully anal,
repressed loner, pic often recalls
Patricia Bardon's 1991 "L'Homme
imagine" ("The Man of Her Imagination"), though without that film's
strain of black comedy and inventiveness. Godreche is on the money
as Benedicte, with good support
from Quester, Demarle and Salinger as the men, but debuting director Sophie Fillieres' script is as boring and uninteresting as her main
character.

Photography by Benoit Delhomme is sharp and nicely composed. At least on a tech level, pic is
confident throughout.

—*Derek Elley*

CRIMINAL

(B&W — 16mm)

A Mallan Film production. Produced
by David Jacobson, Wolfgang Held.
Executive producers, Alex Jacobson,
Beate Veldtrup, Peter Franz Stein-
bach. Directed, written by David Ja-
cobson. Camera (b&w), Held; editor,
David Jacobson; production design,
Manuel Wilhelm; sound, John Murray;
creative consultant, Chaim Bianco; as-
sistant director, Sepideh Farsi. Re-
viewed at Berlin Film Festival (Forum
section), Feb. 16, 1994. Running time:
79 MIN.
Gus .... Ralph Feliciello
Gina .... Liz Sherman
Marjorie .... Sheila York
John .... Eric Reid
Tim .... Gianfranco Piras
Salesman .... Tim Miller
Lover .... Jim Myers
Phyllis .... Mikki Moine

A familiar tale of middle-aged
angst and dislocation is given
assured treatment in this first
feature by David Jacobson, but
there may not be too many paying
customers willing to participate
in the experience. Pic's main
asset is the quite beautiful b&w
photography by co-producer
Wolfgang Held.

Gus (Ralph Feliciello) is a middle-
age man in a dead-end job, married
to the demanding Marjorie (Sheila
York), who wants him to buy an
ugly suburban house he can't afford. On an impulse, he steals
money from his firm and makes the
down payment. When he returns
home to tell Marjorie the good
news, he discovers her in the shower with a lover.

So he hits the road, winding up in
the Niagara Falls area of upper
New York, where he meets Gina
(Liz Sherman), a maid at a hotel
there, who has fallen out with her
boyfriend, John (Eric Reid). Gus
and Gina share a bed and some
dreams of the future for a few hours,

but inevitably Gus, a born loser, is going nowhere.

It's not exactly original material, and the actors are forced to make the best of stock characterizations. But the moody atmosphere of upper New York State, and especially the Niagara Falls region, is evocatively caught.

Tech credits are generally good on what was obviously a low-budget effort. —David Stratton

UVLETSCHENIA
(PASSIONS/AVOCATIONS)
(RUSSIAN)

A Nikola Film production, in association with Roskomkino. Produced by Igor Kalionov. Directed, written by Kira Muratova. Camera (color), Genady Karjuk; editor, Valentina Oleynik; music, Beethoven; production design, Eugeny Golubenko; sound, Emmanuel Segal. Reviewed at Berlin Film Festival (Panorama section), Feb. 20, 1994. Running time: **112 MIN.**

Violetta	Svetlana Kolenda
Nurse Lila	Renata Litvinova
Kasjanov	Mikhail Demidov
Nikolayev	Vassili Rybakin
Milashevski	Alexei Schevtshenko
Amirov	Genagy Tkatshenko

K ira Muratova, the femme helmer who used to get into trouble with Soviet authorities over her very personal films, has become more obscure since the end of communism. It's difficult to fathom what her latest, variously known as "Passions" and "Avocations," is all about. Unless a Muratova cult develops in the West, there'll be few bookings for this one.

The no-plot pic concentrates on people who share a passion for horses. Opening scene takes place on the grounds of a hospital near the sea. An injured jockey is recovering, though still confined to a wheelchair. Lila, a nurse, introduces him to Violetta, a kooky circus performer. The three, plus a couple of smartly dressed men who may be hospital orderlies, talk about the differences between circus horses and racehorses. There are hints of sexual innuendo in the dialogue, but nothing definite emerges.

The scene then shifts to stables and a racetrack, where gunfire is sometimes heard in the background (the scanty synopsis explains we are now in Central Asia). A fashion photographer and his slinky models pose alongside horses. The talk is still of horses, with the dialogue more obscure than ever.

References to classical literature and politics abound, but Muratova keeps her artistic cards close to her chest. Technically professional,

with excellent camera work, "Passions" is a tough sell by any standard. —David Stratton

GUNHED
(JAPANESE)

A Manga Entertainment release (U.K.) of a Toho Co., Sunrise production. Produced by Gunhed Production Committee. Executive producers, Tomoyuki Tanaka, Eiji Yamamura. Directed by Masato Harada. Screenplay, Harada, James Bannon. Camera (color), Junichi Fujisawa; editor, Fumio Ogawa; music, Toshiyuki Honda; special visual effects, Koichi Kawakita; mechanical designs, Masaharu Kamahari. Reviewed at De Lane Lea Preview Theater, London, Feb. 4, 1994. Running time: **99 MIN.**

Brooklyn	Masahiro Takashima
Sgt. Nim	Brenda Bakke
Seven	Yujin Harada
Eleven	Kaori Mizushima
Bebe	Aya Enyoji
Bancho	Mickey Curtis
Balba	James B. Thompson
Boomerang	Doll Nguyen
(English soundtrack)	

"G unhed" is a hokey slab of Nipponese sci-fi that's OK for buffs but not high-key enough to break into wider markets. Five-year-old production, pairing Brenda Bakke alongside local name Masahiro Takashima, looks like a Ridley Scott/James Cameron knockoff and plays like a Japanese comic strip with live actors.

Setting is the Pacific island 8JO in the year 2039, 13 years after a megabattle in which the island's super computer, Chiron 5, successfully defended itself against a battalion of Gunheds (unmanned robots) sent by the World Union Government to curb its global ambitions.

A group of "treasure hunters," led by Japanese mechanic Brooklyn (Takashima), land on 8JO to salvage Chiron 5's computer chips. After bumping into a Texas Air Ranger (Bakke) on a mission of her own, plus two young kids — Seven and Eleven (get it?) — who survived the war there, everyone suddenly discovers Chiron 5 is warming up for another attempt at world domination. Brooklyn manages to repair a damaged Gunhed for a final showdown with the billion-dollar brain.

Pic cruises along in second gear most of the time, with authentically cheesy dialogue, unflashy f/x, good model work, a bland pop-synth soundtrack and light, jokey tone. Hardware-heavy visuals and graybrown color scheme ape any number of futuristic flicks. Compositions mirror comic-strip art rather than being cinematic in their own right.

Things pick up in the final half-hour, which eventually delivers the

action goods without springing any major surprises. Lack of widescreen and Dolby sound is a handicap, however, and a couple of gaping plot holes look like the result of trimming.

As the carrot-chewing mechanic who starts a wimp and ends up a hero, Takashima takes his time but develops an easygoing charm. Bakke, clad in a figure-hugging rubber suit, makes a tough and sexy Texas Ranger but voices her lines as if she can't wait to get home. Pic was reportedly a B.O. hit for Toho on local release in 1989.

—Derek Elley

NEO-TOKYO/ SILENT MOBIUS
(JAPANESE — ANIMATED)

A Streamline Pictures release. Executive producer, Haruki Kadokawa. English version produced, directed by Carl Macek. ADR script, Ardwight Chamberlain ("Neo-Tokyo"), Tom Wyner ("Silent Mobius"); postproduction, Tom Merchant, Scott Narrie; music, Mickey Yoshino ("Neo-Tokyo"). Reviewed at Coolidge Corner Theatre, Brookline, Mass. (In SF/19: Annual 24-Hour Sci-Fi Movie Marathon, Feb. 20-21, 1994.) Running time: **103 MIN.**

NEO-TOKYO:

LABYRINTH

Directed by Rin Taro. Screenplay, Taro; character design, Atsuko Fukushima; art direction, Yamako Ishikawa.

RUNNING MAN

Directed by Yoshiaki Kawajiri. Screenplay, Kawajiri; art direction, Katsushi Aoki; backgrounds, Yuji Ikehata.

THE ORDER TO STOP CONSTRUCTION

Directed by Katsuhiro Otomo. Screenplay, Otomo; art director, Takamuro Mukuo.

SILENT MOBIUS

Produced by Haruki Kadokawa. Directed by Michitaka Kikuchi. Screenplay, Kei Shigema, Kikuchi; music, Kaoru Wada; art direction, Norihiro Hiraki; character design, Kikuchi.

Voices (English version): Robert Axelrod (Sugioka), Jeff Winkless (Robot 444-1), Michael McConnohie (reporter Bob Stone), Cheryl Chase (Sachi), Tom Wyner (Boss), Iona Morris (Katsumi), Alexandra Kenworthy (Miyuka), Joyce Kurtz (Kiddy), Jeff Winkless (Lucifer Hawke), Wendy Lee (Nami), Malora Harte (Rally), Barbara Goodson (Lebia), Julie Donald (Yuki).

S treamline Pictures is billing this as a "spectacular double bill of contemporary Japanese animation," but it's really a featurette and three shorts combined into two separately titled films. Pix will acquire must-see

status among aficionados of Japanese "anime," while more mainstream sci-fi/horror/fantasy genre fans may continue to wonder what all the fuss is about.

"Neo-Tokyo" consists of three films, none of which really have anything to do with Tokyo. Rin Taro's "Labyrinth" and Yoshiaki Kawajiri's "Running Man" are heavy on style and short on character and plot.

In the former, a young girl and a cat are pulled through a mirror into a ghostly world, while in the latter a champion race driver literally races to death. (An edited version of "Running Man" has appeared on MTV's "Liquid TV" series.)

While stylish, the problem is that viewers are simply asked to appreciate effects, since there is no point to either film.

"The Order to Stop Construction" (written and directed by Katsuhiro Otomo, who did the feature-length "Akira") is the standout. A low-level executive for a Japanese firm is sent to a South American country, where the revolutionary government has just canceled the company's contract. His orders are simple: End the project.

The problem is that the project is to build a city with an entirely robot crew, and the robot foreman refuses to let anything interfere with the completion of the job, including human management. The visuals are dramatic and the story is sharply ironic.

Michitaka Kikuchi's "Silent Mobius" also has a narrative, but its problems are connected to its being based on a popular Japanese comic book largely unknown to Western audiences. As a result, the film — which covers the origins of a young woman joining the Abnormal Mystery Police — fails to achieve the resonance it obviously intends.

The story focuses on Katsumi, who, in the year 2024, learns that she has inherited magical powers from her mother and must battle a demon named Lucifer Hawke. While the effects are suitably apocalyptic, audiences without the foreknowledge they bring to, say, the "Superman" or "Batman" films, may find themselves at sea.

They may also be confused by a magical sign that is, in fact, a sixpointed Star of David. No explanation is offered for the changing of the traditional pentagram to the Jewish symbol.

Japanimation tends to sell itself on its look, and the visuals in all four offerings are impressive. But if "anime" is to achieve a Western audience beyond the cultists, "The Order to Stop Construction" shows that it is a tight, coherent story that will get audiences to pay attention.

The American versions were released in 1993, although the Japanese films carry 1986 copyright for "Neo-Tokyo" and 1991 for "Silent Mobius." —*Daniel M. Kimmel*

THE PAPER

A Universal release of an Imagine Entertainment presentation of a Brian Grazer production. Produced by Grazer, Frederick Zollo. Executive producers, Dylan Sellers, Todd Hallowell. Co-producer, David Koepp. Directed by Ron Howard. Screenplay, David Koepp, Stephen Koepp. Camera (Deluxe color), John Seale; editors, Daniel Hanley, Michael Hill; music, Randy Newman; production design, Hallowell; art direction, Maher Ahmad; set decoration, Debra Schutt; costume design, Rita Ryack; sound, Danny Michael; associate producers, Louisa Velis, Aldric La'auli Porter; assistant director, Porter; second unit director, Hallowell; casting, Jane Jenkins, Janet Hirshenson. Reviewed at Universal Studios, Universal City, March 2, 1994. MPAA Rating: R. Running time: **110 MIN.**

Henry Hackett	Michael Keaton
Bernie White	Robert Duvall
Alicia Clark	Glenn Close
Martha Hackett	Marisa Tomei
McDougal	Randy Quaid
Graham Keighley	Jason Robards
Marion Sandusky	Jason Alexander
Paul Bladden	Spalding Gray
Susan	Catherine O'Hara
Janet	Lynne Thigpen
Phil	Jack Kehoe
Carmen	Roma Maffia
Ray Blaisch	Clint Howard
Lou	Geoffrey Owens
Robin	Amelia Campbell
Deanne White	Jill Hennessy
Henry's Father	William Prince
Henry's Mother	Augusta Dabney
Carl	Bruce Altman
Wilder	Jack McGee

A rambunctious look at a day in the life of a struggling New York tabloid, "The Paper" is Paddy Chayefsky lite. With every member of the all-star staff battling personal life crises as they race to put the next edition to bed, Ron Howard's pacy meller can't help but generate a fair share of humor, excitement and involvement, even if it veers off the tracks in the final reels with some contrived, over-the-top theatrics. Good cast and the usual Howard/Brian Grazer instinct for entertainment value should translate into B.O. that rates page one, if perhaps below the fold rather than a banner headline.

Likable, underdog status of nearly the entire cast of characters is fixed from the outset, as the New York Sun is established as a financially precarious sheet (in the mold of the real-life Post and Daily News) desperately trying to hold head above water in tough economic times, even if it remains the sixth-largest daily in the nation.

Setting the wheels and presses in motion this hot summer day is the brutal murder of a pair of white men in a parked car. Two black teens who were glimpsed at the scene are quickly arrested, and the paper's forces mobilize to fan the city's racial tensions by putting the youths on the front page with the headline "Gotcha!"

But, as they used to say, there are 8 million stories in the naked city, and this movie's got a few of them. Under pressure from his mucho pregnant wife, Martha (Marisa Tomei), to get a better-paying job, Sun Metro editor Henry Hackett (Michael Keaton) halfheartedly interviews at the snooty N.Y. Sentinel (read Times), where he sneaks a look at the note pad of his would-be future boss (Spalding Gray) and steals some key info for the Sun.

Crusty old-school editor Bernie White (Robert Duvall) hacks through a staff meeting before getting the bad news about his prostate cancer from his doctor and, after trying to reconcile with his resentful daughter (Jill Hennessy), repairs to a bar for the rest of the day, leaving the paper in the hands of managing editor Alicia Clark (Glenn Close), who finds the time for a hotel quickie with her lover and prepares for a showdown over her contract that night with her publisher (Jason Robards).

Putting together clues based on the filched tip, Henry and rumpled staffer McDougal (Randy Quaid) conclude that the teenagers about to be branded killers are innocent and the hit was actually the work of the mob. This leads to sniffing around for leaks at police h.q., Henry missing a dinner with his wife and in-laws intended to celebrate his new job at the Sentinel and, after deadline has long since passed, a pitched battle between Henry and a royally p.o.'d Alicia over which front-page story will roll off the presses.

It's at this point that David and Stephen Koepp's screenplay begins careening in unsafe directions. Close's intensely physical brawl with Keaton, motivated solely by her desire to save money, brings out her "Fatal Attraction" hissability.

Thereafter, everyone joins their boss in a local bar, as if they were congregating for an episode of "Cheers," where a city official is laying in wait with a gun for McDougal, who made him look bad in print. Everybody goes a little crazy, but somehow the Sun will rise the next day with a measure of tattered glory intact.

At the moments when it becomes most antic and tries to propound truths about journalism and human nature, "The Paper" unavoidably recalls a watered-down version of such Chayefsky classics as "Network" and "The Hospital," in which prominent and pressurized institutions underwent the knife as wielded by one of the day's foremost verbal surgeons. There's nothing here nearly that incisive or outrageous, and the main feeling one comes away with is that what ends up in a newspaper everyday is almost a matter of accident.

But even if the vitriol runs thin, the film does have some juice coursing through its veins along with the ink. Howard keeps the cynical dialogue coming and the scenes punchy (if literally too much so toward the end), making for a generally lively, if somewhat hokey, outing.

He's handsomely helped by his uniformly talented actors, all of whom snap out the lines, good and bad, like the crafty pros they are, even if they aren't hitting any unfamiliar notes. As could be expected, a bunch of cranky individualists fill out the briefly drawn supporting staff of the paper.

Visually, film is kept interesting and airy by virtue of the newsroom's location on a high floor of a Lower Manhattan building that's all windows, which means that almost anywhere lenser John Seale points his very mobile camera, there's a dramatic panorama of New York backdropping the action. All other behind-the-scenes contributions are solid.

—*Todd McCarthy*

LIGHTNING JACK

(AUSTRALIAN)

A Savoy Pictures release of a Lightning Ridge/Village Roadshow production. Produced by Paul Hogan, Greg Coote, Simon Wincer. Executive producers, Graham Burke, Anthony Stewart. Directed by Wincer. Screenplay by Hogan. Camera (Atlab color), David Eggby; editor, O. Nicholas Brown; music, Bruce Rowland; production design, Bernard Hides; art direction, Lisette Thomas, Virginia Bieneman (Australia); set decoration, Lynn Wolverton Parker, Susan Maybury (Australia); costume design, Bruce Finlayson; sound (Dolby), Bud Alper, Lloyd Carrick (Australia); line producer, Grant Hill; assistant director, Bob Donaldson; second unit director/stunt coordinator, Bill Burton; casting, Mike Fenton, Julie Ashton. Reviewed at Savoy Pictures screening room, Santa Monica, March 5, 1994. MPAA Rating: PG-13. Running time: **93 MIN.**

Lightning Jack Kane	Paul Hogan
Ben Doyle	Cuba Gooding Jr.
Lana	Beverly D'Angelo
Pilar	Kamala Dawson
Marshal Kurtz	Pat Hingle
Marcus	Richard Riehle
Mr. Doyle	Frank McRae
John T. Coles	Roger Daltry
Sheriff	L.Q. Jones
Bart	Max Cullen

March 14, 1994 (Cont.)

While it's unlikely to cement a new era for the Western, "Lightning Jack" is a good-natured, if laconic, oater that rides along nicely on the screen persona of writer/actor Paul Hogan. But without the inspired zaniness of earlier Hogan efforts, don't expect "Jack" to "Croc" 'em at the box office. This is a commercial mosey on the range that plays well as a programmer and should go on to decent ancillary and foreign returns.

It would be a stretch to merely pass the effort off as "Crocodile Dundee" goes west and back in time. Hogan's Lightning Jack Kane is not as much of a fish out of water here. There are tinges of national pride, but Jack is passing through town only to elude the law and not to board a steamer headed Down Under.

The fictional outlaw is a minor member of the notorious Younger Brother gang lucky enough to dodge a hail of bullets and escape while his cohorts ride into the history books. He might have disappeared too, save for a newspaper article that dismissed his importance to the criminal consortium. So, he sets out to rob a bank and winds up grabbing a paltry sum and a mute named Ben (Cuba Gooding Jr.) as a hostage.

When it comes time to release his charge, however, Ben makes it clear he'd rather adopt outlaw ways. Jack initially resists but soon finds Ben's camaraderie and usefulness hard to discard.

Hogan's script rides into familiar terrain and pokes fun at convention without establishing a crisp, new spin. There's a foray into the politics of the new frontier, treacherous passage through Indian territory and the requisite whorehouse stop to meet up with long-suffering, good-natured g.f. Lana (Beverly D'Angelo).

Hogan relies on personality rather than narrative. That approach provides him the opportunity to feign cowardice and put the pin in macho posturing when it's revealed vain Jack ought to be wearing spectacles to see his way through trouble. The role fits Hogan like a glove.

The supporting cast isn't provided much to hang a hat upon. D'Angelo, Pat Hingle's blustery lawman and L.Q. Jones' bad-man-turned-peace-officer are to type, albeit given dignity by the performers. Gooding is less fortunate in a sidekick role too reliant on bug-eyed response and lap-dog obedience.

Director Simon Wincer is right at home in the saddle after such forays as "Phar Lap" and "Lonesome Dove." "Lightning Jack" has an easy lope and an uncluttered visual style that works well with the material.

This throwback to the likes of "Cat Ballou" comes up a tad short on hilarity and action. Still, its good-natured joshing carries the audience along for an enjoyable, scenic ride. —*Leonard Klady*

SANTA BARBARA

HANDGUN

A Workin' Man Films production in association with Odessa Films/Shooting Gallery. Produced by Bob Gosse, Larry Meistrich. Exec producers, Richard Abromowitz, Mark Balsam, Mitchell Maxwell. Directed, written by Whitney Ransick. Camera (color), Michael Spiller; editor, Tom McCardle; music, Douglas J. Cuomo; production design, Andras Kanegson; sound, Jeff Pullman; associate producers, David Tuttle, Bill McCutchen; casting, Lina Todd. Reviewed at Santa Barbara Intl. Film Festival, March 5, 1994. Running time: **90 MIN.**

George McCallister	Treat Williams
Jack McCallister	Seymour Cassel
Michael McCallister	Paul Schulze
Ted	Toby Huss
Roy	Angel Caban
Earl	Frank Vincent

As a comic spin on the action/heist genre, "Handgun" resembles a cross between Hal Hartley's "Simple Men" and Quentin Tarantino's "Reservoir Dogs." Whitney Ransick's low-budget feature directorial debut is technically uneven, but its sharp dialogue and superlative performances, particularly by Treat Williams, should insure it a place on the festival circuit. Additional post-production work on the editing and sound might increase chances for theatrical release.

Wounded during a robbery that goes awry, Jack McCallister (Seymour Cassel) escapes with half a million in payroll booty, which he stashes in a locker. But as soon as the news gets around, a gallery of dubious characters, headed by McCallister's two sons, set out on a desperate hunt for the stolen cash.

Like "Simple Men," "Handgun" spins an intergenerational tale of a criminal father and his two strange but endearing sons. McCallister's elder son, George (Williams), is a violent thief who's as quick with words as he is with his gun. Michael (Paul Schulze), his baby brother, is an elegantly dressed, small-time con artist. Estranged for years, the two brothers form an uneasy alliance in hopes of retrieving their father's money. The gimmick is that before dying after a shootout with Earl (Frank Vincent), a ruthless gangster from his past, their father secretly revealed one crucial clue to George and one to Michael. Realizing that they each possess indispensable but partial info about the loot's location, the siblings are compelled to work together.

The intricate labyrinth of kidnaps, escapes, chases and betrayals would do any action pic proud. But following the model of "Reservoir Dogs," Ransick also knows that the only way to treat such familiar turf is by investing it with fresh perspective and shrewd humor — as a spoof of machismo, tough guys, dim-witted cops and family ties. Ransick's deadpan humor mixes idiosyncratic wit with laconic and cryptic dialogue.

Ransick never surrenders to the temptation of making his narrative weird for its own sake. Though the characters are not meant to be conventionally realistic, they always inhabit a recognizable urban locale, one populated by slapstick thugs and dumb cops who seem to appear whenever there's the slightest intimation of action on the streets.

All three lead actors — Williams, Cassel and Schulze — are impressively in tune with Ransick's quirky, offbeat sense of characterization.

But ultimately, "Handgun" belongs to Williams, who here renders one of his most accomplished performances. He gives his deliciously wicked, amoral role sharp, fresh shadings, yet always remains within character.

Tech credits, particularly Michael Spiller's lensing (with additional photography by Jean de Segonzac), are adequate on what appears to be an extremely low budget. Sound mixing and editing, however, suffer.

Despite these shortcomings, "Handgun" exhibits an unmistakably alert intelligence and cinematic sensibility that announce the arrival of an original American filmmaker. —*Emanuel Levy*

LIVING WITH ...

(DOCU — COLOR — 16mm)

A Bardo Films production. Produced, directed by Steven D. Esteb. Camera (color), Sandra Chandler; additional photography, Ulli Bonnekamp; music, Randy Tico; sound, Jose Araujo. Reviewed at Santa Barbara Intl. Film Festival, March 5, 1994. Running time: **66 MIN.**

"Living With ..." is an instructive and uplifting documentary about the residents and volunteers of Heath House, a model AIDS home in Santa Barbara. Though docu lacks artistic shape, its importance lies in showing how people with AIDS could live a more comfortable and emotionally fulfilling existence given the appropriate facilities. As such, "Living With ..." is a natural for public TV and a must for various educational and AIDS-oriented orgs.

There is a lot to be learned from "Living With ...," a docu full of insights and "how-to" guidelines for replicating the Heath House model elsewhere. Accommodating only seven residents at a time, the facility, named after its founder, Alice Heath, is a small operation. But it performs marvels for its residents, who to qualify for admission must be homeless, low-income or living in unsatisfactory conditions.

Pic successfully personalizes the stories of its residents and care givers. The novelty of the Heath House — and docu as a whole — is its emphasis on life, and not death.

While other docus have focused on people with AIDS, it's a pleasure to hear the Heath House's staff and volunteers talk about the positive functions and meaning of their work, be it administration, cooking or cleaning.

Aesthetically, film lacks an interesting structure, and production values are just moderate, but its real significance is political and pragmatic. Without overly stressing it point or preaching, "Living With ..." succeeds with its inspirational message for more compassionate care. —*Emanuel Levy*

HEALER

Produced, directed by John G. Thomas. Executive producer, Billy Bordy. Screenplay, Russ Reina. Camera (CFI color), Maximo Munzi; editor, Dann Cahn; music, Kamen Dranduski, Willy Kazasian; sound (Dolby), Neal Sprutz; casting, Marvin Paige. Reviewed at Santa Barbara Intl. Film Festival, March 4, 1994. Running time: **105 MIN.**

Nickel	Tyrone Power Jr.
Brent	John R. Johnston
The Jackal	David McCallum
Francie	DeLane Matthews
Igor Vostovich	Turhan Bey
Sergeant Gaylor	Lee Patterson

John G. Thomas' "Healer," which received its world premiere as the opener of the ninth Santa Barbara Intl. Film Festival, is a slim, poorly written message movie about the transformation of an irresponsible ex-con into a compassionate paramedic. Though set in the potentially exciting world of paramedics and meant to raise consciousness about the elderly, ineptly made indie may only surface in minor fests or retrospectives of regional cinema.

At the center of the well-intentioned "Healer" is Nickel (Tyrone Power Jr.), an ex-con paroled to an ambulance service at the local hospital, where he must work out the last year of his sentence. As part

March 14, 1994 (Cont.)

of his training, he's partnered with Brent (John R. Johnston), a cynical paramedic who perceives his work as dealing with "lizards, sevens and turkeys" (jargon for old people, dead bodies and charlatans).

Set in a retirement resort called Seabreeze, narrative follows the team's adventures and the various people they encounter on the job. Among them are Igor Vostovich (Turhan Bey), an old Russian immigrant placed in a nursing home against his will, and Francie (DeLane Matthews), a young woman so committed to caring for her ailing grandmother that she neglects to have a life of her own.

Russ Reina's schematic script, which is based on his personal experience as a paramedic, draws on all-too-obvious contrasts between children who neglect their aging parents and those who sacrifice themselves completely to the cause.

As could be expected, Igor soon begins to function as a surrogate father to Nickel, preaching and moralizing about the important things in life, and Nickel pursues an uneasy romance with Francie.

Comic relief in an otherwise stale film is provided by a character named the Jackal (David McCallum), an endearing if opportunistic drifter who seems to be present wherever there are gullible people to be exploited — be they hospital officials or patients.

Regional writer Reina reportedly worked for eight years on his screenplay, though it's hard to tell from the finished product. His characters don't converse so much as they deliver blatant, heavy-handed speeches about human compassion and responsibilities.

Worse yet, though Reina's heart is in the right place, the old people are so awkwardly portrayed and shot in the first part of the film that, ironically, one might draw the wrong conclusion about his attitude toward the elderly.

Despite attempts to avoid TV-movie-like political correctness, Thomas' clumsy direction accentuates even more the script's conventional and didactic structure. Thomas fails to endow the picture with the energy and pacing that would lift the writing from its pedestrian level.

With the exception of McCallum's entertaining performance as the Jackal, the cast lacks color and distinction. This is particularly true of Power, who looks and acts very much like his father, and Matthews. Neither can enliven or personalize their stiff, formulaic roles.

Technical credits are average, though Dann Cahn's inconsistent editing lacks fluidity.

—*Emanuel Levy*

NATURAL CAUSES

A Pacific Rim production. Produced, written by Jake Raymond Needham. Executive producers, Tanong Purananda, Yachitr Yuvaboon. Co-producers, Knit Kounavudhi, Joan Weidman. Directed by James Becket. Camera (Foto-Kem color), Denis Maloney; editor, Richard Fields; music, Nathan Wang; production design, Jan Holt; art direction, Sean Gundlach; set decoration, Tammy Musikadilov; costume design, Mutita Na Songkla; sound (Ultra-Stereo), Bill Robbins; associate producer/assistant director, Christine Fugate; casting, Donald Paul Pemrick. Reviewed at Santa Barbara Intl. Film Festival, March 5, 1994. Running time: **88 MIN.**

Jessie McCarthy	Linda Purl
Somchai	Cary-Hiroyuki Tagawa
Michael Murphy	Will Patton
The Westerner	Tim Thomerson
Mrs. McCarthy	Janis Paige
Fran Jakes	Ali MacGraw

Set in Bangkok, "Natural Causes" is a messy, incoherent political thriller about a young American woman who finds herself in the midst of a plot to assassinate former Secretary of State Henry Kissinger. Pic makes good use of Bangkok's colorful scenery, but its roguish, muddled plot and maladroit, uninvolving direction should take it straight to video domestically, with some possibilities for theatrical release offshore.

Jake Raymond Needham's tale begins rather suspensefully, when Rachel McCarthy (Janis Paige), an American woman, is killed in her limo on the way to the airport to meet her estranged daughter, Jessie (Linda Purl), whom she has not seen for 10 years. Upon arrival at her mother's beautiful estate, the naive Jessie begins to realize that her mother, who lost a husband and son in the Vietnam War, was engaged in a mysterious international scheme involving Vietnamese refugees.

"Natural Causes" aims to be an engaging conspiracy story about an attempt to sabotage the reconciliation treaty between Vietnam and the U.S. Initially, its gallery of characters is colorful enough for a web of deception and international intrigue. Along the way, Jessie meets Fran Jakes (Ali MacGraw), a U.S. State Dept. official, CIA agent Michael Murphy (Will Patton) and Major Somchai (Cary-Hiroyuki Tagawa), a high-ranking Thai detective.

Unfortunately, scripter Needham concocts a hugely improbable, often preposterous stew. Pic is carried forward not by logic but by a relentlessly mechanical outline that defies narrative or political sense. Scant clues are given to the characters' motivations, but ultimately the convoluted plot is of no particular consequence.

Novice director James Becket fails to interweave the various subplots and characters in a dramatically involving manner. And in the midst of tension, he commits a fatal error by inserting a lengthy romantic sequence between Jessie and Somchai, an interlude that literally arrests the film.

As the heroine, Purl acquits herself as a pleasant leading lady, but MacGraw is stiff in what is described as her screen comeback. Patton, usually a good offbeat character actor, is wasted, as is Tagawa.

The only reward in watching "Natural Causes" is its Thai scenery, which is well shot by Denis Maloney. —*Emanuel Levy*

HIGH SCHOOL II

(DOCU)

A Zipporah Films production. Produced, directed by Frederick Wiseman. Camera (color) John Davey; editor, Wiseman. Reviewed at Remis Auditorium, Museum of Fine Arts, Boston, March 1, 1994. (In Cinema du Reel fest, Paris.) Running time: **223 MIN.**

After more than a quarter century of filmmaking and more than two dozen films, documentarian Frederick Wiseman is entitled to make his films any way he wants, especially when he's making them for his own company, Zipporah Films. Still, while his no-narration, no-interviews, *cinema verite* style is effective, "High School II" suggests that some stronger editorial control might have been helpful. Nearly four-hour docu could be reduced to under two hours and attract notice on fest and arthouse circuits. As is, commercial and even PBS prospects are dim.

The title is something of an injoke. Back in 1969, Wiseman did a documentary called "High School" about a lower-middle-class urban school. It ran all of 75 minutes. While the new film is also about a high school, there's really no connection between the two films beyond the title.

"High School II" focuses on the students, teachers, staff and parents involved with the Central Park East Secondary School in New York City. Its inner-city public school students are given the opportunity to learn outside of traditional classroom settings, and the evidence Wiseman presents suggests that much of what they're accomplishing is worth examining.

In one scene, a teacher leads a few students in a discussion of "King Lear." One seems to be dozing and makes a careless remark about the play being "funny." But Wiseman lets the camera roll, and we see the teacher encourage the student to elaborate on his remark. It turns out that he's not out of it, but instead someone offering an insightful comment comparing the characters in "Lear" to a modern-day crime family and contrasting "Lear" with "Macbeth."

There's humor, too, from a raucous debate by students on immigration law, to teachers' deadpan discussion of how to teach the proper use of condoms, complete with lifelike props. But there's also repetition and dead spaces. Pic includes several student-teacher-parent conferences when one or two might have sufficed, and there are stories of disciplinary problems without any background or postscript, so we get only the middle of the story.

No doubt this is all intentional. It's part and parcel of Wiseman's patented style to show us everything a visitor to the school would see without further elaboration. But since even he must shape his work by choosing what to film and how to edit it together, providing a tighter film would make this more user-friendly without interfering with the style or content. In its present form, it feels more like a collection of everything Wiseman shot, with only the very beginning and very ending indicating any editorial control.

Hitchcock once observed that drama is life with the dull bits cut out. Wiseman's film may be true to life by leaving all the dull bits in, but at 223 minutes, it's asking a lot of an audience to stick it out.

Film bowed March 11 at the Cinema du Reel fest in Paris and will have its American debut at the Museum of Fine Arts, Boston, on March 19. —*Daniel M. Kimmel*

PERSONNE NE M'AIME

(NOBODY LOVES ME)

(FRENCH)

A Rezo Films release (France) of a Bloody Mary Prods. presentation of a Bloody Mary Prods./France 2 Cinema/ Cinemanufacture/La Television Suisse Romande production, with participation of Canal Plus and CNC. Produced by Didier Haudepin. Directed by Marion Vernoux. Screenplay, Vernoux, Nicolas Errera. Camera (color), Eric Gautier; editor, Patricia Ardouin; music, Arno; production design, Michel Vandestien; costume design, Marie Vernoux; sound, Jean-Louis Garnier, Francois Musy. Reviewed at Max Linder Panorama Cinema, Paris, Feb. 25, 1994. Running time: **98 MIN.**
Annie .... Bernadette Lafont
Francoise .... Bulle Ogier
Marie .... Lio
CriCri .... Michele Laroque
Dizou .... Maaike Jansen
Lucien ....Jean-Pierre Leaud
With: Judith Vittet, Andre Marcon, Antoine Chappey, Claude Muret.

"**N**obody Loves Me" is a spirited round of emotional hide-and-seek peopled by engagingly flawed women and dorky men. Fests and TV should show some affection.

Bernadette Lafont toplines as the lusty, beer-loving Annie, mother of pretty bartender Marie (Lio), a single mom who has rotten luck with guys. Annie and Marie haven't seen each other in seven years.

Freshly bounced by her latest lover, Annie drops in on her uptight bourgeois sister, Francoise (Bulle Ogier), who suspects that her husband, supposedly at a seaside resort conference, is having an affair.

At Annie's urging, the two set off to surprise Francoise's spouse. Annie befriends attractive hotel manager CriCri (Michele Laroque), who's had it with both her job and her husband. Rounding out the odd quartet is hotel chambermaid Dizou (Maaike Jansen), just shy of 60, who still enjoys conjugal bliss — unlike the other women — and has 11 children to show for it.

Pic's seemingly random structure, of which more than a third is taken up with flashbacks to seven years earlier, is not always easy to follow, but all loose ends are sweetly tied by the end.

Thesps inhabit their roles with a winning array of mannerisms and delivery. Whereas Ogier is delicate and puts on Blanche Dubois airs, Lafont is delightfully crude and direct. Lio conveys the melancholy of a late-20s woman who's kind to men and gets treated like dirt in return.

Jean-Pierre Leaud, in a few fleeting scenes, delivers one of his patented droll perfs as Lafont's long-ago main squeeze and laconic confidant to Lio. Older actors blend nicely with talented newer names.

Up-close, warts-and-all lensing lingers on the characters, who sometimes address the camera when not confiding in each other. Helmer Marion Vernoux and d.p. went for a deliberately grainy, contrasty look that grows irksome in the long run. On the music side, gritty rhythmic ballads are inserted from time to time to good effect.

—*Lisa Nesselson*

APEX

A Republic Pictures release of a Green Communications Inc. presentation in association with Republic. Produced by Talaat Captan. Executive producer, Captan. Line producer, Gary Jude Burkart. Directed by Phillip J. Roth. Written by Roth, Ronald Schmidt, based on a story by Roth, Gian Carlo Scandiuzzi. Camera (FotoKem color), Mark W. Gray; editor, Daniel Lawrence; assistant directors, Craig Connolly, David A. May; music, Jim Goodwin; robot suits and special makeup effects, Altered Anatomy FX; special visual effects, Ultra Matrix; sound (Surround Sound Stereo), Bill Reinhardt; assistant directors, Craig Connolly, David A. May; casting, Elizabeth Weintraub. Reviewed at Loews Westwood Mall 3, Houston, March 4, 1994. MPAA Rating: R. Running time: **103 MIN.**
Nicholas Sinclair .... Richard Keats
Shepherd .... Mitchell Cox
Natasha Sinclair .... Lisa Ann Russell
Taylor .... Marcus Aurelius
Rashad .... Adam Lawson
Dr. Elgin .... David Jean Thomas
Desert Rat .... Brian Richard Peck
Mishima .... Anna B. Choi
Johnson/Rebel .... Kristin Norton
Gunney .... Jay Irwin
1973 Father .... Robert Tossberg
1973 Mother .... Kathy Lambert
Joey .... Kareem H. Captan

"**A**pex" is an unpolished gem of a sci-fi B movie that should find a receptive audience in homevid and pay-cable venues. Pic was dropped into perfunctory theatrical release Friday with little fanfare and no press previews, usually a sure sign of a dog. In this case, though, the mongrel might have gobbled up slightly more B.O. coin had sci-fi fans been aware of its subject matter.

Script by director Phillip J. Roth and Ronald Schmidt is an involving variation on the familiar sci-fi theme of trying to alter the present by messing around with the past.

Richard Keats toplines as a 2073 time-travel researcher who timewarps back to 1973 to retrieve a faulty robot probe. But because he has been infected with a mysterious virus — and, worse, because his fellow scientists send another robot probe to find him — Keats inadvertently lays the groundwork for the living nightmare he encounters when he returns to 2073.

Back in the future, most humans are dead or dying because of the virus, while armies of killer robots hunt down the survivors.

In this parallel universe, Keats is a soldier in a rebel army that wages guerrilla campaigns against the robots. Also in the anti-robot unit: Lisa Ann Russell, Keats' loving wife in the good 2073, a virus-infected kamikaze in the bad 2073.

In setting up the time-travel adventure and man-vs.-machine conflict, Roth (presumably no relation to his more-celebrated literary namesake) borrows more than a few pages from "The Terminator" and "Battlestar Galactica," to name just two of his most obvious sources.

Still, Roth keeps "Apex" moving at a brisk enough pace to skate over whole stretches of thin ice. Made with more imagination than skill, and more resourcefulness than polish, pic makes the absolute most of an obviously limited budget. The computer-generated special effects and robot suits are quite impressive.

Acting is much better than average for the genre, beginning with the surprisingly compelling perf by Keats. He and former Revlon model Russell generate an unexpected poignance in a scene in which he tries to explain to her what she means to him in another life.

Also worth noting: Mitchell Cox as a two-fisted anti-robot guerrilla, and Marcus Aurelius (presumably no relation to his more-celebrated historical namesake) as a hot-tempered, foul-mouthed guerrilla.

Title is supposed to stand for "Advanced Prototype Extermination Unit," but the robots are never referred to as such. —*Joe Leydon*

L'UOMO CHE GUARDA

(THE VOYEUR)

(ITALIAN)

A D.A.R.C. release (Italy) of a Rodeo Drive/Erre Cinematografica production. (International sales: Adriana Chiesa Enterprises, Rome.) Produced by Marco Poccioni, Marco Valsania, Angelo Rizzoli. Directed, written, edited by Tinto Brass. Camera (Cinecitta color), Massimo Di Venanzo; music, Riz Ortolani; art direction, Luigia Battani; costume design, Millina Deodato. Reviewed at America Cinema, Rome, March 6, 1994. Running time: **102 MIN.**
Dodo .... Francesco Casale
Silvia .... Katarina Vasilissa
Alberto .... Franco Branciaroli
Fausta ....Cristina Garavaglia
Pascasie .... Raffaella Offidani

Years back, in orgiastic odysseys like "Caligula" and "Salon Kitty," Tinto Brass spun a semblance of narrative to dress up his elaborate slap-and-tickle sessions. Now, Italy's peerless purveyor of socially acceptable porn has almost stopped bothering. His latest gynecological peep show, "The Voyeur," is as artless an exercise as any of its recent predecessors, but local auds have looked on in steady numbers and oglers in other undemanding markets will probably do likewise.

The title character is a university lit professor (Francesco Casale) dumped by his exhibitionist wife (Katarina Vasilissa), whose repertoire of peekaboo-skirt tricks makes Sharon Stone look like Mary Poppins. While angling to lure her back, he ponders his own behavior, finding sounding boards in his libidinous father (Franco Branciaroli), pa's comely housekeeper (Cristina Garavaglia) and an eager-beaver student (Raffaella Offidani).

Though ostensibly based on Alberto Moravia's novel of the same name, the late novelist goes uncredited apart from an acknowledgment by way of Garavaglia perusing a copy of the tome while airing her nether regions. Brass makes a half-hearted show of lending intellectual substance with featherweight literary references plus some vapid deliberation on father-son phallic envy and the rapport between voyeur and exhibitionist, but flesh-peddling is clearly his main mission. Intermittent dabs of humor are invariably leaden.

Tech work is adequate, but Riz Ortolani's risibly kitsch (and omnipresent) music makes the tired sex fantasies and pedestrian lingerie fetishism look even more like inelegant undergraduate ribaldry. Other than for their physical attributes, performers are unremarkable. Brass himself pops up in an unimaginatively cast cameo as a corpulent faculty member drooling over nubile college girls.

—*David Rooney*

ANGIE

(DUTCH)

A Meteor Film release (Netherlands) of a Lagestee Film, Veronica, Meteor production. (International sales: Hills Entertainment Group, Hilversum.) Produced, directed by Martin Lagestee. Executive producer, San Fu Maltha. Screenplay, Lagestee, with contributions from Michael Belderink, Paul Ruven, Simon de Waal. Camera (color), Tom Erisman; editor, Herman P. Koerts; music, Joop Koopman, Clifford Scholten; title song, Simone Pormes; art direction, Harry Ammerlaan; costume design, Jacqueline Steijlen; sound (Dolby), Victor Dekker; assistant director, Annick Vroom; casting, Jeannette Snik. Reviewed on Hills Entertainment vidcassette, London, Feb. 1, 1994. Running time: **97 MIN.**

With: Annemarie Rottgering, Daniel Boissevain, Hidde Schols, Derek de Lint, Marijke Veugelers, Peter Tuinman, Jack Wouterse.

A mixed-up-siblings crimer capped by a road-movie finale, "Angie" is an OK Dutch semi-actioner that could have a brief offshore career as a dubbed item on ancillary or latenight TV. Pic bowed last fall on its home turf.

Title character (Annemarie Rottgering) is a lanky, sullen teen who leaves a young-offenders institution only to be assaulted by her mother's b.f. soon after settling back home. She moves in with her delinquent elder bro, Alex (Daniel Boissevain), who steals autos, and starts dating a waiter, Frank (Hidde Schols), who has gambling debts with some hoods.

After doing a heist together, the trio later hit the road, pursued by Frank's creditors and (after robbing a gas station) the cops. When they are cornered at a marina by the authorities, the truth about Angie and Alex's incestuous relationship emerges.

Producer/director Martin Lagestee, working from his own script, produces a workmanlike package without delving very deep into the psychology of his characters. Action sequences are fine, with sharp cutting, even though the pic tends to work in fits until the latter stages.

Main fault is there's too much jostling for attention in the slim script (incest, delinquency, youth kicks), and the most interesting character is the steely nerved Alex (well played by the charming Boissevain) rather than the underdrawn Angie (blankly portrayed by the boyish Rottgering). Other perfs are solid.

—*Derek Elley*

THE VELVET UNDERGROUND AND NICO

A film by Andy Warhol. Music by the Velvet Underground. Reviewed at Sundance Film Festival, Park City, Utah, Jan. 28, 1994. Running time: **66 MIN.**

With: Lou Reed, John Cale, Sterling Morrison, Maureen Tucker, Nico, Ari Boulogne.

Revived at the 1994 Sundance Festival as a midnighter, Andy Warhol's 1966 "The Velvet Underground and Nico" records a jam session of the popular Velvet Underground, when the band's main musicians were Lou Reed and John Cale. Centerstage is Nico, a statuesque, blond German model who sits on a stool as the musicians form a semicircle behind her.

Short pic was made during the height of Warhol's creativity as a pop artist and filmmaker; between 1963 and 1967, he made more than 50 films, ranging in length from four minutes to 25 hours. Among other things, this work challenges the myth about Warhol's passive and mechanical aesthetics — as if he just turned on the camera to record what was in front of it.

Film consists of two reels of long, uninterrupted takes. At first, the camera just records, sort of playing with the music, but then it begins to behave erratically, panning and zooming in an arbitrary manner. Changes in speed and camera angles were crucial to the minimalist technique of Warhol who, as painter-turned-director, was interested in exploring the continuity in both space and time of an actual experience.

Footage also includes a glimpse of the police officers who arrived on the scene after neighbors complained, as well as of Warhol himself. Overall, pic attests to Warhol's aversion to editing and his preference for just splicing together reels. As with Warhol's other films, it's impossible to tell where his technical ineptitude ends and innovative philosophy begins.

One can only speculate about the silence that prevailed at the sold-out Sundance screening — and the relatively small number of walkouts. It could be that the audience, which was composed of very young viewers, was simply baffled by Warhol's minimalist, yet audacious technique, the likes of which is almost non-existent today but was integral to the exploratory nature of the 1960s.

—*Emanuel Levy*

STO DNEY DO PRIKAZA

(100 DAYS BEFORE THE COMMAND)

(RUSSIAN)

A Gorki Filmstudio, Mir Workgroup production. (International sales: Erkus Filmstudio, Moscow.) Directed by Hussein Erkenov. Screenplay, Yuri Polyakov, Vladimir Golodov. Camera (color), Vladislav Menshikov; editor, Galina Dmitrieva; music, Yogan Bak; art direction, Sergei Filenko; sound, Viktor Duritsyn. Reviewed at Berlin Film Festival (Panorama section), Feb. 21, 1994. Running time: **68 MIN.**

With: Armen Daigarkanian, Lena Kondulainen, Aleksandr Chislov, Vladimir Zamansky, Oleg Vasilkov.

Though technically poor and dramatically erratic, this metaphoric, slightly surrealistic look at life in the Russian military packs a punch. Pic should raise some interest in arthouse circles and, because of its borderline homoeroticism, among gay and lesbian festivals.

To get Gorki Studios to invest, plus permission to use military locations, director Hussein Erkenov and writers Yuri Polyakov and Vladimir Golodov produced two fake scripts in addition to the real one. Result came as a shock to both the studio and the military. The 1990 pic has been screened in Russia, but its savagely anti-military tone meant it wasn't seen outside Russia until Erkenov formed his own sales company and toted the reels to the Berlin fest this year. Film is less a protest against military life than a metaphor for people doomed to be victims of life rather than its masters. Instead of a plot, pic presents an assemblage of episodes with little or no dialogue. Characters are barracks soldiers without names who, for unexplained reasons, are driven toward darkly repulsive fates like suicide and public humiliation.

Episodes have no motivation or background, nor standard endings: The next one starts just before we learn the end or repercussions of the last. Each serves not to portray real characters or offer insights, but to portray a feeling of impending doom. Result is a kind of existential poem or epitaph to those who seemed doomed from the beginning without knowing why.

Because the actors play types rather than real characters, specific performances do not stand out among the wooden-faced cast. Tech credits are mediocre to poor, especially the lukewarm colors and uninteresting locations.

Still, as a director Erkenov succeeds in invoking a heady atmosphere and a meaty, homoerotic suggestiveness that lend a strange attraction to his characters' piteous roads to self-destruction.

—*Eric Hansen*

ISA MEIDAN

(PATER NOSTER)

(FINNISH — B&W)

A Villealfa Filmprods. production, in association with Finnish Film Foundation, TV1. (International sales: World Sales Christa Saredi, Zurich.) Directed, written by Veikko Aaltonen. Camera (b&w), Olavi Tuomi; editor, Aaltonen; music, Mauri Sumen; art direction, uncredited; sound (Dolby), Risto Iissalo, Tom Forsstrom. Reviewed at Berlin Film Festival (Forum section), Feb. 17, 1994. Running time: **86 MIN.**

Juhani Haavisto .... Hannu Kivioja
Eino, his father .... Martti Katajisto
Marja .... Elina Hurme
Ranatanen .... Heikki Kujanpaa
Eino, as a
    young man .... Matti Onnismaa
Aino .... Aino Aaltonen
Boy .... Antti Mattila

Finnish director Veikko Aaltonen, whose offbeat s&m psychodrama "The Prodigal Son" was a sleeper at last year's Berlin festival, returns in style with his third feature, "Pater Noster." Creepy, oddball examination of a son's dark relationship with his crippled father lacks the previous movie's eye-opening bravura but looks a strong candidate for quality tube sales and further fest dates.

With its look into the stygian depths of human nature, pic has the same cage-rattling quality as "Prodigal," sans latter's contentious sadomasochistic content, which should make it an easier sell to nervous webs. And where "Prodigal" was urban-set and in color, "Pater Noster" is in monochrome (sharply lensed by Olavi Tuomi) and locationed in the backwoods, playing on a whole tradition of rural Finnish cinema going back to the 1950s. Script was written before "Prodigal" commenced shooting. Juhani (Hannu Kivioja), a sailor, returns after 20 years to take his hospitalized father (Martti Katajisto) back to their abandoned family smallholding and reach some kind of understanding with the older man. While there, he meets Marja (Elina Hurme), who has a young daughter.

First 20 minutes function as a prologue to the real story, with Juhani visiting the family farm, reliving memories of his father and finally crying out, "That's not how it was!" Pic, which freely intercuts fantasy flashbacks to his childhood with present-day scenes, demands considerable attention to sort out all the psychology, especially the obscure ending.

Though the drama is played straight, there's still a sense (as in "Prodigal") that Aaltonen delights in manipulating his audience, which adds a blackly comic edge to the serious goings-on. Deliberately melodramatic bursts of music contrast sharply with the hyper-controlled visual style, reminding auds that this is, after all, a movie from the maverick Kaurismaki brothers' Villealfa Filmprods.

The gaunt-looking Kivioja, so good as the hired muscle in "Prodigal," encores strongly in the role of the tortured Juhani. Other roles, essentially support, fit the ticket. Tech credits are clean, with no trace of the rapid 25-day shoot.

—*Derek Elley*

OUT: STORIES OF LESBIAN AND GAY YOUTH

(CANADIAN — DOCU —16mm)

A National Film Board of Canada production. (International sales: National Film Board of Canada, Montreal.) Produced by Silva Basmajian. Executive producer, Dennis Murphy. Directed by David Adkin. Camera (16mm, color), Joan Hutton, John Walker; editor, Steve Weslake; music, Aaron Davis; sound, Paul Durand. Reviewed at Berlin Film Festival (Panorama section), Feb. 17, 1994. Running time: 79 MIN.

Its construction and musical score recalling public school audiovisual programs, the well-meaning "Out" was adrift in the sophisticated international milieu of the Berlin Film Festival. Doc's title, a misnomer reportedly attached by the National Film Board of Canada, has little to do with the broad, unfocused amalgam of subjects pic addresses. Commercial prospects seem limited to Canada, where it opens nationwide in March, with possible educational use in remote outposts and a few gay and lesbian festival screenings the only options outside its native country.

Several likable teens and twenty-somethings recount the pain of being closeted and the difficulty of finally coming out to family and friends. Film broadens to include stories of transvestites, street hustlers and parental support group P-Flag, all of whom have virtually no connection to being "out" but instead fill out this primer on all things homosexual in Canada. Pic itself comes out somewhat conservatively on the side of traditional

coupling. The '70s-style music track with obligatory guitar is irritating. Editing and camera work are pedestrian. —*Howard Feinstein*

SURAT UNTUK BIDADARI
(A LETTER FOR AN ANGEL)
(INDONESIAN)

A Jakarta Institute of the Arts (Faculty of Film & TV)/Cipta Televisi Pendidikan Indonesia/Mutiara Era Nusa Film/Gema Tondoi Barito/Perum Produksi Film Negara production. (International sales: Global Sarana Film, Jakarta.) Produced by A. Alatas Fahmi, Robert S. Sumendap, Benny V. Aboebakar, Amoroso Katamsi. Executive producer, Budiyati Abiyoga. Directed by Garin Nugroho. Screenplay, Nugroho, Armantono. Camera (color), Winaldha E. Melalatoa; editor, Arturo G. Pradjawisastra; music, Tony Prabowo; art direction, Satari SK; costume design, M. Cholis; sound, Hartanto, Icang Zaini. Reviewed at Berlin Film Festival (Forum section), Feb. 12, 1994. Running time: 117 MIN.
Lewa .... Windy
 With: Nurul Arifin, Adi Kurdi, Viva Westi, Fuad Idris, Hotalili, Ibrahim Ibnu, Jajang Pamoncak.
 (Indonesian dialogue — Sumba dialect)

A slyly offbeat blend of docu and village drama, filtered through an over-literal Indonesian boy's eyes, "A Letter for an Angel" marks a bold sophomore effort by 32-year-old director Garin Nugroho that could interest specialized webs. Tightening by about 20 minutes wouldn't hurt either.

The boy is Lewa, 9, an antsy tyke prone to wild temper tantrums, whose mother died when he was very young. He has a warm relationship with Berlian Merah, an attractive young woman in the same village, whose brother, Malaria Tua, is his best friend.

A loner and a dreamer, the kid writes letters to an angel he believes takes care of the land, and is mystified why he never gets any replies. He spends his time cutting classes and playing on the beach with the crazed Malaria Tua.

One day a group of city types, in town for a fashion shoot, lend Lewa a Polaroid camera, and the kid becomes obsessed with recording everything through its lens. His curiosity triggers a bloody feud between neighboring villages.

The movie doesn't stint on ambition. Nugroho's cutting style is consciously jagged, with sequences often begun sans intros, inserted chunks of real-life village rituals (complete with explanatory captions) and weird, semi-mystical scenes of considerable magic.

Just when it seems "Letter" may settle down into a rural kiddie pic, Nugroho either switches styles or shocks the viewer with unexpected violence. (Pic contains much graphic footage of animals being slaughtered in ceremonies.)

Thanks to natural playing by a largely non-pro cast, the formula works most of the time. Apart from the three adult leads (all fine), other thesps are from Sumba, an island east of Bali chosen by Nugroho for its broad mix of cultures and traditions. Some 90% of the dialogue is in local dialect.

Tech credits are OK, given the small ($235,000) budget, which allowed only 30 days' shooting. Color on print caught had a bright, somewhat washed-out look. Pic has yet to open commercially in Indonesia.

—*Derek Elley*

CHEUNG CHIN FUCHAI
(ALWAYS ON MY MIND)
(HONG KONG)

A United Filmmakers Organization production for Hui's Film Prod. Co., Topping Time Films. (International sales: Hui's Film Prod. Co., Hong Kong.) Produced by Eric Tsang, Michael Hui. Executive producer, Claudie Chung. Directed by Jacob C.L. Cheung. Screenplay, James Yuen. Camera (color), Ardy Lam; editor, Henry Cheung; music, Chan Wing-leung; art direction, Ngai Fong-nai; costume design, Vivian Lam; sound, Steve Chan; assistant director, Tang Wing-yiu. Reviewed at Berlin Film Festival (Panorama section), Feb. 17, 1994. Running time: 101 MIN.
Tseung Yau-wai .... Michael Hui
Yin, his wife Josephine Siao Fong-fong
Sze ("Suzanne") .... Chan Siu-ha
Min .... Chor Sze-pui
Chung .... John Tang
 Also with: Cindy Lai, Vivian Lam, Raymond Lui, Rain Lau, Ho-ho Yuen, Joe Junior, Tse Fun-yung, Spencer Chan, Jacob C.L. Cheung, Simon Lo, Lee Wing-man, Tsui Kwok-keung, Wong Ho-sze.
 (Cantonese dialogue)

TV newscasters should be tied down and forced to watch "Always on My Mind," a scabrous black comedy about spin-doctoring on the airwaves that takes a lunatic premise and squeezes it till the juice runs out. Film's plethora of Hong Kong in-jokes and manic humor is likely to limit its play with Western auds, but Sinophiles will relish its sharp scripting and fine lead playing by two of the territory's most accomplished thesps.

Well-known actor/director Michael Hui toplines as a middle-aged editor at fictional web CCN who loses his job and finds he has cancer of the intestine on the same

day. His wife (Josephine Siao Fong-fong) and three kids are so self-absorbed that they hardly notice he has only three months to live.

When Hui accidentally gets an inside scoop on a police coverup, the CCN execs come up with a ratings-boosting wheeze — rehire Hui, go public on his terminal disease and win the public over with "honest" reporting (on the basis that Hui must be telling the truth as he has nothing to lose). Hui and Siao become instant celebs, but problems start when Hui starts going too far in the honesty stakes on air.

Potentially bad-taste idea, which plays like a comic version of "Network" with a dash of "Broadcast News," comes off thanks to Hui's own buoyant performance and his wonderful double-teaming with Siao, whose quietly crazed perf is a minor gem. Hui's final on-air speech, which draws on the comic's standup skills, manages to be both funny and moving.

Script is thick with local refs and in-jokes that don't travel, but the overall good-natured tone is clear enough.

Direction by Jacob Cheung ("Cageman"), who also cameos as a film director, is well paced. Version shown at the Berlin fest was Cheung's preferred "international" one, with an open ending as to whether Hui survives. Hong Kong version, which bowed last December to OK business, had Hui surviving his op. Pic's Chinese title means "The Money-Grabbing Couple."

—*Derek Elley*

OBCY MUSI FRUWAC
(THE STRANGER MUST FLY)
(POLISH-GERMAN)

A Saco Films (Warsaw)/Projekt 4 Film (Berlin) production. (Intl. sales: Odra Film, Wroclaw.) Produced by Wieslaw Saniewski, Christine Hamer. Directed, written by Saniewski. Camera (color), Ryszard Lenczewski; editor, Zygmunt Olejnik; music, Lech Janerka; art direction, Tadeusz Kosarewicz; costume design, Krystyna Swiecznik; sound, Aleksander Golebiowski. Reviewed at Berlin Film Festival (market), Feb. 15, 1994. Running time: 92 MIN.
 With: Piotr Fronczewski, Ewa Blaszczyk, Ewa Zietek, Ewa Wencel, Zbigniew Zapasiewicz, Aleksander Bardini, Krzysztof Bauman, Henryk Niebudek, Milogost Reczek, Frank Ciazynski, Karin Duewel, Boguslaw Linda, Juergen Frohriep.
 (Polish and German dialogue)

Old tensions die hard in "The Stranger Must Fly," an accessible light comedy about a bunch of Polish thesps in the new

March 14, 1994 (Cont.)

March 21, 1994

Germany who find the welcoming West isn't such a hayride after all. With some loss of ballast in the stodgier second half (and a snappier title), this could find a nest in subtitled TV skeds.

Central character, more an observer than mover of events, is Maks (Piotr Fronczewski), a legit director from Wroclaw who journeys to Berlin to help actor friends mount a long-banned revue.

Once in Berlin, Maks finds his pals are on the bread line, state subsidies are verboten to foreigners, and a former Polish apparatchik (memorably played by vet Zbigniew Zapasiewicz) is oiling his way through town on a "cultural" freebie.

There's nothing hugely new here, but writer/director Wieslaw Saniewski marshals a likable, colorful cast, plenty of self-mocking Polish humor, and occasional sequences (like Maks silently witnessing a nocturnal neo-Nazi street demo) that have a dreamlike quality.

Ensemble playing is excellent, and technically the film is fine.

—Derek Elley

LEFTERIS DIMAKOPOULOS

(LEFTERIS)

(GREEK-GERMAN)

A Greek Film Centre-Stefi Film-Attika (Athens)/Ciak Film (Hamburg) co-production. Produced by Pantelis Mitropoulos, Pericles Hoursoglou. Directed, written by Hoursoglou. Camera (color), Stamatis Yannoulis; editor, Takis Yannopoulos; music, Giorgos Papadakis; production design, Anastasia Arseni; sound, Andreas Achladis. Reviewed at Berlin Film Festival (market), Feb. 15, 1994. Running time: **105 MIN.**
Lefteris .... Nikos Georgakis
Dimitra .... Maria Skoula
Panayotis .... Nikos Orphanos
Giorgos .... Manolis Mavromatakis

Winner of the Silver Alexander Award and best-actress prize at last year's Thessaloniki film fest, "Lefteris" is a notable Greek film on the universal theme of an ambitious man who loses sight of the important things in life. First-time director Pericles Hoursoglou and his excellent cast breathe new life into the basically familiar material.

Pic opens on New Year's Eve 1987, with prosperous engineer Lefteris Dimakopoulos (Nikos Georgakis) celebrating with his wife and family in his elegant home.

There's an unexpected visitor, Lefteris' old friend from student days, Panayotis (Nikos Orphanos), who reminds him of Dimitra (Maria Skoula), the woman he'd loved and lost on the road to success.

Flashback to 1973; Lefteris (the name means "freedom") is working as a student in Athens and living with the lovely Dimitra, who is strongly disapproved of by his family back home. He quarrels with his uncle, who pays his bills, when the old man calls Dimitra a whore.

All through his student days (with political unrest touched on also), Dimitra is loyal to Lefteris and neglects her own studies to help him.

Once he graduates, he gets a job in Germany for two years, then does compulsory military service in the navy. On one of his increasingly rare visits to Dimitra, he makes her pregnant and then is furious to discover what's happened. Dimitra has an abortion, and leaves him for good.

The familiar situation is given freshness here thanks to Hoursoglou's sensitive direction and the natural performances of the cast of newcomers.

Tech credits are all excellent, with the camera work of Stamatis Yannoulis especially fine.

—David Stratton

NAKED GUN 33 1/3: THE FINAL INSULT

A Paramount Pictures release of a David Zucker production. Produced by Robert K. Weiss, David Zucker. Executive producers, Jerry Zucker, Jim Abrahams, Gil Netter. Co-producers, Robert LoCash, William C. Gerrity. Directed by Peter Segal. Screenplay by Pat Proft, David Zucker, LoCash. Camera (DeLuxe color), Robert Stevens; editor, Jim Symons; music, Ira Newborn; production design, Lawrence G. Paull; art direction, Bruce Crone; set decoration, Kathe Klopp; costume design, Mary E. Vogt; sound (Dolby), Hank W. Garfield; associate producers, Michael Ewing, Jeff Wright; assistant director, John Hockridge; second unit director, Weiss; casting, Pamela Basker. Reviewed at the Village Theater, L.A., March 14, 1994. MPAA Rating: PG-13. Running time: **82 MIN.**
Lt. Frank Drebin .... Leslie Nielsen
Jane Spencer .... Priscilla Presley
Ed Hocken .... George Kennedy
Nordberg .... O.J. Simpson
Rocco .... Fred Ward
Muriel .... Kathleen Freeman
Tanya .... Anna Nicole Smith
Louise .... Ellen Greene
Ted .... Ed Williams
Papshmir .... Raye Birk

Paramount figures to blast away the competition with its third spin of "The Naked Gun," loaded with the usual barrage of irreverent, politically incorrect and virtually non-stop gags. Even in light of disappointing results for some recent sequels, the new "Gun" should score a bull's eye with the teen and college crowd, rivaling its predecessors' hefty box office take.

The formula for these movies is easy to decipher but difficult to execute. Working from the presumption that if stupid is good, idiotic is better, the filmmakers cram in more jokes per minute than would seem possible, hit the target with enough of them to keep the audience going, and then get out quickly (in this case, a brisk 82 minutes), before the novelty wears off.

The other main element involves a heavy reliance on movie parodies, and this latest platter offers some killers, perhaps the most inspired being its "The Untouchables" spoof that precedes the credits.

Those keeping track, however, will also see references, seldom subtle, to such diverse sources as "Thelma & Louise," "White Heat" and "The Crying Game."

Tracing the plot of one of these romps is virtually pointless, and the latest is thinner in that department than the others. Police squad detective Frank Drebin (Leslie Nielsen) has retired and taken

to the domestic life, while his wife — and a courtroom full of breast-feeding mothers — prosecutes child-support cheats.

Frank gets talked into returning to the force, going under cover to bunk up with a terrorist (Fred Ward) and the terrorist's mob, including his snarling mother (Kathleen Freeman) and bombshell girlfriend (supermodel Anna Nicole Smith).

Director Peter Segal and writers Pat Proft, David Zucker and Robert LoCash succumb to occasional bouts of toilet humor, but there's also extended hilarity in a scene set around the Academy Awards.

By now Nielsen, Priscilla Presley and the other regs can virtually mail in their performances, which give shameless mugging a good name. Ward's an effective bad guy, while Smith's wonder-of-modern-engineering outfits almost prompt one to ignore that, based on this perf, she should probably stick to modeling.

Tech credits evince the attention to detail needed to maintain this sort of farce, while closing credits include the usual scroll of ongoing lunacy.

Considering this series is based on a TV show canceled 12 years ago — after just six episodes — "33⅓" may not be "the final insult," as it indicates, but for the producers, it certainly qualifies as the last laugh.

—Brian Lowry

MONKEY TROUBLE

A New Line Cinema release of a Ridley Scott/Percy Main production in association with Effe Films and Victor Co. of Japan Ltd. Produced by Mimi Polk, Heidi Rufus Isaacs. Executive producer, Ridley Scott. Co-producer, John C. Broderick. Directed by Franco Amurri. Screenplay, Amurri, Stu Krieger. Camera (Technicolor), Luciano Tovoli; editor, Ray Lovejoy, Chris Peppe; music, Mark Mancina; production design, Les Dilley; art direction, Nathan Crowley; set decoration, Denise Pizzini; costume design, Eileen Kennedy; sound (Dolby), Michael Evje, Charles Kelly; associate producer, Christian Halsey Solomon; special effects coordinator, J.D. Street IV; casting, Karen Rea. Reviewed at the Aidikoff Screening Room, Beverly Hills, March 14, 1994. MPAA Rating: PG. Running time: **95 MIN.**
Dodger .... "Finster"
Eva .... Thora Birch
Shorty .... Harvey Keitel
Amy .... Mimi Rogers
Tom .... Christopher McDonald
Peter .... Kevin Scannell

Starring an adorably cute Capuchin monkey, which performs magnificent tricks, "Monkey Trouble" is a touching children's adventure that belongs among the great animal movies. With Harvey Keitel in a refreshingly different role and beautiful child-star Thora Birch, this sentimental family yarn boasts a superlative production. New Line can

March 21, 1994 (Cont.)

start planning a sequel to a film that is likely to score high with children, especially girls.

Nine-year-old Eva Gregory (Birch) desperately wants a pet, but mom (Mimi Rogers) thinks she's not mature and responsible enough to take care of one. Besides, Eva's stepfather (Christopher McDonald) is hyperallergic to animals and the family is too busy with Eva's baby brother.

Opportunity knocks when Shorty Kohn (Harvey Keitel), a gypsy hustler, loses his pet, a Capuchin monkey trained to entertain and lift the wallets and jewelry of the crowds along Venice Beach's boardwalk. Shorty, who's about to pull a big heist with two crooks, has abused his pet so much that the monkey really hates him.

This is the premise to an endearing children's fantasy that can be summed as "girl meets monkey, girl loses monkey, girl finds monkey." Eva sneaks the monkey into her house and gradually a rewarding bond evolves between them. To her parents' amazement, all of a sudden Eva cleans her room, shows concern for them and is even sensitive to her brother. As for Eva, she gets her own surprise upon discovering her pet's felonious skills and dubious past.

So long as monkey, named Dodger by Eva, is centerstage, the tale is charmingly diverting; in one of several hilarious chase scenes, the monkey ends up in a kite hovering over Venice Beach. Lenser Luciano Tovoli performs marvels with his camera, which impressively tracks the pet as it shrewdly moves from one locale to another. Briskly paced by director Franco Amurri, pic makes good use of Venice and other colorful L.A. locations.

Problem is, audiences are always ahead of the yarn, and whenever bits of narrative are used to cement the girl and her pet's escapades, the film becomes a bit stale and uninvolving — though not for long.

As can be expected, the good cast of adult actors mostly plays second banana roles, except for Keitel, whose colorful outfitting extends to a set of bad teeth. Birch ("Hocus Pocus") has the good looks and screen presence of a major child star.

Behind-the-scenes hands can take bows all the way down the line, notably lenser Tovoli, production designer Les Dilley, costume designer Eileen Kennedy — and animal trainer Mark Harden.   —*Emanuel Levy*

ABOVE THE RIM

A New Line Cinema release. Produced by Jeff Pollack, Benny Medina. Executive producer, James D. Brubaker. Directed by Pollack. Screenplay, Barry Michael Cooper, Pollack, story by Pollack, Medina. Camera (Deluxe color), Tom Priestley Jr.; editors, Michael Ripps, James Mitchell; music, Marcus Miller; production design, Ina Mayhew; set decoration, Paul Weathered; costume design, Karen Perry; sound (Dolby), Michael Barosky; associate producers, Mara Manus, Steve Greener, Aaron Meyerson; assistant director, Howard McMaster; stunt coordinator, Jeff Ward; casting, Marie E. Nelson, Ellyn Long Marshall. Reviewed at Raleigh Studios, L.A., March 8, 1994. MPAA Rating: R. Running time: **93 MIN.**

Kyle-Lee	Duane Martin
Shep	Leon
Birdie	Tupac Shakur
Rollins	David Bailey
Mailika	Tonya Pinkins
Bugaloo	Marlon Wayans
Flip	Bernie Mac
Monroe	Byron Minns

Coming at the end of a full-court press of basketball movies, "Above the Rim" has the distinction of being in many ways the most interesting, yet also the most hackneyed. A fine cast and the movie's general energy can't overcome that mix of cliches and technical flaws, which should conspire to prevent any high flying at the box office.

Director/co-writer/producer Jeff Pollack seems to feel compelled to make all the obvious moves in telling this story of a talented high school basketball player torn between two brothers — one a drug-dealing street operator (Tupac Shakur), the other a school security guard (Leon) and former high school standout tormented by his past.

That alone might be enough to sustain a movie, but Pollack and co-writer Barry Michael Cooper keep firing off enough cliches to fill an NBA stat sheet. While that won't necessarily put off urban teens drawn to the subject matter, it should limit room for a crossover to reach a wider audience.

The protagonist, Kyle-Lee (Duane Martin), is awaiting word about a Georgetown scholarship when life starts to get complicated, as he suddenly finds himself torn between his well-meaning coach and the local gangster Birdie (Shakur) over a playground basketball tournament.

He also clearly resents his mother's budding involvement with the security guard who, despite the coach's urging, still frets over the death of a friend and can't bring himself to get involved in basketball again.

The irony is that "Above the Rim" — which in some ways conveys the fresh feel and edge of a low-budget independent production — mirrors so many tired plot elements from other recent efforts to cash in on basketball's popularity, most notably a key wrinkle in "The Air Up There."

The shame of it is that Martin (whose credits include "White Men Can't Jump"), Leon ("Cool Runnings") and rapper Shakur ("Poetic Justice") all exhibit smooth moves in their limited roles, even without much of an assist from the script.

Although the basketball action is reasonably authentic, the director seems too enamored with flashy dunks and spins that ultimately feel overly repetitive and choreographed.

In addition, the movie inadvertently sends a mixed message about violence, falling back on a cold-blooded killing — almost as an afterthought — to tie up its loose ends.

Shakur, who played a similar role in "Juice" and has spent his share of time in court recently offscreen, makes an effectively menacing heavy, while Martin and Leon both seem deserving of better-conceived vehicles.

Tech credits, however, are generally shoddy, with murky photography and occasionally garbled dialogue — drawbacks that contribute to "Above the Rim's" failure to really get off the ground.   —*Brian Lowry*

FOR THE MOMENT

(CANADIAN)

A John Aaron Features II presentation produced with the participation of Rogers Telefund/Telefilm Canada/the Manitoba Cultural Industries Development Office/Canadian Broadcasting Corp. Produced by Jack Clements, Aaron Kim Johnston. Co-producers, Joe McDonald, Ches Yetman. Directed, written by Johnston. Camera (color), Ian Elkin; editor, Rita Roy; music, Victor Davies; production design, Andrew Deskin; art direction, Jim Phillips; set decoration, Mark Andrew Webb; costumes, Charlotte Penner; sound, David Husby; assistant director, Allan James; casting, Anne Tait. Reviewed at Santa Barbara Intl. Film Festival, March 12, 1994. (Also in Vancouver Film Festival.) Running time: **120 MIN.**

Lachlan	Russell Crowe
Lill	Christianne Hirt
Betsy	Wanda Cannon
Zeek	Scott Kraft
Johnny	Peter Outerbridge
Kate	Sara McMillan

A sort of "Yanks" on the Canadian prairie, "For the Moment" is an appealing, nostalgic wartime romance that effectively evokes a specific time and place. Full of noble, fresh-scrubbed faces and manly, grace-under-pressure behavior, stately picture exemplifies an old-fashioned cinematic style that won't be everybody's cup of tea. But older and, particularly, female audiences might respond to the tale's poignance, and stardom-in-the-making lead performance from Russell Crowe could provide a good marketing peg with the right timing.

Set in Manitoba, 1942, yarn centers upon an ill-fated affair between a young married local woman and an Aussie pilot there to take part in the British Commonwealth Air Training Plan of Canada, under which would-be flyers from many Allied nations hit Canada for short spells of training.

Crowe plays Lachlan, a handsome fellow whose understated self-confidence would be right at home in a Hemingway story. Between lectures and practice flights, Lachlan slowly cozies up to Lill (Christianne Hirt), a perky farm girl whose husband is already away at war.

In contrast to this discreet affair is Betsy (Wanda Cannon), a bootlegger with two kids who believes in charging for what a lot of other women give away. She eventually hooks up with Zeek (Scott Kraft), a dashing Yank flight instructor.

These and other little dramas are played out at a measured, occasionally indulgent pace by Winnipeg-based writer-director Aaron Kim Johnston, whose previous effort was the 1990 childhood memoir "The Last Winter."

Few of the plot developments are particularly surprising, and a couple of them seem forced, particularly the arbitrary beating of a black recruit (who's never seen again) and the one-dimensional villainy of some thugs who are dragged in just to create physical conflict once in a while. In general, Johnston could have developed some more imaginative interaction among the soldiers.

But for those who respond to love stories played out under pressurized, time-foreshortened circumstances, "For the Moment" has something to offer. Johnston displays a real feel for the land and for a principled way of life that makes his film resemble something that might have actually been made in the 1950s rather than the 1990s.

Putting the film over most, however, is Crowe. Rugged and solid without seeming too overbearing, Crowe fashions a persona here that, as was often said about Clark Gable, may be equally appealing to men and women.

Hirt makes for a spunky, reasonably appealing partner, and has one dramatically devastating scene, which she plays entirely silent, in which she receives a dreaded tele-

March 21, 1994 (Cont.)

gram. Other perfs are decent but more emblematic than dimensional.

Pic boasts superior production values for its $2.8 million budget, notably Ian Elkin's handsome lensing of the vast Canadian landscapes. Film world-premiered last fall in a longer version at the Vancouver Film Festival, where it won the audience prize for top Canadian feature, and debuted in shorter cut in Santa Barbara. —*Todd McCarthy*

MONA MUST DIE

A Jones & Reiker presentation in association with Rhino Films of an MMD production co-produced by VCL/Carolco Communications GmbH in conjunction with Jugendfilm Verleih and Bernd Gaumer. Produced by Robert Caplain. Executive producers, Harris Tulchin, Stephen Nemeth. Co-producer, Tom Colamaria. Directed by Donald Reiker. Screenplay, Patricia Jones, Reiker. Camera (color), Russ Alsobrook; editor, Nathaniel Burr Smidt; music, Greg O'Connor; production design, Preston Sharp; costume design, Julie Carnahan; sound (Ultra-Stereo), Joe Kenworthy; associate producers, Doug Blake, Floyd Coard; assistant director, Ken Fuchs; casting, Meg Liberman. Reviewed at Santa Barbara Intl. Film Festival, March 12, 1994. Running time: **97 MIN.**
Mona
von Snead .... Marianne Sagebrecht
Eddie von Snead ... Uwe Ochsenknecht
Rachel McSternberg .... Sheila Kelley
Father Stilicato .... Dick Miller
Betty .... Debbie Allen
Irv von Snead .... Norman Nixon
Dr. Shaner .... John Shaner
Grocery Delivery Boy .. Adam Stradlin
TV Repairman .... Tracey Walters
Clarence .... Steve White
Jamal .... Mel Winkler

The old standby crime premise of two lovers disposing of the spouse who's in the way is given a mostly lame black comic tweaking in "Mona Must Die," a curious Germanic-flavored U.S. indie that could find a small niche where oddball bookings have a chance of cultivating an audience, as well as on video and in foreign territories where names of the leading players mean something.

Living in a beautiful home overlooking a secluded Malibu beach, the hefty Mona ("Sugarbaby's" Marianne Sagebrecht) continually badgers her forlorn husband Eddie (Uwe Ochsenknecht) about his unwillingness to have sex with her.

But when Mona departs for liposuction treatment, Eddie has occasion to rescue a would-be suicide from the waves in front of his house. Natch, she turns out to be a beautiful, if rather hysterical, young woman, and in short order, Eddie and Rachel (Sheila Kelley) are packing 9½ weeks of action into a single week.

When Mona returns, Eddie unconvincingly passes Rachel off as a hired nurse. Clearly, the triangular living arrangement isn't going to

last, so the passionate lovers repeatedly try to do poor Mona in — burying her in the sand, throwing her in the garbage, towing her out to sea — but the big lady just won't stay down.

Similar frustrated death scenarios have been played to various comic effect in numerous other films, from "The Ladykillers" to "Harold and Maude" and the Inspector Clouseau series. Here, the couple's strenuously physical efforts to dispose of their formidable prey are generally more exhausting than amusing, although there are a few good gags along the way to keep attention from flagging entirely.

Helping matters are the game performances of the three leads, along with the bright, colorful physical presentation that gives the action an apt cartoon-like quality. But vet TV director Donald Reiker, in his feature debut, mostly hits an arch tone while attempting something stylized. Comic mark he's aiming for isn't easy to hit, and while result isn't precisely bad, pic isn't able to click into a comfortable gear and stay there.

Film's funniest moments are provided by Dick Miller, in briefly as a beleaguered priest who defensively complains, "It's getting very trendy nowadays to accuse priests of sexual improprieties with young boys." Despite heavy sexual element, it's mostly of a caricatured and physically unrevealing nature.
—*Todd McCarthy*

CHUPPA: THE WEDDING CANOPY

(DOCU — COLOR)

A GEO Film production. Produced by Laurie Zemelman Schneider. Executive producers, Sascha Schneider, John Lionel Bandmann. Co-producer, Hanania Baer. Directed by Laurie Zemelman, Sascha Schneider. Camera (color), Baer; editor, Gesa Marten; associate producer, Paul Lawrence. Reviewed at Santa Barbara Intl. Film Festival, March 5, 1994. Running time: **80 MIN.**

At once a formidable tale of survival, a touching love story and an enduring family saga, "Chuppa: The Wedding Canopy" is an original documentary about the wedding of a Jewish couple half a century after they met and got engaged. Celebrating one family's struggle to move beyond the pain of the Holocaust, this truly uplifting docu deserves a theatrical release prior to showings in Jewish film festivals, public TV and other venues.

Helma and Benno Schneider met and fell in love as teenagers in the ghetto of Riga, Latvia, in 1942. Despite humiliating traumas and deni-

grating experiences that would break the spirits of most people, Helma and Benno managed to sustain a relationship that proved nurturing and fulfilling. When their concentration camp was dissolved, the two lived for a year on the run in the Russian forests. By then, they each had lost their entire family, which meant that there were no people to witness a traditional Jewish marriage.

Sascha, the couple's eldest son (and co-director), recalls how he vowed, and always knew, that one day he would give his parents the proper wedding ceremony they never had. As a culmination of dreams and promises, the chuppa also had impact on the interaction of parents and children and on Sascha's marriage to his wife, co-director and producer Laurie Zemelman Schneider.

Although the elder couple, now in their 70s, occasionally break out crying (and switch to Yiddish) while recalling Hitler, their matter-of-fact philosophy of life, which is full of humor and wit, is most impressive.

As a testament to the indefatigable human spirit and to the need to come to terms with one's past — no matter how painful it is — "Chuppa" is one of a kind.
—*Emanuel Levy*

TRADING MOM

A Trimark Pictures release. Produced by Raffaella De Laurentiis. Executive producer, Robert Little. Directed, written by Tia Brelis, based on Nancy Brelis' novel "The Mommy Market." Camera (color), Buzz Feitshans IV; editor, Isaac Sehayek; music, David Kitay; production design, Cynthia Charette; set decoration, Lisa Caperton; makeup, Jennifer Bell; assistant director, Patty Chan Morrison. Reviewed at the Santa Barbara Intl. Film Festival, March 5, 1994. MPAA Rating: PG. Running time: **83 MIN.**
Mommy, Mama, Mom,
  Natasha .... Sissy Spacek
Elizabeth .... Anna Chlumsky
Jeremy .... Aaron Michael Metchik
Harry .... Asher Metchik
Mrs. Cavour .... Maureen Stapleton

A didactic fairy tale for children, "Trading Mom" is an amiable if undistinguished film for the whole family. As a vehicle for Sissy Spacek, who plays four different kinds of mothers, and with the appearance of "My Girl" star Anna Chlumsky, pic will appeal mostly to the very young.

In Tia Brelis' screen adaptation of her mother's 1966 novel, "The Mommy Market," Spacek plays a single, career-oriented mother too busy to give her children "quality time." Unhappy with her inattentiveness, Elizabeth (Chlumsky), Jeremy (Aaron Michael Metchik) and Harry (Asher Metchik) rush to

complain to their friend, Mrs. Cavour (Maureen Stapleton), and the strange, white-haired woman prescribes an ancient magic spell that can erase the memory of their biological mother and allow them to shop for the "ideal" one.

Like a classic fairy tale, "Trading Mom" lets the children select and experience a different kind of mom in each of its three episodes: a selfish, glamorous woman who wants to transform them into decorations, an avid outdoor "scouts" type and a clownish performer who builds a circus right in the back yard.

Playing all four roles, Spacek is most convincing as the real mother and seems to have fun as the outdoor type. But she is not particularly good with accents — her portrayals of the French mama and Russian circus performer are forced and too actorish.

Tech credits, particularly Cynthia Charette's production design of the mommy market, will please toddlers.

Message that the grass is not always greener will be joyfully embraced by single working mothers and may encourage youngsters to appreciate what they have — realizing, as Judy Garland did in "The Wizard of Oz," that "there's no place like home."

Though "Trading Mom" lacks the appeal, charm and look of a great fairy tale like "The Secret Garden," it's an enjoyable experience, a film that can be watched by parents and children together.—*Emanuel Levy*

WUNDBRAND: SARAJEVO, 17 TAGE IN AUGUST

(GANGRENE: SARAJEVO, 17 DAYS IN AUGUST)

(GERMAN — DOCU — B&W)

A Factory 2 production, in associate with Arte. (International sales: Factory 2, Berlin.) Directed, written by Didi Danquart, Johann Feindt. Camera (b&w), Feindt; editor, Danquart; music/sound, Cornelius Schwehr; associate producers, Martin Hagermann, Thomas Kufus. Reviewed at Berlin Film Festival (Forum section), Feb. 13, 1994. Running time: **83 MIN.**

This small b&w docu about Sarajevo under siege works as a touching probe into life during wartime. Though too uneven to leave a lasting impression, it has enough fascinating and moving sections to give an insight into the horrors of the conflict for the civilian population. It will work for specific fest and TV auds.

Best sections are the interviews with young soldiers — some still in their teens — who talk about being shot at and wounded, and shooting and killing. One recounts killing an old woman by mistake. Another tells of being a comedian in civilian life, and is proud to do his John Cleese impression for the camera.

Directors Didi Danquart and Johann Feindt made the film under conditions of extreme danger, which explains the lingering impression that they were thankful for what they got rather than trying to get everything they wanted. Feindt's camerawork is strong and impressive. Switching between arbitrary location shots and interviews, pic provides an atmospheric, everyday portrait of bombed-out Sarajevo without resorting to actual combat footage. —*Eric Hansen*

DAHIL MAHAL KITA
(BECAUSE I LOVE YOU: THE DOLZURA CORTEZ STORY)
(PHILIPPINE)

An OctoArts Films presentation. Produced by Art R. Ilagad, Orly R. Iiagad. Directed by Laurice Guillen. Screenplay, Ricardo Lee. Camera (color), Eduardo Jacinto; editor, Efren Jarlego; music, Nonong Buencamino; production design, Edgar Martin Littava; associate producer, Tess Fuentes. Reviewed on vidcassette, San Francisco, Feb. 24, 1994. (In S.F. Asian-American Intl. Film Festival). Running time: **101 MIN.**
Dolzura Cortez .... Vilma Santos
Paolo .... Christopher DeLeon
Mother .... Charito Solis
Also with: Eula Valdez, Maila Gamila, Jackie Aquino, Mia Guitierrez.

This dramatized life story of the Philippines' first publicly acknowledged AIDS patient takes a classic women's-pic inspirational approach, giving star Vilma Santos ample opportunity to demonstrate spunk and teary histrionics. Obviously intended to educate home auds, pic is lively enough to interest specialized fests abroad.

Initial 40 minutes are a whirlwind tour of Dolzura Cortez's pre-diagnosis adult life. Dolly abandons her small village and nasty husband, leaving with her three kids for the big city where she indulges in love affairs that end her second marriage to a wealthy foreigner. Irrepressible, Dolly starts a femme "contract worker" agency, living the nightclub high life to support her brood.

A sudden collapse on a discotheque floor presages diagnosis of full-blown AIDS. Moved to a Manila hospital ward, Dolly encounters old lover Paulo, now an AIDS researcher. He eventually convinces her to reveal herself via newspaper interviews, lending a "human face" to the hitherto anonymous specter of local AIDS paranoia. Before her

1992 death, Cortez apparently did much to educate Filipinos and alleviate their baseless fears of casual contagion.

Pic engenders sympathy in the right ways, taking pains to counter charges that AIDS is "God's punishment." The identity of Dolly's "infector" is also pointedly left unknown, in line with anti-stigmatizing message. Portrayal of illness (especially Kaposi's sarcoma lesions) is graphic.

Yet while film scoffs at virus-hysterical reactions by the public and the media, it oddly fails to spell out transmission-risking behaviors and safer-sex techniques, beyond passing mention of condoms.

Leading Philippine actress Santos cuts a Susan Hayward-worthy swath early on as the hearty, partying gal who loves being "chased by men," and later in various stalwart/angry/agonized postures. "Nothing can put me down, not even this disease!" she cries. While death throes are melodramatically prolonged, this showy perf gives film its driving force.

Director Laurice Guillen's supporting cast and tech values are above average; smart pace flags occasionally in the second half. As usual with Philippine features, dialogue mixes Tagalog with English phrases. —*Dennis Harvey*

LE VOLEUR ET LA MENTEUSE
(THE THIEF AND THE LIAR)
(FRENCH)

A Bac Films release of a Les Films 13/Les Films Tapon production, in association with Sofiarp and participation of Canal Plus. (Intl. sales: Jean-Paul de Vides, Paris.) Produced by Claude Lelouch. Executive producer, Tania Zazulinsky. Directed, written by Paul Boujenah. Camera (color, widescreen), Philippe Pavans de Ceccatty; editor, Helene de Luze; art direction, Laurent Tesseyre; sound (Dolby), Vincent Arnardi; assistant director, Simon Lelouch. Reviewed at 14 Juillet Odeon Cinema, Paris, Jan. 15, 1994. Running time: **79 MIN.**
Suzanne Henson .... Mathilda May
Paul Salomon .... Gerard Darmon
Jeff .... Philippe Leotard
Solange .... Nathalie Cerda
Restaurant owner ...... Jacques Bonnot
Also with: Christian Charmettant, Charles Gerard.

Bare-bones boy-meets-girl story "The Thief and the Liar" is a modestly engaging tale centering on the visceral connection between an escaped convict and a woman at odds with her surroundings. Intimate widescreen drama produced by Claude Lelouch should do OK at Gallic wickets and on the Euro tube.

Paul Salomon (Gerard Darmon) has flown lockup and hitched to a wintry resort town on the English Channel to recover a briefcase full of dough on his way to Blighty. He hastily buys new clothes in a shop where movie costumer Suzanne (Mathilda May) is also making purchases.

Late that night, Paul invites himself to her restaurant table and tells her the truth about himself. Suzanne, skeptical, invents an imaginary life for herself based on Helena, the traumatized Russian violinist heroine of a pic she was working on. The more Suzanne fibs, the more truthful Paul becomes. The relationship is cemented when Suzanne discovers he really is an escaped thief on the lam. They share a night of torrid romance, but the local police chief (Philippe Leotard) is on their trail.

Though there is nothing earth-shattering about the encounter, the chemistry between Darmon and May works. Former is well cast as the grizzled charmer, and May is more convincing here as a contemporary woman having an extended bad-hair day than in recent period roles as explorer Isabelle Eberhardt or writer Colette.

Shot in 18 days, pic boasts the immediacy and continuity of one long night. A subplot about the restaurant waitress who is having an affair with the married police chief gives Nathalie Cerda a chance to shine. Widescreen lensing alternates formal compositions with hand-held stuff. —*Lisa Nesselson*

TODOS A LA CARCEL
(EVERYONE OFF TO JAIL)
(SPANISH)

A Sogetel S.A., Central de Producciones Audiovisuales, Antea Films S.A. production. Executive producers, Jose Luis Olaizola, Fernando de Garcillan, Pepe Ferrandiz. Directed by Luis G. Berlanga. Screenplay, Jorge Berlanga, Luis G. Berlanga. Camera (color) Alfredo Mayo; editor, Maria Elena Sainz de Rozas, Rori Sainz de Rozas; music, Luis Mendo, Bernardo Fuster; production design, Rafael Palmero. Reviewed at Cine Carlos III, Madrid, Jan. 15, 1994. Running time: **90 MIN.**
With: Jose Sazatornil (Artemio), Jose Luis Lopez Vasquez (Padre Rebollo), Jose Sacristan (Quintanilla), Antonio Resines (Mariano), Juan Luis Galiardo (Munagorri), Agustin Gonzalez (Warden).

As in early Berlanga films, the touches of black humor, gentle ribbing of reds, fascists and modern socialists, and zany goings-on are all present in "Everyone Off to Jail." True to form, helmer again drags out a turbulent, non-stop yackfest, constantly changing the roster of oddball characters. But the oc-

casional laugh is soon overtaken by tedium, and it all finally feels very *deja vu.*

Mostly unfolded in a Valencia prison, plot has an enterprising promoter organizing a day of tribute to erstwhile political prisoners. These, along with the media reps and politicos, have been invited to a gala dinner. Everything goes wrong, as persons with diverse vested interests create continuous droll confusion.

The central character (a throwback to Berlanga's 1978 "National Shotgun") is a nervous, fawning Jose Sazatornil, who tries to collect overdue coin from a government official for a toilet installation.

Berlanga's customary long-sequence shots constantly switch from person to person — transvestites, cooks, politicos, jailbirds — as he bombards the audience with non-stop slangy dialogue and gesticulations.

But what was poignant satire in the 1970s now verges dangerously close to parody of Berlanga's own earlier work. The intended political satire, now set in modern democratic Spain, is rather passe, and the scatological sequences are silly. Pic has been only moderately successful on its home turf. —*Peter Besas*

BELOW 30/ ABOVE 10,000

A Damaged Californians production. Produced by P. James Keitel, D. Scott Hessels. Directed by Keitel. Screenplay, Hessels. Camera (color), Duane Manwiller, John (Culp) Bailey, Brad Rushing; editor, Thomas R. Sanders; original music, Michael Whitmore. Reviewed on vidcassette, San Francisco, Jan. 21, 1994. Running tine: **77 MIN.**
Michael .... David Clayberg
Wendy .... Kathryn Cressida
Robert .... Jeff Glickman
Also with: Lori Heuring, Hanz Maroto, Whitney Schrandt.

This twentysomething road movie ventures off the beaten track for sure, both in literal — via slick wilderness lensing — and figurative ways. But coyly experimental aspects will limit exposure to curious college auds and American indie-focus fests. Pic was launched with unspoolings at Berkeley's Pacific Film Archive.

Clever opening conveys recent bummers in the lives of 26-year-old L.A. protags via select motifs and answering-machine messages. Wiseacre Robert has just been ejected from both job and apartment; earnest Michael's g.f. professes love for an older man; social worker Wendy is feeling vulnerable after a juvenile's violent outburst. Since friends shared Colorado childhoods, the trio impulsively decide to "leave bad luck in the rear-

March 21, 1994 (Cont.)

view mirror" by taking off on a camping expedition.

Their pop-ironic rapport is engaging at first, all the more so for its refreshingly casual depiction of young male-female friendships sans sexual tension. But discussions of love, identity and philosophy soon turn self-consciously literary. Worse, screenplay posits the landscape and ocean as additional "characters" who (in titles) bemoan their ancient separation when not waxing philosophic or planting thoughts in the heads of human figures.

Novelty of this conceit soon wears didactically thin. By the time actors deliver lengthy monologues on solo hiking treks, pic feels like a collegiate writing project foisted upon the filmmakers' backpacking holiday. An abrupt non-ending exacerbates sense of a short-subject concept needlessly stretched to feature length.

Performers are attractive and affable, but their natural rhythms stall as verbiage piles up. Use of songs by Ethyl Meatplow and other bands is judicious, editing lively. Crisp, handsome photography, including underwater footage shot in barrier reefs near Belize, sports some impressive flourishes.

Director P. James Keitel and scenarist D. Scott Hessels won attention for prior vidshorts under production monicker Damaged Californians. If their grasp of narrative cinema doesn't develop past this first feature, they can take heart in what looks like a natural career path toward nature docs. —*Dennis Harvey*

L'ORSO DI PELUCHE

(THE TEDDY BEAR)

(ITALIAN-FRENCH)

A Penta Distribuzione release (Italy) of a Master Movie Distribution (Rome)/ Les Films Alain Sarde (Paris) coproduction. Produced by Giuseppe Auriemma. Directed by Jacques Deray. Screenplay, Dardano Sacchetti, Filippo Ascione, Jean Curtelin, based on the novel by Georges Simenon. Camera (Technicolor), Luciano Tovoli; editor, Nino Baragli; music, Romano Musumarra; art direction, Francois De Lamothe, Enrico Luzzi; costume design, Luzzi; sound (Dolby), Remo Ugolinelli, Corrado Volpicelli. Reviewed at Savoy Cinema, Rome, March 9, 1994. Running time: **89 MIN.**
Jean Riviere .... Alain Delon
Chantal .... Francesca Dellera
   Also with: Regina Bianchi, Paolo Bonacelli, Martine Brochard, Julie Dupage, Valentina Forte, Franco Interlenghi, Claudia Pandolfi, Mattia Sbragia, Alexandra Winisky, Laure Killing, Madeleine Robinson.
   (Italian soundtrack)

With an association spanning 25 years and nine features ("Borsalino" being the best-known), topliner Alain Delon and helmer Jacques Deray might have hoped for a more dignified reunion than "The Teddy Bear." Bland and uninvolving psychothriller is routine fare.

Adapted from a Georges Simenon novel, pic has Delon as an emotionally bankrupt, philandering gynecologist with a plush clinic in Brussels, whose responsibility for two deaths (the first indirectly, the second directly) steers him back to hearth and home.

Build-up to the dubious conclusion is a standard serving of anonymous death threats, circuitous clues (the teddy bear of the title for one), obsessive pursuit, and tormented self-examination after the suicide of a love-struck young nurse bedded and abandoned by the doc. Delon's expressionless remoteness is paired by a wooden turn from Italo sexpot Francesca Dellera, who spouts improbable dialogue seemingly meant to peg her as a self-styled Holly Golightly. Deray directs with a journeyman's efficiency that's matched by competent tech backup. —*David Rooney*

HIGH BOOT BENNY

(IRISH-GERMAN)

A Sandy Films (Ireland)/ZDF (Germany) production, in association with Radio Teilifis Eireann (Ireland)/La Sept-Arte (France)/Televisio de Catalunya (Spain)/Channel 4 (U.K.). (Intl. sales: Stranger Than Fiction, London.) Produced by David Kelly. Executive producers, Joe Comerford, Kelly. Directed, written by Comerford. Camera (Super-16mm, Metrocolor; Technicolor prints), Donal Gilligan; editor, Elen Pierce Lewis; music, Gaye McIntyre; production design, John Lucas; sound, Pat Hayes. Reviewed on videocassette, Mar. 12, 1994. (In Berlin Film Festival, Forum section.) Running time: **82 MIN.**
   With: Frances Tomelty (Matron), Alan Devlin (Manley), Marc O'Shea (Benny), Fiona Nicholas (The Orphan), Annie Farr (Dorothy), Seamus Ball (Father Bergin).

A slim but atmospheric tale of a Belfast teen caught up in IRA-Loyalist retribution, "High Boot Benny" reps a confident turn by Irish filmer Joe Comerford, whose "Reefer and the Model" screened in the Berlin fest's Panorama section in 1988. Commercial chances look mild, but film has a cinematic feel and interesting non-sectarian approach to its subject matter.

Benny (Marc O'Shea) is a 17-year-old delinquent, mistrustful of all sides in the Irish conflict, who takes refuge in a remote village school just across the border in (southern) Ireland. School is run by a woman (Frances Tomelty) who's trying to create a neutral haven for kids, and also has vague sexual stirrings for Benny; she's helped by an ex-priest (Alan Devlin), her sometime lover and sympathizer.

Events escalate when the school janitor, a police informer, is found murdered. Benny is tarred and feathered by IRA men, and one night Loyalists and the Brit army cross over from Northern Ireland with Tomelty and Devlin in their sights.

Dialogue is a tad over-expository at times, but perfs by the three leads mesh well, with Tomelty (the widow in Jim Sheridan's "The Field") economically portraying the schoolmom's idealism and warmth. Photography, cutting and Gaye McIntyre's ethnic-flavored score are all fine. —*Derek Elley*

PERDIAMOCI DI VISTA

(LET'S NOT KEEP IN TOUCH)

(ITALIAN)

A Penta Distribuzione release of a Cecchi Gori Group Tiger Cinematografica production. Produced by Mario and Vittorio Cecchi Gori. Directed by Carlo Verdone. Screenplay, Verdone, Francesca Marciano. Camera (Cinecitta color), Danilo Desideri; editor, Antonio Siciliano; music, Fabio Liberatori; art direction, Francesco Bronzi; costume design, Tatiana Romanoff; sound (Dolby), Benito Alchimede. Reviewed at Intl. Recording screening room, Rome, Jan. 24, 1994. Running time: **115 MIN.**
Gepy Fuxas .... Carlo Verdone
Arianna .... Asia Argento
Antonazzi .... Aldo Maccione
   With: Sonya Gessner, Cosima Costantini, Anita Bartolucci, Edmondo Tieghi, Natalia Bizzi.

Carlo Verdone's "Let's Not Keep in Touch" figures as a major disappointment. Somberly comic tale of a cynical TV star's slow-combustion romance with a young paraplegic is often quietly affecting, but Verdone's 13th outing reps an unlucky venture. The Roman actor/director's staunch following, however, should ensure pic a brisk run locally.

Verdone plays the unscrupulous host of a reality show that trades in human misery. The unlikely lovers meet when a wheelchair-bound member of the studio audience (Asia Argento) attacks him on air for capitalizing on other folks' tragedies. His inept self-defense fires national ire and the show is axed, leaving him to face up to a friendless, empty existence.

Feeling guilty, Argento sets up a rapprochement date. Rest of pic charts the obstacle-strewn course of their budding relationship, although the script establishes no credible basis for duo's attraction.

Verdone's earlier "Curse the Day I Met You" squeezed sweetly awkward comedy from a seemingly mismatched couple's thwarted romance. This one plumbs deeper into similar terrain, gently making a case for unconditional love. However, the two-character focus is muddied by oafish humor in surrounding scenes, plus lame digs at Italo TV via Verdone's attempts to revive his career by refereeing a mud-slinging match between unfaithful partners on a low-rent regional web. Argento is not entirely convincing when required to heat up and register anger, but the young thesp's sullen beauty and unstudied intensity make her a captivating presence. —*David Rooney*

LA NAISSANCE DE L'AMOUR

(THE BIRTH OF LOVE)

(FRENCH-SWISS — B&W)

A Pan Europeene release of a Why Not, La Sept Cinema (Paris)/Vega Films (Zurich) production, with participation of Canal Plus/Ministry of Culture & Francophonie/SACEM/Departement Federal de l'Interieur (Berne)/SSR/RTSI-Televisione Svizzera. (International sales: Why Not, Paris.) Co-executive producers, Christian Paumier, Pierre-Alain Schatzmann, Pascal Caucheteux, Ruth Waldberger. Directed by Philippe Garrel. Screenplay, Garrel, Marc Cholodenko, Muriel Cerf. Camera (b&w), Raoul Coutard; editors, Sophie Coussein, Yann Dedet; music, John Cale; costume design, Laura Travelli; sound, Jean-Pierre Ruh. Reviewed at Club de l'Etoile screening room, Paris, Aug. 27, 1993. (In Rotterdam and Venice (noncompeting) fests.) Running time: **91 MIN.**
Paul .... Lou Castel
Marcus .... Jean-Pierre Leaud
Ulrika .... Johanna Ter Steege
Helene .... Dominique Reymond
Fanchon .... Marie-Paul Laval

A better title for Philippe Garrel's self-indulgent film would be "Sullen, Unappealing Characters Pontificating on Their Lives and Problems." Confessional, intimate look at middle-aged artistic types adrift remains true to the French auteurist tradition, and Garrel's faith in his actors is palpable. However, only hard-core cinephiles will connect with this orbit of helmer's navel.

Narrative unspools in a dreary, workaday Paris (rigorously lensed in b&w by new wave icon Raoul Coutard) against a backdrop of the brewing Gulf War. Basic idea is that love can go out the window from one day to the next, the same way it can fly in without warning.

March 21, 1994 (Cont.)

Paul (Lou Castel), an actor, beds indifferent Ulrika (Johanna Ter Steege), argues with his wife (Marie-Paul Laval), who is about to give birth to their second child, and is a mediocre role model for his adolescent son. Why a dour lunk with nothing going for him should be so attractive to women (including one who's half his age) is a mystery.

The only live wire in the cast is Jean-Pierre Leaud as Paul's friend Marcus, a writer who has abandoned his craft in favor of "thinking." Leaud delivers crazed philosophical monologues and wonders aloud why his g.f. has left him.

Soundtrack is awash with aural distractions in exteriors — a conscious choice by Garrel, who abhors looping and post-syncing. John Cale's music is fleeting.

—*Lisa Nesselson*

DE ESO NO SE HABLA

(I DON'T WANT TO TALK ABOUT IT)

(ARGENTINE-ITALIAN)

An Oscar Kramer SA (Buenos Aires)/Aura Films (Rome) co-production. (International sales: the Sales Co., London). Produced by Kramer, Roberto Cicutto, Vincenzo De Leo. Directed by Maria Luisa Bemberg. Screenplay, Bemberg, Jorge Goldenberg, from a story by Julio Llinas. Camera (color), Felix Monti; editor, Juan Carlos Macias; music, Nicola Piovani; production design, Jorge Sarudiansky; costumes, Graciela Galan; sound, Carlos Abbate; assistant director, Alejandro Maci. Reviewed at Venice Film Festival (competing), Sept. 3, 1993. (Also in Toronto Festival of Festivals.) Running time: 105 MIN.
Ludovico
D'Andrea .... Marcello Mastroianni
Leonor .... Luisina Brando
Charlotte .... Alejandra Podesta
Madam .... Betiana Blum
Dr. Blanes .... Alberto Segado
Signora Zamilidio .... Monica Villa
Widow Schmidt .... Tina Serrano
Father Aurelio .... Roberto Carnaghi
Alcade .... Jorge Luz
Police Chief .... Juan Manuel Tenuta

Argentina's No. 1 femme director, Maria Luisa Bemberg, has come up with a quirky, bizarre comedy-drama in "I Don't Want to Talk About It," based on the sort of left-field premise that has fascinated filmmakers like Luis Bunuel and Marco Ferreri in the past. Production is handsome, off-the-wall, yet at times strangely muted, and should drum up interest on the international arthouse circuit.

This tall tale is set in a small Argentine town in the 1940s. Luisina Brando cuts an imposing figure as Leonor, a respected, well-off widow who is determined that her daugh-

ter, Charlotte, a dwarf, live as normal a life as possible while keeping up a veneer of respectability in the close-knit community.

Most eligible local bachelor is the slightly mysterious Ludovico (Marcello Mastroianni), who has his choice of all the single women in the district. Indeed, Leonor rather fancies he might marry her one day, as he's a regular visitor to her home and is forever telling stories to the delighted Charlotte and giving the adolescent presents.

So Leonor is amazed to discover that it's not her the dapper Ludovico is courting, but Charlotte. Eventually, he marries her, and they appear to be blissfully happy until, one sad day, a circus comes to town.

Bemberg keeps the audience guessing as to how these unusual relationships will be resolved, and imbues the film with a gentle humor. It would be interesting to speculate what fun a more outrageous director — Bunuel, say, or Alejandro Jodorowsky — might have had with the obsessive passion inherent in this subject, but Bemberg is content to handle the theme in a perfectly matter-of-fact style, which makes the strange narrative appear even stranger. Performances are top-notch, with Mastroianni superb as the tormented, ardent lover and Brando imposing as the fiercely proud matriarch. Alejandra Podesta has been perfectly cast as the diminutive Charlotte.

Production values are excellent, and there's a typically catchy score from Italo composer Nicola Piovani.

—*David Stratton*

RAM CSAJ MEG NEM VOLT ILYEN HATASSAL

(NO GIRL EVER HAD THIS EFFECT ON ME)

(HUNGARIAN — B&W)

A Hunnia Filmstudio production with the support of MTV Friz. Produced by Sandor Simo, Judit Kopper. Directed by Peter Reich. Screenplay, Reich, Attila Hazai. Camera (b&w), Tibor Klopfler; editor, Katalin Meszaros; music, Miklos Konrad. Reviewed at Hungarian Film Week, Budapest, Feb. 7, 1994. Running time: 83 MIN.
Miklos .... Miklos Deri
Dora .... Erika Marozsan

An ultra-low-budgeter, filmed in black-and-white, "No Girl Ever Had This Effect on Me" is a promising feature debut for U.S.-trained helmer Peter Reich. Pic has something of the feeling of the French new wave or some of the recent U.S. indie no-budgeters.

Miklos, the sad-sack hero, works as a press photographer and plays guitar in a small jazz band (Reich appears as another of the musicians). He's had a couple of relationships that came to nothing, and now he's keen on Dora, a quiet, attractive girl who hangs around the club where he plays.

Theirs is an unremarkable relationship. The film avoids sex scenes (when they do sleep together, fully clothed, it's because they're tired). But there's an honesty and freshness about Reich's low-key approach, and his young actors are appealing and relaxed.

"No Girl," which relies heavily on v.o. narration, is probably a bit too slight to play the fest route, but it's likely that Reich will be heard from again. —*David Stratton*

ROUEN

DU PAPPA ...

(DADDY BLUE)

(NORWEGIAN)

A Norsk Film production. (International sales: Norsk Film, Oslo.) Produced by Harald Ohrvik, Esben Hoilund Carlsen. Directed, written by Rene Bjerke. Camera (color), Peter Mocrosinski; editor, Trygve Hagen; music, Svein Gurdersen; costume design, Runa Fonne. Reviewed at Rouen Festival of Nordic Cinema (competing), Rouen, France, March 11, 1994. Running time: 89 MIN.
LP .... Hakon Bolstad
Line .... Benedikte Lindbeck
Father .... Nils Ole Oftebro
Mother .... Grethe Ryen

"Daddy Blue" is a sensitively told, wry tale of a taciturn young teen who tests his wings and learns an unspoken lesson or two about grown-up behavior. Feature bow by Rene Bjerke, founder of Oslo's Cinematek, is a spare, fest-ready charmer.

LP, the only child of a comfortably middle-class Norwegian couple, celebrates his junior-high graduation by swiping a sailboat. He's about to crash into a dock when pixie-faced, accomplished sailor Line hops aboard to enjoy a few days of chaste skinny-dipping and sun-bathing until LP's dad catches up with them.

Freed from household patterns — and with the delectable 20-year-old Line aboard — father and son see each other in new and telling ways.

Slight but charming pic, appealingly played, rings true throughout. Comic timing is fine and humor is conveyed more through slow burns, behavioral juxtapositions, and

guilty or knowing expressions than via dialogue. LP doesn't say much, Line strips at every opportunity, and Dad tries to assess the lay of the land even though he's at sea.

Lensing has a summery, timeless bent.

—*Lisa Nesselson*

BALTIC LOVE: THREE STORIES

(FINNISH-ESTONIAN)

A Filminor (Helsinki)/Exit Film (Tallinn) production. Produced by Heikki Takkinen. Directed by Peeter Urbla. Screenplay, Urbla, Heikki Makela, Takkinen. Camera (color), Jukka Lampinen, Mait Lepik, Priit Grepp, Juha-Veli Akras; editor, Elyi Oras. Reviewed at Rouen Festival of Nordic Cinema (competing), Rouen, France, March 13, 1994. Running time: 99 MIN.
With Andres Noormets (Mattias), Carmen Mikiver (Ann), Liana Upeniece (Regina), Sergei Vartschuk (Sergei), Dainius Kazlauskas (Vytautas), Katri Horma (Juozas).

An intermittently touching trio of tales set in the three newly independent Baltic states in 1991, "Baltic Love" is strictly fest fare. Three geographically distinct episodes show the messy repercussions of Soviet occupation on twentysomethings who want only to live and love.

In "Estonian Spring 1991: Mattias and Ann," young Mattias is the last Estonian political prisoner to be freed from a Moscow hoosegow. His wife Ann, an actress at the Tallinn theater where he also worked, has meantime taken up with another man. With disarming candor, Ann delivers a sweet speech about how she remade her life without meaning to.

In "Latvian Summer 1991: Regina and Sergei," Russian paratrooper Sergei is enjoying a sincere cross-cultural idyll with Latvian sweetheart Regina, but two patriotic buddies — who saved his life after he was left for dead in Afghanistan — intercede. Animosity between occupier and occupied is well-conveyed and love is not permitted to conquer all.

Third and clumsiest episode, "Lithuanian Autumn 1991: Vytatutas and Juozas," concerns a virginal seminary student drawn to a stripper from Tallinn when her "Jazz and Sex" revue plays a local hotel. His priest uncle tries counsel, but nephew delivers an embarrassing speech comparing his beloved's body parts to biblical spices.

Film has a washed out, muddy patina which lends an almost home-movie style intimacy. One unifying factor is characters' reluctance to speak Russian. Male and female full-frontal nudity is smoothly integrated and could be a selling point in certain markets, although pic's thrust is political and emotional.

—*Lisa Nesselson*

JIMMY HOLLYWOOD

A Paramount release of a Baltimore Pictures production. Produced by Mark Johnson, Barry Levinson. Executive producer, Peter Giuliano. Directed, written by Levinson. Camera (Deluxe color), Peter Sova; editor, Jay Rabinowitz; music, Robbie Robertson; production design, Linda DeScenna; set decoration, Ric McElvin; costume design, Kirsten Everberg; sound (Dolby), Steve Cantamessa; associate producers, Marie Rowe, James Flamberg, Gerrit Van Der Meer; assistant director, Giuliano; second unit camera, Eric D. Andersen; casting, Louis Di Giaimo. Reviewed at Paramount Studios, L.A., March 23, 1994. MPAA Rating: R. Running time: **109 MIN.**
Jimmy Alto .... Joe Pesci
William .... Christian Slater
Lorraine .... Victoria Abril
Detective .... Jason Beghe
Detective .... John Cothran Jr.

At the critical, defining moment in the life of would-be Hollywood actor Jimmy Alto, he comes up firing blanks. The same can be said of Barry Levinson's oddball attempt to mix offbeat comedy with social commentary and fringe-level character study. However well intentioned, the contrary elements just don't mesh, and pic's only possible B.O. salvation — laughter — never materializes. This look at a showbiz loser will itself be a commercial castoff.

Basically a three-character piece set almost entirely within a few blocks either side of Hollywood Boulevard, production represents a case of the scale and cost of a project being way out of proportion to its story and potential appeal. As a low-budget indie shot on the run and then marketed cleverly, this story of terminal down-and-outers might have made some sense. As a $20 million studio undertaking without major stars, however, it never stood a chance.

As obsessed with Hollywood stardom as any youngster stepping off the bus in the 1930s, Jimmy (Joe Pesci) is no closer to making it now than he was seven years ago when he arrived in L.A. from Jersey. Lucky enough to have a sexy g.f., Lorraine (Spanish star Victoria Abril), who aspires to be hairdresser to the stars, Jimmy spends his time hanging out in dingy Hollywood coffee shops, reading the trades and sitting in front of the self-promotional billboard he's bought for a bus stop bench on Sunset in Bel-Air, always in the company of dimwit grunge puppy William (Christian Slater).

Characters and the picture are going nowhere fast when Jimmy's car radio is stolen. With nothing better to do, Jimmy and William take to the bushes, camcorder in hand, to videotape the culprit in the act next time. They then dump the criminal, along with the incriminating tape and a note, at the doorstep of the Hollywood police station.

Jimmy then makes an effective tape of himself as Jericho, the fearless leader of S.O.S. (Save Our Streets), a self-appointed "watchdog of Hollywood" vigilante group dedicated to targeting the scum that has made the entertainment capital so dangerous.

Local TV stations take notice; exhilarated by the media attention and driven by a romanticized notion of what Hollywood was and should be, Jimmy and William don masks and catch any number of bad guys in the act, always taping them and issuing new proclamations.

In one of life's telling little ironies, the authorities aren't terribly concerned with the vermin Jimmy turns in, but have dozens of cops assigned to track down the dangerous Jericho.

What ultimately seems to have been Levinson's overriding motivation in writing the piece — a love of Hollywood as a place, sorrow over what has become of it and empathy for those who retain, however naively, a purity and innocence in their dreams — is actually rather sweet and sympathetic. The discrepancy between

As a low-budget indie shot on the run and then marketed cleverly, this story of terminal down-and-outers might have made some sense.

myth and reality is perhaps nowhere more extreme than in Hollywood, and the unyielding portrait of it here as a crime-ridden home to hopeless lowlifes is pretty acute.

But the film doesn't work on any level, and, to compound the problem, those levels don't synch up. As the focus of attention, Jimmy is sadly and obnoxiously self-centered and small-minded; nothing exists in his universe outside his own deluded notions of himself as an actor, and society's deterioration bothers him only to the extent that it soils his dream world.

As a view of vigilantism and social activism, film is soft and fuzzyheaded, neither tough-minded or rabble-rousing on the right hand nor analytical or insightful on the left. As comedy, there are enough decent gags to fill out a trailer, but the sound of silence where laughs were meant to be weighs heavily throughout.

In a blond hairpiece almost as awful as his getup in "JFK," Pesci is more antic than engaging, although his former aluminum siding salesman and spiritual cousin to Levinson's characters in "Diner" and "Tin Men" remains entirely believable as an actor who's never even so much as appeared in a commercial.

Slater's thick-headed second-banana role reps the farthest thing from a glamorous star turn as one could imagine, and Abril, in her American film debut, is spirited, even if her character seems rather too blindly supportive of her no-account b.f.

Although Peter Sova's lensing aims to evoke urban blight, production values are still way beyond what was necessary or appropriate for the material. In an unconvincing tag-on, Harrison Ford pops up under the end credits as the unlikely star of a Jimmy Alto biopic. —*Todd McCarthy*

D2: THE MIGHTY DUCKS

A Buena Vista release of a Walt Disney Pictures presentation of an Avnet/Kerner production. Produced by Jordan Kerner, Jon Avnet. Executive producer, Doug Claybourne. Co-producers, Steven Brill, Salli Newman. Directed by Sam Weisman. Screenplay, Brill, based on characters created by Brill. Camera (Astro Color Lab color; Technicolor prints), Mark Irwin; editors, Eric Sears, John F. Link; music, J.A.C. Redford; production design, Gary Frutkoff; art direction, Dawn Snyder; set decoration, Kathryn Peters; costume design, Grania Preston; sound (Dolby), David Kelson; assistant director, David Householter; second unit director, Steve Boyum; second unit camera, Joel King; hockey technical adviser, Jack White; casting, Judy Taylor, Lynda Gordon. Reviewed at El Capitan Theater, L.A., March 18, 1993. MPAA Rating: PG. Running time: **106 MIN.**

Gordon Bombay	Emilio Estevez
Michelle Mackay	Kathryn Erbe
Tibbles	Michael Tucker
Jan	Jan Rubes
Wolf	Carsten Norgaard
Marria	Maria Ellingsen
Charlie	Joshua Jackson
Fulton	Elden Ryan Ratliff
Goldberg	Shaun Weiss
Averman	Matt Doherty
Banks	Vincent Larusso
Julie	Colombe Jacobsen
Portman	Aaron Lohr
Russ	Kenan Thompson
Ken	Justin Wong

Let's just put aside the fact that perennial hockey powers Canada and Russia get eliminated in the early rounds of the international competition that forms the centerpiece of "D2: The Mighty Ducks." Or that a team from Iceland — never a noted threat in the sport — is cast as the heavies in the competition for the cup so dearly cherished by Team USA under the leadership of coach Gordon Bombay (Emilio Estevez). Even disregarding its credibility problems, "D2" is a pretty sorry follow-up to a picture that spawned a National Hockey League franchise and enchanted the box office to the tune of $50 million.

While there are plenty of ideas and ideals floating through this youthful action comedy, it's sorely lacking in anything vaguely resembling a script. The ragtag pucksters get a patchwork palette that results in a tired pastiche of sports cliches. Commercial prospects are fast, down and dirty, and likely to put a real crimp in the bigscreen franchise.

In the new outing, with his ongoing attempt to play in the pros again stymied by injury, Gordo is tipped as the ideal hockeymeister for the upcoming Junior Goodwill Games (winter edition). All he has to do is round up his old Ducks and add some new kids.

But Team USA isn't really a squad, it's a collection of minorities and social causes. There's the Hispanic player who skates like lightning but hasn't learned how to stop. And there's the female goalie who's actually better than the regular Jewish kid, but for some unknown reason he's been granted seniority. By the final faceoff, these and other problems will be resolved.

In truth, it's a wonder these rink rats can outscore the Trinidad team, let alone make the playoffs. Add to the mix Gordon's brief seduction into the world of product endorsement and those Icelandic dirty tricksters, and the lunacy is complete.

Director Sam Weisman's best shots are on the ice, building the excitement of competition to a fever pitch. But that momentum is DOA every time he has to cut to narrative, complete a plot point, include a product placement shot or a nod to the NHL Ducks' Anaheim arena.

Confronted with such overwhelming entertainment obstacles, it's no wonder that the adult players appear so ill at ease. Estevez, who had so much charm and energy in the first, acts as if there was a dark cloud trailing his path. The rest of the cast merely struggles to maintain some shred of dignity.

Strictly matinee fare for the preteen set, "D2: The Mighty Ducks" are fast proving they're simply not quacked up to be in a commercial league of their own.

—Leonard Klady

MAJOR LEAGUE II

A Warner Bros. release of a James G. Robinson presentation of a Morgan Creek production. Produced by Robinson, David S. Ward. Executive producer, Gary Barber. Directed by Ward. Screenplay, R.J. Stewart, story by Stewart, Tom S. Parker, Jim Jennewein, based on characters created by Ward. Camera (Duart color; Technicolor prints), Victor Hammer; editors, Paul Seydor, Donn Cambern; music, Michel Colombier; production design, Stephen Hendrickson; art direction, Gary Diamond; set design, Kyung Chang; set decoration, Leslie Bloom; costume design, Bobbie Read, sound (Dolby), Robert Anderson Jr; technical adviser, Steve Yeager; assistant director, Jerram A. Swartz; line producer/second unit director, Edward D. Markley; second unit camera, John M. Stephens; casting, Ferne Cassel. Reviewed at Warner Bros., Burbank, March 23, 1994. MPAA Rating: PG. Running time: **104 MIN.**

Rick Vaughn	Charlie Sheen
Jake Taylor	Tom Berenger
Roger Dorn	Corbin Bernsen
Pedro Cerrano	Dennis Haysbert
Lou Brown	James Gammon
Willie Mays Hayes	Omar Epps
Rube Baker	Eric Bruskotter
Harry Doyle	Bob Uecker
Jack Parkman	David Keith
Rachel Phelps	Margaret Whitton
Isuro Tanaka	Takaaki Ishibashi
Flannery	Alison Doody
Nikki Reese	Michelle Burke
Johnny	Randy Quaid
Monte	Skip Griparis

It's a fast trip back to the minors for "Major League II," a singularly unfunny, dramatically tepid follow-up to 1989's $50 million theatrical success. Time has not been kind to the franchise, with the second season imposing a straitjacket structure that's in direct opposition to the inspired chaos of the original. Apart from an emotional ninth-inning surge, this is one yarn that unravels into a heap of plot strands all too quickly.

Commercial prospects for the Cinderella squad are other than championship form. Unlike the screen team, the film has fast-start potential but should choke after a couple of innings. Even the addition of a Japanese comic on the field is unlikely to provide much heat in the one offshore market where baseball packs a hefty commercial swing.

Story dives directly into the next season of the fictional Cleveland Indians, who won their onscreen division five years back. They ought to be pumped for bigger and better things. Instead, they return diminished by off-season activity. Rick "Wild Thing" Vaughn (Charlie Sheen) has gone so legit that he's now a sought-after spokesman for chichi products. Knee injuries send Jake Taylor (Tom Berenger) to the coaching ranks, and Roger Dorn (Corbin Bernsen) has stepped off the field to buy the club from former owner Rachel Phelps (Margaret Whitton). Meanwhile, Willie Mays Hayes (Omar Epps) did an action film, and Pedro Cerrano has switched from voodoo to Buddhism.

The thread running through R.J. Stewart's screenplay is that old, feel-good saw about being yourself. The by-the-book plot systematically has each character seeing the light — which, as the team once again becomes whole, transforms the cellar club into a World Series contender.

The predictable device robs the film of a lot of momentum. Devoid of pace, much of the humor comes across as forced and insipid. Peripheral characters and commentators — so integral to the first — emerge as somehow separate and, somewhat ironically, much funnier than the principals. While the original was a true ensemble piece, "Major League II" places its dominant emphasis on Sheen's character. The thankless role he has to play drags him through the movie only vaguely aware that he has a crisis to resolve. When he is transformed, his moment of epiphany occurs offscreen.

The rest of the cast is allowed barely more than a single note to play. That applies to veterans, including Bernsen and Whitton, as well as the hayseed new catcher limned by Eric Bruskotter and the mean, vain heavy embodied by David Keith. Randy Quaid is badly misused in the recurring part of a fan in the stands whose sentiment swings with the Indian's fortunes. So one has to be thankful for the energy Bob Uecker provides as the radio play-by-play man and the truly inspired deadpan of his sidekick (Skip Griparis). The actor who comes off best is Wesley Snipes, who opted not to do the sequel and whose part was recast with Epps.

The dramatic bedrock of both "Leagues" is teamwork, teamwork, teamwork — do your job, work hard and collaborate. It's a good rule of life and something the makers of "League II" appear to have forgotten during the hiatus between these two baseball production seasons.

—Leonard Klady

MOTHER'S BOYS

A Miramax/Dimension Films release in association with CBS Prods. Produced by Jack E. Freedman, Wayne S. Williams, Patricia Herskovic. Executive producers, Bob and Harvey Weinstein, Randall Poster. Directed by Yves Simoneau. Screenplay, Barry Schneider, Richard Hawley, based on Bernard Taylor's novel. Camera (color), Elliot Davis; editor, Michael Ornstein; music, George S. Clinton; art direction, David Bomba; set decoration, Barbara Cassel; costume design, Deena Appel, Simon Tuke; sound (Dolby), Clark King; associate producer, Dan Franklin; assistant director, Steve Danton; casting, Francine Maisler. Reviewed at the Beverly Connection, L.A., March 19, 1994. MPAA Rating: R. Running time: **95 MIN.**

Jude	Jamie Lee Curtis
Robert	Peter Gallagher
Callie	Joanne Whalley-Kilmer
Lydia	Vanessa Redgrave
Kes	Luke Edwards
Michael	Colin Ward
Ben	Joey Zimmerman

Elegant style and amiable cast can't conceal the silliness of "Mother's Boys," an unsuspenseful variation of the yuppie-in-peril thriller. Jamie Lee Curtis stars as the "mother from hell." Miramax/Dimension understandably did not hold advance screenings for this film, which will enjoy a longer life on the video shelf than in movie houses.

Set in L.A., story begins as Jude (Curtis), an attractive woman who deserted her husband (Peter Gallagher) and three sons without any explanation, suddenly returns, determined to win back her family. Jude is convinced that her hubby still loves her, even though he is now attached to Callie (Joanne Whalley-Kilmer), the warm and supportive assistant principal at his son's school.

When begging forgiveness and other "charming" strategies fail, Jude resorts to manipulating eldest son Kes (Luke Edwards), who had suffered the most from her abandonment.

She's not above buying her kids expensive gifts, taking them to a planetarium and, in pic's most controversial scene, demonstrating to Kes in full nudity her scar from his birth, which she sees as a symbol of their special bond.

Not much can be praised about "Mother's Boys," a film that has an uninteresting beginning, an exploitative middle that actually cheats by genre standards, and a ludicrous climax that is borderline laughable. The few suspenseful moments generated

March 28, 1994 (Cont.)

by Canadian helmer Yves Simoneau are unfairly earned.

Elliot Davis' fancy lensing only accentuates the predictably slender plot of the movie.

Fans of former scream queen Curtis might get a kick out of seeing her not as a frightful victim, but as an erotic, manipulative avenger. The attractive Gallagher does what he can with his poorly written role. The only performer who rises above the material is the luminous Vanessa Redgrave, as Curtis' sensitive mother. —*Emanuel Levy*

HANS CHRISTIAN ANDERSEN'S THUMBELINA

A Warner Bros. release of a Don Bluth presentation. Produced by Bluth, Gary Goldman, John Pomeroy. Directed by Bluth, Goldman. Screenplay, Bluth, based on the story by Hans Christian Andersen. Supervising directing animator, John Pomeroy; directing animators, John Hill, Richard Bazley, Jean Morel, Len Simon, Piet Derycker, Dave Kupczyk; Technicolor; editor, Thomas V. Moss; music, William Ross, Barry Manilow; original songs by Manilow, Jack Feldman, Bruce Sussman; production design, Rowland Wilson; art direction, Barry Atkinson; sound (Dolby), John K. Carr; associate producer, Russell Boland; voice casting, Judy Taylor, Lynda Gordon. Reviewed at Plaza Theater, L.A., March 24, 1994. MPAA Rating: G. Running time: **94 MIN.**

Voices:
Thumbelina .... Jodi Benson
Ms. Fieldmouse .... Carol Channing
Mrs. (Ma) Toad .... Charo
Jacquimo .... Gino Conforti
Mother .... Barbara Cook
Baby Bug .... Kendall Cunningham
Queen Tabitha .... June Foray
Gnatty .... Tawny Sunshine Glover
Mr. Beetle .... Gilbert Gottfried
Mr. Mole .... John Hurt

Talented animation maverick Don Bluth's newest outing, "Hans Christian Andersen's Thumbelina," fails to effectively mine the poetic images and characters of the Danish children's classic and instead translates the yarn into a perky contemporary bestiary filled with frenetic, hypercomical creatures woefully lacking in charm or warmth. The chances of "Beast" or "Mermaid"-type dollars for this unaffecting family fare would seem as slight as the film heroine's tiny waist. Respectable theatrical receipts and a solid video life would seem a "happily ever after" for this modestly entertaining family outing from the maker of the 1986 animated B.O. triumph "An American Tail."

Pic employs the vocal talents of a colorful acting crew (including Charo, John Hurt, Carol Channing,

Gilbert Gottfried and animation vet June Foray), the music of Barry Manilow and teams of animators and artists from Ireland to Hungary. But co-producer/director/screenwriter Bluth unfortunately fails to pull these elements together into a dramatic, cohesive movie.

Thumbelina's quest to find the fairy prince of her dreams, and her prince's battle to save her from the creatures of the woods, stop and start, never pausing long enough to create a consistent mood. There's also a vacuum where there should be a memorable nemesis.

The film opens promisingly with Thumbelina's brief encounter with Prince Cornelius, and if both are a tad too '90s in appearance, their first evening together conveys the magic of romance and offers a spectacular nocturnal flight through the countryside, courtesy of an obliging bumblebee. Manilow's music lends a strong emotional lift to the proceedings, but the songs that follow aren't nearly as memorable or as affecting.

As Thumbelina stumbles through a series of threatening encounters with the forest's denizens, her character development is imperceptible. Likewise Prince Cornelius, who knows in the film's first moments that Thumbelina is his true love.

Perhaps preschoolers will find "Thumbelina" an entertaining alternative to "Barney" and others of his ilk, but they'll have a hard time finding older siblings who'll relish the chance to share their adventure. Parents, hoping to share time in the imaginary world of childhood, will instead find their patience strained.

It may sound silly to question the motivation of a lovesick frog or the character arc of a randy beetle, but the best animated fantasy films are chock-full of grumpy dwarves, passionate beasts, loyal crickets and the like, and their creators have wedded solid storytelling skills to their gift for making dreamlike images.

Other than an occasional breathtaking splash of animation, "Thumbelina" adds little to the form's history. In its best moments, it gives a glimpse of the delicate poetry that underlines Andersen's vision of a beautiful spirit outcast in a frightening, oversized world. But those moments are as fragile as a fairy's wing and are quickly overwhelmed by characters like Gottfried's bleating, abrasive Mr. Beetle and Charo's cuchi-cuchi reptile stage mother, Ma Toad. The result is more grim than Grimm.

—*Steven Gaydos*

TOTAL BALALAIKA SHOW

(FINNISH — DOCUMENTARY)

A Sputnik production in association with YLE, TV-1, Eila Werning, Megamania, Atte Blom, Esek, Luses. (International sales: World Sales Christa Saredi, Zurich.) Produced, directed by Aki Kaurismaki. Camera (color), Heikki Ortamo; editor, Timo Linnasalo; stage design, Sakke Jarvenpaa, Ilkka Paloniemi, Erkki Karenaho, Marko Louna; sound (Dolby), Tom Forsstrom; assistant director, Erkki Astala; second unit camera, Pekka Aine, Tahvo Hirvonen, Timo Salminen, Olli Varja. Reviewed at Rouen Festival of Nordic Cinema (non-competing), Rouen, France, March 19, 1994. (Also in Berlin Festival, Panorama section.) Running time: **56 MIN.**

With: The Leningrad Cowboys, the Alexandrov Red Army Chorus & Dance Ensemble, conducted by Igor Agafonnikov.

(English and Russian soundtrack. Titles in English)

Aki Kaurismaki's "Total Balalaika Show" is the most incongruous — and inspired — crosscultural pairing since Nureyev danced with Miss Piggy. Hourlong concert docu, in which Finland's Leningrad Cowboys trade standards with the ex-Red Army Choir, could have auds convulsing with laughter, stamping their feet and clapping their hands from Woodstock to Vladivostok.

Comedy and music webs, as well as specialized, campus and midnight-movie programmers, should delight in this surefire crowdpleaser whose outlandish premise would have been unimaginable just a few years back.

Apart from a staged opening shot of a contract-signing, pic is a straight docu of the June 12, 1993, concert that Kaurismaki helped to initiate. Before a crowd of more than 70,000 in Helsinki's Senate Square, the musically challenged Finnish rock band traded hot licks and bellowed dopey standards with the sometimes baffled, but always sonorous, Russian choir.

From the first note, it's Irony Curtain all the way. A zaftig blonde, with the Cowboys' trademark elongated-eggroll-on-a-diving-board bangs, introduces the show. Whereupon the Ruskies — over 100 strong and in dress uniform — perform "Finlandia" by Sibelius. Cowboychiks then segue into a rip-roaring rendition of "Let's Work Together," including deadpan "ahwoum-ah-woums" from the stentorian ex-Soviets.

Sober title cards announce each musical chestnut. "Volga Boatmen" is followed by the Turtles classic "Happy Together" during which a straight-faced and uniformed Rus-

sian soloist serenades the Cowboys' vocalist while his comrades belt out the chorus.

Another soloist does a serviceable Tom Jones imitation with "Delilah," while lovely damsels in ornate Russian folk garb glide onstage. Other numbers include "Kalinka" (a rhythmic show-stopper), Bob Dylan's "Knockin' on Heaven's Door" (with balalaika chorus) and "Gimme All Your Lovin'" (PDQ Bach-style treatment).

Kaurismaki provides the viewer with better-than-front-row seats, capturing the earnest conductor and his hard-working charges from multiple angles. Sound recording and mixing is crisp and resonant. Russians are frequently lit so their drab, olive uniforms glow red.

Stage decorations include fake palm trees, a bust of Lenin irreverently hunkered down behind the wheel of a convertible, and a full-sized red tractor that houses the Cowboys' drummer.

Closing number is "Those Were the Days," with Ruskie and Cowboy leads trading verses including "We'd live the life we choose/We'd fight and never lose" with their arms around each other's shoulders.

—*Lisa Nesselson*

DELLAMORTE DELLAMORE

(ITALIAN-FRENCH-GERMAN)

A DARC release (Italy) of an Audifilm production in association with Urania Film (Rome)/KG Prods. (Paris)/Bibofilm & TV (Bad Homburg), and with Silvio Berlusconi Communications. Produced by Tilde Corsi, Gianni Romoli, Michele Soavi. Co-producers, Conchita Airoldi, Dino Di Dionisio. Directed by Soavi. Screenplay, Romoli, based on a novel by Tiziano Sclavi. Camera (color), Mauro Marchetti; editor, Franco Fraticelli; music, Manuel De Sica; art direction, Antonello Geleng; costumes, Maurizio Millenotti, Alfonsina Lettieri; in Dolby stereo; special effects, Sergio Stivaletti. Reviewed at Intl. Recording screening room, Rome, March 12, 1994. Running time: **100 MIN.**

Francesco
Dellamorte .... Rupert Everett
Gnaghi .... Francois Hadji Lazaro
She .... Anna Falchi
Mayor .... Stefano Masciarelli
Marshall Straniero .... Mickey Knox
Doctor .... Clive Riche
Valentina .... Fabiana Formica
(English dialogue)

A hip, offbeat horror item floating on a bed of dark philosophy, "Dellamorte Dellamore" is a deceptively easy genre picture with hidden depths. Based on a famous Italian comic strip, film toplines Rupert Everett as a romantic gravedigger more at ease with zombies than human beings. Helmer Michele Soavi (a former assistant to Dario Argento) comes into his own with this personal pic, balancing gore, sex, laughs and youthful despair.

Familiarity with creator Tiziano Sclavi's cultish Dylan Dog character (drawn with Everett in mind) isn't necessary to enjoy the film, which could travel well with careful handling. Pic opened locally to shapely biz.

Everett is the misanthropic Francesco Dellamorte, who's retired from the world to tend a small-town cemetery where the dead have begun climbing out of their graves. He quietly copes with the problem by bashing in the zombies' skulls and shooting them between the eyes, leaving his half-wit assistant Gnaghi (brilliantly played by French singer Francois Hadji Lazaro) to rebury the critters.

Although Francesco has spread the rumor he's impotent, he's not — as a young widow (neophyte Anna Falchi, of Jessica Rabbit dimensions) is pleased to discover. Their idyll, with a healthy dose of attractive, stylized nudity for both, ends badly when her late husband rises from the dead and bites her. Gnaghi has a similar affair with the mayor's daughter, who's been reduced to a disembodied head after a motorcycle accident.

Soavi's visceral connections between love and death (not to mention food and regurgitation) will revolt many, and it takes a strong stomach to watch Everett and Falchi's nude romping on bone-strewn graves. Motif pans out, however, in a final plot turn, when Everett moves from killing the dead to murdering the living, as he can't distinguish between the two.

Everett is physically perfect for the role and moves easily between a stylized comic-strip character and a serial killer with a broken heart. As Gnaghi, Lazaro swings from hilarious to heart-wrenching in the film's mystic finale. As Everett's squeeze, Falchi doesn't make it past level one.

Lensing and dense production design are campy parodies of horror low-budgeters. Apart from its lovely village setting and a few signposts in Italian, pic (shot in English) could be set anywhere.

—*Deborah Young*

MINA TANNENBAUM

(FRENCH)

A UGC release of an Ima Films production, in association with UGC Images, Christian Bourgois Prods., La Sept Cinema, FCC, SFPC (France)/ Les Films de l'Etang (Brussels)/Belbo Film Prods. (Amsterdam), with participation of Canal Plus, Sofinergie 2, Sofinergie 3, CNC, RTBF and Eurimages. (International sales: UGC.) Produced by Georges Benayoun. Co-executive producers, Paul Rozenberg, Oury Milshtein. Directed, written by Martine Dugowson. Camera (color), Dominique Chapuis; editors, Martine Barraque, Dominique Gallieni; music, Peter Chase; production design, Philippe Chiffre; costume design, Marie Lauwers; sound (Dolby), Alain Villeval; associate producer, Yves Marmion; assistant director, Charli Beleteau; casting, Gigi Akoka. Reviewed at UGC screening room, Paris, France, Feb. 15, 1994. Running time: **127 MIN.**
Mina
Tannenbaum ...... Romane Bohringer
Ethel Benegui .... Elsa Zylberstein
The cousin .... Florence Thomassin
Francois .... Nils Tavernier
Didier .... Stephane Slima
Serge .... Eric Defosse
Jacques Dana .... Jean-Philippe Ecoffey
With: Harry Cleven, Hugues Quester.

"**M**ina Tannenbaum" blends visual flair and fine female perfs in a bittersweet meller about the 25-year-long friendship between two Jewish girls in Paris. Wildly uneven but imaginatively told tale, which could rouse offshore arthouse interest, is perfect for women's and Jewish-themed fests.

Although local crix are divided on scattershot but engaging story's merits, the public is turning out. First feature by writer/director Martine Dugowson is lensed with brio, although most of its more flamboyant storytelling devices are lifted from other films.

People who knew painter Mina Tannenbaum (Romane Bohringer), including former best friend Ethel Benegui (Elsa Zylberstein), address the camera docu-style during the opening credits. Mina's chic female cousin (Florence Thomassin) is the de facto narrator, who launches flashbacks that trace the girls' intertwined destinies.

Chubby, fun-loving Ethel and myopic, sternly precocious Mina meet as youngsters, age 7, in ballet class. (Two leads as kids are wonderfully cast.) Narrative fast-forwards to age 16 — surviving first crushes and romances, and enduring tussles with their typically Jewish moms whose dialogue and mannerisms seem to have been bought in bulk at a cliche warehouse.

Art student Mina has the stubborn and impractical courage of her convictions; Ethel is more of an opportunistic chameleon. Their love/hate relationship exerts a powerful pull on their respective actions as they pursue men and happiness.

Pic nicely captures the awkwardness and unspoken rivalry between Mina and Ethel, skillfully depicting little hesitancies due to haircuts, clothes, physical attributes and so on. Ethel insinuates her way into a job at a trendy magazine, while Mina is the starving artist.

Transitions are frequently derivative. Guardian angels matted into the sky are kissin' cousins to Woody Allen's mammoth mom in his seg of "New York Stories." Giant close-ups of a glowing cigarette tip as an unseen smoker inhales echo "Wild at Heart." As adolescents, the girls' shadow alter-egos step out of their real bodies: Ethel is gussied up as a tart in a red dress and Mina squires her in a "Yentl"-style Hassidic boy get-up.

Pic unerringly re-creates decors and garb from 1958 through 1991. Dugowson's training as a d.p. results in assured lensing that interjects poetic license to reinforce states of mind. (When Mina and Ethel are born in 1958, nurses waltz down hospital corridors.) Exact dates of momentous events mark the passing years.

Score is pleasant and wide-ranging. Ending is very drawn out and predictable. —*Lisa Nesselson*

NEW DIRECTORS

THE GIRL IN THE WATERMELON

A Mommy & Daddy production. Produced by Sergio Moskowicz. Executive producer, Andrew Louca. Directed, written by Sergio M. Castilla. Camera (color), Irek Hartowicz; editor, Elizabeth Schwartz; music, Ana Araiz; art direction, Boris Curatolo; costume design, Susan Cannon; sound, Annette Dento. Reviewed at Titus I Theater, Museum of Modern Art, N.Y., March 19, 1994. (In New Directors/New Films.) Running time: **92 MIN.**
Diane Mayerofsky .... Michele Pawk
Eddie Alvarez .... Lazaro Perez
Robert Willbarth .... Steven Stahl
Matt
Carrere ...... James Spencer Thierree
Samantha
Mayerofsky .... Meredith Scott Lynn
Julius .... Michael Allinson
Phil
McGovern ... Steven Mark Friedman
Paul Rosen .... Jon Avner
Lucy .... Jamie Lynn Reif
Coco .... Jose Herrera

As inviting as an open fire hydrant in August, Sergio M. Castilla's "The Girl in the Watermelon" sets a young girl's search for an unknown father against an idealized urban backdrop. Casting New York City as a colorful, multicultural playground, "Watermelon" becomes overripe at points, but the mush is easily overlooked as pic's good nature takes hold.

Pic's position as the opener for the 1994 New Directors/New Films series could prove a mixed blessing: Spotlight might be too harsh for this small, albeit charming, entry. Still, warm audience and critical response should help "Watermelon" find a distrib and a place on the specialized circuit.

Chief among Castilla's accomplishments is discovery of Meredith Scott Lynn, who plays 17-year-old Samantha Mayerofsky. Lynn keeps the smart, precocious Sam from sitcom-brat status, and contributes mightily to the film's considerable warmth.

Sam is a Brooklyn girl on a mission: Find the father she never knew. Getting no answers from her exasperated mother (well-played by Michele Pawk), the teenager steals a peek at mom's 1976 datebook.

She discovers two paternal candidates and, unbeknownst to mom, writes them letters of introduction.

Castilla's rose-colored perspective is in full view as the two men — one a Latino, trumpet-playing ladies man (Lazaro Perez) and the other a WASPy, gay and very wealthy SoHo art dealer (Steven Stahl) — jump at the chance of inviting their newfound "daughter" into their lives.

Much of the film's comedy involves Sam's balancing of her three families — mom, dad and dad — and wandering through the diverse and colorful worlds her new fathers represent.

Writer/director's smart dialogue and knack for detail shows an infatuation with New York comparable to Woody Allen's annual cinematic valentines. He shows a similar compassion to his characters, and luckily so: The gay and Latino characters veer dangerously close to offensive stereotype, collision avoided by the film's big heart.

Castilla isn't quite so fortunate in other areas. Whimsy turns cutesy in a pair of dream sequences — title refers to Sam's dream in which she sees herself as an embryo inside a watermelon — and pic's repeated use of underwater metaphors is obvious and cloying.

Lovingly shot by Irek Hartowicz, pic looks like a lot more than its $1 million budget. Other tech credits are fine, particularly Ana Araiz's well-chosen musical backdrops.

Cast is terrific. Michael Allinson limns the best manservant since John Gielgud donned white gloves for "Arthur." —*Greg Evans*

TWISTING IN POPENGUINE
(TWISTE A POPENGUINE)
(SENEGALESE)

A presentation of Cameras Continentales/France 2. Produced by Moussa Sene Absa, Takis Candilis. Executive producer, Annick Ouvrard. Directed, written by Sene Absa. Camera (color, video transfer), Dominique Gentil; editor, Sene Absa; production design, Yves Brover; art direction, Benedicte Larue; costumes, Caroline De Vivaise. Reviewed at Rotterdam Intl. Film Festival, Feb. 4, 1994. Running time: **95 MIN.**
Johnny Hallyday .... Ousmane Bo
Clo Clo .... Patrice Nassalang
Sylvie Vartan .... Coura Ba
M. Benoit .... Jean Francois Balmer
Sheila .... Marieme Fall
Baac .... Ismael Thiam
Dame Castilor .... Isseu Niang
Jabeel .... Abdoulaye Diop Danny
El Hadj Gora .... Abou Camara

An unusual and vibrant piece set in recent colonial Africa, "Twiste a Poponguine" tackles serious material with an arresting light touch and signals a notable new talent in producer/director/writer Moussa Sene Absa. The mix of cultures old and new produces a universal tale that should break out of the festival circuit and land solidly in arthouse distribution internationally.

Set in the mid-1960s in a small Senegalese village, the story centers on a group of teenagers who've cast off century-old traditions for Western fashions and music. With a nod to "West Side Story," they divide into gangs. The French-influenced Les Ins adopt the names of Gallic pop stars, while the Kings prefer American rhythm and blues.

Granted, it's a small universe, with the gangs consisting of but three members. Johnny Hallyday's group has the monopoly on the town's two girls, but the Kings own the only record player — a Teppaz —outside of the big city.

The elders look on with a combination of amusement and dismay. The shock of the new is never clearer than when one of the wealthy merchants imports a television and puts an end to the local pastime of watching shadow puppets.

Sene Absa packs a lot of history into his script and re-creates the transitional era affectionately. Its comedic tone allows him to weave in some telling issues about cultures intrinsically at odds. Ultimately, it's his confidence in humanity that wins the day and makes "Twiste a Poponguine" a very satisfying entertainment.

The filmmakers overcome modest tech resources with energy and wit. It's a handsome production that one would be hard-pressed to guess had been shot on Beta. The cast is uniformly terrific and the picture is a surprise, a delight and a genuine discovery.

—*Leonard Klady*

NESTOR'S LAST TRIP
(NESTORE L'ULTIMA CORSA)
(ITALIAN-FRENCH)

A Warner Bros. Italia release (Italy) of a Sacha Film Co., Aurelia Cinematografica (Rome)/Florida Movies (Paris) production, in association with Silvio Berlusconi Communications. Produced by Sergio Giussani. Directed by Alberto Sordi. Screenplay, Rodolfo Sonego, Sordi. Camera (color), Armando Nannuzzi; editor, Tatiana Casini; music, Piero Piccioni; art direction, Marco Dentici; costume design, Paola Marchesin. Reviewed at Fiamma Cinema, Rome, Mar. 10, 1994. Running time: **105 MIN.**
With: Alberto Sordi (Gaetano), Matteo Ripaldi (Ferruccio), Cinzia Cannarozzo (Iris), Eros Pagni (Otello), Tatiana Farnese (Cesarina), Simona Caparrini (Wilma).

Veteran Italo comic Alberto Sordi has been directing himself in vehicles for several years with less than brilliant results. Pedestrian helming on this tearjerker, about a 75-year-old Roman cabbie and his horse, hurts a gentle story that harks back to another era. Appealing mainly to nostalgia audiences, pic has underperformed theatrically on home turf.

Gaetano (Sordi) and his horse, Nestor, happily trot tourists around Rome until the buggy's owner (Eros Pagni in a malicious cameo) informs him the jig is up. Next morning, Gaetano is to take his carriage to Cinecitta, drop Nestor off at the slaughterhouse and wend his way to the old folks' home. At the last moment, he rebels and leads Nestor on a (doomed) search for greener pastures.

It takes a consummate thesp like Sordi to make something of this maudlin material, and he pulls it off in a very human and moving perf. Tale at times recalls Vittorio De Sica's classic "Umberto D.", without approaching its emotion. Pic is peppered with slightly out-of-date characters, like the stripteasing mom (Cinzia Cannarozzo) of Gaetano's grandson (Matteo Ripaldi) and her hot-rodding boyfriend.

Tech credits are good.

—*Deborah Young*

THE SNAIL'S STRATEGY
(LA ESTRATEGIA DEL CARACOL)
(COLOMBIAN)

A Caracol TV/FOCINE/Crear TV/Prods. Fotograma/EMME production. Produced, directed by Sergio Cabrera. Executive producer, Salvatore Basile, Sandro Silvestri. Screenplay, Humberto Dorado, based on a script by Cabrera, Ramon Jimeno. Camera (color), Carlos Congote; editor, Manuel Navia, Nicholas Wenworth; music, German Arrieta. Reviewed at Cartagena Film Festival, Colombia, March 9, 1994. (Also in Sundance Film Festival.) Running time: **116 MIN.**
With: Frank Ramirez, Humberto Dorado, Florina Lemaitre, Gustavo Angarita, Vicky Hernandez, Edgardo Roman, Fausto Cabrera, Salvatore Basile, Victor Mallarino.

This second feature by Sergio Cabrera is rife with domestic concerns, including violence, bureaucracy and misuse of power, balanced by a large cast of quirky characters who band together in their fight for justice. The film is Colombia's largest national hit, having drawn almost double the attendance of "Jurassic Park."

An ensemble comedy, "The Snail's Strategy" takes pokes at official corruption in Colombia, and very few people are spared — not politicians, the police, lawyers, judges or the rich.

At the beginning of the century, large mansions in the center of Bogota were abandoned by the wealthy as the city grew northward. These buildings were occupied by squatters, and law stipulates that, after being unclaimed for a determined period, ownership passes into the hands of the residents.

Told in flashback, pic relates the case of the Olive house, a rambling complex of 48 rooms popularly known as "The Coop." When the former owner tries to reclaim the building, the tenants resist.

A lawyer manages to delay eviction while an old theatrical stage manager comes up with a strategy: Using a series of pulleys and levers, the tenants dismantle the building piece by piece until only the facade remains.

As the many residents interact to carry out their strategy, their individual idiosyncrasies are laid bare. On the other side are the villains, who manipulate the law, sometimes violently, for their own ends. Cabrera has a good feeling for directing actors and manages to infuse this complex microcosm of Colombian society with dramatic life.

—*Paul Lenti*

WE ARE ALL STARS
(TODOS SOMOS ESTRELLAS)
(PERUVIAN)

A Torre de Babbel production. Produced, directed by Luis Felipe Degregori. Executive producer, Jenny Valapatino. Screenplay, Ronnie Tenoche. Camera (color), Eduardo Davila; editor, Luis Barrios; music, Miky Gonzalez, Wicho Garcia; art director, Marta Mendez; associate producer, Augusto Navarro. Reviewed at Cartagena Film Festival, Colombia, March 5, 1994. Running time: **87 MIN.**
With: Milena Alva, Mariella Balbi, Elide Brero, Katia Condos, Ricardo Velasquez, Hernan Romero, Ricardo Fernandez, Julian Legaspi, Dante Herrera.

"We Are All Stars" offers a humorous look at Latin life, while examining notions of fame and the power of mass media. Fast-paced commercial venture should do well in other Latin territories.

Tale concerns the dysfunctional family of Carmen Huambachano (Milena Alva), religious viewers of Lima's weekly TV series "We Are All Stars," in which a normal family is selected to be interviewed and then given the chance to win prizes.

When Carmen's clan is chosen and the TV crew appears at the front door, the family must come to grips with how it wants to be viewed by the nation. The house must be repainted and decorated, everyone pulls out their best finery, and a husband must be found to replace the "no good rat" who left Carmen years earlier.

Helmer Luis Felipe Degregori has a good feel for the material and keeps the plot moving. The ensemble cast, especially the youthful actors, is sharp.

Video images from the TV show and the satires of other TV programs vary the texture of the film.

—*Paul Lenti*

THE DEVIL'S PLATES
(LOS PLATOS DEL DIABLO)
(VENEZUELAN)

A Foncine production. Produced by Malena Rocayolo. Directed by Thaelman Urgelles. Screenplay, Urgelles, Edilio Pena. Camera (color), Vitelbo Vasquez; editor, Mario Handler; music, Vinicio Ludovic. Reviewed at Cartagena Film Festival, Columbia, March 9, 1994. Running time: **91 MIN.**

March 28, 1994 (Cont.)

April 4, 1994

With: Gustavo Rodriguez, Mimi Lazo, Marcela Walerstein, Julio Sosa, Victor Cuica, Ana Maria Paredes.

Following an obvious storyline, "The Devil's Plates" offers a shopworn tale of a frustrated writer whose lust for fame drives him to kill and plagiarize the work of a promising author.

Pic is marred by a rather wooden performance by Gustavo Rodriguez, who plays Ricardo Azolar, a man who writes and writes but is unhappy with his literary output.

At a salon where pretty people drape themselves around a garden and discuss literature and the role of the writer, Ricardo meets and falls for a writer groupie who is in love with a promising new scribe named Daniel (played by Julio Sosa, former head of the Venezuelan film institute, Foncine).

Ricardo befriends Daniel, only to kill him, steal his manuscript and basically usurp Daniel's life. Ricardo dyes his hair, discards his glasses, starts smoking cigars and takes up with Daniel's g.f. His eventual fate is obvious. Pic begins with a voiceover, which informs that the film is the autobiographical story of Ricardo's deeds, written in retrospect in prison and destined to be his true masterpiece.

Main problem is that the pivotal role of Ricardo is so disagreeable that one quickly loses interest in him and his situation.

Tech credits are fine but film offers few surprises. —*Paul Lenti*

RORAIMA

(VENEZUELAN)

A Yekuana Films production. Executive producer, Helena M. Bocco. Directed by Carlos Oteyza. Screenplay, Oteyza, Yajaira Gonzalez, Oscar Lucien. Camera (color), Hernan Toro; editor, Freddy Veliz; music, Alejandro Blanco; art direction, Diego Risquez; associate producer, Jose I. Oteyza. Reviewed at Cartagena Film Festival, Columbia, March 8, 1994. Running time: 104 MIN.
With: Isabel Dussinova, Daniel Lopez, Stephen Ellery, Lupe Barrado, Hugo Marquez, Diego Risquez, Andres Scull, Sophia Oteyza, Daniel Giandoni.

A pretentious chronicle of a woman's search for her brother, "Roraima" offers a meandering microcosm of modern Venezuelan society. Second feature by Carlos Oteyza is set in the jungles of Roraima, a no-man's-land inhabited by outlaws and rejects from civilization.

Pic begins when Carlota (Isabel Dussinova) is sent by her father to look for her younger brother, who disappeared years earlier under suspicion of having killed a woman.

The brother was last heard to be living in Roraima, a jungle territory in southern Venezuela off limits to visitors and under international dispute. Area has become a haven for international fugitives in addition to those who illegally pan the rivers for gold and diamonds.

In road movie fashion, Carlota's search brings her in contact with many of the area's eccentric characters, who are preyed upon by a corrupt, all-powerful army unit.

Location shooting tends toward the pretty and at times makes the film look as if it were financed by the tourism department. Acting is OK.
—*Paul Lenti*

PASSIONATE INDUCEMENT

(MOVIL PASIONAL)

(VENEZUELAN)

An E.M. Films (Venezuela)/Cumbre Films (Mexico) production. Produced by Diana Sanchez. Directed by Mauricio Walerstein. Screenplay, David Suarez, Walerstein. Camera (color), Vitelbo Vazquez; editor, Sergio Curiel; music, Carlos Moreau; art direction, Eva Ivanyi. Reviewed at Cartagena Film Festival (MECLA market), Colombia, March 7, 1994. Running time: 100 MIN.
Gyula .... Orlando Urdaneta
Maria .... Maria Rojo
Macabi .... Miguel Angel Rodriguez
Also with: Elvira Valdez, Hugo Marquez, Haydee Balza.

Those who expect plenty of violence and kinky sex in the films of Mauricio Walerstein will not come away disappointed from his latest effort. Even before the credits finish, viewers have already been treated to a grisly murder and a woman's breasts smeared with the blood of her dead husband.

Following a basic murder mystery plot, sleazy story concerns a hardboiled police commissioner, Gyula (Orlando Urdaneta), who is pressured to find the murderer of a wealthy American businessman. Victim's wife (Mexican actress Maria Rojo) is a former prostie who stands to inherit a large sum of money; she is also still in love with her former pimp, Macabi (Miguel Angel Rodriguez).

This shabby premise allows Walerstein to delve into the seamy underbelly of Caracas' demimonde, as the police conduct roundups of hookers and pimps in an effort to find the murderer. Basically, the plot is an excuse to explore a world defined by sex and violence.

Tech credits tend toward very low budget, and acting is OK.
—*Paul Lenti*

I LOVE YOU AND I'LL TAKE YOU TO THE MOVIES

(TE QUIERO Y TE LLEVO AL CINE)

(CUBAN)

An ICAIC-Video Luna production. Produced, directed, edited by Ricardo Vega; interlude music, Juan Pinera; sound, Ricardo Perez. Reviewed at Cartagena Film Festival, Colombia, March 10, 1994. Running time: 65 MIN.
INSOMNIA
Screenplay, Vega, Juan Carlos Tellez, based on a story by Virgilio Pinera. Camera (color), Carlos Madrigal; music, Ulises Hernandez.
With: Rolanda Tarajano.
THE CUIRASS
(LA CORAZA)
Screenplay, Vega, Miguel Fernandez, based on a story by Leonardo Eiriz. Camera (color), Raul Rodriguez; music, Juan Antonio Leyva. With: Jorge Crespo, Leonardo Eiriz.
I LOVE YOU AND I'LL TAKE YOU TO THE MOVIES
(TE QUIERO Y TE LLEVO AL CINE)
Screenplay, Vega, Ramon Garcia. Camera (color), Santiago Yanes; music, Magda Galvan.
With: Niurka Noya, Ricardo Vega, Liliana Reino.

This experimental-short anthology film has the texture and feel of a student effort. Its only interest is that it comes from Cuba, which has been forced to curtail much of its serious film production due to lack of funds.

Made up of a trio of tales, "I Love You" works best when it doesn't strive for narration, as in the second tale, "The Cuirass," which involves a pair of sunglasses that pass from person to person.

First story, "Insomnia," predictably enough deals with the desperation of someone unable to sleep, while final yarn concerns a couple who go to the movies only to find they are pursued by a camera crew filming their every movement.

Given the super low-budget treatment, the obviousness of each of these stories is pathetic and overstated, while acting is strictly amateur.

Film begins with a time-lapse interlude that is repeated between each story in an effort to pad an already very short film.
—*Paul Lenti*

SERIAL MOM

A Savoy release of a Polar Entertainment production. Produced by John Fiedler, Mark Tarlov. Executive producer, Joseph Caracciolo Jr. Directed, written by John Waters. Camera (Technicolor), Robert Stevens; editors, Janice Hampton, Erica Huggins; music, Basil Poledouris; production design, Vincent Peranio; art direction, David J. Bomba; costumes, Van Smith; sound (Dolby), Rick Angelella; associate producer, Pat Moran; assistant director, Mary Ellen Woods; second unit director, Steve M. Davison; casting, Paula Herold, Moran. Reviewed at Savoy screening room, Santa Monica, March 10, 1994. MPAA Rating: R. Running time: 93 MIN.
Beverly Sutphin ..... Kathleen Turner
Eugene Sutphin .... Sam Waterston
Misty Sutphin .... Ricki Lake
Chip Sutphin .... Matthew Lillard
Rosemary
 Ackerman .... Mary Jo Catlett
Scott .... Justin Whalin
Birdie .... Patricia Dunnock
Dottie Hinkle .... Mink Stole
Carl .... Lonnie Horsey
Carl's Date .... Traci Lords
Suzanne Somers .... Herself

"Chip, our mother is Charles Manson!" Ricki Lake exclaims to her brother upon learning of their perfect suburban mom's double life in John Waters' latest exposé of society's hypocrisies, normal people's naughty thoughts and the secrets that lie behind suburbia's well-manicured facades. Fun, almost endearing in its cheeky irreverence, but also rather mild and scattershot in its satiric marksmanship, "Serial Mom" provokes chuckles and the occasional raised eyebrow rather than guffaws and gross-outs. B.O. prospects appear moderate, as pic doesn't have the bite or sustained high comedy to propel this from cultdom to mainstream hitsville.

To all outward appearances, Baltimore hausfrau Beverly Sutphin (Kathleen Turner) is June Cleaver incarnate. An endlessly supportive wife to dentist Eugene (Sam Waterston), she runs the ideal household, keeping the home spotless and serving up a delicious dinner every night to her family, which includes college-student daughter Misty (Lake), who has extensive boy problems, and high-schooler son Chip (Matthew Lillard), a gore-film junkie.

As soon as they all leave for the day, however, Beverly jumps into action, making obscene phone calls to a silly neighborhood woman. Chip's teacher pulls Beverly's chain, daring to suggest that some therapy would help the youngster curb his addiction to horror pix.

Without hesitation, Beverly runs the man over with her car for his impudence and heads home, where she can admire her signed photograph of Richard Speck and tune in Joan Rivers hosting her new TV show, "Serial Hags," devoted to women who love mass murderers.

Once started, there's no stopping Beverly, who runs Misty's impolite boyfriend through with a fire poker and dispatches a couple for not flossing.

In a nifty little Hitchcock homage, she clubs a woman over the head with a leg of lamb as she watches and sings along to the movie "Annie," all for not rewinding the videotapes she rents (any film that can find a way to excerpt both "Annie" and "Blood Feast" has something going for it).

By the time she's arrested and charged with murder, she has killed six people. Firing her attorney for entering an insanity plea, media favorite Beverly argues her case herself and emerges as a feminist heroine who will be played in the TV movie by Suzanne Somers.

Waters' trademark social mockery, campy humor and celebration of the tawdry are all in ample evidence. After an excursion into more benign, PG and PG-13 territory for his last two efforts, "Hairspray" and "Cry-Baby," it's good to see him back where his sick humor and taste for raunch have more room to roam.

But the problem is not only the wispy, clothesline plot that has no more complexity than a series of blackout sketches. Waters' recent, bigger-budget films don't seem subversive in the way that his bargain-basement indies did, because the object of their loving derision is a 1950s white-bread America, derived mostly from television, that has already been parodied to death and seems at too much of a remove from anything vital or on-the-line.

With David Lynch having plumbed this territory in more insidious and disturbing ways in "Blue Velvet" and "Twin Peaks," it's tough to shake audiences up

with any new revelations about nice families of four in homes with two-car garages.

Waters' distinctive humor could also be better amplified and sustained if it were goosed up by more stylized visuals; the decor is right, but if the lensing and technique were as audacious and cockeyed as the ideas and jokes, the material would be socked over more impressively.

With its mockery of America's glorification of celebrity and luridly winking fascination with crime, "Serial Mom" is tolerably amusing as far as it goes, but Waters misses a big opportunity by ending the film as soon as he does.

With all the jokes about the death penalty and legendary murderers, the film seems to be building to a climactic scene in the gas chamber (or lethal injection room), where Beverly could enact a finale worthy of Susan Hayward.

Perhaps Waters didn't want to reprise the conclusion of his "Female Trouble," in which Divine went to the electric chair, but as it is, pic feels oddly truncated.

At one with Waters' charming bad-boy spirit, Turner turns in a game, rambunctious star performance that hits the right note between satire and seriousness and gives the film such weight and grit as it has.

With little to do, Waterston fits less effectively into the Waters universe, while Lake and Lillard as the kids progress from amazement to genuine enthusiasm for their mom's new-found fame.

Supporting cast is peppered with the usual assortment of Waters-world notables, including Mink Stole, Traci Lords and Patricia Hearst. Basil Poledouris' flavorful score no doubt deliberately contains numerous echoes of Bernard Herrmann.

—*Todd McCarthy*

CLIFFORD

An Orion Pictures release of a Morra, Brezner, Steinberg & Tenenbaum Entertainment production. Produced by Larry Brezner, Pieter Jan Brugge. Directed by Paul Flaherty. Screenplay, Jay Dee Rock, Bobby Von Hayes. Camera (Deluxe color), John A. Alonzo; editors, Pembroke Herring, Timothy Board; music, Richard Gibbs; production design, Russell Christian; art direction, Bernie Cutler; set decoration, Catherine Mann; costume design, Robert de Mora; sound (Dolby), Larry Kemp, Lon Bender; assistant director, Douglas E. Wise; second unit director/stunt coordinator, George (Bud) Davis; casting, Lynn Stalmaster. Reviewed at the UA Theaters, L.A., March 17, 1994. MPAA Rating: PG. Running time: **89 MIN.**

Clifford	Martin Short
Martin Daniels	Charles Grodin
Sarah Davis	Mary Steenburgen
Gerald Ellis	Dabney Coleman
Parker Davis	G.D. Spradlin
Annabelle Davis	Anne Jeffreys
Julien Daniels	Richard Kind
Theodora Daniels	Jennifer Savidge
Roger	Ben Savage

Orion serves up another long-on-the-shelf turkey with this gimmicky, poorly conceived comedy, which draws its only inspiration from the short-lived novelty of having Martin Short playing a bratty 10-year-old boy. While pic could do some minor business on the fringe of the live-action youth market, box office prospects appear pint-sized.

The allure of having Short regress to childhood is as mystifying as the movie's tired execution under the direction of Paul Flaherty, a Short colleague at SCTV (the two are also collaborating on an NBC comedy pilot).

Other than having Short slouch — or reversing the old Alan Ladd trick by standing other adults on boxes — no real effects went into creating the not terribly convincing illusion of "getting small."

Relating his story in inexplicable flashback to a wayward boy (Ben Savage, betraying the pic's expiration date by looking considerably younger than in his current TV series), Short plays the nightmarishly bratty title character, who sets the story in motion by forcing his father's Hawaii-bound plane to land in Los Angeles.

Desperate to make it to a convention, Clifford's folks dump the kid on his little-seen Uncle Martin (Charles Grodin), who's out to convince his betrothed, Sarah (Mary Steenburgen), that he likes children.

Disappointed when Martin won't take him to Dinosaurworld (the reason he sabotaged the plane in the first place), Clifford slowly escalates his revenge, as the exasperated Martin tries to hide from Sarah that he has the equivalent of "The Omen" child living under his roof.

If the premise has potential, Flaherty and writers Jay Dee Rock and Bobby Von Hayes squander the opportunity with over-the-top characters mouthing stilted dialogue in predictable situations. Grodin, in particular, gets caught playing an unfortunate twist on his role in "Beethoven," eliminating the actor's trademark slow boil in favor of unpleasant ranting.

Short delivers a few laughs initially as the very bad seed, but never brings anything to the role that justifies casting an adult in this part, other than the fact that the filmmakers could shoot full days and not have to pay an on-set tutor.

"Clifford," in fact, seems caught between worlds, aspiring to be more than children's fare while remaining simple enough to appeal to moppets; it doesn't remotely succeed on either level.

Tech credits actually outshine the material in several places, particularly the inspired theme park attraction created for Dinosaurworld, which looks like a whole lot more fun than sitting through the movie. Richard Gibbs' impish score also conveys the tone for which "Clifford" was striving and, in its eagerness to please, so obviously came up short. —*Brian Lowry*

SXSW

DOC'S FULL SERVICE

A Brazos Films production. Produced, directed by Eagle Pennell. Executive producer, Michael Farrow. Screenplay, Henry Wideman Jr., Pennell, Kim Henkel. Camera (color), Jim Barham; editor, Sheri Galloway; music, Chuck Pinnell, John Sargent; sound, Philip R. Davis. Reviewed at South by Southwest Film and Media Conference, Austin, Texas, March 18, 1994. Running time: **85 MIN.**

Doc	Kevin Wiggins
Ann Boles	Christine McPeters
Clifford "Pee Wee"	
Leyendecker	James Belcher
Cecil	Lynn Miller Jr.
Belma	Jeanette Wiggins
Vernon	Bob Poole
Big Silly	David Born
Little Silly	Travis Baker
Stacy	Branwyn Andrus
Tracy	Paige Witte

Texas filmmaker Eagle Pennell, a cult fave for his raucous low-budgeters "Last Night at the Alamo" (1983) and "The Whole Shootin' Match" (1978), makes a comeback of sorts with "Doc's Full Service," a surprisingly sweet-natured comedy-drama about comings and goings in a small-town service station. Pic is a natural for fest circuit, though its commercial prospects appear limited.

Working from an original screenplay he penned with Henry Wideman Jr. and Kim Henkel, Pennell has come up with a small-scale, low-key indie effort that resembles something adapted from a one-set play. (Script could be presented as a legit production with only minor alterations.) Most of the episodic story takes place within the office of the title location, a service station that has many more casual visitors than paying customers.

Doc (Kevin Wiggins) is a laid-back, even-tempered fellow who has spent most of his life in the same Texas town. He's so comfortable with his lot — or, perhaps, so afraid of change — that he's even willing to remain married to a shrewish wife (Jeanette Wiggins) who's having a not-so-secret affair with the local used-car salesman (Bob Poole).

It's only when Doc takes a hankering to a pretty young barbeque stand operator (Christine McPeters) that Doc begins to consider a life beyond the town limits. Even then, he's slow to make a decision and easily distracted by the colorful characters who wander in and out of his office.

At its frequent best, "Doc's Full Service" plays like an extended episode of a better-than-average sitcom. And like a good sitcom, it's stocked with scene-stealers in the supporting cast: Pee Wee (James Belcher), a hard-drinking but good-hearted mama's boy who wants to stage a play at the local church; Big Silly (David Born) and Little Silly (Travis Baker), telephone installers who want to connect with a pair of stranded floozies; and Cecil (Lynn Miller Jr.), a mechanic who's proud he attended BMW repair school, where he "was taught by real Germans."

Pic as whole is a lightweight charmer, instantly forgettable but genuinely amusing. Things turn heavy in a couple of scenes with Doc and his new love, and there's a noticeable strain in the effort to make these scenes seem important. Pennell's on much safer ground when he's not trying so hard.

As Doc, Wiggins makes an effective straight man for the movie's more broadly comic characters, and a sympathetic loser in his dead-serious affairs of the heart. McPeters is stuck with most of the heavy lifting in the dramatic scenes, but she remains appealing. Belcher finds an effectively melancholy undercurrent in a character that could have been played strictly for laughs.

On a technical level, "Doc's Full Service" makes the absolute most of an obviously limited budget. Pic still needs more work on sound-looping, but Jim Barham's fluid cinematography is impressive.

—*Joe Leydon*

SECOND COUSIN, ONCE REMOVED

An Intrepid Ventures Group production. Produced by John McColpin. Executive producers, George and Nancy Shorney, Andrew and Mary Alice McColpin, Tom Rogers. Directed by John Shorney. Screenplay, John Shorney, John McColpin, Pete Ellis, Dave Bussan. Camera (b&w), Roger Dean; editors, John Shorney, John McColpin; music, Blake Leyh; production design, Helmut Dusek; sound, Chuck Michael; associate producer, Lawrence E. Manierre. Reviewed at the South by Southwest Film and Media Conference, Austin, Texas, March 17, 1994. Running time: 86 MIN.

Clyde Belmondo	Pete Ellis
Natalie	Robyn Sands
Weasel	Kevin Kildow
Laura	Kim Little
Lou	Herb Shorney
Band	Thelonious Monster

Whatever might be left of the midnight movie circuit would be the best place for "Second Cousin, Once Removed," an aggressively hip film noir pastiche. Shot in suitably gritty black-and-white and full of attitude and artifice, pic has all the style and substance of a musicvideo shot by movie buffs.

First-time feature helmer John Shorney takes his cue, and much of his plot, from hardboiled melodramas of the '40s and '50s in which not-so-innocent fall guys were duped into crime by shady ladies. He also tips his hat to other noir-inspired pix, most notably by naming his hero Clyde Belmondo (after Jean-Paul Belmondo in Godard's "Breathless").

Clyde (Pete Ellis), a straight-arrow Chicago ad man, drives his 1966 Chrysler Newport convertible to L.A. to meet a distant cousin who's been writing him flirty letters. The bad news is, Laura (Kim Little) has been taken hostage by some Hollywood sleazoids after stealing a bundle of their cash. The worse news is, the money's now in the safe of some underworld goons who operate a guitar store as a legit front.

And the worst news is, after being framed for murder and roughed up by the sleazoids, Clyde is forced to find some way of stealing the money from the guitar store safe.

It takes a very long time for Clyde to check a newspaper for information about the murder he supposedly committed, and even longer for him to realize why nothing's been printed about it. These are just two of the most obvious holes in a slapdash plot that's credited to four writers.

"Second Cousin" abounds in in-jokes and knowing references keyed to the lower fringes of the Hollywood scene — Laura is a would-be actress, the sleazoids are making a cheapie vampire thriller. The climax is lifted from the crime classic "Kiss Me Deadly," but played for laughs. Pic isn't really funny enough to qualify as a full-fledged comedy, but it has a few laughs, most of them intentional.

As Clyde, Ellis is appropriately buttoned-down and borderline thick-witted. Among the supporting players, Robyn Sands makes the most memorable impression as Natalie, best friend of the missing Laura. She isn't quite what she seems, of course.

Roger Dean's black-and-white lensing and Helmut Dusek's aptly seedy production design are pic's strongest assets. —*Joe Leydon*

CULTIVATING CHARLIE

A GMS Prods. Inc. production. Produced by Mark Glick. Directed, written by Alex Georges, based on Voltaire's "Candide." Camera (color), Jamie Thompson; editor, Bill Moore; production designer, Corey Kaplan; art direction, Jim Kanan; sound, Tom Varga; line producer, Susan Elkins; assistant director, Francis R. Mahoney III; casting, Ellen Parks. Reviewed at South by Southwest Film and Media Conference, Austin, Texas, March 19, 1994. Running time: 113 MIN.

Charles Thundertrunk	Jake Webber
Ed Thundertrunk	David Huddleston
Martin	Vincent Schiavelli
Prescott Putney	Josef Sommer
Katsu	Mako
Dr. Timothy Leary	Himself
Glosser	Richard Libertini

"Cultivating Charlie" is a slick but self-indulgent misfire that recalls the sophomoric excesses of flower-power fables from the late '60s and early '70s. Despite a few recognizable names in the supporting cast, and production values that belie its reported $1.6 million budget, pic will have a hard time finding an audience in any medium.

First-time feature filmmaker Alex Georges has concocted an unappetizing mixture of curdled whimsy and smug New Age blather, supposedly based (very loosely) on Voltaire's "Candide." His actors are much better than the material deserves, but even that doesn't help.

Charles Thundertrunk (Jake Webber), the innocent young hero, is the vegetarian son of a fast-food mogul (David Huddleston). Reluctantly, he agrees to make a cross-country promotional tour for his father's Burger World eateries. But after he witnesses a crazed gunman's massacre of several patrons at a Burger World outlet, he detours to a journey of self-discovery.

Along the way, he's joined by his boyhood hero, Glosser (Richard Libertini), a dreamy-eyed sage who's permanently blissed-out after a near-death experience and whose philosophy dictates that everything, good or evil, always happens for the best.

The travelers set out to find Glosser's journal, which has been stolen by a nihilistic meanie (Vincent Schiavelli) who likes to set fire to libraries. By the time the good guys catch up with him, this baddie has moved up to torching people with his flame thrower. This leads to a climactic confrontation that has lots of fire — but, unfortunately, no enlightenment.

Most of "Cultivating Charlie" is a muddle-headed and interminably picaresque comedy that, while silly, is basically harmless. Sporadically, however, pic reveals a mean-spirited edge, presenting violent deaths that are not at all justified in this lightweight context.

In one of the final scenes, Charlie's father pops up and announces, out of the blue, that Charlie's ex-girlfriend has been fatally shot by a stalker. The revelation serves no dramatic purpose, other than to allow Georges another opportunity to note that, hey, this crazy old world sure is an absurd place sometimes.

Yes, it sure is. In fact, sometimes people actually are able to raise money to make films like "Cultivating Charlie."

—*Joe Leydon*

GOTHENBURG

SEE YOU TOMORROW, MARIO
(I MORGON MARIO)
(SWEDISH-PORTUGUESE)

A Swedish Film Institute presentation of a Torrom Film, Prole Films production, with participation of SFI, Instituto Portugues de Cinema, Radio Televisao Portugues, Fundacao Calouste Gulbenkian. Produced by Henrique E. Santo, Miguel Cardoso, Solveig Nordlund. Directed by Nordlund. Screenplay, Nordlund, Tommy Karlmark, from Grete Roulund's novel. Camera (color), Lisa Hagstrand; music, Jose Mario Branco. Reviewed at Gothenburg Film Festival, Gothenburg, Sweden, Feb. 6, 1994. Running time: 76 MIN.

With: Joao Silva, Paulo Cesar, Jose Candido, Helder Abreu, Victor Norte, Canto e Castro, Figueira Cid, Lilia Hernandes, Miguel Guilherme, Eduardo Luis, Percy Brandt, Ulla Wikander.

Charming low-budgeter about a day in the life of street urchins on the tourist island Madeira is an appealing combo of indignation and humor. Carefully handled, pic could definitely pull in some specialized audiences.

April 4, 1994 (Cont.)

The tykes hustle Swedish tourists, dive for coins and generally try for the best life possible. Main character Mario (Joao Silva) also has to deal with a hospitalized mother who's probably on her last lap.

Helmer Solveig Nordlund, who's used to working with non-pros, draws natural performances from a young cast playing roles close to their own lives. Pic's lack of coin sometimes shows, but Nordlund's careful direction, the film's likable characters and a strain of humor sometimes bordering on plain farce manage to overcome most of the budgetary restraints.

—*Gunnar Rehlin*

A BUSINESS AFFAIR

(FRENCH-BRITISH-GERMAN-SPANISH)

A Films Number One release (France) of an Osby Films (France)/ Film & General Prods. (U.K.)/Connexion Films (Germany)/Cartel (Spain) production, with participation of Canal Plus, Prodeve, Sofiarp 2. (International sales: Capella Intl.) Produced by Xavier Larere, Clive Parsons, Davina Belling. Co-executive producers, Martha Wansbrough, Willy Baer. Directed by Charlotte Brandstrom. Screenplay, William Stadiem, from a story by Stadiem and Brandstrom, based on Barbara Skelton's books "Tears Before Bedtime" and "Weep No More." Additional dialogue, Agnes Caffin. Camera (color), Willy Kurant; editor, Laurence Mery-Clark; music, Didier Vasseur; production design, Sophie Becher; sound (Dolby), Steve Wheeler; associate producer, Diana Costes Brook. Reviewed at Cine Beaubourg Cinema, Paris, March 27, 1994. (In Gothenburg Film Festival.) Running time: **98 MIN.**
Kate Swallow .... Carole Bouquet
Vanni Corso .... Christopher Walken
Alec Bolton .... Jonathan Pryce
Judith .... Sheila Hancock
With: Anna Manahan, Fernando Guillen Cuervo, Tom Wilkinson.
(English dialogue)

"**A** Business Affair" is an unremarkable contemporary dramatic comedy that underutilizes ordinarily fine thesps. Theme of a lovely and talented woman's coming to terms with true independence has potential, but tedious misfire from Paris-born helmer Charlotte Brandstrom is neither here nor there. Cable sales and video rentals are likely on the strength of name cast.

Frenchwoman Kate Swallow (Carole Bouquet) works as a floor model at a London department store to support her adored celeb hubby of four years, grumpy novelist Alec Bolton (Jonathan Pryce), whose creative juices aren't flowing. In her spare time, Kate is swiftly writing her own first novel on a laptop computer whose clicking keyboard drives laborious pen-and-ink Alec nuts.

American mover and shaker Vanni Corso (Christopher Walken), a Sicilian whose maxim is "I figured if my father could sell pizzas in Harlem, I could sell culture in Europe," signs tony Alec to bolster the failing old London publishing firm he's bought. But when Kate submits her book to Corso, Alec takes umbrage and the marriage begins to totter.

Corso courts and wins Kate, who eventually discovers that even he feels threatened by a successful woman.

Script — based on real-life travails of writer Barbara Skelton, but updated from the 1950s — lurches along, with the actors never seeming to inhabit their roles. Dialogue, while sometimes crude and snappy, rarely sounds spontaneous. Only Sheila Hancock acquits herself with dignity as Walken's stiff-upper-lipped secretary.

Subplot of Pryce paying a matador to service Bouquet when she runs off to Spain plays like it was dropped in from another — equally mundane — movie. First scene with real feeling occurs 15 minutes from the end when divorced Pryce and Bouquet meet on the street.

Deliberately deglamorizing lighting is unflattering to all concerned. Even London's Ritz Hotel is made to look pedestrian. Accordion-heavy score, while OK in itself, rarely suits the action. Pic's nudity is tasteful. —*Lisa Nesselson*

GOOD NIGHT, IRENE

(SWEDISH-DANISH)

A Triangelfilm/Kedjan presentation of a MovieMakers, SVT2 (Sweden)/ Danmarks Radio, Kenneth Madsen Filmproduktion (Denmark) production, with participation of Nordic Film & TV Fund. (International sales: MovieMakers, Taby, Sweden.) Produced by Bert Sundberg. Directed, written by Stellan Olsson. Camera (color), Hans Welin; editor, Lasse Lundberg; music, Tomas Elfstadius; production design, Soren Skjaer; costume design, Marianne Lunderquist. Reviewed at Gothenburg Film Festival, Gothenburg, Sweden, Feb. 8, 1994. Running time: **110 MIN.**
With: Lars-Erik Berenett, Christian Gortz, Mikael Strandberg, Nina Gunke, Hampus Medin, Cim Meggerle, Johannes Brost, Ernst Gunther, Birgit Carlsten, Jan Malmsjo, Thor Eggers, Anette Bjarlestam, Gerd Hagnell.

A nostalgic look by helmer Stellan Olsson ("Sven Klang's Combo") at his own childhood, "Good Night, Irene" appealingly mixes touching humor and dark tragedy. Well told and multilayered, pic is definitely worth a look, and could become a minor hit on the fest and international arthouse circuit.

Olsson's alter ego, the Man (Lars-Erik Berenett), returns to the small country town Svalov after many

years. He walks the streets, takes photographs and recalls his youth. Flashbacks limn the Boy's (Christian Gortz) story of teenage sexuality and friendship, plus a view of the adult world full of unfaithfulness, greed, jealousy and still-surviving fascist ideals.

Irene of the title is a strange hardtop-owner (Gerd Hagnell), worshipped by madcap inventor Jóns (Jan Malmsjo) — two trusting, naive people who fall victim to the evils of the world. —*Gunnar Rehlin*

JUST YOU & ME

(BARA DU & JAG)

(SWEDISH-DANISH)

A United Intl. Pictures release (Sweden) of a Mekano Pictures, Swedish Film Institute, FilmTeknik, Getfilm (Sweden)/Per Holst Filmproduktion (Denmark) production, with support from Nordic Film & TV Fund. (International sales: Swedish Film Institute, Stockholm.) Produced by Anders Birkeland. Directed by Suzanne Osten. Screenplay, Osten, Barbro Smeds. Camera (color), Goran Nilsson; editor, Michal Leszczykowski; music, Bengt Berger; production design, Mona Theresia Forsen. Reviewed at Riviera Cinema, Stockholm, Feb. 14, 1994. (In Gothenburg Film Festival.) Running time: **98 MIN.**
Flore Daimon .... Francesca Quartey
Eliel Radon .... Etienne Glaser
Berit Sordin .... Lena T. Hansson
Also with: Bjorn Kjellman, David Jazy, Adam Nilsson, Brahim Elouagari, Maria Simonsson, Malin Bergstrom, Gabriel Hermelin, Reuben Salamander, Bo-Ingvar Ljungqvist, Ann Petren, Rolf Wikstrom.

At times a very funny political satire, "Just You & Me" is flawed by an unbelievable love story that eats up too much screen time. B.O. prospects look shaky.

Director Suzanne Osten's previous film, "Speak Up! It's So Dark," dealt seriously with growing racism and neo-Nazism in Swedish society. Her new pic picks up those themes, though the subject is given more comedic treatment.

Twenty-five-year-old Flore (Francesca Quartey), a black woman born and raised in Sweden, is made minister of schools and at once becomes a media darling. She sees this as a chance to implement her ideas for change in the education system.

Unexpectedly, though, she falls for Eliel (Etienne Glaser), a 50-year-old teacher with five kids. It's difficult for the two to find time together, and this puts a strain on both their love affair and Flore's work.

Pic is often funny and on target when mocking politicians and their not-always-honorable decisions. But the romance doesn't ring true,

and isn't helped by Glaser's boring, one-dimensional portrait.

As Flore, newcomer Quartey is good, as are most of the supporting thesps. Best of the latter is Lena T. Hansson as the prime minister's secretary: a scene in which she throws a hysterical fit and tells everyone "I run things around here" is a mini-classic.

Tech credits are all good.

—*Gunnar Rehlin*

BEYOND THE SKY

(HOYERE ENN HIMMELEN)

(NORWEGIAN)

A Northern Lights production in association with NRK Drama, Schibsted Film. Produced by Axel Helgeland. Co-producer, Karin Bamborough. Directed by Berit Nesheim. Screenplay, Klaus Hagerup, based on his novel. Camera (color), Philip Ogaard; editor, Lillian Fjellvaer; music, Geir Bohren, Bent Aserud; production design, Frode Krogh; costume design, Torkel Ranum. Reviewed at Gothenburg Film Festival, Feb. 9, 1994. Running time: **90 MIN.**
Mari .... Inger Lise Winjevoll
Miss Kjaer .... Harriet Andersson
Morten .... Arne Willy Granli Johnsen
Wenche ..... Birgitte Victoria Svendsen
Also with: Henrik Scheele Aleksander, Joachim Calmeyer, Jorunn Kjellsby, Per Jansen, Gunhild Enger, Nina Helene Andersen.

Predictable but charming, this romantic comedy could become a modest B.O. success with careful handling. New film by Norwegian helmer Berit Nesheim is an unpretentious and entertaining youth drama, though not as striking as her freshman feature, "Frida."

Pic tells of Mari (Inger Lise Winjevoll), a 12-year-old with attitude who rebels against her parents and teachers in both her clothing and her manners. The only adult she really likes is Miss Kjaer (Harriet Andersson), her oddball teacher who's about to retire. During the summer vacation, the two help each other to adopt a more lighthearted view of the world. They also find the teacher's long-lost love (Joachim Calmeyer), leading to an optimistic ending.

It's clear from the beginning that these two voluntary social outcasts are going to find and help each other, so in that sense the pic springs few surprises. But the overall tone is amusing and cheery, and there are some nice comic touches en route.

Both leads are appealing. Swedish thesp Andersson, who worked often with Ingmar Bergman, remains strikingly beautiful in her 60s. —*Gunnar Rehlin*

April 4, 1994 (Cont.)

NINA DARLING

(NINA ALSKLING)

(SWEDISH — DOCU)

A Folkets Bio presentation of a CO.Film/SVT-1 production. Produced, directed, written by Christina Olofson. Camera (color), Lisa Hagstrand; editor, Annette Lykke Lundberg; music, Johan Zachrisson. Reviewed at Gothenburg Film Festival, Gothenburg, Sweden, Feb. 6, 1994. Running time: 60 MIN.

Already a controversial item in Sweden, this docu about a woman sexually molested as a child has a powerful simplicity that makes it a natural for the fest circuit. Co-producer SVT pulled the film from its skeds on legal advice that relatives of the (now dead) offender could be recognized and sue. Director Christina Olofson has cried censorship.

Starting at age 8, and continuing through her childhood, Nina was abused by her foster father. Now in her 40s, she tells the tale straightforwardly and without sentimentality, a harrowing tale of an adult's power over an innocent and trusting child. Though the pic features old photographs from Nina's childhood, the foster father's face is never shown. —*Gunnar Rehlin*

THE HANDS

(HANDERNA)

(SWEDISH)

A Triangelfilm/Kedjan presentation of an SVT2 production. (International sales: SVT Intl., Stockholm.) Produced by Tommy Starck. Directed, written by Richard Hobert. Camera (color), Lars Crepin; editor, Leif Kristiansson; music, Ake Parmerud; production design, Aida Kalnins; costume design, Marie Wallin. Reviewed at Gothenburg Film Festival, Gothenburg, Sweden, Feb. 7, 1994. Running time: 89 MIN.
With: Boman Oscarsson, Sven-Bertil Taube, Camilla Lunden, Tomas Norstrom, Eddie Axberg, Curt Spangberg, Hans Mosesson, Jan Tiselius.

"The Hands" is a low-key thriller that only half succeeds in being scary. B.O. prospects locally are so-so. Pic, originally shot as a telepic, would be better off on the small screen.

Film is the second in writer/director Richard Hobert's series illustrating the seven deadly sins. The first, "Spring of Joy," was a comedy.

A seemingly innocent young man, Tomas (Boman Oscarsson), arrives on a small island off the Swedish coast and is slowly taken up by the community. It then appears

that he has "magic" hands, with the ability to divine water or oil. In fact, it's all part of a scam.

Pic needs a larger dose of shocks and more rapid narrative style to work as a true suspenser. Performances and tech credits, however, are all good. —*Gunnar Rehlin*

THE SCENT OF YVONNE

(LE PARFUM D'YVONNE)

(FRENCH)

A Bac Films release of a Lambart Prods./Zoulou Films/Centre Europeen Cinematographique Rhone-Alpes/M6 Films production, in association with Cofimage 5, Investimage 4, Sofiarp 2, with participation of Canal Plus, CNC. (International sales: President Films, Paris.) Produced by Thierry Ganay. Executive producer, Monique Guerrier. Directed, written by Patrice Leconte, based on Patrick Modiano's novel "Villa Triste." Camera (color, widescreen), Eduardo Serra; editor, Joelle Hache; music, Pascale Esteve; production design, Ivan Maussion; costume design, Annie Perier; sound, Paul Laine, Yves Osmu, Dominique Hennequin; assistant director, Michel Ferry. Reviewed at 14 Juillet Odeon Cinema, Paris, March 26, 1994. Running time: 87 MIN.
Dr. Rene
Meinthe .... Jean-Pierre Marielle
Victor Chmara ...... Hippolyte Girardot
Yvonne Jacquet .... Sandra Majani
Yvonne's Uncle ...... Richard Bohringer

After the delectably crude male buddy humor of "Tango," Patrice Leconte returns in "The Scent of Yvonne" to a variation on the steamy, dreamy melancholy that permeated "The Hairdresser's Husband." International arthouse exposure seems likely for this stunningly lensed widescreen memoir captured at the intersection of insouciance and longing.

Deceptively simple tale concerning one man's haunted reminiscence of an intense romance in the summer of 1958 purrs along thanks to fine performances and Leconte's stylistic assurance.

Pic is told in flashback as Victor (Hippolyte Girardot) gazes into what appears to be a bonfire — but is something else entirely — and thinks back a few years to the fateful day he met lovely young Yvonne (Sandra Majani) in the lobby of a luxury hotel on the shores of Lake Geneva.

Jean-Pierre Marielle makes a terrific entrance as Dr. Meinthe, a classy but flamboyant homosexual physician who provides unstated services in connection with the Algerian war. Because of the war, draft-dodging Victor is living under an assumed identity in a boarding house not far from Switzerland.

Yvonne, Victor and Meinthe form a trio of co-conspirators who enjoy an unhurried life of elegance

and spirited mockery. Pic plumbs an era before the sexual revolution when much was tacitly forbidden and thereby all the more delicious.

Sensual love scenes between Yvonne and Victor are full of leisurely preliminaries and prolonged caresses. Using widescreen to isolate meaningful gestures, Eduardo Serra's camera lingers on evocative details: a silk scarf, a teasingly placed knee, a jukebox tonearm.

A splendidly staged set piece of snotty local prize competition for the best combo of luxury car, male driver and female passenger-with-dog is the very essence of monied leisure, '50s- style.

Dutch-born former model Majani brings an unstudied grace to the flighty Yvonne. Girardot pulls off the laid-back paranoia of a reserved soul who admits that he does "nothing" for a living. Marielle imparts great dignity and tenderness to his tastefully flashy, wide-ranging role. Richard Bohringer makes a down-to-earth contribution as Yvonne's garage-owning uncle.

Beautifully integrated score has an appropriate tinge of melancholy, offset by multiple Celia Cruz songs. Novel by prolific author Patrick Modiano, who co-wrote "Lacombe Lucien" with Louis Malle, dates from 1975. —*Lisa Nesselson*

THE STORY OF A BOY WHO WANTED TO BE KISSED

(L'HISTOIRE DU GARCON QUI VOULAIT QU'ON L'EMBRASSE)

(FRENCH)

An MKL/Lazzenec Diffusion release (France) of a Les Films Pelleas, Glem Film, France 3 Cinema production, in association with Investimage 4 and Cofimage 5, with participation of Canal Plus and CNC. (International sales: WMF, Paris.) Produced by Philippe Martin. Co-producer, Gerard Louvin. Directed, written by Philippe Harel. Camera (color), Olivier Raffet; editor, Benedicte Teiger; music, Philippe Eidel; art direction, Laurent Allaire; costume design, Marie-Christine Lespannier; sound, Laurent Poirier; casting, Kris Portier de Bellair. Reviewed at Club de l'Etoile screening room, Paris, March 2, 1994. Running time: 100 MIN.
Raoul .... Julien Collet
Isabelle .... Helene Medigue
Mathilde .... Marion Cotillard
Virginie .... Marie Pailhes

Title just about sums up the action — or lack of it — in Philippe Harel's well-observed, minimalist "The Story of a Boy Who Wanted to Be Kissed." While pic is ideal for fests concerned with Awk-

ward Young Adulthood, film depicts the mundane so effectively that it's borderline soporific.

Film faithfully records the lackluster routine of Raoul (Julien Collet), a floundering young man who, when asked "What do you do?," freely admits, "Not much." This nondescript cipher, age 20, lives alone in a garret and is ostensibly researching an art history thesis on "The Color White in Painting."

Raoul also diligently observes women in cafes and on the street, sometimes following them but never finding the nerve to speak.

When a suave buddy tells him to visit a prostitute, Raoul replies that he "wants to be kissed." Halfway through the story (which covers six months), Raoul strikes up an indifferent carnal relationship with Isabelle (Helene Medigue). Raoul gets his kiss but also his comeuppance.

Nice stylistic touches include assorted women describing their sex lives directly to the camera — which represents Raoul as he reads "The Hite Report" — and a scene in which Raoul imagines all surrounding sound and movement halting as he approaches a girl in a bar.

As he proved in his deft short films and 65-minute indie pic "Un Ete sans histoires" (1992), scripter/helmer Harel is a kind of social scientist when it comes to nailing existential discomfort. Banality triumphs down to the last detail when Raoul pays a drab and uneventful visit to his parents in the countryside.

Collet does such a good job of fading into the woodwork wherever he goes that the viewer has no difficulty understanding why Raoul's love life is so unsatisfactory. Having a good time is just too laborious. —*Lisa Nesselson*

TARCH TRIP

(JAPANESE — 16mm)

A Jurgen Bruning Filmprods. production. Produced by Jurgen Bruning. Directed, written, edited by Hiroyuki Oki. Camera (color), Oki. Reviewed at Rotterdam Intl. Film Festival, Jan. 29, 1994. Running time: 64 MIN.
With: Tadayuki Kataoka, Masashi Mori, Masamitsu Yamatsu, Kazuhiko Uetake, Takashi Furukawa, Tatsuo Soma, Seiji Otsuta.

Japanese experimental filmmaker Hiroyuki Oki's "Tarch Trip" proposes the Zen answer to Gregg Araki's "Totally F***ed Up." Minimalist and without dialogue, pic is an uncompromisingly oblique riff on being young and gay in the shadow of the rising sun. It's destined for double-edged reception as a bewilderingly unrewarding patience test to some and a highly personal shot of maverick creativity to others. Either way it should be fleet-footed at gay fests and avant-gardist skeds.

Shot in and around Oki's home among the bland, boxlike architecture of provincial Aichi, pic is basically a meditative series of impressionist snapshots broadly distinguishable into two groups dictated by weather and loosely edited to form a non-linear collage.

Sunny skies dominate images of life and growth (sunflowers being the most recurrent of them), with three young friends asserting their visibility in the seemingly unaccommodating suburbs. Rain-darkened skies glower over the trio cut down to two. Its third member (the HIV-positive Tarch) is seen only in photographs.

Pic's sexual charge and fragmented depiction of intimacy are steadily cranked up throughout, giving a coherent thread in retrospect that's not there during viewing time. Oki mixes prolonged static glimpses with freewheeling handheld camera work to produce a rough, undulating texture echoed on the soundtrack by a cocktail of brooding synth music and random ambient noise.　*—David Rooney*

THE SORROW, LIKE A WITHDRAWN DAGGER, LEFT MY HEART

(KOREAN)

A Young Film production. Produced, directed by Hong Ki-Seon. Executive producer, Pak Keon-Seop. Screenplay, Ki-Seon, I Cheon-Hyi. Camera (color), Pak Hyi-Cu; lighting, Kang Sang-Yong; editor, Pak Sun-Tuk; music, Hong Seong-Kyu. Reviewed at the AMC Kabuki 8, San Francisco, March 10, 1994. (In S.F. Asian American Intl. Film Festival.) Running time: **98 MIN.**
With: Co Cae-Hyeon, Kim Cin-Nyeong, Pak Cong-Cheor, Choe Dong-Cun, I Hyi-Seong, Hong Seok-Yeon, Cang Min-Sung, I Yong-Sang, Sin Cong-Thae.

This rare Korean indie production sheds light on a little-known issue of worker exploitation in Asia. While that slant may interest fests looking for human rights themes, wobbly dramatic development will preclude further export potential.

Subject is dire conditions suffered on motorless wooden shrimp barges that have scarcely changed in 300 years. Crews are often abducted for service, then detained for endless, dangerous hauls by unscrupulous bosses.

Handsome but lame young protag Cae-Ho seeks work in port city of Mokpo and is forced aboard a shrimp boat, where fellow "slaves" include a boy barely in his teens, a half-wit and a weary 30-year veteran. Owners regularly deliver food and fresh water, keeping crew safely distant from land. Any signs of rebellion are cruelly punished.

Helmer Hong Ki-Seon captures this harsh existence, but the storyline lurches from one incident to the next. Along the way, escape efforts are betrayed, and Cae-Ho finds improbable romance with a blind prostitute during one brief island stop. (It's unclear why he doesn't take this opportunity to flee.) Offered the position of captain, hero abruptly turns tyrant, then has second thoughts. But a typhoon climax (poorly handled, with stock footage) washes away hopes of freedom. Film is set in 1987, with radio broadcasts providing intermittent background on South Korea's pro-democracy movement.

Conventional chopsocky noises during fight scenes distract amid otherwise realistic presentation. Major problem in current edition are atrociously translated titles, which confuse action via such imponderables as "I can't live with these craps beeping in my ears."
—Dennis Harvey

MONKEYS IN PARADISE

(KORAKU ZARU)

(JAPANESE)

A Vortex Japan production. Produced by Mitsutaka Kubo. Executive producer, Shuichi Ohi. Directed, written by Kenchi Iwamoto. Camera (color), Hideyo Fukuda; editor, Naoki Kaneko; music, Masakosan. Reviewed at Rotterdam Intl. Film Festival, Feb. 4, 1994. (Also in Festival of Festivals, Toronto.) Running time: **82 MIN.**
Papa .... Yuji Kohtari
Mom .... Kurenai Kanda
Yoshiaki .... Takaaki Kurihara
Michiko .... Aiko Murakoshi
Also with: Rina Okada, Chiyochirow Aoki, Hadaka Samuzora, Asako Kobayashi, Takuo Kobayashi.

Former cartoonist/illustrator Kenchi Iwamoto made something of a splash on the festival beat with his 1991 debut "Kikuchi," a minimalist glimpse at the alienation of a Tokyo laundromat attendant. Following with "Monkeys in Paradise," he again throws open the communication gap, this time surfing the mismatched wavelengths between members of a vacationing family in a more freewheeling, resoundingly comical key. Shrewdly marketed, this feverish dose of manga

madness could spark its share of cult B.O. action.

Iwamoto blithely tosses convention aside and introduces a disorderly succession of peripheral characters and narrative threads in the opening reel, some of which are then willfully left dangling. Consequently, pic is mildly confusing at first, but its visual playfulness, deadpan cast and eccentric black humor provide a more than substantial hook until the family nucleus takes center screen.

Their trip kicks off ominously, with a general divergence of interests fueling mutual intolerance. Shrewish Mom (Kurenai Kanda), who'd rather be dallying elsewhere, becomes increasingly tetchy, while cheapskate Papa (Yuji Kohtari) further stokes grievances by haggling for a cut-rate motel room in which sleep is precluded by the glare of a traffic light outside the window.

Secretly traumatized by a brush with a sex fiend, daughter (Aiko Murakoshi) suffers from continual nausea to the unrestrained amusement of her brother (Takaaki Kurihara), who's gripped by girl troubles. Papa attempts to air the subject of marital problems with his wife and lack of communication with the kids, with dismal results.

Shoving the absurdist tone even further off-center are lensman Hideyo Fukuda's delightful compositions, their harmonious symmetry constantly shattered as the characters loom amusingly into view in extreme close-ups.

Color filters — pink for exteriors, blue for interiors — add an additional twist. Visuals repeatedly point up the incongruous meeting of Nipponese and Western cultures.

Entirely recorded in post-production, sound has been cleverly manipulated with unexpectedly funny results. Most notably, locusts buzz musically on the soundtrack in jeering mockery of the hapless vacationers. Novel transitional wipes highlight the episodic comic-strip structure.

A psychedelic floral end-credit sequence paired with composer Masakosan's go-go accompaniment takes a final, dissonant dig at the pathos of the family left locked in silence around the dinner table.
—David Rooney

KING OF THE AIRWAVES

(LOUIS 19, LE ROI DES ONDES)

(CANADIAN-FRENCH)

A Malofilm Distribution (Canada) release of a Les Films Stock International/Eiffel Prods. production, with the participation of Telefilm Canada, SOGIC and Le Ministere de la Culture et de la Communication (Paris). (International sales: Malofilm Intl.) Produced by Richard Sadler. Co-produced by Jacques Dorfmann. Directed by Michel Poulette. Screenplay, Emile Gaudreault, Sylvie Bouchard, Michel Michaud, based on an original idea by Bouchard, Gaudreault. Camera (color), Daniel Jobin; editor, Denis Papillon; music, Jean-Marie Benoit; artistic director, Jean Becotte; costumes, Judy Jonker; sound, Normand Mercier; line producer, Pierre Laberge. Reviewed at the Maisonneuve Theatre of Place des Arts, Montreal, March 24, 1994. Running time: **93 MIN.**
Louis Jobin .... Martin Drainville
Julie .... Agathe de la Fontaine
Aline Jobin .... Dominique Michel
Charlotte Dubreuil .... Patricia Tulasne
Remi .... Gilbert Lachance
Roger .... Jean L'Italien
Also with: Yves Jacques, Rene-Richard Cyr, Chantal Francke, Sonia Laplante, Michel Tremblay, Macha Grenon, Marie-Claude Robitaille, Jean-Pierre Coallier, Yves Desgagnes, Gildor Roy, Marcel Leboeuf, Andree Boucher, Annette Garand, Normand Levesque, Benoit Briere, Jacques Lussier, Sylvie Legault, Gaston Lepage, Guillaume Lemay-Thivierge, Ysabelle Rosa, Rita Bibeau, Johanne-Marie Tremblay.

The wacky, light comedy "King of the Airwaves" is exactly the sort of mass-appeal comic pic with lots of local flavor that tends to generate boffo B.O. action in French Canada, and it will likely be one of the bigger Quebec hits of the year. It opened across the province April 1.

Pic's original storyline and rapid-fire, MTV-like pacing will probably generate good word of mouth, and the presence of a slew of well-known Quebec actors and media personalities in cameo appearances will also help pull in the crowds. This Canadian-French co-production could have a theatrical life in French-speaking Europe but is unlikely to make it to the silver screen in the U.S. The inventive script might pique the curiosity of producers interested in an English-lingo remake.

Louis Jobin (Martin Drainville) is a young, rather downbeat salesman who spends his days working in an electronics store and his nights in couch-potato mode, zapping from channel to channel. His passion for the tube spurs Louis to sign up for a talent contest being run by local

Channel 19, which promises to shoot the winner's every movement, 24 hours a day for the next three months.

Louis, of course, wins the contest, and suddenly he's on the other end of the remote control. This unassuming, ordinary guy becomes the most unlikely media celebrity, as the TV cameras turn his life into a real-life soap opera that has the entire city hooked.

The high-concept script — based on an idea dreamed up by Emile Gaudreault and Sylvie Bouchard, of the popular Quebec comedy troupe Groupe Sanguin — provides lots of yuks in the first half as Louis' fairly mundane existence comes in for some close scrutiny. Pic works as a lighthearted critique of the media's power to pervert whatever it touches.

Seasoned actress Dominique Michel is a delight as the domineering mother who's hellbent on making the most of her son's 15 minutes of fame, but it's Drainville's performance that holds "King of the Airwaves" together.

Best known for a supporting role in the Quebec TV drama "Scoop," Drainville makes an impressive feature-film debut here, and there is something intensely likable about his turn as a lonely nerd trying to deal with his unexpected fame.

The film's one-gag premise begins to wear thin after an hour, though, especially when helmer Michel Poulette slows down the pacing to focus on Louis' on-air romance with Julie (Agathe de la Fontaine). Fortunately, the laughs are soon back in full swing and the manic tempo goes into overdrive for the last 20 minutes, as Louis rebels against his new-found stardom. Climactic scene serves up a hilarious spoof of the famous kitchen sex scene in "9½ Weeks."

Budgeted at \$C3.1 million (\$2.3 million), pic features top-notch production values throughout.

—Brendan Kelly

ON TOUR
(A TURNE)
(HUNGARIAN)

A Hunnia Filmstudio-Duna TV production. (International sales: Cinemagyar). Produced by Sandor Simo. Directed, written by Geza Beremenyi. Camera (color), Sandor Kardos; editor, Teri Losonczi; music, Ferenc Darvas; production design, Gyula Pauer. Reviewed at Hungarian Film Week, Budapest, Feb. 6, 1994. Running time: **93 MIN.**
With: Karoly Eperjes, Mari Torocsik, Miklos Benedek, Iren Bordan, Zoltan Bezeredi, Tamas Cseh, Eniko Borcsok, Zoltan Ternyak.

A modest success at the Hungarian B.O. last year, this breezy comedy, about a group of bickering traveling actors, scores with Magyar-speaking audiences because of a popular cast and funny lines, but probably won't translate.

Director Geza Beremenyi could have worked a little harder on the script to realize concept's premise. Eight members of an acting company dash around Hungary in midsummer in three cars performing one-night stands of musical numbers and sketches in a variety of venues.

Offstage, there's the inevitable quarreling and sexual jealousies, the minor crises. But the show goes on.

Beremenyi seems to have decided that, because his film is about actors, he should encourage his excellent cast to overact; as a result, there are some strident performances from usually reliable players. Yet during a period when Hungarian-produced films face an uphill battle to score at the local wickets, the success of this one is notable.

—David Stratton

HOLY MATRIMONY

A Buena Vista release of a Hollywood Pictures presentation of an Interscope Communications/Polygram Filmed Entertainment production in association with Aurora Prods. Produced by William Stuart, David Madden, Diane Nabatoff. Executive producers, Ted Field, Robert W. Cort. Co-executive producers, Daniel Jason Heffner, Douglas S. Cook. Directed by Leonard Nimoy. Screenplay, David Weisberg, Cook. Camera (CFI color), Bobby Bukowski; editor, Peter E. Berger; music, Bruce Broughton; production design, Edward Pisoni; art direction, David Crank; costumes, Deena Appel; sound (Dolby), Martin Raymond Bolger; assistant director, Benjamin Rosenberg; casting, Owens Hill, Rachel Abroms. Reviewed at Cineplex Odeon Spectrum Theatre, Houston, March 25, 1994. MPAA Rating: PG-13. Running time: **93 MIN.**

Havana	Patricia Arquette
Zeke	Joseph Gordon-Levitt
Wilhelm	Armin Mueller-Stahl
Peter	Tate Donovan
Markowski	John Schuck
Orna	Lois Smith
Cooper	Courtney B. Vance
Link	Jeffrey Nordling
Mr. Greeson	Richard Riehle
Female Officer	Mary Pat Gleason

A sort of humorous variation on "Witness," "Holy Matrimony" appears to exist in a commercial limbo, and Disney has a challenge selling this innocuous but problematic comedy. Pic opened April 8 in a 15-city regional release, not including New York or Los Angeles, indicating some understandable apprehension as to how it will play with critics and ticket buyers.

Basic problem is that any plot synopsis makes the film sound more sordid, and more potentially offensive, than it is. Director Leonard Nimoy and screenwriters David Weisberg and Douglas S. Cook have bent over backwards to avoid sleaziness and overt salaciousness, but their admirable restraint may not be enough to win over the picture's natural constituency, the "family movie" audience.

Pic begins with bosomy sexpot Havana (Patricia Arquette) on the run with boyfriend Peter (Tate Donovan) after they rob a carnival operator's safe. They cross the border into Canada and hide out at the Hutterite religious colony where Peter grew up. Peter is greeted like the returning prodigal son, and the Hutterite elders, led by Uncle Wilhelm (Armin Mueller-Stahl), accept his story that Havana — his "fiancee" — wants to convert to their religion.

Naturally, the vivacious, blunt-spoken Havana feels stifled by the restraints of Hutterite life — no TV, makeup, cigarettes or four-letter words — and she's even more unhappy when, after marrying Peter, she must serve him as a meekly submissive spouse. But she's determined to stick around, since she doesn't know where Peter has hidden the stolen money.

And she remains determined after Peter is killed in an auto accident. Mindful of the colony's strict adherence to biblical law, Havana borrows a page from Deuteronomy and insists on her right to remain with the Hutterites by marrying Peter's younger brother.

Trouble is, the younger brother, Zeke (Joseph Gordon-Levitt), is all of 12 years old.

"Holy Matrimony" plays the second marriage mostly for safe, sitcom-style laughs. There is one scene where Zeke tries to make his buddies believe he's a virile lover, and another scene where Havana doesn't bother to get dressed before chasing Zeke away from her door. (The nudity is implied, with Arquette viewed only above the waist, from the rear.)

Other than that, however, pic steers far away from even implied acknowledgment of what surely will be on the minds of many audience members (especially teens lured by trailers and TV spots). Zeke is depicted as an old-fashioned, unsophisticated youngster — "I'm 12 years old! I still hate girls!" — who's uncomfortable around females in general and openly hostile to Havana in particular. Predictably, he warms to the outsider, and she to him — but in a purely platonic, brother-sister way.

Their budding friendship flowers when they leave the Hutterite community to return the stolen money, with a crooked FBI agent (John Schuck) in hot pursuit, triggering what must be the most contrived and thoroughly unnecessary car-chase scene in recent years.

Arquette sparkles as Havana, making a believable transition from amoral Marilyn Monroe wannabe to relatively honest Big Sister figure. She's at her funniest while trying to fit in as a Hutterite, hiding behind a phony smile and mumbling bitter comments to herself.

Gordon-Levitt (last seen as young Norman in "A River Runs Through It") is unaffected and engaging as Zeke, while Mueller-Stahl plays Uncle Wilhelm with just the right mix of gravity and compassion. Neither Nimoy nor the writers make the mistake of treating the Hutterites with anything but affectionate respect. As a result, pic's humor is never mean-spirited, and often quite pleasant.

On a tech level, pic is everything it should be and more. Bobby Bukowski's nimble color lensing is a definite asset. So is the costume design of Deena Appel, who manages an effective contrast between the simple look of the Hutterites and the more colorful outsiders.

—*Joe Leydon*

DREAM LOVER

A Gramercy release of a Polygram Filmed Entertainment presentation of a Propaganda Films production in association with Nicita/Lloyd Prods. and Edward R. Pressman. Produced by Sigurjon Sighvatsson, Wallis Nicita, Lauren Lloyd. Executive producers, Steve Golin, Pressman. Supervising producer, Tim Clawson. Co-producer, Elon Dershowitz. Directed, written by Nicholas Kazan. Camera (Deluxe color), Jean-Yves Escoffier; editors, Jill Savitt, Susan Crutcher; music, Christopher Young; production design, Richard Hoover; art direction, Bruce Hill; set decoration, Brian Kasch; costume design, Barbara Tfank; sound (Dolby), David Brownlow, Mary Jo Devenney; assistant director, Mary Ellen Woods; casting, Johanna Ray. Reviewed at Raleigh Studios, L.A., Feb. 28, 1994. (In Cleveland Film Festival.) MPAA Rating: R. Running time: **103 MIN.**
Ray Reardon .... James Spader
Lena Reardon .... Madchen Amick
Elaine .... Bess Armstrong
Larry .... Fredric Lehne
Norman .... Larry Miller
Martha .... Kathleen York
Cheryl .... Blair Tefkin
Billy .... Scott Coffey
Judge .... Clyde Kusatsu
Buddy .... William Shockley

An overly abstract mystery about the difficulty of really knowing another person and the unfathomables of amorous attachment, "Dream Lover" is too rarefied for a popular thriller and too dramatically hokey for an art film. Directorial debut of notable screenwriter Nicholas Kazan displays more of an awareness of film's visual possibilities than a flair for them, and while there are any number of interesting ideas bouncing around here, pic falls between stools both artistically and commercially. Gramercy release, which bowed at the Cleveland Film Festival April 9, will have a tough sled theatrically, although prospects on cable and video are somewhat brighter.

Bearing no relation to Alan J. Pakula's 1986 Kristy McNichol starrer of the same name, this Propaganda production slowly generates a moderate amount of interest through the setup but never develops much of what can pass for a plot.

Despite a disastrous first encounter, young divorced L.A. architect Ray (James Spader) manages to quickly win the favor of fashion model-gorgeous Lena (Madchen Amick).

Receptive as she is to his attentions, she warns him that "I'm just a regular screwed-up person," and recognizes that men tend to believe that they know her because they see their fantasies realized in her lovely face and stunning body.

They marry and have kids, but after awhile Ray begins to imagine that his wife might not be true to — or truly with — him.

He catches Lena in some lies, and his suspicions that she may not be who she claims are confirmed when he tracks down her parents in rural Texas and brings them back to California for a confrontation.

Lena plausibly responds that she had to reinvent herself to escape her dismal past, but Ray's jealousy grows by leaps and bounds.

The stakes mount quickly thereafter through accusations and admissions of indiscretions, betrayals and overt manipulations, all leading up to legal proceedings and a climactic murder in a loony bin.

On their first date, Lena suggests that getting to know someone is akin to peeling an onion, and it's true that one never knows how much of her personality has been revealed and how much more remains to be discovered.

But without dramatic adornment or terrific surprises, the character striptease, along with Ray's ever-escalating frustration, isn't enough to compel unstinting viewer interest.

Lena decidedly falls into the femme fatale category, but Kazan is mostly operating far from neo-noir territory.

Rather, he adopts a bright, modern, highly stylized look that emphasizes designer settings, expensive threads, lateral tracking shots, unusual editing devices and a preponderance of close-ups that combine to create an abstract, distanced ambiance.

Idea was no doubt to fashion a kind of dream world for Ray to inhabit with his dream woman, which makes the film interesting to watch but also involves a considerable sacrifice of believability.

A related problem is that, even after being together for some years, Ray and Lena still seem like strangers, so that their relationship hardly feels real.

Unfortunately, the more the onion is peeled, the less of it there is, leaving the picture with little sense of conviction or substance by the end.

After his rewardingly offbeat outing in "The Music of Chance," Spader retreats here to handsome-but-bewildered yuppie territory, to somewhat diminishing returns.

Rather like Christopher Walken, his smooth good looks work best when he's playing edgier or threatening characters rather than nice guys.

Fully looking the part of most men's fantasies, "Twin Peaks" vet Amick does a creditable job with a role whose motivations are probably too convoluted to make sense of.

Kazan pulls off some effective scenes, notably one in Texas in which Ray meets his wife's low-life ex-boyfriend, nicely played by William Shockley.

Visual appointments, including lensing by Jean-Yves Escoffier ("Les Amants du Pont Neuf") and Richard Hoover's production design, are both arty and artful.

—*Todd McCarthy*

AFRICAN FEST

ALMA'S RAINBOW

A Paradise Plum presentation of a Crossgrain Pictures/Rhinoceros Prods. production, in association with Channel 4. (International sales: Red Carnelian, N.Y.) Produced by Ayoka Chenzira, Howard Brickner, Charles Lane. Line producer, Geri Jasper. Directed, written by Chenzira. Camera (color), Ronald K. Gray; editor, Lillian Benson; music, Jean-Paul Bourelly; set design, Peggy Dillard Toone; costume design, Sidney Kai Innis; casting and choreography, Thomas Osha Pinnock. Reviewed at African Film Festival, Milan, Italy, March 18, 1994. Running time: **85 MIN.**
Alma Gold .... Kim Weston-Moran
Rainbow Gold . Victoria Gabriella Platt
Ruby Gold .... Mizan Nunes
Blue .... Lee Dobson
Miles ....Isaiah Washington IV
Babs .... Jennifer Copeland
Pepper .... Keyonn Sheppard
Sea Breeze .... Roger Pickering

A woman's coming-of-age film with a few new twists, "Alma's Rainbow," feature film bow of African-American director Ayoka Chenzira, describes a black girl growing up in Brooklyn with radically diverse role models to choose from. A sparkling perf from young Victoria Gabriella Platt keeps the comedy-drama lively, but real drawing card is pic's realistic female p.o.v. on a black childhood.

Much appreciated by Italian auds when it opened the African Film Festival in Milan, this indie production should appeal particularly to black and women viewers but might find a small offshore niche with careful handling.

Rainbow (Platt) is teetering through that awkward age when girls are torn between being street-dancing tomboys and dressing up for the boys. Each morning, she flattens her growing breasts with a piece of cloth.

Her mom, Alma (Kim Weston-Moran), proud owner of a beauty salon, is little help. Reason for her prim severity is explained upon the surprise arrival of her sister Ruby (Mizan Nunes) from Europe.

In their youth, the two tried to break into showbiz as a singing sister act, but while Ruby took off for a "glamorous" career as a Josephine Baker imitator in gay Paris, Alma got pregnant with Rainbow and decided to play it safe.

Writer/director Chenzira wrings the maximum contrast out of the divided/reunited siblings, tending toward caricatures of the sexually repressed Mother and the freedom-is-bliss Floozy. Naturally, it's Aunt Ruby who piques Rainbow's imagination and draws out her femininity.

Ruby's influence even reaches Alma. In a climactic scene more comic than dramatic, Rainbow returns home after (unsuccessfully) trying to lose her virginity to find her mom on the couch with handyman Blue (Lee Dobson), who's been wooing her for several reels.

Chenzira shows a tendency to skimp on the emotion, preferring to serve a richly reasoned dish with humorous seasoning.

A fresh, all-black cast holds the story together. Weston-Moran throws herself into the thankless role of the hung-up mom, while Nunes is a splendidly tawdry Ruby, a penniless prima donna who insists on arriving at appointments in style, even if it means getting a lift in a hearse.

Platt's Rainbow draws the audience into her world with a melting gaze and mucho presence. Male characters are far less developed.

Produced on a $300,000 shoestring, pic stays mostly indoors, where Ronald K. Gray's warm lensing underlines the self-contained world Alma wishes her beauty parlor/home to be. Film has screened at the Independent Feature Film Market in New York and in several fests as it awaits a U.S. distrib.

—*Deborah Young*

MORE TIME

(ZIMBABWEAN)

A Media for Development Trust release (Zimbabwe) of a John & Louise Riber production. Directed by Isaac Meli Mabhikwa. Screenplay, Andrew Whaley, John Riber. Camera (color), Joao Costa; editor, Louise Riber; music, Peace of Ebony, others. Reviewed at African Film Festival, Milan, Italy (competing), Mar. 22, 1994. Running time: **90 MIN.**
Thandiwe .... Prudence Katomeni
David .... Webster Gonzo
Girl .... Barbara Nkala
   (English dialogue)

"**M**ore Time" is a breezy yet insightful look at teens growing into adult relationships under the specter of AIDS. Pic won top honors at the first Southern Africa Film Festival in Zimbabwe last fall and was prized at Milan's African Film Festival. It could work splendidly at educational venues.

Thandiwe (Prudence Katomeni) is a bobby-soxer ready to take the step from intramural basketball to her first boyfriend. Good-looking David (Webster Gonzo) is tormented by the return of his old girlfriend, who left school when she got pregnant. Now her infant daughter is dying of AIDS, passed on through the girl's clandestine relationship with her uncle. The uncle is already dead, and David is afraid he may be infected.

Thandiwe, meanwhile, chafes at the bit imposed by her strict parents. She sneaks out to see David, gets into fights, and one afternoon gets drunk. In a well-handled scene, Thandiwe's know-it-all girlfriend forces her to buy condoms for future safety, insisting on her right to AIDS protection when the snooty pharmacist says the girls are too young to need them.

From being light and *tres* politically correct, pic evolves into an outright plea for AIDS safety among teens in its closing scene, staged at a concert-dance against the virus.

Debuting helmer Isaac Meli Mabhikwa shows a perceptive touch in dealing with teen problems. Lead actress Katomeni is a charmer, lending conviction to the film's arguments while keeping the entertainment quotient high. Supporting cast is fresh and natural. Local music track is another plus.
           —*Deborah Young*

LOOKING FOR MY WIFE'S HUSBAND

(A LA RECHERCHE DU MARI DE MA FEMME)

(MOROCCAN)

A COE release (Italy) of an Arts & Techniques Audio-Visuels production. Produced, directed by Mohamed Abderrahman Tazi. Screenplay, Aicha Regragui. Camera (color), Federico Ribes; editor, Kahena Attia; art direction, Pierre Gompertz, Abdelkrim Akellach; costumes, Larbi Yacoubi. Reviewed at African Film Festival, Milan, Italy (competing), March 19, 1994. Running time: **100 MIN.**
Hadj Ben Moussa .... Bachir Skirej
Houda .... Mouna Fettou
Lalla Rabea .... Naima Lemcherki
Lalla Hobbi .... Amina Rachid
Tamo .... Fatima Moustaid
   (Arabic dialogue)

A satire on the intricate Islamic law code dealing with polygamy, "Looking for My Wife's Husband" has clicked in Morocco as a hit comedy. Thanks to its extreme local color (story is set in a harem), pic will be a curiosity item offshore for fests and special-interest auds.

Quite a different type of film from "Badis," director Mohamed Abderrahman Tazi's previous fest success, "Husband" could be compared to a Moroccan sitcom set in a middle-class, modern-day harem. Fat but lovable gold merchant Hadj (comic Bachir Skirej, a thesp who worked many years in the U.S.) has three wives, each of a different generation. The women, who are good friends, have divided up their "duties" for Hadj. Everything goes wonderfully well, until Hadj repudiates his beautiful youngest wife, Houda (Mouna Fettou), in a fit of jealous rage.

She calmly moves back in with her parents, cuts her hair and updates her wardrobe. Hadj, on the other hand, is racked by suffering and discovers he can't live without her. Islamic law allows him to remarry Houda only if she first marries another man who then repudiates her.

Aicha Regragui's script brings out the feeling of community among the women, children and servants in the harem, emphasizing the wives' surprising camaraderie and independence of mind. In a sense, it replays "Badis'" theme of women's victimized position in society in a grotesque but affectionate comic key. Crisply lensed within the walls of a magnificent tiled house, pic is a pleasure to watch.   —*Deborah Young*

THE LOTTERY

(WARIKO, LE GROS LOT)

(IVORY COAST)

An Atriascop release (Paris) of a Kramo-Lancine production. Directed, written by Fadika Kramo-Lancine. Camera (color), Lionel Cousin; editor, Kramo-Lancine, Cisse Salimata; music, Cheick M. Smith. Reviewed at African Film Festival, Milan, Italy (competing), March 22, 1994. Running time: **90 MIN.**
Ali .... Allassane Toure
Awa .... Abiba Kabore
   Also with: Rachel Tehi, Losseni Traore, Ahissatou Traore, Adrienne Koutouan, Adama Diarra, Sidiki Traore.

Striving earnestly to be funny, "The Lottery" is too intent on preaching its no-free-lunches message to be amusing. Though director Fadika Kramo-Lancine's sharp eye for detail is illuminating about the lifestyle of the Ivory Coast's urban poor, storyline is monotonous, limiting pic's prospects beyond the fest circuit.

An underpaid policeman, Ali (Allassane Toure), is elated to discover his wife, Awa (Abiba Kabore), has bought the winning lottery ticket. The problem is finding the ticket, which no amount of searching turns up. Tension grows as word spreads back at the village that the family has become rich. Relatives ply Ali with demands for money, which even his wise father can't stop. When the ticket is found at last, Ali realizes with chagrin that the windfall won't begin to buy all the things his extended family needs.

Kramo-Lancine ("Djeli," 1981) has solid notions about shooting and editing, evident in a witty opening montage showing money changing hands in the marketplace. A lively local score keeps things humming.
           —*Deborah Young*

THE GOLDEN BALL

(LE BALLON D'OR)

(FRENCH-GUINEAN)

A Le Studio Canal Plus presentation of a Chrysalide Films production. Produced by Monique Annaud. Directed by Cheick Doukoure. Screenplay, Doukoure, David Carayan. Camera (color), Alain Choquart; music, Loy Erlich, Ismael Isaac. Reviewed at African Film Festival, Milan, Italy (competing), March 23, 1994. Running time: **100 MIN.**
   With: Aboubacar Sidiki Sumah, Agnes Soral, Habib Hammoud.
   (French dialogue)

"**T**he Golden Ball" is a modern-day African fairy tale about Bandian, a 12-year-old whose knack for soccer takes him out of his poor village to play with the pros. Child actor Aboubacar Sidiki Sumah, who appears to do his own remarkable stunts, is an authentic delight in this well-shot offering from Guinea. Easy to watch and absorb, it's a perfect kidpic with a touch of malicious irony behind its cheery Horatio Alger story.

To help Bandian's soccer talent bloom, a witch doctor rubs unguents on his small legs. After his math teacher calculates it will take him 320,000 days of hauling wood after school to afford a real leather soccer ball, a European doctor (Agnes Soral) finds him a used ball. Thereon, there's no stopping the budding champion.

Helmer Cheick Doukoure ("Blanc d'ebene") sets this inventive, upbeat film to the foot-tapping beat of local music. Bandian humorously narrates much of the story offscreen. Following a fight with his folks, the boy runs off to the city, where he spends a night in jail with a friendly dwarf before a fish- and video-dealer who adores soccer "discovers" him.

Tech credits are pro throughout.
           —*Deborah Young*

PUSHING THE LIMITS

(FRENCH)

An MC4 and MGA release of an MC4/MGA/Centre Europeen Cinematographique Rhone-Alpes/Flach Film/NRJ Prods./France 2 Cinema production, with participation of Canal Plus. (International sales: Mercure, Paris.) Produced by Jean-Pierre Bailly. Directed by Thierry Donard. Screenplay, Donard, Philippe Barrassat, Yvan Lopez, Pascaline Simar, Bruno de Champris, Alexandra Deman, from a screen story by Donard. Camera (color), Jerome Nouvelle; editors, Roland Baubeau, Bruno de Champris; music, Marcello Twitti; costume design, Jeanne Berthon, Nadia Chimlewski, Marie-Jose Journou; sound (Dolby), Denis Gautier, Christian Chauvin, Jean-Paul Loublier; free-fall camera, Francois Rickard, Werner Noremberg, Andy Duff; associate producer, Jean-Pierre Saire. Reviewed at Grand Rex Cinema, Paris, March 26, 1994. Running time: **97 MIN.**
Fiona Gelin .... Fiona Gelin
Xigor Copeland .... Marc Twight
Farjonnes .... Edward Meeks
   Also with (as themselves): Eric Fradet, Eric Bellin, Criss Firsberg, Christophe Crettin, Dominique Gleizes, Jean-Louis Lugon-Moulin, David Sharrock, Daniel Gelin.

"**P**ushing the Limits" grafts a make-do plot about greed and commercialism onto scattered sequences of breathtaking athletic feats, performed by top-notch sky-surfers and ski daredevils. Pic, which is drawing young auds in exclusive run on one mammoth Paris screen, is a good candidate for exhibition offshore and should enjoy a healthy life on video.

Told in flashback with tons of v.o., story is framed by scenes of Fiona (Fiona Gelin) releasing a magnificent eagle from a mountain top. She hosts "Extreme Game," a popular derring-do show on private web Castle TV, run by malevolent, ratings-hungry mastermind Farjonnes (Edward Meeks).

Among the risk-takers are mild-mannered Xigor Copeland (Marc Twight), a consummate ice climber and sky-surfer. Rugged colleagues Eric and Christophe are extreme snowboarders, bunny-hopping down sheer inclines. Dominique is a jumper who leaps into voids and skis off cliffs wearing a last-minute parachute. Criss is a radical telemark skier. Jean-Louis skis straight down deadly inclines. Eric Fradet is a gifted sky-surfer rendered mute in an accident.

Story lurches along from stunt to stunt as pic takes fearless friends to dramatic vistas in Chamonix, Mont Blanc, Argentina and Bolivia's Lake Titicaca. Non-pro actors are sometimes awkward with dialogue although they shine on the slopes.

Xigor announces to the world that he thinks he can sky-surf and then land on the slopes without using a parachute to break his fall. To up the ante, he'll do so at night with only flares and a laser beam to light his way. Farjonnes pits the buddies against one another in the weeks leading to the live stunt. Fiona and Xigor's romance suffers from the tension. Will brave Xigor outsmart venal Farjonnes?

Close-ups are always crisp, but footage of exploits from a distance tends toward fuzzy. Cutting is quite good in a snazzy sequence (which took four months to shoot) where Xigor races a plane to a snowy finish line.

The loud rock score suits the action.

Pic is dedicated to athlete/cameraman Francois Rickard, who was killed during aerial filming over Lake Titicaca. —*Lisa Nesselson*

DEATH OF A NATION: THE TIMOR CONSPIRACY

(BRITISH — DOCU)

A Central Independent Television production. Produced, directed by David Munro. Co-producer, Max Stahl. Written, presented by John Pilger. Camera (color), Stahl, Preston Clothier, Simon Fanthorpe, Bob Bolt, Munro; editor, Joe Frost; music, Agio Pereira; sound, Ian Sherry, Caleb Moss; associate producers, Gill Scrine, Ana de Juan. Reviewed at Mandolin Theater, Sydney, March 22, 1994. Running time: **96 MIN.**

Docu filmmakers David Munro and John Pilger filmed secretly in apparently hazardous conditions in Indonesian-occupied East Timor to come up with this devastating accusation of genocide by one large, powerful Asian nation against a tiny neighbor. Docu, which screened February on British TV and has opened in two Sydney cinemas with bookings in other Aussie cities to follow, is unquestionably strong stuff.

Pilger lucidly sets up the background to the 1975 invasion of tiny, Catholic East Timor, which at the time was still a Portuguese colony, by its powerful Muslim neighbor, pointing out that President Gerald Ford and Secretary of State Henry Kissinger visited the Indonesian capital of Jakarta on the eve of the invasion. Two Aussie TV crews, comprising five men, were killed at the time of the invasion; Pilger shows moving footage of the last report filed by one of the victims, Greg Shackleton, as he prepares for an imminent assault on Timor.

In the nearly 20 years since the Indonesian takeover, per Pilger, a campaign amounting to genocide has been waged on the Timorese — who are not ethnically linked to the Javanese of Indonesia — culminating in the infamous 1991 massacre in Dili, which was covered by a film crew. According to the film, one-third of the population of East Timor, or 200,000 men, women and children, have died.

Pilger accuses the U.S., Britain and Australia of complicity. A former CIA man talks about U.S. encouragement of Indonesia, while a former British foreign minister makes the astonishing claim that it doesn't bother him "what one set of foreigners do to another." Australian Foreign Minister Gareth Evans is seen flying above Timor while toasting his Indonesian counterpart over a successful agreement to divide the proceeds from undersea oil fields off the coast of Timor.

The tragic fate of the Timorese (who fought gallantly for the Allies during World War II) is presented via interviews with exiles and residents who are photographed so that they can't be identified.

On a technical level, "Death of a Nation" isn't an outstanding example of the art of documentary; its TV format doesn't entirely suit cinema presentation. But in terms of its disturbing content, which is passionately and even courageously presented, it's a thought-provoking knockout. —*David Stratton*

THE FLOOD
(L'INONDATION)
(FRENCH-RUSSIAN)

A UGC release (France) of an Erato Films/Ima Films production in association with R. Films/La Sept Cinema/Les Films du Camelia/Mosfilm. (International sales: UGC, Paris.) Produced by Daniel Toscan du Plantier. Executive producers, Toscan du Plantier, Jerome Paillard. Directed by Igor Minaiev. Screenplay, Jacques Baynac, Minaiev, from the novel by Yevgyeni Zamyatin. Camera (color), Vladimir Pankov; music, Anatoli Dergachev; art direction, Vladimir Murzin; sound, Igor Urvantsev; assistant director, Tamara Vladimirtseva. Reviewed at Berlin Film Festival (market), Feb. 17, 1994. Running time: **97 MIN.**
Sofia .... Isabelle Huppert
Trofim .... Boris Nevzorov
Ganka .... Masha Lipkina
Pelagia .... Svetlana Kruchkova
With: Andrei Tolubeyev.
(French dialogue)

Isabelle Huppert has one of her best screen roles in some time in "The Flood," a sexually charged, atmospheric yarn of femme vengeance set in the back alleys of '20s Russia. Pic's low-key, semi-stylized approach will limit its theatrical life, but there's much to admire until it slips off the rails in the final reel.

Huppert herself discovered the novel by Russian writer Yevgyeni Zamyatin two years ago and, after personally buying the rights, persuaded Daniel Toscan du Plantier to produce, with Paris-based, Ukrainian director Igor Minaiev taking behind-the-lens duties.

Setting is a dingy apartment block in '20s Petrograd (modern St. Petersburg), where Sofia (Huppert) lives a dutiful existence with laborer hubby Trofim (Boris Nevzorov). Though the couple have an active sex life, and Sofia herself a hyperactive imagination, she's still failed to bear a child.

Afraid of losing Trofim, Sofia agrees to adopt a 13-year-old orphan, Ganka (Masha Lipkina), whose dark-eyed presence immediately adds a sexual frisson to the household. Some years later,

Trofim starts sharing Ganka's bed as well as his wife's, and, when a flood fails to conveniently dispatch her younger rival, Sofia decides to take matters into her own hands.

Minaiev's approach to the basically meller material plays up the story's atmospheric quality, with sparse dialogue, short scenes separated by dissolves, and whole sequences built simply on looks, music and carefully composed visuals.

Though set in newly communizing Russia of the 1920s, pic has a strongly 19th-century, almost Dostoyevskian feel, heightened by a brownish, pastel color scheme and working-class setting. Political content is negligible and, despite the Gallic dialogue, pic is 100% Russo in look and feel.

The flood itself, in which the River Neva breaks its banks, is economically but well staged. Minaiev then delivers the dramatic goods in a shocking murder scene that recalls Roman Polanski's early pix in its dispassionate brutality. Only in a hospital confessional at the very end does the movie finally tip over into needless melodrama.

Huppert is tops in the creepy central role, which plays on her strengths in portraying disturbed normality. Thesp melds comfortably with the Russian cast, and even manages to bring off a potentially risible over-enthusiastic masturbation session.

As her cloddish husband, Nevzorov is fine, despite the handicap of learning his (sparse) French dialogue by rote. Lipkina, as the girl, exudes a natural sensuality that contrasts well with Huppert's more complex portrayal.

Technically, pic is pro, with Mosfilm studio shooting adding to the required sense of irreality, and Anatoli Dergachev's symphonic score a major assist in the whole emotional package. —*Derek Elley*

THE IGUANA
(L'IGUANE)
(FRENCH — B&W — 16mm)

A Les Films du Desordre production. Directed, written by Filip Forgeau. Camera (b&w), Denis Gravouil; editor, Alix Joe; sound, Rodolphe de Jesus Trindade. Reviewed at French-American Film Workshop (competing), Avignon, France, July 2, 1993. (At Cambridge French-American Film Workshop.) Running time: **91 MIN.**
With: Fred Gimenez (Fredo), Dominick Rongere (Frag), Maryel Ferraud (The Girl), Filip Forgeau (The Addict), Denis Imbert (The Dealer), Bo Gaultier de Kermoal (The Bolivian).

If anyone out there is programming a Nihilism Fest, here's the perfect opener. "The Iguana," a dark ballad of alienation punctuated by comic musings, is a long haul for all but the most committed wastrels, but weaves a strange cumulative spell.

Pic gets inside the head of a man who has no particular place to go, following tattooed ex-con Frag (Dominick Rongere) as he meanders through the margins of nowheresville, crossing paths with a dealer, a drug addict, memories of a dead buddy and an exotic beauty (Maryel Ferraud) who morphs depending on the man she's with.

Stage-trained helmer Filip Forgeau, in his first film, may be a talent to watch. His affection for the sometimes wry and often pained observations of loners, losers, ex-cons and druggies is evident in every frame. Atmospheric b&w lensing lends a poetic patina to bleak and grungy settings.

Entire project was written, financed, shot and edited in two months, for some $55,000. Voice-overs are drenched in slang and will require careful subtitling.

"The Iguana" shared the $10,000 Kodak Prix Tournage at the French-American Film Workshop in Avignon last summer and is showing this week at Harvard in the Workshop's Cambridge edition.
—*Lisa Nesselson*

A.R.M. AROUND MOSCOW

(DOCU)

A Finley-Stoeltje production. Produced, directed, written, edited by Jeanne C. Finley, Gretchen Stoeltje. Camera (color, video-to-film), Finley; original music, Marilyn S. Zalkan; sound, Phil Benson; additional camera, Julian Backus, Richard Fox, Morgan Barnard. Reviewed on vidcassette, San Francisco, Jan. 21, 1994. Running time: **75 MIN.**

"**A.** R.M. Around Moscow" explores a bizarre sidelight of post-Iron Curtain "free trade" — the market for Eastern brides whose presumed "traditional feminine values" attract Western men uneasy with the liberated women back home. Unimaginative doc, currently making the rounds in specialized venues, should win over international fests and teleplay by virtue of lurid appeal of its engrossing subject.

A.R.M. stands for "American-Russian Matchmaking," an org that's sprung up to parade the former Soviet Union's eligible femmes past suitors with cash to pony up — $3,000 due on wedding date. U.S. flak Ron Rollbrand brings groups to Moscow four times

a year for cattle-call-like screenings, banquets and dating. Cutting a lowbrow Hefneresque figure, he sums up the lure by snapping, "This is not a debate" at his own (very young, blond, pretty) Russian mate as she tries to air an opinion.

Following one such trek from early beauty contest-like "heats" to various conclusions — one couple does get married — pic shows both sides of a dubious coin. The women are frank about drunken/slothful Russian men and economic hardships; they simply want a chance at a better life, with love as a hopeful bonus. American men, faces often electronically scrambled, range from nerdy, apparent nice guys to scarier sorts.

Vid feature is competently shot and edited with an ambivalent tone that lets viewers draw their own conclusions. But lack of notable style or p.o.v. precludes looking at past grads of the program, stated rumors that some brides became abused domestic slaves, parallels to similar wives-for-sale circuits in Asia and elsewhere.

Neutral take is formally admirable, but there's a fascinating message here about "feminist backlash" and its underlying male insecurities that filmmakers decline to spell out. When some bright docmeister decides to make that movie, "A.R.M. Around Moscow" will provide rich fodder for clips. —*Dennis Harvey*

PRISONER OF TIME

A Prize Prods. production. (International sales: Prize Prods., Berkeley, Calif.) Produced, directed, written by Mark A. Levinson. Camera (color), Boris Gortinski; editors, Levinson, Patrick Dodd; consulting editor, Jay Mason; music, David West; production design, Andrei Anisimov; art direction, Lawrence Hornbeck; costume design, Mary Stutz; sound, Scott Kinzey; assistant director, Joan Bierman; script/art consultant, Sonia Melnikova-Lavigne; story consultant, Patrick Dodd. Reviewed at Berlin Film Festival (market), Feb. 18, 1994. Running time: **95 MIN.**

Chrystina Marr	Elena Koreneva
Peter Wells	Peter Vilkin
Alexander Jadov	Oleg Vidov
Viktor	Stanislaw Staniek
Rosa	Galina Loginova
Elizabeth Fleming	Patricia Brown

S hackled by a novice script, uninteresting direction and actors doing their best in a second language, "Prisoner of Time" is a well-meaning but gauche low-budgeter that doesn't do justice to its theme of former Russian dissidents beached in the U.S. Commercial chances look bleak.

Directorial bow of S.F.-based sound editor Mark A. Levinson is a

timely idea on paper, but demands larger resources and considerably more behind-the-lens experience than helmer can muster at this stage. Despite the presence of experienced thesps Elena Koreneva ("Asya") and Oleg Vidov ("Red Heat"), both transplants themselves, "Prisoner" doesn't look to break out beyond the college circuit.

Brief prologue, set in Moscow, 1982, has Koreneva and Vidov emotionally parting in their apartment, Vidov torching his paintings before heading for the airport. Flash forward to 1992, and Koreneva, billed as "a former dissident writer," arrives stateside to accept a literary award for her long-banned masterpiece "An Invisible City." Meanwhile, Vidov, initially hailed as a hero when he arrived in the U.S. a decade ago, is on the skids, economically and artistically — an angry young Soviet artist dinosaured by political detente and the West's short attention span.

Koreneva tries to find common ground with her old lover but fails, finally accepting some TLC from her American PR man (Peter Vilkin). Melodramatic ending, with Vidov knocked down by a car, doesn't work.

Levinson's script covers all the thematic bases, but is full of clumsy, expository-heavy dialogue. Believability isn't helped by having Koreneva and Vidov (plus other Russians) speak in English to each other, after using their own lingo (subtitled) in the prologue.

Visual style tends toward the static and boxy, with only basic editing. —*Derek Elley*

800 TWO LAP RUNNERS

(JAPANESE)

An Argo Pictures presentation of a Suntory/Pony Canyon/New Century Producers production. (International sales: Herald Ace, Tokyo.) Produced by Isao Yoshihira. Directed by Ryuichi Hiroki. Screenplay, Masato Kato, from the novel by Makoto Kawashima. Camera (color), Naoki Kayano; editor, Kan Suzuki; music, Motohiro Tomita; art direction, Teru Yamazaki. Reviewed at Berlin Film Festival (Panorama section), Feb. 16, 1994. Running time: **109 MIN.**
With: Shunsuke Matsuoka, Yujin Normura, Tsugumi Arimura, Miwako Kawai, Sasamoto Masayuki, Yoshihiko Hakamada, Reiko Shiraishi.

A basically simple tale of on-and off-track rivalry between two college athletes, "800 Two Lap Runners" is given a complex spin by offbeat direction, a script that keeps you guessing and likable perfs by its young cast. Bemusing but strangely watchable result is fest material only.

Ryuji, son of a gangster, is more interested in girls than books, but agrees to help boost his college's rep in track. Kenji, a rich kid, can't seem to make it with girls but is obsessed with beating the record of his late friend, Aihara, a legendary runner with whom Kenji also had a homosexual liaison.

Kenji takes up (unsuccessfully) with Aihara's former g.f., the crippled Kyoko, while Ryuji has been smitten by Shoko, a champion femme athlete in the 100-meter hurdles who's actually more interested in Kenji.

The various sexual crosscurrents work themselves out at a summer camp, although it often takes a road map to work out who's who. But director Ryuichi Hiroki, in his feature bow, maintains interest with striking compositions, a boppy soundtrack of period faves (notably "Just One Look") and a strain of low-key comedy charmingly put over by an attractive cast.

Technically, pic is very fine.
—*Derek Elley*

FEAR CITY: A FAMILY-STYLE COMEDY

(LA CITE DE LA PEUR: UNE COMEDIE FAMILIALE)

(FRENCH)

An AMLF release (France) of a Telema/Le Studio Canal Plus/France 3 Cinema/M6 Films production. Produced by Charles Gassot. Co-executive producers, Gassot, Dominique Brunner. Directed by Alain Berberian. Screenplay, Dominique Farrugia, Chantal Lauby, Alain Chabat ("Les Nuls"). Camera (color, widescreen), Laurent Dailland; editor, Veronique Parnet; music, Philippe Chany; art direction, Jean-Marc Kerdelhue; set decoration, Gilles Budin, Marie-Laure Valla; costume design, Maika Guezel; sound (Dolby SR), Dominique Warnier, Claude Villant; special effects, Didier Roux; assistant director, Robert Kechichian; casting, Pierre Amzallag. Reviewed at Gaumont Marignan Cinema, Paris, March 2, 1994. Running time: **102 MIN.**
Benjamin/TV Journalist/
Simon Jeremi ... Dominique Farrugia
Youri/Serge Karamazov/
TV Journalist .... Alain Chabat
Odile Deray .... Chantal Lauby
Commissioner Bilaes ... Gerard Darmon
Extra Youri/Disquieting Loner/
Emile Gravier .... Sam Karmann
Also with: Marc de Jonge, Valerie Lemercier, Tcheky Karyo, Daniel Gelin, Jean-Pierre Bacri, Eddy Mitchell, Rosanna Arquette.

"**F**ear City," a pioneering but paper-thin Gallic offshoot of the ZAZ school of literal humor, applies deadpan delivery to a sendup of horror and detective pix set during the Cannes Film Festival.

Good local returns seem assured since actor/scripter trio "Les Nuls" (literally, the Nothings) is much-beloved by Gallic auds for its parodies of French TV. In-jokes about the fest scene could spark offshore sales, but, though a handful of gags are truly inspired — and production doesn't skimp on stunts and effects — most reruns of "Get Smart" have more sustained oomph.

At the Cannes fest, earnest publicist Odile (Chantal Lauby) is struggling to promote "Red Is Dead" — a schlocker about a hammer-and-sickle killer in a welder's mask — when a real hammer-and-sickle killer starts slashing projectionists at market screenings. (Hapless projectionists are played by uncredited French celebs.)

Odile milks the gory coincidence by flying in dumpy dork actor Simon Jeremi (Dominique Farrugia) and hiring inept hunk Serge Karamazov (Alain Chabat) as his bodyguard. Meanwhile, the media-savvy police commissioner (Gerard Darmon) romances Odile, while a disquieting loner (Sam Karmann) lurks on the periphery.

Story is modestly fleshed out with literal-minded gags, wacky stunts, plenty of toilet humor and spoofs of such films as "Pretty Woman" and "Basic Instinct," climaxing with well-integrated Steadicam footage of actors on the red-carpeted steps of the Palais last year.

Actors all display good comic timing, with a special nod to Darmon's suave inspector. Canal Plus topper Pierre Lescure and Unifrance topper Daniel Toscan du Plantier appear as themselves.

—*Lisa Nesselson*

A MOMENT OF ROMANCE II
(TIAN RUO YOU QING ER)
(HONG KONG)

A China Entertainment Films Production presentation of a Paka Hill Film production. Produced by Johnny To. Directed by Benny Chan. Screenplay, Susan Chan. Camera (color), Ardy Lam; editor, Ma Chung Yiu; music, William Hu; production design, Catherine Hun. Reviewed at Rotterdam Intl. Film Festival, Jan. 29, 1994. Running time: **95 MIN.**

Frank	Aaron Kwok
Celia	Wu Chien Lien
Jack	Kwok Tsuen On

Contrary to its vaguely misleading monicker, "A Moment of Romance II" is heavi-

er on casualties than courtship. A fast and furious teen flick combining biker action, Triad violence and a dash of amour, this diverting commercial froth may be too insubstantial to woo auds outside the world's Asian screen network.

Original entry (also directed by then-rookie Benny Chan) helped catapult Andy Lau to matinee-idol status. This one enlists another smoldering hunk in newcomer Aaron Kwok.

Kwok plays Frank, a troubled loner astride a requisite angry-young-man motorcycle. Yin to his yang is Celia (Wu Chien Lien), a virtuous mainlander attempting to raise funds for her political-prisoner brother's legal defense by turning tricks. Sticky encounters with both cops and mobsters send her careening into Frank's arms to the strains of a mawkish pop ditty.

Action becomes increasingly frenetic as the thugs close in on Celia. Frank enters a grueling motorcycle race hoping the cash prize will buy Celia a quick exit, and an initially nasty racetrack henchman lends a hand. The cop on Celia's tail also turns sympathetic, but not in time to block some serious bloodletting.

Chan orchestrates the proceedings at an appropriately breathless pace that skims over the odd improbable plot turn. On- and off-camera talent is generally on target.

—*David Rooney*

WE, THE CHILDREN OF THE 20TH CENTURY
(NOUS, LES ENFANTS DU XXEME SICLE)
(FRENCH-RUSSIAN — DOCU)

A Lapsus (Paris) production, with La Sept/Arte (France) and D.A.R. St. Petersberg (Russia), in collaboration with RAI 3 (Italy) and Danmarks Radio (Denmark). (International sales: Lapsus, Paris) Produced by Esther Hoffenberg. Directed by Vitali Kanevski. Written by Kanevski, Varvara Krassilnilova. Camera (color), Valentin Sidorine; editing, Olivier Ducastel. Reviewed at Berlin Film Festival (Forum section), Feb. 16, 1994. Running time: **84 MIN.**

Siberian-born director Vitali Kanevski did not begin making features until he was 55, but belatedly burst onto the fest circuit with Cannes winners "Freeze, Die, Come to Life!" (Camera d'Or, 1990) and "An Independent Life"(Jury prize, 1992). Both pix explored lost youth in a hostile environment and starred the unknown boy Pavel Nazarov.

In this French-financed docu, Kanevski interrogates street kids of

St. Petersburg and Moscow, the kind of youngsters he met in 1989 while casting "Freeze, Die." One of the impoverished subjects turns out to be none other than Pavel Nazarov. Interesting but overlong study should find plenty of fest and specialized TV slots, though theatrical opportunities appear slim.

Shooting the kids straight-on, helmer coaxes them to speak about their crimes, which range from petty theft to murder, and they respond with brutal honesty. "We hate working," says one urchin. "We'd rather steal." Some scenes are tough going: A 14-year-old girl recalls how her mother sold her to men "for a glass of vodka," and a teenage boy describes how he ate the heart and liver of his victim.

Settings range from the street to reform schools and prisons. Kanevski imposes a structure by filming progressively older delinquents, but his too-literal attempts at metaphor — assembly-line bread loaves paralleling the kids' lives — trivialize the serious subject matter.

Beginning in 1966, just before he was to graduate from the Moscow Film School, Kanevski spent eight years in prison for alleged rape, and the strength of his concern for the marginalized is evident onscreen. Somewhat harder to swallow are his unrelenting questions about punishment and redemption, as well as his final query: "Could you, in the name of an ideal, kill your own father?"

Tech credits are fine, and natural sounds add to pic's authentic feel.

—*Howard Feinstein*

FRESH KILL

The Airwaves Project production in association with ITVS, Channel 4, Woo Art Intl. (International sales: Jane Balfour Films, London.) Produced, directed by Shu Lea Cheang. Co-producer, Jennifer Fong. Screenplay, Jessica Hagedorn. Camera (color), Jane Castle; editor, Lauren Zuckerman; music, Vernon Reid; production design, Nancy Deren; art direction, Mike Nino; costume design, Candace Donnelly; sound (Dolby), Mark Deren; assistant director, Jody O'Neil; associate producer, Shari Frilot. Reviewed at Berlin Film Festival (Panorama section), Feb. 17, 1994. Running time: **79 MIN.**
Shareen

Lightfoot	Sarita Choudhury
Claire Mayakovsky	Erin McMurtry
Mimi Mayakovsky	Laurie Carlos
Jiannbin Lui	Abe Lim
Miguel Flores	Jose Zuniga
Stuart Sterling	Will Kempe
Honey	Nelini Stamp
Clayton Lightfoot	Rino Thunder

Not many auds will survive "Fresh Kill." First feature of Gotham-based vid artist Shu Lea Cheang is a jokey dump-bin of eco-paranoia, techno-fright and lesbian parenting that's as ap-

pealing as the Staten Island rubbish dump of the title. This one's for card carriers only.

Sarita Choudhury ("Mississippi Masala") and Erin McMurtry are a couple living in a consumer-hell New York where the airwaves are dominated by the fake-friendly GX Corp. (motto: "We Care"). Choudhury runs a garbage-clearing service; McMurtry works in a terminally hip Manhattan sushi bar called Naga Saki.

In between trying to earn a living to provide their daughter (Nelini Stamp) with an education, the two femmes start to realize GX Corp. is peddling toxic cat food in its commercials. Ending is a post-nuclear new dawn.

Cheang's relentless barrage of vid imagery, painfully unfunny dialogue (especially in the sushi bar scenes) and freewheeling collage of ideas rapidly pall after the first 10 minutes. Lesbian content, mostly limited to lyrical lovemaking scenes, is never developed. The Taiwan-born helmer also throws in some digs at her native country's Orchid Island, a nuclear dump, for good measure.

Tech credits on the pic, which got major funding from the Corp. for Public Broadcasting, are OK. Perfs are harmless.

—*Derek Elley*

THE HEROES
(I MITICI)
(ITALIAN)

A Warner Bros. Italia release of a Video 80/Dean Film production. (International sales: Intrafilm.) Produced by Carlo Vanzina, Enrico Vanzina. Directed by Carlo Vanzina. Screenplay, Leo Benvenuti, Piero De Bernardi, Enrico Vanzina, Carlo Vanzina. Camera (color), Luigi Kuveiller; editor, Sergio Montanari; music, Umberto Smaila; art direction, Tonino Zera; costume design, Roberta Guidi Di Bagno; sound (Dolby), Tommaso Quattrini. Reviewed at Adriano Cinema, Rome, March 8, 1994. Running time: **102 MIN.**

Fabio	Claudio Amendola
Deborah	Monica Bellucci
Enzo	Ricky Memphis
Tonino	Tony Sperandeo
Igor	Ugo Conti
Signora Motta	Mirella Falco
Colombo	Umberto Smaila

The Vanzina brothers' second national release within three months, "The Heroes," revisits Mario Monicelli's 1958 burglary caper "Big Deal on Madonna Street," updating the heist attempt by a bungling band of misfits to '90s Milan, the kingdom of kickback scandals. A congenial cast brings some pep to the well-trodden material, but assembly-line direction and uneven pacing keep matters pretty mundane.

Having tried and failed at being gainfully employed, TV technicians Fabio (Claudio Amendola) and Enzo (Ricky Memphis) plan to crack the safe of a ritzy Milan jewelry store. They rope in a gorgeous but unrefined small-town siren (Monica Bellucci) to case the joint; a sewage worker (Tony Sperandeo) to find an underground entry; and an overweight trapeze artist (Ugo Conti) to bypass the alarm-equipped floor. Also in on the deal is their wily hotelier (Mirella Falco).

Comedy stemming from the interplay between ill-assorted group components from Milan, Rome, Sicily and the Marches will be less immediate outside Italy. But the engaging thesps and broad-based characters communicate readily. Film's only major lapse into heavy-handedness is a witless caricature of gay lasciviousness by Umberto Smaila as a jewelry store boss.

Tech credits are undistinguished, notably the flat, lifeless lensing. Music (by Smaila) maintains a suitably jaunty rhythm, something the script and editing could use.

—*David Rooney*

RAPA NUI

A Warner Bros. release (Hayden Film Distribution release in Australia) of a Tig Prods./Majestic Films production. Produced by Kevin Costner, Jim Wilson. Executive producers, Barrie Osborne, Guy East. Directed by Kevin Reynolds. Screenplay, Reynolds, Tim Rose Price, from a story by Reynolds. Camera (Technicolor; Panavision widescreen), Stephen Windom; editor, Peter Boyle; music, Stewart Copeland; production design, George Liddle; art direction, Ian Allan; costumes, John Bloomfield; stunts, Glenn Boswell; special effects, Steven Richard Courtley; assistant director, K.C. Hodenfield; casting, Elisabeth Leustig. Reviewed at Orpheum theater, Cremorne, Sydney, March 4, 1994. Running time: **107 MIN.**

Noro	Jason Scott Lee
Make	Esai Morales
Ramana	Sandrine Holt
Ariki-mau	Eru Potaka-Dewes
Tupa	George Henare
Haoa	Zac Wallace

"**R**apa Nui" looks very much like an act of cinematic folly, a wacky anthropological adventure staged on a grand scale and filmed in obviously difficult and inhospitable circumstances. It's more of a guilty pleasure than a satisfying movie experience, and though it may open to reasonable figures if given an attractive campaign by Warners, it looks to have stunted legs. It's getting theatrical release in Australia and parts of Europe ahead of U.S. exposure, which is planned for September.

"Robin Hood" director Kevin Reynolds initiated this project after seeing an ethnographic docu about Easter Island, the world's most remote inhabited island, and then visiting the place himself. Screenplay, which he concocted with Britisher Tim Rose Price, speculates on the creation of the moai, the mysterious giant statues scattered over the barren terrain, and on what happened to the original islanders prior to the arrival of the Dutch on Easter Sunday, 1722.

Result is a fiction that brings to mind that other piece of impressive cinematic foolishness, Howard Hawks' "Land of the Pharaohs" (1955), about the creation of the pyramids. Pic unfolds some 40 years before the Europeans landed, when the island's inhabitants were divided between the ruling Long Ear nobility and the enslaved Short Ears. The people believe that the first settler was Hotu Matua, and the moai are built by the Short Ears to encourage his return.

Every year, a contest is held among the Long Ear clans to decide who will rule for the next year. The competition consists of a kind of Ironman race, in which clan reps have to climb down a sheer cliff, swim through shark-infested waters to a neighboring island where sea birds nest, obtain eggs from the nests, swim back and rescale the cliff, with the clan that sponsored the first man to arrive with his egg intact deemed to be the next ruler.

For 20 years, the race has been won by the same clan, led by Ariki-mau (Eru Potaka-Dewes). The old man is now sick but determined to win again via his grandson, Noro (Jason Scott Lee).

Tupa loves a Short Ear girl, Ramana (Sandrine Holt from "Black Robe"), who is in turn loved by another Short Ear, Tupa's boyhood friend Make (Esai Morales). Marrying a Short Ear is taboo for a Long Ear, but Grandfather gives Tupa his blessing provided he wins the race.

When the Short Ears rebel at having to construct a larger moai in record time, Make is given permission to enter the race also; if he wins, he can have Ramana himself.

The race is excitingly staged and filmed, as the contestants battle with each other and the elements, including the inevitable shark attack. The somewhat anticlimactic final reel depicts a civil war between the Long and Short Ears, which anthropologists suggest was the reason for the disappearance of Rapa Nui's original population.

Reynolds decided to shoot on Easter Island, with additional shooting and post-production in Australia. The result certainly looks spectacular, although it's doubtful if the journey was really necessary, as the rugged cliffs and bleak terrain could undoubtedly have been duplicated elsewhere, and most of the moai are clearly models made specifically for the picture. Stephen Windom's Panavision cinematography is impressive, and production and costume design are also imaginative. Stewart Copeland did the fine score.

Dramatically, pic is more problematic, and just as Hawks had problems deciding how ancient Egyptians might talk, so the dialogue for the most part is unconvincing. The members of the diverse cast act in as many styles as they have accents, resulting in sometimes laughable moments.

Still, it could be that there is an audience willing to go along with the exotic melodramatics of this silly but perversely enjoyable epic.

—*David Stratton*

TOM & VIV

(BRITISH-U.S.)

An Entertainment Film Distributors (U.K.)/Miramax (U.S.) release of a Samuelson Prods./Harvey Kass/IRS Media production, with participation of British Screen. (International sales: Samuelson, London.) Produced by Marc Samuelson, Harvey Kass, Peter Samuelson. Executive producers, Miles A. Copeland III, Paul Colichman. Line producer, John Kay. Directed by Brian Gilbert. Screenplay, Michael Hastings, Adrian Hodges, from the play by Hastings. Camera (Technicolor, widescreen), Martin Fuhrer; editor, Tony Lawson; music, Debbie Wiseman; production design, Jamie Leonard; art direction, Mark Raggett; costume design, Phoebe De Gaye; sound (Dolby), Peter Glossop; assistant director, Sean Guest; makeup, Morag Ross; casting (U.K.), Michelle Guish. Reviewed at Plaza 1 Cinema, London, Jan. 25, 1994. Running time: **125 MIN.**

Tom Eliot	Willem Dafoe
Vivienne Haigh-Wood	Miranda Richardson
Viv's mother	Rosemary Harris
Viv's brother, Maurice	Tim Dutton
Berty	Nickolas Grace
Viv's father	Philip Locke

Passion of only the driest and most cerebral kind peeks through the lace curtains of "Tom & Viv," a handsomely appointed but overly starchy love story that attains real clout only in the final reel. Intense but tight-jawed playing by Willem Dafoe as Yank poet T.S. Eliot and an eccentric perf by Miranda Richardson that doesn't jell until its latter stages mark this as a well-meaning but noble failure. Opened April 15 in the U.K., pic is slated for U.S. release via Miramax in the fall.

Commercially, this looks to be a tricky proposition. Besides the "Tom & Viv ... who?" problem, and a script that makes only fleeting reference to Eliot's most famous work, "The Waste Land," about halfway in, this is a small-scale drama at heart, despite the well-laundered period look and occasional larger set pieces. The two-hours-plus study of a doomed love affair between a highly refined poet and an all-out nut case will need terrific reviews to break out beyond arty venues.

Michael Hastings' original play started life at London's Royal Court Theater in February 1984, with Julie Covington and Tom Wilkinson in the leads. Covington also toplined the March 1985 revival. In December 1992, the play was broadcast by BBC Radio 3, with Richardson bowing as Viv and John Duttine as Tom.

Co-scripters Hastings and Adrian Hodges have done a fine job opening up the action without diluting the intensity of individual scenes. Tale opens in 1914, with spoiled socialite

Vivienne Haigh-Wood (Richardson) visiting Merton College, Oxford, with her soppy brother, Maurice (Tim Dutton), to see American student Tom Eliot (Dafoe). We immediately know she's one sandwich short of a picnic when she blithely dances on the college lawns.

Following a whirlwind affair, the couple marry and honeymoon in the southern coastal resort of Eastbourne. But Viv's wild mood swings, not helped by her strange collection of medicines, lead to her wrecking their room during her breakdown.

In London, the impecunious couple share a flat with Tom's friend Bertrand Russell (Nickolas Grace). Tom is barely accepted by Viv's snooty parents, while her own behavioral changes are diagnosed incorrectly and treated with yet more medication. Her sudden outbursts against her husband continue, however, even in public or when with friends.

After taking a job at a bank, Tom begins establishing himself as a poet, and later secures a position at publisher Faber & Faber. Viv, however, is going from bad to worse, one day pouring melted chocolate through the firm's mailbox. Warned by a medic that his wife won't get any better, Tom finally has her committed to an asylum.

Ten years later, unvisited by Tom, she still speaks lovingly of him. Her condition is finally diagnosed by an American researcher as a hormonal imbalance triggered by her menstrual cycle.

Possibly taking its cue from Eliot's own works, there's an almost academic quality to the film that robs it early on of any believable passion. From the first of Viv's attacks, pic essentially becomes a catalogue of her breakdowns and public embarrassments, with Tom an increasingly clench-jawed bystander.

With little feel for Eliot's growing rep as a poet — we hear about his career, but rarely witness its benefits — it's hard to get a handle on Viv's obsessive belief in his talent. Even the first reading *en famille* of "The Waste Land" is deployed more as a podium for Viv's instability than a demonstration of Eliot's gifts as an artist.

Such a controlled approach might have worked if the two leads had any onscreen chemistry; but at times, it's as if Dafoe and Richardson were acting in different movies. Brit director Brian Gilbert holds his thesps on a tight rein.

Adopting a semi-strangled accent clearly modeled on Eliot's own recordings (but not necessarily reflecting the poet's everyday voice), Dafoe gives one of his most desiccated, emotionally withdrawn performances. There's a power and a concentration here that works splendidly in close-ups and solo turns, but there's little emotional arcing when anyone else is around.

Richardson's performance is even more eccentric, with a seemingly deliberate decision to play Viv's mood swings in a semi-comedic vein. For the actress who made such subtle nuances of expression work in "Damage" and "Century," the impulse to play Viv as a '20s airhead seems inexplicable.

Still, if her histrionic breakdowns don't work on a dramatic level, Richardson comes through later in spades, beginning with a wonderfully subtle scene of her deliberately giving the wrong answer to the docs' questions when she sees in Dafoe's eyes that the marriage is over. In her final scenes, in superb, measured dialogue describing Viv's love for Eliot, Richardson gives a glimpse of the emotion "Tom & Viv" attempts to describe but which remains out of reach.

Other performances are reliable, and tech credits throughout are good, with detailed (but unlived-in) costuming by Phoebe De Gaye, ditto production design by Jamie Leonard, fine widescreen exterior lensing by Martin Fuhrer and pungent use of Richard Strauss' "Four Last Songs" and Pergolesi's "Stabat Mater" on the soundtrack.

—*Derek Elley*

WITH HONORS

A Warner Bros. release of a Spring Creek production. Produced by Paula Weinstein, Amy Robinson. Executive producers, Jon Peters, Peter Guber. Co-producers, Abe Milrad, G. Mac Brown. Directed by Alek Keshishian. Screenplay, William Mastrosimone. Camera (Technicolor), Sven Nykvist; editor, Michael R. Miller; music, Patrick Leonard; production design, Barbara Ling; art direction, Bill Arnold; set design, Suzan Wexler; set decoration, Cricket Rowland; costume design, Renee Ehrlich Kalfus; sound (Dolby), Curt Frisk; associate producers, Stacey Lassally, Julie Pitkanen; assistant director, Steve Dunn; casting, Marion Dougherty, Nessa Hyams. Reviewed at Warner Bros. screening room, Burbank, April 6, 1994. MPAA Rating: PG-13. Running time: **100 MIN.**

Simon .... Joe Pesci
Monty .... Brendan Fraser
Courtney .... Moira Kelly
Everett .... Patrick Dempsey
Jeff .... Josh Hamilton
Pitkannan .... Gore Vidal

Wearing its heart and politics on its sleeve, this earnest but sappy drama would be far more compelling if its applause lines weren't so well-lit. Mixing elements from "Down and Out in Beverly Hills" and "The Paper Chase," "With Honors" should win points from the politically correct crowd but earn limited box office laurels.

The movie takes a little while simply to recover from its contrived setup, which has a driven Harvard student, Monty (Brendan Fraser), drop the only copy of his 100-page thesis into the hands of a homeless man, Simon (Joe Pesci), who hangs out under the college library.

Insulted by the way in which the lad dismisses him, and sensing a meal ticket to carry him through the winter, Simon offers a compromise: One page of the thesis returned for each good turn from Monty, who, in desperation, brings Simon home with him — a development treated with responses ranging from encouragement to outrage by his three roommates.

That scenario provides ample time for a bond to form between the two, as well as for Monty to re-examine his cynical and conservative political leanings, which mirror those of his renowned professor (Gore Vidal, in an inspired bit of casting).

Unfortunately, that's about all the inspiration "With Honors" can muster. Pic falls back on situations corny enough to make Nancy Kerrigan blush.

Playwright-turned-screenwriter William Mastrosimone peppers his script with extremely smart dialogue, but the characters and narrative are so narrowly drawn and predictable the movie feels like it's condescending to — indeed, even lecturing — its audience.

Simon, in particular, offers the most idealized Hollywood take on homelessness one could imagine: a sidewalk philosopher who acts daft one moment and then in the next outlectures a pompous Harvard prof. Apparently fearing that the audience won't exhibit the same intelligence, the classroom bursts into applause.

Pesci turns in an uneven, overly mannered performance in the difficult central role, at times speaking in an awkward snapping chirp of a voice, then turning into a fatherly sage to his self-obsessed charges when the situation calls for it.

Symbolic overkill is evident in the surrogate fatherhood issue inherent to the Monty-Simon pairing — the former having been abandoned by his dad, the latter having left a wife and young son three decades earlier.

Director Alek Keshishian, a 1986 Harvard grad who helmed the Madonna docu "Truth or Dare," dives into this maudlin material with obvious zeal and some occasional flair. In the same vein, the integrity of Fraser and the radiant Moira Kelly as Monty's platonic housemate almost sustain the picture through to the end.

Since this is for the most part a two-character piece, Kelly manages to charm despite the screenplay's limitations, but the movie's other characters aren't so lucky. Both Patrick Dempsey and Josh Hamilton ("Alive") have little to do other than serve as Harvard archetypes (snotty rebel, driven med-student-in-waiting) to flesh out this slightly older, apartment-bound "Breakfast Club."

Tech credits, at least, are as crisp as autumn in New England, from Sven Nykvist's photography (part of the shooting was done in Chicago) to the meticulous design of the quartet's college digs.

Continuing her affiliation with Keshishian, Madonna also provides a closing-credit ballad, "I'll Remember," which, if nothing else, promises to make the soundtrack more memorable than the movie itself.

—*Brian Lowry*

WHITE FANG 2: MYTH OF THE WHITE WOLF

A Buena Vista release of a Walt Disney Pictures presentation. Produced by Preston Fischer. Co-producers, Justis Greene, David Fallon. Directed by Ken Olin. Screenplay, Fallon. Camera (Technicolor), Hiro Narita; editor, Elba Sanchez-Short; music, John Debney; production design, Cary White; art direction, Glen W. Pearson; costumes, Trish Keating; sound (Dolby), Rob Young; associate producer, Danielle Weinstock; assistant director, Howard Ellis; head trainers, Joe Camp, Tammy Maples; casting, Gail Levin. Reviewed at AMC Meyer Park 14 Theatre, Houston, April 12, 1994. MPAA rating: PG. Running time: **106 MIN.**

Henry Casey .... Scott Bairstow
Lily Joseph .... Charmaine Craig
Moses Joseph .... Al Harrington
Peter .... Anthony Michael Ruivivar
Katrin .... Victoria Racimo
Rev. Leland Drury .... Alfred Molina
Adam John Hale .... Paul Coeur
Heath .... Geoffrey Lewis
Halverson .... Matthew Cowles
Bad Dog .... Woodrow W. Morrison
Leon .... Reynold Russ
Jack Conroy .... Ethan Hawke

Even though Jack London wouldn't recognize any of it, "White Fang 2: Myth of the White Wolf" should attract a respectable percentage of the family audience that made Disney's "White Fang" (1992) a noteworthy B.O. performer. But this generally satisfying sequel appears an even safer bet as a homevid and pay TV crowd pleaser.

Ethan Hawke, who starred as young prospector Jack Conroy in the previous pic, shows up here only for a brief, unbilled cameo at the start to plausibly introduce Henry Casey (Scott Bairstow) as the new human companion of the titular half-dog, half-wolf. While Conroy is busy in San Francisco after the 1906 earthquake, Casey is working Conroy's gold mine — and romping with White Fang — back in the Alaskan wilderness.

When Casey and White Fang capsize and nearly drown while paddling up-river for supplies, Casey is saved by a Haida Indian princess, Lily Joseph (Charmaine

Craig), who thinks he is the human incarnation of the wolf spirit her uncle glimpsed in a dream. White Fang saves himself and spends some time with a wolf pack before catching up with Casey.

Even after he's dubbed White Wolf, Casey insists he is just a regular guy who happens to keep a wolf as a pet. But tribal leader Moses Joseph (Al Harrington) calmly contends that Casey is indeed the one who will help his hunger-ravaged community by finding out why the caribou that used to provide the community's chief source of meat no longer graze nearby.

Eventually, White Fang returns, alive and well and ready to help Casey find the caribou, uncover secret villainy, win Lily's heart and fight the good fight. All of which leads to corny but entertaining outdoor adventure in the manner of yesteryear's Saturday matinees.

David Fallon's serviceable screenplay keeps the narrative simple and politically correct. The Haida are depicted as noble, compassionate and intelligent, while just about every white man — especially Alfred Molina as a transparently fake preacher who's trying to move the Haida off their land so he can mine for gold — is a rotten, duplicitous exploiter. And to keep things rigorously non-sexist, it's repeatedly emphasized that Lily isn't just a helpless heroine in buckskin, but a bow-and-arrow whiz who trains Casey to hunt.

New agers may be pleased to note that every vision and premonition of the Haida is proven true, even when a young Haida brave predicts that, after his death, his spirit will live on inside a crow. The more traditionally religious may be distressed to see Christianity represented only by the mean Molina. Uncle Walt likely would not have approved.

On the other hand, compared with the credibly faked viciousness of the dog fights in the first "White Fang," there is a marked decrease in violence here. Of the three humans killed, two of them die off-camera. As noted, the third casualty returns as a crow.

There wasn't much time for lovey-dovey stuff in the first "White Fang," but the sequel develops a chaste romance between Casey and Lily, and even allows White Fang to find a mate. Actor-turned-director Ken Olin ("thirty-something") handles these elements with the same sure hand he applies to the action scenes in his feature helming debut.

Newcomers Bairstow and Craig do well in roles that, for the most part, are more physically demanding than emotionally challenging. Molina, as the cliched villain of the piece, comes across with all the subtlety of a silent-movie mustache twirler. Harrington fares much better as Moses Joseph, conveying a winning sincerity even when he's forced to deliver lines — "Let the wolf inside you free!" — that are difficult to take with a straight face.

Five dogs (trained by Joe Camp and Tammy Maples) share the role of White Fang, and each is thoroughly convincing.

On a technical level, "White Fang 2" is extremely impressive. Hiro Narita's sharp lensing of spectacular locations in Colorado and British Columbia is the best single reason to view pic before it's reduced to TV-screen dimensions.

The surprisingly tepid B.O. performance of "Iron Will" — another recent Disney outdoor adventure, and a much better movie overall — might portend some rough sledding for "White Fang 2." If the sequel does even modestly well, however, don't be too surprised to see a TV series spinoff, if not a "White Fang 3."

—Joe Leydon

WIDOWS' PEAK

(BRITISH)

A Fine Line (U.S.)/Rank (U.K.) release of a Rank Film Distributors/Fine Line Features presentation, with participation of British Screen, of a Jo Manuel production. Produced by Manuel. Executive producer, Michael White. Co-producer, Tracey Seaward. Directed by John Irvin. Screenplay, Hugh Leonard, from his original story. Camera (color), Ashley Rowe; editor, Peter Tanner; music, Carl Davis; production design, Leo Austin; costume design, Consolata Boyle; sound (Dolby), Peter Lindsay; assistant director, Martin O'Malley; casting, Nuala Moiselle. Reviewed at MGM Shaftesbury Avenue Theater, Jan. 20, 1994. Running time: **102 MIN.**
Miss O'Hare .... Mia Farrow
Mrs. Doyle Counihan ....Joan Plowright
Edwina
  Broome .... Natasha Richardson
Godfrey .... Adrian Dunbar
Clancy .... Jim Broadbent
With: Anne Kent, John Kavanagh, Rynagh O'Grady, Gerard McSorley, Michael James Ford, Garrett Keogh.

There's more old-fashioned blarney on show in "Widows' Peak" than at a shamrock-growers convention. Comedy-drama about dark deeds in a picturesque Irish village should generate pleasant biz among undemanding folk, despite uneven plotting and featherweight content. One-two-three teaming of **Mia Farrow, Joan Plowright and Natasha Richardson manages to keep the dramatically rickety craft afloat through star power**

alone. Now playing in the U.K., film begins its stateside playoff April 29.

Though pic looks like a shameless endeavor to cash in on the "Enchanted April" crock of gold, Irish scribe Hugh Leonard's story was written years ago for Maureen O'Hara and her daughter Mia Farrow. By a curious twist of cinematic fate, Farrow now ends up playing her mom's role, Richardson Farrow's role, and the whole shebang was shot in County Wicklow, home ground for O'Hara and familiar turf for Farrow.

Yarn is set during the mid-'20s in the spa resort of Kilshannon. Town is a stuffy, parochial, middle-class enclave, socially ruled by a Mrs. Doyle Counihan (Plowright), high priestess of a section of the village dubbed Widows' Peak, whose members also include penurious spinster Miss O'Hare (Farrow), a Brit-hater with a murky past.

Enter American of Brit descent Edwina Broome (Richardson), a superglam World War I widow who soon has D.C.'s son, Godfrey (Adrian Dunbar), dancing on a string but is seemingly loathed by the dowdy O'Hare. Hostility between the feuding femmes leads to Edwina's ramming of O'Hare's boat at the Kilshannon regatta, and the latter's moves to stir up local opinion that Edwina wants her dead.

There's a sudden clanking of dramatic gears 70 minutes in, when all this whimsy takes on a darker edge. Each woman learns the dark truth about the other's background, leading to a dramatic set piece when O'Hare crashes Edwina's engagement lunch. When O'Hare disappears, Edwina is thrown in the clink for her murder — until a final double-twist that's not entirely unexpected.

Forty years ago, "Widows' Peak" would have been shot on an MGM backlot with studio interiors. Here, belief is suspended by the sound of Plowright and Farrow grappling with Irish accents, and Richardson with an American accent. Pic needs a sharper script and pacier direction to counter the earthbound realism of locations on display here.

Unlike, say, "Hear My Song," the pic never takes wing and flies. That's also due to the fact that most of the plotting is crammed into the final 30 minutes after an hour or so of strolling 'round the block. Dramatic imbalance keeps "Peak's" wheels firmly on the ground.

Main pleasure is watching the central trio of thesps have a fine old time. Richardson is nicely insouciant as the glamorous outsider; Plowright does her usual shtick with tart one-liners; and Farrow, though looking a tad young for her role, has a kind of wild believability as a paranoid victim. Dunbar is OK but overshadowed in such company.

Tech credits, from Carl Davis' score to costuming and lensing, all contribute to a pleasant package, though print caught had a slightly washed-out look, with weak greens and too much red. *—Derek Elley*

COPS AND ROBBERSONS

A TriStar release of a Channel production. Produced by Ned Tanen, Nancy Graham Tanen, Ronald Schwary. Directed by Michael Ritchie. Screenplay, Bernie Somers. Camera (Technicolor), Gerry Fisher; editors, Stephen Rotter, William Scharf; music, William Ross; production design, Stephen Lineweaver; art direction, Philip Toolin; costumes, Wayne Finkelman; sound (Dolby), Kim Ornitz; assistant director, Albert Shapiro; casting, Rick Pagano, Sharon Bialy, Debi Manwiller. Reviewed at Sony Studios, Culver City, April 10, 1994. MPAA Rating: PG. Running time: **93 MIN.**
Norman Robberson .... Chevy Chase
Jake Stone .... Jack Palance
Helen Robberson .... Dianne Wiest
Osborn .... Robert Davi
Tony Moore .... David Barry Gray
Kevin
  Robberson .... Jason James Richter
Cindy Robberson .... Fay Masterson
Billy Robberson .... Miko Hughes
Fred Lutz .... Richard Romanus

There's trouble afoot in Pleasant Valley, and the postcard-perfect suburb is about to burst at the seams in "Cops and Robbersons." But the mixture of mischief and mayhem served up in the antic affair is never quite in balance. It's a tale long on intriguing ideas and always a millimeter short in its realization. Trapped in a sitcom sensibility, the film never makes the vital connection with the audience that's necessary to spawn a hit. It should open respectably considering cast and premise, but displays no signs of longevity. Despite trappings of sophistication, "C&R" is best suited to a juvenile crowd who will thrive on the obvious nature of the proceedings.

The complex setup centers on Osborn (Robert Davi), a goon involved in forgery and money laundering. The police know he's about to make a big exchange and have tracked him down to the quiet, residential neighborhood. Assigned to the case are grizzled vet Jake Stone (Jack Palance) and his "90210"-style partner, Tony Moore (David Barry Gray).

They set up their command post in the home of Norman Robberson (Chevy Chase), who lives next door to Osborn. Robberson, a police-show junkie, is ready to do his civic duty and get a first-hand lesson in police procedures. His family — wife Helen (Dianne Wiest) and three children — do not initially share nearly as much zeal for the two new upstairs boarders.

The film's first, and most telling misstep, is its focus. While Robberson is the titular lead, it's really

Stone who takes center stage. Too old for his station, he is a snarling bear who stays on the job rather than face being alone in retirement. Somehow the Robbersons realize that under that curmudgeonly exterior beats the heart of a pussycat and they mean to force that aspect out of him by hook or by crook.

Norman is considerably less interesting. His idea of fun is sitting down to breakfast with the entire family and just talking. He'd be in ecstasy over an afternoon of tossing the old pigskin with his teenage son.

The prospect of suddenly being able to realize his fantasy of being a cop ought to unleash a wild man. But true to his nature, he is either too slow-witted or uncoordinated to effect much of a change. So the fun rests with Jake and Tony, who find themselves "going native" in the proximity of the suburban fold.

Stone offers Palance the opportunity to plumb deep inside his hard-boiled persona and extract a rich vein of humor and pathos. The fact that he eludes the obvious is a testament to four decades of on-the-job training. Those who are able to surprise us do best with their roles, including Wiest as a homemaker with pluck; Davi, who like Palance plays against type; and Gray, who commands quiet authority in a thankless role.

Chase, in another physical role, should get back to more romantic fare a la "Foul Play." He's simply better playing smart rather than dumb.

Tech credits are polished if unremarkable. As with the material, everything's been watered down and homogenized for general consumption. The sad part is that one can taste the bite and satire that must have made the "Cops and Robbersons" script a riveting read. But on the screen it's just another easy-to-prepare, predictable microwavable serving. —*Leonard Klady*

BABYFEVER

A Rainbow Film Co. release of a Jagtoria production. Produced by Judith Wolinsky. Directed, edited by Henry Jaglom. Screenplay, Jaglom, Victoria Foyt. Camera (Deluxe color), Hanania Baer; sound, Sunny Meyer; associate producer, Bonnie Beauregard. Reviewed at Sunset Towers screening room, Beverly Hills, March 24, 1994. MPAA Rating: R. Running time: **110 MIN.**
Gena .... Victoria Foyt
James .... Matt Salinger
Roz .... Dinah Lenney
Anthony .... Eric Roberts
Rosie .... Frances Fisher
Milly .... Elaine Kagan
Mark .... Zack Norman

Henry Jaglom's "Babyfever" is to women and their biological clocks what his 1991 "Eating" was to women and their relation-

ship with food. Aiming to provide an intimate look at women's feelings and thoughts about motherhood, the indie filmmaker fashions a stylistic blend of fictional story, based on his own experience, and documentary, using interviews with many women, that emerges as overly long, fractured and only intermittently entertaining. Prime target audience for this outdated pic is suggested by its subtitle, "For those who hear their clock ticking."

After a series of uneven personal films ("Always," "New Year's Day," "Venice/Venice"), Jaglom seems to be in a feminist phase of his career.

Victoria Foyt (Jaglom's wife) stars as Gena, an attractive middle-aged career woman who can't make up her mind whether she wants to have a baby with James (Matt Salinger), her sensitive b.f. who likes to talk about building a nest and meshing their yuppie careers.

Just when Gena is about to make a commitment, old flame Anthony (Eric Roberts) reappears with a proposition that confuses her even more. Some suspense arises when Foyt suspects she might be pregnant and anxiously awaits test results from her doctor.

Following exactly the same format as "Eating," "Babyfever" consists of interviews with diverse women, all in their 30s and 40s, who talk to the camera about babies, men, sex, motherhood and careers. "Eating's" central event was a birthday party; here it's a baby shower, which provides an occasion for all kinds of biological and psychological sermons.

While "Babyfever" is a more focused film, its anecdotal narrative is not as rich as that of "Eating," where food served as both a metaphor and a substitute for love and sex.

It's too bad that lovely actresses like Frances Fisher ("Unforgiven") are made to ask — straight-faced — about pregnancy and artificial insemination. Pandering to women, the three male characters, who often just interrupt the tale, are conceived as stereotypes. And it doesn't help that they are played by Roberts, Salinger and Zack Norman, who manage to accentuate the narrow definition of their roles.

The most disappointing element of "Babyfever" is how conventional and humorless the material is. The film rehashes ideas that appeared in New York and other magazines in the late 1980s.

Also dissatisfying is the stereotypical casting — for example, an aging, unattractive woman talks about how she has become reconciled to being single for the rest of her life. At the same time, the film will please any affirmative-action committee, as it carefully uses women of every ethnic minority and sexual orientation.

Dedicated to Jaglom's young daughter, "Babyfever" obviously bears strong personal meaning for Jaglom and Foyt, but as a social-issue film it's not very engaging. —*Emanuel Levy*

LEPRECHAUN 2

A Trimark Pictures release. Produced by Donald Borchers. Executive producer, Mark Amin. Co-producers, Mark Jones, Michael Prescott. Directed by Rodman Flender. Screenplay, Turi Meyer, Al Septien, based on characters created by Jones. Camera (CFI color), Jane Castle; editors, Christopher Roth, Richard Gentner; music, Jonathan Elias; production design, Anthony Tremblay; art direction, Claire Kaufman; costumes, Meta Jardine; Leprechaun makeup, Gabe Z. Bartalos; visual effects supervisor, Paulo Mazzucato; sound (Ultra-Stereo), Oliver Moss; assistant director, Eddie Ziv; casting, Linda Francis. Reviewed at the Culver Cinema, Culver City, April 8, 1994. MPAA Rating: R. Running time: **85 MIN.**
The Leprechaun .... Warwick Davis
Cody .... Charlie Heath
Bridget .... Shevonne Durkin
Morty .... Sandy Baron
Ian .... Adam Biesk
William O'Day .... James Lancaster
Tourist .... Clint Howard
Tourist Girlfriend ... Kimmy Robertson

There's no lucky charm, or charm of any kind, to "Leprechaun 2." This malevolent little horror item is a nasty piece of business that revels in chicanery and gore. For the die-hard fan, this may be just the sort of pot o'gold that's eluded him. Otherwise, be forewarned, there's more bile than blarney in this bit of Irish folklore. Commercial prospects for the genre outing are down and dirty. This is strict programmer fare for a niche audience and straight on to video and cable. It should do respectable, if fleeting, business in its limited theatrical run.

Though the character's the same, the sequel bears only oblique reference to its predecessor. Tale begins a thousand years ago in ancient Ireland with the screen Leprechaun (Warwick Davis) in search of a bride.

According to mystic legend, he can have the hand of any damsel who sneezes three times. This hitherto unknown bit of the archaic, of course, is spurred more by convenience than logic.

Just as he's about to have a fetching lass in his clutches, her father (and his slave) foils the scheme. But the evil gnome promises to return in a thousand years and have his way with the man's most alluring ancestor.

It's a mighty slim device for even the most Pyrrhic victory. But true to his word, ole Lep pops up in modern-day California 1,000 St. Patrick's Days later. His intended is Bridget (Shevonne Durkin), and

this time her knight comes in the form of teenage boyfriend Cody (Charlie Heath).

Three ah-choos later, Bridget is captive but hardly captivated. It might all end there, except that Cody has wound up with a piece of the tiny ogre's gold. And nothing drives a leprechaun crazier than being without even the tiniest sliver from his gilded pot.

The makers of this menace have the good sense to steer clear of anything too serious and have a bit of fun while racking up the body count. The accent is cruel and darkly ironic, and brevity rather than wit allows them to skip through the pastiche plot.

Davis brings zest to his role despite having to maneuver through a ton of makeup. There's also a nice turn by Sandy Baron as Charlie's streetwise, alcoholic uncle who's undone by greed. The rest of the cast is merely functional.

"Leprechaun 2" is a reasonably well-made, idle diversion. It may just, but only just, have the pluck to raise its head again slightly sooner than 2994. —*Leonard Klady*

'TIL DEATH
(HASTA MORIR)
(MEXICAN)

An Imcine/Vida Films/FFCC/Ocixem production. Directed by Fernando Sarinana. Screenplay, Marcela Fuentes Berain. Camera (color), Guillermo Granillo; editor, Carlos Bolado; music, Eduardo Gamboa; art direction, Gloria Carrasco. Reviewed at IX Muestra de Cine Mexicano, Guadalajara, Mexico, March 15, 1994. Running time: **90 MIN.**
Mauricio .... Damian Bichir
El Boy .... Juan Manuel Bernal
Victoria .... Veronica Merchant
With: Dolores Beristain, Vanessa Bouche, Maru Duenas, Dino Garcia, Montserrat, Ximena Sarinana.

Bound to attract a measure of international attention, " 'Til Death" concerns the ruthless world of Mexican street kids, those bound by their own code of honor. Drawing parallels to south-of-the-border predecessors like "Los Olvidados" and "Rodrigo D.," pic's schematic script underlines its themes even while the overall approach is definitely arty, with slick production values.

Bold first feature by Fernando Sarinana revolves around the uneasy friendship between two contempo teens, Mauricio (Damian Bichir) and El Boy (Juan Manuel Bernal), both of whom dress in the latest grunge styles. When Mauricio comes from Tijuana to visit, El

Boy initiates him into Mexico City's fringe world of minor holdups and petty larceny.

When he kills the security guard at a convenience store, El Boy flees the capital and goes into hiding. Taking advantage of El Boy's absence, Mauricio gets ahold of El Boy's aunt's mortgage papers, which he sells to a fence, betraying the friendship.

Mauricio ingratiates himself with the young woman who lives at the aunt's property while passing himself off as El Boy. El Boy's return sparks the inevitable confrontation.

Overall, the film admirably manages to conjure up this marginal world of violence and street gangs. Gloria Carrasco's lean art direction is effective, combined with choice location work in and around poor neighborhoods in Mexico City and Tijuana. Rock soundtrack showcases some of Mexico's best contemporary music.

Sarinana could stand to forget a few tricks he learned in film school — such as the jump-cuts used during the sex scenes — which tend to call attention to technique and distract from the storyline. But the modern theme and youth-driven story carry the day, and pic should find considerable offshore interest.

—*Paul Lenti*

BIENVENIDO - WELCOME

(MEXICAN)

A Cooperativa Rio Mixcoac/U. of Guadalajara/Cooperativa Conexion/ Trata Films production. Executive producer, Gonzalo Lora. Directed by Gabriel Retes. Screenplay, Retes, Maria del Pozo. Camera (color), Chuy; editor, Carlos Salces; music/art direction, Miguel Perazas. Reviewed at IX Muestra de Cine Mexicano, Guadalajara, Mexico, March 14, 1994. Running time: **115 MIN.**
With: Lourdes Elizarraras, Luis Felipe Tovar, Gabriel Retes, Juan Claudio Retes, Kenia Gazcon, Fernando Arau, Maria Fernanda Garcia, Lucila Balzaretti, Ignacio Retes, Desire Rios, Jose Manuel Fernandez.

You know something's up when "Bienvenido — Welcome" begins with the final credits and all of the characters speak terribly accented English. When the accents finally become unbearable, filmmaker Gabriel Retes lets us in on the joke and the pic takes on a new dimension.

In order to be both relevant and commercial on the international market, the director of this film-within-a-film tries to make an art pic in English about AIDS. Pic is rife with in-jokes that are hilarious to those familiar with Retes' earlier films, yet can be enjoyed by the uninitiated as well. (At one point Retes' real-life father tells him off for including family members in all his films.)

The film plays off notions of multinational works filmed in English, the making of low-budget "art" films with a message, and general problems on the set.

The main problem is that Retes takes his time in letting the audience in on the joke. (Word is that the film will be re-edited to move up some of this key information.)

Tech credits are above average. A re-edit should find some interest on the international arthouse circuit.

—*Paul Lenti*

DESERTS SEAS

(DESIERTOS MARES)

(MEXICAN)

An Imcine/FFCC/Desiertos Films/ Resonancia/Efeccine production. Produced, directed, written by Jose Luis Garcia Agraz. Executive producer, Gonzalo Infante. Camera (color), Carlos Marovich; editor, Manuel Hinojosa; music, Diego Herrera, Alejandro Giacoman; art direction, Carmen Gimenez Cacho. Reviewed at IX Muestra de Cine Mexicano, Guadalajara, Mexico, March 14, 1994. Running time: **90 MIN.**
Juan Aguirre .... Arturo Rios
Carmen .... Dolores Heredia
With: Juan Carlos Colombo, Veronica Merchant, Lisa Owen, Javier de las Piedras, Luis Octavio Gonzalez, Laura Almela.

Touting a highly personal storyline, "Deserts Seas" recounts three separate tales that weave through the film's narrative. Although pic boasts some interesting elements, they don't add up to a satisfying whole.

Third feature by Jose Luis Garcia Agraz (brother of "Phantoms in Love" helmer Carlos Garcia Agraz) revolves around the contemporary tale of a filmmaker, Juan, whose g.f. leaves him for another man. Stridently played by Arturo Rios, the filmmaker goes from sullen to brooding as he tries to woo her back, basically by staging numerous temper tantrums.

Juan's account is punctuated by the story of the death of his father, which is never recounted in full. We are told that his father died on the same day Juan first saw the sea. We are later shown Juan's first view of the sea but are not told how his father died. The director has lovingly recreated the past and his vision of his parents, giving this world the complexity of life as seen through the eyes of a confused 10-year-old. Unfortunately, the rest of the film lacks this multidimensional vision.

Juan is working on an original screenplay, which gives us a third reality level. This script has something to do with the conquest of Mexico and an angel that represents Juan's father, but it is all very confused, and these scenes go nowhere.

Technically, pic is well made. Title is a pun that alternately means "Deserts Seas" and "From Certain Seas."

—*Paul Lenti*

PHANTOMS IN LOVE

(AMOROSOS FANTASMAS)

(MEXICAN)

A Televicine production. Produced by Ignacio Sada Madero. Directed by Carlos Garcia Agraz. Screenplay, Paco Ignacio Taibo II, based on his novel. Camera (color), Xavier Perez Grobet; editor, Ramon Aupart, Garcia Agraz; music, Alejandro Giacoman; art direction, Marisa Pecanins. Reviewed at IX Muestra de Cine Mexicano, Guadalajara, Mexico, March 15, 1994. Running time: **92 MIN.**
Hector
Belacoaran Shayne .... Sergio Goyri
Laura Ramos .... Mariana Levy
Marquez .... Manuel Ojeda
Fantasma Samudio .. Salvador Sanchez
With: Bruno Bichir, Alberto Rodriguez Estrella, Mercedes Olea.

Televicine, the film production arm of Mexico's TV giant Televisa, has committed to produce a series of about 10 features based on the novels of Paco Ignacio Taibo II. These books highlight the adventures of Hector Belacoaran Shayne, a hardboiled, one-eyed detective played here by Sergio Goyri. (Rather than release the films one by one, the firm is bankrolling the entire series before undertaking their official launch.)

"Phantoms in Love," third pic in the series, refers to a masked wrestler, known as the Phantom, who is killed at the beginning of this film. Shayne is hired to find the killer. He is also hired to discover the truth about a teenage suicide.

As Shayne works on these disparate cases, the audience strives to find a narrative thread that connects the two tales. Both mysteries are eventually resolved despite no interlinking element; there are just two mysteries.

Tech credits are OK, as film takes its lead from a well-explored genre. Goyri does an effective job with the character of the eccentric-yet-attractive detective. There are some fun moments in the dialogue, but overall there is little that is new.

Director Carlos Garcia Agraz is the brother of Jose Luis Garcia Agraz, producer, director and writer of "Deserts Seas" (Desiertos Mares).

—*Paul Lenti*

AMBER

(AMBAR)

(MEXICAN)

An Imcine/Bandidos Films production. Executive producers, Sebastian Silva, Emilia Arau. Directed by Luis Estrada. Screenplay, Hugo Hiriart, Jaime Sampietro, Estrada, based on the play by Hiriart. Camera (color), Emmanuel Lubezki; editor, Estrada; music, Santiago Ojeda; art direction, Monica Chirinos. Reviewed at IX Muestra de Cine Mexicano, Guadalajara, Mexico, March 13, 1994. Running time: **90 MIN.**
Kluski .... Hector Bonilla
Corbett .... Jorge Russeck
Young Max .... Martin Altomaro
Older Max .... Muni Lubezki
Commissioner .... Pedro Armendariz
With: Angelia Aragon, Gabriela Roel, Ana Ofelia Murguia, Emilio Echeverria, Jose Carlos Rodriguez, Diego Luna, Bruno Schwebel.

A fantasy-adventure tale along the lines of "The Adventures of Baron Munchausen" and "1,001 Nights," "Amber" demonstrates a certain ambition to try something different in Mexican cinema. Yet, like Luis Estrada's earlier film "Bandidos," pic doesn't have an audience: It proves too simple for adults, too complicated and sexual for tots.

In a story told in flashback, old Max (Muni Lubezki) recounts his adventures as a young man (Martin Altomaro), when he acquired a precious amber stone. His journey brings him into contact with a variety of adventurous types — from ship captains and commissioners to exotic dancing girls and prostitutes.

The frequent use of miniatures is ingenious, and Monica Chirinos' imaginative art direction is impressive, but the film lacks cohesion. Despite problems, pic should attract some interest for its ambitious effort and novel approach.

—*Paul Lenti*

THE DIRIGIBLE

(EL DIRIGIBLE)

(URUGUAYAN-CUBAN-MEXICAN-BRITISH)

A Nubes Montevideo/ICAIC/Channel 4/U. of Guadalajara/Ibersis/Fondation Montecinemaverita/Centre Intl. Creation Video production. Executive producer, Mariela Besuievsky. Directed, written by Pablo Dotta. Camera (color), Miguel Abal; editor, Samuel Larson; music, Fernando Cabrera. Reviewed at IX Muestra de Cine Mexicano, Guadalajara, Mexico, March 16, 1994. Running time: **90 MIN.**
French Woman .... Laura Schneider
Translator .... Marcelo Bouquet
Julio .... Eduardo Miglionico
El Moco (Snotty) .... Gonzalo Cardozo
Inspector Cardozo .... Ricardo Espalter

April 18, 1994 (Cont.)

Although suggesting a certain weightiness, "The Dirigible" is a lightweight piece of fluff that may make the rounds at a few festivals. Commercial possibilities seem nil, even on the arthouse circuit.

Touted as a rare feature from Uruguay, "The Dirigible" is a pretentious mess that meanders for 1½ hours without going anywhere.

Bookending the film is the story of the dirigible, whose appearance over Montevideo in the early part of the century distracted crowds from the former president Baltasar Brum's public suicide. Confused plot then deals with the supposed return of a Uruguayan writer, the search of a French woman, her translator and a juvenile delinquent named El Moco (Snotty).

Director and writer Pablo Dotta's pic deliberately tries to offend with gross-out scenes such as the woman photocopying her genitals, and El Moco pulling mucus out of the translator's nose and later defecating in the middle of a room.
—*Paul Lenti*

POLICE RESCUE

(AUSTRALIAN)

A UIP release of a Southern Star Xanadu production, in association with Australian Film Finance Corp./Australian Broadcasting Corp./United Intl. Pictures. Produced by Sandra Levy, John Edwards. Executive producers, Errol Sullivan, Penny Chapman. Directed by Michael Carson. Screenplay, Debra Oswald, based on the television series. Camera (color), Russell Bacon; editor, Chris Spurr; music, John Clifford White; production design, Murray Picknett; sound, Peter Grace; stunts, Glenn Boswell; associate producer, Wayne Barry; assistant director, Michael Fanna; casting, Liz Mullinar. Reviewed at UIP screening room, Sydney, March 3, 1994. Running time: **90 MIN.**
Sgt. Mickey McClintock ..... Gary Sweet
Constable
Lorrie Gordon .... Zoe Carides
Sgt. Georgia Rattray .... Sonia Todd
Constable Angel
Angelopoulos .... Steve Bastoni
Insp. Bill Adams .... John Clayton
Constable Kathy
Orland .... Tammy McIntosh
Constable Brian
Morley .... Jeremy Callaghan
Sharyn Elliott .... Belinda Cotterill
Terry .... Jeremy Sims

This mediocre actioner is a disappointing spinoff of a popular Aussie TV series. Not enough thought has been devoted to transforming this cop story into a genuine big-screen experience, the result being an unexciting potboiler. This could generate some initial biz Down Under and in Britain, where original played on BBC-TV, but legs look to be stumpy.

The men and women of Sydney's Police Rescue Squad have thrilled small-screen viewers for three years now, but scripter Debra Oswald and first-time feature director Michael Carson, both alumni of the series, haven't come up with any original ideas for the feature.

Plot has femme squad newcomer Lorrie Gordon (Zoe Carides), ex of the Drug Squad, under suspicion from police Internal Affairs because her former partner, and secret lover, who was killed in the line of duty in pic's confusingly staged opening sequence, has been revealed as corrupt.

As a result, Rescue Squad's Sgt. Mickey McClintock (Gary Sweet) gives her the hostile treatment; then, suddenly and, in plot terms, most unconvincingly, goes to bed with her.

She's relieved from police duty, but becomes a heroine during pic's climactic siege in which a distraught man, with explosives strapped to his waist, holds a group of kindergarten moppets and their teacher hostage high up in a city office building. —*David Stratton*

SCHRAMM

(GERMAN)

A Joerg Buttgereit/Manfred O. Jelinski production. Produced by Buttgereit, Jelinski. Directed, written by Buttgereit, from a screen story by Buttgereit, Franz Rodenkirchen. Camera (color), Jelinski; editor, Jelinski, Buttgereit; music, Max Mueller, Gundula Schmitz, Mutter; makeup, Marianne Drope, Heike Eger; special effects, Michael Romahn. Reviewed at Hof Film Festival, Hof, Germany, Oct. 28, 1993. (Also in Rotterdam fest.) Running time: **75 MIN.**
With: Florian Koerner von Gustorf, Monika M., Micha Brendel, Carolina Harnisch, Xaver Schwarzenberger, Gerd Horvath.

Latest chapter in sex-slasher exploration by cult writer/director Joerg Buttgereit ("Nekromantik") has "fans only" written all over it. Helmer's less interested in telling true-life story of serial killer Lothar Schramm than he is in giving auds a feel of what it might have been like inside the sex killer's mind. Result is boring, except for those with a yen for the latter experience.

Schramm murdered more than a dozen women in his career, painting lipstick on their mouths and raping them posthumously. Then, one day (according to the film), while washing blood off a wall of his apartment, he fell off a ladder and broke his neck.

Buttgereit shows only two victims here. There is little dialogue, no exploration of motives or methods, and only a token look at Schramm's environment. Instead, Buttgereit tries to re-create a kind of visual blood frenzy.

Method is to use a handful of scenes and look at them over and over again from different perspectives. Using out-of-date experimental means (repetition and color distortion), Buttgereit tries to put the audience into the killer's mind, and probably gets as close as a director with limited means can.

That doesn't prevent him from exploiting shock effects. Best is when Schramm nails his penis to a table, with convincing special effects by Michael Romahn.

Though it's hard to judge perfs under circumstances where lensing, lighting and color effects are the most important things, Florian Koerner von Gustorf as Schramm and Monika M. as his prostie neighbor (and only friend) fit the film's requirements perfectly. Blown up from 16mm, pic is good within its budget limitations, especially camera work by co-producer Manfred O. Jelinski. —*Eric Hansen*

IN DARKEST HOLLYWOOD: CINEMA & APARTHEID

(U.S.-CANADIAN — DOCU — VIDEO)

A Nightingale Prods./McKinnon Associates production. (International sales: Daniel Riesenfeld, Chicago.) Directed, written by Peter Davis, Daniel Riesenfeld. Camera (color/b&w; video), editor, Riesenfeld; sound, Davis. Reviewed at Berlin Film Festival (Forum section), Feb. 18, 1994. Running time: **112 MIN.**

Now that white rule is presumably ending in South Africa, "In Darkest Hollywood" provides some sort of closure to the 46 years since the 1948 elections ushered in apartheid. Noted Canadian-based social-activist documentarian Peter Davis ("Hearts and Minds") teamed with Californian Daniel Riesenfeld to make this technically top-notch video about the ideological implications of cinema under apartheid. Created in two 56-minute parts for TV, where it should have legs worldwide, it has been traveling the fest circuit since November in London.

Helmers provide lots of ammo to support the contention that film is never merely experiment, that it does not exist in a political vacuum. Extensive clips from American and South African features, as well as newsreel clips, often quite handsome and harrowing, from the Sharpeville Massacre in 1960 and the Soweto riots in 1976, support the multitude of authoritative talking heads. These include African intellectuals, white producers, black actors and both black and white directors, though occasionally too-

brief clips literalize and trivialize testimony.

Courageous indies like apartheid propagandist-turned-anti-government-documentarian Anthony Thomas and Yank filmmaker Lionel Rogosin ("Come Back Africa") get their due, as do such misguided name directors as Richard Attenborough ("Cry Freedom"), whose shooting structure mirrored the segregated society surrounding him, and the South African Jamie Uys ("The Gods Must Be Crazy"), whose benevolent paternalism is reproached by another speaker. (Contradiction is one of the video's structuring devices.)

Some highlights: clips from first all-black South African film, "African Jim" (1949), a delightful musical made before the white film industry appropriated the genre; actor/director John Kani explaining how Hollywood provided an escape valve for blacks repressed under apartheid, illustrated by clips of young South African males attired in natty film noir duds; a hypocritical all-white world premiere of "Cry, the Beloved Country" in Johannesburg in the early 1950s; and expert testimony about Hollywood's blind eye to apartheid until the 1980s. —*Howard Feinstein*

TREKKING TO UTOPIA

(SOUTH AFRICAN-GERMAN — DOCU)

A Metrofilm production, in association with ZDF-Arte. Produced by Sabine Pfeiffer, Mark Hurwitz. Directed, written by Michael Hammon. Camera (color), Hammon; editor, Mona Brauer; music, Reinhard Scheuregger; sound, Robyn Hofmeyr; assistant director, Mark Lewis. Reviewed at Berlin Film Festival (Forum section), Feb. 19, 1994. Running time: **89 MIN.**

On the verge of South African elections, there could be international interest in this docu, which allows Afrikaners to express their views about the coming of democracy to that troubled country. There are no real surprises here, but the film is still of considerable interest.

That's partly because director/cameraman Michael Hammon, who was born in South Africa, decided to take a small film crew and follow more or less the route taken by thousands of Boers who, in 1838, fled British domination in the Cape Colony. These "Voortrekkers" embarked on what became known as "The Great Trek," planned to establish a Boer republic, and fought the Zulu nation in bloody encounters.

In 1916, a silent feature film was made that recreated the trek on a lavish scale; Hammon uses extensive footage from this epic, which has been forgotten (or more likely, never seen) by film historians. It looks like a pic worth reviving on its own account.

Following the route of the Voortrekkers, Hammon visits small towns and farms in the S.A. hinterland, where some people refuse even to speak English as a matter of principle. Many see the changes happening in the country as a betrayal, others are afraid, and some are angry and willing to fight. Dreams of an independent Afrikaner republic are still alive, and Hammon's film gives voice to the people who harbor those dreams and ambitions.

Film is technically fair, with some inadequate sound recording at times. —*David Stratton*

A CLASS TO REMEMBER

(GAKKO)

(JAPANESE)

A Shochiku Co., Nippon TV, Sumitomo Corp. production. (International sales: Shochiku Co., Tokyo.) Produced by Shigehiro Nakagawa. Directed by Yoji Yamada. Screenplay, Yamada, Yoshitaka Asama. Camera (color), Tetsuo Takaba, Mutsuo Naganuma; editor, Iwao Ishii; music, Isao Tomita; art direction, Mitsuo Degawa, Yutaka Yokoyama; sound (Dolby), Isao Suzuki. Reviewed at Berlin Film Festival (Panorama section), Feb. 16, 1994. Running time: **128 MIN.**

With: Toshiyuki Nishida (Kuroi), Keiko Takeshita (Keiko Tajima), Masato Hagiwara (Kazuo), Yuri Nakae (Eriko), Eiko Shinya (Eomeoni), Weng Huarong (Zhang), Hiroshi Kanbe (Osamu), Nae Yuki (Midori), Kiyoshi Atsumi (Greengrocer), Kunie Tanaka (Inoda).

A cozy, upfront heartwarmer about a Tokyo night-school teacher and his pupils, "A Class to Remember" is a polished big-studio production that won't get much farther offshore than the vid shelf in Nipponese food stores.

Co-produced by Shochiku in commemoration of its 40th anni, pic has didactic family entertainment written all over it. Helmer Yoji Yamada, best known for directing all but two of the features in the 24-year-long "Tora-san" series, made this between cranking out Nos. 45 and 46. His last non-"Tora-san" item was the 1991 "My Sons," also strong on traditional values.

Setting is a night junior high on Tokyo's lower east side where longtime teach Kuroi (Toshiyuki Nishida), known as "Old Fox," turns down his boss's offer of a transfer to another school. While his students pen pre-grad essays on their de-

sires and memories, flashbacks limn their personal stories.

Confection purrs along pleasantly for most of its length. Some nice light comic touches, plus Nishida's unsappy perf as the dedicated teacher, keep the pic from stewing in its own juices. Japanese title simply means "School." —*Derek Elley*

MINOR CRIME

(DELIT MINEUR)

(FRENCH)

An Ariane release (France) of an Oliane Prods., FR1 Films Prods. production, with participation of Canal Plus, Investimage 4, Byimages 2, CNC. (International sales: WMF, Paris.) Produced by Marie-Laure Reyre. Directed by Francis Girod. Screenplay, Girod, Michel Grisolia. Camera (color), William Lubtchansky; editor, Genevieve Winding; music, Romano Musumarra; production design/set decoration, Jacques Bufnoir; costume design, Florence Desouches; sound, Andree Hervee, Claude Villand; assistant director, Jerome Navarro; casting, Pierre Amzallag. Reviewed at 14 Juillet Odeon Cinema, Paris, March 5, 1994. Running time: **106 MIN.**

Claire	Caroline Cellier
Guerin	Claude Brasseur
Claude	Niels Arestrup
Laurent	Christopher Thompson
Madeleine	Macha Meril
Guillaume	Mathieu Crepeau

Also with: Anne-Marie Philipe, Gerard Sety, Pierre Gerard, Maurice Baquet, Claude Winter.

"**M**inor Crime" is a sly, slow-burning tale of adultery and is-it-or-isn't-it patricide in a posh Paris suburb. Patient viewers will enjoy the fine perfs on display in this adult exercise in shifting morality.

Fortyish Claire (Caroline Cellier) is married to once-dashing but self-destructive alcoholic Claude (Niels Arestrup), with whom she has a 15-year-old son, Guillaume (Mathieu Crepeau), and a younger daughter.

Claire trysts every few days with her handsome 24-year-old lover, Laurent (Christopher Thompson), spoiled son of local restaurateur Madeleine (Macha Meril), once Claire's rival for Claude's affections. Guillaume, who reads detective novels and has a knack for sleuthing, is fully aware of his mom's extramarital activities, but Claude isn't.

Not, that is, until the local police inspector (Claude Brasseur) decides to let her husband know the score. Latter ends up dead on the floor and the cop is shown to have an ulterior motive of his own.

Helmer Francis Girod and his longtime writing partner Michel Grisolia carefully establish the day-to-day routines of their emotionally

dissatisfied characters in pic's first half and then — slowly — cut to the chase. There's little traditional action, but the suspense accrues gradually and with a sure hand.

Cellier — in her first screen appearance since starring in late husband Jean Poiret's "Le Zebre" — is aces in a meaty role that lets her be mom, wife, mistress and cashier in a chic eatery. Combo of Cellier's careworn face and smashing figure lends poignance to her character's search for romantic balance.

Young newcomer Crepeau convinces as Guillaume.

Lensing and decor suit the carefully calibrated, morally queasy goings-on, with TV shows and commercials constantly punctuating scenes in cozy homes and hotel rooms. Girod himself cameos as the director of an institution for severely retarded children. Pic's French title literally means "misdemeanor" but also puns on the fact that an under-18 "minor" is involved. —*Lisa Nesselson*

BRIGITTA

(GERMAN-HUNGARIAN — B&W)

A Dagmar Knoepfel Filmproduktion production, in association with MOVI (Budapest), Bavarian Film Fund. Produced by Dagmar Knoepfel, Sandor Buglya. Directed, written by Knoepfel, from the short story by Adalbert Stifter. Camera (b&w), Miklos Gurban; editor, Knoepfel; music, Lajos Wohner; art direction, Istvan Horvath, Sandor Katona. Reviewed at Hungarian Film Week, Budapest, Feb. 6, 1994. Running time: **79 MIN.**

Florian	Karl Achleitner
Istvan	Tamas Jordan
Brigitta	Eva Igo
Gustav	Klaus Haendl

(German and Hungarian dialogue)

Doggedly uncommercial, but made with loving precision, "Brigitta" is a slim costumer about a German artist who becomes intrigued by a mysterious woman when visiting a Hungarian friend in the countryside. Fest circuit beckons.

Based on the 1842 short story by Adalbert Stifter, pic strongly recalls the films of Gallic director Eric Rohmer with its leisurely conversations, large truths drawn from small events and general optimism regarding human nature.

Florian, a young German artist, travels to visit his Magyar pal Istvan, meticulously sketching flora on the way. Directed to his friend's place by a striking woman astride a horse, he gradually pieces together her story during tours round Istvan's capacious estate. Final revelation is warm and satisfying.

German scripter/director Dagmar Knoepfel takes her time unfolding the vignette, but the dialogue is well turned, Miklos Gurban's b&w lensing precise and easy on the eyes, and the tempo attuned to the leisurely classes pic describes. As the cross-cultural friends, Karl Achleitner and Tamas Jordan mesh well, with an easy bonhomie. Hungarian actress Eva Igo handles the shadowy title role with commanding but elegant style.
—*Derek Elley*

IMAGE IN THE RAIN

(AME NO WADACHI)

(JAPANESE — 16mm)

Produced by Furosawa Binbun. Directed by Ito Nobuyuki. Screenplay, Takahashi Ikuo. Camera (color), Tomita Shinji; music, Hieda Hiroshi, Ogino Kiyoko. Reviewed at Rotterdam Intl. Film Festival, Jan. 28, 1994. Running time: **75 MIN.**

With: Kuronuma Hiromi, Kobiyama Yuichi, Sanaya Keiko, Miura Nobuko, Kanegae Siyunta.

A sober essay on the sometimes crippling legacy of childhood events, "Image in the Rain" is like an intricate psychological puzzle, the pieces of which never quite fit together. Despite its persuasive overlying lugubriousness, this unresolved fusion of routine drama, poetic nuance and elliptical symbolism doesn't jell into any form coherent enough for audiences to bite into.

Mishimura, a despondent middle-aged man, moves into an apartment block and immediately finds a kindred spirit in his neighbor's lonely son, Shohei. Mourning a pet dog, the boy sits glued to the window, hypnotized by the mysteries of sun showers. A strange, almost sinister bond links Shohei's father to Mishimura, both of whom lost their brothers at a young age in freak accidents.

Shohei and his father go with Mishimura to the secluded waterfall where his brother was killed, and he initiates the boy into the arcane rites of looking through the water into the next world. Back home, tragedy strikes when Shohei continues the mystic quest alone. Attempting to travel beyond a sun shower to find his dog, the boy is run down by a truck. Unanswered questions regarding the deaths in their pasts fester between Mishimura and his neighbor, drawing the two men into a violent confrontation.

Director Ito Nobuyuki laces the action with vaguely experimental touches such as distorted sound and warped images of nature, enriching the film's murky visual texture but not compensating for its lack of a unifying tone. Though effective at times, music more often runs to heavy-handed overstatement.

—*David Rooney*

ANGEL OF MERCY
(ANJEL MILOSRDENSTVA)
(SLOVAK-CZECH)

A Slovak Television, Ars Media (Bratislava)/Czech Television (Prague) production. (International sales: Filmexport Prague, Prague.) Directed by Miloslav Luther. Screenplay, Vladimir Korner, Luther, Marian Puobis, from a novella by Korner. Camera (color), Vladiminir Hollos; editor, Patrik Pass; music, Beethoven, Dvorak, Brahms; production design, Dusan Fischer; costume design, Maria Sulekova, Maria Miklasova. Reviewed at Berlin Film Festival (market), Feb. 15, 1994. Running time: **95 MIN.**
Anezka .... Ingrid Timkova
Christoph ....Juraj Simko
     Also with: Jozef Vajnar, Peter Simun, Juraj Mokry, Marta Sladeckova.
(Slovak dialogue)

A handsomely upholstered, Mitteleuropa costume meller, "Angel of Mercy" treads familiar ground to solid effect. Story of an affair between a major's wife and a prisoner of war is reliable fodder for foreign-lingo programmers.

The beautiful Anezka (Ingrid Timkova) arrives in the war-torn town of Stryj to visit her husband, dying of third-degree burns from a gasoline attack by an executed saboteur's wife. Event took place in a brothel, but the officer is to be declared a hero all the same.

Disillusioned with the military, Anezka starts work as a nurse in the army hospital and soon falls for a hunky prisoner. Their affair fails to revive any hope in him, and he even rejects her attempt to let him escape. Ending is tragic.

Slovak production has a strong literary feel, shored up by handsome period design and costuming, plus thoughtful performances, especially by Timkova as the strong, grieving widow. Pic evokes any number of earlier Czech-Slovak turn-of-the-century costumers, without adding much new.

Production credits are pro throughout. Largely TV-financed movie preemed in Bratislava last December. —*Derek Elley*

WHEN A MAN LOVES A WOMAN

A Buena Vista release of a Touchstone Pictures production. Produced by Jordan Kerner, Jon Avent. Executive producers, Simon Maslow, Ronald Bass, Al Franken. Coproducers, C. Tad Devlin, Susan Merzbach. Directed by Luis Mandoki. Screenplay by Bass, Franken. Camera (Technicolor), Lajos Koltai; editor, Garth Craven; music, Zbigniew Preisner; production design, Stuart Wurtzel; art direction, Steven A. Saklad; set design, Stan Tropp; set decoration, Kara Lindstrom; costume design, Linda Bass; sound (Dolby), Thomas D. Causey; associate producer, Salli Newman; assistant director, Steve Danton; second unit camera, Frank Holgate; casting, Amanda Mackey, Cathy Sandrich. Reviewed at the Disney Studios, Burbank, April 20, 1994. MPAA Rating: R. Running time: **124 MIN.**
Michael Green .... Andy Garcia
Alice Green .... Meg Ryan
Amy .... Lauren Tom
Gary .... Philip Seymour Hoffman
Jess Green .... Tina Majorino
Casey Green .... Mae Whitman
Emily .... Ellen Burstyn
Walter ....Eugene Roche
Dr. Gina
     Mendez .... Latanya Richardson

There's something terribly askew and misleading in the very title "When a Man Loves a Woman" ("Significant Other," its original name, is no better). This contempo tale of alcoholism and substance abuse does have an underlying tenderness, but its core is sober, vivid and gut-wrenching. Despite the odd lapse into movie logic at film's end, it's a first-class production, accentuated by fine performances and an unflinching script.

Though likely to earn high critical praise, the film is more aptly a *succes d'estime* than 150-proof box office potent. The presence of charismatic actors is an asset, but audiences have been cool toward this particular subject matter of late regardless of cast, quality or emotional wallop.

Michael (Andy Garcia) and Alice (Meg Ryan) Green are the seeming paradigm of the yuppie lifestyle. He's an airplane pilot and she's a high school guidance counselor. They have a snug little San Francisco home and two well-adjusted pre-teen girls.

But the cracks in the veneer soon become obvious. Alice cannot face a social situation without at least one drink too many. After a near-fatal boating incident on a Mexican vacation, she promises to reform — meaning only that she will hide her drinking problem more ferociously and that

Michael will continue to believe in Band-Aid treatment.

The scenario is classic and predictable and has rarely been shown onscreen with such candor or precision. Alice is lucky. She has an accident in the shower that finally wakes everyone up and sends her packing to a detox center.

The ambition of the Ronald Bass-Al Franken screenplay is often staggering. It's more a case study than a traditional three-act movie fable. The film takes on the logic of a bar crawl, veering toward the conventional only in Luis Mandoki's direction and with some much appreciated excursions into levity.

Unlike such seminal works as "The Lost Weekend" and "The Days of Wine and Roses," this new outing eschews the perforce nightmarish look to convey its Dantean trek. The action takes place in broad daylight and is rather like a magic act in which an adept conjurer plays for a willing dupe.

Ryan has one of those rollercoaster roles that demands attention. Her character arc is the more obvious, beginning as the happy lush and going through a series of dark transitions before she's able to stand on her own two feet. It's a testament to her craft and wiles that she's able to keep both viewer attention and sympathy.

Of even greater challenge is Garcia's part as the unexpected villain of the piece. Superficially a caring and concerned partner, he's nonetheless capable of inflicting enormous damage under the veil of good intentions.

He is glib, macho and self-centered. But his intentions (no matter what the effect) are understandable, though misguided. His transformation — more difficult to diagnose and treat — is therefore the more painful of the two.

Supporting roles are largely functional with the exception of Tina Majorino as the couple's older daughter. Philip Seymour Hoffman and Lauren Tom play characters who elicit such bad traits as jealousy and violence from the principals.

Richard Bradford, in an uncredited role, has a nice turn as an angry recovering addict, and Ellen Burstyn is completely wasted as Ryan's mother.

While the conclusion is too pat for all that has preceded it, anything more downbeat would be too devastating to contemplate. "When a Man Loves a Woman" is unquestionably ragged and, in this instance, that bolsters its integrity. Though a grueling expe-

rience, it is refreshing to see serious subject matter handled so deftly in a Hollywood production.

—*Leonard Klady*

THAT'S ENTERTAINMENT! III

An MGM release presented in association with Turner Entertainment Co. Produced, directed, written, edited by Bud Friedgen, Michael J. Sheridan. Executive producer, Peter Fitzgerald; additional music arranged by Marc Shaiman; music supervision, Marilee Bradford; film restoration, Cinetech; new sequences camera (Deluxe color/ b&w), Howard A. Anderson III; production sound (Dolby), Dave Kelson, Bill Teague; assistant director, Ric Rondell. Reviewed at Warner Hollywood screening room, L.A., March 7, 1994. MPAA Rating: G. Running time: **113 MIN.** (including overture).
     Hosts: June Allyson, Cyd Charisse, Lena Horne, Howard Keel, Gene Kelly, Ann Miller, Debbie Reynolds, Mickey Rooney, Esther Williams.

It's been 20 years since the first "That's Entertainment!" proved that there was gold in the MGM vaults, and 18 years since the second installment, which might have suggested that the cupboard had long since been cleaned bare. But by searching a little further into unfamiliar corners and outtake cans, resourceful filmmakers Bud Friedgen and Michael J. Sheridan have come up with a bang-up third anthology of golden-era musical highlights that capably holds its own with its predecessors. The audience for such an undertaking, especially those who experienced the excerpted films at the time of their release, may have dwindled in the intervening two decades, but theatrical B.O. should still be good, on the way to a long life on TV, cable and video.

Metro was reportedly the only major studio to systematically save its outtakes, a policy that has paid off here in spades in some musical gems that surprisingly dwarf many sequences that ended up in pictures. Happily, along with preserving and restoring the films themselves to sparkling condition, Turner Entertainment also saved these exhilarating footnotes to film history, which many buffs will eventually want to savor repeatedly on homevid and laser.

Format is the same as before, as legendary stars from MGM's musical heyday introduce different chapters in the story, which encompasses 62 musical numbers culled from more than 100 films. As June Allyson, Cyd Charisse, Lena Horne, Howard Keel, Ann Miller, Debbie Reynolds, Mickey Rooney and Esther Williams reminisce, mostly in genteel fashion, how it

April 25, 1994 (Cont.)

was in the glory days, filmmakers discreetly conceal that the old MGM lot on which they're photographed now belongs to Sony.

Pic steps quickly, and amusingly, through the first years of sound, neatly disguising that the Metro musical didn't really hit its stride until some years later. Then, bang, the first dynamite sequence, featuring the dazzling hoofer Eleanor Powell, first in "Broadway Melody of 1938," then more spectacularly essaying "Fascinatin' Rhythm" in "Lady Be Good," with the filmmakers providing a revealing split-screen look at the finished number and behind-the-scenes footage showing how the elaborate scene was accomplished. If nothing else, this interlude will introduce quite a few viewers to Powell's protean talents.

Having edited the first two "That's Entertainment" anthologies, Friedgen and Sheridan know well how to pace and balance two hours of clips, and they put their expertise to work by following some classic material with comic relief, such as the forgotten Ross Sisters performing a grotesque contortionist number from "Broadway Rhythm."

Similarly, they manage to maintain a roughly chronological presentation while still deftly juggling solos and production numbers, color and black-and-white, the fresh and the familiar. Remarkably, feature repeats very little footage from the earlier installments, while naturally harking back to many of the same films.

Williams' stupendous and campy aquatic ballets and, perhaps especially, some of the shining moments with Fred Astaire and Judy Garland will prove particular eye-openers to new audiences.

By contrast, buffs will be drawn by the numerous outtakes, beginning with two by Reynolds, one a rendition of "You Are My Lucky Star" cut from "Singin' in the Rain," another an alternate version of "A Lady Loves" from "I Love Melvin."

Horne, who admits that "I never felt like I really belonged in Hollywood," is a big winner here, as repped by a deleted tune, "Ain't it the Truth," which she sang in a bubble bath for "Cabin in the Sky," and her electrifying "Can't Help Lovin' Dat Man," shown after two versions of Ava Gardner performing the same song from "Show Boat," one in the actress's own voice (rather sweet and not bad) and one as dubbed for the finished film by Annette Warren.

Garland's "I'm an Indian Too," lensed before she was fired from "Annie Get Your Gun," proves rather sloppy, shrill and vaguely embarrassing, but her "March of the Doagies" from "The Harvey Girls" was a giant production number to have been dropped. Another previously unseen performance, her rendition of "Mr. Monotony"

shot for "Easter Parade," is a stunner, and marked the first appearance of her subsequent trademark outfit, the half-tuxedo.

But perhaps most amazing of all is the contrast of two versions of the song "Two Faced Woman." The one previously seen by the public, with Joan Crawford in "Torch Song," is a camp atrocity, with the star in hideous "tropical" makeup. The other, with a sizzling Charisse, is shown here for the first time and is great, but was cut from "The Band Wagon." As Reynolds puts it here, "It's been suggested that they may have used the wrong version."

Chronologically, the last pix excerpted are "Jailhouse Rock" and "Gigi," which neatly illustrates the musical fork in the road that appeared by the late 1950s. "Gigi" essentially marked the end of the great MGM musical as it had been known in the Arthur Freed era, and that film, and those before it, belonged to a very different world. But "That's Entertainment! III," like its predecessors, makes it a very agreeable place to visit.

Technically, film is mostly tops, with superior sound and excerpts looking great. One quibble is that, while the original aspect ratios, from the old Academy format to widescreen, are respected most of the time, on occasion the former standard 1.33 ratio is distorted to the modern 1.85. Inconsistency of this application is puzzling.

—*Todd McCarthy*

BAD GIRLS

A 20th Century Fox release of a Ruddy Morgan production. Produced by Albert S. Ruddy, Andre E. Morgan, Charles Finch. Executive producer, Lynda Obst. Co-producer, William Fay. Directed by Jonathan Kaplan. Screenplay, Ken Friedman, Yolande Finch, story by Ruddy, Charles Finch, Gray Frederickson. Camera (CFI color; Deluxe prints), Ralf Bode; editor, Jane Kurson; music, Jerry Goldsmith; production design, Guy Barnes; art direction, M. Nord Haggerty; set decoration, Michael Taylor, Brian Kasch (Sonora); costume design, Susie DeSanto; sound (Dolby), Jose Antonio Garcia; assistant director, Jules Lichtman; second unit director/stunt coordinator, Walter Scott; second unit camera, Phillip Pfeiffer, Dan Turrett, Jamie Anderson; casting, Mike Fenton, Julie Ashton, Julie Selzer. Reviewed at 20th Century Fox Studios, L.A., April 20, 1994. MPAA Rating: R. Running time: **99 MIN.**

Cody Zamora	Madeleine Stowe
Anita Crown	Mary Stuart Masterson
Eileen Spenser	Andie MacDowell
Lilly Laronette	Drew Barrymore
Kid Jarrett	James Russo
William Tucker	James LeGros
Frank Jarrett	Robert Loggia
Josh McCoy	Dermot Mulroney

With Westerns back in fashion and women ready to take the reins, it was inevitable that a

female outlaws pic like "Bad Girls" would get made. But even though the sight of four comely cowgirls strapping on six-guns and thundering across the plains has its undeniable kick, the bad news is that "Bad Girls" drinks from an empty trough of wit and style. Quite promotable in concept, this well-scrubbed, unexciting Fox release might hit the target on opening weekend but looks to misfire in subsequent rounds.

Undertaking such a project, it seems that the two alternatives would have been to make a gritty, truly feminist, "Thelma & Louise"-like Western designed to be dramatically valid within the historical context, or to slyly wink at the audience while applying gender reversal to genre conventions.

"Bad Girls" falls in a bland netherworld, exhibiting no attitude or personality as it strains to come up with enough dramatic twists and confrontations to get it to feature length. The novelty of watching the foxy foursome mount up or square off against assorted bad boys wears off surprisingly quickly, even if interest is sustained by their well-maintained hairdos and the impressive frequency of their costume changes.

With a possible bow to "Unforgiven," tall tale starts with barroom floozy Cody Zamora (Madeleine Stowe) gunning down a prominent lawman when he starts getting too rough with her fellow prostie Anita Crown (Mary Stuart Masterson). Saved from lynching at the hands of local religious reformers, Cody high-tails it out of town with Anita, self-styled Southern belle Eileen Spenser (Andie MacDowell) and blond babe Lilly Laronette (Drew Barrymore).

While Pinkerton goons try to track them down, these ladies of ill repute decide to go straight and open a sawmill on Anita's Oregon homestead plot. But just as Cody is withdrawing her life savings from a bank, old flame Kid Jarrett (James Russo) robs it, thus ensnaring the women in the world of big-stakes outlawry and treachery.

Along the way, the "honky-tonk harlots" hook up with helpful cowboy Josh McCoy (Dermot Mulroney), who takes a shine to Cody and wants revenge on Jarrett for killing his dad, and green rancher William Tucker (James LeGros), who'd love to lasso Eileen. Climactic shootout between the girls and Jarrett's desert scum has the predictable result, and no tension in its staging.

The five script and story writers were unfortunately unable to come up with much interesting for the feisty femmes to do, providing director Jonathan Kaplan, who replaced original helmer Tamra Davis, with an insurmountable problem. Despite

the twist-on-cliches plotting, no humor is brought to the execution, so the film looks like what it is — four Hollywood actresses duded up in Western gear, riding horses and toting pistols.

Which isn't to say that they don't look good doing it, just thoroughly unbelievable. Stowe projects grim, unwavering resolve throughout to leave her old life behind once she recovers her money from the devilish Jarrett. MacDowell is mostly coy smiles and coquettish glances, while Barrymore looks to be the best rider of the bunch. Masterson is stuck with the dullest part, that of a still-grieving widow forced into prostitution, and with the most embarrassingly anachronistic speech, a feminist diatribe against sexist laws.

As for the men, Russo's villain is uninteresting, Robert Loggia does a Gene Hackman as a crusty old coot, while LeGros and Mulroney are on the bland side.

Production looks exceedingly squeaky-clean, with sets and costumes revealing an un-lived-in look. The one inspired stroke in Guy Barnes' production design is Russo's living quarters, a converted outdoor courtyard with boudoir accoutrements.

Poor script and lack of a compelling dramatic arc make the events seem cobbled together and without rhythm. Action is also exceedingly mild, with violence toned down, ample opportunities for nudity averted and any true grit excised. Despite the R rating, it feels more like a PG. —*Todd McCarthy*

BRAINSCAN

A Triumph Release of a Michel Roy production. Produced by Roy. Executive producers, Esther Freifeld, Earl Berman. Co-executive producer, Jeffrey Sudzin. Directed by John Flynn. Screenplay, Andrew Kevin Walker, story by Brian Owens. Camera (color), Francois Protat; editor, Jay Cassidy; music, George S. Clinton; production designer, Paola Ridolfi; sound (Dolby), Don Cohen; visual effects and character design, Rene Daalder; makeup effects, Steve Johnson, XFX Inc.; stunt coordinator, Dave McKeown; assistant director, Pedro Gandol. Reviewed at Cineplex Odeon Spectrum Cinema, Houston, April 19, 1994. MPAA rating: R. Running time: **95 MIN.**

Michael	Edward Furlong
Detective Hayden	Frank Langella
Trickster	T. Ryder Smith
Kimberly	Amy Hargreaves
Kyle	Jamie Marsh
Martin	Victor Ertmanis
Dr. Fromberg	David Hemblen

It's a rare teen horror pic that can be faulted for excessive restraint, but "Brainscan" may be too tame for the creature-feature fans and slasher devotees who will be drawn by its ad campaign. If Triumph can't get the word out that this is more of a feel-good date movie than a gross-out monster rally, distrib can expect a fast B.O. fade after fair-to-good openings in regional release. A similar marketing challenge will arise for homevid release.

Director John Flynn and scripter Andrew Kevin Walker clearly set out to establish a new horror franchise a la "Friday the 13th" and "A Nightmare on Elm Street." Just as clearly, they made a conscious decision to tone down the blood and guts, to make their pic more palatable to a wider audience. At least one murder takes place entirely offscreen, while two other deaths are relatively bloodless and entirely accidental.

In theory, such a novel approach to disreputable genre conventions might strike a responsive chord among moviegoers tired of the flood tide of violence in recent film fare. In practice, however, it's highly doubtful that anybody worried about movie violence would buy a ticket to something called "Brainscan" in the first place.

Edward Furlong of "Terminator 2" fame is well cast as Michael, a 16-year-old horror movie fan, computer whiz and social misfit whose mother died years ago and whose father spends too much time away on business. Michael is quick to respond when he sees an ad in Fangoria magazine for Brainscan, a CD-ROM interactive virtual-reality game that promises to "interface with your unconscious." Unfortunately, this is one case of too much truth in advertising.

The Brainscan display on Michael's computer terminal hypnotizes him. While he's under, he dreams of brutally stabbing a total stranger, then slicing off the dead man's foot, all of which reps the pic's only concession to gore hounds. But when he wakes up, he finds it wasn't really a dream — and the amputated foot is in his refrigerator.

Enter Trickster (T. Ryder Smith), a sardonic bogeyman who looks and dresses like a really ugly '80s glam rocker (imagine Adam Ant in a Halloween mask). Trickster pops out of Michael's computer and warns the teen that the games have only just begun. If Michael wants to cover his tracks and stay a few steps ahead of an inquisitive cop (Frank Langella), he will have to play by Trickster's rules. And rule No. 1 is that Michael must keep playing new Brainscan CDs, for one living nightmare after another.

Once the first murder is out of the way, film becomes an exceedingly tame, only sporadically exciting thriller. The most elaborate special effects are saved until the end, when Michael is literally swallowed up by

Trickster while the computer-generated gremlin tries to make Michael kill a pretty classmate (Amy Hargreaves) who lives nearby and hasn't been too careful about closing her curtains while undressing.

Most of the time, "Brainscan" resembles nothing so much as an undistinguished made-for-cable pic that fails to make the most of a promising high-concept premise. Filmmakers don't even provide enough good wisecracks for Trickster, who comes across like Freddy Krueger Lite. Wrap-up is surprisingly sunny, suggesting that "Brainscan" might have worked better as a segment of Nickelodeon's "Are You Afraid of the Dark?"

Furlong gives a solid and sympathetic performance as Michael. Langella plays it perfectly straight, which works. Smith plays Trickster as a jaded rock star from hell, which works even better. Hargreaves looks and sounds a lot more like the girl next door than actresses in her type of role usually do in this type of movie. Jamie Marsh is aptly Beavis-and-Butt-Headed as Furlong's only friend, a fellow horror movie fan.

Rene Daalder's visual effects and Steve Johnson's makeup effects are everything they need to be. A good thing, too, because that may partially appease horror buffs disappointed by the pic's small body count. Other tech credits are adequate.
                                                    —*Joe Leydon*

SURVIVING THE GAME

A New Line Cinema release of a New Line production in association with David Permut Prods. Produced by Permut. Executive producer, Kevin J. Messick. Co-producer, Fred Caruso. Directed by Ernest Dickerson. Screenplay, Eric Bernt. Camera (Deluxe color), Bojan Bazelli; editor, Sam Pollard; music, Stewart Copeland; production design, Christiaan Wagener; art direction, Madelyne Marcom; set decoration, George Toomer Jr.; costume design, Ruth Carter; sound (Dolby), Felipe Borrero; assistant director, Randy Fletcher; stunt coordinator, Bob Minor; casting, Jodi Rothfield, Katie Ryan. Reviewed at the UA Theater, L.A., April 15, 1994. MPAA Rating: R. Running time: **96 MIN.**

Mason	Ice-T
Burns	Rutger Hauer
Cole	Charles S. Dutton
Hawkins	Gary Busey
Wolfe Sr.	F. Murray Abraham
Griffin	John C. McGinley
Wolfe Jr.	William McNamara
Hank	Jeff Corey

Cinematographer Ernest Dickerson doesn't live up to the promise of his directing debut, "Juice," with this threadbare chase movie, which almost makes surviving the screening its own endurance test. Top-flight cast and pretty outdoor images

can't overcome the pic's many deficiencies, and flat action sequences should leave even genre predators unsatisfied.

Eric Bernt's first produced screenplay is inspired by Richard Connell's short story "The Most Dangerous Game," which has been the basis, both officially and unofficially, for previous features, including John Woo's "Hard Target" just last year. But the script meanders aimlessly — and far too leisurely — through this familiar terrain, and Dickerson seems too preoccupied with gauzy lighting to rev up the action.

Ice-T plays a homeless man, Mason, tapped by a group of hunters to lead them on a Pacific Northwest expedition only to discover that he, in fact, is to be their prey.

The six sportsmen include former CIA operatives (Rutger Hauer, Charles S. Dutton, Gary Busey) who seek out the hunt as recreation, as well as a lanky Texan (John C. McGinley) and a Wall Street tycoon (F. Murray Abraham) who brings along his reluctant son (William McNamara) for a sort of rite of manhood.

Cut loose with a brief head start reminiscent of "The Naked Prey," Mason proves surprisingly resourceful, quickly turning the tables on his pursuers — armed with high-powered rifles — in this bucolic game of cat and mouse.

All this would be more compelling if we knew more about Mason or, for that matter, the hunters. The movie takes more than 30 minutes before it gets into the actual hunt, but all we really learn about the protagonist is that he lost his family and likes stray dogs.

The movie is equally non-commital when it comes to political overtones, other than the wealthy hunters' obvious disdain for the homeless, whom they've preyed upon before. Thankfully, considering the premise, race isn't made an issue.

While there's some lovely photography of the setting, Dickerson doesn't bring any flair or ingenuity to the action sequences. Certain choices are baffling, including a chase through the woods so dark as to be virtually indecipherable that quickly bursts into broad daylight.

Uninspired dialogue doesn't help define any of these characters. Ice-T projects a properly defiant stance, but, through no fault of his, the audience doesn't know anything more about him at the end than they did when the movie started.

The bad guys, meanwhile, are either too over the top or not crazy enough — the exception being a wild-eyed Busey, who provides a rare moment of amusing gallows humor.

Tech credits are uneven, from Stewart Copeland's bizarre score to the special effects, which include one especially gory shot that would be revolting if it weren't so cheesy.

Pic also ends rather abruptly, though it's doubtful anyone will be disappointed when this "Game" is over.
                                                    —*Brian Lowry*

SIOUX CITY

A Cabin Fever Films presentation in association with Facet Films Inc. of a Rix-Ubell production. Produced by Brian Rix, Jane Ubell. Executive producers, Jeff Lawenda, H. Daniel Gross. Directed by Lou Diamond Phillips. Screenplay, L. Virginia Browne. Camera (FotoKem color), James W. Wrenn; editors, Christopher Rouse, Mark Fitzgerald; music, Christopher Lindsey; production design, Rando Schmook; sound (Ultra Stereo), Geoffrey Lucius Patterson; assistant director, Jim Goldthwait. Reviewed at WorldFest/Houston Intl. Film Festival, April 17, 1994. Running time: **100 MIN.**

Jesse Rainfeather Goldman	Lou Diamond Phillips
Chief Drew McDermott	Ralph Waite
Leah Goldman	Melinda Dillon
Jolene	Salli Richardson
Blake Goldman	Adam Roarke
Dan Larkin	Bill Allen
Russell Baker	Gary Farmer
Clifford	Apesanahkwat

Debut theatrical project for Cabin Fever Films is an undistinguished mystery-thriller that's criminally short on mystery and thrills. "Sioux City" will work best as product for company's homevid arm, with Lou Diamond Phillips providing the vid-store equivalent of marquee allure.

Phillips serves as director here, after performing similar double duty for Trimark's "Dangerous Touch." He does a serviceable job on both sides of the camera, but even a seasoned helmer would have a hard time making anything special from L. Virginia Browne's hackneyed and awkwardly contrived script.

Story focuses on Jesse Rainfeather Goldman (Phillips), a Lakota Indian who was adopted in early childhood by a BevHills Jewish couple (Melinda Dillon, Adam Roarke). He has grown up to be a cocksure intern who knows little about Native American ways. But he gets a crash course in multiculturalism when he receives an amulet from his biological mother, who lives on a reservation in Sioux City.

Eager to learn why she has contacted him after so many years, Jesse drives to Sioux City. But he's too late — when he arrives, he's told his mother died in a house fire. Jesse uncovers evidence that his mother was shot before her body was burned. He investigates a little more and incurs the wrath of the local police captain (Ralph Waite) and his junior officer (Bill Allen).

Jesse is brutally beaten and left for dead. But his grandfather, a medicine man named Clifford (Apesanahkwat), and a beautiful Lakota woman (Salli Richardson) nurse him back to health. Once recovered, Jesse immerses himself in Lakota customs and contacts the spirit of his mother. This leads to a climax that will neither surprise nor satisfy anyone.

To give Phillips and Browne credit, they don't fall into the trap of making all palefaces villainous bigots or cultural imperialists. Pic is particularly respectful of Jesse's parents, characters who could easily have been turned into selfish, insensitive clods or worse. The drawn-out ending suggests some serious thought went into finding a way to allow Jesse some hope of reconciling his allegiances to two cultures.

Except for Dillon and Roarke, who make the most of what little they get to do, supporting perfs range from stiffly sincere (Richardson, Apesanahkwat) to overbearingly obvious (Waite, Allen). Tech values are average. —*Joe Leydon*

PLUGHEAD REWIRED: CIRCUITRY MAN II

A Trans Atlantic Entertainment and I.R.S. media presentation. Produced by Steven Reich. Executive producers: Robert M. Bennett, Paul Colichman, Miles Copeland III, Paul Rich. Line producer, John Schouweiler. Directed, written by Steven Lovy, Robert Lovy. Camera (Foto-Kem color), Stephen Timberlake; editor, David Dresher; music, Tim Kelly; production design, Robert Lovy; art direction, Brian F. McCabe; sound (Ultra-Stereo), Patrick M. Griffith; special effects makeup, Sota Effects; special visual effects, Anthony Doublin; assistant director, Jeanine Rohn; casting, Donald Paul Pemric. Reviewed at WorldFest/Houston Intl. Film Festival, April 16, 1994. Running time: **98 MIN.**

Plughead	Vernon Wells
Kyle	Deborah Shelton
Danner	Jim Metzler
Leech	Dennis Christopher
Rock	Nicholas Worth
Norma	Traci Lords
Beany	Paul Willson
Squaid	Andy Goldberg
Guru	Tom Kenny
Senator Riley	George Murdock

"Plughead Rewired: Circuitry Man II" is a silly and self-indulgent sequel to a 1989 sci-fi adventure that was no great shakes in the first place. Pic appears destined for minimal theatrical exposure, though it may enjoy some shelf life as a homevid cult item.

Filmmaking brothers Steven and Robert Lovy once again offer their cheesy-looking vision of a future world where pollution has made the air all but unbreathable, most humans dwell in underground cities, and computer chips have replaced drugs as a source of cheap thrills.

Plughead (Vernon Wells), the haughty bad guy from the first "Circuitry Man," returns with a new chip that's guaranteed to extend human life by 10 years.

The manufacturing process requires torturing innocent victims to death, but Plughead does not view this as a problem. Rather, it's his way of mixing pleasure with business.

Also returning from the original is Danner, the suicidal romantic played by Jim Metzler. Like Plughead, Danner is a "biosynthetic" creature. Unlike Plughead, he's a good guy. He's also much more handsome and has many fewer plug holes in his head.

Danner is drafted by a renegade FBI agent (Deborah Shelton) to help her track down Plughead. Their journey takes them to a desert wasteland that looks just like the desert wasteland in the previous movie. Obviously, the Lovy brothers don't want to tamper with a successful formula.

Very much like "Circuitry Man," "Plughead Rewired" has the fatuous and self-satisfied air of a project cobbled together by people with a misplaced regard for their own cleverness.

The sequel actually manages to be even more annoying with its slapdash mix of mock-serious romanticism, tongue-in-cheek violence, low-rent special effects and in-joke movie references.

The Plughead character gets more screen time in the sequel in an obvious attempt to create a cult villain like Freddy Krueger ("Nightmare on Elm Street") or Pinhead ("Hellraiser"). Wells plays the part with gleeful relish, indicating he may have an eye on future bookings at sci-fi conventions.

Metzler gives pic's best perf, if only because he's the only person onscreen who appears familiar with the concept of underplaying.

Dennis Christopher, another "Circuitry Man" alum, reprises his role as a seedy criminal aptly named Leech. This cannot be viewed as a good career move.

Shelton is strident and unappealing, although, unlike in "Circuitry Man," here she undrapes at times. Traci Lords keeps her clothes on as a scientist kidnapped by Plughead and forced to work on his life-extension chips.

Production values are pretty much what one might expect from a small-budget exploitation pic that's on the fast track to homevid.
—*Joe Leydon*

SEASON OF CHANGE

A Jaguar Pictures presentation of a Sterling Films/Jim Thomasson production. Produced by Charles Lippitz, Robin P. Murray, Robert Spiotta. Executive producers, Jim Thomasson, Zvika Wloch, Jeff Smith Jr. Coproducers, Charlene Campbell, Andy Cannon. Directed by Murray. Screenplay, Shirley Hillard. Camera (color), Steve Slocomb; editors, Alain Jakubowicz, Gerard Jakubowicz; music, Alby Potts; art direction, Bonnie Cannon; sound (Ultra-Stereo), Bob King; associate producers, Tree Many Feathers, Hillard; assistant director, Andy Cannon; casting, Andrea Stone Guttfreund, Laurel Smith. Reviewed at WorldFest/Houston Intl. Film Festival, April 16, 1994. Running time: **98 MIN.**

Randy Parker	Michael Madsen
Sally Mae Parker	Nicholle Tom
Martha Parker	Jo Anderson
Big Upton	Hoyt Axton
Bobby	Ethan Randall

"Season of Change" is a tepid and slackly paced coming-of-age drama bound for quick homevid and pay TV playoff. Awkward direction, cliche-packed script and an ill-at-ease performance by the usually reliable Michael Madsen drag pic down like so much dead weight.

Set in rural Montana circa 1946, "Season" tells the story of 13-year-old Sally Mae Parker (Nicholle Tom of the "Beethoven" comedies), who can't help noticing the tension between her father (Madsen), a recently returned war vet, and her pregnant mother (Jo Anderson), a prudish Bible-thumper. Dad worries about finding a job to provide for his growing family. Sally worries about her blossoming womanhood and her growing attraction to a cocky teen mechanic (Ethan Randall). And mom worries whether both her daughter and her husband are hopelessly hell bound.

It doesn't take long for dad to seek comfort in the arms of a neighboring war widow. And it takes only a little longer for Sally to become aware of her father's adultery. In one of the pic's more unfortunate sequences, Sally finds her father's shirt covered with lipstick stains only slightly smaller than the numbers on a football jersey.

Pic is so ham-handedly obvious that it often becomes inadvertently funny. The low point comes when Sally tosses off the covers one morning to reveal a large blood stain on her sheets, and more blood dripping down her legs.

First-time feature helmer Robin Murray (a vet documentary and TV director) obviously means well, but he winds up turning a sensitive, even magical moment into something coarse.

Tom works hard at conveying sincerity and ebullience. Madsen spends most of his time looking like he wished he were elsewhere. Anderson is sporadically successful at conveying her character's inner anguish and vulnerability.

But the most winning performance comes from Hoyt Axton as Sally's easygoing grandfather. Fine period flavor comes through on what was obviously a limited budget. Steve Slocomb's attractive lensing of the Montana landscapes is another plus. —*Joe Leydon*

ISTANBUL FEST

MARIO, MARIA AND MARIO
(MARIO, MARIA E MARIO)
(ITALIAN-FRENCH)

A Massfilm, Studio El, Matopigia, Sacis (Italy)/Les Films Alain Sarde, Filmtel (France) production. (International sales: Sacis, Rome.) Produced by Franco Committeri, Luciano Ricceri. Directed by Ettore Scola. Screenplay, Ettore Scola, Silvia Scola. Camera (color), Luciano Tovoli; editor, Raimondo Crociani; music, Armando Trovajoli; art direction, Luciano Ricceri; sound, Paolo Venditti; assistant director, Franco Angeli. Reviewed at Istanbul Intl. Film Festival, April 12, 1994. Running time: **115 MIN.**

Mario Boschi	Giulio Scarpati
Maria Boschi	Valeria Cavalli
Mario Della Rocca	Enrico Lo Verso

With: Laura Betti, Willer Bordon, Maria De Rose, Rosa Ferraiolo, Mariangela Fremura.

Veteran Ettore Scola's first pic since his 1989 "What Time Is It?" is a watchable, well-turned, lightweight love-and-politics item centered on three young people affected by the new political atmosphere of post-Iron Curtain Europe. Lack of international star power and rather local subject matter may account for the 1993 release's slow journey

April 25, 1994 (Cont.)

offshore, though this shapes up as a solid item for fests and European TV sales.

Following the collapse of the Berlin Wall in the late '80s, Italy's Communist Party was dissolved and replaced by the softer leftist group, the PDS. Young Roman couple, Mario and Maria Boschi (Giulio Scarpati, Valeria Cavalli), party members since their teens, find cracks in their marriage develop into major fissures when he goes along with the changes and she sticks by her principles.

Enter Mario Della Rocca (Enrico Lo Verso), a party member from Sicily with similar ideas to Maria's. Though also married with a kid, Mario II fills a gap in Maria's increasingly empty life, and when Mario I goes off to a conference in Bologna the two begin a cautious romance.

Traumatized by her loss of one love and discovery of another, Maria falls sick and eventually moves in with her brother, as well as consummating her relationship with Mario II. Time passes, and at another local party meeting the trio, now each living alone, finally work out their personal and political problems.

Like the film's title, there's a slightly cute, over-engineered feel to the whole thing, with the convenient bookending by party meetings and with a coda showing the thirtysomethings as political "derelicts," an object of scorn by a younger generation of far-rightists.

Overall, however, the political content is more a hook for a good old relationships movie than a major component of the script. Characters spend more time worrying about their love lives than sitting around jawing about the end of East Eurostyle socialism, and the latter (as in the final party meeting) generally mirrors the pic's personal relationships rather than purely making political points.

Though occasionally overplaying her character's feyness, legit actress Cavalli, in her first major role, forms a fine female center of quiet strength. Scarpati and Lo Verso chime well in the pic's generally light dramatic key. Surrounding characters, such as two feuding older Communists, satisfyingly bulk out the pivotal players.

Tech credits are pro throughout, with gentle, melodious scoring by Armando Trovajoli and unforced lensing by Luciano Tovoli.

—*Derek Elley*

AN AUTUMN STORY
(BIR SONBAHAR HIKAYESI)
(TURKISH)

A Z Film production. (International sales: Z Film, Istanbul.) Produced by Aycan Cetin. Directed, written by Yavuz Ozkan. Camera (color), Ertunc Senkay Kurgu; editor, Sedat Karadeniz. Reviewed at Istanbul Intl. Film Festival, April 15, 1994. Running time: 105 MIN.
With: Zuhal Olcay, Can Togay, Kaan Girgin, Meltem Cumbul, Sinem Uretmen.

A glossily lensed study of a disintegrating yuppie marriage, forged during Turkey's political tensions of 1978-81, "An Autumn Story" has the heart of a novella that even luminous playing by actress Zuhal Olcay can't disguise. Pic is an OK entry for film weeks, riding on director Yavuz Ozkan's rep for his previous "Two Women."

Olcay plays a 30-year-old college teacher who marries a slick, ambitious economics grad (Can Togay) as the country undergoes military takeover. After the birth of their child, it's downhill slowly, as Togay becomes a career-obsessed banker and soon takes a blonde on the side. Olcay, meanwhile, has a young male student making goo-goo eyes at her in class.

Main problem is accepting how Olcay's beautiful, level-headed prof sticks with such a self-centered smoothie instead of booting him out by reel three. Though Ozkan's script implicitly links the hollowness of the marriage to early-'80s political developments, the parallel isn't sufficiently developed to conquer the familiar *cine-roman* content.

—*Derek Elley*

BLOCK C
(C BLOK)
(TURKISH)

A Mavi Film production. (International sales: Mavi Film, Istanbul.) Produced, directed, written by Zeki Demirkubuz. Camera (color), Ertunc Senkay; editor, Nevzat Disiacik; music, Serdar Keskin. Reviewed at Istanbul Intl. Film Festival, April 12, 1994. Running time: 93 MIN.
With: Fikret Kuskan, Serap Aksoy, Zuhal Gencer, Selcuk Yontem, Ulku Duru.

Metaphysics run riot in "Block C," a posed but strangely watchable slice of femme alienation that's strongly Gallic in flavor. Feature bow of Zeki Demirkubuz, former assistant to director Zeki Okten,

---

shows *beaucoup* style but less in the substance department.

Title refers to the smart new apartment block in which Tulay, chic resident of No. 16, is in the final lap of her marriage to couch potato Selim. Finding her lively maid in the sack one day with janitor's son Halet, Tulay starts to come apart at the seams.

Though fancy crosscutting blurs the structure, pic is mostly framed by heart-to-heart chats between Tulay and her best friend, Fatos. Driving around town, she becomes an observer of her own life, eyeing young men, nearly getting raped by some youths and, finally, exchanging bodily juices with young Halet.

Ending has her striding out in a fresh start. Gliding through the film like a younger Anouk Aimee, Fikret Kuskan makes an always watchable Tulay, and helmer Demirkubuz juggles moods and wispy content with some skill. But repeated sequences of Kuskan in shades musing by the seashore, or gazing through rain-flecked windows, do not a substantial picture make.

Tech credits are smooth. For the record, the Turkish "C" is pronounced like the English "J."

—*Derek Elley*

A BOAT ANCHORED IN THE DESERT
(YOLCU)
(TURKISH)

A Belge Film, TRT production. (International sales: Belge Film, Istanbul.) Produced by Sabahattin Cetin. Directed by Basar Sabuncu. Screenplay, Sabuncu, from the play by Nazim Hikmet. Camera (color), Huseyin Ozsahin; editor, Aytug Aslan; art direction, Mete Yilmaz. Reviewed at Istanbul Intl. Film Festival, April 14, 1994. Running time: 102 MIN.
With: Tarik Akan, Mujde Ar, Halil Ergun, Berhan Simsek.

Fine performances and a strong script buoy "A Boat Anchored in the Desert," an atmospheric, Pinteresque drama set in a remote railroad station in eastern Turkey during the War of Independence. First film in several years by quality helmer Basar Sabuncu is flawed only by lax, over-forward post-synching of dialogue.

Movie is based on the two-act playlet "The Traveler" (Yolcu) by long-exiled writer Nazim Hikmet. Piece was written in 1941 in prison and first staged in 1963, shortly before his death.

Time is 1921, the place a whistle-stop Anatolian station at which trains bringing wounded back from the front never stop. Here, the cen-

---

tral trio of a dour stationmaster, his unsatisfied, scheming wife and a crippled switchman warily circle each other, looking for a way out. Arrival of a mysterious young soldier precipitates the breakup of the closed circle.

Helmer Sabuncu, also a legit director, seamlessly expands the hour play to feature length, with nifty use of limited interiors, simple but striking snowbound vistas, and direction that doesn't cramp his experienced cast. Veteran Tarik Akan is a model of contained frustration as the stationmaster; Mujde Ar, in the pivotal role of the dowdy but feisty wife, carries the pic. Tech credits are OK. —*Derek Elley*

DISINTEGRATION
(COZULMELER)
(TURKISH)

A Film F production. (International sales: Film F, Istanbul.) Produced by Dincer Sipahi. Directed, written by Yusuf Kurcenli, from a story by Cezmi Ersoz. Camera (color), Colin Mounier; editor, Ismail Kalkan; music, Arif Erkin; art direction, Serdar Gunbilen. Reviewed at Istanbul Intl. Film Festival, April 13, 1994. Running time: 103 MIN.
With: Tarik Akan, Nurseli Idiz, Savas Dincer, Tunca Yonder, Tomris Oguzalp, I. Hakki Sen, Duygu Ankara, Omer Colakoglu.

"Disintegration" is an OK relationships drama set against the political and social changes in '80s Turkey. More natural performances and characters put this a notch above the similarly themed "An Autumn Story" (also in this year's Istanbul fest), though background may baffle non-Turkish auds.

Central character, Ugur, an accountant by day and novelist by night, is trying to adjust to the new, market-oriented Turkey, in between divorcing his wife and living out of a hotel. Meanwhile, his longtime friendship with Nihal, wife of political prisoner buddy Kemal, blossoms into a love affair. The two finally decide to leave the country when it looks like Kemal may be released under a government amnesty.

Pic never delves too deep into the central quandary of a man in love with an imprisoned friend's wife, and director Yusuf Kurcenli's script assumes considerable knowledge by viewers of the political background to the main relationships. Memory flashbacks to Ugur's youth in an Islamic school are also puzzling.

Still, the movie is always watchable, especially thanks to Nurseli Idiz's nuanced perf as Nihal and several lively supporting characters. Technically, film is par, and pacing smooth. —*Derek Elley*

ONLY THE BRAVE

(ROMANCE DE VALENTIA)

(DUTCH-BRITISH — DOCU)

A Scorpio Film Prods. (U.K.)/VPRO-TV (Netherlands) co-production. Produced by Kees Rijninks. Directed, written by Sonia Herman Dolz. Camera (color), Ellen Kuras; editor, Andrez de Jong; music, Leo Anemaet. Reviewed at Rotterdam Intl. Film Festival, Feb. 2, 1994. Running time: **89 MIN.**
With: Enrique Ponce, Manuel Tornay, Juan Antonio Maguilla, Jose Sanchez, Antonio Novillo.
(Spanish soundtrack)

"**O**nly the Brave" examines bullfighting as a phenomenon lying somewhere between art, sport, cultural tradition and religious doctrine. Filmmaker Sonia Herman Dolz refrains from directly entering the debate over blood sports, maintaining a cool critical distance and refusing to glorify the *corrida*. Technically accomplished, free-flowing portrait is ideal for worldwide docu fests and TV slots.

Ostensibly an account of one triumphant summer (1992) in the career of 20-year-old matador Enrique Ponce, the film's focus casually fans out to explore components of charisma, artistry, courage, discipline and an awareness of mortality considered fundamental to a worthy torero's formation.

Herman Dolz presents these facets via an unconstrained stream of impressions that avoids didactic fact-feeding. The religious fervor permeating the practice is conveyed by intercutting between gored matadors, funerals, fatherly mentors, baptisms and bull-branding, using both new and archival footage.

Ponce is placed under the spotlight only gradually, as part demigod, part kid next door, and bullfight scenes are an even longer time coming.

But even when the fiery clashes appear, director plays down the crowd's excitement to concentrate on Ponce's balletic turns in the ring. Spectator participation is cranked low under Leo Anemaet's dramatically restrained music, adding to a depiction of the sport that's more psychological than spectacular.

The film's final ring sequence (played as Ponce's ultimate ascension to greatness) is a fierce fight against a bull considered such a noble, determined opponent that the matador spares its life, winning resounding respect from the crowd.

Running parallel to coverage of the torero's dedication are the reflections of bull breeders, who appear even more obsessive in their pursuit of excellence. But their attempts to justify the carnage as an emotional and spiritual reward to the audience are unlikely to sway

detractors and represent the docu's only repetitive element.
—*David Rooney*

THE YEAR OF THE DOG

(GOD SOBAKI)

(RUSSIAN-FRENCH)

A Kinodokument, Lenfilm, Studio Golos (St. Petersburg), Roskomkino (Moscow)/Sodaperaga (Paris) production. (International sales: Sodaperaga, Paris.) Produced by Semyon Aranovich, Frishetta Gukasyan, Vyacheslav Telnov, Guy Seligman. Directed by Aranovich. Screenplay, Aranovich, Albina Shulgina, Vadim Mikhailov, Zoya Kudrya. Camera (color), Yuri Shaigardanov; editor, Tamara Gusevaya; music, Oleg Karavaichuk; art direction, Marksen Gauchman-Sverdlov. Reviewed at Berlin Film Festival (competing), Feb. 19, 1994. Running time: **132 MIN.**
Vera Morozova .... Inna Churikova
Seryozha .... Igor Sklyar
Also with: Aleksandr Feklistov (Lobanov), Mikhail Dorofeyev (Nikolai Ivanovich), Sergei Bobrov (Kuzya), Gennadi Menshchikov (Nikolai), Era Ziganshchina (Mother), Valentina Kovel (Grandmother).

"**T**he Year of the Dog" starts as an offbeat, odd-couple black comedy, takes a left into Slavic philosophizing and just keeps going. Often likable but finally wearing, film scrapes by on the charms of its lead duo but is too distended to raise much of a ruckus outside the fest pound.

Seryozha (Igor Sklyar) is a brash young ex-con who hooks up with shy, middle-aged Vera (Inna Churikova) after stealing her purse on his way home from jail.

Things start humming when Seryozha casually stabs her hostel warden during an argument. After fleeing on a train, they find themselves in a deserted village, realizing only too late that they've wandered into a radioactive-contaminated area.

Tone becomes darker as the pair seem to accept their fate and set up house. When three marauders pass by, Seryozha locks them up in the village jail, tortures them and then releases them after they've formed a loose camaraderie.

Central theme of two loners thrown together by circumstances comes over clear enough, but the pic's flimsy structure starts to creak during the second half under the weight of philosophizing and gabby, uninteresting dialogue.

Still, Churikova, always a highly watchable actress, is excellent as the slightly kooky, cautious spinster, and there's an undercurrent of sadness to her portrayal that could have been better exploited with a tighter script. Sklyar is also very good as the half-charmer Seryozha, whose hidden demons always lurk just beneath the surface.

Tech credits are OK, with a loose style of filming that matches the script.
—*Derek Elley*

THE DECLINE OF THE CENTURY: TESTAMENT L.Z.

(ZALAZAK STOLJECA: TESTAMENT L.Z.)

(CZECH-FRENCH-CROATIAN-AUSTRIAN — DOCU)

A Czech Television/Constellation/ Croatian Television/Sinex production. (International sales: Constellation Prods., Paris.) Directed by Lordan Zafranovic. Written by Zafranovic, Vojdrag Bercic. Camera (color/b&w), Andrija Pivcevic, Branko Janklin; editing, Ivica Drnic, Ljuba Djurkoviceva, Jan Daniel; voiceover, Zafranovic. Reviewed at Berlin Film Festival (Forum section), Feb. 13, 1994. Running time: **201 MIN.**

A seven-year project that uses smashing black-and-white archival footage to illustrate the rise and fall of the Nazi government that ruled Croatia from 1941-45, "The Decline of the Century" unfortunately falls into the trap of director Lordan Zafranovic's own vanity.

Croatian helmer, one of the most noted directors in the former Yugoslavia, interweaves these historical records with far too many excerpts from his own films from the 1960s-1980s, as well as gratuitous inserts of himself mulling over the project. Ultimate impression is of a retrospective of clips from his own works, with old newsreels providing validation for his insights.

Cop-out epilogue that refuses to take a stand on the contempo situation lessens pic's urgency. Commercial prospects are nil, but TV slots in some areas seem likely.

Footage of war-crimes trial of former Croatian Nazi Interior Minister Andrija Artukovic, who was extradited from California in 1986, provides a fascinating anchor to the wealth of material.

To his credit, helmer never backs off from subject of Croatian collaboration with the Nazis, and footage of Croats in Zagreb warmly greeting the Germans offers proof. Now Paris-based, Zafranovic addresses present-day conflicts in the former Yugoslavia through a montage of TV news clips of anonymous bodies and destruction, essentially moaning over the atrocities without analyzing them or those responsible.
—*Howard Feinstein*

THE CROW

A Miramax/Dimension Films release, presented in association with Entertainment Media Investment Corp., of an Edward R. Pressman production in association with Jeff Most Prods. Produced by Pressman, Most. Executive producer, Robert L. Rosen. Co-producers, Caldecot Chubb, James A. Janowitz. Directed by Alex Proyas. Screenplay, David J. Schow, John Shirley, based on the comic book series and comic strip by James O'Barr. Camera (Deluxe color), Dariusz Wolski; editors, Dov Hoenig, Scott Smith; music, Graeme Revell; production design, Alex Mc-Dowell; art direction, Simon Murton; set design, William Barcley; set decoration, Marthe Pineau; costume design, Arianne Phillips; sound (Dolby), Buddy Alper; visual effects supervisor/second unit director, Andrew Mason; special makeup effects artist, Lance Anderson; stunt coordinator, Jeff Imada; miniature photography, Dream Quest Images; associate producers, Gregory A. Gale, Grant Hill; assistant director, Steve Andrews; casting, Billy Hopkins, Suzanne Smith. Reviewed at the Aidikoff Screening Room, Beverly Hills, April 27, 1994. MPAA Rating: R. Running time: **100 MIN.**
Eric Draven .... Brandon Lee
Albrecht .... Ernie Hudson
Top Dollar .... Michael Wincott
T-Bird .... David Patrick Kelly
Skank .... Angel David
Sarah .... Rochelle Davis
Myca .... Bai Ling
Tin Tin .... Lawrence Mason
Funboy .... Michael Massee
Mickey .... Bill Raymond
Torres .... Marco Rodriguez
Shelly .... Sofia Shinas
Darla .... Anna Thomson
Grange .... Tony Todd
Gideon .... Jon Polito

"**T**he Crow" flies high. For a while rumored to be impossible to complete due to the tragic accidental death of star Brandon Lee eight days before lensing was due to wrap, the pic that finally emerges is a seamless, pulsating, dazzlingly visual revenge fantasy that stands as one of the most effective live-actioners derived from a comic strip.

Despite a simplistic script that unfortunately brandishes its cartoon origins rather too obviously, the combo of edgy excitement, stunning design, hot soundtrack and curiosity about Lee will rep an irresistible lure to young audiences in large numbers, giving this very strong commercial wings. As far as Miramax/Dimension is concerned, it's too bad the film isn't moving into the marketplace right now, rather than on May 11, since there's absolutely nothing out there that could compete with it.

Based on James O'Barr's bold comic strip, which has generated a considerable following since he started drawing it in the early 1980s, "The Crow" centers on a

May 2, 1994 (Cont.)

dark angel who literally rises from the dead to settle matters with the gang of thugs who killed him and his fiancee on the eve of their wedding. Tale is more pungent than poignant, however, in that it's set in a generic inner city so hellish it makes Gotham City look like the Emerald City.

Noted Aussie commercials and musicvideo helmer Alex Proyas drenches his debut Yank feature in a claustrophobic, rain-soaked atmosphere that owes more than a little to "Blade Runner," but pic still generates a distinctive personality due to its aggressive narrative vigor, agreeable mixture of sweetness and nastiness, and a technical mastery that ranges from the highly efficient to the inspired.

Tour de force opening brings the viewer in for a slow landing over a bleak urban landscape blighted by fires on Devil's Night, Halloween Eve. The Crow, a girl's narration informs, transports souls to the land of the dead, but if a crime was so heinous that the soul can't rest, the Crow can sometimes bring it back.

That's all the explanation needed for the rebirth, a year later, of Eric Draven (Lee), who, as is shown in brilliant, violent flashes of montage, was murdered by a bunch of drooling hooligans who then raped and mortally injured his bride-to-be. A rock musician by trade (O'Barr patterned his character design on Iggy Pop and Bauhaus' Peter Murphy, while Lee shed pounds to resemble Black Crowes lead singer Chris Robinson), Eric gradually realizes what happened to him, and is led, one by one, to his vile assailants by a large crow that flaps above the desolate streets like a mythic bearer of dread tidings.

Like Robert Patrick's T-1000 in "Terminator 2," Eric recoils from gunshots but instantly heals, lending him plenty of chutzpah in dealing with the baddies. He dispatches them in increasingly imaginative fashion, impaling one with multiple syringes and strapping another with tape into a car that becomes a speeding time bomb. He finally gets to the bottom of things when he bursts in on a crime conference convened by ultimate heavy Top Dollar (Michael Wincott), precipitating an enormously Gothic climax atop an abandoned cathedral.

Pic's main problem is an exceedingly straight, A-B-C-D narrative line with no subplots, twists or turns, which even Proyas' protean direction can't keep comfortably aloft the entire time. Banter and nasty repartee could also have been sharpened up and made more humorous, and some anti-drug and anti-smoking sops seem wimpy in context.

But film creates one of the most imaginatively rendered, impressively sustained artificial worlds seen on film in some time, and the action is riveting to behold. Working extensively with miniatures as well as on existing studio sets in Wilmington, N.C., vet video production designer Alex McDowell has devised a staggering look for the bombed-out cityscape.

McDowell, Proyas, ace lenser Dariusz Wolski ("Romeo Is Bleeding") and costume designer Arianne Phillips have carefully calculated a shadowy, color-drained environment, melding their contributions into a vision worthy of a single visual artist. Special effects, particularly those involving the flying crow, are outstanding (overhead shots taken from behind the bird looking down on the city are particularly breathtaking). Film is entirely nocturnal, save for a brief respite an hour in.

But certainly much of the attention here will rightly focus upon Brandon Lee. The 28-year-old son of the late Bruce Lee had not had a very distinguished career up until this, but there's no doubt that this role would have made him a performer to reckon with, and perhaps a star. His striking looks, sinuous presence and agile moves lock one's attention, and the painful irony of his role as a dead man returning from the grave will not go unnoticed. (The more morbid will concentrate on the flashback shooting scene in which Lee was fatally wounded.)

Most supporting thesps enjoyably seem to be competing for who can be the meanest, nastiest, scummiest villain. Graeme Revell's outstanding, moody score is supplemented by more than a dozen edgy rock songs that promise a fine soundtrack.

A sequel would have seemed like a foregone conclusion. But, so sadly, it would be missing this film's central presence, Brandon Lee. Film is dedicated to him and his fiancee, Eliza.

—*Todd McCarthy*

PCU

A 20th Century Fox release of a Paul Schiff production. Produced by Schiff. Co-producer, Barry Sabath. Directed by Hart Bochner. Screenplay, Adam Leff, Zak Penn. Camera (Deluxe color), Reynaldo Villalobos; editor, Nicholas C. Smith; music, Steve Vai; executive music producer, Ralph Sall; production design, Steven Jordan; art direction, David M. Davis; set decoration, Enrico Campana; costume design, Mary Zophres; sound (Dolby), David Lee; assistant director, Martin Walters; casting, Margery Simkin. Reviewed at 20th Century Fox screening room, L.A., April 27, 1994. MPAA Rating: PG-13. Running time: **79 MIN.**

Droz	Jeremy Piven
Tom	Chris Young
Gutter	Jon Favreau
Rand McPherson	David Spade
Samantha	Sarah Trigger
Mersh	Jake Busey
Garcia-Thompson	Jessica Walter
George Clinton	Himself

Screenwriters Adam Leff and Zak Penn, who garnered some notoriety last year for providing the story for "Last Action Hero," have concocted a rowdy new comedy, "PCU," that's a boisterous if not uproariously funny look at political correctness as it afflicts college campuses today. Though insufficiently stinging, this timely satire could rise above modest B.O. expectations if it connects significantly with the generational group that is its subject.

Leff and Penn have set their yarn at the fictional Port Chester University, no doubt standing in for Wesleyan, their alma mater. It's a campus divided into so many protest groups that students have no time to attend classes. At the center is a coed gang whose anarchic leader, Droz (Jeremy Piven), encourages any form of offensive and bizarre behavior. The gang resides at the Pit, a vibrantly messy dorm that embraces smoking and drinking and dismisses recycling and sympathy for murdered animals.

Into this chaos arrives Tom (Chris Young), a handsome prefreshman totally unprepared for life on the treacherous campus, which is torn apart by Rand ("Saturday Night Live's" David Spade), a spoiled brat who leads the wealthy Republican fraternity; the Womynists, headed by a humorless feminist, and other militant clubs.

Despite diverse causes, however, all factions are united in their hatred of the Pit and their wish to shut it down. And few people on campus, including the board of trustees, can tolerate the stuffy, rigid president (Jessica Walter), who eventually gets her comeuppance during the school's bicentennial ceremonies.

True to form, "PCU" dispenses an exaggerated view of college culture but also reveals a sensitive ear to its current lingo and ambiance. For instance, the feminists, outraged at a student who dared to bed a white male, protest against "penis parties" and demand to be called women instead of girls. Most of the jokes, however, are rather mild.

"PCU" tries to capture the comic energy and surreal fun that pix like "House Party" and "National Lampoon's Animal House" had. But despite some memorable vignettes, the film's climax, a huge party in which George Clinton and Parliament Funkadelic perform, is not very satisfying. Unfortunately, the pranks don't match composer Steve Vai's resourceful and boisterous music.

In his feature directorial debut, Hart Bochner shows some visual flair and a sense of tempo. But whenever pic dawdles, he tries to increase its vitality by inserting chases or scenes of characters running around. Production values are first-rate, particularly Reynaldo Villalobos' snappy lensing.

Most of the ensemble cast is pleasant enough. In the lead, however, Piven lacks the wild charisma of a John Belushi. As the naive youngster, Young wears the same wide-eyed, open-mouthed expression throughout.

Political correctness is such a natural target for satire, it's surprising that it has taken so long to hit the bigscreen. At the same time, given the issue's extensive media coverage, it wouldn't have been too much to expect "PCU" to cut with a sharper and nastier edge.

—*Emanuel Levy*

THE FAVOR

An Orion Pictures release of a Nelson Entertainment presentation. Produced by Lauren Shuler-Donner. Executive producers, Barry Spikings, Rick Finkelstein, Donna Dubrow. Directed by Donald Petrie. Screenplay, Sara Parriott, Josann McGibbon. Camera (Deluxe color), Tim Suhrstedt; editor, Harry Keramidas; music, Thomas Newman; production design, David Chapman; art direction, Mark Haack; costume design, Carol Oditz; sound (Dolby), Stephan Von Hase; assistant director, Marty Elcan; casting, Bonnie Timmerman. Reviewed at the Orion Screening Room, L.A., April 18, 1994. MPAA Rating: R. Running time: **97 MIN.**

Kathy Whiting	Harley Jane Kozak
Emily Embrey	Elizabeth McGovern
Peter Whiting	Bill Pullman
Elliott Fowler	Brad Pitt
Tom Andrews	Ken Wahl
Joe Dubin	Larry Miller
Maggie Sand	Holland Taylor

The premise of "The Favor" recalls the insouciance of some great French moral comedies, but the unfunny moral of this story is, it won't recall many to the B.O.

An almost happily married woman relieves the tedium of her oh-so-perfect marriage and family with somewhat wild fantasies of love-making with her hunky high school beau. But when the prospect of fulfilling that fantasy looms at an upcoming class reunion, the woman opts for a safe-sex solution. She enlists a single friend to do the deed and report back the results.

This is delicate material, and, unfortunately, it's executed by comparative barbarians. The banter makes Neil Simon seem sophisticated. The direction and technical elements are obvious, bright and vapid, while the performers struggle against staggering odds to pro-

May 2, 1994 (Cont.)

vide nuance. Added together, the prospects don't amount to much theatrically or in subsequent exploitation.

Kathy Whiting (Harley Jane Kozak) is the mother of two young girls who's married to Peter (Bill Pullman), a college science professor/researcher. Her life is cozy but downright dull.

In contrast, her best friend, Emily (Elizabeth McGovern), lives a swinging life. Her sometime boyfriend Elliott (Brad Pitt) is a visual artist, and Em is constantly jetting off to places exotic — like Cleveland — on business.

The wild abandon of her friend is what prompts Kathy's proposition. When Emily goes to Denver for a trade show, she is to take Tom (Ken Wahl) — the unconsummated love of Kathy's past — to dinner and bed.

The mission is only partially accomplished. The offscreen union is a success, but the bad news (for Kathy) is that the reality more than lives up to the long-smoldering fantasy.

Sara Parriott and Josann McGibbon's screenplay is like a good joke ineptly related. Somehow the punchline has been positioned in the middle of the story, and all that follows is excess baggage. With the focus obscured, the tale dissolves into a series of non sequiturs that include Emily's unwanted pregnancy and the prospect that Kathy might just want to verify Tom's sexual report card.

The performers barely manage to slink through with their dignity. They, rather than director Donald Petrie, provide whatever shadings "The Favor" has to offer. This is one of those rare instances where the shock troops were sent in and survived, albeit with copious scarring.

Held up in Orion's narrow escape from corporate death, the film, of two-years-plus vintage, has not aged like fine wine. Still, it would be futile to argue that the passage of time is the primary problem of this production. Rather, its fiber is intrinsically threadbare.

Of some interest, though, is the arrival of a third Elwes brother in the credits (following actor Carey and producer Cassian). Damian Elwes is the painter of the work Pitt's character creates.

—*Leonard Klady*

NO ESCAPE

A Savoy Pictures release in association with Allied Filmmakers of a Pacific Western production. Produced by Gale Anne Hurd. Executive producer, Jake Eberts. Co-producers, Michael R. Joyce, James Eastep. Directed by Martin Campbell. Screenplay, Michael Gaylin, Joel Gross, based on Richard Herley's book "The Penal Colony." Camera (color), Phil Meheux; editor, Terry Rawlings; music, Graeme Revell; production design, Allan Cameron; art direction, Ian Gracie; set decoration, Lesley Crawford; costume design, Norma Moriceau; sound (Dolby), Ben Osmo; assistant director, Colin Fletcher; stunt coordinator, Conrad E. Palmisano; casting, Pam Dixon Mickelson. Reviewed at the Aidikoff screening room, Beverly Hills, April 20, 1994. MPAA Rating: R. Running time: **118 MIN.**

Robbins	Ray Liotta
The Father	Lance Henriksen
Marek	Stuart Wilson
Casey	Kevin Dillon
King	Ian McNeice
Dysart	Jack Shepherd
Warden	Michael Lerner
Hawkins	Ernie Hudson

Impressive production values can't redeem the senseless plot of "No Escape," a synthetic pastiche of sci-fi actioners a la the Mad Max films and Hollywood prison dramas. Incoherent mix of genre conventions, dearth of big-name stars and absence of female characters should make the appeal of this mishmash less universal than it might have been. But with the only actioner currently in the movie market, Savoy should take a nibble at the B.O. with the support of younger male action aficionados.

Set in 2022, saga begins in a maximum-security, high-tech prison, where a ruthless warden (Michael Lerner) tortures Robbins (Ray Liotta), a Marine captain convicted of murdering his commanding officer. Robbins is then sent to Absolom, a hidden jungle where the most dangerous inmates are left to die.

On the island, he encounters its two resident but antagonistic communities: the Outsiders, an anarchic group of savages led by Marek (Stuart Wilson), and the Insiders, peaceful colonists whose leader is a compassionate man who calls himself the Father (Lance Henriksen).

After some brutally nasty battles with Marek, the wounded Robbins somehow manages to escape to the Insiders, where he finds a home. Unfortunately, once he lands there, the adventure settles into a moralistic tale of renewal and redemption, with occasional bursts of mechanically engineered violence.

Following the tradition of prison yarns, scripters Michael Gaylin and Joel Gross fashion a diverse group of inmates, including quiet but severe security chief Ernie Hudson, ingenious inventor Jack Shepherd and Ian McNeice, who's in charge of the members' well-being. There's also a subplot concerning male camaraderie, replete with homoerotic overtones, between a young, immature prisoner (Kevin Dillon) and Liotta as his charismatic role model.

Director Martin Campbell, who previously made the disappointing thriller "Defenseless," doesn't furnish his film with the verve, high-strung pace and tension to elevate it above a standard prison-camp escape yarn. Pic is constructed with enough calculation to build a computer, but the story lacks credibility and a meaningful political context.

For an actioner, there are too many lingering close-ups of Liotta's beautiful blue eyes, long shots of the ocean and vast silences.

Liotta makes a valiant effort as the tough but sensitive Marine. But while it's refreshing to see an action hero not in the comic-strip mold of Stallone or Schwarzenegger, Liotta is not very commanding.

As the heavy, Wilson goes for the cynical, malevolent humor that works well for Alan Rickman, but the writing doesn't support his ambition. The rest of the gifted ensemble play stock characters, each marked by one personality trait.

Tech credits are proficient, particularly Phil Meheux's Aussie-location lensing and Allan Cameron's production design of the ultra-electronic prison and primitive colony. But overall, pic is not on a par with producer Gale Anne Hurd's previous genre efforts, like "Alien" and "Terminator."

"No Escape" has its fair share of gun-blazing mayhem and bloody fistfights, as well as some off-putting decapitations, but ultimately the futuristic, prison and action elements don't jell. End result is a hodgepodge with some good moments but no grip or dramatic excitement. —*Emanuel Levy*

BEYOND BEDLAM
(BRITISH)

A Feature Film Co. release (U.K.) of a Metrodome Films production. Produced by Paul Brooks. Executive producer, Alan Martin. Co-executive producers, Alec Georgiadis, Tony Georgiadis. Line producers, Tim Dennison, Jim Groom. Directed by Vadim Jean. Screenplay, Rob Walker, Jean, from the novel by Harry Adam Knight. Camera (Technicolor), Gavin Finney; editor, Liz Webber; music, David A. Hughes, John Murphy; production design, James Helps; art direction, Riette Hayes-Davies; costume design, Jayne Gregory; sound (Dolby), Richard Flynn; makeup, special prosthetics, Jacquetta; associate producer, Simon Brooks; assistant director, Helen Flint; casting, Carl Proctor. Reviewed at MGM Oxford Street 4 Theater, London, April 22, 1994. Running time: **88 MIN.**

Terry Hamilton	Craig Fairbrass
Stephanie Lyell	Elizabeth Hurley
Marc Gilmour	Keith Allen
Judith	Anita Dobson
Matthew Hamilton	Craig Kelly
Scott	Jesse Birdsall
Miss Coope	Faith Kent

Also with: Georgina Hale, Samantha Spiro, Stephen Brand, Zoe Heyes, Annette Badlund, Natasha Humphrey.

"Beyond Bedlam" is an ambitious Brit horror schlocker that seems to have mislaid its script halfway. Careening, often stylish meltdown of everything from Thomas Harris shavings to Elm Street and Clive Barker offshoots starts with a bang but trails off into a whimper as the pic abandons all logic in the second half. Genre nuts may want to check out this curio, but pic's longest lockup will be in the vid bin.

The movie's release on home turf ironically coincides with draconian new guidelines for homevideo enforced on Blighty's censors by politicians responding to a tabloid-led outcry against overly violent home viewing. Pic has had its temporary vid rating withdrawn by the British Board of Film Classification unless cuts are made to certain sequences. Theatrically, however, "Bedlam" uncut got an "18" — Britain's most restrictive rating.

Biggest surprise for auteurists is that the film, based on the novel by Harry Adam Knight ("Carnosaur"), emanates from the same producer/director team (Paul Brooks, Vadim Jean) as the cheeky 1992 low-budget comedy "Leon the Pig Farmer."

As self-professed members of the "multiplex generation," dedicated to making commercial rather than traditional Brit fare, producer Paul Brooks and director Vadim Jean, who co-scripted wtih Rob Walker, here essay solid genre territory, with decidedly mixed, sometimes comic results.

Slickly mounted opening reel has a doctor at a research institute,

May 2, 1994 (Cont.)

Stephanie Lyell (Elizabeth Hurley), injecting herself with a drug, and a man in a sleek apartment building experiencing hallucinations, jumping out a window and self-combusting on the way down. Cop on the case Terry Hamilton (Craig Fairbrass) is still haunted by a psycho he put away seven years ago — Gilmour, dubbed the Bone Man (Keith Allen), who happens to be the doctor's prize patient.

Stephanie has been testing a mind-calming drug, BFND, on herself for possible side effects, and feeding it to Gilmour. Result is some kind of dream transference into which Gilmour can tap, causing the deaths of people in his doctor's dreams.

In a long climax that takes up the whole of the picture's second half, Stephanie and Terry team up to take Gilmour out, working through the institute's labyrinthine corridors in between being menaced by hallucinations generated by the Bone Man in his cell.

If all that sounds like grade-A nonsense, the filmmakers, to their credit, never pretend otherwise. Shot largely in an abandoned sanitarium in north London, the $3 million production has an umbral, high-gloss visual style in its early going that cleverly relies on closeups and spare, lightly dressed settings.

Problems sprout like mushrooms on the way to the final showdown between hero and villain that relegates the supposedly spunky Stephanie to the sidelines and throws overboard the primary asset of Gilmour's character, his Hannibal Lecter-like mind control.

As the leering loon, Allen (gangster Jack Doyle in "The Young Americans") comes off best, if starved of dialogue to match his brain power. Hurley, briefly impressive as a terrorist in "Passenger 57," is photogenic but uneven, rarely living up to the sexy, daring doctor sketched in the opening. Fairbrass ("Prime Suspect," "Cliffhanger") is standard hunk as the cop, too often stranded by the thin script.

Tech credits are largely good given the limited budget, with some stylish lighting by d.p. Gavin Finney and atmospheric, in-your-face music by David A. Hughes and John Murphy, who have clearly done their genre homework. Liz Webber's cutting is trim.

—*Derek Elley*

CHASERS

A Warner Bros. release of a James G. Robinson presentation of a Morgan Creek production. Produced by Robinson. Executive producer, Gary Barber. Co-producer, David Wisnievitz. Directed by Dennis Hopper. Screenplay, Joe Batteer, John Rice, Dan Gilroy, story by Batteer, Rice. Camera (Cinefilm Lab color, Technicolor prints), Ueli Steiger; editor, Christian A. Wagner; music, Dwight Yoakam, Peter Anderson; production design, Robert Pearson; art direction, Natalie Wilson; set decoration, Kate Sullivan; costume design, Michael Boyd; sound (Dolby), Roger Pietschmann; assistant director, Babu Subramaniam; second unit camera, Paul Taylor; casting, Mary Jo Slater. Reviewed at the Beverly Connection, L.A., April 22, 1994. MPAA Rating: R. Running time: **101 MIN.**

Rock Reilly	Tom Berenger
Toni Johnson	Erika Eleniak
Eddie Devane	William McNamara
Howard Finster	Crispin Glover
Rory Blanes	Matthew Glave
Vance Dooly	Grand L. Bush
Salesman Stig	Dean Stockwell
Flo	Bitty Schram
Sgt. Vince Banger	Gary Busey
Master Chief Bogg	Seymour Cassel
Duane	Frederic Forrest
Katie	Marilu Henner
Doggie	Dennis Hopper

Audiences won't be chasing after "Chasers." Snuck into the marketplace by Warner Bros. under cover of night, without advance screenings or even pre-opening print ads, this mangy, dimwitted gender switch on "The Last Detail" won't even have the benefit of trial before being sentenced to the video brig, since it's virtually there already.

This atypically low-profile, low-concept Morgan Creek production has exactly the same premise as Hal Ashby's salty, first-rate 1973 Jack Nicholson starrer about a tough-talking Navy lifer and a partner assigned to prisoner-escort duty. Difference here is that the detainee isn't hapless greenhorn Randy Quaid, but sultry sexpot Erika Eleniak, sentenced to seven to 10 for assault and going AWOL.

Hard-guy vet Rock (Tom Berenger) lays down strict rules for the trip to prison, but his slick, self-confident companion, Eddie (William McNamara), melts instantly at the sight of their voluptuous captive. For her part, Toni (Eleniak) will try every angle in attempting to escape, starting with a highly improbable disguise as a truck-stop waitress and continuing through such supposedly hilarious efforts as stuffing a tampon down the van's gas tank.

With the screenwriters evidently having realized that they'd forgotten to provide such niceties as personalities and motivation, toward the end, the characters suddenly reveal a little something of themselves so as to pave the way for the heart-tugging moment when Toni would finally be led off to the clink. But this is followed by an utterly incredible epilogue, the last word in tacked-on happy endings.

Scattered about are little morsels to keep the desperate viewer attentive: McNamara's early Tom Cruise-like cockiness, Eleniak's incredible physique, a reasonably tasty sex scene between the two of them, some grungy Southeastern seaboard locations, and what basically amounts to cameos by an odd lot of actors, including Gary Busey, Seymour Cassel, Crispin Glover, Dean Stockwell, Frederic Forrest and Marilu Henner. Helmer Dennis Hopper also turns up briefly.

—*Todd McCarthy*

HOUSTON FEST

MEN LIE

A Lexington Pictures production. Produced by Sylvia Caminer, John Ciarcia. Executive producers, John Andrew Gallagher, Jeff Mazzola. Co-producers, Dianne E. Collins, Mary Hickey. Directed, written by Gallagher. Camera (color), Bob Lechterman; editor, Mary Hickey; music, Ernie Mannix; production design, James Bono; sound, Melanie Johnson; associate producer, John Puma; assistant director/casting, Sylvia Caminer. Reviewed at WorldFest/Houston Intl. Film Festival, April 20, 1994. Running time: **87 MIN.**

Scott	Doug DeLuca
Jill	Ellia Thompson
Uncle Frank	Frank Vincent
Peter	Garry Blackwood
Diane	Catherine Landherr
Scott's Dad	Victor Argo
Scott's Mom	Peggy Gormley

With: Aida Turturro, Michael Badalucco, Carolyn McDermott, Catherine Scorsese, Cathy Scorsese, David Faustino, Rainbow Borden, Michael Imperioli, Judith Malina, Isha Beck, Paula Stevens, Nicholas Turturro, Lorraine Marshall, Jeff Mazzola, Johnny (Cha-Cha) Ciarcia, Frank Acquilino, Nelson Vasquez, Sabah Shayan, Lisa Scarola, Mark Scarola, Tony Sirico, Marilyn Sokol, Tina Montalbano, Tony Rigo, Phil Carlo, Paul Herman, Victor Colicchio.

There's probably an audience out there for "Men Lie," but it will take a savvy distrib with niche-marketing skills to find it. Word of mouth could generate pleasing B.O. in urban markets. Vid and pay TV prospects are brighter.

Small-budget, N.Y.-lensed indie is a smartly written and cleverly constructed comedy with just a hint

of early Woody Allen. Basic plotline has two-faced Scott (Doug DeLuca) swearing fidelity to his beautiful fiancee, Jill (Ellia Thompson), even while he attempts to bed every woman who crosses his path. In this amatory pursuit, the young man is greatly encouraged by his heartily sleazy uncle (Frank Vincent), the sort of guy who would try to settle a sexual harassment suit by sending flowers to the complainant.

All this is interesting enough and reasonably well acted, though a trifle stilted at times. But it's not the whole story. Director/writer John Andrew Gallagher repeatedly interrupts the main action for on-camera declarations by "witnesses" (an eclectic mix of New York actors and celebrities) who provide commentaries and counterpoints to the Scott-and-Jill story.

The female witnesses — including Aida Turturro, Judith Malina, Marilyn Sokol and Catherine Scorsese — are especially hilarious as they offer withering put-downs of two-timing men in general and Scott in particular. Think of it as a Greek chorus with attitude.

"Men Lie" doesn't exactly cover new ground. But it does provide some zingy one-liners, a few dead-on insights and enough informed observations on the war between the sexes to keep couples laughing while they're watching the pic, and arguing when discussing it afterward. It has the potential to develop a cult following among women who have heard all the evasions and excuses the men offer here — in other words, among all women.

While no one will accuse the pic of excessive slickness, Gallagher has made the absolute most of what obviously was a limited budget. Ernie Mannix's music is particularly effective.

—*Joe Leydon*

RAVE REVIEW

The Wildebeest Co. presentation of a Gnu Films/Bergman Lustig production. Produced by Jeff Seymour, Ram Bergman, Dana Lustig. Executive producers, Marcy Lafferty Shatner, William T. Elston, Dawn Tilman. Directed, written by Seymour. Camera (color), Richard Crudo; editor, Terry Kelley; music, Amotz Plessner, Tal Bergman; production design, John Marshall; costumes, Kristen Anacker; sound, Carey Lindley; assistant director, Jeffrey January. Reviewed at WorldFest/Houston Intl. Film Festival, April 21, 1994. Running time: **92 MIN.**

May 2, 1994 (Cont.)

Steve Maletti	Jeff Seymour
Abe Weinstein	Carmen Argenziano
Bert	Ed Begley Jr.
Peter Watki	Robert Costanzo
James	James Handy
Milton Mandler	Bruce Kirby
Brian	Leo Rossi
Lou	Joe Spano

Noted L.A. legit director Jeff Seymour makes his feature debut with a project no doubt close to his heart — a dark comedy set in the world of L.A. theater. Pic is neither dark nor funny enough to make the most of its premise, but its sturdy craftsmanship insures vid and cable exposure.

Seymour doesn't stretch himself in the lead role of Steve Maletti, an L.A. stage director whose small theater is forever on the verge of bankruptcy. (Last summer, Seymour cited the economy as a chief reason for closing his North Hollywood Gnu Theatre after eight years.)

But the director/screenwriter strikes the right balance of egotism and idealism in his portrait of the artist as a deficit spender.

Pic begins on a clever note, with Ed Begley Jr. and Joe Spano typecast as TV stars who appear at Maletti's theater between more profitable gigs.

Unfortunately, the TV stars turn in their notices when they land roles in a movie shooting in Africa. Even more unfortunately, the lack of marquee allure means Maletti has to close his production prematurely. Desperate to raise money to save his struggling theater, he obtains the L.A. rights to a still-popular Broadway hit.

"Rave Review" (known as "Acting on Impulse" during filming) reaches its seriocomic high point when Maletti tries to scare a notoriously harsh critic (Bruce Kirby) out of writing a bad review and inadvertently causes the old man to have a fatal heart attack.

When Maletti ascertains that the man really has died — just minutes after writing a highly favorable review — the director scrambles to make sure no one learns of the untimely demise before the review appears in the L.A. Times.

Seymour has a difficult time establishing and sustaining a consistent tone. Some scenes, such as the critic's death, are mildly amusing, though not quite as sardonic as they might be. Later, as Maletti is harassed by a suspicious cop, pic turns dead serious.

Film's final third has a rushed, slapdash quality, suggesting some transitional scenes were left on the cutting-room floor, or never lensed in the first place.

On the plus side, "Rave Review" has some amusingly in-joke observations about small-budget theater in L.A., Hollywood's recruitment of promising talent, overly emotional actors and the uneasy relationship between critics and artists.

Pic turns downright nasty, and perilously close to homophobic, in its depiction of an effeminate theater critic (Robert Costanzo) who comes on to Maletti.

For the most part, however, humor is inoffensive. Perhaps a little too inoffensive. One can only dream of what wonders Paul Bartel could have worked with this plot.

Supporting performances are generally good, with Leo Rossi a hilarious standout as an actor who can't help crying in every role. Tech values are OK. *—Joe Leydon*

OBLIVION

An R.S. Entertainment release of a Full Moon Entertainment presentation. Produced by Vlad Paunescu, Oana Paunescu. Executive producer, Charles Band. Co-producers, Albert Band, Debra Dion, Peter David. Directed by Sam Irvin. Screenplay, David, based on a story idea by Charles Band. Story, John Rheaume, Greg Suddeth, Mark Goldstein. Camera (Fotokem color), Adolfo Bartoli; editor, Margaret-Anne Smith; music, Pino Donaggio; production design, Milo; costume design, Michael Roche, Radu Corciova, Oana Paunescu; visual effects, David Allen Prods.; special makeup effects, Alchemyfx, Michael Deak; sound (UltraStereo), Tiberiu Borcoman; casting, Robert MacDonald, Perry Bullington. Reviewed at Paramount Studios, L.A., April 28, 1994. (In World Fest/Houston Intl. Film Festival.) Running time: 94 MIN.

Zack Stone	Richard Joseph Paul
Mattie Chase	Jackie Swanson
Redeye	Andrew Divoff
Stell Barr	Meg Foster
Buteo	Jimmie Skaggs
Mr. Gaunt	Carel Struycken
Lash	Musetta Vander
Doc Valentine	George Takei
Miss Kitty	Julie Newmar

It's been proffered that the demise of the Western can be paralleled with the ascendancy of science-fiction — one genre literally replacing the other. So, the prospect of literally combining the two ought to pack twice the fun. "Oblivion," which took a top prize at the Houston film fest, does the twining, but the result really isn't an improvement, let alone a logical step forward.

This sagebrush star war provides a pleasant diversion but gets tripped up in parodying the mutation it's in the process of defining. Low-budget item simply doesn't have enough stunts, effects, action or street smarts to zap up the grosses for intended June release. It should play better in the small-format arena. (In a flourish of self-promotion, pic even provides scenes from a forthcoming sequel shot back-to-back with the first venture.)

The town of Oblivion looks like a frame from a 1950s oater that's been retrofitted with some high-tech gizmos (location work was done in Romania). The heavy is the reptilian Redeye (Andrew Divoff), who shoots the sheriff and short-circuits his cyborg deputy (Meg Foster). It's all in the name of some precious metal and, of course, the lust for power.

There appears to be no relief from the new reign of terror save for the return of the lawman's son, Zack Stone (Richard Joseph Paul). The problem is that Zack's top priority is catching the stage-shuttle for the next asteroid. He's an empath, a rare breed that feels the physical pain of others, and therefore has adopted pacifist ways. Of course, he'll be forced to reconsider his stance.

The innate strength of the Western was its simplicity, and "Oblivion" not only eschews that dictum, it adds high camp to the recipe. Its humor is more sophomoric than sly and rears its head in a most unseemly fashion.

Far more effective is its sober side, as director Sam Irvin demonstrates a facility for action set pieces. He's also clever with special-effects stop-motion oddities that include giant scorpions and a vicious horned toad.

But the film is at sea in search of a consistent tone. Paul and femme interest Jackie Swanson play their roles pretty close to the vest, while Redeye's goons are buffoonish cartoons. Somewhere in the middle, just the right balance is provided in Foster, Divoff and Jimmie Skaggs' sidekick.

The physical setting is visually arresting, akin to the spaghetti Westerns that redefined the genre's landscape. It's still too heavily weighted toward six- and not laser-gun conventions, and hopefully the next installment will have rooted out the bothersome tumbleweeds on its horizon.

—Leonard Klady

MAY JEAN

(TAIWANESE)

A New Asian Horizons presentation of a Golden Entertainment Co. Ltd. production in association with Win's Movie Prods. Ltd. (Hong Kong) and Chang-Hong Channel Film & Video Inc. Executive producers, Yang Teng-Kwai, Charles Heung, Mark T. Wu. Directed, written, musical score by Steven C.C. Liu. Camera (color), Chen Yuen-Shiu; editor, Chen Po-Wen; art direction, Wang Tung; costumes, Lo Hsieh-Kuang; sound (Dolby), Du Du-Jy. Reviewed at WorldFest/Houston Intl. Film Festival, April 21, 1994. Running time: 94 MIN.

May Jean	Chin Su-Mei
Communist Army Commander	Wong Huei-Wu
Captain Wong	Ti Lung
Sister Helen	Susan Layton
Henry	Wu Lin-Shan
Hu	Liu Yuen-Tei
Babe	Liu Kwan-Pan
Nono	Liu Di-Shen
Ma	Liu Po-Hon
Tsang Ta-toh	Shiu Hsiao-Shen
Dah-Toh	Li Ying
Uncle Pi	Li Kuen
Sister Fong	Priscilla Barnes
Mr. Platt	James Callahan

Vet Taiwanese filmmaker Steven C.C. Liu returns after a 10-year hiatus with a lavishly mounted but simplistic melodrama that veers perilously close to high camp. Despite obvious sincerity on Liu's part, pic's ponderous pacing and cloying sentimentality will turn off even the most ardent devotees of Asian cinema.

Chin Su-Mei (who starred in Ang Lee's arthouse hit "The Wedding Banquet" billed as May Chin) toplines as May Jean, a beautiful young woman whose life is torn asunder when her village is caught in the cross-fire between nationalist and communist forces in 1947.

After her deserter husband is executed by the local communist commander, May Jean winds up working at a Catholic school where the plucky Sister Helen (Susan Layton) teaches 40 Chinese orphans. When Sister Helen injures herself, it's up to the even pluckier May Jean to lead the children out of harm's way. They set out on a 20-day walk through the war zone, heading to the seacoast where a U.S.-bound ship is due to sail.

Periodically, "May Jean" cuts from the overland misadventures to some heavy-handed scenes of bickering between a feisty American nun (Priscilla Barnes of "Three's Company") and a harried U.S. diplomat (James Callahan). She insists the ship will have to wait for the orphans. He insists the ship can't wait for anyone. And on it goes. Evidently, these English-language scenes were intended to make the pic more interesting for Western audiences. They don't.

May 2, 1994 (Cont.)

"May Jean" offers a few impressive battle scenes, some borderline loony musical interludes and many, many teary-eyed close-ups of May Jean and her orphans. The ending is utterly shameless in the way it milks the tragedy of separation — May Jean can't join the children aboard the ship — for what seems like an eternity. Oddly enough, however, pic never manages to work up much suspense while May Jean and the children are traveling between warring armies. There's no real sense of danger because there's never any serious doubt about the ultimate outcome.

Liu is much too fond of photographing little boys as they urinate into rivers. Other instances of low comedy are even less effective.

Chin is almost as resourceful, and suffers every bit as nobly, as a silent-movie heroine. Her performance is pic's strongest asset, but it's not nearly enough.

Production values, especially Chen Yuen-Shiu's handsome color lensing, are fine. —*Joe Leydon*

TURIN FEST

GLITTERBUG

(BRITISH — B&W/COLOR)

A Basilisk Communications/BBC production in association with Opal/Dangerous to Know. Produced by James Mackay. Directed by Derek Jarman. Associate director, David Lewis. Camera (b&w/color), Jarman; editor, Andy Crabb; music, Brian Eno. Reviewed at From Sodom to Hollywood, Intl. Gay Film Festival, Turin, Italy, April 15, 1994. Running time: **60 MIN.**

Derek Jarman's "Glitterbug" is a perfect companion piece to "Blue," satisfyingly capping off the late English iconoclast's screen work. This lissome montage of Jarman's Super 8 footage fused with a multitextured Brian Eno score constitutes a breathless journey taking in the director's films, friends and favored stomping grounds. It should be welcomed as a fitting final addition to his eclectic output.

Associate director David Lewis and editor Andy Crabb worked with Jarman through the latter half of 1993 to distill "Glitterbug" from some 15 hours of home movies shot between 1970 and 1985. BBC execs added subtitles to identify time, place and people appearing on-screen before airing the film in March, soon after Jarman's death. The definitive version, however, contains no commentary apart from Eno's music.

The film's appropriateness as a farewell legacy derives from the intimate nature of the video-diary format and its affectionate chronicle of Jarman's world prior to its gradual disfigurement by AIDS. It also achieves a yin-yang balance with "Blue" that enhances both films' communicative power.

One is entirely without images while the other is without words. One is a pristine techno creation built to house a lifetime of reflections, the other is a freewheeling lyrical memoir fashioned from what's essentially a slapdash first film, as the initial footage predates Jarman's 1976 debut feature, "Sebastiane."

Shoots of both "Sebastiane" and "Jubilee" are glimpsed. The former amusingly conveys a climate of maverick creativity and untroubled sexuality; the latter recaps the advent of punk, particularly as a London phenomenon.

Despite jaunts to Italy, Spain and the English countryside, London remains an omnipresent factor in "Glitterbug." The film eloquently captures the city's physical presence, from moody, gray Thames scenes to orderly parks and gardens to starkly ugly housing estates. It glances back at the pre-AIDS days of parties, drugs and drag, typified by gutter-glam footage of Andrew Logan's Alternative Miss World contest.

Perhaps the most arresting sequences are those devoted to Tilda Swinton, who appeared in all of Jarman's films beginning with "Caravaggio." She's first seen straddling a boar, heroically brandishing a sword, then playfully darting around a garden maze at her family castle in Scotland.

Crabb's seamless editing cleverly exploits the technical limitations of Super 8, using occasional lack of definition to create the illusion of images melding into one other. Blow-up quality is fine given the footage's origins. —*David Rooney*

ONE FOOT ON A BANANA PEEL, THE OTHER FOOT IN THE GRAVE:

SECRETS FROM THE DOLLY MADISON ROOM

(DOCU — VIDEO)

A Clinica Estetico, Joanne Howard production. Produced by Jonathan Demme, Peter Saraf. Directed by Juan Botas, Lucas Platt. Camera (color), Victoria Leacock, Botas; editor, Platt; music, Anton Sanko. Reviewed at From Sodom to Hollywood, Intl. Gay Film Festival, Turin, Italy, April 17, 1994. Running time: **80 MIN.**

Jonathan Demme-produced docu "One Foot on a Banana Peel, the Other Foot in the Grave" invites its audience, without artifice or affectation, into the day-to-day experience of gay men living with AIDS. Pic eavesdrops in tearoom fashion on patients' conversations at a clinic in New York's West Village, giving as much time to banality as to bravery. Technical poverty will limit exposure, but the film's honesty should secure it a niche on public TV.

Detractors who slammed "Philadelphia" for soft-pedaling the story's gay elements for mass-market consumption may find the reality base they felt was missing in this frank, decosmeticized flip side.

Like "Silverlake Life," this docu wields a devastating emotional impact that comes from watching one of its subjects (co-director Juan Botas) gradually fade and die. In both films, the home-movie immediacy makes the sense of loss even more palpable.

Botas' humor and openness make his hospitalization and subsequent death (recorded primarily via its effect on his fellow patients) a quietly harrowing experience. But "Banana Peel" risks allowing a large chunk of the audience to tune out before they feel its real impact.

The major burden directly follows the main titles. A voiceover relates Botas' initial impulse to film conversations between patients, actively preparing the audience for the funny, life-affirming, heroic exchanges. What comes next is inevitably a letdown — basically a long stretch of engaging but unexceptional banter, compromised by raw sound recording that makes much of it unintelligible.

In the meantime, the visual limitations imposed by a Hi-8 video camera being passed around a drab office interior don't go unnoticed.

But as staff and patients of the clinic become more familiar, and the warmth and solidarity between them is expressed, the film slowly comes into its own. Discussions of love, loss, preparation for death, and attitudes to AIDS are often poignant. Observations about the generation of gay men coming out in the age of AIDS add another somber dimension. The only giveaway of the modest project's Demme-monde citizenship is its astute use of Anton Sanko's delightful music, which starts out jauntily but gradually bends the same basic riff into a more soulful commentary.

—*David Rooney*

REMEMBRANCE OF THINGS FAST: TRUE STORIES VISUAL LIES

(BRITISH — 16MM)

A Maybury/Menage production, in association with the Arts Council of Great Britain and Channel 4. Produced by Chiara Menage. Executive producer, John Maybury. Directed, written by Maybury. Camera (color), John Mathieson; editor, Gavin Burridge; music, Marvin Black; art direction, Alan Macdonald; costume design, Judy Blame; sound design, Black. Reviewed at From Sodom to Hollywood, Intl. Gay Film Festival, Turin, Italy, April 16, 1994. Running time: **60 MIN.**
With: Tilda Swinton, Rupert Everett, Aiden Brady, Mark Lawrence, Shyrene, Lola.

In "Remembrance of Things Fast," video artist John Maybury creates a darkly alluring queer-nation landscape and populates it with enough questioned norms, challenged preconceptions and inescapable associations to more than justify the Proustian allusion of his title. This witty barrage of sexual diversity and media mayhem should energize gay fests and experimental skeds.

Subtitled "True Stories Visual Lies," pic juxtaposes gay self-perception with the view from outside. The control exercised by the media over all aspects of contemporary society is cleverly lampooned via a computer-generated terrain of news flashes, commercials and scrambled soundbites. A merciless stab at U.S.-style, twin-anchor newscasts is especially funny, reducing the format to a duel of gossipy vilification.

An even more tangible presence is AIDS, though like every ingredient in Maybury's food-for-thought smorgasbord, it's dealt with in unexplicit terms.

One of pic's chief strengths is its ability to throw open debate by means of abstract reference. Drugs, sex, rape, gay-bashing, race riots, (dis)education, thought conditioning, transgender experience, S&M, technology and war all surface and ricochet off one another, interspersed with shadowy flashes of homoerotica.

Maybury toys with the star charisma of thesps Tilda Swinton and Rupert Everett by labeling their frequent direct-to-camera discourses with the caption "uncommercial presentation." With a virtually shaved head offsetting his pampered good looks and sleek intensity, Everett shows a decidedly new side to his screen personality. Swinton's chameleonlike gifts and archly humorous intonations are perfectly attuned to Maybury's pursuits, as they were in his previous feature, "Man to Man."

Technically, the film (mostly originated on video, apart from some use of Super 8) is keen, from its brooding, abstract expressionist look to its dazzling use of color, complex soundtrack and Marvin Black's hypnotic music. Production tab, per director, was £25,000 ($37,000), funded by the U.K.'s Arts Council and Channel 4. Pic won the special jury prize in the gay Teddy Bear Awards at this year's Berlin fest.

—*David Rooney*

DARKER SIDE OF BLACK

(BRITISH — DOCU — 16MM)

A Black Audio Film Collective/Normal Films production, in association with BBC-TV and the Arts Council of Great Britain. (International sales: Arts Council, London.). Produced by David Lawson. Directed by Isaac Julien. Camera (color, 16mm), A. Jaffa, David Scott; editor, Joy Chamberlain; music, Trevor Mathison; sound, Mathison. Reviewed at From Sodom to Hollywood, Intl. Gay Film Festival, Turin, Italy, April 16, 1994. Running time: **55 MIN.**
With: Ice Cube, Buju Banton, Brand Nubian, Michael Franti, Shabba Ranks, Cornel West, Trisha Rose, Michael Manley, Monie Love.

Isaac Julien ("Young Soul Rebels") steps into documentary feature territory with surefooted results in "Darker Side of Black," an intelligent overview of black pop culture that examines the social, cultural and political influences of rap and ragga music, with particular emphasis on its growing homophobic content. Public TV and musicvideo webs should make space for this stimulating study, made for British pubcaster BBC's "Arena" docu series.

Julien maintains a healthy critical distance as he addresses a series of issues and their relation to contempo black music. Gun culture, urban violence, drugs, machismo, misogyny, religion, the sexual dynamics of dance-club culture and aggressive power in music as a substitute for societal strength all provide a complex arena for debate.

Docu points out that the emerging anti-gay strain is arguably the black music scene's only flagrant incitement to violence. The can of worms was opened by Jamaican ragga musician Buju Banton's 1992 release "Boom Bye Bye," whose lyrics urge that lesbians and gay men be ferreted out and eliminated. The singer's views are more or less mirrored by Shabba Ranks, a star in

the U.S. and an advocate of crucifixion for gays.

Imaginatively lit talking-head interviews and well-chosen musicvid clips lend the docu a snappy visual texture that takes its heavy diet of facts and opinions beyond the constraints of investigative journalism. An occasional tendency toward poetic rumination in the linking voiceover is the only jarring element.

—*David Rooney*

CROOKLYN

A Universal release of a 40 Acres and a Mule Filmworks production in association with Child Hoods Prods. Produced, directed by Spike Lee. Executive producer, Jon Kilik. Co-producer, Monty Ross. Screenplay, Joie Susannah Lee, Cinque Lee, Spike Lee, story by Joie Susannah Lee. Camera (Duart color; Deluxe prints), Arthur Jafa; editor, Barry Alexander Brown; music, Terence Blanchard; production design, Wynn Thomas; art direction, Chris Shriver; set decoration, Ted Glass; costume design, Ruth E. Carter; sound (Dolby), Rolf Pardula; sound design, Skip Lievsey; associate producers, Joie Susannah Lee, Cinque Lee; assistant director, Michael Ellis; casting, Robi Reed. Reviewed at Universal Studios, Universal City, May 3, 1994. MPAA Rating: PG-13. Running time: **112 MIN.**
Carolyn Carmichael . Alfre Woodard
Woody Carmichael ...... Delroy Lindo
Tony Eyes .... David Patrick Kelly
Troy .... Zelda Harris
Clinton .... Carlton Williams
Wendell .... Sharif Rashed
Joseph .... Tse-Mach Washington
Nate .... Christopher Knowings
Tommy La La .... Jose Zuniga
Vic .... Isaiah Washington
Jessica .... Ivelka Reyes
Snuffy .... Spike Lee
Right Hand Man ...... N. Jeremi Duru
Aunt Song .... Frances Foster
Clem .... Norman Matlock
Viola .... Patriece Nelson
Aunt Maxine .... Joie Susannah Lee
Uncle Brown .... Vondie Curtis-Hall
Minnie .... Tiasha Reyes

Both annoying and vibrant, casually plotted and deeply personal, Spike Lee's "Crooklyn" ends up being as compelling as it is messy. Fictionalized look at the filmmaker's family life during the early 1970s is loud, grating, disorganized and off-putting for more than half its running time, but eventually jells into an exceedingly vivid portrait of a specific household, as well as of a time and place that looks idyllic compared with the urban situation 20 years hence. Crossover appeal of this music-laden comedy-drama is limited, but core audience that has supported Lee's studio features will probably turn out for this, the least ostensibly "controversial" of his efforts to date, resulting in OK early summer B.O.

After the far-reaching and, in many ways, over-reaching ambition and contentious politics of "Malcolm X," it's understandable that Lee would want to retrench in the familiar Brooklyn neighborhood where he grew up and deal with matters close to home. Written with his brother and sister, it's an account of family life loaded with anecdote and bereft of sharp focus until well into the second hour. But the specificity of memory evoked and the feeling of loss

ultimately generated make it not all that far-fetched to consider "Crooklyn" Spike Lee's "Fanny and Alexander," even if it's far less mature and nuanced than Ingmar Bergman's film.

The Carmichaels live in a spacious, eclectically furnished brownstone in Brooklyn. Woody, the patriarch (Delroy Lindo, memorable as West Indian Archie in "Malcolm X"), is a jazz musician at a career standstill during the heyday of rock and pop. His wife, Carolyn (Alfre Woodard), teaches school to pay the bills, and fights a losing battle trying to control her five children, who would rather eat junk food than black-eyed peas and turn on the TV whenever she's not around to forbid it.

Family life consists of almost constant hollering and arguing, something that continues out on the street with the neighbors. The kids constantly dump garbage outside the basement apartment of weird neighbor Tony Eyes (David Patrick Kelly), who deserves it because his countless dogs stink up the whole area; tenants are late with their payments; the electricity gets turned off; two guys (one played by Spike Lee) are constantly sniffing airplane glue out of paper bags, and the Carmichaels' oldest kid and only girl, 10-year-old Troy (Zelda Harris), is caught shoplifting.

Just wanting to be left in peace so he can write his music, Woody doesn't protest when a furious Carolyn kicks him out of the house, but he soon comes back, and the craziness returns as before.

Pic takes a turn, both in narrative and style, when, after an hour, the family packs up the Citroen convertible and heads south, where Troy will spend the summer with a middle-class uncle and aunt. Long section devoted to the girl's unhappy stay there is shot so that the images appear squeezed (as if a widescreen film were to be shown in a normal aspect ratio). Device is clearly meant to emphasize Troy's discomfort in alien surroundings but is constantly distracting; unprepared viewers will probably just assume something's wrong with the projection.

At the same time, however, it's here that the film begins to focus on one character. Troy's growing perceptiveness and preoccupations take center stage from here on, even as another of the major characters suddenly becomes ill and dies. Latter events are admirably treated with restraint and an avoidance of the usual Hollywood heart-tugging, although the death creates a void that helps Lee treat the eternal "you can't go home again" theme in his own way.

Although there's quite a bit of Afro hairstyling going on here, Lee exploits the comic potential of early '70s fashions much less than Matty Rich did in "The Inkwell." Still, there are quite a few amusingly indelible sights and sounds: a family of black kids singing along with the Partridge Family on TV, Carolyn looking like an African princess while behaving like a drill sergeant, the neighbors' volatility contrasted with the orderly city block and, in a visual strategy that does work, Troy dreaming she's on a glue-induced high, lifted above the streets as she remains in close-up.

More than three dozen period tunes are slapped onto the action, skillfully at times, awkwardly and arbitrarily at others. Eerie final credits sport the striking juxtaposition of the title song, an intriguing rap number, over vintage clips from TV's "Soul Train," known for a very different sort of music.

Performances are mostly high voltage, led by Woodard as the mother understandably about to come apart at the seams. Lindo brings an appealing, gentle thoughtfulness to the father whose artistic purity verges on selfishness, and newcomer Harris grows into her role as Troy.

In the end, one is left with a strong sense of tumultuous daily life being lived by flawed but vibrant individuals, and with a sadness at the passing of a way of life that may have seemed pretty unruly at the time but now looks downright innocent.

—*Todd McCarthy*

BEING HUMAN

A Warner Bros. release of an Enigma production in association with Fujisankei Communications Group, British Sky Broadcasting and Natwest Ventures. Produced by Robert F. Colesberry, David Puttnam. Directed, written by Bill Forsyth. Camera (Technicolor), Michael Coulter; editor, Michael Ellis; music, Michael Gibbs; production design, Norman Garwood; art direction, Keith Pain, Andrew Precht (S.F.); costume design, Sandy Powell; sound (Dolby), Louis Kramer, Nelson Stoll (S.F.); assistant director, Jonathan Benson; casting, Susie Figgis, Sharon Howard Field. Reviewed at the Festival Theater, L.A., May 3, 1994. MPAA Rating: PG-13. Running time: **125 MIN.**

Hector	Robin Williams
Lucinnius	John Turturro
Beatrice	Anna Galiena
Priest	Vincent D'Onofrio
Dom Paulo	Hector Elizondo
Anna	Lorraine Bracco
Janet	Lindsay Crouse
Deirdre	Kelly Hunter
Betsy	Helen Miller
Tom	Charles Miller
Boris	William H. Macy
Thalia	Grace Mahlaba
The Storyteller	Theresa Russell

"Being Human" never comes alive. This stillborn series of little fables is so flat and ill-conceived that it could convince the uninitiated that neither Robin Williams nor the highly idiosyncratic Scottish writer/director Bill Forsyth had any talent. Clearly knowing full well what they were stuck with, Warner Bros. kept this one under wraps for at least a year, and distrib's only hope is that a lot of Williams fans anxious to see his first outing after "Mrs. Doubtfire" (although it was filmed earlier) will turn out on opening weekend before the smell gets too bad.

Eleven years ago, Forsyth and producer David Puttnam made "Local Hero" for Warner, an outstanding example of a quirky, independent-minded film made for a major studio. Lightning has decidedly not struck twice, however. "Being Human" is quirky, all right, but to no apparent point. Its most singular achievement, in fact, is to have succeeded in draining any vestige of humor out of Williams. Coming from so many gifted people, film's artistic failure is quite puzzling, and rather sad.

Forsyth has built this curiosity out of five historical vignettes centered upon a character named Hector who's played by Williams. Hector's station in life changes from one episode to the next — he's a caveman in the Bronze Age, a slave during the Roman Empire, a traveler fleeing war in the Middle Ages, a Portuguese adventurer during the Age of Exploration and a hapless divorced man in contempo New York — but in any era he's a meek, ineffectual wimp who can't make a decision or stand up for himself.

In prehistoric times, Hector stands by helplessly as invaders make off with his woman and two daughters. At a Roman outpost, Hector suffers from having a stupid master (John Turturro) who insists that he commit suicide with him.

In the Alps in medieval times, Hector is welcomed into the warm arms and home of a lovely widow (Anna Galiena), but rushes out of her embrace to embark on a long journey home. As a shipwrecked sailor on the African coast, the man seems less concerned over matters of survival than in making up with a former lover.

Finally, in New York, Hector undertakes a timid reunion with his daughter and son, from whom he has been separated for some time for a rather peculiar reason.

Surely, one imagines as the playlets unfold at a groggy clip, Forsyth is working toward some interesting reflections on the human condition, some deeply felt commentary on history and humanity's relative enlightenment or lack of same.

But, after more than two hours of patience-eroding tepid drama and non-comedy, the picture shockingly reveals no philosophical connective tissue, no elements that have been meaningfully placed and built so as to coalesce into rewarding meaning at the end.

The episodes all have something to do with the search for family and home, as well as journeys across land and water, and there are running gags about chickens, but there is no payoff. Forsyth must have had some vision of the human animal's position in the universe to prompt him to undertake such a project, but it became lost somewhere along the way. Indeed, the picture's intellectual fabric proves stunningly thin.

As entertainment, it's equally a washout. Never in a film has Williams' inspired, manic personality been so suppressed, never has he seemed so bland. Hector may be human, but in every instance he's less than a man, as he cowers in the face of any threat and vacillates hopelessly when he must make a decision. Worst is the final Hector's embarrassing sheepishness with his own children on a weekend of forced togetherness.

Pacing is also a problem, as each segment is longer than the one that went before it, concluding with the half-hour New York story. Technical aspects are routine, although location work in Scotland and Morocco adds some color to the proceedings.

Here and there are some odd situations and bits — some Romans offering to assist with a suicide, men being hanged from the ends of a cross that tips in the sand, a woman falling through the floor of a dilapidated apartment while sitting on a toilet — that resonate because of their weirdness. But some circumstances conspired to jointly cancel the well-proven talents of all the participants on this one, proving they're only human.

—*Todd McCarthy*

MR. WRITE

A Shapiro Glickenhaus Entertainment release of a Presto production. Produced by Joan Fishman, Rick Harrington. Executive producers, Leonard Loventhal, Richard Allerton, Buddy Ortale. Directed by Charlie Loventhal. Screenplay, Howard J. Morris, based on his play. Camera (color), Elliot Davis; editor, Eric Beason; music, Miles Roston; production design, Pamela Woodbridge; costume design, Elsa Ward; sound (Dolby), John Nutt; assistant director, Rip Murray; casting, Cheryl Bayer. Reviewed in L.A., May 5, 1994. MPAA Rating: PG-13. Running time: **89 MIN.**

Charlie	Paul Reiser
Nicole	Jessica Tuck
Roger	Doug Davidson
Wylie	Jane Leeves
Mr. Rhett	Calvert De Forest
Shelly	Gigi Rice
Dad	Eddie Barth
Roz	Wendie Jo Sperber
Lawrence	Darryl M. Bell
Billy	Tom Wilson
Dan	Martin Mull

"Mr. Write" could be a likable romantic comedy if it didn't get its milieu and characters so wrong. Set in the oft-satirized world of American advertising, this is a sort of low-budget "Hudsucker Proxy," where modest goals and limited resources would not automatically be vices if they were connected to more inspired material. With an abundance of familiar TV faces, including "Mad About You" star Paul Reiser as an aspiring writer and would-be paramour of former "One Life to Live" soaper Jessica Tuck, "Mr. Write" should go quickly to video, where its quiet virtues and Reiser's recognition factor may make it an OK choice for a stay-at-home date night.

Tale involves aspiring scribe Charlie (Reiser), whose dead-end writing career leads him to try his hand at acting in commercials. Predictably, the world of commercials is a comic mine field, filled with dancing snack foods, a bossy director (Wendie Jo Sperber) and beautiful ad exec Nicole (Tuck), who first spars with Charlie, which naturally leads to true love.

Stock obstacles are Nicole's dim-witted outdoorsman b.f. Roger (Doug Davidson) and smarmy junk-food titan father (Martin Mull), and by fade-out romance has triumphed, Charlie has rejuvenated his dead writing career, and Nicole has climbed out of her father's domineering shadow. Had screenwriter Howard J. Morris, working from his own play, drawn his portraits more sharply and displayed any ear or eye for the commercial production field, "Mr. Write" might have become the fast-paced, frenetic good time that director Charlie Loventhal obviously envisioned.

Loventhal, whose "The First Time" and "My Demon Lover" showed a promising comic talent, has a sure hand with his performers, and some of this film's nicest moments occur in the margins, such as a security guard reading the Economist, or a bimbo who's a fan of Pirandello.

What's missing are characters capable of engaging a bigscreen audience. As hard as Reiser and Tuck try to infuse the film with sincerity and emotion, their one-dimensional, cliched roles undo their work. Add supporting performers to the list of untapped assets — notable "if-onlys" being comic Tom Wilson, as Charlie's scheming lawyer buddy,

May 9, 1994 (Cont.)

and Davidson, as Nicole's eco-fanatic beau. The usually reliable Mull also has little to do, and David Letterman foil Calvert De Forest turns in a pointless one-joke perf.

Aside from a few occasional flashes of wit, and Reiser's warm, good-natured lead turn, pic doesn't distinguish itself from the regular TV programming that its leads normally call home. —*Steven Gaydos*

CLEAN SLATE

A Metro-Goldwyn-Mayer release. Produced by Richard D. Zanuck, Lili Fini Zanuck. Directed by Mick Jackson. Screenplay, Robert King. Camera (Deluxe color), Andrew Dunn; editor, Priscilla Nedd-Friendly; music, Alan Silvestri; production design, Norman Reynolds; art direction, William Hiney; set decoration, Anne Kuljian; costume design, Ruth Myers; sound (Dolby), Willie Burton; associate producer, Gary Daigler; assistant director, Matthew Carlisle; casting, Mindy Marin. Reviewed at the Avco Center Cinema, L.A., May 4, 1994. MPAA Rating: PG-13. Running time: **107 MIN.**
Pogue .... Dana Carvey
Sarah/Beth .... Valeria Golino
Dolby .... James Earl Jones
Rosenheim .... Kevin Pollak
Cornell .... Michael Gambon
Dr. Doover .... Michael Murphy
Paula .... Jayne Brook
Hendrix .... Vyto Ruginis
Judy .... Olivia D'Abo
Baby .... Barkley

Any movie stolen by a dog with a depth-perception problem can't be all bad, and "Clean Slate" isn't without a few inspired comic moments. For the most part, however, this convoluted comedy feels like a pale follow-up to "Groundhog Day" that should test the marquee value of star Dana Carvey, chalking up some modest box office returns before being erased by big-budget summer fare.

More than anything, the movie underscores the challenge "Saturday Night Live" alumni have faced shifting to the bigscreen, forced to play a single character instead of, in Carvey's case, his stable of over-the-top caricatures and impersonations.

On top of that, the clever premise — a guy suffering from a form of amnesia that causes him to forget everything when he goes to sleep — never congeals in the execution, partly because the movie has to keep retracing its steps, grinding to a halt every time Carvey nods off again.

First-time screenwriter Robert King seems to have taken much of his inspiration from '40s film noir in putting together a complex mystery plot with assorted nefarious characters, then dropping his dazed and confused protagonist into the middle.

Carvey plays Pogue, a private detective who's been afflicted with his unique illness after a car explosion. Joined by a mysterious woman (Valeria Golino) who was supposed to have died in the blast, he must try to find a priceless coin while staying alive long enough to testify against the mobster, Cornell (Michael Gambon), who engineered the explosion.

Director Mick Jackson ("The Bodyguard") pulls off some amusing sequences, most of them involving Barkley, a Jack Russell terrier seen occasionally on TV's "Full House," who goes through the movie wearing an eye patch and keeps running into things head first. That the pic's ad campaign gives the dog equal billing with Carvey may indicate where MGM saw the movie's appeal.

Carvey fares reasonably well, though with the exception of a few scenes the role is too restrained to tap into skills he's exhibited elsewhere.

Other than Gambon, who oozes nastiness, no one else in the cast particularly shines.

Tech credits are OK, though the Venice/Santa Monica locales don't do much to capture the potboiler atmosphere the script seems to seek. An animatronic version of Barkley also looks rather ersatz, perhaps to fend off flak about having the critter keep missing his doggy-door. Even so, this is one movie that, quite literally, goes to the dog. —*Brian Lowry*

3 NINJAS KICK BACK

A TriStar release of a Sheen production in association with Ben-Ami/Leeds Prods. Produced by James Kang, Martha Chang, Arthur Leeds. Executive producers, Simon Sheen, Yoram Ben-Ami. Directed by Charles T. Kanganis. Screenplay, Mark Saltzman, based on a screenplay by Sheen. Camera (Technicolor), Christopher Faloona; editor, David Rennie; supervising editor, Jeffrey Reiner; music, Richard Marvin; production design, Hiroyuki Takatsu, Gregory Martin; art direction, Scott Meehan; set decoration, Karin McGaughey; costume design, Takeshi Yamazaki, Miye Matsumoto; sound (Dolby), Clifford Gynn; associate producers, Steven L. Bernstein, Vicki Ellis; assistant director, Edward Licht; second unit camera, Nobuhito Noda; casting, Lucy Boulting. Reviewed at Beverly Connection, L.A., April 30, 1994. MPAA Rating: PG. Running time: **99 MIN.**
Grandpa .... Victor Wong
Colt .... Max Elliott Slade
Rocky .... Sean Fox
Tum Tum .... Evan Bonifant
Miyo .... Caroline Junko King
Koga .... Sab Shimono
Glam .... Dustin Nguyen
Vinnie .... Jason Schombing
Slam .... Angelo Tiffe

"3 Ninjas Kick Back" clearly was made with an eye on the international movie market. Set mostly in Japan and adding a female ninja to the three boys, this high-spirited adventure succeeds in conveying the positive and fun elements of both Japanese and American cultures.

This sequel may not be as big a bonanza as "3 Ninjas," Disney's 1992 sleeper, but TriStar should expect strong response from children of all ages.

The new adventure engages its three cute ninjas, Rocky (Sean Fox), Colt (Max Elliott Slade) and Tum Tum (Evan Bonifant), in two missions. Resourceful siblings have to help Grandpa Mori (Victor Wong) return to Japan to present a ceremonial dagger he had won half a century ago to the new winner of the Ninja tournament. And they have to return to L.A. on time to aid their baseball team, the Dragons, against the rival Mustangs.

In pursuit of the dagger, which is a key to a secret gold cave, Grandpa's old enemy Koga (Sab Shimono) recruits a trio of spaced-out heavy-metal rockers. Broadly played, and sporting outrageous wigs and costumes, they are more bumbling buffoons than villains, and provide the excuse for some hilarious fights and inventive physical comedy.

To broaden story's appeal, scripter Mark Saltzman shrewdly adds a young girl, Miyo (Caroline Junko King), whose skills let her teach the boys a lesson or two in the ninja arts.

A new bicultural, reconciliatory tone underlies pic. Some past U.S. movies have portrayed aggressive competition and hostility toward Japan. This film, however, stresses the similarities of these countries and what kids of both cultures can learn from each other.

Charles T. Kanganis, who has directed a number of serviceable actioners, knows that the crucial factors in such adventures are comic energy and swift tempo. Indeed, excepting a couple of superfluous scenes, like those involving the ninjas' parents, pic benefits from kinetic wit and fast pacing. Tech credits, notably lensing and colorful production design, are most proficient.

Film's moralistic dimensions are so well integrated into the narrative that they're hardly noticeable. Still, as in "The Wizard of Oz," "The Secret Garden" and other classic fairy tales, younger viewers will get a flavor of a new and "dangerous" magical world with a healthy dose of traditional family values, such as security of country and comfort of home. —*Emanuel Levy*

TWO COPS

(SOUTH KOREAN)

A Castalia Pictures release. Produced, directed by Woo-Suk Kang. Executive producer, Young-Rak Kwon. Screenplay, Sung-Hong Kim. Camera (color), Kwang-Suk Chung; editor, Hyun Kim; music, Kyung-Shik Choi; production design, Tae-Wook Kim; sound, Bum Soo Kim, Dae-Ho Yang. Reviewed at the Vista Theatre, L.A., April 30, 1994. Running time: **108 MIN.**
Detective Cho .... Sung Gi Ahn
Detective Kang .... Joong-Hoon Park

"Two Cops," a new Korean comedy, proves that the police genre can easily cross national and language barriers. This character-driven farce, about the relationship of a corrupt, easygoing cop and his rigid partner, has the casual charm and appeal to put the new Korean commercial cinema on the international movie map, very much like that of its neighbors, China and Hong Kong.

Up to a point, "Two Cops" feels like a variation on the 1984 French smash hit "Les Ripoux," released in the U.S. as "My New Partner." But instead of the aging cop that the irresistible Philippe Noiret played, the Korean hero Cho (Sung Gi-Ahn) is a younger, more handsome detective whose expensive lunches and personal lifestyle are just as important as his on-duty chores, though he's an efficient pro when push comes to shove.

Story begins as veteran officer Cho is assigned a new, by-the-book partner, detective Kang (Joong-Hoon Park), a recent academy graduate. The rookie is on his partner's tail whenever he smells a bribe or other shenanigans. But as expected, after some personality clashes, the rigid officer begins to loosen up and enjoy the side benefits of his job — fast money, luxury meals, beautiful women. Eventually, Kang outdoes his more experienced mentor, which generates conflict — and humor.

Though conforming to the time-honored genre, scripter Kim provides enough fresh observations and role reversals to make pic entertaining even for viewers familiar with the formula's conventions. Kang's helming, simple and unobtrusive in the positive sense of these terms, reps neat balancing act between dialogue and action. His unembarrassed love for physical comedy is reflected in inventive visual gags.

Production values, particularly Kwang-Suk Chung's lensing, are mediocre, which could be a function of pic's low budget. But the two leading performers are always attractive and amusing.

May 9, 1994 (Cont.)

With a running time of 108 minutes, "Two Cops" could benefit from a prudent trimming of about 15 minutes, especially in the scenes involving the women in the cops' lives, which ultimately detract attention from the more engaging central interaction. —*Emanuel Levy*

TREAD: THE MOVIE

(DOCU)

An Oak Creek Films and Action Sports Adventure presentation sponsored by Rock Shox, Giro, Mongoose, Cannondale, Suncloud, Diamond Back, Yakima, Duro Tire and Velo News. Produced, directed by Bill Snider. Written by Katrina Sibert. Camera (color), Snider; editing, Snider, Steve Capstick; original music, Tom Wasinger; sound, Deann Snider; associate producer, Capstick. Reviewed on vidcassette, San Francisco, April 27, 1994. Running time: 93 MIN.

Mountain biking is the latest daredevil sport to go the Warren Milleresque screen route with "Tread: The Movie." Squarely aimed at fellow riders, visually gonzo effort will find handy berth at specialty stores and some general vid outlets, fueled by footage showcased on "MTV Sports." It's currently four-walling short gigs in relevant burgs, beginning May 4 in Berkeley.

Pic nods to genre's granddaddy, "Endless Summer," by casually focusing on two pro "legends" — Hans Rey and Greg Herbold, whose Bill & Ted rapport embraces much inscrutable-to-outsiders slang. ("Last cross-country I did was a full hurlfest," says Herbold as he puts straw to Pepto-Bismol bottle following double-cheeseburger engorgement.) Sans narration, "Tread" follows duo around the globe, from urban Ecuador to San Francisco hills and Swedish mountaintops.

Mountain biking can be an extremely hazardous sport — this writer recently witnessed a novice rider's grisly head-breaking wipeout on a medium grade. (Lifted out by 'copter, the kid reportedly later died.) But aside from a few scary spills glimpsed, "Tread" keeps focus strictly on thrilling stunts. If angels can dance on the head of a pin, surely Herbold & Rey could figure out a way to hot-dog there as well.

Terrific lensing puts you right there from every angle, including Dramamine-necessitating handlebar and aerial views. While hyperkinetic pace may exhaust lay audiences after a while, MTV-style editing will keep acolytes stoked. Use of music is especially clever,

ranging from surf/industrial metal sounds to mock-Gregorian vocals (chanting "Latin" phrases like "Insane-o/Terrain-o") and Spike Jones-type sound effects.
—*Dennis Harvey*

DRUNKEN MASTER II

(TSUI KUN II)

(HONG KONG)

A Golden Harvest (H.K.) presentation of a Mou Hip (H.K.) production, in association with China Film Co-production Corp. Produced by Leonard K.C. Ho. Executive producers, Eric Tsang, Tseng King-sang. Directed by Lau Kar-leung. Screenplay, Tseng, Yun Kai-chi. Camera (color), Cheung Yiu-tsou, Wong Man-wan, Jingle Ma, Cheung Tung-leung; editor, Peter Cheung; music, Wu Wai-lap; art direction, Eddie Ma, Ho Chong-sing; costume design, Ching Tin-kiu; martial arts directors, Lau, Jackie Chan's Stunt Group; line directors, Chen Chi-hua, Frankie Chan; assistant directors, Kwan Yiu-wing, Lam Hak-ming, Wan Fat. Reviewed at Prince Charles Theater, London, April 30, 1994. Running time: 102 MIN.
Wong Fei-hong .... Jackie Chan
Madam Wong .... Anita Mui
Wong Kei-ying .... Ti Lung
Master Tsan .... Felix Wong
Fu Min-chi .... Lau Kar-leung
General's son .... Andy Lau
(Cantonese dialogue)

Sixteen years after the pic that trampolined him into the local big time, Hong Kong star Jackie Chan bounces back with a titular sequel that's among the most confident in his oeuvre. Though "Drunken Master II" isn't the unrestrained, daredevil actionfest of some of his '80s movies, it's a well-balanced slab of genre cinema in which Chan is more of an ensemble player than previously. Fans worldwide should respond warmly, and ancillary biz looks hot.

The movie pulled a handsome $22.5 million during first 24 days of release across East and Southeast Asia in February. H.K. B.O. alone touched $5.2 million, proving the 40-year-old star hasn't lost his golden touch. Long-promised pic was actually made to benefit the Hong Kong Stuntmen's Union, with which Chan is closely involved.

In fact, the only connection with the 1978 "Drunken Master" (aka "Drunk Monkey in the Tiger's Eyes") is the name of Chan's character, legendary Cantonese martial artist Wong Fei-hung, recently disinterred in a string of Jet Lee/Tsui Hark pix. Original, made by Ng See-yuen's Seasonal Corp., was a

low-tech comedy actioner with Chan playing pupil to a "drunken fist" master. Present item, partly shot in mainland China, is given the whole Golden Harvest production values, plus a bevy of stars led by songstress Anita Mui and veteran m.a. star Ti Lung.

Set in the early Republican era, movie starts in Changchun, northeast China, with Chan and his stern, righteous father (Ti Lung) taking the train back to Canton in the south. En route, their box containing a ginseng root gets swapped with one containing an imperial jade seal, stolen by some nasty Brits for export to the West.

Rest of the plot, back home in Canton, spins on a dime, with plenty of comic shtick involving the missing ginseng, and the Brits and their Chinese heavies targeting Chan & Co. for the missing jade. Terrific set-piece finale is set in an iron smeltery, where local labor is being exploited and the factory used as a cover for the smuggling op.

The star's blend of boyish charm, comic timing and acrobatic skills are undiminished, and Chan is now confident enough to keep his action guns in their holster until a "drunken fist" set-piece some 30 minutes in.

Less frenetic pacing (by H.K. standards) works, thanks to the fuller surrounding characters. Ti Lung settles well into a strong role as Chan's stern father, but it's Mui, as Chan's scheming, gambling-mad stepmom, who keeps the comic pot bubbling. Local heartthrob Andy Lau cameos briefly at the start.

Tech credits are all fine and, as usual in Chan movies, the end-title crawl includes botched takes, including some dangerous fire stunts in the smeltery finale. Though vet action director Lau Kar-leung (aka Liu Chia-liang) left the pic after a dispute with Chan, he still cops the main directing credit. Chinese title literally means "Drunken Fist II," referring to a style of fighting.
—*Derek Elley*

SAN FRANCISCO

THE SECRET OF ROAN INISH

A Jones Entertainment Group Ltd. presentation in association with Peter Newman Prods. Produced by Sarah Green, Maggie Renzi. Executive producers, John Sloss, Glenn R. Jones, Peter Newman. Directed, written by John Sayles, based on the novel "Secret of the Ron Mor Skerry," by Rosalie K. Fry. Camera (color), Haskell Wexler; editor, Sayles; music, Mason Daring; production design, Adrian Smith; sound, Clive Winter; costumes, Consolata Boyle; sound, Clive Winter; associate producer, R. Paul Miller; casting, John and Ros Hubbard. Reviewed at the AMC Kabuki 8, San Francisco, April 21, 1994. (In S.F. Intl. Film Festival.) Running time: 103 MIN.
Hugh .... Mick Lally
Tess .... Eileen Colgan
Tadhg .... John Lynch
Fiona .... Jeni Courtney
Eamon .... Richard Sheridan
Jamie .... Cillian Byrne
Also with: Pat Slowey, Dave Duffy, Declan Hannigan, Fergal McElherron, Frankie McCafferty, Gerald Rooney, Susan Lynch, Linda Greer.

John Sayles' latest marks his entry into family-pic terrain, a crossing that draws pleasant, albeit unexciting, results. Short on the lush atmospherics its fanciful story cries for, "The Secret of Roan Inish" presents a marketing challenge — like another recent slice of Irish whimsy, "Into the West," it may prove too talky and sophisticated for kids, too mild to lure adult customers.

Story (drawn from Brit author Rosalie K. Fry's juve novel) has plucky 10-year-old Fiona (Jeni Courtney) shipped off by a hard-drinking, widowed dad to her grandparents' coastal home in post-World War II County Donegal. There she and teen cousin Eamon are drawn into their folkloric clan past — especially one ancestor's union with a half-human, half-seal "Selkie" (Susan Lynch).

Strange sights further pique Fiona's curiosity. Her infant brother, Jamie, was presumed dead when his cradle of ship's-hull wood mysteriously drifted out from shoreline to sea. But Fiona glimpses the wild-child toddler scampering along the shore. She finally convinces grandfolk (Mick Lally, Eileen Colgan) to row out to Roan Inish, the nearby island home they've abandoned, in hopes of solving the puzzle.

Film captures hardscrabble life of this remote fishing culture, but low-key direction and Haskell Wexler's handsome yet somber lensing could use more leavening touches to help script's fantastic side take flight.

Some scenes will particularly engage young viewers, like the haunting image of the wave-propelled cradle.

For all its attention to realistic detail, "Roan Inish" seems uneasy with the whimsy more crucial to emotional impact. While individual sequences work well, Sayles doesn't come up with the sort of transforming overall mood in which everyday events meld with other-worldly ones. This leaves the polished adult actors hitting a stereotypical note, with twinkles in each eye as they mouth literary-sounding lines.

Juve performers fare better, with towheaded newcomer Courtney an attractive and convincingly resourceful heroine. Her appeal lends pic much of its value for family auds. Local accents, narrative complexity and a rather unvaried pace may tire customers under 8 or so, however. While "Roan Inish" does beguile, it lacks the full-tilt enchantment that might have rendered this material classic family fare.

Tech work is smooth. Jaunty soundtrack of traditional Celtic sounds sets an appropriate mood.
—*Dennis Harvey*

THE ADVENTURES OF PRISCILLA, QUEEN OF THE DESERT

(AUSTRALIAN)

A Gramercy release of a Polygram Filmed Entertainment presentation, in association with the Australian Film Finance Corp., of a Latent Image-Specific Films production. Produced by Al Clark, Michael Hamlyn. Executive producer, Rebel Penfold-Russell. Directed, written by Stephan Elliott. Camera (color; Arriscope widescreen), Brian J. Breheny; editor, Sue Blainey; music, Guy Gross; production design, Owen Patterson; art director, Colin Gibson; costumes, Lizzy Gardiner, Tim Chappel; sound, Gunter Sics; makeup, hair, Cassie Hanlon; choreography, Mark White; stunts, Robert Simper; associate producer, Sue Seeary; assistant director, Stuart Freeman. Reviewed at Hoyts Centre 7, Sydney, April 17, 1994. (In San Francisco Intl. Film Festival, Cannes Film Festival — Un Certain Regard.) Running time: **102 MIN.**

Bernadette	Terence Stamp
Tick/Mitzi	Hugo Weaving
Adam/Felicia	Guy Pearce
Bob	Bill Hunter
Marion	Sarah Chadwick
Benji	Mark Holmes
Cynthia	Julia Cortez
Frank	Ken Radley
Aboriginal Man	Alan Dargin
Shirley	June Marie Bennett
Logowoman	Rebel Russell
Priest	Al Clark
Adam's Mum	Margaret Pomeranz

I f ever a film flaunted itself, it's "The Adventures of Priscilla, Queen of the Desert." A cheerfully vulgar and bitchy, but essentially warmhearted, road movie

with a difference, which boasts an amazing star turn by Terence Stamp as a transsexual, Stephan Elliott's second feature is a lot of fun, and should appeal to tolerant audiences everywhere. It gets a double festival launch, first in San Francisco and a few days later at a midnight screening in Cannes, and enthusiastic reaction on both sides of the Atlantic should lead to solid sales for the Polygram/Latent Image production.

With, apparently coincidentally, a similar plot to the upcoming Beeban Kidron pic for Amblin/Universal, "To Wong Foo, Thanks for Everything, Julie Newmar," "Priscilla" has a simple narrative that's really just a peg on which to allow its three leads to have a great time in drag.

Stamp plays Bernadette, whose lover has recently died. She decides to team up with gay friends Tick (Hugo Weaving) and Adam (Guy Pearce), who are heading to the central Australian town of Alice Springs to perform a drag act at a casino. The invitation to perform has been offered by Tick's ex-wife, and he's a little ashamed to reveal the fact that he once was married.

The trio purchases a not-very-reliable second-hand bus they name Priscilla, and set out from Sydney on the long journey across the desert. Along the way, they experience a number of adventures, including confronting small-town amazement and prejudice, an encounter with aborigines (one of whom joins them in a spirited performance of "I Will Survive") and the inevitable vehicular breakdown.

They also encounter an aging hippie, Bob (the always reliable Bill Hunter), who is frustrated at life with his Asian wife and who tags along with them, forming an attachment to Bernadette.

The plot of "Priscilla" isn't as important as the outlandish, wicked dialogue, the wild costumes and makeup, and the general high spirits of the entire enterprise. Dressed in femme clothes throughout, Stamp gives one of his best perfs as the bereaved woman whose latent masculinity occasionally shows through her graciously elegant exterior and who throws herself into the drag numbers with enthusiasm. Also excellent are Weaving, as the bisexual Tick, and Pearce as the muscular but fey Adam, whose obsession with Abba manifests itself in a genuinely bizarre fashion.

Pic is just a smidge long, but it would be unfair to say it drags. All production credits are spectacularly good, starting with Brian J. Breheny's widescreen photography, which makes the Australian desert look like the landscape of an alien planet. Special mention must be made of the amazingly elaborate costumes by Lizzy Gardiner and Tim Chappel. The score by Guy Gross also deserves a nod.

Although the film doesn't make concessions to a straight audience, it's so outrageous that it becomes positively disarming. It's hard not to respond to such a cheerfully vulgar and in-your-face entertainment, though this is obviously not for the very strait-laced. It should certainly break out of the cult and gay markets and find comparatively wide acceptance.

Great soundtrack includes standards by Village People, Lena Horne, Patti Page and, of course, Abba.

End credits are filled with joke references; for example, pic was supposedly filmed in "Dragarama," Libby Blainey is credited for Title Design and Bad Acting, and Matt Inglis is Best Naughty Boy.
—*David Stratton*

THE BUDDHA OF SUBURBIA

(BRITISH)

A BBC Television presentation. Produced by Kevin Loader. Executive producer, Michael Wearing. Directed by Roger Michell. Screenplay, Hanif Kureishi, Michell, from Kureishi's novel. Camera (color), John McGlashan; editor, Kate Evans; costume design, Alexandra Byrne; incidental music and title song, David Bowie; makeup, Marilyn MacDonald; associate producer, Anna Kalnars. Reviewed on vidcassette, San Francisco, April 20, 1994. (In S.F. Intl. Film Festival. Running time: **236 MIN.**

Haroon Amir	Roshan Seth
Karim Amir	Naveen Andrews
Eva Kay	Susan Fleetwood
Charlie Kay	Steven Macintosh
Margaret Amir	Brenda Blethyn
Uncle Ted	John McEnery
Auntie Jean	Janet Dale
Jamila	Nisha Nayar
Anwar	Badi Uzzaman
Shadwell	David Bamber
Changez	Harish Patel
Matthew Pyke	Donald Sumpter
Eleanor	Jemma Redgrave

A more corrosive Anglo parallel to "Tales of the City" '70s nostalgia, "The Buddha of Suburbia" easily rates as writer Hanif Kureishi's best screen work since "My Beautiful Laundrette." Already broadcast in series form at home, the consistently entertaining, provocative four-hour effort appears a natural for export.

But just *how* is a big question. With complex narrative (from Kureishi's novel) already packed too tight at four hours, editing to viable theatrical length seems impossible. And given PBS' recent slink away from co-producing the highly rated but conservative-bashed "Tales," most obvious U.S. broadcast route for this considerably gamier entity seems roadblocked. Pic's specialized, hipper-than-thou appeal makes sale to

commercial cablecasters look problematic as well.

If nothing else, "Buddha's" uncertain fate highlights the awesome gulf between viewer tolerance/politics on each side of the Atlantic. (And as evidence of the envelope pushed by "Buddha," note this series did provoke some public outrage during BBC airing, whereas "Tales" coaxed nary a whimper.)

Pic reps a qualified comeback triumph for co-adaptor Kureishi, whose "Sammy and Rosie Get Laid" skirted smug p.c. overkill, while his directorial debut, "London Kills Me," was an unqualified disaster. As "Buddha" spans the Me Decade from hangover hippiedom to dawn of the Thatcher Era, it too sports glib aspects and a somewhat chill heart. But the kaleidoscopic narrative keeps attention riveted.

Story centers on young Karim Amir (Naveen Andrews), a South London suburban teen born to Indian father and English ma. At start, civil-servant pa Haroon (Roshan Seth) is gleefully exploiting the vogue for "Eastern philosophies" he knows nothing about. "Masquerading as a Buddhist," dad delivers banal happy-talk aphorisms to upscale patrons at a premium, while secretly carrying on with wealthy acolyte Eva Kay (Susan Fleetwood). When latter liaison goes overground, Karim's devastated mother retreats with her younger son; he joins dad and Mrs. Kay in their move to central London.

Karim drifts about, eventually finding fledgling success as a stage actor. His parallel number is erstwhile school chum Charlie (Steven Mackintosh), Eva's only child. Charlie's failed grab at glam-rock stardom puts him in a prime position later to dive into the exploding punk music scene.

Other subplots involve the bizarre arranged marriage foisted upon Karim's friend Jamila, henpecked Uncle Ted, and various loyalties forged or abandoned along each leading character's path. Along the way, pretensions of music, theater and New Age scenesters are skewered.

Beyond these satirical digs, "Buddha" lets its characters grow in surprising, even poignant directions. But Kureishi's bent toward hip-flippant strokes sometimes robs them of sufficient depth — the breakneck pace allows director Roger Michell little room to let momentous shifts in behavior and circumstance take shape naturally. Instead, they're too often bomb-dropped for shock value.

It's to the credit of the filmmakers that "Buddha" remains assured and grounded throughout — though an even longer running time would have helped. More problematic in terms of overall empathy is central figure Karim, attractively played by Andrews (who like several thesps here figured in "London Kills Me"). Rootless to the end, Karim may be an apt metaphor for Kureishi's cagey take on '70s "freedoms." But his status as observer to everyone's lives (including his own) leaves the film with a hole at its center.

Performances are uniformly terrific, pacing smart. Michell dives full steam into any number of showy set pieces, from early faux-guru gatherings to later punk clubs and weird episodes amid the hypermethod world of a stage mentor. Karim's embroilment in a seedy orgy scene with said mentor, his wife and an unstable actress g.f. (Jemma Redgrave) is hilarious in ways unlikely to pass U.S. broadcast muster anytime soon. Elsewhere, upfront depiction of drug use, bisexuality and nudity (male and female) keep "Buddha" vivid, but won't help its potential stateside chances.

Tech/design work is excellent all around. David Bowie wrote the bland theme song and contributes incidental music; his '70s hits are more gainfully employed, among many apt period tunes soundtracked. —*Dennis Harvey*

THE COW

(KRAVA)

(CZECH REPUBLIC)

A Czech Television presentation. Produced by Helena Sykorova, Karel Skorpik. Directed by Karel Kachyna. Screenplay, Kachyna, Karel Cabradek, based on the novel by Jan Prochazka. Camera (color), Petr Hohjda; editor, Jan Svoboda; music, Petr Hapka; production design, Jiri Zavrel; costumes, Jana Smetanova; sound, Jaroslav Novak; assistant directors, Renata Kindlova, Katerina Kohut. Reviewed at the AMC Kabuki 8, San Francisco, April 20, 1994. (In S.F. Intl. Film Festival.) Running time: **86 MIN.**
Adam .... Radek Holub
Rosa .... Alena Mihulova
Also with: Valerie Zawadska, Viktorie Knotkova, Antonin Molcik, Zenek Dusek.

Veteran Czech director Karel Kachyna, best known for his long-banned Kafkaesque "The Ear," turns to rural drama with this modest but well-executed effort. Fest berths await.

Opening suggests a fable tenor as solemn young protag Adam sets out to sell the cow that provides livelihood for himself and an ailing, former-prostitute mother. Unlike Jack and the beanstalk, however, Adam's adventures are ruled by harsh reality. He returns with expensive morphine for his (presumably syphilitic) ma, only to find her already dead. Adam must perform backbreaking work at local quarry to survive.

Despite low social skills and his "oddity" status (a childhood fall misaligned his shoulders), Adam attracts interest from the local butcher's mistress. He first chases Rosa off his hillside home with a whip, then rapes her in the barn, yet they soon settle into happy, albeit unwedded, domesticity. Storyline brings things tragically full-circle, though close is reasonably upbeat.

Rather plain tale could use a more distinctive p.o.v. to lend Adam's pawn-of-fate trials greater resonance. Period ambiance (circa 1900) is mild in this time-removed, remote setting; sepia childhood flashbacks don't add much psychological dimension, though Radek Holub as Adam limns a credible mix of gloom and tenacity. Other perfs are adequate.

Made for Czech TV, "The Cow" lands stylistically between pastoral balladry and straight-up realism; results are unmemorable but have quiet appeal. Lovely, delicate photography of the verdant mountain scenery is strongest element in polished tech presentation.
—*Dennis Harvey*

THE BROKEN JOURNEY

(UTTORAN)

(INDIAN)

A CEG Worldwide presentation of a National Film Development Corp. of India/Doordarshan production. Produced, directed by Sandip Ray. Screenplay, story by Satyajit Ray. Camera (color), Barun Raha; editor, Dulal Dutt; music, Sandip Ray; production design, Ashoke Bose; sound, Sujit Sarkar; assistant directors, Ramesh Sen, Subroto Lahiri, Ramen Chatterji. Reviewed at the AMC Kabuki 8, San Francisco, May 4, 1994. (In S.F. Intl. Film Festival). Running time: **82 MIN.**
Dr. Sengupta .... Soumitra Chatterji
Jatin Kundu .... Sadhu Meher
Manashi .... Subhalakshmi Munshi
Haladhar .... Debotosh Ghosh
With: Bina, Minakshi Goswami, Masood Akhtar, Pallavi Roy, Bimal Deb, Subhendu Chatterji, Lily Chakraborty, Soven Lahiri, Ashish Mukherji.

"The Broken Journey" was skedded as scenarist Satyajit Ray's next directorial project when the veteran Indian helmer became ill and died in early 1992. After a delay, his son Sandip resumed production. Finished project is a middling narrative on par with elder Ray's later, lesser but respectable works; how far the family name's residual arthouse clout will carry it abroad is uncertain.

Heavy-handed opening scenes introduce Calcutta general practitioner Dr. Nihar Sengupta (Soumitra Chatterji) as a jaded urbanite out of touch with basic values. He sloughs off wife's worries that their college-age daughter may be involved in drugs; his patients are a wealthy, spoiled lot. But the doc leaves these cares behind to present a paper on last 20 years' med-research progress at a Rotary Club meeting seven hours' drive away.

En route, his car has a flat near a remote village. While his chauffeur replaces the tire, doc is distracted by moans nearby. He discovers a gravely ill man who's been exposed to the elements for two days, developing probable pneumonia.

Sengupta impatiently turns the man over to villagers, then suffers conscience pangs and returns soon after — rescuing said peasant from local witch doctor's harsh "exorcism" ceremony. But when Sengupta rushes back to the remote locale once again the next morning, his guilt-induced renewal of the Hippocratic Oath has come too late.

Implicit critique of urban values is haltingly advanced, and the doctor's final, symbolic gesture doesn't carry full weight intended. (Some story sidelines, like his daughter's alleged drug use and the village girl's harassment by unwanted suitor, likewise feel underdeveloped.) Still, both script and helmer Sandip Ray's work gain strength once film settles on peasant's life-or-death struggle as crux for Sengupta's own moral reawakening.

Performances are solid, though somewhat cramped by script's lack of nuance. While lensing and other tech factors are undistinguished, they improve whenever action sticks to village setting.

Musing on morality and medical ethics make pic an intriguing footnote to Satyajit Ray's career. But even in the helmer's own hands, this modestly engrossing but semi-realized "Broken Journey" would probably not have rated among his major achievements.
—*Dennis Harvey*

THE LAST DAYS OF IMMANUEL KANT

(LES DERNIERS JOURS D'EMMANUEL KANT)

(FRENCH — B&W)

A La Sept, L'Ima. Pierre Grise Prods. and Archipel 33 presentation. Produced by Denis Freyd. Directed by Philippe Collin. Screenplay, Collin, Andre Scala. Camera (b&w), Jacques Bouquin; editor. Martine Bouquin; production design, Doris Renault. Reviewed at the AMC Kabuki 8, San Francisco, April 25, 1994. (In S.F. Intl. Film Festival.) Running time: **70 MIN.**
With: David Warrilow, Andre Wilms, Roland Amstutz.

Director Philippe Collin has taken his title's arid-sounding concept — an imagined view of the famed German philosopher's twilight stretch — and fashioned a droll, perfectly tuned miniature with "The Last Days of Immanuel Kant." While appeal is a bit specialized for wider distribution, heavy fest bookings are assured, with Euro TV sales a potential market.

Based on an 1850s essay by Thomas De Quincey, pic chronicles short period in life of the professor/thinker in his native Konigsberg, leading up to his 1804 demise at age 80. Focus is less on tenets of his "critical philosophy" (referenced in conversational fragments) than on his fussy, eccentric lifestyle.

Positively addicted to a strictly observed, somewhat bizarre daily regimen, Kant comes across here as the classic academic crackpot-genius — one who sleeps in an elaborate mummy-wrap, drinks massive quantities of coffee at precise intervals, and holds the entire town at an awed if politely amused distance during his afternoon strolls. In this minutely detailed canvas, the departure of Kant's servant Lampe after 30 years' service amounts to high melodrama.

Such extreme economy of narrative and tone could easily grow dull. But helmer Collin allows no slack, endowing spare scenario with much sly humor as well as eventual poignancy. A spectral, sustained beyond-this-mortal-coil shot hits the ideal closing note.

English-born U.S. actor David Warrilow limns a Kant who's crotchety and severe yet childlike, especially as infirmity weakens his mental and physical faculties. Roland Amstutz's long-suffering Lampe leads a restrained supporting cast. Period trappings are appropriately subdued. Luminous b&w photography is a big plus among modest but assured tech credits. A former assistant director to Renoir, Rohmer, Malle and others, Collin has worked mostly on French TV docs and series; pic is just his third feature, and first since 1979.
—*Dennis Harvey*

CROATIAN CATHEDRALS

(HRVATSKE KATEDRALE)

(Croatian)

A Hrvatska-Radio Televizija production. Directed, written by Hrvoje Hribar. Camera (color), Miso Orepic; editor, Vladimir Lojen; production design, Dinka Jericevic; costumes, Snjeana Bartolec; music, Dario Bulic. Reviewed May 3, 1994, at the AMC Kabuki 8, San Francisco. (In S.F. Intl. Film Festival.) Running time: **77 MIN.**
With: Rene Medvesek, Cintija Asperger-Eastman, Rajko Minkovic, Branko Berovec, Marko Copor.

A droll if undercomplicated exercise, "Croatian Cathedrals" has undeniable curiosity value as a comedy making only glancing refs to war-torn Balkan territories nearby. Modest impact and subtlety of local humor will limit export potential.

Amusing opener has minor-league thug and soccer fan Janko smooching with trashy g.f. Barbara at Zagren park. Catering to her every whim, he promptly gags and binds an old lady to a tree in order to grab her pet pup as a gift. Meanwhile, laconic art historian Vanja is deadline-tardy with his text for a book on area cathedrals. Fleeing a furious publisher, he holes up at ex-amour Maria's plush digs — the very site pegged by Janko for his next robbery.

Writer and would-be thief collide while Maria is away. Their rancorous encounter (played for laughs, yet with some jarring violence that recurs later on) ends with Vanja knocked out and Janko in possession of the all-important manuscript. Everybody gets in on subsequent retrieval chase.

More pets, Maria's bratty offspring and hip-hop-dancing military police figure in scenario that's longer on amusing details than overall propulsion. Writer/director Hrvoje Hribar has managed nicely with cast and tech aspects on a TV budget, though most of the more biting political and social allusions here are too low-key for understanding outside home auds.

—*Dennis Harvey*

GENSEN-KAN INN

(GENSEN KAN SHUJIN)

(JAPANESE)

A Daiei Co. Ltd. presentation of a Kinoshita Film/Sedic/Tohoku Shinsya production. Produced by Koji Yoshida. Executive producer, Shigesaburo Kinoshita. Directed, written by Teruo Ishii, based on the comics by Yoshiharu Tsuge. Camera (color), Koichi Ishii; lighting, Kenjiro Konaka; editor, Yoshiyuki Okuhara; music, Hajime Kaburagi; art direction, Yuji Maruyama; sound, Mineharu Kitamura. Reviewed at AMC Kabuki 8, San Francisco, May 3, 1994. (In S.F. Intl. Film Festival.) Running time: **98 MIN.**
With: Shiro Sano, Akio Yokoyama, Chika Nakagami, Emu Hisazumi, Junichi Ogino, Kaoru Mizuki, Mayo Kawasaki, Nana Okada, Kitaro.

C omic-book artist Yoshiharu Tsuge was a significant figure in the form's 1960s Nippon transition toward more mature themes/audiences. But screen translation of his works is botched in the indifferently mounted omnibus "Gensen-kan Inn." Foreign prospects are weak.

Four stories here suggest an intriguing range of style and content to Tsuge's art. But helmer Teruo Ishii (an action-pic vet) hasn't found an apt tenor for each, let alone means of linking quartet into a cumulative whole.

First seg is a short, quirkily comic view of bizarre family living above cartoonist's home; second is curious fable of roadside waif whose menstrual cramps release "red flowers" into nearby stream bed.

The longer title story has Tsuge (played throughout by Shiro Sano) visiting ghostlike village where he bears mysterious resemblance to a fellow traveler who'd seduced the local inn's deaf-dumb mistress years before.

Final piece is aimless, depressing look at impoverished boho lifestyle depicting Tsuge's fledgling-artist years.

Poorly assembled framing sequences purport to show Tsuge at mercy of latter-day publishers/editors, who fret his stories are too adult or obscure for wide success. Tag has the artist himself allegedly viewing preceding flick.

Asked his opinion by assembled cast and crew, he politely shrugs, "I'm not an expert on film."

Such low enthusiasm is justified. Varied atmospheric requirements (from zany surrealism to supernatural mystery) are rarely nailed amid often careless compositions and rhythm-free editing.

While title story manages a haunting finale, most other set pieces bungle their rich visual potential — a dismaying flaw given few glimpses we get of Tsuge's own meticulously drawn comic-book frames. One endless attempted-rape scene in a candle-lit bathhouse is especially clumsy and ill-crafted.

Perfs are just fair. Mediocre tech work is lowlighted by often grainy, poorly color-processed lensing.

—*Dennis Harvey*

THE SUM OF US

(AUSTRALIAN)

A Southern Star presentation, in association with the Australian Film Finance Corp., of a Hal McElroy-Southern Star production. Produced by McElroy. Executive producers, McElroy, Errol Sullivan. Co-executive producers, Corky Kessler, Donald Scatena, Kevin Dowling. Directed by Dowling, Geoff Burton. Screenplay, David Stevens, based on his play. Camera (color), Burton; editor, Frans Vandenburg; music, Dave Faulkner; production design, Graham (Grace) Walker; line producer, Rod Allan; casting, Faith Martin; assistant director, Carolyne Cunningham. Reviewed at Village Roadshow screening room, Sydney, April 28, 1994. (In Cannes Film Festival — market.) Running time: **99 MIN.**
Harry Mitchell .... Jack Thompson
Jeff Mitchell .... Russell Crowe
Greg .... John Polson
Joyce .... Deborah Kennedy
Jeff (aged 8) .... Joss Moroney
Gran .... Mitch Mathews
Mary .... Julie Herbert
Jenny .... Rebekah Elmaloglou

T op-flight star turns by Jack Thompson and rising star Russell Crowe, who play a loving father and his gay son, elevate this too-faithful adaptation of David Stevens' stage play. Audiences, straight and gay, should respond to the honesty and warmth of the father-son relationship depicted here, bringing the modestly scaled production positive word of mouth.

A basic decision to retain the stage device of having the two main characters react to the audience, and, at times, talk directly into the camera, will be accepted by some and seen by others as a distracting holdover from the theater, which should have been junked in the screen adaptation. Device is particularly questionable toward the end, when the father is immobilized by a stroke, unable to move or talk, yet still moves out of character to relay his thoughts to the audience.

This reservation aside, the piece works because of the heartfelt script, in-depth characters and classy performers. Thompson is Harry Mitchell, a widower who shares a small inner-Sydney house with his son, Jeff (Crowe). Jeff has never made a secret of the fact that he's gay, and the affable Harry is unquestioningly tolerant and accepting of his son's sexual orientation. Almost too accepting: When Jeff comes home one night with a man (John Polson) he's met in a gay bar, Harry joins them for a drink and a chat and insists on making the newcomer feel at home — until he unwittingly drives the astonished lover away.

Jeff is also unwittingly responsible for disrupting his father's new relationship. Harry has met, via a dating service, and fallen in love with Joyce (Deborah Kennedy), a divorced woman still hurt by the rejection of her husband years before. Things go well until Joyce learns about Jeff, which is something she can't handle. Her abrupt departure triggers Harry's stroke, after which his devoted son gives up everything to care for his father.

Thompson gives one of his best and most controlled performances as the kindly Harry, while Crowe continues to display his maturing talent; his sensitive Jeff is quite a contrast with the monstrous character he played in "Romper Stomper."

Supporting roles are solidly limned, especially Polson as the diffident would-be lover who has to put up with the hostility of his parents.

American Kevin Dowling directed the award-winning New York production of "The Sum of Us," and his co-director, Geoff Burton, is wielding the megaphone for the first time after a distinguished career as cinematographer (most recently on "Sirens"). The theatrical treatment suggests that Dowling dominated the partnership; Burton's cinematography is very professional but unobtrusive.

Given the high level of emotion in the subject matter, it's notable that the most moving scenes in "The Sum of Us" are black-and-white flashbacks in which Jeff recalls that his beloved grandmother (Mitch Mathews) lived for years in a lesbian relationship after her husband died, but was cruelly separated from her companion (Julie Herbert) when it was decided the couple were too frail to care for themselves.

Southern Star should have a winner in Australia with this one, and international sales are also indicated, especially when Crowe's career takes off with a couple of upcoming roles in mainstream U.S. pictures.

—*David Stratton*

IZ

(TURKISH)

A Mine Film production. (International sales: Mine Film, Istanbul/TRE Intl., Munich.) Produced by Kadri Yurdatap. Directed by Yesim Ustaoglu. Screenplay, Tayfun Pirselimoglu. Camera (color), Ugur Icbak; editor, Thomas Balkenhol; music, Aydin Esen; art direction, Pirselimoglu; costume design, Aysen Savaskan; sound, Balkenhol, Christian M. Goetz. Reviewed at Mine Film, Istanbul, April 16, 1994. (In Cannes Film Festival — market.) Running time: **118 MIN.**
With: Aytac Arman, Nur Surer, Derya Alabora, Meral Cetinkaya, Erdinc Akbas, Kutay Kokturk.

The ghosts of a secret policeman's misdeeds come back to haunt him in "Iz," an assured feature bow by Turkish director Yesim Ustaoglu that should travel well on the festival circuit and attract attention from specialist buyers, especially in Europe. Film's acute visual style and quality production values put this several notches above most Turkish fare.

Main character Kemal (Aytac Arman) is a plainclothes cop who's bored with his job and coasting toward retirement. One day he overhears a police call on the radio and goes along to break the monotony. The corpse is of an average musician who's committed suicide — and in the process obliterated his face.

Gradually Kemal becomes obsessed with discovering what the man looked like, an increasingly nightmarish quest that leads him to use his ring of informers, hook up with the dead man's prostitute daughter and finally try to leave the country. Ending, though inconclusive, features a surprise revelation that explains Kemal's obsession with the dead man's looks.

Though the pic deliberately keeps its time setting obscure, the implication is that story takes place during Turkey's period of military rule in the early '80s, with an omnipresent atmosphere of fear and police control. Though several Turkish movies have explored the interior journeys of artists and political prisoners, "Iz" cleverly takes the submerged guilt of the oppressor himself and boomerangs it back on him.

Result is a kind of reverse of Kafka's "The Trial," with the cop gradually entangled in the very snares he used to lay for others. Though the pic would benefit from some tightening in its central section, helmer Ustaoglu, who trained as an architect, keeps a generally tight grip on proceedings, with precision camera work, well-judged lighting and clean editing. Performances are fine, and post-production, done in Germany, is good.

Turkish title translates as anything from "track" to "trace" or "evidence," so producers are sticking with the original for the time being.
—Derek Elley

MAN OF ...

(CZLOWIEK Z ...)

(POLISH)

A Figaro production, in association with Lodz Feature Film Studio, PZU, Studio Beta Film, PAI Film. (International sales: Figaro Film, Warsaw.) Directed by Konrad Szolajski. Screenplay, Jaroslaw Lindenberg, Szolajski, from Szolajski's novel "The Man of Flesh and Blood." Camera (color), Wlodek Glodek; editor, Barbara Fronc; music, Krzesimir Debski; art direction, Jerzy Sajko; costume design, Pawel Grabarczyk. Reviewed at Premiers Plans, European First Film Festival (competing), Angers, France, Jan. 27, 1994. (In Cannes Film Festival — market.) Running time: **103 MIN.**
With: Agata Kulesza, Slawomir Pacek, Ewa Gawryluk, Kazimierz Kaczor, Cezary Pazura.

A sendup of Andrzej Wajda's late '70s classics "Man of Marble" and "Man of Iron," this is a broad parody of Polish political reforms (or lack thereof) in the wake of the Solidarity movement that bludgeons its points with a sledgehammer.

Fest auds savvy to Central European events and the Wajda originals may get a chuckle out of this freewheeling and irreverent tale that takes Polish media, public officials, political agitators and the church to task. Pic could also score in specialized venues and classrooms as a rowdy complement to the Wajda pix.

In Warsaw, 1982, plucky blond film school grad Anna (Agata Kulesza) wants to make a film about censorship but is arrested on trumped-up charges along with hapless hero Marek (Slawomir Pacek). Rather than iron or marble, Marek is wimpiness personified.

Returning from French exile in 1989, Anna is drafted into making a Polish TV docu and decides to get to the bottom of what became of Marek. As Anna conducts interviews with various smooth officials, Marek's utterly minor contribution is illuminated via flashbacks of clandestine meetings, imprisonment and a romance with perky fellow activist Marie.

Tragicomic treatment was prompted by helmer Konrad Szolajski's experiences with censorship and half-baked reform on Polish TV.

Material was first published as a satirical novel, "The Man of Flesh and Blood," in order to give Szolajski leverage with the Ministry of Culture, which was reluctant to fund a pic that Wajda reportedly opposed.
—Lisa Nesselson

SPIDER & ROSE

(AUSTRALIAN)

A Dendy Films production in association with the Australian Film Finance Corp. Produced by Lyn McCarthy, Graeme Tubbenhauer. Directed, written by Bill Bennett. Camera (color; Arriscope widescreen), Andrew Lesnie; editor, Henry Dangar; music, Cruel Sea; production design/costumes, Ross Major; sound, (Dolby) Syd Butterworth, Andrew Plain; line producer, Julia Overton; stunts, Glenn Boswell; casting, Alison Barrett; assistant director, Chris Webb. Reviewed at Dendy George Cinema, Sydney, April 28, 1994. (In Cannes Film Festival — market.) Running time: **90 MIN.**

Rose Dougherty	Ruth Cracknell
Spider McCall	Simon Bossell
Jack	Max Cullen
Robert Dougherty	Lewis Fitz-Gerald
Helen Dougherty	Jennifer Cluff
Sister Abbott	Tina Bursill
Nurse Price	Beth Champion
Ambulance Dispatcher	Marshall Napier
Truck Driver	Bruce Venables
Ambulance Driver	Bob Baines

On paper, the idea of an odd-couple generation-gap road movie hardly seems promising, so it's a minor miracle that writer/director Bill Bennett has managed to inject life into such familiar material. Helped by the popularity in Australia of toplined Ruth Cracknell (she stars in the hit TV series "Mother and Son") and buoyed by a tart screenplay and stylish direction, this first production from the Dendy Films exhib-distrib outfit should be a Down Under hit, with strong possibilities of offshore interest.

It opens with a sequence that evokes Peter Weir's "Fearless." An elderly woman wanders, battered, bloodied and obviously in shock, on a deserted country road; Andrew Lesnie's widescreen camera cranes and circles her to reveal, gradually, a wrecked car and then the body of her husband, who, we learn, caused the accident when he fell asleep at the wheel.

A year later, Rose (Cracknell) is ready to leave hospital to return to her family farm, a six-hour drive from Sydney, to celebrate her 70th birthday. Her ambulance driver, Spider (newcomer Simon Bossell), is an anti-social youth who's furious to be forced to spend his last day on the job driving an old biddy cross country; his only aim is to get back to the city in time for the wild party he's planned.

Naturally, the two get on each other's nerves from the start, with Rose disapproving of Spider's reckless driving and loud heavy metal music, and Spider bored by the crotchety old femme's constant nagging. Thanks to Bennett's sharp script and the top-flight performances, these scenes play with a surprising freshness and very Australian sense of humor.

Inevitably, the two antagonists warm to, and learn from, each other during the long journey, but Bennett manages to keep sentimentality and obviousness at bay, partly because the tragedy of Rose's life is never forgotten. A totally unexpected, and well-staged, scene in which the ambulance hits a kangaroo and crashes, comes as quite a jolt about halfway through.

Inevitably, the pair share a series of encounters, the most important being with Jack (Max Cullen), a laconic old beekeeper. Cullen gives a warm, funny perf — and almost steals the film — while providing a mature love interest for Cracknell. There's also a sexist truck driver (Bruce Venables) who gives Rose and Spider a ride, and Rose's disagreeable son (Lewis Fitz-Gerald) and daughter-in-law (Jennifer Cluff).

Cracknell gives a feisty, acerbic performance as the crotchety Rose and, surprisingly, partakes in not one, but two, nude scenes, one in which she shares a bathtub with Bossell. Bennett, who has made low-budget films until now, has clearly gone to some pains to avoid mushiness, and he's succeeded with a frequently funny picture. He has also handled the material with visual flair, resulting in his best direction to date. Lesnie's camera work deserves high praise for its fluidity, with some intricate and extended shots.

The main problem in selling "Spider & Rose" will be to convince audiences that this isn't the formula picture it appears to be. Word of mouth should be positive for this disarming, witty and, at times, genuinely touching picture.
—David Stratton

POISONOUS WOMEN

(YINEKES ... DILITIRIO)

(GREEK)

A Greek Film Centre/Kineton SA production. Produced, directed by Nikos Zervos. Screenplay, Haris Romas, Athena Hadjigeorgiou. Camera (color), Dinos Katsouridis; editor, Yanna Spyropoulou; production design, Elena Christouli; costumes, Marilee Zarkada. Reviewed at Berlin Film Festival (market), Feb. 15, 1994. (In Cannes Film Festival — market.) Running time: **95 MIN.**

Constantinos	Spyros Papadopoulos
Alexandros	Ilias Logothetis
Father	Costas Rigopoulos
Mother	Anna Kyriakou

Also with: Nadia Mourouzi, Athena Tsilira, Valeria Christodoulidi, Alkis Panayotidis, Yannis Karatzoyannis, Yolanda Balaoura, Andreas Voutsinas, Harry Clean, Vlassis Bonatsos.

May 9, 1994 (Cont.)

As a throwback to sex comedy of a less enlightened era, "Poisonous Women" is a cheerfully bawdy example of an almost forgotten genre. It is undoubtedly politically incorrect and may not travel theatrically outside Greece, but it could have video life if well dubbed into English.

Feverish tale concerns a celebrated psychiatrist who specializes in sexual disorders, and the manic people around him. These include his film director brother (who tries to get slasher pix funded by the Greek government) and his nympho wife; his deranged parents; his businesslike, mannish fiancee; and his secretary, who dresses like a nun and openly lusts after him.

Among his stereotypical patients are a man consumed with lust and a frigid woman. But film's just an excuse for frequent scenes of soft-core sexual activity and simple slapstick.

It sounds utterly unpromising, and yet there are quite a few laughs here, with the filmmakers sending up themselves and their audience. Pacing is frantic, the women are attractive, and the comic characters are drawn with the broadest of strokes.
—*David Stratton*

JIANG-HU: BETWEEN LOVE & GLORY/ THE BRIDE WITH WHITE HAIR

(BAKFAT MONUI CHUN)

(HONG KONG)

A Mandarin Films presentation of a Yes Pictures production. (International sales: Mandarin, H.K.) Produced by Michael Wong, Raymond Wong. Executive producers, Ronny Yu, Clifton Ko. Directed by Yu. Screenplay, David Wu, Lam Kei-tou, Tseng Pik-yin, Yu, from the novel by Leung Yu-sang. Camera (color), Peter Pau; editor, Wu; music, Richard Yuen; production design, Eddie Ma; costume design, Emi Wada; sound supervisor (Dolby), Jacqueline Cristianini; martial arts director, Philip Kwok. Reviewed on Universe Laser & Video Co. vidcassette, London, May 2, 1994. (In Cannes Film Festival — market.) Running time: **92 MIN.**
Lien .... Brigitte Lin
Cho Yi-hung .... Leslie Cheung
Chi Wu-shuang .... Ng Chun-yu, Elaine Lui
Lu-hua .... Nam Kit-ying
(Cantonese dialogue)

Even in the crowded market of Hong Kong costume actioners, "The Bride With White Hair" cuts a classy swath. Highly operatic pic version of a novel based on a classic Chinese fable teams superstar cult faves Brigitte Lin ("The East Is Red") and Leslie Cheung ("Farewell My Concubine") in a no-holds-barred meller that could break out to wider dates than the fest and noodle circuit.

The movie took a solid $HK20 million ($2.5 million) locally and preemed in the international marketplace at Mifed last fall under the title "Jiang-Hu: Between Love & Glory." A sequel, also with Lin and Cheung, opened last December to cooler local biz.

Pic marks a change of pace for director Ronny Yu, who bowed with the tough crime movie "The Servants" in 1979. Yu recently followed action director John Woo into the U.S. with plans to helm the $6 million English-language fantasy "Slayer" this summer for producer Stuart Shapiro.

Original yarn, which bears resemblances to German "mountain" myths (such as Leni Riefenstahl's "The Blue Light") and was even adapted into a ballet during China's Cultural Revolution, concerns a thwarted love affair with a mountain girl whose hair has turned white. Present pic is based on a 1958 novel by well-known Hong Kong martial arts novelist Leung Yusang, which constructs a grand tale about warring clans at the end of the Ming dynasty.

Opening has the emperor's troops scaling a snowy peak to find a fabulous flower that blossoms every 20 years and has the power of rejuvenation. The bloom is guarded by swordsman Cho (Cheung), who's been waiting 10 years for his lost love and relates his tragic story.

When a young man, Cho fell for the so-called "wolf girl" Lien (Lin), member of a wild, sybaritic cult ruled by a sister-brother pair of psychotic Siamese twins (Ng Chun-yu, Elaine Lui) who are still joined at the spine. Cho's master, leader of the Seven Clans, wants to annihilate the cult, and the two lovers get caught in the crossfire, with Cho finally losing Lien after a climactic battle.

Though the action sequences when they come are the equal of anything from the best — especially the final showdown, in which Lien's hair turns white and she develops super powers — the film has a broad-spanned, darkly tragic atmosphere that sets it apart from regular, effects-heavy fare. Aided by a fine score from Richard Yuen and a Dolby soundtrack done in Vancouver, it's as much a tragic romance as a rapid-fire chop-chop actioner.

Lin, who's cornered the market in fantasy super-femmes since "The East Is Red," is perfect casting, with Cheung fine as the lovelorn swordsman. So fluid is Yu's direction that he can move from over-the-top sequences with the horrible Siamese twins to rapturous love scenes in mountain pools with nary a pause.

Production values are all excellent, with Peter Pau's lensing making the most of Eddie Ma's Wagnerian sets and Emi Wada's kill-for costumes.
—*Derek Elley*

LOVE IN THE STRANGEST WAY

(ELLES N'OUBLIENT JAMAIS)

(FRENCH)

An Ariane release of a Fildebroc/ Capac/Ice Films/TF1 Films Prods. production, with participation of Canal Plus, Cofimages, Investimage 4. (International sales: President Films, Paris.) Produced by Michelle De Broca. Executive producer, Jean Nachbaur. Directed, written by Christopher Frank, from a story by Jean-Marc Roberts. Camera (color), Bertrand Chatry; editor, Catherine Dubeau; music, Jean-Marie Senia; art direction, Dominique Andre; costume design, Yvette Frank; sound, Daniel Brisseau; associate producer, Paul Claudon. Reviewed at UGC Danton Cinema, Paris, April 21, 1994. (In Cannes Film Festival — market.) Running time: **105 MIN.**
Julien .... Thierry L'hermitte
Anne .... Maruschka Detmers
Angela .... Nadia Fares
With: Patrick Timsit, Umberto Orsini.

"Love in the Strangest Way" — a posthumous release from scripter/helmer Christopher Frank, who died last November — is a taut but somewhat aloof suspenser about a home-wrecking femme fatale and the dark consequences of her deeds. Enjoyably perverse plot could easily be remade as a TV movie in nearly any language.

Three-character drama stars Thierry L'hermitte as Julien, a self-assured exec at a Paris debt collection firm.

When wife Anne (Maruschka Detmers) and 7-year-old son leave on vacation, Julien invites shapely young Angela (Nadia Fares) to dinner on a whim.

Though he backs away from her aggressive angling for a one-night stand, the impetuous and nosy Angela surreptitiously leaves plenty of evidence of her visit.

In record time, she moves into the same apartment building and is hired by Anne to babysit. As Angela orchestrates compromising scenes, Anne's trust in hubby evaporates by stages.

After accidentally whacking Angela with a shovel at a building renovation site, Julien stashes her body in a hollow wall, and buys and moves into the very apartment.

Cynical script makes insulting one's wife's intelligence seem like a more serious transgression than killing a sexy but annoying acquaintance.

Fares is tantalizing as the crafty tease, and Detmers is fine, if subdued, as the incredulous spouse. L'hermitte goes through the motions as the circumstantial evidence of the husband's misbehavior piles up, although the role calls for only a fraction of the thesp's customary charm and comic timing.

Lensing in summertime Paris is OK. Jean-Marie Senia's pulsing score sets a suitably noirish tone from the first frame.

Producers took the English title from a song included here, although literal translation, "Women Never Forget," would seem more apt and commercial.
—*Lisa Nesselson*

THE CROWS

(WRONY)

(POLISH)

An Oko Film Studio/Polish Television production, in association with Film Production Agency, Animex Export-Import. Directed, written by Dorota Kedzierzawska. Camera (color), Arthur Reinhart; editor, Kedzierzawska, Reinhart; music, Wlodek Pawlik; art direction, Magdalena Kujszczyk; costume design, Magda Biedrzycka; sound, Barbara Domaradzka; assistant director, Malgorzata Scislowicz. Reviewed on Oko Film Studio vidcassette, London, March 25, 1994. (In Boston Intl. Festival of Women's Cinema, Cannes Film Festival — Directors Fortnight.) Running time: **66 MIN.**
With: Karolina Ostrozna, Kasia Szczepanik, Malgorzata Hajewska, Anna Prucnal, Ewa Bukowska, Krzysztof Grabarczyk.

Polish helmer Dorota Kedzierzawska, whose gentle hormone opera "Devils, Devils," was noted at Cannes' 1991 Critics' Week, returns in similar vein with "The Crows," a neatly observed mood piece about a prepubescent tyke's day on the lam. Slim but confident pic is ideally suited in length and scale for small-screen playoff after fest dates.

Main character, who's never named, is a loner and a dreamer, unpopular at school, unfazed by boys' sexual taunts and left to her own resources by a young mother who's always out at work. One day, she meets a girl who's scarcely out of diapers, and the pair spend the day wandering around town and romping by the river Vistula.

The girl tells the younger kid that she's her mom and, in a way, she mothers her throughout their odyssey. Ending, in which she delivers the kid back to her real parents and falls asleep on the floor of her own apartment, is as simple and ingenuous as the rest of the pic.

With only an hourlong running time, there's rarely a feeling of wispy material being stretched too far. A characterful performance by Karolina Ostrozna as the feisty loner, stylish photography that makes play with muted colors and dark interiors, a track rich with the sounds of nature, birds, tolling bells, and a simple, childlike score mixing piano and soprano sax — Kedzierzawska juggles all these elements with discreet skill.

—Derek Elley

BOSTON FEST

ODILE & YVETTE AT THE EDGE OF THE WORLD

A BAM Prods. presentation. Produced by Bridget Murnane. Directed, written by Andre Burke. Camera (Foto-Kem color), Chris Squires; editor, Michael Solinger; music, Blake Leyh; production design, John DiMinico; art direction, Paul Logan; sound, (Ultra-Stereo) Ben Lutin; assistant director, Marc Hoffmeister. Reviewed at the Brattle Theatre, Cambridge, Mass., April 29, 1994. (In Boston Intl. Festival of Women's Cinema.) Running time: **95 MIN.**
Odile .... Karen Skloss
Yvette .... Heather Roheim
Johnny .... Noah Fisher
The Father .... Kim Mundy

Reminiscent of early Peter Weir films, especially "Picnic at Hanging Rock," Andre Burke's "Odile and Yvette at the Edge of the World" is a provocative allegory about the innocence and yearnings of two teenage girls. It premiered at the 1993 Edinburgh Film Festival in advance of the Boston Intl. Festival of Women's Cinema unspooling, and could have limited possibilities on the arthouse circuit.

Two sisters, Odile (Karen Skloss) and Yvette (Heather Roheim), escape from their father during a road trip in Texas, where film was shot. Yvette promises to take Odile someplace where her wishes will come true. Through unexplained magic using mundane novelty items, Yvette prevents their father from catching them.

Eventually they find — or conjure up — Johnny (Noah Fisher), a strapping young man who is at first taken by Odile but is soon drawn to Yvette. Feeling betrayed, Odile has to figure out how she will regain control of her own life.

Writer/director Andre Burke and his crew get the most from both their locations and their young tal-

ent. The settings are shot by Chris Squires to appear at once wholly natural and in some sort of twilight zone where the normal rules don't apply. Skloss handles the more difficult role of Odile with aplomb, ably conveying the desires and resentments of a teenage girl. The find here is newcomer Roheim, who suggests depths of knowledge and power in Yvette with little more than an arched eyebrow or twisted smile.

—Daniel M. Kimmel

SHE LIVES TO RIDE

(DOCU)

An Independent Television Service presentation of a Filkela Films production. Produced, directed, edited by Alice Stone. Narration written by Diane Hendrix. Camera (DuArt color), Maryse Alberti; music, Mason Daring; sound, Scott Breindel; sound design, Ron Bochar; associate producer, Hendrix. Reviewed at the Brattle Theatre, Cambridge, Mass., April 26, 1994. (In Boston Intl. Festival of Women's Cinema.) Running time: **75 MIN.**
Narrator: Wren Ross.

Alice Stone's premiere docu effort is a winner from start to finish, as it demolishes the stereotyped image of "biker chicks." Through newsreel footage and contempo interviews with five women, "She Lives to Ride" presents a portrait of a subculture seriously at odds with the conventional Hollywood take on motorcyclists. This crowd pleaser will click at fests and at commercial venues that can tap into feminist and/or biker audiences.

Film offers profiles of five very different women, along with fascinating archival footage of cross-country trips in the days before paved highways. The one who steals the show is Dot Robinson, an 82-year-old biker who putt-putts around Florida on a pink motorcycle. However, she's not just some biking granny but a vet competitive rider who helped break down the gender barrier in the 1930s.

Another profile is of Jo Giovannoni, a middle-class enthusiast who launched Harley Women magazine when she realized that all the motorcycle publications were either technical journals or skin magazines. She even got the late Malcolm Forbes to pose with the violet cycle he gave to Elizabeth Taylor.

Over the course of the profiles, it becomes evident that, for many women, the lure of the motorcycle is not only the freedom of the open road, but the sense of community formed within the various motorcycle clubs. Robinson's Motor Maids wear a set uniform, right down to white gloves, while the Cobras (a black women's group) help plan family-oriented camping trips.

Jacqui Sturgess, leader of the lesbian motorcycle club the Sirens, is shown coordinating her group's participation in New York's Gay Pride parade and formally sipping tea with her partner and fellow cyclist.

Stone puts her film together with wit and verve, including incorporating clips of Marlon Brando in "The Wild One" to show the popular perception of bikers. Helmer's background as assistant editor on films such as "Homicide" and "The Silence of the Lambs" gives the film a polish not often seen in initial docu efforts.

—Daniel M. Kimmel

TURIN FEST

WALKING AFTER MIDNIGHT

(DUS GEZGINLERI)

(TURKISH)

A Yesilcam Filmcilik production. Directed by Atif Yilmaz. Screenplay, Yilmaz, Yildirim Turker, Osman Calli. Camera (color), Metin Erabaci; editor, Mevlut Kocak; music, Selim Atakan; art direction, Kezban Arca Batibeki. Reviewed in Istanbul, April 14, 1994. (In From Sodom to Hollywood, Intl. Gay Film Festival, Turin, Italy.) Running time: **93 MIN.**
With: Meral Oguz, Lale Mansur, Deniz Turkali, Selcuk Ozer.

A marginally soapy but generally well-intentioned lesbian melodrama from veteran Turkish director Atif Yilmaz, "Walking After Midnight" springs few surprises but is held together by a studied perf from actress Meral Oguz as a middle-aged doc with the hots for a long-lost friend. Well received at its Turin screening, the pic could also stroll into other specialized situations.

Oguz plays Nilgun, a divorced doctor from Istanbul who's posted to a small town, where one of her jobs is giving the local hookers medical checkups. One of them turns out to be Havva (Lale Mansur), her best friend from childhood days who never made it up the career ladder.

When Havva falls sick, Nilgun puts her up at her apartment, and the two eventually become an item. Duo later set up home together in Istanbul, where big-city professional and sexual pressures start to strain the relationship.

Aside from a ridiculous first sex scene (in which a drunken Nilgun asks Havva to show her what men do to her in the cathouse), the script skirts most meller pitfalls without bringing much new to the table.

Pat ending, in which Nilgun returns to the heterosexual fold, and Havva, after being seduced by a

lesbian neighbor, returns to the streets, may grate with some gay auds. Pic's target audience is, however, broadband commercial. Casting of the two leads avoids traditional glamour, with Mansur's unconventional looks paralleling Oguz's middle-aged, career-woman appearance. As in all of Yilmaz's movies, tech credits are handsome on all fronts.

—Derek Elley

DREAM GIRLS

(BRITISH — DOCU — 16MM)

A Twentieth Century Vixen production. (International sales: BBC Enterprises, London.) Produced by Jano Williams. Executive producer, Alan Bookbinder. Directed by Kim Longinotto, Williams. Camera (color), Longinotto; editor, John Mister; sound, Claire Hunt. Reviewed at From Sodom to Hollywood, Intl. Gay Film Festival, Turin, Italy, April 15, 1994. Running time: **50 MIN.**

A savvy little docu portrait of an all-femme Japanese troupe, "Dream Girls" is as bizarre as the most diligently transgressive gender-bender enterprise and as benignly exuberant as any kids-in-showbiz tract. Subject of this straightforward but technically adept docu is guaranteed to hook any audience that tunes in.

Focus of pic directed by Kim Longinotto and Jano Williams is Japan's Takarazuka Revue and the exclusive school where its all-girl cast is put through the rigors of a severely disciplined, almost military existence as they prepare to tread the boards.

The revue stages lavish meller musicals on garish sets before packed auds of devoutly adoring women. Femme players taking male roles have an especially ardent following stoked by the fact that the idealized, sensitive men they portray are the antithesis of traditional Japanese manhood.

Housewives gush that the passionate, attentive, erotically charged nature of "male" Takarazuka stars makes them forget the shortcomings of their work-fixated husbands. An astounding volume of love letters, flowers and other tributes arrives, and fans mob their idols in public appearances.

Most Takarazuka alumnae leave at age 25 to be married, and docu touches on the potentially traumatic adjustment to real male-female roles in Japanese society.

—David Rooney

ISTANBUL FEST

NUDE

(CIPLAK)

(TURKISH-FRENCH-GREEK)

An Asya Film (Turkey)/Dream Factory (France)/Astria Film (Greece) production. (International sales: Asya Film, Istanbul.) Directed by Ali Ozgenturk. Screenplay, Ozgenturk, Sadik Karli. Camera (color), Vilko Filac; editor, Mevlut Kocak; music, various. Reviewed at Istanbul Intl. Film Festival, April 13, 1994. Running time: **91 MIN.**
With: Sumru Yavrucuk, Meral Cetinkaya, Erdal Kucukkomurcu, Hulya Karakas, Adnan Tonel, Sami Hazinses, Kulay Kokturk, Ayten Uncuoglu.

"Nude," first film in six years by Turkish maverick Ali Ozgenturk, is a cheeky, mooning look at male-female relationships through the story of two wives liberated by becoming art-school models. Colorful, paper-thin yarn lacks the edge and depth of Ozgenturk's early pix ("Hazal," "The Horse") but just about goes the distance on invention and energy.

Ayla and Seher are two housewives urged by a friend to try nude modeling at a fine arts academy on the picturesque banks of the Golden Horn. As they become more involved in the work and the artistry, their bozo hubbies become more screwed up and sexually inadequate. An offscreen, godlike voice (Ozgenturk himself) monitors and directs events.

Like Ozgenturk's previous "Water Also Burns" (1987), still banned at home, "Nude" is partly about the act of creation, with a fragmented, '60s Godardian flavor that comes close to performance art. With plentiful music, ranging from jazz to "Turandot," pic is at times almost a musical without songs.

Photography by Emir Kusturica's regular lenser, Vilko Filac, is top-drawer, ranging from the rhapsodic to realistic. Cutting and performances are both lively, with a nice ensemble feel and only a slight dip in the third quarter. Nudity is natural throughout. —*Derek Elley*

THE SERPENT'S TALE

(KARANLIK SULAR)

(U.S.-TURKISH)

An Ataman Prods. (Los Angeles/Istanbul) production. (International sales: Ataman Prods., L.A.) Produced, directed, written by E. Kutlug Ataman. Executive producer, Halil Ataman. Camera (color), Chris Squires; editor, Annabel Ware; music, Blake Leyh; production design, John DiMinico; sound design (Ultra-Stereo), Andre Burke; sound, Mike Gitman; associate producers, Richard Holmes, Stefan Schwartz; assistant director, Ahmet Elhan. Reviewed at Istanbul Intl. Film Festival, April 15, 1994. Running time: **82 MIN.**
With: Gonen Bozbey, Metin Uygun, Daniel Chace, Haluk Kurtoglu, Semiha Berksoy, Eric Pio.
(Turkish and English dialogue)

Part intellectual jape, part mystery-thriller, "The Serpent's Tale" ends up not particularly good on either score. Bilingual feature bow by L.A.-based E. Kutlug Ataman starts falling apart early on, despite its technical confidence, making this of interest only for cross-cultural events.

Intriguing opening posits the pic as a reconstruction of a futuristic novel written long ago by Turkey's first female Islamic calligrapher but since destroyed, eaten by her servant. Arabic writing slowly coalesces to form the image of a face, a definite no-no in Islamic culture.

Confusing story, jerkily unfolded, has Yank-in-Istanbul Richie Hunter (Daniel Chace) given an ancient compass by a young stranger, Haldun (Metin Uygun), and told to visit rich aristocrat Lamia (Gonen Bozbey). The artifact is proof that Haldun, Lamia's bastard son, is still alive.

Lamia is hitched to a boorish businessman (Haluk Kurtoglu) who wants to burn down the family mansion and claim the insurance. Meanwhile, her chauffeur tries to steal an ancient scroll (containing the eternal secrets of "death and love") sought by both a religious sect and a U.S. corporation for which Hunter is secretly working. Though Ataman shows a good eye and reasonably confident handling of action sequences, the whole enterprise is shot in the foot by a silly script and English dialogue segs clumsily handled by the Turkish cast.

Legit star Bozbey has presence as the aristocratic Lamia but makes less impression when stepping outside her own language. As the American, Chace is OK within the confines of his lines. Production values are good on the reported $500,000 budget. —*Derek Elley*

A PASSING SUMMER'S RAIN

(YAZ YAGMURU)

(TURKISH)

A TRT production. (International sales: TRT, Ankara.) Produced by Nilgun Sagyasar. Directed by Tomris Giritlioglu. Screenplay, Umit Unal, Giritlioglu, from the story by Ahmet Hamdi Tanpinar. Camera (color), Yavuz Turkeri; editor, Halit Odek; music, Munir Nurettin Beken; art direction, Esat Tekand; costume design, Deniz Ozen. Reviewed at Istanbul Intl. Film Festival, April 12, 1994. Running time: **98 MIN.**
With: Ahmet Levendoglu, Pitircik Akkerman, Selcuk Yontem, Meral Cetinkaya, Muge Akyamac, Mehmet Guleryuz.

Though it never lives up to its impressive opening, "A Passing Summer's Rain" reps a worthwhile third feature by distaff director Tomris Giritlioglu that's of more than passing interest. Literary vignette of a middle-aged novelist's fascination with a beautiful young woman and her troubled past could attract specialized interest offshore.

Set in the picturesque, old-style Istanbul 'burb of Kucuksu at the end of World War II, movie opens with the writer (Ahmet Levendoglu) visited during a summer downpour by a mysterious looker in a red dress (Pitircik Akkerman) who openly flirts with him. Next day, he takes her out, and a strange romance develops, punctuated by the woman's nightmares of an episode in her youth in which her aunt committed suicide in the family's burning house.

Revelation that the house is the one in which the writer now lives, plus an ending that suggests the whole thing may have been his fantasy based on a novel he's penning, is a tad short-storyish. Latter reels are heavy on dream sequences and symbolism for such a flimsy conceit.

Still, playing by the two principals is well balanced, and Giritlioglu turns in a handsome period package, neatly decorated by Debussy's "Clair de Lune" on the soundtrack. —*Derek Elley*

MOON TIME

(AY VAKTI)

(TURKISH)

A Mine Film production. (International sales: Mine Film, Istanbul.) Produced by Kadri Yurdatap. Directed, written by Mahinur Ergun. Camera (color), Ugur Icbak; editor, Nevzat Disiacik; music, Can Hakguder; art direction, Yavuz Fazlioglu. Reviewed at Istanbul Intl. Film Festival, April 14, 1994. Running time: **81 MIN.**
With: Zuhal Olcay, Musfik Kenter, Fusun Demirel, Ali Taygun, Mehmet Kartal, Serra Yilmaz, Tuncer Necmioglu, Nurettin Sen, Ece Sevgen.

Foggy scripting and some overly modish direction cloud "Moon Time," a potentially interesting movie about a romantic triangle set on Turkey's sunbathed southern coast.

Man in the middle is Agah (Musfik Kenter), a 50-ish former high-liver who's returned from the big city to devote himself to Turkish calligraphy and life with his younger mistress, Yildiz (Zuhal Olcay). But tranquility proves an elusive commodity with the stormy Yildiz, and soon Agah's upper-middle-class wife (Fusun Demirel), installed at a neighboring manse, starts trying to lure him back.

Olcay, so good as the long-suffering wife in Yavuz Ozkan's "An Autumn Story," isn't given much to work on as the fiery red-head, apart from endless temper tantrums. In femme helmer Mahinur Ergun's script, Kenter's character emerges dimly as the long-suffering male, caught between a rock and a hard place.

Best perf, and the most fully drawn characterization, is Demirel as the wife, a conservative, moneyed bourgeoise who bides her time like a black widow spider.

Tech credits are good, led by d.p. Ugur Icbak's beautiful vistas of the summery southern seaboard. —*Derek Elley*

May 9, 1994 (Cont.)

ONCE AT NIGHT

(ODNAZHDI NOCH)

(RUSSIAN — B&W)

An Erevan Studio production. Directed by Boris Barnet. Screenplay, Fedor Knorre (from his story and play). Camera (b&w), Stepan Gevorkyan; production design, S. Safaryan, Y. Erzinkyan, A, Arutchan; sound, Y. Grigoryan. Reviewed at the AMC Kabuki 8, San Francisco, May 2, 1994. (In S.F. Intl. Film Festival.) Running time: **83 MIN.**
With: Irina Radchenko, Boris Adreiev, Ivan Kaznetsov, Boris Barnet.

This 1944 Sovfilm was assumed lost until its discovery in an archive last year. Simply mounted but compelling patriotic melodrama should draw a season of bookings on the cinematheque circuit.

Kinetic opening montage shows a Red Air Force plane crashing in an Armenian village occupied by Nazi forces. Its three soldiers are secreted in a bombed-out school's attic by young student Varia, who stays on to clean the facility downstairs for Nazi-headquarters use. One of the wounded men dies, another escapes; Varia risks her life protecting the third. Close has Russian army reclaiming terrain as the soldier who'd gotten away assures traumatized Varia — i.e., Mother Russia — that "you will be avenged. They will pay for everything."

Film was veteran helmer Boris Barnet's next-to-last project; he also plays a Nazi collaborator. Despite some odd narrative gaps (and one bizarre sequence in which Varia distracts attention from her hidden comrades by operatically trilling a song, with full orchestral accompaniment), pic effects a visceral edge from location shooting and economical presentation. Depiction of ruthless occupiers is brutal at times. One especially stirring scene takes place in a dark circus arena, where assembled villagers refuse to comply with Nazi demands.

There and elsewhere, director Barnet manages some arresting, shadow-laden imagery. Lead actress Irina Radchenko's resemblance to Lillian Gish is underlined by her occasionally over-mannered waif histrionics.

The pristine print (discovered by Russian film scholar Naum Kleiman, an honoree at this year's S.F. fest) arrived late for subtitling; though voiceover translation was provided, dialogue is minimal.
—*Dennis Harvey*

DEADLY ADVICE

(BRITISH)

A Mayfair Entertainment Intl. release (U.K.) of a Zenith production. Produced by Nigel Stafford-Clark. Directed by Mandie Fletcher. Screenplay, Glenn Chandler. Camera (color), Richard Greatrex; editor, John Jarvis; music, Richard Harvey; production design, Christopher Hobbs; art direction, Michael Buchanan; costume design, Emma Porteous; sound (Dolby), Mark Holding; stunt coordinator, Tracey Eddon; assistant director, Melanie Dicks; casting, Sheila Trezise. Reviewed at MGM Oxford Street 2 Theater, London, May 3, 1994. Running time: **90 MIN.**
Jodie Greenwood .... Jane Horrocks
Iris Greenwood .... Brenda Fricker
Beth Greenwood .... Imelda Staunton
Dr. Ted Philips .... Jonathan Pryce
Maj. Herbert
  Armstrong .... Edward Woodward
Kate Webster .... Billie Whitelaw
Dr. Crippen .... Hywel Bennett
George Joseph
  Smith .... Jonathan Hyde
Jack the Ripper .... John Mills
Bunny .... Ian Abbey
Judge .... Eleanor Bron

A black comedy about a small-town kook who can't stop deep-sixing her relatives, "Deadly Advice" squanders a gaggle of British character actors on a nothing script that's desperately in need of a laugh track. Leadenly directed attempt at a "Kind Hearts and Coronets" clone stiffs almost from the word go. B.O. looms likewise.

Jane Horrocks ("Life Is Sweet") toplines as Jodie, a shy oddball in a picture-postcard village on the Welsh border who's dominated by her bossy mom (Brenda Fricker) and rumbustious sister, Beth (Imelda Staunton). Latter starts a carnal affair with a hunky male stripper (Ian Abbey).

Though the script doesn't give much away, Jodie clearly hasn't got all her oars in the water. After being visited by apparitions of a local wife-poisoner (Edward Woodward) and Victorian ax murderer (Billie Whitelaw), Jodie sinks a hatchet in her mom's skull. Beth helps her dispose of the corpse, assisted by advice from a phantom Dr. Crippen (Hywel Bennett). When Beth tries some gentle blackmail, Jodie tops her as well, closely followed by her stripper b.f. At her trial for the latter's murder, Jodie pleads self-defense and gets off. Coda, in which she marries patient suitor Ted (Jonathan Pryce), features a well-telegraphed twist, plus some Freudian mumbo-jumbo to explain Jodie's mind-set.

Black comedy of this sort needs to be done either with brisk pacing or great style, and debuting helmer Mandie Fletcher (from the TV series "Blackadder") shows an alarming lack of both. Plot dawdles along for at least half-hour of family backgrounding before Horrocks starts reaching for the hardware, and Glenn Chandler's script is as short on laughs as a burning orphanage.

Though set in the present, the gallery of Brit stereotypes curiously evokes small-town pix of the '50s, sans their spirit and true eccentricities. Horrocks and company's attempts at Welsh accents seem an unnecessary distraction.

Though Horrocks has built a name in Blighty for playing kooky characters, she needs a stronger script and director to carry a pic of this sort. As her mom and sis, Fricker and Staunton are solid; of the gallery of veteran names as the phantom murderers, only Woodward and Mills make any impression. As Horrocks' milquetoast boyfriend, Pryce is also chopped off at the legs by the nothing script.

Sole spark is provided by Richard Harvey's bombastic, mock-Handelian score. Production design, and Richard Greatrex's exterior lensing in the village of Hay-on-Wye, are both fine. —*Derek Elley*

FATHER AND SON

(PADRE E FIGLIO)

(ITALIAN)

A DARC release of an Erre Cinematografica production, in association with Reteitalia (Italy)/Flach Film (Paris)/K2 Two (Brussels). Produced by Angelo Rizzoli. Executive producer, Alessandro Calosci. Directed by Pasquale Pozzessere. Screenplay, Pozzessere, Roberto Tiraboschi. Camera (Technicolor), Bruno Cascio; editor, Carlo Valerio; art direction, Cinzia Di Mauro; costume design, Marina Campanale. Reviewed at Quirinetta Cinema, Rome, April 22, 1994. Running time: **95 MIN.**
Corrado .... Michele Placido
Gabriele .... Stefano Dionisi
Angela .... Enrica Origa
Anna .... Carlotta Jazzetti
Valeria .... Giusy Consoli
Chiara .... Claudia Gerini
Aldo .... Luciano Federico

Up-and-coming Italo talent Pasquale Pozzessere ("Verso Sud") directs a finely realistic tale of Genoa's working class in "Father and Son." This confident, sure-handed effort is slow but likable. Its very specific setting marks it as an art film built to travel, and pic should turn up in many fest venues. Pace could be an obstacle to foreign pickups, but it's definitely worth a look.

Pozzessere and co-scripter Roberto Tiraboschi meticulously embed the generational conflict between father Corrado (Michele Placido) and son Gabriele (suave newcomer Stefano Dionisi) in the heart of working-class Genoa. The characters are introduced as part of a landscape: the port, the factories and little shops like the dry cleaner's where Corrado's wife works.

Now nearing retirement, Corrado works in the port as a night watchman, but his heart is still in the factory where he spent most of his working life. He manages to procure Gabriele, just out of the army, a job in his old plant, but the youth quits. Decision to find his own path provokes a rift that is only partly healed at film's end.

Film makes several references to politics, particularly via old-fashioned militant Corrado. In one amusing scene, he speaks pidgin Russian to some Ukrainian sailors, who reproachfully remind him they aren't part of the Soviet Union anymore. A young lawyer also reminds Corrado the factories aren't the focal point for class struggle anymore. His son, typical to his generation and much to Corrado's disgust, is apolitical.

While Placido gamely mimes his role of a remarried paterfamilias with an authority complex, it's young Dionisi who strikes a noteworthy balance between a realistic perf (he learned to speak with a Genoese accent for the part) and budding stardom, sporting a very modern type of earnest vulnerability.

Also modern are several understated but sexy scenes in which Dionisi casually trysts with two girlfriends (Claudia Gerini, Giusy Consoli). Like the young stepmother (Enrica Origa), they're nicely individualized characters who hold a few surprises.

Film's painstaking realism consistently earns points, while splendid lensing by Bruno Cascio captures a moody atmosphere and reveals Pozzessere's concern with technique. Many key scenes are filmed at night, by the light of ships in the harbor or the neon of game parlors or discotheques. Music ranges eclectically from a mellow jazz score to an exotic African beat.

Film's downside is a slow, step-by-step pace that lacks forward drive.
—*Deborah Young*

POORLY EXTINGUISHED FIRES
(DES FEUX MAL ETEINTS)
(FRENCH)

A Pan-Europeene release of an Image & Compagnie presentation of an Image & Compagnie/SFP Cinema/France 2 Cinema/GMT Prods./Belvedere Prods. production in association with Sofinergie 1 and 2, Investimage 4 and participation of Canal Plus, CNC, Procirep. Produced by Thierry Forsans, Serge Moati. Co-producer, Boudjemaa Dahmane. Directed by Moati. Screenplay, Didier Decoin, Moati, Jean-Jacques Zilbermann, based on Philippe Labro's novel. Camera (color), Jacques Guerin, Georges Orset; editors, Nicole Dedieu, Jean-Pierre Roques; music, Gabriel Yared; production design, Dominique Treibert; costume design, Francoise Guegan; sound, Norbert Garcia, Joel Faure; associate producer, Jean-Pierre Guerin; assistant director, Patrice Martineau. Reviewed at UGC Danton Cinema, Paris, Jan. 30, 1994. Running time: **98 MIN.**
Jerome .... Manuel Blanc
"Tweedy Bird" .... Maria de Medeiros
Francois .... Emmanuel Salinger
Jeanne ....Helene Vincent
With: Rufus, Francois Negret, Christophe Malavoy, Daniel Gelin, Simon de la Brosse, Fabrice Desplechin, Xavier Thiam, Chick Ortega.

A dynamic retelling of the hectic and violent closing weeks of the Algerian war in 1962 through the eyes of a freshly arrived French army journalist, "Poorly Extinguished Fires" benefits from skillful period production design, lively lensing and multiple points of view. Gallic B.O. looks to be modest, but this visually vivid undertaking is fine for fest, specialized and tube outlets with audiences keen on history, war and youth themes.

Philippe Labro's 1967 novel, on which the movie is based, drew sales and acclaim as a wrenching portrait of a generation scarred by the moral abyss of the Algerian conflict, in which joint casualties totaled nearly 750,000. Title is taken from a verse by turn-of-the-century Gallic writer Apollinaire about the prematurely snuffed light in a comrade's eyes.

Story starts in Paris where, before shipping out to Algiers, Jerome Cartier (Manuel Blanc) is interrogated and beaten up by men who confiscate some politically sensitive photos sent him in confidence by Algiers-stationed friend Francois (Emmanuel Salinger).

As Algerian independence draws near after eight years of war, Francois is working for reconciliation between factions. But, as Jerome sees from day one in the country, carnage is everywhere, as vindictive French forces adopt a scorched-earth policy. The photos make Francois and his associates marked people.

Francois is subsequently murdered, and Jerome is drawn to his g.f. (Maria de Medeiros), a local radio announcer, in the wake of his death.

Abrupt sequences of wholesale slaughter and booby-trapped cars exploding are well-handled. Pic brims with naked, bloody corpses of French soldiers in the morgue and doesn't shy away from showing the aftermath of civilian massacres.

Blanc is good as the curious novice later emboldened by the murder of Francois. De Medeiros shines as the high-spirited g.f. who seems insulated from danger by her smile and style. Christophe Malavoy plays a dashing and enigmatic figure whose true identity is a late-arriving shock.

Helmer Serge Moati is a prolific documaker and miniseries director who's worked primarily for TV since the late 1960s. The almost totally hand-held camera work (blown up to 35mm from Super-16) bristles with nervous energy and often has a washed-out documentary look.

Pic contains only establishing shots of Algiers and the Casbah. Bulk of the movie was shot in Tunis, Marseilles and Paris.

—*Lisa Nesselson*

BLACKOUT
(BRITISH)

A Poker production. (International sales: Poker, London.) Produced, directed by Paulita Sedgwick. Screenplay, Damian Wong. Camera (color), Christopher T. Maris; consulting editor, Maris; editor, Peregrine de la Motte; music, Jake Williams; production design, Angel Sedgwick; art direction, Angel Sedgwick, Abi Manox, Guy Beckett; costume design, Angel Sedgwick, Manox; sound (Dolby), Bob Doyle, Ian Selwyn; assistant director, Merlin Massara. Reviewed at Berlin Film Festival (market), Feb. 14, 1994. Running time: **98 MIN.**
Lola .... Kali
Tamara .... Abi Manox
Jean-Marie .... Jean Marc Ferriere
Guy .... Guy Beckett
Arlette .... Ultra Violet
Komandant .... Byron Thomas
Pardo Turin .... Ian McKay
Brother
Francis .... Eddie Tudor-Pole
Zag .... Angel Sedgwick

A mateur from the word go, "Blackout" is an embarrassingly awkward low-budgeter about three youths in a futuristic, war-zone London. Produced in 1992, this first feature of producer/director Paulita Sedgwick, formerly based in France and the U.S., looks set for a nose dive to commercial oblivion.

Trio are blond rocker Lola (Kali), her b.f. Guy (Guy Beckett) and his sister Tamara (Abi Manox), who leave the 'burbs for some kicks in the Red Zone. There they meet eligible druggy bachelor Jean-Marie (Jean Marc Ferriere), son of Arlette (War-

hol icon Ultra Violet), head of a firm that's invented Eternacream. Arlette's in cahoots with the fascistic authorities, who in turn are being hassled by a gang of street youths.

Pic is holed beneath the waterline early on by clumsy dialogue, summer-camp acting, paceless editing and freshman film-school direction. Only survivors from the wreckage are Manox, serviceable as the kid sister, and d.p. Christopher T. Maris, whose pro exterior lensing offsets pic's grungy look in interiors.

—*Derek Elley*

FOREIGN STUDENT
(FRENCH)

An AMLF (France)/Universal (U.S.) release of a Tarak Ben Ammar/Silvio Berlusconi Communications presentation of a Carthago Films/Libra UK/Holland Coordinator production, in association with Featherstone Prods. Produced by Tarak Ben Ammar, Mark Lombardo. Co-executive producers, Peter Hoffman, Victoria Westhead, Menno Meyjes. Directed by Eva Sereny. Screenplay, Meyjes, based on Philippe Labro's novel "The Foreign Student." Camera (color), Franco Di Giacomo; editor, Peter Hollywood; music, Jean-Claude Petit; production design, Howard Cummings; costume design, Carol Ramsey; Dolby sound; assistant director, Greg Jacobs. Reviewed at UGC Danton Cinema, Paris, April 23, 1994. Running time: **93 MIN.**
Philippe
Le Clerc .... Marco Hofschneider
April .... Robin Givens
Cal Cate .... Rick Johnson
Sue Ann .... Charlotte Ross
Zach Gilmore .... Edward Herrmann
Also with: Jack Coleman, Charles Dutton, Hinton Battle, Anthony Herrera.
(English dialogue)

"F oreign Student" is a borderline trite but basically sweet nostalgic memoir of a French boy's formative semester at a Virginia college and his impossible romance with a bright black girl, circa 1955. Directing debut by still photog Eva Sereny is attractively lensed and leads are appealing, but B.O. prospects for old-fashioned pic look modest.

Based on Philippe Labro's hit 1986 novel, the story of exchange student Philippe Le Clerc (Marco Hofschneider) and April (Robin Givens), the beautiful "Negro girl" who memorizes Byron and speaks correspondence-school French when she's not cleaning faculty houses, is punctuated by references to those aspects of U.S. culture that hold a special place in the collective French heart — blues and jazz, Faulkner, Chandler and Salinger.

In lieu of true bite, pic draws its humor and somewhat forced poignance from the radical differences between *le football* (soccer) and American tackle football, and from Philippe's enthusiastic acceptance

of blacks compared with the segregation practiced in the South.

Straightforward tale is awash in wholesome period details and nicely portrayed stock characters: the hunky quarterback who shows Philippe the ropes (Rick Johnson), the paternal professor who takes the new kid under his wing (Edward Herrmann), the Southern belle on the verge of a nervous breakdown (Charlotte Ross), the crusty coach who wants only what's best for the team (Anthony Herrera) and the worldly blues musicians (Charles Dutton as Howlin' Wolf and Hinton Battle as Sonny Boy Williamson) who help the white boy out of a jam on the "colored" side of town.

Givens is fine as the wise looker who knows her place but yearns for more, and German thesp Hofschneider ("Europa, Europa") convinces as the sensitive Gallic interloper. Voiceover from main character looking back after 40 years ranges from self-consciously literary to downright sappy.

Location lensing in Paris and Virginia is slick, the '50s-era production design evocative, although the turnout for the big game against Alabama Tech is laughably small.

—*Lisa Nesselson*

EAST FROM THE WEST, OR THE DISCREET CHARM OF THE MEDIA
(NYUGATTOL KELETRE, AVAGY A MEDIA DISZKRET BAJA)
(HUNGARIAN)

A Mozgokep Innovacios Tarsulas/Rolling Box production. Produced by Istvan Darday. Directed, written by Darday, Gyorgyi Szalai. Camera (color), Tibor Nemes, Gyorgy Palos, Attila Balazs; editor, Margit Galamb; music, Jozsef Czencz. Reviewed at Hungarian Film Week, Budapest, Feb. 9, 1994. Running time: **99 MIN.**
With: Andras Szoke, Janos Regos, Sandor Badar.

T his muddled comedy doesn't live up to its intriguing title. A heavy-handed satire on post-communist consumerism in Hungary, it's a road movie without energy.

Co-director Istvan Darday made the amusing "Holiday in Britain" 20 years ago, but new effort, made with regular collaborator Gyorgyi Szalai, is a labored item that attacks easy, obvious targets (strident TV ads being the main one).

Slim plot involves the journey of a large-screen TV set, first prize in a competition, from Budapest to the village where the lucky winner resides. Carried on a left-behind Russian military truck, the TV is switched on and a perfect picture can be seen as the truck passes through the Magyar landscape.

Comic Andras Szoke, who usually directs his own material, appears as the truck driver's mate and is the main source of the supposed humor.

Tech credits are basic.

—*David Stratton*

TOO MUCH SUN/ WOMEN ALONE

(TROPPO SOLE)

(ITALIAN)

A Lucky Red release of a La Banda Magnetica, Navert Film production, in association with Reteitalia, presented by Pietro Formentin and Massimo Cortesi. Executive producers, Massimo Cortesi, Alberto Osella. Directed by Giuseppe Bertolucci. Screenplay, Sabina Guzzanti, David Rondino. Camera (Fotocinema color), Fabio Cianchetti; editor, Fiorella Giovannelli; music, Andrea Guerra; art direction, Gianni Silvestri; costume design, Grazia Colombini. Reviewed at Fiamma Cinema, Rome, May 2, 1994. Running time: **94 MIN.**

With: Sabina Guzzanti.

A tour de force for young TV impersonator Sabina Guzzanti, "Too Much Sun/Women Alone" is one sprightly, extended joke, with the star playing 14 different roles, practically every speaking part in the film. Guzzanti's cult following has kept local opening B.O. strong, but the film packs too many local references to make travel easy. Even if they don't get all the gags, however, offshore viewers who stumble on this pic will get a look at a bright new talent in Guzzanti, who also co-scripted.

Title is a pun that can be translated either as "too much sun" or "women too alone." Entire film is peopled with dizzy females, with just a handful of men (who appear as mute, muscle-bound pinups). Helmer Giuseppe Bertolucci, who has directed films chronicling the early stage work of popular comic Roberto Benigni, takes a relaxed approach, letting Guzzanti's talky, tongue-in-cheek routines work on their own.

Main character is a flighty TV reporter named Lalla who takes off in her red convertible and sunglasses to interview reclusive singing star Matilde. She finds her living in a villa that makes Xanadu look like a walkup, surrounded by her kitchen-bound mama, her drug-addict sister and a German shepherd.

Much of pic's comedy depends on recognizing the real-life characters behind the fictional ones. Matilde resembles the legendary Mina, a scientist is the spitting image of Rita Levi Montalcini, and Lalla's

boss and bedmate is a cinch for anyone who knows their Italian TV.

Despite Guzzanti's rapid-fire personality changes and mindboggling collection of accents, the featherweight story starts to drag after a while. Bertolucci shows little interest in realistic special effects when several characters appear together in a scene.

All that's missing are male parts for the pretty Guzzanti, who does a brilliant imitation of Silvio Berlusconi on local TV. —*Deborah Young*

A SAINT IN A TURBULENT AGE

(ZUWUUN ZAGYN BOGD)

(MONGOLIAN)

A Mongolkino production. Directed by Zedendambaagin Zerendorsh, Luvsansharavyn Sharavdorsh. Screenplay, D. Maam, J. Baramsai. Camera (color), Sharavdorsh; music, Sh. Chuluun; art direction, Z. Boldsuche. Reviewed at Berlin Film Festival (Forum section — Mongolian sidebar), Feb. 11, 1994. Running time: **128 MIN.**

With: Ch. Erdeniochir, B. Banzaragts, D. Sosorbaram, Th. Idshinhorloo, M. Dorshdagvaa, Z. Zerendorsh.

Collectors of exotic costumers may want to take a peek at "A Saint in a Turbulent Age," but otherwise this 17th-century Mongolian talkfest is too reminiscent of creaky '50s vehicles from Eastern Europe to conquer auds beyond its borders.

Part 1 ("The Rising Tide," 67 minutes) opens in 1657, when Mongolia was threatened by absorption into the neighboring Manchurian empire. Internally, the country is riven by political battling between the Great Khan, local leaders and scholarly Tsanabatsar (Ch. Erdeniochir), dubbed "The Living Buddha" because of his travels in India and Tibet. The Khan himself is also worried about continuing his family line — a problem solved by dusky maid Amina (Th. Idshinhorloo).

Part 2 ("The Ebbing Tide," 61 minutes) fast-forwards to 1686 and the breakdown in peace talks between two factions. Tsanabatsar, who's invented a way of unifying the country through a second written language, is finally forced to flee to Manchuria.

Viewers without degrees in Mongolian history will likely be baffled by most of the goings-on, clogged by a forest of names, a gabby script and unclear development. Moscow-trained helmers' visual style is conservative, with lots of medium shots and close-ups, and only basic cutting. Action scenes are minimal and boxy-looking (in 1.33).

—*Derek Elley*

THE LAST KLEZMER

LEOPOLD KOZLOWSKI: HIS LIFE AND MUSIC

(DOCU — 16mm)

A Maelstrom Films production. (International sales: Maelstrom, N.Y.) Produced by Bernard Berkin. Directed, written by Yale Strom. Camera (color, 16mm), Oren Rudavsky; editor, David Notowitz; music, Leopold Kozlowski, Strom; production design, Strom. Reviewed at Berlin Film Festival (Forum section), Feb. 14, 1994. Running time: **84 MIN.**

It's hard to call Leopold Kozlowski "the last klezmer," and there's only a minimal amount of the Polish composer's music in this movie. But the film is full of spunk and warmth, and with America and Europe going through a modest revival of klezmer music, this homemade docu should get some play at fests and on TV.

Kozlowski has a lot to say about Klezmer music (the folk tunes often heard at Jewish weddings) and Jewish culture in Poland, where he's lived most of his composing career. He also has many a tale to tell about life during the Nazi occupation, in the resistance and in concentration camps. His lively charm wins over the viewer from the beginning, and some of the impromptu scenes director Yale Strom captures are touching.

Perhaps the best of these is when Kozlowski and a friend recall life in the concentration camp. Kozlowski offers a story he's never told before, in which the Nazis made him play "Lili Marleen" on the violin while naked on the dinner table with a burning candle beneath him on which they lit their cigarettes. His friend's comment, completely free of irony: "Must've looked funny."

Film seems incomplete and uneven. There isn't enough music to get a handle on what kind of a composer Kozlowski is — or, for non-insiders, what klezmer is — or to understand all the historic circumstances. Tech credits are poor. Color and lensing, as well as Strom's high-school narrator's voice, give the impression of a Super-8 home movie, which will be charming to some but annoying to others.

—*Eric Hansen*

ITALY AFTER THE WAR

(SUCCEDE IN QUARANTOTTO)

(ITALIAN — DOCU — B&W)

A Mikado Film release (Italy) of a RAI-3 production in association with Aura Film. (International sales: Sacis.) Produced by Francesca De Vita. Executive producers, Roberto Cicutto, Vincenzo De Leo. Directed, written by Nicola Caracciolo, Valerio E. Marino; editor, Angela Monfortese; music, Benedetto Ghiglia; music adviser, Gianni Borgna; sound, Adriano Torbidone. Reviewed at Greenwich Cinema, Rome, March 10, 1994. Running time: **87 MIN.**

Narrator: Oreste Rizzini.

"Italy After the War" is a whirlwind chronicle of the *bel paese*, 1945-48. Assembled entirely from cine-newsreels and footage from Istituto Luce and the Historical Archive of the Workers' Movement, this dense diet of political, social and cultural tidbits should intrigue historians and Italophiles via exposure on specialist webs.

In their 1991 docu "The 600 Days of Salo," former Luce film archive conservator Valerio E. Marino and political-historical journalist and filmmaker Nicola Caracciolo depicted the short-lived fascist puppet republic set up by Benito Mussolini at the end of World War II. Here they document Italy in the devastated aftermath of war, its deliverance from fascism, abandonment of the monarchy and transition to a democratic republic.

Power divisions between the state, church and Mafia, festering North-South antagonism, shifts between the political right and left, and the emergence from chaos of a new moralism that empowers the Vatican all have '90s relevance, even if commentary is light on analysis.

Italy's then-burgeoning film industry is mentioned only fleetingly in snippets showing Silvana Mangano, Lucia Bose and a crooning Vittorio De Sica. But buffs will recognize a font of inspiration for Fellini in street performers and traveling circus acts, and food for the neo-realists in the forlorn urchins on view.

Footage used is mostly in immaculate condition, though the selection often appears disjointed.

—*David Rooney*

MIST, OR MOONLIGHT SHADOW OVER LEVUBU

(KOD AVAGY HOLDARNYEK LEVUBU FOLOTT)

(HUNGARIAN)

A Hunnia Film Studio/Magyar Televizio production. (International sales: Cinemagyar, Budapest.) Produced by Gyorgy Lendvai, Janos Drabik. Directed by Krisztina Deak. Screenplay, Andor Szilagyi, Deak. Camera (color), Gabor Balog; editor, Mrs. Ferenc Szecsenyi; music, Laszlo Melis; art direction, Jozsef Romvari. Reviewed at Hungarian Film Week, Budapest, Feb. 7, 1994. Running time: **93 MIN.**
With: ldiko Toth, Adel Kovats, Frigyes Funtek, George Tabori, Hedi Temessy.

Nebulous scripting and foggy direction sink "Mist," a pretentious drama about two beautiful sisters haunted by family ghosts and a destructive curse. Pic's a major disappointment after helmer Krisztina Deak's tightly controlled Jewish drama "The Book of Esther" four years ago. Foreign sales look murky.

Siblings Olga (Ildiko Toth) and Marta (Adel Kovats) return with their children to the old family seat, a dilapidated mansion in the country that used to be a Communist Party sanitarium. Olga, widowed, soon gets the hots for Marta's artist husband, Viktor; meanwhile, Marta is haunted by the ghost of her nanny (Hedi Temessy) and also discovers some unsettling truths about her wise old uncle, Gabor (George Tabori). Memory and reality start to intertwine, with apocalyptic results.

In the midst of a lot of sitting around talking and reminiscing, and a fog machine that works overtime, pic wastes several talented players (Kovats and veterans Temessy and Tabori) and gets hopelessly tied up in its convoluted script. Laszlo Melis' overheated score seems written for a drama that never reached the screen. —*Derek Elley*

MAVERICK

A Warner Bros. release of an Icon production in association with Donner/Shuler-Donner Prods. Produced by Bruce Davey, Richard Donner. Co-producer, Jim Van Wyck. Directed by Donner. Screenplay, William Goldman, based on the TV show "Maverick," created by Roy Huggins. Camera (Technicolor; Panavision widescreen), Vilmos Zsigmond; editor, Stuart Baird; music, Randy Newman; production design, Tom Sanders; art direction, Daniel Dorrance; set decoration, Lisa Dean; costume design, April Ferry; sound (Dolby), Clark King; associate producer, Alexander B. Collett; assistant director, Van Wyck; second unit director, Terry Leonard; second unit camera, John Connor; stunt coordinator, Mic Rodgers; casting, Marion Dougherty. Reviewed at Warner Bros. Studio, Burbank, May 8, 1994. MPAA Rating: PG. Running time: **129 MIN.**
Bret Maverick .... Mel Gibson
Annabelle Bransford ..... Jodie Foster
Marshal Zane Cooper . James Garner
Joseph .... Graham Greene
Commodore Duvall ....James Coburn
Angel .... Alfred Molina
The Archduke .... Paul Smith
Eugene .... Geoffrey Lewis
Johnny .... Max Perlich
With: Dub Taylor, Dan Hedeya, Robert Fuller, Doug McClure, Bert Remsen, Denver Pyle, Will Hutchins, Clint Black, Waylon Jennings, Kathy Mattea.

There can be little doubt that a whole new generation is about to discover the charm, wit and fun of "Maverick." This exuberant Western is a crowd-pleaser that remains faithful to the genre while having a roaring good time sending up its conventions. Industry mavens expecting a $100 million domestic box office will not de disappointed. The early summer release should play well through the season and translate readily to foreign climes.

The original "Maverick," which aired on ABC from 1957-62, was a popular television staple with Jack Kelly and newcomer James Garner as lovable rogue gamblers. Garner subsequently dusted off his character in several television movies.

In its new bigscreen incarnation, Mel Gibson takes up the mantle with glee. Jodie Foster as a sometimes treacherous temptress, Garner as a seasoned lawman and a rogues' gallery of characters are along for the ride.

Director Richard Donner serves it all up as one rollicking piece of dumb fun. But thanks to a keen, comical script by William Goldman and a sterling cast, it's smart dumb fun.

The film opens on a high note as Bret Maverick (Gibson) is seen perched on his horse with a noose around his neck. He sanguinely states via voiceover that he's had a lousy week. It all began on his way to the winner-take-all poker championship aboard the paddlewheel Lauren Belle.

Then, in flashback, we see him arriving in a small, scenic town to find a card game and win the remaining few thousand dollars he needs for the tournament fee. He stumbles onto a table where the principals include the demure Annabelle Bransford (Foster) and a mean hombre named Angel (Alfred Molina). The extended section allows us to view his con game, which includes a developed pretense of cowardice and a lot of good humor to mask his skill with guns, fists and cards.

He walks away a winner but not without incurring Angel's wrath and Annabelle's lust ... for his money. She attempts to seduce him away from his winnings, but it's tough to con a con man. As they head off for the high stakes, they share a stage coach with Marshal Zane Cooper (Garner) and along the route experience a runaway stagecoach ride, bandits and supposedly hostile Indians.

Donner conducts with aplomb the high-wire act of balancing vintage Western set pieces with contemporary high jinks. "Maverick" is an authentic oater that eschews shortcuts. You can almost taste the dust rising up from the pristine period re-creations vividly captured on the bigscreen by Vilmos Zsigmond.

It's no mean feat that the actors take the script's myriad improbabilities and conveniences and provide them with a center and logic. Goldman has taken his cue from his own script of "Butch Cassidy and the Sundance Kid" and added dollops of "The Sting" for a tasty confection.

The title role provides Gibson with a cocky, physical character that suits his persona. Unlike his TV predecessor, he loves to fight as much as he likes the banter. Foster — not an obvious choice for his sparring partner — throws herself into the comic, vampish role with abandon. It's an inspired pairing.

Best of all is Garner, an unsung master of this type of droll fare. He seems more a kindred spirit, even father, to Gibson than his competitor or nemesis. In this realm he is definite royalty, and one can see the line continuing handsomely with Gibson.

There are nice supporting turns from Molina as the plot heavy and Graham Greene playing the native version of Maverick. James Coburn pops up as the proprietor of the poker tournament to provide the closing section with zest. An endless stream of familiar movie, television and country music faces dot the landscape. Even Danny Glover shows up uncredited as a bank robber with a symbiotic twitch for the hero.

Though it occasionally falters when the pace slackens, "Maverick" is pretty much satisfying entertainment with all stops pulled out. It would be mere quibbling to cite its wrinkles, though those who loved the series have to be disappointed that its theme song and music have been jettisoned.
—*Leonard Klady*

A MILLION TO JUAN

A Samuel Goldwyn Co. and Crystal Sky Communications presentation in association with Prism Pictures. Produced by Steven Paul, Barry Collier. Executive producers, Barbara Javitz, Gary Binkow, Sherman Baldwin. Directed by Paul Rodriguez. Screenplay, Francisca Matos, Robert Grasmere, based on a story by Mark Twain and characters inspired by Rodriguez. Camera (Foto-Kem), Bruce Johnson; editor, Michael Ripps; music, Steven Johnson, Jeffrey Johnson, Samm Pena; production design, Mary Patvaldnieks; costume design, Jennifer Green; sound (UltraStereo), Tony Smyles; casting, Dorothy Koster. Reviewed at Samuel Goldwyn, L.A., May 5, 1994. MPAA Rating: PG. Running time: **97 MIN.**
Juan Lopez .... Paul Rodriguez
Olivia Smith .... Polly Draper
Jorge/Mr. Ortiz .... Pepe Serna
Alvaro .... Bert Rosario
Alejandro
Lopez .... Jonathan Hernandez
Flaco .... Gerardo
Hector Delgado .... Victor Rivers
Mr. Angel .... Edward James Olmos
Jenkins .... Paul Williams
With: Tony Plana, Ruben Blades, Cheech Marin, David Rasche, Liz Torres.

The odds of "A Million to Juan" breaking out of its inherent niche-market appeal can be summed up in its title. This gentle rags-to-riches tale set in the Los Angeles barrio is a good-natured parable that, unfortunately, doesn't pack much commercial punch. Its positive intentions aren't enough to cross over into the mainstream.

Loosely based on the Mark Twain story "The Million Pound Bank Note" (filmed more traditionally in 1954), it centers on Juan Lopez (Paul Rodriguez), a decent, uneducated guy trying to eke out a living and raise his young son. The task is made more difficult by a bureaucratic snafu that threatens to send the U.S.-born, but undocumented, Lopez packing to Mexico.

At this point fate steps into the picture. On the job selling oranges at a quiet intersection, he's beckoned to a limousine and handed an envelope. When Juan rips it open, inside is a check for $1 million. He's told that it is a loan. He has it for a month and, if used properly, he will receive a reward.

Juan doubts its authenticity, but his immigration case worker and buddies prod him to check it out. When a Beverly Hills banker almost goes into cardiac arrest, there can be little doubt about its genuineness.

The basic premise has weathered the years quite well. But the underlying sweetness of the Francisca Matos/Robert Grasmere screenplay is out of step with contemporary mores. Its major problem is that the central character never succumbs to any of the deadly sins his sudden good fortune would ordinarily offer. Juan remains the soul of decency while almost everyone around him turns into gargoyles of lust, desire and greed.

In the absence of internal or external tension, "A Million to Juan" is no more than a trifle and a paean to hope, faith and good deeds. None of these noble sentiments are enhanced by the style of presentation or the wit of the text.

In addition to starring, Rodriguez makes his directorial debut, demonstrating little more than passing knowledge of the grammar of the craft. Even with a modest budget, the picture ought to have had some visual panache or narrative momentum to quicken a mostly predictable scenario.

He at least comes across as a pleasant hero, and his casting of supporting parts is quite shrewd. Among the large cast are keen turns by Ruben Blades and Edward James Olmos and strong secondary work from Tony Plana and Polly Draper as an unexpected romantic interest.

While Rodriguez adheres to the movie dictum of happy endings, his mix of message and mirth is too soft and mushy to reach a contemporary crowd.
—*Leonard Klady*

CANNES FEST

MRS. PARKER AND THE VICIOUS CIRCLE

A Fine Line Features release presented in association with Miramax of a Robert Altman production, produced in association with Odyssey Entertainment Ltd. Produced by Altman. Executive producers, Scott Bushnell, Ira Deutchman. Co-producer, Allan Nicholls. Directed by Alan Rudolph. Screenplay, Rudolph, Randy Sue Coburn. Camera (color; Panavision widescreen), Jan Kiesser; editor, Suzy Elmiger; music, Mark Isham; production design, Francois Seguin; art direction, James Fox; set decoration, Frances Calder; costume design, John Hay, Renee April; sound (Dolby), Richard Nichol; associate producer, James McLindon; assistant director, Nicholls. Reviewed at the Aidikoff Screening Room, Beverly Hills, May 6, 1994. (In Cannes Film Festival — competing.) Running time: **123 MIN.**
Dorothy
 Parker .... Jennifer Jason Leigh
Charles
 MacArthur .... Matthew Broderick
Robert Benchley .... Campbell Scott
Alan Campbell .... Peter Gallagher
Gertrude Benchley .... Jennifer Beals
Eddie Parker .... Andrew McCarthy
Horatio Byrd .... Wallace Shawn
Jane Grant .... Martha Plimpton
Harold Ross .... Sam Robards
Edna Ferber .... Lili Taylor
Deems Taylor .... James LeGros
Paula Hunt ...... Gwyneth Paltrow
Robert Sherwood ...... Nick Cassavetes
George S. Kaufman ..... David Thornton
Mary Kennedy
 Taylor .... Heather Graham
Alexander Woollcott .... Tom McGowan
Franklin P. Adams .... Chip Zien
Heywood Broun .... Gary Basaraba
Ruth Hale .... Jane Adams
Roger Spalding .... Stephen Baldwin
Marc Connelly .... Matt Malloy
Neysa McMein .... Rebecca Miller
John Peter Toohey .... Jake Johannsen
Mary Brandon
 Sherwood .... Amelia Campbell
Donald Ogden Stewart .... David Gow
Beatrice Kaufman .... Leni Parker
Harpo Marx .... J.M. Henry
Fred Hunter .... Stanley Tucci
Joanie Gerard .... Mina Badie
Alvan Barach .... Randy Lowell
Will Rogers .... Keith Carradine

A striking performance by Jennifer Jason Leigh provides the centerpiece for "Mrs. Parker and the Vicious Circle," a highly absorbing but naggingly patchy look at the acerbic writer Dorothy Parker and her cohorts at the legendary Algonquin Round Table. World premiering at the Cannes Film Festival in advance of its skedded fall commercial bow, Alan Rudolph's latest dramatic mosaic is a natural sibling to "The Moderns," his previous examination of a 1920s artistic milieu, although one with more heart, trenchant drama and deftly realized characterizations.

Like the director's other films, this beautifully made period piece will not be an easy sell commercially, but some strong notices and a push to revive interest in Parker among students and the sophisticated public could serve to put it on the map and thus give it a fighting chance. Miramax owns foreign rights.

Parker was one of the first American female writers to develop a critical voice that was respected equally with those of her illustrious male colleagues among the Gotham literati, and a wit who arguably outshone them all. She left behind a legacy of often lacerating theater and literary reviews, tart poetry and numerous screenplays (including the original 1937 "A Star Is Born") that still makes compelling reading, which is why "The Portable Dorothy Parker" has never been out of print since it was first published in 1944.

But because of her obvious great talent, as well as her own self-deprecating remarks, there has always been the sense of full potential never realized. As she says at one point, "I write do-dahs." It is the contrast between the sadness and disappointment of Parker's personal and creative life, and the exhilaration of important friendships and glittering social swirl, that gives this film its poignance.

Screenplay by Rudolph and journalist Randy Sue Coburn begins with Parker (Leigh) in Hollywood in 1937. Drenched in weariness and evident self-loathing for having sold out (many of her old cohorts would do the same), she is prompted by a young admirer to reflect on the "colorful" days beginning 18 years before, when American cultural life was defined by a relatively small group of artists and writers (quite a few of them critics) in New York City.

And colorful they were, Parker admits, although many other details of her life spoke of messiness and desperation. Returning from the war, her husband, Eddie (Andrew McCarthy), reveals himself to be a morphine addict, and hardly Dorothy's match upstairs. At Vanity Fair, she and the other writers, including Robert Benchley (Campbell Scott) wear their salaries around their necks to protest their measly wages, and she is soon fired.

Rudolph amusingly illustrates the physical formation of the Round Table, which here consists of an ever-growing group of fast-talking pals knocking knees around a tiny table until a waiter (Wallace Shawn) has the bright idea of installing a large table around which they can sit comfortably. Per this telling, out of such a practical maneuver was a legend born.

Against the backdrop of the Jazz Age, and Mark Isham's suitably jazzy score, the ever-changing crowd lunches, drinks and vacations together, attends openings, hangs out at speak-easies and inevitably sports its share of romantic complications. Separated from Eddie, Dorothy launches into a passionate affair with rakish newspaperman Charles MacArthur (Matthew Broderick), but it ends badly for her when he can't curb his appetite for actresses even after they're engaged, and she gets an abortion. This seems to start Dorothy on a downward spiral from which she never recovers.

At the heart of the picture, however, is the intense but carefully platonic friendship between Mrs. Parker and Mr. Benchley, as they nearly always call each other. Married with two sons, Benchley is an editor and drama critic who, as is shown in a beautifully fashioned scene, almost inadvertently became a standup comic of sorts, delivering fractured commentaries on mundane subjects. The lovely relationship between the two lends the film an emotional purity that stands in relief to Parker's unsatisfactory other relationships.

All this is fine as far as it goes, but the picture ends very abruptly, almost as if a third act were missing. The frequently returned-to framing device of the older Parker, which often has her delivering snippets of her corrosive poetry, shows her viciously putting down her second husband, Alan Campbell (Peter Gallagher), and eventually turning into the lonely old lush she always feared becoming.

But the proper connection is never made between her declining condition in New York in the late 1920s and her subsequent Hollywood career. Viewers unfamiliar with Parker are given virtually nothing to work with as far as Campbell and the later years are concerned, and there is a yawning gap in the story that only becomes apparent when the film announces that it is over.

This is frustrating, since a great deal of what is onscreen is intelligent and involving. Like most films about famous personalities ("The Moderns" included), this one suffers a bit from the awkward introduction of too many big names — There's Harpo Marx running around a lawn party, Oh, here's George S. Kaufman, Say howdy to Will Rogers, You know F. Scott, don't you?, What should Harold Ross call his new magazine? — but Rudolph handles this nearly impossible problem in generally acceptable fashion.

Anchoring it all is Leigh's superb performance. With her arch, artificial-sounding accent (patterned after recordings of Parker's own voice), she takes a little getting used to, and some of the readings are sufficiently indistinct that some tweaking or even re-looping could be called for to make her dialogue completely comprehensible.

But the actress gets stronger the older Parker becomes, and her delivery of the writer's acid remarks is stinging but natural, not declaratory. Praised to the skies by critics in recent years, she here hits her career summit thus far.

Scott, who is not as pudgy as Robert Benchley was, still conveys a good idea of one's impression of the humorist, and turns in a sensationally delicate and nuanced characterization of a man primarily defined by Old World reticence and self-control but whose wackiness and abandon seeped out through the cracks.

Offbeat casting of Broderick as the heartbreaker MacArthur works well, and Shawn steals a few moments as the creative waiter. A lively lineup of mostly young thesps fills out the long and illustrious cast of characters.

Shot in Montreal, pic is a real treat physically. Jan Kiesser's outstanding widescreen lensing alternates between intense black-and-white for the framing story and lustrous color for the principal sequences. Francois Seguin's highly resourceful production design, careful location work and notably natural, uncliched costumes by John Hay and Renee April all contribute to an indelible sense of time and place. —*Todd McCarthy*

A CONFUCIAN CONFUSION

(DULI SHIDAI)

(TAIWANESE)

An Atom Films & Theatre production. (International sales: Atom Films & Theatre, Taipei/Warner Bros., Burbank) Produced by Yu Weiyen. Executive producer, David Sun. Directed, written by Edward Yang. Camera (color), Arthur Wong, Zhang Zhan, Li Longyu, Hong Wuxiu; editor, Chen Bowen; music, Antonio Lee; production design, Tsai Chin, Yang, Ernest Guan, Yao Reizhong; sound, Du Duzhi; associate producer, Zhan Hongzhi; assistant director, Chen Yiwen. Reviewed at Cannes Film Festival (competing), May 12, 1994. Running time: **133 MIN.**
Qiqi .... Chen Xiangqi
Molly .... Ni Shujun
Ming .... Wang Weiming
Akeem .... Wang Zhongzheng
Birdy .... Wang Yeming
Larry .... Danny Deng
Molly's brother-in-law ..... Yan Hongya
Feng .... Richie Li
Molly's sister .... Chen Limei
Liren .... Chen Yiwen
(Mandarin and Hokkien dialogue)

Ace Taiwan New Waver Edward Yang's first movie in three years, "A Confucian Confusion," is a dense, talky, often blackly comic brain-tickler that's as likely to confuse as to enlighten. This challenging, multicharactered rondo on aspects of contempo Taiwan society should find plenty of play on the festival circuit but looks unlikely to broaden Yang's B.O. appeal beyond the limited number drawn to his previous "A Brighter Summer Day." Locally, pic is going out under the Warner Asia banner.

Long-in-the-works pic started out as a "little comedy," in the director's words, but underwent a radical rewrite following last year's demand by several East Asian countries (including China and Singapore) for modification of the Intl. Declaration of Human Rights on the basis of cultural differences. Basic message of Yang's movie is that it's time for newly wealthy (Confucian-influenced) Asian societies, like Taiwan, to stop limiting themselves and rethink traditional molds.

First few reels seem deliberately designed to confuse viewers, opening with chaotic rehearsals for avant-garde playwright Birdy's first commercial production and then segueing to a long sequence in the office of rich-kid Molly, head of a PR company funded by rich businessman b.f. Akeem. Almost a dozen characters are introed in the movie's opening reel, with backgrounds, connections and relationships often obscure, despite yards of dialogue.

As the mists slowly part, it's clear everyone's connected by either longtime friendships, sexual partnering or blood ties. Molly's goodhearted assistant, Qiqi, is a lower-middle-class pal from school days who's engaged to fellow classmate Ming, a low-rung government bureaucrat who lives with his parents. Molly's business manager, Larry, is a buddy of Akeem and basically runs the company. Molly's elder sis, once engaged to Akeem but now married to an existential writer, hosts a top-rated TV talkshow. Aspiring actress Feng is biding her time in Molly's company till her big break, in between romancing Larry. And that's just the main players.

Catalyst to events is Molly's firing of Feng over a misunderstanding — an action that causes the former to start questioning her lifestyle and exacerbates her distrust of human relationships. Qiqi quits and worsens things by introducing Feng to Birdy, who's ever keen to take on a new actress. Akeem, meanwhile, is finding it harder and harder to pin down Molly to a wedding date.

Tangled skein of developments, all set during a couple of days, includes Molly bedding the upright Ming, Birdy going through a major artistic crisis (in some of the pic's few overtly comic scenes), and the existentialist scribe undergoing a Road to Damascus conversion after a traffic accident. Latter sequence, played as ripe comedy in a crowded nighttime street with a bozo cab driver, is the movie's philosophical nut — that it's time to cut through the structured Confucianism and go for honest, upfront relating.

It's a tribute to Yang's high-sheen technique and ensemble direction that the movie holds the attention even when the viewer is still grappling with character relationships and the highly refined ideas being tossed around in the script. But whereas the equally complexly constructed "A Brighter Summer Day," set during Taiwan's underdeveloped early '60s, had the bonus of period atmosphere for more general viewers, "Confucian Confusion" pivots on the special characteristics of Taiwan's recent economic miracle and may prove simply too arcane in its resonances for non-specialists.

In feel, Yang's fifth feature partly evokes his 1985 "Taipei Story," though with a lighter tone and a less navel-gazing approach to his favorite subject of modern Taiwanese identity. Though the pic is always solidly cinematic, there's also a legit feel to the loquacious script that perhaps reflects the helmer's detour into penning two plays ("Likely Consequence," 1992; "Period of Growth," 1993) since "Day."

Thesp Ni Shujun, who's had uneven parts since her recent bounceback, is terrific in the key Molly role, all yuppie dress code and uptight insecurities. Newcomer Chen Xiangqi, from Yang's two recent plays, shadows Ni perfectly as her best friend and all-round nice person who's content to go with the flow. There's not a weak link in the rest of the cast, with Wang Weiming solid as the moralistic Ming and Chen Limei strong as Molly's talkshow host sister.

Technically, pic is all of a piece, despite four directors of photography contributing, with immaculate compositions and striking use of light and shadow in interiors that also recall "Taipei Story" and parts of Yang's first feature, "That Day, on the Beach." Production design, by a team including Yang and his wife, Tsai Chin, is clean. Music, sparely used, is pointed. Though sound on mono print unspooled at Cannes is fine, pic will be available with a Dolby soundtrack beginning in August.

Original title literally means "Age of Independence," with the Chinese word for the latter having a political as well as personal connotation. —*Derek Elley*

EXOTICA

Alliance Releasing and ARP present an Ego Film Arts production. Produced by Atom Egoyan, Camelia Frieberg. Directed, written by Egoyan. Camera (color), Paul Sarossy; editor, Susan Shipton; music, Mychael Danna; production design, Linda del Rosario, Richard Paris; costume design, Linda Muir; sound (Dolby), Ross Redfern; assistant director, David Webb. Reviewed at Raleigh Studios, L.A., May 3, 1994. (In Cannes Film Festival — competing.) Running time: **104 MIN.**
Francis .... Bruce Greenwood
Christina .... Mia Kirschner
Thomas .... Don McKellar
Zoe .... Arsinee Khanjian
Eric .... Elias Koteas
Tracey ....Sarah Polley
Harold .... Victor Garber
Customs Officer .... Calvin Green

Iconoclastic Canadian filmmaker Atom Egoyan provides another daunting descent into human despair with his latest, Cannes' competing "Exotica." There's demonstrable growth in his visual and narrative skills here but the writer/director isn't likely to expand his audience with the sometimes oblique, unnerving saga of interwoven lives whose paths cross with alternately comic and tragic results. It's decidedly upscale fare with appeal to a niche core, following fest exposure.

A simple synopsis would be futile. Francis (Bruce Greenwood) is a tax inspector who spends every evening at the otherworldly strip club Exotica. He's obsessed with Christina (Mia Kirschner), who's having a difficult time with her one-time boyfriend, Eric (Elias Koteas), the platter spinner. When it becomes clear that Eric is unhinged by Francis' presence, the tax man coerces Thomas (Don McKellar), a pet-shop owner whose books are under scrutiny, to serve as his eyes and ears.

That, at least, represents the surface story. Underneath, there are many secrets lurking and side stories unique to each player, as well as connective links that provide the film's numerous emotional collisions.

Egoyan constructs the piece like an intricate little thriller, dotted with clues and revelations that draw us along. He's exceedingly clever at presenting seemingly important pieces of the puzzle and then reversing the meaning of the information. Mirrors are an intrinsic part of the film's visual and metaphoric structure.

It's nonetheless a confounding choice for storytelling as he's ultimately not at all interested in genre convention. He undoes a significant part of what he sets out to accomplish with the implication of a conclusion that will tie his plot ends securely together. What he provides is anticlimactic, fuzzy and considerably less than a knockout emotional punch.

That said, "Exotica" is still a haunting, chilling experience. Egoyan enters into an eerie, vaguely off-center universe that inhabits an instinctual rather than realistic realm. It's as vivid — though unique — as something one might expect from David Lynch, thanks to accomplished tech work from cameraman Paul Sarossy and production designers Linda del Rosario and Richard Paris. The latter's title construct is particularly inspired.

The filmmaker also has made significant strides with his casting. He effects an odd mix by using seasoned actors including Koteas and Victor Garber with relatively inexperienced thesps. He has an adroit sense of just how much weight each role requires.

There's little doubt "Exotica" is an apt name for this concoction. There's also no denying that viewers will be split in their reaction to this pic, which demands a fair amount of interactivity in filling out its more sketchy plot elements.

—*Leonard Klady*

NO SKIN

(SENZA PELLE)

(ITALIAN)

An Istituto Luce release (in Italy) of a Rodeo Drive production in association with Istituto Luce, RAI-TV. (International sales: Adriana Chiesa, Rome.) Produced by Marco Poccioni, Marco Valsania. Directed, written by Alessandro D'Alatri. Camera (Cinecitta color), Claudio Collepiccolo; editor, Cecilia Zanuso; music, Moni Olvadia, Alfredo La Cosegliaz; art direction, Francesco Piori; costume design, Paola Bonucci; sound (Dolby), Tullio Morganti; assistant directors, Claudia Bensi, Angelo Vicari. Reviewed at Sala Umberto, Rome, May 3, 1994. (In Cannes Film Festival — Directors Fortnight.) Running time: **90 MIN.**
Gina .... Anna Galiena
Riccardo .... Massimo Ghini
Saverio .... Kim Rossi Stuart
Saverio's
  Mother .... Maria Grazia Grassini
With: Paola Tiziana Cruciani, Renzo Stacchi, Patrizia Piccinini, Leila Durante, Piergiorgio Menichini, Marina Tagliaferri, Sergio Tardioli.

In "No Skin," the static grayness of three lives is jolted by a mentally unstable youth's sentimental assault on his unsuspecting inamorata. Accomplished, warmly human second feature from Alessandro D'Alatri is a delicately played, melancholy but emotionally satisfying drama of behavioral dilemmas that oscillates subtly between light and dark moods. It should strike universal chords among international arthouse habitues.

Catalyst for the roller coaster of emotional upheaval is Saverio (Kim Rossi Stuart), an intelligent, acutely sensitive depressive from a well-heeled Roman family whose condition robs him of the protective outer shell that's necessary to contain and control his feelings (hence film's title).

The object of his affections is post office clerk Gina (Anna Galiena), who's unaware of his existence. She lives with coarse but good-natured bus driver Riccardo (Massimo Ghini) and their infant son. The couple's marriage plans have been blocked by Riccardo's estranged wife's refusal to divorce.

Mystified by the constant arrival of letters, poems, flowers and gifts declaring the love of the unknown Saverio, Gina hides the romantic overtures from Riccardo. When he does find the stash of letters, his resulting anger quickly gives way to trust in her fidelity.

This early section rigs a keen balance between inklings of dramatic developments waiting in the wings and gentle predicament comedy, especially when both Gina and Riccardo independently eye every man they pass as a candidate for the faceless paramour.

Saverio's advances become increasingly bold, allowing him to be traced via his phone number. While Riccardo is torn between rage, concern, indulgent resignation and the worst possible psychopath scenarios, Gina is caught off guard and somewhat flattered by the directness of the boy's amorous protestations.

The couple's desire to help the misfit is fueled by Gina's encounter with Saverio's well-meaning but ill-equipped mother (Maria Grazia Grassini), and Riccardo's with his doctor (Patrizia Piccinini).

Gina encourages his friendship, setting him up with work in a friend's greenhouse. At the same time she begins to refuse his floral tributes and attempts to stop the flow of love letters. She acquiesces to a kiss, which immediately pushes his innocent attentions into the dimensions of a sexual threat, causing her to back off.

The film shifts gears, becoming almost unbearably intense when, subsequently, Saverio overwhelms Gina with anguished affection in a crowded supermarket.

Rossi Stuart, who until now has been mainly limited to playing one-dimensional pretty boys, is both convincing and moving in depicting his character's mental and emotional obsession, which climbs to fever pitch, driving away Gina. Her disappearance literally drains the color from his life, with the film dissolving into increasingly grainy, monochrome footage and then into raw black-and-white.

To both Rossi Stuart's and writer/director D'Alatri's credit, Saverio is not merely another misunderstood, harmlessly eccentric teddy bear. Though clearly a sympathetic character from every angle, his unpredictable nature and unchanneled sexual needs give him a darker, almost menacing edge.

His poetic dialogue — an element that often shoves contempo Italian dramas into ludicrously romantic realms — is amply justified here. The glimmer of hope that illuminates his outcome feels like a well-gauged concession, allowing the film to close on not too downbeat a note, without schlepping gratuitously onto happy-ending turf.

Playing immensely likable but solidly everyday folks, Galiena and Ghini make grade-A contributions. Galiena's growing international stature should get a further boost from her fine work here. Ghini's role is undoubtedly the least showy, but perhaps the meatiest, and he brings it a good deal of depth and humor, moving way beyond his recent screen outings.

Direction is focused and unfussy, blemished only by an intrusive fantasy sequence in which Saverio becomes implanted in Riccardo's mind, possibly a residual dollop of D'Alatri's long experience making commercials.

Claudio Collepiccolo's clean, agile camera work poses no undue distraction from what's essentially a performance film. Editing is brisk and economical, though a mild sense of over-extension nags at some midsection scenes.

The buoyantly folkloric East Euro sounds of Bulgarian-born composer Moni Olvadia's dense and richly ironic score rep a distinct plus.

—*David Rooney*

THE SILENCES OF THE PALACE

(LES SILENCES DU PALAIS)

(TUNISIAN-FRENCH)

An Amorces Diffusion release (in France) of a Cinetelefilms & Magfilm (Tunisia)/Mat Films (France) production, with participation of Tunisian Ministry of Culture, French Ministry of Foreign Affairs, French Ministry of Culture, Channel 4 Television (London), Canal Horizon (Tunisia), Hubert Bals Foundation (Rotterdam), Agency for Cultural and Technical Cooperation. Produced by Ahmed Baha Eddine Attia, Richard Magnien. Directed by Moufida Tlatli. Screenplay, Tlatli, Nouri Bouzid. Camera (color), Youssef Ben Youssef; editor, Tlatli; music, Anouar Brahem; production design, Claude Bennys; sound, Faouzi Thabet. Reviewed at Club de L'Etoile screening room, Paris, May 2, 1994. (In Cannes Film Festival — Directors Fortnight.) Running time: **128 MIN.**
Khedija .... Amel Hedhili
Young Alia .... Hend Sabri
Khalti Hadda .... Najia Ouerghi
Adult Alia .... Ghalia Lacroix
Sidi Ali .... Kamel Fazaa
With: Sami Bouajila, Hichem Rostom, Helene Catzaras, Sonia Meddeb, Mechket Krifa, Kamel Touati.
(Arabic and French dialogue)

"The Silences of the Palace" conveys with leisurely candor the problematic relationship between a servant and her illegitimate daughter. North African programmers and women's fests should take note of this film, set in the repressive atmosphere of the ruling monarch's compound on the eve of Tunisian independence.

Permeated by the importance of music and womanly solidarity, film unspools in gradual increments. Pacing suits the repetitive routine of female kitchen staff cut off from the outside world, but may seem overlong to many viewers. First feature from longtime film editor Moufida Tlatli would benefit from some trimming.

Story is told mostly in flashbacks repping p.o.v. of 25-year-old Alia, who, from birth through puberty, lived in the royal palace with her mother, Khedija, a lifelong servant who was obliged to sleep with her princely masters. Weary Alia is scheduled to undergo the latest in a series of abortions, at the behest of longtime b.f. Lotfi, when she learns that Prince Sid Ali has died.

Her return to the now run-down palace she'd fled 10 years prior triggers repressed memories and forces her to reconsider the fate of the child she is carrying. Though Alia never learns who sired her, she better understands her defeated mother's special concern that Alia not be sucked into the hopeless and demeaning cycle of servitude.

Parallels between the nation's bondage and that of the palace servants are sometimes overstated, but the repercussions on Alia — who ends up trading one form of slavery for another — are fairly well portrayed.

Newcomer Hend Sabri is fine as adolescent Alia, who discovers her singing voice and a measure of defiance as Tunisian nationalist forces battle the French in the streets of Tunis — developments that are conveyed exclusively through radio reports. Various strong-willed women give good perfs as the kitchen staff.

Details of household preparations — sorting beads, sewing, stomping raw textiles, are good. All work and celebration is accompanied by song. An anthem favored by the rebels has the force of a hammer blow when Alia defiantly sings it. —*Lisa Nesselson*

LOVERS

(LES AMOUREUX)

(FRENCH)

A Rezo Films release (in France) of a Rezo Films/M6 Films production with participation of CNC, Gan Cinema Foundation, Procirep, Canal Plus. (International sales: Rezo Films, Paris.) Produced by Jean-Michel Rey. Executive producer, Philippe Liegeois. Directed by Catherine Corsini. Screenplay, Corsini, Pascale Breton, Arlette Langman. Camera (color), Ivan Kozelka; editor, Agnes Guillemot; production design, Laurent Allaire; costume design, Pierre-Yves Gayraud; sound, Laurent Poirier; assistant director, Alain Baudy; casting, Brigitte Moidon, Eve Guillou. Reviewed at Club de l'Etoile screening room, Paris, April 28, 1994. (In Cannes Film Festival — Cinemas En France.) Running time: **91 MIN.**
Vivien .... Nathalie Richard
Marc .... Pascal Cervo
Tomek .... Olaf Lubazenko
Ronan .... Loic Maquin
  With: Xavier Beauvois, Jean-Paul Dermont, Isabelle Nanty.

"Lovers" is the well-acted, affecting story of a handsome 15-year-old who looks to his adventurous older sister for guidance but finally takes charge of his own life. Unflattering but vivid portrait of small-minded, small-town life shifts gears to deliver narrative punch toward end. Fests should bite.

After eight years away, gleefully promiscuous twentysomething Vivien (engaging· Nathalie Richard) returns to her Podunk hometown in northern France. She excels at twisting men around her little finger, and her adoring halfbrother, Marc (Pascal Cervo), watches with awe, then with growing consternation, as sis repeatedly sells herself short.

Model student Marc becomes a less dutiful son under Vivien's tutelage, which veers close to incest. In a skillfully handled swing of the pendulum, Vivien settles down as increasingly self-possessed Marc branches out in search of nonvicarious thrills.

Newcomer Cervo gives a strong, nuanced perf as Marc, investing his metamorphosis with layers of yearning and an unstudied adolescent grace. Richard shines in the spunky, tailor-made role of Vivien. Isabelle Nanty is a standout in a bit as her party-girl friend, and Olaf Lubazenko is sweet as the illegal immigrant whose respectful approach throws Vivien for a loop.

Milieu is neatly nailed in a giddy-cum-queasy scene of provincial types eating mussels and French fries with drunken abandon while a mediocre band provides entertainment.

Director and co-scripter Catherine Corsini's pic is resoundingly French in approach and decor, but the tale of putative misfits whose needs outstrip local mentalities has universal resonance. —*Lisa Nesselson*

BYE BYE AMERICA

(AUF WIEDERSEHEN AMERIKA)

(GERMAN)

A Novoskop Film, WDR, La Sept/ Arte, Casting SF, Pandora Film production. (International sales: Pyramide Intl., Paris.) Directed by Jan Schutte. Screenplay, Thomas Strittmatter, Schutte. Camera (Fujicolor), Thomas Mauch; editor, Renate Merck; music, Claus Bantzer; production design, Katharina Woppermann; sound (Dolby), Ekkehard W. Kuchenbecker. Reviewed at Club de l'Etoile screening room, Paris, May 6, 1994. (In Cannes Film Festival — Directors Fortnight.) Running time: **85 MIN.**
Issac .... Otto Tausig
Moshe .... Jakov Bodo
Genovefa .... Zofia Merle
  With: Christa Berndl, George Tabori, Josh Mostel.
  (Polish, English and German dialogue)

"Bye Bye America" is a charmingly acted amalgam of chutzpah, moxie and tempered resignation. Farfetched and fanciful odyssey of a zaftig Polish cleaning lady who returns to her native village after 30 years in America has offshore arthouse potential, particularly in Jewish and Polish enclaves.

Comic prologue, in which Genovefa (Zofia Merle), still speaking more Polish than English, buys a special purse for her triumphant return, sets the tone. Rotund Merle anchors the pic as a no-nonsense yet strangely girlish force to be reckoned with.

Genovefa is married to diminutive fellow Pole Moshe (Jakov Bodo), with whom she has spent the past three decades living in Brooklyn's Brighton Beach area. Moshe's best friend is Issac (Otto Tausig), a German sad sack who sums up his track record in the business world with "If I were to go into the funeral biz, people would stop dying."

The plan is for Issac to housesit while couple sojourns abroad, but, when the garment district sweatshop where Issac works is raided, he joins Genovefa and Moshe on their journey via Polish freighter. Ship conks out in German port and schleppy trio is forced to continue overland. They finally reach Gdansk after countless individual and group setbacks.

The pic — directed by Jan Schutte, who also scripted with Thomas Strittmatter — sacrifices plausibility in later stages but remains touching and amusing throughout. Male thesps are delightful in their downtrodden acceptance, which women counter with hearty resolve.

Bank manager's appreciation speech to immigrant custodial staff about "inner and outer clarity and cleanliness" is tops. Josh Mostel scores as a New Jersey resident attempting to bury his father on Polish soil.

Pic was lensed in New York, Germany and Poland, and production design perfectly evokes the tone of each locale. Mix of languages and destinations is carried off with aplomb. Spare, slightly melancholy music is ideal. —*Lisa Nesselson*

CURFEW

(HATTA ISHAAR AKHAR)

(DUTCH-PALESTINIAN)

An Ayloul Film Prods. (Amsterdam)/ Argus Film Produktie (Amsterdam) production, in association with WDR, Arte, with support of Dutch Ministry of Foreign Affairs, Stichting Doen/Nationale Postcode Loterij (Holland), Avro Television (Hilversum), Municipality of Nazareth. Co-executive producers, Hany Abu-Assad, Samir Hamed, Henri P.N. Kuipers, Peter van Vogelpoel. Directed, written by Rashid Masharawi. Camera (color), Klaus Juliusburger; editor, Hadara Oren; music, Said Mouraad, Sabreen; art direction, Sharif Waked; sound, Roni Berger. Reviewed at Espace St. Michel cinema, Paris, April 26, 1994. (In Cannes Film Festival — Critics' Week.) Running time: **73 MIN.**
Oum Raji .... Na'ila Zayaad
Radar .... Younis Younis
Akram .... Mahmoud Qadah
Houda .... Areen Omari
Amal .... Rana Saadi
Raji .... Assem Zoabi
Abu Raji .... Salim Daw

"Curfew" follows the stressful routine of an extended family when Israeli authorities declare an open-ended curfew in the Gaza community. Timely first feature from young Palestinian helmer Rashid Masharawi, born and raised in a refugee camp in Gaza, communicates the cumulative pressures of being hemmed in without real options. Naturalistic pic, obviously made with modest means, has the ring of truth but is in for a struggle finding playdates beyond fests and educational settings.

Views of corrugated rooftops in a dusty locality give way to scenes of youngsters playing soccer, including the spunky and resourceful Radar. When curfew is declared, people rush indoors. Troops are represented mostly as loudspeaker voices with a few soldiers thrown in, but evenhanded approach concentrates almost exclusively on one tedious, anxiety-provoking day in the life of Radar's family.

The family shares a fairly spacious, if sparsely furnished household. Patriarch is in poor health. One son is studying in Germany, and the arrival of a letter from abroad is a momentous occasion. Another son is compliant — mellowed by his wife and daughter. Bachelor Akram is a simmering hothead with an expression of permanent indignation.

Women hold the household together, nervously rationing food in case the curfew decree lasts for days. Fleet-footed Radar is dispatched for perishables; his mother weighs the risks of stepping into

May 16, 1994 (Cont.)

her own backyard to hang laundry. In the course of one night, a baby is born, houses are searched, tempers are provoked and the uneasy status quo is maintained.

Pic shows practical details of outsmarting confinement, such as communication from shuttered window to shuttered window or over low walls. Side effects, such as labored breathing after being gassed, are alluded to through dialogue. Pic ends much as it began, reinforcing the established cycle of survival.

—*Lisa Nesselson*

SEE HOW THEY FALL
(REGARDE LES HOMMES TOMBER)
(FRENCH)

A Pan Europeene release (in France) of a Bloody Mary/France 3 Cinema production. (International sales: Pan Europeene.) Produced by Didier Haudepin. Directed by Jacques Audiard. Screenplay, Alain Le Henry, Audiard, based on the novel "Triangle," by Teri White. Camera (color), Gerard Sterin; editor, Juliette Welfling, Monique Dartonne; music, Alexandre Desplat; production design, Jacques Rouxel; costume design, Francoise Lefevre; sound, Francois Waledisch, Dominique Gaborieau; assistant director, Serge Boutleroff. Reviewed at Espace Saint-Michel cinema, Paris, April 26, 1994. (In Cannes Film Festival — Critics' Week.) Running time: **98 MIN.**

Marx ....Jean-Louis Trintignant
Simon .... Jean Yanne
Johnny .... Mathieu Kassovitz
Louise .... Bulle Ogier
Sandrine .... Christine Pascal
With: Yvon Back, Yves Verhoeven, Marc Citti, Roger Mollien.

"**S**ee How They Fall," a deft interlocking tale of two small-time hoods and an unlikely avenger, is morally ambiguous and dosed with irony in the noir tradition. Dark, compelling helming debut by veteran scripter Jacques Audiard should do nicely at Gallic wickets and rack up healthy tube sales.

Carefully layered flashbacks, navigated .via the sparing use of voiceover and lightly mocking title cards, propel this gritty character study-cum-thriller.

Simon Hirsch (Jean Yanne), a salesman having a bout of midlife apathy, reluctantly agrees to monitor a stakeout for his dashing younger pal, Mickey, a cop. When Mickey is rendered comatose in a cryptic shooting that the police have no interest in solving, Simon abandons his job, his wife (Bulle Ogier) and his routine to get to the bottom of the hit, finding a low-key vitality en route.

Story covers three years, but this fact will be lost on all but the most attentive viewers due to the pic's elliptical, not unpleasing editing.

In a narrative realm pegged onscreen as "Well Before All This," Marx (Jean-Louis Trintignant), a grizzled gambler and confirmed loner, ends up with adoring simpleton Johnny (Mathieu Kassovitz) in tow. Marx fails at turning him into a tough guy who can help him shake people down, but Johnny's limited grasp of complex moral issues makes him an ideal hit man.

As Simon pursues his investigation in the present, Marx and Johnny forge their deadly partnership in the past. The two stories run parallel to each other until Simon's sleuthing leads him to the dubious duo, whereupon the time frames converge.

Lead thesps, particularly Yanne, couldn't be better in a script marbled with sardonic humor. Narrative structure is rich in telling, faintly ominous details. Photography is solid. Composer Alexandre Desplat's sometimes jaunty, sometimes eerie themes are fitting.

Pic's unsettling (but well-supported) moral appears to be that — depending on the circumstances — killing people can make one into a better-adjusted member of society.

—*Lisa Nesselson*

THE BUTTERFLY'S DREAM
(IL SOGNO DELLA FARFALLA)
(ITALIAN-SWISS-FRENCH)

An Istituto Luce release (in Italy) of a Filmalbatros (Italy)/Waka Films (Switzerland)/Pierre Grise Prods. (France) production with RAI-2, in association with SSR/TSI Televisione Svizzera, Federal Office of Culture (Switzerland), Istituto Luce, Happy Valley Films Ltd. (International sales: Sacis.) Produced, directed by Marco Bellocchio. Executive producer, Livio Negri. Co-producers, Silvia Voser, Martin Marignac. Screenplay, Massimo Fagioli. Camera (Eastmancolor; Technicolor prints), Yorgos Arvanitis; editor, Francesca Calvelli; music, Carlo Crivelli; art direction, Amedeo Fago; costumes, Lia Morandini. Reviewed at CDS screening room, Rome, May 3, 1994. (In Cannes Film Festival — Un Certain Regard.) Running time: **112 MIN.**

Massimo .... Thierry Blanc
Girlfriend .... Simona Cavallari
Mother .... Bibi Andersson
Father .... Roberto Herlitzka
Carlo .... Henry Arnold
Anna .... Nathalie Boutefeu
Old woman .... Anita Laurenzi
Director .... Michael Seyfried

Marco Bellocchio continues down the artistic path suggested by his psychothera-

pist and, in this case, his screenwriter in "The Butterfly's Dream." Its exploration of existential themes is informed by arcane psychological theory, which calls on viewers to grasp the story intuitively rather than rationally. Strictly for those who like to contemplate philosophical puzzles while they follow a symbolic narrative, pic is a prestige European arthouse entry that will appeal to a very restricted audience.

Massimo (Thierry Blanc) is a young classical actor who has taken a singular vow: Apart from play dialogue, he won't speak a word to anyone. Pic suggests different reasons for his decision.

His thick-skinned father (Roberto Herlitzka) thinks he might be reacting to a disappointment in love. The most plausible explanation seems to be that silence (to which he largely converts girlfriend Simona Cavallari) is his form of rebellion against poet Mom (Bibi Andersson) and classic-lit scholar Dad.

Occasionally, instead of answering a question, Massimo bursts out with a perfectly appropriate citation from "Oedipus at Colonus" or "The Prince of Homburg." It is a tribute to Bellocchio's control (or his lack of a sense of humor) that this eccentricity doesn't cross the line into involuntary comedy.

A bizarre director ("Heimat" vet Michael Seyfried) is struck by Massimo's perf onstage. He appeals to Andersson to write a play about her son and his extraordinary resolution. Deeply worried about the boy, she agrees. But even after acting the part of himself, Massimo refuses to become "normal."

Clearly, everyday logic doesn't go far in "Butterfly." As a man says, throwing his married daughter into the arms of her gypsy suitor: "You just have to be intelligent enough to understand fairy tales." Most viewers, however, are likely to find the film less playful and poetic than plain exasperating.

To dig under his characters' skin, Bellocchio uses all kinds of stylization, such as deliberately stilted dialogue and gestures, theatrically framed shots, a stop-start score by Carlo Crivelli, starkly simple costumes by Lia Morandini and nonlogical editing by Francesca Calvelli, which continually disrupts the narrative thread.

Cast is solidly in synch with Bellocchio's intentions, performing in proper theatrical style. Young Swiss stage thesp Blanc is enigmatically expressive as the semimute hero, forced to construct a character using only glances, gestures and a little Shakespeare and Sophocles.

The same can be said of the whole cast, who overcome screenwriter Massimo Fagioli's unnatural dialogue (every line aims at profundity) through sheer bravura. Particularly good are Andersson and Herlitzka as the parents. Nathalie Boutefeu, playing Massimo's girlishly restless sister-in-law, manages to verge on high villainy when she attempts to seduce him, while Cavallari looks underage and submissive as his adoring g.f.

Breathtaking lighting by cinematographer Yorgos Arvanitis is sensuous in the extreme. Long shadows follow characters like thoughts; faces appear against a totally black background. Pic's natural landscapes — from gorgeous Swiss-lake country to a rocky Greek isle — are surcharged with psychic energy.

—*Deborah Young*

May 23, 1994

THE FLINTSTONES

A Universal release of a Steven Spielrock presentation of a Hanna-Barbera/Amblin Entertainment production. Produced by Bruce Cohen. Executive producers, William Hanna, Joseph Barbera, Kathleen Kennedy, David Kirschner, Gerald R. Molen. Co-producer, Colin Wilson. Directed by Brian Levant. Screenplay, Tom S. Parker, Jim Jennewein, Steven E. de Souza, based on the animated series by Hanna-Barbera Prods. Camera (Deluxe color), Dean Cundey; editor, Kent Beyda; music, David Newman; production design, William Sandell; art direction, Jim Teegarden, Nancy Patton, Christopher Burian-Mohr; set design, Paul Sonski, Elizabeth Lapp, Erin Kemp; set decoration, Rosemary Brandenburg; costume design, Rosanna Norton; sound, Charles Wilborn; special visual effects, Industrial Light & Magic; animatronic creatures, Jim Henson's Creature Shop; assistant director, Marty P. Ewing; casting, Nancy Nayor. Reviewed at Universal Studios, Universal City, May 6, 1994. MPAA Rating: PG. Running time: **92 MIN.**

Fred Flintstone	John Goodman
Wilma Flintstone	Elizabeth Perkins
Barney Rubble	Rick Moranis
Betty Rubble	Rosie O'Donnell
Cliff Vandercave	Kyle MacLachlan
Miss Stone	Halle Berry
Pearl Slaghoople	Elizabeth Taylor
Mr. Slate	Dann Florek
Hoagie	Richard Moll
Joe Rockhead	Irwin (88) Keyes
Grizzled Man	Jonathan Winters
Dictabird	Harvey Korman

Kids of all ages hungry for this summer's dinosaur picture will be more than satisfied with "The Flintstones." With all manner of friendly beasts, a superenergetic John Goodman and a colorful supporting cast inhabiting a Bedrock that resembles a Stone Age version of Steven Spielberg suburbia, this live-action translation of the perennial cartoon favorite is a fine popcorn picture for small fry, and perfectly inoffensive for adults. The strong shoulders of its star, the heavy promotional campaign and household-name title will carry Universal to brontosaurian box office.

Watching this fast-paced, advisedly brief confection is akin to taking a quick spin on the Universal Studios tour with a detour through the City Walk attraction, so loaded is it with technical gizmos, showbiz in-jokes and product plugs. In a day when popular movies have more in common with theme parks than old-school artistic traditions, this one fits right in.

This film's use of at least a dozen writers, of whom only three receive final screen credit, was widely reported, and choice of a storyline involving embezzlement is slightly puzzling given the 7-year-old target audience. Millions of kids will be learning the word for financial trickery if they ask mommy and daddy about it during unspoolings.

Inside humor is tipped from the outset, as opening title announces a "Steven Spielrock" presentation. First reel will keep tykes' eyes popping, as the cast of dinosaurs is introduced in rapid succession along with the human characters.

There are giant reptiles working in the rock quarry where Fred Flintstone (Goodman) and his buddies toil, and dog-and-cat-like pets at home. Fred paddles his car along with his outsized feet and takes his family to the drive-in to see George Lucas' "Tar Wars."

Much of the imagination poured into the pic — production design by William Sandell and his team, the costumes by Rosanna Norton and the special-effects details by many hands — is exhausted very quickly. Bedrock is a town of slanting rock roofs with animals that wash dishes with their trunks and "Bedrock's Most Wanted," hosted by Jay Leno, playing on Stone Age TV.

Fred, of course, is the happy, rock-solid working man, thick of bicep and skull, who shockingly wins a promotion out of the rock pile and into the executive suites of Slate & Co. when his best friend, Barney Rubble (Rick Moranis), substitutes his own exam answers for Fred's.

The boss (Kyle MacLachlan) and his foxy secretary (Halle Berry) easily manipulate the lazy simpleton for their own financial ends, setting him up for a big fall as they plot to make off with ill-gotten gains.

Meanwhile, at home, Fred manages to get in hot water with his sprightly wife, Wilma (Elizabeth Perkins), whose mother (Elizabeth Taylor) keeps harping about how Wilma could have done a lot better in her choice of husband, and still might do so.

After lightly going through the motions of a plot, pic ends up in the quarry, where assorted machinery provides the excuse for a parade of slapstick gags and amusement park-like predicaments that seem mostly lumbering.

After the initial pleasure of seeing a cartoon world reinvented for live action, and well-known toon characters becoming flesh and blood, there is little to compel great interest, but the slew of filmmakers have come up with enough contempo references, little jokes and bits of business to keep things busy.

Pic centers squarely on Goodman, and he brings tremendous energy and enthusiasm to the role of Fred. It's no insult to say that he's quite credible as a caveman, and it's hard to imagine that anyone else could so plausibly convey both the cartoonlike and everyman qualities most needed for the role.

Other performers take a relative back seat but are also well cast. Perkins, Moranis and Rosie O'Donnell are perfectly fine as Wilma, Barney and Betty Rubble. MacLachlan is suitable as the hissable yuppie villain, and Berry is slinky as his seductive aide-de-camp.

Given that it requires her almost exclusively to complain about Fred, the mother role brings out Taylor's coarse side, although she looks beauteous in her first screen appearance in some time and amusingly ends up in the mouth of a dinosaur. Harvey Korman does nicely providing a talking bird with an aristocratic voice.

For adults, one significant point of interest here is that the ostensible attitude of this money machine of a movie, which is so loaded with highly calculated marketing and product plugs, is pro-working stiff and anti-big business. Such are the paradoxes and contradictions of capitalism.

Jokiness extends to the final credits, which feature Flintstone-related tunes in rap, reggae and Sex Pistols styles.

—*Todd McCarthy*

NIGHT OF THE DEMONS 2

A Republic Pictures release of a Blue Rider Pictures production. Produced by Walter Josten, Jeff Geoffray. Executive producer, Henry Seggerman. Directed by Brian Trenchard-Smith. Screenplay, Joe Augustyn; story by James Penzi, Augustyn. Camera, David Lewis; editor, Daniel Duncan; music, Jim Manzie; production design, Wendy Guidery; art direction, Darcy Kaye; set decoration, Marv Gullickson; costume design, Hollywood Raggs; sound (Ultra-Stereo), Bo Harwood; line producer, Bill Berry; assistant director, Lynn D'Angona; prosthetic makeup created by Steve Johnson; stunt coordinator, Shane Dixon; casting, Tedra Gabriel. Reviewed at the Mann Theater, L.A., May 12, 1994. MPAA Rating: R. Running time: **98 MIN.**

Bibi	Cristi Harris
Perry	Bobby Jacoby
Mouse	Merle Kennedy
Angela	Amelia Kinkade
Father Bob	Rod McCary
Johnny	Johnny Moran
Rick	Rick Peters
Sister Gloria	Jennifer Rhodes
Terri	Christine Taylor
Shirley	Zoe Trilling
Kurt	Ladd York
Z-boy	Darin Heames

Blessed with some inspired bits of comic lunacy (would you believe a nun battling Satan's minions with holy water-filled squirt guns and balloons?), this follow-up to a 1988 horror pic rises above most slice-and-dice fare and may tantalize some more discriminating palates in addition to the usual teen suspects. Pic gets limited theatrical release and could marginally cash in on the Friday the 13th calendar before a date with homevideo.

Despite the title and genre cliches — such as frequently disrobed teenage dimwits holding a Halloween bash in a creepy old house — "Demons 2" offers a relatively low body count and reasonably impressive special effects given its obvious budget restrictions.

In addition, director Brian Trenchard-Smith plays the material for laughs wherever possible, and even with a few unintentional giggles, the result is a smarter, gentler movie than most teen-oriented slasher pix.

The lead heavy is again the late Angela (Amelia Kinkade), a one-time disco queen who now hornily haunts her old abode.

Recounting Angela's legend, a new girl at St. Rita's school (Zoe Trilling) drags a half-dozen fellow students — including Angela's reluctant sister, Mouse (Merle Kennedy) — up to the house, inadvertently freeing the demon. On top of that, with each new casualty, the latest victim joins the ranks of the undead.

Fortunately, two people associated with the school rally to battle the demons: the bookish Perry (Bobby Jacoby) and yardstick-wielding Sister Gloria (Jennifer Rhodes).

Rhodes, in fact, is a hoot as the Rambo-ized nun, taking to the challenge with martial skill and intensity. That fresh wrinkle almost makes up for the pic's tired "Exorcist" riffs, from having Angela speak in a hoarse male voice to frequent bouts of spitting up green slime.

The rest of the cast is less flashy, though Trilling deserves kudos as the bad girl who becomes really bad, and the male counterparts all prove appropriately dense and single-minded.

Tech credits are solid given the three-week shooting schedule.

May 23, 1994 (Cont.)

While Angela may not exactly qualify as the femme Freddy Krueger producers talk about in the production notes, don't be surprised if "Demons" rises again. —*Brian Lowry*

CANNES FEST

PULP FICTION

A Miramax (U.S.) release of A Band Apart & Jersey Films production. (International sales: BAC Films, Paris.) Produced by Lawrence Bender. Executive producers, Danny De Vito, Michael Shamberg, Stacey Sher. Co-executive producers, Bob Weinstein, Harvey Weinstein, Richard N. Gladstein. Directed, written by Quentin Tarantino, stories by Tarantino, Roger Avary. Camera (Deluxe color; Panavision widescreen), Andrzej Sekula; editor, Sally Menke; music supervisor, Karyn Rachtman; production design, David Wasco; costume design, Betsy Heimann; casting, Ronnie Yeskel, Gary M. Zuckerbrod. Reviewed at Cannes Film Festival (competing), May 18, 1994. Running time: **153 MIN.**

Vincent Vega	John Travolta
Jules	Samuel L. Jackson
Mia	Uma Thurman
The Wolf	Harvey Keitel
Pumpkin	Tim Roth
Honey Bunny	Amanda Plummer
Fabienne	Maria de Madeiros
Marsellus Wallace	Ving Rhames
Lance	Eric Stoltz
Jody	Rosanna Arquette
Koons	Christopher Walken
Butch	Bruce Willis

A spectacularly entertaining piece of pop culture, "Pulp Fiction" is the "American Graffiti" of violent crime pictures. Following up on his reputation-making debut, "Reservoir Dogs," Quentin Tarantino makes some of the same moves here but on a much larger canvas, ingeniously constructing a series of episodes so that they ultimately knit together, and embedding the always surprising action in a context set by delicious dialogue and several superb performances.

Reviews, cast and heavy anticipation will make this a must-see among buffs and young male viewers, but rough genre, length and bloody mayhem will rep a turnoff for others, creating a real test of Miramax's marketing savvy in turning a niche picture into a crossover item upon late-August release.

Working on a wide screen constantly bulging with boldness, humor and diabolical invention, Tarantino indulges himself with a free hand and a budget several times larger than he had on his first outing.

Some may feel that the film sags in spots due to the director's tendency to try to stretch conceits as far as he can, but Tarantino should be commended for daring to explore the limits of his material, winding up on his feet and beating the sophomore jinx in the process.

As did "Reservoir Dogs," new pic begins in a coffee shop, with a young couple who call each other Pumpkin and Honey Bunny (Tim Roth and Amanda Plummer) chattering away before deciding to hold up the place.

Next sequence also feels like familiar territory, as two hit men, Vincent and Jules (John Travolta and Samuel L. Jackson), are attired just like the hoods in "Dogs," in dark suits, white shirts and ties. At once, Tarantino positions himself as the Preston Sturges of crimeland, putting the most incongruous words and thoughts into the mouths of lowdown, amoral characters.

Recently returned from a drug-happy sojourn in Amsterdam, Vincent speaks knowledgeably about the different varieties of fast food available in Europe, while Jules waxes eloquent on the Bible, vengeance and divinity.

After they bump off some kids who didn't play straight with crime lord Marsellus (Ving Rhames), the cool, self-possessed Vincent, as a courtesy, takes his boss' statuesque wife, Mia (a dark-haired Uma Thurman), out for a night on the town.

This "date" occasions the picture's biggest set piece, an amazing outing to a giant 1950s-themed restaurant/club. Even with all the decorous distractions, the plot gets advanced through some tantalizing verbal tennis between the two hot lookers, and the evening ends shockingly, with Vincent forced to save Mia's life in a way that will initially have many viewers cringing but will leave them laughing with appalled relief.

Here as before, Tarantino builds up tremendous tension, only to spice it with humorous non sequiturs. When his characters draw guns, as they so frequently do, one never knows if they're going to blow others' heads off, make a funny speech (they often do both), have the tables turned on them or make an honorable, peaceful exit.

An hour in, pic becomes even more audacious, as Tarantino leads the audience deeper into uncharted territory with new characters whose relationships to those already seen remain unclear for some time.

After a fantastic monologue by Christopher Walken as a soldier giving a prized gold watch to a little boy, a stripped-down Bruce Willis, as a boxer named Butch, is seen jumping out a window and getting in a cab. On instructions from Marsellus, Butch was supposed to take a fall, but he didn't and is on the run for his life.

Butch's existence over the next few hours is agonizingly unpredictable, horrifying and thoroughly zany. Some of the earlier characters begin to drop back into the story, and gradually a grand design starts falling into place.

Overall structure comes clear only after the two-hour mark with launch of the final stretch, which dovetails beautifully back to the beginning but also embraces a new character, the Wolf (Harvey Keitel), an impeccably organized specialist in literally cleaning up other people's dirty work.

Buffs will have a field day with the bold, confident style of the film and with the cinematic points of reference. Tarantino and lenser Andrzej Sekula's striking widescreen compositions often contain objects in extreme close-up as well as vivid contrasts, sometimes bringing to mind the visual strategies of Sergio Leone.

Performances are sensational. Jackson possibly has the showiest opportunities, and he makes the most of them with a smashing turn that commands attention whenever he's present. Travolta, sporting long hair and an earring, is also terrific, especially during his ambiguous outing with Thurman.

With head shaved in a buzz cut, Willis is all coiled tension and self-control. Keitel has tasty fun as a criminal efficiency expert, Rhames is as menacing as a person can be as the pic's most powerful figure, and Roth and Plummer are the jumpy couple on the low-rent end of the criminal spectrum.

Most of the coin for David Wasco's production design must have gone into the enormous diner, a delirious creation. Sally Menke's editing reps the definition of precision, and score consists of many judiciously selected rock tunes.

On any number of important levels, "Pulp Fiction" is a startling, massive success. —*Todd McCarthy*

THREE COLORS: RED
(TROIS COULEURS: ROUGE)
(FRENCH-SWISS-POLISH)

An MKL release of an MK2 Prods. (Paris)/France 3 Cinema/Cab Prods. (Lausanne)/TOR Production (Warsaw) co-production with the participation of Canal Plus and the support of Eurimages Fund, TSR and the Swiss Ministry of Culture. (Foreign sales: John Kochman, MK2.) Produced by Marin Karmitz. Co-executive producers, Yvon Crenn, Jean-Louis Porchet, Gerard Ruey. Directed by Krzysztof Kieslowski. Screenplay, Krzysztof Piesiewicz, Kieslowski; script consultants, Agnieszka Holland, Edward Zebrowski, Piotr Sobocinski. Camera (Eastmancolor), Piotr Sobocinski; editor, Jacques Witta; music, Zbigniew Preisner; production design, Claude Lenoir; costume design, Corinne Jorry; sound (Dolby), Jean-Claude Laureux, William Flageollet, Brigitte Taillandier; assistant director, Emmanuel Finkiel; casting, Margot Capelier. Reviewed at Cannes Film Festival (competing), May 16, 1994. Running time: **99 MIN.**

Valentine	Irene Jacob
The Judge	Jean-Louis Trintignant
Karin	Frederique Feder
Auguste	Jean-Pierre Lorit

With: Juliette Binoche, Julie Delpy, Benoit Regent, Zbigniew Zamachowski.

"Red," the beautifully spun and splendidly acted tale of a young model's decisive encounter with a retired judge, is another deft, deeply affecting variation on Krzysztof Kieslowski's recurring theme that people are interconnected in ways they can barely fathom. If it's true — as the helmer has announced — that this opus will be his last foray into film directing, Kieslowski retires at a formal and philosophical peak.

Arthouse audiences will feel a proprietary thrill as characters from "Blue" and "White" — the first two films in the director's "Three Colors" trilogy — keep a date with destiny in "Red," although the prior installments are by no means a prerequisite for enjoying this free-standing episode.

Taking its inspiration from the last of the three watchwords of the French Republic (liberty, equality, fraternity), "Red" begins with Swiss law student and judge-to-be Auguste (Jean-Pierre Lorit) dialing a telephone number. The camera then plunges into the innards of the phone network, zipping through wires and cables, dipping under Lake Geneva, only to reach a busy signal.

Meanwhile, Auguste lives across the street from fashion model Valentine (Irene Jacob), who communicates via telephone, sometimes awkwardly, with her boyfriend in England.

Auguste is in love with Karin (Frederique Feder), who runs a "personalized weather service," dispensing tailor-made forecasts by telephone. Auguste and Valentine pass each other on countless occasions but have never noticed each other.

Valentine injures a dog with her car and takes the wounded animal to the address on its collar, where she meets Jean-Louis Trintignant, a former judge who listens in on his neighbors' telephone conversations. Valentine is appalled by the judge's intimate trespassing but is drawn to him.

The sun itself seems to know that these two were meant to meet: It obligingly casts a ray of enlightenment into the judge's study. The innocent, faintly troubled young woman and the resigned older man explore the implications of extending a fraternal hand. Kieslowski demonstrates that life can't really be controlled — nor can its consequences. Fate will bring the protagonists together with gale force.

Location lensing in Geneva is aces. The title color is ever present, from a glass of wine to a bowling ball, from a transit ticket to an automobile. The judge even lives in an area called Carouge.

Jacob — who won best actress honors at Cannes in 1991 for her stunning turn in the director's "Double Life of Veronique" — is photogenic under any circumstances, but she has never been so radiant as in her work with Kieslowski.

Trintignant is fascinating as a man who, in mulling over the verdicts of a lifetime and comparing the rigor of a courtroom with the messy and intricate conversations on which he eavesdrops, recalibrates his moral compass thanks to Jacob.

Zbigniew Preisner's score, augmented by soaring vocals, is a fine ally throughout. Kieslowski is aided and abetted by outstanding tech support.

Narrative has a purposeful randomness — the viewer is assured via countless subtle details that the story is ineluctably headed toward something faintly ominous yet cathartic. Denouement and final image are a satisfying grace note both to this film and the entire trilogy.
—*Lisa Nesselson*

RYABA MY CHICKEN

(KOUROTCHKA RIABA/ RIABA MA POULE)

(RUSSIAN-FRENCH)

A Parimedia/Russian Roulette co-production, with the participation of Centre Nationale de la Cinematographie, Films Committee (Russia), Canal Plus. (International sales: Le Studio Canal Plus.) Produced by Jacky Ouaknine, Andrei Konchalovsky. Directed by Konchalovsky. Screenplay, Konchalovsky, Victor Merejko. Camera (color), Eugeni Gouslinski; editor, Helene Gagarine; music, Boris Basourov; production design, Leonid Platov, Andrei Platov; costumes, Natalia Firsova; sound, Alexander Pogossian; assistant director, Ludmila Vassilieva. Reviewed at Cannes Film Festival (competing), May 13, 1994. Running time: **116 MIN.**
Asya .... Inna Churikova
Stepan .... Alexander Surin
Chirkunov .... Gennadi Iegoritchev
Serioga .... Gennadi Nazarov
Vassili Nikititch ...... Victor Mikhailkov

After directing seven films in the U.S., Andrei Konchalovsky makes an inauspicious return to his native Russia with "Ryaba My Chicken," a forced comedy on the interesting theme of the effects of the new democracy on Russian peasants. Pic will get attention thanks to the director's name and rep, but the

strident tone and sometimes unintentionally risible attempts at comedy will earn it mixed reviews and business at best.

Actually, Konchalovsky is not only returning to Russia here but to his second feature film, the long-banned "Asya's Happiness," which he filmed in the small farming community of Bezvodnoye in 1967. Soviet censors banned the film, apparently because the peasants were presented in an overly naturalistic manner and the collective was shown in a negative light (there was also a childbirth scene that offended the blue noses). Pic was not available for screening until the coming of *glasnost* in the late '80s.

The new film, shot in the same village, reintroduces the feisty peasant woman Asya, though with a different actress in the role: Inna Churikova is the new Asya (Iya Savinna was the original). But the tone of the new film is almost completely different from the earlier one, which was handled in semi-docu style with many non-pro actors and improvised scenes. This time around, the director goes for comedy to depict the changes of the last couple of years.

Pic starts promisingly with Asya herself explaining, in a long monologue as she trudges along a country road, how democracy is, in her view, not working. (There's rampant inflation, increased crime, breakdown of authority, and people are generally worse off.) Her ex-husband (a repeat performance by Alexander Surin) now lives with a gypsy and is a hopeless alcoholic, and their son (the baby born in the first film) is now a selfish black-marketeer involved with the Russian mob and the theft of a priceless golden egg from the Hermitage Museum in St. Petersburg.

For a while, Konchalovsky presents an interesting if depressing and conservative vision of village life. The activities of a local capitalist timber merchant (well played by the late Victor Mikhailkov) upset the locals — noise from his sawmill keeps them awake at night — to the point that they demonstrate against him with pro-Communist banners and photos of past Soviet leaders.

But after a while, fantasy (Asya's pet chicken starts to talk and grows to giant proportions) and some unfortunate attempts at broad slapstick (a number of speeded-up chase sequences) spoil the mood completely. The ultimate message of the film is that despite the enormous events of the last few years, basically nothing in Russia will change.

Apart from Mikhailkov, performances are on the strident side, and production values are modest. The decision to include a few b&w sequences from "Asya's Happiness" proves to be a mistake because the lyrical material from the past is so

much better than anything in "Ryaba My Chicken" itself.
—*David Stratton*

TO LIVE

(CHINESE)

A Samuel Goldwyn Co. release of an Era Intl. (H.K.) production, in association with Shanghai Film Studios. (International sales: Era Intl., H.K.) Produced by Chiu Fu-sheng. Executive producers, Christophe Tseng, Kow Fu-hong. Directed by Zhang Yimou. Screenplay, Yu Hua, Lu Wei, from the novel by Yu. Camera (color), Lu Yue; editor, Du Yuan; music, Zhao Jiping; art direction, Cao Jiuping; costume design, Dong Huamiao; sound (Dolby), Tao Jing; associate producer, Barbara Robinson; assistant directors, Zhang Xleochun, Wang Bin. Reviewed at Cannes Film Festival (competing), May 17, 1994. Running time: **125 MIN.**
Fugui .... Ge You
Jiazhen .... Gong Li
Town Chief .... Niu Ben
Chunsheng .... Guo Tao
Erxi .... Jiang Wu
Long'er .... Ni Dabong
Fengxia, as an adult .... Liu Tianchi
Youqing .... Deng Fei
    (Mandarin Chinese dialogue)

A family drama set across 30 years of modern Chinese history, Zhang Yimou's "To Live" is a well-crafted but in no way earth-shaking entry in the helmer's oeuvre. Topped by finely judged perfs by Gong Li and Ge You as an average couple tossed like corks in a storm by civil war, revolution and political strife, the pic will draw core auds for quality Chinese fare but lacks the special smarts to go as far into the marketplace as showier items like "Farewell My Concubine."

Given that a lot of the background is familiar from recent pix, like "Concubine" and "The Blue Kite," Zhang's movie could also run up against the problem of audience burnout on Chinese hops through 20th-century history. Good reviews and marketing will be crucial in overcoming such resistance.

Story, pruned down by Yu Hua and Lu Wei from a long novel by new wave writer Yu, opens in the '40s in a small village in northern China. Fugui (Ge), eldest son of a prominent family, is hooked on gambling. Wife Jiazhen (Gong) leaves him when Fugui loses the ancestral home to local smoothie Long'er (Ni Dabong), but she returns.

In the second of the movie's five segments, Fugui is now a soldier in the Nationalist (KMT) army fighting the Communists in the late-'40s civil war alongside his buddy Chunsheng (Guo Tao). Pic opens out visually at this stage with several striking set pieces involving troop movements and mass carnage that matures the indolent main character.

Postwar, Fugui returns to his now-

communized native village. In the first of several twists of fate, Long'er is executed as a capitalist. Next jump is to 1958 and the so-called Great Leap Forward, with the whole population mobilized to supply iron for mass industrialization.

Flash forward to 1966, start of the Cultural Revolution, and town chief (Niu Ben) introduces a prospective husband to Fugui's grown daughter (Liu Tianchi, strong in a wordless part). After the 90-minute mark, the movie starts to develop true clout with the news that Fugui's buddy Chunsheng has been branded a "capitalist roadster." What will probably become the movie's most-discussed sequence, for its meld of drama and black comedy, is Fugui's daughter giving birth in a hospital where Little Red Book-bashers misrun the show.

In contrast to many other Chinese family sagas, "To Live" has the major advantage for Western auds of a small number of leading characters and clearly defined relationships.

Scripters Yu and Lu have cut out many of the novel's peripheral roles to throw the central relationship into clearer focus. But in doing this and adopting a relatively cool photographic look and distanced shooting style, Zhang rarely develops a head of steam to roll the story over the political and social changes that impinge on the characters.

Result is a finely but undramatically lensed pic (by cinematographer Lu Yue, rather than Zhang's earlier collaborator, Gu Changwei) that more often parades by rather than engaging the emotions for any significant period.

Though many non-Chinese viewers will be drawn by Gong's name, most of the acting honors go to Ge (the epicene aesthete in "Concubine"). He often brings a quirky, ironic edge to the dialogue that makes one think the picture could also be read as a deep satire on China's recent political history rather than pure (melo)drama. Pic has yet to get official approval by the Beijing authorities, after sneaking out to Japan for post-production just before the authorities decreed negs on foreign-funded films should first get local approval. In a tip of the hat to Beijing, Zhang, who's due to start rolling on the foreign-financed "Shanghai Triad" this fall, stayed away from the Cannes fest.

For the first time in a Zhang movie, Gong plays second fiddle to a strong, accomplished actor. She's very good in a supportive role, but her character doesn't develop many wrinkles or depth.

Supporting perfs, including the children, are all fine, with special mention to Niu Ben as the town chief who makes even the Cultural Revolution seem like an everyday event.

Pic lensed over the second half of last year in a variety of mainland

May 23, 1994 (Cont.)

locations on a reported budget of $3 million-$4 million, from the same Hong Kong affiliate of a Taiwan-based company that funded Zhang's earlier "Raise the Red Lantern." Chinese title literally means "Living"; a recent English title, "Lifetimes," has now been ditched. —*Derek Elley*

A PURE FORMALITY
(UNA PURA FORMALITA)
(ITALIAN-FRENCH)

A Cecchi Gori Group (Italy)/Sony Classics (U.S.) release of a C.G. Group Tiger Cinematografica (Rome)/Film Par Film (Paris) co-production. Produced by Mario and Vittorio Cecchi Gori. Executive producers, Bruno Altissimi, Claudio Saraceni. Directed, written by Giuseppe Tornatore. Camera (Kodak color; Telecolor lab; Panavision widescreen), Blasco Giurato; editor, Tornatore; music, Ennio Morricone; art direction, Andrea Crisanti; costumes, Beatrice Bordone; additional dialogue, Pàscal Quignard; production manager, Giuseppe Giglietti; associate producers, Alexandre Mnouchkine, Jean Louis Livi. Reviewed at Cannes Film Festival (competing), May 15, 1994. Running time: **108 MIN.**
Onoff .... Gerard Depardieu
Inspector .... Roman Polanski
Young Policeman .... Sergio Rubini
Captain .... Nicola Di Pinto
Marshall .... Paolo Lombardi
Servant .... Tano Cimarosa
Paola .... Maria Rosa Spagnolo

Putting aside the sentimental charm of his international hit "Cinema Paradiso," Giuseppe Tornatore turns a corner stylistically in the weird but fascinating "A Pure Formality." Bound to have much narrower appeal than the earlier pic, "Formality" could prove a long row to hoe for Euro distribs, who are releasing it right after its bow in the Cannes competition, and for Sony Classics, which will release it in the U.S. this summer. Pic should earn the director broader critical support, however, and, with careful handling, ought to find appreciative auds.

It's clear from the opening that the film is going to be something out of the ordinary. A man (Gerard Depardieu) appears running through the woods in the pouring rain in a nameless land. Covered with mud and half deranged, he's picked up by the police and taken to a lonesome station to await the arrival of the Inspector.

Tension builds as a gentle young cop (Sergio Rubini) and a kindly old servant (Tano Cimarosa) futilely try to make him feel at home, until the scene explodes in unexpected violence.

Enter the Inspector (Roman Polanski), who begins a witty interrogation that will last the length of the film. Someone has been found mur-dered in the woods, a corpse with a face mutilated beyond recognition.

Claiming to know nothing about any murder, Depardieu insists he's Onoff, a world-famous novelist, playwright and songwriter who's presently in a creative funk. Unfortunately, he can't remember anything he did that afternoon — a nasty admission to make to a suspicious policeman.

The Inspector, an intensely insinuating fellow who looks like a character out of an absurdist East European novel, alternates the carrot and the stick to get his man to confess. Incredibly, he turns out to know Onoff's work by heart, and floors the suspect by reciting entire paragraphs verbatim.

Tornatore exploits the bizarre relationship between cop/fan and suspect/genius from every imaginable angle, first making one grovel to the other and then turning the tables. Onoff pits his staggering obstinacy and a professional gift for lying against the shrewd Inspector's efforts to jog his memory and extract a confession.

A tour de force for the two actors, the pic makes few concessions to the audience and will tend to divide viewers into love-it and leave-it camps. The puzzle at the heart of "A Pure Formality" is basically intellectual, not criminal, and some viewers may find their interest flagging as the interrogation drags on and the literary angst takes over. They should revive watching the ending, which contains a payoff that cannot be revealed.

Although almost the whole film takes place inside an ugly room with a leaky roof and faulty lighting, Tornatore (who did his own editing) breaks out the story in various ways. Subliminal split-second flashbacks offer clues as to what really went on that afternoon, even while Onoff is telling a totally contradictory story.

But "Formality" mainly remains watchable thanks to a strong rhythm created by fast cutting and lots of camera movement.

Unexpected mood shifts keep things rolling. Just as Tornatore's script swings from tragic to ludicrous, his lensing ranges from the supernaturally sublime to a mischievous joke. Some camera work is so obvious it's funny — for example, shots from inside a typewriter or a toilet bowl. The eccentric choice to shoot in widescreen Panavision adds an appropriately bigger-than-life dimension to the huge close-ups looming ominously onscreen.

Perfs are arguably pic's most solid and enjoyable element. Depardieu is amusingly unchained as Onoff; playing an irascible bear, he rants and raves like King Lear, only to gradually emerge as an extremely vulnerable figure.

Polanski has a less flamboyant role but gives an equally complex perf. In his hands, the Inspector swings from naive literary hound to a sadistic fascist; from cunning trapper to an honest cop doing his duty.

Also appealing is Rubini (the director/star of "La Stazione"), whose great mooning eyes and perennial embarrassment never fail to provoke a smile.

Cinematographer Blasco Giurato accomplishes some remarkable technical feats, penetrating rain and gloom with flashes of light that show all that needs to be shown. Pic's palette is monochrome with one narratively significant exception.

Ennio Morricone's intense score for shrieking violins is used without mercy to create strong reactions. Musically, the one out-of-place note is the final song, sung by Depardieu. —*Deborah Young*

QUEEN MARGOT
(LA REINE MARGOT)
(FRENCH-GERMAN-ITALIAN)

A Miramax (U.S.)/AMLF (France) release of a Claude Berri presentation of a Renn Prods., France 2 Cinema, D.A. Films (Paris)/NEF Filmproduktion GmbH, Degeto pour Ard, Wmg (Munich)/R.C.S. Films & TV (Rome) production with the participation of the Centre National de la Cinematographie and Canal Plus. Executive producer, Pierre Grunstein. Directed by Patrice Chereau. Screenplay, Daniele Thompson, Chereau, dialogue by Thompson, based on the novel by Alexandre Dumas. Camera (color), Philippe Rousselot; editors, Francois Gedigier, Helene Viard; music, Goran Bregovic; production design, Richard Peduzzi, Olivier Radot; set decoration, Sophie Martel; costume design, Moidele Bickel; sound design (Dolby), Guillaume Sciama, Dominique Hennequin; hair, makeup, special effects, Kuno Schlegelmilch; assistant director, Jerome Enrico. Reviewed at Cannes Film Festival (competing), May 13, 1994. Running time: **161 MIN.**
Margot .... Isabelle Adjani
Henri of Navarre .... Daniel Auteuil
Charles IX .... Jean-Hugues Anglade
La Mole .... Vincent Perez
Catherine of Medici .... Virna Lisi
Henriette
  of Nevers .... Dominique Blanc
Anjou .... Pascal Greggory
Coconnas .... Claudio Amendola
Guise .... Miguel Bose
Charlotte of Sauve .... Asia Argento
Alencon .... Julien Rassam
Nancay .... Thomas Kretschmann
Coligny .... Jean-Claude Brialy

The grandiose "Queen Margot" aspires to the mantle of Shakespearean tragedy but plays more like bad Grand Guignol theater. Sprawling, bloody costumer about the dastardly deeds of 16th-century French royalty is a frenzy of religious conflict, personal betrayal, raw passion and enough killing for all three parts of "The Godfather." Unlike the gangster epic, however, this adaptation of a historically inspired Alexandre Dumas novel doesn't generate any fascination for its murderous characters, and is a mostly unpleasant chore to slog through. With its star-laden cast and heavy promotion, Claude Berri's latest jumbo-budget period piece may fly commercially in Europe, but U.S. B.O. will undoubtedly be closer to "Germinal" than to "Jean de Florette."

Celebrated theater and opera director Patrice Chereau plays the swirling action to the highest balcony, encouraging his actors to emote and gesticulate without restraint to enact a nasty story of outsized emotions and grisly historical events.

In a France dominated by the Italian exile Catherine de Medici (Virna Lisi) and nominally ruled by her son Charles IX (Jean-Hugues Anglade), a gesture is made toward peace through the arranged marriage of the Catholic Margot (Isabelle Adjani), Charles' sister, and the Protestant Henri of Navarre (Daniel Auteuil).

The beautiful Margot makes no secret of her contempt for her mate, however, announcing that she won't sleep with him and even pursuing an outside assignation on her wedding night.

Almost at once, the rulers at the Louvre decide that the Protestants must be wiped out, resulting in the St. Bartholomew's Day massacre that saw perhaps 6,000 killed in Paris on Aug. 23-24, 1572. Spared the sword, Henri advisedly converts to Catholicism, while Margot is awakened amorously by the dashing Protestant La Mole (Vincent Perez), who is protected by his lover before embarking abroad to gather an army to fight the treacherous papists.

Messy strands of too many plots and subplots begin to pull together in the late going. Things come to a head when some poison Catherine intends for the detested Henri ends up polishing off her son Charles instead, prompting the beginning of the end for the Medici clan, not to mention one of the most protracted death scenes (actually a series of sequences) in film history.

Beyond the disagreeableness of all the characters and their behavior, a chief problem is that Margot is basically a sideline player. Her marriage to one Protestant and affair with another places her in a pivotal position astride two opposing factions, but the greater interest lies in the unpredictable behavior of her mother and three antagonistic brothers. Similarly, Henri is an annoyingly ineffectual type until he surprisingly intervenes on behalf of the king. For his part, La Mole is a standard-issue heroic lover type without a distinctive personality.

Dramatically, Chereau starts things off at a fever pitch with a

May 23, 1994 (Cont.)

chaotic and puzzlingly violent wedding ceremony and cranks it up from there. Drenched in sweat, with stringy hair and ill manners, these nobles never for a moment display the kind of elegance and decorum one normally associates with the historical ruling class, and thus there is no modulation to the storytelling or characterizations. This is murderous melodrama with all the organ stops pulled out.

Thematically, Chereau and his co-scenarist, Daniele Thompson, no doubt had in mind parallels to modern Europe, where Catholics and Protestants still fight and religious intolerance is once again resulting in slaughter and a changing political landscape. But the focus is almost exclusively on the carnage and its immediate motivations, rather than on understanding it or providing any philosophical framework for it.

Performances are almost uniformly over the edge into hysteria. Adjani forever seems to be rushing about to cope with the mad events unfolding around her, Auteuil is hamstrung by a passive character, and Anglade hams it up as the bloodthirsty monarch. With her domed forehead and sinister sneers, Lisi conjures up the ghost of Nosferatu.

Physically, pic has been executed on the grandest scale on locations in France and Portugal. Still, Philippe Rousselot's exceedingly mobile camera stays in claustrophobically tight on the characters much of the time, and the palette is depressingly dark and drained of color. Costumes and production design are splendid. Pic has flashes of both male and female frontal nudity. For U.S. consumption, Miramax could easily be understood if it were to consider some shortening, especially in the hectic, scattershot early going. —*Todd McCarthy*

THE BROWNING VERSION

(BRITISH)

A Paramount release of a Percy Main production. Produced by Ridley Scott, Mimi Polk. Co-producer, Garth Thomas. Directed by Mike Figgis. Screenplay, Ronald Harwood, based on the play by Terence Rattigan. Camera (color, widescreen), Jean-Francois Robin; editor, Herve Schneid; music, Mark Isham; production design, John Beard; costume design, Fotini Dimou; sound (Dolby), Chris Munro; assistant director, John Watson; casting, Susie Figgis. Reviewed at Cannes Film Festival (competing), May 15, 1994. Running time: **97 MIN.**
Andrew
Crocker-Harris .... Albert Finney
Laura Crocker-Harris ... Greta Scacchi
Frank Hunter .... Matthew Modine
Tom Gilbert .... Julian Sands
Dr. Frobisher .... Michael Gambon
Taplow .... Ben Silverston
Diana .... Maryam D'Abo

The themes of Terence Rattigan's play "The Browning Version" seem curiously out of date in a modern context. That proves both a pitfall and a strength for this new "Version." The issues of tradition, classical knowledge and history are all the more potent given the passage of time and changes in attitude, but it is inevitably a rarefied audience that will respond to these themes today. In the best of circumstances, that would mean a comparable commercial response to "The Remains of the Day," which it resembles in tone. More likely, pic's specificity to British academia will translate into modest returns from a decidedly upscale crowd.

It's been more than four decades since Anthony Asquith's original screen adaptation, in which Michael Redgrave assayed the role of Andrew Crocker-Harris, a public school teacher with a bad ticker who's facing a forced, early retirement. Albert Finney puts his unique stamp on the role, effecting a heaviness that suggests a hard crust shielding a marshmallow center. At any moment, that facade could cave in on itself, and herein lies his precarious physical nature.

Crocker-Harris is about to vacate his seat for a less stressful life of teaching English to foreigners. But for two decades he was the stern master of Latin, and he will not succumb to sentimentality in his closing days.

The tragedy of this sometimes ridiculous man is multifold. The discipline he brings to the classroom goes on recess in the outside world. His marriage to Laura (Greta Scacchi) is a sham. Her extra-curricular activity is centered around Frank Hunter (Matthew Modine), the brash, well-liked Yank teaching chemistry. Hunter, however, is increasingly anxious about the situation. Like Crocker-Harris' past students, he's in awe of the man's discipline and decency.

But underneath the oppressive drama there is the beating heart in the form of the student who "gets it." Young Taplow (Ben Silverston) is touched by the humanity of the august scholar who never reached his potential. When he's given Aeschylus, it's not a bunch of tongue-twisting words to memorize but an endearing passion play that speaks to today.

The loving, heartfelt nature of the production reaches to every crevice of the film. The filmmakers are all Taplows, striving desperately to do well in class. The look is just right, elegiac yet cloistered and made of a rich brocade of visual and emotional fabric.

Ronald Harwood's adaptation has abridged the original without diluting its most potent contemporary resonances. It provides Scacchi and Modine with meatier roles than they have more commonly limned. Finney is masterful at the center, and helmer Mike Figgis excels in the traditional setting.

Unquestionably a difficult sell, "The Browning Version" will need some high-powered assistance and imaginative hands to reach its market potential. But it's questionable that this can hope for a better fate than Paramount's last British venture, "Wuthering Heights," which was never released in the U.S. —*Leonard Klady*

THE WHORES

(LE PUTTANE)

(ITALIAN)

A Marco Risi and Maurizio Tedesco presentation of a Trio Cinema e Televisione production with participation from the Ministry of Tourism & Entertainment. (International sales: Intra Films, Rome.) Produced by Tedesco. Directed, written by Aurelio Grimaldi, based on his book. Camera (b&w), Maurizio Calvesi; editor, Mauro Bonanni; art direction, costume design, Claudio Cordaro; sound, Maurizio Argentieri; casting, Nicola Conticello. Reviewed at Cannes Film Festival (competing), May 16, 1994. Running time: **83 MIN.**
Orlanda .... Ida Di Benedetto
Liuccia Bonuccia .... Guia Jelo
Milu .... Lucia Sardo
Blu Blu .... Sandra Sindoni
Veronica .... Paola Pace
Kim .... Alessandra Di Sanzo
Maurizio .... Marco Leonardi
Distinguished
Man .... Adriano Chiaramida

Third feature from Sicilian specialist Aurelio Grimaldi offers a random compendium of prostitution in Palermo that's peppered with luminous moments and casually acute observations. Ultimately, though, this volley of occasionally overlapping but mostly unrelated flesh-trafficking episodes flails about aimlessly and unevenly in the absence of a unifying thread. "The Whores" should turn a trick or two on the odd Euro arthouse beat, but these girls are unlikely to be run off their feet.

The most satisfying narrative track follows the lazy cottage industry of Orlanda (Ida Di Benedetto), a sweetly surly Neapolitan just past her prime. Formerly the self-declared best in the business, she now receives a steady North African clientele at home, who uncomplainingly weather her racist epithets and unceremonious manners.

One of them eventually entertains notions of unpaid romance, stepping in to defend her from a predatory john. His gallantry having taken her by surprise, Orlanda does a florid double take that combines amusement, derision and a sneaking enjoyment of the flattery.

Elsewhere, forays into melodramatic cliches weigh heavily: A streetwalker who's also a doting mother (Lucia Sardo) has some doozies to deal with, from the proud First Communion scene to the solitary Christmas to the tearful vow to one day carve out a better life.

Similarly obvious is the story of a hostile male hooker (Marco Leonardi) who's driven to violence by the kindly attentions of his patron (Adriano Chiaramida). Another line, centering on cocky Liuccia (Guia Jelo), starts out promisingly but lumbers into grotesquerie when she gets a beating instead of a fee.

Grimaldi presents prostitution as a workaday, sometimes literally assembly-line job, taking a detached, non-judgmental and naggingly superficial standpoint.

The five women, one man and a transvestite who are seen plying the trade are simplistically shown, largely controlling their own destinies and toiling without undue complaint. The prevailing mood is mostly a quietly humorous one, with a theatrically contrived Jehovah's Witness encounter the only jarring exception.

Shortcomings are masked chiefly by the subject's enduring fascination and by the engaging cast of primarily non-pros and legit thesps.

The film also travels an admirable tonal range, shifting constantly from playful through somber, aided by the variety of music sources tapped. Italo pop diva Mina warbles over the catchily promising title sequence.

A further boost comes from Maurizio Calvesi's agile black-and-white lensing, which offers a stream of low, skewy angles and seductive, unfettered tracking shots. The camera fetishizes both the beauty and ugliness of the whores' and their customers' bodies. Sex is frequently depicted here, but in matter-of-fact, transactional terms, its erotic charge cranked low. —*David Rooney*

UNDER THE OLIVE TREES

(ZIRE DARAKHTAN ZEYTON)

(IRANIAN)

A Miramax release (U.S.) of an Abbas Kiarostami production. Produced, directed, written by Abbas Kiarostami. Camera (color), Hossein Djafarian, Farhad Saba; editor, Kiarostami; sound, Mahmud Samakbashi, Yadollah Najafi. Reviewed at Cannes Film Festival (competing), May 17, 1994. Running time: **103 MIN.**
Hossein .... Hossein Rezai
Tahereh .... Tahereh Ladanian Film
　Director ..... Mohamad Ali Keshavarz
Mrs. Shiva .... Zarifeh Shiva
Farhad .... Farhad Kheradmand

Iranian master Abbas Kiarostami's fascination with the overlap between cinema and reality provides a surprising backdrop to a touching courtship in "Under the Olive Trees." Highly specialized item should tap his growing international arthouse following, with Miramax releasing the pic in the U.S.

Pic is the third installment in the director's cycle of sublimely simple films set in northern Iran, which began with "Where Is My Friend's Home?" Second pic, "And Life Goes On," returned to the locations of "Home" on the pretense of shooting a documentary about the devastating earthquake that took thousands of lives in the area.

In "Olive Trees" — a film more focused than "Life," which it resembles in many ways — a film crew travels to the same zone to shoot a fictional film. Much of the story falls into the genre of movies about making movies. The twist is that from the opening scene the "director" (played by Mohamad Ali Keshavarz) tells the camera he's an actor, and the only professional one the audience will see in the film. By the next scene, in which Keshavarz chooses a young heroine from a sea of country girls dressed in long Iranian garb, the line between fiction and documentary is already beginning to blur.

This game would soon grow tiresome if strong characters didn't quickly come to the fore. The first to emerge is Mrs. Shiva (Zarifeh Shiva), a tough-as-nails assistant director who keeps the actors in line like a drill sergeant. She argues about the authenticity of the costume with newly chosen leading lady Tahereh (Tahereh Ladanian), whose parents died in the earthquake, like many others whom the "filmmakers" meet.

When a young man chosen to play a simple role proves a disaster, the director tells Mrs. Shiva to rehearse one of the local crew members, Hos-

sein (Hossein Rezai), for the part. But there's a jinx in this choice, too: Hossein has been courting Tahereh but has been refused because he's illiterate and doesn't own a house. The girl, confusing reality with the dialogue she's been given, refuses to say hello to him, as the script calls for.

Hossein confesses his torment to the kindly director in a moving scene that owes its conviction to the boy's non-acting. It's easy to imagine that the real-life Hossein believes that the poor and illiterate, like himself, should marry a spouse who can read and write; otherwise, neither will be able to help their kids when they go to school. (Kiarostami explored the same problem in his docu "Homework.")

Rather than replace the actors, the director changes the script, so Hossein and Tahereh play newlyweds who got married the day after the earthquake. Hossein is simply stunning in his long and oft-repeated shot full of dialogue, which he delivers like a pro. But Tahereh, obstinate about realism, again can't bring herself to say the dialogue, and the director again is forced to give in and change his film.

Pic concludes with one of Kiarostami's trademark long-shot long takes, which captures the simple philosophy behind the film, magically giving the audience a moment of contact with a universal human experience.

Pic's minimal action may put some of the audience to sleep, but it is a risk Kiarostami seems prepared to take. Stripping down the story to the essentials, he makes every detail count. Pic communicates a strong feeling of love for this remote rural land and its afflicted population, whose will to pick up their lives after the earthquake has something heroic about it.

Rather than explore the fiction/reality/documentary conundrum abstractly, as many other films have done, "Olive Trees" uses its naive, non-pro actors to draw a straight line between the audience and the real-life inhabitants of the area. The power of the film lies in the masterful way this is accomplished.

Kiarostami must have lensed the film with a skeleton crew, much the way his director does onscreen. He wrote, produced and edited himself, and there is no art direction or music outside the final scene.

　　　　　　—*Deborah Young*

DEAD TIRED

(GROSSE FATIGUE)

(FRENCH)

A Gaumont/TF1 Films production. Directed, written by Michel Blanc. Story by Bertrand Blier. Camera (color), Eduardo Serra; editor, Maryline Monthieux; music, Rene Marc Bini; production design, Carlos Conti; costume design, Elisabeth Tavernier. Reviewed at Cannes Film Festival (competing), May 18, 1994. Running time: **84 MIN.**
Michel/Patrick Olivier ..... Michel Blanc
Carole .... Carole Bouquet
Philippe .... Philippe Noiret
　With: Josiane Balasko, Charlotte Gainsbourg, Mathilda May, Thierry Lhermite, Roman Polanski, Gilles Jacob.

French thesp Michel Blanc has a lot of fun with his image(s) in "Dead Tired," and the result is an extremely funny insider's look at fame that should be big for the diminutive actor on home turf. However, as the hilarity derives from a knowledge of contempo Gallic fare, the pic's international potential will swing with his popularity from territory to territory.

The simple setup is that Blanc is exhausted from a busy schedule of TV and cinema fare. So, when strange things start happening in his life, he wonders if he's losing his mind.

The balding comic is seen running riot in Cannes, where he puts the make on a string of ingenues. Also present is film festival honcho Gilles Jacob, who's caught off-guard and reluctantly gives Gerard Depardieu's room number at the Hotel Carlton to Blanc.

Blanc, after being accused of rape by actress Josiane Balasko, seeks psychiatric help and is advised to spend some quiet time in the country. His friend, actress Carole Bouquet, takes him to her estate in Provence.

Providence steps in when Blanc and Bouquet discover an impostor. The conniving, lecherous character assumed to be him earlier turns out to be a double. A merry chase ensues that culminates with an agreement in which the exhausted actor will do the "good" roles while his mirror image gets the schlock.

Filmmaker Blanc keeps the tale moving at a breakneck pace that prevents its thinness from showing. And while there are a lot of in-jokes that remind one of the somewhat similar "Stardust Memories" from Woody Allen, both films have serious vibrations under a jocular facade.

The final section finds Blanc usurped by his look-alike, causing a desperate attempt to set things right. Imagine Kafka with a droll sense of humor and you have the picture.

"Dead Tired" is a delightful conceit with a scattergun sensibility. While it's not impossible to enjoy it if you are unfamiliar with the French film scene, such knowledge nonetheless enriches the experience.

　　　　　　—*Leonard Klady*

I LIKE IT LIKE THAT

A Columbia release of a Think Again production. Produced by Ann Carli, Lane Janger. Executive producer, Wendy Finerman. Co-producer, Diana Phillips. Directed, written by Darnell Martin. Camera (DuArt color; Technicolor prints), Alexander Gruszynski; editor, Peter C. Frank; music, Sergio George; production design, Scott Chambliss; art direction, Teresa Carriker-Thayer; set decoration, Susie Goulder; costume design, Sandra Hernandez; sound (Dolby), Rosa Howell-Thornhill; assistant director, H.H. Cooper; casting, Meg Simon. Reviewed at Cannes Film Festival (Un Certain Regard), May 18, 1994. Running time: **105 MIN.**
Lisette Linares .... Lauren Velez
Chino Linares .... Jon Seda
Li'l Chino Linares .... Tomas Melly
Minnie Linares .... Desiree Casado
Pee Wee Linares .... Isaiah Garcia
Alexis .... Jesse Borrego
Magdalena Soto .... Lisa Vidal
Stephen Price .... Griffin Dunne
Rosaria Linares .... Rita Moreno

A thick veneer of happening music, multi-ethnicity, tough attitude and sexual frankness gives a hip feel to what is actually an old-fashioned and conventional story of a bickering family in "I Like It Like That." Debut feature by Darnell Martin, reputedly the first black American woman to write and direct a film for a Hollywood major, displays plenty of energy and an adeptness at staging scenes vividly. It should find a commercial niche on the basis of its colorful, warmhearted look at one family's struggle to hang together in a rambunctious community.

Except for a few excursions to other parts of New York City, story largely stays put within a block of 167th Street in the Bronx, a racially mixed area where the teeming street life is portrayed as volatile, contentious, friendly in an aggressive way and always potentially dangerous, as represented by a memorial mural to a cop recently killed there.

Officer was the brother of Chino (Jon Seda), who in the opening scene defines his Latin macho posturing by proudly timing his sexual endurance with his wife, Lisette (Lauren Velez).

But sex, no matter how prolonged, doesn't provide much of a respite from the couple's chaotic family life, which includes three unruly kids; Lauren's aspiring transsexual brother, Alexis (Jesse Borrego); Chino's critical mother (Rita

May 23, 1994 (Cont.)

Moreno) and constant financial problems.

Further complicating matters is the constant threat posed by Magdalena (Lisa Vidal), the local fox who is still hot for Chino and whose little child may be his.

Crisis is precipitated by a blackout during which Chino steals a stereo, landing him in the slammer. To raise the bail, Lisette tries to get a modeling gig but winds up with a job as assistant to a record label exec (Griffin Dunne).

After some local boys stir up trouble by insinuating that Lisette is putting in overtime with her boss, Chino, once free, takes up again with Magdalena, prompting Lisette to have an affair for real in revenge. Misunderstandings reach a head equal to any "I Love Lucy" episode, but sweet conclusion makes for a feel-good fade-out.

A serious sidelight to the romantic ups and downs concerns the raising of small kids in such a neighborhood. The absence of the father when he's in jail, the hot-and-cold relationship of the parents, the lack of money and lure of the streets clearly do not engender feelings of security and respect in the children, and Chino's attempts to physically discipline his son create further alienation and disobedience.

The poignance generated by this part of the story, aided mightily by the winning performance of 10-year-old Tomas Melly, give these scenes special distinction.

On the other hand, viewers not keen on listening to characters yell at each other at top volume, over important and trivial matters alike, might back off. Many of the attempts at humor are pretty limp; a running gag about Lisette's lack of "tetas" far overstays its welcome, and the material relating to Lisette's female-wannabe brother seems gratuitous and unfunny.

With her taste for the mobile camera and overhead shots, as well as the contempo street material, Martin shows an affinity with Spike Lee, although in most other respects her sensibility feels more mainstream and conventional in the way situations resolve themselves in upbeat, undisturbing ways.

Aside from the immediate threat of drugs and insolvency, the greater ills of society aren't grappled with here, and the emotional extremism of the characters is played as much for laughs as for drama.

Mostly unknown thesps throw themselves into their roles with abandon and emerge appealingly. Velez convinces as she manages to cope while being on the brink most of the time, and Seda is fine as the temperamental young father torn in several directions. Dunne is OK as the music exec, while Moreno has little to do as the haranguing mother.

Pic jumps to a strong urban beat, and tech credits are solid. While de-

livering nothing remarkable, Martin demonstrates that she knows her way around a camera and actors, and will certainly be heard from in the future.

—Todd McCarthy

MURIEL'S WEDDING

(AUSTRALIAN)

A Miramax (U.S.) release of a CIBY 2000 presentation in association with Australian Film Finance Corp. of a House and Moorhouse Films production. (International sales: CIBY Sales, London.) Produced by Lynda House, Jocelyn Moorhouse. Directed, written by P.J. Hogan. Camera (color), Martin McGrath; editor, Jill Bilcock; music, Peter Best; production design, Patrick Reardon; art direction, Hugh Bateup; set decoration, Jane Murphy, Glen W. Johnson; costume design, Terry Ryan; sound (Dolby), David Lee; associate producers, Michael D. Aglion, Tony Mahood; assistant director, Mahood; casting, Alison Barrett. Reviewed at Cannes Film Festival (Directors Fortnight), May 18, 1994. Running time: **105 MIN.**

Muriel Heslop	Toni Collette
Bill Heslop	Bill Hunter
Rhonda	Rachel Griffiths
Betty Heslop	Jeanie Drynan
Deidre	Gennie Nevinson Brice
Matt Day	David Van Arkle
Daniel	Lapaine Tania

"Muriel's Wedding" is an aesthetically crude ugly-duckling fantasy that is shrewdly designed as a lowbrow audience pleaser. This Miramax acquisition from Australia trades on the perennial appeal of the theme of building self-esteem by showing up the people who have always held you down, and finding yourself in the process. Good business, at least in English-language territories, looks likely, with young women as the target audience.

In the most obvious terms, first-time writer/director P.J. Hogan establishes poor Muriel (Toni Collette) as, in her own words, "stupid, fat and useless."

Uncouth and tasteless enough to wear a phony leopard-skin dress to a wedding, the overweight 22-year-old high school dropout is savaged by her father (Bill Hunter) for not even being able to type and, therefore, hold a job. She is viciously victimized by her snooty girlfriends, who excommunicate her from their petty little circle for not being cool enough. After a resort vacation where she hooks up with g.f. Rhonda (Rachel Griffiths) to do a lip-synched Abba routine in a club, the young ladies move to Sydney, where Muriel spends much of her time building a fantasy wedding photo album out of shots she gets taken of herself at bridal salons.

In a series of unlikely and bizarre plot developments, Rhonda con-

tracts cancer, which provides the chance for Muriel to care for her and thus build some self-worth; her father becomes embroiled in a financial scandal as well as an extramarital affair, and Muriel fulfills at least the externals of her fantasy by marrying a hunky South African swimmer who needs official status in Australia in order to compete on the Olympic team.

Most of the action is played for broad laughs, and Hogan demonstrates the ability to generate them, even if the humor is base and often cruel, making fun of people's looks and ineptitude.

Visual style highlights the crassest elements of middle-class Aussie lifestyle, with an emphasis on vulgar color schemes, bad clothes and touristic consumerism. Broadly drawn, performances in varying measure manage to overcome the often humiliating way their characters are presented.

Made to look pathetic and doltish in many scenes, Collette's Muriel will nonetheless serve as an effective conduit for the emotions of viewers who have ever felt unattractive, unwelcome and outcast, which reps quite a few people indeed.

It is here that the potential mass appeal of the film lies. Hunter brings his usual flavor to the part of the sociable but unsupportive father. Best performance by far comes from screen newcomer Griffiths, who, as Rhonda, generates real feeling and shows impressive range in her swing from wild party girl to embittered invalid.

Sporting an active pace early on, pic sags in the latter stages, as script skips around among diverse, far-fetched plot strands after the wedding. The 1970s pop group Abba seems to be the flavor of the season in Aussie films, as another Cannes entry, "The Adventures of Priscilla, Queen of the Desert," climaxes with an Abba tune, and this one is papered with the band's music, with "Dancing Queen" its theme.

In this season of weddings and funerals, this film has both, and should appeal to audiences ready for some simple character identification and easy laughs.

—Todd McCarthy

COLD WATER

(L'EAU FROIDE)

(FRENCH)

A Pan-Europeene release (France) of an Ima Films production in association with Ima Prods., La Sept/Arte, SFP Production, Sony Music Entertainment (France). (International sales: Polygram Film Intl. Classics, London.) Produced by Georges Benayoun. Paul Rozenberg. Executive producers, Francoise Guglielmi, Elisabeth Deviosse, Yannick Casanova. Directed, written by Olivier Assayas. Camera (color), Denis Lenoir; editor, Luc Barnier; art direction, Gilbert Gagneux; costume design, Francoise Clavel; sound (Dolby), Herve Chauvel; associate producer, Chantal Poupaud, assistant director, Francois-Renaud Labarthe; casting, Pierre Amzallag. Reviewed at Cannes Film Festival (Un Certain Regard), May 17, 1994. Running time: **93 MIN.**

Christine	Virginie Ledoyen
Gilles	Cyprien Fouquet
Gilles' Father	Laszlo Szabo
Inspector	Jean-Pierre Darroussin
Christine's Mother	Dominique Faysse
Mourad	Smail Mekki
Christine's Father	Jackie Berroyer

Tough, confrontational and resonantly melancholy, "Cold Water" delivers a sustained emotional pummeling, underscored by a steady whisper of despair. Set in 1972, this compulsive drama of two troubled teenagers is deeply rooted in its time period; as a consequence, those who came of age back then will feel an instant affinity, presenting French writer/director Olivier Assayas with perhaps his best shot yet at widespread arthouse acceptance.

The story centers on Christine (Virginie Ledoyen) and Gilles (Cyprien Fouquet), two 16-year-olds in a town near Paris. Though it's immediately clear the pair are a couple, young love is less of an issue here than alienation from their respective dysfunctional families, school and authority in general.

Concerned for her mental stability, Christine's father (Jackie Berroyer) has been considering admitting her to a clinic. When Gilles steals records from a store and gets away, Christine is hauled in by police, prompting her father to act on his intention. Gilles' father, meanwhile, is eyeing boarding school as a solution to his son's escalating disciplinary problems.

After a day in the clinic, Christine's mood swings from sullen to dangerously depressive. She runs off to attend a party, creating a junction at which the film veers off in a more desolate direction, assuming new textures as it slowly begins to build on its potent momentum.

Before the party, virtually no music is heard on the soundtrack, with Denis Lenoir's prowling camera the only outside force comment-

May 23, 1994 (Cont.)

ing and effectively crowding in on the incisively drawn characters. Then, having rigorously established his concerns, Assayas blitzes the film for almost its entire remaining half with a flood of impeccably chosen '70s songs.

The party sequence extends through various phases. The intimacy of Christine and Gilles' reunion gives way to momentary panic when her parents show up, then to drug-induced nirvana around a bonfire and later to morning-after stillness.

Young leads Ledoyen and Fouquet are remarkably honest and unaffected, not only in shared scenes, but also in a series of tense, unnerving face-offs with adults.

Backup cast members are universally strong, particularly the other kids. Assayas directs his fine script with unerring focus, and tech input shows the customary prowess in all quarters.

Especially shrewd is Lenoir's extensive use of panicky, hand-held camera, which serves clear purposes in terms of character definition and steers clear of undue pyrotechnics.
—*David Rooney*

PICTURE BRIDE

A Miramax (U.S.) release of a Thousand Cranes Filmworks presentation in association with Miramax produced in association with Cecile Co. Ltd. Produced by Lisa Onodera. Executive producer, Diane Mei Lin Mark. Directed by Kayo Hatta. Screenplay, Kayo Hatta, Mari Hatta. Story, Kayo Hatta, Mari Hatta, Diane Mark. Camera (Foto-Kem color), Claudio Rocha; editors, Lynzee Klingman, Mallori Gottlieb; music, Cliff Eidelman; production design, Paul Guncheon; costume design, Ada Akaji; sound (Ultra-Stereo), Susan Moore-Chang; assistant director, Emmett J. Dennis III. Reviewed at Cannes Film Festival (Un Certain Regard), May 17, 1994. Running time: **98 MIN.**

Riyo	Youki Kudoh
Matsuji	Akira Takayama
Kana	Tamlyn Tomita
Kanzaki	Cary-Hiroyuki Tagawa
The Benshi	Toshiro Mifune
Aunt Sode	Yoko Sugi

"**P**icture Bride" tells an immigrant saga the outlines of which are similar to many others, albeit one of some distinction based on its unique historical setting. Apparently the first commercial dramatic feature directed by an Asian-American woman, pic is tasteful, careful and quite lacking in dramatic surprises, but represents a respectable job of ethno-cultural rootsfinding and re-creation. Strongly female-oriented, this Miramax pickup should be able to capture a portion of the "Joy Luck Club" audience, even if the film is much less complex, ambitious and emotionally potent than that recent success.

Although stylistically different, opening sections unavoidably recall "The Piano," as a woman travels across the sea to join an intended husband she's never met, only to find unhappiness due to the man's insensitivity and the primitive physical surroundings.

Time and place here is the territory of Hawaii in 1918, around which time nearly 20,000 Japanese women left their homeland to marry laborers on the islands, thereby helping to build the foundation of the Japanese-American community there.

To leave behind what are only described as her "past" and "bad memories," 17-year-old Riyo (Youki Kudoh, of Jim Jarmusch's "Mystery Train") is sent from Yokohama to Hawaii as a "picture bride" on the basis of an exchange of photographs between her and a sugar-cane worker.

Upon arrival, she is shocked to discover that Matsuji (Akira Takayama) is much older than he looked in his portrait, and at least 25 years her senior. He apologizes for sending an out-of-date photo, and she, with impressive fortitude, refuses to consummate their marriage.

But Riyo is in no position to back off the hard work on the sugar plantation, even though, as a slim city girl, she's not as sturdy as many of the other female workers.

Desperately unhappy but with nowhere to turn, she befriends another Japanese woman, Kana (Tamlyn Tomita), who has a small child, and eventually resolves to work extremely hard, both in the fields and doing laundry, in order to earn enough to pay her way home.

At 65¢ per day, however, it's going to take a long time to save up the necessary $300. Things don't get much better with Matsuji, who tries to take her money for a worker strike fund he's organizing and, upon learning that her parents died of tuberculosis, tells her he wouldn't have accepted the match had he known this before.

For a long time, Riyo is just as stubborn a character as Holly Hunter's in "The Piano." Ultimately, however, after a tragedy involving Kana, Riyo and her husband get together, and some final narration makes it clear that she finally accepted her position as a pioneer of her particular class of Hawaiian residents.

Hawaiian-born helmer Kayo Hatta and her sister Mari based their script on an assortment of true-life experiences of real picture brides, and the film offers numerous interesting cultural details, such as the unique songs the workers sang in the fields, the moderate tensions among Asians from different countries, and the ways in which some old traditions were retained and others were dropped.

Much of the dialogue is in Japanese with English subtitles, although characters frequently fall into pidgin English. One particularly vivid sequence has the great Toshiro Mifune appear briefly as a traveling *benshi*, or narrator of a silent samurai film projected on a sheet outdoors.

All the same, most of the incidents have a familiar ring, as the attitudes, adjustment difficulties, racist policies and assorted injustices are quite typical of colonial-era stories everywhere, and the cultural, ethnic and religious conflict during this period in Hawaii seems to have been rather less severe than in many other places. This in no way minimizes what the pioneers went through, but does make for less than exciting drama.

While paying great attention to composition and detail, Hatta sets a relatively slow pace and, except for the subject, nothing in the film evinces any artistic adventurousness. Pic has been made with evident love but conveys little passion or zeal.

As the long-suffering Riyo, Kudoh is exemplary, although the viewer is never really allowed inside her head. Tomita also delivers as the ill-fated Kana, and acting throughout is solid.

Outfitted with a professional post-production sheen by Miramax after its acquisition, pic looks exceedingly handsome, thanks partly to the exceptional locations, marked notably by the green plant life, red earth and generally overcast skies, and also to Claudio Rocha's lensing. —*Todd McCarthy*

AMATEUR

A UGC presentation in association with American Playhouse Theatrical Films, La Sept Cinema and Channel 4 Films of a Zenith/True Fiction Pictures production. (International sales: UGC DA Intl., Paris.) Produced by Hal Hartley, Ted Hope. Executive producers, Jerome Brownstein, Lindsay Law, Scott Meek, Yves Marion for UGC. Directed, written by Hartley. Camera (DuArt color), Michael Spiller; editor, Steven Hamilton; music, Ned Rifle, Jeffrey Taylor; production design, Steve Rosenzweig; art direction, Ginger Tougas; sound (Dolby), Jeff Pullman; assistant director, Gregory Jacobs. Reviewed at Cannes Film Festival (Directors Fortnight), May 14, 1994. Running time: **105 MIN.**

Isabelle	Isabelle Huppert
Thomas	Martin Donovan
Sofia	Elina Lowensohn
Edward	Damian Young
Jan	Chuck Montgomery
Kurt	David Simonds
Officer Melville	Pamela Stewart

A former nun who writes erotic stories, an amnesiac with a criminal past and "the most notorious porno actress in the world" bounce off each other with

tasty results in Hal Hartley's "Amateur." Just as quirky and idiosyncratic as the Gotham-based writer/director's earlier efforts, this one pushes the spiky humor a bit more to the fore while unfolding a tale loaded with offbeat oppositions and odd character detailing. This outing will do little to expand his public beyond the core specialized audience that has supported his work to date.

Isabelle Huppert, who wrote Hartley a fan letter offering to act in one of his films, plays Isabelle, who recently checked out of convent life after 15 years. A failure at writing about sex, a subject about which she seems to have no personal knowledge, she also claims to be a nymphomaniac to Thomas (Martin Donovan), a man who awakens on a downtown New York street with no memory and is trustingly taken in by Isabelle. So start the odd juxtapositions.

Before long, it becomes clear that Thomas has been pushed out a window (and is presumed dead) by his wife, Sofia (Elina Lowensohn), a porno queen whose desperate financial straits lead her to deal with a powerful arms merchant. This sends the film away from Isabelle and Thomas onto an unexpected tangent involving Thomas' accountant, Edward (Damian Young), and two well-educated goons who are tailing Sofia and Thomas.

The main characters all come together in upstate New York in a tragicomic climax in which nearly surreal humor takes precedence over full character revelation or dramatic closure.

The three principals are all vessels waiting to be filled, and none more so than Thomas, who, through the course of the film, can't remember a thing about his pre-injury life. This creates a bit of an energy-draining cipher at the center, but Hartley has surrounded him with indelible characters that more than hold the interest, and the "mystery" surrounding Thomas provides just enough of a narrative engine to keep things moving.

Viewers not in tune with the filmmaker's approach may find the comic elements forced and contrived, since they are often based on absurd conceits. But Hartley's technique is now so refined and precise that he easily achieves his desired effects; the artistic layering of stylization in performance, timing and visuals pulls the action sufficiently away from reality to induce one to accept the strange string of events. This same self-conscious artistry, however, may also be the major element limiting Hartley to a small audience.

Thematically, the amnesia angle has been explored so often that it emerges as the least interesting element here. But the contrapuntal character traits and plot twists create some interesting contrasts between purity and experience, knowledge and ignorance, reputation and what people actually do. Intellectually, pic is lively and wry without becoming pretentious.

Donovan can't do much with a character who basically doesn't exist, but remainder of the cast is excellent. Looking virtually the same as she did 10 or 15 years ago, Huppert has a sweet gravity underlaid with quietly suggestive humor and, if anything, is onscreen too little. Memorable in a minor role in Hartley's last film, "Simple Men," Lowensohn takes on a much bigger part here, that of the sexpot goddess, and makes the most of it in an eye-catching turn.

Young gives a wild performance as the lanky accountant who comes unglued after some electroshock torture. Film's comic highlight is a long tracking shot of him taking shots at one of the goons on a lawn until latter finally collapses. Chuck Montgomery and David Simonds are deliciously cool, calm and collected as the henchmen, and Pamela Stewart gives a terrific reading in the tiny role of a hopelessly understanding and sentimental cop.

Hartley's films become more impressively designed with each outing. Lenser Michael Spiller is a wizard of precision, deftly focusing the viewer's eye on the desired object. Color schemes in Steve Rosenzweig's production design are exceedingly elegant, and fine score by Ned Rifle and Jeffrey Taylor effectively helps set the cool but enticing tone. —*Todd McCarthy*

EAT DRINK MAN WOMAN

(TAIWANESE)

A Samuel Goldwyn release (U.S.) of a Central Motion Picture Corp./Ang Lee/ Good Machine production. Produced by Li-King Hsu. Executive producer, Feng-Chyi Jiang. Directed by Lee. Screenplay, Lee, James Schamus, Hui-Ling Wang. Camera (DuArt color), Jong Lin; editor, Tim Squyres; music, Mader; production design, Fu-Hsiung Lee; set decoration, Hsi-Chien Lee; sound (Dolby), Tom Paul; line producer, Ta-Peng Lan; associate producers, Schamus, Ted Hope; assistant director, Yang-Sheng Ou. Reviewed at Cannes Film Festival (Directors Fortnight), May 13, 1994. Running time: **123 MIN.**

Chu	Sihung Lung
Jen	Kuei-Mei Yang
Kien	Chien-Lien Wu
Ning	Yu-Wen Wang
Madame Liang	Ah-Leh Gua
Jin-Rong	Sylvia Chang
Li Kai	Winston Chao
Chin-Cheng Lu	Lester Chen

On the heels of the international success of "The Wedding Banquet," Ang Lee has directed the ambitious and entertaining "Eat Drink Man Woman." Again his focus is the family, and the universality of his themes translates well commercially in both Eastern and Western markets.

New tale centers on Chu (Sihung Lung), a master chef who's literally lost his sense of taste. The widower lives in Taipei with his three adult daughters — each of whom, consciously or otherwise, is just itching to leave the nest. Jen (Kuei-Mei Yang), the eldest, teaches school and has skillfully learned to hide her emotions since a failed love affair during her university years. Kien (Chien-Lien Wu), a senior exec with the national airline, has her savings invested in an apartment in a new building complex. The youngest, Ning (Yu-Wen Wang), is still in school and works at a fast-food outlet. She has a slow-building relationship with her best friend's boyfriend. Add to this Chu's seemingly inevitable marriage to Madame Liang (Ah-Leh Gua), the mother of the single mother next door, and the tangle of relationships becomes extremely dense.

While the essential components of the film are serious, even grave, Lee's touch is light and his approach anecdotal. Still, his leisurely laying out of the emotional geography is cause for some initial impatience. With so many characters to identify, an anxiety builds that the plot strands have no core.

But as one of the daughters notes, "We communicate by eating." In fact, the ritual of preparing food is a means to avoid interaction. That's been the father's modus operandi for years, and that irony is not overlooked in the fact that he's lost his capacity for this essential and pleasurable human experience.

The script is steeped in food metaphors and illusions. Considerable strife between Kien and her father can be traced to his kicking her out of the kitchen and pushing her into a professional career. More obvious is Ning's choice of a job in the type of eatery her father abhors.

Neither food nor love is finally enough, and it's the former that prevails and allows the often crushing aspects of life to be unburdened. In one climactic scene the effect is refreshingly hilarious, and that insight into humanity is what makes "Eat Drink Man Woman" such a winning recipe.

One has to assume that commercial and critical kudos have been liberating for the filmmaker. The technical sheen and visual assurance of his latest film is a quantum leap from earlier credits. He also elicits deeper, more textured performances from his actors. The overall result is a cinematic feast that will have audiences returning for Lee's next movie meal.

—*Leonard Klady*

I CAN'T SLEEP
(J'AI PAS SOMMEIL)
(FRENCH-SWISS)

A Pyramide release of an Arena Films/Orsans Prods./Pyramide/Les Films de Mindif/France 3 Cinema/MG Films/Agora Film/Vega Film co-production. (International sales: Pyramide Intl.) Produced by Fabienne Vonier, Ruth Waldburger. Directed by Claire Denis. Screenplay, Denis, Jean-Pol Fargeau. Camera (color), Agnes Godard; editor, Nelly Quettier; music, John Pattison; art direction, Thierry Flamand, Arnaud de Moleron; production manager, Catherine Chouridis. Reviewed at Cannes Film Festival (Un Certain Regard), May 12, 1994. Running time: **110 MIN.**

Daiga	Katherina Golubeva
Camille	Richard Courcet
Theo'	Alex Descas
Mona	Beatrice Dalle
Ninon	Line Renaud
Alice	Sophie Simon
Mina	Irina Grjebina
Ossip	Tolsty
Raphael	Vincent Dupont
Abel	Patrick Grandperret

Claire Denis' "I Can't Sleep" is a probing walk through the expatriate communities of Paris. While its realistic setting is revealing, film lacks an emotional hook to involve the viewer in its characters' fates. Well-made but rather cold picture is unlikely to attract the attention of the director's 1988 "Chocolate" but should be of interest to speciality markets.

Film establishes two storylines that casually overlap from time to time. In one, a plucky young Lithuanian actress, Daiga (Katherina Golubeva), drives into town in her beaten-up Russian car, following the empty promises of a theater director with whom she apparently had an affair. Unable to speak French, she is sheltered by relatives and friends, who find her lodging in a small hotel and a job as a chambermaid.

Second thread involves an extended family from Martinique. The grave Theo (Alex Descas), a musician, supports himself and his small daughter by doing carpentry jobs for snooty Parisians. He is about to move back to the Caribbean, over the strident protests of the child's mother (Beatrice Dalle). His brother Camille (Richard Courcet), who is introed wearing makeup and fishnet stockings, has chosen to live on the wild side. In a scene reminiscent of "The Crying Game," he sings torch songs in drag in a gay club and sleeps in Daiga's hotel with his doctor/lover.

Once she has established sympathy for Camille, considered by everyone a polite nice guy, Denis gradually pulls open a curtain on the underbelly of his life: a drug problem, AIDS treatment and a nasty habit of breaking into apartments and murdering old ladies. He strangles his victims quickly and almost painlessly while an accomplice hunts for loot. Denis chooses to recount these adventures as neutrally and non-judgmentally as if the characters were drinking a cup of coffee, making it strangely difficult to condemn the murderer. On the other hand, helmer does raise sympathy for Camille's victims.

Long before the police hunt down Camille, Daiga realizes who he is, and follows him one day out of curiosity and vague amusement. Even when his mother is called to the police station, her horrified reaction is immediately diluted by pity and sorrow, which seems to reflect the filmmaker's attitude.

The film admirably goes beyond racism (which nevertheless lies menacingly in the background) to show expatriates deeply embedded in their own Parisian milieus. The matter-of-fact way they're viewed is a key to film's exploration of Paris' night denizens and crime, of which they can be perpetrators or victims. Slant is original but has the major disadvantage of being rather dull to watch.

Acting is restrained and unexciting. With the exception of Dalle, who strenuously fights to have her husband and daughter stay with her in Paris, the main thesps are alarmingly inexpressive. Golubeva walks through her role like a beautiful, mysterious, chain-smoking sphinx. Her dialogue is necessarily limited by the language problem (a large part of the film is in subtitled Russian). But even when she gets mad — for example, revenging herself against the stage director who snubs her — she remains distant.

Descas and Courcet, likewise, are men of few words. Their feelings seem to run deep, but Denis and coscripter Jean-Pol Fargeau never explore exactly what those feelings are. A metaphor for the filmmakers' project appears in a brief scene in a hospital morgue, where pathologists view pieces of skin from a corpse (presumably one of Camille's victims) under a microscope. It may be a modern and efficient way to study human beings, but the effect is antiseptic.

On the plus side is Agnes Godard's subtle camera work and an almost subliminal musical comment by John Pattison.—*Deborah Young*

71 FRAGMENTS OF A CHRONOLOGY OF CHANCE

(71 FRAGMENTE EINER CHRONOLOGIE DES ZUFALLS)

(AUSTRIAN)

A WEGA Film in association with Camera Film Co. Berlin and ZDF/Arte production. Produced by Veit Heiduschka. Executive producer, Willi Segler. Co-producers, Paul Bielicki, Michael Boehme. Directed, written by Michael Haneke. Camera (color), Christian Berger; editor, Mariae Homolkova; production design, Christoph Kanter; costume design, Erika Navas; sound, Marc Parisotto, Hannes Eder; computer consultants, Andreas Polz, Martin Schemitsch; assistant director, Ramses Ramsauer. Reviewed at Cannes Film Festival (Directors Fortnight), May 18, 1994. Running time: **96 MIN.**
Romanian Boy .. Gabriel Cosmin Urdes
Max .... Lukas Miko
Tomek .... Otto Grunmandl
Inge Brunner .... Anne Bennent
Paul Brunner .... Udo Samel

The aptly, ironically titled "71 Fragments of a Chronology of Chance" is the third film in avant-garde director Michael Haneke's trilogy that began with "The Seventh Continent" and continued with "Benny's Video," both of which were shown at Cannes. Intellectually demanding and non-commercial film should be embraced in the festival and arthouse circuits by film students and viewers interested in postmodern, deconstructionist cinema.

Haneke is a cerebral filmmaker who believes that cinema's most important function is to disturb and disorient its viewers, shaking them out of their habitually passive ways of perceiving reality.

As in his first two films, the plot (if one can describe it as such) revolves around an act of gratuitous violence that, on the surface, defies logical explanation. Premise of his new film is that on the day before Christmas 1993, a 19-year-old student senselessly murders several people and then commits suicide in his car.

Framed as a mystery, the story unfolds in five asymmetrical chapters, beginning on Oct. 12 and culminating on the day of the murder. About a dozen disparate characters are introduced and then periodically revisited, always in a surprising manner. One of the figures who links the fragments is a homeless adolescent, a Romanian exile who's wandering Vienna's streets begging for money and shoplifting.

Haneke accepts the ubiquitous presence of the visual media in our daily lives, particularly the omni-presence of TV, video and computers. Each chapter begins with TV's evening news, often with reportage about war-torn Sarajevo, then updates on the charges against Michael Jackson, using the same footage over and over. Philosophically bent director stresses the numbing effects of the media's repetition of images and soundbites.

Production values in every department are fine, particularly Christian Berger's crystal-clear lensing and Mariae Homolkova's sharply concise editing, both of which are meant to make viewers aware of the arbitrary and manipulative way in which events are pre-arranged and pre-digested for them to consume.

The most accessible film in Haneke's trilogy, "71 Fragments" offers more illuminating insights about the inherent contradictions and frustrations in our lives than most commercial films today. A cerebral entertainment, it is also one of the few films at the festival this year to provide Cannes its claim for showcasing experimental and cutting-edge cinema. —*Emanuel Levy*

BOSNA!

(FRENCH — DOCU)

A Les Films Du Lendemain production (Sales: MKL). Directed by Bernard-Henri Levy, Alain Ferrari. Screenplay, Levy, Gilles Hertzog. Camera (color), Pierre Boffety; editor, Yann Kassile, Frederic Lossignol; music, Denis Barbier. Reviewed at Cannes Film Festival (Un Certain Regard), May 15, 1994. Running time: **119 MIN.**
Narrator: Bernard-Henri Levy.

"Bosna!" is a zealously powerful film about the bloodshed in Sarajevo. Stirring footage contributes to the authenticity and impact of a docu that never claims or attempts to present a balanced view. Timeliness and global attention to the still-unresolved conflict ensure showings on TV and perhaps even theatrical distribution in major Western markets.

"Bosna!" is not the only docu about the region this year; "MGM Sarajevo — Man, God, the Monster," made by local filmmakers, is being shown in the Directors Fortnight at Cannes. The only similarity between the two works is their filmmakers' goal to make the Western world realize the extent of atrocities in Sarajevo — and to plead for immediate action to terminate them.

"Bosna!" is divided into five loosely chronological segments, from April 4, 1992, when the war began, to the present. On closer examination, however, there's a lot of overlap, which is a problem. No matter how a chapter begins, invariably the reportage and imagery switch to the brutal destruction of Sarajevo's Bosnians by the fanatical Serbian aggressors.

Three clear issues emerge. First is the systematic annihilation of Bosnia's civilian community (schools, churches, homes, etc.). The second theme is the long silence of the West.

Third and most consistent motif is the staunch determination of Bosnians to defend their country, even as their families and friends continue to be massacred. Each section dwells on the Bosnians' moral strength, showing how their makeshift militia (many of them youngsters) are using primitive weapons against the far-better-equipped Serbs. The filmmakers insist on categorizing the Bosnians as victims, while the latter resiliently defy this label.

Some sketchy info is offered about the historical origins and political context of the conflict, but "Bosna!" is unabashedly subjective in its ideology and p.o.v. The narration is spoken by co-director and co-scenarist Bernard-Henri Levy, one of France's most respected philosophers and political commentators.

Docu is at its best when using primary sources and firsthand interviews. The cruelest evidence is provided by a Serbian soldier who matter-of-factly confesses how he slit the throat of a Bosnian "like a pig" and raped seven girls, two of whom he later killed.

Pic points to U.S. State Dept. censorship of repeated messages about the death camps built by the Serbs, drawing an analogy to the Holocaust.

Tech credits are very good, which is a major achievement considering the difficulty and risk of gaining entry into the region; on some occasions, the camera crew is just a few yards from the battlefield.
—*Emanuel Levy*

MGM SARAJEVO — MAN, GOD, THE MONSTER

(MGM SARAJEVO — COVJEK, BOG, MONSTRUM)

(BOSNIAN — DOCU)

Produced by Ismet Arnautalic, Ademir Kenovic for SAGA Prods. (Sarajevo). Directed by Arnautalic, Mirsad Idrizovic, Kenovic, Pjer Zalica. Camera (color/b&w), Ahmed Imamovic, Milenko Uherka, Mirsad Herovic, Miso Knezevic, Sulejman Klokoci; editors, Theodoros Koutsoulis, Almir Kenovic, Oliver Todorovic; post-production, Dana Rotberg. Reviewed at Cannes Film Festival (Directors Fortnight), May 13, 1994. Running time: **93 MIN.**

The collective work of four Bosnian directors who shot in Sarajevo late last year, "MGM Sarajevo — Man, God, the Monster" will, by its very nature, attract the attention of everyone concerned with the war in Bosnia. This unique documentary offers firsthand information as it portrays the tortured capital, Sarajevo. Strangely, however, it is less emotionally compelling than many TV reports from war correspondents. Its main niche will nonetheless be Western TV.

The film was made by the Sarajevo Group of Authors (SAGA), which has been a rallying point for the city's intellectuals since the siege began in April 1992.

"Man, God, the Monster" edits three separate films together in a single, multi-visioned portrait of Bosnia. The most engrossing and anguishing segments come from Ademir Kenovic and Ismet Arnautalic's "The Monster's Confession," in which a 21-year-old Bosnian Serb who fought with the Serbian Chetnik aggressors confesses to his war crimes in front of the camera, seemingly days before he is to be executed. His re-enactment of how he slit throats and raped prisoners is all the more bloodcurdling for being told so matter-of-factly. "Others did worse things" is his line of defense, though he does admit to having a recurring nightmare about a man he slaughtered like a pig.

Pjer Zalica's "Godot-Sarajevo" is a fairly straightforward account of how Susan Sontag came to Sarajevo in 1993 and staged a production of "Waiting for Godot." There is little of interest in Sontag's statements (mostly about the play) or the actors' rehearsals beyond the fact that the play took place at all. One thesp states that the sense of the play is really "waiting for Clinton" to take military action that would save the city.

Mirsad Idrizovic's "Personal Affairs" accounts for the bulk of the film. People patch holes in their broken windows, stand in line to get water and dodge bombs as little kids happily sled down the empty streets. There are moments of savoring a rare hot chocolate and a cigarette that bring home the privations under which people live.

What emerges strongly is the filmmakers' enormous desire to show the outside world what they are living through — not only to propagandize the urgent need for military aid but to overcome an unbearable sense of isolation.

Pic mixes the normal, the banal and the theatrical with sheer horror, leaving a feeling of the war's absurdity. Only a few images are completely new to those who have watched years of TV news reports. Nor is there a solid underlying structure. The film plays mainly on contrast, not only in its visuals but, quite successfully, in a peppy selection of music with a strong, lively beat that gives the images a new twist. —*Deborah Young*

A PIN FOR THE BUTTERFLY

(CZECH-BRITISH)

A Heureka Film Prague & Channel Four presentation of a Skreba Film production. Produced by James Crawford. Executive producer, Ann Skinner. Directed, written by Hannah Kodichek. Camera, Ivan Slapeta; editor, Kant Pan; music, Illona Sekacz; production design, Jiri Matolin; costume design, Jan Ruzicka; casting, Kathleen Mackie. Reviewed at Cannes Film Festival (market), May 14, 1994. Running time: **113 MIN.**
Grandma .... Joan Plowright
Grandpa .... Ian Bannen
Uncle .... Hugh Laurie
Mother .... Imogen Stubbs
Great Uncle .... Ian Hogg
Marushka .... Florence Hoath

A disturbing and affecting experience for those hearty viewers who weather the idiosyncrasies, complexities and stylistic wobbliness of the first half of the film, "A Pin for the Butterfly" is ultimately worth the wade. Pic's arcane politics and downbeat subject matter (Eastern Europe under the Communist yoke) will make it a tough sell in most markets. Highbrow audiences with a taste for challenging fare could carry "Pin" through to slight payoff on cable and video, with a modest chance for arthouse theatrical dollars.

One of the prime oddities of "Pin" is that the film is packed with Brit acting talents, so it takes a while to adjust to the English accents clashing with the Czech locations and East Euro setting of the story.

Set in Stalinist Czechoslovakia, "Pin" chronicles the trials of a petit bourgeois family crumbling under the pressures of the '50s Eastern Bloc version of political correctness, wherein a mere positive mention of anything Western could send one to ruin, prison and total ostracism.

Marushka (played stunningly by newcomer Florence Hoath) is a young schoolgirl with an active imagination and unstifled bravery — something her grandparents (Joan Plowright and Ian Bannen) have in short supply and her mother (Imogen Stubbs) possesses not at all.

A would-be actress in the service of the local socialist-realist theater, Marushka's mom is too busy courting favor with the town Communist powers to tend to her daughter.

That duty falls on her grandparents and uncle (Hugh Laurie), who is deeply conflicted by the current events. His aspirations for a life of free thought draw the family into a deadly conflict with the authorities,

a dilemma from which there is no safe quarter.

Director Hannah Kodichek scores points for earnestness and ambition, but "Pin" suffers from perhaps too much of both, and the uncertain tone of the first half of the film, with its mythical creatures, spry humor and dark undertones, muddies the waters of what is a fairly straightforward tale.

Add to those woes the script's clumsy dramaturgy and the confusion of the English accents in the Iron Curtain setting. In short, the audience may find its desire waning before the story kicks into gear, when Marushka's plight comes into a clearer, if tragic, focus.

Production credits are solid, the Czech locations lovely and evocative. Hoath is a polished child thesper, and the film distinguishes itself by not settling for pat answers.

The film asks what price one will pay for security and acceptance, and how children should deal with a world of adults who have abdicated authority and fled from wisdom.

In a market crammed with bloody vengeance tales and erotica, "Pin" deserves points for its seriousness of purpose and willingness to make a tough family film.
—*Steven Gaydos*

WHITE MAN'S BURDEN

A City Films presentation. Produced by Mark Evan Jacobs, Ron Kastner. Executive producer, Ben Barenholtz. Co-producer, Harvey Waldman. Directed by Gregory Hines. Screenplay, Allison Burnett. Camera (Technicolor), Bernd Heinl; editor, Ray Hubley; music, Stanley Clarke; production design, Nancy Deren; costume design, Karen Perry; sound (Dolby), Mark Weingarten, Tom Paul; assistant director, Todd Pfeiffer; casting, Jaki Brown-Karman, Kimberly Hardin. Reviewed at Cannes Film Festival (market), May 14, 1994. Running time: **93 MIN.**
Lonny Baum .... Mark Evan Jacobs
Denise Sheperd .... Karen Kirkland
Todd .... Ruben Santiago-Hudson
Daphne .... Melina Kanakaredes
Fred Ghosh .... Ranjit Chowdhry
Mel Shankman .... Robert Levine
Donny
  Stewart ...... Charles Malik Whitfield
Enid Sheperd .... Lorraine Toussaint
Mr. Baum .... Elliott Gould
Doctor .... Peter Riegert

"White Man's Burden," the directorial debut of actor Gregory Hines, is a serious-minded tale of interracial relationships that marks a promising but flawed filmmaking debut. A downbeat, literal script makes this polished indie effort a limited audience proposition. It should score some theatrical heat based on content but will likely find its biggest response in ancillaries.

The story centers on Lonny (Mark Evan Jacobs), a paralegal with ambitions to flail against the system in the

searing novel he's been unable to begin. His inability to break through has left him emotionally hollow. Additionally, his work challenges are predictable, his relationship with his girlfriend empty and the fractious encounters with his liberal, work-ethic father tedious.

He's looking for an opportunity and seizes the wrong one. By chance he encounters Denise (Karen Kirkland), a bright, black teenager preparing for scholastic tests. He's taken with her voracity to learn and initially extends his hand in friendship as a tutor. Though he denies it, the relationship is more than that of teacher to student. He's attracted to her and she's overwhelmed by the interest and proximity of a mature man.

Though the scenario is common enough, the racial component takes it another step. More than age is a factor here, although that facet of the situation allows many of the characters — especially those who profess progressive attitudes — to demonstrate a latent fear of sex between the races.

Hines and writer Allison Burnett don't pull any punches in "White Man's Burden." With rare exception, the chorus around Lonny and Denise make it clear to each that the situation is doomed to sour. Passion and obstinacy prevail, however, and the consequences are to varying degrees fatal for the couple.

The arc of the tragedy is set early in the film and never waivers from its appointed trajectory. With no prospect of surprise, the narrative flow is increasingly sluggish: It becomes difficult to wade through the sadness when there's no interest or outcome to root for.

The direction, on the plus side, is seamless, uncluttered and, to its disadvantage, unrelentingly earnest. Pic benefits from an undeniable veracity and strong performances from its leads and supporting players. Particularly chilling is Lorraine Toussaint as Denise's mother.

But despite these bright spots, the mantle of this "Burden" is not easily worn. —*Leonard Klady*

RAMPO

(JAPANESE)

A Shochiku Co. release of a Rampo Production Committee production. Produced by Yoshinobu Nishioka, Yoshihisa Nakagawa. Executive producer, Kazuyoshi Okuyama. Directed by Okuyama. Screenplay, Okuyama, Yuhei Enoki. Camera (color), Yasushi Sasakibara; editor, Akimasa Kawashima; production design, Kyoko Heya; sound, Kenichi Benitani; music, Masahiro Kawasaki. Reviewed at Cannes Film Festival (market), May 15, 1994. Running time: **96 MIN.**
Kogoro Akechi .... Masahiro Motoki
Edogawa Rampo .... Naoto Takenaka
Shizuko .... Michiko Hada
Masashi
  Yokomizo .... Teruyuki Kagawa
Marquis Ogawara .... Mikijiro Hira

The making of this large-scale Japanese production — which is based on the work of thriller writer Edogawa Rampo (1894-1965), whose books were often banned in the '30s — has been extremely problematic, but this version of the film, directed mainly by executive producer Kazuyoshi Okuyama, is certainly exciting and impressive, and should have a fest and arthouse future.

Pic started out under the direction of Rentaro Mayuzumi, but was taken over by Okuyama after he rejected Mayuzumi's version; the exec producer, who had never directed before, reshot 60% of the pic. Interestingly, both versions have been offered to Japanese exhibs for pic's June release, with distrib Shochiku leaving individual exhibs with the choice of which "Rampo" to book.

Pic starts out, per an opening title, in a Japan that has embarked on the path to war, with a scene of the author's latest tome being banned by the authorities.

Later, he's amazed to discover that a man has been killed in a manner he described in the banned book: suffocated in his wife's *nagamochi*, or treasure chest. Rampo meets the widow, Shizuko, and discovers to his astonishment that she's a dead ringer for the fictional heroine he's imagined.

He immediately starts writing a sequel, featuring Shizuko as a woman trapped in the home of a kinky marquis who screens porno movies while ravishing her. Rampo has his detective, Kogoro Akechi (who was the Japanese equivalent of Sherlock Holmes), rescue the damsel in distress, but fiction and reality blend in the bizarre climax.

Okuyama handles this strange, Gothic tale at a breakneck pace, using computer animation to enhance the explosive climax. Pic is a lot of fun, with full-blooded perfs, great set and costume design, a fine music score and tight editing.

May 23, 1994 (Cont.)

It will be interesting to see original film when it, too, is screened.

The overseas version screened in Cannes opens with a brief narration by Bruce Joel Rubin (scripter of "Ghost"). The porno footage looks too hot to pass Japanese censors, unless things have changed radically since "The Crying Game" paved the full-frontal way.

Pic was made to celebrate the centenary of Rampo's birth and, coincidentally, the centenary of the establishment of the Shochiku Co. and of cinema itself. Opening shots consist of vintage archive footage shot in Japan. —*David Stratton*

DEAD BEAT

An Anant Singh and Distant Horizon presentation in association with Christopher Lambert of a George Moffly production. Produced by Moffly, Lambert. Executive producer, Singh. Directed by Adam Dubov. Screenplay, Janice Shapiro, Dubov. Camera (Deluxe color), Nancy Schreiber; editor, Lorraine Salk; music, Anton Sanko; music supervisor, Sharal Churchill; production design, Vincent Jefferds; art direction, Lauren Sharfman; costume design, Alexis Scott; sound (Dolby), Ed White; associate producers, Danielle Segal, Michel Gourmelon; assistant director, Dwayne Shattuck; casting, Johanna Ray. Reviewed at Cannes Film Festival (market), May 14, 1994. Running time: **92 MIN.**
Kit .... Bruce Ramsay
Rudy .... Balthazar Getty
Kirsten .... Natasha Gregson Wagner
Donna .... Meredith Salenger
Mrs. Kurtz .... Deborah Harry
Martha .... Sara Gilbert
Jimmie .... Max Perlich
English Teacher .... Alex Cox

Debuting director Adam Dubov sets out onto apparently familiar terrain, but "Dead Beat" keeps some intriguing cards up its sleeve. Limber indie outing co-produced by thesp Christopher Lambert should see a moderate share of theatrical action with young urbanites.

The pic — whose title will be changed for its release — looks at first glance like one more reckless teen romance built into another retro-chic, rites-of-passage movie. But the film tills fresh ground via its unforced humor and appealingly flip approach while it quietly sows a moody dark side.

Loosely based on a serial-killer case that some believe was an inspiration to Charles Manson, the film is set in Albuquerque in 1965 (Arizona locations stand in), offering an atmospheric mix of wide open spaces, faded kitsch architecture and pastel suburbia.

The story of primping, limping womanizer Kit (Bruce Ramsay) is recounted by his adoring disciple Rudy (Balthazar Getty). A devout believer in the power of deceit, Kit employs makeup, hair dye and height-enhancing boots to achieve his Elvis-modeled looks, and uses tales of anything from terminal illness to a destitute family to score with his dates.

He meets a kindred dynamo in rebellious rich girl Kirsten (Natasha Gregson Wagner) and, as their romance goes into orbit, she demands hard evidence of his love. Obligingly, Kit confides that he murdered a local girl, a secret he earlier entrusted to Rudy, who treated it as another fabrication.

Kirsten uses the knowledge to increasingly tighten her hold on Kit. At the same time, she attempts to force Rudy out of the picture, thwarting his romantic progress with Donna (Meredith Salenger) by attributing sordid sexual practices to him.

Kit and Kirsten turn into short-fused time bombs, and as she spirals out of his reach, he's forced to give in to murderous instincts.

Dubov's direction juggles sweetly hokey romance with lean, mean edginess and a wry streak of malicious fun. Though the film sometimes feels like it can't pin down which road it wants to travel, it remains engaging and avoids the contrived coolness of some of its big-budget brethren. Closing note is a minor weak link that feels somewhat tentative next to what's come before.

Ramsay and Wagner make attractive, vigorous leads, eating up their scene-stealing roles (a little too greedily in the former's case). Getty provides able support.

Offscreen contributions are strong all round, from Anton Sanko's live-wire music to Nancy Schreiber's camera, her astute eye for color and composition lending a slick visual panache that puts the thrifty but amply functional 1960s production design in a good light.
—*David Rooney*

TOLLBOOTH

A Trans Atlantic Entertainment presentation of a Roadkill Films production in association with Sneak Preview productions. Produced by Steven J. Wolfe. Executive producers, Herschel Weingrod, Robert M. Bennett, Paul Rich, Rena Ronson. Directed, written by Salome Breziner. Camera, Henry Vargas; editor, Peter Teschner; music, Adam Gorgoni; production designer, Brenden Barry; costume designer, Kelly Zitrick; associate producer/unit production manager, David Goodman. Reviewed at Cannes Film Festival (market), May 15, 1994. Running time: **108 MIN.**
Doris .... Fairuza Balk
Jack .... Lenny Von Dohlen
Dash .... Will Patton
Lillian .... Louise Fletcher
Larry/Leon .... Seymour Cassel
Vic .... James Wilder
Waggy .... William Katt

"Tollbooth" is a strong first film for director Salome Breziner. Odder than the film's off-kilter depiction of a romantic triangle's roadside life and their entanglement with murder and money laundering is the film's debut in the Cannes market instead of the fest, where it would have fit nicely. Clearly not for every taste, it should garner lots of talk about newcomer Breziner and do decent biz on the international art-film circuit.

Pic is determinedly quirky, atmospheric and cut from the same cloth as David Lynch's "Twin Peaks," CBS' series "Northern Exposure" and the dysfunctional Americana of Lasse Hallstrom's "What's Eating Gilbert Grape," with a dash of Wim Wenders' scenic explorations and Samuel Beckett's absurdist minimalism.

The "Tollbooth" of the title is the center of the universe for young lovers Jack (Lenny Von Dohlen) and Doris (Fairuza Balk). On a funky stretch of highway in the Florida keys, Jack mans the tollbooth, collecting fares and dreaming of becoming a cop and moving to Miami with Doris, his high school sweetheart.

Doris pumps gas down the road at the Gator Gas fuel depot, when she's not trysting with bait salesman Dash (Will Patton) and daydreaming about the return of her long-lost father, Leon (Seymour Cassel), and caring for her chronically depressed mother, Lillian (Louise Fletcher).

Film's modest twists and turns come courtesy of Leon's return, and a slim subplot involving the tollbooth's new collector, Vic (James Wilder), whose shady business is drawing the attention of the state police.

What distinguishes the film is not its story. And it's certainly not the off-the-wall theatrics of vet players like Patton, Cassel and Fletcher, who deserve roles beyond the cartoon oddballs that writer/director Breziner serves up.

The charm of the two leads and Breziner's ability to invent a wholly contained world of fantasy and screwy logic carries pic past the thin plot. Balk fully lives up to the promise she demonstrated in Allison Anders' "Gas Food Lodging" (where she also hung out by the side of the American highway). Her Doris is actually the straightest character in the film, and though the role could have lapsed into whininess, Balk draws the viewer into Doris' dilemma with conviction and compassion.

Viewers may never connect viscerally to characters that are closer to film-student conceits than flesh-and-blood people, but they won't lose interest. The assured, imaginative lensing keeps the landscape alive and full of visual surprises and slyly composed treats.

While owing a debt to filmmakers who have preceded her, Breziner also has an original vision and voice and an ability to bring emotional resonance to her cinematic flights of fancy. —*Steve Gaydos*

SAN FRANCISCO

THE MOST TERRIBLE TIME IN MY LIFE
(WAGA JINSEI SAISKU NO TOKI)
(JAPANESE-TAIWANESE)

A Herald Ace presentation of a Shutter Pictures/Taipei/For Life Records Inc. co-production. Produced by Shunsuke Koga, Kaizo Hayashi, Yu Wei Yen. Executive producer, Yutaka Goto. Directed by Kaizo Hayashi. Screenplay, Daisuke Tengan, Hayashi. Camera (b&w, Cinemascope), Yuichi Nagata; editor, Nobuko Tomita; music, Meina Co.; production design, Takeo Kimura; costumes, Masae Miyamoto; lighting, Tatsuya Osada. Reviewed at AMC Kabuki 8, San Francisco, May 5, 1994. (In S.F. Intl. Film Festival). Running time: **92 MIN.**
Maiku Hama .... Masatoshi Nagase
Hoshino .... Kiyotaka Nambara
Kanno .... Shiro Sano
Yang Haitin .... Yang Haitin
Hou de Jian .... Hou De Jian
With: Yu Wei Yen, Wu Kao, Hsiung, Caroline Lu, Jo Shishido, Kaho Minami.

"The Most Terrible Time in My Life" is posited as the first in a three-part feature series following the adventures of Japanese private eye Maiku (Mike) Hama. Unlike his Western namesake, this "Hammer's" efforts at stone-cold machismo perennially run awry. While narrative takes its time in catching hold, director Kaizo Hayashi ("Circus Boys") has designed a striking package whose mix of hip humor, genre nods and visual oomph should travel quite well.

Title is a pun on "The Best Years of Our Lives" — the movie playing in a cinema whose projection booth doubles as the intrepid Hama's Yokohama office. (Cranky box office personnel downstairs won't let his clients pass unless they've bought a ticket.) With his hair slicked back, omnipresent sunglasses and cool threads, he seems the very model of tough-as-nails suaveness. Yet Hama spends an inordinate amount of time getting punched, kicked and shot by everyone in sight.

First such incident occurs when he steps in to protect a Chinese waiter from a quick-tempered customer in a mah-jongg parlor. His gallantry is admirable, his judgment less so, as a lopped-off finger soon must be retrieved from a dog's mouth before reattachment surgery.

Such gruesome bits startle but work well amid sly, drily comedic tenor Hayashi contrives. Yet humor gradually recedes from centerstage as the real storyline emerges — Hama takes on case of finding the Taiwanese "waiter's" apparently long-lost brother, only to find himself plunged into a dangerous thicket of Japan/China mob rivalries.

Once this scenario gets going, the sleuth himself is almost superfluous to action, despite Masatoshi Nagase's droll performance; attention is riveted instead on the two brothers, played with magnetism to spare by Taiwan stars Yang Haitin and Hou de Jian. Their classic Catch-22 of conflicting family/mob loyalties climaxes in tense gun standoff that takes film into a deadly serious, even tragic new dimension.

Pic looks great, with b&w Cinemascope creating an early-'60s Nippon gangster-flick feel; striking, tilted compositions and chiaroscuro lighting effects add elements of noir homage as well. Use of music is sparing but witty, often reminiscent of themes for '70s TV actioners like "Mannix." All other tech aspects are tops.

While its coating of cineaste irony may make "Most Terrible Thing" less than a sure-fire commercial property, it looks ideal for cult status on the rep circuit. Pic wraps up with kitschy tinted footage ostensibly lifted from the next Mike Hama film, "Stairway to the Distant

Past," then ends on color shot of sleuth outside his cinema-cum-office.
—*Dennis Harvey*

METAL & MELANCHOLY
(METAL & MELANCOLIA)
(NETHERLANDS — DOCU)

A VPRO TV presentation of an Ariel Film production. Produced by Susanne Van Voorst. Directed by Heddy Honigmann. Screenplay, Honigmann, Peter Deipeut. Camera (color, 16mm), Stef Tijdink; editing, Han Hendricks, Danniel Danniel; sound, Piotr van Dijl; Peru production assistance, Inca Films. Reviewed at AMC Kabuki 8, San Francisco, May 7, 1994. (In S.F. Intl. Film Festival.) Running time: **80 MIN.**

This perceptive doc focuses on Lima taxi drivers, capturing both the economic straits and indomitable spirit of Peruvians in general. While subject is hardly an easy sell, humorous, in-depth treatment could win limited exposure outside the fest circuit.

Helmer Heddy Honigmann grew up in Lima, then immigrated to Europe at age 22. Twenty years later she trains camera on a baker's dozen or so cabbies, young, old, male and female, as they opine on dangers and pleasures of the job, their own life stories and their nation's gutted infrastructure. All of them — even a glimpsed man raving on the street — have sharp political insights.

Cruising around, director and her drivers are endlessly solicited by pre-adolescent-to-elderly vendors. Demonstrating his elaborate car theft-thwarting devices, one cabby says, "You have to be ingenious to survive this crisis."

Subjects' anecdotes gradually shift pic from amusing to poignant tenor. One early interviewee discusses his acting career, complete with one role's weepy highlight; tears shed later by a struggling single mother are for real.

Populace's anything-to-survive pluck is illustrated by the cop who stops to sternly check Honigmann's papers, then pipes: "I'm a taxi driver too! You want to film me?" In this society where corruption at the top has rendered the middle class virtually non-existent, everyone's a hustler by necessity.

Despite largely passenger-seat p.o.v., film manages to avoid claustrophobic feel. Tech values are modest but effective, with especially good sound recording under the circumstances.
—*Dennis Harvey*

BEVERLY HILLS COP III

A Paramount release of a Mace Neufeld and Robert Rehme production in association with Eddie Murphy Prods. Produced by Neufeld and Rehme. Executive producer, Mark Lipsky. Co-producer, Leslie Belzberg. Directed by John Landis. Screenplay, Steven E. de Souza, based on characters created by Danilo Bach and Daniel Petrie Jr. Camera (Deluxe color), Mac Ahlberg; editor, Dale Beldin; music, Nile Rodgers; production design, Michael Seymour; art direction, Thomas P. Wilkins; set decoration, Marvin March; costume design, Catherine Adair; sound (Dolby), Joseph Geisinger; associate producer, Ray Murphy Jr.; assistant director, Arthur Anderson; casting, Jackie Burch. Reviewed at the National Theater, L.A., March 19, 1994. MPAA Rating: R. Running time: **109 MIN.**

Axel Foley	Eddie Murphy
Billy Rosewood	Judge Reinhold
Joe Flint	Hector Elizondo
Ellis DeWald	Timothy Carhart
Steve Fulbright	Stephen McHattie
Janice	Theresa Randle
Orris Sanderson	John Saxon
Uncle Dave Thornton	Alan Young
Serge	Bronson Pinchot
Minister	Al Green
Ticket Booth Girl	Tracy Lindsey
Todd	Gil Hill

The third installment of the "Beverly Hills Cop" series boasts a return to form by Eddie Murphy and a breezy and witty first half. And though the film runs out of steam before the end, it should satisfy "B.H. Cop" fans, even if it doesn't provide a full reversal of Murphy's recent box office misfortunes. Competition from two highly visible non-sequels, "Maverick" and "The Flintstones," will give "Cop III" a run for its money, perhaps blunting its ultimate gross potential.

The film gets off to a brisk start with a sting-gone-bad at a Detroit stolen-car chop shop. Director John Landis gets a mighty chuckle out of two overweight thieves mimicking a vintage Supremes tune and then quickly shifts moods with an efficient St. Valentine's Day-style massacre and a chase in which Murphy drives a snazzy sports car that disintegrates piece by piece.

Murphy's trademark grin and lithe acrobatic skills dominate here. Thankfully, he's left behind the air of indifference that permeated many of his recent efforts. When he lets go, which is not often enough here, he reminds us why he became a superstar.

The bad-guy trail inevitably leads to Southern California, where Murphy is reunited with an old Beverly Hills crony, Billy Rosewood (Judge Reinhold), and a new cop buddy played by Hector Elizondo. The focus of the action is a theme park called WonderWorld,

on the order of the Disney and Universal parks (it's actually a dressed-up Great America in Santa Clara, owned by Paramount Communications).

Screenwriter Steven E. de Souza has a lark lampooning the squeaky clean Americana atmosphere of these entertainments as well as those overwrought Universal crash-bam-boom thrill rides. There's even a pseudo-Uncle Walt, here named Uncle Dave Thornton, played by Alan Young, best known as Mr. Ed's straight man. Great in-joke is the park's official theme, "The WonderWorld Song," written by veteran Disney tunesmiths Richard M. and Robert B. Sherman.

Unfortunately, the villains are not as interesting as the milieu in which they thrive, which dissipates the tension. One of the better set pieces in the film occurs on a theme park ride gone haywire in which Murphy adeptly executes some of his own stunts.

Another first-half highlight is the return of the impossibly effete Serge (Bronson Pinchot), who has moved from hawking cappuccino on Rodeo Drive to selling designer guns. Pinchot is given free rein and is hilarious. There's more action in his wrists than in some of the film's climactic moments.

If the ending flattens out, it seems a calculated move to make the film more accessible and genial than its brutally cynical predecessor. The restrained carnage could have been satisfying if it had been offset by a little more cleverness on the order of the sequence in which the Universal-style thrill ride is used to incapacitate several villainous goons.

A lot of top-flight craftsmanship went into the film, particularly Mac Ahlberg's cinematography and Michael Seymour's production design. Aces too are the costumes by Catherine Adair, with deserved special mention to Kelly Kimball, who executed the garb for the park animal characters. The soundtrack is chock-a-block with good tunes, new and old. And Nile Rodgers' score effectively complements the action.
—*Richard Natale*

May 30, 1994 (Cont.)

CANNES FEST

BURNT BY THE SUN

(OUTOMLIONNYE SOLNTSEM)

(RUSSIAN-FRENCH)

A Studio Trite and Camera One presentation. Executive producers, Leonid Verechtchaguine, Jean-Louis Piel, Vladimir Sedov. Directed by Nikita Mikhalkov. Written by Mikhalkov, Roustam Ibraguimbekov. Camera, Vilen Kaluta; editor, Enzo Meniconi; music, Edouard Artemiev; art direction, Vladimir Aronin, Alexandre Samulekine; costume design, Natalia Ivanova; sound (Dolby), Jean Umansky; makeup, Larissa Avdiouchko; associate producers, Mikhalkov, Michel Seydoux; assistant director, Vladimir Krassinsky. Reviewed at Cannes Film Festival (competing), May 21, 1994. Running time: **152 MIN.**
Dimitri (Mitia) .... Oleg Menchikov
Maroussia .... Ingeborga Dapkounaite
Serguei Kotov .... Nikita Mikhalkov
Nadia .... Nadia Mikhalkov
Philippe .... Andre Oumansky
Vsevolod .... Viatcheslav Tikhonov
Mokhava .... Svetlana Krioutchkova
Kirik .... Vladimir Ilyine

A winning return to the themes and form of "Slave of Love," "Burnt by the Sun" is Russian director Nikita Mikhalkov's first post-Soviet-era pic to grapple directly with his country's political legacy. Film, which shared the Grand Jury Prize at Cannes with Zhang Yimou's "To Live," unwinds in a leisurely fashion but achieves tragic grandeur and emotional payoff that make it an engrossing film experience. "Sun" will score with fans of Russian cinema and should collect solid specialty-release dollars internationally.

Just as the filmmaker's "Slave" brilliantly captured the Communist revolutionary era by focusing on a group of people seemingly oblivious to the tumultuous events around them, "Sun" is a masterful evocation of Stalinist Russia of the '30s, as experienced by a small circle of family and friends enjoying an idyllic existence far from the purges and gulags. "Sun's" story, co-written by Mikhalkov, covers a day in the life of a Soviet revolutionary hero, Serguei Kotov (excellently played by the director in a return to screen acting after a long layoff). With his radiant wife, Maroussia (Ingeborga Dapkounaite), and precocious, spirited daughter, Nadia (played by Mikhalkov's daughter Nadia), Kotov relishes his life in the countryside, where the locals treat him as a towering father figure.

Into this paradise comes Dimitri (Oleg Menchikov), a handsome 30ish rogue with a mysterious past that includes an affair with Maroussia that preceded her marriage. Dimitri is clearly on a sinister mission, but

while Conrad's "Heart of Darkness" was a journey of discovery into the dark side of the human soul, Dimitri travels into a heart of gladness, where laughter and love abound.

The first half of the film may belabor this point, especially for American audiences who might expect more plot and less atmosphere. But by midpoint it becomes clear that the tension between Kotov's dreams and the reality of the Stalinist apparatus is the true subject of the film. Second half is a riveting display of bravura filmmaking, as Dimitri and Kotov circle one another, both painfully aware that their fates are bound together by ties to the Communist cause.

Pacing aside, Mikhalkov holds the audience's attention with his shrewd juxtaposition of the Kotov family's fragile beauty and the political terror that is descending in the form of an old friend.

As befits a film from the country of Stanislavsky and Chekhov, "Sun's" performances, from the leads to the colorful supporting characters, are uniformly first-rate. The four main players forge indelible portrayals out of the strongest screenplay Mikhalkov has worked from in years.

The script (co-authored with Roustam Ibraguimbekov, who also co-wrote Mikhalkov's "Urga") steers clear of political posturing, instead focusing on what Mikhalkov is really interested in: The universal human dilemma of lives caught between personal, peaceful dreams and the violent traumas of historical forces.

If Mikhalkov indulges himself in painting the picture of the country lifestyle, and lays on the anti-Communist symbolism with a heavy hand at the end, those are minor complaints about what is clearly a major film.

Cinematography by Vilen Kaluta delicately captures the nuances of light and color from the fields, forests and rivers of the pastoral setting. The film is an astonishingly polished production in light of Mikhalkov's statement in the press notes that he "shot this film very quickly." —*Steven Gaydos*

BAB EL-OUED CITY

(FRENCH-ALGERIAN-GERMAN-SWISS)

A Les Matins Films (France)/Flashback Audiovisuel (Algeria)/La Sept Cinema (France)/ZDF (Germany)/Thelma Film (Switzerland) coproduction. Produced by Jacques Bidou, Jean-Pierre Gallepe. Executive producers, Bidou, Gallepe, Yacine Djadi. Directed, written by Merzak Allouache. Camera (Kodak color), Jean-Jacques Mrejen; editor, Marie Colonna; music, Rachid Bahri; production manager, Tahar Haroura. Reviewed at Cannes Film Festival (Un Certain Regard), May 19, 1994. Running time: **93 MIN.**

Boualem .... Hassan Abdou
Yamina .... Nadia Kaci
Said .... Mohamed Ourdache
Rachid .... Mourad Khen
Mabrouk .... Mabrouk Ait Amara
Ouardya .... Nadia Samir
The Imam .... Ahmed Benaissa

"Bab El-Oued City" is to date the most lucid depiction on film of the rise of Islamic fundamentalism in Algeria and its perils. It's essential viewing for anyone interested in getting insight into the people's reaction to this broad political change. A chilling, well-made Euro coproduction, it could bridge the gap between the Arabic-language market and larger auds attuned to political events. Pic was awarded the Intl. Critics' Prize at Cannes.

Pic, directed by Merzak Allouache, an Algerian living in Paris, is set in early 1993, not long after violent clashes brought death to the streets. It forcefully condemns the violence and secret political agenda of the fundamentalists while it separates them from other Islamic believers.

The story takes place in Bab El-Oued, a poor neighborhood of old Algiers. Fifteen loudspeakers perched on rooftops blare the hate propaganda of the rising fundamentalist group, which is lead by toughie Said (Mohamed Ourdache).

One night, young baker Boualem (Hassan Abdou) can take it no more and rips out a loudspeaker, throwing it into the sea. His gesture sets off a search-and-destroy mission by Said and his black-leather-jacket gang.

Around this central thread, Allouache weaves a dense canvas of characters who represent various ways of thinking in Algeria. Boualem is courting Said's liberal sister, Yamina (Nadia Kaci), forced to wear a veil by her brother but inwardly straining against encroaching oppression.

Boualem visits a sad, rich woman living alone (Nadia Samir) who has taken to drink, and who becomes a target for the moralistic gang. An old baker detests Said's aggressiveness, but when pushed he fires Boualem without a thought.

There are boys attacked for listening to Rai music (the homegrown rock) and families that furtively watch Western movies on their satellite-fed TV sets. There are youths who make their living selling contraband perfume and others who dream of Kim Basinger in "9½ Weeks."

Allouache portrays the local imam as a liberal cleric, totally opposed to turning Islam to violent ends. When the going gets tough, he resigns his

post as spiritual leader of Bab El-Oued, saying he doesn't recognize the neighborhood anymore.

There's a lot crammed into "Bab El-Oued City," and at times the many characters, each going in his or her own direction, overpower the narrative. For Western viewers, some details are almost subliminal, such as the origin of Said's group as mercenaries in Afghanistan, fighting "the Russian Commies."

Said's sinister backers, who appear from time to time in a big black car, are never labeled, though their intentions may be guessed as politically driven.

Overall, pic is a scary and accurate prediction of the rising violence that has, in the past year, swept Algerian society. Its fierce criticism makes it a film that probably would not be allowed to shoot in Algiers today.

Technical work is high quality, as is the work of the very natural cast. Abdou's perf as the brave baker who thinks for himself is worth singling out. —*Deborah Young*

TAKE CARE OF YOUR SCARF, TATIANA

(PIDA HUIVISTA KIINNI, TATJANA)

(FINNISH-GERMAN)

A Sputnik Oy (Helsinki)/Pandora Film (Frankfurt) co-production. (International sales: Christa Saredi, Zurich.) Produced, directed, edited by Aki Kaurismaki. Screenplay, Kaurismaki, Sakke Jarvenpaa. Camera (b&w), Timo Salminen; production design, Kari Laine, Markku Patila, Jukka Salmi; costumes, Tuula Hilkamo; sound, Jouko Lumme. Reviewed at Cannes Film Festival (Directors Fortnight), May 20, 1994. Running time: **62 MIN.**
Reino .... Matti Pellonpaa
Valto .... Mato Valtonen
Tatiana .... Kati Outinen
Klaudia .... Kirsi Tykkylainen
Hotel Receptionist .... Elina Salo
Valto's Mother .... Irma Junnilainen
Vepe .... Veikko Lavi
Pepe .... Pertti Husu

Back in form after his disappointing "Leningrad Cowboys Meet Moses," Finland's Aki Kaurismaki has come up with a typically wayward road movie whose content is almost too slight to support the abbreviated 62-minute running time, but which still should charm the director's fans. Non-fans will be unimpressed, and business will be spotty.

In "Tatiana," the helmer junks plot almost completely in favor of a series of observations on the difficulty of forming personal relationships when you're not very articulate. At the same time, he continues his dissection of the grass-roots Finnish character.

Cigar-chomping, caffeine-addicted Valto works at home for his Mum, but when he discovers she's run out of coffee, he locks her in a cupboard, steals money from her purse and splits.

He teams up with his chum Reino, a greasy-haired auto mechanic and self-styled rocker, and the two misfits set out on what appears to be an aimless drive through the Finnish landscape, with Reino swigging vodka and Valto drinking coffee from a portable dispenser.

Along the way they run into two women, skinny Tatiana, an Estonian trying to get home to Tallinn, and chubby Klaudia, a Russian from Alma Ata. Klaudia doesn't speak Finnish, but Tatiana knows enough to ask for a ride.

The joke here is that these macho Finnish guys don't know what to say to the friendly, and obviously available, women. Hardly a word passes between them throughout the journey, even though they spend a night in a hotel, with Klaudia sharing a room with Valto and Tatiana with Reino (nothing happens, though, because the men simply fall asleep).

And yet Kaurismaki and his fine actors convey a wealth of emotion simmering just below the surface, mainly through body language, furtive glances and occasional smiles. It doesn't sound like charming material, but somehow it is, thanks to the director's perverse sense of humor.

Kaurismaki regular Matti Pellonpaa is a grungy delight as the stupid Reino, who finds himself attracted to Tatiana, and Mato Valtonen's Valto is an almost equally amusing character beneath his uncommunicative exterior. As Klaudia, Finnish Film Foundation exec Kirsi Tykkylainen plays her second role in a Kaurismaki film (she was the highlight of "Moses"), and brings warmth and depth to a character who just can't connect because she doesn't speak the language. Kati Outinen's expressive face does wonders with the character of Tatiana.

It's a pity that Kaurismaki didn't spend a bit more time on the screenplay and give his characters a little more to do, thus coming up with a film of more acceptable commercial length. And the beautiful black-and-white photography, by Timo Salminen, is a challenge for ancillary markets. Still, "Tatiana" deserves to find an audience, because beneath the offhand, casual approach is a moving and funny film about relationships.

—*David Stratton*

BARNABO OF THE MOUNTAINS
(BARNABO DELLE MONTAGNE)
(ITALIAN)

An Istituto Luce release (Italy) of a Nautilus Film production, in association with RAI-1. Produced by Tommaso Dazzi. Producer for RAI, Gabriella Lazzoni. Directed by Mario Brenta. Screenplay, Angelo Pasquini, Brenta, Francesco Alberti, Enrico Soci, based on Dino Buzzati's novel. Camera (color), Vincenzo Marano; editor, Roberto Missiroli; music, Stefano Caprioli; art direction, Giorgio Bertolini; costume design, Paola Rossetti; sound (Dolby), Laurent Barbey. Reviewed at Sala Umberto, Rome, April 29, 1994. (In Cannes Film Festival — competing.) Running time: **124 MIN.**
Barnabo .... Marco Pauletti
Ines .... Alessandra Milan
Darrio .... Marco Tonin
Berton .... Duilio Fontana
Molo .... Carlo Caserotti
Marden .... Antonio Vecellio
Del Colle .... Angelo Chiesura

Idealistic forest rangers square off against faceless poachers in "Barnabo of the Mountains," a cold, uninvolving, albeit rigorously filmed costumer. Mario Brenta's minimalist aesthetic may impress some film specialists, but won't get general audiences out of their log cabins to view it. Pic's fest life, which began in the Cannes competition, will probably terminate in scattered small-screen sales.

Based on a novel by Dino Buzzati, "Barnabo" has a similarly uneventful plot to Buzzati's "Desert of the Tartars," combined with the Christian mountain theme of some Ermanno Olmi films. (Brenta is one of the founders of Olmi's famous film school in the Alps.) The result is a dully portrayed moral fable of little impact.

Story opens in 1919, when a green young ranger (Marco Tonin) is murdered while stalking some poachers through the snowy Dolomites in northern Italy. Not a word is spoken for the first 15 minutes, allowing the grandeur of nature, the wind, the firs and falling snow to transport the viewer into what Brenta hopes (in a prologue) is a "mythic" realm.

Enter Barnabo (Marco Pauletti), a fresh recruit whose simple heart is well suited to a monotonous life. He speaks even less than his fellows, and has a sort of stigmata on his hand that mysteriously bleeds from time to time. He also has a bad relationship with his rifle, suggesting he is unwilling to take life.

But when the rangers' commanding officer is killed by the poachers, everyone agrees something must be done. A patrol is organized but turns up no trace of the murderers. It's Barnabo who stumbles onto them, but when his big moment comes, he doesn't shoot. It's hard to decide whether this is out of pure fear and cowardice, or because of ingrained Christian pacifism. In any case, he's discharged from the service.

Barnabo finds work as a farmhand and meditates on what has happened. His exile offers some temporary relief from mountain metaphysics. This is the most concrete part of the film, containing many historical details of back-breaking farm life in the hemp fields in the immediate postwar years. Barnabo's encounter with poor men headed for Argentina to find work is a moving interlude.

The story ends with a moral struggle within Barnabo and his paradoxical victory over the old taint of cowardice.

Subscribing to the less-is-more school, Brenta has a Bressonian reverence for simple gestures, extreme closeups and wordless images. He opts for simply composed frames, clean camera movements, silent faces meant to speak their humanity.

It's a tall order that only a few directors can pull off and, to Brenta's credit, his rigor does lend depth to the story. Everything is surrounded by the spiritual heights of the mountains, suggesting — a little self-consciously — pic's metaphysical dimension.

Roberto Missiroli's editing succeeds in capturing a frozen-time quality (often reminiscent of Olmi's 1959 mountain classic "Time Stood Still") without dragging shots out unnecessarily. Stefano Caprioli's anonymous, high-classical score has little to add.

The entirely non-pro cast — which includes many real-life rangers (like lead Pauletti) and farm hands — is generally stolid and inexpressive. Exception is a wonderfully natural 11-year-old girl, Alessandra Milan, who has the face of a peasant saint. —*Deborah Young*

RICE PEOPLE
(NEAK SRE)
(FRENCH-SWISS-GERMAN)

A JBA Prod., La Sept Cinema, ARP (France)/Thelma Film, TSR (Switzerland)/ZDF (Germany) production, in association with Canal Plus, Channel 4, Direction du Cinema du Cambodge, CNC, French Ministries of Foreign Affairs & Culture, EDI-DEH, Ecrans du Sud. (International sales: ARP/WMF, Paris.) Executive producer, Jacques Bidiou. Directed by Rithy Panh. Screenplay, Panh, Eve Deboise, from the novel "Ranjau Sepanjang Jalan," by Shahnon Ahmad. Camera (color), Jacques Bouquin; editor, Andree Davanture, Marie-Christine Rougerie; music, Marc Marder; art direction, Nhean Chamnaul; sound, Jean-Claude Brisson; associate producer, Pierre-Alain Meier; assistant directors, Alfred Lot, Catherine Dailleux. Reviewed at Cannes Film Festival (competing), May 19, 1994. Running time: **129 MIN.**
Yim Om .... Peng Phan
Sokha .... Chhim Naline
Vong Poeuv .... Mom Soth
Sokhoeun .... Va Simorn
Pou Mann .... Meas Daniel
Man .... Phang Chamroeun
(Khmer dialogue)

"Rice People" is a delicate, low-key, beautifully lensed study of a rural Cambodian family that has the beauty but emotional distance of a moving tableau. First feature by Paris-based Cambodian director Rithy Panh should raise ripples on the fest circuit and be appreciated by enthusiasts of east Asian cinema, but its theatrical harvest looks iffy.

Ranh has taken a novel by Malay author Shahnon Ahmad and transferred it to a Cambodian setting, using one complete cycle of rice-growing to portray the tragic fragmentation of a poor rural family.

In a remote village, Poeuv lives with his wife, Om, and their seven daughters. Poeuv worries about his declining acreage and Om worries about what would happen if the sole man in the family was incapacitated. The group live permanently on a fragile economic balance dictated by the success or failure of their annual crop.

One day Poeuv is poisoned by a thorn in the foot and eventually dies. Om takes on the burden of working in the rice fields as well as running the family. She becomes increasingly paranoid that her kids aren't pulling their weight.

The other villagers finally decide she needs treatment in town, and lock her in a cage. Eldest daughter Sokha takes over and eventually brings in the crop.

Panh keeps the pic's focus rigidly on his two subjects, the family unit and its umbilical, life-or-death link with rice-growing. There's little attempt to delve deep into individual family tensions: Only the father and mother emerge as distinct (if low-key) personalities, and none of the daughters emerges as an individual in her own right.

Instead, Panh lays out a beautifully lensed portrait of family/village life, work in the fields, upsets along the way and communal relationships.

Pic's exceedingly low on dramatic pulse but manages to engage the attention across its two-hour-plus running time. For those prepared to go with Panh's easy rhythm, "Rice People" brings home the goods. Sole moment of eye-opening drama is a dream sequence of the village being torched by the Khmer Rouge, a minor nod to Southeast Asian realities in a film that consciously exists in a political and time vacuum.

Shooting took place some 30 miles from Phnom Penh in the village of Kamreang under constant guard from Khmer Rouge guerrillas.

Technically, pic is a delight to watch, with the blowup from 16mm almost unnoticeable, smooth editing and an atmospherically monodic score by New York-born, Paris-based Marc Marder. Non-pro cast is fine.

—*Derek Elley*

THE QUEEN OF THE NIGHT

(LA REINA DA LA NOCHE)

(MEXICAN-U.S.-FRENCH)

An Ultra Films, IMCINE (Mexico)/Film Works (L.A.)/Les Films du Nopal (Paris) co-production. (International sales: Mercure Distribution, Paris.) Produced by Jean-Michel Lacor. Executive producers, Gregory Maya, Agnes Lacor, Jeremiah Chechick. Directed by Arturo Ripstein. Screenplay, Paz Alicia Garciadiego. Camera (color), Bruno De Keyzer; editor, Rafael Castanedo; music, Lucia Alvarez; production design, Jose-Luis Aguilar; costumes, Graciela Mason; sound (Dolby), Carlos Aguilar; casting, Claudia Becker. Reviewed at Cannes Film Festival (competing), May 19, 1994. Running time: 117 MIN.

Lucha
Reyes .... Patricia Reyes Spindola
Pedro Calderon .... Alberto Estrella
La Jaira .... Blanca Guerra
Dona Victoria .... Ana Ofelia Murguia
Klaus Eder .... Alex Cox
Onate .... Arturo Alegro
Luzma .... Alejandra Montoya
Balmori .... Marta Aura
Gimeno .... Roberto Sosa
Araujo .... Juan Carlos Colombo

"The Queen of the Night" is Mexican director Arturo Ripstein's "imaginary biography" of a real-life, celebrated chanteuse of the '30s and '40s who committed suicide in 1944. Thanks to a strong lead performance by Patricia Reyes Spindola, Ripstein has created a fascinating portrait of a remarkable woman.

Downbeat item will face a tough marketing challenge on the international arthouse circuit, but critical kudos and fest exposure should help.

Film is labeled "imaginary" because, as Ripstein has stated, this is not a realistic biography. He quotes a line from John Ford's "The Man Who Shot Liberty Valance" in justifying his approach to filming the legend rather than the whole truth.

Lucha Reyes was famous for her lovely voice (singing in the popular *cancion ranchera* style) and unconventional behavior. "Queen" opens in 1939, when she is 33 and still living at home with her formidable mother, Dona Victoria, who ran an infamous Mexico City bordello.

Married to leftist Pedro Calderon, Reyes purchases a beggar's daughter to raise as her own. The girl, Luzma, has a pretty rugged childhood, and is often witness to the constant sexual high jinks of Reyes.

With her songs dubbed by Betsy Pecanins, Reyes Spindola is a fine, fiery Reyes, a fiercely independent woman who is never able to make her dreams come true. Her need for love is constantly betrayed by those around her, except her loving daughter, who's unable to help her at the end. Ana Ofelia Murguia is also impressive as Dona Victoria, whose attitude toward her daughter veers drastically as time goes by.

Among the supporting cast, buffs will spot Brit director Alex Cox, who does an impressive turn as Klaus Eder, a European immigrant who's a fan of Reyes but who is expelled as an illegal alien once the war gets under way.

Despite all the music (Reyes dies to the strains of Puccini), the film is never operatic in the Visconti sense; rather, Ripstein goes for a subdued baroque look, with burnished, cluttered sets and dark lighting (camera work by French ace Bruno De Keyzer). It's a rigorous film that will prove a challenge for auds and will be a tough sell.

Mexico was last repped in competition in Cannes 20 years ago with another Ripstein pic, "The Holy Office." It seems a pity that "The Queen of the Night" was relegated to seemingly minor screening slots by the fest programmers, since it's deserving of maximum attention.

—*David Stratton*

SLEEP WITH ME

An MGM release of an August Entertainment presentation in association with Paribas Film Corp. and Revolution Films of a Joel Castleberg production. Produced by Michael Steinberg, Roger Hedden, Eric Stoltz. Executive producer, Castleberg. Directed by Rory Kelly. Screenplay, Duane Dell'Amico, Hedden, Neal Jimenez, Joe Keenan, Kelly, Steinberg. Camera (Foto-Kem color), Andrzej Sekula; editor, David Moritz; music, David Lawrence; production design, Randy Eriksen; art direction, J. Michael Gorman; set decoration, Adam Mead Faletti; costume design, Isis Mussenden; sound (Dolby), Giovanni Di Simone; line producer, Rana Joy Glickman; assistant director, Fernando Altschul; casting, Ellie Kanner. Reviewed at Cannes Film Festival (Un Certain Regard), May 14, 1994. Running time: 85 MIN.

Joseph .... Eric Stoltz
Sarah .... Meg Tilly
Frank .... Craig Sheffer
Duane .... Todd Field
Deborah .... Susan Traylor
Leo .... Dean Cameron
Nigel .... Thomas Gibson
Rory .... Tegan West
Amy .... Amaryllis Borrego
Athena .... Parker Posey
Lauren .... Joey Lauren Adams
Marianne .... Vanessa Angel
Pamela .... Adrienne Shelly
Sid .... Quentin Tarantino
Caroline .... June Lockhart
Josh .... David Kriegel
Minister .... Lewis Arquette

"Sleep With Me" is as erratic as only a film with six writers can be. Initially cloying and cliched, group portrait of twentysomethings in romantic disarray slowly gathers interest as things build to a dramatic head, and there are probably enough points of identification for young adults to give this MGM pickup a modest following theatrically before going on to a more fruitful life in video.

A film about a group of friends made in a somewhat unorthodox group fashion, Rory Kelly's first feature bears decided similarities to "Bodies, Rest & Motion," with which it shares talent in the producing, writing and acting areas, as well as a lineup of foggy, self-involved characters groping to get on track in life.

At the outset, seemingly more due to the forces of gravity than love or passion, longtime couple Joseph (Eric Stoltz) and Sarah (Meg Tilly) decide to get married. This doesn't much change their L.A. lifestyle, however, as their extended family of friends continues to surround them, and they're still prone to the same temptations that existed before the hitching.

Specifically, Joseph's best friend, Frank (Craig Sheffer), after long suppressing his emotions, decides it's time to declare his overwhelming love for Sarah by kissing her in front of everyone at a dinner party. Sarah ultimately succumbs to

Frank's relentless pursuit, and the fact that they have great sex in their one session together complicates matters considerably.

Conceived by Kelly and "Bodies" writer Roger Hedden, script is structured around several large-scale social events — some parties, a dinner and a couple of poker games — each of which was written by a different writer. Early section at the main couple's wedding rehearsal is the most diffuse, irritating and poorly done, as it indulges the contemporary cinema's latest cliche — the hand-held video p.o.v. in which characters reveal themselves in direct-to-camera speeches — at enormous length, as everyone tries to be cynically funny and mock-sincere.

Dinner party scene is peppered with some good juicy sex talk, capped by Frank's explosive gesture, and poker scenes — the first all-male, the second co-ed — possess enough jagged tension and humor to keep audiences interested.

But the extent to which energy and drama have been missing from the film is almost embarrassingly revealed by the strong final party. A hilarious recurring riff by Quentin Tarantino, in which he delivers a convoluted but coherent interpretation of "Top Gun" as a gay film, packs more punch than anything else in the picture.

Playing out the film's central emotional conflict in a very public way on a front lawn at night before many guests, Kelly hits pay dirt with Joseph's blunt confrontation of his former best friend over his affair with Sarah.

Stoltz, Sheffer and Tilly are competent and amiable without being compelling, while remainder of the all-white-bread characters are played as relatively undifferentiated in terms of attitude.

As entertainment, this is a spotty affair, with some sharp moments poking out of general blandness. As a portrait of one pocket of a generation, it's a bit sad, since the characters have nothing on their minds except themselves but can barely make their personal lives work, much less carve a meaningful place for themselves in society.

Tech credits are reasonably good for a low-budget effort.

—*Todd McCarthy*

May 30, 1994 (Cont.)

XIME

(DUTCH/GUINEA-BISSAU)

Produced by Molenwiek Film (Amsterdam)/Arco Iris (Guinee Bissau). (International sales: Molenwiek.) Directed by Sana Na N'Hada. Screenplay, Na N'Hada, Joop Van Wijk. Camera (color), Melle Van Essen; editor, Anita Fernandez; music, Patricio Wong, Malam Mane'; art direction, Anet Wilgenhof. Reviewed at Cannes Film Festival (Un Certain Regard), May 20, 1994. Running time: **95 MIN.**
Bedan ....Jose Tamba
Raul ....Justino Neto
Iala ....Aful Macka
N'Dai ....Etelvina Gomes
Cunha ....Juan Carlos Tajes
Father Vittorio ....Daniel Smith

"Xime," the third film to be made in Guinea-Bissau, interests not only for its rare locale but for a fresh approach to historical storytelling by debuting helmer Sana Na N'Hada. Tale of a village's reaction to its Portuguese oppressors should rank high on this year's list of African films, though market remains small.

Film is set in Guinea in 1963, when Portuguese colonialists ruled the country in western Africa through indolent administrators like Cunha (Juan Carlos Tajes), ferocious green berets and their native henchmen. The village where Bedan (Jose Tamba) lives with his father, Iala (Aful Macka), is a lush haven of peace. A Catholic priest, Father Vittorio (Daniel Smith), teaches the Christian way of life, while the village elders instruct rambunctious youth like Bedan to follow the path of non-violence.

Not everyone, however, is equally submissive. In a stylish opening scene, Bedan's older brother Raul (Justino Neto) appears as part of a band of revolutionaries in the capital. He announces he will return to his native region of Xime to foment unrest against the European rulers.

In Xime, Raul's mission is discovered, and the authorities are determined to capture him. The manhunt theme gives the film a good forward momentum, while much of the running time is filled with standard African village intrigue: kids at school, boy chasing girl, father against son, conferences of elders.

Finally, script by Na N'Hada and Joop van Wijk makes a sketchy attempt at portraying the Portuguese but, unaided by the stilted actors, they never emerge from gray stereotyping and caricature.

A curious tradition that needs a little more explaining in the film is the habit of dressing young men on the brink of adulthood in women's clothing. The transformation of Bedan and his pals from swaggering, sassy teens to meek, feminine "transvestites" is visually startling and rather comical. Apparently this initiation rite is aimed at making them aware it's time to put aside violence and think like adults.

In a strong finale that pulls together the story's threads, the little-seen Raul stumbles into the midst of a marriage ceremony, fatally wounded. As he dies in front of Bedan, who's still dressed as a woman, the younger man realizes "this time, it's war!"

It's clear that the village will put aside its non-violent traditions and fight against its foreign masters. (Guinea-Bissau overthrew Portuguese rule in 1973.)

Film's intentions are ambitious, and its black characters are interestingly three-dimensional. Tamba is amusing and alarming as the youth who sets his eyes on his father's fiancee and has no respect for authority. The girl, Etelvina Gomes, is a beauty who surprises by preferring Bedan's father to the callow youth.

The rich, smoky lensing by Melle Van Essen is unusually colorful, capturing the beauty of African faces along with the lushness and detail of the landscape. Score by Patricio Wong and Malam Mane' gives film a pleasant local rhythm.
— *Deborah Young*

NO MERCY

(SIN COMPASION)

(PERUVIAN-MEXICAN)

A CIBY 2000 presentation of an Inca Films (Lima)/Amaranta Foundation of New Latin American Cinema (Mexico) production. Produced, directed by Francisco J. Lombardi. Executive producer, Gustavo Sanchez. Screenplay, Augusto Cabada, based on "Crime and Punishment," by Feodor Dostoyevsky. Camera (color), Pili Flores Guerra; editor, Luis Barrios; music, Leopoldo La Rosa; production design, Cecilia Montiel; sound, Daniel Padilla; casting, Monica Dominguez; assistant director, Enrique Moncloa. Reviewed at Cannes Film Festival (Un Certain Regard), May 20, 1994. Running time: **120 MIN.**
With: Diego Bertie, Adriana Davila, Jorge Chiarella, Hernan Romero, Marcello Rivera, Mariella Trejos, Carlos Onetto.

There have been many screen adaptations of Dostoyevsky's "Crime and Punishment" over the years, most recently Aki Kaurismaki's quirky Finnish version a decade ago. Now comes a Peruvian adaptation, and it's a solid variation on the familiar story that should do good business in Latin American markets and may even cross over into arthouses in other territories.

This updating places greater emphasis than did previous interpretations on religious aspects of the timeless yarn. Francisco J. Lombardi, who has emerged as Peru's most consistently interesting director, frames the film around a confession that a Christ-like student, Ramon, reluctantly makes to a priest.

Though set in contemporary Lima, the story is essentially the same. Ramon is an impoverished student, struggling with his own identity and purpose in life. A meeting with Sonia, a child/woman prostitute, fills him with pity and hatred for society.

In a sudden, savage act, he kills a rich, ugly old woman and, when he stumbles on the scene, her husband. Like Raskalnikov in the original, he has a series of slightly eerie encounters with an avuncular police inspector who may or may not suspect him of the murders.

The story unfolds naturally in its new setting. Lombardi's rather stolid pacing, however, bumps up the running time to the two-hour mark, which is a bit long for the material.

Perfs are all top-drawer, especially Diego Bertie as the tormented Ramon and Adriana Davila as the prostitute with a pure soul. Technical credits are good down the line.
— *David Stratton*

THE GLASS SHIELD

A CIBY 2000 and a Byrnes/Schroeder/Walker production. (International sales: CIBY Sales, Paris.) Produced by Tom Byrnes, Carolyn Schroeder. Executive producer, Chet Walker. Directed, written by Charles Burnett, based partially on a screenplay, "One of Us," by Ned Welsh. Camera (Foto-Kem color), Elliot Davis; editor, Curtiss Clayton; music, Stephen Taylor; production design, Penny Barrett; art direction, Joel Carter; costumes, Gaye Burnett; sound (Ultra-Stereo), Veda Campbell; assistant director, Paul Childs; second unit camera, Jacek Laskus. Reviewed at Cannes Film Festival (market), May 16, 1994. Running time: **108 MIN.**
J.J. .... Michael Boatman
Deborah .... Lori Petty
Teddy Woods .... Ice Cube
Baker .... Michael Ironside
Massey .... Richard Anderson
Locket ....Bernie Casey
Greenwall .... Elliott Gould
Hal .... M. Emmet Walsh
Bono.................................... Don Harvey
Mr. Taylor .... Sy Richardson
Judge
    Helen Lewis .... Natalija Nogulich

Although writer/director Charles Burnett throws more weighty social and political issues on the table than he can possibly dramatize coherently in less than two hours, "The Glass Shield" emerges as a powerful moral drama that tries to deal with the racism at the root of many problems in contempo American society. Film's equivocal artistic success makes it questionable as a specialized, review-driven release stateside in the manner of the director's last effort, "To Sleep With Anger." What the film has to say will, however, undoubtedly resonate with certain segments of the public, making for a marketing challenge that could pay off with the right moves.

A director warmly embraced by critics but not yet discovered by a wide audience, Burnett here pushes more elemental and inflammatory buttons than before as he dissects a law enforcement system riddled with corruption from top to bottom.

He frames his corrosive portrait around the story of an enthusiastic black rookie cop whose tragic personal journey sees him move from being part of the solution to part of the problem.

At the outset, the youthful J.J. (Michael Boatman) is not exactly given a warm welcome as the first black recruit at the rough, L.A. inner city Edgemar station.

It's dominated by a good old boys' group, four members of which have recently been under investigation for using excessive force on the job. His sole ally initially is another outcast, Deborah (Lori Petty), the only woman at the station and a Jew.

After a cataloging of subtle and implicit forms of racism on the force, incident that sets the dense plot in motion is the arrest of Teddy Woods (Ice Cube) at a gas station. Woods is obviously pulled over by one of the Southern Cal surfer-type cops only because he's black, but when it turns out he's got a gun hidden under his car seat, he is booked and accused of murdering the wife of the affluent Mr. Greenwall (Elliott Gould) on the basis of the gun ID.

Anxious to fit in and prove himself on the squad, J.J., who was also at the scene, goes along with the lie that Teddy was stopped for a traffic violation, which moves Teddy well along the road to death row.

By the second half, film becomes far too top-heavy with content to retain its dramaturgical balance and artistic grace; Burnett clearly had so much he wanted to get off his chest that it became impossible to find a place for it all within his structure.

At the same time, his burning need to deal with these issues is also what gives the film its urgency and force, so it becomes possible to forgive a lot of the esthetic untidiness for the sake of seeing all this discussed so passionately.

At moments, one can see the seed of a modern "Chinatown" here. In painting all the white cops' actions as racist, Burnett is slanting the argument, but it's part of a general aim to dig to the very bottom of things, and thus defensible.

Along the way, vivid snapshots are offered of an overloaded court system, jails that can be more dangerous than the street, police and city government at sharp odds with one another, and the toll taken on the personal lives of police officers.

Boatman gives a lively, sympathetic perf as the eager cop who does the wrong thing, although his private life is scanted to make room for all the sociological and plot baggage.

Nearly all the white characters are hypocrites or downright meanies. Petty doesn't bring much dimension to her role, which could have served as a more effective contrast to the prevailing toughness of the other characters.

Tech credits are solid, although the style is much more straight-ahead than the more oblique, poetic approach of Burnett's previous work. —*Todd McCarthy*

THE PATRIOTS

(LES PATRIOTES)

(FRENCH)

A Gaumont Buena Vista Intl. release of Les Prods. Lazennec production, with Gaumont/SFP Cinema/Glem Films, with the participation of Canal Plus. Produced by Xavier Amblard. Executive producers, Katriel Schory (Israel), Gene Rosow (U.S.). Co-producers, Boudjemaah (SFPC), Gerard Louvin (Glem Films). Directed, written by Eric Rochant. Camera (color, CinemaScope), Pierre Novion; editor, Pascale Fenouillet; music, Gerard Torikian; art direction, Thierry Francois; costume design, Marie Malterre; sound (Dolby), Dominique Dalmasso; associate producers, Adeline Lecallier, Christophe Rossignon; assistant director, Paolo Trotta. Reviewed at Cannes Film Festival (competing), May 20, 1994. Running time: **144 MIN.**

Ariel	Yvan Attal
Yossi	Yossi Banai
Marie Claude	Sandrine Kiberlain
Jeremy Pelman	Richard Masur
Catherine Pelman	Nancy Allen
Eagleman	Allen Garfield

In his third and most accessible feature, "The Patriots," rising French filmmaker Eric Rochant continues to explore the themes of political commitment and personal integrity, this time situated in Israel's intriguing world of espionage. Large-scale, big-budgeted production aspires to belong to the thrilling milieu of John Le Carre, but its rather conventional ideas and uneven execution make it just a sprawling, intermittently absorbing movie. Opening in France June 1, pic is likely to fly high in Europe, and its international cast signals some commercial potential off-

shore, where Rochant is virtually unknown.

With the demise of the Cold War, declining force of communism and changing realities of Eastern Europe, the Middle East seems to be a natural, still largely unexplored backdrop for new espionage movies.

Yvan Attal stars as Ariel, a young French Jew whose need for a more meaningful identity motivates him to leave his family and volunteer for work in the Mossad, Israel's venerated Institute for Intelligence.

Adventure begins in Tel Aviv in 1983, when Attal's car breaks down and he and another man are arrested and brutally treated by the Israeli police. A flashback quickly establishes that Attal had left his country four years earlier on his 18th birthday.

Initial hour follows Attal as he's recruited by Unit 238, one of the organization's toughest, and is trained in all its necessary procedures by Yossi (Yossi Banai), who in the process becomes his surrogate father. His first mission, involving a French atomic scientist, presents no problems of conscience, as its goal is to protect Israel against a nuclear disaster.

In the second mission, which is set in 1987, Attal gets to work with Pelman (Richard Masur), a Jewish-American agent who's married to a gentile (Nancy Allen) and provides Israel with vital info for its survival. It's in this section that the tale gets more nuanced, the ambience scarier and the tension between what matters personally and politically more overtly pronounced.

As writer, Rochant understands that, in order to be seductive, spy stories need to revolve around power games and issues of manipulation. And for a while, particularly in the second part, his movie shows the nasty, foul work conducted by intelligence officers in the name of absolute ideals.

One suspects that larger issues are on the writer's mind, such as the price a person is willing to pay to gain desirable group membership, or the conflict between the dictates of national service and moral integrity.

But Rochant seems unable to decide whether his pic should be a tightly knit suspense-thriller or a personal chronicle of a young man whose initial idealism is tempered by his maturation and disillusionment; pic is framed with voiceover narration, mostly letters that Attal writes to a friend.

Although Rochant tackles the same themes as Le Carre, "The Patriots" lacks the sophisticated cynicism and moral ambiguity of the noted author's best stories.

Most of what Rochant says about intelligence operations is familiar, such as the contrasts between professionalism and ethics, or the insistence of the Mossad on paying its

agents even if they're willing to work out of idealism. Helmer's naivete also informs his attitude toward the Mossad as a mythically powerful institution.

The handsome Attal, who played the leads in Rochant's former pix, acquits himself with an expressive performance that sensitively indicates the gradual changes in his personality. He is surrounded by an able international cast that includes noted Israeli thesp Banai and Americans Allen Garfield, Masur and Allen. Transition from one language to another is surprisingly efficient and effortless.

Tech credits are excellent, particularly the lensing, which conveys the specific flavor of each locale (Tel Aviv, Paris and Washington).

Chief problem is unmodulated pacing: At times pic plods along monotonously, with the camera taking excessively long rests on the actors' faces. With a running time of almost 2½ hours, "The Patriots" could benefit from a trimming of at least 20 minutes. —*Emanuel Levy*

DALLAS DOLL

(AUSTRALIAN)

A Dallas Doll Prods. production, in association with the Australian Film Finance Corp., Australian Broadcasting Corp. and BBC Films. (International sales: The Sales Co., London.) Produced by Ross Matthews. Executive producer, Penny Chapman. Co-producers, Ann Turner, Tatiana Kennedy. Directed, written by Turner. Camera (Eastmancolor), Paul Murphy; editor, Mike Honey; music, David Hirschfelder; production design, Marcus North; costumes, Rosalea Hood; sound (Dolby), Nicholas Hood; line producer, Barbara Gibbs; associate producer, Ray Brown; assistant director, Adrian Pickersgill; casting, Liz Mullinar. Reviewed at Cannes Film Festival (market), May 20, 1994. Running time: **104 MIN.**

Dallas Adair	Sandra Bernhard
Rosalind Sommers	Victoria Longley
Stephen Sommers	Frank Gallacher
Charlie Sommers	Jake Blundell
Rastus Sommers	Rose Byrne

An intriguing premise — an unofficial reworking of Pier Paolo Pasolini's "Teorema" in an Aussie setting — starts promisingly, then misses its target in this unfulfilled pic. Sandra Bernhard's name and rep will help get initial sales, but mixed critical reaction must be taken into account. Vid sales look more promising.

Bernhard, in good, sassy form, plays Dallas Adair, a consultant brought to Australia to advise on a new golf course project. On the plane from L.A., she coincidentally meets Charlie Sommers (Jake Blundell), son of Stephen Sommers (Frank Gallacher), one of her sponsors. The two strike up a friendship when there's a near crash landing,

and Dallas moves into the Sommers' bourgeois home, which also includes Stephen's frustrated wife, Rosalind (Victoria Longley), and their bright teen daughter, Rastus (Rose Byrne), who's a UFO freak.

Like the mystery character played by Terence Stamp in Pasolini's film, Dallas proceeds to seduce members of the Sommers family one by one, excluding Rastus, who loathes her from the start. Charlie spies on her undressing, then loses his virginity to her; Stephen commits adultery with her; finally, Rosalind escapes her hidebound existence by venturing for the first time into gay sex with her.

Pic may sound steamy, but, under the direction of screenwriter Ann Turner, is quite restrained. Turner, who previously directed the interesting "Celia" and the less successful "Hammers Over the Anvil," has come up with a lovely idea, and the leading role is cleverly cast, but the helmer drops the ball about halfway through. Scenes involving Japanese participation in the golf course and an apparent UFO landing — which may be connected to Dallas — come across as irrelevant to the main storyline when they surely should have been integral to the presumed theme of outside forces molding Aussie lives on both a personal and national level.

Pic had a reportedly troubled production history, which unfortunately shows in the ragged second half, in which all the threads and themes so tantalizingly introduced earlier fail to come together satisfactorily. This is a pity, because when the film does work, its blend of sensuality and sardonic humor is strikingly effective.

Bernhard is sleek and quite sexy as Dallas, though Blundell hardly convinces as a virginal teenager in the early scenes. Pic's best performance comes from the always reliable Longley, who enacts the discovery of sexual gratification with genuine style.

Technical credits are pro, except for the somewhat cheesy UFO sequence. —*David Stratton*

SHALLOW GRAVE

(BRITISH)

A Film Four Intl. presentation in association with the Glasgow Film Fund of a Figment Film production. (International sales: FFI, London.) Produced by Andrew Macdonald. Executive producer, Allan Scott. Directed by Danny Boyle. Screenplay, John Hodge. Camera (color), Brian Tufano; editor, Masahiro Hirakubo; music, Simon Boswell; production design, Kave Quinn; costume design, Cate Karin; sound (Dolby), Colin Nicolson; assistant director, Ian Madden. Reviewed at Cannes Film Festival (market), May 16, 1994. Running time: **91 MIN.**

May 30, 1994 (Cont.)

Juliet Miller	Kerry Fox
David Stevens	Christopher Eccleston
Alex Law	Ewan McGregor
Hugo	Keith Allen
Detective-Inspector	Ken Stott
Detective-Constable	John Hodge

Blighty's new wave of knock-'em-dead filmers has a banner to march under with "Shallow Grave," a tar-black comedy that zings along on a wave of visual and scripting inventiveness. Film Four Intl. looks set to rack up healthy sales on this first feature of English TV director Danny Boyle, which will certainly delight buff audiences and has the potential to break out into wider markets too.

Reaction at its world preem screening in the Cannes market was hot, with many questioning why pic wasn't in any of the fest's sections, despite having been submitted for both competition and Directors Fortnight.

Main surprise is that "Grave" manages to sustain its oddball humor and theatrical style without depending on non-stop eye-whacking tricks. First script by Glasgow-based doctor John Hodge (who cameos as a cop) keeps springing surprises until the final shot, and Boyle's direction, though often hyper, manages to serve up an intelligent movie without sacrificing narrative drive or reducing the actors to characterless pawns.

Story, set in modern-day Scotland, revolves around a trio of unlikely friends sharing a spacious top-floor apartment. Juliet (Kerry Fox) is a seemingly levelheaded nurse; David (Christopher Eccleston), a studiously boring accountant in a stuffy firm, and Alex (Ewan McGregor), a wild-side journalist on a local rag.

From their first appearance, grilling applicants for a fourth lodger, it's clear they've all got several screws loose. The lodger problem is solved when Juliet takes a shine to the rough-looking, mysterious Hugo (Keith Allen, the psycho in "Beyond Bedlam"), who soon takes up residence. A short time later, Hugo is found dead in bed, his drawer stuffed with drugs and a suitcase stuffed with money.

After shilly-shallying over what to do, the trio decides to chop up the cadaver, bury the bits and keep the loot — a sequence that sets the tone for the pic's several grisly comic set pieces. Things almost go wrong when two psychotic thugs burst through the door wanting to know where the stash is. David tops both with a hammer, and two more bodies join Hugo's. Rest of the movie, which might well have had trouble sustaining the first half's momentum, switches to tensions among the group.

Finale in the apartment is a real tour de force of black humor, with multiple double-crosses and twists up to the final fadeout.

Boyle's background in theater before moving over to TV (where his credits include segs of "Inspector Morse") shows in the pic's exaggerated but always actorly approach. In look and feel, however, this is pure moviemaking, with a seamless blend of production design, music, editing, sound and lensing that makes it an ensemble achievement on both sides of the camera.

Playing and casting are strong down the line. Of the central trio, Kiwi actress Fox rates special praise for her disarming portrayal of everyday madness.

Among the tiptop behind-camera credits, production designer Kave Quinn's superb set of the off-center apartment is a constant delight, with its color-coded rooms and its play with light. Reported budget was a mere £1 million ($1.5 million), with every cent up on the screen.

—*Derek Elley*

AN UNFORGETTABLE SUMMER

(UN ETE INOUBLIABLE)

(FRENCH-ROMANIAN)

An MKL release (France) of an MK2 Prods., La Sept Cinema (France)/Le Studio de Creation Cinematographique du Ministere de la Culture de Roumanie (Romania) production, with participation of Canal Plus, CNC and Filmex (Romania). (International sales: MK2, Paris.) Produced by Marin Karmitz, Constantin Popescu. Directed, written by Lucian Pintilie, from Petru Dumitriu's novella "The Salad." Camera (color), Calin Ghibu; editor, Victorita Nae; music, Anton Suteu; production design, Paul Bortnovschi, Calin Papura; costume design, Miruna Boruzescu; sound, Andrei Papp; assistant director, Sanda Iorgulescu. Reviewed at Club 13 screening room, Paris, April 22, 1994. (In Cannes Film Festival — competing.) Running time: **82 MIN.**

Marie-Therese Von Debretsy	Kristin Scott-Thomas
Capt. Petre Dumitriu	Claudiu Bleont
Mme. Vorvoreanu	Olga Tudorache
Gen. Tchilibia	George Constantin
Serban Lascari	Ion Pavlescu
Gen. Ipsilanti	Marcel Iures
Lt. Turtureanu	Razvan Vasilescu

With: Cornel Scripcaru, Tamara Cretulescu, Mihai Constantin.
(Romanian, French and English dialogue.)

"An Unforgettable Summer" is a touching, disturbing account of a Romanian army officer who's caught in an untenable position by his wife's tender regard for wrongly condemned Bulgarian peasants. Pic's topical messages about the pitfalls of rigid ethnic identification and the idiocy of blind retaliation make it a good bet for fests and discerning art-house audiences.

Bracketed by voiceover narration, pic starts out with a sequence that is a mad gallop, with the camera in the saddle, giving viewers a crash course in regional rivalries circa 1925. After this segment, though, the film favors a more stately lensing and editing style, which is a departure from director Lucian Pintilie's rambunctious razzle-dazzle in 1992's "The Oak."

After happily married Marie-Therese Von Debretsy (Kristin Scott-Thomas) snubs Gen. Ipsilanti's (Marcel Iures) advances at a city gala, her husband, Capt. Petre Dumitriu (Claudiu Bleont), is reassigned to a God-forsaken frontier post on the Danube, where they set up housekeeping with their three young children.

When Romanian soldiers are ambushed and slaughtered by roving Macedonian bandits, Dumitriu is ordered to retaliate by executing the harmless Bulgarian locals who tend his family's vegetable garden.

Pic dissects what happens when one man's allegiances to family and career point in different directions.

Marie-Therese, sensitive yet flamboyant in the mold of Zelda Fitzgerald, copes with the moral quandary by acting as if the inevitable can be averted. Scott-Thomas gives a properly flighty dimension to the loving wife and mom whose flair for putting a joyous spin on things is forever impaired by the looming atrocity.

Bleont conveys the problems of weighing duty and honor. Razvan Vasilescu, whose frenzied perf in "The Oak" was a standout, is memorable as an opportunistic soldier who has no compunctions about anything the military life may require.

Via dark humor and flashes of cruelty, pic pins down the inexorable lunacy of the military and the damned-if-you-do, damned-if-you-don't turn that personal history can take as a part of political history.

Period details are a convincing blend of rustic and elegant, and Paul Bortnovschi's production design is a study in contrasts, as if to mirror fair and unfair, mad and sane. Anton Suteu's opening music is a sly mix of Mozart and the can-can.

The frantic crescendo of the final sequence has an eerie resonance, as the narrator's final remarks reframe all that has gone before in a different, deeply ironic light.

—*Lisa Nesselson*

NIGHTWATCH

(NATTEVAGTEN)

(DENMARK)

An All Right Film Distribution release of a Thura Film production, supported by the Danish Film Institute in co-production with Danmarks Radio. (International sales: Nordisk Film TV Distribution.) Produced by Michael Obel. Directed, written by Ole Bornedal. Camera (color), Dan Laustsen; editor, Camilla Skousen; music, Sort Sol, the Sandmen, Joachim Holbek; art direction, Soeren Krag Soerensen; costume design, Margrethe Rasmussen; sound (Dolby), Michael Dela. Reviewed at Espace Saint-Michel cinema, Paris, April 26, 1994. (In Cannes Film Festival — Critics' Week.) Running time: **104 MIN.**

With: Nikolaj Waldau, Sofie Graaboel, Kim Bodnia, Lotte Andresen, Ulf Pilgaard, Rikke Louise Andersson.

"Nightwatch" is the slickly made but fairly conventional tale of a strapping young law student who works as a morgue nightwatchman and may be murdering prostitutes in his spare time. Leisurely suspenser, which topped Danish B.O. chart in March and April, strives to inject humor into unmask-the-stalker genre, and its requisite quotient of red herrings should please teens and horror fans.

Appealing newcomer Nikolaj Waldau plays Martin, who takes over the night rounds at the morgue from a middle-aged fellow who's had enough of unsettling goings-on. A serial killer is snuffing and scalping prostitutes, whose corpses sometimes rise off the slab and roam the corridors. Post-mortem bonking also is a factor.

Martin has a loving and supportive relationship with his girlfriend, Kalinka (Sofie Graaboel), but is lured into misbehaving when he and best buddy Jens (Kim Bodnia) agree to a protracted game of truth or dare. Dark, faintly menacing Jens displays some creepy personality traits and has told a drug-addicted underage prostie that his name is really Martin.

As Martin grows increasingly unnerved at work, sensitive police inspector Wormer (Ulf Pilgaard) collects damning evidence that points to Martin as the killer.

Protracted thriller stretches the intrigue until *deus ex machina* time rolls around. Pic is nicely lit and lensed with flair. Nudity is well incorporated.

Director Ole Bornedal's script self-reflexively makes fun of bad movie conventions ("If I were to say 'I love you,' would it sound like bad movie dialogue?"; "If this were a movie, they should call it 'The Night Guard.'"), but not quite enough for adult tastes. —*Lisa Nesselson*

KILLER

A Keystone Films in association with Worldvision Enterprises presentation of a Robert Vince production. Produced by Robert and William Vince. Executive producers, Robert Sigman, Gary Delfiner, Michael Strange. Directed by Mark Malone. Screenplay, Gordon Melbourne, based on Malone's story. Camera (color), Tobias Schlissler; editor, Robin Russell; music, Graeme Coleman; production design, Lynne Stopkewich; art direction, Eric McNab; set decoration, Elizabeth Patrick; costume design, Maxine Baker; sound (Ultra-stereo), Greg Reely; associate producers, Kelsey T. Howard, Abra Edelman; assistant director, Kelsey T. Howard; casting, Edelman, Elisa Goodman, Marcia Shulman. Reviewed at Cannes Film Festival (market), May 15, 1994. Running time: **95 MIN.**

Mick	Anthony LaPaglia
Fiona	Mimi Rogers
Archie	Matt Craven
George	Peter Boyle
Laura	Monika Schnarre
Dr. Alstricht	Joseph Maher

Equal parts fresh observation and strained contrivance, "Killer," a film noir with a twist, announces the promising directorial debut of Mark Malone. Pic features a mesmerizing central performance by Anthony LaPaglia as a nihilistic hit man and a solid one by Mimi Rogers as the femme fatale. Strong acting and renewed popularity of noir may facilitate limited theatrical release for this moody and accomplished pic.

Mick (LaPaglia), the tough, cool hero (aka Bulletproof Heart), is the ultimate pro, supplying efficient services for big bucks. Real suspense begins when Mick is assigned a rather unusual duty: killing Fiona (Rogers), a mysterious femme who's not only expecting him but is willing to be murdered.

As could be expected by noir conventions, as soon as Mick meets his enigmatic victim, he falls for her. But Mick is not a standard fall guy; his obsessive love for Fiona turns out to be transformational and redemptive.

The unity of the action, which takes place in one night in New York, adds to the film's tightly controlled tension. Most of the scenes are set indoors, which makes the pic appropriately claustrophobic.

Unfortunately, the story falters severely in its mid-section, a long picnic in a cemetery in which Fiona suddenly disappears. But the pic regains its vitality and the tragic closure is satisfyingly coherent.

Noir and crime-gangster yarns have portrayed many acts of killing, but seldom have they conveyed in such precise detail the complex feelings of both hit men and their victims just seconds before execution. It's in these scenes, and in the exploration of macho behavior, camaraderie and trust, that "Killer" achieves its distinction — and humanity.

Gordon Melbourne's script is thoughtfully constructed, with neatly placed shards of humor and irony. Writer creates fluent and occasionally bright dialogue and avoids melodramatic cliches so prevalent in new noir pix.

As director, Malone strikes the right balance between theatrical and cinematic sensibility. Just when dialogue becomes static and ambience stagnant, helmer adds camera movement or cuts to the next scene.

Perfectly cast, LaPaglia's powerful physical presence adds to his piercing interpretation of quite a challenging role. "Killer" brings to the surface LaPaglia's qualities as a leading man, after years of doing superb work as a character actor in lousy pix ("29th Street," "One Good Cop"). Rogers also shines as the doomed femme.

Pic's chief reward is the pleasure of seeing how these two actors command the screen and effortlessly sail through its solemn and uninspired moments. —*Emanuel Levy*

VANISHED

(CHONGBAL)

(SOUTH KOREAN)

A Hap Dong Films Ltd. presentation of a Sheen Prods. Inc. production. Produced by James Kang. Executive producer, Jung Hwan Kwak. Directed by Shin Sang Okk. Screenplay, Akira Dasaka, Kenny Kim. Camera (Foto-Kem color), Eugene D. Shlugleit; editor, Sung Bae Park; music, Stu Goldberg; production design, Gregory Martin; assistant director, Sung Bae Park. Reviewed at Cannes Film Festival (non-competing), May 17, 1994. Running time: **98 MIN.**

Park Jin Yook	Kim Hee La
Lee Sang Kya	Shin Seoung Yil
Han Seoung Tae	George Takei
Kang Soo Kyung	Kang Lee Na
Maria Song	Min Bok Khee
Yu Mee Lee	Lim Okk Kyung
Shin Chong Man	Kim Myung

Unveiled as the annual noncompeting "surprise film" at this year's Cannes fest, this pic by fest jury member Shin Sang Okk is a forceful and courageous condemnation of political corruption inside the top reaches of the South Korean government. Film will have minimal commercial impact outside Asia, but it should play the fest route, which might result in TV sales and video release.

Pic purports to tell the background story of the disappearance of a prominent exiled politico who vanished while visiting Paris and was never seen again.

The director (whose name was spelled on the end credits as Sang Okk Sheen in the print reviewed) knows all about political kidnapping from personal experience: After he fell afoul of the government, he and

his actress wife vanished, apparently kidnapped, only to resurface and continue making films in various countries.

"Vanished," Shin/Sheen's first South Korean film since 1976, is a fierce attack on the conservative government of former President Park Chung Hee, called President Han in the film. The pic opens with a crate arriving in Seoul under diplomatic immunity and opened at the president's residence.

Inside is Park Jin Yook, former head of the country's National Security Agency, who had been kidnapped. Park is given 48 hours to agree not to publish his memoirs, in which he plans to attack Han's government.

During two days of imprisonment, Park recalls the military coup that toppled an elected government 18 years earlier, and his complicity as head of security.

What follows is an intriguing panorama of South Korean politics, with the names of the principals changed, but with strong implications of massive abuse of human rights, including torture and murder, organized from the very top.

Vivid scenes of student riots, police and military attacks on the rioters and the suicide of a woman who ignites herself and falls from a tall building graphically depict the public reaction to government intolerance.

But the events will be confusing to anyone but Koreans or students of contemporary Asian politics. The film lacks the strong dramatic line that made a political thriller like "Z" so effective.

Shin's robust, but at times primitive, style is reminiscent of the work of Samuel Fuller: He's obviously passionate about his subject but sometimes deals with that subject in a manner bordering on melodrama. A handful of sex scenes, seemingly included as a sop to the Korean box office, are on the tawdry side.

But this is an unquestionably daring film that makes a full frontal attack on the government of the country where it was made without a hint of concession.

Pic also clearly implies U.S. involvement: CIA reps are shown as willing to go along with human rights violations as long as the government promises that no nuclear weapons will be developed in South Korea.

Film was shot partly in Korea, with some interiors lensed in L.A. and all post-production in the U.S. Technical credits are pretty good.

None of the actors is likely to win any prizes here, and the film itself would not be of major importance

were it not for the helmer's gutsy handling of his potent theme.
—*David Stratton*

MY OWN

(SWAHAM)

(INDIAN)

A Filmfolk production. Produced, directed by Shaji N. Karun. Screenplay, S. Jayachandran Nair, Reghunath Paleri, Karun. Camera (b&w/color), Hari Nair; editor, Raman Nair; music, K. Raghavan, Issac Thomas Kottukapally; production design, Padmakumar; sound (Dolby), Krishnan Unni. Reviewed at Cannes Film Festival (competing), May 21, 1994. Running time: **153 MIN.**

Annapoorna	Aswani
Kannan	Sarath
Stationmaster	Vishnu
Ramayyar	Hari Dass
Landlord	Gopi
Brother-in-Law	Mullenezhi
(Malayalam dialogue)	

Keralan director Shaji N. Karun scored on the fest circuit a couple of years back with his first feature, "Piravi" (Birth), but his second, "My Own," is unlikely to find the same success. Overlong and repetitive, this story of a widow grieving for her dead husband will have almost no commercial chances outside its home territory, and even fest outings may be difficult to achieve.

It's a pity that such a film was screened so late in the Cannes fest, when exhausted viewers lacked the reserves to penetrate its ultra-slow pacing and discover the riches the film has to offer; there were mass exits at the screening caught.

Pic opens in color as Annapoorna's husband, Ramayyar, dies painfully in hospital as the result of an accident; then color drains from the image, and for the rest of the film the present is depicted in monochrome, with color used only for flashbacks to happier times.

The couple ran a small cafe in a tiny village in Kerala (south India), their only link to the outside world the trains that pass by regularly on their way to the city of Trivandrum. After the funeral ceremony for Ramayyar, Annapoorna finds it almost impossible to make enough money to keep her teenage son and daughter fed and clothed. She loses the cafe when it's torn down to pay debts and is forced to move in with her brother-in-law.

The sensitive son, Kannan, is advised by the kindly stationmaster to enroll in the armed forces; his best friend, meanwhile, opts out by leaving the country altogether to find work in the Middle East, and there's a tearful farewell when he catches the train.

A great many tears are, in fact, shed during the course of the film, and Annapoorna's continual sobbing, amplified in Dolby, becomes grating after a while. Aswani, who plays the role, doesn't exactly give a nuanced performance, though Sarath, as Kannan, is more effective.

But the film is full of tender moments, and the patient viewer will be rewarded by scenes like the one in which the dead man's brother, alone on a country road when a storm breaks out (in black and white) is reminded of being with Ramayyar on the same road during a storm (in color). Karun's background as a cinematographer shows in the consistent beauty of his images.

The film would fare better with considerable pruning. India isn't often repped in competition at Cannes, and it's a shame that the sheer length of "My Own" makes it such a daunting viewing experience. There's a particularly beautiful music score by K. Raghavan and Issac Thomas Kottukapally, and all other technical credits are very good. —*David Stratton*

DOWN TO EARTH
(CASA DE LAVA)
(PORTUGUESE-FRENCH-GERMAN)

A Madragoa Filmes (Portugal)/Gemini Films (France)/Pandora Film (Germany) co-production in association with IPACA, RTP and CNC, with support from the European Script Fund. (International sales: Fortissimo Films, Amsterdam.) Produced by Paolo Branco. Directed, written by Pedro Costa. Camera (color), Emmanuel Machuel; editor, Dominique Auvray; music, Raul Andrade, Paul Hindemith; art direction, Maria Jose Branco; costume design, Rosa Lopes Alves; sound, Henri Maikoff. Reviewed at Cannes Film Festival (Un Certain Regard), May 1, 1994. Running time: 110 MIN.
Mariana .... Ines Medeiros
Leao .... Isaach de Bankole
Edite .... Edith Scob
V .... Pedro Hestnes
Violinist .... Raul Andrade
Tano .... Christiano Andrade Alves
(Portuguese/Creole soundtrack)

Lofty, poetic and strewn with arcane symbolism, Portuguese director Pedro Costa's sophomore feature, "Down to Earth," flies in the face of its English-language title. Beautifully crafted and intensely played out against a brooding volcanic landscape, this meandering hell-on-Earth reverie is nonetheless too frustratingly impenetrable to erupt far beyond the fest circuit.

Opening takes place in Portugal, where immigrant worker Leao (Isaach de Bankole) slips into a coma following an accident. A nurse, Mariana (Ines Medeiros), is assigned to accompany him home to the Cape Verde islands. She embraces the chance to escape from the bleakness of her life and deliver the injured man to a more fulfilling existence. She stays on to tend to him while medical supplies are brought to the ill-equipped local hospital.

As Leao hovers on the edge of consciousness in a deathlike trance, Mariana's encounters with the locals begin to have an oppressive effect on her. She meets a withered violinist with 20 children; a Portuguese widow, who stayed on after her husband's death, completely sapped of her strength; the woman's son, who attempts to latch onto Mariana for the life in her.

Mariana is gradually pulled into the miasma of hopelessness that permeates the barren place, and the hell she fled begins to look comparatively rosy.

The film's indolent rhythm, generally elliptical dialogue and stubbornly cryptic plot development make it a long, demanding sit. Those willing to go with its unforthcoming nature, however, will find considerable visual rewards in Emmanuel Machuel's handsome lensing, capturing the stark geography in light that positively glows.

Though the austere meditation throws out far too few clues to make its narrative completely accessible, Costa's eminently skilled direction sustains an intoxicating, sorrowful mood that finds worthy soul mates in the fine cast. —*David Rooney*

ONCE WERE WARRIORS
(NEW ZEALAND)

A Communicado production, in association with the New Zealand Film Commission, Avalon Studios and NZ on Air. Produced by Robin Scholes. Directed by Lee Tamahori. Screenplay, Riwia Brown, from a novel by Alan Duff. Camera (color), Stuart Dryburgh; editor, Michael Horton; music, Murray Grindlay, Murray McNabb; production design, Michael Kane. Reviewed at Cannes Film Festival (market), May 17, 1994. Running time: 99 MIN.
Beth Heke .... Rena Owen
Jake Heke .... Temuera Morrison
Grace Heke ... Mamaengaroa Kerr-Bell
Nig Heke ...... Julian (Sonny) Arahanga
Boogie Heke .... Taungaroa Emile
Polly Heke .... Rachael Morris
Huata Heke .... Joseph Kairau
Bully .... Cliff Curtis
Toot .... Shannon Williams
Dooley .... Pete Smith

The barren lives of members of an urban Maori family are rigorously exposed in this rugged and painful picture, based on Alan Duff's novel, which was a Kiwi bestseller. Though the film has opened strongly on its home turf via Footprint Films distribbery, it looms as a tough sell elsewhere; non-U.S. films about minority groups have rarely made it with mainstream audiences, and first-time director Lee Tamahori's brave pic is likely to prove too unrelentingly violent for the arthouse crowd.

Pic deserves nurturing, because it's one of the best to emerge from New Zealand in quite a while. Tamahori, working from Riwia Brown's intelligent script, has done a marvelous job in depicting the day-to-day horror of the Heke family, which is held together only by its women, the sorely tried Beth and her eldest daughter, 16-year-old Grace.

Beth comes from a noble Maori family, who disapproved of her marriage to Jake Heke some 18 years earlier; she left her roots to live in the city with her hard-drinking spouse and, over the years, they've had five children.

But the family is falling apart, mainly due to Jake's irresponsibility. Out of work, he spends his welfare money boozing at a bar with his mates and getting into fights, and he regularly brings a crowd home for more drinking and eating.

Jake's fiery temper has estranged him from eldest son Nig, who has left home to join a tough street gang; the younger children despise him, too, because he regularly beats Beth when he's drunk.

Now second son Boogie is also in trouble with the law, but the night before his court appearance, Jake beats Beth so badly that she's unable to support her son at the hearing, as she'd promised. As a result, Boogie is sent to a juvenile detention center.

Meanwhile, Grace occasionally visits her homeless friend, Toot, who lives in an abandoned car under a freeway. During yet another of her father's drunken nights, Grace is raped by one of his drinking mates, which triggers the film's tragic climax.

New Zealand's Maori community has traditionally been better treated than minorities in other countries, notably Australia's Aborigines, so it comes as a shock for viewers to be exposed to this desperately sick environment.

"Once Were Warriors" (the title is a sad reminder of a noble past) would be unrelentingly downbeat if not for the magnetic performances of the lead players and for the fact that, despite the drinking and violence, the relationship between Beth and Jake is, against the odds, a warm one. Scenes in which husband and wife spontaneously sing together are wrenchingly touching when placed alongside the ever-present violence.

It could be argued that Tamahori overdoes the level of violence, overstating his point and risking the alienation of his target audience. But this is an in-your-face slice of realism, and the violence is certainly not exaggerated.

Rena Owen plays Beth with distinction, creating a believably passionate woman whose life hasn't turned out the way she planned. As Jake, Temuera Morrison manages to invest this brutal, shiftless character with charm.

Among the generally excellent supporting cast, Mamaengaroa Kerr-Bell shines as the tragic Grace.

This is a remarkably assured first feature, executed with total confidence. A major asset is the brooding cinematography of Stuart Dryburgh (totally different from his work on "The Piano"), and Michael Horton's editing is a precision job.

Further fest exposure should help build public and critical support for this excellent, but troubling and challenging, film.

—*David Stratton*

THREE PALM TREES
(TRES PALMEIRAS)
(PORTUGUESE)

A Madragoa Filmes production for Lisbon 94. Produced by Paolo Branco. Directed, written by Joao Botelho. Camera (color, b&w), Olivier Gueneau; editor, Carla Bogalheiro; music, Antonio Vitorino d'Almeida; art direction, Fernanda Morais; costume design, Rita Lopes Alves; sound, Francisco Veloso. Reviewed at Cannes Film Festival (Directors Fortnight), May 17, 1994. Running time: 68 MIN.
With: Teresa Roby, Pedro Hestnes, Rita Lopes Alves, Alexandra Lencastre, Diogo Infante, Canto e Castro, Ines Medeiros.

Eight hours in the life of Lisbon are idiosyncratically chronicled in "Three Palm Trees." Making a commanding palette of the city, director Joao Botelho offers a visually seductive series of loosely interlocking metropolitan moments that's by turns tragic, jocular, intense, gripping, teasing and even light-operatic. Almost as cerebral as it is cinematic, the film should figure on European TV slates, but theatrically it's too rarefied an exercise in style and oblique philosophy to go beyond the festival field.

The film is one of a trio of hour-long features depicting different stretches of a single day in the "Lisbon, 24 Hours" project commissioned for the city's year as European Capital of Culture. Time frame here is 6 a.m. to 2 p.m., opening with a suicide and closing with a birth.

A pregnant woman in her 40s (Teresa Roby) is about to go into labor. To distract her from anxieties about her suitability for motherhood, the baby's young father (Pedro Hestnes) tells stories of inhabitants of the city sprawling out beyond the three palms opposite their window.

A young woman throws herself in the river; a pair of nighttime revelers stagger home drunk; a man contemplates killing the woman sleeping in his hotel bed, and then shoots himself; an English-speaking couple have a tiff that gets patched up silently; a ballet student learns that she's not cut out to dance.

The vignettes are fluidly woven together by Hestnes' commentary and Roby's dismissive, often disbelieving reactions. Hestnes is drawn directly into the universe of stories when he steps out for cakes and meets a film-star-turned-bag-lady in the park, who frightens him off with an unsolicited demonstration of onscreen kissing technique.

A cake shop provides the stage for an amusing, fully sung mini-opera involving a woman who begs for cash and makes off with a tray of pastries.

The baby's graphically filmed birth coincides with the recovery of a body (presumably the woman from reel one) from the river. Several characters step over the line into each other's stories, creating a sense of fusion of the city's disparate strands.

Botelho's fascination with the elements continues from his previous feature, "Here on Earth." Water and wind feature heavily on the soundtrack, along with Antonio Vitorino d'Almeida's portentous, often willfully strident music.

Color is heightened dramatically, with rich blood reds, warm sea and sky blues and solar yellows almost leaping off the screen. Olivier Gueneau's handsome lensing is especially alluring in the period before sun-up.
—*David Rooney*

BLIND MAN'S BUFF

(A CAIXA)

(PORTUGUESE-FRENCH)

Produced by Paulo Branco for Madragoa Filmes/Gemini Films/La Sept Cinema. (International sales: Mercure Distribution.) Directed, written by Manoel de Oliveira, based on a play by Prista Monteiro. Camera (color), Mario Barroso; editor, Oliveira, Valerie LoisEleux; art direction, Isabel Branco; sound, Jean Paul Mugel. Reviewed at Cannes Film Festival (Directors Fortnight), May 19, 1994. Running time: **96 MIN.**
Blind Man .... Luis Miguel Cintra
Daughter .... Beatriz Batarda
Friend .... Diogo Doria
With: Isabel Ruth, Filipe Cochofel, Sofia Alves, Glicinia Quartin, Ruy de Carvalho.

I f Portuguese master Manoel de Oliveira expanded his fan club with his last, "Valley of Abra-

ham," the same cannot be said of the small, theatrical "A Caixa" (translated as "Blind Man's Buff" but literally "The Box"). The director's sly wit and wide-angle view on the human condition are still present, but his tale of poverty and misery, set in a back alley, remains earthbound. Oliveira's loyal following will probably assure Euro arthouse release.

An opening tag warns audience not to mistake pic for a documentary but to read it as a fable about anachronisms of today's society. Actually, there is small chance that viewers will think the setting — a hillside, staircased alley, inhabited by characters obviously written for the stage — is meant to represent a real place.

Film opens with a drunken gendarme tottering past a big arrow pointing to a theater, and also contains a scene in which dancing fairies appear on the stairway in a kind of entr'acte.

As the neighborhood leisurely awakens, the characters are introduced: a kindly bartender, an old harridan who uses the street as a latrine, a busybody selling chestnuts, a breezy young streetwalker and an unhappy family.

A blind old man (Luis Miguel Cintra) sits in the doorway, selling thread and begging, while his resentful daughter (Beatriz Batarda) wears herself out ironing for a living and lamenting her lot. He anxiously gropes for his collection box, which has been stolen before, and on which his daughter's live-in boyfriend keeps a close eye.

Everyone in the neighborhood ogles the box enviously as the coins accumulate in the course of the morning. Three wastrels plot to steal it, while two boys wait for their chance. When the old man dozes off, the box disappears, lighting the fuse for tragedy.

This little parable about the human condition, which recalls Bunuel without the savagery, is watchable enough. It's enlivened by an amusing perf from Oliveira regular Cintra, who rolls his eyes irresistibly, even while he gets the short end of the stick from the people who live off him. As the daughter who hates him, Batarda is loathsome, making her sudden conversion to wannabe sainthood at pic's end all the more ironic.

Though all perfs are superior, few thesps are able to break out of the theatrical caricature Oliveira obviously required. Exceptions are the actors playing the bartender, who rightly calls himself a simple man with feelings, and a music prof fallen on hard times who plays an extraordinary rendition of Schubert's "Ave Maria" on his guitar.

Choice of music is imaginative throughout, with space found for a

little Nino Rota/Fellini circus theme as well as local ballads.
—*Deborah Young*

JOHNNIE THE AQUARIUS

(JANCIO WODNIK)

(POLISH)

A Polish Television presentation of a Vacek Film production. (International sales: Polish Television, Warsaw.) Directed, written by Jan Jakub Kolski. Camera (color), Piotr Lenar; editor, Ewa Pakulska; music, Zygmunt Konieczny; art direction, Tadeusz Kosarewicz; costume design, Beata Olszewska. Reviewed at Cannes Film Festival (Un Certain Regard), May 15, 1994. Running time: **105 MIN.**
Jancio .... Franciszek Pieczka
Weronka .... Grazyna Blecka-Kolska
Stigma .... Boguslaw Linda
Wandering
Tramp .... Olgierd Lukaszewicz
Blind
Girl .... Katarzyna Aleksandrowicz

"J ohnnie the Aquarius," an offbeat tale of a philosophical Polish peasant who suddenly finds he can perform miracles, is a slight but unusual charmer sustained by fine perfs and an inventive script. Though overlong, this fourth feature of Jan Jakub Kolski should please festgoers and attract a modicum of small-screen sales.

Johnnie/Jancio (Franciszek Pieczka) is an aging, slightly spaced-out country dweller who's so tuned into the joys of life and nature that he hangs his young wife, Weronka (Grazyna Blecka-Kolska), upside down after they've had sex to make sure gravity does its job.

One day, he watches in amazement as his water pail climbs a ladder and settles into a bird's nest. Taking this as a sign of divine powers, Jancio leaves his now-pregnant wife and sets off to perform healing miracles. He is feted by the locals as a neo-divine figure and quickly builds a harem of camp followers and a lucrative business.

With Weronka about to give birth, Jancio, by now a serious ego case, pays a brief visit home, followed by his massive entourage. When the child arrives, however, it's born with a tail, which even Jancio's powers can't get rid of. He's also slowly deserted by the locals as the afflictions he's supposedly healed start to come back. A curse put on the village by a wandering tramp (Olgierd Lukaszewicz) has finally found its mark.

Recurrent joy of the pic is how all the crazy goings-on are treated as absolutely normal by the peasants. When Jancio heals a girl with festering eyes, maggots crawl out and are snapped up by a hungry crow.

Kolski aims for a form of folk-tale simplicity, with a strong overlay of straight-faced Slavic irony, that hits almost all its targets. Visually, the pic is largely naturalistic; its special flavor derives more from the sparse dialogue, pitched almost at the level of a nativity play at times, fine ensemble playing by all the cast, Zygmunt Konieczny's gentle score and the natural integration of human and animal life.

Pieczka is perfect casting as Jancio, moving from a soft-spoken dreamer to bellicose despot in one easy stride. In a largely blank part, helmer's wife, Blecka-Kolska, performs her own miracles of underplaying. Lukaszewicz and Boguslaw Linda play off well against the two leads. Technically, the Polish TV-financed pic is smooth in all departments.
—*Derek Elley*

KATIA ISMAILOVA

(FRENCH-RUSSIAN)

A Pierre Grise (France) release of a Films du Rivage/Studio TTL/Lumiere co-production with the participation of the CNC, the Russian Cinema Committee, Russian Television, Dekar, Image Ltd. and the Gorki Studios. (International sales: Mercure Distribution — Jacques Leglou.) Produced by Marc Ruscart, Igor Tolstounov. Executive producers, Alexandre Gnedenko, Mikhail Zonenachvili. Directed by Valeri Todorovski. Screenplay, Alla Krinitsina, based on a novella by Marina Cheptounova, Stanislav Govoroukhine; adapted by Francois Guerif, Cecile Vargaftig. Camera (color), Sergeui Kozlov; editors, Helene Gagarine, Alla Strelnikova; music, Leonid Dessiatnikov; set design and costumes, Alexandre Ossipov; sound, Henri Roux, Gleb Kraveski. Reviewed at Cannes Film Festival (Directors Fortnight), May 12, 1994. Running time: **94 MIN.**
Katia .... Ingeborga Dapkounaite
Serguei .... Vladimir Machkov
Irina .... Alice Freindlikh
Mitia .... Alexandre Feklistov
Romanov .... Youri Kouznetov
With: Natali Tchoukina, Avangarde Leontiev.

"K atia Ismailova," the story of a married woman whose personality is transformed by a passionate affair, puts a modern spin on the Russian taste for tragic literary heroines. Style is more potent than the content in young Russian helmer Valeri Todorovski's sophomore outing, but slyly sustained noir atmosphere puts across the classic murder-without-remorse narrative. Pic should be welcome at fests.

Bland, submissive Katia (Ingeborga Dapkounaite) types up manuscripts for her mother-in-law, Irina (Alice Freindlikh), a successful author of romance novels, while Katia's hubby, Mitia (Alexandre

May 30, 1994 (Cont.)

Feklistov), is more deeply devoted to Mom than to his wife.

The threesome repair to Mom's *dacha*, where brooding, seductive handyman Serguei (Vladimir Machkov) awakens Katia's buried passions in a steamy sexual encounter on a windowsill. Mother-in-law, who has a heart condition, catches the illicit lovers in the act.

Katia, besotted with sex, becomes bold and giddy, but Serguei's sexual attention span is limited. A local judge who is intimately familiar with Irina's writing takes a special interest in the peculiar and deadly developments at the *dacha*.

Pic's psychology and several plot points, including the finale, are highly derivative, but the inventive lensing and fine thesping win out. Leonid Dessiatnikov's omnipresent score, at its best when sinister and slightly dissonant, grows intrusive and overbearing and could be toned down to good effect.

Modestly budgeted Franco-Russian pic gives every indication that helmer (whose 1991's "Lioubov" also played in the Directors Fortnight) is a talent to watch.

—Lisa Nesselson

THE GREAT CONQUEROR'S CONCUBINE

(XI CHU BAWANG)

(HONG KONG)

A Great Dragon (H.K.) Films Co. production. (International sales: Sil-Metropole Organisation, Hong Kong.) Executive producer, Zhang Yimou. Directed by Stephen Shin. Screenplay, Shin, Xiao He, Sze Yeung-ping, from a literary screenplay by Liu Heng. Camera (color, widescreen), Cheng Siu-keung; editor, Wong Wing-ming; music, James Wong, Romeo Diaz; production design, Mok Kwan-kit; art direction, Ma Kwong-wing; costume design, Mok; sound, Dolby; action choreographer, Kong Tao-ho; associate producer, Lam Bing-kwan. Reviewed at Cannes Film Festival (market), May 14, 1994. Running time: **178 MIN.**
Xiang Yu .... Ray Lui
Lu Zhi .... Gong Li
Liu Bang .... Zhang Fengyi
Yu Ji .... Rosamund Kwan
Fan Zeng .... Lau Seung
With: Tsui Kam-kong, To Siu-tseun, Tsui Heung-tung, Wu Hsing-kuo, Chen Sung-yung.
(Mandarin Chinese dialogue)

"The Great Conqueror's Concubine" is a rich, 10-course banquet of Chinese historical drama that harks back to the pre-arthouse age of East Asian moviemaking. Good-looking, big-budget ($7 million) production should certainly attract specialized Western interest on the strength of its name players (Gong Li, Zhang Fengyi) and behind-camera talent (Zhang Yimou as exec producer), though trimming would be in order for wider distribution.

Initial three-hour version world-preemed in the Cannes market hot from the labs. Producers are considering a 2½-hour cut for Hong Kong release this summer but plan to keep the full version intact as well. Programmers for fests should take a chance on the latter.

In line with the trend toward cross-border Chinese-lingo production, the movie has been tubthumped in the East for its mixed-territory casting, with players from mainland China (Gong, Zhang), Hong Kong (Rosamund Kwan, Ray Lui) and Taiwan (Wu Hsing-kuo, Chen Sung-yung). Helmer, experienced H.K. director/producer Stephen Shin, shot pic on remote mainland locations during four to five months last winter.

True story, a watershed in Chinese history, is set in the late third century B.C., when the country, united under the Qin (Chin) dynasty, was riven by warring factions. Pic focuses on one of the biggest rebellions that led to the formation of Chu State, later threatened by a rival faction led by the king of Han.

Picture divides cleanly into two halves, with the first a series of battles for supremacy between Qin and Chu forces, and the second more focused on personal rivalries as Chu leaders feud for territorial control.

Script, developed from a "literary screenplay" by well-known mainland writer Liu Heng ("Ju Dou," "The Story of Qiu Ju"), does a good job in simplifying some seven years of tangled events, with explanatory captions peppered through the first half to fill in the gaps. This part could be further simplified for Western auds, though by keeping the dramatic focus on a relatively small number of players, the general thrust is clear enough.

Nut of the story has ruthless schemer Lu Zhi (Gong) and her ambitious husband, Liu Bang (Zhang), joining the Xiang clan, led by Xiang Yu (Ray Lui), in its rebellion against the Qin dynasty but plotting a long-term takeover of power once the initial battle is won.

Second half pits the treacherous couple against Xiang, who's trying to be fair to his enemies in the cause of pan-Chinese peace. Xiang is inspired by the goodly love of Yu Ji (Kwan), who's also been inveigled into a sisterly friendship by Lu.

Helmer Shin, who made his name in the '80s with a string of slick yuppie comedies and more recently directed "Black Cat," a clone of "La Femme Nikita," seems deliberately to evoke the '60s style of Hong Kong/Taiwan costumers with full-throttle direction, a name cast and traditional heroic acting styles. For audiences prepared to go with the flow, the meld works, with plenty of large-scale set pieces, milling extras drawn from China's liberation army and frequently awesome production design.

Gong, who's so far generally fared less well in H.K. movies than in artier fare for mainland director Zhang Yimou, here presses major buttons as the beautiful schemer Lu. Despite lusty perfs by males Ray Lui and Zhang Fengyi as the two antagonists, it's still Gong's movie. (She even sings the closing song.) H.K. actress Kwan is fine as the saintly Yu, but it's a less peachy part.

Widescreen lensing squeezes top visual value from the budget, and production designer Mok Kwan-kit's rich costumes deserve a special nod. Color throughout accentuates reds and yellows, in line with the key hues of the warring Chu and Han factions in the latter half. Pic's Chinese title translates as "The Lord of Western Chu," referring to Ray Lui's tragic character. *—Derek Elley*

BREAD AND POETRY

(NAN VA SHE'R)

(IRANIAN)

A Khaneh (House of Children and Young Adults' Literature and Arts) production. Directed, written by Kiumars Poorahmad, based on a TV series by Hushang Moradi Kermani. Camera (color), Parviz Malekzadeh; editor, Poorahmad. Reviewed at Cannes Film Festival (market), May 20, 1994. Running time: **91 MIN.**
With: Mehdi Bagherbeigi, Pavnindokht Yazdanian, Jamshid Sadri, Mohammad Ali Miandar, Mohsen Maleki.

This Iranian tale of a brash young delivery boy who wants to be a poet at all costs is based on a hit TV series. Outside the local market, it could appeal to children's film fests.

The film is self-contained. Majid, a boy of 15, becomes infatuated with Victor Hugo's "Les Miserables." Too poor to buy a copy, he tires of reading the long book in the public library. One day he switches the library copy for a book that he swipes from his literary-minded but mean-spirited brother-in-law. Unfortunately, there's a big check inside the book.

Majid's grandma is distraught about the loss, and the boy travels to the set of a historical movie in search of the missing book. The check turns up one magical night when Majid is invited to the exclusive Poet's Society and gets to read his first published poem before a TV camera.

Veteran helmer Kiumars Poorahmad was Abbas Kiarostami's assistant on "Where Is My Friend's Home," a connection that shows in a peculiar credits sequence showing Poorahmad shooting "Bread and Poetry." But instead of giving the picture a more complex dimension, it just seems a little egotistical, like young Majid. With his loud, bombastic quotations and insensitivity to his family's distress, the boy doesn't get a high sympathy rating. Some of the old folks, like his granny and a revered elderly artist, win in that department.

Technical credits are sound.

—Deborah Young

A KISS GOODNIGHT

A David C. Raskov presentation of an Exposition Park Pictures production. (International sales: GEL, L.A.) Produced by Lori Miller, Daniel Raskov. Co-producers, Gary Depew, Brad Southwick. Directed, written by Raskov. Camera (color), Glenn Kershaw; editor, Amy Tompkins; music, Chris Caswell; stunts, Scott Ateah; assistant director, Southwick; casting, Karen Margiotta. Reviewed at Cannes Film Festival (market), May 18, 1994. Running time: **88 MIN.**
Kurt Pierson .... Al Corley
Natalie Collins .... Paula Trickey
Michael Turner .... Mark Moses
Sgt. Harwood .... Lawrence Tierney
Marcia .... Sydney Walsh
Carl Jasper .... Brett Cullen
Sam .... James Karen

"Fatal Attraction" is revisited yet again, but although "A Kiss Goodnight" is well crafted and contains a couple of good performances, writer/director Daniel Raskov hasn't come up with anything original enough to make this one stand out from the crowd. Sharper scripting and denser plotting would have made all the difference, because Raskov shows talent as a director and avoids the exploitation route. Average vid sales are indicated.

Drama hinges on a brief but initially satisfying affair enjoyed by Matilda (Paula Trickey), a young advertising exec, with Kurt (Al Corley), a stranger she meets in a bar while her boyfriend is working long hours as a medical resident. For a couple of sexy nights, Matilda has a good time, but then she decides that Michael (Mark Moses) is the one she wants. Naturally, Kurt won't take rejection lying down, and starts harassing and stalking Matilda, eventually killing both her secretary and her best friend.

In the early scenes, Raskov builds up the sexual tension with some skill, but ultimately we've been here before many times, and the helmer doesn't bring any new twists to the material. Lawrence Tierney does a turn as the inevitable skeptical cop (though he's surely too old to be holding down this sort of job).

The best thing the film has going for it is Trickey's neat perf as the threatened heroine; she's obviously capable of bigger and better things.

Technical credits are all pro, with excellent lensing by Glenn Kershaw.　—David Stratton

YANKEE ZULU

(SOUTH AFRICAN)

An Anant Singh and Distant Horizon presentation of a Toron Screen Corp./Koukas Troika production. Produced by Andre Scholtz. Executive producer, Edgar Bold. Directed by Gray Hofmeyr. Screenplay, Leon Schuster, Hofmeyr. Camera (color), James Robb; editor, Johan Lategan; production design, Robert van der Coolwijk; costume design, Jo Katsaras; sound (Dolby), Conrad Kuhne. Reviewed at Cannes Film Festival (market), May 15, 1994. Running time: **88 MIN.**
Rhino .... Leon Schuster
Zulu .... John Matshikize
Diehard .... Wilson Dunster
Rowena .... Terri Treas
Tienke .... Michelle Bowes

All-time top-grossing South African feature "Yankee Zulu" is a rollicking, coarse comedy that thumbs its nose at subtlety or sophistication in favor of broad-based yocks, slapstick excess and infantile vulgarity. This fast-paced fusillade of gags, groans and gross-outs culminates in a well-sustained chain of "Home Alone"-style destruction, adding up to crowd-pleasing fare for undemanding markets, in particular for small-fry auds. Pic was boisterously received at its first Cannes market screening.

Estranged childhood buddies Rhino (Leon Schuster) and Zulu (John Matshikize) are reunited when the latter is deported back home 25 years later from the U.S. after stealing one car too many. Rhino's white-supremacist sweetheart was partly what drove his black friend to leave the country, and in his absence, they've been through a bad marriage and ugly divorce.

Ex-wife Rowena (Terri Treas) is now shacked up with Diehard (Wilson Dunster), a crazed, Nazi assigned to escort the prodigal Zulu to serve out his prison term. But Zulu escapes, making off with a winning lottery ticket and prompting an unrelenting chase. He hooks up with Rhino and his adopted daughter, Tienke (Michelle Bowes).

A TV studio makeup artist disguises the two men by switching their color, giving Zulu a taste of white privilege and Rhino some experience of black servitude.

After infiltrating a shindig at Rowena and Diehard's fortress-like love nest, the duo is discovered and threatened with death unless the lottery winnings are returned. But Tienke steps in with a resourceful attack plan, aided by Prince William of Windsor, gone AWOL from a royal tour.

Comedy is in the "Gods Must Be Crazy" vein, with the somewhat laboriously spelled-out anti-racism message thrown in to bulk it up. Little interest is shown in modulation or keeping events even vaguely within the realms of possibility, but the frenetic rhythm and shrilly hammy perfs will keep kids entertained.　—David Rooney

UNCOVERED

(BRITISH-SPANISH)

A CIBY 2000 presentation of a CIBY UK/Filmania production. (International sales: CIBY Sales, London.) Produced by Enrique Posner. Line producers, Denise O'Dell, Jack Baran. Directed by Jim McBride. Screenplay, Michael Hirst, McBride, Baran, based on the novel "La Tabla de Flandes," by Arturo Perez-Reverte. Camera (Technicolor), Affonso Beato; editor, Eva Gardos; music, Philippe Sarde; production design, Hugo Luczyc-Wyhowski; art direction, Llorenz Miquel; costume design, Tracy Tynan; sound (Dolby), Clive Winter; assistant director, Baran; casting, Celestia Fox. Reviewed at Cannes Film Festival (market), May 20, 1994. Running time: **107 MIN.**
Julia .... Kate Beckinsale
Cesar .... John Wood
Menchu .... Sinead Cusack
Domenec .... Paudge Behan
Alvaro .... Art Malik
Lola .... Helen McCrory
Max .... Peter Wingfield
Don Manuel .... Michael Gough
Inspector .... Anthony Milner

Generous dollops of sex and colorful Barcelona settings dress up but can't disguise the routine and predictable whodunit plot of Jim McBride's "Uncovered." Shot under the title "The Flemish Board," this handsome European production doesn't offer enough in the way of a marquee cast or alluring premise to put it over as a theatrical attraction Stateside, where cable and video release look more suitable.

Kate Beckinsale (the young bride in "Much Ado About Nothing") toplines as Julia, an art restorer who, in the course of cleaning a 15th-century Flemish painting of a duke and a knight playing chess under the watchful eye of a duchess, uncovers a Latin inscription along the bottom that reads, "Who killed the knight?"

No sooner does Julia seek advice from her former lover, art authority Alvaro (Art Malik), than he is found murdered. It doesn't take long for the list of victims to outnumber the suspects: Among those drawn into the intrigue are Julia's gay guardian (John Wood), an art gallery proprietor (Sinead Cusack), the painting's dying, aristocratic owner (Michael Gough), his shady niece (Helen McCrory) and her philandering hubby (Peter Wingfield).

Enlisted to piece together the painting's mystery is an arrogant gypsy chess whiz (Paudge Behan), who by analyzing the position of the chess pieces in the painting can begin to sort out the pattern of the real-life murders.

His eventual hot affair with Julia provides momentary distraction from the procession of toppling bodies. The mystery's resolution is easily predictable and perfunctorily handled.

McBride does everything he can to spice up the routine proceedings, injecting sexual innuendo into every possible encounter and populating the cast with lookers in roles big and small.

Julia's habit of sneezing whenever presented with a sexual threat grows irritating, but sensual atmosphere, augmented by gorgeous settings (Wood's character lives in a Gaudi apartment building), Affonso Beato's lovely lensing and flavorsome score by Philippe Sarde, makes pic easy on the eyes.

Putting Anglo-accented thesps in presumably Spanish roles is a curious choice, but approach is at least consistent and proves acceptable. Beckinsale looks a little young to be an experienced restorer, but she holds her own nicely at center screen.

Irish newcomer Behan seems obnoxiously full of himself initially but gradually becomes an appealing presence. Others have fun within the basically functional limits of their roles.　—Todd McCarthy

MONTAND

(FRENCH — DOCU)

An MJN Prods. presentation of a Mun Sa/TF1 Films/National Audiovisual Institute production. Executive producer, Michel Rotman. Directed by Jean Labib. Based on the book "Tu vois, je n'ai pas oublie" by Herve Hamon, Patrick Rotman. Editor, Bernard Josse; sound, Yannick Chevalier. Reviewed at Cannes Film Festival (noncompeting), May 17, 1994. Running time: **143 MIN.**

Jean Labib's lengthy docu on entertainer Yves Montand (1921-91) is virtually an autobiography, because the narration, culled from various interviews, is spoken by Montand himself. Footage of Montand as singer and actor is somewhat randomly selected, with key omissions, and, despite the length of the film, Montand fans will be left wanting even more. It looms as a TV special, which should rate well in Europe and deserves airtime everywhere. Fest outings also are indicated.

Montand was born Ivo Livi to a poor family of Italian Communists in a Tuscan village. He observes that, whenever he hears Italian spoken, he melts. As a teenager he was a hairdresser, and ogled his lady customers, but his family left for Marseilles to escape fascism, and he gradually became an impersonator, then a singer, in the music hall.

Montand was described as a "swing singer," and early footage of him is reminiscent of the young Sinatra: A skinny young man with boundless energy and a unique singing style. He drifted to Paris during the war and found work on the music hall stage in a bill that included Edith Piaf, with whom he had an affair.

Gradually, he established himself as a serious actor, though one of his most famous early roles, in "The Wages of Fear," is not excerpted here. At about the same time, he fell in love with and married Simone Signoret.

He muses on his foray into Hollywood, including his appearance with Marilyn Monroe in George Cukor's "Let's Make Love," describing his affair with the actress ("What happened, happened") and Signoret's forgiving reaction.

He talks frankly about his Communist Party membership, and there's extensive footage of a tour he and Signoret made to Russia in the '50s: a concert attended by 15,000, visits to a factory and a collective farm. But he broke with communism in 1968 with the invasion of Czechoslovakia, which, he says, made him "shriek with sadness."

The film concentrates more on Montand the singer than on Montand the actor. There are scenes from a number of films, but some, like the trailblazing "Z," mysteriously are unmentioned. Other Costa-Gavras films, such as "The Confession," are included, as is the film of which Montand claims to be most proud, Alain Resnais' "The War Is Over."

A scene from "Manon of the Spring" is used to depict a lonely Montand after Signoret's death, and there's also a sad clip from his final film, Jean-Jacques Beineix's "IP5," in which the actor looks terribly ill.

Despite omissions and the limitations placed on director Jean Labib by the decision to use only Montand's own narration, the film is most impressive.

Technically, the clips are almost all good, with the exception of a sequence from the actor's penultimate film, Jacques Demy's underrated musical "Three Places for the 26th," on which the color is quite muddy.　—David Stratton

May 30, 1994 (Cont.)

THE GARDEN OF EDEN
(EL JARDIN DEL EDEN)
(MEXICAN)

A Macondo Cine Video/Instituto Mexicano de Cinematografia/Verseau Intl. production. Produced by Jorje Sanchez. Co-producer, Lyse Lafontaine. Executive producer, Dulce Kuri. Directed by Maria Novaro. Screenplay, Beatriz and Maria Novaro. Camera (Eastman color), Eric A. Edwards; editor, Sigfrido Barjau; music, Autores Varios; art direction, Brigitte Broch; sound (Dolby), Yvon Benoit. Reviewed at Cannes Film Festival (market), May 16, 1994. Running time: **104 MIN.**
Jane .... Renee Coleman
Felipe .... Bruno Bichir
Serena .... Gabriela Roel
Elizabeth .... Rosario Sagrav
Juana .... Ana Ofelia Murguia
Julian .... Alan Ciangherotti
Frank .... Joseph Culp

Mexican director Maria Novaro, whose lovely "Danzon" was shown in Directors Fortnight at the 1991 Cannes fest, has made another engaging drama that centers on women. Set in the border town of Tijuana, "The Garden of Eden" presents a charming portrait of three women whose paths crisscross and destinies intermingle. Prospects for theatrical release are excellent for a film marked by generosity of spirit and humanist compassion in its depiction of marginal lives.

As in her previous work, a light feminist streak runs through Novaro's new film. Serena (Gabriela Roel), a young widow, arrives at her aunt's home in Tijuana with her three children in her attempt to build a new life for her family. Jane (Renee Coleman), a sexy American, who's looking for her close friend, artist Elizabeth (Rosario Sagrav), also lands in town.

On the surface, the three women seem to be types, as Serena is a native Mexican, Jane a white American and Elizabeth Mexican-American. But it's to Novaro's credit that each woman gradually emerges as a fully fleshed individual with her distinctive traits, needs and problems.

Despite various backgrounds, what unites the three beautiful and intelligent women is their search for a more meaningful life. Obviously, that is most exacting for Elizabeth, an artist of mixed ethnicity who has returned to Mexico in search of her roots.

Pic, which Novaro co-wrote with her sister Beatriz, conveys in enchanting detail the nuanced texture of life in a small border town: the touristy commercial aspects, drug dealings and risky attempts to cross the border in the quest for employment and a better life. But unlike Tony Richardson's American pic "The Border," which had a nasty feel in its portrayal of border crossing, the helicopter patrols, routine arrests and deportations that prevail in Novaro's film are just one of the many issues she examines.

Novaro's attitude toward her characters, male and female, is remarkably open. As writer and director, she shows sensitivity to Jane's brother Frank (Joseph Culp), a man who has given up writing and found a new cause in studying the conduct of whales.

Felipe (Bruno Bichir), the only other male, is a handsome Mexican peasant whose chief ambition is to escape to the American side and who, in the process, has an affair with Jane.

Narrative is loosely structured, and it takes some time for this leisurely paced pic to build its power through the accumulation of details. Eric A. Edwards' atmospheric lensing in Tijuana and San Diego is magnificent, capturing in exquisite long shots the 15-mile steel wall that divides the two countries. The visual imagery stresses the contradictory meanings of a border town: sleazy and fun, refuge for some but prison for others, desert and garden (hence the title). —*Emanuel Levy*

HAPPINESS IS NO JOKE
(FAUT PAS RIRE DU BONHEUR)
(FRENCH)

A Prods. Desmichelle/Groupe TSF/Prod. 7/Ingrid Prod. production, with participation of CNC. Produced by Hugues Desmichelle. (International sales: Les Prods. Desmichelle.) Directed, written by Guillaume Nicloux. Camera (color), Raoul Coutard; editor, Brigitte Benard; music, Marcel Kanche; production design, Gregoire Callens; sound, Erik Menard. Reviewed at Club de l'Etoile screening room, Paris, April 28, 1994. (In Cannes Film Festival — Cinema en France.) Running time: **78 MIN.**
Michel .... Bernard-Pierre Donnadieu
Nadine .... Laura Morante
Andre .... Philippe Nahon

Although it strives to appear fraught with meaning, "Happiness Is No Joke" is a prolonged and morose shaggy-dog story.

Slow-moving nocturnal tale, directed and written by Guillaume Nicloux, follows somber Michel (Bernard-Pierre Donnadieu) on his coincidence-laden peregrinations through Paris and environs late on Christmas Eve.

A dreary lug whose wife died recently in a car accident, Michel shares drinks with Andre (Philippe Nahon) in an escargot-paced prologue, then appropriates and refuses to return a yellow scarf belonging to Nadine (Laura Morante) before enduring a series of random encounters. Some of these show people to be essentially good, others pathetic. Michel and Nadine meet again in the course of the night, tryst, and trade confessions that are supposed to tie up the loose ends. But narrative — and viewer's temper — remain frayed.

Donnadieu, who starred in the original version of "The Vanishing," projects personal resolve and deep-seated unpleasantness in equal measure, and casting of faintly sordid ordinary folks is on the nose. Creepy family gathering at Andre's house is a good portrayal of relatives at their worst.

Raoul Coutard's lensing, in which long takes prevail, is technically competent but lacks distinction. From cello to jew's-harp, score's varied instrumentation conspires to imply that narrative is headed somewhere. It's not.
—*Lisa Nesselson*

RED SCORPION 2

An August Entertainment presentation of a Northwood Pictures production. Produced by Robert Malcolm. Executive producers, Jack Abramoff, Robert Abramoff, Dale A. Andrews. Co-producer, Mary Eilts. Directed by Michael Kennedy. Screenplay, Troy Bolotnick, Barry Victor. Camera (color), Curtis Petersen; editor, Gary Zubeck; music, George Blondheim; production design, Brent Thomas. Reviewed at Cannes Film Festival (market), May 17, 1994. Running time: **90 MIN.**
Nick Stone .... Matt McColm
Kendrick .... John Savage
Sam .... Jennifer Rubin
West .... Michael Ironside
Billy Ryan .... Michael Covert
Winston "Mad Dog"
  Powell .... Real Andrews
Gregori .... George Touliatos

A routine actioner that covers familiar ground, "Red Scorpion 2" can expect a brief theatrical release in urban areas followed by a video career.

This is a sequel that doesn't aim high. Reworking the "Dirty Dozen" theme, it involves a disparate group of characters who are brought together by a government agency (headed by Michael Ironside) to stop the activities of a neo-fascist businessman (John Savage) who uses skinheads to do his dirty work against minority communities.

The good guys are led by Nick Stone (Matt McColm), who goes through the action motions without appearing to enjoy it very much. Supporting cast is your standard, ethnically mixed bunch, with Jennifer Rubin as the gal along for the ride. Savage leers his way through the film as the baddie.

The Vancouver-lensed feature contains almost non-stop fights, explosions, shootings and general mayhem, certainly enough to keep the action crowd moderately happy. Technical credits are all adequate. —*David Stratton*

NANOOK
(KABLOONAK)
(FRENCH-CANADIAN)

A UGC release of an Ima Films (Paris)/Bloom Films (Montreal) co-production, in association with Christian Bourgois Prods., France 3 Cinema, Telefilm Canada. (International sales: UGC Intl., Paris.) Produced by Georges Benayoun, Pierre Gendron, Paul Rozenberg. Executive producers, Angelo Pastore, Ginette Petit. Directed by Claude Massot. Screenplay, Massot, Sebastian Regnier. Camera (color), Jacques Loiseleux, Francois Protat; editor, Claire Pinheiro, Joelle Hache; music, Regnier; production design, Valodia Aronine, Gilles Aird; costumes, Anna Kubik. Reviewed at Cannes Film Festival (market), May 19, 1994. Running time: **105 MIN.**
Robert Flaherty .... Charles Dance
Nanook .... Adamie Quasiak Inukpuk
With: Georges Claisse, Matthew Saviakjuk-Jaw, Natar Ungalaq, Seporah Ungalaq.
(English and Inuit dialogue)

In what appears to have been a labor of love, director Charles Massot's film recreates the amazing expedition made by filmmaker Robert Flaherty to the Arctic in 1919-20, which resulted in the first significantly commercial feature documentary, "Nanook of the North" (1922). Handsome pic, with spectacular location shooting in Arctic Canada and Russia, will be a tough sell but could play the fest route to good results.

Charles Dance is well cast as the dogged Flaherty, who undertook the rugged and dangerous trip on commission from Revillon Freres, the fur company. It was perilous, not only because of the danger from polar bears, but also because of the treacherous ice on which the filmmaker and his team trekked for miles to get their footage. Complications — such as film freezing and breaking — are graphically shown.

But this is also about the friendship between Flaherty and his real-life hero, Nanook, the Inuit who agreed to hunt in the old way — with spear and knife rather than with rifle — for the camera, and who faced many dangers along the way.

There's little action in a conventional sense, yet the film exerts a spell, and the location footage is staggeringly beautiful. A scene in which Nanook approaches a huge walrus herd provides an amazing image.

May 30, 1994 (Cont.)

Massot doesn't delve into Flaherty's post-production on the film (the negative was burnt and much of it had to be reshot later), nor does he include any footage from the original "Nanook." Nevertheless, this is a remarkable achievement in many ways, and the natural performance of Adamie Quasiak Inukpuk, as the cheerful Nanook, is a joy to behold.

Pic is in English and Inuit, with English subtitles for the latter scenes. —*David Stratton*

HAPPY, TOO HAPPY

(TROP DE BONHEUR)

(FRENCH)

A Cine Classic release of a La Sept/Arte, IMA Prods., SFP Prods. co-production with the participation of Sony Music Entertainment (France). Produced by Georges Benayoun and Paul Rozenberg. Co-executive producers, Francoise Guglielmi, Elisabeth Deviosse. Directed by Cedric Kahn. Screenplay, Ismael Ferroukhi, Kahn; Camera (Fujicolor), Antoine Roch; editors, Yann Dedet, Nathalie Hubert; set design, Philippe Combastel; sound (mono), Stephane Thiebaut, Jean-Paul Loublier; associate producer, Chantal Poupaud; assistant director, Aude Cathelin; casting, Antoine Carrard. Reviewed at Cannes Film Festival (Cinemas en France), May 16, 1994. Running time: **84 MIN.**
Valerie .... Estelle Perron
Mathilde .... Caroline Trousselard
Kamel .... Malek Bechar
Didier .... Didier Borga
With: Naguime Bendidi, Salah Bouchouareb, Laetitia Palermo, Emmanuel Gautier.

"**H**appy, Too Happy," which explores the bittersweet high jinks of a coed group of hormone-addled high school classmates, is a well-made, convincingly acted slice of Gallic life that has virtually no prospects beyond French borders. Recipient of the 1994 Jean Vigo Prize is almost certain to appear rambling and pointless to offshore auds.

Pic began as an episode of 12-segment French miniseries "Tous les garcons et les filles de leur age," in which a dozen helmers conjure a tale from their adolescent years with the only requirement being a party scene with music in order to anchor the era in song.

(Olivier Assayas' "L'Eau froide" and Andre Techine's "Les Roseaux sauvages," at Cannes in Un Certain Regard, also figure in the series.)

In a dinky town in the sun-drenched Midi, popular, attractive Valerie has been expelled from high school just a few weeks before final exams. Her girlfriend Mathilde lusts after dopey blond Didier, whose good pal Kamel is stuck on Valerie. In the course of one alcohol-soaked evening, a romantic alliance is consummated that permanently alters the group dynamic.

Slangy, realistic dialogue is full of boast and banter about sex. Pic touches on anti-Arab discrimination via three characters who are the children of Algerian immigrants.

Pic has the sustained energy of kids goofing off on the cusp of adult responsibilities, and ensemble cast of newcomers is fine throughout.
—*Lisa Nesselson*

RENAISSANCE MAN

A Buena Vista release from Touchstone Pictures of an Andrew G. Vajna presentation of a Cinergi-Parkway production. Produced by Sara Colleton, Elliot Abbott, Robert Greenhut. Executive producers, Penny Marshall, Buzz Feitshans. Co-producers, Timothy M. Bourne, Amy Lemisch. Directed by Marshall. Screenplay, Jim Burnstein. Camera (Technicolor), Adam Greenberg; editors, George Bowers, Battle Davis; music, Hans Zimmer; production design, Geoffrey Kirkland; art direction, Richard Johnson; set design, Robert Fechtman; set decoration, Jennifer Williams; costume design, Betsy Heimann; sound (Dolby), Les Lazarowitz; assistant director, Sergio Mimica-Gezzan; casting, Paula Herold. Reviewed at the Mann Bruin Theatre, L.A., May 25, 1994. MPAA Rating: PG-13. Running time: **129 MIN.**
Bill Rago .... Danny DeVito
Sgt. Cass .... Gregory Hines
Capt. Murdoch ....James Remar
Col. James .... Cliff Robertson
Donnie Benitez .... Lillo Brancato Jr.
Miranda Myers .... Stacey Dash
Jamaal
 Montgomery .... Kadeem Hardison
Jackson Leroy .... Richard T. Jones
Roosevelt Hobbs ....Khalil Kain
Brian Davis .... Peter Simmons
Mel Melvin .... Greg Sporleder
Tommy Lee
 Haywood .... Mark Wahlberg

What looks like "Stripes" in its TV campaign actually has more in common with "Dead Poets Society" or even "To Sir With Love," featuring Danny DeVito as the reluctant teacher of eight dense-but-good-hearted Army recruits. As a result, this bittersweet comedy presents a real marketing challenge, one offering plenty of crowd-pleasing elements but also carrying enough fat to weigh down its box office prospects.

Actually, the movie Disney doubtless wants to emulate is "Sister Act," another star-driven, fish-out-of-water comedy that cruised to hit status during summer 1992.

Despite its appealing moments, however, the analogy doesn't quite hold. For one thing, pic runs more than two hours; director Penny Marshall risks overstaying her welcome, pursuing subplots relating to practically each of DeVito's charges, when one or two might have sufficed.

What the pic needed was a clearer focus, or a more ruthless hand in the editing room. As is, highlights are too often followed by lulls of inactivity or feel-good moments that cause the narrative to drag.

DeVito plays Bill Rago, an advertising executive who suddenly loses his job and is forced to take a temporary gig teaching a group of Army underachievers. The idea, not warmed to by the group's sergeant (Gregory Hines), is that having more smarts will make the group better soldiers.

Uncertain where to begin, Rago stumbles onto the idea of teaching the kids Shakespeare, gradually winning them over and becoming involved in their various hard-luck stories. As a civilian, the teacher also has little use for military discipline, providing some broad comedic strokes through his occasional skirmishes with Army brass.

Marshall showed how adept she can be at mixing comedy with poignant moments in "Big," and first-time writer Jim Burnstein's semi-autobiographical script hardly leaves a heart string unplucked or an Army joke unlaunched.

It's often a long trek between those moments, however, making the movie feel more like a stroll in the woods than a forced march. In short, Marshall has tried to do too much, dealing with certain subplots too sparingly to deliver on their promise.

If Rago is agonizing about going back to the advertising world, for example, the conflict isn't fully communicated to the audience. Similarly, a possible relationship with a female officer turns up as an afterthought, to the point where one wonders why it was introduced at all.

That said, DeVito is such an engaging character that "Renaissance Man" generates its share of laughs, and the filmmakers have done a terrific job casting the eight recruits with fresh faces who bring the film an inordinate amount of energy.

Lillo Brancato Jr. emerges as the principal scene-stealer, playing the Brooklyn-born Benitez, but Kadeem Hardison (from TV's "A Different World") is also a hoot, and rapper Mark Wahlberg (aka Marky Mark), making his movie debut, has the properly addled look of a good ol' country boy.

Richard T. Jones and Khalil Kain prove equally effective in more serious turns as a onetime football star and promising student whom Rago tries to take under his wing.

On the flip side, both Hines and James Remar seem miscast (their roles probably could have been flip-flopped) as the stern drill sergeant and overworked captain, failing to provide strong foils for DeVito.

Tech credits are solid, with a particularly strong and eclectic music score. Too bad other drawbacks prevent the pic, despite its various pleasures, from being all that it could be. —*Brian Lowry*

THE BEANS OF EGYPT, MAINE

Live Entertainment presents an American Playhouse Theatrical Films/ I.R.S. Media release. Produced by Rosilyn Heller. Executive producers, Lindsay Law, Miles Copeland III, Paul Colichman. Directed by Jennifer Warren. Screenplay, Bill Phillips, based on the novel by Carolyn Chute. Camera (Foto-Kem), Stevan Larner; editor, Paul Dixon; music, Peter Manning Robinson; production design, Rondi Tucker; costume design, Candace Clements; sound (Dolby), Mark Weingarten; line producer, Amanda DiGiulio; casting, Donald Paul Pemrick, Judi Rothfield, Katie Ryan. Reviewed at Cannes Film Festival (market), May 14, 1994. Running time: **97 MIN.**
Earlene Pomerleau .. Martha Plimpton
Roberta .... Kelly Lynch
Rueben Bean .... Rutger Hauer
Beal Bean .... Patrick McGaw
Mr. Pomerleau .... Richard Sanders

There's a colorful, almost archaic slice of America in which "The Beans of Egypt, Maine" resides; it's akin to "What's Eating Gilbert Grape," only starker and more physically frightening. Pic should appeal to a small, upscale domestic theatrical audience, but prospects beyond that seem dim: Despite its vivid nature, the film is neither relieved by star performers nor compromised by obvious, inappropriate violence or low humor.

The "Beans" of the title are an unsettling brood of loggers of the title outpost (population: 729).

Reuben (Rutger Hauer) is a drinker and brawler who runs afoul of the law and lands a long prison term. He leaves behind Roberta (Kelly Lynch), his companion and mother of a brood of nine. Also part of the extended family is Beal (Patrick McGaw), who becomes Roberta's sometime lover and possesses the famous Bean short fuse.

All this is observed by Earlene (Martha Plimpton), a neighbor under the thumb of a strict religious father. Her dad warns her against any contact, but, despite the Beans' crude ways, the young woman is drawn to them; their earthiness, directness and unity stand in sharp contrast to her oppressive family life.

The spirit of Carolyn Chute's anecdotal novel arrives onscreen with an understandable, even winning, awkwardness. Confusion is an apt byword for the proceedings, and Bill Phillips' screenplay captures the seesaw battle between repulsion and attraction to the characters cast amid a harsh environment.

The context provides Plimpton with a rich opportunity to transform from naif to haggard housewife. Her unique context provides the glue for this ramshackle yarn. Tyro director Jennifer Warren also fares well with the other players: Hauer, Lynch and especially McGaw as the proud, vain and doomed Beal offer rich portraits.

"The Beans of Egypt, Maine" is an effective, if limited-appeal, human drama. One senses the filmmakers' ambivalence toward the principals, but in this instance, that is precisely the right posture.

—*Leonard Klady*

CITY SLICKERS II: THE LEGEND OF CURLY'S GOLD

A Columbia Pictures release of a Castle Rock Entertainment/Face production. Produced by Billy Crystal. Executive producer, Peter Schindler. Directed by Paul Weiland. Screenplay by Crystal, Lowell Ganz, Babaloo Mandel, based on characters created by Ganz and Mandel. Camera (Technicolor; Panavision widescreen), Adrian Biddle; editor, William Anderson; music, Marc Shaiman; production design, Stephen Lineweaver; art direction, Philip Toolin; set design, Richard McKenzie, Nancy Patton; set decoration, Clay A. Griffith; sound (Dolby), Jeff Wexler, Don Coufal, Gary Holland; boss wrangler, Jack Lilley; assistant director, Bill Elvin; second unit director, Mickey Gilbert; second unit camera, Don McCuaig; casting, Naomi Yoelin, Amy Gerber. Reviewed at Sony Studios, Culver City, June 1, 1994. MPAA Rating: PG-13. Running time: 116 min.

Mitch Robbins	Billy Crystal
Phil Berquist	Daniel Stern
Glen Robbins	Jon Lovitz
Duke Washburn	Jack Palance
Barbara Robbins	Patricia Wettig
Bud	Pruitt Taylor Vince
Matt	Bill McKinney
Holly Robbins	Lindsay Crystal
Clay Stone	Noble Willingham
Ira Shalowitz	David Paymer
Barry Shalowitz	Josh Mostel

The gang that couldn't ride straight is back on the commercial trail in "City Slickers II: The Legend of Curly's Gold." The lively sequel to an original that grossed $123.8 million domestically is a sure-shootin' entertainment that shouldn't have much trouble rounding up an audience for the high jinks on the range. The handsome contempo oater is rife with both gags and classic genre lore and the combination is USDA B.O. prime.

Getting once-bitten urbanite Mitch Robbins (Billy Crystal) back in the saddle proves a bit of a sleight of hand for the scripters. He's running a Manhattan radio station and knee deep in tsoris because of his big heart. His hire of buddy Phil (Daniel Stern) in sales is pretty much a wash and when his low-life brother Glen (Jon Lovitz) insists on moving in with the family, wife Barbara (Patricia Wettig) envisions divorce court.

It's easy to see why he's always searching for the nearest exit. But in every door frame, at every window is the image of trail boss Curly (Jack Palance). Mitch is obsessed by the notion that he just may have buried the grisled cowboy a tad prematurely.

So, when he stands in the mirror adjusting Curly's Stetson, providence steps in. Tucked into the lining is a map indicating the way to buried gold. The lure of hidden treasure takes a big bite out of Phil and

when a search of records at the New York Public Library jibes with details on the blotter, an expedition is set in motion. Conveniently, the trail begins just spitting distance from Las Vegas, where Mitch was headed for a trade show.

From the start it's clear where "City Slickers II" is headed and one's willing acceptance of being prodded along forgives much of its initial narrative clunkiness. Crystal's appeal stems from an innate decency and that asset smooths over the sometimes schticky humor and the queasy encounters with Stern and Lovitz's characters.

The film truly transforms and comes alive once it heads into sagebrush territory. It hits full stride with the introduction of Duke (Jack Palance), Curly's twin brother. The long-separated sib had been dogging Mitch, so those haunting images were actually substantive.

The filmmakers nod appreciatively to "The Treasure of the Sierra Madre" and both movies share a fondness for parable and a keen sense of irony. But the "Slickers" sequel is less than obsessive in its lust for lucre. Friendship, family and the manly way are the bonds that comprise its more sober-sided nature. With the exception of some fuzzy attitudes about marriage, they are values tinged with the lachrymose.

At its heart the film is about Crystal's desire to be a cowboy. The pursuit is somewhat vain though thankfully non-oppressive. He simply cannot hide his glee when charging full out on horseback. It's masterfully captured in Adrian Biddle's camerawork, and director Paul Wieland is equally shrewd in framing the iconographic Palance with low-angle shots and tight close-ups. The contrast in every way works to the benefit of the story.

Crystal's character grounds the yarn in the real and humorous. He also reveals a penchant for clasping hands to face and screaming a la an overaged Macaulay Culkin. He's at the service of the material (which he co-wrote with Lowell Ganz and Babaloo Mandel) and generous to a fault with other performers. That proves a tad indulgent in regard to his "Slicker" pardners who, by dint of their screen characters, are meant to be obnoxious and cloying. But it's just fine in response to Palance, who won an Oscar for the 1991 original and can't help but catapult the movie into the mythic. His presence and consummate performing skill elevate and electrify the proceedings. Also worth a note is an uncredited turn by Bob Balaban as a radio shrink with a perfect deadpan delivery and attentiveness.

"City Slickers II" is a welcome sequel, much in the spirit of the original but keen to mosey into new

terrain. It's definitely the yee-hah! film of the season. —*Leonard Klady*

SPEED

A 20th Century Fox release of a Mark Gordon production. Produced by Gordon. Executive producer, Ian Bryce. Coproducer, Allison Lyon. Directed by Jan De Bont. Screenplay, Graham Yost. Camera (Deluxe color; Panavision widescreen), Andrzej Bartkowiak; editor, John Wright; music, Mark Mancina; production design, Jackson De Govia; art direction, John R. Jensen; set design, Louis Mann, Peter Romero, Stan Tropp; set decoration, K.C. Fox; costume design, Ellen Mirojnick; sound (Dolby), David R.B. MacMillan; second unit director, Alexander Witt; special visual effects, Sony Pictures Imageworks; stunt coordinator, Gary Hymes; assistant director, David Sardi; casting, Risa Bramon Garcia, Billy Hopkins. Reviewed at Village Theater, L.A., May 31, 1994. MPAA Rating: R. Running time: **115 MIN.**

Jack Traven	Keanu Reeves
Howard Payne	Dennis Hopper
Annie	Sandra Bullock
Capt. McMahon	Joe Morton
Harry	Jeff Daniels
Stephens	Alan Ruck
Jaguar Owner	Glenn Plummer
Norwood	Richard Lineback
Helen	Beth Grant
Sam	Hawthorne James
Ortiz	Carlos Carrasco
Terry	David Kriegel
Mrs. Kamino	Natsuko Ohama
Ray	Daniel Villarreal

Although it hits any number of gaping credibility potholes on its careening journey around Los Angeles, "Speed" still manages to deliver the goods as a non-stop actioner that scarcely pauses to take a breath. While highly derivative and mechanical in planning and execution, this high-octane thrillathon boasts more twists, turns and obstacles than the most hazardous video arcade road raceway, and provides the kind of mind-boggling stunts and staggering destruction that makes for strong domestic B.O. and even bigger returns overseas.

Drawing upon any number of previous perilous vehicle pix, including "Runaway Train," "The Taking of Pelham One Two Three" "Juggernaut" and the Japanese "Bullet Train" (not to mention the ill-fated "The Big Bus"), with quite a bit of Fox's own "Die Hard" thrown in for good measure, this rollercoaster ride across city streets and freeways carries with it a couple of commercial question marks. Most notably, the sheer manipulativeness and familiarity of the format could turn some viewers against it, and Keanu Reeves as a heroic leading man is an untested concept. But pic's straightforward success as a summer popcorn movie should keep it on a commercial tear for some time.

Story by debuting screenwriter Graham Yost actually offers three disaster pictures rolled into one: 23-minute curtain raiser, which resembles a "Die Hard" offshoot, features passengers in a highrise elevator being terrorized; 67-minute main action is set on board a bus that's rigged to blow up if it slows to under 50 miles-per-hour; and 25-minute climax features the film debut of L.A.'s new, still-under-construction subway. Whatever the means of transportation, Yost has written a stuntman's delight.

No time is wasted on exposition or character grounding, as pic opens with an obviously demented Howard Payne (Dennis Hopper) stabbing a security guard in the ear and imperiling a long-drop elevator with a powerful charge of dynamite. Demanding a large bundle of cash if the passengers are to be spared, the baddie is done in by the fearless aerialist maneuvers of L.A.P.D. SWAT daredevil Jack Traven (Keanu Reeves) and his partner Harry (Jeff Daniels). It appears that Payne is hoist on his own explosive petard.

Appearances are deceiving, however, as Payne is not dead. In fact he soon announces to his nemesis, Jack, that he's wired a Santa Monica bus so that, once it hits 50 on the freeway, it will blow sky high if its speed descends below that level. The implausibilities set in at once, as it would be interesting to learn of the last rush hour morning when traffic was light enough to allow for an unimpeded cruise at 50 from the beach to downtown.

If you can get by that one, things improve. With Jack on board the roaring vehicle, which is populated with the usual assortment of mixed humanity — a few blacks, a hot-headed Latino fearful of being arrested who shoots the driver, an annoying tourist, and so on — the police manage to guide the bus to an empty freeway so it can maintain its fast pace. Replacing the injured man behind the wheel is the feisty Annie (Sandra Bullock), who at least is qualified for the job since her license was recently revoked for speeding.

Under the fierce pressure, and with the help of Harry back at h.q., Jack keeps trying to figure out how to disarm the bomb, lowering himself under the bus in one particularly harrowing sequence to take a close look as the pavement practically scrapes his back. There are also any number of momentary emergencies to deal with, including disputes among the passengers and the death of one woman who disobeys Payne's order that no one leave the bus.

Film's hallmark stunt — which will have audiences everywhere oohing and aahing — has the huge bus building up a big head of steam so that it can bridge a 50-foot gap in a freeway overpass. From there, bus heads for the airport, where it's free to circle the runways until Jack and the other cops on the scene very cleverly figure out how to save the day.

But that's not all, as Payne is able to kidnap Annie and, rather implausibly, take her for a ride on the exceedingly short subway run, where he and Jack enact a final, fatal duel.

First-time helmer Jan De Bont, the ace lenser of most of Paul Verhoeven's films as well as "Die Hard" and numerous other large-scale pix, handles the action with great nimbleness and dexterity; film can hardly be faulted from the point of view of visual presentation of very complex action. All tech aspects, from stunts and special effects to editing and locations, are pro without seeming too heavy or needlessly expensive.

As the action hero, Reeves shows no more expressive range than he has in the past, but he is appealingly, and surprisingly, forceful and commanding in the sort of role he's never tackled before, and there's little doubt that this will bring him new audience identification and open up a new assortment of parts for him.

A prime disappointment, however, is Hopper, who has done this maniac routine before, but much more memorably, in "Blue Velvet" for example. For whatever reason, he brings no new wrinkles or nuances to this willfully evil character, which much more effectively might have been enacted by a veteran actor cast against type, a la Henry Fonda in "Once Upon a Time in the West," or by a relative unknown, such as Alan Rickman in "Die Hard." —*Todd McCarthy*

CANNES FEST

INTIMATE WITH A STRANGER

(BRITISH)

An Independent Intl. Pictures presentation of a Roderick Mangin-Turner production. (International sales: Pilgrim Entertainment, London.) Produced by Mangin-Turner. Directed by Mel Woods. Screenplay, Woods, Mangin-Turner. Camera (color), Nicholas Tebbet; editor, Brian Smedley-Aston; music, Ledsam & Pugh; production design, Graeme Story; sound (Dolby), Barry Reed; associate producer, Ed Harper; assistant director, Rupert Style. Reviewed at Cannes Film Festival (market), May 13, 1994. Running time: 93 MIN.

Jack Hamilton	. Roderick Mangin-Turner
Michelle	Daphne Nayar
Summer	Janis Lee
Carol	Amy Tolsky
Ellen	Lorelei King
Vicki	Ellenor Wilkinson
Barbara	Darcey Ferrer
Woman No. 1	Kaethe Cherney
Woman No. 2	Colleen Passard
Woman No. 3	Sara Mason
Woman No. 4	Francesca Wilde

"**A**merican Gigolo" bumps up against "sex, lies, and videotape" in "Intimate With a Stranger," a generally compelling relationships movie about a burned-out Santa Monica gigolo and his clients. With its strongly written, truthful female characters, this first feature by Brit helmer Mel Woods could attract a solid following among upscale urban women, given careful handling. Those expecting a grindfest will tune out early on.

Main character is Jack (producer/co-scripter Roderick Mangin-Turner), who looks like a beefy, long-haired biker but is actually a dropped-out college prof who's built a lucrative sack business servicing uptight femmes. In private, however, he's living life out of the bottom of a bottle, still scorched by former g.f. Michelle (Daphne Nayar). He now keeps his relationships with the opposite sex "strictly business."

Though Jack is technically the central character, the movie is a showcase for a string of terrific female thumbnails, ranging from a tough career type (Ellenor Wilkinson) who starts by giving Jack a hard time, through a teen virgin (Janis Lee) who wants to kick off her sex life in style, to a Jewish wife (Amy Tolsky) whose marriage is low on mattress activity.

After an opening that shows Jack cruising around Santa Monica on his bike, rest of the pic boils down to a series of one-to-one encounters in his small apartment, with each section prefaced by a straight-to-camera confessional by a woman whose hang-up echoes that of the next featured player. Though there's a definite legit feel to the movie, script is an original by Mangin-Turner and director Woods.

Opening session, between Jack and virgin Summer, sets the tone for subsequent segments, with the women getting the bulk of the dialogue as they work out their frustrations and needs and Jack gently coaxing from the sidelines. Though the dialogue's occasionally raw, sex content is relatively small, nudity discreet. Woods also has a habit of keeping the camera tight on the characters, with long shots reserved for later in an episode.

Running through the pic is the parallel story of Jack's new understanding with former g.f. Michelle, who pops by for talk sessions from time to time and provides a focus for his own struggle to carve out a real life. Happy ending, with Jack ditching his drinking habit and address book, is one of the few too-easy notes in a movie that mostly steers clear of the expected.

Performances by the women are strong down the line, headed by a wonderfully sad-comic and sexy perf by Tolsky as the bruised wife. Lee is also excellent in the tricky part of the California teen, and Wilkinson aces as the hardened career woman. Nayar brings a quiet sophistication to the part of Michelle, and the four unnamed, confessional-to-camera women hew sharply defined characters with economy and precision.

As Jack, Mangin-Turner both looks and sounds the part, despite being Brit to the core. But in solo scenes and more emotional sessions, he's less natural than his surrounding distaff players.

Tech credits are fine, with sharp lensing by Nicholas Tebbet and clean cutting by Brian Smedley-Aston. Only glitch is an uneven soundtrack, with over-intrusive background noise and occasional dropout in Mangin-Turner's lines. Interiors were all shot at the U.K.'s Shepperton Studios, and the posted $1.5 million budget, raised by Mangin-Turner and Woods from British and U.S. sources, is well spent. —*Derek Elley*

HOW TO BE MISERABLE AND ENJOY IT

(COMO SER INFELIZ DISFRUTARLO)

(SPANISH)

An Atrium production. (International sales: Iberoamericana Films). Produced by Enrique Cerezo, Carlos Vasallo. Executive producer, Andres Vicente Gomez. Directed by Enrique Urbizu. Screenplay, Carmen Rico-Godoy, Jose Luis Garcia Sanchez, based on the novel by Rico-Godoy. Camera (color), Angel Luis Fernandez; editor, Pablo Blanco; music, Bingen Mendizabal. Reviewed at Cannes Film Festival (market), May 16, 1994. Running time: **85 MIN.**
Carmen .... Carmen Maura
Antonio .... Antonio Resines
Marta .... Irene Bau
Romualdo .... Ramon Madaula

In this Spanish comedy, the fabulously gifted Carmen Maura plays a role similar to her hilarious turn in Pedro Alomodovar's "Women on the Verge of Nervous Breakdown." There may be an international audience for this commercial crowd-pleaser that could be exploited on the basis of Maura's popularity and congenial humor.

Premise is similar to that of the 1981 French pic "La Vie Continue," which was loosely remade in the U.S. as "Men Don't Leave." In all three films, a middle-aged woman, whose husband suddenly dies, struggles with her newfound widowhood before achieving a new identity.

Since the message of these comedic dramas — life must go on — is simple and familiar, the only amusing element for viewers to observe is the specific experiences and struggles of these women before they finally gain a new sense of independence and self-worth.

Amiable tale begins as the adulterous Carmen (Maura) gets home one morning after having spent the night playing poker and having fun with her male friends. Her jealous husband throws a tantrum, and soon afterward, is stricken with a fatal heart attack.

At first, Carmen feels emotional emptiness, loneliness, and disorientation. She also realizes that her new status signals availability in the eyes of her male boss and colleagues at the newspaper where she works. Things get more complicated when Carmen's teenage daughter, Marta (Irene Bau), who studies ballet in Paris, announces she is pregnant.

Like most Spanish comedies of the last decade, the encounters and humor revolve around the libido.

Most of the situations in "Miserable" are as funny as they are familiar, though overall pic lacks the outrageous wit, high style and camp that mark Alomodovar's best comedies.

Carmen experiences sexual harassment and a couple of dates with men who talk big about sex, but prove impotent. Finally, Carmen meets her new prince, a handsome businessman who treats her like a mature woman. It's one of the comedy's fresh touches that Carmen's anticipation of becoming a grandmother contributes to her autonomy much more than does her career.

It's also clear that without a truly charismatic actress, this slight, rather uneven movie could not exist: Maura's captivating performance is the glue that holds the episodic structure together.

A rare performer, Maura serves commanding notice whenever she's onscreen. Helmer Urbizu must have realized that, for Maura is in every scene. — *Emanuel Levy*

LOVE AND A .45

A Trimark release of a Darin Scott/Trimark production. Produced by Scott. Exec producers, Mark Amin, Andrew Hirsch. Co-producer, Jim Steele. Directed, written by C.M. Talkington. Camera (Foto-Kem color), Tom Richmond; editor, Bob Ducsay; music, Tom Verlaine; production design, Deborah Pastor; art direction, D. Montgomery; costume design, Kari Perkins; sound (Dolby), Bill Fiege; assistant director, Kris Krengel. Reviewed at Cannes Film Festival (market), May 14, 1994. Running time: **101 MIN.**
Watty Watts .... Gil Bellows
Starlene
  Cheatham .... Renee Zelwegger
Billy Mack Black .... Rory Cochrane
Dino Bob .... Jeffrey Combs
Creepy Cody .... Jace Alexander
Ranger X .... Michael Bowen
Justice Thurmar .... Jack Nance
Thaylene .... Anne Wedgeworth
Vergil .... Peter Fonda
Stipper .... Tammy Le Blanc
Young Clerk .... Wiley Wiggins

Jean-Luc Godard's dictum that "all you need to make a movie is a girl and a gun" is proven once again in "Love and a .45," a down 'n' dirty, white-trash Saturday night special with a number of things going for it. Trimark release would have done just fine as a wild and woolly, drive-in-oriented exploitationer back in the 1970s, but the revival of the outlaw-lovers-on-the-run format is getting tired fast, and whatever modest theatrical B.O. pic generates will be superseded by a longer life on video.

Debuting writer/director C.W. Talkington trots out the familiar formula of two attractive kids one step ahead of the law and other criminals while racing toward the Mexican border. At the same time, pic is very much a post-Tarantino creation, with some riffs and comedy-laced violence obviously inspired by "Reservoir Dogs."

Stick-up specialist Watty Watts (Gil Bellows) is a self-proclaimed "artist" at what he does, and tensely amusing opening sequence, in which he makes nice with a sweet kid at a convenience store he's holding up, carefully positions him as a good guy among bad guys.

Another story entirely is Billy Mack Black (Rory Cochrane), a sky-high, lunatic biker and sometime partner of Watty who loses his cool during a subsequent robbery and kills the checkout girl, who happens to be the sheriff's daughter. Watty finds himself forced to shoot Billy for his infraction, but he doesn't finish the job, so while two debt-collector goons chase Watty and his girlfriend, Starlene (Renee Zelweger), across Texas, Billy licks his wounds, waiting to get back at Watty.

Perhaps acknowledging that the desperate-young-lovers format is running out of gas, Talkington takes numerous detours into more scenic dramatic territory, some of them courtesy of Tarantino. Most notable is a sequence, both harrowing and funny, in which Billy is getting an elaborate tattoo etched onto his scalp when the goons walk in, push aside the artist and proceed to torture Billy by repeatedly plunging the tattoo needle into his noggin.

Even more bizarre is a homecoming wherein Watty and Starlene visit her parents, played by Anne Wedgeworth and Peter Fonda. Playing off his eternal 1960s hippie image, the latter is a gas as a perpetually giddy druggie who can speak only with an electronic voice amplifier and, in a classic moment, gifts the young couple with some vintage 1968 acid as if he were giving them a rare bottle of Lafite Rothschild.

Pic is striking for seeming to be not only about, but actually of, the sleazy criminal milieu it depicts. Dialogue is lively and performances mostly sharp, including Bellows as the philosophical small-time criminal and Jeffrey Combs and Jace Alexander as the maniacal hit men. Model Zelwegger is pretty much standard-issue leading lady for this sort of thing.

By far the highlight is Cochrane's crazed performance as the scumbag Billy. Cochrane, who was great as the skinny stoned kid in "Dazed and Confused," has Billy bouncing off the walls even when he's not indoors or tripping, and is endlessly inventive in portraying varying states of paranoia, rage, treachery, delirium and insanity. It's a totally wild, hilarious and convincing characterization.

What holds the film back, however, in addition to its less than compelling schema and central relationship, is its utter lack of visual style. At a time when most pictures feature form almost at the expense of content, this one has an utterly undesigned look that's virtually distinctive in its blandness.

Climax, which also reflects the influence of Tarantino by way of Hong Kong actioners, is rather blah. — *Todd McCarthy*

JONATHAN OF THE BEARS

(ITALIAN-RUSSIAN)

A Viva Cinematografica/Project Campo production, in association with Silvio Berlusconi Communications. (International sales: Overseas Filmgroup, L.A.) Produced by Vittorio Noia, Franco Nero, Alexander Skodo. Executive producers, Cesare Noia, Gabriel Sefarian. Directed by Enzo G. Castellari. Screenplay, Castellari, Lorenzo De Luca; story by Nero, De Luca. Camera (color), Mikhail Agranovich; editor, Alberto Moriano; music, Clive Riche, Alexander Biliaev, Fabio Constantini; original Indian music, Knifewing Segura; art direction, Marxen Gaukman Sverdlov, Marco Dentici; costume design, Paola Nazzaro; sound, Dolby; associate producers, Laura Mazza, Michael Branstetter. Reviewed at Cannes Film Festival (market), May 18, 1994. Running time: **100 MIN.**
Jonathan .... Franco Nero
Chatow .... Knifewing Segura
Chief .... Floyd "Red Crow" Westerman
Fred Goodwin .... John Saxon
Shaya .... Melody Robertson
Maddock .... David Hess
Williamson .... Bobby Rhodes
Musician .... Clive Riche
(English dialogue)

Dubbing itself the first "borscht Western," "Jonathan of the Bears" is a lively Franco Nero genre pic, shot entirely in Russia. A mixed Italian, Russian and U.S. cast and crew blend smoothly in a tale about a loner who takes on a town of evildoers in defense of the Indians who raised him. Pic could do some theatrical biz before passing to TV and video.

Action helmer Enzo G. Castellari ("The Great White") got this cherished project off the ground in the wake of recent hits like "Dances with Wolves" and "The Last of the Mohicans." However, for all its Native American slant, "Jonathan" feels much more like a descendant of the glorious Sergio Leone horse operas, though sans their technical innovations.

Story is told in flashbacks that shuttle back-and-forth from Jonathan's childhood to maturity. After witnessing the cold-blooded murder of his parents by three white robbers, six-year-old Jonathan is befriended first by a playful bear cub, then by a wise Indian chief (Floyd "Red Crow" Westerman).

The chief prefers the blond towhead to his own son, Chatow, and a rivalry develops between the boys. Later in life, grown-up Jonathan (Nero) and Chatow (Knifewing Segura) are still at odds when the chief is laid out in the sacred burial ground.

After years of hunting his parents' killers, revenge has left Jonathan empty. His archery skills and rescues of the weak and oppressed (Indian women, wounded bears), have made him a legend.

Lead by the ruthless Fred Goodwin (John Saxon), a pack of oil-hungry killers descends on a western town. When Goodwin notices black gold bubbling out of the Indian burial ground, he touches off a war consummated in one long action sequence of falling horses and flying arrows.

Following the captured Indian beauty Shaya (an unlikely Melody Robertson) into town, Jonathan is taken prisoner. The godless Goodwin has him "crucified" on the church tower, leaving him to die.

Saved by a remorseful black killer (Bobby Rhodes), Jonathan proceeds to mow down the town's remaining male population in a long, drawn-out stalking sequence.

Though hordes of people die in "Jonathan," Castellari prefers action-packed shootouts to bloody realism. His obvious fondness for the Old West shows in the detailed sets (built on an army base outside Moscow) and lovingly incorporated Indian lore.

Mikhail Agranovich's lensing captures an outdoor sense of stormy skies, forests, rivers and plains — even if there are a suspicious number of Russian birch trees around.

Nero makes a dashing, soulful lone wolf. Though he looks a little overage to be blood-brother to the handsome Segura, thesp has an innate class that saves him from ridicule in many awkward situations, like killing a trapper to save a bear, or hanging on a cross.

Saxon is self-assured as the gentleman-villain. The Indian tribe has a curious Eskimo look, with the exception of the fine Westerman and Segura, both Native Americans, and the attractive but mute Robertson as Jonathan's love interest.
—*Deborah Young*

BANDIT QUEEN

(INDIAN-BRITISH)

A Kaleidoscope production for Channel 4. (International sales: Channel 4, London.) Produced by Sundeep Singh Bedi. Directed by Shekhar Kapur. Screenplay, Mala Sen. Camera (color), Ashok Mehta; additional camera, Giles Nutgens; editor, Renu Saluja; music, Nusrat Fateh Ali Khan; additional music, Roger White; production design, Eve Mavrakis; art direction, Ashok Bhagat; costume design, Dolly Ahluwalia; sound (Dolby), Robert Taylor, Tim Lewiston, Ernest Marsh; associate producer, Varsha Bedi; assistant director, Mike Higgins. Reviewed at Mr. Young's preview theater, London, April 29, 1994. (In Cannes Film Festival (Directors Fortnight). Running time: **121 MIN.**

Phoolan Devi	Seema Biswas
Vikram Mallah	Nirmal Pandey
Man Singh	Manoj Bajpai
Mustaquim	Rajesh Vivek
SriRam	Govind Namdeo
Kailash	Saurabh Shukla
Madho	Raghuvir Yadav

(Hindi dialogue)

True story of a femme bandit who eluded the Indian authorities for five years makes initially leisurely but finally gripping viewing in "Bandit Queen," a slow starter that reserves its biggest punches for the end. This often visually striking movie could have limited theatrical legs beyond the fest circuit, but would stand better commercial chances with the first half back on the editing bench.

Phoolan Devi finally surrendered to the police in the northern state of Uttar Pradesh in January 1983, accused of murder and kidnapping. Pic is based on the dictated prison diaries of the woman herself who, after a change of government, was finally released in February this year to local superstar status.

A long, 15-minute pre-credit sequence opens in 1968, with Devi a feisty young girl burdened by her low-caste background but not prepared to accept a standard rural existence. Married off, she submits to her husband's sexual demands but finally leaves the village in search of an independent life.

Post-main title, she's an assured young woman (Seema Biswas) living with relatives but the target of insults from local studs. One day, she comes across handsome young local bandit Vikram (Nirmal Pandey), and a spark flies.

Later, while back with her parents, she's kidnapped by a bandit gang of which Vikram is a member. When the sleazoid gang head publicly rapes her, Vikram kills him, takes over, and makes her a full-fledged member too.

Things get complicated when the real gang henchman, SriRam (Govind Namdeo), is released from prison and re-assumes leadership.

When Vikram is mysteriously shot in the leg one day, Devi nurses him in the big city, and the two subsequently engage in a growing spiral of violence, starting with her publicly rifle-butting her former husband to death.

It's here, some 75 minutes in, that the pic finally starts to grab the attention, with Vikram declaring her a real bandit at last ("Kill one and they'll hang you. Kill 20, and you're famous") prior to his sudden death at the hands of SriRam.

The dramatic screws tighten with a shocking sequence — all the more powerful for its visual discretion — of Devi gang-raped by SriRam's men and then stripped naked in front of the villagers. Her subsequent revenge, dubbed the Behmai Massacre of February '81, forms the dramatic climax of the pic.

For Western auds unacquainted with either the true story or the intricacies of India's caste system (blamed for all of Devi's actions), the movie's early reels assume too much prior knowledge to exert true dramatic pull. The disarray of the authorities and the woman's growing celebrity among the masses are also thinly sketched, with the movie almost entirely set among the bandit world.

Comprehension isn't helped by sometimes choppy editing in the early going, and helmer Shekhar Kapur's habit (striking in the latter stages but confusing earlier on) of dispensing with intros when moving to a new sequence. Effect is like joining a conversation halfway through and having to piece together what's going on. Date and place captions also seem randomly rather than systematically employed.

Still, once the story moves into high gear, Kapur brings out his big guns to often stunning effect. The gang-rape, set to the sight and sound of a creaking barn door as each male enters, has a shocking casualness. And the final massacre, shot almost entirely from high angles, is paced and staged almost like a western shootout.

Though at times the pic wears its right-on western political credentials too obviously on its sleeve, Kapur keeps pulling the stylistic rug out from beneath the viewer's feet by refs to commercial Hindi productions (notably in the "Bollywood"-style treatment of the Vikram-Phoolan Devi romance) and raw, four-letter expletives issuing from the mouth of the heroine. Scene of Devi stripped naked is a jaw-dropper in Indian cinema terms.

Biswas is terrific in the title role, moving from tough to tender with natural ease. Pandey makes a handsome, sensitive partner, and Namdeo a true villain.

Production values are high, with colorful, crisp location lensing by Ashok Mehta rating a special bouquet.
—*Derek Elley*

TRAPS

(AUSTRALIAN)

A Ronin Films (Australia) release of an Ayer Prods. film, in association with the Australian Film Finance Corp, with the assistance of the Australian Film Commission, Film Queensland. Produced by Jim McElroy. Directed by Pauline Chan. Screenplay, Chan, Robert Carter, based on characters in the book "Dreamhouse" by Kate Grenville. Camera (color), Kevin Hayward; editor, Nicholas Beauman; music, Douglas Stephen Rae; production design, Michael Phillips; costumes, Davie Rowe; sound, John Shiefelbein; line producer, Tim Sanders; assistant director, Chris Short; casting, Alison Barrett. Reviewed at Greater Union screening room, Sydney, Nov. 30, 1993. (In Cannes Film Festival (Market). Running time: **95 MIN.**

Louise Duffield	Saskia Reeves
Michael Duffield	Robert Reynolds
Daniel	Sami Frey
Viola	Jacqueline McKenzie
Tuan	Kiet Lam
Tatie-Chi	Hoa To
Capt. Brochard	Thierry Marquet

Vietnamese-born Pauline Chan, already known on the fest circuit for her short films (especially "The Face Between the Door and the Floor"), has come up with a solid feature debut in "Traps," an interesting, suspenseful pic which takes four intriguing characters and places them in an exotic and dangerous setting: French Indochina (later Vietnam) in 1950. Strong performances from a good cast should earn this quality Australian production critical kudos.

This was a very tricky project to bring off, since the book on which the film is loosely based, Kate Grenville's "Dreamhouse," is not set in Vietnam but in Italy; the drastic shift in locale probably explains some of the oddities in the narrative, notably why an Australian journalist has been assigned to write a favorable piece about life on a French-owned rubber plantation in Southeast Asia (why not a French journalist, since everything written has to be translated into French?)

But these doubts are eventually cast aside, partly because Chan makes her characters so interesting and partly because she seizes the opportunity of filming on location in her homeland to create an intimate and chilling depiction of the beginning of the Communist insurrection that eventually led to the Vietnam War.

The journalist, Michael Duffield (newcomer Robert Reynolds) and his English photographer wife,

June 6, 1994 (Cont.)

Louise (Saskia Reeves), arrive at the plantation managed by a Frenchman, Daniel (Sami Frey) and meet the man's intense and rather strange daughter, Viola (Jacqueline McKenzie). In essence, "Traps" is a four-hander in which the emotions and passions of these characters are placed under the microscope, though the mounting tension of the increasingly militant Viet-Minh rebels, some of whom are employed at the plantation, is a major additional factor in the drama.

It soon becomes obvious that something is wrong with the marriage; Louise and Michael don't have much to say to each other, and Louise often seems distracted. But they do have a healthy sexual relationship, except when Michael becomes unexpectedly violent (in reasonably graphic scenes). Nor does everything seem quite as it should be between Daniel and his daughter. He's arrogant and manipulative, a man of the world who, the film suggests, might have been on intimate terms with the girl, who apparently takes after her mother, whose absence remains unexplained.

The women pair off when Louise befriends the very unsophisticated Viola, even suggesting she return with her to London when the visit comes to an end. But she's shocked by Viola's sluttish behavior toward French soldiers who pick up both women when they're stranded after a tire blow-out in the jungle. The suspenseful climax has the women captured by the Communists and facing what they expect to be imminent death.

Chan pulls the various strands of the film together with skill; "Traps" is a very well-made film, though it lacks the dazzling style of the director's shorts.

Performances are solid, with Jacqueline McKenzie stealing the pic as the sulky, rebellious Viola. Saskia Reeves vividly portrays the unhappy Louise, Robert Reynolds is well cast as the somewhat bland Michael, and Sami Frey brings an edge to his role as the devious Daniel.

"Traps" was filmed on location in Vietnam and in far North Queensland, but looks seamlessly convincing as far as locale and period are concerned. All tech credits are excellent, especially Kevin Hayward's fine photography.

—David Stratton

EROTIQUE

(GERMAN-U.S.)

A Beyond Films presentation of a Brandon Chase production in association with Group 1/Trigon/Tedpoly Films. Reviewed at Cannes Film Festival (market), May 14, 1994. Running time: **93 MIN.**

LET'S TALK ABOUT LOVE
Produced by Christopher Wood, Vicky Herman. Executive producer, Marianne Chase. Directed by Lizzie Borden. Screenplay, Borden, Susie Bright, based on a story by Borden. Camera (color), Larry Banks; editor, Richard Fields; music, Andrew Belling; production design, Jane Ann Stewart; costume design, Jolie Jimenez; sound (Dolby), James Thornton; assistant director, Betsy Pollock; casting, Jerold Franks.
Rosie .... Kamala Lopez-Dawson
Dr. Robert Stern .... Bryan Cranston
Murohy .... Liane Curtis

TABOO PARLOR
Produced by Monika Treut, Michael Sombetzki. Directed, written by Treut. Camera (color), Elfi Mikesch; editor, Steve Brown; production design, Petra Korink; costume design, Susann Klindtwordt; sound (Dolby), Wolfgang Schukrafft; assistant director, Margit Czenki.
Claire .... Priscilla Barnes
Jukia .... Camilla Soeberg
Victor .... Michael Carr
Franz .... Peter Kern
Hilde .... Marianne Sagebrecht

WONTON SOUP
Produced by Teddy Robin Kwan, Eddie Ling-Ching Fong. Directed by Clara Law. Screenplay, Fong. Camera (color), Arthur Wong; editor, Jill Bilcock; music, Tats Lau; production design, Eddie Mok; sound (Dolby), Gary Wilkins; assistant directors, Choi Kwok-Fai, Shek Sui-Lun; casting, Jerold Franks.
Adrian ....Tim Lounibos
Ann .... Hayley Man
Uncle .... Choi Hark-kin

The problems confronting omnibus productions are readily apparent in "Erotique." The trio of female-leaning "sexy" tales suffers from episodes that vary in quality from good to bad to ugly. But even the good isn't enough to carry the weaker components and, finally, all the film has to sell is a novel concept. Mildly titillating, rather than shocking or controversial, it will initially disappoint with its come-on and ultimately disappoint at the box office. It's specialized fare with limited appeal, with best prospects down the road on homevideo.

The initial idea was to give four distaff helmers from different continents the chance to create a modern, female erotic tale (an episode in Brazil was shot but is not included in the completed film). But the carte blanche invitation has failed to stimulate the trio's creative juices. The vignettes can be respectively categorized as not fully conceived, embarrassing and just OK.

First up is Lizzie Borden's "Let's Talk About Love," which centers on Rosie (Kamala Lopez-Dawson), who works a phone sex line. One particular regular sparks her interest with his slightly upscale erotic fantasies. Chief interest in Borden's story is the constant shifting of dominance between the phoner and the phonee. Eventually Rosie uncovers that the caller is a sex therapist (Bryan Cranston) and she sets out, with the help of a friend, to exact the ultimate humiliation on him. Though the setup is intriguing, the confrontation deflates all that has proceeded it.

In Monica Treut's "Taboo Parlor," a lesbian couple (Priscilla Barnes, Camilla Soeberg) plan a night on the town that will culminate in their having their way with a man. They arrive at the club referred to in seg's title, which is run by Peter Kern and in which Marianne Sagebrecht is a sort of social director. The activities of latter actress are more amusing in theory than the rather banal entertainment exacted onscreen.

As with the first section, "Taboo" is rather a single-joke premise. While neither narrator particularly knows how to tell the story, the Treut encounter sags long before the punch line.

The finale takes viewers to Hong Kong for Clara Law's "Wonton Soup." Unlike its sister chapters, the episode doesn't attempt to spin a sexual or sensual yarn. It centers on an Australian-born Chinese man (Tim Lounibos) and his H.K. girlfriend (Hayley Man) in the throes of attempting to bridge cultural friction in the British colony.

Dramatically, it is the most ambitious and textured of the trio. It also has a sweetness that's in sharp contrast to the others. "Erotique" is just the latest in a long line of failed omnibus pix grappling with sexual themes. The prospect of handing an open ticket to filmmakers to let their erotic imaginations go wild onscreen has historically produced a series of cinematic fiascoes. The latest exercise is no exception — an interesting curio for the record books unable to rise to the occasion.

—Leonard Klady

BLUE TIGER

A First Look Pictures release of a Neo Motion Pictures/Ozla Pictures production. Produced by Michael Leahy, Aki Komine. Executive producers, Joel Soisson, W.K. Border, Don Phillips, Taka Ichise. Directed by Norberto Barba. Screenplay, Soisson, story by Ichise. Camera (color), Christopher Walling; editor, Caroline Ross; production design, Markus Canter; set decoration, Anthony Stabley; costume design, Kathryn Shemanek; sound, Larry Scharf; tattoo artist, Michael Bacon; stunt coordinator, Dan Bradley; associate producer, Alicja E. Oleszczuk; assistant director, Michael Cedar; casting, Don Phillips. Reviewed at Cannes Film Festival (Market), May 14, 1994. Running time: **87 MIN.**
Gena Hayes .... Virginia Madsen
Seiji .... Toru Nakamura
Henry Soames .... Dean Hallo
Gan .... Ryo Ishibashi
Luis .... Sal Lopez
Lt. Sakagami .... Yuji Okumoto
Smith .... Harry Dean Stanton
Darin Hayes .... Henry Mortensen

Packed with classy production values and performances that range from first-rate to standard action-pic dramatics, "Blue Tiger" comes tantalizingly close to being a gem among the Cannes market revenge-thriller rubble.

Pic is distinguished by real care to the lensing and main story, which positions Virginia Madsen and Toru Nakamura as doomed lovers, a la "Duel in the Sun," caught in the crossfire of a mob battle for control of a Southern California business operation.

Far from standard in most categories — some strictly B-movie bad guys vs. good guys and pointless mayhem keep threatening to derail pic's core pleasures — this could break out into a surprise crime hit.

Though it never quite overcomes those drawbacks, "Tiger" proves Madsen's acting skills, which are usually lost in this kind of fare, and announces a first-rate directing talent in first-timer Norberto Barba and a real find in charismatic Japanese star Nakamura.

When Madsen loses her son in a bloody Yakuza hit, the all-American mother slowly disintegrates into madness. Her recovery is spurred by the memory of one detail that distinguished her son's killer — an elaborate tattoo of a blue tiger.

Tattoo artist Harry Dean Stanton, a chain-smoking aesthete hooked up to an oxygen tank, cannot provide the name of the killer, but he does offer clues, prompting Madsen to submit to the needle and take up work in a cocktail bar frequented by Japanese mobsters, flaunting her tattoo in hopes of flushing out the killer.

She succeeds in finding the killer's brother, Ryo Ishibashi, but little does she know that the real villain is the

June 6, 1994 (Cont.)

sexy, sensitive Nakamura, who is torn between his Yakuza duties and his soul's desire to escape, perhaps even to find love.

This leads to the fated coupling with Madsen, but not before all hell breaks loose in L.A., with shootouts, bombings, knifings and assorted knee-in-the-groin theatrics.

As long as Madsen and Nakamura are circling each other, drawn in by sexual chemistry and palpable doom, "Tiger" is fun, even riveting fare. But less effective is the Yakuza gang war. Director Barba seems aware of the genre's limitations and does his best to dispose of the less interesting nonsense in order to focus on the nonsense that actually works.

"Tiger" is in the hallowed tradition of B movies that sport more intelligence and craft than the production calls for; perhaps its reward will come, as Nakamura philosophizes, "in the next life," when Barba, Madsen and Nakamura get their hands on material equal to their abilities.

Outstanding cinematography by Christopher Walling should draw attention, and Stanton once again makes something special out of a secondary character with only a few scenes. Buffs will also appreciate Madsen's brother Michael in a cameo as a gun dealer who supplies sis with a weapon — and the film's sharpest line — a .45 that he touts as "the school kids' favorite gun."

—*Steven Gaydos*

THE VIOLIN PLAYER

(LE JOUER DE VIOLON)

(BELGIAN-FRENCH-GERMAN)

A Hachette Premiere et cie production. Produced by Rene Cleitman. Directed by Charlie Van Damme. Screenplay, Jean-Francois Goyet, Van Damme, based the novel "Musikant," by Andre Hodier. Additional dialogue, Francois Dupeyron. Camera (color), Walter Vanden Ende; editor, Emmanuelle Castro; music, Vladimir Mendelssohn; set design, Carlos Conti, Jacques Mollon; costume design, Brigitte Faur-Perdigou; sound (Dolby), William Flageollet, Gerard Rousseau; casting, Jeanne Biras. Reviewed at Cannes Film Festival (competing), May 22, 1994. Running time: **96 MIN.**
Armand .... Richard Berry
Charles .... Francois Berleand
Lydia .... Ines De Medeiros
Ariane .... Geno Lechner
Daraud .... John Dobrynine

Accomplished Belgian cinematographer Charlie Van Damme, who lensed some Alain Resnais and Agnes Varda films, makes his feature directorial debut with "The Violin Player," a pretentious movie that mythologizes "true" musicians as a special species, able to reach out and transform the masses through art.

This laboriously ponderous pic, which exhibits all the cliches of a European art film, may delight users of the Paris metro, where the narrative is set, and of perhaps a few other Continental undergrounds, but it's not likely to excite American passengers.

Tale starts when Armand (Richard Berry), a dark-haired, severelooking classical violinist, decides to parachute out of the orchestra circuit, leaving behind a most promising career. Cutting himself off completely from his chic music milieu, he begins to live a meager existence in the Paris metro, absorbed by the mysterious life there that's created by its random aggregate of passengers and the resident beggars and tramps.

Narrative stretches place over a yearlong period, with time marked by the metro's changing seasons. There, in the "lower depth," Armand befriends Lydia (Ines de Medeiros), a charming employee who becomes intrigued with his conduct. Lydia is contrasted with Ariane (Geno Lechner), a singer who early on reproaches Armand for being too demanding and harsh on himself.

Regrettably, the script offers only vague reasons why Armand forsakes his brilliant career. This is done through a series of flashbacks to his friendship with another genius musician who committed suicide while experiencing a personal and professional crisis. Most of "The Violin Player," however, focuses on Armand's newly gained consciousness and determination to make his gifts accessible to the masses. In its unabashedly populist message, pic aspires to show how the magic of music can touch people in a transcendental, quasi-religious fashion.

Sporting the same cliches of other French pix about artists, most recently "Un Coeur en hiver" and "Tous les Matins du monde," film posits creativity as a solitary phenomenon and "true" artists as tormented souls — as if agony and grief are prerequisites for producing great art.

"The Violin Player" depicts at length Armand's elan while playing to the public, fulfilling his goal of challenging such modern urban maladies as loneliness and indifference. It also draws a distinction between audiences who passively listen to music and those rapturously embracing it.

In the film's most embarrassing sequence, the effect of Armand's music is chronicled through reaction shots of his entranced audience — a young couple become so aroused they leave the metro, a beggar suddenly feels an urge to share his one slice of bread with another miserable fellow, a woman begins to move in an expressive manner.

Reportedly, it took two years and a long uphill battle to finance this co-production, whose visual sheen is far more impressive than its symbolically pregnant narrative. On the

plus side, virtuoso violinist Gideon Kremer, who is credited as technical adviser, performs a radiant version of Johann-Sebastian Bach's "The Chaconne." Use of classical music (by Ysaye, Beethoven) somehow helps to make this stale and unexciting film a bit more tolerable.

—*Emanuel Levy*

THE SHIPWRECKED

(LOS NAUFRAGOS)

(CHILEAN)

A Cine Chile presentation of an ACI Communicaciones/Prods. D'Amerique Francaise/Arion production. Produced by Yvon Provost, Ely Menz. Executive producer, Carlos Alvarez. Directed, written by Miguel Littin. Camera (color), Hans Burmann; editor, Rodolfo Wedeles; music, Jorge Arriagada, Angel Parra, Daniel A. Vermette; production design, Carlos Garrido; assistant director, Christina Littin. Reviewed at Cannes Film Festival (Un Certain Regard), May 14, 1994. Running time: **120 MIN.**
Aron .... Marcelo Romo
Isol .... Valentina Vargas
Sebastian Mola .... Luis Alarcon
Ur .... Bastian Bodenhofer
Rene .... Tennyson Ferrada

Miguel Littin's new political film, "The Shipwrecked," is an ambitious, though ultimately disappointing drama about the pervasive impact of Chile's 1970s military dictatorship on its present-day society. A complex narrative structure, switching back and forth between past and present, along with an often tedious philosophical narration, result in a disjointed film that will intrigue viewers interested in Latin American cinema, but holds little commercial promise for other audiences.

Set in the present, tale begins when Aron (Marcelo Romo), a sensitive middle-aged man, returns home after a two-decade exile in Europe. His journey takes the form of a painful soul-searching, motivated by his deeply felt need to better understand himself, his family, and his country. The psychological journey is framed as a mystery, as Aron tries to unveil the murder of his father and the disappearance of his brother (Bastian Bodenhofer).

To his dismay, Aron discovers that Chile's devastating political events have not only destroyed his family's unity and the personal happiness of its individual members, but have also left an open sore in the country's collective state of mind. It turns out that nobody is excited to see him, including his mother, who's on the verge of severe mental breakdown and hardly recognizes him.

Pic unfolds as a series of encounters, most of which end in a failure to communicate or to bridge past lives with the present. Among the

more touching meetings are a touching one with Isol (Valentina Vargas), the woman who never stopped loving him, and a confrontation with Mola (Luis Alarcon), the brutally corrupt police officer — and family's ideological enemy — who was in charge of many murders.

Writer/director Littin evokes a tragic, often poetic, mood through a multi-layered maze of crucial childhood memories and painful nightmares, all indicating Chile's broken spirits and fragmented history. Chief problem is the tale's excessively multifarious structure, which precludes direct emotional involvement. There is too much narration, too many existential observations, too many biblical allegories, and too many cuts from present to past.

Slow and rather static pacing doesn't help either, though special kudos go to stylized lensing of Hans Burmann, whose nuanced lighting effectively captures the changing tone of the story. In the lead role, Romo's commanding presence and resounding elocution manages to overcome pic's segmental structure.

Though historical footage and flashbacks are used, "The Shipwrecked" doesn't succeed in conveying Chile's political context in the 1970s; vague generalities in the dialogue refer to the past as "chaos and confusion." However, pic works better as an inner psychological exploration, stressing the need of every citizen to achieve continuity with the past on both personal and collective levels, even if the road is turbulent and painful.

—*Emanuel Levy*

CARLO & ESTER

(DANISH)

An Asa Film/Nordisk Film/Rysraes production, with the participation of the Danish Film Institute. (International sales: Nordisk Film.) Produced by Henrik Moller-Sorensen. Directed by Helle Ryslinge. Screenplay, Ryslinge, Sven Omann. Camera (color), Jacob Banke Olesen; editor, Birger Moller Jensen; music, Anders Koppela. Reviewed at Cannes Film Festival (Market), May 14, 1994. Running time: **107 MIN.**
Ester .... Gerda Gilboe
Carlo .... Aksel Rasmussen
Viola .... Birgitte Federspiel
Kamma .... Erni Arneson
Mrs. Nielsen .... Ruth Maisie
Ricard .... Ingolf David
Peter .... Waage Sando
Hanne .... Helle Ryslinge

A film about an elderly couple's love affair doesn't exactly break new ground, but director Helle Ryslinge adds a few fresh elements to the theme in "Carlo & Ester," a generally touching romance that, with

June 6, 1994 (Cont.)

some trimming, could find a modest art-cinema niche.

Ryslinge (whose earlier work includes "Coeurs Flambes" and the Venice prize winner "Sirup") doesn't shrink from the sexual aspect of a love story between 80-year-olds and includes a couple of chaste nude scenes that may be appealing, or troubling, according to taste. She and her fine actors handle these scenes with delicacy.

Carlo (Aksel Rasmussen), a healthy former bricklayer and motor-bike racing champ, lives in a retirement home with his sick wife, Viola, who's suffering from Alzheimer's disease and can't relate to the real world at all. At a funeral, he meets Ester (Gerda Gilboe), widow of a greengrocer, who lives alone in a small apartment.

Romance blossoms, to the horror of their respective children and friends, and eventually the two start spending nights together, with Ester fully accepting that Carlo spends as much time as possible with his wife.

Some of Ryslinge's themes are fairly obvious (that the children of elderly people act like disapproving parents themselves in this kind of situation), and she could certainly reduce the running time since some scenes drag on after they're finished.

But the fine cast, starting with topliners Gilboe and Rasmussen, is uniformly excellent, and the problems facing old people in the '90s are vividly presented. Supporting characters, including Ruth Maisie as a nosy neighbor and Erni Arneson as Ester's best friend, are beautifully scripted and played.

As with most Danish films, production values are excellent. Ryslinge herself appears as Carlo's alcoholic daughter-in-law. *—David Stratton*

FEMME FONTAINE: KILLER BABE FOR THE C.I.A.

A Troma Team release of a Hope Prods./Uniqueness Co. production. (International sales: Troma, N.Y.) Produced, directed, written by Margot Hope. Executive producers, Nancy Hope, Chi-sun Chu. Line producer, Mark Hope. Camera (color), Gary Graver; editor, Graver; additional editing, Larry Maddox; music, Gardner Cole; production design, Cory Arzoumanian; sound, Ultra-Stereo; associate producer, David S. Fralick; assistant director, Richard Gabai. Reviewed at Cannes Film Festival (market), May 13, 1994. Running time: **98 MIN.**
Drew Fontaine .... Margot Hope
Master Sun .... James Hong
Mercedes Lee .... Catherine Dao
Also with: David Shark, Arthur Roberts, Harry Mok, Kevin Fry.

The tease factor runs high in "Femme Fontaine: Killer Babe for the C.I.A.," a Troma

pickup that gives new meaning to the phrase tongue-in-cheek. Showcase for the well-packaged talents of Margot Hope, who also directed, wrote and produced, is a passable time-waster for the freeze-frame crowd.

Plot of sorts has Hope as an agency assassin who's more concerned with tracing her missing father, a spy who disappeared in South America in 1986. Trail leads her to an L.A. porno producer who's laundering money for a Chinatown gangster (Catherine Dao) and then, via her tai chi master (James Hong), to a neo-Nazi org fomenting Aryan supremacy on the streets of California.

Hope, who's stronger on wardrobe than athletic ability, keeps the stew of soft-core t&a and low-thrills action moving along, and the cast of assorted muscleheads and starlets look like they had fun dressing up.

Hong adds a touch of sanity to the proceedings, and Dao overacts wildly as an incompetent Dragon Lady.

Apart from a lazy, disco-beat score by Gardner Cole, production values are mostly superior to regular Troma-produced fare. *—Derek Elley*

WHY IS MOTHER IN MY BED?

(POURQUOI MAMAN EST DANS MON LIT?)

(FRENCH)

A Gaumont Intl. presentation of a Gaumont/K'ien Prods./Le Studio Canal Plus/TF1 Films production. (International sales: Gaumont, Paris.) Produced by Alain Poire. Directed by Patrick Malakian. Screenplay, Catherine Hertault, Jean-Luc Seigle. Camera (color), Regis Blondeau; music, Eric Levi; art direction, Clorinde Mery; sound, Olivier Villette. Reviewed at Cannes Film Festival (market), May 14, 1994. Running time: **92 MIN.**
Pierre .... Gerard Klein
Veronique .... Marie-France Pisier
Antoine .... Benjamin Chevillard
Also with: Sophie Desmarets, Jean-Michel Dupuis, Consuelo de Havilland, Isabelle Nanty.

"Why Is Mother in My Bed?" is an airy but agreeable account of an enterprising tyke's perceived responsibility for his parents' split and his efforts to get them back on a conjugal track. Gently amusing, visually snappy Gallic family offering pushes enough universal buttons to find a home on international tube slates, especially with a less antiquated title.

The rift starts when, feeling resentful about being the only kid in his class whose folks won't cough up for a leather jacket, pre-teen Antoine (Benjamin Chevillard) swipes one from a boutique. With Pa (Ger-

ard Klein) bringing home only a skimpy teacher's wage, Antoine's mother (Marie-France Pisier) determines that they need more cash to stay happy, so she takes a job as an ad agency telephone operator.

She's swiftly upgraded to junior ideas woman, then to exec level, where she vastly out-earns her husband. His sense of inadequacy sparks marital spats and steers him into a dalliance with a private tuition student. Inevitably, he checks out, and Antoine, blaming himself, embarks on Operation Reconciliation.

The film gets off to a confusing start, with some unnecessarily jumbled narrative. But once moving, it breezes along at a sprightly clip, thanks to its spirited cast and stylish, vividly colorful look, which at times seems mildly reminiscent of Belgian breakthrough pic "Toto the Hero." *—David Rooney*

KIM NOVAK IS ON THE PHONE

(C'E KIM NOVAK AL TELEFONO)

(ITALIAN)

A Drer Cinematografica/RAI TV production. Directed, written by Enrico Roseo. Camera (color), Ennio Guarnieri; editor, Nino Baragli; music, Nicola Piovani; art direction, Danilo Donati. Reviewed at Cannes Film Festival (market), May 15, 1994. Running time: **89 MIN.**
Enrico .... Jacques Perrin
Emilia ....Joanna Pacula
Luca .... Joachim Lombard
Enrico's Mother .... Sylva Koscina
"Kim Novak" .... Anna Falchi

A film that will strike a poignant note of recognition in the heart of any movie producer who has ever considered selling his/her grandmother to raise film financing, "Kim Novak Is On the Phone" marks the directing bow of Italian producer Enrico Roseo. An overly slow pace and mishmash of styles will provoke some audience attrition for a film whose pleasant atmosphere and mature theme seem aimed at broader, if older, auds, peacefully watching TV at home.

Though the material would seem a natural for comic treatment, Roseo prefers a wistful key of nostalgia as he looks over his hero's past. Jacques Perrin (a producer in his own right) plays ever-boyish producer Enrico, who has a problem: He has to lay his hands on $250,000 fast to close a deal with Kim Novak for his next movie. (The actress has a special meaning for him, as the audience will discover.) He sets out optimistically for his family house near Parma, intending to sell it quickly. But the stately villa, filled with antique heirlooms,

family portraits and cobwebs, can't be sold without the consent of his wife, Emilia (Joanna Pacula).

Resentfully separated, she has no intention of giving Enrico the time of day. She's made a new life for herself with a steady but dull businessman and has turned their teenage son, Luca (Joachim Lombard), against his father.

A curious feeling of retouched autobiography pervades "Kim Novak." The realistic settings — middle-class apartments, bachelor residences, Parmesan cheese factories — strain against a dreamier, Fellinesque atmosphere.

Enrico embarks on a memory trip back to his gilded adolescence, when he drove a Porsche and organized innocent "orgies" for his pals with a sexy blond barmaid (Anna Falchi) who looked like Kim Novak.

One scene on the beach at daybreak, with a violinist playing Nicola Piovani's plaintive score while Enrico stares with drunken yearning at two naked girls, is clearly inspired by "Amarcord" and "I Vitelloni."

As the couple's teenage son, Lombard embodies the fantasy of a wise youth who, ignoring his harridan mother, sides with his unpresentable father and campaigns to straighten him out. They play squash, wrestle and go to mass together.

This TV-style relationship feels out of place with the cynical details of Enrico's failings. More convincing is Enrico's discovery that all his school buddies have grown old and rich but are as lacking in generosity as he is.

Some of Italy's top technicians worked on the film, and tech quality is fine. *—Deborah Young*

RELATIVE FEAR

A Norstar Entertainment, Allegro and Westwind presentation. Produced by Tom Berry, Stefan Wodoslawsky. Executive producer, William Webb. Co-producer, Franco Battista. Directed by George Mihalka. Screenplay, Kurt Wimmer. Camera (color), Rodney Gibbons; editor, Ion Webster; production design, Patricia Christie; costume design, Trixi Rittenhouse; sound, Richard Nichol; assistant director, John Bradshaw. Reviewed at Cannes Film Festival (market), May 17, 1994. Running time: **89 MIN.**
Linda .... Darlanne Fluegel
Peter .... Martin Neufeld
Earl .... M. Emmet Walsh
Adam .... Matthew Dupuis
Det. Atwater .... James Brolin
Clive .... Bruce Dinsmore
Connie .... Denise Crosby
Margaret .... Linda Sorensen

First came "The Bad Seed," then "The Good Son" and now "Relative Fear," a Canadian-produced knockoff of last year's Macaulay Culkin pic that was a studio knockoff of the '50s Patty McCormack vehicle. Those in search of killer pix featuring kiddies with angelic faces and homicidal souls won't be disappointed.

If the material this time around is essentially routine, there's still fun to be had with "Fear." Video-friendly cast names mean big theatrical bucks are unlikely, but small-screen future should be strong, as the filmmakers deliver a classy, involving domestic drama with some good creepy moments.

Pic kicks into gear when two mothers-to-be, Connie (Denise Crosby) and Linda (Darlanne Fluegel), give birth in the same hospital at the same time. The old switcheroo occurs, and Linda senses there's a problem when her newborn babe gives her a sock on the cheek. The tale's central intrigues kick off right away. Maybe the frightful little tyke's a beast because his real mom, Connie, is a homicidal maniac. And whatever happened to Linda's real son?

Four years later, we meet the mean little guy Linda took home following the switch, Adam (Matthew Dupuis), an autistic child who doesn't speak but glowers impressively when things don't go his way. He's especially unhappy with Grandpa Earl (M. Emmet Walsh), a disabled crank who criticizes Adam for being "dumb as a stump."

His loving daddy, Peter (Martin Neufeld), goes from dreaming of having a rocket scientist son to having a kid "who just says mommy or daddy," but Adam's verbal deficiencies become the least of the family's problems.

Soon people are dropping dead left and right around the house, a circumstance unchanged by the arrival of special education tutor Clive (Bruce Dinsmore), a loving hands-on therapist whom the family hopes will get Adam chattering. Det. Atwater (James Brolin), the local gendarme, starts to get suspicious of the boy, and even mom starts to wonder if her little man is a little monster.

Fluegel stands out in the cast, the members of which, for the most part, deliver serviceable performances.

Film's main disappointment is its inability to rise above average plotting, and Crosby, as a big, bad mama, needs more screen time to get her lethal attitude up to a Hannibal Lecter level. When the two moms finally clash in a prison encounter payoff with Crosby in chains, the opportunity for high-voltage thrills is never realized.

Before fadeout, Linda's real son's whereabouts are worked out, along with a few tasty twists, and film transcends what looks like exploitation of the mentally handicapped to become a sharp comment on prejudice and the fact that psycho-kid genre assumptions can be misleading. —*Steven Gaydos*

JAMILA

(GERMAN-BRITISH)

A Hemlin Media Intl./Cori Films presentation of a Triangle Film production. (International sales: Cori Film Distributors, London.) Produced by Ernst Ritter von Theumer. Executive producers, Helmut Hulsner, Christopher von Gotz. Directed by Monica Teuber. Screenplay, Ruth Rothmann, Christopher McGee, from the novel by Chingiz Aitmatov. Camera (color), Manos Mussaev; editor, Vera Dubesikova; music, Eugen Doga; art direction, Marat Sadigaliev; costume design, Micheline Michel; sound (Dolby), Simon Happ; assistant director, Irina Sidorova; second unit camera, Peter Maiwald. Reviewed at Cannes Film Festival (market), May 14, 1994. Running time: **101 MIN.**
Older Seit .... F. Murray Abraham
Jamila .... Linh Dan Pham
Young Seit .... Nikolai Kinski
Daniyar ....Jason Connery

Striking lensing of the Kirghiz steppes reps the only plus in "Jamila," a flat translation of a 1956 story by w.k. fabulist Chingiz Aitmatov about young love in the Soviet grasslands. Presence of F. Murray Abraham, "Indochine" newcomer Linh Dan Pham as the title character and Jason Connery doesn't elevate the material much above ground level. Small-screen European sales loom brightest.

Pic is framed as a reminiscence by N.Y.-based painter Seit (Abraham) of his first, unconsummated love affair as a youth in the Kirghiz hinterland during the mid-1940s. Journeying back to his homeland, Seit recalls in v.o. his adoration of the beautiful Jamila (Linh), who can give the men in the village a run for their money on horseback but who's parceled off to her brutish elder brother in an arranged marriage.

When the brother gets sent off to the war, the young Seit (Nikolai Kinski) is deputized as Jamila's protector. Enter handsome, wounded soldier Daniyar (Connery), bringing true love and some brave-faced but bruising disappointment for Seit. Coda has the older Seit arriving in the village to find Jamila's a grandmother, but pulling back from meeting her.

On few occasions does the movie attain the ingenuous, fablelike tale of puppy love that the material suggests. Though Manos Mussaev's camera and Eugen Doga's rhapsodic music do their best, pic is floored by a so-so script, lack of narrative thrust and pretty but gauche perfs by both Linh and Kinski as the youngsters.

Connery makes the best of an underwritten part, and Abraham, more heard than seen, is solid at best. German director Monica Teuber's helming is technically competent but uninspired. —*Derek Elley*

TALK

(AUSTRALIAN)

A Suitcase Films production in association with the Australian Film Commission. Produced by Megan McMurchy. Directed by Susan Lambert. Screenplay, Jan Cornall. Camera (color), Ron Hagen; editor, Henry Dangar; music, John Clifford White; production design, Lissa Coote; costumes, Clarrissa Patterson; sound (Dolby), John Dennison, Tony Vaccher; assistant director, Keith Heygate; casting, Liz Mullinar. Reviewed at Cannes Film Festival (Market), May 20, 1994 (also in Seattle Film Festival). Running time: **86 MIN.**
Julia Strong .... Victoria Longley
Stephanie Ness .... Angie Milliken
Jack/Harry .... Richard Roxburgh
The Girl ....Jacqueline McKenzie
Mac ....John Jarratt
Witnesses .... Ella-Mei Wong,
Tenzing Tsewang, Kee Chan

Susan Lambert's first feature, after a number of interesting shorts and medium-length films, is a mixture of reality and fantasy that cogently explores the lives of two thirtysomething women friends during a period of less than 24 hours. The reality works much better than the fantasy, but the net result is positive, and this low-budgeter, which is already sparking fest interest, starting with Seattle, could have a modestly successful arthouse life.

The title is apt; the women in this film certainly do talk. But the talk is interesting, funny and sharply written, and the superb actresses entrusted with all this dialogue never put a foot wrong.

Julia (Victoria Longley) is facing a crisis; for some time she's turned a blind eye to her husband's affair with a younger woman, but now she wants to bring matters to a head. Her best friend, Stephanie (Angie Milliken), is single but desperately wants a baby; she's just come back from Tokyo where she had a frustratingly unfulfilled encounter with a man who might have given her her wish.

The two women work together writing and designing adult comic books. In an early scene, a spunky TV repairman (Richard Roxburgh), brought in to fix Stephanie's TV set, openly eavesdrops on the women as Stephanie tells Julia about her Tokyo adventure in graphic detail.

As the day wears on, the increasingly distraught Julia suspects (for no very good reason) that she's being followed by a girl (a tiny role for Jacqueline McKenzie), and jumps to the conclusion that this must be her husband's mistress. Stephanie, meanwhile, arriving at the TV repair shop to collect her equipment, has a passionate and very satisfying encounter with the repairman.

All these scenes are funny, honest and abrasive, a tart look at career women and their hangups. Less successful are the fantasy scenes, which constantly interrupt the main action. Filmed like a lurid cartoon in hideous greens and reds, these feature the women (Longley with an amazing hairstyle) as detectives involved in a case details of which are never very clear. These scenes are mildly amusing, but detract from the main thrust of the film.

Longley and Milliken are splendid as the female buddies, but the supporting cast, apart from Roxburgh, who mainly has to look spunky, have little to do.

Production values are high for this very inexpensive production, which has been blown up from Super 16mm to 35mm most effectively. Ron Hagen's cinematography is very good, Henry Dangar's editing is sharp, and John Clifford White has provided an exciting music score.

Not by any means a film for everyone, this is still a confident first feature and one many people will enjoy. —*David Stratton*

THE CHILDHOOD FRIEND

(ITALIAN)

A Filmauro release (Italy) of a Duea Film, Filmauro production. Produced by Antonio Avati, Aurelio De Laurentiis. Directed, written by Pupi Avati. Camera (color), Cesare Bastelli; editor, Amedeo Salfa; costume design, Sissi Parravicini; sound (Dolby), Chat Gunther; assistant director, Alberto Lonardii. Reviewed at Cannes Film Festival (market), May 19, 1994. Running time: **95 MIN.**
Arnold Gardner .... Jason Robards III
Norma .... Amy Galper
Eddie "Chuck" Greenberg .Jim Ortlieb
Myers .... Jim Mullins
Owen .... Steve King
Ted Gardner ....Joe Ryan
(English soundtrack)

Italo director Pupi Avati's return to the U.S. Midwest (location for his 1991 jazz biopic "Bix") yields embarrassing results in "The Childhood Friend," a silly MOW-style psychodrama that should have stayed home in Rome. Lensed in English, the movie has already nosedived at

June 6, 1994 (Cont.)

Italian hardtops and looks set for the electronic dumpbin elsewhere.

Jason Robards III plays Arnold Gardner, a tough-talking journalist shaken by an old friend's death in a Chicago hotel room. Gardner blames his pal's demise on selling out to the TV network after his start as a crusading journalist.

Gardner offers to take over his friend's talkshow ("The XXVth Hour") and, though net execs know they're grasping a nettle, they take a chance. Gardner's frank, hardhitting, issue-based style proves popular.

As his ratings rise, so do Gardner's personal problems. Already divorced from his wife (Amy Galper), daughter of a high-up suit, Gardner starts receiving calls and letters from a hometown wacko in Indiana. As the pressure mounts, Gardner offers a live phone-in with the murderer on his show.

Revelation that Gardner and the wacko both raped the same girl 20 years earlier climaxes in a blah shootout finale.

Though the plot has more holes than a golf course, and dialogue is too grounded in simple exposition, Avati at least keeps things moving with restless editing and a mobile camera. But pic's rambling style, which may have worked in a European setting, is too loose to harness a genre item set Stateside with a Yank cast.

Performances are as bland as the script, with Robards glowering and charmless as the ambitious journo and Galper photogenic but flat as his ex-wife. Background score, based on Wagner's "Parsifal" prelude, is wildly inappropriate. Technical credits are OK, though dialogue is noticeably out of synch at several points. —*Derek Elley*

CYBORG COP II

A Nu Image presentation of a New World production. Produced by Danny Lerner. Executive producers, Avi Lerner, Trevor Short. Directed by Sam Firstenberg. Screenplay, Jon Stevens, from a screen story by Firstenberg. Camera (color), Yossi (Joseph) Wein; editor, Marcus Manton; music, Bob Mithoff; production design, John Rosewarne; art direction, Ray Wilson; costume design, Diana Cilliers; sound (Ultra-Stereo), Colin McFarlane; special effects coordinator, Rick Cresswell; assistant director, Mark Roper; casting, Jane Warren. Reviewed at Cannes Film Festival (market), May 16, 1994. Running time: **97 MIN.**

Jack Ryan	David Bradley
Jesse Starkraven	Morgan Hunter
Liz McDowell	Jill Pierce

Loose sequel to last year's "Cyborg Cop" reunites lead David Bradley ("American Ninja") and helmer Sam Firstenberg in a wall-to-wall actioner that's a step down in quality, but still solid rental fodder.

Like the first, pic opens with a warehouse shootout, with loose-cannon cop Jack Ryan (Bradley) this time up against one Jesse Starkraven (Morgan Hunter), lumbering psycho brother of a man Ryan killed "last year." Starkraven is captured, but taken away by secret governmental body ATG (Anti-Terrorist Group) and turned into a new-model cyborg.

Rest of the movie is basically Ryan teaming up with the tough ATG head (Jill Pierce), plus plenty of heavy artillery, to battle Starkraven after he's engineered a cyborg breakout and attempts to wipe out the human race.

Script doesn't bother with things like character development, and even lacks the romantic sparring that gave a smidgen of depth to Bradley's character in the original.

Special effects are OK given the limited budget, but editing is considerably slacker than in the first entry.

Part three of Nu Image's franchise is already in the works, sans Bradley. —*Derek Elley*

DREAM AND MEMORY

A C&A production. (International sales: C&A, c/o Angelika Film, N.Y.) Produced by Ann Hu. Co-producers, William Goins, Cheng Zheng. Directed, written by Hu, based on a story by Zhang Hongnian. Camera (color, 16mm), Brian Clery (U.S.), Tu Jiakuan (China); editors, Debbie Ungar, Zheng Jing; music, Zhang Lida; art direction, Liu Yuan (U.S.); Duan Zhenzhong (China), sound, Stu Deutsch (U.S.), Li Yongjie (China), George Leung, Gu Quanxi; associate producers, Zhang Daxing, Liu Yuan; assistant directors, Jean Heyer, Xu Qiaonan; special consultants, Edward Orshan, Roy Nemerson, Ben Hayeem. Reviewed at Berlin Film Festival (market), Feb. 18, 1994. (In Cannes Film Festival — market.) Running time: **82 MIN.**

Hong Yuan (in U.S.)	Bing Yang
Hong Yuan (in China)	Shao Bing
Village Secretary	Li Wei
Aunt Sara	Kathleen Claypool
Janet	Adina Porter
Ai Cheng	Wang Shuo
Lanzi	Ren Yan
Gaixiu	Shi Ke

(English and Mandarin Chinese dialogue)

Laudable in theory but uneven in practice, "Dream and Memory" is a mixed bag. The reminiscence of a friendship forged during the Cultural Revolution by a Gotham-based Chinese artist will be of interest to Sinophiles and special-interest groups but won't travel far beyond that.

Film is the first of a series of cross-cultural items planned by N.Y.-based C&A Prods. using independent filmmakers from mainland China. Chinese sections of "Dream" were lensed in northern China in fall '92, using mainland technicians; New York segs were shot in spring '93, with a mixed American/Chinese-American crew. Peking-born producer/director Ann Hu herself moved to the U.S. in 1979.

Central character is Hong Yuan (Bing Yang), a blind Chinese man living with his uncle's American widow (Kathleen Claypool) whose memories of the Cultural Revolution are stirred by a letter from an old friend, Ai Cheng (Wang Shuo). Fifteen years earlier, during the late '60s, the two were sent to paint propagandist wall pictures in remote Stone Village.

Film cross-cuts between their life in the village 15 years earlier — when the duo were split by artistic differences and Hong (Shao Bing) fell for a local peasant girl (Ren Yan) — and Hong's aimless existence in New York, reminiscing with his aunt and romanced by a woman (Adina Porter) who can't bring herself to tell him she's black.

Chinese scenes, simply but effectively shot on location, partly evoke old-style mainland pix in their iconography and acting styles. Story is treated episodically but has an ingenuous charm aided by subtitled Chinese dialogue, a feel for landscape and economic detailing of how Mao's policies reached into the remotest corners of the country.

New York sections are less happy, with poor English enunciation by Yang, as the older Hong, stodgy direction and clumsy scripting.

Impression is of two small movies stir-fried together, with no overall dramatic arc and the sum considerably less than the parts. Still, the Chinese segs show Hu as a director of some promise, so long as she delegates producing and scripting chores in the future. Tech credits are OK for a 16mm low-budgeter. Parallel Chinese title, "Shanhe jiuhua," evokes reminiscences of China's landscape. —*Derek Elley*

THE UNGRATEFUL AGE

(MAGARECE GODINE/ L'AGE INGRAT)

(BOSNIAN-FRENCH)

A Profil (Sarajevo)/Igman Prods. (Paris) co-production. Produced by Refik Besirevic, Nenad Dizdarevic, Michel Mavros. Directed by Dizdarevic. Screenplay, Dizdarevic, Tarik Haveric, based on a novel by Branko Copic. Camera (color), Mustafa Mustavic; editor, Milena Arsenijevic; music, Zlatko Arslangic; art direction, Kemal Hrustanovic; associate producer, Frederic Gilbert; production director, Besirevic. Reviewed at Cannes Film Festival (market), May 15, 1994. Running time: **97 MIN.**

"The Ungrateful Age" (aka "The Tough Teens") is the first feature film from Bosnia after the breakup of Yugoslavia. Despite its interest as a Bosnian film, its audience is hard to pinpoint, since pic reads as a light and charming kidpic of yore.

Helmer Nenad Dizdarevic finished lensing at the end of March 1992, a scant week before the war in the former Yugoslavia broke out. The negative was trapped in a lab occupied by Serbian forces and had to be smuggled out for post-production in Zagreb and Paris.

Based on Branko Copic's autobiographical 1950 novel, pic is set on the eve of World War II in a boys' school. This old world environment is peopled by well-dressed, clean-faced kids, ages 13-15, and old fuss-budget teachers more concerned with discipline than teaching.

A long series of schoolboy pranks is followed by an equally long series of punishments. Dizdarevic individualizes his boys carefully, but their practical jokes have a sameness after a while. Despite some miscarriages of justice, such as the expulsion of an imaginative but penniless country boy, the school contains so little real conflict it looks relatively idyllic.

Adult audiences, perhaps unfairly, will comb the film for references to the current Bosnian situation. An uncredited juvenile cast performs with winning sincerity. Tech credits are fine. —*Deborah Young*

PROJECT SHADOWCHASER II

A Nu Image presentation of an EGM Film Intl. production. Produced by Gregory Vanger, John Eyres, Geoff Griffith. Executive producers, Avi Lerner, Trevor Short, Danny Dimbort. Directed by Eyres. Screenplay, Nick Davis. Additional scripting, John Cianetti. Camera (Foto-Kem color), Alan M. Trow; editor, Amanda I. Kirpaul; music, Steve Edwards; production design, Mark Harris; art direction, Ray Wilson; costume design, Leigh Bishop; sound design, Joe Zappala; 2nd unit director, Nick Davis; martial arts coordinator, Bryan Genesse; assistant director, Mark Roper. Reviewed at Cannes Film Festival (market), May 19, 1994. Running time: **94 MIN.**

Android	Frank Zagarino
Frank Mead	Bryan Genesse
Laurie Webber	Beth Toussaint

Ahighly serviceable actioner about terrorists taking over a nuclear base, "Project Shadowchaser II" reps a further budget notch in the belts of L.A.-based Brit duo, helmer John Eyres and producer Geoff Griffith ("Monolith"). Though this second trip to the "Die Hard" well doesn't have anything to keep Joel Silver awake nights, action buffs are assured a smooth ride.

Long-planned followup to the 1991 Eyres-Griffith original finally emerges under the Nu Image banner, with a plot totally different from that previously announced. Only links with the first is (now Nu Image contractee) Frank Zagarino as a terrorist android, and a similar holed-up storyline. Pic is also known as "Night Siege."

Setting this time is Christmas at a privately run nuclear base ordered to dismantle its arsenal by the U.S. prez. When terrorists, led by a blond musclehead (Zagarino), take over the joint and threaten to nuke Washington, D.C., a maintenance engineer (Bryan Genesse), a scientist (Beth Toussaint) and her son pick them off one by one.

Pic is smoothly cut, and has a script that takes time to sketch characters before the last hour of action. Genesse (also doubling as martial arts coordinator) and Toussaint make a good team without too many clever wisecracks, and Zagarino has a ball as the sicko android. Limited effects are solid and thriller elements click neatly into place.
—*Derek Elley*

THE ROLY POLY MAN

(AUSTRALIAN)

A REP (Australia) release of a Rough Nut Pictures production, in association with Kolapore Management, with the participation of the New South Wales Film and Television Office, Australian Film Finance Corp. (International sales: Total Film.) Produced by Peter Green. Executive producer, Jonathon Steinman. Directed by Bill Young. Screenplay, Kym Goldsworthy. Camera (color), Brian J. Breheny; editor, Neil Thumpston; music, Dave Skinner; production design, Robert (Moxy) Moxham; costumes, Margot Wilson; sound (Dolby), Guntis Sics; special effects, David Young; line producer, John Winter; assistant director, Chris Webb; casting, Greg Apps. Reviewed at Cannes Film Festival (Market), May 13, 1994. Running time: **95 MIN.**
Dirk Trent .... Paul Chubb
Mickey .... Les Foxcroft
Sandra Burnett .... Susan Lyons
Laurel Trent .... Zoe Bertram
Dr. Henderson .... Frank Whitten
Prof. Wauchop .... Rowan Woods
Det. Tom McKenzie .. Peter Braunstein
Axel .... John Batchelor
Jane Lewis .... Jane Harders
Motel Manager .... Valerie Bader
Vicki Lane .... Sarah Lambert
Chantal .... Deborah Kennedy
Nun .... Barbara Stephens
Newsreader .... Richard Morecroft
Barfly .... Paul LePetit

A modestly budgeted private eye yarn, with horror and sci-fi frills, "The Roly Poly Man" has an amiable cast and several good scenes, but suffers from sometimes puerile scripting. It should have a life on video, but serious theatrical biz looks iffy.

First-time helmer Bill Young and scripter Kym Goldsworthy stick to the classical shamus formula, complete with sardonic narration and a clutch of mysterious characters, including an attractive femme fatale. Difference is that the private investigator, charmingly played by Paul Chubb, is a pudgy, accident-prone nerd, and the plot — involving a disparate group of victims whose heads have exploded — belongs more in the genre of the horror than mystery.

Dirk Trent, who describes himself as a "no frills" detective, is working for a woman (Jane Harders) whose philandering spouse entertains his pretty secretary in a seedy motel. Shooting the sexual highjinks through the uncurtained motel window with a vidcamera, Trent's loyal assistant (Les Foxcroft) films what appears to be the murder of the secretary by the husband; but later the girl shows up, and, on closer inspection of the tape (a la "Blow Up"), Trent deduces the man's head simply exploded. Other victims with exploded heads turn up, and the trail leads to a suave medico (Frank Whitten) carrying out strange experiments to cure brain tumors.

Pic has a sharp sense of macabre humor. Trent's girlfriend, played with forceful energy by Susan Lyons, is manager of the city morgue, and one scene involving brain remains may have sensitive members of the audience gagging. There's also a funny running gag involving Trent's unwanted ex-wife (Zoe Bertram) and his large brood of children. But at times attempts at humor don't work.

Pic builds to a silly, but exciting and well-staged, climax. Pic could appeal to private eye fans, but the horror elements may be a turnoff for that target aud, and Chubb, while cheerfully ridiculous, is hardly a hero with whom the hip crowd will identify.

Production values are modest but perfectly adequate.
—*David Stratton*

ALL THINGS BRIGHT AND BEAUTIFUL

(BRITISH-IRISH)

A BBC Enterprises presentation, in association with Bord Scannan Na H'Eireann and RTE, of a Good Film Co. production. (International sales: The Sales Co., London.) Produced by Katy McGuinness. Executive producers, Robert Cooper, Paul McGuinness, Mark Shivas. Directed, written by Barry Devlin. Camera (color), Declan Quinn; editor, Maurice Hely; production design, Grant Hicks; costumes, Lindy Hemming; sound (Dolby), Godfrey Kirby; line producer, Donna Grey; associate producer, Michael Garland; assistant director, Ian Madden; casting, John and Ros Hubbard. Reviewed at Cannes Film Festival (market), May 16, 1994. Running time: **90 MIN.**

Barry O'Neill .... Ciaran Fitzgerald
Father McAteer .... Tom Wilkinson
Tommy O'Neill .... Kevin McNally
Maeve O'Neill .... Gabrielle Reidy
Eileen O'Neill .... Lorraine Pilkington
The Good Thief .... Gabriel Byrne

Similar in theme to the 1961 Bryan Forbes film "Whistle Down the Wind," "All Things Bright and Beautiful" is a gentle, modestly affecting, dramatic comedy set in a small Irish village in 1954, about a 10-year-old boy who claims to have witnessed a miracle. This may be just too slight for much theatrical exposure, but TV and vid sales are definitely indicated.

Pic's chief assets are the convincing setting of a tiny backwater in conservative times, and the lead performance of Ciaran Fitzgerald as the bright young Barry.

A choirboy at the local church, Barry has fallen under the influence of the priest, Father McAteer (Tom Wilkinson). When Barry stumbles across a fugitive IRA man in a barn, he takes him to be Barabbas, the criminal from the Christ story. The gullible McAteer drags the boy to the church, where the lad claims to hear the Virgin speak to him.

Convinced that a 10-year-old wouldn't know the words Barry uses, McAteer is determined that a miracle has occurred. Writer/director Barry Devlin might have made more out of this material but is content to keep his story simple. This diminishes the potential drama, but even so, "All Things" is a pleasurable, if very modest, film.

The children are natural and unaffected, production design and costumes are fine, and the use of period songs for children on the soundtrack (Danny Kaye sings "The Ugly Duckling") is charming. Other production values are adequate.
—*David Stratton*

SHORTCUT TO PARADISE

(SPANISH-PUERTO RICAN)

A Tornasol Films (Spain)/Tornacine/ Shortcut to Paradise (Puerto Rico) co-production in association with TVE and Canal Plus (Spain). Produced by Gerardo Herrero, Letvia Arza-Goderich, Juan Gerard Gonzalez. Directed by Herrero. Screenplay, Daniel Monzon, Satiago Tabernero, with additional material by Arza-Goderich and Gonzalez. Camera (color), Alfredo Mayo; editor, Carmen Frias; music, Jose Nieto; production design, Yvonne Belen; sound (Dolby), Felipe Borrero. Reviewed at Cannes Film Festival (Market), May 16, 1994. Running time: **99 MIN.**

Quinn .... Charles Dance
Maria .... Assumpta Serna
Gus .... Morgan Weisser
Sara .... Katrina Gibson
Lona .... Gladys Rodriguez
Clark .... Axel Anderson
Kevin .... Pablo Figueroa
(English dialogue)

The intriguing concept of a murderous, blackmailing building super who rifles through residents' mail and garbage is an urban American nightmare brought to life in "Shortcut to Paradise." Shot in Puerto Rico in English by Spanish helmer Gerardo Herrero, script has a transplanted feel it never quite shakes off. This routine thriller will probably head quickly to TV and video.

Looking for a secure hideaway where he can drop out of sight for a while, a man (Charles Dance) kills a fellow who's on his way to take a job as super at the rundown Paradise Condominium, and assumes his identity. He introduces himself as Quinn to lonely condo manager Lona (Gladys Rodriguez), but when she later sniffs out the truth, she literally ends up in the garbage. Though he smells like a baddie from a mile away, Quinn ingratiates himself with just about everybody except sensitive young gas station attendant Gus (Morgan Weisser). Gus' best friend is Sara (Katrina Gibson), a young teen who attracts Quinn, too. The trusting girl and her mom (Assumpta Serna) don't sense the danger their super represents until it's too late. In a protracted and fairly exciting climax, Gus and Quinn battle over the girl.

Dance makes a scary super, using cunning intelligence to gain power over the neighbors and disarm adversaries like Gus psychologically. His obvious (if ambivalent) affection for Sara at times makes him more sympathetic than Serna's character, a swinging single who comes on to the underage Gus at all the wrong moments. Gibson, who looks like a young Brooke Shields and bursts with joyful energy, is out of step with Weisser's finely subdued perf as the disturbed Gus.

The exotic Puerto Rican backdrop — actually underused and never named — provides attractive visuals for Alfredo Mayo's camerawork.
—*Deborah Young*

THE LAST TATTOO

(NEW ZEALAND)

A Plumb production, in association with Capella Intl., New Zealand Film Commission, Avalon CFU, NZ on Air. Produced by Neville Carson, Bill Gavin. Executive producers, David Korda, Bridget Hedison. Directed by John Reid. Screenplay, Keith Aberdein. Camera (color), John Blick; editor, John Scott; music, John Charles; production design, Ron Highfield; costumes, Barbara Darragh; sound (Dolby), Tony Johnson; line producer, Jan Haynes; assistant directors, David Norris, Stuart Freeman; casting, Mike Fenton. Reviewed at Cannes Film Festival (Market), May 15, 1994. Running time: **109 MIN.**

Kelly Towne	Kerry Fox
Capt. Michael Starwood	Tony Goldwyn
Cmdr. Conrad Dart	Robert Loggia
Gen. Frank Zane	Rod Steiger
Austin Leech	John Bach
Rose Mitchell	Katie Wolf
Patrick Carroll	Tony Barry
McGurk	Desmond Kelly

A thriller about the hunt for the carrier of a virulent strain of venereal disease in World War II-era New Zealand, "The Last Tattoo" doesn't really deliver enough thrills and suspense to overcome its inherently sordid, though intriguing, theme. It may perform on its home turf, but elsewhere probably won't raise a great deal of excitement outside the video market.

Kerry Fox, who has done better work for directors Jane Campion and Gillian Armstrong in the past, plays Kelly, a nurse attached to the Hygiene Dept. Her job is to work with the Americans, many of whom are on leave in Kiwiland after rugged fighting in the Pacific, and with local brothels to keep VD under control.

Story begins with the murder of a Marine and the disappearance of his g.f., an ex-prostitute. Kelly discovers that both the wife of a prominent local politician and the missing girl carry a hitherto unseen strain of gonorrhea. The carrier has to be found, but meanwhile the murderer, a hit man for a local union (played with menace by John Bach) is after the missing girl.

Kelly, who has seen too much of the downside of sex in her daily work, teams with an eager-beaver Marine captain (Tony Goldwyn) to solve the mystery, and the trail eventually leads to high places. Indeed, the plot ultimately hinges on an attempt by a senior American officer to blackmail the politician, who might be the next New Zealand prime minister, presumably to ensure the postwar cooperation of the Kiwi government.

Director John Reid handles some scenes with flair, but editor John Scott's overall pacing is too sluggish, resulting in an overlong run-

ning time. Notably, the inevitable romance between Fox and Goldwyn, which is a long time coming, is pretty tepid.

Performances are variable, with Rod Steiger more controlled than usual as the senior U.S. officer in Wellington and Robert Loggia suave as his No. 2. Fox eases into her role after an awkward start, but never seems entirely at ease with her character, while Goldwyn is an OK hero. In the supporting cast, Tony Barry is a standout as a devious union official.

Production design (Ron Highfield) and costumes (Barbara Darragh) are first-class and lend needed authenticity to the yarn. —*David Stratton*

TALKING ABOUT SEX

A Curb Entertainment Intl. Corp. presentation of a Pegasus Prods. production. (International sales: Curb Organization, Burbank.) Produced by Gary M. Bettman. Executive producer, Aaron Speiser. Directed by Speiser. Screenplay, Speiser, Carl Nelson, from a screen story by Speiser. Camera (color), Tom Jewett; editor, Wayne Schmidt; music, Tim Landers; art direction, Laurence S. James; associate producer, Heath Slane; assistant director, Lee Lankford. Reviewed at Cannes Film Festival (market), May 15, 1994. Running time: **83 MIN.**

Andie Norman	Kim Wayans
Rachel Parsons	Marcy Walker
Doug Penn	Daniel Beer
Carl Morgan	Randy Powell
Michael Columbus	Kerry Ruff
Lou Jacobs	Joe Richards
With: Daria Lynn.	

"Talking About Sex" is a hip, mostly breezy look at the sexual hang-ups of a bunch of well-tailored Los Angelenos that occasionally hits the right spot but doesn't add to up to an earth-moving experience. Lively performances and trim running time are the major pluses of this sexual jawfest that looks destined for specialized playdates.

Group of characters spins around Andie (Kim Wayans), editor of a dry self-help manual penned by terminally smooth shrink Michael (Kerry Ruff) that she's retitled "Talking About Sex." At an all-night party to celebrate the tome's publication, misunderstandings and mismatches proliferate.

Besides Andie, who argues early on with her boring b.f., Doug (Daniel Beer), other characters include publisher Carl (Randy Powell), who wants to spice up Michael's book and his own marriage; blond looker Rachel (Marcy Walker), who's taken to "re-birthing" meditation sessions as a substitute for that elusive orgasm; a late-30s fashion designer (Daria Lynn) whose sex life is on hold; and Andie's neighbor Lou (Joe Richards), who'd like to pair her off with his strangely uninterested grandson.

Bulk of the pic is set during the gathering, with tears, battles, flirtations and slick party talk, which is broken up by b&w doculike sequences of the women exchanging raw confidences about their most private moments. These bits, shot in hand-held, talking-heads style, are among the best in the movie, a truthful counterweight to the often shallow talk elsewhere.

In fairness, director/co-writer Aaron Speiser never pretends he's making major statements in the movie, and the seriocomic tone is mostly kept afloat by the OK, well-differentiated cast. As the much-in-demand, perky copy editor, Wayans motors the movie.

Tech credits on the obviously low-budget production are up to scratch. —*Derek Elley*

THE COWBOY WAY

A Universal release of an Imagine Entertainment presentation of a Brian Grazer production. Produced by Grazer. Executive producers, G. Mac Brown, Karen Kehela, Bill Wittliff. Directed by Gregg Champion. Screenplay, Wittliff; story by Rob Thompson, Wittliff. Camera (DeLuxe color), Dean Semler; editor, Michael Tronick; music, David Newman; production design, John Jay Moore; art direction, William Barclay; set decoration, Leslie Pope; costume design, Aude Bronson-Howard; sound (digital), Tom Brandau; assistant director, Michael B. Steele; second-unit director, Conrad E. Palmisano; stunt coordinator, Palmisano; casting, Billy Hopkins, Suzanne Smith, Kerry Barden. Reviewed at the Directors Guild theater, Hollywood, May 24, 1994. MPAA Rating: PG-13. Running time: **106 MIN.**

Pepper	Woody Harrelson
Sonny	Kiefer Sutherland
Stark	Dylan McDermott
Officer Sam Shaw	Ernie Hudson
Teresa	Cara Buono
Margarette	Marg Helgenberger
Huerta	Tomas Milian

Universal has a horse with a flat tire in "The Cowboy Way," which isn't funny enough to be a comedy or exciting enough to galvanize action fans. Toss in a plot shot full of holes, and this modern Western faces a rough box office ride beyond whatever initial business its stars can corral.

The premise would seem to suggest putting a country twang on the old "Crocodile Dundee" riff, but director Gregg Champion and writer Bill Wittliff ("Lonesome Dove") never really capitalize on the comedic potential of having two New Mexico cowboys truckin' into New York.

The mismatched duo, serious Sonny (Kiefer Sutherland) and fun-loving Pepper (Woody Harrelson), are onetime rodeo partners who, after a falling out, get thrown together again in trying to locate a

friend who vanished while searching for his daughter (Cara Buono).

The girl, a Cuban immigrant, has been brought to New York by a smuggling outfit, whose evil ringleader (Dylan McDermott) is holding her hostage. Sonny and Pepper almost immediately know who the bad guy is but waste a lot of time charging up bills at snooty hotels, befriending a Western-obsessed New York cop (Ernie Hudson) and, in Pepper's case, crashing posh parties, though the filmmakers never really draw a firm bead on any of those obvious targets.

Indeed, the most amusing and heavily marketed moment from the movie — where a naked Harrelson, after his tryst with a married cowgirl gets interrupted, holds a hat up with no hands — roughly serves as the apex of whatever humor the film can muster.

These cowboys also fail to put any more conventional skills to much use, considering the fish-out-of-water possibilities. The climactic sequence, for example, has the pair riding horses through Manhattan in an overlong chase that isn't anywhere nearly as exhilarating as David Newman's hard-charging score tries to make it seem.

Harrelson harvests a few laughs as the randier of the two cowboys, but there's never much chemistry developed between his character and Sutherland's listless, sober sidekick — or, for that matter, the pivotal role of their friend Nacho (Joaquin Martinez), whose disappearance sets the whole adventure into motion.

All of the characters, in fact, are sparsely developed, with McDermott steely as the villain, Stark, but not as menacing as the build-up requires.

Pic does turn into virtually a non-stop chase during the last half-hour but nevertheless manages to feel flat, perhaps because Champion brings nothing fresh to the action. Those who bother to question such things will also find themselves muttering about Hudson's cop, who blithely joins in the destructive festivities; whether the U.S. has changed its policy on illegal immigration; or how the two cowboys suddenly become so adept at navigating their way around the big city.

Tech credits fare a little better, capturing the swank New York locales in contrast to the west's wide-open spaces. —*Brian Lowry*

June 6, 1994 (Cont.)

THE ENDLESS SUMMER II

(DOCU)

A New Line Cinema release and production, in association with Ron Moler and Roger Riddell. Produced by Moler, Riddell. Executive producer, Michael Harpster. Directed by Bruce Brown. Written, edited by Bruce and Dana Brown. Camera (Foto-Kem color), Mike Hoover; music, Gary Hoey, Phil Marshall; executive music producers, Joel and Lonnie Sill; sound (Dolby), Beverly Johnson; associate producer, Dana Brown, Carey Michaels. Reviewed at Aidikoff screening room, Beverly Hills, June 1, 1994. MPAA Rating: PG. Running time: **107 MIN.**
Narrated by Bruce Brown

Bruce Brown's "The Endless Summer II," the sequel to his 1966 sleeper hit, offers everything anyone could want to know about surfing, and more. Exciting, ravishingly photographed surfing sequences are contained within a travelogue format that is part National Geographic, part adventure and part documentary. While high-adrenaline action will keep surfing fans drenched with enthusiasm, rather schematic structure and narration that is not always fresh or funny should keep B.O. at middle levels.

Over the last three decades, the novelty of surfing has worn out: There have been TV programs and narrative films ("Big Wednesday," "Point Break") about this exciting sport, creating the problem of coming up with something new in documenting the endless search for the "perfect wave." This time out, director and co-writer Brown, who popularized surfing for the public in the 1960s, is only partially successful. After 20 minutes of acrobatic surfing in various combos (solo, tandem, trio, even dogs), story begins by introducing its two handsome California heroes: Blond Patrick O'Connell, an expert on the shortboard, and dark-haired Robert "Wingnut" Weaver, a professional longboard surfer.

Travelogue follows youngsters as they move around the globe, visiting some of its most exotic spots: Costa Rica, Hawaii, France, South Africa, Australia, Fiji, Bali, Java and even Alaska, the latter not exactly an ideal setting or climate for the sport.

After visiting three or four sites, pic becomes a bit redundant as it follows the same structure: Some long shots of the local scenery, info and encounters with dangerous animals (Kodiak bears, wild elephants, alligators, poisonous snakes, hungry lions), meetings with local surfers (including some international champions), and more sumptuous footage in and under water.

The young men are appealing and their pyrotechnics are always exciting to watch, but they are seldom given a chance to use their own voices to share personal thoughts and feelings about their passion. Pic offers only tidbits about the psychology of surfing, the motivation to engage in it, the bliss in doing it, the special personality it takes, and the sub-culture it creates.

Enjoying a much bigger budget, larger crew and more sophisticated equipment than the original, "Endless Summer II" boasts more spectacular scenery and a most impressive technical and visual sheen. But the narration is not as diverting and tongue-in-cheek as that of the first film, which admittedly had the advantage of charting new territory. With a running time of 107 minutes, new edition is too long by at least 20 minutes.
—*Emanuel Levy*

HUMAN RIGHTS

CHRONICLE OF THE UPRISING IN THE WARSAW GHETTO ACCORDING TO MAREK EDELMAN

(KRONIKA TOWSTANIA W GETCIE WARSZAWSKAM WEDLUG MARKA EDELMANA)

(POLISH — DOCU)

A Documentary and Features Polish Films production. Directed, written by Jolanta Dylewska. Camera (b&w), Dylewska; editor, Wanda Zeman; music, Arthur Brauner, sung by Alina Swidowska, Jan Kany Pawluskiesicz; sound, Piotr Strzelecki; special effects, Pyzsard Kujawski. Reviewed at Broadway Screening Room, N.Y., April 11, 1994. (In Human Rights Watch Intl. Film Festival.) Running time: **70 MIN.**

An extended opening sequence to the prolixly titled "Chronicle of the Uprising in the Warsaw Ghetto According to Marek Edelman" begins with a beautiful montage of archival b&w footage of people in slow motion set to music, creating an almost ballet-like feel and an arrested sense of movement that transcends its newsreel source. The images give way to slo-mo shots of brutality and people entering railway cars as the scenes move from 1940 to 1943, ending with the final assault on the War-

saw Ghetto. Powerful short docu will find welcome at fests and venues that accommodate Holocaust-themed offerings.

Opening coda is followed by a medium talking-head shot of Edelman, one of the leaders of the Warsaw Uprising, who narrates a day-by-day chronicle of both the defiance and subsequent survival of those who resisted Nazi annihilation.

Also in b&w, Edelman's memories are presented chronologically, marked by dates that appear on the corner of the screen, days that tick past as the survivors look for a getaway. Edelman is one of about 50 Jews who eventually managed to escape through the sewers to another part of the city. Through leisurely timing and skillful use of archival material, Jolanta Dylewska infuses the film with almost hypnotic power as we follow Edelman's tale of death and survival in an act of unparalleled bravery, as the Jews resist deportation to certain death at Treblinka. The film is a testament to this bravery as well as an indictment of man's inhumanity to man.
—*Paul Lenti*

WHY HAVE YOU LEFT ME?

(KAZI ZASTO ME OSTAVI)

(FORMER YUGOSLAVIA)

A Cinema Design (Zinema Dizajn) production. Produced by Ljubisja Samaedizic. Directed Oleg Novkovic. Screenplay, Novkovic, Srdan Koljevic. camera (color), Miladin Colakovic; editor, Marco Glausac; music, Zoran Simjanovic. Reviewed at Broadway Screening Room, N.Y., April 18, 1994. (In Human Rights Watch Intl. Film Festival.) Running time: **90 MIN.**
Pedja .... Zarco Lausevi
Vera .... Milica Mihajlovic
Rabe .... Ljubisa Samardzic
Also with: Katanna Gojkovic, Dragan Jovanovic, Vladan Dujovic, Bata Stojkovic, Stev Zigon, Nidola Pejakovic.

Although not entirely successful, "Why Have You Left Me?" — first-timer Oleg Novkovic's senior thesis film — bears the crux of his youthful existential angst while painting a bleak picture of a country where people have lost faith in the future. Because of its topicality, film should find interest on the fest circuit.

Pic chronicles the effects of Yugoslavia's bloody civil war on a small group of friends, some of whom are conscripted and then tossed onto the front lines. After a few brusque battle scenes, the majority of the film concerns these characters' unsuccessful efforts to reintegrate themselves into daily life.

Pic opens at a Serbian disco, where we meet Pedja (Zarco Lausevi) and Ljuba, the gay lover of Pedja's girlfriend's brother. Then cut to the front lines, as Pedja, Ljuba and their older friend Rabe dodge bullets and view of the horrors of war.

Ljuba is shot, and the trio encounters a young woman who had been raped. They stay with her and her family, caring for Ljuba in his final moments. The woman even gives him a tape of the song "Why Have You Left Me?" to comfort him.

Pedja cannot shake this young woman from his mind. They are both refugees and cannot go back to life as it was before. When he sees her in Zagreb, he goes to look for her on the banks of the Danube and in a cemetery, where she steals flowers from the graves.

She wanders aimlessly around the city singing such eclectic fare as "The Girl From Ipanema" and the Violent Femmes' "Blister In The Sun." Her shell-shocked demeanor draws him to forget his former g.f. Ivana, who has arranged a new life for them in Paris. When his friend Rabe commits suicide by playing pool with a loaded grenade, Pedja and the young woman throw all caution to the wind.

The film's over-earnest message underlines the fact that these characters are all victims of a meaningless war, and that an equally meaningless death is their ultimate fate.

Tech credits and acting are OK.
—*Paul Lenti*

June 13, 1994

THE LION KING

A Buena Vista release of a Walt Disney Pictures presentation. Produced by Don Hahn. Executive producers, Thomas Schumacher, Sarah McArthur. Directed by Roger Allers, Rob Minkoff. Screenplay, Irene Mecchi, Jonathan Roberts, Linda Woolverton. Songs by Tim Rice (lyrics) and Elton John (music). Original score by Hans Zimmer. Technicolor prints; supervising editors, Tom Finan, John Carnochan; production design, Chris Sanders; art direction, Andy Gaskill; artistic coordinator, Randy Fullmer; artistic supervisors, Brenda Chapman (story), Dan St. Pierre (layout), Doug Ball (background), Vera Lanpher (cleanup), Scott Santoro (visual effects), Scott F. Johnston (computer graphics imagery); sound, Dolby. Reviewed at the Beekman Theater, N.Y., June 7, 1994. MPAA Rating: G. Running time: **87 MIN.**

Voices:
Zazu .... Rowan Atkinson
Simba .... Matthew Broderick
Young Nala .... Niketa Calame
Ed .... Jim Cummings
Shenzi .... Whoopi Goldberg
Rafiki .... Robert Guillaume
Scar .... Jeremy Irons
Mufasa .... James Earl Jones
Nala .... Moira Kelly
Timon .... Nathan Lane
Banzai .... Cheech Marin
Pumbaa .... Ernie Sabella
Sarabi .... Madge Sinclair
Young
   Simba ..... Jonathan Taylor Thomas

Set off by some of the richest imagery the studio's animators have produced and held together by a timeless coming-of-age tale, "The Lion King" marks a dazzling — and unexpectedly daring — addition to the Disney canon. There's little doubt that this film, abetted by a marvelous cast of star voices and songs by Elton John and Tim Rice tending toward huge, sonorous choral numbers, will draw huge, sonorous crowds this summer and beyond.

But the film shifts from upbeat sequences, featuring two snappy sidekicks and plenty of good-hearted accomplices in the classic Disney mold, to scenes of truly terrifying animal-kingdom violence that should cause parents to think twice before bringing along the "Little Mermaid" set. And though the songs are well-integrated with a story that's part "Candide," part "Hamlet," they lack the charm and subtle wit of the Alan Menken/Howard Ashman tunes for "The Little Mermaid" and "Beauty and the Beast."

A mesmerizing pre-credits opening sets up the story and establishes an epic tone that carries through much of the movie. As the sun rises over the African jungle, the animals gather in teeming flocks and herds and broods — gazelles, giraffes, birds, zebras — heeding a call to assembly as the anthemic "Circle of Life" builds over the animals' sounds to a roaring crescendo when they come together in a clearing beneath a promontory.

Up there, Mufasa (James Earl Jones), the Lion King, and his Queen, Sarabi (Madge Sinclair) look on approvingly as the mystical baboon Rafiki (Robert Guillaume) presents their cub, Simba (Jonathan Taylor Thomas), as the future Lion King, while Zazu the hornbill (a hilarious Rowan Atkinson) flits about, making sure the King's bidding is attended to (think Sebastian in "Mermaid").

But there's a shadow on the festivities, and it's not feminists seeing red over such grandiose patriarchal partying. It's Mufasa's brother Scar (Jeremy Irons), a dangerous mix of jealousy, murderous intent and bitchiness. With a trio of menacing, snarly and equally bitchy hyenas — Shenzi (Whoopi Goldberg), Banzai (Cheech Marin) and Ed (Jim Cummings) — Scar begins his campaign to kill off his competition for the throne, enticing Simba and his girlfriend, Nala (Niketa Calame), to venture into forbidden territory, which turns out to be a hyena-packed elephant's graveyard.

Saving the teeny couple from being devoured by the pack, Mufasa teaches his son a lesson about leadership. At one point, father and son look into a starry sky — aside from the animals, the film's most ravishing depictions are the deep and brilliant night skies — and Mufasa explains that the stars are the kings of the past watching over them.

That information comes in handy in the movie's most stunning sequence, which finds Mufasa again saving Simba, this time from a swarming stampede of hyenas and wildebeests set in motion by Scar.

The prolonged, charged scene concludes with Mufasa, having saved Simba, crawling up a mountainside, only to be met by Scar, who promptly and brutally commits fratricide and then convinces Simba it was all his fault. As Hans Zimmer's tumultuous score quiets down, the young cub sets out in exile while Scar and the hyenas take over the jungle.

Finally, the fun begins, as Simba ends up in a kind of Shangri-La, where he's befriended by a flatulent, grub-loving wart hog named Pumbaa (Ernie Sabella) and a catty meerkat, Timon (Nathan Lane, stealing the show). They teach him the pleasures of "Hakuna Matata," which basically means, "don't worry, be happy," and is sung by Lane and Sabella with delightful irreverence.

But those stars keep reminding Simba, now grown (and voiced by Matthew Broderick), of his destiny, with an assist from Nala (voiced beautifully by Moira Kelly). Simba returns to a home left barren and wasted by Scar's selfish tyranny, and nephew and uncle battle to the death as volcanic fireworks explode around them. The natural order is restored, and nature responds with almost unseemly generosity.

While the individual animal characters are represented with typical Disney cleverness, the herds are memorable for their unexpected realism, the zebras in particular. And kudos, too, to Irene Mecchi, Jonathan Roberts and Linda Woolverton for an involving screenplay that handles shifts in tone with considerable grace.

Disney has mounted a huge promotional effort with this movie, what with tie-ins to zoos and personal appearances by various emissaries from the animal kingdom.

None of it is necessary. "The Lion King" doesn't need any help standing alone as a tale that should give parents and older children plenty to talk about. Nevertheless, a generation that remembers the death of Bambi's mother as traumatizing should bear that experience in mind when deciding who goes to "The Lion King" — and who stays home with the babysitter.

—*Jeremy Gerard*

WOLF

A Columbia release of a Douglas Wick production. Produced by Wick. Executive producers, Neil Machlis, Robert Greenhut. Directed by Mike Nichols. Screenplay, Jim Harrison, Wesley Strick. Camera (Technicolor), Giuseppe Rotunno; editor, Sam O'Steen; music, Ennio Morricone; production design, Bo Welch; art direction, Tom Duffield, Tom Warren (N.Y.); set design, Jacques Valin, Sean Haworth; set decoration, Linda DeScenna, Susan Bode (N.Y.); costume design, Ann Roth; sound (Dolby), Arthur Rochester, Danny Michael (N.Y.); special makeup effects, Rick Baker; animatronic wolf effects, Tom Woodruff Jr., Alec Gillis; associate producers, Harrison, Michele Imperato; assistant director, Michael Haley; casting, Juliet Taylor. Reviewed at the UA Westwood Theater, L.A., June 3, 1994. MPAA Rating: R. Running time: **125 MIN.**
Will Randall .... Jack Nicholson
Laura Alden .... Michelle Pfeiffer
Stewart Swinton .... James Spader
Charlotte Randall ...... Kate Nelligan
Detective Bridger ...... Richard Jenkins
Raymond
   Alden .... Christopher Plummer
Mary ....Eileen Atkins
Roy .... David Hyde Pierce
Dr. Vijay Alezias .... Om Puri
Doctor .... Ron Rifkin
Maude .... Prunella Scales

"**W**olf" is a decidedly upscale horror film, a tony werewolf movie in which a full roster of fancy talents tries to mate with unavoidably hoary, not to say hairy, material. Offspring of this union is less ungainly than might have been feared, but is also less than entirely convincing, an intriguing thriller more enjoyable for its humor and sophistication than for its scare quotient. Classy production's artistic schizophrenia mirrors the perplexing marketing challenge facing Columbia.

The studio must convince the horror/special-effects crowd to attend a Jack Nicholson/Michelle Pfeiffer/Mike Nichols picture and persuade the filmmakers' fans to see a genre pic. Best guess is that film will attract a portion of the audience that went for the studio's previous lavish, prestige shocker, "Bram Stoker's Dracula," but far from all of it, making recoupment of its reportedly $70 million-plus production cost a dicey matter.

Clearly, no expense has been spared in outfitting this project, which bears comparison to such perennials as "Dr. Jekyll and Mr. Hyde," "Beauty and the Beast" and many mangier monster epics turned out over the decades. But no matter how snazzy the trappings, when you get down to it, this is still, at heart, a werewolf picture — the story of a man who starts growing an abnormal amount of hair, developing acute senses of smell, sight and hearing, and roving out under the full moon to cause all manner of mayhem.

June 13, 1994 (Cont.)

Correctly sensing where this is headed, viewers can derive the most amusement from watching how the clever filmmakers adroitly sidestep many of the form's cobwebs while still trying to deliver the expected goods. Ultimately, they score best where witty dialogue, decorative doodling, character one-upmanship and knowing variations on audience expectations are concerned; they are least successful in developing relevant themes and delivering the down-and-dirty fun, thrills and suspense sought by genre addicts.

Set on a snowy night to the accompaniment of Ennio Morricone's old-fashioned creepy-crawly score, opening sequence has Will Randall (Nicholson) hitting a wolf with his car on a lonely Vermont road. Thinking it's dead, he reaches out to touch it, whereupon the animal suddenly revives and bites him on the hand before lighting out into the woods.

Back in New York, Will is facing the dread midlife prospect of being ousted from his position as editor in chief of a quality book publishing house in the wake of a takeover by billionaire tycoon Raymond Alden (Christopher Plummer). At a swank dinner party at the latter's estate, Will's worst fears are confirmed, but he also has a chance meeting with Raymond's edgy, beautiful daughter, Laura (Michelle Pfeiffer).

The first sign that something is amiss is the thick hair growing around the bite on Will's hand. Pic's best stretch involves Will's bewildered but delighted growing awareness of his heightened sensory powers and increased youthfulness and energy, and his employment of them to scheme against his sniveling, two-faced former protege, Stewart Swinton (James Spader), whom Raymond has promoted into Will's former job.

Will's discovery that Stewart is also having an affair with his wife (Kate Nelligan), which Will amusingly learns courtesy of his acute new sniffing abilities, prompts him to seek solace with Laura, to whom he confesses what happened to him and with whom he eventually starts an affair. On a nocturnal outing, Will attacks a deer, and the ante is upped on each successive night as he is increasingly dominated by the aggressive animal growing inside him.

No doubt highly mindful of the audience's suspension-of-disbelief mechanism, the filmmakers have carefully charted Will's transformation, having chosen an intelligent, skeptical man as their subject and retaining rationality as far as possible. The strong humor injected into the proceedings, at least through the second act, also helps keep one on the film's side.

But as Will's attacks become increasingly savage, the story becomes channeled into a more conventional format, and fact that the Will-Laura relationship has no resonance delivers the picture a body blow that may not knock it out but does put it on the ropes. Laura is presented as a bad little rich girl whose life is mostly devoted to defying Daddy while still enjoying his money. She and Will inhabit different wavelengths, and nothing that happens between them develops any particular rooting interest for the viewer. Ultimate revelation that "Wolf" is supposed to be a transcendent romance almost seems like an afterthought, and one that's hardly prepared for by the treatment of the story up until then.

Script by Jim Harrison and Wesley Strick, which bears no relation to Harrison's novel "Wolf," tries hard to make this shaggy story play plausibly as a modern piece, but still can't avoid such tired devices as full moon fever and the Middle European expert who explains lycanthropy to Will.

A sensible intelligence has been applied to the characterizations. Unlike the case in his previous, over the top horror outing, "The Shining," Nicholson begins his performance in a low key and cranks it up only by degrees. Except for the nocturnal moments when the wolf takes over, the actor holds the line firmly in order to create a tension between his will to normalcy and his helpless transformation into savagery.

By contrast, Pfeiffer's Laura comes across as hard and brittle. It's not a rewarding role and, given the grandly romantic goal the film fails to achieve, her character needs more shading and generosity of heart.

Spader is back playing the sort of loathsome yuppie he excelled at earlier in his career, and doing it just as well as before. Nelligan has little to do as the unfaithful wife, while some of the other supporting perfs, notably those of Eileen Atkins and David Hyde Pierce as Will's loyal publishing underlings, are dead perfect in the venerable Nichols shorthand mode.

New York locations and elaborate soundstage sets are accompanied by fine use of L.A.'s Bradbury Building as the home of the book firm. Rick Baker, who knows his werewolves (numerous credits include "An American Werewolf in London" and "Greystoke"), has once again done ace special makeup effects, and brief scenes in which people run and jump in wolflike fashion are highly effective. Other tech credits represent the best that money can buy.

—Todd McCarthy

THE CLIENT

A Warner Bros. release presented in association with Regency Enterprises and Alcor Films of an Arnon Milchan production. Produced by Milchan, Steven Reuther. Co-producer, Mary McLaglen. Directed by Joel Schumacher. Screenplay, Akiva Goldsman, Robert Getchell, based on the novel by John Grisham. Camera (Technicolor, Panavision widescreen), Tony Pierce-Roberts; editor, Robert Brown; music, Howard Shore; production design, Bruno Rubeo; art direction, P. Michael Johnston; set design, Marco Rubeo, Kevin Cross; set decoration, Anne D. McCulley; costume design, Ingrid Ferrin; sound (Dolby), Petur Hliddal; associate producer, Guy Ferland; assistant director, Yudi Bennett; second unit camera, Robert Wagner; casting, Mali Finn. Reviewed at Warner Bros. Studio, Burbank, June 6, 1994. MPAA rating: PG-13. Running time: **120 MIN.**

Reggie Love .... Susan Sarandon
Roy Foltrigg .... Tommy Lee Jones
Dianne Sway .... Mary-Louise Parker
Barry Muldano .... Anthony LaPaglia
Clint Von Hooser .... Anthony Edwards
Harry Roosevelt .... Ossie Davis
Mark Sway .... Brad Renfro
Ricky Sway .... David Speck
McThune .... J.T. Walsh
Sgt. Hardy .... Will Patton
Thomas Fink .... Bradley Whitford
Trumann .... Anthony Heald
Paul Gronke .... Kim Coates
With: William H. Macy, Micole Mercurio, Kimberly Scott, William Sanderson, Walter Olkewicz, Amy Hathaway, Jo Harvey Allen, Ron Dean, William Richert

"**T**he Client" is a satisfactory, by-the-numbers child-in-jeopardy thriller that will fill the bill as a very commercial hot-weather popcorn picture. Lackluster, if faultlessly professional, in terms of filmmaking and performance, this third adaptation of a John Grisham best-seller to hit the big screen within less than a year's time typically has enough narrative meat on it to pull audiences in and keep them attentive. But unlike "The Firm" and "The Pelican Brief," both of which used superstar casts in addition to the Grisham identity plate to propel them past the $100 million domestic B.O. mark, this one will have to sail somewhat more on the author's rep, spelling business that promises to be strong but perhaps less than towering.

While the tale's hook is powerful and sets up considerable peril for the protagonists and intrigue for the viewer, overriding problem here is the basic lack of suspense. With a child lead, sympathetic female cohort and a chief bad guy who looks like he just walked off a pirate ship, one can safely bet the house that nothing will happen to the heroes. And director Joel Schumacher doesn't stir up any dramatic tension on his own. Nearly every scene advances the story, but in perfunctory fashion, resulting in a film that proves reasonably involving but in no way exciting.

Opening sequence still stands, two hours later, as the best in the picture. Two little brothers, Mark and Ricky Sway (Brad Renfro and David Speck) witness a big, bearded man park his car in a secluded area, attach a hose to the exhaust pipe and stick it through the window. Unable to stand by passively, 11-year-old Mark detaches the hose, not once, but twice, upon which the man throws him in the car and insists that he die with him. Mark manages to save himself, but not before hearing the man's secrets, which involve the whereabouts of the missing body of a U.S. senator who was murdered by the Mob.

With young Ricky lapsed into a coma after watching the violent events, scene shifts to a Memphis hospital, where the boys' single mother (Mary-Louise Parker) frets over losing her job, and Mark becomes the object of relentless attention on the part of the cops, the FBI, the press and, particularly, fierce federal prosecutor Roy Foltrigg (Tommy Lee Jones), who hopes to use the kid's knowledge to further his own political ambitions.

But not if one Reggie Love can help it. Having watched enough TV shows to know that he should have a lawyer, Mark finds one in Ms. Love (Susan Sarandon), a woman who makes up for her limited experience with unflagging tenacity and personal commitment. Warned by Mob henchmen that he's dog meat if he spills the beans to anyone, Mark won't even tell his attorney what he knows, much less the anxious Foltrigg, and the main mystery consists of how long it will take the kid to come across with the goods. The answer is, a long time.

Meanwhile, Mark outwits mobsters who move in on him at the hospital, tries to revive his bedridden brother with funny pranks, has a meeting of the minds with Reggie, who conveniently had a drinking problem just like Mark's dad and has two kids who won't see her, just as Mark has exiled his own father, and boldly takes the Fifth when Foltrigg finally gets him on the stand.

Action finale has Mark and Reggie moving in on the senator's hidden corpse at the same time the gangsters arrive, but even here the only jolt comes from the unexpected entrance of a raccoon. Those deserving of just desserts get them offscreen in this relatively mild PG-13 concoction, and feel-good wrap-up manages to give everyone what they want.

Schumacher's directorial style is strictly presentational, devoted to getting the plot up on the screen in comprehensible fashion with no fuss, no frills, no thrills. Making "The Client" feel so mundane is its mechanical construction, which consists of doling out a little plot, then a little

June 13, 1994 (Cont.)

character revelation, then back to the plot, and the superficial nature of the characters themselves.

Each of the leads is outfitted with one or two significant biographical or motivational traits, and that's seen as enough for the audience to understand them. Reggie has her determination to prove herself in the wake of a broken marriage and subsequent drug and booze addictions, Mark carries around his resentment toward his irresponsible father and resultant mistrust of all adults, and Foltrigg is driven by single-minded ambition.

Story's sympathies are weighted in transparently audience-friendly directions, rooted in the predicaments of an endangered kid and a beleaguered woman fending for themselves against good old boy government types and the scummiest of villains. Given the ambivalent treatment of the Foltrigg character, it is somewhat surprising, and disappointing, that he doesn't become a more insidious force, while the mobsters, repped most prominently by the reptilian Barry Muldano (Anthony LaPaglia), are so grossly caricatured as to be virtual parodies of baddies.

Performances are only OK, given the skin-deep characters. Sarandon is all earnest gumption and resilient dedication, while Jones, with virtually no character to play, executes an assortment of actorly riffs that at least make him entertaining. Young Renfro is similarly acceptable as the victimized Mark, but he doesn't match the exceptional work of numerous other child thesps in recent pix, including Jesse Bradford in "King of the Hill," T.J. Lowther in "A Perfect World" and Max Pomeranc in "Searching for Bobby Fischer."

Technical contributions all contribute unimpeachably to the pro sheen of the entire enterprise.

—*Todd McCarthy*

BARCELONA

A Fine Line Features release from Castle Rock Entertainment of a Westerly Films presentation. Produced, directed, written by Whit Stillman. Camera (Fotofilm color; Technicolor prints), John Thomas; editor, Christopher Tellefsen; music, Marc Suozzo; design, Jose Maria Botines; costume design, Edi Giguere; sound (Dolby), Licio Oliveira; line producers, Victoria Borras, Rosa Romero; associate producers, Edmon Roch, Cecelia Kate Roque; assistant directors, Antonio A. Farre, Sergio Martos; casting, Billy Hopkins, Simone Reynolds. Reviewed at Cannes Film Festival (market), May 15, 1994. (In Seattle Intl. Film Festival.) Running time: **100 MIN.**

Ted	Taylor Nichols
Fred	Chris Eigeman
Montserrat	Tushka Bergen
Marta	Mira Sorvino
Ramone	Pep Munne
Aurora	Nuria Badia
Greta	Hellena Schmied
Frank	Francis Creighton
Dickie	Thomas Gibson
Consul	Jack Gilpin

Four years after his distinctive debut feature, "Metropolitan," Whit Stillman has delivered a superior follow-up in "Barcelona." A verbal tale of two well-spoken young American men posted in the beautiful seaport city during what is described as "the last decade of the Cold War," sophisticated picture possesses a strong authorial voice and an appealing intelligence in its handling of affairs of the heart and its Yanks-abroad theme. By, about and for thoughtful people interested in culture and politics, film will need strong reviews and strategic launch by Fine Line to get past no-name cast and director's limited profile.

But late July release could be a shrewd move to capture the interest of discriminating urban viewers starved for some substance after two months of big-budget summer fare. After just two Cannes market screenings, pic had its official world preem June 12 at the Seattle Film Festival.

In a sensual, Old World setting rocked by sporadic violence directed at such U.S.-identified targets as the American Library, IBM and the USO, the somewhat priggish Ted (Taylor Nichols) nonetheless lives a charmed existence as a sales rep for an American company. His social life is filled with delightful, beautifully attired "trade fair girls" who overflow a seemingly endless round of parties, and Ted's only problem is an inclination toward undue seriousness that prevents him from enjoying the city's pleasure-oriented lifestyle as much as he should.

Hobbled by no such handicaps is his cousin Fred (Chris Eigeman), a U.S. Navy officer who suddenly turns up and camps out in Ted's apartment. With his loud, obnoxious ways and patriotic views, Fred could easily be written off as a typical Ugly American, but he quickly shows himself to be considerably more complex than that. Stillman sets up a temperamental opposition between the two men, who have been antagonistic with each other since they were boys stateside.

Pleasing his cousin with the news that young Spanish women are promiscuous, Ted nonetheless announces that, tired of being a slave to his obsession with physical beauty, he will henceforth go out only with plain girls, and won't sleep with anyone until he's found Miss Right.

Those vows last only until he meets Montserrat (Tushka Bergen), a somewhat sullen blonde who dates Ted but still continues to see a virulently anti-Yank Spanish b.f. Latter provides one of many doors into what is perhaps the film's most singular achievement, the portrayal of the manifold ways — from subtle to overt — in which anti-American sentiments were vented overseas during a certain period in the '70s and '80s.

This line of inquiry may be of limited interest to international viewers, and even to domestic audiences, but Stillman is clearly gripped by the subject and integrates it into his dramatic material in an impressively detailed way that feels fresh in a fictional narrative context. Fred explodes when Spaniards, seeing him in uniform, scorn him as a "fascist," as if they didn't know their own history, and can barely contain himself when one professes to speak knowledgeably of the evils of the "AFL-CIA."

With the Sixth Fleet treading water nearby, however, some locals feel they have just cause for complaint, and Fred himself becomes the victim of a terrorist act. Ted's hospital vigil during his cousin's life-and-death struggle unexpectedly provides the stage for further romantic developments, and an epilogue rounds out the loose ends in satisfactory fashion.

After examining the rarefied world of debutante socialites with wit and obvious expertise in "Metropolitan," Stillman opens up his artistic universe a bit more here, and displays an increased ease with filmmaking craft. Main problem with his first film was a real stiffness in the direction that made it rely almost exclusively on the dialogue and subject matter for its effect. Stillman seems much more comfortable with the visual side of things this time out, as he and lenser John Thomas (one of several "Metropolitan" teammates, along with editor Chris Tellefsen and composer Mark Suozzo, to repeat here) adroitly convey the Barcelona an everyday resident would experience, rather than the tourist version.

Abundant dialogue is tart, informed, often droll and as opinionated as real conversation. Pic's almost extreme literary quality and expatriate characters make one feel that Stillman could be a spiritual brother to the Lost Generation of 1920s writers. The arch, old-school way his Yanks speak takes a little getting used to and may simply sound stilted to some viewers.

Nichols and Eigeman, both from "Metropolitan," seem right at home in Stillman's world, and make their not always easy characters grow on one as things proceed. Supporting cast of many women and a few men is marked by a nice variety of types. The lovely settings and intelligent company make "Barcelona" a welcome place to spend some time. Action sags somewhat in the stretch shortly before the attack on Fred, indicating that a little pruning could make a sharp film even better.

—*Todd McCarthy*

GETTING EVEN WITH DAD

A Metro-Goldwyn-Mayer release of a Jacobs/Gardner production. Produced by Katie Jacobs, Pierce Gardner. Executive producer, Richard Hashimoto. Directed by Howard Deutch. Screenplay, Tom S. Parker, Jim Jennewein. Camera (Deluxe color), Tim Suhrstedt; editor, Richard Halsey; music, Miles Goodman; production design, Virginia L. Randolph; art direction, Clayton R. Hartley; set decoration, Barbara Munch; costume design, Rudy Dillon; sound (Dolby), Bill Phillips, John Phillips; associate producers, Parker, Jennewein, Elena Spiotta; assistant director, K.C. Colwell; second unit director, Jack Gill; casting, Richard Pagano, Sharon Bialy, Debi Manwiller. Reviewed at Skywalker Sound, Santa Monica, May 31, 1994. MPAA Rating: PG. Running time: **108 MIN.**

Timmy	Macaulay Culkin
Ray	Ted Danson
Theresa	Glenne Headly
Bobby	Saul Rubinek
Carl	Gailard Sartain
Alex	Sam McMurray
Lt. Romayko	Hector Elizondo
Kitty	Kathleen Wilhoitte
Wayne	Dann Florek

Neither Macaulay Culkin nor Ted Danson has improved his luck in selecting projects with this schizophrenic comedy, which can't decide if it wants to be broadly farcical or fuzzily heartwarming. While it fares better on the latter front, pic doesn't succeed on either level and should test the patience even among Culkin's peer group. In short, "Dad" should have a hard time getting even where it counts.

At least the movie features Culkin once again outsmarting adults — as he did in the enormously successful "Home Alone" movies — following his bizarre foray into thriller territory with "The Good Son."

June 13, 1994 (Cont.)

A more subtle problem presenting itself is that the moppet icon appears to be entering a somewhat awkward stage, and his near-shoulder-length hair here doesn't help matters any. Then again, hairstyling might be of less concern if the principals had more to work with in Tom S. Parker and Jim Jennewein's script.

Culkin plays an 11-year-old boy dumped on the doorstep of his dad (Danson), an ex-con whom he hasn't seen in years. Timmy, who's been living with his aunt since his mother's death, has the bad timing to show up just when Dad is about to undertake a major theft, seeking a big enough score to go straight and buy the bakery where he works.

Timmy has his own ideas, however, and hides his father's ill-gotten gains, forcing him to squire the kid around town in exchange for finding out where the loot is.

That setup is obviously designed to allow father and son to grudgingly grow to love each other, while milking laughs out of Dad's two partners in crime (Saul Rubinek, Gailard Sartain), who follow Timmy and his father everywhere they go, not wanting to let their share of the booty get away from them.

While that provides the opportunity for "Home Alone"-type skewering of the two bumbling criminals, director Howard Deutch ("Pretty in Pink," "Some Kind of Wonderful") never seems comfortable taking the full plunge into those waters.

As a result, even though the title and marketing imply that this will be a broad comedy, few of the jokes play that way, and the extended sequence where Culkin drags the adult trio to amusement parks, the zoo and elsewhere, falls thuddingly flat.

Deutch does a little better with a cat-and-mouse search for the stash that incorporates the local police, including a femme cop (Glenne Headly) who provides a potential love interest for Dad — the narrative undergoing a real stretch to involve a female character. In fact, that subplot serves only to prolong the movie, which feels like a long sit, especially for small fry.

Culkin's cold, impassive line delivery is getting a bit tired, especially as he slouches toward his teens. While he became a megastar in "Home Alone" playing a kid who gets to live out every kid's fantasy, it's become obvious that it's difficult to expand his appeal beyond that formula.

After his lengthy tenure on "Cheers," meanwhile, Danson could use a part where he doesn't play a borderline moron with a good heart, as he did in "Made in America" as well.

Other performances tend to be too over-the-top, particularly Rubinek as the most annoying of the small-time hoods, while Headly's not terribly believable as a policewoman.

Technically, pic makes only sparse use of its San Francisco locales, suffers from pacing problems and relies too heavily on Miles Goodman's score to provide the sense of impishness to which it so obviously aspires. *—Brian Lowry*

CANNES FEST

THE TROUBLES WE'VE SEEN: A HISTORY OF JOURNALISM IN WARTIME (1ST AND 2ND JOURNEYS)

(VEILLES D'ARMES: LE JOURNALISME EN TEMPS DE GUERRE (1er ET 2eme VOYAGES)

(FRENCH-GERMAN-BRITISH — DOCU)

A Little Bear Prods. (Paris)/Premiere (Germany) production, with participation of Canal Plus and the BBC. Produced by Bertrand Tavernier, Frederic Bourboulon. Directed, written by Marcel Ophuls. Camera (color), Pierre Boffety, Pierre Milon; editor, Sophie Brunet; sound recording, Michel Faure, Eric Devulder; sound editing, Ariane Doublet; sound mixing, Paul Bertault; kinescoping, Swiss Effects; assistant directors, Dominki Moll, Laurent Cantet. Reviewed at Cannes Festival (non-competing), May 23, 1994. Running times: **92 MIN.** ("First Journey"), **137 MIN.** ("Second Journey"). Total running time: **229 MIN.**

With: Marcel Ophuls, Philippe Noiret, John Simpson, John F. Burns, Martha Gellhorn, Nicolas Koljevic, Radovan Karadzic, Slobodan Milosevic, Alain Finkielkraut, Philip Knightley, Patrick Poivre D'Arvor, Romain Goupil, Patrick Chauvel.

(English, French, German, Serbian and Croatian dialogue)

In "The Troubles We've Seen," master documentarian Marcel Ophuls tackles the dangers, rewards and ethical/philosophical underpinnings of war reporting in this century. Helmer's restless probing — and audacious juxtaposing of movie clips with footage culled from four trips to Sarajevo starting January '93 — yields a compellingly sculpted view of ongoing atrocities and ongoing courage, framed by a view of other historical conflicts that is comprehensive only in segments.

These first two free-standing installments of a three-part project preemed, with little advance notice, on final day of the Cannes fest and will be telecast by Brit pubcaster BBC the last two Saturdays in July. Theatrical release in France this autumn should be echoed in major cities worldwide.

Pix are dense, entertaining, informative but also "difficult" for viewers whose level of erudition in the arts and humanities falls beneath that of Ophuls himself — which is just about everybody. Helmer is a major character in both installments.

Ophuls has an unbeatable opening hook in the true story of how World War II was declared on the very day his father, Max Ophuls, was directing a scene in the costumer "From Mayerling to Sarajevo" in which disgruntled Prinzip ("I forget if he was Serb or Croatian," Ophuls tells the camera) shot Archduke Ferdinand, thereby setting off the *first* World War. Ophuls postulates there's no end to meaningful coincidences or to history itself.

Ophuls reiterates historian Philip Knightley's pronouncement that "the first casualty of war is the truth," and posits the journalist's job as trying to get at the truth all the same. He then cuts to mocking military scenes from "Duck Soup," including the Marx Brothers singing "All God's Children Got Guns."

Ophuls documents his efforts to get to Sarajevo in January '93, speaks to intrepid journalists — both novice and seasoned, but all freezing — and relates the efforts of his own tiny crew to get around, which they do mostly by tagging along with the BBC's exemplary men in the field.

Pic is peppered with print, broadcast and photojournalists, with many pertinent observations from Pulitzer Prize-winning New York Times correspondent John F. Burns (both parts) and veteran BBC special envoy John Simpson (first part).

Martha Gellhorn, the crusty no-nonsense reporter who posed as a nurse to sneak aboard a D-Day landing craft, only to have her scoop swiped by former husband Ernest Hemingway, is an unmitigated delight. Gellhorn says boredom is the worst thing in a war setting and contends that "war correspondents are highly privileged and shouldn't be glorified."

Apart from gathering firsthand accounts and letting the camera run long enough for friends and foes alike to reveal telling details, Ophuls has always excelled at the juxtaposition of disparate imagery. Since the Holiday Inn in Sarajevo is home to the foreign press corps, he has a field day with clips from the 1942 Bing Crosby starrer and its classic ditties "White Christmas" and "Happy Holidays."

Clips from Olivier's screen version of "Henry V" comment brilliantly on the folly of ill-considered battle, as Clinton, Major, Mitterand and Kohl are shown going about their non-committal business in the comfort of state occasions.

Although clips — from "His Girl Friday" to "Lola Montes" — make irreverent points throughout, pic's second part employs a highly questionable comparison when footage of James Cagney dancing up a storm is intercut with testimony from a Bosnian stage actor whose legs were blown off.

First part ends with jarring sequence of Ophuls wearing a bathrobe and a fedora in a Vienna hotel room, while a shapely naked woman lolls on the bed. Auds at the Cannes preem were baffled by helmer's intent. Scene could be taken to mean that life goes on outside the besieged war zone, that journalists are "whores" or, better yet, that viewers can rapidly disregard the whole topic of Sarajevo's agony to wonder, "What's Ophuls doing on camera with a naked woman?"

Pic's longer second part is bracketed by shots of Venice, which Ophuls deems to be "another dying city." Back in Sarajevo, docu delves into risks and etiquette of war reporting and the primordial importance of luck. In a series of scathing indictments based on televised news shows hosted by Gallic media honchos, French government officials are shown spinning their wheels with egregious complacency.

Pic examines control of info during the Gulf war, and the president of Serbia assures Ophuls with a straight face that freedom of the press in Serbia is "unparalleled."

Ophuls and Burns conducted lively interviews, weeks prior to the massacre, in the same Sarajevo market where the devastating February '94 bombing took place. (Pre-massacre interviewees all insisted that relief supplies be re-directed to their needier compatriots outside of town.)

Odyssey winds down as a surgeon at an overwhelmed clinic in Sarajevo — a city where one out of every six people was killed in less than a year — sings "Nobody Knows the Trouble I've Seen" in a lovely baritone.

At Cannes fest, "First Journey" was screened in an answer print fresh from the lab; "Second Journey" was shown as video projection. Pierre Boffety and Pierre Milon's no-frills camera work is involving and communicates on the big screen. Sound recording is crisp, editing tops.

More footage of Ophuls sparring with Serb leaders would be welcome and will apparently figure prominently in third and final installment.

Outraged that French trades had given little or no coverage to the Cannes screening, Ophuls canceled his press conference and left town, sending a witty and combative fax to take his place. Latest opus proves that when it comes to much-

June 13, 1994 (Cont.)

needed conceptual chutzpah, Ophuls is irreplaceable.

—*Lisa Nesselson*

WILD REED
(LES ROSEAUX SAUVAGES)
(FRENCH — DRAMA — COLOR)

An IMA and Les Films Alain Sarde release and co-production, with the participation of Le Canal Plus, in association with La Sept/Arte, IMA and SPF. Produced by Alain Sarde, Georges Benayoun. Executive producer, Jean-Jacques Albert. Directed by Andre Techine. Screenplay, Techine, Gilles Taurand; Camera (color), Jeanne Lapoirie; editor, Martine Giordano; set decoration, Pierre Soula; costume design, Brigitte Laleouse; sound (Dolby), Francois Groult; assistant director, Denis Bergonhe. Reviewed at Cannes Film Festival (Un Certain Regard), May 22, 1994. Running time: **110 MIN.**

Maite .... Elodie Bouchez
Francois .... Gael Morel
Serge .... Stephane Rideau
Henri .... Frederic Gorny
Madame Alvarez .... Michele Moretti

Following the disappointing family melodrama "Ma Saison preferee," which opened last year's Cannes festival, Andre Techine is back in top form with "Wild Reed," a poignantly touching coming-of-age saga. Putting his notorious penchant for visual style at the service of a more personal work, Techine has made one of his best and most emotional films. Evocation of universal themes about adolescence and sexual politics, peppered with Gallic charm and popular American songs, should make this film, which could be described as a French "American Graffiti," seductive to offshore audiences with a taste for warm French fare.

Set in 1962, at the end of the Algerian war, tale centers on the inner turmoil of a trio of youngsters at a boarding school. Francois (Gael Morel), a sensitive boy (clearly the helmer's alter ego), is beginning to explore his sexuality when he finds himself attracted to the masculine, working-class Serge (Stephane Rideau), a classmate.

A sexual incident between them in the dorm one night confuses Francois, though it's clear to Serge that it was a one-time occurrence, a release of unbearable sexual tension. In fact, Serge is attracted to Maite (Elodie Bouchez), the pretty daughter of Madame Alvarez (Michele Moretti), their severe, demanding teacher.

Into this stable, rather calm world arrives Henri (Frederic Gorny), a militant French-Algerian boy whose radical politics throw the school into turbulence. "Wild Reed" is wonderfully precise in chroni-

cling how political ideas created bitterly opposing camps over the issue of Algeria's independence and hence tore the country apart.

Pic's first scene, the wedding of Serge's brother, establishes that he, like many of his compatriots, would do anything to avoid going back to war, and his death serves as the dramatic impetus for various personal/political crises.

Structured as a series of interlocking vignettes, "Wild Reed" contains moments that are at once painful and droll. In one touching scene, Francois stands in front of a mirror, repeating over and over, as if to convince himself, "I am a faggot." In another, he storms into the town's shoe store, whose owner is known to be gay, and shocks the bewildered man with a direct question about his lifestyle.

As always, Techine is excellent at exploring "tiny" personal flashes that assume larger meaning when placed against the broader historical context. In the film's last and most important sequence, a picnic by the river, the four main characters are forced to come to terms with their inner crises and emerging identities. In a masterly stroke, with a restlessly swirling camera, helmer skillfully captures that crucial moment that announces the end of innocence and the beginning of adulthood.

Techine is one of few French directors to explore life in the provinces, and here Jeanne Lapoirie's luminous lensing seizes the specific flavor of France's Southwest. Like "American Graffiti," the energetic soundtrack uses popular hits from the era, including the Platters' "Smoke Gets in Your Eyes," Del Shannon's "Runaway" and the Beach Boys' "Barbara Ann."

In its lyrical mood, perceptive scrutiny of rites of passage and fresh, naturalistic acting, "Wild Reed" bears resemblance to Louis Malle's great childhood films, most notably "Murmur of the Heart."

—*Emanuel Levy*

TRACKING DOWN MAGGIE:
THE UNOFFICIAL BIOGRAPHY OF MARGARET THATCHER
(BRITISH — DOCU —16mm)

A Lafayette Film production for Channel 4. Produced by Rieta Oord, Nick Broomfield. Directed by Broomfield. Camera (color), Barry Ackroyd; editors, Rick Vick, Susan Bloom; music, David Bergaud; sound, Matthew Booth. Reviewed at Cannes Film Festival (market), May 19, 1994. Running time: **83 MIN.**

Kamikaze documentarist Nick Broomfield unleashes his bothersome Brit persona on the Iron Lady with hilariously revealing results in "Tracking Down Maggie." Basically 1½ hours of the filmmaker being rigorously denied access to his subject, the outcome exposes sides to Thatcher that more hands-on portraits might never approach. Extensive TV and festival exposure is a cert.

Film opens with Big Ben chiming out a somewhat unceremonious farewell to Britain's former prime minister, given four days to pack her bags and vacate 10 Downing Street after a 15-year stint. Thatcher's business affairs fell immediately into the hands of her pampered son Mark, whose alleged involvement in shady international arms deals becomes Broomfield's most hotly pursued topic.

He trails Thatcher on a U.S. promotional tour for the publication of her autobiography. While attempting without much luck to get past her security team, he digresses into her past to amusingly reassess the grocer's daughter from suburban Grantham via locals and school chums.

An entertaining recap is provided of her cultivation of the Iron Lady image, and the elocution lessons designed to lower her initially off-putting voice.

Standout encounter is a brush with an eccentric former neighbor who salvaged the toilet from chez Thatcher when the bathroom was remodeled. The artifact now sits proudly in the woman's living room, planted with greenery and bearing a plaque that reads, "Margaret Thatcher sat here."

Thatcher's special bond with her son is contrasted with the distinct lack of closeness between her and Mark's twin sister, Carol. Likewise, her father is repeatedly acknowledged as a great influence, while her mother is seldom mentioned. This view is cleverly tied in with the fact that from the moment she broke into the then-stringently male world of politics, Thatcher failed to appoint a single woman to a senior cabinet position.

Mark Thatcher is stealthily brought into the picture by way of allegations over his role in various affairs including a £16 million ($24 million) arms deal between Britain and the Malaysian government, illicit Arab business contracts and the sale of chemical weapons to Iraq. His rapid rise to become one of the richest men in Britain prompted widespread speculation as to the source of his wealth, but the former prime minister acknowledges no taint on his propriety.

Broomfield raises questions as to whether Thatcher knew of her son's operations while she was in office. At the same time, he throws open debate regarding her own interest

in arms trading following the Falklands war, pointing out that Britain became the world's No. 2 arms exporter under her government.

Attempts to pin down Mark Thatcher are even more brusquely truncated, with Broomfield playing it all as some kind of nightmarish farce. Meanwhile, he uncovers an incestuous finance circuit by which Thatcher (both mother and son) initiatives pay dividends to a group of companies who in turn were major contributors to her government and now to her private foundation.

Sharp editing by Rick Vick and Susan Bloom slyly plays up the sinister aspects of the Thatcher entourage's off-limits behavior, milking considerable humor out of the obvious threat posed by Broomfield's two-person crew, especially their attempted ambush of a hairdressing appointment. Also on-target is Barry Ackroyd's gleefully intrusive camera.

—*David Rooney*

GREAT MOMENTS IN AVIATION
(BRITISH-U.S.)

A BBC Films production in association with BBC Enterprises and Miramax Films. (International sales: the Sales Co., London.) Produced by Philippa Giles. Executive producer, Mark Shivas. Directed by Beeban Kidron. Screenplay, Jeanette Winterson. Camera (color), Remi Adefarasin; editor, John Stothart; music, Rachel Portman; production design, Tony Burrough; costume design, Les Lansdown; casting, Leo Davis. Reviewed at Cannes Film Festival (market), May 17, 1994. Running time: **92 MIN.**

Dr. Angela Bead ..... Vanessa Redgrave
Rex Goodyear .... John Hurt
Duncan Stewart .... Jonathan Pryce
Gwendolyne Quim .... Dorothy Tutin
Gabriel Angel .... Rakie Ayola

Beeban Kidron's "Great Moments in Aviation" is a willfully theatrical, sporadically magical romantic comedy embracing three barely compatible narrative strands, not one of which ever gets full flight clearance. Damaged beyond repair by a mannered scripting style and evident recutting, this wingless relic looks commercially to stay confined to its hangar.

After the esoteric charms of her first U.S. pic, "Used People," Kidron's latest is something of a return to the scaled-down dimensions of her idiosyncratic British TV work. While her talent for gently easing inventive comedy out of awkward situations frequently illuminates "Aviation," it offers a beacon in decidedly murky surroundings.

Opening in the West Indies in the '50s, story leaps headlong on to an earthly enchanted plane. A farewell

June 13, 1994 (Cont.)

banquet marks the departure of Gabriel Angel (Rakie Ayola), a young woman setting sail for England, where she dreams of becoming an aviator.

Once on board the cruise ship (a stylish theatrical set, crossing an equally make-believe ocean), the tone shifts jarringly to terrain somewhere between archaic drawing-room comedy and mystery-driven melodrama. Pic gets no help from Brit novelist Jeanette Winterson's preposterous dialogue and comic mistiming that serves up more misses than hits.

A booking mix-up forces Gabriel to share her cabin with Scottish gent Duncan Stewart (Jonathan Pryce), and an unlikely affection slowly begins to blossom.

Thwarting their romantic progress is Rex Goodyear (John Hurt), a snaky art historian who insists Stewart is not the man he claims, but an impostor who stole one of his paintings and murdered his wife. Also on board are a pair of homeward-bound missionary women (Vanessa Redgrave, Dorothy Tutin), rumored to be lovers.

A good hour is taken up with onerous scene-setting before the wheels really start turning, leaving only the shortest stretch to sort events into some semblance of order. Consequently, some potential jewels are squandered. Chief among them is Redgrave and Tutin's mutual revelation that their love for each other goes way beyond companionship. Though it's captivatingly played, with a physical clinch that's by no means shy, the scene is lobbed in and robbed of its impact.

Other outcomes fall afoul of the editing reshuffle, and almost everything that happens does so with inadequate justification. Winterson's script is so crammed with ill-fitting incident that it never loiters long enough to find a focus.

Questions about the line between truth and falsehood, genuine and fake, are too flimsily voiced to mean much. Likewise, the intro of race issues in the closing voiceover only makes the haphazard mix even more lumpy.

Brightest stretches are those repping the most marked departure from Kidron's previous work. Sharply directed opening seg and frequent flashbacks to Gabriel's home soar above the stilted doings on the liner. Considerable help comes from Remi Adefarasin's warmly lit camera work, awash with color, and from Rachel Portman's stirring choral music.

Perfs by the seasoned Brit cast make a deliberate play for overwrought caricature with patchy results. In the film's most naturalistic turn, Ayola is a constant pleasure to watch. Unforced and appealing, she often succeeds in pulling the fanciful fireworks momentarily back down to Earth. *—David Rooney*

DON'T DO IT

A Hess/Lippert Films and Julian R. Film presentation of a Randy Lippert production. Produced by Lippert, Eugene Hess. Executive producers, Marco Weber, Oliver Eberle. Coproducer, Klaus Kaehler. Directed, written by Hess. Camera (Deluxe color), Ian Fox; editor, Marc Grossman; music, Hal Lindes; art director, Jackie McCardle; costume supervisor, Jennifer Levy; sound (Dolby), Ken Hathcock; casting, Maureen A. Arata. Reviewed at Cannes Film Festival (market), May 15, 1994. Running time: **88 MIN.**

Suzanna	Heather Graham
Dodger	James Le Gros
Michelle	Sheryl Lee
Robert	James Marshall
Charles	Esai Morales
Alicia	Sarah Trigger
Jake	Balthazar Getty
Dave	Alexis Arquette
Letticia	Elizabeth Barondes
Anthony	Steven Brill

The folks involved in "Don't Do It" should have heeded the title's explicit warning, or at least held out for a sharper script. Despite a promising cast and a painstakingly hip veneer, reality has neither flavor nor bite in this addition to the Generation X minimalist gabfest canon. A spell in the colorless company of three whining L.A. couples, pic looks likely to saunter straight onto video racks.

Overly schematic setup has one member of each duo hedging about onward commitment as they secretly pine for their former flames. Suzanna (Heather Graham) lobbies for heavier emotional dues from Dodger (James Le Gros). He carries a torch for Alicia (Sarah Trigger), who's having trouble announcing her pregnancy to current partner Robert (James Marshall). He's still hot for career-bent film student Michelle (Sheryl Lee), while she's found script and sack material in pool hall dude Charles (Esai Morales), who in turn is still hankering after Suzanna.

The sextet's romantic ramblings are embroidered to lightly humorous ends with two satellite strands involving a lovelorn airhead (Balthazar Getty) receiving counseling from his clueless buddy (Alexis Arquette), and goof-off cafe staffers (Elizabeth Barondes, Steven Brill) having phone sex while their customers scream for service.

The laboriously orchestrated finale transparently rigs an unexpected encounter among the three couples, in which they face up to the truth about their amorous allegiances.

The able-bodied acting corps takes a stab at making animated fare out of what's basically inconsequential verbosity, but the script's gaping chasm where something called character definition should be leaves them all floundering thanklessly.

After their astute work together in "Drugstore Cowboy," the reteaming of Graham and Le Gros is especially dismal, saddled with easily the most irritating dialogue of the bunch. The Morales-Lee duo comes off slightly better, with a modicum of tension sewn in as he sweats out the wait for HIV test results.

Technically, the film is tidily executed in all departments. Hal Lindes' easygoing music score is agreeably at odds with the overworked plot machinations on which it comments. *—David Rooney*

BACK TO BACK, FACE TO FACE

(BEI KAO BEI, LIAN DUI LIAN)

(HONG KONG)

A Simon Wong/Willy Tsao presentation of a Simpson Communication production, in association with China Film Coproduction Corp. and Xi'an Film Studio. (International sales: Fortissimo Film Sales, Amsterdam.) Executive producers, Willy Tsao, Jacob C.L. Cheung, Li Xudong. Directed by Huang Jianxin. Executive director, Yang Yazhou. Screenplay, Huang Xin, Sun Yuan, from the novel "Qiu feng zuile" ("The Drunken Autumn Wind") by Liu Xinglong. Camera (color), Zhang Xiaoguang, Zhu Shen; editor, Lei Qin; music, Zhang Dalong; art direction, Li Xingzheng; sound, Yan Jun; assistant director, Xu Xuezheng. Reviewed at Cannes Film Festival (Directors Fortnight), May 21, 1992. Running time: **147 MIN.**

Wang Shuangli	Niu Zhenhua
Old Ma	Lei Gesheng
Xiao Yan	Li Qiang
Accountant Li	Ju Hao
Wang's Father	Liu Guoxiang
Luo	Xu Xuezheng
Fanlang, Wang's Wife	Li Haihai
Monkey	Wang Jinsong

Any observer of office politics will get a quiet kick out of "Back to Back, Face to Face," a long but involving satire on bureaucratic trench warfare, modern Chinese style, that boasts wonderful ensemble perfs and a script dripping with subtle ironies. Second pic in mainland helmer Huang Jianxin's loose trilogy on the country's fast-changing urban life is a fine, if more low-key, successor to his 1992 "Stand Up, Don't Bend Over" and will find a solid following at fest screenings. Small-screen sales should be warm, though theatrical more problematic.

Central character is tubby, thirtyish Wang, assistant director of the Cultural Center in Xi'an, one of China's oldest cities, who's liked by his staff, is a master manipulator, but still can't make it to the top rung. To everyone's surprise, the vacant post of director is given to a rustic Communist cadre member, Old Ma, and under the guise of help and cooperation, Wang sets about trying to get him pushed upstairs.

But when Old Ma is finally transferred, another bureaucrat takes his place — the younger, sharper Yan, who's up to Wang's games and not about to roll over. Wang's crafty old father engineers a situation in which Yan is publicly humiliated, but the latter manages to keep his position as director and exact revenge on Wang, who collapses from the strain and is hospitalized.

With Wang temporarily off the field, his colleagues set up Yan for the big fall by suggesting he program laser-disc shows of hotsy foreign movies at the center. The ruse works, but Wang himself has by now decided there's more to life than ladder-climbing.

Director Huang trod some of this ground in earlier works like "The Black Cannon Incident" and "The Stand-In," both acid satires of fumbling bureaucracy and the mindless machinery of Chinese hierarchies. In the meantime, he's discarded the stylistic baggage of such movies and, as in "Stand Up," which satirized the country's new entrepreneurialism, places complete focus on well-cast ensemble playing and solid scripting, both of which catch the nuances of double-edged dialogue and everyday conversation. Visually, pic is cool and unstylized.

There's hardly a character who doesn't emerge as a fully drawn individual, each constantly adapting to shifting circumstances. Even Wang's young wife, initially a shrewish nag, develops sympathetic wrinkles, mostly through the lunatic subplot of her sly old father-in-law quietly trying to poison her daughter (and make her handicapped) so the family can get official dispensation from the state's one-child policy and have a second sprig.

Ensemble playing, led by the wonderful, ever-smiling Niu Zhenhua (the vulgar businessman in "Stand Up") as Wang, is tiptop, with special praise also for Liu Guoxiang as the father, Ju Hao as the Vicar-of-Bray accountant, and Li Haihai as the wife. Tech credits are par.

Movie is one of a slate produced by Hong Kong-based Simpson Communications using helmers from China, Taiwan and H.K. Scenes in the rickety, temple-like Cultural Center were actually shot on Hainan island, with most of the rest in Xi'an itself. Huang is planning to expand the movie into a five-hour miniseries, further developing the characters. Though current version is full of plot, pic could easily be trimmed by half an hour to aid theatrical chances. —*Derek Elley*

A GIFT FROM HEAVEN

A Hatchwell-Lucarelli Prods. production. (International sales: Hills Communications, Hilversum, Netherlands.) Produced by Laurent Hatchwell. Executive producer, Alan D. Jacques. Co-producers, Steve Yaconelli, Steve Mirkovich. Directed by Jack Lucarelli. Screenplay, David Steen. Camera (Foto-Kem color), Yaconelli; editor, Mirkovich; music, Jean-Noel Chaleat; production design, Robert Varney; costume design, Laura Slakey; sound (Dolby), Joe Kenworthy; assistant director, Jamie Hitchcock; casting, Jeannie Wilson. Reviewed at Cannes Film Festival (market), May 15, 1994. Running time: **102 MIN.**
Ma Samuals .... Sharon Farrell
Messy Samuals .... Gigi Rice
Charlie .... David Steen
Cousin Anna .... Sarah Trigger
Hesley .... Gene Lythgow
With: Mark Ruffalo, Nicholas Worth, Molly McClure

Fine scripting and cohesive playing by a trio of female leads gives quality clout to "A Gift From Heaven," an affecting, nuanced chamber drama of conflicting passions set in the North Carolina boonies in the '70s. Though unhurried pacing and lack of big names could limit B.O. stateside, pic reps a striking freshman entry by former actor Jack Lucarelli that, with the right marketing, could find a niche in Europe, pic's source of funding.

Story, originally written as a play by former actor David Steen, is almost entirely set in a remote backwoods dwelling that houses a middle-aged single mother (Sharon Farrell), her simple son, Charlie (Steen), from a union at age 12 with her evangelist uncle, and adopted daughter Messy (Gigi Rice). Mom is an overprotective Bible thumper who's devoted to the taciturn Charlie and gives frequent tongue lashings to the slovenly Messy.

Arrival of pretty, naive Cousin Anna (Sarah Trigger), who's come to stay awhile following the death of her parents, sets off a string of sexual and emotional firecrackers that have smoldered for years.

First half-hour leisurely but never boringly details the women's characters as they fuss around the house, eat dinner and bond on various levels. Though all the players give Steen's dialogue the full "y'all" treatment, and Farrell especially plays the mother in heightened mode, the self-contained setting and scripter's ear for natural voice rhythms sustain interest in the characters even when nothing much is happening onscreen.

Tensions start rising to the surface on the first night, when the two younger women go to a local dance,

Messy stays out most of the night, and mom's passionate love for her son (whom she's dubbed "a gift from heaven") takes an unseemly physical turn in the barn.

Next day, Anna and Charlie, who've been secretly eyeing each other since she arrived, pair off for a river trip. As mom's protective instincts start to run out of control, the ever-neglected Messy opts for a radical solution to the effects of Anna and Charlie's inevitable departure.

There's enough emotional scarring and tangled passion here to fuel a couple of Tennessee Williams plays, but, to filmer's credit, the dramatic reins are kept so tightly controlled that character, rather than backwoods Greek tragedy, is the keynote.

In overall flavor, pic evokes observant, female-led dramas like "Places in the Heart" rather than full-bodied Southern mellers, and, though the setting is solidly American, there's an almost European whiff to both pacing and direction. It's the kind of movie that the late Georges Delerue might have scored.

Onscreen sexual activity is studiously avoided, and it's left vague whether anything actually happens. Only false move in the dramatics department is a late-on physical set-to between mom and Anna that comes over as jarringly melodramatic.

Though Farrell and Trigger ("P.C.U.") neatly etch the story's emotional extremes, pic's standout performance is by Rice as the unloved, supposedly devil-may-care adopted daughter who's terrified of emotional vacuums. In such strong company, scripter Steen's own playing of the simple-headed Charlie is a rung or two lower in believability and technique.

Steve Yaconelli's unforced lensing and Steve Mirkovich's unshowy, fluid editing are major assists throughout. Score by French composer Jean-Noel Chaleat is pleasant. Though set in North Carolina, the movie is totally shot in California, with no loss of credibility. A change of title could benefit the pic's commercial potential. —*Derek Elley*

ANITA

(FINNISH)

A Fantasiafilmi production. (International sales: Fantasiafilmi, Helsinki.) Produced by Asko Apajalahti, Jukka Helle, Johannes Lassila. Directed by Peter Lindholm. Screenplay, Lindholm, Olli-Pekka Parviainen. Camera (color), Kjell Lageroos; editor, Lindholm; music, Jori Sivonen; costume design, Meiju Vaisanen. Reviewed at Cannes Film Festival (market), May 15, 1994. Running time: **85 MIN.**
Anita Virtanen .... Liisa Mustonen
Matti
Harkonen ..... Pirkka-Pekka Petelius
Rotko .... Taneli Makela

Commercials director Peter Lindholm makes a smooth transition to features with "Anita," a high-gloss, fast-paced caper-crimer about a female con artist that's solid, if not socko, entertainment. Finnish production probably won't interest the arthouse market.

Title character (an impressive Liisa Mustonen) is a chic grifter who has become headline news throughout the country for a series of ruthlessly executed scams. Hard-boiled cop Harkonen (Pirkka-Pekka Petelius) has an obsession with catching her, but so far she's eluded his clutches.

Real story starts when Anita meets another super-grifter (Taneli Makela) and the two team up on a major bank-account swindle. Complication is that Anita falls for her partner, who's several notches above her in coldblooded business style.

Helmer Lindholm, who also co-wrote the screenplay, manages to play a few riffs on the crime genre by having voiceover narrations by three of the men involved with the main character, as well as a tight, procedural-like plot that doesn't stand around on street corners. A few spicy sex scenes involving the heroine are stirred in for good measure.

Tech credits are peachy on all levels, and the movie's visuals are never less than classy.

—*Derek Elley*

JOHNNY 100 PESOS

(JOHNNY CIEN PESOS)

(CHILEAN)

An August Entertainment presentation of a Catalina Cinema production. Produced, directed by Gustavo Graef Marino. Screenplay by Gerardo Caceras, Marino. Camera (color), Jose Luis Arredondo; editor, Danielle Fillios; music, Andres Pollak; production design, Juan Carlos Castillo; sound, Marcos de Aguirre. Reviewed at Cannes Film Festival (market), May 19, 1994. Running time: **90 MIN.**
Johnny Garcia .... Armando Araiza
Gloria .... Patricia Rivera
Freddy .... Willy Semler
Alfonso .... Luis Gnecco
Loco .... Armando Silvestre
Patty .... Paulina Urrutia
Journalist .... Sergio Hernandez
Judge .... Luis Alarcon

An unusual political thriller from Chile, "Johnny 100 Pesos" has definite international arthouse appeal thanks to its energetic, original slant on crime and politics in the Third World. A mix of a lot of familiar genre conventions, pic has been popping up on the fest circuit for several months and marks director/co-writer Gustavo Graef Marino as a talent worth watching, a filmmaker who knows how to

twist the conventional into his own unique vision.

Pic takes the heist-gone-wrong premise to new extremes. Johnny (Armando Araiza) is the youngest member of a gang that has earmarked a video club (actually a money-laundering operation) for its current job. Problem is that they take too long to execute their plan, and a silent alarm triggers the arrival of an army of police.

Matters only get worse when the media descend on the scene. Situation reaches its zenith when the crooks pose as terrorists and demand a plane to Cuba as part of their hostage demands.

While the obvious parallel here is to "Dog Day Afternoon," Marino has more complicated turf to explore given the internecine nature of South American politics. He also paints a devastating picture of Latin TV journalists, whose elevation of Johnny to media *cause celebre* goes from the heady to the scabrous as the portrait contorts into the classic good boy gone wrong.

The modest production provides "Johnny" with a gritty, almost docu-like surface that complements the drama. There is a raw, edgy quality to narrative and editing that heightens the implicit sense of danger.

Araiza is a charismatic performer, and ensemble cast works like a well-oiled machine. But mostly it's filmmakers' ability to keep the audience surprised at every plot twist that makes pic unique and refreshing.

A definite crowd pleaser, "Johnny 100 Pesos" will require a bit of clever promotion to lure audiences. But it's exactly the type of smart thriller that can play upscale and cross into the mainstream in U.S. and Euro outlets. —*Leonard Klady*

THE HARD TRUTH

A Promark Entertainment Group, Spectator Films presentation of a Force Majeure production. Produced by Brad Southwick, Gary DePew. Executive producers, Carol M. Rossi, Steve Beswick, Joseph M. Cohen, David Newlon. Directed by Kristine Peterson. Screenplay, Jonathan Tydor. Camera (color), Ross Berryman, editor, Kert Vander Meulen; music, Daniel Licht; production design, Michael Perry; art direction, David Blass; costume design, Yvonne Marie Cervantes; sound (Ultra-Stereo), Brian Bidder; associate producer, Jon Kramer; assistant director, Wade Danielson; casting, Elisa Goodman, Abra Edelman. Reviewed at Cannes Film Festival (market), May 18, 1994. Running time: **100 MIN.**
Dr. Chandler
Etheridge .... Eric Roberts
Jonah Mantz .... Michael Rooker
Lisa Kantrell .... Lysette Anthony
With: Ray Baker, Don Yesso.

A by-the-numbers action thriller with the time-honored ingredients of a gruff, jaded cop, a slick safecracker and a curvaceous, double-crossing femme fatale, "The Hard Truth" provides few surprises but should prove serviceable enough as video fare.

After some drab preamble, the souped-up opening tracks a subway station shootout, which ends with daredevil cop Jonah (Michael Rooker) wiping out a crazed killer. His itchy trigger finger gets him swiftly suspended by Internal Affairs.

Jonah's babe, Lisa (Lysette Anthony), has her own work woes, with her corrupt councilman boss (Ray Baker) insisting on more from her than simple shorthand. When Lisa proposes filching the $3 million mob handout her boss took for pushing through a building contract, Jonah opts in, also blackmailing shifty electronics wiz Dr. Chandler Etheridge (Eric Roberts) to come in on the deal.

But one look at the doc, and formerly sack-happy Lisa has a headache where Jonah's concerned. This spells bad tidings all round.

Action scenes will hardly keep Walter Hill awake nights, but they sustain a reasonably brisk pace — if not brisk enough to disguise a clanging lack of heat in the sexual department.

Chief shortcoming is Brit export Anthony, who looks the ticket and purrs in a convincing Yank accent, but on the smolder-ometer rates somewhere on a par with Sandra Dee. Other thesps deliver less wooden but strictly routine turns. Tech input strikes the same purely functional note. —*David Rooney*

BOULEVARD

A Norstar Entertainment production. Produced by Peter Simpson, Ray Sager. Executive producers, Ilana Frank, Peer Oppenheimer. Directed by Penelope Buitenhuis. Screenplay, Rae Dawn Chong. Camera (color), David Frazee; editor, Bernadette Kelly; music, Ian Thomas; production design, Jasna Stefanovic. Reviewed at Cannes Film Festival (market), May 16, 1994. Running time: **96 MIN.**
Ola .... Rae Dawn Chong
Jennefer .... Kari Wuhrer
J Rod .... Joel Bissonnette
Hassan .... Lou Diamond Phillips
McClaren .... Lance Henriksen

The only novelty of "Boulevard," an otherwise B-grade suspense thriller, written by actress Rae Dawn Chong and directed by Penelope Buitenhuis, is that it takes a distinctly female p.o.v. Focus on women, however, proves superficial and phony, though spectacular, violent scenes, in a sleazy setting populated by pimps and hookers, might prove titillating enough to lure the undemanding video crowd.

Escaping from an abusive husband, Jennefer (Kari Wuhrer) is forced to give up her baby for adoption and fend for herself in the big city. But it's her good fortune to meet Ola (Chong), a street-smart prostie who gives her shelter in her apartment and makes an effort to shield her from the clutches of Hassan (Lou Diamond Phillips), a murderous pimp who controls the neighborhood.

When Ola witnesses the brutal murder of a young hooker by Hassan and refuses to testify, she is interrogated by tough cop McClaren (Lance Henriksen), who then deports her. All alone, Jennefer succumbs to prostitution, falling victim to Hassan's manipulation. In the bloody climax, however, the now tough and invigorated femme gathers enough power to confront her vengeful husband.

The material is routine, particularly the raw, borderline-primitive dialogue, but helmer Buitenhuis shows some proficiency at conveying visually the dynamics of street life. "Boulevard" suggests the importance of female camaraderie, but ultimately the violence against women is so excessive and exploitational that it's shocking to realize pic was written and directed by women.

Chong and Phillips, two attractive performers who have done good work in the past, are wasting their talents in this suspenser. Tech credits aptly summon up the necessary trashy atmosphere.
—*Emanuel Levy*

CARL, MY CHILDHOOD SYMPHONY
(MIN FYNSKE BARNDOM)
(DANISH)

An ASA Film/Film Cooperativet Danmark/Nordisk Film production, in association with Svensk Filmindustri. (International sales: Nordisk Film.) Produced by Henrik Moller-Sorensen. Directed, written by Erik Clausen, based on the autobiography by Carl Nielsen. Camera (color), Claus Loof; editors, Anders Refn, Grete Moldrup, Jesper W. Nielsen; music, Carl Nielsen; production design, Palle Arestrup; costumes, Manon Rasmussen; sound (Dolby), Preben Mortensen; assistant director, Lennart Pasborg; casting, Jette Termann. Reviewed at Cannes Film Festival (market), May 18, 1994. Running time: **130 MIN.**
Carl 1 .... Morten Gundel
Carl 2 .... Anders Forchhammer
Carl 3 .... Nicolaj Kaas
Kirstine (Mother) .... Stina Ekblad
Niels (Father) .... Jesper Milsted
Anna .... Anna Eklund
Outzen .... Frits Helmuth
Jens .... Morten Staugaard
Anne-Sofie .... Sandra Friis
Magda .... Christine Ulrich
With: Steven Pedersen, Soren Hytholm Jensen, Daniel Flosser, Peter Hoffmayer, Rene Hansen, Helene Egelund.

This handsomely staged biography of Carl Nielsen, a celebrated Danish composer of the late 19th century, who rose from the humblest of peasant origins to achieve fame for his much-loved symphonies, is an inspiring pic. Though it may not have what it takes to snag theatrical distribution outside Scandinavian and select Euro territories, it should certainly be seen by quality-TV programmers worldwide.

Based on Nielsen's autobiography, the film, as the title suggests, covers only the musician's formative years and ends as he leaves the provinces to find fame and fortune in Copenhagen. Writer/director Erik Clausen has divided the film into three more or less equal segs, employing three look-alike actors to play Carl at the ages of 7, 15 and 19, much as Jane Campion did in "An Angel at My Table."

Part one, 1871, intros Carl as a bright lad who lives in the countryside with his hard-working but very poor family, which becomes reduced in number due to emigration and a TB scourge. Carl inherits a love of music from his father, who plays the fiddle in a local band and who teaches his son to play the instrument. Still, his brother Albert is a more talented musician until he's sidelined by an accident (for which Carl's unwittingly responsible) that permanently damages his hand.

Part two, 1879, has young Carl taken by his forceful mother to join an army post in provincial Odense, where he becomes the company bugler and teaches himself to play the piano. He falls under the influence of Outzen, an eccentric old man who plays honky-tonk piano in a cheap bar but who prefers to play Mozart whenever he can, and forms a promising relationship with Mormon barmaid Magda, which founders when she turns out to be more interested in his soul than in lovemaking.

Part three, 1883, depicts Carl starting to write his own music and to play at high society soirees. He forms a brief relationship with Anna, a haughty Swedish beauty who eventually rejects him.

This is a richly detailed, acutely observed production, beautifully cast and performed (the three actors who play Carl are all excellent), and several cuts above the average bio of a revered musician. The problem is that Carl himself is, at the ages depicted in the film, still too immature to emerge as a fully rounded character. But as a study of an uneducated and underprivileged child whose burning love of music drives him on despite the odds, the film, which Clausen has dedicated to his own son, is truly inspiring.
—*David Stratton*

TERESA'S TATTOO

A CineTel Films production in association with Yankee Entertainment Group. Produced by Lisa M. Hansen, Philip McKeon. Executive producers, Paul Hertzberg, Marc Rocco. Coproducer, Cataline Knell. Directed by Julie Cypher. Screenplay, Georgie Huntington. Camera (color), Sven Kirsten; editor, Christopher Rouse; music, Andrew Keresztes; original songs by Melissa Etheridge; sound (Ultra-Stereo), Geoffrey Patterson, John S. Coffey; associate producer, Huntington; assistant director, John E. Vohlers; casting, Mary Jo Slater. Reviewed at Cannes Film Festival (market), May 13, 1994. Running time: **88 MIN.**
Gloria/Teresa .... Adrienne Shelly
Carl .... C. Thomas Howell
Sara .... Nancy McKeon
Wheeler .... Lou Diamond Phillips
Michael .... Casey Siemaszko
Rick .... Jonathan Silverman
With: Majel Barrett, Brian Davila, Anthony Clark, Nanette Fabray, Tippi Hedren, k.d. lang, Joe Pantoliano, Mary Kay Place, Mare Winningham, Kiefer Sutherland.

Despite being heavily doused with madcap whimsy, quirky casting and a driving song score, atrophy starts setting in before the main titles of "Teresa's Tattoo" are over. As lifeless as the stiff that turns up in reel one, this titanic misfire may sit a spell on video shelves thanks to its name cast, but the unendearingly harebrained comedy looks destined for a hasty burial.

Plot is uninspired lunacy. Hal Hartley regular Adrienne Shelly plays a brain-dead bimbo with a Chinese dragon tattooed across her chest, who's somehow landed a pair of holograph earrings containing details of the U.S. space program.

Taken hostage by an inept band of thugs headed by greaseball freezer-treat king Carl (C. Thomas Howell), she swiftly drowns in a freak pool accident involving a lethal, untethered beach ball.

Her kidnappers need a look-alike to take over as the bait in their extortionist scam. Enter Shelly again as a college math whiz, this time in a bad wig. She's drugged, tattooed and dewigged during her fast-girl beauty makeover. Her escape leads to a tortuous round of chase scenes, as Carl and company try to get her back before an FBI-employed yokel (Lou Diamond Phillips) or her budding flame (Jonathan Silverman) get to her first.

Script and direction strive so concertedly for loopy comedic anarchy that the film's unwavering flatness and lack of rhythm are never less than excruciating. Timing is way off all around, with Howell looking awkward in weedy sleazebag guise and Phillips and Silverman making resoundingly humorless showings, due in no small part to their witless dialogue. Shelly does a generic flake act that wears thin instantly, and

Nancy McKeon as her unfazable friend fares only marginally better.

Star cameos are thick on the ground, from k.d. lang as a Baptist fundamentalist to Mary Kay Place as a suburban vulgarian to an unbilled Kiefer Sutherland as a cop.

Tech input is on the plus side, and Melissa Etheridge's songs should earn points in youth-oriented vid markets. —*David Rooney*

RADIO INSIDE

A Polar Entertainment production in association with Capitol Films. Produced by John Fielder, Joe Caracciolo Jr., Mark Tarlov. Executive producers, Sharon Harel, Jane Barclay. Co-producers, Margaret Hilliard, Suzanne Smith. Directed, written by Jeffrey Bell. Camera (color), Brian Capener; editor, Jim Clark; music, Gil Goldstein; music supervisor, Bones Howe; production design, John Diminico; associate producers, Glen Trotiner, Dean Garvin; casting, Billy Hopkins, Kerry Barden. Reviewed at Cannes Film Festival (market), May 15, 1994. Running time: **91 MIN.**
Matthew .... William McNamara
Natalie .... Elizabeth Shue
Michael .... Dylan Walsh
With: Ilse Earl, Pee Wee Love, Ara Madzounian, Steve Zurk.

Coming to terms with grief and guilt gives "Radio Inside" a soulful center, around which is spun a sensitive tale of two brothers in love with the same girl. Honesty and emotional insight are frequently on hand, but writer/director Jeffrey Bell (expanding his short graduation film to feature length) is too tender-hearted with his characters to bulk up much dramatic weight, and the result fails to distinguish itself from able but antiseptic small-screen fare.

A year after the drowning of his father during a vacation, Matthew (William McNamara) is still tormented by not having been able to save him. His older brother, Michael (Dylan Walsh), attempts to yank him out of daydreamland by pushing him into an advertising career, but Matthew prefers his undemanding lifeguard job at the local pool.

Michael becomes increasingly work-obsessed, unwittingly (and somewhat predictably) fanning the flames of attraction between his frustrated girlfriend, Natalie (Elizabeth Shue), and his brother. The bond remains relatively innocent, but adds fresh fuel to Matthew's sense of guilt.

Title comes from Matthew's continual retreat into the radio inside his head, switching the dial whenever things become too problematic. But the intermittent fantasy and flashback sequences lack the stylistic flourish to successfully lift the rather bland core narrative out of its commonplace confines.

Matthew's exchanges via phone and in the flesh with Jesus in the guise of a Cuban drifter (Ara Madzounian) feel like a similarly undernourished idea. More effective are the frequent flashes of water imagery, both as comfort and threat, and a more abstract slant in this direction may have given the film some of the textural depth it's lacking.

Brian Capener's crisp lensing catches the Miami setting in an eye-pleasing summer haze. Local color is overplayed, though, with at least one montage too many of neon-swathed city streets, sunstruck deco architecture and carefree beach fauna. Thesps all acquit themselves respectably, but the homogenized lead trio is too scrubbed and vanilla in tone to give their characters' trials much urgency. —*David Rooney*

PLAYMAKER

(U.S.-BRITISH)

An Orion release (U.S.) of an Odyssey Entertainment presentation of a Steinhardt Baer/Samuelson production. (International sales: Odyssey, L.A.) Produced by Thomas Baer, Marc Samuelson, Peter Samuelson. Executive producer, Michael Steinhardt. Line producer, Cheryl L. Cook. Directed, written by Yuri Zeltser, based on a screenplay by Michael Schroeder and a story by Darren Block and Kathryn Nemesh. Camera (Foto-Kem color), Ross Berryman; editor, John Rosenberg; music, Mark Snow; production design, Philip Vasels, Diane Hughes; costume design, Sigrid Insull; sound (Ultra-Stereo), Daniel Monahan; sound design, Eric Williams; associate producer, Anna Godessoff; assistant director, Lisa Campbell; casting, Donald Paul Pernick. Reviewed at Cannes Film Festival (market), May 16, 1994. Running time: **88 MIN.**
Ross .... Colin Firth
Jamie Harris .... Jennifer Rubin
Eddie .... John Getz
Allen .... Jeff Perry

An every-which-way script takes the heat out of "Playmaker," part erotic thriller, part psychodrama, part old-fashioned murder mystery that can't make up its mind which direction it's headed. Despite good chemistry between leads Colin Firth and Jennifer Rubin, and smart-looking direction by Yuri Zeltser, this genre mishmash looks like a tough sell theatrically for Orion in the U.S., with cable and homevid looming as more appropriate destinations.

Pic starts promisingly, with career-stalled actress Jamie (Rubin) hearing about casting sessions for a big-budget movie, "Playmaker," and following the advice of bartender friend Eddie (John Getz) to take a cramming session with reclusive acting coach Ross Talbert.

Arriving at Talbert's remote home in the L.A. hills, Jamie meets a man (Firth) who immediately starts playing bizarre mind games, building up and breaking down her confidence to improve her thespian skills.

These scenes, played with cool, erotic assurance by both leads, climax in a hotsy sequence (shot like "9½ Weeks") of Rubin lying atop a grand piano as Firth slowly scissors off her black dress and scanties.

Just when the movie is shaping up as a psychodrama class act, script takes its first left — into woman-in-jeopardy territory — as Rubin discovers morbid files on other actress clients and shoots Firth in panic.

Next left turn seriously stretches credibility, with Rubin finding out in L.A. that Firth's character faked his death and is actually an out-of-work actor who impersonated Talbert. To get her revenge, she disguises herself as a casting director and sexually humiliates him back at the house.

Pic goes completely off the rails hereon, switching into a murder mystery in which the real villain appears, and a loony coda of Rubin shooting her agent and driving off again to the house in the hills.

Zeltser, who started as a scripter and whose directing bow was the interesting 1992 direct-to-video "Eye of the Storm," shows style to spare but drops the ball early on as a writer. Rubin and Firth, aces in the opening half-hour, gamely struggle on for the rest. Tech credits are fine, with handsome lensing by Aussie cinematographer Ross Berryman. —*Derek Elley*

POLSKI CRASH

(GERMAN)

A Gemini Film production, in association with MS Films (Warsaw)/WDR (Cologne). (International sales: Barbarella Entertainment, Cologne.) Produced by Gerhard Schmidt. Directed by Kaspar Heidelbach. Screenplay, Jost Krueger. Camera (color), Karl Walter Lindenlaub; editor, Hedy Altschiller; art direction, Norbert Scherer; sound, Wolfgang Wirtz. Reviewed on Gemini Film vidcassette, London, Feb. 12, 1994. (In Berlin Film Festival — New German Films section, and Cannes Film Festival — market.) Running time: **94 MIN.**
With: Klaus J. Behrendt, Juergen Vogel, Clotilde Courau, Miroslaw Baka, Susanne Wilhelmina, Heinrich Schafmeister, Wojciech Wysocki.
(German and Polish dialogue)

First theatrical feature by Cologne-based TV director Kaspar Heidelbach is an undemanding mystery-thriller, set in Warsaw, that should slip quietly into latenight Eurotube skeds as a dubbed item.

Womanizing Dortmund insurance agent Tom (Klaus J. Behrendt) gets a message to help his psychotic brother, Piet (Juergen Vogel), in Poland, where he's hiding out from the local mob after double-crossing them on a stolen auto deal. Plot mainly concerns Tom tracking him down, in between being hassled by the police, plus sack time with Piet's sexy g.f., Alina (Clotilde Courau).

Action quotient is low, and script reads like a Cold War spy story update. Performances are OK, and technically pic is pro. —*Derek Elley*

FAST GETAWAY II

A CineTel Films release of a Live Entertainment presentation in association with CineTel Films. (International sales: CineTel.) Produced by Russell D. Markowitz. Executive producer, Paul Hertzberg. Directed by Oley Sassone. Screenplay, Mark Sevi, based on characters created by James Dixon. Camera (Foto-Kem color), Mark Parry; editor, Glenn Garland; music, David Robbins; production design, Jeannie M. Lomma; costume design, Shanna Knecht; sound, Lee Archer; stunt coordinator, Gary Paul; martial arts choreographer, Gregg Brazzell; assistant director, John Wildermuth. Reviewed at Cannes Film Festival (market), May 13, 1994. MPAA Rating: PG-13. Running time: **90 MIN.**
Nelson Potter .... Corey Haim
Lily .... Cynthia Rothrock
Patrice .... Sarah G. Buxton
Sam Potter .... Leo Rossi
Rankin .... Pete Liapis

Cynthia Rothrock fans are likely to feel shortchanged by "Fast Getaway II," an OK crimer that relegates the martial arts star to occasional walk-ons in what's basically a Corey Haim vehicle. Movie is a slicker, more technically polished product than the 1991 first entry and should tick over nicely in ancillary formats, but action buffs won't be busting down the doors for this one.

Cocky bank robber Nelson (Haim) has abandoned his life of crime by opening up a bank insurance business with his tolerant g.f. (Sarah G. Buxton) while his father — and former partner (Leo Rossi) — waits to exit from the stir.

When Lily (Rothrock) breaks into a bank that Nelson has just declared iffy on security, and she later plants a knife with his prints at another crime scene, father and son team up to take her on. Things are further complicated for Nelson by having a sleazoid FBI agent on his case full time.

Though Rothrock gets in her high kicks from time to time, she's essentially a marginal figure in a movie that plays on Haim's boyish charm and his relationships with Buxton and Rossi. Buxton, especially, makes a mark in a role that could have been just a reaction part.

Technically, the Arizona-set and shot pic is smooth under helmer Oley Sassone ("Bloodfist III"). Martial arts choreography is uninspired, but hardware action sequences are up to scratch.

—*Derek Elley*

SARA

(IRANIAN)

Produced by Hashem Seifi, Dariush Mehrjui. (International sales: Farabi Cinema Foundation, Tehran.) Directed, written by Mehrjui. Camera (color), Mahmud Klari; editor, Hassan Hassandoost; art direction, Farlar Javaherian. Reviewed at Cannes Film Festival (market), May 20, 1994. Running time: **102 MIN.**
Sara .... Niki Karimi
Hessam .... Amin Tarokh
Simi .... Yasman Malek-Nasr
Goshtasb .... Khosro Shakibal

Though it's hard to imagine Henrik Ibsen's 19th-century feminist play "A Doll's House" transferred to contemporary Iran, vet filmmaker Dariush Mehrjui boldly takes on the challenge in "Sara." Lively perfs and pro lensing make the result watchable and only a little stagey. Though a specialty item, "Sara" is much indicated for festival pickups.

Mehrjui, an insightful chronicler of the middle class, sets his adaptation in a comfortably wealthy home in Tehran and husband Hessam's (Amin Tarokh) bank. Sara (Niki Karimi) appears to be a submissive, obedient wife, but she confides to her girlfriend Simi (Yasman Malek-Nasr) that 10 years earlier she took out a loan without her husband's knowledge to send him abroad for medical treatment.

Guarding her secret, she spends her evenings embroidering wedding gowns to pay back the lender, Goshtasb (Khosro Shakibal). Goshtasb, now a bank manager, is about to be fired by Hessam for falsifying a signature, and threatens to reveal all to her husband unless he can keep his place at the bank.

Simi, who thinks Hessam should be eternally grateful to Sara for what she's done, declines to stop Goshtasb (her former suitor) from spilling the beans. But Hessam shows his true colors as a vindictive, egotistical bully when Goshtasb threatens to make a scandal. Sara's world crumbles, but in the process she becomes aware of her own rights.

Story follows Ibsen closely, but the somewhat dated chestnut gains new interest from being set in a country that sanctions separate social rules for its female population. In their dark clothes and head coverings, worn at all times, the women in "Sara" seem totally out of synch with the modern city they are a part of.

It isn't hard to imagine Ibsen's tale being plausible there. If Mehrjui had toned down a few set pieces, like Sara's final, theatrical confrontation with Hessam, the film could almost pass for exotic realism.

Fine perfs from all hands bring the story to life. Karimi is alternately gushing and anxiety-ridden as Sara, making the audience share in her plight. Technical work is fine.

—*Deborah Young*

SEAVIEW KNIGHTS

(BRITISH)

Produced by Lois A. Wolffe. Executive producers, Christopher Parkinson, Clifford Davis. (International sales: Stranger Than Fiction Ltd., London.) Directed by Richard Kurti. Screenplay, Kurti, Bev Doyle. Camera (Metrocolor), Ivan Bartos; editor, Timothy Gee; music, Oliver Davis; production design, Mike Grant; costume design, Louise Johnson; sound (Dolby), Ian Leiper, Mike Johnstone; associate producer, Julie Bracewell; assistant directors, Alison Begg, Richard Bird, Will Goss. Reviewed at Cannes Film Festival (market), May 14, 1994. Running time: **101 MIN.**
Merlin .... James Bolam
Arthur .... Clive Darby
Jackie .... Sarah Alexander
The Blind Concierge .... Anita Dobson
The Psychiatrist .... Hildegard Neil

At one point in "Seaview Knights," a modern would-be King Arthur takes a look around his decaying nation and comments that "Britain is indeed in need of a savior." Unfortunately, the hero of this misfired fable can't begin to save the film, much less his country. Commercial outlook for this achingly unfunny piece of British whimsy is bleak even on home turf, much less overseas.

Unpromising opening sequence has young Arthur (Clive Darby) bonked on the head from the fallout of excess vibrations of some neighbors' lovemaking. Scrambled brains cause the bank robber to think he's actually England's legendary king, returned after more than 1,400 years to put things right in England.

Unfortunately, director Richard Kurti and his co-writer, Bev Doyle, can't think of a single interesting way for him to set about doing this. After wandering like a stumblebum around the vast Blackpool amusement park, Arthur becomes the victim of a scheme sewn by his chosen Merlin (James Bolam), a taxi driver who assembles a wayward bunch of misfits and two-bit criminals to make up a new Round Table.

These no-goods try to locate a stash of stolen loot Arthur has hidden, while the man who would be king heads off for London, where he comes upon some Arabs plotting to blow up Parliament. In these sequences, otherwise innocuous film plummets into burlesque-like racial stereotyping, not to mention inept action staging.

Fade-out will provoke anyone making it that far to wonder how this script got a greenlight without being sent back for a rewrite and a request to figure out what it was trying to say.

Attempts at comedy, such as having the new knights being anointed with a cricket bat rather than broad sword, range from the broad to the grotesque, and performances are unengaging. Pro production values make one notice all the more the poverty of imagination elsewhere.

—*Todd McCarthy*

DAUDET'S WINDMILL

(LE MOULIN DE DAUDET)

(FRENCH)

An MKL release of an Anna Films/Uderzo Prods./Les Films du Seraphin production, with aid from the Languedoc-Roussillon region. (International sales: MKL, Paris.) Produced, directed, written by Samy Pavel, based on "Letters From My Windmill" and "La Petite Chose," by Alphonse Daudet; camera (color, widescreen), Nino Celeste; editor, Isabelle Dedieu; music, Klaus Schulze; sound (Dolby), Suzanne Durand; assistant director, Stanley Mangenot; casting, Juliette Thierree. Reviewed at Club de l'Etoile screening room, Paris, March 24, 1994. Running time: **100 MIN.**
With: Jean-Pierre Lorit, Irene Jacob, Louis Lalanne, Robert Ripa, Arnaud Olivari, Christophe Hennes.

"Daudet's Windmill," a fetchingly lensed anthology of tales from the fanciful works of 19th-century writer Alphonse Daudet, takes the Classics Illustrated approach to revered literature. Prospects beyond French-speaking territories and classrooms look slim.

Daudet (Jean-Pierre Lorit, looking like a cross between grunge and dandy) scratches the nib of his pen on parchment in extreme close-up, prompting reminiscences and flights of imagination.

At its best, film resembles Pier Paolo Pasolini's omnibus pix, sans the lascivious edge. Pic's most lyrical passages are Daudet's visit to a friend's elderly grandparents and an extended fantasy about a precocious infant king on his deathbed. Final tale about a priest's nervous visit to hell is a stagy, kitschy vision of corny devils roasting a man on a spit.

Irene Jacob is a pale, fleeting presence as Daudet's mother in childhood flashbacks.

Pavel and d.p. Nino Celeste — who worked wonders in 1990's "The Van Gogh Wake" — obviously relish the opportunity to bring historic tableaux to life. But however lovely the widescreen provincial vistas, too many passages smack of didactic illustration. —*Lisa Nesselson*

DEATH IN SHALLOW WATER

(HALAL A SEKELY VIZBEN)

(HUNGARIAN-GERMAN-AUSTRIAN)

A Mozgokep Innovacios Tarsulas (Budapest)/Satellit Film (Starnberg)/Vega Film (Vienna) co-production, with the support of Eurimages. Produced by Istvan Darday, Barna Kabay, Veit Heiduschka. Directed by Imre Gyongyossy, Kabay. Screenplay, Gyongyossy, Katalin Petenyi. Camera (color), Peter Jankura; editors, Petenyi, Maria Nagy; music, Zoltan Biro; production design, Tamas Vayer. Reviewed at Hungarian Film Week, Budapest, Feb. 8, 1994. Running time: **103 MIN.**
Maria .... Anna Romantowska
Dobos .... Jan Englert
Tibor .... Michael Marwitz
Peter .... Pavel Delag
Hans .... Daniele Legler
Martha .... Katerzyna Walter-Sakowich
Gabor .... Geza Kaszas
Dr. Koslov .... Ivan Darvas
Esther .... Karolina Roszinszka

"Death in Shallow Water" is a political thriller inspired by a real-life mystery: the apparent suicide of a prominent Hungarian intellectual, just one of many such people who died mysteriously or disappeared in Central Europe during the 1980s. It's an intriguing story but is given disappointingly flat treatment by the Hungarian team of Imre Gyongyossy, Barna Kabay and Katalin Petenyi, whose most celebrated pic to date has been the 1983 Oscar-nominated "The Revolt of Job." Arthouse release looks dubious, with chances better in video.

Story centers on Tibor (Michael Marwitz), a chemical researcher who has discovered how poisonous gases can be neutralized in chemical weapons. It's 1988, and Hungary is still a Communist state: The Russians want the details of Tibor's research, and they try to recruit him and his wife, Maria (Anna Romantowska), to no avail. Tibor is secretly arrested by the KGB, who drown him in a bathtub. His body is found in shallow water in Lake Batalon, and the Hungarian police appear convinced it's suicide. But his son Peter (Pavel Delag) won't let the matter rest and

June 13, 1994 (Cont.)

is determined to solve the mystery, with tragic results.

Potential is here for a good, old-fashioned spy thriller, with lots of intrigue and suspense, but Gyongyossy and Kabay (who last made the excellent, underrated semi-docu "Exiled") are steeped in a more cerebral, less energetic style of cinema. Result is that, as a thriller, "Shallow Water" fails to deliver; the ingredients are there, but not the tension and cinematic dash to make it work.

Multinational cast's performances are mixed, with Romantowska coming off best as the dead man's distraught wife. Location photography is effective.

—*David Stratton*

LONDON

(BRITISH — DOCU)

A Zeitgeist release (U.S.)/BFI distribution (U.K.) of a Koninck/British Film Institute production, in association with Channel 4. (International sales: BFI, London.) Produced by Keith Griffiths. Executive producer, Ben Gibson. Executive in charge of production, Angela Topping. Directed, written by Patrick Keiller. Camera (color), Keiller; editor, Larry Sider; music, various; sound design, Sider; sound, Hugh Strain; assistant director, Julie Norris. Reviewed at Berlin Film Festival (Forum), Feb. 19, 1994. Running time: 84 MIN.
Narrator: Paul Scofield.

A new riff on an old town, "London" is an ironic docu portrait of the U.K. capital hung on major events of a single year, 1992. Mildly offbeat item could prove a winner with select offshore auds able to tune into its dry humor. Pic has just entered U.K. commercial release.

Feature-length bow of former architect Patrick Keiller, the film is structured as a continuous commentary by an offscreen character (voiced by actor Paul Scofield) who's returned to the city after seven years to help his former lover, Robinson (never seen or heard), on some unspecified research project into London's artistic past.

Together, they take five journeys across town, sampling the architecture and public spaces, as well as remarking on events of the year, such as premier John Major's re-election, an IRA bombing campaign, the Euro monetary crisis and annual Notting Hill street carnival. The narrator mostly records his friend's lofty views and thoughts on the metropolis.

Cute idea sometimes trips over its own intellectual conceit but generally succeeds, thanks to the quality of thought, cleverly balanced irony and Scofield's fruity voicing. In Keiller's liberal, generally anti-establishment take, London is portrayed as a rigid, unsociable city that punishes individualism, favors the solitary life and has historically discouraged Continental-style public sociability. In short, "a collection of interesting people who'd prefer to be elsewhere."

Pic would benefit from tightening by about 15 minutes, and some thinning of its often statistics-heavy narration. Keiller's 35mm lensing is immaculate, a series of static, well-composed tableaux juxtaposed in leisurely style. Music, mostly from Beethoven's 15th string quartet, is well placed.

—*Derek Elley*

SENTIMENTAL MANIACS

(MANIACI SENTIMENTALI)

(ITALIAN)

A United Intl. Pictures (Italy) release of a DIR Intl., Union PN production. (International sales: Intra Films, Rome.) Produced by Giorgio Leopardi, Renato Izzo, Ricky Tognazzi. Directed by Simona Izzo. Screenplay, Simona Izzo, Graziano Diana, Giuseppe Manfridi. Camera (color), Alessio Gelsini Torresi; editor, Angelo Nicolini; music, Antonio Di Pofi; art direction, Mariangela Capuano. Reviewed at the Barberini Cinema, Rome, April 21, 1994. Running time: 95 MIN.
Luca .... Ricky Tognazzi
Mara .... Barbara De Rossi
Sandro .... Alessandro Benvenuti
Serena .... Monica Scattini
Claudia .... Clelia Rondinella
Giusy .... Veronica Logan
Caterina .... Giuppy Izzo
Mother .... Pat O'Hara
Maurizio .... Alessandro Gianni

Scriptwriter Simona Izzo has hit a home run at the Italian box office with "Sentimental Maniacs," her first directing project. Auds have applauded this buoyant, low-budget local comedy for its dynamic young cast and simple approach to the emotional and sexual problems of several disharmonious couples. But laughs are strongly tied to the non-stop dialogue, and this competently directed but rather ordinary comedy stands small chance of working as well offshore.

Action takes place in a run-down Italian country villa on the weekend when Luca and Mara's two little girls make their first Communion. As relatives gather for the event, storm clouds brew.

The sexually and professionally frustrated Luca (Ricky Tognazzi, son of the late Ugo Tognazzi and spouse of co-star Giuppy Izzo) is ready to leave his family for a flighty young actress (Izzo).

Wife Mara (a tearfully tragic Barbara De Rossi) tries desperately to hold on to him.

Mara's sisters Claudia (Clelia Rondinella) and Giusy (Veronica Logan) are bubbleheads whose woes are of their own doing. Claudia is having a tormented fling with a married man; Giusy is destroying her young love with imaginary illnesses.

The female roles (including De Rossi's) are played with theatrical exaggeration and a cabaret-style emphasis on Mediterranean curves popping out of cut-out sweaters (when worn).

Though main players Tognazzi and De Rossi have a lot of screen presence, perfs are one-note and get a little tiresome.

Most satisfactory members of the cast are an offbeat couple played by Monica Scattini (as Luca's sex-starved sister) and Alessandro Benvenuti (his bachelor friend.)

Theirs is the only happy sexual coupling in the film, perhaps suggesting how bleak most modern relationships are.

Camera work is unobtrusive, and the musical commentary by Antonio Di Pofi irritatingly pat. Angelo Nicolini's cutting leaves ne'er an empty moment. —*Deborah Young*

CLOSING NUMBERS

(BRITISH)

An Arden Films production for Channel 4. Produced by Jennifer Howarth. Directed by Stephen Whittaker. Screenplay, David Cook. Camera (color), Nic Knowland; editor, Max Lemon; production design, Terry Ackland-Snow; music, Ackland-Snow; costumes, Amy Roberts; sound, Moya Burns; makeup/hair, Cherry West; associate producer, Cook; assistant director, Marc Jenny; casting, Noel Davis, Jeremy Zimmermann. Reviewed at Variety Club Screening Room, San Francisco, May 18, 1994. (In San Francisco Intl. Lesbian & Gay Film Festival.) Running time: 95 MIN.
Anna .... Jane Asher
Keith .... Tim Woodward
Steve .... Patrick Pearson
Jim .... Nigel Charnock
Mary .... Hazel Douglas
Frank .... Frank Mills
Anna's Father .... Frederick Treves
Peter .... Jamie Glover

This BBC drama follows U.S. telepic precedent in addressing gay identity/AIDS themes through telescope of an initially shocked, then stalwart "normal" family. Thoughtful and intelligent, if a bit heavy-handed, "Closing Numbers" looks to pub-casters, foreign nets and video as likeliest outlets. A couple of fairly graphic sexual scenes (jarring in this stiff-upper-lip context) may have to go in the pursuit of some potential markets.

Aud p.o.v. rests with middle-class, middle-aged English housewife Anna (Jane Asher), who grows suspicious when husband Keith's (Tim Woodward) lovemaking takes a sudden fervent, adventuresome turn. She suspects infidelity is the spur — and after red-herring pursuit of a suspected femme inamorata, she's stunned to face thirtysomething Steve (Patrick Pearson) as real object of hubby's illicit affections.

David Cook's screenplay grants Asher a tad too much slack in the weepy-histrionics department. Effect sometimes gets silly: She skulks into an adult bookstore for masochistic "research" on homosexual practices, and later angrily hurls a dildo at Keith as challenge to keep his extra-curricular action "at home."

Other plot elements skirt simple-mindedness as well, like Anna's fast conversion from ignorance to activist compassion (re: AIDS consciousness) and stereotypical portrayal of terminal-case queen Jim (Nigel Charnock). Subplots center on AIDS/homophobic terror from Jim's elderly parents, and angry confusion suffered by college-cramming son Peter (Jamie Glover).

Pic ends on note of tentative familial reconciliation, tinged by ambiguous doom — HIV test results are the source of much melodramatic tension here. While Cook manipulates responses baldly, his plot twists score mainly as both clever and character-empathetic. Director Stephen Whittaker (a Brit TV-drama vet) does his part exacting solid performances amid polished if unimaginative presentation.

"Closing Numbers" constantly skirts a maudlin, obvious tenor in its mainstreamed p.c. message. Ultimate transcendence of those terms is gently moving, albeit modest enough to limit potential play in more sophisticated theatrical terrains. Tech values are slick.

—*Dennis Harvey*

UNDER HEAT

A Furious Films production. Produced by Denise Kasell, Frances N. Murdock, Peter Reed. Directed by Reed. Screenplay, Reed, Michael David Brown, based on Brown's novel. Camera (color), Manfred Reiff; editor, Irene Kassow; production design, Carol Strober; music, Elizabeth Swados. Reviewed at Variety Club Screening Room, San Francisco, May 24, 1994. (In San Francisco Intl. Lesbian & Gay Film Festival.) Running time: **91 MIN.**
Jane .... Lee Grant
Milo .... Robert Knepper
Dean .... Eric Swanson
With: David Conrad, Dan Desmond, Deborah Hedwall, Lily Knight.

Former dancer Peter Reed's debut feature is also, sadly, his last — helmer died of AIDS in April at age 40. Sadder still is the fact that this hackneyed, borderline-ludicrous family melodrama occupied his final months. Slick production values and telepic tenor suggest cable broadcast as likeliest outlet.

Based on a novel by Michael David Brown (who co-wrote screenplay with Reed), film mixes retro "Playhouse 90" feel with sub-Tennessee Williams verbosity that translates stiffly to celluloid form. While AIDS plot strand — among too many contrived crises — rates poignancy given its offscreen context, "Under Heat" embraces cliches at every juncture.

Dean (Eric Swanson), 36, has returned to visit his mom (Lee Grant) and older brother, Milo (Robert Knepper). We immediately deduce gay Dean is HIV-positive, though his plans to break that news to the family are interrupted repeatedly (with dim, heart-tugging obviousness). No wonder — this family seems to magnetize trauma. Mom's hit the bottle ever since doctor Dad committed suicide (for no clear reason) 20 years earlier, an act remembered by both sibs in gauzy flashbacks.

She's also diagnosed with a tumor that could be malignant. Meanwhile, bad-boy Milo has an ex-wife and two kids waiting in the wings for reconciliation. His sometime lover and partner in heroin use and dealing, Velma, skulks around, meddling to eventual disastrous effect.

Shot in the countryside around Albany, N.Y., "Under Heat" posits these figures as Souls in Torment. But they're artificial from the get-go, never as witty, wise or profoundly pained as the filmmakers seem to think. (Their posturing also seems laughably disembodied from the rural landscape.) As narrative winds toward its predictable funeral/stiff-upper-lip finale, howls gradually displace intended aud weepage.

Last half-hour, in particular, invites unkind laughter — especially when skimpily clad bad girl Velma chases the funeral procession sobbing, "I loved that son-of-a-bitch!"

Lead perfs are all grandstanding gesture, especially Swanson's over-telegraphing of "gay" and "doomed" signals. Given her heftiest screen role in some time, the normally expert, eerily unaged Grant is miscast. Her smart, sophisticated tenor is all wrong given Mom's history of emotional fragility.

Tech values are smooth. Reed demonstrates a pretty, albeit conventional, camera eye, and full-tilt empathy toward practiced thesps in stale circumstances. It's anyone's guess whether his directorial abilities would have seemed more promising granted less banal material.

—*Dennis Harvey*

BABY'S DAY OUT

A 20th Century Fox release of a John Hughes production. Produced by Hughes, Richard Vane. Executive producer, William Ryan. Co-producer, William S. Beasley. Directed by Patrick Read Johnson. Screenplay, Hughes. Camera (Deluxe color), Thomas Ackerman; editor, David Rawlins; music, Bruce Broughton; production design, Doug Kraner; art direction, Joseph Lucky; set decoration, Beth Rubino; costume design, Lisa Jensen; visual effects supervisor, Michael Fink; sound (Dolby), Ronald Judkins; pigeon wrangler, Mark Jackson; assistant director, Doug Wise; casting, Janet Hirshenson, Jane Jenkins. Reviewed at the Goldwyn Pavilion, L.A., June 14, 1994. MPAA Rating: PG. Running time: **98 MIN.**
Eddie .... Joe Mantegna
Laraine Cottwell .... Lara Flynn Boyle
Norby .... Joe Pantoliano
Veeko .... Brian Haley
Gilbertine .... Cynthia Nixon
Agent
  Grissom .... Fred Dalton Thompson
Mr. Andrews .... John Neville
Bennington Cottwell .... Matthew Glave
Baby Bink .... Adam Robert Worton,
                        Jacob Joseph Worton
Sally .... Brigid Duffy
Mr. Tinsel .... Eddie Bracken

Somewhere, far too late in the plot progression of "Baby's Day Out," one of the befuddled villains eyes the camera and declares: "This isn't funny anymore." The latest offering from writer/producer John Hughes is a tired retread of past comic formulas played a pitch higher, a rhythm faster. It tries too hard to please and fails miserably. Aimed squarely at a very young audience, it should have some initial activity and disappear quickly into the summer mill of commercially disappointing programmers.

The plot is rather like a pre-pubescent spin on O. Henry's "The Ransom of Red Chief." A trio of kidnappers (Joe Mantegna, Joe Pantoliano, Brian Haley) pose as baby photographers to gain access to the home of an old-money Chicago couple (Lara Flynn Boyle and Matthew Glave). At an opportune moment they snatch the infant son and hide out until their ransom demands are met.

The foolproof plan goes awry when 9-month-old Bennington August Cottwell IV, aka Baby Bink, crawls out an apartment window and into the hustle-bustle of downtown. For the ensuing period, the three stooges, the Cottwell household and the authorities are just a few baby steps behind the object of desire and love.

It's a simple enough premise, but neither Hughes nor director Patrick Read Johnson provides much in the way of novelty. The action is either played out for slapstick or dripping

with pathos. Either tack is geared toward obvious results.

In fact, even more than the O. Henry reference, the biggest influence on the tale derives from decades of Looney Tunes, especially those featuring the Road Runner. Baby Bink may be oblivious to malevolent intention, yet by crawling into such perilous spots as a gorilla cage and a construction site, he subjects his pursuers to physical abuse that would ordinarily fell a highly trained SWAT team.

The cartoon sensibility seems simply trite and predictable in the live-action mode. The considerable violence provides neither shock nor humor, each incident just another location where the snatchers can be run over by a literal or figurative steam roller — and, as has become a Hughes signature, an opportunity for characters to be shot in close-up clasping hands to face and screaming into the camera.

The filmmakers' penchant for treacly sentiment is also evident as heartwarming pictures of home and family punctuate the narrative. But real emotion doesn't take root in the highly manipulative entertainment, and a florid score is employed assiduously to coax appropriate response.

"Baby's Day Out" may be deserving of at least one award. It's difficult to recall when so many accomplished performers have worked this far below their professional standard. Mantegna and Pantoliano struggle to maintain some shred of dignity, while Flynn Boyle and John Neville can't quite decide whether to speak up or let their roles fade into the background.

There does appear to be an unwarranted sense of pride among the filmmakers, who drop a very obvious clue about the picture's sequel potential. But opening figures should erase any doubt about possibilities for a franchise.

—*Leonard Klady*

WYATT EARP

A Warner Bros. release of a Tig Prods./Kasdan Pictures production. Produced by Jim Wilson, Kevin Costner, Lawrence Kasdan. Executive producers, Jon Slan, Dan Gordon, Charles Okun, Michael Grillo. Directed by Kasdan. Screenplay, Gordon, Kasdan. Camera (Technicolor; Panavision widescreen), Owen Roizman; editor, Carol Littleton; music, James Newton Howard; production design, Ida Random; art direction, Gary Wissner; set design, Charles Daboub Jr., Tom Reta, Barry Chusid; set decoration, Cheryl Carasik; costume design, Colleen Atwood; sound (Dolby), John Pritchett; assistant director, Stephen Dunn; second unit camera, Richard Bowen; casting, Jennifer Shull. Reviewed at Cineplex Odeon Century City, L.A., June 11, 1994. MPAA Rating: PG-13. Running time: **189 MIN.**

Wyatt Earp .... Kevin Costner
Doc Holliday .... Dennis Quaid
Nicholas Earp .... Gene Hackman
Ike Clanton .... Jeff Fahey
Johnny Behan .... Mark Harmon
Virgil Earp .... Michael Madsen
Allie Earp .... Catherine O'Hara
Ed Masterson .... Bill Pullman
Big Nose Kate ..... Isabella Rossellini
Bat Masterson .... Tom Sizemore
Bessie Earp .... JoBeth Williams
Mattie Blaylock ... Mare Winningham
James Earp .... David Andrews
Morgan Earp .... Linden Ashby
Josie Marcus .... Joanna Going
   With: James Gammon, Rex Linn,
Randle Mell, Adam Baldwin, An-
nabeth Gish, Lewis Smith, Ian
Bohen, Betty Buckley.

I f you're going to ask an audience to sit through a three-
hour, nine-minute rendition
of a story that has been told
many times before, it would help
to have a strong point of view on
your material and an urgent reason to relate it. Such is not sufficiently the case with "Wyatt
Earp," a stately, handsome,
grandiose gentleman's Western
that evenhandedly but too doggedly tries to tell more about the
famous Tombstone lawman
than has ever before been put
onscreen.

Sticking closer to the known
facts than other versions just as it
mounts the Earp saga in terms
more epic than heretofore seen,
Lawrence Kasdan's expansive
and obviously expensive second
oater has more than enough interesting characters and dramatic
scenes, as well as Kevin Costner
back in the Old West, to draw audiences both domestically and
overseas. But undue length poses
a drawback, as do subject's familiarity and lack of sustained excitement, resulting in brawny but less
than brilliant B.O. prospects.

Tale of the laconic, steel-nerved
marshal who prevailed in the legendary gunfight at the O.K. Corral has always been a screen natural. It's greatest, most mythic telling is found in John Ford's "My
Darling Clementine," although
contemporary viewers will draw
primary comparison to the messy
but brassily entertaining "Tombstone," which came out, and performed surprisingly well, just six
months ago.

By contrast with the Disney
version, this new picture is serious and self-important. By spanning many years in the lives of
Earp and his family, the filmmakers are clearly making statements
about the cost of maintaining ideals, the inevitability of loss and the
wages of enforcing the law, but do
so in so discursive a manner as to
take much of the bite out of their
commentary.

The bigger-than-life approach
has some advantages in terms of
sheer scope and pictorial quality,
but everything here that could be
expressed in shorthand instead is
elaborated on, and everything
that could be implied is underlined, especially by the bombastic,
faux ennobling score.

Opening reels, set on the Earp
family farm, are designed to establish the clan's patriarchal nature and dedication to the precepts of justice and family. "Nothing counts as much as blood," intones the boys' lawyer father
(Gene Hackman). "The rest are
strangers." On an initial trek
west, Wyatt loses his lunch after
witnessing his first deadly shootout, and returns to the Midwest
where, dramatized at great
length, he marries, only to lose his
pregnant young wife to typhoid.

Wyatt (Costner) instantly goes
into a drunken, criminal downward spin, and the man's early
loss is heavily credited by Kasdan
as having been responsible for
Wyatt's harsh, unrelenting personality. With his father's help, he
gradually pulls himself out of his
stupor, becomes a buffalo hunter
(scenes of stampeding beasts inevitably recall "Dances With
Wolves") and eventually lands in
Wichita, where he almost inadvertently becomes a lawman.

From here on, pic begins treading on somewhat more familiar
territory, as Bat and Ed Masterson enter the story, followed by
Doc Holliday (Dennis Quaid), the
gunslinging dentist and "sporting
man" who forms an unlikely partnership with the brothers Earp in
trying to tame lawlessness in the
boom towns Dodge City and
Tombstone.

Inevitably, the road leads to the
O.K. Corral. The showdown between the Earps and Holliday on
one side and the Clantons and
McLaurys on the other is staged
with a brutal, startlingly realistic
quickness, rather than with a theatrical buildup of suspense and
elaborate choreography. What
fills out the time before and after
is a detailed portrait of the corrupt
politics of the Arizona Territory,
circa 1881, and a none-too-
flattering picture of Earp family
life, especially where the women
were concerned.

Kasdan misses out by not making
more of the fact that the woman
who eventually became Wyatt's
third and lasting wife, Josie Marcus
(Joanna Going), had actually been
the fiancee of the sheriff who became his arch-enemy, Johnny
Behan (Mark Harmon).

But Behan's duplicitous dealings and anxiousness to put the
Earps on trial for murder after the
gunfight are nicely sketched, and
the strained relations of the Earp
men and their assorted women,
some of them ex-whores and all of
whom basically have to do what
Wyatt says, make for an ironic
commentary on a group that places family ties above all.

"You're a cold man, Wyatt
Earp," charges one of his sisters-
in-law, and pic has to live with the
fact that the figure at its center is,
indeed, an icy, implacable fellow.
It's a role to which Costner is well
suited, as he keeps his distance
from most of the characters and
keeps his word about upholding
laws, particularly the dicey one in
both Dodge and Tombstone not
allowing firearms within city limits (anti-gun legislators take
note). All that's missing is the
tightly coiled quality beneath the
surface that he showed so impressively in "A Perfect World."

Standout performance, in what is
invariably a showy role, comes from
Quaid as Doc Holliday. Looking elegantly gaunt from having shed
more than 40 pounds for the part,
actor delivers a droll, sardonic,
poised reading of this charismatic,
equivocal character, and pic jumps
to life whenever he's around.

Cast is enormous, and the sheer
size of many scenes is startling in
itself. Clearly, no expense has been
spared in this attempt to make the
ultimate Wyatt Earp film, and Ida
Random's production design, which
encompasses dozens of distinctive
sets, Colleen Atwood's countless
costumes and Owen Roizman's expansive cinematography all help
make this a physically imposing
Hollywood production in the way
the world has always expected. Unfortunately, James Newton
Howard's score thunders away almost throughout, giving the film an
extra layer of pretentiousness and
heaviness that it scarcely needs.

To their credit, Kasdan, Costner
and the other key contributors have
sought to present a slightly more
ambiguous reading of one of the
West's key heroes than the public
has come to expect. But inasmuch
as it posits itself as a "dark" Western, it also inadvertently demonstrates just how brilliant "Unforgiven" really was.

—*Todd McCarthy*

LITTLE BIG LEAGUE

A Columbia release of a Castle Rock
Entertainment presentation of a
Lobell/Bergman production. Produced
by Mike Lobell. Executive producers,
Steve Nicolaides, Andrew Bergman.
Directed by Andrew Scheinman.
Screenplay, Gregory K. Pincus, Adam
Scheinman, story by Pincus. Camera
(Technicolor), Donald E. Thorin; editor,
Michael Jablow; music, Stanley Clarke;
production design, Jeffrey Howard; set
decoration, Ethel Robin Richards; cos-
tume design, Erica Edell Phillips;
sound (Dolby), Bob Eber; associate pro-
ducer, Adam Merims; assistant direc-
tor, Mark McGann; second unit direc-
tor, Bill Pohlad; casting, Mary Gail
Artz, Barbara Cohen. Reviewed at
Sony Pictures screening room, Culver
City, June 15, 1994. MPAA Rating: PG.
Running time: **119 MIN.**
Billy Heywood .... Luke Edwards
Lou Collins .... Timothy Busfield
Mac Macnally .... John Ashton
Jenny Heywood .... Ashley Crow
Arthur Goslin .... Kevin Dunn
Thomas Heywood .... Jason Robards
Chuck Lobert .... Billy L. Sullivan
Joey Smith .... Miles Feulner
Jim Bowers .... Jonathan Silverman
George O'Farrell .... Dennis Farina
Spencer Hamilton ... Wolfgang Bodison
Jerry Johnson .... Duane Davis

A nother attempt to cash in on
America's pastime, this perfectly innocuous little baseball comedy has its heart in the
right place but never makes it out
of the infield in terms of laughs or
excitement. As a result, with limited cast appeal and the spotty
performance of recent sports pix,
"Little Big League" figures to lean
more toward that first adjective at
the ticket window.

Like last season's "Rookie of the
Year," the premise centers on a
young boy living out a big-league
baseball fantasy. In this case, 12-
year-old Billy (Luke Edwards) gets
left a major league franchise, the
Minnesota Twins, by his grandfather (Jason Robards), who has faith
in the boy's knowledge of the game
and love of the team. To the initial
chagrin of the players, Billy decides
to make himself manager, not-so-
gradually winning them over as he
tries to teach them to enjoy the
game again, helping the team go on
a winning tear.

Rather than simply follow that
"Major League" riff to its logical
conclusion, however, the script
comes full circle by having Billy
himself become too wrapped up
with winning, straining relations
with his friends until he, too, has to
relearn the value of being a kid.

If that weren't enough, Billy also
must grapple with the idea of the
team's first baseman (Timothy Busfield) courting his single mom (Ashley Crow).

Castle Rock partner Andrew
Scheinman, making his directing
debut, seems to find all of that territory a bit too much to cover. Even
with the movie's leisurely pace and

June 20, 1994 (Cont.)

liberal use of musical montages to chart the Twins' rise and fall, there still isn't enough time to develop any character other than Billy himself. Those montages also help rob the baseball sequences of suspense or excitement, despite their technical authenticity and appearances by real-life major leaguers Ken Griffey Jr., Randy Johnson and Wally Joyner.

To his credit, Scheinman (working from a script by his brother, Adam Scheinman, and Gregory K. Pincus) doesn't swing for the fences in the laughs department, offering more bittersweet or tender moments than big guffaws. The result, though, is a rather muted tone, without the broad strokes or emotional highs that youngsters, in particular, might expect from the genre.

Because of the way it's structured, Edwards has to carry the movie, which is a lot to ask. While he comes off as a real and likable kid, he's not expressive enough to convey some of the turmoil his character seems to be — or should be — experiencing.

Robards is perhaps most effective in his cameo, while the rest of the cast mostly gets stuck swinging at material outside the strike zone. Indeed, several of the Twins players are virtually indistinguishable, and the Busfield-Crow relationship gets especially short shrift.

The pic actually fares best with its clever use of music, from Stanley Clarke's score to the particularly appropriate John Fogerty tune "Centerfield."

Billy's friends also provide some occasionally amusing "Stand by Me"-type rambling about old TV shows, such as why a millionaire would be aboard the Minnow on "Gilligan's Island." Production values are generally sharp, although Scheinman falls into the slow-motion trap that seems to snare most sports-related pix. In fact, with children a big part of the target audience and a two-hour running time, a faster delivery all around probably would have been advisable.   —*Brian Lowry*

NAKED KILLER

(CHIKLO GOUYEUNG)

(HONG KONG)

A Wong Jing's Workshop production. Produced by Wong Jing. Executive producer, Wong. Directed by Clarence Fok Yiu-leung. Screenplay, Wong. Camera (color), William Yim, Peter Pau; editor, Wong Chi-hung; music, Lowell Lo; art direction, Ngai Fong-nay; costume design, Shirley Chan; martial arts director, Lau Shung-fung; choreography, Stephen Lee; associate producer, Dennis Chan; assistant directors, Leung Pak-kin, Ching Sut-tsing. Reviewed on Mei Ah vidcassette, London, May 1, 1994. Running time **91 MIN.**

Kitty .... Chingmy Yau
Tinam .... Simon Yam
Princess .... Carrie Ng
Sister Cindy .... Kelly Yao
(Cantonese soundtrack)

Even jaded palates will get a rush from "Naked Killer," a deliriously over-the-top slice of Hong Kong phooey that's got latenight fest hit and cult video title written all over it. Already a hotly traded item among Asian buffs, this sexy, cartoon-violent yarn about feuding lesbian assassins plays like a modern version of classic costume actioners.

Someone is going around Hong Kong topping horny males and slicing off their genitals. Enter strung-out cop Tinam (Simon Yam), who still suffers from barfing fits over accidentally killing his brother three months earlier.

Tinam (literally, "Iron Man") meets obsessive, long-legged looker Kitty (Chingmy Yau) in a unisex hair salon and is soon giving Michael Douglas lessons in the jitters.

When Kitty shoots up a gangster's office in revenge for her father's death, she's taken home by professional assassin Sister Cindy (Kelly Yao), who keeps rapists chained up in her cellar for martial arts workouts. Sister Cindy takes on Kitty as a pupil.

The mystery killer turns out to be Princess, lesbian ex-pupil of Sister Cindy who has a contract to take out her former teacher. Tinam, meanwhile, is being driven nuts by Kitty's come-ons. When Princess ends Sister Cindy's career, Kitty hits the vengeance trail big time.

Under the practiced hand of producer/scripter Wong Jing and journeyman director Clarence Fok Yiu-leung ("Dragon From Russia"), pic emerges as a juicy blend of martial arts actioners and Hong Kong's so-called Category III (sexpot) movies, with comedy stirred in for good measure.

Movie milks references to everything from early Brian De Palma movies to "Basic Instinct," but its sheer glee in pushing the taste envelope well past its limits marks it as pure Hong Kong.

As the elegant lesbian super-assassin, Carrie Ng walks away with the pic, though she's closely followed in the vamp stakes by both the older Yao and young sex star Yau as mistress and ambitious pupil.

Technically, the film oozes gloss in all departments, including an eye-opening main title shot by ace Hong Kong lenser Peter Pau. Pic took a solid $HK10 million ($1.3 million) on local release in December '92.   —*Derek Elley*

CACHE CASH

(FRENCH)

A Gaumont Buena Vista Intl. release (France) of a Gaumont/Gaumont Prod. 2 production, with participation of Canal Plus. Produced by Alain Poire. Directed by Claude Pinoteau. Screenplay, Guy Lagorce, Pinoteau, Jean Veber, based on the novel "Les Dieux provisoires," by Lagorce. Camera (color), Jean Tournier; editor, Marie-Joseph Yoyotte; music, Vladimir Cosma; production design, Hugues Tissandier; costume design, Annie Quesnal; sound, Bernard Bats; assistant director, Bernard Seitz; casting, Francoise Menidrey. Reviewed at Gaumont Marignan Theater, Paris, June 12, 1994. (In Paris Film Festival, noncompeting.) Running time: **90 MIN.**
Antoine .... Aurelien Wiik
Lisa .... Josephine Serre
Clemence .... Rose Thiery
Claire .... Sophie Broustal
Durandet .... Jean Carmet
Max .... Jean-Claude Dreyfus
With: Georges Wilson, Jean-Pierre Darroussin, Michel Duchaussoy.

"Cache Cash" is a solidly entertaining and sweetly plotted adventure that interweaves a bank heist, cavalier parents, animal friends, strong women, evil men and two resourceful children. Charming suspense tale, convincingly told from youngsters' point of view, is a real find for family-oriented fests and foreign-lingo-friendly theatrical and tube slots. An eventual English-language remake would come as no surprise.

Claude Pinoteau — who launched Sophie Marceau and others on promising careers — scores with two gifted child actors who come across as natural and appealing without a trace of smarm.

From his secret treehouse in the forest, resilient 11-year-old country boy Antoine (Aurelien Wiik) spots bank robbers hiding their 40-million-franc haul. Because one of the conspirators is Jacques (Michel Duchaussoy), father to Antoine's new best friend — adorable 10-year-old Lisa (Josephine Serre), who's visiting for the summer from Canada — Antoine moves the stash instead of blowing the whistle.

The kids share a love of animals and a healthy disdain for hypocritical grown-ups, including their own, mostly absentee, fathers. Antoine and Lisa run away in style to the resort town of Biarritz, discovering that a steady supply of 500-franc notes and a little chutzpah pave the way nicely.

Missing loot infuriates bandit Max (Jean-Claude Dreyfus), who sets off to intercept the kids in a sustained chase peppered with close calls.

Pic has two choice roles for strong women. Slinky Claire (Sophie Broustal) uses her body to get what she wants. Antoine's chief ally, outrageously strong governess Clemence (Rose Thiery), can outlift and outpunch any man, which makes her very handy in a fight.

Nerdy Jean (Jean-Pierre Darroussin) successfully beds Claire when she mistakenly thinks he has the missing loot. Tasteful sex and nudity, which Gallic youngsters take in stride, might be problematic in other markets.

The late Jean Carmet appears briefly as a reluctant veterinarian.

Breathless finale is well staged in a house-of-horrors fairground ride. Jaunty Vladimir Cosma score is pleasing and effective.
     —*Lisa Nesselson*

INSIDE THE GOLDMINE

A Cineville presentation in association with Hugh Pedy. Produced by Adam Stern. Executive producers, Pedy, Uri Zighelboim. Line producer/assistant director, Louis Nader. Directed by Josh Evans. Screenplay, Evans, Zighelboim. Camera (Foto-Kem color), Fernando Aguilles; editor, Nabil Mechi; music, Robin Lemusier; production design, Karen Hasse; art direction, Creston Funk; sound (Cinestereo), Oliver Haycroft, Mike Michaels, Sam Mendelssohn; casting, Tony Markes. Reviewed at Seattle Intl. Film Festival (New Directors), June 9, 1994. Running time: **92 MIN.**
Jordan Dalgren .... Alan Marshall
Clyde Daye .... Josh Evans
Emily .... Alicia Tully Jensen
Sid Dalgren .... Gary Chazen
Stockard .... Charlie Spradling
Waitress ..... Natasha Gregson Wagner
Scarlet Rider .... Ines Misan
Daisy .... Drew Barrymore
Det. Abraham .... Himself

The most devastating view of Generation X yet, "Inside the Goldmine" is a searing first feature emphasizing passion over style. Its raw energy imbues every frame, with the prospect of hope not remotely a part of its vocabulary. That should earn it critical attention but will seriously limit its commercial prospects to fest and arthouse venues.

Unquestionably influenced by the early films of John Cassavetes, director/co-writer and star Josh Evans uses the murder of a young woman to anchor his characters and situations. Jordan (Alan Marshall) is the scion of a famous Hollywood producer, and buddy Clyde (Evans) is both his accomplice and tormentor.

The entertainment industry serves as a backdrop and metaphor for the young people's empty lives (Evans, son of Robert Evans and Ali

McGraw, comes by his Hollywood knowledge honestly). Aimless, unmotivated and from wealthy families, this breed has evolved into textbook nihilists. Given that context, one understands why the police suspect Clyde — who's had earlier brushes with the law — of murdering the girl briefly seen at the beginning offering a rather vile analysis of their crowd.

Played with the nerve endings exposed, scenes unfold in long takes. The dialogue leaves nothing to the imagination. The psychodrama splits audiences into those quickly headed for the door and heartier viewers mesmerized by the honesty and invention of the vision.

Evans' cast is largely composed of non-pros, which further intensifies the vivid nature of the production. As an actor he has an effortless charisma. The script is relentless in keeping its intentions masked and in refusing to let characters or viewers off the hook.

Most potent are the encounters between Jordan and his father (Gary Chazen). The latter is classically abusive toward a son he feels compelled to compete with.

Tech credits demonstrate a precise and unswerving perspective. Particularly striking is Fernando Aguilles' camera work, which borders on the bright and surreal as counterpoint to the action.

The "Goldmine" of the title is elusive and beyond the reach of the principals. Unquestionably intended to wear viewers down, the film is an apt showcase for a unique, emerging hyphenate.

—Leonard Klady

CAPTURE
THE WHITE FLAG

A Seattle Feature Prods. production. Produced, directed, written by Alex Zedicoff. Camera (color), Kyle Bergerson; editor, Ken Rogerson; music, Gregory Nissen; costume design, Bonnie Bodine; sound, Steve Cammarano; assistant director, Shannon Braly; casting, Georgianne Walken (U.S.), Trish Robinson (Canada). Reviewed at Seattle Intl. Film Festival, May 25, 1994. Running time: **84 MIN.**
Daniel .... Chris Harlowe
Ramos .... Jason Collins
Joel .... Seth Sexton
Jane .... Erin Randels
Marty .... Eric Cozens
Susan .... Sarah Buff
Bill .... Jim Dean

A coming-of-age tale with a slight literary twist, this debut venture for helmer Alex Zedicoff captures something about the twilight between adolescence and manhood, but no flags will fly at the B.O., even on the indie circuit.

Title refers to childhood game teenaged Daniel (Chris Harlowe) recalls through innumerable flashbacks as he tries to cope with the onslaught of adult problems. His dad's a self-absorbed weakling, his stepmom a neurotic wreck, and a troubled tough guy (Jason Collins) seems to follow everywhere he goes. The bully even shows up when the scene switches from a working-class Seattle nabe to an out-of-town summer camp.

For a while, Danny boy forms an uneasy alliance with a spoiled younger camper (Seth Sexton), based on their mutual admiration for "The Odyssey."

This Homeric connection is stretched to the max in "Capture the White Flag," via redundant, superficial references and a modern-day Cyclops who appears at least twice too often to have any shock effect.

The Greek classic may be the one source hammered home here — the only book ever written, to hear these folks tell it — but there are also rude hints of "Portnoy's Complaint" when our hero meets Jane Fliegelbaum (wooden Erin Randels), the tease of his dreams.

Naturally, Daniel quietly triumphs against adversity and finds the Inner Strength to grow, but at considerable cost to the narrative and even the most sympathetic auds.

The dramatic arc of long lulls followed by minor explosions soon grows numbing, and perfs generally aren't up to the journey.

Fortunately, the lead is, and whenever the camera rests on Harlowe's expressive face, pic hints at more soulful stuff than it finally delivers. That's partly because Zedicoff shows so little compassion for the other characters. The females are all harridans or shrews, and the language is much too harsh for "Flag" to find a home in school programs that otherwise might have welcomed it. Tech credits are passable for this no-budget production.

—Ken Eisner

PAUL BOWLES:
THE COMPLETE
OUTSIDER

(DOCU — 16mm)

A First Run Features production. Produced, directed by Catherine Warnow, Regina Weinreich. Camera (color), Burleigh Wartes; editors, Jessica Bendiner, Amanda Zinoman; music, Paul Bowles; sound, Samantha Heilweil; narration, Bowles, Brian Woolfenden. Reviewed at Seattle Intl. Film Festival, June 3, 1993. Running time: **57 MIN.**

An unusually complete look at the self-exiled author of "The Sheltering Sky" and other pre-Beat era classics, this docu effectively depicts a surviving enigma in his Tangier retreat, and has some sharp insights into the act of writing itself. This "Outsider" can expect enthusiastic acceptance by pubcasters, educators and literary audiences worldwide.

Pic was undertaken when co-helmer Regina Weinreich went to teach with writer Paul Bowles in Tangier and realized she and fellow English-lit doctorate Catherine Warnow had gone through graduate school scarcely hearing of his work. With help from the National Endowment for the Arts and the Moroccan government, a decade of letter writing resulted in this series of lively interviews, punctuated by archival clips (including a surrealistic '50s piece from Hans Richter), atmospheric travel footage and interviews with friends like Allen Ginsberg, Ned Rorem and Millicent Dillon.

There are plenty of other high-toned names dropped as Bowles and others describe his relationships with Gertrude Stein, W.H. Auden, Benjamin Britten, Leonard Bernstein, Tennessee Williams, William S. Burroughs (who put Bowles at the center of "Naked Lunch") and Jean-Paul Sartre — Bowles titled his translation of "No Exit" after spying a sign in the New York subway.

And, of course, there's the strained competition with wife Jane, who pursued her lesbian affairs while he struggled with his own vague sexuality.

The filmmakers are less interested in his austere romantic life than his rich musical one. Bowles wrote operas and Broadway musicals in the 1940s, and turned his attention to collecting North African music and stories (and smokables) thereafter; the pic's soundtrack is replete with examples of his compositions. He also reads from

his works, and obliges the camera with plenty of curmudgeonly quips.

The emerging portrait is of an artist keenly tuned to his environment but always painfully alien from it — someone who, by the time filming began in 1988, felt strange anywhere outside of his own apartment.

Lensing and sound vary from problematic to very good, but this doesn't interfere with the thoughtful subject. Although Bowles, now 83, remains a quintessential pessimist, the overall tone is of lighthearted introspection, and there are plenty of sardonic laughs from all quarters. *—Ken Eisner*

S.F. GAY FEST

SUPER 8 ½

(CANADIAN — B&W/16m)

A Strand release of a Jurgen Bruning production in association with Gaytown Prods. and Strand Releasing. Executive producers, Jon Gerrans, Marcus Hu, Mike Thomas. Directed, written by Bruce LaBruce. Camera (b&w), Donna Mobbs; editors, Manse James, Robert Kennedy; sound, James. Reviewed at San Francisco Intl. Lesbian & Gay Film Festival, June 11, 1994. Running time: **106 MIN.**
Bruce .... Bruce LaBruce
Googie .... Liza Lamonica
Johnny Eczema .... Mikey Mike
Pierce .... Klaus Von Brucker
Wednesday Friday .... Chris Teen
Jane Friday .... Dirty Pillows
With: Buddy Cole, Ben Weasel, Amy Nitrate, Vaginal Creme Davis, Richard Kern.

Canadian Warholian auteur Bruce LaBruce has risen to a new plateau with this impudent "cautionary biopic." A fake documentary, "Super 8½" marks a leap in performance and technical prowess from his prior feature, the basement Gus Van Sant "No Skin Off My Ass." Midnight-movie appeal stands compromised by numerous segs of hardcore (yet strangely funny/banal) sexual activity, plus need to shave a good half-hour off running time.

First hour is willfully sloppy yet hilarious, as alleged former gay porn actor/director Bruce (LaBruce) scrutinizes his life and career for lens of arty docu-inquisitor Googie (Liza Lamonica). Blackout scenes encompass interviews with Bruce (seen in his faux-Warhol Factory apartment), former lovers and sex cinema co-workers, and scene-fringing lesbian punkette "sisters" Wednesday & Jane Friday. Also glimpsed are Bruce's alleged earlier porn epics, which are graphic yet ridiculously arty, plus broadcast shards of such relatively recent

June 20, 1994 (Cont.)

kitsch epics as "Butterfield 8" and "Play It as It Lays."

Basically formless scenario entertains for a long while until awaited confrontation between Bruce's boozy, edge-of-breakdown persona and "predatory" helmer Googie. But film badly outstays its welcome, rambling through last 45 minutes' "press conference" (only seg shot in color), interminable clips from helmer's ostensible prior porn reels (including "I Am a Fugitive From a Gang Bang" and "My Hustler, My Self") and nonexistent denouement.

This final tedium seems needless, given funky, vibrant performances and savvy aesthetic that surrounds them. One late highlight is unspooling of Googie's own experimental flick "Submit to My Finger," which employs the Friday sisters to "Faster, Pussycat, Kill! Kill!"-type effect. It's frequently difficult to separate flashback, interview and alleged archival sequences into chronological coherence.

Pic's occasional amateurity of lensing just underlines its anti-mainstream position. LaBruce makes ample fun of his own decadent image throughout and coaxes daft/fearless turns from others. "Super 8½" pushes the envelope of acceptable gay indie cinema; it's at once clever, indulgent and perilously beyond the pale of conventional taste. —*Dennis Harvey*

THE CREATION OF ADAM

(COTBOPEHNE AGAMA)

(RUSSIAN)

A D. Kamandar Studio presentation with the participation of NEVA Studio. Produced by Dzhavanshir Kamandar, Anatolli Kasimov. Executive producer, Olga Naidenova. Directed by Yury Pavlov. Screenplay, Vladimir Maslov, Vitaly Moskalenko. Camera (color), Sergei Machilsky; editor, Raisa Lissova; music, Andrei Sigle; production design, Michael Suzdalov; costumes, Andzhela Sapunova; sound, Alexander Bershadsky. Reviewed at Variety Club Screening Room, San Francisco, June 14, 1994 (in S.F. Intl. Lesbian & Gay Film Festival). Running time: **93 MIN.**
With: Saulis Balandis, Sergei Vinogradov, Irina Metlitskaya, Anzhelika Nevolina, Alexander Strizhenov.

Editor/film scholar Yury Pavlov's feature helming debut is a quietly captivating religious parable of sorts with significant homoerotic overtones. Story's cryptic progress will limit exposure beyond fest circuit, though some Euro theatrical is possible.

Handsome protagonist Andrei seems dead-ended both at his design-firm job and in soured marriage to Nina. One female co-worker has an unrequited passion for him, but questions are raised about Andrei's sexual identity when he rescues a young man from street gay-bashers. As his wife announces she's filed for divorce (calling him a "freak ... just a nonentity"), hero faces new source of tension from Philip, a mysterious figure who's ostensibly arrived with a major design-biz project.

With his aggressively sexual presence, Philip at first appears a threatening supernatural force. The two men's odd day trip to a warehouse and beach soon turns surreal, as Philip announces, "I am your patron saint" and declares Andrei the reincarnation of an ancient savior. Latter flees in panic.

But at Philip's apartment, pic's rising mysticism grows benign. When Philip kisses Andrei's arm, a knife wound from the skirmish with bashers vanishes; after a night of ambiguous sexual vibes, this "angel" disappears as well. Andrei wanders around the city, alone and uncertain. Close posits a miraculous new development in the hitherto childless marriage to Nina.

Just what all this means is far from clear, though some visual and dialogue cues suggest Christian and pagan-mythological subtexts (notably in discussion of ancient "androgynes" gender-split by an angry Zeus). Philip's statement — that he's "come here to excite your memory, to teach you the one and only thing: love" — makes "Wings of Desire" seem a likely script inspiration. In any case, ultimate effect is a tender, poetic and refreshingly pansexual (albeit never explicit) fantasia on themes of mercy and faith.

Performers are attractive and low-key, directorial nuances ditto. Solid tech work features handsome, often golden-filtered lensing and sensitive, sparing use of music. Current English subtitles are poorly translated. While press sheet's sales line, "The most romantic film of 1993," seems rather a stretch from any mainstream p.o.v., "The Creation of Adam" does leave a warm, spectral afterglow.
—*Dennis Harvey*

NOT ANGELS BUT ANGELS

(CZECH REPUBLIC-FRENCH — DOCU)

A Mirofilm presentation. Produced by Miro Vostiar with Frank Beauvais. Directed, written, edited by Wiktor Grodecki. Camera (color), Vladimir Holomek; sound, Jan Cenek; associate producer, Michel Klein; line producer, Peter Lencses; assistant director, Beauvais. Reviewed at Variety Club Screening Room, San Francisco, May 31, 1994. (In S.F. Intl. Lesbian & Gay Festival.) Running time: **80 MIN.**

Compromised by the odd disadvantage of being too technically slick for its gritty subject, this docu on boy street hustlers of Prague offers Eastern Euro setting as only novel element in otherwise predictable look at familiar subject. Gay and docu-slanted fests may bite; Euro broadcast is possible, although a couple of gratuitous, explicit bits might require trimming.

Polish-born helmer Wiktor Grodecki immediately catches the eye with his candy-hued lighting and gimmicky compositions for interviews with some dozen lads (most in their late teens). But while visual fuss and jazzy editing do spice up what's essentially a lot of talking-head footage, that approach — rather similar to Diane Keaton's in the more fanciful 1987 docu "Heaven" — calls attention to itself at the expense of investigative depth.

Some additional sequences manipulate to questionable ends, as in flashy cuts to leering johns (presumably actors) and a tasteless bit mixing up footage of a tattoo-laden tramp's strip with hardcore porn stills. Use of borrowed music (mostly classical, plus some clamorous metal & Tibetan sounds) is effective yet employed to levy condescending doomed aura on teen prosties.

Kid subjects are fairly articulate, describing their (largely foreign-tourist) customers and personal backgrounds. But Grodecki rarely strays from the method of approaching a topic (AIDS fears, condom use, favored and disliked sexual acts) and rapidly cutting between all interviewees as they offer basically the same responses.

Sum effect is watchable but unenlightening, with glossy presentation adding shock-value tenor that leaves a sour aftertaste. Weighed against such similar portraits of the disenfranchised as "Paris Is Burning," "Not Angels But Angels" seems more judgmental than compassionate toward its hard-luck protagonists. —*Dennis Harvey*

CHICKEN HAWK

(DOCU — 16mm)

A Stranger Than Fiction Films presentation of a Side Man production. Produced, directed by Adi Sideman. Executive producers, Sam Sideman, Peter Smith. Camera (color), Nadav Harel; editor, Harel; narrators, Barbara Adler, Mimi Turner; associate producers, Andrea Wolf, Annat and Assaf Keller, Gal Gotsegen. Reviewed at San Francisco Intl. Lesbian & Gay Film Festival, June 12, 1994. Running time: **58 MIN.**

Less sensational than its title suggests, this short feature doc examines gay male pedophiles from p.o.v. of both their few activist spokesmen and the many enraged opponents. While intelligently weighed and insightful to a degree, the volatile emotions surrounding any discussion of this subject will limit exposure to some gay fests and educational webs.

Free-form but tightly knit effort revolves mostly around interviews with confessed "boy-lovers" and the hostile reactions their beliefs (most claim celibacy, given legal consequences of acting on desires) draw from surrounding communities. One feels some sympathy for the high school teacher who's canned simply for expressing his ideas re age-of-consent laws. On the other hand, it's easy to understand angry, protective stance taken by parents who'd prefer such men run out of town.

Brief historical background shows that adult-child sexual relations have been permitted in some cultures. Other sidelights depict members of controversial advocacy group the North American Man-Boy Love Assn., and the furious reaction they provoke from other participants at a Gay Pride Day march.

In current climate of heightened child-abuse sensitivity, "coming out" as a pedophile seems an act of daring or lunacy, depending on one's view. Indeed, some of the subjects here are quite creepy — notably the religio-psychobabble-spouting man who gushingly interprets any trivial encounter with local lads in flirtatious terms.

Though pic negotiates heated issue informatively, a longer running time would have permitted deeper scrutiny. Could any clinical evidence of former "boy" subjects be found to buttress NAMBLA's claim that such relationships can be harmless, or even beneficial? The thorniest moral question here — how can "consent" be gauged when emotional/sexual maturity itself is variable? — goes basically uncommented upon.

Good editing and OK lensing and sound lend package feel of a locally produced TV doc. —*Dennis Harvey*

MY ADDICTION

(CANADIAN — COLOR/B&W/16mm)

An Orton Film Corp. presentation. Directed, written, edited by Sky Gilbert. Camera (color/b&w), Gregg Bennett; sound, post-production, Dennis Mohr; assistant director, Stephen Lang. Reviewed on vidcassette, San Francisco, June 4, 1994. (In S.F. Intl. Lesbian & Gay Film Festival.) Running time: **61 MIN.**
With: Caroline Gillis, Ellen-Ray Hennessey, Daniel MacIvor, O'Mara, Tracy Wright.

This shapeless effort at hip comedy hinges on a lopsided client-hustler relationship.

June 20, 1994 (Cont.)

Amateur feel and short running time will limit prospects to unselective gay fests.

Story, such as it is, springs from hysterical housewife Mary Ann's suspicion that her husband, Matt, is cheating. She hires a detective/cameraman to record other half's activities — revealed as fixation on the apparently aptly named younger male prostie Dick.

After declaring his love, Matt faces Dick's get-out-or-I'll-kill-you threats. He sticks around, passing time with latter's bisexual junkie flatmate, Marvette. Dick returns from a trick and, true to his word, beats Matt senseless. Conclusion posits patly ironic "second marriage pact" between man and wife.

Wobbly, variably focused fauxverite lensing (alternating between color and blue-tinged b&w) gets old fast. Likewise seemingly improvised dialogue, delivered by performers void of any transcendent spark. Sound quality is good, which perhaps isn't appropriate, given pic's conceit. Notation of characters' "addictive" behaviors (re sex, drugs, alcohol, nicotine) leads nowhere.

Canuck helmer Sky Gilbert has created several stage shows, some of which — notably "Drag Queens in Outer Space" — have traveled stateside to infinitely more defined, satirical effect than this enervated enterprise can muster. His commitment to this torpid, sub-Gus Van Sant rough-trade scenario can only be explicated as highly personal. And that's no excuse.

—*Dennis Harvey*

KANADA

(CANADIAN — 16m)

A Mike Hoolboom production, produced with the assistance of Canada Council, National Film Board of Canada and Ontario Arts Council. Produced, directed, written, edited by Hoolboom. Camera (color/b&w), Steve Sanguedolce; original music and sound design, Earle Peach; set design, Kika Thorne; sound recording, Ann Marie Fleming, Gary Popovich. Reviewed at San Francisco Intl. Lesbian & Gay Film Festival, June 12, 1994. Running time: **65 MIN.**
Charlie .... Babs Chula
Prime Minister's
Assistant .... Sky Gilbert
The Newscaster .... Mike Hoolboom
The Prime Minister ..... Andrew Scorer
The Bride .... Kika Thorne
Bobbie .... Gabrielle Rose

Aquasi-experimental bore, "Kanada" mixes lesbian drama and political satire to no discernible point. Southern-exposure potential is such that creator Mike Hoolboom might have better luck shopping pic northward, i.e., around the Arctic Circle.

Setting is a fantasy near-future in which national bankruptcy, global

wars and militant Quebec separatism have turned Canada to chaos. A TV newscaster (Hoolboom in death's-head mask) reports absurdist developments while former hockey star Wayne Gretzky, posited as new prime minister, tries to hold the nation together. Intercut are scenes with two chic 30-ish women — prostitute and writer, respectively — as they banter and quarrel through a love affair that ends violently. Additional segs feature enigmatic figure in bridal garb running through desolate urban landscapes.

Struggling for Godardian impudence, none of these elements connect or comment upon one another; they're not so hot on their own, either. Best factor is some amusingly bratty dialogue for the two female lovers (well-played by Babs Chula and Gabrielle Rose), though the pretentiousness and dim scatological humor rampant elsewhere often intrude here as well. Satire of Canuck politics waxes sophomoric at best, unhelped by decision to backdrop those parts with irrelevant "Caligari"-style abstract "sets."

Latter segs are b&w; those featuring the two women, in color. Characters spend most of running time addressing camera directly in close-up. Overexposed images throughout seem intended to artily camouflage micro-budget, yet only exacerbate tedium. Pic's infrequent coherent messages run no deeper than "TV makes us stupid" or pat lovers-vs.-warmongers gender stereotyping ("Life gives women a purpose; death gives men one," intones the prime minister's assistant).

Best line is a (probably borrowed) joke: "You know why they call television 'the medium'? Because it's neither rare nor well-done." "Kanada" provides unneeded further proof that film projects can be half-cooked as well. —*Dennis Harvey*

CANNES FEST

O MARY THIS LONDON

BRITISH

A Samuel Goldwyn release of a BBC Films production. Produced by Helen Greaves. Executive producer, Mark Shivas. Directed by Suri Krishnamma. Screenplay, Shane Connaughton. Camera (color), Sean Van Hales; editor, Sue Wyatt; music, Stephen Warbeck; production design, Brian Sykes. Reviewed at Cannes Film Festival (market), May 19, 1994. Running time: **90 MIN.**
Mickey .... Jason Barry
Mary ....Oba Seagrave
Bimbo .... Dylan Tighe

The tough lives of three Irish youngsters in London are rigorously and painfully exposed

in the vibrant urban drama "O Mary This London," a wildly confrontational and emotionally resonant tale underscored by humor as well as despair. Exquisitely written, directed and acted pic exhibits the same rough sensibility and energetic style that mark the films of Stephen Frears and Ken Loach. This rude and vivid film establishes Suri Krishnamma as a gifted director to watch and should be embraced by fans of new British cinema.

"O Mary This London" joins a recent slate of British films in its ultra-realistic portrait of London as a multicultural, dangerous metropolis, peopled with eccentric and volatile citizens whose anger and frustration often result in catastrophes and tragedies. Pic speaks not in the dignified tone of the Merchant Ivory tradition but in the biting voice of the pubs, streets, immigrants and beggars — in short, authentic working-class denizens.

Tale revolves around an offbeat trio of friends, Mickey, Mary and Bimbo, who arrive in London on a ferry from Dublin, expecting to improve on their dreary, oppressive lot at home. Mary (Oba Seagrave) is depressed over her unwanted pregnancy, presumably a result of her affair with Bimbo (Dylan Tighe), though identity of baby's father becomes one of the film's surprises and a catalyst for personality conflicts.

Gifted scripter Shane Connaughton constructs three fascinating portraits of people who live close to their appetites — and close to the edge. In his compelling screenplay, the characters always confront each other openly and abrasively in a network of relationships that is much more complex than it initially seems.

Underlying the notion that London is a ruthless city to outsiders who don't belong, writer's strategy is to expose the trio to different experiences that first separate but later reunite them. Structured as a road pic about the cruel struggle to survive, story shows how the youngsters learn some tough lessons about life — and about themselves. The intense challenges they face over the course of a few days are sufficient for a lifetime for members of the middle or upper class. But the film is anything but a luck-of-the-Irish saga; in fact, its shockingly tragic ending is well-earned.

A boldly intuitive director, Krishnamma's particular talent seems to lie in creating worlds that appear lunatic but are entirely plausible. A stylishly bleak urban environment is created by Sean Van Hales' vibrant lensing of Elephant and Castle, Westminster and Trafalgar Square, and Sue Wyatt's sharply swift editing.

Disorder and despair are the central metaphors of this unsettling but immensely satisfying movie. Everything here has the aura of gritty spontaneity, particularly the fresh, unactorish performances of leads Jason Barry, Seagrave and Tighe. —*Emanuel Levy*

ANGEL DUST

(TENSHI NO KUZU)

(JAPANESE)

A Twins Japan, Euro Space production. (International sales: Celluloid Dreams, Paris.) Produced by Taro Maki, Kenzo Horikoshi, Eiji Izumi. Executive producer, Satoshi Kanno. Directed by Sogo Ishii. Screenplay, Yorozu Ikuta, Ishii. Camera (color), Norimichi Kasamatu; editors, Hiroshi Matsuo, Ishii; music, Hiroyuki Nagashima; production design, Tomoyuki Maruo; line producer, Atsuyuki Shimoda. Reviewed at Cannes Film Festival (market), May 21, 1994. Running time: **117 MIN.**
Setsuko Suma .... Kaho Minami
Rei Aku .... Takeshi Wakamatsu
Tomoo .... Etsushi Toyokawa
Yuki Takei .... Ryoko Takizawa

Sogo Ishii waives the delirious black comedy of his well-traveled 1984 outing, "Crazy Family," for an altogether more subversively disquieting mood in "Angel Dust." Set against a Tokyo that's part glittering jewel, part computerized monster, this psycho-killer chiller proffers love as the most debilitating, mind-controlling drug of all. Technical dazzler should intoxicate its share of festival junkies and fans of Japanese pix.

Panic spreads when a succession of young females become subway murder victims like clockwork every Monday during peak hour. A police shrink specializing in criminal mental disorders, Setsuko (Kaho Minami), becomes part of the investigating team, and her inquiries lead her to radical former colleague and lover Aku (Takeshi Wakamatsu).

Aku's forte is ironing out the kinks of brainwashed religious-cult recruits, using highly unorthodox, psycho-manipulative methods that have placed him at the center of a heated controversy. The state of alarm crescendos feverishly each week as crime time rolls around, while Setsuko's growing obsession with the case and the mind games of prime suspect Aku threaten to push her over the edge.

En route to the suspenser's surprise solution, an eye-opener of "Crying Game" proportions regarding Setsuko's ill-fated husband (Etsushi Toyokawa) is casually sprung. Plot is at times on the fuzzy side, and several scenes are stretched way beyond their due, but Ishii keeps the heady brew cooking, exercising a steely fascination that doesn't let up.

Performances are persuasive, but the film is in every sense a techno creature, not an acting showcase. Jumpy editing, a rich, composite soundtrack, and Norimichi Kasamatu's glowering camera work make strong contributions.

—*David Rooney*

F.T.W.

A Nu Image presentation of an HKM Film in association with Red Ruby Prods. Produced by Tom Mickel. Executive producers, Avi Lerner, Ron Altbach, Danny Dimbort. Directed by Michael Karbelnikoff. Screenplay, Mari Kornhauser, story by Sir Eddie Cook, Kornhauser. Camera (Foto-Kem color), James L. Carter; editor, Joe D'Augustine; music, Gary Chang; production design, J.K. Reinhart; art direction, Don Dievs; costume design, Jaqueline De La Fontaine; sound (Ultra-Stereo), James Thornton; associate producers, Alexis Magagni, Kornhauser; second unit director, Mickel; second unit camera, Nick Taylor; casting, Danielle Eskinazi. Reviewed at Cannes Film Festival (market), May 15, 1994. Running time: **100 MIN.**
Frank T. Wells .... Mickey Rourke
Scarlett Stuart .... Lori Singer
Sheriff Rudy Morgan .... Brion James
Clem .... Peter Berg
With: Rodney A. Grant, Aaron Neville, Charlie Sexton.

Mickey Rourke does better in the rodeo ring than in the arena of life in "F.T.W.," a mostly ho-hum cross between a modern cowboy yarn and a lovers-on-the-run crime saga. Quiet, even delicate mood set by Rourke's performance is disrupted by cliched scripting and the leading characters' predictably self-destructive downward spiral. Modest pic would no doubt be thrown from the saddle right away in any theatrical ride, and the nasty violence would prove a turnoff for the young, Middle American "8 Seconds" crowd. But star's name will at least provide it with a certain profile in vid and cable release.

All Frank T. Wells (Rourke) wants after 10 years in prison is the usual cowboy dream — ridin' free and havin' a little place of his own. A rodeo champ at 24, he admits that something inside him died after what he claims was an act of self-defense was twisted into a manslaughter conviction. Nevertheless, he hits the circuit again in Montana to see if he can make a buck and recapture something of his former glory.

Scarlett Stuart (Lori Singer) is another story altogether, a wildcat involved in a highly abusive, frankly sexual relationship with her intimidating brother, Clem (Peter Berg). After Clem kills four people in a bank robbery, the cops mow

him down. Scarlett escapes, only to meet Frank on the road.

Bunking in Frank's trailer, Scarlett realizes that fate might be playing its hand here, in that Frank has the same initials that she has tattooed on her hand — F.T.W., as in what the world can go do with itself. Although she's accustomed to much rougher treatment than she gets from Frank, the two inevitably hook up, and remainder of the film parallels his re-emergence as a bronco rider with her misguided attempts to give them financial security by robbing convenience stores and banks.

Although there's no reason, in theory, why rodeo and crime shouldn't mix, they don't match up well in this case, largely because Frank and Scarlett's natures and desires are at such odds. Frank is a throwback, much like Kirk Douglas' naive cowboy in "Lonely Are the Brave," who was born a hundred years too late, while it's impossible to imagine Scarlett settin' out on the porch watching the sunset for one evening, much less a lifetime.

They're both outsiders, to be sure, but they each belong in a different movie with a different partner, not preventing each other from being their true selves. From a dramatic p.o.v., they generate no rooting interest as a couple. Ending is far-fetched, tragically sentimental and hard to swallow. Looking a bit filled out and outfitted with what seem to be ill-fitting dentures, Rourke delivers an appealing portrait of an uncomplicated, mostly gentle man of limited horizons, one who deserves the break he never gets. Singer's character is considerably less sympathetic, especially when she continues to commit stupid crimes against her lover's wishes. Supporting perfs are adequate.

Rodeo footage is kept to a relative minimum, and Big Sky locations rep a major plus. Behind-the-scenes contributions are par.

—*Todd McCarthy*

LOVE CHEAT & STEAL

A Motion Picture Corp. of America presentation of a Brad Krevoy and Steve Stabler production. Produced by Krevoy, Stabler. Co-producer, Chad Oman. Directed, written by William Curran. Camera (color), Kent Wakeford; editor, Monte Hellman; production design, Jane Stewart; casting, Ed Mitchell, Robyn Ray. Reviewed at Cannes Film Festival (market), May 16, 1994. Running time: **96 MIN.**
Paul Harrington .... John Lithgow
Reno Adams .... Eric Roberts
Lauren Harrington .... Madchen Amick
Paul's Father .... Donald Moffat

Common sense, not to mention plausibility, is not the strongest suit of "Love Cheat & Steal," a desperate wannabe film noir that lacks the form's crucial elements of suspenseful ambience and steamy sexuality. Still, proficient production values and decent performances by character actor John Lithgow and the attractive Madchen Amick may make this routine psychological thriller a time-killer for the video crowd that watches movies late at night, when their critical faculties are not quite sharp.

Tale begins with convicted murderer Reno (Eric Roberts) breaking out of prison with a mate (Richard Edson). Angry at being set up, and vengeful, Reno heads toward the mansion of his beautiful ex-wife, Lauren (Madchen Amick), who recently married wealthy financial consultant Paul (John Lithgow). Presenting himself to the surprisingly naive Paul as Lauren's brother, Reno invades their house, threatening to destroy her new life if she won't help him rob Paul's bank — and consent to his sexual advances.

Trying to mix danger with desire and romance, this recycled saga centers on a trio of immoral characters who spend their time scheming, lusting, double-crossing and blackmailing — all to little emotional effect. The film's cynical ending may be shocking but only somewhat decently earned.

In the first half-hour, scripter/helmer William Curran builds familiar but still pleasurable tension, and maintains the necessary calm and seductive surface of a good film noir. But an effective thriller needs more than formulaic characters, the occasional twist and a perverse undertone; it needs some design, shapeliness and logic, elements that are missing here. Fans of the time-honored genre would recognize almost every thematic trick and visual cliche in Curran's handbook.

Roberts, who's beginning to age and lose his rough sexual exterior, gives a monotonous performance as the betrayed husband. The usually reliable Lithgow doesn't have a particularly interesting or plausible role, and as a result his work is just passable. Rising actress Amick ("Twin Peaks," "Dream Lover"), who would seem to possess the looks and talent it takes for stardom, comes across as unduly tough, lacking the electrifying presence that is so crucial to playing a femme fatale.

One wishes the level of plot and quality of writing would match the production's technical prowess, as evidenced in Kent Wakeford's polished lensing and Monte Hellman's precise editing.   —*Emanuel Levy*

THE BLONDE
(LA BIONDA)
(ITALIAN)

A Fandango production. (International sales: Intra Film, Rome.) Produced by Domenico Procacci. Directed by Sergio Rubini. Screenplay, Gian Filippo Ascione, Umberto Marino, Rubini. Camera (Technicolor), Alessio Gelsini; editor, Angelo Nicolini; music, Jurgen Knieper; art direction, Carolina Ferrara, Luca Gobbi; costume design, Nicoletta Ercole; sound (Dolby), Franco Borni, Amedeo Casati; assistant director, Domenick Tambasco. Reviewed at Cannes Film Festival (market), May 17, 1994. Running time: **99 MIN.**
Christine .... Nastassja Kinski
Tommaso .... Sergio Rubini
Alberto .... Ennio Fantastichini
Annibaldi .... Luca Barbareschi
With: Veronica Lazar, Umberto Ratto, Giacomo Piperno.

Nastassja Kinski starrer "The Blonde" retools seasoned film noir staples into a sturdy, well-played but somewhat conventional romantic tragedy. Exalted expectations for Italo actor/director Sergio Rubini's follow-up to his highly regarded 1990 debut, "The Station," led to local critics being generally underwhelmed during last year's national release. Shorn of some 20 minutes and considerably fine-tuned, the film has enough dramatic kick to interest upscale international webs and video labels.

Tommaso (Rubini), a shy southerner with a slight physical disability, endures a stint in fast-track Milan to undertake watchmaking training. Driving home at night, he hits a pedestrian (Kinski), who subsequently lands on his doorstep with amnesia. Irritation at the intrusion of the mysterious blonde with no past soon makes way for attraction, but just as Cupid's arrow hits him hard, the blonde's memory returns and she hightails it.

She steps back into a flash-trash world, in which her unscrupulous lover, Alberto (Ennio Fantastichini), is planning to go big time with a hefty cocaine deal. The blonde has her own plans to take him for a ride and make a fresh start. Lovelorn Tommaso tracks her down, but her attempts to push him away go unheeded.

Rubini is terrific, limning another guileless, earnest-but-awkward type, this time headed for a resoundingly tragic end. His grasping desperation for what looked momentarily like a more fulfilling life cranks up an often wrenching intensity, though attempts to trowel on psychological weight via his disability stigma feel heavy-handed.

Kinski also delivers a sharply double-edged but sympathetic turn. The normally formidable Fantastichini is largely wasted on a standard sleazebag.

Often an eyesore on film, Milan here becomes an effectively cruel presence, shot mostly at night or in harsh artificial light. The constant dose of crowds and traffic functions admirably but highlights the whopping lapse in credibility of a climax played out on an airport freeway that's deserted during rush hour. Tech side is solid. —David Rooney

CHILI'S BLUES

(C'ETAIT LE 12 DU 12 ET CHILI AVAIT LES BLUES)

(FRENCH-CANADIAN)

An Alliance Communications presentation of a Prods. du Cerf production, with participation of Telefilm Canada, La Societe Generale des Industries Culturelles (Quebec), and collaboration of Societe Radio Canada and Quebec government. (International sales: Alliance, Toronto.) Produced by Louise Gendron; executive producer, Madeleine Henrie; director, Charles Biname; screenplay, Jose Frechette; camera (color), Pierre Mignot; editor, Gretan Huot; music, Richard Gregoire; art direction, Francois Seguin; costume design, Renee April; sound (Dolby), Claude Lahaye, Marcel Pothier; associate producer, Josee Mauffette. Reviewed at Cannes Film Festival (market), May 18, 1994. Running time: **99 MIN.**
Pierre-Paul .... Roy Dupuis
Chili .... Lucie Laurier
Also with: Joelle Morin, Julie Deslauriers, Fanny Lauzier, Marie-Josee Bergeron.
(French dialogue)

Low-key treatment of an intriguing premise takes much of the spice out of "Chili's Blues," a charming but over-metaphysical love story set in a Quebecois railroad station just after JFK's assassination. Though festivals could bite, the small screen looks to be the more likely destination for this quietly offbeat movie.

Picture takes the theme of North American loss of innocence after the Dallas shooting and shows both sides of the psychological coin through two characters who meet at a snowbound station on Dec. 12, 1963. One is a teenager (Lucie Laurier) who's screwed up and despondent about life; the other is a door-to-door salesman, Pierre-Paul (Roy Dupuis), whose positive attitude may or may not succeed in winning her over.

Catalyst for the meeting is Pierre-Paul's discovery of a girl with a gun in her mouth slumped in a washroom stall. By the time he's alerted the stationmaster, she's disappeared, and all he can remember is that she was wearing a plaid kilt.

That day, the station happens to be full of a group of schoolgirls, all with the same plaid kilts.

Chili (Laurier) finally comes forward, and a slow, cautious romance develops in the nooks and crannies of the station. Flashbacks limn the girl's troubled youth, but after the pair make love, she says she isn't the girl he was seeking. The truth is revealed only at the very end.

Main star of the picture is the fine set of the station concourse, bustling with stranded passengers. Apart from the brightly lit flashbacks to Chili's youth, photography is mostly shadowy and downbeat, in tune with the central romance.

Dialogue is thick with Gallic metaphysics, but central perfs by Laurier (splendid) and Dupuis (more of a blank page) just about sustain interest. Smaller roles, including other schoolgirls and elders, are much livelier. Period detail shows some care. —Derek Elley

BLOWN AWAY

A Metro-Goldwyn-Mayer release of a Trilogy Entertainment Group production. Produced by John Watson, Richard Lewis, Pen Densham. Executive producer, Lloyd Segan. Co-producer, Dean O'Brien. Directed by Stephen Hopkins. Screenplay, Joe Batteer, John Rice, based on a story by Rice, Batteer, M. Jay Roach. Camera (Deluxe color; Panavision widescreen), Peter Levy; editor, Timothy Wellburn; music, Alan Silvestri; production design, John Graysmark; art direction, Steve Cooper, Lawrence Hubbs; set decoration, Peg Cummings; costume design, Joe I. Tompkins; sound (Dolby), Thomas Causey; special effects coordinator, Clay Pinney; technical advisors, Lt. Bob Molloy, Herb Williams; assistant director, Josh McLaglen; casting, Mike Fenton, Allison Cowitt. Reviewed at MGM Screening Room, Santa Monica, June 17, 1994. MPAA Rating: R. Running time: **121 MIN.**
Jimmy Dove .... Jeff Bridges
Ryan Gaerity .... Tommy Lee Jones
Max O'Bannon .... Lloyd Bridges
Anthony Franklin ..... Forest Whitaker
Kate .... Suzy Amis
Lizzy .... Stephi Lineburg
Capt. Roarke .... John Finn
Rita .... Caitlin Clarke
Cortez .... Chris De Oni
Bama .... Loyd Catlett

The pyrotechnics are the stars of "Blown Away," an overly complex, muddled thriller of politics and revenge. In need of some dynamite to dislodge an often unfathomable story, the film is just too cool and cynical. Die-hard action seekers may be drawn into its technical bag of tricks, but those in search of a gripping, emotional genre pic will be disappointed. That spells bad news in the current, competitive marketplace, so business will be fast and commercially undistinguished.

The adversaries are Jimmy Dove (Jeff Bridges), a veteran of Boston's Bomb Squad, and Ryan Gaerity (Tommy Lee Jones), a mad, Irish explosives expert recently escaped from a security lockup in Northern Ireland. Gaerity has an old bone to pick with Dove that — although masked in both men's dark past — is pretty easy to decipher.

As a young man, Jimmy (then known as Liam) was trained by the other man in bombology. Once allies, the student thwarted one of his teacher's more diabolic efforts when it became clear innocent people would be hurt. Jimmy/Liam escaped to the U.S. abetted by a relative, assumed a new identity and put his skill to positive pursuits, while Gaerity spent 20 years waiting for a chance to escape and wreak havoc on his former pupil.

His wrath is unleashed with a series of explosions that rapidly reduces the bomb squad's manpower. His ultimate goal is Jimmy, but he's plotted a slow, soul-withering death for him. Gaerity schemes to blow up

Dove's new wife (Suzy Amis) and step-daughter at a Boston Pops concert in which the wife plays violin.

Joe Batteer and John Rice's script operates almost exclusively on movie logic and not common sense. Its bigger sins range from a reliance on incessantly sloppy dramatic shorthand and a shockingly careless attitude toward humanity.

"Blown Away's" back story of strife in Northern Ireland and its impact on the central characters has no texture. One can piece together elements of Jimmy's escape from the authorities and his new identity, but it's never clear whether he remains a fugitive at large. After all, it takes Gaerity but seconds of screen time to track him down, while all the resources of Interpol (it's revealed in a tossed-off reference) continue to be befuddled by Liam's disappearance and whereabouts.

There are many more head-scratchers that fray at all efforts to create dramatic tension. Most contemporary thrillers are easy to logically pick apart after the fact. But their visceral energy ought to overcome story lapses during the heat of viewing.

That stated, director Stephen Hopkins continues to be the leading craftsman in the field saddled with bad material. As with the 1993 "Judgment Night," his scripts make little sense and his efforts to prop up the narrative stylistically are noble if futile exercises.

But where "Judgment Night" had some interesting performances, "Blown Away" is crushed by close to career low points for Bridges and Jones.

In the absence of character development or depth, they are reduced to a kind of posturing that borders on the embarrassing; their innate intelligence as actors makes both very bad with characters deprived of real motivation.

Marginally more acceptable are the supporting turns by Forest Whitaker, Lloyd Bridges, Amis and Caitlin Clarke, who are afforded scant opportunity to register in underwritten, barely integrated roles. Finally, there are just too many cheap tricks and not enough substance in this big, explosive enterprise. Its arm's-length stance toward issues and characters cynically reduces the film to statistics rather than emotions, setting off a commercial implosion which bodes ill for its box office.

—Leonard Klady

June 27, 1994 (Cont.)

I LOVE TROUBLE

A Buena Vista release of a Touch-stone Pictures presentation in association with Caravan Pictures. Produced by Nancy Meyers. Co-producer, Bruce A. Block. Directed by Charles Shyer. Screenplay, Meyers, Shyer. Camera (Technicolor), John Lindley; editors, Paul Hirsch, Walter Murch, Adam Bernardi; music, David Newman; production design, Dean Tavoularis; art direction, Alex Tavoularis; set design, Sean Haworth, James J. Murakami, Nick Navarro, William O'Brien, Nancy Tobias; set decoration, Gary Fettis; costume design, Susan Becker; sound (Dolby), Richard Bryce Goodman; stunt coordinator, Jack Gill; additional film editing, Richard Marks, Lynzee Klingman; associate producers, John D. Schofield, Julie B. Crane; assistant director, K.C. Colwell; second unit directors, Block, Charles Picerni; second unit camera, Tom Priestley; casting, Bonnie Timmermann. Reviewed at the Regent Theater, L.A., June 22, 1994. MPAA Rating: PG. Running time: **123 MIN.**

Sabrina Peterson	Julia Roberts
Peter Brackett	Nick Nolte
Sam Smotherman	Saul Rubinek
The Thin Man	James Rebhorn
Matt Greenfield	Robert Loggia
Kim	Kelly Rutherford
Jeannie	Olympia Dukakis
Sen. Gayle Robbins	Marsha Mason
Justice of the Peace	Eugene Levy
Rick	
Medwick	Charles Martin Smith
Wilson Chess	Dan Butler
Kenny Bacon	Paul Gleason
Evans	Jane Adams
Virginia Hervey	Lisa Lu
Lindy	Nora Dunn

As if more evidence were needed, "I Love Trouble" stands as yet further proof of how hard it is to make a souffle, as well as to successfully re-create the pure pleasure of the old movies today's filmmakers so revere. A Cary Grant-Audrey Hepburn vehicle some 30 years too late, this ultrapolished romantic suspenser serves up mild romance, mild suspense and mild humor. But the top-lined duo of Julia Roberts and Nick Nolte in a spiffy package make for passable entertainment that Disney can parlay into solid summer B.O.

Filmmakers Charles Shyer and Nancy Meyers display a sympathetic and understandable nostalgia for the newsroom classics of the 1930s and George Cukor's "Adam's Rib" and "Pat and Mike," Alfred Hitchcock's "North by Northwest" and Stanley Donen's "Charade."

But having one's taste in the right place is not a substitute for originality and zest, both of which are in relatively short supply in this luxuriously appointed yarn of a rugged, legendary scribe who meets his match in a beautiful young cub reporter.

Nolte plays Peter Brackett, a Windy City columnist in the Ben Hecht tradition who's coasting on his reputation at the Chronicle now that his first novel is out. A notorious womanizer, boozer and cynic of the old school, Brackett is temporarily forced back onto the beat as punishment for his laziness and finds himself scooped by competing Globe newcomer Sabrina Peterson (Roberts).

Story in question involves the derailment of a passenger train in which several people are killed, but it quickly builds into a case of corporate intrigue and subterfuge involving missing briefcases, microfilm and something called LDF, a genetically produced hormone that makes cows produce milk much more quickly.

After vying to outdo each other for some time, Brackett and Peterson (who, in good old newspaper fashion, call each other by their last names) agree to team up on research while still filing separate stories. But they continue to bluster about their lack of sexual attraction.

The chase leads them to rural Wisconsin, Las Vegas — where they marry in an act of self-defense against a bad guy — then back to dairyland, where the quickly estranged couple must prove their love by trying to save each other's lives in perilous circumstances reminiscent of any number of romantic thrillers of the past.

Nothing that happens is very surprising, including the outcome, meaning that the film must rely on its moment-to-moment charm to seduce the audience. Roberts and Nolte do their share to supply this, but Meyers and Shyer, who co-wrote the script, with Meyers producing and Shyer directing, have given them more in the way of ticklish situations to contend with than sharp repartee and fizzy dialogue.

Most of the goings-on manage to hold the interest, but they seem a bit slack and lacking in wit and inspiration, making for a tolerably entertaining but far from effervescent sit.

Pic's most exceptional elements are its production values, which are notably top-drawer. Dean Tavoularis' production design is lush and evocative, especially in its newsrooms and the climactic chemical company set that evokes Frank Lloyd Wright's Wisconsin Johnson Wax building.

John Lindley's subtle, appealingly dark lensing not only dis-plays the settings to lustrous effect but provides the stars with glamour lighting unusual in this day and age. David Newman's score helps the proceedings seem a bit less overlong than they are.

—_Todd McCarthy_

IMPROPER CONDUCT

An Everest Pictures presentation of a Victor Bhalla/Jag Mundhra production. Produced by Bhalla, Mundhra. Co-producer, Subhash Bal. Directed by Mundhra. Screenplay, Carl Austin, story by Mundhra. Camera (Crest National Lab color), James Michaels; editors, Wayne Schmidt, David Schulman; music, Alan Dermarderosian; production design, Brian McCabe; art direction, Lincoln Hiatt; set decoration, Nadine Hedera; wardrobe, Ricardo Delgado; sound, Brian Tracy; line producer, Bhalla; assistant director, James LaClair; casting, Lori Cobe. Reviewed on videotape, L.A., June 21, 1994. Running time: **93 min.**

Sam	Steven Bauer
Ashley	Tahnee Welch
Michael Miller	John Laughlin
Bernie	Nia Peeples
Kay	Lee Anne Beaman
Doug	Adrian Smed
Emily	Kathy Shower
Jo Ann	Patsy Pease
Defense Attorney	Matt Roe
Kurtis	Everett Lamar
Gabby	Wendy McDonald
Mark	Stephen Fiachi
Frost	Stuart Whitman

A T&A sexploitationer dressed up in politically correct garb, "Improper Conduct" is a minor league time killer that's neither suspenseful nor erotic. Tale of femme revenge against a boss who demands too much overtime is video fare all the way, although producers are giving it token theatrical exposure.

Jag Mundhra has made more than a dozen steamy thrillers, such as "Night Eyes," "Wild Cactus" and "Last Call," that have generated a certain following on vid. But if "Improper Conduct" is any indication, his plotting and direction will have to become a good deal less formulaic and programmatic if he's going to graduate to solid big screen fare. Beginning with the murder of a blonde secretary in a New York office stairway, pic picks up at an L.A. office party, where ad agency employe Tahnee Welch discreetly gets it on with one of her co-workers. When new marketing head John Laughlin arrives from Gotham with pregnant wife, and boss Stuart Whitman's daughter, Kathy Shower, in tow, he begins taking a special interest in Welch's work, constantly touching her and making untoward remarks.

When he finally goes over the edge and attacks her in an elevator, Welch takes Laughlin to court on sexual harrassment charges, with hunky Steven Bauer as her attorney. But she can't prove anything and, after having been painted as the office slut by the defense and losing the case to boot, she does herself in by cracking up in a car.

Yarn's second half is devoted to revenge extracted by Welch's sister, Lee Anne Beaman, who gets herself hired by Laughlin with the express intent of setting him up for the big fall. Central scene is a motel tryst between the two that's videotaped and repeatedly shown as blackmail.

Helmer has clearly made a special effort to insure that everyone on-screen is attractive, but is less concerned that they be interesting to spend time with. Major liability is Welch's character, who is uniquely sour and dispirited no matter what the occasion. But then every character is allowed only one dimension— Laughlin is lecherous, Beaman determined, Whitman hale and hearty, and so on.

Bauer's cover boy lawyer is particularly ill-defined, although Nia Peeples contributes some welcome spunk as his perky assistant. With the exception of the Peeples, all the younger leads have at least one nude sex scene, although the couplings are quite tame and politely choreographed.

Tech credits are smooth for the most part, although sound mix is a little spotty and Mundhra's moving camera coverage becomes wearisome after the first few scenes.

—_Todd McCarthy_

POLICE ACADEMY: MISSION TO MOSCOW

A Warner Bros. release of a Paul Maslansky production. Produced by Maslansky. Co-producer, Donald L. West. Directed by Alan Metter. Screenplay, Randolph Davis, Michele S. Chodos. Camera (color), Ian Jones; editors, Denise Hill, Suzanne Hines; music, Robert Folk; production design, Frederic Weiler; art director, Ilia Amoorsky; sound (Dolby), Steve Nelson; associate producer, Suzanne Lore; assistant director, Alex Hapsas; producer (Russia), Leonid Vereschagin; casting, Melissa Skoft. Reviewed at MGM Ewell 2, Surrey, England, June 22, 1994. Running time: **83 MIN.**

Commandant	
Lassard	George Gaynes
Sgt. Jones	Michael Winslow
Sgt. Tackleberry	David Graf
Cpt. Callahan	Leslie Easterbrook
Cpt. Harris	G.W. Bailey
Kyle Connors	Charlie Schlatter
Commandant	
Rakov	Christopher Lee
Konstantin Konali	Ron Perlman
Katrina	Claire Forlani
Adam	Richard Israel

It's been five years since Warner last wheeled out the boobs in blue, and the intervening span hasn't been kind. Seventh "Police Academy" stanza, with the gang taking on the Moscow mafia, is an inept, geriatric romp that's for completists only. Rental hell looms for this one, which WB sneaked out

June 27, 1994 (Cont.)

in the U.K., sans press previews on June 17 and is tentatively due for U.S. release in October.

Law and order is breaking down in Moscow, where top mobster Konstantin Konali (Ron Perlman) has made millions from worldwide sales of a computer game. In desperation, top cop Rakov (Christopher Lee) rings his stateside pal Lassard (George Gaynes), who promptly announces, "Team, we're off to Russia — to kick many, many buttskies."

Excuse for a plot has Konali forcing a computer nerd (Richard Israel) to install a device in the game that will give him access to security systems for world domination. While Lassard slides off for some R&R, the troops go undercover.

Jaw-droppingly unfunny antics include Callahan (Leslie Easterbrook) doing a spoof of Michelle Pfeiffer's piano writhe in "The Fabulous Baker Boys" and bad-cop Harris (G.W. Bailey) dressing up in a tutu for "Swan Lake" at the Bolshoi. A belated car chase around Moscow will amuse anyone with a passing knowledge of the city's geography.

Filmers lost the script between LAX and Moscow airport: A subplot about a new recruit (Charlie Schlatter) falling for his cute interpreter (Claire Forlani) doesn't get off the blocks, and the normally reliable Bailey spends most of the pic looking like he's lost his passport. Michael Winslow's regular shtick with sound effects is clumsy this time, and Easterbrook is starting to look a tad matronly for her sexpot role.

Tech credits are on the cheesy side, with dialogue that sounds as if it were recorded in a metal tank.
—*Derek Elley*

THIEVES QUARTET

A Headliner Entertainment Group release of a Mooncoin film. Produced by Colleen Griffen. Executive producer, Michael Legamaro. Directed, written by Joe Chappelle. Camera (DuArt color), Greg Littlewood; editors, Randy Bricker, Scott Taradash; music, John Zorn; sound, Byron Smith; makeup, Linda Samordral-Smith; associate producer, Linda Bergonia; assistant director, Greg Still; casting; Cherie Mann & Associates; Reviewed at Raleigh Studios, L.A., June 23, 1994. Running time: **90 MIN.**

Jimmy Fuqua	Phillip Van Lear
Art Bledsoe	Joe Guastaferro
Jessica Sutter	Michele Cole
Mike Quinn	James "Ike" Eichling
Morgan Luce	Richard Henzel
Ray Higgs	Jamie Denton
Jill Luce	Dawn Maxie

Add first-time writer-director Joe Chappelle to the list of talented young filmmakers (Quentin Tarantino, Nick Gomez, John Dahl, Whitney Ransick) who find neo-noir film's textures and terrains irresistible, and use the genre as their low-budget path to self-expression and gainful em-

ployment. Chappelle's edgy little crime thriller, "Thieves Quartet" drives a familiar road, where quirky, down-and-dirty crooks conspire and connive, and ultimately square-off over their ill-gotten gains. "Thieves" makes a fine showcase for Chappelle's directorial chops and is a sturdy crime drama filled with tension and first-rate performances. But the writer half of Chappelle's hyphenate status delivers a routine, by-the-numbers plot that culminates in a payoff so predictable as to now be beyond cliche for fans of Hong Kong's John Woo, Tarantino's "Reservoir Dogs" and their burgeoning ranks of imitators. Theatrical numbers and good reviews should provide a modest send-off for the video release, and a bigger boost for Chappelle's helming career.

When aging hippie bartender Art Bledsoe (Joe Guastaferro) dreams up a kidnapping plot to score a quick $2 million, he turns to three partners in his hometown Chicago to help him pull off the heist. Jimmy Fuqua (Phillip Van Lear) is susceptible to the lure of fast money, since he seems destined for little more than a nickel-and-dime car wash job. Mike Quinn (James "Ike" Eichling), a disgraced Chicago ex-cop, and Jessica Sutter (Michele Cole), Bledsoe's sleazy girlfriend, are in similarly dreary straits, with no hope for advancement except, as one observes, crime or "hitting the lottery."

Their lottery arrives in the form of an intricate plan to grab Jill Luce (Dawn Maxie,) the daughter of blueblood tycoon Morgan Luce (Richard Henzel). Ostensibly a character study that gets inside the heads of the "Thieves Quartet," film suffers from the fact that once inside their heads, there isn't much of interest and, despite terrific work from all of the leads, there's more gold in the film's tense action moments when the kidnapping scheme gets under way and begins to unravel.

Especially strong sequences involve a chance encounter between gunmoll Sutter and a menacing local cop (Jamie Denton), and a ransom plan that runs pere Luce and several FBI tails through a maze of subway tunnels, el platforms, taxis and trains. When first-rate character players like Eichling and Guastaferro are on screen, the film achieves a powerful believabilty that is riveting, and Van Lear's sad, wistful performance as Fuqua provides the moral center of a criminal universe in collapse.

Effectively and resourcefully shot for minimal bucks on location in Chitown and the Illinois countryside, "Thieves" also boasts moody, atmospheric camerawork by Greg Littlewood, and a dazzling jazz

score by John Zorn that's worth a CD release.
—*Steven Gaydos*

THE WEDDING GIFT

(U.K.)

A Miramax release of a BBC Films/Island World production. Produced by David Lascelles. Executive producers, Richard Broke, Margaret Matheson. Directed by Richard Loncraine. Screenplay, Jack Rosenthal. Camera (color), Remi Adefarasin; editor, Ken Pearce; production design, Tony Burrough. Reviewed at the Carolco screening room, West Hollywood, May 3, 1994. (In AFI Intl. Film Festival.) Running time: **87 MIN.**

Diana Longden	Julie Walters
Deric Longden	Jim Broadbent
Deric's Mother	Thora Hird
Aileen Armitage	Sian Thomas
Nick Longden	Andrew Lancel
Sally Longden	Anastasia Mulrooney

Made for television in the U.K. but getting a U.S. theatrical release, "The Wedding Gift" fits the general description of what TV viewers have come to know as disease-of-the-week movies, although it shines above that genre with its wit, offbeat charm and understated pathos. Even so, prospects of B.O. recovery are probably limited to whatever word-of-mouth treatment can offer, with video likely to be a more natural medium.

Based on a true story, pic relies almost entirely on strong central performances by Julie Walters ("Educating Rita") and Jim Broadbent ("Life Is Sweet"), a couple very much in love but with a very serious problem.

Diana (Walters) is suffering from an unknown, unexplained and deteriorative disease that causes her periodic pain as well as the inability to use her limbs and occasional blackouts. Doctors remain baffled but unwilling to admit they're stumped, as with all doctors in such movies.

While the couple deals with their plight by virtue of their humor and considerable affection, Diana anticipates dying and, through happenstance, comes upon the idea of trying to find someone to replace her once she's gone — in this case, a blind novelist (Sian Thomas) with whom Deric (Broadbent) feels an immediate affinity and who may be able to further his own literary aspirations.

From that description, this undoubtedly sounds like a three-hankie affair, bearing some resemblance to a recent NBC movie, "The Subtitute Wife," which starred Farrah Fawcett.

Much to his credit, director Richard Loncraine doesn't butter up the corn. He and writer Jack Rosenthal manage to bring a distinct feel to the proceedings by looking on these people through such a detached lens — shunning the more maudlin and obvious approach to which the storyline lends itself.

On the down side, Diana's condition isn't exactly pleasant (a problem also faced by a movie like "Lorenzo's Oil"), and the filmmakers do a rather slapdash job developing Deric's budding interest in the writer or his pangs of guilt about those feelings.

There's nevertheless much to savor in the performances, with Walters offering just the right combination of fear and strength as the stricken woman, while Broadbent captures the determination of a man who can't accept his inevitable loss.

Pic was originally titled "Wide-Eyed and Legless" when it aired in the U.K., perhaps more appropriate than its current Hallmark-type handle, given its quirky, bittersweet tone.
—*Brian Lowry*

DON'T PAVE MAIN STREET: CARMEL'S HERITAGE

(DOCU)

A Julian Ludwig production for Carmel Heritage. Produced by Ludwig. Directed by Ludwig, William T. Cartwright. Written, edited by Cartwright. Camera (color), Bruce Nolte; music, David Benoit. Reviewed at AFI screening room, L.A. June 9, 1994. (In AFI Intl. Film Festival.) Running time: **113 MIN.**

Hosted and narrated by Clint Eastwood.

Invaluable information about Carmel's history as a literary and artistic community is related in "Don't Pave Main Street: Carmel's Heritage," a documentary about a fascinating, largely unknown subject done in a tad too conventional manner. Clint Eastwood, Carmel's long-time resident and ex-mayor who serves as host and narrator, will considerably elevate docu's visibility, perhaps even facilitating limited theatrical release before its airing on PBS and other venues.

Most people think of Carmel as a town of outstanding natural beauty and unique charm, but they don't realize its rich cultural heritage. Co-directors Julian Ludwig and William T. Cartwright have therefore wisely decided not to make a National Geographic travelogue, but instead to focus on its importance as an art colony.

June 27, 1994 (Cont.)

Docu begins with a survey of Carmel as a region inhabited by Indians, explorers and missionaries, who founded the famed Carmel Mission in 1771.

The picture follows a historical approach, but becomes quite interesting with its selection of bohemian figures, whose lives and times are then followed in defiance of a narrower chronology.

Through extensive research of published books, private journals, photographs, archival footage, and interviews, scripter Cartwright constructs a colorful collective biography of Carmel as a pioneering center for letters and arts.

Among the leading figures are renowned San Francisco poets Robinson Jeffers and George Sterling. Docu acknowledges Sterling's role in attracting novelists Jack London, Upton Sinclair and Sinclair Lewis to Carmel, the location which inspired them to produce their best-known work.

The sequences dealing with photographers Edward Weston and Arnold Genthe, and with journalist and radical social thinker Lincoln Steffens, are especially illuminating. So is the chapter chronicling the 1910 opening of the Forest Theatre, California's oldest outdoor theater, that in its epic productions could use onstage more than half of the town's residents.

Demonstrating, as Eastwood says, that Carmel is much more than just quaint, docu doesn't neglect the private lives of its celebrated artists, detailing duels and fisticuffs between rival lovers, philandering husbands, suicidal authors, and other accidents and scandals that could easily fill the tabloids, though they are handled by Eastwood in an unsensational, matter-of-fact style.

One of the film's elegiac themes is the notion of Carmel always being at the crossroad of tradition and modernity, increasingly becoming victim to the push toward urban development.

Ending sometime in the 1950s, docu is missing an overview of the last three decades, during which Carmel's — and America's — geographic and social landscapes have rapidly changed.

Chief problem is the impersonation of figures' voices by actors, which creates an unavoidable distance between the viewers and the genuinely emotional stories.

A guest appearance by former movie star and now Carmel resident Doris Day somehow enlivens matters. More primary info about Eastwood's involvement, including his term as mayor, would have resulted in a more personal and exciting work; the famous actor-director just says that he fell in love with Carmel when he shot his first pic as helmer, "Play Misty for Me," there in 1971.

Still, made for the non-profit society Carmel Heritage, "Don't Pave Main Street" may fulfill a vital historical function by encouraging other regional communities to record their own cultural pasts for future generations.

—Emanuel Levy

TO DIE FOR

(BRITISH)

> A Victor Film Company production. Produced by Gary Fitzpatrick. Directed by Peter Mackenzie Litten. Screenplay, Johnny Byrne. Camera (color), John Ward; editor, Jeffrey Arsenault; music, Roger Bolton; art direction, Geoff Sharp; sound (Dolby), Julian Dawton. Reviewed at Raleigh Studios screening room, L.A., June 21, 1994 (In L.A. International Gay & Lesbian Film & Video Festival). Running time: **101 MIN.**
> Simon .... Thomas Arklie
> Mark .... Ian Williams
> Terry .... Tony Slattery
> Siobban .... Dillie Keane
> Mrs. Downs .... Jean Boht

"To Die For," a remarkably forthright film about life in the age of AIDS, features engaging characters, lively dialogue, snappy humor and, above all, affecting emotion. While the drama is marred by an incongruent tone and too many changes in mood that detract attention from the main story, this British movie, which receives its U.S. premiere at the L.A. Gay & Lesbian Film & Video Festival, deserves to be seen by a larger constituency than its primary target audience.**

Focusing on the lifestyle of two lovers, Simon (Thomas Arklie) a handsome man who is HIV-negative, and Mark (Ian Williams), his female-impersonator companion who's positive, screenwriter Byrne offers a new angle to the growing body of films about AIDS. His story, which begins with Mark's deteriorating health, provides a credible chronicle of how the couple, who have an open relationship, react to Mark's impending death.

A homebody while not performing in a club, Mark spends his time watching a video of the AIDS Memorial Quilt while preparing his own. At the same time, the more macho Simon, who works as a TV technician, spends his nights cruising London's gay scene, looking for exciting new encounters.

Unlike most AIDS dramas, "To Die For" is not so much about Mark's struggle with the lethal disease as about Simon's survival after his lover's death, which occurs in an unmelodramatic way in the first half-hour. Indeed, coming back

from the hospital, Simon deposits Mark's box of keepsakes in the closet and continues his flamboyant lifestyle, seemingly unaffected by his loss.

His new, convenient motto is life must go on.

However, in the second — and weakest — part of the film, Mark's ghost returns to haunt his companion, giving him hell for his reckless conduct.

With a nod to Noel Coward's classic "Blithe Spirit," though not as funny, this sequence contains some amusing moments, as Simon is the only one who sees and hears Mark; all others think he's crazy.

Using some special effects, the ghost scenes, which don't add much to the proceedings, manage to shift the film's realistic tone in a jokey, forced direction. This problem is exacerbated by two other characters, Siobban (Dillie Keane), the eccentric upstairs neighbor, and her zany, politically correct do-gooder b.f. Terry (Tony Slattery). Siobban, whom Mark describes as the Irish question, and Terry are meant to provide comic relief, but their one-liners are often coerced and incongruent with the central, much more touching, drama.

Fortunately, the film regains its consistency in the last sequences, in which Simon, a man never able to express his true love for Mark during their life together, is forced to come to terms with his feelings and newly-gained consciousness.

Some candid encounters between Simon and his mother, which result in better understanding of his dead father, also reinforce the film's psychological realism and its rigorous fidelity to ordinary lives.

Scripter Byrne's greatest achievement is his non-judgmental treatment of the characters, allowing for multiple P.O.V. to prevail. This is greatly assisted by the open and balanced tone by helmer Litten, whose compassion is demonstrated in the natural, appealing performances he elicits from his two leads, Arklie and Williams, both of whom make splendid debuts here. Litten is also excellent in capturing the desolate comedy of loneliness in swift, sure strokes.

Excepting Bolton's overbearing music, tech credits of this low-budgeter are impressive, particularly Ward's alert camera, which vividly conveys the nuanced ambiance of cruising bars, sensuous discos and gyms.

Despite its shortcomings, "To Die For" is a film of many positive qualities that is neither smug nor sentimental.

Overall, it is much more satisfying and edifying than the likes of

"Philadelphia," in which all issues readily fit into neat categories and resolutions.

—Emanuel Levy

S.F. GAYFEST

WORLD AND TIME ENOUGH

> A 1 in 10 Films presentation. Produced by Julie Hartley, Andrew Peterson. Directed, written by Eric Mueller. Camera (color), Kyle Bergersen; editor, Laura Stokes; production design, Heather McElhatton; music, Eugene Huddleston; sound, Johnny Hagen; coproducer, David Haugland; associate producer, Emily Stevens; casting, Lynn Blumenthal. Reviewed at Variety Club Screening Room, San Francisco, June 21, 1994. (In S.F. Lesbian & Gay Intl. Film Festival.) Running time: **90 MIN.**
> Mark .... Matt Guidry
> Joey .... Gregory G. Giles
> David .... Kraig Swartz
> Mike .... Peter Macon
> Marie .... Bernadette Sullivan
> Mr. Quincy .... John Patrick Marin
> Young Mark .... Adam Mikelson
> Mrs. Quincy .... Kathleen Fuller

With its two attractive, mildly alienated young gay male protagonists and HIV status/societal homophobia themes, writer-director Eric Mueller's debut "World and Time Enough" plays like a declawed "The Living End" too sweet-natured to bother hitting the road. While tone skirts excess cuteness and story could have been better developed, feature has enough charm to perform well with gay urban auds.**

Leading figures are both in their late 20s: Mark is a conceptual artist whose political (yet incongruously funny) short-lived public projects occupy any time not spent at various despised temp jobs. Joey works as a highway trash collector, which vocation he uses to shore up his fetishistic pile of found junk.

Each are semi-estranged from family: Mark is incommunicado with his widowed dad, while Joey searches for his biological parents in wake of adopted folks' angry response to his coming out. It was love at first sight for the pair, who've lived together for some years in their warehouse-like apartment at pic's start.

Not much happens, though Mueller keeps things bouncy via flashbacks, fantasy scenes, stray bits of pop-culture satire, et al. Viewers know long before Mark does that his father (with whom he's decided to reconcile) has apparently keeled over dead at his home worktable.

Joey, meanwhile, fights for the attention of a stubborn co-worker/former lover, searches in vain for his "real" parents, and resists a married sister's attempts to smooth stormy seas between himself and their adopted mom and dad.

Whimsical tenor is dominated by endearing, puppyish personae of two heroes, with Mark registering as a little daft, Joey a little dim. But deeper exploration of various dramatic currents (especially the seemingly healthy Mark's "doomed" perception re: his HIV-positivity) wouldn't have hurt, especially when scenario reaches for near-tragedy at the close.

Semi-parodic thumbnail sketches of the homophobic "straight" world are pat. While characters' quirkiness mostly beguiles on a light Gen X-fantasy level, it sometimes grows too coy. Least successful element is campy stand-up-style commentary of Mark's best friend David (Kraig Swartz).

Such flaws ultimately do little to muss pic's shaggy appeal, though they limit its lasting impact. The camera-ready looks and charm of leads Matt Guidry and Gregory G. Giles will prove strongest suit for pic's commercial prospects; with "Go Fish" as its lesbian counterpart, this modestly winning package could emerge as the year's pre-eminent date movie for gay male auds. Tech values are good, with creative use of unfamiliar Minneapolis locales and particularly good editing management of script's slight, patchwork nature.

—Dennis Harvey

SEATTLE FEST

GREEN HENRY
(DER GRÜN HEINRICH)
(SWISS)

> A Condor Films (Zurich)/Toro Film/Osby Films production, in co-production with SRG, ZDF, ORF, Canal Plus. Produced by Karl H. Mezinger (German version), Xavier Darere (French version). Directed by Thomas Koerfer. Screenplay, Koerfer, Peter Muller, Barbara Jago, based on a book by Gottfried Keller. Camera (color), Gerard Vandenburg; editor, Marie-Joseph Yoyotte; music, Bruno Coulais; production design, Jan Schlubach; costumes, Monika Jacobs; sound, Johnny Dubach, Jean-Paul Loublier. Reviewed on vidcassette at Seattle Intl. Film Festival, June 10, 1994. Running time: **110 MIN.**
> Green
> Henry .... Thibault de Montalembert
> Anna .... Florence Darel
> Judith .... Assumpta Serna
> Mother .... Dominique Sanda
> Uncle .... Mathias Gnadinger
> Lys .... Arno Chevrier
> Teacher .... Paul Burian
> Painter .... Heribert Sasse
> Young Henry .... Andreas Schmidt
> Young Anna .... Anna Scheschonk

Spectacular sets, a massive cast and torrid sex scenes make this sprawling take of an 1880 novel an easy sell in specialized markets, even if slightly cheesy aura will keep it off the A circuit.

Pic opens in Munich during carnival bacchanalia, and rarely have there been so many tongues thrust, invited or not, into so many mouths. There's even a uvular tango between hulking Lys (Arno Chevrier, doing his best Depardieu imitation) and his sensitive painter pal Henry. Amidst all the polymorphous perversity, the latter — who wears a green suit as a sign of his immaturity and envy — is incensed to find Lys cheating on his virginal fiancee, and challenges the older man to a morning-after duel. What Henry's really steamed about is his own failure to follow through on the lost love of his life. The balance of the tale moves to Switzerland, and a much more sober tone, as we see young Henry (Andreas Schmidt) lose his father, seek the elusive love of his stern mother (Dominique Sanda, impressive in a static role), take Dickensian abuse at school and discover the theater via a seductive actress, Judith (Assumpta Serna). Most important, he fumbles his relationship with cousin Anna (first played by Anna Scheschonk, then by ethereal Florence Darel).

Later, a somewhat older Henry (stoical Thibault de Montalembert) rediscovers his childhood sweetheart, but is distracted once again when Judith, who hasn't aged a day, pops up in the same village. What he doesn't appreciate until too late is Anna's frail condition: She coughs a lot, and since this is the 19th century, she must have TB. Picturesque tragedy ensues, along with much more kissing.

The contrast between serious existential undercurrent and literal, bodice-ripping turmoil is sometimes jarring — a bit like "Kaspar Hauser" meeting "Wide Sargasso Sea." Dialogue looping was dubious in French-lingo version caught (called "Henri le Vert"), but dubbing problems would stymie any package here, considering the polyglot cast. Once it gets going, though, the pic moves briskly, and tech credits are generally sensational, with Gerard Vandenburg's colorful lensing the biggest plus. Bruno Coulais' folkloric score is also attractive, even if it rings about two centuries out of date. *—Ken Eisner*

SEX, DRUGS & DEMOCRACY
(DUTCH — DOCU — 16mm)

> A Red Hat Prods. release of a Barclay Powers production. Produced by Powers, Jonathan Blank. Directed, written, edited by Blank. Camera (color), Blank. Reviewed on vidcassette at Seattle Intl. Film Festival, June 10, 1994. (Also in Cannes Film Festival — market.) Running time: **87 MIN.**

There's more to Holland than tulips and windmills, as this docu attests. Quasi-sensational images of the upfront trade in flesh and cannabis guarantee a ready audience even beyond college circuits, and the deluge of talking heads makes a convincing case for the lowland country as a bastion of libertarian virtues. But formless structure and the absence of a single critical voice give it all the impact of a latenight infomercial.

Many-hatted Jonathan Blank obviously had fun assembling his collage of street scenes, archival footage and interviews — all conducted in English — with sex workers, politicians, minority activists and police, most of whom come across as souls of pure reason.

The testimonials soon grow wearying, however, and Blank's tendency to repeat footage at arbitrary intervals doesn't help. Even worse, he uses porno-club scenes to support a discussion of gay and lesbian lifestyles.

Any questions about hidden costs of freedom are ultimately begged. Tech credits are as rough as the circumstances dictate, and one might wish to see b&w historical images integrated in a more thoughtful way.

Still, slapdash style doesn't exactly run counter to the free-for-all subject, and passages from the Netherlands' startlingly enlightened constitution give pause for thought.

Pic also begins with a terse quote from Dutch philosopher Spinoza: "All things excellent are as difficult as they are rare" — equally apt words for documentaries or nations.

—Ken Eisner

CANNES FEST

LITTLE BLOND DEATH
(DE KLEINE BLONDE DOOD)
(NETHERLANDS)

> A Verenigde Nederlandsche Filmcompagnie production. (International sales: Atlas Intl.) Produced by Rob Houwer. Directed by Jean van de Velde. Screenplay, van de Velde, Houwer, based on the novel by Boudewijn Buch. Camera (color), Jules van den Steenhoven; editor, Victorine Habets; music, Jurre Haanstra, Toots Thielemans; art direction, Freek Biesiot. Reviewed at Cannes Film Festival (market), May 20, 1994. Running Time: **92 MINS.**
> Valentine Boecke .. Antonie Kamerling
> Mieke .... Loes Wouterson
> Mickey .... Olivier Tuinier

Winner of last year's top film prize in Holland, and the country's Oscar submission, "Little Blond Death" is an extraordinary debut film packed with emotion and stylistic panache. Director and co-writer Jean van de Velde navigates seemingly familiar territory and pushes it in novel directions. The result is an exhilarating roller-coaster ride filled with insightful, unexpected turns. Its universally accessible story combined with energy and craft make it a natural for international arthouse exploitation and a critical success that could spell upbeat commercial prospects.

Valentine Boecke (Antonie Kamerling) is a twentysomething poet with an established cult reputation in Dutch coffeehouses. He's equally well-known for living high — a wastrel and druggie who spouts angry rhetoric against anything vaguely conformist.

A product of a stifling home ruled by a martinet war vet father, his rebellion follows a classic curve. He's lucky because his poetry offers him a venue to vent and a means of earning a living. However, he's totally at sea emotionally and sexually.

June 27, 1994 (Cont.)

Adapted from an autobiographical novel, the narrative evolves awkwardly but with a sense of blinding truth that smoothes out all unsightly wrinkles. It's a story propelled by circumstance rather than cliche. The logic is simple and effective — every action will necessitate a reaction. Boecke's life and the manner in which he responds to both the mundane and vital is honest if unconventional.

The incident that will forever change his life is a chance encounter with Mieke (Loes Wouterson), a teacher who encouraged his artistic bent as a young teen. She's obviously fallen on hard times, and a whirlwind of alcohol, pent up emotion and repressed anger lead them to an incendiary moment of passion.

When Mieke pops up several months later, Valentine is horrified to see that she is pregnant. He is livid and confused, unable to come to terms with a paternal instinct at odds with the sense of entrapment he fears most. For him, there is no balance, and his attitude and actions initially are all extremes prompted by either a troubled past or pure emotional reflex.

The director revels in his bitterly conflicted character. It allows for a rather unconventional narrative, pacing and visual style that is synchronous with Valentine's mood swings. The camerawork by Jules van den Steenhoven is truly dazzling, and the music by Jurre Haanstra and harmonica virtuoso Toots Thielemans provides an inspired additional layer for the story.

Kamerling's central performance is remarkable in deftly twining the raveled threads of the film into a continuous string. In a physically demanding role, he makes the challenge appear organic. Wouterson and youngster Olivier Tuinier as the product of the lovers' union are also outstanding.

The conclusion is no less complex than all that proceeds it. There's tremendous veracity in its mix of confrontation, recognition and sorrow that is somehow emotionally appropriate and satisfying, yet wholly unmanipulative.

—Leonard Klady

THE FENCE

A Showcase Entertainment presentation of a Life production. Produced, directed by Peter Pistor. Co-producer, Lisa Zimble. Screenplay, Peter Fedorenko. Camera (Foto-Kem color), John Newby; editor, Margie Goodspeed; music, Jeff Beal; production design, Eric Fraser; art direction, Robert Harris; costumes, Nanette M. Acosta; sound, Thomas G. Varga; line producer/assistant director, Cas Donovan; casting, Judy Claman. Reviewed at Cannes Film Festival (market), May 17, 1994. Running time: **98 MIN.**
Terry Griff .... Billy Wirth
Rudy .... Marc Alaimo
Jackie .... Erica Gimpel
Del .... Paul Benjamin
Arthur Price .... Lorenzo Clemons
With: Suli McCullough, Raynor Scheine.

A dour, if heartfelt, study of a young man dealt a lifelong losing hand, "The Fence" remains too modest in aim and accomplishment to mark off much commercial terrain for itself. First feature by former Berlin-based real estate developer Peter Pistor displays a feel for the underbelly of urban American life but doesn't offer audiences much in the way of edification or entertainment. Minor theatrical prospects internationally will quickly make way for longer vid life.

Peter Fedorenko's semi-autobiographical screenplay charts the sad life story of Terry Griff, who as a teen is bounced into juve detention for killing his abusive dad in self-defense and is subsequently sent to prison for stabbing a guard.

Out on the streets for the first time in 13 years, Terry (Billy Wirth) resolves to go straight, but understandably finds it difficult. Hanging in a Chicago hood, he looks up Jackie (Erica Gimpel), the attractive but defensive sister-in-law of his best friend, who O.D.'d in prison. He soon gets a job in a foundry, but when he half-strangles his parole officer for ripping him off, he finds himself back in the criminal subculture, pulling a heist with a two-bit street hustler. Ending is poignant/fatalistic in 1940s noir fashion.

Pistor relates this downbeat story in suitably muted fashion, and the options open to Terry seem realistically limited. But aside from his momentary flirtation with the workaday world, Terry never develops much as a character, so pic's dramatic range remains constricted and somewhat monotonous.

Interracial aspects are well handled (almost every character aside from Billy and the chief villain is black), and pic cannot be reproached for its sincerity and unblinking view of a bleak urban landscape, only for its small stature in a demanding marketplace.

Up-and-comer Wirth broods and smolders like a young John Cassavetes in conveying Terry's hurt and fear. Other perfs are mostly engaging, while tech contributions are modestly in line with pic's other aspirations.

—Todd McCarthy

BLACK BOX

(ISRAELI)

A Look Films production. Produced by Gideon Kolirin. Directed by Yeud Levanon. Screenplay, Nomi Sharron, Levanon, based on the novel by Amos Oz. Camera (color), Avi Koren; editor, Tali Halter; music, Adi Renart; production design, Ariel Roshko. Reviewed at Cannes Film Festival (market), May 13, 1994. Running time: **90 MIN.**
Ilana .... Bruria Albek
Alex .... Ami Traub
Sommo .... Mati Seri
Zakheim .... Amnon Meskin

A dapting to the screen "Black Box," the epistolary novel by Amos Oz, arguably Israel's most accomplished living writer, presents a major challenge that is only partially met by director Yeud Levanon. This tale of obsessive love and wrecked marriage, which unfolds against Israel's complex political setting, should prove intriguing to viewers interested in the new Israeli cinema, but it holds limited commercial allure for other audiences.

Story's heroine is Ilana (Bruria Albek), a beautiful woman divorced from her first husband, Alex (Ami Traub), for seven years, but still madly in love with him. Though remarried to the understanding Sommo (Mati Seri), with whom she has a young daughter, Ilana's body, heart and soul yearn for Alex, an internationally famous scholar who lives in London. As a result of their painful divorce, their teenage son has become rebellious and keeps running away in an effort to be independent.

Using Ilana's voiceover narration, tale is structured as a series of flashbacks interwoven with episodes from the present. Ilana's recollections of her fervid marriage on a gorgeous Jerusalem estate (now deserted) are contrasted with her contempo routine life with Sommo. For personal and political reasons, both Alex's manipulative lawyer (Amnon Meskin) and Sommo conspire to keep the lovers apart.

Chief problem is the almost unbridgeable chasm between the book's subtle complexity of ideas and their onscreen translation. Regrettably, what survives of Oz's lyrical novel is only the bare bones.

As the internally tortured, obsessively passionate woman, Albek gives a creditable, if not distinguished, performance, though pic calls for a major actress with a wider range of expressive behavior. Of the

three men, only Meskin, as the sly lawyer, stands out, using his deep voice to give his lines sharp shadings.

Tech credits, particularly Avi Koren's precise lensing, are adequate, but readers who got a terrific charge from Oz's highly romantic book, which was immensely popular both in and outside Israel, will be disappointed by the more realistic and rather flat film version.

—Emanuel Levy

OH GOD, WOMEN ARE SO LOVING

(DIEU QUE LES FEMMES SONT AMOUREUSES)

(FRENCH)

An AMLF release (France) of an MDG Prods./Films 7/Centre Europeen Cinematographique Rhone-Alpes production with participation of Canal Plus and Sofiarp 2. (International sales: President Films, Paris.) Produced by Marie-Dominique Girodet. Directed, written by Magali Clement. Camera (color), Pierre Lhomme; editor, Amina Mazini; music, Jean-Jacques Lemetre; art direction, Bruno Bruneau; set decoration, Frederique Hurpeau; costume design, Clementine Joya; sound, Henri Morelle; assistant director, Michel Cheyko; casting, Francoise Menidrey. Reviewed at 14 Juillet Cinema, Paris, June 3, 1994. (In Cannes Film Festival — market.) Running time: **87 MIN.**
Anne .... Catherine Jacob
Arthur .... Etienne Chicot
Daniel .... Mathieu Carriere
Jacques .... Yves Beneyton
Mama .... Pascale Audret
Regis .... Jean-Pierre Malo
With: Grace de Capitani, Fiona Gelin, Judith Remy.

D espite a large cast and frenetic intentions, "Oh God, Women Are So Loving" is a stillborn and uninvolving look at a single, working mother of three and the non-stop parade of friends, relatives and men in her life. Quick theatrical exposure and tube dates await this forced semi-comedy.

Pleasingly plump Catherine Jacob portrays Anne, who works as a TV series editor while raising her teenage son by ex-hubby Daniel (Mathieu Carriere) and 8-year-old twin daughters by unnamed dad.

When carefree musician Arthur — who left Anne in the lurch a tell-tale eight years prior — shows up again and insists on courting her, Anne is ultra-hostile. Arthur's presence confuses Anne's ongoing affair with self-centered married doc Regis and her approach to a new love interest, soon-to-be-divorced Jacques.

Bland dialogue and contrived situations never convince, although harried households of fortyish French professionals probably resemble the places on display here. Director and scripter Magali Clement's underdeveloped characters orbit around Jacob, who gamely plugs away, although her character's behavior is frequently arbitrary.

Pleasant snippets of classically inflected music almost make up for scattershot pacing. Lensing is claustrophobic and workmanlike.
—*Lisa Nesselson*

MESSENGER

A Norman Loftis production. Produced, directed, written by Norman Loftis. Camera (color), Joe Di Gennaro; editor, John Walters; music, Joe Loduca; sound, David Alvaraz; assistant director, David Giardina. Reviewed at Cannes Film Festival (market), May 18, 1994. Running time: **84 MIN.**
Jeff .... Richard Barboza
Tina .... Carolyn Kinebrew
John .... Scott Ferguson
Lois .... Malika Davis

Norman Loftis' 1990 outing "Small Time" tracked a lowlife loser's doomed descent in pungent but sympathetic New York neorealist terms. His new feature works a similar beat with more technical polish but a less refined cutting edge. Refashioning a "Bicycle Thief" riff around a young black family man's attempts to stick to the straight and narrow, "Messenger" struggles under the weight of academic intent. Marginal fest dates look to be the limit.

In an upfront homage to Vittorio De Sica's 1948 milestone, the drama of "Messenger" hinges on a stolen bicycle. A former petty criminal determined to provide legit support for his growing family, Jeff (Richard Barboza) lies about having a bike in order to land a job with a courier service. Reluctantly, he allows his pregnant wife, Tina (Carolyn Kinebrew), to pawn her wedding ring to buy one.

Once mobile, he works hard, embracing the do-right existence while Tina laughs off some mild derision from the girls in the hood, most of whom visit their men in the slammer. But a moment's distraction leads to the bike being swiped. In strict De Sica style, a search ensues, most of it with Tina and their rapper chum John (Scott Ferguson) in tow, while frustration and hopelessness shove the already hotheaded Jeff increasingly off kilter.

Skillfully crafted within its no-budget frame (reportedly well under $100,000), the dramatically intense scenario is stifled by excessive talkiness, without whipping up the anxiety necessary to convey the fact that survival, self-sufficiency and the salvation of the family unit all hang in the balance.

The three leads (all of them "Small Time" alumni) adopt a naturalistic approach that generally sits well, but in the most demanding role, Barboza doesn't show the range to convincingly limn his char-

acter's edge-of-violence/hysteria/breakdown behavior. Loftis appears as a civic-minded but ultimately ineffectual cop.
—*David Rooney*

FUNNY MAN

(BRITISH)

A Nomad Pictures production. (International sales: Victor Film Co., London.) Produced by Nigel Odell. Executive producers, Gareth Wiley, Steve Parsons. Co-producers, Tim James, David Redman. Directed, written by Simon Sprackling. Camera (Technicolor), Tom Ingle Jr.; editor, Ryan L. Driscoll; music, Parsons/Haines; production design, David Endley; costume design, Alex Westover; sound (Dolby), Patrick Boland; special effects, Neill Gorton, Jim Francis; assistant director, Toby Duckett. Reviewed at Cannes Film Festival (market), May 18, 1994. Running time: **93 MIN.**
Funny Man .... Tim James
Callum Chance .... Christopher Lee
Max Taylor .... Benny Young
Tina Taylor .... Ingrid Lacey
Psychic Commando .... Pauline Chan
Johnny Taylor .... Matthew Devitt
Hard Man .... Chris Walker
Crap Puppeteer .... George Morton
Thelma Fudd .... Rhona Cameron
  With: Hary Heard, Jamie Heard, Bob Sessions, Ed Bishop, John Chancer.

A nutty truffle of fairground antics and over-the-top bad taste, "Funny Man" isn't half as funny as it thinks it is, but has enough chuckles to draw the six-pack and frozen-dinner contingent. Sophomoric humor of this low-budget horror-comedy is unlikely to travel far beyond the British Commonwealth, with ancillary its biggest market.

Pic is basically a variation on that old chestnut, the haunted house yarn, with a variety of wackos meeting grisly ends at the hands of a pesky visitor from hell, a blend of the Joker in the deck and the court Fool.

Setting is an ancestral pile won by record producer Max (Benny Young) from the mysterious Callum Chance (Christopher Lee) in a poker game. As Max's family and a bunch of hitchhikers stop over, Chance summons up the "Funny Man" (Tim James), who turns them into pig slop one by one.

Pic ditches any pretense at plotting early on and settles into a showcase for James' entertainingly athletic antics (and comic asides to the camera) as he takes on each victim in blackly comic two-handers. Largely unknown cast go the abattoir in reasonable style. Only one to make a sizable impression is Pauline Chan as a black psychic whose hand turns into a rocket launcher. Lee is in only briefly.

Tech credits are OK, and special effects passable. Prosthetics for James rate a special nod.
—*Derek Elley*

THE RETURN OF TOMMY TRICKER
(LE RETOUR DES AVENTURIERS DU TIMBRE PERDU)
(Canadian)

A Malofilm release (Canada) of a Rock Demers and Kevin Tierney production (Les Productions la Fete) with the participation of Telefilm Canada, Sogic Quebec, Government of Quebec (Programme credits d'impot), The Movie Network (First Choice), Super Ecran, and the collaboration of Canada Post Corp., La Societe Radio-Canada, CFCF Television Inc., Radio-Quebec, Endeavour Tucker Ltd. (Murray Newey and Judith Trye). (International sales: Productions la Fete.) Directed, written by Michael Rubbo. Camera (color) Thomas Vamos; editor, Jean-Pierre Cereghetti; music, Kate, Anna and Jane McGarrigle; art direction, Guy Lalande; costumes, Suzanne Ferland; sound, Louis Dupire; line producer, Lorraine Du Hamel; associate producer, Ina Fichman; casting, Lois Siegel, Agence Elite. Reviewed at Cannes Film Festival (Market) May 21, 1994. Running time: **100 MIN.**
Tommy Tricker .... Michael Stevens
Cass .... Joshawa Mathers
Nancy .... Heather Goodsell
Albert .... Paul Nocholls
Ralph .... Andrew Bauer-Gador
Molly .... Adele Gray

A welcome antidote to the many vulgar and often violent films made for younger audiences, this imaginative sequel to the 1987 "Tommy Tricker and the Stamp Traveller" should have no difficulty following in the successful path of its 14 predecessors in Rock Demers' 10-year-old "Tales for All" series.

Tommy Tricker, his sister and friends return in a new philatelic adventure to free Charles Merriweather, the mysterious lad imprisoned for 60 years on Canada's famous Bluenose sailing ship stamp.

Two companions see this as a humanitarian cause, but Tommy intends to ask Charles to partner in a stamp collecting biz. Working their magic spells, the children bring back Charles, but he surprisingly turns out to be pretty Molly Merriweather, Charles' younger sister.

But Molly, back from her lost horizon, is aging visibly. Conjuring up their magic methods, the kids hie to the exotic Cook Islands, where potent layers of Bluenose stamps plastered all over Molly restore her youth and beauty. Tommy falls in love with her, Charles returns, and all ends happily with the suggestion that Tommy may well be traveling again in another sequel.

Michael Rubbo deftly handles writing and direction. Tech credits are first-class, young thesps are beguilingly natural. —*Gerald Pratley*

SOUVENIR
(SPANISH)

A Lauren Films release (Spain) of an Avanti Films production in association with Canal Plus Espana, Television Espanola, Television de Catalunya, Ministry of Culture, Generalitat de Catalunya, with support from the European Script Fund. (International sales: Europex, Paris.) Produced by Rosa Romero, Victoria Borras. Directed by Rosa Verges. Screenplay, Jordi Beltran, Verges. Camera (color), Flavio Labiano; editors, Quim Boix, Marisa Aguinaga; music, J.M. Pagan; art direction, Rosa Ros; costume design, Maria Gil; sound (Dolby), Miguel Rejas; assistant director, Alexandra Palau; casting, Teresa Estrada. Reviewed at Cannes Film Festival (market), May 16, 1994. Running time: **89 MIN.**
Yoshio .... Futoshi Kasagawa
Rita .... Emma Suarez
Elvira .... Anna Lizaran
  With: Pepa Lopez, Emilio Gutierrez Caba, Merce Pons, Simon Andreu, Enric Majo, Eulalia Ramon.

Catalan director Rosa Verges made some ripples in the festival and arthouse pond with her breezy 1990 debut, "Boom Boom." She mines similar territory in "Souvenir," a well-choreographed chain of comedic coincidences that's sold short by its halting rhythm. Congenial but sluggish romantic comedy is reportedly headed for an editing rethink, and with tightening to increase its verve and accelerate its momentum, it should make a toothsome tube item.

Flying into Barcelona, Japanese tourist Yoshio (Futoshi Kasagawa) takes a fancy to stewardess Rita (Emma Suarez). Following their arrival, they reclaim identical suitcases, and after he persuades her to pose for a souvenir photo, she unwittingly flits off with his luggage.

Before he can track her down to switch suitcases, Yoshio is hit by a car, leaving him with no memory aside from the name Rita, and no grasp of Spanish. The road to rehabilitation becomes an escalating spiral of misadventures (including virtual adoption by Rita's unsuspecting mother), inexorably steering the helpless visitor toward love.

Sweetly amusing upshot identifies the amnesiac as a humble postman who won the suitcase, camera and European jaunt on a TV gameshow.

Kasagawa provides an affable comic anchor, but Suarez reps something of a weak link, her lack of establishing scenes and shortage of screen time cheating the film of an adequate romantic target.

Despite frequent injections of the same freshness Verges brought to her first feature, there's a fatigued quaintness about her material here

that stymies its theatrical chances. Tech input is generally fine.
—David Rooney

REVENGE OF THE RED BARON

A Concorde Films release of a New Horizons production. Produced by Mike Elliott. Executive producer, Roger Corman. Co-producer, Scott Levy. Directed by Robert Gordon. Screenplay, Michael J. McDonald. Camera (Foto-Kem color), Christian Sebaldt; editor, Kagan Ertiscan; music, Robert Randles; visual effects, Ken Solomon; sound (Ultra-Stereo), Bill Robbins; assistant director, Burgess Steinberg; casting, Laura Schiff. Reviewed at Cannes Film Festival (Market), May 17, 1994. Running time: **86 MIN.**
Grandpa James .... Mickey Rooney
Jimmy Spencer .... Tobey Maguire
Carol Spencer .... Laraine Newman
Richard Spencer .... Cliff De Young
Lou .... Ronnie Schell
Det. Lewis .... Ronnie Schell
Voice of Red Baron ..... John McDonnell

The infamous Red Baron, featured in Roger Corman's 1971 "Von Richtofen and Brown" returns as a lethal toy, a sort of cousin to Chucky in "Child's Play," in this underwhelming effort from Concorde. Target audience of pre-pubescent males would do better to hunt for the original on vid shelves.

Pic opens with scene of an air battle over France in 1918 in which Spencer (not Brown) downs the Baron, then segues to present-day California where Spencer's grandson, Jimmy (Tobey Maguire), is in trouble at school and is suspended for a week. His divorced mom (Laraine Newman) sends him off to the country to bond with his surly father (Cliff De Young) and almost senile granddad (Mickey Rooney, playing most of his nothing role in a wheelchair).

Granddad proudly shows the boy remote control model planes patterned on his own aircraft and that of the Baron's, and while playing with these devices a flash of lightning reactivates the Baron, who manages to get some bullets for his tiny machine guns and starts killing people while at the same time spouting a string of truly excruciating puns: "Your security's full of holes," after blasting a security guard, is a reasonable sample.

This is a distinctly unexciting vehicle, handled without imagination and with a totally unthreatening villain in the doll-like Baron. It has little or no chance of theatrical exposure, and will be a modest video attraction.

Tech credits are on the cheesy side.
—David Stratton

BEG!

(BRITISH)

A Robert Golden Pictures presentation of a Beg Ltd. production. (International sales: Pilgrim Entertainment, London.) Produced by Sandra Yarwood. Executive producer, Robert Golden. Directed by Golden. Associate director, David Glass. Screenplay, Peta Lily, Glass, Golden, from the play by Lily, Glass. Camera (color), Chris Middleton; editors, Terry Jones, Dean Wyles; music, Steve Parsons, David Pearl; additional music, Francis Haines; production design, Harry Metcalf; art direction, Sue Ferguson; costume design, Jochien Van Schuppen; sound (Dolby), Steve Taylor; associate producer, Andrea Marsh; assistant director, Steve Lincoln; casting, Suzy Korel. Reviewed at Cannes Film Festival (market), May 17, 1994. Running time: **108 MIN.**
Penny Second .... Peta Lily
Det.-Sgt. Stiltskin .... Philip Pellew
Dr. Rogers .... Julian Bleach
Hal .... Oleg Fedorov
Dr. Second Senior .... Chris Banks
Dr. Melplash .... Jeremy Wilkin

British grunge hits rock bottom in "Beg!," a chaotic mishmash of physical theater and grossout schlocker that's as entertaining as a night in the morgue. Though avant-garde gatherings may bite, this first production of Chicagoborn U.K. commercials director Robert Golden looks set for a long career on the shelf. Wicket chances are zip.

Story is set in a dreary private hospital, St. Caninus, in which order has broken down and the well-heeled management is pondering further cuts. Someone has murdered the head of research, which sets off a power struggle for the vacant post between women's ward head Penny (Peta Lily) and the oily Dr. Rogers (Julian Bleach).

Opening reel, full of blackly comic gross-out fare and a raft of undefined characters, sets the tone. By the time the plot comes vaguely into view around reel three, the mix of sophomore antics, bargain-basement production values and watch-me-shock effects is well on the road to nowhere.

Brit mime artiste Lily, who co-wrote/directed the recent fringe production on which pic is based, is serviceable as the femme doctor battling a cynical management. (Film can also be read as a satire on the U.K.'s privatizing health system.) Other roles are played at full tilt.

Technically, pic is adequate.
—Derek Elley

NIGHTFIRE

A Triboro Entertainment presentation of a Miklen Entertainment production. Produced, directed by Mike Sedan. Executive producer, Steven Mackler. Screenplay, Catherine Tavel, Helen Haxton, from a story by Sedan. Camera (Foto-Kem color), Zoran Hochstatter; editor, Thomas Meshelski; music, Miriam Cutler; sound, Brent Beckett; assistant director, Eric Davies. Reviewed at Cannes Film Festival (market), May 14, 1994. Running time: **93 MIN.**
With Shannon Tweed, John Laughlin, Rochelle Swanson, Martin Hewitt

A slickly tooled erotic suspense story with a quartet of personable leads, "Nightfire" delivers the soft-core goods but falters in the last reel with some underwhelming thriller elements. Pruning would sharpen the product, which should have a decent life on vid shelves.

The simple plot has Shannon Tweed and John Laughlin as an unhappily married couple who live on a spectacularly appointed, remote ranch. Tweed's a high-powered businesswoman who neglects her spouse, who becomes increasingly into kinky sex while she remains frigid.

Enter Martin Hewitt and Rochelle Swanson, a couple who like to walk on the wild side. They drop in at the ranch claiming a car breakdown, but it soon becomes clear that Laughlin's hired them to behave sexily in front of Tweed in an attempt to turn her on.

So there are frequent scenes in which the well-built duo fondle each other in the jacuzzi, or anywhere else that's handy.

Tweed is just disgusted by all the carrying on, however, so Laughlin turns even nastier.

Pic unfolds in a predictable manner, but fans of the genre shouldn't be disappointed, especially when the formidable Tweed and Swanson do their thing, which is most of the time. Tech credits are fine.
—David Stratton

FORREST GUMP

A Paramount release of a Steve Tisch/Wendy Finerman production. Produced by Finerman, Tisch, Steve Starkey. Co-producer, Charles Newirth. Directed by Robert Zemeckis. Screenplay, Eric Roth, based on the novel by Winston Groom. Camera (DuArt, Technicolor; Deluxe prints; Panavision widescreen), Don Burgess; editor, Arthur Schmidt; music, Alan Silvestri; executive music producer, Joel Sill; production design, Rick Carter; art direction, Leslie McDonald, Jim Teegarden; set design, Erin Kemp, James C. Feng, Elizabeth Lapp, Lauren E. Polizzi; set decoration, Nancy Haigh; costume design, Joanna Johnston; sound (Dolby), William B. Kaplan; visual effects supervisor, Ken Ralston; special visual effects, Industrial Light & Magic; assistant director, Bruce Moriarty; second unit director, Starkey; second unit camera, David M. Dunlap; casting, Ellen Lewis. Reviewed at the Bruin Theater, L.A., June 27, 1994. MPAA Rating: PG-13. Running time: **142 MIN.**
Forrest Gump .... Tom Hanks
Jenny Curran .... Robin Wright
Lt. Dan Taylor .... Gary Sinise
Bubba Blue .... Mykelti Williamson
Mrs. Gump .... Sally Field
Young Forrest .... Michael Conner Humphreys
Young Jenny .... Hanna R. Hall

A picaresque story of a simpleton's charmed odyssey through 30 years of tumultuous American history, "Forrest Gump" is whimsy with a strong cultural spine. Elegantly made and winningly acted by Tom Hanks in his first outing since his Oscar-winning "Philadelphia" performance, Robert Zemeckis' technically dazzling new film is also shrewdly packaged to hit baby boomers where they live. Pic offers up a non-stop barrage of emotional and iconographic identification points that will make the postwar generation feel they're seeing their lives passing by onscreen. Paramount's target audience is obvious, and boffo B.O. should ensue.

In a part Dustin Hoffman might once have killed for, Hanks plays a kind of semi-imbecile whose very blankness makes him an ideal audience prism through which many of the key events of the '50s through early '80s can be viewed. Lacking any ideology or analytical powers, Gump is the immutable innocent moving in a state of grace through a nation in the process of losing its innocence, an Everyman who acts instinctively in an age defined by political divisiveness.

Although hard to pigeonhole, the picture unavoidably recalls the idiot-savant classic "Being There," and significantly resembles "The World According to Garp" in tone. Most often mentioned, however, will be its similarity to Woody Allen's "Zelig," as some of the biggest laughs stem from wizardly interpolations of the Gump character

July 11, 1994 (Cont.)

into newsreel and TV footage of several U.S. presidents and other leading figures.

As Gump narrates his story to a succession of listeners at a Savannah, Ga., bus stop, a most curious life is revealed in evocative, often jokey flashbacks. Gump is raised in an old plantation mansion, now a boarding house, by his abandoned mother (Sally Field), who tells the boy that he's no different from anyone else despite his 75 I.Q. Outfitted with leg braces and shunned by other boys, young Forrest finds his only friend in a beautiful little girl, Jenny, herself the victim of abuse at home.

Once Forrest, in a startling scene, literally breaks free of his leg shackles, he becomes "a running fool," darting about wherever he goes at terrific speed. Even though he doesn't understand the rules, he becomes a star running back on the high school and college football teams, and it's at the U. of Alabama that the grown-up Forrest has his first date with destiny, as a dopey-looking bystander next to Gov. George Wallace as the first black students are admitted through the school's doors.

After another encounter, with JFK, Forrest heads for Vietnam, where his dim-wittedness makes him the ideal Army soldier. On the way, he meets Bubba Blue (Mykelti Williamson), another not especially swift fellow who's like Forrest's black brother, a man whose dreams of a shrimping life give Forrest something to aspire to once they're back.

After an intense battle, Forrest saves the lives of several men, including his commanding officer, Lt. Dan (Gary Sinise), who nonetheless loses his legs, and Forrest returns home to receive the Medal of Honor from LBJ and have a chance reunion with Jenny (Robin Wright), who's become a camp follower of SDS and Black Panther types.

Through it all, Forrest retains his love and idealized image of Jenny. She, however, indulges in the try-it-all excesses of the era, becoming a stripper, hippie, activist, druggie and more. Jenny keeps popping into Forrest's life at intervals, never quite ready to settle for his unquestioning love until it's almost too late.

Meanwhile, Forrest's eventful life comes to embrace a stint as a champ ping-pong player, a down-and-out period with Lt. Dan in New York, a hilarious key role in the Watergate saga, amazing success as a shrimp boat captain, the resumption of his life as a runner, which sees him be-

come a sort of mystical guru figure to the jogging set, and finally the unexpected arrival of fatherhood.

In covering so much ground, literally and figuratively, Eric Roth's intelligently structured, finely tuned screenplay also serves up innumerable cultural touchstones that will have most viewers in the 30-50 age range melting in recognition. Main themes here have to do with the impulse to recapture the past; the wish to return to one's childhood, or at least the site of it; the desire to fulfill your life with your original true love; the need to refashion the simple feeling of home after many aimless years; and assuming the responsibilities of parenthood after much delay.

At just short of 2½ hours, pic is a bit indulgent, long and excessive at times, but this is more than compensated for by its humor and sharp-witted storytelling. For the minority of nay-sayers the film will encounter, pic's key problem will be its preoccupation with lost innocence and certain other self-centered hang-ups.

Pic is weakest in the Forrest-Jenny relationship; the characters have nothing but their childhood connection going for them. Changes in Jenny's life are mostly marked by the alterations to Wright's coiffure and costumes, and the actress has little to play until the late moments.

On the other hand, Gump reps another career triumph for Hanks after his Oscar turn. Affecting a Southern drawl and affable sweetness, the actor draws the viewer close to his curious character immediately, and manages to keep one intrigued and amused throughout. His comic timing is as sharp as ever, even when interacting with real-life figures in docu footage, and his malleable physicality contributes a great deal to the intermittent hilarity.

In the key supporting roles, Sinise and Williamson are excellent, while Field pops up as Forrest's loving mom at the beginning and near the end.

Zemeckis' direction is supple, and in this instance he has well balanced his long-term interest in technical matters with concern over performance and content. From the extraordinary, descending opening shot on through a vivid ground-level Vietnam firestorm and the documentary facsimiles, the film is a superior example of Hollywood craftsmanship, with outstanding contributions from lenser Don Burgess, production designer Rick

Carter, costume designer Joanna Johnston and numerous special-effects hands.

The film has been very well worked out on all levels, and manages the difficult feat of being an intimate, even delicate tale played with an appealingly light touch against an epic backdrop.

—*Todd McCarthy*

TRUE LIES

A 20th Century Fox release of a Lightstorm Entertainment production. Produced by James Cameron, Stephanie Austin. Executive producers, Rae Sanchini, Robert Shriver, Lawrence Kasanoff. Directed, written by Cameron, based on a screenplay by Claude Zidi, Simon Michael, Didier Kaminka. Camera (CFI color), Russell Carpenter; editors, Mark Goldblatt, Conrad Buff, Richard A. Harris; music, Brad Fiedel; production design, Peter Lamont; art direction, Robert Laing, Michael Novotny; set design, Joseph Hodges; set decoration, Cindy Carr; costume design, Marlene Stewart; sound (Dolby), Lee Orloff; unit production managers, Scott Thaler, Patricia Whitcher; Digital Domain visual effects supervisor, John Bruno; special effects coordinator, Thomas L. Fisher; stunt coordinator, Joel Kramer; associate producer, Pamela Easley; first assistant directors, J. Michael Haynie, Aldric La'Auli Porter; casting, Mali Finn. Reviewed at the Mann Festival Theater, L.A., July 7, 1994. MPAA Rating: R. Running time: 141 MIN.
Harry .... Arnold Schwarzenegger
Helen .... Jamie Lee Curtis
Gib .... Tom Arnold
Simon .... Bill Paxton
Juno .... Tia Carrere
Aziz .... Art Malik
Dana .... Eliza Dushku
Faisil .... Grant Heslov
Spencer Trilby .... Charlton Heston

A reunion of "Terminator 2" star Arnold Schwarzenegger and writer/director James Cameron creates obvious expectations, and this 2½-hour action comedy tries way too hard to live up to them. Providing its share of fun in stretches, pic ultimately overstays its welcome with a level of mayhem that will simply feel like too much for any marginal fan of the genre. "Lies" should prove a big draw initially but will have to hustle just to reach its $100 million-plus price tag.

This certainly isn't the movie Schwarzenegger needed to redeem himself after the disappointment of "Last Action Hero." Indeed, while not as soulless, "True Lies" shares more similarities to that film than it would care to admit in the overtime department — that is, being overlong, overproduced and over budget.

Such considerations won't necessarily bother teenagers, but

that demographic alone can't sustain an enterprise like this, and writer/director/co-producer Cameron will doubtless put off more discerning palates with the pic's sheer bloat.

In its best moments, "True Lies" comes closest to Schwarzenegger's earlier vehicle "Commando," which also mixed plenty of humor with a cartoonish level of destruction.

Yet even with its ribald laughs and spectacular action sequences (clearly seeking to up the ante on the latter front), the movie gets mired in a comedic midsection that wears the audience down, sapping their energy before the film shifts to a chaotic third act that doesn't know when to quit.

"Lies" is really two movies in one. An impressive Bondian opening sequence introduces us to secret agent Harry Tasker (Schwarzenegger), who infiltrates a heavily guarded compound, mixes it up with partygoers (among them the stunning Tia Carrere) and then beats a sensational retreat.

Tasker, it turns out, leads a double life, having convinced his wife (Jamie Lee Curtis) and teenage daughter (Eliza Dushku) that he's a staid computer salesman. Back in Washington, Harry and sidekick Gib (Tom Arnold) get on the trail of an Arab terrorist (Art Malik) who's acquired four nuclear weapons. They pursue the felon in an elaborate horse-and-motorcycle chase through the city.

So far, so good, until the script (based very loosely on a French film, "La Totale") veers into a periodically amusing but staggeringly drawn-out tangent that has Harry suspecting his wife of infidelity and using all his agenting wiles to investigate. Roughly an hour long on its own, this foray into romantic comedy offers some crowd-pleasingly broad flourishes — including an over-the-top turn by Bill Paxton — but doesn't jibe with what precedes or follows it.

Schwarzenegger does get to play a family man as well as a glib action hero, showing off the innate likability that prompts audiences to root for him. Curtis is also provided some juicy moments as the buttoned-up, soon-to-be-awakened wife, while Arnold launches his solo career (assuming that lasts) with a scene-stealing performance as Harry's affable and foul-mouthed sidekick.

In short, this stew has the right ingredients, and Cameron (to understate matters considerably) overcooks it — bogging down in comedy before offering a barrage of pyrotechnics.

There's plenty of jaw-dropping stuntwork, terrific fight choreography and breathtaking use of the

Florida Keys as a background locale; but there are also some noteworthy glitches, including easily spotted doubles during a few chase sequences — a minor distraction, yet surprising given the overall technical wizardry involved.

Sets, costumes and production design are all impressive and opulent, and "T2" alumnus Brad Fiedel provides another muscular score in the mode of that earlier effort.

Add it up, however, and the result is 141 minutes of extravagant fodder for an enticing three-minute trailer. And that, unfortunately, is no lie. —*Brian Lowry*

THE SHADOW

A Universal Pictures release of a Bregman/Baer production. Produced by Martin Bregman, Willi Baer, Michael S. Bregman. Executive producers, Louis A. Stroller, Rolf Deyhle. Coexecutive producer, Stan Weston. Directed by Russell Mulcahy. Screenplay, David Koepp, based on Advance Magazine Publishers Inc.'s character "The Shadow." Camera (Deluxe color), Stephen H. Burum; editor, Peter Honess; music, Jerry Goldsmith; production design, Joseph Nemec III; art direction, Dan Olexiewicz, Steve Wolff, Jack Johnson; set decoration, Garrett Lewis; costume design, Bob Ringwood; sound (Digital Experience), Keith Wester; visual effects supervisor, Alison Savitch; special makeup effects supervisor, Carl Fullerton; special makeup effects, Greg Cannom; stunt coordinator, Dick Ziker; associate producer, Patricia Churchill; assistant director, Louis D'Esposito; second unit director, Ziker; casting, Mary Colquhoun. Reviewed at the Directors Guild of America Theater, L.A., June 28, 1994. MPAA Rating: PG-13. Running time: **107 MIN.**
Lamont Cranston/
The Shadow .... Alec Baldwin
Shiwan Khan .... John Lone
Margo Lane .... Penelope Ann Miller
Moe Shrevnitz .... Peter Boyle
Reinhardt Lane .... Ian McKellen
Farley Claymore .... Tim Curry
Barth .... Jonathan Winters
Dr. Tam .... Sab Shimono
Burbank .... Andre Gregory

From a box office standpoint, the more pertinent question than "Who knows what evil lurks in the hearts of men?" may be "Who knows or cares anything about the Shadow?" — a character whose heyday came in the '30s. Despite the film's visual opulence, that factor alone should prevent "The Shadow" from covering much summer audience once those predisposed to see it have run their course.

Starting with the main title credits backed by Jerry Goldsmith's brooding score, "The Shadow" is clearly trying to mine the "Batman"

lode, down to its impressive production design, somber tone and occasional flashes of high camp.

Despite similarities as a vigilante creature of the night, however, the Shadow — a character that enjoyed its greatest success in radio after being created in pulp novels — lacks the visceral appeal of Batman and won't strike the same chord with moviegoers. Indeed, those familiar with the character are more likely to be 70 than 17.

That leaves the movie in its own shadow world, desperately trying to sell itself to teenagers without alienating its core of fans. While it may offer scant consolation to Universal, in the latter regard, at least, "The Shadow" is more satisfying than an effort like "Dick Tracy," though the end result is a hollow production design showcase.

Pic opens with its worst sequence, set in Tibet, illustrating how Lamont Cranston (Alec Baldwin) acquires his Shadowy powers. Director Russell Mulcahy recovers with a stylish introduction of the character in New York, as the Shadow rescues a scientist (Sab Shimono) and recruits him as one of his many operatives.

The heart of the story involves a comic-book nemesis, Shiwan Khan (John Lone), a descendant of Genghis Khan who possesses the same mental powers as the Shadow and harbors his ancestor's world-conquering ambitions.

Influencing the mind of noted if slightly daft scientist Reinhardt Lane (Ian McKellen), Khan decides to start his quest by destroying New York, fashioning a pre-nuclear facsimile of an atomic bomb. Cranston, meanwhile, finds himself entangled with Lane's daughter, Margo (Penelope Ann Miller), who unknowingly possesses a natural facility that forges a psychic link between the two.

Mulcahy, principally known as a commercial and musicvideo director before helming "Highlander" and its sequel, remains a gifted visual stylist but struggles with character and meanders when it comes to advancing a story — a challenge made more difficult thanks to the underdeveloped script by David Koepp ("Jurassic Park").

The movie does offer its share of action, making the most of the character's creepy power to slink into and out of shadows. Those flourishes and the efforts of the special-effects team, production designer Joseph Nemec III and costume de-

signer Bob Ringwood are the pic's real stars.

That said, Baldwin turns in a sturdy central performance, putting his steely tough-guy act to good use while managing to bring some dimension and self-effacing humor to his role regarding the character's tormented past. Lone also provides a shrewd and formidable adversary, despite having to overcome such near-laughable camp trappings as walking down Broadway in full Mongol armor.

Other performances, however, are either uneven or wildly over-the-top, particularly Miller's shameless vamping as the female lead. Her lack of chemistry with Baldwin represents one of the many obstacles that even the powers of the Shadow can't quite overcome.

Tech credits, as noted, are superb, particularly the combination of matte shots and miniatures used to create Gotham, or rather, New York City. —*Brian Lowry*

AVIGNON FEST

LOOSE SCREWS
(LA FOLIE DOUCE)
(FRENCH)

A Pan-Europeenne release (France) of a Sara Films/Investimage 4/Cofimage 5 production, with participation of Canal Plus and Procirep. Produced by Alain Sarde. Directed by Frederic Jardin. Screenplay, Jardin, Fabrice Roger-Lacan. Camera (color), Christophe Pollock; editor, Catherine Quesemand; sound, Stephane Thiebaut, Jean-Francois Auger; assistant director, Fabrice Roger-Lacan. Reviewed at French-American Film Workshop (competing), Avignon, France, June 23, 1994. Running time: **90 MIN.**
Louise .... Geraldine Pailhas
Landrieu .... Bernard Verley
Edouard .... Edouard Baer
Gloria .... Isabelle Nanty
Josef .... Joseph Malerba
Lotte .... Emmanuelle Lepoutre
Vera .... Cristina Cascardo
Julie .... Aude Amiot
Franck .... Franck Bussi
Roman .... Benjamin Kraatz

"Loose Screws" is a vibrant, freewheeling first film whose large cast, zingy thesping and technical polish belie a mere three-week shooting schedule. Twenty-five-year old helmer Frederic Jardin — who has picked up a useful trick or two as assistant director for Godard, Doillon and Sautet — is a talent to watch.

A slick, intense and humorous examination of a petulant band of self-centered young Parisians, pic is an appealing if improbable look at the rigors of sex and love as seen from the vantage of Gallic baby-boomer bellybuttons. If that sounds like familiar territory, pic's saving grace is that it orbits its characters's navels rather than helmer's. Pacing is a cut above the norm and lensing is airy and assured.

Dashingly cynical Edouard hosts a lonely-hearts confessional show on a hip Paris radio station and, as the only romantically unattached member of his circle of pals, gives unsolicited advice to his twenty-something cohorts.

Edouard was an item with spacey Lotte, but she's now completely taken with strong silent type Roman. Boyish Eric and womanly Louise break up when Louise falls for fiftyish intellectual Landrieu, and Eric takes up with sexy shoe saleswoman Vera.

Slightly older Gloria and Josef are married and working themselves to death, but Josef is cheating with Julie, and Gloria has found spectacular carnal delight in the arms of the manager of a local coffee shop, Franck.

Characters tryst, gossip, go to work and barrel toward their respective romantic crises. Pretty girls take their shirts off, everyone pouts, ponders, expounds and exchanges occasionally snappy dialogue.

Dolores Chaplin cameos in a horror movie that is being promoted by a PR firm where some characters work.

Summery location lensing in typical Paris streets is as pleasantly giddy as the fine performances and competently interwoven vignettes. The camera leans in close to get the juicy details of couplings and uncouplings. —*Lisa Nesselson*

THE UPSTAIRS NEIGHBOR

A Brandon Foley and Matt Devlen production. Produced by Devlen. Executive producer, Foley. Line producer, Danny Kuchuck. Directed, written by James Merendino. Camera (color, 16mm), Greg Littlewood; editor, Esther P. Russell; music, Bruce Langhorne; art direction, Charlotte Malmlof. Reviewed at French-American Film Workshop (competing), Avignon, France, June 25, 1994. Running time: **91 MIN.**
With: Sebastian Gutierrez, Rustam Branamen, Christina Fulton, Kane Picoy.

"The Upstairs Neighbor," a darkly humorous study of a young novelist's rampant and possibly justified paranoia,

July 11, 1994 (Cont.)

puts a resolutely L.A. spin on Polanski's "The Tenant." Low-budget indie, shot in two weeks, parlays good perfs and a dollop of Satanic ritual into an effective, if derivative slice of mood-driven entertainment. Fests and midnight programmers should nibble.

Semi-productive writer Eric, who lives on the ground floor of a duplex, is convinced that the guy upstairs — a fit fellow with arched eyebrows who also writes for a living — is tapping his phone. Eric's anxiety mounts when he sights what appears to be a human sacrifice in progress. After boning up on the topic of the occult, Eric improvises a radical means of escape from the evil eye.

Action is opened out into a few other locations, including a trendy coffeehouse and a used bookshop, but mostly revolves around Eric's apartment building, whose stucco walls and ceiling offer scant comfort.

Pace is measured but never dull. Some transitions are abrupt and arbitrary. Lensing nicely suggests Eric's deteriorating state of mind.

Performances are all fine, with an L.A. underground spin. Eerie, mournful score has the desired edgy effect. —*Lisa Nesselson*

VENIAL SIN ...
MORTAL SIN ...

(PECHE VENIEL ...
PECHE MORTEL ...)

(FRENCH)

A Prods. Desmichelle Groupe TSF/ Images & Trames/Test production, with participation of CNC. (International sales: CGR Intl., Paris.) Produced by Hugues Desmichelle. Directed, written by Pomme Meffre, from her novel. Camera (color), Guy Chabanis; editor, Francoise Berger-Garnault; music, Jean-Pierre Stora, Georges Rabol; production design, Gisele Cavali; set decoration, Henri Meffre; costume design, Nicole Bize; sound, Pascal Ribier; associate producer, Aurele Giraud; assistant director, Francois Vantrou. Reviewed at French-American Film Workshop (competing), Avignon, France, June 24, 1994. (Also in Cannes Film Festival — market.) Running time: **73 MIN.**
With: Nini Crepon, Philippe Adrien, Isabelle Sadoyan, Brigitte Rouan, Anny Romand.

An 11-year-old girl's sexual awakening via a 50-year-old man is detailed in the same casual tone as more girlish pursuits in "Venial Sin ... Mortal Sin ...," Pomme Meffre's partly autobiographical construct — strung together from evocative bric-a-brac and nostalgic tableaux — is from the love-it-or-hate-it memoirs school of filming mastered by Terence Davies, but told from a resolutely female p.o.v.

Highly stylized portrait of post-World War II small-town life is the cumulative result of lovingly recreated details juxtaposed with literary but never stilted narration as a dapper gent who has happened upon the girl's illustrated diary reads it cover to cover.

Helmer plunges into the past via colorized postcards and formal camera work, which examines objects and settings — with and without people — to build a sort of voyeuristic bond with the viewer. Actors go about their business to illustrate the diary's revelations, but there is no synchronized dialogue.

From simple, pithy, often amusing observations, an indelible portrait emerges of one child's curiosity, imagination and sexual awakening in a specific time and place.

Celine — portrayed only as a photo glued into the diary — recounts the delicious pleasure of being intimately caressed by the local hairdresser, whose wife recently died. She writes of how yummy it is to eat rabbit heads, of seeing her first black G.I., about attending confession after making out with a local boy, of her beloved grandmother and her perky aunt.

There is a healthy patina to Celine's desire for additional sexual stimulation, which she describes in glowing terms between clandestine visits to the hairdresser. Camera lingers on the setting but never the act itself.

Pic is completely successful at examining the world through a child's eyes, but despite brief running time, the relatively static stills-and-ambient-sounds presentation grows tiresome before film's surprise conclusion.

Period production design is aces and musical passages are splendid. (Pic's title comes from a sing-song kids' tune about confession.)

Pic's buoyant mood runs counter to conventional wisdom about sexual molestation of children. Helmer's point — that sex for girls can be consensual and pleasurable at a very early age — is sure to spark lively debate wherever pic is shown. —*Lisa Nesselson*

MARSEILLES

TALES FROM
A HARD CITY

(FRENCH-BRITISH — DOCU — VIDEO)

A La Sept/Arte, Channel 4 production. (International sales: Picture Palace North.) Produced by Alex Usborne, Jacques Bidou. Directed by Kim Flitcroft. Camera (color, Betacam SP), Paul Otter, Richard Ranken, John Warwick, Mike Wilkie; editors, David Hill, Yann Dedet; music, Dan Carey; sound, Jane Barnet, Marc Hatch. Reviewed at Vue sur les Docs festival (competing), Marseilles, France, June 17, 1994. Running time: **81 MIN.**

"Tales from a Hard City" follows the mostly deluded showbiz aspirations of several plucky young residents of economically depressed Sheffield, England. Closer to scripted drama than straight docu, pic was finished on June 16 and world preemed the next day at the Marseilles docu fest, where it took top honors to mixed response.

Spirited petty thief Glen has a knack for karaoke. Paul, an ex-boxer-turned-actor, spars verbally with his "image consultant" and tries to sweet-talk local auto dealers into a free car in exchange for his charisma. Foxy young mother Sarah tries to parlay the "Greek incident" — she was jailed while on holiday in Greece for alleged lewd dancing — from tabloid fodder into a recording career under the gung-ho but questionable guidance of various entrepreneurial types, including local bar owner Wayne Chadwick.

Casual, somewhat indulgent account has its comic moments but remains a slight piece of work about basically likable young people trying to make a buck against the odds.

Suspiciously neat evolution of pic's narrative and its aura of partial re-enactment fueled debate at the Mareilles unspooling about where the true boundaries of documentary currently lie.
—*Lisa Nesselson*

BETRAYAL

(FORRADERI)

(SWEDISH-BRITISH-DANISH — DOCU)

A Charon Film/Channel 4 Television/ Swedish Film Institute/Swedish Television/National Film Board of Denmark/Nordic Film & TV Fund production. Produced, directed by Fredrik von Krusenstjerna. Co-executive producer, Michael Darlow. Camera (color), Jan Roed; editor, Niels Pagh Andersen; sound, Dolby. Reviewed at Vue sur les Docs festival (competing), Marseilles, France, June 17, 1994. Running time: **58 MIN.**
Interviewer: Bjorn Cederberg.
Narrator: John Hurt.
(German dialogue, English narration)

A dense, info-laden and handsomely produced docu, "Betrayal" charts the firsthand efforts of a former friend to get at the inner workings of enigmatic Sascha Anderson who, for 20 years, led a double life as a leading cultural figure in the East German dissident underground and as a high-ranking informer to the Stasi. Involving pic, which has been shown in Denmark and is slated for Swedish TV and Channel 4 airings in the fall, is a tasty morsel that raises more questions than it answers.

On-camera interviewer Bjorn Cederberg — a German-speaking Swede whose investigative reflections are spoken to excellent dramatic effect by British thesp John Hurt — met Sascha in 1983 in Prenzlauer Berg, the district of East Berlin where he and his dissident artist friends hung out, and believed that he knew him fairly well. So his shock mirrored that of Sascha's immediate circle upon discovering that the man they all knew as "a fearless and magnetic figure in the illegal underground" was a compulsive liar and accomplished spy. Three chief informers emerge in secret police Stasi files: All of them are cover names for Anderson.

Cederberg speaks to Sascha's former pals, ex-girlfriends, erstwhile contacts in the Stasi hierarchy (lensed only as shadows) and Sascha himself, trying to piece together Anderson's peculiar and exceedingly active past.

Anderson apparently got his start as an informer by ingratiating himself into the script department of the Film Academy at DEFA-Studio (now Babelsberg) in the mid-1970s. A publisher by trade who agreed to appear in the film and was always aware of the camera, Anderson says, "In my view I never worked for the Stasi. According to their files, I worked for them. But that's not my opinion."

Close to one-fifth of East Germans ended up in Stasi files, whose extensiveness, per helmer, puts the Pentagon's or the FBI's holdings to shame. The camera tags along as Conny, a long-standing friend of Sascha's, goes to read her files after introductory counseling by a social worker.

Filmmakers arranged a surprise on-camera confrontation between Conny and Sascha in Rome two years after the scandal broke. Sascha is briefly flustered, surprised that the docu crew was prepared to fork out the money for Conny's plane ticket. "Documentaries are expensive these days," says Conny. The awkward but incisive confrontation leaves no doubt that Anderson ratted on his friends for two decades yet fails to see the harm in his actions.

Tech credits are pro. A longer version of the story would be welcome. —*Lisa Nesselson*

OTAKU

(FRENCH — DOCU — VIDEO)

A Cargo Films/France 2 production, with participation of Television Suisse Romande. Produced, directed by Jean-Jacques Beineix. In color. Editor, Jackie Bastide; interviewer, Etienne Barral. Reviewed at Vue Sur les Docs festival (Sunny Side of the Doc market), Marseilles, France, June 18, 1994. Running time: **52 MIN.**

A coolly fascinating look at the techno-cocooning, gizmo-worshipping and obsessive doll-collecting of a substantial slice of urban male Japanese society, Jean-Jacques Beineix's "Otaku" suggests that nerds and dweebs — who are in the vanguard of "virtual relationships" — may inherit the Earth.

Visually snappy and intellectually intriguing docu — which exists in 52-, 77- and 168-minute cuts — is a natural for TV slots and a potential tool for students concerned with alienation, sublimation and cracks in the Unified Front of Salarymen.

The word "otaku" is a polite form of address for obsessed hobbyists who prefer pixels to people and who stay at home pursuing their compulsive special interests to the exclusion of all other activities.

Subjects are lucid about their stunted emotional growth and failure to make the transition to adult human relationships. One nocturnal otaku compares himself to the anti-social young clerk who's obsessed with an opera singer in helmer's "Diva."

Many otaku fixate on so-called "idols" — primped-to-order young female pop stars whose photos they stock on home computers to fuel daydreams and masturbatory fantasies.

The only teen in a group of three video-porn enthusiasts who's actually experienced sex says he found it "a bit painful" and it gave him a backache.

One of pic's best segs shows how dewy schoolgirls are photographed and then mass-produced as miniature doll replicas available in kits to be snapped up by thousands of collectors. One 34-year-old vice president of a magazine firm solemnly admits to owning 200 such dolls, one of which he confides in. Stumped by a question about how he would interact with "a real woman," he replies, "You have to meet one first."

Docu presents plenty of professional opinions to go with the frank confessions of otaku. Voiceover translation in British- and Japanese-accented English is clear and concise if a bit sterile.
—*Lisa Nesselson*

BUCCANEER SOUL

(ALMA CORSARIA)

(BRAZILIAN)

A Serene Prods./Dezenove Some Imagens production. Produced by Sara Silveira. Co-producer, Donald Ranvaud. Directed, written by Carlos Reichenbach. Camera (color, b&w), Reichenbach; editor, Cristina Amaral; music, Reichenbach; art direction, Renato Theobaldo; sound, Jose Luiz Sasso. Reviewed at Pesaro Intl. Festival of New Cinema (competing), June 18, 1994. Running time: **116 MIN.**
Rivaldo Torres .... Bertrand Duarte
Teodoro Xavier .... Jandir Ferrari
Anesia .... Andrea Richa
Eliana .... Mariana De Moraes
Verinha .... Flor
Magalhaes .... Jorge Fernando
With: Emilio Di Biasi, Carolina Ferraz, Abrahao Farc, Roberto Miranda, Ricardo Pettine, Paulo Marrafao, David Y Pond, Amaziles Almeida, Rosana Seligmann, Raul Figueiredo.

Brazilian auteur Carlos Reichenbach's "Buccaneer Soul" presents a dense jungle of personal and political history nourished by a steady stream of references-cum-homages to literature, cinema, music, poetry and philosophy. Fragmented, freewheeling story of a Sao Paolo intellectual and his long-standing sidekick ranges from absolute lucidity to opaque symbolism to playful digression, but remains at all times a seductive, almost hallucinatory trip that should figure widely on the festival trail.

The central duo is introspective, death-obsessed Torres (Bertrand Duarte) and his more outgoing, moneyed friend Xavier (Jandir Ferrari). Encasing recollections of the chums' adolescence and early adulthood is a party in a seedy pastry bar to launch their volume of poetry.

Flashing back to 1957, the film tracks the birth of their friendship,

then moves into the '60s to recap their first amorous encounters and visits to the local movie house. Frequent returns to the party tie past to present. The arrival of hooker Anesia (Andrea Richa) sparks a memory in which Torres accompanies her on a parental visit posing as her fiance at her bullying pimp's request.

Reichenbach tosses in surreal elements with a liberal hand. Most bizarre passage is one in which a pianist plays Debussy at the poetry book launch, setting off a volley of image associations and memory flashes. The Chinese bar proprietor mind-travels to Hong Kong, while the publisher's floozy dreams of hula-dancing in Hawaii.

Footage for this reportedly comes from Super-8 movies shot by Reichenbach's father in the early '50s. The sequence plays a little like a short film spliced into the larger frame, but despite the choppy structure throughout, the film never loses its flow.

Aficionados of cinema *novo*, and of Brazilian culture in general will get their teeth into Reichenbach's cult-of-the-dead concerns, his paean to Sao Paolo and his sprawling canvas splashed with national influences.

Even more wide-ranging are his nods to international filmmaking inspirations, from jokey asides (Samuel Fuller being casually handed an Oscar he's owed as he leaves a theater) to direct citations evoking Godard, Vigo and Mizoguchi.

Virtually a one-man show technically, the film is smartly shot and scored by Reichenbach. Music is deftly but subtly used to set a different tone with each change of period. Perfs are on-target. Pic shared main prize honors in the traditionally non-competitive Pesaro fest's 30th anniversary feature competition. —*David Rooney*

THE LULLABY

(IAVNANA)

(GEORGIAN)

An Arci Studio/Georgia Film Concern/Sameba Studios production. Directed by Nana Dzanelidze. Screenplay, Nino Natrosvili, Dzanelidze, based on stories by Jacob Gogebasvili. Camera (color), George Beridze; editor, Tata Tvalechrelidze; music, Dzansug Kachidze, Vachtang Kachidze; art direction, Nikolai Zandukeli, Giya Bagadze; sound, Michail Kilasonidze, Guram Gogua. Reviewed at Pesaro Intl. Festival of New Cinema (competing), June 23, 1994. Running time: **76 MIN.**
With: Nata Murvanidze, Nino Abuladze, Maja Bagrationi, Niko Tavadze, Archil Tsitisvili, Kachi Kavsadze, Zeinab Botsvadze, Ediser Magalasvili.

Debut feature from Georgian femme helmer Nana Dzanelidze is a handsomely filmed

but indigestibly syrupy fable about reaffirming national and cultural identity. Earnest humanistic quality could usher this leisurely folkloric froth into the odd festival or quality tube berth, but ultimately "The Lullaby" will sing most audiences to sleep.

A good half-hour of the slim running time is taken up with an ambling prologue in which familial bliss is established to saturation point. The sun-drenched idyll shows an aristocratic couple in rural Georgia in an unspecified historical period. With their beloved infant daughter, Keto, the group prays and plays together, spontaneously breaking into rapturous choral recitals like some kind of Pre-Raphaelite Von Trapp family.

Enter two scruffy vagabonds, who partake of the saintly family's hospitality and then kidnap Keto. Though not explicitly tagged by nationality, the villains appear to be Muslims from Georgia's neighboring republic Azerbaijan, lending the film a decidedly propagandistic political subtext.

Beautifully shot and lit, and edited with a succession of quick cuts, the film overdoses on its greeting-card visual splendors. Intense playing from the adult thesps can't ward off a stolid, dramatically flat feeling, while kid cast members push cutesiness to the limit. Pic was a contentious choice to split the best film prize at Pesaro. —*David Rooney*

JLG/JLG — SELF-PORTRAIT IN DECEMBER

(JLG/JLG — AUTOPORTRAIT DE DECEMBRE)

(FRENCH-SWISS)

A Gaumont/Peripheria production. Produced, directed, written by Jean-Luc Godard. In color and Dolby SR. No further credits available. Reviewed at Pesaro Intl. Festival of New Cinema (non-competing), June 25, 1994. Running time: **54 MIN.**

An inebriating dialectical diary of words, sounds, images and landscapes, Jean-Luc Godard's "Self-Portrait in December" sees the Nouvelle Vague's most enduring *enfant terrible* focus on his own life and work by focusing on everything around him. Festivals, cinematheques and cultural webs should welcome this galloping reflection on the filmmaker's rapport with art, nature, politics, philosophy, history, and most of all, cinema.

Shot in and around Godard's home in Switzerland last winter, the film maneuvers adroitly between personal assessment by abstraction and by association. Solemn, snow-covered fields and frozen lakes are juxtaposed with darkly glowing interiors, evocatively lit by single lamps or insistently featured windows.

Godard himself comes into view only gradually, beginning as a disembodied voice, then as a shadowy profile, then shot from behind or from large distances, before eventually moving into the light. Seen in his production offices and editing suite, or at home idly conversing with his nubile housekeeper, he portrays himself as something of a misanthrope, seeming to simultaneously play up and debunk his living-legend status.

His thoughts emerge as an uninterrupted, chaotic train of ideas, from studied reflections to spontaneous responses, restlessly questioning the nature of creativity, culture and learning like some kind of wily high-art channel-surfer.

Along with light-flooded windows and doors, Godard uses screens within the screen as a minor motif, running occasional clips and snatches of dialogue from films by contemporaries and admired directors such as Jacques Demy, Nicholas Ray, and Roberto Rossellini.

Soundtrack is a vigorous melange of overlapping, often unintelligible dialogue, multifarious sound sources and sonorously clanging musical chords. The elements are featured to great effect, with wind, rain, storms and lapping waves all cranked up to a thunderous level.

Superlative technical contributions go unacknowledged, however, since the film carries no credits at either end. —*David Rooney*

PESHAVAR WALTZ

(RUSSIAN)

An Iskona Studio production. Directed, written by Timur Bekmambetov, Gennadij Kajumov. Camera, Alexander Aranysev, Sergej Trofimov; music, Alexander Vojtinskij. Reviewed at Karlovy Vary Film Festival (competing), July 5, 1994. Running time: **87 MIN.**
Charlie Palmer .... Barry Kushner
Dubois .... Viktor Verzbickij

One of the strongest contenders for recognition in what has been an otherwise modestly meritorious pack, "Peshavar Waltz" is a startling, gripping anti-war manifesto from Russian first-time directors Timur Bekmambetov and Gennadij Kajumov. Tagged by one jury member as "a Russian 'Platoon' " and by another admirer as "Tarkovsky meets Tarantino," "Peshavar" examines a bloody incident from the former Soviet Union's Vietnam: the war in Afghanistan.

Resourcefully and powerfully shot by the young directing duo for an astonishing $50,000, violent war pic puts to shame most Hollywood actioners with hundreds of times the meager budget and will gain film world's attention both for its raw force and exhumation of facts that have heretofore gained little notice in the Western press.

Though confusing at times and technically rough around the edges (especially the sound), like "Terminator" for James Cameron, "sex, lies, and videotape" for Steven Soderbergh and "Reservoir Dogs" for Quentin Tarantino, "Peshavar" will provide a launching pad for unknown filmmakers' careers once pic gets eyed outside this sleepy Bohemian village fest.

At a military base in Pakistan's Peshavar region, a group of Russian prisoners of war grab control of the base, unwittingly aided by British journalist Charlie Palmer (Barry Kushner), who is being assisted by French medic Dubois (Viktor Verzbickij) in his documentation of the camp conditions.

Once the Russians wipe out their captors, seize control of the radio transmitter and barricade themselves in, Palmer and Dubois find themselves hostages and witnesses to a barbaric insurrection where the lines between friends, allies, deserters, warriors and various ethnicities are blurred or smashed. The film feels so authentic that at times its freewheeling narrative seems like a reconstruction of doc footage of an actual event. The Russian thesps who play the P.O.W.s are completely convincing, their faces wracked with pain and terror that haunt long after the film wraps up.

Dubois is forced to attend to the wounded and dying, and Palmer weaves in and out of the bloodshed with his camera capturing every moment of heroism, betrayal and confusion. The story, reportedly fact-based and revealed only by Russian dissident Andrei Sakharov, indicts not only the brutal Pakistani collaborators who held the men in subhuman conditions, but the Russian invaders and the cynical geopolitics of American advisers who look on as the rebellion is wiped out by a helicopter bombing raid courtesy of the P.O.W. military command.

Although the story fails to develop a clear narrative or establish characters in a conventional manner, and though the details of the event get lost in the mud, blood and smoke, and key dialogue moments are garbled, "Peshavar" nonetheless creates memorable, passionate images.

It's easier to believe that the film could gain a following from war film fans who will find it a low-budget "Das Boot" than it is to read that it won first prize at a "student" film festival last year. If this is a "student" film and Oliver Stone's "Heaven and Earth" a big-budget studio pic, perhaps it's time for our top action helmers to check into a Russian night school class.
—*Steven Gaydos*

MAKAROV

(RUSSIAN)

Directed by Vladimir Chotinenko. Screenplay, Valerij Zalotucha. Camera (color) Jevgenij Grebnev; music, Alexandr Pantykin. Reviewed at Karlovy Vary Film Festival (After Revolution), July 4, 1994. Running time: **95 MIN.**
Makarov .... Sergej Makoveckij
With: Jelena Majórava, Irina Metlidkaja, Vladimir Iljin, Sergej Parsin, Leonid Okunev, Jevgenij Steblov.

Like its double-entendre title, "Makarov" is a richly layered film that juxtaposes the tradition of image-laden Russian poetry against gritty, crime-infested, post-revolutionary Moscow. Guns have replaced language as the forbidden source of power. Whispers in dark corners and encounters with back-alley thugs create an edgy mood that sets the story on its well-paced spiraling descent. Discomfort factor limits film's international appeal beyond the arthouse circuit.

Makarov is the name of both central characters: a Russian poet (Sergej Makoveckij) with writer's block and the hand pistol he buys. "Need a Makarov?" hisses a black marketeer to the surprised poet.

And the question reverberates throughout the film: Does Russia need its poets? Or its guns? Echoing sounds build a tension and fear that overcome the poet's initial resistance, and he pays the demanded 10,000 rubles — the payment from his just-published book of poetry. So begins his deception.

At their home, Makarov's wife reads him a poem about a bullet destined to find its target. "Maybe it's better when ignorance is bliss," she recites as Makarov hides his Makarov in the toilet tank. This technique runs throughout the film, with characters quoting poetry that enhances or comments ironically on the action. And, in a recurring image, Makarov catches sight of himself in the mirror, forcing him to reflect on what he is becoming.

While family, friends, even strangers urge him to go on with his writing, Makarov becomes more obsessed with the gun, which seems to take on a life of its own, He sculpts the gun's impression from the pages of a poetry book and hides it there, the gun literally replacing poetry.

Jagged, pulse-driven music and crashing glass accompany Makarov's tensed-wire emotions. Fine score and solid technical credits enhance the film, but Russian poetry steals the movie.
—*Cathy Meils*

THE SANDMAN

(DER SANDMANN)

(GERMAN)

A Raphaela-Filmverleih production. Produced by Anja Schmidt-Zaringer, Karl Margraf. Directed, written by Eckhart Schmidt. Based on the novel by E.T.A. Hoffmann. Camera, Johannes Kirchlechner; editor, Raoul Sternberg; music, Chopin, Vivaldi; costume design, Sibilla Pavenstedt; sound, Feona Marshall; makeup, Dorothea Goldfuss. Reviewed at Karlovy Vary Film Festival (competing), July 4, 1994. Running time: **104 MIN.**
Daniel .... Lorenzo Flaherty
Olimpia .... Stella Vordemann
Clara .... Sabrina Paravicini
Coppola .... Erik Schumann

A cool-toned adult fairy tale about a young man's obsessive quest to discover his exceedingly strange childhood roots, German director Eckhart Schmidt's "The Sandman" (based on the E.T.A. Hoffmann story) uses a trio of attractive young leads and dreamlike Italian locations to deliver a stylish entertainment that could grab international art circuit auds. Though a German production with Euro thespers, pic is in English, an important asset for this arty, offbeat fable involving an autoerotic *menage a trois.*

On a romantic vacation visit to his Italian hometown, Daniel (Lorenzo Flaherty) troubles his lover, Clara (Sabrina Paravicini), by incessantly wandering off and exhibiting such odd behavior as breaking and entering the luxurious estate of mysterious tycoon Coppola (Erik Schumann). Seems Daniel is having flashbacks to his unhappy childhood, which we discover included an industrial accident that killed his father, an event he somehow connects to Coppola.

But the real object of his attention is Coppola's glacially beautiful daughter Olimpia (Stella Vordemann), a stunner given to wandering the estate clad in a number of costumes worthy of a Victoria's Secret catalog. As Daniel grows more and more aroused by Olimpia, and increasingly convinced of Coppola's guilt, Clara's frustration finally drives her to split for Venice.

Once left to his devices with Olimpia, Daniel discovers that there's much more to her and his childhood memories than he ever imagined. Turns out that Olimpia isn't a normal sweetheart in any sense of the word, but is in fact a bionic babe created by Coppola in the factory of Daniel's nightmares from his youth. Quest becomes both a desire to get under Olimpia's skin to see what makes her tick, and a fierce battle to kill Coppola.

Tale unfolds like source material for "Blade Runner" and plays with Daniel's repetitive pursuits in a fashion as detached as Resnais' "Last Year at Marienbad." Smart handlers will steer this theatrically toward young intelligentsia who could find it a compelling date-night diversion sure to stimulate controversy as well as hormones. Seriousness of purpose and icy airs keep it far from the sleaze category, though, and pic could develop cult following and perform well for vid and cable.　　　　*—Steven Gaydos*

THE BEGINNING AND THE END

(PRINCIPO Y FIN)

(MEXICAN)

An IMCINE/Fondo de Fomento a la Calidad Cinematografica/Alameda Films production. Produced by Alfredo Ripstein. Directed by Arturo Ripstein. Scre enplay, Pal Alicia Garciadiego, based on the novel by Naguib Mahfouz. Camera (color, Panavision widescreen), Claudio Rocha; editor, Rafael Castanedo; music, Lucia Alvarez; sound, Antonio Diego, David Baksht; production manager, Gerardo Barrera; postproduction manager, Daniel Birman Ripstein. Reviewed April 11, 1994, at the AMC Kabuki 8. (In San Francisco Intl. Film Festival.) Running time: **183 MIN.**

Gabriel Botero	Ernesto Laguardia
Ignacia Botero	Julieta Egurrola
Nicolas Botero	Bruno Bicher
Mireya Botero	Lucia Munoz
Guama Botero	Alberto Estrella
Julia	Blanca Guerra
Carinoso	Alonso Echanove
Natalia	Veronica Merchant
Cesat	Luis Felipe Tovar
Polvoron	Ernesto Yanez
Isabel	Luisa Huertas

Veteran director Arturo Ripstein has transferred Nobel Prize-winning Egyptian author Naguib Mahfouz's 1940s novel to a contemporary Mexican

setting with "The Beginning and the End." While switch does essentially no harm, this somber, somewhat emotionally distant effort lacks the operatic sweep its tragic family-epic material seems to cry for. Pic, which has been making the fest rounds for the past several months, will prove a tough sell outside Spanish-speaking territories.

At start, the middle-class Botero clan is left unexpectedly impoverished by the father's abrupt demise. Matriarch Ignacia settles affairs with coldblooded speed, tossing out ne'er-do-well eldest son Guama to cut household expenses. (Still, the family is soon forced out, relocating in a basement flop.) He tumbles into substance-abusive lifestyle as bar bouncer and sometime pimp, later drifting toward an ill-fated liaison with drug dealers.

Aspiring law student Gabriel is Dona Ignacia's favored offspring. Demanding that all-too-pliant remaining children Nicolas and Mireya sacrifice their futures to ensure his, she calls Gabriel "our high card, and we have to place all our bets on him." Thus reduced to drudge work, Nicolas loses his own shot at further schooling; then Mama steps in to ruin romance with a sympathetic divorcee. Mireya fares even worse. Desperate for any diversion from sewing-shop slavery, her sexual exploitation at hands of a caddish neighborhood baker leads to the risky solace that streetwalking affords.

Slow-moving narrative builds toward a suitably shocking denouement, when the ruthlessly self-centered Gabriel — now facing possible disaster en route to bourgeois success — convinces one sibling to cover his tracks by committing suicide.

Story brings to mind such epics of familial collapse as "Rocco and His Brothers" (especially in the good/bad brother dynamic between callous Gabriel and saintly Nicolas), with Ignacia a fearsome Iphigenia-Medea figure of heedless matriarchal ambition.

But there's little cinematic grandeur or profound depth of sympathy in Ripstein's grim, tightly focused account, leaving intended mythic dimensions at a remove from what becomes a grotesque pileup of slum-life catastrophes. More impassioned treatment could have heightened several scenes to much greater impact, as when Ignacia disgustedly pours Guama's stolen heroin stash down the sink — realizing seconds later that she's probably sealed its doom. Yet pic draws scant suspense from such twists; the bleak atmosphere suggests these characters are lost from the start.

Performances are uniformly good, albeit reigned in by director's insistence on low-key realism. Lensing's preponderance of close-

ups similarly adds to a mood that, however intendedly claustrophobic, ends up sapping the power of a potentially devastating sage. Tech work in other departments is pro.

While a respectably crafted downer, "The Beginning and the End's" cold progress belies Ripstein's avowed aim to explore "the wound of mankind" in an "operatic tone." His glum restraint results in something closer to overblown conventional melodrama.

—Dennis Harvey

REFLECTIONS ON A CRIME

A Roger Corman presentation of a Concorde Films/Saban Pictures production in association with Forrester Films. (International sales: Saban Pictures, L.A.) Produced by Gwen Field, Barbara Klein, Carol Dunn Trussel, Alida Camp. Executive producers, Corman, Lance H. Robbins, Mike Elliott. Directed, written by Jon Purdy. Camera (Foto-Kem color), Teresa Medina; editor, Norman Buckley; music, Parmer Fuller; production design, Arlan Jay Vetter; art direction, Roger Belk; costume design, Denna Appel; sound (Ultra-Stereo), Christopher Taylor; associate producer/casting, Billy DaMota; assistant director, Marco Black. Reviewed at Seattle Intl. Film Festival, June 10, 1994. Running time: **96 MIN.**

Regina	Mimi Rogers
Colin	Billy Zane
James	John Terry
Howard	Kurt Fuller
Tina	Lee Garlington
Ellen	Nancy Fish
Doctor	Frank Birney
Attorney	Adrienne Regard
Daniel	Alain Ohanian
Haircutter	Ina Parker

A full-bore star turn by Mimi Rogers, playing a glamorous killer about to take the chair, is the main selling point for this slickly made, intellectually empty character study. Sharp style on a mini-budget and uncompromising seriousness lend some distinction to Jon Purdy's first feature. Fests might take note, but pic's cloistered, two-character-play nature and self-importance make this a tough prospect theatrically.

College-thesis title is the first tip-off to pretensions far outstripping by-the-numbers dialogue and telepic plotting. Rogers, who won an audience award in Seattle for her work here, toplines as Regina, convicted of killing her pompous husband because "divorce would have broken his heart." From this flimsy bit of moral ambiguity, writer/helmer Purdy fashions a claustrophobic, execution-eve faceoff between Rogers and young "media junky" guard Colin (Billy Zane), who has bribed his way into her holding cell.

Rogers then spins her tale of the events leading up to the fatal en-

counter, some repeated from every angle, with the only twist that hubby is dispatched by different means each time.

That sounds intriguing on paper, but Purdy's leaden hand guarantees hard labor for all involved. Problems begin with the casting of John Terry as the rich, overbearing spouse: His thesping is so soapy that the many marital-banter scenes veer dangerously close to "SCTV"-type parody.

Although "Reflections" boasts plenty of women behind the camera, the man in charge is more than capable of decimating any claim the pic makes for probing female psychology. B-meister Roger Corman exec produced, and the gratuitous ogling of Rogers' body (or her body double) is certainly more Russ Meyer than Chantal Akerman. The upscale effects of Teresa Medina's stylish lensing and Denna Appel's smooth clothing (some people would kill for Rogers' prison garb) serve only to undercut Purdy's serious intent.

Even the tough-talking lead can't resist hyping her part for relentless meller effect, although Rogers' character's resolute acceptance of responsibility for her deed and fate is refreshing, even bracing. Zane's steady restraint, while generous, sometimes leaves her hanging with too much ham on display.

—Ken Eisner

FAUST

(FRENCH-CZECH REPUBLIC-BRITISH-GERMAN)

A Heart of Europe (Prague)/Lumen Films (Paris) presentation, in co-production with BBC Bristol, Koninck (U.K.) and Pandora Film (Hamburg), of an Athanor production, with participation of CNC (France) and Czech Ministry of Culture. (International sales: Celluloid Dreams, Paris.) Produced by Jaromir Kallista. Executive producers, Colin Rose (for BBC), Karl Baumgartner, Keith Griffiths, Michael Havas, Hengameh Panahi. Directed, written by Jan Svankmajer. Camera (color), Svatopluk Maly; editor, Marie Zemanova; art direction, Eva Svankmajerova; costume design, Ruzena Blahova; sound (Dolby), Ivo Spalj; choreography, Daria Vobornikova; animation, Bedrich Glaser. Reviewed at Carre Seita screening room, Paris, May 3, 1994. (In Cannes Film Festival — Un Certain Regard.) Running time: **95 MIN.**

Faust	Petr Cepek

In "Faust," master stop-action animator Jan Svankmajer interjects joltingly surreal animated imagery into a live-action treatment of the legend of a man who signs a deal with the devil without consulting agent or lawyer. Fest and tube programmers will want to check it out.

As in vet surrealist's prior feature-length pic, "Alice," animated passages are so startling and inventive that the narrative tissue between bursts of stop-action animation, pixilation and puppetry enchants far less in comparison.

Faust (Petr Cepek) at first shrugs off lures from Mephistopheles' henchmen — which begin as cryptic photocopied maps handed out to commuters at a Prague subway exit — but ends up summoning the devil's helper.

Faust declares that Lucifer can have his soul if he guarantees 24 years of pleasure-filled life in exchange. The deal works out differently. Faust finds himself an actor and then, literally, a puppet on a theater stage.

Outstanding animated set pieces include a clay fetus growing in a test tube that, once "born," sits up and retains its baby body while its head goes through all the stages of aging, until it turns into a clone of Faust's head, only to decay and die. Wonderfully expressive miniature puppet scribes issue forth when the time comes for Faust to sign his soul away in blood: Marionettes representing the devil get into a pixilated rumble with angel marionettes.

Evocative live-action silliness includes a corps de ballet performing with rakes in the great outdoors.

—*Lisa Nesselson*

SQUADRON
(SWADRON)
(POLISH)

A Warsaw Film Studios production in association with Zebra Films, Arkadia, High Speed Films, AK Prods. Produced by Julisuz Machulski, Jacek Moczydlowski. Directed, written by Machulski, based on short stories by Stanislaw Rembek. Camera (color), Witold Adamek; editor, Jadwiga Zajicek; music, Krzesimir Debski; production design, Dorota Ignaczak, Valentin Gidulianov; costume design, Magdalena Biernawska; sound, Nikodem Wolk-Laniewski. Reviewed at Cannes Film Festival (market), May 21, 1994. Running time: **101 MIN.**
With: Radoslaw Pazura, Janusz Gajos, Sergei Szakurov, Jan Machulski, Katarzyna Lochowska, Bernard Pierre Donnadieu, Tomasz Stockinger, Jerzy Nowak.

The anti-war sentiments of the Polish-produced "Squadron" provide the lavish period costumer with a universal resonance and appeal. Yet the familiarity of the story and an ambivalent conclusion work against the material's commercialism. It should spark some critical interest, but international theatrical prospects are tepid.

Set during an insurrection of Polish peasants in 1863, the tale focuses on Fydor (Radoslaw Pazura), a young officer in a regiment of Russian dragoons sent to quell the unrest. He initially confronts his commission with zeal, but the reality of the war zone turns his passion into confusion. The brutality of his fellow soldiers in quashing the rebellion appears hopelessly out of balance with the modest demands of the Poles.

It's no coincidence that writer/director Julisuz Machulski slaps his film with a title that recalls "Platoon." Though set a century apart, the themes and situations have strong parallels. The confrontation between military and native factions also echoes the more recent "Geronimo."

"Squadron's" vantage point is a little too cold and distant. Its protagonist is a cipher who's troubled, though detached, as he witnesses racism, sadism and other horrors of war. His inability to take action or respond may ring true to life but produces a less than compelling emotional conclusion.

While Machulski leaves us short of a catharsis, he does engage the mind and provides a stunning pictorial display. The production values and period detail of the film are peerless. It is provocative, if unconsummated, material that's too heavily weighted toward the cerebral. —*Leonard Klady*

DREAMPLAY
(DROMSPEL)
(NORWEGIAN-SWEDISH)

An Unni Straume Filmproduksjon (Norway)/Trust AB (Sweden)/Nordic Film & Television Fund production, with support of Swedish and Norwegian Film Institutes. Line produced by Imagine Prods. (England). (International sales: SlotMaschine, Paris.) Produced by Unni Straume, Bente Erichsen. Co-executive producers, Lars Jonsson, Peter Aalbaek Jensen. Directed, written by Straume, based on August Strindberg's play "Ett Dromspel." Camera (b&w), Harald Paalgaard; editor, Mikael Leschilowsky; music, Rolf Wallin; art direction, Carle Lange; costume design, Runna Fonne; sound (Dolby), Sturla Einarson; consultant, Wojciech Marczewski. Reviewed at Carre Seita screening room, Paris, May 4, 1994. (In Cannes Film Festival — Un Certain Regard.) Running time: **89 MIN.**
Agnes .... Ingvild Holm
Lawyer .... Bjorn Wilberg Andersen
Poet .... Bjorn Sundquist
Ticket Seller .... Liv Ullmann
Victoria .... Bibi Andersson
Blind Man .... Erland Josephson
Man in Cinema .... Finn Schau
(Norwegian dialogue)

In "Dreamplay," a heady smattering of philosophical and rhetorical issues is lensed with cinematic and intellectual rigor in fine-grained black-and-white. Arty drama — adapted from Swedish playwright August Strindberg's 1902 "A Dream Play" — mixes elements from the Bible, mythology and poetry into a disjointed and mostly dreary meditation on the human condition as investigated by God's daughter.

Although arresting faces of top Scandi thesps hold the screen, pic demands the kind of attentive patience that is rare beyond fest and educational settings.

Heavenly visitor Agnes (Ingvild Holm, who bears a deliberate resemblance to the young Bibi Andersson) descends to Earth to sound out a cross-section of mortals on the sources of their pains and sorrows.

Agnes, who has a gamin charm that becomes more careworn in the "mud and dust" of Earth, ends up married to a penniless lawyer, a killjoy with whom she lives in a stuffy basement with their infant.

In a classy nod that works on several levels, Liv Ullmann is the cashier at a cinema where a film starring an actress named Victoria is showing. Victoria is none other than Bibi Andersson, and the unidentified film is Bergman's "Persona" (in which Ullmann and Andersson starred.)

One male repeat customer is so enamored of his personal screen goddess that he tells Agnes he knows only one woman — Victoria. He gets the chance to meet his now middle-aged idol, with interesting results.

Agnes hooks up with a moody poet who, contending that all beauty must be dragged through the mud, warns angelic Agnes that her thoughts will no longer fly if she gets too much clay on her wings.

Pic is chock-full of dialogue — much of it ponderous — yet its lensing, much of which is in dark subterranean settings, or rain and murk, is resplendent. Excellent sound design adds to the ethereal atmosphere, and meditative pace fits the moody material. Thesps, most of whom take a theatrical tack, are fine throughout. —*Lisa Nesselson*

IT COULD HAPPEN TO YOU

A TriStar Pictures release of an Adelson/Baumgarten and Lobell/Bergman production. Produced by Mike Lobell. Executive producers, Gary Adelson, Craig Baumgarten, Joseph Hartwick. Directed by Andrew Bergman. Screenplay, Jane Anderson. Camera (Technicolor), Caleb Deschanel; editor, Barry Malkin; music, Carter Burwell; production design, Bill Groom; art direction, Dennis Bradford; set decoration, George DeTitta Jr.; costume design, Julie Weiss; sound (Dolby), Gary Alper; assistant director, Henry Bronchtein; casting, John Lyons. Reviewed at the Beverly Connection, L.A., July 13, 1994. MPAA Rating: PG. Running time: **101 MIN.**
Charlie Lang .... Nicolas Cage
Yvonne Biasi .... Bridget Fonda
Muriel Lang .... Rosie Perez
Bo Williams .... Wendell Pierce
Angel .... Isaac Hayes
Jesu .... Victor Rojas
Jack Gross .... Seymour Cassel
Eddie Biasi .... Stanley Tucci
Walter Zakuto .... Red Buttons

Clearly out to tap the same heartline reached by last year's "Sleepless in Seattle," TriStar looks to have another summertime hit with this charming romantic comedy — one that's less gushy than "Sleepless" and will probably be a bit less flashy at the box office. Even so, the "Honeymoon in Vegas" team of director Andrew Bergman and star Nicolas Cage again find themselves holding a winning ticket.

Presented in fairy tale form — down to its awkward, "once upon a time" narrated introduction — "It Could Happen to You" cultivates and actually merits the designation "Capra-esque."

The simple premise (very loosely inspired by a true story) has affable New York cop Charlie (Cage) finding himself short of cash and promising hard-luck, recently bankrupted waitress Yvonne (Bridget Fonda) that he'll split anything he wins from the lottery with her in lieu of a tip. The ticket turns out to be a $4 million winner and, much to the chagrin of his avaricious wife, Muriel (Rosie Perez), Charlie decides to honor his pledge.

As Muriel proceeds to ostentatiously spend the loot, the bond between Charlie and Yvonne grows, with the two sharing good deeds that range from doling out free subway tokens to entertaining neighborhood kids.

In that respect, Bergman and writer Jane Anderson (who wrote

HBO's satiric "The Positively True Adventures of the Alleged Texas Cheerleader-Murdering Mom") wring a nice twist on the premise of "Indecent Proposal" — namely, the power of money not only to bring people together but to drive them apart.

What really make the film, however, are Bergman's general restraint despite the nature of the material, and the strong central performances. Cage and Fonda are extremely natural as the good-hearted lug and goodbye girl, while the squawking, raging Perez only needs to be fitted for a broomstick. Wendell Pierce also proves particularly likable as Charlie's partner, a cop with an affinity for the Knicks and carbohydrates.

While less obvious than "Sleepless" in terms of dripping romance, "It Could Happen to You" does emulate some of its formula, from the classic song score (which includes a new rendition of "Always" by Tony Bennett) to Caleb Deschanel's loving cinematography of the Big Apple.

Pic does have a balancing darker side, however, in Perez's character and its clever spoofing of

---

Cage and Fonda are extremely natural as the good-hearted lug and goodbye girl.

tabloid fascination in the central couple, which seems particularly timely in light of recent events. Bergman then really brings home the homage to Capra with the pic's warm, bordering-on-irresistible finale.

Other tech credits are fine, with particular kudos to Perez's laugh-out-loud wardrobe. As romances go, it should be noted the title works better than the initial "Cop Tips Waitress $2 Million" — a phrase that remains in the form of a front-page headline in the New York Post, which plays a fairly significant supporting role in the movie. —*Brian Lowry*

ANGELS IN THE OUTFIELD

A Buena Vista release of a Walt Disney Pictures presentation in association with Caravan Pictures. Produced by Irby Smith, Joe Roth, Roger Birnbaum. Executive producer, Gary Stutman. Directed by William Dear. Screenplay, Dorothy Kingsley, George Wells, Holly Goldberg Sloan, based on the motion picture "Angels in the Outfield," from the Turner Entertainment Co. library. Camera (Technicolor), Matthew F. Leonetti; editor, Bruce Green; music, Randy Edelman; production design, Dennis Washington; art direction, Thomas T. Targownik; set decoration, John Anderson; costume design, Rosanna Norton; sound (Dolby), Willie Burton; visual effects supervisor, Giedra Rackauskas; associate producer, Sloan; production manager/associate producer, Richard H. Prince; assistant director, L. Dean Jones Jr.; second unit director, Smith; casting, Pam Dixon Mickelson. Reviewed at the Mann Village Theatre, L.A., July 9, 1994. MPAA Rating: PG. Running time: **102 MIN.**

George Knox	Danny Glover
Mel Clark	Tony Danza
Maggie Nelson	Brenda Fricker
Al the Angel	Christopher Lloyd
Hank Murphy	Ben Johnson
Ranch Wilder	Jay O. Sanders
Roger	Joseph Gordon-Levitt
J.P.	Milton Davis Jr.
David Montagne	Taylor Negron

The term "crowd-pleasing" is frequently overused, but it applies to this — the latest in a line of so-so baseball movies, which serves up its corn so unabashedly it's hard to take offense at its sappiness. Most of its appeal is strictly for tykes, but as the roar of Disney's "The Lion King" gradually fades, this soft pop-up to the family audience could do some purring for the studio as well.

"Angels in the Outfield" shows scant devotion to the 1951 film on which it's based, changing the gender of its child lead and augmenting its implied magic with gauzily shot angels and other special effects — clearly aimed at a new generation of moviegoers that isn't trusted to appreciate subtlety or possess much imagination.

Updated for non-nuclear families of the '90s, the story centers on a foster child, Roger (Joseph Gordon-Levitt), whose shiftless father says he may be able to reclaim him when the boy's favorite team, the last-place California Angels, wins the pennant.

Roger offers up a prayer to make it so, and the stars twinkle in response — sending down a wild-eyed, honest-to-you-know-who angel, Al (Christopher Lloyd), whom only Roger can see.

Circumstances bring Roger and his friend J.P. (Milton Davis Jr., the tot made famous by bantering with Shaquille O'Neal in a Pepsi commercial) into contact with the Angels' sour manager, George Knox (Danny Glover), who ultimately

---

comes to believe the boy and uses his heavenly advice to lift the team out of the cellar.

William Dear, who directed the equally warm and fuzzy "Harry and the Hendersons," doesn't shy away from overblown sentimentality after a rather slow and grim first act, as glowing winged figures pop up all over the field. The script by Dorothy Kingsley, George Wells and Holly Goldberg Sloan also provides enough broad sight gags to entertain the moppet set.

In fact, "Angels" is so soft there's barely a Snidely Whiplash in the piece, other than a smarmy radio announcer (Jay O. Sanders) who's rooting for Knox to fail.

Glover brings the requisite mix of exasperation and reluctant warmth to his role, while Tony Danza has what amounts to an extended cameo as a washed-up pitcher given a second chance — enjoying the pic's most moving scene, but one that also demonstrates the depths to which the movie will sink in leaving no heartstring unplucked.

Tech credits are sound, if a little overdone in visualizing the angelic visitors. —*Brian Lowry*

NORTH

A Columbia Pictures release of a Castle Rock Entertainment production in association with New Line Cinema. Produced by Rob Reiner, Alan Zweibel. Executive producers, Jeffrey Stott, Andrew Scheinman. Directed by Reiner. Screenplay, Zweibel, Scheinman, based on the novel by Zweibel. Camera (Technicolor), Adam Greenberg; editor, Robert Leighton; music, Marc Shaiman; production design, J. Michael Riva; art direction, David Klassen; set decoration, Michael Taylor; costume design, Gloria Gresham; sound (Dolby), Bob Eber; assistant director, Frank Capra III; casting, Jane Jenkins, Janet Hirshenson. Reviewed at Sony Studios, Culver City, July 13, 1994. MPAA Rating: PG. Running time: **88 MIN.**

North	Elijah Wood
Narrator	Bruce Willis
Arthur Belt	Jon Lovitz
Winchell	Matthew McCurley
Judge Buckle	Alan Arkin
Barker	Richard Belzer
Grandpa	Abe Vigoda
North's Mom	Julia Louis-Dreyfus
North's Dad	Jason Alexander
Alaskan Mom	Kathy Bates
Alaskan Dad	Graham Greene
Ma Tex	Reba McEntire
Pa Tex	Dan Aykroyd
Amish Mom	Kelly McGillis
Amish Dad	Alexander Godunov
Donna Nelson	Faith Ford
Ward Nelson	John Ritter
Mrs. Ho	Lauren Tom
Governor Ho	Keone Young
Al	Robert Costanza

Rob Reiner's "North" is a shaggy-dog tale of a boy who "divorces" his parents and goes on an arduous trek to find his ideal mother and father. Ultimately, its message is the familiar "there's no place like home." But

---

rather than creating a modern "Wizard of Oz," this noble misfire just barely manages to pull back the curtain and reveal the man manipulating the image. Not quite a mature comedy nor an antic adventure for kids, the effort falls through the commercial cracks. B.O. prospects are soft here and abroad, despite the presence of name talent in front of and behind the camera.

The single-named title character (Elijah Wood) is the perfect preteen. He excels academically, at sports and in extracurricular activities. But his interaction with work-obsessed parents (Jason Alexander, Julia Louis-Dreyfus) is increasingly having a negative impact on his psyche.

So he goes to his "private place" — a chair store in a mall — to think it out. There he meets a man dressed in an Easter bunny suit (Bruce Willis) who listens to his problem and offers the sage advice that people just don't have any control when it comes to parents.

Rather than shrugging off the obvious, it gets North's mind working. Why can't he be a "free agent"? He bounces the idea off Winchell (Matthew McCurley) — the unctuous pint-sized *provocateur* who edits the school paper — who sets the wheels in motion for a precedent-setting court case.

Seemingly an extreme variation on recent child emancipation suits, "North" wades through the issue with guns blazing. The action throws his parents into simultaneous comas, and an eccentric judge (Alan Arkin) rules in favor of the lad. He adds the rider that North must reconcile with his family or find suitable new parents within two months. Otherwise he will be remanded to an orphanage.

While the boy travels the globe in his quest, Winchell fashions a children's revolution aimed at bringing grown-ups to their knees in servitude to their spawn.

This split focus diminishes the story's impact. There's a gentle quality to the little truths North uncovers as he screen-tests couples from such places as Texas and Alaska, and refugees from a 1950s sitcom. On the other hand, his schoolmate's fiendish manipulation of North's exploits chafes at an otherwise benign soul.

So, when the two elements collide in the finale, the result is a bloody draw unrelieved even by an upbeat ending.

The intrinsic failure of Alan Zweibel and Andrew Scheinman's script is that it tips its hand from the start. There are myriad clues that the boy's path will lead right back to his front yard. In the absence of tension, there ought to be more profound truths in the material.

July 18, 1994 (Cont.)

Reiner effected a deft touch with similar filigree stuff in "The Princess Bride," but in this outing fails to find the balance or tone that would make the parable work. Wood is the sane voice meant to glue the pieces together, and that burden proves too weighty for his small shoulders. Surrounded by human gargoyles, too often he's simply drowned out.

Tech credits are smooth, and Reiner even pulls off a fantasy song-and-dance sequence that suggests "North" might have made a dandy musical. The large ensemble cast is given no more than the opportunity to provide a glimpse of its talent. Wood and Willis, as a kind of guru conscience, wind up as observers when they should be pushing the story along.

"North's" prospects defy directional logic. It truly is that unique breed of misconceived entertainment that only a filmmaker of talent is capable of making.

—*Leonard Klady*

LIFE'S TOO GOOD

A Kind Stranger Production presentation. Executive producers, Amy Lee, Jerry Levine, Marilyn Root, Bob Root, Anne Paradis. Directed, written by Hilary Weisman. Camera (color), Frank Coleman; editor, Jim Ohm; music, Harry Fix; art direction, Keely Flow; sound, Lenny Manzo; assistant director, Donna De Angelis. Reviewed at Remis Auditorium, Museum of Fine Arts, Boston, June 25, 1994. Running time: **74 MIN.**

Tasha	Claudia Arenas
Victor	Michael Medico
Linda	Marjorie Burren
Ted	Paul Horn
Dani	Kathleen Cullen
Henry	Doug Miller
Grandma	Betsy White
Grandpa	John Blood

First feature by writer/director Hilary Weisman is a domestic comedy shot locally in Chelmsford, Mass. Knowing take on family relationships overcomes technical rough edges, resulting in a contender for fests and venues seeking indie product, especially from a femme p.o.v.

Story focuses on the mother and two daughters of the Rosen family. Mom Linda (Marjorie Burren) is a middle-aged widow perfectly happy to live with the comfy but passionless Ted (Paul Horn). Tasha (Claudia Arenas) and aspiring artist Victor (Michael Medico) are twentysomethings living with her mother while trying to figure out what they want to be when they grow up. Younger daughter Dani (Kathleen Cullen) is class valedictorian facing the upcoming graduation while goofing off with b.f. Henry (Doug Miller).

Film follows days leading up to graduation, as each of these couples tries to make sense of their relationships and their lives. Much of the focus is on Tasha and Victor, who talk out everything in their lives, sometimes to the detriment of the short feature's momentum. Best scenes show the family dynamics, such as when all six sit down to dinner eating different things (the grown-ups want steak while Gen X-ers prefer "healthier" fare).

Weisman has a good feel for how family members talk — and often don't listen — to each other. Best scene is when mother is called to her own parents' home on the night before graduation because her mother (Betsy White) has chosen this moment to rehash memories of her father (John Blood) having an affair 40 years earlier.

Visual tech credits are solid, with good use of locations, and belie ultralow budget. Sound work reveals pic's limitations, especially when overlapping conversations result in a muddy soundtrack.

—*Daniel M. Kimmel*

STAGGERED

(BRITISH — COMEDY)

An Entertainment Film Distributors release (U.K.) of a Big Deal Pictures production. Produced by Philippa Braithwaite. Executive producers, Chris Parkinson, Clifford Davis. Line producer, Helen Booth. Directed by Martin Clunes. Screenplay, Paul Alexander, Simon Braithwaite. Camera (Technicolor), Simon Kossoff; editor, Peter Delfgou; music, Peter Brewis; production design, Iain Andrews; art direction, Steve Ritchie; costume design, Ralph Holes; sound (Dolby), Geoff Neate; associate producers, Alexander, Braithwaite; assistant director, Richard Lingard. Reviewed at MGM Trocadero 2, London, July 12, 1994. Running time: **94 MIN.**

Neil Price	Martin Clunes
Gary	Michael Praed
Carmen	Anna Chancellor
Margaret	Sylvia Syms
Graham	Griff Rhys Jones
Flora	Virginia McKenna
Hilary	Sarah Winman
Sarah's Father	Michael Medwin

An oddball comedy about a mild-mannered geek who's shafted by his best friend on his stag night, "Staggered" is a likable Brit item that's average multiplex fodder. Good-looking but unevenly paced low-budgeter lacks the smarts to travel very far beyond home base but should tick over in ancillary.

Pic is first feature outing of TV comedy writer Paul Alexander and Simon Braithwaite, brother of producer Philippa and former ad sales manager of Brit movie mag Empire. Sitcom-style humor, peopled by a large gallery of British eccentrics, produces a steady flow of mild gags

but doesn't build a proper head of steam to go the distance as a feature.

TV comic Martin Clunes (who also helms, after experience in legit directing) stars as toy demonstrator Neil, due to marry pretty, middle-class Hilary (Sarah Winman). At his stag party, supposed best friend Gary (Michael Praed) slips a mickey in his beer, and next day Neil wakes up on a remote Scottish beach wearing only his watch.

Bulk of the pic consists of Neil's efforts to get back to London in the three days before his nuptials, while Gary, who arranged the whole diversion, insinuates himself into the favor of Hilary and her snooty mom (the reliable Sylvia Syms) to get his hands on the bride's money.

Characters encountered on the way include a Scottish recluse (a winning Virginia McKenna) who only wants to know whether Andy Williams is still alive; a traveling Welsh salesman, Graham (Griff Rhys Jones, working overtime), who's into suburban S&M sessions; and an apocalyptic medical researcher, Carmen (Anna Chancellor), who curiously proves Neil's salvation. En route, he also fractures his arm, gets arrested for jewel fencing and provokes a small amount of mayhem.

Though the episodic pic starts well, as a kind of accident-prone reverse road movie, it starts to run out of gas midway as the journey idea is dropped in favor of Neil's developing relationship with Carmen, and to focus on a cop (John Forgeham) who's permanently on Clunes' case. An outrageous dream sequence, in which Carmen performs an autopsy on the still-conscious Neil, sits strangely here.

Best of the supporting cast is Chancellor, as the psychologist with more dark currents than a buttered bun.

The vacant-looking Clunes (one of the stars of the BBC sitcom "Men Behaving Badly") is OK in the central role, though light on big-screen presence. As director, he's hit-and-miss, dropping the ball completely in some sequences (the revelation of Graham's secret; the weak finale) but scoring in others, especially in the early going.

Simon Kossoff's generally smart lensing is an asset throughout. More music by Peter Brewis would have helped to nudge things along.

—*Derek Elley*

3,000 SCENARIOS TO COMBAT A VIRUS

(3000 SCENARIOS CONTRE UN VIRUS)

(FRENCH)

A CRIPS/Medecins du Monde/APS/AESSA presentation of a Blue Films/Bernard Verley Films/Frouma Films Intl./Les Prods. de 3eme Etage production, with support of CNC, Procirep and AFLS, and participation of TF1, France 2, France 3, Canal Plus, Arte and M6, in partnership with Agfa. Directed by Jean Achache, Philippe Berenger, Richard Berry, Jane Birkin, Paul Boujenah, Patrice Cazes, Caroline Champetier, Jacky Cukier, Jacques Deray, Xavier Durringer, Sebastien Graal, Laurent Heynemann, Benoit Jacquot, Gerard Jugnot, Cedric Klapisch, Philippe Lioret, Jean Marboeuf, Tonie Marshall, Ivana Massetti, Laetitia Masson, Michel Meyer, Fernand Moskowicz, Jean-Daniel Pillault, Jacques Renard, Charlotte Silvera, Florence Strauss, Virginie Thevenet, Bernard Verley, Daniel Vigne, Patrick Volson. Screenplays based on ideas submitted by French school kids under age 20. Reviewed at Gaumont Marignan, Paris, June 11, 1994. (In Paris Film Festival — non-competing.) Running time: **109 MIN.**

With: Anemone, Daniel Gelin, Patachou, Francois Cluzet, Valeria Bruni-Tedeschi, Chiara Mastroianni, Melvil Poupaud, Martin Lamotte, Mathieu Kassovitz, Michel Boujenah, Mathieu Demy, Lola Doillon, Michel Duchaussoy, Jessica Forde, Nils Tavernier.

Thirty short films, based on ideas culled from over 3,000 proposals submitted by French students aged under 20, and directed by a cross-section of volunteer helmers and celebs make up "3,000 Scenarios to Combat a Virus." Spots — produced with the help of all six Gallic channels — will be telecast and coupled with high-profile theatrical releases (including Palme d'Or winner "Pulp Fiction") before touring schools and prisons.

A few of the mini-pix are standouts with international potential, in which humor and/or well-channeled emotions create vivid, thought-provoking cinematic worlds. But, overall, this omnibus collection, initiated by humanitarian organization Medecins du Monde, points up how difficult it is to translate the reality of AIDS into an engaging, uncontrived and non-maudlin short.

Four production houses divvied up the winning submissions and helmers were assigned a script. Project — which is a great template for youth involvement in other countries — took three years to mount.

Emphasis is on heterosexual transmission; only one seg addresses intravenous drug use, and one other deals with male homosexuality.

Strident rap and moody classical are the two prevailing musical choices. Lensing styles run the gamut.

In Virginie Thevenet's seg, Melvil Poupaud sets the wheels of doubt spinning in Chiara Mastroianni's head with news that her boyfriend is cheating on her with an infected female classmate.

In excellent seg helmed by Tonie Marshall, Mathieu Kassovitz gives a compact, knockout perf as the schoolyard cut-up who flamboyantly buys condoms for a shy buddy who's about to lose his virginity.

Jacky Cukier helms a wacky but unnerving look at a self-involved hippie family so far behind the times that they're completely oblivious to the existence of AIDS. When distraught daughter informs astrology enthusiast Anemone that she's HIV-positive, Mom says, "That's wonderful, dear" and Mom's current b.f. adds, "It's good to be positive about things."

When a 122-year-old teacher leads youngsters through the Paris natural history museum in the year 2080, they get a historic overview of AIDS and, muddling 20th-century trailblazers, ask if the Beatles discovered the vaccine.

Laurent Heynemann's dialogue-free saga of a loving, infected couple is quietly powerful. Jacques Deray helms a sternly moving account of classmates mourning a deceased buddy at his funeral.

Several spots deal with pharmacies. Daniel Gelin stars as a senior citizen who bothers a pharmacist for countless items in order to mask his purchase of condoms — as demanded by the elderly woman (Patachou) he's courting.

In the Cedric Klapisch-helmed comic gem that's sure to travel the world, flustered Valeria Bruni-Tedeschi is transporting her adored goldfish, Kiki, in its bowl, which shatters. Thesp races to a pharmacy, storms the crowded counter and demands a condom. Another client adds bottled water and Kiki paddles in new latex home, brilliantly illustrating the slogan "A Condom Can Save a Life."

Another, more controversial Klapisch contribution shows a series of lively nude couples — straight, gay, interracial — having sex in the same hotel room to a Philip Glass tune from "The Photographer" while offscreen voices describe how the existence of AIDS must modify behavior. A man applies a condom to his erect penis as a woman caresses him. Result is tasteful and informative.

—*Lisa Nesselson*

KARLOVY VARY

THE CASE OF BRONEK PEKOSINSKI
(PRZYPADEK PEKOSINSKIEGO)
(POLISH)

A Studio Filmove "N" production. Produced, directed, written by Grzegorz Krolikiewicz. Camera (color), Ryszard Lennzewski; editors, Halina Nawrocka, Tereza Miziolek. Reviewed at Karlovy Vary Film Festival, July 4, 1994. Running time: **90 MIN.**
With: Bronislav (Bronek) Pekosinski, Maria Klejdysz, Anna Seniuk, Jolanta Rychlewska, Franciszek Trzeciak, Franciszek Pieczka, Aleksander Fogiel.

In a bold chess move that triumphs, director Grzegorz Krolikiewicz casts aging and crippled Bronek Pekosinski in his own biography. The Alzheimer-diagnosed Pole takes a dry-eyed journey through his life story in a search for his identity. Its semi-docu style and affecting subject matter grab the audience early on, and its unresolved ending will jab at puzzle solvers long beyond the closing credits. This second-place prize winner at Karlovy Vary could play out well with serious cinema-goers far beyond Poland's borders.

Like a pawn in the game of chess that he once mastered, Bronek gazes with a bland smile as his handlers — guardians or Communist Party ruffians — and events determine his path. Now frail and decrepit, crippled by a stroke, he is often literally picked up and set in place. The framework for the film is a chess match during which Bronek tells what he remembers of his past to his opponent, who urges him to delve deeper. In flashbacks, and without any change of demeanor or clothing, Bronek replays his history.

It begins with his falling on a pile of potatoes, thrown over a concentration camp fence by his mother. Because he has no identity, the authorities invent a genealogy of sorts for him: his birth date the day Germany invaded Poland, his name derived from the acronym of the orphanage where he spends his childhood. The potato landing damages the child, his hunchback malformation adding to his misfortunes.

Though surrounded by a solid cast of actors, Bronek's simplicity and honesty stand out. A glowing blank slate, a cipher patiently being buffeted by the winds of fate, in the end this ancient infant seems fazed by only one thing: the search for his mother's, and therefore his own, identity. The brilliant choice to use Pekosinski as himself in every scene, from infancy through the chess-match narration, lends a universal resonance: The old man is present in the child; the child lives in the old man.

Bronek's one interest in life is chess, which he masters. This provides keys for the director in unlocking Pekosinski himself and his past. One can't help but care for this fragile man, but the unsentimental eye of the camera and the unromanticized visual style refuse to provide easy emotional outlets. They don't have to. The image of Bronek Pekosinski's hopeful face in a cynical world is haunting enough.

—*Cathy Meils*

HORROR STORY
(KRVAVY ROMAN)
(CZECH)

An AB Barrandov production in co-production with the Czech Ministry of Culture, Czech Television, Filmexport, Mirofilm, Jaroslav Brabec. Produced by Jan Suster. Executive producers, Lucie Hertlova, Viktor Mayer. Directed, written by Brabec, based on the novel by Josef Vachal. Screenplay collaboration, Jiri Soukup, Georgi Ivanov, Jiri Brozek. Camera (b&w/tinted color), Brabec; editor, Brozek; music, Jiri Sust; set design, Katarina Holla; sound, Jiri Hora, Ivo Spalj. Reviewed at Karlovy Vary Film Festival, July 2, 1994. Running time: **99 MIN.**
Paseka, Master,

Fragonard	Ondrej Pavelka
Elzevira	Klara Jirsakova
Pedro de Rudibanera	Raoul Schranil
Kurt	Jakub Saic
Ignac	Vladimir Marek
Kubova	Veronika Freimanova
Father Bruna	Jirina Jelenska
Kuba	Rudolf Hrusinsky
Hanicka	Barbora Leichnerova

Cinematographer-turned-director Jaroslav Brabec cleverly melds early movie techniques with postmodern tongue-in-cheek flair in a fresh, original homage to black-and-white movies. It's a picaresque effort worthy of Steve Martin, with innocent sexpot heroines and a jumble of incongruous stories that, incidentally, journeys technically through the birth of talkies. That's a start at describing the fun and inventiveness in "Horror Story." University and yuppie colonies should love it.

The movie might better be titled "Bloody Novel." The source, Josef Vachal's 1924 tome, is a surrealistic kaleidoscope of bizarre plot developments. The glue of the film is the character of the author (Ondrej Pavelka), who introduces and comments on his novels and life. "The events of everyday life are much more terrible than any bloody novel," he intones. "No suffering goes unrewarded; no crime goes unpunished."

Brabec uses black-and-white film and pacing techniques to recreate the quality of early silent films. Broad action styles and obviously painted scenery contribute to the affectionate parody. Giant ants with fake butterfly wings swing across the foreground. A naive farm girl twirls her skirts in happiness as the camera cuts to a sassy close-up of her bare bottom. Fingers chopped off a hand in melodramatic fury clatter to the floor, obvious plaster fakes.

As the story hops from scene to scene, stretching credulity to the breaking point, Brabec enhances the monochrome with a rainbow of tones. Forest scenes have a greenish cast, an Amsterdam pirates' pub bears a purple hue, and Hawaiian island natives are bathed in orange. Even the writer's narrative scenes seem to be enhanced with gray.

Editing techniques range from circular fade-outs to jump cuts, and sound is used to hilarious effect. Advancing from purely silent movie, pic adds grossly inappropriate noises and then dialogue, a la the first talkies, while continuing to supply subtitles.

The wildly undulating story links characters in improbable ways, managing by the end to entwine the loose threads in a complicated but acceptable manner.

Near the film's end, the author declares, "In every trash novel, blood isn't very real." When he closes his finished novel, the only solid color in the film appears in the red blood that oozes from the book's pages. Pic is a film teacher's — and student's — delight. —*Cathy Meils*

AMERIKA

(CZECH REPUBLIC)

A Simply Cinema/Czech Television production. Produced by Jaroslav Boucek. Executive producer, Boucek. Directed by Vladimir Michalek. Screenplay, Michalek, Martin Duba, based on the novel by Franz Kafka. Camera (color), Duba; editor, Jiri Brozek; music, Michael Dvorak, David Koller; set design, Jindrich Goetz; costume design, Monika Drapalova, Petra Jachymova, Vera Linhartova; sound (Dolby), Michal Dvorak, Koller. Reviewed at Karlovy Vary Film Festival (competing), July 5, 1994. Running time: **90 MIN.**

Karel Rossmann	Martin Dejdar
Uncle Jacob/	
Father Rossmann	Jiri Labus
Klara	Jjarka Rytychova
Tereza	Katerina Kozakova
Topic	Jiri Schmitzer
Delamarche	Oldrich Kaiser
Robinson	Pavel Landovsky
Brunelda	Liduse Tomanova
Mack	Tomas Vorel
Green	Pavel Novy
Pollunder	Minal Riehs
Subal	Jan Schmid

Debuting Czech director Vladimir Michalek brings countryman Franz Kafka's unfinished novel "Amerika" to the screen with care and imagination. But as has previously been the problem in rendering the Czech literary master's schematic nightmarish vision on film, from Orson Welles' "The Trial" to Steven Soderbergh's fictional thriller "Kafka," the cold existential terrain of his work makes for a rather distancing cinematic experience. Best bet is scholastic and pubcaster airings where pic can serve as a perfectly respectable intro to the term "Kafkaesque."

Derived from a production by the Czech Republic's Prague Ypsilon Theatre, screenplay by director Michalek and cinematographer Martin Duba takes a fairly straightforward approach to the material, charting the journey of Karel Rossmann (Martin Dejdar) from Europe to the mythical land of the title. Just as Kafka wrote the piece from his imagination and not from a first-hand look at the Promised Land, there's no attempt to treat the story realistically, and the film boasts a lovely art-deco-inspired theatrical look with painted skyline backdrops and mattes of overpowering urban landscapes.

Karel's journey begins with his delivery to the good graces of his industrialist Uncle Jacob (Jiri Labus), but after a lengthy period of testing, characterized by typically Kafkaesque paranoia-inducing incidents, Karel falls into a trap set by the sexually aggressive daughter (Katerina Kozakova) of one of his father's associates.

Cast out as undeserving of a place in his uncle's empire, Karel falls in with alcoholic tramp Topic (Jiri Schmitzer) and angelic barmaid Klara (Jjarka Rytychova), who serves the heady brews that lighten their dark world of poverty and hopelessness.

After Topic goads him into a quarrel, Karel, thinking he has killed the tramp, is forced to go underground under the protection of Green (Pavel Novy), a toady old graybeard, and Mack (Tomas Vorel), a tough young thug. His benefactors turn out to be emissaries of destruction, and as in Quentin Tarantino's "Pulp Fiction," the protagonist becomes the prey of these two darkly perverse and sadistic monsters. Ultimately, however, there is a brighter lining than one might expect after all the angst that precedes the payoff.

Tech credits for this stylish, well-crafted pic only somewhat redeem its overall staginess and stodginess.
—*Steven Gaydos*

QUAM MIRABILIS

(ITALIAN — B&W — 16mm)

An Alberto Rondalli production, in association with Ipotesi Cinema, Metropolis Teatro & Altro. Produced, directed, written by Rondalli. Camera (b&w), Rondalli; editors, Giulia Ciniselli, Rondalli; sound, Paolo Centoni. Reviewed at Pesaro Intl. Festival of New Cinema (competing), June 19, 1994. Running time: **56 MIN.**

Anna	Giada Balestrini
Sister Natalie	Valeria Bugatto
Mother Superior	Elisabetta Faleni
Sister Amalia	Anna Sivelli

With: Rocio Cuadrelli, Barbara Santoni, Maite Lozano, Georgette Cavestri, Laura Castelli, Alberto Bargetto.

Rigorously monastic in both setting and execution, "Quam Mirabilis" spins a story of Bressonian simplicity about two cloistered nuns whose love flowers only to be crushed. Made for a meager $32,000, first feature by Alberto Rondalli (a student of Ermanno Olmi's film school) brings a hint of scholarliness to its austere formality but is a solemnly affecting, potent ensemble piece that should accrue admiration at festival showings.

Imposingly lensed by Rondalli in black-and-white, and punctuated by a series of unaccompanied 12th- and 13th-century religious chants sung by a single female voice (pic's Latin title comes from the first line of one of them), the film's most resounding merit is its ability to travel the tortuous contours of souls and minds using rarely more then a murmur of dialogue.

The narrative unfolds as a sustained flashback from the deathbed of Anna (Giada Balestrini), revealing her first inklings of religious conviction while praying with her mother as a child, her entry into the convent and her rapport with the other nuns, a group presence that hovers uncertainly somewhere between solidarity and insidiousness.

The suicide of a mentally unstable nun signals the end of Anna's novitiate serenity and her first manifestations of spiritual doubt. The gloomy, taciturn spell lasts until the arrival of new recruit Sister Natalie (Valeria Bugatto). The slow-kindling passion between them is delicately sketched, but conveys the longing beneath their stilted behavior.

When convent tongues start wagging, Anna is reprimanded, and Natalie looks set to be shunted off to another nunnery. The lovers take flight for one night of ecstasy (seen only in luminous afterglow) before being rounded up the next morning.

The film opens and closes with the same series of shots in and around the rustic convent, framing windows, doors, alcoves and a tree-lined lane as mournfully expressive, if somewhat studied, bookends. Though the stark setting is brought too heavily into play in establishing the characters' emotional states, Rondalli's compositions are consistently arresting without being overly structured.

Cast is uniformly strong, with all seven thesps playing nuns admirably eschewing performance in favor of veiled suggestion.
—*David Rooney*

BODIES AND SOULS

(CORPS ET AMES)

(SWISS — 16mm)

A Prods. Vermillon production. Director of production, Joseph Paleni. Directed, written by Aude Vermeil. Camera (color), Axel Brandt; editor, Frederic Berney; art direction, Nicole Conus; sound, Etienne Cuppens. Reviewed at Pesaro Intl. Festival of New Cinema (competing), June 24, 1994. Running time: **78 MIN.**

Clara	Catia Riccabonni
Lou	Philippe Reymondin
The Professor	Antoine Guinand
Sybile	Bernadette Patois
Lou's Mother	Monica Goux
Lou's Father	Daniel Vermeil
Lou's Brother	Joseph Paleni
Lou's Sister	Nicole Conus

"Bodies and Souls" conducts a stream-of-consciousness scrutiny of the role of sex in an average heterosexual relationship observed via the couple's own exchanges and those with friends and family. This ponderous exercise in psychosexual politicking may land scattered fest dates on the strength of its subject, but most auds will feel their desire thoroughly extinguished before reel one is over.

Approach lies somewhere between *cinema verite* documentary, Warholian minimalism and Dr. Ruth-style couples counseling without the humor. Clara (Catia Riccabonni) and Lou (Philippe Reymondin) are intro'd in bed, musing on everything from sodomy to penetration politics to her lesbian experiences.

The discussion fans out to touch on larger issues such as fidelity, cohabitation, the ebbing of desire in a relationship and the importance of communication in facilitating sex. Politics and male vs. female attitudes are also explored. The less than scintillating banter shifts gears momentarily when the couple are seen fully clothed, locked in a sustained kiss, while their voiceovers recount assorted down-and-dirty episodes.

Mixing scripted scenes with monologues and improvisations, writer/director Aude Vermeil's tack fails to establish flesh-and-blood base elements for her intended Everycouple. Consequently, their ramblings inhabit a lifeless (not to mention sexless) theoretical plane.

The visually dreary effort would require considerably more animated editing to shake off its academic fustiness. —*David Rooney*

July 25, 1994

LASSIE

A Paramount release of a Broadway Pictures production. Produced by Lorne Michaels. Executive producer, Michael Rachmil. Co-producers, Dinah Minot, Barnaby Thompson. Directed by Daniel Petrie. Screenplay, Matthew Jacobs, Gary Ross, Elizabeth Anderson, based upon the character Lassie created by Eric Knight. Camera (Cine Film color; Deluxe prints), Kenneth MacMillan; editor, Steve Mirkovich; music, Basil Poledouris; production design, Paul Peters; art direction, David Crank; costume design, Ingrid Price; sound (Dolby), Stacy Brownrigg; assistant director, Christine L. Larson; Lassie's owner/trainer, Robert Weatherwax; casting, Gretchen Rennell. Reviewed at National Theater, L.A., July 19, 1994. MPAA Rating: PG. Running time: **92 MIN.**

Matthew Turner	Thomas Guiry
Laura Turner	Helen Slater
Steve Turner	Jon Tenney
Jennifer Turner	Brittany Boyd
Sam Garland	Frederic Forrest
Len Collins	Richard Farnsworth
April	Michelle Williams
Jim Garland	Charlie Hofheimer
Josh Garland	Clayton Barclay Jones

Since Hollywood of late finds itself continually going to the TV well for bigscreen source material, it was probably inevitable that a tube and film evergreen like "Lassie" would get a '90s update. New telling is a well-wrought, affecting adventure, thanks to the steady hand of vet helmsman Daniel Petrie and a sensitive, insightful screenplay that focuses on the human drama while providing a long leash to the famed collie's canine charisma, cunning and athletic prowess. This "Lassie" is classy, and B.O. should be the same.

Those in search of surprises in a "Lassie" update are barking up the wrong tree, but the virtues of this outing should satisfy both small fry and accompanying grown-ups. Strongest appeal lies in the sharply observed and emotionally rich portrayal of a family confronting challenges together. When contractor Steve Turner (Jon Tenney) decides to move his family from Baltimore to the ancestral country home of his late wife, in the Shenandoah Valley, least thrilled is teen son Matthew (Thomas Guiry), a pint-sized rebel on a skateboard, hiding behind metal-blasting headphones and lots of attitude. Little sister Jennifer (Brittany Boyd) is more enthusiastic, and step-mom Laura (Helen Slater) is supportive, if overwhelmed by the prospect of raising the kids and following her man to the boondocks.

On the way to their old Virginia home, a spry four-pawed friend named Lassie leaps into their car and their lives, and helps them face the challenges of living on the land.

It doesn't hurt that their best shot at a livelihood involves sheep ranching, and Lassie just happens to be a pro sheep wrangler, as well as a tremendously loving, caring and wise dog. Matthew's icy resolve quickly melts under the collie's warm gaze, and the entire family begins to acclimate to country life.

Also helping speed their transition from the fast lane to the molasses-paced rural lifestyle is grizzled father-in-law Len Collins (Richard Farnsworth), whose love for the children of his late daughter is a palpable, anchoring influence.

There are a few thorns in the garden, however, including rival sheep rancher Sam Garland (Frederic Forrest, convincing in his take on the bullying character) and his sons Jim (Charlie Hofheimer) and Josh (Clayton Barclay Jones). The Garlands have had an undisputed run of the countryside, which has included some prime grazing land that just happens to be part of the Turner spread, and Garland's prosperity is suddenly threatened.

One of the strongest elements of this "Lassie" is the authenticity of the Garland clan and their modern farming ethos, which includes spiffy ATVs for the boys, a posh mansion with solar panels, an indoor pool and lots of Santa Fe-chic furnishings. The two sons are particularly well-cast and believable as contemporary rural American kids, and the script by Matthew Jacobs, Gary Ross and Elizabeth Anderson skillfully weaves the details and psychological nuances of these other key characters.

Less satisfying is Tenney's role, which seems uncertainly drawn, and he settles into playing a by-the-numbers almost-perfect dad, a deficiency that's exacerbated by some of the tale's predictable developments. Slater gets more out of her character, and particularly affecting are her moments of growing appreciation and love from the children.

Guiry is a pleasant juvenile lead, taking on the "Lassie" sidekick role that has been handed down from Roddy McDowell to Tom Rettig to Jon Provost, and Michelle Williams gives a winning performance as his love interest. But what makes "Lassie" work is the craftsmanship and thoughtfulness that director Petrie and his creative team bring to the task. Particularly strong is Kenneth MacMillan's economical lensing, which is understated yet capable of delivering a touch of grandeur when required.

While some cynics may scoff at the validity of yet another "Lassie," the pros involved clearly took the assignment seriously, and looked past the story's rather mixed recent TV history toward its classic elements. This "Lassie" may be short on new tricks, but for an old dog it still has plenty of smarts.

—*Steven Gaydos*

BLACK BEAUTY

A Warner Bros. release of a Robert Shapiro production. Produced by Shapiro, Peter Macgregor-Scott. Directed, written by Caroline Thompson, based on the novel by Anna Sewell. Camera (Technicolor), Alex Thomson; editor, Claire Simpson; music, Danny Elfman; production design, John Box; supervising art director, Les Tomkins; art direction, Kevin Phipps; set decoration, Eddie Fowlie; costume design, Jenny Beavan; sound (Dolby), Simon Kaye; chief horse trainer, Rex Peterson; assistant director, Chris Carreras; second unit director, Vic Armstrong; second unit camera, David Feig, Tony Spratling; casting, Mary Selway. Reviewed at Warner Bros. Studios, Burbank, July 18, 1994. MPAA Rating: G. Running time: **85 MIN.**

Farmer Grey	Sean Bean
Jerry Barker	David Thewlis
John Manly	Jim Carter
Squire Gordon	Peter Davison
Reuben Smith	Alun Armstrong
Mr. York	John McEnery
Lady Wexmire	Eleanor Bron
Lord Wexmire	Peter Cook
Joe Green	Andrew Knott
Voice of	
Black Beauty	Alan Cumming

Although already filmed three times in the sound era, "Black Beauty" has never been put onscreen faithfully or well, a situation partially remedied by this affecting, rather grave rendition of the children's perennial. After making her mark over the last several years as one of the most distinctive young screenwriters in Hollywood, debuting director Caroline Thompson has brought considerable feeling and care to this story of a fine horse's often difficult life in Victorian England. Still, a lack of poetry and nuance in the visual storytelling, as well as a somewhat hasty, rushed feel in the pacing from event to event, keeps this at an artistic distance from such modern kids' classics as "The Black Stallion" and "The Secret Garden," the latter of which Thompson penned. Good B.O. looms.

Anna Sewell's original motivation in writing the 1877 book was to bring to light the cruel treatment of horses prevalent in the England of her day. Indeed, the tome, long wrongly thought of as a benign young girls' favorite, is a veritable catalogue of the sadnesses and painful horrors that mankind can visit upon its faithful, spirited servants, and as such was long published under the imprimatur of the anti-cruelty societies in the U.K. and U.S.

Work's other most notable feature is its first-person narration from the point of view of Black Beauty. Unlike the previous adaptors, Thompson, who wrote from the animals' p.o.v. in "Homeward Bound: The Incredible Journey," has retained this device, which some viewers may find off-putting at first but which soon proves charming and lends the film what world view it has.

"We don't get to choose the people in our lives. For us it's all chance," observes Black Beauty at one point, and entire film illustrates how a horse's fate rests wholly upon whether it lands in the hands of good or evil human beings, who here seem to exist in equal measure.

Like an old man sitting under a tree ruminating about his long life, an aged Black Beauty (voiced enthusiastically with a light Brit accent by Alan Cumming) casts a look back to his idyllic youth on a gorgeous country estate, where he could gambol with other horses, notably the frisky filly Ginger, and was broken and well trained by a fine man whose life he saves during a storm.

Illness comes, as does a horrible stable fire, but these are more easily survived than life under his aristocratic new owners, whose callous mistreatment of Black Beauty and Ginger starts them both on a rocky, downward path.

So badly injured that he's no longer presentable in high society, Black Beauty becomes a horse for rent and, later, a taxi horse in darkest working-class London.

Fortunately, his driver (David Thewlis, in his first bigscreen outing since "Naked") is sensitive to his charge's well-being, and the newly renamed Black Jack does as well as can be hoped for under trying circumstances. But the worst is yet to come, as two years of pulling heavy grain wagons leave the once-splendid animal a forlorn sack of skin and bones. A late, serendipitous encounter allows Black Beauty the calm of a peaceful rural retirement.

Previous versions of the story have invented human romances and melodramas to provide a focus, but here nothing of the sort intrudes upon the rather unvaried account of Black Beauty's checkered, often sorrowful life. By closely following the book, Thompson has had to face its extremely episodic nature, a problem that has not entirely been surmounted either in the scripting, which is more functional than deeply developed in terms of theme and character, or the editing, which pushes along from one key point to another without finding those pauses or grace notes where emotion and meaning can grow.

The "Black Beauty" story provides all the dramatic material necessary for a profound meditation on the rigors and pain of life on Earth, whether human or animal, along the lines of Robert Bresson's devastating "Au Hasard Balthazar." Thompson doesn't take the tale that far, and goes just halfway toward establishing a strong equine p.o.v., doing well with the narration but never providing a consistent visual correlative.

Still, pic has been done with a tasteful intelligence that respects its source and has plenty to offer youngsters as well as adults, although small children could be especially disturbed by the rough treatment, sad separations and death that are part of the story.

While much of the action is set in rural areas, the mid-Victorian setting comes to vivid life in the crowded London sections courtesy of John Box's production design and Jenny Beavan's costumes. Alex Thomson's lensing is characteristically handsome, but having horses as one's main camera subject often means following them rather than adhering to fixed compositions, and variable weather also seems to have contributed to a somewhat inconsistent visual quality. Danny Elfman's vigorous score helps maintain pic's high energy.

Demands on the performers are moderate, although Thewlis weighs in sympathetically, and '60s British film icons Peter Cook and Eleanor Bron are welcome presences as the snooty aristocrats. Lead horses are truly beauties, and some wonderful flirting and sporting between Black and Ginger are among the film's quiet highlights. —*Todd McCarthy*

CHEYENNE WARRIOR

A Concorde/New Horizons release of a Roger Corman presentation. Produced by Mike Elliott. Executive producers, Corman, Lance H. Robbins. Coproducer, Alba Francesca. Directed by Mark Griffiths. Screenplay, Michael B. Druxman. Camera (Foto-Kem color), Blake T. Evans; editor, Roderick Davis; music, Arthur Kempel; production design, Aaron Osborne; set decoration, Jeanne Lusignan; costume design, Tami Mor; sound (Ultra-Stereo), Christopher Taylor; associate producer, Mike Upton; assistant director, Michael A. Allowitz; second unit director, Francesca; second unit camera, David Pierro; casting, Mark Sikes. Reviewed at Foto-Kem Labs screening room, Burbank, July 19, 1994. MPAA Rating: PG. Running time: **90 MIN.**

Rebecca Carver	Kelly Preston
Hawk	Pato Hoffmann
Andrews	Bo Hopkins
Kearney	Rick Dean
Otto Nielsen	Clint Howard
Matthew Carver	Charles Powell
Red Knife	Dan Clark
Tall Elk	Winterhawk
Running Wolf	Joseph Wolves Kill
Barkley	Dan Haggerty

A non-exploitation title from the Roger Corman shop, "Cheyenne Warrior" flirts with becoming a low-budget female "Dances With Wolves," but settles in as a respectable, if unexciting, consideration of the difficulties of interracial romance in the Old West. With negligible action or sex, handsomely made pic has few selling points for theatrical situations, unless a way were found to tap the '70s auds of "Wilderness Family"-type fare. Regional playoff began in Florida July 22.

Blonde-tressed Kelly Preston plays a pregnant young bride making her way out West with callow Civil War draft dodger hubby Matthew Carver (Charles Powell).

Stopping over at genial Barkley's (Dan Haggerty) isolated trading post, the couple is vaguely threatened by two Irish outlaws and three Indians who happen by, and Carver proves himself a bad bet for survival on the range when he stupidly rides out to warn the Irish that the Indians are after them and is murdered for the favor.

After several further killings, Preston's Rebecca, now alone at the compound, takes in injured young Cheyenne warrior Hawk (Pato Hoffmann) and nurses him back to health. Together, they withstand an attack by some hostile Pawnee, but when Hawk asks Rebecca to join his tribe to have her baby, she declines, deciding to deliver it alone.

Rather too soon after Hawk returns with help just in time to assist in the birth, a very reserved romance blooms between the two, setting the stage for a fairly lengthy to-and-fro about the possibilities of the attractive twosome getting together on a more permanent basis.

Michael B. Druxman's script takes a '60s-liberal slant on these matters, but finally heeds the realities of the time and place in forcing the characters to make the hard but only possible decision. Some of the dialogue is awkwardly declamatory, and there are a few clinkers. When Hawk proudly insists that "I don't wish to live as a white man," Rebecca queries, "Couldn't you come visit?"

Material is ultimately too lean and lacking in dramatic tension, but director Mark Griffiths has put it up onscreen in competent, sober fashion. Settings and costumes look too well-scrubbed for the remote outpost location, and attitudes in general seem more 20th than 19th century, but it's a reasonable effort on a limited budget.

Thesping is agreeable without being incisive. Grit, violence and impact are kept strictly within PG range. —*Todd McCarthy*

THE SILENCE OF THE HAMS

(ITALIAN)

A UGC release (in France) of a Film Office Cinema presentation of a Thirtieth Century Wolf/Silvio Berlusconi Communications production. Produced by Ezio Greggio, Julie Corman. Executive producer, Greggio. Directed, written by Greggio. Camera (color), Jacques Haitkin; editors, Robert Barrere, Andy Horvich; music, Parmer Fuller; production design, Jim Newport, Russell Smith; set decoration, Natali Kendrick Pope; costume design, Leesa Evans; sound, James R. Einolf; mechanical effects, Ultimate Effects; special effects makeup, Dave Barton, Modus EFX; casting, Craig Campobasso. Reviewed at UGC screening room, Paris, July 7, 1994. Running time: **81 MIN.**

Antonio Motel	Ezio Greggio
Dr. Animal Cannibal Pizza	Dom DeLuise
Jo Dee Fostar	Billy Zane
Lily	Joanna Pacula
Jane	Charlene Tilton
Inspector Balsam	Martin Balsam

With: Stuart Pankin, John Astin, Larry Storch, Bubba Smith, Rip Taylor, Phyllis Diller, Shelley Winters, Mel Brooks, John Landis, John Carpenter, Joe Dante.
(English dialogue)

As its title suggests, "The Silence of the Hams" is a very distant (and slightly retarded) cousin to the genre-parody pix of Mel Brooks and the Zucker-Abrahams-Zucker gang. There's a sophomoric glee to Italo one-man-band Ezio Greggio's endeavor, but the pic — which tanked in its home territory — remains a feeble grab bag of scattershot and stale gags. Still, brand-name cast is sure to attract video rentals, and undemanding substance-abusing adolescents may actually get a kick out of the earnest but lame proceedings.

Greggio's love of Hollywood oozes off the screen as "Psycho," "Basic Instinct," "Night of the Living Dead," "Dracula" and, of course, "The Silence of the Lambs," among other pix, get lampooned. Ham-fisted "Hams," however, will leave most viewers pining for the originals.

Pic opens with helmer being stabbed to death in the shower, which is about as sharp as the proceedings get. Narrating in his crisp Italian accent, Greggio backtracks to explain how he came to be offed by an unseen assailant whose identity is revealed in the final scene.

In a pastiche of L.A. where Rodney King is seen beating the police, FBI recruit Jo Dee Fostar (Billy Zane, sporting the somewhat plastic makeup popularized by Sean Connery in the early James Bond pix) gets his first big case, which takes him to the Hollywood Nuthouse to interview inmate Dr. Animal Cannibal Pizza (Dom DeLuise, doing a way-over-the-top Hannibal Lecter impression).

When Fostar's girlfriend, Jane (Charlene Tilton), steals $400,000 from her employer (Rip Taylor) and holes up at the Cemetery Motel — a run-down Bates Motel clone run by edgy Antonio Motel (Greggio) — Jane's exotic sister, Lily (Joanna Pacula), enters Fostar's life.

Martin Balsam, from the original cast of "Psycho," plays Inspector Balsam, who checks into hotel guests who check out for good.

Finale — in which the true culprit is unmasked and unmasked and unmasked — has a smidgen more oomph than the paper-thin silliness that precedes it.

Highly idiomatic, literal dialogue abounds ("May I be frank?" "I thought you were Jo") and the script's command of colloquial American English is excellent.

But apart from a handful of genuinely funny sight gags and a few on-target snippets of literal humor, pic's major accomplishment is having lured so many erstwhile, current and demi-celebrities into playing along.

John Astin addresses a disembodied foot in a table-top box as "Smelly Thing," and everyone does the distinctive Addams Family theme-song finger-snap whenever thesp is around. Phyllis Diller, as a secretary, tries to foist cups of coffee on everyone she meets.

Pic also provides plenty of work for celebrity look-alikes. Bill Clinton and George Bush duke it out while jogging with Zane. A dead ringer for Hillary Clinton appears, and pic features a "Thriller" spinoff in a graveyard with a Michael Jackson clone.

Production design conveys enough key elements to readily identify the sources being spoofed. Lensing and editing are OK.

Ominous score — heralded at one point by a voiceover that says, "The tension was so thick and the music so pretentious they knew they must be getting close" — is the one consistently fine production element. —*Lisa Nesselson*

LA PEINTRE

(HUA HUN)

(TAIWANESE-CHINESE)

A Golden Tripod (Taiwan)/Shanghai Film Studio (China) co-production. Produced by Yu Shu, Zhang Pengcheng. Directed by Huang Shuqin. Supervising director, Zhang Yimou. Screenplay, Lin Liyin, Wang Shuying, from the book by Shi Nan. Camera (color), Lu Le; music, Liu Yuan; production design, Zheng Changfu, Chen Chunlin; associate producers, Huang Sungyi, Wang Shuying. Reviewed at Hoover Theater 2, Sydney, April 21, 1994. Running time: **88 MIN.**
Pan Yuliang .... Gong Li
Pan Zanhua .... Yee Tung-shing
Chief Prostitute .... Zhang Qiongzi
Wang Shouxin .... Da Shichang

China's most celebrated actress, Gong Li, crops up playing the leading role in this Taiwanese-Chinese co-production, which opened recently in Hong Kong and is making the rounds of Chinatown cinema circuits internationally. Biography of a real-life, controversial Chinese woman painter, who rose from life as a bordello prostitute to celebrity on the Paris art scene, is fascinating but low-key. Based on Gong's rep, however, it could crop up at fests and segue to wider exposure.

Pan Yuliang (1899-1977) is first seen at age 12, working in a brothel in a small provincial town. When the establishment's most celebrated prostie tries to retire, she's promptly murdered and Yuliang is in the running to take her place.

But on her first night, she meets local official Zanhua. They fall in love and marry, despite the fact that he has a wife already.

The couple move to the big city, and at the Shanghai Arts Institute Yuliang quickly becomes an accomplished painter. But the institute becomes the focus of demonstrations against foreign influences on Chinese art, particularly regarding the use of nude models, and the place is closed down.

Yuliang, however, wants to continue with her nude portraits and is forced to use herself as a model, sitting naked by a mirror to do so. One self-portrait, "Bathing Woman," brings her international attention when it wins a prestigious French prize.

Now separated from Zanhua, who has returned to his other wife, Yuliang moves to Paris and spends most of her life there. Back home, she's accused of "depravity" and her work is never recognized.

Pic looks like a modest production, and pretty much stands or falls on Gong's central performance. Fortunately, she makes the most of a flatly written role, and ages surprisingly convincingly from a young girl to an elderly woman.

The early scenes are reminiscent of many other Chinese films, but once the heroine establishes herself in Paris an altogether different, more mellow, tone is prevalent. This is one Chinese film to cover a 60-year time span without even mentioning the Cultural Revolution.

Gong's longtime collaborator Zhang Yimou gets a slightly mysterious credit, which translates as either "directorial planning" or "supervising director."

Though Zhang was reportedly on the set during filming, pic is the work of femme helmer Huang Shuqin, best known for "Woman, Demon, Human."

While "La Peintre" is the only title for the film outside Chinese territories, the original title translates as "Soul of a Painter," and pic is also known as "Pan Yuliang, a Woman Painter." —*David Stratton*

MYSTERY OF THE PUZZLE

(ZAHADA HLAVOLAMU)

(CZECH)

A Filmexport Prague presentation of an AB Barrandov production. Produced by Jan Suster. Executive producer, Pavel Novy. Co-producers, Czech Ministry of Culture, Lucernafilm, Petr Kotek. Directed by Kotek. Screenplay, Ivan Arsenjev, Kotek, based on the novel by Jaroslav Folgar. Camera (color/b&w), Miro Gabor; editor, Michal Cingros; music, Petr Malasek; set design, Michal Krska; costume design, Martin Kurel; sound (Dolby), Karel Janos, Jiri Kejr, Ivo Spalj. Reviewed at Karlovy Vary Film Festival, July 8, 1994. Running time: **95 MIN.**
Mirek Dusin .... Ondrej Host
Jaroslav Metelka .... Martin Voldrich
Jindra Hooyer .... David Divis
Rychlonozka .... Martin Vlasak
Cervenacek .... Jaroslav Richter
Long Bidlo .... Karel Zima
Bohous .... Jaromir Krizek
Stetinac .... Josef Dufek
Losna .... Matej Hadek

Spies, rival neighborhood newspapers and a mystery from the past figure in this 1930s boy's adventure. "Mystery of the Puzzle," based on a book and popular but short-lived comics series, is a somberly hued, energetic film akin to a less than spanking-clean Hardy Boys escapade. Slightly gritty story pits a small band of nice boys against a committee-dominated gang of hooligans. Film should appeal on both sides of the Atlantic, especially to boys.

The Fleet Arrows are five upstanding pre-teens who hand-print the "Tom-Tom," a news sheet for kids. On the other side of town, the leather-jacketed Vonts rule the streets. Chalk drawings of their secret symbol, a mystery puzzle, appear on stone walls. The Fleet Arrows, having discovered the diary of a boy who died under suspicious circumstances years before, set out to find the puzzle and learn the message it holds. When their discoveries are printed by a rival paper, the Fleet Arrows expel one of their members as a suspected traitor.

In a series of grainy black-and-white flashbacks, the story of the hapless orphan boy unfolds through the pages of his diary. The plan of his wonderful invention, a bike that flies, is hidden inside the mystery puzzle. Chases through back alleys and church catacombs ensue, as the Vonts try to steal the diary, which reveals that the orphan was stalked by the unknown M.

Non-violent chase scenes, plenty of adventure and a mystery to think through have a universal appeal for grade-schoolers not yet past the age of innocence. The appealing urchin quality of the orphan boy draws sympathy and interest in his fate. Music and camera work turn this into a film noir for kids.
—*Cathy Meils*

SATURNIN

(CZECH)

A Czech Television release of a Jupiter film production. Produced by Capek-Borovan. Executive producer, Hana Stefanova. Directed by Jiri Vercak. Screenplay, Magdelena Wagnerova, Vercak, based on the novel by Zdenek Jirotka. Camera (color), Josef Spelda; editor, Zdenek Patocka; set design, Michal Krska; costume design, Ivana Bradkova; music, Jiri Spitzer. Reviewed at Karlovy Vary Film Festival, July 9, 1994. Running time: **97 MIN.**
Saturnin .... Oldrich Vizner
Jiri Oulicky .... Ondrej Havelka
Barbora .... Lucie Zednickova
Grandfather .... Lubomir Lipsky
Doctor .... Milan Lasica
Aunt Katerina .... Jana Synkova
Milous .... Petr Vacek

A Czech version of a "Masterpiece Theatre"-style production, "Saturnin" is a 1920s period comedy that might have come from the pen of a Central European P.G. Wodehouse. Well-mannered and technically correct, it ambles through its amusing, inconsequential entertainment at a relaxed pace. Too slight for a far-flung cinema life, it could nonetheless find a slot on upscale cable or public TV.

Saturnin (Oldrich Vizner) is a quirky though perfectly proper butler who manages to change the humdrum life of his wimpy master, Jiri (Ondrej Havelka). Jiri, one of the planet's less-than-adequate inhabitants, creates minor disasters at every turn. Under Saturnin's control, he gains a reputation as a big game hunter and sets off for adventure on a houseboat.

Jiri's self-centered, widowed Aunt Katerina (Jana Synkova) and boorish, spoiled Cousin Milous (Petr Vacek) turn up as uninvited house guests sponging off all available relatives. Also on the scene is the lovely, poised Barbora (Lucie Zednickova), who captures Jiri's fancy.

The loyal Saturnin intervenes whenever Jiri's interests are threatened, creatively improvising whatever actions are necessary to look after his master's comfort.

By film's end, Jiri has become a suitable match for Barbora, Aunt Katerina has been married to a wealthy man, and Milous has been put in his place. All loose ends are neatly tied up in this entertaining bit of Czech fluff. Solid tech credits, mildly broadened characters and a soupcon of slapstick add to the film's undemanding pleasure quotient. —*Cathy Meils*

HELIMADOE

(CZECH)

A Czech Television production in co-production with KF a.s./Studio 1. Produced by Vera Lastuvkova, Helena Sykorova, Karel Skorpik. Executive producers, Frantisek Karoch, Sarka Podlipna. Directed by Jaromil Jires. Screenplay, Vaclav Sasek, based on the novel by Jaroslav Havlicek. Camera (color), Petr Polak; editor, Milan Justin; music, Lubos Fiser; set design, Milos Ditrich; costume design, Jarmila Konecna; sound, Pavel Dvorak, Jan Kacian. Reviewed at Karlovy Vary Film Festival, July 3, 1994. Running time: **90 MIN.**

Doctor Hanzelin	Josef Somr
Helena	Jana Dolanska
Lida	Zuzana Bydzovska
Marie	Ljuba Krbova
Dora	Lucie Zednickova
Ema	Jana Konecna
Young Emil	Jakub Marek
Adult Emil	Petr Pelzer

Anostalgic look back at an adolescent boy's summer of first love, "Helimadoe" has the look and feel of a quality cable or PBS show. A gentler take on the "Belle Epoque" theme, but without the Oscar winner's originality or verve, "Helimadoe" is a pleasant and undemanding effort by vet helmer Jaromil Jires.

The puzzle of a title derives from the names of a country doctor's (Josef Somr) daughters. Emil (Jakub Marek), a 15-year-old with the face and red curly hair of a cherub, spends a summer following the doctor and his daughters on their rounds, as a sort of apprenticeship in spite of his mother's disapproval. Her haughty beau stands in contrast to the five daughters, whose spontaneity and warmth immediately enfold Emil. Each of the five reacts to Emil differently, nurturing or flirting with him. The youngest, Ema (Jana Konecna), jealously watches Emil's growing infatuation with sexy Dora (Lucie Zednickova).

The coquetry continues harmlessly until a traveling magician and his dying wife stop in the sleepy town. While the doctor is unable to save the wife, Dora begins an affair with the magician, using the lovesick Emil as her go-between. When she runs off with the magician, Emil is all too ready to leave the town with his parents and turn his back on Ema's affection.

The sentimental reminiscence of youthful folly is well served by pic's warmly muted colors and the tender, all-the-time-in-the-world pace of the film. The movie's production values are fine, and Jires captures an atmosphere found in Czech studio films of an earlier era, a world touched by warmth, graciousness and a lust for life.

Although "Helimadoe" doesn't burn itself into the memory, it should find an appreciative audience among nostalgic viewers and family auds. —*Cathy Meils*

THE PRINCESS FROM THE MILL

(PRINCEZNA ZE MLEJNA)

(CZECH)

A Nero/Czech Television production. Executive producer, Etamp Film Production. Directed by Zdenek Troska. Screenplay, Vratislav Marek, Troska. Camera (color), Ervin Sanders; editor, Ivana Kacirkova; music, Milos Krkoska; production design, Martin Maly; costume design, Jan Ruzicka; sound (Dolby), Vlastimil Kulisek. Reviewed at Karlovy Vary Film Festival, July 3, 1994. Running time: **105 MIN.**

Eliska	Andrea Cerna
Jindrich	Radek Valenta
Imp	Yvetta Blanarovicova
Water Sprite	Jakub Zindulka
Witch	Lucie Bila
Father	Alois Svehlik
Count	Ota Sevcik
Servant	Ladislav Zupanic

"The Princess From the Mill" radiates an innocence, honesty and love for its story that will make this charming Czech fairy tale a bull's-eye hit with the primary school set and their parents. Beautifully filmed in crayon-bright colors, the tale blends romance and fantasy in an idyllic countryside setting. Sweet folk songs and a romantically pretty score move the film along at a gentle pace. Film should carry over well to a wider European market.

Daydreaming Jindrich (Radek Valenta) leaves his village, determined to find and marry a princess. A witch (Lucie Bila) transports him to a mill pond where Eliska (Andrea Cerna) lives with her father (Alois Svehlik). Their only neighbors, a green-skinned water sprite (Jakub Zindulka) and a furry, horned imp (Yvetta Blanarovicova), are a rustic Mutt and Jeff. Both love Eliska and immediately spot Jindrich as serious competition. Hoping to divert the princess-obsessed intruder, the two transform into frog and cat awaiting the magic kisses from Jindrich that turn them into a pair of ugly bickering sisters.

When a wealthy, aged nobleman (Ota Sevcik) joins the queue of contenders for Eliska's hand, the maid, in time-honored fairy tale tradition, sets a trio of tasks for her suitors. Heavy doses of magic and comedy get the three bumblers over the hurdles, while Jindrich sails through the tasks easily and unknowingly. But — big problem — Eliska is no princess and Jindrich wants nothing less. Using her suitors' gifts, Eliska appears in crown and gown, walking on the pond, and Jindrich at last recognizes her as the princess of his dreams.

Performances are broad and energetic. Jindrich's hard-working and appealing character and Eliska's spirited, level-headed nature rescue the two from vacuousness. In a role that has already earned her an acting award, Blanarovicova as the adorably naughty imp bolts and scampers across the screen with non-stop squirrely chatter and disappears as a spiraling blue twinkle.

Director Zdenek Troska builds on a Czech tradition of period costume fairy tale films, while bolstering his own reputation with this well-drafted movie. —*Cathy Meils*

FORTRESS

(PEVNOST)

(CZECH-FRENCH — B&W)

A KF a.s./Synergia production in association with Margo Films (France). Produced by Ales Hudsky. Executive producer, Hudsky. Directed by Drahomira Vihanova. Screenplay, Vihanova, Alexandr Kliment. Camera (b&w), Jiri Macak; editor, Vihanova; music, Jiri Stivin; set design, Vladimir Labsky; costume design, Olga Vylefalova; sound, Libor Sedlacek. Reviewed at Karlovy Vary Film Festival, July 8, 1994. Running time: **102 MIN.**

Evald	Georgy Cserhalmi
Officer	Miroslav Donutil
Lydie	Zuzana Kocurikova
Petrasek	Josef Kemr

"Fortress" could have been titled "Kafka Slept Here," or rather tossed and turned, since vet Czech filmmaker Drahomira Vihanova has fashioned a cleanly etched black-and-white nightmare vision about the crushing power of blind authority. Despite its lucid, somber camera work by Jiri Macak, a strong central performance by Georgy Cserhalmi as Evald, a kind of oppressed, tortured Everyman, and nice dollops of humor to leaven the heavy thematics, "Fortress" fails to distinguish itself sufficiently from other cinematic trips down an overly familiar road.

Pic's repetitious plotting and overall dreariness checkmate chances for more than limited specialty fest screenings. University unwindings and pubcaster play for auds curious about new post-bloc East Euro fare are best-case fate.

Mood is established immediately when Evald arrives in a sleepy rural village where he's assigned to measure water levels. The town leaders are uniformly sinister and secretive, and the fortress of the title is a strange, sprawling Gothic affair where an unnamed military force is ensconced, entertaining themselves with prostitutes and lots of sharpshooting and munitions hi-jinks. But the purpose of their mission — supposedly to guard a top secret installation — remains elusive.

After consorting with a local woman and one of the prosties, Evald befriends the garrison's tough main officer (Miroslav Donutil), who lets down his guard to reveal the true mandate of the soldiers stationed at the fortress. As Gertrude Stein famously observed about Oakland, "There's no there there."

The townspeople are conspirators in keeping this secret, a deal that Evald, for still mysterious reasons, is unwilling to sanction. Without a clearer understanding of the source of his rebellion, and an involving relationship to provide a counterpoint to this somewhat standard tract against totalitarianism, pic must get by on stunning visuals and shaggy-dog unraveling of the tale.

Unfortunately, this isn't enough, and this creepy home-grown reaction to the abuses of state is slower going than it should be. Even with its drawbacks, though, the haunting images and eerie mood stay in the mind like a disturbing dream. —*Steven Gaydos*

MARSEILLES

PICTURES OF A KINGDOM

(BILDER VON ANDERSWO)

(GERMAN — DOCU — B&W)

A Ralf Zoller Filmproduction/Gunther Bolley Film production, with assistance of Hochschule fur Fernsehen und Film (Munich). Executive producer, Dieter Horres. Directed, written by Ralf Zoller. Camera (b&w), Benedict Neuenfels; editor, Gunvor E. Morte; music, Roberto Murolo. Reviewed at Vue sur les Docs Festival (competing), Marseilles, France, June 18, 1994. Running time: **91 MIN.**

With: Evgen Bavcar.

(German and French dialogue)

Afascinating impressionistic portrait of blind Slovenian photographer Evgen Bavcar, "Pictures of a Kingdom" is a sort of yellow brick road for the mind's eye. Docu melds its subject's voice-over observations, helmer's sly choice of visuals and intelligent sound design with flair and originality. Imaginative result would be

July 25, 1994 (Cont.)

an excellent classroom tool for students of photography, cinema and visual perception. Tightening in final third, which devolves into slightly indulgent repetition, could make pic a fest sleeper.

Self-described as a philosopher, aesthete and writer, "but not a photographer," Bavcar — who lost his sight in two separate childhood accidents at ages 10 and 11 — has been blind for 38 years, 19 of which he has spent in Paris. Since the 1980s, he has exhibited his carefully constructed photos to international acclaim.

Bavcar is an engaging raconteur whose pithy philosophizing is keenly underlined by inventive b&w visuals in the streets of Paris and Venice and inside art museums, where an inspired friend describes paintings and sculptures in terms of sounds and colors.

Emphasizing, in a playful and unpretentious manner, that cameras and lenses, as well as people, require light in order to "see," Benedict Neuenfels' monochrome lensing is a perfect fit. Helmer toys with focus and sometimes presents a completely white or completely black screen, effectively sharpening the viewer's reliance on other senses. Bavcar's eerie photos are integrated as freeze frames.

Pic, blown up from Super-16, has many dim nocturnal passages that communicate beautifully on the big screen but may register poorly on TV and video.

Winner of the Prix du Public at Marseilles docu fest, effort loses steam at about the one-hour mark during real-time episode of Bavcar photographing a young woman.

—*Lisa Nesselson*

JUPITER'S WIFE

(DOCU — VIDEO)

Produced, directed, edited by Michel Negroponte. (International sales: Films Transit, Montreal.) Co-producers, Jane Weiner, Doug Block. Written by Gabriel Morgan, Negroponte. Camera (color), Negroponte; music, Brooks Williams, Beo Morales; sound design, Harmonic Ranch. Reviewed at Vue sur les Docs Festival, Marseilles, France (competing), June 18, 1994. Running time: **87 MIN.**

"Jupiter's Wife," the engaging portrait of a spirited and articulate homeless woman whose stomping ground is New York's Central Park, is a wonderful piece of sociological detective work

in which fate, persistence, the upheaval of the '60s and the enduring shorthand of Greek mythology all play a role. Suspenseful, strangely heartening account of a fractured and partially mended life world preemed at the Marseilles docu fest and should enjoy a long career on the fest circuit and in discerning tube slots.

In summery Central Park, a few blocks from where he grew up, one-man filmer Michel Negroponte encounters Maggie, a fit, jovial woman in her mid-40s with a large back-pack and half-a-dozen dogs. Helmer records his deepening, almost conspiratorial friendship with his resourceful subject, who projects an aura of well-being and relishes words, puns, linguistic coincidences and etymology.

Maggie, who became homeless in 1986, claims to be the late actor Robert Ryan's daughter, says she has six children and reports that she receives regular radio transmissions from her hubby, the Greek god Jupiter.

As helmer gradually discovers, there are substantial — if coded — grains of truth in all of Maggie's matter-of-fact claims. Negroponte eventually deciphers Maggie's crypto-poetic language, piecing together the itinerary via which she began hearing voices and scrounging for survival.

Although "it can be complicated to visit someone who roams 840 acres," Negroponte traces Maggie's fortunes for two years, during which time she braves the coldest December in New York's recorded history, parts with some of her beloved dogs and achieves a more conventional housing solution.

Filmmaker is an integral part of the proceedings, taking the initiative to investigate the strangely fertile Ryan family connection and to dig up both a Universal newsreel and a segment of "What's My Line?," circa 1968, that features 22-year-old Maggie plying her trailblazing trade. (With symbolic prescience worthy of a novel, the show's host cheerfully asked, "So, Maggie, your future is in Central Park?")

Helmer's unwavering respect for his subject contributes to the intriguing but never exploitative tone. Project was originated on Betacam tape for a mere $400 and is destined for transfer to 35mm.

—*Lisa Nesselson*

SYDNEY FEST

THE ROMANOV STONES

(ROMANOVIN KIVET)

(FINNISH)

A Spede-Tuotanto Oy production. Produced by Pertti Pasanen. Directed by Aleksi Makela. Screenplay, Kalle Chydenius, Santeri Kinnunen, Makela. Camera (color), Kari Sohlberg; editor, Jari Innanen; music, Hannu Korkeamaki; production design, Pertti Hilkamo; sound (Dolby), Paul Jyrala. Reviewed at Leura screening room, Leura, Australia, April 30, 1994. (In Sydney Film Festival.) Running time: **93 MIN.**

Patrick	Samuli Edelman
Tony	Santeri Kinnunen
Edvard Roivas	Stig Fransman
Valto	Kari-Pekka Toivonen
Kaarina	Katarina Kaitus
Julia	Minna Sanchez
Marco	Pekka Valkeejarvi
Niki	Juha Veijonen
Ahma	Kari Hietalahti

"The Romanov Stones" is an unabashed Hollywood-style thriller filled with action, shootings and stunts. It would be a calling-card pic for director Aleksi Makela, if anyone ever gets to see it.

The son of established actor Vesa Makela, who has a small role here, Aleksi Makela is a talented newcomer who has simply re-created the staple American action-formula film in Finnish settings with Finnish heroes.

Simple plot has a couple of fresh-faced buddies, Patrick and Tony, hired by a villainous millionaire gambling czar to steal priceless Russian jewels known as the Romanov stones. The lads are double-crossed and nearly killed, but they return later to exact a revenge on the villain, winding up not only with all his money, but his wife and daughter, too.

Pic has a few dull patches, and there are lots of holes in the plot. But the action scenes are vigorously staged, on an obviously limited budget, suspense is effectively generated, location scenery (shot partly in Lapland) is spectacular and pacing is brisk.

Dialogue contains the Finnish equivalent of such cliches as "Cut to the chase" and "Let's rock 'n' roll," but it's all in good fun and marks Makela as a director to watch.

—*David Stratton*

LEX AND RORY

(AUSTRALIAN)

A Colorim Intl. Releasing Corp. presentation of a Globe Film Co. production. Produced by Scott Andrews, Dean Murphy. Directed, written by Murphy. Camera (color), Tim Smart; editor, John Leonard; music, Frank Strangio; production design, Katie Wright, Dallas Olsen; sound (Dolby), Michael Slater; associate producer/director, Mal Bryning; assistant director, Brendan Campbell. Reviewed at Hoyts Center 2, Sydney, June 2, 1994. (In Sydney Film Festival.) Running time: **95 MIN.**

Lex	Angus Benfield
Dai	Fiona MacGregor
Rory	Paul Robertson
Nikki	Wendy Holics
Jamie	Ashley Bindon
Gary Bryson	Stewart Fainchey
Sue Bryson	Carol Brand
Thomas McKenzie	Scott Goddard

A wholly indie pic, produced without government funding (though the Australian Film Commission came up with a marketing grant after completion), "Lex and Rory" rates an A for the effort and dedication of its twenty-something creators, writer/director/producer Dean Murphy and producer Scott Andrews. Aimed at a teen audience, film has charming moments and generally lively performances from a fresh-faced cast but is too slight to make much of a dent in the market. Offshore sales are unlikely.

Eschewing sex and violence, this is a study of hormone-driven teens who can talk to each other only by telephone. In fact, the awkward construction has prospective lovers Lex and Dai meet for a clinch only at the very end, their romance having taken place at a distance until then.

Set in the provincial city of Albury, home base of the filmmakers, pic explores the world of affluent teens who have been indulged by their parents but still have all the usual emotional problems. Lex has a crush on the spunky Dai, who already has a devoted boyfriend, but he's too shy to approach her. One night he calls her, and over a series of increasingly lengthy and romantic phone conversations, he persuades her to pursue her dream of applying for a design course (against the wishes of her bullying father).

Pic should really be titled "Lex and Dai," since Lex's buddy Rory is a marginal character at best. More footage is devoted to Dai's supposedly cute kid brother, Jamie, and a b&w, silent-style epilogue featuring him is a pointless indulgence.

Message is that teenagers should follow their dreams and not be swayed by their parents or school teachers. Touchy subject of teen suicide is also a factor, via a scene in which the dispirited Dai contemplates taking an overdose of sleeping pills.

Main assets are the young actors. Angus Benfield is a personable Lex and Fiona MacGregor a foxy Dai, with Paul Robertson and Wendy Holics less effective as the secondary couple. Pic has moments of charm and insight. Its production values are modest but adequate.

—*David Stratton*

MASTER OF ZEN

(DATMO TSOUSI)

(HONG KONG)

A Brandy Film production. Produced, directed by Brandy Yuen. Screenplay, Yuen, Johnny Li, Chan Koo-fong, Sam Shum. Camera (color), Steven Pun; editor, Ma Yu; music, Lowell Lo; production design, Luk Manwah; costumes, Silver Cheung; martial arts directors, Yuen, Chow Yuen-mo; associate producer, Shum; assistant director, Garry Chan. Reviewed at Leura screening room, Leura, Australia, May 26, 1994. (In Sydney Film Festival.) Running time: **90 MIN.**
Master Dharma .... Derek Yee
Master Prajna Tara ... Chen Sung-yung
With: Fan Siu-wong, Wu Ma, Austin Wei, Fan Mui-sung, Ko Hung, Brandy Yuen, Chow Yuen-mo, Silver Cheung, Garry Chan.

This intriguing companion piece to "Little Buddha," shot mostly on location in mainland China, sets out to depict how Buddhism arrived in China from India. Handsomely produced Hong Kong indie pic did modest business ($HK2 million) at home this spring and is unlikely to fare better elsewhere.

According to Brandy Yuen's lowkey epic, an Indian prince, Dharma (Derek Yee), whose snaky brothers are plotting to assassinate him, sees a vision of his future self. He reacts by renouncing future rights to his father's throne and becomes a wandering monk, who travels east into China spreading the word of Buddha to all who are willing to listen. He winds up meditating in a cave from which no one is able to remove him, passes his religious message onto a disciple, and lives until the venerable age of 150.

Yuen beefs up this meditative saga with bursts of martial arts action and explores his themes with a clarity that is sometimes absent from Bernardo Bertolucci's far more lavish exploration of Buddhism. Yet the net result is strange-

ly uncompelling, and Yuen's direction is strictly functional.

Production credits are solid.

—*David Stratton*

HARJUNPAA AND THE PERSECUTORS

(HARJUNPAA JA KIUSANTEKIJAT)

(FINNISH)

An Ake Lindman Film production. Produced, directed by Ake Lindman. Screenplay, Lindman, Esko Salervo, based on a novel by Matti Yrjana Joensuuu. Camera (color), Pertti Mutanen; editor, Pipsa Valasvaara; music, Lasse Martenson; sound, Jussi Olkinuora; line producer, Raili Salmi; assistant director, Liisa Rauteva. Reviewed at Leura screening room, Leura, Australia, April 30, 1994. (In Sydney Film Festival.) Running time: **100 MIN.**
Harjunpaa .... Kari Heiskanen
Onerva .... Riitta Havukainen
Jari Lahikoinen .... Mats Langbacka
Sanna Lahikoinen .... Sari Havas
Dodo .... Antti Virmavirta
Anttu .... Tom Poysti
Thurman .... Svante Martin

This gloomy urban thriller, filmed mostly at night, is about a couple of malcontents who harass a yuppie couple. Sluggish yarn looks unlikely to spark interest outside its home turf.

A policeman, Harjunpaa, and his female partner investigate the persecution, which mostly takes the form of ordering unwanted deliveries to the home of the couple, such as a huge pile of coal, which is dumped on their cherished rose garden. The constant worry eventually drives the yuppie husband off his rocker, and dour tale ends with a couple of suicides.

It's hard to get engrossed in these basically uninteresting characters. Direction is flat, pacing slow. Otherwise, credits are OK.

—*David Stratton*

I'M NOT COOKING TONIGHT

A Cinema Island production. Produced by Betsy Yamazaki. Directed, written, edited by Takaya Yamazaki. Camera (Duart color), Tamar Stone; music, Hideaki Tokunaga; sound, Mark Paperno. Reviewed at AFI/L.A. Film Festival, July 7, 1994. Running time: **70 MIN.**
Ken .... Katsuo Nagasawa
Meg .... Julia Gibson
Man with Gun .... Aaron Mendelson
Wife .... Celvia Jones
Todd .... Stephen Nunns
Amy .... Marilyn Salinger
With: Betsy and Takaya Yamazaki as themselves.

Attempting to make a virtue of its non-budget, "I'm Not Cooking Tonight" stumbles along, fitfully clever, often painfully awkward. The slim nature of this first-person fictionalization improves somewhat by dint of its tongue-in-cheek self-consciousness. But in the absence of raw energy or a truly vibrant story, the picture is no more than a sketch for a potentially better-conceived project. It could attract modest specialized interest but most likely will serve as a calling card for the filmmakers' future efforts.

From the first frame, Japaneseborn writer/director Takaya Yamazaki attempts to co-opt the audience and enlist it as an accomplice in the making of his movie. He admits that his plight — and the one of his American producer wife

— is how to make a film in the absence of money. So, the guerrilla approach they will take is to beg, borrow and steal film, rely on friends for services and tell a simple story dear to their hearts — the incident that was the turning point in their relationship.

Getting there turns out to be half (or less) the fun of the amusingly presented premise. Takaya introduces the actors who will be playing characters based on himself (Katsuo Nagasawa) and his wife (Julia Gibson). Later, all four sit around and discuss how the story is developing. But rather than providing wry commentary, the quartet fidget and squirm as they attempt to introduce or clarify key plot points.

The seminal moment alluded to at the outset is a bizarre evening in which a presumed burglar (Aaron Mendelson), brandishing a revolver, holds the couple hostage in their New York apartment. Rather than money, he's actually looking for a place to camp out and a way to reunite with his estranged wife.

Sadly, the filmmaker lacks the skill to make this unexpected twist

poignant or revelatory to a degree that would overcome pic's technical and artistic weaknesses.

"I'm Not Cooking Tonight" is pretty much a parboiled effort. Perhaps next time the Yamazakis will have the fixings with a more substantive meal.

—*Leonard Klady*

LAST STATION

(ARMENIAN)

Parev Films presents an Armenfilm Studios production. Produced by Nora Armani. Directed by Haroutiun Katchatrian. Co-director, Armani. Screenplay, Katchatrian, Armani, Gerald Papasian, Mikayel Stamboltsian. Camera (color), Vrej Petrossian, Arto Melkoumian; editors, Sophie Gabrielian, Lena Saroyan; music, Avet Terterian; art direction, Samuel Nahatakian. Reviewed at AFI/L.A. Film Festival, July 6, 1994. Running time: **93 MIN.**
Gerald .... Gerald Papasian
Nora .... Nora Armani
Armen .... Armen Djigarkhanian
Marie .... Marie Pailhes
Shirley .... Bonnie Moore
(English soundtrack)

Somewhere in the meanderings of "Last Station" is an interesting saga of people who are physically and emotionally displaced in society. However, its filmmakers fail to find the core or focus of that idea. Add extremely modest to poor production values, and the Armenianproduced, English-language venture appears doomed to special screenings far from the commercial mainstream.

Relayed in flashback, this is the story of Gerald (Gerald Papasian) and Nora (Nora Armani), a couple of Egyptian-born Armenian performers who achieve brief notoriety when they stage a drama about themselves and their heritage. It's a show born out of desperation, professional disappointment and, obliquely, a need to find links with a culture they have known only on a secondhand basis.

It's intriguing material related in the most banal fashion. Gerald recounts the personal odyssey in the process of writing a letter to Nora. He's also trying to make some sense of their failed marriage and the complacent lifestyle he's adopted as a journeyman actor in Paris.

The paucity of technical resources for "Last Station" is all too obvious. Direct-sound scenes suffer from thin, hollow looping, and drab, static visuals exacerbate the leaden pace. Virtually the entire story is prodded along by voiceover narration that often foreshadows what director Haroutiun Katchatrian is about to convey visually.

Katchatrian further diminishes the effort with an unconvincing conclusion that inadvertently mocks

July 25, 1994 (Cont.)

his very approach. The film is frustrating, offering the prospect of some meaty issues but delivering an unpalatable hash.

—*Leonard Klady*

COMING TO TERMS WITH THE DEAD
(PETITS ARRANGEMENTS AVEC LES MORTS)
(FRENCH)

A Pan-Europeene release of an Eclipsa Films/La Sept Cinema/Pan-Europeene production. Produced by Aline Mehouel. Directed by Pascale Ferran. Screenplay, Pierre Trividic, Ferran. Camera (color), Jean-Claude Larrieu; editor, Guy Lecorne; music, Beatrice Thiriet; production design, Philippe Chiffre; sound, Jean-Jacques Ferran; visual effects, Pierre Planckaert. Reviewed at Club de l'Etoile screening room, Paris, April 28, 1994. (In Cannes Film Festival — Cinemas en France.) Running time: **108 MIN.**
Vincent .... Didier Sandre
Zaza .... Catherine Ferran
Francois .... Charles Berling
Suzanne .... Sabrina Leurquin
Jumbo .... Guillaume Charras

"**C**oming to Terms with the Dead" is a haunting three-part puzzle about the unspoken legacy shared by four grown siblings. Helmed with stylistic assurance by 34-year-old co-scripter Pascale Ferran, pic's artful, three-pronged approach is a bit too long. But fest auds and arthouse denizens are likely to be forgiving, as cunningly layered loose threads gradually yield a satisfying tapestry.

Ferran collaborated with Arnaud Desplechin on "La Sentinelle," and her concerns here mine similar territory: death, memory and responsibility as they rattle in the human psyche.

A Brittany beach in August serves as launch pad for interlocking flashbacks. The words "A Triptych" appear onscreen, followed by a prologue in which an engagingly precocious 8-year-old boy agrees to guard a magnificent sand castle for the 40-ish man who built it. The camera settles on various objects washed up on the shore, then examines three different wristwatches as their hands approach noon.

Using a strategy not unlike that of Fons Rademakers' "The Assault," bits and pieces of a traumatic childhood event are doled out until the narrative coalesces. But only the viewer — not the protagonists — ever gets the full picture.

"Part I — Jumbo" is a lyrical and trenchant look at the goings-on in a Brittany port from the p.o.v. of an obstinate and imaginative youngster who has given himself the code name "Jumbo." Jumbo comments on his caring but ineffectual parents while trying to make sense of the death of an admired playmate. Guillaume Charras is a real find in the role. Jumbo is a sort of updated Greek chorus to the self-contained segments that follow.

In "Part II — Francois," 32-year-old Francois (Charles Berling), a specialist in insect classification, harbors ancient resentments toward Vincent (Didier Sandre), who's building an exquisitely elaborate sand castle, and is buffeted by his discomfort, which alternates with pleasant thoughts of an attractive journalist who recently came to interview him. Through sharp editing, pic captures the ways in which minds wander, settle on a thought, then wander anew.

In "Part III — Zaza," Zaza (Catherine Ferran), a nurse burnt out by job stress, lolls in the sunshine and thinks back to her childhood, to the drawbacks of being perceived as a tower of strength and emotional stability and to a dinner date with a former suitor 20 years after the fact. Seg features pleasing special effects of energy radiating through actress's body as she repeats yoga-inflected relaxation exercises in a b&w nether world.

Overall, pic has a literary feel for detail while exploiting snippets of sound and arresting visual flourishes to replicate shifting states of consciousness and concentration. Script explores the residue of emotional discomfort with sometimes startling imagery (a satchel hurtling through space, a dog snared in a churning escalator).

Thesps are fine throughout. Conclusion is a bit long in coming, but extended stretches of narrative mastery announce a filmmaker to watch. —*Lisa Nesselson*

MUSCLE
(KURUTTA BUYOKAI)
(JAPANESE)

A Strand Releasing presentation of an Enk production. Produced by Syuji Kataoka. Executive producer, Taturo Komada. Directed by Hisayasu Sato. Screenplay, Shiro Yumeno. Camera (color), Fumio Sato; lighting, Hiromi Kato; editor, Seiji Sakai; music, So Hayakawa; assistant directors, Takashi Zeze, Tadami Ohara. Reviewed at the Castro Theater, San Francisco, June 9, 1994. (In S.F. Lesbian & Gay Film Festival.) Running time: **60 MIN.**
Ryuzaki .... Takeshi Ito
Kitami .... Simonn Kumai
Tida .... You Suzuki
Yoko .... Kiyomi Ito
June .... Koyoma Hageki
Maze .... Hiroshi Makoto

This slick Nippon effort treads into extreme sex-and-violence fantasy terrain that seems unlikely to find many fans offshore.

While similarly outre pix like "Iron Man" or "Wicked City" have won limited midnight play in the West, short running time and queasy gay-sadism theme make "Muscle" (somewhat misleadingly retitled from its original "Lunatic Theatre") best suited for specialty vid stores.

Somber young hero Ryuzaki, once editor of a bodybuilding magazine, is obsessed with two things: locating a print of late Italo helmer Pasolini's notorious Sade-based swan song, "Salo," and reuniting with ex-lover Kitami. Seems he'd missed the flick's original run — due to a prison sentence incurred when the duo's increasingly over-the-top sex sessions resulted in one lopped-off limb. Now he's back on the street, scoping for a "one-armed man" whose severed part has been preserved in a long jar.

Mysterious events occur en route to final score-settling at the Lunatic Theatre cinema. A dominatrix offers up her abusive services to the disinterested protag; a young male prostitute and older man at the waterfront (later rattling off a personal history borrowed from Pasolini's "Teorema") likewise annoy hero.

Sexual sequences (including fantasies and flashbacks) stop just short of hardcore. Strenuous tumbling is rendered a bit silly by visibly inert male genitalia, while bizarre aspects — including one episode that involves margarine (an homage to Bertolucci?) and chest-knifing — will strike most as a mixture of the grotesque and the ludicrous. Director Hisayasu Sato suggests black-comedy tenor at times, as when hero goes around posting "Missing" flyers for his lover, each illustrated with a single silhouetted arm.

But mostly "Muscle" is solemnly, rather pretentiously serious. Dreamlike mood recalls such classic underground fetish scenarios as "The Story of O." Lensing is sharp, often formally composed to a sterile degree. Additional tech qualities and perfs are OK. S&M tastes in the U.S. seem tilted toward more harmless power-balance role playing; "Muscle's" leap to actual dismemberment, et al. had the S.F. Gay Fest's packed opening night aud exiting in droves throughout.

—*Dennis Harvey*

WHISPERING PAGES
(TIKHIYE STRANITSY)
(RUSSIAN-GERMAN)

A North Foundation, Eskomfilm (Russia)/Zero Film (Germany) production, with participation of Hamburg Film Office. (International sales: Zero Film, Berlin.) Produced by Vladimir Fotiev. Co-producers, Martin Hagemann, Thomas Kufus. Directed, written by Aleksandr Sokurov, based on 19th-century Russian prose themes. Camera (color/b&w), Aleksandr Burov; editor, Leda Semyonova; music, excerpts from Gustav Mahler's "Kindertotenlieder"; production design, Vera Zelinskaya; set decoration, A. Glushpak; costume design, L. Kryukova; color printing, A.A. Polyanin. Reviewed at Berlin Film Festival (competing), Feb. 12, 1994. Running time: **80 MIN.**
Hero .... Aleksandr Cherednik
Girl .... Elizaveta Korolyova
Official .... Sergei Barkovsky

Fans of abstract helmer Aleksandr Sokurov ("Stone," "The Second Circle") will find much to admire in "Whispering Pages," a mesmeric journey through 19th-century Russian literary themes that looks like Dostoevsky on acid. Most other auds will head for the exit fast. Commercially, this doesn't have a prayer.

Though Sokurov's name is often linked with that of the late Andrei Tarkovsky, who supported him from abroad at a time when his works were banned in the Soviet Union, there's little stylistically to link the two. "Pages" is pure abstract filming, which adherents will prefer to experience prone and under the influence of chemicals, with strong crossover potential for avant-garde art galleries.

In tone, and trawling of thematic material, pic is more down-in-the-depths Dostoevsky, Gogol and Gorky than up-market Pushkin or Tolstoy. Dreamlike opening evokes dock lands, drab buildings and a murky river before seguing to a series of long sequences set among street beggars, a loony bin and dark underground passages.

Central character parallels Raskolnikov, the anti-hero of "Crime and Punishment," while an urchin-like female recalls Sonya, the prostitute in the same novel. Dialogue is minimal, with excerpts from Mahler's song cycle "Kindertotenlieder" supplying atmosphere.

Most interesting conceit of the film is a technical one, with printing perpetually balanced on a fine line between pure b&w and hints of color. When the pic briefly blossoms into an unadulterated red, it's a major event. —*Derek Elley*

OUDE TONGEN

(DUTCH)

A Bergen/NOS/Toneelgroep production. Produced by Hans de Wolf, Hans de Weers. Directed, written by Gerardjan Rijnders. Camera (color), Maarten Kramer; editor, Wim Louwrier; music, Boudewijn Tarenskeen; art direction, Rikke Jelier, Alfred Schaaf, Dirk Debou; sound, Marcel de Hoogd. Reviewed at Cannes Film Festival (market), May 19, 1994. Running time: **91 MIN.**

Bartje Mossel	Jasper Kraaij
Ab Mossel	Fred Goessens
Ria Mossel	Lieneke le Roux
Babs	Hanna Risselada
Nicole	Rosa Risselada
Dr. Peter Ligt	Mark Reitman
Dr. Jannie Ligt	Catherine ten Bruggencate
Oma	Nora Kretz

There's more than a nodding resemblance between the Dutch "Oude Tongen" and the work of David Lynch, particularly his "Twin Peaks'" cycle. Unfortunately, that comparison works against this quirky venture by theater-based writer/director Gerardjan Rijnders. Imitation rather than inspiration prevails in this tale of a small town come unglued when a child porn ring is uncovered in God-fearing country.

Culled from a three-part television venture, the theatrical version appears to have intensified the oblique nature of an already obscurely related drama. Theatrical prospects are severely limited by the pic's specialized nature, and the producers would be better advised to go back to the original and exploit it for the small screen, where it should rack up sales in upscale territories.

Oude Tongen is a quiet agricultural village dominated by church and family where the brothels and beer halls exist just outside the city limits. But something is amiss. For some mysterious reason a chicken coop has been raided and its layers have had their necks broken.

The planets here are definitely out of alignment, and there's no disputing that Rijnders has a keen sense of how to visually convey the off-kilter environment. He's considerably less skilled in tying in key plot points.

The haphazard manner in which the case snowballs from a prank into a sociopolitical scandal is rich, ironic material. But the humor gets lost in the mix. One needs a road map to sort out the host of characters, situations and allusions crammed into the abbreviated version of the series. It emerges as weighty and un-fathomable rather than the deft, organic sleight-of-hand intended.
—*Leonard Klady*

TO THE STARRY ISLAND

(KEU SOME GAGO SIPTA)

(SOUTH KOREAN)

A Park Kwang-su Film production, in association with Samsung Nices and Channel 4 (U.K). (International sales: Fortissimo Films, Amsterdam.) Produced by Park Kwang-su. Executive producer, Park Ki-yong. Directed by Park Kwang-su. Screenplay, Im Chul-woo, Lee Chang-dong, Park Kwang-su, based on Im's novel "I Want to Go to the Island." Camera (color; widescreen), Yoo Young-gil; editor, Kim Hyun; music, Song Hong-sup; art direction, Cho Yung-sam; costume design, Kwon Yoo-jin; sound (Dolby), Lee Byung-ha; special effects, Kim Chul-suk; associate producer, Park Keon-seop. Reviewed at Cannes Film Festival (market), May 20, 1994. (In Melbourne Film Festival.) Running time: **99 MIN.**

Kim Senior/ Kim Chul	Ahn Sung-ki
Moon Duk-bae/ Moon Chae-ku	Moon Sung-keun
Oknim	Shim Hae-jin
Poltoknyeo	Ahn So-young
Opsunne	Lee Young-yi

With: Kim Young-man, Choi Hyung-in, Hur June-ho, Min Kyeong-jin, Kim Il-woo, Kang Sun-sook, Choi Woo-hyeok.

An evocative childhood reflection of events that shaped, scandalized and embittered the population of a small island off the South Korean coast in the 1950s, new Korean cinema exponent Park Kwang-su's "To the Starry Island" makes a plaintive bid for reunification. Handsome production's episodic narrative is somewhat short on exposition and cohesiveness, making wide arthouse impact doubtful, but fest and quality TV programmers should make space.

Present-day opening has Moon Chae-ku (Moon Sung-keun) and Kim Chul (Ahn Sung-ki), chums since childhood, accompanying the body of Moon's father to his native Kwisong Island to be buried. But resentment for the dead man runs high, and the locals refuse to let the boat dock. Going ashore without the coffin, Moon attempts to talk the islanders round while his friend's mind wanders back 40 years to their childhood.

With no significant tonal shift to mark the time distinction, the flashback initially poses some confusion. But once the period relocation is established, and the infant Chul steps in as an almost silently expressive observer, the island inhabitants (with the women at center stage) provide a delicate range of human drama.

Most affecting is the story of simple-minded villager Oknim (Shim Hae-jin), forced into marriage with no idea of what's expected of her. Oknim's exchanges with the sorrowful, motherless Chul about dead souls becoming stars give the film its title. Other tracks follow an adulteress and a manhandled wife invested with shaman's powers.

Somewhat belatedly, Moon Duk-bae (the dead man of the present) steps back into focus as a disloyal neighbor, an indifferent father to Chae-ku and his sickly sister Pan-nim, and an unfaithful husband. When Pan-nim dies, her mother becomes insane with grief. Moon dispatches her, supposedly to a mainland hospital, but in reality to an early grave, and is consequently banished from the island.

The far-off specter of war becomes more immediate with the arrival of a Nationalist Army platoon. Remoteness of the island dictates a general neutrality among the population, but by posing as northern Communists, the troops deceitfully root out supposed Communist sympathizers for execution. The revelation that Moon is architect of the ruse cements the islanders' hatred of him.

Story closes back in the present, with the old shaman (Lee Young-yi) mediating reconciliation arrangements between locals and Moon's body, anchored offshore in a boat that becomes a funeral pyre in a ceremonial send-off.

Though a more linear editing hand could be imposed to cut down on excessive convolution, the drama remains a commanding one. Technically, pic is a prestige job right down the line, especially Yoo Young-gil's warm-hued widescreen lensing, and sparingly used music by Song Hong-sup, which mixes a traditional Eastern flavor with Western synth sounds.

Released locally in December '93, "Island" reportedly clocked around 400,000 admissions in Seoul, putting it well ahead of most other local art films.
—*David Rooney*

WOMEN HAVE ONLY ONE THING ON THEIR MINDS …

(ELLES NE PENSENT QU'A CA …)

(FRENCH)

An AFMD release of a Flach Film/France 2 Cinema/Alhena Films/Erre Cinematografica/M6 production. (International sales: Mercure, Paris.) Produced by Jean-Francois Lepetit. Directed by Charlotte Dubreuil. Screenplay, Dubreuil, Georges Wolinski. Camera (color, Technovision widescreen), Carlo Varini; editor, Luc Barnier; music, Jacques Davidovici; art direction, Bernard L'Herminier; costume design, Michele Cerf; sound, Alix Comte; assistant director, Patrick Poubel. Reviewed at UGC Montparnasse Cinema, Paris, March 29, 1994. Running time: **92 MIN.**

Margaux	Claudia Cardinale
Jess	Carole Laure
Mario	Roland Blanche
Pierre	Bernard Le Coq
Leon	Heinz Bennent
Vic	Bernard Yerles
Olga	Diane Pierens
Lucille	Patrick Mille

Also with: Camille Bruyere, Bernard Giraudeau.

"Women Have Only One Thing on Their Minds …" is an ultra-light-weight comedy of manners that follows the romantic fortunes of a loosely federated band of relatives and lovers. Offshore prospects are limited for this item, which strives to be hip but comes up pedestrian.

Pic covers one week in Paris, bracketed by the arrival from and departure for NYC by Margaux (Claudia Cardinale). It's been 20 years since she left her older hubby, a painter (Heinz Bennent). Daughter Jess (Carole Laure), who buys and sells classic cars with klutzy partner Mario (Roland Blanche), accidentally OD'd on sleeping pills and is hospitalized.

Jess' live-in b.f. is a sensitive younger musician who cares more about music than sex. She has a strapping 17-year-old son by ex-hubby restauranteur Pierre (Bernard Le Coq), who lives with a sexy black African student half his age. Jess' hospital psychologist initiates a jolly affair with her teen son.

Running gag is that the flaky Jess experiences three more unintentional brushes with death in short order. This keeps the cast in constant contact, musing about sex and sometimes indulging in it.

Occasionally clever, often crude dialogue is adequate. Thesps are OK — with Cardinale a strange mix of raunch and class — and assorted characters remain distinct.

At one point, Cardinale and Laure, decked out in gloves and sleeveless gowns, perform the Marilyn Monroe standard "Bye Bye Baby" in English. —*Lisa Nesselson*

THE WEDDING PHOTOGRAPHER

(BRYLLUPSFOTOGRAFEN)

(DANISH)

A Such Much Movies production. Produced by Peter Norgarrd. Directed by Johan Bergenstrahle. Screenplay, Dag Solstad, Bergenstrahle. Camera (color), Erling Thurmann-Andersen; editor, Peter Englesson; music, Pierre Dorge, Irene Becker; production design, Tove Robert Rasmussen; sound (Dolby), Morten Bottzauw; casting, Jacob Kielland. Reviewed at Cannes Film Festival (market), May 21, 1994. Running time: **85 MIN.**

Daniel Svare	Kurt Ravn
Maria Galaxe	Nonny Sand
Vera Berg	Ilse Rande
Tarik	Kadhim Faraj
Max	Anders Peter Bro
Christoffer Berg	Niels Skousen
Ahmed	Runi Lewerissa

Swedish theater and film director Johan Bergenstrahle made something of a name for himself in the '70s with pix that touched on ingrained Scandi racism ("Made in Sweden," "Foreigners," "A Baltic Tragedy"). Now he's back with a tale revealing that racists remain menacingly active in the Danish provinces in the '90s.

Pic's main theme, however, is a familiar tale of a middle-aged man, a former revolutionary and top TV journalist known for his hard-hitting programs from the world's trouble spots. He retires to his hometown and has an affair with an actress young enough to be his daughter. Modest outing is basically a small-screen experience.

Kurt Ravn plays the burnt-out Daniel, who comes home and takes over the photography business where he served an apprenticeship as a boy. An old flame (Ilse Rande) wants to reignite their relationship, but Daniel is more interested in the alluring Maria (Nonny Sand), a young actress who's playing a nude scene with an Arab actor in an updated production of Strindberg's "Miss Julie" on the local boards. The night Daniel checks out her per-

formance, Maria and her co-star are literally tarred and feathered by racist louts in midperformance.

Production values are modest for this low-budgeter, which is decently acted but really doesn't say anything new about its subjects. —*David Stratton*

SATIN STEEL

(CHUNGGAMSUK)

(HONG KONG)

A Mandarin Films production. (International sales: Mandarin Films, H.K.) Produced by Michael Ng, Raymond Wong. Executive producers, Clifton Ko, Ronny Yu. Directed by Alex Leung Siu-hung. Screenplay, Roman Cheung, Vincent Kok. Camera (color), Sander Lee; editor, Kam Ma; music, Lee Han-kam; costume design, Vivian Lam; action director, Leung Siu-hung. Reviewed at Cannes Film Festival (market), May 17, 1994. Running time: **84 MIN.**

Jade	Jade Leung
Ellen Chan	Anita Lee
Ken	Russell Wong
With: Kent Chan.	

(English soundtrack version)

"Satin Steel," third outing of H.K. wannabe fighting femme Jade Leung, is an uneven but passable entry that should amuse auds tuned into East Asian actioners. Leung, who scored a small cult following with her debut in "Femme Nikita" rip-off "Black Cat," generally delivers the goods in a variety of Singapore and Indonesian locations.

Hand-me-down plotline has Leung as a cop with attitude — hubby was shot dead on their wedding night — dispatched to Singapore to help snare a Yank Mafioso arms dealer. In the trim island republic, she's partnered with feisty cop Ellen (Anita Lee), who's thinking of retiring and marrying her dorky b.f.

The scenery picks up when the action moves to Java, where Leung gets involved with the Yank's lawyer (Russell Wong), who finally realizes he's being used by his boss. After some soppy comedy-romance involving the distaff duo, last half-hour is a solid actionfest set in the jungle and atop some volcanoes near Surabaya.

Statuesque ex-model Leung, as a cop with a death wish, partners well with the ditzier Lee. Action se-

quences and tech credits are solid. On English dubbed print caught, direction is credited to Clifton Ko and Tony Leung, though Chinese sources solely credit Alex Leung Siu-hung, one of several co-directors on the classic "Angel" (1987). Original Chinese title means "Heavy Metal." —*Derek Elley*

THE MASK

A New Line Cinema release in association with Dark Horse Entertainment. Produced by Bob Engelman. Executive producers, Mike Richardson, Charles Russell, Michael De Luca. Directed by Russell. Screenplay, Mike Werb, story by Michael Fallon, Mark Verheiden. Camera (Foto-Kem color), John Leonetti; editor, Arthur Coburn; music, Randy Edelman; production design, Craig Stearns; art direction, Randy Moore; set decoration, Ellen Totleben; costume design, Ha Nguyen; special makeup effects, Greg Cannom; visual effects consultant, Ken Ralston; choreography, Jerry Evans; sound (Dolby), Mark Hopkins McNabb; associate producer, Carla Fry; assistant director, Denis L. Stewart; casting, Fern Champion, Mark Paladini. Reviewed at Broadway Cinema, Santa Monica, July 21, 1994. MPAA Rating: PG-13. Running time: **101 MIN.**
The Mask/

Stanley Ipkiss	Jim Carrey
Tina Carlyle	Cameron Diaz
Lt. Mitch Kellaway	Peter Riegert
Dorian Tyrel	Peter Greene
Peggy Brandt	Amy Yasbeck
Charlie Schumacher	Richard Jeni
Niko	Orestes Matacena
Irv	Timothy Bagley
Mrs. Peeman	Nancy Fish
Burt	Johnny Williams
Milo	Max

Lean, mean and green, "The Mask" is unquestionably a money-making movie machine. But there's nothing mechanical or rote about the offbeat romantic adventure. This showcase for the talents of Jim Carrey is adroitly directed, viscerally and visually dynamic and just plain fun. The box office will be booming just like the title character's heart, and the film should easily emerge as one of the year's biggest commercial successes.

The comic-book refugee arrives with a nod to "Dr. Jekyll and Mr. Hyde." In the fictional burg of Edge City, good-hearted Stanley Ipkiss (Carrey) works doggedly as a loan officer at a major bank. He's a very nice guy and, true to the old saw, has wound up at the appropriate lower rung of the ladder.

Then comes that fateful night.

While his buddy and a couple of babes glide into the exclusive Coco Bongo Club, Stan gets the proverbial heave-ho. Driving back to his dreary apartment, the dejected sap spies what he thinks is a body floating in the river. He dives into the polluted waters only to discover a carved face mask attached to a mass of flotsam.

But when he returns home and tries on the relic, the fit is frightening. Drab, mild-mannered Stanley morphs into a confident whirlwind

of color with a grin on his green face revealing a set of pearly whites that's blinding. In his new guise, the Mask, he definitely provides the edge in Edge City.

Though there's little doubt where the tale is headed, Mike Werb's script and Charles Russell's direction effectively manage to mask obvious intentions with crisp, witty banter and visual bravura.

The usual pitfall of the drab guy providing long, colorless narrative is cleverly sidestepped by means of colorful supporting characters, Carrey's innate charisma and a truly extraordinary dog named Max as Stanley's intrepid, industrious and perplexed pet, Milo.

Meanwhile, the dazzling special effects come as close as humanly possible to replicating the mayhem and invention of '40s Warner Bros. cartoons. The title character literally bounces off walls, and when he spies his dream girl, his jaw puts a dent in the floor boards.

Because Stanley is such a nice, albeit uptight, guy, he can only daydream about knockout Tina Carlyle (Cameron Diaz). The Mask is another matter. Nothing is going to stop him from romancing her and dancing up a storm in one of the film's inventive bits of pyrotechnic choreography.

The glitch is that Tina is the moll of gangster Dorian Tyrel (Peter Greene). So, somewhat inadvertently, the green-complected Mask winds up putting a monkey wrench in Tyrel's power-hungry plans.

In addition, Lt. Kellaway (Peter Riegert) of the ECPD is in pursuit, convinced the Mask is the criminal mastermind behind the city's current spate of lawlessness.

It's inconceivable to imagine anyone but the dexterous Carrey as the Mask. And the film sports a uniformly strong support cast with very good villains, including Greene and Orestes Matacena, and a droll goodcop turn from Riegert. Diaz is a real find as the femme fatale who's just looking for the decent thing to do.

Applying a deft touch, Russell, hitherto a genre director, maintains a cartoon style to the violence that's quite suitable for all audiences. At the same time, pic has a hip sensibility that will attract young adults as well as older ones for a late summer B.O. deluge.

It may only be coincidence that the green-skinned character sports a yellow-gold suit and fedora. In the commercial academy, "The Mask's" colors are definitely green and gold.
—*Leonard Klady*

CLEAR AND PRESENT DANGER

A Paramount release of a Mace Neufeld and Robert Rehme production. Produced by Neufeld, Rehme. Co-producer, Ralph Singleton. Directed by Phillip Noyce. Screenplay, Donald Stewart, Steven Zaillian, John Milius, based on the novel by Tom Clancy. Camera (Deluxe color; Panavision widescreen), Donald M. McAlpine; editor, Neil Travis; music, James Horner; production design, Terence Marsh; art direction, William Cruse; set decoration, Mickey S. Michaels, Jay R. Hart; set design, Dawn Snyder; costume design, Bernie Pollack; sound (Dolby), Arthur Rochester; special effects coordinators, Joe Lombardi, Paul Lombardi; visual effects supervisor, Robert Grasmere; stunt coordinator, Dick Ziker; associate producer, Lis Kern; assistant director, Alan B. Curtiss; second unit director, David R. Ellis; second unit camera, Michael A. Benson; casting, Mindy Marin. Reviewed at Paramount Studios, L.A., July 22, 1994. MPAA Rating: PG-13. Running time: 141 MIN.
Jack Ryan .... Harrison Ford
Clark .... Willem Dafoe
Cathy Ryan .... Anne Archer
Felix Cortez .... Joaquim de Almeida
Robert Ritter .... Henry Czerny
James Cutter .... Harris Yulin
President Bennett .... Donald Moffat
Ernesto Escobedo ..... Miguel Sandoval
  With: Benjamin Bratt, Raymond Cruz, Dean Jones, Thora Birch, Ann Magnuson, Hope Lange, Tom Tammi, Tim Grimm, Belita Moreno, James Earl Jones.

Jack Ryan takes on the Colombian drug cartels and some nefarious members of a duplicitous U.S. government in "Clear and Present Danger," the third entry in Paramount's Tom Clancy franchise. Narrative complexity and momentum make this a true cinematic equivalent of an absorbing page-turner. Even if the excitement only occasionally reaches thrilling levels, its bestseller profile, action quotient and Harrison Ford as a can-do hero assure muscular late summer B.O. for this well-tooled entertainment.

Although the format is familiar and filmmakers sometimes work up a sweat just getting all the necessary exposition and info up on-screen, pic's complex plot, double-edged characters and political relevance to recent history help make this the most interesting of the three Clancy adaptations, at least from a content p.o.v. Despite Ryan's moral uprightness and the presence of some undiluted villains, many of the issues here are painted in shades of gray rather than simplistic black-and-white, which is all to the good in terms of creating dramatic ambiguity if not for providing elemental cheap thrills.

Setting the nasty chain of events in motion is the murder of a prominent U.S. businessman and friend of the president who, it turns out, has been in league with the cartels. Embarrassed and awakened to the ineffectiveness of the country's war on drugs, the prez (Donald Moffat) has Ryan (Ford), now acting CIA deputy director of intelligence due to the illness of his boss (James Earl Jones), pursue the matter, while secretly setting loose national security adviser James Cutter (Harris Yulin) and CIA hard-liner Robert Ritter (Henry Czerny) to send a paramilitary force against the drug lords.

To this end, they hire CIA cowboy Clark (Willem Dafoe), who leads a unit of Latino guerrilla fighters into the jungle to hit the operations of drug kingpin Ernesto Escobedo (Miguel Sandoval). Latter is none too pleased the U.S. is laying claim to the $650 million stash he shared with the president's late friend. His response is to launch a rocket attack on a convoy of Yank politicos and operatives, including Ryan, trapped in a narrow Bogota street, which makes for the film's most eventful and original action set piece.

Ryan is kept in the dark as long as possible about the extra-legal combat mission, as well as about private discussions between Cutter and Escobedo's suave lawyer, Felix Cortez (Joaquim de Almeida), a former Castro aide who harbors ambitions of replacing his boss as top dog in Colombia. When Ryan finds out, the straight-arrow patriot becomes damn mad, and is forced to fight rear-guard battles with the president's men just as he attempts to rescue what's left of the abandoned guerrilla unit and settle matters once and for all with Escobedo and Cortez.

It's a lot of incident to pack into a feature, and the talents of three top Hollywood screenwriters — Donald Stewart, Steven Zaillian and John Milius — have been well, if not deeply, used to ensure that the story is coherent and the characters have at least a semblance of plausibility. To their credit, and that of director Phillip Noyce, repeating from "Patriot Games," the far-ranging plot isn't confusing, and many characters who are allotted only a few moments of screen time manage to make the required impression.

On an action level, pic is less highcharged than numerous other efforts of its ilk, although a sequence in which the U.S. drops a smart bomb on a drug lord conclave is vivid and will prompt some wishful thinking on the part of those who imagine there's an easy solution to the drug problem out there somewhere. Final action scene feels a bit flat and anti-climactic, in that it's mainly routine chase and gunplay stuff between Ryan and Cortez, with a predictable outcome.

More interesting is the harsh take on the way the U.S. government, and the president in particular, conducts foreign policy. With Moffat cutting a Reagan/Bush-like figure of a leader with untold links to shady businessmen and a way of letting his underlings know what he wants done without assuming personal responsibility himself, yarn ultimately forces its hero, Ryan, to choose between covering up for the men who have misled and lied to him, and embarrassing the country by standing up for the truth.

Anxious to express his character's confusion, reticence and wariness whenever possible, Ford still can't help but be the noble stalwart for what he sees as the nation's traditional virtues. Dafoe seems to enjoy playing an action part and might have been given more to do. The villains shine, particularly de Almeida as the smooth, amoral Latin counselor, Czerny as the crafty CIA deputy and Yulin as the president's dirty operator. As the Escobar figure, Sandoval neatly conveys how such vicious criminals can also be family men adored by those around them.

As before, Anne Archer, as Ryan's wife, is asked to be supportive and worried in equal measure. Incisive character sketches are provided by Ann Magnuson, as a government secretary duped and betrayed by her lover Cortez, and Hope Lange, as a determined senator.

Production values are customarily expensive-looking and professional, with an assortment of Mexican locations attractively standing in for South American settings. James Horner's score goes in some interesting and unusual directions for this sort of genre item.
—*Todd McCarthy*

AIRHEADS

A 20th Century Fox release of an Island World/Robert Simonds production. Produced by Simonds, Mark Burg. Executive producer, Todd Baker. Co-producer, Ira Shuman. Directed by Michael Lehmann. Screenplay, Rich Wilkes. Camera (Deluxe color), John Schwartzman; editor, Stephen Semel; music, Carter Burwell; production design, David Nichols; art direction, Edward McAvoy; costume design, Bridget Kelly; sound (Dolby), Douglas Axtell, Russell Fager; assistant director, Joe Camp III; casting, Billy Hopkins, Suzanne Smith. Reviewed at the Mann Westwood, L.A., July 27, 1994. MPAA Rating: PG-13. Running time: 91 MIN.
Chazz Darby .... Brendan Fraser
Rex .... Steve Buscemi
Pip .... Adam Sandler
Ian the Shark .... Joe Mantegna
Wilson .... Chris Farley
Milo .... Michael McKean
Kayla .... Amy Locane
Doug Beech .... Michael Richards
Jimmie Wing .... Judd Nelson
O'Malley .... Ernie Hudson
Suzzi .... Nina Siemaszko

There's plenty of sound and fury in "Airheads," and while it would be extreme to say it adds up to nothing, the antic musical lark certainly doesn't have a lot on its mind. An absurdist variation on "Dog Day Afternoon," the picture is a rather good-natured view of Generation X and the pursuit of rock 'n' roll stardom. While it hits the right chord for a niche audience, don't expect better than modest domestic returns.

The slim premise finds a trio of "we don't want to be labeled" musicians desperately trying to get a little bit of attention. Club dates have yet to produce interest from major (or minor) companies, and attempts to get music execs to listen to a demo tape have landed on deaf ears.

So, after ringleader Chazz (Brendan Fraser) gets turfed out by his girlfriend, Kayla (Amy Locane), he tells cronies Rex (Steve Buscemi) and Pip (Adam Sandler) that it's time to be more aggressive. His plan is to storm rebel radio station KPPX and get their tape played on the air. They all agree that it's a good plan.

But execution proves more troublesome. After lucking into the security building, their pleas to D.J. Ian the Shark (Joe Mantegna) are returned with dripping cynicism. Further disdain from the station manager gets Chazz downright crazy and he pulls out a semi-automatic. Suddenly the spinners are all ears and ready to comply.

It doesn't really matter that the boys are packing water pistols — they look real enough. More to the point, the station's vintage reel-to-reel machine isn't working quite right, and the moment of glory lasts about five seconds before the tape gets ground up in the works. But attempts at a hasty retreat come to naught, as the police have already surrounded the station. The only recourse for the rockers is to take KPPX hostage and bask in instant media attention.

The logic may be fuzzy-headed to an extreme, but so are the film's protagonists. Though it's little more than a one-joke premise, director Michael Lehmann gets maximum mileage from the low-octane script by Rich Wilkes. Wisely, there's minimal interest accorded the narrative, with the emphasis placed on the off-kilter characters and their social milieu.

Slick and energetic in execution, "Airheads" comes off as a goof that will leave mainstream audiences cold. But somewhere in the margins it hits a nerve that could echo for years in cult heaven and create brisk business in ancillaries.

Though Fraser looks the role, his attitude is a tad too earnest to effect the kind of whacky vision called for in the material. Cohorts Buscemi and Sandler drift more naturally to the required zaniness. The large supporting cast are a weird and wonderful melange; there are eccentric perfs by the likes of Michael Richards, Michael McKean, Nina Siemaszko,

and, with wildly unctuous glee, Judd Nelson as a record exec more than ready to capitalize on the trio's instant media celebrity.

The anarchic saga could have used more bite or the hint of a threat just to keep things interesting. As it is, it lacks that vital edge that means the difference between merely winding up on the charts and having lasting resonance.

—*Leonard Klady*

CORRINA, CORRINA

A New Line Cinema release of a Steve Tisch production. Produced by Paula Mazur, Steve Tisch, Jessie Nelson. Executive producers, Ruth Vitale, Bernie Goldmann. Line producer, Eric McLeod. Directed, written by Nelson. Camera (Film House, Foto-Kem color), Bruce Surtees; editor, Lee Percy; music, Rick Cox; production design, Jeannine Claudia Oppewall; art direction, Dina Lipton; set design, Louisa Bonnie; set decoration, Lauren M. Gabor; costume design, Francine Jamison-Tanchuck; Whoopi Goldberg's costumes, John Hayles; sound (Dolby), David Kelson; associate producer, Joseph Fineman; assistant director, Phillip Christon; casting, Mary Gail Artz, Barbara Cohen. Reviewed at the Warner Hollywood Studios, L.A., July 18, 1994. MPAA Rating: PG. Running time: **114 MIN.**
Corrina

Manny Singer	Ray Liotta
Molly Singer	Tina Majorino
Jenny Davis	Wendy Crewson
Sid	Larry Miller
Grandma Eva	Erica Yohn
Jevina	Jenifer Lewis
Jonesy	Joan Cusack
Frank	Harold Sylvester
Anthony T.	
Williams	Steven Williams
Wilma	Patrika Darbo
Grandpa Harry	Don Ameche
With: Lucy Webb, Courtland Mead, Asher Metchik.

"Corrina, Corrina," starring Whoopi Goldberg as a perky housekeeper who brings solace and joy to a depressed '50s Jewish household, is a schmaltzy if entertaining comedy-drama. Strong chemistry between Goldberg and Ray Liotta, and a winning performance by child actress Tina Majorino, happily triumph over old-fashioned material and mediocre production values. New Line should expect a favorable B.O. response.**

Basing her story loosely on personal experience, writer/director Jessie Nelson examines the life of a Jewish family after the mother has suddenly died of cancer. Manny Singer (Liotta) is an ad jingle writer who throws himself into work as a way of dealing with his depression. But his 9-year-old daughter, Molly (Majorino), is so traumatized by the event that she becomes mute.

Tale begins with the desperate Manny interviewing for a maid in a

sequence that recalls "Mrs. Doubtfire." A parade of eccentric women passes through (including a funny turn by Joan Cusack) before Corrina Washington (Goldberg) lands the job. Corrina can't cook, but she possesses a sassy, quirky personality that Manny thinks will be good for the child. Scripter makes sure to establish that Corrina is a Renaissance woman with knowledge of poetry and music; her talk is peppered with references to Gertrude Stein, Erik Satie (whose music is used here) and Louis Armstrong.

The film moves predictably through all the paces — and moods — of its three characters. After a long silence and enormous efforts by Corrina, Molly utters her first word and grants her first smile. From there, she builds a special rapport with the housekeeper, who becomes a surrogate mom.

As it's the conservative 1950s, some complications ensue once an interracial romance evolves between Manny and Corrina. And, as if to remind the audience that the broader political context has not been forgotten, a darker tone invades the tale occasionally, as in a restaurant scene in which Corrina is mistaken for a waitress, or when her bitter sister Jevina (Jenifer Lewis) persistently reminds her after each affront that, after all, she is a black woman. The overall mood, however, is sunny and upbeat, as befits the material.

As could be expected, the supporting characters, especially Manny's *yenta* mother (Erica Yohn) and Jenny (Wendy Crewson), a divorcee with an eye on Manny, are drawn with a broad brush.

Novice helmer Nelson shows no instinct for pacing and exhibits little skill at interesting visual presentation or framing.

With these flaws, the best thing the film has going for it is the first-rate acting of its three leads. Goldberg delivers a restrained yet emotional turn, while Liotta renders a sensitive, multi-shaded perf as the bereaved dad.

Majorino seems to be an acting natural, excelling again in a role that is more central and demanding than her previous turn as Meg Ryan's daughter in "When a Man Loves a Woman." It's probably not her fault that she becomes too cute in the last reel, as the whole movie progressively tries too hard to be a crowd-pleaser with its increasing reliance on montage and cross-cutting.

Fortunately, the lively soundtrack uses old pop songs to cue the varying moods, giving some rhythm to a picture that suffers from unmodulated pacing and fumbled editing.

"Corrina, Corrina" features the final performance of veteran actor Don Ameche, who plays Liotta's dying father. —*Emanuel Levy*

ONLY THE BRAVE

(AUSTRALIAN — 16mm)

A Pickpocket Production. Produced by Fiona Eagger. Directed by Ana Kokkinos. Screenplay, Kokkinos, Mira Robertson. Camera (color), Jaems Grant; sound, James Currie. Reviewed at Raleigh Studios screening room, L.A., June 22, 1994. (In L.A. Intl. Gay & Lesbian Film & Video Festival.) Running time: **60 MIN.**

Alex	Elena Mandalis
Vicki	Dora Kaskanis
Kate	Moudo Davey
Rog	Bob Bright

A harrowing, ultra-realistic coming-of-age portrait of a group of tough teenage girls, "Only the Brave" is a new Australian film of astonishing, raw power. One-hour running time will limit theatrical prospects, but pic provides a bold calling card for director Ana Kokkinos.

Set in the seedy, barren outskirts of Melbourne, story centers on two working-class girls, Alex and Vicki, who live on the edge and are desperate to get out of their desolate, dead-end surroundings. Residing with her dad, Alex (Elena Mandalis) dreams of reuniting with her alcoholic mother, a singer who now lives in the North. The equally wild Vicki (Dora Kaskanis), who aspires to become a singer, is Alex's pal and object of her growing and unsettling affection.

Sharply observant script relates the tragic spiral of events, at school and at home, that dooms Alex, Vicki and their clique of troubled teenagers. The harsh realism of physical fights at school and sexual abuse at home is contrasted with dreamy sequences, such as flashbacks of Alex's mother or fantasies of finding her singing in another city.

Film has the novelty of portraying alienation and rites of passage among girls whose ethnic minority (Australians of Greek descent) accentuates their marginal positions and feelings. Dressed in heavy trench coats, these "bad" girls spend their time smoking dope, setting fire to hedges, hanging out at abandoned houses and deserted train stations — in short, engaging in behavioral patterns that, in U.S. movies, are strictly boys' domain.

Though dominant tone is dark and brooding, there's also tenderness, best exemplified in Alex's relationship with her sensitive school teacher Kate (Moudo Davey), who encourages her literary talent and even begins to respond to her sexual yearnings. In film's most lyrical scene, Vicki lays her head in Alex's lap, aching for a caress that her terrified friend is afraid — or perhaps incapable — of giving.

Tech credits of the very low-budget 16mm effort are modest.

But in congruence with her brilliantly naturalistic direction, Kokkinos imbues the picture with alert intelligence and depth, successfully resisting the more clinical strategy of American movies of the week.

—Emanuel Levy

KILLER KID

(FRENCH)

An AFMD release (France) of a Flach Film/Tetra Medias/SFP Cinema/M6 Films production with participation of Canal Plus and in association with Sofiarp 2, Investimage 4 and Procinep. (International sales: Mercure Distribution.) Produced by Catherine Mazieres, Jean-Francois Lepetit. Co-producer for SFPC, Boudjemma Dahmane. Directed by Gilles de Maistre. Screenplay, de Maistre, Miguel Courtois, based on Claude Klotz's novel. Camera (color, widescreen), Jean-Bernard Aurouet; editor, Robert Coursez; music, Rene Aubry; art direction, Jimmy Vansteenskiste; costume design, Michele Bouty; sound, Michel Picardat, Eric Tisserand; assistant director, Denis Seurat; casting, Bruno Delahaye, Marie-Christine Lafosse, Eric Daviron. Reviewed at Gaumont Marignan Cinema, Paris, June 10, 1994. (In Paris Film Festival, Panorama section; also in Cannes Junior fest.). Running time: **95 MIN.**
Laid .... Teufik Jallab
Karim .... Younesse Boudache
Isabelle .... Agathe de la Fontaine
Hans .... Marc de Jonge
(French and Arabic dialogue)

Snappy plotting and heartfelt perfs by two youngsters make "Killer Kid" an involving account of an improbable friendship between two 11-year-old Arab youths. One, trained in Lebanon to be an efficient killer, will take the other, the plucky France-raised son of immigrants, as a role model in Paris before carrying out a deadly mission. Pace never flags in this widescreen adventure that won the Jury Prize and Grand Prix du Public at the 1994 Cannes Junior sidebar.

First fiction outing from Emmy-winning documaker Gilles de Maistre, whose prior pix covered child soldiers and child labor exploitation, is set in 1986, when a wave of terrorist bombings rocked Paris.

Through a series of no-nonsense training exercises in a secret guerrilla camp in Lebanon, stern Laid (Teufik Jallab) is indoctrinated into being a calculating and unfeeling assassin, bent on waging holy war. His levelheadedness and soldierly devotion get him chosen for a vital mission in Paris. But to blend in, Laid — who speaks fluent if somewhat formal French — needs to study the behavior of a typical French kid.

Karim (Younesse Boudache), raised in the immigrant-heavy projects outside Paris, is an irreverent, fun-loving boy who skateboards, break dances, listens to rap, plays videogames and has a soft spot for a pretty 16-year-old junkie. A terrorist unit commanded by Hans (Marc de Jonge) forces Karim's dad to "loan him out."

Tight-lipped Laid, who gets up at 6 a.m. to pray, at first baffles Karim, whose infectious enthusiasm gives him a glimpse of the childhood he never had. The two boys form a friendship pact that will alter the course of French history when an assassination plot backfires in an unlikely but interesting way.

As junior gunman Laid, Jallab has the cold posture and undercurrent of distress befitting his role. Peppy Boudache, as Karim, speaks exclusively in punchy hipster slang.

Non-political pic, in which fanaticism is vividly evoked, is a harsh but engaging introduction to child exploitation.

Lensing has a restless documentary feel that propels the narrative. Score has sinister verve.

—Lisa Nesselson

MOLOM, A MONGOLIAN TALE

(MOLOM, CONTE DE MONGOLIE)

(FRENCH)

A Lung Ta/Films de la Pagode/France 2 Cinema production, with participation of Canal Plus, France 2, CNC, Fondation Elf, Fondation Gan. Produced, directed, written by Marie Jaoul de Poncheville. Executive producers, Fabien Ouaki, Franz-Christoph Giercke. Screenplay, Pierre Joffroy, Patrick Laurent. Camera (color), Jacques Besse; editor, Danielle Anezin; music, John McLaughlin, Trilok Gurtu; art direction, Abderrahmane Sissako; sound (Dolby), Jean-Pierre Laforce, Laurent Dreyer; sound design, Pierre Choukroun; associate producer, Elisabeth Dauchy. Reviewed at Gaumont Marignan Cinema, Paris, June 7, 1994. (In Paris Film Festival, competing; also in Cannes Junior fest.) Running time: **96 MIN.**
Molom .... Tseded
Yonden .... Yonde Junai
(Mongolian dialogue)

"Molom" is the splendidly lensed, free-form tale of an adorable young boy who, under the leisurely tutelage of a wizened spiritual guide, trades life with wolves on the Mongolian steppes for the lessons of Buddha. Serene, non-violent pic brims with exotic vistas and should appeal to kids of all ages whose attention spans haven't been eroded by Western distractions.

In voiceover, Yonden (Yonde Junai) explains that Molom (Tseded) changed from an eagle into a man to teach him to seek the pearl at the heart of life.

Tyke and shaman form a playful partnership as they hike across the majestic steppes. Yonden's casual apprenticeship makes "The Karate Kid" look like the boot-camp sequences of "Full Metal Jacket" — lessons, such as they are, penetrate by osmosis in natural settings.

The ethereal, spacey story is carried by the lensing, which boasts an unerring feel for the protagonists' faces and the knockout landscape. Loose script took form as crew accompanied duo on trek.

When teacher and pupil reach civilization, the contrasts of Nikita Mikhalkov's "Close to Eden" come to mind, although helmer does little more than present city life and monastery rituals and let viewers draw their own conclusions.

Pic was lensed in Mongolia and at Lake Baikal in the autonomous region of Buryat (in Siberia) by Marie Jaoul de Poncheville, a former documaker whose previous pix dealt with Tibet, Nepal and Mongolia. Traditional Mongolian folk tunes are pleasing, but John McLaughlin's jazzier contributions are sometimes a tad too contemporary-sounding to mesh.

—Lisa Nesselson

THE LITTLE RASCALS

A Universal Pictures release of a Universal and King World presentation. Produced by Michael King, Bill Oakes. Executive producers, Gerald R. Molen, Deborah Jelin Newmyer, Roger King. Co-producer, Mark Allan. Directed by Penelope Spheeris. Screenplay, Paul Guay, Stephen Mazur, Spheeris, story by Spheeris, Robert Wolterstorff, Mike Scott, Guay, Mazur. Camera (Deluxe color), Richard Bowen; editor, Ross Albert; music, William Ross; production design, Larry Fulton; art direction, Gae Buckley; set decoration, Linda Spheeris; costume design, Jami Burrows; sound (DTS), Susumu Tokunow; assistant director, Matt Earl Beesley; second unit director, Beesley; stunt coordinator, Shane Dixon; casting, Judy Taylor, Lynda Gordon. Reviewed at the Cineplex Odeon Universal City Cinema, Universal City, July 30, 1994. MPAA Rating: PG. Running time: **82 MIN.**
Spanky .... Travis Tedford
Alfalfa .... Bug Hall
Darla .... Brittany Ashton Holmes
Stymie .... Kevin Jamal Woods
Porky .... Zachary Mabry
Buckwheat .... Ross Elliot Bagley
Butch .... Sam Saletta
Woim .... Blake Jeremy Collins
Waldo .... Blake McIver Ewing
Froggy .... Jordan Warkol
Uh-Huh .... Courtland Mead
Mary Ann .... Juliette Brewer
Jane .... Heather Karasek
Petey .... Himself
Mr. Welling .... Mel Brooks
Buckwheat's
  Mom .... Whoopi Goldberg
Miss Crabtree .... Daryl Hannah
A.J. Ferguson .... Reba McEntire

Those who grew up watching "The Little Rascals" on murky UHF TV stations may well be intrigued by the idea of introducing their kids to this full-color, bigscreen version. Still, the challenge of stretching those mildly diverting shorts to feature length remains formidable, and one has to wonder whether an audience exists beyond nostalgic parents and their young children — in short, anyone between the ages of 10 and 30. Sporadically clever and thoroughly inoffensive, this Universal release at best seems destined for returns along "Beethoven"/"Problem Child" lines.

One has to admire director Penelope Spheeris' perseverance in dealing with revered TV material, having last tackled "The Beverly Hillbillies" and, before that, the neoclassic "Wayne's World."

As with "Hillbillies," this movie's principal achievement may be its slavish devotion to the original and the remarkable casting done in terms of finding tots who closely resemble their rascally forebears.

One gains a real appreciation for what the filmmakers have undertaken only during outtakes that roll over the closing credits, providing some indication of what it must have been like to work with a cast composed almost entirely of 5- to 9-year-olds, as plaintive voices intone, "Don't look at the camera, honey" from offscreen.

After the initial kick associated with seeing the characters, "Rascals" goes about the business of setting up a rather conventional plot, as love-smitten Alfalfa (Bug Hall) violates the rules of the all-male He-Man Womun-Haters Club by wooing the decidedly feminine Darla (cherubic Brittany Ashton Holmes).

This irks his pal, Spanky (Travis Tedford), and inadvertently results in the destruction of their clubhouse. Needing $350 to rebuild, the group embarks on various efforts to raise the money, ultimately getting its chance via a go-cart race that also includes the new object of Darla's affection, rich kid Waldo (Blake McIver Ewing, who bears an uncanny resemblance to the Culkin clan).

It's hard to believe that input from five writers was needed to come up with that premise. As with "The Flintstones," which had the advantage of ample visual gimmickry, the quintet struggles at spreading the material over 80 minutes, turning in amusing moments but also some rather arid stretches.

The real problem involves finding a steady source of laughs, as opposed to mild grins. While much of the fun involves hearing moppets deliver lines like "You took the best years of my life," it's a novelty that tends to yield gradually diminishing returns.

The filmmakers do make clever use of adult cameos, from Donald Trump as the rich kid's father to Whoopi Goldberg as Buckwheat's mom. TV tykes Mary-Kate and Ashley Olsen ("Full House") and Raven-Symone ("The Cosby Show") also appear in blink-and-miss-them scenes.

For the most part, though, this is the kids' show, and they acquit themselves reasonably well. Difficult as it is to single any of them out, Holmes proves a real scene-stealer as Darla, while Kevin Jamal Woods, as Stymie, may be the most natural actor in the bunch.

Credit Spheeris at least with bringing a certain energy to the simple proceedings, and the technical crew with creating a world that looks modern yet still feels comfortably enmeshed in a 1930s sensibility.

William Ross helps by deftly weaving his own score around the recognizable "Little Rascals" theme, while the song score appropriately includes Randy Newman's "Short People."

—*Brian Lowry*

BROTHER MINISTER:
THE ASSASSINATION OF MALCOLM X
(DOCU — B&W/COLOR)

An X-Ceptional Prods. in association with Illuminati Entertainment Group Inc. and Why Prods. Inc. production. Produced, directed by Jack Baxter, Jefri Aalmuhammed. Executive producer, Lewis Kesten. Screenplay, Baxter, Aalmuhammed, Joan Claire Chabriel. Photographic consultant, Robert Haggins; editor, Mitchell Kress; music, Richie Havens, Annie Lennox. Viewed on videocassette, L.A., July 27, 1994. Running time: **117 MIN.**
Narrator: Roscoe Lee Browne.

"**B**rother Minister: The Assassination of Malcolm X" is an interesting documentary that raises more than it answers provocative questions about the forces involved in the 1965 killing of the charismatic black leader. At its present two-hour length, level of discourse and visual form, docu seems to be a likely candidate for airings on public TV and cable, although there's probably room for theatrical runs in urban centers and college towns. Pic just finished a commercial engagement in L.A.

Central allegation here is that the FBI, New York Police Dept. and the Nation of Islam, led by Louis Farrakhan, attempted to undermine Malcolm X's credibility after his split from NOI's founder, Elijah Mohammed. At the time, Malcolm X charged Mohammed with immoral conduct, claiming that he sired several children by his secretaries.

Docu reconstructs in fascinating detail the suspension of Malcolm X from NOI, his rejection of its doctrine of racial separatism, his pilgrimage to Mecca, his close ties with some African nations and attempts to win official U.N. recognition for his new organization.

Film asserts effectively that death threats were issued by NOI leaders. It also outlines how Malcolm's new political org was infiltrated by undercover cops and how the FBI sent fake letters to NOI in order to splinter the various black factions.

Reportedly, just months before his death, Malcolm X was working on the formation of a coalition with Dr. Martin Luther King, whose agenda called for King to organize blacks in the South while Malcolm X worked in the North.

This "suspicious" and "threatening" coalition is described by New York Post journalist Jack Newfield as "J. Edgar Hoover's worst nightmare."

Docu has its own peculiarities: It's unclear why Malcolm's widow, Betty Shabazz, was not interviewed, as she is the only person who straightforwardly implicates Farrakhan in the murder, in an excerpt from CBS' "News Forum" that precedes the docu proper.

In general, the clips used at the outset, about the press reaction to the docu's making, raise provocative and challenging claims that the filmmakers sometimes find hard to substantiate.

Technically, film is quite conventional, alternating lengthy interviews with authentic historical footage, and could advisedly be cut by 15-20 minutes. On the plus side, narration by Roscoe Lee Browne is kept to a minimum, letting the material speak for itself.

"Brother Minister" lacks conclusive evidence or coherent theory as to who ordered the assassination of Malcolm X, but it certainly adds new pieces of crucial info to the puzzle. With some luck, and beneficial response by key media figures, docu might lead to the reopening of the case, which is undoubtedly its aim.

—*Emanuel Levy*

BOY MEETS GIRL
(BRITISH — 16mm)

A Kino Eye production. Produced by Ray Brady, Chris Read. Line producer, Ray Tang. Directed by Brady. Screenplay, Brady, Jim Crosbie, from an idea by Brady. Camera (color), Kevin McMorrow; editor, Russell Fenton; music, Crosbie, Geoff Southall; production design, Brady; costume design, Pam Hogg; sound, "Alan Smithee" (Crosbie), John Salcini; special makeup effects, Sunil Chandragiri; assistant director, Minou Norouzi. Reviewed at National Film Theatre, London, July 30, 1994. Running time: **90 MIN.**
Tevin .... Tim Poole
Julia .... Danielle Sanderson
Anne Marie .... Margot Steinberg
Woman in chair .... Susan Warren

Ambition fatally exceeds reach in "Boy Meets Girl," a laudable attempt to push the envelope of British filmmaking that doesn't get much farther than first base. Chamber drama about a woman who keeps a man prisoner in her cellar and slowly tortures him to death is done in by performances and scripting that aren't up to snuff. Combo of disagreeable subject matter and weak execution will limit this party pooper to rendezvous on the latenight fest circuit. Theatrical and ancillary chances look virtually non-existent.

Film world preemed at London's National Film Theatre as part of its Fantasm '94 minifest. Despite the pic's advance rep as a brain-bending shocker, reaction from the buff audience was muted, with no noticeable walkouts.

Action starts with supposedly French looker Anne Marie (Margot Steinberg) taking bar pickup Tevin (Tim Poole) back to her apartment for some rough and tumble. After passing out from a spiked drink, he wakes up strapped to a dentist's chair in nothing but his jockey shorts. Anne Marie, meanwhile, who turns out to be Yank, has slipped into some dominatrix duds and begins a program of physical and mental torture, homevideoed by an unseen third party.

A plot switch around the 40-minute mark has Tevin waking up to confront the real mastermind, serial killer Julia (Danielle Sanderson), a soft-spoken young English woman who was the unseen vidtaper and has since added Anne Marie's head to her collection in the cellar.

Tevin's catalogue of humiliations (including having his hand fried in a microwave) continues, with lots of sexual psychobabble from Julia, occasional glimpses of her snuff-movie collection and an attempted escape by the hapless protagonist prior to the ritualistic conclusion.

Pic's major flaw is its failure to develop an atmosphere of threat or menace between captor and victim. Single-set chamber drama of this kind needs top-flight dialogue, strong playing and confident technique to go the distance. Although "Boy Meets Girl" has its moments in each of these departments, they're fleeting indeed, and any buildup in atmosphere isn't helped by frequent (and frequently obscure) chapter divisions like "I Lied," "The American Dream" and "Just an Average Victim."

By opting for a "serious" approach, with its exaggerated role-reversal commentary on everyday domestic violence, the movie has none of the fantastic, over-the-top qualities of low-budgeters by, say, Germany's Jorg Buttgereit ("Nekromantik," "Schramm").

Result is an unengaging, often sophomoric exercise that doesn't really work on any level. Direction by co-writer/producer Ray Brady is deliberately unflashy, which unfortunately serves to spotlight further the shortcomings in dialogue and performances. Tech credits are reasonable, given the budget.

—*Derek Elley*

LOST IN AFRICA

(BRITISH)

A Pyramide release (France) of a JLDE Image Intl. presentation of a Duke of Northumberland/Hotspur Prods. production. Produced by Gerald Green. Co-executive producers, the Duke of Northumberland, Gerry Levy. Directed, written by Stewart Raffill. Camera (color; widescreen), Roger Olkowski; editor, Peter Zinner; costume design, Diane Kirman; sound (Ultra-Stereo), Arnold Braun; special effects/makeup, Everett Burrell; animal wrangler, Hubert Wells; big tusker trainer, Randall J. Moore; stunts, Fernando Celis; assistant director, Roger Lapage; second unit director, Hubert Wells; casting, Leroy Wilson, Konga Mb Andau. Reviewed at Gaumont Marignan Cinema, Paris, June 7, 1994. (In Paris Film Festival, competing.) Running time: **101 MIN.**

Elisabeth	Jennifer McComb
Michael	Ashley Hamilton
Rabar	Mohamed Nangurai
Charles	Timothy Ackroyd

"**L**ost in Africa" is a contrived but basically enjoyable adventure tale that plunks two white tenderfoots into the wilds of black Africa, with an angry native tracker on their tail and only a protective 100-year-old elephant on their side. Attractive location lensing with wildlife galore makes this a modest B.O. prospect for family outings, although youngsters may be spooked by a few vivid examples of the law of the jungle in action.

Black poachers hijack a handful of hostages from a group of American, English and Japanese tourists. U.S. teen Michael (Ashley Hamilton) escapes with Elisabeth (Jennifer McComb), the English woman he's been harassing for 10 days, and an English gent, Charles (Timothy Ackroyd), but shoots and kills the tribal chieftain in the process.

Chief's handsome young son Rabar (Mohamed Nangurai) sets out to avenge the dead leader. Meanwhile, Charles is mauled to death by a lion, leaving the at-first-antagonistic young couple to fend for themselves against scorpions, crocodiles, vultures and fleas, forming a romantic bond en route.

Michael and Elisabeth remain suspiciously pale and well-groomed, despite their struggles to survive in hostile territory. Whenever they're about to die of thirst or fall prey to enemies, a wise old tusker — "the last of the great elephants," as people utter at every opportunity — provides the hint or warning they need.

Widescreen lensing well serves locations in Kenya, Botswana, Tanzania and Zimbabwe, although some encounters with animals are more convincing than others. Continuity in terms of time and distance is a bit wobbly, but confrontation between tracker and his human prey affords some late-arriving thrills. A subplot about an orphaned baby elephant is genuinely touching.

American thesp McComb's British accent comes and goes. As Michael, 17-year-old Hamilton, son of George Hamilton and Alana Stewart, makes his screen debut.

The John Williams-style score sounds ridiculously overblown in spare, natural settings.

—*Lisa Nesselson*

COUNTRY LIFE

(AUSTRALIAN)

A UIP (Australia) release of an Australian Film Finance Corp./Dalton Films production. (International sales: Southern Star Film Sales.) Produced by Robin Dalton. Directed, written by Michael Blakemore, suggested by "Uncle Vanya" by Anton Chekhov. Camera (color), Stephen Windon; editor, Nicholas Beauman; music, Peter Best; production design, Laurence Eastwood; costumes, Wendy Chuck; sound (Dolby), Ben Osmo, Phil Judd; assistant director, Colin Fletcher; casting, Alison Barrett. Reviewed at UIP screening room, Sydney, July 26, 1994. (In Brisbane Film Festival.) Running time: **114 MIN.**

Dr. Max Askey	Sam Neill
Deborah Voysey	Greta Scacchi
Jack Dickens	John Hargreaves
Sally Voysey	Kerry Fox
Alexander Voysey	Michael Blakemore
Maude Dickens	Patricia Kennedy
Fred Livingstone	Maurie Fields
Wally Wells	Ron Blanchard
Hannah	Googie Withers
Violet	Robyn Cruze
Mr. Pettinger	Bryan Marshall
Logger	Tony Barry

Latest entry in the upmarket Merchant-Ivory school of cinema is the Australian "Country Life," which has been cunningly adapted from Chekhov's "Uncle Vanya" by writer/director/thesp Michael Blakemore. Result is a classy item, steeped in a kind of melancholy nostalgia, with solid perfs and a good dose of down-to-earth humor. Robin Dalton's production breaks no new ground but does what it does with impeccable precision. Result should do well with its target audience in arthouse cinemas worldwide.

Blakemore, who left his native Australia decades ago for a successful career as theater director in Britain, has skillfully transposed the Russian characters of the original into a convincing group of rural Aussies just after World War I. Jack Dickens (John Hargreaves) has abandoned his own literary ambitions to run the farm he inherited from his father; his elderly mother (Patricia Kennedy) lives in the house, as does his niece, Sally Voysey (Kerry Fox). Sally was abandoned by her feckless father, Alexander Voysey, after her mother, Jack's sister, died.

Every month, Jack sends hard-earned money to his brother-in-law to support him in his career as a literary critic in London. Sally, a good-hearted plain Jane, is hopelessly in love with local doctor Max Askey (Sam Neill), who is hardly aware she's around.

Story revolves around the return of the long-absent Alexander (Blakemore) and his much younger wife, Deborah (Greta Scacchi). It is quickly apparent that Alexander is a pompous bore (he has, in fact, left the London literary scene in disgrace) and that Deborah isn't especially happy. Jack and Askey hover around the alluring stranger, to the distress of poor, ignored Sally.

Blakemore's screenplay contains a subtext about Australians starting to sever ties with Mother England, a theme familiar from several Aussie films these days, most recently "Sirens." Chief motif here is the English-style garden that used to be a showpiece of the Dickens farm but has now fallen into decay, echoing Jack's discovery that the European fame of his supposedly celebrated brother-in-law is nothing more than a piece of arrogant self-promotion.

Actors, for the most part, rise to the occasion, with Hargreaves as the naive, betrayed Jack, and Fox as the lonely, loveless Sally particular standouts. Neill brings some complexity to the role of Askey, who's a pacifist and leftist at a time when such beliefs were decidedly unfashionable and who has a secret drinking problem. Blakemore himself makes the arrogant Alexander a splendidly unlikable snob. Of the major thesps, Scacchi is saddled with the least interesting role and can't do much with the character of the flirtatious Deborah.

Supporting players are on the mark, and it's especially good to see vet actress Googie Withers again, after many years' absence from the screen, playing a strong-willed Irish servant in the Dickens household.

Production values are top-drawer, notably Stephen Windon's attractive lensing on location in the Hunter Valley of New South Wales, Laurence Eastwood's sumptuous production design, Nicholas Beauman's pro editing and Peter Best's apt score.

Fact that story is essentially a downer in which none of the characters winds up fulfilled or happy is leavened by the prevalent humor, which takes the edge off the pain. It's a major advance over Blakemore's only previous feature film, the British-made "Privates on Parade" (1982).

Pic's Oz preem at the Brisbane film fest was in advance of an October release via UIP.

—*David Stratton*

GIRLS WITH GUNS

(LES BRAQUEUSES)

(FRENCH)

A Chrysalide Films release of a Chrysalide Films/Studio Canal Plus/CEC Rhone-Alpes/TF1 Films Prod./M6 Films production. (International sales: Le Studio Canal Plus.) Produced by Monique Annaud. Executive producers, Gilles Sacuto, Milena Poylo. Directed by Jean-Paul Salome. Screenplay, Salome, Laurent Benegui, Gerard Mordillat, Joelle Goron. Camera (color), Patrick Duroux; editor, Michele Robert-Laulliac; art direction, Sylvie Olive; costume design, Charlotte David; sound, Jerome Thiault; boxing consultant, Michel Gibert. Reviewed at UGC Opera Cinema, Paris, July 23, 1994. Running time: **94 MIN.**

Cecile	Catherine Jacob
Bijou	Clementine Celarie
Muriel	Alexandra Kazan
Lola	Nanou Garcia

With: Annie Girardot, Laurent Spielvogel, Jacques Gamblin, Jean-Claude Adelin.

"**G**irls with Guns" is a jaunty little comedy about four resourceful girlfriends who turn their luck around by robbing banks. Somewhat vulgar, fairly inventive pic should stir up some commercial interest, and sitcom-style format could facilitate a remake in any country where thirtysomething women are fed up with dead-end jobs and meager earnings.

Matronly Cecile (Catherine Jacob), who teaches electrical repair to teenage boys, is severely overdrawn at the bank, while Bijou (Clementine Celarie) is abandoned by her abusive hubby, a military man, mere days after giving birth to their third child.

Sexy but none-too-bright waitress Muriel (Alexandra Kazan) is in debt to her restaurant manager and is desperately trying to conceive a child with her hunky wheelchair-bound hubby. Lola (Nanou Garcia), fresh out of prison, lands a job as a bus driver but can't afford a place to live.

When they walk in on a holdup in progress, Lola and Bijou spontaneously empty the till after the clerk abandons the store to chase the original robber. Following this impromptu theft, their first target is a local sex shop to which inexperienced Bijou brings along stockings — the opaque variety — to wear over their heads.

Quartet studies Belmondo pix for tips on how to wield a gun and how to treat a hostage. Cleverly staged bank jobs are lensed with verve.

Whereas movie heists traditionally drive the perps apart, this gang grows closer. And unlike Thelma and Louise or the desperadoes in "Bad Girls," these ladies aren't on the run. They empty safes on their lunch breaks and go home to cook supper.

August 8, 1994 (Cont.)

Bad guys who cross the heroines get their carefully orchestrated comeuppance, and the good guys get their reward. Spirited thesps strike the right system-snubbing tone throughout, in line with the immoral but fun approach.

Pic was lensed off the beaten path in the suburbs of Montelimar, where the distinctive concrete stacks of a nuclear power plant are a stone's throw from the bus terminal. —*Lisa Nesselson*

VEVEY FEST

FALSE PREGNANCY

(GROSSESSE NERVEUSE)

(FRENCH-SWISS)

A Bloody Mary Prods., France 2 (Paris)/Prods. Crittin & Thiebaud (Geneva)/TSR, Afitec Valais production. Produced by Didier Haudepin. Executive co-producer (Switzerland), Pierre-Andre Thiebaud. Directed, written by Denis Rabaglia. Camera (color), Pierluigi Zaretti; editor, Monique Dartonne; music, Louis Crelier; production design, Michel Vandestien; costume design, Nathalie Du Roscoat; sound, Daniel Ollivier. Reviewed at Vevey Comedy Film Festival (noncompeting), Vevey, Switzerland, July 27, 1994. (Also in Locarno Film Festival.) Running time: **84 MIN.**
Martin .... Tom Novembre
Genevieve .... Sabine Haudepin
Sally .... Isabelle Townsend
Antoinette .... Catherine Samie
Julien .... Patrick Braoude
Veronique .... Clotilde Baudon
With: Jean Rougerie, Marie-Laure Dougnac, Anne Kreis, Caroline Gasser.

"**F**alse Pregnancy" is an intelligent, fast-paced, French-lingo comedy with something for everyone: people who dote on dogs and babies, and folks who shudder at the sight of 'em. Clever first feature by scripter/helmer Denis Rabaglia eyes the implications of a gestating tyke from a masculine p.o.v. Upbeat fest/tube/arthouse item has good commercial potential and could lend itself to a U.S. remake.

Thirty-five-year-old Martin (Tom Novembre) is halfheartedly conjuring ad campaigns for the Floppy dog-food empire — a job secured for him by his ambitious ex-wife (Sabine Haudepin) — when he discovers that 23-year-old English *au pair* Sally (Isabelle Townsend) is pregnant via their one-night stand three months prior. Sally intends to keep the baby but dismisses Martin as an irrelevant component.

As mild-mannered Martin seeks guidance from friends and family, pic explores a broad spectrum of attitudes toward bundles of joy.

His militant do-gooder mom (Catherine Samie) decries the im-

pending birth and threatens to disown Martin if the pregnancy isn't terminated, since each European baby consumes enough food to nourish 10 Ethiopians.

His best buddy, Julien ("Nine Months" helmer Patrick Braoude) — a committed househusband to five youngsters — threatens to cancel their friendship if Martin so much as alludes to abortion.

While his childless ex-wife conspires to influence Sally, Martin befriends a freshly minted teenage mom who, thanks to an entertainingly cynical midwife, delivers under unexpected circumstances.

Comic and reflective touches abound as pic examines romantically ambivalent Martin's existential anxiety. Humor is grounded in human interactions rather than the crass buffoonery on display in recent pregnancy farce "Nine Months," now in the U.S. remake pipeline.

Sweetly nuanced comic thesping is well served by snappy lensing, punchy editing, visually varied settings and a jokingly sinister score.

Samie as Martin's crusading mom delivers a rock-solid perf in a role reminiscent of Glenn Close's screen debut in "The World According to Garp."

Crowd-pleasing pic has racked up several international honors including Germany's Max Ophuls Prize. —*Lisa Nesselson*

AFI/L.A. FEST

DEFICIENCY

(CARENCES)

(FRENCH)

A Tokuma Communication/Strudel Films co-production. Produced by Jean-Stephanie Michaux. Directed, written by David Rozenberg. Camera (color), Erwan Elies; editor, Bertrand Boutillier; music, Philippe Haim; production design, Jean-Paul Bernard; sound, Gilles Benefice. Reviewed at AFI/L.A. Film Festival, July 6, 1994. Running time: **91 MIN.**
Roland Resse .... Christophe Garcia
Madame Martin .... Isabelle Sadoyan
Roger .... Jerome Frey
Viviane .... Barbara Tissier
Madame Dietrich .... Arlette Balkis
Mr. Jules .... Phillippe Nahon
Raymond .... Daniel Millgram

The rise of neo-Nazism in France forms the backdrop for first-timer David Rozenberg's "Deficiency." The quiet, brooding piece reflects an assured hand behind the camera that should find an appreciative arthouse response. The restraint with which he tells the fact-based tale, however, is a bit too subdued to grab audiences by the jugular and give pic must-see status.

At the outset, Roland Resse (Christophe Garcia) is behind bars and the victim of a brutal beating by fellow inmates. Withholding the nature of the crime he's committed, writer/director establishes a sense of sympathy for Resse before laying out his story.

Resse arrives in a rural community in answer to an ad for farm workers. He's introverted, socially awkward and somehow pitiable, dressed up like an overgrown boy scout. Madame Dietrich (Arlette Balkis) agrees to a trial period and arranges for him to rent a room in the village from Madame Martin (Isabelle Sadoyan).

Martin attempts to draw the young man out of his shell, and it proves a slow, difficult process.

At work, Reese keeps to himself until Dietrich insists he eat with his fellow workers because they must work as a family. At the table he reveals he's a vegetarian and believes in a pure mind and body. He finds a kindred soul in Roger (Jerome Frey), a racist who cautions him to keep his beliefs to himself. Later, Resse is taken into the local neo-Nazi party and given work.

Told in a simple, disquieting fashion, "Deficiency" emerges as a latter-day variation on "Lacombe Lucien." But while Louis Malle's film benefits from the inherent conflict of its World War II setting, this effort simmers for a long time before boiling over to its tragic conclusion.

Garcia effects a chilling, almost creepy, manner for his character that signals a major acting talent. It is a superbly acted piece by major and supporting thesps.

Elegantly directed by Rozenberg, the film has much to applaud artistically and technically. Its minor sin is that, by its very nature, the material leans toward the cerebral rather than the visceral and keeps the audience at arm's length. —*Leonard Klady*

GATHER AT THE RIVER

(MUSICAL DOCU — 16mm)

A Mug-Shot production. Produced, directed, edited by Robert Mugge. Camera (color), Christopher Li, Bill Burke; sound, William Barth. Reviewed at AFI/L.A. Film Festival, June 28, 1994. Running time: **101 MIN.**
With: Bill Munroe, Doug McCurry, others.

This edition among filmmaker Robert Mugge's odes to musical expression finds him deep in bluegrass country. Though the title — "Gather at the River" — suggests something with a gospel beat, it is the "high lonesome"

style of banjo pickers like Bill Munroe that is the focus of this non-analytic homage. It should provide a tuneful return from specialized and TV dates.

Mugge focuses on contemporary artists in the field. His obvious delight with the musical form comes across effortlessly, while historical background is weaved in on the most casual basis.

There are also some intriguing sidebars in which he films unlikely devotees from Japan and Eastern Europe who have come to America to perform their variation on the theme. One seg finds him in a workshop where youngsters are taking up the cause, proving the traditions aren't quite ready to give up the ghost.

Theatrical prospects are blunted by Rachel Liebling's recent "High Lonesome," which explored the territory more earnestly and with a bite better suited to the bigscreen. "Gather at the River" is a more leisurely view for those looking to lean back and tap their feet in rhythm. —*Leonard Klady*

THE KINGDOM OF ZYDECO

(DOCU — 16mm)

A Mug-Shot production. Produced, directed, edited by Robert Mugge. Executive producer, David Steffan. Line producer, Robert Maier. Camera (color), David Sperling; sound, William Barth; second unit camera, Bill Burke. Reviewed at AFI/L.A. Film Festival, June 28, 1994. Running time: **71 MIN.**
With: Boozoo Chavis, Beau Jocque, others.

Director Robert Mugge attempts to give structure to his appreciation of Zydeco music by pitting two of its proponents in a competition in which one will be crowned king of the rhythmic form. While the music remains uniquely infectious, the electioneering format proves neither dramatic nor of particular interest to the filmmaker. Still, the performance segments have enough appeal to ensure small-screen interest and some specialized theatrical play.

Typical of past outings, Mugge focuses on the music. In "The Kingdom of Zydeco," background is at its most ethereal.

The so-called rivals for the throne are the veteran Boozoo Chavis and a popular newcomer named Beau Jocque. Neither has a great deal to say about what makes his brand of music unique. Both would much rather just play and let the fans decide.

There is some brief reference to the whole affair being a publicity stunt by "outsiders." And while questions of race pop up, Mugge has no intention of making them an issue in the film. After belaboring the whole idea of a contest, he perfunctorily reveals the winner without even a courtesy trumpet blast or drumroll.

Though the filmmaker's work has never displayed a fluid style, "The Kingdom of Zydeco" is decidedly more self-conscious and awkward than past outings. It's definitely best to tune out the dialogue and tune in the Cajun beat.

—*Leonard Klady*

PARAJANOV

(GERMAN — DOCU — 16mm)

A Kino production. Produced by Frank Loprich, Katrin Schlosser, Dorothea Holloway. Directed by Ron Holloway. Camera (DuArt color), Thomas Schwan; editor, Monika Schindler; sound, Markus Stoffell. Reviewed on videocassette, L.A., July 27, 1994. (In AFI/L.A. Film Festival.) Running time: **57 MIN.**

Iconoclastic Armenian-born filmmaker Sergei Parajanov is the subject of this documentary, which is more primer than textbook to a remarkable and unique cinematic vision. Essentially content to record the subject's thoughts and buttress with selected clips, it proves disappointing for its lack of analysis or the conviction to place him in the movie pantheon. As such, it has limited theatrical, television and classroom prospects.

Director Ron Holloway bases the film on a series of interviews he conducted with Parajanov at a 1988 retrospective in Munich (Parajanov died in 1990). Those discussions fail to coalesce in a dramatic fashion, providing only odd bits of insight into his working methods, themes, influences and the general working conditions in the Soviet Union.

The subject notes that it was not until his 1964 "Shadows of Our Forgotten Ancestors" that he "found his theme." But he doesn't explain further, nor does Holloway step forward or bring in a scholar to examine the films. Clips, although visually striking, do not advance a perspective, either.

Finally, "Parajanov's" most memorable moments are its glimpses of the political realities endemic to the government-controlled cultural industry. Imprisoned several times during his career, Parajanov paints a portrait of contemporaries who never fulfilled their promise. His generation of Soviet filmmakers suffered, he says, living with constant fear.   —*Leonard Klady*

WACKO

(PARANO)

(FRENCH)

A Manitou Prods./Ex Nihilo/Phase Films/Les Films Eric Atlan/France 3 Cinema production, with participation of Investimage 4 and Canal Plus. (International sales: Mainstream, Paris.) Produced by Yann Piquer. Executive producer, Eric Atlan. Directed, written by Piquer, Alain Robak, Manuel Fleche, Anita Assal, John Hudson. Camera (color), Bernard Dechet, Remy Chevrin, Darius Khondji, Jean Poisson; editors, Pierre Didier, Elisabeth Moulinier, Marc Cave, Nathalie Le Guay; music, Alain Guelis, Scoop!, Richard Gili; associate producers, Yves Chevalier, Patrick Giminez, Patrick Sobelman, Takis Veremis. Reviewed at French-American Film Workshop (competing), Avignon, France, June 22, 1994. Running time: **81 MIN.**

With: Smain, Jacques Villeret, Patrick Bouchitey, Jean-Francois Stevenin, Alain Chabat, Christine Combe, Jean-Francois Gallotte, Jean-Marie Maddeddu, Gustave Parking, Nathalie Presles, Marina Rodriguez-Tome, Cecile Sanz De Alba.

"**W**acko" features five self-contained, over-the-top tales — linked by the conversations of a mismatched couple who meet through a personals ad — in the time-honored tradition of "The Twilight Zone" and horror movies. An ordeal for viewers who aren't on the helmers' humor wavelength, and an entertaining series of distractions for those who are, slick pic's a natural for teenage auds and cable TV.

In "Burning Revenge," a man douses a gas station with gasoline in the middle of the night and threatens the attendant with a cigarette lighter.

"Panic FM" follows a pizza delivery cyclist (popular comic Smain) who sees unnerving "Jacob's Ladder"-style apparitions as he pedals through the streets listening to a grisly radio show.

In "Dead End," a couple driving along a country road keeps experiencing the same near-fatal accident.

In the comically extreme "Sado's Blues," a woman with deep masochistic needs, and the paraphernalia to match, invites a wimp up to her apartment and demands that he service her.

"Happy Birthday" is a creative twist on wife and lover killing hubby, nimbly assisted by a scuba outfit and a forest fire.

Punch lines are, for the most part, predictable, which puts the burden of pleasure on the telling.

Visual execution — all episodes are lensed and edited with skill and efficiency — far outstrips the merit of the gags themselves. Sound effects and musical accompaniment are on the nose and mostly aggressive thesping suits each seg.

—*Lisa Nesselson*

THE TRANSPARENT WOODS

(LES BOIS TRANSPARENTS)

(FRENCH)

A France 3 presentation of a Mediterranee Film Prod./France 3 Grand Sud Ouest production. Produced by Louis Leblanc. Directed, written by Pierre Sullice. Camera (color), Ariane Damain; editor, Jean-Baptiste de Battista; music, Michel Ghuzel; production design, Michele Susini; sound, Alain Duprat; assistant director, Dominique Delroche. Reviewed at French-American Film Workshop (competing), Avignon, France, June 23, 1994. Running time: **87 MIN.**

Alex	Didier Agostini
Vero	Maria De Medeiros
Leo	Philippe Ducroizet
Patrice	Jean-Philippe Puymartin

With: Claude Aufaure, Marianne Groves, Veronique Silver.

A charming student finds the company of a young man with Down's Syndrome more satisfying than that of a dour painter in "The Transparent Woods," an ultra-leisurely ode to nature and tolerance marred by its cliched central portrait of a blocked artist. Valiant but ultimately tedious pic is admirably sensitive to issues concerning mental retardation and could be of great interest to people involved with special education.

When radiant Vero (Maria De Medeiros) comes to visit her painter boyfriend Alex (Didier Agostini) in the remote country house where he's just burned his latest canvases, she meets and becomes friendly with Leo, a 24-year-old man with Down's Syndrome who tends to wander away from the special camp for the mentally retarded where he's spending the summer.

After curmudgeonly Alex banishes Vero so he can concentrate on work for a gallery show, Leo makes a nuisance of himself.

Outcome is telegraphed from the outset: Contact with mentally impaired but emotionally vibrant Leo will help Alex surmount his artistic block.

Alex's occasional v.o. musings are heavy-handed. It's difficult to fathom why a woman as bright and vivacious as Vero would continue to live with ornery, malicious Alex.

Philippe Ducroizet is endearing as Leo, who strives to reconcile his attraction to Vero with the limits of his capabilities.

Lensing communicates the wild vegetation of the Cevennes region. Syncopated score by Michel Ghuzel is a plus, although sappy song lyrics intercede.   —*Lisa Nesselson*

August 15, 1994

NATURAL BORN KILLERS

A Warner Bros. release presented in association with Regency Enterprises and Alcor Films of an Ixtlan/New Regency production in association with J D Prods. Produced by Jane Hamsher, Don Murphy, Clayton Townsend. Executive producers, Arnon Milchan, Thom Mount. Coproducer, Rand Vossler. Directed by Oliver Stone. Screenplay, David Veloz, Richard Rutowski, Stone, story by Quentin Tarantino. Camera (Technicolor), Robert Richardson; editors, Hank Corwin, Brian Berdan; executive music producer, Budd Carr; production design, Victor Kempster; supervising art director, Alan R. Tomkins; art direction, Margery Zweizig; set design, John Perry Goldsmith, Stella Furner; set decoration, Merideth Boswell; costume design, Richard Hornung; sound (Dolby), David Macmillan; visual effects, Pacific Data Images; animation sequences, Colossal Pictures; animation designer, Mike Smith; associate producers, Risa Bramon Garcia, Rutowski; assistant director, Herb Gains; second unit director, Philip Pfeiffer; casting, Garcia, Billy Hopkins, Heidi Levitt. Reviewed at Skywalker Sound, Santa Monica, Aug. 5, 1994. MPAA Rating: R. Running time: **119 MIN.**

Mickey	Woody Harrelson
Mallory	Juliette Lewis
Wayne Gale	Robert Downey Jr.
Dwight McClusky	Tommy Lee Jones
Jack Scagnetti	Tom Sizemore
Mallory's dad	Rodney Dangerfield
Old Indian	Russell Means
Mallory's mom	Edie McClurg
Gas Station Attendant	Balthazar Getty
Duncan Homolka	Joe Grifasi
Mabel	O-Lan Jones

'**N**atural Born Killers" is a heavy duty acid trip, quite possibly the most hallucinatory and anarchic picture made at a major Hollywood studio in at least 20 years. As a scabrous look at a society that promotes murderers as pop culture icons, as well as a scathing indictment of a mass media establishment that caters to and profits from such starmaking, the film has a contemporary relevance that no one can miss. It also happens to be Oliver Stone's most exciting work to date strictly from a filmmaking point of view.

Served up in a highly stylized manner, this almost laughably bloody pic will once again stir up the old op-ed page arguments about violence in the cinema that date back to the late '60s. Ensuing controversy will combine with the sheer exhilaration of the piece to provide the marketing upside, while heavy gore quotient will keep many away, resulting in strong B.O. in certain situations, but something less than widespread appeal.

A rare Stone film in that it's neither historically rooted nor written originally by him, "Natural Born Killers" still shows the bloody fingerprints of its original author, Quentin Tarantino, although Stone has made the material his own (Tarantino receives story credit only) and supplied a thick layer of sociopolitical commentary readily recognizable as his. Using the standby "Gun Crazy"/"Bonnie And Clyde" young-lovers-on-a-killing-spree format but traveling further down that road than anyone has before, the director has made a fiction that might be said to resemble a psychedelic documentary about the American cult of sex, violence and celebrity.

Film is divided into two halves, the first of which vividly, and often outrageously, lays out the crazy three weeks during which the lead couple gun down 52 people out west. The second half presents the insane media circus which surrounds their incarceration, a live in-prison TV interview, a riot and their subsequent amazing escape. The glorification of Bonnie and Clyde that Arthur Penn's film made note of 27 years ago is shown here to have magnified into a virtual definition of a vulgar culture, and seems quite appropriate to an age dominated by such figures as Amy Fisher, the Menendez brothers, Tonya Harding and, yes, O.J. Simpson. Stylistic and thematic motifs are established at once, as some stunningly off-kilter, floating shots, intercut with black-and-white alternates and inserts of animals living and dead, lead up to Mickey (Woody Harrelson) and Mallory (Juliette Lewis) shooting up a roadside cafe. They kill for the sake of their great love for each other, they say, and the film's psychological ambitions never get much deeper than that. But the wild stylistics will be a turn-on for viewers ready for a visceral ride with the feel of an elaborate, souped-up '60s exploitation road picture.

In an audacious comic conceit, flashbacks show Mallory's family life heretofore in literally sitcom terms, as meanie dad (Rodney Dangerfield) bullies and molests her before hunky escaped con Mickey comes along to rescue her and launch their killing spree, a la "Badlands," by knocking off her folks.

As the two leave a trail of blood on New Mexico's infamous Route 666, blowing away people whenever they feel like it, for no reason, but normally leaving one survivor to tell the tale, the killers quickly become the celebs of the moment, in large part due to the spotlighting provided by a show called "American Maniacs," hosted by the fatuous Wayne Gale (Robert Downey Jr.).

After two particularly disturbing episodes, one in which Mallory roughly seduces an innocent teenager (Balthazar Getty) before killing him, and another in which Mickey reflexively murders a wise Indian (Russell Means) who has been hospitable to them, the pair are finally cornered by police in Gallup and are taken away.

Their capture, however, merely sends the picture into an even higher gear, as the irrepressible Wayne Gale sets out to capture his highest ratings ever via a live interview with the nation's most prolific killer on Super Bowl Sunday.

At the same time, the unhinged good old boy warden (Tommy Lee Jones) has brought in a tough cop (Tom Sizemore) to quietly eliminate Mickey and Mallory in-house. But during the TV interview, Mickey's survival instincts come to the fore, and he manages to incite a volcanic prison riot that allows the reunited couple to escape, with the hyion, resembling a demonically clever light show at a late '60s rock concert. Picking up technically where he left off on "JFK," Stone, along with his exceptional collaborators, including cinematographer Robert Richardson, editors Hank Corwin and Brian Berdan, production designer Victor Kempster and assorted visual and animation design hands, has served up a dazzling array of images that rivets the attention for two hours.

The narrative is related in color 35mm, black-and-white, Super 8 and video, and at different speeds. As the couple zooms off to some new bloody destination, the backgrounds are shown via blatantly artifi them entertaining, if uniformly repellent. Harrelson and Lewis are all lust (blood and sex) and no conscience as the pretty couple "naturally born bad." Jones is broader than he's ever been as the sweaty, lip-smacking warden none too good at his job. Standout perf comes from Downey, whose imitation of Robin Leach's distinctive cockney accent is hilariously dead-on, and who deftly conveys the true extent to which his character admires his lethal subjects.

A wrap-up montage of celebrity criminals and suspects includes a shot of O.J. Simpson, which merely nails home the timeliness of Stone's dizzying diatribe against a vulture-like media and the irresponsibility of modern culture. Film's style may be akin to a shotgun blast, but it still manages to hit the bull's eye.

—*Todd McCarthy*

A GOOD MAN IN AFRICA

A Gramercy Pictures release of a Southern Sun presentation of a Polar Entertainment production in association with Capitol Films. Produced by John Fiedler, John Tarlov. Executive producers, Joe Carracciolo Jr., Avi Lerner, Sharon Harel, Jane Barclay. Directed by Bruce Beresford. Screenplay by William Boyd, based on his novel. Camera (Technicolor), Andrzej Bartkowiak; editor, Jim Clark; music, John Du Prez; production design, Herbert Pinter; art direction, Graeme Orwin; set decoration, Vic Botha; costume design, Rosemary Burrows; sound (Dolby), Hank Garfield; assistant director, Mark Egerton; casting, Billy Hopkins, Susie Figgis. Reviewed at Sony Studios, Culver City, Aug. 10, 1994. MPAA Rating: R. Running Time: **95 MINS.**

Morgan Leafy	Colin Friels
Celia Adekunle	Joanne Whalley-Kilmer
Dr. Alex Murray	Sean Connery
Prof. Sam Adekunle	Louis Gossett Jr.
Arthur Fanshawe	John Lithgow
Chloe Fanshawe	Diana Rigg
Priscilla Fanshawe	Sarah Jane Fenton
Friday	Maynard Eziashi
Hazel	Jackie Mofokeng
Kojo	Themba Ndaba

Although it was written of a bygone era, Noel Coward must have had "A Good Man in Africa" in mind when he declared "mad dogs and Englishmen go out in the noonday sun." William Boyd's novel forms the basis of the contemporary yarn in which the British stiff upper lip sags lower in the West as statehood arrives in a distant outpost. It stakes out "Our Man in Havana" territory in its ironic tone, but it's not nearly as humorous or as successful in delivering up a satisfying soupcon of caustic wit. Commercial prospects are tepid for what's essentially a shaggy dog story.

Sean Connery's name may spark some initial biz, he doesn't play the title character per se. The film's just too cerebral for the mainstream, and specialized audiences demand a more vigorous, edgy spin to this type of material. Item has already opened in Germany.

The picture's "good man" is Morgan Leafy (Colin Friels), a member of the Brit diplomatic corps in Kinjanja, a fictional emerging nation. Coming by his underachievement honestly, Leafy is unfocused, slow to catch the colonial drift and spurred on by adrenalin rather than common sense. It's difficult to feel sympathy for his plight (flies, exotic viral strains) or prospects (terminal outback postings).

Still, he does muster a shred of dignity in the company of preening, incompetent commission superior Fanshawe (John Lithgow), corrupt local politician Adekunle (Louis Gossett Jr.) and Celia (Joanne

Whalley-Kilmer), the latter's predatory wife. Leafy is the servant of other people's needs, vanity and brutishness.

Basically, it's a combination of his own lack of judgment and others' recognition that he can be pushed around that puts him in contact with Dr. Alex Murray (Connery). The Scot physician adopted Africa 23 years earlier and has selflessly, if rigidly, ministered to the locals ever since. He is a bona fide legend.

Leafy's task is to win favor for British interests with Adekunle. And what the new nation's future president wants is a lucrative construction contract. Trouble is that Murray is on the board which says yea or nay, and he can spot a hypocrite across the veldt.

Boyd's story is rife with incident that makes for a good read but a slim movie. There's never any question of Murray's position or the possibility of compromise. Additionally, Leafy's fate has more to do with circumstance than character.

Considering the dramatic thinness, one can understand director Bruce Beresford's fascination with secondary characters and in creating mood and physical atmosphere. Despite Adekunle's less-than-altruistic nature, the sentiment is clearly pro-native and extremely anti-colonial without stooping to obvious caricature.

Matters are not enhanced by the casting of Friels. Role calls for a deft comic actor less mannered in his awkwardness and limited intelligence. He simply does not come across as someone capable of even bumbling onto the right conclusion. Hence, the authority Connery and Gossett bring to their parts drowns the hapless Leafy and unbalances the film.

The subject matter of "A Good Man in Africa" has emotional and intellectual resonance. It's the stuff of good movies, as evidenced by "Our Man in Havana" or "The Mouse That Roared," but yet to be cultivated on the former dark continent. —*Leonard Klady*

IN THE ARMY NOW

A Buena Vista Pictures release of a Hollywood Pictures presentation. Produced by Michael Rotenberg. Executive producers, Nicholas Hassitt, Cyrus Yavneh. Directed by Daniel Petrie Jr. Screenplay, Ken Kaufman, Stu Krieger, Petrie, Fax Bahr, Adam Small, story by Steve Zacharias, Jeff Buhai, Robbie Fox. Camera (Technicolor), William Wages; editor, O. Nicholas Brown; music, Robert Folk; production design, Craig Stearns; art direction, Randy Moore; set design, Thomas Reta; set decoration, Ellen Totleben; costume design, Michael T. Boyd; sound (Dolby), Mark Hopkins McNabb; assistant director, Josh King; second unit director, Yavneh; casting, Mary Jo Slater, Steve Brooksbank. Reviewed at the Avco Cinema Center, L.A., Aug. 12, 1994. MPAA Rating: PG. Running time: **93 MIN.**

Bones Conway	Pauly Shore
Jack Kaufman	Andy Dick
Christine Jones	Lori Petty
Fred Ostroff	David Alan Grier
Sgt. Stern	Esai Morales
Sgt. Ladd	Lynn Whitfield
Sgt. Williams	Art LaFleur
Gabriella	Fabiana Udenio

Targeted at the "Beavis and Butt-head" generation, this simpleminded military comedy should appeal to those who consider "Stripes" a classic oldie. At best, marginally amusing, with comic Pauly Shore demonstrating his limited acting skills as well as the finer points of "dudespeak," Hollywood Pictures' march into boot camp figures to pack up moderate boxoffice rations.

A regiment of writers participated in putting together this harmless romp, which — with one free-spirited goof dragging his buddy into the Army — certainly doesn't shy away from the "Stripes" comparison, down to Shore's character at one point delivering an inspiring if incomprehensible pep talk.

Shore plays Bones, who dreams of leaving the "Crazy Boys" stereo superstore where he works and opening his own business with buddy Jack (Andy Dick, of "Reality Bites" and "The Ben Stiller Show").

Bones talks Jack into joining the Army reserve, and after a brief boot camp sequence (with Lynn Whitfield, of all people, as their tough-as-nails sergeant), the pair end up being called into active service in Chad because of the specialty Bones has chosen: water purification.

Through a series of ridiculous circumstances, Bones' outfit — which includes tomboyish Christine ("A League of Their Own's" Lori Petty) and the omniphobic Fred ("In Living Color" alumnus David Alan Grier) — find themselves behind enemy lines, taking up the challenge of fending off a bunch of inept Libyan soldiers.

Perhaps the most amusing aspect of "In the Army Now" is unintentional — namely, that the Arizona and California desert locations used as stand-ins for Africa look suspiciously like Arizona and California.

That notwithstanding, Shore's toned-down shtick does offer a few chuckles in its unrelenting stupidity, though he's such a one-note performer it's difficult to do much with him beyond that.

Director Daniel Petrie Jr. (whose writing credits include "Beverly Hills Cop" and his directing debut, "Toy Soldiers") manages to maintain the lightweight tone even when bullets are flying. A more annoying aspect of the screenplay involves constant and casual harassment of women, from Bones repeatedly coming on to his female instructor to Jack's inept and constant propositioning of Christine.

Dick proves rather bland even by sidekick standards, while Petty, Grier and Art LaFleur — as another snarling officer — each generate a few laughs with thinly written material. Esai Morales, however, is under-used as a tough, special forces commando, while Brendan Fraser appears in a very brief cameo for those, again, who consider "Encino Man" a lost classic.

Tech credits are okay, with plenty of impressive Army hardware showcased. Filmmakers no doubt received ample cooperation based on the pic's favorable portrayal of military service, dude.

—*Brian Lowry*

BROKEN HARVEST

(IRISH)

A Destiny Films production. (International sales: Destiny, Stillorgan, Ireland.) Produced by Jerry O'Callaghan. Executive producer, Maurice O'Callaghan. Directed by Maurice O'Callaghan. Screenplay, Maurice O'Callaghan, Kate O'Callaghan, from the former's story "The Shilling." Camera (Technicolor), Jack Conroy; editor, J. Patrick Duffner; music, Patrick Cassidy; production design, Alan Galett; set design, Laura Bowe; costume design, Maeve Paterson; sound (Dolby), Trevor O'Connor, Liam Saurin; assistant director, Nick McCarthy; associate producers, Jack Conroy, Grainne Ferris. Reviewed on Destiny Films vidcassette, London, Aug. 3, 1994. (In Cambridge Film Festival.) Running time: **101 MIN.**

Arthur O'Leary	Colin Lane
Josie McCarthy	Niall O'Brien
Catherine O'Leary	Marian Quinn
Jimmy O'Leary	Darren McHugh
Mary Finnegan	Joy Florish
Willie Hogan	Joe Jeffers
Adult Jimmy	Pete O'Reilly
Adult Willie	Michael Crowley
(English dialogue)	

Part rites-of-passage movie, part meditation on the "new" Ireland forged from the War of

Independence and subsequent Civil War, "Broken Harvest" is a beautifully lensed but dramatically static pic that falls short of its aspirations. Long-gestated work by writer/director Maurice O'Callaghan may work theatrically on home turf — where Buena Vista Intl. is putting it out Aug. 26 — but offshore chances look stronger on the fest trail and the small screen.

Story opens in present-day New York, where businessman Jimmy O'Leary (Pete O'Reilly) hears of the death of his mother, Catherine (Marian Quinn, sister of Aidan). The news cues a long flashback to growing up in rural West Cork during the '50s, where old tensions still linger from the anti-Brit struggles of the '20s and later divisions.

Young Jimmy (Darren McHugh) lives a carefree life of comic books, rock 'n' roll, escapades with pal Willie (Joe Jeffers), and growing attention from the pubescent Mary (Joy Florish). For the adults, things are more complicated: the farm Mom and Dad have inherited is burdened with debt, and the latter (Colin Lane), an idealist still consumed with anti-Brit hatred, is obsessed with his expensive hobby of horse-rearing.

A deep-seated feud between Jimmy's dad and Willie's easygoing uncle, Josie (Niall O'Brien), leads to violence when Josie (rightly) accuses Jimmy of pilfering money from the church collection. To add salt to old wounds, Josie still carries a torch for Jimmy's mom, who gave him the heave-ho years earlier.

O'Callaghan's script, from his own story "The Shilling," is a rich brew of political currents, adolescent growing pains, historical refs (including brief b&w sequences of the father fighting the British in the '20s), and an inbred love for the Irish landscape and rural way of life. Though the elements are all in place for a potentially involving drama, and many individual sequences work well, the whole obstinately fails to cohere into an engaging package.

Blame that mostly on dialogue that's over-spare and often awkward, and a directorial style that's too first-gear and stiff. Though O'Callaghan has a solid grasp of the basics and could develop into a helmer of worth, "Harvest" too often shows signs of the labor of love at the expense of real dramatic momentum.

Performances are generally OK, led by a fine showing from Quinn, who deserves more screen time as the devoted-mom-in-the-middle. Lane and O'Brien are well-contrasted as the proud father and relaxed Josie, though the basis for their enmity needs more explanation. The kids are all solid.

Tech credits are pro, with special praise for Jack Conroy's loving photography of the beautiful West Cork and Wicklow locations.

August 15, 1994 (Cont.)

Patrick Cassidy's pastoral/religioso score is pleasant but somewhat added-on in feel.

Pic's title equates the family's poor wheat harvest, which leads to their financial demise, with the broken dreams of the Irish-for-Ireland, "before it all went wrong." Black-and-white sequences were actually shot 10 years ago, when the 100% indie-financed movie first got off the ground. —*Derek Elley*

ANDRE

A Paramount release of a Kushner-Locke production. Produced by Annette Handley, Adam Shapiro. Executive producers, Peter Locke, Donald Kushner. Co-executive producer, Lawrence Mortoff. Co-producers, Sue Baden-Powell, Dana Baratta. Directed by George Miller. Screenplay, Baratta, based on the novel "A Seal Called Andre" by Harry Goodridge, Lew Dietz. Camera (color), Thomas Burstyn; editors, Harry Hitner, Patrick Kennedy; music, Bruce Rowland; production design, William Elliot; art direction, Sheila Haley; set decoration, Barry Kemp; costume design, Maya Mani; sound (Dolby) Michael McGee; assistant director, Brian Giddens; second unit director, Ernie Orsatti; stunt coordinator, Danny Virtue; animal coordinator, Bruce McMillan; animatronic seals, Image Animation; casting, Annette Benson, Lindsay Walker. Reviewed at Paramount Studios, Aug. 10, 1994. MPAA Rating: PG. Running time: **94 MIN.**
Harry Whitney .... Keith Carradine
Toni Whitney .... Tina Majorino
Thalice Whitney .... Chelsea Field
Paula Whitney .... Aidan Pendleton
Steve Whitney .... Shane Meier
Billy Baker .... Keith Szarabajka
Mark Baker .... Joshua Jackson
Andre the Seal .... Tory the Sea Lion

The first theatrical feature from the Kushner-Locke TV producing outfit, "Andre" is a good-natured family yarn with colorful seacoast locales, an amiable, pet-loving clan and a crafty, comical seal with more tricks up his fin than you can shake a herring at. Though quality kids 'n' animal pix "Lassie" and "Black Beauty" have been hitting tough surf this summer, Paramount may find the B.O. waters less challenging now that the seasonal megahits have been launched. Strong kiddie interest built from savvy promo efforts highlighting "Andre's" aquatic acrobatics should put this ahead of both the dog and pony shows.

Based on a true story and set in Rockport, Maine, in the early '60s, "Andre" charts the fantastic experiences of harbor master Harry Whitney (Keith Carradine), a soft-hearted animal lover who has instilled his fondness for beasties in all members of his clan, including super-mom wife Thalice (Chelsea

Field), teenagers Steve (Shane Meier) and Paula (Aidan Pendleton), and especially grade-schooler Toni (Tina Majorino).

Their lovely, rustic seaside home is packed with chickens, rabbits, pigeons and other critters, and both Dad and daughter Toni seem to prefer their furry friends to the two-legged variety.

While Dad grapples with work-related problems, such as seal-hating fishermen, led by disgruntled, boozy angler Billy Baker (Keith Szarabajka), Toni battles cruel classmates who taunt her for her country ways, causing her to withdraw further into the world of wildlife. Enter the eponymous Andre, "played" with astonishing range and skills by Tory the Sea Lion.

Separated from his brood, then rescued by pere Whitney and nursed back to health with the loving help of Toni, Andre proves to be more of a friend and a challenge than the family could imagine.

Essentially an old-fashioned morality play about the healing powers of love and community, "Andre" is most interesting when exploring family dynamics and local politics, with an eye on the growing pains of the human players' collective moral development.

Rather than serving up a gallery of cliched heroes and villains, Aussie helmer George Miller ("The Man From Snowy River") steers his able cast through screenwriter Dana Baratta's more complex weaving of old hometown rivalries, issues of conflicting commitments to family, community and nature, and the difficulties encountered on the path from childhood to maturity.

Though it never rises above the conventional to achieve the visionary quality of a true children's film classic like "The Black Stallion," "Andre" is a light-hearted, entertaining diversion with more on its mind than just capitalizing on the tricks and treats of its raspberry-blowing, basketball-balancing star.

And while many of "Andre's" antics are clearly pitched comically beyond the realm of reality, pic's PG rating is sillier than anything in the film, and defies logic unless one is a Luddite farmer whose "parental guidance" includes protecting children from life-affirming movies containing no sex, no nudity, no swearing and no violence. As Andre would say, "BLLLPPPPP-PHHHH!" —*Steven Gaydos*

LOCARNO FEST

ERMO

(HONG KONG — CHINA)

An Ocean Films Co. presentation, in association with Shanghai Film Studio. (International sales: Shu Kei's Creative Workshop, Hong Kong.) Produced by Chen Kunming, Jimmy Tan. Executive producer Li Ran. Directed by Zhou Xiaowen. Screenplay, Lang Yun, from the novella of the same name by Xu Baoqi. Camera (color), Lu Gengxin; editor, Zhong Furong; music, Zhou; art direction, Zhang Daqian; costume design, Liu Qingli; sound (Dolby), Hong Yi; assistant director, Liu Jing. Reviewed at Locarno Film Festival (competing), Aug. 6, 1994. Running time: **107 MINS.**
Ermo .... Ailiya
Blindman .... Liu Peiqui
Ermo's husband .... Ge Zhijun
Blindman's wife .... Zhang Haiyan

A beautifully lensed, piquantly acted tragi-comedy about a gutsy young peasant wife's equal love for her bankroll and b.f., "Ermo" confidently stakes out its own ground in the increasingly crowded field of Chinese rural movies. Offshore arthouse sales look promising for this assured entry by director Zhou Xiaowen, previously known in Sinophile circles for his (still banned) first pic, "In Their Prime" (1986), and the commercial thrillers "Desperation" and "Obsession." A host of other fests are already standing in line for this hotly fought-over Locarno world preem.

Despite surface similarities with Zhang Yimou's plucky peasant pic, "The Story of Qiuji," present item has none of that movie's ironic take on China's still-monolithic justice and social systems. Instead, Zhou has amplified a 1992 novella, focusing on a young woman's affair with her neighbor and coming up with a slyly comic journey of the heart that's truthfully grounded in "new" attitudes toward money and sex in '90s China. Title character (played in unexaggerated style by Inner Mongolian actress Ailiya) is a coin-obsessed peasant in a remote village in northern Hebei province who labors night and day on the family's handmade noodle business. Her elderly husband is a sickly, now-impotent ex-village chief; their neighbors are the kindly "Blindman," who drives her to market every day, and his sharp-tongued wife, whose prize possession is a TV.

Jealous of their lifestyle and starved of affection, Ermo channels her energies into stashing away enough loot to buy the biggest TV set around, a 29-incher. Getting a better-paid job in town at a new restaurant, she even resorts to sell-

ing her blood on the side. Meanwhile, her friendship with Blindman is consummated one night in his battered truck.

Ermo's husband knows, and Blindman's wife suspects, what's going on. Blindman breaks off the affair and deliberately has a relationship (unshown) with a prostitute to throw his wife off the scent. The two families patch things up, and finally the great day arrives for Ermo and her husband to regain their local standing by purchasing the giant TV.

In changing the focus of the original novella — in which the TV has no special emphasis, and which has a conventional happy-lovers ending — Zhou comes up with a fresh furrow in the well-ploughed field of Chinese rural dramas focusing on lonesome young wives (most recently, "The Story of Xinghua"). Ermo is also no passive victim: driven, tunnel-visioned, and with a strong peasant feel for the bottom line, she's like a truck careening toward a cliff-edge she can't see coming. Pic's ending is a neat, ironic study in emotional emptiness.

Small-name cast meshes well, with each of the four principals sympathetically handled and with a balance of strengths and weaknesses. Rural flavor, from details of noodle-making to vignettes such as Blindman paying off an old peasant he's accidentally run over, is well caught without being self-consciously "exotic."

Standout photography by Lu Gengxin employs a rich palette of autumnal reds and yellows, with interiors a study in chiaroscuro lighting. Direct-sound soundtrack (still a rarity in Chinese filmmaking) is immaculate, with a discreet Dolby dub. All postproduction was done in Beijing, rather than offshore. Pic carries a Hong Kong producers' banner, as Ocean Films stepped in with financing when Zhou and others finally ran out of money during postproduction. —*Derek Elley*

THE ABADANIS

(ABADANI-HA)

(IRANIAN — B&W)

An Ali-Akbar Kasra/M.Jazayeri/Kiyanush Ayyari production. (International sales: Farabi Cinema Foundation, Tehran). Directed, written by Ayyari. Camera (b&w), Ali-Reza Zarrindast; music, Saeed Shahram; sound, Jahangir Mirshekari. Reviewed at Locarno Film Festival (competing), Aug. 6, 1994. Running time: **94 MIN.**
Darvish .... Saeed Pursamimi
Hassan Khouf .... Hassan Rezai
Borna .... Saeed Sheikhzadeh
Darvish's wife ..... Afsaneh Mohammadi

Tale of a poor cabdriver's search for his stolen auto amid the flotsam of '80s Tehran, "The Abadanis" is a warm and wonderfully human pic that consistently delights with its canny blend of Italian Neo-Realist refs and subtly blended modern techniques. Sixth feature of Iranian filmer Kiyanush Ayyari, after a long career in 8mm and 16mm, should prove a popular item on the fest circuit and with specialist buyers.

Like the Italo classic "The Bicycle Thief" (to whose makers the movie is unabashedly dedicated), "The Abadanis" is a portrait of a city and society via a journey through its nether regions. Refugees from the bombed port of Abadan during the Iran-Iraq War, the humble Darvish and his family eke out a living in Tehran with his battered jalopy. When the car is stolen in broad daylight, Darvish and young son Borna set out on a hunt that leads them into a twilight world of scrap dealers and black marketeers, with their guide the crafty but basically warm-hearted trader, Hassan Khouf.

Despite its seemingly downbeat subject matter and b&w photography, pic is an engaging ride from scene one, thanks to a script and performances that strike a neat balance between observation and ironic comedy, and cutting that never lingers for purely arty effect. On paper, Ayyari's portrait of a city riddled with petty crime and subject to constant air-raid warnings is a depressing affair; onscreen, he communicates a basically optimistic view of a bickering, hotheaded society that, bottom line, looks after its own.

The movie's major achievement is in cleverly incorporating sophisticated camera techniques to enhance its appeal without compromising the low-budget, neo-realist feel. From opening closeups of an anti-theft device being removed from the car, through discreet crane shots, to striking compositions of industrial landscapes, lensing by Ali-Reza Zarrindast is consistently on the money.

Perfs are fully-drawn and engaging, led by Hassan Rezai's gnarled, one-eye-on-the-main-chance Khouf, and Saeed Pursamimi's hunched, increasingly desperate father, an out-of-towner who's a stranger in his own land. As the kid Borna, Saeed Sheikhzadeh is cute but savvy.

Plentiful use of atmospheric music by Saeed Shahram is a dramatic plus. —*Derek Elley*

BORDERLINE
(METECHMIO)
(GREEK)

A Greek Film Centre production, in association with ZDF/Arte, Channel 4, ET1, Panos Karkanevatos, RTBF, Stefi, Metron, Forever Films. (International sales; Greek Film Centre, Athens.) Directed by Panos Karkanevatos. Screenplay, Karkanevatos, Yannis Xanthopoulos. Camera (color), Andreas Sinanos; editor, Yannis Tsitsopoulos; music, Nikos Kypourgos; art direction-costume design, Anthi Karafilli; sound, Dinos Kittou. Reviewed at Locarno Film Festival (competing), Aug. 5, 1994. Running time: 81 MIN.
Yannis Markou ..... Aris Lebassopoulos
Father .... Christos Kalavrouzos
Stelios .... Stavros Zalmas
 Also with : Takis Moschos, Maria Kiriaki, Dinos Karydis, Patis Koutsaftis, Efi Drossou, Alexandros Moukanos, Babis Tigas, Yannis Bofilios, Yannis Stathis.

A brother's search for his elder sibling turns into a voyage of self-discovery in "Borderline," an affecting slice of metaphysical drama that plays like an Angelopoulos pic without the longeurs. First feature of young Greek director Panos Karkanevatos should get his name into festival catalogs before segueing to the small screen.

Yannis (Aris Lebessopoulos) is an insecure cop who stumbles across an illegal immigrant's forged papers bearing the name of his father and home village. He then finds his long-lost brother Stelios' photo in police files under a false identity. Realizing that Stelios (Stavros Zalmas), who supposedly drowned when he deserted the army, may still be alive, Yannis sets out in search of him under the guise of police business.

Yannis is soon called off the job, but by then his search has become an obsession. Eluding his superiors, he goes into hiding and finally tracks down the man who arranged for Stelios to flee the country. The big question is whether he follows his brother's lead.

With its theme of ordinary Greeks liberating themselves from authoritarianism (Stelios from the army, Yannis from the police force and the shadows of his strong father and brother), the film could as well be set in the days of the country's military junta as in the present. Karkanevatos seems to keep the setting deliberately vague, concentrating more on the young brother's emotional changes as a fresh start slowly presents itself.

Dialogue is spare and to the point, with much of the movie in meditative style accompanied by Nikos Kypourgos' melancholy, highly effective, Morricone-like score. Trim running time, fine lensing by An-

dreas Sinanos, and fistfuls of flashbacks to the brothers' youth, all help to maintain attention, even when nothing much is happening on screen. Performances are all OK, given the movie's introverted style.
—*Derek Elley*

VIVA CASTRO!
(RUSSIAN)

A Star Kino Video, Lenfilm production. (International sales: Star Kino Video, St. Petersberg.) Directed, written by Boris Frumin. Camera (color), Sergei Yurizditsky; editor, Irina Gorokovskaya; music, Viktor Lebedev; costume design, Sergei Chizhov. Reviewed at Locarno Film Festival (competing), Aug. 7, 1994. Running time: 82 MINS.
 With: Pavel Zharkov, Yulia Sobolevskaya, Sergei Dontsov, Natalia Kononova, Anastasia Vesneva.

Mid-'60s Russia gets the rosy-tinted treatment in "Viva Castro!" a loose, laidback assemblage of autobiographical experiences by recent returnee Boris Frumin, whose New York-lensed "Black and White" played the fest circuit two years ago. Likable but ambling movie, very much in the light, breezy "St. Petersburg school" style, lacks theatrical legs but could be of interest in certain Euro and specialized markets.

Main story, set in the small town of Gachina, revolves round Kolya, a high school teen with a crush on his sexy singing teacher, who keeps giving him the come-on. Kolya's home life is a mess: his father skips town over some stolen museum coins, and his mother is sent to a labor camp as punishment. A year later, Pa returns, dying of cancer, and Kolya becomes involved with a pretty young woman hired to nurse him. Taking part in a "Viva Cuba" concert, Kolya tries to fix a final meeting between his imprisoned mother and ailing dad. Another diversion also rears its head: the concert's musical director is Kolya's former singing teacher, for whom he still has the hots.

Frumin embellishes the basically simple central story with a mass of other characters, small incidents, and anecdotal episodes often shot in a consciously eccentric style and without bridging scenes. As in many recent Russo pix, it takes a while to work out who's who and what's going on.

Though the movie dips in its final reels, it just about goes the distance on performances and Frumin's brand of black Slavic comedy. Music is well placed in maintaining interest, and tech credits are okay, including some use of direct sound rather than the usual loose postsynching. —*Derek Elley*

MOVIE DAYS
(ICELANDIC)

An Icelandic Film Corporation/Peter Rommel Filmproduction/Zentropa Entertainments coproduction. Produced by Fridrik Thor Fridriksson, Rommel, Peter Aalbaek Jensen. Directed by Fridriksson. Screenplay, Einar Gudmundsson, Fridriksson. Camera (color), Ari Kristinsson; editor, Steingrimur Karlsson; production design, Arni Paull Johannson; costume design, Karl Aspelund; sound (Dolby), Kjartan Kjartansson. Reviewed at Cannes film festival (Market), May 16, 1994. (In Locarno Film Festival — competing.) Running time: 85 MINS.
Thomas .... Orvar Jens Arnarsson
Nicholas .... Orri Helgason
Father .... Rurik Haraldsson
Mother .... Sigrun Hjalmtysdottir
Grandmother ..... Asta Esper Andersen
Toni .... Jon Sigurbjornsson
Briet .... Gudrun Asmundsdottir
Stranger .... Otto Sander

Fridrik Fridriksson's follow-up to his exceptional "Children of Nature" (1991) is a youthful semi-autobiographical saga of a boy growing up in Iceland, circa 1960. Though heartfelt and keenly observed, "Movie Days" lacks bite and focus, rambling through loosely cobbled episodes and eventually just running out of steam. It should find some interest on the fest circuit, but commercial prospects will be extremely rarified.

Young Thomas' (Orvar Jens Arnarsson) life is ineffably shaped by the movies. His parents shepherd him to tony fare like "King of Kings," he spends his Saturdays at Roy Rogers matinees and creates make-believe scenarios culled from the images he has seen. The tale seems superficially sweet, anecdotal and aimless. However, Fridriksson has slyer intents. He takes great delight in poking fun at the subtle and not-so-subtle influence American film and TV has on the population of Reykjavik.

The tale turns darker when Thomas is sent to spend the summer on a relative's farm. In the absence of a celluloid security blanket, he relates to the odd environment as if it were the setting of a genre thriller. Ultimately, the situation is inverted by bringing the young boy back home to real tragedy and the imaginary horror of the big screen.

Though the saga's ambitions are lofty, the portrayal is mute and oblique. It replicates the warm memories of films such as "Cinema Paradiso," but struggles to provide a more realistic perspective to the coming-of-age story.

Handsomely produced on a modest budget, "Movie Days" demonstrates a deft artistic hand, particularly with talent and locale. The fact that it just misses emotionally is all the more disappointing, considering the craft and sincerity so organic to the piece. —*Leonard Klady*

BLANKMAN

A Columbia Pictures release of a Wife 'N' Kids production. Produced by Eric L. Gold, C.O. Erickson. Executive producer, Damon Wayans. Co-producer, Jack Binder. Directed by Mike Binder. Screenplay, Wayans, J.F. Lawton, based on Wayans' story. Camera (Technicolor), Tom Sigel; editor, Adam Weiss; music, Miles Goodman; production design, James Spencer; art direction, Keith Burns; set design, Stephanie J. Gordon; set decoration, Michael C. Claypool; costume design, Michelle Cole; sound (Dolby), Simon Kaye, Jonathan Bates; associate producer, Tracy Carness; assistant director, Patrick Clayton; casting, Lucy Boulting. Reviewed in Los Angeles. MPAA Rating: PG-13. Running time: **92 MIN.**

Darryl Walker	Damon Wayans
Kevin Walker	David Alan Grier
Kimberly Jonz	Robin Givens
Mayor Harris	Christopher Lawford
Grandma Walker	Lynne Thigpen
Michael Minelli	Jon Polito
Mr. Stone	Jason Alexander

In a follow-up to his appearance in "Mo' Money," Damon Wayans stars in "Blankman," a superhero adventure-comedy that reunites him with his "In Living Color" sidekick David Alan Grier. Young viewers will rejoice at a comic-book fable that celebrates a self-appointed neighborhood crime fighter in the "Superman" mold. Adults, however, may find the film too goofy, too loud and vastly uneven in humor and execution, which may explain why Columbia decided not to hold advance press screenings. Still, this kinetically nutty pic should take a healthier bite at the B.O. than Robert Townsend's "Meteor Man," which had a similar premise.

After a childhood prologue, pic finds Darryl Walker (Wayans) as an eccentric inventor who thinks he can make a difference in Metro City, Ill., to the chagrin of his protective older brother, Kevin (Grier). When crime reaches unbearable proportions — the police go on strike, the mob holds the mayor hostage — Darryl decides to take action. Garbed in a cape fashioned from his grandmother's housecoat and armed with an arsenal of homemade crime-stopping gizmos, he transforms himself into a mythic, vigilant hero, whom the puzzled media name Blankman.

As a comic-book fable, "Blankman" is populated with all the usual suspects: the sleazy newsman (Jason Alexander) who tries to get the scoop on Blankman; the mayor (Christopher Lawford) thwarted by the mob; the underworld kingpin (Jon Polito). There's also unexpected romance with a beautiful TV reporter (Robin Givens) who breaks the story of Blankman's escapades and catapults him to national celebrity.

In a change of tone, Mike Binder, whose two previous pix ("Crossing the Bridge," "Indian Summer") were semi-autobiographical, imbues "Blankman" with hyperactive slapstick, turning the film's assaultiveness into a comic style that is only intermittently effective or funny. But he succeeds in orchestrating a visual corollary to the narrative, using set pieces with realistic earth tones which later change into brighter, fantasy colors. James Spencer's production design accentuates the childlike p.o.v. of the film: Blankwheel, a modified motorcycle used by Blankman to ride the subway system, and Blankstation, his hideaway, are simple but enchanting visual treats.

Pic is a showcase for the chameleonic Wayans and his straight-from-the-hip humor. Many scenes are played for broad and naive laughs that kids may find charming but mature viewers will consider dumb.

Secondary cast members all hit their marks: As the older brother and reluctant sidekick, Grier lends sanity and reliable support; Polito plays the mob boss to the hilt; and the sexy Givens adds a much needed touch of grace.

In contrast to the coarse "Mo' Money," the playfully naive "Blankman," which Wayans executive produced and co-wrote with J.F. Lawton, doesn't conceal its feel-good nature and old-fashioned values of faith, sincerity, idealism and communal responsibility. Pic has many shortcomings, but it's also a rarity: an inner-city adventure devoid of high-tech bloodshed and gratuitous violence. —*Emanuel Levy*

THE NEXT KARATE KID

A Columbia release of a Jerry Weintraub production. Produced by Weintraub. Executive producer, R.J. Louis. Directed by Christopher Cain. Screenplay, Mark Lee. Camera (Technicolor), Laszlo Kovacs; editor, Ronald Roose; music, Bill Conti; production design, Walter P. Martishius; set decoration, Tracey A. Doyle; sound (Dolby), Andy Wiskes; stunt coordinator/martial arts choreographer, Pat E. Johnson; associate producer, Susan Ekines; assistant director, Nick Mastandrea; casting, Joy Todd. Reviewed at UCG Forum Horizon Cinema, Paris, Aug. 8, 1994. MPAA rating: PG. Running time: **104 MIN.**

Mr. Miyagi	Noriyuki (Pat) Morita
Julie Pierce	Hilary Swank
Colonel Dugan	Michael Ironside
Louisa	Constance Towers
Eric	Chris Conrad
Abbot Monk	Arsenio Trinidad
Ned	Michael Cavalieri

The franchise is still kicking — but not very high — in "The Next Karate Kid," in which a troubled teenage girl is transformed from bratty rebel into confident martial artist. Leisurely and overly familiar pic should appeal to young teen girls, but won't be breaking any B.O. bricks with its bare hands. Pic opened in France, as well as Quebec, in advance of its U.S. opening, pushed back a few weeks to Sept. 9.

Boston dweller Louisa (Constance Towers) has her hands full with granddaughter Julie (Hilary Swank), whose parents were killed in a car crash. An indifferent student, Julie is permanently angry.

Having witnessed Julie's swift reflexes in averting a near-accident, wise Mr. Miyagi, played again by Noriyuki (Pat) Morita, embarks on a low-key mission to rescue the floundering 17-year-old via karate. Wholesome apprenticeship tale has its scattered moments of humor and insight but lacks sustained verve.

Miyagi discovers that not only is "girl different than boy," but Julie is a much more fully formed — and negative — personality than Ralph Macchio's Daniel was when he came under Miyagi's tutelage in the original installment.

Pic's laudable values — always try to avoid a fight, respect yourself and all living things — are hammered home through solid if unscintillating examples that adapt serene Asian wisdom to modern Western dilemmas.

Thesps all hold their often stereotypic ground, but Morita excels as one cool, compassionate dude who always finds a way to recycle conflict and adversity into spiritual growth.

Athletic Swank is gratingly cranky at the outset and a tad too enthusiastic once she shapes up. Chris Conrad is appealing as the kindly hunk who admires Julie's independent spirit.

Although there's not much karate action compared with previous three pix, final showdown on prom night gives Julie the opportunity to artfully deck the jerk who's been baiting her at school.

Nominally set in Boston, locations have a generic this-could-be-anywhere feel. Tech credits are fine. —*Lisa Nesselson*

MILK MONEY

A Paramount Pictures release of a Kennedy/Marshall production. Produced by Kathleen Kennedy, Frank Marshall. Executive producers, Patrick Palmer, Michael Finnell. Directed by Richard Benjamin. Screenplay, John Mattson. Camera (Deluxe color), David Watkin; editor, Jacqueline Cambas; music, Michael Convertino; production design, Paul Sylbert; set design, Antoinette J. Gordon; set decoration, Casey Hallenbeck; costume design, Theoni V. Aldredge; sound (Dolby), Richard Lightstone; assistant directors, Cara Giallanza, Vincent Agostino; second unit directors, Marshall, Palmer; second unit camera, Robin Browne; casting, Mary Goldberg, Amy Lippens. Reviewed at Raleigh Studios, L.A., Aug. 17, 1994. MPAA Rating: PG-13. Running time: **108 MIN.**
V .... Melanie Griffith
Tom Wheeler .... Ed Harris
Frank
   Wheeler .... Michael Patrick Carter
Waltzer .... Malcolm McDowell
Betty .... Anne Heche
Cash .... Casey Siemaszko
Jerry the Pope .... Philip Bosco
Kevin Clean .... Brian Christopher
Brad .... Adam LaVorgna
Mr. Clean .... Kevin Scannell
Stacey .... Jessica Wesson
Holly .... Amanda Sharkey

The premise of "Milk Money" could curdle in your stomach, and the execution of the idea is just plain rancid. With a tip of the hat to the performers, this is a misguided comedy with Hall of Shame pedigree. Its commercial prospects are quick, down and dirty.

Representing the worst in hybrid sensibility, the picture attempts to meld an adult romantic comedy with a coming-of-age tale. The collision of upscale and lowbrow humor is a twisted mess that's not pretty to watch. The film tries hard to be likable even if it means lying like a Trojan — so much for honesty as the best policy.

Curiosity is the operative word for the script. Three boys on the cusp of puberty decide they had better start their own sex education program because their families and school are doing an inadequate job. So they raid their piggy banks and sell their vintage comic books to raise $103.26 and head for the big city to pay to see a real live naked lady.

To the credit of first-time scribbler John Mattson and director Dick Benjamin, they pursue the preposterous with alacrity. The naifs fall right into an urban scam but are saved from robbery at gunpoint by a good-hearted prostitute — yes, cinema's venerable hooker with a heart of gold.

V (Melanie Griffith) goes one step further. For the cache of nickels and quarters, she provides the trio with a peak at her pulchritude. It might

all end there, save for the fact that the boys discover their bikes have been lifted, and they are literally left out in the rain.

Fortunately, they are destitute and shivering within plain sight of V's apartment window. She puts the tykes into her pimp's car and escorts them back to the suburbs. But after she drops off Frank (Michael Patrick Carter), the car stalls and she's stuck. Luckily, there just happens to be a vacancy in the lad's treehouse.

Barely 20 minutes into the movie, "Milk Money" has erected a house of cards taller than the Empire State Building. But there's simply no stopping the filmmakers' lust for contrivance and coincidence. Frank's dad, Tom (Ed Harris), is, of course, a lonely widower, and V is in mortal danger because she's inadvertently run off with a tankful of ill-gotten lucre that's already resulted in the murder of her "manager."

The film is obvious, loud, mean-spirited and has its mind in the gutter. The shame is that it needn't have been any of those things. At its core are two excellent performances by Griffith and Harris, real screen chemistry and the basis for a heartwarming union between two societal oddballs.

Griffith remains luminescent in an essentially impossible role. There's no one better at playing a character who's both vulnerable and street smart. The pity is the leering context of this particular yarn.

Similarly, Harris shines in this rare opportunity to play against type. It's an endearing, unselfconscious performance right down to his thinning, spiky hairline. Newcomer Carter is a winning child performer. Usually effective performers, including Malcolm McDowell and Casey Siemaszko, have little to do but strike a pose or convey an attitude.

Benjamin effects a breezy style and adopts easy visual cliches of city and suburban life. He proves once again to be a functional helmsman who steps out of the way and lets his artistes do their job. Unfortunately, this is an instance when the material needed more of an iron fist.

The laissez faire direction has turned what's unique and effective about the drama into something cheap. "Milk Money's" humanity and observation is reduced to a dirty joke indifferently related.

—*Leonard Klady*

COLOR OF NIGHT

A Buena Vista release from Hollywood Pictures of an Andrew G. Vajna presentation from Cinergi. Produced by Buzz Feitshans, David Matalon. Executive producer, Vajna. Co-producers, Carmine Zozzora, David Willis. Directed by Richard Rush. Screenplay, Matthew Chapman, Billy Ray, story by Ray. Camera (Technicolor), Dietrich Lohmann; editor, Jack Hofstra; music, Dominic Frontiere; production design, James L. Schoppe; supervising art director, Gary A. Lee; art direction, Jack Morrisey; set design, Sydney Z. Litwack; set decoration, Cynthia McCormac; costume design, Jacki Arthur; sound (Dolby), David Kelson; assistant director, Jack Frost Sanders; second unit camera, John Connor, George Mooradian; casting, Wendy Kurtzman. Reviewed at the Bruin Theater, L.A., Aug. 17, 1994. MPAA Rating: R. Running time: **121 MIN.**
Bill Capa .... Bruce Willis
Rose .... Jane March
Martinez .... Ruben Blades
Sondra .... Lesley Ann Warren
Bob Moore .... Scott Bakula
Clark .... Brad Dourif
Buck .... Lance Henriksen
Casey .... Kevin J. O'Connor
Dale .... Andrew Lowery
Anderson .... Eriq La Salle
Ashland .... Jeff Corey
Michelle .... Kathleen Wilhoite
Edith Niedelmeyer . Shirley Knight

"Color of Night" is a knuckleheaded thriller that means to get a rise out of audiences but will merely make them see red. It's confounding and sad that director Richard Rush waited 14 years to make another film after his striking "The Stunt Man," only to choose a script as dismal as this. The allure of Bruce Willis in a sexy thriller might be enough to generate some good initial numbers, but pic is a commercial short-termer.

One doesn't like to spoil the fun of a surprise ending, but "Color of Night" aspires to a "Crying Game"-like twist that doesn't work for one minute. Since it's clear from very early on that at least one character isn't what he or she appears to be, the two hours during which the film sweats heavily to build up intrigue and suspense just seem like wasted motion.

Tone edges increasingly into the faintly ridiculous as the film inches along, leading to a conclusion that had a preview audience issuing hoots and catcalls.

Pokey script by Matthew Chapman and Billy Ray centers upon New York shrink Bill Capa (Bruce Willis), who hies to L.A. after one of his patients takes a swan dive out of his high-rise window.

When Capa arrives in L.A., his best friend, fellow head doctor Bob Moore (Scott Bakula), pulls him into a group therapy session

populated by nympho Sondra (Lesley Ann Warren), uptight hypochondriac Clark (Brad Dourif), bereaved widower Buck (Lance Henriksen), twisted artist Casey (Kevin J. O'Connor) and a weird, uncommunicative teenager named Richie.

After Dr. Bob is gruesomely stabbed to death in his office, irreverent detective Martinez (Ruben Blades) comes onto the case, while Capa continues to hang out at his friend's ultra-lavish Malibu home and drive his Mercedes.

Since Bob reported receiving threats before his death, suspicion naturally falls on his patients, and much tedium ensues when Capa makes the rounds, visiting each group member in an effort to piece together the puzzle.

To spice matters up, a lithe young thing name Rose (Jane March) conveniently rear-ends Capa one day, starting a hot affair that, in its original cut, earned the film an NC-17 rating, but now consists of a lot of twisting and turning in a pool, shower and bed. Sex scenes are steamy and unclothed, but too brief for anyone to get hot and bothered.

At the same time, numerous nasty murder attempts are made upon Capa, in the form of a rattlesnake in his mailbox and a mysterious red car that tries to ram him off the road. At least one more member of the group meets a grisly fate, leading to the "revelation" that will have any remotely observant viewer groaning in knowing anticipation.

Among the plausibility problems are the murdered doctor's lack of relatives or friends other than Capa, the fact that he necessarily had dozens of other patients, aside from those in the depicted group, who might be suspects, and Capa's continued presence in his house.

Motivation behind the murders is obscure at best, and melodramatic climax, with its pathetic echoes of "Vertigo," is a joke.

From the leads through the supporting cast, performances are serviceable and sometimes amusing, but only standout is Blades, who brings a lot of salt and pepper to his role of the skeptical, sassy investigator.

Willis is watchable if not deep in a psychologically motivated piece, while March, who made her mark in "The Lover," displays a demure yet quicksilver personality here.

Technically, considerable effort has gone into giving this a lush veneer, notably in James L. Schoppe's expensive-looking production design.

But the lensing is on the dark and soft side, the score is more conventional and less seductive than it might have been, and director Rush seems to have taken both the moth-eaten plot and psychological gobbledygook far too seriously. As Hitchcock would have said, it's only a movie — and one he wouldn't have made.
—*Todd McCarthy*

EROTIC TALES

(GERMAN)

A Regina Ziegler Filmproduktion in co-production with Tele-Munchen and Westdeutschel Rundfunk. (International sales: Mercure Distribution, Paris.) Executive producer, Ziegler. Associate producer, Hartmut Koehler. In color. Reviewed on vidcassette, L.A., Aug. 12, 15, 16, 1994. (In AFI/L.A., Montreal fests.). Total running time: **170 MIN.**

WET
Produced by Noah Golden. Line producer, Michael Mandaville. Directed, written by Bob Rafelson. Camera, Theo Van de Sande; editor, Michael Elliot; music, David McHugh; production design, Brian Eatwell; costume design, Julie Rae Engelsman; sound (Dolby), Mary Jo Devenney; assistant director, Nancy Stone; casting, Jakki Fink, Jory Weitz. Running time: **27 MIN.**
Bruce Lomann .... Arliss Howard
Davida Urked .... Cynda Williams
Jolene Wolff .... Kathleen Wilhoite
William .... John Toles-Bey

THE DUTCH MASTER
Produced by Jonathan Brett. Directed by Susan Seidelman. Screenplay, Brett, Seidelman. Camera, Maryse Alberti; editor, Mona Davis; music, Wendy Blackstone; production design, Lester Cohen; set decoration, Judy Rhee; costume design, Ellen Lutter; sound, Tony Cowans; assistant director, Charles Zalien; casting, Jill Greenberg. Running time: **32 MIN.**
Teresa .... Mila Solvino
Kim .... Aida Turturro
Dorothy .... Sharon Angela
Joey .... Rick Pasqualone

THE INSATIABLE MRS. KIRSCH
Produced by Ronaldo Vasconcellos. Directed, written by Ken Russell. Camera, Hong Manley; editor, Xavier Russell; wardrobe, Rosie Russon; Dolby sound; assistant director, Rupert Style. Running time: **27 MIN.**
Mrs. Kirsch .... Hetty Baynes
Writer .... Simon Shepherd

VROOOM, VROOOM, VROOOM
Produced, directed, written, edited by Melvin Van Peebles. Camera, Igor Sunara; supervising editor, Victor Kanefsky (Valkun); music, Van Peebles; art direction, James Sherman; sound, John McCormick; visual effects produced by Balsmeyer & Everett; visual effects supervisor, Randall Balsmeyer; visual effects production design, Michael Shaw; morphing sequences produced by Syzygy Digital Cinema; assistant director, Derrick Boatner. Running time: **28 MIN.**
Leroy .... Richard Barboza
With: Laura Lane, Dewar Zazee, Kim Smith, William (Spaceman) Patterson, Ted Hayes, Asha Jenkins, "New Image," Reggie Osse.

TOUCH ME
Line producer, Illumination Films. Directed by Paul Cox. Screenplay, Cox, Barry Dickins, Margot Wiburd. Camera, Nino Martinetti; music, Ranjit Saha et al.; art direction, Neil Angwin; sound, Rochelle Oshlack. Running time: **26 MIN.**
Sarah .... Gosia Dobrowolska
Christine .... Claudia Karvan
Claude ....Chris Haywood
Stewart .... Barry Otto
Roderick .... David Field
Charles .... Norman Kaye

THE CLOUD DOOR
Directed, written by Mani Kaul. Camera, Anil Mehta; editor, Lalitha Krishna; music, Ustad Zia Fariduddin Dagar; costumes, Bhanu Athaiya; sound, Vikram Joglekar. Running time: **30 MIN.**
With: Anu Arya Aggarwal, Murad Ali, Vasudeva Bhatt, Shashi, Yusuf Khurram, Shambhavi, Irfan, Bahauddin Dagar.

The usual scenario of an episodic project looking tantalizing on paper but proving disappointing in the actual sampling plays itself out in "Erotic Tales." An intriguing group of six diverse international directors has produced a grab bag of half-hour vignettes that is almost uniformly undercharged sexually and, with a couple of exceptions, cutesy in plot resolution. Most have trouble simply telling a structurally coherent, involving story. Unsatisfying as a group, but with one stunner in the bunch, German-produced collection can play at fests and in specialized urban and campus slots, but is better suited to cable playoff stateside and tube situations overseas.

The Bob Rafelson and Susan Seidelman entries debuted at Cannes (after the latter had been nominated for a short-subject Oscar), and the entire six-pack was served up for the first time on two programs, one U.S., the other international, at the recent AFI/L.A. fest.

Rafelson has a bit of slippery fun with "Wet," which depicts an after-hours encounter between an upscale bathroom-fixtures salesman and a provocative would-be customer for the ultimate in whirlpool bathtubs.

Popping into the store right at closing time, the playful Cynda Williams checks out the merchandise lonely guy Arliss Howard has to offer, building up to her nude plunge in the bubbles and invitation to the unsuspecting fellow to join her. Explanatory coda is harmlessly silly.

Comedy, sexual tension and voyeuristic elements are all there in light but agreeable doses. The voluptuous Williams ("One False Move") and Howard play off each other nicely, and pic has been elegantly mounted under modest circumstances.

Coincidentally, Seidelman's "The Dutch Master" also involves after-hours entry and a bathtub, but concerns not a casual encounter but a romantic fixation across the centuries. Mila Solvino plays a working-class dental assistant who, on a chance visit to New York's Metropolitan Museum, becomes fascinated with a beautiful young man depicted in a 17th-century Dutch painting.

As her boss, friends, parents and fiance become perplexed by her behavior, Solvino is able to enter the world of the painting as an unseen spectator to the events being played out by its inhabitants, which she does repeatedly, finally donning period garb and offering herself to her dream man.

Played out almost entirely behind v.o. commentary by assorted onlookers, pic is pleasantly observant about the transforming qualities of art, but is mostly interesting as a technical exercise, as the transition of the painting into a three-dimensional dramatic setting proves quite effective. Maryse Alberti's lensing is sensitive to its inspirational source, while erotic content per se is minimal.

"The Insatiable Mrs. Kirsch" represents Ken Russell at low tide. Coarse and staggeringly silly up to its bizarrely sweet surprise ending, this is another largely voiceover tale in which a young male writer (Simon Shepherd) becomes obsessed with a tarty-looking woman (Hetty Baynes) at a remote Dorset seaside inn.

As both sit at separate tables at meals, the novelist goes bananas watching the woman lasciviously eating corn on the cob, sausage, asparagus and an eclair. Following her to her door, he listens as she wears out three vibrators, then secretly pursues her on jaunts across the countryside, where she is similarly auto-erotic.

By making the object of the fellow's lust so overtly vulgar and crude, Russell would seem to be having a little fun with the whole notion of erotic obsession, but it's all very one-note and gross. Final twist is downright goofy, even benign, especially coming from the past master of lust and kink. Compared with the other entries, technical aspects here are rather threadbare.

Better technically, but equally bereft of ideas, is Melvin Van Peebles' inane "Vrooom, Vrooom, Vrooom," a fantasy in which a horny young man's wishes for a slick motorcycle and a hot woman are satisfied in one go by a voodoo woman.

Leaving his father's country shack behind, Richard Barboza zooms off each night on his bike, which under the moonlight transforms magically into a gorgeous woman positioned strategically between his legs. Blissful state of affairs lasts until Barboza makes the mistake of giving a flirtatious woman a ride, at which point the chopper rebels and gives its driver the heave-ho.

With its very broad acting and simplistic story, entry is notable only for the slick morphing effects that turn the bike's exhaust pipes into legs, headlight into a head and gas tank into a woman's torso.

Paul Cox's Aussie contribution, "Touch Me," at least offers up some distinctive textures and a reasonably adult sensibility. Loaded with femme nudity and tentative homoeroticism, this study of female friendship bordering on the amorous doesn't know where it's going but remains intriguing and quite watchable while it's onscreen.

Gosia Dobrowolska plays an art teacher whose warm feelings for her class' sexy model, Claudia Karvan, prompt her to dump her b.f., at least for the weekend, and join her female friend for a few days in the mountains.

The duo's three sessions of intense physicality — a fireside, full-body oil massage, a romp in the fields with two horses, and a sponging Dobrowolska gives Karvan — are dwelled upon at length and are hardly painful to watch. But the action, which is punctuated by some explicit messages and drawings that keep rolling out of the teacher's fax machine, never builds to a comprehensible conclusion, so that, despite its crisp dialogue and good performances, episode has little weight.

By far, the most striking erotic tale comes from India and the group's least-known director, Mani Kaul. Although its narrative is somewhat unclear, "The Cloud Door" features pictorial beauty, slow-building sensuality and surprising humor that combine to rich effect.

Uniquely funny opening has a pet parrot delivering an erotic commentary to an exquisitely beautiful, palace-bound princess. After a voyeuristically bountiful scene of several gorgeous women cavorting in a pool, the bird flies off to the home of a handsome young fellow and guides him to its mistress's palace to take revenge against a local religious fanatic "who is against Eros."

A poetic, enigmatic love scene ensues that is certainly quite explicit by Indian standards. From this point on, action becomes increasingly obscure, but the performers' dancelike movements, the precise camera moves, extraordinary orchestration of colors and musical detailing are seductive throughout and, as filmmaking, are on a level well beyond that displayed in the other installments. As a dividend, performance by the talking parrot is downright hilarious.
—*Todd McCarthy*

MARIE

(BELGIAN-FRENCH-PORTUGUESE)

An Oviri Films release of a Saga Film, RTL TVI (Brussels)/MSBA Prods. (Paris)/Vermedia (Lisbon) production, with support of Eurimages and participation of Canal Plus and CNC. Produced by Hubert Toint. Executive producer, Saga Film. Directed by Marian Handwerker. Screenplay, Luc Jabon, Catherine Verougstraete, Pascal Lonhay, Handwerker. Camera (color), Patrice Payen; editor, Denise Vindevogel; music, Dirk Brosse; art direction, Pierre Francois Limbosch; set decoration, Marie Lauwers; costume design, Guy Cantraine; sound, Ricardo Castro; associate producers, Maurice Brover, Paolo De Sousa; assistant director, Paul Fonteyn. Reviewed at UGC George V Cinema, Paris, Aug. 11, 1994. (In Paris Film Festival — competing.) Running time: **89 MIN.**
Marie .... Marie Gillain
Tonio .... Alessandro Sigona
Marie's mother .... Aurore Clement
With: Sabrina Leurquin, Stephane Ferrara, Jorge Sousa Costa, Margarida Marinho.
(French and Portuguese dialogue)

Marie Gillain gives a radiant, sensitive perf as a contemporary Belgian teenager with problems to spare in "Marie." Socially conscious road movie is practically Dickensian in its compound misfortunes, but stands on the side of love, hope and commitment in a cruel world. Fest and TV exposure are indicated.

Teenage Marie, whose previous boyfriend committed suicide, unsuccessfully combs her small Belgian town to let her current b.f. know she's pregnant and her mother is making her get an abortion. En route to the clinic, Mom — whose husband split for good the day Marie was born — admits that, given the chance, she would have aborted Marie.

Just prior to the operation, Marie bolts from the clinic table and takes refuge in a pool hall where the father of the fetus tells Marie he doesn't love her and she's a slut. Nearby Paulo (Stephane Ferrara), a kindly drug dealer, seems like a step up, but while escaping to Brussels with him, police flag down his car. After they set up a rendezvous at his apartment, Paulo jettisons Marie before embarking on a chase that — unbeknownst to her — ends in his death.

Keeping the appointment, Marie discovers Paulo's ultra-independent 7-year-old son, Tonio, holding down the fort. (Young actor Alessandro Sigona is every bit as lovable as Salvatore Cascio, the winning tyke in "Cinema Paradiso.") Tonio's mom returned to her native Portugal after he was born. Following a police raid in which Paulo's death is revealed, Marie decides to trek from Brussels to Lisbon to deliver Tonio to the mother he's never met.

A few unacceptably abrupt transitions mar the otherwise chronological tale. Musical score is almost unforgivably sappy and cloying; pic would probably play better without it. Other tech credits are fine.

Gillain, who made her screen debut as Gerard Depardieu's daughter in the original French version of "My Father, the Hero," is a lovely, spontaneous actress. At pic's end she is pregnant and unwed in a foreign country, but the film achieves an open-ended aura of solidarity and hope.

Film won the Grand Prix at the Paris Film Festival, along with best actress honors for Gillain.
—*Lisa Nesselson*

THE SMILE

(LE SOURIRE)

(FRENCH)

An AMLF release (in France) of a Les Films de la Boissiere/Film Par Film/TF1 Films Prod. production, with participation of Canal Plus, Investimage 3 and BNP Images. Produced by Annie Miller, Jean-Louis Livi. Co-executive producers, Miller, Jean-Jose Richer. Directed, written by Claude Miller. Camera (color), Guillaume Schiffman; editor, Anne Lafarge; music, Pierre Boscheron, Antoine Ouvrier, Vincent Glenn; art direction, Jean-Pierre Kohut Svelko; set decoration, Pierre Gompertz, Alain Veissier; costume design, Jacqueline Bouchard; sound (Dolby), Paul Laine, Gerard Lamps, Sylvie Liebeaux; assistant director, Valerie Othenin-Girard; casting, Sherif Scouri, Amelie Berard. Reviewed at AMLF screening room, Paris, Aug. 4, 1994. Running time: **89 MIN.**
Le Clainche .... Jean-Pierre Marielle
Jeanjean .... Richard Bohringer
Odile .... Emmanuelle Seigner
With: Chantal Banlier, Nadia Barentin, Nathalie Cardone, Bernard Verley, Maite Nahyr, Christine Pascal.

Scripter/helmer Claude Miller manipulates time and desire with complete filmic assurance for the lion's share of "The Smile." But his arrestingly sensual tale of a fantasy-perfect woman who appears on the horizon of male mortality peters out just shy of its melancholy conclusion. Keenly acted mood piece is a good bet for the international arthouse circuit, provided political correctness regarding women-as-sex-objects hasn't got patrons by the throat. Just opened in Paris, film will have its North American preem at the Montreal Film Festival.

With Duke Ellington's "Jump for Joy" setting the tone, form and content mesh with near-giddy mastery as three protagonists are introduced through intercut opening sequences.

An onscreen electrocardiogram administered to Le Clainche (Jean-Pierre Marielle), the sixtyish medical director of a countryside clinic, reveals that he's headed for a second, almost certainly fatal, heart attack. Dapper, cranky and endearing, Le Clainche is physically and emotionally antsy. He's weary but determined to sexually possess "one last woman."

Meanwhile, at a carnival fairground, Odile (Emmanuelle Seigner) delights in the adrenalin rush of a roller coaster ride. Men undress her with their eyes as she strides down the midway aware of her own earthy appeal and reveling in her youth.

Odile is inexplicably drawn to a striptease attraction whose charismatic barker, Jeanjean (Richard Bohringer), boldly yet sweetly invites her to join the show. Although she's a tennis pro by profession, the offer tempts her on a mysterious, primal level.

Le Clainche's somnolent testosterone bolts to the surface when he becomes smitten with Odile, whose prone form he first encounters in a railway compartment. He mounts a gentlemanly, but desperate, campaign to conquer her.

Le Clainche's approach would worry or offend many women, but Odile is an idealized creature who gives serious consideration to trysting with Le Clainche's old carcass, as surely as she plans to audition for Jeanjean's all-nude enterprise.

Seigner, whose somewhat stiff but compelling beauty helped keep "Frantic" and "Bitter Moon" hurtling along, here retains a secretive aura as an unpretentious country gal meant to project health and vitality.

A strange symbiosis emerges between Odile and Le Clainche. By turns tender and harsh, pic is an ode to male vanity marbled with the uncertainty of encroaching death.

Marielle's performance is aces. His sexual need, cloaked in civility, abuts the no-nonsense, oggle-away atmosphere of Jeanjean's strip joint.

Cinematography has gusto, and sound design is highly effective at conveying states of mind. There's a sort of out-of-body feel to the editing that transports the viewer, the better to bring the narrative crashing back to reality.

A fake-docu passage about the offstage lives of peripatetic carnival strippers, based on a book-length photo essay by Susan Meiselas, is a bit jarring. Pic's shortcoming is that, after bringing the central trio together, its otherwise superb rhythm falters in the process of prying them apart. Ending comes across as desultory rather than devastating.

French title means "the smile," but is also a playful expression for the cleft in a woman's posterior.
—*Lisa Nesselson*

LIMITA

(RUSSIAN)

A Studio 29 production. Produced by Serge Magarow. Directed by Denis Evstigneev. Screenplay, Irakly Kvirikadze, Pyotr Lutzik, Alexei Samoryadov. Camera (color), Sergei Kozlov; music, Eduard Artenyev; production design, Pavel Kaplevich; choreography; Alla Sigalova. Reviewed at Cinema Center, Moscow, June 29, 1994. Running time: **105 MIN.**
With: Vladimir Mashkov (Ivan), Yevgeny Mironov, Kristina Orbakaite, Maxim Sukhanov.

A fast-paced thriller set in the world of Russia's "new rich," that conspicuous consumer society of nightclubs and foreign cars that sprang up in the '90s, Denis Evstigneev's directing debut has a sense of style that sets it apart from other new Russian releases this year.

Its title, which translates most literally as "hicks," refers to the film's two central characters, Ivan and Misha, who have made it to Moscow from the provinces in time to catch the rising boom of perestroika's economic opportunity. All we see of their past are an intercut series of hand-held, black-and-white sequences of carefree camaraderie, set against their present-day world of stylishly decorated apartments, nightclubs, fast cars and indulgence.

Ivan (Vladimir Mashkov) has struck it rich as a computer codebreaker, and the film's plot revolves around a disk that's brought to him for decoding. He sets about to perform what turns out to be the hardest job of his life, only to discover that the code has been set by his friend, who's working as a technical specialist for a bank. Eventually, out of loyalty, he interrupts the decoding program — but with fatal results for Misha, who is killed by Ivan's client as the only person with the key to the disk.

The film's twist comes at its very end, when Ivan sets out to take vengeance and discovers that the information on the disk had incriminated him too, thus leaving him with empty ideals about loyalty, and marking the end of a simple world in which he'd do anything for a friend.

"Limita" is edited with a speed and fluency unusual for Russian cinema, and Sergei Kozlov's camerawork, with its night-drive sequences (reminiscent of "Diva") and stylized club scenes, catches the bizarre newness of pic's world. Evstigneev was himself a cameraman, working on films like Vadim Abrashitov and Alexander Mindadze's 1989 "The Servant," as well as Pavel Lungin's "Taxi Blues" and "Luna Park" — and it shows in his directorial debut.

August 22, 1994 (Cont.)

This is new Russian filmmaking, with one foot in Europe: Post-production was done in Paris, with an overall budget at close to $1 million. Only two things may complicate the film for the foreign viewer. First, the exact meaning of the title, a term used by Muscovites with a strong hint of scorn about those who came to try to make it in the capital, doesn't translate. Second, the final plot twist comes in just one sentence — blink and you've missed it. —*Tom Birchenough*

VEVEY FEST

LE PERIL JEUNE

(FRENCH)

A Vertigo Prods., La Sept/Arte, Cameras Continentales production. Produced by Aissa Djabri, Farid Lahoussa. Directed by Cedric Klapisch. Screenplay, Klapisch, Santiago Amigorena, Alexis Galmot, Daniel Thieux. Camera (color), Dominique Colin; editor, Francine Sandberg; art direction, Francois Emmanuelli; costume design, Pierre Yves Gayraud; sound, Francois Waledisch; casting, Bruno Levy. Reviewed at Vevey Comedy Film Festival (non-competing), Switzerland, July 29, 1994. (Also in Chamrousse and Paris fests — competing.) Running time: **102 MIN.**
With: Julien Lambroschini, Nicolas Koretzy, Vincent Elbaz, Joachim Lombard, Romain Duris, Lisa Faulkner, Christine Sandre.

The sheer anticonformist exuberance of a group of five young men during their senior year of high school in 1975 anchors "Le Peril Jeune," the involving account of four surviving buddies reunited five years later for the birth of a child fathered by their recently deceased friend. Nostalgic slice of life, told mostly in flashback, is a natural for fests that value good ensemble perfs and assured helming.

During their all-night vigil in a Paris hospital, the four pals — who have drifted apart in the five years since graduation — reminisce together, trying to retrace the moments that set the once-carefree Tomasi on the path of drug use that would lead to his fatal overdose.

Despite the bittersweet circumstances, their banter is laced with humor and confessions as the guys sort through the puzzle pieces of their relationships with girls, teachers, parents and drugs. The perceptual oddities of tripping on acid are nicely conveyed, as is the diffuse macho pride that costs one of the gang his one true love.

Sets, clothing, music and hairstyles are on the nose. The atmosphere of the budding feminist movement, of a student demonstration de-

volving into a tear-gas-clouded combat zone, and of the barely contained hysteria of joking in class are all captured with fly-in-amber accuracy. Protagonists' encounters with the class slut and the lovely British girl who arrives from London to teach English are nicely etched.

Originally commissioned as part of the made-for-TV series of pix that spawned Andre Techine's "Wild Reeds" and Olivier Assayas' "Cold Water," "Le Peril Jeune" — which took the top prize at the Chamrousse Comedy Fest and nabbed the Jury Prize at the Paris Film Festival — will have its Gallic theatrical release in November.

Pic's title, which translates as "The Youth Peril," is also a pun on the expression for "yellow peril," and a direct reference to a famous mid-'70s cover story in the irreverent magazine "Charlie Hebdo," which mocked establishment fears about Gallic youth. —*Lisa Nesselson*

LOCARNO FEST

LIKE TWO CROCODILES

(COME DUE COCCODRILLI)

(ITALIAN-FRENCH)

An Istituto Luce release (Italy) of a Fandango (Rome)/Ki'en Prod. (France) production, in association with Portobello Pictures, Bellatrix Pictures, RAI-1. (International sales: Intrafilms, Rome.) Produced by Domenico Procacci. Directed by Giacomo Campiotti. Screenplay, Alexander Adabachan, Campiotti, Marco Piatti. Camera (Technicolor), Raffaele Mertes; editor, Roberto Missiroli; music, Stefano Caprioli; art direction, Antonia Rubeo; (Dolby). Reviewed at Locarno Film Festival (competing), Aug. 12, 1994. Running time: **100 MIN.**
Gabriele .... Fabrizio Bentivoglio
Young Gabriele .... Ignazio Oliva
Father ....Giancarlo Giannini
Mother .... Valeria Golino
Claire .... Sandrine Dumas
Antonella .... Angela Baraldi

Rising Italian star Fabrizio Bentivoglio is a big-league art dealer with a family score to settle in "Like Two Crocodiles," which grips the viewer in a personal drama that spans a generation. After its Locarno preem, this second feature by Giacomo Campiotti ("Corsa di primavera") should be a fest favorite.

Skillfully narrated, gorgeously lensed by Raffaele Mertes ("Flight of the Innocent"), with intriguing characters and many fine perfs (several by child thesps), pic could also be one of this season's big Italo attractions for offshore quality distribs.

Gabriele (Fabrizio Bentivoglio) is introduced in his Parisian lairs: a Christie's-type antique appraisal firm, and an automated apartment that suits his bachelor lifestyle. As his girlfriend, Claire (Sandrine Dumas), points out, he lives in a box that no one can penetrate.

Flashbacks introduce the history of his problem. He and his infant brother, Martino, are bastard children, a second family that *pere* Giancarlo Giannini has secreted away in the country. When his beloved, high-spirited mother (Valeria Golino) dies, he and Martino are transferred to his father's official family.

In a fabulous villa on a lake, they grow up in luxury. But teenage Gabriele (Ignazio Oliva) is hated and despised by his two half-brothers, who eventually drive him away.

Now a suave, successful antique dealer in Paris, adult Gabriele seizes a chance to return to Italy and revenge himself on his evil brothers by ruining them financially. But his trip home is also a journey into his past.

The mark of Russian screenwriter Alexander Adabashan, a longtime writer for Nikita Mikhalkov, is visible in the film's clever, complex plot, whose mythic roots lie in the biblical tale of Joseph and his brothers. At the same time, film has a modern concreteness — and a sense of humor — that makes the story credible as well as engrossing.

As Gabriele, Bentivoglio has a buried childlike wistfulness under his cold exterior that perfectly segues from Oliva's eagerness to please. His motives are carefully established, and he remains an appealing hero even at his most scheming and nefarious.

Giannini has the distant look of a 19th-century patriarch whose will, however absurd and inconvenient, is family law. Golino is fresh and strong as his self-sacrificing mistress. Ditto Dumas as Gabriele's mistreated French lover and Angela Baraldi as his first love and defender.

Mertes' sweeping cinematography gives the settings an almost fairy-tale quality, particularly the castle-like villa.

Despite a few initial jolts as the b&w flashbacks (unnecessarily printed in a retro sepia tone) begin, Roberto Missiroli ends up smoothly blending past into present in what must have been a complicated editing job. —*Deborah Young*

CHUNG KING EXPRESS

(CHUNGHING SAMLAM)

(HONG KONG)

A Jet Tone Production Co. production. (International sales: Fortissimo Film Sales, Amsterdam.) Produced by Chan Yi-kan. Executive producer, Chan Pui-wah. Directed, written by Wong Kar-wai. Camera (color), Christopher Doyle, Lau wai-keung; editors, William Chang, Hai Kit-wai, Kwong Chi-leung; music, Frankie Chan, Roel A. Garcia; art direction-costume design, William Chang. Reviewed at Locarno Film Festival (competing), August 10, 1994. Running time: **103 MIN.**
Drug dealer ..... Brigitte Lin Ching-hsia
He Quiwu,
Cop 223 .... Takeshi Kaneshiro
Cop 663 .... Tony Leung Chiu-wai
Faye .... Faye Wang
Air hostess .... Valerie Chow
(Cantonese and Mandarin dialogue)

Four years after his cult classic "Days of Being Wild," Hong Kong maverick stylist Wong Kar-wai trampolines back with "Chung King Express," a quicksilver magical mystery tour through the lives of a bunch of young downtown loners. Hip pic, drenched in neo-'60s nostalgia, should delight sinophiles and prove an intriguing addition to the fest repertoire, though its appeal may prove too specialized for broad sales.

Wong made the moderately budgeted, HK$15m ($2 million) movie in only three months, between the end of shooting and start of post-production on his mammoth martial arts costumer "Ashes of Time," already two years in the works. With its plentiful use of hand-held camera, fast-cutting, and collage-like approach to story-telling, "Wild" has a fresh, risk-taking feel very different from the rigorous "Days," even though its romantic undercurrent and quartet of urban dreamers are not far removed from the earlier pic. Effect is a little like watching an early Godard movie set in contempo Hong Kong, though with a technical slickness from employing two megastars (Brigitte Lin Ching-hsia, Tony Leung Chiu-wai) and top technicians (lenser Christopher Doyle, production designer William Chang).

First story (42 minutes), set around the labyrinthine tenement building Chung King House in downtown Kowloon, spins on a romantic young cop (Takeshi Kaneshiro), recently ditched by his g.f. As he mopes around, devouring cans of pineapple and calling up old flames, destiny leads him to cross paths with a cold-hearted drug dealer (Lin) in a blond wig and designer shades.

Second, more involving story (61 minutes) centers on another young cop (Leung), also ditched by his air hostess g.f. (Valerie Chow), who's the unwitting fixation of a dotty worker (Faye Wang) at Midnight Express, a fast-food joint.

First seg, almost entirely shot at night, and much showier technically, is the lesser of the two halves, but establishes the movie's overall tone of urban forlornness. There's enough energy in the direction and loopy humor in the piece to just about fill the running time.

Longer seg has more going for it, with an engagingly wide-eyed perf by Wang (in a Jean Seberg, "Breathless" haircut) whose body language and facial expressions are wonders to behold. Matinee idol Leung, all boyish incomprehension, is as fresh and relaxed as he's ever been in his multi-pic career. These are two people you just want to see get together.

Overall, Wong's movie doesn't leave as big a wash behind it as the more ambitious "Days" and his "Mean Streets"-like debut, "As Tears Go By," but it's an enjoyable cruise. A richly detailed soundtrack, including classics such as "California Dreamer," accompanies the many dialogue-free montage sequences.   —*Derek Elley*

ROSINE

(FRENCH)

Produced by Bernard Verley, Alain Sarde for BVF. Directed, written by Christine Carriere. Camera (color), Christophe Pollock; editor, Raymonde Guyot; music, Elisabeth Anseutter. Reviewed at Locarno Film Festival (competing), Aug. 10, 1994. Running time: 102 MIN.

Rosine	Eloise Charretier
Marie	Mathilde Seigner
Pierre	Laurent Olmedo
Chantal	Christine Murillo
Yasmina	Aurelie Verillon
Francine	Maite Maille

A 14-year-old girl from a French factory town fights a touching if losing battle to win her indifferent mom's heart in "Rosine," a first feature by Christine Carriere. A convincing cast of unknowns lends weight to this small but on-target pic, which touches on the trauma of incest with psychological realism but no sensationalism. Film generates an intimacy that could come across well on the small screen.

The nowhere locale — a community of row houses near a highway in northern France where it's always cold and raining — sets the scene for Rosine's (Eloise Charretier) bleak family life. An unwed mother at 16, Marie (Mathilde Seigner) is now an irresponsible, unmotherly 30. She spends her nights on dates in singles bars and discos, leaving Rosine to pine for her at home.

Absorbed by her own problems, Marie brushes Rosine off cruelly. But Rosine's adoration, which bor-

ders on the unhealthy, never flags. Then one day a young man appears out of nowhere: It's Rosine's father, Pierre (Laurent Olmedo). Marie is only too happy to take him back in, and Rosine initially responds well to his kindly interest.

But Pierre soon reveals a violent streak, beating Marie and finally raping Rosine in an off-camera scene that is nonetheless psychologically explicit. Battered but not destroyed, the girl tries to force Marie to acknowledge what has happened. But her insinuations are met with defensive indifference, and all that is left for Rosine is to run away. In a curious symbolic finale, society itself seems to put on blinders to the grim injustice done to kids like Rosine. Though uncompromising ending is downbeat, it leaves space to believe that plucky Rosine will fight on.

Carriere re-creates an emotionally empty working-class world of barely hidden violence, yet glances affectionately at even her most flawed characters. As Rosine's selfish, unhappy mom, Seigner has an innocent pathos that makes one feel she's as much a victim of circumstance as her daughter. Newcomer Charretier bubbles with life and energy as Rosine, wise beyond her years but with a big emotional hole in the center. Music track relies heavily on contempo teen rock, whose blast is used to drown out the anguish of real life.
                    —*Deborah Young*

ORGANIZED CRIME & TRIAD BUREAU

(CHUNGON SATLUK LINGGEI)

(HONG KONG)

A Unidan Investments production for Magnum Films. Executive producer, Danny Lee. Directed by Kirk Wong. Screenplay, Winky Wong. Camera (color), Wong Wing-hang, Chan Kwong-hung; editor, Choi Hung; music, Tsung Ding-yat; art direction, Hau Wing-choi; assistant director, Lam Kam-kong. Reviewed at Locarno Film Festival, Aug. 11, 1994. Running time: 93 MIN.

Lee	Danny Lee
Cindy	Cecilia Yip
Tung	Antony Wong
Female cop	Elisabeth Lee
Fan Tsi-tsing	Cheung Yiu-yeung
(Cantonese dialogue)	

Despite its clumsy English title, "Organized Crime & Triad Bureau" is a crackerjack Hong Kong actioner that just keeps on coming. Pic forms the central seg of a loose, fact-based trilogy begun with the Jackie Chan starrer "Crime Story" and concluding with "Rock n' Roll Cop," all directed by ex-New Waver Kirk Wong. Trio unspooled at Locarno and should

blast a hole in other fests' midnight skeds.

Bulk of the action is set on Cheung Chai, one of Hong Kong's many neighboring islets, whither sleazy Tung (Antony Wong) and his mistress (Cecilia Yip) have holed up prior to escaping to mainland China. Unconventional cop Lee (Danny Lee) seals off the island and finally captures Tung; back in Hong Kong, Cindy busts him out for a final showdown in the colony's streets.

Simple storyline is merely an excuse for a succession of terrific *verismo* set pieces that rival the classic money-transfer sequence in "Crime Story." Made on a smaller budget and with lower-league stars, "Bureau" hints at what "Crime Story" might have looked like before Jackie Chan and major studio Golden Harvest became attached: grittier, almost docu-drama in feel, with a preponderance of hand-held camera work and less flashy lighting.

Wong's skill at building excitement through editing, sound and music, rather than spectacular stunts or effects, pays dividends in both the Cheung Chai section and the final street battle.

Lead performances are all on the button, with a granite-faced Lee, wild-eyed Wong and designer-looker Yip. Flashbacks to Yip's character's troubled sexual past could easily be snipped. Pic did reasonable business on local release last January.   —*Derek Elley*

ROCK N' ROLL COP

(SANG GONG YATHO TUNGCHAP FAN)

(HONG KONG)

A Sky Point Film Investment production. Executive producer, Kirk Wong. Directed by Wong. Screenplay, Lou Bing. Camera (color), Ko Tsiu-lam; editor, Kam Ma; music, Tsung Ding-yat; art direction, Eddie Ma; assistant director, Lui Ka-wah; action director, Lo Lai-yin. Reviewed at Locarno Film Festival (midnight screenings), Aug. 13, 1994. Running time: 93 MIN.

Inspector Hung	Antony Wong
Wang Jun	Wu Hsing-kuo
Hou-yee	Carrie Ng
Shum Chi-hung	Yu Wing-kwong
Singer	Chan Ming-tsing
(Cantonese and Mandarin dialogue)	

The shadow of Hong Kong's 1997 handover to China forms an intriguing background to "Rock n' Roll Cop," a trans-border actioner that teams a guitar-strumming honky with his besuited mainland counterpart in pursuit of a felon hiding out in the People's Republic.

Film wraps up a trio of movies all directed by Kirk Wong and based on stories told him by a real-life cop.

Last is the weakest of the three but more similar in style to the docudrama-like "Organized Crime & Triad Bureau" than the high-sheen opener "Crime Story," with Jackie Chan. The three pix have no characters in common.

Antony Wong (the villain in "Bureau") here plays Hung, a maverick plainclothes cop who pursues a psychotic villain (Yu Wing-kwong) and his gang across the border to Shenzhen after a sickening crime in a Kowloon gambling joint. He and hard-nosed mainlander Wang (played by Taiwan star Wu Hsing-kuo) wait for the villain's squeeze, Hou-yee (the striking Carrie Ng), to lead them to his hiding place.

"Cop" lacks the hard-driven, all-out procedural style of "Bureau." When they come, however, the action sequences deliver.

Performances are fine, and location shooting in China natural and uncramped.   —*Derek Elley*

August 29, 1994

MONTREAL

THERE GOES MY BABY

An Orion Pictures release of a Nelson Entertainment presentation of a Robert Shapiro production. Produced by Shapiro. Executive producers, Barry Spikings, Rick Finkelstein. Directed, written by Floyd Mutrux. Camera (Deluxe color), William Fraker; editors, Danford Greene, Maysie Hoy; executive music producer, Budd Carr; production design, Richard Sawyer; art direction, Louis Mann; set decoration, Peg Cummings; costume design, Molly Maginnis; sound (Dolby), William Randall; assistant directors, Stephen Fisher, George Fortmuller; casting, Lynn Stalmaster, Janet Hirshenson, Jane Jenkins. Reviewed at Orion screening room, L.A., Aug. 23, 1994. (In World Film Festival, Montreal — competing.) MPAA Rating: R. Running time: **99 MIN.**

Pirate	Dermot Mulroney
Stick	Rick Schroder
Sunshine	Kelli Williams
Finnegan	Noah Wyle
Babette	Jill Schoelen
Tracy	Kristin Minter
Mary Beth	Lucy Deakins
Calvin	Kenny Ransom
Pop	Seymour Cassel
Burton	Paul Gleason
Maran	Frederick Coffin
Frank	Andrew Robinson
The Beard	Humble Harve Miller
Morrisey	Shon Greenblatt
George	J. E. Freeman

It may not be intentional, but "There Goes My Baby" is a virtual companion piece to "American Graffiti." Set in 1965, three years after the George Lucas pic, it's also an episodic character piece in which eight high school grads confront their future on two fateful nights as the soundtrack counterpoints the action with the music of the day. Lost in the shuffle of Orion's bankruptcy for two years, it's been retrieved from the shelf and is competing at the Montreal fest. Ripe for discovery, the riveting, infectious comic drama has a real shot at sleeper success with proper support.

This good-natured, emotion-charged memory piece has a lot to say about the era's political and social landscape. It rarely stoops to preaching; rather, its wallop comes from the key personalities and the way pivotal historic events are absorbed into the mundane and unsullied lives of American teenagers.

Narrated by Anne Archer, the look back is told from the p.o.v. of class valedictorian Mary Beth (Lucy Deakins). In 1961, her class at Westwood High, in California, was chronicled by Look magazine as the country's future. It's a mantle they did not seek; nor do they desire it four years later.

In the interval, JFK was assassinated, the civil rights movement took root, the country began a "police action" in Vietnam and rock 'n' roll lost a lot of its inanity. The class has evolved, too. Some have developed a keen social conscience and others simply want to be on the road or in the surf.

The last night of school and its immediate aftermath bring all these elements to the fore, as well as such deeply personal issues as teenage pregnancy and career and college options.

Initially, pic seems no more than a goof. But writer/director Floyd Mutrux has a lot more on his plate. A classmate who lost a brother in Vietnam is mercilessly clubbed and taken to jail by police for his schoolyard protest. Later, at the height of a final celebration, word wafts in that across town the Watts riots have ignited.

Filmed prior to the '92 L.A. riots, "There Goes My Baby" takes on an eerily prophetic tone. Yet the events never overpower the characters, whose lives are elegantly interwoven. Whether they're arguing about Vietnam, coming to blows over studying at the radical haven of Berkeley or simply confronting the breakup of a relationship, the characters dominate.

Mutrux and his young cast deserve enormous credit for keeping the loosely knit tale emotionally absorbing. It's a real sleight-of-hand to balance the comic and dramatic elements, invoking both the serious and the goofy sides of the recent past.

The younger performers are down to earth and credible. Particular standouts are Rick Schroder as a surfer headed for Vietnam, Kelli Williams as an original flower child, Jill Schoelen as an aspiring rock star and Kenny Ransom as the school's lone black student.

Add to the high-level talent mix a soundtrack with an ironic bite and cinematographer William Fraker's poetic eye, and the result is a unique and highly entertaining pic. This time capsule is about rites of passage and the loss of innocence. It captures the moment with wit and affection, and while it treats its subjects fondly, the tone is not nostalgic or maudlin.

"There Goes My Baby" is a genuine find of supreme simplicity and skill. Like the era it relives, it seems an anachronism among the current crop of films. Yet its sincerity and craft set it apart, and that difference makes it all the more potent.
— *Leonard Klady*

PRINCESS CARABOO

A TriStar release and Beacon presentation of a Longfellow Pictures/Artisan Films production. Produced by Andrew Karsch, Simon Bosanquet. Executive producers, Armyan Bernstein, Tom Rosenberg, Marc Abraham. Directed by Michael Austin. Screenplay, Austin, John Wells. Camera (Rank Film Labs color; Technicolor prints), Freddie Francis; editor, George Akers; music, Richard Hartley; production design, Michael Howells; art direction, Sam Riley; set decoration, Sasha Schwertd; costume design, Tom Rand; sound (Dolby), Peter Glossop; assistant director, Jonathan Benson; second unit director, Bosanquet; second unit camera, Kelvin Pike, Eddie Collins; casting, Lucy Boulting. Reviewed at Loews Copley Place, Boston, Aug. 18, 1994. (In Montreal, Boston fests.) MPAA Rating: PG. Running time: **96 MIN.**

Princess Caraboo	Phoebe Cates
Mr. Worrall	Jim Broadbent
Mrs. Worrall	Wendy Hughes
Frixos	Kevin Kline
Professor Wilkinson	John Lithgow
Gutch	Stephen Rea
Lord Apthorpe	Peter Eyre
Lady Apthorpe	Jacqueline Pearce
Magistrate	
Haythorne	Roger Lloyd Pack
Reverend Hunt	John Wells
Amon McCarthy	John Lynch
Prince Regent	John Sessions
Betty	Arkie Whiteley

"Princess Caraboo" is an airy bit of historical fluff. Based on a true story, the romantic comedy about a Pacific island princess in 1817 England who may not be for real could be considered Merchant Ivory Lite. The great costumes and sets are more substantial than the plot and characters. Frothy diversion, which world-preemed at the Montreal fest over the weekend and will follow up at the Boston fest, is inoffensive and will entertain those who enjoy period romances, but it's questionable whether that is enough to draw a sizable public.

Princess Caraboo (Phoebe Cates) shows up in a country village unable to speak or write English, but slowly conveys a story of her kidnapping from a royal household and her swimming for safety from a pirate ship off the English coast. The Worralls (Jim Broadbent, Wendy Hughes) — at the bottom of the upper classes — see the princess as a means to increase their wealth and prestige. Their problem is Gutch (Stephen Rea), a local reporter who is suspicious of the princess even as he finds himself falling in love. Central plot point concerns whether Caraboo is on the level.

The chief attractions here are away from center stage. Kevin Kline milks a supporting role as the Worrall's Greek butler for all it's worth, while John Lithgow is a standout in a featured turn as a skeptical academic who begins to succumb to the princess's charms.

Equally striking is the location shooting in Wales and western England, which brings the early 19th century to life. A ball planned to introduce the princess to England's Prince Regent (John Sessions) is a gem of art design and choreography. In addition to production designer Michael Howells and his team, credit is due to Anthony van Laast for staging the period dances.

But the central story is cotton candy. Caraboo's story is suspicious from the beginning, and is not helped by the casting of Cates, who is charming but looks far too modern for the role. Rea glides through the part of the muckraking reporter, but with nothing really at stake he has nothing to play against. The predicament that Caraboo's fraud — if fraud it be — can be punishable by death never seems a possible outcome of the story. Her ultimate romance with the reporter is wholly an invention of the filmmakers.
— *Daniel M. Kimmel*

CAMP NOWHERE

A Buena Vista release of a Hollywood Pictures presentation of a Michael Peyser production. Produced by Michael Peyser. Executive producers, Andrew Kurtzman, Eliot Wald. Co-producers, David Streit, Janet Graham. Directed by Jonathan Prince. Screenplay, Kurtzman, Wald. Camera (Technicolor), Sandi Sissel; editor, Jon Poll; music, David Lawrence; production design, Rusty Smith; art direction, James I. Samson; set design, Christopher S. Nushawg; set decoration, Mona Personius; costume design, Shery Thompson; sound, (Dolby) David Kelson; associate producer, Gloria Lopez; assistant directors, Richard Hawley, Timothy Lonsdale; casting, Amy Lippens. Reviewed at Avco Cinema, L.A., Aug. 24, 1994. MPAA Rating: PG. Running time: **96 MIN.**

Morris	
"Mud" Himmel	Jonathan Jackson
Dennis	
Van Welker	Christopher Lloyd
Zack Dell	Andrew Keegan
Trish Prescott	Marne Patterson
Gaby Nowicki	Melody Kay
Norris Prescott	Ray Baker
Rachel Prescott	Kate Mulgrew
Dr. Celeste	
Dunbar	Wendy Makkena
Donald Himmel	Peter Scolari
Nancy Himmel	Romy Walthall
Karl Dell	Peter Onorati
M. Emmett Walsh	T.R. Polk
Lt. Eliot Hendricks	Tom Wilson
Fein	Burgess Meredith

Like poor little "Mud" Himmel, the hero of "Camp Nowhere" who is constantly upbraided by his nerdy parents for not realizing his "potential," this Hollywood Pictures youth comedy about a group of misfit kids who create a secret summer camp squanders its potential. Moderate B.O. looks limited to the braces-and-Barbie set.

When Mud (Jonathan Jackson) is faced with another summer of computer camp, he rebels and enlists three friends in a wild plan to create their own summer camp.

Since Zack (Andrew Keegan) is being shipped off by his war-loving father to a military camp, Trish (Marne Patterson) looks to be dispatched to theater camp by her culturally challenged folks, and Gaby (Melody Kay) will be sent to fat camp by her weight-obsessed mom, this gang of four share a quest for freedom from neurotic parental expectations.

They find the perfect adult co-conspirator in wild and crazy ex-high school drama instructor Dennis Van Welker (Christopher Lloyd). Their summer of fun is to be financed by the dough their parents plan to spend on their respective camps, but then another two dozen school pals get wind of the plan. Suddenly there's a busload of free-spirited adolescent revelers ready to party hearty until September.

At this point, "Camp Nowhere" serves up a truly interesting situation which the filmmakers generally leave wilting in the sun. Van Welker, it turns out, isn't so much a broken-down loser as an idealist who believes in mining the youths' energy and vitality.

And the kids, who gorge themselves on junk food and fulfill their every consumer fantasy on a shopping spree, are revealed to be surprisingly introspective and thoughtful. Their own summer camp turns into the kind of learning experience sought by their well-meaning but blockheaded parents.

Elements of "Dead Poets Society," "Zero de Conduit" and "Lord of the Flies" appear, only to disappear under the weight of rushing forward the more traditional plot points.

For instance, when director Jonathan Prince gently glides the film toward visual lyricism, as in a wonderful scene of nighttime revelry, the action is abruptly cut short in order to return to standard TV sitcom speechifying and corny comedic histrionics.

Prince gets some decent performances out of the kiddie cast and keeps the action lightly bubbling along, but interesting premise needed more than the so-so treatment delivered here.

Pic's forced, frenetic payoff yields some funny wish fulfillment as the kids lure their parents to a family visiting day, run like a military operation to maintain the illusion of the conspirators' respective camp experiences.

But the material is handled safely: The dangerous implications of the unsupervised and hormonally supercharged kids, their purchase of several cases of beer and the specter of Woodstock-like orgiastic partying are all shortchanged or never addressed.

Perfs range from so-so to special, with newcomer Jackson a standout, and Wendy Makkena, as an unlikely love interest for Lloyd, gamely striving to pump some romance and adult appeal into the juvenile proceedings.

Pic boasts savvy use of Southern California wilderness locations standing in for the Adirondacks, but the often harsh, glaring lighting of outdoor scenes wastes the ample pictorial opportunities of kids in paradise. —*Steven Gaydos*

S.F.W.

A Gramercy Pictures release. Produced by Dale Pollock. Executive producer, Sigurjon Sighvatsson. Co-producer, Mike Nelson. Directed by Jefery Levy. Screenplay, Danny Rubin, Levy, based on the novel by Andrew Wellman. Camera (color), Peter Deming; editor, Lauren Zuckerman; music, Graeme Revell; production design, Eve Cauley; art direction, Philip Messina; set decoration, Sandy Struth; costume design, Debra McGuire; sound, David B. Chornow; associate producer, Gloria Lopez; assistant director, John E. Vohlers; casting, Owens Hill, Rachel Abroms. Reviewed at Skywalker Sound, Santa Monica, Aug. 18, 1994. (In Edinburgh Film Festival.) MPAA Rating: R. Running time: **92 MIN.**

Cliff Spab	Stephen Dorff
Wendy Pfister	Reese Witherspoon
Morrow Streeter	Jake Busey
Monica Dice	Joey Lauren Adams
Janet Streeter	Pamela Gidley
Scott Spab	David Barry Gray
Joe Dice	Jack Noseworthy
Gerald Parsley	Richard Portnow
Mr. Spab	Edward Wiley
Mrs. Spab	Lela Ivey

A satirical spin through America's oft-reported fascination with celebrities, no matter how empty or facile, "S.F.W." tries hard to juice up a subject that feels done to death, even before Oliver Stone's similarly themed "Natural Born Killers" hits the theaters. This summer's youth pic "Airheads," a B.O. bellyflop, walked the same side of the street. Despite "S.F.W.'s" teen rebellion subtext and appealing, youthful leads, this loud, tough satire will likely draw no more than an appreciative cult following and modest receipts.

Billy Wilder made essentially the same film and scored the same topical points with his dark classic "Ace in the Hole" decades before the "Slacker" generation was spawned, and Martin Scorsese scored artistic if not commercial points with his comic satire of moronic American celebrityhood, "The King of Comedy," more than a decade ago.

When suburban teen buddies Cliff Spab ("Backbeat's" Stephen Dorff) and Joe Dice (Jack Noseworthy) zip into their local convenience store for a couple of brewskis, their typical night out on the 'burb is turned upside down. Waiting inside is a group of video camera-wielding terrorists who hold the two boys and three other customers hostage.

The gang demands that TV networks broadcast the tapes they're creating, but the lack of a political or financial explanation for their actions is only one of several key weaknesses of Danny Rubin and director Jefery Levy's caricature-laden adaptation of Andrew Wellman's novel.

Pic instead focuses on the after-effects of what turns into a 36-day ordeal that claims the lives of all the hostages except Spab and winsome uppercrust teen Wendy Pfister (Reese Witherspoon).

Spab, the film suggests, becomes a hero to America's young because of his defiance and sardonic view of his drab, small-town life more than his success at blowing away the bad guys. His resistance in the face of captivity is exemplified by his personal slogan, "So fucking what" (hence the film's acronymic title).

When Spab barks this at his captors, and explains why his dreary life has fostered this nihilistic attitude, his foul-mouthed mantra turns into a national slogan, and Spab videos, T-shirts, mugs, CDs and fan clubs are created. Along the way, Spab discovers his own values are growing clearer, even as the world is viewing him as a kind of walking cliche.

While Levy, whose previous pix were "Drive" (1991) and "Inside Monkey Zetterland" (1992), clearly sympathizes with his protagonist's ennui and confusion, "S.F.W." fails to develop flesh-and-blood characters, and instead trades on tired filmic tricks that stack the deck at every turn. These range from the characters' obviously parodistic names, to stock shots of the Spab home with obligatory factory smokestacks in the background, to over-the-top performances in virtually all of the supporting roles.

Pic unevenly switches back and forth between sincere teen romance and a directorial heavy-handedness matched only by the crashing, obvious sound design and heavy-metal musical score. Levy's over-the-top approach bludgeons material that's thin and arch to begin with.

In its least successful passages, pic recalls not Wilder or Scorsese, but AIP '60s sociopolitical teenpix like "Wild in the Streets." While that take may be good for a few laughs, pop kitsch has a nasty habit of turning back on itself and undermining the opportunities for emotional resonance and more serious points buried beneath the excess and artifice. —*Steven Gaydos*

WAGONS EAST!

A TriStar release from Carolco of an Outlaw production in association with Goodman-Rosen Prods. Produced by Gary Goodman, Barry Rosen, Robert Newmyer, Jeffrey Silver. Executive producer, Lynwood Spinks. Co-producer, Jim Davidson. Directed by Peter Markle. Screenplay, Matthew Carlson, story by Jerry Abrahamson. Camera (Technicolor), Frank Tidy; editor, Scott Conrad; music, Michael Small; production design, Vince J. Cresciman; art direction, Hector Romero C.; set design, Miguel Angel Gonzalez B.; set decoration, Enrique Estevez L.; costume design, Adolfo "Fito" Ramirez; sound (Dolby), Pud Cusak; assistant director, Gary Marcus; second unit camera, Angel Goded, Henner Hoffman; casting, Richard Pagano, Sharon Bialy, Debi Manwiller, Tory Herald. Reviewed at TriStar screening room, Culver City, Aug. 16, 1994. MPAA Rating: PG-13. Running time: **106 MIN.**

James Harlow	John Candy
Phil Taylor	Richard Lewis
Julian	John C. McGinley
Belle	Ellen Greene
Ben Wheeler	Robert Picardo
John Slade	Ed Lauter
Little Feather	Rodney A. Grant
Zeke	William Sanderson
Constance Taylor	Melinda Culea
Lindsey Thurlow	Robin McKee
The Chief	Russell Means
Gen. Larchmont	Charles Rocket

"Wagons East!" records John Candy's final hours spent before the cameras, and, unfortunately, they were far from his finest. Tepid one-joke comedy could provide a few yuks for kids, but everyone's creative burners were on low heat for this woeful outing, which won't be around much past Labor Day.

Gag here is completely related by the title: A bunch of Old West pioneers who have had enough of bank robbers, cattle rustlers, drunken boors and intolerant know-nothings decide to head back from whence they came.

To guide them east, they hire wagonmaster James Harlow (Candy), who, they learn too late, happened to have been trail guide for the Donner Party and still has a pretty shaky sense of direction.

In ultra-politically correct fashion, the Indians are only too happy to oblige and escort the palefaces out of their territory, but the trek is vehemently opposed by the big-money rail interests, who fear bad publicity if word of the malcontents gets around. Fat cats hire an inept gunslinger and, finally, the Cavalry to make sure the bumbling crew doesn't make it back.

There's a very mild analogy here, perhaps, to those modern California transplants who, in the wake of earthquakes, riots, fires and assorted other calamities, are retreating to imagined paradises elsewhere, but it remains undeveloped.

The dialogue and the characters' neuroses, however, are insistently contemporary, with colloquialisms and '90s urban lingo cascading out of everyone's mouths. The one archaic touch is John C. McGinley's overtly gay characterization, which plays like an effeminate caricature from olden days.

Candy looks heavier than ever and seems rather listless, but there was clearly little in the material to inspire him to any heights of lunacy. Although filmed earlier, his picture for Michael Moore, "Canadian Bacon," will be the final release starring the late actor, and it can be hoped that it will serve as a more fitting testament to his talent than this uninspired comedy.

—*Todd McCarthy*

IT'S PAT

A Buena Vista release of a Touchstone Pictures presentation of a Charles B. Wessler production. Produced by Wessler. Executive producer, Teri Schwartz. Co-producers, Cyrus Yavneh, Richard Wright. Directed by Adam Bernstein. Screenplay, Jim Emerson, Stephen Hibbert, Julia Sweeney, based on characters created by Sweeney. Camera (Technicolor), Jeffrey Jur; editor, Norman D. Hollyn; music, Mark Mothersbaugh; production design, Michelle Minch; art direction, Mark Worthington; set decoration, Beth De Sort; costume design, Tom Bronson; sound (Dolby), Russell Williams II; associate producers, Christine M. Zander, Philip E. Thomas; assistant director, Josh King; casting, Carol Lewis. Reviewed at AMC Meyer Park 14, Houston, Aug. 10, 1994. MPAA Rating: PG-13. Running time: **77 MIN.**
Pat .... Julia Sweeney
Chris .... David Foley
Kyle .... Charles Rocket
Kathy .... Kathy Griffin
Stacy .... Julie Hayden
Doctor .... Timothy Stack
Nurse .... Mary Scheer
Mrs. Riley .... Beverly Leech
Postal Supervisor .... Larry Hankin
Tippy .... Kathy Najimy
Arlenn Sorken .... Herself
Camille Paglia .... Herself
Station Manager .... Tim Meadows

Ever hear the one about the pic that was too bad to be released, so it escaped? Well, that old joke now has a new punch line: "It's Pat," a shockingly unfunny "Saturday Night Live" spinoff that Disney plans to unleash Aug. 26 in limited regional engagements. A quick fade to homevid is likely.

Julia Sweeney is co-writer as well as the star of this no-joke comedy based on her one-joke "SNL" sketches about an androgynous eccentric. But Sweeney, who first invented the character while a member of the L.A.-based "Groundlings" comedy troupe, has almost perversely turned the relatively harmless TV-sketch regular into a boorish, egotistical creep for the bigscreen. Fans of the "SNL" sketches will be disappointed. Nonfans won't bother.

Under the inconspicuous direction of musicvid veteran Adam Bernstein in his feature debut, "It's Pat" plays very much like what it is, an extended version of a variety show sketch.

Pic, like the "SNL" sketches, rests entirely on a single running gag: Neighbors, co-workers and casual acquaintances find it hard to decide, and impossible to ask, whether Pat — a frumpish figure in short-cropped hair and asexual attire — is male or female.

Pat finds a soul mate in Chris (David Foley of TV's "Kids in the Hall"), whose hippie-ish clothing and hairstyling is every bit as gender-unspecific as Pat's, while a straight-arrow neighbor, Kyle (Charles Rocket), becomes so obsessed with Pat that he doesn't even care whether the object of his affection is a he or a she.

Film relies heavily on verbal and visual gags that run the gamut from the painfully obvious to the grossly crude. Typical of the pic's humor is a scene in which Pat, briefly employed in a sushi restaurant, sneezes messy mucus onto a diner's order.

What little plot there is involves Kyle's efforts to uncover just who — or what — Pat is. One stunt leads to Kyle's videotaping Pat for a segment of a TV show called "America's Creepiest People." And that leads to pic's only really funny bit — "Sexual Personae" author Camille Paglia, deftly playing (and parodying) herself, appears on camera to comment on the significance of Pat's androgyny.

Sweeney whines and snorts her way through as Pat, while Foley is easier to take as a much more engaging character. Rocket chews up the scenery and his lines with shameless gusto. Among the supporting players, Kathy Najimy makes the most amusing impression as a drugstore clerk who's understandably rattled each time Pat appears in her store.

Michelle Minch's production design is genuinely clever, particularly in the realization of Chris's neo-hippie pad. Other tech credits are average. —*Joe Leydon*

THE SECRET JOURNEY: LIVES OF SAINTS AND SINNERS

(IL VIAGGIO CLANDESTINO: VITE DI SANTI E PECCATORI)

(ITALIAN)

A Fiumara d'Arte production. Produced by Matteo Bavera. Directed, written by Raul Ruiz. Camera (color, 16mm), Francois Ede, Renaud Personaz; editor, Valeria Sarmiento; music, Gianni Gebbia, Miriam Palma, Vittorio Villa. Reviewed at Taormina Film Festival, Italy, July 31, 1994. Running time: **60 MIN.**
With: Enzo Moscato, Marco Manchisi, Marco Cavicchioli, Enzo Vetrano, Donato Castellaneta.
(Italian dialogue)

Raul Ruiz's hourlong "Lives of Saints and Sinners" is a joyful, consistently entertaining allegory about human types. Lensed in Sicily, no-budget pic displays the Chilean director's erudite wit at its condensed best.

A very accessible work, "Saints" may run into programming problems outside adventurous TV nets because of its length, but could easily be combined with other short Ruiz productions, which he has been cranking out at the rate of about three a year. (The five-minute "The Dark Night of the Inquisitor," made in defense of Salman Rushdie, and the 26-minute "Promenade," made with Costa Gavras, are also 1994 productions.)

Non-stop dialogue gives momentum to "Saints," structured like a picaresque tale (Don Quixote even turns up briefly, as a sailor). Trudging around the Sicilian countryside, a kaleidoscope of characters collide and exchange humorous one-liners of irreverent theological intent. Yet beneath its irony, pic has a disturbing resonance.

Playing Christ in a perversely incomprehensible Neapolitan dialect is Enzo Moscato. He explains to Mario (Marco Manchisi), a kind of Everyman, that he never ascended into heaven after the Crucifixion, but has been wandering the Earth on a secret journey, hiding out from the angels (whom he fears). He helps mankind out with the occasional miracle, and makes his living predicting the weather.

Mario ventures into a labyrinth — a bizarre sculpture that is actually part of a permanent exhibit put up by the artists' colony Fiumara d'Arte, which produced the pic. There he meets an angel who tells half-truths, a sinful woman who

dreams of tempting a saint, and San Gil (Enzo Vetrano).

Film's imagination never flags. The game of salvation and damnation continues at a fast clip. Each time a pair meets, one asks, "Saint or sinner?" and a new round of paradoxical, teasing reasoning begins.

The all-Italian cast comes mostly from the stage and looks like they had a great time shooting with Ruiz in the harsh Sicilian landscape. This is one case where the film's minuscule budget is a plus, making it seem light as a feather technically, and putting the emphasis on dialogue rather than plain but effective fixed-camera visuals.

—*Deborah Young*

WONDERBOY

(DE SUEUR ET DU SANG)

(FRENCH)

An Ultramarine/Kristian Kuhn Film Prod./SFP Cinema/Diagonale production. Produced by Philippe Goldfain. Directed by Paul Vecchiali. Screenplay, Frederick Leroy, Vecchiali, based on Leroy's novel. Camera (color), Georges Strouve; editor, Cathy Charmorey, Vecchiali; music, Roland Vincent; art direction, Jean-Jacques Gernolle. Reviewed at Taormina Film Festival (competing), Italy, Aug. 1, 1994. Running time: **116 MIN.**
With: Sam Job, Fabienne Babe, Jacques Martial, Jean-Marc Thibault, Kader Bouchanef, Judith Reval, Rudiger Vogeler.

The original French title of "Wonderboy" translates as "Sweat and Blood," which ably expresses what it is that the hero, nicknamed Wonderboy, can't stand about the boxing profession. This unconventional anti-boxing/romance picture by veteran Paul Vecchiali is a curiosity item with enough oomph to break into regular release.

Maurice (Sam Job), a chubby but muscular 18-year-old black teenager, has been pushed into professional boxing by his crippled father (Jacques Martial), a former champ. But Maurice has an artistic soul and, a la "Golden Boy," dreams of becoming a violinist.

To encourage his son (who still sleeps with teddy bears) in this masculine profession, Maurice fixes him up with older, white femme fatale Nora (Fabienne Babe). Before the two can do anything, Nora's nasty husband barges in and Maurice accidentally kills him. Circling of the cops brings Nora and Maurice together, and the young man rises to the top in one knockout match after another.

Nora, the offbeat heroine, shows an iron will to get the man she loves against all obstacles. Frequently undressed, or photographed in shock-value Madonna-like underwear, her

August 29, 1994 (Cont.)

tough, slutty beauty contrasts strongly with Wonderboy's softness. One explicit bedroom scene between the couple is quite hot.

Boxing fans will be disappointed by "Wonderboy's" lack of realism. Reversing stereotypes at every turn, Vecchiali strives for novelty in shooting the fight scenes, which are more stylized than violent or exciting. Similarly, the poor but scenic, racially mixed neighborhood looks about as realistic as a musical set, and characters even burst into song at one point.

African music track is fine listening.
—*Deborah Young*

IN THE NAME OF THE DUCE

(NEL NOME DEL DUCE)

(ITALIAN-FRENCH — DOCU)

An IPS (Rome)/Agav Films (Paris) production, in association with Channel 4, La Sept/Arte, RAI-3, Kershet Broadcasting (Israel), CNC. Produced by Amos Gitai, Francesco Tomelli. Directed, written by Gitai. Camera (color, video), Aldo Cimaglia; editor, Manuela Ciucci; music, Simon Stockhausen. Reviewed at Taormina Film Festival, Italy, July 28, 1994. (Also in Locarno Film Festival.) Running time: **60 MIN.**
(Italian soundtrack)

Part of a trilogy about the rise of racism in Europe by Israeli filmmaker Amos Gitai, "In the Name of the Duce" made headlines when docu's subject, Italian legislator Alessandra Mussolini, tried to have it banned for slurring her image. No authority seems to have taken her grievances seriously, and pic was screened at the Taormina Film Festival and later at Locarno.

Hourlong docu aims to expose how closely connected the neofascist Alleanza Nazionale party is to the dangerous old-style fascism of Alessandra's grandfather, Benito Mussolini. Pic, which looks like it was shot and put together very quickly, is far from a polished work, and its message is certainly diluted by the lack of rigor.

But at a time when Italy's neofascist party has entered the government and is making political overtures to Israel, this is one of the most direct challenges on film to those who choose to forget the past. Juxtaposition of Jews who lived through World War II with the neo-fascists' "new look" of modern pragmatism is a simple but effective ploy.

Pic dwells on Alessandra Mussolini's unsuccessful campaign to become mayor of Naples last year, and most of the unexceptional material is far less eye-catching than the TV news. Gitai has only one brief, polite encounter with Mussolini in a hotel lobby. Pic's key sequence is a visit by

Gitai and his Italian crew to the Alleanza Nazionale headquarters in Naples, where they're firmly refused entry into a locked room (the hangout of party old-timers) where a poster of Benito hangs.

Other entries in Gitai's trilogy are "Queen Mary '87" and "In the Valley of the Wupper," set in Germany.
—*Deborah Young*

THE PRIVATE EYE BLUES

(FEISEUNG TSINGTAM)

(HONG KONG)

A Tedpoly Films production. Produced by Teddy Robin Kwan. Directed, written by Eddie Fong Ling-ching. Camera (color), Jingle Ma; editor, Fong; music, John Landon, Kwan, Michael Au; art direction, William Lygratte; sound (Dolby), Roger Savage; visual consultant, Clara Law; associate producer, Kay Wong; assistant director, Lo Tsi-leung. Reviewed at Locarno Film Festival (surprise film), Aug. 14, 1994. Running time: **99 MIN.**
With: Jacky Cheung, Kathy Chow, Fan Hsiao-hsuan, Lee Hiu-tung.
(Cantonese and Mandarin dialogue)

"The Private Eye Blues" is a loopy, likable gumshoe yarn that rolls along in high style for about an hour but starts getting footsore in its final reels. Though this black comedy on Hong Kong/China relations in the run-up to the colony's 1997 communist takeover is a treasure trove of in-jokes for sinophiles, its appeal looks limited to specialized slots.

Writer/director Eddie Fong Ling-ching is known for his previous "The Last Princess of Manchuria" (1990; aka "Kawashima Yoshiko"), though perhaps best known for his striking sex-and-swordplay classic "An Amorous Woman of Tang Dynasty" (1984). Fong and partner Clara Law, who cops a "visual consultant" credit here, can afford to be bold in their satire on mainlanders: Both are emigrating to Australia. "Blues" showed as the surprise film at this year's Locarno fest, where Law was a jury member.

Popular actor/singer Jacky Cheung stars as a seedy, beer-swigging private dick hired by a rich mainland businessman to find a kook from Beijing who's gone missing in H.K. Said kook turns out to have powers of foresight and healing, of great use to Beijing's gerontocracy.

Pic adopts a neo-bluesy style, with lots of tilted shots and a verbal humor poised somewhere between "The Late Show" and "The Long Goodbye."

As in many recent H.K. comedies, mainlanders are portrayed as vulgar, boozy, woman-chasing bumpkins, though as one menacingly reminds Cheung, "In a few years, we'll all be under the same roof."

Performances are all sprightly and well drawn, and technically the pic is slick (final stages of post-production were done in Australia). Production company Tedpoly is linked to Polygram, for whom Cheung records.
—*Derek Elley*

MARIE'S SONG: I WAS I KNOW NOT WHERE

(MARIES LIED: ICH WAR, ICH WEISS NICHT WO)

(GERMAN)

A Palladio Film production, in association with WDR, SWF, Arte. (International sales: Palladio Film, Cologne.) Produced by Niko Bruecher, Ulrich Felsberg. Executive producer, Felsberg. Directed, written by Bruecher. Camera (color), Jolanta Dylewska; editor, Wanda Zeman; music, Andreas Schilling; production design, Alexander Scherer; costume design, Daniele Schneider-Wessling. Reviewed at Locarno Film Festival (competing), Aug. 8, 1994. Running time: **92 MIN.**
With: Sylvie Testud, Bastian Trost, Martin Feifel, Veronica Quilligan, Jean-Francois Perrier, Carola Regnier.

"Marie's Song" is an immaculately made, labor-of-love Euro art movie that would have been even better at half its length. Crystalline portrait of a teenage girl's dreams in 19th-century Prussia should garner debuting Cologne-based director Niko Bruecher attention on the fest circuit. Small-screen sales outside the U.S. look possible.

Setting is a large country estate in 1813, where 16-year-old Marie (Sylvie Testud) is bullied by her governess (Veronica Quilligan) and ignored by her reclusive mother (Carola Regnier). Enter Mom's merchant friend (Jean-Francois Perrier) and his shy nephew (Bastian Trost), who when he's not being caned by his disciplinarian uncle stirs vague desires in Marie.

She, however, becomes more attached to a passing, soldier-like ruffian (Martin Feifel). After he rapes Marie and his gang kills her mother, Marie coolly gets her revenge.

Bruecher's description of an age in which casual brutality coexisted with the highest refinement in arts and manners is beautifully caught with pinpoint photography by Polish lenser Jolanta Dylewska, one of the subtlest effects tracks in recent memory and a classic-flavored score by Andreas Schilling that propels the sparsely dialogued movie.

Lacking, however, is the more involving, meditative beauty of other exercises in period style like Rohmer's "The Marquise of O ..." and Kubrick's word-heavier "Barry Lyndon." Despite charming playing by 23-year-old newcomer Testud as Marie, "Song" remains a stanza masquerading as a full-length poem, in which more increasingly becomes less.
—*Derek Elley*

CINEMA, OF OUR TIME: ABBAS KIAROSTAMI

(CINEMA, DE NOTRE TEMPS: ABBAS KIAROSTAMI)

(FRENCH — DOCU)

An AMIP production. Directed by Jean-Pierre Limosin. In color; music, Georges Delerue. Reviewed at Locarno Film Festival, Aug. 14, 1994. Running time: **57 MIN.**
(Farsi soundtrack)

Part of a French TV series called "Cinema, of Our Time," this hourlong docu on the thoughts and work of Iran's best-known filmmaker, Abbas Kiarostami, will be of sure interest to international cinephiles. It would also make a neat program item to double-bill with any of his films.

"All cinema," says Kiarostami, an articulate, good-humored man in dark glasses, "whether documentary or fiction, is based on lies. We make the audience believe lies to reach a higher truth."

His own films blend fiction and docu elements with deceptive simplicity. Key scenes from all the pictures — puzzlingly, not identified — are skillfully excerpted and intercut with interviews of Kiarostami and his actors.

Director Jean-Pierre Limosin, who never appears on camera, shoots Kiarostami on the road in the earthquake-damaged area of northern Iran featured in Kiarostami's trilogy "Where Is My Friend's House?" (1987), "Life and Nothing More" (1992) and "Under the Olive Trees" (preemed at Cannes this year).

At times it seems as if Kiarostami was directing Limosin's film. In any case, pic raises issues that are close to Kiarostami's own artistic concerns. He proves a willing and eager subject, brimming with ideas about cinema and discussing his work with non-pro actors and child thesps.
—*Deborah Young*

September 5, 1994

TELLURIDE

THE NEW AGE

A Warner Bros. release of a Regency Enterprises and Alcor Films presentation of an Ixtlan/Addis-Wechsler production. Produced by Nick Wechsler, Keith Addis. Executive producers, Oliver Stone, Arnon Milchan. Co-producers, Iya Labunka, Janet Yang. Directed, written by Michael Tolkin. Camera (Technicolor), John H. Campbell; editor, Suzanne Fenn; music, Mark Mothersbaugh; production design, Robin Standefer; art direction, Kenneth A. Hardy; set design, Barbara Ann Jaeckel; set decoration, Claire Jenora Bowin; costume design, Richard Shissler; sound (Dolby), Stephen Halbert; associate producer, Alison Balian; assistant director, Christine Larson; casting, Deborah Aquila. Reviewed at the Directors Guild of America, L.A., Aug. 18, 1994. (In Telluride, Toronto fests.) MPAA Rating: R. Running time: **110 MIN.**

Peter Witner	Peter Weller
Katherine Witner	Judy Davis
Jean Levy	Patrick Bauchau
Kevin Bulasky	Corbin Bernsen
Paul Hartmann	Jonathan Hadary
Anna	Patricia Heaton
Dale Deveaux	Samuel L. Jackson
Sandi Rego	Audra Lindley
Alison Gale	Paula Marshall
Laura	Maureen Mueller
Bettina	Tanya Pohlkotte
Misha	Bruce Ramsay
Sarah Friedberg	Rachel Rosenthal
Mary Netter	Sandra Seacat
Ellen Saltonstall	Susan Traylor
Jeff Witner	Adam West

At one point in "The New Age," the terminally stylish post-yuppie couple played by Peter Weller and Judy Davis put on their fanciest threads in order to commit double suicide, but can't go through with it. Like them, Michael Tolkin's new film gets all dressed up but doesn't quite know where to go. Pic's ambitions, sporadic wit and fashionable surfaces will be enough to attract a certain slice of the hip upscale crowd, but regular folks will tune out very early on the empty, emotionally troubled characters on view here, resulting in spotty B.O.

As in his first directorial outing, "The Rapture," Tolkin once again focuses on people who have lost their way in a society defined principally by appearances and sales pitches. Earlier film was provocative in its surprising look at religious fanaticism, but lingering doubts about Tolkin's p.o.v. on his material are exacerbated by the seemingly all-pervasive cynicism on the loose in "The New Age": It's easy to make fun of an obsession with materialism, as well as of the religious cults people may pursue in reaction, but it's a lot tougher to offer up a viable alternative that makes sense in the face of the daily bombardment of sensation, information and opinion. Tolkin wears an intelligent smirk, but a smirk is the most superficial of reactions, covering any lack of your own values.

Peppy opening scenes have upscale El Lay denizens Peter and Katherine Witner (Weller and Davis) losing the big-buck jobs that have enabled them to live the high life in the Hollywood Hills through the face-the-music early '90s. When bummed, what better to do than throw a huge party, one that features the usual black-draped models, arch artistes, studio types and mystical, quasi-religious weirdos who have always found Los Angeles to be their happiest hunting ground.

In bad shape as a couple, Peter and Katherine begin fooling around openly and then agree to separate while still living under the same roof. Their proximity allows them to continue arguing, and Tolkin occasionally gets off a bon mot, such as when Katherine sarcastically asks her selfish husband, "Why don't you get in touch with your inner adult?"

But prolonged exposure to their emotional and spiritual exhaustion doesn't bring the viewer any closer to these angst-ridden moderns, who compound their folly by opening a chic clothing store that's minimalist in both its merchandise and volume of business.

So as their lives collapse around them, the two seek salvation elsewhere; Katherine in New Age spirituality (sought, as in "The Rapture," in the California desert), Peter tentatively in the kinky club scene and ultimately in phone sales.

Through sharing their feelings of being lost and getting on each other's nerves, the pair comes together again in a certain way, but the dramatic trajectory and satiric purpose become fuzzier as the finish line approaches, leaving the film less than coherent in articulating its attitudes.

Part of picture's sourness is reflected by the name of the store the couple open — Hipocracy. A strained attempt at sophisticated humor, such a choice would seem to doom almost any enterprise to failure.

Together again after their outstanding pairing in "Naked Lunch," Weller and Davis search for as many nuances to nerve-wracked edginess as they can while remaining remote at their cores. For someone who seems to care so little, it is mysterious why Weller's occasionally wacky character isn't willing to take more risks; he's blase, yet tightly coiled. Davis is compelling to watch, as always, but it would have been helpful if there were at least one thing her Katherine really wanted in life; she's such a lost soul one can't get any kind of handle on her.

Most of the supporting characters wander in and out of the Witners' lives without much in the way of visible connections, save for Peter's playboy father, nicely etched by Adam West (father and son share the same pickup line for ladies — "How are your morals?"). Lots of attention has been lavished on ultra-trendy locations, sets and clothes, although John Campbell's lensing manages to make everyone look pretty wasted and unattractive, which might be part of the point but doesn't prove inviting.

—*Todd McCarthy*

MONTREAL

A SIMPLE TWIST OF FATE

A Buena Vista release of a Touchstone Pictures production. Produced by Ric Kidney. Executive producer, Steve Martin. Directed by Gillies MacKinnon. Screenplay, Martin, suggested by the novel "Silas Marner" by George Eliot. Camera (Technicolor), Andrew Dunn; editor, Humphrey Dixon; music, Cliff Edelman; production design, Andy Harris; art director, Tim Galvin; set decorator, Maria Nay; costume design, Hope Hanafin; sound (Dolby), Mary Ellis; assistant director, Vebe Borge; casting, Dianne Crittenden. Reviewed at World Film Festival, Montreal (noncompeting), Aug. 26, 1994. MPAA Rating: PG-13. Running time: **106 MIN.**

Michael McCann	Steve Martin
John Newland	Gabriel Byrne
Nancy Newland	Laura Linney
April Simon	Catharine O'Hara
Mathilda McCann (age 11)	Alana Austin
Mathilda McCann (age 5)	Alyssa Austin
Tanny Newland	Stephen Baldwin
Keating	Byron Jennings
Bryce	Michael des Barres
Marsha Swanson	Amelia Campbell
Lawrence Simon	Kellen Crosby

The pairing of Steve Martin and 19th-century novelist George Eliot seems about as likely an artistic union as Oliver Stone adapting Louisa May Alcott. Yet the resulting film, "A Simple Twist of Fate" — inspired by "Silas Marner" — betrays no telltale strains of clashing sensibilities. Martin leavens the material somewhat, but this is a faithful, heartfelt, somber piece about family and responsibility. It's upscale fare on the order of the company's recent "When a Man Loves a Woman," but without the dramatic bite that would ensure more than a quick dip into the commercial mainstream.

Clearly a modest proposal, the film is not quite a comfortable stretch for the artists involved. The marketing challenge will be selling Martin in a subdued persona. In that respect, pic recalls Bill Murray's blighted "The Razor's Edge." Still, the new outing is considerably more successful and entertaining, and that should arouse initial interest.

Pic's twist involves the proverbial child abandoned at the doorstep. The irony is that the man who becomes the surrogate father, Michael McCann (Martin), is recently divorced after leaving his wife when she revealed the child she was expecting was sired by someone else. The dour, reclusive furniture-maker finds meaning in his life through his care of an infant girl.

The baby's biological dad is John Newland (Gabriel Byrne), the wealthiest man in the county, who is primed for a political career. His indiscretion with a frail drug addict doesn't fit with the image of a family man and a paragon of public virtue. So he keeps his own counsel when circumstance brings the girl to McCann and quietly, behind the scenes, arranges for him to become the legal guardian.

Over the course of a decade, we see the girl, Mathilda (Alana Austin), evolve into a bright, precocious child. Her blossoming also brings out the best in McCann. But Newland finds himself becoming increasingly possessive. He seeks her affection through attention and gifts and, when he can no longer be quiet, reveals the truth to his barren wife.

Eventually, he goes to court to win back custody in a bitterly contested trial. And, as with so many like hearings, the issue tells more about the adult combatants than the child they seek to gain.

The repressed nature of Martin's character may be logical, but it tends to keep the emotional component of the tale at bay. Odd incidents throughout the film do reveal his humanity, but they remain footnotes rather than organic developments that would have drawn us into the ultimate dilemma.

Byrne, on the other hand, gives a multitextured performance as the villain of the piece. He's truly chilling as a character who will say and do virtually anything to get what he wants. The frightening aspect is that Newland comes to believe his own spiel and is so convincing that one cannot tell when he's acting or being sincere.

Austin is genuinely winning as the girl, and Laura Linney, as Byrne's show wife, conveys a much-appreciated intelligence and depth.

Overall, it is a polished, adult film. But the cerebral approach is off-putting. The cool tone director Gillies MacKinnon uniformly applies to

September 5, 1994 (Cont.)

Martin's script refuses to make distinctions between asides and key character and plot points. That may not matter on an intellectual level, but clearly falls short dramatically.

The absence of real tension and an all too-neat conclusion removes the audience from the type of cathartic high one expects when all the skeletons are exposed and justice finally done. The absence of a simple manipulation or two leaves the film limp and disappointing.
—*Leonard Klady*

THE DAUGHTER OF D'ARTAGNAN
(LA FILLE DE D'ARTAGNAN)
(FRENCH)

A Bac Films release (France) of a Ciby 2000/Little Bear production. (Intl. sales: Ciby Sales, London.) Executive producer, Frederic Bourboulon. Directed by Bertrand Tavernier. Screenplay, Michel Leviant, based on an idea by Riccardo Freda, Eric Poindron, adapted by Leviant, Tavernier, Jean Cosmos. Camera (color), Patrick Blossier; editor, Ariane Boeglin; music, Philippe Sarde; costumes, Jacqueline Moreau; sound, Michel Desrois, Gerard Lamps. Reviewed at World Film Festival, Montreal (non-competing), Sept. 1, 1994. Running time: **125 MIN.**

Eloise	Sophie Marceau
Quentin	Nils Tavernier
D'Artagnan	Philippe Noiret
Athos	Jean-Luc Bideau
Porthos	Raoul Billerey
Aramis	Sami Frey
Lady in Red	Charlotte Kady
Mazarin	Luigi Proietti
Duke of Crassac	Claude Rich
Planchet	Jean-Paul Roussillon

Bertrand Tavernier's "The Daughter of D'Artagnan" is an unabashedly old-fashioned, swashbuckling action-comedy that will likely surprise longtime fans of the French helmer's more weighty work. The salty costume drama will do boffo biz with French-speaking auds in Europe and Canada and will generate interest in the U.S. among viewers looking for light, entertaining foreign fare.

In an unusual move, France's Bac Films released the pic in the main coastal vacation areas of France in early August and opened it in Paris a couple of weeks later. It is already ringing up strong action at the box office in Tavernier's home country.

"Daughter" received a wildly enthusiastic response at its North American preem at the Montreal film fest. Malofilm Distribution, which has French rights in Canada, will open the pic in Quebec Oct. 7. Miramax has U.S. rights to the film.

This is a sexy, often very funny sequel to the Alexandre Dumas classic "The Three Musketeers"; Tavernier has said it is a tribute to the action pix he grew up with, and the film's strength comes from its ability to deliver the thrills 'n' spills of the Errol Flynn-style actioners without being self-consciously nostalgic.

Set in 1650s France, fast-paced story opens with a slave escaping through the woods from the estate of the evil Duke of Crassac (Claude Rich). The Mother Superior of a nearby convent gives refuge to the slave and is murdered by the Duke's henchman in retaliation.

Eloise (Sophie Marceau), who is studying at the convent, is shocked by the murder, and the spunky, rebellious girl immediately sets off for Paris hoping to enlist her famous dad, D'Artagnan (Philippe Noiret), to help seek revenge.

Along the way, she meets up with flaky, romantic poet Quentin (Nils Tavernier, the director's son) and gets involved in the first of pic's many bench-clearing brawls featuring implausibly comic punch-ups and neatly choreographed sword duels. She arrives in Paris to find her aging father is a shadow of his former swashbuckling self and isn't exactly crazy about jumping back into the musketeer biz.

Eloise is convinced that the Mother Superior's murder is part of a larger, nefarious plot to destabilize the country, and so she heads off to the royal court to warn the powers-that-be of the impending insurrection.

D'Artagnan finally reveals his old fighting spirit and reluctantly agrees to help out his daughter. He rounds up his three old musketeer pals — Athos, Porthos and Aramis — to embark on one last adventure.

The plot then takes a series of convoluted twists involving everything from competing conspiracy theories to the amorous exploits of the young king, but the fast-moving action sequences and always-witty dialogue keep the viewer entertained throughout.

All-star French thesps are uniformly first-rate. Marceau is captivating and sexy as the spirited female musketeer, and Noiret adds a poignant edge to pic with his portrayal of D'Artagnan as an almost-washed-up hero. Actors look like they're having fun, particularly Rich, who turns in an over-the-top comic turn as the low-IQ bad guy.

Philippe Sarde's wonderfully warm score and Jacqueline Moreau's sumptuous period costumes add to pic's flavor and elegance.

"The Daughter of D'Artagnan" is light years removed from well-known Tavernier pix like "Round Midnight" and "Daddy Nostalgie," and the helmer has said lensing the film was like a vacation for him. That sense of lighthearted pleasure is precisely what makes the film so viewer-friendly. —*Brendan Kelly*

MESMER

A Cineplex Odeon (Canada)/Mayfair (foreign) release of a Levergreen/Accent/Studio Babelsberg production. Produced by Weiland Schulz-Keil, Lance Reynolds, Robert Goodale. Co-producers, Andras Hamori, Susan Cavan. Directed by Roger Spottiswoode. Screenplay, Dennis Potter. Camera (color), Elemer Ragalyi; editor, Susan Shipton; music, Michael Nyman; production design, Jan Schulbach; costume design, Birgit Hutter; sound (Dolby), Karl Laabs; assistant director, Michael Zenon. Reviewed at World Film Festival, Montreal (competing), Aug. 28, 1994. Running time: **107 MIN.**

Franz Anton Mesmer	Alan Rickman
Maria Theresa	
Paradies	Amanda Ooms
Frau Mesmer	Gillian Barge
Prof. Stoerk	Jan Rubes
Dr. Ingehousz	David Hemben
Francisca	Anna Thalbach
Franz	Simon McBurney
Herr Paradies	Martin Schwab
Duchess DuBarry	Shirley Douglas
Dr. Deslon	Peter Dvorsky

The wild, impressionistic view with which writer Dennis Potter assails the so-called age of reason in "Mesmer" seems barely containable on the bigscreen. And if it were not for the grounded, eccentric title performance by Alan Rickman, one imagines the entire film might defy gravity and spin out of earthly orbit. The film is a non-stop assault of contradictory tones, wicked asides and outrageous style. It's a viewing challenge akin to an obstacle course, and that will surely limit its theatrical prospects — especially stateside — though it unquestionably has a strong, rarefied appeal.

Biography is the least of concerns in the film, which focuses on a few short years in the life of the 18th-century medical radical who ventured into such areas as hypnosis and harmonics before they had names.

The drama and humor come from the threat he poses to the establishment. Mesmer truly has the esteemed Viennese doctors working overtime to explain away his success with supposedly hopeless cases, employing methods the "enlightened" folk feel are only a short step away from devil worship.

It's evident at the same time that the good doctor is no saint. His code about suffering is simple and goes against the grain of his era, which lived (and died) by the practice of bleeding when all else failed. He intrinsically likes the notion of being the square peg in the round hole. There's no doubt his vanity can amply withstand the attention — both good and bad.

Aside from the cat-and-mouse game that structures the piece, Potter sullies the notion of reason and passion being wholly separate entities in Mesmer's questionable doctor-patient relationship with Maria Theresa (Amanda Ooms).

The blind daughter of a wealthy businessman, she is a local celebrity for her almost professional recitals. She's also prone to seizures, and when Mesmer calms her at a concert by will and the laying on of hands, she insists he pay her further attention.

The healer's own loveless marriage only enhances the situation. His growing attraction — perhaps influenced by the moon and tides — to Maria Theresa provides the excuse to finally banish Mesmer. Ironically, his next stop is Paris where, rather than a clientele of beggars and the poor, he becomes a court favorite.

Rickman effects an eerie, otherworldly quality in his role. It's all a front, though, for the man is from humble origins and totally breaks down in the face of love. He is, excuse the expression, mesmerizing.

Support cast is uniformly strong, with Jan Rubes, normally cast in fatherly roles, chilling as the chief nemesis. Ooms is a striking presence in her first major English-speaking film.

Director Roger Spottiswoode wisely sticks to the themes and ironies of Potter's script. The approach is more poetic than narrative, held together by the central performance. Tech credits are strong, though the images tend to lean toward the dark side.

A fitting testament to the late writer, "Mesmer's" tale is rife with contemporary resonance that makes the already unsettling material even more haunting. It should hit just the right bell in arthouses and ancillary markets.
—*Leonard Klady*

LIGHT MY PASSION
(ENCIENDE MI PASION)
(SPANISH)

A Producciones Cinematograficas Penelope/S.L. production. (International sales: RTVE, Madrid.) Produced by Jose Maria Calleja, Juan Luis Galiardo. Directed by Jose Miguel Ganga. Screenplay, Victoria Calero, Ganga. Camera (color), Antonio Pueche; editor, Pablo Blanco; music, Bernardo Bonezzi. Reviewed at World Film Festival, Montreal (competing), Aug. 29, 1994. Running time: **87 MIN.**

With: Miguel Bose, Juan Luis Galiardo, Emma Suarez, Karra Elejalde, Ana Alvarez.

A bizarre comedy of sexual and social manners, Jose Miguel Ganga's "Light My Passion" is a spirited, very funny, very odd tale jam-packed with enough twisted sex scenes, Freudian psychology and caustic class conflict to keep any Luis Bunuel fan happy. It's all good, steamy fun and should do well with sophisticated auds looking for offbeat foreign fare.

In a nod to Bunuel's "Diary of a Chambermaid," botanist Angel (Miguel Bose) has an uncontrollable foot fetish and is first drawn to Luisa (Emma Suarez) when he catches a glimpse of her bare feet in the flower shop. She also looks more than a little like his mother — which she discovers only after they've married and moved to his mansion in the Spanish countryside.

That's when the plot takes off into wacky overdrive. Luisa keeps waking up in the middle of the night to find her husband in various compromising positions with her feet. Even worse, that's the only attention she gets from him. Mostly, Angel holes up in his lab and Luisa is left alone.

Angel's mad old professor Lucas (Juan Luis Galiardo) arrives to supply Luisa with a little erotic instruction and somehow finds time to embezzle money from the household. There is also an even weirder subplot about a psychopathic one-eyed pimp, a desperate hooker and a wild nightclub that just happens to be quite near Angel's mansion.

It's all entirely implausible, and that's a big part of the film's charm. Lead thesps don't go overboard hamming it up, preferring to let the zany plot provide most of the laughs. Galiardo, in particular, stands out as the stylishly suave professor-turned-con-man.

"Light My Passion" is rooted in the classic Spanish cinematic themes of repressed sexuality and class conflict, but pic works precisely because it never stops long enough to take any of this too seriously. Tech credits are first-rate throughout. —*Brendan Kelly*

DUST OF LIFE

(POUSIERRES DE VIE)

(FRENCH-ALGERIAN)

A Swift (Paris) production in association with 3B Prods., Hamster Prods., La Sept Films (France), IVP (Algeria), TeleMunchen (Germany), Paradise Film (Belgium) and Salon Films (Hong Kong). Produced by Jean Brehat. Executive producer, Charles Wang. Directed by Rachid Bouchareb. Screenplay, Bouchareb, Bernard Gesbert, from Duyen Ahn's novel "La Colline de Fanta." Camera (color), Youcef Sahraoui; editor, Helene Ducret; music, Safy Boutella. Reviewed at World Film Festival, Montreal (competing), Aug. 28, 1994. Running time: **87 MIN.**

With: Daniel Guyant, Gilles Chitlaphone, Leon Outtrabady, Jehan Pages, Siu Lin Lam, Eric Nguyen, Yann Roussel, William Low.

Along with a wholly fresh view of post-Yankee Vietnam, "Dust of Life" is a coming-of-age tale that is both poetically universal and harrowingly personal. It should play well in fest and French-lingo situations, although

pic's polyglot nature may prove a marketing puzzle for arthouses.

Pic begins with footage of the 1975 fall of Saigon scissored into the struggles of young Son (Daniel Guyant), whose mother frantically tries to reunite him with his father, a black American officer. She fails, and Son is picked up by the new regime in a sweep of beggars, orphans and — worst of all — Amerasians.

"Dust" settles into details of his adjustment to a tough work camp in a remote mountain region near Cambodia. Surrounded by guards, booby traps and hostile Montagnards, the boys know that escape only brings death, or at least a long stay in an underground tiger cage. Son finds a firm friend and protector in Bob (Gilles Chitlaphone), an older boy, and a sympathetic camp instructor (Eric Nguyen) allows him paper for poems and letters.

After the two friends fall in with smart little Shrimp (Leon Outtrabady), they make a break, and the subsequent raft trip downriver toward what was Saigon proves the pic's dramatic highlight. But even when things aren't moving, Youcef Sahraoui's imaginative widescreen lensing makes the most of lush landscapes and anxious young faces. Moody, propulsive music also helps, and helmer Rachid Bouchareb gets consistently honest work from his large cast of newcomers — with Algerian, Thai and Indochinese actors making a surprisingly convincing showing as mixed-race prisoners.

—*Ken Eisner*

MAGIC HUNTER

(BUVOS VADAS)

(HUNGARIAN-SWISS-FRENCH)

Accent/Gargantua Motion Pictures presents an Alliance International release of a Budapest Filmstudio/UGC Images/Vega Film production in co-operation with Studio Babelsberg. Produced by Andras Hamori, Wieland Schulz-Keil. Executive producers, Susan Cavan, David Bowie, Robert Goodale. Co-producers, Ferenc Kardos, Yves Marmion, Ruth Waldburger. Directed by Ildiko Enyedi. Screenplay, Enyedi, Laszlo Laszlo Revesz. Camera (color), Tibor Mathe; editor, Maria Rigo; music, Gregorio Paniagua; production design, Attila Ferenczfy-Kovacs; sound, Istvan Sipos; Reviewed at World Film Festival, Montreal (non-competing), Aug. 31, 1994. (Also in Venice fest.) Running time: **103 MIN.**

Max	Gary Kemp
Eva	Sadie Frost
Maxim	Alexander Kaidanovsky
Kaspar	Peter Vallai
Lili	Alexandra Wasscher
Lina	Ildiko Toth
Police Chief	Mathias Gnadinger
Virgin Mary	Natalie Conde

The second feature of Hungarian Ildiko Enyedi, "Magic Hunter" is an unsettling pas-

tiche of thriller and fantasy elements that will require a willingness to let oneself enter the heart of the material. Slow to reveal its true intentions, the film evolves into an original vision as distinctive as it is unlike her debut effort, "My 20th Century."

Essentially, pic expresses a child's perception of an adult world. It's sophisticated, upscale fare that should score well in specialized release.

Tale begins in an unstated time during a fierce bomb attack. In the recesses of an underground shelter, a young mother tells her daughter the story of a hunter whose luck is about to run out.

Main story centers on Max (Gary Kemp), a police marksman who's lost his confidence after accidentally shooting a hostage. An associate offers him bullets that are guaranteed to give him a high score on a target-shooting exercise.

The initial series of events appear to be some macabre setup rather than pure coincidence. The mystery intensifies when the protagonist is assigned to protect Maxim (Alexander Kaidanovsky), a Russian chess grandmaster, and told the endangered man cannot know that he's being protected.

It doesn't help matters that Maxim encounters Max's wife, Eva (Sadie Frost), and their daughter, Lili (Alexandra Wasscher), in a park. The sniper can see that there's an attraction between his wife and Maxim. Eva and Lili are the same two who were taking refuge from the bombs at the picture's outset.

Woven into the main narrative is a parallel story set in medieval times in which Max, Kaspar (the magic bullet man) and others are involved in a fairy tale concerning good and evil. Eventually, the separate threads are tied together in a rather outrageous conclusion plucked from Lili's innocent perspective.

Some may want to plumb for profound meaning in the often elliptical storytelling. It seems more likely that the film's ideas are connected by a child's naivete and uncomplicated appreciation for basic human emotion.

The international cast fit squarely into what's referred to as modern Budapest. Kemp is riveting in an essentially heroic role, and Frost and Kaidanovsky give themselves over completely to the director's gestalt.

The edgy, uncertain nature of the material is nicely complemented technically. Particularly noteworthy are Tibor Mathe's camerawork, which goes for saturated images, and the music score from Gregorio Paniagua that hearkens back to classical opera but injects a modern tempo.

"Magic Hunter" is an enchanting, original vision. The assurance and playfulness of the work suggests a rich treasure trove to come from Enyedi. —*Leonard Klady*

THE DARLING FAMILY

(CANADIAN)

A Cineplex Odeon Films (Canada) release of a Darling Family Inc. production, with participation of OFDC, the Canada Council and the National Film Board of Canada. Produced by Hadley Obiac, Alan Zweig. Executive producer, Linda Griffiths. Directed by Zweig. Screenplay, Griffiths, from her play. Camera (color), Gerald Packer; editor, Michael Pacek; music, Mychael Danna; art direction, Taavo Sooder; sound, Steve Munro. Reviewed at World Film Festival, Montreal (non-competing), Aug. 26, 1994. Running time: **86 MIN.**

She	Linda Griffiths
He	Alan Williams

Well-conceived two-hander is a dynamic showcase for top Canadian thesp Linda Griffiths ("Lianna"), who also scripted and exec produced. As the suddenly pregnant half of a new couple struggling to decide if they even like each other, she's a magnetic figure, even if the pic doesn't quite live up to its fertile premise. Despite universal issues it raises, no-budget prod has little chance of flying off Festival Island.

Opened-up version of Griffiths' theatrical study of an unnamed twosome is also marked by a barrage of Big Questions for folks approaching middle age — title refers to the legendary "Peter Pan" clan, and the pic ponders myths and realities of maturity.

Here, the faraway dreamers are a thirtysomething Toronto woman whose mantra is "Tell me what you're feeling" (Griffiths) and an older, more cynical ex-Brit (Alan Williams), complete with leather jacket, electric guitar and an endless supply of conversation stoppers.

Mismatched from the start, they manage to make a commitment — at least to keep talking. The chatter's incessant, taxing lenser Gerald Packer's impressively left-field methods of thwarting filmed-play syndrome (which are unhelped by harsh lighting and ugly music) and daring auds to keep up with staccato patter. Witticisms arise often enough to reward attention, and the decision to mix inner thoughts and asides to the camera produces challenging and layered verbal effects.

It's too bad the pic's all head and no heat. With his wonderfully modulated tones, Williams is at home as the male part of the romantic tongue-twisting, though not a terribly appealing screen presence. The lovers don't generate enough sparks to explain meeting for coffee, let alone contemplating a child together. This lack of visceral motivation makes it hard to care about the outcome of the relationship.

—*Ken Eisner*

AILSA

(IRISH-GERMAN-FRENCH)

> A Temple Films production. (International sales: Cine Electra, London.) Produced by Ed Guiney. Directed by Paddy Breathnach. Screenplay, Joe O'Connor, based on his short story. Camera (color), Cian de Buitglar; editor, Emer Reynolds; music, Dario Marianelli; art direction, Padraig O'Neill. Reviewed at World Film Festival, Montreal, Aug. 29, 1994. Running time: **78 MIN.**
> Miles .... Brendan Coyle
> Sara .... Andrea Irvine
> Campbell .... Juliette Gruber
> Sean .... Darragh Kelly
> Vera .... Blanaid Irvine
> Old Mr. Johnson .... Des Spillane
> Jack .... Gary Lydon

"**A**ilsa," first feature from Irish docu helmer Paddy Breathnach, is a moody, morose tale of obsessive love that could attract some arthouse attention and will pique the curiosity of specialty auds looking for Anglo-Irish literary fare. Pic is scripted by young Dublin novelist Joe O'Connor and is based on one of his short stories. But "Ailsa" is just too relentlessly downbeat and self-consciously bookish to cross over to a wider public.

Miles Butler (Brendan Coyle), who works in an office charting family trees, comes home one night with his girlfriend, Sara (Andrea Irvine), to discover that the power has been cut in their Georgian apartment building. When Miles goes up to see the landlord about the problem, he discovers Mr. Johnson electrocuted in his bathtub.

Eventually a young woman, Campbell Rourke (Juliette Gruber), moves into the landlord's old apartment and Miles slowly becomes fascinated by the intriguing new tenant. He starts stealing her mail but never gets up the nerve to talk to his neighbor, and that's one of the frustrations of the pic: He never acts on his obsession, and O'Connor's script doesn't do enough to articulate why Miles is willing to alienate his g.f. and lose his job over a woman he hardly knows. Miles finally goes completely over the edge when he learns the news that Campbell has given birth to a baby girl, Ailsa.

Coyle's sullen visage sets the tone for this dark drama and he gives a strong performance, which is essential since he's in nearly every frame. Tragic finale underscores pic's bleak mood and won't help its commercial prospects.

Lensing is suitably shadowy and somber throughout, as is musical score. Other tech credits are excellent.

—*Brendan Kelly*

TOTOR

(CAMEROON-FRENCH)

> A DK7-Communications production. (International sales: DK7-Communications, Paris.) Produced, directed, written by Daniel Kamwa. Camera (color), Henri Czap; editor, Philippe Gosselet; music, Guy Boulanger; art direction, Alain Tenenbaum; costumes, Marthe Njeuyi. Reviewed at World Film Festival, Montreal, Aug. 26, 1994. Running time: **90 MIN.**
> With: Gaylord, Edna, Marcel Bokalli, Helianne Manzouer, Mapeta Bolitchitchi, Daniel Kamwa, Louise Moungui, Marthe Bouambo, Jean Djamani, Marie Kedi, Julia Mensah, Aloys Mahouwa, Henriette Nyamba, Claude Santonga.

A story of a young boy and his pet turtle, this Cameroon-lensed pic is likely to stretch the patience of even the most ardent fan of African cinema and is unlikely to travel far internationally. "Totor" is a film that lurches from graphic violence to wacko surrealism without making much of an attempt to explain the radical mood swings.

Things start off fairly seriously, with a man breaking into a hut in the middle of the night demanding to see his child. He gets into a big fight with the mother, who vigorously denies the child is his, and the guy ends up torching the hut. The boy, Mentse, flees and ends up being adopted in a nearby village. Then comes a graphic circumcision scene that will have auds running for the exits. Equally inexplicably, script turns sentimental with the arrival of the cute turtle named Totor and then descends into goofy comedy, with everyone fighting over the turtle. Finale is a slice of offbeat magical realism that has little connection to the rest of the film. It has its endearing moments, but "Totor" will leave most viewers scratching their heads in consternation.

—*Brendan Kelly*

ZINAT

(IRANIAN)

> A Farabi Cinema Foundation production. (International sales: Farabi Cinema Foundation, Tehran.) Produced by Farhang-Sara Bahman. Executive producer, Behruz Gharibpour. Directed, written by Ebrahim Mokhtari. Camera (color) Homayun Pievar; editor, Shirin Vahidi; music, Ahmad Pejman; art direction, Gholamreza Nami. Reviewed at World Film Festival, Montreal, Aug. 27, 1994. Running time: **87 MIN.**

> Zinat .... Atefeh Razavi
> Zinat's Father .... Mehdi Fat'hi
> Salehe .... Niku Kheradmand
> Zinat's Mother .... Shahin Alizadeh
> Hamed .... Hassan Joharchi

"**Z**inat" is an engaging drama about one woman's attempt to break free of the male-dominated rules and regulations that govern life in rural Iran. The feminist message is universal, but slow pacing will restrict interest to the fest circuit.

Zinat (Atefeh Razavi) is working in a public health clinic in a small town in southern Iran and is set to be married to Hamed (Hassan Joharchi). Hitch is that Hamed's parents are adamant that Zinat quit her job as soon as she weds their son, so she can devote herself full-time to household duties.

This doesn't sit well with the otherwise mild-mannered Zinat, who is committed to providing medical care for the community. Under intense pressure from Hamed's and her own family, Zinat finally caves in and leaves the job to settle down as a full-time housewife. But her former patients keep showing up on the doorstep with horrific health problems and Zinat finds it impossible to turn them away, even though her quintessential mother-in-law from hell does her best to keep Zinat locked up in the home.

Razavi does well as the confused but tough young woman, but the script overdoses on the sociology at the expense of the real-life drama. Tech credits are fine.

—*Brendan Kelly*

DIRTY MONEY

> A Bruce/Deane production. Produced, directed by James Bruce. Co-produced, written by Frederick Deane. Camera (Foto-Kem color), Christian Faber, Rick DiGregorio, Michael Meyers; editor, Bruce, Robert Barrere; music, Paul Barrere, Bill Payne; costume design, Alexandra Welker; sound, Rick Scheexnayder, Vladimir Tukan, J.A.C., Luis Alvarez. Reviewed on vidcassette, Boston, Aug. 26, 1994. (In Montreal, Boston fests. Running time: **81 MIN.**
> With: Frederick Deane, Timothy Patrick Cavanaugh, Biff Yeager, Charmagne Eckert, David Jean Thomas, Dagmar Stansora, Delaune Michel, Jorge "Maromero" Paez.

"**D**irty Money" is a throwback to the classic Hollywood B picture, especially low-budget cult favorites like Edgar G. Ulmer's "Detour." Unfortunately, there isn't much market for such films outside of cable, so this indie effort figures to serve mostly as a calling card for participants seeking further work.

A heist unfolds during the opening credits. Through no fault of his own, non-participant Sam (Frederick Deane) lands in the middle of a dispute that leaves one of the crooks dead and two of them (Timothy Patrick Cavanaugh, Biff Yeager) after him. They kill his wife before his eyes and proceed to chase him from L.A. to San Diego and on to a circus in Mexico for the final showdown. Plot, acting and tech credits don't rise above the adequate. As Sam, Deane (who also wrote and co-produced) seems to bounce back a bit too quickly from his character's situation. Cavanaugh is the standout as the more vicious of the crooks.

With no stars and no real novelty to the story, helmer James Bruce does what he can to keep it moving, and result should prove diverting for undemanding audiences, as well as enable Bruce to get an opportunity to show what he can do with more complex material.

—*Daniel M. Kimmel*

LEAVES AND THORNS

(ILAYUM MULLUM)

(INDIAN)

> An Alcom-Madhyam production. Produced by K. Satish. Directed by K. P. Sasi. Screenplay, Sasi, P. Baburaj, Satheesh Poduval. Camera (color), R. V. Ramani; music, Ramesh Narayan; editor, P. Raman Nair. Reviewed at World Film Festival, Montreal, Aug. 27, 1994. (Also in Venice fest — Critics Week.) Running time: **91 MIN.**
> With: Pallavi Joshi, Shanti Krishna, Kanya, Shabnam, Shammi Thilakan, Nedumudi Venu, Thilakan.

K. P. Sasi's drama about spirit-crushing sexism in a rural Kerala town is best suited for global fest circuit and film programs dealing with women's issues. Unimpressive tech values and didactic storytelling are major drawbacks.

Sasi's script, loosely based on real events, focuses on four spirited young women in a village where most males are domineering swine who regularly engage in sexual harassment and spousal abuse. The heroines are repeatedly warned by parents and neighbors to be submissive to men in all matters.

When her father refuses to pay her dowry after her marriage, Pavarthi (Shanti Krishna) is cruelly mistreated by her husband and commits suicide. Her surviving friends are radicalized by her death, to the point of publicly humiliating a local bureaucrat who tries to molest Santha (Pallavi Joshi) on a bus. The bureaucrat's mean-spirited flunky responds by spreading rumors that the three women are heavy-drinking harlots. Nothing good comes of this.

Acting is fine, with particularly strong work from Joshi. Pic makes many valid points, but pushes them so hard that their impact often is blunted.

—*Joe Leydon*

LOCARNO

GIRL WITH A BOOK
(LA JEUNE FILLE AU LIVRE)
(FRENCH)

An Institut National de l'Audiovisuel production. (Intl. sales: INA, Bry-sur-Marne, France.) Directed by Jean-Louis Comolli. Screenplay/libretto, Michel Beretti. Music, Andre Bon. Camera (color), Jacques Pamart; editor, Anne Baudry. Reviewed at Locarno Film Festival (special programs), Aug. 9, 1994. Running time: **64 MIN.**
Saskia .... Sophie Marin Degor
Hugo Sierra .... Jean-Marc Salzmann
Gallery Owner .... Christine Schweitzer
Collector .... Monte Jaffe
Eva .... Consuelo Caroli
(French, English, German and Italian dialogue)

A brief, fully orchestrated opera about the art world, sung in a mixture of French, English, German and Italian, "Girl With a Book" is a sparkling and unexpected treat, brimming over with mischievous wit and pleasurable erudition.

Made for a new series of opera films created specifically for TV, pic (splendidly shot on 35mm) pairs French critic/director Jean-Louis Comolli with composer Andre Bon and librettist Michel Beretti in a fresh, fast-paced, mixed-genre work that will interest cinephiles as much as opera buffs, not to mention art mavens with a sense of humor.

It may take a daring TV programmer to find the right slot, but pic ought to be preceded by good word-of-mouth from the festival circuit.

There is rarely a dull moment in the story, which proceeds by a series of esthetic, and often comic, jolts. First shock is the contrast between the corny subject matter — an artist and his model struggling in a garret to survive — and seriousness of the singing actors.

While bohemian artist Hugo Sierra (baritone Jean-Marc Salzmann) immortalizes her on canvas, model Saskia (soprano Sophie Marin Degor) strikes a suggestive pose. "You moved!" he booms. "No I didn't!" she trills. Session dissolves in a passionate embrace.

Next scene is a futuristic art gallery, where a sultry gallery owner (soprano Christine Schweitzer) hosts a *vernissage* featuring Hugo's "Girl With a Book."

She sings about how the artist's market share is unvaried, but she has an American collector on the line for him. Said collector (bass Monte Jaffe) is a gangster type who has never appreciated art until he is bewitched by the painting of Saskia.

The shrewd gallery owner organizes a heist of the painting so Hugo's market value will rise. She throws a party to celebrate the theft, "a sign of success!"

In his luxurious home, the collector pines for the secret he thinks the painting holds. He tries having a fling with Saskia, precipitating her tragic breakup with Hugo, but realizes she's just a model and that it's the painting-woman who enchants him.

Though it seems constantly to risk becoming boring and pedantic, pic almost always comes up with a new invention when the going gets rough. In a spoof of certain art historians, a bevy of policemen called in to investigate the theft look for hidden meanings in the painting.

Toward the end, scenes begin to dawdle. But these are the exception, and most of "Girl With a Book" warbles on at a fast andante.

Singing is professional, and cast members turn out to be surprisingly good actors, too. Joke is that each sings in a different language, but in a world of artistic conventions, it doesn't make any difference. (Subtitles are essential for all markets.) Costumes and decor are modern and witty, and Jacques Pamart's cinematography skillfully quotes all kinds of atmospheres, from garret to gallery to church, with a knowing wink.

—*Deborah Young*

TAKE ME AWAY
(EMMENE-MOI)
(FRENCH)

A Persona Films/La Sept Cinema production. Directed by Michel Spinosa. Screenplay, Spinosa, Gilles Bourdos. Camera (color), Antoine Roch; editor, Stephanie Mahe; music, Peter Hammill. Reviewed at Locarno Film Festival (competing), Aug. 14, 1994. Running time: **80 MIN.**
Sophie .... Karin Viard
Vincent .... Antoine Basler
Anna .... Ines de Medeiros
Gardet .... Didier Benureau

"Take Me Away," first feature by Michel Spinosa, follows the tormented relationship between two former lovers. Low-budget talkfest, set almost entirely in a two-star hotel, quickly grows stale despite energetic acting and a fast pace. Commercial life looks limited to hardcore art-film lovers.

Sophie (Karin Viard) bursts back into the life of her ex, glum hotel receptionist Vincent (Antoine Basler). She provokes Vincent into renewing their romance, and he willingly abandons his current male lover to take up the challenge.

As the heroine, Viard belongs to the Isabelle Adjani school of hysterical, long-haired beauties who hypnotize the viewer by talking and moving at the speed of light. Sophie's pizazz carries the first scenes along well enough, aided by Antoine Roch's nervous camerawork and its nonstop swish-pans in close-up. (High-profile lensing won a technical award at the Locarno fest.)

But the technical and thespian fireworks soon begin looking repetitive, and pic settles down into a numbing study of two eccentrics without a goal in life.

A new character appears with the arrival of provincial mouse Anna (a practically invisible Ines de Medeiros), who tiptoes in from Romania determined to unite with another hotel employee (Didier Benureau). But this subplot doesn't go very far, as he promptly has a heart attack and is taken to hospital.

To his credit, Spinosa succeeds in giving this unlikely tale a certain cohesiveness around Sophie's anxieties and her uncontrolled talent for spreading misery all around her. The eye-catching Viard generates some degree of sympathy (as well as exasperation), and Basler holds his own as her doormat.

—*Deborah Young*

JOE & MARIE
(SWISS-GERMAN-FRENCH)

An Artimage (Geneva)/Interimages (Paris)/Apollo Film (Munich)/TSR/SF DRS production. (International sales: Artimage, Geneva.) Produced by Andre Martin. Directed by Tania Stocklin. Screenplay, Stocklin, Cyrille Rey-Coquais. Camera (color), Ciro Capellari; editors, Stocklin, Barbara Weber; music, Martin Meisonnier. Reviewed at Locarno Film Festival (competing), Aug. 11, 1994. Running time: **94 MIN.**
Marie .... Estelle Vincent
Joe .... Gay Etgar
Marie's father .... Mathias Gnadinger
Marie's mother .... Viktor Lazlo
Joe's father .... Rufus
Joe's mother .... Aurore Clement
(French dialogue)

"Joe & Marie" celebrates the socially doomed love affair between two 14-year-old kids, a poor black girl and a middle-class white student. Depthless characters make for a familiar story, slickly lensed and directed by Swiss helmer Tania Stocklin. Pic's pretty kids, cool music track and studied dose of rebellion might tune in Euro teen auds.

Marie (Estelle Vincent) is a tough beauty who has stopped going to school and has begun stealing wallets, watches and mopeds. Joe (Gay Etgar) is an awkward, curly-haired model student. They meet literally by accident, and their young love blossoms in secret, far from the eyes of their parents and peers.

Marie is the child of a hard-working black woman (Viktor Lazlo) and a failed, boozing writer (Mathias Gnadinger), whose basic humanity and poverty makes an easy contrast to Joe's redneck family. His butcher father (Rufus) and Bible-thumping mom (Aurore Clement) are two insufferable bigots, their house a prison.

Marie and Joe turn a cemetery vault into a love nest and meeting point. It comes in handy after a shoplifting escapade and later, when Marie kills a man during a holdup. The local papers call them monsters, but all they want is to love each other and maybe find a quiet place where Marie can give birth to the baby she's expecting.

Stocklin, who co-directed the award-winning "Georgette Meunier" with Cyrille Rey-Coquais (here credited as a scripter), leaves the ending open. Against all odds, film suggests that the pair may one day sail to Africa and find happiness.

Pro lensing and cutting give pic a pedicured look. Thesping tends to be stereotyped and slightly over-the-top, though Lazlo and Gnadinger have some good moments as Marie's unconventional parents.

As Marie, Vincent has the beauty and poise of a ghetto Lolita. Etgar's lovelorn, poetry-writing schoolboy in baggy jeans and striped pajamas comes from another planet. Told from the kids' p.o.v., the story holds up as standard romantic entertainment for the younger set.

—*Deborah Young*

PAX
(PORTUGUESE)

A GER production for Lisboa 94, with support from Ipaca. Produced by Joachim Pinto. Directed by Eduardo Guedes. Screenplay, Bruno Heller. Camera (color), Dominique Chapuis; editor, Claudio Martinez; music, Carlos Cainha Martins. Reviewed at Locarno Film Festival (competing), Aug. 13, 1994. Running time: **73 MIN.**
Franny .... Amanda Plummer
Esmeralda .... Isabel Ruth
Rui .... Joao Lagarto
Pedro .... Paulo Guilherme
With: Carlos Cainha Martins, Marcia Brea, Patricia Abreu, Manuel Mendes, Manuel Joao Vieira, Tony Lima, Candido Ferreira.
(English and Portuguese dialogue)

Though it wandered into competition at the Locarno festival as a late entry, "Pax" looks like a simple, TV-style Portuguese comedy, nicely lensed but not especially funny. Despite the presence of "Pulp Fiction's"

September 5, 1994 (Cont.)

Amanda Plummer in a repeat scatterbrain role, this feather-weight pic set in nighttime Lisbon is unlikely to travel far beyond its local borders.

"Pax" is part of a trilogy about Lisbon commissioned by the city, which is the European cultural capital for 1994. (Joao Botelho's "Tres Palmeiras," seen at Cannes, is another segment.) Slight storyline, however, reveals little about the town and its dwellers.

Plummer plays a dippy American girl, Franny, who has come to Lisbon to deliver a precious parcel, although she's lost the address of the person she's supposed to give it to, recalling only that his name is Joao. Aging hooker Esmeralda (Isabel Ruth) decides to help her find him, and they tool around town all night, stopping off in bars. What's inside parcel is pic's one real surprise.

Helmer Eduardo Guedes, who has worked in the U.K. and likes using English-speaking thesps (John Hurt and Ian Dury in "Rocinante," Tom Waits in "Bearskin"), simply unleashes Plummer to be as hammy as she likes. Unfortunately, she has neither witty dialogue nor wild plot twists to sail away on.

Local cast shows good esprit de corps and creates a pleasantly un-threatening world of down-and-outers who live and love by night. Dominique Chapuis' attractive lensing bathes the city in a cleansing rain. —*Deborah Young*

GINO

(AUSTRALIAN)

A Filmside production, in association with the Australian Film Finance Corp. (International sales: Southern Star.) Produced by Ross Matthews. Directed by Jackie McKimmie. Screenplay, Vince Sorrenti, Larry Buttrose. Camera (color), Ellery Ryan; editor, Emma Hay; music, Roger Mason; production design, Chris Kennedy; costumes, Anna Borghesi. Reviewed at Brisbane Film Festival, Aug. 6, 1994. Running time: **89 MIN.**
Gino Palizetti .... Nicholas Bufalo
Lucia Petri .... Zoe Carides
Mr. Palizetti .... Bruno Lawrence
Mrs. Palizetti .... Rose Clemente
Rocco Petri .... Nico Lathouris
Maria .... Fiona Martinelli
Angelina .... Maria Venuti
Nonno .... Lucky Fordali
Stan .... John Polson
Larry Stone .... Graeme Blundell

"**G**ino," third feature from Jackie McKimmie ("Australian Dream," "Waiting"), is a small-scale, amiable comedy about a young Italo-Australian who wants to be a standup comic. Modest returns may be expected for this offering, which has plenty of pleasant scenes but in the end isn't very memorable.

Newcomer Nicholas Bufalo is likable as Gino, whose hard-working dad (Bruno Lawrence) is a builder but who wants a different life for himself. He's in love with Lucia (Zoe Carides), only daughter of a rich developer (Nico Lathouris), and has made the mistake of getting her pregnant. While working through this dilemma, he prepares to audition for a popular TV variety show.

Screenplay, co-written by stand-up comic Vince Sorrenti, rings amusingly true in depicting the life-styles of these two Italo-Aussie families, one still struggling, the other wealthy.

McKimmie's affection for her characters is evident, and performances are natural and unaffected, even though Kiwi actor Lawrence, badly miscast, has an uphill battle with his accent. Not so successful are the scenes in which Gino performs his comic act; although the TV audience seems to find him hilarious, and although several noted Australian wits worked on his material, his so-called comic routine is pitifully unfunny, undermining the point of the film. —*David Stratton*

PLAY IT ALL

(KAIKKI PELISSA)

(FINNISH)

A Wonderfilm production. (International sales: Finnkino, Helsinki.) Produced by Matti Ollila. Executive producer, Jukka Makela. Directed by Matti Kassila. Screenplay, Kassila, Ollila, from an original story by Kassila. Camera (color), Henrik Paersch; editor, Irma Taina; music, Jukka Linkola; production design, Minna Santakari; sound (Dolby), Johan Hake; associate producer, Paivi Hartzell. Reviewed on Wonderfilm vidcassette, London, Aug. 21, 1994. (In Edinburgh Film Festival.) Running time: **100 MIN.**
With: Esko Salminen, Hannele Lauri, Satu Silvo, Jukka Puotila, Allu Tuppurainen, Kari Heiskanen, Aake Kalliala, Antti Litja, Pentti Siimes, Esko Nikkari, Kati Outinen.

A good-looking, smoothly packaged Finnish whodunit, "Play It All" won't blaze much of a theatrical trail beyond home base but could catch on with internationally minded buffs. Film is a surprisingly fresh and youthful entry from veteran helmer Matti Kassila, 70, best known offshore for the 1955 rural classic "Harvest Month."

Pic opens in pacy style with a young woman at a country railroad station bidding farewell to her older husband and dashing indoors for some rumpy-pumpy with her lover. This turns out to be a scene from a meller ("Sin") being shot in the actual site, in central Finland, where the real events took place decades earlier.

At a press conference, the script-writer turns up, threatening revenge for a past injustice by the producer (Hannele Lauri), and later that night he's stabbed to death after a sauna. Aside from the producer, who'd screwed him out of profits on a previous pic, suspects include the horny main actress (Satu Silvo), the cool location manager (Jukka Puotila) and various glowering locals, unhappy at a film crew raking over dead coals.

There's nothing very original here, but the movie's straight-arrow procedural style follows the rules of the genre with enough varied suspects to keep one guessing. Reliable thesp Esko Salminen holds things together as the gruff, straight-talking cop on the case, and there's even a political cover-up for good measure.

Playing is in a slightly heightened style that fits the genre. Action sequences, including a finale on a speeding train, are pro if hardly breathtaking. Handsome tech credits include a moody score by Jukka Linkola and atmospheric stereo dub. —*Derek Elley*

EVERYNIGHT ... EVERYNIGHT

(AUSTRALIAN)

A Rescued Films production. Produced, directed by Alkinos Tsilimidos. Screenplay, Ray Mooney, Tsilimidos, based on Mooney's play. Camera (b&w), Toby Oliver; editors, Cindy Clarkson, Tsilimidos; music, Paul Kelly, Shane O'Mara; production design, Steven Meier. Reviewed at Leura screening room, Leura, Australia, Aug. 1, 1994. (In Melbourne Film Festival.) Running time: **92 MIN.**
Dale .... David Field
Berriman .... Bill Hunter
Best .... Robert Morgan
Bryant .... Phil Motherwell
Barrett .... Jim Daly
Governor .... Jim Shaw
Gavat .... Simon Woodward
Driscoll .... Theodore Zakos
Gilchrist .... Bill Tisdall

An extremely grim, though undeniably impressive, prison picture, starkly filmed in black-and-white, "Everynight ... Everynight" should impress critics and be seen on the fest route, but it's such a downer that it's hard to imagine the film finding much of a paying audience. First-time director Alkinos Tsilimidos certainly hasn't compromised, and deserves credit for what is, in many ways, a remarkable piece of work.

Tsilimidos penned the screenplay with ex-con-turned-playwright Ray Mooney, who knew Christopher Dale Flannery, a criminal who served as the basis for the character of Dale, brilliantly played by David Field.

At a press conference, the script-writer turns up, threatening re Action never moves outside the prison setting, and the only characters are staff and prisoners in the top-security H Division. For hitting a prison guard, Dale winds up in this nightmare environment even before he's been sentenced.

Guards regularly beat and humiliate prisoners. Yet Dale, through his independence and courage, manages to lead a kind of revolt that culminates in a government inquiry into the prison.

This is not a film for the squeamish, as Tsilimidos spares the viewer nothing in depicting the guards' violence. Soundtrack is an almost non-stop stream of four-letter words, and regular arthouse auds will likely be scared off by the filmmaker's relentless approach.

Beautifully lit by cinematographer Toby Oliver, pic's monochrome images and director's fondness for very long takes give the pic an austerity at times reminiscent of French master Robert Bresson.

Pic had its world preem at the Melbourne fest. —*David Stratton*

THE KITE

(PATANG)

(INDIAN)

A GNS Motion Pictures production. (International sales: GNS, Gaya, India.) Directed by Goutam Ghose. Screenplay, Ghose, Ain Rasheed Khan. Camera (color), Ghose; editor, Moloy Banerjee; music, Ghose; art direction, Ashoke Bose. Reviewed at Taormina Film Festival (competing), Italy, Aug. 2, 1994. Running time: **104 MIN.**
Jitni .... Shabana Azmi
Somra .... Sayed Shafique
With: Om Puri, Robi Ghost, Mohan Agashe, Ashad, Shatrughan Sinha.

In "The Kite," Bengali filmmaker Goutam Ghose ably combines an eye for India's disenfranchised poor with a gift for storytelling. Tale, set around a lonesome desert train stop, assumes thriller overtones as deadly destiny approaches the main characters. Starring internationally known actress Shabana Azmi and cut at a normal Western pace, pic is worth a look for programmers of Indian fare.

Jitni (Azmi) is a tough unwed mother who works as a house maid but still turns heads in the shabby village where she lives with her teenage son, Somra (Sayed Shafique), and young daughter. All the houses have been illegally constructed on land belonging to the railroad, and have no water or electricity.

The station chief turns a blind eye on the stealing that goes on when trains slow down near the town. Under the cover of darkness, boys clamber aboard the moving trains and toss out goods to adult accomplices. This practice furnishes a living to men like Jitni's lover, Mathura, who must contend with an idealistic new commissioner repping the Railway Protection Force.

Ghose, who also lensed, uses two distinct styles of shooting. Most of the film is beautiful, with people and their hovels standing out against a majestic natural background and the ever-present railroad track, which dominates the town. In the scenes involving the crooks, politicos and rail authorities, however, pic throws sophistication to the wind and has a flat, amateurish look. Luckily, these scenes are few and far between.

Boyish Somra, whose passion is flying kites, finds himself drawn ever deeper into Mathura's ring of child thieves. When Mathura becomes convinced that Somra despises him for sleeping with his mother, he decides to sacrifice him to the railroad guards on the next heist. Denouement is a surprise.

One leaves "The Kite" feeling outraged both at adults' callous exploitation of kids, the enormous gap between the nouveau riche and the perpetually poor, and the pervasive sense of futility. Ghose also composed pic's subdued score.
                        —*Deborah Young*

THE INDECISIVE GUY

(L'IRRESOLU)

(FRENCH)

A Bac Films release of a Salome/Bac Films/M6 Films/Generale d'Images/Duende production, with support of Sofica Sofinergie 3 and participation of Canal Plus and CNC. Produced by Maurice Benart. Executive producer, Alain Centonze. Directed by Jean-Pierre Ronssin. Screenplay, Jean-Charles Le Roux, Ronssin. Camera (color), Benoit Delhomme; editor, Joelle Van Effenterre; music, Pascal Esteve; costume design, Fabienne Katany; sound, Pierre Excoffier, Claude Villand; associate producer, Jean Labadie; assistant director, Catherine Bernstein. Reviewed at UGC Biarritz Cinema, Paris, July 18, 1994. Running time: **85 MIN.**
Francois .... Vincent Lindon
Gaelle .... Sandrine Kiberlain
Christine .... Thiam
Marianne .... Barbara Schulz
Marie-France .... Beatrice Agenin
    With: Paul Pavel, Christine Murillo.

"The Indecisive Guy" is the uncompelling story of a nerdy playwright whose love life is riddled with interesting women for no apparent reason other than that the script has placed them in his path. Tedious helming debut by co-scripter of 1990 local hit "La Discrete" barely sustains a dramatic pulse as the charismatically challenged protagonist is buffeted by women who know exactly what they want.

Thirty-five-year-old playwright Francois (Vincent Lindon), a low-key cipher, finally has a hit play running in Paris, an autobiographical item called "The Indecisive Guy." Francois has great sex with emotionally fragile Gaelle, 25, who yearns to be valued for more than her comely bod. He also has great sex with Christine, 29, a gorgeous self-assured black doctor who wants to start a family and is mere weeks away from returning to Africa for good. He lets himself be seduced into sexually initiating 18-year-old Marianne, the perky daughter of his impresario, whose 45-year-old wife, Marie-France, has also been throwing herself at him.

Unable to decide which, if any, of these women he wants to bond with for good, Francois coasts. Since he has no discernible personality, it's almost impossible to care about what he does or doesn't do on a personal or professional level. A potentially interesting theme — how a contemporary man can assert himself without misinterpreting his mate's signals — is lost along the way.

Although female thesps valiantly inhabit their underwritten roles, Lindon — a popular Everyman whose hangdog expression has worked in his favor in previous screen outings — comes across as a sort of Woody Allen without the frantic energy or the gags, though the script does feature some nicely turned phrases.

Lensing is efficient. A jazzy, melancholy score is used occasionally to good effect.   —*Lisa Nesselson*

ALONE, GEORGIA

(SEULE, GEORGIE)

(FRENCH — DOCU — VIDEO)

An Arte TV production. Produced by Hans Robert Eisenhauer. Directed, written by Otar Ioseliani. Camera (color video), Nugsar Ercomaichvili; editors, Ioseliani, Marie Agnes Blum. Reviewed at Taormina Film Festival, Italy, Aug. 2, 1994. (Also in Locarno fest.) Running time: **240 MIN.**
    (French and Georgian soundtrack)

Award-winning Georgian-born helmer Otar Ioseliani, who has worked most recently in France ("Minions of the Moon," "The Butterfly Hunt"), returns to shoot a four-hour docu about his native land. "Alone, Georgia," made for French television, will long remain the definitive film compendium about the history, legends, culture and lifestyles of the former Soviet republic, now an independent state. The sheer breadth and length of the project may give prospective TV viewers

pause, yet docu contains scarcely a dull moment.

Pic opens with a recent image of soldiers exchanging rifle fire. Often in the news because of its coups and civil war, Georgia has a long history of conflict and invasions, as well as a rich cultural tradition.

The film is divided into three parts. In the first, "Prelude," Ioseliani traces Georgian history through the 18th century and Russia's annexation of the country in 1801. The emphasis is on Georgia's unique culture, which includes its own alphabet, literature, art and wines. None of this, the director points out, was suppressed by the Russians.

But part two, "Temptation," shows the bitter consequences of the Russian revolution. The Soviet takeover is depicted in archival footage, while a voiceover describes the ensuing purges, mass deportations and the results of Stalin's collectivization policies.

Russian culture makes forcible inroads in this period, while freedom of thought, expression and religion disappear.

Ioseliani presents the parade of Russian leaders from Lenin to Andropov with the maximum irony and scorn. With Gorbachev and perestroika, Georgia recovers its political autonomy. But local conflicts — particularly the separatist movement in Abkhazia, on the Black Sea — almost immediately end the festivities. Shots of bombed-out buildings in the capital, Tbilisi, are heart-wrenching.

Docu's third part, "The Ordeal," addresses the dramatic situation the country faces today.

Film is informative and literate, as might be expected of a director of Ioseliani's caliber. Highlights include many clips from Georgian films by Nikoloz Shengalaya, Tenghiz Abuladze and others. Several filmmakers are interviewed on-camera, along with politicos like Eduard Shevardnadze.
                        —*Deborah Young*

QUIZ SHOW

A Buena Vista release of a Hollywood Pictures presentation of a Wildwood Enterprises/Baltimore Pictures production. Produced by Robert Redford, Michael Jacobs, Julian Krainin, Michael Nozik. Executive producers, Fred Zollo, Richard Dreyfuss, Judith James. Co-producers, Gail Mutrux, Jeff McCracken, Richard N. Goodwin. Directed by Redford. Screenplay, Paul Attanasio, based on the book "Remembering America: A Voice From the Sixties" by Goodwin. Camera (DuArt color; Technicolor prints), Michael Ballhaus; editor, Stu Linder; music, Mark Isham; production design, Jon Hutman; art direction, Tim Galvin; set decoration, Samara Schafer; costume design, Kathy O'Rear; sound (Dolby), Tod A. Maitland; sound design, Gary Rydstrom; associate producer, Susan Moore; assistant director, Joseph Reidy; casting, Bonnie Timmermann. Reviewed at Walt Disney Studios, Burbank, Aug. 30, 1994. MPAA Rating: PG-13. Running time: **130 MIN.**
Herbie Stempel .... John Turturro
Dick Goodwin .... Rob Morrow
Charles Van Doren .... Ralph Fiennes
Mark Van Doren .... Paul Scofield
Dan Enright .... David Paymer
Albert Freedman .... Hank Azaria
Jack Barry .....Christopher McDonald
Toby Stempel .... Johann Carlo
Dorothy
    Van Doren .... Elizabeth Wilson
Robert Kintner .... Allan Rich
Sandra Goodwin .... Mira Sorvino
Chairman .... George Martin
Lishman .... Paul Guilfoyle
Account Guy .... Griffin Dunne
Sponsor .... Martin Scorsese
Dave Garroway .... Barry Levinson

A national scandal that arguably inflicted an early wound on the American postwar moral fiber is smoothly dramatized in "Quiz Show." With colorful, bright characters playing out a lamentable true-life scenario against the lively backdrop of '50s television and the vibrant New York City of the era, Robert Redford's handsome, smartly constructed new film stands likely to capture the imagination of the educated, culturally inclined public. Difference between good B.O. results in more upscale markets and wider acceptance will be determined by whether pic's marketing can make younger audiences curious about a popular phenomenon from four decades ago.

While constantly applying ethical, political and intellectual shadings in order to deepen the context and implications of the episode, Redford and screenwriter Paul Attanasio telescope history rather severely in squeezing the events of three years into a matter of months. But their points are well and carefully made, and if the film lacks an edge of excitement and daring, the story still proves strongly engrossing.

September 12, 1994 (Cont.)

Set in 1958, pic sweeps the viewer into a live broadcast of the NBC game show "Twenty-One." At the time, it was the first among many knowledge-oriented programs that enthralled the nation, a refined match in which two contestants confined to "isolation booths" seemed to wrack their brains to answer relatively difficult questions.

At the outset, the king of "Twenty-One" is Herbie Stempel (John Turturro), a brainy, ill-mannered Jewish grad student from Queens who has fended off all opponents for weeks and earned a small fortune in the process. Finally, the show's producer, Dan Enright (David Paymer), asks Stempel to take a dive for a large fee, thus allowing a new champion, the handsome, brilliant, patrician Charles Van Doren (Ralph Fiennes), to be crowned.

Although Van Doren, along with the rest of the nation, believes that the show features honest competition, Enright makes it clear to him from the beginning that the show's staff will feed him answers. After initially wavering, Van Doren goes along with the ruse, persuaded that it's been done that way all along and no one will ever know.

Before long, Van Doren is anointed "the egghead turned national hero." A prince from one of the country's most distinguished intellectual and literary families, this Columbia literature instructor becomes a heartthrob as well as an inspiration to students to bone up on their studies; it's suddenly cool to be smart thanks to this Time magazine cover boy.

But shadowing it all is young Dick Goodwin (Rob Morrow), a similarly bright Harvard grad holding down a Washington entry-level job on the House Subcommittee on Legislative Oversight. Getting wind of a grand jury's quashing of a probe into alleged quiz show fraud, Goodwin scours Gotham checking things out for himself until Stempel finally spills the beans that he was supplied with his answers. It all ends in congressional hearings at which Van Doren at long last admits his complicity in the scandal.

Applying an evenhanded approach that gives all the principals more or less equal time and weight, and extending both sympathy and skepticism to the wrong-doers, filmmakers show the shocking ease with which otherwise decent, even exemplary people were capable of such monumental lapses in ethics and morality. As the whistle-blower who raised a stink mainly because he felt shortchanged by the show's producer, Stempel is granted a full measure of obnoxiousness,

while with Van Doren one gets the feeling that this seemingly splendid gentleman should simply have known better.

Even Goodwin, a precocious troubleshooter and tenacious investigator, is painted as a less than full-fledged hero, in that he hoped to nail the network and the sponsor, not Van Doren, whom he had come to like enormously. Fact that the big boys got off scot-free seems like the first blow to a future '60s liberal's idealism.

Quiz show sequences are craftily done, and New York in the city's heyday of the '50s is deftly evoked. But the film's best scenes are those that bring to life the now all-but-vanished elite intellectual ruling class. Highlights in this area are a summer birthday party at the Connecticut country home of Van Doren's Pulitzer Prize-winning father, Mark (Paul Scofield), where Goodwin marvels at the family's effortless erudition and sparring with Shakespearean quotations, and a climactic scene in which the son admits his transgressions to his father.

On the flip side, Stempel points out to Goodwin the anti-Semitism promoted by the show's Jewish producers when they had Jews lose to WASPs. In general, the pursuit of truths hidden behind official postures and the loss-of-innocence themes that have regularly popped up in films by and starring Redford are on view here, gracefully expressed without grandstanding.

Cast members make the characters register strongly, even if the simple matter of accents suspends full credibility at numerous moments. Turturro, who put on considerable poundage for the role, is a perfect Stempel — pushy, nervous, uncouth and, finally, unwilling to be shoved aside. Morrow captures a quiet wryness along with Goodwin's intelligence and drive, but his aimed-for Boston accent ranges all up and down the Eastern seaboard. Similarly, Fiennes, now drastically slimmed down from "Schindler's List," cuts a winning figure as Van Doren, but he can't keep his English accent suppressed for long.

Supporting turns are excellent, including Paymer's unapologetic Dan Enright, Christopher McDonald's slick TV host Jack Barry and Mira Sorvino's feisty wife of Goodwin. But best of all is Scofield, who, as the poet and professor Mark Van Doren, single-handedly sums up the feeling of privilege, irreproachable intellectual superiority and distractedness of the mid-century academic elite.

Redford's cool, analytical directorial style well suits this probing cultural critique, although the film is a

tad overlong and might have profited from a bit more dash at times. Splendid locations, lensing, production and costume design and music help bring to life a period that lives in many people's memories but is still long gone. —*Todd McCarthy*

TELLURIDE

ED WOOD

A Buena Vista release of a Touchstone Pictures presentation of a Burton/Di Novi production. Produced by Denise Di Novi, Tim Burton. Executive producer, Michael Lehmann. Co-producer, Michael Flynn. Directed by Burton. Screenplay, Scott Alexander, Larry Karaszewski, based on the book "Nightmare of Ecstasy: The Life and Art of Edward D. Wood Jr." by Rudolph Grey. Camera (DuArt b&w; Technicolor prints), Stefan Czapsky; editor, Chris Lebenzon; music, Howard Shore; production design, Tom Duffield; art direction, Okowita; set design, Chris Nushuang, Bruce Hill; set decoration, Crickett Rowland; visual consultant, Richard Hoover; sound (Dolby), Edward Tise; assistant director, Michael Topoozian; casting, Victoria Thomas. Reviewed at Telluride Film Festival, Sept. 3, 1994. (Also in New York Film Festival.) MPAA Rating: R. Running time: **124 MIN.**

Ed Wood	Johnny Depp
Bela Lugosi	Martin Landau
Dolores Fuller	Sarah Jessica Parker
Kathy O'Hara	Patricia Arquette
Criswell	Jeffrey Jones
Reverend Lemon	G. D. Spradlin
Orson Welles	Vincent D'Onofrio
Vampira	Lisa Marie
Bunny Breckinridge	Bill Murray
Georgie Weiss	Mike Starr
Paul Marco	Max Casella
Conrad Brooks	Brent Hinkley
Loretta King	Juliet Landau
Tor Johnson	George "The Animal" Steele

Tim Burton pays elaborate tribute to the maverick creative spirit in "Ed Wood," a fanciful, sweet-tempered biopic about the man often described as the worst film director of all time. Always engaging to watch and often dazzling in its imagination and technique, picture is also a bit distended, and lacking in weight at its center. Result is beguiling rather than thrilling, oddly charming instead of transporting, meaning that Disney will have its work cut out for it trying to capture the full "Edward Scissorhands" audience for what is at heart a cult movie and a film buff's dream.

Only Burton could have made this film, in at least two ways: Only Burton, who has never had a flop, would have used his clout to make such a personal film about a fringe figure like Wood (to the point of walking from Columbia to Disney in order to make it in black-and-white), and only he could have given

such an amiable, sympathetic twist to what could just as easily have been portrayed as a life of abject failure, desperation and trashiness.

Virtually unknown during his lifetime and for some time after his death in 1978, Wood started gaining notoriety as an auteur of the lower depths when his beyond-bad 1950s epics "Glen or Glenda" and "Plan 9 From Outer Space" developed followings in the 1980s. He made several other films, with titles such as "Jail Bait," "Bride of the Monster" and "The Sinister Urge," all shot in a matter of days on home-movie budgets.

Wood's other claim to fame was that, although apparently straight, he was an avid transvestite, with a particular taste for Angora sweaters. This predilection was dramatized, if that is the word, in "Glen or Glenda," in which Wood himself starred as a young man seeking understanding for his odd habit.

The context for Burton's take on this curious career is the Hollywood nether world of 40 years ago, a world that existed in the shadows of the major studios and was populated by characters who can be called both colorful and freakish and can still, to an extent, be seen dragging along Hollywood Boulevard today.

Following one of the all-time great opening credit sequences, in which the cast members' names appear on tombstones, scene-setting finds Wood (Johnny Depp) and his motley crew dejected following a desultory little theater opening. "Orson Welles was only 26 when he made 'Citizen Kane' and I'm already 30," Wood realizes, so it's high time for him to get moving on his highly personal first opus, "I Changed My Sex," very loosely based on Christine Jorgensen's sex change, which was later retitled "Glen or Glenda."

Wood is able to raise his meager financing by proposing to topline Bela Lugosi, the old "Dracula" star whom Wood meets by chance in Hollywood. "I'm just an ex-boogeyman," admits Lugosi (Martin Landau), who hasn't worked in four years and has been addicted to morphine for 20. Living in a dismal tract house straight out of "Edward Scissorhands," Lugosi is grateful for the work and becomes a friend and sort of spiritual mentor to Wood.

By contrast, Wood's girlfriend and appallingly bad lead actress Dolores Fuller (Sarah Jessica Parker) bolts in revulsion at her man's sartorial tastes and weird colleagues. Along the way, Wood's entourage comes to include aspiring transsexual Bunny Breckinridge (Bill Murray), faux TV psychic Criswell (Jeffrey Jones), TV horror hostess Vampira (Lisa Marie), hulking pro wrestler Tor Johnson (George "The Animal" Steele), actress and would-be film financier Loretta King (Juliet Landau) and new g.f. Kathy

September 12, 1994 (Cont.)

O'Hara (Patricia Arquette), who wound up marrying him.

Much of the running time is spent recounting the cock-eyed, disrupted shoots of "Bride of the Monster" and "Plan 9," with Burton and company taking great pains to reproduce the indelibly flat look of the Wood originals. Although the financing and production details of these immortal works are amusing, they do become somewhat repetitive after awhile, with Wood and his colleagues scrambling to get the cameras rolling and the director signing off on every setup after one take, regardless.

Giving the story its principal weight is the Wood-Lugosi relationship. Initially, the young director willingly pays the old star the obsequious homage the actor believes he deserves. But when Lugosi needs serious help with his addiction, Wood is the only one there for him, checking him into a clinic and, later, filming some footage that ended up as Lugosi's posthumous appearance in "Plan 9."

Lifting all this enormously is Landau's astounding performance as the old Hungarian. Looking (thanks to a terrific makeup job) and sounding very much like the real thing, Landau brilliantly conveys the ego, pride, hurt and gratitude of the man in his twilight and, despite his character's grand theatricality, gives the film its most human moments.

One could well ask why anyone would want to make a biography of such a disreputable figure as Ed Wood. The answer for Burton and screenwriters Scott Alexander and Larry Karaszewski lies in the film's key scene, a no-doubt fictional encounter between Wood and his hero, Orson Welles (Vincent D'Onofrio), at Musso & Frank's. A despondent Wood speaks to Welles, who's got troubles of his own, about his problems, and is told to tenaciously follow his own vision in his work. "Visions are worth fighting for," Welles insists, inspiring Wood to rush out and finish "Plan 9" according to his own designs.

(D'Onofrio, a virtual dead ringer for Welles when the latter was in his 30s, is the perfect choice for the role — even if the voice sounds vaguely electronic — but he is given a quip which, even though it's a good line, is highly unfair to Charlton Heston. Welles complains that Universal is obliging him to use Heston to play a Mexican in a picture, while the truth is that Heston was essentially responsible for forcing Universal to let Welles direct, and not only co-star in, "Touch of Evil.")

Once Wood finishes "Plan 9," biopic flies into purest fantasy, even if many viewers won't recognize it as such. Wood and his wife arrive at Hollywood Boulevard's illustrious Pantages Theater, where "Plan 9" is cheered to the rafters by a well-appointed packed house. Scene conveys the recognition and respect Wood always sought but never achieved in a career that eventually degenerated into pornography and alcoholism.

As Wood, Depp is more animated and less interiorized than he has ever been onscreen before, and no doubt a number of fans will be curious to see how he looks in drag. He does everything possible to create audience interest in this strange fellow, but Wood, perhaps unavoidably, remains a lightweight both as a talent and a man. There's never any sense of private assessment about his life, no feeling that he thinks about what he does.

Remainder of the cast delightfully fill out a roster of nicely individualized Hollywood weirdos, with Parker niftily pulling off some deliberately bad acting, Arquette expressing great understanding as the only woman who would put up with Wood's eccentricities, and Jones a perfect Criswell.

Technically, "Ed Wood" is a feast on a par with Burton's previous films, but in black-and-white. Sensational models and Tom Duffield's production design brilliantly conjure up a Hollywood in transition between illustrious past and seedy present, and cinematographer Stefan Czapsky has pulled off the difficult trick of echoing the laughably poor lighting of Wood's own films while still shooting a beautiful-looking picture. Howard Shore, replacing Danny Elfman as composer on Burton's films, has come up with an excitingly varied, pacing-helpful score. —*Todd McCarthy*

THE BUDDY FACTOR

A Cineville presentation in association with NeoFight Film and Mama'z Boy Entertainment. Produced by Steve Alexander, Joanne Moore. Executive producers, Jay Cohen, Stephen Israel. Co-producers, Kevin Spacey, Buzz Hays. Line producer, Louis Nader. Directed, written by George Huang. Camera (Foto-Kem color), Steven Finestone; editor, Ed Marx; music, Tom Heil; production design, Veronika Merlin, Cecil Gentry; art direction, Karen Haase; costume design, Kirsten Everberg; sound (Dolby), Giovanni DiSimone; associate producer, Kevin Reidy; assistant director, Michael Proust; casting, Andrea Stone Guttfreund, Laurel Smith. Reviewed at Telluride Film Festival, Sept. 4, 1994. Running time: **93 MIN.**

Buddy Ackerman	Kevin Spacey
Guy	Frank Whaley
Dawn	Michelle Forbes
Rex	Benicio Del Toro

With: Jerry Levine, T. E. Russell, Roy Dotrice.

"The Buddy Factor" will become this year's must-see primer for aspiring producers and studio execs. Borrowing a page from "The Player" with a tip of the hat to "Reservoir Dogs," George Huang's sharp first feature reps the latest diving expedition to attempt to measure the true depths of venality and cynicism in contempo Hollywood. Narrow focus on the relationship between a selfish, macho exec and his green assistant will limit audience interest to in-the-know urbanites, but an aces performance by Kevin Spacey and smart take on industry ways should generate sufficient critical support to give this very dark comedy a shot at solid cult status.

A revenge fantasy in which a much put-upon flunky gets some of his own back when he holds his insufferable boss hostage and tortures him over all "the indignities and hardships" he's suffered, pic charts a recent Hollywood arrival's quick trip from idealism to murderous me-firstism.

Hip opening scene has 25-year-old film school grad Guy (Frank Whaley) reeling in disgust when his young dinner mates at a trendy eatery react with utter blankness when he mentions Shelley Winters and her credits. Guy, it would seem, got lucky in town right away, landing a fast-track job as personal assistant to high-powered studio production exec Buddy Ackerman (Spacey), a man known for reveling in power, babes and abuse of his employees.

Not only does Buddy humiliate the naive Guy in front of other workers, throw things at him and make him remove from local newsstands every copy of a Time issue that includes a derogatory mention of him, he even prevents the kid from ever taking lunch, which means Guy must meet foxy young producer Dawn (Michelle Forbes) one evening.

That such a tough cookie as Dawn would immediately make a play for gullible little Guy is the script's least believable ploy, but she does it mostly to improve her position with Buddy so he'll move on her new project. Buddy initially responds to the script with an utter lack of enthusiasm, but Guy is eventually able to turn him around, thereby linking his fate in town directly to that of the project and his detested boss.

But in the meantime, Guy must endure an endless cascade of verbal and sometimes physical abuse, and the many scenes of Buddy grinding his peon into the carpet, then digging a hole so he can push him further down, have an insidious, mordant humor that is greatly enhanced by Spacey's incisive, fundamentally serious performance.

Buddy's favorite lines are, "Shut up, listen and learn" and, courtesy of John Wayne, "Do not apologize, it's a sign of weakness." Spacey never tries to cozy up to the audience to suggest that Buddy's secretly a nice guy under it all. (Once the film is seen in Hollywood, speculation will ensue as to who inspired the character; Huang once worked as an assistant to Barry Josephson, and such names as Don Simpson, Joel Silver and Scott Rudin have already come up.)

Intercut with the office action are "current" scenes in which an enraged Guy, having tied up Buddy in the latter's house, forces him to confront his own childish sadism, all the while torturing him and threatening worse. Escalating face-off is climaxed by an unexpected arrival, and surprise ending truly does "The Player" one better in its evaluation of how self-centered, amoral and insular Hollywood may be.

Film's perspective remains small, as few other characters enter into the fray and Huang devotes nearly all of his energy to keeping the narrative afloat. But within its limited range, pic has verve, a fine control of tone and a stylish look given its low budget and three-week sked. Lensing, production design, editing and music are all excellent.

Most important, the three main roles are well-cast and performed. Spacey dominates, but Whaley makes a convincing transition from goody-goody to icy insider, and Forbes manages well despite being forced to flip-flop on command between sarcastic bitchiness and softer intimacy.

Short of serving up a B.O. bonanza with your first feature, the best way to get Hollywood to know your name is to make a film industryites will talk about, and Huang has craftily done that.
—*Todd McCarthy*

September 12, 1994 (Cont.)

BULLETS OVER BROADWAY

A Miramax release from Sweetland Films of a Jean Doumanian production. Produced by Robert Greenhut. Executive producers, Doumanian, J.E. Beaucaire. Co-producer, Helen Robin. Co-executive producers, Jack Rollins, Charles H. Joffe, Letty Aronson. Directed by Woody Allen. Screenplay, Allen, Douglas McGrath. Camera (DuArt color; Technicolor prints), Carlo Di Palma; editor, Susan E. Morse; production design, Santo Loquasto; art direction, Tom Warren; set decoration, Susan Bode, Amy Marshall; costume design, Jeffrey Kurland; sound (Dolby), Frank Graziadei; associate producer/assistant director, Thomas Reilly; casting, Juliet Taylor. Reviewed at Sony Studios, Culver City, Aug. 31, 1994. (In Telluride, Venice, Toronto, New York fests.) Running time: **99 MIN.**

David Shayne .... John Cusack
Julian Marx .... Jack Warden
Cheech .... Chazz Palminteri
Nick Valenti .... Joe Viterelli
Olive Neal .... Jennifer Tilly
Sheldon Flender .... Rob Reiner
Ellen .... Mary-Louise Parker
Helen Sinclair .... Dianne Wiest
Sid Loomis .... Harvey Fierstein
Warner Purcell .... Jim Broadbent
Eden Brent .... Tracey Ullman

Woody Allen works a clever twist on the Cyrano theme in "Bullets Over Broadway," a backstage comedy bolstered by healthy shots of prohibition gangster melodrama and romantic entanglements. Not all the characters in the colorful ensemble cast are well developed, and some of the subplots peter out, but constantly amusing confection keeps improving as it scoots along and result should please the Woodman's fans, even if breakout with a wider public is unlikely.

This is Allen's first indie venture away from his longtime studio affiliations, although nothing has changed aesthetically or productionwise in this Miramax release, as longtime behind-the-scenes collaborators are still on board to turn out an unusually handsome 1920s period piece.

Casting lends the film a slightly different feel, however, as Allen is absent onscreen, and, for the first time since "Stardust Memories" (with the exception of "Oedipus Wrecks" in "New York Stories"), neither Diane Keaton nor Mia Farrow turns up in an important female role.

The neurotic, hypochondriacal Allen personality is present nonetheless in the form of David Shayne (John Cusack), a young Greenwich Village playwright who rants, "I'm an artist!" and swears to his bohemian friends that he'll brook no compromise in the production of his new play.

Shayne quickly changes his tune, however, when producer Julian Marx (Jack Warden) informs him that he's found a backer for a Broad-

way opening of "God of Our Fathers," with the proviso that the man's girlfriend play a prominent role.

Persuaded of the wisdom of this course, Shayne, who also insists on directing, goes along with the arrangement, but practically has a seizure when he meets the "actress," Olive Neal (Jennifer Tilly), a goo-voiced bimbo who's supposed to play a psychiatrist even though she doesn't know what "masochistic" means and her only qualification for the stage is that she's the mistress of bigtime mobster Nick Valenti (Joe Viterelli).

Faced with the consequences of his decision, Shayne wakes up at night shrieking, "I sold out! I'm a whore!" and must also tolerate the critical barbs of Olive's thuggish bodyguard, Cheech (Chazz Palminteri), who sits in on all rehearsals to keep an eye on Olive.

The shenanigans of these characters, as well as the rest of the play's cast, including Jim Broadbent, Tracey Ullman and grande dame leading lady Dianne Wiest, who takes an intense personal interest in Shayne, consume most of the seriocomic attention as the play wends its way, first to Boston, then back to New York.

Giving the confection some unexpected resonance are, initially, some surprising sparks between fastidious leading man Warner Purcell (Broadbent, in what might once have been called the Denholm Elliott role) and Olive, and, much more important, the evolution of Palminteri's character.

A street hoodlum and hit man, Cheech begins by telling Shayne, "You don't write like people talk," and gradually makes secret contributions to the play-in-progress that end up saving it from major flopdom. The discovery of one man's artistry with the simultaneous uncovering of another's lack of same gives the largely artificial piece some pleasing weight, something aided immeasurably by Palminteri's thoroughly delightful performance.

Cusack functions as the director's stand-in right down to the frantic complaining and flailing mannerisms, and Tilly, Viterelli, Warden and Broadbent all deliver expert comic turns.

Wiest is initially on the money as the theatrical prima donna with a creeping Norma Desmond complex, but role acquires no further dimension as matters progress, and her romance with Shayne seems rote. Ullman's part is even more sketchily written, and Mary-Louise Parker does what little she can on the sidelines as Shayne's g.f. Rob Reiner has a couple of good scenes as a Village philosopher.

Santo Loquasto's opulent production design creates magnificent period backdrops for the careening

action, Jeffrey Kurland's costumes complement them perfectly, and Carlo Di Palma's warm lensing bathes everything in a red-and-yellow glow. In its mixing of show-biz and gangsters, this is a nice companion piece to Allen's "Broadway Danny Rose," and about as amusing.
                                    —_Todd McCarthy_

VANYA ON 42ND STREET

A Sony Pictures Classics release of a Fred Berner presentation produced in association with Laura Pels Prods. and New Media Finance. Produced by Berner. Directed by Louis Malle. Theater director, Andre Gregory. Adapted from Anton Chekhov's "Uncle Vanya" by David Mamet. Camera (DuArt color), Declan Quinn; editor, Nancy Baker; music, Joshua Redman; production design, Eugene Lee; costume design, Gary Jones; sound, Tod A. Maitland; associate producer, Alysse Bezahler; assistant director, Gary Marcus. Reviewed at Telluride Film Festival, Sept. 3, 1994. (Also in Venice, Toronto fests.) Running time: **119 MIN.**

Vanya .... Wallace Shawn
Yelena .... Julianne Moore
Sonya .... Brooke Smith
Dr. Astrov .... Larry Pine
Serybryakov .... George Gaynes
Maman .... Lynn Cohen
Marina .... Phoebe Brand
Waffles .... Jerry Mayer
Mrs. Chao .... Madhur Jaffrey
Himself .... Andre Gregory

The performances are precise, the language is alive and well spoken and the setting is striking, but "Vanya on 42nd Street" still suffers rather heavily from the limitations of filmed theater. It's a prestige item for the fest and arthouse circuit and, later, a strong cable, video and public TV attraction.

Reuniting with Andre Gregory 13 years after their surprise success "My Dinner With Andre," Louis Malle has unobtrusively recorded a theater piece that Gregory and this cast rehearsed and performed, on and off, for more than four years. Working from an adaptation of Chekhov's classic drama done by David Mamet from a literal translation, Gregory and his actors continued to explore the depths of the timeless work through periodic rehearsals, improvisations and informal performances before limited audiences at the decaying Victory Theater off Times Square.

To make the film, the company moved to the nearby New Amsterdam Theater, the former home of the "Ziegfeld Follies," now being renovated at enormous cost by Disney. As seen here, however, the facility couldn't be more of a wreck, an utterly dilapidated shell so dangerous they weren't even allowed on-

stage, and were forced to clear a performance area in the orchestra.

As it happens, the exquisite ruin provides a clever background correlative to the play's theme of faded splendor and lost possibilities. Initial footage of the cast arriving amidst the squalor of 42nd Street segues with beguiling seamlessness into a run-through of the play, which depicts the fraying of a landed Russian family around the turn of the century.

Wallace Shawn is the 47-year-old Vanya, who declares, "I've squandered my past on nonsense" and vainly pursues the affections of the beautiful Yelena (Julianne Moore), who is faithfully married to aging scientist and writer Serybryakov (George Gaynes). Latter's daughter by his first marriage, Sonya (Brooke Smith), pines for a frequent visitor to the estate, Dr. Astrov (Larry Pine), while other members of the family and staff have their say about the unhappy goings-on at key moments along the way.

Mamet's dialogue, while not as modern as that of his own plays, spills nicely out of the mouths of these actors, all of whom seem quite at home with their characters. Students of the theater and acting will find plenty here that's absorbing, while Chekhov purists will no doubt take exception to certain abridgements and liberties with the text, which carries potent parallels to current times in its thematic concern for the environment and, more broadly, the collapse of civilization as its characters have known it.

But more casually interested viewers may well find this simply too dry an exercise, too much a staged piece and not enough of a movie. No matter how articulate the performances and clever the setting, the lack of a true visual dimension robs the film not only of scenic elements but of an interpretive dimension in cinema terms. What may well have been mesmerizing in live performance becomes increasingly claustrophobic and even exasperating on the screen, and one is finally left with the impression of a highly skilled run-through rather than a fully realized production.

Less mannered than usual, Shawn is a convincingly self-loathing Vanya, and Moore is a vibrant Yelena, full of laughter and assured self-justification. Gaynes impressively brings equal measures of egotism, impatience and decay to bear on his Serybryakov, Pine proves an appealing Astrov, and Smith provides the piece with its most poignant moments as Sonya.

Shot in two weeks last May, film looks and sounds good, although Declan Quinn's very mobile camerawork displays some curious wavering at times. —_Todd McCarthy_

BLUE SKY

An Orion release of a Robert H. Solo production. Produced by Solo. Co-producer, Lynn Arost. Directed by Tony Richardson. Screenplay, Rama Laurie Stagner, Arlene Sarner, Jerry Leichtling, story by Stagner. Camera (CFI color; Deluxe prints), Steve Yaconelli; editor, Robert K. Lambert; music, Jack Nitzsche; production design, Timian Alsaker; art direction, Gary John Constable; set decoration, Leslie Rollins; costume design, Jane Robinson; sound (Dolby), Jacob Goldstein, Susumu Tokunow; supervising producer, John G. Wilson; associate producer, Stagner; assistant director, Thomas J. Mack; second unit director, Lambert; casting, Lynn Stalmaster. Reviewed at Orion screening room, L.A., Aug. 24, 1994. (In Toronto Film Festival.) MPAA Rating: PG-13. Running time: **101 MIN.**

Carly Marshall	Jessica Lange
Hank Marshall	Tommy Lee Jones
Vince Johnson	Powers Boothe
Vera Johnson	Carrie Snodgress
Alex Marshall	Amy Locane
Glenn Johnson	Chris O'Donnell
Ray Stevens	Mitchell Ryan
Colonel Mike Anwalt	Dale Dye
Ned Owens	Tim Scott
Lydia	Annie Ross
Becky Marshall	Anna Klemp

Two fine actors give among the best performances of their careers in "Blue Sky," a long-on-the-shelf Orion picture that deserves a good shot at a theatrical life before being put out to video pasture. This 1991 production was the last film directed by Tony Richardson, and it happens to be one of the more creditable efforts of the latter part of his career. The old-fashioned but lively character study of a long-married military couple having midlife trouble will go nowhere without distrib support and some fine reviews, but a lucky break would give it a chance at sleeper status.

Jessica Lange makes the most of an opportunity at a full-blown star turn as Carly Marshall, the wife of Army scientist Hank Marshall (Tommy Lee Jones), whose irrepressible sensuality and wild spirit can't be reined in even by the military. It's the early 1960s, and at the outset she friskily teases and tempts the local officers in Hawaii with her Brigitte Bardot get-up, only to shortly move into a Marilyn Monroe phase.

In fact, Bardot and Monroe are about the only other actresses one can imagine pulling off such a role as well as Lange has. Bardot, in fact, did it in "And God Created Woman," laying to waste every man on the horizon, and Monroe could easily have been the object of the comment made by another military wife about Carly: "Women like you are the reason men like women in the first place."

When Hank, Carly and their two girls are transferred to a base in Alabama, the "litter box" they are forced to live in sends Carly into a deep funk. It becomes clear that the even-keeled Hank is the only person who understands Carly and can calm her down, but her violent mood swings are nevertheless alarming, especially to older daughter Alex (Amy Locane), who's just entered troublesome teendom.

While Hank is forced to cope with the Army's gung-ho nuclear-test fanatics, Carly tries to integrate herself into femme life on the base, but she's a blond bombshell at a tea party and bound to cause trouble. Sure enough, when Hank bows out of twirling her around at a big social, Carly gets carried away on the dance floor with the camp's commanding officer, Vince Johnson (Powers Boothe), and the seeds are surely planted for future trouble.

Taking care of a life force such as Carly is clearly a full-time job, so when Hank is sent to Nevada for two weeks to observe an underground nuclear test, the door is opened for Vince to prey upon Carly's obvious weakness. Unfortunately, their late-night tryst is witnessed by Alex and her new beau, Vince's son Glenn (Chris O'Donnell), and all hell breaks loose on the base.

Rama Laurie Stagner's semi-autobiographical original story, which she cooked into a lively screenplay with help from Arlene Sarner and Jerry Leichtling, pushes into rather more dubious and murky territory from this point on. When Hank tries to reveal the fact that two civilians were exposed to radiation during the test explosion, the Army comes down hard, committing him to a hospital for "observation" and threatening him with court-martial. Carly then takes matters into her own hands, suddenly becoming a crusader for full disclosure of military secrets and coverups and fighting to save her husband from career oblivion or worse. Melodramatic contrivances of the last act are somewhat hard to swallow, but the lead characters have generated such good will up to this point that the tendency is to grant them the benefit of the doubt and wish them the best.

Richardson, who died in 1991 shortly after completing the picture, mounted the action in a visually straightforward, unflashy manner, concentrating his attention where it counted, on the performances. Result is very much like a solid melodrama from the 1950s, and gratifyingly so — a sharply focused piece in which a small number of characters define themselves in terms of their interaction within well-proscribed physical and social limits. Pic feels like a throwback, but in a refreshing way.

While Lange has the showy role, with almost unlimited opportunities to emote and strut her stuff, which she does magnificently and with total abandon, Jones must let his characterization take shape more gradually. But his Hank ultimately emerges as fully three-dimensional as does his wife, with the actor demonstrating terrific control and nuance on a tight rein.

Boothe and Carrie Snodgress are very good as the base's first couple, while Locane and O'Donnell, both of whom have matured significantly since the pic was made, fill the bill nicely as the sparking adolescents.

Production values are modest but serviceable. —*Todd McCarthy*

TIMECOP

A Universal release of a Largo Entertainment presentation in association with JVC Entertainment of a Signature/Renaissance/Dark Horse production. Produced by Moshe Diamant, Sam Raimi, Robert Tapert. Executive producer, Mike Richardson. Co-producers, Todd Moyer, Marilyn Vance. Line producer, David A. Shepherd. Directed by Peter Hyams. Screenplay, Mark Verheiden; story by Richardson, Verheiden, based upon the comic series created by Richardson, Verheiden. Camera (Deluxe color), Hyams; editor, Steven Kemper; music, Mark Isham; production design, Philip Harrison; art direction, Richard Hudolin; set decoration, Rose Marie McSherry, Ann Marie Corbett; costume design, Dan Lester; sound (DTS), Eric Batut; visual effects supervisor, Gregory L. McMurry; special effects coordinator, John Thomas; visual consultant, Syd Mead; stunt coordinator, Glenn Randall; associate producers, Mark Scoon, Richard G. Murphy; casting, Penny Perry. Reviewed at Universal Studios screening room, Universal City, Sept. 6, 1994. MPAA Rating: R. Running time: **98 MIN.**

Walker	Jean-Claude Van Damme
Melissa	Mia Sara
McComb	Ron Silver
Matuzak	Bruce McGill
Fielding	Gloria Reuben
Ricky	Scott Bellis
Atwood	Jason Schombing

Despite a marketable concept and first-rate production values, director Peter Hyams delivers a curiously flat sci-fi comic-book actioner starring the ever limber Jean-Claude Van Damme. While an eye-catching trailer and plenty of fancy footwork for Van Damme fans suggest a strong opening, "Timecop" seems unlikely to cross over beyond that audience and get more casual genre fans to give it the time of day.

That's something of a disappointment for those who harbored high expectations for the movie, especially after the strong summer haul by Dark Horse Entertainment's previous creation, "The Mask."

Like most time-travel stories, this one must grapple with the usual absurdities and contradictions about changing the past to affect the present — a head-scratcher that certainly didn't inhibit the enjoyability of the "Terminator" movies, from which the filmmakers have obviously drawn some inspiration.

Still, for the most part, Hyams' lackluster direction and the repetitive quality of the action sequences squander an intriguing premise and impressive production design, leaving few moments that elicit the sort of "Wow!" response such fare needs to prosper.

Van Damme plays Max Walker, a D.C. cop whose wife (Mia Sara) is apparently murdered in an explosion. Ten years later, in 2004, we find Walker functioning as a "timecop," policing those who have gone back in time to strike it rich or influence the course of history.

Walker busts his former partner, for example, trying to cash in on the Depression, in the process discovering that the real mastermind behind the time-crime wave is the U.S. senator (Ron Silver) responsible for overseeing the enforcement program — a slick operator seeking to use his ill-gotten gains to finance a run for the presidency.

That crisscrossing, cat-and-mouse chase through time has its moments, but the script by comic creator Mark Verheiden (from a story crafted with exec producer Mike Richardson) has a hard time connecting the strands. In the same vein, while there's no shortage of mayhem, the time-traveling conundrum actually ends up deadening the movie's suspense, since the playing field and stakes keep changing.

Strictly in terms of the action, Hyams also milks the fight scenes too long (how many kicks to the face can one person take?), drawing out sequence after sequence in which someone walks down a corridor waiting to get rapped over the head.

In addition, Hyams (who as usual functioned as his own cinematographer) ends up shooting too much action in the dark, filming one brawl in a driving rainstorm so murky it's difficult to keep track of who's pummeling whom.

The same largely goes for the movie's particular sci-fi rules, with talk about the ramifications of altering the past seemingly tossed aside as soon as those guidelines become inconvenient. Verheiden does provide a few clever quips and twists in his screenplay, but nothing to match the closing-credit flourish of playing the song "Time Won't Let Me."

Van Damme acquits himself well, though the more acting he gets to do the more violence his accent inflicts on the English language. Silver proves a glib but not particularly menacing villain through no fault of his own, while Sara and newcomer Gloria Reuben are attractive if sparsely used as the female leads.

Aside from Van Damme's calisthenics, pic's principal attributes are

September 12, 1994 (Cont.)

its special effects and visual style, including a ripple-like wave caused as travelers pop in and out of time. But the technique bears a striking resemblance to the liquid cyborg in "Terminator 2: Judgment Day," somewhat diminishing its impact.

—Brian Lowry

IMAGINARY CRIMES

A Warner Bros. release of a Morgan Creek production. Produced by James G. Robinson. Executive producers, Gary Barber, Ted Field, Robert W. Cort. Co-producers, Stan Wlodkowski, Kristine Johnson, Davia Nelson. Directed by Anthony Drazen. Screenplay, Johnson, Nelson, based on the book by Sheila Ballantyne. Camera (Technicolor), John J. Campbell; editor, Elizabeth Kling; music, Stephen Endelman; production design, Joseph T. Garrity; art direction, Pat Tagliaferro; costume design, Susan Lyall; sound (Dolby), Mark Ulano; assistant director, Linda Fox; casting, Deborah Aquila, Jane Shannon. Reviewed at Loews Copley Place, Boston, Aug. 24, 1994. (In Boston Film Festival.) MPAA Rating: PG. Running time: **104 MIN.**

Ray Weiler	Harvey Keitel
Sonya	Fairuza Balk
Valery	Kelly Lynch
Mr. Webster	Vincent D'Onofrio
Abigail Tate	Diane Baker
Jarvis	Chris Penn
Margaret	Amber Benson
Greta	Elisabeth Moss
Eddie	Seymour Cassel
Ginny Rucklehaus	Annette O'Toole

This teenage girl coming-of-age story boasts some fine performances, but is weakened by an overly familiar plot. Lukewarm reviews and lack of audience hook for this Boston Film Festival opener will lead to rough sledding at the fall B.O.

Tale opens with Sonya Weiler (Fairuza Balk) looking back on her senior year of high school in 1962 Portland, Ore. Her mother (played by Kelly Lynch in flashback) has succumbed to cancer. Her father, Ray (Harvey Keitel), is a well-meaning ne'er-do-well whose get-rich-quick schemes leave a lot of angry people in their wake.

Keeping a promise to his wife, Ray enrolls Sonya at an exclusive girl's school for her senior year, even though it's questionable whether he will be able to pay for it. There she falls under the tutelage of a well-meaning English teacher (Vincent D'Onofrio) who encourages her writing as well as her ambitions to go to college.

Between the bill collectors and the trouble that Ray creates for himself and a young sister (Elisabeth Moss) with her own history of problems, Sonya has her hands full. Story concerns how she endures her travails and eventually emerges a stronger person. We've seen all this before in countless dramas, right down to the sympathetic teacher — who invariably teaches English rather than math or science.

Film's key asset is the acting, particularly the perfs by Balk and Lynch. Balk is clearly up to the demands of the role, and continues to make the transition from child actress ("Return to Oz") to young adult parts. Lynch is superb in her few scenes as the mother who has been dealt several bad hands by life.

Keitel is stuck with the thankless role of a man who begins as a well-intentioned lout and somehow manages to save himself from his worst mistake at story's end, but is otherwise unchanged. The most remarkable achievement in his performance is his accent, scrubbed of every trace of New York and the big city. He successfully portrays a small-time, small-town hustler who, for all his tough talk, would be eaten alive on the real mean streets.

Good use is made of the Oregon locale, and John Campbell's cinematography captures the damp of the seasons and grimness of the Weiler family's series of homes. Graduation scene, though, is obviously shot in fall, with autumn trees incongruous during a springtime ritual.

—Daniel M. Kimmel

TRIAL BY JURY

James G. Robinson presents a Warner Bros. release of a Morgan Creek production. Produced by Robinson, Chris Meledandri, Mark Gordon. Executive producer, Gary Barber. Directed by Heywood Gould. Screenplay, Jordan Katz, Gould. Camera, Frederick Elmes; editor, Joel Goodman; music, Terence Blanchard; production design, David Chapman; art direction, Barbra Matis; set decoration, Steve Shewchuk; sound, (Dolby) Bill Daly; line producer, Michael MacDonald; assistant director, Albert Shapiro; casting, Heidi Levitt. Reviewed at Technicolor, L.A., Sept. 8, 1994. MPAA Rating: R. Running time: **92 MIN.**

Valerie	Joanne Whalley-Kilmer
Pirone	Armand Assante
Graham	Gabriel Byrne
Vesey	William Hurt
Wanda	Kathleen Quinlan
Jane Lyle	Margaret Whitton
John Boyle	Ed Lauter
Leo Greco	Richard Portnow
Johnny Verona	Joe Santos
Emmett	Stuart Whitman

Earlier this year, Morgan Creek hit the jackpot with the Jim Carrey breakthrough "Ace Ventura: Pet Detective." Whatever the secret of that film's appeal, B.O. lightning will not strike again with Morgan Creek's courtroom melodrama "Trial by Jury," even if at times the pic draws bigger laughs than "Ace."

Unfortunately, the howls elicited by "Jury" are all unintentional, the result of a preposterous, cliche-ridden screenplay co-authored by Jordan Katz and director Heywood Gould. Even charismatic top-rank stars like William Hurt, Gabriel

Byrne and Joanne Whalley-Kilmer can't resuscitate this leaden-paced legal thriller. The script's troubles begin immediately, when the key government witness in the murder and racketeering trial of John Gotti-like crime boss Rusty Pirone (Armand Assante) is murdered in an unbelievable fashion. Either the cops protecting the witness are the worst boys in blue since the Keystone days, or the writers can't find a way to jump-start a story that seems belabored only minutes after the opening credits.

The only saving grace at the outset is Kathleen Quinlan's nice 'n' nasty turn as Wanda, a hard-bitten hooker/contract killer. That her character is never developed beyond her leather mini, tattoos and stiletto is only one of the pic's wasted assets.

Trying hard to put Pirone away is Byrne's U.S. Attorney Daniel Graham, laboring in a stock role as a crusading good boy from the same bad neighborhood as Pirone. All that's missing is Pat O'Brien as the kindly priest and the Bowery Boys for local color and comic relief. Sad to report, help like Leo Gorcey and Huntz Hall never arrives.

Instead, Valerie Alston (Whalley-Kilmer) strolls into the trial, an idealistic single mom who runs an antique clothing store in Manhattan, oblivious to the fact that she's been picked for the most dangerous jury duty assignment since, well, the John Gotti trial. She wakes up to the possibility that sending a mob boss to the gas chamber could be hazardous to her health only after disgraced ex-cop Tommy Vesey (Hurt) and a gang of thugs straight out of "Mod Squad" kidnap her in broad daylight. The plan is to scare Alston into hanging up the jury.

An unrequited love story of sorts develops between Vesey and Alston, and Pirone also falls for the pert brunette, though his affection is deadly and propelled by self-interest. To prove his power over her, he pays a nocturnal visit to her apartment, and he's so over-the-top evil that he could have turned into a bat as he left.

By the pic's draggy third act, the legal tables are turned upside down, and the denouement involves Alston's conversion from well-meaning citizen into the hit-mom from hell.

With cinematographer Frederick Elmes' atmospheric lensing, Hurt and Quinlan's dark turns as menacing mob torpedoes, and enough laughable dialogue to fill a camp film festival, all "Jury" needed was a director willing to take the film all the way into the realm of courtroom-thriller parody. Director Gould, the writer behind the Tom Cruise starrer "Cocktail," apparently didn't see the possibilities in the frothy concoction he's cooked up here with co-writer Katz. Just

imagine the opportunities in a pic with a crime boss named Rusty.

Compared with some of television's dramatically compelling, diligently researched courtroom dramas like "Law & Order," film auds will send this pic straight to the video slammer. *—Steven Gaydos*

THE SHAWSHANK REDEMPTION

A Columbia release of a Castle Rock Entertainment production. Produced by Niki Marvin. Executive producers, Liz Glotzer, David Lester. Directed by Frank Darabont. Screenplay, Darabont, based on the short novel by Stephen King. Camera (Technicolor), Roger Deakins; editor, Richard Francis-Bruce; music, Thomas Newman; production design, Terence Marsh; art direction, Peter Smith; set decoration, Michael Sierton; costume design, Elizabeth McBride; sound (Dolby), Willie Burton; assistant director, John R. Woodward; casting, Deborah Aquila. Reviewed at AMC Century City, L.A., Aug. 24, 1994. (In Toronto Film Festival.) MPAA Rating: R. Running time: **142 MIN.**

Andy Dufresne	Tim Robbins
Ellis Boy "Red" Redding	Morgan Freeman
Warden Samuel Norton	Bob Gunton
Heywood	William Sadler
Capt. Byron Hadley	Clancy Brown
Tommy Williams	Gil Bellows
Brooks Hatlen	James Whitmore
Bogs Diamond	Mark Rolston
D.A.	Jeffrey DeMunn

There's a painstaking exactness to "The Shawshank Redemption" that is both laudable and exhausting. The 19 years that the film's protagonist spends behind prison walls is a term shared by the audience. It's vivid, grueling and painful, and passes with the appropriate tedium and sudden bursts of horror that one imagines reflect the true nature of incarceration.

Mostly one is drawn along by the fascinating portrait and the innate humanity of its inmate principals. But it's a long, serious haul (albeit leavened by humor and the unexpected) that will put a crimp in the pic's mainstream acceptance. Definitely a film requiring careful nurturing, "Shawshank" will need critical kudos and year-end honors to maintain slow but consistent box office.

The saga begins in 1947, when bank vice president Andy Dufresne (Tim Robbins) goes on trial for the murder of his wife and her lover. Though he strenuously maintains his innocence, his dispassionate demeanor grates on the court. Circumstantial evidence proves enough to land him in Shawshank Prison with two concurrent life sentences.

September 12, 1994 (Cont.)

While it's unquestionably Andy's story, the chronicle is related in voiceover by "Red" (Morgan Freeman), a lifer who's set himself up as someone who can get "things" from the outside. He marvels at the new man's tenacity, knowing intrinsically that Andy is different and that he likes him, quirks and all.

While the film pays close attention to such requisite matters as sexual assault, staff brutality and the human capacity to survive, it has something quite different on its mind. It's consumed by circumstance and life's little ironies, which occur even in prison.

The turning point for Andy and his cronies is a bit of conversation captured during a work detail. A guard bemoans the fact that Uncle Sam will take a healthy bite of a recently deceased relative's legacy. The ex-banker plucks up his courage and tells him how to keep the windfall. For a moment it's like Androcles pulling the thorn from the lion's paw.

Soon Andy is put to work in all manner of financial activity. He is Warden Norton's (Bob Gunton) crown jewel and the source of both an enhanced public image for the man and a quietly acquired personal fortune. It's not lost on the convicted murderer that he had to enter prison to learn dishonesty.

Gaining a more comfortable life behind bars proves a double-edged sword. The warden cannot afford to have Andy paroled. The man knows too much, and he is too valuable an asset. So, when the prospect of the truth rears its head, extreme measures come into play.

Ultimately, "The Shawshank Redemption" is about the dominance of real justice. That element of the narrative keeps the movie from descending into abject resignation.

Writer/director Frank Darabont adapts his source material with sly acuity. It's a fiendishly clever construct in which seemingly oblique words or incidents prove to have fierce resonance. Darabont errs only when he digresses too long on a supporting character or embellishes a secondary story.

Central to the film's success is a riveting, unfussy performance from Robbins. Precise, honest and seamless, it appears virtually uncalculated. It is the anchor keeping the piece from foundering.

Freeman has the showier role, allowing him a grace and dignity that come naturally. It's a testament to his craft that the performance is never banal. Supporting work is uniformly strong, with Gunton and Clancy Brown, as a vicious guard, extremely credible in their villainy.

Tech credits are strong, with Roger Deakins' images and Thomas Newman's original score providing just the right balance between the somber and the absurd. Terence Marsh's sets — on an actual prison location — capture the mustiness and permanence of the environment with aplomb.

A testament to the human spirit, the film is a rough diamond. Its languors are small quibbles in an otherwise estimable and haunting entertainment. —*Leonard Klady*

THE EAGLE SHOOTING HEROES: DONG CHENG XI JIU
(SEDIU YINGHUNG TSUN TSI DUNG SING SAI TSAU)
(HONG KONG)

A Jet Tone Prod./Scholar Films production. Produced by Tsai Sung-lin. Executive producer, Wong Kar-wai. Directed by Jeff Lau. Action director, Sammo Hung. Screenplay, uncredited, based on characters from the novel "The Eagle Shooting Heroes" by Louis Cha. Camera (color), Peter Pau; editor, Kai Kit-wai; music, James Wong; production design, William Chang; art direction, Alfred Lau; costume design, Charles Leung, Grace Lu; sound, Leung Kar-leun; special effects, Ting Yuen-tai, Tang Wai-yuk; associate producers, Norman, Jacky Pang; assistant directors, Shek Siu-lun, Law Chi-leung; second unit camera, Lau Wai-keung. Reviewed on vidcassette, Aug. 20, 1994. (In Toronto Film Festival.) Running time: **116 MIN.**

Wang Yao-shih .... Leslie Cheung
Third
  Princess .... Brigitte Lin Ching-hsia
Tuan Wang-yeh ... Tony Leung Kar-fai
Hung Chi .... Jacky Cheung
Ou-yang Feng ... Tony Leung Chiu-wai
Chou Po-tung .... Carina Liu
Imperial Master .... Maggie Cheung
Wang's Sweetheart .... Joey Wang
Ou-yang Feng's Cousin ... Veronica Yip
Wang Chung-yang,
  the Taoist .... Kenny Bee
(Cantonese and Taiwanese dialogue)

This crazed, hyperactive takeoff of Hong Kong martial arts costumers will entertain Asian buffs and leave most others slack-jawed at its anything-goes chutzpah. Central Asian-set extravaganza could easily be retitled "Carry On Up the Seraglio."

Cast with some of the biggest names in the H.K. industry, and trading on every cliche of the genre, the movie takes a handful of well-known characters from Louis Cha's late-'50s classic swordplay novel "The Eagle Shooting Heroes" and spins a loony story around their exploits when younger.

As in the sleeper "92 Legendary La Rose Noire," on which helmer Jeff Lau worked uncredited, most of the in-jokes and refs will pass non-buffs by, but there's enough lunacy on hand for latenight fest auds to groove on. Pic was exec produced by Lau's partner in Jet Tone, cult fave Wong Kar-wai, and the star lineup is virtually identical to Wong's long-awaited martial arts magnum opus, "Ashes of Time."

Multistrand plot spins on two mad Taiwanese (Tony Leung Chiu-wai, Veronica Yip) who are after the imperial jade seal held by Third Princess (Brigitte Lin Ching-hsia). She teams up with a handsome young swordsman (Leslie Cheung) to find an all-powerful kung fu manual; shadowing them is his jealous sweetheart (Joey Wang), herself pursued by a beggar king (Jacky Cheung) claiming to be her long-lost cousin.

Also wandering around the plot is an effete Indian Buddhist (Tony Leung Kar-fai, from "The Lover") in search of true love and nirvana; a horny gay Taoist (played in male drag by actress Carina Liu) out to revenge the death of his adored master (Kenny Bee); and a glam court magician (Maggie Cheung).

Complex story, in which everyone seems related to everyone else, also finds time for gay in-jokes, satire of '50s swordplay movies and a witty riff on classics like "Dragon Gate Inn," with all the cast gathering at the same hostelry.

Most of the fun for buffs is seeing big names sending up their image with pratfalls and other shtick. For general viewers, the action sequences (directed by veteran Sammo Hung) are entertaining enough, with more wire work and trampolining than Barnum & Bailey.

After a fast-moving first half-hour, movie bogs down with two extended sequences that overstay their welcome. Pic later recovers its breath, but still pushes its luck at almost two hours.

Technically, the film lacks the polish of the best H.K. fare, and English subtitles poorly render the jokey dialogue.

Pic clocked a tony $HK22 million ($3 million) on local release at the peak of the costume martial arts boom in early '93. —*Derek Elley*

WHALE MUSIC

An Alliance release of an Alliance/Cape Scott Motion Pictures production. Produced by Raymond Massey, Steven DeNure. Executive producers, Robert Lantos, David Hauka. Directed by Richard J. Lewis. Screenplay, Paul Quarrington, Lewis, based upon the novel by Quarrington. Camera (Alpha Cine), Vic Sarin; underwater photography, Craig Ibbotson; editor, Richard Martin; music, George Blondheim; whale music, Rheostatics; production design, Rex Raglan; art direction, Charles Leitrants; costume design, Toni Burroughs-Rutter; sound (Ultra-Stereo), Daryl Powell; assistant director, Laurence Horricks; casting, John Buchan, Michelle Allan. Reviewed at Toronto Film Festival, Sept. 8, 1994. Running time: **100 MIN.**

Desmond Howl .... Maury Chaykin
Claire Lowe .... Cyndy Preston
Fay Ginzburg-Howl .... Jennifer Dale
Kenneth Sexston .... Kenneth Welsh
Daniel Howl .... Paul Gross
Mookie Saunders .... Blu Mankuma
Sal Goneau .... Alan Jordan

Curtain raiser for the Toronto film fest, "Whale Music" is an offbeat, tuneful romance just a shade too quirky to swim in the mainstream. The oddball saga of a burned-out rock star and the tough runaway who invades his tumble-down estate has decided artistic assets but doesn't connect on an emotional level. Best theatrical prospects are in the margins, with offshore appeal likely to outperform domestic returns.

Somewhere in the Pacific Northwest, Desmond Howl (Maury Chaykin) has retreated from the grind of recording studios and concert tours. The run-down manor he inhabits (thanks to rich residual checks) mirrors his own unkempt appearance. But in the midst of decay, the childlike music genius has installed a state-of-the-art recording studio and devotes himself to creating a masterwork — a symphonic piece for whales. The ramshackle harmony threatens to come undone with the arrival of Claire (Cyndy Preston), a rather frank young woman on the run from the law. The surprise is that Howl allows her into his realm and, slowly but steadily, finds her presence a refreshing, almost compulsory aspect of his life.

The film painstakingly details not only the evolution of Howl's composition but also the growing attachment between two seemingly unsuited people. It's truly an instance where you can't help but cheer on these unlikely partners in extraordinary circumstances.

September 12, 1994 (Cont.)

The potential union is muddied by the myriad demons who haunt Desmond — people both living and dead who are fighting for a piece of him. They include Fay (Jennifer Dale), his ex-wife bent on getting him to sell the house, and Kenneth (Kenneth Welsh), the recording exec who owns every note he creates. Most disturbing is an unresolved problem between Howl and his brother (Paul Gross), his singing partner who died in an auto accident that may or may not have been a suicide. He pops up repeatedly in chilling, provocative hallucinations.

While the elements of "Whale Music" are promising, they never coalesce with enough impact to reach a broad audience, although the two central performers work hard to make us care about their plight. Chaykin is a particular standout in a role that literally and figuratively strips him naked for the camera. It's his work that elevates the film from minor appeal to soul-stirring material.

But even Chaykin cannot overcome several key shortcomings. The film's song score just isn't of a quality to convince viewers Howl is a major talent. The narrative, too, is diluted by a split focus in which the filmmaker feels compelled to give inordinate weight to secondary concerns.

While modest in budget, the film has a first-rate look and exceptional, effective sound design. But first-time feature director Richard J. Lewis fails to maintain a distinct focus and allows his pacing to falter. It's the goodwill generated by Chaykin's virtually defenseless character that keeps our interest through the narrative lulls.

An unquestionable marketing challenge, "Whale Music" will hit a chord with a select audience. Its commercial prospects, however, are as fragile as the characters it portrays. *—Leonard Klady*

BEFORE THE RAIN

(BRITISH-FRENCH-MACEDONIAN)

> A Mikado release (Italy) of an Aim Prods. (U.K.)/Noe Prods. (France)/Vardar Film (Macedonia) coproduction, in association with British Screen Finance, the European Coproduction Fund (UK). (International sales: PolyGram Film Intl. Classics.) Produced by Judy Counihan, Cedomir Kolar, Sam Taylor, Cat Villiers. Coproducers, Frederique Dumas, Marc Baschet, Gorjan Tozija. Directed, written by Milcho Manchevski. Camera (color; Technovision widescreen), Manuel Teran; editor, Nick Gaster; music, Anastasia; production design, Sharon Lamofsky, David Munns; associate producers, Sheila Fraser Milne, David Redman. Reviewed at Venice Film Festival (competing), Sept. 5, 1994. Running time: **115 MIN.**
> Anne .... Katrin Cartlidge
> Aleksandar .... Rade Serbedzija
> Kiril .... Gregoire Colin
> Zamira .... Labina Mitevska
> Hana .... Silvija Stojanovska

"**B**efore the Rain" is a visually and narratively stunning tale in three parts, set between modern London and the timeless hills of Macedonia, in the former Yugoslavia. Through a parable of intertwined lives, it attempts to answer the tragic riddle of why the Balkan states are perpetually at war. High production values, and the fact that a third of the film is shot in good Queen's English, should help this heartfelt, poetic and violently anti-violent film find its way to appreciative Western arthouse auds.

"Rain," the first feature directed by Macedonian-born helmer Milcho Manchevski (now a New York resident and director of music vids), is also the first film made in the newly declared republic of Macedonia.

Bordering Greece (which hotly disputes its very name), Albania, Bulgaria and Serbia, the mountainous country is shown to be in danger of becoming the site of the next Balkan bloodbath. But unlike many observers who blame the war in the former Yugoslavia on political pressures, Manchevski depicts senseless ethnic hatred as endemic to the region.

Film is divided into three parts. In "Words," the young Greek Orthodox monk Kiril (Gregoire Colin), living in an ancient monastery, shelters and hides an Albanian girl, Zamira (Labina Mitevska), even though they can't understand each other's language.

A band of machine-gun-wielding roughnecks bursts into the monastery looking for her, claiming she killed their brother. Kiril and Zamira escape together, but are intercepted by the girl's Muslim relatives. They shoot her down in cold blood, rather than let her go off with a Christian.

After the aching beauty of the Macedonian landscape with its monasteries, churches and people who appear lifted from another century, the modernity of the second episode, "Faces," comes as a shock.

Anne (Katrin Cartlidge), who works in a London photo agency, is torn between her Macedonian lover, Aleksandar (Rade Serbedzija), a Pulitzer Prize-winning war photographer, and her sweet, boring husband, Nick (Jay Villiers.)

Before she can make up her mind between them, Aleksandar takes off for Macedonia and Nick dies in an absurd shootout in a restaurant.

"Pictures" takes the story back to Macedonia and brings the threads together. Aleksandar returns to his native village, where he's determined to spend the rest of his life forgetting the horrors of taking photographs on the front line.

But the rumblings of war have already infected the once-peaceful Christian villagers: They treat their Albanian neighbors, who are Muslims, as enemies now. Trigger-happy boys with automatic weapons bar Aleksandar's way when he goes to see his boyhood love, Hana (Silvija Stojanovska).

Pic owes part of its disturbing magic to its challenging structure. All the events seem to take place at the same time, until the surprising and clever ending.

Without beating around the bush, "Rain" accuses the people themselves of starting a fratricidal war, rather than blaming politicians or the U.N.

The Macedonian part has an urgency that spills over into the London sequence, where a normal restaurant becomes the site of a massacre. It suggests that no war is limited by man-made boundaries, and no place is so far away that it is safe from danger and violence.

There is a piercing sadness in the fanaticism of hating one's neighbor which "Rain" captures very clearly. The monks who have sheltered Bosnian refugees tell the bloodthirsty avengers to turn the other cheek. "We already have," they reply. "An eye for an eye." "Might is right." "He's not one of us — I'll cut his throat." "It's time to revenge five centuries of our blood."

Actors have a strong iconic presence, in which faces are as important as speeches. Dialogue is kept to a realistic minimum. A passionate soundtrack by Anastasia provides a powerful driving force in the film. Manuel Teran's breathtaking cinematography imparts a tragic natural beauty to the landscape which, the film implies, may soon be torn apart by war. *—Deborah Young*

LITTLE ODESSA

> A Fine Line Features release (U.S.) of a New Line Cinema presentation of a Paul Webster/Addis-Wechsler production. Produced by Webster. Executive producers, Nick Wechsler, Claudia Lewis, Rolf Mittweg. Coproducer, Kerry Orent. Directed, written by James Gray. Camera (Technicolor, Foto-Kem prints; widescreen), Tom Richmond; editor, Dorian Harris; music supervisor, Dana Sano; production design, Kevin Thompson; art direction, Judy Rhee; set decoration, Charles Ford; costume design, Michael Clancy; sound (Dolby), Tom Paul; assistant director, Steve Apicella; casting, Douglas Abiel. Reviewed at Venice Film Festival (competing), Sept. 1, 1994. Running time: **98 MIN.**
> Joshua Shapira .... Tim Roth
> Reuben Shapira .... Edward Furlong
> Alla Shustervich .... Moira Kelly
> Irina Shapira .... Vanessa Redgrave
> Arkady Shapira .... Maximilian Schell
> Boris Volkoff .... Paul Guilfoyle
> Natasha .... Natasha Andreichenko
> Sasha .... David Vadim

A highly charged, coolly assured directorial bow graced by riveting work from a trio of accomplished leads, "Little Odessa" immediately etches a firm place on the map for 25-year-old New York newcomer (and University of Southern California alum) James Gray. With critical support and savvy marketing, this somberly explosive family tragedy, set against the brooding backdrop of the Mafia-plagued Russian-Jewish emigre community in Brooklyn's Brighton Beach, has the dramatic potency to stake a significant claim on upscale urban markets. Fine Line pickup world-preemed at the Venice Film Festival and is slated for U.S. release next spring.

Unlike "Reservoir Dogs," "Laws of Gravity" and any number of Scorsese-spun U.S. indie brethren that stalk parallel crime beats, Gray's mob opera eschews a canvas of aggressively drawn violence and hip dialogue constructions to focus more intently on character. The impact of its devastating denouement is consequently of a quieter, though no less visceral nature.

Contracted to erase an Iranian jeweler, Brooklyn-bred hit man Joshua Shapira (Tim Roth) returns reluctantly to the childhood neighborhood he abandoned years earlier to avoid Mafia score-settling from a previous job.

Despite having no contact with his family, word of his arrival reaches his kid brother Reuben (Edward Furlong), who eagerly tracks him down.

On learning that his mother (Vanessa Redgrave) is slowly dying from a brain tumor, Joshua goes to see her, provoking a violent reaction from his rancorous father (Maximilian Schell).

But he uses knowledge of his father's long-standing affair to force his

September 12, 1994 (Cont.)

way back into the family. While he lays plans for the hit, he almost indifferently rekindles something approaching romance with hardened neighborhood girl Alla (Moira Kelly).

As the reunited brothers' friendship evolves, Gray swiftly sets and sustains a dark-hued mood and eases in the early rumblings of momentous catastrophe to come.

Joshua's protectiveness toward his brother takes an almost envious edge as he weighs notions of his own Russian-Jewish ethnicity against what he sees as Reuben's Americanness and, perhaps, redeemability. Scripting of these ideas is at times a little fanciful, but nevertheless is successful in enhancing the complexity of both characters.

Also well developed is Joshua's relationship with Alla. Kelly stays off the obvious tough-girl route, playing her with a quiet kind of hostile moroseness.

As they lurch from a not entirely tender exchange into their initial love scene, accompanied only by ambient noise, Gray effectively conveys that both characters have little time for romantic illusions.

The Iranian contract is carried out (again with only harsh ambient noise heightening the job's cold efficiency) while Reuben watches unseen, and he later retrieves the gun. He is badly beaten by his father, who sees him heading inexorably down the same path as Joshua.

Conflict among the three cranks up menacingly to a higher wattage, further driven by the father's knowledge that the mobsters out to repay Joshua are getting closer to their target.

When Reuben gets wind of this, events build quickly to a short, sharp, annihilating climax that keeps its violence on a surprisingly low level visually. The fact that much of it can be seen coming doesn't lessen the operatically tragic scene's capacity to stun the audience.

Aside from the sometimes overemphatic use of richly portentous Russian choral music, ethnic scene-setting is subtly rendered. As the immigrant parents, both Schell and Redgrave work smoothly into the context, the former especially so, with his character covering an extended emotional field.

But their roles are secondary to those of the younger characters, and the three lead thesps turn in acutely observed work. Roth appears as a man who, in many ways, is already dead, yet with nothing more than fleeting displays of compassion he makes the character resonantly sympathetic.

Kelly also makes an indelible impression during her brief screen time. But perhaps the most striking is Furlong, whose intense gaze and fragile grace push his character under the audience's skin without artifice. His fine work here stands to beam the young thesp into a new casting orbit.

Tom Richmond's arresting widescreen lensing is high on compositional poise and low on fussy camera tricks. Frequently shot under a blanket of snow, the faded setting is given a bleak old-worldliness, and the film's look profits heavily from the constant tonal shifts brought into play via keenly judged lighting.
—*David Rooney*

HEAVENLY CREATURES
(NEW ZEALAND)

A Miramax Intl. presentation of a WingNut Films/Fontana Film Prods. co-production in association with the New Zealand Film Commission. Produced by Jim Booth. Executive producer, Hanno Huth. Co-producer, Peter Jackson. Directed by Jackson. Screenplay, Jackson, Frances Walsh. Camera (Eastman color, Cinemascope), Alun Bollinger; editor, James Selkirk; music, Peter Dasent; production design, Grant Major; art direction, Jill Cormack; costume design, Ngila Dickson; sound (Dolby), Michael Hedges; prosthetic effects, Richard Taylor; digital effects, George Port; assistant director, Carolynne Cunningham; casting, John and Ros Hubbard (U.K.), Liz Mullane (New Zealand). Reviewed at Venice Film Festival (competing), Sept. 7, 1994. Running time: **99 MIN.**
Pauline Parker .... Melanie Lynsky
Juliet Hulme .... Kate Winslet
Honora Parker .... Sarah Peirse
Hilda Hulme .... Diana Kent
Henry Hulme .... Clive Merrison
Herbert Rieper .... Simon O'Connor

Having flirted with cult favor for some time via inventively witty sci-fi and splatter excursions like "Bad Taste" and "Braindead," New Zealander Peter Jackson positions himself to be catapulted far beyond that with his startling fourth feature, "Heavenly Creatures." An exhilarating retelling of a 1950s tabloid murder, it combines original vision, a drop-dead command of the medium and a successful marriage between a dazzling, kinetic techno-show and a complex, credible portrait of the out-of-control relationship between the crime's two schoolgirl perpetrators. The sum total should prompt celestial B.O. in exclusive-release situations pitched at the young hipster bracket, with breakthrough potential hinging on stellar reviews.

The film stands to cleave auds neatly into love-it and leave-it camps, and will no doubt encounter opposition for its unrelentingly flashy bag of tricks, which some may feel crowds out psychological depth. But what's rejected in some circles as being hammered by showiness and style will be embraced in others as an adrenalin-pumping rush of inexhaustible visual creativity.

Opening with the panicked aftermath of the killing itself, Jackson makes an attention-grabbing leap from a fusty Brit newsreel of sedate downtown Christchurch, replete with cheery commentary, to a frenetic Sam Raimiesque tracking sequence in which the blood-spattered teenage girls emerge hysterical from a secluded wood.

He then backtracks to reveal the somewhat morose and short-on-self-confidence Pauline (Melanie Lynsky) being snapped out of her shell by the arrival at school of imperious English girl Juliet (Kate Winslet), who briskly provides her with a role model by mercilessly correcting the French teacher's grammar just minutes after entering the class. Voiceovers of entries from the real Pauline's diaries link the story.

The friendship quickly spirals to the level of passionate interdependence, tracking the pair's hyperactive pursuit of pleasure with manic, often menacing vigor, and sweeping the audience along to the rollicking sound of tunes sung by the girls' favorite tenor, Mario Lanza. They soon begin seeing themselves on an intellectually superior plane to everyone around them, creating an Arthurian fantasyland which is home to two lovers and their remorseless, mass-murdering son.

Jackson slips into the realm of their imagination in a gorgeous sequence that morphs rolling countryside into sculpted gardens, with frolicking unicorns and giant butterflies swooping overhead. Subsequent segs take them to a castle (in the kingdom they call Borovnia), peopled by life-size versions of the modeling-clay likenesses they make of their heroes.

The boundaries of their fantasies begin intruding on real life, amusingly so in a classroom scene in which a monarchy-mad teacher is shocked by Juliet's account of a debauched Borovnia in place of the required essay on the royal family. Much later, when their grip on reality has been severely warped, the girls go to see "The Third Man," and after revealing the mix of fascination and repulsion Orson Welles exerts over them, they run screaming as he pursues them out of the theater and into Juliet's home. Their idyll hits an obstacle when Juliet is hospitalized for tuberculosis, the enforced separation making them more hostile to outsiders. A priest pushing Jesus on Juliet is dragged off and beheaded by an imaginary Borovnian. After displaying a too-precocious proclivity for sex with a student boarder, Pauline is sent for psychiatric counseling to temper her intense friendship with Juliet. Another fantasy figure swiftly disembowels the shrink.

Both girls become more distanced from their families, with Pauline resentful of her hokey folks' unworldliness and Juliet's disdainful, well-heeled parents too preoccupied with each other to pay attention to her. When their marital split threatens to definitively separate the girls, a lethal plan is hatched. The real strength of the characterization by scripters Jackson and Frances Walsh, and the two instinctive young thesps, is that despite their deadly purposefulness, Juliet and Pauline are never transformed into monsters. Played with infinite sympathy, they instead give the impression of being drawn into a vortex in which the terms of survival dictate the harshest course of action.

Their bond falls into unclassifiable territory, being neither an innocent, misconstrued friendship, nor an acknowledged lesbian relationship. This ambiguity is deftly shown in a scene where they make love, imagining each other as their Borovnian idols. A postscript revealing that the terms of their prison release years later included that they could never see each other again lends the conclusion an acute pang.

Backup from the adult cast is strong, with Diana Kent and Clive Merrison on the chill, remote side as Juliet's parents. Simon O'Connor is touching as Pauline's father, at something of a loss to understand what's happening to her, but valiantly keeping his chin up with a run of innocuously dumb comments intended to lighten the situation. As her quietly tragic mother, gradually revealed to be a less-than-perfect take on the '50s suburban housewife, Sarah Peirse is terrific. Eccentricity amongst the school's teaching body sometimes feels like it's plied on a little thickly.

Alun Bollinger's lensing has barely a stationary moment, invigorating the events visually with an impressive barrage of aggressive shooting techniques and frequent, effective filtering of color and light. Widescreen format is impeccably filled with eye-catching compositions. Peter Dasent's forceful music, James Selkirk's editing and a large quota of effects ranging from sophistication to deliberate jokiness all contribute significantly.
—*David Rooney*

SOMEBODY TO LOVE

A Lumiere Pictures presentation of a Lila Cazes production. Produced by Lila Cazes. Executive producer, Jean Cazes. Co-executive producer, Marie Cantin. Directed by Alexandre Rockwell. Screenplay, Sergei Bodrov, Rockwell. Camera (Foto-Kem color), Robert Yeoman; editor, Elena Maganini; music, Mader; music supervisor, Charlie Midnight; songs, Tito Larriva; production design, J. Rae Fox; art direction, Erik Polczwartek; costume design, Alexandra Welker; sound (Dolby), Pawel Wdowczak; choreography, Alexandre Magno; associate producer, Bodrov; assistant director, Cas Donovan; casting, Georgianne Walken, Sheila Jaffe. Reviewed at Venice Film Festival (competing), Sept. 6, 1994. (Also in Toronto fest.) Running time: **103 MIN.**

Mercedes	Rosie Perez
Harry Harrelson	Harvey Keitel
Emillio	Anthony Quinn
Ernesto	Michael DeLorenzo
Mickey	Steve Buscemi
Sam Silverman	Sam Fuller
George	Stanley Tucci
Armando	Gerardo
Nick	Steve Randazzo

With: Paul Herman, Angel Aviles, Lorelei Leslie, Quentin Tarantino, Lelia Goldoni.

Rosie Perez shines as a spunky Latino taxi dancer with showbiz in her eyes in "Somebody to Love," but she's too often a lone beacon in a dramatically foggy and curiously unaffecting pic. Despite some treasurable moments, and a largely reliable cast, Alexandre Rockwell's first pic since his off-the-wall cult comedy "In the Soup" rarely fires on more than one cylinder at a time. Specialized business could start off warm but looks unlikely to break out into any major salsas. Pic drew OK critical reaction at its Venice fest world preem.

Rockwell wrote the main role of a dollar-a-dance babe in a tacky L.A. club with Perez in mind, after discovering taxi dancing was still flourishing in the barrio of East Los Angeles and subsequently meeting the actress at a screening of "Soup." Pic was inspired by the Giulietta Masina character in Fellini's "Nights of Cabiria," and carries a final dedication "In Memory of Federico and Giulietta."

Though occasional scenes recall the 1957 Italo classic, Rockwell's movie is sufficiently rooted in a West Coast milieu for any comparisons to be meaningless. Mercedes (Perez) is a tough-talking Brooklyn transplant who spends her days being rejected at casting calls even when the part calls for a short, dark Latin woman. Her lover, Harry (Harvey Keitel), also from the East Coast, is a passed-over star who's going through mid-age career and marital crises.

Enter Ernesto (Michael DeLorenzo), a dewy-eyed Latin kid who falls for Mercedes at the dance club and starts following her around like a faithful dog. She finds him cute and kind, but not bed material; career opportunities and Harry are the only things she has in her headlights.

In a couple of funny scenes, Rockwell makes the point that both Mercedes and Harry are actually pretty rotten actors. Harry is so bad that he even gets fired from playing a gorilla in a Tarzan movie.

Keen to make an impression on his new love, Ernesto takes a job as a runner for local racketeer Emillio (Anthony Quinn). After finally being invited into Mercedes' bed, Ernesto takes on a contract hit from Emillio to earn the $10,000 she and Harry need to return to Gotham and start over. Ending is bloody and tragic, but with an upbeat coda similar to the ending of Fellini's "Cabiria."

Pic's biggest problem is establishing a thoroughgoing tone. Opening scenes, with Perez involved in some machine-gun repartee with a hustler-agent (Stanley Tucci), and later attending the club and some disastrous casting sessions, have a zing and pace and off-the-wall characters that recall the best bits of "In the Soup." When the Mercedes-Ernesto story hoves into view, however, the movie starts on another path that never really jells.

Given that Mercedes clearly is a loser and her relationship with Ernesto is a non-starter, pic's flat dialogue drags down a movie that initially seemed to celebrate the wackier side of day-to-day life among the showbiz fringe of modern L.A.

In between, Rockwell lards the film with a host of referential injokes that sometimes work but increasingly backfire. Here's Steve Buscemi, camping it up as a drag queen at the dance joint; there's Quentin Tarantino (briefly) as a fast-talking bartender. And, yes, that's Sam Fuller as a famous director who crashes his auto and dispenses words of career wisdom to Perez on the roadside one night before dropping dead.

Keitel himself, in a come-and-go part, is strangely low-key, even when misquoting Shakespeare in leopard-skin briefs and propping up the bar at Perez's niterie. Quinn, who starts well in an unfamiliarly melancholy role, later disappears for most of the movie until yanked back into the plot to provide a dramatic resolution to the Ernesto-Mercedes story.

The movie's one constant is Perez, who acquits herself well. Almost wearing a succession of tacky, figure-hugging clothes, she single-handedly creates a character of superficial hopes and half-understood desires who deserves a sharper script and company than she gets.

J. Rae Fox's production design fits Perez's role like a glove, from the low-rent dance club that's a symphony of kitsch to her own chaotic apartment. Lensing by Robert Yeoman ("Drugstore Cowboy") is sharp and clean in exteriors and richly colored in interiors. Sole technical blip is a sometimes misbalanced soundtrack, which in dance hall sequences makes dialogue difficult to hear against music and effects.

—*Derek Elley*

LAMERICA

(ITALIAN-FRENCH)

A Cecchi Gori Group release (Italy) of a C.G.G. Tiger Cinematografica (Rome)/Arena Films (Paris) co-production in association with RAI-TV Channel 1, Vega Films (Zurich), Canal Plus and the Centre National de la Cinematographie. Produced by Mario and Vittorio Cecchi Gori. Executive producer, Enzo Porcelli. Directed by Gianni Amelio. Screenplay, Amelio, Andrea Porporati, Alessandro Sermoneta. Camera (color, Cinemascope), Luca Bigazzi; editor, Simona Paggi; music, Franco Piersanti; art direction, Giuseppe M. Gaudino. Reviewed at Venice Film Festival (competing), Sept. 4, 1994. Running time: **125 MIN.**

Gino	Enrico Lo Verso
Fiore	Michele Placido
Spiro	Carmelo Di Mazzarelli
Selimi	Piro Milkani

Two tough Italian con artists come face to face with the nightmarish despair of post-Communist Albania in "Lamerica," a hard-hitting, often moving film by top Italo helmer Gianni Amelio. Pic's uncompromising scorn for the two exploiters is matched by its hellish vision of a starving nation desperately searching for an escape hatch. Much tougher than Amelio's previous "The Stolen Children," pic could encounter resistance from more delicate filmgoers. But its evangelical sincerity and the sweeping emotion of its finale could win the director new admirers abroad with well-targeted handling.

Enrico Lo Verso, the swarthy young carabineer from "Children," returns as Gino, an apprentice swindler who comes to Albania with the more experienced Fiore (Michele Placido) to buy a shoe factory they never intend to run. Their get-rich-quick scheme is to cash in on Italian government aid to Albania's devastated post-Communist economy, but first they need to find a local majority partner to play the role of the company's puppet president.

The choice falls on 80-year-old Spiro (Carmelo Di Mazzarelli), a helpless senior who has been driven mad by 20 years of hard labor in the Communist prisons. Now the prison doors have been flung open, but Spiro has no place to go. He still lives in the labor camp, filmed as a living hell, with other lost souls.

The story takes its first turn when Spiro disappears. Gino's angry search for the old man offers Amelio a chance to take his camera on the road and meet roving bands of barefoot children and hungry, hollow-eyed citizens traveling on run-down trains and dusty buses. On the way, Gino begins a frightening descent into the world of no-way-out poverty. His arrogance and cruelty melt away as he is dispossessed of everything he owns: his Suzuki jeep, his chic Italian sunglasses and, finally, his clothes, his passport and what remains of his self-confidence.

In the end, Gino is indistinguishable from the penniless, unwashed, desperate Albanians who cram into a rusty ship bound for Italy. Their faces, some blank, some full of hope, blend into the faces of thousands of Italian immigrants from the past. The film ends here, but Italian viewers remember well the fate of the Albanian refugees on that voyage of hope in the summer of 1991: When they reached Italy, they were herded into soccer stadiums, where they remained for days before being forced to go back home.

Despite its grounding in recent history, there's nothing documentary about "Lamerica's" carefully planned and paced scenes, lensed in chillingly desaturated color and epic widescreen by Luca Bigazzi. At the film's center is the relationship between Gino and the deranged old man, who, much to Gino's surprise, turns out to be Italian, a Sicilian like himself who deserted Mussolini's army in 1939 and went into hiding under an Albanian name. Played by a non-pro, Spiro has the unreal presence of a concentration camp victim come back to life. A lifetime of humiliation hasn't robbed him of his dignity and kindness. In his innocent madness, he believes he's still a young soldier, and imagines Gino is taking him home to Sicily.

Lo Verso is at the height of his powers here, lending intensity to the cocky, despicably self-serving Gino, who gets a comeuppance of biblical proportions. But even this strong a perf can't erase a feeling that the character is schematically drawn, and Gino's slow progress toward human feeling is all too predictable. Placido is on target in a small role as his totally cynical business partner.

Title comes from Amelio's metaphoric connection between the Albanians straining to reach the promised land of Italy, and the impoverished generation of Italians who left their country behind to go to America.

—*Deborah Young*

THE BULL

(IL TORO)

(ITALIAN)

A Cecchi Gori Group release (in Italy) of a Penta Film/Mario and Vittorio Cecchi Gori presentation of a Penta Film/Officina Cinematografica production. Produced by Mario and Vittorio Cecchi Gori, Luciano Luna. Executive producer, Rita Cecchi Gori. Directed by Carlo Mazzacurati. Screenplay, Umberto Contarello, Mazzacurati, Stefano Rulli, Sandro Petraglia. Camera (Cinecitta color), Alessandro Pesci; editor, Mirco Garrone; music, Ivano Fossati; art direction, Leonardo Scarpa; costume design, Lina Nerli Taviani; sound (Dolby), Franco Borni; assistant director, Marina Zangirolami. Reviewed at Venice Film Festival (competing), Sept. 3, 1994. Running time: **104 MIN.**

Franco	Diego Abatantuono
Loris	Roberto Citran
Tantini	Marco Messeri
Danilo	Marco Paolini
Nocchi	Paolo Veronica
Tiziano	Roberto Zamengo
Antonio	Ugo Conti
Colombani	Alberto Lattuada

With: Boris Dvornik, Mirta Zetevic, Zlato Crnkovic, Zoltan Gera, Zoltan Benkoczy, Janos Bata, Peter Kertesz.

T he story of two Italians doggedly trying to turn a profit on a stolen champion breeding bull in the new Central Europe isn't exactly high on the common experience agenda for most folks. But in the hands of director Carlo Mazzacurati, a resourceful scripting team and a winning duo of contrasting but complementary actors, the characters' dilemmas are invested with enough gentle humor, pathos and unexpected immediacy to transform them into a universally human struggle. A quiet charmer in a seductively mellow key, "The Bull" looks to be a strong contender to horn in on international arthouse markets.

With no undue wringing of hands, the film's opening reel quickly sketches a melancholy portrait of a basically honest man driven by frustration to drastic measures. Burly co-op stud-farm worker Franco (Diego Abatantuono) loses his job due to staff cutbacks. When his employers refuse to cough up his settlement money, he breaks into their offices at night to confiscate legal proof of what he's owed. But while he's foraging, the farm's prize bull, Corinto, sidles up, and the animal itself seemingly initiates the idea of the theft.

Having coaxed the massive beast off the premises, he goes looking for help from his good-heartedly meek chum Loris (Roberto Citran), who's battling to get by raising calves. Franco's plan is to transport the valuable bull to Hungary, where it's less readily identifiable, and hence more easily salable.

Having established its singular central quest, the film then switches gears, taking on an appealing, indolent rhythm as the protagonists' problem-strewn journey gets under way. Traveling sequences are given a lilting gait by Ivano Fossati's lush, richly melodic tunes, with the duo's various encounters — of both the helpful and hindering kind — casually rooted in the sober social, political and economic realities of the region. That said, the drama remains primarily a human one.

At a Croatian railway station, a Samaritan stationmaster takes possession of Corinto, eyeing the bull as food for the hoards of war-zone evacuees camped in an unused train. With some remorse, Franco and Loris hightail it, taking shelter with a humble family when their truck breaks down in the middle of rural nowhere.

This interlude is arguably the best of many warmly effective feel-good moments. As in most of the film, the humor stays well clear of the easy-laughs territory, remaining easy and unforced as the Italians cook for their hosts and later lazily romance the young mother whose husband is presumably a war absentee.

Franco and Loris eventually orchestrate a deal for Corinto with a group of kindly dairy farmers. It's a genuinely uplifting ending that comes as a refreshingly uncynical surprise.

Having begun some time back to play minor variations on the type of character that earned him popularity in pix like "Mediterraneo," Abatantuono is considerably more contained here. Perhaps because of the competition, he's less bullish, balancing his towering physical presence and natural aggression with a good dose of introspective sensitivity. Citran backs him up faultlessly, tapping immense audience sympathy almost from his first moments onscreen.

In his customarily uncluttered style, director Mazzacurati tinkles away at the emotional keyboard with no sign of manipulation. The fine script touches on notions of humanity, compassion and dignity, along with sporting a strong feel for the land and the animals raised on it. Only weak link is the early, careful intro of Franco's family, who are subsequently never referred to or even advised when he takes to the road.

Alessandro Pesci's agreeably loose camerawork makes a handsome palette of the vast landscapes. Mirco Garrone's editing strings the journey's many legs together at a breezy, fluid pace, taking only a minor dip in the central section, which could be cured with tightening by a further 10 minutes.

—David Rooney

CAPTIVES

(BRITISH)

A BBC Films/Distant Horizon production. Produced by David M. Thompson. Executive producers, Anant Singh, Mark Shivas. Directed by Angela Pope. Screenplay, Frank Deasy. Camera (color), Remi Adefarasin; editor, Dave King; music, Colin Towns; production design, Stuart Walker; art direction, Diane Dancklefsen; costume design, Odile Dicks-Mireaux; sound (Dolby), Richard Manton; assistant director, Melanie Dicks; associate producer, Ian Hopkins. Reviewed at Venice Film Festival (Venetian Nights), Aug. 31, 1994. (Also in Toronto fest.) Running time: **100 MIN.**

Philip Chaney	Tim Roth
Rachel Clifford	Julia Ormond
Lenny	Keith Allen
Sue	Siobhan Redmond
Simon	Peter Capaldi
Towler	Colin Salmon
Sexton	Richard Hawley
Maggie	Annette Badland
Harold	Jeff Nuttal

S harp direction and on-the-nose central performances by Tim Roth and Julia Ormond put some shine into "Captives," a dramatic love story between a con and a middle-class rebel that reps an interesting feature debut by British helmer Angela Pope. Though scripting falls a tad short of its opening ambitions, pic has enough going for it to break out into small-time theatrical biz on the strength of Roth's name.

Ormond plays Rachel, a young dentist recently separated from her husband (Peter Capaldi) who takes a two-day-a-week job at a prison. One of her patients is tough but charming Philip (Roth), who's coming to the end of a 10-year stint in stir and soon starts coming on to Rachel.

Sexual chemistry gradually wears down Rachel's professional qualms and, in an energetic sex scene in a diner's washroom stall, the duo consummate their mutual craving on one of Philip's day-release outings. Their growing attraction, however, has been noted by Philip's fellow cons, one of whom, a black drug dealer named Towler (Colin Salmon), uses the info to blackmail Rachel into smuggling a package into jail.

Though shaken by her discovery that Philip was convicted of murdering his girlfriend, Rachel agrees to Towler's terms, especially when he starts threatening her best friend (Siobhan Redmond). The package turns out to contain a gun, not drugs, and at the last moment Rachel leaves the jail with the hardware still on her. Followed by Towler's psychotic henchman Lenny (Keith Allen), she becomes the focus of a final shootout.

The opening reels of "Captives" have a taut, thriller-*manque* feel that, combined with the offbeat nature of the love story, holds the attention. Roth (returning to his native accent after a spell playing Yanks) and Ormond ("Young Catherine," "Stalin") click fast as screen partners, the former's hard-edged Cockney charm playing off well against the latter's middle-class poise.

Surrounding perfs by stalwarts like Redmond (excellent in the Brit internal affairs series "Between the Lines") and Allen ("Young Americans," "Beyond Bedlam") provide solid background.

It's in the development of the Philip-Rachel relationship, following their initial hots for each other, that the script starts to hang fire, with some below-par dialogue and uncertain rhythm. Latter half of the pic, though OK, never quite fulfills the opening promise of an obsessive cross-tracks love story, and the thriller elements lack the sheer oomph needed to carry the viewer into different territory.

Pope, whose background has been mostly in docus over the past 20-odd years, shows good command of resources. Though chiefly funded by the BBC, pic (which shot late last year under the title "The Prisoner") has none of the usual telepic feel, thanks to good production values, studio work at Shepperton, and a fuller, $3 million budget.

Remi Adefarasin's lensing is consistently rich and interesting, tweaked by Colin Towns' pacey score and pro cutting by Dave King. "Captives" is no earth-shaker, but announces a director of promise, plus an actress of considerable presence in the assured Ormond.

—Derek Elley

THAT EYE, THE SKY

(AUSTRALIAN)

A Beyond Films/Australian Film Finance Corp./Film Victoria presentation of an Entertainment Media/Working Title Films production. (International sales: Beyond Films.) Produced by Peter Beilby, Grainne Marmion. Executive producers, Robert Le Tet, Tim Bevan, Fred Schepisi. Directed by John Ruane. Screenplay, Ruane, Jim Barton, based on the book by Tim Winton. Camera (Eastmancolor), Ellery Ryan; editor, Ken Sallows; music, David Bridie, John Philips; production design, Chris Kennedy; art director, Brian Dusting; sound (Dolby), Lloyd Carrick; casting, Maura Fay, Rob Bailey; assistant director, Phil Jones. Reviewed at Village Roadshow screening room, Sydney, Aug. 26, 1994. (In Venice Film Festival — Critics Week). Running time: **105 MIN.**

September 12, 1994 (Cont.)

Henry Warburton	Peter Coyote
Alice Flack	Lisa Harrow
Morton "Ort" Flack	Jamie Croft
Tegwyn Flack	Amanda Douge
Sam Flack	Mark Fairall
Grammar Flack	Alethea McGrath
Mr. Cherry	Paul Sonkkila
Mrs. Cherry	Louise Siversen
Fat Cherry	Jeremy Dridan

"That Eye, The Sky" is a lyrical, faithful screen adaptation of 33-year-old Tim Winton's mystical book, which has already been the basis of a successful legit production in Australia. Like the source material, John Ruane's film, which is sumptuously photographed by Ellery Ryan, offers subtle pleasures but no obvious dramatic highlights, and will have to be handled with great care in order to find a receptive audience.

The mood created here is somewhat akin to that of "The Rainmaker," with the setting a small, troubled community visited by a stranger who promises help and salvation but who may well be a phony.

The Flack family lives in harmony in a small farmhouse by a river. Alice (Lisa Harrow) and Sam (Mark Fairall) have two children, Tegwyn (Amanda Douge), a blossoming teen, and Morton (Jamie Croft), known as Ort, an inquisitive, sensitive 12-year-old. The fifth member of the family is a senile grandmother (Alethea McGrath.)

The peace of the Flack household is rudely disrupted when Sam is involved in an offscreen motor accident and, after a spell in the hospital, is returned home still in a deep coma: Alice tries to cope for a while, but is only too happy when a stranger, Harry Warburton (Peter Coyote), arrives on the doorstep, offering help and apparently knowing all about the family's situation. It seems that Harry is a wandering evangelist, and he is soon accepted as a new father figure by Ort. Alice seems attracted to the stranger, but Tegwyn remains suspicious and hostile, suspecting, with some justification, that Harry's interests in the family are as much sexual as spiritual.

This is very different from Ruane's first feature, the engaging black comedy "Death in Brunswick," and indeed seems quite a risky project. It's a film about mysticism and a miracle that is handled in a totally realistic style, a film in which little overt action takes place and even the dramatic climax is deliberately muted.

Audiences looking for more robust filmmaking will stay away, but Ruane's gentle pic could find appreciative supporters who will be moved by the simple story and situations.

The cast is uniformly excellent, starting with young Croft as Ort, the wide-eyed boy who is a familiar enough figure in this kind of story but who is given an edge here by the young actor. Douge is bewitching as the frustrated teenager trying to cope with mixed emotions, and Harrow brings dignity and strength to the character of Alice. As the mysterious stranger, Coyote gives the story its intriguing centerpiece, though no great demands are placed upon the actor.

But the star of "That Eye, The Sky" is undoubtedly Ryan's glorious cinematography, which is marred only by the rather cheesy special-effects shots — in which the farmhouse is bathed with a golden glow seen only by Ort.

Fest exposure is indicated for this challenging, but ultimately rewarding, lyric experience.

—David Stratton

THE POSTMAN

(IL POSTINO)

(ITALIAN-FRENCH-BELGIAN)

A Cecchi Gori Group release (in Italy) of a Penta Film, Esterno Mediterraneo Film/Blue Dahlia Prods./K2T production. Produced by Mario and Vittorio Cecchi Gori, Gaetano Daniele. Executive producer, Alberto Passone. Directed by Michael Radford, in collaboration with Massimo Troisi. Screenplay, Anna Pavignano, Radford, Furio Scarpelli, Giacomo Scarpelli, Massimo Troisi, freely adapted from the novel "Ardiente Paciencia" by Antonio Skarmeta. Camera (color), Franco Di Giacomo; editor, Roberto Perpignani; music, Luis Enrique Bacalov; production design, Lorenzo Baraldi; costume design, Gianna Gissi; sound (Dolby), Massimo Loffredi, Alessandra Perpignani; assistant director, Gaia Gorrini. Reviewed at Venice Film Festival (non-competing), Aug. 31, 1994. Running time: **116 MIN.**
Mario Ruoppolo	Massimo Troisi
Pablo Neruda	Philippe Noiret
Beatrice	
Russo	Maria Grazia Cucinotta
Donna Rosa	Linda Moretti
Telegrapher	Renato Scarpa
Matilde	Anna Buonaiuto
Di Cosimo	Mariana Rigillo
(Italian dialogue)

Late Italo actor Massimo Troisi bows out with an affecting performance in "The Postman," a sad-sweet tale of a simple Mediterranean islander whose life is forever changed by his friendship with an exiled Chilean poet. Though pic looks set to reap emotional B.O. on home turf, where Troisi's name is a marquee draw, offshore chances look decidedly iffier for this first feature by British director Michael Radford since "White Mischief" in 1987. Pic's potentially inspiring story too often remains grounded by a problematic script and unshapely direction.

Film was preemed as the opening night attraction at this year's Venice festival, doubling as an homage to Troisi. The popular Neapolitan comic died in his sleep June 4 at the age of 41, a day after shooting wrapped at Cinecitta Studios.

Chilean writer Antonio Skarmeta's original novel, "Burning Patience," inspired by his own exile in Berlin during the 1980s, was set off the coast of Chile. Present version transfers the action to an unnamed Italian island during the early '50s, and makes several other major changes.

Troisi plays Mario, son of a fisherman, who dreams of wider horizons but lacks the intellectual ticket to reach them. When communist Chilean poet Pablo Neruda (Philippe Noiret) arrives on the island after being granted sanctuary by the Italian government, Mario is hired as his personal postman and slowly gains the aloof man's confidence during daily mail deliveries.

Neruda slowly warms to Mario's uneducated innocence and his interest in discovering the delights of poetry. When Mario falls for sexy local barmaid Beatrice (Maria Grazia Cucinotta) Neruda becomes his counselor/father-confessor, smoothing the way past the girl's overprotective aunt (Linda Moretti) and trying to teach him to pen love poetry.

At the couple's wedding feast, Neruda announces he can return to Chile. His sudden departure leaves Mario stoked with ambitions but still without the means to achieve them. He's even adopted Neruda's communist beliefs in a half-baked way.

As time passes, and his life and marriage stagnate, Mario is forced to face the truth that the poet has forgotten him, and he makes a final desperate effort to attract attention on the mainland. A coda, set five years later, has Neruda returning to the island.

Pic is essentially a two-hander between Troisi and Noiret, spending much of its length flip-flopping between chats at Neruda's cottage and Mario's musings back in the village. Aside from the diverting (but dramatically distracting) subplot of the busybody aunt and the voluptuous Beatrice, no other characters get much of a look in.

Noiret is well cast as Neruda, but it's not a performance that develops much depth as the film progresses.

The Gallic thesp (here dubbed into Italian) is fine at showing the poet's elevated world-weariness and initially condescending treatment of his uneducated "pupil," but the script rarely taps into his own emotions to create a sympathetic character.

It's Troisi's show, and, at that level, the movie offers plenty of moments to savor.

Gaunt and unshaven, and with sad-dog eyes, Troisi gives a warm, ironic performance to treasure. But with little assistance from Radford's by-the-numbers direction, and a script that starts to become very diffused about halfway through, the bottom line is that it's a performance in a vacuum. When Noiret effectively exits the picture two-thirds of the way through, the movie's structure starts to flounder.

Luis Enrique Bacalov's warm, tuneful score is a big help in giving the pic some emotional shape. Other technical credits are par.

—Derek Elley

MONTREAL

CRADLE SONG

(CANCION DE CUNA)

(SPANISH)

A Nickel Odeon Dos (Madrid) production. (International sales: Enrique Herreros, Madrid). Executive producer, Mario Morales. Produced, directed by Jos Luis Garci. Screenplay, Garci, Horacio Volcarcel, based on the book by Gregorio Martinez Sierra. Camera (color), Manuel Rojas; editor, Miguel Gonzales-Sinde; music, Manuel Balboa; production design, Gil Parrondo; costume design, Yvonne Blake; sound, Jose Antonio Bermudez. Reviewed at World Film Festival, Montreal (competing), Sept. 4, 1994. Running time: **103 MIN.**
With: Fiorella Faltoyano, Alfredo Landa, Maria Massip, Diana Pecalver, Maribel Verde, Carmelo Gomez, Virginia Mataix, Maria Louisa Ponte.

For those who've been waiting for a high-quality nun movie, "Cradle Song" will be blessed relief. Winner of special prizes from two juries in Montreal, this fourth Spanish-lingo version of Gregorio Martinez Sierra's 1941 classic of earthly love and heavenly faith is class-A arthouse fare.

If God is really in the details, this deluxe production, with its burnished ochers and luminous blues, is a holy, satisfying experience. Set in a 19th-century convent, the tale follows a gaggle of Spanish nuns whose cloistered habits are first threatened and then uplifted by the

September 12, 1994 (Cont.)

arrival of an abandoned baby girl. The local doctor (terrific Alfredo Landa), an irreverent breath of fresh air — "in vino veritas" is his most pious pronouncement — and best friend to the order's level-headed Mother Superior (Fiorella Faltoyano), agrees to adopt the child and let the group raise her collectively, with heartwarming results.

Title refers to a tune heard by the most maternal sister (Diana Pecalver), as a child, from "a red-haired foreign girl with a face full of freckles." The song is actually "An Irish Lullabye," and its sentimental "tura-lura-lura" refrain forms the core of the pic's lush but measured score. United by the illusory "birth without sin" of their charge, named Teresa after the ailing Mother Superior, veteran helmer Jos Luis Garci's nuns make subtle comment on the limits of monastic life and the rewards of spiritual pursuit. Except for the jarringly over-recorded voices and an abundance of makeup designed to indicate aging, the production captures what one woman calls "the poetry of the small and everyday."

Only caveat is pic's slow pace and sustained tone of hushed reverence in a market cool to religious themes. But the presence of lovely Maribel Verde — when the story flashes forward to the marriage of grown-up Teresa — will help remind cosmopolitan auds of the intelligent pleasures of "Belle Epoque," whose exhib path "Cradle" could follow, with some divine nurturance.

—*Ken Eisner*

SKALLAGRIGG

(BRITISH)

An In Pictures presentation of a BBC production. Produced by John Chapman. Directed by Richard Spence. Screenplay, Nigel Williams, based on the novel by William Harwood. Camera (color), Chris Seager; editor, Gregg Miller; music, Stephen Warbeck; production design, Grenville Horner; sound, Roger Slater. Reviewed at World Film Festival, Montreal, Sept. 1, 1994. Running time: **87 MIN.**

John	Bernard Hill
Esther	Kerry Noble
Raj	Tom Tomalin
Tom	Karl Purden
Young Arthur	Adam Walker
Middle Arthur	Jamie Beddard
Old Arthur/George	Richard Briers
Margaret	Billie Whitelaw
Dilke	John McArdle
Rendle	Ian Dury
Frank	Nick Brimble

"Skallagrigg" is a well-crafted and beautifully acted BBC production with solid the-

atrical potential. The marketing challenge will be to convince audiences this is not a story about disabled characters, but rather a story about characters who happen to be disabled.

Focus is the edgy relationship between John (Bernard Hill), a widowed, newly bankrupt businessman, and Esther (Kerry Noble), his palsied 16-year-old daughter. Years earlier, John turned Esther over to the care of a rehab center for the handicapped. Now he's eager — and more than a little guilt-driven — to re-establish family ties. But Esther is too embittered to quickly accept a reconciliation.

So John agrees to take Esther and her two friends — Raj (Tom Tomalin), a dry-witted, wheelchair-bound cynic, and Tom (Karl Purden), a sweet-tempered fellow with Down's syndrome — on a cross-country van trip. Esther wants to investigate the legends of "Skallagrigg," a mythical protector of disabled people.

The travelers learn the legends have a real-life basis in the misadventures of Arthur, a palsied young man who, in flashbacks, suffers abuse in a residential center that makes Bedlam seem a model of enlightenment. The more John and Esther learn about Arthur, the closer they become. Eventually, their investigation leads them to the nursing home where Arthur is still alive, but just barely, and still under the domination of a sadistic brute.

Director Richard Spence and screenwriter Nigel Williams (working from a novel by William Harwood) do a terrific job of balancing the seriocomic realism of the present-day scenes with the fable-like heightened reality of the flashbacks. More important, they rigorously avoid cheap sentiment and facile romanticizing in dealing with their disabled characters, who are allowed to be crabby, short-tempered and, occasionally, witheringly sarcastic.

Spence has cast disabled nonpros in most of the supporting roles, which pays off handsomely. Noble is a genuine find, and Tomalin is deliciously sardonic. Despite their obvious speech impediments, they are always understandable, and often quite funny.

As John, Hill gives a performance rich in telling nuances and precisely chosen details, and Billie Whitelaw makes the absolute most of her small role as Esther's grandmother.

"Skallagrigg" lets a couple of loose plot threads dangle, and owes a bit too much to "Rain Man" when the time comes to explain its title. Tech credits — especially Chris Seager's lensing — are first-class.

—*Joe Leydon*

SUMMER OF LOVE

(LATO MILOSKI)

(POLISH-BELARUSSIAN)

A Fokus Film (Warsaw) production. Directed, written by Feliks Falk, based on the short story "Nathalie" by Ivan Bunin. Camera (color), Krzysztof Tusiewicz; editor, Alicia Torbus-Wasinska; music, Henryk Kuzniak; sound, Andrzej Lewandowski. Reviewed at World Film Festival, Montreal (non-competing), Sept. 4, 1994. Running time: **85 MIN.**
With: Siergiej Sznyriew, Daria Powieriennowa, Ewa Bukowska, Alona Lisowskaja, Ernest Romanow, Anatolij Tierpicki.
(Russian dialogue, with English subtitles)

Like something straight out of Tolstoy, this old-fashioned tale of late-czarist Russia captures the first blush of post-adolescent romance, and says something deeper and sadder about human nature. Perfectly cast and deliciously mounted, "Summer of Love" will be worth seeking out, even if exhibs have a hard time finding it.

The story is classic: Handsome young medical student Alexander (Siergiej Sznyriew) is whiling away his last summer of freedom at the summer estate of his cousin Sonia Cherkasov (Ewa Bukowska). The two have always had a low-flame thing for each other, and he figures this is a good time to experience "love without responsibility" before hitting the books. What he doesn't expect is that she has also invited her Polish pal Nathalie (Daria Powieriennowa). Predicting her cousin will fall for this introspective beauty, Sonia further confuses the arrangement by asking Alexander to *pretend* to be interested in her friend in order to throw her father, the suspicious Count Cherkasov (Ernest Romanow), off the incestuous scent.

Then there's the problem of the women's two older, and potentially dangerous, suitors. But even without these complications, Sonia is a serious handful, intent on controlling everyone in sight, and never completely sure of her own feelings in the bargain. For a while, the young man is content to stew in the amorous quagmire, but the stakes get higher as he realizes the depth of his interest in Nathalie.

Veteran Polish helmer Feliks Falk (his made-for-TV "Samowolka" was also in Montreal) couldn't have handled his small ensemble any better, and he manages to con-

jure their world nostalgically, with a fitting classical music score, but no undue fussiness in the art direction. Likewise, lenser Krzysztof Tusiewicz establishes a palpable sense of faded place without overwhelming his frail subjects with pictorial melancholy. Unsurpassed fest fare, this "Summer" should be invited to linger well into 1995.

—*Ken Eisner*

WIND FROM WYOMING

(LE VENT DU WYOMING)

(CANADIAN-FRENCH)

A Malofilm release (Quebec) of an EGM/Transfilm/Eiffel production. Produced by Nardo Castillo, Claude Leger. Co-producer, Jacques Dorfmann. Directed, written by Andre Forcier. Camera (color), Georges Dufaux; editor, Jacques Gagne; music, Christian Gaubert; production design, Serge Bureau; costume design, Francois Laplante; sound (Dolby), Patrick Rousseau. Reviewed at World Film Festival, Montreal (competing), Aug. 27, 1994. Running time: **100 MIN.**

Chester Celine	Francois Cluzet
Lea Mentha	Sarah-Jeanne Salvy
Marcel Mentha	Michel Cote
Albert Mouton	Marc Messier
Lizette Mentha	France Castel
Manon Mentha	Celine Bonnier
Father Lachaise	Marcel Sabourin
Romeo	Donald Pilon
Assourhampel	Marc Gelinas
Johnny Bowsky	Jean-Marie Lapointe
Nicole Piaf	Leo Munger
Reo	Martin Randez

The characters of Andre Forcier's "Wind From Wyoming" inhabit a truly bizarre world. His easy melange of high and low-brow sensibilities is rather like a Brechtian soap opera. While unquestionably a daunting challenge for the mainstream, pic hits a vital nerve with partisan auds and should carve a comfortable niche in upscale markets.

In a milieu of punch-drunk boxers and their handlers, Lea (Sarah-Jeanne Salvy) is in love with up-and-comer Reo (Martin Randez). But he breaks her heart by taking up with her mother, Lizette (France Castel), and that puts papa (Michel Cote) — his trainer — into a spin. Meanwhile, sister Manon (Celine Bonnier) has become infatuated with celebrated New Age author Chester Celine (Francois Cluzet), who's about to make a personal appearance in Montreal.

Add to the mix a hypnotist (Marc Messier) brought in to alter affections and a collection of oddballs who gravitate about Motel Oscar, and you have a busy, intelligent and unpredictable crew.

Forcier aggressively assaults the audience with images and incidents. No laugh is too crude, and the outrageous is *de rigueur*. It's a pretty bleak vision of the human condition, with much humor wrung out of adversity.

Every aspect of the production is pitched into high gear, and overall effect leaves one gasping. But it's all kept in control and the plot threads tie together neatly at the end.

Abetted by a superb ensemble cast and a beautifully polished production, "Wind From Wyoming" (a reference to a mythical breeze with erotic powers) is a wacky, good-natured and skillful piece that succeeds by studiously avoiding judging its characters.

—*Leonard Klady*

NASTAZJA

(POLISH-JAPANESE)

A Comstock presentation of a HIT/ Say-To Workshop Inc. production in association with Television Tokyo Channel 12 Ltd. Produced by Hisashi Ito, Masato Sakakibara, Teruhiko Abe. Directed by Andrzej Wajda. Screenplay, Wajda, Maciej Karpinski, based on Fyodor Dostoevsky's "The Idiot." Camera (color), Pawet Edelman; editor, Ewa Small; production design, Krystyna Zachwatowicz; sound, Malgorzata Lewandowska, Fumio Hashimoto; music, Malgorzata Przedpelska-Bieniek. Reviewed at World Film Festival, Montreal, Sept. 2, 1994. (Also in Toronto fest.) Running time: **97 MIN.**

With: Tamasaburo Bando, Toshiyuki Nagashima.

Andrzej Wajda's "Nastazja" is the sort of jaw-dropping folly that only a great filmmaker would attempt. Indeed, only someone with Wajda's international prestige would likely be able to convince financiers to back something this audaciously bizarre. Global fest exposure is virtually guaranteed, even though pic will eventually be remembered as a curious footnote in Wajda's career.

To get some idea how off-the-wall it is, imagine this pitch: Polish-born Wajda directs Kabuki-trained actors in a two-person, Japanese-language dramatization of the final chapter of Dostoevsky's classic Russian novel "The Idiot."

No kidding.

Wajda, reportedly an ardent devotee of Kabuki, filmed "Nastazja" in 13 days, on location in Warsaw's picturesque Pac Palace. Most of the action (for want of a better term) takes place in a single, lushly appointed den where the mercurially virile Rogozhin (Toshiyuki Nagashima) and the frail, epileptic Myshkin (Tamasaburo Bando) confront each other in a long series of free-form conversations about Nastazja, the enigmatic woman they both love.

Pic begins with Rogozhin's helping the beautiful Nastazja flee the church where she was to wed Myshkin. Once the conversations begin, however, time and space are artfully scrambled, so that the two men re-enact past encounters and clashes. Occasionally, specific exchanges are repeated like recurring movements in a symphony. At other times, Bando (one of Japan's leading Kabuki stars) dons earrings and a shawl and becomes Nastazja, all the better for his co-star to converse with "her" as well.

Even audiences accustomed to stylized Kabuki traditions will find "Nastazja" fairly tough sledding. Pic is static to an uncomfortable extreme, and bloodless in its abstract storytelling. Some critics will be tempted to make comparisons with "My Dinner With Andre" or "What Happened Was ...," but "Nastazja" makes both those pix seem as thrill-packed as "True Lies."

And yet, for all that, "Nastazja" often exerts an almost mesmerizing fascination. The bluish-green, smoke-shrouded visual design enhances the pic's dreamlike quality. For long periods, the eye is captured, the mind enchanted. Pic will, quite literally, put some people to sleep. But others will find themselves riveted by the visual and verbal rhythms. If ever a pic deserved the label "acquired taste," here it is.

The understated performances of the two leads are more impressive than affecting, but they are everything they should be in this context. Pawet Edelman's fluid cinematography and Krystyna Zachwatowicz's evocative production design are strong assets.

"Nastazja" is, if nothing else, a one-of-a-kind experience. Both its harshest critics and its greatest admirers will have no trouble agreeing on that. Unfortunately for Wajda, the former will far outnumber the latter. —*Joe Leydon*

WES CRAVEN'S NEW NIGHTMARE

A New Line Cinema production. Produced by Marianne Maddalena. Executive producers: Robert Shaye, Wes Craven. Co-executive producer, Sara Risher. Co-producer, Jay Roewe. Directed, written by Craven, based on characters created by Craven. Camera (Foto-Kem color, Filmhouse prints), Mark Irwin; editor, Patrick Lussier; music, J. Peter Robinson; production design, Cynthia Charette; art direction, Troy Sizemore, Diane McKinnon; set design, Stephen Alesch; costume design, Mary Jane Fort; sound (Digital DTS), Jim Steube; supervisor of visual effects, William Mesa; assistant director, Nick Mastandrea; casting, Gary Zuckerbrod. Reviewed at Toronto Film Festival, Sept. 9, 1994. MPAA rating: R. Running time: **112 MIN.**

Freddy Krueger/Robert Englund	Robert Englund
Heather Langenkamp	Herself
Dylan	Miko Hughes
Chase Porter	David Newsom
Julie	Tracy Middendorf
Dr. Heffner	Fran Bennett
John Saxon	Himself
Wes Craven	Himself
Robert Shaye	Himself
Sara Risher	Herself
Marianne Maddalena	Herself

Freddy Krueger is alive and well and raising hell one more time in "Wes Craven's New Nightmare," an ingeniously conceived and devilishly clever opus that proves "Freddy's Dead — The Final Nightmare" wasn't so aptly named after all. Franchise creator Craven returns to the scene of the crime with an amusing self-referential thriller that promises to scare up a B.O. bonanza, and maybe even earn some admiring reviews.

Craven's audacious conceit is that his first "Nightmare on Elm Street" (1984) and the five sequels directed by others were works of fiction that inadvertently summoned, and briefly contained, a real supernaturally evil force. Unfortunately, after the sharp-fingered bogeyman Krueger was decisively killed in the series finale, the evil force was freed to wreak havoc — while still in the form of Freddy — on an unsuspecting world.

For that reason, Craven explains while playing himself in the pic's most darkly comical sequence, he simply *must* make another "Nightmare" pic.

What springs from this fanciful premise is an inspired scramble of "reality" and role-playing that would impress Pirandello himself. Gore hounds and other seekers of cheap thrills may be disappointed by Craven's wise decision to tone down the carnage here. But just about everyone else will have a great time with the in-jokes and cross-references. Better still, "New Nightmare" is a self-contained work that can be enjoyed by auds unfamiliar with the earlier pix. It should provide a wild roller-coaster ride for anyone game enough to get on board.

Heather Langenkamp, star of the first "Nightmare," returns to star as Heather Langenkamp, an actress who has a devoted cult following for her performance in "Nightmare on Elm Street." She's still on good terms with her "Nightmare" co-stars (including Robert Englund and John Saxon, also cast as themselves). But she's extremely reluctant to appear in a brand-new "Nightmare" sequel, despite lucrative offers made by real-life New Line Cinema exec Robert Shaye and producer Sara Risher.

Unfortunately, even though she wants no part of another Freddy pic, Freddy just won't stay out of her life. And her dreams.

First, the bogeyman disposes of her special-f/x artist husband (David Newsom). Then Freddy sets his sights on Langenkamp's little boy, Dylan (Miko Hughes), whose worst fears about a monster lurking beneath his bed are entirely justified. When Langenkamp seeks help from Craven, the writer/director admits that the "real" horrors are exactly like those he has glimpsed in his own nightmares. That's the bad news. The worse news is, Craven is transforming those nightmares into a new script. And the work-in-progress doesn't look like it's building to a happy ending.

When he isn't playing fast and loose with what's real and what isn't, Craven drops a few intriguing hints that he's had mixed feelings about the influence of his and other people's horror pix. The stern-faced doctor (Fran Bennett) who diagnoses Langenkamp's seizure-prone child speaks disapprovingly of the ways violent horror pix can harm impressionable kids. On the other hand, the name Craven gives the doctor — Heffner, a clear reference to the former MPAA ratings board chief — may be taken as a satirical jab at such criticism.

In the end, it's clear that Craven views his grisly art as no more dangerous for children than fairy tales, a point he hammers home with verbal and visual references to "Hansel and Gretel." As Langenkamp herself notes, "Every child knows who Freddy is. He's like Santa Claus."

Englund once again is in bravura form as Freddy, playing the flame-scarred, blade-fingered creep as much for nasty laughs as unnerving shocks. He has far less screen time as himself, but he's very effective in that role, too.

Langenkamp proves she is still one of cinema's most resourceful scream queens here. Newcomer Hughes is adept at maneuvering through Dylan's bizarre personality swings. It is more than mildly unsettling, however, to see this small child stick a sharp blade into Freddy's back during the inevitable Armageddon that climaxes "New Nightmare." This will only provide fresh ammunition for those who would brand Craven and other horrormeisters as irresponsible.

"New Nightmare" works best when it takes a straight-faced but gleefully fang-in-cheek approach to genre conventions. Surprisingly, it is least distinctive during what is normally the high point of a "Nightmare" pic, the fiery good-vs.-evil climax. This sort of thing has been done too many times already, both in the "Nightmare" series and the "Hellraiser" pix, to have the effect it once had.

The special effects team supervised by William Mesa perform far beyond the call of duty. Advances in computer-generated imagery and assorted other innovations make "New Nightmare" far more dazzling — and, at times, even scarier — than the 10-year-old original. Other tech credits are solid.

Don't be too surprised if "Wes Craven's Newer Nightmare" goes into production real soon. But it will have a tough act to follow.

— *Joe Leydon*

ONLY YOU

A TriStar release of a Fried/Woods Films and Yorktown Prods. Ltd. production. Produced by Norman Jewison, Cary Woods, Robert N. Fried, Charles Mulvehill. Directed by Jewison. Screenplay, Diane Drake. Camera (Technicolor), Sven Nykvist; editor, Stephen Rivkin; music, Rachel Portman; production design, Luciana Arrighi; art direction, Stephano Ortolani, Maria Teresa Barbasso, Gary Kosko (Pittsburgh); set decoration, Ian Whittaker, Alessandra Querzola (Italy), Diana Stoughton (Pittsburgh); costume design, Milena Canonero; sound (Dolby), Ken Weston; associate producer, Michael Jewison; assistant director, Tony Brandt; casting, Howard Feuer. Reviewed at Toronto Film Festival, Sept. 15, 1994. MPAA Rating: PG. Running time: **108 MIN.**

Faith Corvatch	Marisa Tomei
Peter Wright	Robert Downey Jr.
Kate	Bonnie Hunt
Giovanni	Joaquim De Almeida
Larry	Fisher Stevens
The False Damon Bradley	Billy Zane
Damon Bradley	Adam LeFevre
Dwayne	John Benjamin Hickey
Leslie	Siobhan Fallon
Fortune Teller	Antonia Rey
Faith's Mother	Phyllis Newman

Norman Jewison tries to revive some of the "Moonstruck" magic, via a side trip through "Sleepless in Seattle," in "Only You." A puff of a romantic comedy set in a storybook Italy and populated by characters who believe in pursuing their amorous destinies as long as it involves staying in five-star hotels, handsomely turned-out trifle has a healthy dose of highly calculated commercial appeal, especially to those who are ready to swallow cornball romance without worrying about excess sweets. But the real B.O. story will rest upon whether topliners Marisa Tomei and Robert Downey Jr., both previously successful mainly as supporting names, are capable of opening and sustaining a picture.

With acknowledged bows to "Roman Holiday," as well as to "South Pacific," this impossibly romantic concoction has two main characters who believe in "the stars and the moon" and who chase across some of the world's most picturesque scenery and fabled cityscapes because of their commitment to the idea that there's one true soulmate out there just made to match up with them. An enthusiastic sales pitch for hanging onto your dream until you find it, as well as one giant valentine to Italy, film serves up enough mildly amusing situational comedy along the way to keep general audiences engaged. But sophisticated it's not.

Quick prologue establishes the premise that drives first-time screenwriter Diane Drake's story: As a child, Faith is informed by both a Ouija board and a fortuneteller

that her man of destiny will be named Damon Bradley. Fourteen years later, Faith (Tomei) hasn't forgotten this prediction but has also become realistic. A Pittsburgh schoolteacher, she's set to marry straight-and-narrow podiatrist Dwayne (John Benjamin Hickey) in 10 days when an old friend of Dwayne's calls in his regrets for not being able to attend the wedding, since he's leaving for Venice that very day. Oh yes, his name is Damon Bradley.

Faith immediately spins into orbit at this and rushes to the airport with best friend Kate (Bonnie Hunt). Latter is unhappy in her long-term marriage, suspecting that hubby Larry (Fisher Stevens) is fooling around, so she decides to fly to Italy with Faith to get away.

Checking first at the Hotel Danieli in Venice, pair proceed through San Gimignano and on to Rome, where through a mix-up and a lie, Faith comes to believe that a friendly Yank (Downey) is Damon Bradley. Faith is delirious over having met the object of her eternal desire, while through the course of "Some Enchanted Evening" (pic's repeated theme song), "Damon" falls in love with her.

By morning, the smitten young man has to admit that he's not who he said he was, but is actually named Peter. Furious and disappointed, Faith decides to return to Pittsburgh and keep her wedding date, even though Kate is now making time with a local Romeo named Giovanni (Joaquim De Almeida). After protracted arguments to the effect that it shouldn't matter what his name is, Peter realizes that the only way he can keep Faith in the country, and his chances alive, is to help her find the real Damon and hope for the best.

They head down the coast for the stunning seaside town of Positano, where another possible Damon Bradley is found in the hunky form of Billy Zane, who wines and dines Faith as Peter agonizingly looks on. Road has a couple more twists before the anticipated feel-good ending.

Jewison knows exactly where the laugh and welling-up buttons are that will hook the audience into this middle-class fairy-tale-come-true, and has smartly cast it with engaging personalities. Cast at least partly for her Audrey Hepburn gamin quality, Tomei comes on a little strong for some tastes, but her enthusiasm and ordinary-gal quality will get most viewers rooting for her.

Downey is spirited and winning in one of the more conventional roles he's played to date, displaying both his quicksilver inventiveness and hangdog self-deprecation. As the wilted housewife brought back to full bloom by a little Latin loving, Hunt has most of the good lines and delivers them with expert timing. De Almeida is all charm and smooth moves, and Stevens and Zane both make the most of brief roles.

Productionwise, pic looks to have been one of the choice crew assignments in recent times, with the fabulous locations caught in peak season. Sven Nykvist's lensing, heavy on travelogue, bathes the exquisite settings, and Luciana Arrighi's production design, in rosy warmth. Rachel Portman's able score is abetted by any number of standard and classical tunes. — *Todd McCarthy*

NOSTRADAMUS

An Orion Classics release of an Allied Entertainments and Vereinigte Film Partners production. Produced by Edward Simons, Harold Reichebner. Executive producers, Peter Mcrae, Kent Walwin, David Mintz. Directed by Roger Christian. Screenplay, Knut Boeser, Piers Ashworth, based on a story by Boeser, Ashworth, Christian. Camera (Deluxe, color), Denis Crossan; editor, Alan Strachan; music, Barrington Pheloung; production design, Peter J. Hampton; art direction, Christian Nicul; set decoration, Michael D. Ford; sound (Dolby), James Corcoran; associate producer, Gerry Levy. Reviewed at Orion screening room, Beverly Hills, Aug. 18, 1994. MPAA Rating: R. Running time: **118 MIN.**

Nostradamus	Tcheky Karyo
Sclainger	F. Murray Abraham
Monk	Rutger Hauer
Catherine De Medici	Amanda Plummer
Marie	Julia Ormond
Anne	Assumpta Serna
King Henry II	Anthony Higgins

A gaudy tableau on an epic scale, "Nostradamus" is a disappointingly conventional biopic about the noted medieval scholar/prophet. Designed as a monument, this costume drama exhibits most of the sorrows of international productions: a rambling narrative, anachronistic language and an unsuccessful blend of accents and acting styles. Like "1492: Conquest of Paradise" and, more recently, "La Reine Margot," "Nostradamus" is the kind of extravaganza that Americans tend to steer away from but that is embraced by offshore audiences, particularly in Europe.

While focusing on the life of the famous philosopher/scientist, Michel de Nostradame (1503-1566), there's no doubt that the filmmakers see strong contemporary relevance in the tale of a man who devoted his life to fighting the ravaging ills of 16th-century Europe: uncontrollable plagues, a conservative medical establishment and the terror of the Inquisition.

The story establishes right away the curious, unorthodox persona of Nostradamus who, as a boy, began experiencing visions of the future. He went on to study new forms of medicine, hoping to find a cure for the plague, but his nonconformist personality and unorthodox methods irritated the Catholic Church as well as the medical profession.

Using the paradigm of classic mythology, the filmmakers perceive Nostradamus as a misunderstood hero — and survivor. Born Jewish, he managed to survive the Inquisition, the plague and the devastating death of his first wife, Marie (Julia Ormond), who shared his interest in science, to marry a second wife, Anne (Assumpta Serna), and establish another family.

Scripters Knut Boeser and Piers Ashworth fail the challenge of writing literate yet credible dialogue for historical characters and placing them in authentic political contexts. At times, the narrative feels like a synopsis for a movie yet to be made.

Filming in Romania, France and England, novice director Roger Christian (the accomplished art director on "Alien" and "Star Wars") endows his pic with lush visuals (kudos to lenser Denis Crossan), but he's unable to find the core of the story, and, after the first reel, pic loses its dramatic focus and momentum.

Despite its humanitarian intentions, "Nostradamus" is neither involving nor seriously informative. The flashes forward of the hero's prophetic visions of Hitler, World War II and Kennedy don't work; they puncture a script that is already too episodic.

Conforming to its genre requirements, "Nostradamus" is a big, amorphous picture with the normal complement of stunning storms, spectacular fights, multicolored pageantry — and naked bodies. Almost every encounter with a woman — be she a patient, sister-in-law or the queen — has erotic overtones and ends up in seduction, which trivializes both historical events and personae.

In the lead, handsome French thesp Karyo acquits himself with a decent performance, which, considering the script's limitations, is an achievement. Of the large international cast, Rutger Hauer is effective as a mad monk, F. Murray Abraham is for once effectively cast as the hero's mentor, and Amanda Plummer is so weird as Catherine de Medici that her lines almost sound campy.

It might be faint praise, but "Nostradamus" is easier to watch than the beautiful but vapid "1492" or the obnoxiously pretentious "La Reine Margot." —*Emanuel Levy*

ART DECO DETECTIVE

A Trident Releasing Inc. release. Produced by Philippe Mora, Bruce Critchley. Directed, written by Mora. Camera (Eastmancolor), Walter Bal; editor, Janet Wilcox-Morton; music, Allan Zavod; production design, Pamela Krause Mora; costume design, Sarah Hackett; sound (Dolby), Kermit Samples; associate producers, Jim and Laura Kirsner, Jen Lin, Joe Taetle; assistant director, Dan Allingham. Reviewed on videocassette, L.A., Sept. 1, 1994. Running time: 102 MIN.

Arthur	
Decowitz	John Dennis Johnston
Hyena	Stephen McHattie
Jim Wexler	Brion James
Detective Guy Lean	Joe Santos
Julie/Meg Hudson	Rena Riffel
Irina Bordat	Sonia Cole
Lana Torrido	Max John-James

If you didn't know the credits of director Philippe Mora, you'd think this intellectually pretentious, failed campy satire about the "crazy" state of the world was made by a novice. Though showing some facility for fast dialogue, this verbose pic — by the same helmer of "Communion," "Howling II: Your Sister Is a Werewolf," "Howling III" and the upcoming ecological thriller "A Breed Apart" — is just eccentric. It lacks the zest, fun or disturbing provocation that one would expect from midnight fare. Short theatrical release is a warm-up en route to video.

Writer/helmer Mora concocts a potpourri that mixes elements of classic noir, international political thrillers and sex satires. At its center is Arthur Decowitz (John Dennis Johnston), nicknamed Art Deco, an aging, burnt-out detective in the mold of Raymond Chandler's heroes, who becomes a pawn in an international scheme, motivated by conspiracy and paranoia that might even surprise Oliver Stone. Deco is set up as the fall guy in a CIA plan to trap Hyena (Stephen McHattie), a mad terrorist threatening to blow up L.A. and incriminate the Middle East.

Tale is somewhat leavened by Deco's encounters with a gallery of zany, if stereotypical, characters: a sleazy British filmmaker, a Hollywood sex goddess, a Washington call girl, undercover agents, manipulative diplomats, and so on. Unfortunately, pic is too derivative in its recycling of noir conventions and types, including a subplot about twin sisters (played by Rena Riffel), one of whom is believed to be murdered.

Lenser Walter Bal, who years back worked on Truffaut's films, keeps the camera close to the characters, as dialogue is the crucial element — and chief problem — in this film. There are probably no more than a dozen witty lines and a dozen moments that justify the film's claim to being a relevant political satire. The rest is just mumbo jumbo.

Though it contains S&M sex and cross-dressing, "Art Deco" qualifies as camp in intent rather than execution. You keep hoping for pic, which ideally should have been a short, to pass into the realm of camp, but it stubbornly refuses.—*Emanuel Levy*

THE PROFESSIONAL
(LEON)
(FRENCH)

A Columbia (U.S.)/Gaumont Buena Vista Intl. (France) release of a Gaumont/Les Films du Dauphin production. Executive producer, Claude Besson. Directed, written by Luc Besson. Camera (color, Technovision widescreen), Thierry Arbogast; editor, Sylvie Landra; music, Eric Serra; production design, Dan Weil; art direction, Carol Nast, Gerard Drolon; set decoration, Carolyn Cartwright, Francoise Benoit-Fresco; costume design, Magali Guidasci; sound (Dolby), Pierre Excoffier, Gerard Lamps, Francois Groult, Bruno Tarriere; special effects supervisor, Nicky Allder; assistant director, Pascal Chaumeil; casting, Todd Thaler (U.S.), Nathalie Cheron (France). Reviewed at Publicis Elysees cinema, Paris, Sept. 14, 1994. Running time: 106 MIN.

Leon	Jean Reno
Stansfield	Gary Oldman
Mathilda	Natalie Portman
Tony	Danny Aiello
Malky	Peter Appel
Mathilda's Father	Michael Badalucco
Mathilda's Mother	Ellen Greene

With: Elizabeth Regen, Carl J. Matusovich, Randolph Scott.
(English dialogue)

A dour and illiterate Italian hit man finds redemption in the company of a headstrong, orphaned girl in Luc Besson's "The Professional." Shooting entirely in English for the first time since his runaway local hit "The Big Blue," Besson delivers a naive fairy tale splattered with blood. Mix of cynicism and sentiment will ring hollow to cine-literate sophisticates but may play well to the gallery.

Pic was released Sept. 14 in France, where the biggest screen in Paris, the Gaumont Grand Ecran Italie, ran round-the-clock weekend screenings to meet expected demand. Movie bows stateside Oct. 21.

Offshore audiences who enjoyed the ricocheting narrative improbabilities of Besson's "La Femme Nikita" will discover a less exotic blend here. In much the same way that the roadway antics of "Speed" seem most plausible to folks with no firsthand experience of L.A.'s true traffic patterns, so this New York-set tale will be most credible to viewers who have never set foot in Gotham.

Tale dawdles to the half-hour mark when Mathilda (Natalie Portman), a bright but abused 12-year-old truant, whose wardrobe seems to come from the same haberdashery as Jodie Foster's in "Taxi Driver," returns from the grocery store to find that Stans-

field (Gary Oldman) and his trigger-happy crew have used her entire family for target practice.

Mathilda is reluctantly taken in by her towering and taciturn neighbor, Leon (Jean Reno), a self-described "cleaner" (Bessonian slang for "hit man"). The ambitious, only mildly bereaved waif thinks that's "cool" and begs 40-ish Leon to teach her his trade.

The utter isolation of Leon's life — his one true love is a carefully tended house plant — is conveyed by his inability to identify Mathilda's obvious dress-up impressions of Madonna, Marilyn Monroe and Charlie Chaplin.

The mismatched couple bonds, and the formerly invincible hit man becomes vulnerable. Reno — as strongly linked to Besson's screen career as De Niro is to Scorsese's — finds a way to prove his love for Mathilda 10 minutes before the closing credits roll.

Dialogue is adequate but lacks a single quotable or memorable line. Fortunately, the visuals — shot on location in Little Italy and Spanish Harlem, with eight weeks of studio interiors in France — put the story across. Widescreen lensing favors tight close-ups, and multiple shoot-'em-ups are edited with panache. Portrayal of elapsed time, however, is very wobbly.

Newcomer Portman shows an appealing spontaneity although she never registers as a real child. Danny Aiello is good, if familiar, as a restaurateur.

Oldman's edgy perf as a drug- and power-crazed turncoat, while not one of his best, is by far the most interesting characterization on display.

Eric Serra's occasionally imaginative and faintly Oriental wall-to-wall score sometimes tries too hard to imbue sequences with intensity or suspense, but is not unduly invasive.
—*Lisa Nesselson*

TORONTO

DESTINY IN SPACE
(U.S.-CANADIAN — DOCU)

An Imax Space Technology production. Produced by Graeme Ferguson. Co-director, astronaut training manager, James Neihouse. Screenplay, editor, Toni Meyers. Camera (IMAX color), Neihouse, David Douglas, various astronauts; music, Maribeth Solomon, Micky Erbe; sound, Peter Thillaye; associate producer, Phyllis Ferguson. Reviewed July 25, 1994, at Space Center Houston. (In Toronto Film Festival). Running time: 40 MIN.
Narrator: Leonard Nimoy.

Forget the expensive pyrotechnics of "True Lies" and the high-tech time-tripping of

September 19, 1994 (Cont.)

"Forrest Gump." The most amazing special effects in any contemporary pic are those in "Destiny in Space," a spectacular Imax docu given a special presentation at the Toronto Film Festival. Pic should find large and appreciative audiences as it slowly rolls out to Imax houses in urban markets.

Rarely has the adjective "awesome" been more appropriate than it is for this docu, which showcases space footage collected by astronauts during nine shuttle missions over four years.

In any format, such sights would be impressive. In Imax — a format with frames 10 times the size of conventional 35mm — they are downright astonishing.

"Destiny" is both an exciting voyage to the far reaches of the known universe and a provocative speculation on the mysteries that lie beyond our present knowledge.

The computer-generated visualizations of Venus, Mars and Jupiter — drawn from data gathered from space probes and interpreted by NASA Jet Propulsion Lab scientists — are nothing short of eye-popping.

And the clips from Stanley Kubrick's classic "2001: A Space Odyssey," used to illustrate theories about long-term space flight, are cleverly selected. But even these segments are upstaged by the Imax footage shot during missions of the Atlantis, Discovery and Endeavor space shuttles.

Some of the Imax-scale extraterrestrial imagery is so overwhelming, more than a few viewers will instinctively shut their eyes as a precaution against vertigo.

Indeed, it is frequently dizzying, and not a little scary, to gaze at the space shuttles, the floating astronauts and their deployed cargo — most notably, the Galileo probe and the Hubble Space Telescope — against the immense black nothingness of space.

Pic, produced by Graeme Ferguson, is the product of a public-private partnership involving the National Air and Space Museum, Lockheed Corp., NASA and the Imax Corp.

Leonard Nimoy (yes, Mr. Spock himself) delivers the narration by writer/editor Toni Meyers in an aptly grave, slightly sandpapered voice. Occasionally, the words have an edge of advocacy, emphasizing the need for manned flights to Mars.

But even viewers who have serious reservations about financing big-ticket NASA programs will savor "Destiny in Space" as a real-life adventure that's more amazing that anything Arnold Schwarzenegger has ever attempted. —Joe Leydon

PRIEST

(BRITISH)

A BBC production. (International sales: the Sales Co., London.) Produced by George Faber, Josephine Ward. Executive producer, Mark Shivas. Directed by Antonia Bird. Screenplay, Jimmy McGovern. Camera (color), Fred Tammes; editor, Sue Spivey; music, Andy Roberts; art direction, Ray Langhorn. Reviewed at Toronto Film Festival, Sept. 12, 1994. Running time: **105 MIN.**
Father Greg .... Linus Roache
Father Matthew .... Tom Wilkinson
Maria Kerrigan .... Cathy Tyson
Father Ellerton .... James Ellis
Graham .... Robert Carlyle
With: John Bennett, Rio Fanning, Jimmy Coleman, Lesley Sharp, Robert Pugh, Christine Tremarco.

"**P**riest" is an absolutely riveting, made-for-BBC slice-of-life drama that could generate strong, upscale action theatrically if promoted properly. A controversial look at incest, gay love and the Catholic Church, the pic screened as a "work-in-progress" at the Edinburgh Intl. Film Festival, where it took home the Michael Powell Award as best British feature film, and film had its official world preem to a rousing reaction at the Toronto fest.

"Priest" is the first full-length feature from theater and TV vet Antonia Bird, and Bird impresses with an ability to maintain an entertaining pace while never neglecting the weighty issues raised by Liverpool writer Jimmy McGovern's script. Bird has clearly already attracted attention in Hollywood: She is currently in post-production on the Touchstone Pictures release "Mad Love," starring Drew Barrymore and Chris O'Donnell.

Father Greg (Linus Roache), a young priest brimming with lofty ideals, is in for a rude shock to his value system when he arrives in a tough, inner-city Liverpool parish. First there's his colleague Father Matthew (Tom Wilkinson), a middle-aged social activist prone to giving rabble-rousing, left-wing speeches from the pulpit. Even worse — from Father Greg's point of view — is the fact that Father Matthew is openly breaking his vows of celibacy and living with a woman.

But the young priest's naive sense of right-and-wrong soon begins to come apart at the seams. One night, he switches from his day-job robes into a leather jacket and heads out to a local gay bar, where he picks up a guy. His own transgression of church protocol induces a major guilt trip for Father Greg, and the ethical horizon becomes even more cloudy when a young girl tells him in the confessional that her father is sexually abusing her.

The priest feels he can't help the girl because it would break the seal of silence of the confession. There is an electrifying scene in which Father Greg confronts the unrepentant, abusive father in the confessional. Things go from bad to worse when Father Greg's lover, Graham (Robert Carlyle), refuses to disappear from sight, and the two conflicts come to a head in an inspirational finale that manages to criticize the hypocrisy of Catholic doctrine without resorting to a blanket condemnation of the church.

Roache will turn heads with his intense perf in a difficult role, and the rest of the cast get the job done with gritty flair. McGovern's script is refreshingly down-to-earth, and it's his willingness to generate laughs from even the direst situations that makes the pic so accessible.

Shot with the sort of gutsy street style associated with early Stephen Frears or recent Ken Loach, "Priest" is a fine example of how to craft an issues pic that isn't just preaching the same old sermon.
—Brendan Kelly

COLONEL CHABERT

(LE COLONEL CHABERT)

(FRENCH)

October Films (U.S.) release of a Film Par Film production. Produced by Jean-Louis Livi. Executive producer, Bernard Marescot. Directed by Yves Angelo. Screenplay, Jean Cosmos, Veronique Lagrange, Angelo, based on the novel by Honore de Balzac. Camera (color), Bernard Lutic; editor, Thiery Derocles; art direction, Bernard Vezat; costumes, Franca Squarciapino; sound (Dolby), Pierre Gamet; assistant director, Frederic Blum. Reviewed at Toronto Film Festival, Sept. 9, 1994. Running time: **110 MIN.**
Chabert .... Gerard Depardieu
Countess Ferraud .... Fanny Ardant
Derville .... Fabrice Luchini
Count Ferraud .... Andre Dussollier
Boucard .... Daniel Prevost
Hure .... Olivier Saladin
Godeschal .... Maxime Leroux
Desroches .... Eric Elmosnino
Simonnin .... Guillaume Romain
Boutin .... Patrick Bordier
Chamblin ....:.. Claude Rich
With: Jean Cosmos, Jacky Nercessian, Albert Delpy, Marc Maidenberg, Romane Bohringer, Valerie Bettencourt, Florence Guerfy, Julie Depardieu, Isabelle Wolfe.

Acclaimed French cinematographer Yves Angelo ("Germinal," "Tous Les Matins du monde") makes a self-assured and uncommonly satisfying directorial debut with "Colonel Chabert," a fascinating period drama that boasts the star power of Gerard Depardieu and Fanny Ardant and literary pedigree of Balzac. It's a winning combination that should help U.S. distrib October Films score a critical and commercial hit on the arthouse circuit when pic begins platform release at year's end.

Angelo boldly establishes his command of the medium in drama's mesmerizing opening sequence, a haunting depiction of the sorting out of fatalities after the 1807 Battle of Eylau. The soundtrack swells with the mournful second movement of Beethoven's Trio in D Major, Op. 70 (the "Ghost" trio) — the only sound heard during the otherwise silent sequence — while bodies are stripped of uniforms and valuables and prepared for mass burial. But in that group of nameless, faceless dead lies a man who is still alive, if just barely.

Trouble is, it takes Colonel Chabert (Depardieu) a decade to recover and make his way back to Paris. When he returns, he finds he is officially listed as dead. His "widow" (Ardant) has claimed his fortune and taken a new husband, the politically ambitious Count Ferraud (Andre Dussollier). Not surprisingly, Countess Ferraud — who has two children by her second spouse — refuses to acknowledge the disheveled and wild-eyed stranger as her late husband.

The source material is Balzac's classic novel, but the mood is deliciously Dickensian in the law office where Chabert goes to file a lawsuit to regain his name, wife and fortune. His case is accepted by Derville (Fabrice Luchini), a brilliant and much-admired lawyer who could teach modern-day attorneys a thing or two about the fine art of legal hardball.

It may be difficult to imagine anyone stealing a pic from Depardieu and Ardant, but Luchini comes impressively close to such grand larceny with his stylish, sharp-witted portrayal of Derville.

But Depardieu is the one who ultimately dominates "Colonel Chabert." His performance and the pic itself may remind many of another case of dubious identity, "The Return of Martin Guerre." But Depardieu, looking appreciably trimmer than he has in quite some time, does not attempt to repeat his earlier triumph. His work here is a fresh, carefully calibrated mix of enigmatic brooding, volcanic rage and obsessive cunning.

Ardant is equally effective as Countess Ferraud, a woman who has risen from squalid beginnings by thoroughly reinventing herself.

Ardant and Depardieu (reunited onscreen for the first time since Francois Truffaut's second-to-last feature, 1981's "The Woman Next Door") develop an emotionally diverse give and take that is rich with anger, irony and ambiguity. A scene in which Derville vainly attempts to get the couple to agree to an out-of-court settlement is only the most obvious of several scenes that resound with a provocative contemporary relevance.

Except for the stunning opening and a few briefly glimpsed battlefield panoramas, Angelo keeps the action up-close and personal. Some auds may find the early scenes excessively talky. But many more ticketbuyers will appreciate Angelo's willingness to emphasize the harsh poetry he and co-screenwriters Jean Cosmos and Veronique Lagrange have adapted from Balzac.

As Count Ferraud, Dussollier has relatively few scenes, but he makes the absolute most of his character's ambiguities. Other supporting players, including budding French star Romane Bohringer ("The Accompanist") in a cameo bit as a maid, are excellent.

Technically, "Colonel Chabert" is outstanding across the board. Bernard Lutic's cinematography, Franca Squarciapino's costumes and Bernard Vezat's art direction vividly enhance the period flavor. The musical score consists entirely of classic selections aptly chosen by Angelo. Expect strong sales for a soundtrack album. —*Joe Leydon*

A MAN OF NO IMPORTANCE

(BRITISH)

A Sony Pictures Classics release of a Majestic/Newcomm/BBC Films presentation of a Little Bird production. Produced by Jonathan Cavendish. Executive producers, James Mitchell, Guy East, Robert Cooper, Mark Shivas. Directed by Suri Krishnamma. Screenplay, Barry Devlin. Camera (Technicolor), Ashley Rowe; editor, David Freeman; music, Julian Nott; production design, Jamie Leonard; art direction, Frank Flood; costume design, Phoebe De Gaye; sound (Dolby), David Stephenson; assistant director, Lisa Mulcahy; casting, Michelle Guish. Reviewed at Toronto Film Festival, Aug. 9, 1994. Running time: **98 MIN.**
Alfie Byrne .... Albert Finney
Lily Byrne .... Brenda Fricker
Ivor Carney .... Michael Gambon
Adele Rice .... Tara Fitzgerald
Robbie Fay .... Rufus Sewell
Inspector Carson ...... Patrick Malahide
Christy Ward .... David Kelly
Father Ignatius Kenny .... Mick Lally

Deception is the key element in the early-1960s, Dublin-set "A Man of No Importance." While it initially reveals itself as a larkish, romantic ode to a bygone time, it evolves darker tones and comes perilously close to full-bore tragedy by fade-out. Commercially, it's an uneasy mix, requiring very special handling to reach a niche audience. Critical response will play a crucial part in acceptance internationally.

Unquestionably, the emotional roller-coaster ride is kept under control by another full-blooded performance by Albert Finney. He's Alfie Byrne, a fiftysomething bus conductor with a glint of the poet. His route is a magical mystery tour in which the regular riders have been conscripted into a play circle.

He's been toying with the idea of staging Oscar Wilde's "Salome" (following last season's "The Importance of Being Earnest") when Adele Rice (Tara Fitzgerald) climbs aboard — his idealized vision of the temptress. It also appears that the never-married man fancies her away from the rehearsal hall. But, sad to say, she has a boyfriend back in her village.

Barry Devlin's screenplay recreates Dublin as a small, provincial town where everyone has their nose in their neighbor's business and the church is the cornerstone of social life. Alfie, of course, wants to put on his show at the church, and the good father, upon hearing the play's about John the Baptist, assumes it's of the highest piety.

But the intimacy of the environment is certain to be Alfie's undoing. His sister (Brenda Fricker) finds his immersion in books and "art" unhealthy. Carney (Michael Gambon), the local butcher and King Herod of the piece, is shocked that words such as "virgin" appear in the play, and that Alfie, the director, has his attention focused on Adele.

When romance with his star is cut short, the conductor invokes the playwright, asking her if she's heard of "the love that dare not speak its name." The man, so devoted to the works of Wilde, begins to wonder whether his fatherly attitude toward his driver Robbie (Rufus Sewell) might actually have a sexual connotation.

Finney plays the role like a finely tuned fiddle. His character's elfin quality masks not worldliness but naivete. His ability to draw us along in the wrong direction and surprise us with the same revelations he experiences is masterful.

The support cast, from vets such as Gambon, Fricker and David Kelly to tyros Fitzgerald and Sewell, is superlative. They provide a rich texture and authenticity which elevate the proceedings.

Still, director Suri Krishnamma can't quite accommodate the abrupt shifts in tone that infuse the narrative. Despite fine work from his actors and smooth technical polish, the more provocative elements of the tale arise awkwardly and grate against the early section's almost whimsical nature. It's an odd melange, decidedly for the more rigorous moviegoer. —*Leonard Klady*

DANCE ME OUTSIDE

(CANADIAN)

A Cineplex/Odeon release of a Yorktown/Shadow Shows production. Sales: Alliance. Produced by Brian Dennis, Bruce McDonald. Executive producers, Norman Jewison, Sarah Hayward. Directed by McDonald. Screenplay, McDonald, Don McKellar, based on the book by W. P. Kinsella. Camera (Film House), Miroslaw Baszak; editor, Michael Pacek; music, Mychael Danna; production design, John Dondertman; costume design, Beth Pasternak; sound (Dolby), Ross Redfern; assistant director, David Webb; casting, Clare Walker. Reviewed at Toronto Film Festival, Sept. 9, 1994. Running time: **84 MIN.**
Silas Crow .... Ryan Rajendra Black
Frank Fencepost .... Adam Beach
Sadie Maracle .... Jennifer Podemski
Gooch .... Michael Greyeyes
Illianna .... Lisa LaCroix
Robert McVey .... Kevin Hicks
Ma Crow .... Rose Marie Trudeau
Robert Coyote .... Selim
Running Bear Sandoval
Poppy .... Sandrine Holt
Clarance Gaskill .... Hugh Dillon

Director Bruce McDonald has concocted a feisty adaptation of novelist W.P. Kinsella's "Dance Me Outside" — a contemporary look at life on an Indian reservation and its environs. Bolstered by a winning, youthful cast, the film is a droll ensemble piece that makes its serious points skillfully and effortlessly. The unique perspective of the milieu alone should provide a solid commercial hook, and the consummate craft of the production ensures strong specialized returns domestically and in upscale foreign outings.

Central to the story is Silas Crow (Ryan Rajendra Black), a teen living on a Northern Ontario reserve whose goal is to take a mechanic's course in Toronto with his buddy Frank Fencepost (Adam Beach). Part of his entrance requirement is to write a story about his home, and the film's narrative serves as the basis of that tale.

The incident that focuses the array of characters is the rape and murder of Little Margaret Wolfchild. The killer, Clarance Gaskill (Hugh Dillon), is a rowdy who hangs out at the Blue Quill pool hall. His conviction for manslaughter, for which he's sentenced to two years, has a powerful impact on individuals and the community as a whole.

The orbiting vignettes tend to be humorous or poignant. When Silas' sister Illianna (Lisa LaCroix) returns home with her Anglo husband, Robert (Kevin Hicks), the ensuing tension is less about cultural differences than their childlessness.

When it's revealed that Robert has a low sperm count, a plan is hatched to couple Illianna with an ex-boyfriend while the buddies enlist friends to stage a bogus ritual in

which Robert will be inducted into the tribe. The latter section is a comic delight as he dons war paint and proclaims himself the spirit of the wolverine.

Without wearing its sentiment on its sleeve, "Dance Me Outside" subtly conveys the nature of Indian-white tension from the natives' perspective. They are neither noble nor savage, but an abused minority with quite understandable and deep-seated resentment toward the colonists.

McDonald and co-scenarist Don McKellar construct an ingenious script from the novel by Kinsella (best known for "Shoeless Joe," which was made for the screen as "Field of Dreams").

Seemingly episodic and anecdotal, there's actually little dross to be found. Even the most arcane incident ultimately proves to have profound significance to the central story.

The cast of newcomers is a knockout, with Black and Beach expressing a "Bill & Ted"-type camaraderie textured with more profound considerations. Both are extremely charismatic, and Beach reveals a natural comic flair.

There's not a weak link among the supporting cast, with special nods to Jennifer Podemski as Silas' serious, on-and-off-again girlfriend, LaCroix as the sister and Michael Greyeyes as a former reservation bad boy who's reformed by the harsher realities of life.

An extremely handsome production, "Dance Me Outside" has a stunning sheen thanks to the camerawork of Miroslaw Baszak and John Dondertman's design. Mychael Danna's score and the song selections provide the film with a gritty authenticity. —*Leonard Klady*

DOUBLE HAPPINESS

(CANADIAN)

A First Generation/New Views Films production. Produced by Stephen Hegyes, Rose Lam Waddell. Directed, written by Mina Shum. Camera (color), Peter Wunstorf; editor, Alison Grace; music, Shadowy Men on a Shadowy Planet; production design, Michael Bjornson; costume design, Cynthia Summers; sound (Dolby), Tim Richardson; assistant director, Shirley-Anne Parsons; casting, Ann Anderson, Carmen Ruiz-Laza. Reviewed at Toronto Film Festival, Sept. 7, 1994. Running time: **92 MIN.**
Jade Li .... Sandra Oh
Dad Li .... Stephen Chang
Mom Li .... Alannah Ong
Pearl Li .... Frances You
Andrew Chau .... Johnny Mah
Mark .... Callum Rennie
Sau Wan Chin .... Donald Fong
Lisa Chan .... Claudette Carracedo
Mrs. Mar .... Barbara Tse

The debut feature of writer/director Mina Shum, "Double Happiness," immediately tags her as a kind of distaff Ang Lee and a definite budding talent with a bright future. The low-budget saga of a young Chinese-Canadian woman caught between two cultures is an appealing, feisty yarn enlivened by a sharp cast and unaffected direction. It's an unquestionable audience pleaser with strong specialized potential both domestically and in offshore locales.

The title invokes a philosophical belief that it's possible to find balance between traditional and modern societies. But for aspiring twentysomething actress Jade Li (Sandra Oh), the world of her father (Stephen Chang) is rife with rules that run counter to her pursuits.

Still, she wants to please him. So she endures arranged dates with prospective husbands and puts on a phony facade to give credibility to a harmonious life in Canada when his old crony from China comes calling.

It's pretty weighty stuff at its core. But Shum prefers to invoke the humor and pathos of each incident and therein lies the film's strength and offbeat flavor. Rather than dismiss one caller — who's even less keen about the arrangement — she rubs him off the family list by feigning indignity because she claims he had her pick up the check at a restaurant. The raised eyebrows from this revelation say it all.

The stifling nature of raw-boned traditions is having a detrimental effect on Jade. She must keep her relationship with Mark (Callum Rennie), a non-Asian, a guarded secret, and when the family catches wind of the situation, it's blood relationships that prevail.

Shum employs some potentially dangerous devices — such as having characters address the camera — and she favors a candy-box color scheme that gives the proceedings an air of unreality. But her work is generally assured, and with a bit of careful tweaking, the picture's few lulls could be erased.

The performances are a delight, with Chang deftly creating a character imprisoned by ancestral dictates. Although he's capable of unnecessary cruelty, his motivations are completely understandable.

But the film's highlight is Oh's mesmerizing performance. She's a stunning discovery.

—*Leonard Klady*

SECOND BEST

(BRITISH-U.S.)

A Warner Bros. release of a Regency Enterprises and Alcor Films presentation of a Sarah Radclyffe/Fron Film production. Produced by Radclyffe. Executive producer, Arnon Milchan. Directed by Chris Menges. Screenplay, David Cook, based on his novel. Camera (Technicolor), Ashley Rowe; editor, George Akers; music, Simon Boswell; production design, Michael Howells; art direction, Roger Thomas; set decoration, Sam Riley; costume design, Nic Ede; sound (Dolby), Peter Glossop; associate producer, Judy Freeman; assistant director, Waldo Roeg; casting, Susie Figgis. Reviewed at Warner Bros. Studios, Burbank, Sept. 7, 1994. (In Toronto Film Festival.) MPAA Rating: PG-13. Running time: **105 MIN.**

Graham Holt	William Hurt
James	Chris Cleary Miles
John	Keith Allen
Margery	Prunella Scales
Debbie	Jane Horrocks
Bernard	Alan Cumming
Uncle Turpin	John Hurt

The agonizing process by which a withdrawn man and his troubled adopted son grow to know and love each other is minutely charted in "Second Best." Nicely acted and dramatized in all its particulars, the film is nevertheless so modest in its aim and achievement that it will be exceedingly difficult to drum up much audience interest in seeing it, at least theatrically.

Indeed, it is hard to remember the last time either Warner Bros. or exec producer Arnon Milchan was involved in such a small-scale production. One just doesn't see the major studios these days making pictures about the emotional problems of two difficult people living in a cramped house in a tiny village in Wales, much less one where there's neither romance nor action. More's the pity, but that's the way it is.

Told with the aid of many quick flashbacks and a change in narrative voice, novelist and screenwriter David Cook's acutely felt story revolves around the deprived emotional lives of 10-year-old James (Chris Cleary Miles) and the 42-year-old man who would adopt him, Graham Holt (William Hurt). James' mother is dead and his father, John (Keith Allen), is a long-term jailbird. Living a sad childhood in an orphanage, James holds dearly to the memory of his father and the hope that their bond will somehow bring them together again.

For his part, Graham is also motherless, and his father (Alan Cumming) is bedridden due to a stroke. A rumpled, withdrawn village postmaster, Graham has never had a significant emotional contact or sexual experience, but now has the sudden impulse to adopt a boy,

which would be the first assertive thing he's done in his life.

On a bureaucratic level alone, the process is not easy, but Graham receives permission to have James stay with him at his little home. Graham initially proposes a kind of partnership arrangement, and James is clever enough to take advantage of this, testing how far he can go and sometimes erupting into violent and rebellious fits.

James lets Graham know in no uncertain terms that he'll never truly replace his real dad, and conquering this attitude becomes Graham's uphill battle. After his own father dies, Graham is officially allowed to foster James, at which point the boy's old man suddenly turns up, looking terrible and stricken with AIDS.

This development is clearly designed to bring matters to a head and resolve them, a tad too conveniently. The final reel becomes a bit murky and incipiently sentimental, with director Chris Menges trying to understate the feel-good ending but also underplaying the dramatic payoff.

To a large extent, pic depends upon performance to put it over. A seemingly unlikely choice to play an unworldly Welshman, Hurt lets his inwardness work to great benefit and creates a completely convincing and often touching characterization of a man who tries, with great difficulty, to come out of his shell in an uncommon way.

Miles is an excellent match as the deprived, temperamental James, expressing the many faces of boyhood from fearful defensiveness and rebellion to startling precociousness.

Former cinematographer Menges, in his third directorial outing, evinces a great sympathy with Cook's material and exercises restraint in the most blatantly emotional moments. It's adept work on a small canvas. In line with this, behind-the-scenes contributions are correct but unobtrusive.

—*Todd McCarthy*

ECLIPSE

(CANADIAN-GERMAN)

A Malofilm Distribution release (Canada) of a Fire Dog Films/TiMe Medienvertieb production, with the participation of Telefilm Canada, Ontario Film Development Corp., the National Film Board of Canada, PAFPS Program, the Canada Council, LIFT. (International sales: Malofilm Intl., Montreal.) Produced by Camelia Frieberg, Jeremy Podeswa. Executive producer, Wolfram Tichy. Directed, written by Podeswa. Camera (color/b&w), Miroslaw Baszak; editor, Susan Maggi; music, Ernie Tollar; art direction, Tamara Deverell; sound, Jane Tattersal; associate producer, Regine Schmid. Reviewed at Toronto Film Festival, Sept. 11, 1994. Running time: **95 MIN.**

Henry	Von Flores
Brian	John Gilbert
Sylvie	Pascale Montpetit
Gabriel	Manuel Aranguiz
Sarah	Maria Del Mar
Norman	Greg Ellwand
Angelo	Matthew Ferguson
Michael	Earl Pastko
Jim	Daniel MacIvor
Carlotta	Kirsten Johnson

"Eclipse" is an impressive debut feature from Toronto helmer Jeremy Podeswa that will elicit strong response on the arthouse circuit with its powerful blend of casual sex, eye-catching, arty camera work and witty, sophisticated dialogue. Eclectic variety of gay and straight sexual encounters may scare off some mainstream auds, but Podeswa's assured sense of style will appeal to those looking for sexy, hip, upscale fare.

Innovative pic updates "sex, lies, and videotape" turf by capturing a series of lusty liaisons featuring 10 interconnected characters who are all part of a complex network of friends, lovers and casual acquaintances. Podeswa's nontraditional narrative ties together this web of desire by having one participant from each encounter appear in the next intimate rendezvous, where he or she steams up the screen with another newcomer.

All these couplings are shot in stylish black-and-white, with connecting sequences about Toronto's preparation for the upcoming solar eclipse lensed in color. High school student Angelo (Matthew Ferguson) is videotaping a documentary on eclipse fever for a school project, and his color images of people talking about the event are intercut with sex scenes in an assortment of settings, including a hotel room, an artist's loft, a suburban living room and a crowded nightclub bathroom.

First close encounter of the erotic kind has middle-aged, middle-class Brian (John Gilbert) picking up a young hustler (Von Flores) at night, and, shortly thereafter, Brian is seen getting it on with Sylvie (Pascale Montpetit), his French-Canadian domestic. Next scene features Sylvie rolling around the floor at her English-as-a-second-language school with Gabriel, a Central American refugee (Manuel Aranguiz), and Gabriel passes the amorous torch to Sarah (Maria Del Mar), who is the wife of his immigration lawyer.

This carnal game of musical chairs includes everything from a poignant moment of passion between two gay friends to a funny morning-after conversation where two lovers try to piece together what happened a few hours earlier. In spite of the content, pic isn't really about steamy thrills. Podeswa's intelligent script is more concerned with the fleeting pleasures that desire offers and how difficult it is to maintain passionate relationships.

Canadian thesps deliver uniformly strong performances, particularly Montpetit as the tough-talking domestic and Ferguson as the precocious kid with the video camera and seductive looks. Miroslaw Baszak's camerawork is a beautiful mix of moody, black-and-white portraits, grainy video images and colorful footage of the moon and sun crossing paths, which was shot in Mexico during a 1991 solar eclipse. Ernie Tollar's worldbeat-flavored score adds an exotic edge to the impassioned proceedings. Despite modest budget, all other tech credits are excellent.

It won't be an easy sell, but "Eclipse" will click with same urbane auds who enjoy fellow Toronto helmer Atom Egoyan's work. Pic serves notice that Podeswa is a visual stylist to keep an eye on.

—*Brendan Kelly*

CRUMB

(DOCU)

A David Lynch presentation of a Superior Pictures production. Produced by Lynn O'Donnell, Terry Zwigoff. Executive producers, Lawrence Wilkinson, Albert Berger, Lianne Halfon. Coproducer, Neal Halfon. Directed by Zwigoff. Camera (DuArt color; 16mm), Maryse Allberti; editor, Victor Livingston; sound, Scott Breindel. Reviewed at Toronto Film Festival, Sept. 9, 1994. (Also in New York Film Festival.) Running time: **119 MIN.**

A frank, intimate look at a phenomenal popular artist and his extraordinarily dysfunctional family, "Crumb" is an excellent countercultural documentary. Made by a longtime friend of the subject, pic goes a good way toward explaining the whys and wherefores of the twisted, biting, extremely funny comic-book art of Robert Crumb, just as it puts a positively weird American family up onscreen with the cooperation of at least some of its members. Film is ideal for specialized theatrical slots and should have a good life on video and selected cable outlets, although it is no doubt too racy and politically incorrect for PBS. Somewhere, someday it will have to be shown on a double bill with "Brother's Keeper."

R. Crumb is still the best and most enduring artist to have emerged from the world of underground comics, a mordant satirist and drug-inspired fabulist who rode the wave of anti-establishment irreverence to cult popularity in the mid-1960s. A social misfit of the first order, Crumb draws characters and outrageous, lewd events with such exaggerated precision that art critic Robert Hughes herein aptly calls him "the Breughel of the 20th century," so that his work alone justi-

fies the extended attention the film lavishes upon him.

But the man's singular personality and unimaginable family background take this way behind a mere study of a pop culture figure. A slouching, weed-like figure in thick glasses and '40s-style hat who looks like a gunsel from some cheap vintage Hollywood crime film, the Zap Comix king skulks in and out of encounters with ex-girlfriends and wife, his kids, sex mag models and, most of all, his mother and two brothers (two sisters refused to participate).

Enough is seen of the family's earlier years to spot the Crumb boys as nerds and outcasts. All three were talented artists, however, especially brothers Robert and Charles. But the latter stopped drawing early on and is seen in the film living with his mother as a medicated recluse, albeit an insightful and willing participant and narrator of the Crumb family saga, as well as a strangely effective camera subject.

Not only do the brothers talk about their intense artistic rivalry and "sadistic bully" of a father, but they dwell extensively on their youthful sex fantasies and practices, which had considerable bearing on Robert's later work (his first sex object was Bugs Bunny).

At a lecture, Crumb explains how he feels ripped off in the cases of perhaps his three most famous creations — the "Keep on Truckin'" slogan and drawings, the "Cheap Thrills" Janis Joplin album cover and "Fritz the Cat" in its movie incarnation. Drawing all the while, he visits the Haight in San Francisco where, despite having been such a local hero, he says he could never fit in with the hippie crowd; expresses his disgust at commercialization; drops in on his brother Max, living a marginal existence in S.F.; attends a New York gallery opening, where Hughes and others hold forth on his work, and explains how he traded six of his sketchbooks for a chateau in the South of France, where he has now lived for two years in an attempt to escape what he considers the horrors of modern American life.

Although it's clear that drugs — LSD in particular — played a major role in Crumb's creative breakthrough, pic could have used more analytical commentary on this score. Film doesn't ignore the controversial and, to some people, disturbing misogyny in Crumb's work; he himself fesses up to it, but isn't about to start censoring himself as an artist.

But the film keeps coming back to the family, and rewardingly so. Their eccentricities represent a source of easy laughs at the outset, but director Terry Zwigoff spends enough time at the homestead with Robert, Charles and Mom for the viewer to feel deeply how genuinely

disturbed they are, and info on certain family members' fates in the final crawl proves truly upsetting.

Zwigoff has used his enduring friendship with Crumb and knowledge of his work and family to no doubt get closer to the core than anyone else could have, and has also structured his film intelligently. It may be slightly overlong at two hours, but Crumb fans, who will probably increase in number in the wake of the attention the picture will generate, shouldn't mind at all.

—*Todd McCarthy*

POSTCARDS FROM AMERICA

An Islet presentation in association with Channel Four Films of a Normal production. (International sales: the Sales Co., London.) Produced by Christine Vachon, Craig Paull. Executive producer, Mark Nash. Directed, written by Steve McLean, adapted from the writings of David Wojnarowicz. Camera (color), Ellen Kuras; editor, Elizabeth Gazzara; music, Stephen Endelman; production design, Therese Deprez; art direction, Scott Pask; costume design, Sara Clotnick; sound, Neil Danziger, Jan McLaughlin; coproducer, McLean; associate producers, Philip Yenswine, Olivier Renaud-Clement, Joel Hinman, Pamela Koffler; assistant directors, Elizabeth Gill, Chris Hoover; casting, Daniel Haughey. Reviewed at Toronto Film Festival, Sept. 11, 1994. (Also in New York Film Festival.) Running time: **89 MIN.**

Adult David	James Lyons
Teenage David	Michael Tighe
Young David	Olmo Tighe
The Hustler	Michael Imperioli
Father	Michael Ringer
Mother	Maggie Low

"**P**ostcards From America" is an inert, experimental indie feature that sends out stylized impressions of a difficult, disturbed life. Based on the rage-filled autobiographical writings of artist David Wojnarowicz, who died of AIDS two years ago, first feature by Brit musicvideo helmer Steve McLean is decked out in many avant-garde trappings that make its impact on the viewer remote and secondhand despite the primal nature of the material. A downer without much compensatory insight or dramatic power, this won't travel far beyond the fest circuit and core gay audiences.

Wojnarowicz railed about the horrors of AIDS and recounted aspects of his rough life as an abused child and Times Square hustler in print, on video and as a performance artist, as well as on film for Rosa von Praunheim. Present pic is based on two books, "Close to the Knives" and "Memories That Smell Like Gasoline," but is strangely stripped of any identification of the leading character, named David, as a potential or actual artist.

This is just one of several strategies that drains the fragmented story of the strength it might have had, as McLean shuffles and deals the cards from his deck in a highly selective manner and leaves far too many of them face down. Here as elsewhere displaying the influence of Todd Haynes' "Poison," also produced by Christine Vachon, three aspects of David's life are presented in different visual styles: a depressing suburban childhood that included regular beatings from his violent alcoholic father, his stint as a New York street hustler and petty criminal, and an abstract section that finds David wandering, and sometimes at risk, in the desert.

Most of the action, such as it is, is deliberately distanced via David's ongoing voiceover narration and monologues by various characters, notably the father, who is more enraged than David. This sort of approach can work if the language and accompanying visuals are poetic enough to cut to the heart by a different route than can be accomplished by conventional dramatics, but neither the writing nor the images are bracing or haunting. The circumstances of the kid's upbringing may have been deplorable, but the film bestows upon them no special dimension to compel the audience's indulgent attention.

From a sexual p.o.v., pic assumes a gay perspective even from childhood, as the youthful David is provoked by an older masochist in one vividly peculiar scene, and goes on to recount numerous pickups, quickies, make-out sessions and anonymous encounters without getting very graphic.

Indeed, film is so dry that it sacrifices any power to disturb, jolt or make the viewer see anything in a new way. If "Postcards" was meant to express Wojnarowicz's howl of anguish, it has failed by muffling it with too many self-consciously artistic distancing devices.

Acting and technical aspects of this low-budgeter are so-so.

—*Todd McCarthy*

CURSE OF THE STARVING CLASS

A Trimark release and production. Produced by William S. Gilmore, Harel Goldstein. Executive producers, Bruce Beresford, David Goldstein. Directed by Michael McClary. Screenplay, Beresford, based on Sam Shepard's play. Camera (color), Dick Quinlan; editor, Dean Goodhill; production design, Ladislav Wilheim; set decoration, Grey Smith; costume design, Kathryn Morrison; sound (Ultra Stereo), Robert Wald; associate producer, Fran Roy; assistant director, Tom Herod; casting, Shari Rodes, Joseph Middleton. Reviewed at Toronto Film Festival, Sept. 10, 1994. Running time: **101 MIN.**
Weston .... James Woods
Ella .... Kathy Bates
Wesley .... Henry Thomas
Emma .... Kristin Fiorella
Ellis .... Lou Gossett Jr.
Taylor .... Randy Quaid

A stellar, eccentric cast brings class but no emotional resonance to "Curse of the Starving Class," a peculiarly ineffective rendition of Sam Shepard's 1977 award-winning play. An ironic dissection of the American Dream as it affects and destroys one farming family, pic signals a curse at the box office, though video prospects may be better due to Shepard's name and recognition value of James Woods and Kathy Bates.

If the piece seems outdated and familiar, it is not because its issues are no longer relevant, but rather a result of Shepard's obsessive exploration of the same myths and conflicts in such subsequent works as "Buried Child," "True West" and "Fool for Love."

The usual Shepard themes of commitment to the land, disintegration of the nuclear family and intergenerational strife between father and son are all here — along with the typical iconography of dilapidated houses, shabby motels and sleazy bars.

Woods plays Weston, the alcoholic, irresponsible patriarch of a down-on-its-luck family whose members keep reminding themselves they do not belong to the starving class. Weston's wife, Ella (Bates), a feisty if disenchanted woman, can barely manage the run-down farm and feed her children, Wesley (Henry Thomas) and Emma (Kristin Fiorella).

Each member of this dysfunctional family engages in daydreams and fantasies to escape a gloomy, hopeless fate.

Desperate to visit Paris before it's too late, Ella tries to sell the farm to Taylor (Randy Quaid), a greedy land developer, even if it means going to bed with him.

Eluding his collectors and still haunted by nightmares from his combat days in Vietnam, Weston has his own plan for the land.

With no guidance from their parents, Wesley and Emma are lost souls, confronted with the fact that they are doomed inheritors of the family curse.

Scripter Beresford, better known as a director, has worked hard to open up the play. It backfires: Shepard's offbeat, ironic humor, so integral to the magic of theater, is missing from the writing — and direction.

Pic is also unsuccessful in conveying the poetic quality of the language — onscreen, actors appear bizarre when talking to an empty refrigerator, their sheep or themselves.

First-time director Michael McClary doesn't trust his material, and subsequently his style hysterically vacillates between outdoor and indoor scenes. With all his effort, however, the narrative remains theatrical in its structure, with well-timed exits and entrances.

Helmer uses too many "cinematic" cuts and intercuts, and the actors have no opportunity to build coherent characters or to sustain any emotion beyond the few seconds they are given in brief scenes that are erratically paced and edited.

Under these circumstances, Woods gives one of his weaker performances, particularly in the first half, when he's over-the-top.

Bates, who reprises her acclaimed Off Broadway role, is no more than OK. Unfortunately, the director inflicts on her close-ups that are not only unflattering but don't do much to register the emotions of her complex character as both victim and survivor.

Thomas and Fiorella have a few good moments, but Quaid and Lou Gossett Jr. (as the local bar owner) are defeated by one-dimensional roles.

This is a miss on several levels, proving again that what works on stage doesn't necessarily translate to the screen. —*Emanuel Levy*

VIVE L'AMOUR
(AIQING WANSUI)
(TAIWANESE)

A Sunny Overseas Corp./Shiung Fa Corp. production for Central Motion Picture Corp. (International sales: CMPC, Taipei.) Produced by Chung Hu-pin. Executive producer, Jiang Feng-chy. Executive in charge of production, Hsu Li-kung. Line producer, Tzon Wei-hua. Directed by Tsai Ming-liang. Screenplay, Tsai, Yang Pi-ying, Tsai Yi-chun. Camera (color), Liao Pen-jung, Lin Ming-kuo; editor, Sung Fan-chen; art direction, Li Pao-lin; set decoration, Chen Chien-hsun; costume design, Luo Chung-hung; sound design, Hsin Chiang-sheng; sound, Yang Ching-an, Hu Ding-yi; assistant director, Yu Cheng-wei, Tsai Yi-chun. Reviewed on vidcassette, London, Aug. 19, 1994. (In Venice Film Festival — competing.) Running time: **118 MIN.**
May Lin .... Yang Kuei-mei
Hsiao-kang .... Lee Kang-sheng
Ah-jung .... Chen Chao-jung
(Mandarin dialogue)

A nother in the lengthening line of Taiwanese urban alienation movies, "Vive L'Amour" is a severe letdown after young director Tsai Ming-liang's promising, multi-layered debut on the same theme, "Rebels of the Neon God." Poscy, anti-dramatic pic about three lost souls in contempo Taipei looks like it will lose most of its audience as well, though mild homoerotic undercurrents could find this a few friends in gay situations. Venice fest awarded pic the Gold Lion, which it shared with Macedonia's "Before the Rain."

First two reels (virtually sans dialogue) intro the three protagonists in downbeat style. Boyish, blank-faced salesman Hsiao-kang steals the key to a vacant apartment and halfheartedly slashes his wrist. Elsewhere in the city, smooth-looking Ah-jung picks up an older woman, May, and the two have sex in the same apartment.

Hsiao-kang, it turns out, sells indoor niches for crematorium urns. May is a real-estate agent, perpetually on the phone to clients and running from property to property. Ah-jung is a sidewalk vendor of clothing.

Though far from the bread line, all are "homeless" in their own ways, living off the rump of an affluent society but not a part of it. The two men meet and pal up, and when Ah-jung and May meet at the apartment for more sex, Hsiao-kang is an accidental witness under the bed. Long final sequence follows May as she breaks down in tears on the way to work.

Tsai's cool, immaculately framed style is occasionally effective (as black comedy) but mostly maddeningly mannered and empty, evoking little sympathy or engagement with the characters. Dialogue is flatly delivered, and Hsiao-kang's sexual confusion (explicit only near the end, when he minces around the apartment in femme clothes) seems more tacked on than integrated into the pic's emotional fabric.

Performances by the two males, both from "Rebels," are OK within pic's limits. As the sidelined woman, the experienced Yang Kuei-mei does her best with a thankless part. Technically, pic is fine, with clean lensing by its two cinematographers, but basically this is a so-what movie in spades. —*Derek Elley*

TWO BROTHERS, MY SISTER
(TRES IRMAOS)
(PORTUGUESE-FRENCH)

A Joaquim Pinto presentation of a Grupo de Estudos & Realizacoes (Lisbon)/Arion Prods. (Paris) production, with participation of ZDF, CNC, RTP, IPACA and the European Script Fund. (International sales: GER, Lisbon.) Executive producer, Pinto. Directed, written by Teresa Villaverde. Camera (color), Volker Tittel; editors, Vasco Pimentel, Villaverde; art direction, Joao Calvario; costume design, Rosa Almeida, Miguel Mendes; sound (Dolby), Pimentel. Reviewed at Venice Film Festival (competing), Sept. 1, 1994. Running time: **108 MIN.**
Maria .... Maria de Medeiros
Mario .... Marcello Urgeghe
Joao .... Evgeni Sidihin
Teresa .... Laura del Sol
The teacher .... Mireille Perrier
The father .... Fernando Reis Jr.
The mother .... Olimpia Carlisi
With: Luis Miguel Cintra.

S haking off her flimsy Euro-babe persona from "Pulp Fiction," Portuguese thesp Maria de Medeiros hauntingly plays a doomed waif bearing passive witness to her family's slow dissolution and her own destruction in "Two Brothers, My Sister." Sophomore feature by Teresa Villaverde balances stylishness with sobriety as it stealthily drums up a wrenching crescendo of despair. Though wide arthouse exposure may remain elusive, this elegantly constructed drama should make a considerable mark via festival and quality TV showings outside the U.S.

Villaverde eases straight into the anguished heart of her story, with a series of extended glimpses showing the crumbling process already well under way. The family's fragile figureheads are a blind, often drunkenly violent father (Fernando Reis Jr.) and his deeply unhappy wife (Olimpia Carlisi). Pushed into motherhood too young, she shrugs off the running of

September 19, 1994 (Cont.)

the house onto introspective, pathetically self-effacing Maria (Medeiros), who cooks, cleans, studies and holds down a job.

Violence erupts when Maria's brothers retaliate against their father for brutalizing his wife. They move out, adding family go-between to Maria's daunting duty roster. Having lost his job, the youngest brother, Mario (Marcello Urgeghe), turns despondently to an admiring older man (Luis Miguel Cintra) for support.

Without explicitly recounting her inner conflict, Villaverde and Medeiros mold Maria into a puzzling, almost self-sacrificing victim. Her love for her brothers is intensified to emotionally ambiguous extremes, traced back to the shared intimacy of their childhood.

Even a potentially liberating moment, such as a night out with her brothers, assumes a dark edge, with Maria giving herself over to a punishing sexual encounter. A glimmer of extra-familial communication with her teacher (Mireille Perrier) also fades quickly when Maria slips into her role as a dumping ground for other people's woes.

As the drama takes an increasingly grievous turn, Maria's precarious balance gets pushed further off-kilter. She distractedly stabs her boss while he attempts to rape her. Then she deals with her mother's matter-of-fact suicide in a squalid rented room, alone.

Villaverde sidesteps the grim story's plethora of melodramatic openings, instead using an imposing, finely modulated atmosphere as her driving force. She gets inside her characters' ruptured emotional states taking mainly furtive steps, and the approach is echoed by the solid, unerringly controlled cast.

Playing an intricate character who's crippled by solitude, Medeiros wields an intensity that so far remains untapped in her English-lingo outings. (Role won her a best actress nod at the Venice fest.) As the young brother, Urgeghe stands out in a strong supporting field.

Volker Tittel's handsome lensing of Lisbon's shadowy contours is persuasively in-synch with the film's doleful nature. —*David Rooney*

ASHES OF TIME

(DUNG CHE SAI DUK)

(HONG KONG)

A Scholar Films Co. (H.K.) presentation of a Jet Tone Prod. production, in association with Tsui Siu-ming Prod. Co., Beijing Film Studio, Pony Canyon. (International sales: Fortissimo, Amsterdam.) Produced by Tsai Sung-lin. Executive producer, Jeff Lau. Supervising producers, Norman Law, Tsui Siu-ming, Jacky Pang. Directed, written by Wong Kar-wai, based on characters from Louis Cha's novel "The Eagle Shooting Heroes." Camera (Agfacolor), Christopher Doyle; editors, Patrick Tam, William Chang, Hai Kit-wai, Kwong Chi-leung; music, Frankie Chan; production design, William Chang; art direction (Peking), Yang Zhanjia; costume design, Luk Ha-fong; sound, Leung Tat, Leung Lik-chi; martial arts supervisor, Sammo Hung; associate producers, Shu Kei (H.K.), Chen Zhigu (Peking). Reviewed at Venice Film Festival (competing), Sept. 10, 1994. Running time: **95 MIN.**
Ou-yang Feng .... Leslie Cheung
Huang Yao-shi ..... Tony Leung Kar-fai
Mu-rong Yin/
    Mu-rong
    Yang .... Brigitte Lin Ching-hsia
Blind
    Swordsman .... Tony Leung Chiu-wai
The Woman .... Maggie Cheung
Hung Chi .... Jacky Cheung
Peach Blossom .... Carina Liu
Young Girl .... Charlie Young
Hung Chi's Wife .... Bai Li
    (Cantonese dialogue)

Hong Kong sword 'n' sandal cinema gets its first art movie with the long-awaited "Ashes of Time," a rousing elegy to the heroic dark side that stabs straight to the emotional heart of the Chinese swordplay tradition. Frequently breathtaking, and never less than audacious, this complex, highly referential genre-bender could, however, prove a challenging sell in the international marketplace. Reaction at its Venice world preem swung from passionate support to total confusion, depending on individual ability to tune into its dense style and plotting.

A last-minute competition entry at Venice, pic was already a legend before it hit the screen, with a massive $HK40 million ($5.5 million) budget, a clutch of missed fest dates, and the attached name of cult director Wong Kar-wai ("Days of Being Wild," "Chung King Express"). The East Asian version, some five minutes longer with more action front and back, opened recently in Hong Kong.

"Ashes" began as the first of a two-pic production deal (with the same megastar cast and story basis) between Wong's company Jet Tone and the H.K. affil of Taiwan's Scholar Films. Under pressure to produce a B.O. winner for Chinese New Year '93, the second pic was brought forward, turned into a comedy (directed by Wong's partner

Jeff Lau) and emerged as "The Eagle Shooting Heroes: Dong Cheng Xi Jiu," scoring a healthy $HK22 million ($3 million).

By then, the skeds of the cast had changed, so Wong waited till summer '93 to complete the first movie, of which only a fifth had been shot in H.K. studios. Remainder of pic was shot on mainland China.

Like "Heroes," pic takes its inspiration from a popular late-'50s novel by Louis Cha (aka Chin Yung/Jin Yong), extracting a couple of aged characters and spinning a yarn around their earlier days.

Ou-yang Feng (Leslie Cheung), after youthful adventures and losing his love (Maggie Cheung) to his brother, runs a trouble-shooting business from a remote desert inn, agenting swordsmen for dirty work. Every year, he's visited by his pal, Huang (Tony Leung Kar-fai), who's also lovelorn; Huang later visits Ou-yang's pining ex at her home in White Camel Mountain.

Ou-yang is hired by a man, Murong Yang (Brigitte Lin Ching-hsia), to kill Huang, who once ditched Murong's sister, Yin. Yin also hires Ou-yang to kill her brother. Yin and Yang turn out to be the same person.

Other characters in the interlocking stories include a half-blind swordsman (Tony Leung Chiu-wai), whose wife (Carina Liu) fell in love with Huang; and a barefoot swordsman (Jacky Cheung) who avenges the death of the brother of a penniless young girl (Charlie Young). Pic ends with Ou-yang and Huang — the characters from Cha's novel — moving on to their separate destinies.

Plotting is no more or less labyrinthine than usual martial arts movies. But Wong throws an extra wrench in the works by giving over most of the movie to either voiceover soliloquizing (by both Ou-yang and Huang) or melancholic two-way dialogues; action sequences are more brief intermissions than narrative components.

Aside from a couple of large-scale action sequences, the pic doesn't flaunt its budget (50% of which went to above-the-line costs). For much of the time Wong's visual style has a pregnant simplicity, with plentiful use of close-ups, stark desert vistas and half-obscured faces. There's generally only one or two players onscreen, and the accent is always on the dialogue.

Action sequences (choreographed by veteran Sammo Hung) erupt almost unannounced, each taking its style from the main participant: Mu-rong's is over before it's started, and the half-blind swordsman's is only dimly perceived. Wong puts to striking effect an innovation (first used in his debut, "As Tears Go By") of shooting at 10 frames per second and double-printing each frame: Effect is like blurred, jerky slo-mo.

Most striking of all, however, is the movie's color palette, for which

Wong and Australian-born lenser Christopher Doyle copped a Venice Fest award. Mixing filters, reverse printing and pinpoint timing, the film often has an unreal, almost video-originated look, heavy on sepias and the like. Frankie Chan's epic melancholy score and Luk Ha-fong's realistic, lived-in costume design are further pluses.

Performances are on the money all round, and running time sensibly tight. Chinese title literally means "Evil East, Poisonous West," nicknames for the Huang and Ou-yang characters. —*Derek Elley*

JASON'S LYRIC

A Gramercy Pictures release of a Jackson/McHenry Co. presentation, in association with Propaganda Films. (International sales: Polygram Film Intl., London.) Produced by Doug McHenry, George Jackson. Executive producers, Suzanne Broderick, Clarence Avant. Co-executive producer, Marilla Ross. Executive in charge of production (Propaganda Films), Tim Clawson. Co-producers, Dwight Williams, Bobby Smith Jr. Directed by McHenry. Screenplay, Smith. Camera (color), Francis Kenny; editor, Andrew Mondshein; additional editing, William Scharf; music, Afrika, Matt Noble; music supervision, Adam Kidron; production design, Simon Dobbin; art direction, David Lazan; costume supervisor, Craig Anthony; sound (Dolby), David Yaffe; associate producer, Bill Carraro; assistant director, Thomas Smith; casting, Jaki Brown-Karman, Kimberly Hardin. Reviewed at Venice Film Festival (Special Events), Sept. 8, 1994. Running time: **119 MIN.**
Jason .... Allen Payne
Lyric .... Jada Pinkett
Joshua .... Bokeem Woodbine
Alonzo .... Treach
Marti .... Lisa Carson
Gloria .... Suzzanne Douglas
Maddog .... Forest Whitaker

A film that starts promisingly as the unsentimental portrayal of a rural black community, "Jason's Lyric" stumbles into a lame love story and ends in a conventional shootout and bloodbath. Pic's something-for-everyone philosophy could backfire into a meager B.O. harvest for helmer Doug McHenry, who co-produced with partner George Jackson ("New Jack City," "House Party 2"). Venice fest screening attracted little buzz.

Most convincing part is the prelude, in which Maddog (Forest Whitaker) comes home from Vietnam with one leg and a heart full of bitterness. His beloved wife, Gloria (Suzzanne Douglas), bars him from the house to protect herself and their two small boys from his violent temper. In a tragic scuffle, he is fatally shot by one of the boys.

Years later, little Jason (Allen Payne) has grown up into a clean-cut TV salesman with aspirations, while his black-sheep brother Joshua (Bokeem Woodbine) is a cokehead ne'er-do-well who's in and out of jail. Father's death has left its mark on Jason, too, in recurring nightmares and a paralyzing guilt complex.

He falls for a high-spirited waitress, Lyric (Jada Pinkett), and spends much screen time courting her and talking about their dreams for the future. Meanwhile, Joshua falls in with a bad gang planning a bank robbery. When he botches it, they string him up in a garage and torture him Tarantino-style (mostly off-camera).

Violent finale is an old-fashioned, at-home shootout that pits the two brothers against each other and resolves the original family tragedy with more tragedy.

Whitaker is moving as the crippled father, whose hopeless passion for Gloria touches depths of sorrow. Payne ("New Jack City") is a serious, straight-arrow hero who's easy to sympathize with. As the bad seed, Woodbine never loses his little-boy tenderness, even at his most frightening and demented. As the poetic Lyric, Pinkett is bright and attractive but lacks the convincing roughness that would correspond to her environment.

McHenry keeps the story moving smoothly and at a good pace. Abundant aerial shots give perspective to the setting — a run-down black area on the outskirts of Houston, with the city skyline rising in the background like a faraway dream. Francis Kenny's lensing is high-quality throughout. Soundtrack by Afrika and Matt Noble is easy listening. —*Deborah Young*

PIGALLE

(FRENCH-SWISS)

A Premiere Heure LM, UGC, FCC (France)/Delfilm (Switzerland) production, with participation of Canal Plus, Sofinergie 3, Federal Office of Culture of the Federal Dept. of the Interior (Switzerland). (International sales: UGC Intl., Neuilly.) Produced by Romain Bremond, Patrice Haddad. Directed, written by Karim Dridi. Camera (color), John Mathieson; editor, Lise Beaulieu; art direction, Gilles Bontemps; costume design, Jean-Louis Mazabraud; sound, Jean-Pierre Laforce; assistant director, Jean-Jacques Jauffret. Reviewed at Venice Film Festival (competing), Sept. 2, 1994. Running time: **93 MIN.**
Vera .... Vera Briole
Fifi .... Francois Renaud
Fernande .... Raymond Gil
Malfait .... Philippe Ambrosini
Divine .... Blanca Li
The Emperor ...... Jean-Claude Grenier
Pacha .... Bobby Pacha
Mustaf .... Younesse Boudache
Jesus le Gitan .... Patrick Chauvel
Forceps .... Jacky Bapps
Elegant Roger .... Roger Desprez

Gallic newcomer Karim Dridi checks in with an arresting first feature in "Pigalle." As it cruises strip joints, peep shows, sex shops, drug dens and prostitution beats — in the company of pimps, pushers, junkies, whores, transvestites and murderers — this bruising but unexpectedly redemptive tract perhaps piles on one or two tragedies too many. But it remains a punchy, smartly executed nocturnal narco-trip, which should bump and grind its way into festival beds before turning limited arthouse tricks.

Opening seg loosely weaves its way among a series of characters connected by ties that are only gradually clarified. At the center is pickpocket Fifi (Francis Renaud), romantically involved with both transvestite hooker Divine (Blanca Li) and Vera (Vera Briole), a peepshow dancer resisting the push to become a prostitute. Vera's live-in career counselor, a small-time dealer known as Jesus le Gitan (Patrick Chauvel), rounds out the picture.

Having ushered in his main characters, writer/director Dridi then proceeds to rub them out as hostility steps up between the quarter's shady operators. First to go is Divine. Sent by a lewd dwarf and his corpulent cohort to entertain the sadistic Malfait (Philippe Ambrosini), she dies in the gutter after a particularly gruesome session. Next up is le Gitan, whose severed head gets dumped in Vera's bed.

But with the exception of one or two peripheral figures who teeter on the edge of grotesquerie, all characters are treated with dignity. Pushed by Divine's death into a desperate course of action, Fifi is especially well drawn, and deftly played with a kind of sullen indifference by Renaud. Rest of the mainly non-pro cast is also on-target, shunning histrionic fireworks despite the opportunities provided.

Though some of the film's many narrative twists are less than crystal-clear, Dridi keeps a tight grip on the material and sustains energy at virtually peak level throughout. Scenes are cut fast and lean by ace editor Lise Beaulieu ("Savage Nights"), with a fragmented quality that ditches preamble to go straight to the core.

Brit lensman John Mathieson's work ably serves the film's mix of narrative and docu styles, scanning the various dives and sticking close to the characters, given a harsh glow by the artificial light of nighttime Pigalle. When daylight is seen for the first time, in the pic's unforced, upbeat ending, it almost comes as a shock. Blowup from Super-16mm creates a serviceably scruffy, edgy look that befits the filmmaker's aims. —*David Rooney*

METAL SKIN

(AUSTRALIAN)

A Daniel Scharf Prods. presentation. (International sales: Southern Star Film Sales, L.A.) Produced by Scharf. Line producer, Elisa Argenzio. Directed, written by Geoffrey Wright. Camera (Cinevex Film Lab color; widescreen), Ron Hagen; editors, Bill Murphy, Jane Usher; music, John Clifford White; production design, Steven Jones-Evans; art direction, Graham Blackmore; costume design, Anna Borghesi; sound (Dolby), David Lee; sound design, Frank Lipson; associate producer, Jonathan Shteinman; assistant director, Chris Odgers; casting, Prototype Casting, Greg Apps. Reviewed at Raleigh Studios, L.A., Aug. 30, 1994. (In Venice, Toronto fests.) Running time: **115 MIN.**
Joe .... Aden Young
Savina .... Tara Morice
Roslyn .... Nadine Garner
Dazey .... Ben Mendelsohn
Savina's Mother .... Chantal Contouri
Pop .... Petru Gheorghiu

This look at young down-and-outers living an Australian industrial-park nightmare is so overwrought and unrelievedly grim that it comes close to playing like a parody of teenage angst movies. Goosed up with car-smashing violence, Satanism and plenty of fancy editing tricks, Geoffrey Wright's follow-up to his controversial 1992 "Romper Stomper" sports the sort of fashionably nihilistic gear to put it over with a certain segment of hip young moviegoers, but its lack of appeal on virtually all aesthetic levels will mostly limit its commercial prospects to a hard-core heavy-metal and leather set.

Joe (Aden Young) represents perhaps the extreme definition of an underprivileged kid: Unemployed for four years, he lives in a squalid home on the barren outskirts of Melbourne that's half-shack, half-fortress, with a lunatic father whose only companion is a shrieking parrot. Joe shows signs of sensitivity in his feelings for the cute but guarded Roslyn (Nadine Garner), but he never gets anywhere with either her or Savina (Tara Morice), a co-worker at his new job at a grocery store, because local Romeo Dazey (Ben Mendelsohn) has in both cases gotten there first.

Nevertheless, the smooth Dazey takes Joe under his wing after a fashion, showing him the racing cars at his dad's shop and hanging out with him at an illicit latenight drag race. This sequence reps the film's major set piece, as hundreds of tough-acting teens gather in an abandoned rail yard to see who's got the hottest rod. Unfortunately, the evening doesn't go well for Joe, who's beaten behind the wheel and smashes up the car of the gathering's biggest maniac, who labels him "Psycho Joe."

Meanwhile, Savina puts a voodoo hex on Dazey for spurning her, and Joe tries to take advantage of Savina's vulnerability by being nice to her, but it all backfires in tragedy when she takes her devil worship to a fatal extreme.

When Joe's house then gets trashed, the youngster becomes unhinged and undertakes a shooting spree that threatens Dazey, his family and Roslyn. A less-than-convincing metal-on-metal battle between the two kids in hot rods brings things to an unedifying end.

Wright works overtime trying to supply the film with the kind of blindly destructive visceral force that's *de rigueur* these days for stories of angry, alienated youth, relying upon jump cuts within the frame to speed up the action and tossing in lots of violent rage and engine revving.

But only the two male characters, Joe and Dazey, are remotely interesting and, unfortunately, the more Wright chooses to concentrate upon Joe and his many problems, the more ordinary and less interesting he becomes; conversely, just as Dazey begins seeming more complex, the less is seen of him.

As for the females, Roslyn remains a one-dimensional object of the boys' desire, while Savina, with her sullen temper and unabated appetite for demonism, is a royal pain throughout.

Despite the hyped-up technique, aggressive style becomes trying after a while, and pacing through the midsection is sluggish. Some trimming wouldn't hurt a bit. Tech credits are serviceable.
—*Todd McCarthy*

MONTREAL

TWO FLAGS

(MAN MU BANG)

(SOUTH KOREAN)

A Dae-Jong Film Co. Ltd. production. Produced by Byun Jang Ho. Directed by Aum Jong Sun. Screenplay, Hong Ji Un, based on the story "The Cabin" by Oh Yu Kwon. Camera (color), Lee Sung Sup; editor, Lee Kyong Ja; music, Lee Chul Hyok; art direction, Lee Myong Su; costumes, Sin Kyong Sim; sound (Dolby), Lee Jae Wung, Kang Dae Sung. Reviewed at World Film Festival, Montreal (competing), Aug. 31, 1994. Running time: **110 MIN.**
With: Chang Dong Hwi, Yun Chong Hee, Kim Hyong Ill, Shin Young Jin.

Vet South Korean helmer Aum Jong Sun has a good chance to move beyond the global fest circuit with "Two Flags," an affecting wartime drama that could click with arthouse ticket buyers.

Pic has the earthy humor, narrative simplicity and tragic inevitability of a peasant folk tale. Acting is strong across the board, with particularly impressive work coming from Yun Chong Hee, one of South Korea's top B.O. draws.

Yun plays a middle-aged farm widow whose thatched cottage is unfortunately situated on the front line of the Korean War. She carefully follows the movements of the opposing armies, and always flies the flag of whichever side has troops in the area.

An elderly farmer (Chang Dong Hwi) appears on her doorstep and blusters his way into her bed. But he's exiled to the unheated guest house when another stranger — a younger, stronger war survivor (Kim Hyong Ill) — shows up. The widow figures she's better off as the bed mate of the younger man, who's hearty enough to cut down trees for firewood. He's also better, apparently, at other household chores.

Then another refugee, a young woman (Shin Young Jin), arrives. She takes up with the old farmer, immediately arousing the jealousy of the widow and her young lover. One thing leads to another, and the four characters wind up fighting in the barnyard — a small-scale version of the civil war that's raging around them.

"Two Flags" is immensely satisfying both as darkly ironic metaphor and emotionally involving tragedy. It easily achieves a universal resonance by being scrupulously specific about its period, setting and characters.

Lee Sung Sup's sharp cinematography and Lee Myong Su's evocative art direction greatly enhance the dead-of-winter ambiance. Other tech credits are first-rate.
—Joe Leydon

RHYTHM THIEF

(16mm — B&W)

A Film Crash (New York) production. Produced by Jonathan Starch. Directed, edited by Matthew Harrison. Screenplay, Harrison, Christopher Grimm. Camera (b&w), Howard Krupa; music, Danny Brenner, Hugh O'Donovan, John L. Horn, Kevin Okurland; art direction, Daniel Fisher, costume design, Nina Canter; sound, Charles Hunt; associate producers, Pier Paolo Piccoli, Trula and Gary Marcus; casting, Meredith Jacobson. Reviewed at World Film Festival, Montreal (non-competing), Sept. 3, 1994. (Also in Toronto Film Festival.) Running time: **88 MIN.**
With: Jason Andrews, Eddie Daniels, Kimberly Flynn, Kevin Corrigan, Sean Haggerty, Mark Alfred, Paul Rodriguez, Cynthia Sley.

No-budget New York item gets stronger as it moves confidently forward, weaving together the lives of some very desperate Lower East Siders before reaching a quietly devastating close.

You couldn't ask for a more marginal existence than that of Simon (impressive Jason Andrews), a tightly wound hustler who ekes out a living by sneakily recording underground bands and selling the dubs. Mostly, he wants to be left alone in his virtually empty flat, although he's frequently pestered by sexy g.f. Cyd (Kimberly Flynn) who won't take the hint, admiring street dude Fuller (Kevin Corrigan) who wants to be Simon's "prototype" and a pathetic junkie called Shayme (Sean Haggerty) who keeps crowding onto his corner. Then there are those leather-metal band members hot on his trail.

Much of the harsh-contrast black-and-white pic studies the emptiness of Simon's low-rent life, with his meditative bouts of eating peanut butter and ignoring the phone interrupted by the darkly funny aggressions of his neighbors — he spends a lot of time cleaning up plaster dust from overhead shotgun blasts.

This routine is seriously upended by the arrival of a strange young woman (Eddie Daniels) from his Long Island hometown. Turns out, she was in the same mental hospital as Simon's mother — she even has some of ma's poetry written on her arms — and her presence releases long-suppressed feelings of abandonment. The pair heads out

to Far Rockaway for a seaside respite, but Simon's self-loathing and quirky code of honor drag him back to the city, with unhappy results.

Helmer Matthew Harrison shot the pic in 11 days, and it has appropriately slapdash energy without sacrificing the more layered rewards of a thoughtful script (although lenser Howard Krupa could let his camera rest a little longer on grungily enigmatic subjects). The results are considerably tighter than such readily comparable, improv-heavy efforts as "Laws of Gravity" and "Amongst Friends." All-pro cast helps, as does super-hip score, combining hip-hop, reggae and alternative tunes in a tension-building soundtrack. Pic's 16mm lensing will pose initial problems, but timely transfer could bring "Rhythm" to selected urban auds.
—Ken Eisner

THE RIVER WILD

A Universal release of a Turman-Foster Co. production. Produced by David Foster, Lawrence Turman. Executive producers, Ilona Herzberg, Ray Hartwick. Directed by Curtis Hanson. Screenplay, Denis O'Neill. Camera (Deluxe color; Panavision widescreen), Robert Elswit; editors, Joe Hutshing, David Brenner; music, Jerry Goldsmith; production design, Bill Kenney; art direction, Mark Mansbridge; set design, William Hiney; set decoration, Rick T. Gentz; costume design, Marlene Stewart; sound (DTS Stereo), Ivan Sharrock, Kirk Francis; co-producer, O'Neill; assistant director, Tom Mack; stunt coordinator/second unit director, Max Kleven; casting, Nancy Klopper. Reviewed at the Hollywood Galaxy, L.A., Sept. 19, 1994. MPAA Rating: PG-13. Running time: **111 MIN.**
Gail .... Meryl Streep
Wade .... Kevin Bacon
Tom .... David Strathairn
Roarke .... Joseph Mazzello
Terry .... John C. Reilly
Ranger Johnny .... Benjamin Bratt

The characters and the audience take a wild ride in "The River Wild," a tense, sharply made thriller about a family held hostage during a river rafting vacation. A rare actioner in which a woman gets the lion's share of the heroics, pic marks a career watershed for Meryl Streep, outstanding as a buff white-water rafter who has it all over the men around her. With few other high-profile action films in the marketplace in the early fall, this should have clear sailing to strong B.O., with equal appeal to men and women, and can even end up as an attraction on the Universal tour.

The number of successful action dramas with women center stage can practically be tallied on one hand, and that's with the "Alien" epics accounting for three of them. Linda Hamilton flexed some muscle in the "Terminator" sci-fiers, and perhaps "La Femme Nikita" and its Yank remake could be counted, but the list is pathetically short however you draw it up.

"The River Wild," then, is refreshing on this level as well as several others, in that it's reasonably intelligent for a formulaic nuclear-family-in-jeopardy suspenser, well acted and seemingly authentic in its detailing of the characters' imposing physical challenges.

Looking robust and glowing with healthy color, Streep is first glimpsed sculling at sunset in Boston, where her character, Gail, lives with architect hubby Tom (David Strathairn), two kids and a dog. The night before, the too-busy Tom bails on the rafting trip they're due to take out West, revealing fissures in the family that will both deepen and close later on.

September 26, 1994 (Cont.)

Leaving her little daughter with her folks, Gail, son Roarke (Joseph Mazzello), whose 10th birthday the vacation is celebrating, and Fido are virtually hopping aboard their raft when Tom belatedly joins them. Not exactly the aquatic equal of Strathairn's memorable Cajun river rat in "Passion Fish," Tom sits rigidly in the vessel while Gail expertly navigates it downstream.

Gail, who grew up amidst these spectacular mountains, used to be a river guide and knows its every twist and turn, a fact seized upon by a trio of supposed fishermen led by the friendly Wade (Kevin Bacon). When their guide mysteriously disappears, Gail can hardly refuse to help Wade and his creepy-looking buddy, Terry (John C. Reilly), get down the river, just as she can't ignore the young gent's cocky self-confidence in the face of her husband's stiff distractedness.

Film's first half is given over to building some solid characters and relationships, establishing Gail's mastery of the river and laying unmistakable hints that "something's off" about the two guys, which only Tom, among the family, picks up on.

Second half suddenly explodes into violent and open conflict. It turns out that the pack Wade is carrying contains $250,000 that he and Terry robbed from a cattle auction. They've also already killed two men. With the authorities expecting them to try to slip over the nearby border to Canada, they've decided to head the opposite way, past the normal rafting destination and over some almost impossible rapids called the Gauntlet. Beyond there, they figure, no one will look for them. And who better to take them there but Gail, one of the few to have run the Gauntlet before?

First-time screenwriter Denis O'Neill and director Curtis Hanson tighten the screws skillfully after Wade takes charge. Wielding a gun and threatening the family members to varying degrees, Wade still likes to think of himself as a nice guy who might yet have a chance with Gail, whom he admires for her gumption and talent. By contrast, he has no use whatsoever for Tom, who luckily escapes from the raft just in time, giving him a chance to prove his manhood when the lives of his wife and son are at stake.

The cat-and-mouse game continues suspensefully until the climactic encounter with the Gauntlet, where Nature effectively becomes an unknown third force in the battle of wits. Numerous twists and turns adroitly postpone full audience satisfaction and relief until the very last.

Hanson, undertaking by far his biggest production to date, nicely balances the assorted elements of action, good guys vs. bad guys, family drama, sentiment and humor, and all other hands carry their weight impressively. Crisply lensed in widescreen by Robert Elswit mostly in Oregon and Montana, film is exceedingly handsome, and the on-water footage is about as exciting and rough-and-tumble as it could be. Joe Hutshing and David Brenner's editing is tight, while Jerry Goldsmith's score is conventionally effective.

Production materials state that Streep did 90% of the rapids work herself, but film makes it look as though she did it all. Spunky, determined, emotional, resilient and powerfully physical, her Gail seems every bit the grown-up girl raised on the river. Role allows Streep to explore new dimensions (and a bit of normalcy) not covered by her diverse previous parts, and could position her for a new phase of public acceptance.

Bacon proves insidiously effective as a boyish baddie, Strathairn is ideal as the reserved but ultimately resourceful husband, and Mazzello has a lot more opportunity to show his range than he did as one of the kids in "Jurassic Park." Reilly's white trash sidekick reps the film's most forceful reminder of its closest precursor, "Deliverance."

Some incidental bits involving Gail's deaf father and her family's ability to sign are neatly and unobtrusively worked into the drama. Only unnecessary baggage is some hocus-pocus involving the old Indian tradition of visionquest. —*Todd McCarthy*

THE SCOUT

A 20th Century Fox release of a Ruddy Morgan production. Produced by Albert S. Ruddy, Andre E. Morgan. Executive producers, Herbert S. Nanas, Jack Cummins. Directed by Michael Ritchie. Screenplay, Andrew Bergman, Albert Brooks, Monica Johnson, based upon the New Yorker article by Roger Angell. Camera (Deluxe color), Laszlo Kovacs; editors, Don Zimmerman, Pembroke Herring; music, Bill Conti; production design, Stephen Hendrickson; art direction, Okowita; set decoration, Merideth Boswell; set design, Thomas Betts, Gina B. Cranham; costume design, Luke Reichle; sound (Dolby), Kim Ornitz; associate producer/assistant director, Thomas Mack; casting, Richard Pagano, Sharon Bialy, Debi Manwiller. Reviewed at 20th Century Fox screening room, L.A., Sept. 21, 1994. MPAA Rating: PG-13. Running time: **101 MIN.**

Al Percolo .... Albert Brooks
Steve Nebraska .... Brendan Fraser
Doctor Aaron .... Dianne Wiest
Ron Wilson .... Lane Smith
Jennifer .... Anne Twomey
Tommy Lacy .... Michael Rapaport

Baseball fans lamenting a strike-shortened season won't get their needed fix with this virtually baseball-free baseball movie — an odd hybrid of broad comedy and a darker undercurrent of psychological drama. Even with the modest allure of Albert Brooks in what amounts to a mainstream effort, "The Scout" should get a quick trip to the showers.

Brooks both wrote (with Andrew Bergman and Monica Johnson) and stars in the film — inspired by a New Yorker magazine article — about a down-on-his-luck talent scout who discovers a combination of Sandy Koufax and Mickey Mantle playing ball in the inner wilds of Mexico.

What Al (Brooks) has found is Steve Nebraska (Brendan Fraser), a fireball-throwing, ambidextrous dream come true — albeit one with a childlike mentality, a disconcerting temper and a purposefully murky past.

After some badgering, Al inks the kid to a multimillion-dollar deal with the New York Yankees, mentioning offhandedly that he'll allow him to pitch the first game of the World Series if the team gets there.

What follows, however, is less about baseball than a sort of awkward reworking of "Of Mice and Men," with Fraser as the potentially dangerous innocent and Brooks cast as the reluctant father figure, trying to keep the kid's head together just long enough to cash in on that lucrative contract.

Still, Brooks and director Michael Ritchie (who last visited the ballpark with "The Bad News Bears") never quite commit to either of the movie's disparate chords — bailing out of the batter's box in terms of the psychological drama and, after some amusing moments at the outset, generally steering clear of broad comedy.

At last, inexplicably, "The Scout" seems to remember that it's supposed to be a baseball movie, throwing in an anticlimactic ending with a "Rocky" riff, right down to Bill Conti's score. By then, Elvis may have left the stadium.

At his best playing the self-obsessed characters he wrote and directed in "Modern Romance" and "Lost in America," Brooks may have learned the hard way here that playing warm and fuzzy isn't exactly his thing. Through much of the story, Al's indifference to Steve's obvious psychological problems, while the source of some laughs, doesn't elicit much sympathy, making any epiphany feel forced at best.

Fraser is appropriately impish and waiflike, but he's pretty much left to toss out the same emotional pitch over and over again — not unlike his 109-mile-an-hour fastball, which ceases to impress the fourth or fifth time the ball bowls over the catcher.

Dianne Wiest, as a caring psychologist, is about the only other performer of note in this two-character piece, also peppered with clever cameos by the likes of Yankee owner George Steinbrenner, Tony Bennett and NBC announcer Bob Costas.

Tech credits don't always hit the strike zone either, leaving the unmistakable sense that "The Scout" underwent extensive editing and abandoned potential subplots. Pic does score in terms of Brooks' tacky wardrobe, while suffering a bad case of late-inning bluster with Conti's score. —*Brian Lowry*

TERMINAL VELOCITY

A Buena Vista release of a Hollywood Pictures presentation of an Interscope Communications/Polygram Filmed Entertainment production. Produced by Scott Kroopf, Tom Engelman. Executive producers, Ted Field, David Twohy, Robert W. Cort. Co-producer, Joan Bradshaw. Directed by Deran Serafian. Screenplay, Twohy. Camera (Technicolor), Oliver Wood; editors, Frank J. Urioste, Peck Prior; music, Joel McNeely; production design, David L. Snyder; art direction, Sarah Knowles; set decoration, Beth A. Rubino; costume design, Poppy Cannon-Reese; sound (Dolby), Stephan Von Hase Mihalik; visual effects design and supervision/second unit visual effects director, Christopher F. Woods; aerial coordinator, Kevin Donnelly; aerial stunt coordinator, Jerry Meyers; aerial camera, Frank Holgate, Donald M. Morgan; land-based second unit director, Buddy Joe Hooker; land-based second unit camera, Bill Roe; additional camera, Charles Minsky; assistant director, George Parra; casting, Terry Liebling. Reviewed at the Cinerama Dome, L.A., Sept. 19, 1994. MPAA Rating: PG-13. Running time: **100 MIN.**

Ditch Brodie .... Charlie Sheen
Chris Morrow .... Nastassja Kinski
Ben Pinkwater .... James Gandolfini
Kerr .... Christopher McDonald
Lex .... Gary Bullock
Sam .... Hans R. Howes
Noble .... Melvin Van Peebles
Karen .... Cathryn de Prume
Dominic .... Richard Sarafian Jr.

Since Hitchcock shuffled off this mortal coil and the James Bond pix lost their Cold War raison d'etre, the void for witty and romantic actioners has yawned wide. Earlier this summer, "True Lies" produced strong B.O. results on its $100 million-plus investment, but for less than a quarter of that price, "Terminal Velocity," a snappy, thrill-packed political espionage/heist picture, should deliver more bang for the buck.

Set in the spectacularly cinematic world of skydiving, "Velocity" starts in high gear, with an intrigue involving damsels in distress and midnight landings of jumbo jets in a desolate Arizona desert. Faster

September 26, 1994 (Cont.)

than you can yell "Jump!" skydiving instructor Ditch Brodie (Charlie Sheen) is taking a winsome novice jumper named Chris (Nastassja Kinski) on a danger-filled leap into post-Cold War politics, murder and a bounty of tongue-in-cheek homages to Hitch and Ian Fleming.

Starting with a body switcheroo straight out of "Vertigo," the romp turns into a "From Russia With Love"-meets-"North by Northwest" political thriller before landing firmly in "Goldfinger" heist-of-the-century territory. But rather than feeling stitched together from cribbed sources, "Velocity" is a thoroughly amusing and exhilarating cliffhanger.

Sheen finds himself a classically Hitchcockian wrong man, employed as the ultimate fall guy (pun intended) for Kinski's earnest KGB agent, who's trying to save Russia from a massive hit on its already shaky treasury. The unlikely scenario is no obstacle to a rousing good time: As Ditch and Chris chase the evildoers and in turn are chased by same, pic is filled with punchy gag-filled dialogue and sensational action bits, both in the air and on the ground.

Though opening minutes are less than sure-footed, by the time sinister baddies — peroxided killer Kerr (Christopher McDonald) and slippery D.A. investigator Ben Pinkwater (wink-wink) (James Gandolfini) — are in pursuit, the kicks have begun, with wild stunts involving jet-propelled vehicles, night drops into industrial smokestacks, shootouts and the jaw-dropping finale involving two planes, a Cadillac and an unwieldy locked car trunk.

Pic's pleasures come as a welcome surprise, given the uninspired title, director Deran Serafian's previous feature credits ("Death Warrant," "Roadflower," "Gunmen"), Sheen's somewhat worn-out welcome in the action genre after clinkers like "Navy SEALS," "The Rookie" and, especially, "The Chase," and Kinski's uncertain status after a virtual disappearance from Hollywood. "Velocity" is filled with good news on all their accounts.

Serafian's sharp, lean direction is perfectly matched to David Twohy's clever, well-paced script, and should put the helmer onto the A list of actioner talents. Romantic leads are in on the jokes and up to pic's physical demands. Kinski will win kudos for a solid femme fatale turn, while Sheen's glib, sexy persona suits the befuddled but courageous flyboy.

Southwest locations provide a colorful backdrop, and Oliver Wood's action-intense lensing keeps up with the imposing challenges of the stunt-heavy material. Picture stays impressively aloft until fade-out. —*Steven Gaydos*

TORONTO

LOOK ME IN THE EYE

(BRITISH)

A Skreba-Creon Films production for the BBC. Produced by Simon Relph. Executive producer, George Faber. Directed, written, edited by Nick Ward. Camera (color), Seamus McGarvey; music, Nicholas Russell-Pavier, David Chilton; production design, Teresa McCann; art direction, Casey Dobie; set decoration, Ray Chan; costume design, Michael O'Connor; sound, Danny Hambrook; associate producers, Jane Headland, Anita Overland; casting, Fran Robertson. Reviewed at Toronto Film Festival, Sept. 13, 1994. Running time: **85 MIN.**

Ruth/Sian	Caroline Catz
Luke	Seamus Gubbins
Thomas	Barnaby Stone
Mick	Mat Patresi
Maureen	Kelly Hunter

Split identity, the eternal threat of the libido to break loose, and the power of the human imagination are some of the themes explored in "Look Me in the Eye," Nick Ward's visually striking, postmodern psychosexual thriller. Though borrowing elements from two quintessential 1960s movies, Antonioni's "Blowup" and Bunuel's "Belle de jour," pic succeeds in establishing its individuality. Prospects for theatrical release are excellent for this innovative art film, which can be enjoyed on a number of levels.

Ruth (Caroline Catz) is neither as stunningly beautiful as "Belle de jour's" Catherine Deneuve nor as intriguingly mysterious as "Blowup's" Vanessa Redgrave. But like those heroines, she's a complex woman, clearly dissatisfied with her teaching job and recent marriage to a rather conservative hubby (Seamus Gubbins).

One day, sitting in a coffee shop, Ruth encounters Thomas (Barnaby Stone), a brilliant photographer. Instantly intrigued, she asks him to take some erotic pictures of her. But when she realizes that Thomas has secretly been photographing her for two years — at her wedding, at school, on the train she rides to work — she sneaks into his studio and destroys all his photos and negatives.

This daring act puts her in a state of perpetual anxiety, fearing that Thomas will come back for revenge. Sure enough, 18 months later he reappears, and it's hardly a surprise that this rendezvous occurs during a nasty rainstorm.

Understanding that the manner in which the story is told is far more important than its contents — or even plausibility — writer/director Ward constructs a fascinating, dark

world, one grounded in reality but also benefitting from Ruth's extraordinary imagination and sexual fantasies.

Ward contrasts Ruth's ordinary existence as a wife and mother in the 'burbs with the potentially dangerous games she plays on her own in the city. Gradually, the noirish erotic tale takes the shape of an obsessive love affair, set against the bleak urban landscape of London's King's Cross, which is wonderfully captured by Seamus McGarvey's stylish lensing.

In the dual role of Ruth and Sian, the prostitute Thomas befriends, Catz renders an inspired, always sympathetic performance, based on physical grace as well as verbal charm. Catz's attractive, though non-glamorous, appearance lends the film a credible focus, reinforcing the universality of sexual fantasies.

Ward's ingenious cutting and sharp editing are full of tricky shots that bring snap to the story's suspense. A voyeuristic scene in which Ruth watches Thomas making love through a keyhole in his studio is shot and cut with great wit and precision.

In its consistently mysterious mood, multi-layered narrative and intricate storytelling devices, "Look Me in the Eye" bears some resemblance to "Blowup" and David Hare's "Wetherby." It's a tribute to the director's assurance and integrity that only seldom do the film's sensory impressions outweigh his thematic insights into Ruth's tormented persona. For connoisseurs of style and technique, pic's look and sound provide pleasures of a high cinematic order.

—*Emanuel Levy*

NADJA

David Lynch presents a Kino Link production. Produced by Mary Sweeney, Amy Hobby. Executive producer, Lynch. Directed, written by Michael Almereyda. Camera (DuArt b&w), Jim Denault; editor, David Leonard; music, Simon Fisher Turner; production design, Kurt Ossenfort; costume design, Prudence Moriarty; sound (Dolby), William Kozy; sound design, Stewart Levy; second unit camera, Ed Talavera; casting, Billy Hopkins, Suzanne Smith, Kerry Barden. Reviewed at Toronto Film Festival, Sept. 13, 1994. Running time: **95 MIN.**

Cassandra	Suzy Amis
Lucy	Galaxy Craze
Jim	Martin Donovan
Dr. Van Helsing	Peter Fonda
Renfield	Karl Geary
Edgar	Jared Harris
Nadja	Elina Lowensohn
Morgue Security Guard	David Lynch

Vampires stalk the netherworld of the downtown New York scene in "Nadja," a lovely idea for a film that's been beautifully executed but slips too far off its narra-

tive tracks to get where it wants to go. Stunningly lensed in a mixture of black-and-white 35mm and Pixelvision and featuring one of the sexiest female vampires ever to bare her teeth onscreen, Michael Almereyda's low-budgeter will develop a certain critical and cult following, but isn't quite exotic, bold or exciting enough to edge from the commercial shadows into B.O. daylight.

Thoughtful and humorous pic gets off to a rousing start, as the darkly mysterious, extravagantly beautiful Nadja (Elina Lowensohn) picks up a guy in a bar with some disarmingly direct talk, and later feasts upon him. A wealthy Romanian, Nadja has just lost her father (Transylvania's most illustrious citizen) and, rather than carry on his bloody legacy for countless more centuries, she is wearily determined to set a new course for her life.

Nadja next meets young Lucy (Galaxy Craze), whom she seduces in a tantalizing scene and with whom she unexpectedly falls in love. Lucy, it turns out, is married to Jim (Martin Donovan), whose uncle, Dr. Van Helsing (Peter Fonda), has killed Nadja's father and is now after the alluring young woman and her twin brother, Edgar (Jared Harris), who is in the care of private nurse Cassandra (Suzy Amis).

After creating such promise through the intriguing setup of stunning twin vampires in trendy, nocturnal Gotham, it's disappointing that Almereyda develops narrative butterfingers, letting the storyline become too diffuse and cutting among too many principal characters. Having established Nadja as the main focus of interest, tale splinters off to follow too many tangents and less intriguing figures in a half-baked attempt to paint a portrait of a dysfunctional vampire family, until Nadja ultimately reassumes center stage with a fateful decision that provides a distinctive and satisfying denouement.

Despite the dramatic problems, pic maintains a certain hold throughout due to the peculiar atmosphere, lovely style and flavorsome dialogue, which often hits weirdly campy, facetious notes. In his last film, "Another Girl, Another Planet," Almereyda pioneered the use of the toy Pixelvision video camera, and he has reprised its use here in scenes that relate to the vampire state of mind; blowing these images up to 35mm makes for grainy, impressionistic glimpses that contrast vividly with the beautiful sheen of lenser Jim Denault's coverage of the main action. Technical work overall, notably the sound design, as well as the diverse score, is fancy and impressive.

September 26, 1994 (Cont.)

Tone is set by the commanding performance of Lowensohn, previously seen in "Another Girl" as well as several Hal Hartley films. Physically imposing, sometimes garbed in a cape and utterly self-possessed, she's the definitive modern vampire, and it's too bad the script wasn't shaped to use her more powerfully.

Fonda brings a manic humor to his role of the vampire killer, while other thesps turn in more straightforward jobs. Exec producer David Lynch pops in briefly as a security guard at a New York morgue.

—*Todd McCarthy*

ROY COHN/ JACK SMITH

A Jonathan Demme presentation of Good Machine/Pomodori Foundation/ Laboratory for Icon & Idiom production. Produced by Ted Hope, James Schamus, Marianne Weems. Directed by Jill Godmilow. Screenplay based on the plays "Roy Cohn" by Gary Indiana and "What's Underground About Marshmallows" by Jack Smith. Camera (color), Ellen Kuras; editor, Merrill Stern; music, Michael Sahl; sound, Larry Loewinger; associate producer, Anthony Bregman, Mary Jane Skalski; assistant director, Anita Thacher. Reviewed at Toronto Film Festival, Sept. 13, 1994. Running time: **90 MIN.**
Roy Cohn/
Jack Smith .... Ron Vawter
Chica .... Coco McPherson

Ron Vawter, an icon of New York's downtown theater scene who died of AIDS in April, delivers a mesmerizing performance in "Roy Cohn/Jack Smith," a splendid theatrical piece that examines the lives of two infamous homosexuals. This challenging, avant-garde picture begs for major release to unleash its full potential, though it's mostly for upscale, sophisticated audiences and the festival circuit.

Roy Cohn, the homophobic rightwing lawyer and sleazy backroom politico, and Jack Smith, the notorious underground filmmaker, had nothing in common except for being white homosexuals who lived in an oppressive society, contemptuous of any sexual deviation. Yet the fact that both died of AIDS (in the late 1980s) lends an ironic as well as tragic note to their opposing lifestyles.

Cohn, who's also a central figure in Tony Kushner's drama "Angels in America," was a closeted homosexual who went out of his way to thunder against the "Sodom and Gomorrah" of openly gay life.

In diametric opposition, avant-garde filmmaker Smith ("Flaming Creatures") flaunted his homosexuality in public, and even established a fleeting fame as a result of it. Both men were political, albeit in different ways: Cohn used overt politics as a drag (a mask to conceal his sexual orientation), while Smith turned drag into a form of sexual politics.

In this film, Cohn's tortured personality and hypocrisy emerge during a lecture he gives at a banquet for the American Society for the Protection of the Family. As the lecture's exact text couldn't be retrieved, writer Gary Indiana takes some liberties, but always stays true to the essence of the man.

Smith, often credited as a founder of performance art, mixed flamboyant drag, fragments of Arabian Nights kitsch and B-movie camp, calling attention to the artifice of both theatre and film.

Pic was entirely shot at the theatrical space the Kitchen on Oct. 31-Nov. 1, 1993. Director Jill Godmilow ("Waiting for the Moon") uses subtle intercutting between two pieces that in the theater were presented as separate acts. Material's revelatory richness and Vawter's magnificently modulated portraits make both sections unusually entertaining.

Assisted by the sharp, elegant lensing of Ellen Kuras ("Swoon") and Merrill Stern's precise and astute editing, "Roy Cohn/Jack Smith" meets the often impossible task of chronicling a theatrical production while making it visually interesting through shrewd manipulation of time, space — and audience reaction. The smooth transitions between Vawter's rehearsals and his actual performance illuminate the magical quality of his acting.

Whether intended or not, this film serves as a most eloquent tribute to Vawter, a founding member of the Wooster Group, whose postmodern, deconstructionist works have made a major mark on the theater world.

—*Emanuel Levy*

WINDIGO

(CANADIAN)

An Allegro Films Distribution release (Canada) of a Lux Films production, with the participation of Telefilm Canada and SOGIC. (Intl. sales: Allegro Films, Montreal.) Produced by Nicole Robert. Directed, written by Robert Morin. Camera (color), James Gray; editor, Lorraine Dufour; production design, Marie-Carole de Beaumont; costume design, Nicoletta Massone; sound, Marcel Chouinard. Reviewed at Toronto Film Festival, Sept. 9, 1994. Running time: **97 MIN.**
Eddy Laroche .... Donald Morin
Jean Fontaine .... Guy Nadon
Conrad Volant .... Richard Kistabish
Christine Bastien .... Nathalie Coupal
Rogatien Cote .... Yvon Leroux
Yves St-Hilaire .... Michel Laperriere
Luc Labrecque .... Michel Albert
Odilas (Dilas) Paquette ...... Paul Berval
Louis (Bleu) Rozon .... Gaston Caron
Lucas Tomassine .... Alex Cheezo
Freddy Hook .... Serge Roberge

Clearly inspired by the violent land dispute that shook up Quebec in the summer of 1990, Montreal helmer Robert Morin's "Windigo" is an intelligent, thought-provoking look at the strained relations between white Canadians and the country's original inhabitants. Morin's first pic, "Requiem pour un beau sans-coeur," was a fest favorite, winning the best Canadian feature prize at the 1992 Toronto event and screening as part of Critics' Week in Cannes. "Windigo" is likely to repeat that success on the fest circuit.

But Morin's supportive stance toward first-nation gripes may temper pic's B.O. performance in French Canada, where the population has been generally unsympathetic to native demands. "Windigo" opens commercially in Quebec in late October. Outside Canada, this nuanced political potboiler is more likely to find a home in specialized theatrical settings and on the small screen.

Renegade native leader Eddy Laroche (Donald Morin) sparks a political crisis in Canada when he holes up in a remote region of northern Quebec and unilaterally declares the independence of the Aki territory. Most of the action takes place on board a dilapidated old ship, the Pickle, which is carrying a group of government and native negotiators up the river to meet with Laroche and his tribe of rebels.

But Laroche has also demanded that a TV crew accompany the group, and much of the story is told from the p.o.v. of cynical veteran TV reporter Jean Fontaine (Guy Nadon), who feels he's drawn the short straw with this assignment.

Fontaine and his cameraman begin a series of interviews with the people on the boat, as the journalist tries to understand the roots of the native insurrection, and it quickly becomes clear to Fontaine that the 30-second news byte isn't adequate to capture the complexities of the issue.

By the time they reach the rebel camp, the journalist is having great difficulty maintaining his usual, objective distance from the story he's covering, and the classic media quandary is at the heart of this subtle pic.

"Windigo" falters somewhat with a finale that borrows too heavily and obviously from "Heart of Darkness"/ "Apocalypse Now" territory, with Laroche as the crazed Kurtz character who's gone off the deep end. Also, some thesps don't deliver the goods. Nadon is completely believable as the troubled journalist, but some members of the supporting cast — particularly Morin as the native leader — don't seem up to expressing the complexities of their characters.

All tech credits are first-rate, especially cinematographer James Gray's mix of scenic film footage and grainier video images for the TV interviews. —*Brendan Kelly*

THE RED LOTUS SOCIETY

(FEIXIA AHDA)

(TAIWANESE)

A Performance Workshop/Long Shong Films production. Produced by Wang Ying-hsiang, Nai-chu Ding. Executive producers, Xie Mingchang, Chen Qiyuan. Directed, written by Stan Lai. Camera (color), Christopher Doyle; editor, Chen Bowen; music, Fumio Itabashi; art direction, Samuel Wang; costume design, Li Weihui; sound (Dolby), Annette Danto; assistant director, Zhou Xinming. Reviewed at Toronto Film Festival, Sept. 14, 1994. Running time: **120 MIN.**
Ahda .... Ying Zhaode
Dan .... Chen Wenming
Kuei .... Na Weixun
Mr. Mao .... Li Tongcun
Ahda's Father .... Lee Lichun
Blind Man Lu .... Lu Lu Yuzhou
Miss Sung .... Lo Manfei

Drama, fantasy, martial arts and romance are the ingredients of the not quite filling Taiwanese pic "The Red Lotus Society." Lacking the zip of recent Hong Kong genre pix, the gentle, cerebral nature of this outing will limit commercial acceptance outside ethnic situations. Nonetheless, it demonstrates real talent on the cusp of commercial and critical acceptance.

At the core of the drama is the Asian martial art of "vaulting" — the ability to leap, glide and seemingly defy gravity. Ahda (Ying Zhaode) has spent years training with bags of iron powder to transcend mortal bounds and find the spiritual enlightenment to lift into the heavens.

Though tales of the mythical group who practiced the art fill his head, there are more practical problems at hand. His father, a healer, is in trouble with racketeers involved in the jade trade. His boss, the Taipei wheeler-dealer Miss Sung (Lo Manfei), may also be the mortal link to the secret of the Red Lotus.

Throw in some colorful mentors and psychics and a problematic romance with a woman named Dan (Chen Wenming) and result is a film too heavily weighted with plot. Focus, so important to vaulting, strays constantly, and ultimately all the loose ends do not tie into a pretty knot.

Still, writer/director Stan Lai keeps things interesting with visual dash and colorful characters. Mainly a rumination, "The Red Lotus Society" feels constrained when it really desires to fly. When spurts of action do occur, they feel anticlimatic.

Zhaode lends a charismatic presence to the proceedings, and the lensing is slick, if too obviously somber. This intriguing follow-up to helmer's 1992 "The Peach Blossom

Land" is ideal fest fodder but hardly vanguard material.

—*Leonard Klady*

PAINT CANS

(CANADIAN)

A Libra Films release of a Salter Street production. Produced by Paul Donovan, Michael Mahoney. Directed, written by Donovan, based upon his book. Camera (color), Les Krizsan; editor, David Ostry; music, Marty Simon; art direction, Shelley Nieder; sound, Allan Scarth, Alec Salter; associate producers, Benedict O'Halloran, Alan MacGillivray; assistant director, Cordell Wynne. Reviewed at Toronto Film Festival, Sept. 13, 1994. Running time: **100 MIN.**
Wick Burns	Chas Lawther
Arundel Merton	Robyn Stevan
Vittorio Musso	Bruce Greenwood
Bryson Vautour	Nigel Bennett
Maitland Burns	Don Francks
Neville Lewis	Andy Jones
Morton Ridgewell	Paul Gross
Inge Von Nerthus	Ann Marie MacDonald

How to navigate the pitfalls of a government film fund and make your little screen gem is the theme of "Paint Cans." While it speaks the universal language of bureaucratese, pic is a little too close to the truth and lacks the comic outrage to connect in a significant way outside its Canadian milieu. Still, it has a nice deadpan quality that could appeal in specialized release in selected markets.

Wick Burns (Chas Lawther) is a career government official who fully understands that appearing to be busy and attentive is even better than actually being in the fray. His latest dilemma is an arty little ditty entitled "Paint Cans." The project marks the theatrical directing debut of Vittorio Russo (Bruce Greenwood), who went to film school with Wick, and is produced by the sleazy but politically effective Neville Lewis (Andy Jones). No one in the Film Finance Office of Canada particularly likes the proposal, but a simple denial would be too fast and simple.

So, they hedge their bets by checking out the response at other funding agencies. The prospect of script development money is tossed around and, like shifting political winds, the attitude to fund or not to fund blows hot and cold.

Writer/director Paul Donovan is also guilty of playing too many angles. The internecine maneuvers within the agency are ample grist for the narrative mill. He delineates Burns quite well by showing the way he operates. But he then dilutes the broth by entering into Burns' home life and his bizarre relationship with a cantankerous dad (Don Francks) who considers him a professional and moral washout.

More effective is the official's budding romance with Arundel (Robyn Stevan), a journalist he meets in Cannes. It indicates his vulnerability and how love might humanize even someone trained to be a government automaton.

Lawther, in his unflappable role, is an interesting centerpiece to the action. Supporting characters are familiar types given little new spin or oddball quirks, which creates a certain sameness that teeters on the deadly and flattens any possibility of tension, danger or hilarity.

A polished if modest production, the film has a pleasant quality. That might be a step up from the efforts backed by the somewhat fictional agency. Still, it's a long shot from the cure to mediocrity it so obviously disdains. —*Leonard Klady*

BOCA

(U.S.-BRAZILIAN)

A Zalman King Collection presentation of a J.N. Producoes Culturais production. (International sales: 10dB Inc., Canoga Park, Calif.) Produced by Jeff Young, Joffre Rodrigues. Executive producer, Zalman King. Screenplay, Ed Silverstein. Camera (color), Pedro Farkas; editor, Andy Horvitch; music, Richard Feldman, Midge Ure, Adam Gargoni; production design, Annie Young; art direction, Gioconda Coelho, Claudia Medesto, Wilma Garcia; sound (Ultra-Stereo), Juarez Dagaberto; associate producers, Caigue Martin Ferriera, Linda Clark; contributing directors, Walter Avancini, Sandra Werneck; assistant director, Tania Lamarca; additional camera, Eagle Egilsson; casting, Denise Del Queto. Reviewed at Toronto Film Festival, Sept. 14, 1994. Running time: **93 MIN.**
JJ	Rae Dawn Chong
Reb	Martin Kemp
Boca	Tarcisio Meira
Jesse James Montgomery	Martin Sheen
Moema	Denise Milfont
Fonseca	Carlos Dellabella

Zalman King has invented a new genre with "Boca": soft-core social consciousness. A slick-looking "expose" about the epidemic of street children in Brazil conducted by a sexy young American journalist, pic resembles "Pixote" intercut with "Wild Orchid." Clearly made with the utmost seriousness of intent (filmmakers claim Bunuel's "Los Olvidados" as their inspiration), this aesthetic hodgepodge would meet with critical slaughter if released theatrically, so cable and video look like the natural destination.

Listed in the Toronto fest catalog as the work of one Rene Manzor, film in fact has no director of record and is a mongrel creation culled from numerous sources. Considerable footage was included from a 1990 Brazilian film, "Boca de ouro" ("Golden Mouth"), first feature by

TV director Walter Avancini (who receives a "contributing director" credit here), adapted from a Nelson Rodrigues play staged in 1962 by Nelson Pereira dos Santos, who originally intended to helm the film version. Additional material came from a local documentary as well as from "Wild Orchid," and new scenes were shot with the principal actors, including Brazilian star Tarcisio Meira, who here repeats his performance in the title role of the 1990 film, only this time in English.

Despite the multitude of parents, there can be no doubt as to the identity of the film's true auteur. No matter how passionately (and naively) the cause of Rio's orphans is argued, it's as if King can't help himself, as he constantly returns to such diversions as Rae Dawn Chong in the throes of wild sex, a debauched orgiastic ritual, or a "best tits" contest between a gangster's tarts and some local women conducted at an enormous garbage dump. Rarely has a filmmaker had such a mixed-up idea of what his intended audience might be.

Surviving a bloody massacre, shaken U.S. TV reporter JJ (Chong) sits down to record on tape the story of what's happened to her. In flashback, she's shown joining a former flame, photog Reb (Martin Kemp), and trying to find out who's behind the death squads who are killing the city's street kids.

After uselessly interviewing government authorities, she heads into the *favela* to meet Boca (Meira), a slum native who raised himself up to become a crime king-pin. Decked out with a full set of gold choppers, Boca is a ruthless killer without a conscience, but seems to be fighting his own battle to save the children from the thugs enlisted by local businessmen to get rid of the ragamuffins, who scare away visitors and customers.

Subject is certainly urgent and dramatic, but material has been shaped by King and "Red Shoe Diaries" scripter Ed Silverstein into something that's both sensationalistic and soft-minded. Killings and sex scenes are replayed repeated in slo-mo and wallowing detail, while the righteous U.S. liberal played by Chong lectures every Brazilian she can corner about how awful it is that they're not personally solving the problem of the children.

Naturally, all this unfolds during carnival, providing even more opportunity to show skin. But it's not all travelogue stuff; one major plus is the location lensing way up the hillsides in Rio's impoverished *favelas*, which can't have been easy to pull off.

Chong throws herself into her role with deadly earnest, while Meira projects unshakable authority as the crime lord. Martin Sheen is in for a couple of scenes as the knowing local CIA operative.

—*Todd McCarthy*

THE ASCENT

An RHI Entertainment production in association with Cabin Fever Entertainment. Produced by Njeri Karago. Executive producers, Robert Halmi Jr., Thomas Molito, Robert Bantle. Directed by Donald Shebib. Screenplay, David Wiltse. Camera (Film House color; Panavision widescreen), David Connell; editor, Ronald Wisman; music, Irwin Fisch; production design, Michael Baugh; costume design, Elizabeth Ryrie; sound (Ultra-Stereo), Walter P. Anderson; stunts, Duncan Ferguson; associate producer, Tim Harbert; assistant director, Myron Hoffert; second unit director, Rick Ridgeway; second unit camera, Scott Ranson; casting, Lynn Kressel. Reviewed at Toronto Film Festival, Sept. 13, 1994. Running time: **96 MIN.**
Franco Distassi	Vincent Spano
Maj. David Farrell	Ben Cross
Enzo	Tony Lo Bianco
Patricia	Rachel Ward
Sgt. Thomas	Mark Ingall
Maj. Quinn	John De Veillers

A remote anecdote from World War II is given the bigscreen treatment in "The Ascent," a handsomely produced but dramatically routine indie about an Italian POW in 1942 British East Africa who challenges his English captor in a climb of Mount Kenya. Once upon a time, this passable but instantly forgettable wartime actioner would have been reasonable double-bill fodder. These days, however, the theatrical marketplace has no room for this sort of mid-range fare, spelling a video/cable/TV fate. Italy reps the one market where it could do well theatrically.

The film's main attraction, the unique setting and scenery, is instantly apparent. A low-maintenance prisoner-of-war camp, commanded by Brits but staffed by African subjects, sits on a dusty plain in the shadow of imposing Mount Kenya. Said to be one of the most difficult mountains in the world to scale, peak gives the camp's chief officer, Maj. David Farrell (Ben Cross), something to occupy his time beyond his Italian and German prisoners and a lovely local widow, Patricia (Rachel Ward).

At the outset, however, the rigid, dour Farrell, who's lost his wife and child in the war, is an underachiever, having failed to conquer either Mount Kenya or Patricia. Leave it to a dark and handsome Italian, Franco Distassi (Vincent Spano), to take up the slack, even if he has to escape from the camp to do so.

September 26, 1994 (Cont.)

The Italians hatch a plan for Franco and Enzo (Tony Lo Bianco) to climb the mountain, plant the Italian flag at the summit and return to camp. Franco can't abide the last part of the scheme, but when Enzo is forced to drop out, the younger man pushes on alone, with Farrell in hot, and jealous, pursuit.

Based on a true incident, David Wiltse's screenplay is straightforward and devoid of ironies or complexity. With a host of potential sources of tension to draw upon, from the mixture of English, Italians, Germans and Africans confined to tight quarters, script mostly trades in stock national characterizations — the uptight Englishman, condescending Nazi, hot-blooded Latin, and so on.

Climactic couple of reels depicting the two men's chase up the mountain are scenically diverting, but even the Rockyesque ending seems rather perfunctory and less than rousing, except perhaps to Italian patriots. Problem with the story is that there is virtually nothing at stake, giving the viewer little reason to invest much emotional interest in the characters.

Canadian helmer Donald Shebib has mounted the proceedings in presentable fashion and the performances are agreeable enough, but it's the unbeatable locations that provide the greatest diversion here.
—*Todd McCarthy*

VENICE

LIVING IT UP

(LA BELLA VITA)

(ITALIAN)

A Life Intl. release of a Time Intl. Film production. Produced by Roberto Cimpanelli. Executive producer, Paolo Vandini. Directed by Paolo Virzi. Screenplay, Virzi, Francesco Bruni. Camera (color), Paolo Carnera; editor, Sergio Montanari; music, Claudio Cimpanelli; production design, Attilio Caselli. Reviewed at Isonzo screening room, Rome, Aug. 31, 1994. (In Venice Film Festival — Panorama.) Running time: **95 MIN.**

Bruno Nardelli	Claudio Bigagli
Mirella	Sabrina Ferilli
Gerry Fumo	Massimo Ghini
Renato	Giorgio Algranti
Luciano	Emanuele Barresi
Rossella	Paola Tiziana Cruciani

Working-class life in today's Tuscany is at the center of "**Living It Up**," a romantic comedy of rare naturalness, set in **a rural world of steel mills and supermarkets. A likable film with a strong social background, Paolo Virzi's directing debut, which preemed in the Venice fest's Panorama section, promises to be a fest fave, though its lack of big comic stars may cramp domestic B.O. revenue.**

When Bruno (Claudio Bigagli of "Mediterraneo" fame) and Mirella (Sabrina Ferilli) get married in 1989, things are going well at the steel mill. Three years later, the mill is in trouble and Bruno is one of hundreds to be laid off his job. "The easy life" of pic's Italian title ironically refers to what is waiting for workers who get the pink slip.

At the same time, Bruno's marriage hits the skids when Mirella lets herself be seduced by a regional TV host who goes by the moniker Gerry Fumo (Massimo Ghini). Bruno is the last to find out. In a painful confrontation, Bruno faces his wife and asks her to leave. She moves in with the handsome, babyish Fumo, while secretly pining for Bruno.

Bruno's plans to open a small steel plant with some friends fizzle out, and he suffers a serious heart attack. It brings him back together with Mirella, but their reunion is only temporary. In the end they amicably agree to go their own ways, and begin rebuilding their lives at a distance.

Though the story sounds downbeat, pic's tone is generally light. Script by Virzi and Francesco Bruni anchors the dramatic events in such a tightly woven social context that the characters seem protected from their own fatal mistakes. Bruno has the solidarity of his buddies at the plant, as well as the unrequited love of co-worker Rossella (Paola Tiziana Cruciani), a labor organizer and party militant.

Red flags fly proudly over Tuscany's leftist workers, who nevertheless have a hard time adapting to changing times and job cutbacks. By leaving Bruno and her job in the supermarket for a middle-class life with Fumo, Sabrina loses the relaxed camaraderie of the old gang. Without hammering his point, Virzi makes it clear that she has taken a step into boredom and emptiness.

Newcomer Ferilli (last seen in Marco Ferreri's "Diary of a Madman") makes a sparkling, larger-than-life heroine. Her innocent voluptuousness, recalling Italo actresses of Sophia Loren and Gina Lollobrigida's day, is cloaked in modest attire, revealed at most in a tacky see-through bra. Yet Sabrina conquers less through her looks than with her good humor and moral scruples.

Bigagli plays up Bruno's gentle side, which explains both his attraction for Sabrina and why the passion has drained out of their marriage. The explosion, when it comes, is all the more dramatic.

Virzi shows good directing control in this first stint, and his background in screenwriting is evident in pic's smooth narrative.
—*Deborah Young*

THE KINGDOM

(RIGET)

(DANISH)

A Zentropa Entertainments/Danmarks Radio production, in association with Swedish Television, WDR, Arte and the Coproduction Office. (International sales: the Coproduction Office, Berlin.) Produced by Ole Reim. Executive producers, Svend Abrahamsen, Peter Aalbaek Jensen. Co-producer, Ib Tardini. Directed by Lars von Trier. Screenplay, Tomas Gislason, von Trier, from a screen story by Niels Vorsel, von Trier. Camera (color), Eric Kress; editors, Jacob Thuesen, Molly Malene Stensgaard; music, Joachim Holbek; art direction, Jette Lehmann; costume design, Annelise Bailey; sound design (Dolby), Per Streit; associate producer, Philippe Bober; assistant director, Morten Arnfred. Reviewed at Venice Film Festival (Window on Images), Sept. 6, 1994. Running time: **279 MIN.** (Part one: **133 MIN.**, part two: **146 MIN.**)

Helmer	Ernst Hugo Jaregard
Mrs. Drusse	Kirsten Rolffes
Rigmor	Ghita Norby
Hook	Soren Pilmark
Aage Kroger	Udo Kier
Hansen	Otto Brandenburg
Bulder	Jens Okking
Moesgaard	Holger Juul Hansen
Mona	Laura Christensen
Judith	Birgitte Raabjerg
Bondo	Baard Owe
Mogge	Peter Mygind
(Danish and Swedish dialogue)	

Danish helmer Lars von Trier's first film since "Zentropa" (1990) is a lunatic, "Twin Peaks"-like meld of black-comedy soap and Z-grade horror flick that looks like an instant cult item among auds willing to go the stretch. Though the 4½-hour running time places it beyond the pale for anything but ultra-specialized theatrical distribution, this strikingly realized work is a natural for festivals and specialized TV sales outside the U.S.

Shot on video for Danish TV, pic unspooled at Venice in a 35mm transfer divided into two parts, each containing two episodes. Though pic's vid origins remain obvious, the quirky nature of the material (mostly printed in orange-sepia tones, recalling von Trier's first feature, "The Element of Crime") lends itself to such a look, and von Trier's impressive use of Dolby translates into a thoroughly theatrical experience.

Tone is set from the very beginning with a mock-lugubrious voice-over detailing the history of a giant Copenhagen hospital known as the Kingdom, built on ancient marshland once used as bleaching ponds. Over murky shots of chlorine vapors and a hand groping upward, audience is told that "cracks are starting to appear in the edifice," with the broader message that the spirit world is ready to do battle with the arrogance of 20th-century science. Blood bursting through a wall, followed by rock 'n' roll-backed main titles, kicks the yarn off in punchy style.

Episode one ("The Unheavenly Host," 66 minutes) starts slowly, with intimations that the labyrinthine building is haunted by a dead child as the large cast is intro'd in mock-soap style.

Characters include an arrogant Swedish neurosurgeon, Helmer, who loathes Danes and has turned a young girl, Mona, into a vegetable through a bungled brain operation; his lover, anesthetist Rigmor, who's into Haitian voodooism; Mrs. Drusse, an old spiritualist who fakes illnesses to stay in the hospital and solve the haunting; a doctor, Hook, who runs a black market in medical supplies from the basement; Bondo, an obsessed head of pathology; Moesgaard, hopeless head of the whole place; and Mogge, jilted in his love for a sexy doctor. Two retarded dishwashers in the kitchen function as a kind of Greek chorus.

With an eye on the pic's epic length, von Trier lets the black comedy seep out slowly, but some 30 minutes in, it's clear something is rotten in the Kingdom of Denmark. Despite its high-tech facade, the hospital is peopled by obsessives: Mogge saws a head off a corpse and presents it to his inamorata, senior staff are bound together by some kind of obscure Masonic brotherhood, Helmer is covering his tracks over the mismanaged op, and the sidewalk is cracking as the spirit world forces its way up.

By episode two ("Thy Kingdom Come," 67 minutes), Mona's alter ego is haunting the building in a major way, the severed head has gone AWOL, and the Masonic group is planning an illegal organ transplant from a dying patient. Most of episode three ("A Foreign Body," 70 minutes) revolves round various parties secretly raiding the

September 26, 1994 (Cont.)

hospital archives for incriminating documents. Meanwhile, a doctor, Judith, is suddenly heavily pregnant with a strange fetus, and old Mrs. Drusse has made contact with the ghost, a young girl murdered in 1919 by her father (Udo Kier), one of the original building's founders.

Pic's grand finale ("The Living Dead," 76 minutes) has Helmer jetting off to Haiti to practice voodoo on his enemy, Moesgaard; Mrs. Drusse exorcising the dead girl's spirit in the basement; and Judith giving birth to a huge alien form while a group of politicians tour the building.

Shooting in a semi-docu, handheld style, with antsy cutting, von Trier lets the lunacy slowly grow out of the complex web of escalating events, all played in straight-faced manner by the excellent cast. As the corrupt, overweening Swede, Ernst Hugo Jaregard carries the pic in grand style; veteran actress Ghita Norby hits just the right note as his quietly loony lover; and, as Mrs. Drusse, Kirsten Rolffes trots steadily through the pic like some spiritualist Miss Marple. All other players are on the button. Most of the filming took place in the actual hospital of the title. —*Derek Elley*

47 RONIN
(SHIJUSHICHININ NO SHIKAKU)
(JAPANESE)

A Toho Eiga production for Toho, NTV, Suntory. (International sales: Toho Intl., Tokyo.) Produced by Jitsuzo Horiuchi, Seiji Urushido, Kiyoshi Nagai. Executive producers, Toshiaki Hashimoto, Hiroshi Takahashi. Directed by Kon Ichikawa. Screenplay, Kaneo Ikegami, Yo Takeyama, Ichikawa, from the 1748 kabuki play cycle "Kanadehon Chushingura" by Shoichiro Ikemiya. Camera (color), Yukio Isohata; editor, Chizuko Osada; music, Kensaku Tanigawa; production design, Hisao Nabeshima, Makiko Goto; art direction, Toshiro Muraki; costume design, Yoshio Ninomiya, Yasunao Inui, Ikuko Saito; sound (Dolby), Teiichi Saito, Tetsuya Ohashi; fighting choreography, Shinpachi Miyama; associate producer, Hidehiko Takei; assistant director, Masaaki Tezuka. Reviewed at Venice Film Festival (Venetian Nights), Sept. 7, 1994. Running time: **132 MIN.**
Kuranosuke Oishi .... Ken Takakura
Karu .... Rie Miyazawa
Matashiro Irobe .... Kiichi Nakai
Riku .... Ruriko Asaoka
Yoshiyasu
  Yanagisawa .... Koji Ishizaka
Hyobu Chisaka .... Hisaya Morishige
Kozukenosuke Kira .... Ko Nishimura

In his 70th feature, "47 Ronin," veteran Kon Ichikawa takes his first stab at an oft-filmed "Chushingura," about clan revenge in 18th-century feudal Japan. Good-looking, precision

piece of work will appeal to Japan specialists familiar with the historical tale and interpretive subtleties, but more general buffs drawn by Ichikawa's name are likely to be turned off by the pic's dry, largely undramatic style and confusing, character-heavy narrative.

Ken Takakura ("Black Rain," "Mr. Baseball") toplines as Oishi, chamberlain of the Ako clan, who plans revenge on government official Lord Kira for a contretemps that led to the Ako clan head's execution. Oishi suspects a coverup and gathers around him a group of like-minded *ronin*.

After assembling war funds by selling vast quantities of salt, Oishi fabricates graft rumors that force Kira to retire and later move out of Edo Castle into a private manse. Kira's relative, Irobe, helps Kira to fortify his dwelling and also to outsmart Oishi in the rumor game. On Dec. 14, 1702, exactly 21 months after the original contretemps, Oishi leads his 47 *ronin* in a nighttime attack on the snow-covered mansion.

Ichikawa's storytelling style, which reportedly sticks closer to the historical events than other versions have, is clean and uninflected, with the action zipping back and forth between a series of indoor locations (denoted by captions). Even from the early going, however, the amount of information foreign audiences are asked to retain in terms of who's who makes following events virtually impossible without a detailed synopsis.

Though the film's look is always pristinely beautiful, and performances vivid, without an understanding of the story's crosscurrents it's hard to become emotionally involved. Pic's 10-minute finale of Oishi and company slicing their way through the mansion's surrounding labyrinth and warren of connecting rooms is impressive, however. But for most viewers it will be too little too late.

Tech credits are all immaculate, and there's a cute performance by model/singer/actress Rie Miyazawa as Oishi's love interest. Of the dozen or so other versions of the tale, the best known is Kenji Mizoguchi's mammoth, two-part "The Loyal Forty-Seven Ronin of the Genroku Era" (1942-42). —*Derek Elley*

GENESIS:
THE CREATION
AND THE FLOOD
(GENESI: LA CREAZIONE
E IL DILUVIO)
(ITALIAN-GERMAN)

An Istituto Luce release (in Italy) of a RAI-TV Channel 1/Lux co-production in association with Lube-Betafilm. (International sales: Betafilm.) Executive producer, Franco Bollati. Associate producer, Paolo Piria. Directed, written by Ermanno Olmi. Camera (color, 35mm), not credited; editor, Paolo Cottignola, Fabio Olmi; music, Ennio Morricone; art direction, Paolo Biagetti; costumes, Enrico Sabbatini; sound, Dolby. Reviewed at Venice Film Festival (non-competing), Sept. 5, 1994. Running time: **101 MIN.**
Storyteller/Noah ...... Omero Antonutti

The Bible may be the most plundered text in film history, but, before this project, no one has ever attempted to systematically shoot it for TV. For this first episode of the mammoth, 20-episode adaptation, director Ermanno Olmi ("The Tree of Wooden Clogs") sticks closely to the text. Reverent without being cloying, beautifully lensed but deliberately without spectacular scenes, "Genesis: The Creation and the Flood" won't set the world on fire but should prove nicely serviceable for worldwide small-screen use.

"Genesis" is the only episode in the series that producers plan to release theatrically. Preemed out of competition at the Venice fest, it looked uncomfortably out of place as an art film. Distrib Istituto Luce will give pic a try in Italian venues, but box office is likely to be thin.

Shot in the Moroccan desert with a non-pro cast of local Bedouins (except for Italian lead Omero Antonutti), pic tells a familiar story with minimum embellishment. An old nomadic sage (Antonutti) recounts the creation and the flood to his big-eyed grandson and other silent listeners gathered around a campfire. Apart from the boy's simple questions and his grandfather's reassurances, dialogue is taken word for word from the Bible. Simple modern Italian was read in the version screened at Venice, suggesting that foreign-language versions will also opt for a modern rendition of the sacred text.

Olmi has a humble, non-institutional brand of religion closely tied to nature, the land and the common people. Pic opens with images of birds in flight, fish in the sea, sheep at pasture, the faces of young women, old men and children. Nothing supernatural appears in "Genesis" — no serpents, angels with

flaming swords or images of the Creator at work. This undoubtedly robs the tale of some of its entertainment quotient, but what's lost in special effects is gained in focusing on the text's inherent poetry.

The Cain and Abel story is told through the angry glances of the boy Cain at his placid shepherd brother. The murder takes place offscreen, but God's interrogation of Cain, as read by Antonutti, is terrifying enough. Antonutti reappears in the second half as Noah, a part with no speaking lines but much worried frowning. Again, the big scenes one would expect — the lions and elephants tramping onto the Ark, the Ark floating on turbulent flood waters — Olmi leaves to John Huston. All we see is Noah and his relatives slapping timber and thatch together, and sharing the barnlike interior with domestic farm animals.

Pic has a slow, reverent rhythm that requires getting used to. Its images of the Moroccan desert and some ancient structures are finely shot and cut but lack the visual fireworks that a director like Werner Herzog might have injected. An excellent choice of ethnic music accompanies the film. Ennio Morricone composed the series' opening and closing music. —*Deborah Young*

THE HEART'S CRY
(LE CRI DU COEUR)
(FRENCH)

A Les Films de la Plaine/Les Films de l'Avenir/Centre Europeen Cinematographique Rhone-Alpes production. Executive producer, Sophie Salbot. Directed by Idrissa Ouedraogo. Screenplay, Ouedraogo, Robert Gardner, Jacques Akchoti. Camera (color), Jean Monsigny; editor, Luc Barnier; music, Henri Texier; art direction, Olivier Paultre; sound, Dominique Levert, Dominique Hennequin. Reviewed at Venice Film Festival (competing), Sept. 8, 1994. Running time: **86 MIN.**
With: Richard Bohringer, Said Diarra, Felicite Wouassi, Alex Descas, Clementine Celarie, Jean-Yves Gautier.
(French dialogue)

Leading Burkina Faso director Idrissa Ouedraogo transplants an African family to Paris in "The Heart's Cry," a well-made, dignified, French-funded production. Presence of Gallic star Richard Bohringer in a supporting role should boost local interest, though pic's main audience will be viewers interested in African cinema, plus some younger auds. A good fest run is assured.

Moctar (Said Diarra), an 11-year-old boy living in Mali, leaves his village and sick grandfather to go to Paris with his mother Saffi (Felicite Wouassi) to join his father, Ibrahim Sow (Alex Descas). After years of

September 26, 1994 (Cont.)

hard work as an emigrant laborer, Ibrahim now owns his own garage. He has prepared a nice home for his family, and aspires for his son to become a doctor.

Moctar seems to be adapting well to his new environment, until one day he begins seeing (or hallucinating?) a scary hyena trotting down the street. His schoolmates laugh at him and the school psychiatrist alarms his parents about the boy's mental health. Everybody tries to persuade him he's imagining things. Only Paulo (Bohringer), an outsider who befriends him, is willing to take him seriously and help him overcome his fears.

Film's interest lies in the way Ouedraogo (director of the prize-winning "Yaaba," "Tilai" and "Samba Traore") sidesteps the usual African-immigrant plot issues of racism and marginalization to concentrate on the psychological adjustment problems of a child.

As Moctar, newcomer Diarra is a serious, plucky hero who courageously engages the hyena in a fiery showdown in pic's climactic scene.
—*Deborah Young*

THE LIFE AND EXTRAORDINARY ADVENTURES OF PRIVATE IVAN CHONKIN

(BRITISH-FRENCH)

An Artificial Eye (U.K.)/MK2 (France) release of a Portobello Pictures/MK2 Prods. co-production, in association with Fandango (Rome), La Sept Cinema, Canal Plus, Centre National de la Cinematographie (France), Channel Four Films, the European Co-Production Fund (U.K.), Cable Plus, KF, EFA, Studio 89 (Czech Republic), Studio Trite (Russia.) Produced by Eric Abraham. Co-producer, Katya Krausova. Directed by Jiri Menzel. Screenplay, Zdenek Sverak, based on a novel by Vladimir Voinovic. Camera (color), Jaromir Sofr; editor, Jiri Brozek; music, Jiri Sust; art direction, Milan Bycek; associate producer, Domenico Procacci. Reviewed at Venice Film Festival (competing), Sept. 4, 1994. Running time: **106 MIN.**
Ivan Chonkin .... Gennady Nazarov
Niura .... Zoya Buryak
Golubev .... Vladimir Ilyin
Kilin............................ Valeri Zolotukhin
Stalin .... Zinovi Gerdt
With: Alexei Zharkov, Yuri Dubrovin, Sergei Garmash, Marian Labuda, Maria Vinogradova.
(Russian dialogue)

A satire on Stalinism and Soviet bureaucracy, "The Life and Extraordinary Adventures of Private Ivan Chonkin" was made a decade too late to have political impact. **A British-French co-production featuring an all-Russian cast directed by Czech helmer Jiri Menzel, pic is an exemplary East/West European art-house offering that will probably do limited business theatrically in quality markets.**

The story is based on a famous banned Russian novel, written by Vladimir Voinovic in 1969 (just two years after Menzel's masterful "Closely Watched Trains" won an Oscar for best foreign film.) Voinovic was expelled from the Writers' Union in 1974 and exiled from the USSR a few years later. In Czechoslovakia, meanwhile, Menzel was banned from filmmaking for five years after his 1969 "Larks on a String."

"Chonkin" was finally published in Russia in 1989, after the adventure of perestroika. Menzel, too, benefited from the new winds blowing in the East, and won a belated Gold Bear in Berlin for "Larks on a String" in 1990.

Menzel and Voinovic's common experiences make "Chonkin" a natural fit, even if pic's tone has a very un-Russian lightness and gentle humor that recalls Menzel's "My Sweet Little Village." Ivan Chonkin (Gennady Nazarov) is a doltish soldier, the laughingstock of his company. Assigned to stand guard over a broken airplane in a remote village called Red, he is forgotten by his superiors as World War II breaks out.

A simple soul with a heart of gold and an insatiable appetite for sex, Chonkin shacks up with the town postal clerk, Niura (Zoya Buryak), and the two spend joyous weeks rolling in the hay on her farm. The idyll ends when some jealous neighbors write an anonymous letter denouncing Ivan as a spy. It sets off a very funny chain of misunderstandings, which culminates in a party of NKVD secret service police setting off for Red.

Pic carefully balances comic and tragic tones. While the secretary files her nails, a sadistic NKVD officer tortures innocent citizens chosen at random. He meets his match only once, when he arrests a little Jewish craftsman (Zinovi Gerdt) whose name turns out — providentially — to be Stalin.

But Ivan proves a tough customer, too. Insisting that only a general can relieve him of guard duty, he refuses to be arrested. His blind insubordination leads to a grotesque and quite successful comic finale in which he stymies both the feared secret police and the Soviet war machine.

High-flying fantasy ending, which is not in the book, offers viewers an exhilarating happy ending, and is no more far-fetched than the rest of the tale. —*Deborah Young*

A SHADOW YOU SOON WILL BE

(UNA SOMBRA YA PRONTO SERAS)

(ARGENTINE)

A Hector Olivera/Tercer Milenio, Instituto Nacional de Cinematografia production. (International sales: Aries Cinematografica, Buenos Aires.) Produced by Fernando Ayala. Directed by Hector Olivera. Screenplay, Olivera, Osvaldo Soriano, based on Soriano's novel. Camera (color) Felix Monti; editor, Eduardo Lopez; music, Osvaldo Montes; art direction, Emilio Basaldua; costume design, Margarita Jusid; sound (Dolby), Jorge Stavropulos. Reviewed at Venice Film Festival (competing), Sept. 10, 1994. (Also in Toronto fest.) Running time: **105 MIN.**
The Engineer .... Miguel Angel Sola
Coluccini .... Pepe Soriano
Nadia .... Alicia Bruzzo
Lem .... Eusebio Poncela
Barrante .... Luis Brandoni
Boris .... Diego Torres
Rita .... Gloria Carra

Veteran helmer Hector Olivera's lonesome road movie set in the southern pampas of Argentina, "A Shadow You Soon Will Be," metaphorically describes a pervasive feeling of emptiness and desolation in the years following the end of military rule in 1983. Gently amusing and specifically Argentine, it will probably hover on the fringes of the international fest and art-film circuit, winning over limited auds with its honesty and charm.

A man in his 40s known only as "the engineer" (Miguel Angel Sola) has just returned from Europe, where he lived in exile during the long military dictatorship. Bereft of family and friends, he travels with nothing but the clothes on his back. Claiming to be a computer expert on his way to a job in the south, he wanders aimlessly through the flat, deserted but magical countryside, where railway tracks end in the middle of the pampas and only a few antique cars roll down an endless highway.

On the road, in motels and ghost towns, he meets eccentrics like himself who become momentary traveling companions. He has a comic fling with a buxom, gun-toting medium, Nadia (Alicia Bruzzo). He gets a ride in a Rolls with a mysterious millionaire, Lem (Eusebio Poncela). He befriends Barrante (a touching perf by Luis Brandoni), a vagabond who earns his bread hosing down farm laborers with a portable shower.

Most interesting character is Coluccini (Pepe Soriano), a former circus owner who has gone broke. He involves the hero in a rigged card game that backfires. Soriano's perf as the shyster with a heart of gold is reminiscent of a character out of a Fellini film.

Based on a 1990 novel by Osvaldo Soriano, who co-scripted, the story ends where it begins. Argentina is shown as a broken-down country with no future in sight and no memory of the years of bloody repression that have recently ended.

Felix Monti's masterful lensing has a simple, pleasant clarity. In the main role, Sola is a cool guy who watches the world go by with restrained indignation and some amusement — which are more or less the feelings this good-natured, unsentimental pic communicates to its audience. —*Deborah Young*

GERMAINE AND BENJAMIN

(DU FOND DU COEUR: GERMAINE ET BENJAMIN)

(FRENCH)

A GMT Prods. production, in association with La Sept/Arte, SFP, Home Made Movies, Club d'Investissement Media, Babelsberg Studio (Germany). (International sales: Marathon Intl., Paris.) Produced by Jean-Pierre Guerin. Executive producer, Beatrice Caufman. Directed by Jacques Doillon. Screenplay, Jean-Francois Goyet. Camera (color), William Lubtchansky; editor, Francois Dufau; art direction and costumes, Anais Romand; sound, Jean-Pierre Duret. Reviewed at Venice Film Festival (Special Events), Sept. 7, 1994. Running time: **138 MIN.**
Germaine de Stael .... Anne Brochet
Benjamin Constant ...... Benoit Regent
Anna Lindsay .... Frances Barber
Juliette Recamier .... Sophie Broustal
Prosper
de Barante .... Thibault
de Montalembert
Albertine .... Louise-Laure Mariani
Charlotte
de Hardenberg ..... Catherine Bidaut
Monsieur de Stael .... Hans Zischler

Fans of cerebral French helmer Jacques Doillon will adore "Germaine and Benjamin," a splendid dramatization of the historic love affair between Franco-Swiss author and statesman Benjamin Constant and the brilliant Madame de Stael. A discursive talkfest rolling over two hours, pic is aimed squarely at arthouse regulars who are willing to read non-stop subtitles and revel in the subtle S&M games couples played in Napoleon's day.

Pic has a technical claim to fame: It's the first feature shot entirely in high-definition digital video, then transferred to 35mm. The vid tapings allowed Doillon and cinematographer William Lubtchansky to indulge in extraordinarily lengthy takes that give the film a distinctive, rather theatrical style.

The technique's touted ability to offer great depth of field without much lighting may be debated, since most scenes indoors are shallow two-shots. But the overall beauty of the lensing will convert many skeptics to the esthetic possibilities of video. Production manager Serge Roux says the process was cheaper than shooting in 35mm.

Constant (Benoit Regent) and Germaine de Stael (Anne Brochet) began their tempestuous liaison in 1794. There are no bedroom scenes in pic, but there is much passion, tears and theorizing about love. Doillon emphasizes both de Stahl's brilliant, febrile mind and the dominating influence she exerted over those around her, first of all Constant. She pushed him into a political career after the French Revolution, and later urged him to have the courage of his convictions and publish her own anti-Napoleon book.

The characters change costume but don't age. After nearly 20 years, they meet for the last time. Constant has remarried, de Stahl's children are grown, but they're still emotionally involved in a masochistic love-hate relationship that has nowhere to go but in circles.

Brochet is riveting as the impetuous, selfish and emotional Germaine, upstaging even Regent's strongly likable, modern Constant. The chemistry between the two thesps is a pleasure, even when the characters' emotional life becomes repetitive.

Most scenes are variations on the two lovers closeted together in richly decorated Empire interiors, Brochet in eye-catching gowns and turbans, the less secure Regent figuratively at her feet. Jean-Francois Goyet's dialogue is sophisticated, often impassioned, and barely pauses for an embrace.

—Deborah Young

IRON HORSEMEN

(FINNISH-FRENCH-ITALIAN)

A Villealfa Filmprods. (Finland)/UGC, Noe Prods. (France)/Film Master Film (Italy) production. Produced by Aki Kaurismaki, Cedomir Kolar, Sergio Castellani. Executive producers, Klaus Heydemann, Marc Baschet. Co-producers, Yves Marmion, Frederique Dumas-Zajdela, Carlos Pasini Hansen. Directed, written by Gilles Charmant. Camera (color), Timo Salminen; editor, Veikko Aaltonen; music, Wouter Zoon; production design, John Ebden; art direction, Mark Lavis; costume design, Marilyn Fitoussi; sound (Dolby), Jouko Lumme; assistant director, Pauli Pentti. Reviewed at Venice Film Festival (Critics' Week), Sept. 9, 1994. Running time: **84 MIN.**

Bad Trip .... Dominic Gould
Rhonda .... Laura Favali
Darling .... Kari Vaananen
Candy .... Nicky Tesco
Seeker .... Matti Pellonpaa
Genghis Khan .... Saku Kuosmanen
Guzzler .... Puntii Valtonen
Zipper .... Antti Reini
With: Jean-Marc Barr, Jim Jarmusch, Aki Kaurismaki.
(English dialogue)

A satirical spin on late-'60s biker movies, with rural Finland effectively standing in for California, "Iron Horsemen" (aka "Bad Trip") tips its helmet to B-movie maestros like Roger Corman, Monte Hellman, Herschell Gordon Lewis and, naturally, Dennis Hopper. Though it's little more than a scant attempt to put a new slant on an old genre, this droll parody from the production stable of Aki Kaurismaki has enough hokey horsepower and retro-pop savvy on its side to lure a modest share of young urbanites and college crowds.

Bad Trip (Dominic Gould), an acid-head member of motorcycle gang the Cannibals, steals a bike belonging to group leader Candy (Nicky Tesco). Tracked down at his parents' house, he soon learns the ruthless bikers live up to their name, serving his father for lunch, and tagging Ma as Candy's personal plaything. Sentenced to death, Bad Trip is given 30 minutes to hotfoot it before the gang gives chase.

His weird encounters and narrow escapes flesh out the rest of the threadbare plot. Among the former are a wandering Russian with stars and stripes in his eyes (Kaurismaki); Trip's flaky brother, who eats bugs in his tropical greenhouse (Jean-Marc Barr); and a biker with a calling for the priesthood who aids his escape (Matti Pellonpaa). A ro-

mantic interlude of sorts comes via a machine gun-toting, bank-robbing Che Guevara devotee, Rhonda (Laura Favali), who eventually dumps him for his lack of class consciousness.

From out of Trip's dreams or acid-induced hallucinations comes the Silver Rider (Jim Jarmusch), a white-knight biker who helps him shake off his pursuers by rigging a decapitation trap. Pic sidesteps into Monty Python territory when the bikers' dismembered heads keep talking.

Debuting writer/director Gilles Charmant (assistant director on Kaurismaki's 1992 "La Vie de Boheme") neatly captures the feel of the B movies he eulogizes and (somewhat smugly) derides by laying tinny pop tunes over the slapdash action, heightening color to garish extremes and drawing large, untethered performances from the cast. His main departure is in production values, creating a clean look and sound that many of the originals didn't have. *—David Rooney*

MONTREAL

THE LAST SUPPER

(CANADIAN)

A Hryhory Yulyan Motion Pictures production, in association with DNA Theatre. (International sales: Hryhory Yulyan Motion Pictures Inc., Toronto.) Produced by Greg Klymkiw. Co-producers, Hillar Liitoja, Cynthia Roberts. Directed by Roberts. Screenplay, Liitoja, Klymkiw, Roberts, based on Liitoja's play. Camera (color), Harald Bachmann; editors, Roberts, Su Rynard; music, Nicholas Stirling; sound, Phil Strong, Roberts. Reviewed at World Film Festival, Montreal, Aug. 28, 1994. (Also in Vancouver fest.) Running time: **96 MIN.**

Chris .... Ken McDougall
Val .... Jack Nicholsen
Dr. Parthens .... Daniel MacIvor

Based on the award-winning Toronto play of the same name, "The Last Supper" is an important addition to the growing body of pix about AIDS-related issues, but this painfully realistic feature will be too grueling for most auds and may even be tough to handle for viewers close to the topic. It will, however, attract interest at fest and other specialized screenings.

Ultra-claustrophobic pic is shot entirely in one room, where dancer/choreographer Chris (Ken McDougall) lies on his sickbed awaiting death. Helmer Cynthia Roberts has shot film in real time, with minimal editing and no shortage of long, laborious silences. Chris has decided to end his life via a doctor-assisted

suicide, and film covers his last moments with his lover, Val (Jack Nicholsen). They eat a final meal together and reminisce about happier times. Chris performs one last deathbed dance, and even the lethal injection is choreographed to music.

McDougall, a well-known Canadian theater and dance personality here recreating his stage role, died from AIDS-related causes four days after shooting wrapped on "The Last Supper." Shot on a shoestring budget, pic's camerawork is deliberately shadowy and other tech credits are just as low-fi. Producer Greg Klymkiw was involved in several key, recent indie Canuck features — notably "Careful" and "Tales from the Gimli Hospital" — but his latest production isn't likely to win the same cult auds as those earlier pix. *—Brendan Kelly*

MISS AMERIGUA

(PARAGUAYAN-SWEDISH)

A PBN/Filmteknik/Latin Films (Stockholm) production. Produced, directed by Luis R. Vera. Screenplay, Vera, Andres Colman. Camera (color), Martin Nilsson; editor, Lisskulla Moltke-Hoff; music, Jan Tolf; production design, Carlos Dos Santos; art direction, Ricardo Migliorisi; costumes, Rocio Sienra; sound, Jaime Villanueva; associate producers, Oscar Elizeche, Pascual Rubiani, Enrique Hellmers, Pablo Jara. Reviewed at World Film Festival, Montreal (non-competing), Aug. 31, 1994. Running time: **93 MIN.**

Maria Desamparo .... Sonia Marchewka
Rosa Pasion .... Raquel Baeza
Carmen Banderas .... Ayesa Frutos
Evaristo .... Hector Silva
Col. Banderas .... Jesus Perez
Inocencio Periodista .... Jorge Baez
Reencarnacion .... Carlos Cristaldo
Amelia, la Bruja .... Graciela Canepa

The first feature from Paraguay in 30 years, "Miss Amerigua" is no great earth-shaker but a mild political satire with touches of magical realism that paints an agreeably sketchy portrait of a fictional South American town.

Pic starts with a hint of a childhood bond between black-haired Evaristo and fair-skinned Maria in an idyllic waterfall setting. This reverie is shaken when the boy witnesses the murder of his activist father at the hands of Amerigua's resident fascist, Col. Banderas. Years later, the grown Evaristo (Hector Silva) returns from revolutionary training in Nicaragua with revenge and Maria on his mind.

At first, the town doesn't notice his arrival, since everyone's caught up in the annual bathing-babe contest. This time, there's unusually stiff competition between the very

September 26, 1994 (Cont.)

grown-up Maria (Sonia Marchewka), Evaristo's sexy sister Rosa Pasion and Carmen Banderas, haughty daughter of the colonel, who by now owns most of the verdant region. Leftists eventually confront the right, love triumphs, and there are literal fireworks to abruptly, and rather haphazardly, end the semi-farcical proceedings.

Chilean-born, Swedish-based helmer Luis Vera is better at handling light comedy and tender moments than holding narrative together, and auds may have trouble differentiating principal characters or caring about their aspirations, let alone finding allegorical meanings in their exaggerated actions. Much of the expository dialogue is perfunctory, but peripheral business, as with an inept young journalist (Jorge Baez) and a philosophical hairdresser (Carlos Cristaldo), is reliably amusing.

Tech credits are adequate, with Vera and lenser Martin Nilsson excelling only in isolated vignettes that drop plot in favor of a gently supernatural texture. Aggressive marketing, based on attractive female troika, could bring "Like Water for Chocolate" fans sniffing. Pic, however, is too slight and fragmentary to sustain non-Spanish-lingo interest. —*Ken Eisner*

CROSSINGS

(HONG KONG-U.S.)

A Riverdrive Prods. Ltd. (New York) production. Produced by Willy Tsao. Executive producer, Jessinta Liu. Directed by Evans Chan. Screenplay, Evans Chan, Joyce Chan. Camera (color) Jamie Silverstein; editor, Henry Chang; music, Kung Chi Shing, Cui Jan; production, costume design, William Chang (Hong Kong), Deana Sidney (New York); sound, Coll Anderson. Reviewed at World Film Festival, Montreal (non-competing), Sept. 1, 1994. Running time: **102 MIN.**
With: Anita Yuen (Mo-yung), Simon Yam (Benny), Lindzay Chan (Rubie), Ted Brunetti, Monica Ha, Monica Ha, Elizabeth Flax, Toshiro Chan Yamamoto, Philip Meng Miou.

A veritable hot pot of not-totally-compatible ingredients, "Crossings" is an overambitious study of the points at which Chinese and American cultures intersect, or don't. Pic will reward those with committed interest in the subject and repel others.

Hong Kong beauty Anita Yuen toplines as Mo-yung, a young middle-class woman whose family wants her to marry a sight-unseen Toronto man so she can leave the British colony before 1997. Those plans fly out the window when she meets Benny (Simon Yam), an ultra-cool photographer who may

be peddling other goods on his shuttles between New York and H.K. Eventually, Mo-yung follows him to the Big Apple with something he wanted mailed; she has a hard time finding him, although his "clients" are soon looking for her.

Along the way, she runs into Rubie (serene Lindzay Chan), a part-white health worker who is being followed by a possibly psychotic schoolteacher with a fixation on Asian women.

Some scenes are alarmingly clumsy, but the script has wit ("Marco Polo," says one character, "brought two things home from China: pasta and the Mafia") and occasional moments — particularly those between the two female leads — are simply and touchingly handled.

Helmer Evans Chan was inspired by a real, mid-'80s incident in which a H.K. immigrant was pushed off a N.Y. subway platform by a crazed Caucasian (scary Ted Brunetti). "Crossings" smacks of calculated agenda, with ideas usually outstripping execution. Pic is chaotic and rough, but it moves swiftly, with at least one display of talent for every fumble. —*Ken Eisner*

PEPE & FIFI

(PEPE SI FIFI)

(ROMANIAN)

A Solaris Film Production. (International sales: Romaniafilm, Bucharest.) Produced by Vily Auerbach. Directed by Dan Pita. Screenplay, Pita, Ioana Eliad. Camera (color) Dan Alexandru; editor, Cristina Ionescu; music, Adrian Enescu; art direction, Nicolae Dragan, Georgeta Solomon. Reviewed at World Film Festival, Montreal (competing), Sept. 3, 1994. Running time: **105 MIN.**
With: Cristian Iacob, Irina Movila, Mihai Calin, Costel Constantin, Charles Maquignon, Liliana Biclea, Damian Crismaru.

A harrowing portrait of the dead-end lives of a couple of young Romanians in turbulent, post-Communist Bucharest, veteran helmer Dan Pita's "Pepe & Fifi" is simply too relentlessly downbeat to appeal to international auds. It is a moving, slice-of-life drama, but bleak tone eventually overwhelms pic.

Mood is set in the first moment, as a scruffy beggar predicts the imminent apocalypse, and atmosphere only toughens further with introduction of Pepe (Cristian Iacob), an up-and-coming boxer who gets beaten up badly in a jolting fight scene. His sister Fifi (Irina Movila) spends most of her time cruising Bucharest's trashy nightclub scene, where she meets an ultra-sleazy pimp/mobster named the Baron.

Shot in grainy, low-budget style in the seedier parts of Bucharest,

"Pepe & Fifi" makes it clear that toppling the Communist dictatorship was hardly a panacea for Romania's social ills.

But the point is driven home with all the subtlety of a pneumatic drill. Throughout the film, Pepe's best friend, the wheelchair-bound Carol, shouts out a steady stream of political commentary through a megaphone, and homeless people deliver wordy, politically aware speeches.

Sound quality is a bit dodgy at moments and Dan Alexandru's camerawork mirrors the dark temper of the story. —*Brendan Kelly*

THE STORY OF YUNNAN

(YUN NAN QIU SHI)

(CHINESE)

A Beijing Film Studio production. (International sales: Zhang Shong Film Co., Tapei, Taiwan.) Produced by Cheng Zhigu, Dou Yaoling, Ye Li Pei. Directed by Zhang Nuanxing. Screenplay, Tian Sheng, Xie Tieng. Camera (color), Wang Xiaole; music, Lin Wai Zhe, Li Xinyun; production design, Shu Gang; sound, Li Bojian. Reviewed at World Film Festival, Montreal (competing), Aug. 29, 1994. Running time: **97 MIN.**
With: Lu Xiuling, Lin Jianhua, Pu Cunxin.

The Chinese March of Time continues in "The Story of Yunnan," yet another family saga showing how to survive revolutions, rural isolation and too much aging makeup. Twist is that the heroine is Japanese-born and ends up in a part of China whose colorful folk life is rarely seen in the West. A limited international arthouse life is possible after fest rounds are over.

Like many other Beijing-blessed pix, "Yunnan" begins at the end of the Sino-Japanese War (aka World War II). Raised in occupied Manchuria, teenaged Zyuko (lovely Lu Xiuling) is left behind when her father's regiment suddenly retreats. Captured on the Great Wall, the young woman is renamed Zhuzi and protected by a Chinese officer (Lin Jianhua), whom she eventually marries and accompanies to his remote village in central Yunnan Province. Unfortunately, the husband has some unnamed disease and doesn't survive the harsh trek.

That leaves her in the hands of his compassionate mother and confused younger brother, Xia Lou (Pu Cunxin), who tells Zhuzi that tribal tradition makes her *his* wife now. She throws a fit, and it takes Lou much sucking on his bong to figure

that he's still got an inside track. After establishing herself in the village — her brief training as a nurse comes in handy with the local population, presented here as quaintly backward — she lets him stake his claim, and they have several wonderful children.

Of course, their path is not entirely smooth. Triumphant Communists threaten to throw her out of the country in 1949, and area youths turn on her during the Cultural Revolution. Still, there are no crises that a heartfelt word or a kindly cadre can't dispel.

Pic is equally ambivalent about Zhuzi's eventual trip to her homeland. Japan sequence is tenderly handled, with the plethora of material goods both attractive and repellent. But fact that the heroine hasn't *really* gotten 40 years older becomes painfully obvious when she's shoved up against actual oldsters in an awkward class reunion.

Helmer Zhang Nuanxing is better at capturing anthropological oddities than keeping narrative sharp, but she gets plenty from Lu Xiuling, who moves from passive damsel to hearty village elder. —*Ken Eisner*

THE REVENGE OF ITZIK FINKELSTEIN

(NIKMATO SHEL ITZIK FINKELSTEIN)

(ISRAELI)

A Revenge of Itzik Finkelstein Ltd. production. Produced, directed by Enrique Rottenberg. Screenplay, Rottenberg, Esteban Gottfried, from Ricardo Talesnik's "La Venganza de Beto Sanchez." Camera (color), Jorge Gurvitz; editors, Tali Halter-Shenkarusic, Shlomo Idov; art direction, Danni Leifschitz; sound, Shabtai Sarig. Reviewed at World Film Festival, Montreal (non-competing), Aug. 29, 1994. Running time: **83 MIN.**
With: Moshe Ivgi, Esteban Gottfried, Dvora Kedar, Shmil Ben-Ari, Ayelet Sorer, Alexander Cohen, Cesar Ulmer, Shiri Golan, Gilat Ankori, Ezra Kafri, Bat-Sheba Noam, Moska Alkalai.

Filled with old-fashioned humor and the nebbishy appeal of its Jerry-Lewis-on-Prozac star, Moshe Ivgi ("Cup Final"), this "Revenge" will be sweet to selected auds while leaving others sour. It's currently making the rounds in the U.S. as part of the traveling Israel Film Festival.

Small-time hustler Itzik Finkelstein still lives with his aged mother in suburban Tel Aviv, but figures his ship has come in with a foolproof novelty — who wouldn't want a key-chain monk with a red-tipped erection? He orders 50,000 units, but for some reason he has a tough time moving the merchandise.

His despair is relieved only when one of the monk-lets comes suddenly to life in the form of a dour six-foot friar, sans sexual apparatus, but with a South American accent (Daniel Stern-ish Esteban Gottfried) and the promise that he'll grant Itzik some wishes.

Although it's not clear what powers this brown-robed genie, invisible to everyone else, actually offers, Itzik is nudged into action and sets out to punish those he figures made him such a loser. The greasy-haired schlemiel confronts a bossy fourth-grade teacher, a sadistic army officer, his slimily successful cousin and, finally — who else? — his Yiddishe mama (Dvora Kedar) before realizing he's his own worst enemy.

Along the way, Argentina-born helmer Enrique Rottenberg mounts some amusing set pieces, many based on the standard talking-to-thin-air premise, in between some mildly cruel moments and flashes of wit (when Itzik confronts his mother, in the pic's best scene, she blows up at Freud's pernicious influence). Tech credits are adequate and include some crude special effects.

Auds at Montreal preem were evenly divided between oldsters, who guffawed mightily, and youthful viewers, who walked. That split also reflects the pic's antediluvian sexual politics: Younger female characters are casually abused or stripped for no reason. This mindless misogyny in the otherwise funny "Itzik" will probably relegate pic to video status. —*Ken Eisner*

A HERO'S LIFE
(LA VIE D'UN HEROS)
(CANADIAN)

A Malofilm Distribution release (Canada) of a Prods. La Fete production, with the participation of Telefilm Canada, the National Film Board of Canada, Quebec government (tax credit program) and Stopfilm Inc. (International sales: Malofilm Intl., Montreal). Produced by Rock Demers. Directed, written by Micheline Lanctot. Camera (color), Thomas Vamos; editor, Gaetan Huot; music, Milan Kymlicka; art direction, Gaudeline Sauriol; sound, Richard Besse; costumes, Christiane Tessier; line producer, Lorraine Du Hamel; associate producers, Yves Rivard (National Film Board), Andre Gagnon. Reviewed at World Film Festival, Montreal (competing), Sept. 4, 1994. (Also in Toronto fest.) Running time: **103 MIN.**
Bertin .... Gilbert Sicotte
Agathe .... Veronique Le Flaguais
Evelyne .... Marie Cantin
Hanibal
   (Young) .... Christopher B. MacCabe
Hanibal (Old) .... Erwin Potitt
Amelie .... Marie-Eve Champagne
   With: Diane Robitaille, Onil Melancon, Andre Lacoste, Jacques Languirand, Manuel Aranguiz.

"A Hero's Life," the latest feature from Quebec actress-helmer Micheline Lanctot, is an intriguing drama exploring lost love, the tricks that memory plays and the ties that bind three generations of a French-Canadian family. The warm, often humorous tone will help pic ring up decent B.O. returns in French Canada, where it opened commercially Sept. 23. But the wordy v.o. narration and the woolly, isolationist view of World War II will limit its international appeal.

Lanctot's script is based on an interesting, little-known slice of local history: In the 1940s, some German POWs were shipped to Canada, and rural Quebecois routinely enlisted these prisoners to help them out on their farms.

Agathe (Veronique Le Flaguais) and Bertin Chevalier (Gilbert Sicotte) are a young couple living on a farm outside Montreal, and their rather uneasy marriage is strained with the arrival of the German prisoner Hanibal (Christopher B. Mac-Cabe). The film presents an almost idyllic portrait of his forced stay in Quebec. The Chevalier clan seems strangely unconcerned about his ties to the Nazis. Narrative is told from several perspectives, which makes for a fairly muddled first hour.

Agathe's daughter Evelyne (Marie Cantin), now a middle-aged mother herself, is retelling a somewhat mythologized version of the Hanibal story to her own child, Amelie, as they drive toward the Chevalier farmhouse for a family reunion with the former German prisoner.

Pic features first-class Quebec thesps, but script fails to give any of them much room for character development. All tech credits are topnotch, particularly the lush scenic camerawork of vet lenser Thomas Vamos. —*Brendan Kelly*

AU PAIR
(GERMAN-BRITISH)

An Angelika Films release of a Hermes Film GmbH (Munich) production, for Bayerischer Rudfunk and Teliesyn, Wales. Produced by Angelika Weber, Thomas Hernadi. Directed by Weber. Screenplay, Hernadi, Greg Dinner. Camera (color) Marian Sloboda; editor, Alexander Rupp; music, Gerhard Daum; sound, David Heinemann. Reviewed at World Film Festival, Montreal (non-competing), Sept. 1, 1994. Running time: **92 MIN.**
   With: Clare Woodgate, Justin Chadwick, Elizabeth Schofield, Karl Tessler, Dale Rapley, Anna Nieland, Wilke Durant, Myriam Weber.

Idiotic in the extreme, "Au Pair" gives its nanny heroine the full Harlequin Romance treatment, effectively bumping it out of fest and arthouse circuits. Still, it boasts the salable combo of snazzy leads, glossy lensing and a hooky premise. Look for a long life in vid rentals and dub-happy Euro webs.

Opening scenes in Wales detail the disaffection of 17-year-old Susan (Clare Woodgate) with her quiet seaside village, busy veterinarian mom and loutish b.f. (Justin Chadwick). Learning of a job in Germany, Susan goes Continental, and the rest takes place in a Munich where no one (except lowly workers) speaks German. Nominally looking after the oddly voiceless child of narcissistic TV executive Barbara (Elizabeth Schofield) and dorky architect Ivo (Dale Ripley), the Welsh lass tumbles for Barbara's "assistant," Walter, a coldfish cad whose job appears to consist of smoking cigarettes and taking off his sunglasses just so.

Susan and the others fall in and out of "love," but they all remain ciphers, with relentless soap-opera music to pump up unearned emotions (minorkey synths drone even when characters order coffee). Chadwick makes the best impression: His adolescent rock-singer role is written as a working-class buffoon, but he provides the only discernible heart. Schofield is simply awful, with flat Sandra Bernhard mannerisms grating against a supposedly elegant role.

It's a creaky bodice-ripper in which no bodices are ever ripped, but the pic is slickly shot. And Woodgate's pretty, pudgy face is a conveniently blank screen upon which unformed adolescent minds can project vague stirrings without the intrusion of pesky reality or modern politics. —*Ken Eisner*

October 3, 1994

THE ROAD TO WELLVILLE

A Columbia release of a Beacon and Columbia presentation of a Dirty Hands production. Produced by Alan Parker, Armyan Bernstein, Robert F. Colesberry. Executive producer, Tom Rosenberg, Marc Abraham. Directed, written by Parker, based on the novel by T. Coraghessan Boyle. Camera (Duart color; Technicolor prints), Peter Biziou; editor, Gerry Hambling; music, Rachel Portman; production design, Brian Morris; art direction, John Willett, Richard Earl (U.K.); set decoration, Claudette Didul; costume design, Penny Rose; sound (Dolby), Nelson Stoll; associate producer, Lisa Moran; assistant director, Peter Kohn; casting, Howard Feuer, Juliet Taylor. Reviewed at Sony Pictures Studios, Culver City, Sept. 27, 1994. (In Tokyo Film Festival.) MPAA Rating: R. Running time: **120 MIN.**
Dr. John Harvey

Kellogg	Anthony Hopkins
Eleanor Lightbody	Bridget Fonda
Will Lightbody	Matthew Broderick
Charles Ossining	John Cusack
George Kellogg	Dana Carvey
Goodloe Bender	Michael Lerner
Dr. Lionel Badger	Colm Meaney
Endymion Hart-Jones	John Neville
Ida Muntz	Lara Flynn Boyle
Nurse Irene Graves	Traci Lind
Virginia Cranehill	Camryn Manheim
Poultney Dab	Roy Brocksmith
Dr. Spitzvogel	Norbert Weisser

A satire of health fanaticism in turn-of-the-century America, "The Road to Wellville" is a curiosity of the first order. Amusing without being particularly funny, and not especially involving in terms of its characters or melodrama, Alan Parker's unzipped cereal comedy is more something to gape at in wonderment, so persistently odd and unusual are its setting and tone. Broadly acted one-of-a-kind offering will probably receive enough critical support from some quarters to give it a good send-off in upscale urban situations, but wider potential is uncertain.

Based on T. Coraghessan Boyle's 1992 historically based novel, physically resplendent picture takes a comical look at the shenanigans perpetrated in the name of good health at the Battle Creek Sanitarium, circa 1907. Founded by the Seventh Day Adventists, the impeccably appointed lakeside spa has become the personal laboratory of Dr. John Harvey Kellogg (Anthony Hopkins), a righteous physician, inventor and philosophical crusader who thunders on to his affluent clients about the evils of meat, smoking, alcohol and sex, and the virtues of Bulgarian yogurt and frequent enemas.

Among those arriving to take the cure this fall season are Will and Eleanor Lightbody (Matthew Broderick and Bridget Fonda), an attractive young couple who could use a little time alone to sort out their problems. Instead, they are assigned to separate rooms ("Sex," Dr. Kellogg insists, "is the sewer drain of a healthy body.") and put on rigorous regimes to cure what ails them. Will finds himself sexually stimulated by many of the esoteric treatments to which he's submitted, particularly the enemas as administered by lovely Nurse Graves (Traci Lind).

Also turning up in the Michigan boom town is Charles Ossining (John Cusack), who hopes to strike it rich by producing a successful new cornflake breakfast food. His crooked partner, Bender (Michael Lerner), however, has squandered the investment money, so the pair recruit Kellogg's derelict adopted son, George (a practically unrecognizable Dana Carvey), to make a reckless stab at cashing in on the famous name.

A fair amount of the running time is devoted to the rather extraordinary detailing of the assorted treatments at "the San," from the bizarre to the mundane. Opening on a gleeful and enchanting note, with a row of mostly older and overweight ladies laughing in orchestrated unison, the film proves as energetic as its central character as it documents the vibrating machines, electric blankets, dunkings and dousings, current-fed baths and rear-end probings endorsed by Kellogg, as well as the genitally stimulating belt and "womb manipulation" practiced by the doctor's more erotically inclined competitors. Many cast members, notably Broderick, perform much of the film in a state of virtual undress.

The sheer novelty of all this, as well as the rare and tantalizing depiction of Teddy Roosevelt's America and the unstressed but obvious parallels of these health fads to those of modern times, maintain a kind of grinning interest through pic's first half.

But the lack of compelling or inventive narrative incidents, coupled with characters who uniformly inspire no more than lukewarm enthusiasm, leaves the second half flailing about in an increasingly desperate search for comic cappers and dramatic resolution.

As eccentric and magnetic as he is, Hopkins' Kellogg, decked out in white finery, wire-rimmed glasses, close-cropped hair, moustache and goatee, goofy rabbit-like buck teeth and an accent that ranges from Southern riverboat captain to John Huston, remains a one-dimensional figure devoid of character development or personal quest. The only burr in his saddle is his anarchic son, who keeps turning up to demand money and terrorize his guests.

Subplot involving Ossining's attempt to crack the cornflake market involves a lot of broad venality and humor that doesn't really come off. By contrast, the running gag of Will's constant sexual excitement in a repressed environment should probably have been played more for out-and-out bedroom farce; as it is, there's a degree of hesitancy to his furtive dalliances with his nurse and fellow patient Ida Muntz (Lara Flynn Boyle) that deflates the potential hilarity.

Faring a bit better is Fonda's Eleanor, who is awakened to the notion of liberated female sexuality by her hefty friend Virginia (jovial, insinuating Camryn Manheim) and attracts the attention of therapists Dr. Lionel Badger (Colm Meaney) and the Teutonic Dr. Spitzvogel (Norbert Weisser), whose notions of keeping bodily systems flowing run directly contrary to Kellogg's.

While Parker keeps the proceedings zippy and colorful, only at moments is he able to hit what feels like the precise tone required for this unusual piece. There is too great a gap between the period re-creation — its detail and richness splendidly attended to by production designer Brian Morris, costume designer Penny Rose, lenser Peter Biziou, composer Rachel Portman and others — and the broad, one-note nature of the characterizations.

Curiously, plot at one point focuses intently on four mysterious deaths that occur simultaneously at the San, but film then just as mysteriously drops them, making nothing of the development.

Parker deserves quite a few points for heading way off the beaten path here, but his compass unfortunately hasn't given him the exact coordinates he needed to reach his seriocomic destination.

—*Todd McCarthy*

TSAHAL

(ISRAELI — DOCU)

Les Productions Dussart/Les Films Aleph/France 2 Cinema/Bavaria Films production (International sales, President Films, Paris). Produced by Bertrand Dussart. Directed by Claude Lanzmann. Camera (color), Dominique Chapuis, Pierre-Laurent Chenieux, Jean-Michel Humeau; art direction, Sabine Mamou; sound, Bernard Aubouy. Reviewed at Toronto Film Festival, Sept. 12, 1994. Running time: **300 MIN.**
With: Arik Sharon, Ehud Barak, Avihu Bin-Nun, Amos Oz, David Grossman, Avigdor Feldman, others.

A microscopic look at the Israel Defense Force is offered in "Tsahal," Claude Lanzmann's unabashedly epic documentary, a logical follow-up to his landmark 1985 "Shoah." Though not as emotionally gripping and awesome as that Holocaust docu, "Tsahal" is equally remarkable in its unrelenting attempt to understand the ideological foundations of the Israeli Army as one of the most celebrated in the world. The five-hour docu deserves a major theatrical release, as it raises relevant issues that go beyond Israel and its army, such as conduct during combat, the fear of death, militarism as a value and the cost of living in a society dominated by wars.

Lanzmann has devoted his career to the painstaking documentation of modern Jewish and Israeli history. His cumulative efforts have resulted in a trilogy ("Pourquoi Israel?" in 1973, "Shoah" and now "Tsahal") that has contributed not only to the understanding of the Jewish experience, but also changed the conventions of the docu genre in terms of scope, method and style.

The centrality of the army as a sacred institution in Israel's political culture derives from the fact that in 46 years of independence, the country has engaged in five major wars. This makes "Tsahal" a much more ambitious and encompassing work than if it were strictly about combat and warfare. Indeed, despite diversity of opinion, the most consistent theme here is the crucial link between the Holocaust and the very existence of Israel as a Zionist state.

Using his famed challenging mode, Lanzmann begins by plunging right into the fascinating question of feelings during combat, specifically the fear of death and the guilt of survivors. In the first hour, helmer scrutinizes the 1973 Yom Kippur War and its meaning for the men who fought its battles as well as for the county at

October 3, 1994 (Cont.)

large. This war marked a turning point in Israel's history, as one witness says: "It was like a big fire burning society, a massive execution of a whole generation."

Docu's chief strategy is similar to that used in "Shoah" — complete reliance on direct interviews and reconstructed memories, and avoidance of historical footage. As Lanzmann conducts his interviews, his camera tracks Israel's borders, offering a good sense of the country's tiny size and its alarming proximity to neighboring Lebanon, Syria, Jordan and Egypt.

Among the many priceless scenes are interviews with would-be pilots, Israel's elite force, before and after their test flights. Lanzmann's cameras are fortuitously present when the weeding-out process takes place, evidencing the immediate, spontaneous reaction to success — and failure.

"Tsahal" focuses its attention on the younger generation ("Israel's jewel in the crown") — teenagers who are obliged to serve a term in the armed forces before going into the reserves. While deeply committed to and proud of their service, the youngsters are also aware of the price — no fun, no dating, the entire energy of adolescence spent on preparation for the army.

At times, docu is morbid and depressing, as in a cemetery scene, where Lanzmann shockingly realizes that the buried soldiers lost their lives at the age of 18 or 19.

In its first part, "Tsahal" seems like a tribute to the indefatigable spirit of the Israeli soldier. But then Lanzmann switches to the dissenting voices of writers David Grossman and Amos Oz and civil rights lawyer Avigdor Feldman, who criticize Israel's militarism and its treatment of Arabs in the occupied territories. Docu's last hour is particularly strong in juxtaposing the irreconcilable left-wing and right-wing views on the issue of Israeli settlements in the West Bank.

"Tsahal" is by no means flawless. Some viewers will find it exceedingly long. And not all the information is equally absorbing: The sequences dealing with Israeli tanks and other machinery may be too technical for the lay public. Out of respect for his witnesses, many of whom are members of the military elite, Lanzmann neither interrupts nor forces cuts, letting them conclude their stories well beyond making the crucial point.

There's also one glaring omission: Lanzmann didn't interview any women in the military, which is peculiar considering Israel's pride in initiating compulsory service for women and their representation in almost every branch.

Helmer gathered his info in 1992, and recent developments in the Middle East have contextualized "Tsahal" in ways that couldn't have

been anticipated by Lanzmann — or Israel's power elite.

Nonetheless, as in "Shoah," Lanzmann's persistent, tireless probing hammers away at details that initially appear isolated, but later have an enormously cumulative power. After five hours of lengthy interviews with officers and rank-and-file, military and civilians, one gets a good grasp of what makes the Israeli army tick.

—*Emanuel Levy*

JEROME'S SECRET
(LE SECRET DE JEROME)
(CANADIAN)

An Allegro Films Distribution release (Canada) of a Cine Groupe/Citadel Films/National Film Board of Canada production, with the participation of Telefilm Canada, SOGIC, Quebec government, New Brunswick government and the Nova Scotia Film Development Corp. (International sales, Allegro Films, Montreal.) Produced by Marie-Andree Vinet, Barry Cowling. Directed by Phil Comeau. Screenplay, Jean Barbeau, Comeau. Camera (color), Eric Cayla; editor, Helene Girard; music, Marcel Aymar; art direction, Luc J. Beland; costume design, Jacinthe Demers; sound, Claude Hazanavicius; associate producer, Yves Rivard. Reviewed at the Berri Cinema, Montreal, Sept. 23, 1994. Running time: **100 MIN.**

Julitte	Myriam Cyr
Jean Nicholas	Germain Houde
Cyrille	Remy Girard
Jerome	Denis Lapalme
Molidje	Andrea Parro
Modeste	Viola Leger
Antoine	Bernard Leblanc
Elizabeth	Isabelle Roy
Didier	Bertrand Dugas
Father Daly	Lionel Doucette

"Jerome's Secret" is the first fictional feature by and about Acadians, the French-speaking people from the Maritime Provinces of eastern Canada, and the historical drama had a popular run in the area in August. Pic will not ignite the same B.O. fever in Quebec, where it just opened, and despite potential appeal of theme of displaced francophone culture in French-lingo Europe, slow pace and uneven cast will limit appeal outside Canada.

Based on a real-life slice of Acadian history, strange story is built around a mysterious young man with no legs who washes ashore in Baie Ste-Marie, Nova Scotia, in 1863. The handsome cripple (Denis Lapalme), who appears to be mute, is adopted by a young couple, Corsican expatriate Jean Nicholas (Germain Houde) and his feisty Acadian wife, Julitte (Myriam Cyr), and is given the name Jerome.

Clearly, the shipwrecked amputee is intended as a symbol of the isolation and oppression that has marked Acadian history. But

Jerome's sorry lot in life is only a sideline to the main drama in the film, which has more to do with Jean Nicholas and Julitte's tortured relationship than anything else. The husband is ostracized by his xenophobic neighbors, and he takes out his frustrations on his young wife.

He desperately wants kids, but the couple is unable to produce a child, which makes matters even worse.

The biggest problem with "Jerome's Secret" is Houde's inability to bring this sense of anger and futility to the screen. Cyr is much better as the stoic, unhappy wife, and, as usual, popular Quebec star Remy Girard sparkles in a supporting role as an enigmatic traveling dentist/doctor/fugitive from justice.

Pic was lensed in the historic Acadian village of Caraquet, and Eric Cayla's shots of the rugged coastal landscape provide an evocative snapshot of the rural region. All other tech credits are top-notch.

—*Brendan Kelly*

OCTOBER
(OCTOBRE)
(CANADIAN)

A C/FP Distribution release (Canada) of an ACPAV production, in association with the National Film Board of Canada and with the participation of Telefilm Canada. (International sales, C/FP Distribution, Montreal.) Produced by Bernadette Payeur, Marc Daigle. Directed, written by Pierre Falardeau, based on the short story "Pour en finir avec octobre" by Francis Simard. Camera (color), Alain Dostie; editor, Michel Arcand; music, Richard Gregoire; costume design, Michele Hamel; sound, Michel Arcand; line producer, Andre Dupuy; associate producer, Yves Rivard; assistant director, Rene Pothier. Reviewed at the Eaton Centre Cinema, Montreal, Sept. 26, 1994. (In Vancouver Film Festival.) Running time: **97 MIN.**

With: Hugo Dube, Luc Picard, Pierre Rivard, Denis Trudel, Serge Houde.

Maverick helmer Pierre Falardeau's sympathetic view of French-Canadian terrorism guarantees that "October" will spark all kinds of controversy and will almost certainly be one of the most talked-about Canadian pix of the year. The film, which is based on the true story of the kidnapping of a Quebec cabinet minister in October 1970, already provoked an acrimonious public debate when Falardeau's script was leaked to a federal senator last year, and the rhetoric is bound to heat up once again when "October" hits screens across the country this month.

C/FP Distribution opened the pic throughout Quebec Sept. 30 and, in an unusual move, distrib is rushing subtitled prints of the French-lingo

film into theaters in English-speaking Canada over the next couple of weeks. (Normally franco Quebec pix open outside the province several months after the Montreal preem, if at all.) It also will screen at the Vancouver Film Festival.

Idea is obviously to try to cash in on the media controversy, but pic is unlikely to spark much demand with English-Canadian filmgoers, who'll be turned off by Falardeau's partisan take on Canada's October Crisis. That didactic approach and script's unfortunate tendency to lapse into dated, Marxist rhetoric also will deter international auds. It will do well on its home turf, though, where there's more support for helmer's radical politics.

When script is not assaulting the audience with agitprop dialogue, "October" works surprisingly well as a gripping, suspenseful psychological thriller. Falardeau shows a real knack for sustaining a taut, tense pace, even though there's little in the way of high-powered action here.

Story opens with members of the Front de Liberation du Quebec dumping the dead body of Quebec Labor Minister Pierre Laporte into a car trunk and fleeing the scene.

The rest of the film recounts the week leading up to Laporte's murder by the revolutionary Quebec nationalists. Instead of focusing on all the tumultuous events of the October Crisis, Falardeau attempts to tell story from the p.o.v. of the four FLQ hard-liners who took Laporte hostage and later killed him. They snatch him at gunpoint from his suburban front lawn and soon have him holed up in a nondescript bungalow.

Claustrophobic drama unfolds almost entirely in this house, as these young idealists grapple with the harsh reality of their actions. Suspense is heightened by intelligent use of radio and TV clips from October 1970. Falardeau's script aptly captures the moral conundrums the kidnappers face over the course of the harrowing week, but those subtle touches are all too often followed by slices of dogmatic dialogue that sound out of place.

Hugo Dube, Luc Picard, Pierre Rivard and Denis Trudel deliver standout performances as the troubled terrorists, and Serge Houde is also top-notch as the kidnap victim, in a tough role that requires him to spend much of the film blindfolded and strapped to a bed.

All other tech credits are fine, though Richard Gregoire's score tends toward the overly melodramatic.

—*Brendan Kelly*

TORONTO

MOVING THE MOUNTAIN

(BRITISH — DOCU)

A Xingu Films production. Produced by Trudie Styler. Directed by Michael Apted. Camera (color), Maryse Alberti; editor, Susanne Rostock; sound, Scott Breindel; music, Liu Sola. Reviewed at Toronto Film Festival, Sept. 17, 1994. (Also at Heartland Film Festival.) Running time: 83 MIN.

Director Michael Apted ("35 Up," "Coal Miner's Daughter") adds another impressive credit to his singularly diverse resume with "Moving the Mountain," a fascinating BBC production that could score in theatrical runs. Global fest and TV exposure is a virtual certainty.

Docu examines the Chinese democracy movement that was crushed — temporarily, at least — by the 1989 massacre in Tiananmen Square. Apted finds a fresh perspective, and an inspired method for placing events in historical context, by focusing primarily on student dissident Li Lu, once No. 18 on the Chinese government's most-wanted list.

Interviewed in the U.S., where he now resides as an emigre, Li recalls his formative years during the Cultural Revolution, his difficult childhood as the son of politically incorrect parents, and his sudden surge of hope as the 1989 democracy movement began to flower in Tiananmen Square. Apted uses, sparingly but effectively, dramatized re-creations of scenes from the dissident's youth. But pic consists mainly of archival footage, most of it never before used, and interviews with Li and other student leaders (including, amazingly, some who still live in China).

With the benefit of hindsight, Li and other dissident leaders acknowledge they vastly underestimated the willingness of Chinese leaders to violently repress their protests. They also admit guilt-racked suspicions that they may have acted too impetuously in agitating events that resulted in so many deaths.

Pic is admirably frank in dealing with tensions between the dissidents who fled to other countries, and those who remained behind. The articulately passionate Li Lu insists that he left China "to make myself ready for when the time comes" to begin the movement anew. Back in China, however, another student dissident says of Li and company: "If they really want

to work for democracy, only when they come back will it be possible."

On a tech level, "Moving the Mountain" is first-rate across the board. Liu Sola's musical score is occasionally overbearing, but more often thunderously effective. Susanne Rostock's editing is razor-sharp.

Pic's title comes from a Chinese proverb about a farmer's efforts to remove, stone by stone, a mountain from his land. The farmer admits he might not live long enough to see the task completed. But his children's children's children may see the day when the mountain is moved.
—Joe Leydon

PICTURE OF LIGHT

(CANADIAN-SWISS — DOCU)

A Grimthorpe Film/Andreas Zust presentation. (International sales: Grimthrope Film, Toronto.) Produced by Peter Mettler, Alexandra Gill. Executive producer, Zust. Directed by Mettler. Camera (color), Mettler; editors, Mettler, Mike Munn; music, Jim O'Rourke; sound, Leon Johnson, Gaston Kyriazi, Peter Braker, Gill, Mettler. Reviewed at Toronto Film Festival, Sept. 10, 1994. Running time: 86 MIN.

As do many good documentaries, "Picture of Light" takes viewers to a place they otherwise would probably never go. In this case, destination is the Canadian Arctic Circle to witness the northern lights, and while the sight is worth the trip, film decidedly overstays its welcome by about half. Item could achieve a limited theatrical life sold as a head trip, but it's not really dazzling or hallucinatory enough to become a major entry. Pic should be a good bet down the road on cable, public TV and video.

Director/lenser Peter Mettler traveled by train to the edge of the world, 3,000 miles north of Toronto, to capture the mystical beauty of the aurora borealis in dead of winter. Filmmaker's deadpan philosophical narration gives the proceedings a certain charm at first, as the tracks dead-end at Churchill, Manitoba, and the hardy crew hole up at a wasteland motel to await the chance to photograph the magical lights.

Most memorable scene occurs shortly after arrival, as Mettler sets out at night across deeply piled snow. With a single flashlight illuminating the scene and the crunch of his footsteps cranked up amusingly high, narration offers many of the 170 different words and definitions in the native Inuit language for snow and ice.

Although it is nothing compared with what the crew went through, the wait at the motel nonetheless proves tiresome for the viewer, and much of the material feels like filler

before the inevitable climactic light show. Even then, just as a succession of interviewees admits how hard it is to describe the northern lights, one feels that seeing them on film doesn't really do them justice, either.
—Todd McCarthy

BAR GIRLS

A Lavender Hill Mob production. Produced by Laura Hoffman, Marita Giovanni. Co-producer, Doug Lindemann. Directed by Giovanni. Screenplay, Hoffman, based on her stage play. Camera (Foto-Kem color), Michael Ferris; editor, Carter Dehaven; music, Lenny Meyers; art direction, Darryl Fong, Keith Brunsmann; set decoration, Lia Niskanen, Andrew Rosen; costume design, Houston Sams; sound, Jessie Bender. Reviewed at Toronto Film Festival, Sept. 18, 1994. Running time: 95 MIN.
Loretta	Nancy Allison Wolfe
Rachel	Liza D'Agostino
J.R.	Camila Griggs
Noah	Michael Harris
Veronica	Justine Slater
Tracy	Paula Sorge
Sandy	Cece Tsou

Though lacking the comic verve and savvy wit of "Go Fish," "Bar Girls" situates itself in similar territory, as a seriocomic look at the lifestyles of eight lesbians who frequent the same bar. Marita Giovanni's smooth direction and a good ensemble cast, which happily overcome the film's overly theatrical melodramatics, should put pic over in urban markets with gay and lesbian viewers and hip, open-minded crowds.

Unlike "Go Fish," which was stylistically innovative and politically subversive, "Bar Girls" does for lesbians what numerous American movies have done for heterosexuals, examining courtship and dating, attraction and jealousy, separation and reconciliation. Adapting her stage play to the screen, Laura Hoffman has transplanted the familiar locale and interactions of a neighborhood bar to a specifically lesbian milieu.

As the story begins, Loretta (Nancy Allison Wolfe) is leaving Girl Bar for what appears to be another solitary night, when she spots the beautiful Rachel (Liza D'Agostino) walking in. She bets a friend that within 10 minutes Rachel will be in her car — and, miraculously, this time her come-on works.

At Loretta's house, the two nervous women begin to share their pasts and soon realize that neither is completely free to start a new involvement. Loretta is still attached to Annie (Lisa Parker), "a psych-jock from Bakersfield," who's now attracted to an unavailable, heterosexual woman. For her part, Rachel confides that she's hitched to a man, though the mar-

riage is disintegrating and she's now seeing Sandy (Cece Tsou).

Despite it all, Loretta and Rachel get involved, move in together and even vow monogamy and eternal love. But their bliss is interrupted by various complications: Former attachments turn out to be unresolved, and new players are determined to position themselves between the two lovers.

Regrettably, what makes "Bar Girls" rather conventional is that, except for the fully fleshed-out Loretta, the characters are types marked by just one or two traits. Rachel demands monogamy because her father always cheated on her mother; Sandy is virtuous; Veronica is a beautiful heterosexual who's now willing to experiment with alternative lifestyles; Tracy is a tough customer who can fix trucks; J.R. is an aggressive cop.

Pic's format, particularly in the first reel, is a bit rigid. As Loretta and Rachel recollect their affairs, flashbacks are inserted in an obvious manner that breaks the flow of the realistic dialogue. Scripter's efforts to open up her play by including street, beach and office scenes are only partially successful, and her humor is often forced, not quite concealing a preachy layer of self-taught "relationship" lessons.

On the plus side, novice helmer Giovanni manages to keep the theatrical proceedings smooth and light most of the time. One can sense her affinity for the material and love of staging the romantic intrigues that beguile her characters. She's also good with the actresses, all of whom reprise their stage roles.

Wolfe is a standout as Loretta in a performance that highlights the complexity of her character as a bright and attractive career woman who's also slightly neurotic about relationships.

Tech credits, particularly Michael Ferris' fluent lensing and Lenny Meyers' buoyant music, are more than adequate for a modestly budgeted indie. —Emanuel Levy

ETERNITY

(AUSTRALIAN — DOCU — B&W/COLOR)

A Vivid Pictures Pty. Ltd. production, in association with the Australian Film Commission and the New South Wales Film and Television Office. Produced by Susan MacKinnon. Directed, written by Lawrence Johnston. Camera (b&w, color), Dion Beebe; editor, Annette Davey; music, Ross Edwards; art direction, Tony Campbell; sound, Liam Egan. Reviewed at Toronto Film Festival, Sept. 13, 1994. (Also in Telluride, Vancouver fests.) Running time: **56 MIN.**
Arthur Stace .... Les Foxcroft
Witnesses: Dorothy Hewett, Martin Sharp, George Gittoes, Colin Anderson, Ruth Ridley, others.

The Australian documentary "Eternity" proves that it's possible to make an engrossing film by exploring the meanings and effects of a single word — eternity. A biographical account of an eccentric credited for being the father of graffiti, pic is perfect material for festivals, TV and other markets that exhibit short-form features.

Docu unravels as a puzzle: For 40 years, the word *eternity* mysteriously appeared on Sydney's streets and sidewalks. Written in yellow chalk, in elegant copperplate script, it always followed the same pattern, appearing overnight in the most unusual spots. In 1956, after 20 years, the author's identity was revealed. Renamed by the media "Mr. Eternity," Arthur Stace became an instant celebrity, but he continued his routine task until he died in 1967, at the age of 83.

A dozen witnesses reconstruct Stace's terrible life as an uneducated petty criminal with a severe drinking problem. Deeply depressed and "out of kilter" by his own admission, Stace dramatically changed his life in 1930, when he decided to go to church for salvation.

Ruth Ridley claims that writing the word was a religious mission for her father. Other witnesses hold that it's not only the word, but also the manner and places where it was written that made his simple sermon so inspirational. Says writer Dorothy Hewett: "It was like one of those archetypal messages that come from outer space."

Reportedly, Stace didn't enjoy his fame, always stressing that his message was far more important than himself. And though committed to his calling, Stace wasn't perceived as fanatic or obsessive.

Writer/director Lawrence Johnston, whose 1990 "Night Out" was well-received in Cannes, endows his film with the right balance of matter-of-fact reportage and the humor one expects of an eccentric chronicle. He adroitly broadens pic's scope to provide relevant observations on the role of urban myths in modern life and the function of religious transformation for loners and misfits.

Dion Beebe's crisp b&w lensing and Annette Davey's sharp editing make this original film visually engrossing. —*Emanuel Levy*

LUCKY BREAK

(AUSTRALIAN)

A UIP (Australia) release of a Generation Films/Lewin Films/Australian Film Finance Corp. production. (International sales: Pandora Cinema.) Produced by Bob Weis. Co-producer, Judy Levine. Directed, written by Ben Lewin. Camera (color), Vincent Monton; editor, Peter Carrodus; music, Paul Grabowsky; production design, Peta Lawson; costumes, Anna Borghesi; sound, Gary Wilkins; line producer, Lesley Parker; assistant director, Brendan Campbell; casting, Liz Mullinar. Reviewed at Hoyts Center, Sydney, Aug. 15, 1994. (In Toronto Film Festival.) Running time: **93 MIN.**
Sophie .... Gia Carides
Eddie .... Anthony LaPaglia
Gloria .... Rebecca Gibney
Anne-Marie LePine .... Robyn Nevin
George LePine .... Marshall Napier
Yuri .... Jacek Koman
Myra .... Mary-Anne Fahey
Kate .... Sioban Tuke
Doctor .... Nicholas Bell

"Lucky Break" adds a few new wrinkles to the venerable and resurgent formula of romantic comedy. Writer/director Ben Lewin, whose last effort was "The Favor, the Watch and the Very Big Fish," comes up with some oddball ideas again, but his screenplay lacks the wit and zaniness that might have propelled this modest offering into wider distribution. Moderate results can be expected.

Film harks back to the Rock Hudson-Doris Day comedies of the late '50s and early '60s. Partly based on the director's own experiences, pic opens promisingly with a sequence that intros attractive Gia Carides as Sophie, a young writer with a vivid, sensual imagination. Working alone in a public library, she's overheard reading her raunchy material out loud by Eddie (Anthony LaPaglia), a slick jeweler and practiced womanizer who already has his hands full with a demanding fiancee (Rebecca Gibney). Sophie falls heavily for Eddie, and he's obviously interested in her. However, since she was sitting at a desk when they met, he doesn't know her secret: As a result of childhood polio, one of Sophie's legs is paralyzed.

Convinced he'll be put off when he discovers she's crippled, Sophie spies on Eddie from a distance. When she breaks her paralyzed leg in a freak accident, an opportunity for happiness presents itself, and she pretends her leg is in plaster as the result of a skiing mishap.

The two embark on a brief relationship that's complicated by a nebulous subplot involving stolen jewelry and a Russian cop (Jacek Koman) who also fancies Sophie. But Lewin, despite his tantalizingly offbeat premise, has come up with a screenplay that never really sparkles. Carides, the spiteful rival from "Strictly Ballroom," is a delight as Sophie, but LaPaglia (her real-life fiance) seems to be taking it all too seriously. A major miscalculation is a sequence in which the amorous Eddie cuts his tongue on Sophie's plaster-encased leg and is forced to undergo painful surgery.

Production values are all elegant, with Vincent Monton's photography taking full advantage of the attractive people and settings. Paul Grabowsky's music adds needed zest to the proceedings.
—*David Stratton*

VENICE

THE TRUE LIFE OF ANTONIO H.

(LA VERA VITA DI ANTONIO H.)

(ITALIAN)

An Istituto Luce release of a Piccioli Film/Istituto Luce co-production in association with Bellatrix Pictures. Produced by Gianfranco Piccioli. Directed, written by Enzo Monteleone. Camera (color), Arnaldo Catinari; editor, Cecilia Zanuso; music, Mimmo Locasciulli; art direction, Francesco Priori; costumes, Mari Caselli. Reviewed at the Alcazar Cinema, Aug. 3, 1994. (In Venice Film Festival — Panorama.) Running time: **94 MIN.**
Antonio Hutter .... Alessandro Haber
Mother .... Adriawa Innocenti
Father ....Giancarlo Maestri
Terrorists .... Beatrice Kruger, Doris von Thury
With: Giuliana De Sio, Bernardo Bertolucci, Mario Monicelli, Gabriele Salvatores, Paolo and Vittorio Taviani, Marcello Mastroianni, Nanni Loy.

Posing as a fake documentary/biography of veteran character actor Alessandro Haber, "The True Life of Antonio H." is actually a joyful celebration of Italian cinema and the acting profession. Multiple guest appearances by filmmaking icons like Bertolucci and Mastroianni, well-chosen film clips and pic's recurrent theme of acting as obsession should delight film buffs. This witty directing debut by screenwriter Enzo Monteleone ("Mediterraneo") preemed at the Venice fest and should work fine domestically for producer/distrib Istituto Luce. It also looks promising for specialized offshore release.

"Antonio H." represents Haber's apotheosis and possibly his well-deserved introduction to a wider audience. As pic underscores, this stage, screen and TV thesp has worked with virtually every significant Italo director since he cameoed in Marco Bellocchio's "China Is Near" in 1967. He has a passion overflowing into neurosis for the acting profession. A consummate comedian, the "Zelig" of Italian cinema has a reputation for never turning down a role, of whatever type or importance.

But there is a gap of uncharted size between the real-life actor and his fictional double, Antonio Hutter. Using a strategy similar to Nanni Moretti's "Dear Diary," pic deliberately shuffles the reality/fiction deck to keep viewers guessing where one leaves off and the other begins.

While it's true that Haber lived with actress Giuliana De Sio and appeared in famous films, the story of how he narrowly missed snagging the Joe Pesci role in Martin Scorsese's "Raging Bull" is a fabrication. In any case, it's all great fun, especially because Haber is awesomely honest and ironic about himself.

Haber/Hutter always knew he wanted to be an actor. After moving to Rome, Italy's filmmaking capital, he chases after Jean-Luc Godard, Orson Welles and Dustin Hoffman until they shake him off. (Hoffman is his idol, he says, because "The Graduate" made him realize there was room in the movies for short, ugly actors.)

He calls famous directors to beg for a role, or lies in wait outside their houses. Throughout the film, Monteleone inserts (possibly spurious) interviews with directors whom Haber/Hutter persecuted, like Monicelli, the Taviani brothers, Bertolucci, Nanni Loy, Michele Placido. "He was devastating!" insists Mastroianni. "Once he found you, he never left you in peace."

His career began when he forced his way into spaghetti Westerns like "A Fistful of Dollars" and Roman toga operas like "The Aeneid." He had a near-brush with success when Bertolucci cast him in "The Conformist." But as he recounts with tragic irony, his scene — the blind men's ball — got left on the cutting room floor, never to appear until the restored director's cut was released 20 years later.

The portrait that ultimately emerges is a complex blend of talent, stubbornness, neurosis and bad luck. In real life, Haber continues to work nonstop. His perf as St. Joseph's mute helper in "For Love, Only for Love" won him Italy's two top industry awards last year.

Cecilia Zanuso's excellent cutting gives the film a snappy pace.
—*Deborah Young*

TAKE ME AWAY
(PORTAMI VIA)
(ITALIAN)

A Nemo release (in Italy) of an Ax-elotil Film/Tea Film production. Produced by Gianluca Arcopinto. Directed by Gianluca Maria Tavarelli. Screenplay, Leonardo Fasoli, Tavarelli. Camera (color), Pietro Sciortino; editor, Marco Spoletini; music, Paolo Lasazio, Roberto Padovan; art direction/costume design, Stefano Giambanco; sound, Mario Jaquone. Reviewed at Venice Film Festival (Italian Panorama), Sept. 8, 1994. Running time: **105 MIN.**

Cinzia .... Stefania Orsola Garello
Cristina .... France Demoulin
Alberto .... Sergio Troiano
Luigi .... Michele Di Mauro
Paolo .... Fabrizio Monetti
Mario .... Riccardo Montanaro

Two local losers and a pair of East European call girls stumble through life in a cold, uncaring Italian city in "Take Me Away." First feature by the promising Gianluca Maria Tavarelli has a sophisticated new-wave look and carefully drawn characters. Its market outside Italy can only be quite specialized, though fest outings should earn pic supporters.

The two parallel stories take place in Turin, given a grubby contemporary look by Pietro Sciortino's harsh, unglamorous lensing. It's a world of loneliness and violence, in which happiness is elusive. Alberto (Sergio Troiano), a 30-year-old door-to-door appliance salesman, and his best friend Luigi (Michele Di Mauro), a social worker, spend their evenings bar- and disco-hopping, hunting for girls.

They hate their jobs, are perpetually broke, and fight a losing battle against loneliness and depression. Somehow the nuanced, sympathetic perfs by Di Mauro and Troiano make these dead-end lives interesting.

Bulgarian-born Cinzia (Stefania Orsola Garello) and Russian blonde Cristina (France Demoulin) are high-priced call girls who spend their nights servicing clients (off-screen) in hotel rooms.

They also hate their jobs, but are more desperate and rebellious than Alberto and Luigi, for whom they are unreachable objects of fantasy. The four characters finally hook up in pic's dramatic finale, which is surprisingly upbeat.

Tavarelli describes boredom through repetition: The boys keep returning to the same dull discos, the girls keep knocking on hotel doors. This is a dangerous strategy, and film's leisurely pace needs tightening. So does the dialogue.

The intense Orsola Garello and Demoulin offer a fresh view of the anxieties of the unhappy hooker in some memorable conversations, including a parable about salmon that merited spontaneous applause at pic's Venice preem. Also of note are supporting thesps in poignant marginal roles, such as Alberto's UFO-obsessed neighbor Mario (Riccardo Montanaro) and Luigi's mentally unbalanced patient Paolo (Fabrizio Monetti).
—*Deborah Young*

LOVE BURNS
(ANIME FIAMMEGGIANTI)
(ITALIAN)

A Dinosaura release (in Italy) of a Brooklyn Films/PFA Films production. Produced by Agnese Fontana Rancan, Pier Francesco Aiello. Executive producers, Marco Isoli, Rancan. Directed, written by Davide Ferrario. Camera (Technicolor), Gherardo Gossi; editor, Claudio Cormio; music, Ivo Papasov; art direction/costume design, Franca Bertagnolli, Alessandra Montagna; sound (Dolby), Tiziano Crotti. Reviewed at Venice Film Festival (Italian Panorama), Sept. 3, 1994. Running time: **95 MIN.**

With: Giuseppe Cederna, Elena Sofia Ricci, Alessandro Haber, Monica Scattini, Flavio Bonacci, Francesca Prandi, Maria Elena Bannino, Doris von Thury.

Love makes the world go round — in circles — in "Love Burns," an offbeat, rather surreal Italian comedy featuring a strong young cast but no high-grossing comics. Preemed at Venice, Davide Ferrario's second feature won fans among hip young auds, who should make up a healthy onshore market. Foreign viewers may find the comedy more a local flavor.

Rosario (Giuseppe Cederna) is a depressed high school teacher who has lost both his left-wing political convictions and, recently, his wife, Elena (the versatile Elena Sofia Ricci), a beautiful, temperamental private eye. He begins having visions of the Virgin Mary (Monica Scattini), who appears to be in love with him. Also infatuated with the short, pony-tailed Rosario are his fellow teacher Amelia (Doris von Thury) and his burly gangster neighbor Salvatore (the ever-inventive Alessandro Haber).

Flubbing a suicide attempt, Rosario decides it's time to tune in with the real world — i.e., to become a criminal. He steals a car, gets hold of a gun and plunges ever deeper into the murky depths. Everything bad he does is rewarded, and when Elena (thrown out by her sister) comes back to him, he becomes firmly convinced crime pays.

Ferrario, a former film critic and distributor, has fun playing with his characters, getting them to confuse good and evil and chase after each other in a hopeless *ronde* of unrequited love.

A film largely based on actors, pic showcases rising talents like Cederna, Ricci and Haber (subject of recent movie "The Real Life of Antonio H."). As an amusing contrast, the Bulgarian music score by Ivo Papasov is a plus. —*Deborah Young*

ROAD TO PARADISE
(DOROGA V RAY)
(RUSSIAN-GERMAN)

A Frist Film Co. (Russia)/Jonas Film, Trans Media Film (Germany) production. Produced by Aleksei Guskov, Sergei Moskalenko, Ulrich John. Directed, written by Vitali Moskalenko. Camera (color), Sergei Makhilski; editor, Valentina Yankovskaya; music, Yuri Pryalkin; art direction, Svetlana Sosnina. Reviewed at Venice Film Festival (Critics' Week), Sept. 8, 1994. Running time: **107 MIN.**

With: Ivan Volkov, Natalya Petrova, Bogdan Stupka, Aleksei Guskov, Aleksei Kortnev, Svetlana Korkoshko.

A romantic thriller with a quirky indie flavor, "Road to Paradise" reps an interesting attempt by freshman writer-director Vitali Moskalenko to push the fabric of Russo filmmaking away from multicharacter family yarns and grim portraits of neo-capitalist chaos. Though some may not buy into its mix of fancifulness and romantic whimsy, pic is worth a look for fests and small-screen buyers outside the U.S.

Setting is Moscow, 1957. University student-cum-jazz musician Igor meets French looker Michelle at an international youth festival. A spy for the French secret service, she's after documents held by Igor's scientist uncle. The KGB, wise to the setup, encourage Igor to seduce her, accompany her back to France, and infiltrate the business of her father, a munitions manufacturer.

Twist is that the youngsters genuinely fall in love, and Michelle's background is not what it appears. Reunited at a concert in Denmark, the lovers hightail it to freedom, pursued by KGB goons.

Shot in a loose, occasionally confusing style, but cleverly evoking the period with fine, budget art direction, the movie boasts genuinely likable performances, a measure of self-irony and convincing detail about its subject (helmer's father was a KGB op). Pic's spirit is pro-youth and genuinely independent, thumbing its nose at both East and West Europe. It's no accident that the late-'80s coda is set in sun-drenched Barbados.

Tech contributions are good, with Sergei Makhilski's photography especially eye-catching.
—*Derek Elley*

SOMEWHERE IN THE CITY
(DA QUALCHE PARTE IN CITTA)
(ITALIAN)

An Arcadia production. Executive producer, Riccardo Rovescalli. Directed by Michele Sordillo. Screenplay, Sordillo, with dialogue collaboration by Gaetano Sansone. Camera (Telecolor), Luciano Baresi; editor, Gianni Lari; music, Ludovico Einaudi; art direction/costume design, Stefania Sordillo; sound, Roberto Mozzarelli; assistant director, Jorgelina Pochintesta. Reviewed at Venice Film Festival (Italian Panorama), Sept. 6, 1994. Running time: **75 MIN.**

Enrico .... Ivano Marescotti
Anna .... Carlina Torta
Aghim .... Fatos Haxhiraj
Giulia .... Carolina Salome
Morini .... Eugenio Canton
Giovanni .... Massimo Gallerani

"Somewhere in the City" relates the disruption to marital inertia caused by the arrival of a stranger. Contrary to most other visitations of this well-trodden theme, the stranger's departure leaves behind neither emotional wreckage nor moral cleansing, but rather a return to the reassuring grayness. Though the film's undernourished visuals conspire to shortchange its sober examination of human shortcomings, sophomore director Michele Sordillo's honest, focused approach should guide this modestly budgeted entry to scattered festival dates.

The suicide of a former friend who came looking for help and didn't get it sits heavily on the conscience of Milanese management consultant Enrico (Ivano Marescotti), prompting him to help down-and-out Albanian immigrant Aghim (Fatos Haxhiraj) by setting him up in a small apartment adjoining his own and lining up some manual labor for him.

Outsider's presence initially bothers Enrico's wife Anna (Carlina Torta). A failed concert pianist, her dissatisfaction over career frustration, weight gain and middle-age blues is further aggravated by the bottled-up certainty that her husband is having an affair.

Gradually, the balance shifts, with Anna's sympathy for Aghim growing, while Enrico's gives way to resentment of his constant intrusions, and eventually to suspicion of dishonesty.

October 3, 1994 (Cont.)

Sordillo's generally astute script contains no easy lessons. Instead, it edgily plays on Italy's relative youth as a destination for numbers of immigrants. The conflicting ideas that arise are well developed, particularly in the examination of distrust as a part of human nature.

Sordillo keeps his cast focused. Albanian legit actor/director Haxjiraj furnishes the narrative with a solid pivotal force. Marescotti and Torta sketch a credible, unadorned portrait of married malaise, though the soullessness of his job feels a little overstated.

—*David Rooney*

THE FILM THIEF
(LADRI DI CINEMA)
(ITALIAN)

An Istituto Luce release (in Italy) of an Azione Cinematografica production. Produced, directed, written by Piero Natoli. Camera (Telecolor), Carlo Cerchio; editor, Mimmo Varone; music, Luigi Ceccarelli; art direction/costume design, Natoli; sound, Marco Grillo. Reviewed at Venice Film Festival (Italian Panorama), Sept. 11, 1994. Running time: **95 MIN.**
Mercurio .... Piero Natoli
Josephine .... Joanna Chatton
Aristide .... Pier Francesco Aiello
Carlotta .... Čarlotta Natoli
Paola .... Vera Gemma
Valerio .... Valerio Mastandrea
Marco .... Neri Marcore
Claudia .... Claudia Poggiani

Piero Natoli, Italy's eternal independent filmmaker, transforms his years of struggle into enjoyable comedy in "The Film Thief." Pic's subject matter and honest self-irony should give it an edge with fest audiences.

It's painfully clear that Natoli's inside knowledge of Rome's indie film scene comes from personal experience, and the fact that pic is his fifth feature is itself a tribute to his perseverance. He wrote, produced, directed, stars in, and handled art direction and costumes on present item.

Mercurio (Natoli) is a good-natured indie filmer used to adversity. His loyal crew, which includes his daughter Carlotta (played by Natoli's real-life offspring, actress Carlotta Natoli) as cinematographer, is ready to shoot whenever and wherever necessary.

Mercurio's immediate problem is to close a deal with "Italy's only film producer and distributor" to release his latest opus. The distrib's assistant, Aristide (Pier Francesco Aiello), suggests Mercurio screen the film at his own expense at Cannes, where his busy boss is bound to see it.

Natoli steals a lot of shots from the last Cannes meet, including a doorman's refusal to let Mercurio into a party because he's improperly dressed (captured by a hidden camera). His market screening has an audience of one: the attractive French girl Josephine (Joanna Chatton, the indies' answer to Kim Basinger).

She follows the disappointed but undefeated director back to Rome, where he hatches a plot to force the big-shot distrib to send his movie to Venice.

Story is quickly paced, inventive and always ironic. In the main role, Natoli is a likable ham, backed by a low-rent cast that fills the bill nicely. The slight home-movie aura that hangs over "Thief" actually works in its favor, reinforcing sympathy for the little guys on no-budgets who also make movies.

—*Deborah Young*

YOU DRIVE ME CRAZY
(DU BRINGST MICH NOCH UM)
(AUSTRIAN)

An SK Film & Television production, in association with MR Film Kurt J. Mrkwicka and with participation of Austrian Film Production Fund, Austrian Radio, Vienna Film Financing Fund. Produced by Josef Koschier. Directed, written, edited by Wolfram Paulus. Camera (color), Wolfgang Simon; music, Peter Valentin; art direction, Alois Ellmauer; costume design, Vasitti Magnus; sound (Dolby), Johannes Paiha; assistant director, Hamdi Doker. Reviewed at Venice Film Festival (non-competing), Sept. 5, 1994. Running time: **98 MIN.**
Simon Halm .... August Zirner
Helga Thaler .... Katja Flint
Helmut Thaler .... Georg Schuchter
Anette Halm .... Gabriela Benesch
   With: Ute Cremer, Louise Martini, Nino Kratzer, Thomas Kristmann, Theresa Perrer, Ferdinand Pfleger.

While it boasts only a few fresh kinks rather than innovative twists on a generic infidelity comedy-drama, Austrian item "You Drive Me Crazy" is a spry, intelligent, intimate look at a brief but beatific respite from two stale marriages. Dramatic clout and laughs are both a little gentle to facilitate much theatrical exposure, but a sizable field of Euro TV berths awaits.

The affair in question sparks slowly, as Simon (August Zirner) and Helga (Katja Flint) cross paths each day while dropping their two kids apiece at nursery school. He's married to somewhat self-centered Anette (Gabriela Benesch), who corners him into virtual house-husband status despite his teaching job, and she to careerist medic Helmut (Georg Schuchter).

Writer-director Wolfram Paulus prods the action along unobtrusively, as love burgeons faster than the pair can handle it. Turning point comes at a party, where the clandestine lovers let down their guard, cutting a passionate figure on the dance floor, and considerably riling their unamused spouses.

A tight, unfussy production both in front of and behind the camera, this unassumingly amiable pic could benefit from a less pedestrian title.

—*David Rooney*

WORDS UPON THE WINDOW PANE
(IRISH)

A Pembridge Pictures production, in association with Calypso Film (Cologne), Delux Prods. (Luxembourg), Northpro (U.K.), with participation of British Screen, Irish Film Board, NRW, WDF. (International sales: Pembridge, Dublin.) Produced, directed, written by Mary McGuckian, based on the one-act play "The Words Upon the Window Pane" by W.B. Yeats. Executive producers, Uwe Franke, Tom Reeve, Romain Schroeder, Peter Flood. Co-producer, Anna J. Devlin. Camera (color), Des Whelan; editor, Kant Pan; music, Niall Byrne; production design, Christopher Hobbs; art direction, Andrew Munrow; costume design, Monica Howe; sound (Dolby), Rick Dunford; casting, John & Ros Hubbard. Reviewed at Venice Film Festival (Special Events section), Sept. 2, 1994. Running time: **99 MIN.**
Miss McKenna .... Geraldine Chaplin
Mrs. Henderson .... Geraldine James
Dr. Trench .... Ian Richardson
John Corbet .... John Lynch
Abraham Johnson ..... Gerard McSorley
Cornelius Patterson .... Donal Donnelly
Mrs. Mallet .... Gemma Craven
Stella .... Brid Brennan
Vanessa .... Orla Brady
Jonathan Swift .... Jim Sheridan
   With: Hugh O'Connor, Kate Flynn, Brendan Conroy, Mikel Murfi, Mal Whyte.

Strong down-the-line casting adds flavor but not much life to "Words Upon the Window Pane," an umbral screen version of the W. B. Yeats one-acter about Dublin spiritualists visited by the ghosts of Jonathan Swift and his two women. Legit enthusiasts will relish correspondences with the original playlet, but others will spend most of the time baffled. Theatrically, this de facto teleplay doesn't stand a prayer.

Tone of the movie, shot in deep blacks and blues, is set by an opening quote: "I reckon no man thoroughly miserable unless he be condemned to live in Ireland." Verging on the thoroughly miserable is repressed spinster Miss McKenna (Geraldine Chaplin), head of the Dublin Spiritual Society, circa 1928, who invites Mrs. Henderson (Geraldine James) over from Blighty to be guest medium at an attempt to communicate with 18th-century scribe Swift.

With dialogue tending toward the literary and courteous (in both time frames), perfs generally low-key and lensing nocturnal, it's left to Niall Byrne's Philip Glass-like score and occasional bursts of machine-gun cutting to bring any life to the proceedings.

As the visiting medium, the ever-reliable James dominates scenes she's in. Chaplin, mostly tight-jawed and grim-faced, makes less impression.

Other actors are all skilled and reliable within the limits of their parts, and there's an extended cameo by Irish director-scripter Jim Sheridan as Swift that's more buffoonish than dramatically valid amid such pro casting. Running time is on the leisurely side.

—*Derek Elley*

WEIRD TALES
(STRANE STORIE)
(ITALIAN)

A Film Master Film production in association with Pasodoble, Green Movie, Film Master Clip. Associate producers, Johnny Dell'Orto, Luciano Beretta, Marco Balich, Ambrogio Lo Giudice. Executive producers, Sergio Castellavi, Stefano Coffa, Giorgio Marino, Carlos Pasini. Directed by Sandro Baldoni. Screenplay, Baldoni, Dell'Orto; camera (color), Renato Alfarano; editor, Dede Dedevitiis; art direction, Giancarlo Basili. Reviewed at Venice Film Festival (Window on Images), Sept. 10, 1994. Running time: **82 MIN.**
Narrator .... Flavio Bonacci
Man on Train .... Ivano Marescotti
Single Woman .... Silvia Cohen
Housewife .... Mariella Valentini
Effete Husband .... Alfredo Pea

In "Weird Tales," a father tells his teenage daughter three surreal tall tales on a train, involving the other passengers in his bizarre imaginings. Though basically funny, the episodes are linked by an anguishing sense of building global doom. Handicapped by an uncertain pace, this first directorial effort by Sandro Baldoni (based on his own short stories published in Il Manifesto) nonetheless provokes many a chuckle of recognition at our absurd world, where nothing is too far-fetched to be partly true. Lack of stars as well as its eccentric viewpoint may keep it from scoring high onshore, but it could work as an offbeat fest item.

Thesp Ivano Marescotti is showcased in four different roles, which he fills like a chameleon. In the frame story, he is a grumpy, aloof businessman who categorically refuses to believe that scruffy narrator Flavio Bonacci's tales are plausible. In the first tale, he is an average victimized citizen who wakes up wheezing one morning. Workmen tell him that his air has been cut off because he didn't pay his bill. He embarks on a life-or-death dash through a Kafkaesque bureaucracy (painfully hilarious to anyone who has ever paid bills in Italy) to get his air turned back on.

In episode two, Marescotti is on sale at the neighborhood supermarket. He is bought by redheaded, single Silvia Cohen, who likes him because he's so "tender." But when he refuses to go to bed on command, she returns him to the supermarket manager as out-of-date merchandise.

The last and longest tale depicts the war between two neighboring families, one rich snobs, the other poor churls. This basic tension, aggravated by proximity, turns to open hostility. The escalating violence is punctuated by chilling TV news reports about Bosnia, Cuba and Rwanda. Mariella Valentini cameos as the slatternly companion of belching Marescotti, while Cohen plays the wickedly bitchy wife of preening Alfredo Pea. Film ends mysteriously with the passengers wandering around a bombed-out train. Its reference to the Italicus tragedy, a fascist train bombing that took many lives and was never solved, will be clear only to Italians.

Baldoni has good film instincts, and when his stories get rolling they catch the viewer up. Rhythm is marred, however, by repetition, which drags out the story unduly.

Despite its low-budget look, Giancarlo Basili's art direction makes some visual points (as in the two apartments facing each other in the family war story). —*Deborah Young*

JERUSALEM

COFFEE WITH LEMON
(CAFFE IM LEMON)
(ISRAELI)

A Zvi Shapira-Gady Castel production, in association with the Fund of the Promotion of Israeli Quality Films, Israel Broadcast Authority. Directed by Leonid Gorovets. Screenplay, Gorovets, Semyon Vinokur. Camera (color), Valentin Belonogov; editor, Alan Yakobovich; music, Haim Frank Elfman; art direction, Sasha Ganelin. Reviewed at Jerusalem Film Festival, July 1, 1994. Running time: **94 MIN.**
Valery Ostrovsky . Alexander Abdulov
Jana .... Tatiana Vasilyeva
Michal .... Bruria Albec

The tragic and all-too-common dilemma of a new immigrant to Israel — in this case, a famous Russian actor — who can't find work because he can't speak Hebrew is explored in "Coffee With Lemon." Like his hero, director Leonid Gorovets ("The Ladies' Tailor") immigrated only three years ago, and this crossover film, lensed partly in Moscow, has an authentic ring. Some offshore possibilities are indicated.

Russian thesp Alexander Abdulov is a natural as the famed, self-centered thespian Valery Ostrovsky, who has just won the best actor award at the Berlin Film Festival. Story catches his last appearance onstage in Moscow, before he, wife Jana (Tatiana Vasilyeva) and their son leave their luxurious apartment and set off for Israel. Contrary to expectations, the land of milk and honey translates into a major setback in the family's quality of life. Their first home, a ratty pre-fab trailer in the middle of nowhere, surrounded by equally maladjusted neighbors, is a shock.

Even worse is Valery's belated discovery that he can't survive as a Russian-language actor. His half-hearted attempts to learn Hebrew throw him into the arms of his son's beautiful teacher, Michal (Bruria Albec), who has also made herself indispensable to his lonely wife. The reason for Michal's disruptive involvement with the Ostrovsky family is never explained, however. Abdulov's posturing bravura rescues the plot from many dangerous twists, as with his near-involvement in the lucrative business his old buddy Alex develops as a stage hypnotist and crank. Pic ends disappointingly with an abrupt fatality, while Moscow explodes in its brief civil war. At its best, film offers real insight into the life of the new Israelis from Russia. Cast is a plus, pacing is good and lensing pro. —*Deborah Young*

THE DISTANCE
(HAMERHAK)
(ISRAELI)

A Lonely Spy Ltd. production. Produced, directed, written by Dan Wolman. Camera (color), Victor Bilokopitov; editor, Shoshi Wolman; music, Slava Ganelin. Reviewed at the Jerusalem Film Festival, July 3, 1994. Running time: **85 MIN.**
Oded .... Chaim Hadaya
Svetlana .... Genia Chernik
Mother .... Ruth Farchi
Father .... Isaac Shilo
With: Miriam Nevo, Bat-Sheva Noam.

Dan Wolman's no-budget look at the quiet desperation of family relationships, "The Distance," won the Wolgin award for best Israeli film of the year. Wolman's first feature in nine years has a close-up intimacy, as his camera follows a handful of characters and their homey drama. Apart from festivals, pic is a choice candidate for arthouse release and would translate well onto the small screen.

Oded (Chaim Hadaya) is a young Israeli architect who now lives in Chicago with his wife and kids. His career is in full bloom, but his sick and aging parents in Tel Aviv want him to move back home where they can see him often.

Oded's week-long visit home is quietly momentous. Almost accidentally, he manages to create a painful rift between his folks and Svetlana (the sprightly Genia Chernik), a Russian girl who has become their live-in maid and confidante. With effortless subtlety, Wolman suggests multiple reasons for Oded's behavior, including attraction to Svetlana and jealousy over her taking his place in the family.

As though inspired by his budget restrictions, Wolman leaves nothing superfluous in this subtly shot, well-cut film. He concisely portrays Oded's parents as warmhearted and understanding people who make unconscious but effective use of emotional blackmail to get their only child back to Israel.

Chernik turns in a superb perf as a dignified Russian divorcee, whose normal friendship with a man sets off Oded's paranoia and the family's mini-calamity. Only Hadaya, as the indecisive, self-centered but guilt-torn son is inexpressive, creating a gap in the film's central role.

Technical work is fine.
—*Deborah Young*

DREAMS OF INNOCENCE
(SIPUR SHEMATCHIL BELEVAYA SHEL NACHASH)
(ISRAELI)

Produced by Marek Rozenbaum, Katriel Schory. Directed by Dina Zvi-Riklis. Screenplay, Avi Mugrabi, based on a novel by Ronit Matalon. Camera (color), Danny Schneur; editor, Rachel Yagil, Anat Lubersky; music, Shem Tov Levy; art direction, Avi Avivi. Reviewed at Jerusalem Film Festival, July 2, 1994. Running time: **85 MIN.**
Monsieur Robert .... Moshe Ivgy
Mother .... Rita Shukrun
Neighbor .... Levana Finkelstein
Benjamin .... Nessim Sisso
Margalit .... Efrat Aviv

Going by the more fetching title in Hebrew of "A Tale That Begins with the Funeral of a Snake" (from the Ronit Matalon source novel), "Dreams of Innocence" describes the life of a family living in a poor country village. Quite a charming film, pic's gentle humor and warm characters could appeal to younger auds wherever foreign-lingo pix are accepted.

Tale is narrated by 10-year-old Margalit (the engaging Efrat Aviv), who ironically views the misadventures of her 13-year-old brother Benjamin (Nessim Sisso) and her ne'er-do-well father (Moshe Ivgy). Styling himself "Monsieur Robert," the father takes off for Africa just before Benjamin's bar mitzvah.

When the family dog is kidnapped, the kids secretly take a train to Tel Aviv to find him. They spend the night camping out with a traveling circus that seems to have something magical about it. Though they don't find their dog, they do stumble onto Monsieur Robert. For the first time, his adoring son sees him as the pathetic loser he really is, living in a world of dreams.

The story skips around a lot, as though trying to cover too many episodes in the book. Another problem is the lack of a clear central character, since Margalit drops out of the narrative for long stretches.

Director Dina Zvi-Riklis communicates her amused affection for the characters with all their pluses and minuses. Rita Shukrun stands out as the kids' plucky mother who keeps the family going. As her irresponsible mate, the fine Moshe Izgy has a wistful Charlie Chaplin look that softens his execrable behavior. —*Deborah Young*

NEWLAND

(ERETZ HADASHA)

(ISRAELI)

Produced by Chaim Sharir. Directed by Orna Ben-Dor Niv. Screenplay, Kobi Niv. Camera (color), Amnon Zlayet; editor, Einat Glazer; music, Uri Widislavssi. Reviewed at Jerusalem Film Festival, July 7, 1994. Running time: **105 MIN.**

Anna	Ania Bukstein
Jan	Michael Phelman
Roza	Eti Ankri
Malul	Shuli Rand
Bardugo	Rami Dannon
Zadiko	Asher Zarfati

This first feature by award-winning docu-maker Orna Ben-Dor Niv fails to convince in its glossy tale about plucky orphans and transit camps in 1949 Israel. Preferring photogenic tykes and TV-style plotting to realism, with an occasional bout of fantasy thrown in, "Newland" might find a niche on the small screen.

Two beautiful children, 8-year-old Anna (Ania Bukstein) and her older brother Jan (Michael Phelman), have been separated from their parents during the war, which sent them across half of Europe. They arrive in Israel on an immigrant boat, hoping to locate their mother.

The hardships of the transit camp and terrifying memories of the war are lightened by the camaraderie of the immigrants. There is an upright young man who has lost his wife, a couple expecting a baby, a sick old prof cared for by his young Catholic wife.

There are also bad elements, like the small-time gangsters who prostitute young girls and steal food. Anna, who longs for her mother and refuses to speak, and Jan, determined to forge his way in the world and never look back, are united in their misery.

Then, Jan finds a job on a neighboring kibbutz. Too young to come with him, Anna now finds herself alone in the camp, which is closing down, with only her teddy bear for company and solace.

Containing more than one nod to Hollywood, "Newland" is so packed with stereotyped characters and situations, it never gets off the ground — until the kids literally fly off with their teddy bear in an ending that's a cross between "E.T." and "Peter Pan."

Perfs are standard but acceptable. —*Deborah Young*

LOVE AFFAIR

A Warner Bros. release of a Mulholland production. Produced by Warren Beatty. Executive producer, Andrew Z. Davis. Directed by Glenn Gordon Caron. Screenplay, Robert Towne, Beatty, based on the motion picture "Love Affair," screenplay by Delmer Daves, Donald Ogden Stewart, story by Mildred Cram, Leo Mc-Carey. Camera (Technicolor), Conrad L. Hall; editor, Robert C. Jones; music, Ennio Morricone; production design, Ferdinando Scarfiotti; art direction, Edward Richardson; set design, Al Manzer, James Murakami; set decoration, Dan L. May; costume design, Milena Canonero; sound (Dolby), Jim Tannenbaum; visual effects supervisor, John Richardson; associate producer, Mark Ovitz; assistant director, Jimmy Simons; Tahiti second unit director, Hall; casting, Marion Dougherty. Reviewed at Warner Bros. Studios, Burbank, Oct. 5, 1994. MPAA Rating: PG-13. Running time: **108 MIN.**

Mike Gambril	Warren Beatty
Terry McKay	Annette Bening
Ginny	Katharine Hepburn
Kip DeMay	Garry Shandling
Tina Wilson	Chloe Webb
Ken Allen	Pierce Brosnan
Lynn Weaver	Kate Capshaw
Herb Stillman	Paul Mazursky
Nora Stillman	Brenda Vaccaro
Anthony Rotundo	Glenn Shadix
Robert Crosley	Barry Miller
Sheldon Blumenthal	Harold Ramis

The appeal of this "Love Affair" is only skin deep. A film of gorgeous surfaces and negligible emotional resonance, this third rendition of a perennial sentimental favorite is easy on the eyes and has its share of beguiling moments in the early going, but crucially lacks a compelling climax and any sense of urgency in its storytelling. Big promotional push and lack of much competition should translate into some good opening numbers, but audiences won't likely give a hoot in the long run.

Leo McCarey's two versions of this star-crossed romance, "Love Affair," starring Charles Boyer and Irene Dunne in 1939, and "An Affair to Remember," toplining Cary Grant and Deborah Kerr in 1957, were favorites to their respective generations. Contempo audiences will recall that "Sleepless in Seattle" paid extended homage to the latter as the epitome of romance, making it one of the hot video rental titles of last summer.

Main hook of this telling is the matchup of Warren Beatty and Annette Bening as jet-setters who, already engaged to others, become irresistibly attracted to each other and, after an intense tryst, resolve to meet at the top of the Empire State Building in three months if they are serious about each other. Beyond that, there is the curiosity of seeing Katharine Hepburn on the bigscreen

in a major film for the first time in 13 years.

Setup is jauntily and briskly done, with Beatty plausibly cast as a former L.A. football star (shades of "Heaven Can Wait")-turned-broadcaster engaged to a talkshow doyenne (Kate Capshaw), and glamorous Bening as Terry, the fiancee of a high-finance magnate (Pierce Brosnan). Pair meet in the upstairs first-class cabin on a flight to Sydney, and self-referential lines abound as Beatty's well-known sports stud, Mike, eagerly puts the make on Terry to the scarcely concealed fascination of the other passengers.

An emergency landing on a tiny South Pacific island fatefully pits the characters together for longer than anticipated, as the travelers board a Russian cruise ship for a brief drunken voyage to Tahiti. Again, Mike does his best to get to know the quick-witted, elegantly sophisticated object of his desire, but it's only upon a visit to his aunt (Katharine Hepburn) at her splendid home in the hills of Bora Bora that, spurred by a heart-to-heart between the women, the possibility of something meaningful between the two sparring partners becomes apparent. Flying back to New York after a torrid two-day fling that's seen only in a banal ship montage, they set their Empire State rendezvous

and check out their respective fiances at the gate after landing. With both set on breaking their engagements, pic treads water in mid-section, with Beatty lamely informing his L.A. agent (Garry Shandling) that "I want to simplify my life" and taking a football coaching job at a remote state college, and Bening making the rounds in Gotham as a jingles singer and music teacher.

On her way to her appointment with destiny, Bening meets with a tragic accident that sends her to the hospital and leaves Beatty holding the bag. It's here that the emotional tension should build, but instead, the story stalls in a holding pattern until the long-awaited reunion. Played in Bening's unaccountably cold, tiny apartment, the scene is muffed in the writing, direction and playing, turning what should be a cornily irresistible romantic climax into a no-impact ending.

As he has in other films, notably "Shampoo," Beatty has fun with his own image here, but in a mild and innocuous way. There are plenty of references to his character's irrepressible flirtatiousness and past conquests ("You know that I've never been faithful to anyone in my life," he warns Bening), as well as offhand remarks about his advancing age, new-found like of children

and desire to settle down. But unlike some of his previous roue characters, this one just isn't very interesting, so even though Beatty looks great and has his patter down, the inner needs of his aging jock aren't conveyed to the viewer with any conviction.

It's not even that the motives behind making the film aren't heartfelt, as there's no reason to doubt that Beatty, who produced and co-wrote with Robert Towne, didn't intend this as a lavish and sincere valentine to his wife. But dramatically, there's no keen edge or passion to it, and pic doesn't do enough to make the audience care about characters who would seem to have everything, whether they end up together or not. Ultimate effect is of a beautiful package with nothing much inside.

Bening is enchantingly vivacious and sparkling, a fine match in looks, wit and sophistication to her leading man. At first, it's disconcerting to see Hepburn truly looking like a little old lady, puttering about with a cane and clearly afflicted by her long-term neurological disease. But it must also be said that the conclusion of her 10-minute turn results in the only moving moment in the picture, as Mike, and then Terry, say goodbye to the great lady, leaving her alone on her mountaintop.

Shandling proves lively as Beatty's toady, while Capshaw and Brosnan are given short shrift as the cast-off prospective mates.

Although some wry humor is sprinkled throughout, script could have been funnier, and there's a lack of unified visual style and directorial approach by Glenn Gordon Caron despite rich lensing by Conrad L. Hall, opulent production design by the late Ferdinando Scarfiotti (who receives an "in memorium" end credit) and a lushly romantic score by Ennio Morricone that betrays more than a hint of his "Once Upon a Time in America" theme.

Several TV personalities appear on-air as themselves, as does Ray Charles in a concert sequence. Film is dedicated to Time Warner's late topper, Steve Ross.

—*Todd McCarthy*

October 10, 1994 (Cont.)

THE SPECIALIST

A Warner Bros. release of a Jerry Weintraub production. Produced by Weintraub. Executive producers, Steve Barron, Jeff Most, Chuck Binder. Co-producer, R. J. Louis. Directed by Luis Llosa. Screenplay, Alexandra Seros, suggested by the "Specialist" novels by John Shirley. Camera (Technicolor), Jeffrey L. Kimball; editor, Jack Hofstra; music, John Barry; production design, Walter P. Martishius; art direction, Alan Muraoka; set decoration, Scott Jacobson; costume design for Sharon Stone, Judianna Makovsky; sound (Dolby), Andy Wiskes; associate producers, Tony Munafo, Susan Ekins; assistant director, Dennis Maguire; second unit director/stunt coordinator, Allan Graf; second unit camera, Michael O'Shea; casting, Jackie Burch. Reviewed at the Gemini Theater, N.Y., Oct. 6, 1994. MPAA Rating: R. Running time: **109 MIN.**
Ray Quick .... Sylvester Stallone
May Munro .... Sharon Stone
Ned Trent .... James Woods
Joe Leon .... Rod Steiger
Tomas Leon .... Eric Roberts

The year's third big explosives orgy (after "Speed" and "Blown Away"), Luis Llosa's "The Specialist" delivers plenty of bright fireballs while agreeably dispensing with the genre cliche of mad bomber fighting iron-willed hero amid a terrified populace. But pic demonstrably fails to make good on the potential chemistry of Sylvester Stallone and Sharon Stone, who oddly spend most of their screen time communicating by phone. Since the result is to romantic thrillerdom what phone sex is to the real thing, B.O. prospects look iffy after initial curiosity about stars' teaming is defused.

Notably lacking in forward momentum until very late in the game, story opens with a prologue in which CIA explosives specialists Ray Quick (Stallone) and Ned Trent (James Woods) come to blows while trying to assassinate a Colombian drug lord. Though the targeted car also carries a little girl, psycho Ned, the "rigger," is eager to blow it to kingdom come anyway. Humane Ray, the "trigger," tries to abort the mission. After his effort proves unsuccessful enough to provide pic its first big bang, Ray retaliates by giving Ned a whaling and later getting him booted from the agency.

Subsequent grudge feud moves to the back burner when tale shifts to present-day Miami. Ray, now apparently not connected with a government agency, though with a conscience that must be a serious career handicap, makes phone contact with a potential client, May Munro (Stone), who is looking to eradicate three Cuban-American gangsters led by Tomas Leon (Eric Roberts).

Flashback explains that May as a child watched the trio brutally murder her parents. She's now bent on revenge, but with Ray initially refusing to lend his services, she must proceed alone. He is, however, sufficiently intrigued to follow her actions from a safely voyeuristic distance.

She begins by making herself available to Tomas, capably incarnated by Roberts, who projects no ethnicity whatsoever but again proves his aptitude at oozing sleaze from every pore.

The killer's affair transpires under the increasingly watchful eyes of his crime boss father, Joe Leon (Rod Steiger), and Ned, who now appears to be simultaneously employed by the Leon family and the Miami police, a bizarre if advantageous dual career that is never sufficiently explained.

Ray continues to observe May's relationship with Tomas, which leads only to implicit sex, until disgust gets the better of him. This is the story's most plausible turn, since Tomas is nothing less than repulsiveness in human form, with the wardrobe to prove it.

So Ray finally agrees to execute May's wishes, and does so quite literally: Via his incendiary expertise, Tomas' two accomplices are soon transformed into grilled gangster.

Ray warns May before setting out to bomb one, "If this is a setup, I'll kill you." The threat leads, with no small obviousness, to the tale's second half, where May's ulterior motives fuse with Ned's and Ray must extricate himself from a tangle of malevolent schemings.

Director Llosa, abetted by cinematographer Jeffrey Kimball, gives pic a polished look and handles the action scenes competently. He faces a thankless task, though, in trying to breathe life into Alexandra Seros' script (derived from the "Specialist" novels of John Shirley), which not only serves up cliched characters with cartoon motives but fails to connect these main players dramatically.

Through much of the pic Stallone, Stone and Woods seem to be appearing in separate movies. If so, the best is the one inhabited by Woods, who attacks his somewhat absurd part with exuberant, scenery-devouring gusto.

Stallone and Stone turn in solid if unremarkable work, but can hardly overcome the script's staggering mistake in not setting them face-to-face until 70 minutes in. Their subsequent sex scene, which features lots of steam, unwanted dialogue and the arty compositions of a perfume ad, will make most viewers yearn for another building to go to blazes.

An additional liability is the mannered, unconvincing work of Steiger, whose misguided stab at a Latino accent results in many unintentionally comic verbal tics, such as constantly pronouncing "you" as "jew."

Most tech credits are fine, with Miami contributing the Fountainbleu Hotel and other appealing scenery, and John Barry's score inappropriately but enjoyably evoking 007's Caribbean adventures.

—*Godfrey Cheshire*

KILIAN'S CHRONICLE

A Lara Classics production. Produced by Pamela Berger, Mark Donadio. Directed, written by Berger. Executive producer, Barbara Hartwell. Camera (color), John Hoover; editor, Jon Neuburger; music, R. Carlos Nakai; Bevan Manson; production design, John Demeo; art direction, Sophie Carlhian; costume design, Dena Popienko; sound, Coll Anderson; associate producer, Krista Thomas; assistant director, David Arndt. Reviewed at the Coolidge Corner Theater, Brookline, Mass., Sept. 19, 1994. Running time: **112 MIN.**
Kilian .... Christopher Johnson
Ivar .... Robert McDonough
Turtle .... Eva Kim
Contacook .... Gino Montesinos
Kitchi .... Jonah Ming Lee
White Eagle .... Robert Mason Ham

Beautifully shot tale of a confrontation between a European man and a New England Indian tribe has a twist that makes "Kilian's Chronicle" a true original — it's set 500 years *before* Columbus reached the New World. Writer/director Pamela Berger has based her story on Viking legends as well as recent archeological discoveries. The result, world-preemed in Boston Oct. 5, is a domestic arthouse pic that could take off with proper handling and strong word of mouth.

Berger is an art history professor at Boston College with a second career as a filmmaker. She first wrote and produced Suzanne Schiffman's 1987 directorial debut, "Sorceress," and two years later made her own helming debut with "The Imported Bridegroom." Although set in different locales and time periods, all three pix involve the theme of cultures clashing as individuals try to accommodate one another.

Here she relies on recent findings confirming legends of Viking visits to North America 1,000 years ago. Berger has created a story based on one such legend about a Celtic slave leaving his ship to explore the territory. Kilian (Christopher Johnson) has been captured by Norsemen, yet hopes to win freedom and return to his homeland.

Instead, he finds himself alone on the New England coast, where he is befriended by the local tribe who rescue him from a snake bite. Eventually he must decide if he is better off taking his chances getting back to Ireland or staying with Turtle (Eva Kim), the Indian girl with whom he has been trying to avoid falling in love.

Berger shows his growing identification with the tribal people through language. At first their speech is unintelligible to him and to the audience. Later, as he becomes more fluent, subtitles translate the conversations. Finally, Kilian and the Indians converse easily in their language, which comes across as English to the viewer.

Performances are on the mark, with Johnson an appealing hero and Kim a comely presence who keeps Turtle on an equal footing with Kilian. Robert McDonough is a suitably frightening adversary as the Viking who vows that Kilian will be recaptured, while Gino Montesinos and Jonah Ming Lee provide able support as the tribe members closest to Kilian.

Among the selling points here are the simplicity of the tale and the effectiveness of John Hoover's camerawork and John Demeo's production design in making Massachusetts and Connecticut locales convincing as virgin wilderness. Tech credits are nearly flawless. Only problem is Kilian's perfect grooming throughout the pic, especially since we never see him cut his hair.

For Berger, this represents a quantum leap over "The Imported Bridegroom," which played best to audiences willing to forgive the rough edges. With "Kilian's Chronicle," no apologies are necessary.

—*Daniel M. Kimmel*

THE LOST WORDS

A Scopix (New York) production. Produced by Scott Saunders, Vanessa Baran, Katrina Charmatz. Directed, edited by Saunders. Screenplay, Dan Koeppel, Saunders, Michael Kaniecki. Camera (color; Hi-8 video/16mm blow-up), Marc Kroll, Saunders; music, Kaniecki, Chris Burke, Neal Sugarman, George M, Red Sedan; art direction and paintings, Carmen Einfinger; lighting, Karl Nussbaum; production sound, Michael Greene. Reviewed on vidcassette, N.Y., Oct. 2, 1994. Running time: **90 MIN.**
With: Michael Kaniecki, Bob McGrath, Zelda Gergel, Brian O'Neill, Deborah McDowell, Rini Stahl, Fred Tietz, Salley May, George M, Joe Litto.

Romantic hassles among New York's boho/yuppie crowd get a sharp, kaleidoscopic treatment by first-time helmer Scott Saunders, whose no-budget feature should provide grins for hip urban auds in limited situations.

Satiric comedy focuses on the often self-created travails of Charles (Michael Kaniecki), a neurotically frazzled filmmaker, musician and video editor. Like most of his 30ish pals, Charles is unnerved by competing work and domestic demands, but decides to try to make sense of things by filming his life. While drawing amiable scoffs from his poker circle, the enterprise gets a cooler reception from his patient

October 10, 1994 (Cont.)

g.f., Marcie (Zelda Gergel), who understandably balks at discussing intimate details with a cameraman only feet away.

Charles, an acrophobe, can't even walk across the Brooklyn Bridge to see his much-needed shrink without Marcie's support, so it's little wonder that he inches toward a crackup when she sets off for a brief French holiday. Convinced by her belated return that she's been unfaithful, he explodes in a fit of jealousy, sundering the relationship.

During her absence and following the breakup, story limns not only Charles' solitary miseries and job woes but also the male-female difficulties of various friends, sometimes via interview-style footage interwoven with impressionistic views of Manhattan.

Like a Woody Allen tale for younger, less affluent New Yorkers, pic has the disadvantage of covering well-trod thematic territory, with endless chatter about relationships (the word itself crops up repeatedly) and potshots at such familiar satiric targets as performance artists. But a bit of viewer indulgence pays off, because the writing of Dan Koeppel, Saunders and Kaniecki, smoothly meshed with improvisation, produces a milieu well worth caring about, along with a smattering of genuinely hilarious scenes.

Shot on Hi-8 video and blown up to 16mm for theatrical, pic makes the most of technical limitations with its wittily handled faux-docu premise. An added plus is the casual, naturalistic ensemble feel of the cast, especially actor/musician Kaniecki's appealing turn as the charmingly screwed-up hero.

—*Godfrey Cheshire*

TORONTO

FAMILY

(BRITISH)

A BBC production. Produced by Andrew Eaton. Executive producer, Michael Wearing. Directed by Michael Winterbottom. Screenplay, Roddy Doyle. Camera (color), Daf Hobson; editor, Trevor Waite; music, Elvis Costello, John Harle; art direction, Mark Geraghty; sound, Kieran Horgan. Reviewed at Toronto Film Festival, Sept. 14, 1994. (Also in Telluride fest.) Running time: **119 MIN.**
Charlo .... Sean McGinley
Paula .... Ger Ryan
Nicola .... Neili Conroy
John Paul .... Barry Ward

Made for the BBC, "Family," a dark portrait of a working-class family, shows again the gap between the quality and diversity of British and American TV. The last segment of Roddy Doyle's Barrytown trilogy, "Family" is a perfect companion piece

to "The Snapper," as the two films complement each other in sensibility and tone. A startling piece of writing and filmmaking, this two-hour feature, compressed from the original four-hour TV version, should first get a theatrical release, but entire work deserves a slot on PBS or cable.

By now it's quite evident that author Doyle is also the auteur of films based on his work, for no matter who directs his stories — Alan Parker ("The Commitments"), Stephen Frears ("The Snapper") and now Michael Winterbottom — his distinctive voice always emerges clearly.

Thematically, "Family" can be perceived as a dark mirror image to "The Snapper," as both films focus on the routine, everyday lives of one struggling working-class family.

Social workers would have no problem labeling the Spencers as a dysfunctional family, as the clan is dominated by Charlo (Sean McGinley), a brutish, overbearing patriarch who physically and emotionally abuses his wife Paula (Ger Ryan) and their children. A petty thief, he makes a living out of stealing video equipment. When not at home, Charlo can be loving and charming.

Paula begins as a long-suffering wife, hoping for a better future that will terminate her hubby's incessant philandering and violent domestic outbursts. But when push comes to shove, she's resilient enough to fight back, take matters in her hands and even kick her hubby out of the house.

Lacking an appropriate role model, young son John Paul faces the danger of following in his dad's footsteps. Nicola, the teenage daughter who works in a factory, is beginning to experience her emerging sexuality, which is noticed by her too watchful dad.

It's a tribute to Doyle's multilayered, nuanced writing that he doesn't treat the Spencers as a clinical case in need of counseling and therapy. His non-linear narrative has no climaxes, no melodramatic contrivances — rather, it's composed of natural events and conversations that take place in every family.

The division of the narrative into four chapters, each devoted to a different member of the family, provides multiple perspectives on this group. The characters move from center stage to the periphery and back with the smooth ease that only a gifted writer and director can achieve.

First-time helmer Winterbottom conveys in great detail the wrenching experience of residing in the Spencer household. There are many "tiny" moments that in their fidelity to ordinary life are priceless. It's as if the actors got caught by the camera, which observes unobtrusively, refraining from editorializing on the characters and their problems.

Daf Hobson's restless camera and Trevor Waite's finely modulated editing underline energy when it's called for and quiet restraint in other episodes. At times, the boil-down from four hours to two is manifest in abrupt transitions and truncated editing.

This "Family" is so richly observed and so emotionally satisfying that, with some luck, it should follow the pattern of Ingmar Bergman's "Scenes From a Marriage," a masterwork shown in different lengths and versions, theatrically and on TV.

—*Emanuel Levy*

MY LIFE AND TIMES WITH ANTONIN ARTAUD

(EN COMPAGNIE D'ANTONIN ARTAUD)

(FRENCH — B&W)

An Archipal 33/Laura Prods./La Septe-Arte/France 2 production. Produced by Denis Freyd. Directed by Gerard Mordillat. Screenplay, Mordillat, Jerome Prieur, based on Jacques Prevel's "En compagnie d'Antonin Artaud." Camera (b&w), Francois Catonne; editor, Sophie Rouffio; music, Jean-Claude Petit; art direction, Jean-Pierre Clech; sound, Pierre Lorrain, Dominique Dalmasso. Reviewed at Toronto Film Festival, Sept. 12, 1994. Running time: **93 MIN.**
Antonin Artaud .... Sami Frey
Jacques Prevel .... Marc Barbe

In Gerard Mordillat's "My Life and Times With Antonin Artaud," Sami Frey gives such an astonishingly intense performance that his portrait of the genius and madness of the famed French poet/intellectual is far more insightful than that offered in the current documentary "The True Story of Artaud the Momo," co-directed by Mordillat and Jerome Prieur.

In its chronicle of a peculiar, obsessive friendship, evocative mood and stylized black-and-white cinematography, this fictionalized drama bears some resemblance to Christopher Munch's "The Hours and Times." Appealing in an idiosyncratic way, special pic deserves fest exposure and arthouse attention, especially in the U.S., where Artaud's name is virtually unknown except to theater students.

Narrative begins in May 1946, when Artaud returns to Paris after spending nine years in a Rodez asylum. His return is eagerly anticipated by Jacques Prevel (Marc Barbe), an ambitious young poet determined to follow his mentor in all his wanderings, be it to nursing homes or Saint Germain-des-Pres.

A complex relationship and intimate bond evolve between the two, with Prevel becoming Artaud's dis-

ciple, companion — and supplier of drugs. Prevel's postwar existence, marked by misery and suffering, is brightened by interactions with his wife and longtime mistress.

Fictionalized journal is narrated by Prevel, centering on the last two years of Artaud's life. The film captures not only the creative persona of Artaud, for whom "words were bombs," but also the artistic milieu that surrounded him in the 1940s.

There have been too many cliched movies about suffering poets, but this one sheds fresh light on the effects of pain — and mental disorder — on creativity. Illustrating Artaud's self-rationalizing motto that "sickness makes you stronger," pic is excellent at showing the hallucinatory sensibility and wounds of a man who, confined to asylums, was ravaged for most of his life by the excruciating pain of cancer and the effects of drugs.

Ultimately, pic derives its emotional power from Frey's dominating portrayal of Artaud's contradictory personality, by turns shocking and magnificent, cruel and sensitive. Frey, who bears a physical resemblance to Artaud, has borrowed some of the artist's notorious gestures without imitating him. Strong chemistry between Frey and Barbe, as the young and handsome, but also less talented, poet makes their intense encounters credible.

Technical credits are impressive on all levels: Resourceful lensing and production design and mindful location work contribute to an indelible sense of time and place. In some scenes, pic's visual style approximates surrealist cinema as well as Theater of the Absurd, two schools of which Artaud was a founder, as evidenced in his seminal treatise, "The Theater and Its Double."

—*Emanuel Levy*

THE TRUE STORY OF ARTAUD THE MOMO

(LA VERITABLE HISTOIRE D'ARTAUD LE MOMO)

(FRENCH — DOCU)

A Laura Prods./Les Films d'Ici/La Septe-Arte/Arcanal/Centre Georges Pompidou production. Directed by Gerard Mordillat, Jerome Prieur. Camera (color), Francois Catonne; editor, Sophie Rouffio; music, Jean-Claude Petit. Reviewed at Toronto Film Festival, Sept. 11, 1994. Running time: **170 MIN.**
With: Paule Thevenin, Henri Thomas, Marthe Robert, Anie Besnard, Rolande Prevel, Jacqueline Adamov.

"The True Story of Artaud the Momo" is an exceedingly long, often indulgent documentary about Antonin Artaud,

October 10, 1994 (Cont.)

the famed French actor, poet and intellectual who died in 1948 at the age of 50. Though less insightful, less provocative and less entertaining than the portrait offered in the 93-minute feature "My Life and Times With Antonin Artaud," made by the same filmmakers, docu should appeal to intellectual viewers on fest and arthouse circuits interested in French arts and letters.

While researching Artaud's life for their dramatic feature, co-directors/writers Gerard Mordillat and Jerome Prieur thought it would be a good idea to make a docu about Artaud's last years, which were marked by madness, insufferable misery and excruciating pain.

Artaud was a man of many talents, leaving his mark as an actor (as Marat in Abel Gance's "Napoleon"), playwright ("The Cenci"), screenwriter (Germaine Dulac's "Le Coquille et le clergyman") and philosopher ("The Theatre and Its Double"). But above all, he was a visionary intellectual who devoted his entire life to the exploration of the meaning and power of words: "Language was life's energy to him," says a poet-friend.

Despite rich archival footage — recitation of Artaud's poems, display of his drawings, photos of his intellectual circle and interviews with some of his friends — docu is only partially successful, as it lacks analytic focus as well as interesting structure. For the most part, it's a talking-heads docu.

Docu's chief problem, in addition to its near-three-hour running time, is the emphasis placed on Artaud's personality at the expense of his creative genius and body of work. Moreover, despite contradictory reports, most witnesses can't conceal their admiration for Artaud as "bigger than life," and result is a mythical portrait, devoid of sufficient critical, dispassionate evaluation.

Some sections are quite dull, notably the detailed reactions of Artaud's friends to his death and the controversy over his burial.

Highlights include a discussion of Artaud's theatrical philosophy, vis-a-vis the Greek tragedies that he admired, and a detailed reconstruction of a 1947 lecture that Artaud gave, which was meant to revive interest in his work but badly misfired as a result of Artaud's anxiety and inability to deliver.

Given his decade of institutionalization in various asylums, engaging issues related to his "madness" emerge, such as the difficulty of diagnosing it. One witness, claiming that Artaud overreacted to his illness and was not insane, blames Artaud himself and bourgeois society for stigmatizing the artist. There's also some humor: While hospitalized, Artaud would take long walks, then grab a taxicab, instructing the driver in a most dramatic way, "To the madhouse!"

Despite serious shortcomings, docu succeeds at conveying Artaud's intensely vibrant personality, and the genius and madness that informed his life.

—*Emanuel Levy*

MR. SARDINE
(GUOQI SHADIANYU)
(HONG KONG)

A Simpson Communications production. (International sales: Simpson Communication Ltd., Hong Kong.) Executive producers, Jacob Cheung Chi Leung. Directed by Derek Chiu. Screenplay, Chan Kam Cheong. Camera (color), Kai Shek; editor, Yiu Tin Hung; art direction, Fok Tat Wah. Reviewed at Toronto Film Festival, Sept. 10, 1994. Running time: **108 MIN.**
With: Wong Chi Wah, Irene Wan, Liu Kai Chi, Poon Fong Fong.

The insecurity of life in Hong Kong today provides the prickly thematic backbone of "Mr. Sardine," a strange little comedy of mild amusement value and elusive political import. Shot independently on a low budget (about $300,000), pic will hold some interest for Asiaphiles with an eye on 1997 (when China takes over government of Hong Kong), but is too haphazard in its storytelling and modest in achievement to have much offshore commercial impact.

Mr. Sardine (Wong Chi Wah) is a first-class dork so klutzy he can barely manage his job as a supermarket clerk. Unaccountably, he has a girlfriend who wants to marry him, but he doesn't seem capable of a relationship with her, physically or otherwise.

Sardine has stockpiled his apartment with hundreds of cans of food and, when his crazy landlady, Mrs. Pei, dies in his flat with a stupid grin on her face, he feels responsible and bunglingly tries to dispose of the body. At the same time, Sardine must contend with the dead woman's foxy daughter, Anna, as well as with a cop who seems to have nothing better to do than pester the hapless young man.

In its portrayal of Sardine's hording and other motifs, pic takes some potshots at the island's unbridled consumer society, and the police are set up for some particularly heavy hits. Key line comes from the materialistic Anna, who says, "In this life, many things are out of our control," an obvious reference to the uncertainty of things three years hence, although how such a nerdy leading character and the death of Mrs. Pei relate to other aspects of Hong Kong remains fuzzy.

ENGLISH, AUGUST
(INDIAN)

A Tropicfilm production. Produced, directed by Dev Benegal. Screenplay, Benegal, Upamanyu Chatterjee, based on the novel by Chatterjee. Camera (color), Anoop Jotwani, K.U. Mohanan; editor, Benegal; editorial consultant, Thom Noble; music, Vikram Joglekar, D. Wood; production design, Anuradha Parikh-Benegal; costumes, Pia Benegal; sound, Joglekar; assistant director, Sopan Maler; casting, Uma Da Cunha. Reviewed at Toronto Film Festival, Sept. 17, 1994. Running time: **126 MIN.**
With: Rahul Bose, Salim Shah, Shivaji Satham, Veerendra Saxena, Tanvi Azmi, Mita Vashisht.

A confident first feature that explores the intriguing subject of the way grassroots India is administered, "English, August" should crop up at fests in the coming months but is unlikely to cross over into arthouses in the West.

For anyone interested in life on the subcontinent, Dev Benegal's film gives lucid insight into the "middling" corruption of low-level government bureaucrats in the boondocks. Agastya Sen, portrayed with humor and sensitivity by Rahul Bose, is a well-educated Bengali who joins the public service and is sent to work as an assistant to the collector in a tiny village where he doesn't speak the language.

Billeted in appalling quarters without proper plumbing facilities (and soon joined by a persistent frog that simply won't go away), Sen is lonely and bored away from his city friends.

Benegal's convincing depiction of the little village, with its absurd ceremonies and meetings and its deeply ingrained poverty, is the principal attraction of this languid film, which, like its indolent hero, just drifts along observing life.

The soundtrack is mostly in English, the language in which bureaucrats from different parts of the country converse, and, unusual for an Indian film, it is peppered with four-letter words.

Pic looks good, with top-quality cinematography. Cast members are all fine, with Bose's deadpan delivery of the often humorous dialogue a major asset. Tighter pacing would have helped this likable pic find a far wider audience than it probably will.

—*David Stratton*

THE DEVIL NEVER SLEEPS
(EL DIABLO NUNCA DUERME)
(U.S.-MEXICAN — DOCU — 16mm)

A Xochitl Films production. Produced, directed, written by Lourdes Portillo. Co-producer, Michelle Valladares. Camera (color, 16mm), Kyle Kibbe; editor, Vivian Hillgrove Gilliam; music, Mark Adler, Lola Beltran; sound, Jose Araujo. Reviewed at Toronto Film Festival, Sept. 16, 1994. Running time: **87 MIN.**

The slightly fictionalized documentary "The Devil Never Sleeps" concerns the journey of Chicana filmmaker Lourdes Portillo back to Mexico to investigate the mysterious death of her uncle. Graced with a healthy dose of humor and some introspective commentary, pic attempts to be deeply personal and also revelatory of Mexico's family mores, but ultimately its limited scope and crude execution will restrict its appeal to fans of docus.

All Portillo knows when she begins her investigation is the "official story," which is that her uncle Oscar committed suicide. His widow (and second wife), whom the family never liked or accepted and suspected of gold-digging, claims that he took his life because he was ridden with cancer.

But everyone suspects there's more to the case, which prompts the filmmaker to examine police reports and press coverage of his death. Thus is constructed a portrait of a successful, affluent entrepreneur and politician, with hints that a lot of people owed him money and that he had family problems.

Docu's most intriguing dimension is its Pirandellian illustration of the notion that human reality is subjectively perceived and constructed. Indeed, despite her use of various methods to solve the puzzle — personal interviews, police reports, background surveys, family gossip — Lourdes is only slightly more informed at the end of her inquiry than she had been at the start. Lacking depth, docu suffers from the director's exercise of restraint and detachment.

It doesn't help that visually the film is shapeless, consisting of a series of talking heads, and that tech credits are on the raw side.

Still, "The Devil Never Sleeps" is mildly entertaining, particularly in the sections that try to make sense of the radically contradictory accounts of the same events or issues given by different members of Oscar's family. —*Emanuel Levy*

October 10, 1994 (Cont.)

DUTCH FEST

06

(DUTCH)

A Dino Filmprodukties production. (International sales: Dino, Amsterdam.) Produced, directed by Theo van Gogh. Screenplay, Johan Doesburg, Ariane Schluter, Ad van Kempen, from the 1994 play directed by Doesburg. Camera (color), Tom Erisman; editor, Ot Louw; music, Ruud Bos; art direction, Ruud van Dijk; sound, Ben Zijlstra; assistant director, Maria de Haas. Reviewed at Dutch Film Festival (competing), Utrecht, Sept. 26, 1994. Running time: **90 MIN.**
Sarah .... Ariane Schluter
Thomas .... Ad van Kempen

The sex talk comes down-and-dirty in "06," a rendering of the controversial Dutch legit piece that charts the truth-and-lies relationship between a man and a woman in a series of phone conversations. Though the format and content feel the same after a while, this offbeater has enough going for it in the two lead performances to cause a ripple on the fest circuit, with small-screen sales for cable and bold Euro webs a possibility. Pic drew critical plaudits at the Dutch Film Festival.

Original play, performed in spring 1994, was dubbed "interactive." Members of the audience, in individual cubicles with video monitors, could switch between actors and actresses. The term "06" is the Dutch equivalent of premium-rate 900 numbers in the U.S.

Maverick director Theo van Gogh's pic settles for a single pair, cross-cutting between them. She is always in her living room, more questioned than questioner; he in his workroom, not far from his architect's drawing board. Each chat is supposedly separated from the previous one by a week.

The subtext concerning lies that each sex spins to the other is mainly implied rather than laid on with a sociological trowel. A good number of the 11 episodes turn on verbal stimulation of the other's fantasies, with one or both heavily masturbating. Thanks to light, witty playing by both actors, and unembarrassed frankness in the dialogue, the effect is intriguing, funny and sexy, without being remotely pornographic.

Though limited to two sets, van Gogh serves up a richly colored supply of visuals, either tracking around the characters as they talk or holding on them for more contained effect. Ariane Schluter, especially, is aces in her multifaceted role. —*Derek Elley*

HOUSE CALL

(DE FLAT)

(DUTCH)

A Polygram release (Netherlands) of a Movies Filmprods./TROS production. Produced by Chris Brouwer, Haig Balian. Directed by Ben Verbong. Screenplay, Jean van de Velde, from an idea by Gijs Versluys. Camera (color), Theo Bierkens; editors, Brouwer, Verbong, Bert Rijkelijkhuizen; music, Patrick Seymour; art direction, Rikke Jelier, Alfred Schaaf; sound (Dolby), Peter Flamman; assistant director, Natasa Hanusova. Reviewed at Dutch Film Festival (competing), Utrecht, Sept. 26, 1994. Running time: **106 MIN.**
Roos Hartman .... Renee Soutendijk
Eric Coenen .... Victor Low
Jacy .... Hans Hoes
Davy .... Jaimy Siebel

"House Call" would be ripe for a stateside remake if "Sliver" hadn't snuck in there first. That's a pity, as this watchable Dutch erotic thriller about a professional woman who falls for a maybe-murderer in the same apartment block scores on almost all levels on which the overblown Yank pic bombs, even if it can't match the Paramount production's star power and high-gloss look.

In ordinary circumstances, this could have picked up some offshore coin following the trail of other Dutch genre items like Dick Maas' "The Lift" and "Amsterdamned." Without some highly inventive marketing, its future is more likely to be buff events, hooked by actress Renee Soutendijk's name, and as a dubbed vid item. Helmer Ben Verbong is best known for his debut "The Girl with Red Hair" and the more recent erotic drama "The Indecent Woman."

Soutendijk ("The Fourth Man") plays Roos, an attractive divorced doctor who's just moved into a glass-and-white-tiles apartment building by the sea with her young son, Davy. An early caller is handsome young copywriter Eric (Victor Low), who suspects all is not well with another tenant, Roos' housekeeper. They break into her apartment and find her murdered.

Roos is already being pestered by a heavy breather on the phone, and (unknown to her) by a peeping tom with binoculars. Eric pals up with her son and starts making direct moves on her, and despite warnings from other tenants, she slowly becomes attracted to him.

Meanwhile, the police haul in Eric on suspicion of the housekeeper's murder. There's also the unresolved problem of whether he killed his late wife. Roos' paranoia moves up a couple more notches when another woman in the block is strangled.

Though the film equally recalls other genre items like John Carpenter's 1977 telepic "Someone's Watching Me!" and the producers claim the script was kicking around long before "Sliver," finished item contains at least a couple of scenes that recall the latter pic. One is even played for laughs, with Soutendijk turning herself on in a bathtub and being suddenly interrupted by her son.

Script makes little attempt to spread suspicion much beyond Eric, but manages to juggle the is-he/isn't-he moods with some skill, helped by fine, equivocal playing by Low. Soutendijk is excellent, bringing mature character to the role of the doc without trying to overreach the script's genre limitations. Sex scenes between the two are hot, and visually frank on Soutendijk's part.

Apart from occasionally muddy processing in some interiors, the movie is technically fine, with classy lensing by Theo Bierkens and atmospheric scoring by Patrick Seymour. Cutting is smooth.

Despite great expectations, pic performed disappointingly on local release. Dutch title translates as "The Apartment Block." —*Derek Elley*

ONCE BEATEN, TWICE SHY

(EENMAAL GESLAGEN, NOOIT MEER BEWOGEN)

(DUTCH)

A Studio Nieuwe Gronden production, in association with NOS-TV. (International sales: Cinemien, Amsterdam.) Produced by Rene Scholten. Directed by Gerrard Verhage. Screenplay, Ger Beukenkamp, from the novel "La Meche" (The Game) by Lucie Veldhuyzen-Marchal. Camera (color), Nils Post; editors, Stefan Kamp, Hens van Rooy; music, Fons Merkies; art direction, Harry Ammerlaan; costume design, Bernadette Cörstens; sound, Marcel de Hoogd; assistant director, Bart Reddingius. Reviewed at Dutch Film Festival (competing), Utrecht, Sept. 26, 1994. Running time: **82 MIN.**
Mother .... Ineke Veenhoven
Charles .... Jack Wouterse
Gina .... Ariane Schluter
Mary .... Kathenka Woudenberg
Jozef .... Stefan de Walle

Solid direction and strong performances hold the attention in "Once Beaten, Twice Shy," a black comedy centered on a dysfunctional Dutch family. Pic's only real faults are some fuzziness in the development and a lack of dramatic highs. Reliance on dialogue consigns the pic to small-screen sales within Europe, but it's good quality gab for most of the way.

Story, set in the '50s and based on a Belgian novel, is mostly set in a rambling, book-laden house in southern Amsterdam, wherein live a domineering mother (Ineke Veenhoven), her bookish son, Charles (Jack Wouterse), and sexually enigmatic daughter, Gina (Ariane Schluter). Their lodger-cousin, Jozef (Stefan de Walle), fantasizes over girlie mags when he's not pacing the room trying to think up a good plot for his novel.

Inspiration comes with the news that Charles is hooked on a glamorous woman across the street (Kathenka Woudenberg) who is suspected of murder (never explained). Charles' introduction of this intellectual featherweight into the household spurs a family breakdown, ending with the mother hurling the woman's dog through the window and Gina coming out of the closet as a lesbian.

Most of the pic is well-played dialogue scenes between various combinations of the quintet as they play intellectual games and work out long-buried tensions. There's also the chance that the whole thing is imagined by the slightly crazed, over-imaginative writer.

Performances are all nicely in tune with the low-key, Grand Guignol atmosphere, with notable turns by Schluter (so good in Theo van Gogh's sex-talk pic "06") as the repressed, chain-smoking daughter, and Jack Wouterse as her lumbering bro. Helmer Gerrard Verhage gets good mileage from the antique-heavy mansion, and all tech credits are smooth and confident. —*Derek Elley*

1,000 ROSES

(1000 ROSEN)

(DUTCH)

A Sigma Filmproductions/NOS-TV production. Produced by Matthijs van Heijningen. Directed by Theu Boermans. Screenplay, Gustav Ernst, from his own play. Camera (color), Theo Bierkens; editor, Rene Wiegmans; music, Lodewijk de Boer; art direction, Ben van Os, Jan Roelfs; sound, Marcel de Hoogd, Jan van Sandwijk; special effects, Hans Voors; assistant director, Paula van der Oest. Reviewed at Dutch Film Festival (competing), Utrecht, Sept. 23, 1994. (Also in Toronto fest.) Running time: **96 MIN.**
Gina .... Marieke Heebink
Harry .... Jaap Spijkers
Liesje .... Tessa Lilly Windham
Gina's Mother .... Marianne Rogee
Rita .... Marisa van Eyle
Kernstock .... Bert Geurkink
With: Rik Launspach, Hennes Demming.

"1,000 Roses" is an ambitious but muddled attempt by theater director Theu Boermans to meld reality and a fairy-tale allegory in some sort of commentary on material pursuits. Mixture of styles, shot through with nods to David Lynch, has its moments but will end up mystifying rather than entertaining its limited public.

Setting is a dreary industrial town whose economy depends on a monolithic wire factory. When the complex goes bankrupt, the working-class community loses its sense of certainty until some Yanks move in and give the place a second lease on life.

At the same time, a young woman, Gina (Marieke Heebink), seizes her chance at independence from her doltish lover, Harry (Jaap Spijkers), and hits the entrepreneurial trail with a local computer expert (Bert Geurkink) as her tutor.

Adapted from a play by Gustav Ernst, film is framed as a kind of anti-industrial, pro-green allegory, mutely observed by the woman's young daughter (Tessa Lilly Windham) and set in a vague time period.

As the main characters expend their energy on either money-making or sex, nature slowly reclaims the town in a jungle of green shoots and red roses. This fantasy angle sits uncomfortably alongside a blood-drenched finale of Harry running amok with a chain saw and forklift, and the wire factory exploding across town.

Lead players give it their best shot, and the copious coupling is earthy and good for some chuckles. End result, however, is a lot of time and care spent on a confused, and confusing, text. —*Derek Elley*

CROSSING BORDERS

(RIT OVER DE GRENS)

(DUTCH-GERMAN — B&W)

A Casa Film (Netherlands)/ZDF (Germany) production, in association with Wuste Film. (International sales: NFM/IAF, Amsterdam.) Produced by Rosemarie Blank, Stefan Schubert. Directed, written by Blank. Camera (b&w), Martin Gressmann; editor, Mara Loytved-Hardegg, Blank; art direction, Marieken Verheyen, Olga Delgado-Lopes, Lars Betko; sound, Klaus Klingler, Jac Vleeshouwers. Reviewed at Dutch Film Festival (competing), Utrecht, Sept. 25, 1994. Running time: **95 MIN.**
  With: Christien Vroegop, Anke van 't Hof, Medi van 't Hof.
  (Dutch and German dialogue)

A young woman's vagrant wanderings around the Netherlands and Germany make curiously involving viewing in this first feature of Euro documaker Rosemarie Blank. "Crossing Borders" may not rate a theatrical passport, but festivals and specialized tube buyers should take note.

The mysterious, sullenly attractive Nele (Christien Vroegop) is intro'd scavenging garbage from an Amsterdam street market. On an impulse, she leaves the caravan she lives in and sets out with her dog to find a friend in Germany.

The nomadic trek leads her to Berlin, Dresden, Hamburg and East Friesland, in cold, wintry landscapes where her only, fleeting companionship is with an old relative and a young student, Leo. Upbeat ending celebrates her independence.

Pic lacks the structured, feature-film feel of, say, Agnes Varda's Sandrine Bonnaire starrer "Vagabond," and settles for a looser, more restless format like Wim Wenders' "Kings of the Road," with a poetic-realist edge. The point of the odyssey is soon lost, but thanks to tip-top B&W lensing (deep blacks, careful compositions) and a hypnotic perf by Vroegop as the girl, the potentially dreary, going-nowhere subject takes on a strangely watchable quality. —*Derek Elley*

IT WILL NEVER BE SPRING

(WILDGROEI)

(DUTCH)

A Sigma Filmproductions production. (International sales: Concorde Film Nederland, the Hague.) Produced by Matthijs van Heijningen. Directed, written by Frouke Fokkema. Camera (color), Gerard Vandenberg; supervising editor, Ot Louw; editor, Peppijn Kortbeek; music, Maurits Overdulve, Hans Otten; production design, Rikke Jelier, Alfred Schaaf; sound, Marcel de Hoogd, Huud Nijhuis; assistant director, Anouk Sluizer. Reviewed at Dutch Film Festival (competing), Utrecht, Sept. 23, 1994. (Also in Toronto fest.) Running time: **95 MIN.**
Lin Lammerse .... Hilde van Mieghem
Emile Lombardo .... Thom Hoffman
Marot .... Ellen ten Damme

In her second feature after the dour but poised farming drama "Vigour," Frouke Fokkema trips up badly with "It Will Never Be Spring," a literary-based stab at high style about a one-sided *amour fou* between a femme writer and a well-heeled publisher. Commercial chances look wintry in the extreme.

Central character is the glamorous Lin (Hilde van Mieghem), who's written a bestseller about her affair called "Wildgroei" ("Wild Growth," pic's Dutch title). After she's hauled out of a canal by two riverboat men, flashbacks detail the various phases of her obsessive love for smoothie Emile (Thom Hoffman), a publisher who later takes up with Lin's sexy sister, Marot (Ellen ten Damme).

Though the film occasionally hits its target of stylish game-playing and glossy lensing, it more often falls flat on its face with uninteresting direction and such ludicrous exchanges as "You're like a peeping tom in my solitude" and "Shut up, we've already fantasized ourselves to death." Switches between color

and B&W in the latter half are the final nails in the pic's coffin.

Hoffman is monochrome in the male role, and van Mieghem variable as the writer. The striking ten Damme contributes lithe support as the hotsy sister. Technically, pic is OK but not up to its ambitions.
—*Derek Elley*

VENUS IN FURS

(DUTCH)

A Moskito Film production. (International sales: NFM/IAF, Amsterdam.) Produced by Victor Nieuwenhuijs. Directed by Maartje Seyferth, Nieuwenhuijs. Screenplay, Seyferth, Nieuwenhuijs, Ian Kerkhof, from Leopold von Sacher-Masoch's 1869 novel "Venus im Pelz." Camera (B&W), Nieuwenhuijs; editors, Herbert van Drongelen, Seyferth; music, Tchaikovsky, Mahler, Grieg; art direction, Peter Paul Oort; sound, Peter Burghout, Volfango Pecoraio, Jan van Sandwijk. Reviewed at Dutch Film Festival (competing), Utrecht, Sept. 25, 1994. (Also in Sao Paulo fest.) Running time: **65 MIN.**
Wanda ....Anne van de Ven
Severin .... Andre Arend van Noord
  With: Raymond Thiry, Hilt de Vos, Claire Mijnals.
  (English soundtrack)

Inappropriate American dubbing takes the sting out of "Venus in Furs," an arty, updated take on the 19th-century classic S&M novel that fails to stimulate anything except the occasional giggle. Even Euro tube sales look soft for this one.

Relationship between dominatrix Wanda and lap dog Severin is boiled down to a series of posy encounters — in an old manse, a stable, a kind of crypt — in which she humiliates, whips and generally walks all over him, thereby encouraging his masochistic love. Ending has him branded by another man while she walks off with a woman friend.

Best bits are lingering, poetic closeups of bodies in well-lit B&W while chunks of Mahler's and Tchaikovsky's fifth symphonies resound. Alas, when the young thesps occasionally open their mouths to voice high-falutin' dialogue, they sound more like spoiled kids out of "Beverly Hills, 90210." Both actors are clearly mouthing Dutch.

The blond Anne van de Ven is too girlish as the woman, and Andre Arend van Noord comes over as sulky and uninteresting as the man. His voiceovers harking back to youthful S&M fantasies add little depth to the so-what proceedings. Full-frontal nudity is unblinking but natural. —*Derek Elley*

EXIT TO EDEN

A Savoy Pictures release of an Alex Rose/Henderson production. Produced by Alex Rose, Garry Marshall. Executive producers, Edward Milkis, Nick Abdo. Directed by Marshall. Screenplay, Deborah Amelon, Bob Brunner, based on the novel by Anne Rice. Camera (Technicolor), Theo Van de Sande; editor, David Finfer; music, Patrick Doyle; production design, Peter Jamison; art direction, Margie McShirley; set decoration, Linda Spheeris; costume design, Ellen Mirojnick; sound (Dolby), Jim Webb; assistant director, Ellen Schwartz; casting, Valorie Massalas. Reviewed at the UA Westwood, Oct. 12, 1994. MPAA Rating: R. Running time: **113 MIN.**
Lisa Emerson .... Dana Delany
Elliot Slater .... Paul Mercurio
Sheila Kingston .... Rosie O'Donnell
Fred Lavery .... Dan Aykroyd
Dr. Martin Halifax ..... Hector Elizondo
Omar .... Stuart Wilson
Nina Blackstone .... Iman
Tommy Miller .... Sean O'Bryan
Diana .... Stephanie Niznik

There's something essentially dishonest in "Exit to Eden" that eats away at the fabric of the picture. The mix of erotic, comic and thriller elements diminishes whatever the original intention might have been for this melange.

Nonetheless, pic has a great come-on, and initial curiosity should generate decent box office. But once word gets out that it's all sizzle and no substance, commercial prospects will evaporate.

The thread of the story is the track-down of Omar (Stuart Wilson), a notorious diamond smuggler, and his accomplice Nina (Iman). LAPD undercover detectives Sheila Kingston (Rosie O'Donnell) and Fred Lavery (Dan Aykroyd) have been one step away from apprehending them, stymied because no one knows what Omar looks like.

Luck intercedes when it's learned that photographer Elliot Slater (Paul Mercurio), on a hunch, snapped the villain in action. But before the cops can get their hands on his negatives, Slater whisks away for a therapeutic vacation on the sexual fantasy island of Eden.

Built on a series of shaky coincidences, "Eden" descends further into the abyss of the preposterous as the cops and crooks both don disguises and try to meld into the scenery at the remote retreat in order to nab the visual evidence.

Director Garry Marshall might have been better served had he kept the dominance and submission antics as a backdrop rather than making them the focus of the film.

Elliot has come to the spa to confront his "aberrant" sexual inclinations and learn to commit. Somehow he's redeemed through his contact with camp commander Mistress Lisa (Dana Delany). And, in true fairy tale fashion, the woman's stern veneer is stripped away by true love and the good girl rises to the surface.

Marshall — who truly believes in such pap, as evidenced by "Pretty Woman" — is undone by an inferior script and what would appear to be self-doubt. He is a sucker for dumb jokes, and they diminish the credibility of the Eden locale. He also renders the situation toothless by assiduously avoiding the use of a single discouraging or four-letter word.

The irony is that in addressing American queasiness toward sexual matters, "Exit to Eden" reinforces the hoariest of stereotypes. In addition to righting the good-girl-gone-bad, he recreates the female buddy character via O'Donnell. She's not classically attractive, just honest about what she observes. The rest of the principal cast can't make much of the material.

Filmed in a slick, bright fashion, the picture is too visually obvious. It has the sophistication of an adolescent bathroom joke indifferently told. Saddled with a misguided sense of propriety, the lack of nerve or audacity in the endeavor renders shameful results.

— *Leonard Klady*

LITTLE GIANTS

A Warner Bros. release of an Amblin Entertainment production. Produced by Arne L. Schmidt. Executive producers, Walter F. Parkes, Gerald R. Molen. Directed by Duwayne Dunham. Screenplay, James Ferguson, Robert Shallcross, Tommy Swerdlow, Michael Goldberg, based on a story by Ferguson, Shallcross. Camera (color), Janusz Kaminski; production design, Bill Kenney; editor, Donn Cambern; music, John Debney; costumes, April Ferry; sound (Dolby), J. Paul Huntsman; assistant director, David McGiffert; second unit director, D. Michael (Micky) Moore. Reviewed at General Cinema Meyerland 3, Houston, Oct. 8, 1994. MPAA Rating: PG. Running time: 105 MIN.

Danny O'Shea	Rick Moranis
Kevin O'Shea	Ed O'Neill
John Madden	Himself
Becky O'Shea	Shawna Waldron
Karen O'Shea	Mary Ellen Trainor
Nubie	Matthew McCurley
Patty Floyd	Susanna Thompson
Mike Hammersmith	Brian Haley
Spike Hammersmith	Sam Horrigan

With: Todd Bosley, Eddie Derham, Danny Pritchett, Devon Sawa, Troy Simmons, Joe Paul Steuer, Marcus Toji, Christopher Walberg, Michael Zwiener.

Imagine "The Bad News Bears" in Pop Warner football togs, and you'll have a good idea what to expect from "Little Giants." The Warners release from

Amblin is a familiar but funny sports comedy that likely will score impressive numbers as a mid-autumn B.O. contender.

Rick Moranis heads the fine cast as Danny O'Shea, a small-town single father who wants to help his tomboyish daughter (Shawna Waldron) — and maybe upstage Kevin (Ed O'Neill), his cocky older brother — by coaching a team of kids who have been rejected by Kevin for the town's Pop Warner junior team.

Kevin, a former high-school star and Heisman Trophy winner, is the town's local hero and doesn't want to risk his standing in the community. So when he's asked to coach the Pop Warner team, he chooses only the very best athletes. Becky, his brother's daughter, would seem to fall into that category. But Kevin refuses to choose her because, hey, she's a girl.

Rather than get mad, Becky decides to get even by tricking her father — owner and operator of a service station — into coaching a team of rejects. At first, Danny is reluctant, mainly because he never was much of a football player. But when Kevin pointedly reminds Danny of his inadequacies, Danny decides it's high time to step outside his older brother's shadow.

No fewer than four screenwriters are credited with cobbling together a scenario that seems cribbed from bits and pieces of other pix about children and their games. Director Duwayne Dunham ("Homeward Bound: The Incredible Journey") keeps things moving at an acceptably brisk pace. Still, film might be too long for very young audiences.

In addition to Becky, the well-cast players on Danny's Little Giants team include Rudy (Michael Zwiener), a corpulent youngster whose flatulence is overused as a running gag; Rasheed (Troy Simmons), an eager-beaver receiver; Nubie (Matthew McCurley), a brainy nerd who uses his computer expertise to plot football plays; Jake (Todd Bosley), whose mother thinks football will improve his self-esteem; and Junior (Devon Sawa), a trigger-armed quarterback who's just hunky enough to make Becky think boys aren't so yucky after all.

Story is pat and predictable, as Danny whips his team into shape for a big practice game against his brother's Cowboys team. On the other hand, pic is never less than engaging, and often manages to be genuinely amusing.

Moranis' expert performance here is up to past standards. He is especially good in scenes with newcomer Waldron, who's a real find.

Among supporting players, Brian Haley is a standout as a gung-ho Cowboys player's father. Also worthy of note is Mary Ellen Trainor as Kevin's not entirely supportive wife, and Sam Horrigan as the Cowboys' most ferociously intimidating player.

Tech values are much better than they have to be. How much better? The attractive color lensing is by Janusz Kaminski, the Oscar-winning cinematographer of "Schindler's List." And the second-unit director is D. Michael (Micky) Moore ("Butch Cassidy and the Sundance Kid," "Raiders of the Lost Ark"). To paraphrase the Hallmark slogan, Amblin cares enough to provide the very best.

— *Joe Leydon*

RADIOLAND MURDERS

A Universal Pictures release of a Lucasfilm Ltd. production. Produced by Rick McCallum, Fred Roos. Executive producer, George Lucas. Directed by Mel Smith. Screenplay, Willard Huyck, Gloria Katz, Jeff Reno, Ron Osborn; story, Lucas. Camera (Rank Laboratories color), David Tattersall; editor, Paul Trejo; music, Joel McNeely; production design, Gavin Bocquet; art direction, Peter Russell; set decoration, Jim Ferrell; costume design, Peggy Farrell; sound (DTS), Carl Rudisill; stunt coordinator, Leon Delaney; assistant director, Waldo Roeg; second unit director, Vic Armstrong; unit production manager, David Hartley. Reviewed at Universal Studios screening room, Universal City, Calif., Oct. 13, 1994. MPAA Rating: PG. Running time: 108 MIN.

Roger	Brian Benben
Penny	Mary Stuart Masterson
General Whalen	Ned Beatty
Milt Lackey	George Burns
Billy	Scott Michael Campbell
Bernie King	Brion James
Lieutenant Cross	Michael Lerner
Rick Rochester	Michael McKean
Walt Whalen Jr.	Jeffrey Tambor
Max Applewhite	Stephen Tobolowsky
Zoltan	Christopher Lloyd
Katzenback	Larry Miller
Claudette	Anita Morris
Dexter Morris	Corbin Bernsen

George Lucas collaborated previously with screenwriters Willard Huyck and Gloria Katz on "Howard the Duck," and in terms of recalling that fiasco, "Radioland Murders" does pretty much everything but quack. A wild farce with more than 100 speaking parts, pic offers scant appeal to the MTV generation and is too frenetic for anyone who might appreciate its Golden-Age-of-radio setting. The result should be a static-ridden, one-note box office tune.

As a rule, you know a movie is in trouble when psycho comic Bobcat Goldthwait — among the lengthy roster of celebrity cameos — provides one of the movie's more restrained performances.

Billed as a "romantic mystery-comedy," "Radioland" wants to be a cross between "Clue" and a Marx Bros. movie, with perhaps a pinch of "Radio Days" and the short-lived TV show "On the Air" thrown in for good measure.

The result, however, is a well-intentioned but annoyingly shrill exercise virtually devoid of romance, suspense or wit. Director Mel Smith ("The Tall Guy") struggles to make sense of the scattershot screenplay, written by "Howard" and "Indiana Jones and the Temple of Doom" scribes Huyck and Katz as well as the team of Jeff Reno and Ron Osborn, working from a story by Lucas.

Set in 1939, all the action takes place during the debut night of a new radio network, WBN, emanating from a Chicago studio. One of the writers (Brian Benben) is seeking to woo back his estranged wife (Mary Stuart Masterson), the owner's assistant, in the midst of the startup chaos.

Soon, however, matters become a bit grim, as various staffers turn up dead, each time preceded by a cackling, "Shadow"-like voice coming from somewhere in the building. Roger (Benben) soon finds himself a suspect, trying to solve the mystery while everyone else struggles to keep the station on the air.

Sadly, that synopsis is more coherent than the movie seems most of the time, as the narrative caroms between scenes slavishly recreating the radio shows and all the behind-the-scenes mayhem using fast-cut editing techniques.

Though the period feel may inspire comparison to Lucas' early directorial effort "American Graffiti" (which Huyck and Katz also co-wrote), this effort only resembles that film in its generous use of nostalgic songs. For the most part, "Radioland" feels like a theme-park ride without an exit — rolling out a non-stop barrage of stale sight gags and snappy repartee that's both cliche-ridden and sorely lacking in snap.

Masterson gets to be plucky and not much else, while Benben plays a character similar to his persona in the HBO series "Dream On" and discovers that the role is easier to endure in that less-expansive format.

October 17, 1994 (Cont.)

Beyond that, a dizzying array of performers (including Robert Klein, George Burns, Harvey Korman, Peter MacNicol and Christopher Lloyd) show up for the party and find themselves with practically nothing to do.

Tech credits are generally impressive, though the Industrial Light & Magic effects and stunts seem a bit much, given the storyline, and the jazzy, non-stop score grows equally tiresome. If the movie itself laments a lost era, any youngsters inclined to judge the period based on "Radioland" will doubtless be glad that television came along. —*Brian Lowry*

A TROLL IN CENTRAL PARK

A Warner Bros. presentation in association with Don Bluth Ltd. Produced by Don Bluth, Gary Goldman, John Pomeroy. Directed by Bluth, Goldman. Screenplay, Stu Krieger; music, Robert Folk; original songs, Barry Mann, Cynthia Weil, Norman Gimbel, Folk; production design, Dave Goetz; sound (Dolby), Brian Masterson. Reviewed at General Cinema Galleria II, Houston, Oct. 8, 1994. MPAA Rating: G. Running time: **76 MIN.**

Voices:

Stanley	Dom DeLuise
Queen Gnorga	Cloris Leachman
Gus	Phillip Glasser
Rosie	Tawney Sunshine Glover
Hilary	Hayley Mills
Alan	Jonathan Pryce
King Llort	Charles Nelson Reilly

The latest from animator Don Bluth ("An American Tail," "The Land Before Time") likely will fade from theaters even quicker than his recent "Thumbelina." Warner Bros., clearly wary of the pic's prospects, opened it Oct. 7 in limited regional release. Vid chances can only be brighter.

Scripted by Stu Krieger ("Monkey Business"), "A Troll in Central Park" is the story of Stanley (voice by Dom DeLuise), the most good-hearted fellow in Troll Land, a kingdom where good-heartedness is highly suspect.

Because he has, quite literally, a green thumb, Stanley can make lovely flowers grow wherever he places his enchanted digit.

Unfortunately, this behavior makes him extremely unpopular with Gnorga, the gleefully wicked troll queen, who thinks beautiful flowers are even more repulsive than good-heartedness. So she banishes Stanley to the worst place she can think of — New York City.

As it turns out, however, this is not quite a fate worse than death. While living in a Central Park cave, Stanley is able to beautify his environs. He also befriends the two young children of neglectful, workaholic parents, and teaches them that, if you believe in yourself, anything is possible.

These are words that Stanley himself must learn to live by when Gnorga shows up to wreak havoc, uproot flowers and terrify small children.

"Troll" is a sweet and sunny fantasy that, like Bluth's "Thumbelina," is aimed at youngsters too young, or too nightmare-prone, to appreciate "Teenage Mutant Ninja Turtles" or "Mighty Morphin Power Rangers."

Older viewers (i.e., anyone over the age of 12) may find it too pokey and bland, and yearn for the visceral excitement and pictorial splendor of "The Lion King."

To be fair, Bluth's new pic features animation by his Dublin-based production house that is more imaginative, and far less greeting-card banal, than "Thumbelina." (It ranks several notches below "American Tail" and "Land Before Time," however.) And the vocal talents are all they should be.

DeLuise is aptly excitable and lovable as Stanley, while Leachman is amusingly over-the-top as the wicked Gnorga. The original songs by Barry Mann, Cynthia Weil, Norman Gimbel and Robert Folk are instantly forgettable, but they serve the story agreeably well.

—*Joe Leydon*

WAR OF THE BUTTONS

(BRITISH-FRENCH)

A Warner Bros. release (U.K.) of a Warner Bros. presentation, in association with Fujisankei Communications Group, of an Enigma production, in association with La Gueville and Hugo Films. Produced by David Puttnam. Executive producers, Xavier Gelin, Stephane Marsil, David Nichols. Directed by John Roberts. Screenplay, Colin Welland, adapted from the 1962 film "La Guerre des boutons," directed by Yves Robert, from the novel by Louis Pergaud. Camera (Eastmancolor; Technicolor prints), Bruno De Keyzer; editor, David Freeman; consulting editor, Jim Clark; music, Rachel Portman; conductor, David Snell; production design, Jim Clay; art direction, Chris Seagers; costume design, Louise Frogley; sound (Dolby), David John; associate producer, Steve Norris; assistant director, Mark Egerton; second unit director, Margy Kinmonth; casting, Ros and John Hubbard. Reviewed at Warner West End 7, London, Oct. 10, 1994. (Also in Tokyo fest.) Running time: **90 MIN.**

Schoolmaster	Liam Cunningham
Fergus	Gregg Fitzgerald
Geronimo's Dad	Colm Meaney
Geronimo	John Coffey
Marie	Eveanna Ryan
Gorilla	Paul Batt
Riley	Thomas Kavanagh
Jonjo	John Murphy
Adult Marie's voice	Dervla Kirwan

With: Brendan McNamara, Gerard Kearney, Kevin O'Malley, Anthony Cunningham, John Cleere, Daragh Naughton, John Crowley, Stuart Dannell-Foran, Karl Byrne, Barry Walsh, Derek O'Leary, Niall Collins.

Though no one seems to have stopped and asked if the world really needs it, this remake of the 1962 Gallic kidpic about warring tykes is a light, often charming transplant to Irish soil that's old-fashioned in the best sense and manages to avoid almost every obstacle that time and changing values can throw in its path. But whether a theatrical audience still exists in mature Western markets for this kind of up-market Saturday-matinee fare is something that Warners will need to ponder territory by territory. The David Puttnam production opened in the U.K. on Oct. 14, following its world preem in Dublin in late August.

Original director/co-scripter Yves Robert, who owned the rights to Louis Pergaud's novel, reportedly resisted all offers for a remake for a long time. Given that any transposition to contempo Britain would have been incongruous, Puttnam and writer Colin Welland's ingenious solution of setting it deep in rural Ireland, in an unspecified period, and virtually excluding all signs of modern, everyday, adult life, gives the movie a sense of timelessness and (for non-Irish auds) a slightly whimsical edge that just about makes the goings-on acceptable.

Interestingly, the reworking is much softer than the Gallic B&W original, which featured some salty language from the kids, considerably more passionate playing and an ending in which the two gang leaders embraced each other in a reform school. At the time, the pic played as an adults-only arthouse release.

Standing in for the rural Brittany of the original is a sleepy corner of southwest Ireland, where two villages, Carrickdowse and Ballydowse, straddle a stretch of tidal water. Welland's adaptation is framed as a v.o. reminiscence by the adult Marie, a girl once attached to the "Ballys" gang and, it turns out, stuck on its young leader, Fergus (Gregg Fitzgerald).

The scruffy Ballys are engaged in a permanent kids' war with the neighboring "Carricks," whose leader is the more upscale-looking Geronimo (John Coffey) and who are never seen out of school uniform and neckties.

Following a set-to on a bridge, in which one of their number is insulted, the Ballys graffiti a Carrickdowse church, precipitating a head-to-head in which they capture Geronimo's thuggish sidekick (Paul Batt) and remove all the buttons from his clothing. In revenge, the Carricks later do the same thing to Fergus.

In the next battle, the Ballys surprise the opposition by jumping up stark naked, retrieve their buttons and start to build a war chest for a final showdown. Set in a ruined castle, this ends with Geronimo beaten and de-buttoned.

Last half-hour, which has a kind of tagged-on feel as the pic searches for a resolution, centers on the repercussions after a turncoat from the Ballys guts the gang's forest h.q. with a tractor. Last reel has both Fergus and Geronimo fleeing to the hills to escape the wrath of their parents, and buddying up in a somewhat low-voltage finale.

To the movie's credit, any allegory to the present Irish troubles is simply there for the taking rather than being forced centerstage. By keeping the focus tight on his young players, all non-pros and mostly in their early teens, debuting director John Roberts constructs a self-sufficient world. Preachiness is kept to a minimum.

A measure of Roberts' success is that the nude battle (the original's most famous sequence) skirts embarrassment through swift handling and a playful tone. Likewise, the pic's least successful moments are in the final stretch, where the adult world and modern hardware (which would seem to place the movie somewhere in the '80s) intrude.

Casting and playing are on the button. As the two gang leaders, the rougher-looking Fitzgerald and finer-featured Coffey fit their roles like gloves, and there's flavorsome support, notably from Eveanna Ryan as the hero-worshipping Marie and Batt as Coffey's tree-swinging lieutenant. On the adult side, Liam Cunningham is fine as the Ballys' sympathetic teacher, and the experienced Colm Meaney ("The Snapper") solid as Coffey's dad.

Tech contributions are led by an upbeat, Irish-tinged score from ace composer Rachel Portman, who once again gives shape and emotional substance to potentially loose material, not least in her handling of the young Marie's pre-hormonal admiration for Fergus. Bruno De Keyzer's lensing of the verdant West Cork locations is sometimes ill-served by poor color grading in the print caught. —*Derek Elley*

VANCOUVER

ACROSS THE MOON

A Hemdale release of a Robert Mickelson production in association with Airstream Films (L.A.). Produced by Robert Mickelson. Directed by Lisa Gottlieb. Screenplay, Stephen Schneck. Camera (color), Andrzej Sekula; editor, Daniel Loewenthal; music, Christopher Tyng, Exene Cervenka; production design, Andrzej Sekula; art direction, Ken Larson; costume design, Giovanna Ottobre Melton; sound, William Fiege; casting, Cathy Henderson Blake, Tom McSweeny. Reviewed at Vancouver Film Festival (non-competing), Oct. 1, 1994. Running time: **100 MIN.**

Carmen .... Elizabeth Pena
Kathy .... Christina Applegate
Ritchie .... Tony Fields
Lyle .... Peter Berg
Paco .... Michael Aniel Mundra
Rattlesnake Jim .... James Remar
Frank .... Michael McKean
Barney .... Burgess Meredith
Old Cowboy .... Jack Nance
Lawyer .... Richard Portnoy

This peripatetic tale of women on the road doesn't quite live up to its freewheeling indie promise, but it serves as a long-awaited star vehicle for the varied talents of Elizabeth Pena.

Pena and Christina Applegate topline as barrio-bred Carmen and Beverly Hills deb Kathy, who have nothing in common except their men, Ritchie and Lyle (Tony Fields and Peter Berg), the lamest crooks in San Jose, Calif. When the lads' latest scam goes sour, they're sent to a correctional facility deep in the Mojave Desert. Despite their chalk-and-*queso* backgrounds, the women, plus Carmen's young son, Paco (impressive newcomer Michael Aniel Mundra), decide to pitch in together and head south — in a photogenic red convertible, natch.

The end of the dusty road is rougher than expected, but they soon convert an abandoned trailer into something like home. Personality conflicts persist, though, and Carmen hooks up with a local hunk called Rattlesnake Jim (James Remar) while Kathy meets increasing resistance from the prison system in her attempts to be with Lyle. Meanwhile, little Paco skips school to hang with Frank (Michael McKean), a hard-luck wild-animal wrangler waiting for tinseltown to call. Burgess Meredith shows up briefly as an extra-crotchety prospector, and David Lynch regular Jack Nance, as an ornery cattle rancher, adds to the collection of odd small-town characters.

Helmer Lisa Gottlieb (who grabbed an Oscar for her short "Murder in the Mist") tries hard — too hard — for a quirky, "Bagdad Cafe"-style mix of harsh facts and magic realism. The results are mildly engaging. Biggest problem is Stephen Schneck's script, which centers on femme chemistry, then fails to give leads anything interesting to say to each other. Most of what Carmen and Kathy do and talk about is connected with the menfolk in their life, draining the pic of gals-on-their-own audaciousness.

Though likable enough, Applegate seems to be too-consciously playing against her "Married ... With Children" rep, and her part lacks memorable edge. Songs from Exene Cervenka also fail to generate expected energy.

What "Moon" does boast, besides color-rich lensing from "Reservoir Dogs" cinematographer Andrzej Sekula, is a *very* sexy perf from Pena, who is more than ready to break out of the nice best friend/tough-talking secretary ghetto. Her scenes with Remar — particularly one in a high-desert hot tub — will get tongues wagging, and vidbiz is assured down the line. Theatrical B.O. may be slight, but the pic serves timely notice to Hollywood to take Pena seriously as a leading lady. —*Ken Eisner*

HIGHWAY OF HEARTACHE

(CANADIAN — 16MM)

A Scorn-a-Rama Pictures (Vancouver) production. Produced, directed, written by Gregory Wild. Camera (16mm), Brian Pearson; editor, Reginald Dean Harkema; music, Barbara Chamberlin; production design, Gregory Wild, Darcy Wild; costume and wig design, Druh Ireland, Dean Ryane; sound, Hal Beckett; casting, Wild, Janet Morris-Reade; assistant director, Patricia Barry. Reviewed at Vancouver Film Festival, Oct. 1, 1994. (Also in Chicago Gay Fest.) Running time: **86 MIN.**

With: Barbara Chamberlin, Pat Patterson, Serge Houde, Klaus Kohlmeyer, Sean Pritchard, Willie Taylor, Dusty Ryane, Christy Russell, Manfred Janssen, Sidney Morozoff, Jana White, the Big Wigs, plus voices of Rondel Reynoldson, Betsy Plamer, Marlene Franks, Arlene Belcastro, Philip Maurice Hayes.

Easily the weirdest feature yet to come out of Canada, "Highway of Heartache" is a scrappy cult item that pokes relentless fun at country music, the Christian right, tabloid TV and what debut helmer Gregory Wild calls "victimology."

The mega-victim here is Wynona-Sue Turnpike (Barbara Chamberlin), a would-be country star, complete with beehive 'do and cat's-eye glasses, whose career keeps getting sidetracked by things like steady abuse from her heartless mother, the Ku Klux Klan's kidnapping of her interracial child, and the sundry betrayals of various menfolk — whom she has a habit of shooting on live TV.

Wynona-Sue whines constantly, even after she marries the man of her dreams, a chatshow host called Crawfish (funny Pat Patterson), but everything's fodder for her bottomless bag of hurtin' tunes. Anyway, her truest love relationship is with her "beautiful little cigarettes."

In the well-named Wild's demented hands, there's not a scrap of naturalism — or even daylight — on display. The sets are wholly artificial, right down to brightly painted shadows and cartoon windows. Tacky animation, choruses of obese drag queens and loose lip-syncing add to a carnival atmosphere marrying John Waters' taste to a beyond-Douglas Sirk plot. Fortunately, the script — though often puerile in the extreme — is consistently funny, and manages to drive home the helmer's social agenda without collapsing the narrative into utter silliness.

Most surprising of all is that the music, penned and performed by Chamberlin herself, is actually catchy enough to stand on its own. The Seattle thesp also is appealing

enough to give her grotesque character some needed sympathetic depth.

Pic, shot in 16mm, is guaranteed to offend general auds, and scatological lingo makes network and regular 'plex berths impossible, but this "Highway" will head to a happy camp in gay fests, and at midnight screenings, where it's easy to imagine rhinestone-encrusted fans chanting along with "Ring on My Finger, Stiff on My Hands." —*Ken Eisner*

TOKYO COWBOY

(CANADIAN)

A C/FP (Canada) release of a Big Space Films Prods. production, with participation of Telefilm Canada and British Columbia Film. Produced by Lodi Butler, Richard Davis. Directed by Kathy Garneau. Screenplay, Caroline Adderson. Camera (color, B&W), Kenneth Hewlett; editor, Debra Rurak; music, Ari Wise; sound, Tim Richardson, Jacqueline Christianini; production design, Richard St. John Harrison; set decorator, Brian Davie; casting, Stuart Aikens; assistant director, Sandra Mayo. Reviewed at Vancouver Film Festival, Sept. 12, 1994. Running time: **94 MIN.**

With: Hiromoto Ida, Christianne Hirt, Janne Mortil, Anna Ferguson, Alec Willows, Michael Ironside, Christine Lippa, Dwight McFee, Sharon Heath, Brent Strait, Karen Steinebach, Denalda Williams.

This frequently delightful culture-clash comedy boasts a stunning performance in the title role and a clever hook in the concept of a young Japanese who heads to the rolling hills of Canada and finds the West wilder than he'd imagined.

A natural talent who enlivens even the smallest bits of business, actor/dancer Hiromoto Ida toplines as No Ogawa, a Tokyo burger-flipper who realizes his dream of visiting a place where people still rope dogies and wear cowboy hats.

The casting of Christianne Hirt as No's childhood pen pal Kate is less felicitous. Now an artist and semi-open lesbian struggling against rural narrow-mindedness and her own self-doubt, Kate's got a lot on her plate when he shows up, spurs in hand. Too bad everyone forgot to make her likable.

Scripter Caroline Adderson puts lots of zing in the pic's small talk, but transition to Big Issues is clunky, and whenever the brittle Hirt's in charge, the screen goes dead.

Fortunately, Janne Mortil, as Kate's open-hearted mate, and Anna Ferguson, as her crotchety, chain-smoking mother, bring it back to life, and Ida handles a gender-bending kabuki climax beauti-fully, giving the film an unexpect-edly memorable twist.

Fresh-looking effort was shot near Vancouver (with some B&W movie-parody scenes shot on the set of the "Bordertown" series), and first-time helmer Kathy Garneau captures the oddball rhythm of small-town life, peopling the tale with whimsical side characters — most notably Alec Willows' self-impressed postman — who are funny without turning into gross caricatures.

Project was lensed in Super-16 and blown up to 35mm with little harm to rich color or quirky compo-sitions. Uninspired score, sporadic plotting and lack of names make theatrical playoff unlikely, but this unusual "Cowboy" can expect to ride numerous offshore webs, in-cluding those in Tokyo.

—*Ken Eisner*

GREEN SNAKE

(CHING SE)

(HONG KONG)

A Film Workshop production for Seasonal Film Corp. Produced by Ng See-yuen. Executive producer, Tsui Hark. Directed by Tsui. Screenplay, Tsui, Lilian Lee, based on Lee's novel. Camera (color, Panavision widescreen), Ko Tsiu; editor, Ah Tsik; music, James Wong, Lui Tsung-tak; art direction, Lui Cho-hung; costume design, Ng Po-ling; action choreography, Yuen Pan, Tang Chia; snake concept, William Chang. Reviewed on Mei Ah vidcassette, Lon-don, Oct. 3, 1994. (In Vancouver Film Festival.) Running time: **102 MIN.**
Green Snake .... Maggie Cheung
White Snake .... Joey Wang
Hsu Hsien, the Teacher Wu Hsing-kuo
Fa-hai, the Monk .... Zhao Wenzhuo
With: Ma Tsing-mou, Tien Feng, Lau Seun, Luk Kar-tseun, Chan Tung-mui.
(Cantonese dialogue)

Seductive art direction and slinky performances can't quite hide the cracks in the script of "Green Snake." This splashy variation on the old Chi-nese fable of a scholar bewitched by two snake women is an enjoy-able enough f/x ride but lacks the substance to slither far beyond specialized screenings.

Big-budget, HK$33 million ($4.25 million) item bills itself as the 20th anni production of Ng See-yuen's Seasonal Film Corp., which pros-pered on early Jacky Chan starrers "Snake in the Eagle's Shadow" and "Drunken Master."

Here, Ng pairs fantasy meister Tsui Hark and author Lilian Lee

("Rouge," "Farewell, My Concu-bine") in latter's riff on the oft-filmed yarn.

Taiwanese actor Wu Hsing-kuo ("Temptation of a Monk") plays Hsu Hsien, a hapless male who falls for White Snake (Joey Wang), who's mastered the art of human form after 1,000 years' training.

Her mischievous sister, Green Snake (Maggie Cheung), has had only 500 years' practice and still can't get her lower half right.

On their trail are a Buddhist monk (Zhao Wenzhuo) halfway to nirvana, and a mad Taoist who's out to cleanse canal-riddled Hangzhou of nasty rep-tilians.

Hsu becomes a secular bystander as the forces of religion, and the human and non-human worlds, do battle, finally trashing the town and everyone in it.

Though the religious mumbo-jumbo comes thick and fast, the basic plotline is easy enough to follow, and Cheung especially throws herself into the part of the pesky younger sister.

Model work is obvious but suitably fairytale-like, and the production boasts a sensual play with color and sexuality that's new to Tsui's *oeuvre*. Pic's look often recalls the early '60s works of Italian *fantastique* maestro Mario Bava.

Local B.O. was a disappointing HK$9.5 million ($1.3 million) on re-lease in November '93.

—*Derek Elley*

THE SILENCE OF NETO

(EL SILENCIO DE NETO)

(U.S.-GUATEMALAN)

A Morningside Movies (New York)/ Buenos Dias (Antigua) production. (In-ternational sales: Morningside Movies, N.Y.) Executive producer, Luis Argue-ta. Directed by Argueta. Screenplay, Justo Chang, Argueta. Camera (color), Ramon Suarez; editor, David Tedeschi, Gloria Pineyro; music, Jose Gallegos, Maurice Gallegos; production design, Justo Chang; art direction, Ana So-lares; set decoration, Vivian Rivas; cos-tume design, Gloria Wurmser; sound, Antonio Arroyo; associate producer, Abigail Hunt; assistant director, Jorge Ramirez Suarez. Reviewed at San Se-bastian Film Festival (non-competing), Sept. 21, 1994. Running time: **106 MIN.**
Neto Yepes ..... Oscar Javier Almengor
Ernesto Yepes .... Herbert Meneses
Eduardo Yepes .... Julio Diaz
Elena Yepes .... Eva Tamargo Lemus
German .... Eduardo Jose Guerrero
Alberto .... Sergio Paz
Nidia .... Indira Chinchilla

"The Silence of Neto" sets a pre-teen boy's efforts to put childhood behind him against the U.S.-orchestrated coup that overthrew Guatemalan president Jacobo Arbenz's lib-eral, left-wing government in 1954. Though the film's political agenda lapses in and out of focus, debuting director Luis Argueta keeps the human drama squarely within his sights. Result is a hand-somely produced, engagingly played first feature from Guate-mala's fledgling film industry that should land theatrical dates in Spanish-lingo territories and ex-posure through specialist cul-tural outlets beyond that.

Concise glimpses during the opening credits fluidly intro the tyke of the title, Neto (Oscar Javier Almengor), and the death of his fa-vorite uncle, Ernesto (Herbert Meneses). Neto converses with Ernesto's ghost during the funeral service, ushering in a prolonged flashback to six months earlier.

U.S. and local military interven-tion is chronicled first as a distant rumble, anxiously followed on radio broadcasts promoting a red-scare campaign to protect U.S. interests in the Guatemalan fruit export in-dustry that were compromised by Arbenz's land reforms.

Gradually, the conflict's tentacles take hold of everyday life. Evening curfews become routine; govern-ment employees, including Neto's father and the teaching staff at his school, lose their jobs to army per-sonnel; Neto's classmate sweet-heart and her family disappear overnight; and his own family is

forced by the threat of bombings to leave the city.

The war zone also extends to Neto's family life. His father, Edu-ardo (Julio Diaz), raises him with a firm hand, instilling ties to hearth and home, while his uncle pushes the boy in free-spirited, inquisitive directions. Hostility between the two men is fueled by their shared passion for Neto's mother (Eva Tamargo Lemus).

Argueta opts for a rather straightforward narrative ap-proach, but his strongest suit is a breezy handle on the innocent pur-suits of adolescence. Slightly chubby Neto's halfhearted attempts at exer-cise, his observation of the passion-ate clinches between the family's Indian maid and her revolutionary lover, and trips with his chums to ogle a girls' ballet class are all given captivating treatment. Neto's long-standing ambition to fly a hot-air balloon without his father's help provides a satisfying cap-off.

The film's technical polish far out-shines its modest $500,000 budget. The' cast, culled mainly from the ranks of Guatemalan theater, is generally fine. —*David Rooney*

THE CHESS GAME

(LA PARTIE D'ECHECS)

(BELGIAN)

A Les Films de l'Etang (Brussels)/ Les Films des Tournelles (Paris)/Cab Prod. (Switzerland)/FR 3 (Paris)/TBF (Brussels) co-production. Produced by Anne-Dominique Toussaint, Pascal Jedelewicz. Directed by Yves Hanchar. Screenplay, Josiane Morand. Camera, Denis Lenoir; editor, Laurent Uhler; music, Frederic Devreese; art direc-tion, Pierre-Francois Limbosch; cos-tumes, Suzanne Van Well; sound, Olivi-er Hespel; associate producers, Jacque-line Pierreux, Jean-Louis Porchet, Ger-ard Ruey. Reviewed at San Sebastian Film Festival (competing), Sept. 17, 1994. Running time: **110 MIN.**
Ambroise .... Pierre Richard
Max .... Denis Lavant
Marquise .... Catherine Deneuve
Lord Staunton .... James Wilby
Suzanne .... Delphine Bibet
Anne-Lise .... Hilde Heijnen
With: Pascal Crochet, Antoine Gold-schmidt, Alexandre Von Sivers, Olivier Maes.

This handsomely produced and skillfully directed period piece about a child chess mas-ter who grows into a kind of Quasimodo torn between his ob-session for the game and his search for a deeper human reality should appeal to discriminating audiences, though commercial prospects may be limited by the central theme of chess.

Certainly, Hanchar has drama-tized the links with the venerable game to the maximum. But what quickens the pace is the extraordi-

October 17, 1994 (Cont.)

nary performance of Denis Lavant as the tortured prodigy of humble origin. His histrionic tour de force will seem excessive to some and superb to others.

Set in 1828, most of the story unfolds in the elegant country mansion of a marquise who is obsessed with the arcane and almost mystical implications of chess and whose dream it is to host the yearly world chess championships in her sumptuous villa. She is even willing to sacrifice her daughter in marriage as a trophy. Max, the slightly unbalanced prodigy, is pitted in a series of three games against the haughty British world master. Hanchar weaves in subplots as the tension between the opposing players builds, and the intrigues thicken as Max lurches from moments of high insanity to reassuring confidence that he will win the match, helped by a servant girl and his mentor, a Protestant minister, who try to steady him.

Thanks to a tight script, superb thesping and top-notch technical credits, pic never slackens for a moment as the audience watches with fascination at what Max's next quirky move, in life and on the chess board, will be. The playing of the games may be far removed from that of a real chess match, but they work well in building the drama.

—Peter Besas

THE DETECTIVE AND DEATH

(EL DETECTIVE Y LA MUERTE)

(SPANISH)

A UIP release (Spain) of a Ditirambo Films/Lola Films production, in association with Studio Tor, Sigma, with the participation of TVE and Canal Plus. (International sales: Iberoamericana Films, Madrid.) Produced by Andres Vicente Gomez. Executive producer, Miguel Angel Barbero. Directed by Gonzalo Suarez. Screenplay, Suarez, with the collaboration of Azucena Rodriguez. Camera (color), Carlos Suarez; editor, Jose Salcedo; music, Suso Saiz; production design, Alain Bainee; set decoration, Allan Starsky; costume design, Yvonne Blake; sound (Dolby), Krzysztof Grabowski; associate producers, Sylvia Suarez, Manuel Lombardero, Ignacio Martinez; assistant director, Fernando Pacheco; casting, Magda Szwarcbart. Reviewed at San Sebastian Film Festival (competing), Sept. 22, 1994. Running time: **109 MIN.**
Detective (Cornelio) ..... Javier Bardem
Maria .... Maria de Medeiros
Dark Man .... Carmelo Gomez
G.M. .... Hector Alterio
Duchess .... Charo Lopez
Laura .... Mapi Galan
Donluis .... Francis Lorenzo
Ofelia .... Paulina Gomez

Commanding perfs and arresting visuals are put to work on a bizarre meeting between film noir and gruesome fairytale in "The Detective and Death." But seasoned Spanish helmer Gonzalo Suarez takes on a load of fabulist, philosophical baggage and distracting peripheral characters that encumber the lugubrious thriller with pretentious hokum. Keen craftsmanship might see this one to some festival play, but theatrically it looks far too esoteric to make a killing.

Suarez reworks Hans Christian Andersen's fable "The Story of a Mother" in a modern but no less surreal setting. The original recounts a mother's trek through a labyrinthine forest to reclaim her child from Death. This version charts a nightmarish odyssey across a nameless European city wracked by crime and racial violence, with an unscrupulous business magnate known as G.M. (for *Grande Mierda*) holding the power to grant or deny life.

In his fortress-like blue headquarters, G.M. (Hector Alterio) is facing his own imminent death from illness. Before he goes, however, he determines to satisfy the birthday wish of his comely daughter and lover, Laura (Mapi Galan), to have her estranged mother (Charo Lopez) killed.

G.M.'s wayward employee, the Detective (Javier Bardem), lands the job of bringing her in. Knowing the love-struck Detective will try to save his intended victim, his admiring adversary, the Dark Man (Carmelo Gomez), tails him.

Having painstakingly constructed a fanciful thriller premise, Suarez hauls in the fairytale brigade. A forlorn mother with an ailing baby, Maria (Maria de Medeiros), crosses paths with the Dark Man and the Detective. She latches onto the Detective, believing he can lead her to G.M., with whom she plans to bargain for her son's life.

The central section is particularly tough going, with a barrage of superfluous characters laboriously drawn.

Looking uncannily alike at times, Bardem and Gomez are well paired as the story's good and evil travelers. Bardem won the San Sebastian fest's best actor honors for his roles here and in main prize winner "Numbered Days." Both pix flaunt a darker side of the actor than his beefcake turns in Bigas Luna's "Jamon, Jamon" and "Golden Balls." Medeiros' edge-of-madness act is occasionally overwrought, but she effectively builds the desperate ferocity of a mother's love into a force to be reckoned with.

Alain Bainee's stylish production design, and the bleak, wintry Polish locations, are given a grim allure by lenser Carlos Suarez (the director's brother). But the film's gloomy, deeply tonal look could have benefited from widescreen. *—David Rooney*

THE DAUGHTER OF THE PUMA

(PUMAENS DATTER)

(DANISH-SWEDISH)

A Domino Film & TV production, in association with Danish Film Institute, Red Barnet, Danida (Denmark)/SIDA, Radda Barnen, Ulf Hultberg Film (Sweden). (International sales: Domino, Copenhagen.) Produced by Peter Ringgaard. Executive producer, Tom Winther. Directed by Asa Faringer, Ulf Hultberg. Screenplay, Bob Foss, Faringer, Hultberg, based on the novel by Monica Zak. Camera (color), Dirk Bruel; editor, Leif Axel Kjeldsen; music, Jacob Groth; sound (Dolby), Henrik Langkilde; casting, Alejandro Laballero. Reviewed at San Sebastian Film Festival (non-competing), Sept. 22, 1994. Running time: **85 MIN.**
Aschlop .... Angela Cruz
Mateo .... Gerardo Taracena
Kuschin .... Alfonso Lopez S.
Catarina .... Dolores Heredia
Maria .... Elpidia Carrillo
Juana .... Nora Aguirre
Pascual .... Damian Zavala
Grandfather Juan .... Jose Pedrero
(Spanish dialogue)

Based on a novel inspired by the achievements of Guatemalan Nobel Peace Prize recipient Rigoberta Menchu Tum, "The Daughter of the Puma" recounts a woman's clandestine return from a Mexican refugee camp to search for her missing brother in their country, under oppressive military rule. The occasional didacticism of Swedish directing duo Asa Faringer and Ulf Hultberg cramps this polished Danish-Swedish co-production's hopes of wide theatrical playoff, but its forceful dramatic and political foundation, and its harrowing re-enactment of the extermination of an entire village, should carry the film to extensive exposure on cultural webs.

A slightly cluttered preamble outlines the powerful bond linking Aschlop (Angela Cruz) to her brother Mateo (Gerardo Taracena). They were separated when she fled with her parents to Mexico and he joined the guerrillas fighting to restore Guatemala to its Indian population. The birth of Mateo's son in the camp spurs Aschlop to undertake the dangerous journey to her homeland, entrusting her life to her guiding spirit, the puma.

The sight of her native village occupied by soldiers triggers Aschlop's horrific recollections. The quick crescendo from warning signs of the military's approach to their brutal onslaught is well-rendered, starting with the rumble of helicopters, stomping boots and the loading of weapons, and building to the bloody massacre of the population.

The directors' grip on the engrossing material slips when, having narrowly avoided arrest for being without documents, Aschlop falls into the hands of some sadistic torturers. When she escapes with the aid of her guardian puma, the film regains its footing.

Aside from some opening-reel uncertainty, the drama is solidly structured, with the universal themes of courage, resilience, pride in one's cultural heritage and the struggle for freedom stirringly fleshed out.

Straightforward, natural performances are backed by keen production values, moving music and crisp lensing of the imposing landscapes and noble, wounded faces. End credits list the many similar villages wiped out during Guatemala's 30-year civil war. *—David Rooney*

NUMBERED DAYS

(DIAS CONTADOS)

(SPANISH)

An Aiete Films/Ariane Films production, in collaboration with the ICAA, Sogepaq and Canal Plus Espana. Produced by Imanol Uribe, Andres Santana. Directed, written by Uribe, based on the novel by Juan Madrid. Camera, Javier Aguirresarobe; editor, Teresa Font; set design, Felix Murcia; costumes, Helena Sanchis; sound, Gilles Ortion; music, Jose Nieto; production manager, Andres Santana. Reviewed at Cine Princesa, Madrid, Aug. 25, 1994. (In San Sebastian Festival — competing.) Running time: **93 MIN.**
Antonio .... Carmelo Gomez
Charo .... Ruth Gabriel
Vanesa .... Candela Pena
Rafa .... Karra Elejalde
Lisardo .... Javier Bardem
With: Elvira Minguez, Joseba Apaolaza, Pepon Nieto, Chacho Carreras, Raquel Sanchis.

It's hard to muster up any sympathy for the assorted terrorists, pimps, sluts, junkies and other Basque lowlifes that infest this sordid and dull exercise in profanity.

Instead of any attempt to explain or even justify the motives of ETA separationist thugs, helmer/scripter Imanol Uribe prefers to lense a tedious succession of off-putting sex and drug scenes that are mostly irrelevant to the vague plot.

Antonio, a member of an ETA commando, is more interested in his slutty, unattractive neighbor than in his terrorist mission: to set off a bomb in front of a Madrid police station.

The cops, portrayed as little better than the terrorists, never get wise to him, as the scene shifts between somewhere in the north of Spain and Madrid, and even briefly to Granada for a "romantic" sequence. Along the way, Antonio shoots an inoffensive traffic cop standing on a street corner in Madrid, just to show he's tough.

Carmelo Gomez is rather bland as the terrorist; Ruth Gabriel is unsexy as the slut; and Javier Bardem, as the drugged-up tipster, is just revolting. Pic won the San Sebastian fest's top prize, the Golden Shell. —*Peter Besas*

TENDER HEART

(ALCIZ SHUREK/ COEUR FRAGILE)

(KAZAKH-FRENCH)

A Kazakhfilm Studios (Alma-Ata)/ ACC (Paris) production. (International sales: ACC.) Produced by Anar Kachaganova, Ken Legargeant, Romaine Legargeant. Executive producer, Nina Lavrik. Directed by Ermek Shinarbaev. Screenplay, Leila Akhinjanova. Camera (color), Sergei Kosmanev; editors, Marie-France Poulizac, Khadisha Ourmourzina; art direction, Vladimir Trapeznikof; costume design, Elena Svavilnayo; sound, Sergei Lobanov, Thierry Delor. Reviewed at San Sebastian Film Festival (competing), Sept. 23, 1994. Running time: **84 MIN.**
Aijan .... Natalya Arinbassarova
Adik .... Adilkhan Essenboulatov
Saoule .... Saoule Souleymenova

An aimless 25-year-old's obsessive love for a former ballet star may sound like the stuff of cloying sentimentality, but in "Tender Heart" it's sketched with an emotional starkness and unsettling, melancholy undercurrent that shift it into a less obvious, more acutely felt register. The same poise and control that distinguished Kazakh new wave figure Ermek Shinarbaev's previous work should guide this modest but compelling feature to a run of festival slots.

The first co-production between Kazakhstan and France, film is the fruit of a pact firmed at the 1993 Locarno fest, where Shinarbaev's "A Place on the Tricorne" took the top award.

Graceful opening sequence presents aging ballerina Aijan (Natalya Arinbassarova) giving dance classes in an Alma-Ata theater. Her son is away studying in Paris, and her troubled daughter (Saoule Souleymenova) is on the verge of moving out of their apartment, leaving her mother alone. Returning home one evening, Aijan is assailed by a down-and-out youth, Adik (Adilkhan Essenboulatov), who tries to rape her.

Perhaps sensing a kindred victim of solitude, Aijan takes no legal action, and Adik soon becomes a regular fixture in the apartment building and theater. His advances begin to seem more driven by desperation, and when he lands dead drunk and ill on her doorstep, she finally lets him into her apartment and her life.

From then on, Aijan's reaction wavers between compassion and fear, one minute stabbing Adik after a too-heated display of passion, the next minute dressing the wound. But, certain of eventual humiliation due to their pronounced age difference, she gently pushes him away.

As in "Tricorne," Shinarbaev is less concerned with narrative explicitness than with establishing a climate permeated with sorrow in which writer Leila Akhinjanova's characters are piteously suspended. Some auds may find his style too inert, and his sideline focus on Aijan's daughter as she hits the emotional skids feels distracted. But on the whole, the director's tack of uncovering emotional shadings by maintaining a cool distance from his characters pays dividends.

The same distance is mirrored in Sergei Kosmanev's sedately composed camerawork, frequently framing subjects from the opposite end of dark corridors, or through windows or doors.

Both leads are consistently impressive, with Arinbassarova's regal mix of dignified detachment and pained longing giving the film a potent center. —*David Rooney*

...AND THE EARTH DID NOT SWALLOW HIM

An American Playhouse Theatrical Films presentation of a KPBS/Severo Perez production. Produced by Paul Espinosa. Executive producers, Lindsay Law, Espinosa. Co-producer, Perez. Directed, written by Perez, based on the novel by Tomas Rivera. Camera (color), Virgil Harper; editor, Susan Heick; music, Marcos Loya; production design, Armin Ganz; art direction, Kirk M. Petruccelli, Russell Smith, Peter Stolz; set decoration, Sharon Reed, Norine Joy Francis; costume design, Yvonne Cervantes; sound (Ultra-stereo), Susumu Tokunow; associate producer, Bob Morones; assistant director, John Acevedo; casting, Morones. Reviewed at San Sebastian Film Festival (non-competing), Sept. 19, 1994. Running time: **99 MIN.**
Marcos .... Jose Alcala
Bartolo .... Daniel Valdez
Florentina .... Rose Portillo
Joaquin .... Marco Rodriguez
Dona Rosa .... Lupe Ontiveros
Lupita .... Evelyn Guerrero
Don Cleto .... Sam Vlahos
Lalo .... Art Bonilla
El Mohado .... Sal Lopez
Narrator .... Miguel Rodriguez

The fragmented recollections of a Chicano boy whose family scrapes out a meager living as agricultural laborers in 1950s rural America, "...And the Earth Did Not Swallow Him" strums an absorbing, accomplished but over-familiar riff on immigrant hardship. Soft-pedaling of the story's social injustices, along with slim character definition and a shortage of real dramatic sparks tag this squeaky-clean, innocuous production as unchallenging, easy-viewing fare for general tube situations.

Adapted from Tomas Rivera's autobiographical novel, the film deals primarily with the importance of memory in determining a sense of roots, place and family. Through the eyes of 12-year-old Marcos (Jose Alcala), the members of his family are kept down by their arcane superstitions and by others' exploitation of them. His mother (Rose Portillo) cultivates the spirits of the house and attempts to bargain with God for the return of her beloved son Julian, missing in Korea. His father (Daniel Valdez) takes seasonal work in the orange orchards, trying to retain some dignity despite low pay and appalling conditions.

Because annual trips north for harvesting jobs make it difficult to get a regular education, Marcos is left with an aunt and uncle so he can stay in one school. The grotesque, boozing couple barely feed him and work him into the ground, eventually frightening him into silence after they commit a crime. At school, bullied by WASP boys, Marcos retaliates and is victimized by the principal.

Gradually, pic pieces together a quietly aggrieved mosaic of the family's dismal lot. But the well-performed, rambling reflection lacks an adequate mooring. The anxious wait for Julian goes only halfway toward filling that role. Likewise the exploration of Marcos' rapport with death, his tested faith and his railing against the devil. The stamp of sanitized small-screen entertainment is sealed by pic's mundane narration. —*David Rooney*

LIFE AND DEATH OF THE HOLLYWOOD KID

(HOLLYWOOD KID EU SAENG-AE)

(SOUTH KOREAN)

An Ahn's World Prod. film. Produced by Ahn Dongkyu. Directed, written by Chung Jiyoung, based on a novel by Ahn Junghyo. Camera, Shin Ok-Hyun; editor, Park Sun-Duck; music, Shin Bung-Ha; set design, Cho Youn-Sam; sound, Kim Won-Young. Reviewed at San Sebastian Film Festival (competing), Sept. 21, 1994. Running time: **114 MIN.**
The Hollywood Kid .... Choe Minsu
Yun Myonggil .... Yoko Yongjae
Hyonsuk .... Shin Hyesu
Also Kim Chung-Hyun, Youn Soo-Jin.

This familiar but nonetheless charmingly handled and often poignant yarn is about the adventures of a group of schoolboy film buffs and how cinema evolves into something more important than life itself.

Story starts in the regimented and censored Korea of the 1950s and '60s as a group of boys from a film club sneak into films banned for minors. First half of pic has some touching vignettes, as the boys defy school authorities and even stowaway on a freight train to undertake the first leg of an intended trip to their mecca: Hollywood. The ringleader is henceforth known as the "Hollywood Kid."

But when the filmic aficionados mature, pic takes a different dramatic tack. One of the boys becomes a successful producer, but the Hollywood Kid loses his bearings, managing to pen one script.

The final melodramatics detract from the early part of the film, as pic's sincerity evolves into contrived situations. Pic could garner some interest on the fest circuit and perhaps even draw a small audience in select arthouses. —*Peter Besas*

RIMINI

TEN MONOLOGUES FROM THE LIVES OF THE SERIAL KILLERS

(DUTCH)

A Stichting Zapruder production. (International sales: Rieks Hadders, Amsterdam.) Produced by Ian Kerkhof, Joost van Gelder. Directed, written by Kerkhof, partly based on the writings of Charles Manson, J.G. Ballard, Roberta Lannes, Henry Rollins. Camera (color), Joost van Gelder; editors, Rene A. Hazekamp, Herbert van Drongelen; sound, Fokke van Saane. Reviewed at RiminiCinema Film Festival, Italy (competing), Sept. 29, 1994. (Also in Chicago fest.) Running time: **58 MIN.**
With: Rodney Beddal, Kain, Lorand Sarna, Ian Kerkhof, Mark Bellamy, Pieternel Pouwels, Liz Savage.
Voices: Edmund Emil Kemper, Geto Boys, David Swatling, Ted Bundy, Colman Hogan, Kenneth Bianchi.
(English dialogue)

Drawn from a mix of fictional and factual writings, "Ten Monologues From the Lives of the Serial Killers" brews a heady cocktail of psychopathic and sociopathic experience. Director Ian Kerkhof applies a medley of styles to material that runs from unsettling, purely textual rants to blasts of discomforting imagery. Though it makes no pretense of offering real insight into the mind of a murderer, this killer compendium is a guaranteed attention-getter for festival lineups.

Most disquieting and penetrating of the 10 episodes is one featuring a scratchy home movie of a child playing in a park. Accompanying the seemingly happy footage is an almost tender voiceover in which a sexually abused son recounts how

October 17, 1994 (Cont.)

his need for his father turned to revulsion. His darkening recollections culminate in the father's being slain in the same secluded park, and the son's confession of feeling closer to the butchered corpse than to the living man.

Parental hatred is also a driving force for the opening piece, "Mother's Day." The camera dances a slow, probing circle around the expressionless figure of a chain-smoking convicted killer as his off-screen voice recalls how he beheaded his belittling mother, and the remorse he felt afterward.

Other sequences are more abstract, with the standout a passage from English author J.G. Ballard's "Crash." The excerpt, which fuses love and morbidity in the aftermath of an auto accident, is read against a black screen flashing to a succession of brutal images.

Ballard's "The Atrocity Exhibition" is the source of a murderous litany recited by an inmate as a soul chant, and later as a solemn death count. The Geto Boys' Jeffrey Dahmer-inspired rap, "Murder Avenue," provides a more explicit linguistic shocker, sure to incite adverse reactions.

Also provocative is a murderer's discussion of pornography, and his condemnation of the entry of graphic violence into the average home via television. The diatribe is laid over footage of a naked man (Kerkhof) masturbating while watching an S&M video.

Kerkhof's one foray into slightly more conventional narrative terms — a bitter, soft-spoken Brit's ruminations as he follows a potential victim across a park — reps the film's least distinctive chapter.

Lenser Joost van Gelder's work takes a different approach to each episode, at times stalking his subject from a distance and at others observing from a static position, with shifting light patterns. Editing travels from jumpiness to fluidity, in line with the shifting tones of the monologues. —*David Rooney*

A SILENT TRAVELER
(DE ZWIJGENDE REIZIGER)
(DUTCH — 16mm)

A DNU Film production, in association with NOS-TV. (International sales: Jan Rofekamp/Films Transit, Montreal.) Produced by Rolf Orthel, Fransjoris de Graaf. Directed, written by Ibrahim Selman, in collaboration with Hugo Heinen, Orthel. Camera (color, 16mm), Peter Brugman; editor, Kees Linthorst; music, Dalshad Said, Serbest Zozan, Democrat Taha; art direction, Rebecca Geskus; costume design, Heleen Verhelst; sound, Jac Vleeshouwers. Reviewed at RiminiCinema Film Festival, Italy (competing), Sept. 30, 1994. (Also in Dutch fest.) Running time: **91 MIN.**
Silo .... Abdulkadir Yousif
Simko .... Walid Hadji
Kurde .... Halima Sadik
Moho .... Umet Ali
Azid .... Bangin Abdulkadir
Taho .... Said Ali
    (Kurdish dialogue)

A Dutch production of a Kurdish film shot in Greece, "A Silent Traveler" offers a modest but admirable reaffirmation of the national identity of a people displaced by war. Destined to be applauded more for its rendering of the plight of the Kurds than for its fairly indifferent cinematic qualities, this sincere act of mourning for a nation's independence looks tipped for cultural-institution circuits and fests focusing on human rights issues.

Debuting Iraq-born, Netherlands-based writer/director Ibrahim Selman starts out on docu ground, with a voiceover explaining his objectives and the film's stand-in location, and recalling Kurdistan before the advent of war. He then shifts into narrative mode, with glimpses of life in a mountain village caught in the conflict between Iraqi military authorities and *peshmergas* (guerrilla freedom fighters).

The hostilities touch village shepherd Silo (Abdulkadir Yousif) when soldiers humiliate him and his son, Simko (Walid Hadji), forcing them to slaughter one of their sheep and carry it to the military camp. Reasoning that it's a short step from sheep to human lives, Silo buys a rifle to protect his family.

The weapon, and Simko's violent hatred of the soldiers, don't escape the attention of Moho (Umet Ali), a former villager returned as a police officer. But he refrains from taking action, primarily because of his marital designs on Silo's daughter, Kurde (Halima Sadik). Moho's conflicting feelings of personal loyalty and official duty create an even more volatile situation.

The characters are never quite three-dimensional (thesps are all Kurdish refugees in Athens), but the well-written scenario encapsulates its political and cultural con-

---

cerns most of the time. Only occasionally does Selman's agenda become transparent, as in the forced political consciousness and vaguely feminist tone of an exchange between an assertive Kurd and her uneducated mother. Film's technical level is purely functional.
—*David Rooney*

TORONTO

THE QUALITY OF MERCY
(VOR LAUTER FEIGHEIT GIBT ES KEIN ERBARMEN)
(AUSTRIAN)

A Provinzfilm Intl. production in association with Daniel Zuta Film and Rattlesnake Pictures. Produced by Daniel Zuta, Andreas Gruber. Directed, written by Gruber. Camera (color), Hermann Dunzendorfer; editor, Eva Schneider; music, Peter Androsch; art direction, Susanne Quendler-Kopf; sound, Rudiger Payrhuber. Reviewed at Toronto Film Festival, Sept. 17, 1994. Running time: **100 MIN.**
Frau Karner .... Elfriede Irrall
Fredl Karner .... Rainer Egger
Michail .... Oliver Broumis
Nikolai .... Merab Ninidze
Mitzi Karner .... Kirsten Nehberg
Berghammer ..... Thierry van Werveke
Gendarm Birker .... Rudiger Vogler

Austrian helmer Andreas Gruber takes a distanced, almost academic approach to what might seem like sure-fire dramatic material in "The Quality of Mercy," a fact-based World War II pic that lacks the extra spark necessary to carry it beyond the fest circuit.

At its infrequent best, "The Quality of Mercy" recalls "Schindler's List" in its thoughtful consideration of the ways that war brings out unexpected and inexplicable extremes of good and evil in the least likely people. Unfortunately, there is little that is moving, exciting or enlightening about Gruber's cool, matter-of-fact presentation. Pic is based on a 1945 incident that occurred in the Mauthausen region, where it is still referred to as the Muhlviertler Rabbit Hunt. Only 150 of 500 Russian inmates survive an escape from the Mauthausen concentration camp, and they must contend with the harsh winter, the unfamiliar landscape and, worst of all, the blood lust of nearby villagers pressed into service by the local SS commanders.

Most of the villagers don't need much encouragement by the SS to take part in a take-no-prisoners hunt for the escaped Russian soldiers. Indeed, the majority of the hunters appear to enjoy their work thoroughly.

Fortunately for two fugitive Russians, Michail (Oliver Broumis) and Nikolai (Merab Ninidze), not every villager follows the SS directives. The taciturn but good-hearted Frau Karner (Elfriede Irrall) allows the two men to hide in her family's barn. And her adult son (Rainer Egger), rejected for military duty because of nearsightedness, sees enough of what's going on to help as many Russians as he can.

Pic's first half is so relentlessly dark and repetitiously violent that it nearly numbs the audience with its overkill. Second half, which focuses primarily on the Karners and their efforts to hide the two Russians from SS search parties, is much easier to take. Surprisingly, however, neither half generates much suspense. Best performance comes from Rudiger Vogler as the village police chief who's too decent to take part in the hunt but too ineffectual to act when another villager — appropriately enough, a butcher — marches Russian prisoners out of the jail and summarily executes them. The look of self-disgust on Vogler's face speaks volumes about the impotence of weak-willed virtue in the face of resolute evil.

Hermann Dunzendorfer's excellent color lensing enhances the wintry ambiance. Other tech credits are fine. —*Joe Leydon*

LAMARCA
(BRAZILIAN)

A Producao da Cinema Filmes/Morena Filmes production. (International Sales: Riofilme, Rio de Janeiro.) Produced by Jose Joffily, Mariza Leao. Directed by Sergio Rezende. Screenplay, Rezende, Alfredo Oroz, based on the book "Lamarca Guerilla Captain" by Emiliano Jose Oldack Miranda. Camera (color), Antonio Luiz Mendez; editor, Isabelle Rathery; music, David Tygel; production design, Clovis Bueno; sound, Jorge Saldanha. Reviewed at Toronto Film Festival, Sept. 14, 1994. Running time: **129 MIN.**
Carlos Lamarca .... Paulo Betti
Iara .... Carla Camurati
Fio .... Jose de Abreu
Marcia .... Deborah Evelyn
Zequinha .... Eliezer de Almeida

A basically simple tale of a manhunt in the lush landscape of Brazil's Bahia region some 23 years ago when security forces hunted down a renegade army officer who had become the charismatic leader of a revolutionary group, "Lamarca" is standard fare which has little chance of finding international arthouse acceptance. Co-scripter and director Sergio Rezende handles his theme in a totally straightforward fashion, which makes for surprisingly dull viewing given the potent nature of the material.

Carlos Lamarca, stoically portrayed by Paulo Betti, was a captain in the Brazilian Army who served with the U.N. forces in Suez and returned home a hero. But as he became politicized as the Brazilian government of the day moved further to the right, he eventually deserted the army and joined a revolutionary force dedicated to the violent overthrow of the very establishment he'd previously served.

For about nine months — between December 1970 and September 1971 — following an incident in which the Swiss ambassador to Brazil was kidnapped by Lamarca's group, Lamarca and his followers were relentlessly hunted down. One by one, the members of his unit are either shot down or arrested and viciously tortured to make them reveal their leader's hiding place. Even Lamarca's mistress falls victim to the security crackdown.

Eventually, the defeated revolutionary hightails it to a remote part of Bahia with just one companion, but escape proves impossible.

A few flashbacks, awkwardly positioned at times, flesh out this simple tale with information about Lamarca's past, but otherwise Rezende's film is a flat and overly linear effort. Ironically, when these events were actually taking place, Brazil's *cinema nuovo* movement, led by the late Glauber Rocha, was dazzling the world with its revolutionary pix; a poster for Rocha's "Land in a Trance" is prominently displayed at one point, reminding one how much better Rezende's film might have been.

The numerous gunfights are prosaically staged and seem strangely unconvincing, while true insight into Lamarca's undoubtedly courageous life is lacking. Perfs and production values are adequate, though editor Isabelle Rathery might profitably have tightened the material. —*David Stratton*

HENRY & VERLIN

(CANADIAN)

An Original Motion Picture Co./Act of God Prods. presentation. Produced by John Board. Executive producer, Simon Board. Directed, written by Gary Ledbetter, based on Ken Ledbetter's stories. Camera (color), Paul van der Linden; editor, Miume Jan Eramo; music, Mark Korven; production design, Lillian Sarafinchan; costume design, Nancy McHugh; sound, Eramo; associate producer, Jean Stawarz; casting, Dorothy Gardner. Reviewed at Toronto Film Festival, Sept. 11, 1994. Running time: **87 MIN.**

Henry	Gary Farmer
Verlin	Keegan Macintosh
Minnie	Nancy Beatty
Ferris	Robert Joy
Agnes	Joan Orenstein
Lovejoy	Eric Peterson
Mabel	Margot Kidder
Doc Fisher	David Cronenberg

Sensitive handling of touchy issues and superb acting elevate "Henry & Verlin," a compassionate story of the unusual friendship between a childlike uncle and his equally problematic nephew, a notch or two above the level of sentimental American TV movie melodramas. Though predictable, film's inspirational human values, preaching for greater tolerance and acceptance, should make it accessible to audiences beyond Canadian borders.

Set in rural Ontario during the Great Depression, tale revolves around Verlin (Keegan Macintosh) a 9-year-old boy who doesn't talk. Annoyed by his inability to communicate, Verlin's mother, Minnie (Nancy Beatty), takes the boy to a doctor (self-effacingly played by David Cronenberg), all the while accusing her husband, Ferris (Robert Joy), of passivity and indifference. Things change when Ferris' brother Henry (Gary Farmer) befriends Verlin and pulls him away from his overly protective family. In pic's best sequences, Henry teaches Verlin the small pleasures of life, like rolling cigarettes, stealing chickens and running in the open fields.

Together, they visit Mabel (Margot Kidder), a retired, physically disabled prostitute who lives on the outskirts of town. Soon the three form the kind of intimate bond that exists among social outcasts, much to the resentment of the small town's reactionary forces.

Adapting his father's stories to the screen, writer/director Gary Ledbetter piles up a large number of melodramatic events and obstacles, such as Henry accidentally setting a barn on fire or being beaten by town thugs, to prevent the two misfits from developing their unique attachment.

Pic's emotional convulsions are decisively structured and, happily, only a few scenes have the tear-jerking desperation associated with the genre.

The big, childlike Henry, who bears a resemblance to Lenny in Steinbeck's "Of Mice and Men," is superbly embodied by Farmer, who's particularly effective at conveying the innocent naivete of such a man. The strong chemistry between Farmer and Macintosh, who plays Verlin in a natural manner, promotes the story's likability.

Kidder gives one of her more impressive performances in a flashy role that's extremely well-written. As the parents, Joy and Beatty are stuck with the plot's unconvincing portion, which they carry modestly and credibly.

Handsome tech credits compensate for film's predictability and overly broad brush strokes. Paul van der Linden's crisp lensing and Lillian Sarafinchan's imaginative design are lush and evocative, especially in the big nature scenes that contribute to the feel of a specific time and place. Mark Korven's rousing score also helps.

—*Emanuel Levy*

BOLLYWOOD

(INDIAN)

A Soni-Khan/Cine Creations production. Produced, directed, written by B.J. Khan, based on the book "Show Business" by Shashi Tharoor. Executive producers, John Tu, David Sun, Vimal Soni. Camera (color), Jayvant Pathare; editor, Renu Saluja; music, Tushar Parte; lyrics, Tharoor; production design, Khan; co-producer, Rajinder Singh. Reviewed at Toronto Film Festival, Sept. 16, 1994. Running time: **140 MIN.**

With: Chunky Pandey, Saeed Jaffrey, Dipti Naval, Veena Bidasha, Meera Verma, Mukeshi Rishi, Tariq Yunus.

(English dialogue)

India, which claims to have the world's biggest film industry, produces about 800 features a year, even though audiences are largely confined to Indian communities around the world. The average Indian film is, by Western standards, a cliched combination of corny action sequences and clunky musical routines, hardly worth spoofing in a pic running two hours and 20 minutes. "Bollywood," which sets out to do just that, quickly runs out of comic steam, and, despite being made in English, is unlikely to play outside Indian theaters.

Writer/producer/director/production designer B.J. Khan (mysteriously named Bikramjit "Blondie" Singh in the Toronto fest catalaog) sets out to parody something that's beyond parody, and his evident de-

light at mocking the conventions of mainstream Indian cinema is at best modestly amusing. Result prompted significant walkouts at screening caught.

Based on a book, "Show Business," by Shashi Tharoor, pic establishes a "serious" actor, Ashok, played in the Victor Mature tradition by Chunky Pandey, who decides to go for the money and become a movie star.

All too soon, Ashok is starring in the lavish actioner "Godambo," opposite an aging femme star, and is currying favor with a sex-starved gossip columnist, who likes to interview up-and-coming male talent in her boudoir.

Ashok has a series of mistresses, his wife gives birth to triplets, he becomes involved in a political scandal, and he's involved in an accident during some stunt riding. His story is fleshed out with overly generous samples of the dreadful films in which he appears, which are followed by titles explaining that, in the name of "stamina," sub-plots and numerous songs have already been omitted. A lot more could have been left on the cutting room floor.

Thesping is suitably broad, with well-known actor Saeed Jaffrey slumming it as a self-styled guru. Production values are handsome, although a faulty camera lens seems to have been used in some scenes. Biggest drawback of version caught is the English soundtrack, which is not only inauthentic but often incomprehensible, sounding as if it was recorded at the bottom of a well. —*David Stratton*

FATE

(GERMAN — 16mm)

A German Film and Television Academy (DEFB) production. Executive producer, Christian Hohoff. Co-producer, Fred Kelemen. Directed, written, edited by Kelemen. Camera (color, 16mm), Kelemen; assistant camera, Ann-Katrin Schaffner, Martina Radwan; sound, Alejandra Carmona; assistant director, Regina Krah. Reviewed at Toronto Film Festival, Sept. 12, 1994. Running time: **76 MIN.**

With: Sanja Spengler, Valerij Fedorenko.

The intellectually pretentious "Fate" marks the directorial debut of Fred Kelemen, whose vision of the world is congruent with the notoriously gloomy, angst-ridden tone of earlier German cinema. Though intensely personal, this ponderous pic registers more as an academic exercise than a fully worked-out narrative, mandating strict confinement to the fest and arthouse circuits.

Narrative is made to demonstrate the director's epistemology, announced in the opening title card,

October 17, 1994 (Cont.)

that "the distance between our present life and hell can be as short as a single breath." To this end, story is set on one continuous — and interminable — night, in which the paths of several lonely individuals crisscross.

After being kicked out of another man's house, an accordion player wanders through dark, empty streets, goes into a fountain and issues a shrieking *cri de coeur*, a la Harvey Keitel in "Bad Lieutenant."

When his g.f. refuses to let him into her apartment, he forces his way in, only to discover she was having sex with another man. Shooting the other man, he beats her, while the camera zeros in on her trembling knees. Later on in a bar, a man courts this woman, while another makes sexual advances to her under the table.

Kelemen overstretches the "no communication" thesis — his characters come from different countries, speak different languages and uphold different traditions. But he also wants to show that, despite their marginal solitude, the characters are all bound together by fate and the eternal quest for happiness and moral redemption.

The film's bleak imagery is far more impressive than its minimalist, broken dialogue. Long takes, meant to preserve real time, lend the picture some realism but also make it more tedious.

Ultimately, pic's message — that almost every gesture of love and friendship can turn into misunderstanding, humiliation and defeat — may be more reflective of the director's immature sensibility than of the logical state of his characters and their social networks.

—*Emanuel Levy*

VENICE

SIX DAYS, SIX NIGHTS
(A LA FOLIE)
(FRENCH)

A Lumiere Pictures presentation of a New Light Films/France 3 Cinema production. (International sales: Lumiere Pictures, London.) Produced by Alexandre Arcady. Executive producer, Robert Benmussa. Directed by Diane Kurys. Screenplay, Kurys, Antoine Lacomblez. Camera (color), Fabio Conversi; editor, Luc Barnier; music, Michael Nyman; production design, Tony Egry; costume design, Mic Cheminal; sound (Dolby), Pierre Befve, Claude Villand; paintings, Alain Kleinmann, Ofer Lellouch; works on glass, Bernard Moninot; associate producer, Philippe Lievre; assistant director, Marc Angelo; casting, Pierre Amzallag. Reviewed at Venice Film Festival (competing), Sept. 10, 1994. Running time: **96 MIN.**

Alice	Anne Parillaud
Elsa	Beatrice Dalle
Franck	Patrick Aurignac
Sanders	Bernard Verley
Thomas	Alain Chabat
Raymond	Jean-Claude de Goros
Betty	Marie Guillard

Potentially hot teaming of Gallic stars Anne Parillaud and Beatrice Dalle fails to ignite in "Six Days, Six Nights," a bland triangular drama that ambles along and finally self-destructs. Seventh feature of Diane Kurys, an often sensitive chronicler of female emotions, is a shadow of earlier works like "Entre Nous" and "Love After Love." Offshore arthouse sales loom cool.

Parillaud and Dalle play sisters, Alice and Elsa, who haven't seen each other for two years. One day, Elsa leaves her husband and two kids, and turns up on the Paris doorstep of Alice, a painter with a warm live-in relationship with Franck (newcomer Patrick Aurignac).

Franck doesn't take to Elsa, who starts by tossing her mom's ashes out the window and shows a startling lack of concern for the couple's privacy. When her unfaithful husband, Thomas (Alain Chabat, from comedy group Les Nuls), shows up for a reconciliation, Elsa loses it and almost smashes up the apartment.

Tensions reach a point where even Alice stops defending her sister and makes it clear she must leave. At the last minute, the couple let her stay on, and Elsa starts coming on to Franck, as well as wrecking Alice's studio to prevent her leaving for an exhibition in New York.

After convincing Franck that Alice is emotionally unstable, and bedding him to seal their alliance, Elsa has Alice tied up in her own apartment. A silly coda in Gotham (with Jerryka Soukwell warbling "Here We Go Again" on the soundtrack) finally torpedoes the movie.

For a film that starts out promising an emotional examination of sibling domination, the result is pretty thin stuff. Intimations that the two women may be lesbian ex-lovers rather than sisters (far more plausible given the chalk-and-cheese casting of Parillaud and Dalle) are left tantalizingly hanging, despite several scenes of more-than-sisterly affection.

Also left undeveloped is the midway hint that Alice rather than Elsa may be the more barking of the pair. As the man in the middle, Franck is simply a bouncing ball between the two women, with little to do but look sulky and handsome.

Though Kurys' direction is strangely slack, the main fault lies with the script, which has no clear idea where it's headed and fails to develop either emotional tension or a clear bead on its characters. Dialogue is generally lackluster, with even the mental bond between the two women more taken for granted than clearly spelled out.

Parillaud, looking sweetly sexy throughout, is low-key. Dalle, easily slipping into a white-trash role, pouts a lot. Aurignac looks confused by the whole affair.

Though Fabio Conversi's bright, glossy lensing is always a treat for the eyes, it's wrong for a pic supposedly concerned with destructive passions. Ditto Michael Nyman's music, which is unresponsive to the currents onscreen.

English title is virtually meaningless, given the movie's disregard of any fixed time span. The French original, "A La Folie," gets closer to describing things, though not in the sense that Kurys presumably intended.

—*Derek Elley*

LOADED
(BRITISH-NEW ZEALAND)

A British Screen/New Zealand Film Commission presentation, in association with the British Film Institute, Channel 4 and Geissendorfer Film, of a Strawberry Vale (London)/The Movie Partners (Auckland) production. (International sales: BFI, London.) Produced by David Hazlett, Caroline Hewitt (U.K.), John Maynard, Bridget Ikin (N.Z.). Executive producers, Ben Gibson, Hans W. Geissendorfer. Directed, written by Anna Campion. Camera (Fujicolor; prints by Metrocolor), Alan Almond; editor, John Gilbert; music, Simon Fisher Turner; additional music, Angela Conway, Bruce Gilbert; production design, Alistair Kay; art direction, James Hambidge; costume design, Stewart Meacham; sound (Dolby), Peter Lindsay; assistant director, Max Keene. Reviewed at Venice Film Festival (Window on Images), Sept. 4, 1994. Running time: **104 MIN.**

Neil	Oliver Milburn
Giles	Nick Patrick
Rose	Catherine McCormack
Zita	Thandie Newton
Lionel	Matthew Eggleton
Lance	Danny Cunningham
Charlotte	Biddy Hodson

With: Dearbhla Molloy, Caleb Lloyd, Joe Gecks.

"Loaded" falls flat on its face early on and lies there for 100-odd minutes. Weakly scripted, lacklusterly acted tale of a bunch of young, disillusioned Brits flounders around as much as its characters. Commercial chances look grim.

Pic, which shot under the title "Bloody Weekend," is first feature by U.K.-based Anna Campion, sibling of Kiwi director Jane, following two shorts. Billed as the first Anglo-N.Z. co-production, it's produced on the latter side by Bridget Ikin ("An Angel at My Table," "Crush") and John Maynard ("The Navigator," "Sweetie"), who came in after the movie was developed by the British Film Institute. Post-production was done in New Zealand.

Central character of the sextet is Neil (Oliver Milburn), who's meeting a group of friends at a country house for a weekend of moviemaking. There's Neil's insecure g.f., Rose, who's deciding when to lose her virginity; an independent young black woman, Zita; bespectacled Giles, who collects pix of psychos; and Lance and his self-assured squeeze, Charlotte. They're later joined by the earnest Lionel, who sees the video as his passport to a career.

Aside from Neil, who's alienated from his mother's affections, and Zita (Thandie Newton), who's the strongest of the group, most of the kids are vapidly drawn, with few distinctive characteristics, and come over as unattractive and spoiled. The video they work on — some kind of Celtic horror-fantasy — looks as feeble as their lives.

After some sophomoric experimentation with acid, Neil and Lance drive out for cigarettes and accidentally kill Lionel on his motorbike. Rest of the pic is taken up with the kids burying his body in the woods and moping around in an orgy of self-pity.

Campion's failure to evoke any sympathy or interest in her characters holes the movie below the waterline early on. Coupled with direction best described as loose, and a generally flat visual style, there's not much for audiences to hang onto when the drama cranks up later on.

Aside from Newton ("Flirting," "Young Americans"), as the self-possessed Zita, and Catherine McCormack as Rose, both of whom make small impressions, performances by the rest of the freshman cast are blah. —*Derek Elley*

THE TIT AND THE MOON
(LA TETA I LA LUNA)
(SPANISH-FRENCH)

A Lolafilms (Barcelona), Cartel (Madrid)/Hugo Films (Paris) production. (International sales: Iberoamericana Films, Madrid.) Executive producer, Andres Vicente Gomez. Co-producers, Xavier Gelin, Stephane Marsil. Directed by Bigas Luna. Screenplay, Cuca Canals, Luna. Camera (color, Panavision widescreen), Jose Luis Alcaine; editor, Carmen Frias; music, Nicola Piovani; art direction, Aime Deude; costume design, Patricia Monne; sound (Dolby), Marc Antoine Beldent; special effects, Juan Ramon Molina; associate producers, Manuel Lombardero, Eduardo Campoy; casting, Consol Tura. Reviewed at Venice Film Festival (competing), Sept. 7, 1994. Running time: **88 MIN.**

With: Mathilda May, Gerard Darmon, Miguel Poveda, Biel Duran, Abel Folk, Laura Mana, Genis Sanchez.

October 17, 1994 (Cont.)

Mammaries light the corners of Catalan director Bigas Luna's mind if this paean to womanly orbs is any indication. A featherweight but frequently charming fairy tale about three men enamored of the same woman, "The Tit and the Moon" initially promises something of a return, after the lame bawdiness of "Golden Balls," to the wit and verve of "Jamon, Jamon," arguably Luna's best film to date. Though the promise goes a little awry along the way, this good-natured romp packs enough piquancy and earthy humor to help it bust in on selected international markets.

Opening sequence is an attention-getter, taking in the climactic moments of the Catalan sport of forming a human tower. The job of 9-year-old Tete (Biel Duran) is to climb to the top tier. Despite a fierce pep talk from his machismo-spouting father (Abel Folk), Tete can't muster the courage to scale the final rungs, and the tower topples.

Providing the story's narrative voice, Tete amusingly bemoans the arrival of his baby brother as something akin to a greedy piglet lapping up his mother's milk, which he feels should be going his way. Determined to find a replacement, he makes a plaintive appeal to the moon to find him a breast to call his own. A suitable pair hits town attached to French cabaret performer Estrellita (Mathilda May), the so-called Queen of Stuttgart, who has an act with her besotted, jealous husband Maurice (Gerard Darmon).

Romantic competition comes from serenading trailer-park electrician Miquel (Miguel Poveda). But Tete's gift to Estrellita of a pet frog prompts her — in the pic's most outrageous moment — literally to open her maternal faucet and quench the boy's thirst.

When the French couple's act is unveiled — a symphony of flaming flatulence and rectal cannon tricks from Maurice, with Estrellita as ballerina backup — the pic's gentle equilibrium and vaguely magical air take a tumble, from which it never fully recovers.

Though the cast is uniformly agreeable, with the frequently disrobed May a breezy delight, diminutive Duran provides pic's most winning element. His innocently funny running commentary shifts attention from the story's insubstantial nature and encourages audiences to go with its libertarian spirit as it pushes the case for all-out pursuit of sensual pleasure.

Similar to his work on "Jamon, Jamon," cinematographer Jose Luis Alcaine creates a glowing widescreen canvas of vivid color. Visual invention is consistently on view, from a clothesline strung with Estrellita's rainbow of lingerie, through the garish circus atmosphere of the cabaret, to the sea of red, white and black team colors in the prologue and triumphant coda, in which Tete shimmies up the human tower.

—*David Rooney*

IN THE HEAT OF THE SUN

(YANGGUANG CANLAN DE RIZI)

(HONG KONG-TAIWANESE-CHINESE)

A King's Video (Taiwan)/Star City Film & TV Development (China) presentation of a Dragon Film Intl. (Hong Kong) production, in association with China Film Co-production Corp. (International sales: Golden Harvest, H.K.) Produced by Ki Po, Hsu An-chin, Guo Youliang. Executive producers, Manfred Wong, Liu Xiaoqing. Directed, written by Jiang Wen, from the novella "Dongwu Xiongmeng" ("Wild Beasts") by Wang Shuo. Camera (color), Gu Changwei; editor, Zhou Ying; music, Guo Wenjing; art direction, Chen Haozhong; costume design, Liu Huiping; sound (Dolby), Gu Changning, Manfred Arbter; associate producers, Fan Chien-kung, Tsang Hing-sun, Zhao Jingwei; assistant directors, Zhang Hua, Ma Wenzhong. Reviewed at Venice Film Festival (competing), Sept. 9, 1994. Running time: 139 MIN.

Ma Xiaojun (Monkey)	Xia Yu
Mi Lan	Ning Jing
Liu Yiku	Geng Le
Liu Sitian	Shang Nan
Yu Beipei	Tao Hong

With: Dai Xiaopo, Wang Hai, Siqin Gaowa, Wang Xueqin, Fang Xiaogang, Wang Shuo.
(Mandarin Chinese dialogue)

Mainland Chinese star Jiang Wen ("Red Sorghum," "Hibiscus Town") makes an engaging directing bow with "In the Heat of the Sun," a semi-autobiographical coming-of-age pic set in Cultural Revolution China whose only major fault is its fulsome running time. Full of well-observed characters, and actorly to a degree, "Sun" could cast a modest shadow over arty wickets with half an hour sheared.

Movie is based on a 1991 novella by well-known bad-boy writer Wang Shuo, though Jiang's script is more of a free interpretation, changing some 70% of the original and mixing in a mass of personal memories. (Even the central character/narrator's nickname, "Monkey," was Jiang's own teenage moniker.) It's not Jiang's first shot at scripting: He previously worked uncredited on some pix in which he starred — "Red Sorghum," "Li Lianying, the Imperial Eunuch" and "Black Snow."

Characters are intro'd in 1969, as the boys' military fathers are shipped out in a troop plane to spread Chairman Mao's doctrine. Cut to the early '70s, and a hot summer in Peking: The bunch are in their mid-teens, living in a military compound with time on their hands for skipping school, getting into brawls and eyeing girls.

Leader is the assured Liu Yiku (Geng Le), who seems to be sleeping with the devil-may-care Yu Beipei (Tao Hong). The younger Monkey Ma (Xia Yu) also gets the come-on from her, but is obsessed with an older girl, Mi Lan (Ning Jing).

Pic's main problem is that its episodic structure, which essentially boils down to a last-summer, rite-of-passage movie, is too fragile to go two-hours plus. (Initial cut was 220 minutes, enough for a miniseries, which remains an option, according to producers.) Jiang consciously avoids the cliches of Cultural Revolution-set movies, with virtually none of the usual Maoist book-waving and demos, but he doesn't come up with a strong enough central narrative on which to hang the series of vignettes.

Though the pic has a hazy feel, as if this is how Ma remembers things rather than how they actually happened, a Brechtian device in which the action freezes while the narrator clears his mind comes too late for proper assimilation.

Still, there's a freshness to the characters (especially the two independent-minded girls), and sexual frankness (a shower scene with the boys, a brief topless shot of actress Ning), that tread new ground for a Mainland China-shot movie. Scenes of rival-gang hooliganism, plus a bold sequence of cadres privately viewing a Western t&a movie, are also eye-opening in the same context.

As in many actor-helmed items, thesps are given plenty of rein, sometimes at the expense of overall pacing and structure. But on an individual level, perfs are fine and casting top-drawer. As Monkey Ma, 17-year-old high school student Xia has both an uncanny resemblance to Jiang himself and a likable combination of insolence and innocence.

Standout perf comes from Ning (the striking lead in "Red Firecracker, Green Firecracker"), enigmatic as the object of Ma's infatuation. Newcomer Tao etches memorable support as the free-thinking tease Yu. Well-known Siqin Gaowa pops up in two scenes as Ma's mom.

Ace lenser Gu Changwei ("Judou," "Farewell My Concubine") bathes the pic in a gorgeous late-afternoon, summery glow, with play of light and shadow. (Chinese title literally means "Days of Brilliant Sunlight.") Romantic scoring, based on a well-known theme from Italo opera "Cavalleria Rusticana," may send mixed signals to Western auds, though the director says music of this kind was an essential component of his youth.

End crawl bears a special thanks to Volker Schloendorff, boss of Germany's Babelsberg Studios, where final mixing was done. Most of the $2 million budget on the three-way Chinese co-production was raised from Hong Kong. —*Derek Elley*

THE NIGHT AND THE MOMENT

(BRITISH-FRENCH-ITALIAN)

A Miramax release (in U.S.) of a Ulysse Entertainment presentation of an Arthur Pictures (U.K.)/SFP Cinema (France)/Cecchi Gori Group Tiger Cinematografica (Italy) production, with participation of Paca Finance Conseils and Canal Plus. (International sales: MCEG Sterling, Los Angeles.) Produced by Pierre Novat, Boudjemaa Dahmane. Executive producers, Philippe Martinez, Ernst Goldschmidt. Directed by Anna Maria Tato. Screenplay, Jean-Claude Carriere, Tato, based on the novel "La Nuit et le moment" by Claude-Prosper de Jolyot Crebillon. Camera (color), Giuseppe Rotunno; editor, Ruggero Mastroianni; music, Ennio Morricone; production design, Richard Cunin, Arianna Attaom; costume design, Gabriella Pescucci; sound (Dolby), David Stephenson; associate producers, Bernard Vilgrain, Marina Gefter; assistant director, Patrick Nicolini. Reviewed at Venice Film Festival (Venetian Nights), Sept. 4, 1994. Running time: 90 MIN.

The Writer	Willem Dafoe
The Marquise	Lena Olin
Julie	Miranda Richardson
The Governor	Jean-Claude Carriere
Armande	Carole Richert
Justine	Christine Sireyzol
Official	Guy Verame
Prison Guard	Ivan Bacciocchi

(English dialogue)

Presenting ample evidence of the margin for disaster in filmic Europuddings, "The Night and the Moment" throws together an Italian director, French source material and a high-caliber English-speaking cast with no sign of the various sensibilities ever becoming acquainted. Battling against turgid repartee, glaring miscasting and a directorial void, stars Willem Dafoe, Lena Olin and Miranda Richardson can do little to bring this moribund erotic frock piece to life. Theatrical light of day looks to be momentary at best.

Comparison with Stephen Frears' "Dangerous Liaisons" will be inevitable and brutal. Taken from a novel by licentious 18th-century scribe Crebillon, the story is basically a duel of words between a wily, libertine writer (Dafoe) and

October 17, 1994 (Cont.)

an alluring noblewoman (Olin), with seduction the unhurried goal.

A guest at her chateau, the writer slips into her boudoir after lights-out and launches into the first of numbing discourses on the nature of love. In no rush to hit the hay, she coaxes him to recount some of his amorous escapades with the other guests. To Ennio Morricone's monotonously rambunctious, faux-classical score, the pic recaps his conquest of over-eager Armande (Carole Richert), followed by a more diverting hit on high-minded Julie (Miranda Richardson).

More interesting are his recollections of time spent in prison for his immoral writings and dangerous acquaintances. Pic stokes a modicum of curiosity as to the identity of the woman in the next cell. Communicating with him unseen through a hole in the wall, her mysteriousness sparks something closer to love than to the conquering spirit in him.

A further sign of life comes by way of the prison governor (playfully limned by Jean-Claude Carriere, long-term Luis Bunuel collaborator and co-scripter of this doozy).

The writer's gradual seduction of the marquise is ploddingly charted in lifeless, literary dialogue. When the pair finally make whoopee, high-art lensing helps kill whatever shreds of credible passion have been worked up.

Aside from Carriere, Olin emerges with the lion's share of dignity. Her regal bearing goes a long way toward masking her unsuitability for the role. Appearing stifled by his wardrobe and dialogue, Dafoe often seems to be winking at the audience, with little concern for keeping his contempo demeanor locked away. Richardson looks no less out of place, but even more uncomfortable.

Italo director/co-writer Anna Maria Tato brings no definitive stamp to the material, and little guidance to the actors. Instead, she surrounds herself with prestige contributors like Morricone and lensman Giuseppe Rotunno, both of whom work under par. Costumer Gabriella Pescucci's threads are impressive, but largely squandered within a production design that's short on scope, giving the whole outing a pinched, theatrical feel.

—*David Rooney*

FORGET ME

(OUBLIE-MOI)

(FRENCH)

A Les Films Alain Sarde production. (International sales: Studio Canal Plus, France.) Produced by Sarde. Directed by Noemie Lvovsky. Screenplay, Sophie Fillieres, Emmanuel Salinger, Marc Cholodenko, from a story by Lvovsky. Camera (color), Jean-Marc Fabre; editor, Jennifer Auge; music, Andrew Dickson; art direction, Emmanuel de Chauvigny; costume design, Francoise Clavel; sound, Ludovic Henault. Reviewed at Venice Film Festival (Window on Images), Sept. 10, 1994. Running time: **95 MIN.**

Nathalie .... Valeria Bruni Tedeschi
Christelle .... Emmanuelle Devos
Eric .... Laurent Grevill
Antoine .... Emmanuel Salinger
Fabrice .... Philippe Torreton
Denis .... Olivier Pinalie

"**F**orget Me" will divide viewers into two camps: Those who find the heroine, played by Valeria Bruni Tedeschi, an unbearably tiresome neurotic inventing passionate love affairs, and those who find her a sincerely befuddled woman in love, worthy of sympathy. Perf is eye-catching in either case. This first feature by Noemie Lvovsky shows great energy in capturing the world of young Parisians living life to the hilt on a shoestring. The Alain Sarde production could become a minor cult item among believers, though its reception offshore remains a question mark.

Nathalie (Bruni Tedeschi) is obsessed with Eric (Laurent Grevill), a hospital orderly who has had enough of her. She refuses to be cast off, and persecutes him at home and at work. Meanwhile, she dumps the nice boy she lives with, Antoine (Emmanuel Salinger). He's deeply hurt and, when she leaves him, tells her he'll never see her again.

Rebuffed by Eric, Nathalie next alienates her best (and only) friend, Christelle (Emmanuelle Devos), by making a covert play for her boyfriend, Fabrice (Philippe Torreton). But Fabrice is as neurotic as she is, and kicks her out of bed before their betrayal is consummated. Brokenhearted and confused, Nathalie begins to sink into the depths of depravity. Only part of the audience will feel sorry about her decline.

Love or hate her character, Bruni Tedeschi (who bears little resemblance to her sister, Italian model Carla Bruni) is what makes "Forget Me" tick. She injects the hip script with nonstop nervous energy and turns in a shrill but believable perf as a middle-class girl who makes love her life. Her pestering phone calls to friends and lovers have a comic edge just this side of pathos, an ambiguity that Lvovsky plays on skillfully.

Rest of cast is on target, and technical credits are fine.

—*Deborah Young*

ACCUMULATOR 1

(AKUMULATOR 1)

(CZECH)

A Heureka Film production. Produced by Petr Soukup. Executive producer, Premysl Prazsky. Directed by Jan Sverak. Screenplay, Jan Slovak, Jan Sverak, Zdenek Sverak. Camera (color), F. A. Brabec; editor, Alois Fisarek; music, Ondrej Soukup, Jiri Svoboda; art direction, Milos Kohout; costume design, Jaroslava Pecharova; sound (Dolby), Zbynek Mikulik. Reviewed at Venice Film Festival (Critics' Week), Sept. 5, 1994. Running time: **102 MIN.**

Olda .... Petr Forman
Anna .... Edita Brychta
Fisarek .... Zdenek Sverak
With: Marian Labuda, Boleslav Polivka, Tereza Pergnerova, Jiri Kodet.

Young Czech helmer Jan Sverak radically changes direction after his Oscar-nominated debut feature, "The Elementary School," with the distinctive techno-vampire yarn "Accumulator 1." Though its tongue-in-cheekiness sometimes runs to the absurd, this cautionary tale about the horror lurking behind the average TV screen should connect with festival audiences and possibly score some fringe play on the arthouse circuit. The film is also a solid showcase for Czech f/x expertise.

Soon after being interviewed on a TV current affairs show, couch potato Olda (Petr Forman, son of director Milos) is overcome by a massive wave of lethargy. Whisked to hospital, he stumps doctors, but a mysterious natural healer, Fisarek (Zdenek Sverak, co-scripter and father of helmer Jan), diagnoses his ailment as chronic loss of energy.

Fisarek trains Olda to recharge his energy levels by sapping the life force from trees, art and people, with children tapped as especially powerful conduits.

He encourages him to bolster his strength through sex, sending him to a ritzy, Turkish bath-type establishment for some tantric instruction from nubile women. But his energy keeps dissipating any time he gets close to a TV screen.

Olda takes up with comely dentist Anna (Edita Brychta), whose father died of the same affliction, and their first sack session proves an earth-shaker when a mouse trap sets off a TV remote. Olda's energy is sucked out and beamed into the stratosphere where it's bounced off a satellite to give a surge of power to a porn program spoofing Snow White.

Now with love on his mind, Olda fights back, transforming himself into an anti-tube terrorist and buying up remote controls, which he handles like pistols.

Using skills he learned from Fisarek, he embarks on a plan to flood the evil screen with more energy than it can handle.

Sverak orchestrates the giddy plot twists at a sufficiently brisk clip to ensure that occasional dips in narrative clarity are relatively unnoticed. Humor is often on the clutzy side, but appealing nonetheless, and pic's message, pushing the pursuit of human contact and cultural wealth over facile entertainment, should find wide acceptance.

One of the script's best and most frequent devices is to travel inside its subject. Olda's erratic heartbeat is monitored via a roller-coaster tour of his arteries, while a journey beyond the small screen wittily reveals a world populated by alter egos of the energy vampire's victims, where newscasts, nature docus, talkshows, action movies and porno pix all co-exist in cramped quarters.

F. A. Brabec's keen camera and moody lighting, alternating blues and oranges, do ample justice to the crafty production design. Other tech contributions, including a thunderous, symphonic score, are pro.

—*David Rooney*

THE PEACOCKS

(I PAVONI)

(ITALIAN)

An Istituto Luce release of an A.M.A. Film production, in association with Sacis and Silvio Berlusconi Communications. Produced by Gianni Minervini. Directed by Luciano Manuzzi. Screenplay, Claudio Lizza, Manuzzi; camera (color), Claudio Cirillo; editor, Nino Baragli; art direction, Gianni Silvestri; costumes, Francesco Panni. Reviewed at Cinecitta, Aug. 25, 1994. In the Venice Film Festival — Special Events. Running time: **104 MIN.**
 With: Rinaldo Rocco, Nicola Russo, Sabrina Knaflitz, Vincenzo Crivello, Max Malatesta, Flavio Albanese, Victor Cavallo, Benedetta Buccellato, Ivano Marescotti.

"The Peacocks" reconstructs, on a barely fictionalized level, a bloodcurdling crime that captured media attention in Italy a few years ago: The brutal slaying of a well-to-do couple by their teenage son, whose only aim was to collect his inheritance early. Helmer Luciano Manuzzi meticulously dramatizes the crime from the boy's p.o.v. without, however, attempting a deep psychological reading of his personality. The film is as intriguing as a news story, but also curiously distant from its distasteful subject. After bowing in Venice's Special Events sidebar, it could make a profitable run in Italy based on the story's notoriety and relative freshness. Offshore, fests and arthouse programmers will find it worth a look.

Vittorio (Rinaldo Rocco) is a snobbish layabout whose main interest in life is spending money on clothes. His father has grown rich through hard work at the family's fish-processing plant. Foolishly, he has spared his son the rigors of work, and together with the boy's loving, slavish mother spoiled him rotten.

For fun, Vittorio takes his pals to an expensive eatery and pays the bill with a gold watch. His band of latter-day "vitelloni" includes a gas station attendant and a young fisherman. Under Vittorio's diabolic goading, Paolo, a gentle innocent (Nicola Russo), leaves his job, buys a car he can't afford, attempts to rape a schoolmate and generally sinks into perdition.

Vittorio and his band amble from bar to disco, shoe store to restaurant. Pic communicates the numbing boredom of their lives all too well. Inevitably, the money runs out, and Vittorio hits on a daring plan to bump off his harmless folks and collect the inheritance he arrogantly considers his own.

For sheer audacity, the scheme is staggering. Manuzzi records no emotion or hesitation on Vittorio's part as the appointed night approaches. His three buddies, who have agreed to help him for $7,000 each, crack under the strain of waiting for his unsuspecting parents to come home, but Vittorio has the conscience of a Nazi exterminator. The dark deed is done in a long, sickening scuffle, and the boys take off for the disco to unwind.

Despite a sharp, surprisingly mature perf by newcomer Rocco as the dandyish parent-killer, Vittorio is basically an unredeemed negative figure with whom no sane viewer can identify. By concentrating more on Vittorio's social environment than his inner workings, "Peacocks" is left with a big black hole at its center. Not even his lady lawyer — called in after he has been arrested and jailed — can bear him, and director Manuzzi doesn't try to hide his repugnance.

Film concludes with Vittorio behind bars, implying that justice, at least, has been served. Interestingly, no mention is made of the scandal that rocked the public shortly after the real-life murderer's arrest, when it was discovered that he had become a hero to scores of youngsters (who still regularly write admiring letters to him).

Shot on Italy's Adriatic coast, pic is heavy on atmosphere, conjured up by Claudio Cirillo's tasteful cinematography and Gianni Silvestri's rich but soulless sets.

—*Deborah Young*

TOKYO

MUEN AND RID

(AMDAENG MUEN KAB NAI RID)

(THAI)

A Five Stars Production Co. Ltd./ Cherdchai Prods. production. Executive producer, Chareon Iamphungporn. Directed by Cherd Songsri. Screenplay, Thom Thathree, Channipa. Camera (color), Anupap Buachand; editor, M.L. Warapa Ukris; music, Chamras Sewatapom; art direction, Songsri; sound (Dolby), Niwat Samniangsanor. Reviewed at Tokyo Film Festival, Kyoto, Sept. 25, 1994. Running time: **129 MIN.**
 With: Jintara Sukaphat, Santisuk Promsiri, Ron Rittichai, Duangdao Charuchinda, Man Theerapol.

Thailand's premier director, Cherd Songsri, has surpassed himself with "Muen and Rid," a film of such high quality it deserves much more than the limited release it is likely to have. Songsri's story of true love and one woman's eventually successful struggle for women's rights in Thailand in 1865 is based on a true story. Despite a two-hour plus running time and a few technical glitches, pic is convincingly and charmingly acted, with lovely scenery, crisp photography and a compelling plotline. Film is already the biggest hit in Thai history.

The story revolves around Amdang Muen, the real-life women's rights advocate portrayed with innocence, sincerity and strength by actress Jintara Sukaphat (Thailand's most popular actress, seen by Western audiences in "Good Morning Vietnam").

Muen's first victory is winning the right (from both her family and the head monk) to learn to read.

When she falls in love, and later refuses to be sold by her family to become an extra wife (essentially a concubine) of rich, married man Poo, the consequences change not only her life but the status of all contemporary and future Thai women. Having already professed her love to Buddhist monk Rid, who will not renounce his vows — which include celibacy — she violently refuses advances by her "owner" (it is pointed out later that she is, in fact, property), runs away from him several times and ultimately fakes her own drowning in order to escape.

Rid hears of Muen's drowning and becomes desolate when he believes her dead. He decides — too late, he thinks — to renounce his vows and returns home to find Muen there. The two get married. Problem is that Muen is technically already married, though the marriage has never been consummated. She fights the legal system to gain her freedom from the arrangement and winds up in jail. Eventually she petitions King Rama IV, and he not only pardons her and validates her marriage to Rid, but also changes the law whereby men are allowed to sell or own girls and women.

As Rid, Santisuk Promsiri conveys Buddhist tranquility without being boring, and discovers earthly love and passion without being campy. Supporting roles are strong as well.

Tech aspects contain a few subpar glitches, but for the lion's share of the film are nearly impeccable.

—*Karen Regelman*

DROP SQUAD

A Gramercy Pictures release of a Spike Lee presentation of a 40 Acres & a Mule Filmworks production. Produced by Shelby Stone, Butch Robinson. Executive producer, Lee. Directed by D. Clark Johnson. Screenplay by Johnson and Robinson, based on a story by David Taylor. Camera (color), Ken Kelsch; editor, Kevin Lee; music, Mike Bearden; production design, Ina Mayhew; art director, Paul Weathered; costume design, Darlene Jackson; sound (Dolby), Matthew Price; assistant director, David Taylor; casting, Jaki Brown-Carmen. Reviewed at Sunset Screening Room, L.A., Oct. 18, 1994. MPAA Rating: R. Running time: **86 MIN.**

Bruford Jackson Jr.	Eriq LaSalle
Rocky Seavers	Vondie Curtis-Hall
Garvey	Ving Rhames
June Vanderpool	Kasi Lemmons
XB	Leonard Thomas
Stokely	Eric A. Payne
Mali	Vanessa Williams
Trevor	Michael Ralph
Huey	Billy Williams
Lenora Jamison	Nicole Powell
Berl (Flip) Mangum	Afemo Omilami
Spike Lee	himself

Part thriller, part social satire, "Drop Squad" is never quite on secure enough ground to translate ambition into entertainment. The decidedly Afrocentric tale tries hard to reach a wider audience, but falls short of finding the channel to make its themes universal. Without obvious appeal to a non-ethnic audience, pic should score some initial niche interest in fast playoff and promptly segue into domestic ancillary exploitation.

The title refers to a mythical band whose edict is to grab black brothers and sisters who've lost their way and turned their backs on their heritage. It's an acronym for Deprogramming and Restoration of Pride.

The latest candidate is an ad exec named Bruford Jamison (Eric LaSalle). His sister is alarmed that his campaigns for products aimed at blacks use gross stereotypes insensitive to women, men and decency. She's not wrong.

One, a fast-food promo, enlists two obese choir members, and no less than "Drop" exec producer Spike Lee, to shuck and jive for a chicken franchise and its product, the Gospelpak. It leaves friends and relatives gasping, but Bruford simply sees it as a way to sell a product.

The problem is not so much the issue as the tone. The obviousness of the situation cries out for some humor, but director/co-writer David Johnson approaches the text as if it were sacred. The rich opportunities for irony are totally squandered.

This problem is further demonstrated by the group doing the "brain cleansing." Apparently in operation for eight years, its initial methods and philosophy have been sullied with time.

Rocky (Vondie Curtis-Hall), its founder, is concerned that the group's approach is becoming increasingly violent and sloppy. Garvey (Ving Rhames) responds that the times dictate the more aggressive behavior. The parallel crisis surely harks back to the biblical adage, "Physician, heal thyself."

While specifically centered on the black community, the situations in which a culture is subsumed are relevant to any minority besieged by the American melting-pot mindset. Ultimately, Bruford's sin has less to do with color than just plain friendship. His attitude and demeanor toward a childhood buddy are far more offensive than any of the crimes he's committed in the name of advertising.

Director Johnson has an adroit style when his story is on the move. However, when confronted with relatively static exposition, the drama goes flat. The absence of wit, at times, is truly deadly to the story's texture.

The ensemble cast is uniformly good despite roles of limited dimension. LaSalle quite effectively gets across his bewilderment at being singled out for the treatment. Additionally, there's a nice interplay between Curtis-Hall and Rhames as comrades separated by the process, but not the intent, of "Drop" activities.

"Drop Squad's" gritty, documentary style is deceiving. The currents running beneath its surface are much deeper than the filmmakers' ability to convey them, and that is its crime. —*Leonard Klady*

STARGATE

An MGM release of a Mario Kassar presentation of a Studio Canal Plus/ Centropolis production in association with Carolco Pictures. Produced by Joel Michaels, Oliver Eberle, Dean Devlin. Executive producer, Kassar. Co-producer, Ute Emmerich. Directed by Roland Emmerich. Screenplay, Devlin, Roland Emmerich. Camera (Deluxe, widescreen), Karl Walter Lindenlaub; editors, Michael Duthie, Derek Brechin; music, David Arnold; production design, Holger Gross; art direction, Peter Murton, Frank Bollinger; costume design, Joseph Porro; sound (Dolby), David Ronne; digital/visual effects supervisor, Jeffrey Okun; special creature effects, Patrick Tatopoulos; Egyptology consultant, Dr. Stuart Smith; assistant director, Steve Love; casting, April Webster. Reviewed at Avco Cinema, Westwood, Oct. 14, 1994. MPAA Rating: PG-13. Running time: **120 MIN.**

Col. Jack O'Neil	Kurt Russell
Dr. Daniel Jackson	James Spader
Ra	Jaye Davidson
Catherine	Viveca Lindfors
Skaara	Alexis Cruz
Sha'uri	Mili Avital
General W.O. West	Leon Rippy
Lt. Kawalsky	John Diehl
Kasuf	Erick Avari

"Stargate" has one of those plots that naturally causes people to roll their

eyes. **Commercial prospects for this curiously unabsorbing yarn border on the dire.**

What this juvenile adventure has in spades is special effects and picturesque locations. What it lacks is an emotional link to make the Saturday afternoon he-man posturing palatable, or at least bearable. Its core appeal is to preteens, and considering its mammoth budget ($60 million-$70 million), half-price tickets won't be enough to part the enveloping sea of red ink.

The setup occurs in Giza, Egypt, circa 1928. An archaeological expedition unearths a giant ring inscribed with hieroglyphs of unknown origin and meaning. We're promptly propelled into the present, where Egyptologist Dr. Daniel Jackson (James Spader) is telling a learned, if disbelieving, crowd that the pyramids could not possibly have been built by man. Only one listener stays behind, offering him the job of translating an ancient stone lodged in a secret and remote military complex. It is, of course, the piece seen at the beginning. Never mind how it was transported across the ocean or its whereabouts for most of this century.

Suffice it to say that the symbols turn out to be a map rather than a language. The ring is a portal to another dimension — an entrance to the land of the true builders of one of the seven wonders. Are your eyes spinning yet?

Breaking the impenetrable code leads to a military probe commanded by former basket case Col. Jack O'Neil (Kurt Russell). Jackson tags along as interpreter and on the other side discovers something akin to "Lawrence of Arabia" outtakes with a pinch of "The Ten Commandments" and a dash of the "Star Wars" trilogy.

The inhabitants of this world are biblical-style slaves, the ruler a galactic hermaphrodite (Jaye Davidson). It's all downhill from there. The oppressed workers, with the help of the soldiers and scientist, rise up to quell the evil oppressor. It's pretty standard, predictable stuff.

Director Roland Emmerich pushes the obvious plot buttons, turns up the florid score and injects appropriate panoramas. It's a textbook scenario that creaks with age and whose lack of originality cannot be obscured with visual craft.

Pic should be more visceral. But every time the story gets perilously close to an emotional moment, the focus shifts abruptly to some corny bit of action. O'Neil never truly confronts the dark past of a dead son, and Jackson's

budding relationship with a slave (Mili Avital) is chaste beyond belief.

The acting challenge is simply to keep a straight face and not look like a total imbecile. It's arguable that anyone succeeds at the task.

And despite the ever-present, state-of-the-art technology, there's hardly a single indelible image in the course of two hours. One walks away uncertain whether there is a film called "Stargate," or if it was merely a dream composed of badly remembered movie cliches.

—*Leonard Klady*

A PASSION TO KILL

An A-Pix Entertainment release of a Rysher Entertainment presentation of a Bruce Cohn Curtis production. Produced by Bruce Cohn Curtis. Executive producers, Keith Saples, William Hart. Directed by Rick King. Screenplay, William Delligan. Camera, Paul Ryan; editor, David H. Lloyd; music, Robert Sprayberry; production design, Ivo Cristante; costume design, Barbara Palmer; line producer, Jim Lotfi; casting, Denise Chamian. Reviewed October 18, 1994. Rating: R. Running time: **93 MIN.**

David	Scott Bakula
Diana	Chelsea Field
Beth	Sheila Kelley
Jerry	John Getz
Ted	Rex Smith
Lou	France Nuyen
Morales	Eddie Valez
Martindale	Michael Warren

To paraphrase the World War II-era query, "Was this pic really necessary?" "A Passion to Kill" is an entirely formulaic soft-sex soap 'n' slasher indistinguishable from the hundreds of cable-ready pix already clogging up the airwaves. With a by-the-numbers script from former soap scribe William Delligan and standard-issue helming from Rick King, pressure falls on lovely Chelsea Field's nude scenes to keep viewers awake. Pic will hit theaters and disappear faster than a channel-surfed station.**

Diana (Field) responds to her abusive husband (Rex Smith) by burying a kitchen knife between his shoulder blades. Seven years later, the fetching but lethal lass has married hard-charging entertainment mouthpiece Jerry (John Getz) whose best friend, David (Scott Bakula), strives to beat him on the squash court and, it turns out, in the bedroom as well.

David should know better, being a pleasant New Age shrink who regularly visits his own guru, Lou (France Nuyen), an exotic psychologist with a penchant for pithy phrases.

But love and lust know no bounds, and soon David is involved in a wearily obsessive romance with

his best pal's gal, and Jerry has become the poster boy for Ginzu. The predictability of the dilemma would be instantly solved if only Bakula could make a "Quantum Leap" out of this potboiler and into another winning TV series.

Is Diana really a husband-killer? Has her ex Rex set her up for a fall? Or is assistant D.A. Beth (Sheila Kelley), who has pined for David since their college days, really the fatal attraction here? These questions pale beside a more pressing mystery: Who on earth will pay for a ticket to this determinedly small-screen diversion?

—*Steven Gaydos*

THE PUPPET MASTERS

A Buena Vista release of a Hollywood Pictures production. Produced by Ralph Winter. Executive producer, Michael Engelberg. Directed by Stuart Orme. Screenplay, Ted Elliot, Terry Rossio, David S. Goyer. Based upon the novel by Robert A. Heinlein. Camera, Clive Tickner; editor, William Goldenberg; music, Colin Towns; production design, Daniel A. Lomino; costume design, Tom Bronson; art director, James C. Hegedus; set designer, Alan Manzer; set decorator, Cloudia; sound (Dolby), Robert Anderson Jr.; unit production manager, Andrew G. La Marca; assistant director, Michael Grossman; visual effects supervisor, Peter Montgomery; stunt coordinator, Jeffrey Dashnaw; casting, Sharon Howard-Field;. Reviewed at Avco Cinemas, L.A., October 19, 1994. Rating: R. Running time: **108 MIN.**

Andrew Nivens	Donald Sutherland
Sam Nivens	Eric Thal
Mary Sefton	Julie Warner
Holland	Keith David
Graves	Will Patton
Jarvis	Richard Belzer
Ressler	Yaphet Kotto

Fans of sci-fi master Robert A. Heinlein may turn out for the bigscreen spinning of his 1951 tale "The Puppet Masters," but only the most undiscriminating monster-pic buff will come away satisfied. A thoroughly undistinguished if inoffensive telling of Heinlein's classic tale of parasitic outer-space creatures who threaten to control our planet, "Puppet Masters" should creep into the marketplace and leave the box office virtually undisturbed.

Set in the same bucolic Iowa locations that worked so effectively in "Field of Dreams," "Masters" makes an ironic counterpoint to that pic's placid spiritualism. But instead of magical ballplayers imparting a beatific calm to all who encounter them, here a particularly nasty brand of interplanetary gremlins turn humans into lethal zombies willing to kill in order to do their masters' bidding.

Like the 1956 Don Siegel classic thriller "Invasion of the Body Snatchers" — and by extension the

October 24, 1994 (Cont.)

two "Body Snatchers" remakes — and the 1953 space spooker "Invaders from Mars," "Masters" plays out a familiar scenario pitting heroic scientists against forces determined to plunder our planet while plucking out and chucking away our personalities.

In what's almost a reprise of his role in Philip Kaufman's 1978 "Body Snatchers," Donald Sutherland plays Andrew Nivens, an earnest CIA-type foe to the ornery critters. He's aided by his son Sam (Eric Thal), a handsome martial arts expert who just happens to work for Dad and the Company.

Sam's love interest is Mary (Julie Warner), a perky exobiologist brought in to uncover some Achilles gill to the slimy little bloodsuckers, whose preferred method of dominance is to attach themselves to humans' backs. Assisting her is quirky scientist Graves (Will Patton), who's odd enough to provide the pic with tension over his state of mind. Is he a pod guy, or isn't he? Only his extraterrestrial knows for sure.

By the pic's third act, when Sam has to go into the gooky hive where the space invaders replenish their human hosts with a kind of plasma battery recharge, clunky dramatics and low-rent art direction have caused pic to lapse into a slumber more numbing than anything that might descend from the skies. Though Heinlein's novel preceded most of the pix that have made the alien invasion and human somnolence scenario so overly familiar, the filmmakers have proceeded as if it were still the early '50s and all of this were revelatory, not timeworn.

What directors like Siegel made horrifyingly effective is here delivered straight-faced and winds up pedestrian at the hands of Brit helmer Stuart Orme. Along with the laughable creature effects, Orme ignores the fact that the material doesn't offer the common citizens' perspective of the invasion, which Siegel mined so effectively. The audience is forced to stay with the less compelling super-heroic characters as they fight the invasion inside their tech labs and Pentagon berths.

Worst of all, Orme misses the chance to explore the difference between alien-induced stupors and the everyday Midwest existence. What a difference it could have made if someone had said, "Is this Hell?" and someone answered, "No, it's Iowa." —*Steven Gaydos*

THE DAY THE SUN TURNED COLD

(TIANGUO NIEZI)

(HONG KONG)

A Pineast Pictures Ltd. (Hong Kong) production. Produced by Ann Hui, Yim Ho. Directed by Yim. Screenplay by Yim, Wong Hing-Dong. Camera (color), Hou Young; editor Chao Ying-Wu, Wong Yi-Sun; music, Yoshihide Otomo. Reviewed at Vancouver Film Festival (non-competing), Oct. 12, 1994. Running time: **99 MIN.**
With: Siqin Gaowa, Tao Chung-Hua, Ma Jingwu, Wei Zhi.
(Mandarin dialogue)

Freud comes to China in the Grand Prize winner of this year's Tokyo Fest, a sumptuously shot study of filial loyalty and "Hamlet"-like angst. Top tech values, a provocative plot hook, and the star-power of Siqin Gaowa ("The Women of the Lake of Scented Souls") assure offshore fest berths and healthy arthouse respect.

Although nominally a Hong Kong production, "The Day the Sun Turned Cold" is set in the same bleak northern China territory as "Ermo" and "The Story of Qiu Ju." Vet mainland helmer Yim Ho's stylish conceit rests on 24-year-old Guan Jian (Tao Chung-Hua), who seeks to bring city police evidence that mom (Siqin) may have murdered his father 10 years earlier. At first, the chain-smoking captain he accosts figures the lad to be either an over-imaginative reader of dimestore crime novels, or a would-be Raskolnikov, but eventually he accompanies Guan to his frozen homeland to help unravel the mystery.

The pic unfolds with time-jumping self-assurance, and the first third is particularly rich in ambiguity, with young Guan's emotional alliances constantly shifting between his hard-working mother, his cruel-tempered schoolteacher father (Ma Jingwu), and the handsome young woodsman (Wei Zhi) who befriends him and falls for mama. Guan's betrayal of their affair has tragic consequences, and many layers of guilt and resentment serve to both suppress and revive his memories. By the time mom is formally charged, Guan's still not sure about his own motives.

Thesping is superb throughout, and Hou Young's widescreen compositions keep things interesting even when the pic's energy flags near the end (a switch to mom's P.O.V. might have added balance and insight). Exceptionally naturalistic sound is a big plus, as is the subtle dovetailing of Yoshihide Otomo's orchestral score with regional Chinese folk music. All told, the days ahead for this "Sun" look warm indeed. —*Ken Eisner*

THIS WINDOW IS YOURS

(KONO MADO WA KIMI NO MONO)

(JAPANESE — 16MM)

A PIA Corp./Japan Satellite Broadcasting Inc. production. (International sales: PIA Filme Festival Office, Tokyo). Produced by Takenori Sento, Tamotsu Kanamori. Directed, written by Tomoyuki Furumaya. Camera (color, 16mm), Kazuhiro Suzuki; editor, Mari Kishi; music, Isao Yamada; sound, Masami Nishioka; art direction, Toshihiro Isogai. Reviewed at Vancouver Film Festival (in competition), Sept. 23, 1994. Running time: **95 MIN.**
With: Yukako Shimuzo, Hideo Sakai, Toshio Kamiaki, Yoshiyuki Kubota, Hirome Kurose, Ayako Noma, Toru Yamaguchi.

Its aims may be slight, but it's hard to think of a film that more exactly captures the precise moment adolescents become young adults. First-time feature helmer Tomoyuki Furumaya's wry eye and restrained hand won "This Window Is Yours" the inaugural Dragons & Tigers prize for new Asian cinema at the just-wrapped Vancouver fest.

Pic centers on six youngsters who spend their last summer together in rural northeastern Japan before heading off in separate directions. Soon, the focus rests on a pair who don't quite know they're a pair. Pugnacious Taro (Hideo Sakai) is sidelined with a broken leg, which gives pretty Yoko (Yukako Shimuzo) — staying just a window away — plenty of chance to tease Taro back to health and open his eyes to the possibilities of grown-up pleasures.

Although their affections grow steadily, neither is ready for a serious move, making this probably the first teenage-crush tale in which both parties say "I love you" but never get around to kissing each other. Ironically, the sex-free sensuality of this summer romance may be startling to Western auds, but a languorous, hesitant pulse is its chief appeal, along with effortlessly attractive young actors — non-pros all — who drift through the happily parentless reverie to the sound of twangy surf guitars.

Helmer claims "American Graffiti" was the pic's chief inspiration, but an episode of Canadian sketchcom "The Kids in the Hall" directed by Ozu comes closer to its gently wacky sensibility.

Tech credits are appropriately rough, with a purposely phony rear-projected fireworks sequence underscoring a no-budget approach to the fleeting joys of youthful confusion. Pic's 16mm format is problematic for theaters, but this "Window" is so universal, it easily could open on any web. —*Ken Eisner*

CANARY SEASON

(BULGARIAN)

A Boyana Films production. Directed by Eugeny Mihaylov. Screenplay, Nikolay Valchinov. Camera (color), Eli M. Yonova; music, Kiril Dontchev. Reviewed at Denver Film Festival, Oct. 17, 1994. Running time: **133 MIN.**
With: Plamena Getova, Paraskeva Djukelova, Petar Popyordanov.

The savagery imposed on Bulgarians by a closed system tore families apart, shredding hope in their drab lives and making truth the first victim. "Canary Season," a prize winner in Bulgaria last year, depicts dire lives without blinkers in a film of shattering power.

This is the tragic account of a woman's brutalization by forces set loose by the Communist regime, which stresses its power in a twisted kind of masculine bravery. The title comes from the expressed hope of a principal character that "someday we'll get two canaries." Although that wish is never realized, hopes are renewed with the breakup of the totalitarian government.

After Lily's love is taken into the army, she is raped by a scion of Communist officials, becomes pregnant and is forced to marry her attacker. Her mother-in-law finds letters from Lily's love, and uses her power to have Lily sent to a labor camp where she suffers cruelly. The trials she endures finally break her, and she is put in an asylum from which she is eventually rescued.

This awful life is described in flashbacks as Lily tells her misbegotten, failure-prone son, Malina, of the events that have kept her from being a good mother. Malina has been shifted from place to place and has grown up an uncomprehending tough in detention, torn with hatred of Lily.

Lensed entirely on location in Sofia and on the shores of the Black Sea, the film has an immediacy due to director Eugeny Mihaylov's acute sense of drama and the fluid, sensitive camerawork of Eli Yonova.

October 24, 1994 (Cont.)

Performances are outstanding. Both Plamena Getova and Paraskeva Djukelova, who play, respectively, the young and the old Lily, were honored as best actresses by the Bulgarian Film Society for their work in this film. The two women bear an extraordinary likeness of face and character, and give shining, heartbreaking performances. Petar Popyordanov, who plays the dark role of the boy's father, was awarded the best actor prize by the society, and helmer Mihaylov was named best director.

Grim as the film is, it is an important account of a terrible time.
—*Allen Young*

VUKOVAR POSTE RESTANTE

(FORMER YUGOSLAVIA)

> Dan Films Prods. Producer, Danka Muzdeka Mandzuka. Executive producer, Steven North. Directed by Boro Draskovic. Screenplay, Maja Draskovic, Boro Draskovic. Camera (color), Aleksander Petkovic. Reviewed at Denver Film Festival, Oct. 16, 1994. (Also in Vienna fest.) Running time: 96 MIN.
> With: Mirjana Jokovic, Boris Isakovic.

Exploring the tragic events in the former Yugoslavia, "Vukovar Poste Restante" sears the eye with images of mindless ethnic conflict, as it ranges from an idyllic rose garden to the concluding panoramas of a devastated land.

Just as the Berlin Wall falls and hopes for peace arise, a wedding takes place between a Croat woman and a Serbian man in Vukovar; once this would have been unexceptional. The marriage becomes a Capulet-Montague combat even before the wedding party reaches the reception, with marching columns of Croats and Serbs sending the celebrants running.

The neighbors write nasty graffiti on the walls of the bride's family's home, as Serbs and Croats reject those they had always lived with. The newlyweds are divided when the Serbian husband goes off to the army, and the conflict succeeds in destroying home, city and nation.

The subject of the film is "What's true at one time is false at another," and its depiction of a beautiful country's loss of its moral compass is a terrifying, dazzling achievement. Director Boro Draskovic has an acute eye, open to sudden and stark imagery. There are unforgettable images of the once beautiful Vukovar area turned into a land of skeletons. Helmer manages to establish a sense of family among his well-to-

do, sophisticated principals, and the ensuing barbarous events show the thin line between civilization and chaos.

Poignant and meaningful images stay with the viewer. A white pet bird symbolizes peace, and from its perch in the rose garden it flies with increasing desperation, ending up amidst the smoke and flame of a destroyed city. A tank crashes through the garden wall; three crones stir a hellish broth in a replay of the witches in "Macbeth." Anna, whose husband is a Serb, is the victim of a savage rape by Serbians.

There is blame enough for all parties to the conflict in a final aerial sweep over a tortured landscape. Draskovic says to his people, look at what you have done.

A viewer can be excused for feeling futility. —*Allen Young*

TRUE BELIEVERS: THE MUSICAL FAMILY OF ROUNDER RECORDS

(DOCU)

> A Mug Shot release. Produced, directed by Robert Mugge. Camera (color), Bill Burke. Reviewed at Denver Film Festival, Oct. 15, 1994. Running time: 85 MIN.

The richly diverse tracks of Rounder Records provide vibrant music in Robert Mugge's "True Believers: The Musical Family of Rounder Records," one of three films made by Mugge over a 10-day stay in Louisiana.

In what might have been a series of disconnected musical vignettes, Mugge weaves a rare series of performances into the enlivening history of Rounder Records to provide an exhilarating entertainment.

Rounder Records makes no effort to lead the mass-consumption charts, concerned instead with little-noticed but worthy varieties of the music of America — the folk music that comes in such different packages. Mugge introduces the three Rounder founders but does not overdo facts. The music itself gives the film its kick. And it resounds.

Major delights are top-flight bluegrass from young Alison Krauss, adept on violin as in singing; more bluegrass from the Johnson Mountain Boys; a lilting Mexican folk song of the 1940s from Tish Hinojosa; wildly pungent, accordion-flavored zydeco from Beau Jocques; and more energetic Creole stuff from Steve Reilly and Bruce Daigrepont. With great piano riffs, Marcia Ball struts her brash, sure singing; Bill Morrissey's ballads are fresh and true, and his final number about the joys of heaven is a comic delight. Irma Tho-

mas is a great find, a blues singer of top rank — a discovery by Rounder Records, "the little label that could."

The bright, clean sound of the exceptional recording and fluid, colorful camerawork enhance every moment of this choice bit of Americana.
—*Allen Young*

MILL VALLEY

DREAMS
(CHBI)
(RUSSIAN)

> A Courier Studio (subsidiary of Mosfilm Studios) presentation of a Karen Shakhnazarov/Alexander Borodyansky film. Produced, directed, written by Shakhnazarov, Borodyansky. Executive producer, Galina Shadur. Camera (color), Borid Brojovsky; editors, Lyudmila Mordvinova, Irina Kozhemyakina; music, Anatoly Kroll; production design, Leonid Swintsitsky; sound engineer, Igor Mayorov; sound mixer, Evgeny Bazonov. Reviewed at the Sequoia I, Mill Valley, Calif., Oct. 11, 1994. (In Mill Valley Film Festival.) Running time: 78 MIN.
> With: Oleg Basilashvili, Lyudmila Mordovinova, Armen Djigarhanyan, Arnold Ides, Peter Merculov, Alexey Jarcov, Valery Nosic, Yury Sherstnev, Andrey Vertogradov.

"Dreams" ventures yet another satirical look at post-Soviet Russia in economic/moral disarray, albeit through an offbeat prism: Its heroine is a 19th-century aristocrat whose "nightmares" foresee chaos 100 years hence. Funny, imaginative pic could find limited theatrical interest abroad.

Nubile young countess Masha (Lyudmila Mordovinova) is disturbed by bizarre nocturnal visions in which she's a lowly Moscow cafeteria worker. Modern-day "dreams" find her perennially chased by a randy coworker, amid some outrageous scenarios. They include her unlikely appointment as minister of the economy, in which role she must literally seduce Western money men into making high-risk loans; a stint as a backup singer for a cheesy rock act; and competing topless in a "Best Bust" variety spectacular.

At first skeptical, Masha's hubby (a high-ranking Tsarist official), doctor and hypnotist soon grow terrified by this vision of the nation's upcoming "complete cretinization." But Tsar and cabinet vehemently reject the count's preventive socialist proposals. A future they can scarcely comprehend is thus sealed. The empire will fall, be rebuilt under communist auspices, then crumble again.

Pic has some of the anarchist zip of early Woody Allen efforts like "Bananas," albeit in a gentler, less wildly inspired mode. Still, major

set pieces (including court ball in which the countess, under clairvoyant fashion influence, creates a scandal with Mother Russia's first miniskirt) hit the comic bull's eye. Satire of sexploitation rife in Russia's current marketplace is witty and generally good-natured. Close could be punchier, as it bypasses climactic laughs in favor of mild "mystical" suggestion that latter-day protagonist is her dreaming predecessor's reincarnation.

Despite some slow stretches in period segs, writing/directing team keeps the ball rolling. Production values are smooth in both the 1893 and 1993 milieus, with solid tech work. The actors — who keep resurfacing in crass modern roles far flung from their dignified court personae — are droll throughout.
—*Dennis Harvey*

MR. 247

> A Tribe Production of a Vern Oakley film. Executive producer, Marc Bailin. Co-producers, Melanie Webber, Jennifer Wilkinson. Produced, directed by Oakley. Screenplay, Paul Zimmerman, story by Oakley, Zimmerman. Camera (color), Rex Nicholson; editor, Suzanne Pillsbury; music, Jan Hammer; music supervisor, Harvey Shield; production design, Cathy T. Marshall; costumes, Gayle Alden Robbins; associate producers, Ernest Kalman, Marc Garland; casting, Bernard Telsey. Reviewed at the Sequoia I, Mill Valley, Calif., Oct. 8, 1994. (In Mill Valley Festival.) Running time: 89 MIN.
> Grace Rhodes .... Lisa Eichhorn
> Peter Kessler .... Stanley Tucci
> Elaine .... Caroline Aaron
> With: Robert LuPone, Vincent Young, Len Stanger, Tammy Grimes, Wesley Addy, Cynthia Martells, Robert Joy, J. Smith-Cameron, Mary Jo Salerno, Gary Lahti.

"Mr. 247" (re-titled from "#247," still on the credits at its preem screening) is a traditional romantic comedy/weepie "women's pic" in the Hollywood Golden Age sense, albeit with a modern sperm-donor hook. Sans benefit of B.O. headliners, charming but low-key feature looks to land where most femme issue-slanted efforts do these days — as a broadcast premiere.

Grace (Lisa Eichhorn) is a Manhattan corporate exec facing onset of middle age sans mate or children. String of broken romantic commitments has left her sour on romance. Her more upbeat pal Elaine (Caroline Aaron) suggests she skip the "life-partner" worry and go straight to motherhood, via artificial insemination. At first appalled, biologically ticking Grace gives in and buys her "anonymous" pregnancy. She's then seized with a need to know the identity of the "father." Using Elaine as spy, she circumvents anonymity strictures to uncover donor 247.

October 24, 1994 (Cont.)

He's upstate gallery owner/photographer Peter Kessler (Stanley Tucci), who considers twice-weekly sperm bank contribution his lucrative "other job," and carries on an affair with a married woman for purely carnal purposes that don't impinge on his misanthropic/commitment-wary mindset.

Out of curiosity, Grace and Elaine road-trip to check out this "stud." To her acute embarrassment, Grace and the man hit it off. When the awkward truth comes out, Peter misreads the situation as entrapment. Teary episodes ensue, followed at length by a qualified reconciliation.

Scenarist Paul Zimmerman and producer/director Vern Oakley hew to a slightly bland, empathetic tenor, albeit one mitigated by bright dialogue and resistance to full-on movie-of-the-week sentimentality. Problem is, Peter and Elaine are fairly tongue-tied by mutual attraction, which means their characters fail to deepen when the relationship should. Eichhorn (who was terrif in Ivan Passer's underrated "Cutter's Way") is intelligent, attractive and likable here. But she doesn't provide the sparkle that might lift this sweet but ordinary vehicle onto another commercial plateau. Nonetheless, rapport with Tucci lends their scenes an nervously comedic tilt.

Other perfs are smart, from Aaron's brash gal pal to Robert Joy's Russian sperm-bank administrator. Cast as Grace's therapist, vet actress Tammy Grimes is less effective in scenes that too baldly echo promo material's boast that this is "'An Unmarried Woman' for the '90s."

Gently humorous touches lift "Mr. 247" a bit. But approach is ultimately conventional in mix of contempo urban knowingness, watered-down feminism and reluctant-Prince-Charming romance. Pretty cinematography exploits countryside and New York City skylines for postcard effects. Other tech efforts are pro. Pic should translate nicely to cable, where current marketplace deems it belongs. —*Dennis Harvey*

TOKYO

OF LOVE
AND SHADOWS

A Betka Film Ltd. production. Produced by Richard Goodwin, Betty Kaplan, Paul F. Mayersohn. Executive producers, Ernst Goldschmidt, Isidro Miguel, Herve Hachuel. Directed by Kaplan. Screenplay, Donald Freed, Kaplan, based on the novel by Isabel Allende. Camera (color), Felix Monti; editors, Kathy Himoff, Bill Butler; music, Jose Nieto; art direction, Abel Faccello. Reviewed at Tokyo Film Festival, Kyoto (competing), Sept. 26, 1994. Running time: **109 MIN.**

Irene	Jennifer Connelly
Francisco	Antonio Banderas
Beatriz	Stefania Sandrelli
Gustavo	Camilo Gallardo
Mario	Patricio Contreras
Rosa	Susana Cortinez

Betty Kaplan's intriguing first feature is a story of love, politics and truth set after Chile's military coup in 1973. It's based on the novel Isabel Allende wrote after "The House of the Spirits" — and could do some specialized arthouse business internationally.

Performed in English by an almost entirely native Spanish-speaking cast, the film is accessible by international audiences, yet retains the Hispanic flavor that audiences will expect. It does this without being condescending or stereotyped, and its wide range of quirky characters (from a gay makeup artist to a heavyset house maid who speaks only in rhyming verse) are believable despite their eccentricities.

Jennifer Connelly is Irene, an upper-crust Chilean woman, engaged to be married to her cousin Gustavo (Camilo Gallardo), an elite army captain. One day, a handsome, actively liberal photographer named Francisco (Antonio Banderas) comes in for a job at the fashion magazine where Irene works as a reporter. They go to research a fluff-piece on a self-proclaimed living saint, Angelina. Some soldiers come as well, interrupting Angelina's religious trance, and she hurls one into the mud.

Angelina then becomes one of Chile's "missing," taken by the insulted military. Irene tells Angelina's distraught mother, "I will help you." Her journey takes her closer to Francisco, but en route both of them learn up-close and firsthand about the excesses of the Chilean military. Pic is based on a true incident that started the long process of stemming the military's power.

Performances are top-notch. Connelly is convincing in her evolution from a frivolous young woman to one willing to take risks for the sake of compassion and freedom.

Banderas' characterization of Francisco is passionate and heart-winning.

Also deserving of special kudos are Patricio Contreras as Mario, a gay makeup artist, and Susana Cortinez as the humorous housekeeper.

Shot on location in Argentina, near the border of Chile, the film boasts impeccable technical credits and slick editing.
—*Karen Regelman*

CREST OF BETRAYAL
(CHUSHINGURA GAIDEN YOTSUYA KAIDAN)
(JAPANESE)

A Shochiku Co. Ltd. production. Produced by Tetsuo Sasho, Ryuta Saito. Executive producer, Yozo Sakurai. Directed by Kinji Fukasaku. Screenplay, Motomu Furuta, Fukasaku. Camera (color), Shigeru Ishihara; editor, Koichi Soni; music, Kaoru Wada; art direction, Yoshinobu Nishioka; sound (Dolby), Koichi Hirose. Reviewed at Tokyo Film Festival, Kyoto, Sept. 25, 1994. Running time: **105 MIN.**

Iemon Tamiya	Koichi Sato
Oiwa	Saki Takaoka
O-ume	Keiko Oginome
Kihei Ito	Renji Ishibashi
Omaki	Eriko Watanabe
Ichigaku Shimizu	Keizo Kanie
Yasubei Horibe	Tsunehiko Watase

In "Crest of Betrayal," director Kinji Fukasaku tackles the traditions and history of his homeland through the innovative combining of two oft-told local legends: "Chushingura" (better known as "The Loyal Forty-Seven Ronin"), the story of 18th-century shogunate intrigue and loyalty, and "Yotsuya Kaidan," a chilling ghost story about a beautiful woman who falls victim to passion and evil.

Beautiful scenes and the clever weaving of the two story lines should ensure a solid showing with the Japanese public and Japan buffs, despite somewhat flat perfs. But helmer's cleverness in mixing the tales will be all but lost on the uninitiated.

The link between the stories is Iemon Tamiya (Koichi Sato), an Edo-era samurai caught in a world of paradoxes: poor even though he's a samurai, a cultured musician who has murdered women for money, a lonely orphan yet a member of several groups.

After a long time wandering, he finally finds acceptance as a samurai for the Asano family — a feudal lord under the Shogun. The "Chushingura" plot revolves around the fact that Asano is forced to commit hara-kiri by his superior, Lord Kira. Traditionally, 47 of Asano's samurai remain loyal and become *ronin* (or wandering samurai with no master), secretly hatching and eventually executing a plan to avenge their former master. In this telling, though, Iemon

has been added as the would-be 48th, who seems loyal only to himself.

He's lulled into inactivity by the appearance of a beautiful prostitute named Oiwa, played with too much cuteness by Saki Takaoka. Suddenly, a third party enters the scene, eventually causing the demise of their illicit but happy affair.

The intruder is a mute, noble girl called O-ume, whose portrayal by Keiko Oginome is flat and falls short on believability. O-ume also happens to be the granddaughter of a samurai employed by Lord Kira. Ultimately Oiwa and Iemon, both ghosts, witness the 47 ronins' successful attack against Lord Kira.

The film is colorful and grandiose, full of the sights and sounds of traditional Japan, with a consistently high technical quality, and special nods to costuming, photography, art direction and music. Fukasaku was one of two co-directors of the Japanese sequences of Fox's Pearl Harbor epic "Tora! Tora! Tora!" (1969).

Though both stories have been produced innumerable times for stage, TV and film, "Crest of Betrayal's" biggest competitor will be "47 Ronin," a huge effort by rival production house Toho Eiga with a more famous cast that includes Ken Takakura, directed by Kon Ichikawa. Both are set for release in Japan on Oct. 22.
—*Karen Regelman*

THE CONFINED
(ANTAREEN)
(INDIAN)

A National Film Development Corp./Doordarshan production. (International sales: NFDC, Bombay.) Directed, written by Mrinal Sen, based on a story by Sadat Hasan Manto. Camera (color), Shashi Anand; editor, Mrinmoy Chakraborty; music, Anand; art direction, Goutam Bose; sound, Anup Mukherjee, Sudipta Bose. Reviewed at San Sebastian Film Festival (competing). Running time: **91 MIN.**

The Woman	Dimple Kapadia
The Writer	Anjan Dutt
With: Tathagata Sanyal.	

Having seemingly put aside the political and social vocation of his more prolific filmmaking days, veteran Bengali director Mrinal Sen is again in a meditative, allegorical frame of mind with "The Confined." Though it's deftly composed, and almost compelling in an overworked, theatrical fashion, this rarefied account of an intense telephone relationship between two strangers appears likely to find a direct line to only a finite group of devoted festfollowers.

Basically an elaborate reflection on the difficulty of communication within a large city, the film sets up its two characters in self-imposed exile on opposite sides of a teeming

October 24, 1994 (Cont.)

Calcutta, then allows them briefly to interconnect.

A writer (Anjan Dutt) takes up temporary residence in a stately mansion. Elegant, sustained shots of its empty, dilapidated corridors, courtyards and staircases establish a climate of expectation that comes to fruition when the telephone rings. The caller is a woman (Dimple Kapadia) in a large, modern apartment, who fills her nights of insomnia by phoning random numbers. Refusing to speak at first, she breaks the silence on the second call, having sensed a receptive listener in the writer.

Each consecutive conversation defines a game that strays from playful banter through flirtation to attempts to get under each other's skin by feeling around for hidden truths. Each party's concrete knowledge of the other's life is kept to a minimum, but boundaries are eventually crossed, irrevocably breaking the line that links them.

Sen creates a potent spell from the situation but quickly lets it become ponderous and repetitive. More congenial are the framing sequences, with a manservant royally escorting the audience (and the initially unseen writer) into the mansion at the front end, and a fleeting, wordless face-to-face encounter at the back.

As lensman and composer, Shashi Anand brings the slender premise some much-needed dimension, establishing two distinct poles as the camera prowls the shadowy recesses of the writer's world and bathes in the pristine brightness of the woman's.　*—David Rooney*

LIBERATION

(DOCU — B&W/COLOR)

A Simon Wiesenthal Center presentation of a Moriah Films production. Produced by Marvin Hier, Arnold Schwartzman. Executive producer, Richard Trank. Directed by Schwartzman. Screenplay, Martin Gilbert, Hier, Schwartzman. Editor, David Dresher; additional editing, Steve Nielson; music, Carl Davis; production design, Schwartzman; sound (Dolby), Mark Friedman; associate producer, Isolde Schwartzman. Reviewed at Deauville American Film Festival, France, Sept. 8, 1994. Running time: **98 MIN.**
Narrators: Ben Kingsley, Whoopi Goldberg, Patrick Stewart, Miriam Margolyes, Jean Boht.

Using archival footage and intelligent, accessible narration, "Liberation" packs an enormous amount of information into a manageable package on Hitler's attempts to eradicate the Jews. Educators across the religious spectrum will appreciate the film's balanced secular approach and keenly researched narrative clarity. Despite its ambitious scope — starting in September '39 and concluding after the concentration camps were liberated at war's end — at no time does the presentation overwhelm or confuse.

Following its world preem at the Deauville fest in September, the handsomely mounted docu, produced by the newly formed Moriah Films arm of the Simon Wiesenthal Center, preemed stateside Oct. 18 at the Academy of Motion Picture Arts & Sciences. It unspools in Gotham on Nov. 9.

Helmer Arnold Schwartzman, who won a docu Oscar in 1982 with "Genocide," utilizes mostly B&W footage with a smattering of color documents. Special dates are signaled onscreen with four "Resistance knock" drumbeats, repping the dot-dot-dot-dash of the letter "V" (for victory) in Morse code.

Spoken by accomplished actors, voiceovers bring to life first-person anecdotes, some wrenching and some providing memorable comic relief.

An English woman, who when extending a luncheon invitation to Yank soldiers billeted nearby had specified "No Jews, please," was horrified to discover six black soldiers at her door. "There must be some mistake," she sputtered. "No, ma'am," a soldier replied. "Col. Cohen doesn't make mistakes."

Pic champions Allied ingenuity in fooling the German army while deploring the gaps in leadership that might have saved more Jews. Other revelations are fascinating. Pope Pius XII refused to join in a public renunciation of the Nazis. Four hundred European rabbis marched on Washington but were informed that Roosevelt was not free to meet with them, after the president had been so advised by two American Jewish organizations. And the British government declined to make public a speech in which Goebbels announced he would exterminate the 48,000 Jews still living in Berlin.

Whoopi Goldberg, who narrates the "Hollywood Canteen" seg, explains that black soldiers were welcome to fight and die for their country but met with prejudice at every turn.

Pic is particularly effective in showing the stress and anxiety when war-weary Britain was pelted with V-1 rockets a week after the Normandy landings. The account of the oft-told liberation of Paris also resonates with suspense.

Optical quality of newsreel shots and period imagery is aces throughout. Popular songs, often far mellower than the images they underline, augment Carl Davis' excellent score.　*—Lisa Nesselson*

SCENES FROM THE NEW WORLD

An RKGM production, in association with Filmhaus, Austria. (International sales: RKGM, N.Y.) Produced by Karol Martesko, Gordon Eriksen, Heather Johnston. Executive producer, Ronald Guttman. Directed, written by Eriksen, Johnston. Camera (color), Armando Basulto; editors, Tim Squyres, Eriksen, Johnston; music, Tony Silbert, Laurie Fitzgerald; art direction, Jana Cisar, Manuela Strihavka; sound, Neil Danziger; associate producers, Wolfgang Ramml, Gernot Schaffler; assistant director, Wendy Jo Cohen. Reviewed at San Sebastian Film Festival (competing), Sept. 21, 1994. (Also in Hamptons fest.) Running time: **104 MIN.**

Myles	Michael Ralph
Stephanie	Christine Clementson
Alex	David Chan
Lee	Paula D. Ralph
Mirabel	Lidia Ramirez
Billy	Michael Imperioli
Wing	Stephen Xavier Lee
Nicky	Grant Chang
Bob	Alvin Eng
Organa	Organa Della Eve
Mrs. Thatcher	Laurie Cohen
Old man	Jimmy Leong

Aiming to redress the balance after Hollywood's rash of all-white my-generation comedies, tandem directors Gordon Eriksen and Heather Johnston ("The Big Dis") have concocted a multicultural variation on the theme in "Scenes From the New World." But inept scripting makes their PC pretext little more than a strained infomercial for interracial good-neighborliness, played out by an ensemble cast that finds unison only in its self-conscious, sitcom-style mugging. These scenes look destined to remain unseen.

Container for the racially mixed bag is a house in suburban Queens owned by an old Chinese businessman (Jimmy Leong) intent on keeping up cultural barriers. But grandson Alex (David Chan), who lives there, and his Latino girlfriend (Lidia Ramirez) have other ideas.

They recruit their own tenants, starting with African-American Myles (Michael Ralph), who wants to stay footloose while awaiting a transfer to Europe. The designs of manhunting roommate Stephanie (Christine Clementson) cut in on his plans, and the unexpected arrival of his kid sister, Lee (Paula D. Ralph), creates an additional glitch. Grandpa stirs up further trouble by renting space to a trio of Hong Kong students.

Tension inside the house and out gets fired up rather mechanically to fever pitch, with contributions coming from a gang of white slackers and a nosy, condescending neighbor. A sympathetic lesbian couple still clinging to '60s ideals complete the already crowded picture.

Attempts to ruminate on issues of commitment, trust and, above all, race are unsupported in lighter moments by comic mistiming and wooden delivery, and at more earnest junctures by a script that lumbers straight in with its labored points rather than paving the way for them with motivation or credible buildup.

Ultimately, the casting conceit has no more depth (and considerably less entertainment value) than the gaggle of ethnic extractions among the crew members on vintage "Star Trek."

Technical input is several notches above the film's creative side, but not so high as to make it of interest to anyone outside cast and crew.
—David Rooney

THE SEXUAL LIFE OF THE BELGIANS

(LA VIE SEXUELLE DES BELGES)

(BELGIAN)

A Transatlantic Films production. Produced, directed, written by Jan Bucquoy. Executive producer, Francoise Hoste. Camera (Agfacolor), Michel Baudour; editor, Matyas Veress; production design, Nathalie Andre; sound, Jean-Gregoire Mekhitarian. Reviewed at Cannes Festival (market), May 13, 1994. Running time: **80 MIN.**

Jan Bucquoy	Jean-Henri Compere
Jan as a child	Noe Francq
Noella Bucquoy	Isabelle Legros
Therese	Sophie Schneider
Ariane Bucquoy	Pascale Binneri
Aunt Martha	Michele Shor
Mia	Dorothee Capelluto

This autobiographical first feature by a well-known and slightly notorious Belgian writer, designer, producer and conceptual artist turns out to be a quite charming and often funny satire of sexual manners and mores between 1950 and 1978. Not as harsh as Belgians apparently expected from Jan Bucquoy, the film is funny and sexy enough to find some arthouse approval.

According to the narration, spoken by Bucquoy himself, his interest in sex began at his mother's breast, but growing up in a small provincial town with bickering, ineffectual parents proved stultifying. One escape was an immensely romantic visit to the cinema with his sister to see "Johnny Guitar" (the Victor Young theme music for Nicholas Ray's film crops up occasionally, and Peggy Lee sings the brief title song at the end of Bucquoy's pic).

His first sexual experience was with a schoolgirl who allowed him to look but not touch; later, on a drab seaside holiday in a caravan, an older boy furthered his sex education during the screening of a Laurel and Hardy two-reeler.

October 24, 1994 (Cont.)

Jan's life is filled with beautiful women, including the teacher who kept crossing and uncrossing her legs, and a beautiful aunt who showed him her body because she felt it was no secret.

Eventually, Jan winds up in Brussels and becomes a political activist of the '60s. Here there are sexual encounters galore before he winds up in a disastrous, short-lived marriage that results in two children. After this is over, the affairs with women continue; one night he finds himself involved with both a mother and her free-thinking daughter.

There's a charming insouciance to all of this, as Bucquoy tells his story candidly and with a sharp sense of humor that mocks Belgian stuffiness and parochialism.

Jean-Henri Compere is fine as the soulful hero. Among the parade of women who pass by, standouts are Sophie Schneider as the woman he marries and Michele Shor as his ultra-liberated aunt.

—*David Stratton*

JUSTINO, A SENIOR CITIZEN KILLER

(JUSTINO, UN ASESINO DE LA TERCERA EDAD)

(SPANISH)

A Jose Maria Lara P.C. production. Directed, written by Luis Guridi, Santiago Aguilar. Camera· (16mm, B&W sepia tinted), Flavio Martinez Labiano; editor, Cristina Otero; set design, J.L. Arrizabalaga y Biaffra; music, Jose Carlos Mac; sound, Pablo Sanz. Reviewed at Sitges Film Festival, Spain, Oct. 13, 1994. Running time: **94 MIN.**
Justino .... Saturnino Garcia
Sansoncito .... Carlos Lucas
Renco .... Francisco Maestre
Reme .... Carmen Segarra
With: Concha Salinas, Mara Fernandez-Muro, Alicia Hermida, Carlos de Gabriel, Rosario Santesmasa, Fausto Talon.

Grainy and amateurish, shot on a Spanish shoestring, "Justino" nonetheless has such a mixture of endearing humanity, humor and outrageous situations that it beguiles the viewer. This quirky but charming little opus by two unknown directors is a real find, and if carefully handled could garner ducats aplenty in select release. Told with refreshing economy and simplicity, this sleeper drew big kudos at the Sitges fest, and walked away with two awards, including best film.

The tongue-in-cheek yarn concerns a *puntillero* (the man who finishes off the dying bull in the ring with a stab in the neck) who, at 62, is retired from the *corrida*. Being a widower who lives with his grown son, he

becomes the quintessential superannuated man, drinking with his picturesque, somewhat disreputable cronies at the local bar.

Plot then takes a sudden twist when, in a moment of peeve, he stabs his son and daughter-in-law and stuffs them into the freezer. Justino's career as a serial killer flowers forth. After polishing off a bothersome beggar, and a landlady who complains about the noise of a party he is throwing for his cronies, he decides to give himself up. But the police in the squad car only laugh, and it is their last laugh. Pic ends in a mass murder in an old-age home, but instead of Justino being blamed, the police shoot someone else as the culprit.

Pic being in black-and-white, the blood is never very striking, and the murders are schematized so as to be non-violent. Saturnino Garcia, who was named best actor at Sitges, is a virtually unknown bit actor and puts in a wonderful performance as the deadpan killer who is nevertheless endearing. Carlos Lucas, another unknown, is superb as Justino's ragged companion. —*Peter Besas*

DECLARATIONS OF LOVE

(DICHIARAZIONI D'AMORE)

(ITALIAN)

A Filmauro Distribuzione release (in Italy) of a Duea Film/Filmauro production. (International sales: Sacis, Rome.) Produced by Antonio Avati, Aurelio De Laurentiis. Directed, written by Pupi Avati. Camera (Cinecitta color), Cesare Bastelli; editor, Amedeo Salfa; music, Stefano Caprioli; production design, Giuseppe Pirrotta; costume design, Steno Tonelli; sound (Dolby), Raffaele De Luca; assistant director, Gianni Amadei. Reviewed at Venice Film Festival (non-competing), Sept. 6, 1994. Running time: **91 MIN.**
Dado .... Alessio Modica
Dado's father .... Arnaldo Ninchi
Dado's mother .... Angiola Baggi
Piera .... Valeria Fabrizi
Superintendent .... Carlo Delle Piane
Ito Marenchi .... Dino Sarti
Adult Sandra .... Delia Boccardo
Silvi .... Andrea Scorzoni
Professor Colli .... Ivano Marescotti
Gaby .... Antonella Attili
Young Sandra .... Carlotta Miti

In "Declarations of Love," Pupi Avati returns to the warmly affectionate evocations of bygone Bologna that were his earlier staple. He obtains affably entertaining results, but clutters his subject with a clumsily executed flashback/forward structure that sullies the action in both time frames. Handsome production is unlikely to inspire the amorous odes of its title, but could court attention at fests and as choice TV.

The openly autobiographical recollection of Avati's stately hometown in 1948 centers on 15-year-old Dado

(Alessio Modica), his school chums, extended family and bungled attempts to strike up a romance with a series of uninterested candidates. Individual, loosely interlaced stories are picked up, then brushed aside with a captivatingly light touch.

Classroom scenes jauntily recapture the agonizing ritual of being drilled by a stern teacher (Ivano Marescotti), and the satisfaction of shrewdly escaping that fate. Home life is awash with eccentric relatives.

While there's little of any significant dramatic weight, the delicate mosaic of characters and vignettes arranged over an undulating emotional panorama is fully functional in its own right, similar to Woody Allen's "Radio Days." But Avati also saddles it with a heavy-handed dramatic frame that he fails to integrate into the narrative.

Opening with B&W footage of a woman's violent death, he attempts to tell her story both then and now. As the target of one of Dado's failed romantic overtures, the character gels seamlessly into her surroundings. But as a menopause-stricken adult slipping awkwardly in and out of past and present, the character stands to leave most auds scratching their heads in confusion.

Large, able cast, including several Avati regulars, puts in fine work all round, with Marescotti's teacher and Angiola Baggi as Dado's mother among the most memorable. Cesare Bastelli's warm lensing, suffused with a nostalgic glow, ably reflects Avati's sentimental mood. —*David Rooney*

THE PACK

(IL BRANCO)

(ITALIAN)

A Cecchi Gori Group release (in Italy) of a Cecchi Gori Group Tiger Cinematografica, Sorpasso Film production. Produced by Mario and Vittorio Cecchi Gori, Marco Risi, Maurizio Tedesco. Directed by Risi. Screenplay, Andrea Carraro, based on his novel. Camera (color), Massimo Pau; editor, Franco Fraticelli; music, Franco Piersanti; art direction, Claudio Cinini; costume design, Metella Raboni; sound (Dolby), Tommaso Quattrini. Reviewed at Venice Film Festival (competing), Sept. 9, 1994. Running time: **90 MIN.**
Raniero .... Giampiero Lisarelli
Pallesecche .... Ricky Memphis
Ciccio .... Salvatore Spada
Sylvia .... Tamara Simunovic
Marion .... Angelika Krautzberger
Brunello .... Roberto Caprari
Ottorino .... Luca Zingaretti
Sola .... Giorgio Tirabassi
Sorquinto .... Natale Tulli
Esterina .... Sasha Altea

Based on two different real-life episodes of violent gang rape in the Italian provinces, Marco Risi's "The Pack" makes the fatal mistake of trying to tell a brutal tale from the p.o.v. of one of

the rapists. **The result is off-key and highly alienating, particularly for female viewers.**

Risi has tackled delicate social themes in all his films, from the Palermo ghetto in "Forever Mery" to the Ustica tragedy in "The Invisible Wall." His intention here is clearly noble: to expose the underlying inhumanity of the average Giovanni.

Pic opens with a replay from a famous call-in radio show, in which northern Italians bitterly insult southerners and vice versa. The point is that people identify "otherness" as alien and enemy. This is the cultural level of the jobless teenage boys who hang out in the pool hall of a small town outside Rome.

Raniero (newcomer Giampiero Lisarelli) is the best-looking and most innocent of the lot; "Dry Balls" (Ricky Memphis) is the meanest and most sadistic. But when word spreads that some pals have got hold of two German hitchhikers in an isolated shack in the woods, everyone hops on their mopeds to take part in the fun.

By the time the boys get there, Sylvia (Tamara Simunovic) has already been raped repeatedly. Her reactions are oddly muted, and she seems more concerned about the fate of her friend, Marion (Angelika Krautzberger), who is a virgin.

Though the level of psychological violence is high, none of the rapes are shown on-screen, and nudity is kept to a minimum. As the unfortunate tourists, Simunovic and Krautzberger under-act and underreact, portraying the girls as helpless victims who don't connect emotionally with the viewer.

Of the boys, Memphis (who normally plays ghetto heroes) leaves the strongest impression of mindless evil. Lisarelli's Raniero inspires mostly contempt when he flashes back to his churchgoing days as a child, or tearfully frets about how the rapes are going to affect his career goals.

On his fifth feature, Risi has a serviceable technique well in hand. Franco Piersanti's music and Massimo Pau's foggy lighting heighten the tale's anguish without going for subtlety. —*Deborah Young*

October 24, 1994 (Cont.)

BLACK MOUNTAIN
(HEI SHAN LU)
(CHINESE)

A Xi'an Film Studio production. Directed by Zhou Xiaowen. Screenplay, Zhu Jianxin, Zhou. Camera (color), Zhou; editor, Zhong Furong; music, Zhao Jiping; art direction, Dou Guoxiang; costume design, Ren Zhiwen; sound, Hui Dongzhi; assistant camera, Cao Jiuping; assistant director, Wang Dawei. Reviewed on vidcassette, Locarno, Aug. 14, 1994. (In World Film Festival, Montreal.) Running time: **97 MIN.**
The woman ....Ailiya
"Sixth Brother" .... Xie Yuan
"Elder Brother" .... Zhao Xiaorui
With: Han Guichen, Wang Anqing, Jin Lianhua, Zhao Gang, Wang Dawei, Guo Zhiqiang.
(Mandarin dialogue)

"**B**lack Mountain" is a beautifully shot tale of elemental passion between two roughnecks and a lone woman in a remote country inn. Quality, mainland Chinese item should be well received on the fest trail and in specialized Sino-friendly theatrical and tube slots.

Fourth feature of director Zhou Xiaowen was shot in 1990 but (apparently because of its sexual content) passed by the Chinese authorities only last year. The movie, which is getting its first offshore exposure at the Montreal fest, forms an interesting reference item to Zhou's latest (ninth) feature, "Ermo," also rural-set but with a very different, contemporary feel.

Setting is a heavily wooded, bandit-infested mountain pass somewhere in northern China during the Sino-Japanese War. In a dilapidated church lives a sullen young woman (Ailiya) and her ferocious mutt. Passing through are strong, silent traders and porters, to whom she dispenses food, foot care and occasional sexual favors.

Following an attack by bandits, a brutish porter (Zhao Xiaorui) stays on to tend his injuries and make moves on the woman. She, meanwhile, has the mutual hots for another porter, the handsome, kindlier "Sixth Brother" (Xie Yuan). As tensions rise between the two men, the Japanese arrive to take the place by force.

With its spare dialogue, glowing interiors and rugged landscape, pic is basically an atmosphere piece. Photography by Zhou himself and Zhao Jiping's eerie, woodwindy score keep the irreal, mystical edge ever-present. Both turn up the heat in the two major sex scenes (sweaty, but mild by Western standards), which are shot and cut like something out of Zalman King.

Striking Inner Mongolian actress Ailiya, who plays the gutsy lead in Zhou's "Ermo," gives a fine, earthy perf as the much-abused mountain femme. The bull-like Zhao and scrawnier Xie are on the money as the yin and yang in her life.

Tech credits are handsome in all departments. Chinese title literally means "Black Mountain Road."
—*Derek Elley*

MIDNIGHT DANCERS
(FILIPINO)

A Tangent Films production. Executive producer, Richard Wong Tang. Directed by Mel Chionglo. Screenplay, Ricardo Lee. Camera (color), George Tutanes; editor, Jess Navarro; music, Nonong Buenoamino; production design, Edgar Martin Littaua; sound, Ramon Reyes. Reviewed at Toronto Film Festival, Sept. 13, 1994. Running time: **100 MIN.**
With: Alex Del Rosario, Grandong Cervantes, Lawrence David, Luis Cortez, Richard Cassity, Danny Ramos, Perla Bautista.

Macho dancers and call boys, prostitutes and pimps, flamboyant queens and closeted homosexuals populate Mel Chionglo's "Midnight Dancers," a compassionate portrait of Manila's gay subculture and its relation to mainstream society. Tale's specific setting and handsome lead characters will obviously make it a likable experience for gay viewers, though depiction of broader family issues might extend pic's appeal beyond its primary target audience.

Story centers on three brothers from Cebu as they function in Manila's gay world as "macho dancers" or "sibak" (gay slang for male prostitutes). The youngest and most naive brother, Sonny, provides the film's emotional focus and point of view. Manila's gay world is presented from his perspective, as he slowly assimilates into its culture to the point of taking a transvestite lover.

The oldest sibling, Joel, who's only 23 but has been working for seven years, attempts to balance his relationships with a wife and a gay lover. Tougher brother Dennis represents yet a different type, favoring the edgy excitement of the streets over intimate family life.

Chionglo's liberal, almost too-good-to-be-true philosophy is informed by the notion that love can not be constricted by gender or sexual orientation.

Writer Ricardo Lee and director Chionglo stress Manila's depressed economy, showing how a lean job market often necessitates male prostitution. To illustrate their thesis, the filmmakers opt for a docudrama style, one that observes all members of the family, male and female, as they go about their daily existence.

Nonetheless, in the last reel, melodramatic events come fast and furious — police arrests, brutal killings, scandalous adultery, family feuds, emotional reconciliations — and subsequently pic loses its balanced tone and, to some extent, its humor.

Another major problem is helmer's inability to decide how much sexual titillation and voyeurism the story should encourage.

The actors who play the three brothers are newcomers, but they all acquit themselves with natural, relaxed performances. Though the shows' choreography is unimpressive, the camera seems to caress the handsome boys and their almost nude bodies. Pic's erotic charge is undeniably its major selling point, particularly for the audiences for which it was made. —*Emanuel Levy*

BLUE HELMET
(CASQUE BLEU)
(FRENCH)

An AMLF release of a Ciby 2000/Novo Arturo Films/TF1 Films production, with participation of BNP Images and Canal Plus. Executive producer, Alain Depardieu. Directed by Gerard Jugnot. Screenplay, Jugnot, Christian Biegalski, Philippe Lopes-Curval. Camera (color), Gerard de Battista; editor, Catherine Kelber; music, Yves de Bujadoux; production design, Jean-Louis Poveda; costume design, Martine Rapin; sound (Dolby), Didier Lize; assistant director, Laurent Laubier. Reviewed at Pathe Palace Cinema, Avignon, France, June 20, 1994. Running time: **95 MIN.**
Patrick .... Gerard Jugnot
Alicia .... Victoria Abril
Laurette .... Valerie Lemercier
Nicolas .... Jean-Pierre Cassel
Gisele .... Micheline Presle
Pierre .... Claude Pieplu
With: Jean-Noel Broute, Roland Marchisio, Hubert Saint Macary.

A strained, uninvolving attempt to straddle comedy and tragedy, "Blue Helmet" is a total misfire in terms of script and tone. But tale of armed insurrection at a vacation retreat is sure to start off strong on home turf due to presence of writer/director/star Gerard Jugnot, plus well-liked thesps such as Valerie Lemercier and Victoria Abril. Jugnot's previous outing, "Une Epoque formidable," was one of the top-grossing Gallic pix of 1991.

In order to atone for one episode of infidelity in 13 years of marriage, French wine grower Patrick (Jugnot) takes his wife, Alicia (Abril), back to the unnamed Mediterranean island resort where the couple met and fell in love at the Peace Inn Hotel.

Tedium sets in immediately as other — mostly French — vacationers and staff are introduced: gracious hotel owner Nicolas (Jean-Pierre Cassel) and his affected lover, Freddy (Roland Marchisio); gauche secretary Laurette (Lemercier), who falls for gay Nicolas; a young man with low self-esteem and a sleeping-pill habit (Jean-Noel Broute); camcorder enthusiast Pierre (Claude Pieplu) and his wife, Gisele (Micheline Presle), a seventyish woman on overly intimate terms with her pet dog; and a young foreign couple in heat.

Alicia refuses to forgive Patrick, and the paying customer is likely to feel likewise. After 45 minutes of weak prelims, civil war breaks out on the island, and Nicolas and his guests are taken hostage by the insurgents.

Gags are feeble, and few and far between, and crises are contrived. Thesping is adequate but characters' dilemmas are never the least bit involving or convincing. Pic was competently lensed in Malta.
—*Lisa Nesselson*

October 31, 1994

MARY SHELLEY'S FRANKENSTEIN

A TriStar Pictures release presented in association with Japan Satellite Broadcasting and the IndieProd Co. of an American Zoetrope production. Produced by Francis Ford Coppola, James V. Hart, John Veitch. Co-producers, Kenneth Branagh, David Parfitt. Executive producer, Fred Fuchs. Directed by Branagh. Screenplay, Steph Lady, Frank Darabont. Camera (Technicolor color), Roger Pratt; editor, Andrew Marcus; music, Patrick Doyle; production design, Tim Harvey; supervising art direction, Martin Childs; art direction, John Fenner, Desmond Crowe; costume design, James Acheson; sound (Dolby, SDDS), Ivan Sharrock; associate producer, David Barron; assistant director, Chris Newman; second-unit director, Marcus; unit production manager, Barron; creature makeup and effects designed by Daniel Parker; visual effects supervisor, Richard Conway; casting, Priscilla John. Reviewed at the Mann Village Theater, L.A., Oct. 27, 1994. MPAA Rating: R. Running time: **123 MIN.**

Creature/Sharp Featured
Man .... Robert De Niro
Victor .... Kenneth Branagh
Henry .... Tom Hulce
Elizabeth ...... Helena Bonham Carter
Walton .... Aidan Quinn
Victor's Father .... Ian Holm
Grandfather .... Richard Briers
Professor Waldman .... John Cleese
Professor Krempe ...... Robert Hardy
Victor's Mother .... Cherie Lunghi
Mrs. Moritz .... Celia Imrie
Justine .... Trevyn McDowell

Kenneth Branagh has indeed created a monster, but not the kind he originally envisioned. A major disappointment creatively, the film still has the makings of a box office brute for TriStar, based on alluring marquee elements and the success of "Bram Stoker's Dracula." However, it doesn't look to be the money-making hulk a more electrifying telling might have produced.

Far from the definitive version of the tale, this lavish but overwrought melodrama is in many ways less compelling than even a recent made-for-cable movie and a 1973 miniseries starring Michael Sarrazin that was less faithful to the source material.

Tackling a Gothic epic as director/co-producer/star, Branagh seems to overreach himself, playing every aspect at an almost operatic level that's too feverish for its own good.

In addition, the director and writers Steph Lady and Frank Darabont seem to get carried away in playing up the story's romance, at the expense of the horror-action elements that a large segment of the audience doubtless anticipates. Yet more grisly aspects of the film could be off-putting to some of those the filmmakers are courting with the Branagh-Helena Bonham Carter pairing.

Perhaps including the author's name in a classic horror story invites pretentiousness, but "Mary Shelley's Frankenstein" hews close enough to the original to only demonstrate where it misses the mark.

The beginning proves effective and true to the novel, as a sea captain (Aidan Quinn) exploring the arctic stumbles upon the crazed Victor Frankenstein (Branagh), who recounts his cautionary tale about scientific obsession in detailed flashback.

Seeking to get inside Frankenstein's head, as it were, the account begins with the death of his mother in childbirth, and Victor's own longings for his adopted sister (Carter). Moving on to a university, Victor encounters an elder doctor (an almost unrecognizable John Cleese) and seizes on his work to try to thwart death, using parts of corpses to create his monster.

It's nearly an hour into the film before the creature emerges from the tank, and despite the overamplified tone, there's still hope for the movie at that juncture.

Assuming the monster has died, Frankenstein returns to Geneva, while the Creature — after demonstrating his prodigious strength in escaping the townsfolk — befriends a simple country family, learning (or as he puts it, remembering) how to speak and read before ultimately going after his creator to seek vengeance.

At this point, however, the movie begins to spin wildly out of control, unable to strike the delicate balance needed between pathos, romance and horror. When a key sequence involving the doctor, his bride and the monster is greeted with more than a few unintentional laughs, it's clear "Frankenstein" has strayed into dangerous territory.

Curiosity about Robert De Niro's performance will almost certainly fuel box office, yet the prospect of one of the screen's greatest actors in such a notorious role doesn't live up to expectations. Despite the hoopla, De Niro's creature doesn't even approach the terror factor of his role in "Cape Fear," while failing to inspire the empathy that even Boris Karloff — bolts and all — engendered.

De Niro's makeup doesn't help matters, appearing grotesque but not particularly jarring. One can see too much of De Niro behind those scars, never really letting the actor lose himself within the character.

Branagh's own performance is appropriately crazed, while Carter as always proves radiant and engaging. Among the capable supporting cast, Thomas Hulce provides the only humor in what's otherwise a rather grim, severe exercise.

Opulent sets and costumes abound, but the curiously designed lab scenes don't establish the standard one might have anticipated, and Patrick Doyle's relentlessly bombastic score is simply overbearing.

Other tech credits are generally impressive but not a complete success by any means, and certainly not as breathtakingly florid as the most recent "Dracula," which also counted producers Francis Ford Coppola and James V. Hart as part of its team.

As with that film, based on the anticipation here, there's a strong yearning to send "Frankenstein" back to the drawing board.

—Brian Lowry

THE WAR

A Universal Pictures release of an Island World picture. An Avnet/Kerner production. Produced by Jon Avnet, Jordan Kerner. Executive producers, Eric Eisner, Todd Baker. Co-executive producer, Kathy McWorter. Co-producers, Martin Huberty, Lisa Lindstrom. Directed by Avnet. Screenplay, McWorter. Camera (DeLuxe color), Geoffrey Simpson; editor, Debra Neil; music, Thomas Newman; production design, Kristi Zea; art direction, Jeremy Conway; set decoration, Karen O'Hara; costume design, Molly Maginnis; sound (DTS), Mary H. Ellis; associate producer, Deborah Love; unit production manager, Alma Kuttruff; assistant director, Love; casting, David Zubin, Debra Zane. Reviewed at the Universal Pictures screening room, Universal City, Oct. 21, 1994. MPAA Rating: PG-13. Running time: **125 MIN.**

Stu .... Elijah Wood
Stephen .... Kevin Costner
Lois .... Mare Winningham
Lidia .... Lexi Randall
Miss Strapford ...... Christine Baranski
Mr. Lipnicki .... Raynor Scheine
Moe .... Bruce A. Young
Elvadine .... LaToya Chisholm
Amber .... Charlette Lewis

Director Jon Avnet's attempt to recapture the flavor of his "Fried Green Tomatoes" comes out of the oven a bit squishy in "The War," an earnest but over-cooked stew. The main ingredient is actually a big slice of "Stand By Me," but there are sprinkles from various Vietnam war movies and even "Places in the Heart." A strong marketing campaign may help early box office pickings, but long-term prospects suggest a modest harvest.

Despite Kevin Costner's presence — in a role that's nearly the opposite of his turn in "A Perfect World" — "The War" really belongs to its child cast, headed by Elijah Wood and newcomer Lexi Randall.

Still, the parallel between the Vietnam war and the children's feud with a local clan of kids feels heavy-handed even by Oliver Stone-type standards, and attempts to infuse the narrative with a sense of spirituality are so blatantly manipulative that they lack the wallop Avnet and screenwriter Kathy McWorter are clearly going after.

Set in Mississippi during the summer of 1970, the story focuses on a poor family whose patriarch (Costner) has returned from Vietnam bearing emotional scars that make it difficult for him to hold a job.

His wife (Mare Winningham) struggles to keep the family afloat, while the kids set about the task of building a tree fort, all the while feuding with the despised Lipnickis — an almost feral family of dirt-poor bullies who clearly take their lead from an alcoholic, abusive father.

Along the way, Costner's wounded vet seeks to teach his son a sort of "Coward of the County"-esque message about what is or isn't worth fighting for, illustrating the point with his own story — told in sporadic flashback episodes — about a particularly haunting episode from the war.

Still, Avnet and McWorter lose the battle for credibility on the home front, especially in the over-the-top battle sequence for the tree fort that feels as forced and stilted as its resolution. The filmmakers invest too much time demonizing the Lipnickis to allow for the sort of pat ending they've devised.

"The War" does yield memorable moments of a smaller variety, such as the scenes of Lidia (Randall) and friends crooning their own versions of Supremes tunes, down to the garish choreography. There's also a particularly strong scene in which the girls stand up to a bigoted teacher.

Unfortunately, the movie wrestles with too many demons of its own to be completely effective, reaching too far and trying too hard to uplift the audience. Too many movies have been down this road before.

Wood remains a gifted child actor and also proves to be about the only cast member who doesn't find himself stumbling over his Southern drawl. (Indeed, some of the children's speech is so thick that many who live north of the Mason-Dixon line or west of Galveston will find themselves in need of a translator.)

Costner proves earnest and sincere in his latest good ol' boy performance, lending marquee value to a movie whose focus is on the kids. Even so, he seems somewhat miscast in the pivotal supporting role, almost inadvertently projecting too much movie-star charm for the tortured soul he's supposed to be playing.

Winningham (Costner's put-upon missus in "Wyatt Earp" as well) is used sparingly as the mother. Casting of the kids is impeccable.

Tech credits deftly evoke the period, augmented by an omnipresent song score that begins with "Who'll Stop the Rain?" and concludes with Cat Stevens' "Peace Train" — selections that say it all, with about the same subtlety, about the rail "The War" is riding.

—*Brian Lowry*

SQUANTO: A WARRIOR'S TALE

A Buena Vista release of a Walt Disney Pictures production. Produced by Kathryn Galan. Executive producer, Don Carmody. Directed by Xavier Koller. Screenplay, Darlene Craviotto. Camera (Technicolor), Robbie Greenberg; editor, Lisa Day. music, Joel McNeely; production design, Gemma Jackson; art direction, Claude Pare; costume design, Olga Dimitrov; sound (Dolby), Patrick Rousseau; native consultants, Russell Peters, Howard Jeddore; assistant directors, Michael Williams, Christopher Stoia; casting, Lynn Stalmaster. Reviewed at the Festival Cinema, Westwood, Oct. 24, 1994. MPAA Rating: PG. Running time: **101 MIN.**
Squanto .... Adam Beach
Brother Daniel .... Mandy Patinkin
Sir George .... Michael Gambon
Thomas Dermer .... Nathaniel Parker
Epenow .... Eric Schweig
Brother Paul .... Donal Donnelly
Brother Timothy .... Stuart Pankin
Harding .... Alex Norton
Nakooma .... Irene Bedard

Though subtitled "A Warrior's Tale," Disney's "Squanto" more aptly should be viewed as "The Legend of Thanksgiving." While that prospect might sound particularly dire, the intelligence and craft of this period drama quickly overcome any qualms about subject matter or interpretation.

The rich tapestry is definitely a cut above the company's most recent family outings, and that will be a decided asset at the box office. Its historic nature and ethnographic flavor are likely to draw its strongest commercial action offshore, particularly in European environs where "White Fang" was a howling success.

The central character, a 17th century Native American, is derived from the history books. However, while the broad facts of his life remain intact, the script has fashioned an effective speculative storyline to fill in the unrecorded passages.

Squanto (Adam Beach) has recently married when a band of British traders arrives in his village to exchange trinkets for furs. The friendly transactions sour as the sailors forcibly take him and others aboard their ship and back to England for display and sport.

Shortly after arriving in Plymouth, England, Squanto escapes during a public contest pitting him against a bear. His flight fortuitously takes him into the protective care of a band of learned monks.

The pith of the film is the confrontation between Squanto — representing centuries of Indian culture — and the band of religious recluses. The brothers are initially fascinated by their "noble savage." But as they learn to communicate, the exchange takes on greater equilibrium. Though certain values are intrinsically at odds, they share a belief in the human spirit and the essential desire to do the right and humane thing.

Darlene Craviotto's screenplay is a classic confrontation of good vs. evil. On the one hand there's Squanto, a man plucked from his people, and the monks, a brotherhood that has separated itself from the wider society. The black hats are represented by Sir George (Michael Gambon), the tyrannical overlord of the Plymouth Shipping Co., and his minions.

And there's a nice counterbalance in gray provided by Dermer (Nathaniel Parker), an interpreter who embodies a more modern business attitude; and Epenow (Eric Schweig), another native captive who harbors tremendous antagonism toward the Brits.

Director Xavier Koller effects a keen sense of detail and observation in the story, which subtly deflects some inherent narrative clunkiness. The daring manner in which Squanto manages a return to America, for instance, provides such a tremendous emotional catharsis that much of what follows with the Pilgrims becomes anti-climactic.

Filmed in historic locations in Canada, the picture has a seamless historic quality. Tech credits are sterling, including Robbie Greenberg's camerawork and production design by Gemma Jackson. Overall it is a graceful, simple saga that skirts the obvious for a more textured view of a bygone time, without falling into the pit of docudrama.

Beach invests Squanto with a physical dynamism and nascent intelligence. It's an unaffected performance that's robust and riveting, and the successful core of the film. Supporting players range from colorful turns by Mandy Patinkin and Donal Donnelly as holy brothers, and Gambon's effete magnate, to more layered and disturbing resonances from Schweig and Parker.

Obviously a great deal of care was invested in "Squanto," and that breathes integrity into every frame. Yet, it remains mythic and timeless and vastly entertaining.

—*Leonard Klady*

DER BEWEGTE MANN

(GERMAN)

A Neue Constantin release (in Germany) of a Bernd Eichinger production. (International sales: Atlas Intl., Munich.) Produced by Eichinger. Line producer, Harry Kuegler. Directed, written by Soenke Wortmann, based on the comics "Der bewegte Mann" and "Pretty Baby" by Ralf Koenig. Camera (color), Gernot Roll; editor, Ueli Christen; music, Torsten Breuer; songs performed by Palast Orchester, sung by Max Raabe; production design, Monika Bauert; costume design, Katharina von Martius; sound (Dolby), Simon Happ; assistant director, Heike Hempel; associate producers, Martin Moszkowicz, Molly von Fuerstenberg, Kuegler, Elvira Senft. Reviewed at Film Palast, Berlin, Sept. 13, 1994. Running Time: **93 MIN.**
Axel .... Til Schweiger
Doro .... Katja Riemann
Norbert .... Joachim Krol
Walter/Waltraud .... Rufus Beck
Butcher .... Armin Rohde

Also with: Nico van der Knaap, Antonia Lang, Martina Gedeck, Kai Wiesinger, Christof Wackernagel, Heinrich Schafmeister, Martin Armknecht.

"Der bewegte Mann" is Germany's funniest date movie in a long time and, like its hero, does a risky balancing act between the sexes. Though based on two gay comic books by cult cartoonist Ralf Koenig, this romantic comedy is angled towards heterosexual couples. Following a powerful opening in Germany Oct. 6, pic looks set to become the most successful German film of the year, with some international potential indicated. Producer Bernd Eichinger and director Soenke Wortmann are already mulling an American remake.

Title refers to a man who can be "moved" (bewegt) back and forth across the line of sexual preference. The main character, Axel (Til Schweiger), is such a man, a macho hunk who's cheated one too many times on g.f. Doro (Katja Riemann). When Doro throws him out of the house, the only place he can find to stay is the apartment of homosexual Norbert (Joachim Krol).

Norbert wants Axel badly, but he's much too shy to make any obvious moves, preferring to suffer under Axel's insensitivity. Doro, however, picks up right away on what's going on and panics that Axel is really gay. Even when she discovers she's pregnant and takes Axel back to marry him, her suspicions continue.

Film has an uneven feel that derives from being based on two separate comic books, each with its own climax. Several episodes are fine on their own terms — like Norbert showing up in drag at Axel's wedding, Axel hiring Norbert's apartment to have sex with another woman when Doro is heavily pregnant, and Doro finding him in Norbert's apartment naked — but what makes the film work is its dry, sophisticated dialogue, taken almost word for word from the originals.

The comics' gay perspective has been "straightened" for the movie, with Axel no longer sexually undecided but simply a naive fish out of water exploring the bizarre environment of his new landlord. However, the script's incidental comments on men and sex from a largely gay vantage point are insightful. Koenig's dialogue has a quality that also allows his many women readers (and filmgoers) to feel like eavesdroppers, listening to men talk about men in a blatantly sexual way.

Schweiger makes a handsome lead, but that's almost all he does. The show is stolen by Katja Riemann (from "Making Up!"), who shows strong camera presence as Doro, and most of all by Krol ("No More Mr. Nice Guy") as Norbert, whose sad, puppy-dog face would break the heart of even the biggest homophobe. Rufus Beck is perfect as Norbert's cross-dressing, screechy friend Walter/Waltraud.

Fine lensing by Gernot Roll gives the pic a comfortable, classy warmth and the Palast Orchester with vocalist Max Raabe provides a Fred Astaire class with songs from the '20s and '30s (currently en vogue in Germany).

Wortmann's direction is tight and pro, with a feel for holding and manipulating his audience's attention. Since leaping to fame with the 1992 "Alone Among Women," young turk Wortmann has badly needed another hit. This is it.

—*Eric Hansen*

THE MONSTER

(IL MOSTRO)

(ITALIAN-FRENCH)

A Filmauro Distribuzione release (in Italy) of a UGC Image (Paris) production of a Melampro (Rome)/Iris Film, with participation of Canal Plus, La Sept Cinema, Sofinergie. (International sales: UGC, France.) Produced by Roberto Benigni, Yves Attal. Executive producer, Elda Ferri. Directed by Benigni. Screenplay, Vincenzo Cerami, Benigni. Camera (Technicolor), Carlo Di Palma; editor, Nino Baragli; music, Evan Lurie; production design, Giantito Burchiellaro; costume design, Danilo Donati; sound (Dolby), Jean-Paul Mugel; associate producer, Gianluigi Braschi; assistant director, Gianni Arduini. Reviewed at Anica screening room, Rome, Oct. 21, 1994. Running time: **110 MIN.**

Loris	Roberto Benigni
Jessica	Nicoletta Braschi
Taccone	Michel Blanc
Jolanda	Dominique Lavanant
Roccarotta	Jean-Claude Brialy
Pascucci	Ivano Marescotti
Chinese teacher	Franco Mescolini
Frustalupi	Laurent Spielvogel
Distinguished resident	Massimo Girotti

A relatively harmless but by no means angelic social misfit gets mistaken for a serial killer in "The Monster," the first actor-director outing by leading Italian comedy star Roberto Benigni since his 1991 domestic record-breaker, "Johnny Stecchino." Though the irreverent Tuscan rib-tickler's work behind the cameras fails to match the heights of his onscreen presence, the laughs come thick and fast, guaranteeing colossal biz at home, and at least a modest assault on offshore markets.

After the less-than-rapturous reception given his Hollywood excursion in Blake Edwards' "Son of the Pink Panther," here Benigni ironically echoes Edwards' work with Peter Sellers, showcasing his singular gifts as both physical comedian and crazed babbler.

Benigni plays Loris, a shifty, sexually overwound petty shyster who's not the least bit interested in getting along with his fellow residents in a gargantuan apartment block. At a party, he gets a tip-off about an easy conquest, but approaches the wrong woman.

Attempting to apologize later for his groping hands, he makes matters worse with an out-of-control chainsaw. The terrified victim's police report convinces head cop Frustalupi (Laurent Spielvogel) that Loris is "the Mozart of vice," the violent sex killer he's spent 12 years stalking.

Hoping to surprise him in the act, Frustalupi and police shrink Taccone (Michel Blanc) tail Loris. The cleverly orchestrated, misconstrued circumstances they catch on film seemingly tag him as a depraved sex fiend who even strangles cats. Eager to pounce, the cops send in policewoman Jessica (Nicoletta Braschi) as bait.

Braschi (Benigni's real-life wife) makes a tasty, extremely amusing foil as she nervously flaunts her charms, falling in love in the process.

Though the pic's comic concerns are far from new, Benigni's verve and inventiveness make them fresh, often skating tantalizingly along the edge of offensiveness.

Standout scenes are numerous, from Loris' attempts to improve his career prospects by learning Chinese, through him setting up a decoy in the local supermarket to facilitate shoplifting, to his ruses to discourage buyers of the apartment he's renting. Benigni also tosses in a witty dig at the Italian political circus via an overblown condominium meeting.

On the down side, the film suffers from an uneven rhythm. (Prints being touted for international sale are reportedly shorn of 10 minutes, which could eliminate lulls.) Benigni's direction is rather flat overall, especially in the more frenetic final reels where cops begin to close in on Loris. However, given that the performing energy is kept at full steam, this presents no major problem.

Alongside the delightful leading duo, Gallic actor-director Blanc ("Dead Tired") gels seamlessly as the barely sane medic, especially in a funny scene where Loris has the doc and his jittery wife (Dominique Lavanant) over to dinner.

Lavanant and Jean-Claude Brialy as the building's distraught administrator also earn their share of laughs. As a distinguished gent unfazed by Loris and Jessica's increasingly eccentric behavior, Massimo Girotti adds a welcome running joke.

Despite some of the names on hand, the film's tech slate is unremarkable, aside from Evan Lurie's jaunty score. Biggest disappointment is Carlo Di Palma's lensing, which is frequently less than sharp and does little to alleviate the blandness of the suburban setting.

—*David Rooney*

THE LAST GOOD TIME

A Samuel Goldwyn release of an Apogee Films production. Produced by Dean Silvers and Bob Balaban. Executive producer, Klaus Volkenborn. Directed by Balaban. Screenplay, Balaban, John McLaughlin, based on Richard Bausch's novel. Camera (color), Claudia Raschke; editor, Hughes Winborne; music, Jonathan Tunick; production design, Wing Lee; art direction, Michael Shaw; set decoration, Betsy Alton; costume design, Kimberly A. Tillman; sound, Antonio L. Arroyo; associate producers, Ricardo Freixa, Todd Scott Brody; casting, Billy Hopkins, Susanne Smith, Kerry Barden. Reviewed at the Hamptons Film Festival, Oct. 19, 1994. Running time: **90 MIN.**

Joseph Kopple	Armin Mueller-Stahl
Ida Cutler	Maureen Stapleton
Howard Singer	Lionel Stander
Charlotte Zwicki	Olivia D'Abo
Eddie	Adrian Pasdar

Armin Mueller-Stahl delivers a towering performance in Bob Balaban's "The Last Good Time," an unusually poignant, finely observed comedy-drama about an old man whose life changes dramatically as a result of a fateful encounter with a young woman. Goldwyn faces a tough challenge in marketing an intimate, often slow film that not only lacks conventional action or drama, but also features three of four characters who are senior citizens.

Mueller-Stahl plays Joseph Kopple, an elegant 70-year-old widower who still clings to the memories of his beautiful wife, whose untimely death also signaled mental dissolution for him. A retired musician, he's being hounded by the IRS for failure to pay taxes on his pension. The only grace in his lonely, fastidious life, mostly spent in his walk-up Brooklyn apartment, is nightly violin-playing.

One evening, Joseph witnesses a nasty fight between a young couple upstairs, which ends with Charlotte (Olivia D'Abo) being kicked out of the apartment by boyfriend Eddie (Adrian Pasdar). With all of her belongings thrown out the window, Joseph picks up her lipstick and key, two symbolic items that will later prove crucial. The freezing Charlotte has no place to go, so Joseph takes her in and gradually they develop a strange friendship.

On the surface, pic centers on the bittersweet relationship between two very different individuals. Indeed, the script, co-written by Balaban and McLaughlin, stresses the huge gaps in the characters' age, education and lifestyle. But after the first reel, it becomes clear the film's goal is to challenge our preconceived notions and stereotypes about aging.

Director Balaban succeeds in steering away from sentimental melodrama and from imposing obvious turning points on the central relationship, which grows naturally. Leaving aside the crude sitcom humor of a commercial hit like "Grumpy Old Men," the filmmakers refuse to judge or pander to any of their characters.

Pic is excellent in chronicling the importance that Joseph attaches to order and routine, particularly his daily visits to a nursing home, where Howard Singer (Lionel Stander), his 89-year-old friend, resides. Most of the humor is based on the interaction between Joseph and Howard, a dying man who hasn't lost his sharp tongue or his mental vigor. The scene where the two men smoke cigars, get drunk and reminisce about sex is as funny as it is touching.

As the film's emotional center, Mueller-Stahl renders a splendid lyrical performance — he's a rare actor who, by projecting inner verve and not just dialogue, always serves notice. That D'Abo is less impressive may be a result of her less developed role, as story is told from Joseph's p.o.v. What Charlotte brings to Joseph's dreary existence is well-established, but it's not always clear how she feels toward him.

A stellar supporting cast includes the irascible Stander and the magnificent Maureen Stapleton, as a chatty neighbor whose friendly gestures are at first rejected by Joseph.

Lenser Claudia Raschke and editor Hughes Winborne imbue the film with an arresting visual style, using uninterrupted long takes and radiant panning to convey the changing physical, and emotional, space between Joseph and Charlotte.

The filmmakers struggle a bit too hard to end the story on an uplifting note, which undermines the more ambiguous tone, but this doesn't mar the emotional impact of a quiet, resonant film that is as sparing in words as it is abundant in meanings.

—*Emanuel Levy*

October 31, 1994 (Cont.)

SILENT FALL

A Warner Bros. release of a Morgan Creek Production. Produced by James A. Robinson. Executive producer, Gary Barber. Co-producers, Penelope L. Foster, Jim Kouf and Lynn Bigelow. Directed by Bruce Beresford. Screenplay, Akiva Goldsman. Camera (Duart, prints by Technicolor), Peter James; editor, Ian Crafford; music, Stewart Copeland; art direction, David Bomba; set decoration, Patty Malone; costume design, Colleen Kelsall; sound (Dolby), Chris Newman; assistant director, Katterli A. Frauenfelder; casting, Shari Rhodes, Joseph Middleton. Reviewed at Hamptons Film Festival, Oct. 23, 1994. MPAA Rating: R. Running time: **100 MIN.**
Jake Rainer .... Richard Dreyfuss
Karen Rainer .... Linda Hamilton
Dr. Harlinger .... John Lithgow
Sheriff Mitch Rivers .... J.T. Walsh
Tim Warden .... Ben Faulkner
Sylvie Warden .... Liv Tyler

An awkward synthesis of autism as a clinical problem and family abuse as a social issue, Bruce Beresford's "Silent Fall" is a well-crafted murder mystery that unfortunately is short on excitement and genuine suspense. Downbeat word-of-mouth and competition from several major films in the next two weeks will spell box office disappointment for Warners' earnest psychological drama.

Richard Dreyfuss plays Jake Rainer, a once-prominent psychiatrist whose successful work with autistic children drew on his unique mix of warmth, humor and personal methods. But a disastrous incident, for which he was indicted and then acquitted, has made him a man haunted by guilt and anguish, one who refuses to practice — or share intimacy with his wife — anymore.

Jake is forced out of his professional and emotional stupor when a bizarre double murder occurs at the Wardens' estate. There are no obvious clues, but there are two witnesses: Tim Warden (Ben Faulkner), an autistic 9-year-old boy, and his overly protective sister Sylvie (Liv Tyler). When Jake arrives at the scene of the crime, Tim is holding a bloody knife, and Sylvie is hiding in the closet.

At first, he's reluctant to get involved, which gives his wife (Linda Hamilton) plenty of ammunition for accusing him of being a failure. It's only when his rival, the stern Dr. Harlinger (John Lithgow), subjects Tim to his notorious authoritarian treatment that Jake takes the child under his wing.

The first — and more interesting — part of the narrative focuses on the symptoms of autism. As is often the case with such movies, Jake provides all kinds of medical explanations so that every viewer will understand what autism is or isn't.

Some viewers are likely to find these meticulously observed sequences, in which Tim speaks in different voices or reacts in unpredictable manner, not terribly absorbing.

However, after an hour or so, pic changes gears and turns into a rather conventional thriller. As such, it depends on offering twists and revelations, and the chief problem is that pic provides so many clues that it's possible to unravel the killer's identity long before the finale.

Helmer Beresford, who has made forceful courtroom ("Breaker Morant") and social issue movies ("Driving Miss Daisy"), shows smooth adeptness with the requirements of the suspense genre. As always, though, he's more interested in character development than plot, which here gets progressively contrived — and banal.

In the lead role of a man who had emotionally "withdrawn" from the world, Dreyfuss renders one of his more restrained and effective performances. Holding the entire picture together, he has some excellent moments in his one-to-one interactions with the kid.

It's refreshing to see the muscled Hamilton in a non-action pic, but as Jake's suffering wife, she plays a thankless role whose main purpose is to remind Jake that he's a quitter. Tyler and Faulkner, two attractive newcomers, are well cast as the troubled siblings.

Technical input, which benefits from Beresford's longtime collaborations, shows prowess in all quarters, particularly James' crisp lensing of Maryland's countryside and Stoddart's impressive production design.

"Silent Fall" doesn't sentimentalize autistic children, but, like "Rain Man" and "Awakenings," it trivializes autism for entertainment purposes, which may be morally dubious.
—*Emanuel Levy*

JUDICIAL CONSENT

A Rysher Entertainment production in association with Prelude Pictures. Produced by Douglas Curtis, Mark W. Koch. Executive producers, Keith Samples, William Hart. Co-producers, Michael and Atanas Ilitch. Directed, written by William Bindley. Camera (Foto-Kem, color), James Glennon; editor, William Hoy; music, Christopher Young; production design, Dorian Vernacchio, Deborah Raymond; costume design, Eleanor Nyquist Patton; casting, Fern Orenstein. Reviewed at Hamptons Film Festival, Oct. 21, 1994. Running time: **101 MIN.**
Gwen Warwick .... Bonnie Bedelia
Alan Warwick .... Will Patton
Charles Mayron .... Dabney Coleman
Martin .... Billy Wirth
District attorney .... Lisa Blount

"Judicial Consent" aspires to belong to the A league of suspense thrillers about female lawyers, like "Jagged Edge" with Glenn Close or Cher's vehicle, "Suspect." Its star, the always graceful Bonnie Bedelia, does an honorable job, but the film's B plot and its lack of sustained suspense reduce it to just a pleasant generic item. Technically polished entry may enjoy a limited theatrical release, but it seems best suited to the tube, with good prospects on video.

Gwen Warwick (Bedelia) is a stern, accomplished criminal court judge, soon to be appointed to the Michigan Supreme Court. Seemingly curious and sexually unfulfilled, one night she follows Martin (Billy Wirth), a sexy law clerk, into his office, and a steamy affair evolves.

When Gwen's roguish colleague, Charles Matron (Dabney Coleman), "a chronic flirt," is found dead in his office, she's asked to preside over the case. Soon, what seemed "circumstantial" evidence turns out to be a well-planned murder, with Gwen as the prime suspect. Realizing she's been set up, Gwen begins a desperate race against time to prove her innocence.

The courtroom format relies heavily on finely tuned dialogue and unanticipated revelations, but Bindley's writing, specifically in the court sequences, is borderline banal and the disclosures aren't particularly suspenseful.

Though a first-time helmer, Bindley gives his picture a smooth and polished look, displaying some mastery over the genre's tricks — and visual cliches. Dark lofts, swinging doors, empty parking lots and so on are all nicely handled, but they're also familiar to an audience that always seems to be ahead of the pic's characters.

Bedelia gives a charming, dominating performance, but the woman she plays is too intelligent and too bright to behave in such a senseless manner. For instance, lawyers, particularly women, might find offensive a sex scene in Gwen's office in which she's shown reaching orgasm while negotiating an important assignment on the telephone. Will Patton, usually brilliant in small, offbeat roles, is miscast here in the underwritten role of Gwen's bland husband; we never get a sense of the kind of marriage the Warwicks have. As Martin, gifted character actor Coleman is wasted in an unrewarding role, while Wirth is there mostly to look good as the stranger with a "mysterious" motive.

Movies that know how to mix the dangerous and the erotic often make edgy, highly diverting thrillers, but "Judicial Consent" is too obvious and too conscious of its form.
—*Emanuel Levy*

THE DESPERATE TRAIL

A Turner Entertainment film of Motion Picture Corp. of America production. Produced by Brad Krevoy and Steven Stabler. Co-producer, Chad Oman. Directed by P.J. Pesce. Screenplay, Pesce, Tom Abrams. Camera (Foto-Kem, color), Michael Bonvillain; editor, Bill Johnson; music, Stephen Endelman; production design, Jonathan A. Carlson; sound (Dolby), Rick Waddiell; casting, Sarah C. Koeppe. Reviewed at Hamptons Film Festival, Oct. 20, 1994. Running time: **93 MIN.**
Marshall Speakes .... Sam Elliott
Jack .... Craig Sheffer
Sarah .... Linda Fiorentino
Walter .... Frank Whaley

The shadows of spaghetti Westerns maestro Sergio Leone and Sam Peckinpah loom large over the imagery of "The Desperate Trail," a new oater with a strong heroine played by Linda Fiorentino. Tale's quality and its characters never match helmer P.J. Pesce's technical savvy, speedy pacing and thrilling shootouts. Despite splashy directorial debut, lack of narrative originality and uneven writing will keep enthusiasm at a moderate level. There are also serious questions whether Turner Pictures will air the Western on TNT, or just send it straight to video.

There's little doubt that Pesce has talent to burn, but it's also clear that he's a more proficient director than writer. You wish Pesce's penchant for grand, operatic style were matched by a truly fresh narrative, instead of the second-rate tale that is presented as a "feminist" Western, though in actuality it's not revisionist.

Fiorentino is felicitously cast as Sarah, a tough, foul-mouthed woman who is being escorted by Marshall Speakes (Sam Elliott) to the nearest town, where he plans to hang her for killing a young man who was sexually abusive. Sharing their stagecoach is a mousy older woman, whose bullying hubby gave her a black eye, and Jack, a young man (Craig Sheffer) clutching a mysterious box in his lap.

As the stagecoach rides through New Mexico, vivid memories of John Ford's 1939 masterpiece "Stagecoach," come to mind, though the references to it and other classic Westerns seem rather formal and stylistic, since "Desperate Trail" doesn't have classic depth or tension.

As the story unfolds, it turns out that the man Sarah killed was Speakes' son, which means that his obsessive pursuit may be more a matter of personal vendetta than justice restored. As scripter, Pesce entertains the idea of a good lawman turned evil, but Speakes comes across as a mechanical.

Still, structured as a caper, "Desperate Trail" displays the requisite twists and turns. It's a mouse-and-cat chase in which the roles of captor and captive are often reversed.

The acting, however, is not as uniformly high as one would expect. Elliott projects his usual macho bravado, but his performance is quite monotonous. Fiorentino and Sheffer acquit themselves better with straightforward, natural performances, greatly assisted by some sharp dialogue.

The acting, however, is not as uniformly high as one would expect. Elliott projects his usual macho bravado, but his performance is monotonous. Fiorentino and Sheffer acquit themselves better with straightforward performances, greatly assisted by some sharp dialogue.

What the film has going for it are three or four rousing set-pieces, beginning with the stagecoach's hold-up and continuing with shoot-outs that would make Sergio Leone proud. Displaying a sustained tempo, most of the action flies fast, hurtling the audience along with it. Editor Johnson shrewdly keeps the pace zipping, seldom allowing the story to sag in its more sentimental moments.

Helmer Pesce should be commended for his well-orchestrated, strikingly shot and framed climax, a corker that provides both dramatic and visual satisfaction, keeping the pic at least two cuts above the usual Hollywood Western.

—Emanuel Levy

OUT OF IRELAND

(Docu)

An American Focus production. Produced by Paul Wagner, Ellen Casey Wagner. Co-producer, Dorothy Peterson. Directed by Paul Wagner. Screenplay, Wagner, Kerby Miller. Camera (color) Erich Roland; editor, Neil Means, Reid Oechslim, Wagner; music direction, Mick Moloney; sound, O. J. O'Connell, Patrick Doyle. Reviewed on videotape, Oct. 23, 1994. No MPAA Rating. Running time: **111 MIN.**
With the voices of Kelly McGillis (narration), Aidan Quinn, Liam Neeson, Gabriel Byrne, Brenda Fricker.

Docu on the Irish-American experience is a solid bit of filmmaking sure to score on fest circuit and in limited runs catering to ethnic Irish audiences. Such bookings, like the premiere engagement at Dedham Community Theatre outside Boston, will allow for theatrical playoff before film finds a home on public television and on homevid.

Filmmaker Paul Wagner, 1985 Oscar winner in the docu short category, expounds at feature length on two centuries of Irish immigration to the U.S. Narrative deftly combines personal stories — including those of Irish actors Aidan Quinn and Liam Neeson — with background ranging from William of Orange's conquest of Ireland to John F. Kennedy's visit to his family's ancestral town.

With much of the history taking place pre-motion pictures, Wagner does what he can to bring the film to life, with Erich Roland's exquisite location photography in Ireland mixing with countless still photos and drawings. Several historians and commentators appear on camera including Mick Moloney, who put together the period and traditional musical score for the film.

Film will click with Irish-Americans who will see themselves and their ancestors reflected in the story. Wagner endeavors to appeal to a larger audience, contending that the history of the Irish in America is really the history of America.

At film's end, one immigrant returns to Ireland for a visit, and realizes that for him, "home" has become America. In focusing on one immigrant group's experience, "Out of Ireland" could not be more universal — nor, given the current debate over immigration in general, more timely.

—Daniel M. Kimmel

HEAD ABOVE WATER

(HODET OVER VANNET)

(NORWEGIAN)

A Filmkameratene production in association with Svensk Filmindustri (Sweden). (International sales: Majestic Films, London.) Produced by John M. Jacobsen. Directed by Nils Gaup. Screenplay, Geir Eriksen, Eirik Ildahl. Camera (color), Erling Thurmann-Andersen; editor, Malte Wadman; music, Kjetil Bjerkestrand; production design, Harald Egende-Nissen; sound, in Dolby. Reviewed at Svensk Filmindustri screening room, Stockholm, Aug. 28, 1994. Running time: 100 MIN.
Lene .... Lene Elise Bergum
Einar .... Svein Roger Karlsen
Bjorn .... Morten Abel
Gaute .... Reidar Sorensen
Cop .... Jon Skolmen

Agory comedy-thriller with a high body count, "Head Above Water" is an unevenly acted but OK treat for those not turned off by such black slapstick humor. Pic marks a change of tone for Lapp director Nils Gaup, who made the Oscar-nommed "Pathfinder" (1988), and subsequently the pirate yarn "Shipwrecked" (1990) for Disney.

Setting is an island off the Norwegian coast during summer where a couple are vacationing. When husband Einar goes off on a fishing trip with friend Bjorn, wife Lene is visited by former lover Gaute. Gaute gets drunk, undresses, and falls asleep, but when Lene wakes up next morning, he's dead.

In a panic, Lene hides the body in a potato cellar before her jealous hubby returns. In doing so, however, its neck gets broken. Chain of events grows, with murders, attempted murders and suspicion on all sides.

Gaup mixes horror and laughs, with the former frequently grisly. Nudity is also explicit, with lovely Lene Elise Bergum shedding her garments for the slightest reasons. On the acting side, however, Bergum (a non-pro in her first role) is the weak point in the movie.

—Gunnar Rehlin

ZORN

(SWEDISH)

A Sandrews presentation of a Swedish Television Channel 1 Drama production, in association with Nordisk Film & TV-Fund, NRK, FST, YLE, RUV, Nordic Coproduction Fund, Artistfilm. Produced by Lars Safstrom, Gunnar Hellstrom. Directed, written by Hellstrom. Camera (color), Jorgen Persson; editors, Louise Brattberg, Helene Berlin; music, Hans Arnbom, others; production design, Henny Noremark-Haskel; costume design, Ann-Mari Anttila; sound (Dolby), Lennart Gentzel, Erik Forslund, Johnny Ljungberg. Reviewed at Royal Cinema, Gothenburg, Sweden, Sept. 26, 1994. Running time: **126 MIN.**
Anders Zorn .... Gunnar Hellstrom
Emilie Bartlett .... Linda Kozlowski
Emma Zorn .... Liv Ullmann
Albert Engstrom .... Stig Grybe
Paul W. Bartlett .... Rupert Frazer
Oscar II .... Jarl Kulle
Mrs. Gardner .... Yvonne Lombard
Also with: Rikard Wolff, Kristina Tornqvist, Cecilia Ljung, Birgitte Sondergaard, Ulf Eklund, Axel Duberg, Ingvar Kjellsson.

Lavish but cliched, Gunnar Hellstrom's biopic of turn-of-the-century Swedish painter Anders Zorn comes across as an empty shell with no insight into the man it depicts. It could, however, find an international audience on the strength of its production values. Pic has been a moderate success in Sweden.

Hellstrom, who for years has lived in the U.S. (where he's directed TV, including "Dallas"), fought for a long time to make his movie on Zorn. The painter was famous for his nudes and womanizing, and his works now sell for millions of dollars.

When the pic opens, Zorn (played by Hellstrom himself) is already famous and, among other things, has been commissioned to do a portrait of the Swedish king. However, his personal life is a mess: he's over-weight, drinks too much, and is constantly unfaithful to his wife (sensitively played by Liv Ullmann), sleeping with his models.

Driven by a constant need to be praised, he goes to the U.S. for a series of exhibitions. There, he settles into an on-and-off affair with Emilie Bartlett (Linda Kozlowski), wife of Yank sculptor Paul W. Bartlett who eventually commits suicide. Emilie and Zorn move to Sweden, where Zorn makes no attempt to hide from his wife what is going on under their own roof.

Pic mostly looks exquisite. Cameraman Jorgen Persson ("Pelle the Conqueror," "The Best Intentions") captures the beauty of the Swedish landscape in both winter and summer, and re-enactments of motifs in Zorn's paintings are well done.

The problem is that the script deals only in the cliches of Zorn's life, with no new insights or depth. Why, for instance, was he so attractive to a string of young women? Instead of providing an answer, Hellstrom is content to spend a lot of screentime simply focusing on shapely female flesh.

Pic also falls back on cliches when establishing foreign atmosphere. When Zorn meets Emilie in Paris en route to Sweden, the scene is established with a closeup of a French accordion player, with the camera then moving up to a window in which the lovers meet. If they'd met in Africa, maybe the shot would have started with bongo drums.

Aside from Ullmann, who gives one of the best performances of her career, other acting is lackluster. Kozlowski (working in English) is bland as the Yank mistress, and Hellstrom lacks depth in the title role. Pic was shot entirely in Sweden.

—Gunnar Rehlin

AMNESIA

(CHILEAN)

An Arca production. (International sales: Cine Chile, Santiago.) Executive producers, Carlo Bettin, Luis Justiniano. Directed by Gonzalo Justiniano. Screenplay, Gustavo Frias, Gonzalo Justiniano. Camera (color), Hans Burmann; editor, Danielle Fillios; music, Jose Miguel Tobar, Miguel Miranda; art direction, Carlos Garrido; costume design, Iseda Sepulveda; sound (stereo), Eugenio Gutierrez; assistant directors, Enzo Blondel, Ivan Sanhueza. Reviewed at Venice Film Festival (Special Events), Sept. 1, 1994. (Also in San Sebastian fest.) Running time: **90 MIN.**
Zuniga .... Julio Jung
Ramirez .... Pedro Vicuna
The captain .... Nelson Villagra
Carrasco .... Jose Secall
With: Marcela Osorio, Myriam Palacios.

An offbeat, sometimes nightmarish black comedy about a soldier's revenge on his psychotic commanding officer when both are back in civvy street, "Amnesia" is an interesting

October 31, 1994 (Cont.)

enough entry for Latino gatherings but isn't likely to remain long in foreign buyers' memories.

Though set in an unnamed South American country that previously experienced a ruthless junta, story's resonances clearly include the pic's country of origin, Chile. But specifics aren't crucial to enjoying the slim, off-center yarn.

Ramirez (Pedro Vicuna), a weird-looking guy with glasses, spots a face he remembers in the street and tracks him down to a bar. The man is the slug-like Zuniga (Julio Jung), formerly a sergeant at a detention camp in the desert who ruled with a rod of iron and casually shot any of his charges on a whim.

Feigning friendship, and a desire to forget past injustices, Ramirez chats up Zuniga over a few beers. Flashbacks limn their times in the desert, during which Ramirez was a guard, on one occasion letting a prisoner escape and on another being a witness to Zuniga's callous shooting of a pregnant woman. After seeming to win Zuniga's confidence, he invites him back to his house for dinner. Meanwhile, however, he calls the man who escaped years back for an elaborate revenge on the still-remorseless Zuniga.

Chilean helmer Gonzalo Justiniano, in his fourth feature, maintains interest in the often-grotesque comedy of events by adopting a slightly heightened visual style and emphasizing the more surreal elements of the story.

Small cast of players meshes well, with the cartoonish-looking Jung and vacant-looking Vicuna both fine as villain and hero. Technically, film is pro.
—*Derek Elley*

VANCOUVER

HELL BENT

(CANADIAN)

A WinterRode Films Inc. (Winnipeg) production, with the participation of Telefilm Canada, CIDO, and Canada Council. Produced by Ken Rodeck, Phyllis Laing. Directed, written by John Kozak. Camera (color), Charles Lavack; music, Steve Hegyi; production design, Kim Forrest; casting, Shelagh Carter. Reviewed at Vancouver film fest (out of competition), October 13, 1994. Running time: **83 MINS.**
Marty .... Danial Sprintz
Andy .... Kevin Doerksen
Leslie .... Alison Northcott
Old Woman .... Dorothy Montpetit
Old Man .... Edward Raethorne

Hard-hitting and all-too-timely, "Hell Bent" looks unflinchingly in the eyes of especially aberrant offspring of a lost generation. It finds very little staring back. Far from sensationalistic, pic presents preteen violence as a blunt expression of empty values and simple boredom.

Winnipeg helmer-scripter John Kozak makes only token attempts to detail family and social backgrounds of three junior-high-age kids on a path straight to you-know-where. Instead, we take for granted that these unreachable adolescents are way past caring about the consequences of their mostly mindless actions. Hyperactive Marty (Danial Sprintz), in particular, looks for violence in almost every confrontation, from taunting a grumpy convenience-store clerk, to picking on a local grade-schooler, and urinating in a businesswoman's fancy Mercedes.

Tiring of this "kids' stuff," he convinces his dorky sidekick (Kevin Doerkson) and their ultra-stoical, chain-smoking pal (Alison Northcott) — to join him in the impromptu sacking of an old house by the railroad tracks. Next thing you know, they're holding a tiny woman and her wheelchair-bound husband captive while they smash decades of the couple's precious memories. It's grim material, but Kozak keeps a cool head and draws no moralistic conclusions.

Tech credits look better than the pic's half-million-dollar budget, and he gets memorable perfs from the non-professional cast, even with an excess of screaming from Sprintz. The camera has a real find in the ethereal young Northcott, although the helmer may depend a little too much on her coldly angelic face for ironic resonance. Metal-guitar score is effective, if somewhat predictable.

Expect much action as an educational discussion-starter and, with some language clean-up, "Hell" is bent for lengthy web play.
—*Ken Eisner*

A BORROWED LIFE
(DUO-SANG)
(TAIWANESE)

A Chang Su A&V Company, Long Shong Films (Tapei) production. Executive producer, Hou Hsiao-Hsien. Produced by Wang Ying-Hsiang, Chou Chun-Yu, Jan Hung-Tze, Hsieh Ping-Han. Directed, written by Wu Nien-Jen. Camera (color), Liu Cheng-Chuan; editor, Liao Ching-Song; music, Jiang Hsiao-Wen, Liu Hui-Ling, Chen Che-Cheng; sound, Tu Tu-Che; art direction, Liu Che-Hua; costume design, Wei Lin, Lee Chung; assistant director, Jiang Pao-Teh. Reviewed at Vancouver film fest (in competition), October 13, 1994. Running time: **165 MINS.**
With: Tsai Chen-Nan, Tsai Chiou-Fong, Fu Jun, Peng Wan-Chun, Chang Li-Shu, Chen Mu-yi, Huang Chine-Ho, Chen Shu-Fang, Mei Fang, Chen Hsi-Wang, Kao Tong-Hsio.
(Mandarin, Japanese, and regional dialogue)

This almost-three-hour helming debut from Wu Nien-Jen, who scripted such Hou Hsiao-Hsien epics as "A City of Sadness" and "The Puppetmaster" taxes the viewer's interest with obscure Taiwanese history, and hands out sparse, if tasty, dividends in return. A healthy trim and some well-placed explanations could still change that ratio, resulting in specialized fest and arthouse playoffs for this father-son saga.

Those who know that Tokyo once controlled and developed the northern tip of Taiwan will be better equipped to understand the generational conflict between Sega (Tsai Chen-Nan), whose mining-town peers hold none-too-secret affections for Japanese language and culture, and his son, Wen-Jian (played by three young thesps, including twentysomething Fu Jun), raised in postwar, anti-Japan fervor. Bulk of the autobiopic outlines the son's mixed memories of his difficult old man, who worked like a dog, but often went off boozing and gambling.

Best scenes are hazy, child's-eye recreations of the 1950s, as when dad dumps his tyke at a theater featuring a corny Japanese movie with a live Mandarin translator who makes running comments on the plot and the crowd. By the middle section, when Sega's job is threatened and the town starts falling apart, the problems get too monotonous to sustain serious interest, although Wu's eye for poignant detail remains visually rewarding. The final third, in which Wen-Jian, now a married Tapei writer, watches helplessly as his uncommunicative father slowly dies of black-lung disease, is needlessly gruelling.

Wu could have stuck to the early stuff, with a quick death-bed coda, or switched the focus to female members of the family. Instead, the patriarchal pas-de-deux is played out well beyond audience endurance. Leisurely pace is not the real problem, since protracted scenes often pay off emotionally.

Especially sweet is the restriction of incidental music to period radio tunes, singalongs, and section bookends. The pic's form, though, is ultimately impenetrable, with boundless room given to repetitive business while crucial facts and potentially fascinating characters get short shrift. What this "Life" needs is a borrowed knife. —*Ken Eisner*

DINNER IN PURGATORY
(BRITISH)

A Dinner in Purgatory Prods. Ltd. production. Produced by Kerry Kiernan, Stefan C. Linn. Executive producers, Xavier Azalbert, Theo Duchen, Barbara and Edward Kiernan, Gertrud and Antonius Linn, Stefan C. Linn, Eddy Pirard, Mary and Teddy Prendergast, Gordon Robertson, Tyke and John Toler. Directed, written by Kerry Kiernan. Camera (Eastmancolor), Billy Malone; editor, Sally Hilton; music, David Hughes, John Murphy; production design, Sarah Loftus; sound, John Marchbank, casting, Kerry Kiernan. Reviewed on videocassette, Boston, Aug. 29, 1994. Running time: **79 MIN.**
Simone de Beauvoir ... Yvonne Bonnamy
Saint Paul .... Edward Halsted
Eve .... Elizabeth Jasicki
Socrates .... Chris Johnston
Machiavelli .... James Reynard

Basically a film about five people talking in a room, "Dinner in Purgatory" (billed as "a philosophical comedy") is an experiment that almost works. It's a near miss, but unique nature of the material should ensure fest activity and some appeal in the right art venues. Ancillary action (especially on Bravo or PBS, and college use) seems assured.

Premise is that modern young woman Eve (comely Elizabeth Jasicki) dies and wakes up in purgatory, where she passes time with Christian Saint Paul (Edward Halsted), Greek philosopher Socrates (Chris Johnston), Renaissance politician Machiavelli (James Reynard) and French feminist/existentialist Simone de Beauvoir (Yvonne Bonnamy). While one doesn't need a philosophy degree to follow the discussion, if the names don't ring a bell, the film obviously won't work.

No explanation is given as to why these five people are thrown together, or why Saint Paul isn't in heaven. Instead, during champagne and then dinner, the five debate theology, history, politics and the equality of the sexes. Saint Paul comes in for a lot of grief since Socrates is a

October 31, 1994 (Cont.) **November 7, 1994**

pagan, Machiavelli a blasphemer and de Beauvoir an atheist, but he manages to hold his own.

But writer/director Kerry Kiernan paints himself into a philosophical corner since the five ultimately debate the meaning of life, and, inevitably, whatever answer they come up with to this eternal mystery will strike the viewer as banal.

Audience has to be willing to play along, and it takes a good 10 or 15 minutes before the film finds its level, but then the chat becomes quite engaging. Able cast manages to create characters beyond simply mouthing positions, with Johnston's genial Socrates and Bonnamy's worldly de Beauvoir coming off best.

Tech credits are up to snuff, with limited funds concentrated on the set and costumes, so that claustrophobic nature of the enterprise doesn't become overwhelming.
—*Daniel M. Kimmel*

ONCE A YEAR, EVERY YEAR

(TUTTI GLI ANNI UNA VOLTA L'ANNO)

(ITALIAN-FRENCH-BELGIAN)

An Academy Pictures release (Italy) of a DDS Cinematografica (Rome) production, in association with Les Films Auramax (Paris)/Alain Keytsman Prod. (Brussels). (International sales: Sacis, Rome.) Produced by Donatella Senatore, Andrea Marzari. Directed by Gianfrancesco Lazotti. Screenplay, Lazotti, Cecilia Calvi, from a story by Paola Scola. Camera (Telecolor), Sebasiano Celeste; editor, Carlo Fontana; music, Giovanni Venosta; art direction, Fabio Vitale; costume design, Gianna Gissi; sound (Dolby), Luciano Muratori. Reviewed at Venice Film Festival (Italian Panorama), Sept. 4, 1994. Running time: **88 MIN.**

Lorenzo	Giorgio Albertazzi
Romano	Paolo Bonacelli
Mario	Lando Buzzanca
Annamaria	Carla Cassola
Francesco	Paolo Ferrari
Ginevra	Paola Pitagora
Laura	Giovanna Ralli
Raffaele	Jean Rochefort
Giulia	Alexandra La Capria
Davide	Gianmarco Tognazzi
Giuseppe	Vittorio Gassman
(Italian dialogue)	

With most neophyte directors eager to distance themselves from the moth-eaten comedy vehicles that kept Italo cinema in the creative doldrums through the '70s and '80s, "Once a Year, Every Year" figures as an exception. Second-time helmer Gianfrancesco Lazotti steers a veteran cast through their paces in an ensemble comedy that might have been made two decades back. Surprisingly, the result is relatively buoyant, with

snappy dialogue and able performers helping to smooth out the fusty undertaking's wrinkles. Less surprisingly, its most receptive audience will be Euro oldsters parked comfortably in front of their TVs.

Set during an annual reunion dinner of lifelong friends now at retirement age, the film's conflict turns on a letter from a recently deceased group member proposing the rest live out their twilight years together in a disused convent. Initially, the friends scoff at the notion. But as the evening rolls on and the imperfections in each of their seemingly cushy lives are exposed, the proposal takes on a certain appeal.

The octet is a lively group of characters, from the dinner's officious organizer (Giorgio Albertazzi), rudely awakened to his wife's unhappiness, through the group clown (shoddily dubbed French thesp Jean Rochefort), to the overworked, underloved lush (Carla Cassola). The group's traditional leader, Giuseppe (Vittorio Gassman), arrives after dessert and confesses to being under house arrest on fraud charges.

Perfs are sharp across the board, but more appealing when characters are bantering than when they are dealing with the script's flimsily justified explosive moments.

Though the potentially static, theatrically staged situation remains mobile, the merit rests more with the actors and script than with Lazotti's purely functional direction or the film's modest, TV-bound look.
—*David Rooney*

INTERVIEW WITH THE VAMPIRE

A Warner Bros./Geffen Pictures release of a Geffen Pictures presentation. Produced by David Geffen, Stephen Woolley. Co-producer, Redmond Morris. Directed by Neil Jordan. Screenplay, Anne Rice, based on her novel. Camera (Technicolor), Philippe Rousselot; editors, Mick Audsley, Joke Van Wijk; music, Elliot Goldenthal; production design, Dante Ferretti; supervising art director, Malcolm Middleton; art direction, Alan Tomkins (New Orleans), Jim Tocci (San Francisco), Jean-Michel Hugon (Paris); set design (New Orleans), Stella Furner, Munroe Kelly; set decoration, Francesca Lo Schiavo; costume design, Sandy Powell; sound (Dolby), Clive Winter; vampire makeup and effects, Stan Winston; visual effects supervisor/ second unit director, Rob Legato; assistant director, Patrick Clayton; casting, Juliet Taylor, Susie Figgis. Reviewed at the United Artists North Theater, Santa Fe, N.M., Nov. 2, 1994. MPAA Rating: R. Running time: **122 MIN.**

Lestat	Tom Cruise
Louis	Brad Pitt
Armand	Antonio Banderas
Santiago	Stephen Rea
Malloy	Christian Slater
Claudia	Kirsten Dunst
Madeleine	Domiziana Giordano
Yvette	Thandie Newton
New Orleans Whore	Indra Ove
Mortal Woman on Stage	Laure Marsac

Mortals will be lured but probably not smitten by the handsome bloodsuckers in "Interview With the Vampire." Finally onscreen after innumerable failed attempts over nearly two decades, Anne Rice's perennially popular novel has been given an intelligent, darkly voluptuous reading that rises to pulsating life numerous times during the course of its deadly journey. But the film also has its turgid, dialogue-heavy stretches, and the leading performances, if acceptable, are not everything they needed to be to fully flesh out these elegant immortals. High want-to-see and curiosity factor, Tom Cruise, Rice's reputation and a highly fueled marketing drive will deliver toothsome B.O. through the holiday season.

The author's recent self-publicized change of heart notwithstanding, the controversy over Cruise's casting as the commanding vampire Lestat will certainly heat up again once the film comes out. But what fans of the book will see is just about as faithful a rendition of the narrative as could possibly be managed in a two-hour film. All the main characters and crucial events are here, given vivid dimension against a sumptuous backdrop.

What unsuspecting viewers will get is a bloody, often dour period piece in which an assort-

ment of tortured characters struggle with their vampire natures and each other as they test the limits of immortality and lack of morality. On a pure visceral level of thrills for a modern audience, the picture has its share of riveting moments, although it tends to back off from displays of heavy gore and excess.

Regardless of one's familiarity with the source, what's missing is a strong sense of emotional exchange and development among the main characters. The intense bonds of love, resentment and hatred that arc through the centuries among Lestat, Louis, the vampire he creates, and their "daughter," Claudia, are only lightly felt due to the compressed series of events, reduced motivations and lack of thesp chemistry.

The viewer happily rides along with the story because of the innate interest of these unusual characters and the rush of startling events, but the emotional and thematic depth that might have given the piece substance and resonance is only indicated, not indelibly etched.

Director Neil Jordan and his richly talented team set a wonderfully evocative mood from the outset, as the camera swoops over the Bay Bridge and down into nocturnal San Francisco to light upon the exquisite, immaculate Louis (Brad Pitt), who is ready to tell his life story into a tape recorder for an interviewer (Christian Slater) in an empty room on Market Street. "I'm flesh and blood, but not human," Louis declares to his startled interlocutor. "I haven't been human in 200 years."

How he became so sends the story back to 1791 Louisiana, where the 24-year-old widower Louis is singled out by the devilishly handsome, courtly Lestat (Cruise). Instead of just sucking Louis' blood and killing him, Lestat takes him to the brink of death and then has Louis drink from him, thus giving the victim the gift of ageless, endless life.

So, after a look at his last sunrise, Louis joins Lestat on the ceaseless nightly prowl for prey. Whereas Lestat is relentless and remorseless, favoring tasty young men and women and especially aristocrats, Louis retains a regard for human life and mostly picks on little animals for sustenance. Not fully comprehending or accepting his new nature, the tortured Louis burns down his grand plantation house and moves to New Orleans with Lestat, where they continue to operate out of a lavishly appointed apartment.

But their debauched bachelor existence suddenly changes with the arrival of Claudia. Finding a young girl grieving next to her plague-victim mother, Louis uncharacteristically decides to take her. But Lestat gives her the same treatment he gave Louis years before, and Claudia (Kirsten Dunst) becomes their vampire daughter and partner, possessing a hunting instinct to rival Lestat's while enjoying a special affair of the heart with Louis that includes bunking with him in his coffin.

But even after many years, Claudia cannot forgive Lestat for locking her into the body of a child, with no hope of maturing into a grown woman. Diabolically, she arranges the difficult feat of killing, or seeming to kill, a master vampire, as Louis ambivalently watches.

Tale's second half takes Louis and Claudia to Europe, where their search for others like them leads them to the sinister Theatre des Vampires in Paris, 1870. Here, jaded upper-class audiences thrill as vampires enact little skits before getting down to the main event, the killing of a sacrificial victim. Leader of this macabre troupe is the magnetic Armand (Antonio Banderas), who quickly becomes the sort of mentor Louis has always sought to teach him the secrets of vampire life in the way Lestat never did.

But just as Louis creates for Claudia the mother she always needed, vampire revenge brings tragedy to the little group, forcing Louis to take matters into his own hands before heading off into the centuries for a rendezvous with his past and future.

All of this is enacted in a world of unyielding darkness — punctuated only by the colorful costumes, blood, fire and unnaturally light skin of the vampires — which comes to seem like both a blessing and a curse. The night belongs to the blood hunters, to be sure, but it also enslaves them, dooming them to an existence of secrecy, stealth and loneliness.

Brad Pitt's Louis is handsome and personable, but there is no depth to his melancholy, no pungency to his sense of loss. He also doesn't seem to connect in a meaningful way with any of the other actors except, perhaps, to Slater's interviewer. This is unfortunate because his profound feelings for Claudia, Lestat and Armand are meant to be among the primary driving forces of the story.

Also coming up short of ideal is Cruise's Lestat. While not as physically imposing as one imagines the character on the printed page, it's easy to get used to his looks. The bigger problem is that Lestat has been stripped of much of his meanness, his sarcastic, bullying manner and threatening force, which seriously lessens the reasons for Louis' unhappiness and Claudia's revenge.

When Banderas strides upon the stage in the second half, one suddenly witnesses the kind of compelling, charismatic presence a master vampire should have. This type of natural dominance and superiority

doesn't come through in Cruise's Lestat.

Dunst is just right in the difficult part of the child vampire, while Stephen Rea oozes and sneers his way around as Armand's evil henchman. Slater brings welcome energy and humor to the inquisitor role that River Phoenix was going to play (the film is dedicated to the late actor), and Laure Marsac registers briefly but strongly as the centerpiece of the Paris vampires' theatrical spectacle.

The production, which seductively combines location shooting in three of the world's most beautiful cities with exemplary studio work, is superb. Dante Ferretti's production design respects both the realism of the locales and the fantastic demands of the vampire milieu, particularly when the story enters the quasi-religious, catacomb-like world of the theater company. Ferretti and costume designer Sandy Powell have outdone themselves in the entirely appropriate lavishness of their work, and Philippe Rousselot's exceedingly dark lensing makes both sets and costumes appear as the only visual relief in a world otherwise cloaked in unending gloom.

Stan Winston's vampire makeup and effects are also among the picture's highlights. These monsters are distinguishable from humans most notably by the tiny blue veins visible beneath their pale skin, and the transformation scenes of Louis and Claudia are stunning and even moving because of the expertness and utter believability with which they are done.

Final jewel in the crown of artistic contributions is Elliot Goldenthal's outstanding score, which hints at the diverse influences of Bernard Herrmann, Danny Elfman and Erik Satie while developing a rambunctious life of its own that adds immeasurably to the film's character. Ending provides a little twist on that of the book that easily sets up a sequel if one proves warranted. Rice's "Vampire" story has made it securely onto the screen, even if its blood has been somewhat diluted in the process.

—*Todd McCarthy*

PONTIAC MOON

A Paramount Pictures release of a Robert Schaffel/Youssef Vahabzadeh production. Produced by Schaffel, Vahabzadeh. Executive producers, Jeffrey Brown, Ted Danson, Bob Benedetti. Co-producer, Sharon Roesler. Directed by Peter Medak. Screenplay, Finn Taylor, Brown; story by Taylor. Camera (Deluxe color), Thomas Kloss; editor, Anne V. Coates; music, Randy Edelman; production design, Jeffrey Beecroft; art direction, Wm Ladd Skinner; set decoration, Robert J. Franco; costume design, Ruth Myers; sound (Dolby), Kim Ornitz, Ric Waddell; associate producer, Taylor; assistant directors, Cellin Gluck, Robin Oliver; unit production managers, Steve Barnett, George Goodman; casting, Jane Jenkins, Janet Hirshenson. Reviewed at the Paramount screening room, Nov. 2, 1994. MPAA Rating: PG-13. Running time: **107 MIN.**

Washington Bellamy .... Ted Danson
Katherine
  Bellamy .... Mary Steenburgen
Andy Bellamy .... Ryan Todd
Ernest Ironplume .... Eric Schweig
Lorraine .... Cathy Moriarty
Jerome Bellamy .... Max Gail
Alicia Frook .... Lisa Jane Persky

Ted Danson's box office star may wane a little further with "Pontiac Moon," a sincere but tedious road movie that derives its title and inspiration from the Apollo landing/moonwalk in 1969. Pic's quirky, almost European flavor lends itself to a small, sensitive scale, but the filmmakers shoot for the stars and end up with a story that's more mundane than magical.

That's more bad news for fans of Danson, whose last effort, "Getting Even With Dad," also failed to lift off commercially. "Moon" shares certain elements with that film, focusing on the relationship between a father and son, as well as the family's emotionally scarred, polyphobic mother (Mary Steenburgen).

Katherine (Steenburgen) hasn't ventured outside the house for seven years, and her husband, Washington, an eccentric teacher, fears her phobias may be extending to their 11-year-old son (Ryan Todd, a dead ringer for Brandon Cruz circa "The Courtship of Eddie's Father"), who isn't even allowed to ride in a car.

Seizing on the imminent moon landing to create "one perfect act," Washington decides to take the boy and his vintage Pontiac the 1,776 miles (no doubt additional symbolism regarding his declaration of independence) to Spires of the Moon National Park, which would push the car's mileage to 238,857 — equaling the distance between the earth and the moon.

That flimsy if somewhat romanticized premise provides the basis for a journey of self-discovery that meanders at times, and never quite makes it onto the emotional highway.

For starters, nearly the entire movie is rendered anti-climactic after Steenburgen's character chal-

lenges her fears — the source of which are also revealed fairly early on — and takes off after the pair, leaving scant suspense as to the inevitable reunion.

The script by Finn Taylor and Jeffrey Brown also does a half-baked job of developing the period, as father and son encounter a Vietnam veteran Native American (Eric Schweig of "Last of the Mohicans"), hostile rednecks, a flirty waitress (Cathy Moriarty) and a bumbling local sheriff (John Schuck), the last sequence threatening to turn the pic into a lightweight "Thelma & Louise."

Director Peter Medak, whose recent directorial offerings include grittier fare like "The Krays" and "Romeo Is Bleeding," offers some nice touches but also hits some potholes along the road. Cutting back and forth between the Apollo landing and the story, the director tries too hard to create a sense of wonder — an overreaching also exemplified by Randy Edelman's score.

At first overly mannered, Danson eventually settles into his character and offers a fairly convincing performance as the frustrated intellectual, a stretch the studio probably owed him after 11 years of yeoman service on "Cheers."

Similarly, Steenburgen is a tangled mass of nerves as the frantic wife, and Moriarty provides a much-needed injection of vitality in what amounts to an extended cameo. Todd's youth, however, isn't afforded much depth, nor does the story bother to develop Schweig's intriguing character.

Tech credits are solid, though Thomas Kloss' cinematography of the sweeping desert vistas is pretty but not breathtaking — just another area where "Moon" doesn't quite shine. —*Brian Lowry*

OLEANNA

A Samuel Goldwyn Co. release in association with Channel 4 Films of a Bay Kinescope production. Produced by Patricia Wolff, Sarah Green. Directed, written by David Mamet, based on his play. Camera (DuArt), Andrzej Sekula; editor, Barbara Tulliver, music, Rebecca Pidgeon; set decoration, Kate Conklin; costume design, Jane Greenwood; sound (Dolby), Peter Kurland, Freddy Potatohead, Ryan Weiss; fight coordinator; B.H. Barry; assistant director; Cara Giallanza. Reviewed at Samuel Goldwyn Pavilion, Westwood, Oct. 23, 1994. Running time: **89 MIN.**

John .... William H. Macy
Carol .... Debra Eisenstadt

David Mamet's "Oleanna" comes with all the trappings of political correctness that the playwright and filmmaker so obviously abhors. It's a tale of sexual tension in the workplace (here, academia) in which a common situation is propelled into the stuff of tragedy. While the core issue of sexual harrassment is vital and potent, the story has an unbalanced perspective that severely blunts its emotional and sociological points.

November 7, 1994 (Cont.)

Add to that a barrage of gab and weak performances, and commercial prospects are dim. The picture is more *cause celebre* than commercial celebration, with no more than OK upscale domestic prospects.

Hewing to the structure of his play, Mamet's first act finds a professor, John (William H. Macy), in conference in his office with Carol (Debra Eisenstadt), a failing student. There's a tentative quality to the encounter as phone calls relating to the close of a house sale routinely interrupt the flow and focus of the meeting.

The intrusion of grim household realities aggravates a simmering rage constrained only by manners and civility. John is burned out. His teaching prowess is spent and he feels hopelessly shackled to family and convention but afraid to confront the fact that he wants to bail and start over, unencumbered.

So Carol is a challenge, a conceit and a diversion. He spends more time grappling with her inability to comprehend than he should. Her twitchy behavior is somehow relaxing in his present state of mind, and he feels safe and liberated venting his frustration and contempt for the teaching process.

It is, of course, a huge mistake.

In the second act, John has asked Carol to his office. In the brief interim, she's made accusations of sexual harrassment against him to the tenure committee. He's now in jeopardy of losing all those material things he railed against in the first act. He's ready to apologize.

But as low as he's willing to stoop, John isn't ready to accept — as Carol insists — that the accusations are fact simply because the committee has accepted them.

John's not guilty of anything on Carol's hysterical laundry list. While by no means a paragon of anything, his chief crimes are vanity and self-delusion. It's true that the attention he paid Carol was ill-placed, but it was not sexual. Mamet makes that very clear — too clear, in fact, leaving little dramatic ambiguity.

Rather than a full-blown assault on changing social values, "Oleanna" is more like a horror film, with Carol a freshman "Bad Seed." "Oleanna" is apparently a reference to a bygone utopian community. Still, one can't help suspect a more perverse derivation — an opaque reference to oleander, the poisonous shrub.

With such an obvious villain in Carol, the subject of sexual harassment gets hopelessly lost. The real concern is whether something remotely resembling justice will prevail. Unlike, for instance, "Fatal Attraction," this film never finds the magic balance between genre convention and sociopolitical currents. Its relevance to sexual harassment is on the same level as "The Hand That Rocks the Cradle's" analysis of contemporary babysitting.

Mamet doesn't help matters by eliciting unshaded performances from his actors. Eisenstadt is shrill and obvious as Carol. Her characterization eliminates any possibility for sympathy.

Macy fares little better in a part that largely demands a lot of preening. And though he is so obviously wronged, his thick-headedness makes his victimization logical rather than reprehensible.

The best that can be said for this missed opportunity is that Mamet does yeomanlike work in transferring his work from stage to screen. As filmed plays go, "Oleanna" effectively opens up the action without betraying the essence of its origins.
—*Leonard Klady*

DOUBLE DRAGON

A Gramercy Pictures release of an Imperial Entertainment and Scanbox presentation of a Greenleaf production. Produced by Sunil R. Shah, Ash R. Shah, Alan Schechter, Jan Hamsher, Don Murphy. Executive producers, Sundip R. Shah, Anders P. Jensen. Directed by James Yukich. Screenplay, Michael Davis, Peter Gould. Camera (CFI color), Gary Kibbe; editor, Florent Retz; music, Jay Ferguson; production design, Mayne Berke; art direction, Maya Shimoguchi; set decoration, Kristan Andrews; costume design, Fiona Spence; sound (DTS), Patrick Hanson; special effects technical adviser, Joe Lombardi; associate producers, Tom Karnowski, Paul Lombardi; assistant directors, Robert M. Williams Jr., George Fortmuller; unit production manager, Karnowski; second unit director/stunt coordinator, Jeff Imada; casting, Harriet Greenspan, Annette Benson. Reviewed at the Raleigh Studios screening room, L.A., Oct. 26, 1994. MPAA Rating: PG-13. Running time: **95 MIN.**

Koga Shuko	Robert Patrick
Jimmy Lee	Mark Dacascos
Billy Lee	Scott Wolf
Linda	
Lash	Kristina Malandro Wagner
Satori Imada	Julia Nickson
Marian Delario	Alyssa Milano
Bo Abobo No. 1	Nils Allen Stewart
Bo Abobo No. 2	Henry Kingi

Even kids won't get much of a kick out of this high-energy, low-IQ futuristic slugfest, which plays down to, and, in many ways, below the level of some Saturday-morning cartoons. While "Double Dragon" has a hit videogame in its corner, "Super Mario Bros." proved that's no assurance of box office success, and more discerning tykes will likely bypass this hyperactive romp, squirreling away their cash for more game cartridges.

Beyond name recognition, the best things "Dragon" has going for it are the appealing leads, though both Mark Dacascos (who starred in Fox's martial arter "Only the Strong") and Scott Wolf (from Fox Broadcasting's "Party of Five") are rendered so dopey by the script that teen heartthrob status will have to wait for better vehicles.

Yet another sci-fi story set in earthquake-ravaged Los Angeles (the big joke is that the Hollywood sign is up to its "H" in water), under musicvideo director James Yukich's pacing, "Dragon" never slows down long enough to explain half of what's going on. That would be OK if the dialogue were more palatable, the nonstop action more inventive or the sets and special effects less cheesy.

Dacascos and Wolf play Jimmy and Billy Lee, teenage brothers whose mentor (Julia Nickson) possesses half of a dragon amulet that bestows certain powers on its holder.

The other half has been stolen by Koga Shuko, a power-obsessed mogul played so campily by Robert Patrick that even his bad haircut seems appropriate. Shuko spends the entire movie chasing the boys to get their half of the charm, using the gangs who rule New Angeles by night as his minions.

The Lees, meanwhile, are befriended by a band of vigilante teens whose leader (Alyssa Milano, a long way from "Who's the Boss?") has a haircut almost as bad as Koga Shuko's.

Yukich and writers Michael Davis and Peter Gould shoot for a sense of camp fun, but dialogue like "My whole life just flashed before my eyes. Dude, I sleep a lot!" makes it difficult not to laugh at them rather than with them.

"Dragon" does manage a few chuckles, if only for absurdity's sake, with cameos by Vanna White and George Hamilton as newscasters, but unlike "RoboCop," there's no satirical bite behind the idea. Similarly, one of the few amusing moments — where the brothers let loose with a "Home Alone"-esque scream — is undercut by going back to the gag at least a half-dozen times.

Patrick, best-known as the evil cyborg in "Terminator 2," proves a toothless villain here, and the brothers are surprisingly cavalier about effecting revenge upon him, indicative of the whole production's lightweight and lighthearted tone. Another cheat is the fact that the dragon amulet isn't made whole until the final reel, and even then, its power is anti-climactic.

On the tech side, sets frequently look like something out of "Peewee's Playhouse." Matte shots of Hollywood under water are quaint, but a bit too obvious to enthrall sophisticated kids, who will recognize that this "Dragon" is, itself, a little wet behind the ears.
—*Brian Lowry*

SISTER MY SISTER

(BRITISH)

A Film Four Intl. presentation in association with British Screen of an NFH production. Produced by Norma Heyman. Directed by Nancy Meckler. Screenplay, Wendy Kesselman. Camera (color), Ashley Rowe; editor, David Stiven; music, Stephen Warbeck; production design, Caroline Amies. Reviewed at Hamptons Film Festival, Oct. 23, 1994. Running time: **102 MIN.**

Madame Danzard	Julie Walters
Christine	Joely Richardson
Lea	Jodhi May
Isabelle	Sophie Thursfield

A dramatization of the real story upon which Jean Genet's play "The Maids" is based, "Sister My Sister" is a small-scale film with some powerful moments. The film's claustrophobic ambience, overt lesbian overtones and formal artistic sensibility might restrict the appeal of this intense chamber piece to the arthouse and festival circuits.

Set in 1932, in a French provincial town, the drama concerns Madame Danzard (Julie Walters), a strict, authoritarian mother who domineers her clumsy daughter, Isabelle (Sophie Thursfield), to the point of emotional suffocation. As her major concerns are immaculate appearance, respectability and order, she's also extremely harsh with her two maids, Christine (Joely Richardson) and her younger sister, Lea (Jodhi May).

During the first hour, there's hardly any communication between the upstairs and downstairs in the rigidly stratified household. Through cross-cutting, the narrative draws parallels between the two sets of relationships, both based on unequal power and unhealthy emotional dependency. The tensions between the four women gradually reach breaking point, and in the horrific climax, an act of shocking violence erupts.

The insecure Christine resents the fact that sister Lea is their mother's favorite, and she still suffers from a bad experience at her convent. In contrast, Lea is the more sensitive and forgiving one. The sisters' isolation from the outside world and their sense of humiliation make them too reliant on each other. Soon, an explicitly sexual dimension is added to their already charged emotional encounters.

While the core situation is clearly established by writer Wendy Kesselman, her undernourished script doesn't offer much in the way of narrative surprises or in-depth characterizations. Lacking in specifics, the script doesn't achieve good dramatic construction; for long stretches, there's no dialogue and the interaction consists of exchanged looks.

Under these circumstances, chief problems may be pic's excessive running time and deliberate pacing. Attempting to overcome the screenplay's shortcomings, director Nancy Meckler focuses on the performances of her four talented actresses. But her use of flashbacks, which don't add much to the proceedings, the slow tempo and detached staging all indicate that ideally this should have been a one-hour play.

Walters, usually a reliable pro, gives a one-note performance, but the fault lies in her narrowly conceived role. As the sisters, Richardson and May fare better, displaying a greater range of emotions and giving some sharp shadings to their lean dialogue.

Proficient production values, particularly Ashley Rowe's crisp lensing and Caroline Amies' impressive production design, show alert intelligence behind the camera.

—*Emanuel Levy*

WHEN I WAS 5, I KILLED MYSELF

(QUAND J'AVAIS 5 ANS JE M'AI TUE)

(FRENCH)

A PCC/M6 Films/Lumiere/Les Films Galaxie/Aliceleo production in association with La Sofica Cofimage 5 and Canal Plus. Produced by Patrick Godeau. Directed by Jean-Claude Sussfeld. Screenplay, Sussfeld, Jean-Pierre Carasso, based on Howard Buten's novel. Camera (color), Jean-Paul Rosa Da Costa; music, Pierre Delas, Amaury Blanchard, Fabrice Aboulker; costume design, Caroline De Vivaise; sound, Julien Cloquet. Reviewed at Hamptons Film Festival, Oct. 22, 1994, Running time: **100 MIN.**

Gil .... Dimitri Rougeul
Jessica .... Salome
Edouart .... Hippolyte Girardot
Dr. Nevele .... Patrick Bouchitey

Unlike most American movies, which usually portray children as cute, precocious and asexual, the French drama "When I Was 5, I Killed Myself" has the distinction of acknowledging children's sexual drives and romantic needs. This forceful drama, which is decorated with an impressive visual design, deserves limited theatrical release, though it lacks the overt commercial appeal of more sentimental pix about children, like "Cinema Paradiso" and "My Life as a Dog."

The French film industry probably makes more and better movies about children than any other national cinema. Though not in the tradition of Truffaut's films, "When I Was 5, I Killed Myself," in its thematic focus, serious approach and intensity, bears some resemblance to Rene Clement's 1951 classic "Forbidden Games," as both films depict private worlds that adults cannot understand.

Set in 1962, tale involves Gil (Dimitri Rougeul), a precocious boy blessed with a creative imagination, who falls hopelessly in love with Jessica (Salome), his beautiful classmate who's as eccentric as he is. Predictably, their love is perceived as "unhealthy" and disruptive, deviating from mainstream society's definitions of how children should or shouldn't behave, and Gil is sent to a center for problem children.

At the rigid institution, Gil is subjected to the methods of the stern educator Dr. Nevele (Patrick Bouchitey) and the more flexible and modern ones of Edouart (Hippolyte Girardot), a young, open-minded intern. While the contrast between the two men and their respective philosophies is too schematic, the scripters succeed in making their point about the damaging effects of outdated, restrictive methods in dealing with children.

Director Jean-Claude Sussfeld and his co-writer Jean-Pierre Carasso are sensitive to the way children communicate and behave, particularly when there are no adults around them. Taking the kids' p.o.v., some scenes at school are charming in their fresh authenticity.

Sussfeld employs a corollary visual style to accentuate the drama's motifs. The long shots of the institution's empty corridors convey Gil's physical and emotional isolation and the place's cold, impersonal nature. And there's one priceless scene at a zoo in which Gil and Jessica, defying the rules, jump over the fence to get a closer look at the animals.

A good deal of the film's allure derives from its depiction of children's mistrust of any form of authority — family, school, medical profession or psychiatric institute. But, vacillating between a serious clinical case and a spontaneous children's adventure, pic sometimes has a hard time finding the right tone.

Ultimately, though, "When I Was 5" makes a strong case for greater understanding, permissiveness and tolerance toward children. This explicit message makes the film's finale both emotionally effective and satisfying from narrative and ideological standpoints. —*Emanuel Levy*

THE CREW

A Cineville Inc. production. Produced by Daniel Hassid, Adam Stern, Dan Ireland. Directed by Carl-Jan Colpaert. Screenplay, Colpaert, Lance Smith. Camera (color), Geza Sinkovics; editor, Emma E. Hickox; music, Alex Wurman. Reviewed at Hamptons Film Festival, Oct. 22, 1994. Running time: **99 MIN.**

Bill .... Donal Logue
Phillip .... Viggo Mortensen
Jennifer .... Pamela Gidley
Tim .... Jeremy Sisto
Camilla .... Laura del Sol
Bill's mother .... Grace Zabriskie
Alex .... John Phibin
Catherine .... Sam Jenkins

In its dramatic tensions and forced conflicts, U.S. indie "The Crew" feels like an exercise in group dynamics rather than a fully worked out narrative. Well-intentioned but uneven tale of a pleasurable yacht cruise that turns into a nightmare might be of some interest to minor film festivals, though it lacks commercial potential.

Five young people go on what is expected to be a relaxing, enjoyable cruise in the Bahamas. The protagonist, Bill (Donal Logue), is still tormented by the suicide of his alcoholic mother (Grace Zabriskie), but he decides to join his wife, Jennifer (Pamela Gidley), on a yacht owned by her brother Phillip (Viggo Mortensen), an uptight yuppie lawyer. Phillip's client Alex (John Phibin), a rock musician, and his "mysterious" date, Catherine (Sam Jenkins), round out the group.

The anticipated fun is all but dashed when the yacht is taken over by two stranded passengers whose boat caught on fire. They are Tim (Jeremy Sisto), a man who's recently undergone a sex-change operation, and Camilla (Laura del Sol), a Latina immigrant he's smuggling into the U.S. to get cash to pay for his operation.

Though set outdoors, this overbaked melodrama has the brooding intensity and claustrophobic ambience of an intimate play. Indeed, the encounter with outsider Tim brings to the surface marital, familial and other tensions that make apparent the ugly biases of the more privileged characters. Central conflict is between the nasty, bigoted Phillip and "misunderstood deviant" Tim.

The blatantly preachy, poorly written group interaction is intercut with scenes of Tim phoning his lover, which will remind viewers of Sidney Lumet's "Dog Day Afternoon."

As constructed by writers Carl-Jan Colpaert and Lance Smith, the characters don't communicate so much as scream at each other — the dialogue consists of brief scenes and nasty one-liners.

There are some truthful, compassionate moments between Bill and Tim, two outcasts, but they are contained in a schematic story that telegraphs its humanistic messages about tolerance for alternative lifestyles without subtlety.

Under Colpaert's misguided direction, none of the actors, even the gifted Gidley, can build a coherent, let alone sympathetic character.

Mediocre technical credits make the pedestrian quality of "The Crew" all the more noticeable.

—*Emanuel Levy*

AT RISK

A Visualiner presentation. Produced by Kari Nevil and David E. Pyle. Directed by Elana K. Pyle. Screenplay, Elana and David Pyle. Camera (color), David Scardina; editor, Robert Graham Jones; music, Kevin Hedges; production design, David E. Pyle. Reviewed at the Hamptons Film Festival, Oct. 20, 1994. Running time: **95 MIN.**

Lara .... Elana K. Pyle
Steven .... Daniel McDonald
Jennifer .... Kim Myers
Max .... Vince Vaugh
Mrs. Nolan .... Shirley Anne Field

There's a huge gap between the bold intent and undistinguished execution of Elana Pyle's feature debut, a noir melodrama that also positions itself as a relevant cautionary tale. Unfortunately, pic's disjointed narrative, unevenly played core drama and crude production values would rule out any possibility of theatrical release.

It's hard to tell whether it was naivete, vanity or just misjudgment that led writer/director Pyle to cast herself as a femme fatale, for she not only lacks the alluring presence but also the talent to play a woman whom men find irresistible.

As the story begins, Lara returns from Mexico, where she spent a year unsuccessfully trying to unravel her marital problems with Steven (Daniel McDonald), her selfish, career-oriented, philandering hubby. Now, with plenty of time on her hands, she tries to locate her lover, Max (Vince Vaughn), a photographer who has mysteriously disappeared.

Through flashback, we learn that Lara met Max while going to see a private eye and that they practiced unsafe sex. To further complicate matters, Lara's paintings are destroyed by custom officers tipped off that the paintings contain hidden drugs. About 15 minutes before pic is over the Pyles introduce the specter of AIDS over the proceedings in a desperate attempt to make their yarn socially conscious, one with blatant messages about promiscuous sex and the risk of contracting the HIV virus.

November 7, 1994 (Cont.)

As most Hollywood movies about AIDS have focused on gay men, a morality tale about the lethal virus in the heterosexual community is more than welcome. Yet, the whole thing is done in such haphazard manner that it's doubtful whether the message will be taken seriously in this particular context.

In its present form and shape, "At Risk" is so underdeveloped that it needs substantial work before it's shown to the public again. Helmer Pyle seems to lack technical knowledge of such vital points as camera placement and movement, lighting and framing. The acting is almost uniformly unpolished and, except for Hedges' serviceable music, tech credits are on the raw side. —*Emanuel Levy*

VIENNA

JONAS IN THE DESERT

(DOCU — COLOR/B&W)

A Black Sun Flower production. Produced, directed by Peter Sempel. Screenplay, Jonas Mekas, Sempel. Camera (color, B&W), Jonas Scholz; editor, Sempel. Reviewed at Vienna Film Festival, Oct. 24, 1994. Running time: **123 MIN.**

Peter Sempel's docu tribute to experimental filmmaker and cinema guru Jonas Mekas is weakened by derivative, everything-but-the-kitchen-sink technique that looks inferior next to the original material included. Still, Mekas — best known for his '60s pic "The Brig" and being the brother of Adolfas Mekas, director of "Hallelujah the Hills" — and the famous eccentrics who surround him easily hold the attention for two hours.

German director Sempel follows Mekas on a tour of his Anthology Film Archives, run with a one-man-band enthusiasm and single-mindedness. Samples of avant-garde film are included along the way, and a substantial chunk of the docu is given over to the experimental artists, musicians and filmers who make up Mekas' rarefied, downtown New York, mutual-admiration society. Pic never identifies the speakers and performers.

Amid icons like Andy Warhol, Allen Ginsberg, Yoko Ono and Kenneth Anger, Mekas comes across as a humble, unaffected figure. Warhol appears fatuous, Ono shallow, silly and vain. Even Sempel suffers in comparison: His off-camera questions have the depth of a Barbara Walters interview. —*Cathy Meils*

I PROMISE

(ICH GELOBE)

(AUSTRIAN)

A Filmladen release (Austria) of a DorFilm production. Produced by Danny Krausz, Milan Dor. Directed, written by Wolfgang Murnberger. Camera (color, B&W), Fabian Eder; editor, Maria Homolkova; music, Robert Stiegler, Mischa Krausz; production design, Renate Martin, Andreas Donhauser; costume design, Thomas Olah; sound, Reinhold Kaiser. Reviewed at Vienna Film Festival, Oct. 26, 1994. Running time: **115 MIN.**
Berger .... Christoph Dostal
Rumpler .... Andreas Lust
Moser .... Andreas Simma
Kernstock .... Marcus J. Carney
Tomschitz .... Leopold Altenburg

"I Promise" is writer/director Wolfgang Murnberger's personal view of a young man's required army service and his meditations on life and God. Dreams, daydreams and reality merge in a seamless blend of the conscious and subconscious. Pic, which closed the recent Vienna Film Festival, is Austria's entry for the Oscars and has already won the Austrian Film Commission's prize for best film of the year. However, its richly textured dialogue will require first-class translation to work offshore.

Berger (Christoph Dostal), a quiet, less than enthusiastic soldier, spends most of his free time in a latrine stall (his "one square meter of freedom"), counting the days and etching a medieval fantasy on the back of the door.

The plot, which follows Berger and his buddies through their unexceptional training and soulless search for weekend sex, is the framework for the pic's real substance — Berger's thoughts and dreams, and helmer Murnberger's quirky vision of army life.

Movie's opening sequence, in moody B&W, is like something out of Ingmar Bergman's "The Seventh Seal." A knight enters a ravaged castle, where two women survive. One squirts him with breast milk; the other, Berger runs through with his lance. Sequence turns out to be a dream, from which Berger awakens to the shouts of his drill sergeant and ordinary life, in color.

Images from the dream reappear through the film in their real contexts. The castle is a nearby factory, the soldiers get lost in the dream's birch woods one night, and the women underscore Berger's conflict between his romantic, medieval ideal of love and his obsession with sex.

Fabian Eder's lensing and Maria Homolkova's editing enhance Murnberger's vision in scenes where daydreams melt in and out of reality. The 33-year-old director's previous feature, "Heaven or Hell,"

racked up a handful of international awards in 1990-91. —*Cathy Meils*

AKTION K

(AUSTRIAN — DOCU — COLOR/B&W — VIDEO)

A Provinz Film production. Produced by Andreas Gruber. Directed, written by Bernhard Bamberger, from an idea by Gruber. Camera (color, B&W; Beta SP), Jerzy Palacz, Karl Kremsmuller; editor, Evi Romen; sound, Stephan Wagner. Reviewed at Vienna Film Festival, Oct. 22, 1994. Running time: **60 MIN.**

When Andreas Gruber was shooting his POW escape pic "The Quality of Mercy" he invited Bernhard Bamberger to make a behind-the-scenes docu comparing the movie with actual events and the current attitudes of residents in the area. "Aktion K" perhaps unintentionally undercuts Gruber's movie by showing it for the play-acting it is, but also removes the blinders from anyone who thinks Nazism was vanquished in 1945.

Sobering, well-made film (aside from some heavy-handed use of music) looks ripe for exposure on serious international webs. Fiftieth anni of the escape is Feb. 2.

Of the 519 Russians who escaped from Mauthausen concentration camp, only nine survived. One of these, Mikhail Ribchinsky, returned during filming to retrace his path to safety.

Gruesome archive footage shows barely alive, skeletal men paraded naked before the camera, a far cry from the slim young actors in Gruber's pic. Docu plays on such contradictions by showing actors in boots and blankets sitting down to plates of warm food after filming a scene of shivering prisoners sipping watery soup. In a nearby bar, actors portraying Nazis discuss how easy it would have been to follow orders.

Ugliest moment in Bamberger's interviews of local Austrians comes when a cadaverous old man in national costume sits in his comfortable home lecturing Bamberger on Hitler's intrinsic correctness.
—*Cathy Meils*

JOINT VENTURE

(AUSTRIAN)

An Epo-Film production. Produced by Dieter Pochlatko. Directed by Dieter Berner. Screenplay, Hilde Berger. Camera (color), Walter Kindler; editor, Irene Tomschik; music, George Berner; costume design, Heidi Melinc; sound, Heinz Ebner. Reviewed at Vienna Film Festival, Oct. 20, 1994. Running time: **90 MIN.**

Eva .... Michaela Kuklova
Christian .... Gregor Bloeb
Liane .... Nina Franoszek
Adamec .... Jiri Menzel
Pavel .... Jan Novotny
Harada .... Tad Horino

A bright, well-made comedy on East European cross-border business, "Joint Venture" is a clever and entertaining update of *commedia dell'arte* characters and plot complications with just enough twists to keep auds engrossed. Pic is itself a joint venture of Austrian and Czech actors and locations, and looks set to move offshore into limited venues.

Eva (Michaela Kuklova), a hotel bar dancer, agrees to marry Harada (Tad Horino), an octogenarian Japanese businessman with a teenager's sex drive, and act as his front to acquire real estate in Prague. When Harada collapses from overstimulation, Eva is left without a meal ticket. She cajoles a more desirable young Austrian, Christian (Gregor Bloeb), into taking Harada's place at the altar.

Christian, who's been sent to Prague by his business partner/lover Liane (Nina Franoszek) to buy the same property, spots an opportunity. But the adorable Eva follows him back to Vienna, where a farcical *menage a trois* ensues. When Harada's associates show up, the entire cast ends up in a bidding war that pits Eva against her equally penniless ex-husband (Jan Novotny).

The movie clips along at a bright pace, and Kuklova is spunky and enchanting as Eva. Vet Czech helmer Jiri Menzel pops up in a supporting role as a Prague gangster. Tech credits are fine. —*Cathy Meils*

AN IMAGINED AUTOBIOGRAPHY

(ISRAELI)

A Transfax Film production. Produced by Marek Rosenbaum. Directed, written by Michal Bat-Adam. Camera (color), Yoav Kosh; editor, Boaz Leon; music, Amos Hadani; art direction, David Varod; costume design, Sharona Cohen; sound, Israel David. Reviewed on videocassette, Oct. 24, 1994. (In Boston Jewish Film Festival, Israel Film Festival, N.Y.) Running time: **89 MIN.**
Aya .... Michal Bat-Adam
Teenage Aya .... Michal Zoartz
Child Aya .... Shira Lew-Munk
Father .... Gedalia Besser
Mother .... Liat Goren

Top Israeli femme director Michal Bat-Adam turns introspective for "An Imagined Autobiography," but prospects abroad are dim beyond specialty fest showings. Story concerns a film director (Bat-Adam) who is making a movie about her childhood and adolescence while dealing with her father's decline. Film bows stateside at New York's Israel Film Festival on Nov. 10, and

November 7, 1994 (Cont.)

screens at the Boston Jewish Film Festival on Nov. 15.

The clash between film and reality is really the core of the movie, with scenes from the autobiographical film clashing with scenes from Aya's memory. Sometimes the memory is harsher and sometimes the film is, as if Bat-Adam doesn't trust either as a source of truth.

Her character's childhood was a rough one, with a distant father (Gedalia Besser) and a mentally disturbed mother (Liat Goren) who was in and out of institutions. However, the point of it all seems to be for the adult character to feel sorry for herself, and the ultimate resolution — when she realizes that the mystery of life will never be fully revealed to her — falls flat.

Femme performances are good, with Goren touching as the mother losing her grip on reality, and Michal Zoartz and Shira Lew-Munk on target as Aya at different ages. Gedalia Besser's father is more problematical, especially in flashbacks where his hair is dyed in a failed attempt to make him look younger.

Tech values are also a problem in a film where movies, reality and fantasies mix together. Some scenes have such harsh lighting that it appears characters are being followed around by spotlights.

Pic is being shown as part of retro of Bat-Adam's films. That's probably the best showcase for it.
—*Daniel M. Kimmel*

THE SERVILE

(VIDHEYAN)

(INDIAN)

A General Pictures/Quillon/Kerala production. Produced by K. Ravindranathan Nair. Directed, written by Adoor Gopalakrishnan, based on a story by Zachariah. Camera, Ravi Verma; editor, Mani; music, Vijaya Bhaskar; art direction, Sivan. In London Film Festival. Running time: **112 MIN.**

Bhaska Patelar .... Mammooty
Thommie .... Gopha Kumar
Saroja .... Tanvi Ajmi
Omana .... Sabita Anand
  Malayalam dialogue

The nature of servility within the individual, society and politics is closely observed in Adoor Gopalakrishnan's latest film, "The Servile." His rigid adherence to his roots (Kerala) and language (Malayalam) and his tight cinematic control continue to make him a sought-after director on the fest circuit, and pic's pacing and length are attuned to international tastes.

Although set in the '60s in a secluded, traditional village in South India, "The Servile" is tinged with remnants of British colonization. During World War II, the scarcity of food drove impoverished Christian Kerala farmers to seek a living in the bordering state of Karnataka. On arrival, they found that their only hope was to encroach on forested land, which the British entrusted to the village chiefs, empowering them to collect taxes and enforce law, a practice that persisted into the 1960s. One such migrant is Thommie (Gopha Kumar), a cringing good-hearted slob who typifies the downtrodden. Thommie enjoys a close relationship with his lovely young wife, Omana (Sabita Anand), and their little son. The scheming village chief Bhaskar Patelar (Mammooty) sees in him a prime opportunity to validate his authority before his resentful "subjects." He whips the poor man into subjugation, making him his willing and unquestioning ally. Thommie, although aware of being manipulated, is fascinated all the same by the prospect of being a confidante of someone so powerful. Bhaskar subjugates him swiftly into total submission — by raping his wife and making her his mistress, by forcing him to witness the murder of his own wife, Saroja (Tanvi Ajmi), who has dared to question his actions, and by making Thommie his accomplice on mindless little acts of self-aggrandizement.

When the chief's domination of the village goes too far, the villagers unite and turn against him. Almost to the end, Thommie remains faithful to his feudal lord. Only when Bhaskar has been hunted to death by the villagers does Thommie realize that his spirit and person are now free, in a way he had never experienced.

Gopalakrishnan's sense of *mise en scene* is impeccable. The performances, although over-stressed, are powerful, particularly that of Mammooty, who manages to give his negative character nuances that make him appear alternately childish, stunted and mean. Gopalakrishnan's canvas opens up large, disturbing issues. In his own Kerala state, where he enjoys critical and commercial success, his films invariably create political controversy, as this one has done. In "The Servile," the levels of meaning have been subtly woven into a strong narrative.
—*Uma da Cunha*

GOOD VIBRATIONS, BAD SITUATIONS

(GUT DRAUF, SCHLECHT DRAN)

(GERMAN — 16mm)

A Lothar Lambert production. Produced, directed, written, edited by Lambert. Camera (color)/music, Albert Kittler; sound, Kittler, Lambert. Reviewed at Toronto Film Festival, Sept. 14, 1994. Running time: **70 MIN.**
With: Dagmar Beiersdorf, Dorothea Moritz, Stephanie Hofmeister, Klaus Redlich, Renata Soleymany, Baduri, Lothar Lambert.

Lothar Lambert, whose entire film *oeuvre* has been shown at the Toronto festival over the years, attempts to capture the liberated spirit of the new Berlin in "Good Vibrations, Bad Situations," an uneven sex farce that is only intermittently entertaining. Though only half of the sketches are truly funny, pic should enjoy the support of the festival circuit, where most of Lambert's previous films have premiered.

Unfolding as a series of comic sketches, "Good Vibrations" is meant to show, as one character says, that "Berlin is a nightmare since the Wall is gone." Yarn begins with a conversation between two middle-aged housewives, who meet in the famous Kurfurstendamm square and complain that Berlin has become a center for queers, foreigners and anti-social types. The women are utterly humorless, their discourse dominated by gossip and quips about sex. As is often the case with such structures, some episodes are more amusing than others. One of the strongest sketches is "Tomb Song," in which a young boy and his mother visit the cemetery where Marlene Dietrich is buried. In another brief segment, a handsome foreigner is interviewed for a gardening job by an older gentleman and it turns out that they have met before in less than respectable circumstances.

In moments, but only in moments, "Good Vibrations" reveals sharp tongue and lucid mind, uncluttered by "politically correct" or "culturally accepted" norms. But for such a confection to work, the humor needs to be outrageous and biting — and it is not. For example, a gag in which a young man cannot get sexually aroused, while his girl tries every strategy possible to excite him, goes far too long before making its point.

This film is in color and, for a change, helmer is not the lenser, but its look and feel are similar to Lambert's former outings, displaying his distinct sensibility. Though a pleasant viewing for the most part, "Good Vibrations" is not as risque or original as Lambert's "Fucking City" or "All You Never Wanted to Know About Women."
—*Emanuel Levy*

UNCONDITIONAL LOVE

A Prodigy production. Produced, directed by Arthur Bjorn Egeli. Executive producer, David Ellsworth. Co-producer, Ted Collins. Screenplay, Egeli, Ian Bowater. Camera (Colorlab), Teresa Medina; editor, Barbara Boguski; music, Michael Errington; production design, Stephen J. Lattimer; art direction, Lee Trask; costume design, Jacqueline Saint Anne; sound (Dolby), Sean Sullivan; associate producers, Joan E. Lenos, Hank Gans; assistant director, William Clark; casting, Ted Collins. Reviewed on videocassette, Boston, Sept. 1, 1994. Running time: **85 MIN.**

Steven Buchanan .... Pablo Bryant
Mary Chambers .... Aleksandra Kaniak
Melissa Gardner .... Isabelle Dahlin
Robert Hoffman .... David Ellsworth
Theresa .... Jessica Brytn Flannery
Ron Chambers .... Joe Estevez
Hal Wilson .... Hal Streit
Anne Melon .... Adrienne Newberg

Middlebrow tale of young artist freeing himself of various mentors to find his own style is beautiful to look at but not terribly profound. Fests and venues looking for something that seems deep, sexy and knowing while serving up easy-to-digest ideas may draw some business with this pic.

Chief among the film's virtues are the well-used locations in Provincetown, on the tip of Cape Cod, stunningly captured by cinematographer Teresa Medina. The images are often as attractive as the paintings we see, several of them done by producer/director/co-writer Arthur Bjorn Egeli.

Story concerns Steven (Pablo Bryant) who has been under the tutelage of older painter Robert Hoffman (David Ellsworth), adopting his impressionistic style. Steven is on the verge of his first professional showing but isn't sure if he's ready.

Fighting for his affections and attentions are his mentor, his model and lover (Jessica Brytn Flannery) and another young painter (Isabelle Dahlin) who looks up to him. Into this comes a new distraction in the person of a married next-door neighbor (Aleksandra Kaniak), who becomes model, lover *and* tutor, encouraging him to forgo representational painting for abstraction.

Strength of Egeli's script (written with Ian Bowater) is its depiction of young artists' doubts about whether they can really paint for a living. Most touching is Steven's friend (Hal Streit), whose youth is behind him but who hasn't yet had his big break.

Pic falls flat in its debates on impressionism vs. abstraction, an issue that was settled in the art world in the early part of this century. For the folks in the story it would be like arguing with a young filmmaker as to whether he should make a talkie or a silent film. Indeed, in this post-modern era, the dispute seems positively quaint.

Thesping is decidedly uneven, with several performers seemingly reciting speeches rather than speaking in character. Faring best are Bryant as the young artist and Streit as his older friend.

Egeli makes a valiant attempt to present what is largely his central character's internal struggle for a personal vision, but in oversimplifying the issues he ends up losing the arthouse audiences that would have been his best bet for giving the film a shot.
—*Daniel M. Kimmel*

EAGLES DON'T HUNT FLIES

(AGUILAS NO CAZAN MOSCAS)

(COLOMBIAN-ITALIAN)

A Caracol Television/Producciones Fotograma (Colombia)/Emme (Italy) production. Produced by Sandro Silvestri. Executive producers, Salvatore Basile, Marianella Cabrera, Abelardo Quintero. Directed by Sergio Cabrera. Screenplay, Humberto Dorado, with collaboration of Jorge Goldemberg, Jorge Fraga, Frank Ramirez, Jasha Gelabert, Cabrera. Camera (color), Jose Medeiros, Juan Cristobal Cobo; editor, Sergio Nuti; music, German Arrieta, Juan Marquez; art direction, Enrique Linero; costume design, Sandra Kasparone, Herbert Manzano; sound, Gregory Valtierra, Heriberto Garcia, Fausto Achilli; associate producers, Sergio Cabrera, Mabel Garcia De Angel, Camillo Vives, Maura Vespini. Reviewed at Venice Film Festival (Special Events), Sept. 9, 1994. Running time: **110 MIN.**
With: Frank Ramirez, Humberto Dorado, Florina Lemaitre, Angelo Javier Lozano, Fausto Cabrera, Vicky Hernandez.

A grotesque duel to the death between two old friends is told lightly and well in "Eagles Don't Hunt Flies," a likable, unpretentious slice of Latin American folklore with comic and political overtones.

Colombian film and TV helmer Sergio Cabrera has built an international reputation on his two much-prized features — "Dueling Techniques" (1988) and "The Snail's Strategy" (1993) — released in Europe. "Eagles" is an attempt to revive the disappointing commercial fortunes of "Dueling" by intercutting a newly shot framing story into the old film (reviewed in *Variety*, Oct. 19, 1988).

But the frame is completely superfluous to the fine original, whose satirical meditation on the uselessness of violence shines through the makeover. Fests that already programmed "Dueling" will probably pass on "Eagles" on grounds that the films are too similar. But pic should please auds who cottoned to "Snail."

The core film describes the preparations for a gruesome duel between two pals over a never-quite-explained question of honor. Oquendo, a butcher (played by scripter Humberto Dorado), and Albarracin, a schoolteacher (Frank Ramirez), are both members of the left-wing opposition and have many noble memories in common. One involves their absurdly botched attempt to blow up a train on which the president of the country is riding.

Another possible object of the feud is Miriam (Florina Lemaitre), Oquendo's pretty wife, who once massaged the shoulders of bachelor Albarracin. Miriam floats blithely around the small, dusty town with her laundry basket, the only citizen unaware of the encroaching duel.

Instead of stopping the bloodshed, the authorities place bets on who will live and die. The church, personified by Father Troncoso (Fausto Cabrera), is no less cynical in charging for prayers.

The new framing story has Oquendo and Miriam's teenage son Vladimir getting kicked out of military academy when the old story of the duel resurfaces. His search for the truth unfortunately reveals too soon that his father survived the event, spoiling the ending and adding no new dimension to the tale.

—*Deborah Young*

LAURA: THE REBEL YEARS

(ANNI RIBELLI)

(ITALIAN-ARGENTINE)

An Istituto Luce Italnoleggio Cinematografico release (Italy) of a Sintra (Rome)/Division Producciones (Buenos Aires) production, in association with RAI-2, Istituto Luce, Presidency of the Council of Ministers — Main Office of Entertainment, Argentine National Film Institute. (International sales: Intra Films, Rome.) Produced by Rosanna Seregni, Eduardo Nunez. RAI producer, Loredana Rotondo. Directed by Rosalia Polizzi. Screenplay, Polizzi, Mario Prosperi. Camera (Cinecitta color), Juan Carlos Lenardi; editor, Alfredo Muschietti; music, Luis Bacalov; art direction, Santiago Elder; costume design, Michela Gisotti, Trini Munoz; sound, Pedro Marra; assistant director, Raul Rodriguez. Reviewed at Venice Film Festival (Italian Panorama), Sept. 5, 1994. Running time: **103 MIN.**
With: Massimo Dapporto, Alessandra Acciai, Leticia Bredice, Esther Gross, Adelaide Alessi, Inda Ledesma, Juan Cruz Bordeu, Eva Burgos, Adriana Russo, Vanina Fabiak, Daniele Tedeschi.

In "Laura: The Rebel Years," the fall of Peron coincides with the rise of a turbulent teen struggling to buck the constraints of her Sicilian origins in fast-changing 1950s Argentina. First feature by Italo-Argentinian Rosalia Polizzi is a solidly, somewhat unimaginatively directed rites-of-passage yarn, whose weaknesses are a shortage of script muscle and an inconsistent greenhorn turn in the title role. Robust small-screen fare should figure on non-U.S. tube slates.

Giving the film some central ballast is Massimo Dapporto's harsh characterization of Francesco, tradition-bound father of Laura (Leticia Bredice). Overbearing and bitterly resentful on the surface, he displays a more-than-occasional flicker of empathy for the needs of his plucky daughter, which lifts his character out of the realm of stock tyrants.

The friction of family life is conveyed with confident strokes, its emotional power steadily accelerated throughout the film. As Francesco becomes increasingly ill with TB, the family of mute, ineffectual women recedes into the background, leaving the angry father-daughter duo out front with crossed swords.

Less fully rounded is Laura's life outside the familial walls, especially her politically enlightening rapport with communist schoolteacher Dora, played with affectation by Alessandra Acciai. Stilted dialogue makes these scenes sit leadenly and artificially among their looser surroundings. A romantic track with a politically committed lawyer (Juan Cruz Bordeu) is more successful.

Onscreen in virtually every scene, Bredice is spirited and likable, but she lacks the dramatic reach to build the two-dimensional character into a headstrong force of nature capable of carrying the film. A nod to "The Little Foxes," where she stands by watching her dying father grasp for his medication, provides an unnecessary reminder that the novice thesp is no Bette Davis. Like a number of the principals, Bredice is not helped by poor dubbing into Italian.

Tech side is generally tidy, and '50s period re-creation is more than functional.   —*David Rooney*

A THOUSAND AND ONE

(MIL E UMA)

(BRAZILIAN-PORTUGUESE)

A 1001 Filmes (Rio de Janeiro)/Mandragoa Filmes (Lisbon) production. (International sales: Gemini Films, Paris.) Produced by Paulo Branco, Miguel Faria Jr. Executive producer, Carlos A. Diniz. Directed, written by Susana Moraes. Camera (color), Affonso Beato; editor, Marta Luz; music, Pericles Cavalcanti; art direction, Mari Stokler, Gualter Pupo; costume design, Marcelo Pies; sound, Bruno Fernandes. Reviewed at Venice Film Festival (Window on Images), Sept. 2, 1994. Running time: **74 MIN.**
With: Giovana Gold, Alexandre Borges, Hamilton Vaz Pereira, Jose Rubens Xaxa, Cristiana Guinle, Jose Mayer, Fabio Namakamy, Cecil Thire, Claudio Mamberti, Jose Lewgoy, Lelia Abramo, Miguel Faria Jr., Vera Holtz, Walmor Chagas.

First feature by Brazilian documaker Susana Moraes orchestrates a busy union between absurdist comedy, soap opera and Godardian rumination on the filmmaking process. Despite its lofty pretensions, "A Thousand and One" is rarely more than a middling success in any of its three guises. This largely uninvolving tract about a woman's struggle to commit an arcane idea to celluloid may encounter admirers on the European fest circuit, but life beyond that looks negligible.

Following the death of her father, Alice (Giovana Gold) quits her marriage to dumbstruck David (Jose Rubens Xaxa) and scouts financing for her feature on artist Marcel Duchamp's imaginary journey to Brazil. She spots an ideal leading man in musician Antonio (Alexandre Borges), but comes up empty-handed in the coin department, hooking up with cocaine trafficker the Baron (Jose Mayer) to produce her film.

Moraes tosses in a surfeit of plot digressions and underdeveloped peripheral characters that add further clutter to the already overburdened yarn. Distractions such as a flirtatious lesbian, and the Baron's Asian flunky, who hovers about like a bargain-basement James Bond villain, go nowhere. Snippets of the laboriously mounted Duchamp pic provide additional baggage, as does a maddening, intrusive music score, with frequent vocal tunes giving the lowdown on each character.

—*David Rooney*

LIKE A ROLLING STONE

(BO NO KANASHIMI)

(JAPANESE)

An Excellent Film production. Produced by Hidehiro Ito, Yasuhide Kidota, Kinya Yagi, Misa Okatsu. Directed by Tatsumi Kumashiro. Screenplay, Kumashiro, Ito. Camera (color), Junichiro Hayashi; editor, Masaru Iizuka; music, Tatsunori Oda; art direction, Kiyotaka Sawada; sound (Dolby), Kiyoshi Kakizawa; lighting, Nobuo Maehara. Reviewed at Tokyo Film Festival, Kyoto (competing), Sept. 25, 1994. Running time: **118 MIN.**
With: Eiji Okuda, Eiko Nagashima, Reiko Takashima, Hakuryu.

"Like a Rolling Stone" is yet another entry in the ranks of the already overpopulated Japanese yakuza film repertoire. The solid performances are not as overly dramatic as is often the case in the genre, but the film is disjointed and confusing, with little in the way of plot advancement. Pic will likely do moderately well in Japan based on the fame of lead actor Eiji Okuda and director Tatsumi Kumashiro, who made his reputation with soft-porn pix.

The film is about Tanaka (played well by Okuda), a drug-dealing, chain-smoking, knife-wielding, scar-riddled lackey for the big crime boss. He spends much of his time purposely getting stabbed or injured to prove his loyalty to his boss and get out of other, bigger confrontations. One of the more gruesome but interesting scenes is several minutes of silence while he sews a huge knife gash on his stomach.

The rest of his time is devoted to women. Helmer's soft-porn background is put to good use in the love scenes, which include man-girl, man-woman and woman-girl combos. Perhaps the film's most entertaining quirk does not appear till it's almost over: One of the mistresses reveals a predilection for Tanaka's scars, and he discovers that he can bring her to orgasm just by telling about his battle wounds.

Pic's apparent philosophy is summed up by Tanaka: "Women are evil. Men only kill."

A few interesting moments and clean technical credits make the film acceptable but cannot overcome the shortcomings in plot.

—*Karen Regelman*

FAMILY MATTERS

(DET BLI'R I FAMILIEN)

(DANISH)

A Zentropa Entertainments production, in association with Nordisk Film-TV, Svensk Filmindustri (Sweden), GER (Portugal). (International sales: Nordisk Film-TV Distribution, Stockholm.) Produced by Vibeke Windelov, Peter Albaek Jensen. Directed by Susanne Bier. Screenplay, Lars Kjeldgaard, Philip Zanden. Camera (color), Erik Zappon; editor, Pernille Bech Christensen; music, Johan Soderkvist, Joachim Holbek; production design, Birgitte Mellentin; sound (Dolby), Per Streit. Reviewed at Svensk Filmindustri screening room, Stockholm, Sept. 26, 1994. Running time: **98 MIN.**
With: Philip Zanden, Ghita Norby, Ernst-Hugo Jaregard, Ana Padrao, Anna Wing, Bodil Udsen, Filipe Ferrer, Claus Nissen.

This offbeat black comedy about a Dane who sets off to find his biological father in Portugal is not without merit. However, lack of balance in construction, resulting in some untidy side stories, weakens its impact.

Director Susanne Bier, whose first feature was the laureled but overpraised "Freud's Leaving Home" (1991), here tells the story of Jan (co-scripter Philip Zanden, Bier's real-life partner), who in his mid-30s suddenly finds he was adopted. After seeking out his biological mother (Ghita Norby), a former cabaret artiste, the two set off by cab to a small Portuguese town to track down Jan's true dad.

When they arrive, mom locks herself in her hotel room and forces Jan to conduct his own inquiry. On the way, he falls for the beautiful Constanca (Ana Padrao).

Pic mixes comedy and tragedy, with the emphasis on the former at the beginning and the latter at the conclusion. However, despite some interesting plot twists and good performances down the line, the result is still dramatically unsatisfying, mainly due to the relationship between Jan and his mother being swept to one side in the later stages.

—*Gunnar Rehlin*

CRACKING UP

A Foolish Mortal Films production. (International sales: Foolish Mortal, N.Y.) Produced by Matt Mitler. Co-producer, Lilli Mitler. Directed by Matt Mitler. Screenplay, Matt Mitler, Theodore P. LoRusso, from a story by Matt Mitler. Camera (color), Mark Traver; editor, Matt Mitler; music, Arthur Rosen; art direction, Shawn Sullivan, Ben Dulong; costume design, Carol Brys; sound, Rob Taz; associate producers, Robert Prichard, Jennifer Prichard, William Otterson; assistant director, Judy Gorjane. Reviewed at Venice Film Festival (Critics' Week), Sept. 8, 1994. Running time: **92 MIN.**

Danny Gold	Matt Mitler
Jake	Jason Brill
Alan	David Wells
Dack	Kevin Brown
Hazel	Debra K. Lynn
Carolyn	Carolyn McDermott
Kimberly	Kimberly Flynn

"**C**racking Up" falls to pieces almost immediately but keeps on going. Manic, antipathetic portrait of a manic, antipathetic Lower East Side performance artist won't get much farther than screenings for cast and crew.

New York standup comic Matt Mitler, who produced, helmed, co-wrote and edited, plays Danny Gold, a cross between Lenny Bruce and Jerry Lewis on speed. Between segs of his and others' acts at a nitery in the East Village, pic charts his chaotic personal relationships (with a waitress and chiropractor) and self-destructive professional life (with his agent, colleagues and TV denizens) in a torrent of dialogue and restless camerawork.

With no shading to the unlikable central character, and unfunny repartee that palls fast (even Gold's agent has better gags than his client), the movie is already a major turnoff by reel two. Unlike, say, in Arthur Penn's similarly themed "Mickey One" (1965), there's no attempt to broaden the movie's focus into more ambitious spheres.

Performances by large roster of Gothamites are all solid, including the manic Mitler. Tech credits on the low-budgeter are fine, and blowup from Super-16mm acceptable.

—*Derek Elley*

STAR TREK GENERATIONS

A Paramount Pictures release of a Rick Berman production. Produced by Berman. Executive producer, Bernie Williams. Co-producer, Peter Lauritson. Directed by David Carson. Screenplay, Ronald D. Moore, Brannon Braga, story by Berman, Moore, Braga, based upon "Star Trek," created by Gene Roddenberry. Camera (Deluxe, widescreen), John Alonzo; editor, Peter Berger; music, Dennis McCarthy; production design, Herman Zimmerman; art direction, Sandy Veneziano; costume design, Robert Blackman; special visual effects supervisors, Ronald B. Moore, John Knoll; special makeup effects, Michael Westmore; sound (Dolby), Thomas Causey; assistant directors, Yudi Bennett, Chris Soldo. Reviewed at Paramount Studios, Hollywood, Nov. 7, 1994. MPAA Rating: PG. Running time: **118 MIN.**

Capt. Jean-Luc Picard	Patrick Stewart
Capt. James T. Kirk	William Shatner
Dr. Soran	Malcolm McDowell
Cmdr. William Riker	Jonathan Frakes
Lt. Cmdr. Data	Brent Spiner
Lt. Cmdr. Geordi La Forge	LeVar Burton
Lt. Cmdr. Worf	Michael Dorn
Dr. Beverly Crusher	Gates McFadden
Counselor Deanna Troy	Marina Sirtis
Montgomery Scott	James Doohan
Cmdr. Pavel Chekov	Walter Koenig
Guinan	Whoopi Goldberg
Lura	Barbara March
B'Etor	Gwynth Walsh
Capt. Harriman	Alan Ruck

It may not "boldly go where no one has gone before," but "Star Trek Generations" has enough verve, imagination and familiarity to satisfy three decades' worth of Trekkers raised on several incarnations of the television skein. The first bigscreen outing for the "Next Generation" crew should soar at the box office and handsomely revive the theatrical franchise much in the way that the reinvented series blasted off with fans old and new. Expect a smooth flight into early 1995 with solid prospects overseas.

In order to facilitate the return of several members of the original Starship Enterprise, a rather convoluted plot has been fashioned. The story begins at a PR-event maiden voyage of a "New" Enterprise, with Kirk (William Shatner), engineer Scott (James Doohan) and Chekov (Walter Koenig) aboard as honored guests and living relics of the Starfleet.

(Leonard Nimoy opted out of this latest vogage.)

The smooth-sailing media voyage gets jettisoned when a distress signal summons the craft into action — two cargo ships are engulfed by a ribbon of electrical energy. In Kirk's heyday it would have been a no-brainer rescue assignment. But the combination of an inexperienced captain and a not yet fully equipped craft add up to catastrophe and the end, albeit heroic, of Kirk. But more on that later.

Four generations after the disaster, the "Next" crew receives an emergency call to throw a lifeline to scientists on an experimental probe. Actually, there's only one left breathing, the human-like El Aurian Dr. Soran (Malcolm McDowell), who not so coincidentally was a survivor of the almost century-old incident on the New Enterprise. Another survivor happens to be aboard — rec center barkeep Guinan (Whoopi Goldberg).

She tells Capt. Picard (Patrick Stewart) of the Nexus, that mysterious ribbon of energy. Guinan says it induces consuming joy. To regain its nirvana, Soran is willing to do anything, including aligning with malevolent Klingons.

"Star Trek Generations" is primarily about stopping the proverbial mad scientist run amok. Its secondary concern, which makes Kirk's resuscitation necessary, is Picard's personal crisis in weighing duty against the need for family — blood-related and otherwise. One can also point to themes of addiction and seduction.

But there's more, keeping in the "Trek" tradition of plot-heavy yarns. While the abundance of

> 'Star Trek Generations' should handsomely revive the theatrical franchise much in the way that the reinvented series blasted off with fans old and new.

narrative thread tends to slow matters to less than warp speed, that's offset by a lot of character detail. The levity in this episode, for instance, revolves around android Data (Brent Spiner) coping with the effects of injecting an "emotion" chip into his circuitry.

November 14, 1994 (Cont.)

The script by Ronald D. Moore and Brannon Braga is so chock-a-block with scientific detail one begins to lose a sense of present, past and future. The story would fail utterly if not for its human dimension.

Advantages to having such familiar characters aboard are the ease of the interplay and the fact that audiences already know the personalities. Shatner and Doohan have mastered the art of playing their roles while providing sly self-commentary. The others have not quite reached that level of acting enlightenment, but give them a few more voyages and they'll be able to make the Vulcan yellow pages entertaining.

Director David Carson, a small-screen "Trek" vet, does well, not brilliantly, in the widescreen arena. Only a couple of earlier movie editions have truly managed to find the right balance of gadgetry and story, science and fun. Carson scores best in capturing the "Star Trek" look, though he tends to linger too long in recording those achievements.

A review of the logbook of "Star Trek Generations" reveals some fractures, bruises and abrasions. One certainly shouldn't have expected less. In the end the ship may not be pristine, but even without Spock, the franchise appears likely to live long and prosper. —*Leonard Klady*

THE SANTA CLAUSE

A Buena Vista release in association with Hollywood Pictures of an Outlaw production. Produced by Brian Reilly, Jeffrey Silver, Robert Newmyer. Executive producers, Richard Baker, Rick Messina, James Miller. Co-producers, William Wilson III, Caroline Baron. Directed by John Pasquin. Screenplay, Leo Benvenuti, Steve Rudnick. Camera (Technicolor), Walt Lloyd; editor, Larry Bock; music, Michael Convertino; production design, Carol Spier; art direction, James McAteer; costume design, Carol Ramsey; sound (Dolby), David Lee; elf wrangler, Christy Garland; special makeup/animatronic effects, Alec Gillis, Tom Woodruff Jr; visual effects supervisor, John Sullivan; assistant director, Bill Elvin; casting, Renee Rousselot. Reviewed at Mann National, Westwood, Nov. 5, 1994. MPAA Rating: PG. Running time: **97 MIN.**

Scott Calvin .... Tim Allen
Dr. Neal Miller .... Judge Reinhold
Laura Calvin .... Wendy Crewson
Charlie Calvin .... Eric Lloyd
Bernard .... David Krumholtz
Mr. Whittle .... Peter Boyle
Det. Nunzio .... Larry Brandenburg
Ms. Daniels .... Mary Gross
Judy .... Paige Tamada

T he sticky legal question of Disney's holiday movie boils down to the validity of the fine print on Old St. Nick's business card. It states that if you put on the "suit," you're stuck with the reindeer, the cookie-and-milk diet, the suite at the North Pole and, of course, delivering the gifts. That's "The Santa Clause."

Unlike the other Santa pic, the drama doesn't wind up in the courtroom. This is a hip, likable spin on the seasonal icon told with a deft mixture of comedy and sentimentality. The mixture should mint some fast Xmas coin and play into the New Year with upbeat returns. Offshore prospects aren't as bright because of the uniquely American flavor to this rendering.

The hapless hero of the piece is ad exec Scott Calvin (Tim Allen), divorced from his wife and doing the split-custody holiday scene with son Charlie (Eric Lloyd). Christmas Eve, they get the traditional Yule meal at Denny's, followed by a reading of "The Night Before Christmas," eggnog and a cozy tuck into bed.

Except this year, a clatter arises from the roof, and when Scott investigates, he startles a red-suited gent who falls with a thud. That's when he passes along his card and Scott reluctantly dons the costume and, with Charlie, climbs aboard the Reindeermobile, grabs the List and goes to work.

The deed done, Comet and crew take the duo to the North Pole where the head elf explains the significant implications of the title clause. Scott reacts by pondering the implications of not believing. When he wakes up the following morning in his suburban bed, he assumes the events of the previous night were all a dream.

The humor in the Leo Benvenuti/ Steve Rudnick screenplay centers on characters' reactions to the preposterous premise. Laura (Wendy Crewson), the ex-spouse, and her cloying new mate, head shrinker Neal Miller (Judge Reinhold), assume Scott's tall tale is a sort of revenge scenario. They turn the tables and have the court suspend Santa dad's visitation rights. But Scott's not lying, for once, so logic is turned on its head.

Director John Pasquin, in his feature debut, has the precarious task of rooting the tale, minimally, in movie reality. Additionally, there's a delicate balance to effect between the gags and seasonal emotion. Then, just to complicate matters, he has an arsenal of special effects and makeup to weave into the plot. In other words, it's a foolhardy task.

While the tyro talent demonstrates no great flair or invention, he does get the job done. This is abetted in no small measure by Allen, who is just as personable and likable on the bigscreen as he is on the tube. Lloyd also turns out to be an engaging kid.

"The Santa Clause" also offers one of those rare instances where the gadgetry and effects don't overwhelm the story. They remain functional and organic, handsomely complemented by the sterling production design of Carol Spier.

Though no paragon, it's definitely nice, with a splash of wit and a nod to the contemporary stumbling blocks on the path to holiday cheer. —*Leonard Klady*

MIRACLE ON 34TH STREET

A 20th Century Fox release of a Hughes Entertainment production. Produced by John Hughes. Executive producers, William Ryan, William Beasley. Directed by Les Mayfield. Screenplay, George Seaton, Hughes, story by Valentine Davis, based on the 1947 motion picture screenplay by Seaton. Camera (Deluxe), Julio Macat; editor, Raja Gosnell; music, Bruce Broughton; production design, Doug Kraner; art direction, Steve Arnold; set decoration, Leslie Rollins; costume design, Kathy O'Rear; sound (Dolby), Ronald Judkins; visual effects supervisor, Gregory McMurry; assistant director, Randy Suhr; casting, Jane Jenkins, Janet Hirshenson. Reviewed at Fairfax Cinema, Los Angeles, Nov. 4, 1994. MPAA Rating: PG. Running time: **114 MIN.**

Kriss Kringle ... Richard Attenborough
Dorey Walker .... Elizabeth Perkins
Bryan Bedford .... Dylan McDermott
Susan Walker .... Mara Wilson
Judge Harper .... Robert Prosky
Ed Collins .... J.T. Walsh
Jack Duff .... James Remar
Alberta Leonard .... Jane Leeves
Shellhammer .... Simon Jones
C.F. Cole .... William Windom

T here's no lack of Santa mentality in the remake of the Christmas chestnut "Miracle on 34th Street." Writer/producer John Hughes has done minor and subtle tampering with the 1947 vintage holiday yarn, and that proves both an asset and a hindrance. Pic should score upbeat, not quite boffo, seasonal returns and join the Christmas club of movies in perpetual year-end television rotation.

What remain enduring and heartwarming about the tale are its themes of hope and belief. More problematic is that while the time is now, Hughes and company have done little to contemporize the story's setting or attitude.

The background tug of war has shifted from Macy's vs. Gimbel's to Cole's — a Macy's clone — and the generic discount Shopper's Express chain. Otherwise, the portrait of a middle-class, affluent, non-ethnic America is unaltered.

Through happenstance, one Kriss Kringle (Richard Attenborough) becomes the official Cole's Santa. Not only does he resemble the yuletide icon, he genuinely loves children and embodies the spirit of giving. And, oh yes, he just happens to be the real McCoy, so he says.

The trouble is that there are still folks who refuse to recognize the obvious. Dorey Walker (Elizabeth Perkins), the Cole's exec who hired him, is a prime example. Her steadfast belief that "truth is the most important thing" has also made her daughter, Susan (Mara Wilson), a 5-year-old doubter.

Mother and child become a significant test case for Kriss Kringle.

When forces of evil at the discount store conspire to discredit him, his attorney (and Dorey devotee), Brian Bedford (Dylan McDermott), must prove him mentally sound. The bigger issue is whether the court is willing to suspend its disbelief.

Hughes and director Les Mayfield have wisely shifted focus to the Santa figure and have a superb St. Nick in Attenborough. Not only is he the embodiment of decency, he's having a crackling good time bringing the character to Earth.

The young Wilson is the other stellar standout, displaying a wisdom and precociousness that enliven material with a tendency toward the cute. Support work from Perkins, McDermott and J.T. Walsh as the prosecuting attorney elevates their otherwise familiar roles.

Though the direction tends to be predictable, this "Miracle" comes with very handsome wrapping. Doug Kraner's production design balances contemporary gloss with timeworn hues. It's all lovingly bathed in light by cameraman Julio Macat.

The overall effect is enjoyable and cozy like a warm fire on a cold night. It also harks back to a bygone, simpler time. For those diehard believers, it's a bit disappointing that the filmmakers huddle in the past rather than press on optimistically into the future. —*Leonard Klady*

WHITE BADGE

(KOREAN)

A Morning Calm Cinema release of a Deil Film production. Produced by Jong Nam Cook. Executive producers, Hak Hun Kim, Dong Kyu Ahn. Directed by Ji Young Chung. Screenplay, Su Young Gong, Young Chel Jo, Seung Bo Shim, Chung, based on the novel by Jung Hyo Ahn. Camera (color), Young Gil Yu; editor, Soon Duck Bark; music, Byung Ha Sin. Reviewed at the Laemmle Grande, Nov. 3, 1994. (In Tokyo Film Festival, Kyoto.) Running time: **125 MIN.**

Kiju Han .... Sung Ki Ahn
Chinsu Pyon .... Kyung Young Lee
Yongok Kim .... Hae Jin Shim
Munki Kim .... Yongjae Tokko
Hisik Chon .... Sejun Kim
Bangjang Hong .... Junho Huh

T he "White Badge" of the Tokyo fest-winning Korean pic is a reference to the designation worn by that nation's soldiers fighting in Vietnam. A rumination on war, it falls short of hitting a universal chord. The maiden release of a new U.S. distrib should score some upscale response but will need to enlist ethnic support until inroads can be made for the virtually unknown national cinema stateside.

Story opens at the time of president Park's assassination in 1979. Han (Sung Ki Ahn), a reporter and war vet, is assigned to write a series about the Vietnamese conflict, which still looms large in the national conscience. Coincidental with the task is a phone call from Pyon (Kyung Young Lee), a member of his platoon.

The nature of the story is simple and familiar. The present is infected by the past. The emotionally scarred journalist revisits, in his mind (and onscreen), the tour of duty. What begins as a relatively easy way to collect a soldier's salary evolves into a living nightmare in which less than a handful manage to get out alive.

More complex and less certain is the aftermath. Han has interiorized his problems, while Pyon's are all too readily apparent. For starters, Pyon has adopted a childlike demeanor and is hopelessly rapped in fantasy, incapable of holding a job or sustaining a relationship.

"White Badge" has first-class production values and an exceptionally fine cast. What it lacks are dramatic answers. Director Ji Young Chung provides an assured sense of time and mood. But the character's actions are drawn from movie cliche rather than an outgrowth of the narrative.

—*Leonard Klady*

LONDON

MIDNIGHT MOVIE

(BRITISH)

A BBC Films production, in association with Whistling Gypsy Prods. Produced by Dennis Potter. Executive producers, Ruth Caleb, Mark Shivas. Co-producer, Rosemarie Whitman. Directed by Renny Rye. Screenplay, Potter, inspired by Rosalind Ashe's novel "Moths." Camera (color), Remi Adefarasin; editor, Clare Douglas; music, Christopher Gunning, production design, Gary Williamson; art direction, Paul Cross; costume design, James Keast; sound (Dolby), John Pritchard; associate producer, Alison Barnett; assistant director, Dermot Boyd. Reviewed on vidcassette, London, Oct. 31, 1994. (In London Film Festival.) Running time: **100 MIN.**
Henry Harris ....Jim Carter
Amber Boyce/
 Mandy Mason .... Louise Germaine
James Boyce .... Brian Dennehy
Mrs. Morrey .... Anna Cropper
Bertie .... Steven Mackintosh
Bob Maclean .... Colin Salmon
Ann Maclean .... Lucinda Ann Galloway
 With: David Curtiz, Gerard Horan, Anthony Pedley.

Dennis Potter's last work shot under his own supervision, "Midnight Movie," is a hit-and-miss blend of the late telly scribe's familiar trademarks, mixing film refs, femme exploitation and larky wordplay in a mock-thriller format. Intended for theatrical release, but on the shelf for the past year, this curate's egg looks destined to unspool on the small screen and at specialized gatherings rather than find any career on the big sheet.

Pic is more successful than the overwritten, convoluted "Secret Friends," the previous feature made by Potter's company, Whistling Gypsy Prods., which bombed in a brief stateside release in early '92. "Movie" is more of a movie, thanks to OK direction by Renny Rye and a trio of lead performances that mesh well. The problem is more Potter's script — a jokey conceit stretched to feature length which, despite incidental pleasures, never really gets under the blanket with its subject matter.

Pic plunges straight into Potterland with a dark voiceover by a lovesick, middle-aged lawyer and scenes of a blonde in a negligee screaming outside an English country mansion one dark and stormy night. Latter turn out to be the first of several intercut sequences from a bad British horror movie shot 20 years earlier, in the pile now rented by American producer James Boyce (Brian Dennehy) and his bimbo Cockney wife, Amber (Louise Germaine).

The movie, "Smoke Rings," is the all-time favorite of the lawyer, Harris (Jim Carter), who's arranged the property rental for Boyce. Harris is still besotted with the pic's late actress, '60s starlet Mandy Mason, an ambitious, sex-obsessed model who died under mysterious circumstances. The nervy Amber just happens to be her daughter. When Boyce invites Harris for dinner, the midnight movie showing on TV is "Smoke Rings." In the days that follow, Amber's increasingly schizophrenic behavior seems to parallel both her mom's life and the plot of the movie, with Harris also drawn into events.

The film is at its best when in the realm of pure parody, either recreating chunks of the amazingly tacky "Smoke Rings" or letting Germaine and Dennehy have fun with their characters, the bullheaded U.S. producer and airhead actress/model. Christopher Gunning's moody, noir score, with lazy sax solos by Stan Sultzman, and Remi Adefarasin's colorful lensing are major assists here.

Weak point is the character of the lawyer, Harris, nominally the pivotal role but often more a bystander to events. Carter's hangdog performance is fine, but his character's obsession with Mandy/Amber is never fully explained and, by the

time the twist ending puts everything in perspective, it's too late.

Germaine, from Potter's six-part TV series "Lipstick on Your Collar" (also helmed by Rye), is good in the double role of Mandy/Amber, especially the former, all '60s blond bob and heavy eye makeup. Dennehy is solid in an easy part.

—*Derek Elley*

TIME HAS COME

(ANA EL-AWAN)

(LEBANESE)

An Aflam Films (Beirut) production, in association with Cinema Earth Co. (Moscow), ADR Prods. (Paris). (International sales: Aflam Films, Paris.) Produced, directed by Jean-Claude Codsi. Screenplay, Codsi, Talal Haidar. Camera (color), Milad Tauk; editor, Nathalie Goepfert, Elvire Lerner; music, Toufic Farroukh; art direction, Hamzi Nasrallah; costume design, Louloua Abdel-Baki; sound, Dirk Bombey, Henri Morelle; associate producers, Oleg Chudnesov, Alexander Taoufik, Alain Rozanes; assistant director, Elie Adabachi. Reviewed on vidcassette, London, Oct. 20, 1994. (In London Film Festival.) Running time: **86 MIN.**
Raya Farah .... Darina el-Joundi
Kamil Nahas .... Simon Abkarian
Kamil's Mother .... Rida Khoury
Uncle Georges .... Antoine Moultaka
 With: Nogi Souraly, Gabriel Yammine, Carole Abboud, Majdi Machmouche.
 (Arabic and French dialogue)

"**T**ime Has Come" (aka "Histoire d'un retour") is an interesting but fairly lightweight look at Lebanon's so-called "lost generation," framed as a love story between two returnees in the late '80s when the worst of the war was over. First feature by French director Jean-Claude Codsi has a strong Gallic flavor in its mix of politics and personal emotions, and is fuzzily developed in its latter stages, but could find slots on discriminating Eurowebs.

Central duo are failed musician Kamil (Simon Abkarian) and rich bourgeoise Raya (Darina el-Joundi), who meet on a boat to Beirut. He's on an assignment from Paris to make a musicvideo about the country; she's returning to find her long lost son. Both had left Lebanon in 1975 at the start of the war, Raya after an arranged marriage to a French surgeon.

Kamil pretends to his mother that he's made a success abroad, but as time goes by he becomes more interested in Raya's mysterious past than knuckling down to composing. As the truth about her son and political past slowly emerges, Kamil finds himself an outsider in his own country, with no shared experience of the war that wrecked lives and shattered a generation.

Considering the weighty matters under the microscope, pic has a generally light, reflective tone that is refreshing in the early stages but later serves to rob the denouement of emotional power. Perfs by the two leads are well-matched, with el-Joundi's Christian upper-class reserve playing off well against the looser Abkarian.

Tech credits are fine, led by Milad Tauk's handsome lensing of sun-drenched Beirut and its verdant, still dangerous environs.

—*Derek Elley*

MAIRI MHOR:
HER LIFE AND SONGS

(MAIRI MHOR:
NA H-ORAIN 'SA BEATHA)

(BRITISH)

A Freeway Films production for BBC Scotland. Produced by John McGrath. Executive producer, John Archer. Directed by Mike Alexander. Screenplay, McGrath, Sim Mac Coinnich. Camera (color), Mark Littlewood; editor, Bert Eeles; musical director, Jim Sutherland; production design, Graham Rose; costume design, Lynn Aitken; sound, Phil Croal, Peter Smith; assistant director, Eric Coulter. Reviewed on vidcassette, London, Oct. 20, 1994. (In London Film Festival.) Running time: **62 MIN.**
Mairi Mhor .... Alyxis Daly
Young Mairi .... Ceit Kearney
John Murdoch .... Sim Mac Coinnich
Captain Turner .... Andrew Stanson
Nell .... Pauline Lockhart
Donald .... Artair Donald
Bailie Simpson .... Derek Anders
 (Gaelic dialogue)

A small but well-formed feather in the hat of non-English-speaking British cinema, "Mairi Mhor" is not so much a feature film as an illustrated song cycle-cum-political pamphlet. This immaculately laundered celebration of the life and works of the 19th-century Gaelic songstress should find a ready berth in discerning Eurowebs' schedules.

Title character was a middle-aged Scottish woman from Skye who, while nursing an English army officer's wife in Inverness, was falsely jailed in 1871 for stealing. Anger at the mistreatment by the Brits unleashed from her a string of nationalist songs over the next 25 years, and she played a leading role in the Highland Land League, struggling for Gaels' home rights.

Pic has no real dramatic conflict, as all the Scots are goody-two-shoes and all the English speakers villains. Playing, too. is more impersonation than real performance.

Still, by re-staging key moments in Mairi's life and melding copious examples of her songs (hauntingly sung by Caitriona-Anna Nic a Phi) with striking lensing of the Scottish landscape, director Mike Alexander (who previously made the low-key Gaelic drama "From the Island") comes up with a kind of illustrated songbook that just about lasts the course.

Tech credits are immaculate, and period detail, though avoiding a lived-in look, seems accurate.

—*Derek Elley*

SARASOTA

THE FAVORITE SON

(LE FILS PREFERE)

(FRENCH)

An AMLF release of a Cinea/Les Films Alain Sarde/France 3 Cinema/Angel's Co. co-production with the participation of CNC, Sofinergie 3, Sofiarp 2, Investimage 3 and Canal Plus. (International sales: Le Studio Canal Plus, Paris.) Produced by Philippe Carcassonne, Alain Sarde. Directed by Nicole Garcia. Screenplay, Garcia, Francois Dupeyron, Jacques Fieschi, Jerome Tonnerre. Camera (color), Eric Gautier; editor, Agnes Guillemot, Yann Dedet; music, Philippe Sarde; production design, Antoine Platteau; sound (Dolby), Pierre Donnadieu, Vincent Arnardi; assistant director, Emmanuel Gust. Reviewed at AMLF screening room, Paris, Nov. 4, 1994. (In Sarasota French Film Festival, Florida.) Running time: **100 MIN.**
Jean-Paul .... Gerard Lanvin
Francis .... Bernard Giraudeau
Philippe .... Jean-Marc Barr
Raphael .... Roberto Herlitzka
Anna Maria .... Margherita Buy
With: Pierre Mondy, Antoinette Moya, Jean-Pierre Becker, Marc Berman, Karine Viard, Philippe Duclos.

With a sure hand guiding excellent perfs, actress-turned-helmer Nicole Garcia investigates the troubled history that both links and divides three grown French brothers and their Italian immigrant father in "The Favorite Son." Emotionally complex and satisfying narrative should do well at Gallic wickets and could attract offshore arthouse audiences.

Jean-Paul (Gerard Lanvin), who manages a hotel in Nice, is heavily in debt. While an auditor perches over the hotel's crooked accounts, Jean-Paul's loan shark gives him three days to come up with 300,000 francs ($60,000). Jean-Paul dutifully

pays regular visits to his elderly father, Raphael (Roberto Herlitzka), a desiccated former boxer whose past, pic gradually reveals, is riddled with passion and mystery. Desperate for cash, Jean-Paul approaches his estranged younger brother, Philippe (Jean-Marc Barr), a wealthy lawyer in Milan. They've barely spoken in the 10 years since Philippe married one of Jean-Paul's former lovers, Anna Maria, and Philippe is loath to help his sibling. Their older brother, Francis (Bernard Giraudeau), a serene schoolteacher who was rejected by Raphael for his homosexuality, can't contribute much money.

In hopes of appeasing his creditors, Jean-Paul takes out a life insurance policy on his father, naming himself as beneficiary. When their dad unexpectedly disappears, the three brothers reluctantly form an awkward search party haunted by spoken and unspoken resentments.

Pic succeeds admirably as both a character study and a detective story. Femme helmer penetrates the world of men with admirable finesse, incorporating scenes in boxing rings, locker rooms and smoky back rooms. The escalating pressures of Jean-Paul's iffy business dealings and his core doubts about posing as a smooth operator on rocky turf are convincingly etched.

Casting is excellent. Lanvin, in a solid central perf, has the posture of a winner and the haunted eyes of a loser. Italo thesp Herlitzka is effective as the father whose mixed legacy of pride and humiliation has been transmitted to his sons.

Other thesps are fine across the board, with special mention for Giraudeau as a self-assured gay man whose sexuality is an evenly incorporated facet of his broader identity.

Lensing in the south of France and in Milan captures the distinctive light of those regions without succumbing to storybook views. Poignant treatment of adult concerns speaks well for Garcia's future as a director. —*Lisa Nesselson*

PRAY FOR US

(PRIEZ POUR NOUS)

(FRENCH)

A Les Films du Losange release of a Telema/France 3 Cinema/M6 Films/Generale d'Images production, with participation of Canal Plus, Investimage 3 & 4 and Cofimage 4 & 5. (International sales: Pyramide Intl., Paris.) Produced by Charles Gassot. Executive producer, Jacques Hinstin. Directed by Jean-Pierre Vergne. Screenplay, Gassot, Vergne, based on the novel by Lionel Duroy. Camera (color), Willy Kurant; editor, Marie Coulais; music, Raymond Alessandrini; art direction, Frederic Duru; costume design, Jacqueline Bouchard; sound, Daniel Ollivier, Paul Bertault. Reviewed at UGC Danton, Paris, July 17, 1994. (In Sarasota French Film Festival, Florida.) Running time: **88 MIN.**
Suzanne Guidon
de Repeygnac .... Delphine Rich
Raoul Guidon
de Repeygnac .... Samuel Labarthe
Annick .... Helene Scott
Christine .... Delphine Legoff
William .... Gaston Dolle

In the mild comedy "Pray for Us," an upper-class Catholic family lands in working-class commie digs in Paris, circa 1960. More bemusing than amusing, this sweetly crafted but ultra-leisurely pic will have to pray for sales beyond French-lingo territories.

Following massive losses in a stock swindle, the Baron Guidon de Repeygnac, his wife the baroness, and their eight perfectly groomed children are abruptly evicted from their elegant apartment in a snooty Paris suburb. Thanks to the baron's army buddy, family and maid move into a tiny utilitarian apartment in a government-subsidized low-income housing project.

The demanding baroness — for whom appearances are everything — has a series of nervous breakdowns. But, after a few initial scrapes with local toughs, the kids learn to steal hubcaps, barter dirty magazines and illegally siphon electricity. While the broke baron valiantly struggles at a series of travelling salesman jobs, the kids trade snobbish Catholic school for egalitarian public school and learn to prefer resourceful low life to the socially regimented high life.

Period details are nicely evoked, and seemingly endless brood is well cast. But the fallen aristocrats' plight is delicately toyed with rather than lampooned. Adversity comes in measured increments that defeat any sustained feeling of conflict or suspense. Result is a quaint, diluted comedy, in which countless possibilities are left underexplored.

Lensing is good, thesps are fine across the board, and jaunty score is just right. —*Lisa Nesselson*

WE LOVE YOU LIKE A ROCK: THE DIXIE HUMMINGBIRDS

(DOCU)

A City Lore Inc./Film Arts Foundation presentation of a Searchlight Films production. Produced by Ray Allen, Ashley James. Directed by James. Camera (color, video-to-16mm), James; additional camera, George Spies, Antoine Vareille, Leonard Levy; editor, Yasha Aginsky; sound, Clive Henderson, Spies, Edward Haber, Allen; production manager, Dolores Elliott. Reviewed Nov. 1 at Castro Theatre, San Francisco. (In Film Arts Festival). Running time: **77 MIN.**

Technically unprepossessing, this doc nonetheless channels its subject and audience to inspirational heights. Portrait of legendary gospel quartet celebrates its music and history in terms bound to excite telecast interest after limited theatrical exposure.

The Dixie Hummingbirds were founded in 1928 by South Carolinian James B. Davis. A decade later, they made their first recordings, then moved to Philly, where they soon headlined a stellar gospel music scene. Personnel changes (numbering some 19 'birds so far) didn't dispel the group's harmonic brilliance, nor weaken its resistance to pop trends — a '50s offer to "go secular" was declined, though the Hummingbirds did accept Paul Simon's invite to sing on his pop hit "Love Me Like a Rock," which won Grammies for both original and Hummingbirds versions.

This legacy is lauded by the likes of Simon, Otis Williams (of the Temptations) and Stevie Wonder in interview segs. But most of pic centers on Hummingbirds' long history (via stills and B&W broadcast clips), elderly current members' home and rehearsal habits, and concert sequences. Traversing from traditional hymns to original songs, this changeable unit remains constant in several respects — i.e., offering "the finest harmonies in the world" (as one admirer claims), complex arrangements (once a cappella, now augmented by instrumental accompaniment), and utterly affable demeanors both onstage and off.

On latter count, dirt is sifted to a perhaps excessive degree. We never learn why prior crucial 'birds left the nest (aside from one recent death). No internal conflicts are

November 14, 1994 (Cont.)

noted, past or present. Are their working days always as sunny as the magically intuitive "rehearsals" glimpsed here? If so, musicians around the globe ought to pay attention. Issues of societal and show-biz racism are likewise skimmed, though within its church-bound circuit the group probably suffered less abuse than most.

Pic limns a significant chapter in African-American culture to strong effect, aided by principals' personal charm. While routine vid lensing is color-soft, all-important sound recording is terrif, editing of disparate elements ditto. "We Love You Like a Rock" is modern ethnography at its most accessible — joyous and intimate, with a soundtrack worth marketing right away.

—Dennis Harvey

A DREAMSCAPE: GAMBLING IN AMERICA

(DUTCH — DOCU)

A Bernie IJdis production in association with Nederlands Fonds voor de Film, NCRV, Binnenlandse Omroep. Produced, directed by IJdis. Camera (color, 16mm), Edwin Verstegen, Deen van der Zaken, Dirk Teenstra; sound, Jane Snijders; editing, Emile Bensdorp; music, Hugo van Neck; re-recording, Stephan Warnas; production coordination, Mariette Friedheim. Reviewed on vidcassette, San Francisco, Nov. 4, 1994. (In Cinequest San Jose Film Festival.) Running time: **80 MIN.**

One of our nation's biggest — and most depressing — "growth industries" is scrutinized in this fascinating English-language doc. While subject will probably merit more conventional treatment by U.S. talents soon, Dutch helmer Bernie IJdis' impressionist survey leaves analysis up to the viewer. Provocative results could find limited theatrical and broadcast play stateside.

Pic is a structureless series of blackout-separated episodes scoping the full breadth of current U.S. "gaming." We visit Vegas and Atlantic City glitterdomes, as well as the new wave of Indian-reservation casinos. A Publishers' Clearing House Sweepstakes spokesman offers the smarmy notion that he provides some sort of Santa Claus-like public service. A PCH television commercial chirps, "Miracles can happen to you/(We're) the house where dreams come true!" Various state lotto ads glimpsed make ticket buying seem like a patriotic act.

One limo-riding high roller admits, "The agony of losing is almost as exhilarating as winning ... it makes people feel they're alive." But most gamblers seen here illustrate that statement in more desperate terms. The poor, infirm and elderly overwhelmingly dominate casino spending and lotto purchases.

In one powerful scene, a gambling-addiction counselor tells us (just after making a suicide intervention on the phone) that some 450,000 Americans are "compulsive" players, with precious few treatment options. He muses that if bus tickets to Atlantic City were sold to routinely bankrupted visitors as one-ways, the burg "would have the U.S.'s biggest homeless problem within two days."

IJdis forgoes any narration or other overt editorial devices. Yet a thesis does emerge: While drug and crime "epidemics" occupy center stage in the press and politics, gambling is proving an equal drain on underclass resources — albeit one that wins little attention because it's so profitable to government and business interests. Result is an exploitation ladder where enormous wealth for a few on top directly fosters the proliferation of pawn shops, homelessness, et al. on the bottom rungs.

View is not without its happy winners and humorous moments. But overall effect is bleak. Helmer's approach grows heavy-handed only in recurrent visual motif of "apocalyptic" flames. Otherwise, editing keeps things lively, even if episodic format does tire eventually. Lensing is slick. *—Dennis Harvey*

CAUGHT IN THE ACTS
(DELITS FLAGRANTS)
(FRENCH — DOCU — 35mm)

A Connaissance du Cinema release of a Pascale Dauman presentation of a La Sept Cinema/Double D Copyright Films co-production with the participation of the CNC, Canal Plus and West-deutscher Rundfunk Koln. Directed by Raymond Depardon. Camera (color), Nathalie Credou; editors, Roger Ikhlef, Camille Cotte, Georges-Henri Mauchant; sound recording (Dolby), Claudine Nougaret, Sophie Chiabaut; sound mixing, Dominique Hennequin. Reviewed at Saint-Andre-des-Arts cinema, Paris, Nov. 2, 1994. Running time: **107 MIN.**

By turns hilarious and touching, "Caught in the Acts" is populated by a riveting array of petty criminals who have been caught red-handed and taken to Paris police headquarters where their often fanciful version of events is recorded by legal specialists. Clearly guilty of entertainment in the first degree, engrossing docu should be sentenced to a long life of fests, tube dates and educational sales.

Opening text explains the steps that follow an arrest. French law allows a suspect to be held for observation without bail for up to 48 hours, before meeting the *substitut de procurer*, whose job it is to take down an accurate first-person statement. The *substitut* is crucial because he or she can decide whether to let someone go, schedule a court date months later or send the suspect to appear before a judge for immediate sentencing.

Ace photographer and documaker Raymond Depardon was granted special permission to film real detainees: Of the 86 suspects who agreed to be filmed, 14 appear in the finished docu. Skeleton crew, shooting in crisp 35mm and recording in Dolby stereo, was permitted to lens suspect and *substitut* only in a two-shot, in profile. Rigorous, no-nonsense framing and long takes, sans close-ups or zooms, perfectly echo the sober reality of captivity and heighten the often ludicrous exchanges.

Audience has ringside seats as legal reps — who have certainly heard and seen it all before — weigh the circumstances and humor, sometimes chastising their delinquent customers. Helmer captures priceless moments with universal appeal, as suspects play innocent only to be presented with detailed lists of the prior arrests and convictions that seem to have slipped their minds.

A sign that says "Do not disturb: interrogation in progress" is chained to the door — presumably to discourage kleptomaniacs. In a nondescript room, suspect and *substitut* communicate across a utilitarian desk. A slightly deaf teenager who recently turned 18 is bowled over by the news that he can now go to prison for the same sorts of infractions he committed as a minor. "Gosh, I'll have to stop now, otherwise I'll get in trouble," is his amazed reaction.

Some repeat offenders evidently live in a world of their own. A woman who was nabbed outside a Paris department store with over $1,000 worth of shoplifted garments and accessories complains, "They could have asked to see my receipt," then babbles on about how it's not as if she'd taken a radio or a camera or "something that you can re-sell."

A young man insists that he would *never* punch a woman — women you merely slap, *men* you punch. Informed that the woman he "slapped" required five stitches and will have a scar, he replies that scars are no big deal and starts to display his own.

Interview sequences, though never dull, are broken up by a few roving shots of suspects being led down endless subterranean corridors, of *substituts* conducting phone business and of the lovely views outside the Palais de Justice in central Paris.

Parade of human dramas leaves viewers with the impression that justice is sometimes served and that, given the right circumstances, anyone can end up in handcuffs.

—Lisa Nesselson

PRESTAZIONE STRAORDINARIA
(ITALIAN)

A Cecchi Gori Group Distribuzione release (in Italy) of a Mario and Vittorio Cecchi Gori/Penta Film presentation of a Cecchi Gori Group/Tiger Cinematografica/Videomaura production. Produced by Mario and Vittorio Cecchi Gori. Directed by Sergio Rubini. Screenplay, Filippo Ascione, Fabrizio Bettelli, Angelo Pasquini, Rubini; camera (Cinecitta color), Alessio Gelsini; editor, Angelo Nicolini; music, Antonio Di Pofi, art direction, Ezio Altieri; costume design, Raffaella Fantasia, Camilla Righi; sound (Dolby), Franco Borni; associate producers, Bruno Altissimi, Claudio Saraceni. Reviewed at CDS screening room, Rome, Nov. 2, 1994. Running time: **105 MIN.**

Clara	Margherita Buy
Aldo	Sergio Rubini
Sgro	Alessandro Haber
Silvana	Simona Izzo
Grisaglia	Gianrico Tedeschi
Olga	Michetta Farinelli
Ornella	Mariella Valentini
Giraldi	Michael Reale

Actor-turned-director Sergio Rubini's "Prestazione Straordinaria" pulls an ineffectual gender switch on a classic sexual-harassment scenario. Despite its slick look and appealing cast, this story of a strait-laced book editor being pursued by a predatory publishing virago is neither funny enough to cut it as comedy, beguiling enough to register as romance or incisive enough to say anything much about sexual politics. Leading duo of Rubini ("The Station") and his wife, Margherita Buy, should goose up some local trade, but offshore trysts will likely end with the odd Euro screen.

The subject here is a diluted version of the theme tackled in the Michael Crichton tome (and forthcoming Barry Levinson film) "Disclosure," which Rubini's character is seen reading at one point.

A secretarial mix-up gets copy editor Aldo (Rubini) mistakenly summoned for some between-the-sheets overtime with ruthless maven Clara (Buy), who's swooped down from Milan to drastically streamline personnel in the company's Rome office. Though he's not quite the hunky junior exec she had in mind, something about Aldo's old-fashioned, romantic nature sets off Clara's urge to conquer.

After first promoting him to a cushy editorial position, Clara swiftly demotes Aldo to the erotica department, playing on his aversion to overt sexuality. She then brings the ambitions of his sweetheart, aspiring writer Silvana (Simona Izzo), into play, before threatening to fire his buddy (Alessandro Haber), who's buckling under debt and the expense of his extended family. Having him cornered, Clara whisks Aldo off to Greece to combine business with pleasure while tracking down a renegade author.

Though the rosy outcome is evident from scene one, and the dialogue at times lumbers into obviousness, the duo's contorted path to passion is sufficiently engaging.

Where the film stumbles badly is in the Greek jaunt. Aldo's rejection of Clara just as romance appears to be warming up is an excruciatingly miscalculated scene, and Clara's inevitable humanizing is far too mechanical. A barbed comment via the embittered scribe about Italy's fate at the hands of Silvio Berlusconi is so forced it's meaningless.

The leads go some distance toward making the uneven script work and covering for the director's failure to settle on a tone that fits. Rubini's honest underachiever provides an appealing anchor. Playing a more aggressive type than her usually timid turns, Buy acts as a winning distraction to the material's flimsiness. The one off-key thesping element is Mariella Valentini's ditzy blond secretary, who seems to have wandered in from a much broader comedy.

Alessio Gelsini's adroit lensing and Ezio Altieri's sharp art direction give the film a handsome, urbane sheen. Antonio Di Pofi's music frequently adds bounce to the proceedings. Pic's untranslatable title basically means overtime, with sexual-favor connotations.

—*David Rooney*

SIXTEN

(SWEDISH)

A Svensk Filmindustri release (in Sweden) of a Svensk Filmindustri/ Swedish Film Institute production. (International sales: Nordisk Film-TV Distribution, Stockholm.) Produced by Waldemar Bergendahl. Directed by Catti Edfelt. Screenplay, Ulf Stark, based on his novel. Camera (color), Rolf Lindstrom; editor, Christer Furubrand; music, Bjorn Isfalt; production design, Lasse Westfelt; costume design, Carina Dalunde; sound (Dolby), Wille Peterson-Berger, Jean-Frederic Axelsson. Reviewed at Svensk Filmindustri screening room, Stockholm, Sept. 6, 1994. Running time: **78 MIN.**

Sixten	Peter Viitanen
Sixten's Dad	Hans Henriksson
Jonte	Jonas Magnusson
Emma	Marie Thulin
"Dancing Feet"	Ing-Marie Carlsson

With: Kalle Stridbeck, Erik Lagerstrom.

A sensitive and multilayered pic about the pains of growing up, "Sixten" has enough going for it to appeal to adult auds as well as teens. Specialized offshore sales look possible.

Title character, in his early teens, lives with his divorced father; his mom lives in Copenhagen and never visits them. To help his dad find a new wife (so he'll also stop being overprotective), Sixten answers lonely-hearts ads in the papers under his father's name, which leads to some unexpected meetings with strange women. At the same time, the kid starts to discover his own sexuality and has a summer romance with a girl at school.

Helmer Catti Edfelt, making her feature bow after directing shorts, gets good performances from her young cast and maintains a balance between comedy and drama. Pic is also loaded with cinema refs, from ever-present film posters to Bjorn Isfalt's music, reminiscent of Nino Rota scores.

One sequence, in which Sixten and his friend Jonte watch an explicit sex scene on homevideo, could cause the pic ratings problems abroad. In Sweden, the film was passed uncut for general audiences.

—*Gunnar Rehlin*

VANCOUVER

THOSE WHO WOULD BE EINSTEIN

(TASOGARE NO EINSTEIN)

(JAPANESE — 16mm)

A Hachisuka Prods. (Tokyo) production. (International Sales: Eizo Seisaka Group). Executive producer, Mitsuhiro Ogata. Produced, directed, written by Kentaro Hachisuka. Camera (color — 16mm), Koshiro Otsu; editor, Takako Kuwahara; music, Chiku Kobayashi; sound, Toyohiko Kuribayashi. Reviewed at Vancouver Film Festival (competing), Oct. 14, 1994. Running time: **70 MIN.**

With: part one: Megu Nomura, Chika Nomura; part two: Osamu Ohtomo, Yuko Uehara, Aya Akahori, Reiko Nakane, Minako Ban, Seiji Rokkaku; part three: Mayumi Suzuki, Sadayuki Ikeda, Motomi Makiguchi, Junko Mashina, Hiroaki Watanabe, Shinichi Minami; epilogue: Mickey Curtis, William Jack Hancock.

This odd three-parter purports to map the metaphysics of the interpersonal universe, dividing its trio of tales into three, different-toned "planets." Festgoers are likely to find it out-there (although some parts look like they take place on planets Campion and Jarmusch), and variable quality may keep it from attracting serious explorers.

"Children of the Sun" features Japanese TV favorites Megu and Chika Nomura as deadpan schoolgirls who ponder sunspots, mirrors and playground equipment. It's slight stuff, and would be slighter still without the identically dressed sisters. Things pick up with "The Matrix of Express Trains, Romance and Weight Loss," the quietly touching, smoothly stylized saga of skinny student Junichi (Osamu Ohtomo), who has relationships only with women on his commuter train line. He makes many fruitless roundtrips before realizing he's missed a good bet with one of his own classmates (Yuko Uehara). "The Simple Treasures of My Ancestors" is the most straightforward seg, following a young, modern woman (Mayumi Suzuki) as she travels to pay tribute to her late father and bumps into one of her long-dead ancestors along the way.

The last is the most conventional, and most confidently handled, saga (with lovely, simple lensing and gingerly, understated perfs), but it's followed by an epilogue, featuring two Caucasians as a father-and-son duo lost in a desert expanse that's as silly as it is baffling. The linking bits between segs, as the camera pans a dull mural to annoying bongo music, are also less than impressive. Young helmer Kentaro Hachisuka went into heavy debt to finish this short opus, and it's hard to picture it breaking even. There's some real talent tucked away here, though, not the least of which is coming up with clever titles. —*Ken Eisner*

MOD FUCK EXPLOSION

(16mm)

An Apathy Prods., Complex Corp. (San Francisco) production. Executive producer, Marcus Hu. Produced by Henry S. Rosenthal, Andrea Sperling. Directed, written, edited by Jon Moritsugu. Camera (color, 16mm), production design, art direction, Jennifer Gentile, Todd Verow; music, Unrest, Karyo, Tengoku, the SF Seals and others; sound, Alberto Garcia; costume design, Jason Rail; associate producer, Timothy Innes. Reviewed at Vancouver film fest (non-competing), Oct. 8, 1994. Running time: **75 MINS.**

With: Amy Davis, Desi Del Valle, Bonnie Steiger, Jacques Boyreau, Jon Moritsugu, Victor of Aquitaine, Alyssa Wendt, Bonnie Dickenson, Lain McLain, Issa Bowser, Elizabeth Canning, Lisa Guay, Christine Wada.

A biker comedy for the Beavis and Butt-head generation, this beyond-bad exercise in underground filmmaking is designed to offend, but there's just enough consistency to its demented world view and no-tech acting to raise a few cynical chuckles, and maybe even the (distant) specter of talent.

Certainly, helmer Jon Moritsugu, who also shows up as the squirrely leader of a pack of "Nipponese" bikers, doesn't care about normal aesthetics. (The pic didn't make its intended preem in S.F. because of sound problems.) He frequently positions the camera so far away from his characters and loops them so loosely that it's hard to tell who's talking.

His leading lady, Amy Davis, is on record as having "no interest in acting," and it shows. She plays a bleached-blond teen called London who considers giving up her virginity for a black leather jacket, or maybe just making out with M-16 (Desi Del Valle), a dropout of indeterminate gender who tends to throw up in the clutch. With its moony voiceovers and mock-poetic tone, London's part of the saga reads like an episode of "My So-Called Life" on bad acid. The rest aspires to sub-Roger Corman glories, with the least scary gang leader of all time (Jacques Boyreau) and his pill-popping mods pitted against said Asian-American cyclists, whom he taunts with such vicious ethnic slurs as "rice jockeys" and "Hunan chickens." Naturally, it all ends in tears — and ketchup — and no one is quite able to express his/ her cool adolescent feelings.

Fueled by an appropriately thrashy soundtrack, pic's a guaranteed hoot for like-minded youths at midnight screenings, although it won't be exploding into suburban venues anytime soon. And given its asterisky title, the complete absence of nudity or sex may shock vid-renters in an unexpected way.

—*Ken Eisner*

November 21, 1994

THE PAGEMASTER

A 20th Century Fox release, presented in association with Turner Pictures Inc., of a David Kirschner production. Produced by Kirschner, Paul Gertz. Live-action scenes produced by Michael R. Joyce. Animation co-producers, David Steinberg, Barry Weiss. Animation directed by Maurice Hunt. Live-action scenes directed by Joe Johnston. Screenplay, David Casci, Kirschner, Ernie Contreras; story by Kirschner, Casci. Live-action camera (Technicolor color, Deluxe prints), Alexandra Gruszynski; editor, Roy Forge Smith; music, James Horner; sound (Dolby), Steve Nelson; supervising animator, Bruce Smith; production design, Gay Lawrence, Valeria Ventura; art direction, Pixote; visual effects supervisor, Richard T. Sullivan; animation sequence director, Glenn Chaika; animation supervisors: story, Robert Lence; layout, Don Morgan; background, Jim Hickey; editor, Jeffrey Patch. Associate producers, Claire Glidden, Roxy Novotny Steven; assistant director, Betsy Magruder; casting, Amy Kimmelman. Reviewed at the 20th Century Fox screening room, Los Angeles, Nov. 16, 1994. MPAA Rating: G. Running time: **75 MIN.**

Richard Tyler	Macaulay Culkin
Mr. Dewey/The Pagemaster	Christopher Lloyd
Alan Tyler	Ed Begley Jr.
Claire Tyler	Mel Harris

Voices

Adventure	Patrick Stewart
Fantasy	Whoopi Goldberg
Horror	Frank Welker
Dr. Jekyll & Mr. Hyde	Leonard Nimoy

Built on a wispy premise better suited to the realm of TV, "The Pagemaster" plays like a slickly produced afternoon special and should be limited in its appeal to the youngest of kids. Macaulay Culkin in an animated fantasy should be some kind of box office draw, but probably not a major hit, with much of the "Barney" crowd more likely to check it out on homevideo.

More than anything else, "Pagemaster" comes off as propaganda for the public library, with even its most hummable song providing a pro-social message about reading and using one's imagination.

The simplest of childhood fantasies, the story begins in the world of live action before our chronically frightened hero, Richard (Culkin), with the help of a mysterious librarian (Christopher Lloyd), gets transported into an animated world where fictional characters come to life — led on his journey by book-sized companions Adventure (voiced by Patrick Stewart), Fantasy (Whoopi Goldberg) and Horror (Frank Welker).

Through the world of books, Richard encounters an array of famous fictional characters and perils while trying to make it to the "Exit" sign, which will provide his means of escape.

The problem is that after introducing these characters — Captain Ahab, Long John Silver, Dr. Jekyll/Mr. Hyde, etc. — the filmmakers don't have anything creative or special to do with them, other than the sort of madcap chase with Mr. Hyde that feels plucked from an old Bugs Bunny cartoon.

A more inspired moment has Richard using a book, "Jack and the Beanstalk," to escape from the belly of a dragon. Unfortunately, such moments are few and far between.

Producer and co-writer David Kirschner (sharing the latter chore with David Casci and Ernie Contreras), whose credits include "An American Tail," has made a reasonably diverting confection for children — with a frenetic pace and plenty of visual stimuli — whose principal appeal for adults will be its abbreviated running time.

Technically, the animation, overseen by one-time Disney animator Maurice Hunt ("The Black Cauldron"), is fluid if perhaps a bit too dark and brooding, though it does offer some impressive flourishes to go with James Horner's typically rousing score. Straying from the "Star Trek" bridge, Stewart hams it up regally as Adventure, while appearances by the live-action performers are extremely brief.

As for Culkin, if he's still looking for a vehicle to prove his drawing power outside of "Home Alone," this probably isn't it, though rest easy: Another Mac attack — Warner Bros.' "Richie Rich" — is just around the corner. —*Brian Lowry*

THE SWAN PRINCESS

A New Line Cinema release of a Nest Entertainment presentation of a Rich Animation Studios production. Produced by Richard Rich, Jared F. Brown. Executive producers, Brown, Seldon Young. Co-executive producer, Matt Mazer. Co-producers, Terry L. Noss, Thomas J. Tobin. Directed by Rich. Screenplay, Brian Nissen; story by Rich, Nissen. Original score, Lex de Azevedo; songs by David Zippel, Azevedo; Technicolor prints; editors, James Koford, Armetta Jackson-Hamlett; character design, Steven E. Gordon; art direction, Mike Hodgson, James Coleman; animation director, Gordon; layout supervisor, Hodgson; sound, DTS; casting, Geoffrey Johnson, Vincent G. Liff, Tara Jayne Rubin. Reviewed at the UA Westwood Theater, L.A., Nov. 12, 1994. MPAA Rating: G. Running time: **90 MIN.**

Voices

Rothbart	Jack Palance
Prince Derek	Howard McGillin
Princess Odette	Michelle Nicastro
Jean-Bob	John Cleese
Speed	Steven Wright
Puffin	Steve Vinovich
Lord Rogers	Mark Harelik
Chamberlain	James Arrington
Queen Uberta	Sandy Duncan

Technically impressive but rather flat and languid story-wise, Richard Rich's first feature since leaving Disney only serves to reinforce the stranglehold his old studio still has on the animation market. While a perfectly serviceable confection for small fry, "The Swan Princess" will likely have its neck wrung commercially by all the high-profile competition aimed at the children's/family market this holiday season, as well as Disney's sabotage in reissuing "The Lion King."

Based loosely on Swan Lake, "Princess" shows up wearing the same accoutrements as recent Disney fare, including a half-dozen original songs, a spunky female lead, elaborate production numbers and comic supporting characters.

Take another look, however, and the film's blemishes begin to show, most notably a decided lack of humor (not for lack of trying), action sequences that are madcap but not especially clever, and songs that for the most part sound like something out of a Las Vegas revue.

The story has all the requisite fairy-tale trappings, as a king and queen decide to unite their separate kingdoms through a royal marriage, bringing their reluctant kids together each summer hoping they'll fall in love.

Just as the kids flower to adulthood, an evil sorcerer banished by the king, Rothbart (voiced by Jack Palance), slays the king and kidnaps his daughter.

Until she agrees to marry him, Princess Odette must live under a curse that turns her into a swan — receiving help from a frog who believes himself to be a prince (John Cleese), a wisecracking turtle (Steven Wright) and a slightly overstuffed bird (Steve Vinovich).

Rich, a veteran animator whose Disney credits include the relatively undistinguished "The Fox and the Hound," calls upon the same influences as Disney's recent blockbusters, but with less impressive results.

On the plus side, the animation is fluid and fast, the layouts and backdrops lush and detailed. Lex de Azevedo's score is also sumptuous and generates one memorable song, the ballad "Far Longer Than Forever."

Still, an old adage says that such movies are only as good as their villain, and despite Palance's sinister mutterings, Rothbart is largely a toothless absentee whose efforts at dark comedy consistently fall flat. That contributes to the lack of suspense, and even with the well-cast voices (particularly Cleese) the character design proves generally uninspired.

In the same vein, Rich and company have the physical elements of a big-budget animated feature down but can't lift the material to that magical level that enthralls adults as well as children.
—*Brian Lowry*

JUNIOR

A Universal Pictures release of a Northern Lights production. Produced, directed by Ivan Reitman. Executive producers, Joe Medjuck, Daniel Goldberg, Beverly Camhe. Co-producers, Neal Nordlinger, Gordon Webb. Screenplay, Kevin Wade, Chris Conrad. Camera (Deluxe), Adam Greenberg, Sheldon Kahn, Wendy Greene Bricmont; music, James Newton Howard; production design, Stephen Lineweaver; art direction, Gary Wissner; set decoration, Clay A. Griffith; costume design, Albert Wolsky; prosthetics makeup, Matthew Mungle; sound (Dolby), Gene Steven Cantamessa; assistant director, David Sosna; technical consultant, Dr. Richard Buyalos; casting, Michael Chinich, Alan Berger. Reviewed at the Beverly Connection, Los Angeles, Nov. 9, 1994. MPAA Rating: PG-13. Running time: **109 MIN.**

Dr. Alexander Hesse	Arnold Schwarzenegger
Dr. Larry Arbogast	Danny DeVito
Dr. Diana Reddin	Emma Thompson
Noah Banes	Frank Langella
Angela	Pamela Reed
Naomi	Judy Collins
Dr. Ned Sneller	James Eckhouse
Louise	Aida Turturro

No one can touch Ivan Reitman's record for turning high concepts into popular entertainment — really popular entertainment. His latest, the pregnant-man comedy "Junior," is no exception. What separates this straightforward chuckler from the pack is its shrewd reliance on character rather than plot, and that human dimension proves surprisingly poignant. Commercial response should result in the seasonal box office crown.

The accent is on the outrageous, and all involved get away with murder, artistically speaking. It's a potent package and, if it can sustain in the marketplace, could well go on to the worldwide heights of last year's "Mrs. Doubtfire."

In a cloistered lab on an ivy-shrouded campus, researchers Dr. Alex Hesse (Arnold Schwarzenegger) and Dr. Larry Arbogast (Danny DeVito) have been working on a "wonder" drug for safer pregnancies. It's a potential gold mine and a boon to women. But the FDA concludes that it's not quite ready for the marketplace. So, faster than you can say loss leader, the duo get turfed and top Brit cryogenicist Dr. Diana Reddin (Emma Thompson) is ensconced in their former digs.

What's disturbing to Arbogast is the small fortune he's personally committed to the project and that a Canadian consortium is ready to bankroll him and the drug dubbed Expectane. What would really cement the deal is data from a human guinea pig.

November 21, 1994 (Cont.)

The level of desperation is so high and the stakes so great, Arbogast fast-talks Hesse into being that test case. All Al has to do is carry the egg through the first trimester. It's preposterous ... but it's for science.

"Junior" harks back to "Bringing Up Baby" rather than to past attempts with like material such as "Rabbit Test." It's intrinsically funny to watch serious, sober scientists involved in totally goofy pursuits.

The plot turns on one very subtle factor — hormones. The female hormone estrogen that Alex is compelled to take with Expectane may or may not be the reason he refuses to abort after 90 days. Diana needs no chemical stimulant to induce her progressively gooey sentimentality.

It's tough to top the casting of Schwarzenegger. Who expects to see the Terminator getting in touch with his female side? Reitman delights — as he did in "Twins" and "Kindergarten Cop" — in sending up Mr. Mooscles' persona, and Schwarzenegger's performance is relaxed and assured.

The picture also affords Thompson the opportunity to poke fun at her prim, proper image. Not quite kooky but certainly scatterbrained, her character is a bit of an emotional and physical klutz. Her pairing with Arnold seems unlikely, but it's obvious the two performers reveled in the challenge. DeVito and Frank Langella (as the villainous department administrator) nicely round out the cast, albeit in familiar roles — the compulsive salesman and the slick hit man, respectively.

Reitman has an unfussy visual style that at its worst emulates the flatness of television sitcom, complete with inane musical accompaniment. But his sense of storytelling is keen and breezy and his instinct about laying it on with a trowel or tossing it off in sublime fashion is virtually unerring. "Junior" is certain to spawn a lot of laughs and a lot of dough. It's simple and clever and satisfying — an entertainment trio indeed rare, and highly appreciated.

—*Leonard Klady*

FINAL COMBINATION

A Rank Film Distributors release (U.K.) of a Polygram Filmed Entertainment presentation of a Propaganda Films production. Produced by Joni Sighvatsson, Steve Golin, Gregg Fienberg. Executive producer, Gary Milkis. Line producer, Gregory Goodman. Directed by Nigel Dick. Screenplay, Larry Golin, from a screen story by Jonathan Tydor. Camera (Foto-Kem color), David Bridges; editors, Henry Richardson, Jonathan Shaw; music, Rolfe Kent; production design, Jon Gary Steele; art direction, Douglas Hill; set decoration, Nancy Arnold; costume design, Alexandra Welker; sound (Ultra-Stereo), Jim Stuebe; stunt coordinator, Dan Bradley; assistant director, Thomas Patrick Smith; casting, Johanna Ray. Reviewed at Rank Preview Theater, London, Jan. 31, 1994. Running time: **92 MIN.**

Det. Matt Dickson	Michael Madsen
Catherine Briggs	Lisa Bonet
Richard Welton	Gary Stretch
Det. Chuck Rowland	Tim Russ
Donato	Damian Chapa
Lt. Stein	Carmen Argenziano
Ike (Point Man)	
Pointer	Clarence Landry
Sara	Susan Byun
Art Robinson	Alan Toy

Headed straight to vidbins is "Final Combination," a so-what serial-killer low-budgeter that manages to squander the combined talents of Michael Madsen and Lisa Bonet on a back-of-a-coaster script. The Propaganda Films production finally gets a token theatrical airing in the U.K. starting Nov. 18, almost a year after its initial press screening.

A blond Madsen plays Matt Dickson, a hockey player-turned-hard-bitten L.A. cop whose wife has walked and who now gets his kicks from a bottle and one-night stands. Roaming the streets is psycho boxer Welton (Brit actor Gary Stretch, a former pugilist) who batters girls to death in seedy motel rooms and uses the names of famous sluggers as aliases.

Enter journalist Catherine Briggs (Bonet), who points Dickson to a string of similar murders and soon jumps in the sack with him. Dickson, who's mighty slow on the uptake, is alerted to the boxing connection by an old ex-pro (Clarence Landry) who runs the motel where the initial murders took place. Catherine, meanwhile, is pursuing her own agenda: Her sister was popped by Welton a while ago.

Madsen has trod these mean, noirish sets before, and here seems to be giving Robert Mitchum lessons in minimalist acting. Bonet briefly injects some life into the proceedings, but much of her dialogue sits awkwardly on her lips. Stretch is suitably menacing as the hard-as-nails serial wacko.

Director Nigel Dick, a founding director of Propaganda with a solid background in musicvids, brings a measure of style to the largely inte-

rior-shot movie, but can't summon up much tension from a cornball script that is terminally light on plot. A final car chase comes too late to appease even genre fans.

—*Derek Elley*

ONE FOR YOU, ONE FOR ME AND ONE FOR RAPHAEL
(UNO A TE, UNO A ME E UNO A RAFFAELE)
(ITALIAN)

An Alia Film production, in association with RAI-3. Produced by Enzo Porcelli. RAI producer, Anna Albanese. Directed by Jon Jost. Screenplay, Jost, in collaboration with Edoardo Albinati; camera (Technicolor), Jost; editor, Benni Atria; music, Jon A. English; sound, Theo Eshetu, assistant director, Eric Black. Reviewed on vidcassette, Rome, Nov. 10, 1994. (In Venice, Vienna fests.) Running time: **85 MIN.**

Costanza	Eliana Miglio
Lucia	Lucia Gardin
Cecilia	Vittoria Arenillas
The Lawyer	Pier Paolo Capponi
Carlo	Lino Salemme
The Porter	Nicola Pistoia
The Worker	Daniele Formica

This Italian-language turn by eternal maverick Jon Jost presents a far from definitive lowdown on the country's kickback phenomenon. Stalwart devotees might admire the film's technique, but most auds will find its messianic tone and stolid rhythms hard to swallow.

Jost's elegant but dramatically comatose meditation on dishonesty more or less fingers the entire Italo population for the decades of graft and thievery that brought Italy to its knees. The idea of innate venality and the look-out-for-No. 1 mentality is hardly new, and its exploration here is limited to a stream of supercilious, often trite pontification. The film drew a hostile response from Italian critics at this fall's Venice fest.

Jost eschews a delineated narrative, preferring to create a rapport between his actors and steer them in whatever improvisational direction he chooses. But what works in his impressive U.S. indie pix doesn't work here: The rudderless cast shows little sign of connecting with one another, their director or the material.

The closest thing to a narrative thrust comes from the plight of Costanza (Eliana Miglio). Due to her infringement of laws on the declaration of rent as income, she is unable to throw non-paying Argentine tenant Cecilia (Vittoria Arenillas) out of her apartment. After an opening 50 minutes virtually without incident, things threaten to start moving when house-bound, depressive Cecilia gets dressed and heads outdoors.

A pair of misjudged dramatic set pieces follows. The first has Cecilia's disgruntled b.f. (Lino Salemme) cycling out to the site of Pasolini's murder to rant about the sorry state of Italy. The leaden scene is a far cry from the understated eloquence of Nanni Moretti's similar pilgrimage in "Dear Diary."

Next up, Costanza goes with her chum (Lucia Gardin) to the legal office of the latter's uncle (Pier Paolo Capponi). After pulling strings to budge Cecilia, the corrupt lawyer takes out a pistol and shoots himself before the barely startled girls.

Not one figure is established as a character. As a consequence, their laborious spiels on various aspects of the central theme, in excruciatingly long sequences, seem disconnected and superficial, delivering faux profundity instead of valid reflection.

The film's grounding in recent political events comes via snippets of radio broadcasts detailing kickback arrests and terrorist attacks. More subtle is the geographical scene-setting: Jost's loose-limbed camerawork ably avoids cliche in capturing Rome and its surrounds, with an architectural focus that's frequently more illuminating than its human one. Jon A. English's constant blitz of music over almost every scene quickly grates.

—*David Rooney*

LONDON

GETTING ANY?
(MINA YATTERUKA!)
(JAPANESE)

An Office Kitano/Bandi Visual/Right Vision production. Produced by Masayuki Mori, Hisao Nabeshima, Yasushi Tsuge, Takio Yoshida. Directed, written by Takeshi Kitano. Camera (color), Katsumi Yanagishima; editor, Kitano, Yoshinori Oota; music, Hidehiko Koike; production design, Norihiro Isoda; costume design, Fumio Iwasaka; sound (Dolby), Senji Horiuchi. Reviewed at London Film Festival, Nov. 16, 1994. Running time: **76 MIN.**

Asao	Dannkann
World Defense Force Chief	Shouji Kobayashi
Head Yakuza #1	Tetsuya Yuuki
Head Yakuza #2	Yuuji Minakata
Head Yakuza #3	Renn Oosugi
Injured Yakuza	Susumu Terajima
Russian Actor	Masumi Okada
Mother	Tokie Hidari
Scientist	Takeshi Kitano

Great sex, and how to get it, is the single joke behind "Getting Any?," fifth feature of Japanese maverick Takeshi Kitano that's unlikely to find much action beyond home base. This one-note collection of comic turns built around popular talkshow host/entertainer Dannkann runs out of gas halfway and motors on for another 40 minutes without anyone at the wheel. Arthouse

November 21, 1994 (Cont.)

auds wired into Kitano's splendidly offbeat gangster pix like "Violent Cop" and "Sonatine" won't be shooting for this one.

Pic kicks off promisingly with an excerpt from a mock-"Miami Vice" TV show called "Miami P.D. Special Task Force," wherein a smooth Japanese hero picks up a girl curbside and segues to strenuous rumpy-pumpy in his swanky convertible. Cut to nerdy, impressionable couch potato Asao (Dannkann), who immediately reckons a set of smart wheels is the open-sesame to great sex.

Initial gags are very funny, with Asao cruising in a dinky-sized car and trying to pick up a variety of women. When that doesn't work, and he's ripped off by a smooth auto dealer, he next fantasizes that first-class travel by air always includes sex with a hostess. But to buy a first-class ticket, he needs some serious money — which means robbing a bank, which means first finding a gun.

When a yakuza drops dead in front of him one day, Asao gets his shooter, but every attempt to rob a bank ends in abject failure. Even when he hijacks a security truck, he accidentally sets fire to the loot inside. Next fantasy is that famous actors have great sex on planes, so Asao joins a studio as an extra and attempts to become a star of samurai movies.

And so it goes on. Final seg finds Asao fantasizing about being invisible so he can play peekaboo in a femme bathhouse. Enter a mad scientist (played by Kitano himself), who fouls up the conversion process by letting a fly in the equipment and turns Asao into a monstrous insect.

Aside from being a virtual one-man show for the hangdog talents of Dannkann, the pic appears in its early stages to be a satire on the persuasive power of TV and popular genres therein. That's soon negated, however, by a rondo-like structure that becomes progressively more tiresome and leads to no conclusion or final twist.

Individual gags, some lasting only a few seconds, are funny in the early going, with an absurdist sense of humor pitched somewhere between Monty Python, Inspector Clouseau and the anarchic comedies of Sogo Ishii ("Crazy Family"). But without even a developing plotline to hang the gags on, the movie soon spirals down its own drain.

Technically, it's a good-looking piece of work, with clean color lensing, careful composition and trim cutting. For the record, running time of the print screened at the London world preem was 30 minutes shorter than that advertised; judging by stills in the festival's catalogues, at least one whole episode involving yakuza gangs has mysteriously disappeared. But at 76 minutes, it's plenty long enough already. *—Derek Elley*

THE EMIGRANT

(AL-MOHAGER)

(EGYPTIAN-FRENCH)

A Misr Intl. Films (Egypt)/Ognon Pictures, FR3, La Sept/Arte (France) production. (International sales: Misr Intl., Cairo.) Produced by Gabriel Khoury, Humbert Balsan. Directed, written by Youssef Chahine. Script collaborators, Rafik el-Sabban, Ahmed Kassem, Khaled Youssef. Camera (color), Ramses Marzouk; editor, Rachida Abdel-Salam; music, Mohamed Nouh; art direction, Hamed Hemdan; costume design, Nahed Nasrallah; sound, Dominique Hennequin; special effects, Excalibur; choreography, Walid Aouni; assistant director, Ahmed Kassem. Reviewed at London Film Festival, Nov. 15, 1994. (Also in Locarno, Montpellier fests.) Running time: **128 MIN.**

Ram	Khaled el-Nabaoui
Simihit	Yousra
Amihar	Mahmoud Hemida
Adam	Michel Piccoli
Basma	Safia el-Emari
Hati	Hanan al-Torki
Tut	Ahmed Bedir

With: Seif Abdel-Rahman, Ahmed Salama, Sayed Abdel-Kerim, Amr Abdel-Guelil, Sid Aly Kouiret.

Veteran Egyptian director Youssef Chahine comes up trumps with "The Emigrant," a fascinating retelling of the Genesis tale of Joseph, shorn of both Judeo-Christian preaching and Hollywood razzmatazz. Though the relatively low-key pic is an almost impossible marketing proposition theatrically, festivals and specialized Eurowebs should give this space in their skeds.

Historical movie buffs will find Chahine's version particularly rewarding, told as it is from an Egyptian rather than Hebraic perspective. The only previous version of the Joseph tale is Irving Rapper's 1961 Italo "Sold Into Egypt" (Giuseppe venduto dai fratelli), with Belinda Lee and Robert Morley, a straight telling of the biblical yarn, set some 3,000 years ago.

The Joseph character is here called Ram (Khaled el-Nabaoui). He's a dreamer and proto-intellectual who's bullied by his elder brothers and wants only to travel to Egypt, seat of learning, to study agriculture.

Ram basically has had it with the superstition-riddled nomadic lifestyle of his family, presided over by his father (French thesp Michel Piccoli, sporting a Moses-like beard).

Ram is escorted across Sinai by his brothers and promptly sold to an Egyptian, Ozir (Sayed Abdel-Kerim), who works for the military head of Thebes, Amihar (Mahmoud Hemida).

Through a combo of charm and *cojones*, Ram is virtually adopted by Amihar and given a chance to develop a barren stretch of land outside the capital.

Unwittingly, he becomes caught up in various sexual and political intrigues, first catching the eye of the impotent Amihar's sex-starved wife, Simihit (Yousra), and later becoming a pawn in Amihar's plot to foment famine and unseat Thebes' aged ruler.

Simihit, high priestess of the Cult of Amun, has also secretly switched to the rival Cult of Aten. (This religious struggle also forms the basis of Michael Curtiz's 1954 Fox epic "The Egyptian.")

There's enough going on in Chahine's two-hour movie to fuel a miniseries, and the abrupt plot transitions, which sometimes impede full understanding, often make the pic play like a cut-down theatrical version.

But thanks to Chahine's stress on character rather than spectacle, the characters slowly emerge as fully drawn beings, with notable playing by Hemida as the ascetic soldier, Yousra as his lovelorn wife and, especially, el-Nabaoui as Ram, who brings charm and even a measure of comedy to the central role.

As Ram's g.f., looker Hanan al-Torki is a perky support. A dubbed Piccoli melds OK into the Arab cast, despite being there for the sake of co-production coin.

Technically, the movie is fine, with good, clear photography, fine locations, a rhapsodic symphonic score by Mohamed Nouh, and clever mixing of sets and Egyptian ruins. Occasional f/x are OK, too. *—Derek Elley*

23:58

(23 H 58)

(FRENCH)

An MW Prods. production. (International sales: Motion Media, Paris.) Produced by Pierre-William Glenn, Martine Benveniste. Directed by Glenn. Screenplay, Glenn, Frederic Leroy, Edith Vergne; camera (Fujicolor), Jean-Claude Vicquery; editor, Anita Perez; music, Laurent Cugny; art direction, Jacques Voizot; costume design, Magali Guidasci; sound, Henri Roux, Adrien Nataf; assistant director, Olivier Peray; second unit director, Alain-Michel Blanc. Reviewed at London Film Festival, Nov. 15, 1994. Running time: **83 MIN.**

Bernard	Jean-Francois Stevenin
Supt. Paul (Steve) Morin	Jean-Pierre Malo
Thierry	Gerard Garnier
Inspector Jean-Marie	Yan Epstein
Momo	Kader Boukanef
Florence	Amelie Glenn
Didi	Sophie Tellier
Inspector Bertrand	Isabelle Maltese
Inspector Mathieu	Octave Arrighi

Tale of a stadium holdup during the Le Mans 24-hour motor-bike race, "23:58" freely mixes movie-buff in-jokes and solid genre elements to generally satisfying results, despite coming unglued in the final reels. This fourth helming excursion by French cameraman Pierre-William Glenn (who's worked with Tavernier, Truffaut, Losey and Fuller) is too ingrown to win general offshore auds' interest but reps his best feature to date, following uneven earlier works and the dismal futuristic actioner "Terminus" (1987).

The running joke throughout "23:58" is that the robbery reminds the investigating cop (Jean-Pierre Malo) of a heist movie. After running through titles like "The Anderson Tapes," "Melodie en sous-sol" and "L'Amour braque," he finally realizes it's Stanley Kubrick's 1956 "The Killing," also set at a racetrack.

It's here, about an hour in, that the buff element starts to derail the film. After a series of stills from the Kubrick pic, the cop says he's decided "to change the ending" and even gives the main robber (Jean-Francois Stevenin) a vidcassette of the movie.

Apart from minor details like the robbers wearing masks and a fight diversion near the start, Glenn's film bears no resemblance to Kubrick's B&W classic, with its complex cutting and grittier, '50s feel. On its own terms, however, "23:58" is a neat time-passer.

Pic is framed as a reminiscence by ex-racer Bernard (Stevenin) in a letter to the young daughter (helmer's own sprig, Amelie Glenn) of a late colleague, in whose memory he's arranged the heist. With another former biker, Thierry (Gerard Garnier), and a host of well-placed help-

November 21, 1994 (Cont.)

ers, Bernard steals 6 million francs of gate money and hides out in the track area till the race is over.

Things go wrong early on, with two karate colleagues trying to cut themselves in on the loot, the g.f. (Sophie Tellier) of one associate blabbing to the police, and an Arab helper (Kader Boukanef) killed on the track. Meanwhile, the chief cop, who's a motorbike and movie buff, slowly pieces together the scenario.

Glenn cleverly mixes in footage shot at the 14th Le Mans race to give the film a *verismo* feel. Less certain is the pic's pacing, which, like the occasional sax solos on the soundtrack, has a loose feel that doesn't build any tension.

Still, performances by a seasoned cast keep things ticking, led by Malo's wondrously laid-back, long-haired cop and Stevenin's grizzled ex-racer. Tech credits are smooth.

Film's title stems from a remark by Malo's character that the 24-hour race lasts only 23 hours and 58 minutes, as the last lap is never run because of spectators' invasion of the track.   —*Derek Elley*

MONTPELLIER

AL-KOMPARS

(THE EXTRAS)

(SYRIAN)

A National Film Organization of Syria production. (International sales: Ebla Prods., Damascus.) Directed, written by Nabil Maleh. Camera (color), Hana Ward; editor, Mohamed Ali Maleh; music, Vahe Demerjian, Samir Hilmi; art direction, Labib Ruslan, Rida Hoshos; sound, Emil Saade. Reviewed at Montpellier Festival of Mediterranean Cinema (competing), France, Oct. 27, 1994. (Also in London fest.) Running time: **94 MIN.**
With: Samar Sami, Bassam Kousa, Mohamed Esh-Sheikh Naguib, Wafaa Mouselly.

In "The Extras," Syrian scripter/helmer Nabil Maleh delivers an often funny and ultimately devastating viewing experience propelled by two standout performances in the lead roles. This engaging account of a poor young couple who find peace away from prying eyes for the first time in their eight-month courtship will have its most powerful impact in Arabic-speaking countries, but also has potential for offshore arthouses.

Salem (Bassam Kousa), a pleasant fellow who stutters when nervous, works a full shift at a service station before attending rehearsals at Damascus' National Theater, where he's been an extra for five years. As his extended family lives in crushingly small quarters, he meets his girlfriend, Nada (Samar Sami) — a widow who sews in a factory and is kept on a tight leash

by her tradition-minded brothers — only in public spots.

Salem's bachelor friend has agreed to loan the lovebirds his apartment for two hours. Comic situations abound until Salem finally gets his benefactor out the door.

Tightly paced pic takes place entirely in the apartment, exploring the would-be lovers' often justified paranoia via a punchy series of exchanges. These start with Nada's arrival: When she removes her head scarf, Salem realizes that until now he has never seen his beloved's hair.

Director Maleh creates an atmosphere of love and longing beset by anxiety. Salem's p.o.v. is played out to good effect via mostly amusing fantasy sequences. Sound effects and incidental music mesh with the ever-shifting mood; photography and editing are effective. Aside from a few overly ominous chords, pic steers clear of cliche.

With four awards from three previous fests to its credit, pic played Montpellier the week it was banned by Syria's censors. They reportedly petitioned for the return of the print, but a subsequent screening at the London Film Festival in mid-November went ahead as planned.
—*Lisa Nesselson*

ON THE FAR SIDE OF THE TUNNEL

(AL OTRO LADO DEL TUNEL)

(SPANISH)

A Serva Films production. (International sales: Sogepaq, Madrid.) Directed by Jaime de Arminan. Screenplay, de Arminan, Eduardo Arminan. Camera (color), Teo Escamilla; editor, Jose Luis Matesanz; art direction, Julio Esteban; sound (Dolby), Miguel Polo. Reviewed at Montpellier Festival of Mediterranean Cinema, France, Oct. 24, 1994. Running time: **97 MIN.**
With: Fernando Rey, Maribel Verdu, Gonzalo Vega, Amparo Baro, Rafael Alonso, Luis Barbero, Gabriel Latorre, Pedro Alvarez-Ossorio, Jorge Calvo, Asuncion Sanchez.

In "On the Far Side of the Tunnel," the late Fernando Rey gives a crusty, convincing perf as a charmingly grumpy screenwriter who ends up sequestered in a monastery with his younger writing partner to finish an overdue script for an uninspired European co-prod. Pic's first half is light and amusing, but it subsequently veers toward darker territory. Fests and tube sales should shed a little light on this tunnel.

The lure of showbiz, even in the most remote outposts, is gently lampooned as the five monks at the off-season retreat stick their ecclesiastical noses into the penning of what is meant to be a Sean Connery vehicle set in 19th-century Scotland. With the help of an alluring and over-imaginative young female baker,

supporting players drop plentiful hints that the story would play far better as a contemporary Spanish-language love story, set in some of the lovely local locations.

Script-in-progress concerns an elderly musician, his young protege and a young woman with a death wish. Unsolicited input from the baker pulls the lackluster melodrama into the present, where the three protagonists play out a potentially risky variation on the period triangle.

Wry comic timing and a conspiratorial tone sustain the pic until it wobbles toward its dramatic conclusion. Some viewers will regret the shift in tone, while others will appreciate the literary sense of closure. Location lensing in Spain's picturesque Huesca region is easy on the eye. Playing is sweet and assured.
—*Lisa Nesselson*

HAWAII

RED LOTUS

(BUA DENG)

(LAOTIAN — B&W)

A Laos Film presentation of a State Cinematographic Co. production. Directed by Som-ok Southiphone. Camera (B&W), Padit Lattanaboungnang, Dalavanh Lasavong; editor, Dara Kanlagna; music, Douangmysay Lykaya. Reviewed at Hawaii Film Festival, Honolulu, Nov. 9. 1994. Running time: **83 MIN.**
With: Somchit Vongsamang, Vongdeuane Phonsavan, Amkha Ouparasane, Khanthaly.

Reportedly one of only three Laotian movies preserved of the dozen made to date, "Red Lotus" is no masterpiece but is a fascinating glimpse of a culture and cinematography almost unknown outside its borders. This 1988 production, which received its U.S. preem at the Hawaii fest, recalls Vietnamese pix of the period and deserves exposure at other Asian-specific events.

Setting is a small northern village in Vientiane province in the early '70s. The country's brief 20-year period of independence, following longtime French rule, is coming to an end, as pro-Communist troops gain the upper hand over the U.S.-backed royal Laotian army. The government wants to use the village as a bridgehead in its war against the guerrillas, and utilizes a cease-fire to build up troops there.

Simple story is told from the p.o.v. of country girl Bua Deng (Somchit Vongsamang), whose fiance, Man, has run off to join the Reds. Her mother urges her to marry the capitalistic Siang instead, and, despite her objections, the wedding takes place, alongside her sister Kamwan's to a sympathetic government supporter.

Finale has Man and company attacking the village, routing government troops and rescuing Bua Deng after her lecherous stepfather kills Siang and drags her into the woods.

Though performances generally steer clear of broad caricature, scripting is only functional, with the best sequences those in which dialogue is at a minimum. Still, helmer Som-ok Southiphone shows a basic grasp of camera style, and editing is OK. In the title role, Somchit shows some screen presence as the strong but compliant heroine.   —*Derek Elley*

DESTINY

(TOOROG)

(MONGOLIAN)

An ARD Cinema Co. production. (International sales: ARD, Ulaanbaatar.) Produced, directed by Y. Tserendolgor. Screenplay, M. Togmid, based on the opera "Three Meaningful Mountains" by Dashdorjiin Natsagdorj. Camera (color), J.A. Salbai; editor, D. Batgerel; music, D. Luvsansharav; art direction, Kh. Enhtuvshin; consultant, Kh. Nyambuu. Reviewed at Hawaii Film Festival, Honolulu, Nov. 9, 1994. Running time: **95 MIN.**
Yunden .... G. Basbayar
Nansalmaa .... S. Bolormaa
Balgan .... B. Batsuuri
Khorolmaa .... O. Delgertsetseg

Though you need a road map to follow the plot, this lively reworking of a famous 1934 Mongolian opera has enough going for it to work as a curio item on the Asian circuit. Mixture of straight dialogue, occasional songs, costumes to die for and tiptop color processing add up to an exotic package.

Basic love story, set at the turn of the 20th century, concerns handsome Yunden, betrothed to sweetheart Nansalmaa. Snake in the steppe grass is Khorolmaa, who also has the hots for Yunden and deliberately recommends nobleman Balgan should marry Nansalmaa instead. Yunden rescues Nansalmaa from Balgan's palace and the two lovebirds expire during their flight.

Performances are surprisingly fresh and natural, and femme helmer Y. Tserendolgor (who has produced Western as well as Mongolian operas) keeps things moving at a merry clip. Ethnic-flavored songs are easy on the ear, and spacious outdoor locations always a treat for the eyes.   —*Derek Elley*

November 28, 1994

COBB

A Warner Bros. release of a Regency Enterprises/Alcor Films production. Produced by David Lester. Executive producer, Arnon Milchan. Directed, written by Ron Shelton, based on the book "Cobb: A Biography" by Al Stump. Camera (Technicolor), Russell Boyd; editors, Paul Seydor, Kimberly Ray; music, Elliot Goldenthal; production design, Armin Ganz, Scott Ritenour; art direction, Troy Sizemore, Charles Butcher; set decoration, Claire Jenora Bowin; costume design, Ruth Carter; makeup, Ve Neill; sound (Dolby), Kirk Francis; baseball coordinator Rob Ryder; special effects supervisor, Jim Fredburg; assistant director, H. Gordon Boos; casting, Victoria Thomas. Reviewed at the Warner Studios, Burbank, Nov. 16, 1994. MPAA Rating: R. Running time: **128 MIN.**

Ty Cobb	Tommy Lee Jones
Al Stump	Robert Wuhl
Ramona	Lolita Davidovich
Willie	Lou Myers
Mickey Cochrane	Stephen Mendillo
Jameson	William Utay
Prof. Cobb	J. Kenneth Campbell
Ty's Mother	Rhoda Griffis
Mud	Allan Malamud

Tyrus Raymond Cobb was the **stuff of legend. Baseball's premier hitter, he was a ferocious player on and off the field. He was self-possessed, meanspirited, a bigot and embodied just about every lowly human quality imaginable. In short, he's an ideal movie subject.**

So, the wonder of wonders of "Cobb" is why writer/director Ron Shelton made a movie that more accurately should be titled "Stump." The film is essentially the chronicle of how sports scribe Al Stump (Robert Wuhl) was summoned to the bedside of the ailing Ty Cobb (Tommy Lee Jones) to write the official bio of the Baseball Hall of Fame's first inductee.

The two stories aren't complementary, and Shelton's periodic shifts of focus result in an ambivalent, conflicted drama. Cobb is a peacock and flamboyant scene stealer while Stump's dilemma is a crisis of conscience — whether to write the naked truth or print the legend.

Audiences will be confused by what the picture is not. It's not really about Cobb or baseball or a bygone era. It's neither character study nor historic drama. It's ambitious but oblique and unfocused, and only the most generous of viewers will forgive its numerous lapses and vagaries. The film's prospects of breaking out of a specialized niche are remote.

When Stump arrives at the snowbound Tahoe residence of the great man in 1960, he encounters a pistol-waving, decaying relic. The one-time Detroit Tiger effortlessly demonstrates that he earned his hateful reputation honestly. He browbeats his chosen Boswell, drags him on a drinking and carousing spree through Reno and expects him to be grateful for a nonstop stream of abuse.

It's unclear just how much sympathy we are to extend the unrepentant and bullying title character. Glimmers of humanity flicker through, and pop-psych references provide hints about the origins of his bad behavior.

But if Cobb is secondary, or merely a catalyst, Shelton fumbles just as badly with Stump. His groveling is beneath contempt. It's tough to get behind a guy whose justification for being a toady is that it will enable him to secretly write the "real" story while he feeds his subject pages of the sanitized version.

With such a blighted concept, one can well understand why the two principal actors appear to be struggling with their characters. Jones plays Cobb on a Shakespearean scale, with obvious parallels between the Georgia Peach and King Lear. But bigger isn't better, and the outsized nature of the interpretation lends the proceedings an unwarranted theatricality.

Wuhl is simply no match for his charismatic co-star. He's a dedicated second banana, and, when all else fails, he mugs.

Shelton gropes for a visual style to fit his material, but winds up with a hodgepodge reflecting different eras and moods. One can sense a keenly personal allegory for the filmmaker in this subject. It's also likely too painful for him to address head on, ultimately rendering a remote and impenetrable drama. —*Leonard Klady*

A LOW DOWN DIRTY SHAME

A Buena Vista Pictures release of a Caravan Pictures presentation. Produced by Joe Roth, Roger Birnbaum. Executive producers, Eric L. Gold, Lee R. Mayes. Directed, written by Keenen Ivory Wayans. Camera (Technicolor), Matthew F. Leonetti; editor, John F. Link; music, Marcus Miller; production design, Robb Wilson King; art direction, Richard L. Johnson; set decoration, Lance Lombardo; costume design, Francine Jamison-Tanchuck; sound (Dolby), Willie Burton; stunt coordinators, Picerni, Billy Burton; associate producer/assistant director, Michael Waxman; second unit director, Charles Picerni; casting, Robi Reed-Humes. Reviewed at the GCC Beverly Connection, L.A., Nov. 18, 1994. MPAA Rating: R. Running time: **100 MIN.**

Shame	Keenen Ivory Wayans
Rothmiller	Charles S. Dutton
Peaches	Jada Pinkett
Angela	Salli Richardson
Mendoza	Andrew Divoff
Wayman	Corwin Hawkins
Luis	Gary Cervantes
Captain Nunez	Gregory Sierra

True to its hybrid billing as an **action-comedy, this writer/director/star turn by "In Living Color" creator Keenen Ivory Wayans isn't flat-out funny enough to completely work as a comedy and doesn't pack enough action to thrive in that genre. Pic nevertheless has its moments and probably won't dishonor itself as a holiday alternative in big urban markets, though crossover appeal figures to be limited.**

In a sense, Wayans has returned to his first feature, "I'm Gonna Git You Sucka," with a different attitude. Where that film was a clever if rather broad spoof of the black action movies of the '70s, "A Low Down Dirty Shame" takes itself and its star far more seriously. That would be effective if Wayans were a more accomplished actor, but as is, the dramatic material largely falls flat and the best laughs come courtesy of Jada Pinkett in a brash, fun performance as the title character's trash-talking, soap opera-obsessed assistant, Peaches. Loaded with cliches, the story features Wayans as Shame, a former L.A. cop trying to make it as a private eye after a case involving a Latin American drug lord (Andrew Divoff) and his entanglement with a beautiful woman (Salli Richardson) ended his career.

Shame is drawn back into those events by a former colleague (Charles S. Dutton) who's now working for the DEA. The drug lord, thought dead, is still alive, and Shame hooks up again with his long-lost girlfriend, irking the possessive Peaches.

All of this ranks as by-the-numbers cop stuff, and plenty of holes have been shot through the script, such as how the down-on-his-luck shamus quickly transforms himself into an overdressed James Bond.

The not-quite-saving grace resides in a handful of genuinely funny moments and the appealing female leads. In terms of action, Wayans the director relies too much on slow-motion in shooting action scenes — a tiresome habit that undercuts the potential excitement of some sequences.

"Shame" also falls victim to certain comedic excesses, and as with "In Living Color's" "Men On ..." sketch, its over-the-top portrayal of Peaches' snap-queen roommate (the late Corwin Hawkins) isn't likely to endear itself to the gay community.

Tall and physically imposing, Wayans has the presence to be an action star but, in keeping with his roots in standup and sketch comedy, seems to be more comfortable trying to generate laughs. While fellow "Living Color" alums Jim Carrey and Wayans' brother, Damon, have established their feature credentials, Keenen appears to be in need of a more finely tuned vehicle.

Richardson oozes sex appeal as the femme fatale, while Dutton and Divoff are at best adequate villains. Pinkett, meanwhile, continues to impress with her versatility after more serious roles in "Menace II Society" and "Jason's Lyric," while Kim Wayans turns up in an amusing cameo.

Tech credits are otherwise OK, and the song score adds some spice to the film — particularly the title track, providing an energy that the production can't sustain.

—*Brian Lowry*

CAMILLA

(CANADIAN-BRITISH)

A Miramax (U.S.) presentation of a Shaftesbury Films/Skreba production, with the participation of Telefilm Canada, Ontario Film Development Corp., Foundation Fund to Underwrite New Drama for Pay Television, Norstar and British Screen. (International sales: Majestic Films Intl., London.) Produced by Christina Jennings, Simon Relph. Executive producer, Jonathan Barker. Directed by Deepa Mehta. Screenplay, Paul Quarrington, based on an original story by Ali Jennings. Camera (color), Guy Dufaux; editor, Barry Farrell; music, Daniel Lanois; production design, Sandra Kybartas; costume design, Milena Canonero, Elisabetta Beraldo; sound, Bruce Nyznik; associate producer, Suzanne Colvin; assistant director, Gareth Tandy. Reviewed at the Palace Cinema, Montreal, Nov. 16, 1994. Running time: **95 MIN.**

Camilla Cara	Jessica Tandy
Freda Lopez	Bridget Fonda
Vincent Lopez	Elias Koteas
Harold Cara	Maury Chaykin
Hunt Weller	Graham Greene
Ewald	Hume Cronyn

With: Ranjit Chowdhry, George Harris, Sandi Ross, Gerry Quigley, Atom Egoyan, Devyani Saltzman, Camille Spence, Martha Cronyn, Sheilanne Lindsay, Don McKellar.

Featuring a standout perform- **ance from Jessica Tandy in her last starring bigscreen role, "Camilla" is a warm, funny road movie that will likely generate strong action with upscale auds looking for smart and entertaining fare. Tandy and co-star Bridget Fonda will help spark initial interest, and Canuck novelist/screenwriter Paul Quarrington's witty script, coupled with a solid ensemble cast, should help create good word of mouth. But this adult drama will need lots of media support to cross over to a wider audience.**

This is particularly true in Canada, where the film is hitting the screen during the hyper-competitive pre-Christmas season. Norstar Entertainment released "Camilla" in Canada's major markets Nov. 25 and Miramax will follow with a launch across the U.S. in mid-December.

Pic opens with Freda Lopez (Fonda) strumming on her electric guitar, and it's soon clear that she's a frustrated singer/songwriter whose husband, Vincent (Elias Koteas), is more than a little skeptical of her musical talents. The less-than-happily-married couple head out from Toronto to a cottage somewhere near Savannah, Ga., for a much-needed vacation.

That's where they meet neighbor Camilla Cara (Tandy), a wacky old woman prone to tall tales, tippling sherry and reminiscing about her exploits as a concert violinist. Camilla's son, Harold (Maury Chaykin), a high-strung, soft-core porn producer, convinces Vincent to help him market his films, and this partnership leaves the two women by themselves.

Freda and Camilla, who hit it off immediately, decide to go back to Toronto to catch a special performance of a Brahms concerto.

Film soon turns into a May-December female buddy pic over a series of rather improbable adventures that include an encounter with a suave con artist (Graham Greene). Along the way, Camilla sets off a nationwide manhunt by calling her son to say she's been kidnapped and orchestrates a reunion with a long-lost lover (Hume Cronyn).

Tandy is terrific as the spirited-but-lonely Camilla, a role that seems tailor-made for the late actress, and Fonda also delivers a nuanced, affecting performance. The Canadian supporting thesps are first-rate too, particularly Chaykin, who always looks like he's nanoseconds away from a panic attack, and Koteas, who plays against type as an insecure guy.

Quarrington — who also wrote "Whale Music" — has penned a script that neatly captures the bittersweet tone of the story without slipping into syrupy sentimentality. Toronto-based helmer Deepa Mehta maintains a quick pace, moving back and forth between comedy and pathos.

Veteran Quebec lenser Guy Dufaux contributes subtle, scenic visuals throughout, and Daniel Lanois' New Orleans-tinged soundtrack adds immeasurably to the Southern atmosphere. The domestic release will have a different score.

—*Brendan Kelly*

SHRUNKEN HEADS

A Full Moon Entertainment production and release. Produced by Charles Band. Executive producer, Debra Dion. Directed by Richard Elfman. Screenplay, Matthew Bright, based on an idea by Band. Camera (Foto-Kem color), Stephen McNutt; editor, Charles Simmons; music, Richard Band; main title theme music, Danny Elfman; production design, Milo; costume design, Greg Lavoi; makeup effects, Alchemyfx; visual effects, Paul Gentry; casting, Macdonald/Bullington, Tolley Casparis. Reviewed at the Royal Theatre, L.A., Nov. 11, 1994. Running time: **86 MIN.**
Big Moe .... Meg Foster
Mr. Sumatra .... Julius Harris
Tommy .... Aeryk Egan
Sally .... Becky Herbst

"Shrunken Heads," a new horror-comedy about revenge and justice in a crime-ridden urban neighborhood, is only mildly entertaining. Pic is neither very scary, very zany nor goofy enough for midnight fare, though it delivers some joyous visual effects for its targeted juvenile audience.

Tommy (Aeryk Egan), a youngster who works at his dad's grocery store, and his two pals are constantly harassed by the punks who terrorize the working-class neighborhood under the malevolent supervision of Big Moe (Meg Foster), their tough female crime boss. When the trio lose their lives in one of these fights, local news vendor Mr. Sumatra (Julius Harris) decides to take action and draw upon his specialty, which is shrinking severed heads and reanimating them into flying demons.

Pic's premise is a lame, familiar excuse for a revenge tale — and some diverting special effects. Young viewers may get a kick out of seeing Sumatra, a Haitian witch doctor with a taste for evil, plucking the heroes' heads and dropping them into a steaming voodoo brew. And they are certain to rejoice at the sight of the tiny heads exercising their magic as avenging angels who watchfully fly above the city.

Helmer Richard Elfman (brother of noted composer/Boingo frontman Danny), whose 1980 flick, "The Forbidden Zone," was far more bizarre and campy, tries to insert some humor into Bright's pedestrian script, but his pacing in the first hour is tedious and unmodulated.

The youngsters, particularly Egan as Tommy and Becky Herbst as his love interest, have some charm, though the one actress who seems determined to have fun with her role is Foster, as the lesbian mobster.

The special effects, which involve the intricate use of motion control, digital effects and masterful puppetry, are impressive, and so is Richard Band's buoyant music. But pic's earlier sequences, shot on a studio backlot, have no semblance of an authentic urban locale.

—*Emanuel Levy*

THE MACHINE
(LA MACHINE)
(FRENCH-GERMAN)

A Pan-Europeenne release (in France) of a Hachette Premiere, DD Prods., Prima, M6 Films, France 2 Cinema (France)/Studio Babelsberg (Germany) production, with the participation of Polygram Filmed Entertainment, Studio Images, Studio Canal Plus, CNC, French Ministry of Culture, Filmfoerderung Berlin, Filmfoerderungsanstalt. (International sales: Polygram Film Intl., London.) Produced by Rene Cleitman. Co-executive producers, Branard Bouix (France), Ingrid Windisch (Germany). Directed, written by Francois Dupeyron, based on the novel by Rene Belletto. Camera (color), Dietrich Lohmann; editor, Noelle Boisson; music, Michel Portal; production design, Carlos Conti; costumes, Elisabeth Tavernier; sound (Dolby), Pierre Gamet, Gerard Lamps, Anne Lecampion; special optical and digital effects, Frederic Moreau; assistant director, Cathy Joube; casting, Jeanne Biras. Reviewed at Club Gaumont screening room, Paris, Nov. 17, 1994. Running time: **96 MIN.**
Marc .... Gerard Depardieu
Marie .... Nathalie Baye
Zyto .... Didier Bourdon
Marianne .... Natalia Woerner
Leonard .... Erwan Baynaud
Hugues .... Claude Berri

A psycho-horror thriller about a switcheroo gone haywire, "The Machine" is an efficiently told tale about a respected contemporary scientist who, in what he intends as a fleeting experiment, trades minds and bodies with a psychotic murderer. Keen playing of compelling premise by a cast led by Gerard Depardieu and Nathalie Baye leads to a dark conclusion that should please conventional horror fans and tonier auds alike.

A creepy-crawly score and off-kilter atmosphere pull viewers into an opening seg in which a sinister young boy comes to his mother's bedroom door armed with a knife and a gun. Action then backtracks "18 Months Earlier," whereupon Depardieu's dense voiceover explains that he's Dr. Marc Lacroix, a brain specialist and shrink whose obsession with discovering how the mind and spirit form within the brain has led him to work with the criminally insane.

Hoping to show twisted patients that there are healthier alternatives to evil thoughts — and yearning to sample a depraved mind-set for himself — Marc secretly builds a machine that can swap minds between two humans. Perfect guinea pig is Zyto (Didier Bourdon), a squat, unsavory-looking fellow described as "the devil himself," who's been locked up for stabbing at least three women to death.

As Marc has lost interest in communicating with his wife Marie (Baye), only his shapely young mistress Marianne (Natalia Woerner)

knows of the machine's existence in an isolated country house.

The trial transfer is nicely accomplished via a "2001"-style voyage through the pupil of an eye. Once installed in Marc's body, Zyto rebels, refusing to help reverse the process and return to his own bod. Marc's oversight in not building a fail-safe or override mechanism is glossed over, and pic roars at full speed into an edgy tussle between good and evil in which the latter has a comfortable head start.

Based on a novel by Rene Belletto, the script reworks timeless elements from pix like "Frankenstein," "Dr. Jekyll and Mr. Hyde" and even a bit of "Shock Corridor." Fluid, urgent lensing and snappy editing propel characters through a kind of speed-chess game, with their own bodies as the playing pieces.

Marc ends up at his asylum in Zyto's body, while Zyto (in Marc's body) inherits the doctor's wife, son and job, the last requiring constant improvisation to avoid detection.

Buffs will note intriguing echoes of "The Return of Martin Guerre," in which Baye and Depardieu were also paired, as Baye is again playing a role in which she must decide if Depardieu's character is her husband or an impostor.

By the time the plot catches up with opening seg, viewers have been on a cleverly choreographed roller-coaster ride of identity and appearances — with a stomach-churning dip yet to come.

Helmer Francois Dupeyron elicits on-the-nose perfs in what could have been a confusing mess if executed with less control. As doc and psycho, Depardieu and Bourdon skillfully modulate their voices and body language. Well-known producer/director Claude Berri contributes a fine acting turn as the asylum's director.

Production design by Carlos Conti· manages to emphasize the fact that characters are trapped, even though they transit through wide-open, spacious dwellings.

According to production notes, both the pic's producer and the author of the original book say they'd hoped to enlist an American director to make a Hollywood film but gave in to scripter/helmer Dupeyron's passion for the material. They have no reason to regret their decision.

—*Lisa Nesselson*

November 28, 1994 (Cont.)

SARASOTA

DAISY AND MONA

(DAISY ET MONA)

(FRENCH)

An A.K. Prods./France 2 Cinema production. Produced by Alain Queffelean. Directed, written by Claude D'Anna. Camera (color), Denys Clerval; editor, Kenout Peltier; art direction, Pierre Queffelean; music, Francois-Xavier Decraene; sound, Jean-Luc Rault-Cheynet; assistant director, Christophe Cheysson. Reviewed at Sarasota French Film Festival, Fla., Nov. 12, 1994. Running time: **91 MIN.**
Daisy .... Marina Golovine
Mona .... Dyna Gauzy
Sami .... Lilah Dadi
Maryse .... Valerie Baurens
Milou
Dujardin .... Jacques Le Carpenter
Thierry Corsaro .... Philippe Seurin
Jacky .... Emmanuel Quatra
Chloe .... Caroline Thery

Director/writer Claude D'Anna's "Daisy and Mona" is a convincingly hard-edged but appealingly sentimental drama with offshore potential and crossover appeal. Pic was notably well received by audience at Florida's recent Sarasota French Film Festival. With proper handling, it could generate respectable numbers in urban markets.

Marina Golovine (the skeptical daughter in Agnieszka Holland's "Olivier, Olivier") plays Daisy, a street-smart Generation X-er with a spiky hairdo and a prickly attitude. She still bears the emotional scars of an abusive childhood, and conducts herself with equal measures of devil-may-care bravado and self-destructive impetuousness. Only when she's forced to accept responsibility for her long-neglected daughter does she begin to find some purpose for her life.

The mother-and-child reunion does not begin very promisingly. Seven-year-old Mona (talented newcomer Dyna Gauzy) has been raised by her father, who got Daisy pregnant when she was still a child herself. But when the father is sent to prison, and his girlfriend rejects Mona, Daisy must claim the child. Neither Daisy nor Mona is particularly happy about this.

An uncomfortable situation gets even worse when Sami (Lilah Dadi), Daisy's small-time-crook lover, is arrested for shooting a racist barroom brawler. Daisy and Mona take flight, relying on scams and petty larcenies for traveling money.

While on the road, they slowly break through their industrial-strength emotional defenses and reach out to each other. But they're never far from danger. Things come to a head when Daisy discovers that her new employer has tricked her into delivering child-porn videos.

D'Anna does a fine job of avoiding the off-puttingly lurid while still maintaining a gritty realism. The film is rich in vivid and persuasive details, particularly as it depicts the squalor of the lower depths to which Daisy and Mona sink. But pic is neither exploitative nor sensational.

The lead performers bring out the best in each other. Golovine is excellent as the wounded young woman whose dreams are too troubling to allow her much sleep. And Gauzy is every bit as compelling when it comes to balancing rude feistiness with emotional vulnerability.

There is a bit too much ersatz "poetry" in the dialogue of the opening scenes, and the upbeat ending goes on too long by half. Otherwise, "Daisy and Mona" is an accomplished and affecting piece of work. Tech values are fine. *—Joe Leydon*

SEVEN SUNDAYS

(FRENCH-ITALIAN)

An Erato Films/Filmtre production in association with TF1 Films Production, ICE Films, JCT Prods. Produced by Jean Bodon, Jerome Paillard. Executive producer, Daniel Toscan du Plantier. Directed, written by Jean Charles Tacchella. Camera (color), Martial Thury; music, Raymond Alessandrini; production designer, Serge Douy; sound (Dolby), Michel Kharat; costumes, Sylvie de Segonzac. Reviewed at Sarasota French Film Festival, Fla., Nov. 13, 1994. Running time: **102 MIN.**
Dodo .... Thierry Lhermitte
Jesus .... Maurizio Nichetti
Benjamin .... Rod Steiger
Marion .... Marie-France Pisier
Janet .... Molly Ringwald
Alice .... Susan Blakely
Nicky .... Nancy Valen
English and French dialogue.

Jean Charles Tacchella's "Seven Sundays" is an amiably inconsequential comedy that appears to be the work of people who simply made things up as they went along. Tissue-thin plotting and flat-footed pacing are major drawbacks. Even so, leads Thierry Lhermitte ("My New Partner") and Maurizio Nichetti ("Volere Volare") are charming enough to make pic a painless time-killer for homevid and pay cable.

Filmed mostly in English in and around Sarasota, Fla., where producer (and Unifrance topper) Daniel Toscan du Plantier is a prime mover behind the annual French Film Festival, comedy owes a bit to the Bob Hope-Bing Crosby romps of yesteryear.

Lhermitte is Dodo, a transplanted Frenchman who avoids work by living off the kindness of women. Nichetti is Jesus, an Italian violinist who has followed his sweetheart to Sarasota with marriage in mind. Very quickly, Jesus discovers that his sweetie has been passing his money on to Dodo. Almost as quickly, both men discover the mystery woman has taken off to parts unknown. Thus, a close friendship is born.

Rod Steiger shows up for a couple of scenes as a con artist who relieves Jesus of his savings. After Steiger completes his scam, there isn't much else in the way of plot. "Seven Sundays" simply drifts from one pointless episode to the next, following the buddies as they half-heartedly woo women while strenuously avoiding steady work.

Little of what happens is genuinely funny, in large measure because of Tacchella's tin-eared dialogue and off-key comic rhythms.

Lhermitte and Nichetti give "Seven Sundays" much more than it gives them. Occasionally, they are visibly uncomfortable as they crack wise in what, for them, is a foreign language. But, then again, even the actors who claim English as their mother tongue — including Molly Ringwald as a Sarasota policewoman and Susan Blakely as one of Lhermitte's wealthy conquests — do not sound entirely at ease here.

Marie-France Pisier (every bit as lovely as she was 20 years ago in Tacchella's "Cousin, Cousine") has a few bright moments in the nothing part of a much-married beauty-shop owner. But she's the only one at this party who isn't trying too hard for too little.

Martial Thury's attractive color lensing makes the most of the Sarasota locations. Other tech credits are unremarkable. *—Joe Leydon*

BLIND SPOT

(LA POUDRE AUX YEUX)

(FRENCH)

An SFP Cinema production. Produced by Boudjemaa Dahmane. Directed by Maurice Dugowson. Screenplay, Jacques Dugowson, Maurice Dugowson, Odile Barski, based on the novel by Maurice Achard. Camera (color), Jacques Guerin; editor, Marie-France Ghilbert; music, Jean-Claude Vannier; set design, Valerie Grall; costumes, Pascaline Suty; sound, Norbert Garcia; assistant director, Pablo Freville. Reviewed at Sarasota French Film Festival, Fla., Nov. 10, 1994. Running time: **95 MIN.**
Arnold .... Robin Renucci
Juliette .... Marilyne Canto
Shakespeare .... Marc Jolivert
Isabelle .... Emmanuell Lepoutre
Leonard .... Pierre-Loup Rajot
Eye Doctor .... Myriam Boyer

Vet TV and pic helmer Maurice Dugowson does disappointingly little with a potentially fascinating premise in "Blind Spot." After promising first reels, drama bogs down and never fully recovers. Pic appears destined for playoff as global fest item.

Robin Renucci is well cast and convincing as Arnold, an ace TV reporter who's eager to cover a revolutionary uprising in northern Sri Lanka. On the eve of his departure, however, he decides to check with a doctor about his recent headaches and eyestrain. The diagnosis is grim: The strain of the Sri Lanka assignment could cause the reporter to go blind.

Arnold doesn't want to risk his eyesight. On the other hand, he doesn't want to turn his assignment over to a despised rival. So he tells everyone he's leaving town, then holes up in his Paris apartment. There, he assembles footage left over from a previous overseas assignment and combines it with updated video material provided by Paris-based Sri Lankan militants. An edit here, a voiceover there, and presto — Arnold has the material for a hard-hitting, first-person documentary.

Unfortunately, "Blind Spot" becomes tedious as soon as Arnold locks his front door and draws the curtains. Alone for weeks, he begins to crack under the pressure of his pretense and the loneliness — which leads to many long, repetitious scenes depicting Arnold in various stages of emotional distress.

Story picks up considerably when Arnold "returns" to Paris and goes to his news agency's studio to complete his documentary. There's a clever latenight sequence in which Arnold, using high-tech trickery that recalls "Forrest Gump," manages to insert himself into a Sri Lankan street scene. The kicker is, his editor suggests that this difficult-to-fake shot should be discarded, for reasons of pacing.

A few more details about the fakery and a lot less emotional frenzy would have helped "Blind Spot" immeasurably. Dugowson, working from a novel by Maurice Achard, obviously wants to offer a cautionary tale about the ways that truth can be twisted in the electronic age. Pic scores some salient points at the very beginning, when Arnold, addressing college students, explains the not-so-hidden meanings of imagery employed by presidents Reagan and Clinton.

Dugowson could cut another five or 10 minutes. The supporting performances are everything they should be. *—Joe Leydon*

November 28, 1994 (Cont.)

THE BLACK ANGEL

(L'ANGE NOIR)

(FRENCH)

A UGC (France) release of a Les Films Alain Sarde/La Sorciere Rouge production. Produced by Alain Sarde. Executive producer, Jean-Claude Brisseau. Directed, written by Brisseau. Camera (color), Romain Winding; editor/first assistant director, Maria-Luisa Garcia; sound, Georges Prat; costumes, Lyvia D'Alche. Reviewed at Sarasota French Film Festival, Fla., Nov. 13, 1994. Running time: **99 MIN.**

Stephane Feuvrier	Sylvie Vartan
Georges Feuvrier	Michel Piccoli
Paul Delorme	Tcheky Karyo
Cecile	Alexandra Winisky
Madeleine	Lisa Heredia
Christophe	Philippe Torreton
Aslanian	Claude Faraldo
Pitot	Bernard Verley
Mme. Pitot	Claude Winter

High style takes precedence over thin substance in Jean-Claude Brisseau's "The Black Angel," a glossy but hollow noir drama that's notable only for its attempt to transform French singer Sylvie Vartan into the Kim Novak of her generation. Pic may click domestically, but offshore prospects are dim.

Vartan plays Stephane, the wife of an older, prominent magistrate (Michel Piccoli). She coldbloodedly shoots a male visitor in her upscale home, then claims she was defending herself against a rapist. Victim turns out to be Wadek Aslanian (Claude Faraldo), a gangster who's viewed as a modern-day Robin Hood.

Paul (Tcheky Karyo), the lawyer hired by Stephane's husband, learns more than he really cares to know about his client, thanks to a series of anonymous letters. The notes provide a road map through the sordid areas of Stephane's past, allowing Paul to discover her history as an ex-prostitute, a porno movie performer — and a frequent cohort of Aslanian.

Naturally, Stephane's husband knows nothing about her past. Just as naturally, nothing that Paul discovers keeps him from falling in love with this mysterious woman.

Plot may not be terribly original, but it certainly could have been played for more suspense and passion than it is here. Brisseau hints that he wants to make a socially conscious point about the power that comes only with money and position, and the false respectability that comes with that power. But this doesn't make his slow-paced pic any more animated or involving.

Vartan does as well as she can in a role that is more of an archetype than a character. But even though she works hard at being an alluring femme fatale, she never strikes any sparks with Karyo. Their mutual attraction — if, indeed, it is mutual — must be taken on faith.

Supporting performances (especially Claude Winter's touching bit as Stephane's long-abandoned mother) are fine. Romain Winding's handsome color lensing gives pic a richly burnished look. Too bad there isn't much going on beneath the attractive surface. —*Joe Leydon*

LONDON

OSAKA STORY: A DOCUMENTARY

(BRITISH — DOCU)

A National Film & Television School production. (International sales: NFTS, U.K.) Produced by Ichiro Matsumoto, Toichi Nakata. Directed by Nakata. Camera (16mm, Metrocolor prints), Simon Atkins; editor, Nakata; sound, Nakata, Mike Billing; associate director, Atkins. Reviewed on vidcassette, London, Nov. 22, 1994. (In London Film Festival.) Running time: **77 MIN.**

A deceptively simple docu that starts out as a family portrait but soon develops real teeth, "Osaka Story" is an impressive bow by Japanese-born, Western-based Toichi Nakata, an alum of the U.K.'s National Film & Television School. Drawing material of universal appeal from specifically Asian subject matter, result could well attract cable and specialized Euroweb sales.

Narrated (sometimes not too distinctly) by Nakata himself, film starts as seemingly yet another diary-of-self-discovery by a sibling returning to the nest after a spell abroad. It soon turns out, though, that this is no run-of-the-mill Japanese family.

Nakata's father is, in fact, Korean (traditionally discriminated against in Japan) and, despite having raised a family of seven in Osaka, also has a wife and two kids back in South Korea. Thanks to his success as a moneylender and owner of three pachinko (pinball machine) parlors, the family is well off; but he now hardly speaks to his Japanese wife, has disowned one daughter for marrying a Nipponese, and once disowned his second son for marrying a Korean Moonie.

Surprise of the film is the growing frankness with which family members, including Nakata's long-suffering mother, talk about papasan, on one occasion even when he's in earshot. To his credit, Nakata, though shocked by some of the discoveries, is careful not to villainize his dad, who in interviews is revealed as a rather sad figure, effectively at home in neither Korea nor Japan, which have a long tradition as enemies.

Nakata's quiet, transparent style, with himself on camera much of the time, lugging around sound equipment, builds to some moving moments, notably at a birthday party for his mother and in solo interviews with his parents. Biggest surprise is saved for the end, when the director reveals his true reason for not fulfilling his duties as eldest son by returning home, marrying, having kids and joining the family biz. —*Derek Elley*

NO PETS

A Braddock Films production. (International sales: Braddock Films, Braddock, Pa.) Produced by Tony Buba, M. Heather Hartley. Executive producer, Buba. Directed by Buba. Screenplay, Jim Daniels, from his short story. Camera (color, 16mm), John Rice; editor, John Stuart Bick; sound design, Wayne Gaines; assistant director, Natalka Voslakov; associate producer, Harish Saluja. Reviewed on vidcassette, London, Nov. 22, 1994. (In London Film Festival.) Running time: **71 MIN.**

Eddie Buford	John Amplas
Lorraine Turner	Lori Cardille
B.J.	Larry John Meyers
Fred Turner	Rick Applegate
Professor	Mark Tierno
Caroline	Holly Thuma
Connie	Eve Marie Piccioni

"No Pets" is a likable slice of blue-collar indie filmmaking that lacks the vital spark to propel it into the quality league. Ambling, well-observed portrait of a Pittsburgh factory worker's day-to-day existence reps a developing talent in Pennsylvania-based filmmaker Tony Buba.

Eddie (John Amplas) is an ordinary Joe who boards with his dog in a suburban couple's home, works a metal-pressing machine by day and drinks at the local bar by night. He's unmarried, is halfheartedly studying at a community college, goes to his quarrelsome parents for a haircut and spends a lot of the movie trying to track down a girl, Connie, who came on to him at a wedding party.

Pic has no plot as such, more a series of parallel threads. Strongest of these is Eddie's growing relationship with his sexy landlady, Lorraine (Lori Cardille), a former swinger now married to a lawyer creep. Eddie slowly bonds with her in a series of chats on the porch.

If all this sounds pretty low-key, it is. But Buba never pretends the movie is more than its lead characters' ambitions, all of which are firmly stuck in neutral. Trim running time and minimal technique get by on a quiet strain of humor, easy, natural dialogue and interesting characters, especially a standout perf by Cardille as the espresso-voiced Lorraine, a volcano of repressed sexuality in a nurse's uniform.

Tech credits are fine within low-budget limits. —*Derek Elley*

DON'T GET ME STARTED

(BRITISH-GERMAN)

A British Film Institute release (U.K.) of a BFI/TiMe Medienvertriebs presentation of a Skyline production, in association with Frankfurter Filmproduktion (Frankfurt), with participation of Channel 4 (London), Filmstiftung NRW (Dusseldorf) and Martest Film (Cologne). (International sales: BFI, London.) Produced by Steve Clark-Hall. Executive producers, Ben Gibson, Wolfram Tichy. Co-producer (Germany), Michael Smeaton. Executive in charge of production, Angela Topping. Directed, written by Arthur Ellis. Additional shooting and post-production, Paul Cowan, Martin Walsh. Camera (color), Gil Taylor; editor, Mike Bradsell; music, Roger Bolton; production design, Caroline Amies; art direction, Knuth Loewe; costume design, Peri De Braganca; sound (Dolby), George Richards; fight arranger, Bill Weston; assistant director, Gary White; associate producer, Beate Balser; casting, Marilyn Johnstone. Reviewed at MGM Trocadero 7, London, Oct. 13, 1994. (In London Film Festival; also in Venice Festival — Critics' Week.) Running time: **76 MIN.**

Jack Lane	Trevor Eve
Jerry Hoff	Steven Waddington
Gill Lane	Marion Bailey
Larry Swift	Ralph Brown
Pauline Lewis	Marcia Warren
Barry Lewis	Alan David
Joe Kean	Patrick O'Connell
Alice Kay	Lorna Heilbron

"Don't Get Me Started" is a neat idea on paper that doesn't survive its journey to the screen. Feature bow by British commercials and rockvid director Arthur Ellis about a hitman's unsuccessful attempts to turn over a new leaf in suburbia too often plays like a half-hour short stretched to feature length. Theatrical chances loom equally unsuccessful.

The U.K.-German co-production, with locations in Cologne and Dusseldorf reasonably doubling for London, has had a troubled passage to the screen. Following a disastrous preem in the Cannes market in May '93 in a 98-minute version under the title "Psychotherapy," pic was hastily withdrawn and recut, with additional shooting patched in (supervised by Paul Cowan and Martin Walsh). New version debuted in the Critics' Week at this fall's Venice festival.

At 76 minutes, the movie is a much tighter piece of work, more focused, and benefits from better sound mixing and being relieved of its original deafening score. However, it's still a cute idea that hasn't been fully realized as a feature film.

British TV thesp Trevor Eve plays Jack, who's moved to the U.K. and just started a new marriage and a new job as an insurance salesman. Also, it's almost a year since he quit smoking, and the strain is almost

November 28, 1994 (Cont.)

unbearable whenever friends or colleagues light up.

Jack's desire to quit the leaf and become a "perfect" member of middle-class society slowly emerges as a metaphor for something much darker. Tracked down by investigative journalist Jerry (Steven Waddington), he's exposed as Michael Grillo/Peter Neill, a hit man who may also have murdered his first wife. Jack's scarcely bottled psychosis, which has already led to him killing a work colleague, is put to the ultimate test.

Eve is excellent as the enigmatic Jack, suggesting murky currents lying just below the surface of a buttoned-down personality. Beyond that, though, the pic flounders around with a host of stereotyped supports who add little to the story. Overall tone is also shaky, flirting with both film noir and black comedy but settling down with neither.

Technically, pic is OK but has a low-budget look. —*Derek Elley*

THE FLYING CAMEL
(HAGAMAL HMEOFEF)
(ISRAELI)

A Transfax Film Prods. production. Produced by Marik Rozenbaum. Directed, written by Rami Na'aman. Camera (color), Yoav Kosh; editor, Tovah Asher; music, Shem Tov Levy; art direction, Ariel Roshko. Reviewed at Jerusalem Film Festival, July 4, 1994. (Also in London fest.) Running time: **92 MIN.**
Professor Bauman .... Gidon Zinger
Phares .... Salim Dau
Sister Gina .... Laurence Bouvard
Geula .... Gilat Ankori
With: Gaby Amrani, Moscu Alkalai.
(Hebrew and English dialogue)

This Israeli comedy brings together three symbolic characters — a Jewish prof, an Arab trash collector and a Catholic novitiate nun — and sets their ethnocentricities in motion. First film by Rami Na'aman is an entertaining audience pleaser with festival appeal, given its clear, simpleminded, optimistic rendition of the country's religious conflicts.

Professor Bauman (Gidon Zinger) is a cultivated old historian who takes a keen interest in Bauhaus architecture and furniture. Forced to live in a junkyard shack, Bauman is not pleased to find Phares (Salim Dau), a Palestinian garbage collector, sleeping in his antique bed one day.

Phares has discovered that his father's orange grove was once located on Bauman's run-down property, and doggedly sticks to his moral right to be there.

The arrival of sexy Sister Gina (Laurence Bouvard) in a camper puts a temporary end to their quarreling, as they vie for her attention.

The trio unite to reconstruct a '30s statue of a camel with wings, the symbol of Tel Aviv's renewal at the 1934 Eastern Fair. Idealistic image of Jewish-Arab harmony perfectly reflects the film's liberal credo but, despite fine perfs from Dau and Zinger, the characters are too stereotyped to run deeper than an amusing gag or two. As the would-be missionary who sleeps in the nude, Bouvard is embarrassingly far off-target.

—*Deborah Young*

WOMAN AS THE DEVIL
(LE DEMON AU FEMININ)
(ALGERIAN)

An Etablissement National de Productions Audiovisuelles production. Directed, written by Hafsa Zinai Koudil. Camera (color), A. Messaad; editor, A. Cherigui; music, Safy Boutella; art direction, K. Krim; sound, A. Moulahcene. Reviewed at Amiens Film Festival (competing), France, Nov. 10, 1994. Running time: **84 MIN.**
With: Ahmed Benaissa, Djamila Haddadi, Fatiha Berber, Doudja Achaichi, Said Amrane, Mustapha Kesdarli.

Based on a 1991 incident in Algiers in which a woman was tortured senseless during an exorcism condoned by her husband and son, "Woman as the Devil" has rough edges and overstated passages but emerges as a useful tool for addressing the threat of rampant fundamentalism.

An accomplished novelist and activist for humanitarian causes in her native Algeria, scripter/helmer Hafsa Zinai Koudil lives in the shadow of death threats that necessitated a police escort during her stay at the Amiens fest, where pic shared the Prix du Public.

Pic is subtle but firm in making the essential distinction between followers of Islam, "a religion of love and tolerance," and the faith as appropriated by fanatics bent on seizing absolute control. But the melodramatic pic forgoes shades of gray in conveying its central narrative.

Salima, a schoolteacher, and Ali, an overworked architect, lead modern secular lives with their two young daughters and grown son, Habib. Humorless Habib spends long hours at the mosque, coming home only long enough to declare that head scarves must be worn, profane (i.e. "pop") music must not be played and everyone should engage in constant prayer. Independent-minded Salima suggests Habib approach his faith through getting a job and acting civil.

Ali begins to experience paranoid delusions, hearing voices and seeing visions — depicted via clumsy p.o.v. fantasies — that portray his wife possessed by the devil. Increasingly embroiled in backward teachings that make women the scapegoats for all of society's ills, Ali invites three fanatics into his home to exorcise Salima. The ordeal leaves her mute and paralyzed.

Outraged, Salima's brother brings formal charges. The case makes it to court, but the judge, on orders from shady higher-ups, releases the culprits with a slap on the wrists.

In broad strokes, Koudil shows how discontented youth (nearly 75% of Algeria's population is under 25) can be boondoggled into cultish obedience, and how omnipresent pressures can make rigid doctrine an appealing refuge even for educated males of the professional classes.

Thesps get the job done, with Salima the most three-dimensional character. Blowup from Super-16 to 35mm is muddy, and tech credits are merely adequate, but raw look does not detract from the story.

The deliberately provocative pic was financed by Algeria's national audiovisual production board after a hard-won battle between members of the grant committee. It's more than likely that this sometimes awkward but heartfelt battle cry will remain banned on home turf. —*Lisa Nesselson*

QUEEN AND KING
(REINA Y REY)
(CUBAN-SPANISH-MEXICAN)

An ICAC (Cuba)/Tele Madrid, SGAE, TVC (Spain)/Imcine (Mexico) production. Produced by Avelio Delgado. Directed, written by Julio Garcia Espinosa. Camera (color), Angel Alderefe; music, Pablo Milanes; art direction, Pedro Garcia Espinosa; costume design, Liz Alvarez; sound (UltraStereo), Carlos Fernandez. Reviewed at Amiens Film Festival (competing), France, Nov. 11, 1994. Running time: **90 MIN.**
With: Consuelo Vidal, Capuli, Coralia Veloz, Rogelio Blain.

In "Queen and King," vet Cuban helmer Julio Garcia Espinosa crafts a sweet fable about an elderly woman and her devoted dog in contemporary Havana. Laced with just enough social and political bite concerning daily privations in Cuba, understated pic will be welcome at fests and in Spanish-lingo territories.

Queen (Consuelo Vidal), a retired servant, lives in a spacious house left by her employers when they split for Miami 20 years earlier. A widow, she keeps the place spic 'n' span with the help of her dog, King, who helps her make the bed before accompanying her on fanciful walks to the beach and day-dreaming excursions to an abandoned railway car.

But times are hard. The local butcher no longer has scraps for King, and the wily pooch starts looking elsewhere for sustenance.

Charming comic interludes comment on the social and material realities of trying to sort out one's allegiances and provide for loved ones in today's Cuba. Pic's pleasant score and expressive location lensing augment the tender complicity between the woman and her dog. Vidal's sterling central performance won her a best actor trophy at the Amiens festival. —*Lisa Nesselson*

THE BAPTISM
(LE BAPTEME)
(GEORGIAN-FRENCH)

A Gruzia Film Studios (Georgia)/Studio Noe, Les Films du Rivage (France) production, with participation of French Ministry of Foreign Affairs and the CNC. (International sales: Les Films du Rivage, Paris.) Produced by Marc Ruscart, Nodar Managadze. Directed by Managadze. Screenplay, Managadze, Sosso Ramichvili, David Djavakhichvili. Camera (color), Victor Pischalnikov; music, Gogui Tchlaidze; art direction/costumes, Guia Laperadze; sound, Zourab Padaraya. Reviewed at Montpellier Festival of Mediterranean Cinema, France, Oct. 25, 1994. Running time: **74 MIN.**
With: Georgi Machaidze, David Djavakhichvili, Nana Kiknadze, Mimi Gabrichidze.

Pleasantly heavy on atmosphere but veiled in content, "The Baptism" is a stylish, visually arresting tale of a hunky young profiteer who gets more than he bargained for when he begins to spy on a middle-aged blind man. Moody, intriguing pic is a natural for fests and specialized playdates.

Georgi, a handsome and shiftless no-goodnik, steals from his well-heeled dad and adoring girlfriends when he's not cruising with his drug-addled friends. But once he becomes obsessed with the routine of a self-sufficient blind man named Irakli, Georgi spends long stretches lurking in his apartment.

Georgi clandestinely observes Irakli's dart games and dinner parties with other blind men. Then a strange transference begins when Georgi is secretly beside Irakli during a solar eclipse.

Pic sustains an ominous mood, nicely reinforced by music and decor. Post-synched dialogue prevents pic from seeming completely polished, but exotic locales compensate somewhat. Arty lensing, sprinkled with reflections, flamboyant camera angles and upside-down shots, suits the off-kilter tale of a flawed protagonist tempting fate.
—*Lisa Nesselson*

VISIT OF THE PRESIDENT

(ZEYARET EL-SAYED EL-RAIS)

(EGYPTIAN)

A Rady Keler release. (International sales: Mounir Rady, Cairo.) Produced by Rady Keler, Maher Rady. Directed by Mounir Rady. Screenplay, Bechir Eldik, Ahmed Metwaly. Camera (color), Maher Rady; editor, Ahmed Metwaly; music, Ragueh Daoud; art direction, Salah Marei. Reviewed at Montpellier Festival of Mediterranean Cinema, France, Oct. 26, 1994. Running time: **115 MIN.**
With: Mahmoud Abdel Aziz, Nagah El-Mogui, Ahmed Rateb, Hayatem, Gihane Nasr, Hassan Al-Asmar, Youssef Daoud.

Spirited ensemble playing and local color galore make "Visit of the President" an engaging, ultimately bittersweet account of a small Egyptian village's frantic preparations for a whistle-stop visit from the U.S. president. The comic and tragic implications of U.S. aid are explored with a light touch, making this a good candidate for social studies and history classes after it travels the fest route.

In El-Dahryia in the Nile delta, local council president Allalah (Mahmoud Abdel Aziz) has reason to believe that the Egyptian and U.S. presidents will pause in his humble village en route from Cairo to Alexandria by train. When the council decides that only pregnant women will be eligible to receive food aid, frenzied mating results. (Rumor has it that an American device can determine if a woman is pregnant the very night she has sex.)

Hammy but entertaining array of loquacious characters, including the local doctor, his zaftig assistant, the barber and the mayor, bicker and scheme as the great day approaches. Village beautification — in which, for example, a modest food stand becomes a "supermarket" — builds to fever pitch.

Photography and editing possess verve. Jaunty musical interludes feel tacked on.   —*Lisa Nesselson*

MAX

(CANADIAN)

An Astral Films release (Canada) of an Apple Pie Pictures production, with the participation of Telefilm Canada and British Columbia Film. (International sales: Norstar, Toronto.) Produced by Charles Wilkinson, Tobias Schliessler, Armand Leo. Directed, written by Wilkinson. Camera (color) Schliessler; editor, Gary Zubeck; music, Graeme Coleman; art direction, David Birdsall; associate producers, Tom Lightburn, Stephen Johnston; assistant director, James Marshall. Reviewed at World Film Festival, Montreal, Aug. 23, 1994. (Also in Toronto, Vancouver fests.) Running time: **94 MIN.**

Andy Blake	R.H. Thomson
Jayne Blake	Denise Crosby
Jayne's Dad	Walter Dalton
Doctor Kaye	Garwin Sanford
Earl	Don Davis
Max	Fabio Wilkinson
Sophie	Colleen Rennison

Vancouver-based helmer Charles Wilkinson's "Max" is a family drama that takes a predictable look at the transformation of former '60s idealists into '90s yuppies. Film, which opens Dec. 2 in Canada, will likely have a short life span in theaters before moving to the small screen.

Andy (R. H. Thomson) and Jayne Blake (Denise Crosby) are a thirty-something couple who used to be VW van-driving, card-carrying hippies but have now settled down in the Vancouver 'burbs with good jobs, two kids and lots of dashed ideals.

Then their son Max is diagnosed with a rare immune disorder and given six months to live.

Medics mention in passing that Max's blood disease is probably due to something toxic in the environment, but they don't go into details. It's just one of several key dramatic moments that is not properly explained in the script.

In a rage, Andy packs up the car and drags his family along to start up a new life in rural B.C., far from the insidious influence of the big city.

It's back to the farm '90s-style, with Andy trying to re-create his hippie youth and provide a natural cure for Max in the process. His wife isn't so sure about all this, and much of the dramatic tension derives from her attempts to tone down his increasingly fanatical idealism.

Thomson does an admirable job of capturing Andy's descent into near madness, but it's Fabio Wilkinson, the helmer's 3-year-old son, who steals most of the scenes with a charming presence that helps lighten the somewhat overwrought melodrama of his father's writing.

Tech credits are fine throughout.
—*Brendan Kelly*

NELL

A 20th Century Fox release of an Egg Pictures production. Produced by Renee Missel, Jodie Foster. Coproducer, Graham Place. Directed by Michael Apted. Screenplay, William Nicholson, Mark Handley, based on Handley's play "Idioglossia." Camera (Rank Film Labs color; Panavision widescreen), Dante Spinotti; editor, Jim Clark; music, Mark Isham; production design, Jon Hutman; art direction, Tim Galvin; set decoration, Samara Hutman; costume design, Susan Lyall; sound (Dolby), Chris Newman; assistant director, David Sardi; casting, Linda Lowy. Reviewed at 20th Century Fox Studios, L.A., Nov. 29, 1994. MPAA Rating: PG-13. Running time: **113 MIN.**

Nell	Jodie Foster
Jerome Lovell	Liam Neeson
Paula Olsen	Natasha Richardson
Alexander Paley	Richard Libertini
Todd Peterson	Nick Searcy
Mary Peterson	Robin Mullins
Billy Fisher	Jeremy Davies
Don Fontana	O'Neal Compton

A cocoon of somber self-seriousness envelopes some fine performances and intelligent craftsmanship in "Nell." The unusual but somewhat dramatically proscribed story of a young woman raised apart from civilization in the North Carolina backwoods, the picture seems rather too aware of its studied artfulness and sensitivity as it dramatizes the effort of two doctors to establish a connection with the outcast, who speaks her own language. Jump-started by prestige stars Jodie Foster and Liam Neeson, the Fox release should enjoy a certain success with audiences seeking serious fare.

Working in his semi-anthropological "Gorillas in the Mist" mode, director Michael Apted moves deep into the Smoky Mountains to unfold the story of Nell (Foster), who at the outset is left alone in a remote lakeside cabin when her mother dies. As is soon explained, Nell speaks in a unique way due to her mother's stroke-induced speech impediments.

Nell is fortunate in being found by an independent-minded doctor, Jerome Lovell (Neeson), who takes to observing her secretly when he realizes that she's not the same around strangers. On her own, Nell is taken to almost ecstatic reveries of emotional swooning and impulsive movement, but becomes belligerent and babbles incomprehensibly when approached.

Naturally, the medical authorities at Charlotte University want to hospitalize this prize specimen for extended observation and treatment, but Lovell manages to win a stay of three months. But no sooner does he pitch a tent near Nell's cabin than psychologist Paula Olsen (Natasha Richardson) turns up in a houseboat to do her own monitoring of Nell's behavior. Stemming their competitiveness, the two enter into

December 5, 1994 (Cont.)

a makeshift collaboration, with Lovell, the only person Nell trusts, interacting with her and trying to crack her language while Olsen tapes it all via remote video.

Although the delivery of the invented language has its own fascination, and becomes tantalizingly more understandable (and seemingly closer to normal English) as the story progresses, Foster's performance relies in great measure upon techniques of movement, dance and mime. Nowhere is this more apparent than in some of the film's most haunting sequences, which have the two visitors spying on her while she cavorts nude in Isadora Duncan fashion on rocks and in the water under the moonlight (but Foster's ultra-trim aerobicized body seems a bit unrealistic). Dante Spinotti's precisely calibrated, silhouetted lensing plays a crucial role in making these scenes come off.

As the two doctors patiently strive to allay Nell's fears of people, daylight and, ultimately, "the big bad world," they also make tiny strides in breaking down the barriers to a possible connection between them. Lovell clearly has spent his life running away, first from his native land, then from big-city practice, and is placing all his chips on the prospect of succeeding at being Nell's teacher and protector. In fits of scarcely concealed jealous anger, Olsen accuses Lovell of having unnatural motives in his feelings for the emotionally needy Nell. She must relax her regimented, learned knowledge to accommodate the singular challenges of dealing with Nell's case.

Forced out of seclusion by prying media, the doctors must ultimately take Nell to town, where she becomes an inert zombie in the hospital. Infuriated, Lovell spirits her out, and it all ends in a somewhat improbable courtroom sequence designed to demonstrate the wisdom of innocence.

Part of the problem with stories of so-called primitive spirits being exposed to "civilization" is that the dramatic trajectory is almost unavoidably predictable, as are the emotions one is expected to feel: There is the wonder of discovering such a being at all, the excitement of finding a person in a raw state, followed by the inevitable sense of sadness and even tragedy as the individual is contaminated by the poison of society, its rules and structures. Invariably, the debate over "artificial" education vs. "natural" instinct rears its head in some form, with a prejudice toward the latter almost always prevailing.

"Nell" can't avoid this, of course, but fortunately, the script by William Nicholson and Mark Handley, based on the latter's play, generally sidesteps overly didactic melodrama. All the same, the film bogs

down a bit in the late stages when resolution is required, when the sense of excitement and discovery is supplanted by a kind of resignation and release.

Foster's Nell represents a one-of-a-kind change of pace for the actress, whose company produced the film, and she delivers with full credibility except for the courthouse climax. But the major weight of the film falls upon Neeson's broad shoulders, and he carries it splendidly, moving the film along while juggling certainties and doubt, hope and apprehension. Richardson does as well as anyone could in a relatively functional, less well-written role.

Outstanding among the film's subtleties is a virtually unspoken connection between Nell and the local sheriff's disturbed wife, nicely etched by Robin Mullins.

Apted's naturalistic approach is insightful and awkward by turns, but a strong atmosphere comes through thanks to the striking mountain setting and Jon Hutman's rustic production design.

—*Todd McCarthy*

DISCLOSURE

A Warner Bros. release of a Baltimore Pictures/Constant c production. Produced by Barry Levinson, Michael Crichton. Executive producer, Peter Giuliano. Co-producer, Andrew Wald. Directed by Levinson. Screenplay, Paul Attanasio, based on the novel by Crichton. Camera (Technicolor; Panavision widescreen), Anthony Pierce-Roberts; editor, Stu Linder; music, Ennio Morricone; production design, Neil Spisak; art direction, Richard Yanez-Toyon, Charles William Breen; set decoration, Garrett Lewis; costume design, Gloria Gresham; sound (Dolby), Steve Cantamessa; special visual effects, Industrial Light & Magic; visual effects supervisor, Eric Brevig; associate producers, Patricia Churchill, James Flamberg; assistant director, Kate Davey; casting, Ellen Chenoweth. Reviewed at Warner Bros. Studios, Burbank, Nov. 28, 1994. MPAA Rating: R. Running time: **127 MIN.**

Tom Sanders .... Michael Douglas
Meredith Johnson .... Demi Moore
Bob Garvin .... Donald Sutherland
Susan Hendler .... Caroline Goodall
Philip Blackburn .... Dylan Baker
Catherine Alvarez .... Roma Maffia
Marc Lewyn .... Dennis Miller
Ben Heller .... Allan Rich
Don Cherry .... Nicholas Sadler
Stephanie
 Kaplan .... Rosemary Forsyth
Mary Anne Hunter ..... Suzie Plakson
Cindy Chang .... Jacqueline Kim
John Conley Jr. ....Joe Urla

"Disclosure" is polite pulp fiction, a reasonable rendition of potentially risible material. Fueled by the high-voltage star power of **Michael Douglas and Demi Moore**, this lavishly appointed screen version of Michael Crich-

ton's page-turner about sexual harassment and corporate power has what it takes to deliver plenty of year-end bounty into Warner Bros.' coffers, although it might have been even more commercial had it been more shamelessly trashy.

The novel was an attempt at a zeitgeist grabber, with the twist that a man accused of sexual harassment in the workplace is, in fact, the "victim" himself. Although this element reps an important plot point, the story actually falls rather easily into the tradition of corporate melodramas sparked by manipulation, power plays, deceit and greed. The sex element is ever-present, but ultimately becomes something of a secondary issue to the computerese and techno-babble that is Crichton's first language.

In this sense, those expecting another "Fatal Attraction" or "Indecent Proposal" might be somewhat disappointed by director Barry Levinson's refusal to emphasize the sleaziest elements of the story and to work the audience up into a primal emotional frenzy. On the other hand, those dreading that approach might be pleasantly surprised to find a tolerably involving story of office intrigue told in the high Hollywood manner.

Paul Attanasio's dense, carefully constructed script swiftly presents Tom Sanders (Michael Douglas) as a respectably reformed '60s type who's gone the yuppie, corporate route but still wears longish hair and a backpack. Cozily ensconced a ferry ride away from Seattle with his lawyer wife (Caroline Goodall) and two kids, Tom is fully expecting a promotion at his high-tech firm, DigiCom, now that a big merger is imminent. But he's laid low by the news that boss Bob Garvin (Donald Sutherland) instead decides to bring in outsider Meredith Johnson (Demi Moore) for the big job.

In his free-swinging single days, Tom had a hot and heavy thing with Meredith, which she seems intent upon reviving during a wine-enhanced private evening meeting. The Big Scene takes place a half-hour in, as Meredith gets Tom to give her a massage as a prelude to quite literally devouring him sexually. He keeps saying no while his body is saying yes, but when he abruptly retreats from fully consummating the act, Meredith, her body fairly popping out of her black lingerie, erupts in full fury, promising a wrathful vengeance on her fleeing ex-lover and professional underling.

The next day, Meredith drops the bombshell, claiming that Tom sexually harassed her at their meeting. Offered a transfer to Texas as a way of avoiding unpleasantness, Tom instantly engages a smart, feisty woman law-

yer (Roma Maffia) while issuing faintly heard denials and threats of a lawsuit, which Garvin wants to avoid so as not to upset his $100 million merger.

The stickiest part for Tom is telling his wife, which one of his co-workers does instead, and the film's worst written, most unconvincing scenes are those in which Tom tries to explain it all to his mate.

On Wednesday in the Monday-to-Friday time frame, the parties move into private mediation before a judge, where the principals regurgitate, in clinical detail, their versions of what and who went down in Meredith's office. As the film is told entirely from Tom's p.o.v., he tells the truth according to the way the encounter has been shown, while Meredith flagrantly lies, playing the victim and the one with cause to be afraid.

When Garvin sees that Tom is effectively standing his ground, he offers to let him stay at Digi-Com, with a bonus thrown in for good measure. But an E-mail message from "A Friend" warns him, "Nothing is as it seems," and only through the marvels of high-tech communication and virtual reality experiences is Tom able to combat the high-stakes warfare that his adversaries initiate in the endgame before the merger.

In typical Crichton fashion, it's a story designed to push the audience's buttons in elemental ways and, like "Rising Sun," weighted to make people's blood boil about the inequities at large today in the big bad business world. Levinson and Attanasio don't ignore the basics of the tale, but don't indulge them either, subjectively approaching Tom's character to maximize dramatic involvement and treating the most explosive aspects of the story more rationally than emotionally. This makes for a cooler film than the one that, say, Adrian Lyne might have made from the same material, but one that's also a bit more dramatically credible given the overall concocted feel.

Back in the familiar "Fatal Attraction"-"Basic Instinct" arena with a predatory female, Douglas is very good indeed as the put-upon man forced to play hardball for the first time with the big boys and girls. Moore's dragon lady is strictly a one-dimensional creation defined by manipulativeness and greed, as no attempt is made to delve into her psychology, but her ripe black-widow looks and malevolent demeanor work perfectly for the intent of the film.

Sutherland and Goodall are good in the largest supporting roles, while many other secondary parts have been exceedingly well cast and acted, notably by Maffia as Tom's resourceful attorney, Dylan Baker as Garvin's two-faced hatchet man,

Dennis Miller and Nicholas Sadler as Tom's techo-geniuses and Allan Rich as Meredith's old-pro lawyer.

Production designer Neil Spisak's main office set is a splendid creation that gives the film much of its character; it's got the look of an old space completely renovated for high-tech purposes, although one could argue that its open, all-glass expanse creates an utterly impossible setting for sexual harassment, or secrets of any kind. Anthony Pierce-Roberts' lensing of atmospheric Seattle locations is lustrous, Stu Linder's editing is clamped down tight, and Ennio Morricone's score builds tension wherever possible.
—*Todd McCarthy*

TRAPPED IN PARADISE

A 20th Century Fox release of a Jon Davison/George Gallo production. Produced by Davison, Gallo. Executive producer, David Permut. Co-producers, Ellen Erwin, David Coatsworth. Directed, written by Gallo. Camera (Deluxe color; Panavision widescreen), Jack N. Green; editor, Terry Rawlings; music, Robert Folk; production design, Bob Ziembicki; art direction, Gregory P. Keen; set decoration, Gord Sim; costume design, Mary E. McLeod; sound (Dolby), Bruce Carwardine; assistant director, Martin Walters; second unit director/stunt coordinator, Glenn R. Wilder; second unit camera, Harald Ortenburger; casting, Donna Isaacson. Reviewed at the United Artists North Theater, Santa Fe, N.M., Nov. 17, 1994. MPAA Rating: PG-13. Running time: **112 MIN.**
Bill Firpo	Nicolas Cage
Dave Firpo	Jon Lovitz
Alvin Firpo	Dana Carvey
Ed Dawson	John Ashton
Sarah Collins	Madchen Amick
Clifford Anderson	Donald Moffat
Shaddus Peyser	Richard Jenkins
Ma Firpo	Florence Stanley
Hattie Anderson	Angela Paton
Vic Mazzucci	Vic Manni
Caesar Spinoza	Frank Pesce
Chief Burnell	Sean McCann
Deputy Timmy Burnell	Paul Lazar
Clovis Minor	John Bergantine
Dick Anderson	Sean O'Bryan
Father Ritter	Richard B. Shull

Whatever else one can say about it, "Trapped in Paradise" is undoubtedly the first movie in which a horsedrawn sleigh is chased by a cop car on Christmas Eve. An agreeable Middle American comedy intent upon reviving oldfashioned virtues in both filmmaking and real life, George Gallo's second feature doesn't serve up the big yocks needed to make it a breakout sleeper, but has enough in the way of sentiment and goofy situational predicaments to put it over as a serviceable family holiday attraction.

The film harks back to a time in life and movies when small-town America represented the ultimate in cozy togetherness, warmth and security.

In such a context, selfishness assumes the dimensions of a mortal sin, and what could be more selfish than crime for personal gain? This is where the Brothers Firpo come in.

An ungainly trio from New York, these boys, although well into their 30s, have yet to acquire any social or career smarts, especially Dave (Jon Lovitz), a congenital liar, and Alvin (Dana Carvey), a helpless kleptomaniac.

Bill (Nicolas Cage) is making an effort to go straight, but when he picks up his brothers upon their release from the pen he's drawn straight back into their harebrained schemes. After a skirmish with the cops, the bozos land in Paradise, Pa., where the annual Christmas Eve Winterfest is getting under way.

But they may as well have traveled by time machine as by stolen car, as the locals seem to be living in a Frank Capra or Leo McCarey film from the 1930s or 1940s. Upon spying $275,000 being deposited in the bank, the Firpos don their ski masks and make off with the loot.

Film's central gag is that the boys simply can't make their getaway due to the overwhelming kindness of the inhabitants. Despite mounting circumstantial evidence, the townsfolk just can't bring themselves to believe that these bumbling simpletons, who are criminals of the "Home Alone" school, could possibly have pulled such a heinous crime, especially when the money was destined for the church.

While being pursued by some dense deputies and a couple of escaped cons, the hapless brothers try to leave town by car, Greyhound, rowboat and sleigh, but keep being "rescued" in spite of themselves, even to the point of being invited to Christmas Eve dinner at the unwitting banker's home.

It comes as absolutely no surprise when everything gets sorted out to general satisfaction even if, at nearly two hours, it takes a little longer than necessary.

But Gallo and his three leading men keep things merrily buoyant most of the time. Cage's character is eternally split between his desire to keep the loot and determination to do the right thing, Lovitz's Dave is a study in exasperation at his brother's indecisiveness, and Alvin, with Carvey looking like Gary Oldman's diminutive sibling, is the loose cannon, forever foraging around and, like Harpo Marx, pulling things out of his coat.

The politics of the piece, which can hardly be ignored, can be read either as a charmingly idealized portrait of an America that probably existed more in people's imaginations than in real life or as an unrealistic impulse to turn back the clock.

One area where the picture gets the short end in the inevitable comparison with the old Hollywood is in supporting performances. Studio-era films were rife with great contract players who only had to show up onscreen to conjure up an array of aspects of, and attitudes toward, society. The community here pales in comparison to those on view in nearly any film produced during the period "Trapped in Paradise" is meant to evoke.

Ironically, pic was actually shot in Canada, and mostly at night in what looks to have been quite frigid conditions. Tech contributions are pro.
—*Todd McCarthy*

FELIDAE
(GERMAN — ANIMATED)

A Senator release (in Germany) of a Senator Film/Trickcompany/Fontana production. Produced by Hanno Huth. Directed by Michael Schaack. Screenplay, Martin Kluger, Stefaan Schieder, Akif Pirincci, based on the novel by Pirincci. Camera (color), Werner Loss; editor, Klaus Basler; music, Anne Dudley; art direction, Desmond Downes; sound, Dolby; character design, Paul Bolger; layout design, Armen Melkonian; direction assistant, Veit Vollmer; animation director, Bernie Denk; layout supervisor, Mark Marren; dialogue director, Angelika Schaack; Reviewed at Film Palast, Berlin, Oct. 19, 1994. Running time: **81 MIN.**

Voices:	
Francis	Ulrich Turkur
Blaubart	Mario Adorf
Pascal/	
Claudandus	Klaus Maria Brandauer
Kong	Wolfgang Hess
Jesaja	Helge Schneider
Archie	Uwe Ochsenknecht
Deep Purple	Michael Habeck
Felicitas	Mona Seefried

Though it doesn't fit into any existing category of toon, "Felidae" is one of the best animated films to come out of Germany, and certainly the most daring. The theatrical potential of this adult thriller about a master race of cats plotting to take over the world is limited only by the imagination of marketing departments. B.O. results in its native land have been potent.

The cats here aren't wisecracking upright-walkers as in Ralph Bakshi's X-rated "Fritz the Cat" (1972) nor cuddly and chaste anthropomorphs as in Disney's "The Aristocats" (1970). These felines prowl, fight, urinate, have sex and otherwise come as close as possible to real animals. The only difference is they speak a human language and solve mysteries.

"Felidae" (Latin for "cats") is based on a 1989 bestselling novel by young Bonn-based writer Akif Pirincci. Seriously written, and angled not just at cat lovers, the result was a fast-paced, engaging adult thriller that caught on with the college crowd. Book has since been translated into 14 languages, with total sales of 1.5 million copies. Pirincci has also penned several follow-ups.

Pic tells the tale of a sharp-witted male cat named Francis who investigates a series of murders. The victims tend to be cats in heat, a fact that soon leads Francis to a plot to force-breed a new race of super-cats to take over the world from humans. The females are allowed to breed only with the best males; inferior male suitors are killed when they get too close.

The infernal plot, which starts out in Sherlock Holmes vein and ends in James Bond style (the evil cat mastermind has even learned to use a computer), touches on many major issues in Germany today: race, euthanasia, the Holocaust, experiments on animals, sects and even sly bits of S&M.

Several scenes are surprisingly explicit. One of Francis' nightmares evolves into a brutal symphony of tortured cat bodies reminiscent of emaciated prisoners in Nazi death camps. Coupling is also bluntly animalistic: When Francis is beckoned by a nameless feline *fatale* in heat, the ensuing scene is pure barnyard sex, including a feline bite to the neck and concluding orgasmic howl.

Plotwise, however, 81 minutes of screen time is not enough for the complex yarn, with some characters and twists getting lost in the confusion. Producers also skimped a little on the charming personality of their hero.

Francis, suavely voiced by the multifaceted Ulrich Turkur, is intelligent and articulate, closer to Cary Grant than Sylvester Stallone. But more of his alert observations and sly comments (like calling his obese human owner a "can-opener") would have been welcome. Francis' rough-and-tumble sidekick, Blaubart (Bluebeard), voiced by one of Germany's best character actors, Mario Adorf, makes a lovably vulgar, endearingly hedonistic buddy.

Other voices are not as inspired. Well-known thesp Klaus Maria Brandauer, as Francis' mentor, Pascal, mumbles away in a by-the-numbers performance. Voice cameos by film star Uwe Ochsenknecht and star comedian Helge Schneider are never more than just that.

Still, all technical and animation credits are superb. Though some of the cats appear a little too exotic or mutated, their look fits the characters well. In most cases, familiar Disney-like cliches are avoided, giving the film a non-American look.
—*Eric Hansen*

HIGHLANDER III: THE SORCERER

(CANADIAN-FRENCH-BRITISH)

An Entertainment Film Distributors (U.K.)/Miramax (U.S.) release of a Peter S. Davis/William Panzer presentation of a Transfilm/Lumiere/Falling Cloud production. Produced by Claude Leger. Executive producers, Guy Collins, Charles L. Smiley. Co-producers, Jean Cazes, Eric Altmayer, James Daly. Line producer, Mychele Boudrios. Directed by Andy Morahan. Screenplay, Paul Ohl, from a screen story by Panzer and Brad Mirman, based on characters created by Gregory Widen. Camera (color, widescreen), Steven Chivers; editor, Yves Langlois; additional editing, Brett Sullivan, Mark Alchin; music, J. Peter Robinson; production design, Gilles Aird, Ben Morahan; sound, Dolby; special visual effects, Brian Johnson; special effects supervisor, Louis Craig; stunt supervisor, Dave McKeown; associate producer, Stephen Key; assistant director, Pedro Gandol; second unit director, Pierre Magny. Reviewed at MGM Ewell, London, Nov. 28, 1994. Running time: **99 MIN.**
Connor MacLeod/
  Russell Nash ... Christopher Lambert
Kane .... Mario Van Peebles
Alex Johnson/
  Sarah .... Deborah Unger
Nakano .... Mako
Stenn .... Mark Neufeld
  With: Raoul Trujillo.

An unbelievably trashy meltdown of the tartan warrior franchise, "Highlander III: The Sorcerer" checks in as a breakneck, roller-coaster genre ride that's brainless fodder for undiscriminating auds. Despite a 1995 copyright date, this Canadian-French-British co-production got fast theatrical playoff in Blighty starting Nov. 25, without advance press previews.

Pic starts with a 15-minute, "Conan"-like prologue in which evil warrior Kane (Mario Van Peebles) surprises Connor MacLeod (Christopher Lambert) and his teacher Nakano (Mako) at the latter's Japanese lair inside Mt. Niri. After decapitating Nakano, Kane and his two sidekicks are buried under the collapsing mountain, and Nakano's super powers pass instead to Connor.

Fast-forward 400 years to 1994, and no sooner has Yank archaeologist Alex (Deborah Unger) flown in to verify some artifacts that could confirm the site of the legendary mountain than Kane breaks out and sets off in search of Connor, killing one of his own sidekicks to get a surge of super power.

Spotting the special effects on the horizon while riding in the Moroccan desert with his adopted son, Connor hightails it to New York to work out what on Earth is going on. He's promptly gunned down by some muggers and locked up in a psycho ward.

While Alex analyzes a scrap of 400-year-old tartan, Connor breaks out and decapitates Kane's other side-kick, getting his own fix of super power. An amazingly smart N.Y. cop who remembers similar events "eight years ago" (year of the first pic's release) realizes Connor must be in town and tracks him down under his modern alias, antique dealer Russell Nash.

Kane also finds Connor and, after a trapeze sword fight that ends with Connor's blade shattered, he morphs into a bird and flies off. Meanwhile, Alex gives Connor a severe case of the flashbacks, as she reminds him of his second wife, Sarah, circa the French Revolution.

Connor beetles off to the Scottish highlands, "where it all began," forges a new sword, is tracked down by Alex, and finally makes it with her in a brief T&A sequence. Final showdown has all parties (plus Connor's son) flying into Newark and dueling it out in a deserted N.J. refinery.

Given there's enough material here for a four-hour miniseries, it's hardly surprising the plot jumps more lights than a runaway ambulance. Lumbered with Lambert's largely incomprehensible accent (not helped by an indistinct soundtrack), British video director Andy Morahan wisely keeps dialogue pared to the bone and lets his five separate units (in Canada, Morocco, Scotland, France and New York) and f/x team get on with the job.

Acting is video caliber, ranging from Van Peebles' manic hamming as the nose-ringed baddie to Unger's straighter playing of the double role of Brit Sarah and Yank Alex. Lambert remains charmlessly wooden throughout.

Color ranges from sharp and attractive in the Scottish and Moroccan scenes to often cheesy or ruddy elsewhere. Effects are OK but repetitive, and scoring veers wildly between mock-heroic orchestral to deafening hard rock. —*Derek Elley*

THE SEPARATION
(LA SEPARATION)
(FRENCH)

An AMLF release (France) of a Claude Berri presentation of a Renn Prods./France 2 Cinema/DA Films/CMV Prods. production, with participation of Canal Plus. Produced by Berri. Executive producer, Pierre Grunstein. Directed by Christian Vincent. Screenplay, Dan Franck, Vincent, based on Franck's novel. Camera (color), Denis Lenoir; editor, Francois Ceppi; art direction, Christian Vallerin; costume design, Sylvie Gautrelet; sound, Claude Bertrand, Jean-Paul Loublier; casting, Frederique Moidon. Reviewed at 14 Juillet Odeon Cinema, Paris, Nov. 28, 1994. Running time: **85 MIN.**
Anne .... Isabelle Huppert
Pierre .... Daniel Auteuil
Victor .... Jerome Deschamps
Claire .... Karin Viard
Laurence .... Laurence Lerel

Two of the finest Gallic thesps of their generation, Isabelle Huppert and Daniel Auteuil, give outstanding performances in "The Separation" as a couple whose relationship disintegrates over three months. Their characters, however, are such self-absorbed ciphers that it's likely few offshore viewers beyond hardcore Francophiles will care. This third feature by director Christian Vincent, whose bow, "La Discrete," was a surprise hit back in 1990, plays like sub-Cassavetes on Quaaludes.

Anne (Huppert) and Pierre (Auteuil) live together in Paris and are parents of a 15-month-old boy, whom Pierre videotapes as part of his ongoing diary. Anne goes off to an unspecified job every day, and illustrator Pierre works on a children's book. They frequently socialize with friends Victor and Claire, who provide comic relief as bumbling, leftover student radicals who are romantically involved but live apart.

Pierre senses something is bothering Anne, and one day she offhandedly announces she's fallen in love with another guy. She doesn't see why this should be hurtful to her current mate, or awkward for their home life, and proceeds to date her new (unseen) love interest while Pierre quietly goes to pieces.

As the title indicates, they eventually call it quits. Pierre, who's done nothing that could be construed as "wrong," loses his mate and his son. The end.

Gallic crix were divided over whether the pic, from a novel by Dan Franck, is a brilliant portrait of contemporary life or another superfluous entry in the intimate "look-ma-I'm-suffering" tradition.

Lots of lengthy close-up two-shots give the uncomfortable impression of eavesdropping on private exchanges. But as the pair aren't given to talking about their problems, all their emotions remain cloaked in reasonableness, with silences and twitches taking the place of insightful dialogue.

Despite a thin plot, Huppert and Auteuil elevate the material to an often riveting plane. Auteuil is outstanding as Pierre, and Huppert, who's cornered the market in smug and selfish, conveys these qualities with beauty and economy.

Occasional extracts from Glenn Gould performing Bach's Goldberg Variations are the only music in the pic.
—*Lisa Nesselson*

U.S. GO HOME
(FRENCH)

A La Sept/Arte, IMA Prods., SFP Prod. production, in association with Sony Music Entertainment (France). (International sales: M5, Paris.) Produced by Georges Benayoun, Paul Rozenberg. Executive producers, Francoise Guglielmi, Elisabeth Deviosse, Yannick Casanova. Directed by Claire Denis. Screenplay, Denis, Anne Wiazemsky. Camera (color), Agnes Godard; editor, Dominique Auvray; music, Yarol; art direction, Arnaud de Moleron; costume design, Rosine Venin; sound, Herve Chauvel; series artistic director, Chantal Poupaud. Reviewed at Turin Intl. Young Cinema Festival, Nov. 20, 1994. Running time: **68 MIN.**
Martine .... Alice Houri
Marlene .... Jessica Tharaud
Alain .... Gregoire Colin
G.I. .... Vincent Gallo

In "U.S. Go Home," Claire Denis brings both toughness and tenderness to bear on the potentially touchy scenario of three teens determined to bid farewell to their virginity. Though it was made for French TV, this warmly satisfying spin along the tortuous path of adolescence is a small jewel with more than enough sparkle for bigscreen showcasing via specialized theatrical distribution.

The film is part of IMA Prods.' "Tous les Garcons et les Filles de Leur Age" series (for Euro cultural web Arte) conceived by former publicist Chantal Poupaud. Nine directors were each commissioned to make a film about teenagers, set in the period of their own youth. A party, and a soundtrack bulging with chart successes of the day, are central to each pic. The series begins chronologically with Andre Techine's 1962-set "Wild Reeds" (premiered last spring at Cannes) and wraps with Olivier Dahan's "Brothers," set in 1990.

Taking place in 1965, Denis' film clocks less than 24 hours in the lives of two midteens, Martine and Marlene (Alice Houri, Jessica Tharaud), and the former's slightly

December 5, 1994 (Cont.)

older brother, Alain (Gregoire Colin). The kids are stuck in a nowhere town that's close enough to Paris to make it tantalizing but far enough away to keep it out of reach.

Via unexplicit, affectionate observation, Denis and co-scripter Anne Wiazemsky create likable, believable characters out of the teen trio as they prepare for a hot night out. During the girls' pre-party makeup session, Martine pledges to get herself deflowered, while upstairs (in one of the pic's most memorable and audaciously extended sequences), Alain dances alone in his room like a tightly coiled sexual spring.

The party brings a swift, almost brutal change of mood as vivid splashes of color against pallid suburbia give way to alluring semi-darkness and some serious making out, splendidly shot by Agnes Godard, whose clinging camera gets determinedly in on the heavy petting.

Martine, a cruelly humbled wallflower, is soothed later in an affectingly sweet moment, when Alain consoles her with an almost sexual embrace. He in turn has been somewhat wounded by an abortive bedroom foray with Marlene.

The final act brings a further about-face in mood. Despite local anti-American feeling, Martine accepts a ride home from a Yank soldier (Vincent Gallo) stationed at a nearby air base. Her cockiness quickly returns in a beautiful sequence in which desire slowly begins to flicker in the lonely, initially uptight soldier as the car travels underneath an atmospheric wash of ghostly trees and sky.

Dialogue is fresh and unembellished, and Denis' acute directorial judgment is echoed to perfection by the remarkable young cast, especially by Houri, who has no previous acting experience. The stellar selection of '60s tunes provides additional pleasures, not least among them the Shangri-Las' hit "Leader of the Pack," sung in French as "Le Chef de la bande." —David Rooney

PEACE AND LOVE
(PAIX ET AMOUR)
(FRENCH — 16mm)

A La Sept/Arte, IMA Prods., SFP Prod. production, in association with Sony Music Entertainment (France). Produced by Georges Benayoun, Paul Rozenberg. Executive producers, Francoise Guglielmi, Elisabeth Deviosse, Yannick Casanova. Directed by Laurence Ferreira Barbosa. Screenplay, Barbosa, Stephane Touitou. Camera (color, 16mm), Antoine Heberle; editors, Yann Dedet, Nathalie Hubert; music, Yarol; art direction, Yves Fournier; sound, Herve Chauvel; series artistic director, Chantal Poupaud. Reviewed at Turin Intl. Young Cinema Festival, Nov. 23, 1994. Running time: 64 MIN.
Alain .... Gil Novi
Fabio .... Emmanuel Mari
Irene .... Yvonne Kerouedan
Odile .... Marianne Papasseudi
Edmond .... David Rossi
Laetitia .... Emilie Ben Guigi

Set in the mid-'70s amongst the residue of the hippy era, "Peace and Love" offers a low-key, sweetly derisive take on the revolutionary pipe dreams, inchoate ideology and doleful compromises of youth. Slim but engaging adolescent excerpt from Laurence Ferreira Barbosa, who scored recently with her debut feature, "There's Nothing Special About Normal People," should charm festgoers as it goes the rounds.

The story charts a brief friendship between Fabio (Emmanuel Mari) and Alain (Gil Novi), two teenage boys with little in common. The former's family is bottom-end working class, with a mother on the stupid side and a right-wing father whose passion is his collection of fascist army figurines. Fabio aspires to be a rock musician but doesn't get much further than playing air guitar to Jimi Hendrix records. His dreams of leftist terrorism are almost a reflex reaction to his father's politics.

While Fabio quotes Stalin, introspective, middle-class Alain quotes Plato, but he is drawn in, almost against his will, by his friend's rather abstract activist enthusiasm. They smash a window at the local town hall and are thrilled when newspapers report the incident as a terrorist act. But the pair quickly lose heart when it looks like they could be fingered for the real terrorist doings around town.

Political rumblings of the time are well established, as is the youthful ennui that stokes kids' disdain for their provincial surroundings (in this case, seaside Nice). A vaguely romantic subplot with a more worldly flower child (Yvonne Kerouedan) feels slightly incomplete.

Perfs are unaffected and appealing. Antoine Heberle's unfussy 16mm lensing lends a rough sheen that's suitably in tune with the project's dimensions.
—David Rooney

PORTRAIT OF A YOUNG GIRL AT THE END OF THE 1960s IN BRUSSELS
(PORTRAIT D'UNE JEUNE FILLE DE LA FIN DES ANNEES 60 A BRUXELLES)
(FRENCH)

A La Sept/Arte, IMA Prods., SFP Prod. production in association with Sony Music Entertainment (France). (International sales: M5, Paris.) Produced by Georges Benayoun, Paul Rozenberg. Executive producers, Francoise Guglielmi, Elisabeth Deviosse, Yannick Casanova, Marilyn Watelet. Directors of production, Pierre-Alain Schatzmann, Mylene Azria. Directed, written by Chantal Akerman. Camera (color), Raymond Fromont; editor, Martine Lebon; music, Yarol; costume design, Sophie Vanhaecke; sound, Pierre Mertens; series artistic director, Chantal Poupaud. Reviewed at Turin Intl. Young Cinema Festival, Nov. 21, 1994. Running time: 63 MIN.
Michelle .... Circe
Paul .... Julien Rassam
Danielle .... Joelle Marlier
Mireille .... Cynthia Rodberg

In "Portrait of a Young Girl ...," Belgium's arbiter of minimalist chic, Chantal Akerman, takes a leisurely stroll through the capital, casting a casual but revealing glance at adolescent anxiety and unspoken love along the way. Thumbing her nose at period authenticity, Akerman instead incites a climate of political consciousness and social change using minor nuances of character, indirect dialogue and a freewheeling filmmaking style. Result is a film of surprising subtlety, intimacy and economy, sure to attract admirers along the festival trail.

Opening scene succinctly establishes Akerman's light, almost playful tone, and the contrasting sadness of the title character, 15-year-old Michelle (Circe). Having decided to quit school, the girl sits at a train station, idly forging absentee notes, with excuses ranging from an illness in the family to her own death.

She goes to the movies and succumbs with no qualms, but with no particular enthusiasm, to the amorous advances of Parisian army deserter Paul (Julien Rassam). They wander the streets for hours, while lenser Raymond Fromont's camera ambles along with them, mimicking their pleasurably unhurried gait.

Just when the film's motor begins to slow down, Akerman abruptly strips away her characters' defenses by robbing them of the insulation offered by the city and its traffic noises, and placing the couple alone in an empty apartment. In an almost plaintive scene, they dance (to Leonard Cohen's "Suzanne"), and then slip between the sheets.

But the film's real emotional thrust comes in the final reels, where Michelle keeps a prearranged appointment with Danielle (Joelle Marlier), clearly the true object of her affections.

Akerman's double-edged approach is complemented with effortless precision by Circe, who counters her character's youthful coolness with unstoppable sincerity and a melancholy undertow. Rassam is also impressive, playing Paul with a generous share of sympathy and sensitivity. —David Rooney

TOKAREV
(TOKAREFU)
(JAPANESE)

A Japan Foundation Film Library/Herald/Argo Pictures presentation of a Suntory Bandai Visual Co. production. (International sales: Herald Ace, Tokyo.) Produced by Genjiro Arato. Directed by Junji Sakamoto. Screenplay, Haruko Imamura, from a story by Iroshi Tokuda. Camera (color), Isao Ishii; editor, Ken-ichi Takashima; music, Shigeru Umebayashi; art direction, Koichi Kanakatsu; sound, Fumio Hashimoto, Kiyoshi Kakizawa. Reviewed at Turin Intl. Young Cinema Festival, Nov. 24, 1994. Running time: 97 MIN.
Michio Nishiumi .... Takeshi Yamato
Ayako Nishiumi .... Yumi Nishiyama
Kei Matsumura .... Koichi Sato

Japanese director Junji Sakamoto's "Tokarev" spins a riveting tale of a mild-mannered suburbanite driven to kamikaze-like extremes by his obsessive desire for revenge. Invigorated by stylish direction, startling shifts in rhythm and a cataclysmic final showdown, this steely, incendiary thriller could slay its share of victims in uptown urban situations with the right push.

Still legally manufactured in Russia and China, the Tokarev gun (with the firepower of a Magnum .45) was originally designed for the Soviet military in 1930. Outlawed in Japan, it continues to figure in criminal circles.

The weapon is used here to hold up a bus load of cheerful tykes. Helpless driver Michio (former Japanese middleweight boxing champ Takeshi Yamato) looks on while his son, Takashi, is snatched by the masked bandit. A neighbor, Matsumura (Koichi Sato), appears at the crime scene, apparently wounded by the kidnapper, who took off on his motorbike.

The kidnapping operation comes as a galvanizing jolt after a tranquil, almost dialogue-free opening, tracking snatches of routine daily life in Michio's neighborhood.

A video arrives in which Takashi himself relays the demand for 10 million yen. The ransom is handed over, but the boy turns up dead in a rubbish bag. Michio and his wife, Ayako (Yumi Nishiyama), are annihilated by the loss, and the sudden gap in their lives causes marital friction.

Watching a video of Takashi at a school sports meet, Michio spots Matsumura studying his son. His suspicions aroused, he approaches the neighbor, and in another stunning lurch from a measured, static pace to feverish action, he gets a severe pummeling and a mouthful of Tokarev for his trouble.

Michio miraculously survives the bullet wound but gives cops false information and further alienates his wife, preferring to track Matsumura himself.

Psychological twists are as bizarre as they are unpredictable, with the characters' impulsive behavior well played by a cast that invests heavily in piercing gazes and strong silences. Tension is strung out to maximum effect with the aid of Shigeru Umebayashi's somber synth music, a diverse bag of editing tricks and some gorgeous slow-motion work. —*David Rooney*

OUT TO THE WORLD
(SAE SANG BAKURO)
(SOUTH KOREAN)

An Ik Young Film Co. production. (International sales: Ik Young, Seoul.) Produced by Park Sang-in. Executive producer, Kim Hyun-taek. Directed, written by Yeo Kyun-dong. Camera (color), You Yong-kil; editor, Kim Hyun; music, Kim Jong-seo; art direction, Shin Bo-kyung; costume design, Kim Yoo-sun; sound (Dolby), Yi Byung-ha. Reviewed at Turin Intl. Young Cinema Festival (competing), Nov. 21, 1994. Running time: **98 MIN.**
Sung-kin .... Moon Sung-kin
Kyung-yong .... Yi Kyung-yong
Hye-jin .... Shim Hye-jin
Gas Station
Attendant .... Yang Hee-kyung
Lieutenant .... Myong Kue-nam
Old Woman .... Kim Ae-ra
Storekeeper .... Park Young-pal
Congressman .... Yi Dong-jin

Despite working as an assistant to eminent Korean director Park Kwang-su, first-time director Yeo Kyun-dong appears to have a more intent eye on the badlands of Hollywood cinema than the vast expanses of South Korea where "Out to the World" unfolds. A blackly comic political allegory about shaking off the debris of dictatorship, this fugitive road movie was a hit in its home territory. Its slick production values, however, are unmatched by its uneven pace and way-too-broad sense of

humor, probably restricting it to Asian circuits.

During transfer to another prison, two mismatched jail mates (Moon Sung-kin, Yi Kyung-yong, who go by their own names in the film) unwittingly become escapees after hardened criminals take charge of the bus. Their plans to turn themselves in go astray when a flighty thrill-seeker (Shim Hye-jin) dumps her tyrannical lover to team up with the luckless duo, seeing herself as the femme counterpart to their Butch Cassidy and the Sundance Kid.

With their relatively innocuous exploits trumped up to outlaw status on the evening news, the trio head for Seoul. After a bungled bank robbery, they escape in an armored truck, distractedly leaving a huge cash stash untouched. Defeated by their own ineptness, they decide to head over the border to North Korea and the false hope of a fresh start.

Until the fugitives hit Seoul, Yeo keeps things moving at a frenetic clip, tossing in plenty of action, laughs and liberal citations from Yank films. But when the story needs to go deeper and expand on its underlying theme of escape from a constrictive conspiracy, the director doesn't adequately rise to the occasion.

In tech terms, however, the film shows considerable polish, with moody lighting, dynamic use of color, sharp shooting of the often inhospitable-looking locations and a lively music score peppered with Korean pop tunes. —*David Rooney*

LIES TO LIVE BY (BABYLON)
(BABYLON: LA PAURA E LA MIGLIORE AMICA DELL'UOMO)
(ITALIAN)

A Brooklyn Films/Palomar production. (International sales: Brooklyn/Palomar, Rome.) Produced by Carlo Degli Esposti, Agnese Fontana. Executive producers, Fontana, Marco Iseli. Directed by Guido Chiesa. Screenplay, Chiesa, Antonio Leotti. Camera (Telecolor, B&W), Gherardo Gossi; editor, Anna Napoli; music, Giuseppe Napoli, Marlene Kuntz; art direction, Vera Castrovilli; costume design, Laura Mazza; sound design (Dolby), Gianfranco Zorzi; sound, Mario Iaquone; assistant director, Luca Gasparini. Reviewed at Locarno Film Festival (competing), Aug. 8, 1994. (Also in N.I.C.E. and Turin fests.) Running time: **100 MIN.**
Charles Forrester .... Bill Sage
Francesco .... Paolo Lorimer
Carla .... Valeria Milillo
Gabrielle .... Sophie Bernhard
Tonino .... Andrea Prodan
(Italian, English and French dialogue)

"Lies to Live By (Babylon)" is a borderline silly Italo low-budgeter whose few

flashes of real talent aren't enough to rescue an uninteresting script and characters. This portrait of four young people's emotional problems in industrial Turin looks unlikely to travel beyond its borders, except to more experimental gatherings.

Setting is summertime in the northern Italian city's bleaker quarters. Factory worker Francesco, a still rebellious thirty-something, can't get over his wife Carla's having slept with a hotel detective on a trip to New York. When the hapless Yank, Charles, arrives on vacation in Turin, Carla deliberately disappears for a few days and gets her friend Gabrielle, a French student, to put him up.

Francesco, by now a serious head case in his "F*** Corporate Rock" T-shirt, mopes around a lot, beats up a guy in the street and threatens Charles that he's next. With Gabrielle's help, the men finally face off in an abandoned warehouse.

Shot on Super-16mm, with 8mm B&W inserts, pic is at its best when not trying too hard for angry, rock 'n' roll effects and veering off in other directions (like the thriller *manque* finale). Unfortunately, the quieter moments serve mainly to spotlight the script's limitations.

Performances range from dire (Bill Sage, flat and lost-looking as the American) to promising (striking newcomer Sophie Bernhard, a Jodie Foster look-alike, as Gabrielle). Tech credits, including blowup to 35mm, are par. —*Derek Elley*

THE THREE SISTERS

A co-production by Russian Television (RTR), the Actor, Krug & Patmos Studios, Delta Film, Russian Committee for Cinema. Produced by Nathan Fedorovsky. Directed by Sergei Solovev. Based on the play by Anton Chekhov. Camera (color), Yury Klimenko; music, Sergei Kuryokhin. Reviewed at Kinocenter, Moscow, Nov. 23, 1994. Running time: **98 MIN.**
With: Otto Zander, Ksenia Kachalina, Olga Belyaeva, Elena Korikova.

Sergei Solovev, director of new cult Russian films such as "Assa," returns to the classics with a quirkily atmospheric version of Chekhov's classic.

When Solovev denies any trace of postmodernism in the film, he must have his tongue firmly in his cheek: This "Three Sisters" is as willfully composed as they come. It starts with framing devices and onscreen quotes, and continues in a selection of elaborate, but obviously theatrical, sets in soft focus.

The result is a beautiful-looking film, with a series of opulent interiors — spacious rooms flooded with dry ice, swept by autumn leaves and even the occasional fall of snow — plus a score by St. Petersburg's

avant-gardist Sergei Kuryokhin that is a work of art in itself.

It's far less an adaptation of the play than a series of snatches of scenes from within it that are short on dramatic content, creating moments when the sheer sameness of the proceedings begins to jar. In this context, Solovev's choice of cast — all, except German actor Otto Zander, playing Vershinin, are students of his film course at Moscow's Institute of Cinematography — shows its inexperience.

The three sisters themselves may look the parts, but there are stretches when they can't manage the depth. The male roles, except for Zander's, are even more ill-filled. The long takes, single sets and stylized language don't help bring out any range of acting styles. When the thesps do branch out, the results too often come close to hysteria.

For languid visuals, this "Sisters" scores highly, but the style leaves time hanging as heavily on the audience as it does on the characters themselves.
—*Tom Birchenough*

December 12, 1994

READY TO WEAR (PRET-A-PORTER)

A Miramax release. Produced, directed by Robert Altman. Executive producers, Bob Weinstein, Harvey Weinstein, Ian Jessel. Co-producers, Scott Bushnell, Jon Kilik. Screenplay, Altman, Barbara Shulgasser. Camera (Technicolor; Panavision widescreen), Pierre Mignot, Jean Lepine; editor, Geraldine Peroni; film editor, Suzy Elmiger; music, Michel Legrand; music supervisor, Allan Nicholls; production design, Stephen Altman; art direction, William Amello; set design, Jean Canovas; set decoration, Francoise Dupertois; costume design, Catherine Leterrier; sound (Dolby), Alain Curvelier; associate producer, Brian D. Leitch; assistant directors, Jerome Enrico, Philippe Landoulsi; second unit director, Nicholls. Reviewed at Sony Studios screening room, Culver City, Dec. 6, 1994. MPAA Rating: R. Running time: **132 MIN.**

With: Sophia Loren (Isabella de la Fontaine), Marcello Mastroianni (Sergei/Sergio), Julia Roberts (Anne Eisenhower), Tim Robbins (Joe Flynn), Kim Basinger (Kitty Potter), Stephen Rea (Milo O'Brannagan), Anouk Aimee (Simone Lowenthal), Lauren Bacall (Slim Chrysler), Lili Taylor (Fiona Ulrich), Sally Kellerman (Sissy Wanamaker), Tracey Ullman (Nina Scant), Linda Hunt (Regina Krumm), Rupert Everett (Jack Lowenthal), Forest Whitaker (Cy Bianco), Richard E. Grant (Cort Romney), Danny Aiello (Major Hamilton), Teri Garr (Louise Hamilton), Lyle Lovett (Clint Lammeraux), Jean Rochefort (Inspector Tantpis), Michel Blanc (Inspector Forget), Anne Canovas (Violetta Romney), Jean-Pierre Cassel (Olivier de la Fontaine), Francois Cluzet (Jean-Pierre), Rossy de Palma (Pilar), Kasia Figura (Vivienne), Ute Lemper (Albertine), Tara Leon (Kiki Simpson), Chiara Mastroianni (Sophie), Tom Novembre (Reggie), Sam Robards (Craig), Georgianna Robertson (Dane Simpson).

B y whichever title you prefer, Robert Altman's latest ensemble extravaganza, "Ready to Wear (Pret-a-Porter)," has all the style, glitz and head-turning star power of an A-list party — and about as much substance. With its focus fragmented among 31 featured players and countless background figures, the film relies upon surface tics and bits of business to sketch the hectic week when fashion designers trot out their latest collections in Paris. While pic is eye-catching and fitfully amusing, net effect proves frivolous and ephemeral, closer to the director's "Health" and "A Wedding" than to "Nashville" or "Short Cuts." No doubt recognizing that critics aren't likely to rally around this Altman opus, Miramax is hoping for the best by opening wide at Christmas. Heavy promo push may stimulate some early rush buying but prospective customers will more likely window shop than make the purchase, resulting in B.O. as durable as last year's fashions.

Shot like a luxuriant documentary in a world of boundless style, attitude and money, the film sets dramatic inventions of consummate artifice and silliness against a milieu that is evoked with a maximum of verisimilitude. Freewheeling director's strategy was to mix his actors with real designers, models and other scenesters with hoped-for lively and combustible results. But while the surfaces, backgrounds and sense of constant motion are authentic to their tinselly cores, what goes on among the fictional participants resembles gag-reliant improv routines that haven't been entirely worked out.

For the record, the "Pret-a-Porter" title appears onscreen in logo form with "Ready-to-Wear" laid underneath in a parenthetical subtitle.

Pic's first joke is writing out the upfront Miramax and Altman credits in Russian against a backdrop of Marcello Mastroianni scurrying across Red Square. Remainder of the action is set in a very visible Paris, and Mastroianni's mysteriously furtive character provides the springboard for what passes for a dramatic thread in Altman and Barbara Shulgasser's checkerboard scenario designed to create a mosaic of the denizens of the fashion world.

Mastroianni flits through the action, quietly disrupting the lives of many of the participants in the week's hectic events. Most significantly, he hops out of a limo when his companion, Jean-Pierre Cassel, head of the host French fashion commission, gags to death on a sandwich. The unknown man's flight and jump into the Seine lead people to suspect that Cassel has been deliberately killed, setting up a fabricated "murder" plot that is so much nonsense. Although the show must go on despite the industry leader's death, his loss naturally has its repercussions. His glamorous widow, Sophia Loren, who hated him, becomes the figurehead of the week's events while his mistress, top designer Anouk Aimee, and her son, Rupert Everett, are facing the prospect of selling their label to Texas boot tycoon Lyle Lovett.

Sneaking around one of the hotels, Mastroianni makes off with the suitcase of American sports reporter Tim Robbins, who is kept in Paris to cover the Cassel murder case and, poor fellow, is forced to share a room with another reporter, Julia Roberts. After a shaky start they decide to make the best of it and never leave the bed for the entire week.

Supplying the scorecard for the rest of the assembled tastemakers is fashion reporter Kim Basinger, who interviews everyone as they arrive and, microphone in hand, covers the shows

for the folks back home. Among those checking in are magazine editors Linda Hunt, Sally Kellerman and Tracey Ullman, all of whom spend most of their time pursuing and being humiliated by top fashion photographer Stephen Rea; ex-magazine doyenne Lauren Bacall, here named "Slim" after her character in her "To Have and Have Not" screen bow; retailer Danny Aiello, who likes to dress in drag and whose wife, Teri Garr, likes to shop; New York Times photojournalist Lili Taylor, whose professed preference for girls is never followed up; and Ute Lemper, a supermodel who shocks everyone by turning up looking ready for the delivery room rather than the runway.

Designers and models themselves get relatively short shrift, with the exception of Richard E. Grant's ultra-effete hand-waver and Forest Whitaker's down-to-earth designer, who happen to be an item. Most prominent mannequins are twin stunners Kiki and Dane Simpson, one of whom is married to Everett while the other is his mistress.

The Mastroianni subplot culminates, unsurprisingly, in his reunion with Loren, and longtime admirers of these two screen greats will get a kick out of the restaging of Loren's boudoir striptease from "Yesterday, Today and Tomorrow" with her man crowing like a rooster as she flicks lingerie items in his direction. Not many stars would dare attempt such a scene 30 years after they first did it, and fewer could get away with it, but Loren proves herself to be in a special category virtually all by herself.

On the other hand, few of the other performers add any luster to their images by virtue of their appearances here. As the trendy photog, Rea is rather amusing in his smug sadism but at the expense of Hunt, Kellerman and Ullman, whom he deliberately snaps in embarrassingly compromising positions. Robbins and Roberts had the tough job of spending the whole shoot in the sack and seem utterly disconnected from the rest of the movie. Aiello wouldn't make anyone's short list of men who would look good in a dress, and not much thought seems to have been given to how to work Bacall, Taylor or Lovett more meaningfully into the proceedings.

Serving as the film's spectacle, of course, are the fashion shows themselves, which have a fascination all their own. Several major designers were responsible for the creations on view, contributing to the pic's authenticity. Real and occasionally famous fashion models pop up parading them for the onlookers and, as if this film needed it, a pinch of extra glamour is added by party scene cameos by Cher, Harry Belafonte and a host of w.k. designers.

Altman has indisputably come up with a one-of-a-kind finale, a fashion show in the buff that was sprung unannounced upon the audience-

within-the-film and will leave film auds gaping in wonderment.

The picture's luminous surfaces represent its most appealing points, from the ritzy Paris settings and cutting-edge clothes to the dozens-of-songs score and, above all, the beautiful people who make for terrific people-watching. But one is left knowing little more about the fashion industry or the people who make it go than can be gleaned by flipping through an issue of Vogue.

—*Todd McCarthy*

DEATH AND THE MAIDEN

(U.S-FRENCH-BRITISH)

A Fine Line Features release presented in association with Capitol Films of a Mount/Kramer production in association with Channel 4 Films and Flach Films with the participation of Canal Plus. Produced by Thom Mount, Josh Kramer. Executive producers, Sharon Harel, Jane Barclay. Co-producers, Bonnie Timmermann, Ariel Dorfman. Directed by Roman Polanski. Screenplay, Rafael Yglesias, Dorfman, based on Dorfman's play. Camera (color), Tonino Delli Colli; editor, Herve De Luze; music, Wojciech Kilar; production design, Pierre Guffroy; art direction, Claude Moesching; costume design, Milena Canonero; sound (Dolby), Daniel Brisseau; associate producer, Gladys Nederlander; assistant director, Michel Cheyko; casting, Mary Selway, Patsy Pollock. Reviewed at Culver Studios screening room, Culver City, Dec. 2, 1994. MPAA Rating: R. Running time: **103 MIN.**

Paulina Escobar ..... Sigourney Weaver
Dr. Roberto Miranda .... Ben Kingsley
Gerardo Escobar .... Stuart Wilson

T hree fine actors and a top director give a very good account of Ariel Dorfman's "Death and the Maiden" in this tense, adroit film version of the play, so any significant reservations about it must stem from the material itself. As vivid and suspenseful as Roman Polanski has made this claustrophobic tale of a torture victim turning the tables on her putative tormentor, one is still left with a film in which each character represents a mouthpiece for an ideology. Chamber drama nature of the enterprise, as well as its roots in foreign politics, tag this as a specialized release domestically, where Fine Line should be able to generate decent results based on good reviews and the names involved.

Dorfman's play, which was produced on Broadway in 1992 with Glenn Close, Richard Dreyfuss and Gene Hackman (directed by Mike Nichols), was clearly based on the contemporary history of his native Chile, but took the universal route by not identifying its locale or specific events. Similarly, the film is set in "a country in South America ... after the fall of the dictatorship,"

December 12, 1994 (Cont.)

and the actions described could reasonably apply to any nation where the regimes have alternated dramatically between left and right.

All the same, the film builds its considerable tension through the accumulation of concrete specifics, not generalities. The early scene-setting has Paulina Escobar (Sigourney Weaver) nervously pacing about a remote beach house during a rainstorm, finally retreating to a closet to eat her dinner. At length, a car pulls up through the darkness and Dr. Roberto Miranda (Ben Kingsley) drops off Paulina's husband, Gerardo (Stuart Wilson), whose car has broken down.

A leftist lawyer, Gerardo has been named to chair the new president's commission on human-rights violations that occurred under the toppled fascist regime. As chance would have it, one of the many victims was Paulina, who as a student 15 years earlier was held prisoner and repeatedly tortured and raped by a man she never saw due to her blindfold.

It doesn't take long for Paulina, who has remained in the bedroom, to tell that the stranger's voice belongs to the man who brutalized her long ago. As the men proceed to get drunk, she sneaks outside and pushes Miranda's car over a cliff, then returns to pistol-whip the visitor and bind him to a chair, her panties neatly stuffed in his mouth.

Thus is Miranda put on trial, with the audience as jury. Gerardo becomes Miranda's defender, a role he embraces a tad too earnestly for Paulina's taste, as he is rather anxious to believe the man's protestations of innocence and is appalled at the idea of his wife taking justice into her own hands.

Revenge is impossible for her, she admits. All she wants from Miranda is an honest confession, upon which she says she'll let him go. If he refuses, she will kill him.

Dorfman, who has expanded but not opened up his play with the help of Rafael Yglesias ("Fearless"), keeps the audience guessing about whether Miranda is the right man up to the very end. Paulina might be just unhinged enough to throw doubt on her credibility, while Miranda's claim that he was out of the country during the period in question increasingly holds water. Script presents its moral and dramatic quandary effectively, even if the strategic coincidences of the characters' opposing ideologies and viewpoints are concocted in a terminally calculated manner.

Fully employing the house set, adroitly designed by Pierre Guffroy, with barren exteriors shot on Spain's northwest coast, Polanski succeeds in establishing a creepy atmosphere. He uses every device at his disposal to keep the tension and ambiguity ratcheted high. Still, the work feels like a skillfully executed assignment rather than a highly personal effort, as it lacks the

perverse, humorous and genuinely idiosyncratic stamp of his most memorable pictures.

Cast is excellent, though having Anglo-American actors portray South Americans will bother some people. Always good at projecting resilience, Weaver is a bundle of raw nerve endings here, and her hair-trigger impulsiveness helps keep one on edge. Kingsley shrewdly tantalizes the viewer about his identity, and gets to deliver the text's most riveting monologue at the end. The lesser-known Wilson may be the first among equals, impressing strongly as the equivocating husband.

Behind-the-scenes talents have contributed mightily. Veteran lenser Tonino Delli Colli's accomplishment looks deceptively simple, but, in fact, with the electricity out in the house most of the night, he has been forced to light the picture largely with candles and the odd lantern or flashlight. His work indoors is superlative, as is his night shooting on location.

Herve De Luze's cutting is very tight, while Wojciech Kilar's original score deftly helps build mood and suspense.   —*Todd McCarthy*

NOBODY'S FOOL

A Paramount release presented in association with Capella Intl. of a Scott Rudin/Cinehaus production. Produced by Rudin, Arlene Donovan. Executive producer, Michael Hausman. Directed, written by Robert Benton, based on the novel by Richard Russo: Camera (DuArt color; Deluxe prints), John Bailey; editor, John Bloom; music, Howard Shore; production design, David Gropman; art direction, Dan Davis; set decoration, Gretchen Rau; costume design, Joseph G. Aulisi; sound (Dolby), Danny Michael; associate producer, Scott Ferguson; assistant director, Joe Camp III; casting, Ellen Chenoweth. Reviewed at Paramount Studios screening room, L.A., Dec. 5, 1994. MPAA Rating: R. Running time: **110 MIN.**
Sully .... Paul Newman
Miss Beryl .... Jessica Tandy
Carl Roebuck .... Bruce Willis
Toby Roebuck .... Melanie Griffith
Peter .... Dylan Walsh
Rub Squeers .... Pruitt Taylor Vince
Wirf .... Gene Saks
Clive Peoples Jr. .... Josef Sommer
Officer
  Raymer .... Philip Seymour Hoffman
Judge Flatt .... Philip Bosco
Birdy .... Margo Martindale
Jocko .... Jay Patterson

"**N**obody's Fool" is a gentle, flavorsome story of a loose-knit dysfunctional family whose members essentially include every glimpsed citizen of a small New York town. Fronted by a splendid performance from Paul Newman as a spirited man who has made nothing of his life, Robert Benton's character-driven film is sprinkled with small pleasures, and the dra-

matic developments here don't take place in the noisy, calamitous manner that is customary these days. Inherent modesty of the undertaking, rare in a studio project, will make it difficult for Paramount to carve out a prominent profile for it in the Christmas rush. But with some luck it could coast quietly through the holidays and, if encouraged, possibly build an audience in midwinter.

Newman's Sully is the odd man out in North Bath, N.Y., a fitfully employed, 60-year-old construction worker and handyman who is reduced to boarding with his elderly eighth-grade teacher, Miss Beryl (Jessica Tandy), pursuing futile legal action assisted by a lawyer, Wirf (Gene Saks), who never wins a case and having the village idiot, Rub Squeers (Pruitt Taylor Vince), as his best friend. His closest soul mate is probably the sexy Toby (Melanie Griffith), and Sully still fancies himself enough of a ladies' man to half-seriously imagine that he might have a chance of a tumble with her. But she's married, however unhappily, to Carl (Bruce Willis), the stingy manager of Tip Top Construction, and this, along with the rather gaping age difference, might just be too much to overcome.

Narrative bridges the holidays beginning at Thanksgiving, which accentuates the aloneness, not only of Sully, but of many other individuals in the run-down town. Miss Beryl is at increasing odds with her son Clive Jr. (Josef Sommer), a businessman who hopes to build a huge, economy-spurting theme park nearby. Toby, Wirf and Rub are mostly left to their own devices, and even Sully's college professor son, Peter (Dylan Walsh), who arrives in town married with two boys, not having seen his father in three years, is soon cast out of his family nest.

Unemployable in any serious way due to a bum knee and irascible manner, Sully begs Carl for work and, when he is refused, takes to stealing the younger man's snow blower, which he must do repeatedly since Carl always takes it back. Whether dealing with his would-be boss or blood kin, Sully wears his reputation for irresponsibility lightly. But no one has suffered nearly as much due to his immature behavior as he has: He's come this far in life without taking care of business, notably his own, and it soon appears that he may have but one more chance.

After the apparent randomness of the opening reels, which portray Sully's cheerfully adversarial relationship with much of life, Benton has adapted Richard Russo's novel in such a way that the film accrues strength through the sprouting of carefully planted seeds. Sully's long-running feud with the local cop finally lands him in jail, and a visit to what had been his father's home,

now boarded up, ends up providing some hope for the future.

As things turn out, events and people's fates become determined by small but decisive acts of generosity that make all the difference. Sully's entirely unwarranted optimism is rewarded in unexpected ways, which does not excuse the laxness with which he's lived his life up until now but does support the theory that change for the better is always possible, that hope should never be extinguished. This theme is not laid on with a trowel in typical Hollywood inspirational fashion, but understatedly. Film's impact is thus light, but appealing all the same.

Playing 10 years younger than his real age with no problem, Newman delivers one of his most engaging performances in years. Portraying the sort of old coot to be found in every small town, the actor brings great zest to his unusual role of a man who refuses to consider himself a loser despite six decades of evidence to the contrary, someone who still takes adolescent delight in behaving like a prankish bad boy, a misfit whose spirit has somehow not been chopped down by life's disappointments. It's a strong role Newman makes even richer.

Just about everyone else on hand shines as well. In her second-to-last role, Tandy, as Sully's thoughtful landlady, has some ominous initial lines, saying "I've got a feeling God's creeping in on me. I've got a feeling this is the year he'll lower the boom." She's very good, as always, and the film is dedicated to her. Willis, who curiously is not billed in the front credits nor in the print art, is the highlight of the strong supporting cast, delivering a tangy turn as the exasperated company boss who's awfully good at saying no. Griffith is appealingly relaxed and easygoing under Benton's direction as Willis' departing wife; Saks has some amusing moments as the sad-sack attorney; and Elizabeth Wilson turns up uncredited as Newman's ex-wife.

The gray atmosphere of an Eastern town in dead of winter is unerringly captured with the help of locations in various towns, David Gropman's deliberately tattered production design and John Bailey's elegant, unfussy lensing. Howard Shore's score is also a solid plus.
     —*Todd McCarthy*

SPEECHLESS

A Metro-Goldwyn-Mayer release of a Forge production. Produced by Renny Harlin, Geena Davis. Executive producer, Harry Colomby. Line producer, Mary Kane. Directed by Ron Underwood. Screenplay, Robert King. Camera (Deluxe color), Don Peterman; editor, Richard Francis-Bruce; music, Marc Shaiman; production design, Dennis Washington; art direction, Tom Targownik; set decoration, Marvin March; costume design, Jane Robinson; sound (Dolby), Richard Bryce Goodman; assistant director, Terry Miller; casting, Howard Feuer. Reviewed at the MGM screening room, Santa Monica, Dec. 7, 1994. MPAA Rating: PG-13. Running time: **99 MIN.**

Kevin	Michael Keaton
Julia	Geena Davis
Freed	Christopher Reeve
Nanette	Bonnie Bedelia
Ventura	Ernie Hudson
Kratz	Charles Martin Smith
Cutler	Gailard Sartain
Garvin	Ray Baker
Wannamaker	Mitchell Ryan

Likable but uneven, this romantic comedy about sparring speechwriters features appealing performances by Michael Keaton and Geena Davis and hits the box office trail at a good time to generate some early returns. After initial turnout, however, many may file absentee ballots and wait for homevideo.

While much may be made of similarities to dueling campaign advisers James Carville and Mary Matalin, the filmmakers have stressed that Robert King's script pre-dated those events. The more telling link with reality, based on recent mudslinging campaigns, is the jaundiced eye the movie turns toward bigtime politics.

Davis and Keaton play warring speechwriters (she's a Democrat, he's a Republican) who have a chance encounter before realizing they're on opposite sides of the same New Mexico Senate race. Concern about fraternizing with the enemy creates tension between the pair even though they're perfect for each other — both hyperactive insomniacs (they meet over a box of Nytol), though Davis' Julia is more the idealist, Keaton's Kevin the gun-for-hire.

Aside from the campaign's ebb and flow, played out in the relentless pursuit of TV news sound bites, another wrinkle gets thrown into the budding relationship when Julia's absentee boyfriend (Christopher Reeve) returns to try to sweep her away.

Director Ron Underwood ("City Slickers") and writer King tend to be more clever than laugh-out-loud funny, with a few notable exceptions, such as the two scribes venting their hostility in front of a group of horrified schoolchildren.

But "Speechless" never achieves the madcap hilarity of the '40s romantic comedies it seeks to emulate, and some of the dramatic moments feel a bit forced.

That said, Davis continues to radiate movie-star appeal beyond the confines of her vehicles (the last being "Angie"), and Keaton remains a gifted smart aleck, delivering a fine comic turn even though the material is often about as slight as the average stump speech.

King does a good job of skewering the political process, from the blustering campaign hacks to the local newscasters who keep leading their broadcasts with the story of a trapped bear cub, but like a politician, the screenwriter has generally trained his sights on fairly easy targets.

Few of the supporting players get the opportunity to shine, with Reeve appropriately smarmy as the globe-trotting reporter and Mitchell Ryan and Ray Baker looking their parts as the two candidates.

Tech credits take sparse advantage of the New Mexico vistas, while Marc Shaiman's score and the song roster prove a bit heavy-handed. Still, held up against the recent spate of uninspired romantic comedies, "less" is, for the most part, a little bit more.

—*Brian Lowry*

DROP ZONE

A Paramount release of a Nicita/Lloyd production. Produced by D.J. Caruso, Wallis Nicita, Lauren Lloyd. Executive producer, John Badham. Coproducer, Doug Claybourne. Directed by Badham. Screenplay, Peter Barsocchini, John Bishop, story by Tony Griffin, Guy Manos, Barsocchini. Camera (Deluxe color), Roy H. Wagner; editor, Frank Morriss; music, Hans Zimmer; production design, Joe Alves; costume design, May Vogt; sound (Dolby), Russell Williams II; sky-diving supervisor, Guy Manos; aerial stunt coordinator, B.J. Worth; casting, Carol Lewis; second unit director, Caruso. Reviewed at Sony Memorial City Cinema, Houston, Dec. 7, 1994. MPAA rating: R. Running time: **101 MIN.**

Pete Nessip	Wesley Snipes
Ty Moncrief	Gary Busey
Jessie Crossman	Yancy Butler
Earl Leedy	Michael Jeter
Selkirk	Corin Nemec
Swoop	Kyle Secor
Jagger	Luca Bercovici
Terry Nessip	Malcolm-Jamal Warner
Bobby	Rex Linn
Winona	Grace Zabriskie
Torski	Sam Hennings
Kara	Claire Stansfield
Deuce	Mickey Jones
Tom McCracken	Andy Romano

Given the dearth of similar product among this year's holiday releases, "Drop Zone" should benefit from being in the right place at the right time. As the only R-rated, hard-action thriller set for wide release before year's end, it is neatly poised for a hit-and-run B.O. grab. Some impressive midair action sequences and Wesley Snipes' marquee allure should help in foreign, homevid and pay cable venues.

Pic is little more than a by-the-numbers programmer, reasonably diverting and briskly paced but thinly written and utterly predictable. To be sure, it's more coherent and much better acted than "Terminal Velocity," another recent skydiving thriller that crashed and burned. But the comparisons aren't all in the new pic's favor. As good as the stunt work is here, there's nothing to match Charlie Sheen's midair rescue of Nastassja Kinski from a car trunk in "Terminal."

Snipes gives a self-assured star performance as Pete Nessip, a U.S. marshal who, with his brother and fellow lawman (Malcolm-Jamal Warner), is assigned guard duty for the transfer of a drug-cartel snitch (Michael Jeter). When their 747 is hijacked by alleged terrorists, Pete's brother is killed, the plane is badly damaged by an explosion and the "terrorists" — along with the snitch — appear to take a fatal free-fall.

The FBI theorizes that Pete's brother caused the explosion, but Pete heatedly disagrees and further insists that the hijackers and prisoner jumped out of the plane and escaped with parachutes. Not surprisingly, this claim is given as much credence as an Elvis sighting. So, while on suspension pending an FBI investigation, Pete goes undercover to prove his theory and clear his late brother's name.

Of course, Pete is absolutely right: The hijackers, led by an unusually subdued (by his standards) Gary Busey, are crack sky-divers who kidnapped the snitch because of his hacking expertise. They plan to use him to break into Drug Enforcement Administration computer files so they can sell the names and locations of undercover agents to drug lords for hefty fees.

As the bad guys prepare to invade the DEA's Washington, D.C., headquarters under cover of a massive July 4 celebration, Pete dogs their trail. He drafts sky-diver Jessie Crossman (Yancy Butler), a beautiful ex-con, to help him gain entry into the sky-diving subculture. This triggers the pic's funniest moment, when Jessie abruptly drops Pete from her airplane, sans parachute, then follows him in freefall so he can share her rig before they hit the ground.

That's as close as Butler and Snipes get during the entire pic. Much like last year's "The Pelican Brief," "Drop Zone" is gutlessly timid about showing any sign of sexual attraction between a black hero and a white heroine. Here, however, the color-consciousness is appreciably less annoying, if only because there is a lot more high-velocity action to distract the audience.

Director John Badham is an old hand at this kind of full-tilt entertainment, and he brings a straight-shooting professionalism to the enterprise. Come to think of it, he's also an old hand at movies about computer hacking — remember

"War Games"? — which might explain why the high-tech elements are, if not entirely believable, at least plausible.

"Drop Zone" contains no fewer than three midair rescues of people who don't have parachutes by people who do. Each is suitably thrilling and vertigo-inducing, and all serve as a testimonial to the skill of aerial stunt coordinator B.J. Worth.

Between the high-flying highlights, the actors are hard-pressed to invest much personality in their stock roles. Snipes brings a welcome touch of self-effacing humor to his heroics and handles the serious rough stuff with aplomb. It's not much of a stretch for an actor who's capable of more complex things, but it's more than enough to propel this pic.

Butler holds his own in the action sequences, particularly in a climactic fistfight with the only woman among the bad guys, and she laces her perf with a wisecracking edge.

Standouts in the supporting cast include Kyle Secor as an eccentric sky-diver who joins Snipes' team, Grace Zabriskie as a cantankerous pilot and newcomer Claire Stansfield in the small but attention-grabbing part of Busey's right-hand woman. Stansfield has the graceful moves of a cat burglar and a bright smile that suggests complicity with every dirty trick in the book. More will be heard from her.

Tech values are strong across the board. Of particular note are Frank Morriss' razor-sharp editing and Hans Zimmer's effectively thunderous musical score. —*Joe Leydon*

MUTUAL CONSENT
(CONSENTEMENT MUTUEL)
(FRENCH)

A Les Productions Lazennec presentation of an MKL release of a Les Productions Lazennec, France 3 Cinema production, with participation of Canal Plus, Sofica, Sofinergie 3 and CNC. (International sales: President Films, Paris.) Produced by Adeline Lecallier. Directed by Bernard Stora. Screenplay, Stora, Philippe Delannoy, based on an idea by Marie Dedale. Camera (color), Romain Winding; editor, Jacques Comets; music, Jeff Cohen; art direction; Arnaud de Moleron; costume design, Jacqueline Bouchard; sound, Georges Prat, Jean-Pierre Laforce; associate producers, Alain Rocca, Christophe Rossignon; assistant director, Gabriel-Julien Laferriere; casting, Christiane Lebrima. Reviewed at Club de l'Etoile screening room, Paris, Dec. 6, 1994. Running time: **109 MIN.**

Romain	Richard Berry
Jeanne	Anne Brochet
Mado	Adrienne Winling
Jeanne's mother	Christiane Cohendy
Ingrid	Marine Delterme
Judith	Emmanuelle Devos

With: Jean-Claude Bouillon, Charles Berling, Christian Bujeau, Christine Citti.

"Mutual Consent" is a superb rendering of the increasingly insidious af-

December 12, 1994 (Cont.)

termath of a friendly divorce. Winningly structured and sharply acted, pic gets in under the wire as one of 1994's most convincing and engaging contemporary dramas. Although ready for the international arthouse circuit as is, this intelligent and often funny film could certainly lend itself to a remake in any country where couples with children call it quits.

Wearing a double halo of reasonableness, Jeanne (Anne Brochet) and Romain (Richard Berry) agree to divorce after a decade of marriage. Their 10-year-old daughter, Mado, is to live with Mom in Paris, and suburb-dwelling Dad is to see the girl twice a week.

Both parties appear cordial and cooperative, and Mado takes the new arrangement in stride. But Romain — whose true nature as a perfectionist and control freak emerges in gradual, keenly choreographed increments — can't abide the smooth transition or his ex-wife's ability to cope.

Romain slyly retaliates by mounting a subtle-but-effective "Gaslight"-style campaign of insinuation to discredit Jeanne at their daughter's school, at work and even with her own well-meaning but malleable parents.

Tight, always entertaining script shows how small incidents get blown out of proportion, how a few well-placed remarks can foster doubt, and how standing up for oneself can be made to look like flightiness rather than strength.

This sure-fire conversation starter will have viewers taking sides, with some folks concluding Jeanne is doing a darn good job juggling work and parenthood, and others sympathizing with Romain's far stricter but apparently sincere take on child rearing.

Thesps are outstanding. Brochet, in a nuanced performance, creates a credible, three-dimensional portrait of a spontaneous, easygoing woman whose every move is potential ammunition for her crafty ex-spouse. Berry's effortless charm mutates into heavy artillery when people or institutions fall short of his character's sometimes preposterous standards. Supporting cast fills the proceedings with pertinent shades of gray.

Mostly summery lensing in Paris and Nimes is aces. The white-on-white decor of Romain's compulsively neat home perfectly reflects his aggressively meticulous mindset. Brochet's makeup and wardrobe underscore her changing moods. Incidental music is just right. —*Lisa Nesselson*

IMMORTAL BELOVED

A Columbia release of an Icon production. Produced by Bruce Davey. Executive producer, Stephen McEveety. Directed, written by Bernard Rose. Camera (Rank color, Technicolor prints; Panavision widescreen), Peter Suschitzky; editor, Dan Rae; music director, Sir Georg Solti; music supervisor, John Stronach; production design, Jiri Hlupy; supervising art director, John Myhre; art direction, Olga Rosenfelderova; costume design, Maurizio Millenotti; sound (Dolby), Peter Glossop; sound design and supervision, Nigel Holland; assistant director, Lee Cleary; casting, Marion Dougherty. Reviewed at Sony Studios screening room, Culver City, Dec. 5, 1994. MPAA Rating: R. Running time: **121 MIN.**

Ludwig van Beethoven	Gary Oldman
Anton Felix Schindler	Jeroen Krabbe
Anna Marie Erdody	Isabella Rossellini
Johanna Reiss	Johanna Ter Steege
Karl van Beethoven	Marco Hofschneider
Nanette Streicher	Miriam Margolyes
Clemens Metternich	Barry Humphries
Giulietta Guicciardi	Valeria Golino
Nikolaus Johann van Beethoven	Gerard Horan
Casper Anton Carl van Beethoven	Christopher Fulford
Therese Obermayer	Alexandra Pigg
Franz Josef Guicciardi	Luigi Diberti
Jakob Hotscevar	Michael Culkin
Karl Holz	Donal Gibson
Young Karl van Beethoven	Matthew North

"Immortal Beloved" attempts to travel the "Citizen Kane" route of using a death's door clue left by a difficult great man to penetrate his secret self. The man in question here is Ludwig van Beethoven, and the result is less than compelling due to the fragmentary telling of the story, off-putting nature of the main character and failure of the filmmakers to make their investigation seem of any particular consequence. Columbia may have hoped that "Amadeus"-like lightning would strike twice for this heavy classical goulash, but domestic audiences aren't likely to belly up in any sizable numbers. Offshore prospects would appear brighter.**

The Rosebud here is a letter from Beethoven found soon after his death addressed to an unnamed Immortal Beloved in which he wrote, among other things, that "I can live only completely with you or not at all." As the brilliant composer never married and was not known to have had any deep romantic attachments toward the end of his life, the identity of his beloved has stumped all biographers over the years.

With a confidence born of dramatic exigency, however, British writer/director Bernard Rose purports to have solved the mystery at long last. Taking a big step in ambition from his last picture, the crafty thriller "Candyman," Rose sets up an inves-

tigatory structure full of flashbacks, multiple narrators and jumps through time that seems more complicated than it is. Crucially, however, he fails to drum up much suspense or even interest in the solution to the puzzle, poking a hole in his own balloon even before he fills it with air to try to make it fly.

Beginning with the hero's death in 1827 and his lavish funeral, film follows the travels throughout Middle Europe of Anton Schindler (Jeroen Krabbe), Beethoven's loyal factotum, as he pursues all his leads in the Immortal Beloved mystery. He first visits a hotel in Karlsbad where he knows his boss (played by Gary Oldman) had an assignation many years before. This lands him an interview with the Countess Giulietta Guicciardi (Valeria Golino), who dramatically claims to have been Beethoven's great love.

Rose uses flashback glimpses of this romance to illustrate how, even at an early age, the composer's encroaching deafness made him even more arrogant, rude and impossible to other people than he already was, and how he felt and cavalierly behaved as if the usual proprieties didn't apply to him. Also sketched is his destructive relationship with his youngest brother and the latter's peasant wife, Johanna (Johanna Ter Steege), which was to have an unpleasant aftermath.

Another line of inquiry takes Schindler to Hungary, where the Countess Anna Marie Erdody (Isabella Rossellini) represents his greatest hope of finding the true Immortal Beloved. Over drinks at an inn, she tells of her great love affair with the composer, which began when she rescued him from the stage when his utter deafness resulted in a conducting fiasco before a glittering audience and endured through Napoleon's attack on her palatial estate and the death of one of her children.

Longest digression involves the stubborn Beethoven's taking over of the rearing of his young nephew Karl for five years, during which he composed nothing, instead vainly trying to make the boy a piano prodigy. This effort ends in tragedy for all concerned, and the subplot has the effect of exposing the story's fundamental weakness: The search for Beethoven's secret love is not a sufficiently strong premise upon which to base an entire film, thus requiring offshoots and tangents to fill out the running time.

At the same time, Beethoven's brusque, high-handed, irrational personality is never made either palatable or accessible. Granted, he is given the dual excuses of genius and deafness to set him apart from the rest of humanity, but neither Rose nor Oldman provide the necessary opening into his character that would give an audience a handle on him, even as a coldly formidable protagonist. Oldman strikes a lot of commanding poses, both as

maestro and lover, but a cohesive, full-bodied characterization never emerges.

Musical climax comes with the rapturously received premiere of the Ninth Symphony, whereupon, in a sort of sub-Ken Russell intergalactic orgasm, Beethoven is literally positioned as a star in the firmament. Pic then presents a solution to the mystery that seems as plausible as any other it might have offered, although it can scarcely be one that no one else has proposed over the past 165 years.

Shot mostly around Prague, Icon production has a polished, early 19th-century look thanks to the colorful locations, Jiri Hlupy's sumptuous production design, Maurizio Millenotti's lavish costumes and Peter Suschitzky's lustrous lensing. Musical side is impeccably handled by Sir Georg Solti and the London Symphony Orchestra, whose performances of assorted Beethoven works dominate the soundtrack.

An interesting technical attempt is made to render a subjective impression of the composer's deafness, in which barely detectable ambient sounds are overwhelmed by a pervasive low din. But even this lends more of an impression of what was not in Beethoven's head than what was. —*Todd McCarthy*

TURIN

ALONE IN THE NIGHT
(YORU GA MATA KURU)
(JAPANESE)

An Argo Pictures presentation of a Video Champ/King Records Co. production, in association with Argo Pictures and New Century Prods. (International sales: Argo Pictures, Tokyo.) Produced by Takuto Niizu. Directed, written by Takashi Ishii. Camera (color), Norichimi Kasamatsu; editor, Yoshio Kitazawa; music, Goro Yasukawa; art direction, Teru Yamazaki, Koichi Kanakatsu; sound, Atsushi Sugiyama. Reviewed at Turin Intl. Young Cinema Festival, Nov. 23, 1994. Running time: **108 MIN.**

Nami Tsuchiya	Yui Natsukawa
Muraki	Jinpachi Nezu
Mitsuru Tsuchiya	Toshiyuki Nagashima
Ikejima	Minoru Terada
Kazuya Shibata	Kippei Shiina

Idiosyncratic Japanese helmer Takashi Ishii pumps his staples of convulsive violence, Grand Guignol carnage, fierce eroticism and weird emotional bonds into a punchy, wronged-woman scenario in "Alone in the Night." Though it's more of a straight genre turn, and a little less striking than some of his previous pix like "Original Sin" and "A Night in Nude," this virtuoso thriller should make a showing in modish midnight-screening setups.**

December 12, 1994 (Cont.)

Tender opening has devoted wife Nami (Yui Natsukawa) painting a heart in pink nail polish on the handle of her cop husband's gun while fretting about the danger of his assignment to infiltrate a gang of drug-dealing yakuza scum. Her fears prove justified when his bullet-ridden body is hauled out of the sea.

Nami's mourning is interrupted when the drug thugs come looking for a confiscated stash of speed. They smash the urn holding the dead cop's ashes, then rape Nami. She attempts suicide, downing pills and floating out to sea in an arrestingly shot sequence, but is saved by Muraki (Jinpachi Nezu), a mystery yakuza with major tattoo work.

Nami poses as a hooker to get close enough to kill mob boss Ikejima (Minoru Terada). But after enduring the sexually sadistic criminal's rough-and-tumble bedroom antics, she fumbles her attempt. Her life is spared through Muraki's intervention, but she is sold off to an out-of-town brothel, where Muraki finds her in a drug-induced stupor. She goes on to kick her drug habit and pursue her revenge.

Ishii's penchant for the bizarre is gleefully indulged in a bloody rooftop face-off with Ikejima around what looks like a neon junk heap. Norichimi Kasamatsu's camera gives the action a suitably sinister, stylized look, with the blue-hued brooding night skies and cityscapes frequently cloaked in amusingly cheesy veils of sea spray, stardust, snowfalls and blowing blossoms.

As in Ishii's earlier pix, water is a constant factor, from lashing rain and stagnant pools to the water beds and steamy bathrooms in which Ikejima's sordid sexual rites are performed.

Keen sound effects are complemented by Goro Yasukawa's music, which runs from solemn pipe tunes to melodic piano to frenzied drumming. —*David Rooney*

BROTHERS: RED ROULETTE

(FRERES: LA ROULETTE ROUGE)

(FRENCH)

A La Sept/Arte, IMA Prods., SFP Prod. production, in association with Sony Music Entertainment (France). (International sales: IMA, Paris.) Produced by Georges Benayoun, Paul Rozenberg. Executive producers, Francoise Guglielmi, Elisabeth Deviosse, Yannick Casanova. Directed by Olivier Dahan. Screenplay, Dahan, Olivier Massart, Gilles Taurand. Camera (color), Alex Lamarque; editor, Zofia Menuet; music, Yarol; art direction, Jann Houllevigue; sound, Louis Foropon; series artistic director, Chantal Poupaud; assistant director, Mathias Honore; casting, Bruno Delahaye. Reviewed at Turin Intl. Young Cinema Festival, Nov. 25, 1994. Running time: **85 MIN.**

Paul	Said Taghmaoui
Samy	Samy Naceri
Max-Laure	Veronique Octon
Maya	Maureen Diot
Zakari	Nabil El Bouhairi
Marco	Romain Duris
Henri	Kader Hemissi
Taxi driver	Denis Seurat

After an apprenticeship in commercials and musicvid factory of Gallic style-merchant Jean Baptiste Mondino, director Olivier Dahan weighs in with a head-turner in "Brothers: Red Roulette." A kind of "Boyz N the Arrondissement," this hip, violent, urban grunge drama set in the 'burbs of Paris is a little too knowing in its endorsement of U.S. indie conventions and in its impressive cannonade of editing and camera tricks. But the film's cool assurance should open up limited playdates, planting Dahan on the list of names to watch.

The film is the last in IMA Prods.' "Tous les Garcons et les Filles de Leur Age" series (for Euro cultural web Arte) conceived by former publicist Chantal Poupaud. Nine directors were each commissioned to make a film about teenagers, set in the period of their own youth. A party and a soundtrack bulging with chart successes of the day are central to each pic. The series begins chronologically with Andre Techine's 1962-set "Wild Reeds" (premiered last spring at Cannes) and wraps with Dahan's pic, set in 1990.

While being taunted with a gun by neighborhood thugs, 13-year-old Zakari (Nabil El Bouhairi) grabs the weapon in a panic and accidentally shoots one of them. A night of desperate flight and pursuit follows, with Zak's strung-out older sister, Max-Laure (Veronique Octon), trying to get to him before the victim's seemingly vengeful brother Paul (Said Taghmaoui) does.

As Zak wanders the streets in a stunned delirium, his brother Samy (Samy Naceri) prepares for a suicidal round of red roulette, a contest that entails running a long series of red lights at high speed.

Coming in furious, fragmentary bursts, the narrative provides a grim tour of an unforgiving environment, rife with drugs, crime and multiethnic tension. Dahan engages in overkill, however, with a series of monochrome talking-head portraits in which youths spell out the harsh urban jungle laws already implicit in the story.

Grainy shots of ugly tower blocks, frantic hand-held tracking sequences, anemic B&W segs and patches of vivid, searing color give things a fired-up edginess. This is matched by electric editing, especially nimble in the climactic driving stretch when Samy takes the wheel.

Dahan's prior training has a hand in the terrific musical spectrum brought into play, from rap and reggae to traditional jazz and blues. Particularly effective is Wynton Marsalis' New Orleans-style funereal riff preceding the violence that kick-starts Zak's night of terror, and Nina Simone belting out "Feeling Good" over the tragic final act.

The young cast hits the right note of sober intensity. Adult presences are shrewdly limited to distant, vaguely disapproving glances, with the exception of a taxi driver who attempts to reach out to Max-Laure. Pic also exists in a 60-minute TV version. —*David Rooney*

INFILTRATE

(L'INCRUSTE)

(FRENCH)

A La Sept/Arte, IMA Prods., SFP Prod. production, in association with Sony Music Entertainment (France). (International sales: M5, Paris.) Produced by Georges Benayoun, Paul Rozenberg. Executive producers, Francoise Guglielmi, Elisabeth Deviosse, Yannick Casanova. Directed by Emilie Deleuze. Screenplay, Deleuze, Laurent Guyot. Camera (color), Antoine Heberle; editors, Dominique Galieni, Eager Di Goute; music, Yarol; art direction, Bernard Madelenat; sound, Michel Brethez, Eric Tisserand; series artistic director, Chantal Poupaud. Reviewed at Turin Intl. Young Cinema Festival, Nov. 24, 1994. Running time: **59 MIN.**
With: Claire Keim, Benoit Majmel, Yann Boudaud, Mathieu Busson, Marcel Bozonnet.

Gate-crashing parties and starting trouble is the preferred Saturday-night pastime of the rowdy teens in "Infiltrate." Charting a week in the life of a high school girl forced by one such party to face up to her obsession with orderliness, the film has an easy appeal that largely masks its lack of a tangible center. Festivals and Eurotubes should make space.

Setting her story in the early 1980s, tyro helmer Emilie Deleuze effectively evokes a time when youth culture had all but cast off the flamboyant frivolousness of disco for the aggressiveness of punk, a passage heavily echoed on the soundtrack.

Undergoing a quiet rebellion against the direction her life is taking, Ariane (Claire Keim) argues with her lax father (Marcel Bozonnet) and attempts to pull away from b.f. Pierre (Benoit Majmel). Against her better judgment, she agrees to throw a party at home, during which the inevitable crowd of hostile outsiders shows up.

Deleuze observes the insidious crescendo of violence with a curious balance of humor and horror, and skillful help from Antoine Heberle's claustrophobic camerawork. The intruders begin by threateningly hitting on Ariane, then bully her guests and steal their wallets before wrecking the place. In the aftermath, Ariane punctiliously lines up shards of broken glass.

As the party is the film's weightiest narrative component, the pic fails to satisfy entirely, being more an intriguing episode than a story in its own right. The larger portrait of adolescent unease never fully emerges, and the most sympathetic character, Pierre, all but dissolves into the party fray.

Limber perfs, tight editing and Deleuze's tough, sometimes frenetic direction are all well synchronized with the material. What's missing is a little more meat on the narrative bones. —*David Rooney*

HEY STRANGER

(BELGIAN-GERMAN)

An Alert Film (Berlin)/Sophimages (Brussels) production, in association with Studio Hamburg, Dokfilm, RTBF. (International sales: Cine Electra, London.) Produced by Alfred Hurmer, Sophie Schoukens. Line producer, Frank Dragun. Directed by Peter Woditsch. Screenplay, Sophie Simon, Woditsch. Camera (color), Elfi Mikesch; editor, Ludo Troch; music, Marc Verhaegen; art direction, Pierre Decraen; costume design, Riccarda Merten Eicher; sound (Dolby), Henri Morelle; assistant director, Pierrot de Heusch. Reviewed at Turin Intl. Young Cinema Festival, Nov. 24, 1994. (Also in Thessaloniki fest.) Running time: **112 MIN.**

Orf	Vincent Rouche
Sarka	Benedicte Loyen
Tania	Hanna Schygulla
Major-domo	William Hickey
Skolimowski	Guy Trejan
Frans	Jacques Seiler
Gabriel	Philippe Van Kessel
(French dialogue)	

German-born, Brussels-based Peter Woditsch pays laborious homage to Fassbinder with his ambitious debut feature, "Hey Stranger." Prague's old-world grandeur may seem the ideal fairytale setting, but this muddled, exasperating flight of fancy barely gets off the ground, despite polished production values.

December 12, 1994 (Cont.)

Woditsch offhandedly brews a fey love story, concocts a mystery about a secret art treasure, comments on the dilemmas inherent in freedom following the demise of the Communist state, and lobs in some charmless musical whimsy — without establishing a clear enough focus to bind these disparate strands together.

A tune whistled by sprightly nymph Sarka (Benedicte Loyen) as she skips about the city's rooftops strikes romance in the heart of Orf (Vincent Rouche). No sooner are the flames ignited than they are put on the back burner when Orf inherits his rich uncle's mansion. In it is a secret store of valuable erotic art, concealed over the years from the Nazis and the Red army, and now guarded by a wizened major-domo (William Hickey, speaking English for no apparent reason while everyone around him speaks French).

The major-domo is killed, and the paintings vanish. Orf tracks the missing artwork to Brussels, where other forces also after them frame him for murder. He gets a hand escaping from a pair of decadent musicians (Hanna Schygulla, Philippe Van Kessel) who help him smuggle the paintings back to Prague, where he rekindles his passion for Sarka.

Perfs are all respectable enough, but thesps like Schygulla and Hickey are squandered on formless characters. Tech expertise also is overshadowed by the incoherent plot.

—*David Rooney*

LONDON

CHASING DREAMS

(BRITISH — 16mm)

A Buffalo Prods. production. Produced, directed, written by Caleb Lindsay. Camera (color, Super-16mm), Lindsay, Dusan Todorovic; editor, Lindsay; sound, Stewart Williams; associate producer, Darrell Lockhart; assistant director, Freya Billington. Reviewed on vidcassette, London, Nov. 30, 1994. (In London Film Festival.) Running time: **83 MIN.**
Alex .... Ian Prince
Patrick .... Luke Shaw
David .... Adam Russ
Chris .... Dominic Knutton
Frankie .... Francis Victor
Mark .... Shola Dale
Alex's Father .... Tom Fahy
Also with: Sara Dee, Alex Howlett, Lucy Sapte, Geraldine Lynch, Sue Walker, Melissa Radcliffe, Zacharee Lee, Alex Dave, Fay Hilliar.

Though "Chasing Dreams" doesn't look to get far beyond fest and Euroweb showings, this likable Brit low-budgeter announces a potentially considerable talent in 22-year-old filmer Caleb Lindsay, who manages the tricky task of consigning his own X-generation's lifestyle and dreams to celluloid in an upbeat,

lightly comic mode. Rejecting both vid-style flash and kitchen-sink grunge, this truly independent production is a slight but quietly impressive calling card that should win friends at specialized unspoolings.

A self-taught filmmaker who came up via video promos for bands, Lindsay made "Dreams" for a mere £18,000 ($27,000) that was put up by a computer company on the basis of the script. Shot on Super-16mm, pic betrays no sign of its impoverished budget, aside from some occasionally indistinct sound recording. Visually alert lensing and smooth editing combine with generally good performances to rep an assured bow.

Virtually plotless film focuses on a group of young guys ambling through their youth with no jobs or visible means of support. Central character is Alex (Ian Prince), who leaves his mom and her new boyfriend and travels south to hook up with his divorced dad and two brothers, Patrick (Luke Shaw) and Frankie (Francis Victor).

Patrick and his buddy David (Adam Russ) are two no-talent musicians who survive on low-rent gigs and dreams of making it in the music biz big time. In practice, they spend most of their time driving around in a camper and trying various ruses (all unsuccessful) to get laid.

Alex and friends Chris (Dominic Knutton) and Mark (Shola Dale) are into nabbing cars and joyriding. After being knifed in a bar one night, Chris survives to steal another day; Mark, however, is killed one night when one of their autos crashes. Film ends with Alex buying a '60s E-Type Jaguar cheap and making a bundle on a trade.

Pic's freshness stems from the fact that it beats no political or judgmental drums about its characters' reapthe-day existence (apart from a brief, awkwardly scripted scene of Alex with a probation officer) and simply presents the group of youths as they are. Performances by the nonpro cast translate well to film and, aside from a few dud scenes, the film has a lightly comic edge that relies totally on character for its effect.

As Alex, Prince is low-key and largely overshadowed in the personality stakes by the other players. Shaw is excellent as his eye-rolling, Belushi-like brother, and teams well with Russ as his sex-obsessed partner. Dialogue is street-level, four-letter most of the way, but played lightly rather than in anger. Brit slang should present no problem for North American auds.

—*Derek Elley*

BRANWEN

(BRITISH)

A Teliesyn Ty Helwick production for S4C (Wales). (International sales: S4C, Cardiff.) Produced by Angela Graham. Directed by Ceri Sherlock. Screenplay, Gareth Miles, Graham, Sherlock, developed from a play by Miles. Camera (color), Ray Orton; editor, Trevor Keates; music, Cliff Norman; production design, Stage Works; sound (Dolby), Alan Jones. Reviewed at London Film Festival, Nov. 13, 1994. Running time: **102 MIN.**
Branwen Roberts ..... Morfudd Hughes
Kevin McCarthy .... Richard Lynch
Llion Roberts .... J.O. Roberts
Mathonwy
  Roberts .... Robert Gwyn Davies
Peredur Roberts .... Allin Elidyr
(Welsh, Irish and English dialogue)

A brave shot at hitching the two Celtic societies of Wales and Northern Ireland under an umbrella of anti-English nationalism, "Branwen" misses its target through shaky development, revealing the stretch marks on its central thesis. This controversial attempt to take Welsh-lingo filmmaking into the contemporary political arena looks set to go not much wider than airings to the already convinced.

Title character (Morfudd Hughes) is a militant Welsh teacher, daughter of a churchman. Despite the objections of her adopted soldier brother, Mathonwy (Robert Gwyn Davies), Branwen marries her b.f., Kevin (Richard Lynch), a Welshman raised in Northern Ireland by whom she's pregnant. The nonpartisan, peaceable Kevin gives in to her demands to raise their kid in Belfast, which Branwen idealistically views as the front line in the anti-English struggle.

While there, the couple become involved in an IRA killing of a soldier, and Kevin, fed up with Branwen's politicking, kicks her out of their house. Back home in Wales, Branwen bonds closer with Mathonwy (who's about to go off and serve in Bosnia), eventually making love with him. When Mathonwy returns wounded, and Kevin reappears from Belfast, the scene is set for a (literal) final conflagration.

Though performances and dialogue are generally on-key, the first half of the pic suffers from confusing exposition in which characters and their relationships are often unclear and considerable prior knowledge of the societies is taken for granted. (Script is developed from a play based on the legend of how the two Celtic nations split apart.) Subtleties in switching between the Welsh and Irish languages will also be missed by non-speakers.

A bigger fault is the dramatic focus, which at first centers on Kevin (as the voice of conciliation) and only later switches to Branwen. Between the two extremes, a convincing case is never made for ex-

tending Irish armed nationalism to the Welsh cause.

Though most of the characters are defined more by their politics than by their personalities, performances are OK within those limits. Technically, the production is pro, with the blowup from Super-16mm bright and strongly colored, if less than ideally sharp in long shots. For the record, freshman director Ceri Sherlock is Welsh-born and producer Angela Graham a Northern Irelander now resident in Wales.

—*Derek Elley*

WILD JUSTICE

(DIAL)

(BRITISH)

A Pendefig production for S4C (Wales). (International sales: S4C, Cardiff.) Produced by Shan Davies. Directed by Paul Turner. Screenplay, Geraint Jones, Eiry Palfrey, Turner. Camera (color), Brian Morgan; editor, Chris Lawrence; music, Mark Thomas; production design, Jane Roberts; costume design, Maxine Brown; sound (Dolby), Jeff Mathews. Reviewed at London Film Festival, Nov. 14, 1994. Running time: **100 MIN.**
With: Nia Medi, Dafydd Emyr, Nick McGaughey, Christine Pritchard, Trevor Selway.
(Welsh dialogue)

Billing itself as "an action-packed, psychological thriller," the Welsh-lingo "Wild Justice" is no such thing. This flatly scripted, and even more flatly directed treatment of the subject of lightly punished female rape is a major letdown after director Paul Turner's impressive, well-considered World War I elegy, the Oscar-nominated "Hedd Wyn."

Dramatic spark is lit when when the youngest daughter of the Hughes family is beaten, raped and left for dead one night. When the perpetrator, Griffith (Nick McGaughey), is released from stir after only three years for manslaughter, the dead girl's elder brother sets out to wreak his own idea of justice on the man.

Milling around in the plot is a sister, Rhiannon (Nia Medi), who's fled back home from London after catching her boyfriend in bed with another woman. She just happens to be a karate student and, while trying to stop her brother's revenge plan, ends up with the rapist in a remote mansion.

Most of the central section of the film is composed of endless sequences of people driving around the countryside in cars. With little dramatic glue, thinly drawn characters and almost no sustained tension, the pic falls apart early on.

Tech credits and performances are standard. An English-language version, shot side-by-side, is reportedly in the works. —*Derek Elley*

THE IMPOSTORS

(LES FAUSSAIRES)

(FRENCH)

An AFMD release of an Adelaide Prod./Lumiere/France 2 Cinema production, with participation of Canal Plus, Cofimage 5, Bymages 3 and CNC. (International sales: WMF, Paris.) Produced by Marc Chayette, Marjorie Israel. Directed by Frederic Blum. Screenplay, Pierre Chossan, Olivier Dazat, Blum, based on the novel "La Tete coupable" by Romain Gary. Camera (color), Bernard Lutic, Sabine Lancelin; editors, Claire Pinheiro, Annie Baronnet; art direction, Jean Louis Poveda, Jean Pierre Lemoine; costume design, Ceceile Balme; sound, Pierre Gamet, Pierre Lenoir, Gerard Lamps, Bernard Chaumeil; associate producers, Eric Altmayer, Eric Mammeja; assistant directors, Gil Descoings, Tamara Dhieux; casting, Richard Rousseau. Reviewed at Forum Horizon Cinema, Paris, Nov. 27, 1994. Running time: **92 MIN.**

Cohn .... Gerard Jugnot
Baker .... Jean-Marc Barr
Meeva .... Viktor Lazlo
Ryckmans .... Claude Pieplu
With: Francois Perrot, Daniel Prevost, Yvon Arai.
(French and English dialogue)

Hampered by a mopey pace offset by only a handful of chuckles, "The Impostors" registers as a tedious exercise in which the natural splendor of Tahiti outdoes a contrived plot at every turn. B.O. prospects look tepid despite (Euro-)marquee value of the two leads, Gerard Jugnot and Jean-Marc Barr.

Cohn (Jugnot), a tubby ex-Parisian and chronic liar, has robbed, swindled or just plain annoyed most of the population of Tahiti and yet, quite literally, cannot get arrested. American scholar Jack Baker (Barr) arrives to write the umpteenth book on the painter Paul Gauguin and is drawn in by the rumor that con man Cohn owns an authentic Gauguin canvas.

The two men form an adversarial relationship that ripens into complicitous friendship once Baker discovers Cohn's true identity.

First pic helmed by experienced assistant director Frederic Blum aims to investigate the perils and pleasures of reinventing oneself, but dawdles so thoroughly in execution as to cancel out script's potential merits. Jugnot acts up a storm, and bilingual Barr — who keeps a tape-recorded diary in English in the otherwise French-lingo pic — is charming but detached. Claude Pieplu amuses as the local police chief whose hands are tied concerning the nuisance-in-residence.

Constant use of swing standards, performed by Benny Goodman, Duke Ellington and Sydney Bechet, only serves to accentuate the distance between their enduring talent and this ephemeral film. Tech credits are OK. —*Lisa Nesselson*

HITS!

A Walron Films Ltd./LLC in association with Symphony Pictures presentation. Produced by William R. Greenblatt, Martha D. Humphreys. Co-executive producer, James Bulleit. Co-producer, Jeffrey S. Malesovas. Directed by Greenblatt. Screenplay, Jeff Monahan, story by Monahan, Luke Toma. Camera (color), Jon Kranhouse; editor, Pam Wish; music, David Lawrence; production design, Shay Austin; costumes, Carolyn Grifel; line producer, Dolly Hall; associate producers, Toma, Gary Caroroso; casting, Todd Thaler. Reviewed at Mill Valley Film Festival, Calif., Oct. 7, 1994. Running time: **85 MIN.**

Mickey .... James Monahan
Dommy .... James Marshall
Kelly .... Martin Sheen
Angie .... Alanna Ubach
Doozie .... Shae D'Lyn

A drab talkfest about two would-be mob thugs trailing a target, "Hits!" invades Scorsese/Cassavetes terrain with no discernible idea of just what it wants to do there. Best chance lies in hyping scant action elements toward ancillary markets.

There have been lots of variations on this "Mean Streets" young-Turks-of-petty-crime theme lately. "Federal Hill," "Laws of Gravity," "Amongst Friends," et al. each brought something distinctive to familiar outlines. As written by lead actor Jeff Monahan, "Hits!" imagines itself a seriocomic character study above all else. But figures and situations here are almost perversely generic.

Introspective Mickey (Monahan) and volatile Dommy (James Marshall, of "Twin Peaks") are thrown together on a "freelance job" by local syndicate boss Kelly (Martin Sheen, appearing just briefly). They're to follow an unnamed man until a mysterious briefcase surfaces, at which point it must be seized by whatever violent means. Most of pic has bumbling novice duo sitting in their car, as "the Mark" (James Bulleit) rides his white limo from restaurant to hotel to cemetery, ad finitum.

After a long, mostly idle night, morning-after shootout leaves protagonists absurdly unscathed. But tag finds them victims of reprisal. Abrupt, so-what impact of this event is underlined by final credits deploying tragic Samuel Barber theme best recalled from "Platoon." Perhaps it's meant as an inside joke. One hopes.

Tedious progress leans heavily on rote evolution between Mickey and Dommy from early antagonism to tentative friendship. Actors are OK but have precious little to work with. Dialogue is routinely gruff, jokey, background-thin. Things liven slightly with arrival of Dommy's g.f. and pal (Alanna Ubach, Shae D'Lyn), whom he invites to break up the waiting game with an unlikely double date. Girls are written and played as stereotyped bimbos.

Making his directorial bow, producer William Greenblatt draws little verve or imagination from a torpid script. Editing sometimes tries to force a jaunty rhythm on scenes, to little avail. Other tech elements are routine. —*Dennis Harvey*

THE CIRCLE GAME

(CANADIAN)

A Shadowlife Film presentation. (International sales: Shadowlife Film, Toronto.) Produced by Brigitte Berman, Joan Cohl. Executive producers, Dusty Cohl, Michael Cohl. Directed by Berman. Screenplay, Berman, Marie-Lynn Hammond, story by Berman. Camera (Film House color), Mitchell Ness; editor, Bruce Lange; music, Gordie Johnson; piano score, John Henry Nyenhuis; production design, Bill Layton; set decoration, Lisa Amaral, Maya Ishiura; sound, Paul Barr; line producer, Robert Appelbe; associate producer, Janet-Laine Green; assistant director, John Pace. Reviewed at Toronto Film Festival, Sept. 10, 1994. Running time: **112 MIN.**

Monika .... Marnie McPhail
Anna .... Janet-Laine Green
Andrea .... Renessa Blitz
Frank .... Tom McCamus
Carl .... David Fox
Marie ....Jayne Eastwood
Evelyn .... Dawn Greenhalgh
Richard .... Albert Schultz

"The Circle Game" painfully demonstrates the downside potential of applying a documentary aesthetic to narrative fiction. First feature by Canadian helmer Brigitte Berman, who won an Oscar for her 1985 docu "Artie Shaw: Time Is All You've Got," goes around in circles without a clue as to how to shape material to dramatic ends, belaboring all its points and subjecting the viewer to unsympathetic characters well beyond the point of endurance. It's a commercial strikeout.

Plot concerns Toronto blues singer and pianist Monika (Marnie McPhail) who, while trying to break into the big time with her band, comes to blows with her mother, Anna (Janet-Laine Green), over the guardianship of 12-year-old Andrea (Renessa Blitz). Latter has been raised by the snooty Anna, but it comes as no surprise when her parentage is revealed, in highly melodramatic terms, to have been otherwise. The selfish, very untogether women continually outdo each other trying to prove who is the less fit mother, and audiences will want to tune out the whole mess.

Part of the problem is Berman's lack of any restraining hand on the performers, who are uniformly way over the top. Other major flaws are her impulse to spell everything out in capital letters and the hand-held *cinema verite* style that flattens everything rather than lending it dramatic punch.

Even musically, pic is of marginal interest, although some extended sequences are devoted to rehearsals and club dates. —*Todd McCarthy*

LA VIE EN ROSE

(CHANGMI BIT INSAENG)

(SOUTH KOREAN)

A Taehung Pictures (Seoul) production. (International sales: Korean Motion Picture Promotion Co.) Produced by Le Tae-Won. Directed by Kim Hong-Joon. Screenplay, Yook Sang-Hyo. Camera (color), Park Seoung-Bai; editor, Park Soon-Duk; music, Cho Dong-Ik; production design, Kim Yoo-Joon. Reviewed at Vancouver Film Festival (competing), Oct. 14, 1994. Running time: **95 MIN.**

With: Choi Myung-Kil, Choi Jae-Sung, Cha Gwang-Soo, Lee Jee-Hyung, Hwang Mee-Sun.

Good locations and a fizzy, what-the-hell attitude save this messy mix of genre parody, class consciousness and arty intentions from withering. Pic could find a grudging home in some commercially minded Asian cinemas, but won't smell sweet enough for offshore arthouse picking.

Set in working-class Seoul in the months leading up to the 1988 Olympics, pic narrows in on a small group of misfits, drawn together at an all-night comic-book shop, which doubles as a super-cheap crash pad. The madam of this open-house "library" is a lovely, introspective woman (Choi Myung-Kil) who handles the roughest elements with relaxed ease. She does, however, become somewhat unnerved by the arrival of handsome gangster Dongpal (Choi Jae-Sung), on the lam from a frame-up charge.

Unfortunately, Dongpal pursues Madam's attentions by raping her in a troubling, if ultimately well-handled scene. The woman responds by refusing to acknowledge his presence, sending him into an existential tailspin that has him following her day and night. He harasses her customers, including her brother (Cha Gwang-Soo), who's a labor leader in hiding, and a young writer (Lee Jee-Hyung) wanting to learn about life. Eventually, though, the toughie begins to fit into their odd little family.

It's an admittedly quirky kind of love story, one that Jean Renoir could have tossed off handily in the politically charged 1930s (or maybe Juzo Itami today, albeit with a more farcical edge). When first-time helmer Kim Hong-Joon tries to throw political commentary into the pulpy romance the attempt is clumsy and too late in coming. Similarly, outright chopsocky sequences lack the necessary flair to justify their rhythm-breaking intrusions — especially when some fights crack with cartoon abandon and others thud realistically.

The problem is one of overambition leavened with a surplus of good taste. Pic is neither rigorous nor cheesy enough to satisfy the various audiences it's gunning for, although good perfs, effective lensing and a snappy pop score make it easy to sit through. —*Ken Eisner*

LOU DIDN'T SAY NO

(LOU N'A PAS DIT NON)

(FRENCH-SWISS)

A Sara Films, Peripheria (Paris)/ Vega Film (Zurich) production. Directed, written by Anne-Marie Mieville. Camera (color), Jean-Paul Rosa Da Costa, Edwin Horak; editor, Mieville; art direction, Yvan Niclass; sound, Pierre-Alain Besse. Reviewed at Locarno Film Festival (competing), Aug. 13, 1994. Running time: **78 MIN.**
Lou .... Marie Bunel
Pierre .... Manuel Blanc
Isabelle .... Caroline Micla
Suzanne .... Genevieve Pasquier
Florence .... Metilde Weyergans
Theo .... Harry Cleven
Francois .... Wilfred Benaiche
(French dialogue)

"Lou Didn't Say No" is a quintessential Euro art film that examines a couple's relationship with great cinematic sophistication and almost no emotion. Strictly for the more cerebral elements of the fest crowd, this pic — written, directed and edited by Godard's close collaborator, Anne-Marie Mieville — is a hothouse flower unlikely to survive on reallife circuits.

The Lou of the title (the beautiful Marie Bunel) is directing a film set in a museum while she holds down a steady job answering a lonelyhearts hotline. Lou spends most of her screen time, however, with her former lover, a passionate, younger actor named Pierre (Manuel Blanc), discussing their relationship.

While he's moody, at times violent, and romantically in love, she's cool, analytical and ready to explore friendship as an alternative to a traditional man-woman relationship. Although Pierre is crazy about Lou, he's seeing another girl (Genevieve Pasquier) whom he may marry. Lou claims she's not the jealous type. Pierre is, and when he sees her kissing a rival, he explodes.

Despite all the tears and teethgnashing, audience is offered little chance to care about the characters, and much of the dialogue is deliberately stagy and unrealistic.

Pic seems hypnotized by high bourgeois culture. At one point Mieville indulges in a lengthy scene showing an anguishing modern dance that continues long after it makes its point. There's also a stage rehearsal, the museum and Lou's film set there, not to mention a refined classical music soundtrack, expensive apartments, exquisite lighting and uniformly attractive actors.

Film concludes with some thoughtful dialogue between a pair of talking Greek statues who seem perfectly in tune with Mieville's style. —*Deborah Young*

SIMPLY LOVE

(EINFACH NUR LIEBE)

(GERMAN)

An Avista Film/Relevant Film GmbH production, in association with Westdeutscher Rundfunk (Cologne). (International sales: Cinepool, Munich.) Produced by Alena Rimbach, Heike Wiehle-Timm. Executive producer, Herbert Rimbach. Directed by Peter Timm. Screenplay, Timm, Michael Arnal, Xao Seffcheque. Camera (color) Fritz Seeman; editor, Helga Borsche; music, Detlef Peterson; production design, Josef Sank Sanktjohanser; sound, Gunter Knon, Eckhard Kuchenbecker. Reviewed at World Film Festival, Montreal (competing), Sept. 2, 1994. Running time: **95 MIN.**
Mamba .... Benno Formann
Pilgrim .... Uwe Ochsenknecht
Thommy .... Steffen Wink
Yuksel .... Moritz Bleibtreu
Nadja .... Regula Grauwiller
Lydia .... Eva Hassmann

A Teutonic "Blackboard Jungle," "Simply Love" starts out exploring hardcore ennui in modern German schools but soon settles into standard teen action. Swift pace, good music and winsome leads make it an agreeably commercial venture.

"Men" star Uwe Ochsenknecht, Germany's answer to Kelsey Grammer, nominally toplines as Pilgrim, a tough-minded high school teacher whose mission is to bring language skills and a twinge of political consciousness to a disaffected crowd of Dortmunder youths. The kids have drifted into two crowds, each with a representative rock band: The Smashers are skinhead-metal bullies, led by rich kid Thommy (Steffen Wink) whose family is intended to be the local version of the Krupps, while the multicultural Fresh Familee boasts Turkish-German rappers and other auslanders.

Into this setup steps Mamba (Benno Formann), a James Deanlike transfer student who doesn't like to be forced into choosing sides. The lines are drawn for him, however, when he's attracted to Thommy's onetime gal pal Nadja, who's no skinhead (Regula Grauwiller looks remarkably like a young Hannah Schygulla).

Meanwhile, Herr Pilgrim decides the only way to pull everyone together is to have them mount a production of "Romeo and Juliet." Montagues and Capulets, get it? It's worth asking, since helmer Peter Timm drops the Shakespeare about two-thirds of the way in and goes for straight Aaron Spelling the rest of the way, also skipping the teacher-in-distress angle.

Pic's conflicts seem artificial from the start, with buffoonish administrators and Wink's swank villain straining credulity. It's got the verve of an old-style exploitationer, though, with bright lensing, fast pacing and upbeat hip-hop score making up for disjointed storytelling. Decent B.O. in dubbed international versions is more likely than continued life on fest circuit.

Originally titled "The Power of Love," the pic flopped at home during Germany's record summer heat wave and is slated for re-release this fall. —*Ken Eisner*

MACEDONIAN SAGA

(MACEDONIAN)

A Pegasus Film production. Produced by Panta Mizimakov. Directed by Branko Gapo. Screenplay, Simon Drakul. Camera (color), Vladimir Samoilovski; editor, Dimitar Grbevski; music, Ljupcho Konstantinov; sound, Gligor Pakovski. Reviewed at World Film Festival, Montreal, Aug. 30, 1994. Running time: **111 MIN.**
With: Biljana Taneska, Meto Jovanovski, Kiril Pop Hristov.

The sheer novelty of a pic from the beleaguered Republic of Macedonia may be enough to guarantee a few stops on the global fest circuit for Branko Gapo's "Macedonian Saga." But this lackluster reworking of the "Romeo and Juliet" scenario will be a tough commercial sell.

Plot deals with a Christian schoolteacher, newly arrived in the Muslim village of Velekorab, who falls for a Muslim beauty who's engaged to a man of her own ethnic and religious background. Dzemile (Biljana Taneska) gives her heart — and body — to Damian (Meto Jovanovski), but is pressured by local mores, her parents and her overbearing older brother to end the scandalous romance. She winds up committing suicide, and he is left a broken man who wanders the snowy countryside.

Director Gapo rarely generates much suspense as the star-crossed romance develops. Indeed, the lovers are never very circumspect and seldom behave as though their love affair is the risky undertaking it is supposed to be. It doesn't help much that their tragic story is told by a minor supporting character who doesn't figure prominently in what's presented onscreen.

Chief point of interest is the characterization of Christian and Muslim clerics, who come off as reasonable and sympathetic even as they warn the young lovers to end their relationship. Other characters are neither written nor acted with notable complexity.

Tech credits are average.
—*Joe Leydon*

FADO, MAJOR AND MINOR

(FADO MAJEUR ET MINEUR)

(FRENCH-PORTUGUESE)

A Gemini Films (Paris)/Madragoa films (Lisbon) co-production. Produced by Paulo Branco. Directed, written by Raul Ruiz. Camera (color), Jean-Yves Coic; editor, Denise de Casablanca. Reviewed at San Sebastian Film Festival (competing), Sept. 20, 1994. Running time: **110 MIN.**
With: Jean-Luc Bideau, Melvil Poupaud, Ana Padrao, Jean-Yves Gautier. (French soundtrack)

Aficionados of quirky underground helmer Raul Ruiz may find something to cheer about in this filmic mishmash, but ordinary mortals will merely yawn or walk out of the show. As usual with Ruiz, there is no apparent story, and scenes and exchanges of dialogue trip over each other with no seeming connection, all served up in mock solemnity, occasionally trailing into drollness and cheap B&W film stock.

Characters may babble about someone's hat, or a boy may sing fado in a nightclub, or a prostitute may fall under the table, or the camera may just linger on a seascape. In this case, the purpose of it all can probably be clear only to Ruiz himself. —*Peter Besas*

OMAHA (THE MOVIE)

A Dana Altman & Bugeater Films Ltd. presentation. Produced by Altman, Dan Mirvish. Directed, written by Mirvish. Camera (color), Oslo Anderson; editors, Alexandra Komisaruk, Larry Maddox; music, Andrew McPherson, M.J. Greenberg; production design, A. Craig Florian, Kristin A. Landis; costumes, Nancy Ross; assistant director, Adam Hyman. Reviewed at Roxie Cinema, San Francisco, Sept. 14, 1994. (In Mill Valley Film Festival.) Running time: 85 min.
With: Hughston Walkinshaw, Jill Anderson, Frankie Bee, Christopher M. Dukes, Lars Erik Madsen.

Writer/director Dan Mirvish created this 35mm indie feature as his USC grad thesis project on a $40,000 budget. For that kind of dough, "Omaha (The Movie)" is a model of tech resourcefulness. But this silly, straining-to-be-quirky comedy is strictly undergraduate in content, and will serve best as a calling card for bigger, better projects.

Prologue introduces Simon (Hughston Walkinshaw) and his nightmare-sitcom Nebraska family. Understandably, Simon decides to flee to the "farthest destination from here." Post-credits, he's back from a year in Nepal and other ex-

December 12, 1994 (Cont.)

otic locales, having run out of money during his "spiritual quest."

Monks gave him a parting gift of Buddhist prayer stones, which wacky ex-g.f. Gina (Jill Anderson) promptly recognizes as valuable emeralds. Awkward readjustment to Midwestern life is further complicated by various Colombian thugs, a kickboxing gang and tabloid TV news team, all hot on the trail of those gems. Climactic chase ends up at junk-car novelty spot Carhenge, a Stonehenge mockup 400 miles outside Omaha.

Milking home-state support for all it's worth, Mirvish includes tongue-in-cheek boosterism cameos by real-life governor, sheriff, mayor, etc. Other eccentric touches include hand-held "subtitle" translations for the Colombian characters, a stockyard foot chase, lots of local sites and in-jokes. Hyperactive editing, gimmicky camerawork and busy soundtrack work hard to make a whiz-bang impression.

Problem is that none of this is very funny, with irksome (albeit fairly well-played) characters and verbal/visual gags that are obvious despite their calculated weirdness. You have to give Mirvish credit for gumption. With this kind of energy and determination on tap, he might be worth watching as artistic maturity — one quality definitely not on display here — takes hold.

—Dennis Harvey

LES AMOUREUSES

(CANADIAN)

An Alliance release of a Les Productions du Cerf production in association with the National Film Board of Canada. Produced by Louise Gendron. Directed, written by Johanne Pregent. Camera (color), Francois Protat; editor, Dominique Fortin; music, Pierre Desrochers; art direction/costume design, Louise Jobin; set design, Pierre Perrault; sound recordist, Richard Besse; sound design, Marie-Claude Gagne; associate producer, Doris Girard; line producers, Madeleine Henrie, Leon G. Arcand; assistant director, Louis-Philippe Rochon; casting, Lucie Robitaille. Reviewed at Mill Valley Film Festival, Calif., Oct. 16, 1994. Running time: **99 MIN.**

Lea	Louise Portal
David	Kenneth Walsh
Marianne	Lea Marie Cantin
Nino	Tony Nardi

This absorbing French-Canadian drama tracks two couples as they grapple with issues of commitment and desire on the brink of middle age. Sans notable marquee names or stylistic panache, insightful but modest effort looks toward Euro TV for best prospects outside home turf.

Theater costume designer Lea (Louise Portal) is shaken at outset by walkout of novelist b.f. David (Kenneth Walsh), who breaks off their 10-year relationship in the wake of an affair with one of his university pro-

tegees. While David soon returns, the episode plagues Lea with lingering doubts. Best friend Marianne (Lea Marie Cantin), an acupuncturist/masseuse, has resigned herself to single status when charming Italian emigre Nino (Tony Nardi) walks into her office. At first his ardor seems a pure come-on. The slow-dawning sincerity of this suit proves challenging for reluctant Marianne.

Pic lacks the authorial insight or filmic style that would transcend basic soap format. Still, story's progress rarely feels untrue, and issues concerning passion in long-term hetero relationships, seldom seriously explored in cinema, are handled with intelligence and sympathy toward all protagonists. Secondary couple tends to be more entertaining, allowing greater room for humor and passion.

All perfs are sensitive. As the least emotionally blocked character (Nino says that others "think too much" to be happy), the ingratiating Nardi gets to steal numerous scenes.

Johanne Pregent earns more praise for her low-key, deft scenario than her direction, which manages actors with care but demonstrates little interest in overall look or cumulative pacing. Still, the sum is restrained, involving adult drama. Tech aspects are pro if routine.

—Dennis Harvey

SALVATION

(VIMUKTHI)

(SRI LANKAN)

An Aloka Films (Private) Ltd. production. Executive producer, Dr. Nimal Jinadasa. Directed by Priyantha Colombage. Screenplay, Jayantha Colombage. Camera (color), Suminda Weerasinghe; editor, Stanley de Alwis; art director, Athula Sulthanagoda; makeup, Samarisi Kadanage; sound, Lionel Gunarathna; assistant director, Donald Jayantha. Reviewed at Roxie Cinema, San Francisco, Sept. 26, 1994. (In Mill Valley Film Festival.) Running time: **110 MIN.**
With: Joe Abeywickrama, Sanath Gunathilaka, Sabitha Perara, Veena Jayakody, H.A. Perera, Sriyantha Mendis, Avantha Mahatanila.

This attractively lensed Sri Lankan feature — the first by producing Aloka Films org — offers a moral lesson or three in the emotionally straightforward, humanist tradition of Satyajit Ray. But as the narrative soon overloads to confusing/hokey effect, pic has appeal limited to global-diversity-leaning fests and highly specialized bookers.

Central figure is Sagara, a good-natured rural lad who grows up emotionally abused and beaten by his alcoholic stepfather. As an adult, he rekindles a childhood crush on beauteous visiting Kumari, whose

orphaned status necessitated an urban move years before. He follows her to the city, where a conscientious journalist rescues him from thugs and provides shelter.

Once they locate Kumari, it is suggested (in murky narrative terms) that she's been reduced to prostitution. Her apparent pimp embroils Sagara in various lurid shenanigans that stretch from pickpocketry to violent strike-breaking and, finally, murder. Latter action is attempt to both break Kumari's downward moral spiral and save the journalist from politically motivated assassination.

But tag (which fudges chronology, like much else here) posits her as an elderly slave to secreted cash a la ZaSu Pitts in "Greed," while seemingly now-middle-aged Sagara plays a humble guru amid serene countryside imagery to the still-young and inexplicably pregnant servant girl he'd rescued earlier from city exploitation.

Unflattering contrast of urban vs. rural moral values is limned simplistically here. One weird scene shows naive Sagara's "hallucinations" on hemp or hash as a delusional view of the city's slum-dwellers in upscale clothing. It's not exactly terrifying.

Elsewhere, crucial plot details are passed over as being presumably too vulgar for depiction. A sense of narrative cluelessness results. Worst, however, is first-half's poor structuring, which at one point allows a flashback-within-flashback-within-flashback. Second half, centered on Sagara's unbelievably slow conscience-stirring, has its own problems.

Perfs tend toward the stilted. Despite poor editing and some zoom-lensing, best attribute here is soph feature director Priyantha Colombage's handsome exploitation of both verdant rural locales and vivid cityscapes. *—Dennis Harvey*

THE ROOK

An Ecco Films Inc. (New York) production. Produced by Eran Palatnik, Alan J. Abrams. Directed by Palatnik. Screenplay, Richard Lee Purvis. Camera (color), Zack Winestine; editor, Ahmad Shirazi; production design, Sebastian Schroder; music, Robert Een; sound, Jan McLaughlin. Reviewed at World Film Festival, Montreal (non-competing), Sept. 4, 1994. Running time: **85 MIN.**
With: Martin Donovan, John A. MacKay, Michael Finesilver, Fritz Fox, David P. Dawson, Diane Grotke, Alice Connorton, Douglas Stone, Karen Abrahams, Damon Rice.

This sluggish bundle of stylized anachronisms is intended as a genre-leaping mind puzzle, but even the most patient auds will give up the game long before

its drawn-out denouement. Look for a quick move to video.

Set in an unspecified country, in a vaguely 19th-century milieu mixing starched collars and horse-drawn buggies with fluorescent lamps and bulbous, "Brazil"-like machinery, "The Rook" follows by-the-book police detective John Abbott (played by Hal Hartley fave Martin Donovan at his most humorless) in his attempts to unravel a creepy murder case.

A young woman has been found with her head shaved and a strange spiral design painted on her belly. Abbott thinks this indicates some connection with unexplained revolutionaries who are threatening the God-fearing order of wherever this is happening. On his way to unfortunate enlightenment, the copper encounters a weaselly printer, a prickly painter and a slinky doctor straight out of '40s film noir, with politics and place names giving no further sense of time or geography. Not that anyone will care after the characters mumble their way through the 20th murkily lit interior.

Film school Kafka at its most tedious, pic shows no interest in its people or their world except as an exercise in overall design. And that's where the talent is, with elaborately detailed sets, clever editing and jazzy chamber music giving viewers something to think about while the story evaporates.

—Ken Eisner

THE SILENT MOVIE LOVER

(EL AMANTE DE LAS PELICULAS MUDAS)

(ARGENTINE)

A Fundacion Leopoldo Torre Nilsson (Buenos Aires) production. Produced by Marilyn Torre. Directed, written by Pablo Torre. Camera (color/b&w) Marcelo Iacarino; editor, Miguel Perez; music, Luis Maria Serra; production design, Eliseo Zanusso; art direction, Pepe Uria; sound, Mario Calabrese; assistant director, Rodolfo Mortola. Reviewed at World Film Festival, Montreal (non-competing), Aug. 31, 1994. (Also in Toronto fest.) Running time: **92 MIN.**
With: Alfredo Alcon (Ralph de Palma), Roberto de Vitta (Paolo), Carola Reyna (Clara), Laura Novao, Gerardo Romano, Sofia Torre.

After a dazzling opening sequence, "The Silent Movie Lover" quickly deteriorates into a series of disconnected tableaux, giving viewers plenty of time to ponder the sleepy pic's many logical and technical flaws. Pic offers a nice hook to arthouse exhibs, a la "Cinema Paradiso," but real movie lovers will stay away.

Tale starts with nuns and orphans listening to a histrionic radio soap as a passing cyclist catches the eye of one teenage girl. That sets the campy atmosphere in which the adult narrator, explaining via v.o., was conceived. Flashbacks then reveal little Paolo (Roberto de Vitta) and his young mother (Carola Reyna) moving to the mausoleum-like household of Ralph de Palma (Alfredo Alcon). Apparently, El Ralph-o was a big Hollywood star in the Latin Lover era, but talking pictures did him in, and now, in the 1950s, he runs a funeral parlor.

Early scenes are beautifully staged and shot, with the blond, big-eyed Paolo focusing the baroque proceedings. But as soon as the pic delves into Ralph's silent-movie history, the narrative breaks down and never recovers. Archival images of Keystone Kops, Charles Chaplin and Pearl White are nonsensically mixed with "re-created" B&W footage in which the Argentinian actor looks, oh, about five years younger than he does now.

We're also supposed to believe that Paolo's mom is a terrific pianist, but when she sits down to play a Schubert trio at de Palma's white grand piano, an unseen cello dominates the soundtrack, along with the unmistakable hiss of vinyl. It's not magic realism but bad sound editing that colors much of the film, with goopy synthesizers competing with booming voices throughout, and sloppy editing prevalent. At the end, helmer Pablo Torre tries to clean up his messy package by staging a forced repetition of the beginning, but the rot is too deep for formal tricks to work.

—*Ken Eisner*

TOWARD THE WITHIN

(BRITISH — DOCU)

A Magidson Films (Culver City) production. Executive producers, Robin Hucler, Ivo Russell. Produced, directed by Mark Magidson. Camera (color), David Aubrey; editors, Magidson, Aubrey; music, Dead Can Dance; sound, Gilles Charbonneau. Reviewed at World Film Festival, Montreal (noncompeting), Sept. 1, 1994. Running time: **78 MIN.**

Disappointing concert pic captures the mysterious sound of Anglo World Beaters Dead Can Dance, but fails to give it any visual interpretation. Despite good transfer from 16mm, "Toward the Within" will head straight toward the video store.

Helmer Mark Magidson used music of the Anglo-Irish duo Dead Can Dance for his work on impressionistic "Baraka" and then culled outtakes for their video "Yulunga." That shot-on-70mm sequence opens "Within" (in letterboxed form), before the pic reverts to performance footage. The movie then settles into a dull song-chat-song-chat format that does little to build on band's

mystical pulse and entrenches their too-sober self-image.

Prosaic lensing points up DCD's lack of visual presence, as well as emphasizing the disparity between powerhouse singer Lisa Gerrard, who invents Slavic-sounding syllables, and her partner Brendan Perry, who talks a good line but croons mundane lyrics like a New Age Vic Damone. Duo's five-piece backup is celluloid window-dressing.

"Within" does offer spectacular Dolby sound and points up the possibility of Gerrard going solo in the near future.

—*Ken Eisner*

THE FOURTH GREEN FIELD

(DOCU — Color/B&W)

A Canoe Prods. production. Directed, written, edited by Margaret Bruen. Camera, Sean Hulsebosch; music, Tommy Makem, the Chieftains; sound, Betty Bruen. Reviewed at World Film Festival, Montreal, Sept. 2, 1994. Running time: **96 MIN.**

Margaret Bruen's "The Fourth Green Field" is a sincere and well-researched docu about the human-rights abuses that have been "justified" (legally, if not morally) in Northern Ireland under the Prevention of Terrorism Act. But the pic's impact is seriously undercut by Bruen's unfortunate tendency to keep hammering away at points long after they are made. Some judicious editing would help pic get exposure in public and cable TV outlets.

Bruen deftly provides historical context in opening scenes, relying heavily on period BBC news reports of civil rights protests by Catholics in Northern Ireland during the 1960s. (The BBC narrator sounds snidely condescending as he refers to the need for authorities to "discipline an obstreperous population.") One thing leads to another, British security forces arrive, and the long years of repression begin.

Bulk of pic is a montage of talking-heads interviews with local and international human rights activists, victims of abuse by British and Irish forces, and relatives of those who have been killed or arrested by what the docu depicts as an occupying army. Irish firebrand Bernadette McAliskey (nee Devlin) is bitterly sardonic as she describes how British forces go about patrolling so-called subversive neighborhoods: "The very fact that you're breathing means you're up to no good."

Pic emphasizes the arbitrary but absolute powers given to police officials by the Prevention of Terrorism Act. Suspected "subversives" can be interrogated and imprisoned

for indefinite terms without trial or legal counsel. An unofficial "shoot to kill" policy has resulted in a suspiciously high body count. At least one innocent bystander was struck and blinded in her own living room by a plastic bullet fired through her window by a patrolman.

"Field" is notably short on reportage of IRA violence. But Protestant vigilantes are persuasively linked to the British officials. "Field" is too didactic and one-sided to be taken as completely objective, and too repetitious for its own good. At its frequent best, however, it works effectively as thought-provoking advocacy journalism.

—*Joe Leydon*

THE DOVE'S BELL-RINGER

(GOLUBINY ZVONAR)

(KAZAKH)

A Kazakhfilm Studio production. Directed by Amir Karakulov. Screenplay, Karakulov, Elena Gordeeva. Camera (color), Fedor Aranyshev; art direction, Rustem Abdrashev. Reviewed at Taormina Film Festival (competing), Italy, July 28, 1994. Running time: **70 MIN.**
Timur .... Chingiz Nogalbaev
Elya .... Elmira Makhmutova

Slow-moving and ponderously elegiac, "The Dove's Bell-Ringer" sets its tale of star-crossed lovers on the lonesome plains of Kazakhstan. New Wave director Amir Karakulov (whose "Woman Between Two Brothers" made the fest rounds in 1991) recounts his minimalist tale in elegant, fixed-camera long takes that follow one another with little variation. Pic shared first prize at the Taormina fest, but its B.O. chances outside fests look remote.

Timur (Chingiz Nogalbaev), a young man who does little besides raising doves, is dumped by his g.f. but soon falls in love with a beautiful young neighbor, Elya (Elmira Makhmutova). They marry, but she dies during childbirth. Driven mad with heartbreak, Timur kills a man in a fight and is thrown into a local jail. He breaks out and wanders back to the dovecote and his memories.

Although plenty of momentous things happen, they are shot with such deliberate casualness and lack of emphasis that the film feels static and uneventful. Minimal dialogue is mirrored by minimal information about the characters. Shots are carefully composed but given little rhythm through editing.   —*Deborah Young*

IT'S ALL LIES

(TODO ES MENTIRA)

(SPANISH)

An Atrium Productions S.A. film, with the participation of Television Espanola S.A. Produced by Enrique Cerezo and Carlos Vasallo. Directed, written by Alvaro Fernandez Armero. Camera, Antonio Cuevas; editor, Ivan Aledo; music, Coque Malla; sets, Jon Arrentxe; sound, Julio Recuero. Reviewed at San Sebastian Film Festival (competing), Sept. 16, 1994. Running time: **103 MIN.**
Lucia .... Penelope Cruz
Pablo .... Coque Malla
Ariel .... Jordi Molla
Claudio .... Gustavo Salmeron
With: Irene Bau, Cristina Rosse Vinge, Fernando Colomo, Monica Lopez, Ariadna Gil, Patricia Garcia Menendez.

This bittersweet local comedy about the lives, loves and problems of four couples shows considerable promise for neophyte helmer Armero, even though much of the dialogue falls flat and some of the situations are forced. Pic may do OK in its home market, but probably won't make a ripple elsewhere.

Item is centered around Pablo, who has a negative slant on life and a new bedmate. The stresses in their relationship parallel those of three other couples who are Pablo's friends, all of whom are not satisfied with their partners but too fearful to change their lives.

At the end of the film, all that seems to remain is the disenchantment and alienation of a sector of Spanish society which has lost its bearings—if it ever had any.

—*Peter Besas*

December 19, 1994

THE MADNESS OF KING GEORGE

A Samuel Goldwyn release in association with Channel 4 Films of a Close Call Films production. Produced by Stephen Evans, David Parfitt. Directed by Nicholas Hytner. Screenplay, Alan Bennett, based on his play "The Madness of George III." Camera (Technicolor), Andrew Dunn; editor, Tariq Anwar; music adapted by George Fenton; production design, Ken Adam; art direction, John Fenner; set decoration, Carolyn Scott; costume design, Mark Thompson; sound (Dolby), David Crozier; assistant director, Mary Sloan; casting, Celestia Fox. Reviewed at Sony Studios screening room, Culver City, Dec. 9, 1994. Running time: **107 MIN.**

George III	Nigel Hawthorne
Queen Charlotte	Helen Mirren
Dr. Willis	Ian Holm
Prince of Wales	Rupert Everett
Greville	Rupert Graves
Thurlow	John Wood
Lady Pembroke	Amanda Donohoe
Duke of York	Julian Rhind-Tutt

Nicholas Hytner, the Tony Award-winning director who dazzled Broadway with his production of "Miss Saigon" and brilliant revival of "Carousel," makes a stunning screen directorial debut in "The Madness of King George," Alan Bennett's comic-tragic drama of the tormented king who almost lost his mind. A towering performance by Nigel Hawthorne, a stellar supporting cast and a boldly lavish production should make this costume epic intriguing viewing for the upscale audience that supported Goldwyn's 1989 "Henry V," Kenneth Branagh's debut.

"The Madness of King George" confirms that power games, family scandals and personal intrigues have always been integral to the British crown, an institution at once revered and reviled by its citizenry. The effective strategy of Bennett, who adapted his 1991 play for the screen, is to demythologize the members of the royal family without trivializing their lives in the silly, banal manner of other works like "The Lion in Winter."

The tale begins in 1788, with King George III (Hawthorne) a vibrant, robust leader, almost 30 years into his reign. He's happily married to his devoted Queen Charlotte (Helen Mirren), who has borne him 15 children, including the Prince of Wales (Rupert Everett) and the Duke of York (Julian Rhind-Tutt).

To most English countrymen, the royal couple represents a desirable political order, based on a solid and stable family life. Yet here, almost from the beginning, the king behaves in a strange, eccentric way. He is the kind of energetic leader who insists on knowing — and interfering in — every aspect of his monarchy.

The king's veneer of respectability is shattered in a series of brief scenes that disclose his "darker side," as he spews obscenities at the queen or sexually assaults her attractive Mistress of the Robes, Lady. Pembroke (Amanda Donohoe). In one of many well-executed, disturbing scenes, the king interrupts a royal concert with an arrogant demonstration of his own mastery of the keyboard.

Through his increasingly irrational conduct, it soon becomes evident that the king is ill, though the specific nature of his ailment is unclear. When the team of royal physicians, portrayed here as inept, barbaric buffoons, can't help, a strong-willed physician, Dr. Willis (Ian Holm), takes the king under his wing and subjects him to a strict psychotherapeutic discipline.

With the exception of a few excessively theatrical scenes, Bennett's poignantly touching script doesn't betray its stage origins. Helmer Hytner moves the action smoothly from tightly controlled indoor settings to gloriously staged outdoor scenes, such as one showing the hyperactive king rampaging through the fields of Windsor at sunrise with his hysterical staff behind him.

Though Bennett and Hytner provide a sharply focused, behind-the-scenes look at King George, they don't neglect the broader political context, most notably his loss of the American colonies. Some of the sharpest dialogue concerns the king's obsession with the rebellious territory; "Give us the wisdom of America," says an observer in a line that bears contemporary relevance.

Reprising the role he created at the Royal National Theatre and played extensively on tour, Hawthorne displays a wide range of emotion, passion and intellect in a performance that sparkles with unusual ebullience. Dominating every scene, Hawthorne brings to his complex part a strong screen presence, light self-mockery and pathos that set divergent moods throughout the film.

Under Hytner's guidance, the entire cast, composed of some of the best actors in British cinema today, rises to the occasion. Mirren is most touching as the devoted queen who is denied access to her husband, Everett is outright marvelous in the juicy role of the conniving son who schemes to become a regent, and Holm shines as the unconventional psychiatrist.

Boasting a rich period look, almost every shot is filled with a handsome, emotionally charged composition. Andrew Dunn's sumptuous lensing, Ken Adam's magnificently resourceful production design, Mark Thompson's opulent costumes, Tariq Anwar's vibrant editing and George Fenton's evocative score reflect an alert intelligence, all contributing to an indelible sense of time and place. —*Emanuel Levy*

LITTLE WOMEN

A Columbia release of a Di Novi Pictures production. Produced by Denise Di Novi. Co-producer, Robin Swicord. Directed by Gillian Armstrong. Screenplay, Swicord, based on the book by Louisa May Alcott. Camera (Technicolor), Geoffrey Simpson; editor, Nicholas Beauman; music, Thomas Newman; production design, Jan Roelfs; art direction, Richard Hudolin; set design, Richard St. John Harrison; set decoration, Jim Erickson; costume design, Colleen Atwood; sound (Dolby), Eric Batut; sound design, Lee Smith; associate producer, Warren Carr; assistant director, Mark Turnbull; second unit director, Mark Lewis; second unit camera, Peter Levy; casting, Carrie Frazier, Shani Ginsberg. Reviewed at Sony Pictures screening room, Culver City, Dec. 8, 1994. MPAA Rating: PG. Running time: **118 MIN.**

Jo March	Winona Ryder
Friedrich Bhaer	Gabriel Byrne
Meg March	Trini Alvarado
Older Amy March	Samantha Mathis
Younger Amy March	Kirsten Dunst
Beth March	Claire Danes
Laurie	Christian Bale
John Brooke	Eric Stoltz
Mr. Laurence	John Neville
Aunt March	Mary Wickes
Mrs. March	Susan Sarandon

Since sound pictures came in, every generation has gotten its own "Little Women." What the modern public has done to deserve it is unclear, but 1990s audiences are the beneficiaries of an outstanding version of Louisa May Alcott's perennial, one that surpasses even the best previous rendition, George Cukor's 1933 outing starring Katharine Hepburn. A moving, passionately told story about the connections among four generations of a family's women — and, more telling, the way women had to struggle to make a mark in a society in which their roles were heavily proscribed — this handsomely produced period piece is easily the most emotionally effective bigscreen melodrama since "The Joy Luck Club," as well as the most intelligent. Even if many men, particularly younger ones, may choose to resist the picture's charms, it will be warmly embraced by most viewers, including women of all ages, and it is easy to imagine some returning repeatedly. If the film is smartly marketed, Columbia has a long-running winner here.

One measure of the film's effectiveness is that it can stand equally well as a beautifully judged adaptation of a famous book, a personal work by director Gillian Armstrong that is very much a companion piece to her first film, "My Brilliant Career," and a 19th-century bookend for Winona Ryder to the late 20th-century characterization with which she started the year in "Reality Bites."

Alcott's enduring 1868 novel about the growing up of four sisters in Concord, Mass., during and after the Civil War has been filmed four times previously, the first time as a silent in 1918. Cukor's 1933 version is notable primarily for Hepburn's luminous performance in the central role of Jo March and for the giddily conspiratorial feeling generated among the sisters, although the picture seems rather starchy today. By contrast, Mervyn LeRoy's 1949 remake starring June Allyson and Elizabeth Taylor and a 1978 TV movie featuring Meredith Baxter were notable for very little at all.

One significant hurdle for the filmmakers was to take contemporary audiences over the threshold of vastly different mores and social conventions to a time when earnestness, family solidarity and sexual reserve were unquestioned standards of behavior, and cynicism and the doubting of authority had scarcely been heard of. They have been notably successful in this regard, thanks to the breezily conversational quality of Robin Swicord's dialogue, the warm informality of the young actresses and the firm concentration on dramatic essentials displayed by director Armstrong.

The four March "little women" are Meg (Trini Alvarado), Jo (Winona Ryder), Beth (Claire Danes) and Amy (initially Kirsten Dunst, then Samantha Mathis). Presided over by their mother, Marmee (Susan Sarandon), while their father is off fighting in the Union Army, the Marches were "once one of our finest families," in the snide opinion of a neighbor, but have come to live in somewhat reduced circumstances in what is nevertheless a beautiful New England home.

The spirited girls are enthralled with dressing up for their own little theatricals and zealously throw themselves into their projects, which include helping the truly disadvantaged, with irrepressible abandon. In addition, the central character, Jo, is an aspiring writer who precociously spins melodramatic tales of adventure and crime.

In due course, in a period that atmospherically spans the seasons, the Marches forge a strong friendship with the young man across the way, Laurie (Christian Bale), whose dreams of a musical career would appear threatened by the call of the family firm. Beth catches scarlet fever as a result of her charitable work with the poor and is never the same again, while the very traditional Meg begins a courtship with stolid tutor John Brooke (Eric Stoltz).

Halfway through, the story jumps ahead four years to Meg's wedding to Brooke. Devastating Laurie by rejecting his marriage

December 19, 1994 (Cont.)

proposal, Jo is encouraged by her mother to "embrace your liberty" and moves to New York City. The contrast between the highly feminine Concord and heavily masculine Manhattan is vividly expressed, and Jo is only able to publish her sensationalist fiction under the name Joseph.

But at her boarding house she meets a German immigrant philosophy professor, Friedrich Bhaer (Gabriel Byrne), with whom she has an instant accord. They quote Walt Whitman together and discuss women's suffrage with other men, and he introduces her to the world of opera, which allows a tentative romance to bloom. At the same time, Amy pursues her interest in painting in Europe, where she becomes reacquainted with Laurie, who has become something of a dissolute playboy.

Spurred on by a family tragedy and Bhaer's admonition that she "should be writing from life, from the depths of your soul," Jo drops her formulaic fiction and fulfills her destiny by metamorphosing into Louisa May Alcott, writing a novel about her family life.

The ending, which rather neatly wraps everything up, still satisfies as a comparative view of how the various sisters are able to achieve something meaningful to each of them.

Armstrong paces her scenes at about half the speed that Cukor did, and they are all the better for it in terms of emotional resonance. Scenes are not milked for easy sentiment but build power from the integrity of the writing and performances. However thwarted Jo may be at various stages, artistically and personally, she perseveres and, happily, a late 20th-century feminist veneer has not been unnaturally imposed upon the material.

Performances by the actresses are all at least very good, with Ryder, Alvarado and Dunst making the strongest impressions. The male roles in the story have always been a bit thankless, but Bale does a creditable job as the spurned suitor.

Shot mostly in British Columbia, film has a splendid period look, thanks in good part to Jan Roelfs' resourceful production design, Colleen Atwood's impeccably detailed costumes and Geoffrey Simpson's burnished lensing. Thomas Newman's score is richly emotional without pandering.

Pic is dedicated to kidnap-murder victim Polly Klaas, from Ryder's hometown of Petaluma, Calif., and the late agent Judy Fox-Scott. —*Todd McCarthy*

LEGENDS OF THE FALL

A Sony Pictures release of a TriStar Pictures presentation of a Bedford Falls/Pangaea production. Produced by Edward Zwick, Bill Wittliff, Marshall Herskovitz. Executive producer, Patrick Crowley. Co-producers, Jane Bartelme, Sarah Caplan. Directed by Zwick. Screenplay, Susan Shilliday, Wittliff, based on the novella by Jim Harrison. Camera (Technicolor), John Toll; editor, Steven Rosenblum; music, James Horner; production design, Lilly Kilvert; art direction, Rick Roberts, Andrew Precht; costume design, Deborah Scott; sound (Dolby), Douglas Ganton; head wrangler, John Scott; assistant director, Nilo Otero; casting, Mary Colquhoun. Reviewed at the Bruin Theater, L.A., Nov. 17, 1994. MPAA Rating: R. Running time: **134 MIN.**

Tristan Ludlow	Brad Pitt
Col. William Ludlow	Anthony Hopkins
Alfred Ludlow	Aidan Quinn
Susannah Finncannon	Julia Ormond
Samuel Ludlow	Henry Thomas
Isabel Two	Karina Lombard
One Stab	Gordon Tootoosis
Pet	Tantoo Cardinal
Decker	Paul Desmond

Novelist Jim Harrison's fascination with the primal forces that influence civilized behavior found its apotheosis in his novella "Legends of the Fall." The sweeping, melodramatic saga is a complex tale with elements both ideal and problematic for the big-screen. The Edward Zwick version is intelligent, emotional and largely succeeds in its transference of the tale to screen.

Primed as the first major release of 1995 (it gets a late-year Oscar-qualifying opening), "Legends" should benefit from year-end attention and its positioning as an awards contender. In a period largely bereft of epic fare, it fills a major void deftly. Its combination of an attractive cast and panoramic settings indicates upbeat commercial prospects.

The story, set during the early 20th century, focuses on the three sons of retired cavalry officer William Ludlow (Anthony Hopkins). A renegade with a moral stripe, Ludlow left the military at issue with government treatment of plains Indians. He settled in the Montana foothills, much to the chagrin of his blue-blooded wife, who retreated one autumn never to return.

The ranch household prefigures the modern nuclear family: in this instance a single parent who creates a family by enlisting a seasoned native scout (Gordon Tootoosis), a native woman (Tantoo Cardinal) and her white ex-criminal mate (Paul Desmond) and young daughter. The boys evolve decently, if differently, in this environment.

As the spring thaw of 1913 arrives, the youngest son, Samuel (Henry Thomas), returns from an Eastern school with his fiancee, Susannah Finncannon (Julia Ormond). His older brothers have taken over key areas of the ranch business. Alfred

(Aidan Quinn) is a sort of operating manager and Tristan (Brad Pitt) is the barely housebroken head wrangler. What all three share is a seemingly resolute fraternal bond.

What Harrison detailed, and Zwick and screen adapters Susan Shilliday and Bill Wittliff ably chronicle, are the forces — internal and external — that erode the family unit. It's a story steeped in tragedy, relieved only by relationships that evolve to a higher plateau.

The distant thunder of the European World War beckons the idealistic Samuel to the call of duty in spite of his father's dissent. Alfred and Tristan go along more as protectors than philosophic comrades. But despite their watchful gaze, Samuel dies on the battlefield, signaling the strife to come.

Reunited in Montana, Tristan and Susannah become lovers. But he is tormented by his failure to save Samuel and departs for parts unknown, allowing Alfred to confess his true feelings to the young woman. When she cannot reciprocate, he too departs, for a new life in cattle futures and, later, politics in Helena.

As densely plotted as "Legends of the Fall" is, it's to the credit of the performers and craftsmen that the film escapes the abyss of melodrama and sentimentality.

Zwick imbues the story with an easy, poetic quality that mostly sidesteps the precious. While emotionally intense, it's neither hurried nor charged with false drama. It's also one of the most handsome of recent films, with sterling work by cameraman John Toll and production designer Lilly Kilvert. It falters in the obvious emphasis of James Horner's musical score.

The actors, working as an ensemble, are near perfect in the service of the material. Pitt is effortlessly charismatic, but Quinn has the film's biggest challenge — delineating the slow dissolution and corruption of decency. He is the reflection and opposite of his father, who after all sinks into madness.

A visceral, thoughtful and emotionally exhausting saga, "Legends of the Fall" recalls sprawling dramas of the 1950s such as "Giant." The genre has evolved with the times but remains a comforting and satisfying style of entertainment.
—*Leonard Klady*

DUMB AND DUMBER

A New Line Cinema release of a Motion Picture Corp. of America production. Produced by Charles Wessler, Brad Krevoy, Steve Stabler. Executive producers, Gerald Olson, Aaron Meyerson. Directed by Peter Farrelly. Screenplay, Farrelly, Bennett Yellin, Bobby Farrelly. Camera (Film House color), Mark Irwin; editor, Christopher Greenbury; music, Todd Rundgren; production design, Sidney Bartholomew Jr.; art direction, Arlan Jay Vetter; costume design, Mary Zophres; sound (Dolby), Jonathan Stein; assistant director, J.B. Rogers; casting, Rick Montgomery, Dan Parada. Reviewed at the Royal Oak Theater, Encino, Dec. 11, 1994. MPAA Rating: PG-13. Running time: **106 MIN.**

Lloyd Christmas	Jim Carrey
Harry Dunne	Jeff Daniels
Mary Swanson	Lauren Holly
Helen Swanson	Teri Garr
J.P. Shay	Karen Duffy
Joe Mentalino	Mike Starr
Nicholas Andre	Charles Rocket
Beth Jordan	Victoria Rowell
Sea Bass	Cam Neely
Detective Dale	Felton Perry

There's not a lot of brain work involved in "Dumb and Dumber," a flat-out celebration of stupidity, bodily functions and pratfalls. Yet the wholeheartedness of this descent into crude and rude humor is so good-natured and precise that it's hard not to partake in the guilty pleasures of the exercise. From its first frames to fade-out, the film is high-gloss, lowbrow comedy that will have general audiences doubled up with laughter. The unapologetic nature of the movie, combined with a strong cast and slick production values, smells decidedly like money.

"D&D" should be one of the big hits of the season and play well especially with a young crowd. It may also, like "Airplane!," be the upscale antidote film — the goofy pressure valve release that kicks in after a season of sober-sided fare.

Harry Dunne (Jeff Daniels) is a rather inept dog groomer who has transformed his van exterior to resemble a sheep dog. Lloyd Christmas (Jim Carrey), who resembles a latter-day Carl "Alfalfa" Switzer, is a limo driver with higher aspirations — he's saving to open a worm supply warehouse he's imaginatively dubbed "I Got Worms."

When Mary Swanson (Lauren Holly) enters Lloyd's limo for a ride to the airport, his heart flies out the sun roof. He's really struck dumb, and bids her a tearful goodbye at the curb. As he pulls away — smack into another vehicle — he notices that his charge has left her briefcase right in the middle of the terminal. Ever gallant, he retrieves it, but not quite in time to get it aboard Mary's flight to Aspen.

It doesn't take a genius to figure where the story is going … the slopes of Colorado, dummy. The slight variation is that Mary doesn't want the

December 19, 1994 (Cont.)

valise; it's filled with $100,000 in ransom money that her husband's kidnappers are supposed to retrieve. But Lloyd got there first and is blissfully unaware of the contents as he and Harry speed cross-country in the flea-infested van.

Needless to say, the plot is no more than a loose device on which to hang an endless supply of well-executed, if sophomoric, jokes, with an emphasis on scatological humor.

The entire affair escapes the gutter thanks to Daniels, Carrey, Holly and a string of very good supporting players. Daniels is particularly adroit in his role, willingly giving himself up to his character's inanity without winking to the audience. Both Daniels and Carrey retain a gleeful innocence and spontaneity that's infectious.

Tyro filmmaker Peter Farrelly (who also co-wrote) displays a natural flair for comedy and pacing. A key element of pic's success is its refusal to overplay its crudeness. Farrelly also dilutes the vulgarity with strong tech credits and highly imaginative wardrobe by Mary Zophres.

The film is about as canny, hip and commercial as comedies come. It's ideal fare for those who want to laugh themselves sick.

—*Leonard Klady*

RUDYARD KIPLING'S THE JUNGLE BOOK

A Buena Vista release of a Walt Disney Pictures presentation of a Sharad Patel production in association with Edward S. Feldman. Produced by Feldman, Raju Patel. Executive producers, Sharad Patel, Mark Damon, Lawrence Mortorff. Co-executive producer, Rajendra Kumar. Co-producer, Michael J. Kagan. Directed by Stephen Sommers. Screenplay, Sommers, Ronald Yanover, Mark D. Geldman; story by Yanover, Geldman, based on characters from "The Jungle Book" by Rudyard Kipling. Camera (Technicolor), Juan Ruiz Anchia; editor, Bob Ducsay; music, Basil Poledouris; production design, Allan Cameron; set decoration, Crispian Sallis; costume design, John Mollo; sound (Dolby), Joseph Geisinger; assistant director, Artist Robinson; second unit directors, Greg Michael, David Ellis; visual effects supervisor, Peter Montgomery; stunt coordinators, Gerry Crampton, Ellis, Tim Davison; head animal trainer, Steve Martin; casting, Celestia Fox. Reviewed at the Avco Cinema Center, L.A., Dec. 9, 1994. MPAA Rating: PG. Running time: **110 MIN.**

Mowgli	Jason Scott Lee
Boone	Cary Elwes
Kitty	Lena Headey
Brydon	Sam Neill
Dr. Plumford	John Cleese
Wilkins	Jason Flemyng
Buldeo	Stefan Kalipha
Harley	Ron Donachie

Disney must tame a major marketing challenge — a title people associate with a children's story, which here comes across as an ambitious hybrid of "Greystoke" and "Indiana Jones and the Temple of Doom." That means adults will have to turn out for this opulent, action-packed production, which, based on the recent track record of remakes, should prove an uphill battle, leaving homevideo as the most successful hunting ground for "Rudyard Kipling's The Jungle Book."

Unlike the 1942 version starring Sabu, or Disney's animated '60s classic, this latest "Jungle Book" seeks a more modern tone, with the imposing Jason Scott Lee as Mowgli — a boy raised in the jungle whose four-footed pals include a bear, a wolf and a panther.

These animals don't talk or sing, however, and one wonders where the movie is going before it dramatically shifts gears into a full-throttled, technically superb adventure — with more bite than most Disney live-action fare — that offers some winning moments but, ultimately, isn't as involving as it needs to be.

For one thing, the narrative keeps changing gears — from nature film to love story to actioner. At the age of 5, Mowgli, the son of an Indian guide, gets lost in the jungle and is raised by animals. Soon he becomes a young man, the lithesome Lee (star of "Dragon: The Bruce Lee Story"), again encountering Kitty (Lena Headey), the young British girl with whom he'd played as a boy.

In section two, Kitty tries to incorporate Mowgli into society, angering Boone (Cary Elwes), a suitor who's also an officer in her father's regiment. Finally, and most effectively, a quest begins to find a lost city filled with treasure, as Mowgli seeks to save his beloved from Boone and her captors.

What ultimately drives the movie is the love story — as Hugh Hudson sought to do in "Greystoke: The Legend of Tarzan, Lord of the Apes" — in true beauty-and-the-beast fashion. As with that film, there's also an environmental conscience, celebrating Mowgli's childlike innocence and the "jungle law" that says to kill only to survive.

Director Stephen Sommers (who steered another Disney live-action revival, "The Adventures of Huck Finn," and scripted here with Ronald Yanover and Mark D. Geldman) serves up a visual feast of beautiful animals and spectacular vistas, often mixed with a somewhat less appetizing soundtrack of grunts and growls.

There is some humor and charm, but until the impressive, "Raiders"-esque last half-hour, the movie straddles the line between children's fare and adult-oriented material; indeed, parents may want to know that the bad guys meet some rather grisly, if not graphic, ends.

Lee is such a striking presence physically that he needn't do much but look happy or baffled, while Headey is at best a passable lure to bring the boy out of the jungle. Elwes fares better as the piece's Snidely Whiplash, while Sam Neill and John Cleese are amusing in small roles.

Technically, "Jungle Book" is an encyclopedia of wonders, from the dazzling scenery (shot largely in Jodhpur, India), cinematography, costumes and sets, to the animals, who frequently out-emote their two-legged counterparts. Even so, "Book" may have been more effective had its story stayed on one page.

—*Brian Lowry*

I.Q.

A Paramount Pictures release of a Sandollar production. Produced by Carol Baum, Fred Schepisi. Executive producers, Scott Rudin, Sandy Gallin. Co-producer, Neil Machlis. Directed by Schepisi. Screenplay, Andy Breckman, Michael Leeson. Camera (Deluxe color), Ian Baker; editor, Jill Bilcock; music, Jerry Goldsmith; production design, Stuart Wurtzel; art direction, Wray Steven Graham; costume design, Ruth Myers; sound (Dolby), Danny Michael; assistant director, John Wildermuth; casting, David Rubin. Reviewed at Paramount Studios, L.A., Dec. 6, 1994. MPAA Rating: PG. Running time: **95 MIN.**

Ed Walters	Tim Robbins
Catherine Boyd	Meg Ryan
Albert Einstein	Walter Matthau
Kurt Godel	Lou Jacobi
Boris Podolsky	Gene Saks
Nathan Liebknecht	Joseph Maher
James Moreland	Stephen Fry
Bob Rosetti	Tony Shalhoub
Frank	Frank Whaley

The conjunction of the stars can be a most unscientific phenomenon. Sometimes, as in the romantic comedy "I.Q.," it's the heartstrings, not the tides, that are being tugged.

This whirlwind affair is a delight that effectively combines a sweet romanticism with a screwball twist. There's definite chemistry — romantic and comic — between its participants that should spontaneously combust into charged box office returns. Prospects are for a healthy holiday frame that may well extend into the new year.

The conceit of this 1950s-set yarn is that the world's most famous scientist, Albert Einstein (Walter Matthau), realizes that his egghead niece is in need of some heart massaging. She has a stuffy tenured beau who bores the pants off Al and his German cadre at Princeton.

The promising spark occurs when the niece, Catherine (Meg Ryan), sputters into a garage and encounters mechanic Ed Walters (Tim Robbins). He experiences love at first sight while she fumbles around for keys, registration and the like.

She also absent-mindedly leaves her watch, and Ed seizes the opportunity it presents.

It's his good fortune that Einstein, not Catherine, opens the door. The old professor and his cronies are well versed in theories of amorousness. They also quickly establish that Ed is no ordinary grease monkey; he has a natural, if unschooled, scientific mind.

A paean to movies past, "I.Q." recalls the style and attitude of a bygone era while retaining a contemporary spirit and polish. Memory dictates that personal and professional options were simpler in the 1950s and that a naif could be propelled into the national consciousness quickly and indelibly.

To win the girl for the young man, the collective *herr* professors create an elaborate ruse that extends to refashioning Ed in tweeds and a meerschaum. They also school him in "cold fusion," a failed Einsteinian principle, and trot him out to deliver a learned paper for a symposium of physicists. The effect is earth-shaking, extending to the Oval Office where Ike declares it a major leap in the space race against the Russkies.

The much ado belies the simplicity of the pic's hopeless romanticism. In that respect it recalls the vintage screwball "Ball of Fire," in which a gun moll hides out with seven jolly, dotty professors and falls in love with the youngest. It also captures the anarchic zaniness long absent from screen comedy.

Director Fred Schepisi had similar fun with "Roxanne," a contemporized "Cyrano." He's created a fantasyland to accommodate the Andy Breckman-Michael Leeson screenplay. It's warm and unbelievable and definitely comforting. You can bet it has a happy ending.

The material provides Robbins with the kind of likable, charismatic role that gained him early recognition. It's his most poised and natural performance since "Bull Durham." Ryan beautifully plays on her pixie persona and the two create a hot fusion that has you cheering on the inevitable.

Despite extensive hair and make-up, enough of that familiar Matthau twinkle is evident in his fanciful take on Einstein. Pic also has a colorful supporting cast and sumptuous tech work from the likes of cameraman Ian Baker and tunesmith Jerry Goldsmith.

"I.Q." is an audience yes-brainer with a heart only the steeliest curmudgeon would deny. It's the kind of entertainment conspiracy that makes one smile knowingly.

—*Leonard Klady*

SAFE PASSAGE

A New Line Cinema release of a Pacific Western production. Produced by Gale Anne Hurd. Executive producers, David Gale, Betsy Beers, Ruth Vitale. Directed by Robert Allan Ackerman. Screenplay, Deena Goldstone, based on the novel by Ellyn Bache. Camera (Deluxe color, Film House prints), Ralf Bode; editor, Rick Shaine; music, Mark Isham; production design, Dan Bishop; art direction, Jefferson Sage; set decoration, Dianna Freas; costume design, Renee Ehrlich; sound (Dolby), Tod Maitland; line producer, Diana Pokorny; casting, Pam Dixon Mickelson. Reviewed at Sony Studios screening room, Culver City, Dec. 1, 1994. MPAA Rating: PG-13. Running time: 96 MIN.

Mag Singer	Susan Sarandon
Patrick Singer	Sam Shepard
Alfred Singer	Robert Sean Leonard
Izzy Singer	Sean Astin
Cynthia	Marcia Gay Harden
Simon Singer	Nick Stahl
Gideon Singer	Jason London
Percival Singer	Matt Keeslar
Mort	Philip Bosco

It's stormy commercial waters ahead for "Safe Passage," a grueling family drama that juxtaposes a family holiday reunion with potential human tragedy. The kitchen sink material — a major staple of television movies — suffers from a severe case of earnestness. That, and the absence of marquee talent beyond Susan Sarandon, diminishes already limited theatrical prospects. Domestic potential is in upscale situations, and it's likely to go the small-screen route abroad.

The unconventional Singers are an estranged couple living in a New Jersey bedroom community. Mag (Sarandon), after raising seven sons (only one is still at home), is troubled by no longer having a brood to care for and no obvious purpose in sight. Patrick (Sam Shepard), an inventor of sorts, now lives in his office and grapples with a mysterious stress ailment that renders him periodically blind. Situation's rife with allegory.

Story proper kicks off with Mag awaking in a sweat from a dream. She's had a premonition that one of her boys is in trouble. Sometime after sunrise she discovers that it's Percival (Matt Keeslar), who's stationed in the Sinai with American peace-keeping forces. He may have been quartered in a Marine barracks bombed by terrorists.

One by one her boys arrive, and Patrick joins them around the table and in front of the television as they ride out the period of uncertainty. A lot of drama unfolds. There's virtually no family relationship that's on an even keel. There's a son who always felt less loved by his father, the brother who felt he quashed another sibling's dreams and a litany of unresolved matters between the couple ranging from his slovenliness to accusations that he was too easygoing and she was too overbearing.

While short of *sturm und drang*, "Safe Passage" has a decided theatrical pitch. Characters exclaim, and Robert Allan Ackerman's heavy-handed direction emphasizes every word as if it were gospel. The simplest of actions take on an outsize quality.

Despite a general dour atmosphere, the cast struggles mightily to provide a human dimension to their roles. Sarandon is workwoman-like as the latter-day Mother Courage, and Shepard effortlessly conveys Patrick's effortless rambling through life. Best of the boys is Sean Astin, the square peg in relation to the rest of the group.

Tech credits are strong, but there's limited opportunity for the crafts to break out of the confinement dictated by the tale. One can also be thankful that the eventual outcome is upbeat, relatively speaking. *—Leonard Klady*

MARIO AND THE MAGICIAN

(MARIO UND DER ZAUBERER)

(GERMAN)

A Senator release (Germany) of a Provobis/Juergen Haase production. Produced by Juergen Haase. Co-producer, Peter Hahne. Directed by Klaus Maria Brandauer. Screenplay, Burt Weinshanker, based on the novella by Thomas Mann. Camera (color), Lajos Koltai; editor, Tanja Schmidbauer; music, Christian Brandauer; production design/costume design, Peter Pabst; sound, Walter Amann; makeup, Gerlinde Kunz, Paul Schmidt, Friedrike Reimer, Marga Bothilla Bergschmidt; assistant directors, Petra Kaethe Niemeyer, Marco Guidone; casting, Risa Kes. Reviewed at Notausgang Theater, Berlin, Dec. 15, 1994. Running time: 127 MIN.

Bernhard Fuhrmann	Julian Sands
Rachel Fuhrmann	Anna Galiena
Cipolla	Klaus Maria Brandauer
Mario	Pavel Greco
Silvestra	Valentina Chico
Graziano	Philippe Leroy Beaulieu
Pastore	Ivano Marescotti
Angiolieri	Rolf Hoppe
Sofronia	
Angiolieri	Elisabeth Trissenaar
Stephan Fuhrmann	Jan Wachtel
Sophie Fuhrmann	Nina Schweser
With: Petra Reinhardt, Franco Concilio.	

(German soundtrack version)

The long-awaited second directorial effort of thesp Klaus Maria Brandauer checks in as a conventional European arthouse film that's stronger on pretty images than story or substance. Based on the autobiographical novella by Thomas Mann, this costumer is too much a collage of Italian snapshots between the wars to touch a wide audience. Pic could, however, do some business among its film-buff target audience, based on name leads and stunning photography alone.

Story limns the holiday visit by a well-known liberal German writer, Bernhard Fuhrmann (Julian Sands), and his family of three to the Italian seaside resort town Torre di Venere in the '20s. While there, he encounters fascism's creeping intolerance and the sad decline of liberal European values into a vulgar kind of barbarism.

Italian guests at the luxury hotel want Fuhrmann and his family moved to an outer building: His 8-year-old daughter caused a scandal when she took her clothes off on the beach. Subsequently, the hotel director (Philippe Leroy Beaulieu) is killed and replaced by a younger man with fascist leanings. And the local police chief (Rolf Hoppe) is an infantile idiot who senses future openings for his tyrannical tendencies.

Amid all this pops up the crippled but mesmerizing magician, Cipolla (Brandauer), who gradually fascinates — and even changes the lives of — some of the characters. There's also the side story of the tragic, unfulfilled love of a waiter, Mario (Pavel Greco), for the police chief's beautiful niece, Silvestra (Valentina Chico).

Unfortunately, the various anecdotes never come together and, in a film entirely peopled by supporting characters, none really gets a chance to tell his or her story.

Brandauer has translated Mann's collection of snapshots into a series of beautiful images, and Hungarian lenser Lajos Koltai's beautiful photography makes every scene a small pleasure. But though the pic's theme is the encroachment of fascism on European culture, the audience is left in the dark about the subject by film's end.

In his first pic as a director, "Georg Elser: Einer aus Deutschland" (1989), Brandauer succeeded in telling the human and intimate tale of Hitler's failed assassin. "Mario," though bigger in both budget and artistic ambition, is more like a cinematic coffee-table book.

Most impressive scene comes early on — the annual waiters' race in which servers run through town carrying trays with wine and spaghetti. Most of the sequence is shot above the heads of observers on the street. Irritatingly, Brandauer maintains this distance between camera and action throughout the film, shying away from closeups or scenes that give the actors a chance to show their stripes.

Brandauer's own (relatively small) part as the magician also falls victim to this distancing: Though the character is seemingly tailored to the Austrian thesp's diabolical style, he performs in an indirect manner, with little visible effort — understatement that doesn't work. Sands' inhibited, stiff Fuhrmann, ostensibly an observer, remains so much a part of the background that it's hard to imagine he sees much. British thesp seems lost in a role that mostly requires him to utter functional lines such as "We leave tomorrow." The film moves on without him, the camera following one minor character after another, but never long enough to give any of them depth.

Within these limitations, however, most other perfs are good, especially Leroy Beaulieu as the hotel director, played with precision and elan.

Tech credits are excellent, though editing by Tanja Schmidbauer could be tighter. Scoring by Brandauer's son, Christian, is functional.

Pic was shot with actors using their native languages. In the German-lingo version caught, Brandauer, who acted in English, dubs his own role. An English version reportedly is planned. *—Eric Hansen*

MIXED NUTS

A Sony Pictures release of a TriStar presentation of a Witt-Thomas production. Produced by Paul Junger Witt, Tony Thomas, Joseph Hartwick. Executive producers, Delia Ephron, James Skotchdopole. Directed by Nora Ephron. Screenplay, Nora Ephron, Delia Ephron, based on the film "Le Pere Noel est une ordure." Camera (Technicolor), Sven Nykvist; editor, Robert Reitano; music, George Fenton; production design, Bill Groom; art direction, Dennis Bradford; costume design, Jeffrey Kurland; sound (Dolby), James Sabat; assistant director, Skotchdopole; casting, Juliet Taylor, Laura Rosenthal. Reviewed at the Samuel Goldwyn Theater, Beverly Hills, Dec. 4, 1994. MPAA Rating: PG-13. Running time: 97 MIN.

Philip	Steve Martin
Blanche Munchnik	Madeline Kahn
Mr. Lobel	Robert Klein
Felix	Anthony LaPaglia
Gracie Barzini	Juliette Lewis
Dr. Kinsky	Rob Reiner
Louie	Adam Sandler
Chris	Liev Schreiber
Catherine O'Shaughnessy	Rita Wilson
Stanley Tannenbaum	Garry Shandling

The holiday spirit goes into life-threatening cardiac arrest with the Christmas-themed comedy "Mixed Nuts." This yarn, set in the wacky world of a telephone crisis center, will be pecan into theaters for a limited time and exiting with a minimum amount of cashew. It's a total misfire with no commercial vital signs registering onscreen.

Based on a French hit, it's lost something crucial in translation. The Americanization provides no clue to the original's appeal. Nor can one fathom why the material attracted a pedigree cast or the writing/directing talents of Nora Ephron.

Philip (Steve Martin) operates the Venice, Calif., help line Lifesavers. The ramshackle office has a tote board that proudly proclaims: "Now Saving 1,423." Judging from his staff, it's a grossly inflated figure. In fact, fhe crew manning the phones could stand a little bit of counseling. Blanche Munchnik (Madeline Kahn) is a tart-tongued widow and Catherine (Rita Wilson) is repressed, living with her mom and dreaming of that white knight. She finds it difficult to be dry-eyed when callers unbridle their woes.

The holiday season isn't so cheery because the landlord has served notice on the service unless it can come up with a large chunk of dough. Somewhere in the mix, there's a parade of weirdos on the line and in the office. A pregnant woman (Juliette Lewis) blows hot and cold about her goof-off, ex-con boyfriend (Anthony LaPaglia), an Amazonian transvestite (Liev Schreiber) is looking for a dance partner, and a ukulele-playing delivery boy (Adam Sandler) is just plain irritating.

Ephron pitches the humor at a cacophonous level and displays the comedic equivalent of two left feet in evolving an absurdist, slapstick yarn. Truly alarming is watching some fine performers, including Kahn and LaPaglia, at their very worst. The best the ensemble members can do is escape with a smattering of dignity.

The patent phoniness of the film seeps right down to its craft. Cameraman Sven Nykvist's work is markedly better on location than on the soundstages, and the production design is as loud, gaudy and unpleasant as the text.

—Leonard Klady

THE NEVERENDING STORY III

(GERMAN)

A Warner Bros. release (U.K.) of a CineVox Filmproduktion/Studio Babelsberg/Dieter Geissler Filmproduktion production, in association with Videal, Bibo TV and Media Investment Club. (International sales: CineVox Intl., L.A.) Produced by Dieter Geissler, Tim Hampton. Line producers, Harry Nap, Harold Tichenor. Directed by Peter Macdonald. Screenplay, Jeff Lieberman, from a screen story by Karin Howard, based on characters from the novel "The Neverending Story" by Michael Ende. Camera (Agfacolor prints in Germany, France and U.K.), Robin Vidgeon; editor, Michael Bradsell; music, Peter Wolf; production design, Rolf Zehetbauer; location art director, Jill Scott; costume design, Monique Prudhomme, Vin Burnham; sound (Dolby), Axel Arft; visual effects supervisor, Derek Meddings; animatronics creatures, Jim Henson's Creature Shop; digital visual effects, Toccata New Image Production; visual/optical effects, Cinemagic; stunt coordinators, Marc Boyle, Bill Ferguson; associate producer, Klaus Kaehler; assistant director, David Tringham; second unit camera, Paul Wilson; casting (U.S.), Mike Fenton, Allison Cowitt. Reviewed at Warner West End 5, London, Dec. 12, 1994. Running time: **95 MIN.**

Bastian
Balthazar Bux ... Jason James Richter
Nicole Baxter .... Melody Kay
Mr. Coreander/
Old Man of
Wandering Mountain .... Freddie Jones
Slip .... Jack Black
Dog .... Ryan Bollman
Mookie .... Carole Finn
Jane Baxter .... Tracey Ellis
Barney .... Kevin McNulty
The Empress .... Julie Cox
Urgl .... Moya Brady
Engywook .... Tony Robinson
Nasty #1 .... Nicole Parker
Nasty #2 .... P. Adrien Dorval
(English dialogue)

"The Neverending Story" lives up to its title in the worst way possible with this third outing, a charmless, desperate reworking of the franchise that might just as well be subtitled "Bastian Goes to High School." Clearly aimed at a generation of moppets with one finger on the fast-forward button, lame effort throws over the magical charm of the 1984 original and darker fantasy of the 1990 sequel for a semi-hip yarn patched together by a marketing committee.

Pic, which has no U.S. distributor, has already taken a middling $5 million in Germany since its late October release, and looks set to garner reasonable biz on ancillary worldwide. Theatrically, however, this every-which-way mishmash looks unlikely to scale the major peaks of its two predecessors, which have grossed a combined $150 million-plus worldwide to date.

Central character, Bastian (Jason James Richter, from "Free Willy"), is now on the edge of puberty and moved home with his father. Dad's new wife Jane (Tracey Ellis) is an eager-to-please happy homemaker with a sharp-tongued pubescent daughter, Nicole (Melody Kay), who reckons her fresh-faced stepbrother is just "weird."

At school, Bastian is bullied by a bunch of senior punks called the Nasties. Bastian takes refuge in the school library, coincidentally run by

Mr. Coreander (Freddie Jones, taking over Thomas Hill's role in the first two pix), the antiquarian bookseller who first intro'd the kid to the wonders of the "Neverending Story" tome, which automatically writes the dreams of whoever is reading it.

Turning its pages, Bastian wishes himself back into the dream world of Fantasia, courtesy of Jim Henson's Creature Shop. But when the Nasties get a hold of the tome and start filling it with their own warped imagination, Fantasia starts to crumble. Bastian locates Fantasia's child empress (now blossomed into the shapely Julie Cox), who begs him to get the book back from the bad guys.

First, however, he has to track down a variety of Fantasians who accidentally beamed back to the real world with him and are wandering round the U.S. in total confusion.

The magic of the original pic lay in its gossamer-light creation of a dream world entirely constructed from the imagination of a lonely, motherless kid living in Washington state. Though considerably darker in tone, and kitted out with a "Star Wars"-type score, the sequel maintained the fiction while directly involving the growing kid in the adventures.

Showing every sign of lack of confidence in its original premise, this latest installment tries to have it all ways, thoroughly Americanizing the modern setting (of minor importance in the previous pix), stirring in a heap of hip, high school dialogue, and relegating the Fantasia sequences to little more than a collection of cuddly toys pitched somewhere between "The Wizard of Oz" and "Return of the Jedi." As one of the dream-world characters says upon hitting the human world, "I've a feeling we're not in Fantasia anymore."

Originality is in short supply throughout. The Fantasian walking tree, Bark Troll, is an arboreal version of "Oz's" Tin Man; the rock-chewers, whose appeal fades fast, behave like lapidary clones of Fred and Wilma Flintstone; and even the most charming of the original constructs, the flying dog, now talks in wisecracks. Product placement for a German airline and U.S. parcel service is particularly naked.

Helmer Peter Macdonald ("Rambo III") does a pro job, and effects (supervised by Brit veteran Derek Meddings) are generally good, on a par with the earlier entries though not this time in widescreen. On the performance side, 14-year-old Richter is OK in a largely reactive role, Ellis mostly restricted to double-takes as his mom, and Jack Black good as a high school heavy straight out of an '80s John Hughes pic. Stealing most of the best lines as a snooty mall-princess is Kay, also 14, an assured presence worth watching.

Other tech credits are up to scratch, though Peter Wolf's music, which veers wildly from the symphonic to disco fodder, fails to impart any consistent atmosphere on the proceedings. Like those of its predecessors, all interiors were shot in Germany (this time at Berlin's Babelsberg Studio rather than Munich's Bavaria Studio), with Vancouver doubling for the unnamed U.S. town.

For the record, Coreander's ominous final words to Bastian are, "The story's not over yet, young man."

—Derek Elley

BLACK LIGHT

(LUMIERE NOIRE)

(FRENCH)

An MH Films release (in France) of an MH Films Prods. production, with support of Peripherie Prod., Record Films, Ecrans du Sud Foundation and participation of French Ministry of Culture, Ministry of Cooperation and Development, Channel 4, Canal Horizons, ACCT and National Center for Film Production of Mali (CNPC). (International sales: MH Films, Paris). Produced, directed by Med Hondo. Screenplay, Hondo, Didier Daeninckx, based on Daeninckx's novel. Camera (color), Ricardo Aronovich; editor, Christine Lack; music, Avanos, Manu Dibango, Aziza, Toure Kunda, others; production design/costume design, Patrick Durand, Laure Clerc Villemer; sound, Philippe Lecocq, Pascal Armand. Reviewed at Elysees Lincoln Cinema, Paris, Dec. 13, 1994. Running time: **107 MIN.**

Yves Guyot .... Patrick Poivey
Ghislaine Guyot .... Ines de Medeiros
Detective Londrin .... Charlie Bauer
Inspector Cadin .... Gilles Segal
Judge Berthier .... Roland Bertin
La Bricole .... Pascal Legitimus
With: Gerard Hernandez, Serge Sauvion, Marc Francois, Michel Vigne, Siaka Kane, Selou Ba, James Campbell, El Haj Fousseynou.

Virtue and determination are exhibited but not rewarded in "Black Light," a refreshingly pessimistic political thriller whose scruffy protagonists are outmaneuvered by French powers-that-be. Mauritania-born helmer Med Hondo's conviction yields a gritty detective yarn with pertinent social underpinnings that fests, as well as cable and issue-oriented programmers, should beam in on.

Paris is plagued by a wave of random terrorist attacks. Guyot (Patrick Poivey), a hologram engineer with a semi-shady past, works for Air France. During a nighttime drive near a Paris airport, Guyot's best friend is shot down in cold blood, and the incident becomes a matter of Guyot's word against two lying policemen who claim to have fired in self-defense.

While Internal Affairs conducts its own, possibly tainted, investigation, Guyot learns of an eye witness: an illegal immigrant from Mali who was being held on the top floor of a hotel overlooking the crime scene and who has since been deported.

Guyot covers a good chunk of French-speaking Africa until he finds the witness and tape records his testimony. Soon thereafter, Guyot is iced in his lab while he's making a hologram that may reveal the assailant's identity. A burned-out but honest police inspector near retirement (played to gruff perfection by former convict and prison activist Charlie Bauer) continues to pursue the truth, which leads to a few baroque touches and a sinister denouement.

Narrative blends questions about democracy under fire, manipulation of the press, human rights violations and police brutality into a detective tale that unfolds in dreary utilitarian Paris suburbs and the sunny reaches of Mali. Thesps do a good, if mostly low-key, job. Broad selection of African music fits well, and tech credits are OK.

Hondo — who dubs the voices of Eddie Murphy and Danny Glover into French to make ends meet — collaborated with popular detective novelist Didier Daeninckx to adapt latter's book, then spent six years scraping together the $2 million budget. President Mitterrand personally interceded when airport authorities refused to allow the production to shoot on location. Title is taken from Victor Hugo's dying words.

—*Lisa Nesselson*

FARINELLI
THE CASTRATO
(FARINELLI IL CASTRATO)
(FRENCH-BELGIAN-ITALIAN)

A Bac Films release (France) of a Vera Belmont presentation of a Stephan Films, Alinea Films, UGC Images, Studio Canal Plus, France 2 Cinema, Studio Images (Paris)/K2 Prods., RTL, TVI production, with aid from the Government of French-Speaking Belgium, MG, Italian Intl. Film and Filmstiftung NRW and participation of Canal Plus, CNC and Procirep. (International sales: UGC Intl., Paris.) Produced by Vera Belmont. Co-executive producers, Linda Gutenberg, Aldo Lado, Dominique Janne, Stephane Thenoz. Directed by Gerard Corbiau. Screenplay, Marcel Beaulieu, Andree Corbiau, Gerard Corbiau. Camera (color), Walther Vanden Ende; editor, Joelle Hache; musical direction, Christophe Rousset; production design, Gianni Quaranta; costume design, Olga Berluti, Anne de Laugardiere; special makeup and hair, Kuno Schlegelmilch; sound (Dolby), Jean-Paul Muguel, Dominique Hennequin; sound design, Richard Shorr; IRCAM sound engineers, Philippe Depalle, Guillermo Garcia, Xavier Rodet, Boris Duval; vocalists, Derek Lee Ragin, Ewa Mallas Godlewska; casting, Gerard Moulevrier, Jose Villaverde. Reviewed at Max Linder Panorama Cinema, Paris, Dec. 12, 1994. Running time: **110 MIN.**

Farinelli/	
Carlo Broschi	Stefano Dionisi
Riccardo Broschi	Enrico Lo Verso
Alexandra	Elsa Zylberstein
Margareth Hunter	Caroline Cellier
Handel	Jeroen Krabbe
Philippe V	Jacques Boudet
Porpora	Omero Antonutti
Countess Mauer	Marianne Basler
The child	Renaud du Peloux de Saint Romain

With: Graham Valentine, Pier Paolo Capponi, Delphine Zentout.
(French and Italian dialogue)

"**F**arinelli" is a lavish, literally baroque account of the triumphant stage career and tortured private life of the 18th century's greatest castrato singer. Somewhat contrived costume meller boasts a technically thrilling re-creation of the vocal prowess needed to perform the now unsingable compositions written for the long-lost voice. Pic will require special handling to attract international arthouse auds beyond hard-core music lovers, but handsome leads, potent sex scenes and strong women's roles help put across the visually compelling package.

No one knows exactly what castrati sounded like, but Farinelli in his prime boasted a range of 3½ octaves and could sing a dazzling 250 notes in a row or sustain a single note for a full minute. For the pic's soundtrack, the voices of countertenor Derek Lee Ragin and soprano Ewa Mallas Godlewska were edited together and digitally enhanced at Paris' IRCAM sound lab. Results are convincingly lip-synched by Stefano Dionisi as Carlo Broschi (1705-82), who achieved spectacular renown across Europe under the stage name Farinelli.

Pic gets off to a dramatic start in Naples with a recently castrated youth plunging to his death during choir practice after warning prepubescent Carlo not to let the music establishment sever his testicles. Young Carlo is understandably upset by the prospect, but his father tells him that he must always put his exceptional voice in the service of his older brother, Riccardo, a composer.

Riccardo writes florid music for his sibling to perform and the two share everything, down to the women who swoon over Carlo: He conducts the foreplay until genitally complete Riccardo (Enrico Lo Verso) takes over. Pic addresses audience curiosity about sex sans *cojones* without making it entirely clear whether Carlo derives any physical satisfaction from his bedroom exploits.

Many years after an unfortunate encounter with the composer Handel (Jeroen Krabbe), who tried unsuccessfully to separate the brothers, Farinelli is lured to London, where two theaters — Covent Garden, directed by Handel, and a rival house directed by Farinelli's former voice teacher Porpora — are having the 18th-century equivalent of a cutthroat ratings war.

Farinelli is a smash at the rival house but becomes obsessed with winning Handel's respect and decides to aim for pure expression in lieu of frills. His breakthrough as an artist leaves no room for Riccardo.

Muscular Italian thesp Dionisi, who from certain angles bears a strong resemblance to Tom Cruise, has the bearing and stage persona of an adulated performer weighed down by the knowledge that he'll never father a child, but he lacks the hairless, doughy demeanor ascribed to castrati. Krabbe cuts a demanding and imperious figure as the vindictive Handel. The soulful Lo Verso sparkles and mugs a bit too vehemently as Farinelli's brother.

Elsa Zylberstein and Caroline Cellier register strongly as bold, caring women. Renaud du Peloux de Saint Romain gives a brief but wrenching perf as Cellier's crippled son, a sort of knowing old soul trapped in the infirm body of a 12-year-old.

Lensing and editing are aces, as are the lush period details of costumes and settings, from velvety theaters and rocky carriage rides to a royal garden during a solar eclipse. Musical performances are shown to cause fainting and spasms of pleasure in listeners.

Pic bounces around in time, and Farinelli's real-life decision to retire at age 32 to perform exclusively for the king of Spain is sketchily presented. French and Italian are used interchangeably to appropriate effect.

Helmer Gerard Corbiau, whose 1987 feature "The Music Teacher" was a foreign-language Oscar nominee, delivers patches of heady emotion but allows them to disperse, due more to the somewhat scattered script than to any errors in presentation. Still, whatever the pic's structural flaws and historical license, its raw material is intellectually intriguing and succeeds in communicating a melancholy sense of triumph tinged with loss.

—*Lisa Nesselson*

GIORGINO
(FRENCH)

An AMLF release (in France) of a Heathcliff/Polygram production. Produced, directed by Laurent Boutonnat. Co-producer, Jose Covo. Screenplay, Gilles Laurent, Boutonnat. Camera (color; widescreen), Jean-Pierre Sauvaire; editing, Agnes Mouchel, Boutonnat; music, Boutonnat; production design, Pierre Guffroy; costume design, Carine Sarfati; sound (Dolby), Jean-Philippe Le Roux, Thierry Rogen; casting, Rose Tobias Shaw (London), Johanna Ray (L.A.), Jessica Horvathova (Prague). Reviewed at Forum Horizon Cinema, Paris, Oct. 9, 1994. Running time: **179 MIN.**

Giorgio/Giorgino	Jeff Dahlgren
Catherine	Mylene Farmer
Father Glaise	Joss Ackland
Innkeeper	Louise Fletcher
Marie	Francis Barber
Sebastien	Jean-Pierre Aumont

(English dialogue)

The lavishly mounted "Giorgino" is the protracted tale of a handsome young French lieutenant who, in October 1918, visits a creepy village in search of a group of retarded children he tended before the war. Everyone in the town is doomed, and so, alas, is the pic, which boasts ominous atmosphere to spare and enough loose ends to weave a sweater. This ambitious oddity crashed and burned at Gallic wickets but could be salvageable in the hands of an inspired editor.

Beautifully designed by ace art director Pierre Guffroy and stunningly lensed on location in the misty and remote reaches of the Czech Republic and Slovakia, widescreen tale has the visual trappings and eerie mood of an "important" film but soon begins to feel like a cross between "Doctor Zhivago" and Visconti's "The Damned" as directed by Ed Wood after he'd been exposed to MTV.

Juicy plot elements, which include madness, revenge, ostracism, infantile behavior, drug addiction, sex-starved harridans, frozen landscapes and the specter of wolves, never coalesce. The kids disappeared under suspicious circumstances that may or may not include foul play by a lovely and mysterious redheaded woman (Canadian songbird Mylene Farmer).

Handsome, semi-narcoleptic newcomer Jeff Dahlgren as the title character is easy on the eye, the ethereal Farmer exudes a disquieting childishness, Joss Ackland is solid as a man of the cloth, and Louise Fletcher and Jean-Pierre Aumont are plain miscast.

As producer, co-writer, director, co-editor and composer of the pitching and rolling wall-to-wall score, Laurent Boutonnat exercised complete creative control, arriving at a three-hour cut that failed dismally in France. Still, there is so much craft on display that one is left with the impression that there may be a far shorter Gothic tale screaming to get out from the visually intriguing but dramatically stultifying footage. —*Lisa Nesselson*

SALZBURG

RADETZKY MARCH

(RADETZKYMARSCH)

(AUSTRIAN-FRENCH-GERMAN — VIDEO)

A Satel, ORF (Vienna)/Progefi (Paris)/Taurus Film, BR (Munich) production. Produced by Michael Wolkenstein. Directed by Axel Corti, Gernot Roll. Screenplay, Georges Conchon, based on the novel by Joseph Roth. Camera (color, Betacam), Roll; editor, Ulrike Pahl; music, Zbigniew Preisner; production design, Karel Vacek, Jiri Matolin; costume design, Uli Fessler; sound, Ian Voigt. Reviewed at Salzburg Film Festival, Dec. 6, 1994. Running time: **301 MIN.**
Franz von Trotta .... Max von Sydow
Carl Joseph
  von Trotta .... Tilman Gunther
Valerie
  von Taussig .... Charlotte Rampling
Dr. Max Demant .... Claude Rich
Eva Demant .... Julia Stemberger
Chojnicki .... Gert Voss
Katharina Slama .... Elena Sofia Ricci
Slama .... Bruno Dallansky
  With: Jean-Louis Richard, Fritz Muliar, Michael Schoenborn, Ernst Stankovski, Karlheinz Hackl, Friedrich Bauschulte.
  (German, French and Italian dialogue)

A sometimes slow-moving but faithful version of Joseph Roth's classic novel about the downfall of the Austrian empire from the perspective of a gentleman-officer's family, "Radetzky March" is as much a triumph for cameraman Gernot Roll as for director Axel Corti; Roll took over the reins when Corti died late last year in mid-filming. In its five-hour, three-part fest version, the leisurely paced pic stands as a seamless, artistic vision. If anything, however, Roll has been over-reverent, letting the planned four-hour epic extend into an hour of overtime.

Lack of English-language performances in the film could hinder sales outside Continental Europe, which is too bad. The rest of the world could use a palatably presented history lesson about conflicts originating in Central Europe.

Franz von Trotta (Max von Sydow), son of an officer, rises to the position of district captain. Franz is the kind of man who kills a fly with his thumb, just as he emotionally squashes his sensitive son, Carl Joseph (Tilman Gunther), fated to carry on the family tradition of military service to the emperor.

Film follows C.J.'s army career and adventures in an increasingly dissolute life. He betrays the three men who offer help and friendship by having affairs with their women. First love, Katharina (Elena Sofia Ricci), is the wife of his riding coach (Bruno Dallansky). Next up is Eva (Julia Stemberger), beautiful wife of his mentor, Max Demant (Claude Rich). By the time he moves in on Valerie (Charlotte Rampling), mistress of his father's friend Chojnicki (Gert Voss), C.J. is caught up in a life of drink and gambling.

Production values are first rate, the leading ladies beautiful and several of the performances outstanding. Rich gives an intelligent, humane portrait of Demant; as Chojnicki, Voss transforms himself into a worldly realist who descends into eerie madness; and Karlheinz Hackl visibly relishes his showy role as a drunken gambler.

Rampling brings sophisticated womanly charm to her role as one of C.J.'s lovers, and von Sydow is perfect as the elder von Trotta, a cold shell of a man who crumbles in the pic's single emotionally involving scene. Next to such players, Gunther is unfortunately not compelling enough to carry the film. —*Cathy Meils*

FEAR OF HEIGHTS

(HOEHENANGST)

(AUSTRIAN)

An Epo-Film production. Produced by Dieter Pochlatko. Directed by Houchang Allahyari. Screenplay, Houchang Allahyari, Tom D. Allahyari. Camera (color), Helmut Pirnat; editor, Charlotte Muellner; music, Michael Lichtenwallner; art direction, Katharina Woeppermann; sound, Moshan Nasiri. Reviewed at Salzburg Film Festival, Dec. 6, 1994. Running time: **101 MIN.**
Mario .... Fritz Karl
Frau
  Gusenleitner ... Dolores Schmidinger
Her father .... Leon Askin
Paul .... Michael Niavarani
Mario's father .... Hanno Poeschl

Refusing to give its story or audience a comfortable way out, "Fear of Heights" is an edgy film with a dark lining that puts an unexpected spin on a seemingly pleasant pastoral comedy about a young man who escapes troubled family and city life to find happiness with a farmer's daughter.

Flashbacks show pic's vulnerable anti-hero, Mario (Fritz Karl), victimized by an abusive father (Hanno Poeschl) and enduring a prison stint, during which time he is gang raped. An immigrant "guest worker" consigned to menial jobs, he unwittingly befriends a transvestite and is thrown out by his father. Fleeing to the countryside, he's grudgingly taken in by an old farmer (Leon Askin) and his middle-aged spinster daughter (Dolores Schmidinger).

Her brittle reserve gradually melts, and romance blossoms. Compared with Mario's other possibilities (his vulgar former g.f., the transvestite and the local innkeeper's fat, greasy-haired daughter), the spinster begins to look positively desirable. When Mario's father shows up demanding money and threatening to expose him to the police, she intervenes.

Director Houchang Allahyari guides the often sad and moody pic with a sure hand. A feeling of existential nausea permeates scenes of the guest-workers' grim urban existence; sunlight breaks through the clouds of anxiety in Mario's life as he experiences a lighthearted security in the routines of farm life.

Karl is appealing and believable as the disturbed Mario, and Schmidinger gives a moving and convincing perf as his rock of salvation. Tech credits are solid. Pic's title stems from Mario's acrophobia, used as a dramatic device in the somewhat imposed finale.
—*Cathy Meils*

TONINO AND TOINETTE

(TONINO UND TOINETTE)

(AUSTRIAN — B&W)

An ORF production. Directed by Xaver Schwarzenberger. Screenplay, Ulli Schwarzenberger. Camera (B&W), Schwarzenberger; editor, Schwarzenberger; art direction, Georg Resetschnig; costume design, Claudia Bobsin; sound, Roland Winke. Reviewed at Salzburg Film Festival, Dec. 6, 1994. Running time: **95 MIN.**
Toinette .... Julia Stemberger
Tonino .... Giulio Ricciarelli
Robert
  Hammer ..... Miguel Herz-Kestranek
Robbi .... George McCoy
Countess Marie
  Kentrovic .... Nicole Heesters
Father Cecco .... Wolfgang Gasser

An old-fashioned romance whose attractive leads are faced with daunting obstacles, "Tonino and Toinette" is set on the eve of World War I but stylistically is planted in the final days of black-and-white dramas, with deep-focus camerawork and detailed interiors recalling the visual appeal of Orson Welles pix. Curious combination of arthouse style and populist plot could make this one hard to slot.

Tall, dark and handsome Tonino (Giulio Ricciarelli) is an Italian fisherman who lost his wife and child during an epidemic. Toinette (Julia Stemberger) is an aristocrat married to an older, hard-hearted munitions manufacturer (Miguel Herz-Kestranek). Their young son, Robbi (George McCoy), is the center of her life.

Toinette takes Robbi to spend the summer with her lively aunt, a countess who arranges daily visits for him to the island home of Tonino, who dreams of going to America and selling spaghetti. When Robbi's father suddenly packs him off to school, Toinette moves in with Tonino and refuses to return home. After a final showdown, the lovers sail off to America with Robbi to start their dream pasta factory.

Ricciarelli and Stemberger have the kind of beautifully sad and sensitive faces that allow them to play the drama honestly. Director Xaver Schwarzenberger's camerawork, with its attention-drawing use of high-contrast B&W, parallels the material's delineation of its characters. Pic's more melodramatic moments, however, often border on the laughable. —*Cathy Meils*

MONTPELLIER

THE WOODEN GUN

(LE FUSIL DE BOIS)

(FRENCH)

A Les Films Princesse, Alizas Film, Roitfeld Prods. (France)/Atlantis Film (Romania)/Channel Films (Spain)/Cinevision (Brussels) production, with participation of CNC. Produced by Denis Karvil, Pierre Roitfeld. Directed, written by Pierre Delerive. Camera (color), Ion Marinescu; editor, Marine Deleu; costume design, Charles Wayenberg; sound, Thomas Gauder; weapons and special effects, Mihai Reti, Victor Ieremia; associate producers, Alain Coffier, Jose-Antonio Romero, Marinescu, Boris Szulzinger; assistant director, Mircea Plangau; casting, Lidia Slavu. Reviewed at Montpellier Festival of Mediterranean Cinema (competing), France, Oct. 26, 1994. Running time: **85 MIN.**

Dallers .... Samuel Le Bihan
Lagrange .... Jordi Molla
Morin .... Jean-Francois Garreaud
With: Philippe Frecon, Yves Collignon, Frederic Saurel.

Though it builds to a genuinely touching catharsis involving a retarded recruit and a protective officer during the Algerian War in 1961, "The Wooden Gun" is a little too accurate in its portrayal of the tedium of army life. Despite an excellent perf by Jordi Molla as the low-I.Q. soldier, earnest pic is strictly fest and Eurotube material.

Gallic scripter/helmer Pierre Delerive makes his feature debut at age 55 with a semi-autobiographical tale that gently illustrates the ironies and idiocy of war while positing that every human soul has a rich purpose.

When well-educated young Parisian Sgt. Dallers (Samuel Le Bihan) arrives in a rustic Algerian outpost to patrol the border with Tunisia, Lagrange (Molla), a certified village idiot who should never have been conscripted let alone assigned to active duty, is the butt of practical jokes from his bored companions in arms. The ultra-gruff ranking officer (Jean-Francois Garreaud) has supplied Lagrange with a wooden replica of a machine gun to prevent accidental firing.

Dallers at first resents being saddled with Lagrange in his unit, but gradually comes to appreciate his sub-intelligent charge, growing more compassionate in the process.

Molla is aces as the terrorized simpleton who craves acceptance and becomes a hero through the serendipitous timing of a trip to the latrine.

Although the pic's late-arriving emotional payoff is strong, the surrounding exposition amounts to little more than a string of vignettes with no compelling narrative motor. The punchy style that distinguishes the opening credits is not carried through to the body of the film.

Stark, rocky landscapes in Romania convincingly stand in for Algeria.
—*Lisa Nesselson*

NECROLOGY

(NEKROLOGJI)

(ALBANIAN — B&W)

An Albafilm Studios production. (International sales: Albafilm, Tirana.) Directed, written by Fatmir Koci. Camera (B&W), Mihal Rama; editor, Shazi Kapoli; production design, Ilia Xhokaxhi; sound, Niko Shallo. Reviewed at Montpellier Festival of Mediterranean Cinema, France, Oct. 25, 1994. Running time: **105 MIN.**

With: Rajmonda Bulku, Enver Petrovici, Guljelm Radoja, Vetiola Mani, Erjona Teme, Medi Malka.

"Necrology" is a lumbering Albanian fiasco about an ancient kingdom whose queen declares that all her subjects are immortal. Budding filmmakers wishing for a crash course in how to learn from someone else's mistakes need look no further than this authentic oddity.

The royal sculptor — who has just completed a monumental Trojan-style horse sans belly — is on hand when the king croaks. The widowed queen denies the ruler's demise by eating double his 'n' hers portions at every meal, while the defunct king decomposes into a skeleton. (Her claim that her dead hubby is "sleeping" recalls the immortal Monty Python "dead parrot" sketch.)

As the visually impressive giant horse dominates the parched Albanian landscape, the nutsy and gluttonous queen grows obese, mischievous monks grow mate with visiting prostitutes, and extracts from Sibelius and Satie thunder away on the soundtrack. The actors studiously emote, while carefully framed, stark B&W images amount to naught.
—*Lisa Nesselson*

HAWAII

HERITAGE

(UV)

(MONGOLIAN)

A Mongolkino production. (International sales: ARD Cinema Co., Ulaanbaatar.) Produced, directed by D. Khatanbaatar, B. Nagnaidorj. Screenplay, Khatanbaatar. Camera (color), N. Zoondui; music, Altankhuyag. Reviewed at Hawaii Film Festival, Honolulu, Nov. 5, 1994. Running time: **73 MIN.**

With: G. Baasankhuu, N. Dugarsanjaa, G. Dashkhuu, G. Battsetseg.
(Mongolian dialogue; English voiceover)

Marred by variable technique but lifted by a cheeky central perf from its 7-year-old star, "Heritage" is a Mongolian kidpic with charm to spare. Pint-sized story of a tyke from the steppes who finds big-city life not to his liking, pic could conceivably travel as a dubbed item in TV kids' slots.

First half-hour intros ankle-biter G. Baasankhuu frolicking on the plains, wrangling horses and generally having a merry old time with his grandpa prior to being sent to the city to live with his uncle for a spell. Urban life, however, turns out to be drab apartment blocks, frequent power outages and a nascent market economy in which he and a friend make a bundle selling bottled lemonade on the streets.

Tensions soon erupt as the naive kid ends up accidentally trashing his relations' apartment and giving away all his earnings to a blind musician. Such selflessness, notes his uncle, doesn't work in today's society. Pic ends with the kid dreaming of returning to his carefree life on the steppes.

Scenes of Baasankhuu wandering round the city in full national dress with his uncle have an almost docu flavor, and are the best in the movie. Elsewhere, development is more jerky, not helped by an English voiceover translation that's confusing in dialogue sequences. Color is variable, and other tech credits basic.
—*Derek Elley*

THE ELDEST DAUGHTER

(LOKUDUWA)

(SRI LANKAN)

A GSK Films production. Produced by Geetha Kumarasinghe. Directed by Sumitra Peries. Screenplay, Tissa Abeysekera, from a story by Edward Mallawarachchi. Camera (color), Willie Blake; editor, Gladwin Fernando; music, Premasiri Kemadasa; art direction, Hemalapa Dharmasena; sound, Lionel Gunaratne. Reviewed at Hawaii Film Festival, Honolulu, Nov. 7, 1994. Running time: **150 MIN.**

With: Geetha Kumarasinghe, Joe Abeywickrama, Iranganie Serasinghe, Jackson Anthony, Kamal Addaraarachchi, Nadika Gunasekera, Trilicia Gunewardene, Veena Jayakody, Rex Codippily, Daya De Alwis, Peter Almeida, Anosha Sonali, Ama Wijesekere.

Shorn of a good half-hour and with much tighter editing in individual sequences, "The Eldest Daughter" could be an OK drama of a woman finding her position in modern Sri Lankan society. As it stands, however, this seventh (and first urban-set) feature of Sumitra Peries — best known for her tender 1978 bow, "The Girls" — is too often marred by the very cliches it sets out to reject.

Pic's producer, Geetha Kumarasinghe, plays Punna, eldest daughter of a government clerk who is forced into retirement by ill health. Punna's suitors are all put off by the family's failure to provide a decent dowry.

Enter Wickrama, who claims not to be interested in a dowry but asks to borrow one to complete his new house. Though he returns the cash, he later disappears and turns out to be a con man pursued by the cops.

Shattered by the experience, Punna gets a job at the clothing firm of a rich friend's father, subsequently rising to the top as his mistress. Further shaken by Wickrama's reappearance, Punna eventually quits her job in an effort to recover her self-esteem and her family's respect.

Strength of the movie is Kumarasinghe's central perf, sliding with assurance from the docile daughter to the tough femme exec. But dramatic situations, acting styles and characters are too grounded in the conventions of South Asian commercial cinema to support Peries' low-key approach, despite some scenes (mostly in the early stages) that possess considerable delicacy.

Tech credits are functional, with poor color processing in print caught.
—*Derek Elley*

FLASHFIRE

A Silver Lion Films and Avondale Pictures presentation of a Lance Hool production. Produced by Hool. Executive producers, Paul L. Newman, James M. Gould. Co-producers, Conrad Hool, John Warren. Directed by Elliot Silverstein. Screenplay, Warren, Dan York. Camera (color), Bert Dunk; editor, Mark Conte; music, Sylvester Levay; production design, Gregory Melton. Reviewed at Cannes Film Festival (market), May 17, 1994. Running time: **90 MIN.**
Jack Flinder .... Billy Zane
Ben Durand .... Louis Gossett Jr.
Lisa .... Kristin Minter

Pleasant and inoffensive, but decidedly unexciting, "Flashfire" is yet another formula thriller about conspiracy and corruption in the police force. Though directed by vet Elliot Silverstein, still best known for his 1965 spoof Western "Cat Ballou," and graced by the presence of Oscar-winning Louis Gossett Jr. and rising star Billy Zane, this cliched item will head to video with no theatrical stops en route.

Pic's hero, Jack Flinder (Zane), rejects his family's wealth, status and power for the brass badge of a police detective. When an insidious firebug is on the loose, Jack and partner Art are called to investigate, which leads to a conspiracy of big-time arson and murder.

When Art is executed in cold blood, Jack and femme fatale Lisa (Kristin Minter), Art's g.f., who witnessed his murder, risk their lives in disclosing a conspiracy of deceit and fraud in the force's highest levels.

Most of "Flashfire's" plot is taken up with clunky, overly familiar ideas, and helmer Silverstein is unable to transform the cliched material into a thrilling actioner. Climax, in which Jack confronts his own superior and mentor, Capt. Ben Durand (Gossett), is predictable and fails to excite.

Zane and Minter are attractive performers, and tech credits are far more polished than the routine plot deserves, but "Flashfire" is stamped, from first frame to last, a genre item of the most conventional kind. —*Emanuel Levy*

BALAGAN

(GERMAN — DOCU)

A Journalfilm Klaus Volkenborn KG production. Produced by Volkenborn. Directed, written by Andres Veiel. Camera (color), Hans Romach; editor, Bernd Euscher; sound, Horst Zinsmeister. Reviewed at the Castro Theatre, San Francisco, July 27, 1994. (In S.F. Jewish Film Festival.) Running time: **97 MIN.**

German-produced doc examines an Israeli theater group's controversial performance, and a few of the leading personalities behind it. Though slickly made, pic's lack of coherent p.o.v. on its subjects (who appear wanting on that score themselves) soon turns matters formless and enervating. Politically slanted fests may find redeeming value.

Religiously observant Iraqi Jew Moni Yosef, Czech camp survivor's daughter Madi Maayan and Muslim Palestinian Khaled Abu Ali founded the Akko Theatre Center. Their play "Arbeit macht fret" evidently incited much interest for its caustic take on contemporary Israeli fixations with the Holocaust. Offstage, Madi says, "The Holocaust is the new religion, the opiate for the masses in Israel ... It's untouchable. (We) go to the extreme on purpose, to provocate."

Presumably that provocation suggests Israeli Jews have increasingly employed the Holocaust as means to morally justify any subsequent actions, including West Bank occupation. But much-needed further articulation of that message is absent here.

Excerpts from the multi-site "Arbeit" performance suggest no cogent thesis at work, as the miscellaneous ranting, nudity and sensationalism look like stock "shocking" avant-garde posturing out of their original context.

Director Andres Veiel unwittingly lets actors' comments suggest a dubious assumption of the artist's inherent moral superiority amid corrupted society. Audience sympathy is hardly with Madi when she strikes a righteous pose re her fake concentration camp arm ID tattoo. "I have a number like the girl in your show, but a real one!" says a play attendee with understandable anger.

There's no insight on the creative process that begat "Arbeit," whose cathartic virtues are taken for granted by the helmer, yet fail screen translation in this unfocused docu. Result is unintentionally unflattering view of agitprop thespians who are meant to be seen as bold and uncompromising. Instead, they seem egotistically insensitive to much-bruised cultures on both sides.

Balagan is a Hebrew expression meaning "productive chaos" — a headache that perhaps induces fresh illumination. The film does not.

Tech work is solid all around.
—*Dennis Harvey*

KANA-KANA: THE SUMMER THAT NEVER WAS

(KANA-KANA)

(JAPANESE — 16mm)

A Taku Oshima Prods. (Tokyo) production. Produced, directed, written, edited by Oshima. Camera (B&W Super-8/color 16mm), Hiroki Miyano; music, Jon Bray; sound, Tutomu Takase. Reviewed at World Film Festival, Montreal (non-competing), Sept. 2, 1994. Running time: **105 MIN.**
With: Noriko Agata, Kenji Matuzaki, Mihoko Naritomi, Kiyoshi Kawatubo, Chie Iwasaki, Ryohei Homna.

Another installment in the new Japanese wave of European-style slices of life, "Kana-Kana" is a piquant and leisurely character study for more than an hour before drifting into obscurity, both in content and style.

Pic centers on Noriko (Noriko Agata), a perky 30-year-old translator who has recently ditched her actor b.f. to move back in with her parents in suburban Tokyo. The folks want her out again, and keep pointing out suitable husband material, but she's more interested in her work, and in a jazzy singing group she and a teacher pal have formed. When the pal stops off to visit a truant student, Noriko becomes intrigued by 15-year-old Takato (Kenji Matuzaki), who appears to have been abandoned by his single mother and is living off shoplifted goods.

Soon, she's helping him tidy up the place and bringing him food and money. Before really thinking about it, she moves in and, after an interlude of playing house, things turn sexual, much to their mutual bewilderment. Problem is, Takato is a very terse kid, and the odd couple's non-conversations and tentative actions aren't likely to engage most auds past initial curiosity, despite Agata's considerable charm. Side trip to a rural cabin isn't much help, since lensing there is even darker than the urban interiors that predominate, and tonal variety is utterly lost.

More adept with actors than *mise-en-scene*, first-time helmer Taku Oshima calls pic "The Summer That Never Was" because of the exploratory, almost accidental, nature of the central relationship, and because 1993 saw more storms than sunshine. He also places Noriko — literally, via Super-8 — within the celebrations of the emperor's wedding, and attempts to draw parallels between her life and that of the same-age empress. That thread is quickly lost, however, and "Kana-Kana" stands little chance of surviving a few festival seasons.
—*Ken Eisner*

FATHERLAND

(VATERLAND)

(GERMAN — 16mm)

A Trans-Film production, in association with UMS Produktion. ZDF. (International sales: Trans-Film, Berlin.) Produced by Albert Kitzler. Directed, written by Uli M. Schuppel. Camera (color, 16mm), Ciro Cappellari; editor, Inge Schneider; music, Alex Hacke, Mick Harvey; sound, Jorg Bohlmann, Nanett Creuzberg. Reviewed at Rimini Cinema Film Festival, Italy (competing), Oct. 2, 1994. Running time: **89 MIN.**
Kadir .... Olivier Picot
Louis .... Ferdinand Bottker
Frieda .... Heide Bartolomaus
Wojtek .... Miroslav Baka
Heidrun .... Christin Konig
With: Thomas Verrlich, Myriam Abbas, Gudrun Okras, Jercy Gotzko, Werner Godemann.

German musicvid and documaker Uli M. Schuppel's first feature is a chilly father-son journey toward an uncertain homeland. Pic is soundly constructed and atmospherically melancholic, but too austere and low on momentum to attract many fellow travelers beyond fest fringes.

Released after two years in a Berlin psychiatric clinic, Algerian immigrant Kadir (Olivier Picot) learns he has a son, Louis (Ferdinand Bottker), born soon after he was institutionalized. His frosty ex-wife tries to deny him access to the boy. His efforts to start afresh in Germany with a factory job are undone by the racist taunts of his co-workers and, in desperation, Kadir kidnaps his son.

As he heads south through a bleak wasteland, it becomes clear Kadir's destination is Algeria. En route, father and son cross paths with a series of misfits, and every sign of hardship Kadir encounters unleashes another childhood memory of his tyrannical father. The harsh winter takes its toll on the son, and his illness forces the pair to stop.

Given the climate of doom from which Schuppel rarely strays, the final-act tragedy is far too inevitable. Adding to the stolid feel are characters who fail to engage on an emotional level. Picot makes a suitably grave centerpiece but is too one-note wounded to evoke sympathy. Miroslav Baka (from Kieslowski's "A Short Film About Killing") is underutilized as a Polish friend who helps Kadir get out of Berlin.

Ciro Cappellari's energized camerawork lends a tough, gritty look, milking the contrasts between the murky factory, the desolate expanses the pair cross and the startling whites and blues of Kadir's Algerian memory flashes.
—*David Rooney*

6 OPEN, 21 CLOSED

(ISRAELI — DOCU)

Produced by Amit Goren, Eitan Harris for Goren-Harris Films. Directed, written by Goren. Camera (color), Harris; editor, Tali Halter-Shenkar. Reviewed at Jerusalem Film Festival, July 4, 1994. Running time: **62 MIN.**

Beer Sheva prison has a reputation as Israel's most dreaded penitentiary. In "6 Open, 21 Closed," director Amit Goren ferrets out some admirable human elements in this living hell. Finely shot and edited, the docu is compelling viewing and looks good for selected fest and tube slots.

The prisoners singled out by Goren are a startling bunch. One burly, half-mad brute is a masochist who vents his rage by slashing his own body with razors. There is a son who wants to share a cell with his father, and a young con man named Amnon who gets married to a policewoman while still in prison.

Pic's star, however, is Shlomo Tweezer, the new prison commander. Though he makes it clear he won't be messed with, Tweezer is an unshakable progressive who tries to practice a policy of rehabilitation. Goren depicts this strong but modest man in truly heroic terms. Particularly moving is a visit to Tweezer's home in the slums of Beer Sheva, with its hint of a family tragedy that marked his life.

Eitan Harris' ever-inventive cinematography adds strong visual interest to this absorbing documentary. Shots of the sand-colored prison in the desert recall the last outpost of civilization in "Desert of the Tartars."
—*Deborah Young*

INDEPENDENCE

(ISTEQLALL)

(PALESTINIAN — DOCU)

Produced by Nurith Keidar for Keshet Broadcasting (Tel Aviv). Directed, written by Nizar Hassan. Camera (color), Nily Aslan; editor, Dani Itzhaki. Reviewed at Jerusalem Film Festival, July 6, 1994. Running time: **55 MIN.** (Arabic soundtrack)

"Independence" is a landmark documentary, not only because it's one of the first to be made for Israeli TV by a Palestinian director, but because it poses an awkward dilemma in the clearest possible terms. Why should Palestinians living in Israel celebrate the national Independence Day, since it marks the day they lost their fatherland? Helmer Nizar Hassan makes a timely, honest, partisan and fascinating attempt to explore the implications of this question.

Filming in his native village of El Mashad, near Nazareth, Hassan asks a wide range of Palestinians how they feel about Independence Day. What is their flag? Where are their loyalties? Mohamed, a truck driver, brushes him off and begs him not to even pose certain sensitive questions. He's equally at a loss to explain why he observes a minute of standing still to commemorate victims of the Holocaust.

Nothing is simple or black-and-white in this world of mixed ethnic groups and contradictory politics. In the village schools (many built by the Israeli government), Arab kids learn nationalist songs in Hebrew. The sympathetic town mayor vaunts his close contact with Israeli pols and amusingly demonstrates it by phoning Yitzak Rabin on camera.

Hassan recites his own first-person voiceover, giving pic an appealing personal touch and immediacy.
—*Deborah Young*

LITTLE HORRORS

(PICCOLI ORRORI)

(ITALIAN)

A Mikado release (Italy) of a Lontane Province Film production. Produced by Massimo Cortesi. Directed, written by Tonino De Bernardi. Camera (color), Tommaso Borgstrom; editor, Fiorella Giovanelli; music, Ciro Buttari. Reviewed at Taormina Film Festival (competing), Italy, July 31, 1994. Running time: **89 MIN.**

Housewife/Angel/ Cabaret Singer	Iaia Forte
Fedra	Anna Bonaiuto
Guitar player	Roberto De Francesco

With: Galatea Ranzi, Enrica Brizzi, Renata Palminiello, Gilda Postiglione, Enrico Ghezzi.

The most serious attempt at experimental filmmaking to come out of Italy in many moons, "Little Horrors" marks the first 35mm feature by Tonino De Bernardi, considered the dean of Italian experimental filmers. This curiosity item, likely to get mainly fest exposure, is a poetic compendium of symbolic incidents and elusive meanings. Some of pic's 15-odd "chapters" are disturbing pinpricks of melancholy. Overall effect, however, is highly abstract and too cerebral for most auds.

De Bernardi's very personal work unspools like a painstakingly composed poem. One tenuous thread running through many episodes is the (mostly female) characters' attempts to establish a relationship with God or the unknown, or at least with other people.

Shot on a shoestring, pic is graced with above-average lensing and perfs by several interesting new actors. De Bernardi has an eerie talent for exploring the female face with his camera. Faces and places (fields, stone farmhouses) have a timeless, archetypal quality.

Pic runs the gamut of theatrical gestures and classical references, from Phaedra and Eurydice to old women baking bread and actors washing their bloody hands in clear streams. All is set to the refined sounds of Bellini, Schubert and Mozart.
—*Deborah Young*

EAST AND WEST

(OST UND WEST)

(AUSTRIAN — B&W — 1923)

A National Center for Jewish Film release. Produced by Listo/Picon Films. Directed by Sidney M. Goldin, Ivan Abramson. Reviewed at the Castro Theatre, San Francisco, July 27, 1884. (In S.F. Jewish Film Festival.) Running time: **65 MIN.**
With: Molly Picon, Jacob Kalish, Sidney M. Goldin, Saul Nathan, Laura Glucksman, Eugen Neufeld, Johannes Roth.

Despite successful original European plays, this early Austrian vehicle for New York-born vaudevillian (and later Broadway/Hollywood actress) Molly Picon eluded *Variety* reviewers of the 1920s. Delightful comedy merits new scrutiny from cinematheque programmers.

Theme is age-old, though no grayer than Joan Miklin Silver's 1988 "Crossing Delancey" update: i.e., the conflicting values between fully "Westernized" immigrant Jews and their relatives still set in traditional *shtetl* ways. Invitation to prim cousin Zelda's Austrian wedding propels "bee-stung"-lipped, bob-haired, saucer-eyed Mollie (Picon) across the Atlantic, alongside now-prosperous Daddy (played by co-director Sidney M. Goldin).

But Mollie's ignorant, breezy disapproval of tradition soon results in a sequence of humorous scandals. First, she breaks Yom Kippur fasting with a scarf-fest that deprives everyone else. Then she teaches the cantor's male flock how to do the flapper shimmy. Finally, she arranges a "mock" wedding with Talmud student Jacob, an act whose religio-legal repercussions she scarcely understands.

Love-struck Jacob refuses to disavow the unconsummated marriage, instead demanding five years' wait before divorce. At the end of that period, he's transformed himself into an acclaimed author sans orthodox spit curls and beard. Mollie falls before realizing the object of desire is her husband.

Interestingly, the tradition-minded man here remakes himself to accommodate an up-to-the-moment femme. As recently as "Delancey," the rare cinematic Jewish heroine was expected to toss her liberated New World ethos and embrace a more gender-restrictive role.

Picon's persona will have none of that. Her amusingly brash Mollie may bear a close resemblance at this point to Zasu Pitts, but her bearing anticipates Clara Bow; such imp naughtiness is tacitly approved when Dad sends her into the cantor's lair with the faint warning, "Remember, they're nice boys. Don't get too rough with them."

Picon's tomboy appeal — glimpsed here in feisty boxing/weight-lifting garb and brief male drag — remains charming. Situational laughs successfully walk a thin line between dissing traditional Judaic culture and its assimilationist U.S. translations. Production is par for then-reigning standards. Fairly fast pace slows somewhat in latter half. Current print is excellent given probably less than ideal source materials.
—*Dennis Harvey*

VEGAS VICE

A Blue Ridge Entertainment/Raejoe Prods. release, in association with Good Doctor Prods. Produced, directed by Joey Travolta. Executive producers, Tom Daniels, Robert Baruc, H. Michael Miller. Co-producer, Pat Davis Lass. Screenplay, Travolta, Rich Dillon. Camera (Foto-Kem color), F. Martin Smith; editor, Rich Cowan; music, Jeff Lass; production design, Joe Sabella; costumes, Kim Ryusaki; sound, Sergio Bandera; associate producer, Jeff Lass; assistant director, Addison Randall; casting, Jean Levine, Doreen Lane. Reviewed at Cannes Film Festival (market), May 13, 1994. Running time: **83 MIN.**

Joe Owens	Sam Jones
Andrea Thompson	Shannon Tweed
Chief Dan Bronski	James Gammon
Bugs	Miguel Nunez
Mike	Tom Fridley
Allison	Rebecca Ferrati
Tony	Branscombe Richmond

An utterly mundane and meretricious actioner, "Vegas Vice" is bottom-rung video fare. Sam Jones and Shannon Tweed topline as Las Vegas cops trying in desultory fashion to nab a serial killer, apparently a hooker who rewards her clients with a bullet in the head, leaving a $100 bill as signature.

No one, least of all co-writer/director/producer Joey Travolta, seems at all inspired by this material, which, though routine, could have at least made for an exciting and sexy thriller. But a by-the-numbers screenplay, routine performances and listlessly staged, almost laughable, action scenes are the kiss of death.

To its credit, there's one reasonably effective auto-crash stunt.

The identity of the killer comes as no surprise, given the overemphatic style of the actor involved.

Pointlessly repeated shots of the exterior of the Vegas cop shop and chopper views of the familiar cityscape add nothing.

End credits reveal that pic's shooting was interrupted by the L.A. earthquake, but the movie itself is devoid of shocks.

—*David Stratton*

STARRY DOME

(ENASTROS THOLOS)

(GREEK)

A Greek Film Centre/Stefi Films production. (International sales: Greek Film Centre, Athens.) Produced, directed by Kostas Aristopoulos. Screenplay, Aristopoulos, Achilleas Kyriakides. Camera (color, widescreen), Stamatis Yannoulis; editor, Despina Maroulakou; art direction/costume design, Anastasia Arseni; sound, Thanasis Georgiades; choreography, Anniuska Economou. Reviewed at Venice Film Festival (Window on Images), Sept. 2, 1994. Running time: **87 MIN.**
With: Sophokles Peppas, Irene Iglesi, Maria Kechagioglou, Smaragda Karydi, Aglaia Pappa, Alexandros Logothetis, Constantinos Markoulakis, Johnny Theodorides.

"**S**tarry Dome" is a good-looking slice of performance theater-cinema that would make an intriguing set text at any respectable university. Free adaptation of the Antigone-Oedipus myth, shot in Venice, Italy, with Greek thesps and late 19th-century garb, is a brainbender for anyone else, though enthusiasts of Manuel de Oliveira and Peter Greenaway's work may feel the odd *frisson*. Adventurous Eurotube buyers may bite.

In this version, Antigone accompanies her father Oedipus on a journey outside Greece, working with a group of traveling players. Her sister Ismene arrives and begs her to return, as their brothers Eteocles and Polynices are at loggerheads. She finds them both dead, berates King Creon for his indifference, and hangs herself.

Even those with vague recall of the Ancient Greek myth may have difficulty matching the onscreen antics with the various versions of the myth. Dialogue, lifted from writers like Shakespeare, Pound, Dostoevsky, Duras and Tolstoy, is rarefied, with copious stirred-in references from Western literature and history; every now and then a pretty ballerina (choreographer Anniuska Economou) does a solo in a Venetian courtyard.

Tech credits are peachy, and costumes eye-catching. Enunciation, especially by the female players, is clear and poised, and choices in classical music, notably from Gounod's "Sappho" and Berlioz's "The Trojans," uplifting. What it all means is anyone's guess. Pic won five prizes at last year's Thessaloniki fest.

—*Derek Elley*

AMERICAN MATCHMAKER

(AMERICANER SHADCHEN)

(B&W — 1940)

A National Center for Jewish Film release, originally released by Fame Films. Produced, directed by Edgar G. Ulmer. Screenplay, S. Castle (Shirley Ulmer), from an original story by G. Heimo. Camera (B&W), Ulmer; editor, Hans E. Mandl; music, Sam Morgenstern, lyrics, William Mercur; production design, Ulmer. Reviewed at the Castro Theatre, San Francisco, July 21, 1991. (In S.F. Jewish Film Festival.) Running time: **87 MIN.**
With: Leo Fuchs, Judith Abarbanel, Rosetta Bialis, Judel Dubinsky, Anna Guskin, Celia Brodkin.

One of Viennese emigre Edgar G. Ulmer's several Yiddish-language pix, "American Matchmaker" eluded *Variety* coverage in both its original run 54 years ago and its late-'70s revival. Late helmer's widow/scenarist, Shirley Ulmer, has just sold Paramount the remake rights to this modest but appealing curio.

Vehicle for stage star Leo Fuchs (still active, with recent roles in "Avalon" and on "thirtysomething") casts him as Nat Silver, one-time sweatshop worker turned manufacturing magnate. Despite — or because of — his wealth, Nat has no luck finding a suitable wife. When the eighth successive fiancee turns out to be a gold digger, he adopts the persona "Nat Gold" and opens an upscale matchmaking service to help others. Not surprisingly, Nat ends up tying the knot with one attractive "client."

This predictable happy close is somewhat undermined by a puzzlingly snobbish characterization of his love object by Judith Abarbanel, who has the odd tendency to avoid direct eye contact with Fuchs in their scenes together. Supporting players, however, hit zesty comic notes, while Fuchs (who sings several songs) limns the protagonist with subdued charm.

Players hold attention during somewhat slow-moving narrative. Stylistic flourishes that distinguished cult director Ulmer's better-known U.S. efforts ("Detour," "Bluebeard") are largely absent here, though low-budget production is resourceful enough.

Interestingly, effort at portraying fully "assimilated" second-generation Manhattan Jewish culture wraps characters in fantasy landscape of champagne, penthouse apartments, tuxedos and glittering gowns.

Original negative was lost; current print, cobbled together from best available sources, is OK, if visually soft. Unfortunately, original English subtitles translate only about 60% of dialogue, depriving most viewers of much verbal wit.

—*Dennis Harvey*

DARK SIDE OF GENIUS

A Pacific Shores Pictures production. Produced by Ray Haboush. Directed by Phedon Papamichael. Screenplay, Frederick J. Stroppel. Camera (color), Papamichael; editor, Britton J. Petrucelli; music, Tom Hiel; costumes, Julie Rae Engelsman; sound, Leonard Marcel; assistant director, Dwayne Shattuck. Reviewed at World Film Festival, Montreal, Sept. 1, 1994. Running time: **87 MIN.**

Julian Jons	Brent Fraser
Jennifer Cole	Finola Hughes
Leon Bennini	Glenn Shadix
Carrie	Moon Zappa
John Barnard	Patrick Richwood
Anna/Kristi	Tina Cote
Sherman McPhee	Patrick Bauchau
Samuel Rourke	Seymour Cassel

"**D**ark Side of Genius" is destined for the bargain bin of the vid store. Ace cinematographer Phedon Papamichael ("Cool Runnings," "Wild Palms") works hard at offering evocatively portentous visuals for his second directorial effort, following his better-than-average Showtime original, "Sketch Artist." But neither he nor a fine cast can do much with the idiocies and inconsistencies of Frederick Stroppel's ludicrously contrived script. If pic were any sillier, it might qualify as camp. But it isn't even that diverting.

Finola Hughes stars as trendy L.A. art critic Jennifer Cole. She's fascinated by the lurid works of a moody artist, Julian Jons (Brent Fraser), who just completed a seven-year lockup for the crime-of-passion murder of his model/girlfriend (Tina Cote). Despite the urgent warnings of her ditzy roommate (Moon Zappa) and her suave editor (Patrick Bauchau), she falls in love with Julian. She dismisses others' fears about Julian, insisting that he's all better now.

Or is he? Julian obviously is still obsessed with his late girlfriend, whose image appears in all of his new paintings. And his precarious mental state only gets worse when a wealthy art collector (Seymour Cassel) commissions Julian to paint the collector's young girlfriend. Naturally, the girlfriend is a dead ringer for Julian's late lover. Just as naturally, she, too, is played by Tina Cote.

If someone were to write a book titled "Smart Women Who Do Stupid Things in Bad Movies," Jennifer would merit at least a footnote. Hughes deserves some credit for not coming across as a complete imbecile, as her character remains willfully blind to danger for so long.

Fraser deserves a similar backhanded compliment for remaining marginally credible even as Julian's psyche is arbitrarily bent and reshaped by the script's incredible twists.

Bauchau has the pic's best line: "A critic should never fall for an artist. Conflict of interest, babe." But artist William Quigley gives the best supporting performance. He's the one responsible for the suitably spooky-looking paintings supposedly done by Julian.

—*Joe Leydon*

'66 WAS A GOOD YEAR FOR TOURISM

(ISRAELI — DOCU)

A National Center for Jewish Film release. Produced by Amit Goren Prods. Directed, written by Amit Goren. Camera (color, video-to-16mm transfer), Eitan Harris; editing, Tali Halter; music, Yo-Go; sound, Ofer Webman. Reviewed at the Castro Theatre, San Francisco, July 27, 1994. (In S.F. Jewish Film Festival.) Running time: **66 MIN.**

Helmer Amit Goren ponders the idea and necessity of a national identity in this journal-like doc; his own powerful pull toward re-adopted Israeli homeland stands at one end of the spectrum, his family's Americanized lifestyles at another. Engaging if diffuse, "'66" will primarily interest showcases for Judaic themes and select educational webs.

At 9 years old in 1966, Goren and two younger sibs moved from Israel to NYC. While the others embraced their new digs as "home," Amit never lost the sense he'd left his behind, and so moved back.

Much of film is spent visiting family members still stateside. Middle brother Yoav, an L.A. musician engaged to a Chinese-American woman (source of some maternal consternation) admits he's in love with pursuing "the American dream" of success. Youngest sib Yuvie identifies as a Jew just tangentially. Tending bar at a Queens topless joint, toning his buffed bod or tuning his motorcycle, Yuvie is so assimilated he's a near-cartoon of Noo Yawk he-maleness.

Nor has Egyptian-born Dad ever missed the years spent in Israel. His Tel Aviv-bred wife, however, has never stopped resenting the separation from her homeland. Significant element omitted here is the impact this bitter wound had on parents' marriage and their relationship to now-adult children. Could resulting tension be one reason why most concerned seem so casual regarding family ties, or about their shared Jewish identity?

To helmer's dismay, they're always too individually "busy" to come together for a meal or even a single shot during course of film, despite simultaneous NYC visits. Goren's sorrow over this blood-knot indifference becomes pic's underlying theme.

Intriguing, disparate personalities on display make this an enjoyable if not especially penetrating dig into cultural/geographic routes to selfhood.

Transfer from vid to film is OK, though "'66" will look best on the small screen. Lensing and sound are adequate. —*Dennis Harvey*

FILM TITLE INDEX
1993-1994

Film Title Index
1993-1994

A

FILM TITLE INDEX

FILM TITLE INDEX

FILM TITLE INDEX

C

FILM TITLE INDEX

FILM TITLE INDEX

FILM TITLE INDEX

FILM TITLE INDEX

FILM TITLE INDEX

FILM TITLE INDEX

FILM TITLE INDEX

FILM TITLE INDEX

FILM TITLE INDEX

FILM TITLE INDEX

FILM TITLE INDEX

FILM TITLE INDEX

Lumiere des Etoiles Mortes, La (The Light From Dead Stars) **FRENCH-GERMAN**
   d. Charles Matton . . . . Jan. 24, 1994
Lumiere Noire (Black Light) **FRENCH** *d. Med Hondo* . . . . Dec. 19, 1994
Lung Min (Cageman) **HONG KONG** *d. Jacob C.L. Cheung* . . . . Apr. 5, 1993
Lungo Silenzio, Il (The Long Silence) **ITALIAN-FRENCH-GERMAN** *d. Margarethe Von Trotta* . . . . Sep. 13, 1993
Lush Life *d. Michael Elias* . . . . Dec. 6, 1993
(Lyrics and Lace) Pikkuja Ja Pikkuhousuja . . . . May 17, 1993

ℳ

M. Butterfly *d. David Cronenberg* . . . . Sep. 20, 1993
Ma Saison Préférée (My Favorite Season) **FRENCH** *d. André Téchiné* . . . . . May 17, 1993
Macedonian Saga **MACEDONIAN** *d. Branko Gapo* . . . . Dec. 12, 1994
Machine, La (The Machine **FRENCH-GERMAN** *d. François Dupeyron* . . . . . Nov. 28, 1994
(Machine, The) La Machine . . . . Nov. 28, 1994
Macht der Biler: Leni Riefenstahl, Die (The Power of the Image: Leni Riefenstahl)
   GERMAN-BRITISH-FRENCH *d. Ray Muller* . . . . Sep. 13, 1993
Mad Dog and Glory *d. John McNaughton* . . . . Mar. 1, 1993
Madadayo (Not Yet) **JAPANESE** *d. Akira Kurosawa* . . . . May 24, 1993
(Madam Water) Madame l'Eau . . . . Mar. 15, 1993
Madame l'Eau (Madam Water) **DUTCH-FRENCH** *d. Jean Rouch* . . . . Mar. 15, 1993
Made In America *d. Richard Benjamin* . . . . Jun. 7, 1993
Madness of King George, The *d. Nicholas Hytner* . . . . Dec. 19, 1994
Madre Muerta, La (The Dead Mother) **SPANISH** *d. Bajo Ulloa* . . . . Nov. 1, 1993
Madregilda **SPANISH** *d. Francisco Regueiro* . . . . Nov. 1, 1993
Magarece Godine/L'Age Ingrat (The Ungrateful Age) **BOSNIAN-FRENCH** *d. Nenad Dizdarevic* . . . . Jun. 6, 1994
(Magic - Stronger Than Life) Karlekens Himmelska Helvete . . . . Jan. 3, 1994
(Magic Hunter) Buvos Vadas . . . . Sep. 5, 1994
Magnificat **ITALIAN** *d. Pupi Avati* . . . . May 24, 1993
Magzat, A (Foetus) **HUNGARIAN-POLISH** *d. Marta Meszaros* . . . . Feb. 21, 1994
Mairi Mhor: Her Life and Songs (Mairi Mhor: Na H-Orain 'Sa Beatha) **BRITISH** *d. Mike Alexander* . . . . . Nov. 14, 1994
(Mairi Mhor: Na H-Orain 'Sa Beatha) Mairi Mhor: Her Life and Songs . . . . . . Nov. 14, 1994
Major League II *d. David S. Ward* . . . . Mar. 28, 1994
Makarov **RUSSIAN** *d. Vladimir Chotinenko* . . . . Jul. 11, 1994
Making Of...And God Spoke, The *d. Arthur Borman* . . . . Oct. 11, 1993
(Making Up!) Abgeschminkt! . . . . Nov. 15, 1993
Malenky Gigant Bolshogo Sexa (A Small Giant of Big Sex) **RUSSIAN** *d. Nikolai Dostal* . . . . Mar. 1, 1993
Malice *d. Harold Becker* . . . . Oct. 4, 1993
Mama Awethu! *d. Bethany Yarrow* . . . . Mar. 7, 1994
Man Mu Bang (Two Flags) **SOUTH KOREAN** *d. Aum Jong Sun* . . . . Sep. 19, 1994
(Man Named Benito, A) Il Giovane Mussolini . . . . Jul. 12, 1993
Man of No Importance, A **BRITISH** *d. Suri Krishnamma* . . . . Sep. 19, 1994
(Man of...) Czlowiek Z... . . . . May 9, 1994
(Man on the Balcony, The) Manen pa Balkongen . . . . Jan. 3, 1994
(Man on the Shore, The) L'Homme sur les Quais . . . . Jun. 7, 1993
Man Without a Face, The *d. Mel Gibson* . . . . Aug. 30, 1993
Man's Best Friend *d. John Lafia* . . . . Dec. 6, 1993
Manen pa Balkongen (The Man on the Balcony) **SWEDISH** *d. Daniel Alfredson* . . . . Jan. 3, 1994
Manhattan by Numbers *d. Amir Naderi* . . . . Apr. 5, 1993
Manhattan Murder Mystery *d. Woody Allen* . . . . Aug. 16, 1993
Maniaci Sentimentali (Sentimental Maniacs) **ITALIAN** *d. Simona Izzo* . . . . Jun. 13, 1994
Manila Paloma Blanca **ITALIAN** *d. Daniele Segre* . . . . Nov. 1, 1993
Manoushe: The Legend of Gypsy Love **BRAZILIAN** *d. Luiz Begazo* . . . . . Nov. 1, 1993
(Many Happy Returns) Kyoso Tanjo . . . . Nov. 1, 1993
Map of the Human Heart **BRITISH-AUSTRALIAN-FRENCH-CANADIAN** *d. Vincent Ward* . . . . Jan. 11, 1993

FILM TITLE INDEX

FILM TITLE INDEX

FILM TITLE INDEX

FILM TITLE INDEX

FILM TITLE INDEX

FILM TITLE INDEX

FILM TITLE INDEX

S

FILM TITLE INDEX

FILM TITLE INDEX

FILM TITLE INDEX

FILM TITLE INDEX

FILM TITLE INDEX

FILM TITLE INDEX

FILM TITLE INDEX

INDEX
994

Director Index
1993-1994

A

Aalmuhammed, Jefri; Baxter, Jack: Brother Minister: The Assassination of Malcolm X

Aaltonen, Veikko: Isa Meidan (Pater Noster); Tuhlaajapoika (The Prodigal Son)

Abdelhamid, Abdellatif: Rassaèlle Chafahyia (Verbal Messages)

Abrahams, Jim: Hot Shots! Part Deux

Abramson, Ivan; Goldin, Sidney M.: Ost und West (East and West)

Absa, Sene: Twiste a Popenguine (Twisting In Popenguine)

Achache, Jean; Berenger, Philippe; Berry, Richard; Birkin, Jane; Boujenah, Paul; Cazes, Patrice; Champetier, Caroline; Cukier, Jacky; Deray, Jacques; Durringer, Xavier; Graal, Sabestien; Heynemann, Laurent; Jacquot, Benoit; Jugnot, Gerard; Klapisch, Cedric; Lioret, Philippe; Marboeuf, Jean; Marshall, Tonie; Massetti, Ivana; Masson, Laetitia; Meyer, Michel; Moskowicz, Fernand; Pillault, Jean-Daniel; Renard, Jacques; Silvera, Charlotte; Strauss, Florence; Thevenet, Virginie; Verley, Bernard; Vigne, Daniel; Volson, Patrick: 3000 Scenarios Contre un Virus (3,000 Scenarios to Combat a Virus)

Achkar, David: Allah Tantou (God's Will)

Achten, Irma: Belle

Ackerman, Robert Allan: Safe Passage

Adkin, David: Out: Stories of Lesbian and Gay Youth

Adlon, Percy: Younger and Younger

Agraz, Jose Luis Garcia: Desiertos Mares (Deserts Seas)

Agraz, Carlos Garcia: Amorosos Fantasmas (Phantoms in Love)

Agresti, Alejandro: El Acto en Cuestion (The Act in Question)

Aguilar, Santiago; Guridi, Luis: Justino, un Asesino de la Tercera Edad (Justino, a Senior Citizen Killer)

Akerman, Chantal: D'Est (From the East); Portrait d'une Jeune Fille de la Fin des Annees 60 a Bruxelles (Portrait of a Young Girl at the End of the 1960s in Brussels)

Akomfrah, John: Seven Songs for Malcolm X

al-Haggar, Khalid: Ahlam Saghira (Little Dreams)

Alcázar, Rafael: El Laberinto Griego (The Greek Labyrinth)

Alea, Tomas Gutierrez; Tabio, Juan Carlos: Fresa y Chocolate (Strawberry and Chocolate)

Alexander, Mike: As An Eilean (From the Island); Mairi Mhor: Na H-Orain 'Sa Beatha (Mairi Mhor: Her Life and Songs)

Alfredson, Daniel: Manen Pa Balkongen (The Man on the Balcony); Roseanna

Algrant, Daniel: Naked in New York

Aljure, Felipe: La Gente de la Universal (The People at Universal)

Allahyari, Houchang: Hoehenangst (Fear of Heights)

Allen, Woody: Bullets Over Broadway; Manhattan Murder Mystery

Allers, Roger; Minkoff, Rob: The Lion King

Allouache, Merzak: Bab El-Oued City

DIRECTOR INDEX

Almereyda, Michael: Nadja

Almodovar, Pedro: Kika

Altman, Robert: Ready to Wear (Pret-a-Porter); Short Cuts

Amelio, Gianni: Lamerica

Améris, Jean-Pierre: Le Bateau de Mariage (The Marriage Boat)

Amiel, Jon: Sommersby

Amurri, Franco: Monkey Trouble

Anders, Allison: Mi Vida Loca

Anderson, Lindsay: Is That All There Is?

Anderson, Paul: Shopping

Anderssen, Kjell-Ake: Min Store Tjocke Far (My Big Fat Father)

Angelo, Yves: Le Colonel Chabert (Colonel Chabert)

Anspaugh, David: Rudy

Anzalone, Francesco: Stelle di Cartone (Cardboard Stars)

Anzola, Alfredo J.: El Misterio de Los Ojos Escarlata (The Mystery of The Scarlet Eyes)

Apted, Michael: Blink; Moving the Mountain; Nell

Arafa, Sherif: Al-Irhab Wal Kabab (Terrorism and Kebob)

Araki, Gregg: Totally F***ed Up

Aranda, Vicente: El Amante Bilingüe (The Bilingual Lover); Intruso (Intruder)

Aranovich, Semyon: The Year of the Dog (God Sobaki)

Arcady, Alexandre: Le Grand Pardon II (Day of Atonement)

Arcand, Denys: Love and Human Remains

Archibugi, Francesca: Il Grande Cocomero (The Great Pumpkin)

Ardolino, Emile: George Balanchine's The Nutcracker

Argento, Dario: Trauma

Argueta, Luis: El Silencio de Neto (The Silence of Neto)

Aristpoulos, Kostas: Enastros Tholos (Starry Dome)

Armero, Alvaro Fernandez: Todo es Mentira (It's All Lies)

Armstrong, Gillian: Little Women

Arnautalic, Ismet; Idrizovic, Mirsad; Kenovic, Ademir; Zalica, Pjer: MGM Sarajevo—Covjek, Bog, Monstrum (MGM Sarajevo—Man, God, The Monster)

Arnfred, Morten: Den Russiske Sangerinde (The Russian Singer)

Aronson, Jerry: The Life and Times of Allen Ginsberg

Arsenault, Jeffrey: Night Owl

Arslan, Yilmaz: Langer Gang (Passages)

Assal, Anita; Fleche, Manuel; Hudson, John; Piquer, Yann; Robak, Alain: Parano (Wacko)

Assayas, Olivier: L'Eau Froide (Cold Water) ; Une Nouvelle Vie (A New Life)

Astrakhan, Dmitrij: Te y Menya Odna (You Are My One and Only)

Ataman, E. Kutlug: Karanlik Sular (The Serpent's Tale)

Athié, Francisco: Lolo

Attenborough, Richard: Shadowlands

Audiard, Jacques: Regarde les Hommes Tomber (See How They Fall)

August, Bille: The House of the Spirits

Austin, Michael: Princess Caraboo

Avancini, Walter; Werneck, Sandra: Boca

Avary, Roger: Killing Zoe

Avati, Pupi: Dichiarazioni d'Amore; Magnificat (The Childhood Friend; Declarations of Love)

Aviad, Michal: Hanashim Mimul (The Woman Next Door)

Avildsen, John G.: 8 Seconds

Avnet, Jon: The War

Axel, Gabriel: Prince of Jutland

Ayyari, Kiyanush: Abadani-Ha (The Abadanis)

Azatian, Arsen V. jt. directorship *see* **Mkrtchian, Nariné**

Azzopardi, Anthony: Latin Nights

Babluani, Temur: Udzinarta Mse (The Sun of the Wakeful)

Badham, John: Another Stakeout; Drop Zone; Point of No Return

Bailey, John: China Moon

Baillargeon, Paule: Le Sexe des Etoiles (The Sex of the Stars)

Baily, Edwin: Faut-Il Aimer Mathilde? (Should Mathilde Be Loved?)

Bajic, Darko: Black Bomber

Balaban, Bob: My Boyfriend's Back; The Last Good Time

Baldoni, Sandro: Strane Storie (Weird Tales)

Bamberger, Bernhard: Aktion K

Bando, Tamasaburo: Yume No Onna (Yearning)

Barba, Norberto: Blue Tiger

Barbosa, Laurence Ferreira: Les Gens Normaux N'Ont Rien D'Exceptionnel (There's Nothing Special About Normal People); Peace and Love (Paix et Amour)

Barden, James H.: The Judas Project

Barkin, Edward S.: Rift

Barnet, Boris: Odnazhdi Noch (Once at Night)

Barrera, Olegario: Fin de Round (End of the Round)

Barron, Steve: Coneheads

Barroso, Mariano: Mi Hermano del Alma (My Soul Brother)

Bartabas: Mazeppa

Bartel, Paul: Shelf Life

Barzman, Paolo: Time is Money

Bat-Adam, Michal: La Femme du Deserteur (The Deserter's Wife); An Imagined Autobiography

Baxter, Jack jt. directorship see **Aalmuhammed, Jefri**

Becker, Harold: Malice

Becker, Jens: Adamski

Becket, James: Natural Causes

Begazo, Luiz: Manoushe: The Legend of Gypsy Love

Begeja, Liria: Loin des Barbares (Far From Barbary)

Beineix, Jean-Jacques: Otaku

Bekmambetov, Timur; Kajumov, Gennadij: Peshavar Waltz

Bell, Jeffrey: Radio Inside

Bell, Neal: Two Small Bodies

Bellocchio, Marco: Il Sogno Della Farfalla (The Butterfly's Dream)

Bemberg, Maria Luisa: De Eso No Se Habla (I Don't Want to Talk About It)

Benegal, Dev: English, August

Benegal, Shyam: Suraj Ka Satvan Ghoda (Seventh Horse of the Sun)

Benhadj, Rachid: Touchia (Song of Algerian Women)

Benigni, Roberto: Il Mostro (The Monster)

Benjamin, Mark; Levin, Marc: The Last Party

Benjamin, Richard: Made In America; Milk Money

Bennett, Bill: Spider & Rose

Benton, Robert: Nobody's Fool

Benvenuti, Alessandro: Caino e Caino (Cain vs. Cain)

Berberian, Alain: La Cite de la Peur: Une Comedie Familiale (Fear City: A Family-Style Comedy)

Beremenyi, Geza: A Turne (On Tour)

Berenger, Philippe jt. directorship see **Achache, Jean, et al.**

Beresford, Bruce: A Good Man in Africa; Silent Fall

Bergenstrahle, Johan: Bryllupsfotografen (The Wedding Photographer)

Berger, Pamela: Kilian's Chronicle

Berglund, Pelle: Polis Polis Potatismos (Murder at the Savoy)

Bergman, Andrew: It Could Happen to You

DIRECTOR INDEX

Branagh, Kenneth: Mary Shelley's Frankenstein; Much Ado About Nothing
Brandauer, Maria: Mario und der Zauberer (Mario and the Magician)
Brandstrom, Charlotte: A Business Affair
Braoude, Patrick: Neuf Mois (Nine Months)
Brass, Tinto: L'Uomo Che Guarda (The Voyeur)
Brault, Michel: Mon Amie Max
Bravo, Edward Michael: I'll Love You Forever...Tonight
Breathnach, Paddy: Ailsa
Brelis, Tia: Trading Mom
Brenta, Mario: Barnabo delle Montagne (Barnabo of the Mountains)
Breziner, Salome: Tollbooth
Brisseau, Jean-Claude: L'Ange Noir (The Black Angel)
Brooks, James L.: I'll Do Anything
Brooks, Mel: Robin Hood: Men In Tights
Broomfield, Nick: Tracking Down Maggie: The Unofficial Biography of Margaret Thatcher
Brophy, Philip: Body Melt
Brown, Bruce: The Endless Summer II
Bruce, James: Dirty Money
Bruecher, Niko: Maries Lied: Ich War, Ich Weiss Nicht Wo(Marie's Song: I Was I Know Not Where)
Bruen, Margaret: The Fourth Green Field
Buba, Tony: No Pets
Buch, Franzuska: Die Ungewisse Lage Des Paradieses (In Search of Paradise)
Buck, Detlev: Wir Konnen Auch Anders... (No More Mr. Nice Guy)
Bucquoy, Jan: La Vie Sexuelle des Belges (The Sexual Life of the Belgians)
Buitenhuis, Penelope: Boulevard
Burke, Andre: Odile & Yvette at the Edge of the World
Burnett, Charles: The Glass Shield
Burr, Jeff: Eddie Presley
Burton, Geoff; Dowling, Kevin: The Sum of Us
Burton, Tim: Ed Wood
Bush, Kate: The Line, The Cross & The Curve
Bushala, Dean; Heaslip, Deirdre: Green on Thursdays
Buttgereit, Joerg: Schramm
Byington, Robert: Sin Verguenza (Shameless)

Cabrera, Sergio: Aguilas No Cazan Moscas (Eagles Don't Hunt Flies); La Estrategia del Caracol (The Snail's Strategy)
Cacoyannis, Michael: Pano Kato Ke Plagios (Up, Down, and Sideways)
Cain, Christopher: The Next Karate Kid
Calderone, Gianluigi: Il Giovane Mussolini (A Man Named Benito)
Cameron, James: The Abyss: Special Edition; True Lies
Campbell, Martin: No Escape
Campion, Anna: Loaded
Campion, Jane: The Piano
Campiotti, Giacomo: Come Due Coccodrilli (Like Two Crocodiles)
Camus, Mario: Sombras en una Batalla (Shadows in a Conflict)
Canawati, Alex: Inevitable Grace
Cannon, Danny: The Young Americans
Cantin, Roger: Matusalem
Caracciolo, Nicola; Marino, Valerio E.: Succede In Quarantotto (Italy After The War)
Caranfil, Nicolae: E Pericoloso Sporgersi (Don't Lean Out the Window)
Carcélès, Laurent: La Brune (Dusk)
Cardona, Dominique jt. directorship *see* **Colbert, Laurie**

DIRECTOR INDEX

DIRECTOR INDEX

Dahl, John: The Last Seduction; Red Rock West

D'Alatri, Alessandro: Senza Pelle (No Skin)

Dalle, Peter: Dromkaken (The Dream House)

Dan, Le: Xuong Rong Den (Black Cactus)

Daneliuc, Mircea: Patul Conjugal (The Conjugal Bed)

D'Angiolillo, Luis Cesar: Matar Al Abuelito (Killing Granddad)

Daniel, Rod: Beethoven's 2nd

D'Anna, Claude: Daisy et Mona (Daisy and Mona)

Danquart, Didi; Feindt, Johann: Wundbrand: Sarajevo, 17 Tage In August (Gangrene: Sarajevo, 17 Days in August)

Dante, Joe: Matinee

Darabont, Frank: The Shawshank Redemption

Darday, Istvan; Szalai, Gyorgyi: Nyugattol Keletre, Avagy A Media Diszkret Baja (East From the West, or the Discreet Charm of the Media)

Dasgupta, Buddhadeb: Charachar (Shelter of the Wings)

D'Auria, Mark: Smoke

Davidson, Boaz: American Cyborg: Steel Warrior

Davies, Howard: The Secret Rapture

Davis, Andrew: The Fugitive

Davis, Peter; Riesenfeld, Daniel: In Darkest Hollywood: Cinema & Apartheid

Davis, Tamra: CB4

Davudi, Abolhassan: Jib-Borha Be Behesht Nemiravand (Pickpockets Don't Go to Heaven)

Day, Bill: Saviors of the Forest

Dayan, Assi: Ha Chayim Alpy Agfa (Life According to Agfa)

de Almeida Prado, Guilherme: Perfume de Gardenias (Scent of Gardenias)

de Arminan, Jaime: Al Otro Lado del Tunel (On the Far Side of the Tunnel)

De Bernardi, Tonino: Piccoli Orrori (Little Horrors)

De Bont, Jan: Speed

De Heer, Rolf: Bad Boy Bubby

de Jong, Mijke: Hartverscheurend (Love Hurts)

de la Iglesia, Alex: Accion Mutante (Mutant Action)

de la Torre, Raúl: Funes, un Gran Amor (Funes, a Great Love)

de Latour, Eliane: Contes et Comptes de la Cour (Accounts and Accounting From the Courtyard)

de Maistre, Gilles: Killer Kid

De Niro, Robert: A Bronx Tale

de Oliveira, Manoel: A Caixa (Blind Man's Buff); Vale Abrao (Valley of Abraham)

De Palma, Brian: Carlito's Way

de Paula, Francisco: Oceano Atlantis (Atlantis Ocean)

de Poncheville, Marie Jaoul: Molom, Conte de Mongolie (Molom, A Mongolian Tale)

De Pree, Tod jt. directorship *see* **Chapman, Dina Marie**

de Putter, Jos: Het Is Een Schone Dag Geweest (It's Been a Lovely Day)

De Sica, Christian: Ricky e Barabba (Ricky and Barrabas)

de Soliers, Bertrand jt. directorship *see* **Muxel, Paule**

Deak, Krisztina: Kod Avagy Holdarnyek Levubu Folott (Mist, or Moonlight Shadow Over Levubu)

Dear, William: Angels in the Outfield

Degregori, Luis Felipe: Todos Somos Estrellas (We Are All Stars)

Dekker, Fred: Robocop 3

del Toro, Guillermo: Cronos (Chronos)

Delerive, Pierre: Le Fusil de Bois (The Wooden Gun)

Deleuze, Emilie: L'Incruste (Infiltrate)

Delpeut, Peter: Forbidden Quest

Demirkubuz, Zeki: C Blok (Block C)

Demme, Jonathan: Philadelphia

Demme, Ted: The Ref; Who's the Man?

Denecke, Gabriele jt. directorship *see* **Kohlhaase, Wolfgang**

Denis, Claire: J'ai Pas Sommeil (I Can't Sleep); U.S. Go Home

Depardon, Raymond: Delits Flagrants (Caught in the Acts)

Deray, Jacques: L'Orso Di Peluche (The Teddy Bear)

Deray, Jacques jt. directorship *see* **Achache, Jean, et al.**

Desrosieres, Antoine: A la Belle Etoile (Under the Stars)

Deutch, Howard: Getting Even With Dad

Deville, Michel: Aux Petits Bonheurs (Life's Little Treasures)

Devlin, Barry: All Things Bright and Beautiful

di Robilant, Alessandro: Il Giudice Ragazzino (Law of Courage)

Dick, Nigel: Final Combination

Dickerson, Ernest: Surviving the Game

Diego, Constante "Rapi": Mascaro, el Cazador Americano (Mascaro, Hunter of the Americas)

Dingwall, John: The Custodian

Dizdarevic, Nenad: The Ungrateful Age (Magarece Godine/L'Age Ingrat)

Doillon, Jacques: Du Fond du Coeur: Germaine et Benjamin (Germaine and Benjamin); Le Jeune Werther (Young Werther)

Dolgin, Gail; Franco, Vicente: Cuba Va: The Challenge of the Next Generation

Dolz, Sonia Herman: Romance de Valentia (Only the Brave)

Donaldson, Roger: The Getaway

Donard, Thierry: Pushing the Limits

Dong, Arthur: Coming Out Under Fire

Donner, Richard: Maverick

Donovan, Paul: Paint Cans

Dorfmann: Shadow of the Wolf (a.k.a. Agaguk)

Dostal, Nikolai: Malenky Gigant Bolshogo Sexa (A Small Giant of Big Sex)

Dotta, Pablo: El Dirigible (The Dirigible)

Doukoure, Cheick: Le Ballon D'Or (The Golden Ball)

Dowling, Kevin jt. directorship *see* **Burton, Geoff**

Dragojevic, Srdjan: Mi Nismo Andjeli (We Are Not Angels)

Draskovic, Boro: Vukovar Poste Restante

Drawe, Matthias: Der Elfenbienturm (The Ivory Tower)

Drazen, Anthony: Imaginary Crimes

Dress, Evelyne: Pas d'Amour sans Amour (S.O.S. Woman in Distress)

Dridi, Karim: Pigalle

Driver, Sara: When Pigs Fly

Duarte, Jorge Marecos: Encontros Imperfeitos (Light Trap)

Dubini, Donatello; Dubini, Fosco: Ludwig 1881

Dubini, Fosco jt. directorship *see* **Dubini, Donatello**

Dubov, Adam: Dead Beat

Dubreuil, Charlotte: Elles Ne Pensent Qu'a Ca... (Women Have Only One Thing on Their Minds...)

Duchemin, Rémy: Fausto

Dugowson, Martine: Mina Tannenbaum

Dugowson, Maurice: La Poudre Aux Yeux (Blind Spot)

Duigan, John: Sirens; Wide Sargasso Sea

Duke, Bill: The Cemetery Club; Sister Act 2: Back In the Habit

Dumitrescu, Bogdan: Unde la Soare e Frig (Outback)

Duncan, Patrick Sheane: The Pornographer

Dunham, Duwayne: Homeward Bound: The Incredible Journey; Little Giants

Dupeyron, François: La Machine (The Machine)

Durringer, Xavier: La Nage Indienne (Heads Above Water)

Durringer, Xavier jt. directorship *see* **Achache, Jean, et al.**

Dylewska, Jolanta: Kronika Towstania W Getcie Warszawskam Wedlug Marka Edelmana (Chronicle of the Uprising in the Warsaw Ghetto According to Marek Edelman)

Dzanelidze, Nana: Iavnana (The Lullaby)

Eastwood, Clint: A Perfect World

Edel, Uli: Body of Evidence

DIRECTOR INDEX

Fernie, Lynne jt. directorship *see* **Weissman, Aerlyn**
Ferran, Pascale: Petits Arrangements Avec les Morts (Coming to Terms With the Dead)
Ferrara, Abel: Body Snatchers; Snake Eyes
Ferrara, Giuseppe: Giovanni Falcone
Ferrari, Alain jt. directorship *see* **Ravalat, Thierry**
Ferrari, Alain; Levy, Bernard-Henri: Bosna!
Ferrario, Davide: Anime Fiammeggianti (Love Burns)
Ferreri, Marco: Diario di un Vizio (Diary of a Maniac)
Feuerzeig, Jeff: Half Japanese: The Band That Would Be King
Field, Connie; Mulford, Marilyn: Freedom on My Mind
Figgis, Mike: The Browning Version; Mr. Jones
Fillieres, Sophie: Grande Petite (The Tall Little One)
Finley, Jeanne C.; Stoeltje, Gretchen: A.R.M. Around Moscow
Firstenberg, Sam: Cyborg Cop II
Fishel, Deirdre: Risk
Fishman, Bill: Car 54, Where Are You?
Flaherty, Paul: Clifford
Fleche, Manuel jt. directorship *see* **Assal, Anita, et al.**
Fleming, Andrew: Threesome
Flender, Rodman: Leprechaun 2
Fletcher, Mandie: Deadly Advice
Flicker, Florian: Halbe Welt (Half World)
Flitcroft, Kim: Tales From a Hard City
Flynn, John: Brainscan
Flynn, Tom: Watch It
Fockele, Jörg jt. directorship *see* **van Diepenbroick, Dorothee, et al.**
Fokkema, Frouke: Wildgroei (It Will Never Be Spring)
Fontaine, Anne: Les Histoires d'Amour Finissent Mal En General (Love Affairs Usually End Badly)
Forcier, Andre: Le Vent du Wyoming (Wind From Wyoming)
Forder, Timothy: The Mystery of Edwin Drood
Forgeau, Filip: L'Iguane (The Iguana)
Forsyth, Bill: Being Human
Fragasso, Claudio: Teste Rasate (Skinheads)
Franco, Vicente jt. directorship *see* **Dolgin, Gail**
Frank, Christopher: Elles N'Oublient Jamais (Love in the Strangest Way)
Frankenberg, Pia: Nie Weider Schlaffen (Never Sleep Again)
Frears, Stephen: The Snapper
Freedman, Gordon: Marilyn Monroe: Life After Death
Freeman, Morgan: Bopha!
Fridell, Daniel: Sökarna (The Searchers)
Fridriksson, Fridrik Thor: Movie Days
Friedgen, Bud; Sheridan, Michael J.: That's Entertainment! III
Friedkin, William: Blue Chips
Friedman, Adam: To Sleep With a Vampire
Frumin, Boris: Viva Castro!
Frye, E. Max: Amos & Andrew
Fucci, Thomas A.: Don't Call Me Frankie
Fukasaku, Kinji: Chushingura Gaiden Yotsuya Kaidan (Crest of Betrayal)
Furumaya, Tomoyuki: Kono Mado Wa Kimi No Mono (This Window is Yours)

Gallagher, John Andrew: Men Lie
Gallo, George: Trapped in Paradise

DIRECTOR INDEX

Gang, Han: Ge Lao Ye Zi (Old Man Ge)
Gang, Xia: Wuren Hegai (No More Applause)
Ganga, Jose Miguel: Enciende Mi Pasion (Light My Passion)
Gans, Christophe; Kaneko, Shu; Yuzna, Brian: Necronomicon
Gapo, Branko: Macedonian Saga
Garay, Jesus: Els de Davant (The Window Across the Way)
Garci, Jos Luis: Cancion de Cuna (Cradle Song)
García, Andy: Cachao...Como Si Ritmo No Hay Dos (Cachao...Like His Rhythm There Is No Other)
Garcia, Nicole: Le Fils Prefere (The Favorite Son)
Garneau, Kathy: Tokyo Cowboy
Garrel, Philippe: La Naissance de L'Amour (The Birth of Love)
Gasiorowski, Jacek: Tak Tak (Yes, Yes)
Gatlif, Tony: Latcho Drom (Safe Journey)
Gaup, Nils: Hodet Over Vannet (Head Above Water)
Gavidia, Danny: Reportaje a la Muerte (Reports of Death)
Geissendorfer, Hans: Justiz (Justice)
Geller, Daniel; Goldfine, Danya: Frosh: Nine Months in a Freshman Dorm
Gémes, József: A Hercegnö és a Kobold (The Princess and the Goblin)
George, Peter: Young Goodman Brown
Georges, Alex: Cultivating Charlie
Gerardo: Un Año Perdido (A Lost Year)
Gerima, Haile: Sankofa
Ghose, Goutam: Padma Nadir Majhi (The Padma Boatmen); Patang (The Kite)
Gibbons, Joe: The Genius
Gibson, Brian: What's Love Got to Do With It
Gibson, Mel: The Man Without a Face
Gies, Hajo: Brandbilen Som Försvann (The Fire Engine That Disappeared)
Gilbert, Brian: Tom & Viv
Gilbert, Sky: My Addiction
Gillard, Stuart: Teenage Mutant Ninja Turtles III: The Turtles are Back...In Time
Giovanni, Marita: Bar Girls
Girard, François: Thirty-Two Short Films About Glenn Gould
Giritlioglu, Tomris: Yaz Yagmuru (A Passing Summer's Rain)
Girod, Francis: Delit Mineur (Minor Crime)
Gitai, Amos: In the Name of the Duce (Nel Nome Del Duce); In the Valley of the Wupper (Dans la Vallee du Wupper); Petrified Graden
Glaser, Paul M.: The Air Up There
Glatzer, Richard: Grief
Glenn, Pierre-William: 23:58 (23 H 58)
Glinski, Robert: Wszystko Co Najwazniejsze... (All That Really Matters...)
Godard, Jean-Luc: Helas Pour Moi (Oh, Woe Is Me); JLG/JLG—Autoportrait de Decembre (JLG/JLG—Self-Portrait in December)
Godmilow, Jill: Roy Cohn/Jack Smith
Godros, Frigyes; Horvath, Dr. Putyi: Privathorvat es Wolframbarat (Private Horvath and Friend Wolfram)
Gök, Sahin: Siyabend û Xecê (Siyabend and Xecê)
Golan, Menahem: Silent Victim
Golden, Robert: Beg!
Goldfine, Danya jt. directorship *see* **Geller, Daniel**
Goldin, Sidney M. jt. directorship *see* **Abramson, Ivan**
Goldman, Gary jt. directorship *see* **Bluth, Don**
Goldstein, Allan A.: Death Wish V: The Face of Death
Golombek, Jens jt. directorship *see* **van Diepenbroick, Dorothee, et al.**
Gomer, Steve: Fly by Night
Gong, Xia: Da Sa Ba (After Separation)
Gopalakrishnan, Adoor: Vidheyan (The Servile)
Gordon, Robert: Revenge of the Red Baron
Gordon, Stuart: Fortress
Goren, Amit: 6 Open, 21 Closed; '66 Was a Good Year for Tourism

Hofmeyr, Gray: Sweet 'N' Short; Yankee Zulu
Hogan, P.J.: Muriel's Wedding
Holland, Agnieszka: The Secret Garden
Holland, Randy: The Fire This Time
Holland, Tom: The Temp
Hollibaugh, Amber; Reticker, Gini: The Heart of the Matter
Holloway, Ron: Parajanov
Hondo, Med: Lumiere Noire (Black Light)
Hong-Joon, Kim: Changmi Bit Insaeng (La Vie en Rose)
Honigmann, Heddy: Metal & Melancolia (Metal & Melancholy)
Hoolboom, Mike: Kanada
Hope, Margot: Femme Fontaine: Killer Babe for the C.I.A.
Hopkins, Stephen: Blown Away; Judgement Night
Hopper, Dennis: Chasers
Hornecker, William E.: Two Brothers, a Girl and a Gun
Hoursoglou. Pericles: Lefteris Dimakopoulos (Lefteris)
Horvath, Dr. Putyi jt. directorship *see* **Godros, Frigyes**
Howard, Ron: The Paper
Howson, Frank: My Forgotten Man
Hribar, Hrvoje: Hrvatske Katedrale (Croatian Cathedrals)
Hsiaohsien, Hou: Hsimeng Jensheng (The Puppetmaster)
Hu, Ann: Dream and Memory
Huang, George: The Buddy Factor
Hubert, Jean-Loup: A Cause d'Elle (Because of Her)
Hudson, John jt. directorship *see* **Assal, Anita, et al.**
Huestis, Marc: Sex Is...
Huettner, Ralf: Der Papagei (The Parrot)
Hughes, Allen & Albert: Menace II Society
Hung, Tran Anh: Mui Du Du Xanh (The Scent of the Green Papaya)
Hunter, Tim: The Saint of Fort Washington
Hussein, Waris: The Summer House
Hyams, Peter: Timecop
Hylkema, Hans: Oeroeg (Going Home)
Hytner, Nicholas: The Madness of King George

ن

Ichaso, Leon: Sugar Hill
Ichikawa, Jun: Byoin de Shinuto Iukoto (Dying in a Hospital)
Ichikawa, Kon: Fusa; Shijushichinin No Shikaku (47 Ronin)
Idrizovic, Mirsad jt. directorship *see* **Arnautalic, Ismet, et al.**
Ijas, Matti: Pikkuja Ja Pikkuhousuja (Lyrics and Lace)
Ijdis, Bernie: A Dreamscape: Gambling in America
Ioseliani, Otar: Seule, Georgie (Alone, Georgia)
Irvin, John: Widow's Peak
Irvin, Sam: Acting on Impulse; Oblivion
Isaksen, Eva: Det Perfekte Mord (The Perfect Murder)
Ishii, Sogo: Tenshi No Kuzu (Angel Dust)
Ishii, Takashi: Nudo No Yoru (A Night in Nude); Yoru Ga Mata Kuru (Alone in the Night)
Ishii, Teruo: Gensen Kan Shujin (Gensen-Kan Inn)
Iskakov, Bulat jt. directorship *see* **Kalymbetov, Bolat**
Islam, Morshedul: Chaka (The Wheel)

DIRECTOR INDEX

J

Jones, David: The Trial
Jones, Mark: Leprechaun
Jordan, Neil: Interview With the Vampire
Joslin, Tom: Silverlake Life: The View from Here
Jost, Jon: The Bed You Sleep In; Frameup; Uno a Te, Uno a Me e Uno a Raffaele
   (One for You, One for Me and One for Raphael)
Jud, Reinhard: James Elroy: Demon Dog of American Crime Fiction
Jugnot, Gerard: Casque Bleu (Blue Helmet)
Jugnot, Gerard jt. directorship *see* **Achache, Jean, et al.**
Julien, Isaac: Darker Side of Black
Jumel, Gérard: Ce Que Femme Veut... (What a Woman Wants...)
Justiniano, Gonzalo: Amnesia

Kabay, Barna jt. directorship *see* **Gyöngyössy, Imre**
Kabay, Barna jt. directorship *see* **Petényi, Katalin, et al.**
Kaboré, Gaston J.M.: Rabi
Kachyna, Karel: The Cow (Krava); Mestem Chodi Mikulas (St. Nicholas is in Town)
Kahn, Cedric: Trop de Bonheur (Happy, Too Happy)
Kaige, Chen: Bawang Bie Ji (Farewell to My Concubine)
Kajumov, Gennadij jt. directorship *see* **Bekmambetov, Timur**
Kalatozov, Mikhail: Soy Cuba/Ja Kuba (I Am Cuba)
Káldor, Elemér: Blue Box
Kalik, Michail: I Vozrascaetsja Veter (And the Wind Returneth)
Kaltenbach, Claudia jt. directorship *see* **van Diepenbroick, Dorothee, et al.**
Kalymbetov, Bolat; Iskakov, Bulat: Posledniye Kholoda (The Last Cold Days)
Kamwa, Daniel: Totor
Kaneko, Shu jt. directorship *see* **Gans, Christophe, et al.**
Kanevski, Vitali: Nous, Les Enfants du XXeme Sicle (We, The Children of The 20th Century)
Kang, Woo-Suk: Two Cops
Kanganis, Charles T.: 3 Ninjas Kick Back
Kaplan, Betty: Of Love and Shadows
Kaplan, Jonathan: Bad Girls
Kapur, Shekhar: Bandit Queen
Kar-leung, Lau: Tsui Kun II (Drunken Master II)
Kar-wai, Wong: Ashes of Time (Dung Che Sai Duk); Chunghing Samlam (Chung King Express)
Karakulov, Amir: Golubiny Zvonar (The Dove's Bell-Ringer)
Karbelnikoff, Michael: F.T.W.
Karkanevatos, Panos: Metechmio (Borderline)
Karmakar, Romuald: Warheads
Karun, Shaji N.: Swaham (My Own)
Kasdan, Lawrence: Wyatt Earp
Kassila, Matti: Kaikki Pelissa (Play It All)
Kassovitz, Mathieu: Metisse
Katchatrian, Haroutiun: Last Station
Kato, Tetsu: Tada Hito Tabi No Hito (The Singing Bamboo)
Kaufman, Philip: Rising Sun
Kaul, Mani jt. directorship *see* **Cox, Paul, et al.**
Kaurismaki, Aki: Leningrad Cowboys Meet Moses; Pida Huivista Kiinni, Tatjana (Take Care of Your Scarf, Tatiana); Total
   Balalaika Show
Kaurismaki, Mika: The Last Border; Tigrero: A Film That Was Never Made

DIRECTOR INDEX

Kramo-Lancine, Fadika: Wariko, Le Gros Lot (The Lottery)
Krishna, Srinivas: Masala
Krishnamma, Suri: Man of No Importance, A; O Mary This London
Krolikiewicz, Grzegorz: Przypadek Pekosinskiego (The Case of Bronek Pekosinski)
Kroske, Gerd jt. directorship *see* **Gröning, Philip, et al.**
Kumashiro, Tatsumi: Bo No Kanashimi (Like a Rolling Stone)
Kuo-fu, Chen: Zhi Yao Wei Ni Huo Yitian (Treasure Island)
Kurosawa, Akira: Madadayo (Not Yet)
Kurti, Richard: Seaview Knights
Kurys, Diane: A la Folie (Six Days, Six Nights)
Kusturica, Emir: Arizona Dream
Kwai, Yuen: Fong Sai-Yuk
Kwang-su, Park: Keu Some Gago Sipta (To the Starry Island)
Kwon-Taek, Im: Seo-Pyon-Jae (Sopyonje)
Kyun-dong, Yeo: Sae Sang Bakuro (Out to the World)

L

Labib, Jean: Montand
LaBruce, Bruce: Super 8
Ladoge, Dominique: Comme un Bateau la Mer en Moins (Like a Boat Out of Water)
Lafia, John: Man's Best Friend
Lagestee, Martin: Angie
Lai, Stan: Feixia Ahda (The Red Lotus Society)
Laing, John: Absent Without Leave
Lakhdar-Hamina, Malik: Automne: Octobre a Alger (Autumn: October in Algiers)
Lam, Ringo: Full Contact
Lambert, Lothar: Gut Drauf, Schlecht Dran (Good Vibrations, Bad Situations)
Lambert, Susan: Talk
Lamm, Staffan: Morfars Resa (Grandfather's Journey)
Lanctot, Micheline: Deux Actrices (Two Can Play); La Vie d'un Heros (A Hero's Life)
Landis, John: Beverly Hills Cops III
Lang, Krzysztof: Paper Marriage
Langhans, Rainer jt. directorship *see* **Ritter, Christa**
Langlois, Michel: Cap Tourmente
Lanzmann, Claude: Tsahal
Lapine, James: Life With Mikey
Lau, Jeff: Sediu Yinghung Tsun Tsi Dung Sing Sai Tsau (The Eagle Shooting Heroes: Dong Cheng Xi Jiu)
Lautner, Georges: L'Inconnu dans La Maison (Stranger in the House)
Law, Clara: You Seng (Temptation of a Monk)
Law, Clara jt. directorship *see* **Borden, Lizzie, et al.**
Lazcano, Arantxa: Los Anos Oscuros (Urte Ilunak/The Dark Days)
Lazotti, Gianfrancesco: Tutti Gli Anni una Volta l'Anno (Once a Year, Every Year)
Le Roux, Hervé: Grand Bonheur (Great Happiness)
Lecchi, Alberto: Perdido por Perdido (Nothing to Loose)
Leconte, Patrice: Le Parfum d'Yvonne (The Scent of Yvonne); Tango
Ledbetter, Gary: Henry & Verlin
Leduc, Paul: Dollar Mambo
Lee, Ang: Eat Drink Man Woman; Hsi Yen (The Wedding Banquet)
Lee, Raymond jt. directorship *see* **Siu-Tung, Ching**
Lee, Spike: Crooklyn
Leeson, Lynn Hershmann: Virtual Love

DIRECTOR INDEX

Loy, Nanni: Pacco, Doppio Pacco e Contropaccotto (Package, Double Package and Counterpackage)
Lozinski, Pavel: Birthplace
Lucarelli, Jack: A Gift From Heaven
Lucio, Paco: El Aliento del Diablo (The Devil's Breath)
Ludwig, Julian jt. directorship *see* **Cartwright, William T.**
Lumet, Sidney: Guilty As Sin
Luna, Bigas: Huevos de Oro (Golden Balls); La Teta i la Luna (The Tit and the Moon)
Lunerti, Lucio: Il Tempo del Ritorno (Time of the Return)
Luther, Miloslav: Anjel Milosrdenstva (Angel of Mercy)
Lvoff, John: Couples et Amants (Couples and Lovers)
Lvovsky, Noemie: Oublie-Moi (Forget Me)
Lynd, Laurie jt directorship *see* **Christopher, Mark, et al.**
Lyne, Adrian: Indecent Proposal
Lynn, Jonathan: Greedy
Lynton, Adam: Tempting a Married Man

Maár, Gyula: Balkan! Balkan! (Balkans! Balkans!); Hoppá (Whoops)
Maas, Dick: Flodder In Amerika (Flodder Does Manhattan!)
Mabhikwa, Isaac Meli: More Time
Macdonald, Peter: The Neverending Story III
MacDougall, David: Tempus de Baristas (Time of the Barmen)
Macek, Carl: Neo-Tokyo/Silent Mobius
Machulski, Julisuz: Swadron (Squadron)
MacKinnon, Gillies: A Simple Twist of Fate
Madden, John: Ethan Frome; Golden Gate
Magar, Guy: Lookin' Italian
Magidson, Mark: Toward the Within
Magnoli, Albert: Street Knight
Magocsi, Deborah: New! Improved! Real-Life American Fairy Tale
Main, Stewart; Wells, Peter: Desperate Remedies
Maira, Salvatore: Donne in un Giorno de Festa (Women on a Holiday)
Mak, Michael: Sex and Zen
Mak, Peter: Yiu Sau Dousi (The Wicked City)
Makavejev, Dusan: Gorilla Bathes at Noon
Makela, Aleksi: Romanovin Kivet (The Romanov Stones)
Makhmalbaf, Mohsen: Honarpisheh (The Actor)
Makoto, Satoh: Aga Ni Ikiru (Living on the River Agano)
Malakian, Patrick: Pourquoi Maman est dans Mon Lit? (Why Is Mother in My Bed?)
Malas, Mohamed: Al-Lail (The Night)
Maleh, Nabil: Al-Kompars (The Extras)
Malle, Louis: Vanya on 42nd Street
Malmros, Nils: Kaerlighedens Smerte (Pain of Love)
Malone, Mark: Killer
Mamet, David: Oleanna
Mamin, Yuri: Okno v Parizh (Window to Paris)
Managadze, Nodar: Le Bapteme (The Baptism)
Manchevski, Milcho: Before the Rain
Mandoki, Luis: Born Yesterday; When a Man Loves a Woman
Maniaci, Teodoro; Rzeznik, Francine: One Nation Under God
Manuzzi, Lucanio: I Pavoni (The Peacocks)

DIRECTOR INDEX

Mapitigama, Chandraratne: Surabi Dena (Womb for Hire)
Marboeuf, Jean: Pétain
Marboeuf, Jean jt. directorship *see* **Achache, Jean, et al.**
Marconi, David: The Harvest; Lilly
Marcus, Adam: Jason Goes to Hell: The Final Friday
Marcus, Erica jt. directorship *see* **Munoz Blaustein, Susan**
Margineanu, Nicolae: Priveste Inainte Cu Minie (Look Forward In Anger)
Margolin, François: Lie (Mensonge)
Marinkovic, Dragan: Byzantine Blue
Marino, Gustavo Graef: Johnny Cien PesosJ (ohnny 100 Pesos)
Marino, Umberto: Comincio Tutto Per Caso (It All Started by Chance)
Marino, Valerio E. jt. directorship *see* **Caracciolo, Nicola**
Marker, Chris: Le Tombeau d'Alexandre (The Last Bolshevik)
Markle, Peter: Wagons East!
Marlowe, Brad: The Webbers
Marshall, Frank: Alive
Marshall, Garry: Exit to Eden
Marshall, Penny: Renaissance Man
Marshall, Tonie: Pas Tres Catholique (Something Fishy)
Marshall, Tonie jt. directorship *see* **Achache, Jean, et al.**
Martella, Massimo: Il Tuffo (The Dive)
Martin, Darnell: I Like it Like That
Martin, Steven M.: Theremin: An Electronic Odyssey
Martin, Wrye; Poltermann, Barry: Aswang
Martinelli, Renzo: Sarahsara (The Waterbaby)
Martinez, Rico: Glamazon: A Different Kind of Girl
Martinotti, Francesco: Abissinia (Abyssinia)
Masayesva Jr., Victor: Imagining Indians
Masharawi, Rashid: Hatta Ishaar Akhar (Curfew)
Massetti, Ivana jt. directorship *see* **Achache, Jean, et al.**
Masson, Laetitia jt. directorship *see* **Achache, Jean, et al.**
Massot, Claude: Nanook (Kabloonak)
Mastilla, Sergio M.: The Girl in the Watermelon
Matalon Eddy: Sweet Killing
Matsuoka, George: Kira Kira Hikaru (Twinkle)
Matton, Charles: La Lumiere des Etoiles Mortes (The Light From Dead Stars)
Maugg, Gordian: Der Olympische Sommer (The Olympic Summer)
Mawuru, Godwin: Neria
Maxwell, Garth: Jack Be Nimble
Maxwell, Ronald F.: Gettysburg
Maybury, John: Rememberance of Things Fast: True Stories Visual Lies
Mayfield, Les: Miracle on 34th Street
Maysles, Albert jt. directorship *see* **Corra, Henry, et al.**
Mayson, Michael jt directorship *see* **Christopher, Mark, et al.**
Mazursky, Paul: The Pickle
Mazuy, Patricia: Travolta et Moi (Travolta and Me)
Mazzacurati, Carlo: Il Toro (The Bull)
M'Bala, Roger Gnoan: Au Nom du Christ (In the Name of Christ)
McBride, Jim: Uncovered; The Wrong Man
McCall, Rod: Paper Hearts
McCarthy, Peter: Floundering
McClary, Michael: Curse of the Starving Class
McCormack, Dan: Minotaur
McDonald, Bruce: Dance Me Outside
McElwee, Ross: Time Indefinite
McGehee, Scott; Siegel, David: Suture
McGuckian, Mary: Words Upon the Window Pane

McHenry, Doug: Jason's Lyric

McInnes, Laurie: Broken Highway

McKay, Malcolm: Maria's Child

McKimmie, Jackie: Gino

McLean, Steve: Postcards From America

McNaughton, John: Mad Dog and Glory

McTiernan, John: Last Action Hero

Mead, Nick: Bank Robber

Meckler, Nancy: Sister My Sister

Medak, Peter: Pontiac Moon; Romeo Is Bleeding

Medem, Julio: La Ardilla Roja (The Red Squirrel)

Meerapfel, Jeanine jt. directorship *see* **Chiesa, Alcides**

Meffre, Pomme: Venial Sin... Mortal Sin... (Peche Veniel... Peche Mortel...)

Megahey, Leslie: The Hour of the Pig

Mehrjui, Dariush: Sara

Mehta, Ketan: Maya Memsaab (Maya: The Enchanting Illusion)

Mehta, Deepa: Camilla

Meinecke, Tobias: The Contenders

Meio, Jorge Silva: Coitado do Jorge (Poor Jorge)

Menahemi, Ayelet; Yaron, Nirit: Tel-Aviv Stories

Menendez, Ramon: Money for Nothing

Menges, Chris: Second Best

Menzel, Jiri: The Life and Extraordinary Adventures of Private Ivan Chonkin

Merchant, Ismail: Hifazaat (In Custody)

Merendino, James: The Upstairs Neighbor

Merlet, Agnes: Le Fils du Requin (The Son of the Shark)

Meshekoff, Matthew: The Opposite Sex...And How to Live With Them

Meskhiev, Dmitri: Nad Tyomnoy Vodoy (Over the Dark Water)

Meszaros, Marta: A Magzat (Foetus)

Metter, Alan: Police Academy: Mission to Moscow

Mettler, Peter: Picture of Light

Meyer, Michel jt. directorship *see* **Achache, Jean, et al.**

Meza, Eric: House Party 3

Miaomiao, Liu: Mati Sheng Sui (Distance Trampling of Horses); Za Zui Zi (Chatterbox)

Michalek, Vladimir: Amerika

Michell, Roger: The Buddha of Suburbia

Mieville, Anne-Marie: Lou N'A Pas Dit Non (Lou Didn't Say No)

Mihaileanu, Radu: Trahir (Betrayal)

Mihalka, Georges: La Florida

Mihalka, George: Relative Fear

Mihalyfi, Sandor: Abel a Rengetegben (Abel in the Forest)

Mihaylov, Eugeny: Canary Season

Mikhalkov, Nikita: Anna 6-18; Outomlionnye Solntsem (Burnt By the Sun)

Milburn, Lynn-Maree: Memories and Dreams

Miller, Claude: Le Sourire (The Smile)

Miller, David Lee: Breakfast of Aliens

Miller, George: Andre; Gross Misconduct

Minaiev, Igor: L'Inondation (The Flood)

Miner, Steve: My Father, The Hero

Ming-liang, Tsai: Aiqing Wansui (Vive L'Amour); Ch'ing Shaonien Na Cha (Rebels of the Neon God)

Mingchuan, Huang: Baodao Da Meng (Bodo)

Minghella, Anthony: Mr. Wonderful

Minkoff, Rob jt. directorship *see* **Allers, Roger**

Minnott, Berry: Harry Bridges: A Man and His Union

Mire, Soraya: Fire Eyes

Miró, Pilar: El Pajaro de la Felicidad (The Bird of Happiness)

Miroslav, Lekic: Better Than Escape

DIRECTOR INDEX

Mirvish, Dan: Omaha (The Movie)
Mitler, Matt: Cracking Up
Mitscherlich, Thomas: Die Denunziantin (The Denunciation)
Miyazaki, Hayao: My Neighbor Totoro
Mkrtchian, Nariné; Azatian, Arsen V.: Radio Yerevan
Moati, Serge: Des Feux Mal Eteints (Poorly Extinguished Fires)
Mocky, Jean-Pierre: Le Mari de Léon (Leon's Husband)
Moffatt, Tracey: Bedevil
Mokhtari, Ebrahim: Zinat
Moland, Hans Petter: Secondlojtnanten (The Second Lieutenant)
Molinaro, Edouard: Le Souper (The Supper)
Moll, Dominik: Intimite (Intimacy)
Molnár, György: Anna Filmje (Anna's Film)
Moniclli, Mario: Cari Fottutissimi Amici (Dear Goddamned Friends)
Monteleone, Enzo: La Vera Vita di Antonio H. (The True Life of Antonio H.)
Mora, Philippe: Art Deco Detective
Moraes, Susana: Mil e Uma (A Thousand and One)
Morahan, Andy: Highlander III: The Sorcerer
Mordillat, Gerard; Prieur, Jerome: En Compagnie D'Antonin Artaud (My Life and Times With Antonin Artaud);
   La Veritable Histoire D'Artaud Le Momo (The True Story of Artaud The Momo)
Moretti, Nanni: Caro Diario (Dear Diary)
Morin, Robert: Requiem pour un Beau Sans-Couer (Requiem for a Handsome Bastard); Windigo
Moritsugu, Jon: Mod Fuck Explosion; Terminal USA
Morris, Emma Joan: Something Within Me
Morton, Rocky: Super Mario Bros.
Mosher, Gregory: A Life In the Theatre
Moshinsky, Elijah: Genghis Cohn
Moskalenko, Vitali: Doroga v Ray (Road to Paradise)
Moskowicz,Fernand jt. directorship *see* **Achache, Jean, et al.**
Motta, Camila: Secuestro: A Story of Kidnapping
Mugge, Robert: Gather at the River; Kingdom of Zydeco, The; True Believers: The Musical Family of Rounder Records
Mulcahy, Russell: The Real McCoy; The Shadow
Mulford, Marilyn jt. directorship *see* **Field, Connie**
Muller, Eric: World and Time Enough
Muller, Ray: Macht der Biler: Leni Riefenstahl, Der (Power of the Image: Leni Riefenstahl, The)
Mundhra, Jag: Improper Conduct
Munic, Robert: The Pros and Cons of Breathing
Munoz Blaustein, Susan; Marcus, Erica: My Home , My Prison
Munro, David: Death of A Nation: The Timor Conspiracy
Munster, Reinhard: Alles Auf Anfang (Back to Square One)
Muratova, Kira: Uvletschenia (Passions/Avocations)
Murnberger, Wolfgang: Ich Gelobe (I Promise)
Murphy, Dean: Lex and Rory
Murphy, Maurice: Exchange Lifeguards
Murray, Robin P.: Season of Change
Mutrux, Floyd: There Goes My Baby
Muxel, Paule; de Soliers, Bertrand: SIDA, Paroles de L'Un A L'Autre (AIDS: Talking to One Another)
Muyl, Philippe: Cuisine et Dependances (Kitchen With Apartment)
Myung-Se, Lee: Chut Sarang (First Love)

Na'aman, Rami: Hagamal Hmeofef (The Flying Camel)
Naderi, Amir: Manhattan by Numbers
Nagnaidorj, B. jt. directorship *see* **Khatanbaatar, D.**

Nakajima, Takehiro: Okoge (Fag Hag)
Nakata, Toichi: Osaka Story: A Documentary
Narahashi, Yoko: Winds of God
Nasrallah, Yousry: Marcides (Mercedes)
Natoli, Piero: Ladri di Cinema (The Film Thief)
Negroponte, Michel: Jupiter's Wife
Neihouse, James: Destiny in Space
Nelson, Jessie: Corrina, Corrina
Neri, Gregory: A Weekend with Barbara Und Ingrid
Nesheim, Berit: Hoyere enn Himmelen (Beyond the Sky)
Newby, Chris: Anchoress
Newby, Christopher jt directorship *see* **Christopher, Mark, et al.**
Newell, Mike: Four Weddings and a Funeral
N'Hada, Sana Na: Xime
Nibbelink, Phil; Wells, Simon; Zondag, Dick; Zondag, Ralph: We're Back! A Dinosaur's Story
Nichetti, Maurizio: Stefano Quantestorie
Nichols, Mike: Wolf
Nicloux, Guillaume: Faut Pas Rire du Bonheur (Happiness is No Joke)
Nicoara, Radu: Lolul Sud (The South Pole)
Nien-Jen, Wu: Duo-Sang (A Borrowed Life)
Nieuwenhuijs, Victor; Seyferth, Maartje: Venus in Furs
Nimoy, Leonard: Holy Matrimony
Niv, Orna Ben-Dor: Eretz Hadasha (Newland)
Nobuyuki, Ito: Ame No Wadachi (Image in the Rain)
Noonan, Tom: What Happened Was
Nordlund, Solveig: See You Tomorrow, Mario (I Morgon Mario)
Norris, Aaron: Sidekicks
Nougmanov, Rashid: Diki Vostok (The Wild East)
Novakovic, Tomislav: Are They Still Shooting?
Novaro, Maria: El Jardin del Eden (The Garden of Eden)
Novkovic, Oleg: Why Have You Left Me? (Kazi Zasto Me Ostavi)
Noyce, Phillip: Clear and Present Danger; Sliver
Nuanxing, Zhang: Yun Nan Qiu Shi (The Story of Yunnan)
Nugroho, Garin: Surat Untuk Bidadari (A Letter for an Angel)
Nunez, Victor: Ruby in Paradise
Nutley, Colin: Sista Dansen (The Last Dance)
Nyamdawaa, N.: An Unfortunate Fortune

Oakley, Vern: Mr. 247
Obomsawin, Alanis: Kanehsatake: 270 Years of Resistance
O'Callaghan, Maurice: Broken Harvest
Oguz, Orhan: Donersen Islik Cal (Whistle If You Come Back)
Ohayon, Michele: It Was a Wonderful Life
Okazaki, Steven: The Lisa Theory
Oki, Hiroyuki: Tarch Trip
Okk, Shin Sang: Chongbal (Vanished)
Okuyama, Kazuyoshi: Rampo
Olhovich, Sergio: Bartolome de las Casas
Olin, Ken: White Fang 2: Myth of the White Wolf
Oliver, Leslie: You Can't Push the River

DIRECTOR INDEX

P

DIRECTOR INDEX

Prior, David A.: Double Threat; Night Trap (Mardi Gras for the Devil)
Proctor, Elaine: Friends
Protazanov, Jakov: Aelita
Proyas, Alex: The Crow
Purdy, Jon: Reflections on a Crime
Puszt, Tibor: A Golyák Mindig Visszatérnek (The Storks Always Return)
Pyle, Elana K.: At Risk
Pyun, Albert: Brain Smasher; Nemesis

Quartullo, Pino: Le Donne Non Vogliono Piu (Women Don't Want To)
Querejeta, Gracia: Una Estacion de Paso (Whistle Stop)
Quintanos, Gene: National Lampoon's Loaded Weapon 1
Quinterio, Carlo U.: Night Train to Venice

Rabaglia, Denis: Grossesse Nerveuse (False Pregnancy)
Radford, Michael: Il Postino (The Postman)
Radler, Robert: Best of the Best II
Radomski, Timm: Batman: Mask of the Phantasm
Rady, Mounir: Zeyaret el-Sayed el-Rais (Visit of the President)
Rafelson, Bob jt. directorship see **Cox, Paul, et al.**
Raffill, Stewart: Lost in Africa
Ramis, Harold: Groundhog Day
Randel, Tony: Ticks
Rangel, Alejandro Pelayo: Miroslava
Ransick, Whitney: Handgun
Rappaport, Mark: Rock Hudson's Home Movies
Rash, Steve: Son-In-Law
Raskov, David C.: A Kiss Goodnight
Rasmussen, Steen jt. directorship see **Wikke, Michael**
Ravalat, Thierry; Ferrari, Alain: Un Jour dans la Mort de Sarajevo (A Day in the Death of Sarajevo)
Ray, Sandip: Uttoran (The Broken Journey)
Redford, Robert: Quiz Show
Reed, Fiona Cunningham: Feed Them to the Canibals!
Reed, Peter: Under Heat
Refn, Anders: Sort Host (Black Harvest)
Reggiani, Simon: De Force Avec d'Autres (Forced to be With Others)
Regueiro, Francisco: Madregilda
Reich, Peter: Ram Csaj Meg Nem Volt Ilyen Hatassal (No Girl Ever Had This Effect on Me)
Reichardt, Kelly: River of Grass
Reichenbach, Carlos: Alma Corsaria (Buccaneer Soul)
Reid, John: The Last Tattoo
Reiker, Donald: Mona Must Die
Reiner, Carl: Fatal Instinct

DIRECTOR INDEX

DIRECTOR INDEX

DIRECTOR INDEX

U

V

DIRECTOR INDEX

W

Weisz, Frans: Op Afbetaling (The Betrayed)
Wellington, David: I Love a Man in Uniform
Wells, Peter jt. directorship *see* **Main, Stewart**
Wells, Simon jt. directorship *see* **Nibbelink, Phil, et al.**
Wen, Jiang: Yangguang Canlan De Rizi (In the Heat of the Sun)
Wenders, Wim: In Weiter Ferne, So Nah! (Faraway, So Close)
Werneck, Sandra jt. directorship *see* **Avancini, Walter**
Wertmuller, Lina: Io Speriamo Che Me la Cavo (Me Let's Hope I Make It)
Whitesell, John: Calendar Girl
Whittaker, Stephen: Closing Numbers
Wiederhorn, Ken: A House in the Hills
Wikke, Michael; Rasmussen, Steen: Russian Pizza Blues
Wild, Nettie: Blockade
Wild, Gregory: Highway of Heartache
Wilkinson, Charles: Max
William, Jano jt. directorship *see* **Longinotto, Kim**
Williams, David D.: Lillian
Williams, Paul: The November Men
Willpower *see* **Berliner, Will**
Wilson, Hugh: Guarding Tess
Wilson, Richard: It's All True
Wilson, Sandy: Harmony Cats
Wincer, Simon: Free Willy; Lightning Jack
Winkelmann, Adolf: Norkurev (North Curve)
Winkler, Henry: Cop and a Half
Winter, Alex jt. directorship *see* **Stern, Tom**
Winner, Michael: Dirty Weekend
Winterbottom, Michael: Family
Wiseman, Frederick: High School II; Zoo
Wiström, Mikael: Den Andra Stranden (The Second Shore)
Woditsch, Peter: Hey Stranger
Wolman, Dan: Hamerhak (The Distance)
Wong, Kirk: Chung On Tsou (Crime Story); Chungon Satluk Linggei (Organized Crime & Triad Bureau); Sang Gong Yatho Tungchap Fan (Rock N' Roll Cop)
Woo, John: Hard Target
Woo-ping, Yuen: Siunin Wong Fei-Hung Tsi Titmalau (The Iron Monkey)
Woods, Mel: Intimate With a Stranger
Wooping, Yuen: Taigik Cheung Sam-Fung (The Tai Chi Master)
Wortmann, Sonke: Acting It Out; Der Bewegte Mann
Wright, Geoffrey: Metal Skin
Wright, Thomas Lee: Eight-Tray Gangster: The Making of a Crip

Xiaoshuai, Wang: Dong-Chun De Rizi (The Days)
Xiaowen, Zhou: Ermo; Hei Shan Lu (Black Mountain)

DIRECTOR INDEX

Yagushi, Shinobu: Hadashi No Picnic (Down the Drain)
Yakin, Boaz: Fresh
Yamada, Yoji: Gakko (A Class to Remember)
Yamaguchi, Takayoshi: Koi No Tasogare (Breakable)
Yamazaki, Takaya: I'm Not Cooking Tonight
Yameogo, S. Pierre: Laafi; Wendemi, l'Enfant du Bon Dieu (Wendemi)
Yang, Edward: Duli Shidai (A Confucian Confusion)
Yaron, Nirit jt. directorship *see* **Menahemi, Ayelet**
Yarrow, Bethany: Mama Awethu!
Yatzouzakis, Dimitrios: Phanouropitta (Saint Phanourios' Pie)
Yi, He: Xuan Lian (Red Beads)
Yilmaz, Atif: Dus Gezginleri (Walking After Midnight)
Yimou, Zhang: To Live
Yimou, Zhang jt. directorship *see* **Fengliang, Yang**
Ying, Ning: Zhao Le (For Fun)
Yiu-leung, Clarence Fok: Chiklo Gouyeung (Naked Killer)
Yorick, John jt. directorship *see* **Kay, Joseph**
Young, Andrew jt. directorship *see* **Todd, Susan**
Young, Bill: The Roly Poly Man
Young, Robert: Splitting Heirs
Young, Robert M.: Roosters
Yu, Ronny: Bakfat Monui Chun (Jiang-Hu: Between Love and Glory/The Bride With White Hair)
Yuan, Zhang: Beijing Zazhong (Beijing Bastards)
Yuen, Brandy: Datmo Tsousi (Master of Zen)
Yuen, Cory: Fong Sai-Yuk Tsuktsap (Fong Sai-Yuk II)
Yukich, James: Double Dragon
Yurcenli, Yusuf: Cozulmeler (Disintegration)
Yuzna, Brian: Return of the Living Dead 3
Yuzna, Brian jt. directorship *see* **Gans, Christophe, et al.**

Zaccaro, Maurizio: L'Articolo 2 (Article 2)
Zafranovic, Lordan: Zalazak Stoljeca: Testament L.Z. (The Decline of the Century: Testament L.Z.)
Zagarrio, Vito: Bonus Malus
Zahavi, Dror: Der Besucher (The Visitor)
Zahedi, Caveh: I Don't Hate Las Vegas Anymore
Zaillian, Steven: Search for Bobby Fischer
Zalica, Pjer jt. directorship *see* **Arnautalic, Ismet, et al.**
Zauberman, Yolande: Moi Ivan, Toi Abraham (Me Ivan, You Abraham)
Zedicoff, Alex: Capture the White Flag
Zeffirelli, Franco: Sparrow
Zehrer, Paul: Blessing
Zeitoun, Ariel: Le Nombril du Monde (I, Bajou)
Zeltser, Yuri: Playmaker
Zemeckis, Robert: Forrest Gump